Mayflower Deeds & Probates

George Ernest Bowman, ca. 1897

Mayflower

Deeds & Probates

FROM THE FILES OF GEORGE ERNEST BOWMAN

At the Massachusetts Society of Mayflower Descendants

by

Susan E. Roser

Genealogical Publishing Co., Inc.

by Genealogical Publishing Co., Inc.
1001 N. Calvert Street, Baltimore, MD 21202

Library of Congress Catalogue Card Number 94-77222
International Standard Book Number 0-8063-1423-0
Made in the United States of America

Contents

Preface

George Ernest Bowman** (1860–1941) is a well known and respected name in the field of Mayflower research. In 1896 he founded the Massachusetts Society of Mayflower Descendants and served as Secretary, Genealogist and Editor for 45 years, until 1941. He was the Editor of the **Mayflower Descendant,** a quarterly genealogical magazine specializing in primary source material, published between 1899 and 1937. In his book, **Plymouth Colony, Its History & People, 1620–1691,** Eugene A. Stratton, FASG, former Historian General of the General Society of Mayflower Descendants, pays tribute to Bowman:

> *The greatest genealogical scholar of Plymouth Colony was George Ernest Bowman . . . He left a living legacy in the Mayflower Descendant, a timeless and unsurpassed collection of original records of the people of colonial Plymouth. Moreover, he left a methodology for precision in acquiring data that has been all too little appreciated in the past, but has been gaining recognition with time.*

Mr. Bowman was a dedicated and disciplined genealogist whose goal was to trace the ancestry of each Mayflower family right up to present-day descendants. Either he did not fully appreciate the enormity of the research involved or he had extremely high expectations of himself (probably the latter), in any case, his goal was never realized although he spent almost half a century trying. Referring to his work as The Mayflower Genealogies, he did manage to accumulate approximately 20,600 pages containing probate, court, church and bible records, cemetery inscriptions, wills, charts, lineages and documentation. His work remains the largest documented manuscript collection on Mayflower genealogy.

In 1983 the Society filmed the collection on microfiche. The Bowman Files, as it is now referred to, consists of 229 microfiche cards, grouped by family name, with each card containing approximately 96 handwritten and typed pages.

Mayflower Deeds & Probates is a compilation of deeds and probate records extracted and transcribed from these Files. It is hoped that by printing Mr. Bowman's research it will be more accessible to researchers and therefore provide assistance in the advancement of Mayflower research; after all, wasn't that Mr. Bowman's lifelong objective?

Introduction

Mayflower Deeds & Probates (MDP) is the last of a three-book series, a companion volume to **Mayflower Marriages (MM)** (1990), and the two-volume **Mayflower Births & Deaths (MBD) (1992).** These four volumes provide a complete account of the births, deaths, marriages, deeds and probate records as found in the research files of noted genealogist George E. Bowman.

This book contains records dealing with Mayflower passengers and their descendants, but the reader may be pleasantly surprised to find wills and deeds pertaining to their non-Mayflower lines as well. Bowman was very thorough in his research and usually undertook the task of locating records pertaining to the family of the person who married into the Mayflower family. Also, in the case of deeds, non-Mayflower lines can be found selling/buying to/from Mayflower lines. Non-Mayflower lines are also found throughout the probate records where, along with their own records, they are found in the Mayflower records as witnesses, appraisers, and administrators. So, although the emphasis is definitely on Mayflower families, this book has an appeal to anyone whose lines originate in the counties of Plymouth, Barnstable, Bristol, Middlesex, etc.

To fully appreciate the data in this book you must not limit yourself to searching out the records of your ancestors only. There are some very interesting deeds and wills within that will give you an insight into how your ancestors lived, while others will entertain you. You will also find depositions, personal letters, affidavits, court judgments and executions, and petitions—four centuries of records are represented in this book.

Primary sources are provided for virtually every record within. Unlike birth, death, or marriage data where the source can be either primary or an unreliable secondary source, deeds and probate records have only one source—the primary record itself. And, as one might expect with someone as meticulous as Bowman, he provided these primary sources throughout. The rare instances he did not cite a source are usually those in which he had the original in his possession or copied the original.

GUIDELINES

1. Format

The format within is very easy to follow and is compatible with **MM & MBD.** I have again included the microfiche numbers to afford the reader quick reference to the **Bowman Files** themselves and to the three companion volumes. Thus, if you found your ancestor's marriage in **MM** under Alden Micro #1 and their children in **MBD** under Alden Micro #1, you would again look under Alden Micro #1 for any deeds and probate records pertaining to this family. Second generation headings (e.g., Constance Hopkins[2], Stephen[1]) within each family indicate that the data following pertains to this branch of the Mayflower family. To increase the usefulness of these sub-headings, they are included in the table of contents.

2. Deeds

The deeds have not been transcribed in their entirety, and you can well imagine the wasted space taken up by these wordy transactions. Full particulars are given—the source, name, occupation and residence of the parties, date, sale price, acreage and location of the land, witnesses, date of acknowledgment, and date of recording in the record office. If the parties were related the relationship is usually (but not always) stated. Quite often additional genealogical data is given, family members may be dividing land, a grantor may name his/her parents and/or grandparents from whom he/she originally received the land. You will learn who your ancestors' neighbors were, see how the family homestead or other lands were passed down through the family—and out of the family as they moved to other areas. The amount of data to be found here depends on what was found in the Files. Some deeds were very lengthy while others were sketchy or contained no details.

3. Probates

As with the deeds, the very wordy wills were transcribed to include information of value and interest. I have tried to keep to the original wording and spelling (as with the deeds) for the sake of accuracy and to give the reader a feel for the time period. Transcriptions include the date written, bequests to friends and family, descriptions of personal and real estate, and names of witnesses. The name of a person who was shown to be related to the deceased is given in bold print. The amount of data to be found here depends entirely on what was found in Bowman's research. Some wills he transcribed fully, others were sketchy, while with some he merely listed the source. I have gone into more detail with some wills because of their interesting nature. I was amazed at how some husbands detailed exactly what their wives were to receive and the instructions as to how they were to be maintained (e.g., 100 lbs. beef yearly, cut firewood at the door, etc.). You will find out if your ancestors made a pre-nuptial agreement, their financial status, family heirlooms passed on, family differences (e.g., "I leave nothing to . . ."), and insights into their death (e.g., aged or infirm, embarking on a sea voyage, going off to war). Wills can often provide the missing link in establishing parentage and family relationships. Parents and grandparents are sometimes named, children and siblings, aunts, uncles, cousins and grandchildren. Children are usually listed in the order of birth, e.g., eldest first (the eldest son receiving a double portion) or sometimes all the sons are listed (in order) followed by all the daughters (in order).

After the decease of the testator the will was probated and letters of administration granted, estates inventoried and accounts rendered, usually ending with the settlement or distribution of the personal and real estate among the heirs. An approximate date of death would be between the date of the will (or codicil) and the earliest date given in the probate records. You will find the probate records particularly useful if your ancestor died intestate (without making a will). Inventories detail the personal and real estate holdings and their values (pounds "£" were used until the late 1700s when dollars took over). I have included the lengthier inventories as it is interesting to see, for example, the items one would find in a 1750 household. The accounts of the administrators are sometimes lengthy in listing the names of all those who were indebted to the estate or were owed from the estate. I have included these lists of names because some ancestors are elusive and cannot be found in probate records of their own; to leave them out would be to ignore their existence. The distribution and settlement of the estate names the heirs of the deceased. If there were minor children (under twenty-one), guardians were appointed. Children between the ages of 14–21 were allowed to choose a suitable guardian. If you find a father appointed guardian of his children it usually means the mother had died. Guardianship records will also be found for those who were judged "non compos mentis"—unable to care for themselves because of age, infirmity, or mental instability. Probate records can also provide ages of the children, exact or approximate death date of the deceased (e.g., last May), residences of the heirs (e.g., now living in New York), and occupations.

4. Indexing

The spelling variations of surnames can be frustrating. When checking the index for a particular name be certain to look for every conceivable spelling. You may be disappointed at not finding your ancestor William Hughes under the

Hughes listings, and unless you look under the name Hewes you may miss him completely. In many instances the spelling of one person's (or family's) surname varies within the same record; for some (e.g., Hathaway, Delano) I have combined all the variations under one heading for easier reference.

Interpretation of family relationships is important. The use of father, mother, brother, sister, etc. sometimes refers to in-laws. The term mother-in-law may refer to step-mother. Senior and Junior are used to designate father and son and mother and daughter as well as to distinguish between two unrelated people of the same name (senior being the elder of the two). Married women are sometimes referred to as spinster while unmarried women could be termed Mrs.

Indexing married women was a challenge. If the record states she was Mrs. Mary Brown or Mary Brown wf of Nathan, but the same record clearly identifies her as the daughter of John Allen, she will be found in the index as both "Brown, Mary (Allen)" and "Allen, Mary." I have done this to make identification of the women easier; but remember, although the index may show her as "Brown, Mary (Allen)," you may find her in the text as "Mrs. Mary Brown." However, if a daughter is listed in the records of her *mother,* I could not make this same identification in the index. If Phebe Harlow mentions her daughter Sarah Hunt with no indication as to her marital status, there could be several scenarios. Sarah could be a single daughter by a previous marriage (Sarah Hunt), a married daughter by a previous marriage (Sarah (   ) Hunt), or simply a married daughter (Sarah (Harlow) Hunt). Therefore, in these cases she will appear exactly as found in the text—Sarah Hunt. Also keep in mind that in cases where marital status is not specified, a married woman may show up in the index as simply "Mercy Snow." If you find an entry in the index such as "William Brown, 127/8," you would find William at the bottom of p. 127 with Brown following at the top of p. 128.

5. Abbreviations

Abbreviations have been used throughout to conserve space. You will find the following throughout: daughter (dau), husband (hus), wife (wf), probate (Pr., prob.), inventory (inv.), administration (adm.), administrator (admr.), administratrix (admx.), executor (exr.), executrix (exx.), recorded (rec.), acknowledged (ack.).

THE BOWMAN FILES

I feel I must use this opportunity to defend some "bad press" the Bowman Files have received, largely due to reviews of my books. Too much emphasis has been placed on the phrase "much of Bowman's work has been superseded by recent research." This is not entirely true. It is Bowman's research that is the foundation for the continuing research that has been ongoing for the past twenty-five years. It is because of Bowman's fifty years of diligent and careful research that today's genealogists have advanced as far as they have with Mayflower research. Are there errors in Bowman's research? Of course there are. You cannot amass 20,000 pages of research on twenty-three different families and not expect to find errors; however, the number of errors is minimal when compared to his research as a whole. (I have pointed out and corrected any errors that I have found.) The false impression has been given that "recent research" has surpassed Bowman's in accuracy. However, anyone familiar with Mayflower genealogical books published in the last twenty-five years knows first-hand the countless errors that have been committed to print. The bottom line here is this: no matter how qualified or careful the researcher is, genealogical research is not infallible; accuracy improves with time, and as new records are discovered, errors are corrected.

ACKNOWLEDGMENTS

As my transcription of **The Bowman Files** comes to an end I would once again like to thank the **Massachusetts Society of Mayflower Descendants** for allowing me to put these records into print.

I would also like to thank Donald Stacy of Sudbury, MA, for it was he who "introduced" me to my Mayflower ancestors in 1976 which has resulted in my passion for Mayflower research.

Finally to my parents, Vince and Ruth Richardson, my heartfelt thanks for that afternoon in 1975 when my genealogical pursuits sprang to life with their words, "Why don't you find out something about our family history?" That day was truly the beginning of a wondrous adventure into the past.

Susan E. Rosner

ADDENDA TO MAYFLOWER BIRTHS & DEATHS

Vol. 1

Pg. 95–Elizabeth Grafton[4] died 26 Mar. 1734 (not 1754). Although the handwriting in the Files looks like a "5", MFIP, Allerton #29 states she died in 1734 with her will probated 3 Apr. 1734.

Pg. 65–<79> should read: His year of *birth* (not death).

Pg. 102–<23> the source should read Kingman:14 (not:10).

Pg. 369–The line should read: Joseph Mosher[3] (Hugh[2–1]), d. betw. 15 Nov. 1743 (will)–23 Mar. 1754 (widow's petition). The date of 7 May 1754 was the date the will was probated.

Index–Jemima Hall, 29 (not 30)
Sarah Perry, 367 (not 368)
William Wood, (not 410)

Vol. 2

Pg. 78–8th line, Stephen Smith[5]–reference to footnote <235> belongs 3 lines below to brother Seth Smith[5].

Pg. 97–<152>–2nd paragraph which reads from left margin "the Elizabeth born 1737 in Rochester as Bowman wondered?"–change Rochester to Sandwich.

Pg. 214–There are two footnotes for <60>–take out the first one.

Pg. 240–<36>–The division of the estate was carried out 25 July 1698 (it was not the date of a will).

Pg. 241–<61>–First line, the line of descent for Lydia (Sparrow[3]) Freeman should read (Jonathan[2], Richard[1]) (not Jonathan[3]).

Pg. 442–Children of Thomas Gibbs & Alice Warren[3] (8) (not 3 of 8).

Pg. 244–Under 21:135–42–Will of Wiliam Makepeace, the line should read "Note: correction on p. 142" (not p. 192).

Index–Add Lydia Cushman, 437

JOHN ALDEN

Micro #1 of 16

PLYMOUTH COUNTY PROBATE, Re: ALDEN

1687	John	Duxbury	#126, 1:10
1696/7	Jonathan	Duxbury	#134, 1:255, 2:28
1696/7	Joseph	Bridgewater	#138, 1:256, 257
1719	David	Duxbury	#76, 4:186
1727	Isaac	Bridgewater	#111, 5:344, 345
1730	John	Middleboro	#132, 5:829, 842, 845, 10:298
1732	Hannah	Middleboro	#101, 6:279, 280
1732	John et al	Middleboro	#133, 6:267,268,282, 8:449, 9:46
1739	Hannah	Duxbury	#102, 8:153,154
1739	John	Duxbury	#127, 8:119,183,380,384,385
1740	Abigail et al	Duxbury	#54, 8:166,176
1741	Benjamin	Duxbury	#63, 8:371,375,410,431, 19:77
1741	Judah	Duxbury	#142, 8:344,424,492, 9:133,134,135
1741	Wrestling et al	Duxbury	#191, 8:417,8:482, 11:110, 15:156
1748	Ebenezer	Middleboro	#83, 11:86,539
1759	John	Bridgewater	#131, 15:284,285, 16:26
1763	David	Middleboro	#77, 16:503,504,535
1764	Silas	Middleboro	#180, 17:135, 19:207, 20:331
1768	Ezra	Bridgewater	#95, 20:8,125,127, 25:82
1769	Joseph et al	Bridgewater	#140, 20:196
1770	Silence et al	Middleboro	#181, 20:409
1771	Susanna et al	Bridgewater	#186, 21:33, 25:83,544,545, 26:361,363, 28:63, 29:152,243
1772	Elizabeth	Duxbury	#92, 21:128
1773	Ebenezer	Middleboro	#82, 21:222,224,336,360, 25:306, 28:99,100
1773	Eleazer	Bridgewater	#87, 21:228,229
1776	Seth Jr.	Bridgewater	#176, 24:18,113, 30:4
1779	Ichabod	Duxbury	#110, 25:282, 27:4, 28:528, 29:300
1779	John et al	Duxbury	#130, 26:66,67
1781	Isaac	Bridgewater	#112, 28:214,216, 27:487, 28:260
1781	Samuel	Duxbury	#168, 28:38,41
1783	Seth	Bridgewater	#178, 26:177
1784	Seth	Bridgewater	#177, 29:203,204
1787	Joseph	Middleboro	#136, 27:224, 30:372,522
1788	Ebenezer et al	Middleboro	#84, 26:454,455
1790	Abiathar	Duxbury	#52, 27:334, 31:484,485
1796	Briggs	Duxbury	#69, 36:17,19
1799	Daniel	Bridgewater	#73, 37:131,441,442, 43:4
1799	Samuel	Duxbury	#169, 34:181, 37:67,164,165, 40:209
1801	Otis et al	Bridgewater	#159, 32:169 (gdn.)
1803	Bezaleel	Duxbury	#68, 34:371 (adm.)
1803	Eleazer	Duxbury	#88, 38:349,351 (adm.)
1803	Joseph	Bridgewater	#137, 38:318,321 (will)
1805	Amherst	Duxbury	#60, 40:152,153 (will)
1808	Seth	Bridgewater	#179, 41:92 (gdn.)
1809	Joshua	Bridgewater	#141, 42:458,459,460, 43:5,88,89, 44:275 (will)
1812	Mercy	Duxbury	#154, 44:224,225 (will)
1812	Mary	Bridgewater	#152, 44:74,75,282,283 (will)
1814	David	Middleboro	#78, 45:260,261, 45:486 (will)
1814	Samuel	Bridgewater	#174, 45:457,458, 46:55 (adm.)
1814	Solomon	Bridgewater	#182, 45:231,232, 47:188 (will)
1815	Edith	Duxbury	#85, 47:58,59,269 (will)
1816	Samuel	Abington	#171, 46:187, 48:204,407, 49:266 (adm.)
1818	Samuel et al	Bridgewater	#175, 41:339, 63:60, 64:135 (gdn.)
1822	Edward U.	Bridgewater	#86, 52:116,128, 56:210,211,525 (adm.)
1825	Job	Middleboro	#124, 52:352, 59:56,173,438, 60:252,535, 61:252 63:170,228,523,541, 66:173,174, 67:13 (adm)
1825	Jonathan	E.Bridgewater	#135, 52:342, 55:292, 59:58,146,147, 60:123, 63:105 (adm.)
1825	Lucy	Middleboro	#146, 51:284, 59:166,406,407, 63:116 (gdn.)
1825	Oliver	Bridgewater	#157, 55:369, 59:423,424, 60:93,94 (will)
1825	Rufus	Middleboro	#162, 59:398,500, 62:2 (will)

PLYMOUTH COUNTY PROBATE, Re: ALDEN (cont-d)

1826	Jedediah	Middleboro	#123, 60:182,183, 61:9, 63:381, 64:178 (adm.)
1827	Oliver	Bridgewater	#158, 64:296,311,317, 65:5, 6?:199, 66:426, 67: 423,552, 77:358,360 (gdn.)
1828	Southworth	( )	#185, 65:74 (gdn.)
1829	Israel	Middleboro	#119, 65:108, 67:559
1830	Eunice	Bridgewater	#94, 55,56, 68:112, 69:165
1831	Isaiah	Scituate	#118, 68:234, 71:13, 72:3,401, 73:54, 74:212, 337, 76:8,9 (adm.)
1835	Benjamin	Duxbury	#64, 71:289 (adm.)
1835	Isaac	Bridgewater	#114, 2:80, 75:319, 77:526, 78:112, 79:92(will)
1835	Rufus	Middleboro	#163, 65:387, 75:197, 77:89, 78:117 (gdn.)
1835	Thomas R.	E.Bridgewater	#188, 71:297, 73:136, 75:222, 77:156,157,342, 78:14,16 (adm.)
1836	Andrew	Middleboro	#61, 1:283**A**, 75:329, 78:195 (will)
1836	Elizabeth	Duxbury	#93, 10:21**A**, 75:383, 78:507, 79:154 (adm.)
1837	Amasa	Bridgewater	#58, 10:92**A**, 75:441, 79:264,409, 80:157
1837	Hosea	Abington	#109, 2:66**O**, 10:72**A**, 75:438, 79:260, 86:568, 589 (adm.)
1837	Isaac F. et al	Bridgewater	#115, 1:29**R**,39**R**, 4:478**O**,498**O**, 8:65**L**,323**L**, 79: 457, 85:296, 86:505 (gdn.)
1838	Betsey W. et al	Middleboro	#67, 8:93**L** (gdn.)
1840	Elijah	W.Bridgewater	#90, 6:83**U**, 8:447**L**,448**L**, 82:141, 83:92, 86:135 (gdn.)
1842	Sabra	Duxbury	#165, 6:336**U**, 11:151**B**, 84:226,588 (adm.)
1843	Betsey	Middleboro	#66, 11:167**B**, 85:238
1844	Isaac	E.Bridgewater	#113, 6:511**U**, 11:229**B**, 86:291 (adm.)
1844	Luther E.	Abington	#147, 9:12**M**, 86:569, 87:419 (gdn.)
1844	Rebecca	W.Bridgewater	#161, 6:526**U**, 8:498**L**,500**L**, 86:497 (gdn.)
1845	Isaiah	Duxbury	#117, 1:433**G**, 87:337 (will)
1845	Judah	Duxbury	#143, 2:30**H**,232**O**, 6:614**U**, 87:111,325, 88:262, 89:244 (will)
1845	Sally H.	Bridgewater	#166, 2:45**H**, 7:41**V**, 87:304,434, 88:457, 90:124, 136,137, 104:204 (will)
1845	Samuel B. et al	Duxbury	#170, 9:40**M**, 89:221 (gdn.)
1848	Abner	Duxbury	#55, 7:409, 12:37**C**, 91:3 (adm.)
1848	James	N.Bridgewater	#120, 1:486**R**, 3:563**P**, 9:136**M**, 91:4,5 (gdn.)
1849	Cyrus et al	Middleboro	#72, 1:292**R**, 3:407**P**, 9:199**M**, 92:152 (gdn.)
1849	Gustavus L. et al	Middleboro	#100, 9:187**M**, 97:171, 110:481 (gdn.)
1849	Mary	Duxbury	#150, 1:510**G**, 8:28**W**, 91:611 (will)
1850	David	Middleboro	#79, 2:231**H**, 3:160**P**, 8:59**W**, 92:150,285, 93:1, 96:116,117 (will)
1850	Hannah	Duxbury	#103, 1:133**R**, 3:158**P**, 8:68**W**, 12:207**C**, 92:320, 98:71 (adm.)
1850	Job	Middleboro	#125, 3:188**P**, 8:83**W**, 12:231**C**, 92:489, 93:27, 94:1,143 (adm.)
1850	Thomas	Bridgewater	#187, 8:89**W**, 12:241**C**, 92:420,421, 94:114, 96: 62 (adm.)

==

Will of **Daniel ALDEN.** <Stafford CT PR #20>
...dated 15 Nov. 1764...wife Rebecca, what she brought from Hanover; four sons, Joseph, Daniel, Zephaniah, Barnabas, Daus. Abigail WHITMAN, Hannah BLOGGETT. Witnesses: Lieut. Timothy EDSON Jr., Mary EDSON, Huldah EDSON. Probated 12 May 1767.

==

Will of **Zephaniah ALDEN.** <Stafford CT PR #28>
...dated 2 Feb. 1796...mentions wife Ann, heirs of brother Joseph, heirs of brother Daniel, sister Abigail WHITMAN wf. of Eleazer WHITMAN, sister Hannah BLODGETT, brother Barnabas, nephews Zephaniah & Abishai sons of Joseph ALDEN. Probated 6 Feb. 1801.

==

Ezra ALDEN, of Greenwich, Hampshire co., Mass. named as guardian to Ezra ALDEN Jr. of Greenwich, heir to his grandfather Uriah RICHARDS of Stafford, 1786. <Stafford CT PR #23>

==

CONNECTICUT PROBATE INDEX:

1756 - Rufus ALDEN, bond, inventory & misc. Ashford. <Pomfret #65.>
1779 - Joab ALDEN, bond & distribution. <Norwich #145>
1785 - John ALDEN, bond only, Lebanon. <Windham #63-6>
1785 - Judah ALDEN, bond only, Lebanon. <Windham #63-7>
1801 - Zephaniah ALDEN, will, etc. <Stafford #28>
1826 - Elisha ALDEN, will, etc. <Stafford #22>
1832 - Eliab ALDEN, bond & distribution. <Stafford #21>
1841 - Howard ALDEN, will. <Suffield #27>

==

Estate of **Joseph ALDEN.** <Stafford CT PR #24>
...Adm. 23 Feb. 1769 to Susanna ALDEN. Surety: Daniel ALDEN. Inventory dated 9 Feb. 1769 by Isaac PHINNEY, John BLODGETT, total: £895.0.6. Distribution by John BLOGGETT, Timothy EDSON, Epheram HIDE, dated 18 Nov. 1772. Heirs: widow Susanna ALDEN, sons Zenos (?sp), Eliab, Joseph, Benjamin, Zephaniah, Abishai and daughter Martha ALDEN.

==

Estate of **John ALDEN** of Lebanon CT. <Windham CT PR #63-5>
...Inventory dated 17 June 1765 by widow Elizabeth, admx., taken by Ebenezer B( ), Azel FITCH, B. SOUTHWORTH. Insolvent.

==

Will of **Elizabeth ALDEN** of Lebanon CT. <Windham CT PR #63-3>
...dated 13 Dec. 1784. Heirs: dau Violette FITCH wf of Isaac FITCH; son Roger ALDEN; dau Elizabeth ALDEN Jr.; dau Parthena LITTLE wf of Woodbridge LITTLE; granddaughters Elizabeth & Parthena FITCH. Gown to Violette that was her grandmother RIPLEY's.

==

Estate of **James GEER** of Groton. <New London CT PR #2191>
Adm. bond dated 8 Apr. 1755 by Sarah GEER, admx. Surety: Robert GEER. Division dated 7 Sept. 1775, heirs: Widow, children: Zipporah, Molly, Lydia, Lucy, James, Samuel. Distribution of widow's dower, 31 ( ) 1787, heirs: son James; dau of Samuel GEER; Molly wf of Elisha SATTERLEE; Lydia, wf of James AVERY 2nd; Lucy, wf of Sanford BILLINGS.

==

Estate of **John SEABURY Jr.** of Groton CT. <New London CT PR #4720>
Bond dated 15 Jan. 1744/5 by Esther SEABURY admx. Surety: Nathaniel GEER. Insolvent.

==

Estate of **Rev. Samuel SEABURY.** <New London CT PR #4722>
Bond dated 10 Oct. 1796 by Rev. Charles SEABURY, admx. Surety: Jared STARR. Division of Heirs: dated 27 Apr. 1799 at N.Y., Violetta R. TAYLOR, Abigail M. CAMPBELL, Edward SEABURY, Maria SEABURY, Charles SEABURY.

==

Estate of **Jabin ALDEN** of Lebanon CT. <Windham CT PR #63-4>
Bond dated 9 Aug. 1808 by Hannah ALDEN, admx. Surety: Andrew WILLIAMS. Receipt of Andrew ALDEN for $51.32 dated 16 Feb. 1809, at Franklin.

==

Will of **Joseph HEWITT** of Stonington CT. <Stonington CT PR #1632>
...dated 18 Nov. 1784...mentions wife Mehitable, son Joseph HEWITT, daus Hannah WHELLER, Prudence LEWIS, Anne WHIPPLE, grandson Josiah HEWITT.

==

Will of **Jabez CHESEBROUGH** of Stonington CT. <Stonington CT PR #1166>
Noncupitive will by Edward HANCOCK and Lucy his wife. Sworn to 30 Dec. 1754.
...dated Nov. 1753, Jabez C. CHESEBROUGH of Stonington...being bound to sea in employ of Col. SALTONSTALL of New London. Estate to brother James CHESEBROUGH. Adm. to Phineas STANTON. Receipt 10 Mar. 1758 by James CHESEBROUGH in full from P. STANTON who was my guardian and also adm. of estate of my brother Jabez.

==

Estate of **Thomas PALMER** of Stonington CT. <New London CT PR #3939>
Bond dated 12 Dec. 1752, by Mary PALMER admx. Surety: Samuel UTLY. At New London, 5 Sept. 1769, order of court to divide real estate between the two daughters, Elizabeth and Mary. Elizabeth now wife of Mr. Thompson WELLS of Hopkinton R.I. Widow's dower set off 23 Sept. 1771.

DAVID ALDEN[2] (John[1])

PLYMOUTH COLONY DEEDS, Re: DAVID ALDEN[2]: (source numbers not cited)

6 Oct. 1725 - Samuel & Priscilla CHEESEBROUGH sell 1/4 of David ALDEN's rights to John SEABURY.
14 Dec. 1725 - John & Elizabeth SEABURY sell 1/2 of David ALDEN's rights to Ebenezer HATHAWAY.
14 Jan. 1727/8 - Samuel & Ruth SPRAGUE owning 1/4 of David ALDEN's rights; Judah & Alice PADDOCK owning 1/4 and Ebenezer HATHAWAY owning 1/2, make division with Sprague & Paddock on one part, Hathaway on other part.
1 July 1730 - Judah & Alice PADDOCK sell lands, 16 Shilling Purchase, Middleboro...Father David ALDEN's rights, to Noah SPRAGUE of Rochester.
20 Sep. 1739 - Samuel & Ruth SPRAGUE sell 1/2 of 20th lot in 2nd allotment of 16 Shilling Purch. in David ALDEN's right to Elkanah LEONARD.
( ) 1739 - Samuel & Ruth SPRAGUE sell all their undisposed of rights in 16 Shilling Purchase in Father David ALDEN's right to their son Noah SPRAGUE.

==

David ALDEN of Duxbury to son **Samuel ALDEN** of Duxbury. <Plymouth Co.Deeds 14:12,13>
...26 Mar. 1717...David ALDEN, husbandman gives to Samuel ALDEN...all my lands...near a place called Rooty Brook...two hundred acres more or less in Middleboro...given to me by my Honoured Father **John ALDEN,** late of sd Duxborough dec'd...as may appear by a deed under his hand & seal bearing date ye 8th Day of July 1674 Recorded in ye late Colony of New-Plymouth together with my whole right or share in ye Great Cedar Swamp in sd Middleborough. Witnesses: Benjamin ALDEN, Samuel RICKARD. Ack. 13 Mar. 1717/8. Rec. 25 Mar. 1718.

==

Nathan SEARS of Rochester to son **Stephen SEARS** of Rochester. <No source cited>
...dated 29 May 1819...I Nathan Sears...for the consideration of the love & goodwill...to my son Stephen SEARS, mariner, quitclaim to him...all the lands of every kind which I own in the town of Liverpool in the Province of Nova Scotia...Reference being had to the Province Grant and to the Proprietor's Records for a more particular description...Dated 29 May 1819. Witnesses: Bethiah HOLMES, Abraham HOLMES. Ack. same day before Abraham Holmes, Justice of the Peace.

==

Wrestling ALDEN et al, of Duxbury. <Plymouth Co.PR #191, 8:417,482, 11:110, 15:156>

(Original) Bond dated 12 Aug. 1741, Wrestling BREWSTER of Kingston app'td. guardian of **Wrastling ALDEN**, son of **Benjamin ALDEN** late of Duxbury dec'd. Surety: John BREWSTER. Witnesses: David ALDEN, Bezaleel ALDEN.

(8:417) Nomination of Guardian: **Wrestling ALDEN** names his uncle Wrestling BREWSTER as his guardian. Dated 12 Aug. 1741 in presence of Jno. WADSWORTH Jr. & Abiell FULLER.

(Original) Bond dated 22 Mar. 1748, Wrestling Alden of Duxbury app'td. Guardian of **Abiather ALDEN** son of **Benjamin ALDEN**. Surety: Samuel ALDEN. Witnesses: Briggs ALDEN, Edward WINSLOW.

(8:482) Nomination of Guardian: **Bezaleel ALDEN** of Duxbury, son of **Benjamin ALDEN**, appoints Ransom JACKSON of Duxbury guardian in presence of Abiel FULLER, David ALDEN.

(11:110) Nomination of Guardian: **Abiather ALDEN** names his brother **Wrestling ALDEN** to be his guardian. Dated 22 Mar. 1748 in presence of Briggs ALDEN, Edward WINSLOW.

(15:156) Account of Joshua BREWSTER who was bondsman to Ransom JACKSON, guardian of **Bezaleel ALDEN**; allowed 27 Apr. 1759; Creditor of estate of Miles STANDISH "The sum of twenty-seven pounds four shillings & two farthings...is now due **Bezaleel ALDEN** from sd Ransom JACKSON & Joshua BREWSTER which they are hereby ordered to pay to discharge the same."

==

Estate of **Elizabeth ALDEN** of Duxbury. <Plymouth Co.PR #92, 21:128>

(Original) Bond dated 16 May 1772, Abiathar ALDEN of Bedeford in the County of York app't. adm. on the estate of Elizabeth ALDEN, Spinster. Sureties: Ebenezer CHANDLER, Calvin PARTRIDGE, both of Duxbury. Witnesses: Briggs ALDEN & Judah DELANO

(21:128) Adm. dated 16 May 1772, Abiathar ALDEN, app'td.

(21:128) Inventory sworn by Isaac PARTRIDGE, Ebenezer CHANDLER, Calvin PARTRIDGE, appraisers 19 May 1772 and by adm. 22 May 1772. Total amount of estate incl. bonds & note against David ALDEN, John ROBINSON, Samuel CATES, the latter dated 8 Dec. 1758, Ł133.2.10

==

Estate of **Deacon Benjamin ALDEN**, of Duxbury. <Plymouth Co.PR #63, 8:371,375,410,431, 19:77>

(Original) Bond dated 21 May 1741, David ALDEN, Hannah ALDEN, app't. adms. Sureties: Edward ARNOLD & Benjamin LORING of Duxbury. Witnesses: Gershom BRADFORD, Daniel LEWIS Jr.

(8:371) Letter dated 21 May 1741, appointing David ALDEN & Hannah ALDEN, widow, admrs.

(8:375) Inventory taken 9 June 1741 by Edward ARNOLD, Ransom JACKSON, Isaac PARTRIDGE. Sworn by David ALDEN 10 June 1741. Amount of property incl. homestead, Ł1100 and 1/4 part of sawmill, "not footed up."

(8:410) Account allowed 12 Aug. 1741, paid & received as follows: from est. of Jacob DINGLEY, Benjamin PRIOR, Benjamin PETERSON, Dr. OTIS, Sherack KEEN, Isaac LITTLE, Joseph BARTLETT, Ephraim NORCUTT, William CARVER, Israel HATCH, Nicholas SEVER, Lucy LITTLE (Ł108, largest creditor), John BREWSTER, Francis ADAMS, Joshua BREWSTER, Philip CHANDLER, Isaac LOTHROP Jr., Samuel BARTLETT, John MURDOCK, Dr. LeBARON, Robert BROWN, Amos FORD, Isaac KEEN, John THOMAS, ( ) WATERMAN, David SAMSON, Jedediah BOURNE, Edward ARNOLD, Josiah BISHOP, Lazarus SAMSON, Samuel FORD, Joseph DEANO, David SAMSON, Joshua DELANO, James THOMAS, Keziah HOLMES, Thomas CROAD, Jeremiah CROOKER, David ALDEN, Mary WADSWORTH, Elizabeth ALDEN.

(8:431) Division of estate, 5 Oct. 1741. Real estate settled on eldest son, **David ALDEN**, he, having paid their shares to his brothers & sisters, viz: Bezaleel, Wrestling, Abiathar & Elizabeth ALDEN and Mary WADSWORTH.

(19:77) Dower set off to **Hannah ALDEN**, widow of Benjamin, by Samuel ALDEN, George PARTRIDGE, Israel SYLVESTER, Nathaniel SIMMONS, of Duxbury and Nathaniel LORING of Pembroke. Land adjoining Isaac PARTRIDGE's and near South River, salt meadow at Bumps Neck lying adjacent to the Mill River and Duck Hill River. Dated 1 May 1759.

==

Estate of **Abiathar ALDEN**, Mariner, of Duxbury. <Plymouth Co.PR #52, 27:334, 41:484,485>

(Original) Bond dated 29 Oct. 1790, Wrestling ALDEN app'td. adm. of estate. Sureties: Isaiah ALDEN, Jacob DINGLY, both of Duxbury. Witnesses: Benjamin CUSHING, Deborah CUSHING.

(27:334) Letter of adm. dated 29 Oct. 1790, Wrestling ALDEN app'td.

(31:484) Inventory taken ( ) Feb. 1792, by Beza ALDEN, Jacob DINGLEY, Isaiah ALDEN. Sworn by Wrestling ALDEN, 28 Feb. 1792. Real estate Ł5.0.0., total Ł83.5.8.

(31:485) Representation of Insolvency dated 28 Feb. 1792.

==

MICRO #2 of 16

Estate of **Joseph LATHAM** of Groton CT. <New London CT PR #A:332-3, 379-381>
Inventory taken 14 Mar. 1705/6 by James MORGAN, Nehemiah SMITH, Walter BODDINGTON. Division dated 25 Feb. 1706/7, heirs: wife Mary, sons Cary (eldest), William, John, Jasper, Joseph, Samuel, Thomas; to John KENEY in right of his wife Elizabeth deceased, eldest daughter of dec'd; to Benjamin STARR in right of his wife Lydia.

Will of **Joseph LATHAM**, of Lyme CT. <New London CT PR #E:435-6>
...dated 18 Sept. 1746...mentions wife Patience; sons: David, John; daughters: (eldest unnamed), Mary, Abigail (under 18); brother Jasper LATHAM, brother-in-law Benjamin STARR.

Will of **Samuel CHESEBROUGH**, of Stonington CT. <New London CT PR #D:248,319>
...dated 19 Jan. 1735/6...wife Priscilla; son Amos; daus Mary HEWIT, Priscilla PALMER, Hannah SHAW, Sarah, Prudence (under 18); grandchildren Nathaniel HEWIT, Mary & Priscilla CHESEBROUGH; most of wearing apparel to go to Thomas PALMER. Witnesses: James DEAN, Samuel CHESEBROUGH Jr., Nathan CHESEBROUGH. Inv. taken 6 May 1736 by Joseph PALMER, William THOMPSON. (Inv. states Samuel d. 2 Mar. 1735/6.)

Estate of **Jabez CHESEBROUGH**, of Stonington CT. <New London CT PR #C:508,509>
Adm. 6 July 1731 by Samuel CHESEBROUGH. Inventory of Jabez CHESEBROUGH who died 13 June 1731. Presented 11 Aug. 1731 by Samuel CHESEBROUGH of Stonington CT.

Estate of **Samuel SPRAGUE**, of Rochester MA. <Plymouth Co.PR #19114, 8:344,480>
(Original) Bond dated 17 Sept. 1740, Ruth SPRAGUE, widow & Noah SPRAGUE app'td. adms. of estate. Sureties: Caleb BLACKWELL, David NYE, yeomen of Rochester. Witnesses: Jacob TOMSON, John TOMSON 3rd.
(8:480) Inventory taken 12 Dec. 1740 by Isaac HOLMES, Nathaniel SNOW, Nathaniel GOODSPEED. Pew in meeting house valued at £2.10s, total estate, £601.1s.

Priscilla HAMMOND of Rochester to **Ebenezer CLAP Jr.** of Rochester <Plymouth Co.Deeds 48:260>
...3 Nov. 1763...Priscilla HAMMOND, widow...for £8 sold to Ebenezer CLAP Jr., tanner...one sixth part of all the Lands & Cedar Swamps in Rochester aforesaid that our hon'd. Father Samuel SPRAGUE late of said Rochester deceased dyed seized of and left intestate. Dated 3 Nov. 1763. Witnesses: Nathaniel SPRAGUE, Nathaniel BASSETT. Ack. 5 Nov. 1763. Rec. 6 Jan. 1764.

Estate of **Samuel SPRAGUE**, of Rochester MA. <Plymouth Co.Deeds 48:260>
...10 Dec. 1763...division of lands...which descends to his children by heirship in the following manner...to Noah SPRAGUE (eldest son); children of Nathaniel SPRAGUE; children of Micah SPRAGUE; children of Elisabeth CHAPMAN, Priscilla HAMMOND. Noah SPRAGUE has bot right of Elizabeth CHAPMAN, Ebenezer CLAP Jr. has bot right of Priscilla HAMMOND, Melatiah WHITE has bot right of the children of Micah SPRAGUE.

Benjamin & Ruth BUMPAS of Wareham to Melatiah White of Rochester <Plymouth Co.Deeds 52:79>
...12 Jan. 1763... 1/6 of all lands & cedar swamp that our hon'd Grandfather Samuel SPRAGUE late of said Rochester deceased dyed seized of...(Ruth's 1/6 part).

Ichabod ALDEN, of Duxbury MA. <Plymouth Co.PR #110, 25:282, 27:4, 28:528, 29:300>
(Original) Bond dated 12 Feb. 1779, Mary ALDEN, widow, app'td. adm. Sureties: C. PARTRIDGE, John HOUSE. Witnesses: Joshua BARSTOW, Elizabeth CUSHING.
(25:282) Inventory by Judah DELANO, Bezaleel ALDEN, C. PARTRIDGE, sworn 7 June 1779.
(29:300) Creditors dated 6 June 1785, "late company of Richard CLARKE & Sons", Pelham WINSLOW, George UFFEL, Nathaniel GOODWIN, Edward WINSLOW, Capt. John GRAY, Dr. Isaac WINSLOW, Hon. George PARTRIDGE, Bezaleel ALDEN, Dr. Eleazer HARLOW, Calvin PARTRIDGE, Warren WESTON, Dr. Ezekiel BROWN, Capt. Robert ALLEN.

Guardianship of **John ALDEN, Rebecca ALDEN**, of Duxbury MA. <Plymouth Co.PR #130, 26:66,67>
(Original) Bond dated 7 June 1779, Mary ALDEN, widow, app'td. guardian to John & Rebecca ALDEN, minors under 14, children of Ichabod ALDEN, dec'd. Sureties: Eliphez PRIOR, Samuel ALDEN Jr. Witnesses: Seth BRADFORD, Isaac LOTHROP.
(26:66) Letter dated 7 June 1779, Mary ALDEN app'td. guardian of son John ALDEN, age 4 years.
(26:67) Letter dated 7 June 1779, Mary ALDEN app'td. guardian of dau. Rebecca Partridge ALDEN, age 2 years.

Estate of **Samuel ALDEN**, of Duxbury MA. <Plymouth Co.PR #169, 34:181, 37:67,164-165, 40:209>
(Original) Bond dated 12 Apr. 1799, George PARTRIDGE of Duxbury app'td. adm. Sureties: Isaac BARKER of Pembroke, George B. NYE of Rochester. Witnesses: Zebulon HASKELL, Isaac LOTHROP.
(37:67) Inventory taken by Samuel LORING, Philip CHANDLER, Isaiah ALDEN, sworn 18 July 1799, total $1918.75, incl. marsh in Kerswell Meadow.
(37:164) Dower warrent 17 Aug. 1799, assigned 18 Nov. 1799, allowed 25 Nov. 1799, to widow Abigail ALDEN.
(40:209) Account by George PARTRIDGE allowed 13 Apr. 1805, land sold to following: Howland SAMPSON, Seva CHANDLER, Abner SAMPSON, Perez BRADFORD, Uriah SPRAGUE, Asa CHANDLER; paid following creditors: Oliver DELANO, Samuel CHANDLER, Nathaniel WINSOR, Abigail WESTON, Dr. FULLER, Benjamin ALDEN, Eliphaz PRIOR, Luke WADSWORTH, John ALDEN, William

FREEMAN, Rebecca FRAZAR, Amos BROWN, Isaac SAMPSON, Constant SAMPSON, Samuel DARLING, Judah ALDEN, Joseph CUSHMAN, William LORING, Frederick PETERSON, John SAMPSON, Amherst ALDEN, Joshua WINSOR, Nehemiah PETERSON, Seth SPRAGUE, Jo. WADSWORTH, Robert CUSHMAN, Nat. HODGES, Charles CUSHMAN, Samuel LORING, Elijah SAMSON, Ezra MORTON, Seth DREW, Benjamin PRIOR, Jo. ADAMS, Joshua CUSHMAN, John RANDELL, Thomas BAKER, Jo. BREWSTER, Philip CHANDLER, Joshua WINSLOW, Mallica DELANO, Jethro TAYLOR, Bildad WASHBURN, Isaiah ALDEN, Gideon HARLOW, Peleg CHANDLER, Asa CHANDLER, Seth WASHBURN, Jed. HOLMES, Samuel LORING, Peleg GULLIVERS, S. RUSSELL.

ELIZABETH ALDEN[2] (John[1])

Will of **George GRENELL/GRINNELL** of Saybrook CT. <Guilford CT PR #8:105,112>
...29 Apr. 1755...wife **Mary**...to **William GRENELL** my eldest son all my lands... where he now liveth which I bought of **Jonathan SPENCER**...also one half of my fifty pound right in Oyster River Quarter...To my son **Daniel GRENELL**...the other half of the fifty pound right ...To my seven daughters **Mary, Anne, Phebe, Rebeckah, Lydia, Lucy** and **Temperance** ...62 ounces of good coined silver a piece...to be paid to them the day they shall come to the age of 18 years ...to my two sons **William** and **Daniel**...all of my husbandry utensils... Witnesses: Rev. William WORTHINGTON, Abraham POST, Temperance WORTHINGTON. Pr. 23 Nov. 1759, Inv. 25 Dec. 1759.

Will of **Samuel SEABURY** of Duxbury MA. <Plymouth Co.Wills 4:1:93,94>
...21 Sept. 1680...To my wife **Martha** my best bed together with all the furniture therof...To my eldest daughter **Elizabeth,** the second best bed with the beding belonging to it...To my second daughter **Sarah** a cow if shee return into New England...To my son **Samuell** my fowling peice and my Cuttler axe and all my surjean bookes and instruments...To my third daughter **Hannah** my third best bed and the furniture...To my second son **John** my birding peice and my muskett...To my son **Joseph** those great silver buttons which I usually weare...To my daughter **Martha** my fourth bed...also To my eldest son **Samuell** my house and all my housing in Duxburrow...viz: ninety acres att home, forty att the iland Creeke pond, six acres of Meddow Ground att the said pond, four att home, two and an halfe att the Gurnett, two acres bought of **Phillip WASHBURNE,** two bought of **Caleb COOKE,** seaven acres nye the dwelling house of **John ROUSE Sen,** provided that hee allow his present mother in law ffree liberty peaceably to inhabite the said house during the whole tearm of her widdow hood...To my son **John** seaventy acres of upland and seaven acres of meddow, lying nye the North River att a place called the brick kills...To my son **Joseph** halfe a parte of a parsell of land which I had of my father **William PAYBODY** which land lyeth nye Pinguen hole on the backside of Sandwich...I will that my negro servant Nimrod be disposed off either by heir or sale. Codicil ...8 Oct. 1680 the abovesaid **Samuell SABERREY** did declare that hee had, att his former wives death given a negro gerle called Jane, now dwelling with **John Rouse Jr.** to his daughter **Elizabeth,** which former gift hee now confeirmed...and alsoe upon further considerations, hee did judge his prsent wife **Martha Saberrey,** to be with child. Will & codicil witnessed by: Ichabod WISWAL, Ralph THACHER. Inventory taken 27 Oct. 1681, no real estate mentioned, items: "Baxters Christian Directory", Ł1.10s; "Nicholas Culpeppers Practice of Phisick", Ł1.4s; Culpepers Annotomy", 3s; "The Phesitions Practice", 1s; "A Latten Herball", Ł1.10s; "A Greek Lexecon", 2s; "Peltons Abstract of the Statutes", 4s; "Serjeants Clossett", 2s6d; 1 silver seale, 1s; Surjeans Instruments, 12s; 1 latten bible, 4s; 1 negroe called Nimrod, Ł26; 1 negro man 7 years; his wife and three children for ever, not valued.

MICRO #3 of 16

Joseph CHILES/CHILDS of Marshfield to **Samuel SEABURY** of Duxbury. <Plymouth Co.Deeds, 12:4>
...1 May 1707...Joseph CHILES, mason and Elizabeth his wife for Ł20 sold to Ensign Samuel SEABURY ...all our or either of our Right...farm whereon the sd Samuel SEABURY now dwells containing in the whole about one hundred acres of upland meadow pasture & woodland...in Duxborough aforesd and also of and into seven acres of salt marsh meadow land in two parcells at or near Duckhill in Duxborough aforesd and also of and into one piece of swamp land meadow containing about two acres lying and being at ye southward end of Island Creek Pond in Duxborough...all which farm, meadows and premisses were formerly ye lands of **Mr. Samuel SEABURY** and **Patience** his wife in ye right of her ye sd Patience Seabury of Duxborough both deceased parents of the abovesd Ensign **Samuel SEABURY** & **Elizabeth CHILES.** Signed by Joseph & Elizabeth Chiles. Witnesses: Isaac THOMAS, Abraham HOWLAND. Ack. by both grantors 4 July 1707. Rec. 17 May 1716.

Joseph CHILES/CHILDS and wife **Elizabeth (SEABURY) Chiles** against **John SEABURY** <Plymouth Co.PR>
...26 Feb. 1709...Joseph CHILES of Marshfield in the county of Plimouth aforesd bricklayer and Elizabeth his wife who is the daughter of **Mr. Samuel Seabery** & **Patience** his wife late of Duxbury ... deceased which said Patience was the daughter & sole heire of **Mr. William KEMP** formerly of Duxbury aforesd deceased...Against Mr. **John SEABURY** son of the aforesd **Samuel SEABERY** late of Duxbury aforesd but now of Norwich in the Colony of Conecticott...Joseph Chiles & Elizabeth his wife allegeth, complaneth & propoundeth as followeth...That the said William KEMP (together with other lands) dyed seized of fourscore acres of upland & a parcell of meadow land sittuate lying & being at the North River at a place called the Brickills in Mattakeset in Duxbury...Patience, as sole heir to her father, the said William KEMP...married the said Samuel SEABERY by whom she had **Samuel SEABERY, John SEABERY** the defendt, **Elizabeth** the plaintiff & **Hannah**...That according to

the Laws of the Colony of Plimoth...one fift part...doth belong to the said Elizabeth CHILES the Plaintiff as descended to her from her mother the aforesd Patience...the plantiffs...pray that the said...acres...be devided into five eaquall parts...the said John SEABERY the Defendt...doth unjustly gainsay & will not permitt the same to be done. Dated 26 Feb. 1709 before Hon. Nathaniel Thomas, Judge of Probate. John SEABERRY served at Groton CT 6 June 1710.

Will of **William FOBES**, of Little Compton RI. <Bristol Co.PR 3:111,112,114,115,187,535-538, 8:133> <3:112>...4 Nov. 1712...To my son in Law **Joseph SEABERY**...fifteen acres of land in the first 24 acre lott in sd Little Compton on the south side of said lot...To my son in Law **Josiah SAWER** and to his now wife **Martha SAWYER**...all the remainder of the foresaid twenty four acre lott on the north side...To my daughter **Elizabeth BRIGGS** the wife of **William BRIGGS** the bed and furniture which is now in her possession which I lent her & the great Brass Kettle. Further I give to her Eldest son **Louet BRIGGS** and to my Daughter **Constant LITTLE** and to my Grandson **Fobes SOUTHWORTH** and to my Grandson **Samuel SEABERY** and to my Grandson **John SAWYER** that acre of land which I have lyeing near the Meeting house in said Little Compton in the north east corner of that land that was formerly **Daniel BUTLER's** land...to my son in Law **John LITTLE** and to my daughter his now wife **Constant**...all my land lyeing on the west side of the great high way being part of the eleventh great lott in...Little Compton...my said Daughter in her life time may bequeath to my Grand Daughter **Rebeccah SOUTHWORTH** or to any other of my Grand children one hundred pounds out of said estate...To my Grandson **Fobes SOUTHWORTH** the westward end of the fourth Great lot...from the great Highway to the sea & pond with the Ferry boat, Wharffe & houseing and all...land lyeing between the said land and creek which land I had in leiu of a meadow Lot lyeing in Sacconet Neck with halfe the third twenty four acre lott in said Little Compton...I further will and order that my sd Grandson **Fobes SOUTHWORTH** shall pay...unto my Grand Daughter **Rebecca SOUTHWORTH** his sisser (sic) one hundred pound in good silver money or in Bills of Credit if then passable at the day of her Marriage or when she shall arive to the age of twenty one years...And I Further will and appoint Justice **Thomas CHURCH** of Little Compton to take that part of this estate which I have herein given to my Grandson **Fobes SOUTHWORTH** and to be his Gaurdian...till he shall come to the age of Twenty one years. And further desire that my son in law **Joseph SEABERY** and **Silvester RICHMOND** be overseers...Witnesses: Thomas GRAY, Joseph BLACKMAN, Thomas CHURCH. <3:115> <u>Inventory</u> taken 12 Nov. 1712:...of the Estate of **Lt. William FOBES** who decased the 6th day of Novembr 1712 by Thomas GRAY, Edward RICHMOND and John WOOD...Among the items: a cane and gloves, 14s; a brace of pistols & houlsters, £2; a ferry boat & wharf, £18; about 30 acers of land be it more or less lying in the 4th great Lott att the west end of sd lott with two smaull housses, £180; halfe the old windmill, £12; 50 acers of land more or less lying on the west side the highway in the eleventh great lott with the housing, £350; the est end of the same lott on the est side the highway being 60 acers more or less, £270; one acer of land lying by the old meeting hous, £8; one 24 acer lott & halfe of land, £30; an Negro woman & child, £15; two Indian boys with their clothing, £10. Total amount of inventory: £1085.4s. <3:111,114> <u>Will Contested</u>: Bristol 14 Nov. 1712 by **Edward SOUTHWORTH** of Little Compton...against any will pretended to be made by the sd Mr. **William FOBES**... <3:187> Pr. 4 Dec. 1712. <3:535-38> <u>Account</u>: by Thomas CHURCH, betw. 1713-16, lengthy, debts incl. £3 to John Stephens for grave stones. <8:133> <u>Receipt</u>: 27 Sept. 1731 **Rebecca SOUTHWORTH** of Scituate...received of my brother **Fobes SOUTHWORTH**...one hundred pounds...legacy by my honoured Grandfather Mr. **William FOBES**. Witnesses: David LITTLE Jr., David LITTLE.

<u>PLYMOUTH COUNTY DEEDS, Grantors & Grantees:</u>

<9:283> - 23 May 1712 - Joseph CHILDS & Timothy ROGERS both of Marshfield (land exchange).
<9:11> - 20 June 1711 - Joseph CHILDS of Marshfield to Charles LITTLE of Plymouth.
<9:213> - 9 May 1712 - Joseph CHILDS & John BARKER both of Marshfield to Ephraim LITTLE of Marshfield.
<10:1:134> - 1 Apr. 1712 - Joseph CHILDS of Marshfield.
<12:4> - 1 May 1707 - Joseph CHILES & wf. Elizabeth of Marshfield.
<14:36> - 14 July 1716 - Joseph CHILES to Anthony EAMES, both of Marshfield.

William FOBES of Little Compton to son in law William BRIGGS, and dau. Elizabeth BRIGGS, his wf. Deed dated 10 June 1708. <Bristol Co.Deeds 6:64>

William KEMP, adm. 2 Nov. 1641 by Mrs. Elizabeth KEMP, admx. Inv. dated 5 Apr. 1642. <Plymouth Co.Court Orders 2:31,47> (See MD 4:75-82)

Joseph SEABURY of Tiverton to **Josiah SAWER** of Tiverton. <Bristol Co.RI Deeds 13:278> ...30 June 1720, Joseph SEABURY, yeoman, for £15 sold to Josiah SAWER, wheelwright...A certain peice of land...in Little Compton...which lott did Originally belong unto **William FOBES** deceased. Ack. 13 July 1720. Rec. 18 July 1720.

Joseph SEABURY of Tiverton to **Daniel EARLE** of Tiverton. <Bristol Co.RI Deeds 31:106> ...16 Apr. 1722, Joseph SEABURY, yeoman, for £65 sold to Daniel EARLE, yeoman...land in Tiverton containing twenty acres...reserving a rod in breadth upon ye north side ye whole length of ye sd twenty acres which was excepted in a deed from William MANCHESTER/MAYSTER. Ack. 14 Aug. 1727. Rec. 16 Sept. 1742.

William FOBES of Little Compton to **Joseph SEABERY** of Little Compton. <Bristol Co.Deeds 4:395> ...1 Feb. 1704/5, William FOBES for £200 sold to Joseph SEABERY...land in Little Compton amongst the hundred accre lotts so called. Contayning seventy accres...being ye fourth lot in number bounded westerly by the wind-mill...southerly by a drift High way, northward by the land of Peter COLLOMER, eastward by a High way...together with the fulling mill... Ack. 22 Feb. 1704/5.

Joseph SEABURY of Tiverton to **Samuel WILLBUR** of Little Compton. <Bristol Co.Deeds 17:512>
...25 Jan. 1717/8...Joseph SEABURY, yeoman, for £36 sold to Samuel WILBUR Sr....land at sd Little Compton containing by estimation Eighteen acres...on the Eastward of a place called Cole Broock within a tract of land which the proprietors of the Land of sd Little Compton surrendered up to Capt. Edward RICHMOND deceast...being the sixth lott in number...north by the fifth eighteen acre lott belonging to John PALLMER...south by the seventh <17:513> eighteen acre lott formerly belonging to Silvester RICHMOND. Ack. 8 May 1725. Rec. 12 Oct. 1727.

Joseph SEABURY of Tiverton to **Nathaniel PAINE, Samuel GALLOP, Nathaniel BLAGROVE, John ROGERS, William SOUTHWORTH.** <Bristol Co.Deeds 11:52>
...13 Feb. 1717...indenture made between Joseph SEABURY of the one part and Nathaniel PAINE, Samuel GALLOP, Nathaniel BLAGROVE, John ROGERS, William SOUTHWORTH Commissioners...witnesseth that the said Joseph SEABERY for £100 sold fifty acres of land...in Little Compton...together with all ...houses...buildings... on a mortgage of £100.

Thomas LAKE of Tiverton to **Joseph SEABURY** of Tiverton. <Bristol Co.Deeds 13:397>
...6 Mar. 1717/8...Thomas LAKE, cooper, for £48, sold to Joseph SEABURY, yeoman, a certain tract of land...in Tiverton...containing twenty acres more or less... Witnesses: John Lake, Benjamin Lake. Ack. 2d Tues. Apr. 1721 by Benjamin LAKE. Rec. 1 May 1721.

Bartholomew HUNT of Tiverton to **Joseph SEABURY** of Little Compton RI. <Bristol Co.Deeds 10:493>
...20 Mar. 1716/7...Bartholomew HUNT, yeoman for £900 sold to Joseph SEABURY, yeoman...the first percell...in sd Tiverton containing eight acres...the second tract...part of the said first great lott and part of the second great lott of land in number amongst the first Division of great lotts of land in said Little Compton...the whole containing one hundred & sixty acres more or less. Ack. 23 Mar. 1716/7 by Bartholomew & Martha HUNT.

Joseph SEABURY of Tiverton & **Thomas DRING, Peter HORSWELL.** <Bristol Co.Deeds 11:178>
...8 Aug. 1717...Jonathan HEAD and Thomas CHURCH of Little Compton and Philip TABER of Tiverton, chosen to arbitrate between Joseph SEABURY as Guardian to Benjamin LAKE of Tiverton...& Peter HORSSWEL and Thomas DRING of Little Compton...for Damages that the sd Benjamin LAKE Received at Robert WOODMAN's husking in October 1715...ordered Horsswell and Dring to pay Joseph SEABURY £5 and to pay the costs. Ack. 30 Sept. 1717. Rec. 9 Oct. 1717.

Joseph SEABURY of Tiverton to **John HUNT** of Little Compton. <Bristol Co.Deeds 13:107>
...19 Feb. 1719...Joseph SEABURY for £4 sold to John HUNT, yeoman...a lot of land in Little Compton containing about seventy acres... in consideration that the said John HUNT doth for Ever here after quitt all his claime in and to a percell of land containing about eighty acres which my Honoured Father gave me by deed of gift. Ack. 24 Feb. 1719/20.

John HUNT of Little Compton to **Leiut. Joseph SEABERY** of Tiverton. <Bristol Co.Deeds 13:156>
...20 Feb. 1719...John HUNT surrendered to Leiut. Joseph SEABERY...all my Right in a Tract...of land in Little Compton...now in the Possession of the said Joseph SEABURY it being the south half of that tract of land my Father HUNT sold to ye sd Joseph SEABURY which south half my father had formerly given me a deed of Gift of. Ack. 24 Feb. 1719/20. Rec. 23 Apr. 1720.

Joseph SEABURY of Tiverton to son **Benjamin SEABURY** of Little Compton. <Bristol Co.Deeds 27:178>
...16 Feb. 1735/6...Joseph SEABURY, yeoman, to son Benjamin SEABURY, tanner...land...partly in Tiverton & partly in Little Compton where is now Dwelling house standeth with severall other Buildings convenient for his Tanning Business...which sd tract contains by measure three acres & sixty one rods. Ack. in Mar. 1735/6. Rec. 13 Mar. 1737.

Joseph SEABURY of Tiverton to son **Samuel SEABURY** of Little Compton. <Bristol Co.Deeds 31:28>
15 Oct. 1739, Joseph SEABURY, yeoman to son Samuel SEABURY, labourer...land in Little Compton ...being ye easterly end of my homstead farm...bounded easterly on land belonging to John SOYER partly & partly on land of Samuel TOMKINS, southerly partly on land of Isaac CASE partly on land of William RICHMOND...westerly on ye remaining part of sd homstead, northerly on land belonging to William BRIGGS. Ack. 8 June 1742. Rec. 9 June 1742.

Daniel SMITH of Bristol to **Joseph SEABERRY** of Tiverton. <Bristol Co.Deeds 17:503>
...18 Mar. 1726/7...Daniel SMITH for £100, sold to Joseph SEABERRY, gentleman...in Bristol...one dwelling house and one eighth part of an acre of land...bounded easterly by Nathaniel BYFIELD late of Bristol, southerly by a street...westerly & northerly by sd Smiths own land...also free Liberty...to fetch water from the well belonging to sd Smith...for the space of four years. Ack. 30 Oct. 1727 by Daniel & Elizabeth SMITH. Rec. 30 Oct. 1727.

Will of **Daniel ALLEN.** <Bristol Co.PR 59:414, 111:209, 130:81, 148:200>
...16 Mar. 1807...mentions wife Betty, sons Wesson, Humphrey, Pardon, Joseph, Gideon, John and two daughters Mary CORNELL and Rhoda MACOMBER; granddaughter Sarah WILLCOX, dau of my dau Ruth SHEARMAN deceased; the other children of said daughter deceased, viz: Nancy EARL, Barbary SHEAR-, MAN, Robert SHEARMAN, Patience SHEARMAN, Matilda SHEARMAN. Pr. 30 July 1822.

Will of **Josiah SAWYER** of Tiverton, yeoman. <Bristol Co.PR 8:27,30,34>
...15 Sept 1733...To my son John SAWYER...my thirty acre lott of land in Little Compton & on the west side of the pine swompt & part of the first six acre lott in number in sd Tiverton...fifteen acres...and twenty acres of the same lott begining at that peice of land I sold to **Richard HEART**

Junr....and also part of the twenty four acre lott the first in number in sd Little Compton... containing about three acres...& also the liveing in my dwelling house till my son **Josiah** comes of age...To my son **Josiah SAWYER**...all the rest of my land...my son **John SAWYER** pay...unto his sister **Hannah WILLISTONE** ten shillings & five pound a year...after her deceas to pay her heirs eighty pounds...& one good feather bed...To daughters **Mercy, Mary, Abigail, Priscilla**, one good feather bed each...To wife Martha one good feather bed & beding & fifty pound in Housal Stuf... my son **John** shall pay his Mother five pound in bills of Credit yearly...my son **Josiah** shall pay his Mother five pound yearly...my four daughters shall pay their sd Mother forty shillings a peice...yearly. Witnesses: Samuel CRANDALL, Isaac CASE, Joseph TOMPKINS. <u>Inventory</u> 15 Nov. 1733, by Nathaniel SEARLE, Gorge PEARSE, Samuel TOMPKINS. Items incl. one negroh man, £100; housing and land in Tiverton, £600; land in Little Compton, £810. Pr. 20 Nov. 1733.

William FOBES of Little Compton to **Martha SEBURY.** <Bristol Co.Deeds 3:248>
...19 Jan. 1700/01...William FOBES, yeoman for love & affection unto my Daughter in Law Martha SEBURY...six pounds...and land in Little Compton...being about twelve acres. Rec. 10 Apr.1701

Zaccheus BUTT of Little Compton to **Martha SEBERRY** of Little Compton. <Bristol Co.Deeds 4:281>
...14 Feb. 1703/4...Zaccheus BUTT, carpenter for £10,12s mortgaged to Martha SEBERRY, a certain tract of land...twenty eight acres...in Little Compton. Ack. 20 Mar. 1704. Rec. 20 May 1704.

<u>MICRO #4 of 16</u>

Will of **Isaac SIMMONS**, yeoman of Duxbury. <Plymouth Co.PR #18330, 19:543>
...31 Aug. 1764...wife Lydia; sons Levi, Jehiel; daughters Zenijah, wf of Samuel HOLMES, Martha LOWDEN, Lusanna (under 18), Lydia (under 15); grandson Isaac, son of Jehiel; sister Priscilla to be maintained by Lydia & Levi. Pr. 9 Sept. 1767.

Will of **Levi SIMMONS**, of Duxbury. <Plymouth Co.PR 36:395,465>
...28 June 1798...wife Lydia; sons Levi, James, Lewis; daughters Sarah RANDALL, Lydia BARSTOW. Witnesses: Josiah HATCH, Benjamin SIMMONS Jr., Asa WATERMAN. <u>Inv.</u> ordered 17 July 1798, including homestead in Duxbury, 1/2 pew in South Meeting house in Marshfield. Pr. 17 July 1798.

Estate of **John SIMMONS**, yeoman of Duxbury. <Plymouth Co.PR 8:43,125,180>
<u>Adm.</u> 6 Aug. 1739 to Susanna Simmons, widow. <u>Inv.</u> taken 23 Aug. 1739 by Pelatiah WEST, Samuel WESTON both of Duxbury and Thomas TRACY of Marshfield. <u>Div.</u> 17 Dec. 1739 as follows: to the widow, her thirds; eldest son John, dau Ruth, son Joel, dau Leah; all five swore to div. 7 Jan. 1740.

Will of **Joseph SIMMONS**, yeoman, of Duxbury. <Plymouth Co.PR 10:152>**<1>**
...14 Mar. 1754...wife Mary; eldest son Nathaniel; son Jedediah; dau Rebeckah PETERSON; grandson Joseph SIMMONS. Witnesses: Samuel WESTON, Elnathan WESTON, Judah DELINO. Pr. 1 June (1761?).

Nathaniel SIMMONS, of Duxbury to **Briggs ALDEN**, of Duxbury. <Plymouth Co.Deeds 51:121>
...22 Oct. 1765...Nathaniel SIMMONS for £39.17.4. sold to Briggs ALDEN...salt marsh in Duxbury... being the whole of said Nathaniel SIMMONS right in a certain Island called Long Island and also a ...cedar swamp...bounded by Glass' ten acre lot and land of Benjamin CHANDLER, Thomas HUNT and Judah DELANO. Witnesses: Jedidiah SIMMONS, Benjamin PRIOR Jr. Rec. 26 Oct. 1765.

Nathaniel SIMMONS & **Jedidiah SIMMONS** of Duxbury to **Joshua STANFORD.** <Plymouth Co.Deeds 52:37>
...22 Oct. 1765...Nathaniel SIMMONS & Jedidiah SIMMONS for £16 sold to Joshua STANFORD of Duxbury ...wood land...a part of the thirteenth & sixteenth lots of upland in the second division of the Comons of said Duxborough & Pembroke...bounded by land of Eliphaz PRIOR, Joshua CHANDLER, Capt. Wait WADSWORTH. Witnesses: Eliphaz PRIOR, Benjamin PRIOR Jr. Rec. 29 Oct. 1765.

Nathaniel SIMMONS of Duxbury to **Joshua CUSHMAN** of Duxbury. <Plymouth Co.Deeds 85:134>
...8 May 1767...Nathaniel SIMMONS, yeoman, for £7.13.4. sold to Joshua CUSHMAN, housewright... seven acres more or less...part of the nineteenth lot in the second division of the Commons...of Duxbury & Pembroke...bounded by land of Phinehas SPRAGUE, Thomas HUNT. Witnesses: Andrew BRADFORD, John WADSWORTH Jr. Rec. 30 Mar. 1799.

Nathaniel SIMMONS of Pembroke to **Nathan SOUL** of Duxbury. <Plymouth Co.Deeds 53:260>
...22 Oct. 1767...Nathaniel SIMMONS, yeoman, for £40 sold to Nathan SOUL, mariner...saltmarsh in Duxbury...bounded by land of Benjamin SOUTHWORTH, Nathan SOUL...four acres more or less...formerly belonging to Joseph BREWSTER. Witnesses: Judah DELANO, James SOULE. Rec. 10 Dec. 1767.

Nathaniel SIMMONS of Waldoboro to **Elijah DAMON** of Plymouth. <Plymouth Co.Deeds 58:51>
...13 Sept. 1773...Nathaniel SIMMONS, husbandman, for £133.6.8 sold to Elijah DAMON, husbandman ...farm and land in Pembroke...the easterly part of the farm that I bought of Josiah KEEN Esq. ...thirty six acres more or less...bounded by...John BONNEY's land which he bought of Elijah FAXON...Josiah CUSHING's land...John BONNEY's land which he bought of Solomon LEVITT...William PHILLIPS'...land (I) sold to Blany PHILLIPS... Witnesses: John HUNT, Paul CASH. Ack. 6 Nov. 1773 by Nathaniel & Mercy SIMMONS. Rec. 13 May 1774.

Nathaniel SIMMONS of Duxbury to **Judah DELANO** of Duxbury. <Plymouth Co.Deeds 54:233>
...7 July 1766...Nathaniel Simmons, yeoman for £300 sold to Judah Delano, yeoman...all my homestead farm...with my cedar swamp laying in North Hill Marsh...also a small piece of wood land

laying at a place called Stanford's Neck. Reference may be had to the records of Nathaniel SIMMON's deeds for the bounds of said lands. Witnesses: Micah SOULE, Josiah SOULE. Ack. 7 July 1766 by Nathaniel & Mercy SIMMONS. Rec. 12 Apr. 1769.

Nathaniel SIMMONS of Pembroke to **Blaney PHILLIPS.** <Plymouth Co.Deeds 58:119>
...3 Sept. 1770...Nathaniel SIMMONS, husbandman, for £226.13.4 sold to Blaney PHILLIPS, husbandman...forty one acres in Pembroke bounded by land of...John BONNEY which he bought of Elijah FAXON...Deacon PHILLIPS'...Blaney PHILLIPS'...land Gideon BISBE deceased dyed seized of...and Jabesh COLE's...being the whole of that which we now call the Great Pasture, which I the said Nathaniel SIMMONS bought of Josiah KEEN Esqr. And also a drift way through the land Jesse THOMAS bought of John GOULD...Witnesses: Jacob READ, Dorothy SIMMONS. Signed by Nathaniel & Mercy SIMMONS. Ack. 13 Oct. 1770 by Nathaniel SIMMONS.[2]

Joseph SIMMONS of Waldoborough to **Thomas SIMMONS** of Waldoborough. <Lincoln Co.Deeds 94:202>
...2 May 1805...Joseph SIMMONS, yeoman, for $300.00 sold to Thomas SIMMONS, housewright...forty acres in Waldoborough...bounded by land of...Matthias STORERS, Job SIMMONS. Signed by Joseph SIMMONS. Ack. 10 July 1806. Rec. 11 June 1816.

Joseph SIMMONS of Waldoborough to **Job SIMMONS** of Waldoborough. <Lincoln Co.Deeds 76:35>
...10 July 1806...Joseph SIMMONS, yeoman, for $200.00 sold to Job SIMMONS...12 acres in Waldoborough bounded by land of Matthias STORERS, Job SIMMONS, James SIMMONS. Witnesses: Thomas SIMMONS, James SIMMONS. Ack. 10 July 1806. Rec. 28 Dec. 1810.

Joseph SIMMONS, James Simmons of Waldoboro to **Frederick CASTNER.** <Lincoln Co.Deeds 72:5>
...23 Aug. 1809...Joseph SIMMONS & James SIMMONS, yeomen for $1150.00 sold to Frederick CASTNER of Waldoboro...forty acres in Waldoborough beginning at Miscongus River, bounded by land of... Matthia STORERS...land lately owned by Job SIMMONS & Zebedee SIMMONS...also one other piece of land bounded...by edge of Sleigo brook in John FEYLER's...by land of Edward MANNING...meaning to convey one half of the land formerly owned by Nathaniel SIMMONS. Signed by Joseph SIMMONS, James SIMMONS and Christiana SIMMONS. Ack. 23 Aug. 1809. Rec. 2 Sept. 1809.

Philip DELANO of Duxbury to **Joshua DELANO.** <Plymouth Co.Deeds 7:255>
...17 May 1706...Philip DELANO, son of Philip DELANO of Duxbury deceased had promised to deed to son Ebenezer DELANO of Duxbury deceased...now deeds to grandson Joshua DELANO, only son of Ebenezer...Martha, wf of Ebenezer, still living. Thomas DELANO, brother of Philip the grantor owns the other half.

Probate of **Joshua DELANO** of Kingston. Will dated 27 June 1750. <Plymouth Co.PR #6283, 12:167>
Inventory <12:264>; Division <12:15:126,128>. (not transcribed in files)

Will of **Moses SIMMONS** of Duxbury, yeoman. <Plymouth Co.PR 16:208,209>
...10 Apr. 1758...wife Rachel, eldest son Ichabod, son William; daughters Mercy, wf of Nathaniel SIMMONS, Lydia, wf of Judah DELANO, Deborah, wf of Jacob WESTON and Anna. Codicil 24 Feb. 1761. Pr. 3 Aug. 1761.

Moses SIMMONS, John WESTON of Duxbury to **Nathaniel THOMAS** of Plymouth <Plymouth Co.Deeds 15:93>
...(31 Feb.?) 1717/8...Moses SIMMONS & John WESTON sell to Nathaniel THOMAS, Gentleman, each 1 share the 2 shares being 1/5 of the 14th lot in Duxbury Beach. Ack. 3 Mar. 1718/9 by Moses SIMMONS, 14 Mar. 1718/9 by John WESTON.

MICRO #5 of 16

Will of **William BRIGGS** of Little Compton RI. <Newport RI Co.PR 1:114>
...2 Nov. 1750...To my well beloved daughter **Mary BRIGGS** & To my well beloved son **William BRIGGS** all my homestead farm where I now live...to be equally divided...my sd daughter shall take her choice of ye halves of ye sd land & housing...To daughter **Mary** all that part of my farm (which lyeth in Tiverton at ye place called Pachet Brook where my Honoured Father **John BRIGGS** formerly lived) which lyeth to the westward of the Cross Wall...To my well beloved son **Lovet BRIGGS**...the part of said farm which lyeth to the eastward of the Cross Wall...also to son **Lovet** twenty acers of land which lyeth in Tiverton & in ye Westward end of ye Seventh & eighth six score acer lotts formerly laid out between ye head of Puncatest out( ) & Dartmouth line...To my well beloved daughter **Judah WILLCOCK** that fifty pounds which she already had of me in Bills of Credit of ye old Tenour which is set down upon my Book of Accounts together also with three hundred & fifty pounds in Bills of Credit of ye old tenour which is due to me from my son **Fobes BRIGGS** upon a bond... morever I give to her my sd daughter my Negro Girl named Rose for term of life...To my well beloved daughter **Elizabeth SHIPPE** the sum of ten pounds in good passable Bills of publick Credit in New England old tenour...To my well beloved daughter **Cathron SISSON**, the sum of ten pounds...To my well beloved daughter **Sarah SHAW** the sum of ten pounds...To my well beloved daughter **Phebe ALMY** one hundred pounds...one good feather bed & beding...also my Negro Girl named Jenne...To son **Lovet** two cows, one mair & colt, two two year old steers & twenty sheep...To son **William** one good feather bed & beding, two cows & twenty sheep...To son **Fobes BRIGGS** the sum of five shillings... To my well beloved wife **Elisabeth BRIGGS** a good & sufficiant maintainance of all sorts of necessaries suiteble for such an aged woman...daughter **Mary** all the rest & residue of estate. Witnesses: Peter Horswell, Constant WOODMAN, Restcome SANFORD. Rec. 22 Dec. 1751.

Will of **Priscilla SOUTHWORTH** of Duxbury, spinster. <Plymouth Co.PR 16:204,205>
...5 June 1761...cousin William SOUTHWORTH & his children; brother John SOUTHWORTH; Alice SOUTHWORTH, dau. of William; Ruma SOUTHWORTH. The following Cousins: Ruth SOUL (dau. of Moses); Deborah (SOULE) Hunt, wf of John; Alice (SOULE)(Perry) King, wf of Edward; Mary WESTON (dau of Elizabeth (SOUTHWORTH) Weston); Mercy (SOUTHWORTH) Soul, wf of Micah; Mary (SOUTHWORTH) Weston, wf of Thomas; Mary SOUTHWORTH, wf of William; Hannah (SOUTHWORTH) Herrenton, widow; Elizabeth SOUTHWORTH; Deborah (SOUTHWORTH) Delano, wf of Reuben. Pr. 3 Aug. 1761.

Will of **Benjamin SOUTHWORTH** of Duxbury. <Plymouth Co.PR #18907, 14:141,144,158>
...1 Oct. 1751...wf Rebecca, eldest son Thomas, sons Constant, Obed, Jasher, daughters Hannah HERRINGTON, Elizabeth, Deborah. Inv. 21 July 1756, pr. 5 July 1756.

Estate of **Constant SOUTHWORTH** of Duxbury. <Plymouth Co.PR #18910, 6:76,101>
...10 Sept. 1731 Rebekah SOUTHWORTH, widow was appt'd. adm. John SOUTHWORTH and Moses SIMONS, yeomen, of Duxbury, gave bond for ₤500 as sureties. Witnesses: James WARREN, Penelope WARREN. Inv. dated 26 Oct. 1731 taken by John ALDEN, John CHANDLER; real estate consisted of farm, half a grist mill with one acre, valued at ₤580. Rebekah swore to inv. 1 Nov. 1731.

Will of **Thomas WESTON** of Duxbury, yeoman. <Plymouth Co.PR #22449, 25:7-10>
...22 Apr. 1776...wf Martha, sons Joseph & Thomas & daus Mary & Jane (the children of first wife) to receive woodland which was their mother's; daus Marcy, Rebecca, son Peleg. Witnesses: William SIMMONS, Abel CHANDLER, Judah DELANO. Inv. taken 19 June 1776 by Judah DELANO, Edward WINSLOW, William SIMMONS, all of Duxbury. Div. dated 23 May 1777. Agreement betw. heirs dated 10 Apr. 1780 between Warren WESTON & Martha WESTON, his wife on the one part and Joseph WESTON and the Guardian to Thomas & Peleg WESTON on the other part. That Martha WESTON, wife to Warren WESTON, shall hold 1/3 of real estate of Thomas WESTON, dec'd, exclusive of what came by his first wife. Signed by Warren WESTON, Martha WESTON, Joseph WESTON and Guardians Judah DELANO & Simeon SOULE. Witnesses: James SOULE, Reuben PETERSON.

Will of **Samuel WESTON** of Duxbury, yeoman. <Plymouth Co.PR #22440, 12:447,448,537>
...12 May 1750...wf Elizabeth, eldest son Samuel to receive home farm and 2/3 salt marsh, son Elnathan to receive 20 acres in Duxbury called Pine Brooke and 1/3 salt marsh, daus. Mary & Priscilla. Witnesses: Joshua CUSHMAN, Thomas WESTON, Jonathan PETERSON. Inv. taken 17 July 1752 by Jonathan PETERSON, Ezra ARNOLD, Nathaniel SIMONS, incl. 10 acres at Pine Brooke, meadow at Wood Island, home farm. Pr. 2 Mar. 1752.

Estate of **Thomas LORING** of Duxbury. <Plymouth Co.PR #13213, 8:242,9:169,10:222,291>
<8:242> 7 Jan. 1739, Capt. Gamaliel BRADFORD, Samuel SEABURY, Joseph FREEMAN, all of Duxbury, appt'd. to appraise the estate of Thomas LORING. <10:222> 20 May 1746, real estate divided among children, viz: Thomas, Simeon, Perez, Levi, Joshua, Deborah...to each one seventh part save to said Thomas the eldest son a double share or two seventh parts.
Guardianship of Children of **Thomas LORING**. <Plymouth Co.PR #13214>
<8:414> 12 Aug. 1741, **Simeon LORING**, chose...my Uncle Joshua LOREING of sd Duxbury...guardian.
<8:416> 12 Aug. 1741, Benjamin LOREING, of Duxbury, app'td. guardian of **Levi LORING**, minor.
<8:443> 28 Jan. 1741, Nathaniel LORING, of Duxbury, app'td. guardian of **Perez LORING**.

Estate of **Braddock LORING** of Boston. <Suffolk Co.PR #26369, 119:265>
...26 Mar. 1821...To the Honorable Thomas DAWES, Esquire, Judge of the Court of Probate within the County of Suffolk Humbly shows **Peres LORING** of Cambridge in the County of Middlesex, surveyor that **Braddock LORING**, late of Boston in the County of Suffolk, surveyor, was last an inhabitant of Boston ...leaving goods and estate of which administration is necessary; that your petitioner is the oldest son of said deceased and requests that administration on the estate... may be granted. Petition for administration granted.

Estate of **John SIMMONS** of Duxbury. <Plymouth Co.PR #18343, 3:388,400>
<3:388> Adm. 9 Feb. 1715 to widow Mercy SIMMONS, admx.
<3:400> Division 11 Feb. 1715/6, widow Mercy, Moses (youngest son) to receive 2/3 of all personal estate, mother's thirds on her death, and all lands, he to pay all debts and to pay his two hundred pounds to six brothers & two sisters, viz: John (eldest, double share), William, Isaac, Benjamin, Joseph & Joshua, Martha the wife of Samuel WEST, Rebeckah, the wife of Constant SOUTHWORTH. Signed by all. Witnesses: Elizabeth THOMAS, Elizabeth WADE.

Will of **Mercy SIMMONS**, widow of Duxbury. <Plymouth Co.PR #18371, 5:487-89>
...26 Sept. 1728...7 sons, John, William, Isaac, Benjamin, Joseph, Joshua; 2 daus Martha, Rebecca. Witnesses: John CHANDLER, John FULLERTON, Philip DELANO. Inv. 8 Nov. 1728, pr.26 Nov. 1728.

Benjamin ALDEN, Samuel ALDEN, Moses SIMMONS to **Benjamin CHANDLER**. <Plymouth Co.Deeds 27:37>
...8 Feb. 1731/2...Benjamin ALDEN, Samuel ALDEN, Moses SIMMONS, yeomen, all of Duxbury to **Benjamin CHANDLER**, housewright, of Duxbury, 3/10 of the 5th & 29th lots of Cedar Swamp in 2nd Division of Commons of Duxbury & Pembroke, sd lots being in Pembroke. Ack. 1 Mar. 1731/2.

Moses SIMMONS, husbandman of Duxbury to **John SOUTHWORTH**, yeoman of Duxbury. Dated 4 Mar. 1736/7, ack. 1 Dec. 1737. <Plymouth Co.Deeds 33:220> (Deed not specified.)

References to Benjamin SIMMONS, grantor & grantee: <Plymouth Co.Deeds>

10:348 - from Samuel SPRAGUE

110:69 - from Benjamin SIMMONS

References to Benjamin SIMMONS (cont-d) <Plymouth Co.Deeds>

10:350 - from Pelatiah WEST et al
11:61 - from John SIMMONS
11:145 - from John WADSWORTH
48:52 - from Indian woman
52:164 - from Esther ANTHONY, Indian
67:253 - from Abijah THOMAS
80:43 - from Joseph HEWET et al
80:50 - from James SPRAGUE et al
82:131 - from Peleg FORD
87:80 - from Benjamin SIMMONS Jr.
87:106 - with Abraham SIMMONS
110:69 - from Benjamin SIMMONS

12:83 - to John WADSWORTH
12:86 - to John WADSWORTH
13:204 - to Essex Trustees
39:61 - to William RICHARDS et al
83:219 - to Dean BRIGGS
83:220 - to Dean BRIGGS
84:190 - to Nathaniel FOSTER Jr.
87:80 - to Benjamin SIMMONS
87:106 - with Abraham SIMMONS
89:262 - to Joseph WHITE et al
89:265 - to Joseph WHITE

Benjamin SIMMONS, Guardianship of Children. <Plymouth Co.PR 5:321,322>
...25 Sept. 1727...Benjamin SIMMONS app'td. guardian of son Benjamin SIMMONS Jr. (minor betw. 14-21) son Abraham SIMMONS (minor betw. 14-21), son Zachariah SIMMONS (minor betw. 14-21), dau. Content SIMMONS (under 14).

Will of **Abraham SIMMONS** of Duxbury. <Plymouth Co.PR 8:435,436,465>
<8:435> 13 Sept. 1740...I Abraham SIMMONS...cordwainer, being bound on an Expedition to the West Indies...to my Brother **Zachariah SIMMONS** & his heirs...one fourth part of all my Estate...to my Brother **Benjamin SIMMONS** & his heirs one quarter part of all my Estate...to my sister **Mercy SIMMONS** one fourth part of my Estate...to my sister **Content SIMMONS** & her heirs one quarter part of all my Estate. Samuel WESTON app'td. Executor. Witnesses: Nathaniel SIMMONS, Mercy SIMMONS, Samuel WESTON Jr. <8:436> Pr. 2 Nov. 1741. <8:465> Inv. presented 6 May 1742.

Estate of **Benjamin SIMMONS** of Duxbury. <Plymouth Co.PR 11:50,170,172,206; 10:534>

<11:50> Adm. dated 2 May 1748, Benjamin SIMMONS, husbandman, of Duxborough, app'td. administrator of estate of Benjamin SIMMONS, yeoman, of Duxborough, deceased.
Bond dated 2 May 1748, signed by Aaron SIMMONS, Josiah KEEN, Isaac TAYOR. Witnesses: Simeon BRETT, Edward WINSOW.

<11:170> Inv. appraised 11 May 1748 by Joseph DELANO, Jonathan PETERSON, Aaron SOUL Jr. 13 July 1748, Aaron SIMMONS, executor, made oath. Items incl. Shoe leather, £8.14; hides & skins, £5.10; Shoemakers tools, £3; 70 acres of land, £880. Total £1547.5.9.

<11:172> Account sworn to 3 Apr. 1749 by Aaron SIMMONS. Debts due the estate from: Isaac WALKER, Elijah CUSHING, Reuben CARVER, Jonathan PETERSON, Eleazer HARLOW, Moses SIMMONS, Micah SOULE, William RICHARDS, Proprs. Committee. Payments made to: Samuel SPRAGUE, Abiah SIMMONS, Silas STETSON, Jonathan SOULE, Coroners & Jury of Inquest, Isaac WALKER, John McFARLAND, Samuel WESTON, Joshua DELANO, Nehemiah THOMAS, Abigail MAGONNE, David ALLEN, John SPRAGUE, Thomas WEST, John CHANDLER, Comfort BATES, John MURDOCK, Esq., William LAUT, Jacob DINGLEY, John WADSWORTH, Benjamin BESTOW.

<11:206> Div. 5 June 1749...widow Hannah SIMMONS, £393.19.2.; Children of Zachariah SIMMONS, eldest son dec'd, £23.15.4. lawfull silver money of New England or £49.0s7. in bills of credit; £7.2.1. silver or £14.13.4. bills to be paid at the decease of the widow to Benjamin SIMMONS, Mercy SIMMONS, Content SIMMONS, Hannah RICHARDS, wf of William RICHARDS, Betty SIMMONS, Priscilla SIMMONS, Abiah SIMMONS. Estate was settled on Aaron SIMMONS with he agreeing to pay out his siblings.

<10:534> Guardianship 3 Apr. 1749...Abiah SIMMONS, minor daughter of Benjamin SIMMONS, named Jonathan PETERSON of Duxborough as her guardian.

Estate of **Mercy SIMMONS** of Duxbury. <Plymouth Co.PR 12:112,113,116>
...24 Feb. 1750/1...nuncupative will in presence of Fear SIMMONS, Lydia SIMMONS & Abiah SIMMONS, but not written out at time dictated as no "Scribuor" was at hand. 1 Apr. 1751 Lydia SIMMONS & Abiah SIMMONS made oath that they heard said Mercy SIMMONS declare her will about two days before she died and it was written out within twelve hours after her death. Everything went to sister **Content SIMMONS.** Executors: Uncle Moses SIMMONS, Mr. Ebenezer FISH. Heirs: 28 Mar. 1751 the following brothers & sisters consent to will, viz: **Aaron SIMMONS, Abiah SIMMONS, Priscilla TAYLOR, Samuel TAYLOR, Betty SIMMONS.**

Will of **Aaron SIMMONS** of Duxbury. <Plymouth Co.PR 31:185-87>
...16 Mar. 1790...loving wife (unnamed); To son Jesse SIMMONS the whole of real and personal estate, he paying...one hundred pounds to sister Mary SHERMAN. Witnesses: Elijah PETERSON, Jabez PETERSON, Reuben DELANO. Pr. 29 May 1790, no inventory indexed.

Benjamin SIMMONS Jr. of Duxbury. Guardianship of Children. <Plymouth Co.PR 11:202-205,133>
Five bonds...22 Mar. 1748, Moses SIMMONS of Duxbury app'td. guardian of: <11:202> Lucy SIMMONS, minor; <11:203> Mica SIMMONS; <11:204> Benjamin & Elizabeth SIMMONS; <11:205> Keturah SIMMONS. <11:133> 1 Aug. 1748, Isaac PARTRIDGE of Duxbury app'td. guardian of Peres SIMMONS, minor.

Benjamin SIMMONS of Duxbury to **William & Hannah RICHARDS** of Duxbury. <Plymouth Co.Deeds 39:61>
...28 Mar. 1739...Benjamin SIMMONS, cordwainer...in consideration of ye parental love and good will and affection...towards my wel beloved Son and Daughter **William RICHARDS** and **Hannah** his wife ...ten acres...within ye Township of Duxborough...part of first Division of ye Common Lands belonging to ye Township of sd Duxborough & Pembroke...Witnesses: Betty SIMMONS, Jonathan PETERSON.

Ack. 21 May 1739 by Benjamin Simmons, rec. 7 Jan. 1747.

William & Hannah RICHARDS, of Pembroke to **Aaron SIMMONS,** of Duxbury. <Plymouth Co.Deeds 47:271> 23 Jan. 1762...William RICHARDS, husbandman & Hannah RICHARDS, tayloress...for ₤13.6.8. sold to Aaron SIMMONS, husbandman...ten acres...in the first Division of the common lands belonging to the Township of said Duxborough & Pembroke... Witnesses: Erastus RICHARDS, Keziah RICHARDS. Ack. 20 Mar. 1762 by William & Hannah RICHARDS. Rec. 28 Dec. 1762.

Zachariah SIMMONS of Duxbury. Guardianship of Children. <Plymouth Co.PR #18408, 11:61,62,10:184> <10:184> 21 May 1746, Nathan SIMMONS, minor son, chooses George PARTRIDGE. <11:61> 13 July 1748 George PARTRIDGE app'td. guardian of (name worn). <11:62> 13 July 1748 George PARTRIDGE app'td. guardian of Zachariah SIMMONS.

Estate of **Zachariah SIMMONS** of Duxbury. <Plymouth Co.PR 17:32>
Adm. dated 25 Apr. 1761, Eleazer SIMMONS, husbandman of Duxbury, appt'd. admr. of Zachariah SIMMONS, late of Duxborough...Labourer, deceased intestate. Bond dated 25 Apr. 1761, of Eleazer SIMMONS, John SPRAGUE, both of Duxborough and Stephen SAMSON of Plimouth, blacksmith. Witnesses: Edward WINSLOW, Penelope WINSLOW.

MICRO #6 of 16

William SIMMONS of Duxbury to **Ichabod SIMMONS** of Duxbury. <Plymouth Co.Deeds 59:175> ...1 June 1768...William SIMMONS, yeoman, for ₤50 sells to Ichabod SIMMONS, yeoman...

Ichabod SIMMONS of Duxbury to **Nathaniel SIMMONS** of Duxbury. <Plymouth Co.Deeds 78:53> ...12 Feb. 1794...Ichabod SIMMONS, Gentleman, on consideration that his son Nathaniel SIMMONS, cordwainer, supports him for the rest of his life & pays his debts & funeral charges, conveys to sd Nathaniel SIMMONS all his real estate in Duxbury...bounded by land of Ichabod WESTON, Abel CHANDLER, Deacon William WESTON. Witnesses: William WESTON, Abel CHANDLER.

References to Consider SIMMONS (grantor & grantee) of Duxbury. <Plymouth Co.Deeds>

54:111 - 2 July 1768, Jonathan SOULE, son of Josiah, to nephew Consider SIMMONS, cordwainer.
66:40 - 5 June 1784, to Aaron SIMMONS. (Nephele Simmons signs, releases dower.) <See below>
100:74 - 24 June 1783, to Gideon HARLOW. (Nephele releases dower.)
139:113 - 3 Jan. 1820, to Whittemore PETERSON. (Naphela signs by mark, releases dower.)
139:135 - 3 Jan. 1820, to Isaiah ALDEN. (Nephela signs, releases dower.)
140:266 - 13 July 1820, to Wadsworth CHANDLER. (Nephele signs, releases dower.)
149:133 - 3 Jan. 1820, to Thomas W. PETERSON. (Nephele signs, releases dower.)
150:98 - 2 May 1823, to Whittemore PETERSON. (Nephele releases dower.)
152:25 - 3 Jan. 1820, to Ichabod SAMPSON, Jr. (Nephela signs by mark, releases dower.)

Consider SIMMONS of Duxbury to **Aaron SIMMONS** of Duxbury. <Plymouth Co.Deeds 66:40> ...5 June 1784...Consider SIMMONS, yeoman, for ₤6 sold to Aaron SIMMONS, yeoman...all my right to a certain piece of land in Duxborough...the easterly corner of 75 acres which Seth ARNOLD, John PARTRIDGE & Thomas LORING, Agents of the Town of Duxborough...sold to my Honored Grandfather Mr. **Josiah SOULE** of Duxborough dec'd...bounded by Phillips Brook, Black Friars Brook by Nathaniel SOUL's. Nephele SIMMONS, wf of Consider releases Dower. Witnesses: Gideon HARLOW, Jabez PETERSON. Ack. 14 Feb. 1786 by Consider SIMMONS. Rec. 28 Mar. 1786.

Will of **Edward SIMMONS** of Newport, RI. <Newport PR 4:89,90,102,198,292,693> <4:89>...22 Aug. 1803...my now wife; son James SIMMONS; grandsons Edward SIMMONS & Robert M. SIMMONS...if my son James or either of my grandsons shall decease without leaving issue...the Estate...shall be equally divided among the surviving children of my son Jonathan SIMMONS, dec'd. Witnesses: John GRELEA, Giles SANFORD, Abigail GRELEA. Pr. 3 Oct. 1803, div. 19 Feb. 1810. (Codicil <4:90> and inv. <4:102> not included here.)

Will of **Jonathan SIMMONS,** blacksmith of Newport, RI. <Newport PR 4:77,79,80,188,197,198, 5:360> <4:77>...19 May 1800...To wife Elizabeth, choice of one bed & bedding; To son **Edward SIMMONS** one dollar; To son **Henry SIMMONS,** the hay scales and the land they stand on; To daughter **Mary SIMMONS** twenty five dollars drawn in the Presbyterian Lottery and likewise eight dollars given by a friend. Nevertheless if my said daughter should choose my clock in lieu of said sums...also one bed and beding...To daughter **Elizabeth SIMMONS** one bed & bedding...To daughter **Desire SIMMONS** one bed & bedding...To son **William SIMMONS** one hundred silver dollars to be paid him at the age of twenty one years...To daughter **Rachel SIMMONS** one bed & bedding...To sons **Robert SIMMONS, Nathan SIMMONS** and **John SIMMONS,** one hundred silver dollars to be paid to each at the age of twenty one years...To wife **Elisabeth** the improvement of all my Estate Real & Personal...so long as she shall remain my widow...then to be equally divided...between my ten children...if my wife should be like to have a child at the time of my decease... Wife named Executrix. Witnesses: Stephen HAWKINGS, Joseph Jacob ROBINSON, Joseph PEABODY. Codicil (no date)...to my two sons **Edward SIMMONS** and **Henry SIMMONS**...hay scales in Newport...blacksmiths tools...all my stock in the shop shall be sold to pay debts...my said son **Edward** shall be joint Executor with his Mother. Witnesses: John GRELEA, Henry BULL, Horace SENTER. Pr. 5 Sept. 1803.

<Plymouth Co.Deeds 12:3> 4 July 1706...Priscilla WISWALL, Peleg WISWALL & John ROBINSON sell land formerly granted to Ichabod WISWALL & John ROBINSON, to Samuel SEABURY of Duxbury.

Estate of **Uriah WADSWORTH** of Duxbury. <Plymouth Co.PR #21764, 27:157,29:166>

<27:157> - Adm. dated 3 May 1784, **Peleg WADSWORTH** of Duxbury, yeoman, app'td. administrator on estate of Uriah WADSWORTH, yeoman, deceased intestate.

<unrec.> - Bond dated 3 May 1784, **Peleg WADSWORTH**, adm.; Sureties: Joseph BARTLETT, mariner & Nicholas DAVIS Jr., cordwainer, both of Kingston. Witnesses: James Leach, Isaac LOTHROP.

<29:166 - Inv. dated 14 May 1784 taken by Judah DELANO, Joseph SOUL, Peres LORING. Incl. thirty five acre lot £298; Cedar Swamp £64; piece of Salt meadow at ye high pines £20; ye old homsted farm with a piece of Salt meadow £200; half a wood wharf £40; a ware house at wharf £2.8s

---

Guardianship of **Benjamin CHANDLER** of Duxbury. <Plymouth Co.PR #3746, 32:143, 38:326>

<32:143> - Bond dated 4 Apr. 1800, **Seth CHANDLER**, Physician, of Hebron, Cumberland co. app'td. guardian of Benjamin CHANDLER, above 14, son of **Peres CHANDLER**, dec'd. Sureties: Sceva CHANDLER, Zenas DELANO. Witnesses: Wadsworth CHANDER, Peres CHANDLER.

<38:326> - Account dated 23 Mar. 1803, Seth CHANDLER charges himself to part of a journey from the province of Maine to attend to the division of the estate and to one year nine months board and tuition in the study & practice of physic.

Estate of **Philip CHANDLER** of Duxbury. <Plymouth Co.PR #3808, 34:58, 35:455,456>

<34:58> - Bond dated 3 Feb. 1795, Sarah CHANDLER, widow, app'td. adm. on estate of Philip CHANDLER, mariner. Sureties: Jotham LORING of Duxbury, Jacob ALBERTSON of Plymouth. Witnesses: Luna LORING, Elisha K. JOSSELYN, J. JOSSELYN.

<35:455> - Inv. taken 9 Apr. 1795 by Jotham LORING, Samuel CHANDLER, Seth CHANDLER, sworn to by widow 11 Dec. 1795. Value of personal estate, £50.

<35:456> - Insolvency dated 11 Dec. 1795.

<orig.> - Memoranda dated 26 June 1797 by widow.

Will of **Perez CHANDLER** of Duxbury. <Plymouth Co.PR #3805, 37:195,196, 241,246,378>
<37:195> 10 Jan. 1800...sons **Peres, Seth, Wadsworth** (named executor), **Daniel, Benjamin** and daus. **Betty, Welthea, Asenath** and granddaughter **Mary CHANDLER**. Witnesses: Philip CHANDLER, Stephen RUSSELL, Jesse CHANDLER. <37:196> Pr. 8 Feb. 1800. <37:196> Inv. 29 Mar. 1800. Total amount of estate $5394.07, incl. real estate in Pembroke. <37:241> Div. 9 May 1800: **Perez, Seth** & **Wadsworth** each one share, **Daniel** & **Benjamin** each one half a share, **Betsey, Welthy** & **Asenath** each one third a share. **Perez** also to receive land bought from Sarah WADSWORTH known as the Mill lot. <37:378> Account dated 31 Dec. 1800, received from the following: Benjamin BOSWORTH, Widow BROWN, Joshua CUSHING, Philip DELANO, John OBRIEN, John WOTSEN, Howland SAMSON, Joshua BREWSTER, Wm. PHILIPS, John RANDAL, Perez CHANDLER, Ezra MICHELL, Ezekiel GLASS, Japhahth DELANO, Benjamin SMITH, Seth CHANDLER, Judah HUNT, Luther DELANO, Daniel CHANDLER, Zenas DELANO, Sceva CHANDLER. Payments made to the following: Sally CHANDLER "guardian", Philip CHANDLER, Asa CHANDLER, "the heirs" Sceva CHANDLER, Zenas DELANO & Nathaniel HOLMES, Seth CHANDLER, Perez CHANDLER, Jotham LORING, Lucy RUSSELL, Lusana RUSSELL, Colson SAMSON, Zilpah CHANDLER, Jedediah HOLMES, Gideon Thomas WHITE, Bildad WASHBURN, Peleg GULLFER, Abner DINGLEY, Samuel LORING, Seth CHANDLER, Abigail SAMPSON, Andrew SAMSON, Elizabeth SNOW, Marcy CHANDLER, Joseph FOORD, Betsey SAMSON, Ichabod SAMSON, Joseph WHITE, Stephen RUSSELL, Deborah SAMSON, John GLASS, Benjamin SMITH, Seth SPRAGUE, Sally CHANDLER, Anthony SAMSON.

Will of **Peleg WADSWORTH** of Duxbury. <Plymouth Co.PR #21757, 37:76-78,128>
...3 June 1799, eldest son Cephas; Silvanus SMITH, son of my dau. Lucia SMITH dec'd; children Uriah, Peleg, Welthea, wf of Judah ALDEN, Ira and Dura.

Will of **William SOUTHWORTH** of Little Compton. <Bristol Co.PR 3:575,576,4:96>
<3:575>...8 May 1719, To wife Martha one nedgrow garle caled Cate togathre with her right of Dowrey as the law directs...To son **Benjamin SOUTHWORTH** ten shilings and former deed of gift...To son **Joseph SOUTHWORTH** twenty pounds and one head...To son **Edward SOUTHWORTH** twenty pounds and one cow...To son **Samuel SOUTHWORTH**, five pound which I lent him with a deed of gift..To son **Nathaniel SOUTHWORTH** £400...To son **Thomas SOUTHWORTH** 20 shillings and a deed of gift...To son **Stephen SOUTHWORTH** halfe my negora man caled Cuffe & one cow & a deed of gift...To son **Gideon SOUTHWORTH** 20 shillings and a deed of gift...To son **Andrew SOUTHWORTH** halfe my negora man caled Cuffe and a deed of gift...To daughter **Elizabeth LITTLE** £60 in goods or chattels...To daughter **Ales/Alice COOKE** £70 in money or land...any estate not disposed of to be divided between grandsons **William SOUTHWORTH** and **Constant SOUTHWORTH** and the rest of my children except Joseph and Benjamin... friend Lt. John WOOD and sons Joseph and Samuel named Executors. Witnesses: Jonathan THURSTON, Richard GRENELL, Nathaniel SEARLE who made oath 24 Aug. 1719. <3:576> Inventory taken 31 July 1719 by John WOOD, Peter TAYLOR and Silvester RICHMOND, incl. two houses and 200 acres, £2000, one negrow man called Cuffe, £50, one negorow woman called Rose, £50, a negorow girl called Kate, £20. Account allowed 7 Feb. 1721/2, payment received from: Symond DAVENPORT, William BRIGGS and Nathaniel SOUTHWORTH. Payments made to: Guardian of Samuel BLAGUE, Joseph SOUTHWORTH, Nicholas MIMS, Nathaniel SEARLE, John CAMBELL, Peter TAYLER, Peter COLLEMORE, Mr. WILLISTON, Thomas BURGES, Joseph WILBORE, Joseph TILLENHAST, John WILBORE, Joseph WOODWORTH, Elisha WOODWORTH, Joseph DAVENPORT, William SYMON, Jonathan GREENHILL, Jonathan STODDER, Silvester RICHMOND, David LITTLE for keeping negro girl 8 years, James DYER, Capt. Symond DAVIS, Capt. William ELY of

Conetikett, Mrs. Elizabeth WILLARD in Boston, Lieut. WOOD, Justice CHURCH, John COOK, John COE, Timothy BAYLY, Joseph SEABERY, Thomas STODDER, George PEIRCE, Edward SOUTHWORTH his legacy, Benjamin & Tho. SOUTHWORTH their legacies, Joseph SOUTHWORTH his legacy, Stephen SOUTHWORTH, Nathaniel SOUTHWORTH, Dr. ARNOLD, Jonathan RECORDS, William PALMER, Nathaniel SOUTHWORTH in part of his legacy, David LITTLE his legacy given by widow, Gideon SOUTHWORTH his legacy, John COOK in part of his legacy, Aaron DAVIS, Josiah SAWYER, Capt. DAVIS, Samuel HOWLAND, ye Trusties of Bristol for one hundred thousand pound loane money, John CARY, Nathaniel BLAGROVE, sundries expended in defending an action commenced by David LITTLE against ye estate on ye account of a negro girl, Joseph SOUTHWORTH for two journeys to Plymouth Courts, Samuel SOUTHWORTH going to Seconet <4:96>.

Will of **Martha SOUTHWORTH,** widow of Little Compton. <Bristol Co.PR 9:22>
...dated 13 June 1729...To my son **Joseph BLAGUE,** 5 shillings...To my son **Andrew SOUTHWORTH** my negro girl named Kate and my Silver Tankerd and brass mortar and pestle...To my daughter **Mary SOUTHWORTH** all my wearing apparril and one small trunk...To my grandson **William SOUTHWORTH** a young heiffer from the cow I had of Stephen WICOX...To my granddaughter **Mary BLAGUE** my Sattinet Gound and short apron...To my sons **Gideon SOUTHWORTH** and **Andrew SOUTHWORTH** the remainder of my estate. Son-in-law **Joseph SOUTHWORTH** appointed sole executor. Witnesses: Elihu WOODWORTH, Benjamin CHURCH, Timothy GLASON. The will of Martha SOUTHWORTH late of "Ceabrook"/Saybrook,, Conneticut was probated 8 Apr. 1738.

MICRO #7 OF 16

Will of **John COE,** husbandman of Little Compton. <Bristol Co.PR 6:195,198,199>
<6:198>...dated 4 Dec. 1728...To wife **Sarah** all household goods, one third of personal estate and profits of real estate...To eldest son **Samuel COE** one half of all lands and housing within the township of Little Compton after the death of my wife, and my sea chest, books and instruments... To my third son **Joseph COE,** one half of all my lands & housing...To my second son **John COE** all my Right of Lands near Casco Bay, one hundred pounds, one feather bed and beding, one cow...To my eldest daughter **Lydia BAILEY,** wife of John BAILEY Jr., my second daughter **Sarah TOMKINS,** wife of Samuel TOMKINS and my third daughter **Elizabeth BURGESS,** the wife of Edward BURGESS, besides what they hath already had, Ł10 each...To my youngest daughter **Hannah COE,** one bed & beding, one milk cow, ten pounds money...sons Joseph & Samuel named Executors. Witnesses: Thomas CHURCH, John PABODIE, William RICHMOND. <6:195> Pr. 21 Jan. 1728/9. Inventory taken 6 Jan. 1728, including seventy acres of land with houses, Ł1400, sea chest, sea books & Instruments, Ł4.

William & Jerusha PEABODY of Little Compton to **Benjamin STARR.** <Worcester Co.Deeds 5:325>
...30 Oct. 1734, William & Jerusha PEABODY for Ł10 sold to Benjamin STARR of New London CT...all our Right and title...unto one certain grant of land granted by the General Court held at Boston ...the 19th of Oct. 1658 to the widow of Thomas STARR late of Charlestown dec'd for four hundred acres of land which was ordered by said Court att their sessions...Witnesses: Thomas CHURCH, John BURGESS. Ack. 30 Oct. 1734, Little Compton by William PEABODY Jr. and wf. Jerusha PEABODY.

Joseph WATERMAN Jr. of Norwich CT to **Nathaniel FISH** of Stonington CT.<Norwich Co.CT Deeds 9:36>
...19 Nov. 1743, Joseph WATERMAN Jr. for Ł1000 old tenor, sold to Nathaniel FISH 120 acres in Norwich near the southwest corner of the town partly bounded by lands of Stephen GARDNER, Isaac WILLIAMS and Josiah EAMS.

Samuel GAY of Norwich to **Nathaniel FISH** of Stonington CT. <Norwich Co.CT Deeds 9:322>
...21 Feb. 1745/6, Samuel GAY for Ł1500 old tenor sold to Nathaniel FISH 100 acres in Norwich being all he purchased of David WOODWORTH partly bounded by lands formerly of Job BARSTOW by land formerly of John COLVER, by the township line...also one acre on which my dwelling house now stands.

Robert DENISON of New London CT and **Andrew DENISON** of Norwich CT sell to **Nathaniel FISH** and **Isaac WOODWORTH,** both of Norwich CT. <Norwich Co.CT Deeds 10:308> (deed not specified)

Isaac WOODWORTH, of Norwich sells his half of above to **Nathaniel FISH.** <Norwich CT Deeds 11:248>

Estate of **Miller FISH** of Norwich CT. Inventory taken 23 Mar. 1763 by Daniel RUDD, Benjamin WOODWORTH, mentions side saddle & pillion. <Norwich CT PR 3:142>

Miller FISH of Norwich CT. Guardianship of Children. <Norwich CT Court Rec.3:112>
...2 Sept. 1777 **John FISH** and **Miller FISH,** sons of Miller FISH, late of Norwich, deceased, minors of age to choose guardians have chosen **Nathaniel FISH Jr.** of Norwich.

NORWICH CT DEEDS:

8:310 - 23 Oct. 1741, Aaron FISH of Groton to Joseph BELTON of Groton, land in Norwich.
11:133 - 14 July 1752, Nathaniel FISH of Norwich to Jabez BIGELOW of Colchester, land in Norwich.
13:397 - 11 Jan. 1757, Nathaniel FISH of Norwich to Samuel WHITING of Norwich, land in Norwich.
13:554 - 26 Mar. 1759, Nathaniel FISH of Norwich to Samuel WHITING of Norwich, land in Norwich.
13:555 - 18 Apr. 1759, Nathaniel FISH of Norwich to Samuel WHITING of Norwich, land in Norwich.
14:86 - 30 Dec. 1756, Nathaniel FISH of Norwich to Nathaniel STARK, of Lebanon, land in Norwich.
19:234 - 1 May 1771, William FISH of Norwich to John M'CALL of Norwich, land in Norwich.
21:306 - 28 Apr. 1773, William FISH of Norwich to Jacob FOX of Norwich, land near my old house.

NORWICH CT DEEDS: (cont-d)

21:308 - 21 Mar. 1772, William FISH of Norwich to Valentine WIGHTMAN, same, land in New Concord.
24:127 - 1 May 1781, William FISH of Norwich to Christopher FRINK, of same, land in Norwich.
24:244 - 21 Jan. 1783, William FISH of Norwich to John GARDNER, of same, land in Norwich. Witnesses: Molly FISH, Nehemiah WATERMAN Jr.
26:303 - 1 June 1772, Nathaniel FISH Jr. of Norwich for Ł8 sold to Joseph OTIS and wife Lucy of Norwich one and a half acres in New Concord in Norwich, west of my dwelling house. Witnesses: Nathaniel FISH, Richard HYDE.
30:44 - ( )Apr. 1795, Christopher STARR of Norwich, judgement against William FISH of Bozrah.
32:28 - 9 Sept. 1801, Lodowich FISH & wife Susan (she under 21), of Norwich to Robert MANWARING of same, land set out to Susan in settlement of estate of her father, Samuel POST, dec'd, his widow Dorcas POST now occupying a house adjacent to granted land.
33:289 - 20 Nov. 1806, Dorcas POST, of Norwich, widow of Samuel, and Ludowick FISH & wife Susan, the daughter of Samuel, both of Litchfield, to Caleb BACON of Litchfield.
36:450 - 15 Oct. 1808, "same to Elisha TRACY of Norwich".

Will of **Martha FISH**, widow of Norwich. <Norwich CT PR 5:14>
...dated 26 June 1773...Martha FISH, widow of Capt. Moses FISH of Groton...only daughter Abigail now the wife of Andrew LATHROP...four sons Moses, Thomas, Elisha & Jonathan FISH. Pr. 4 Oct. 1773

NORWICH CT DEEDS:

11:272 - 27 Apr. 1749, Isaac TRACY, of Norwich to Nathaniel FISH, of Stonington.
15:626 - 10 July 1761, Nathaniel FISH, of Norwich for Ł175 sold to Miller FISH & wife Margret of Norwich, land in New Concord in Norwich.
16:215 - 13 Sept 1763, Jabez POST, of Norwich to Aaron FISH, of Lebanon.
16:144 - 19 Jan. 1762, Nathaniel FISH, of Norwich for Ł230 sold to William FISH, of Norwich, land in New Concord in Norwich, being part of the land he bought of Joseph WATERMAN.
17:269 - 1 May 1766, Nathaniel FISH, of Norwich, to Nathaniel FISH Jr., of Norwich, for Ł105, land in New Concord, bounds partly on Lebanon line.
17:268 - 27 Apr. 1767, Nathaniel FISH, of Norwich, to William FISH, of Norwich, for Ł60, land where bound line runs through middle of Nathaniel's house.
19:330 - 11 May 1769, William FISH, of Norwich to Nathaniel FISH Jr., of Norwich, 53 acres, 153 rods, bounded as follows: beginning at the middle of the house that my father Nathaniel & I live in.
19:331 - 11 May 1769, Nathaniel FISH Jr., of Norwich to William FISH, of Norwich, land bought of Nathaniel FISH 1 May 1766, bound partly on Lebanon line.
19:341 - 23 Oct. 1771, Wheler BROWN, of New London, to William FISH, of Norwich, land at New Concord with a mansion house on it.
20:51 - 28 Sept 1772, Jonas RIPPLETON, of New York City to William FISH, of Norwich.
21:28 - 16 Apr. 1772, Nathaniel FISH, of Norwich, to Nathaniel FISH Jr., of Norwich, 19 acres in New Concord, New London co. Witnesses: Nathan BINGHAM, Joseph FISH.
21:29 - 16 Apr. 1772, "same to same", 24 acres in New Concord.
23:10 - 2 July 1777, William FISH of Norwich, for Ł180 rec'd. of Nathaniel FISH Jr. & his wife Mary, conveys to said Mary FISH, 32 acres, 97 rods in New Concord in Norwich, beginning near door stone, south side the house where my father now lives, partly bounded by Nathaniel FISH Jr.'s land. Witnesses: Mary FISH, Elizabeth SOUTHWORTH.
21:278 - 12 Mar. 1779, Elijah ABEL, of Chatham CT & Oliver ABEL & Alpheus ABEL both of Norwich to Nathaniel FISH Jr., of Norwich, land near latter's house at New Concord.
24:211 - 28 Dec. 1782, William FISH, of Norwich, by judgement on account of debt from Samuel STOCKWELL, of Norwich, cooper's shop in Norwich.
25:94 - 4 Dec. 1783, William FISH, by execution against Moses CLEVELAND, of Norwich.
25:367 - 1 Apr. 1785, Nathaniel FISH Jr., of Norwich, to William FISH, of Norwich, land in New Concord.
25:440 - 10 June 1785, Sherman GARDNER, of Norwich, to William FISH, of Norwich, land in Norwich.

JOHN ALDEN[2] (John[1])

Probate of **Benjamin ALDEN**, Physician, of Boston. 16 Oct. 1749, John CLARK, Physician, of Boston, appointed administrator of estate. <Suffolk PR #9383, 43:162>

Estate of **Simeon STODDARD** and heirs of **John ALDEN**. <Superior Court of Judicature, 1733-1736,p.43>
...23 Apr. 1734...Superior Court held at Plymouth...**Anthony STODDARD** Esq., **William STODDARD**, merchant and **Wiliam CLARK**, Esq. all of Boston...as they are the surviving Executors of the last Will...of **Simeon STODDARD** late of Boston, Esq. dec'd....appellants viz: **Capt. John JONES**, Gent. & **Hannah** his wife of Hopkinton, **Elizabeth WILLARD, Hephzibah MORTIMER, "Mary ALDEN** and **Mary ALDEN"**, **Thomas ALDEN, Elizabeth ALDEN, Anne ALDEN, Mary BRIGHTMAN, Nathaniel HOWARD** & his wife **Hephzibah, Elizabeth BETTERLY, Peter BRITTON** & his wife **Lydia, Mary ALDEN, Zachariah ALDEN, Samuel KNEELAND** and his wife **Mary, Timothy GREEN** & his wife **Elizabeth,** and **Nathaniel ALDEN,** all of Boston, heirs of **John ALDEN,** late of Boston, dec'd, appellees from judgment of Inferior Court of Conn. Pleas at Plymouth 3d Tues. Sept. last part. (Accompanying note reads: "John & wife Elizabeth had mtgd.-claim not pd., verdict for Alden heirs")

Will of **Samuel DOWSE,** of Charlestown MA. <Middlesex Co.PR #4399, 24:282,283,285>
<24:182>...dated 25 Oct. 1746...To brother **Nathaniel DOWSE** land on Bunker's Hill given me by my Honoured Father in his Will...To my brother **Joseph DOWSE,** provided said Joseph shall honourably and comfortably maintain and support my late wife's Aunt **Rachel PAPOT** during her Life and decently bury her...To my well beloved friend **Elisabeth SEWALL** with whom I have engaged to marry, ₤5000 old tenor...To sisters **Katharine WYER** and **Elisabeth SARRAZIN,** ₤500 old tenor each...To my neice **Isabella DOWSE,** daughter of my brother **Joseph DOWSE,** furniture, etc...To **Mrs. Susanna ALDEN** in token of my regard for her great kindness to me and to my late wife in our sickness, ₤100 old tenor... To **Rev. Mr. Hull ABBOT** and **Rev. Mr. Thomas PRENTICE,** Pastors of the Church in Charlestown, ₤10 each old tenor...To **Henry NEWMAN** ₤200 old tenor. <24:285> Pr. 8 Nov. 1746. Inv. taken 27 Nov. 1746.

Guardianship for **Samuel DOWSE.** <Middlesex Co.PR>
Original bond for guardianship for **Samuel DOWSE,** above 14, son of **Samuel DOWSE,** late of Charlestown, dated 13 Apr. 1752. Guardian: Richard SUTTON, leather draper of Charlestown. Witnesses: Andrew BORDMAN, Francis JOHNSON.

---

13 Feb. 1722...**Susanna ALDEN** witnessed mortgage of **Joseph BURRILL** and wife Susanna, of Boston. <Suffolk Co.Deeds 37:199>

Susanna ALDEN of Boston and **Nathaniel ALDEN** of Boston. <Suffolk Co.Deeds 61:287>
...12 July 1731...Susannah Alden, widow for ₤500 "good Publick Bills of Credit" sells to Nathaniel ALDEN, mariner, one half part of dwelling house and land situate...in Milk Street in Boston... Rec. 1 Oct. 1741.<3>

Heirs of **John ALDEN** to **John JONES,** Power of Attorney. <Middlesex Co.PR #122/#247>
...15 Apr. 1736...We, **Elisabeth WILLARD,** widow, daughter to **John ALDEN** of Boston Deceased Mariner, **Hephzibeth MORTIMORE,** late wife to **Nathaniel ALDEN, Mary ALDEN** widow to **Zachariah ALDEN,** sons to the abovesaid **John ALDEN, Nathaniel ALDEN, Mary ALDEN, Thomas ALDEN, Elisabeth ALDEN, Ann ALDEN,** single woman, **Mary BRIGHTMAN, Nathaniel HAYWARD** and **Hephzibeth HAYWARD, Elisabeth BETTERLY, Peter BRITTON** and **Lydia BRITTON, Mary ALDEN, Zachariah ALDEN, Samuel KNEELAND, Mary KNEELAND, Timothy GREEN** and **Elisabeth GREEN,** grandchildren to the aforesaid **John ALDEN,** deceased, all of Boston... do hereby appoint **John JONES** of Hopkinton in the County of Middlesex...our Lawfull Attorney in all causes moved or to be moved for or against us to Prosecute them to finall judgement...Witnesses: Daniel FOWLE, Nathaniel GREEN.<4>

Nathaniel ALDEN of Boston. <Suffolk Co.Deeds 50:22>
...2 Jan. 1735...Nathaniel ALDEN, mariner of Boston, and wife Mary, mortgage land and house on Milk St. to James BOWDOIN. (See above)

Estate of **Nathaniel ALDEN** of Boston. <Suffolk Co.PR 35:80,243,248, 37:488>
<35:80>...10 July 1740...Adm. granted to John JONES of Hopkinton and Timothy GREEN, printer, of Boston. <35:343> Estate declared insolvent, claims examined between 1741-1744. <35:248> Inventory dated 31 Dec. 1740, taken by William YOUNG, Charles COFFIN, Joseph GALE. Items incl. 11/12th of a house, land and barn on Milk St., negro woman, half a pew, one right in Phillipstown, books. Total amount of estate, ₤1661.19s. <37:488> Creditors mentioned: Elizabeth GREEN estate, Elizabeth ALDEN, Ann ALDEN, John JONES, Esq., Dr. Simpson JONES, total paid ₤1358.

MICRO #8 of 16

Estate of **John WALLEY** of Boston. <Suffolk Co.PR #2750, 15:14,56>
...30 Apr. 1702...Elizabeth WALLEY, relict widow of John WALLEY, late of Boston, mariner, deceased intestate, appointed admx. of estate. Inventory allowed 31 July 1702. (He then being called John WALLEY Jr.)

Will of **Simon WILLARD,** of Boston. <Suffolk Co.PR 18:220>
...13 Nov. 1709...Simon WILLARD, shopkeeper, shortly designing a voyage by Sea and not knowing how it may please God to dispose of me therein...to my welbeloved wife Elizabeth, three children Samuel, Abigail and Katherine WILLARD...mentions timber tenement near the Town Dock in Boston. Pr. 11 Jan. 1713, adm. granted to widow.

SUFFOLK CO. DEEDS:

21:653	- ( ) 1704,	John ALDEN et al Exrs. to Simon WILLARD.
21:670	- ( ) 1704,	Joshebeth WING et Exrs. to Simon WILLARD et al.
22:140	- 1 Nov. 1704,	Simon WILLARD to Benjamin PEMBERTON, land inherited from John ALDEN.
22:142	- 25 Nov. 1704,	Benjamin PEMBERTON to Simon WILLARD, land & wooden tenement in Conduit St. near head of Town Dock.
22:145	- ( ) 1704,	Simon WILLARD to Samuel WILLARD, property bought of Benjamin PEMBERTON.
43:173	- 3 May 1729,	Elizabeth WILLARD of Boston, to Joseph SCOTT of Boston, her brick tenement and land given her in will of husband, Simon WILLARD.
28:82	- 6 Mar. 1713,	David & Mary MERRILL, late Mary WILLARD, dau. of Samuel WILLARD of Boston Clerk, late dec'd, sell to Elizabeth WILLARD of Boston, widow, Mary's share in housing & lands of her said father in Groton & Boston.

SUFFOK CO. DEEDS (cont-d):

30:172 - 11 Apr. 1715, William & Hannah LITTLE, of Plymouth, sell to our Honoured Mother Eunice WILLARD of Boston, our right in the lands of our Honoured Father the Reverend Mr. Samuel WILLARD, in Boston, Groton and elsewhere.

Joseph BRIDGHAM of Plimpton to **William BOARDMAN**, of Boston. <Suffolk Co.Deeds 75:233>
22 Nov. 1748...Joseph BRIDGHAM, Physician and wife Abigail, sell to William BOARDMAN, feltmaker, all that wooden tenement...with the land thereto...in Conduit St. near the head of the Town Dock in said Boston.

William BOARDMAN of Boston to **Joseph BRIDGHAM** of Plimpton. <Suffolk Co.Deeds 78:69,70>
...22 Nov. 1748...Indenture between William BOARDMAN, feltmaker and Joseph BRIDGHAM, Physician... Whereas the said William BOARDMAN stands justly indebted unto the said Joseph BRIDGHAM in the sum of Ł250...as a colateral and further security...hath sold unto the said Joseph BRIDGHAM all that wooden tenement or dwelling house with the land...in Conduit St. near the head of the Town Dock in said Boston, bounded as follows: southerly upon Conduit St.; westerly partly on the brick tenement and land of the heirs of **Simon WILLARD** dec'd and partly on land of heirs of Mr. **THOMPSON**, dec'd; northerly upon land of said Thompson's heirs; easterly on housing and land of heirs of **Thomas GROSS**, dec'd. Also, half part of parcel of land behind Conduit St. bounded as follows: easterly, on land of **Samuel WALKER'S** heirs and partly by land formerly in possession of **Thomas SAVAGE** & partly by land of the heirs of **Thomas GROSS**, dec'd; westerly partly by land of said **THOMPSON** dec'd and partly by land of heirs of **Nathaniel WILLIAMS**; northerly by land of heirs of **Joseph PEIRCE**, dec'd. Ack. 22 Nov. 1748, Plymouth County. Rec. 17 Apr. 1750.
<78:70> On 1 Sept. 1761, **Mrs. Abigail BRIDGHAM**, Executrix of the last Will of **Joseph BRIDGHAM** deceased the Mortgagee...acknowledged that she had received full satisfaction for the therein Mortgaged premises and did Quit Claim all her Right Title & Interest therein.

Katharine CAMPBELL of Tiverton to **William BOARDMAN** of Boston. <Suffolk Co.Deeds 93:56>
...29 May 1759...Katharine CAMPBELL, Spinster sold to William BOARDMAN, feltmaker, all rights in wooden tenement or dwelling house with land on Conduit St. near the head of the Town Dock in Boston...on the westerly side partly on the Brick tenement of the heirs of Simon WILLARD, dec'd. Ack. same day, Middleboro. Rec. 1 June 1759.

Thomas ALDEN et al, of Boston to **Nathaniel ALDEN** of Boston. <Suffolk Co.Deeds 61:288>
...19 Feb. 1732...Thomas ALDEN, mariner & wife Jane, Elizabeth ALDEN & Anne ALDEN, spinsters, all of Boston, and John JONES, Gentleman, & wife Hannah of Hopkinton, for Ł333.6.8 sell to our Brother Nathaniel ALDEN, mariner, their rights in house & land on Milk St.

Will of **Dr. Henry BURCHSTEAD** of Lynn. <Essex Co.PR #4020, 333:121,123,173>
...5 Sept. 1753...wife Anna named executrix...children Sarah, Henry, Benjamin, John Henry, Elizabeth, Katharine, Joanna & Rebecca BURCHSTEAD; granddaughter Mary NEWHALL, to John BURRILL, son of Samuel & Anna BURRILL, ye sum of Ł6.13s4d within one year. Pr. 16 June 1755, inv. 16 June 1755.

Guardianship of **Samuel BURRILL** of Lynn. <Essex Co.PR>
...6 Feb. 1797...To the Hon. Samuel HOLTEN Esq., Judge of Probate in & for the County of Essex...We the Subscribers, the Friends and Relations towit the Children of **Samuel BURRILL** of Lynn in said County yeoman beg leave to represent that the said Samuel is advanced to the eightieth year of his age and that by reason of his great age and bodily infirmities he has become and is non compos and incapable to take care of himself or Estate. We further represent to your Honour that he is seized of valuable real & personal Estate in Lynn. We do therefore request your Honor to direct the Select Men of the Town of Lynn to make Inquisition into the Premises (and if said **Samuel BURRILL** shall be adjudged by them or the major part of them to be incapable to take care of himself) to certify the same to your Honour under their hands, in order that some suitable person or persons may be legally appointed Guardian or Guardians to said **Samuel BURRILL** to take care of his person and Estate. Signed by **John BURRILL, Alden BURRILL, Ebenezer BURRILL, Joseph HART.**

Estate of **Samuel BURRILL** of Lynn. <Essex Co.PR #4264, 365:221,266,366:78,311,371:546>
...5 June 1797...**Ebenezer BURRILL**, housewright, **Alden BURRILL**, housewright, both of Salem and **John BURRILL**, cordwainer of Lynn, gave bond of $5000.00, said Ebenezer having been app'td administrator on estate of **Samuel BURRILL**, yeoman, deceased. (Brother **Samuel BURRILL**, blacksmith of Boston, had declined to administer the estate on 3 June.) <371:546> Account: May 1798 (no day), **Joseph HART** receipts to **Ebenezer BURRILL** for $574.00 for the consideration of my deed to **Robert HOOPER**, of my one seventh part of the real estate of my deceased father, **Samuel BURRILL** which sum was paid by the said Hooper to the said Ebenezer for me. In May 1798, **Samuel BURRILL, Elisabeth BENSON, John BURRILL** & **Alden BURRILL** each "receipts for $574 for one seventh as above"

Samuel GRAVES et al, to **John GLOVER** of Marshfield. <Essex Co.Deeds 139:120>
...16 Apr. 1782...Samuel GRAVES, yeoman of Salem & wife Elizabeth, and Jacob COLLINS & wife Lydia, and Hannah Bla( )ey, sell to John GLOVER, Gentleman, the dwelling house & barn where Samuel GRAVES dwells with various land. Witnesses: Caleb COLLINS, R. GRAVES. Ack. by Samuel GRAVES only on 20 May 1782. Rec. 31 May 1782.

ESSEX CO. DEEDS:

142:24 - 10 Apr. 1782, Samuel GRAVES, yeoman of Salem, buys land. Rec. 26 Nov. 1783
142:24 - 24 Nov. 1783, Samuel GRAVES, yeoman of Boston, wife Elizabeth consenting mortgages.

ESSEX CO. DEEDS: (cont-d)

142:127 - 2 Apr. 1784, **Samuel GRAVES**, yeoman of Boston, wife Elizabeth consenting, sells house and land in Lynn. Witnesses: Samuel BURRILL, James WALKER.

Estate of **Samuel B. GRAVES**, mariner of Salem, 1826. <Essex Co.PR #1150, 47:49,31:661,34:148, 32:159,37:258,52:132,53:63,72:51,55:59>
<55:59> On 5 Jan. 1830, Grace GRAVES as legal guardian receipted for shares of Edward GRAVES, Caroline GRAVES, Samuel O. GRAVES, Anne W. GRAVES, William B. GRAVES, Elizabeth GRAVES and Pierce L.W. GRAVES. (Note: Although the above Probate sources are given, they are not further referred to in the files.)

MIDDLESEX CO. DEEDS:

92:538 - 1786, Anthony JONES, grantor.
101:223 - 1789, Anthony JONES, grantor.
110:168 - 3 Dec. 1777, Anthony JONES, Gentleman, of Hopkinton, & wife Elizabeth, to John JONES Jr., husbandman, of Hopkinton.
110:170 - 20 Aug. 1782, Anthony JONES, yeoman, of Hopkinton, to John JONES Jr., yeoman, of Hopkinton, 22 1/2 acres in Hopkinton received by will of father Anthony JONES, dec'd.

Will of **Anthony JONES**, of Hopkinton. <Middlesex Co.PR #12792, 62:89,92,69:123,71:502>
<62:89>...dated 26 July 1781, in the sixth year of American Independance...to wife Elizabeth, horse and chaise with harness, two cows, south lower-room & bed-room in dwelling house with a priviledge in the oven, cellars and well, a sufficiency of good fire-wood...one hundred & twenty pounds pork, eighty pound of beef, ten bushels good Indian meal...sufficiency of sause, both dry and green, ten pounds of sheeps wool...two barrels of good cyder, one bushel and a half of malt ...all my household furniture during her life and the Rev'd. Mr. Samuel Willard's Body of Divinity...the use of my part in a pew in said Hopkinton meeting house...at the decease of my said wife, I give my right in said pew to my two sons, **Nathaniel Alden** and **Anthony**...to son **Nathaniel Alden JONES** a note of hand payable to me for Ł20, dated 12 Feb. 1777, also seventeen pounds lawful money at the rate of Indian corn, at three shillings & four pence per bushel, and my great coat, silver shoe buckles...to my two sons **John JONES** and **Isaac JONES** Ł12 each...to my son **Samuel JONES** Ł12 and my fire arm...to my son **Elisha JONES** Ł38.10s, my silver stock-buckle and knee buckles...to my daughter **Hannah** Ł19...to my daughter **Elizabeth,** Ł15.10S...to my three daughters, **Sarah, Lydia** and **Mehetabel,** Ł24.10s each...to my said son **Anthony**...the whole remainder of my Estate that is not herein disposed of...my great Bible in perticular...the residue of my books... not herein disposed of to be equally divided among all my children (Anthony only excepted)...son **Anthony** appointed executor. Witnesses: Elijah FITCH, Hannah FITCH, Jeremy STIMSON. Consent of heirs dated 7 May 1782 at Hopkinton, signed by Elisabeth JONES, John JONES, James GREENWOOD Jr., Samuel JONES, William VALENTINE, Lydia JONES. <62:92> Probated 9 May 1782. <69:123> Receipt of heirs dated 24 Dec. 1785 at Hopkinton, signed by William VALENTINE, James GREENWOOD, Hannah GREENWOOD, James GREENWOOD guardian to Mehetable JONES, Mathew METCALF guardian to Elisha JONES, John JONES Jr., Samuel JONES, Aaron BUTLER, Isaac JONES, John STONE.

Heirs of **John JONES,** of Hopkinton to **Reuben EAMES,** of Holliston. <Middlesex Co.Deeds 139:111>
1 Feb. 1798...heirs of John Jones, dec'd, for $113.00 sold to Reuben Eames, gentleman...all our rights or shares in a certain tract of land...being in Holliston and containing by estimation ten acres...bounded southeasterly with land of said Reuben Eames, southwesterly with land of Joseph BIGLOW and on all other parts bounded with certain Town ways. Signed by: Mary JONES, Lawson BUCKMINSTER, Samuel VALENTINE, Jeremy STIMSON, Isaac CLARK, Nathaniel HOWE, Rebecca JONES, Gilbert MARSHALL, Mary BUCKMINSTER, Elizabeth VALENTINE, Nancy STIMSON, Nabby CLARK, Jenny MARSHALL, Olive HOWE, JOhn LARNED, Thomas CHAPMAN, Mary CHAPMAN, Ezra EAMES, Sarah EAMES, Abigail COZZENS, Elizabeth WELCH.

Guardianship of Children of **Elijah JONES,** of Sudbury. <Middlesex Co.PR #12819, 258:138>
12 Apr. 1825...guardian app'td. to **Meshach, Avary & Anthony JONES,** minors above the age of 14 years, children of Elijah JONES, late of Sudbury, dec'd.

Will of **John JONES,** of Hopkinton. <Middlesex Co.PR>
...dated 10 Apr. 1823...to my beloved wife Hannah...household furniture...east half of the house where I now live with a right of using the oven in the west part...privilege in the cellar and well and out buildings...my chaise and harness and two cows such as she may choose out of all my cows...she be allowed yearly two hundred pounds of pork, one hundred pounds of beef, eighteen bushels of Indian corn, nine bushels of rye, vegetables, apples, cider...wood at the door of the house cut and prepared...also that she receive from my executor the annual sum of fifteen dollars ...to my daughter **Sally JONES** the sum of four hundred and ninety dollars to be paid in four equal payments (over four years)...to my son **Lawson JONES** the sum of three hundred and eighty five dollars (over three years)...the further sum of fifty dollars to be paid (him) after the decease of my said wife...to my daughter **Mary JONES** the sum of two hundred and fifty dollars (over two years)...to my son **Washington JONES** the sum of two hundred and fifty dollars after he shall arrive at the age of twenty one years (over three years)...the further sum of fifty dollars to be paid (him) at the decease of my said wife...to my daughter **Ann JONES** the sum of two hundred and fifty dollars when she arrives at the age of twenty one years or on her marriage...Whereas at the marriage of my daughters **Betsey BALLARD, Melicent LORING** and **Emily BLISS** I made advances to them ...it would operate unequally to give them any thing more...my six daughters...shall at the decease of my said wife...receive all the household furniture...to my son **John H. JONES** all my real

estate...and remainder of my personal estate...the said **John H. JONES** shall pay all my just debts and funeral charges and expenses also to see that the bodies of me and my wife are decently interred and decent grave stones are erected at each of our graves at his charge and expense...John H. named sole executor. Witnesses: Abraham HARRINGTON, Milton RUGGLES, Thomas FARRAR. Probated 9 Dec. 1824.

==

MIDDLESEX CO. DEEDS:[5]

136:234 - 15 Nov. 1762, Samuel JONES of Acton, yeoman, and Jonas PRESCOTT, of Westford, gentleman with wife Rebecca, sell to Joseph LEE of Concord, physician, all our right...by purchase of any of the heirs or by virtue of the last will and testament of our honoured father Mr. Samuel JONES late of Concord, dec'd. Rec. 28 May 1800.

82:197 - 20 Apr. 1765, John JONES Jr., blacksmith, of Concord sells to Samuel JONES, blacksmith, of Concord, land in Concord. Signed by John Jones, Phebe Jones. Rec. 14 Mar. 1781.

82:197 - 15 June 1767, Thomas JONES, gentleman, of Concord & wife Mary, sell to their son Samuel JONES, yeoman, of Concord, land in Concord. Rec. 14 Mar. 1781.

82:199 - 27 Oct. 1777, Thomas HUBBARD, gentleman, of Concord, sells to Samuel JONES, gentleman, of Concord, land in Concord. Rec. 14 Mar. 1781.

92:156 - 21 Feb. 1785, Jonathan HAYNES, of Sudbury, yeoman, sells to Samuel JONES, of Sudbury, housewright, all my homestead lands & meadows in Sudbury. Milicent HAYNES, wife of Jonathan, releases dower. Rec. 27 Jan. 1786.

90:409 - 26 Mar. 1787, Land in Concord set off to Samuel JONES of Concord, gentleman, to settle judgement against Ezra CONANT of Concord, yeoman. Rec. 13 July 1787.

96:33 - 29 Mar. 1787, Samuel JONES of Acton, yeoman, sells to son Aaron JONES of Acton, yeoman, land in Acton. Rec. 4 July 1787.

102:185 - 1 Dec. 1789, Thomas BRATTLE of Cambridge, esquire, sells to Samuel JONES of Concord, gentleman, land in Concord. Rec. 1 Apr. 1790.

104:14 - 6 Dec. 1790, Ephraim JONES of Concord, trader, sells to Samuel JONES of Concord, gentleman, all his right in the real estate of which my late Father Ephraim JONES late of said Concord, gentleman, deceased died seized...all which real estate...lies in common & undivided with the shares & rights of the other heirs & widow of said deceased. Lucy JONES, wife of Ephraim, releases dower. Rec. 12 Jan. 1791.

114:182 - 24 Oct. 1793, Ephraim JONES of Concord, trader, sells land in Concord to Samuel JONES of Concord, gentleman. Lucy JONES, wife of Ephraim, releases dower.

122:129 - 3 Jan. 1774, Eleazer BROOKS of Lincoln and Francis FAULKNER of Acton, gentlemen, administors on estate of Mr. Daniel BROOKS, late of Acton deceased intestate, sell to Samuel JONES Jr. of Acton, yeoman, land in Acton and Littleton. Rec. 5 Apr. 1796.

82:392 - 27 Oct. 1777, Samuel JONES of Concord, gentleman, sells to Thomas HUBBARD of Concord, gentleman, land in Concord. Rec. 14 Sept. 1781.

131:27 - () Jan. 1794, Samuel JONES of Concord, gentleman, sells to Ephraim JONES of Concord, trader, all the right which I have, claim & hold by purchase from the said Ephraim...in...the real estate which my late father in law Ephraim JONES, late of said Concord, gentleman, deceased, intestate, died seized. Hepzibah JONES, wife of Samuel, releases dower. Rec. 4 Dec. 1798.

126:247 - 1 Apr. 1797, Samuel JONES of Concord, gentleman, sells to Ephraim JONES of Concord, trader, all rights in land in Concord. Hepzibah JONES, wife of Samuel releases dower. Rec. 20 Sept. 1797.

130:382 - 13 Feb. 1798, Nehemiah EASTABROOK of Cambridge, house carpenter, sells to Samuel JONES of Cambridge, cooper, land in Cambridge. Elizabeth EASTABROOKS, wife of Nehemiah releases dower. Rec. 25 Dec. 1798.

133:133 - 29 July 1799, James MILES Jr. of Concord, yeoman, sells to Samuel JONES of Concord, gentleman, land in Concord. Rec. 5 Aug. 1799.

149:269 - 5 Feb. 1803, Samuel JONES of Cambridge, cooper, sells to Ephraim COOK of Cambridge, yeoman, land & buildings in Cambridge conveyed to Jones by Nehemiah Easterbrooks by a deed dated 13 Feb. 1798. Lydia JONES, wife of Samuel releases dower. Rec. same day.

159:515 - 11 Apr. 1804, Samuel JONES of Acton, student of law, sells to Aaron JONES of Acton, guardian of James JONES and Elizabeth JONES of the same Acton, minors, on a mortgage all the real estate of Samuel JONES Jr. late of Acton, deceased, excepting what has been set off to the widow. Mortgage discharged 31 July 1807 by Elizabeth JONES.

159:514 - 21 May 1804, Samuel JONES of Acton, student of the law, sells to Aaron JONES of Acton, trader, all his interest in land and buildings of Samuel JONES who was my grandfather, late of Acton, yeoman, dec'd. Rec. 3 Oct. 1804.

168:439 - 11 Oct. 1805, Samuel JONES of Acton, gentleman, sells to David BARNARD of Acton, gentleman.

169:393 - 5 Dec. 1806, Samuel JONES of Acton, gentleman, sells to James JONES of Acton, trader. Anna JONES, wife of Samuel releases dower.

179:274 - 25 Dec. 1806, Samuel JONES of Acton, gentleman, sells to Aaron JONES of Acton, trader, land in Acton. Anna JONES, wife of Samuel releases dower.

190:268 - 20 July 1810, Samuel JONES of Acton, gentleman, sells to James JONES of Acton, trader, land in Acton. Ack. at Providence RI 20 July 1810.

214:352 - 15 June 1815, Samuel JONES of Sudbury, yeoman, with Rachel his wife, in her right as

MIDDLESEX CO. DEEDS (cont-):

heir at law to the estate of her father Joshua HAYNES, late of Sudbury, gentleman, deceased, intestate, sell to John HAYNES of Sudbury, yeoman, all their right in the estate. Rec. 6 Dec. 1815.

214:350 - 28 Oct. 1815, Levina JONES of Sudbury, widow, heir at law of Joshua HAYNES, late of Sudbury, gentleman, dec'd, sells to John HAYNES.

259:65 - 19 Jan. 1822, Samuel JONES of Sudbury, housewright, sells to John JONES of Sudbury, yeoman, land in Sudbury. Rachel JONES, wife of Samuel, releases dower. Rec. 23 Mar. 1825.

260:522 - 30 Jan. 1822, Indenture between John JONES of Sudbury, yeoman and Samuel JONES of Sudbury, housewright & Rachel his wife, lease of land in Sudbury (formerly deeded to John by Samuel) during life of Samuel for fifty cents a year. Rec. 27 May 1825.

252:157 - 31 Jan. 1824, Samuel JONES of West Cambridge, cooper, to Peter JONES of West Cambridge, yeoman, half of land & dwelling house in W. Cambridge. Rec. 7 Feb. 1824.

252:158 - 31 Jan. 1824, Samuel JONES of West Cambridge, cooper, to Lucy H. GAY, of West Cambridge the wife of John GAY, the other half of above land & house.

321:391 - 10 Apr. 1833, Samuel JONES of Sudbury, gentleman, sells to John JONES of Sudbury, yeoman, land in Sudbury, provided...the said Samuel JONES...pay to the said John JONES...the sum of $300 on demand with interest...then this deed... be void. Rec. 15 Apr. 1833.

139:109 - 7 Jan. 1799, Isaac BURNAP, adm. on estate of Anthony JONES late of Hopkinton, husbandman, deceased, sells to Reuben EAMES of Holliston, gentleman, one undivided ninth part of a ten acre lot of land in Holliston...being the place where Isaac FOSTER now lives. Rec. 20 Nov. 1800.

149:426 - 17 Nov. 1789, Isaac BURNAP, of Hopkinton, gentleman, adm. on estate of Anthony JONES late of said Hopkinton, deceased, sold to Samuel VALENTINE of Hopkinton, gentleman, land & buildings in Hopkinton. Rec. 24 Mar. 1803.

MICRO #9 of 16

Estate of **Anthony JONES** of Hopkinton. <Middlesex Co.PR #12795, 69:404,70:214,215,72:406,409,418, 468,503,515,84:121,85:332-34, 195:124>
8 Nov. 1786, Isaac BURNAP, who is appointed administrator (at widow's request), with Deacon Samuel STOW of Marlborough and Samuel JONES of Concord, housewright, as sureties, gave a bond for £10,000. <70:214> Inv. taken 14 Nov. 1786 by Nathan PERRY, Matthew METCALF & Samuel HAVEN, incl. sixty eight acres of land with building, £250 and one great Bible, 12s. <70:215> Dower set off to widow, Lydia. <84:121> Additional Inv. dated 1797, incl. 8 acres & 50 rods of woodland in Hopkinton...it having heretofore been in common with the shares of the other heirs of the deceased's grandfather and is now separated...and one ninth part of ten acres of improved land in Holliston lying in common. <85:332> Third account of the administrator in 1794 mentions the widow's dower was sold to Capt. Daniel EMES and three rights in a pew were sold to John JONES.

Zachariah ALDEN of Boston and **Edward ADAMS**. <Suffolk Co.Deeds 46:97>
1 Nov. 1731...Zachariah ALDEN, printer, and Lydia his wife discharge the said Edward ADAMS, his heirs, etc...mentions land of Tabitha CRANE, sister of said Lydia ALDEN, the daughters of Ebenezer CRANE, late of Milton, dec'd. Rec. 2 Nov. 1731.

JONATHAN ALDEN[2] (John[1])

Jonathan ALDEN of Marshfield. <Plymouth Co.Deeds 22:61>
3 Apr. 1727...Jonathan ALDEN and wife Elizabeth who was the daughter of Seth ARNOLD of Duxbury, deceased. (Deed not specified.)

Jonathan ALDEN of Marshfield to **Isaac BARKER** of Pembroke. <Plymouth Co.Deeds 25:95>
4 June 1718...Jonathan ALDEN, house carpenter to Isaac BARKER, cordwainer...1/4 of the 18th and 39th lots in upland in Majors Purchase, about 12 acres. Ack. 8 Jan. 1724.

Will of **Pelatiah WEST** of Duxbury. <Plymouth Co.PR 14:330,332,15:254>
...dated 31 Jan. 1731/2...to wife Elizabeth one third...to brother **Samuel WEST** of Lebanon CT all wearing cloaths...to kindsman **Benjamin SOUTHWORTH Jr.** of Duxbury the son of my sister **Abigail COLE**, the wife of **Nathaniel COLE** of Duxbury, all the rest and residue of estate. Witnesses: Philip DELANO, Joseph WESTON, Ezra ARNOLD. Pr. 2 May 1757. <15:254> Inv. dated 13 May 1759, by Briggs ALDEN, Nathaniel SIMMONS, Elnathan WESTON, incl the homestead farm, £200, the salt marsh, £35, seat in the meeting house, £1.

PLYMOUTH CO. DEEDS:

5:238 - 1704, Thomas SNELL to daughters Anne SNELL, Mary SNELL, Martha SNELL.

12:164 - 1708, Anna SNELL to Amos SNELL.

20:106 - 1725, Josiah SNELL et al to John KEITH.

33:154 - 1726/7, Josiah SNELL Sr. to John PACKARD Jr.

42:72 - 21 July 1727, Josiah SNELL Sr. to Josiah SNELL Jr.

PLYMOUTH CO. DEEDS (cont-d):

46:11 - 31 July 1727, Josiah SNELL Sr. to Zachariah SNELL.
7:284 - 1728, Josiah SNELL of Bridgewater to David PACKARD.
24:73 - 1728/9, Josiah SNELL to Josiah EDSON.
34:149 - 1728/9, Josiah SNELL Jr. et al to Recompence CARY.
27:186 - 1729, Josiah SNELL Jr. & wife Abigail (dau of John Fobes) to Edward FOBES Jr.
33:153 - 1735, Josiah SNELL Sr. to John PACKARD Jr.
46:12 - 1 Mar. 1748, Josiah SNELL (son of Thomas) to Zachariah SNELL.
42:66 - 10 Mar. 1753, Josiah SNELL Sr. to daughter Abigail SILVESTER of Duxbury.
48:268 - 16 May 1763, Josiah SNELL, gentleman to Zacharish SNELL, yeoman, both of Bridgewater, sons of Josiah late of Bridgewater.
70:136 - 1789, Anna SNELL, wife of Joseph, to Elijah HAYWARD, 3d.

Pelatiah WEST of Duxbury to **Capt. Thomas BARKER** of Pembroke. <Plymouth Co.Deeds 22:142> ...11 Mar. 1724/5...Pelatiah WEST, yeoman & Elizabeth his wife, for £18 in money sell to Capt. Thomas BARKER ...forty acres within the Township of Pembroke...sd lot is one of the lots of land belonging to the first Division of ye Common Lands which belonged to the Town of Duxborough abovesd and was laid out anno Dom 1710...the twenty eighth lot in ye sd division...Witnesses: Thomas BURTON, Thomas LORING. Rec. 29 Jan. 1727.

Estate of **Edmund CHANDLER** of Duxbury. <Plymouth Co.PR #3754, 4:299,356,357> <4:299>... 5 Feb. 1721...Elisabeth CHANDLER, widow appointed adm.; John ALDEN and widow gave bond of £200. Witnesses: Joseph BRIDGHAM, Thomas FISH. <4:356> Inv. taken 26 Feb. 1721 by John PARTRIDGE, Thomas SOUTHWORTH, Edward ARNOLD. Widow made oath to inventory 20 Apr. 1722. Real estate included: forty acre lot, #28 in Pembroke, £20; one half of 84th lot in second division, £10; one half of 96th lot in second division, £10; meadow at Blue Fish River, £10; share of meadow in second division, £6; house & barn with small piece of land, £70. <4:357> Undated account of debts due from Estate, creditors incl. Nathaniel THOMAS, John WATSON, Mr. MURDOCH, Charles LITTLE, Mrs. EDWARDS of Boston, John WADSWORTH, Samuel SEABURY, Thomas LORING, Mrs. Ruth SILVESTER, Jonathan ALDEN, Jonathan DELANO, Thomas FISH, Samuel FISHER, William BREWSTER Jr., John SPRAGUE, Mr. BURTON, Joseph CHANDLER.

Joseph CHANDLER of N. Yarmouth, **Pelatiah WEST** of Duxbury to **Joshua DELANO** of Duxbury. <Plymouth Co.Deeds 27:178>...20 Feb. 1728/9...Joseph CHANDLER, blacksmith & Pelatiah WEST, yeoman & Elizabeth his wife, for £30 sell to Joshua DELANO,housewright....<179>...all our right in about forty three acres, 84th lot in upland in the second division of Commons belonged to the Towns of Duxborough & Pembroke...Joseph CHANDLER's right being one half and Pelatiah WEST & wife's right being one half...said lot was laid out in 1713...Witnesses: Joshua CUSHMAN, Benjamin SIMMONS Jr., Philip CHANDLER, Joshua CHANDLER. Ack. by all three 4 June 1730. Rec. 30 Jan. 1732.

Pelatiah WEST of Duxbury to **Thomas PRINCE** of Duxbury. <Plymouth Co.Deeds 28:212> ...10 Aug. 1729...Pelatiah WEST, yeoman & Elisabeth his wife as adm. to ye Estate of Edmond CHANDLER late of sd Duxborough deceased, for £10 sold to Thomas PRINCE, shipwright one whole share or fifth part of 29th lot in the second division of ye Commons which belonged to ye Towns of Duxboro and Pembroke laid out in 1712...Witnesses: Joseph SIMMONS, Nathaniel SIMMONS. Rec. 21 May 1734.

Pelatiah WEST of Duxbury to **Philip CHANDLER** of Duxbury. <Plymouth Co.Deeds 34:199,200> ...21 Nov. 1737...Pelatiah WEST, husbandman & Elizabeth his wife for £10 sell to Philip CHANDLER, blacksmith one half of ye whole of the 96th lot in ye upland in Duxbury...ye Second Division of the Common Land of Duxborough & Pembroke...about thirty eight acres <200> laid out in 1713... Witnesses: Thomas PHILLIPS, Joshua SAMSON. Ack. 21 Feb. 1738. Rec. 25 Dec. 1741.

Pelatiah WEST of Duxbury to **Blaney PHILLIPS** of Duxbury. <Plymouth Co.Deeds 45:131> ...23 May 1755...Pelatiah WEST, yeoman for £8.13s4d sold to Blaney PHILLIPS, yeoman...salt meadow...one acre more or less...bounded by Wadsworth's Meadow...Amaziah DELANO's...Wests Krick/ Creek...Witnesses: Ebenezer CHANDLER, Jabesh COLE. Rec. 26 Feb. 1759.

DUXBURY RECORDS (printed):

p.226 - 11 Dec. 1713 - Last division of upland & swampy lots
- 51st & 53rd lots fell to Ebenezer BISHOP & John CHANDLER

p.230 - 29 June 1714 - Division of Cedar Swamp
- 9th & 24th lots fell to Israel SILVESTER, Joseph CHANDLER Sr., Edmund CHANDLER, John CHANDLER, Elisha WADSWORTH, proprietor of farm of Joseph WADSWORTH deceased, James THOMAS, Samuel BRADFORD, William SPRAGUE, Pelatiah WEST.

p.232 - 5 June 1710 - Names of those having rights in town's commons, upland & meadow:
- John CHANDLER, Edmund CHANDLER, (last 4 names together) Samuel CHANDLER, Benjamin CHANDLER, Joseph CHANDLER Sr., Joseph CHANDLER Jr.

p.241 - 17 Jan. 1730/1 - John CHANDLER chosen petty juror.

p.288/9 - 9 May 1748 - In list of voters in 2nd Division with number of rights entitled to:
- Heirs of Joseph CHANDLER Sr. 1, John CHANDLER 1, heirs of Joseph CHANDLER Jr. 1, John CHANDLER 1, Joshua CHANDLER 1, heirs of Samuel CHANDLER 1, Benjamin CHANDLER 2 1/2.

p.321 - 29 Aug. 1757 - Town owes John CHANDLER 2nd for keeping old Jane DELANOE 14 weeks, £1.9.10

p.324 - 1 Mar. 1758 - John CHANLER/CHANDLER 5th, chosen a selectman.

PLYMOUTH CO. DEEDS:

11:146 - 17 Oct. 1715, John CHANDLER, yeoman, of Duxbury to John SIMMONS Jr., yeoman, of Duxbury, 51st lot, 39 acres, 2nd division of Duxbury & Pembroke.

29:134 - 29 Sept. 1726, John CHANDLER & wife Bethiah, of Duxbury to our Brother Elkanah RICKARD of Plympton, husbandman (son of our Honoured Father Henry RICKARD deceased) all rights in estate of Henry. Rec. 20 Feb. 1734.

27:172 - 12 Sept. 1729, Samuel CHANDLER & John CHANDLER of Duxbury, division rec. 23 Dec. 1732.

27:23 - 17 Dec. 1731, John CHANDLER, Sr., yeoman of Duxbury from John SOUTHWORTH, 1 1/4 acre salt meadow in Duxbury; Duck Hill at west end of wharf there bounded by land of said John CHANDLER Sr. and by Mill River. Rec. 10 Feb. 1731/2

41:12 - 20 Dec. 1749, John CHANDLER 3rd, of Duxbury, yeoman, from Thomas CHANDLER, David DELANO & wife Abigail, all of Duxbury, 2 acres land joining land of John CHANDLER 1st, at Duck Hill. Ack. 25 July 1750.

41:248 - 15 July 1751, Joseph CHANDLER of Cornwall CT, to son John CHANDLER of Duxbury, yeoman, half the 39th lot in 2nd Division of Duxbury & Pembroke.

51:123 - 6 June 1764, Judah DELANO, as guardian of Elnathan WESTON, non comp., to John CHANDLER, yeoman, of Duxbury.

67:150 - 12 Mar. 1779, Joseph FREEMAN Jr. et al to John CHANDLER Jr. of Duxbury.

63:74 - 7 June 1780, John CHANDLER, yeoman, of Duxbury, to Jacob WESTON, housewright, east end of his (J.C.) homestead, part in Duxbury, part in Marshfield.

62:269 - 2 Mar. 1784, John CHANDLER, yeoman, & wife Mercy, of Duxbury, to Seth SPRAGUE, of Duxbury, their rights in homestead form of our Father Mr. Phinehas SPRAGUE of Duxbury, deceased, being 1/4 of same.

68:33 - 14 Dec. 1787, John CHANDLER, yeoman, of Duxbury, to Isaac SAMSON, all I bought of heirs of Zeruiah CHANDLER. Wife Mercy signs. Ack. 14 Mar. 1788. Rec. 22 Mar. 1788.

75:67 - 16 Oct. 1788, John CHANDLER, yeoman, & wife Mercy, of Duxbury, to Peleg GU( )LFOR of Duxbury, yeoman, re: division of heirs of Phineas SPRAGUE.

==========

Will of **Briggs ALDEN** of Duxbury. <Plymouth Co.PR #69, 36:17,19>
<36:17>...23 Dec. 1793...wife Mercy, to son Judah ALDEN land on Common Island, to son Nathaniel ALDEN all land in N. Yarmouth & Freeport, unmarried daughters Edith ALDEN, Abigail ALDEN, deceased daughter Deborough, her children to receive furniture which Deborough had of her father at the time of her first marriage, to son Amherst ALDEN all estate in Duxbury & Pembroke. Witnesses: George PARTRIDGE, Benjamin ALDEN, Hannah SOUTHWORTH. Will approved 8 Oct. 1796. <36:19> Probate & bond dated 9 Dec. 1796, Amherst ALDEN app'td. Executor. Sureties: George PARTRIDGE, Benjamin ALDEN. Witnesses: Nathaniel LOTHROP, Isaac LOTHROP.

MICRO #10 of 16

Estate of **Judah ALDEN**, mariner, of Duxbury. <Plymouth Co.PR #142, 8:344,424,492,9:133-35>
<8:344>...21 May 1741, Joshua DELANO app'td. adm. Sureties: Benjamin LORING, Nathaniel SIMMONS. Witnesses: Abraham BOOTH, Samuel ALDEN. <8:424> Inventory taken at Boston 22 July 1741 by William PALFREY, William BAKER, Jonathan PETERSON. Personal estate valued at £47.6. <8:492> Inventory taken 27 Jan. 1741 by John WADSWORTH, Gamaliel BRADFORD, Samuel WESTON. Sworn by Judah DELANO same day. Incl. bond from his brother Samuel ALDEN and Joshua LORING of Duxbury dated 10th June 1741, "248.17.10", land at Ashford which was his father's, land at Ashford which was his mother's viz one half of all her lands at Ashford, "130.0". <9:133> Account of Joshua DELANO allowed 23 Sept. 1743, debts due incl. Samuel BARTLETT, Thomas GARDNER, Jedediah SOUL, Samuel WESTON, Daniel SWINERTON, Micah SAMSON, Samuel STURGIS, Jonathan PETERSON, James BODOIN, Nathaniel DONHAM, Pelatiah WEST, Joshua CUSHING Jr., Thomas GARDNER & WETHERELL in right of Silva CURTIS, Peter ROE of Boston, Benjamin LORING, Hezekiah RIPLEY, Samuel ALDEN Jr., Joshua SOUL, John WADSWORTH. To the **Widow Dolton** right of dower settled. To Peter ROE bill for widow's mourning apparel. To what Ashford land sold at vendue short of the apraisal. <9:134> Insolvency and leave to sell real estate dated second Tuesday of July 1742. <9:135> Receipt of Jas. HOVEY dated 22 Sept. 1743 in full of a judgment Thomas GARDNER recovered against said DELANO in his capacity at ye Inferior Court held at Plymouth on the third Tuesday of Sept. 1742. £49,05.1. Witnesses: Samuel WESTON, Thomas WETHERELL.

==========

Jonathan ALDEN of Marshfield. <Plymouth Co.Deeds 22:61>
...3 Apr. 1727, Jonathan Alden & wife Elizabeth who was the daughter of Seth ARNOLD, Esq. late of Duxbury, release to brothers Edward ARNOLD & James ARNOLD all right to land of father Seth ARNOLD and brother Benjamin ARNOLD, dec'd.

==========

PLYMOUTH CO. DEEDS:

26:44 - 4 Jan. 1730, Jonathan ALDEN of Marshfield to Thomas WATERMAN, step-son.

28:44 - 23 July 1733, Jonathan ALDEN of Duxbury, housewright to Peltiah WEST.

28:115 - 13 Aug. 1733, Jonathan ALDEN of Duxbury, housewright to Peltiah WEST.

30:12 - 3 July 1735, Jonathan ALDEN of Duxbury, gentleman to William HARLOW.

30:29 - 11 Mar. 1735, Jonathan ALDEN of Duxbury to Josiah CUSHMAN.

JOSEPH ALDEN[2] (John[1])

David ALDEN of Middleboro to **John ALDEN** of Middleboro. <Plymouth Co.Deeds 40:120>
Dated 18 Feb. 1743, no particulars given. Witnesses: Jacob GREEN, Joshua WHITE. Ack. 11 Mar. 1744 ("The original deed is owned (Oct. 1909) by Mrs. Bertha Lincoln Heustis, Dubugne, Iowa.)

==

Estate of **Nathaniel SHAW** of Raynham. <"Taunton PR 40:535" (Bristol Co.)>
Will dated 14 Aug. 1795...mentions among others daughter **Sarah ALDEN**...pew in Baptist meeting house...probated 22 Sept 1804. (Not transcribed in files.)

==

Will of **Ezra ALDEN** of Bridgewater. <Plymouth Co.PR #95, 20:8,125;21:127;25:82>

<20:8> Will dated 16 Oct. 1767...wife Rebecca...to underage son **Isaac ALDEN** half of estate... to daughters **Abigail ALDEN** and **Susanna ALDEN** (both in their minority) half of estate. Witnesses: Ebenezer ALDEN, John ORCUT, Content PACKARD. Will probated 4 Jan. 1768, **Nathan ALDEN**, brother of testator app'td. Executor.

<20:125> Inventory taken 11 Dec. 1767 by John ORCUTT, Isaac ALLEN, David KINGMAN Jr. Total amount of estate Ł896.19.1, incl. homestead & buildings Ł380.13.4, lands at Beaver Brook, house & 3/8ths of a sawmill Ł356.13.4. Account of **Nathan ALDEN** allowed 10 Oct. 1768, debts received of: Zachariah SHAW, David KINGMAN, Benjamin BYRAM, Jonathan ALDEN, David KEITH, Jona. BASS, Nathan ORCUTT, Isaac ALDEN, William BARREL, E. WILLIS. Debts paid to: Abisha STETSON, Jacob WHITMARSH, Isaac LAZELL, Joseph KEITH, Samuel CRANE, Nathan ALDEN, David HILL, William BONNEY, Joseph ( ), Caleb KINGMAN, Jacob ALLEN, Josiah RICHARDS, Daniel SHAW, Josiah PERKINS, Eliab FOBES, Dr. HOWARD, Dr. OTIS, Dr. BRYANT.

<21:127> Division of Dower to Rebecca, wife of John BISBEE (late widow of dec'd.), 1/3 of estate incl. real estate leased by said deceased to his father **Capt. Ebenezer ALDEN** during his life...Rebecca to have the improvement at the decease of said Capt. Alden. Dated 21 Apr. 1772, allowed 4 May 1772.

<Orig.> Petition of George VINING & Abigail his wife, for division of estate, 28 Sept. 1778.

<25:82> Warrant & Division of Estate: 12 Nov. 1778, two parts to **Isaac ALDEN**, one part each to **Abigail VINING** and **Susanna ALDEN.**

==

Guardianship of Children of **Ezra ALDEN.** <Plymouth Co.PR #186, 21:33,25:83,25:544,545, 26:361,26:363, 28:63,29:152,29:243>

<Original> Declination dated 30 Nov. 1717, **Nathan ALDEN** declines, having been named guardian in will of Ezra ALDEN.

<21:33> Bonds dated 2 Dec. 1771, David KINGMAN appointed guardian of **Susannah ALDEN, Isaac ALDEN** and **Abigail ALDEN,** all under fourteen. Sureties: John BISBE, Thomas MORE. Witnesses: Thomas LORING, Edward WINSLOW Jr.

<25:83> Account dated 7 Dec. 1778, of David KINGMAN, guardian of the three children. He charges himself with the remainder of the personal estate of **Ezra ALDEN** deceased (widow's dower excepted); paid John BISBEE for supporting **Susanna** from five to seven years old, paid Isaac ALLEN for nursing & boarding of **Abigail** when sick of smallpox, paid for boarding & schooling of **Isaac,** three months.

<25:544> Account dated 1 May 1780 of David KINGMAN, guar. of **Isaac ALDEN,** allowed 2 Oct. 1780.

<25:545> Receipt dated 1 May 1780 of **Nathan ALDEN,** received of Capt. David KINGMAN, Ł7,15,11 in full of the within balance allowed by Hon. Judge of Probate.

<Original> Bond dated 1 May 1780, **Nathan ALDEN** of Bridgewater app'td. guardian of **Isaac ALDEN,** minor over 14. Sureties: David KINGMAN, Hezekiah HOOPER. Witnesses: Melatiah WHITE, John WATERMAN Jr.

<26:361> Nomination dated 1 May 1780, of **Nathan ALDEN** guardian, by **Isaac ALDEN.** Witnesses: Nathan ALDEN Jr., Sarah ALDEN

<26:363> Nomination dated 5 Mar. 1781, of **Nathan ALDEN** guardian, by **Susanna ALDEN** above 14. Witnesses: Elisha BISBE, Isaac ALDEN.

<Original> Petition dated 3 Feb. 1781, of **Susanna ALDEN** for the appointment of **Capt. Nathan ALDEN** to be her guardian. Witnesses: George VINING, Nathan ALDEN Jr.

<Original> Bond dated 5 Mar. 1781, **Nathan ALDEN** app'td. guardian of **Susanna ALDEN,** minor above 14. Sureties: Elijah SNELL, John HUDSON. Witnesses: Jona. CRANE, Isaac LOTHROP.

<28:63> Account dated 9 Apr. 1781, of David KINGMAN, guardian of **Susanna ALDEN.**

<29:152> Account dated 7 June 1784, of **Nathan ALDEN,** guardian to **Isaac ALDEN,** charges himself with money received from Capt. David KINGMAN and Nathan ORCUT.

<29:243> Account dated 7 Mar. 1785 of **Nathan ALDEN,** guardian of **Susanna ALDEN.**

==

Will of **John ALDEN** of Bridgewater. <Plymouth Co.PR #131, 15:284,285,16:26>

<15:284> Will dated 28 Mar. 1759...Rebecca, wife, son John ALDEN, granddaughter Nabby ALDEN. Wife has improvement of estate until son John arrives at the age of twenty one and then to be divided among "my then surviving children". Witnesses: Recompence CARY, William BURREL, Ichabod CARY.

<16:26> Inventory taken 24 May 1759 by Ebenezer ALDEN, Nathan BEAL, Zacharias SHAW. Sworn by Rebecca ALDEN 3 Nov. 1760, real estate valued at Ł266.13.04.

<Orig.> Warrant dated 26 Apr. 1759. Appraisers: Ebenezer ALDEN, Zachariah SHAW, Nathan BEALS.

==

Guardianship of Children of **John ALDEN** of Bridgewater. <Plymouth Co.PR #140, 20:196>

<20:196> Bonds dated 6 Mar. 1769, Hugh ORR appointed guardian of Joseph, James, Adam, Benjamin & Nabbe/Nabby ALDEN, the first four, children of John ALDEN late of Bridgewater, **Nabbe** being the daughter of Isaac ALDEN late of Bridgewater. James & Adam over 14, Joseph, Adam and Nabbe under. Sureties: Ephraim CARY, Benjamin WHITMAN. Witnesses: Shubael TINKHAM, Edward WINSLOW Jr.

Estate of **Jonathan ALDEN** of E. Bridgewater. <Plymouth Co.PR #135>
...24 Feb. 1825, adm. requested by sons **Isaac ALDEN 2nd, Ezra ALDEN...Isaac ALDEN 3rd** named. Bond dated 1 Mar. 1825, $4,000.00 signed by **Isaac ALDEN 3rd** of E. Bridgewater, gentleman, Jesse PERKINS of W. Bridgewater, yeoman, Nathan GURNEY of Abington, Esq. Inventory (no date) incl. homestead, $1,375, Woodland, $420, Personal, $58, Total: $1815.00 Petition dated 21 Mar. 1825 to sell real estate at public auction. First Account dated 20 Feb. 1826, "notes paid to": Isaac ALDEN 2nd, $200; Ezra ALDEN, $200; John ALDEN, $200; Cyrus ALDEN, $200; Jonathan ALDEN, $121; Mehetabel JACKSON, $200; Mary BARRELL, $200. Second Account dated 3 Oct. 1826, "portions distributed to": Ezra ALDEN, 11.76; Isaac ALDEN, 11.76; Edward VINTON, Cyrus ALDEN's portion, 11.76; Edward VINTON, John ALDEN's portion, 11.76; Edward VINTON, Mehetable JACKSON's portion, 11.76; Christopher FRENCH, Jonathan ALDEN's portion, 11.76; Widow Rhoda ALDEN, Samuel ALDEN's heirs' portion, 11.76; Abel BARRELL, Mary BARRELL's portion, 11.76; Daniel ALDEN, 11.76.

Will of **Benjamin RICHARDS** of Bridgewater. <Plymouth Co.PR #16790, 8:373,374>
...dated 24 Jan. 1740/1...mentions wife Lydia and following children: Joseph RICHARDS, Daniel RICHARDS (to get land bought of Hannah BRADFORD), John RICHARDS, Josiah RICHARDS, Ezra RICHARDS, Mehitable PACKARD (wf of David), Sarah PACKARD (wf of William), Lydia RICHARDS and Hannah RICHARDS (both under 18). Probated 20 May 1741.

Will of **David ALDEN** of Middleboro. <Plymouth Co.PR #77, 16:503,504,535>
<16:503>...dated 14 May 1763...mentions wife Judith, and following children: **Solomon ALDEN, David ALDEN, Job ALDEN, Abigail ALDEN** (under 21, to have improvement of old part of the house so long as she needs it), **Silas ALDEN**; brothers **Joseph ALDEN, John ALDEN.** <16:535> Inventory dated 5 Nov. 1763. Appraisers: Abiezer EDSON, Benjamin WHITE, Joshua WHITE. Sworn by Job ALDEN, Ex. Estate incl.: homestead farm Ł600, out meadow Ł53.6.8., farm at Ashford Ł120. Total: Ł953.19.8.
<16:504> Will probated 14 May 1763. (Same day as will written???)

David ALDEN of Middleboro to **John ALDEN** of Middleboro. <Plymouth Co.Deeds 40:120>
...18 Feb. 1743...David ALDEN, for the sum of sixty pounds paid by John ALDEN...a certain piece of meadow containing three acres more or less...lying and being in the purchase caled the sixteen shilling purchase in the town ship of Middleborough...being part of the meadow that I purchased of Joseph WARREN and the other part of that meadow that was formerly John HAWARD's...southwesterly side of Pachade Brook. Witnesses: Jacob GREEN, Joshua WHITE.

Estate of **Silas ALDEN** of Middleboro. <Plymouth Co.PR #180, 17:135,19:207,20:331>
<Orig.> Bond dated 5 Nov. 1764, Silence ALDEN, widow, appointed adm. Sureties: David ALDEN of Middleboro, Edmond HALL of Raynham. Witnesses: Abel STETSON, Edward WINSLOW Jr.
<17:135> Letter of Adm. dated 5 Nov. 1764, Silence ALDEN, widow, appointed.
<19:207> Inventory taken 4 Feb. 1765 by Benjamin WHITE, Joseph ALDEN, Joshua WHITE. Sworn by Executrix 23 May 1765. Real estate valued at Ł774.2.4.
<20:331> Account of Silence LEONARD, adm., allowed 18 May 1768. Received of Solomon ALDEN for land sold at Ashford, Ł24.0.0. Paid to Zephaniah LEONARD, Ephraim OTIS, widow Judah ALDEN, Robert CALDWELL, Thomas DARLING Jr., Thomas HOOPER, Job ALDEN, Jabez CUSHMAN, David KINGMAN, Nathan THOMAS, Lieut. Benjamin WHITE, Josiah BRADFORD, Silvanus EATON, Solomon BEALS, Noah WISWAL, Joshua WHITE, James KEITH, Hugh ORR, Dr. Isaac OTIS, Joseph LUCAS, John PERRY, Jonathan FARMAN.

Guardianship of Children of **Silas ALDEN** of Middleboro. <Plymouth Co.PR #181, 20:409>
<Orig.> Bond dated 22 Nov 1770, Job ALDEN appt'd. guardian of **Roscinda ALDEN,** under 14. Surety: Ephraim SPOONER. Witnesses: Sarah WINSLOW, Edward WINSLOW Jr.
<Orig.> Bond dated 10 Dec. 1770, Job ALDEN appt'd. guardian of **Silence ALDEN,** under 14. Surety: Ephraim SPOONER. Witnesses: Sarah WINSLOW, Edward WINSLOW Jr.
<Orig.> Request (no date) of Solomon ALDEN and David ALDEN for the appointment of their brother as guardian of the children of our brother Silas ALDEN, deceased.

Estate of **Thomas WOOD** of Middleboro. <Plymouth Co.PR 9:414,479,496-500, 15:213>
<9:414> Administration dated 12 Feb. 1744. <15:213> Division dated 1 May 1756, the following appointed to divide estate: John TOMSON, David ALDEN, Benjamin HAYFORD, William CUSHMAN, Benjamin WHITE; nine shares to following heirs: Thomas WOOD, double share (eldest son), Priscilla WOOD, Amaziah WOOD, Zephaniah WOOD, Lemuel WOOD, Abigail WOOD, heirs of Abner WOOD dec'd, heirs of Hannah WOOD, dec'd. Division of 3 Apr. 1758 mentions: **Thomas WOOD, Zephaniah WOOD, Lemuel WOOD, Abigail WOOD, Hannah WOOD, Abner WOOD, Amaser/Amaziah WOOD, Priscilla PRATT** wf of John. Signed by David ALDEN, John TOMSON, William CUSHMAN, Benjamin WHITE. <9:496> Guardianship of Children: 27 June 1745, Elnathan WOOD was appointed guardian of minor children, viz: Amasa/Amaziah, Lemuel, Abigail, Hannah, Thomas and Abner.

Estate of **Thomas WOOD.** <Plymouth Co.Wills 39:178>
Administration dated 25 Feb. 1809. Inventory dated 11 Mar. 1809. Division "mentions Lucinda and Thomas". (not transcribed further in files)

MICRO #11 of 16

Estate of **Joseph ALDEN** of Middleborough. <Plymouth Co.PR #136, 27:224,30:372,522>

<27:224> - Bond dated 4 Apr. 1787, **Abner ALDEN** app'td. adm. Sureties: Seth EATON, Silas WHITE (all of Middleboro). Witnesses: William THOMPSON, Isaac LOTHROP.

<30:372> - Inventory taken 4 July 1788 by Joshua WHITE, Seth EATON, Silas WHITE; sworn by **Abner ALDEN** on 7 July 1788; estate incl. seven acres pasturage which belonged to the estate of **Ebenezer ALDEN**, late of Middleboro, deceased.

<30:522> - Account dated 2 Mar. 1789. Creditors: Dr. Thomas STURTEVANT, Dr. Jonathan FULLER, Dr. Lewis LEPRILETE, Dr. Samuel PERRY, Dr. Joseph CLARK, Class tax paid Jeptha RIPLEY, State tax No.4 paid Abner PRATT, State tax No.5 paid Job ALDEN, John RICKARD, Elijah HACKET, Andrew LEACH, Benjamin & Seth SILVESTER, William BROWN, Seth EATON, Silas WHITE, Nathan EATON, Rufus WESTON, Abner SHAW, Joshua WHTE Esq., Robert LUSCOMBE Esq, Job ALDEN, Seth PADDLEFORD, Samuel RICKARD, Perez LEONARD.

Deborah ALDEN, widow of Middleborough et al. <No source>

...29 Aug. 1789...I **Deborah ALDEN**, widow to **Joseph ALDEN**, late of Middleborough...in consideration of thirty four pounds, seventeen shillings and two pence...paid by **Abner ALDEN** & **Eliab ALDEN** both of Middleboro, yeomen, **Lewis HALL**, yeoman and **Fear** his wife, **Lois ALDEN**, **Orpah ALDEN** & **Polly ALDEN**, all of Raynham; and **Hannah ALDEN**, of Bridgewater, **Abner ALDEN** & **Joshua FOBES**, Guardians to **Joseph**, **Ruth** and **Ebenezer ALDEN**, minors, Heirs to the Estate of said **Joseph ALDEN**, deceased, Do hereby Remit, release and forever quit claim unto them...all my Right of Dower & Power of Thirds in...the estate of **Joseph ALDEN**, deceased. Witnesses: Thomas LEACH, Elisabeth LEACH

Estate of **Ebenezer ALDEN** of Middleboro. <Plymouth Co.PR #82, 21:222,224,336,460;25:306;28:99,100>

<Orig.> - Petition of **Ruth ALDEN**, wife of **Ebenezer ALDEN**, representing that she is left with a number of small children & asking for the appointment of her father **Joseph ALDEN** as administrator. Dated 3 Mar. 1773.

<Orig.> - Bond dated 3 Mar. 1773, **Joseph ALDEN** of Middleboro app'td. adm. of estate of **Ebenezer ALDEN**, trader. Sureties: John JACKSON, Isaac WILLSON.

<21:222> - Appointment of **Joseph ALDEN**, adm., 3 Mar. 1773.

<21:224> - Inventory taken 30 Apr 1773 by Benjamin WHITE, Solomon ALDEN, Joseph EATON, sworn by **Joseph ALDEN** 3 May 1773; real estate £88.6.8, total £181.3.5.

<21:336> - Estate insolvent by **Joseph ALDEN** 3 Dec. 1773, Benjamin WHTE and Abner KINGMAN app'td. Commissioners.

<21:360> - Debts: Silas WOOD, John SHAW, estate of Samuel KINSLEY, Nathaniel TUCKER, Thomas HOOPER, Calvin HOOPER, William WHITE, John JONES, Joseph LEONARD 2d, McWHORTER & STEVENSON, Elias MILLER, Seth ALDEN, Aaron LOPES of Newport, Benjamin SHAW, Gershom RICHMOND, John SHAW Jr., Samuel DUNBAR Jr., Joseph BARDEN, George SHOVE, James KEITH, William PRATT, Calvin EDSON, Nathaniel BUMPUS, Shadrach WILBORE, Isaac SWIFT, William CLARK, Jabez CUSHMAN, Abiel EDSON, Gershom RICHMOND, William RICHMOND, Wiliam BROWN, Joseph LEONARD 3d, Joseph CLARK, Elijah SNOW, Jesse BRYANT, Joshua WHITE, John HILL of Brookfield, Joseph BUMPUS, William TUPPER, Jedediah LYON, Isaac SHAW, Timothy FOSTER, Joshua ALLEN of Dartmouth, Zebulon KING, William TOMSON, Benjamin DARLING, Henry BOWERS of Swanzy, Joseph ALDEN, Isaac TINKHAM, Thomas BRIGGS, Stephen BURT, Zebulon WHITE, Samuel SHAW of New Salem, Ebenezer BAKER, Noah PHINNEY, Joshua FOBES, John HAYWARD, Peter HUNT, Peter CLARK, Thomas WOOD, Zephaniah SHAW, James DUNBAR, Moses EDDY, Samuel SNOW, Hushai THOMAS, John ALDEN. Dated 2 July 1774.

<25:306> - Account of **Joseph ALDEN** allowed 5 July 1779, incl. a journey to Ashfield to pay rates for the land £1.1.5.

<28:99> - Account of **Joseph ALDEN** allowed 5 Aug. 1782.

<28:100> - Order to pay creditors of the estate, dated 5 Aug. 1782.

Ebenezer ALDEN, Guardianship of Children. <Plymouth Co.PR #84, 26:454,455>

<Orig.> - Bond dated 4 Aug. 1788, **Abner ALDEN** app'td. guardian of **Joseph ALDEN** above 14, son of **Ebenezer ALDEN** deceased: Sureties: Isaac TOMSON, Joshua WHITE both of Middleboro. Witnesses: Enoch THOMAS 2d, Rowland LEONARD.

<26:454> - Power of Guardian signed by **Joseph ALDEN**, above 14. Witnesses: Eliab ALDEN, Ichabod EATON. Dated 6 Oct. 1788.

<Orig.> - Bond dated 6 Oct. 1788, Joshua FOBES app'td guardian of **Ruth & Ebenezer ALDEN**, minors above 14 and children of **Ebenzer ALDEN.** Sureties: Daniel FOBES, Robert FOBES. Witnesses: Abner ALDEN, Isaac LOTHROP, Joshua FOBES, all of Bridgewater.

<26:455> - Power of Guardian signed by **Ruth & Ebenezer ALDEN.** Witnesses: Robert FOBES, Solomon FOBES, dated 3 Nov. 1788...all estate that accrues to said minors in right of father and in right of grandfather **Joseph ALDEN** late of Middleboro, deceased.

Will of **Noah THOMAS** of Middleboro. <Plymouth Co.PR 15:278>

...16 Dec. 1758...wife Mary, sons Daniel THOMAS & Abial THOMAS, daughters Lucy ALDEN, Fear SHAW, Mary THOMAS, Hannah THOMAS (under 21), Priscila THOMAS (under 21). Witnesses: Ephraim WOOD, Daniel VAUGHN, Jonah WASHBURN. Prob. 26 Apr. 1759.

Joseph ALDEN, Joseph HAYWARD to **Samuel LUCAS.** <Plymouth Co.Deeds 11:125,126>

...16 Nov. 1713...Joseph ALDEN & Hannah his wife and Joseph HAYWARD & Mehetabel his wife, all of the town of Bridgewater for thirty shillings paid by Samuel LUCAS of the town of Plymouth sold to him thirty acres of undivided <p.126> land within the town of Plymouth belonging to Daniel DONHAM of Plymouth deceased, his children by vertue of their being freeholders in the town of Plymouth

and was granted February the 9th 1701/2. Signed by Joseph ALDEN, Hannah ALDEN, Joseph HAYWARD with Mehetabel HAYWARD making her mark. Witnesses: James SHAW, John PRATT Sr. Rec. 13 May 1715.

Will of **Barnabas ALDEN** of Ashfield. <Hampshire co.PR>
...4 Oct. 1793...to my beloved wife **Elisabeth** all my moveable estate...excepting one gun which I give to my eldest son **Barnabas ALDEN**...To my son **Zephaniah ALDEN** twenty five acres of land on the east end of the hundred acre lot number twenty eight in the second division of land in said Ashfield to be his when he arrives at the age of twenty one years...To my beloved wife the Improvement of all my real estate during her natural life, at her decease I order that my real estate be equally divided between **Barnabas ADEN, Mary GOULD, Lydia GOULD, Susanna HOWES, Deborah SMITH, Esther ALDEN, Abigail ALDEN & Zephaniah ALDEN** all my natural children. Witnesses: Benjamin ROGERS, Justus SMITH, Sibbel FULLER.

Will of **Eleazer ALDEN** of Bridgewater. <Plymouth Co.PR #87, 21:228,229>
<21:228>...dated 2 May 1769 by **Eleazer ALDEN**, advanced in years...sons **Jonathan ALDEN, Eleazer ALDEN, David ALDEN, Ezra ALDEN, Joshua ALDEN, Timothy ALDEN. Eleazer & Joshua** to receive real estate incl. homestead, others to receive personal estate only. <21:22> Probate dated 1 Feb. 1773 **Joshua ALDEN** named executor & appointed. Bond dated 1 Feb. 1773, **Joshua ALDEN** of Bridgewater appointed executor Sureties: Josiah RICHARDS, Christopher SEVER. Witnesses: Samuel BALDWIN, Edward WINSLOW Jr.

References to Simeon & Solomon ALDEN: <Plymouth Co.Deeds>

49:239 -	7 June 1764,	Simeon ALDEN, tanner, of Bridgewater to Richard WILLIAMS of Raynham, land and house in Titicut.
54:98 -	17 Mar. 1767,	Samuel ALDEN, yeoman, of Bridgewater to Simeon ALDEN, tanner, of Bridgewater, land in Titicut my father gave to me.
-	8 Apr. 1768,	Simeon ALDEN, tanner of Bridgewater to Eliphaz PRIOR of Duxborough, wife Mary releases dower.
65:143 -	15 July 1784,	Solomon ALDEN Jr., yeoman, of Bridgewater to Asahel SHAW of Bridgewater.
87:82 -	22 Feb. 1799,	Solomon ALDEN Jr., gentleman, of Bridgewater to Jeremiah KEITH of Bridgewater, land in Pembroke, wife Polly releases dower.
87:177 -	7 Mar. 1799,	Solomon ALDEN Jr., gentleman, of Bridgewater to Asahiel SHAW.
98:69 -	29 June 1799,	Solomon ALDEN Jr., gentleman, of Bridgewater to Noah ALDEN and Amasa ALDEN, land in Pembroke, "Polly signs also".
102:169 -	1805,	Solomon ALDEN Jr. to Joseph WHITE.
108:224 -	1808,	to Solomon ALDEN Jr.
108:240 -	1808,	Solomon ALDEN to Amasa ALDEN.
116:14 -	1809,	Solomon ALDEN to Alexander SHAW.
122:28 -	1813,	Solomon ALDEN to Noah ALDEN.
122:65 -	1814,	Solomon ALDEN to Amasa ALDEN.

Estate of **Daniel ALDEN** of Bridgewater. <Plymouth Co.PR #73, 37:131,441,442;43:46>

<37:131> - Will dated 29 Aug. 1799, wife **Sarah**, children **Otis ALDEN, Daniel ALDEN, Sally ALDEN, Alpheus ALDEN.** Wife **Sarah** and brother **Joseph ALDEN** appoointed executors.
- Declination of **Sarah ALDEN** to act as joint executor with **Joseph ALDEN**, 5 Oct. 1799.
- Probate dated 7 Oct. 1799.

<Orig.> - Bond dated 7 Oct. 1799, **Joseph ALDEN** app'td. executor. Sureties: Moses CARY, Abiel HARRIS. Witnesses: Daniel HOWARD, Isaac LOTHROP.

<37:441> - Inventory taken 21 Oct. 1799 by Moses CARY, Samuel BRETT Jr., Abial HARRIS. Sworn by Joseph ALDEN 4 May 1801; real estate $1600.00, personal $715.97.

<37:442> - Order of notice filed by **Joseph ALDEN** 4 May 1801.
- Account of **Joseph ALDEN** dated & allowed 4 May 1801. Due from the following: Benjamin GLOVER, Fobes FIELD, Richard FIELD, Jonathan CARY, James CARY, Lt. Samuel BRETT, Nathaniel SNELL, Noah AMES. Paid to the following: Samuel ALDEN, Dr. Gridley THAXTER Noah AMES, Moses CARY, Abial HARRIS, Zenas FRENCH, Capt. Jesse PERKINS, Zadoc PERKINS, Ichabod HOWARD, Thomas MACOMBER, "due to the widow Susanna HARRIS", Elisha EAMES, Solomon HILL, Mr. HOOPER, Mercy WARREN, Adin PACKARD, Nathaniel SPEAR, Silas ALDEN, Jonathan CARY Jr., James CARY, Richard FIELD, Williams ALDEN, Oliver HARRIS, Joseph ALDEN, Dr. ALDEN.

<43:46> - Division dated 16 Dec. 1809, by Dea. Daniel SHAW, Howard CARY & Perez SOUTHWORTH; accepted 22 Dec. 1809. One fourth of estate each to **Otis ALDEN** (eldest son), **Daniel ALDEN** (second son), **Sally ALDEN** (daughter), **Alpheus ALDEN** (youngest son).

Estate of **Seth ALDEN** of Bridgewater. <Plymouth Co.PR #177, 29:203,204>
<29:203>...will dated 7 Apr. 1784...three sons **Joseph ALDEN** (named executor), **Oliver ALDEN, Joseph ALDEN**; grandson under 21, **Seth ALDEN.** <29:204> Probate of will dated 4 Oct. 1784. Bond dated 4 Oct. 1784, **Joseph ALDEN** appointed executor. Sureties: Benjamin WILLIS, Moses LEONARD all of Bridgewater. Witnesses: Jesse STURTEVANT, Isaac LOTHROP.

Estate of **Seth ALDEN Jr.** of Bridgewater. <Plymouth Co.PR #176, 24:18,113;30:4>
<24:18> Will dated 24 Aug. 1775 by **Seth ALDEN Jr.**, blacksmith, mentions wife **Mary**, father **Seth ALDEN**, brothers **Oliver ALDEN** and **Joseph ALDEN**; leaves entire estate to wife **Mary** who is named executor with his brother **Oliver ALDEN.** <24:113> Inventory taken 24 Nov. 1775 by Josiah EDSON, Solomon LEONARD, Hezekiah HOOPER. Sworn by **Oliver ALDEN** 25 May 1776; real estate £341.5.0., total amount of estate £487.8.1. <30:4> Account of **Oliver ALDEN** and **Mary ALDEN** dated 3 July 1786.

Charges themselves with cash paid to following: Ephraim ALLEN, George KEITH, Ebenezer PERKINS, James PERKINS, John KEITH, Mary PERKINS, Ezra EDSON, Daniel COPELAND, Josiah EDSON, John WILLIS, Benjamin WASHBURN 2d, Thomas LAWRENCE, Jona than WATERMAN, Jonathan LEACH, Moses SIMMONS, Silas WOOD, John WASHBURN, Henry BASS, Dr. Eleazer CARVER, James ALLEN, Solomon AMES, Adam PACKARD, Zephaniah SMITH, Enoch PERKINS, John RICHHUE, Jonathan RUSSELL, Joseph COPELAND, Eli HUDSON, John PORTER, Abraham PERKINS Jr., Benjamin SAMPSON, Abijah DYER, Joseph SHURBURN, Eliphalet SAWING, Joshua ALDEN, Abisha WILLIS, Joseph BASSETT, Deborah RIPLEY, John CARVER 2d, Solomon ALDEN, James PERKINS Jr., Joseph KEITH, Abraham WASHBURN, Jacob WASHBURN, Samuel SHAW, John PITTS, Joseph WEBB, Benjamin ANDREAS, Benjamin PHILIPS, John WILLIS, Hannah & Sarah HAYWARD on notes, Joab WILLIS Jr., Jonathan WILLIS, Gershom CONANT, Jason FOBES, Simeon AMES, Eliphalet CARY, Luther KEITH, Josiah WASHBURN 2d, Jonathan BENSON, Simeon LEONARD, Eliphalet CARY, John PRATT, Simeon LEONARD, Samuel SALYBURY, estate of Ebenezer KEITH, Jirai SWIFT, Solomon PRATT, Daniel HAYWARD, William GILES, Robert CROSMAN, estate of Francis PERKINS, John ANDREWS, Ezra CONANT, Benjamin KEITH, "John SCOTT & GILL", to Eleazer CARVER as executor of the will of Lev^t PERKINS on note, gravestones for <u>him & children</u>, Eliab HAYWARD, Luther RENSLEY, Hezekiah HOOPER.[6]

Guardianship for **Seth ALDEN 2d** of Bridgewater. <Plymouth Co.PR #178, 26:177>
<u>Bond</u> dated 2 June 1783...**Oliver ALDEN** of Bridgewater app'td. guardian of **Seth ALDEN 2d**, minor under 14, son of **Seth ALDEN Jr.**, late of Bridgewater, deceased, blacksmith. Sureties: Adams BAILEY of Bridgewater, Thomas GANNETT of Plymton. Witnesses: Elijah BISBE Jr., Isaac LOTHROP. <u>Letter of Guardianship</u> appointed **Oliver ALDEN** guardian of **Seth ALDEN** the second, aged seven years.[7]

Will of **John BURRILL**, husbandman, of Weymouth. <Suffolk Co.PR #6180, 29:320,321>
<29:321>...28 July 1727...wife Mercy...To daughter **Mary RIPEY** Ł100...To son **John BURREL** all my Salt meddow at buring/burying island...Witnesses: Benjamin LUDDEN, Abiezer HOLBROOK, Zachariah GURNEY...<29:320> Will probated 13 Dec. 1731.

<u>MICRO #12 of 16</u>

<u>REBECCA ALDEN</u>^{2} (John^1)

Thomas DELANO to Town of Bridgewater, re: brother **John DELANO**. <Bridgewater Rcds.1:49>
...1 Apr. 1667...I **Thomas DELANO** the sonn of **Phillip DELANO** of Duxburrough in the Patten of New Plimouth, taylor/tailor doe heare Ingage and bind...for my brother **John DELANO** now an apprentise to **John HILL**, shoemaker in Bridgewater...fully to discharge the aforesaid towne of Bridgewater of all Losses and Detriments Damages and charges whatsoever that may any way arise by my aforesaid brother **John DELANO** either by impotency or any other casuall providence that my fall out In reference to charge after his apprentiseshipp shall be expired till such time that my brother **John** shallbe received legally as an Inhabitant of another town And then the said **Thomas DELANO** is to be freed from his ingagement...Signed by **Thomas DELANO**. Witness: **John HILL.**

Philip DELANO Sr. & Thomas DELANO Sr. to **John MILLER.** <Plymouth Co.Deeds 7:85>
...3 Mar. 1704...Phillip DILLENO Sen. & Thomas DILLENO Sen. both of Duxboro for...fifteen pounds ...paid by John MILLER Jr. of ye towne of Middleboro...sell...our eighty foure acres of land...on ye northeast side of Raven Brook in ye township of Middleboro...bounded by 25 acres belonging to John COBB, 100 acres belonging to Elder Thomas FAUNCE and 25 acres belonging to Benjamin NYE... Witnesses: John WESTON, Joseph DILLENO. Rec. 28 Nov. 1706.

Deposition of **Nathaniel TURNER** of Shirley. <Worcester Co.Deeds 207:41>
...22 May 1817...I Nathaniel TURNER of Shirley in the county of Middlesex of eighty years of age do testify and say that my father **Amasa TURNER** bought a farm in the southerly part of the town of Lancaster about sixty eight years since, as I was then twelve years of age, that the only road went north of the dwelling house on said farm that I was absent as an apprentice about five years, and I was at my fathers during that period five or six times, that while I was absent the road now travelled was made about six rods south of the dwelling house on said farm, and on land of my fathers, and my father told me that he had agreed with his neighbour **Bezallel SAWYER**, who lived a little west of him, and who had occasion to use the old road to make the alteration for the accommodation of my father, that on my return from my apprenticeship the old road was improved by my father, so far as it went through his land. The old road above mentioned turned out of the now travelled road, near the foot of the hill about eighteen roads westerly of the Berlin road, thence westerly through land now owned by **Timothy WHITING** Esqr. to what was my fathers land, now said Whiting's, about eleven rods northerly of the now travelled road, thence through said land northerly of the house aforesaid, to **Bezallel SAWYER's Jr.** house thence to the southwest corner of **Bezallel SAWYER's** blacksmith shop. Deposition taken at the request of Timothy WHITING. Rec. 30 July 1817.

Isaac SOLINDINE of Leonminster to **Nathaniel TURNER** of Leonminster. <Worcester Co.Deeds 113:353>
...25 May 1789...Isaac SOLINDINE, yeoman for Ł200 sold to Nathaniel TURNER, yeoman, house and land in east part of Leonminster and a saw mill on it bounded by town line of Lancaster & Leonminster. Rec. 25 Jan. 1792.

Thomas BURRAGE of Leonminster to **Nathaniel TURNER** of Leonminster. <Worcester Co.Deeds 113:354>
...9 Sept. 1788...Thomas BURRAGE, husbandman, for Ł12 sold to Nathaniel TURNER, husbandman, six acres in N.E. part of Leonminster. Rec. 25 Jan. 1792.

Nathaniel TURNER of Leonminster to **Obadiah HOLT** of Leonminster. <Worcester Co.Deeds 189:627> ...25 May 1789, Nathaniel TURNER, yeoman and Anna TURNER for 20s sold to Obadiah HOLT, yeoman, three acres in east part of Leonminster on easterly line of town, with house thereon.

Ivory WILDS of Shirley to **Nathaniel TURNER** of Lancaster. <Worcester Co.Deeds 183:3> ...29 Aug. 1801, Ivory WILDS and wife Hannah, for $100.00 sold to Nathaniel TURNER, yeoman, 57 acres in north part of Lancaster.

Nathaniel TURNER of Lancaster to the Shakers in Shirley. <Worcester Co.Deeds 178:282> ...14 Jan. 1808, Nathaniel TURNER, yeoman, for love, etc. deeds to the Shakers of Shirley, about 57 acres in Lancaster, same that he bought of Ivory WILDS. Rec. 19 Jan. 1811.

Nathaniel TURNER of Shirley to **Bezaleel LAWRENCE** of Leonminster. <Worcester Co.Deeds 178:546> ...12 Feb. 1811, Nathaniel TURNER, yeoman for $10.00 sold to Bezaleel LAWRENCE, 1/2 acre in Leonminster, bounded easterly by Lancaster line, near White's Pond, part of his Leonminster farm. Rec. 5 Mar. 1811.

Estate of **Beriah DELANO** of Duxbury. <Plymouth Co. PR #6233, 11:124,399; 12:349; 15:106>
<15:106> Division dated 10 Mar. 1759, names six children, viz: Ichabod DELANO (eldest son, deceased since probate), William DELANO (next eldest son), Silvanus DELANO, Lemuel DELANO, Elizabeth DELANO, Benjamin DELANO.

Josiah, Paul, Thomas SAWYER to **Ichabod TURNER** of Lancaster. <Worcester Co.Deeds 47:206> ...9 Sept. 1760, Josiah SAWYER, Paul SAWYER and Thomas SAWYER Jr. all of Lancaster, yeomen, for L20.8s sold to Ichabod TURNER, cordwainer, ten acres & eighty rods of meadow and two acres and one hundred & thirty three rods of upland in Lancaster at a place known by the name of Whits/ White's Meadow & the upland lyeth between said meadow & ye road that leads from Lancaster to Harvard...Witnesses: Bezaleel SAWYER, Hannah SAWYER (both signed by mark). Rec. 18 Aug. 1762.

Ichabod TURNER of Lancaster to **Paul SAWYER** of Lancaster. <Worcester Co.Deeds 63:569> ...17 Nov. 1761, Ichabod TURNER, cordwainer for 50s sold to Paul SAWYER, yeoman, two acres and fifty rods of land in Lancaster, it lieth on the Scar Hill on the east side of Lancaster South River...said land was laid out to Francis BUTTRICK as may more fully appear by Lancaster Proprietors Book of Records. Witnesses: William RICHARDSON, Josiah SAWYER. Rec. 25 Feb. 1771.

Ichabod TURNER of Killingly CT to **Stanton PRENTICE** of Lancaster. <Worcester Co.Deeds 47:212> ...30 June 1762, Ichabod TURNER , cordwainer, for £40, sold to Stanton PRENTICE, physitian, ten acres and half of Meadow land more or less in them bounds and two acres and one hundred and thirty three rods of upland scituate in said Bolton at a Place called Whites Meadow...bounded partly by Zilpah & David WILDER...premises being formerly ye property of Bezaleel SAWYER, late of Lancaster dec'd. Witnesses: Moses BAYLEY, William HOUGHTON. Rec. 18 Aug. 1762.

Will of **Jonathan DELANO** of Duxbury. <Plymouth Co.PR 19:164>
...2 Dec. 1763...mentions wife Hannah; eldest son **John DELANO**, sole executor; children of 2nd son **Jonathan DELANO**, dec'd; grandson **Samuel DELANO**, son of said son Jonathan; 3rd son **Nathan DELANO**; 4th son **Amasa DELANO**; 5th son **Ebenezer DELANO**; 2 grandsons, **Jonathan DELANO** & **Oliver DELANO**, the sons of youngest son **David DELANO**, dec'd; granddaughter **Zilpha DELANO**, dau. of son David dec'd; daughter **Ruth PETERSON**; daughter **Hannah SOULE**; daughter **Dorothy CURTIS**, dec'd, mother of grandchildren **Silvanus CURTIS** and **Hannah CURTIS**. Witnesses: Abner WESTON, Joshua STANFORD, John WADSWORTH. Prob. 4 Feb. 1765. Inv. 29 Mar. 1765.

Will of **Jonathan DELANO** of Rochester. <Plymouth Co.PR 9:456>
...7 Mar. 1744...mentions father-in-law **Samuel WINSLOW**, wife Rachel, son **Jonathan DELANO** (under age), daughters **Hannah** and **Eliza**...remainder of moveable estate to be equally divided between all my children which I had by my second wife, viz: **Amasa**, **Samuel** and **Irana** excepting what I had by my last wife and that I give what of it shall remain after my debts are paid unto my daughters **Joanna** and **Martha**. Executors: Samuel WINSLOW, Elisha BARROWS. Witnesses: Ebenezer SPOONER, Sarah ROBINSON, Timothy RUGGLES. Probated 20 May 1745, Inv. 24 Apr. 1745.

<Plymouth Co.Deeds 43:144>...13 June 1755, **John DREW** and wife **Susanna** of Halifax sell 12 1/2 acres in 16 Shilling Purchase in Middleboro, 8th share in 21st lost belonging to Susanna.
<Plymouth Co.Deeds 45:70>...27 Apr. 1758, **John DREW** of Halifax sells land.

<Plymouth Co.Deeds 58:229>...2 Nov. 1773, **Dr. Stephen POWERS** and wife **Lydia** of Middleboro sell land to **Isaac TINKHAM.**

Estate of **Thomas DREW**, shipwright, of Halifax. <Plymouth Co.PR #6741, 20:431,21:41>
<20:431>...**Abigail DREW** petitioned court to appoint son **Thomas DREW** of Plimton, cordwainer, administrator on late husband's estate. <unrecorded bond>...13 Nov. 1770, **Thomas DREW**, Ephraim FULLER, yeoman of Halifax and Joseph LUCAS of Plymouth, as sureties gave a bond for £400. <21:41> ...Inventory taken at Halifax 20 Nov. 1770, by Moses INGLEE, Ebenezer TOMSON and Zadock BOSWORTH. Real estate valued at £240; total inventory at £308.1s.10d. Ack. by **Thomas DREW**, administrator, 1 Oct. 1771.

Samuel LUCAS et al of Halifax to **Thomas DREW** of Plimpton. <Plymouth Co.Deeds 64:5>
...12 July 1784, **Samuel LUCAS** & **Abigail LUCAS, Mary DREW**, spinster of Halifax, **Isaac DREW**, cordwainder of Halifax, **John DREW**, cordwain er of Halifax, **Peleg BARROWS Jr.**, yeoman of Plimpton and wife **Jemima BARROWS**...for £150 sold to **Thomas DREW**, gentleman...all our right title and interest in and unto the real and personal estate of **Thomas DREW**, our deceased father of Halifax. Witnesses: Samuel THACHER, Peleg BRYANT. Ack. by **Mary DREW** 24 Jan. 1785, ack. by rest 12 July 1784. Rec. 26 Jan. 1785.

Thomas DREW of Plympton to **Samuel LUCAS** of Plympton. <Plymouth Co.Deeds 64:6>
...28 Sept. 1784...Thomas DREW, gentleman, for £200 sold to Samuel LUCAS, gentleman, all that my lost of land which fell to me and my heirs of the home farm which was owned by my Father Mr. **Thomas DREW** of Halifax...being the estate which he dyed seized of, as also other shares which I bot of the heirs of said estate, being eight shares out of nine, with all the meadows, woods, under wood houses, out houses and barn fences and buildings thereon, always reserving the improvement of my Honoured Mother's Mrs. **Abigail DREW**'s thirds of the whole dureing her natural life. **Lucy DREW** wife of Thomas signs also. Witnesses: John ATWOOD, John DREW. Ack. by Thomas DREW 12 Jan. 1785. Rec. 26 Jan. 1785.

Estate of **Peleg BARROWS** of Carver, 1835. <Plymouth Co.PR #1129>
<71:305> Letter; <75:200> Notice of Appointment; <77:186> Inventory; <73:140> Petition to sell real estate; <78:175> Account.

PLYMOUTH COLONY DEEDS:

63:159 - 4 June 1785, Barzillai DELANO, blacksmith, of Duxbury buys land.
75:273 - 8 Oct. 1793, Barzillai DELANO, blacksmith, of Duxbury buys land.
75:270 - 27 Nov. 1793, Barzillai DELANO & wife Elizabeth sell land bought 4 June 1785 <62:159>
78:165 - 23 Nov. 1795, Barzillai DELANO buys land in Duxbury from Sarah Carver/Caneer?, widow of Marshfield.
84:188 - 3 Apr. 1798, Barzillai DELANO, blacksmith, of Duxbury & wife Elizabeth sell land.
84:205 - 3 Apr. 1798, Barzillai DELANO, blacksmith, of Duxbury & wife Elizabeth sell land.
86:23 - Aug. 1798, Barzillai DELANO, blacksmith, of Duxbury & wife Elizabeth sell land.
87:193 - 3 Apr. 1798, Barzillai DELANO, blacksmith, of Duxbury & wife Elizabeth sell land.
88:176 - 21 Aug. 1798, Barzillai DELANO, blacksmith, of Duxbury & wife Elizabeth sell land.

Samuel DYER et al of Cape Elizabeth to **Barzillai DELANO** of Cape Elizabeth. <Cumberland Co.Maine Deeds 13:244>
...3 July 1769...**Samuel DYER**, yeoman and wf Thankful; **Humphry RICHARDS**, shipwright and wf Sarah; **Daniel STROUT**, yeoman and wf Mary; **James SMALL**, mariner and wf Hannah; **Abigail DELANO**, spinster, all of Cape Elizabeth in the County of Cumberland...in consideration of the sum of twenty pounds lawfullmoney paid us by **Barzilla DELANO** of Cape Elizabeth, blacksmith...convey all our right, title and interest of the real estate of our Father **Thomas DELANO** late of Falmouth, deceased. Signed by: Thankful DYER (mark), Daniel STROUT, Humphry RICHARDS, Mary STROUT, James SMALL, Hannah SMALL, Sarah RICHARDS, John BAILEY, Abigail BAYLEY (mark), Ephraim CLARK, William WEBSTER, Loring CUSHING, Lucy MILLBANK (mark). Falmouth, 4th Mar. 1775, we subscribers set our hands & seal in the presence of the Witnesses: James PURRINGTON, Joseph MORSE, Clement JORDON.
Ack. 30 May 1781: Daniel & Mary STROUT, Humphrey & Sarah RICHARDS, Abigail BAYLEY. Ack. 25 Aug. 1781: James & Hannah SMALL, Thankfull DYER. Ack. 19 Mar. 1782: Samuel DYER. Rec. 12 May 1785.

RUTH ALDEN[2] (John[1])

Will of **Richard FAXON** of Braintree. <Plymouth Co.PR #718, 6:78,79; 5:227>
...29 Nov. 1674...wife Elizabeth, sons Josiah and Richard when they reach 21 years, son Thomas, daughters Mary, Sarah, Hannah, Abigail all at age 21 or marriage, father Thomas FAXON. Witnesses: Christopher WEBB, John BASS.

SUFFOLK CO. DEEDS: (BASS):

183:135 - 1 June 1796, Elisha BASS est. to John DRISCOLL, Boston.
1700:573 - 11 Nov. 1885, John BASS et al to City of Boston.
1717:205 - 1 Apr. 1886, John BASS et ux to Nathaniel P. BATCHELDER, Dorchester (mortgage).
1731:54 - 2 July 1886, John BASS et ux to Home Savings Bank, Dorchester (mortgage).
1754:218 - 23 Dec. 1886, John BASS et ux to Charles H. ALLEN, Dorchester (mortgage).
1759:458 - 14 Feb. 1887, John BASS to Home Savings Bank, Dorchester (mortage).
1761:434 - 5 Mar. 1887, John BASS et ux to Ezra MALLOCH, Dorchester.
1785:481 - 25 Aug. 1887, John BASS to Charles M. BUGBEE, Dorchester.
1788:268 - 9 Sept 1887, John BASS est. to William BRAMHALL, Dorchester.
1821:410 - 15 May 1888, John BASS et ux to Joseph E. BERTRAND, Dorchester.
1830:273 - 10 July 1888, John BASS et al (agreement).
1830:275 - 10 July 1888, John BASS to Henry MAIS, Dorchester.
1830:276 - 10 July 1888, John BASS est. to Henry MAIS, Dorchester.
1879:98 - 27 May 1889, John BASS to Home Savings Bank (mortgage).

MICRO #12 OF 16

SUFFOLK CO. DEEDS 1800-1899 (BASS): (cont-d)

1696:532 - 12 Oct. 1885, John BASS et ux from Home Savings Bank, Dorchester.
1731:52 - 2 July 1886, John BASS et ux from Home Savings Bank, Dorchester.
1759:457 - 14 Feb. 1887, John BASS from Home Savings Bank, Dorchester.
1761:433 - 5 Mar. 1887, John BASS's Wife from Home Savings Bank, Dorchester.
1830:273 - 10 July 1888, John BASS et al (agreement).
1879:97,101,106 - 27 May 1889, John BASS from Home Savings Bank, Dorchester.
1879:103 - 27 May 1889, John BASS to Home Savings Bank, Dorchester (mortgage).
1879:107 - 27 May 1889, John BASS to Home Savings Bank, Dorchester (mortgage).
1909:91 - 19 Nov. 1889, John BASS to Walter B. ROSS, Dorchester.
1911:282 - 3 Dec. 1889, John BASS from Home Savings Bank, Dorchester.
1911:283 - 3 Dec. 1889, John BASS to Home Savings Bank, Dorchester (mortgage).
1922:359 - 21 Feb. 1890, John BASS to Charles E. NUTTER, Dorchester (mortgage).
1945:174 - 3 July 1890, John BASS's Wife from Nathaniel P. BALCHELDER.
1950:157 - 1 Aug. 1890, John BASS to Pauline JOSEPHIE, Dorchester.
1988:449 - 8 Apr. 1891, John BASS et ux to Home Savings Bank, Dorchester (mortgage).
2015:351 - 10 Sept 1891, John BASS to John C. CALVAN, Dorchester.
2025:557 - 3 Nov. 1891, John BASS et al to City of Boston, Dorchester.
2350:501 - 14 Apr. 1896, John BASS's Wife from Nathaniel P. BALCHELDER (discharge of mortgage).
2350:502 - 14 Apr. 1896, John BASS et ux to Home Savings Bank, Dorchester (mortgage).
2353:611 - 28 Apr. 1896, John BASS's Wife from Home Savings Bank, Dorchester.
2353:612 - 28 Apr. 1896, John BASS et ux to Jane H. MURPHY, Dorchester.
2435:489 - 22 Apr. 1897, John BASS et ux to Rosa B. STONE, Dorchester.

SUFFOLK CO. DEEDS 1639-1799 (BASS):

29:122 - 6 Apr. 1715, John BASS, grantee.
30:212 - 13 Sept 1716, John BASS, grantee.
159:92 - 29 Nov. 1786, John BASS from Benjamin BASS, Braintree.
138:172 - 3 May 1783, Samuel BASS et al, guardians to Jacob DAVIS, Roxbury.
139:115 - 30 July 1783, Samuel BASS et al to Andrew SYMMES, Boston.
144:86 - 26 July 1784, Samuel BASS et al to Samuel BABCOCK, Braintree.
148:243 - 9 May 1785, Samuel BASS to Joseph BAXTER, Braintree.
158:232 - 12 Sept 1786, Samuel BASS est. to Samuel BASS, Braintree.
158:232 - 12 Sept 1786, Samuel BASS from Edward BASS, Braintree
162:91 - 23 Feb. 1788, Samuel BASS to Jesse FENNO, Braintree.
162:238 - 8 May 1788, Samuel BASS et al to John PRAY, Braintree.
164:74 - 1 Jan. 1789, Samuel BASS from Seth BASS, Braintree.
164:160 - 18 Feb. 1789, Samuel BASS from William LINFIELD, Braintree.
164:233 - 21 Mar. 1789, Samuel BASS et al to Nathaniel SPEAR, Braintree.
164:283 - 15 Apr. 1789, Samuel BASS from Samuel BASS et al, Braintree.
167:70 - 25 Dec. 1789, Samuel BASS from Joshua HOWARD Jr. et ux, Braintree.
167:70 - 25 Dec. 1789, Samuel BASS from MOSES BAKER, Braintree.
167:70 - 25 Dec. 1789, Samuel BASS from Thomas PENNIMAN et ux, Braintree.
169:25 - 20 Jan. 1791, Samuel BASS from Jonathan DAMON, Weymouth.
171:169 - 17 Dec. 1791, Samuel BASS from John VINTON, Braintree.
172:21 - 3 Feb. 1792, Samuel BASS from Ephraim WALES, Braintree.
172:22 - 3 Feb. 1792, Samuel BASS from John HOLBROOK, Braintree.
172:23 - 3 Feb. 1792, Samuel BASS from Edward HOWARD, admx., Braintree.
172:25 - 3 Feb. 1792, Samuel BASS from Nathaniel WALES, Stoughton.
172:25 - 3 Feb. 1792, Samuel BASS from Seth TURNER, Braintree.
172:26 - 3 Feb. 1792, Samuel BASS from Thomas TEMPLE, Braintree.
172:27 - 3 Feb. 1792, Samuel BASS from Cornelius WHITE, Braintree.
172:27 - 3 Feb. 1792, Samuel BASS from Samuel NILES, Braintree.
172:28 - 3 Feb. 1792, Samuel BASS from Jeremiah NILES, Braintree.

41:12 - 1 May 1727, Seth BASS, grantee.
47:54 - 28 Nov. 1732, Seth BASS, grantee.
79:247 - 16 May 1751, Seth BASS, grantee.
81:274 - 3 Feb. 1753, Seth BASS, grantee.
83:244 - 23 Nov. 1753, Seth BASS, grantee.
94:224 - 2 July 1760, Seth BASS, grantee.
103:144 - 6 Feb. 1765, Seth BASS to David BASS, Braintree.
108:188 - 23 Apr. 1766, Seth BASS to John BORLAND, Braintree.
149:17 - 21 May 1785, Seth BASS from Samuel BASS 2d, Braintree.
149:73 - 1 June 1785, Seth BASS to Joseph CLEVERLY, Braintree.
162:223 - 2 May 1788, Seth BASS to Richard THAYER, Braintree.
163:173 - 15 Sept 1788, Seth BASS to James BRACKETT et al, Braintree.
163:183 - 20 Sept 1788, Seth BASS to Alice BASS, Braintree.
163:191 - 26 Sept 1788, Seth BASS to Nedebiah BENT, Braintree.
164:70 - 30 Dec. 1788, Seth BASS to John ADAMS, Braintree.
164:70 - 30 Dec. 1788, Seth BASS from Samuel BASS Jr. et ux, Braintree.
164:74 - 1 Jan. 1789, Seth BASS to Samuel BASS, Braintree.

SUFFOLK CO. DEEDS 1800-1899 (BASS):

197:207 - 19 May 1801, Samuel BASS to William STACKPOLE, Boston.
214:110 - 10 Dec. 1805, Samuel BASS et al to Samuel ROGERS, Boston.
214:140 - 26 Dec. 1805, Seth BASS Jr. to Redford WEBSTER, Boston (Wood Land, mortgage).
241:177 - 26 Dec. 1812, Seth BASS to Nathaniel FAXON, Boston, (Wood Lane, mortgage).
272:168 - 14 July 1821, Samuel BASS est. to Ebenezer T. ANDREWS, Boston.
279:63 - 12 Sept 1822, Samuel BASS est. to Ebenezer T. ANDREWS, Boston.
306:265 - 6 Jan. 1826, Samuel BASS est. to Ebenezer T. ANDREWS, Boston.
309:274 - 13 May 1826, Samuel BASS est. to Ebenezer T. ANDREWS, Boston.
499:265 - 26 Apr. 1843, Lucretia B. BASS et al to Ebenezer MILLIKEM (Pine St.).
499:271 - 26 Apr. 1843, Lucretia B. BASS from Elizabeth BASS, admx., Boston (Pine St.).
499:272 - 26 Apr. 1843, Lucretia B. BASS et al to Aaron D. WEBBER (Pine St.).
499:277 - 26 Apr. 1843, Lucretia B. BASS et al to Aaron D. WEBBER (Pine St.).
510:86 - 23 Oct. 1843, Lucretia B. BASS et al to Ezra TRULL (Alden's Lane & Court).
603:26 - 18 Aug. 1849, Lucretia B. BASS est. to George L. RICHARDSON (Washington & Pine St.).

PLYMOUTH COUNTY PROBATES:

1750	Jonathan BASS	Bridgewater	#1412, 12:24,143,145 (will)
1750	Sarah BASS et al	Bridgewater	#1414, 444 (guardianship)
1756	Benjamin BASS	Hanover	#1407, 14:77,148 (adm.)
1804	Ziba BASS	Bridgewater	#1415, 34:386, 40:162 (adm.)
1821	Benjamin BASS	Hanover	#1408, 52:44, 54:12,13 (adm.)
1824	Benjamin BASS	Hanover	#1409, 52:269 (adm.)
1825	Benjamin BASS	HANOVER	#1410, 52:379, 55:322, 59:387 (adm.)

NORFOLK COUNTY PROBATES:

1794, David BASS, Quincy, #1155
1807, Abigail BASS, Quincy, #1150
1807, Samuel BASS, Quincy, #1169
1808, Benjamin BASS, Quincy, #1153
1809, David BASS, Quincy, #1155 1/2
1815, Asa BASS, Quincy, #1152
1824, Mary A., Samuel, Peter B., George BASS, Quincy, guardianship, #1168
1825, David BASS, Quincy, #1156
1837, John BASS, Quincy, #1161
1842, Samuel BASS, Randolph, #1170
1849, Isaac BASS, Quincy, #1159
1850, Hezekiah BASS, Quincy, #1158
1850, Josiah BASS, Quincy, #1163
1850, Isaac, Horace, Benjamin, Abigail, Samuel BASS, Quincy, gdnship, chil. of Isaac,dec. Lewis BASS app'td. guardian, #1160
1852, Lydia BASS, Quincy, #1167
1855, Isaac BASS, Quincy, #1164
1859, Jonathan BASS, Quincy, #1162
1863, Andrewetta BASS, Dorchester, #1151
1872, Samuel H., Francis E. BASS, Boston, guard. #1171
1873, Lewis BASS, Quincy, #1166
1875, Grace H. BASS, Quincy, #1157
1877, Benjamin BASS, Quincy, #1154

Will of **Samuel BASS** of Quincy. <Norfolk Co.PR #1169, 14:30,482>
...8 July 1805...sons Samuel BASS, Edward BASS, daughters Mary HAYWARD, Esther SAVIL, grandsons Edmund CLARK, Samuel BASS, son Josiah BASS all real & personal estate. Pr. 12 May 1807.

Will of **John BASS** of Quincy. <Norfolk Co.PR #1161, 67:115-117,421>
...1 Jan. 1836...friend John FOWLE of Quincy, Innholder, given all estate and appointed executor. Pr. 14 Feb. 1837.

Estate of **Samuel BASS** of Randolph. <Norfolk Co.PR #1170, 75:267,268,988,76:877,77:1420,1431,81:1211,652, 84:659,336>
...Mar. 1842...Intestate...left widow Abigail BASS and six children; sons Samuel L. BASS and Henry BASS appointed adm.

NORFOLK COUNTY DEEDS: To Samuel BASS from:

14:150 - 1801, Elijah WILD
14:152 - 1801, Nathaniel HUNT Jr.
14:153 - 1801, Barnabas CLARK
14:154 - 1801, Ebenezer ALDEN et ux
14:155 - 1801, Barnabas CLARK
14:155 - 1801, Ebenezer THAYER, admr.
14:156 - 1801, Caleb HOWARD
14:156 - 1801, Ebenezer CRANE
14:157 - 1801, Stephen CHEESMAN
14:158 - 1801, Joshua HOWARD Jr.
14:158 - 1801, John FRENCH et al
14:158 - 1801, Jacob SPEAR
14:159 - 1801, A. FRENCH
15:69 - 1801, Jacob WHITCOMB
15:77 - 1801, Seth TURNER
15:77 - 1801, Joseph RICHARDS
15:78 - 1801, Thomas HOLLIS
15:78 - 1801, J.T. APTHORP
15:79 - 1801, Eliphalet SAWEN, admr.
15:79 - 1801, Nehemiah FRENCH
15:80 - 1801, L. FRENCH et al
27:262 - 1807, Esther FRENCH
28:68 - 1807, Samuel BASS Jr.
52:211 - 1816, S.M. THAYER et al
61:295 - 1820, Jonathan BASS
66:351 - 1822, Samuel L. BASS
68:92 - 1822, Thomas FRENCH
68:240 - 1823, Barnabas CLARK
68:240 - 1823, Barnabas CLARK
83:249 - 1827, John MANN
96:181 - 1832, Eleazer BEALS
111:228 - Samuel BASS Jr. from Town of Braintree

(Entries to Samuel BASS continue up to 1854, no names given.)

MICRO #13 OF 16

NORFOLK COUNTY DEEDS: From Samuel BASS to:

14:90 - 1801, Barnabas CLARK
18:182 - 1803, Gideon TOWER Jr.
27:156 - 1807, Elisha GLOVER
26:189 - 1807, Seth TURNER Jr.
32:70 - 1808, Aaron LITTLEFIELD
33:152 - 1809, Thomas CURTIS.
36:218 - 1810, Nathan HOLMES.
45:209 - 1814, Thomas CURTIS.
49:72 - 1814, Theophilus THAYER.
49:133 - 1814, Ephraim LINCOLN.
52:132 - 1816, Isaac WHITE.
54:122 - 1817, Elisha MANN/MANER?
59:86 - 1818, Ephraim LINCOLN.
59:135 - 1818, S.L. BASS.
65:107 - 1821, Elisha HOLBROOK, Braintree.
68:36 - 1822, Silas PAINE Jr.
68:96 - 1822, Simeon WHITE.
68:183 - 1823, Rodolphus PORTER.
70:237 - 1824, Ephraim LINCOLN.
70:323 - 1824, Samuel CURTIS.
73:113 - 1824, Joseph LINFIELD.
73:116 - 1824, Samuel PAINE et al.
72:172 - 1824, Mass. Life Ins. Co. (mortgage).
73:267 - 1824, Jedediah FRENCH
75:259 - 1825, Thomas CURTIS.
76:209 - 1826, Chester GUILD.
76:258 - 1826, Richard BELCHER, Jr.
63:147 - 1820, S.H. NEWCOMB.

14:151 - 1801, Samuel BASS et al est. to Jonathan BASS.
18:77 - 1802, Samuel BASS 2d to Seth BASS Jr.
28:68 - 1807, Samuel BASS Jr (or 3rd) to Samuel BASS.
29:167 - 1808, Samuel BASS est. to Josiah BASS.
31:36 - 1808, Samuel BASS est. to Josiah BASS.
67:199 - 1824, Samuel BASS et al to Barnabas CLARK.

NORFOLK COUNTY DEEDS:

18:77 - 1802, Seth BASS Jr. from Samuel BASS 2d.
31:258 - 1808, John BASS to Mary & Hannah BASS (his sisters), Quincy.
51:110 - 1815, John BASS to David BURRILL, Randolph.
66:22 - 1822, Seth BASS of Salem, doctor of medicine, sells land in Quincy to Nathaniel FAXON.
88:28 - 1829, John BASS to Isaac BASS, Quincy.
88:32 - 1829, John BASS et al to Lewis BASS, Quincy.
89:44 - 1829, John BASS (& sister Mary BASS) from Lewis BASS, Quincy.
89:244 - 1830, John BASS et al to Isaac BASS, Quincy.
97:94 - 1832, John BASS from Isaac BASS.
104:63 - 1834, John BASS et al to John FOWLES, Quincy.
104:63 - 1834, John BASS to John FOWLES, Quincy.
103:90 - 1834, John BASS to John FOWLES, Quincy.
106:77 - 1835, John BASS et al to J.H. ROGERS, Quincy.
108:22 - 1835, John BASS et al to Asaph CHURCHILL, Quincy.
108:290- 1835, John BASS et al to Daniel FRENCH, Quincy.
108:228- 1835, Mary BASS from John FOWLE.
131:259- 1841, Mary BASS from Seth MANN et al.

Will of **Ebenezer ADAMS.** <Suffolk Co.PR #14539, 68:227-229>
...9 Jan. 1769...wife Ann...to son **Ebenezer ADAMS** old homestead, silver hilted sword; son **Zabdiel ADAMS**; to son **Micajah ADAMS** my now dwelling house, shop and land formerly belonging to **Baxter VESEY**, also my clock and old casks; dau **Ann SAVELL**; three grandchildren, heirs to my son **Boyls-ton ADAMS**, deceased, viz: **Molly ADAMS, Ann ADAMS** and **Elizabeth ADAMS.** Witnesses: Benjamin HAYDEN, Ebenezer PENNIMAN, Zebuk HAYDEN. Pr. 29 Aug. 1769. <Numerous citations without details referring to probate, bonds, adm., accounts, inventory, etc., viz: 70:43,72:638,73:230,355,356,359,412. 83:267,268 - Divison of estate dated 21 Apr. 1770 mentions children of **Micajah ADAMS**, dec'd.>

Estate of **Elisha SAVEL/SAVIL** of Braintree. <Suffolk Co.PR #14253, 67:32>
...3 June 1768...adm. to widow **Ann SAVIL** of Braintree, widow of Elisha SAVEL, physician, deceased intestate. Eldest son **Edward SAVIL**; daus **Susanna MARSH** and **Lucretia SAVIL**; son **Samuel SAVIL**; dau. **Ann SANDERS.** Bondsmen: Ebenezer ADAMS of Braintree, Gentleman and John ADAMS, Esq. of Boston. <Other citations without details: 67:110 (inv.), 67:399 (debts), 85:313 (account).> Note: widow Ann SAVIL married second Thomas THAYER below.

Estate of **Thomas THAYER** of Braintree. <Suffolk Co.PR #17117, 78:527,601;79:207,208,224,558,559>
<78:601>...3 Dec. 1779, Gaines THAYER, eldest son, app'td. adm.; Ann, widow; children: Gaines, Elkanah, Mary, Lydia and Susanna THAYER. <78:527> Inv. dated 11 Dec. 1779. <79:224> 1780, Release of Dower. <79:559> Division of estate.

Estate of **Ann THAYER** of Boston, 1819. <Suffolk Co.PR #25909, 170:102;117:329,342,363;118:74;191: 240;205:238;312:118>
<170:102> Petition for Administration; John TUCKER petitioned by mother of deceased. <117:342> Inventory. <118:74> Account. <No details given in files.>

Estate of **Micajah ADAMS** of Braintree. <Suffolk Co.PR #15052, 70:514;71:159>
<70:514> 27 Dec. 1771, Elizabeth ADAMS, widow, app'td. admx. <71:159> Inventory.

Charles BAXTER of Braintree to **Samuel BASS 2d** of Braintree, dated 9 Nov. 1788. Witness: Jeriah BASS. <Suffolk Co.Deeds 142:135>

Edward SAVIL of Braintree to **Elijah VEAZIE Jr.** of Braintree, dated 30 Dec. 1788. Witness: Jeriah BASS. <Suffolk Co.Deeds 142:321>

Will of **John BASS** of Braintree. <Suffolk Co.PR #12924, 60:251,250>
<60:251>...dated 7 Aug. 1761...sons **John BASS** of Providence, **Jedediah BASS, Joseph BASS, Jonathan BASS, Benjamin BASS**; daughter **RAWSON** of Grafton; granddaughter **Hannah RAWSON**, under 18. <60:250> Probated 2 Apr. 1762.

Guardianship of **Hannah BASS**. <Suffolk Co.PR #9057, 41:339>
...2 Aug. 1748...Hannah BASS a minor aged about sixteen years named my Honoured Father **John BASS** of Braintree, husbandman, to be my Guardian...to recover...such part and portion of estate as accrues to me in right of my Honoured Uncle **Benjamin NEAL** of Boston.

Will of **Benjamin NEAL**, shopkeeper of Boston. <Suffolk Co.PR #8903, 40:366,367,407;42:199,262,263>
...dated 24 Nov. 1747...wife Zibiah; friend **Rev. Mather BYLES**; brothers **Jonathan NEAL, Joseph NEAL, Abijah NEAL**; Kinsmen **Joseph BASS** of Boston, **Benjamin FIELD** of Braintree, a minor; Mother **Lydia NEAL**; Kinsmen **Joseph VEAZY** of Boston, **Elijah VEAZY** of Braintree; Kinswomen **Hannah BASS** and **Mary FIELD** both of Braintree 1/4 part of real estate and trading stock when they marry or reach 21 years. <40:407> Inventory dated 26 Jan. 1747. <42:199> Account dated 16 Feb. 1748. <42:262> Warrant for Division dated 16 Feb. 1748 <Note: At this time widow Zibiah was the wife of Thomas FOSTER of Boston.>. <42:263> Division of estate dated 15 Mar. 1748. Pr. 12 Jan. 1747.

Will of **Jonathan BASS** of Braintree. <Suffolk Co.PR #16676, 77:526,527>
...4 July 1778, mentions wife Hannah, my two children Jonathan and Susannah. Pr. 25 Sept. 1778.

Susanna BASS of Quincy to **Jonathan BASS** of Quincy. <Norfolk Co.Deeds 21:167>
...22 Nov. 1792...Susanna BASS, spinster for Ł24 sold to Jonathan BASS, cordwainer...all the right, title, inheritance...in both real and personal estate...which our late Father **Jonathan BASS** died seized. Ack. 7 Feb. 1793. Rec. 7 Feb. 1804.

Jonathan BASS of Quincy to **Lewis BASS**. <Norfolk Co.Deeds 277:36>
...12 May 1859...Jonathan BASS of Quincy...in consideration of having been supported during many past years and kindly provided for during my sickness and infirmities of old age by my son Lewis BASS and his wife and family...sell and convey unto the said Lewis BASS about one acre of salt marsh situated in Quincy...also pew #27 in the stone meeting house which I bought of my son **Jonathan Howard BASS**.

Will of **Jonathan BASS** of Quincy. <Norfolk Co.PR #1162, 102:841,103:39>
<103:40>...25 December 1855...As for many years and in my old age and sickness I have resided with my said son **Lewis BASS** and have received from him and his family great and unremitting care and attention for a very inadequate compensation and as I am now indebted to him in a considerable sum of money and the whole amount of my property is but small and as I expect he will continue to provide and care for me...during the residue of my life; now then not being forgetful of, but well remembering my other five children and my grandchildren the children of a deceased son and daughter to any of whom or to any deceased son or daughter I am not or have been under the same obligations. <102:842> Presented for probate 1 Oct. 1859 by **Lewis BASS**, executor. <103:39> Probated on the second Tuesday of Feb. 1860. 24 Sept. 1859, **Lewis BASS**, executor, with **Lewis BASS Jr.** and **Stephen MORSE Jr.** as sureties, gave bond for $100. <Original> The petition of **Lewis BASS** of Quincy...goods and estate valued at $50.00...the widow of deceased, **Susanna BURRELL** wife of Seth BURRELL, **Benjamin BASS, Jonathan H. BASS, Mary B. REED, Mary EDSON, Hannah M. NOTTAGE, Isaac BASS, Horace BASS, Benjamin F. BASS, Abby BASS and Samuel BASS** are his heirs, of whom **Samuel BASS** is minor.

NORFOLK COUNTY DEEDS:

2:147 - 1794, Samuel BASS, Esq., adm. on estate of Jonathan BASS, Esq., late of Randolph, dec'd. from John DYER.
4:14 - 1795, Jonathan BASS from James FAXON.
14:92 - 1801, Jonathan BASS to Zacheus TAYLOR.
14:151 - 1801, Jonathan BASS from Thomas BASS.
20:111 - 1804, Jonathan BASS to Nathaniel COBB.
21:167 - 1804, Jonathan BASS, est. to Jonathan BASS all interest of Susanna BASS in real and personal estate of Jonathan BASS.
32:192 - 1809, Jonathan BASS to James BRACKETT.
49:133 - 1814, Jonathan BASS, est. to Ephraim LINCOLN.
61:295 - 1820, Jonathan BASS to Samuel BASS.
88:60 - 1829, Jonathan BASS, cordwainer, of Quincy from Seth BURRELL 2d, wf Susanna signs.
116:172 -1831, Jonathan BASS from Benjamin BASS.
201:241 -1851, Jonathan BASS et al to Ebenezer ALDEN, all interest of Jonathan BASS et al in real estate of Samuel BASS in Randolph.
277:36 - 1859, Jonathan BASS to Lewis BASS.

MICRO #14 of 16

Will of **Benjamin BASS** of Quincy. <Norfolk Co.PR #1154, 138:109;139:618;143:256,732> <138:109>...9 Sept. 1875...to my daughter **Mary Jane ADAMS**, wife of William ADAMS of Foxboro, $1000...all the rest and residue of my estate I give to my sons **John B. BASS, Joseph A. BASS** and **Edward W.H. BASS** all of said Quincy...sthe portion of the said **Mary Jane ADAMS** to be to her own sole and separate use, free from the interference and control of any husband...son **Joseph A. BASS** appointed executor. Witnesses: E. Granville PRATT, George L. GILL, Louisa BURRELL. <138:109> The will of **Benjamin BASS**, boot manufacturer, was probated 14 Nov. 1877. <139:618> Estate appraised: real estate valued at $4,100., personal estate at $1313.61. <143:256> Acount of **Joseph A. BASS** allowed 9 June 1880. **John B. BASS, J.A. BASS, E.W.H. BASS, Grace Hall ADAMS** by her Guardian **Edward H. BASS**, being all parties interested. <143:732> 23 June 1880, **Joseph A. BASS** petitioned for licence to sell the whole of the real estate for the payment of a legacy.

Thomas J. NIGHTINGALE of Quincy against **Benjamin BASS** of Quincy. <Norfolk Co.Deeds 283:275> ...whereas Thomas J. NIGHTINGALE, victualler, of Quincy, upon the third Monday of Sept. 1859... recovered judgment rendered on 3 Oct. 1859, for his title and possession of and in a certain parcel of land containing one half acre with all the buildings thereon...situated in Quincy...against **Benjamin BASS**, boot maker, of Quincy and **Grace H. BASS**, his wife...who had unjustly with held, put out, or removed the said **Thomas J. NIGHTINGALE** from his possession thereof...we command you, that without delay, you cause the said Thomas J. NIGHTINGALE to have possession of and in the said above described premises. Rec. 24 Jan. 1860.

NORFOLK COUNTY DEEDS:

86:277 - 1829, Benjamin BASS & wf Grace to George VEAZIE.
89:35 - 1829, Benjamin BASS & wf Grace to J.Q. ADAMS.
116:172 - 1837, Benjamin BASS & wf Grace to Jonathan BASS.
120:21 - 1838, Benjamin BASS & wf Grace to T.J. NIGHTINGALE.
240:136 - 1855, Benjamin BASS to S.H. LEWIS.
283:275 - 1860, Benjamin BASS & wf Grace (& ux. est.) to T.J. NIGHTINGALE.

Will of **Lucy H. EATON**, of Boston. <No reference cited.> ...9 Apr. 1930...**1.** I direct that my name with the date of my birth, 30 Nov. 1844, and the date of my death be cut upon the back of the monument of the lot numbered 4576 in Mount Aubourn Cemetery. **2.** All baskets of Indian, foreign or unusual make I give to the Peabody Museum of Archeology and Ethnology, Cambridge, Mass. **3.** I give to the Mass. Society of Mayflower Descendants a Framed Broadside - Lines on Death of John Alden, 1687, a blue brocaded vest worn by my great grandfather **Captain Alden BASS** at his wedding in 1766, and a pair of high heeled brocaded slippers belonging to his wife. **4.** I give to the Mass. Historical Society a Framed Letter from said **Captain Alden BASS** to his wife from Three Rivers in 1776, together with an account of his capture by the British & his return from Quebec to Sudbury St., Boston, written by **Mary Elizabeth Bass KENDALL. 5.** I give to the Boston Museum of Fine Arts a Wax Portrait by Rauschman of my grandfather **Joseph EATON** who died 8 Feb. 1809 at the age of thirty-five; a Framed Embroidery of the 18th Century "Absence Killeth" under medallion; and the pair of bronze mantel lamps and a gilt clock now in the corner room of my apartment. **6.** All my wearing apparel, jewelry and silver, all books, pictures, bronzes, foreign embroideries, household furniture and all other like articles of domestic or personal use...I give and bequeath to **Martha H. MORSS** of Newton, Mass. and **Katherine S. BRADLEE**, wife of **John R. BRADLEE**, of New York........**7.** To said **Martha H. MORSS** and **Katherine S. BRADLEE** and to their brother **James H. REED** of Chestnut Hill, ten thousand dollars each. **8.** to **Henry P. KENDALL, Richard I. KENDALL** and **Edith KENDALL**, children of the late **Henry A. KENDALL** of Brookline...a mortgage note for thirty thousand dollars belonging to me and secured by real estate on the corner of Sudbury and Alden St. in Boston. **9.** To **William S. HASELTINE** of Brookline, eight thousand dollars. **10.** To **Walter I. SWANTON, Henry A. SWANTON** and **Frederick W. SWANTON** of Washington D.C., eight thousand dollars to each of them... **11.** To **Mrs. Ellen J. DIKE,** daughter of the late **B.T. LORING** of Braintree, ten thousand dollars... **12.** To **Elsie B. TAYLOR,** wife of **Dr. E. Wyllys TAYLOR,** of Boston, and to **Mary R. HOWE,** daughters of **Mrs. Kate B. HOWE,** ten thousand dollars to each of them; to **Frances E. EMERSON** and **Margaret L. THOMAS,** daughters of said **Ellen J. DIKE,** five thousand dollars to each of them... **13.** To **Clara E. FULLER,** now in my employ, five thousand dollars. **14.** To **Sabra BRADLEE,** daughter of said **John R. BRADLEE,** two thousand dollars...If she has died leaving no issue living, then I give said sum to her mother, **Katherine S. BRADLEE.** I give to **Marian MORRIS,** daughter of said **Martha H. MORSS,** two thousand dollars...I give to **Rosamond Eaton SNOW,** daughter of said **James H. REED,** two thousand dollars...I give to **Ruth W. ROBINSON** and **Katherine TAYLOR,** daughters of said **Dr. E. Wyllys TAYLOR** two thousand dollars to each of them...**15.** To my former maid, **Annie T. HOWES,** wife of **Walter HOWES** of Cambridge and to **Michael J. MERRICK** of Brookline, two thousand dollars to each in recognition of their faithful services. **16.** To **Clift Rogers CLAPP** of Newton, twenty-five thousand dollars In Trust to invest and reinvest the same and to pay **Clara E. FULLER,** now in my employ, from the net income thereof and if necessary from the principal, twelve hundred dollars per annum during her life...and on her death: a/ To pay one-half of the principal of said trust fund then remaining to the Young Men's Christian Union of said Boston...to be used for the Christmas Festivities for poor children, for the Country Week, and for Rides for invalids. b/ To pay the other half to the Unitarian Service Pension Society, the income to be used for pensions to ministers... **21.** To the Children's Mission, to Children Incorporated, to the Farm and Trades School Inc., to North End Union now located at 20 Parmenter St., Boston, and to Arlington St. Church of Boston for its Endowment Fund, ten thousand dollars. **22.** All the rest and residue of my estate...to the

Massachusetts General Hospital, established in 1811; one part to the Massachusetts Charitable Eye and Ear Infirmary; one part to the American Unitarian Ass.; one part to the Museum of Fine Arts of Boston; one part to the Women's Educational and Industrial Union in Boston; one part to the Community Health Ass. of Boston; one part to the Children's Hospital, formerly on Huntington Ave., now on Longwood Ave., Boston; and one part to the Society for the Prevention of Cruelty to Children, Boston...Witnesses: Benjamin M. ANNABLE of Beverly, Mass., Emil W. MILLER of Boston, Ethel G. GLOVER, of Malden, Mass.

==

Estate of **Alden BASS** of Boston. <Suffolk Co.PR #21927, 101:435>
...18 July 1803, distribution of estate to children: **Deborah CHAPIN**, wife of Amariah; **Hannah EATON**, wife of Joseph; **Moses BASS**, **Mercy BASS**. <See also 101:397,420,446,437,438>

==

Estate of **Joseph BASS** of Dorchester. <Suffolk Co.PR #9939, 48:158-160>
...1 June 1753, Warrant for division of estate. 5 June 1753 estate settled on following heirs: widow **Hannah**, eldest son **Joseph BASS**; sons **Edward BASS**, **Benjamin BASS**, **John BASS**; heirs of son **William BASS** dec'd; daughter **Hannah BASS**; heirs of daughters **Elizabeth** & **Susanna BASS** dec'd. <Note: Bowman questions the name of daughter Susanna as an error for Mary.>

==

Estate of **Moses BASS** of Boston. <Suffolk Co.PR #19799, 90:556>
<90:556>...27 Sept. 1791...**Moses Belcher BASS**, upholster, app'td. administrator on estate of **Moses BASS**, late of Boston, dec'd. <90:561> Inventory dated 17 Oct. 1791, one horse and land the late Mansion of the deceased now occupied by **Henry BASS**, £300. One other house and land now occupied by **Mrs. Moses BASS** and **Gillam BASS**, £280., total £580. <92:69> Account. <92:324> Warrant for Dower. <92:326> Warrant for Division. <92:327> Division.

==

Estate of **Moses Belcher BASS** of Boston. <Suffolk Co.PR #25169>
<115:88> Will dated 10 Feb. 1817. <250:190> Bond. <246:269> Letter. <115:294> Inventory dated 19 May 1817. <311:147> Evidence perpetuated. <No details given in files.>

==

Estate of **William COPELAND** of Braintree. <Suffolk Co.PR #3802, 19:239>
...31 Dec. 1716, Mary COPELAND, widow appointed admx.

==

Will of **David ARNOLD** of Norton. <Bristol Co.PR 46:140,184,299;47:173;48:121;109:425>
<46:140>...dated 28 Mar. 1803, mentions wife **Phebe**; son **David ARNOLD**; dau. **Phebe HODGES**, wf of George; sons **John ARNOLD**, **Samuel ARNOLD**, **Asa ARNOLD**, **Salmon ARNOLD**, **William ARNOLD**, **Lemuel ARNOLD** and dau. **Sarah ARNOLD.** <46:184> Inventory dated 12 Jan. 1811. <46:299> Divison. <47:173,48:121> Accounts. Probated 1 Jan. 1811.

==

Samuel ARNOLD, Esq. of Londonderry VT to **Barnard WHEELER** of Rehoboth MA.<Bristol Co.Deeds 93:443>
...17 Feb. 1812, Samuel ARNOLD for $550 sold to Barnard WHEELER...all my right in and unto the real estate whereof **Jeremiah WHEELER** late of Rehoboth died seized, which estate is undivided and hold in common among the heirs of said **Jeremiah WHEELER** deceased. **Nancy ARNOLD** wife of the said Samuel releases dower. Ack. 17 Feb. 1812. Rec. 12 Mar. 1812.

==

Samuel ARNOLD, Esq. of Londonderry VT to **Lemuel ARNOLD** of Norton MA. <Bristol Co.Deeds 97:344>
...19 Feb. 1812, Samuel ARNOLD for $200 sold to Lemuel ARNOLD, gentleman, four certain pieces of land...that was set off to me the said Samuel in the Division of my father's, **David ARNOLD** late of Norton, deceased, estate. Ack. 19 Feb. 1812. Rec. 26 Nov. 1814.

==

Samuel ARNOLD, of Attleboro, yeoman, and wife Mindwell, sell land in Attleboro to **Mary ARNOLD.** Dated 21 Dec. 1814. <Bristol Co.Deeds 105:132>

MICRO #15 of 16

Estate of **Elijah COPELAND** of Easton. <Bristol Co.PR 151:351;54:160;55:154,242;57:532,540;59:118>
<151:351> 4 Nov. 1817, **Josiah COPELAND**, yeoman of Easton, appointed adm. <54:160> Inventory taken 29 Oct. 1817. <55:154,242> Settlement of estate 4 Sept. 1818. <57:532,540> Real estate appraised. <59:118> 5 Jan. 1819, Real estate divided, viz: **Elijah COPELAND**, **Josiah COPELAND**, **Rhoda COPELAND** (widow of dec'd.), **Martin COPELAND**, heirs of **Abigail GUILD**, daughter of dec'd., **Mary DUNBAR**, dau. of dec'd. Probated 8 Feb. 1822. <201:12> 9 Oct. 1818 Administrator states personal estate is insufficient by $846.00 to pay debts and desires to sell real estate at public auction to raise money.

==

Estate of **William BOWDITCH** of Braintree. <Suffolk Co.PR #8986, 41:124,206,215>
<41:124>...10 May 1748, **Samuel BASS** of Braintree, yeoman, appointed administrator of estate of brother-in-law, **William BOWDITCH**, clothier, dec'd. <41:206> Inventory taken 13 May 1748, incl. one half part of dwelling house & barn, half a corn mill, fulling mill & shop with half of all implements, half the priviledge of the stream & dams, half an acre of land where they stand, £512.10; six acres orchard, mowing & planting land, £210; 32 acres pasture land, £540; £90 old tenor allowed the widow out of the moveables. <42:215> 24 Feb. 1748, setting off the widow's thirds. <43:462> Further accounting of **Samuel BASS**, adm., dated 3 Apr. 1750, incl. money rec'd. from **Jonathan BASS** for seventeen and three quarters acres; "sundry small things in the widow's sickness, £5; two iron utensils which belonged to deceased's daughter, **Ruth**, £3,15.

===

Guardianship of Children of **William BOWDITCH**. <Suffolk Co.PR>
Dated 30 Aug. 1748: <41:400>...**Jonathan BASS** of Bridgewater, gentleman, appointed guardian of **Jonathan BOWDITCH**, a minor aged about ten years. <41:401>...**Samuel BASS** of Braintree, yeoman, appointed guardian of **Bathsheba BOWDITCH**, a minor aged about twelve years. <41:401>...**Susannah BOWDITCH**, minor aged about fifteen years, choses her Uncle, **Jonathan BASS**, of Bridgewater as her guardian. <41:402>...**Abigail BOWDITCH**, minor aged about seventeen years, choses her Uncle, **Samuel BASS** of Braintree, yeoman, as her guardian.

Estate of **William BOWDITCH** of Braintree. <Norfolk Co.PR #2245, 1:104,195,522;3:164,438,440>
<1:104>...27 Nov. 1793, **Susanna BOWDITCH**, widow, declines adm. and asks son **William BOWDITCH** to be appointed adm. <1:195>...Inventory dated 14 Apr. 1794, incl.: half a pew in meeting house, half a dwelling house & barn on six acres, half a grist mill & priviledge, sixteen and a half acres pasture land, total: Ł316.2. <3:438>...4 Apr. 1797, Widow's thirds set off. <3:164,440>... Division of estate dated 6 May 1797, viz: to widow **Susanna BOWDITCH**; children **William BOWDITCH, Jonathan BOWDITCH, James BOWDITCH, Benjamin BOWDITCH, Susanna HUNT**, wife of Ebenezer Jr., **Mary HUNT**, wife of Elihu, **Abigail BOWDITCH**. Guardianship of Children: <1:522>...12 May 1795, **Abigail BOWDITCH**, above 14, chose **William BOWDITCH**, yeoman, of Braintree; **Benjamin BOWDITCH**, above 14, chose **Barnabas THAYER**, tailor, of Braintree.

Estate of **Jonathan WILD** of Randolph. <Norfolk Co.PR #20334, 1:52,171,256>
<1:171>...3 June 1794, adm. granted to **John WILD** of Randolph, gentleman. <1:256> Inventory dated 30 Oct. 1794, incl.: mansion house, barn, corn house with all the land lying in Randolph with a small orchard and piece of land lying in Stoughton, Ł110; about eight acres joining the house lot in Stoughton, Ł28,16s; about forty two acres of pasture land incl. bair swamp lying in Stoughton, Ł58,4s; about twenty acres of pasture and unimproved land in Stoughton adjoining land of **Atherton WALES**, Ł36; about two acres fresh meadow in Randolph bounded by **Capt. Eliphalet SAWEN's** meadow & others, Ł18. <1:52> Account dated 7 July 1795, **John WILD** asks allowance for his time tending his Father in last sickness and for cash paid to mother.

Jonathan WILD et al to **John WILD**. <Norfolk Co.Deeds 27:110>
...12 Feb. 1796, **Thomas FRENCH** of Randolph, gentleman, and wife **Hannah; Jonathan WILD** of Walpole, Physician; **Edmund WILD** of Roxbury and wife **Sarah; Eunice SAWEN** of Randolph, widow, **Daniel WILD** of Boston, merchant, **Samuel V. TURNER** of Randolph, yeoman, and **Abigail** his wife...all heirs of Deacon **Jonathan WILD**, late of Randolph, gentleman, dec'd...for $500 quit claim to **John WILD** of Randolph...all the real estate of which Deacon **Jonathan WILD** died posessed.

Will of **John WILD** of Randolph. <Norfolk Co.PR #20331, 56:317-8,440-1;57:155-8,214;58:92-3,177-8>
<56:318>...dated 19 Dec. 1807, mentions wife **Jemima**, sons **Joshua WILD, Simon Willard WILD**, daughters **Jemima WILD, Sally CURTIS, Polly CODMAN, Eunice WILD**, grandson **Daniel CURTIS** ($50 at twenty, one years of age), granddaughter **Sally CURTIS** (one good cow at the age of eighteen), heirs of daughter **Betsey VINTON**, dec'd. Thomas FRENCH, Jonathan WALES Jr. appointed executors. Witnesses: Seth TURNER, Silas ALDEN Jr., Calvin ALDEN. <56:440> Inventory dated 13 Oct. 1831, incl. homestead in Randolph and Canton, 70 acres, $1330.00. <56:317> Pr. 4 Oct. 1831.

NORFOLK COUNTY DEEDS:

54:314 - (no date), John WILD to Daniel CURTIS.
59:41 - 13 Dec. 1813, John WILD & wife Jemima to Simon Willard WILD of Canton, yeoman, land in Canton. Ack. 11 Feb. 1818.
76:142 - 22 Apr. 1823, John WILD of Randolph & wife Jemima, gentleman to Daniel CURTIS of Randolph, yeoman, woodland in Canton.
115:61 - 7 May 1832, Jonathan WALES Jr. of Randolph, executor of will of John WILD, late of Randolph, dec'd. sells at public auction to Daniel CURTIS of Canton, yeoman, about ( )teen acres of pasture and woodland.

Estate of **Jonathan BASS** of Braintree. <Suffolk Co.PR #19512, 89:190>
...8 June 1790, Samuel BASS of Braintree, appointed adm. of estate of Jonathan BASS, dec'd.

MICRO #16 of 16

Samuel BASS of Randolph to **Ephraim LINCOLN** of Randolph. <Norfolk Co.Deeds 49:133>
...12 July 1814, Samuel BASS, Esq. for $1000 sold to Ephraim LINCOLN, merchant, once acre of land lying in Randolph...it being a piece of the farm belonging to **Colonel Jonathan BASS**, dec'd.

Jonathan BASS of Braintree VT and **Samuel BASS** of Randolph. <Norfolk Co.Deeds 61:295>
...21 Mar. 1811, Jonathan BASS of Braintree in the County of Orange and State of Vermont, Esq. for $7800 sold to Samuel BASS, Esq...a farm with a dwelling house and barn thereon containing... one hundred and twenty acres lying in Randolph...bounded by land of Joseph PORTER, Zenas FRENCH, John ADAMS, Jacob WHITCOMB, Asa BELCHER, Billy BELCHER, Simeon WHITE...also ten acres...fresh meadow...bounded by land of Sarah ALDEN...also twenty acres wood land in Rocky Woods...bounded by land of Joseph PORTER, Simeon WHITE and others unknown. Rec. 26 Feb. 1820.

Jonathan BASS et al of Braintree VT to **Ebenezer ALDEN** of Randolph. <Norfolk Co.Deeds 201:241>
...5 Oct. 1850, Jonathan BASS of Braintree in the County of Orange and State of Vermont by Henry BASS his attorney, Allen PUTNAM of Roxbury and wife Sarah B., in her right; Samuel BASS, Mary

BASS, James L. BASS, children and heirs at law of Samuel BASS late of Boston, dec'd. and one of the heirs at law of Samuel BASS late of Randolph, Esq., dec'd. and Henry BASS of said Boston sold to Ebenezer ALDEN of Randolph all the right we have in...lands situated in Randolph...of which Samuel BASS late of Randolph, Esq. deceased died seized. Rec. 14 May 1851.

==

Estate of **Naphthali THAYER** of Braintree. <Suffolk Co.PR #12481, 57:251,341;59:339-41,454>
<57:251>...Administrators, widow Bathsheba and Naphtali THAYER, husbandman, both of Braintree.
<57:341>...Inventory dated 10 Nov. 1760, house & land, £267.13.4, mentions bedding delivered to Bathsheba BEALS, total £372.9.7. <59:339-40> Widow's dower dated 27 Apr. 1761. <59:454> Division of estate dated 29 Oct. 1761 to heirs: widow Bathsheba; four children, viz: **Naphtali THAYER** (only son), **Bathsheba BEALS, Bethiah THAYER, Susanna THAYER.**

==

Heirs of **Naphthali THAYER** of Braintree. <Suffolk Co.Deeds 113:122>
...5 May 1768, Agreement made between **Nathan BEAL** of Mendon & wf **Bathsheba; Naphtali THAYER** of Braintree, yeoman; **Bethiah THAYER** and **Susanna THAYER,** singlewomen of Braintree, divide dower set off to **Bathsheba THAYER** our honoured mother now deceased. Rec. 16 Sept. 1768.

==

Nathan BEAL of Mendon and **David WHITE** of Braintree. <Suffolk Co.Deeds 125:268>
...5 May 1774, Nathan BEAL, blacksmith and wf Bathsheba...for eighteen pounds two shillings and eight pence...sell to David WHITE, yeoman...land in Braintree containing three acres...bounded by land of Joseph PORTER, heirs of Daniel BASS, Bethiah THAYER, heirs of Naphthali THAYER, dec'd.

FOOTNOTES

<1> p.9, The probate date of 1761 is questionable as Bowman states Joseph SIMMONS[4] (Mercy Pabodie[3], Elizabeth Alden[2]) died 20 May 1768 ae 78 <no source stated>.
<2> p.10, A note on this page states "Blaney PHILLIPS once lived in Hanson MA, then Pembroke MA (1760) on the site of the house now owned (1912) by Richard EVERSON.
<3> p.17, Susanna ALDEN, widow, appears to be Susanna (WINSLOW) Alden, wife of Capt. John ALDEN[3-2]. At this point in the files, little is written regarding this Alden line, except for a list of children showing division of real estate, with no dates or sources. Capt. John's estate was divided into twelve shares with widow Susanna receiving six shares which she sold to son Nathaniel, 12 July 1731. The following five children each received one share: Nathaniel ALDEN; Thomas ALDEN and wife Jane; Elizabeth ALDEN; Hannah JONES, wife of John; Anne ALDEN. (All four sold their shares to Nathaniel 19 Feb. 1732.) The last share went to the children of son John ALDEN, dec'd. See p.18 for deed from siblings to Nathaniel ALDEN.
<4> p.18, On the back of this document in a different hand & ink is written: "Mary GAIL dafter/ daughter to William ALDEN Grand Childrin to Capt. John ALDEN Elizabeth Bettely Sister to Mrs.Gail".
<5> p.20, The following Middlesex deeds were found at the end of Microfiche #8 and beginning of Microfiche #9 but have been placed here in chronological order.
<6> p.28, The mention of gravestones, both for himself and his children is particularly touching given the circumstances. Seth ALDEN died 29 Aug. 1775 in his 34th yr. He lost his three children the same month: Seth, age 7 on 10 Aug.; Mehitable, age 5 on 11 Aug. and Betsey, age 2 on 8 Aug. See <7> for a possible son born after his death.
<7> p.28, Bowman suggests this seven year old Seth ALDEN 2d is the son of Seth ALDEN[5] (Seth[4], Joseph[3-2]) and Mary CARVER, born after his father's death in 1775.

==

==

ISAAC ALLERTON

MICRO #1 OF 9

John HOLMES of Plympton to **Jacob CHIPMAN** of Barnstable. <Plymouth Co.Deeds 21:92>
...7 Jan. 1726/7, John HOLMES for L800 sold to Jacob CHIPMAN, husbandman, the farm tenement where I now dwell in Plympton...about 200 acres upland, meadow and swampy land.

Will of **Jeremiah THOMAS** of Middleboro. <Plymouth Co.PR 7:267>
...dated 29 Sept. 1735, mentions wife **Mary**; sons **Nathaniel THOMAS** (eldest), **Jeremiah THOMAS, Jedediah THOMAS,** daughters **Sary WOOD, Elizabeth THOMSON, Mary BLACK, Lydia HACKETT, Thankful COBB, Bethiah CHIPMAN, Priscilla THOMAS**, son **Ebenezer THOMAS** executor.

MARY ALLERTON^{2} (Isaac^{1})

PLYMOUTH COUNTY DEEDS:

3:162 - 1699, Eleazer CUSHMAN to Thomas CUSHMAN.
7:161 - 1706, Eleazer CUSHMAN to Samuel BRADFORD.
10:1:26 - 1713, Eleazer CUSHMAN to Benjamin EATON.
10:2:374- 1714, Eleazer CUSHMAN to David BOSWORTH.
14:6 - 7 Mar. 1717/8, Eleazer CUSHMAN of Plymouth and son John CUSHMAN to Joseph MITCHELL.
15:139 - 5 May 1718, Eleazer CUSHMAN from Richard WAITE, land in Plympton.
16:115 - 1722, Eleazer CUSHMAN of Plymouth to son Moses CUSHMAN. Ack. 10 Dec. 1722.
18:140 - 14 Oct. 1723, Eleazer CUSHMAN Sr. of Plimpton gift to son Eleazer CUSHMAN of Plimpton, reserving improvement to self & wife for life.
41:190 - 7 Oct. 1748, Eleazer CUSHMAN, husbandman of Plympton to Nathaniel COBB.
41:225 - 7 Oct. 1748, Eleazer CUSHMAN, husbandman of Plympton (wf Eunice releases dower) to Samuel BARROWS.
44:136 - 21 Mar. 1750, Eleazer CUSHMAN, husbandman of Plympton to Jonathan PARKER.
45:97 - 2 Nov. 1758, Eunice CUSHMAN, widow of Eleazer, of Plympton, to John RICKARD.

26:169 - 1731, James CUSHMAN, cordwainer of Plymouth (brother of Elkanah) to Nathaniel JACKSON.
33:118 - 27 May 1736, James CUSHMAN, Josiah CUSHMAN, Allerton CUSHMAN, division.
33:118 - 13 Aug. 1739, James CUSHMAN, blacksmith of Plimpton from Allerton CUSHMAN.
33:35 - 1739, James CUSHMAN, blacksmith of Plympton & Allerton CUSHMAN, sons of Allerton, dec'd division.
35:126 - 1742, James CUSHMAN, order to sell.
36:156 - 1744, James CUSHMAN (brother of Elkanah; mother Hester now wf of Capt. Benjamin WARREN; widow now wife of Joseph RUGGLES of Hardwick) by J. HOVEY, administrator, to Lazarus LEBARON.
38:13(-)- 1746, James CUSHMAN to Allerton CUSHMAN.
53:228 - 1767, James CUSHMAN to Elkanah CUSHMAN, division.
64:16 - 1785, James CUSHMAN to John FAUNCE.
70:192 - 1790, James CUSHMAN, Mercy CUSHMAN to Ichabod MORTON et al.
71:74 - 8 Feb. 1790, James CUSHMAN, tanner of Kingston & G. COBB, division.
72:51 - 1791, James CUSHMAN, Mercy CUSHMAN to Joseph WHITON.
72:268 - 1792, James CUSHMAN to Jonathan HOLMES et al.
79:126 - 1796, James CUSHMAN to Ichabod HOLMES.
91:52 - 1801, James CUSHMAN to Lemuel MORTON.

16:51 - 1722, John CUSHMAN to Richard DWELLEY.
17:88 - 1723, John CUSHMAN to Jabez PRATT.
19:115 - 1725, John CUSHMAN to Joseph LUCAS.
55:222 - 1771, John CUSHMAN to Samuel TILSON
61:72 - 15 Apr. 1782, John CUSHMAN to James CUSHMAN, son of Thomas dec'd.

29:100 - 1734, Moses CUSHMAN to Francis PUMMERY.
29:179 - 1735, Moses CUSHMAN to Abiel LEACH.
46:240 - 1761, Moses CUSHMAN to Daniel DUNBAR
53:129 - 1767, Moses CUSHMAN to Abner CUSHMAN

Will of **Eleazer CUSHMAN** of Plympton. <Plymouth Co.PR #5806, 14:509,510>
...dated 22 Feb. 1758, everything to wife Eunis/Eunice. Pr. 2 May 1758.

Will of **James CUSHMAN** of Dartmouth. <Bristol Co.PR 25:265,267>
...dated 14 Mar. 1775, son **Elisha CUSHMAN**; dau. **Temperance CUSHMAN**; sons **James CUSHMAN, Seth CUSHMAN, Ebenezer CUSHMAN, Thomas CUSHMAN**; my five daughters including **Lydia JENNEY** (dec'd. wf of Ephraim and her two daughters), daughter **Patience CORNISH**. Pr. 6 Oct. 1778.

James CUSHMAN, cordwainer, 20 Mar. 1732/3, surety on executor's bond, estate of **Capt. Thomas TABER** of Dartmouth. <MD 16:234>

Barnabas SPOONER of Dartmouth to **James CUSHMAN** of Dartmouth. <Bristol Co.Deeds 20:166>
...28 Feb. 1731/2, Barnabas SPOONER, yeoman, for £20 in bills of good publick credit sold to James CUSHMAN, cordwainer...part of Spooner's homestead in Dartmouth containing about three and a half acres, bounded by land of John JENNEY. Witnesses: Zaccheus TOBEY, Stephen WEST Jr.

Benjamin BURGES of Dartmouth to **James CUSHMAN** of Dartmouth. <Bristol Co.Deeds 30:86>
...15 Aug. 1740, Benjamin BURGIS, Practitioner of Physick, for £30 sold to James CUSHMAN, cordwainer, upland in Dartmouth, bounded by said Cushman's homestead, about ten acres.

James CUSHMAN of New Bedford to **Elisha CUSHMAN** of New Bedford. <Bristol Co.Deeds 81:436>
...14 Sept. 1796, James CUSHMAN, yeoman, for $170.00 sold to Elisha CUSHMAN, yeoman...lands that fell to me in ye Division of ye homestead estate of my honoured Father **James CUSHMAN** late of New Bedford, dec'd according to ye Division between my two brothers, **Seth & Elisha CUSHMAN** and myself together with my dwelling house...also signed by **Hannah CUSHMAN** (mark). Witnesses: John CUSHMAN, Mary CUSHMAN. Rec. 16 Sept. 1802.

Will of **Anthony WATERMAN** of Halifax. <Plymouth Co.PR #22126, 20:348,349,545,546>
<20:348>...dated 28 Oct. 1769, to my sons **Anthony WATERMAN** and **Elisha WATERMAN;** to my three daughters **Joanna STURTEVANT, Sarah WASHBURN** and **Phoebe WATERMAN** a piece of meadow lying above the dam on the north side of Monpouset meadow-brook (so called), bounded by land of Capt. Josiah STURTEVANT & Eleazer WATERMAN; my well beloved wife (not named); my honoured mother **Lidia WATERMAN;** my two grandchildren **Paul STURTEVANT** and **Eliphalet STURTEVANT** at the age of twenty one years. Witnesses: Ephraim BRIGGS, Samuel PALMER, Jesse STURTEVANT. <20:349>...5 Mar. 1770 will probated. <20:349>...Inventory dated 21 Mar. 1770 by Moses INGLEE, Samuel PALMER and Ignatius LORING, real estate valued at £314.13s4d, total £388.14s6d. <20:545> **Hannah WATERMAN** presented account which was approved 20 May 1771.

Will of **Hannah WATERMAN** of Halifax. <Plymouth Co.PR 34:347;36:425,495>
<36:425>...dated 26 Sept. 1782, mentions son **Elisha WATERMAN;** two grandsons **Paul STURTEVANT** and **Lifelet/Eliphalet STURTEVANT,** sons to my daughter **Hannah STURTEVANT** deceased; three daughters **Joanna STURTEVANT, Sarah WASHBURN** and **Phebe TOMSON. William STURTEVANT** son-in-law appointed executor. Witnesses: Samuel Stafford STURTEVANT, Jesse STURTEVANT, Susanna STURTEVANT and Priscilla STURTEVANT. <34:347,36:425>...1 Oct. 1798, will of **Hannah WATERMAN,** widow, was presented for probate by **Zebadiah TOMSON** of Halifax, gentleman, **William STURTEVANT** the executor in said will being dec'd. <36:495>...Inventory dated 3 Jan. 1799, taken by **Zebadiah TOMSON, Samuel Stafford STURTEVANT** and **Adam TOMSON,** total $95.69.

Estate of **Anthony WATERMAN** of Halifax. <Plymouth Co.PR #22125, 20:395,557>
<20:395>...6 Aug. 1770, Calvin CURTIS of Scituate, yeoman, appointed administrator. <unrecorded bond>...6 Aug. 1770, Calvin CURTIS, Abiel TURNER, of Scituate, gentleman and Cornelius TURNER of Hanover, shipwright, gave a bond for £300. Witnesses: Jonah EDSON, Edward WINSLOW Jr. <20:557>... Inventory taken 6 Nov. 1770 by Eleazer WATERMAN, William STURTEVANT & Jacob CHIPMAN, real estate valued at £123.4s, total, £152.1d.

Guardianship of Children of **Anthony WATERMAN.** <Plymouth Co.PR #22149, 20:395>
...6 Aug. 1770, **Sarah WATERMAN,** of Halifax, widow, with Jonathan CUSHMAN of Kingston, yeoman and Calvin CURTIS of Scituate, yeoman, as sureties, gave a bond of £100 as guardian unto **James WATERMAN,** a minor about four years of age, son of **Anthony WATERMAN,** late of Halifax, dec'd. Witness: Edward WINSLOW Jr. 6 Aug. 1770, same as above for **Calvin WATERMAN,** minor about two years of age.

Nathan ALLEN Jr. of Brookfield to **Jonathan WATERMAN** of Bridgewater. <no reference cited>
...6 May 1776...Nathan ALLEN Jr., housewright for one hundred & fifty pounds sold to Jonathan WATERMAN, cordwainer...land in Brookfield.

Othniel & Pelatiah GILBERT of Brookfield to **Jonathan WATERMAN.** <Worcester Co.Deeds 110:503>
...7 June 1784...Othniel GILBERT and Pelatiah GILBERT, yeomen, for twelve pounds sold to Jonathan WATERMAN, cordwainer...two acres in Brookfield bounded by land of Levi GILBERT, Theophilus WATERMAN...this seventh day of June in the year of our Lord one thousand seven hundred and eighty four and the eighth year of the Independence of America. Witnesses: Nathan ALLEN, William ALLEN Jr.

Jonathan WATERMAN of Brookfield to **Jacob KENT Jr.** of Brookfield. <Worcester Co.Deeds>
...10 Apr. 1815, Jonathan WATERMAN, cordwainer, for ninety dollars sold to Jacob KENT Jr., yeoman fifteen acres in Brookfield bounded by land of Paul CROWEL and Ephraim ADDAMS. Witnesses: Joseph WOOD, Foster DAVIS. Rec. 25 May 1816.

Jonathan WATERMAN of Brookfield to **John GILBERT** of Brookfield. <Worcester Co.Deeds>
...Aug. 1833, Jonathan WATERMAN, yeoman, for forty dollars sold to John GILBERT, two acres in Brookfield bounded by land of Linus BA(   )OTER, Thomas SANFORD and Rice SANFORD...said land was deeded to Jonathan WATERMAN by Othniel GILBERT and Pelatiah GILBERT in 1784. Witnesses: Daniel SAMPSON, Liberty SAMPSON. Rec. 7 Mar. 1837.

Jonathan WATERMAN of Brookfield to **Thomas SANFORD, Coleman W. GILBERT** of Brookfield. <no ref.>
...12 June 1834, Jonathan WATERMAN, yeoman, for two hundred and seventy five dollars sold to Thomas SANFORD and Coleman W. GILBERT, yeomen, twenty five acres in the West Parish of Brookfield bounded by land of MAKEPEACE, BARROW, CROWEL. Witnesses: Josiah SANFORD, Calvin SANFORD.

Jonathan WATERMAN of Brookfield to **Rice SANFORD.**
...4 May 1836, Jonathan WATERMAN, gentleman, for six hundred dollars sold to Rice SANFORD, yeoman ...forty acres in Brookfield bounded by land of Adolphus HAMILTON, William FOSTER, Levi ROSS, Coleman W. GILBERT, Dexter BRUICE, Samuel GILBERT Jr. Witnesses: Joseph W. WOOD, Jesse BLISS.

MICRO #2 OF 9

Estate of **Abner CUSHMAN** of Halifax. <Plymouth Co.PR #5781, 17:173;19:437-8,519,557>
...1766...<no details given in files>.

==========

William DONHAM of Halifax to **Nathaniel GOODWIN** of Plymouth. <Plymouth Co.Deeds 79:6>
...29 Oct. 1795, William DONHAM and wife Deborah for £3.12s sold to Nathaniel GOODWIN, Esq....our right & interest in the seventh share in the fourth great lot and last division of Plymouth and Plimton Commons lying in Plymouth to the westward of the Great South Pond, reference to said proprietors of Plymouth & Plimton's Second Book of Records page 144 for the bounds thereof, and was laid out to our grandfather **Eleazer CUSHMAN** and decended to us from him by heir ship. Witnesses: Josiah TOMSON, Mercy WATERMAN. Rec. 9 Nov. 1795.

==========

Rachel CUSHMAN of Halifax to **Thomas HOBART.** <Plymouth Co.Deeds 146:50>
...4 Oct. 1822, Rachel CUSHMAN, widow of **Jotham CUSHMAN,** Esq. of Halifax, sells her thirds in house and land in Hanover, 4 corners, to Thomas HOBART.

==========

Estate of **Jotham CUSHMAN** of Halifax. <Plymouth Co.PR #5865, 46:207;48:487-9;49:246>
<46:207>...3 Mar. 1817, Nathaniel COLLAMORE, gentleman, of Pembroke, appointed administrator.
<48:488>...2 June 1817, estate insolvent, widow to receive allowance with nothing left to distribute.

==========

Will of **Allerton CUSHMAN** of Plympton. <Plymouth Co.PR #5786, 6:2-4,12>
<6:2>...dated Oct. 1730, mentions sons **Allerton CUSHMAN** (under age) and **Joseph CUSHMAN** (under age), brother **Josiah CUSHMAN** executor; wife **Elizabeth.** Pr. Mar. 1730/1. <6:12> Account mentions daughter **Mary CUSHMAN,** sons **James CUSHMAN, Allerton CUSHMAN** (all under age).

==========

James, Josiah & Allerton CUSHMAN. <Plymouth Co.Deeds 33:118 (same ref. as below)>
...27 May 1736, division of the fourth lot of Cedar Swamp between the three.

==========

Allerton CUSHMAN of Plimton to **James CUSHMAN** of Plimton. <Plymouth Co.Deeds 33:118>
...13 Aug. 1739, Allerton CUSHMAN, yeoman, for £25 sold to James CUSHMAN, blacksmith, one acre of meadow lying in Plimton adjoyning Jones River Meadows and is known by the name of Cookes Point and also a piece of swamp adjoyning my homestead containing one acre and half...it being the same that my Honoured Grandfather **Elkanah CUSHMAN** bought of **Adam WRIGHT** deceased known by the name of Watson's Meadow.

==========

Allerton CUSHMAN Jr. et al to **Thomas WATERMAN** and **Gideon SAMSON.** <Plymouth Co.Deeds 53:237>
...22 Sept. 1766, **Allerton CUSHMAN Jr.** and wife **Harmony, Ephraim CUSHMAN** and wife **Sarah, Joseph DOWNER** and wife **Asenath,** all of Coventry CT for twenty four pounds sold to **Thomas WATERMAN** and **Gideon SAMSON** three fifths part of a lot of saltmeadow in Duxbury in Lot #1 of the 2nd Division of Commons belonging to Duxbury and Pembroke laid out in 1712.

==========

Will of **Robert CUSHMAN** of Kingston. <Plymouth Co.PR 14:410>
...dated 9 Feb. 1746/7, mentions daughter **Hannah WASHBURN.** Codicil 9 May 1749. Pr. 7 Nov. 1757. <The files do not transcribe the will. Bowman appeared to be trying to prove the parentage of the Hannah CUSHMAN who married Moses WASHBURN.>[<1>]

==========

Estate of **Elkanah CUSHMAN** of Plymouth. <Plymouth Co.PR 4:20>
...22 June 1717, division of estate; widow **Hester** now the wife of Benjamin WARREN; children **Elkanah CUSHMAN, James CUSHMAN, Elizabeth CUSHMAN** and **Hannah CUSHMAN**; Hannah to receive her father's share in the seventh great lot in the last Division of Common.

==========

Will of **Elkanah CUSHMAN** of Plympton. <Plymouth Co.PR 5:330>
...dated 14 Oct. 1725, mentions son **Allerton CUSHMAN,** daughter **Martha HOLMES,** two granddaughters **Elizabeth DELANOE, Hannah CUSHMAN,** son **Josiah CUSHMAN.** Pr. 26 Sept. 1727.

==========

John WATERMAN of Plymouth to **Joseph WARREN.** <Plymouth Co.Deeds 33:89>
...1 May 1739, John WATERMAN, housewright and wife Hannah sell to Joseph WARREN, yeoman...lot in Plymouth which was laid out to our Honoured Father **Elkanah CUSHMAN Jr.** of Plymouth, deceased and is the fourth lot in the seventh great lot in ye last Division of Common lands.[<2>]

==========

James CUSHMAN of Plymouth to **Nathaniel JACKSON** et al of Plymouth. <Plymouth Co.Deeds 26:169>
...26 June 1731, James CUSHMAN, cordwainer for £13.6s8d sold to Nathaniel JACKSON, Samuel JACKSON & Josiah CUSHMAN both of Plimton...a certain parcell of Cedar Swamp being the fifth division in the eighth great lot in the South Meadow Cedar Swamp in Plimton...sixth part of said lot... being ye same that my brother **Elkanah CUSHMAN** of said Plymouth sold to said three by deed dated 3 Feb. 1727/8. Witnesses: John DYER, Elkanah CUSHMAN.

==========

Estate of **James CUSHMAN** of Plymouth. <Plymouth Co.PR #5847, 8:471-73>
<original bond>...6 Mar. 1741, James HOVEY, joiner, of Plymouth administrator on estate of **James CUSHMAN**, mariner, dec'd, gave bond of £800 with Thomas MURDOCH, merchant and Elkanah CUSHMAN, mariner, both of Plymouth as sureties. Witnesses: John WATERMAN, Edward WINSLOW. <8:471>...6 Mar. 1741, Nathaniel THOMAS, Esq., Thomas SPOONER and Thomas MAYHEW, all of Plymouth were appointed to appraise the real and personal estate. Inventory taken 14 Apr. 1742, incl.: one half of seven and a half acres swamp in Plympton, £4.13s,9d; one half of about three acres meadow & upland in Plymton at £7.10 per acre, £11.5s; his third of about one and a half acre salt meadow in Kingston incumbered with his mother's dower dureing her life, £4; his third of twenty acres of upland in Kingston under the same incumbrance, £3.6s8d; his half of thirty acres of land in Kingston, at £3.6.8 an acre, £50. <8:472>...20 Apr. 1742, **Hannah CUSHMAN** receipted to James HOVEY, admr., on estate of my deceased husband for necessaries set off to her. <8:473>...Account dated 14 July 1742, payments made to: John BREWSTER; Robert CUSHMAN & Josiah CUSHMAN for showing ye land; Mr. HOWLAND; Samuel WRIGHT for searching the meadow for iron ore; Isaac LOTHROP, Esq.; Robert BROWN, Esq.; Samuel BARTLETT, Esq.; Thomas MURDOCH; Lazarus Le BARON; Elkanah CUSHMAN; Lemuel COBB; Silvanus COBB; Jonathan DARLING; WATSON & MAYHEW; Thomas HOLMES; John WATERMAN; Nathaniel SHURTLEFF; Hannah CUSHMAN, for mourning; Thomas WETHERELL; William DYER's administrators; Dr. THOMAS; George HOLMES.

Will of **William STURTEVANT** of Halifax. <Plymouth Co.PR #19806, 13:130-1,154,369,454-6>
...dated 7 Aug. 1753, mentions two daughters **Hannah RIPLEY** and **Fear WATERMAN**; grandchildren, the children of my late son **Isaac STURTEVANT**, viz: **William, Isaac, Simeon, Samuel, Jesse, Nathaniel, Deborah** and **Martha**; wife **Joanna**; son-in-law **John WATERMAN Jr.** app'td. sole executor. Witnesses: Thomas CROADE, Nathaniel CROADE, John TILLSON. Pr. 3 Sept. 1753. <13:154> Inventory taken 8 Sept. 1753 by Robert WATERMAN, Noah CUSHMAN, Samuel WATERMAN. <13:369> Account allowed 2 Dec. 1754. <13:454>...1 Feb. 1755, **William STURTEVANT** of Halifax, grandson of **William STURTEVANT** late of Halifax, dec'd and Hezekiah BEARCE of Halifax, guardian to **Isaac, Simeon, Samuel, Jesse** and **Nathaniel STURTEVANT**, grandsons of **William**, dec'd, petition the court for permission to sell land and part of saw mill bequeathed to them. <13:455> Petition granted 12 Feb. 1755. <13:456>...23 Apr. 1755, William STURTEVANT, Hezekiah BEARCE and Austin BEARCE gave bond for £500 for sale of the land and saw mill.

Estate of **Ichabod CUSHMAN** of Middleboro. <Plymouth Co.PR #5835, 6:245,263,295;7:313,317,320>
...1732...<no details given in files>

Jabez VAUGHAN of Pomfret VT. <Plymouth Co.Deeds 68:127>
...1 Dec. 1784, Jabez VAUGHAN & wife Lois sell rights in one eighth of real estate of **James SOULE** of Plympton, dec'd. <63:28>...31 Aug. 1770, Jabez VAUGHAN Jr. of Middleboro, wife Lois signs.

Will of **Isaac CUSHMAN Jr.** of Plympton. <Plymouth Co.PR #5842, 5:317,580;7:20,24;8:301>
<unrecorded original>...noncupative will dated 13 Sept. 1727, mentions beloved wife; son **Nathaniel CUSHMAN** (under 21); daughter **Phebe;** land to son **Nathaniel** excepting and reserving my Father and my wife's improvement; my five daughters (unnamed). Witnesses: John BELL, Benjamin CUSHMAN, Ruth CHURCHEL.

Will of **Mercy CUSHMAN**, of Plympton. <Plymouth Co.PR #5875, 8:215,299,301>
...dated 16 Dec. 1728, widow of **Isaac CUSHMAN** of Plympton; mentions son **Jonathan FREEMAN**; dau. **Marcy WATERMAN**; son **Bradford FREEMAN** (under 21); son **Ichabod FREEMAN** (under 21); heirs of dau. **Marcy** ("she still living & no heirs then"); daus. **Fear CUSHMAN, Priscilla CUSHMAN** and **Abigail CUSHMAN**; brother **Samuel BRADFORD** of Plimpton, executor. <8:215> adm. 2 June 1740. <8:301> Inventory dated 17 Apr. 1741.

MICRO #3 OF 9

Nehemiah STURTEVANT of Plympton. <Plymouth Co.Deeds 40:190>
...11 Mar. 1747, Nehemiah STURTEVANT, yeoman and wife **Fear**, sell land in Plympton settled on the said **Fear** in the settlement of her Honoured Father **Isaac CUSHMAN**, dec'd, estate.

Nehemiah STURTEVANT of Plympton. <Plymouth Co.Deeds 62:81>
...15 Mar. 1783, Nehemiah STURTEVANT, yeoman, (wf Huldah joins), sells land of grandfather, **Nehemiah STURTEVANT** received through father **Noah STURTEVANT.** The following deeds (with no data) are also cited with Nehemiah & Huldah as grantors: <63:75> 1 July 1783; <69:98> 4 Aug. 1789; <81:262> 1790.

Joseph JOSSELYN of E. Bridgewater to **Marquis F. JOSSELYN** of Boston. <Plymouth Co.Deeds 152:251>
...7 Mar. 1825, Joseph JOSSELYN, with wf Deborah releasing, sells land in E. Bridgewater to Marquis F. JOSSELYN, housewright. Also <154:1>...7 Mar. 1825, Marquis F. JOSSELYN, houswright of Boston to support Joseph JOSSEYLN & wf Deborah for life. <168:8>...3 Feb. 1830, Marquis F. JOSSELYN, housewright, of Boston and wf Eunice.

John HAWKS of Lynn to **Walter WHITFORD.** <Essex Co.Deeds 52:7>
...7 Mar. 1728/9, John HAWKES, husbandman, and wf Mary, sell Common Right in Salem, said right is for Walter WHITFORD's dwelling house erected before the year 1661 and is not yet...recorded by Salem proprietors.

John HAWKS Jr.of Lynn to **Samuel WHITFORD** of Salem. <Essex Co.Deeds 65:115>
...9 Nov. 1733, John HAWKS Jr., husbandman, and wf Mary, the daughter of **John WHITFORD,** late of Salem, mariner, dec'd, sell to our brother Samuel WHITFORD, fisherman... <no details in files>

John HAWKS of Lynn. <Essex Co.Deeds 62:191>
...14 May 1734, John HAWKS, husbandman, and wf Mary, sell half Common Right...in Salem...of our Father **John WHITFORD,** dec'd. <purchaser not named>

Estate of **John HAWKES** of Lynn. <Essex Co.PR #12922, 318:184;324:270,271,348;335:468,469>
<318:184>...11 Sept. 1738, **Adam HAWKES 3d** of Lynn, app'td. administrator on estate of father, John HAWKES. <324:348> Inventory taken 19 Sept. 1738 by **Jno. HAWKES 3d** et al, about 80 acres, L660. <324:270> Account dated 10 Nov. 1740. Warrant to set off dower to widow **Mary HAWKES** and divide remainder into seven parts. <324:271> Division dated 8 Oct. 1740, one third to widow, remaining two thirds cannot be divided. <324:271> Guardianship of Children, 10 Nov. 1740: David NEWHALL app'td. guardian of **Eunice HAWKES,** dau. of John dec'd; Ebenezer BANCROFT app'td. guardian of **Elizabeth HAWKES,** dau. of John dec'd. <335:468> Appraisal dated 22 May 1758 by William COLLINS, L. COLLINS, Moses HAWKES, Samuel GOWING and Josiah WALTON all of Lynn, of real estate of **John HAWKES** late of Lynn, dec'd (which was formerly set out to his widow) into seven equal parts. <335:469> Settlement dated 29 May 1758, estate cannot be divided, the whole is assigned to **Adam HAWKES,** son of deceased, he to pay: legal representatives of **Mary FELTCH,** dec'd; **Eve BANCROFT,** wf of John; **Lydia NORWOOD,** wf of Thomas NORWOOD; **Eunice WALTON,** wf of Jacob; **Elizabeth MEAD,** wf of John.

Will of **Josiah BROWN** of Reading. <Middlesex Co.PR #3121>
...dated 5 Oct. 1752, mentions wife **Susanna**; sons **Nathaniel BROWN, Jonathan BROWN, Abel BROWN**; children of deceased son **Ephraim BROWN,** viz: **Josiah, Dorothy, Jacob, Hannah; Huldah HAWKS,** dau of my daughter **Huldah,** dec'd; **Susanna BACHEL(OR),** dau of my daughter **Susanna,** dec'd. Inventory valued at Ⱡ129, personal and Ⱡ3295, real estate.

Estate of **Adam HAWKS** of Reading. <Middlesex Co.PR #10822>
...4 Jan. 1774, **Lydia HAWKS,** widow, app'td. administrator on estate of husband, dec'd intestate. Inventory including farm at Lynn settled 9 Sept. 1777. Children mentioned: **John HAWKS, Benjamin HAWKS, Adam HAWKS, Huldah BROWN, Lydia PERKINS, Mary PUTNAM.**

Will of **Ebenezer HAWKES** of Marblehead. <Essex Co.PR #12913, 343:369;344:146;345:120;348:347>
<343:369>...dated 2 Sept. 1761; to grandchildren, children of son **Ebenezer HAWKES,** dec'd, half of all real and personal estate incl. half of what I have of the estate that belonged to **John ESTES,** dec'd that was given him by his grandfather **Matthew ESTES**; daughter **Elisabeth GRIFFEN**; son **Samuel HAWKES**; two grandsons, **Ebenezer HAWKES** and **Joseph HAWKES,** sons of my son **Samuel,** at the decease of my son **Samuel,** their father, they to pay several bequests to their brothers and sisters, viz: **John HAWKES, Matthew HAWKES, Philedilphia HAWKES, Sarah HAWKES, Deliverance HAWKES** and **Patience HAWKES**; to my grandson **Ebenezer HAWKES** the over sight care and management of the estate I have willed to his father, my said son **Samuel,** during the term of Samuel's life; **Ebenezer** and **Benjamin** appointed executors. Codicil dated 29 June 1765: to daughter **Elizabeth GRIFFIN** and husband **Joseph** the dwelling house where we now dwell with garden and blacksmith shop, after their decease it to go to my three grandchildren, viz: **Benjamin GRIFFIN, Ebenezer GRIFFIN** and **Elisabeth GRIFFEN.** Witnesses: Mary GRIFFEN, Joseph STRIKER, Zaccheus COLLINS. Pr. 3 Feb. 1767. Inventory dated 9 June 1767 (various real estate holdings) and 2 July 1773. Inventory presented 6 Apr. 1784 by **Ebenezer HAWKES,** administrator, Quaker, "he affirmed".

Ebenezer HAWKES of Lynn to **Thomas HAWKES** of Lynn. <Essex Co.Deeds 13:239>
...19 Dec. 1699, Ebenezer HAWKES, blacksmith, sells to Thomas HAWKES, husbandman, land on Saugus River obtained by my Honoured father Master **John HAWKES** of Lynn; **Moses HAWKES** and **John HAWKES,** brothers of said **Thomas HAWKES** release their rights. Ack. 23 Feb. 1699/1700

Ebenezer HAWKES of Lynn to **John BURRELL** of Lynn. <Essex Co.Deeds 20:176>
...9 Apr. 1708, Ebenezer HAWKES, blacksmith sells to John BURRELL, yeoman; wf Elizabeth releases dower. <no details given>

Ebenezer HAWKES of Lynn to **Thomas CHE(V)ER.** <Essex Co.Deeds 32:286>
...4 Aug. 1709, Ebenezer HAWKES and wife sell to Thomas CHE(V)ER. Ack. 3 Mar. 1717/18.

Ebenezer HAWKES of Lynn to **Isaac LARRABE Jr.** <Essex Co.Deeds 43:112>
...13 Jan. 1714/5, Ebenezer HAWKES, blacksmith, to Isaac LARRABE Jr., lands laid out to John HAWKS and other lands.

Ebenezer HAWKES of Marblehead to **Joseph BREAD/BREED** of Lynn. <Essex Co.Deeds 41:202>
...30 Dec. 1720, Ebenezer HAWKES, blacksmith, to Joseph BREAD/BREED, land laid out to my brother **John HAWKS** on Lynn Town Commons, being the 2d lot in 3d range in 4th division in the ox pasture. Witnesses: John COIT, Elizabeth HAWKES. Ack. 25 Dec. 1721.

Ebenezer HAWKES of Marblehead to **Thomas KIMBALL** of Marblehead. <Essex Co.Deeds 43:146>
...21 Jan. 1722/3, Ebenezer HAWKES, blacksmith and wf Sarah sell to Thomas KIMBALL, house etc. he bought of George CHINN and his sister.

Ebenezer HAWKES et al, of Lynn. <Essex Co.Deeds 50:226>
...25 Apr. 1709, Hannah HUTCHINSON, Ebenezer HAWKES and Margaret HAWKES, as executors of will of Moses HAWKES of Lynn...

Ebenezer HAWKES of Lynn. <Essex Co.Deeds 57:105>
...7 May 1718, Ebenezer HAWKES, blacksmith, wf Elizabeth releasing dower, land laid out to my brother John HAWKS and other lands...

Ebenezer HAWKES of Marblehead. <Essex Co.Deeds 42:17>
...5 Dec. 1723, agreement between Ebenezer HAWKES, blacksmith, "et al".

Ebenezer HAWKES of Marblehead. <Essex Co.Deeds 45:79>
...29 July 1725, Ebenezer HAWKES, blacksmith, with wf Sarah releasing dower...

Ebenezer HAWKES of Marblehead. <Essex Co.Deeds 42:17>
...25 Apr. 1728, Ebenezer HAWKES, blacksmith, with wf Sarah releasing dower, et al...

Ebenezer HAWKES of Marblehead. <Essex Co.Deeds 55:49>
...4 Sept. 1729, Ebenezer HAWKES, blacksmith, with wf Sarah releasing dower...

Ebenezer HAWKES of Marblehead. <Essex Co.Deeds 65:125>
...2 Oct. 1729, Ebenezer HAWKES, blacksmith, with wf Sarah releasing dower...

Ebenezer HAWKES of Marblehead. <Essex Co.Deeds 69:119>
...12 Apr. 1733, Ebenezer HAWKES, blacksmith, with wf Ruth releasing dower...

Ebenezer HAWKES of Marblehead. <Essex Co.Deeds 64:74>
...10 Oct. 1733, Ebenezer HAWKES, blacksmith, with wf Ruth releasing dower...

Ebenezer HAWKES of Marblehead. <Essex co.Deeds 64:92>
...5 Nov. 1733, Ebenezer HAWKES, blacksmith, with wf Ruth releasing dower...

Ebenezer HAWKES et al of Marblehead to **Samuel HOLTON** of Salem. <Essex Co.Deeds 68:261>
...5 Jan. 1735, Ebenezer HAWKES, blacksmith, with consent of wf Ruth, and Samuel POPE of Salem, with wf Sarah consenting, to Samuel HOLTON, land in Salem.

Ebenezer HAWKES et al of Marblehead to **Bartholomew REA.** <Essex Co.Deeds 68:262>
...5 Jan. 1735, Ebenezer HAWKES, blacksmith, with wf Ruth, and Samuel POPE of Salem with wf Sarah to Bartholomew REA, land in Salem.

Ebenezer HAWKES et al of Marblehead. <Essex Co.Deeds 71:79>
...23 Mar. 1735, Ebenezer HAWKES, blacksmith, with wf Ruth releasing, and Samuel POPE, with wf Sarah releasing, of Salem, land in Salem.

Ebenezer HAWKES et al of Marblehead to **Joseph CROSS.** <Essex Co.Deeds 71:277>
...31 Jan. 1736, Ebenezer HAWKES, blacksmith, with wf Ruth, and Samuel POPE, with wf Sarah, to Joseph CROSS, land in Salem.

Estate of **Ebenezer HAWKES Jr.** of Marblehead. <Essex Co.PR #12912, 323:86;324:645;341:8>
<323:86>...11 Feb. 1741, **Ebenezer HAWKES** and **Anna HAWKES**, widow, both of Marblehead, appointed administrators. <324:645> Inventory taken 2 Feb. 1741. <341:8> Account dated 24 Nov. 1763, of **Ebenezer HAWKS**, administrator on estate of his son, **Ebenezer HAWKS Jr.**; mentions land with house & garden sold to Widow MEEKS for £33.6.8, land sold to Ebenezer, Amos & Benjamin HAWKS for £246.

Ebenezer HAWKES of Marblehead et al. <Essex Co.Deeds 108:269>
...10 Oct. 1759, Ebenezer HAWKES, blacksmith & **Anna HAWKES**, widow, as administrators on estate of **Ebenezer HAWKES Jr.**, of Marblehead, blacksmith, for £246 sell to **Ebenezer HAWKES Jr.**, blacksmith, **Benjamin HAWKES**, cordwainer and **Amos HAWKES**, fisherman, one third of mansion house of said dec'd, also other lands and land in Cumberland Co. ME.

Ebenezer, Amos & Benjamin HAWKES to **Ebenezer HAWKES.** <Essex Co.Deeds 112:255>
...30 Nov. 1764, Ebenezer HAWKES of Windham, Cumberland Co., Amos HAWKES, of Windham, farmer and Benjamin HAWKES of Marblehead, shoemaker, for £53.6.8 sell to our Grandfather Ebenezer HAWKES of Marblehead, blacksmith, all their rights to a piece of land or rocks with an old shop on it near Nick's Cove. Witnesses: Joseph GRIFFEN, Elizabeth GRIFFEN. Rec. 22 Dec. 1764.

Ebenezer HAWKES & Amos HAWKES to **Benjamin HAWKES** of Marblehead. <Essex Co.Deeds 112:261>
...1 Dec. 1764, Ebenezer HAWKES, blacksmith and Amos HAWKES, farmer, both of Windham, Cumberland Co., for £10.13.4 sell to our brother Benjamin HAWKES, cordwainer, two thirds of land in Marblehead near Nicks Cove. Witness: Joseph GRIFFIN.

Estate of **Benjamin HAWKES** of Marblehead. <Essex Co.PR #12907, 347:443;348:278;351:71;359:241,518>
<347:443>...5 May 1772, **Deborah HAWKES** appointed admx. <348:278> Inventory dated 15 June 1772, (Ebenezer called a shoreman), incl. 100 acres of land in Windham ME, piece of pasture land on Great Neck at Marblehead.

Estate of **Benjamin HAWKES** of Marblehead. <Essex Co.PR #12908, 375:139,281,522;376:315-6,330-1> <375:139>...22 Apr. 1807, **Mrs. Mehitable HAWKES** appointed admx. of estate of Benjamin HAWKES, mariner, dec'd. Sureties: Nathan BOWEN, Esq., William ROGERS. <375:281> Inventory taken 27 June 1807, real estate $1100.00, personal $122.91. <375:522> List of debts, allowance to widow. <376:315> 19 Jan. 1808, Widow's thirds set off, mentions mansion house, small dwelling house, shop. <376:330> Account of Admx. dated 21 Apr. 1808, mentions part of real estate sold by order of Court of Common Pleas at Ipswich last Mon. Dec. 1807.

MICRO #4 of 9

Estate of **Dr. Thomas HAWKES** of Lynn. <Essex Co.PR #12943, 313:450,480> <313:450>...4 June 1722, **Sarah HAWKES**, widow, appointed admx. on estate of husband who died intestate. Sureties: William GIDDINGS of Ipswich and John BRINTNALL gave bond of £800. <313:480> Inventory taken 15 June 1722 by Nathaniel GOWING, Joseph HAVEN and John BRINTNALL, incl. Doctor Books, Lancits & Druggs, £2.10s; housing & land together with common lott, £255.8s.

Will of **Joseph HAVEN** of Lynn. <Essex Co.PR 328:430,431; 331:305> ...dated 7 Mar. 1748/9, "kindsmen" **Elkanah HAWKES** and **Jonathan HAWKES** both of Lynn appointed sole executors. Bequests made to: children & grandchildren of my deceased sister **Hannah PARKER**, viz: **Joseph PARKER**, surviving children of **Hannah** & **Mary**, daughters of my said sister **PARKER**; my sister **Sarah HAWKES**, of Lynn, widow; kindswoman **Sarah GREY**, wf of Benjamin of Lynn; kinswoman **Hannah WAITE**, wf of Jonathan Jr. of Lynn; housekeeper, **Abigail EDMUNDS**; remaining estate to **Elkanah HAWKES** and **Jonathan HAWKES**. Witnesses: Timothy HITCHINGS, Aaron FELT and Francis SMITH. Pr. 20 Mar. 1748. <331:305> Inventory taken 30 Apr. 1753 by Timothy HITCHINGS, Aaron FELT and Francis SMITH.

Estate of **Thomas HAWKS** of Lynn. <Essex Co.PR #12944, 318:154> <318:114>...5 Oct. 1736, **Elkanah HAWKES** appointed administrator. Sureties: Jonathan HAWKS of Lynn and Daniel GIDDIN of Ipswich gave bond of £100.

Will of **Elkanah HAWKS** of Lynn. <Essex Co.PR 353:144> ...dated 16 Jan. 1778, mentions wife **Eunice**; children: **Thomas HAWKS, Elkanah HAWKS, Ezra HAWKS, Eunice HITCH, Sarah MARRET, Elizabeth HAWKS, Love HAWKS** (dau), **Grace HAWKS**. Witnesses: Francis SMITH, Samuel WILLSON, Adam HAWKS.

Will of **James BLAKE** of Boston. <Suffolk Co.PR #37379, 149:70> ...dated 10 Dec. 1847, mentions wf **Elizabeth**; sister **Rachel BLAKE**; children: **James Gorham BLAKE, Charles BLAKE, George Thacher BLAKE, Elizabeth WOOD**; children of my late sister **Susannah MARSHALL** and the issue of her deceased children; niece **Adaline O. GRAY**; **Mrs. Mary CLARKE**, widow of the late **Joseph Elliott CLARKE**; **Miss Elizabeth Elliot CLARKE** dau of said **Mary CLARKE**; American Home Missionary Society. The estate and dwelling house on Charles St., Boston, now occupied by my dau **Elizabeth WOOD**, the estate and buildings on West Cedar St. and the estate and buildings on Bridge St., Boston to be sold, along with ten thousand dollars in stocks and cash, all to be put in trust for the comfortable support of daughter **Elizabeth WOOD** and for the support and education of her children.<3>

Estate of **Jonathan HAWKS** of Chelsea. <Suffolk Co.PR #12911, 60:182,546,548-9,561> <60:192>...12 Mar. 1762, **Abigail HAWKS**, widow, appointed admx. of estate of Jonathan HAWKS, cordwainer, dec'd intestate, with Elkanah HAWKS, gentleman and William FARRINGTON, cordwainer, both of Lynn. <60:546> Inventory taken 26 May 1762 by Thomas PRATT, Samuel SPRAGUE & Jonathan PORTER. <60:548> 4 June 1762, real estate appraised and dower set off to widow; extensive real estate including: dwelling house in Chelsea; "the barn"; 18 acres; 11 acres called the Barn lot; 16 acres called northeast pasture; 40 acres; house lot; 20 acres pasture; 9 acres bounded by land of Mr. FERINTON/FARRINGTON; 5 acres; 7 acres bounded by land of Mr. BERRY; 3 acres woodland in the 600 acres so called bound by land of Esq. HALL of Boston; half an acre woodland in Lynn in partnership with Elkanah HAWKS and in the 600 acres so called; half a 7 acre lot of salt marsh in partnership with said Elkanah HAWKS and bounded on said Elkanah HAWKS own marsh; an old house & yard room in Lynn; 6 acres woodland in Malden bounded by land of the Widow HASEY; two acres salt marsh in Chelsea bounded by marsh of Samuel SERGENT. <60:561> Account of **Abigail HAWKS** dated 21 Aug. 1762. Debts due the estate from: John FARRINGTON, Jonathan BARREY, Mr. BEARD, William FARRINGTON, John TUTHILL.

Abigail HAWKES of Boston to **Peter THACHER et al.** <Suffolk Co.Deeds 136:166,167> ...30 Sept. 1782, Abigail HAWKS, widow, for £100, sold to Peter THACHER of Malden, clerk, and wf Elizabeth, Samuel CHENEY of Roxbury and wf Hannah, and Thomas RUGGLES of Boston, merchant and wf Abigail, the said Thomas acting as attorney to William HAWKES...all my right unto the real estate of my late beloved husband Jonathan HAWKES of Chelsea, gentleman, dec'd, lying in Chelsea whether by right of Dower or otherwise. Witnesses: Rebecca WYER, Peggy CUSHING. Ack. & rec. 20 Dec. 1782.

Peter THACHER of Malden **et al** to **John BUCKMAN** of Boston **et al.** <Suffolk Co.Deeds 136:167> ...30 Sept. 1782, Peter THACHER, clerk and wf Elizabeth, Samuel CHENEY of Roxbury and wf Hannah, and Thomas RUGGLES of Boston, merchant and wf Abigail, said Thomas acting as attorney to William HAWKES, mariner, for £630, sold to John BUCKMAN of Boston, trader and Thomas SACK of Chelsea, gentleman...house and lot of land lying in Chelsea late belonging to Jonathan HAWKES, gentleman, dec'd containing 40 acres....bounded by land of James STOWERS, land late belonging to Jonathan WILLIAMS commonly called the Dudley Farm. Also a Barn and 30 acres bounded by land sold to

Jonathan HAWKES and land of Samuel PRATT, Samuel SPRAGUE. Witnesses: Rebecca WYER, Peggy CUSHING, Simeon WHITMAN Jr., David WHITMAN. Rec. 20 Dec. 1782.

Estate of **Jonathan HAWKES** of Chelsea. <Suffolk Co.PR #18774-#18776, 85:657>
...31 Oct. 1786, Guardianship of Children: **Abigail HAWKES, Elizabeth HAWKES, Rachel HAWKES**, children of Jonathan HAWKES, cordwainer, dec'd.

PLYMOUTH COUNTY DEEDS:

1:212 - 18 Dec. 1689, Thomas CUSHMAN of Plimouth to John ALLEN of Middleboro.
4:104 - 8 July 1695, Thomas CUSHMAN of Plymouth, yeoman to John WATERMAN of Plymouth. Rec.1702.
4:167 - 3 Feb. 1702/3, Thomas CUSHMAN of Plymouth & wf Abigail to Thomas LORING of Plymouth, land on which my son Thomas hath built.
5:217 - 16 Feb. 1702/3, Thomas CUSHMAN of Plymouth to Abiel FULLER of Plymouth.
10:1:221 - 4 Feb 1702/2, Thomas CUSHMAN, Duxbury & Thomas LORING of Plym. to Maj. John BRADFORD.
10:1:421 - 18 Nov. 1712, Thomas CUSHMAN of Plympton to Benjamin WARREN of Plymouth, land bought of Deacon John RICKARD.
11:187 - 21 Oct. 1713, Thomas CUSHMAN of Plympton, yeoman, to Dr. Caleb LORING of Plymouth, land bought of Deacon John RICKARD in 1713.
11:134 - 21 Dec. 1713, Thomas CUSHMAN of Plympton, yeoman to Benjamin EATON Sr. of Plympton.
11:95 - 21 Dec. 1713, Thomas CUSHMAN of Plympton, yeoman, to Samuel BRADFORD of Plympton.
11:29 - 1 Mar. 1714/5, Thomas CUSHMAN of Plympton to son Robert CUSHMAN of Plymouth, part of land where I formerly lived.
11:214 - 22 June 1715, Thomas CUSHMAN of Plympton, yeoman, to son Job CUSHMAN of Plymouth.
12:194 - 5 Sept 1715, Thomas CUSHMAN, Sr., of Plympton to Jacob TOMSON.
15:188 - 31 May 1721, Thomas CUSHMAN Sr., of Plympton, yeoman to son Samuel CUSHMAN.
15:179 - 31 May 1721, Thomas CUSHMAN Sr., of Plympton, yeoman to son Benjamin CUSHMAN.
15:211 - 28 Dec. 1721, Thomas CUSHMAN, of Plympton, yeoman to sons Samuel & Benjamin CUSHMAN.
19:29 - 27 Feb. 1721/2, Thomas CUSHMAN, of Plympton, yeoman, to sons Samuel & Benjamin CUSHMAN.
19:29 - 12 Feb. 1724/5, Thomas CUSHMAN, of Plympton, yeoman, & wf, to sons Samuel & Benjamin CUSHMAN of Plympton.
50:44 - 16 May 1765, Thomas CUSHMAN of Plympton and Thomas CUSHMAN of Bridgewater.
53:219 - 20 May 1765, Thomas CUSHMAN of Plympton, yeoman to Isaac CHURCHELL of Plympton.
54:34 - 11 Sept 1767, Thomas CUSHMAN of Kingston, innholder, as admr. on estate of Robert CUSHMAN of Kingston, dec'd.
57:112 - 24 Mar. 1773, Thomas CUSHMAN of Plympton, yeoman, to Benjamin CUSHMAN of Plympton, quit claim to house and land Benjamin lives on.
75:48 - 13 Jan. 1772, Thomas CUSHMAN, Benjamin CUSHMAN & Timothy RIPLEY - bounds settled, on Dunham's Neck, Winnatuxet River.

Estate of **Job CUSHMAN** of Plymouth, mariner. <Plymouth Co.PR 8:165;9:101-3>
<8:165>...5 Mar. 1739, **Lydia CUSHMAN**, widow, and Edward ARNOLD, Esq. of Duxbury, appointed admrs. <9:101> Inventory dated 21 May 1740, same day widow receives allowance for necessaries. <9:103> Account of admrs. (not dated).

Will of **Lydia CUSHMAN** of Plymouth. <Plymouth Co.PR 11:216;12:366>
...dated 27 Sept. 1744, "aged sixty three years", mentions eldest daughter **Maria BARKER**, youngest daughter **Lydia CUSHMAN** as sole executrix, brother **Edward ARNOLD.** Witnesses: Experience LOTHROP, Elizabeth HOWLAND, Benjamin LOTHROP. Pr. 11 May 1749. Letter issued to **Lydia ATWOOD**, wf of Solomon, sole executrix. <12:366> Bond dated 16 Mar. 1749.

Will of **Robert CUSHMAN** of Kingston. <Plymouth Co.PR #5883, 14:410,412,527;15:46;16:44>
<14:410>...dated 9 Feb. 1746/7, mentions wife **Prudence**, children: **Robert CUSHMAN, Thomas CUSHMAN, Joshua CUSHMAN, Jonathan CUSHMAN, Ruth PERKINS, Abigail LEONARD, Hannah WASHBURN.** Codicil dated 9 May 1749. Pr. 7 Nov. 1757. <14:412> Letter. <14:527> Inventory. <15:46,16:44> Account.

MICRO #5 OF 9

Will of **Robert CUSHMAN Jr.** of Kingston, yeoman. <Plymouth Co.PR 12:387;15:497>
<12:387>...dated 2 Sept. 1751, mentions wife **Marcy** and unnamed children. Pr. 7 Oct. 1751.
<15:497> Distribution of Real Estate by father of dec'd, **Robert CUSHMAN**; mentions eldest son **Robert CUSHMAN** to have the whole, reserving his mother's dower and paying their shares to his brothers & sisters as follows: **Lydia FULLER, Jerusha COBB, Rebecca FULLER, Mercy HARLOW, Hannah COBB, Ruth RICKARD, Abigail ROBENS/ROBBINS, Isaac CUSHMAN.**

Heirs of **Robert CUSHMAN** to **Ebenezer COBB** of Kingston. <Plymouth Co.Deeds 53:129>
...3 Nov. 1766, **Robert CUSHMAN, Josiah FULLER & wf Lydia, Ebenezer COBB Jr. & wf Jerusha, Barnabas FULLER & wf Rebecca, James HARLOW & wf Mercy, John COBB** in right of wf **Hannah** dec'd, **Samuel RICKARD & wf Ruth, Abigail ROBBINS, widow of Benjamin ROBBINS** and **Isaac CUSHMAN**, all children and heirs of **Robert CUSHMAN**, late of Kingston, dec'd, sell to **Ebenezer COBB**, 7 acres in Kingston.

<60:149> - 18 Nov. 1766, The above heirs (except Robert CUSHMAN) sell to **Robert CUSHMAN.**
<60:150> - 4 May 1781, **Robert CUSHMAN**, sells land bought of other heirs 18 Nov. 1766.

James ROBBINS of Yarmouth N.S. to **Abigail ROBBINS.** <Plymouth Co.Deeds 52:243>
...1 Apr. 1765, James ROBBINS, yeoman, sells to Abigail ROBBINS, widow, land in Cedar Swamp in Plympton, part of Beaver Dam Swamp, received by him in will of his father **Jeduthan ROBBINS.**

Eleazer ROBBINS of Plympton to **Abigail ROBBINS** of Kingston. <Plymouth Co.Deeds 52:244>
...25 Nov. 1766, Eleazer ROBBINS sells to Abigail ROBBINS, widow of Benjamin ROBBINS, his share in Beaver Dam Swamp.

Abigail ROBBINS of Kingston. <Plymouth Co.Deeds 82:13>
...13 Feb. 1767, Abigail ROBBINS, widow, sold land she bought of Eleazer ROBBINS & James ROBBINS of Plympton which was given them in their father's last will.

Thomas CUSHMAN of Kingston to **Abigail ROBBINS** of Kingston. <Plymouth Co.Deeds 54:34>
...11 Sept. 1767, Thomas CUSHMAN, admr. of estate of Robert CUSHMAN, of Kingston, dec'd, sells to Abigail ROBBINS, spinster, 10 acres.

Abigail ROBBINS of Kingston. <Plymouth Co.Deeds 63:140>
...13 Sept. 1767, Abigail ROBBINS, spinster, (sells?) 10 acres, part of land formerly laid out to Mr. Robert CUSHMAN, of Kingston, dec'd.

Joseph ROBBINS of Yarmouth N.S. to **William STEVENS** of Plymouth. <Plymouth Co.Deeds 91:71>
...12 May 1798, Joseph ROBBINS, blacksmith & wf Elizabeth for $7.00 sell to William STEVENS, trader, all rights and interest in real estate of our mother **Phebe STEPHENS,** late of Carver, dec'd, which she died seized of lying in Plymouth or else where and which descended to her from her father **William HARLOW,** late of Plymouth, dec'd. Witnesses: Joseph ROBBINS Jr., Mercy TORREY. Ack. at Yarmouth N.S. by both (no date).

PLYMOUTH COUNTY DEEDS: (References to **ROBBINS.**)

47:147,153; 52:243; 53:129; 54:34; 60:149; 63:140; 70:201; 79:252; 82:13,221,222; 91:71; 92:36; 97:20; 105:11,151; 132:137; 143:132; 145:222; 149:43,76; 154:246.

Joseph ROBBINS of Plymouth. <Plymouth Co.Deeds 66:276>
...5 Dec. 1787, Joseph ROBBINS, blacksmith, mortgages his right, one eighth, in Swan Hole Grist Mill at Plympton.

Joseph ROBBINS of Yarmouth N.S. to **Stephen SAMPSON** of Plymouth. <Plymouth Co.Deeds 69:137>
...27 July 1789, Joseph ROBBINS, blacksmith sells to Stephen SAMPSON, blacksmith shop in Plymouth being the same he bought of Stephen SAMPSON, 5 Nov. 1783 <63:44>.

Lemuel CROOKER of Plympton to **David HERSEY** of Yarmouth N.S. <Yarmouth Co.N.S.Deeds 1:169>
...9 May 1780, Lemuel CROOKER, yeoman and wf Abigail, for £13.10s quit claim to David HERSEY, all rights in land laid out to **Benjamin ROBBINS,** dec'd in 1763...Ack. Plymouth co. 12 May 1780.

David HERSEY of Yarmouth N.S. to **Joseph ROBBINS** of Plymouth. <Yarmouth Co.N.S.Deeds 1:220>
...1 Apr. 1782, David HERSEY sells above to Joseph ROBBINS for £17.10s.

Will of **Thomas HAYWARD** of Bridgewater. <Plymouth Co.PR 8:367>
...dated 18 July 1740, mentions wife **Bethiah;** son **Seth HAYWARD;** daughter **Alice** and her son **Thomas CUSHMAN;** daughters **Bethiah, Mary** and **Phebe.** Pr. 6 June 1741.

Will of **Samuel CUSHMAN** of Attleborough. <Bristol Co.PR 19:397,448;20:420>
<19:397>...dated 3 Aug. 1763, mentions wife **Fear;** daughters **Desire FOSTER, Mercy FULLER;** son **Jacob CUSHMAN** named executor; livestock, wearing apparell, books to be divided between wife and "three" children; grandsons **Samuel CUSHMAN, Noah FULLER.** Witnesses: Benjamin ROBINSON, Jemima FULLER, Stephen FULLER. <19:399> Pr. 21 Mar. 1766. <19:448> Inventory dated 1 Apr. 1766 by Benjamin DAY, Ebenezer ROBINSON, George ROBINSON, all of Attleborough. <20:420> Account dated 12 Dec. 1768, payments made to Thomas DAGGET; Dr. Bezabel MAN; David DAY; John STEPHENS; for coffin and digging of grave, 13 shillings.

Will of **Jacob CUSHMAN** of Attleborough. <Bristol Co.PR 34:170,173,385>
<34:170>...dated 19 Nov. 1792, mentions wife **Hannah;** children: **Samuel CUSHMAN; Joseph CUSHMAN; Rowland CUSHMAN; Cynthia ROBBINS** the wf of Job; **Elisabeth CUSHING** the wf of Jacob; **Lois THOMPSON** the wf of John; **Mary AVERY** the wf of John; children of **Rebecca TINGLEY** late wife of Samuel (when they arrive at lawful age); **Eunice IDE** the wf of Ichabod; **Lucy ROBINSON** the wf of Nathaniel; **Joseph CUSHMAN** (appointed executor). Witnesses: Elisha MAY, Ebenezer TIFFANY Jr., William READ. Pr. 2 Aug. 1796.

Will of **Noah FULLER** of Attleborough. <Bristol Co.PR 29:153;30:11;29:306>
<29:153>...dated 11 Oct. 1785, mentions wife **Mercy;** son **Noah FULLER;** son **Comfort FULLER; Mercy CLAFFLIN** the wf of Phineas and **Chloe BATES** the wf of John, "my two surviving daughters"; granddaughters **Filena TINGLEY** and **Sabria TINGLEY,** the two daughters of **Benjamin TINGLEY** and **Isabel** his wife; to grandson **Caleb FULLER,** my Great Bible; grandson **Noah FULLER** (at the age of 21); to grandson **Kenez FULLER** one pair silver buckels. Executors: sons **Noah FULLER,** yeoman and **Comfort FULLER,** physician. Witnesses: Ruth MAY, Jesse RICHARDS, Elisha MAY. Pr. 5 Sept. 1786. <unrecorded document>...5 Sept. 1786, at Taunton, **Phinehas CLAFFLIN/CLAFLEN** and **John BATES** stated objections

against the will: That said Fuller was not in his right mind, as appears by his disposing of his estate as he has done. 1st By his not disposing of the improvement of the one half his real estate during his widow's life. 2nd By his not giving anything to four heirs, viz: **Molly TINGLY, Nancy TINGLY, Benjamin TINGLY Jr.** and **Sally TINGLY**...heirs by their mother being said Fuller's daughter. 3rd By his giving one third of the indoor moveables to **Philene TINGLY** and **Sabra TINGLY**, as daughters of **Benjamin TINGLY** and **Issabella** his wife...**Cybil TINGLY** was not said Tingly's wife (she being dead). 4th By his not disposing of his out door moveables, cash in hand and debts due to his estate. <29:306> Inventory taken 5 Sept. 1706 at Taunton by Elisha MAY, Esq., Elkanah WILLMARTH and Ebenezer TYLER, sworn to by **Noah FULLER**, executor, 7 Aug. 1787. No real estate mentioned; notes of hand due from: **Noah FULLER Jr.**, £3.17s, dated 1 Feb. 1786; **Phineas CLAFFLEN**, L2, dated 22 Nov. 1784; **Benoni WILMARTH**, £1.5s, dated 31 Oct. 1785; **Nathaniel READ**, £3, dated Sept. 1785. <30:11>...5 Aug. 1788, at Rehoboth, **Rebecca FULLER** of Attleborough, widow, appointed admx. of estate...not administered upon by **Noah FULLER** the executor who is also deceased. Sureties: Stephen FULLER, Gibson SWEET, yeomen of Attleborough. Witnesses: Samuel MOREY Jr., W. BAYLIES.<4>

Estate of **John BATES** of Thompson CT. <Thompson CT PR>
...(no date in files), mentions sons **Alanson BATES** and **John BATES Jr.** as executors; granddaughters **Nancy GEORGE**, wf of John Jr. and **Polly TOURTELLOTTE**, wf of Jacob; daughter "Ballard"; Sybil JOSLIN wf of Jesse (no relationship). Pr. 15 Dec. 1834.

Will of **Thomas CUSHMAN** of Lebanon CT. <no reference>
...dated 9 Jan. 1726/7, mentions children: **William CUSHMAN, Thomas CUSHMAN, Eleazer CUSHMAN** (under 21), **Zibiah CUSHMAN** (eldest dau), **Ruth CUSHMAN** (under 18), **Lydia CUSHMAN** (under 18). Witnesses sworn 28 Feb. 1726/7, pr. 7 Mar. 1726/7.

Estate of **Josiah COOK** of Tolland CT. <Hartford CT PR #1379>
...Bond dated 18 Sept. 1752, **Jesse COOK** of Coventry, adm. Surety: Samuel WEST of Tolland. Distribution of estate to children: **Sarah HARRIS, Lydia COOKE, Submit COOKE, Zibiah COOKE, Ruth COOKE** and **Josiah COOKE.**

REMEMBER ALLERTON[2] (Isaac[1])

James FERGUSON of Marblehead to **Archibald FERGUSON** of Marblehead. <Essex Co.Deeds 48:102>
...1 Feb. 1709/10, James FERGUSON...in consideration of the filial love towards my Honored Father Archibald FERGUSON, as also for the great charge...he hath been out upon me & for divers other goods causes...convey all my goods, lands, tenements, wares, merchandizes, wages due...or other things...which I may justly claime as in right my own or...by my Honoured Grandfather **Moses MAVERICK**, late of Marblehead, dec'd or by my Honoured Mother the daughter of my said Grandfather, the late wife of my abovesaid father Archibald FERGUSON. Witnesses: Joshua ORNE, William JILL. Rec. 20 July 1726.

Archibald FERGUSON of Marblehead to **Samuel BRIMBLE** of Marblehead. <Essex Co.Deeds 48:101>
...27 May 1726, Archibald FERGUSON for £50 sold to Samuel BRIMBLE, shoreman...a certain cows commonage...in Marblehead...laid out to me in the Lower Division being the lott number ten, bounded by lotts of Ebenezer HAWKES and "BLACKLER & SLADEN"...my wife Patience renouncing all her right of dower and my daughter Mary having freely signed with me. Signed by Archibald FERGUSON, Mary BOO (by mark) and Patience FERGUSON (by mark). Witnesses: Ebenezer HAWKES, Richard REITH.

Will of **John RIDDAN** of Marblehead. <Essex Co.PR #23416, 334:85,86,254>
<334:85>...dated 30 Sept. 1756 ("so recorded"), mentions wife **Sarah**, children: **Ezra RIDDAN, John RIDDAN, Ebenezer RIDDAN, Joseph RIDDAN, Mary, Hannah** and **Sarah.** <334:86> Pr. 12 Sept. 1756 ("so recorded"). <334:254> Inventory dated 14 Jan. 1757.

Will of **John REDDING** of Marblehead. <Essex Co.PR #23417, 39:861,873;73:568,776;75:99;76:347,558, 82:71,349;83:145;89:18;408:304>
<408:304>...dated 24 Mar. 1806, all real and personal estate to wife **Mary** for life, then to his heirs (not named in files). Pr. 3 Apr. 1831.

ESSEX COUNTY DEEDS:

107:260 - 11 Jan. 1760, Moses HAWKES Jr., husbandman of Lynn, sells land. Mary signs also.
110:257 - 2 Dec. 1762, Moses HAWKES of Lynn, husbandman, wf Mary signs, sells to Thomas RIDDAN.
115:82 - 31 Oct. 1764, Abijah HAWKES of Lynn, blacksmith, & wf Hannah, mortgage to Thomas MANSFIELD, clothier, his right in real estate of father Moses HAWKES, dec'd.
160:277 - 1795, Benjamin HAWKES, of Marblehead, mariner, sells land.
183:164 - 4 Feb. 1808, Mehitable HAWKES, widow of Benjamin, of Marblehead, sells land.
200:46 - 5 Jan. 1813, Benjamin HAWKES, of Salem, boat builder, & wf Abigail, sells land.

Estate of **Moses HAWKES** of Lynn. <Essex Co.PR #12934, 347:141,259,260;349:207-8;360:148,219,306, 539,540>...1771 (no details given in files).

Guardianship of Child of **Moses HAWKES.** <Essex Co.PR #12945, 351:59>
...31 Dec. 1774...Guardianship of **Thomas HAWKS**, minor aged seventeen, son of Moses HAWKS, late of

Lynn, dec'd, was granted to Abner CHEEVER who gave bond with Jacob NEWHALL and Benjamin GOLDHWAIT as sureties.

Estate of **Nathan HAWKES** of Sangus. <Essex Co.PR #12937, 16:234;404:228;43:3;31:387;34:55;24:679> <404:228>...will dated 1824 (no details given in files).

Will of **Moses MAVERICK** of Marblehead. <Essex Co.PR #1472, 9:293,295>
...dated Jan. 1685/6, mentions wife **Eunice**, executrix; **Moses HAWKS** ye only surviving child of my daughter **Rebecca**, dec'd; the four children of my daughter **Abigail**, dec'd, viz: **Samuel WARD, Abigail HINDS, Mary DOLLABER** and **Martha WARD**; four daughters, **Elizabeth SKINNER, Remember WOODMAN, Mary FERGUSON** and **Sarah NORMAN**; son-in-law **Archibald FERGUSON**, executor, Samuel CHEEVER and Ambrose GALE, overseers. Depositions: dated 16 July 1686 of Archibald FERGUSON age about 37, John NORMAN, age about 26; dated 29 Mar. 1685/6 of Ambrose GALE age about 55. Pr. 30 Mar. 1686.**<5>**

MICRO #6 OF 9

Estate of **Stephen HODGEKINS Jr.** of Ipswich. <Essex Co.PR #13517, 336:352>
...1760, Stephen HODGEKINS Jr., son of Hezekiah. (no details given in files)

Estate of **Stephen HODGEKINS Jr.** of Ipswich. <Essex Co.PR #13518, 337:37>
...3 Mar. 1760, widcw **Elizabeth** appointed admx. <#13519, 338:16> Guardianship of son **Stephen HODGEKINS**, minor above 14 granted to mother.

Estate of **Stephen HODGEKINS** of Ipswich. <Essex Co.PR #13520, 364:288>
...1796...(no details given in files).

Estate of **Capt. Thomas HODGEKINS** of Ipswich. <Essex Co.PR #13522, 365:337,428>
...1797...(no details given in files).

Estate of **Abigail HODGEKINS** of Ipswich. <Essex Co.PR #13486, 410:119>
...1837, Abigail HODGEKINS, widow, Rev. pensioner. (no details given in files).

ESSEX COUNTY PROBATE:

337:375 - 1760, Capt. John FRIEND of Newbury.
340:508 - 1763, Sarah FRIEND.
349:267 - 1773, James FRIEND of Wenham.
357:388 - 1785, Deacon John FRIEND of Wenham.

Will of **Maj. Samuel WARD** of Ipswich. <Essex Co.PR #28928>
...29 July 1689, Whearas the Governer and Counsill have orderid me upon an expeditian to Cannade/ Canada by gods asistans agaienst the Comon enemie...I therfor declaer this as my last will and testement if I faiell in this expedition...to wife **Sarah**...all that which I gave her at my day of mariag and for an adition to it god having given me a living child by her I give herr my negroe Ceser during my daughters lieff/life or day of mariage to be improved for the bringing up and help of her maientenance but at my daughter **Mercy**'s death or day of mariage I leave him to be disposed of amongs all my children each to have thear equall proportion of what he is then worth; to son (in law) **John TUTTELL** the leggasie which my daughter **Martha** had given her from herr grandfather...; daughter **Marie DOLIVER** of Marblehead; honoured father **BRADSTRETT**; houses & lands in Charlestown and small parcel of land given me by the Towne of Marblehead to son **Samuel WARD**; surviving children of daughter **Abigail HINDS**; children of daughter **Remember WILSON**;...Lastly I constitutt and apoient my belovid wieff **Sarah WARD** to be my sooll execetrixe and intrett herr to be as kiend to my Children as I have ben to herr Children. Witnesses: Thomas WADE, Joseph BROWNE, Daniel HOVEY Jr. verified the will which was left with them "on his goeing to Canada on ye 30th of July 1690...at that time he was a disposeing mind and...was well composed, being seriously melancholy in haste to looke after his souldiers". Pr. 22 Apr. 1691. Inventory taken 12 Mar. 1690/1 by John DANE and Richrd WALKER, incl. a negro valued at Ł25; total Ł209.18s3d. Account of debts due from the estate, total Ł256.9s9d.**<6>**

Estate of **John HINDS** of Marblehead. <Essex Co.PR #13375, 346:248,323,531;347:1b>
...1770...<346:248> Administration. <346:323> Inventory. <346:531> Insolvency. <347:1b> Warrant, widow Mary.

Will of **Capt. William HINDS** of Marblehead. <Essex Co.PR #13381, 320:335-7;324:110>
<320:335>...dated 9 Feb. 1735, mentions wife **Lydia**; children: **Rebecca GROSS, William HINDS, Joseph HINDS, Benjamin HINDS, Elizabeth MAYNE, Hannah DODD**; grandchildren: **Joseph HOLMAN, Abigail ROLLS, Susanna NORTHY**. Pr. 30 June 1736. <320:337> Inventory, 1 July 1736.

Estate of **William HINDS** of Marblehead. <Essex Co.PR #13382>
<350:86>...1774, Administration. <351:117> Inventory. (no further details in files)

Estate of **William HINDS** of Marblehead. <Essex Co.PR #13383>
<362:367>...1793, Will. <362:368> Probate. <362:458> Inventory. (no further details in files)

Estate of **William HINDS** of Marblehead. <Essex Co.PR #13384>
<378:208>...1809, Will, probate. (no further details)

Estate of **John HOLMAN** of Salem. <Essex Co.PR #13576, 303:169>
<original>...1693, Will. <303:169> Administration.

Estate of **William HOLMAN** of Marblehead. <Essex Co.PR #13587, 312:198,386>
<312:198>...1718, Administration. <312:386> Account.

Estate of **Samuel HOLMAN** of Marblehead. <Essex Co.PR #13583>
<322:121>...1737, Will. <322:496,497> Inventory, Account.

Estate of **Gabriel HOLMAN** of Salem. <Essex Co.PR 334:158>
...1756, Will. ("many more refs." - not cited)

Estate of **John NORTHY**, glazier of Marblehead. <Essex Co.PR #19601, 326:139-141>
<326:139>...will dated 20 Dec. 1744, wife **Susanna** sole executrix, son **Joseph NORTHY**, daughter **Sarah NORTHY**. Pr. 28 Jan. 1744. No inventory indexed.

Thomas ROLES Jr., **John NORTHY** of Marblehead to **William HINDE** of same. <Essex Co.Deeds 85:235>
...19 Apr. 1740, Thomas ROLES Jr., fisherman, & wf Abigail, and John NORTHY, glazier, & wf Susanna, to William HINDE, shoreman, land given to them in will of our Father, William HINDE, dec'd.

Roger VICKERY et al of Marblehead. <Essex Co.Deeds 90:145>
...2 Feb. 1747, Roger VICKERY, fisherman & Susanna his wife, late Susannah NORTHEY, and Abigail ROLES/ROALS, widow. (no details)

ESSEX COUNTY DEEDS:

<125:150> - 8 Oct. 1768, Richard STACEY of Marblehead, mariner, & wf Rebecca to Joseph NORTHEY, mariner, of Marblehead, house & land bordering on land owned lately of my father John STACEY.
<160:140> - 9 Jan. 1796, Edward NORTHEY & wf Susanna sell land.
<161:252> - 15 June 1797, Susanna NORTHEY, spinster sells land rec'd as heir to mother & brother (not named in deed).
<162:218> - 9 Aug. 1797, Joseph HART of Salem, mortg. to Susanna NORTHEY, single, of Manchester.
<175:18> - 6 June 1804, Mortgage to Susanna NORTHEY, single, of Manchester.

Estate of **John NORTHEY** of Marblehead. <Essex Co.PR #19600>
<319:177>...1732, Administration. <318:64> Letter.

Estate of **Joseph NORTHEY** of Marblehead. <Essex Co.PR #19602, 366:558;367:177-8>
<366:558>...25 June 1799, adm. granted to **Hannah NORTHEY**. <367:177> Inventory dated 9 Aug. 1799, no real estate; total $73.75. <367:178> Account dated 7 Nov. 1799 mentions allowance to widow.

ESSEX COUNTY DEEDS:

<149:193> - 14 Feb. 1789, Samuel BARTOLL, painter, of Marblehead, & wf Mercy, mortgages house & land to Sarah CLOUGH, wf of Ebenezer, barber, of Marblehead.
<153:237> - 27 June 1789, Samuel BARTOLL, painter, of Marblehead, & wf Mercy, sell half of house & land in Marblehead to Benjamin Tyler REED, gentleman, of same.
<153:146> - 4 Aug. 1791, Samuel BARTOLL, painter, of Marblehead, mortgages land received from grandfather, John BARTOL; mentions Uncle William BARTOL's land. Discharged 9 Nov. 1821.
<189:51> - 5 Sept 1793, Samuel BARTOL & wf Mercy, sell to Sarah CLOUGH, land mortgaged 14 Feb. 1789. Rec. 6 Dec. 1809.
<164:123> - June 1798, Samuel BARTOL, painter, of Marblehead, obtained judgement against Jonathan GLOVER, Esq. and William BARTOL, both of Marblehead.

Estate of **Samuel BARTOL** of Salem. <Essex Co.PR #2004>
<409:229>...3 Mar. 1835, "Court ordered, on her petition, that Samuel BARTOLL, late of Salem, gentleman, deceased intestate, was a revolutionary pensioner, that he died 23 Feb. 1835 leaving a widow, Hannah BARTOLL, who is now living."**<7>**

Estate of **John TUTTLE** of Ipswich. <Essex Co.PR #28391, 311:365;313:686>
<311:365>...2 Apr. 1716, administration granted to widow **Martha TUTTLE**. Sureties: Simon TUTTLE, Abram FOSTER, both of Ipswich. Witnesses: Cutting NOYES, Daniel ROGERS. <313:686> Release of heirs: Daughters: **Martha HASKALL**, wf of Mark, of Glocester; **Mary WARNER**, wf of Nathaniel, of Ipswich; **Abigail HASKALL**, wf of William, of Glocester; **Remember HARRIS**, wf of Job, of Ipswich.

Heirs of **John TUTTLE**. <Essex Co.Deeds 51:53>
...13 Apr. 1727, we **Nathaniel WARNER**, yeoman & **Mary** his now wife; **Job HARRIS**, shoreman & **Remember** his wife, all of Ipswich...and **William HASKALL**, shoresman, of Glocester and **Abigail** his wife, for £600 sold to our Brother in Law **Mark HASKALL** of Glocester, yeoman...the full three fifths of the real estate of our Late Brother **William TUTTLE**, late of Ipswich, dec'd; also mentions our Uncle **Symon TUTTLE** and our grandmother TUTTLE. Witnesses: Thomas BERRY, Sarah HODGKINS.

Estate of **Simon TUTTLE** of Ipswich. <Essex Co.PR #28396, 304:414,5; 308:243,248>
<304:414> Administration. <304:415> Inventory. <308:243,248> Settlement dated 28 Oct. 1701, names

widow **Sarah**, and children: **John TUTTLE, Simon TUTTLE, Elizabeth AYRES** wf of Samual, **Joanna PICKARD, Abigail WARNER** wf of Philemon, **Sarah WARD** wf of Samuel, **Charles TUTTLE, Susanna TUTTLE.**

Estate of **William TUTTLE** of Ipswich. <Essex Co.PR #20399>
<314:315> Letter. <315:445> Inventory. <316:150> Account. Brother in law of **Job HARRIS** and **Mark HASKALL.** (no date or details) Guardianship of Children: **William TUTTLE** and **Sarah TUTTLE**, both minors. <#20398, 313:687; #28295, 314:543>

Will of **Joanna PICKARD.** <Essex Co.PR 331:47;328:165-7,440-1>
<328:165>...dated 15 July 1746, mentions oldest dau **Ruth JEWETT**, wf of Eliphalet; youngest dau **Lucy PICKARD**; dau **Joanna BURPE**; dau **Sarah NOYES** wf of Benjamin; son **Jonathan PICKARD.** <328:440> Pr. 26 Sept. 1748.

Estate of **Nathaniel WARNER** of Ipswich. <Essex Co.PR #28970>
<340:428>...5 Sept. 1763, adm. granted to widow **Mary WARNER.** Sureties: Mark HASKELL, Nathaniel CROSS. <341:19>...Inventory dated 21 Nov. 1763, incl. 90 acres upland meadows, woodland & buildings there on, exclusive of what was sold to son **John WARNER**, £350.; pew in ye old Parish meeting House, £13.6.8.; total £572. <341:430>...Account dated 5 Nov. 1764. <341:493>...Division dated 6 Dec. 1764, to following children as heirs: **Nathaniel WARNER and John WARNER**, children of eldest son **Nathaniel WARNER**, dec'd; **Mary BUZWELL, Abigail HEARD, John WARNER, William WARNER, Martha BURROWS, Sarah STEVENS, Joseph WARNER, Susanna HODGE, Lucy CROSS.**

John WARNER of Ipswich to **Isaac DODGE** of Ipswich. <Essex Co.Deeds 142:141>
...22 Jan. 1779, John WARNER, yeoman, & wf Susanna, for £900 sells to Isaac DODGE, dwelling house with two acres of land in Ipswich, bordered by land of William WARNER, Henry RUSSELL, Thomas SMITH, widow Abigail HEARD, Isaac DODGE and other lands bordered by Dr. John CALF, Mary BUSWELL, Charles BOLLS, heirs of Robert POTTER, dec'd; three acres received from estate of father **Nathaniel WARNER** of Ipswich dec'd. Witnesses: Ephraim KENDALL, Nathaniel DAY Jr.

ESSEX COUNTY DEEDS: (re: HARRIS)

92:70 - 3 June 173(0), John HARRIS the 6th, of Ipswich, yeoman & wf Mary to brother in law Samuel WAITE of Ipswich, clothier. Ack. 16 Nov. 1743.
77:91 - 25 June 1733, Job HARRIS & wf Remember.
74:10 - 5 Feb. 1735, Job HARRIS of Ipswich, shoreman, & wf Ruth to Daniel HERD.
81:164 - 7 Mar. 1738, Job HARRIS of Ipswich, shopkeeper, & wf Ruth.
75:263 - 23 May 1738, John DENNIS & wf Sarah, Mark HASKALL & wf Martha, Job HARRIS, joiner and Thomas DENNIS, joiner, all of Ipswich, sell land drawn by heirs of Simon TUTTLE.
92:69 - 25 Apr. 1742, Job HARRIS of Ipswich, yeoman & wf Ruth to Thomas TREADWELL 3d.
92:113 - 22 Mar. 1747, Job HARRIS of Ipswich & wf Ruth quit claim to Jacob GOODALE, rights in land deeded to Jacob by Ruth GOODALE, singlewoman of Ipswich 21 Mar. 1747 land lately estate of John GOODALE, dec'd of Salem.
120:41 - , Job HARRIS of Ipswich, shopkeeper & wf Ruth to Caleb LORD & Daniel LORD, land at northerly corner of homestead. Ack. 25 Mar. 1751.
101:30 - 11 May 1753, Job HARRIS, of Ipswich, yeoman & wf Ruth.
129:29 - 13 Sept 1770, John CALEF to John HARRIS 3d, cooper.
129:29 - 6 Jan. 1770, Job HARRIS of Ipswich, yeoman to son John HARRIS, cooper, half his dwelling house. Witnesses: James HARRIS, John HART.
131:124 - 4 Apr. 1772, James HARRIS of Ipswich, hatter, & wf Susanna, for a quit claim of land in Ipswich, part of estate of father Job HARRIS dec'd to John HARRIS, of Ipswich, cooper, rights in other land of their father Job HARRIS.
132:124 - 17 Sept 1773, Nathaniel HARRIS, of Portsmouth NH, merchant, to sister Sally CALDER, wf of Robert of Newburyport, all right in estate of Remember, late wife of Job HARRIS dec'd.
132:124 - 30 Sept 1773, Robert CALDER, of Newburyport, innholder, & wf Sally, in right of our grandmother HARRIS formerly TUTTLE, by our Father Nathaniel HARRIS, dec'd to James HARRIS of Ipswich, hatter.
241:226 - 29 Dec. 1818, Joseph LORD, adm. of Job HARRIS of Portsmouth NH, licensed to sell to pay debts, sells to David LORD one undivided fifth part of various pieces of land in Ipswich, all subject to rights of widow of James HARRIS of Ipswich, dec'd.
241:227 - 21 Dec. 1819, Mark HARRIS of Portland, Esq. & wf Ruth; William HARRIS of Portland, trader & wf Betsey; and James HARRIS of Boston, trader quit claim to David LORD right in house & homestead above <241:226>.
241:227 - 15 May 1826, David LORD of Salem & wf Lucy, house & homestead formerly of James HARRIS dec'd; three fifths bought of Mark HARRIS and others in the settlement and division of the real estate of the said James HARRIS dec'd, they being part of the heirs at law by deed 21 Dec. 1819, and one fifth by Joseph LORD, adm. of Job HARRIS, another heir at law of said James as by deed and remaining fifth descended to said Lucy as a dau of James, dec'd.

Will of **Job HARRIS** of Ipswich. <Essex Co.PR #12490, 347:226,389>
<347:226>...dated 9 Mar. 1771, mentions wife **Ruth**; grandson **Nathaniel HARRIS** son of my son **Nathaniel HARRIS**, dec'd, twenty five pounds lawfull money which I look upon as a full portion in my estate together with what will lawfully derive to him from his Grandmother **Remember HARRIS** as her

share in her Grandmother **TUTTLE**'s thirds of the estate of **Simon TUTTLE,** dec'd; grand daughter **Sarah HARRIS,** dau of my late son **Nathaniel,** dec'd; grandson **John FRIEND** (under 21); son **Edward HARRIS,** sons **James HARRIS** and **John HARRIS** joint executors. Witnesses: Samuel LORD Jr., Caleb LORD and Daniel NOYES. <347:226> Pr. 28 Oct. 1771. <347:389> Inventory taken 12 Dec. 1771 by Samuel LORD Jr., Daniel ROGERS, Daniel NOYES. Various real estate holdings, including pew in Rev. Mr. Roger's Meeting House.

Will of **James HARRIS** of Ipswich, hatter. <Essex Co.PR 387:433>
...dated 8 Apr. 1815, mentions wife, all my children, son **Job HARRIS** executor.

MICRO #7 OF 9

Guardianship of **Sarah WARD, Abigail WARD.** <Essex Co.PR 313:12>
...14 July 1719, Sarah WARD, upwards of 14 years and Abigail WARD, minor children of **Samuel WARD** of Ipswich, dec'd, chose their mother **Sarah DENNIS** alias WARD as guardian.

Guardianship of **Abigail SKINNER**, Boston. <Suffolk Co.PR 8:305>
...3 Nov. 1698, Thomas JACKSON of Boston, appt'd. guardian of Abigail SKINNER, dau of **Thomas SKINNER,** late of Boston, baker, dec'd, she being a minor under the age of fourteen years.

Thomas SKINNER of Boston to **Samuel SHRIMPTON.** <Suffolk Co.PR 16:259>
...17 Nov. 1687, Thomas SKINNER and wf Elizabeth for £600 sell to Samuel SHRIMPTON, their tenement in Boston situated near the head of the Great Dock known as Bendall's Dock. Witnesses: J. ADDINGTON, Thomas JACKSON, Eliezer MOODEY, Samuel HOBART.

William HEWES, Thomas JACKSON of Boston to **John TURNER** of Salem. <Essex Co.PR 11:227>
...25 June 1695, William HEWES, physitian & wf Elizabeth, and Thomas JACKSON, merchant, & wf Priscilla, which said Elizabeth & Priscilla are ye two only surviving daughters and co-heirs of **Nathaniel GRAFTON,** late of Salem, mariner, dec'd, for £50 sell to John TURNER, merchant, land in Salem appertaining to ye estate of **Nathaniel GRAFTON,** bounded by land of William WEST, Richard FLINDER, John TURNER. Witnesses: Elizur HOLYOKE Jr., Elezer MOODEY Sr.

John TURNER of Salem to **Samuel BROWNE** of Salem. <Essex Co.PR 11:227>
...2 Mar. 1696/7, John TURNER conveys to Samuel BROWNE & wf Eunice, all his right in the above deed. Witnesses: John CROAD, Abigail Mansfield.

Estate of **Moses HAWKES,** Sangus, farmer. <Essex Co.PR #41972>
<279:605>...1879, Administration. <282:7> Notice.

Will of **Moses HAWKES** of Lynn. <Essex Co.PR #12932, 310:107-9; 313:66>
...dated 8 Dec. 1708, mentions wf **Margaret**; brother **John HAWKS**; children (all under 21): **Moses HAWKS** & **Adam HAWKS** (eldest sons), **John HAWKS, Margaritt, Rebeckah;** wf **Margaret,** brother **Ebenezer HAWKS** and cousin **Hananiah HUCHASON** executors. Pr. 18 Apr. 1709. Inventory 11 Jan. 1708/9.

Estate of **Daniel HITCHINGS** of Lynn. <Essex Co.PR 318:64;319:96>
<318:64>...10 June 1731, **Daniel HITCHINGS** of Lynn appointed administrator of estate of father, Daniel HITCHINGS. <319:96> Inventory 7 July 1731.

Estate of **Adam HAWKES** of Lynn. <Essex Co.PR 318:33>
...6 Oct. 1729, **Moses HAWKES** of Lynn, appointed administrator of estate of brother Adam HAWKES.

Estate of **John HAWKES** of Lynn. <Essex Co.PR #12923, 328:239;329:116;331:252;335:353;342:48,158>
<328:239>...14 Nov. 1748, Administration granted to widow **Hannah HAWKES.** <329:116> Inventory taken 25 Nov. 1748 by Elisha NEWHALL, Ebenezer NEWHALL, Samuel HALLOWELL; real estate, £1102, personal, £292. <331:252> Account dated 2 Apr. 1752, incl. the widow for lying in after her husband's death, £50; bringing up three young children, £150. <335:353> Account dated 12 June 1758, of **Hannah HAWKES** alias **FULLER,** for bringing up one young child three years since last account,£1. 10s. <342:48> Account & Distribution dated 18 Feb. 1765, of **Hannah HAWKES** alias **FULLER,** incl. to widow now Fuller, £29.15.8; to **Adam HAWKES,** eldest son, £14.18.4; to **Mary, Lydia, Sarah, Rebecca** and **John,** all children of the dec'd, £7.9s2d; to **LAZELL** descendants of **Hannah,** £7.9s2d. <342:158> Division of Real Estate dated 17 Apr. 1765, by William COLLINS, Zacheus COLLINS, Thomas RIDDEN; one third to widow **Hannah HAWKES** now **FULLER,** remainder to eldest son **Adam HAWKES Jr.,** he to pay brothers & sisters. 22 Apr. 1765, **Adam HAWKES Jr.** paid £40.16s7d to each: **John HAWKES** (minor above 14), **Mary SMITH, Lydia SWEETSER, Sarah JOHNSON, Rebecca TUFTS, Hannah FARRINGTON** (only child of **Hannah FARRINGTON**).

Adam HAWKES Jr. of Lynn to **William SWITCHER** of Lynn. <Essex Co.Deeds 113:137>
...23 Apr. 1765, Adam HAWKES Jr., cordwainer, for £400 sold to William SWITCHER, husbandman, land with house & barn in Lynn, formerly belonging to "Hawkes Farm & Townsends Land" lately possessed by John HAWKES, dec'd...with **Thomas FULLER** and wife **Hannah** surrendering all their right of dower. Witnesses: Abraham SMITH, Samuel SWEETSER.

Will of **Thomas FULLER** of Lynn. <Essex Co.PR #10424, 343:194,270,272;344:235>
<343:194>...dated 22 Mar. 1763, mentions wf **Hannah**; eldest son **Thomas FULLER;** son **Edward FULLER;**

remaining children: **Elizabeth BREEDEN, Elisha FULLER, David FULLER** (fourth son), **Abigail BOLER, Ebenezer FULLER, Jonathan FULLER** (youngest son); sons David & Jonathan executors. Pr. 1 Sept. 1766. <343:194> Inventory taken 17 Sept. 1766. <343:272> Warrant for dower dated 1 Sept. 1766. <344:235> Account of executors dated 26 Oct. 1767.

Estate of **John HAWKES** of Lynn. <Essex Co.PR #12922>
<318:184>...1738, Administration. <324:348> Inventory. <324:270> Account. <324:271> Warrant for Division. <335:468> Warrant. <335:469> Division. (Files mention widow Mary only.)

WORCESTER COUNTY PROBATE, Series A, 1731-1881: (re: HAWKES)

1837	Daniel	Southbridge	#28423, Guardianship
1839	Benjamin	Ashburnham	#28419, Will
1846	Phebe	Ashburnham	#28426, Guardianship
1847	John	Lancaster	#28424, Will
1848	Phebe	Ashburnham	#28426, Administration
1848	Phebe	Ashburnham	#28427, Pension
1856	Alice	Lancaster	#28418, Administration
1860	Benjamin	Templeton	#28420, Will
1869	Laura A.	Templeton	#28425, Administration
1874	Achsah	Westminster	#28417, Will
1877	Caroline E.	Petersham	#28421, Guardianship
1880	Celia	Northbridge	#28422, Will

WORCESTER COUNTY DEEDS: (re: John HAWKES)

<64:500> - 10 June 1771, John HAWKES of Lancaster, cordwainer from John BRADSTREET.
<73:272> - 31 Jan. 1775, John HAWKES of Lancaster, & wf Hannah to Michael NEWHALL of Bolton.
<82:373> - 6 Jan. 1779, John HAWKES of Bolton, cordwainer, to John JAMES of Southboro, land in Lancaster.
<82:516> - 1780, John HAWKES from "States Committee".
<102:432> - 7 Nov. 1785, John HAWKES of Lancaster, yeoman to John WILLARD of Lancaster, gent.
<103:168> - 11 July 1787, John HAWKES of Lancaster, yeoman, mortgage to Elizabeth CHASE, house bought from John JAMES. Discharged 19 Apr. 1794.
<108:234> - 13 Aug. 1789, John HAWKES, cordwainer & wf Hannah to Abel BECKWITH, land bought from John WILLARD.
<124:56> - 21 Jan. 1794, John HAWKES of Lancaster, yeoman, from Joseph CARTER. (see 126:315)
<126:315> - 11 Mar. 1796, John HAWKES of Lancaster, yeoman, & wf Hannah, mortgage to John SPRAGUE land bought from John JAMES and land bought from State Committee.
<139:168> - 23 Aug. 1796, John HAWKES of Lancaster, Physician, & wf Hannah to Jonathan WHITNEY.
<134:200> - 5 Apr. 1797, John HAWKES, Physician from Amos FARRINGTON
<134:201> - 5 Apr. 1797, John HAWKES, Physician from Amos FARRINGTON.
<144:408> - 6 Apr. 1797, John HAWKES, of Lancaster, Physician, to Silas WILLARD of Lancaster.
<134:199> - 1798, John HAWKES from Seth SARGEANT.
<139:387> - 1800, John HAWKES from Samuel JONES.
<151:657> - 22 Jan. 1800, John HAWKES, Physician, & wf Hannah to John HAWKES Jr. of Lancaster.
<142:573> - 1801, John HAWKES from Josiah WILLARD.
<150:563> - 1803, John HAWKES to Samuel DAMON.
<151:657> - 1803, John HAWKES, Physician, & wf Hannah to John HAWKES Jr., yeoman, both of Lancaster, land in Lancaster.
<152:213> - 1803, John HAWKES from Samuel DAMON.
<152:152> - 24 Aug. 1803, John HAWKES, Physician, & wf Hannah, mortgage to Boston Bank.
<154:466> - 1804, John HAWKES to Job HOWARD.
<160:499> - 1806, John HAWKES from Silas WILLARD.
<169:138> - 1808, John HAWKES to Benjamin FARNSWORTH.
<225:236> - 21 Nov. 1810, John HAWKES of Lancaster, gent., & wf Hannah to Benjamin FARNSWORTH.
<191:199> - 1814, John HAWKES from Boston Bank.

Will of **John HAWKES** of Lancaster. <Worcester Co.PR #A28424, 89:425-6;90:426>
<89:425>...25 Mar. 1844, mentions wife **Alice** and following nine children: **Alice HOUGHTON**, wf of Phineas; **John HAWKES; Sally RICHARDS**, wf of John; **Daniel A. HAWKES; James HAWKES; Harriet WHITNEY** wf of William D.; **Benjamin HAWKES; Rebeccah PARKER** wf of Edmund; **Cynthia A. FARNSWORTH**, wf of Benjamin F. Witnesses: H.A. HASTINGS, E.A. NURSE, James RUGG Jr. Pr. 4 Jan. 1848. Citation 7 Dec. 1847. Account of Adm. (no date given), accepted by all heirs.

MICRO #8 of 9

Will of **Daniel HITCHINS** of Lynn. <Essex Co.PR #13392>
<320:208>...dated 1 Mar. 1734/5, mentions wife **Susanna**; children: **Daniel HITCHINS** (eldest son & executor), **Elkanah HITCHINS, Timothy HITCHINS, Susanna HAWKS**. Witness: Thomas HAWKES. <320:209> Pr. 7 Apr. 1735. <320:210> Inventory dated 19 June 1735.

Will of **Moses HAWKS** of Lynn. <Essex Co.PR #12933, 337:478; 338:126>
<337:478>...dated 3 Nov. 1760, mentions wife **Susanna**; children: **Moses HAWKS** (eldest son), **Abijah HAWKS, Nathan HAWKS, Daniel HAWKS, James HAWKS, Mary MANSFIELD, Susanna HAWKS, Anna HAWKS, Lois**

HAWKS. Pr. 26 Jan. 1761. Inventory dated 10 Mar. 1761.

Estate of **Abijah HAWKS** of Richfield NY. <Otsego Co.NY PR>
...11 Apr. 1843...Whereas my late husband, Abijah HAWKS, died on the 13th day of Mar. last (intestate) I therefore request that you will constitute & appoint Seldan CHURCHILL, administrator. Signed by **Lois HAWKS** (because of age & infirmity she signed by cross). 25 Apr. 1843, **Abijah HAWKS** one of the children, made oath to mother's request.

John CUNNINGHAM of Richfield NY to **Abijah HAWKS** of Richfield NY. <Otsego Co.NY Deeds 00:361>
...15 Aug. 1826, John CUNNINGHAM & wf Louisa for $215.25 sell all rights in land in Richfield, being part of great lot No.17 in Schuylers patent, bounded by land of John STOVER, David TAFT, said John CUNNINGHAM. Witness: Daniel ANDREWS.

Moses HAWKES Jr. of Lynn to **Abraham SMITH** of Lynn. <Essex Co.Deeds 111:68>
...12 Oct. 1757, Moses HAWKES Jr., yeoman, & wf Mary, for £57.8s sold to Abraham SMITH, cordwainer...part of lands in Lynn called Tallers Farm lately in possesion of Capt. William ROBY, dec'd, containing fifteen and a half acres called Burch Plain bounded by land of Moses HAWKES, Jr., HUTCHERSON, MANSFIELD. Witnesses: Abijah HAWKES, Benjamin Bullerd RIDDAN. Ack. 3 Mar. 1760.

Moses HAWKES et al of Lynn to **Benjamin EATON** of Marblehead. <Essex Co.Deeds 109:132>
...23 Feb. 1761, **Thomas RIDDAN**, yeoman; **Moses HAWKES**, yeoman, & wf Mary; **Jonathan BERRY**, cordwainer & wf Joanna and **Elizabeth RIDDAN** of Marblehead, singlewoman, for £6917s10d and the further sum of £59.3s already paid, sold to Benjamin EATON, gentleman...all our right which we each of us have in the estate both real and personal of Sarah, the dec'd wife of the said Benjamin EATON... incl. the dwelling house of the said Benjamin and the land whereon it stands in said Marblehead and adjoyning thereto which land was sold by me the said Thomas RIDDAN to the said Sarah by deed bearing date of 23 Nov. 1758...and also all the right which **Benjamin RIDDAN** the son of the said Thomas has in the premises...**Jerusha RIDDAN**, wf of Thomas releases dower. Rec. 4 Mar. 1761.

Abijah HAWKES of Lynn to **Nathan HAWKES & Daniel HAWKES** of Lynn. <Essex Co.Deeds 144:218>
...3 Jan. 1772, Abijah HAWKES, blacksmith, one of the sons of **Moses HAWKS**, late of Lynn, yeoman, dec'd, for £90 sold to Nathan HAWKS, husbandman and Daniel HAWKS, cordwainer...without benefit of senorship...his share in real estate of father. Witnesses: Daniel BAKER, Elizabeth MEARS.

James HAWKS of Petersham to **Nathan HAWKS** of Lynn. <Essex Co.Deeds 202:242>
...21 Mar. 1775, James HAWKS, cordwainer, one of the sons of **Moses HAWKS**, late of Lynn, yeoman, dec'd, for £97.13a8d sold to Nathan HAWKS, husbandman...all my share in the real estate of the said Moses HAWKS. Witnesses: Mary BRUCE, Sarah BLANEY. Rec. 5 Jan. 1814.

Thomas MANSFIELD of Lynn to **Nathan HAWKS** of Lynn. <Essex Co.Deeds 202:243>
...18 Mar. 1783, Thomas MANSFIELD, clothier, & wf Mary, for £100 sold to Nathan HAWKS, gentleman, all our rights in real estate of our Father **Moses HAWKES**, late of Lynn, yeoman, dec'd. Witnesses: Mary MANSFIELD, Margaret MANSFIELD. Rec. 5 Jan. 1814.

John HITCHINGS of Lynn to **Nathan HAWKS** of Lynn. <Essex Co.Deeds 202:243>
...7 Apr. 1783, John HITCHINGS, cordwainer, & wf Lois, for £220 sold to Nathan HAWKS, gentleman, all rights in real estate of our Father **Moses HAWKES**, late of Lynn, yeoman, died seized which right of ours is just five sixteenths of the same estate excepting the interest which our mother **Susanna HAWKES** hath. The premises are situate and lying in Lynn aforesaid and in common and undivided. Witnesses: Abijah HAWKS, Ebenezer EATON. Rec. 5 Jan. 1814.

Abijah HAWKS of Petersham to **Anna HAWKS** of Petersham. <Worcester Co.Deeds 122:348>
...17 June 1785, Abijah HAWKS, blacksmith, for £30 sells to Anna HAWKS, spinster...three acres in Petersham. Witnesses: John HITCHINGS, Abijah HAWKS. Rec. 13 Aug. 1794.

Anna HAWKS of Brookfield to **Moses WILSON** of Petersham. <Worcester Co.Deeds 122:349>
...4 Aug. 1794, Anna HAWKS, spinster, for £30 sells to Moses WILSON...three acres in Petersham bought 17 June 1785 from Abijah Hawks. Witnesses: Cornelius WHITE, Asa WHITE. Rec. 13 Aug. 1794.

Anna HAWKES of Lynn to **Nathan HAWKES** of Lynn. <Essex Co.Deeds 202:243>
...9 Dec. 1784, Anna HAWKS, spinster, for £80 sold to Nathan HAWKES, gentleman...all rights in real estate of my honoured Father **Moses HAWKS**, late of Lynn, yeoman, died siezed, being just one eighth part of the said estate...excepting the right and interest which my mother **Susanna HAWKES** hath. Witnesses: Daniel HAWKES, Nathan HITCHINGS. Rec. 5 Jan. 1814.

<u>MICRO #9 of 9</u>

Benjamin HAWKES et al of Salem to **Jonathan BECKETT** of Salem. <Essex Co.Deeds 179:80>
...21 Feb. 1794, **Mary BECKETT**, widow; **Retier BECKETT**, shipwright; **James BECKETT**, gentleman & wf Deborah; **Thomas ROWELL**, boat builder & wf Hannah; **Benjamin HAWKES**, boat builder & wf Abigail; **Joseph BROWN**, mariner & wf Mary; **Ebenezer SLOCUM**, mariner & wf Sarah; **Samuel LEACH**, boat builder & wf Lydia, for £22 sold to **Jonathan BECKETT**, shipwright...all our right to two common rights in the Great Pasture so called in Salem, the said two rights being the same that did belong to **William BECKETT** late of Salem, dec'd and came to us as part of his real estate. Rec. 1 Sept. 1806.

Joseph HITCHINGS of Lynn to **Nathan HAWKES** of Lynn. <Essex Co.Deeds 202:242>
...6 Apr. 1778, Joseph HITCHINGS, cordwainer, one of the sons of **Daniel HITCHINGS**, late of Lynn, yeoman, dec'd, for £60 sold to Nathan HAWKS, gentleman...all my share in the real estate and personal estate of Daniel HITCHINGS. Witnesses: James HITCHENS, John HITCHINGS. Rec. 5 Jan. 1814.

Will of **Nathan HAWKS** of Saugus. <Essex Co.PR #12937>
<404:228>...31 Dec. 1818, mentions wf **Sarah**; children: **Nathan HAWKS Jr.**, **James HAWKS**, **Daniel HAWKS**, **Hannah HAWKS**, **Susanna HAWKS** and **Mary HAWKS**. <New Series 43:3> 16 Nov. 1824, **Daniel HAWKS** and **Susanna HAWKS** (dau) executors and adms. on estate of Nathan HAWKES who died in October last past ...<43:3> Pr. first Wed. in Jan. 1825. <31:387> Warrant. <34:55> Inventory. <24:679> Affidavit.

Will of **Sarah HAWKS**, widow, of Saugus. <Essex Co.PR #12942, 410:204>
...7 June 1837, mentions daughters **Hannah HAWKES** (sole executrix), **Susanna HAWKES** & **Mary HAWKES**. Signed by mark. Witnesses: Asa T. NEWHALL, Sally M. NEWHALL, Sarah A. HAWKES. <103:80> Pr. 3d Tues. May 1838. <79:366> Order notice. <94:749> Warrant. <104:58> Inventory. <100:86> Affidavit.

Will of **Susanna HAWKES**, singlewoman, of Saugus. <Essex Co.PR #41983, 417:480>
...30 Sept. 1842...I Susanna HAWKES do give and devise to my sisters **Hannah** and **Mary** all my estate, real and personal, forever. I appoint **Mary** my executrix. Signed **Mary HAWKES**. <417:480> Saugus, 28 July 1854, Whereas I the subscriber (Mary) was appointed executrix...of my sister, **Susanna HAWKES** of Saugus...I find myself unable by reason of sickness. Benjamin F. NEWHALL of Saugus appointed. <146:630> Order notice. <206:3> Pr. 1st Tues. Sept. 1854. <205:185> Administration. <207:805> Warrant. <214:85> Inventory. <174:1213> Affidavit. <209:640> Account.

Will of **Hannah HAWKES**, singlewoman, of Saugus. <Essex Co.PR #41963, 421:132>
...15 Dec. 1857, mentions sister **Mary HAWKES**; Melzer AVERY; sister in law **Rachel HAWKES**; Thomas SWEETSER of Chelsea; neices **Elizabeth C. HAWKES**, **Sarah Ann HAWKES**, **Hannah HAWKES** and **Susannah HAWKES**; Sarah R. EVANS, Caroline STEVENS, Francis Merriam AVERY and John Quincy Adams AVERY. Benjamin F. NEWHALL named executor. "Before signing I revoke so much of this will as relates to **Rachel HAWKES** and Sarah R. EVANS and give them nothing." Witnesses: Benjamin B. BROWN, Ebenezer BUTTERFIELD, Abby J. AUSTIN, Benjamin F. NEWHALL. <227:108> Pr. 1st Tues. Feb. 1861. <220:306> Order notice. <229:355> Warrant & Inventory. <230:251> Affidavit. <240:400> Account.

Will of **Mary HAWKES**, singlewoman, of Saugus. <Essex Co.PR #41969, 423:34>
...1 Mar. 1861, mentions neices **Elizabeth C. HAWKES**, **Sarah Ann HAWKES**, **Hannah HAWKES** and **Susannah HAWKES**; nephew **Moses HAWKES**; legal representatives of Melzer AVERY, dec'd; Thomas SWEETSER of Chelsea; Caroline STEVENS; Francis Merrick AVERY, son of Melzer; John Quincy Adams AVERY. Benjamin F. NEWHALL named executor. <234:407> Pr. 2 Feb. 1864. <237:703> Warrant & Inventory. <238:558> Affidavit. <240:1371> Account.

Will of **Nathan HAWKES** of Saugus. <Essex Co.PR #41973, 422:339>
...22 Feb. 1861, mentions grandchildren **Nathan Mortimer HAWKES**, **Henry Cook HAWKES**, **Albert Douglas HAWKES**, **Tacy Pratt HAWKES**; daughters **Susannah HAWKES**, **Elizabeth C. HAWKES**, **Sarah Ann HAWKES**, **Hannah HAWKES** (named executor). <234:253> Pr. 2 June 1863. <238:316> Affidavit. <424:87> Receipts.

Estate of **Thomas PERKINS**, iron monger, of Boston. <Suffolk Co.PR #2648>
<14:319>...27 Mar. 1701, **Remember PERKINS**, widow, appointed admx. <New series 5:327> Bond dated 27 Mar. 1701 by Henry FRANKLIN, taverner and Thomas PHILLIPS, tailor, both of Boston. <14:428> Inventory taken at Boston 13 Apr. 1701 by Jarvis BALLARD and Richard DRAPER. No real estate mentioned. <15:109> 31 Dec. 1702, administration granted to Benjamin PEMBERTON, brewer, of Boston, as **Remember PERKINS**, widow is also lately dec'd. <original> 2nd Inventory taken 30 Jan. 1702 by Arthur JEFFRY, Jonathan EVERAI( ), James SMITH. <New series 5:329> Account dated 31 Aug. 1714, mentions children **Elizabeth PERKINS** and **Mary PERKINS** to receive clothing & linen when they come of age or marry, and who are under the care and education of Joseph HUMPHREYS of Hingham. <21:218> Account of Edward WINSLOW and Benjamin PEMBERTON, executors of Benjamin PEMBERTON late of Boston, dec'd, relating to an administration of said Benjamin PEMBERTON dec'd upon the estate of Thomas PERKINS, approved 5 Jan. 1718. Account includes the following items:
24 Dec. 1702 - 11 pairs gloves for his wife's funeral, £1.6s; 25 Mar. 1703 - nursing the children 16 weeks at 5s, £4; 8 yds damask for the childrens' coats, £1.4s; 3 yds linnen for aprons, 8s3d; May 1703 - 3 caps, 2 pettycoats, 1 sheet, 1 apron, 1 pair stays delivered to Joseph HUMPHRYS for the children; 11 July 1703 - to Joseph HUMPHRIES, one year's board of the children, £14.6s; for keeping Elizabeth before Mary, 6s; 1704 - schooling for Elizabeth, 6s; 6 Dec. 1705 to Joseph HUMPHRIES, one year's board of the children to April last, £13.8...<8>

Estate of **David HERSEY** of Abington. <Plymouth Co.PR (originals)>
Bond dated 4 Dec. 1827, William TORREY appointed administrator. 4 Dec. 1827, **Mary HEARSY** declines to adm. on estate of father. Division dated 4 Mar. 1828, James BATES, Micah POOL and Nathan STUDLEY, all of Abington, appointed to divide real estate among children **Mary HERSEY**; **Elizabeth TORREY**, wf of William; **Desire STODDARD**, wf of Nathan; **Lydia JENKINS**, wf of Isaiah; and **Martha DAWES**, wf of Jacob. Actual division dated 12 Apr. 1828.

Estate of **Nathan STODDARD** of Abington. <Plymouth Co.PR #19585, D13:200;X9:109;97:351;99:79>
...3 Dec. 1856, following heirs at law of the estate have accepted account of estate: **Edward ESTES**, **Betsey J. ESTES**, **Gilman C. WHITING**, **Diantha WHITING**, **Jenkins LANE**, guardian of **Adaline STODDARD**, **George HAMMAN**, **Lydia HAMMAN**.

FOOTNOTES

<1> p.41, Bowman was undoubtedly trying to separate two women - Hannah CUSHMAN (daughter of Elkanah) and Hannah CUSHMAN (daughter of Robert). He shows that the Cushman Genealogy:131 has Hannah (daughter of Robert) marrying John WATERMAN; Howland Genealogy:269 states she married Moses WASHBURN and Davis' Landmarks:276 states she married John WATERMAN while on p.78 Davis states she married Moses WASHBURN. Bowman concludes that Hannah (daughter of Robert) married Moses WASHBURN, and Hannah (daughter of Elkanah) married John WATERMAN. A good example of the discrepency of data that can be found in published materials and why secondary sources should be used with caution and always be verified.
<2> p.41, The files state that in Plymouth Co.Deeds 39:28, there are two deeds showing that in 1747, John WATERMAN and wife Hannah were alive and her sister had a second husband, she being called Elizabeth MURDOCK.
<3> p.45, The files contain two pages of citations to probate records but no details are given. Since these records may very well contain data of interest to researchers, these numerous reference numbers with limited data & dates will be given here. Note that the date of the last entry is 1904.

<264:315> Petition for Probate, Bond, Letter. <244:38> Order of notice. <149:74> Probate. <288:258> Inventory. <432:165> Widow's Allowance. <151:64> 1st Account. <370:383> Notice of Appointment. <330:185> Elizabeth BLAKE et al, Petition for Trusteeship. <339:81> Bond. <334:164> Letter. <289:286> Inventory. <151:194> 1st Account (Elizabeth WOOD, G.T. BLAKE, Elizabeth BLAKE). <154:305> 2nd Account (Elizabeth BLAKE, G.T. BLAKE). <486:25> Petition for Citation. <483:80> 2nd Account Allowed. <493:52> Petition for Removal of Trustee. <499:504> Trustees Bond. <508:353> Notice of Appeal. <543:441> Bond, Letter, Petition for Trust by Linus M. CHILD (1883). <544:226> Inventory of real estate (G.T. BLAKE), 1883. <548:293> Trustees final account allowed, 1883. <697:321> Trustees final account allowed, 1894. <742:344> Letter, decree, bond, Petition of Trust by Amos L. WOOD, 1898. <760:94> Petition & decree for compromise, 1899. <806:104> Petition for release of contingent interest, 1902. <849:122> Releases, 1904. <849:304> Trustees' 1st and final account allowed, 1904.
<4> p.48, The reference to "Rebecca Fuller, widow" probably refers to the wife of Noah Fuller Jr. The wife of Noah Fuller Sr., Mercy (Cushman) Fuller, was still alive so he could not have had a second wife named Rebecca.
<5> p.49, "To the Honoured County Court beholden at Ipwitch, 22 Apr. 1691, by adjournment from ye 31 of March last, The Humble Petition of Edward WOODMAN of Boston who married Remember MAVERICK, daughter of Moses MAVERICK, late of Marblehead, In behalfe of the seaven children of said Remember, his wife, Humbly sheweth..." The court petition goes on to state that administration of the estate of Moses MAVERICK, dec'd, was granted to his widow, Eunice MAVERICK, 15 July 1686, but that to date, she had not settled the estate. <Essex Co.Court Papers 50:70>
<6> p.49, The deposition of the witnesses state Samuel's will was sealed & delivered to them "and this was don on his goeing to Canda on ye 30th July 1690". Although his will is said to be dated 29 July 1689, it would seem more probable that he wrote his will the day before he left, not one year before, particularly since he was so anxious about his soldiers.
<7> p.50, The pension record of Samuel BARTOLL is included in the files. Samuel enlisted as a drummer in the Revolutionary War, 25 June 1775 and served for nine months and five days. He served in Col. Thompson's Rifle Regiment under Capt. Craig in Pennsylvania. Samuel applied for pension 2 Apr. 1818, age 54, and his claim was allowed. In 1820 he gave the following info: "He was formerly a marine but has lost his right leg by amputation and is now a painter. His wife was then living and her daughter, widow Cloutman and her son 3 years old". The record also states Samuel died 23 Jan. 1835. See **MBD 1:103 (#73)** for a discussion on the discrepency in death dates for Samuel.
<8> p.55, Both Thomas & Remember PERKINS died quite young, when they were about 28 years of age and within one year of each other. They had been married only seven years and had lost four of their six children to infant deaths.

==

==

JOHN BILLINGTON

MICRO #1 of 2

Estate of **Thomas BILLINGTON** of Taunton. <NEHGR 6:93>
...1 May 1662, Inventory taken by Richard WILLIAMS, George HALL. Isaac HALL, ae 24 and John WOOD, ae 42, depose they heard Thomas BILLINGTON on his death bed, 3-4 days before his death, say that he gave all his property to James LEONARD Sr.

Estate of **Francis BILLINGTON,** labourer of Middleborough. <Plymouth Co.PR #2000>
<34:207> Letter 12 Nov. 1799, Samuel TUCKER, yeoman, of Middleboro, appointed administrator. <Original> Bond 12 Nov. 1799 by Samuel TUCKER. Sureties: Wilkes WOOD, John TINKHAM, of Middleboro Witnesses: Thomas THOMSON, Isaac LOTHROP. <Original> Request 12 Nov. 1799, **Jedidah BILLINGTON,** widow of Francis BILLINGTON, declines adm. <37:227> Warrant 12 Nov. 1799 to John MORTON, John TINKHAM, Zephaniah SHAW, of Middleboro. Inventory 12 Dec. 1799. <37:228> Account of Samuel TUCKER dated 18 Apr. 1800. Representation of Insolvency 18 Apr. 1800.

PLYMOUTH COUNTY PROBATE:

1703	Francis & Christian BILLINGTON	Middleboro	#2001
1712	Isaac BILLINGTON	Middleboro	#2002, 3:156
1718	Seth BILLINGTON	Middleboro	#2003, 4:96,99,100

Estate of **Francis BILLINGTON** of Fairhaven. <"Taunton PR" 58:424,426>
...2 Oct. 1821, **Reliance BILLINGTON,** widow, appointed admx.

FRANCIS BILLINGTON[2] (John[1])

Petition of **Isaac BILLINGTON.** <Plymouth Co.PR #2001>
...1 Mar. 1703/4...A true Narrative or Relation or A Bill of Changes drawn up by Isaac BILLINGTON and his wife Hannah...concerning the great expence & charge they were at, in keeping their aged parents, **Francis & Christian BILLINGTON,** late of Middleborough in the County of Plymouth in New England, deceased; for the space of 7 years, even to their Death & Burial. They were near 80 years old when they dyed; & it is now 18 years since. Soon after ye former, never to be forgotten, impoverishing indian Warrs, my aged Father, Francis BILLINGTON, came to me and told me he must return again to Middleborough for he could no longer subsist at Plymouth, & urged me with ye greatest importunity to goe with him, alledging that he should perish if I did not, for there his lands & livings were; whereupon (tho then I lived comfortably at Marshfield) I removed with my family to Middleborough to take care off & provide for my aged Parents, according to their request. And did for near ye space of 7 years provide both house, food and apparal for them & kept them both in sickness & health; & at death was at ye charge of ye funerall; And Lieut. TOMPSON then Selectman of ye Town promised me that if I would take care of them & not suffer them to want, I should have all ye estate that my father left at his decease & whatever divisions & allotments of lands might fall to him & his heirs, should be mine; And if I did not take care of them all must be sold by ye Selectmen for their relief. And indeed what my Parents left at their decease was but a small recompence, for ye great charge and trouble that I was at, for near seaven years together; which if I should reckon by six shillings pr week would amount to above ten times ye value of all the lands. Now my humble request to ye honoured Court is, that (seeing I can have no other recompence but ye lands) it may be settled upon me & mine; That none of ye rest of ye relation, seing they never did any thing towards releiving them in their wants, may trouble me or mine in our peaceable & quiet possession of those late divisions of lands, falling to my deceased father, which I have purchased at so dear a rate...Signed by Isaac & Hannah BILLINGTON.

Francis BILLINGTON of Plymouth to **Samuel EATON.** <Plymouth Co.Deeds 3:47>
...3 Jan. 1663, Francis BILLINGTON gives to son in law Samuel EATON and daughter Martha, land on Namasket River; after their deaths land to go to their daughter **Sarah EATON.**

Francis BILLINGTON to **Richard BULLOCK.** <Plymouth Co.Deeds 3:122>
...13 Feb. 1663, Francis BILLINGTON deeds gift to son in law Richard BULLOCK, daughter Elizabeth and grandson Israel BULLOCK.

Francis BILLINGTON of Plymouth to **Isaac BILLINGTON.** <Plymouth Co.Deeds 3:31>
...11 May 1665, Francis BILLINGTON, living in the jurisdiction of Plymouth and in the place called Namasskett or otherwise called Namasquocomaquist, to son Isaac BILLINGTON...after my wife's decease and mine I doe freely give all the land that I have lying att the place called by the Indians, Namasquocomaquist, bounded by land of Joseph BUMPAS, Samuel EATON and Namasskett River ... fifty acres...and if in case that...he doe marry, that if...hee should leave her a widdow that

shee should enjoy it for her life...Witnesses: Samuel STURTIVANT, William CROW, William HOSKINS.

Francis BILLINGTON to **William CROW.** <Plymouth Co.Deeds 3:59>
...30 July 1666, Francis & Christian BILLINGTON deed land to William CROW.

Francis BILLINGTON of Plymouth to **John BARROWS** of Plymouth. <Plymouth Co.Deeds 3:129>
...25 Dec. 1668, Francis BILLINGTON, planter, deeds to John BARROWS, his dwelling house & land... bounded on the west end with the upland that is on the west side of the swamp called Bradford's Marsh, the which upland the aforesaid Francis BILLINGTON gave unto Benjamin EATON. (Also mentions land given to Richard BULLOCK of Rehoboth, his wife Elizabeth and their son Israel - see pg.57.)

Francis BILLINGTON of Middlebury to **Gershom COBB** of Middlebury. <Plymouth Co.Deeds 39:250>
...2 June 1675, Francis BILLINGTON sells to Gershom COBB, land in Middlebury. Witnesses: John BRYANT Jr., William CROWE. 6 Mar. 1685/6, John BRYANT Jr. took oath to witnessing the signatures. Rec. 30 Dec. 1748.

Estate of **Isaac BILLINGTON** of Middleboro. <Plymouth Co.PR #2002>
<3:156> Inventory taken 16 Apr. 1712 by Lieut. Joseph VAUGHAN, Henry WOOD; mentions 25 acres in Middlebury. 21 June 1721, **Seth BILLINGTON,** son of Isaac, appointed administrator. Bond dated 21 June 1721. Surety: Joseph BUMPAS of Middleborough. Witness:Thomas CROADE.

Estate of **Seth BILLINGTON** of Middleboro. <Plymouth Co.PR #2003>
<4:96> Inventory taken 27 May 1718 by Elisha VAUGHAN, Henry WOOD. Samuel WARREN, admr., made oath on 18 June 1718. No real estate mentioned. <4:95> 11 June 1718, Samuel WARREN, brother-in-law to Seth BILLINGTON, app'td. administrator. <4:99> Appraisal of Estate 18 June 1718 by Jacob TOMSON, Elisha VAUGHAN, Samuel WOOD; real estate: one half of the hundred acre lot formerly belonging to William BARDEN's right in Pachade Neck...with one eighth part of the sawmill, £88; meadow on Namasket River, £2.10s; one sixteenth part of 80 acres formerly set out to the proprietors of Pachade, £4; one quarter part of two lots (#89 & #139) in the sixteen shilling purchase...£4.10s; two and a half acres of meadow, one quarter part of a meadow and one quarter part of a cedar swamp, £8; total £107. <4:100> Division & Settlement 20 June 1718, to brother & sisters of Seth BILLINGTON; the lands were settled upon Samuel WARREN who married one of the sisters and is administrator of the estate, he to pay the brother & sisters their share. The whole estate amounted to £152 which was divided five ways, viz: **Isaac BILLINGTON; Desire BONNEY;** children of **Lydia WASHBOURN,** dec'd; **Elinor WARREN** and **Mary WOOD,** who each received £30.8s.

Francis BILLINGTON of Plymouth to **James BONNEY** of Pembrooke. <Plymouth Co.Deeds 14:255>
...3 Dec. 1719, Francis BILLINGTON for £5 sold to James BONNEY, all rights in lands both uplands, meadows and swamps, divided & undivided which belonged to my Honoured Father **( ) BILLINGTON,** dec'd and did of right belong to my Honoured Grandfather dec'd at ye time of his decease lying & being within ye Township of Middleborough...Witnesses: Josiah COTTON, Thomas HOWLAND.<1>

<Plymouth Co.Deeds 24:199>...6 Nov. 1729, **Francis MILLER** sells part of a lot that belonged to **Francis BILLINGTON.**

Estate of **Samuel BULLOCK** of Rehoboth. <Taunton PR 11:118>
...14 Apr. 1746, **William BULLOCK** of Rehoboth, appointed administrator on estate of his father.

Guardianship of **Keziah BULLOCK.** <Taunton PR 11:674>
...4 Apr. 1749, Richard BULLOCK of Bristol appointed guardian of Keziah BULLOCK, over 14, daughter of "Thomas HORTON", late of Rehoboth.

Will of **John BULLOCK,** weaver, of Barrington MA. <Taunton PR 9:231>
...10 Mar. 1735/6, mentions wife **Elizabeth;** children: **Israel BULLOCK, John BULLOCK, Richard BULLOCK, Elizabeth BULLOCK, Prudence BULLOCK, Mary BULLOCK;** granddaughter **Anne BROWN,** under age. Pr. 17 July 1739.

Estate of **Matthew LEMOTE,** sail maker, of Plymouth. <Plymouth Co.PR #12568>
<17:178> Bond 20 Feb. 1767, George LEMOTE & Richard HOLMES, sail makers, Benjamin CHURCHELL & Charles CHURCHELL, coopers, all of Plymouth signed. George LEMOTE & Richard HOLMES, administrators. Witnesses: Penelope WINSLOW, Edward WINSLOW Jr. <19:560> Decree 1 Feb. 1768, **George LEMOTE,** only son and Richard HOLMES, husband to **Mercy,** eldest daughter of dec'd to have estate settled on them. To **Mercy HOLMES, Susanna CHAMBERS, Mary PAPPOON, Abigail MAXWELL,** their sixth part. <19:436> Inventory. <19:558> Account.

Estate of **Isaac BILLINGTON** of Middlebury. <Plymouth Co.PR #2002>
<3:156>...16 Apr. 1712, Inventory of estate, appraised by Lieut. Joseph VAUGHAN, Henry WOOD; incl. 25 acres land in Middlebury, total of estate: £7.17s.6d. Bond 21 June 1712, **Seth BILLINGTON,** son of dec'd, administrator. Surety: Joseph BUMPUS of Middleboro. Witness: Thomas CROADE.

John WASHBURN of Plymouth to **Samuel BRADFORD** of Duxborough. <Plymouth Co.Deeds 10:1:466>
...8 Dec. 1708, John WASHBURN, yeoman for L20 sold to Samuel BRADFORD, gentleman, twenty acres in Duxborough...upon which my Honoured Grandfather **John IRISH** dec'd formerly dwelt being near Duxborough Mill and commonly known by ye name of Irish's Orchard...bounded lands of Edward SOUTHWORTH & lands formerly of Samuel HUNT. Witnesses: Ephraim LITTLE, Elisha HOLMES. Rec. 1 Jan 1713.

Guardianship of Children of **John WASHBURN** of Plymouth. <Plymouth Co.PR #21961, 4:288-291> ...22 Sept. 1721, Francis ADAMS, clothier, of Plymouth, appointed guardian of the seven children of John WASHBURN, viz: **Barnabas WASHBURN** (betw. 14-21); **Elisha WASHBURN** (betw. 14-21); **Ephraim WASHBURN** (betw. 14-21); **Thankful WASHBURN** (under 14); **Ebenezer WASHBURN** (under 14); **Ichabod WASHBURN** (betw. 14-21); **Jabez WASHBURN** (under 14). Bond 22 Sept. 1721, of Francis ADAMS with **John WASHBURN**, husbandman, of Plymouth, as surety. Witnesses: Benoni LUCAS, Thomas CROADE.

Will of **Barnabas WASHBURN**, husbandman, of Kingston. <Plymouth Co.PR #21923> <20:396>...dated 20 Mar. 1770, mentions wf **Hannah** and sons **Barnabas WASHBURN** & **Elkanah WASHBURN**; brother-in-law **John ADAMS**, clothier, of Kingston, named executor. Witnesses: Jabez WASHBURN, Ezekiel WASHBURN, Francis ADAMS. <20:397> Inventory taken 24 Aug. 1770 by Ephraim WASHBURN, Benjamin COOK, John GRAY. <21:283> Account allowed 2 Aug. 1773. Received from: Micah THOMAS, Consider FULLER, Samuel FOSTER. Paid to: Molly HOLMES, William SEVER, Esq., John FULLER, Josiah WASHBURN, Jabez WASHBURN, Silvanus COOK, Nathaniel LITTLE, Capt. John WADSWORTH, William DREW, executor of estate of William RAND Jr., John THOMAS, Esq., James COBB, Dr. Loring's executor, Thadeus RANSOM, Nathan PERKINS, Elisha STETSON, Cornelius SAMPSON, Barnabas BRIGGE, Stetson BRADFORD, Ephraim WASHBURN, Job DREW, Joshua ADAMS, John FULLER, John ADAMS Jr., Edward WINSLOW Jr..

Estate of **Ebenezer WASHBURN** of Kingston. <Plymouth Co.PR #21949> <7:436> Letter of administration, dated 3 Oct. 1738, granted to widow **Lydia WASHBURN**. Bond dated 3 Oct. 1738. Sureties: John FAUNCE, yeoman of Kingston, Benjamin SAMPSON, dealer, of Kingston. Witnesses: John FULLARTON, Mary WINSLOW. <14:102> Division: 5 Mar. 1756 the following were appointed to divide real estate, viz: John WADSWORTH of Duxborough, Jabez WASHBURN, John FAUNCE, Ephraim WASHBURN, Josiah HOLMES (all of Kingston). Real estate was divided into four parts among the following children: **Ebenezer WASHBURN** (double portion), **Simeon WASHBURN** and **Lydia DAVIS**, wf of Nicholas.

Will of **Lydia (WASHBURN) Waterman** of Kingston. <Plymouth Co.PR #22049> <29:147>...dated 1 July 1765, mentions son **Ebenezer WASHBURN**; son **Simeon WASHBURN** dec'd; children of dau **Lydia DAVIS**, dec'd, viz: **Nicholas DAVIS Jr.**, **John DAVIS**, **Zenas DAVIS**; brother **John FAUNCE** to be guardian of my three grandsons. Witnesses: Reuben BISBE, John FAUNCE Jr., Hannah FAUNCE Jr. <29:172> Inventory dated 3 May 1784 by John FAUNCE, yeoman, Kimball PRINCE, yeoman, Judah WASHBURN, gentleman, all of Kingston. <29:173> Division dated 24 June 1784...real estate of **Lydia WASHBURN**, late of Kingston, dec'd, who was at time of her death wife of Thomas WATERMAN of Halifax, divided into four equal parts, viz: **Ebenezer WASHBURN** (double share), **Nicholas DAVIS Jr.**, **John DAVIS**. Oath by John FAUNCE, Kimbal PRINCE, 5 July 1784.

Will of **Simeon WASHBURN**, blacksmith, of Kingston. <Plymouth Co.PR #22099> <19:68>...dated 23 Feb. 1764, mentions brother **Ebenezer WASHBURN**; nephews **Nicholas DAVIS**, **John DAVIS**, **Zenas DAVIS** (all under 21); mother **Lidia WASHBURN**; uncle **John ADAMS**. Witnesses: Uriah BARTLETT, Josiah COOK, Gamaliel BRADFORD. <19:69> Bond dated 2 Mar. 1764 by **Lidia WASHBURN**, widow & **John ADAMS**, clothier, both of Kingston. Sureties: Nathaniel SIMMONS, yeoman and Gamaliel BRADFORD Esq., both of Duxbury. Witnesses: Thomas WESTON, Edward WINSLOW Jr.

Estate of **Elisha WASHBURN** of Kingston. <Plymouth Co.PR #21960> <7:52> Administration granted 19 Aug. 1734 to **Martha WASHBURN**, widow, of Kingston. Sureties: Luke PERKINS, Isaac CHURCHILL. Witnesses: Sarah WINSLOW, Margaret ROGERS. <7:63> Inventory taken 3 Sept. 1734 by Gershom BRADFORD, Joseph MITCHELL, William RIPLEY. <original> Account dated 4 Mar. 1734/5. <7:128> Widow's Allowance dated 2 May 1735.

Estate of **Ephraim WASHBURN**, yeoman, of Kingston. <Plymouth Co.PR #21966> <original> Bond dated 4 Dec. 1775 by Ebenezer WASHBURN, yeoman, admr. Sureties: Ebenezer THOMPSON of Halifax, Hopestill SOUTHWORTH of Rochester. Witnesses: Nathaniel SOUTHWORTH, J. CUSHING. <24:271> Inventory dated 4 Dec. 1775 by Benjamin COOKE, Simeon COOKE, Judah HALL all of Kingston. <24:272> Widow's dower 7 Apr. 1777 to **Eglah WASHBURN**, widow, part of homestead farm, six acres bounded by land of Robert COOK, dec'd; ten acres meadow & woodlands, adjoining land of Barnabas WASHBURN, dec'd; seven acres at Pond Pasture. <24:274> List of claims dated 28 Feb. 1777. Debts: Estate of Ephraim WASHBURN Jr.; Joseph ADAMS; Thadeus RANSOM; Elkanah WASHBURN; Dr. Samuel NUTTING; Sarah WASHBURN; Deborah WASHBURN; Crocker SAMPSON; John ADAMS; Ebenezer WASHBURN; Ebenezer ADAMS; Jabez WASHBURN; Ezekiel WASHBURN; Abner BISBEY; Hon. John THOMAS, Esq.; Robert CUSHMAN; Widow Mary LORING; John TILSON; James EVERSON; Isaac BREWSTER; Jabez EATON; Stetson BRADFORD; Keziah THOMAS; Wrestling BREWSTER; William DREW; Hon. William Sever, Esq.; Peleg BRADFORD; Elisha STETSON; Capt. Peleg WASHBURN. Due from: Simeon COOK; James BRADFORD; Ephraim EVERSON, Zadoc THOMAS; Elijah CHANDLER; Thomas DILINGHAM; James COBB; Consider ORCUT; Isacher BISBY; John WESTON; Judah WASHBURN; John BRADFORD; Nathaniel GILBERT; Francis ADAMS; Job DREW; Lot EATON; Micha THOMAS; Seth WASHBURN. <24:238> Account dated 8 Apr. 1777.

Estate of **Ephraim WASHBURN Jr.**, yeoman, of Kingston. <Plymouth Co.PR #21967> <23:76> Letter dated 4 Dec. 1775, Hopestill BISBEE of Rochester, yeoman, appointed admr. <24:113> Inventory dated 5 Dec. 1775 by Benjamin COOKE, Gideon SAMSON, Simeon COOKE. <original> Bond dated 4 Dec. 1775 by Hopestill BISBEE of Rochester. Sureties: Seth CUSHING, yeoman, of Plympton and Ebenezer WASHBURN, yeoman, of Kingston. Witnesses: Ebenezer TOMSON, J. CUSHING.

Joseph MICHELL of Plymouth to **Ephraim WASHBURN**. <Plymouth Co.Deeds> ...3 Feb. 1725, Joseph MICHELL, tanner, for £10 paid by John WASHBURN of Plymouth, yeoman, do give to Ephraim WASHBURN, son of said John, a certain parcell of salt marsh in Plymouth.

Witnesses: Mariah BRADBURY, Hannah COTTON. Rec. 3 Feb. 1724/5

John FAUNCE of Kingston to **Ephraim & Barnabas WASHBURN** of Kingston. <Plymouth Co.Deeds 26:167> ...10 Jan. 1730/31, John FAUNCE for £13 sells to Ephraim WASHBURN and Barnabas WASHBURN, 6 acres adjoining land of Deacon John WASHBURN whereupon his house now stands, which said 6 acres Faunce formerly purchased of Gershom BRADFORD....joining lands which Gershom BRADFORD lately sold unto Deacon John WASHBURN. Witnesses: Judith FAUNCE, Lydia FAUNCE.

John WASHBURN of Kingston to **Ephraim WASHBURN** of Kingston. <Plymouth Co.Deeds 36:160> ...20 Mar. 1743/4, John WASHBURN, husbandman, for love I have to my dutifull son, Ephraim WASHBURN, yeoman, give 36 acres in Kingston being part of ye farm of land whereon I now dwell, bounded by land of Gershom BRADFORD and Barnabas WASHBURN, also land and meadow in Kingston which I bought of Gershom BRADFORD, 22 Apr. 1739. Witnesses: Robert BRADFORD, Daniel BRADFORD.

Ephraim & Barnabas WASHBURN of Kingston to **John WASHBURN** of Kingston. <Plymouth Co.Deeds 36:161> ...4 Apr. 1744, Ephraim WASHBURN and Barnabas WASHBURN, yeomen, for & in consideration of the duty we owe and love & good will & respect to our Honored Father John WASHBURN, husbandman, have leased & made over to said father all that farm of land in Kingston whereon he now dwelleth... farm which was given to us by our abovesaid father as may appear by deeds. Witnesses: Robert BRADFORD, Daniel BRADFORD.

Estate of **Ephraim WASHBURN**, yeoman of Kingston. <Plymouth Co.PR>
<24:238>...8 Apr. 1776, **Ebenezer WASHBURN** of Kingston, app'td administrator. <24:271> Inventory taken 3 Jan. 1776 by Judah HALL, Benjamin COOK, Simeon COOKE. Inventory of real estate taken 7 Apr. 1777 by John GRAY, Robert BRADFORD, Benjamin COOKE. Land all in Kingston, adjoins estate of **Barnabas WASHBURN. Eglah WASHBURN**, widow.

Ephraim WASHBURN of Kingston to **Nicholas SEVER** of Kingston. <Plymouth Co.Deeds 45:117> ...1 Jan. 1739, Ephraim WASHBURN, yeoman, for £100 sells to NIcholas SEVER, Esq., 87 acres in Kingston, being the homestead on which I now live, part of which was given me by my father John WASHBURN, late of Kingston and the other part I purchased of Robert COOKE, Elisha WASHBURN, Rev. William RAND and the widow Hannah BRADFORD. Witnesses: George RING, William SEVER.

MICRO #2 of 2

Susanna WASHBURN et al to **Judah WASHBURN** of Kingston. <Plymouth Co.Deeds 110:161> ...7 Apr. 1790, Rebecca WASHBURN, Susanna WASHBURN, Silvester HOLMES, yeoman & wf Molly, all of Kingston, for £161, sold to Judah WASHBURN, gentleman...all our right...in the real estate whereof Deacon Jabez WASHBURN, late of Kingston, died seized of except the one half of the deceased dwelling house, like wise the said Susanna WASHBURN does...forever quit all her right...in said premises given her by the heirs of Jabez WASHBURN Jr., dec'd. Witnesses: Isaac WASHBURN, William SIMMONS. Ack. by all 7 June 1809. Rec. 8 June 1809.

Will of **Jabez WASHBURN** of Kingston. <Plymouth Co.PR #22001, 35:120-2>
...dated 4 Nov. 1791, mentions wife **Deborah**; children **Judah WASHBURN** (sole executor); **Rebecca WASHBURN; Susanna WASHBURN**; chil. of son **Jabez WASHBURN**; granddaughter **Molly HOLMES**. Witnesses: John FAUNCE, Elijah FAUNCE, John COOK. Bond 7 Jul 1794 by **Judah WASHBURN**. Sureties: John FAUNCE, John COOK, yeomen of Kingston. Witnesses: Caleb LORING, Isaac LOTHROP. <35:122> Inventory 12 July 1794; homestead farm, salt meadow at Duxbury, half pew in Meeting house.

Estate of **Jabez WASHBURN Jr.** of Kingston. <Plymouth Co.PR #22003>
<23:74> Bond 4 Dec. 1775, **Ebenezer WASHBURN**, yeoman, of Kingston, administrator. Sureties: Ebenezer THOMPSON, yeoman, of Halifax, Hopestill BISBEE, yeoman, of Rochester. Witness: Nathaniel SOUTHWORTH. <24:65> Inventory taken 4 Dec. 1775 by John GRAY, Ebenezer COBB Jr., both of Kingston and Benjamin WHITE of Marshfield. Real estate incl. dwelling house, barn, shoemakers shop, tan house, tan works, wood lot. <28:526> 2nd Inventory taken 2 Sept. 1782 by John GRAY, Esq., Robert COOKE, gentleman, Nicholas DAVIS Jr., cordwainer, all of Kingston. <28:526> Settlement of Real Estate 6 Jan. 1783. Estate settled on eldest son **Elisha WASHBURN**, he to pay siblings their share, viz: **Bildad WASHBURN, John WASHBURN, Judith WASHBURN, Lucy WASHBURN, Jabez WASHBURN, Abiel WASHBURN.** Memorandum dated 6 Jan. 1783 states there was no widow. <31:6> Account dated 15 Apr. 1789, by **Ebenezer WASHBURN**, adm. Debts due from: Simeon COOK, Isaac CUSHMAN, Zachariah STANDISH, Widow Hannah COOK, Eliezer FAUNCE, Mrs. Hannah THOMAS, Deacon Jabez WASHBURN, Jesse FULLER, Capt. Judah WASHBURN, Desiah GRAY, Nicholas DAVIS Jr., Elisha WASHBURN, Seth WASHBURN, Salvenus COOKE, James CUSHMAN, Josiah FULLER, James EVERSON Jr., Lydia EVERSON, Nathaniel BONEY, Kimbel PRINCE. Debts paid to: Job DREW, Theophlas STETSON, Elisha CUSHMAN, Hon. William SEVER, Elisha WATERMAN, Salvenus COBB, Capt. George BRYANT, Benjamin WHITE Jr., Nicholas DAVIS, John LEACH, Seth COBB, Ginne SILLEVINE, Bezalal HOWARD, Rev. William RAND, Jerusha COBB, John ADAMS, John ADAMS Jr., Jedidah HOLMES, Ammeriah CUSHMAN, Benjamin COOKE, Dr. Jabez FULLER, Josiah COOKE, Capt. Benjamin LOTHROP, Jabez EATON, James COBB, William DREW, Esq., Elisha WASHBURN the guardian of three of the heirs, John FAUNCE the guardian of three of the heirs.

Guardianship of Children of **Jabez WASHBURN Jr.** of Kingston. <Plymouth Co.PR #22004>
<26:103> 4 Dec. 1780, **Elisha WASHBURN**, cordwainer, of Kingston, app'td. guardian of **Abiel, Jabez Lucy WASHBURN**, minors under 14. <26:380> 4 Dec. 1780, John FAUNCE, yeoman, of Kingston, chosen by **John & Bildad WASHBURN**, minors above 14. <26:405> 13 Nov. 1780, John FAUNCE chosen by **Judiath**

WASHBURN, minor above 14.

==========

Estate of **Jabez WASHBURN**, housewright, of Kingston. <Plymouth Co.PR #22002>
<34:174> Letter 16 Jan. 1799, Cephas WADSWORTH, housewright, of Kingston, app'td. administrator. Bond 16 Jan. 1799 by Cephas WADSWORTH. Sureties: Elisha WASHBURN, cordwainer, of Kingston and David BARON, gentleman, of Plymouth. Witnesses: John COTTON, Noah GALE. <36:496> Inventory 16 Jan 1799 by John FAUNCE, Rufus WASHBURN, Samuel STETSON, all of Kingston. <38:363> Account 19 Aug. 1803. Debts paid to: Fear FOSTER, Stephen COBB, Samuel STETSON, Judah ALDEN, John SEVER, George RUSSELL, Seth DREW, Esq., Bildad WASHBURN, Abiel WASHBURN, Rev. Mr. WILLIS, Micah BARTLETT, Joseph EVERSON, Robert COOK, Mark KEEN, Pelham BREWSTER, Isaac CHURCHILL, Wrestling BREWSTER Jr., Stetson BRADFORD, Mary HARLOW, Sylvanus COOK, David BEAL, Peleg BRYANT, Francis ADAMS, Ezra MORTON, Thomas STETSON, Silas MORTON, John FAUNCE, Abel KINGMAN, Lemuel DREW Jr., Dr. Jabez FULLER, Josiah WEST, Melzar ADAMS, Charles HOLMES, Mr. BONNEY, Francis KING, Judah WASHBURN. Allowance paid to widow.

==========

Estate of **John WASHBURN**, blacksmith, of Plymouth. <Plymouth Co.PR #22016>
<20:213> Letter 9 May 1769, **Abigail WASHBURN**, widow, app'td. administratrix. Inventory taken 18 May 1769 by Thomas FOSTER and Eleazer STEPHENS. <20:344> Account of widow allowed 14 May 1770; estate declared insolvent. <original> Bond 9 May 1769. Sureties: Eleazer DUNHAM, yeoman and Josiah JOHNSON, blacksmith. Witnesses: Edward WINSLOW Jr., Hannah WINSLOW.

FOOTNOTES

<1> p.58, Since there has arisen some question as to the accuracy of the clerk's copy of this deed, I have left out the name in question so as not to compound the error and confuse the family researcher. While the clerk's copy says "my Honoured Father Francis BILLINGTON" and does not name the Grandfather, it should probably be the other way around - "my Honoured Father" and "my Honoured Grandfather Francis BILLINGTON". The grandfather in question, Francis[2] had only two sons, Isaac & Joseph, he did not have a son Francis. See MF5G 5:50 and MQ 52:133.

==========

WILLIAM BRADFORD

MICRO #1 of 15

BARNSTABLE COUNTY DEEDS: (re: BRADFORD)

<2:128> - 6 May 1803, Edward BRADFORD, yeoman of Falmouth & wf Sarah to Joseph LAWRENCE.
<2:40> - 3 Mar. 1809, Edward BRADFORD, mariner of Falmouth & wf Sarah to John TOBEY, mortgage of house & land on Davis' Neck in Falmouth.
<4:124> - 26 July 1819, Noah BRADFORD, potter of Barnstable from Prince NYE, yeoman of Barnst., land with a potter shop on road to Nye's dock.
<1:233> - 1820, Susanna BRADFORD to Seth ROBINSON.
<2:118> - 1820, Noah BRADFORD to Daniel PARKER.
<3:115> - 1822, Noah BRADFORD to John DOANE.
<4:124> - 13 May 1822, Noah BRADFORD, potter of Barnstable from Daniel PARKER, yeoman of Barns.
<1:223> - 30 Sept 1822, Noah BRADFORD, potter of Barnstable from Joseph BLISH, Esq. of Barns.
<4:125> - 28 Nov. 1822, Noah BRADFORD from "Doanes, Smith, Taylors, Hortons, Rogers" land in Barnstable bordering on N. Bradford's other land.
<4:123> - 7 May 1825, Noah BRADFORD, potter, of Barnstable, from Joseph BLISH, Esq. of same.
<1:223> - 31 July 1826, Noah BRADFORD, yeoman, of Barnstable from John DOANE, Esq., of Orleans, sells back land bought 6 Nov. 1822.
<4:131> - 1827, Noah BRADFORD to (Ammiel?) JENKINS.
<3:266> - 1829, Cornelius BRADFORD to Joseph WINSLOW, land in Brewster.
<4:214> - 1830, William BRADFORD to Benjamin BURGESS, land in Sandwich.
<15:204> - 1836, Noah BRADFORD by administration to Lloyd CHASE, land in Barnstable.
<34:30> - 1844, James BRADFORD, et al to Ebenezer HOLWAY, land in Provincetown.
<34:465> - 1845, James BRADFORD, et al to James CHANDLER, land in Provincetown.

Susanna BRADFORD of Falmouth to **John DAVIS** of Falmouth. <Barnstable Co.Deeds, Falmouth 1:130> ...26 Mar. 1816, Susanna BRADFORD, widow, for support & maintenance & for $50.00, sold to John DAVIS, yeoman, all her real estate in Falmouth, half acre & house, near West Cong. Meeting House; being land set off to her et al from land of her mother Anner WICKS.
<1:233>...5 Apr. 1824, John DAVIS as assignee of Susanna BRADFORD, widow, of Falmouth...refers to Francis WICKS, Esq., former assignee and land at Woods Hole.

PLYMOUTH COUNTY PROBATES: (re: BRADFORD)

1687	William	Plymouth	#2625, 1:6
1700	William et al	Plymouth	#2628, 1:328
1703	William	Plymouth	#2626, 2:42,240
1714	Samuel	Duxbury	#2599, 3:301,304
1724	John Jr.	Plymouth	#2552, 4:439,440
1728	William Jr.	Kingston	#2622, 5:403,5:601,6:22,14:90,29:293
1730	Jael	Kingston	#2545, 5:753,755,803
1730	William	Kingston	#2621, 5:665,714,7:437,440
1733	Nathan et al	Kingston	#2582, 6:395-397
1736	John	Kingston	#2553, 7:260,261,274,10:421,438
1740	Samuel	Plympton	#2605, 8:199,201,202,236,9:441-7
1742	Samuel et al	Plympton	#2606, 9:34-7,14:10,11,427,12:388-90
1745	Zadoc	Kingston	#2635, 10:85
1746	Ephraim	Kingston	#2524, 10:343,345,374,13:75
1746	Noah	Plymouth	#2585, 10:363-4,424,426,11:168,264, 12:368
1747	Simeon et al	Kingston	#2612, 10:523,11:76-77
1750	Elisha	Kingston	#2518, 11:446,12:354
1751	Lemuel & Nathaniel	Plymouth	#2563, 12:205,206,18:50-52,16:222
1751	Nathaniel	Plymouth	#2583, 12:151,12:365,522,16:219
1770	John	Plympton	#2555, 20:408,466,24:116-27,24:119, 42:141
1776	Sarah et al	Plympton	#2610, 22:72,73,194-96
1778	Gamaliel	Duxbury	#2527, 25:17,19,285
1778	Grace et al	Duxbury	#2536, 22:224,26:4-6
1779	Samuel	Duxbury	#2600, 23,220,25:463,40:104,50:201
1782	Peabody	Duxbury	#2588, 27:330,29:34,31:185,33:10,33: 36,41
1782	Robert	Kingston	#2595, 28:460-1,514,535,29:30-2,135
1783	Ira et al	Duxbury	#2542, 26:413,242,248,316,473
1784	Benjamin	Kingston	#2502, 27:146,29:193
1787	Nathan	Kingston	#2581, 30:273,274
1788	Susannah et al	Plympton	#2617, 26:219

1790	Mary	Kingston	#2576, 26:494,31:301,389
1791	Joseph	Plympton	#2559, 27:357
1793	Gideon	Plympton	#2533, 27:537,33:467,470,529,530
1794	Jane	Plympton	#2550
1802	Perez	Duxbury	#2590, 38:96,97,244 (will)
1802	William	Plympton	#2629, 34:311,38:144,39:448,43:521,45:57,60 (adm)
1803	Mary	Duxbury	#2579, 38:461-3 (will)
1805	Gideon	Plympton	#2534, 40:224,226,316 (will)
1806	Polly et al	Plympton	#2591, 32:291,41:74,183,45:119 (gdn.)
1807	Elizabeth	Plympton	#2520, 39:97,42:64 (adm.)
1807	Gamaliel	Duxbury	#2528, 42:19,21,22 (will)
1807	John	Plympton	#2556, 42:130 (will)
1811	David	Plymouth	#2513, 41:79 (gdn.)
1811	Silvanus	Kingston	#2611, 39:278,43:399,44:19,20,39,348 (adm.)
1813	Ruth	Plymouth	#2597, 39:419,45:414-16 (adm.)
1813	William	Plymouth	#2627, 39:427,45:417 (adm.)
1814	Mary	Plympton	#2577, 41:183,47:417,50:98 (gdn.)
1814	Winslow	Plympton	#2633, 45:251,252,488,489,46:24(adm.)
1815	Hitty A. et al	Plymouth	#2541, 41:201 (gdn.)
1816	Jane	Kingston	#2549, 46:444,48:206-7,315,49:161-162 (will)
1816	Samuel	Duxbury	#2601, 46:153,48:153,442 (adm.)
1818	Josiah	Plymouth	#2560, 41:357,49:290-1,54:163,57:512,58:536,60:483, 64:446,67:217 (gdn.)
1818	Robert	Kingston	#2596, 46:276,49:363,50:134,134,292-3 (adm.)
1821	Bartlett	Plymouth	#2500, 52:37,53:476,477,479,56:233,57:313,59:105 (adm)
1822	Lucy et al	Plymouth	#2567, 51:173 (gdn.)
1822	Sarah	Plymouth	#2607, 52:102 (adm.)
1824	Hannah	Plymouth	#2537, 55:242,58:301,382 (will)
1825	Consider	Kingston	#2508, 52:404,55:364,59:493,60:91,92,330-2,485 (adm.)
1826	Stetson	Kingston	#2616, 63:84,86 (will)
1828	Abraham	Plympton	#2494, 61:186,66:112-3,228,312
1831	John	Plympton	#2557, 70:469,71:7,72:544,73:85,76:51 (adm.)
1832	Hannah et al	Plympton	#2538, 65:215-7,229,73:372-74,80:349,81:152,**2O**:353,396 **8L**:117,**1R**:80 (gdn.)
1834	Julia et al	Kingston	#2561, 65:374 (gdn.)
1834	Sarah	Kingston	#2608, 71:255,73:441,75:153,76:444 (adm.)
1836	James	Plymouth	#2547, 71:395,75:357,78:135,319,79:35,140,79:365,**2O**:37 (adm.)
1836	Prince	Duxbury	#2592, 71:377,75:356,78:38,79:19,320,322,89:566,**2O**:12 (adm.)
1837	Charles	Plympton	#2504, **10A**:79,75:500,79:543,82:247 (adm.)
1837	George A.	Kingston	#2529, **8L**:43 (gdn.)
1837	Gershom et al	Duxbury	#2532, **8L**:48,49 (gdn.)
1837	Hezekiah	Plympton	#2540, **10A**:484,75:440,79:22,260,81:206 (will)
1838	Abigail	Duxbury	#2493, **8L**:417-8,80:459,**2O**:385,**1R**:63 (gdn.)
1838	William	Plympton	#2630, **10A**:176,80:289,**5T**:50,**2O**:88,**1R**:64,81:261,**11B**:489 **7V**:240 (adm.)
1839	William et al	Plympton	#2632, **8L**:127-8, 83:36,88:313-5,92:294 (gdn.)
1840	David	Kingston	#2512, **1G**:134,82:140,304,83:335,**6U**:85 (will)
1840	Eleanor et al	Plymouth	#2517, **8L**:193,83:25,86:378,**9M**:1,86:379 (gdn.)
1840	Lyman	Duxbury	#2573, **10A**:315 (adm.)
1841	Martha D.	Duxbury	#2575, **8L**:207 (gdn.)
1843	William L.	Plympton	#2631, **11B**:152,85:341,**6U**:393 (adm.)
1844	Gershom	Duxbury	#2531, **11B**:274,86:566,**6U**:558,87:117 (adm.)
1848	Ellis	Kingston	#2522, **12C**:34,**7U**:407,91:7,92:1,2 (adm.)
1849	Charles	Plymouth	#2503, **12C**:39,92:4 (adm.)
1849	Bartlett	Plymouth	#2499, **12C**:77,94:573,95:155 (adm.)
1850	James et al	Plymouth	#2548, **9M**:251 (gdn.)
1850	Priscilla	Kingston	#2593, **12C**:198,92:186,93:224,94:548 (adm.)

Mary BRADFORD of Kingston, non-compos-mentis. <Plymouth Co.PR #2576>
<31:301>...4 Oct. 1790, Mary BRADFORD of Kingston, singlewoman, represented non-compos-mentis by friends, relatives and neighbors, viz: David BRADFORD, Levi BRADFORD, Gershom COBB, Charles FOSTER, James FOSTER, Elisha BRADFORD, Wait BRADFORD, John ADAMS Jr., Seth DREW, Nicholas DAVIS Jr., Isaac BREWSTER, Ichabod BRADFORD, Levi HOLMES, Joseph HOLMES, Stetson BRADFORD, Joseph FULLER, John WASHBURN, Oliver SAMPSON. 16 Oct. 1790, Mary BRADFORD represented non-compos-mentis by John GRAY, John FAUNCE, Jedediah HOLMES, the selectmen of Kingston. <26:494> 1 Nov. 1790, Jedediah HOLMES, of Kingston, appointed guardian. Sureties: Lewis BRADFORD of Kingston, Josiah SOULE of Duxbury. Witnesses: James LEACH, Isaac LOTHROP. <31:389> 11 Apr. 1791, The subscribers represent that Mary BRADFORD is of sound mind, viz: William DREW, William SEVER, (Gamaliel BRADFORD, Philip CHANDLER, selectman of Duxbury), Asa CHANDLER, Amos PHILLIPS, Joshua BREWSTER, William BREWSTER, Luther SAMSON, Peres CHANDLER, Perez CHANDLER Jr., Ezra MICHELL, John MICHELL, Wadsworth CHANDLER Seth CHANDLER, Stephen RUSSELL, William SAMSON, Thomas PHILLIPS, Ephraim CHANDLER, Nathan BREWSTER, Nathan CHANDLER. <31:389> 6 June 1791, Guardianship revoked.

Will of **Mary BRADFORD** of Duxbury. <Plymouth Co.PR #2579>
<38:461>...21 Dec. 1792, by Mary BRADFORD, single woman, advanced in years, mentions Joseph CHANDLER, oldest son of Nathan CHANDLER of Duxbury by his second wife; Ira CHANDLER, younger brother of said Joseph. Joseph CHANDLER named executor; in case he should not survive me I appoint his said brother Ira CHANDLER sole executor. Witnesses: Philip CHANDLER, Amos PHILLIPS, Joshua BREWSTER. <38:462> Probate 18 Nov. 1803 by Ira CHANDLER, executor. At this time Philip CHANDLER was deceased and Amos PHILLIPS had removed from the Commonwealth. <38:463> Bond 18 Nov. 1803 by Ira CHANDLER, yeoman of Duxbury. Sureties: Joshua BREWSTER, gentleman and Benjamin SMITH, cordwainer, both of Duxbury. Witnesses: Nathaniel LOTHROP, Isaac LOTHROP.

Guardianship of Children of **Samuel BRADFORD** of Plympton. <Plymouth Co.PR #2617>
<26:219>...Letter 7 July 1788, Samuel BRADFORD app'td. guardian of his children, viz: **Susanna BRADFORD, Abigail BRADFORD, Samuel BRADFORD, Winslow BRADFORD**, all minors under 14...estate which accrues to them in right of their Grandfather **Daniel VAUGHN**, late of Plymton, dec'd. Sureties: Ebenezer BRIGGS of Middleborough, Joshua LORING of Plymton. Witnesses: Jno. DAVIS, Isaac LOTHROP.

Estate of **Joseph BRADFORD**, Physician, of Plympton. <Plymouth Co.PR #2559>
<27:357> Letter 17 Oct. 1791, Gideon BRADFORD Jr., of Plymton, gentleman, app'td administrator. Sureties: Calvin BRADFORD of Plymton, Samuel LUCAS of Carver. Witnesses: Marlbry TURNER Jr., Joseph WRIGHT.

Guardianship of Children of **Sarah BRADFORD** of Kingston. <Plymouth Co.PR #2561>
<65:374> Letter 7 Oct. 1834, Charles BRADFORD, yeoman of Kingston, app'td guardian of **Julia BRADford** and **George A. BRADFORD**, above 14, children of Sarah BRADFORD, widow, dec'd. Sureties: David CROOKER of Plympton, Ezra MITCHELL of Kingston. Witness: J.H. LOUD. (Julia chose her brother Charles, 10 Sept. 1834, George chose his brother Charles, 1 Sept. 1834.)

Guardianship of Children of **William BRADFORD** of Plympton. <Plymouth Co.PR #2591>
<32:291> Letter & Bond 22 Mar. 1806, **Polly BRADFORD**, widow, app'td guardian of children of William BRADFORD, yeoman, viz: **Saba BRADFORD, William BRADFORD, Polly BRADFORD, Mercy BRADFORD**, all under 14. Sureties: Asaph SOULE, Asaph SOULE Jr. Witnesses: Zephaniah PERKINS, William PERKINS <41:74> Letter 2 Apr. 1811, Oliver CHURCHILL, yeoman of Plympton, app'td guardian of **Saba Soule BRADFORD & William BRADFORD** (over 14) and **Molly BRADFORD & Mercy BRADFORD** (under 14). Sureties: Jeremiah SAMPSON, John PRINCE, both of Kingston. Witnesses: Nathan ALDEN, Lot WHITMARSH. <41:183> Letter 5 Apr. 1814, Jonathan PARKER Jr., gentleman of Plympton, app'td guardian of **Mercy BRADFORD** (minor above 14). <45:119> Warrant for Division 21 Sept. 1813, Elijah BISBE, Esq., Jonathan PARKER Jr., trader and Martin HAYWARD, gentleman, all of Plympton, app'td to make division & partition of real estate whereof **Polly BRADFORD**, late of Plympton, minor, died seized... to her brother **William BRADFORD**, and sisters **Saba SHERMAN** wf of Asa Jr. & **Mercy BRADFORD.** Division 4 Oct. 1813: to **Saba SHERMAN** part of homestead bounded by land of Silvanus RIPLEY & Bela STURTEVANT; to **William BRADFORD** remaining part of homestead, woodland near Ichabod PHINNEY's and bounded by land of Hopestill BISBEE and one third of nine acre lot in Turkey Cedar Swamp; to **Mercy BRADFORD** two and a half acre meadow in Jones River Meadow, one third of above lot in Turkey Cedar Swamp.

Estate of **Priscilla BRADFORD** of Kingston. <Plymouth Co.PR #2593>
<original> 6 May 1850, Martin L. TUPPER, being one of the heirs-at-law requests that Seth TUPPER be app'td adm. <12:198> Petition 6 May 1850, by Seth TUPPER of Duxbury to be app'td adm. of estate of his sister Priscilla BRADFORD. Bond 6 May 1850. Sureties: Seth DREW, Horace L. COLLAMORE, both of Kingston. Witnesses: Henry COBB, Lysander BARTLETT Jr., David BEAL. <92:186> Inventory 7 May 1850, Seth DREW, Horace L. COLLAMORE, Joseph STETSON, all of Kingston, app'td appraisers. Real estate: one quarter part of undivided house formerly occupied by Peleg TUPPER. <93:224> Account 3rd Monday May 1851. Received from: Nathan BROOKS. Paid to: E. CUSHMAN, Nathan BROOKES; H.N. JONES, M.D.; James PRATT; John PORTER, M.D.; H.L. COLLAMORE; Seth DREW; Joseph STETSON; Joseph STETSON, adm.; William BRADFORD. <94:548> 2nd Account 1st Mon. May 1852. Paid to: Edwin CUSHMAN; N. BROOKS; Dr. JONES; James PRATT; John PORTER; H.L. COLLAMORE; Seth DREW; Joseph STETSON; Joseph STETSON, adm.; William BRADFORD; Seth TUPPER; W. & F.A. GRENELL; Martin & S. TUPPER; Grenvill BROOKS; W. JOHNSON; F.M. JOHNSON; John PERKINS, Mary T. JOHNSON.

Estate of **Prince BRADFORD**, shipwright, of Duxbury. <Plymouth Co.PR #2592>
<original> 18 Jan. 1836, **Hariet BRADFORD**, widow, requests Samuel BRADFORD be app'td administrator of estate. <71:377> Letter 18 Jan. 1836, Samuel BRADFORD, yeoman of Duxbury, app'td. Bond 18 Jan. 1836. Sureties: Levi LORING, Edward LORING, both of Duxbury. Witness: J.H. LOUD. <78:38> Inventory: 12 Feb. 1836. Real estate: homestead farm; nine acre woodland south of Fronore Brook; three acres woodland north of Dead Swamp; three acres woodland west of Plymouth Road; four acres English meadow east of Island Creek Brook; two & quarter acres salt marsh adjoining Island Creek. <2:120> Petition 8 Aug. 1836, to sell real estate to pay debts...order of notice to all persons interested to be published in the Old Colony Memorial. <79:19> Account 16 Jan. 1837. Due from: John SEVER, Lysander BARTLETT, George HUMPHREY, James SOULE. Paid: James N. SEVER, Weston FREEMAN, Levy CHANDLER, Morling GARDNER, Samuel CHANDLER, Asaph HOLMES, Samuel LORING, Allin DANFORD, Ezra PERKINS, W. STUDSON, George ADAMS, George FULLAR, Nayham BAILEY, Seth WASHBURN, Seth DREW, T. ADAMS, John GRAY Jr., Ezra CUSHMAN, Melzar WHITTIN, William FREEMAN, Nathaniel FAUNCE, Hiram TREBBLE, Joseph SIMONS, Jonathan GLASS, Rufus BRADFORD, David BEAL, John GLASS, Joseph HOLMES, John PORTER, Asa WESTON, Joseph WHITE, Levy LORING, Samuel BRADFORD, Nathaniel HOLMES. <79:320> Dower set off 15 May 1837 to **Harriet BRADFORD**, widow, viz: three acres bounded by land of Samuel BRADFORD, Bisbee CHANDLER and Levi LORING; one acre English meadow bounded by land of Arnold

FREEMAN, John GLASS and heirs of said dec'd; two and one quarter acres of Black Grass Meadow on east side of Island creek bounded by land of Samuel BRADFORD, Seth SPRAGUE Jr.; three acres wood land near dead swamp bounded by land of Asa WESTON, Wadworth CHANDLER, Seth SPRAGUE Jr., Briggs PETERSON. <79:322> Division of Real Estate 15 May 1837 by Levi LORING, Samuel BRADFORD, Joseph CHANDLER. The subscribers having notified all the heirs...set off to **Gershom BRADFORD 2d** as his full share of his Father's land. Witnesses: **Harriet BRADFORD,** Otis CHURCHILL. <89:566> Petition by **Otis C. BRADFORD** of Duxbury that he is interested, claiming, as one of the children & heirs at law, one sixteenth part or share as tenant in common with **Gershom BRADFORD, Harriet BRADFORD, Hannah BRADFORD, Lydia BRADFORD, Susan BRADFORD** - all of Duxbury, in the real estate not set off to the widow as dower. Order of Notice 1st Mon. Dec. 1846 and 3rd Mon. Jan. 1847, Levi LORING, Joseph CHANDLER and Joshua BREWSTER, all of Duxbury, app'td. Commissioners. <89:568> Warrant to Commissioners 18 Jan. 1847. Division as follows: except the widow's dower and a share which has previously been set off to **Gershom BRADFORD,** to **Otis BRADFORD,** and to **Harriet BRADFORD, Hannah BRADFORD, Lydia BRADFORD & Susan BRADFORD** who choose to hold their share together.

Estate of **Robert BRADFORD,** yeoman of Kingston. <Plymouth Co.PR #2596>
<46:276>...Letter 6 July 1818, Silvanus BRADFORD, of Gloucester RI, trader, app'td administrator. Sureties: Jeremiah SAMPSON, Benjamin WATERMAN, both of Kingston. Witnesses: Nathaniel BRADFORD, Beza HAYWARD. <49:363> Inventory. <50:134> Insolvency. <50:32> Petition to sell real estate 18 Jan. 1819. <50:292> Claims on estate examined. Order of Notice. <50:293> Claims 17 July 1819, viz: Dr. Paul L. NICHOLS, Bildad WASHBURN, Sarah CUSHING, J. & J. SEVER, Daniel BRADFORD, Ruth STAPLES, Sylvanus BRADFORD. Signed by Otis WATERMAN, Stephen BRADFORD. Account allowed.

Estate of **Ruth BRADFORD,** widow of Plymouth. <Plymouth Co.PR #2597>
<39:419>...Letter 26 June 1813, William BRADFORD, mariner of Plymouth, app'td administrator. Sureties: Josiah BRADFORD, mariner and Zacheus BARTLETT, both of Plymouth. Witnesses: Beza HAYWARD, Beza HAYWARD Jr. <45:416> Warrant 20 June 1814 to Jonathan TUFTS, yeoman, Lemuel BROWN, gentleman and Thomas PATY, mariner to appraise real estate whereof **William BRADFORD,** late of Plymouth, cordwainer, died seized and also the real estate whereof his widow **Ruth BRADFORD** died seized, and settle on one or more of their children. <45:414> Inventory 26 June 1813 (warrant), 10 July 1813 (oath of appraisers), 25 June 1814 (oath of adm.). <45:415> Account 25 June 1814.

Estate of **Samuel BRADFORD,** housewright of Duxbury. <Plymouth Co.PR #2601>
<46:153>...27 May 1816, **Prince BRADFORD,** gentleman, of Duxbury and son of dec'd app'td. adm., the widow, **Lydia BRADFORD** having declined. Sureties: Samuel BRADFORD, housewright of Duxbury, John DIXON, painter, of Plymouth. Witnesses: Beza HAYWARD, Experience HAYWARD. <48:153> Warrant to Appraise 27 May 1816 to Abijah FREEMAN & Isaiah ALDEN, yeomen of Duxbury, Melzar ADAMS, gentleman of Kingston. Inventory 1 July 1816, incl. half a pew in Rev. John Allyn's meeting house. <48:442> Account 15 Apr. 1817 by **Prince BRADFORD.** Paid: estate of Dr. Isaac BARTLETT, Samuel LORING's bill delivered to my mother the widow of said deceased, to my brother **Samuel BRADFORD,** to my sister **Eunice WESTON,** to my brother **George BRADFORD.**

Estate of **Sarah BRADFORD,** widow of Plymouth. <Plymouth Co.PR #2607>
<52:102>...Letter 21 Jan. 1822, LeBaron BRADFORD, gentleman, of Plymouth app'td adm. <original> Bond 21 Jan. 1822. Sureties: William DAVIS Jr., gentleman and Nathaniel M. DAVIS, Esq. both of Plymouth. Witnesses: N. HAYWARD, Beza HAYWARD.

Estate of **Sarah BRADFORD,** widow of Kingston. <Plymouth Co.PR #2608>
<71:255>...Letter 11 Aug. 1834, Charles BRADFORD, yeoman, of Kingston app'td adm. Sureties: Samual RING of Kingston, William BRADFORD of Plympton. Witness: J.H. LOUD. <75:153> Affidavit. <76:444> Inventory 21 Aug. 1834 by Peleg BRADFORD, Samuel RING, Ezra FULLER, of Kingston. <73:441> Petition to sell real estate 21 Jan. 1835, for payment of debts.

Estate of **Silvanus BRADFORD,** yeoman of Kingston. <Plymouth Co.PR #2611>
<original>...4 Jan. 1811, **Jane BRADFORD,** widow, asks to have John FAUNCE app'td adm. <39278>... Letter 7 Jan. 1811, John FAUNCE, Esq. of Kingston app'td. Sureties: Joel WHITE, Thomas FULLER, yeomen of Halifax. Witness: David BEAL. <43:399> Notice. <43:399> Estate insolvent 2 Apr. 1811. <43:399> Warrant to appraise 7 Jan. 1811 to Josiah COOK, Jeremiah SAMPSON, Robert COOK Jr., yeomen of Kingston. Inventory 2 Apr. 1811. <44:19> Warrant 7 Oct. 1811 to Judah WASHBURN, gentleman, Josiah COOK & Jeremiah SAMPSON, yeomen, all of Kingston, to assign dower to **Jane BRADFORD,** widow of dec'd. <44:40> Claims on estate 2 Apr. 1811. Paid: George RUSSELL, David BEAL Jr., Hezekiah RIPLEY, Samuel STETSON, Joseph ADAMS, Stafford STURTEVANT, David SMITH, Elkanah WASHBURN, Seth PERKINS, Elkanah COOK, Jacob FISH, Daniel CUSHMAN, John BARTLETT, Nathaniel CUSHMAN, Amos COOK, Caleb COOK, Rufus RING, James CUSHMAN, Zachariah BRIGDEN, Thomas BREWSTER, Cornelius DREW, Ezra D. MORTON, Charles HOLMES, Eunice COOK, Lemuel HOLMES, Henry HOLMES, Elisha STETSON, Zadock PACKARD, John FAUNCE, Josiah COOK. <44:20> Account 1 Nov. 1811. <44:348> Order of sale at public auction 2nd Mon. Jan. 1812. <original> Bond 6 Jan. 1812 of John FAUNCE, adm., to secure sale. Sureties: Ebenezer CUSHMAN, Eliezer FAUNCE, of Kingston. Witnesses: Robert CUSHMAN, Asa COOKE.

Will of **Stetson BRADFORD,** yeoman of Kingston. <Plymouth Co.PR #2616>
<63:84>...dated 14 Mar. 1810, being advanced in years; mentions wf **Lurana;** sister **Orpha;** children **William BRADFORD, Charles BRADFORD, Spencer BRADFORD, Betsey BRADFORD, Peleg BRADFORD, Zilpah WATERMAN.** Wife and son Peleg named executors. Witnesses: Martin PARRIS, Zenas FAUNCE, Elkanah CUSHMAN. <original> Consent of heirs signed by **Spencer BRADFORD, Zilpah WATERMAN, Levi WATERMAN, Betsey BRADFORD.** <63:86> Letter 16 Oct. 1826 appointing **Peleg BRADFORD** executor, he being the only surviving executor therein named. Bond 16 Oct. 1826. Sureties: Elkanah CUSHMAN, Robert

HOLMES, both of Kingston. Witness: P.W. WARREN.

Estate of **William BRADFORD**, cordwainer of Plymouth. <Plymouth Co.PR #2627> <39:427>...Letter 14 July 1813, William BRADFORD, mariner, of Plymouth app'td. administrator. Sureties: Zacheus BARTLETT, Esq., Josiah BRADFORD, mariner, both of Plymouth. Witnesses: Beza HAYWARD, Experience HAYWARD. <45:417> Division 25 June 1814. Real estate set off to children, viz: **William BRADFORD, Josiah BRADFORD Jr., Jesse BRADFORD, Deborah THOMAS** wf of Benjamin, they paying to **Abner HOLMES**, only heir of **Mary HOLMES**, dec'd, their sister.

Estate of **William BRADFORD**, yeoman of Plympton. <Plymouth Co.PR #2629> <original>...6 Apr. 1802, **Polly BRADFORD**, widow, requests that Asaph SOULE Jr. be app'td. adm. <34:311> Letter 6 Apr. 1802, Asaph SOULE Jr., yeoman of Plympton app'td. Sureties: Asaph SOULE Sr and John BRADFORD, yeomen of Plympton. Witnesses: Daniel MANLEY Jr., Zebedee SNELL. <38:134> Inventory 6 Apr. 1802, appraised by George SAMPSON, Zephaniah PERKINS, Oliver CHURCHILL, all of Plympton. <39:448> Letter 2 Apr. 1811, Oliver CHURCHILL app'td. adm., Asaph SOULE Jr. being disabled by infirmity of body. Sureties: Jeremiah SAMPSON, John PRINCE, yeomen of Kingston. Witness: Nathan ALDEN, Lot WHITMARSH. <43:421> Inventory 2 Apr. 1811 taken by Elijah BISBE, Esq., Perez BRADFORD, yeoman and Jonathan PARKER Jr., trader, all of Plympton. <45:57> Division 3 May 1813 of estate among children & heirs, viz: **Saba SHERMAN**, wf of Asa Jr., **William BRADFORD, Polly BRADFORD, Mercy BRADFORD**; incl. dwelling house; corn mill near John BRADFORD's; saw mill on Colchester Brook, Plympton; two and a half acres meadow adjoining land set off to John CHURCHILL, late of Plympton, now resident in Pittsfield, County of Berkshire; woodland; homestead farm & four acres in turkey swamp. <45:60> Order of Notice, 3 May 1813.

Estate of **William BRADFORD**, millwright of Plympton. <Plymouth Co.PR #2630> <10:176A>...Petition 29 May 1838 by **Salome BRADFORD**, widow. Decree appointing **Salome BRADFORD** administratrix. Bond 29 May 1838. Sureties: William H. SOULE of Plympton, Peter H. PEIRCE, of Middleboro. Witnesses: J.H. LOUD, Sidney TUCKER. <80:289> Inventory taken 18 June 1838 by Martin HAYWARD, William H. SOULE, Asa SHERMAN, all of Plympton. Real estate incl. homestead farm; 27 acres & buildings; Jones River Meadow, 4 acres; 6 acre wood lot near Barnabas Phinney; 9 acre wood lot near Asa SHERMAN; pew in Congregational Meeting House in Plympton. <5:50-J> Notice of appointment of administatrix posted 13 Aug. 1838. <2:88-O> Petition to sell real estate 25 Feb. 1839. <1:64-R> Bond to secure sale, 25 Feb. 1839. <81:261> 1st Account 28 May 1839 by admx. Paid to: Alexander HOLMES; Zadock CHURCHILL's note & interest; M. HAYWARD; William PERKINS; R.B. BRADFORD; J. PARKER; Z. SHERMAN; Z. PARKER; S. RING; N. BRIGGS; D. DOTEN; J. ADAMS; SAMPSON & PARKER; John T. ELLIS; Jas. THURBER; Dr. T.L. NICHOLS; Lydia BRADFORD; Asa SHERMAN; Isaac WRIGHT; J.H. LOUD. <11:489-B> Petition 7 July 1846, by William H. SOULE of Plympton to be appointed administrator, **Salome BRADFORD** having intermarried. Decree, Bond & Letter 6 Apr. 1847, William H. SOULE app'td. adm. Sureties: Jonathan PARKER, Isaiah CHURCHILL, both of Plympton. Witnesses: John T. ELLIS, Ira PARKER. <7:240> Notice 9 Aug. 1847, of appointment of adm.

Guardianship of Children of **William BRADFORD**, millwright, of Plympton. <Plymouth Co.PR #2632> <8:127-L>...Decree appointing William H. SOULE guardian of **Minerva BRADFORD & Mary M. BRADFORD**, minors under 14. <8:126-L> 7 Feb. 1839, **William BRADFORD**, minor above 14, chooses William H. SOULE as guardian. <86:36> Warrant 8 Dec. 1840, Isaac WRIGHT, Jonathan PARKER, Josiah T. ELLIS app'td. to appraise estate of **William, Minerva & Mary M. BRADFORD**, minors. Inventory 9 Jan. 1841, incl. interest received on Francis SOULE's note. <88:313> 1st Account 7 July 1846, of William H. SOULE, gdn. of **Minerva BRADFORD**, late of Plympton, who has recently become 21 years of age; incl. one half the amount of balance due from the estate of your brother **William BRADFORD**, dec'd; Dr. A.W. KINGMAN's bill, 7 Mar. 1844; certified to on 7 July 1846 by the widow and heir at law of the estate of **William BRADFORD**, millwright, late of Plympton. Signed by **Salome PACKARD, Apollos PACKARD, Minerva BRADFORD**. <88:315> 1st Account 7 July 1846 of William H. SOULE, gdn. of **William BRADFORD**, late of Plympton, minor, dec'd, incl. 25 Mar. 1844, SAMPSON & PARKER's bill; 2 July 1846, Deacon Ch. BUMPUS' bill. <92:294> Account 6 Aug. 1850 of William H. SOULE, gdn. of **Mary M. BRADFORD** now **Mary M. JOHNSON** of North Bridgewater, signed by **Mary M. JOHNSON, Edwin JOHNSON**.

Estate of **William L. BRADFORD**, mariner of Plymouth. <Plymouth Co.PR #2631> <11:152-B>...Petition 10 Apr. 1843. Decree, Letter & Bond 10 Apr. 1843, Zacheus SHERMAN app'td. adm. Sureties: Jonathan PARKER, Erastus LEACH, both of Plympton. Witness: J.H. LOUD. <85:341> Inventory 27 May 1843 by Martin HAYWARD, Asa SHERMAN, Earl STURTEVANT. <6:393-U> Notice of appointment published in the Old Colony Memorial.

Estate of **Winslow BRADFORD**, trader of Plympton. <Plymouth Co.PR #2633> <46:24>...Letter,Bond 9 Feb. 1814, Benjamin LUCAS, housewright, of Carver, app'td. adm. Sureties: Hamblen TILSON, cordwainer of Plymouth and Zillah BRADFORD, widow, of Plympton. Witness: Edward MILLER. <45:251> Warrant to appraise, 3 Feb. 1814 to Daniel SOULE, yeoman, of Plympton, Joshua COLE, gentleman & Ebenezer DOTEN, yeoman, both of Carver. Inventory 5 Feb. 1814 incl. two notes of hand with interest against Samuel BRADFORD. <45:252> Insolvency 9 Feb. 1814. <45:489> Account 13 Sept. 1814, incl. expenses of the funeral paid to Samuel BRADFORD, allowance to widow.

Guardianship of Children of **Capt. Lemuel BRADFORD Jr.** of Plymouth. <Plymouth Co.PR #2541> <41:201> Letter 3 Feb. 1815, Lemuel BRADFORD, gentleman, of Plymouth app'td. guardian of **Hitty Amelia BRADFORD** and **George Frederick BRADFORD**, minors uner the age of 14, children & heirs of **Lemuel BRADFORD Jr.**, late of Plymouth and lately a Captain in the Service of the United States, dec'd. Bond 3 Feb. 1815. Sureties: Nathaniel BRADFORD, Isaac LeBaron, both of Plymouth.

Estate of **James BRADFORD**, housewright, of Plymouth. <Plymouth Co.PR #2547> <71:395>...Letter/Bond 5 Apr. 1836, **Eleanor BRADFORD**, widow, app'td. admx. Sureties: Nathaniel C. COVINGTON mariner and Ellis DREW, both of Plymouth. Witnesses: Sarah P. DREW, Catherine D. COVINGTON. <78:135> Inventory taken 8 Apr. 1836 by Nathaniel WOOD, Nathaniel C. COVINGTON, Barnabas CHURCHILL, all of Plymouth. <75:357> Notice of app'td. of **Eleanor BRADFORD** as admx. published in Old Colony Memorial. <78:319> Insolvency 8 Aug. 1836. <79:35> List of Claims 20 Feb. 1837 by William Morton JACKSON and Anthony MORSE. Claimants: John TRIBBLE, NELSON & HARLOW, Samuel DOTEN, Lucy BRADFORD, John TRIBBLE & Co., Nathaniel RUSSELL & Co., Phineas LEACH, George W. VIRGIN, Freeman BARTLETT, Oliver T. WOOD, John BARTLETT, Benjamin BULLARD, Ruben PETERSON, Alvin VAUGHAN, Nathaniel CARVER, Hayward & WARREN, Silas REED, William J. BARTLETT, Zacheus BARTLETT, George P. FOWLER, Joseph W. HODGKINS, Thomas MAY, Lucas HOLMES & Co., John SANDERS, George ADAMS, John PERKINS, Simeon DYKE. <79:40> Dower assigned 20 Feb. 1837 to widow, one third part real estate, confirmed 15 May 1837. <2:37-O> Petition/Order to sell land 20 Feb. 1837. <79:365> Account 14 Aug. 1837, allowed by admx. Real estate sold to John BARTLETT, Seth BENSON, Henry SEYMORE, George HARLOW. Reversion of widow's dower to Nathaniel C. COVINGTON.

Guardianship of Children of **James M. BRADFORD** of Plymouth. <Plymouth Co.PR #2548> <original> Petition 8 Apr. 1850 by Joseph BRADFORD and Samuel D. HOLMES, both of Plymouth, praying for the appointment of a guardian of **James M. BRADFORD Jr.**, minor over 14, that his father is now without this Commonwealth & that his mother has recently deceased. <9:251-M> Decree 3rd Mon. May 1850, John PERKINS of Plymouth app'td. guardian of **James M. BRADFORD Jr.**, minor above 14 and **Johnson BRADFORD**, minor under 14, children of **James M. BRADFORD**. <9:251-M> Bond 20 May 1850 by John PERKINS. Sureties: Joseph BRADFORD, Samuel D. HOLMES, both of Plymouth. Witness: J.H. LOUD. Order for Citation to be served on **James M. BRADFORD Jr.**.

Will of **Jane BRADFORD**, singlewoman, of Kingston. <Plymouth Co.PR #2549> <48:206>...5 Apr. 1816, mentions brothers **Sylvanus BRADFORD, Robert BRADFORD, Noah BRADFORD** (youngest brother), sister **Ruth**; Mrs. Seth EVERSON, Sally WATERMAN, Mrs. SIMMONS, Selah BRADFORD. Witnesses: Sarah CUSHING, Sarah SAMSON, Hannah WATERMAN. <46:444> Letter/Bond 7 Oct. 1816, **Robert BRADFORD** of Kingston app'td. admr. Sureties: Stephen BRADFORD, potter and Benjamin WATERMAN,yeoman. Witnesses: Jeremiah SAMPSON, Beza HAYWARD. <48:207> Warrant to appraise 22 Aug. 1816. Inventory 7 Oct. 1816. <48:315> Affidavit of notice 7 Oct. 1816. <49:161> Account 5 Dec. 1817 by Robert BRADFORD, admr. Received from: Ichabod WATERMAN, Thomas BRADFORD, James BRADFORD. Paid to: Dr. NICKOLS, Levi COOK, B. WATERMAN, D. COOK, George THOMAS, R.C. & W. Man. Co., Spencer BRADFORD Josiah COOK, M. PARRIS, Stephen BRADFORD, Jeremiah SAMPSON, Peleg BRADFORD, N. CUSHMAN, Sally CUSHING, Sally WATERMAN, Cash to pay Ruth's legacy. <49:162> Receipts 26 Nov. 1817.

Will of **John BRADFORD**, gentleman, of Plympton. <Plymouth Co.PR #2556> <42:130>...30 May 1807, mentions wife **Eunice**; son **John BRADFORD**; eldest dau **Polly STANDISH**, wf of Ellis; 2nd dau **Eunice WASHBURN**, wf of Asa; daus. **Nancy BRADFORD, Suke BRADFORD, Sophe BRADFORD, Jane BRADFORD.** Witnesses: Caleb STETSON, Zadock CHURCHILL, Isaac CHURCHILL. <original> Bond 6 Jul 1807 by **John BRADFORD** of Plympton as executor. Sureties: Isaac CHURCHLL, yeoman and Jabez LORING, gentleman, both of Plympton. Witnesses: Jesse PERKINS, Nathan ALDEN.

Estate of **John BRADFORD**, gentleman, of Plympton. <Plymouth Co.PR #2557> <original>...1 Nov. 1831, **Betsey BRADFORD**, widow, declines administration and wishes Jonathan PARKER be appointed. <71:7> Letter/Bond 1 Nov. 1831, Jonathan PARKER app'td. Sureties: John BRADFORD, Zacheus PARKER, both of Plympton. Witnesses: Asa SHERMAN Jr., Polly S. PARKER. <70:469> Inventory taken 8 Nov. 1831 by Martin HAYWARD, Ebenezer WRIGHT, Zenas BRYANT Jr., of Plympton. Real estate incl. homestead farm in Plympton, 55 acres; 15 acre Bump lot; 23 acre sawmill lot; five sixteenths of a sawmill; Mack lot; half of 9 acre lot in Turkey Swamp; half of 5 acre salt marsh in Marshfield; two and a half acres of Cedar Swamp in Carver; Curchill Meadow, two and three quarter acres; 4 acres wood land by PHINNEY's; 7 acres swamp & meadow adjoining Stephen BONNEY's land; pew in Meeting house in Plympton. <72:544> Division 24 Apr. 1832 among eight children, viz: **Eunice FULLER**, wf of Philemon; **John BRADFORD; Daniel P. BRADFORD; Maria BRADFORD** (now **Maria LEACH**); **Patience P. BRADFORD; Thomas G. BRADFORD; William L. BRADFORD; Hannah BRADFORD.** <73:85> Petition to sell real estate 17 Feb. 1834. <76:51> Account 17 Feb. 1834. Real estate delivered to heirs, furniture to widow. Sold to: John BRADFORD, Joseph NYE, Jonah WELCH, Zaccheus SHERMAN, Jonathan PARKER, Hobart, Michell & Co., Lemuel RICKARD, Columbus TOMSON, Arnold LEACH, Ebenezer DEANE, Oliver PARKER Jr., Zenas CUSHMAN, Jeddediah HOLMES, Solomon RICHMOND, Nathaniel RUSSELL, James ELLIS, George C. WRIGHT, William TAYLOR, John A. PARKER, Southworth WRIGHT, Zenas CUSHMAN, Wennslow/Winslow WRIGHT, Otis WATERMAN. Paid to: Nathaniel SYLVESTER, Thomas LORING, Rufus WRIGHT, Daniel CHURCHILL Jr., Allen HOWLAND, George RUSSELL, Rufus BRADFORD, Elijah BISBE, Asa SHERMAN Jr., Isaac WRIGHT Jr., Barsillia WRIGHT, Josiah PERKINS, Jabez P. TOMSON, Polly GRAY, Zebedee CHANDLER, Isaac CHURCHILL, James ELLIS, Ezra PHINNEY, Cy( ) BUMPUS, John P. ELLIS, Leban OLNEY, Frederick JACKSON, HARLOW & NELSON, Thomas ADDAMS, George VIRGIN, Phineas WELLS, Jacob H. LOUD, Martin COOK, Joseph SHERMAN's wf, William H. SAMPSON & Co., Caleb LORING, Henry B. RODGERS, Lot THATCHER, Ezra S. WHITE, Samuel BRYANT, Isaac VAUGHAN, William WRIGHT, Thomas CUSHMAN, Nathan PERKINS, Philemon FULLER, Zenas CUSHMAN, Joseph ALLEN, James WADSWORTH, Bartlett ELLIS, Melvin BAILEY, Lemuel RICKARD, Joseph BATES, Daniel CHURCHILL, SHERMAN & LUCAS, George C. WRIGHT, Susannah ELLIS 2d, Ebenezer WRIGHT, Jonah WILLIS, William BRADFORD, Martin PERKINS, John BRADFORD, Martin HAYWARD, Samuel NICHOLS, George ADAMS, Hezekiah BRADFORD, Isaac BONNEY, Seth CHURCHILL, Ezekiel LORING, Zadock CHURCHILL, Zachariah EDDY, Nathan PERKINS of Halifax, Isaac PHILLIPS, Eleanah BARTLETT, Henry L. THOMAS, William PERKINS, Charles SHERMAN, Hiram STURTEVANT, Levi FISH, Erastus LEACH, Ezra D. MARTIN, Seth ALLEN, Dr. Paul NICHOLS, Josiah T. ELLIS, Warren LUCAS, Bela BOSWORTH, Ebenezer LOBDELL, Daniel RING, John A. PARKER, Josiah WRIGHT, Jonathan PARKER, John

BRADFORD, Daniel VICKERY, Widow Betsey BRADFORD, William BRADFORD 2d, Martin HAYWARD, Josiah T. ELLIS, Isaiah CHURCHILL, Martin HAYWARD, Zenas BRYANT, Ebenezer WRIGHT, Allen DANFORTH.

Guardianship of **Josiah BRADFORD**, labourer, of Plymouth. <Plymouth Co.PR #2560>
<49:290>...10 Apr. 1818, N. HAYWARD and Ichabod DAVIE, Overseers of the Poor of Plymouth, represent that **Josiah BRADFORD**, by reason of his imbecility, both of body & mind, is incapable of taking care of himself and family, pray that inquisition be made and a Guardian appointed. Warrant 11 Apr. 1818 by Judge of Probate, Joshua THOMAS, to Selectmen of the Town of Plymouth, viz: William HAMMATT, Nathan REED & William P. RIPLEY who adjudge **Josiah BRADFORD** incapable of taking care of himself. <41:357> Letter/Decree/Bond 18 Apr. 1818, Nathan HAYWARD app'td. guardian. Sureties: James THACHER, Physician and William S. RUSSELL, merchant, both of Plymouth. Witnesses: Beza HAYWARD, John S. HAYWARD. <54:163> Account 31 Dec. 1821, of Nathan HAYWARD, Guardian of **Josiah BRADFORD**, a United States Pensioner. Paid to: N. RIPLEY & Co., Mary DREW, T. COVINGTON and sundries & cash delivered to **Josiah BRADFORD** & wife. <57:512> Account 31 Dec. 1823. <58:536> 3nd Account 1 Jan. 1825. <60:483> 4th Account 1 July 1826. <64:446> 5th Account 1 Jan. 1828. <67:217> 6th Account 15 Nov. 1828.

Estate of **Bartlett BRADFORD**, gentleman of Plymouth. <Plymouth Co.PR #2500>
<original>...Request 16 Apr. 1821 by **Lucy BRADFORD**, widow, that W. James BRADFORD, housewright and Samuel BRADFORD, cooper, be app'td. admrs. Bond 16 Apr. 1821. Sureties: Solomon RICHMOND, tanner and Nathaniel RUSSELL, Esq., both of Plymouth. <52:37> Letter 16 Apr. 1821. <53:476> Warrant to appraise, 16 Apr. 1821, to Simeon DIKE, blacksmith, Rufus ALBERTSON, clothier and Solomon RICHMOND, tanner, all of Plymouth. <53:479> Order of notice posted 19 June 1821. Order to sell such personal estate of dec'd as the widow shall judge unnecessary to be retained for her own use & for use of her children. <original> Bond 30 Oct. 1822 by Samuel BRADFORD to convey real estate belonging to **Lewis G. BRADFORD, Bartlett BRADFORD, Barnes W. BRADFORD, Lucy B. BRADFORD** and **Eveline BRADFORD**, minors, as described in Petition of **Lucy BRADFORD**, their guardian. Sureties: William DAVIS, Nathaniel RUSSELL, Esq., both of Plymouth. Witnesses: N. HAYWARD, Beza HAYWARD, Experience HAYWARD, Susan HAYWARD. <56:233> Account allowed 20 May 1822, by James & Samuel BRADFORD. Received from John SAMPSON & Co. Paid to: Zack BARTLETT, Lot HASCAL, Charles BREWSTER, Ezra FINNEY, J.B. BATES, NELSON & HARLOW , DAVIS & RUSSELL, F. COBB, Esther ALBERTSON, Seth BENSON, J. SPOONER, J. AVERY, Dr. A. MACKIE, Elias THOMAS, Salsberry JACKSON, Ezra LUCAS, Dr. NICCOLS/NICHOLS, George SAMPSON, S. RICHMOND, Lucy HARLOW, H. TILESON, J. TRIBEL/TRIBBLE, James VAUGHAN, J. HARLOW, Silvanus BRETT, James MORTON, Brackley CUSHING, N. HAYWARD, S. DYKE, Elias THOMAS, Ellis BRADFORD, A.S. SILVESTER, Widow. <57:313> Oath of Samuel Bradford advertizing sale. <57:313> Account 15 Sept. 1823, of Samuel BRADFORD as agent on sale, in interest of minor children. <59:105> 2nd Account 15 Apr. 1825, of James & Samuel BRADFORD. Paid to: N. WOOD, William SPOONER, N. HAYWARD, John THOMAS, S. SPOONER, I.B. HEDGE, N. RUSSELL & Co., Richard HOLMES, William HARVEY.

Guardianship of Children of **Bartlett BRADFORD**, gentleman of Plymouth. <Plymouth Co.PR #2567>
<51:173>...Letter/Bond 21 May 1822, **Lucy BRADFORD**, widow, app'td. guardian of minors under 14, the children and heirs of **Bartlett BRADFORD**, dec'd., viz: **Lucy B. BRADFORD, Lewis G. BRADFORD, Evelina BRADFORD, Bartlett BRADFORD, James W. BRADFORD**. Sureties: Southworth SHAW, gentleman and Simeon DIKE, blacksmith, both of Plymouth. Witnesses: William S. RUSSELL, George F. COBB.

Estate of **Lyman BRADFORD**, sparmaker, of Duxbury. <Plymouth Co.PR #2573>
<10:315-**A**>...Petition 20 Jan. 1840 of **Isaiah BRADFORD** of Duxbury, sole heir-at-law, that William BRADFORD of Duxbury be app'td. admr. Decree/Bond 20 Jan. 1840, William BRADFORD app'td. Sureties: Gorham EMERSON of Duxbury and William R. DREW of Plymouth. Witness: Jabez P. THOMPSON.

Guardianship of Child of **George B. BRADFORD** of Kingston. <Plymouth Co.PR #2575>
<8:207-**L**>...18 Jan. 1841, **George B. BRADFORD** app'td. guardian of his dau **Martha D. BRADFORD**, minor under 14. Bond 18 Jan. 1841. Sureties: Rufus B. BRADFORD, William BRADFORD, both of Kingston. Witness: Joseph LOVERING.

Guardianship of Children of **William BRADFORD** of Plympton. <Plymouth Co.PR #2577>
<41:183>...Letter/Bond 5 Apr. 1814, Jonathan PARKER Jr., gentleman of Plympton, app'td. guardian of **Mary/Mercy BRADFORD**, minor above 14, (who chose him). <50:98> Account beginning 27 Jan. 1814/5 and allowed 18 Jan. 1819. Incl. paying Asa SHERMAN's share of the expense of **Polly BRADFORD** in her last sickness, 30 Jan. 1815; paying Hudson SOULE for gravestones for **Polly.** <47:417> Notice of Real Estate sale, Monday 30 Jan. 1815, at one o'clock P.M. at the house of Asa SHERMAN Jr., land belonging to **Mary BRADFORD**, a minor. <original> Bond to secure sale, 28 Dec. 1814 by Jonathan PARKER Jr., guardian. Sureties: Martin HAYWARD, Asa SHERMAN, both of Plympton. Witnesses: Cornelius CHURCHILL, Polly PARKER.

Will of **Perez BRADFORD**, gentleman of Duxbury. <Plymouth Co.PR #2590>
<38:96>...25 May 1802; mentions children **Samuel Cooper BRADFORD** and **Judith Cooper BRADFORD**, both under age; Gamaliel BRADFORD of Boston named executor and guardian of children; Sophia BRADFORD to have the care of my daughters; Seth BRADFORD. Witnesses: Daniel BRADFORD, Louisa DAWES, David SANDRAS. <original> Bond 2 June 1802 by Gamaliel BRADFORD. Sureties: Daniel BRADFORD, gentleman of Duxbury and William HICKLING, merchant of Boston. Witnesses: Elkanah WATSON, Isaac LOTHROP. <38:244> Inventory 16 June 1802 by Daniel BRADFORD, Enoch FREEMAN, William FREEMAN. Oath of Capt. Gamaliel BRADFORD 19 Jan. 1803.

Estate of **Bartlett BRADFORD** of Plymouth. <Plymouth Co.PR #2499>
<12:77-**C**>...Petition 1 May 1849 by **Caleb RIDER** of Plymouth, brother-in-law of dec'd. Decree/Bond

1 May 1849, **Caleb RIDER** app'td. admr. Sureties: Ellis DREW, Samuel C. BALDWIN, both of Plymouth. Witness: Lucy B. RIDER. <94:573> Account 1st Mon. Dec. 1852. Received from: L.G. BRADFORD, CADWELL, COGSHALL, S. BURBANKS, COLBY & CLARK, Southworth BARNES, D. MAYBURY. Paid to: H. MAGOUN, S. & J. BROWN, Dr. HUBBARD, James MORTON, LEXTON, Dr. WARREN, D. THURBER, Benjamin BRAMHALL, L.G. BRADFORD, J.H. LOUD, William H. JACKSON, William R. DREW, G. GARDNER, Ephraim WARD, M. BATES Jr. <95:155> Account allowed 2nd Mon. Apr. 1853.

Will of **Hezekiah BRADFORD**, mason of Plympton. <Plymouth Co.PR #2540>
<79:22>...26 Oct. 1836, mentions wife **Margaret** (named executrix), mother-in-law **Lydia BRADFORD.** Witnesses: Jonathan PARKER, Lewis BRADFORD, William PERKINS. <original> Declination 9 Jan. 1837, **Margaret BRADFORD** requests that Jonathan PARKER, Esq., of Plympton, be appointed executor. <10:484-**A**> Bond 16 Jan. 1837 by Jonathan PARKER, admr. Sureties: Joshua EDDY of Middleboro and Cephas WATERMAN of Kingston. Witness: J.H. LOUD. <75:440> Notice of appointment, 4 July 1837. Warrant for inventory 16 Jan. 1837, Ebenezer WRIGHT, William PERKINS, Zacheus SHERMAN, all of Plympton app'td. appraisers. <79:260> Inventory 3 Apr. 1837. <81:206> Account 20 May 1839 of Jonathan PARKER. Received from: Josiah PERKINS, Ebenezer LOBDELL, Zanus CUSHMAN, Samuel BRYANT, William S. EDDY, Martin PERKINS, William TAYLOR, Timothy CHURCHILL, Abial WASHBURN, Margaret BRADFORD, Nathan PERKINS. Paid to: Alexander CHURCHILL, Martin HAYWARD, William PERKINS, Oliver PARKER, Winslow WRIGHT, SAMPSON & ELLIS, George FULLER, Columbus THOMPSON, Elijah BISBE, Josiah T. ELLIS, Daniel CHURCHILL, Gracy BRADFORD, Isaiah CHURCHILL, Amus FULLER, Dr. Paul NICKOLS, Ebenezer WRIGHT, Z. SHERMAN, Zacheus PARKER, Zacheus SHERMAN.

Estate of **Charles BRADFORD**, mariner, of Plymouth. <Plymouth Co.PR #2503>
<12:39-**C**>...Petition 22 Jan. 1849 by Lemuel BRADFORD Jr. of Plymouth, who is requested by the sole heir-at-law to act as admr. Decree/Bond/Letter 22 Jan. 1849. Sureties: Lemuel BRADFORD, Harvey P. COLE, both of Plymouth. Witnesses: Lydia N. BRADFORD, William S. HOLMES. <92:4> Account 30 Jan. 1850 of admr. Balance paid to **Lemuel BRADFORD**, the sole heir-at-law.

Estate of **Charles BRADFORD**, nailer, of Plympton. <Plymouth Co.PR #2504>
<10:79-**A**>...Petition/Letter 10 Apr. 1837, **Caleb C. BRADFORD** of Kingston, asks to be app'td. admr. on his brother's estate. <original> Decree/Bond 10 Apr. 1837. Sureties: Lewis RIPLEY, Thomas S. CUSHMAN. Witness: J.H. LOUD. <79:543> Inventory taken 15 May 1837 by John BRADFORD, William BRADFORD, both of Plympton, and Timothy FRENCH of Kingston. <75:500> Affidavit 4 Dec. 1837. <82:247> Account by **Caleb C. BRADFORD.** Paid to: Alexander HOLMES, George RUSSELL, Paul L. NICHOLS, Bartlett BRADFORD, David DOTEN, HAYWARD & STURTEVANT, Martin HAYWARD, George A. BRADFORD, David CHURCHILL, Asaph HOLMES, R.B. BRADFORD, C.C. BRADFORD, Oliver EVERSON, Elkanah CUSHMAN, William BRADFORD, N. RUSSELL, Noah PRENCE, Julia BRADFORD.

Guardianship of **Abigail BRADFORD** of Duxbury. <Plymouth Co.PR #2493>
<8:4:7**L**>...Petition 2 Oct. 1838 by Benjamin ALDEN, J.F. WADSWORTH and Z. FAUNCE, Selectmen of Duxbury for a guardian for **Abigail BRADFORD,** insane person. Decree 1st Tues. Nov. 1838 appointing Silvanus SMITH, of Duxbury, guardian. <8:418-**L**> Bond 6 Nov. 1838. Sureties: George FRAZAR, Joseph A. SAMPSON, both of Duxbury. Witness: J.A. LOUD. <80:459> Inventory taken 20 Nov. 1838 by Benjamin ALDEN, Joseph F. WADSWORTH, Samuel CHANDLER, all of Duxbury. Real estate: about 2 acres salt & English meadow. <2:385> Petition to sell real estate, 1st Mon. Dec. 1838. <80:459> Order to sell real estate 3 Dec. 1838. <1:63-**R**> Bond to secure sale 21 Jan. 1839.

Estate of **Abraham/Abram BRADFORD**, yeoman of Plympton. <Plymouth Co.PR #2494>
<61:186>...Letter 14 Apr. 1828, **Deborah BRADFORD,** widow, app'td. admx. Bond 14 Apr. 1828. Sureties: Pelham HOLMES, Cephas BUMPUS, both of Plympton. Witness: P.W. WARREN. <66:113> Insolvency 19 May 1828. <66:112> Inventory taken 19 May 1828 by Zenas BRYANT Jr., Cephas BUMPUS and Pelham HOLMES. <66:312> Warrant to appraise 14 Apr. 1828. <66:228> Account 11 Aug. 1828. Paid to: Martin HAYWARD, Joseph SHERMAN, Cephas BUMPUS, Pelham HOLMES, balance to widow.

Guardianship of Children of **John BRADFORD**, yeoman of Plympton. <Plymouth Co.PR #2538>
<65:215>...Letter 20 Feb. 1832 appointing William PERKINS, yeoman, of Plymouth, guardian of the minor children of **John BRADFORD**, dec'd, viz: **Patience P. BRADFORD** (over 14), **Thomas G. BRADFORD** (over 14) and **William BRADFORD** (under 14). <65:216> Letter 20 Feb. 1832, appointing Erastus LEACH, yeoman, of Plympton, guardian of **Maria BRADFORD**, minor dau above 14. <65:217> Letter 20 Feb. 1832 appointing **Betsey BRADFORD**, widow, of Plympton, guardian of **Hannah BRADFORD**, minor dau under 14. "Revoked". <65:229> Letter 9 Apr. 1832 appointing William PERKINS guardian of **Hannah BRADFORD** above. <original> Bond 20 Feb. 1832 by William PERKINS, gdn. of **Patience P. BRADFORD, Thomas G. BRADFORD** and **William BRADFORD.** Sureties: Erastus LEACH, Martin HAYWARD, both of Plympton. Witnesses: Obadiah LYON, Jabez P. THOMSON. <original> Bond 20 Feb. 1832 by Erastus LEACH, gdn. of **Maria BRADFORD.** Sureties: Martin HAYWARD, William PERKINS, both of Plympton. Witnesses: Obadiah LYON, Jabez P. THOMSON. <original> Bond 20 Feb. 1832 by **Betsey BRADFORD** gdn. of **Hannah BRADFORD.** Sureties: Josiah T. ELLIS, Barzilla E. WRIGHT, both of Plympton. Witness: Jonathan PARKER. <original> Bond 9 Apr. 1832 by William PERKINS, gdn. of **Hannah BRADFORD.** Sureties: Jonathan PARKER, Erastus LEACH, both of Plympton. Witness: Samuel LEONARD Jr. <73:372> Petition to sell real estate allowed 9 Apr. 1832. <2:353-**O**> Petition to sell 20 Feb. 1837 by William PERKINS, gdn. of **William BRADFORD & Hannah BRADFORD,** to sell half of a dwelling house in Plympton. <8:117-**L**> Letter 2nd Mon. Aug. 1838 appointing Samuel W. TILLSON of E. Bridgewater, gdn. of **Hannah BRADFORD** minor over 14. Sureties: Isaac HATCH, Welcome YOUNG, both of E. Bridgewater. Witness: J.H. LOUD. <80:349> Account allowed 2 Oct. 1838 of William PERKINS, gdn. of **Hannah BRADFORD.** Received from: Erastus LEACH, Josiah WRIGHT, Martin BOSWORTH. Paid to: Jonathan PARKER, debts of **John BRADFORD**'s estate, Henry L. THOMAS, Isaac WRIGHT, John BRADFORD, Alexander CHURCHILL, Joseph NYE, Josiah T.

ELLIS, Hezekiah BRADFORD, Zacheus PARKER, Martin HAYWARD, Peter H. PEIRCE, Erastus LEACH, Otis WATERMAN, Aliab WASHBURN, Josiah WRIGHT, Joseph SHERMAN, James THURBER, Ebenezer WRIGHT. <81:52> Inventory taken 30 Dec. 1838 by Josiah T. ELLIS, Barzilla E. WRIGHT, Jonathan PARKER, all of Plympton, of estate of **Hannah BRADFORD**, minor. <1:80-**R**> Bond to secure sale, 2 July 1837 by Samuel TILLSON, gdn. of **Hannah BRADFORD**, minor under 21. Sureties: David KINGMAN, gentleman, Welcome YOUNG, Esq., both of E. Bridgewater. Witness: Spencer CUSHMAN. <2:396-**O**> Petition to sell real estate, 2 July 1839, one quarter of a dwelling house owned in common with **William BRADFORD**.

Estate of **Elizabeth BRADFORD**, widow, of Plympton. <Plymouth Co.PR #2520>
<39:97>...Bond/Letter 2 Jan. 1807 by Perez BRADFORD, admr. Sureties: Kimball PRINCE, John PRINCE, yeomen, of Kingston. Witnesses: Nathan ALDEN Jr., Isaac LOTHROP. <42:64> Inventory taken 7 Apr. 1807 by George SAMPSON, Isaac WRIGHT, Peleg WRIGHT, all of Plympton.

Estate of **Capt. Ellis BRADFORD**, master mariner, of Kingston. <Plymouth Co.PR #2522>
<original>...Request 30 Nov. 1848 to have Thomas RUSSELL app'td. administrator by the heirs at law, viz: **Priscilla BRADFORD, Dolly B. BRYANT, George B. BRADFORD, Rufus B. BRADFORD.** <12:34-**C**> Petition 4 Dec. 1848 for appointment of admr. Bond/Letter 4 Dec. 1848 by Thomas RUSSELL, admr. Sureties: J.N. SEVER, Joseph STETSON. Witness: Uriah BARTLETT. <7:407-**V**> Notice. Oath 15 Jan. 1849. <12:134-**C**> Warrant to appraise. <91:7> Inventory taken 7 Jan. 1849 by Thomas E. HOLMES, Samuel ADAMS, Joseph STETSON, all of Kingston. <92:1> Dower 12 May 1849 assigned to **Priscilla BRADFORD**, widow. <92:2> Account 30 Jan. 1850 by admr. Received from: William BRADFORD, George B. BRADFORD. Paid to: Charles ROBBINS, S. DREW, Edwin CUSHMAN, James PRATT, Seth TUPPER, R.B. BRADFORD, George T. ADAMS, F.C. ADAMS, Abigail TUPPER, P.L. NICHOLS, John PORTER, Thomas C. HOLMES, Samuel ADAMS, Joseph STETSON.

Guardianship of Child of **Nathaniel BRADFORD**, of Kingston. <Plymouth Co.PR #2529>
<8:43-**L**>...Decree 10 Apr. 1837, Caleb C. BRADFORD of Kingston, app'td. gdn. of **George A. BRADFORD** minor over 14, son of **Nathaniel BRADFORD**, late of Kingston, dec'd, said minor having declared his choice. Bond/Letter 10 Apr. 1837 by guardian. Sureties: James N. SEVER, Lewis GRAY, both of Kingston. Witness: J.H. LOUD.

Estate of **Gershom BRADFORD**, Esq. of Duxbury. <Plymouth Co.PR #2531>
<original>...Request 24 Aug. 1844 to have Gershom B. WESTON of Duxbury app'td. administrator by the widow and heirs, viz: **Sarah B. BRADFORD, Lucia A. BRADFORD, Elizabeth H. BRADFORD, Charlotte BRADFORD, Maria W. BRADFORD.** <11:274-**B**> Decree/Bond 27 Aug. 1844 of admr. Sureties: William ELLISON of Duxbury, Alden B. WESTON of Boston. Witnesses: W.H. FAIRFIELD, George C. WESTON. <11:274-**B**> Warrant to appraise 27 Aug. 1844. <86:566> Inventory taken last Tues. Nov. 1844 by John HICKS, William ELLISON, Josiah MOORE, all of Duxbury. <6:558-**U**> Notice of appointment 26 Nov. 1844. <87:117> Account 14 Apr. 1845 by admr. Received from: J.S. THOMAS, Nathaniel WINSOR. Paid to: Martin SAMPSON, Nathan C. BREWSTER, James WESTON Jr., Otis WESTON, William FREEMAN, Barker HUNT; one third balance to widow, one quarter each to **Maria W. BRADFORD, Lucia A. BRADFORD, Elizabeth H. BRADFORD, Charlotte BRADFORD.** Receipt signed 5 Mar. 1845 by all five.

Guardianship of Children of **Prince BRADFORD** of Duxbury. <Plymouth Co.PR #2532>
<8:49-**L**>...Decree 10 Apr. 1837 appointing **Harriet BRADFORD** gdn. of her children, **Harriet BRADFORD** and **Otis BRADFORD**, minors over 14 (they having chosen their mother), and **Hannah B. BRADFORD, Lydia BRADFORD, Susan BRADFORD**, minors under 14, the children of **Prince BRADFORD**, late of Duxbury, dec'd. Bond/Letter 10 Apr. 1837 of gdn. Sureties: Otis CHURCHILL of Plymouth, Samuel BRADFORD of Duxbury. Witness: Gershom BRADFORD. <8:48-**L**> Decree 10 Apr. 1837 appointing Otis CHURCHILL of Plymouth gdn. of **Gershom BRADFORD**, minor over 14, said minor having declared his choice. Bond/Letter of gdn. 10 Apr. 1837. Sureties: Oliver SAMPSON of Kingston, Sylvanus PRIOR of Duxbury. Witness: J.H. LOUD.

Will of **Gideon BRADFORD**, gentleman of Plympton. <Plymouth Co.PR #2534>
<40:224>...22 Mar. 1805, mentions wife **Abigail**, seven children: **Zabdiel BRADFORD; Abram BRADFORD; Isaac BRADFORD;** to **Gideon BRADFORD** (land I bought of my brother **Calvin BRADFORD**, two lots of land I bought of Isaac JACKSON and a piece of wood land between **Calvin BRADFORD's** and Isaac JACKSON's land); **Abigail BRADFORD, Sampson BRADFORD, William BRADFORD.** Wife **Abigail** and son **Zabdiel** named executors. Witnesses: George SAMPSON, Elijah BISBE, Huldah STURTEVANT. <40:226> Pr. 6 May 1805. <original> Bond 6 May 1805 by executors. Sureties: Elijah BISBE, Esq., George SAMPSON, yeoman, both of Plympton. Witnesses: Job DREW, Isaac LOTHROP. <40:316> Inventory taken 4 Nov. 1805 by Elijah BISBE, Esq., George SAMPSON, Isaac WRIGHT, all of Plympton. Notes of Henry KNOX, Esq., Peleg SAVERY.

Will of **Hannah BRADFORD**, widow/single woman of Plymouth. <Plymouth Co.PR #2537>
<58:301>...6 Jan. 1821, mentions nephew **Nathan PERKINS**; sisters **Lois PERKINS, Mercy PERKINS**; nephew **Solomon BRADFORD**; nieces **Mercy PERKINS, Priscilla PERKINS.** William P. RIPLEY named executor. Witnesses: Nathaniel RIPLEY Jr., John S. PAINE, William P. RIPLEY. Pr. 9 Aug. 1824. <original> Bond 10 Aug. 1824 by William Putnam RIPLEY, merchant (executor). Sureties: Henry JACKSON, blacksmith, Ezra COLLIER, book seller, both of Plymouth. Witnesses: Beza HAYWARD, William S. RUSSELL. <55:242> Order of notice 9 Aug. 1824. <58:382> Inventory taken 9 Aug. 1824 by Ichabod DAVIE merchant, Lemuel BROWN, gentleman and elnathan S. HOLMES, gentleman, all of Plymouth.
(**Note:** Hannah BRADFORD is called both widow and single woman in the probate records.)

MICRO #2 of 15

Will of **Gamaliel BRADFORD**, Esq. of Duxbury. <Plymouth Co.PR #2528>
<42:19>...7 Mar. 1796, mentions unnamed wife, children: **Perez BRADFORD, Sophia BRADFORD, Gamaliel BRADFORD, Alden BRADFORD, Daniel BRADFORD, Gershom BRADFORD, Sarah BRADFORD, Jerusha WESTON**; sons **Perez & Gamaliel** named executors. Witnesses: John ALLYN, George PARTRIDGE, Enoch FREEMAN. Codicil 15 June 1802 names wife, sons **Alden** and **Gamaliel**, son **Perez** dec'd, to grandchildren **Samuel Cooper BRADFORD** and **Judith Cooper BRADFORD** the four shares of my estate which I gave their father in my foregoing will; son **Gamaliel** named executor. Witnesses: Rev. John ALLYN, Enoch FREEMAN, George PARTRIDGE. <43:21> Probate 31 Jan. 1807. <original> Bond 26 Feb. 1807 by **Gamaliel BRADFORD**, gentleman, of Boston, executor. Sureties: Ezra WESTON Jr., merchant, of Duxbury and James THACHER, Physician, of Plymouth. Witnesses: John B. THOMAS, Isaac LOTHROP. <42:21> Notice 17 July 1807. <42:22> Inventory taken 26 Apr. 1807 by Samuel LORING, Enoch FREEMAN, David SAUNDRES/SANDERS. Receipt dated 10 May 1807, signed by executor.

Guardianship of Children of **James BRADFORD** of Plymouth. <Plymouth Co.PR #2517>
<8:193-L> Appointment 2nd Mon. Aug. 1840 of Ellis DREW of Plymouth, as guardian of **Eleanor BRADFORD** and **James H. BRADFORD**, minors above 14, and **Nathaniel BRADFORD**, minor under 14, the children of **James BRADFORD** of Plymouth. <8:193-L> Bond/Letter 10 Aug. 1840. Sureties: Nathaniel RUSSELL Jr. and Henry SEYMORER, both of Plymouth. Witness: Willard WOOD. <83:25> Inventory taken 3rd Mon. Jan. 1841 by Simeon DIKE, John WASHBURN, Barnabas CHURCHILL, all of Plymouth, incl. all the interest in the dwelling house bought of Nathaniel COVINGTON by **Eleanor BRADFORD.** <86:378> Account 12 Aug. 1844 by Ellis DREW, gdn. Paid to: Clement BATES, L. HUBBARD, L. BARNES, N. WOOD, HAYWARD & WARREN, T. GORDON, N. RUSSELL, P. MORTON, A.G. NYE, Eleanor BRADFORD, A. COVINGTON, S. BARNES, J.W. HODGKINS, S.D. HOLMES. <9:1-M> Appointment 2nd Mon. Aug. 1844 of **James H. BRADFORD**, of Roxbury as guardian of **Nathaniel BRADFORD**, minor under 14. Bond/Letter 12 Aug. 1844. Sureties: Nathaniel C. COVINGTON, Ellis DREW, both of Plymouth. Witness: **Eleanor BRADFORD.** <86:379> Inventory taken 13 Aug. 1844 by Nathaniel C. COVINGTON, Ellis DREW, Nathaniel WOOD.

Will of **David BRADFORD**, yeoman, of Kingston. <Plymouth Co.PR #2512>
<1:134-G>...27 Aug. 1839...to Francis DREW of Kingston, my English & Black grass meadow lying on Tussock Brook together with my wood lot near Howland SAMPSON's; Sarah BAILEY, wife of Wood BAILEY of Kingston; Thomas B. DREW, son of Job W. DREW of Kingston; parents of said Thomas DREW; Julius G. GLYNN, grandson of Joseph BARTLETT of Kingston. Eli COOK named executor. Witnesses: Samuel E. CUSHMAN, Daniel F. JOSSELYN, Deborah S. COOK. Pr. 3rd Mon. May 1840. <82:304> Inventory sworn to 10 Aug. 1840 by Seth DREW, George ADAMS, Samuel E. CUSHMAN, all of Kingston. <6:85-U> Notice 10 Aug. 1840. <83:335> Account 31 May 1841 of executor. Received from: Francis DREW. Paid to: David B. BARTLETT, Elkanah CUSHMAN, Ward BAILEY, Dr. P.L. NICHOLS, S.E. CUSHMAN, D.F. JOCELYN, George STETSON, Hiram TRIBBLE, Joseph BAILEY, Joseph BARTLETT, Sarah BAILEY.

Guardianship of Child of **Charles BRADFORD**, mariner, of Plymouth. <Plymouth Co.PR #2513>
<41:79> Letter 10 Apr. 1811 appointing Isaac DUNHAM, mariner, of Plymouth, guardian of **David BRADFORD**, minor above 14, son of **Charles BRADFORD**, late of Plymouth, dec'd. <original> Bond 10 Apr. 1811 by guardian. Sureties: Salisbury JACKSON, Charles BRADFORD, rope makers of Plymouth. Witnesses: Beza HAYWARD, Experience HAYWARD.

Estate of **Consider BRADFORD**, mariner, of Kingston. <Plymouth Co.PR #2508>
<52:404> Bond/letter 17 Oct. 1825 by **Betsey BRADFORD**, widow, as admx. Sureties: James BRADFORD, housewright, Southworth SHAW, blacksmith, both of Plymouth. Witnesses: Pelham W. WARREN, Lucy BRADFORD. <59:493> Insolvency 17 Oct. 1825. <60:330> Appointment of Commissioners 17 Oct. 1825, viz: Jedediah HOLMES, Anchor SMITH, George RUSSELL, of Kingston. <60:91> Inventory taken 11 Dec. 1825 by Jedediah HOLMES, Josiah COOK, brick layer, Thomas BRADFORD, housewright, all of Kingston. <55:364> Notice 3 Jan. 1825. <60:92> Widow's Allowance 3 Jan. 1826, $142.00. <60:331> Warrant to assign dower 3 Jan. 1826 to Jedediah HOLMES Jr., blacksmith, Josiah COOK Jr., brick layer and Thomas BRADFORD, housewright. <60:332> Dower 27 Mar. 1825. <60:330> List of Claims 15 May 1826, to Wiswal S. STETSON, Paul L. NICHOLS, Thomas BRADFORD, Ellis BRADFORD, Gains HOLMES, Seth EVERSON, Melzar WHITTON, Benjamin DELANO, Thomas WINSOR & Co., Josiah WILLIS. <60:332> Sale of real estate 15 May 1826 by admx. <60:485> Account allowed 17 July 1826. Received from: James SPOONER, James BRADFORD Jr. Paid to: Jedediah HOLMES Jr., J. COOK Jr., Thomas BRADFORD, J. MELAUTHLIN, Allen DANFORTH.

Will of **Noah BRADFORD**, mariner, of Plymouth. <Plymouth Co.PR #2585>
<10:363>...16 Apr. 1746, everything to wife **Hannah**, executrix. Witnesses: Nathaniel DUNHAM Jr., Ezekiel DUNHAM, James RICHARD. Pr. 3 Mar. 1746. <10:424> Inventory taken 23 May 1747 by Thomas FOSTER, Nathan DELANO, Thomas DOTEY. <10:426> Insolvency 26 May 1747. <11:264> List of Claims 26 May 1747, viz: Samuel CLARK, Capt. Gershom BRADFORD, Timothy TRUMBALL of Charlestown, Joseph MORTON Jr. <11:168> Dower to widow 19 Aug. 1748. <12:368> Account of **Hannah POTTER**, late **Hannah BRADFORD**, executrix, 22 July 1749.

SUFFOLK COUNTY PROBATE: (re: BRADFORD)

1739	Abigail	#7383, gdn.	1876	Ann	#27405, adm.
1843	Alden	#33808, adm.	1891	Arthur R.	#88231, adm.
1645	Alexander	#36, will	1876	Augustus	#59304, adm.
1824	Ann	#27405, adm.	1731	Benjamin	#6067, will

SUFFOLK COUNTY PROBATE, cont-d: (re: BRADFORD)

1845	Charles	#34447, adm.	1739	Joseph	#7385, gdn.
1852	Charles	#37697, adm.	1782	Joseph	#17757, will
1887	Charles F.	#78277, adm.	1787	Joseph	#18980, will
1874	Clara	#55775, trust	1847	Joseph	#35335, will
1886	Daniel L.	#75097, will	1808	Joseph N.	#23276, gdn.
1887	Duncan	#77431, will	1849	Joseph N.	#35939, gdn.
1882	Edwin M.	#67210, gdn.	1867	Joseph N.	#47593, adm.
1739	Elizabeth	#7384, gdn.	1825	Julia C.	#27456, gdn.
1789	Elizabeth	#19274, adm.	1886	Julia E.	#76092, will
1789	Elizabeth	#19411, gdn.	1856	Justus F.	#40773, adm.
1852	Elizabeth	#37809, adoption	1825	Katherine B.	#27542, adm.
1885	Elviza	#73163, will	1846	LeBaron	#34922, will
1867	Emeline T.	#47861, will	1792	Margaret	#19867, adm.
1866	Frank T.	#47416, adm.	1852	Margaret	#38751, adm.
1857	Franklin M.	#41021, gdn.	1825	Martin L.	#27457, gdn.
1858	Frederick A.	#41832, adm.	1878	Rebecca	#62194, will
1882	Frederick J.	#67210, gdn.	1852	Rebecca E.	#37915, gdn.
1839	Gamaliel	#32316, will	1853	Rebecca E.	#38334, adm.
1890	George H.	#84220, adm.	1680	Robert	#-----, will
1884	George R.	#72302, adm.	1792	Rufus	#19883, adm.
1851	Granville W.	#37127, will	1815	Samuel	#24633, "cancelled"
1754	Hannah	#12505, will	1818	Samuel	#25649, adm.
1869	Hannah	#49610, will	1810	Samuel C.	#23516, adm.
1878	Harriet M.	#61437, will	1886	Samuel D.	#75069, gdn.
1891	Henry W.	#88817, gdn.	1825	Sarah	#27772, adm.
1742	Hepzibah	#7699, gdn.	1874	Sarah	#56273, gdn.
1874	Isabella T.	#55667, adm.	1885	Sarah	#72808, will
1740	James	#7510, adm.	1888	Sarah	#79036, adm.
1742	James	#7700, gdn.	1875	Susan	#56564, adm.
1789	Job	#19275, adm.	1762	Thomas	#13069, adm.
1735	John	#6708, will	1887	Thomas G.	#77418, will
1784	John	#18227, will	1825	William B.	#27458, gdn.
1828	John H.	#28642, will	1835	William B.	#30783, will
1885	John H. Jr.	#73293, gdn.	1865	William B.	#46209, will
1865	John R.	#46086, will	1742	Williams	#7701, gdn.
1867	John R.	#47733, adm.	1871	Willie Harrison	#51938, adoption

---

JOHN BRADFORD[2] (William[1])

Will of **Thomas BOURNE**, draper, of Marshfield. <Plymouth Co.PR 2:2:20>
...2 May 1664...I give unto my daughter **BRADFORD** according to my promise, twenty pounds to be payed her in corne or cattle or goods and also I give her my wifes gould ringe. Pr. 2 June 1664.

Gov. William BRADFORD to **John BRADFORD.** <Plymouth Co.Deeds 3:1>
...1649...I have given unto my son John BRADFORD, and alreddy possesed him therof; all that land I bought of Constant SOUTHWORTH for which I have payed Ł12...and since have built an house theron which cost mee upward of Ł34...since confeirmed unto the said John BRADFORD by Mistris **Allis BRADFORD Sr.**, 1658.

Alice BRADFORD Sr. of Plymouth to **Ralph ALLEN** of Sandwich. <Plymouth Co.Deeds 2:2:131B>
...1663, Alice BRADFORD Sr. to Ralph ALLEN, half of certain lands of which she had given half to son **John BRADFORD.** Signed by "A B" (her mark).

MERCY BRADFORD[2] (William[1])

Estate of **Benjamin VERMAYES/FEIRMAYES.** <Essex Co.PR 1:514>
Inventory taken 26 9th mth 1666 by the desire of the widow **ESTWICK**; land in Marblehead between John GIDNEY's and Goodman POTER ...**Esther ESTWICK** did intrust in the hands of Benjamin VERMAYES one cowe valued at five pounds.<1>

1668, 23 12th mth, Esther EASTWICK, admx. on estate of Edward EASTWICK. <Essex Co.Deeds 3:50>
1669, 8 4th mth, Edward EASTWICK, estate. <Essex Co.Deeds 3:61>
1668, 23 12th mth, Esther EASTWICK, adm. <Essex Co.Deeds 3:50>
1669, 8 4th mth, Esther EASTWICK, adm. <Essex Co.Deeds 3:61>
1696, 17 Feb. , Esther EASTWICK et al, adm. <Essex Co.Deeds 11:204>
1705, 15 Aug. , Esther EASTWICK et al. <Essex Co.Deeds 18:99>
17-5, 11 Feb. , Esther EASTWICK, estate. <Essex Co.Deeds 88:57>

WILLIAM BRADFORD[2] (William[1])

Will of **James FITCH Sr.** of Norwich. <New London CT PR #2013>
...7 Feb. 1695/6, mentions unnamed wife, children: **James FITCH, Abigail, Elizabeth, Hannah, Samuel FITCH; Nathaniel BISSELL,** hus of dau **Dorothy; Daniel FITCH, John FITCH, Jabez FITCH, Nathaniel FITCH, Joseph FITCH, Eliezer FITCH, Anne.** Capt. Samuel MASON and Lt. Daniel MASON, brothers of wife, named executors. Codicil July 1697. Pr. 4 Dec. 1702. Inventory sworn to 2 Dec. 1702 by **Mrs. Priscilla FITCH.**

William BRADFORD of Plymouth to **Elisha & Timothy BOURNE** of Sandwich.<2>
...4 Jan. 1688. To All People unto whom these presents shall Come Greeting etc.: whereas the Honorable the Councill established at plimoth in the County of Devon for the planting Ruling ordering and Governing of New England in America, by vertue and authority of Letters pattents under the great seale of England from our late Sovreign lord King James the first Bearing Date At Westminster in the Eighteenth yeare of his said Majetis Reign of England etc. ffor and in consideration that **William BRADFORD** Esq. and his assosciats had att their own proper Cost and Charges planted and inhabited a Town Called by the Name of New plimoth in New England aforesd and for their better subsistence and incouragement to proceed in so pious a work especially tending to the propagation of Religion and the great incouragment of Trade to his Majtis Realme and the advancement to the publique plantation: The said Councill by their patent or Grant under their Comon seale signed by the Right Honorable Robert Earle of Warwick president of said Councill Bearing date the thirteenth day of January in the fifth year of the Reign of our late Soveraign lord King Charls the first Annoque Domini 1629 did give grant enfeoffe Assign and Confirm unto the said **William BRADFORD** his heires assosciats and assigns for ever all that part of New England in America aforesaid and Tract and Tracts of Land that lys within or between a certeyn Rivolet or Rundlet there comonly called Cohasset Alias Conihassitt towards the north and the River Comonly Called Narragansett River towards the sourth and the great weastern Ocean toward the east and Betweene and within other lyns and limitts in said pattent or Grant more at large expressed and all lands Rivers waters havens creeks ports ffishings, and all heridittaments proffitts and Comodites scituate lying being, or arising within or betweene any the sd limitts and bounds togeather with all Rights Royalties priviledgis etc. as in and by the said grant whereinto Reference being had doth and may more at larg appear And whereas Divers percells of said Lands have for the ends aforesaid Been Granted by the said **William BRADFORD** or his Declared assosciats or assigns by power Dirived from him unto sundry perticuler persons who by virtue of said Grants have had for many years the quiet and peacable possession thereof And yet for want of some Niceties and formalities of law not so precisely observed in their first and new beginings Divers questions and Debaits may arise about the title of the severall Grantees unto the lands granted as aforesd amongst others a certeyn percell and percells of Lands Granted to **Elisha BOURNE** and **Timothy BOURNE** Both of Sandwich or to their predicessors (whose Right therein hath for many years been quietly and peaceably possessed by them the said **Eisha BOURNE** and **Timothy BOURNE** and their predicessors and is now in the quiet possession of the said **Elisha BOURNE** and **Timothy BOURNE**) for the more sure making whereof now KNOW YEE That I **William BRADFORD** of New plimoth In the County of plimoth and In the Collony of plimoth In New England aforesd Esq. son and heire of the above named **William BRADFORD** Esq., Deceased as well in performance of the true Intent and meaning of the said **William BRADFORD** my ffather in the said Grant and for the ends abovementioned as for Divers other good Causes and Considerations me at this time especially moving HAVE granted remised released and for ever quitt Claimed and by these presents for me and my heires do grant remise release and for ever quitt Claime unto the said **Elisha BOURNE** and **Timothy BOURNE** in their full and peaceable possession and seisin now being and to their heires and assigns for ever All such right estate Title interest possession and demand whatsoever which I the said **William BRADFORD** ever had now have, or ought to have, in, or to, All and singuler the Messuages land Tenements Grounds Soyles waters rivers Creeks ffishings Hereditaments royalties mineralls proffits priveledgis and comodities whatsoever scituate lying and being arising happening or Acreuing or which shall arise happen or acrue in or within the limitts and Bounds of a certaine percell and percells of land lying and being on both sides of the River called the Herring river alies Maniment river within the Township of Sandwich aforesd and In the Colony aforesaid and are limmeted and bounded as followeth, viz: one percell of land lying and being on the westerly side of said Herring river being by estemation three hundred acres be it more or less bounded northerly by a straight lyne extending from the month of the hering river pond so called westerly unto the most westerly end of ye pond that is nearest to the place called naquansitt and westerly is bounded partly by a straight line extending from the westerly end of the pond last mentioned southerly unto a little Brook that runs into said naquansitt bay and partly by the salt water from that said Brooke unto the lower end of the Neck called Maniment Neck and Southerly bounded by maniment river or the Hering river aforesd and easterly by sd Herring river unto the mouth of the pond first mentioned called the herring river pond only saving the Indyans rights in the land on the sd neck called maniment neck and one small percell of lands more lying and being on the most southerly side of said river being by estimation threescore acres be it more or less, bounded northerly by the high way called road Island way from a marked oak tree standing near said High way as the way goes unto the said Hering river and so bounded westerly by sd river untill it comes to a little Brooke that issus into said river near maniment westerly from the now dwelling house of said **Elisha BOURNE,** and southerly is bounded from said Brook by the edg of the hills untill it come to the head of a little Brooke issuing out below sd hills and easterly is bounded from the head of said Brooke on a straight line unto the the first mentioned marked oak tree: so that is to say. That neither I the said **William BRADFORD** nor my heires from henceforth shall or may have or claime any right title estate interest or demand, of, in, or to, the said pmises or any of them, but thereof shall for

ever hereafter be and excluded by these presents. KNOW YEE further also that I the said **William BRADFORD** for the considerations and ends aforesaid HAVE Approved and by these pres(ents) do for me and my heires as much as in me lyeth ratifie and confirme unto the said **Elisha BOURNE** and **Timothy BOURNE** in their full and peaceable possession and seisen and (to) their and each of their heires and assigns for ever, All and singuler the aforesaid lands and other the premises with their and every their appurtinances: within the said bounds and limitts TO HAVE AND TO HOLD to the said **Elisha BOURNE** and **Timothy BOURNE** and to each of them their & eche of their heires and assigns for ever in maner and forme following viz: TO HOLD in comon all such wast lands within the said limitts as yet lye in comon and undivided for herbage firewood or such like comon use untill they shall see cause otherwise to order the same. And to hold in seaveralty and not joyntly to each of them All and every such Messuage Teniment and lands as eche or either of them are severally and perticulerly possessed of in eche one of their perticuler and severall right and interest therein respectively according to the known and accustomed bounderies thereof, and accordingly to eche and every of their heires and assigns for ever and to the only proper use and beheofe of them and eche of them their heires and assigns respectively for ever TO BE HOLDEN of his Majetis as of his manner of East Greenwich in the County of Kent In the Realm of England in free and Comon Soccage and not in Capite nor Knights service YEILDING and paying to our soveraign Lord & King his heires and successors for ever one fifth part of the care of the mines of Gold and silver, and one other fifth part thereof to the said president and Concill which shall be had possessed and obteyned within the limits afforesaid for all services and demands whatsoever as is expressed in said patent or Grant of said Councill. And I the said **William BRADFORD** and my heires all and singuler the said premises with the appurtinances to the aforesaid **Elisha BOURNE** and **Timothy BOURNE** their and each of their heires and assigns respectively, against me the said **William BRADFORD** and my heires will for ever hereafter warrant and Defend by those presents. (only two small percels of meadow ground lying and being on the northerly side of said maniment river within limitts aforesd excepted one percell thereof being in the occupation of **Jacob BURG** lying for two acres, and the other percell is in the occupation of **Ezra PERRY Jr.** lying for three acres according to the known and accustomed bounderies of eche (percell) In WITNESS whereof I have hereunto set my hand and seale the fourth day of january Anno Domd 1688 Annoque R:Rs Jacobi secundi quarto...with the words "only saving the Indyans right in the land on the said Neck called maniment Neck" enterlined over the one and thirtieth line before the sealling & delivering hereof Signed by **William BRADFORD.** Witnesses: John HATHWAY Sr., Rowland COTTON, William BASSITT.

MICRO #3 OF 15

Will of **Daniel STEEL** of Hartford CT. <Hartford CT PR #5173>
...7 July 1785, stricken in years, mentions wife **Mary**, children: **Timothy STEEL; Lemuel STEEL; Thomas STEEL; Mary GOODWIN; Welthey**, late wife of Asher SHELDON; **Submit BURR**, wf of William. Pr. 1 Apr. 1788. 4 Mar. 1811...That part of real estate of **Daniel STEEL** late of Hartford, dec'd that lies in common between his two sons **Lemuel STEEL** and **Thomas STEEL** and the heirs of **Roswell STEEL.**

Estate of **Capt. John WEBSTER** of Farmington CT. <Hartford CT PR #5767>
Inventory taken 6 Sept. 1753 by Jared LEE and John BELL. (no record of will).

Will of **Thomas HOSMER** of Hartford CT. <Hartford CT PR #2914>
...1 Jan. 1777, mentions wife **Susanna**, children: **Susanna KELLOGG**, wf of Joel; **Ruth KELLOGG**, wf of Ephraim; **Jerusha HOSMER; Thomas HOSMER; Eldad HOSMER; Daniel HOSMER; Elisha HOSMER; Simeon HOSMER** and **Ashbel HOSMER**; to grand-daughter **Susanna KELLOGG** when 18, if she lives with her grand-mother. Pr. 24 Feb. 1777. Inventory taken 5 Mar. 1777 by Benjamin COTTON, John WHITMAN Jr., (Morgin?) GOODWIN, total Ł1277.8.10.

Estate of **Samuel STEEL Sr.** <Hartford CT PR #5198>
Bond 2 Jan. 1709/10 by administrators **Thomas STEEL** and **William STEEL.** Surety: **James STEEL.** Inventory taken 21 Feb. 1709/10. Sworn to 3 Apr. 1710 by admrs. on estate of their late Father **Samuel STEEL Sr.** Distribution 28 Feb. 1711/2 to **Thomas STEEL**, eldest son, Ł234; **William STEEL**, Ł117; **Daniel STEEL**, Ł117; **Eliphalet STEEL**, Ł117; widow **Mercy STEEL**, Ł47.15.2; **Abiel STEEL**, Ł117. Account 5 Feb. 1710/1 leaves Ł702.0.3. to be divided among eldest son (double part) and the three sons and the daughter.

Estate of **Samuel STEEL Jr.** <Hartford CT PR #5199>
Inventory taken 22 Feb. 1709/10, total Ł105. Sworn to 3 Apr. 1710 by **Thomas STEEL** and **William STEEL**, administrators of their late brother **Samuel STEEL Jr.**

Estate of **Mercy STEEL** of Hartford CT. <Hartford CT PR #5196>
Bond 5 Apr. 1720 by administrator **Thomas STEEL.** Surety: **John WEBSTER.** Inventory taken 24 May 1720 by Samuel SEDGEWICK, Caleb BALL. Agreement Apr. 1724 to divide estate of mother **Mercy** and brother **William STEEL**, made by **Thomas STEEL, Daniel STEEL, Eliphalet STEEL, John WEBSTER** in right of wife **Abiell.**

Estate of **John STEEL** of Hartford. <Hartford CT PR #5188>
Ivnentory taken 30 Mar. 1698 of estate of **John STEEL** who deceased the sixth of this instant March by Joseph EASTON, Thomas BUNCE. Sworn to 14 Apr. 1698 by **James STEEL.**

Estate of **William STEEL** of Hartford CT. <Hartford CT PR #5209>
Bond 2 Feb. 1712/3 by **Thomas STEEL**, admr. Surety: Samuel HOWARD. Inventory taken 30 Mar. 1713 by

Samuel SEDGWICK, Thomas ENSIGNE, on estate of **William STEEL** who deceased 25 Nov. 1712; total, £105.14.4

Will of **Ebenezer STEEL** of Hartford CT. <Hartford CT PR #5176>
...26 June 1745, mentions wf **Susanna**, children: **John STEEL, Daniel STEEL, Bradford STEEL, Elisha STEEL, Mary, Susannah, Huldah, Melatiah.** Witnesses: Thomas SEYMOUR, Jared SEYMOUR, Eunice SEYMOUR Pr. 20 Jan. 1746/7. Inventory taken 20 June 1746 by Stephen HOSMER, Thomas HOSMER. Sworn to by **Susanna STEEL**, executrix, 20 Jan. 1746/7.

Will of **Thomas STEEL** of Hartford CT. <Hartford CT PR #5208>
...20 Sept. 1737, mentions wf **Susanna**, children: **Samuel STEEL, William STEEL, Nathaniel STEEL, James STEEL, Jerusha WELLS, Susanna HOSMER, John STEEL.** Pr. 5 Feb. 1739/40. Inventory taken 29 Jan. 1739/40.

Will of **Eliphalet STEEL** of Hartford CT. <Hartford CT PR #5178>
...16 July 1773, mentions wf **Catharine** (to receive whole estate), eldest son **Josiah STEEL.** Pr. 13 Dec. 1773.

Will of **Samuel STEELE** of Hartford CT. <Hartford CT PR #5201>
..7 Feb. 1777, mentions wf **Martha**, children: **Allyn STEELE, Joel STEELE, Thomas STEELE, Elizabeth, Mary, Martha, Lucretia, Sybil.** Pr. 6 Oct. 1779.

Will of **William STEEL** of New Hartford CT. <Farmington CT PR #2620>
...20 Feb. 1777, mentions widow of son **Timothy STEEL** (called Abigail in distribution), son **William STEEL**, son **Isaac STEEL**, son **Seth STEEL**, children of son **Timothy**, daus. **Lydia, Huldah.** Pr. 22 Apr. 1777.

Will of **Theophilus STEELE** of Hartford CT. <Hartford CT PR #5206>
...19 June 1775, mentions unnamed wife, son **Theophilus STEELE** when he reaches 21. Pr. 25 July 1775. Inventory sworn to 23 Oct. 1775 by **Marienne STEEL**, widow & executrix.

Will of **John STEEL** of Washington MA. <Hartford CT PR #5191>
...21 Jan. 1785, mentions wf **Christian**, children: **Ebenezer STEEL, Moses STEEL, Christian STEEL, Ruth STEEL, Timothy STEEL, Aaron STEEL, Pitt STEEL.** Pr. 5 Apr. 1785 at Stockbridge MA.

Estate of **Elisha STEEL** of Derby. <New Haven CT PR #9844>
Bond 17 June 1805 by **Norman STEEL**, admr. Surety: Eleazer PATCHIN. Inventory taken June 1805 by Philo HOLBROOK, Jesse SMITH, total: $875.13. Widow **Eunice STEEL** quitclaims to **Norman STEEL**, 1 July 1805.

Will of **John STEEL Jr.** of Hartford CT. <Hartford CT PR #5190>
...4 Dec. 1760...wf **Lydia**, to my brothers and sisters to be equally divided...Pr. 14 Apr. 1761.

Estate of **Bradford STEELE** of Derby. <New Haven CT PR #9839>
Bond 7 May 1804 by George STEELE, Nathan WHEELER, admrs. Surety: William KENNEY. Inventory taken 4 June 1804 by Levi TOMLINSON, Philo HOLBROOK, total: $3312.04. Distribution 9 Feb. 1805 to: widow **Sarah**, son **Ashbel STEEL**, son **Bradford STEEL**, son **Daniel STEEL**, son **George STEEL**, heirs of **Susanna FLOWERS**, dau **Nelle KENEY** wf of William, dau **Mary WAREN** wf of Edward, dau **Hannah WHITNEY**, widow.

Estate of **James STEEL** of New Hartford. <Hartford CT PR #5184>
Bond 20 Jan. 1767 by Lois STEEL, James STEEL. Surety: Stephen CHUBB. Inventory taken 4 Dec. 1766, total: £244.9.11. Distribution 30 Apr. 1771 by Israel LOOMIS, Stephen CHUBB, to: widow **Lois**, children: **James STEEL** (eldest son), **Sarah NICKELSON, Lois SPENCER, Elizabeth STEEL, Susanna STEEL Ann STEEL, John STEEL, Jesse STEEL.** Account 25 Apr. 1771...There was one child that was but one year and eleven month old at the decease of the father and another that was but three year and six months.

Will of **Col. Jabez FITCH** of Canterbury CT. <Plainfield CT PR>
...10 Dec. 1783, to son **Jabez FITCH** one hundred pounds to be deducted out of note of hand for one hundred and ten pounds, dated 20 Mar. 1777; son **Asahel FITCH**; daus. **Jerusha, Lydia, Lucy**; son **Pever FITCH**, dec'd, of Stanford; dau **Alice**, dec'd, wf of Rev. James COGSWELL. Witnesses: Capt. James DYAR, Lucy GALUSHA, Eliashib ADAMS. Pr. 10 Feb. 1784.

Will of **Nathan BRADFORD**, husbandman, of Kingston. <Plymouth Co.PR #2581>
<30:273>...11 Sept. 1787, mentions wf **Sarah**, sons **Jonathan BRADFORD, David BRADFORD.** Witnesses: Zedekiah SANGER, Charles FOSTER. Pr. 5 Dec. 1787. <original> Petition & Agreement 28 Nov. 1787 by **Sarah BRADFORD**, widow, **Jonathan & David BRADFORD**, sons and only heirs at law...said will being defective by reason of only two witnesses signing...heirs agree that will shall be proved notwithstanding. Witnesses: Seth WASHBURN, Seth WASHBURN Jr., Sarah BRADFORD.

MICRO #4 of 15

Estate of **Nathaniel BRADFORD**, housewright of Plymouth. <Plymouth Co.PR #2583>
<12:151> Letter/Bond 16 May 1751, **Sarah BRADFORD**, widow, app'td. admx. Sureties: Thomas SPOONER, gentleman, Ebenezer SPOONER, cordwainer, both of Plymouth. Witnesses: James OTIS Jr, Edward WINSLOW. <12:365> Inventory taken June 1751 by James HOVEY, Thomas JACKSON, Samuel FOSTER; incl. his shop standing on Cole's Land - land bought of his mother in Kingston, interest in lands in common with **Nathan BRADFORD.** <12:522> Petition 27 May 1752 of **Sarah BRADFORD**, widow and guardian of his children, to sell real estate that said Nathaniel died seized of, lands in Kingston as tenant-in-common with Nathan BRADFORD of Kingston & Lydia, wf of Lazarus LEBARRON of Plymouth, Physician, that she is left with two small children the oldest of which is little more than three years. Bond for sale 15 Sept. 1752. Sureties: Thomas SPOONER, Ebenezer SPOONER. <16:219> Account 7 Dec. 1761 by **Sarah BRADFORD**, Ephraim SPOONER. Witnesses: Edward WINSLOW, Thomas SPOONER Jr. Due to: Lazarus LeBARON, Hannah THOMAS, WARREN & GOODWIN, MURDOCK & TILLSON, Ebenezer SPOONER, Nathaniel SHURTLEFF, Josiah CARVER, Barnabas HEDGE, Ruben CARVER, Matthew LEMOTE, Benjamin BARNES, Nathan BRADFORD, Elizabeth LUDDIN; clothing for children **Lemuel BRADFORD** & **Nathaniel BRADFORD** from date of father's death, eleven years.

==========

Guardianship of Children of **Nathaniel BRADFORD**, housewright of Plymouth. <Plymouth Co.PR #2563>
<12:205> Letter/Bond 13 July 1751, **Sarah BRADFORD**, widow, app'td. guardian of **Lemuel BRADFORD** and **Nathaniel BRADFORD**, minor sons. Surety: Ebenezer SPOONER of Plymouth. Witnesses: Edward WINSLOW, John LOTHROP. <18:50,52> Letter/Bond 7 Dec. 1761, Ephraim SPOONER, trader of Plymouth, app'td. guardian of **Nathaniel & Lemuel BRADFORD**, minors. Sureties: Thomas SPOONER, Thomas SPOONER Jr., both of Plymouth. Witnesses: Ebenezer ROBBINS, Edward WINSLOW, both of Plymouth. <16:222> Receipt & Discharge 16 Dec. 1761, Ephraim SPOONER being guardian to **Nathaniel & Lemuel**, children of said deceased, discharges **Sarah BRADFORD.**

==========

Peleg HOLMES, yeoman of Kingston to **Josiah HOLMES**, yeoman of Kingston. <Plymouth Co.Deeds 47:236>
...1 June 1762, Peleg HOLMES for £173.6s8d sold to Josiah HOLMES...all my lands in Kingston with the sixty fourth part of the furnace in Kingston...I said Abigail HOLMES hereafter mentioned have rec'd the contents. Witnesses: William RIPLEY, John FAUNCE, Deborah TINKCOM, Elizabeth CUSHMAN.

MICRO #5 of 15

Will of **Nathan CHANDLER**, yeoman of Duxbury. <Plymouth Co.PR #3795>
<35:324>...26 Feb. 1795, mentions wife **Esther; Nathan CHANDLER** & **Isaac CHANDLER** the two oldest sons of my eldest son who is dec'd; **Ephraim CHANDLER** & **John CHANDLER** the two youngest sons of my eldest son who is dec'd; children: **Ruth, Lucy, Hannah, Ira CHANDLER.** Witnesses: Philip CHANDLER, Stephen RUSSELL, Peres CHANDLER. <35:325> Bond 27 Oct. 1795 by Ira CHANDLER as exec.. Sureties: Perez CHANDLER, Philip CHANDLER. Witnesses: Isaac LOTHROP, John ADAMS Jr.

==========

Estate of **Ephraim CHANDLER** of Kingston. <Plymouth Co.PR #3759>
<original> Request 27 Feb. 1794 by **Mollie CHANDLER** that John FAUNCE be app'td admr. <27:472> Bond /Letter 5 Mar. 1794, John FAUNCE of Kingston app'td. Sureties: Samuel Stafford STURTEVANT, Jabez STURTEVANT, both of Halifax. Witnesses: Joseph THOMAS, Isaac LOTHROP. <35:32> Inventory taken 19 Mar. 1794 by Noah SIMMONS, Levi BRADFORD, Ichabod CHURCHILL, all of Kingston; incl. three lots of land in Duxborough, one lot cedar swamp at Carver, homestead and other land in Kingston. <35:209> Order of notice 5 Mar. 1794. <35:541> Account 1 Aug. 1796 of John FAUNCE, admr. Paid to: Phebe ROGERS, Jothan LORING, Dr. Jabez FULLER, Amos COOK, David LUCAS, David BEAL, Jonathan HOLMES & sons, Francis ADAMS Jr., Seth WASHBURN Jr., Noah SIMMONS, Ichabod CHURCHILL, Dr. James THATCHER, Uriah BARTLETT, Mrs. Hannah THOMAS, John ADAMS, John SIMMONS, John FULLER, Hannah CHANDLER, Mr. COTTON, Mr. Zephanah WILLIS, Isaiah ALDEN. <36:278> Division 1 Jan. 1798 by John GRAY, Noah SIMMONS, both of Kingston, and Phillip CHANDLER of Duxbury; one third set off to **Molly CHANDLER**, widow; one sixth of remainder to each of children, viz: **Selah RUSSELL** wf of Melzar, **Nathan CHANDLER** (eldest son), **Isaac CHANDLER** (2nd son), **Ephraim CHANDLER** (3rd son), **John CHANDLER** (youngest son), **Rispa CHANDLER** (youngest dau). <36:285> Account 1 Jan. 1798 of admr. Debts paid to: Ira CHANDLER, John FULLER, Joseph RIPLEY, Melzia RUSSELL. <47:53> Division of Dower 1 July 1808 by Jedediah HOLMES & Noah SIMMONS, both of Kingston, and Wadsworth CHANDLER of Duxbury. Widow **Mary CHANDLER**'s dower divided to above six children. Confirmed 9 Jan. 1815.

==========

Guardianship of Children of **Ephraim CHANDLER** of Kingston. <Plymouth Co.PR>
<32:48> Bond/Letter 1 Aug. 1796, **Molly CHANDLER**, widow, app'td. guardian of **Nathan CHANDLER** (above 14), **Isaac, Ephraim, John** & **Rispa CHANDLER**, minors under 14. Sureties: John FAUNCE of Kingston, Ira CHANDLER of Duxbury. Witnesses: Josiah WOTTSON, Ezra NICHOLL. <32:339> Bond/Letter 3 June 1808, Joshua BREWSTER of Duxbury app'td. guardian of **Ephraim** & **John CHANDLER**, minors above 14. Sureties: Jedediah HOLMES, Nathan CHANDLER, both of Kingston. Witnesses: Ephraim CHANDLER, Isaac LOTHROP.

==========

William HUNT of Chilmark. <Plymouth Co.Deeds 40:243>
...10 July 1750...William HUNT & wf Sarah, as she is executrix of estate of **Samuel BRADFORD**, late of Plympton, gentleman, dec'd, releases to **Ezekiel BRADFORD, Simeon BRADFORD** and **Waite BRADFORD**, sons of **Ephraim BRADFORD** dec'd.

==========

Division of Land: **BRADFORD, BONNEY, CHURCHILL.** <Plymouth Co.Deeds 45:253>
...24 Mar. 1759, **Elisha BRADFORD**, cooper, **Benjamin BRADFORD**,yeoman, **Ezekiel BRADFORD**, yeoman and

Simeon BRADFORD, yeoman, all of Kingston, owners of one quarter of first lot cedar swamp in Colchester Swamp in Plympton. **William BONNEY** & **Isaac BONNEY**, both of Plympton own one quarter; **William CHURCHILL, Isaac CHURCHILL, David CHURCHILL,** all of Plympton own one half. (**Simeon BRADFORD** does not sign or acknowledge.)

Estate of **Simeon BRADFORD** of Springfield VT. <Windsor VT PR>[3]
...16 Nov. 1793, adm. granted to **Asa BRADFORD.** Inventory taken (no date given) by Simon STEVENS, Hezekiah HOLMES, Simeon BROWN; total £469.10s3p. Division (no date given) among following heirs: **Phebe BRADFORD,** widow, **Joel BRADFORD, Simeon BRADFORD, Ephraim BRADFORD, Asa BRADFORD, Hosea BRADFORD, Lucy M. ROBERTS** wf of John W., **Nabby HOLMES** wf of Walter, **Cynthia BRADFORD, Deborah BRADFORD, Ruth SMITH** wf of James.

Simeon BRADFORD to **Ezekiel BRADFORD,** yeomen of Kingston. <Plymouth Co.Deeds 53:10>
...21 Sept. 1765, Simeon BRADFORD for £120 sold to Ezekiel BRADFORD all my right in the real estate that was given to me by my Late Worthy Father **Ephraim BRADFORD** deceased by his last will... it being the Homestead whereon my Father Last Dwelt and my part with my Brother's the said Ezekiel's lyeth in common between us and undivided and my said Brother Ezekiel is to take it in the condition it now lyes without any charge to me. Witnesses: Samuel FOSTER, Andrew BRADFORD.[4]

Will of **Joshua RIPLEY** of Windham CT. <Windham CT PR>
<2:204>...6 Jan. 1738/9, mentions sons **Joshua RIPLEY, Hezekiah RIPLEY, David RIPLEY,** dau **Jerusha RIPLEY,** grandchildren **Ann BINGHAM, Abigail MANNING, Samuel MANNING,** daus. **Alice EGERTON, Hannah WEBB, Leah COOK, Rachel TRACEY, Faith BINGHAM** dec'd (leaving a daughter), **Margaret SEABURY, Irene MANNING** dec'd (leaving daughters), **Ann WHEAT.** <2:205> Pr. 27 June 1739. <2:212> Inventory 16 July 1739.

Will of **Judith RIPLEY** of Windham CT. <Windham CT PR 15:77,84,90,123>
...1 July 1803... (no details given except for pencilled note "widow of Gamaliel who d. 1799".)

CHESHIRE CO. NH DEEDS:

<1:484> - 1772, Abner BINGHAM from Elisha ELY, of Marlow.
<1:485> - 1772, Abner BINGHAM to Daniel CLARK Jr., of Marlow.
<140:115> - 6 May 1840, Abner C. BINGHAM & wf Adaline to Eliot R. OSGOOD, of Springfield VT.
<141:204> - 6 May 1840, Abner C. BINGHAM, mortgage from Eliot R. OSGOOD of Rockingham VT.

Will of **Joshua RIPLEY** of Windham CT. <Windham CT PR 12:208,225,336,366,423>
<12:208>...10 Nov. 1787, to wife **Deborah;** to my four sons **Eliphalet RIPLEY, Ralph RIPLEY, Nathaniel RIPLEY, Erastus RIPLEY** all my land lying on Bushnell's Plain between the road leading from Windham to Mansfield and the parsonage belonging to the first Society in Windham, about eighty acres; to son **Erastus** the house in which I now dwell...also one yoak of oxen, three cows & twenty sheep when he arrives at the age of twenty one or on the first day of April next; to my son **Nathaniel** one pair of two year old steers to be delivered to him the next spring after he shall arrive at the age of twenty one; to dau **Polly RIPLEY** one acre of land at the south end of my home lot, also all my houshold furniture, excepting what articles came by my **present wife**...also a three year old cow now in the keeping of James SAWYER...untill she arrive at the age of eighteen years...and also an obligation against John GENNINGS Jr. for six good sheep to be delivered me in the month of Jan. 1790; my three daughters **Elizabeth, Olive, Lydia;** to my son **Ralph** one pair yearling steers, also six sheep now in the possession of Daniel LINKON, one cow now in the possession of Zerviah DINGLEY, the use of said cow and sheep ...apply to the benefit of my daughter **Lydia** and her children; son **Ralph** named executor. Witnesses: Hezekiah RIPLEY, Methias SAWYER, Shubael FITCH. Pr. 17 Jan. 1787/8. <12:225> Inventory taken 18 Feb. 1788 by Hezekiah RIPLEY, Ebenezer BACKUS; 75 acres at Bushnell's plain, £48,15s; 25 Acres, £62.10s; 16 acres homelot, incl house & barn, £104.

Will of **Joshua ABBE** of Windham CT. <Windham CT PR 15:280,285,453,539;6:214,217,270>
<15:280>...7 Apr. 1804, mentions four daughters, viz: **Zibah WALES, Mary HEBARD, Zerviah WEBB, Lucretia BADGER.** Witnesses sworn 21 Jan. 1807. Pr. 3 Feb. 1807.

Will of **Samuel COOK** of Windham CT. <Windham CT PR>
<3:231>...17 Aug. 1745, to wife **Leah;** to eldest daughter **Rebeckah** ye sume of five shilings oald Tenour haveing given hur hur proportion of my Estate heare to fore; to daughter **Jerusha** one hundred pounds oald Tenor; to daughter **Welthean** five shilings oald Tenour have given hur hur proportin heare to fore; to daughter **Mary** ye sume of one hundred pounds oald Tenour; to my two sons **Samuel COOK** and **Phinias COOK** all my lands. Wife **Leah** and her brother **Hezekiah RIPLEY** named executors. Witnesses: Jonathan BREWSTER, Jonathan RUDD, Isaac WOODWARD. Witnesses sworn 9 Sept. 1745. Pr. 11 Sept. 1745. <3:368> Inventory taken 27 Aug. 1745 by Edward WALDO, John CARY, John MANING, incl. a brown wigg, £2; a gray wigg, £1.5s; sword & belt, £1.5s; silver spoon, £2.14s4d; 2 large pewter platters, £2; old deep pewter platter, £1; Bible, 5s; bond for money Isaac WOODWARD's, £30; note of Jonathan LUCE, £10.5s; note of Daniel CLARK, 30s lawful money or £6 old tenour; pair of silver sleeve buttons, 10s; money due by notes, £5.4s. <Special 2:195> 13 Sept. 1748, **Samuel COOK** a minor son to **Samuel COOK** of Canterbury, dec'd made choise of **Mrs. Leah COOK** to be his guardian, said minor being 16 years old ye 25 day of August last. <Special 2:274> 5 Feb. 1750/1, **Mrs. Leah COOK** of Windham, elected guardian to **Phineas COOK,** minor

MICRO #6 OF 15

Will of **Leah BRADFORD** of Windham CT. <Windham CT PR #1346>
...9 Sept. 1772...advanced in years; to daughters of my eldest daughter **Rebecca**; to grandaughter **Jerusha WHEAT**; to dau **Welthy PARDY**...my gold ring which hath my former husband's name theiron; to dau **Mary MANNING**...my gold necklace; to **Samuel, Sibbel** and **Leah** the children of son **Samuel COOK**, dec'd, **Leah** to receive gold ring; son **Phinehas COOK**. Witnesses: Edward BROWN, Asa BREWSTER, Rebecca KILLBOURN. Pr. 9 May 1775. (original will in files)

Estate of **Samuel COOK** of Plainfield CT. <Plainfield CT PR #517>
Inventory taken 18 May 1758 by Israel UNDERWOOD, Curtis SPAULDING. Sworn to by unnamed administrator 30 June 1758.

Will of **Elisha BRADFORD** of Cheshire MA. <Berkshire Co.PR 14:407>
...28 Mar. 1809, mentions wf **Eunice**; daughters **Susannah BROWN, Lucy SAYLES, Salley BRADFORD**; six sons, viz: **William BRADFORD, Joseph BRADFORD, Hopstill BRADFORD, Levi BRADFORD, Simeon BRADFORD, George BRADFORD.** Wife **Eunice BRADFORD** and Jonathan RICHARDSON named executors. Witnesses: Edward MARTIN, Ephraim FERINGTON, Samuel MARTIN, Esther RICHARDSON. Pr. 4 July 1809.

Will of **Isaac BROWN** of Adams MA. <Berkshire Co.PR 11:390>
...14 Mar. 1864, mentions wf **Susannah**; children: **Jerome B. BROWN** (executor), **Albert G. BROWN, Mariah A. LAPHAM, Eunice B. COLE, Eliza B. BROWN, Daniel BROWN**; grandson **Edwin F. JENKS**. Witnesses: Henry J. BLISS, Alvah C. PRINCE, Abbie S. RICHMOND. Pr. 25 Apr. 1866.

Calvin RIPLEY of Swanzey to **Levi BRADFORD** of S. Kingston RI. <Bristol Co.Deeds 91:268>
...27 May 1810, Calivn RIPLEY, gentleman for $2000.00 sold to Levi BRADFORD, yeoman, 35 acres in Swanzey...Peggy RIPLEY, wife of the said Calvin RIPLEY in token of her consent...

...Sept. 1811...Judgement against **Charles RIPLEY** of Somerset, rope maker, and **Calvin RIPLEY**, of Swansea, yeoman... <Bristol Co.Deeds 93:183>

Estate of **Calvin RIPLEY** of Swansea MA. <Bristol Co.PR>
<84:402> Administration 6 Sept. 1842, Henry GARDNER 2nd of Swansea, app'td. <115:326> Notice 6 Sept. 1842. <155:84> Letter 6 Sept. 1842. <161:84> Bond 6 Sept. 1842. Bondsmen: John B. GARDNER, William TRIPP, both of Fall River.

Estate of **Benjamin BRADFORD**, yeoman of Kingston. <Plymouth Co.PR #2502>
<27:146> Letter/Bond 7 Apr. 1784, Levi HOLMES of Kingston, app'td admr. Sureties: Jedediah HOLMES of Kingston, Zacheus FISH of Pembroke. Witnesses: David KINGMAN, Isaac LOTHROP.<29:193> Inventory taken 3 Sept. 1784 by Peter WEST, Noah SIMMONS, Jedediah HOLMES, all of Kingston.

Estate of **Elisha BRADFORD** of Kingston. <Plymouth Co.PR #2518>
<11:446> Letter/Bond 26 June 1750, Samuel FOSTER, gentleman, of Kingston, app'td admr. Surety: Jedediah BOURNE, cordwainer, of Marshfield. Witnesses: Edward WINSLOW, Hannah WINSLOW. <12:354> Inventory taken 28 June 1750 by Elisha STETSON, Samuel KENT, Evon SKINNER. <original> Account taken July 1750. To: Samuel FOSTER, William BARNES, Deborah PETERSON, Elijah MACKFALING, Dr. LORING, Grace DAVIS, Elisha STETSON Jr., Phebe COOK, Deacon BREWSTER, Dr. ASTIN, Elisha STETSON; mourning clothes for the widow; maintenance of three small children till they were put out.

MICRO #7 OF 15

Will of **John BRADFORD Jr.** of Plymouth. <Plymouth Co.PR #2552>
<4:429>...(Mar. 1724)...Oath by Caleb LORING, Gershom BRADFORD, Seth CHIPMAN taken 28 Apr. 1724 that sometime about the latter end of March last they did see the within named **John BRADFORD** sign, seal & heard him declare the within written to be his last will. Will mentions wf **Rebecca**, (executrix); son **Robert BRADFORD**, dau **Rebeckah BRADFORD**; Joseph STACEY, pastor. Witnesses: Caleb LORING, Gershom BRADFORD, Seth CHIPMAN. Inventory taken 6 May 1724 by Isaac CUSHMAN Jr., Jacob MICHELL, Gershom BRADFORD. Pr. 8 June 1724. Oath by **Rebecca BRADFORD** 20 June 1724.

Will of **Capt. Robert BRADFORD** of Kingston. <Plymouth Co.PR #2595>
<28:460>...8 Aug. 1782, mentions unnamed wf; children: **Orpah, Stetson BRADFORD, Robert BRADFORD, Peleg BRADFORD, Zilpah BRADFORD, Rebecca** (dec'd), **John BRADFORD**; friend William DREW of Kingston, executor. Witnesses: Robert COOK, James WATERMAN, Benjamin WATERMAN. <28:514> Inventory taken 29 Nov. 1782 by John GRAY, Ebenezer WASHBURNE, Robert COOK, all of Kingston; incl lands in Kingston, Pembroke, Duxbury and Halifax. <28:535> Insolvency 6 Jan. 1783 by William DREW, Esq. <29:30> Account 6 July 1783 by Ebenezer WASHBURNE, Jedediah HOLMES, both of Kingston. List of Claims: Barnabas BRIGGS, Josiah COOK, Jabez FULLER, Jabez WASHBURN, John ADAMS, Judah WASHBURN, Estate of Benjamin LORING, dec'd, Isaiah THOMAS, Susannah CHAMBERLIN, Micah HOLMES, William SEVER; taxes paid Eliezer WATERMAN, Judah DELANO & Increase ROBINSON. Paid to: Silvanus BRADFORD, Jonas WHITMAN, Elkanah WASHBURN, Lot EATON, Zenas WATERMAN, Elisha STETSON, Keziah THOMAS, Joseph THOMAS, Elisha BREWSTER, Estate of John BREWSTER, Capt. Robert BRADFORD, Stetson BRADFORD, Thaddeus RANSOM, Estate of Policarpus LORING, Gideon BRADFORD, Est. of Capt. John BRADFORD, Elisha BRADFORD, Orpha BRADFORD, Dr. Isaac WINSLOW, Levi LORING. <29:135> Dower assigned 14 Apr. 1784 by Nathaniel LITTLE, Jno. ADAMS, Judah WASHBURN. <39:32> Account of William DREW 4 Aug. 1783.<original> Letter from heirs, 2 June 1788, Micah HOLMES Jr. having made application for division of real estate.

Heirs: Widow (age 80, unnamed), **Orpha BRADFORD, Robert BRADFORD, John BRADFORD, Stetson BRADFORD.**

PLYMOUTH COUNTY DEEDS:

<116:83> 1785, John BRADFORD to Sylvanus BRADFORD.
<90:21> 1798, John & Hannah BRADFORD to Stephen BRADFORD.
<94:261> 1803, John & Hannah BRADFORD to son Stephen BRADFORD of Kingston
<114:166> 1810, John BRADFORD to Stephen BRADFORD, potter, homestead.
<173:200> 1832, John BRADFORD of Plympton...
<245:8> 1834, Stephen & Martha BRADFORD to Jason BRADFORD.

Will of **William HUNT** of Chilmark MA. <Dukes Co.PR 6:14>
...19 Mar. 1760, to wf **Sarah** dwelling house and land in Chillmark at a place called Monamsha, wood land north of the Mill owned by Thomas TILLTON; to son **Samuel HUNT** 160 acres in Chillmark adjoining in part the lands of said son...which I had formerly a dwelling house standing near the place called the Sugar Loaf...also one fifth part of all my estate; to grandson **Beriah NICKERSON**, son of my daughter **Jane**, 20 acres in Chillmark...which I last purchased of Mr. William CLARK... one acre salt marsh at Menamsha; grandchildren **Jane NICKERSON** and **Nathaniel NICKERSON**, children of my late daughter **Jane**; daus **Mary HUNT, Sarah HATCH, Hannah HUNT.** Son **Samuel** named executor. Witnesses: Cornelius BASSETT, Jonathan LOOK, David HILLMAN. Pr. 19 July 1769 at Tisbury and administration granted to **Samuel HUNT**, yeoman of Liverpool, Nova Scotia.

Estate of **Sarah HUNT**, widow of Chilmark MA. <Dukes Co.PR 6:38,39>
<6:38>...9 Jan. 1771, Samuel BRADFORD, Physitian, of Chillmark, app'td. admr. <6:39> Inventory taken 4 Feb. 1771 by Samuel MAYHEW, David TILLMAN, Matthew CLARK, total: £59.6s8d.

Will of **Gideon BRADFORD** of Plympton MA. <Plymouth Co.PR #2533>
<33:467>...11 May 1784, mentions wf **Jane**, children: **Levi BRADFORD, Samuel BRADFORD, Joseph BRADFORD, Gideon BRADFORD, Calvin BRADFORD, Sarah ELLIS** wf of Freeman, **Jane BISBEE** wf of Noah. Witnesses: Samuel WRIGHT, Samuel WRIGHT Jr., Sarah WRIGHT Jr. <33:470> Declination 11 Nov. 1793 of **Jane BRADFORD** as executrix. <27:537> Letter/Bond 11 Nov. 1793, **Levi BRADFORD, Gideon BRADFORD** app'td admrs. Sureties: Calvin BRADFORD, Samuel WRIGHT, both of Plympton. Witnesses: Nathaniel LOTHROP, Isaac LOTHROP. <33:539> Inventory taken 17 Dec. 1793 by James CHURCHELL, George SAMPSON, of Plympton, Samuel LUCAS of Carver. Oath 7 Jan. 1794 by **Levi & Gideon BRADFORD.**

Will of **Jane BRADFORD**, widow, of Plympton MA. <Plymouth Co.PR #2550>
<original>...31 May 1794, mentions son **Levi BRADFORD,** daus **Jenny BISBEE** wf of Noah, **Sarah ELLIS** wf of Freeman. Witnesses: Lewis BRADFORD, Levi BRADFORD Jr., Ezra BRADFORD. (1st & 3rd witnesses sworn 4 Jan. 1796.) Will not probated.

Will of **Luther BRADFORD** of Plympton. <Plymouth Co.PR>[<5>]
<original>...23 Mar. 1858, mentions wf **Mary**; sister **Mary BRADFORD**; children: **Joseph Warren BRADFORD, DeWitt Clinton BRADFORD, William Harrison BRADFORD, Mary Angeline BRADFORD, Clara Lorett BRADFORD, Lydia Holmes BARROWS, Ruth Cook PRATT, Irene Shaw PRATT, Sarah Ann WATERMAN, Aroline Bartlett PENNIMAN.** Petition of heirs for probating 2 July 1861 states **Luther** died 28 June 1861 at Plympton and names the heirs as follows: widow **Mary**, children: **Lydia H. BARROWS** wf of Jacob of Middleboro; **Ruth C. PRATT** wf of Thomas A. of Middleboro; **Irene S. PRATT** wf of Simeon of Middleboro; **Sarah A. WATERMAN** wf of Jonathan B. of Halifax; **Aroline B. PENNIMAN** wf of Prince E. of Plympton; **Mary A. THOMAS** wf of A.C. of Middleboro; **Clara L. BRADFORD**, minor, of Plympton; **Joseph W. BRADFORD** of Carver; **Dewitt C. BRADFORD** of Middleboro; **William H. BRADFORD**, minor, of Plympton.

Estate of **John BRADFORD**, gentleman, of Plympton. <Plymouth Co.PR #2555>
<20:409> Letter/Bond 22 Nov. 1770, **Elizabeth BRADFORD**, widow and **John BRADFORD**, yeoman, app'td. admrs. Sureties: Ichabod HOLMES, Ephraim SPOONER, both of Plymouth. Witnesses: Thomas BARRISTER, Edward WINSLOW Jr. <20:466> Inventory taken 28 Jan. 1771 by William BONNEY, Timothy RIPLEY, Gideon SAMSON. <24:116> Division dated 31 May 1776 by John BRYANT, Samuel LUCAS both of Plympton, Noah CUSHING of Halifax. Real estate divided into 12 shares, viz: **Capt. John BRADFORD** (eldest son), **Perez BRADFORD, Oliver BRADFORD, William BRADFORD, Elizabeth MAGOUN, Mary CHURCHILL, Priscilla RIDER, Hannah WATERMAN, Lydia BRADFORD, Mercy BRADFORD, Sarah BRADFORD.** <24:119> Dower assigned 31 May 1776 to **Elizabeth BRADFORD,** widow. <24:127> Account 4 Apr. 1776. Received from: Nathaniel PRENTICE, Isachar BISBE, Seth WATERMAN, Isaac CHURCHEL, Nathaniel BONNEY, Silas STURTEVANT, Ephraim MORSE, Robert BRADFORD, William BONNEY, William CHURCHEL, Abner BISBE, George BRYANT, Kimbal PRINCE, David CHURCHEL, Josiah WEST, Deborah EATON, Simeon BONEY, Nathaniel HARLOW, James HARLOW, Seth CUSHING, David MAGOUN, Ichabod CHURCHEL, Nathaniel CHANDLER, Nathaniel BRYANT, Benjamin CUSHMAN, Ebenezer BONNEY, Ephraim BRYANT, Thomas LORING, Josiah PERKINS. Paid to: Robert FORSTER, George WATSON, Josiah STURTEVANT, Pelham WINSLOW, Benjamin BLOSSOM, William BONNEY, James HOVEY, John ADAMS, John MAXAM, Zephaniah PERKINS, Ebenezer DEAN, William CHURCHEL, Micah ALLEN, James FAUNCE, Jabez HOWLAND, Thomas CUSHMAN, Nathaniel CHURCHEL, Ignatius LORING, Robert COOKE, Jabez WASHBURN, Timothy RIPLEY, Zebdiel SAMPSON, Thomas GANNET, John BRYANT, Thomas SAMSON, Nathan PERKINS, Widow Mary LORING, Zadock THOMAS, James MORTON, Edward WINSLOW, Samuel BRADSTREET, Ebenezer SOUL, John PERKINS, Gideon SAMSON, William SEVER. <original> Complaint 30 Jan. 1783 by **Nathaniel & Priscilla RIDER**, being heirs, against admrs. <original> Complaint 28 Mar. 1792 by **Levi BRYANT** of Plympton, in right of his wife **Lydia**, heir. <original> Citation 28 Mar. 1792 to **Elizabeth BRADFORD**, widow and **John BRADFORD**, admrs. <original> Division of dower 20 Apr. 1807 by Peleg WRIGHT, Timothy RIPLEY, Adam TOMSON, between **John BRADFORD,** heirs of **Elizabeth MAGOUN**, dec'd, **Lydia BRYANT**, heirs of **William BRADFORD**, dec'd, **Mary CHURCHILL, Priscilla RYDER,**

Marcy SEARS, Oliver BRADFORD, Perez BRADFORD, Hannah WATERMAN, Sarah BOSWORTH.

Guardianship of Children of **John BRADFORD** of Plympton. <Plymouth Co.PR #2610>
<22:72> Letters 6 May 1776, Gideon SAMSON, yeoman, of Plympton, app'td. guardian of **Sarah BRADFORD** aged 16, **William BRADFORD** aged 11. Sureties: Joseph WRIGHT, Thomas SAMSON, both of Plympton. <22:194> 6 May 1776, **Mercy BRADFORD, Lydia BRADFORD, Oliver BRADFORD** made choice of Gideon SAMSON as guardian. Witnesses: John BRADFORD, Mary CHURCHILL.

Will of **John BRADFORD,** gentleman, of Plympton. <Plymouth Co.PR>
<42:130>...13 May 1807, mentions wf **Eunice,** children: **John BRADFORD, Polly STANDISH** (eldest dau) wf of Ellis, **Eunice WASHBURN** (2nd dau) wf of Asa, **Nancy BRADFORD, Suke BRADFORD, Sopha BRADFORD, Jane BRADFORD.** Witnesses: Caleb STETSON, Zadock CHURCHILL, Isaac CHURCHILL. Pr. 6 July 1807.

MICRO #8 OF 15

Estate of **William BRADFORD Jr.** of Kingston. <Plymouth Co.PR #2622>
<5:403> Letter/Bond 22 June 1728, **Hannah BRADFORD,** widow, app'td. admx. Sureties: John BRADFORD, Samuel FOSTER, both of Kingston. Witnesses: Sarah LITTLE, Marcy CUSHMAN. <5:601> Inventory taken 2 July 1727 by Francis ADAMS, Elisha STETSON, Wrastling BREWSTER, all of Kingston. <6:22> Account 20 May 1731 by admx. Owed to: Mr. Benjamin SAMSON, Elisha STETSON, Thomas CROADE, Ichabod WASHBURN, Ebenezer COB, Joshua LORING, Thomas WITHERELL, Dr. LeBARON, Dr. LORING, Mr. SEVER, Mr. MURDOCK, Cornelius DREW, Seth CHIPMAN, Josiah THOMAS. <14:90> Division 24 Feb. 1756 by Samuel SEABURY, John WADSWORTH, Jonathan PETERSON, John HUNT, all of Duxbury and John COOPER of Kingston; Heirs: **Hannah PARTRIDGE** (formerly the widow of dec'd); children: **James BRADFORD** (eldest son); heirs of **Samuel BRADFORD,** dec'd; heirs of **Zadock BRADFORD,** dec'd; **Eliphalet BRADFORD;** heirs of **William BRADFORD,** dec'd; **Hannah BRADFORD.** <29:293> Division of Dower 9 Nov. 1784 by John GRAY, John ADAMS, Benjamin COOK, to divide dower set off to **Hannah PARTRIDGE,** late widow of George PARTRIDGE, dec'd, formerly widow of **William BRADFORD.** To heirs: **James BRADFORD;** heirs of **Zadock BRADFORD,** dec'd; **Eliphalet BRADFORD;** heirs of **William BRADFORD,** dec'd; heirs of **Hannah SPAULDING,** dec'd; heirs of **Samuel BRADFORD,** dec'd. Division of real estate whereof **Samuel BRADFORD** died seized (who was son of **William BRADFORD,** dec'd, and died under the age of twenty-one years, without issue), between the above mentioned heirs, dated 6 June 1785.

Guardianship of Children of **William BRADFORD** of Kingston. <Plymouth Co.PR #2506>
<7:276> Letters/Bonds 17 Mar. 1736, George PARTRIDGE of Duxbury, app'td. guardian of **James BRADFORD** (betw 14-21), **Eliphalet BRADFORD** (betw 14-21), **Zadock BRADFORD** (betw 14-21) and **William BRADFORD** (under 14), sons of **William BRADFORD,** dec'd. Surety: Isaac SIMMONS Jr. Witnesses: Anthony THOMAS, Edward WINSLOW. <original> Bond 12 Mar. 1745 by Samuel FOSTER of Kingston as gdn. of **William BRADFORD,** minor. Surety: Stephen CHURCHILL of Plymouth. Witnesses: James WARREN, Edward WINSLOW.

Estate of **Zadock BRADFORD** of Kingston. <Plymouth Co.PR #2635>
<10:85> Administration granted 12 Mar. 1745 to Samuel FOSTER, gentleman, of Kingston. Sureties: Stephen CHURCHEL, gentleman, Josiah CARVER, mariner, both of Plymouth. Witnesses: James WARREN, Edward WINSLOW. (See James BRADFORD deed below for reference to a 1744 will.)

Willard SPAULDING of Killingsley CT to **John BREWSTER** of Kingston MA. <Plymouth Co.Deeds 41:58>
...15 Mar. 1749/50, Willard SPAULDING, husbandman, and wf Hannah SPAULDING, for Ŀ20 sold to John BREWSTER, innholder...all our right...unto a certain tract or piece of land in Kingstown...that did belong to our Honoured Father **William BRADFORD** of said Kingstown, deceased. Witnesses: James DANIELSON, Joseph SPAULDING. (Kingston/Kingstown)

Willard SPAULDING of Killingsly CT to **Samuel FOSTER** of Kingston MA. <Plymouth Co.Deeds 40:167>
...10 Nov. 1749, Willard SPALDING, yeoman, and wf Hannah, for Ŀ100 sold to Samuel FOSTER, gentleman...all the right...in the estate that fell to my said wife Hannah by the deceased of her brother **Samuel BRADFORD.** Witnesses: William MARSH, Priscilla MARSH.

James BRADFORD of Plainfield CT to **Samuel FOSTER** of Kingston MA. <Plymouth Co.Deeds 38:71>
...12 May 1746, James BRADFORD, house carpenter, for Ŀ400 sold to Samuel FOSTER, gentleman... lands belonging to brother **Zadock BRADFORD** now deceased, lying in Kingston, Duxborough, Plimton or Pembroke...or whatsoever Right or Interest he had at the time of his Deceased in any of said Towns It being what I bought on one Mercy POWER of New Port RI which Estate was given to her the said Mercy POWER by said **Zadock BRADFORD**'s last Will and Testament in writing dated 8 Feb. 1744. Witnesses: John FOSTER, Issacher FULLER.

James BRADFORD of Preston CT to **John BREWSTER** of Kingston MA. <Plymouth Co.Deeds 35:53>
...24 June 1742, James BRADFORD, housewright, for Ŀ500 sold to John BREWSTER, innholder...all rights in real estate given me by my Honoured Grandfather **John BRADFORD,** dec'd and my Honoured Father **William BRADFORD,** late of Kingston, dec'd...the said BREWSTER being at the charge of dividing with the rest of the Proprietors in the said Estate And Whereas my Grandmother is now in possession of one half of my said Grandfather's estate...Witnesses: Elisha STETSON, Samuel FOSTER.

William BRADFORD of Kingston MA to **Seth CHIPMAN Jr.** of Kingston MA. <Plymouth Co.Deeds 40:60>
...19 June 1749, William BRADFORD, cordwainer, for Ŀ800 sold to Seth CHIPMAN Jr., mariner...real and personal estate ...that came to me by my Honoured Grandfather **Major John BRADFORD** and my Hon-

oured Father **Mr. William BRADFORD**, dec'd, and by my Brother **Samuel BRADFORD**, dec'd, only excepting and reserving my right and titles of land in the eastern parts of this countrey. Witnesses: John WADSWORTH, John WADSWORTH Jr.

Zadock BRADFORD of Duxbury to **Lucy BRADFORD** of Duxbury. <Plymouth Co.Deeds 178:176>
...1 Aug. 1833, Zadock BRADFORD, mariner, to mother Lucy BRADFORD, one third of house, barn and lot given to Zadock by his father Zadock BRADFORD 23 July 1828.

Will of **Joseph BRADFORD** of New London CT. <New London CT PR #667>
<7:93>...14 Sept. 1731, mentions wf **Mary,** children: **Joseph BRADFORD** (eldest son), **John BRADFORD, Anne DEMICK/DIMMOCK** (eldest dau), **Priscilla HIDE, Sarah TUTHILL, Hannah BUELL, Elizabeth BRADFORD, Alithea BRADFORD, Irene BRADFORD.** Witnesses: Col. William WHITING, James HARRIS, John RICHARDS. <5:53> Pr. 10 Mar. 1746/7. <5:57> Inventory 20 Apr. 1747. Acquittance 18 June 1747 to **Mrs. Mary BRADFORD**, signed by: **Samuel & Priscilla HIDE** of Lebanon, **David & Alithea HIDE** of Lebanon, **Jonathan & Irene JAMES**, of Lebanon, **Andrew & Elizabeth LISK** of Lebanon, **Israel & Sarah LOTHROP** of Norwich, **Timothy & Hannah BUELL** of Hebron. <5:84> Account 10 Oct. 1749 by **Mrs. Mary BRADFORD**, executrix. (original will in files)

Estate of **Samuel HYDE** of Canterbury CT. <Plainfield CT PR #1161>
Inventory taken 5 July 1763, £15.6.0.

Estate of **Samuel HIDE** of Lebanon CT. <Windham CT PR #2144>
Receipt 16 Sept. 1748 from **Adonijah FITCH, (   ) FITCH, David HIDE,** of Lebanon, for £100 legacy from will of our honoured father Mr. Samuel HIDE. Receipt 17 Sept. 1748 from **Ebenezer BROWN** and **Sarah BROWN** for same.

Estate of **David HYDE** of Canterbury CT. <Plainfield CT PR #1145>
Inventory 4 Feb. 1817. Account 4 Nov. 1817 of **Alba HYDE**, executor.

Will of **Lieut. Daniel MOULTON** of Mansfield CT. <Windham CT PR #2788>
...19 Mar. 1767, mentions wf **Hannah,** sons **Gurdon MOULTON** & **Daniel MOULTON,** mother **Mehitable MOULTON,** brother in law **Samuel HIDE Jr.** Inventory 27 May 1767.

Will of **Samuel HIDE** of Lebanon CT. <Windham CT PR #2145>
...30 Jan. 1775, mentions wf **Priscilla,** children: **Ann HINKLEY** wf of Jared; **Sibel METCALF** wf of Jabez; **Zerviah METCEL** wf of Andrew; **Abigail HIDE**; grandchildren **Mary & Priscilla,** daughters of my said daughter dec'd (not named); grandsons **Gurden & David** the only children of my dau **Hannah,** dec'd; son **Samuel HIDE,** executor. Pr. 30 Apr. 1776. Inventory 1 May 1776, total £319.18.2.

Will of **Joseph BRADFORD.** <New London CT PR #667>
...25 Mar. 1811, mentions wf **Eunice,** children: to **Joseph BRADFORD,** $1.00 (he being absent many years); to **Stephen BRADFORD,** $100.00; **Benjamin BRADFORD** to maintain his unfortunate sister **Patience; Sarah BRADFORD**; granddaughter **Eunice BRADFORD.** Pr. 2 May 1815.

Col. William WHITING et al to **John SPRAGUE** of Lebanon CT. <Lebanon CT Deeds 3:243>
...7 Aug. 1819, **William WHITING** of Hartford, **Samuel WHITING** of Windham and **Lt. Joseph BRADFORD** of New London, for £5 quitclaim to **John SPRAGUE**...50 acres more or less, bounded partly on road to Hartford and partly on Henry WOODWARD's lane.

MICRO #9 OF 15

Estate of **Capt. Joseph BRADFORD** of Haddam CT. <Middletown CT PR>
<4:192> 5 Jan. 1778, **William BRADFORD** app'td. admr. <4:193> Inventory 24 Jan. 1778 by Phinehas BRAINERD, Charles SEARS, Jeremiah BRADFORD; incl. 35 acre home lot, £105; 60 acres out land, £70; an old Bible, 20s. <4:217> Account 6 Apr. 1778 by **William BRADFORD,** admr., £223 to be divided among heirs. <4:248> Distribution of estate 7 Apr. 1778 to following children: **William BRADFORD** (eldest son), **Robert BRADFORD, Henry BRADFORD, Elizabeth MAYO, Ann LYMAN, Hannah RUSSEL.**

MIDDLETOWN COUNTY CT DEEDS:

<21:261> 24 Nov. 1768, William BRADFORD to Stephen SEARS, both of Middletown.
<21:354> 24 Nov. 1768, William BRADFORD of Middletwon to Joel ARNOLD of Haddam.
<26:183> 4 May 1781, William BRADFORD of Chatham to Solomon HUBBARD of Middletown.
<27:295> 6 Sept 1785, William BRADFORD of Chatham to John HUBBARD of Middletown.

Will of **Robert BRADFORD** of Haddam CT. <Middletown CT PR>
<9:61>...26 Sept. 1803, mentions wf **Penelope,** eldest son **Joseph BRADFORD** of Westfield MA, second son **Perss/Perez BRADFORD** (named executor). Witnesses: Daniel BRAINERD, Susan BRAINERD, Abigail BRAINERD. Pr. 7 Feb. 1808.

Estate of **Penelope BRADFORD** of Haddam CT. <Middletown CT PR 12:268,289,296,319>
<12:268>...1822, son **Perez BRADFORD** appointed administrator.

Will of **Ebenezer STEELE** of Hartford CT. <Early Conneticut PR 3:655>
...26 June 1745, mentions wf **Susanna,** children: **John STEELE, Daniel STEELE, Bradford STEELE,**

Elisha STEELE, Mary (evidently married), **Susanna, Huldah, Melatiah.** Pr. 3 Mar. 1746/7.

Estate of **John STEELE** of Hartford. <Early CT PR 1:587>**<6>**
...John STEELE d. 6 Mar. 1698, father **James STEELE,** wf **Melatiah,** children: **Bethiah, John** (died a minor), **Ebenezer** (minor in 1715). (Distribution of estate?) 15 Dec. 1715, **Samuel SHEPHARD** of Hartford, in right of wf **Betthiah,** dau of John STEELE and **Melatiah STEVENS** of Killingsworth. 7 Feb. 1715/6 **Ebenezer STEELE,** minor about 19, chose **Thomas STEELE,** guardian.

Estate of **Charles WHITING** of New London CT. <New London CT PR #5691>
...Bond 12 Dec. 1738 by Joseph BRADFORD Jr., admr. Surety: Thomas FARGOE(sp). Inventory 8 Jan. 1738/9 by Adonijah FITCH, Daniel FITCH, total £49.5.0; 23 Jan. 1738/9 articles set off to widow, **Elizabeth,** as necessary to her support. Petition 11 Dec. 1738 of widow **Elizabeth** that Joseph BRADFORD Jr. administer estate.

Will of **Col. Gamaliel BRADFORD** of Duxbury. <Plymouth Co.PR #2527>
<25:17>..24 Apr. 1778, mentions children: **Samuel BRADFORD** (eldest son, dec'd), **Gamaliel BRADFORD, Seth BRADFORD, Peabody BRADFORD, Peter BRADFORD, Andrew BRADFORD, Abagail WADSWORTH, Hannah STANFORD, Ruth SAMSON;** unnamed grandchildren, the children of son Samuel; lands in Kingston & Winslow in County of Cumberland. Witnesses: Peres LORING, Isaac WINSLOW, Rebekah FRAZER. <25:19> Inventory 28 July 1778 by Peleg WADSWORTH, Perez LORING, Joseph SOUL, all of Duxbury. <25:285> Warrant for Division 15 Sept. 1778. Real estate divided into 5 shares between: heirs of **Samuel,** eldest son dec'd; **Gamaliel,** second son; **Seth,** third son; **Peabody,** fourth son and **Peter,** fifth son, reserving to **Andrew BRADFORD** the right to cut wood as long as he lives.

Estate of **Peabody BRADFORD,** yeoman of Duxbury. <Plymouth Co.PR #2588>**<6a>**
<27:330> Letter/Bond 7 Oct. 1782, **Welthea BRADFORD,** widow and **Lewis BRADFORD,** yeoman, both of Duxbury, app'td. admrs. Sureties: Charles FOSTER of Kingston, Levi LORING of Duxbury. Witnesses: William SHAW, Isaac LOTHROP. <29:34> Inventory taken 1 Sept. 1783 by Peres LORING, Levi LORING, Charles FOSTER. <31:185> Account of **Lewis BRADFORD,** surviving admr., allowed 1 May 1790. Received from: Jesse BARLOW, Francis KING, Barney BRIGGS, William TILSON, Isaac WATERMAN, James CHURCHEL. Paid to: Calvin RIPLEY, Isaac CHURCHEL, William SEVER, Josiah WEST, John PHILLIPS, Elisha FREEMAN Jno. ADAMS, Timothy RIPLEY, Caleb CHURCHEL, Samuel SAMPSON, Jonas WHITMAN, Caleb LORING, Oliver BRADFORD, Kimbal PRINCE. <33:10> 2nd Account 5 Apr. 1792, expenses incl. supporting brother **Ira BRADFORD** and sister **Lucy BRADFORD** for seven years, to women's apparel equally divided among my five sisters. <33:36> Division 10 Apr. 1792 by John GRAY, Joseph SAMPSON, both of Kingston and Samuel LORING of Duxbury. Real estate divided into nine parts to following children: **Lewis BRADFORD** (eldest son), **Pamela LITTLE** wf of Nathaniel Jr., **Cynthia BRADFORD, Charles BRADFORD, Joanna BRADFORD, Sylvia BRADFORD, Lucy Foster BRADFORD, Ira BRADFORD.** <33:41> 3rd Account 28 Apr. 1792. Paid: Nehemiah PETERSON, Nathan BREWSTER, John SAMPSON (for taxes), Bildad WASHBURN (for gravestones).

Guardianship of Children of **Peabody BRADFORD,** yeoman of Duxbury. <Plymouth Co.PR #2542>
<26:413> 5 May 1783, **Charles BRADFORD,** minor above 14, makes choice of Samuel LORING of Duxbury as guardian. Witnesses: Peres LORING, Michael SPRAGUE. Bond 5 May 1783 by Samuel LORING. Sureties: Charles FOSTER of Kingston, Lewis BRADFORD of Duxbury. Witnesses: James LEACH, William SNELL. <26:473> 7 Mar. 1791, **Joah/Joanna BRADFORD, Silvia BRADFORD,** minors above 14, make choice of James FOSTER of Kingston, as guardian. Witnesses: Judith BRADFORD, Pamela BRADFORD, Charles FOSTER, Benjamin ALLEN. Bond 7 Mar. 1791 by James FOSTER. Sureties: Nicholas DAVIS Jr., Bildad WASHBURN, both of Kingston. Witnesses: Gideon BRADFORD Jr., Isaac LOTHROP. <26:242> Letter/Bond 6 Apr. 1791, James FOSTER app'td. guardian of **Ira BRADFORD,** minor under 14. Sureties: John FAUNCE of Kingston, Nathaniel FOSTER Jr. of Middleboro. Witnesses: Thomas SHERMAN, Seth WESTON. <26:248> Letter/Bond 31 Mar. 1792, David BRADFORD of Kingston, app'td. guardian of **Lucy BRADFORD,** minor under 14. Sureties: James FOSTER of Kingston, Lewis BRADFORD of Duxbury. Witnesses: Nathaniel LITTLE Jr., Isaac LOTHROP. <26:316> Letter/Bond 28 Jan. 1795, Charles FOSTER of Kingston app'td. guardian of **Ira BRADFORD,** minor under 14. Sureties: Ichabod WASHBURN, David BRADFORD, both of Kingston. Witnesses: Levi BRADFORD, Cynthia BRADFORD.

Estate of **Samuel BRADFORD,** yeoman of Duxbury. <Plymouth Co.PR #2600>
<23:220> Letter/Bond 1 Feb. 1779, son **Samuel BRADFORD** of Duxbury app'td. admr. Sureties: Peter BRADFORD, Amos PHILLIPS. Witnesses: David KINGMAN, George BISBEE. <25:463> Inventory 30 Mar. 1779 by Peleg WADSWORTH, Seth BRADFORD, Peter BRADFORD; incl. part of farm given him by his father in his lifetime. <40:140> Account 2 Oct. 1804 by **Samuel BRADFORD,** incl. to supporting my mother and the family 5 years. <50:201> Warrant for Division 4 May 1803, by Samuel LORING, Levi LORING, Benjamin ALDEN, all of Duxbury, to set off to **Isaiah BRADFORD** and **Grace BRADFORD,** two of the children, their shares being two eighths parts and to set off real estate which **Gamaliel BRADFORD,** late of Duxbury, dec'd devised to his grandchildren, the children of his son **Samuel BRADFORD,** dec'd to - **Isaiah BRADFORD** and **Grace BRADFORD** (two of said grandchildren). Division 11 June 1803, one seventh each to **Grace BRADFORD** and **Isaiah BRADFORD.** Ratified and confirmed 17 May 1819.

Guardianship of Children of **Samuel BRADFORD,** yeoman of Duxbury. <Plymouth Co.PR #2536>
<26:4> Letters 7 Sept. 1778, **Samuel BRADFORD,** yeoman of Duxbury, guardian of children of **Samuel BRADFORD,** dec'd, viz: **Elihu BRADFORD** age 13, **George BRADFORD** age 11, **Isaiah BRADFORD** age 9. <22:224> 7 Sept. 1778, **Samuel BRADFORD** chosen guardian by **Grace BRADFORD Jr.** ae 15. Witnesses: Peter BRADFORD, Samuel BRADFORD. Bonds 7 Sept. 1778 by **Samuel BRADFORD** as gdn. of above minors. Sureties: Peter BRADFORD of Duxbury, Melzar ADAMS of Kingston. Witnesses: Seth BRADFORD, Asa BEARCE.

Stephen PAINE of Bristol RI to **Gershom BRADFORD** of Kingston MA. <Bristol RI Deeds 1:8>
...21 Mar. 1746/7, Stephen PAINE, Esq. for £3100 old tenor sold to Gershom BRADFORD, gentleman of Kingstown, in the County of Plimouth...ninety acres in Bristol, bounded by land belonging to heirs of Mr. Constant CHURCH, dec'd; heirs of Charles CHURCH Esq., dec'd. **Priscilla PAINE**, wf of Stephen, releases right of dower. Witnesses: Lydia POTTER, Thomas THROOPE Jr.

Gershom BRADFORD of Bristol RI to **Daniel BRADFORD** of Bristol RI. <Bristol RI Deeds 1:176>
...28 Sept. 1749, Gershom BRADFORD, gentleman, for and in consideration of ye Love and good will I bare to my Beloved Son Daniel BRADFORD, yeoman and Divers other good Causes...have given unto him ye one moiety or the one half part of my Homestead farm in Bristol, containing about ninty acres...bounds set forth in a deed from Coll. Stephen PAINE to me baring date ye twenty first day of march 1746/7. Witnesses: Joseph RAYNOLDS Jr., Jonathan RAYNOLDS.

Estate of **Capt. Gershom BRADFORD** of Bristol RI. <Bristol RI PR>
<1:243,306> Administration 2 May 1757 granted to son **Daniel BRADFORD. Priscilla BRADFORD**, widow, having refused. <1:247,305> Inventory 6 June 1757 by Mr. Thomas THROOPE, Capt. Joseph RAYNOLDS.

Gershom BRADFORD of Plymouth MA to **Francis COOKE** of Plympton MA. <Plymouth Co.Deeds 12:49>
...13 Mar. 1715/6, Gershom BRADFORD to Francis COOKE, 30 acres...which was granted to my Father **Samuel BRADFORD**, dec'd, by the Town of Plymouth.

Gershom BRADFORD of Plymouth MA to **Samuel RING** of Plympton MA. <Plymouth Co.Deeds 12:110>
...18 Mar. 1716/7, Gershom BRADFORD to Samuel RING...land bought of Thomas BARKER of Pembroke, 19 Dec. 1716.

Gershom BRADFORD of Plymouth MA to **Isaac LOTHROP** of Plymouth MA. <Plymouth Co.Deeds 15:110>
...22 Feb. 1720/1, Gershom BRADFORD, yeoman to Isaac LOTHORP, gentleman...mentions several pieces of land in Plymouth...part of land given me by my Honoured Father **Samuel BRADFORD,** dec'd, by his last will; mentions the following: Elisha BRADFORD, Maj. John BRADFORD, Joseph BRADFORD, dec'd, Jael BRADFORD.

Gershom BRADFORD of Plymouth MA to **Charles LITTLE** of Plymouth MA. <Plymouth Co.Deeds 15:181>
...22 July 1721, Gershom BRADFORD to Charles LITTLE...all that part of my ffarm & Tenement whereon I now dwell both upland swamp and meadow land which was given me by my Honoured Father...(Excepting a thirty acre lot of land I lately sold to Francis COOKE) with all the farm whereon John WASHBURN now dwells, and land where Ebenezer EATON now dwells.

MICRO #10 OF 15

Gershom BRADFORD of Plymouth MA to **Joseph BARSTOW** of Scituate MA. <Plymouth Co.Deeds 15:104>
...7 Feb. 1720/1, Gershom BRADFORD, yeoman, to Joseph BARSTOW...land given me by my father's will, where my dwelling house now stands.

Gershom BRADFORD of Plymouth MA to **Jacob COOKE** of Plymouth MA. <Plymouth Co.Deeds 15:133>
...15 Mar. 1720/1, Gershom BRADFORD, yeoman to Jacob COOKE, husbandman...Witnesses: Jacob MITCHELL, Joseph MITCHELL.

Gershom BRADFORD of Plymouth MA to **John WASHBURN** of Plymouth MA. <Plymouth Co.Deeds 16:126>
...29 Dec. 1722, Gershom BRADFORD to John WASHBURN...**Priscilla BRADFORD** releases right of dower. Witnesses: Gamaliel BRADFORD, Benjamin SAMSON.

Gershom BRADFORD of Plymouth MA to **John FAUNCE Jr.** of Plymouth. <Plymouth Co.Deeds 16:126>
...29 Dec. 1722, Gershom BRADFORD to John FAUNCE Jr....my 20 acre lot of land which was formerly given unto me by my Honoured Father **Samuel BRADFORD**, dec'd. **Priscilla BRADFORD** releases right of dower. (Bowman's note says "other Bradfords are mentioned".)

Gershom BRADFORD of Plymouth MA to **John FAUNCE Jr.** of Plymouth MA. <Plymouth Co.Deeds 16:127>
...29 Dec. 1722, Gershom BRADFORD to John FAUNCE Jr....land of Father **Samuel BRADFORD,** dec'd. (Bowman's note says "other Bradfords are mentioned".)

Gershom BRADFORD of Plymouth MA to **John FAUNCE Jr.** of Plymouth MA. <Plymouth Co.Deeds 16:147>
...22 Dec. 1722, Gershom BRADFORD to John FAUNCE Jr...land given me by my Father **Samuel BRADFORD,** dec'd. Witnesses: Gamaliel BRADFORD, Benjamin SAMSON.

Gershom BRADFORD of Plymouth MA to **Samuel BRADFORD** of Plympton MA. <Plymouth Co.Deeds 17:133>
...27 Feb. 1723/4, Gershom BRADFORD & wf Priscilla to Samuel BRADFORD...Witnesses: Robert BRADFORD, Priscilla WISWALL. (Bowman's note says "several other Bradfords mentioned".)

Gershom BRADFORD of Plymouth MA to **John ROGERS** of Swansea MA. <Plymouth Co.Deeds 18:169>
...3 Oct. 1724, Gershom BRADFORD, yeoman to John ROGERS, Esq...

Gershom BRADFORD et al to **James BEARSE Sr.** of Plympton MA. <Plymouth Co.Deeds 18:209>
...10 Oct. 1716...**Hannah BRADFORD,** widow, of Duxborough and Gershom BRADFORD of Plymouth, to James BEARSE Sr...Witnesses: Elizabeth BRADFORD et al. Rec. 29 Mar. 1725.

Gershom BRADFORD of Kingston MA to **Deacon John WASHBURN** of Kingston MA. <Plymouth Co.Deeds 24:99> ...(not dated), Gershom BRADFORD, husbandman to Deacon John WASHBURN, husbandman...Ack. 22 Apr. 1729. Rec. 21 May 1729.

Gershom BRADFORD of Kingston MA to **Samuel BRADFORD** of Plympton MA. <Plymouth Co.Deeds 26:195> ...21 Aug. 1731, Gershom BRADFORD, yeoman, to Samuel BRADFORD, gentleman...Witness: Elisha BRADFORD. (Bowman's note says "other Bradfords mentioned".)

Robert CUSHMAN Jr. to **Gershom BRADFORD** of Kingston MA. <Plymouth Co.Deeds 35:66> ...6 Oct. 1741, Robert CUSHMAN Jr. to Gershom BRADFORD, gentleman...

Gershom BRADFORD of Kingston MA to **William RAND** of Kingston MA. <Plymouth Co.Deeds 38:194> ...8 Apr. 1747, Gershom BRADFORD, gentleman to William RAND, clerk...land in Kingston bounded west upon land of Robert BRADFORD...being part of the homestead given to me by Father in his last Will...together with my dwelling house...**Priscilla BRADFORD**, wf, releases dower.

Gershom BRADFORD of Kingston MA to **John FAUNCE** of Kingston MA. <Plymouth Co.Deeds 39:21> ...30 June 1747, Gershom BRADFORD, gentleman, to John FAUNCE, yeoman...liberty to cart from said swamp as was given me from my Honoured Father **Samuel BRADFORD**, dec'd.

Gershom BRADFORD of Bristol RI to **Richard ADAMS** of Kingston MA. <Plymouth Co.Deeds 43:46> ...27 Nov. 1754, Gershom BRADFORD, gentleman, to Richard ADAMS, mariner.

Gershom BRADFORD of Bristol RI to **Peter LANE** of Hingham MA. <Plymouth Co.Deeds 46:166> ...25 Nov. 1754, Gershom BRADFORD, gentleman, to Peter LANE, executor to the last will & testament of my honoured Mother **Hannah BRADFORD**, dec'd...land given me in her said Testament out of land given me by my honoured Father **Samuel BRADFORD** and by me sold to my Grandfather **John ROGERS**, Esq. and by him given to my said mother. Deed subject to division among daughters of said Hannah.

Gershom BRADFORD of Bristol RI to **Ephraim WASHBURN** of Kingston MA. <Plymouth Co.Deeds 59:48> ...4 Feb. 1756, Gershom BRADFORD, gentleman to Ephraim WASHBURN, yeoman; mentions Mrs. Hannah BRADFORD, dec'd and land he gave to Jonathan WESTON. Rec. 5 July 1777.

The following reference numbers only are found in the files pertaining to **Gershom BRADFORD** as a grantee: Plymouth Co.Deeds 12:81; 13:106; 15:78; 16:125; 17:132; 20:10; 115:235; 117:4,22; 136:211; 139:173,200; 142:99; 152:83,84; 162:157; 172:60; 181:273; 184:152; 188:233; 192:61; 193:14; 217:263; 224:142; 227:174; 260:39; 275:215; 285:85; 289:124; 290:36,231; 296:49; 297:34.

Alexander BRADFORD of Stonington CT to **John FAUNCE** of Kingston MA. <Plymouth Co.Deeds 49:34> ...4 Nov. 1763, Alexander BRADFORD, gentleman, for £3.6s8d sold to John FAUNCE, yeoman, one eight part of a lot of meadow the whole whereof contains about fourteen acres more or less and lays in Plimpton...and was formerly the Estate of **Gershom BRADFORD** late of Bristol & Colony of Rhode Island, gentleman, dec'd. Witnesses: Benjamin TURNER, David STOCKBRIDGE.

Estate of **Daniel BRADFORD**, Esq. of Bristol RI. <Bristol RI PR>
<2:737> Probate 6 Aug. 1810, last will & testament was exhibited. Witnesses: Joseph REYNOLDS, Samuel REYNOLD & Sarah FALES 2d. William COX, Samuel REYNOLDS, John PECK app'td appraisers. <2:738> Estate rendered insolvent. Sureties on bond: **Leonard J. BRADFORD, Samuel BRADFORD..** <3:207> Inventory 7 Jan. 1811; incl pew in Cong.Cath. Meeting House, $35.00. <2:26> Account 2 Nov. 1812, of **Daniel BRADFORD**, executor, incl. legacy to widow $200.00, legacy to Priscilla CHILD $50.00.

Estate of **Leonard Jarvis BRADFORD.** <Bristol RI>
<4:29> Will. <2:43,3:270> Inventory. <3:26,30,55,57> Probate. (No dates or details given in files other than his death date - 27 July 1812.)

BRISTOL RI DEEDS: (re: Daniel BRADFORD)

<1:176> - , Daniel BRADFORD from Gershom BRADFORD.
<2:137> - 1 June 1758, Daniel BRADFORD, yeoman of Bristol RI from Simon DAVIS. Witness: Charles CHURCH. Rec. 12 Mar. 1760.
<3:83> - 31 Oct. 1764, Daniel BRADFORD, Esq. of Bristol as "com.", insolvency.
<3:140> - 16 June 1766, Daniel BRADFORD, Esq. to Peter CHURCH, gentleman, both of Bristol. Wife Mary releases dower.
<2:269> - 31 May 1769, Daniel BRADFORD, Esq. to Peter CHURCH, gentleman, both of Bristol. Wife Mary releases dower. Ack. 3 Aug. 1770 by Daniel BRADFORD (wf not ment.)
<4:296> - 24 May 1792, Daniel BRADFORD, Esq. to Nathaniel FALES Jr., yeoman, both of Bristol. Wife Susanna joins.
<6:34> - 15 May 1798, Daniel BRADFORD, Esq. to son Daniel BRADFORD Jr., gentleman, both of Bristol. No wife mentioned.
<6:282> - 13 Aug. 1801, Daniel BRADFORD Jr., gentleman, of Bristol from CHAPIN.
<8:359> - 14 Nov. 1803, Daniel BRADFORD Jr. & Leonard J. BRADFORD, of Bristol.
<8:360> - 22 Oct. 1803, Daniel BRADFORD Jr. & Leonard J. BRADFORD, of Bristol.

Daniel BRADFORD of Bristol RI to **Samuel BRADFORD** of Bristol RI. <Bristol RI Deeds 7:164> ...15 Nov. 1808, Daniel BRADFORD, Esq. to son Samuel BRADFORD, mariner, land bounded south on land of **Daniel & Leonard J. BRADFORD**, west on Narragansett Bay. Witnesses: Daniel BRADFORD Jr.,

Peter CHURCH Jr. Ack. same day before **Daniel BRADFORD Jr.**, J.P.

Daniel BRADFORD of Bristol RI to **Lenoard J. BRADFORD** of Bristol RI. <Bristol RI Deeds 8:173>
...17 Jan. 1811, Daniel BRADFORD, Esq. to Leonard J. BRADFORD, merchant, land partly on land of heirs of **Daniel BRADFORD**, Esq., dec'd. Wife Sarah releases dower. Ack. 19 Jan. 1811 by D.B. only. Witnesses: Susanna BRADFORD, Jonathan RUSSELL.

Daniel BRADFORD of Bristol RI from Town of Bristol RI. <Bristol RI Deeds 9:59>
...15 Apr. 1812, Town of Bristol RI to Daniel BRADFORD, Esq., Farm let: land in Bristol being part of the school lot, bounded as follows: west by land rented to Sheajashub BOWIN, north by road to a cross road, east by said cross road to land of heirs of Benjamin BOSWORTH, dec'd, south by land of Benjamin BOSWORTH to land of Sheajashub BOWIN, $18.68 to be paid on 25 Mar. for 50 yrs

---

Nathan BARDIN, Samuel N. BLAKE to **Daniel BRADFORD, Nathaniel BULLOCK.** <Bristol RI Deeds 9:117>
...2 Dec. 1814, Nathan BARDIN, Samuel N. BLAKE, gentleman, both of Bristol RI to Daniel BRADFORD, Nathaniel BULLOCK, land in Bristol with dwelling house.

Thomas SWAN of Bristol to **Daniel BRADFORD** of Bristol. <Bristol RI Deeds 9:267>
...29 Apr. 1816, Thomas SWAN, mariner to Daniel BRADFORD, Esq., land with dwelling house & other buildings in Bristol, bounded by Bradford St., N.P. SWAN, Thomas RICHMOND, Thames St. Witnesses: Samuel BRADFORD, John HOWLAND.

William THROOP to **Daniel BRADFORD, John W. BOURNE** of Bristol RI. <Bristol RI Deeds 9:289>
...24 Mar. 1817, William THROOP, Esq. of Bristol to Daniel BRADFORD, John W. BOURNE, Esqrs., two thirds of all my right in a lot of land with dwelling house in Bristol, bounded as follows: Union St., land of William FALES & Joseph WALDRON, land of Richard SMITH, land of Nathan BISHOP. Two thirds part of same estate conveyed to Grantor by deed from said BRADFORD & BOURNE on 20 Mar. 1817 as commissioners on estate of Nathan BARDIN & Samuel N. BLAKE, insolvent debtors.

Dr. Jeremiah BRADFORD of Middletown CT to **Jacob HURD** of Middletown. <Middletown CT Deeds 14:310>
...24 Feb. 1757, Dr. Jeremiah BRADFORD for £19.10s sold to Jacob HURD, ten acres in Middletown on the east side of Connecticut River in the Parish of Middlehaddam being part of the lands of Jonathan COLLENS of Wallingford. (<14:309> 21 Feb. 1757 Jeremiah bought land from Jonathan Collens.)

Jeremiah BRADFORD of Chatham CT to **Rebeckah, Joel BRADFORD** of Chatham. <Chatham CT Deeds 13:483>
...4 Apr. 1811, Jeremiah BRADFORD, for...the love and good will & affection that I have and bear unto my Wife Rebeckah and my third son Joel BRADFORD...quitclaim all rights in fifty acres in Chatham in the Society of Middlehaddam with the house & barn...Witnesses: Ezra BRAINARD, J.P., Thomas LELAM Jr.

Jeremiah BRADFORD Jr. et al. <Chatham CT Deeds 6:154>
...(no date), **Chauncy BULKLEY, Nathaniel DOAN 2d, Ralph SMITH 2d** of Chatham for £15 sold to **Jeremiah BRADFORD Jr., Joel BRADFORD** both of Chatham, and **William BRADFORD** of Weathersfield...three quarters of a piece of land the whole piece containing about one quarter acre. Witnesses: Jonathan PENFIELD, Mary BRADFORD. Rec. 19 July 1792.

Jeremiah BRADFORD et al. <Chatham CT Deeds 14:157>
...28 Oct. 1807, Jeremiah BRADFORD Jr., **Joel BRADFORD**, of Chatham, **William BRADFORD** of Wethersfield and **Jeremiah BRADFORD Jr.** of Berlin VT, for $800.00 sold to **Barnabas DUNHAM** of Berlin... land in Chatham near Middlehaddem landing containing about one quarter acre...bounded north on Ralph SMITH's land, with the Distillery thereon standing. Witnesses: Asahel H. STRONG, Harry "BRAFORD", Horace BRADFORD, Joseph BUCKLEY. Rec. 5 Apr. 1810.

William & Joel BRADFORD to **Newel BRAINERD** of Chatham CT. <Chatham CT Deeds 19:197>
...30 May 1821, William BRADFORD of Wethersfield and Joel BRADFORD of Chatham, for $130 sold to Newel BRAINERD...one quarter part of seven acre lot in Chatham, bounded by land of Jesse HURD & Jeremiah TAYLOR...together with one quarter part of dwelling house...belonging together with one quarter part of land lying near the aforesaid land...about one acre. Witnesses: Ralph SMITH, Harriet STEWART. Rec. 8 Mar. 1824.

Jeremiah BRADFORD of Berlin VT to **Newel BRAINERD** of Chatham CT. <Chatham CT Deeds 16:564>
...10 Feb. 1824, Jeremiah BRADFORD for $65.00 sold to Newel BRAINERD...one undivided eighth part of seven acres in Chatham, bounded by land of Jesse HURD & Jeremiah TAYLOR...together with one eighth part of dwelling house...together with one eighth part of land lying near the aforesaid land...about one acre. Witnesses: "Diah" RICHARDSON, Charles BULKLEY.

Nathaniel DOAN of Chatham CT to **Jeremiah BRADFORD, Ralph SMITH 2d.** <Chatham CT Deeds 11:448>
...19 Mar. 1805, Nathaniel DOAN for $800 sold to Jeremiah BRADFORD and Ralph SMITH 2d, both of Chatham...a certain piece of land in Chatham bounded by land of Russel DOAN, Noadiah TAYLOR and land now or late belonging to Chauncy BULKLEY...The condition of this deed is such that whereas the said BRADFORD and SMITH did on the 18th day of March 1805 promise and engage in writing to Stephen GRIFFITH Esq. of said Chatham to indemnify the said GRIFFITH from certain promisory notes whereon the said GRIFFITH is liable as a maker or indorser, viz: one note executed by...Nathaniel DOAN in favor of the Hartford Insurance Company for $270.00 and indorsed by the said GRIFFITH, also a note executed by the said DOAN in favor of Charles L. SMITH for $300.00 and indorsed by the said GRIFFITH, also a note for $188.95 executed by the said GRIFFITH to the said SMITH and by

him indorsed over to Jonathan BROWN of Chatham which note was executed and indorsed as aforesaid to secure the said BROWN a sum due from the said DOAN to the said BROWN...If Nathaniel DOAN pays note, this deed to be void. Witnesses: Cyrus BILL, Asahel H. STRONG.

==========

Jeremiah BRADFORD of Chatham CT et al to **David SELDEN** & Co. <Chatham CT Deeds 11:401>
...29 Mar. 1802, **Samuel DUDLEY, Joseph DUDLEY, Asa GOFF, Robert BRAINERD, Ebenezer THOMAS 2d** all of Haddam & **Jeremiah BRADFORD,** for $120 received of **David SELDEN** & Co...quitclaim a certain fish place...(See Below). Witnesses: Edward SELDEN, Mary SELDEN.

==========

Jeremiah BRADFORD of Chatham CT to **David SELDEN** & Co. <Chatham CT Deeds 11:400>
...19 Sept. 1803, Jeremiah BRADFORD for $30.00 paid by David SELDEN & Co...quit claim all rights to a certain fish place on the east side of Connecticut River...bounded by Parsonage lot and Thomas SELDEN's house lot...reserving to myself the Liberty to go up northerly as far as an ash stump near the uper end of the Meadow the usual place where the Company with Whom I am Conserned set out for a hall. Witnesses: Seth OVERTON, Thomas CHILD.

==========

Nathaniel & Job DOAN of Chatham CT to **Jeremiah BRADFORD Jr.** of Chatham. <Chatham CT Deeds 10:141>
...5 Feb. 1801, Nathaniel DOAN & Job DOAN, for £8 sold to Jeremiah BRADFORD Jr...one equal fourth part of a certain piece of land containing about one quarter acre, it being the piece of land where said BRADFORD's distillery stands...bounded by highway, river and Capt. Ralph SMITH's land, it being the whole of the right of said land which James BRAINARD, dec'd, formerly owned. Witnesses: William TALBUT, Daniel SHEPHARD.

==========

Joel BRADFORD of Chatham CT to **Noadiah TAYLOR** of Chatham CT. <Chatham CT Deeds 19:529>
...29 Mar. 1827, Joel BRADFORD for $210 sold to Noadiah TAYLOR...forty five acres in Chatham in the Society of Middlehaddam...bounded on north by land of the heirs of the Rev. David SELDEN, west on Connecticut River, south on Benjamin HURD & David SELDEN's heirs, east on highway...provided that mortgage note is paid before 29 Mar. 1829. Witnesses: Abigail BUNCE, Ira LEE.

==========

Estate of **William BRADFORD** of Wethersfield CT. <Hartford CT PR>
<35:50> Letter 22 Oct. 1824, **Nancy BRADFORD** app'td. admx. <35:67> Inventory taken (no date) by Walter BULKLEY, Archibald ROBBINS, incl. 6 feather beds, $180; 6 tables, $20; 5 looking glasses, $30; 1 piana forte, $70; 1 brass clock, $25; carpeting & rug, $35; 42 chairs, $50; 2 stoes, $45; 23 silver spoons & sugar tongs, $25; watch, $8; window curtains, $10; cow, $18; store & lot, $340 and house & lot, $1025. Total: $9,534.49. <original> Bond 22 Oct. 1824 by **Nancy BRADFORD** of Wethersfield and **Elizabeth BRADFORD,** widow of William BRADFORD, dec'd.

==========

Will of **Eilzabeth BRADFORD,** widow of Wethersfield CT. <Hartford CT PR>
<37:4>...4 Jan. 1828, to Henry BULKLEY, Esq. of Wethersfield, $800 of the Capital Stock of the Bank of America in the City of New York, in sacred trust, to pay to my daughter **Betsey...**as long as she remains the wife of Ralph BULKLEY; son **George BRADFORD;** to the said Henry BULKLEY $200 in sacred trust...until my Granddaughter **Susan,** the daughter of my late son **Horace BRADFORD,** shall become of full age; daughters **Fanny BRADFORD** and **Sophia BRADFORD;** daughters **Nancy** and **Charlotte;** sons **William BRADFORD** (named executor), **George BRADFORD** (who receives nothing). Witnesses: Joshua L. WILLIAMS, Thomas STOW, Ursula SMITH. <37:8> Pr. 25 Mar. 1829. <37:10> Inventory 24 Mar. 1829. <37:220> Agreement. <37:279> Agreement approved. <original> Declination of **William BRADFORD** to serve as executor, requests that sister **Fanny** be named. <original> Release 22 Aug. 1831, the following heirs have received from **Fanny BRADFORD** $885.49 as their share of estate, viz: **William BRADFORD** (New York, NY), **Sylvester BULKLEY & Nancy B. BULKLEY** (Berlin CT), **Charles H. HILL, Sophia HILL, Richard GRIMES, Charlotte GRIMES.**

==========

Job BRADFORD et al of Boston MA against **Jesse HIGGINS** of Chatham CT. <Chatham CT Deeds 2:253>
...4th Tues. Jan. 1772, Job BRADFORD and Thomas LOYD, both of Boston...recovered judgment against Jesse HIGGINS...for the sum of £20.19.1 damages and £1.7.3. cost of suit. Writ was ussued to levy on goods or lands of said Jesse HIGGINS.

MICRO #11 OF 15

Estate of **John TUFTS** of Boston MA. <Suffolk Co.PR #20741, 95:362>
Will 8 June 1797, mentions wf **Mary,** half brother & sister, cousins. Pr. 8 Aug. 1797. (Names are given in the files but the pencilled handwriting is difficult to make out.)

==========

Estate of **Mary TUFTS** of Boston MA. <Suffolk Co.PR #21075, 97:372>
Will 11 Aug. 1796, leaves all to children. Pr. 10 or 16 July 1799.

==========

Will of **Abigail TUFTS,** widow of Medford MA. <Middlesex Co.PR #16350>
...12 Apr. 1776, mentions granddaughter **Lucy JONES;** estate to be divided into seven equal parts among children, viz: **Simon TUFTS, Abigail BISHOP, Cotton TUFTS, Samuel TUFTS, Mercy BROOKS,** heirs of son **William TUFTS,** heirs of dau **Anna JONES.** Simon & Cotton named executors (Cotton refused 7 Sept. 1790). Witnesses: Nathaniel RAND, Richard BOYLSTON, Nathaniel RAND Jr.

==========

Will of **Simon TUFTS** of Medford MA. <Middlesex Co.PR #16423>
...14 Nov. 1786, mentions wf **Elizabeth;** brother **William TUFTS,** dec'd; children: **Lucy, Simon TUFTS** (to receive all his mother's patrimonial estates), **Turrell TUFTS, Cotton TUFTS, Hall TUFTS.** Witnesses: Gardner GREENLEAF, Moses BILLINGS, Ebenezer HALL. Division of estate 8 Dec. 1790; dau

Lucy is called **Mrs. Lucy HALL.** Codicil 12 Dec. 1786, to wife **Elizabeth** her portion of the estate of her late father **Stephen HALL,** Esq.

Will of **James TUFTS**, yeoman of Medford MA. <Middlesex Co.PR #16378>
...Oct. 1810, mentions wf **Elizabeth**, children: **Mary REED, James TUFTS Jr., Elizabeth (MENDALLsp), Lucretia RICHARDSON, Sally TOWNSEND, Elias TUFTS, Marcy TUFTS, Fanny TUFTS, Lucy TUFTS, Nancy TUFTS**; children of my dau **Mary** & dau **Elizabeth.**

Will of **Lucy TUFTS**, widow of Charlestown MA. <Middlesex Co.PR #16397>
...24 June 1826, mentions Jacob & Lucretia PROCTOR and their children: Ardila M. PROCTOR (eldest dau) & Lucretia AUGUSTA PROCTOR (2nd dau), under 21, eldest sons Charles PROCTOR, John PROCTOR; (Som--?) FISKE & his wf Ardila LOUISE FISKE.

SUFFOLK COUNTY PROBATE: (re: TUFTS)

1797	John	will	#20741, 95:367	1826	Ebenezer	will	#27095, 124:296
1799	Mary	will	#21075, 97:372	1832	Susanna	will	#29918, 130:-57
1807	William	adm.	#22874, 105:202	1838	Ann	adm.	#32012, 442:249
1818	(sp)	gdn.	#25739, 374:20	1838	Asa	adm.	#31934, 201:176
1823	M(sp)	will	#27059, 121:158	1844	Hannah	will	#33929, 142:205

(Although there is no source cited for the above they appear to be from Suffolk Co.PR. The pencilled handwriting is hard to make out in places. On the following page in the same handwriting and format are the following:

1808	Joseph N. BRADFORD	gdn.	#23276	1849	Joseph N. BRADFORD	gdn.	#35939
1824	Ann BRADFORD	adm.	#27405	1867	Joseph N. BRADFORD	adm.	#47593

Estate of **Ann BRADFORD**, widow of Boston MA. <Suffolk? Co.PR #27405>
...15 Nov. 1824, Samuel BRADFORD, merchant of Boston, app'td. adm.; mentioned are Daniel BRADFORD merchant, Kathren B. BRADFORD, Lucy BRADFORD. Inventory 28 Mar. 1825.(very difficult to decipher)

Estate of **Joseph Nash BRADFORD.** <Suffolk? Co.PR #23276>
Petition 26 Dec. 1808 by his brother **William Barnes BRADFORD.** (Additional dates of 9 Jan. 1809 and 11 Dec. 1809 are given but handwriting too faint to make out details.)

Estate of **John MERCHANT** of Boston MA. <Suffolk Co.PR #18475>
...July 1785, **Anne MERCHANT**, widow, app'td. admr. Sureties: William FOSTER, Simeon MAYHEW, merchants of Boston. Deposition 22 Aug. 1785 mentions a sister who should occupy the house she lives in for life. Inventory taken 10 July 1787 by Thomas DAVIES, Bossensar(sp) FOSTER, Jacob COOPER. Oath of **Ann MERCHANT**, widow, admx., 9 Mar. 1790.

Estate of **Moses NORMAN**, block maker of Newport RI. <Newport RI PR>
<4:347> Petition 1 Dec. 1806, **Sarah NORMAN**, widow, app'td. admx. <4:381> Inventory 6 Apr. 1807, total $38.04. <4:407> Receipts 1 June 1807.

Moses THURSTON, Wm. THURSTON of Newport RI to **Henry BULL** of Newport. <Newport RI Deeds 13:34>
...11 May 1812, Moses THURSTON & wf Elizabeth and William THURSTON sell to Henry BULL land on Bull St. (Additional THURSTON deeds are cited but not transcribed, viz: 17:66, 19:63, 22:114, 22:218, 36:37.)

Estate of **Capt. Nathaniel GILBERT**, gentleman of Taunton MA. <Bristol Co.PR>
<14:555> Will 18 June 1755, mentions wf **Deborah**, children: **Nathaniel GILBERT** (eldest son), **George GILBERT, Welthea GILBERT, Abigail GILBERT, Joanna GILBERT**, all under age. <14:558> Pr. 7 Oct. 1755. <15:66> Inventory, 1755. <125:135-39> Guardianship 16 Mar. 1757, **Deborah**, widow, app'td. gdn. of the five children, all under 14. <18:97> Account 1762, of **Deborah TISDALE**, late **Deborah GILBERT**, as gdn. of the children. <127:75> Guardianship 9 July 1762, Benjamin WILLIAMS, Esq. of Taunton app'td. gdn. of the children with **Welthy & Abigail** now above 14.

Estate of **Capt. Samuel GILBERT** of Berkley MA. <Britol Co.PR><7>
<original> 10 May 1777...Samuel GILBERT...Inhabitant of Berkley has absented himself for near two year leaving...an Estate both real and personal...said Samuel GILBERT volenterily went to our enimies and is still absent from his habitation...therefore pray for appointment of agent for his estate. Signed by four Selectman of Berkley. <147:163> Letter 7 July 1777, John BABBIT, gentleman of Berkley app'td. agent. <original> Inventory 20 Apr. 1778, incl. 198 acres, £1980; 20 acres, £80; 100 acres in Mansfield, £600. <original> Division 23 Mar. 1779 of real estate of Samuel GILBERT, absentee; 3 Apr. 1779, one third set off to wife, **Sarah GILBERT.** <original> Confiscation 12 Sept. 1780, 198 acre homestead in Berkley. <original> Bond 6 Sept. 1796 by widow **Sarah GILBERT**, admx. Inventory 6 Sept. 1796, estate of **Capt. Samuel GILBERT**, late of Berkley, gentleman, dec'd. <original> Account 5 Aug. 1800 of **Sarah GILBERT**, admx...all estate which came into her hands on or before 28 July 1797. Paid: **Ebenezer PIERCE Jr.** & wf **Sally** her part and **Ezra CHASE** & wf **Jerusha** her part. <42:493> Insolency 3 Mar. 1807, **Sarah GILBERT**, widow. <42:506> Inventory 14 Mar. 1807. <43:311> Division 4 Aug. 1807 to **Jerusha CHASE** wf of Ezra and **Sally PIERCE** wf of Ebenezer. <109:175> Order of notice 3 Mar. 1807, Ebenezer PIERCE Jr. of Berkley. <150:204> Letter 3 Mar. 1807, Ebenezer PIERCE Jr., yeoman, adm. of **Sarah GILBERT**, widow, late of Berkley.

BRISTOL COUNTY DEEDS: (re: Samuel GILBERT)

38:269 - 26 Feb. 1752, Samuel GILBERT from Bezaleel THRASHER.
39:216 - 8 Dec. 1752, Samuel GILBERT to Nathaniel GILBERT.
40:568 - 7 Apr. 1755, Samuel GILBERT from George SANFORD.
41:312 - 7 Apr. 1755, Samuel GILBERT from Nathaniel GILBERT (at Norton).
41:312 - 7 Apr. 1755, Samuel GILBERT from John BRIGGS Jr.
41:313 - 7 Apr. 1755, Samuel GILBERT from Nathan MIRICK.
42:337 - 2 July 1757, Samuel GILBERT from Ebenezer CRANE.
43:139 - 20 June 1758, Samuel GILBERT to Ebenezer PAUL.
44:449 - 15 Oct. 1760, Samuel GILBERT to Benjamin TIFFANY.
44:449 - 15 Oct. 1760, Samuel GILBERT to Thomas GROVER.
44:450 - 15 Oct. 1760, Samuel GILBERT to Edward PAINE.
45:508 - 14 June 1762, Samuel GILBERT from Ebenezer PAUL.
46:98 - 1 Oct. 1762, Samuel GILBERT to Jacob STAPLE Jr.
47:234 - 14 Sept 1764, Samuel GILBERT from Joseph DEAN.
47:235 - 14 Sept 1764, Samuel GILBERT from Ephraim PRAY.
47:383 - 28 Feb. 1765, Samuel GILBERT to Ebenezer FRENCH
49:81 - 29 Oct. 1765, Samuel GILBERT to Samuel WELLMAN.
50:488 - 29 July 1767, Samuel GILBERT from Seth WHITE.
50:551 - 14 Oct. 1767, Samuel GILBERT to Timothy TINGLEY.
55:85 - 1 May 1769, Samuel GILBERT from Job ANTHONY Jr. & wf.
55:85 - 25 Dec. 1772, Samuel GILBERT from John BABBITT.
55:149 - 20 Mar. 1773, Samuel GILBERT, gentleman of Berkley, to John BRETTUN.
55:150 - 20 Mar. 1773, Samuel GILBERT, gentleman of Berkley, to Abiel DRAKE.
61:374 - 13 Mar. 1783, Samuel GILBERT to Joseph ATWOOD (confiscated estate).
63:265 - 14 Sept 1785, Samuel GILBERT to Nathaniel TOBEY (confiscated estate).
67:183 - 26 July 1786, Samuel GILBERT to Samuel PAULL (confiscated estate).
71:104 - 18 July 1792, Samuel GILBERT, gentleman of Berkley, to John ROBINSON, yeoman of Raynham land in Taunton.
71:104 - 18 July 1792, Samuel GILBERT from Ebenezer MIRICK.

Estate of **Ebenezer HATHAWAY** of Freetown MA. <Bristol Co.PR>
<original> Petition for Dower 12 Mar. 1792 of **Welthe HATHEWAY**, widow...Whereas my Late husband **Ebenezer HATHAWAY**...on 4 August 1790 did by his Deed of Gift convaye to my son **Gilburt HATHAWAY** our Dwelling house and a part of our homestead farm and as it has pleasied God to lay me under sum bodely infermeteys...<original> Petition 15 Mar. 1792 by **Gilbert HATHEWAY** to have Ephraim WINSLOW and Col. Benjamin WEAVER, both of Freetown, set off dower. <148:443> Bond 4 Sept. 1792, by **Gilbert HATHEWAY**, yeoman, as administrator. Sureties: Ambrose BARNABY, William REED, gentlemen of Freetown. Witnesses: Samuel S. WILDE, William BAYLIES. <original> Warrant 4 June 1793 to appraise estate by Benjamin WEAVER, William REED, Benjamin PORTER. <32:312> Inventory 11 June 1793. Personal estate included notes against Calvin HATHAWAY, Benjamin DEAN, Zebulon WHITE and Godfrey BRIGGS.

Ebenezer HATHAWAY, gentleman of Freetown to **Calvin HATHAWAY**. <Bristol Co.Deeds 70:52>
...4 Aug. 1790, Ebenezer HATHAWAY gives to son Calven HATHAWAY, yeoman of Freetown, land in Freetown and Middleborough, including part of homestead.

Ebenezer HATHAWAY, gentleman of Freetown to **Gilbert HATHAWAY**. <Bristol Co.Deeds 70:19>
...4 Aug. 1790, Ebenezer HATHAWAY gives to son Gilbert HATHAWAY, yeoman of Freetown, homestead & land in Freetown, land in Berkeley and Middleborough; mentions land to be deeded to son Calven same day.

Benjamin CRANE, mariner of Berkeley against **Ebenezer HATHAWAY Jr.** <Bristol Co.Deeds 65:503>
...21 June 1786, Judgement against Ebenezer HATHAWAY Jr., gentleman, late of Freetown in favor of Benjamin CRANE; Ebenezer called "an absentee".

Ebenezer HATHAWAY, gentleman of Freetown against **Ebenezer HATHAWAY Jr.** <Bristol Co.Deeds 65:504>
...26 June 1786, Judgement against Ebenezer HATHAWAY Jr., gentleman, late of Freetown in favor of Ebenezer HATHAWAY; Ebenezer Jr. called "an absentee".

Ebenezer HATHAWAY of Freetown to **Ebenezer HATHAWAY Jr.** of Burton N.B. <Bristol Co.Deeds 66:243>
...25 July 1787, Ebenezer HATHAWAY, gentleman, sells to Ebenezer HATHAWAY Jr. land and part of house in Freetown; same description as that of land given to creditors in Deed 65:504.

Ebenezer HATHAWAY Jr. by Attorney to **Theophilus CLARK, Oliver GRINNELL.** <Bristol Co.Deeds 72:90>
...16 July 1793, Ephraim WINSLOW and Calven HATHWAY, both of Freetown...Attorneys to Ebenezer HATHWAY, farmer of Burton N.B., for £75 sold to Theophilus CLARK Jr., shop joiner and Oliver GRENNELL, seaman, both of Freetown...dwelling house and about half an acre of land in Freetown...for a more perticular discription of ye boundaries of said Land to ye Deed from **Capt. Ebenezer HATHWAY** to ye said Ebenezer.

Ebenezer HATHAWAY, gentleman of Freetown to **Hannah HATHAWAY** of Freetown. <Bristol Co.Deeds 70:52>
...4 Aug. 1790, Ebenezer HATHAWAY gives to daughter Hannah HATHAWAY, single, half of gristmill in Freetown in common with James WINSLOW to have possession after grantor's decease.

Will of **Hannah HATHAWAY**, singlewoman of Berkley MA. <Bristol Co.PR 61:224> ...12 Nov. 1823...I do not give nor bequeath anything to my sister **Welthea RUGGLES**. I also do not give nor bequeath anything to my three brothers, viz: **Gilbert HATHAWAY, Calvin HATHAWAY** and **Luther HATHAWAY**. I do not give nor bequeath anything to the children of my two brothers, viz: **Ebenezer HATHAWAY** and **Shadrach HATHAWAY**. I give and bequeath to Celia FRENCH, wife of Capt. Samuel FRENCH Jr. my bed and bed furniture. I do not give nor bequeath anything to the following children of my sister **Tryphena CRANE**, viz: **Weltha NICHOLS, Tryphena HATHAWAY, Nathaniel CRANE, Henry CRANE, Phebe BABBIT, Abi BABBIT, Hannah CRANE, Lydia BABBIT, Rebekah NICHOLS** and **James CRANE**. Lastly I give and bequeath all the rest residue and remainder of my personal estate...to Adoniram CRANE Esq. (named executor) and Celia FRENCH, wife of Capt. Samuel FRENCH Jr. Witnesses: William S. CRANE, Levi L. CRANE, John C. CRANE. <61:180> Citation for probate 2 Dec. 1823. <61:225> Pr. 9 Jan. 1824. <original> Bond 9 Jan. 1824 by Adoniram CRANE, Esq. Sureties: Levi L. CRANE and William S. CRANE. Witnesses: Edward ANTHONY, D.G.W. COBB. <61:573> Receipt 16 Dec. 1824, two hundred dollars in full for my share of estate...signed by Celia FRENCH, Samuel FRENCH Jr.

Ebenezer HATHAWAY of Freetown to **Ebenezer HATHAWAY Jr.** of Freetown MA. <Bristol Co.Deeds 62:545> ...26 Oct. 1770, Ebenezer HATHAWAY, gentleman, for £10 sold to Ebenezer HATHAWAY Jr., blacksmith ...land in Freetown, part of the twenty fourth lot in ye freemans purchase...bounded by my homestead farm which was given to me by my Honoured Father Ebenezer HATHAWAY deceased...together with the blacksmith shop and Cole House thereon standing. Rec. 16 Aug. 1784. (no witnesses mentioned)

Will of **Ebenezer HATHAWAY** of Burton, N.B. <Sunbury Co., N.B. PR A:159>[8] ...16 Jan. 1811, mentions wf **Mary**, children: **Ebenezer HATHEWAY, Warren HATHEWAY, Cushi HATHEWAY, Calvin Luther HATHEWAY, Charles Reed HATHEWAY, James Gilbert HATHEWAY, Thomas Gilbert HATHEWAY**; executors to maintain the Widow Mary GARISH according to the tenor of the Bond given to her by me. Witnesses: Peres GILBERT, Lucretia GILBERT, Deborah SCOVIL.

MICRO #12 OF 15

Ebenezer HATHAWAY of Freetown MA to **Gilbert HATHAWAY** of Freetown MA. <Bristol Co.Deeds 70:19> ...4 Aug. 1790, Ebenezer HATHAWAY, gentleman sold to son Gilbert HATHAWAY, yeoman...my homestead farm in Freetown; land in Freetown purchased by deed of James EDMINSTER & John WINSLOW; land in Berkley; half part of salt meadow; other land in Freetown purchased by deed of Samuel TISDALE.

Gilbert HATHAWAY of Freetown MA to **Samuel TUBBS** of Berkley MA. <Bristol Co.Deeds 77:443> ...2 Jan. 1797, Gilbert HATHAWAY, yeoman sells to Samuel TUBBS, yeoman, land in Berkley. Mary HATHAWAY signs.

Gilbert HATHAWAY of Freetown MA to **Philip HATHAWAY 2d** of Freetown MA. <Bristol Co.Deeds 84:405> ...5 Mar. 1801, Gilbert HATHAWAY, yeoman, for $2800.00 sold to Phillip HATHAWAY 2d, clerk...all the real estate I have in said Freetown except ten acres of land off of the east end of my Edminister farm...another piece of land my Tisdale lot...also a piece of salt meadow which came to me by my honoured Father **Ebenezer HATHAWAY**, decd. Mary HATHAWAY signs also. Witnesses: Gilbert HATHAWAY Jr., Luther HATHAWAY. Rec. 5 Mar. 1805.

Gilbert HATHAWAY of Freetown MA to **Calvin HATHAWAY** of Freetown MA. <Bristol Co.Deeds 82:180> ...15 June 1801, Gilbert HATHAWAY, yeoman for $20.00 release to Calven HATHAWAY, yeoman...all my right in five of ye Taunton Proprietors Land, which were laid out on 28 Dec. 1770 to ye heirs of **Ebenezer HATHAWAY** Esq. Witnesses: Benjamin BROWN, Benjamin WEAVER. Rec. 14 Mar. 1803.

Will of **Peres BRADFORD** of Attleboro MA. <Bristol Co.PR 11:168> ...12 June 1746, mentions wf **Abigail**, children: **Peres BRADFORD** (eldest son, under 21), **Joel BRADFORD, George BRADFORD, John BRADFORD, Joseph BRADFORD, Abigail LEE** wf of Samuel Jr., **Hannah BRADFORD, Mary BRADFORD, Elizabeth BRADFORD**. Witnesses: Benjamin MAY, Ebenezer FOSTER, John ROBBINS Jr. Pr. 5 Aug. 1746. <11:229> 24 Dec. 1746, Samuel LEE Jr., shipwrite, of Swanzey and dau **Hannah BRADFORD**, spinster, of Attleboro, app'td administrators of estate as widow **Abigail BRADFORD** is deceased. <11:481> Account 7 June 1748 of Samuel LEE and **Hannah GAY**, admrs., paid legacies to **Abigail LEE** and **Mary GOULD**. <17:602> Account 7 Aug. 1753 of admrs., paid legacies to **Hannah GAY** and **Elizabeth SWEETLAND**.

Guardianship of Children of **Peres BRADFORD** of Attleboro MA. <Bristol Co.PR>
<11:230> 24 Dec. 1746, Gershom BRADFORD of Kingston app'td gdn. of **Joel BRADFORD**, minor over 14. <11:232> 3 Mar. 1746 (1747), Samuel LEE Jr. app'td gdn. of **Peres BRADFORD**, minor over 14. <11:475> 7 June 1748 Gershom BRADFORD app'td gdn. of **George BRADFORD** (above 14), **John & Joseph BRADFORD** (under 14).

Benjamin WISE, yeoman of Attleborough to **Peres BRADFORD**, Esq. of Swanzey.<Bristol Co.Deeds 34:46> ...6 Sept. 1745, Benjamin WISE & wf Prudence for £1300 old tenor bills sold to Peres BRADFORD... all their homestead farm in Attleborough, containing 70 acres as described in deed 40:488.

Perez BRADFORD of Lynn MA to **Daniel DAVIS Jr.** of Swanzey MA. <Bristol Co.Deeds 43:486> ...24 Mar. 1759, Peres BRADFORD, laborer, for £13.10s sold to Daniel DAVIS Jr., yeoman...one eighth part of a certain piece of land and meadow in Swanzey...being what was given by ye last will and testament of Peres BRADFORD Esq., deceased, to his son Joel.

BRISTOL COUNTY PROBATE (re: Perez BRADFORD)

23:69 - 1733/4, P.B. to George LEONARD.
23:267 - 1734/5, P.B. to Benjamin HODGES.
32:402 - 1744, P.B. to Edward LUTHER.
33:14 - 1744, P.B. to Edward GRAY et al.
34:45 - 1745, P.B. from mother Hannah BRADFORD, part of estate of her father John ROGERS.
34:90 - 1745, P.B. to Benjamin COLE Jr.
35:289 - 1748, P.B. to Hezekiah BOWEN.
40:488 - 1754, P.B. & wf to Samuel PITCHER.
41:225 - 22 Oct. 1754, P.B., shoreman of Marblehead against Benjamin COLE.
41:278 - 1755, P.B. et al to Stephen PECK.
43:486 - 1759, P.B. to Daniel DAVIS Jr.
44:506 - 1761, P.B., Swansea to Samuel CHACE.
48:368 - 1765, P.B. et al to Samuel LEE Jr.

PROVIDENCE REGISTRY OF DEEDS:

20:145 - 28 Apr. 1773, Charles LEE of Providence, shipwright, buys land on Great Road to Plainfield from William & Mary HOYLE.
21:589 - 29 July 1788, Charles LEE, yeoman, buys land from Thomas & Abigail AUGELL.

Will of **Jabes GAY** of Attleborough MA <Bristol Co.PR 38:392>
...(no date given), mentions daughters **Hannah CHURCH, Selah GAY,** children of **Filena WHITAKER** (minors), **Monica BAKER, Molly METCALF, Lucy METCALF,** heirs of **Eleana BA()N.** Pr. 26 Oct. 1801.

Will of **Perez BRADFORD** of Attleborough MA. <Bristol Co.PR>
<original>...12 June 1746, mentions wife **Abigail,** eldest son **Peres BRADFORD** (under 21) to receive homestead farm and four acres salt meadow in Swanzey which was purchased of Jonathan KINSLEY; son **Joel BRADFORD** to receive land purchased from Benjamin WISE lying in Attleborough adjoyning land of Nathaniel METCALF; sons **George BRADFORD, John BRADFORD, Joseph BRADFORD** to receive all lands in North Yarmouth and Plymouth; wife to receive dwelling houses, orchading outhouses & lands purchased from Samuel LEE. (also cited but not detailed: 11:168,170,229,232,393,481,17:602,603)

Perez BRADFORD et al of Attleborough MA to **Samuel LEE Jr.** of Swanzey. <Bristol Co.Deeds 48:368>
...24 Oct. 1749, **Jabez GAY** & wf **Hannah, Mary GOULD** (of Cumberland RI), **Elisabeth BRADFORD, Peres BRADFORD, Joel BRADFORD, George BRADFORD, John BRADFORD, Joseph BRADFORD,** all of Attleborough, for £600 old tenor sold to **Samuel LEE Jr.,** shipwright, all their right by vertue of a certain deed of sale...of Samuel BONNEY date ye 11th Apr. 1745...eleven acres being ye homestead whereon ye said Samuel LEE now dwells, bounded by land of Samuel LEE, Eber SHERMAN, highway to Sleads ferry...being ye same lands that was conveyed to **Peres BRADFORD,** Esq. deceased by said deed. Acknowledged at Attleborough 14 Dec. 1749 by Jabez GAY, Hannah GAY, Mary GOULD, Elizabeth BRADFORD; at Attleborough 25 Sept. 1757 by Perez BRADFORD, Joel BRADFORD; at Swansea 9 Mar. 1758 by John BRADFORD; at Providence 9 Feb. 1764 by George BRADFORD, Joseph BRADFORD. Rec. 14 Oct. 1765.

Perez BRADFORD et al to **Stephen PECK** of Rehoboth MA. <Bristol Co.Deeds 41:278>
...31 Mar. 1750, **Samuel LEE** & wf **Abigail** of Swanzey, **Jabez GAY** & wf **Hannah, Samuel SWEETLAND** & wf **Elisabeth, Mary GOULD** widow and **Peres BRADFORD,** all of Attleborough, for £100...we being some of the heirs of ye Honourable **Peres BRADFORD,** Esq. deceased, quit claim unto **Stephen** of Rehoboth all rights in three pieces of land which our said Honoured father purchased of said Stephen as by a deed on file dated July ye 12th 1744...and that ye said **Stephen PECK**...Rec. 31 Mar. 1755.

Perez BRADFORD of Attleborough MA to **Samuel PITCHER** of Attleborough MA. <Bristol Co.Deeds 40:488>
...28 Dec. 1752, Peres BRADFORD, yeoman & wf Mary for £466.13s4d sold to Samuel PITCHER, yeoman, homestead farm in Attleborough containing seventy acres, bounded by land of Benjamin CRABTREE, Samuel DAY, John ROBBINS Jr., Benjamin MAY, Nathaniel ROBBINSON. Ack. by Perez BRADFORD at Cumberland RI 29 Oct. 1753. Rec. 2 Oct. 1754.

Estate of **Elijah DAMON Sr.,** yeoman of Pembroke MA. <Plymouth Co.PR>
<43:353> Dower set off 1 Oct. 1810 to widow **Anna DAMON.** <45:52> Order for division 1 May 1813, to and among his children & heirs, viz: heirs of son **Elijah DAMON,** dec'd; heirs of **Abigail HOLMES,** dec'd; heirs of **Nancy HOLMES,** dec'd; heirs of **Mercy BRIGGS; Elizabeth ELDRIDGE** wf of Joshua of Salem, to each one share, the whole to be divided into five shares.

Will of **Kenelm BAKER,** yeoman of Marshfield MA. <Plymouth Co.PR>
<20:496>...13 Apr. 1770, mentions wf **Patience;** to son **John BAKER** land I bought of Samuel BAKER bounded by land of Samuel THOMAS, James SPRAGUE together with the old farm that my father gave me bounded by land of Ephraim FOORD, heirs of Michael FOORD, James SPRAGUE...with the meadow by wharf-creek that I bought of Noah THOMAS with a quarter of the grist-mill; to son **Kenelm BAKER Jr...** together with one third of my fresh-meadow and one half of my meadow in the neck that I bought of Thomas BOURN and half the meadow that lieth in Duxborough & in Marshfield that my father gave me...; to son **William BAKER** all my homestead farm that I bought of Robert HOWLAND, William HOWLAND and Zenas THOMAS together with a piece of land & swamp that my father gave me with that I bot of Fobes LITTLE together with my pew in the meeting-house, reserving a right for **Lucy FISHER**...to sit in so long as she shall see fit...and further I give to my son William all my farming tools with my sword & gun together with my part in the saw-mill; to my four daughters **Alice LITTLE** wf of Ephraim; **Sarah LITTLE** wf of Thomas; **Betty TURNER** wf of Abner; **Lucy FISHER** wf of Daniel, my pine wood lot that I bot of Samuel KENT lying near the land of Adam HALL. Sons John & William named executors. Witnesses: John DINGLEY, Gideon Thomas WHITE, Benjamin WHITE. <20:497> Pr. 3 June 1771. <21:9> Inventory 10 June 1771, total £1356,8s3d. <21:184> Account 5 Oct. 1772, incl. "a desperate debt due from Josiah KEEN". Payments to: Nathaniel Ray THOMAS, Esq., Mary

DORING, Orphan FOORD, Lemuel DELANO, Mark KEEN, John BAKER Jr., John DINGLEY, Ebenezer SHERMAN, James SPRAGUE, Abiah THOMAS, Gershom THOMAS, Zenas THOMAS, Nehemiah THOMAS, Elisha FOORD, Abijah WHITE, Jeremiah PHILLIPS, Jeremiah LOW, Abraham PETERSON, Abraham WALKER, Isaac KEEN, Samuel TAYLOR, Benjamin WHITE, Solomon LEAVIT, John HOLMES, Jacob DINGLEY, Abigail SHURTLEFF; g.s. Ł1.4s.

MICRO #13 OF 15

John BRADFORD of Plymouth to **Thomas BRADFORD.** <Norwich CT Deeds 2A:201>
...10 June 1690, John BRADFORD...whereas my respected aunt Martha formerly the widow of my uncle John BRADFORD late of Norwich deceased by her will left me all her real & personal estate in New London CT, for Ł15 sell to my brother Thomas BRADFORD all my said nineth part of said estate. Witnesses: William BRADFORD, Joseph BRADFORD.

William BRADFORD of Plymouth to **Thomas BRADFORD** of Norwich CT. <Norwich CT Deeds 2A:202>
...12 Apr. 1690, William BRADFORD to son Thomas BRADFORD the one nineth received from my sister Martha BRADFORD widow of my brother John BRADFORD by her will. Witnesses: Samuel SPRAGUE, Josiah HOLMES, Kenelm BAKER.

Thomas WATERMAN of Norwich CT to **Thomas BRADFORD** of Norwich CT. <Norwich CT Deeds 2A:49>
...1 Apr. 1691, Ensign Thomas WATERMAN to Mr. Thomas BRADFORD ten acres, also his right & interest in the house & home lot of Mr. John BRADFORD deceased be it a third more or less except what belonged to the worshipfull William BRADFORD, Mr. Joseph BRADFORD and Mr. John BRADFORD...said Waterman having received Ł45 and Thomas BRADFORD having paid Ł79 to his father, his uncle Joseph and his brother John who were legatees unto Mrs. Martha TRACY deceased (formerly BRADFORD).

Estate of **Lieut. James BRADFORD** of Canterbury CT. <Original in files, #229>[<9>]
Bond/Letter 31 Mar. 1762 by **Thomas BRADFORD** and **William BRADFORD.** Sureties: Samuel WOODARD, Aaron CLEAVELAND. Distribution of estate 12 June 1762 to children: **Mary WOODARD** wf of Joseph; **Jerusha PELLET** wf of Jonathan (eldest dau); **Sarah ADAMS** wf of Joseph (2nd dau); **Anna CLEAVELAND** (3rd dau); **Thomas BRADFORD** (eldest son); **William BRADFORD** (2nd son). Signed by John CURTIS, Obadiah JOHNSON, Jabez FITCH Jr. Inventory 5 Apr. 1762, by Samuel HUNTINGTON, Obadiah JOHNSON, Stephen FROST. Incl. Notes of hand on: Joseph WOODARD, Enos WOODARD, Timothy BACKUS Jr., Josiah BRETT, Timothy WARNER, Joseph ALLEN, Benjamin BACON, Josiah MANING, Hezekiah PELLET, John BROWN, Joseph ADAMS of Killingley, John ADAMS, Asher FLINT, Simon FOBES, Samuel WILLIAMS, Elihu ADAMS, Jacob BURNAP, Nathan HEBBARD, Mr. James COGSWELL, Eliashib ADAMS, Josiah HIDE, William SHAW, Ezra CLEAVLAND, Phinehas ADAMS of Norwich, John HEBBARD, Joseph LEACH, Caleb HIDE, Capt. James (LASEL?sp), Eliphalet FARNUM, Capt. Elijah BYAR, Capt. John FISH, Silas CLEAVLAND, David RIPLEY, John ORMSBY, Parker ADAMS, Samuel CLEAVLAND, Jedediah BENJAMIN, (Ah)ariah ADAMS, Stephen FROST, Matthias BUTTON, Aaron MARSH (desperate debt), Phinehas TRACY, John MANING Jr., John HOWARD, Ezekiel SPAULDING, Hezekiah RIPLEY, Benjamin BAKER, Timothy TUPPER (desperate debt), John BACKUS. Notes of hand against: Benjamin CLEAVLAND, Nehemiah PARRISH, William BOND, John DURFEE, Jonathan PELLET, Solomon ADAMS, Abijah BROWNE, William EARL, John HUBBARD, John ORMSBY, (Ah)ariah ADAMS, Joseph ADAMS, Josiah HIDE, John ADAMS, Caleb HIDE, William BRADFORD, Cornelius WALDO, John BROWN, Jonathan RAYNFORD, Richard RAYNFORD, Joseph BACON, Stephen BOND, Deliverence BROWN, Timothy WINTER.

William BARNES of Plymouth MA to **Robert STANDFORD** of Duxborough MA. <Plymouth Co.Deeds 35:48>
...3 June 1742, William BARNES, yeoman & wf Alice for Ł300 old tenor sold to Robert STANDFORD, yeoman...all that our farm or parcel of upland swampy land and fresh meadow...partly the said Alice BARNES' right & partly our sister Sarah BARNES' right derived from our Grandfather Benjamin BARTLETT deceased who had it from Mr. **William COLLYARE** by a deed dated 28 June 1666.

Will of **William BARNES** of Plymouth MA. <Plymouth Co.PR #1048>
<12:197>...23 Jan. 1749, mentions wife **Elce/Alice**, dau **Marcy HEDGE**, brother **John BARNES** dec'd, two sons **Lemuel BARNES** & **Benjamin BARNES**; mentions lands at Hebron CT in partnership with Capt. HINCKLEY, heirs of Isaac LOTHROP Esq. and heirs of brother John BARNES. <12:199,16:93> Pr. 6 May 1751. <12:461> Inventory sworn to 5 Apr. 1752. <25:203> Warrant to divide, 22 Nov. 1775 by John GRAY of Kingston, Silvanus BARTLETT & Thomas JACKSON of Plymouth, to heirs of **Lemuel BARNES** and **Benjamin BARNES.** Division 21 July 1777.

Bradford BARNES of Danby VT to **Benjamin & Isaac BARNES** of Plymouth. <Plymouth Co.Deeds 196:240>
...22 Sept. 1798, Bradford BARNES, yeoman & wf Sarah sell to Benjamin BARNES & Isaac BARNES, yeomen...all rights in real estate of father Benjamin BARNES, late of Plymouth dec'd. Ack. same day but not recorded until 2 Nov. 1838.

Estate of **Benjamin BARNES** of Plymouth MA. <Plymouth Co.PR>
<25:408> Receipt 9 Nov. 1778, **Samuel BATTLES** & wf **Alice, Benjamin BARNES, Isaac BARNES, Josiah BARNES** all of Plymouth and **Elisha CORBIN Jr.** & wf **Experience, Bradford BARNES, Mercy BARNES** all of Dudley in the County of Worcester, children & heirs of **Benjamin BARNES**, dec'd, do acknowledge that we have received of **Elisha CORBIN** & **Experience** his wife (our mother), administrators on the estate of said **Benjamin BARNES** our full part, etc. <30:128> Warrant to divide 26 Mar. 1787 by Sylvanus HOLMES, Ebenezer SAMPSON, Seth HARLOW, yeomen, (saving part to sett off to **Experience CORBAN,** the widow of said dec'd as dower) divided into nine equal parts, viz: to **Bradford BARNES** (eldest son), **Benjamin BARNES, Josiah BARNES, Isaac BARNES, Alice BATTLES, Mercy BARNES** heirs, **Experience CORBAN, Sarah BARNES** heirs.

Estate of **Mercy BARNES**, singlewoman of Plymouth MA. <Plymouth Co.PR #1036>
...7 Mar. 1786, Andrew CROSWELL, gentleman, app'td. administrator. <original> Inventory 17 May 1786 of estate of Mercy BARNES late daughter of **Benjamin BARNES** late of Plymouth dec'd. (Also cited but not detailed: 27:211, 29:533, 30:94, 31:480.)

Andrew CROSSWELL of Plymouth MA to **Benjamin Jr. & Isaac BARNES** of Plymouth. <Plymouth Co.Deeds> <77:266>...31 Jan. 1795, Andrew CROSSWELL...administrator on the estate of Mrs. **Mercy BARNES** late of said Plymouth dec'd authorized to sell real estate to pay debts, for £39 sold to Benjamin BARNES Jr. & Isaac BARNES, yeomen...four acres of pasture land in Plymouth near the old farm house and was set off to Mercy in the division of the estate, also a piece of wood land containing about four acres...bounded by White's pasture at Deep Water. Rec. 22 Sept. 1795.

MICRO #14 OF 15

PLYMOUTH COUNTY DEEDS:

125:138 - 22 Feb. 1814, Benjamin BARNES & Isaac BARNES, of Plymouth, divide; mentions land of brother, Bradford BARNES.
129:154 - 13 Aug. 1816, Benjamin BARNES & Isaac BARNES, gentlemen of Plymouth, divide.
129:155 - 12 Feb. 1817, Benjamin BARNES & Isaac BARNES, divide.
204:236 - 8 June 1842, Lucy HARLOW, widow, et al.
219:46 - 12 Jan. 1846, Isaac BARNES & wf Lucy of Plymouth to Lucy HARLOW, widow of Plymouth, "half interest of Isaac BARNES at time of death rcd. by grantor as heir of said Isaac BARNES his father the other half was assigned to my sister Lucy HARLOW. Deceased owned same in com. with Ellis BARNES."
225:218 - (no date) , Leander LOWELL & wf Mercy B. of Plymouth to Lucy HARLOW, widow of Lowell, one third of house of Ivory HARLOW, dec'd.

Estate of **Benjamin BARNES** of Plymouth MA. <Plymouth Co.PR #974, 10A:207>
<81:72> Inventory 17 Jan. 1839. <81:171> Division 6 Apr. 1839, $6259.00 each to heirs, viz: **Benjamin BARNES, Bradford BARNES, Ellis BARNES, Deborah GOODING** wf of John, grandson **Samuel BARNES.**

Benjamin BARNES of Plymouth MA to **Isaac BARNES** of Plymouth MA. <Plymouth Co.Deeds 60:90>
...1 Jan. 1780, Benjamin BARNES & Isaac BARNES, yeomen, sell land in Plympton bordered by land that fell to Experience CORBIN & Mercy BARNES in the division of their father, Benjamin BARNES' estate.

Isaac BARNES of Plymouth MA. <Plymouth Co.Deeds 61:163>
...4 Oct. 1782, Isaac BARNES, yeoman, sells land in Plympton he bought of Josiah FINNEY Jr. & wf Alice on 31 Jan. 1778 recorded 59:96, set off to Alice in division of her grandfather, William BARNES', estate being fourth share assigned to Lemuel BARNES' heirs.

PLYMOUTH COUNTY DEEDS:

74:203 - 8 July 1793, Isaac BARNES, yeoman of Plymouth & wf Lucy sell land at (Saquish?) bought from John WATERMAN in 1785.
77:3 - 8 Oct. 1794, Isaac BARNES & wf Lucy sell land bought from Amariah HARLOW.
77:75 - 24 Oct. 1794, Isaac BARNES, yeoman of Plymouth & wf Lucy sell half his lands at Little Town bought from Jacob ALBERTSON in 1791, see 71:8.
78:52 - 20 Mar. 17(?), Ansel HARLOW, Jonathan HARLOW, Isaac BARNES & wf Lucy, Seth LUCE & wf Jedediah, Mary HARLOW, Clarisse HARLOW, children of Jonathan HARLOW of Plymouth, dec'd.
79:138 - 31 Dec. 1794, Ansel HARLOW, Isaac BARNES & wf Lucy, Seth LUCE, mariner & wf Jedediah and Polly HARLOW, spinster, all of Plymouth and Jonathan HARLOW of Halifax, sold to Henry BARTLETT, mariner of Plymouth, all their right in dower in estate of our father Jonathan HARLOW of Plymouth, set off to our mother Sarah HARLOW, dec'd.
87:58 - 30 Apr. 1796, Isaac BARNES & wf Lucy and Seth LUCE & wf Jedediah, said Lucy & Jedediah daughters of Jonathan HARLOW dec'd.
87:250 - 5 May 1800, Isaac BARNES & wf Lucy sell land.

Estate of **Samuel COLE** of Plymouth MA. <Plymouth Co.PR>**<10>**
<6:123> 31 Jan. 1731, **Mercy COLE,** widow, appointed administratrix. <6:178> Inventory 10 Apr. 1732 by John DYER, Thomas HOLMES, Stephen CHURCHELL; incl. an Indian girl, £6; half a dwelling house Mrs. Cole dwells in, £285; half a house wherein Samuel Cole's widow dwells in, £150. <6:435> Guardianship 11 Mar. 1733/4, Barnabas HEDGE of Plymouth appointed guardian of **Samuel COLE,** son of Samuel COLE, dec'd, a minor under 14.

Estate of **Barnabas HEDGE**, gentleman of Plymouth MA. <Plymouth Co.PR 17:88>
...18 Nov. 1762, **Mercy HEDGE**, widow, appointed administratrix.

Estate of **Barnabas HEDGE**, Esq. of Plymouth MA. <Plymouth Co.PR>
<10:386A> 10 Aug. 1840, **Isaac L. HEDGE** of Plymouth and George WARREN of N.Y. app'td. admrs. Surety: **Eunice D. HEDGE,** widow. (Also cited but not detailed: 83:158,159, 6:148U.)

Will of **Eunice Dennie HEDGE** of Plymouth MA. <Plymouth Co.PR>
<92:12>...2 Apr. 1843, mentions **Tryphena HEDGE,** widow of my son **Barnabas HEDGE Jr.**, dec'd; five

daughters, viz: **Abby B. WARREN** wf of Charles H. WARREN, Esq. of New Bedford; **Unice D. ROBBINS**, widow of Dr. Chandler ROBBINS; **Ellen H. LUNT** wf of Rev. William LUNT of Quincy; **Elizabeth WARREN**, wf of George WARREN of N.Y.; two sons, viz: **Isaac L. HEDGE** and **Thomas HEDGE**; grandchildren: **James G. HEDGE, Sarah T. CUSHMAN** wf of Joseph CUSHMAN Jr. and **Nathaniel T. HEDGE**, children of son **Barnabas**. Pr. 30 Jan. 1850.

Estate of **Jonathan BARNES**, seafaring man, of Plymouth MA. <Plymouth Co.PR #1012>
<7:248>...27 Dec. 1736, Thomas DOANE of Chatham, mariner, app'td administrator on estate of father in law Jonathan BARNES. <8:283> Petition 10 Mar. 1740 of Stephen CHURCHILL Jr., cooper, of Plymouth and Joseph SMITH, seafaring man, of Plymouth...whereas Thomas DOANE Jr. of Chatham, mariner, on the 27 Dec. 1736 took out Letters of Administration on the estate of our Honoured father in law, Jonathan BARNES...but said Doane has been out of this Government most of the time since & has made no progress in the settlement And being now gone to Holland & no prospect of his doing anything towards settlement, they pray that Mr. Thomas FOSTER, blacksmith of Plymouth be app'td administrator. Request was granted. <8:285> Inventory taken 16 Apr. 1741 by Nathaniel THOMAS, Esq., Samuel BARTLETT Sr., Thomas SPOONER, all of Plymouth. <8:286> List of debts 18 Apr. 1741. <9:171> Account 23 Dec. 1743.

Estate of **Stephen CHURCHILL** of Plymouth MA. <Plymouth Co.PR #4100>
<12:356> Letter/Bond 26 Sept. 1751, **Hannah CHURCHEL**, widow, app'td administratrix. Sureties: Nathaniel SHURTLIFF, tailor & John BARTLETT, innholder. Witnesses: John LOTHROP, Hannah WINSLOW. <12:513-5> Guardianship 20 Aug. 1752, **Hannah CHURCHELL**, widow, app'td gdn. of minor children: **Stephen CHURCHELL, Zadock CHURCHELL, Hannah CHURCHELL.** Surety: Benjamin CHURCHILL, cordwainer. <13:106> Inventory taken 9 Oct. 1751 by John HARLOW, Benjamin BARTLETT, Joseph BARTLETT Jr.; incl coopers stock at Mr. Lothrop's shop; Indian servant, 120s; one eighth part of the Schooner, Dove, £15; one eighth part of the Schooner, Frindship, £32.10s; half pew in new meeting house in first Precinct, £4.14s4d; total £446.7s7d.

Thomas LONG of Middleborough MA to **Stephen CHURCHILL** of Plymouth MA. <Plymouth Co.Deeds 102:120> ...7 Apr. 1798, Thomas LONG, cordwainer & wf Batsheba/Bathsheba, for $16.66 convey to Stephen CHURCHILL, gentleman, all our right...in a pew in the Meeting House of the first precinct in Plymouth whereof Doctor Chandler ROBBINS is pastor and is on the lower floor in said meeting house on the northerly side of said house being a part of the same pew now improved by said Stephen CHURCHILL and the whole right the said Batsheba owns in said pew by heirship from her father **Zadock CHURCHILL** late of said Plymouth, dec'd. Witnesses: Nehemiah COBB, Miles HOLMES.

Guardianship of Child of **Zadock CHURCHILL**, cooper, of Plymouth MA. <Plymouth Co.PR #3995>
<original> 10 Oct. 1793, **Bathsheba CHURCHILL**, now residing in Bridgewater, minor, seventeen years of age, chose her mother **Bathsheba CHURCHILL**, widow, of Plymouth. Signed: "Bethshe" CHURCHILL. <26:281> 16 Oct. 1793, **Bathsheba CHURCHILL**, widow, app'td. gdn. of daughter. <original> Bond 15 Oct. 1793. Sureties: Andrew CROSWELL, gentleman and Nathaniel THOMAS, housewright, both of Plymouth. (Zadock called a mariner in the bond.)

Bathsheba CHURCHILL of Plymouth to **Stephen CHURCHILL** of Plymouth MA. <Plymouth Co.Deeds 78:37> ...2 Mar. 1795, Bathsheba CHURCHILL, widow, guardian to Barthsheba CHURCHILL Jr., a minor, being licenced by the Supreme Judicial Court to sell the real estate of said minor...for £17 sell to Stephen CHURCHILL, gentleman, all minor's rights in real estate lately belonging to Hannah HOWES, widow, dec'd...excepting & reserving a right to one seat in a pew on the lower floor of the Rev. Mr. Robbins Meeting House. Witnesses: Bathsheba CHURCHILL Jr., Joshua THOMAS.

Estate of **Elizabeth BRADFORD**, widow, of Plymouth MA. <Plymouth Co.PR #2521>
<23:186> Letter/Bond 15 July 1778, Sarah HOLMES, widow, of Plymouth app'td admx. Sureties: Joshua THOMAS, gentleman and William HARLOW Jr., of Plymouth. Witnesses: Thomas S. HOWLAND, Isaac LOTHROP. <25:84> Inventory taken Aug. 1778 by Sylvanus BARTLETT, James DOTEN, William CROMBIE. Oath by Sarah HOLMES 19 Aug. 1778. <25:306> Account 7 July 1779; paid Josiah CARVER's bill for maintaining the deceased, and Josiah FINNEY. <25:324> Account 24 May 1780 by admx.

Estate of **William BRADFORD**, yeoman of Kingston MA. <Plymouth Co.PR #2621>
<5:665> Letter 1 Apr. 1730, **Elizabeth BRADFORD**, widow, app'td admx. <5:714> Inventory taken 13 Apr. 1730 by Francis ADAMS, Samuel FOSTER, Seth CHIPMAN. <7:437> Division 15 Dec. 1737..."real estate of William BRADFORD (the son of William BRADFORD) late of Kingston..."; mentions widow **Elizabeth BRADFORD** and children: **Charles BRADFORD**, eldest son (one share to John BREWSTER in the right of Charles BRADFORD, one share to Thomas ADAMS in the right of Charles BRADFORD); **Sarah BRADFORD, Jerusha BRADFORD, Josiah BRADFORD, Mercy BRADFORD.** Oath 22 Dec. 1737 by John WADSWORTH, Joseph MITCHELL, Samuel FOSTER, Gamaliel BRADFORD, John WINSLOW, Commissioners. <7:440> Division of real estate 24 Mar. 1737 to above heirs. <original> Discharge 27 Dec. 1739, John ADAMS of Kingston binds himself to deliver to **Elizabeth BRADFORD**, widow, half cord of wood annually and discharges Zephaniah HOLMES & wf Sarah from demands of Elizabeth. Witnesses: Ann THOMAS, James HOVEY

Guardianship of Children of **William BRADFORD** of Kingston MA. <Plymouth Co.PR #2506>
<5:839> Letter/Bond 11 Mar. 1730/1, John FINNEY of Plymouth app'td gdn. of **Charles BRADFORD**, minor betw. 14-21. Surety: Jonathan EAMES of Plymouth. Witnesses: Mary WINSLOW, Penelope WARREN. <7:249> Letters 29 Nov. 1736, George PARTRIDGE of Duxbury app'td gdn. of **Sarah BRADFORD & Jerusha BRADFORD** (betw. 14-21) and **Mercy BRADFORD & Josiah BRADFORD** (under 14). Surety: James ARNOLD of Duxbury. Witnesses: Edward WINSLOW, Hopestill ARNOLD. <8:342> Letter 21 May 1741, Gershom BRADFORD app'td gdn. of **Josiah BRADFORD**, minor. Surety: Benjamin LORING of Duxbury. Witnesses: Daniel

LEWIS Jr., Samuel ALDEN.

William BRADFORD Sr. of Kingston MA et al to **Josiah & John FINNEY.** <Plymouth Co.Deeds 22:70> ...6 June 1727, William BRADFORD Sr., yeoman & wf Elizabeth, **Samuel MARSHALL**, cooper of Plymouth & wf Priscilla, **Jonathan BARROWS Jr.**, cordwainer of Plymouth & wf Phebe...receive from our brothers Josiah FINNEY & John FINNEY, yeomen of Plymouth...a certain lot of land that was our Honoured Father's, Josiah FINNEY dec'd.

Elizabeth BRADFORD, widow of David, of Kingston from **Thomas CROADE.** <Plymouth Co.Deeds 26:56> ...8 Jan. 1730/31. (No details.)

Josiah FINNEY of Plymouth MA to **Elizabeth BRADFORD** of Kingston MA. <Plymouth Co.Deeds 30:9> ...1 May 1735, Elizabeth BRADFORD, widow of William dec'd, buys land from Josiah FINNEY, yeoman.. upland & salt marsh being part of ye estate left to Josiah by Honoured Father Josiah FINNEY, dec.

Edward SPARROW of Plymouth MA to **Elizabeth BRADFORD** of Plymouth MA. <Plymouth Co.Deeds 36:212> ...20 June 1744, Edward SPARROW, mariner, & wf Jerusha, for £31.5s old tenour bills of credit, sells to Mrs. Elizabeth BRADFORD, widow of Plymouth...the northerly front lower room in ye dwelling house where I now dwell in Plymouth...

Oliver BRADFORD of Plympton MA to **Elizabeth BRADFORD** of Plympton MA. <Plymouth Co.Deeds 81:64> ...30 May 1795, Oliver BRADFORD sells to Elizabeth BRADFORD, widow...the eighth share in the division of the estate of my honoured father John BRADFORD, late of Plympton, dec'd.

PLYMOUTH COUNTY DEEDS:

35:196 - 1743, Plymouth, Elizabeth BRADFORD to Lemuel MORTON.
38:194 - 1747, Kingston, Elizabeth BRADFORD to Thomas ADAMS.
77:77 - 12 May 1758, Elizabeth BRADFORD, wf of John, and Eleazer HOLMES (heirs, division). Rec. 1794.
45:245 - 1759, Kingston, Elizabeth BRADFORD to Thomas ADAMS.
57:44 - 1772, , Elizabeth BRADFORD to Josiah BRADFORD.
77:69 - 18 June 1794, Plymouth, Elizabeth BRADFORD of Plympton, widow of John to Ichabod HOLMES.
85:77 - 1797, Plymouth, Elizabeth BRADFORD to Oliver BRADFORD.
91:113 - 1801, Plympton, Elizabeth BRADFORD to George COBB.

31:149 - 19 Dec. 1737, John BREWSTER & Thomas ADAMS sell land bought of Charles BRADFORD son of William dec'd.
32:138 - 18 July 1738, Charles BRADFORD, seafaring man of Kingston to Thomas ADAMS, mariner.
35:157 - 25 Jan. 1742/3, John BREWSTER, housewright of Kingston to Thomas ADAMS.
36:77 - 29 Oct. 1743, Richard WAITE & wf Mary to Edward SPARROW, mariner of Plymouth.
37:146 - 17 Apr. 1745, Josiah BRADFORD, cordwainer of Plymouth to Thomas ADAMS, land in Kingston.

Charles BRADFORD of Kingston MA to **John BREWSTER** of Kingston MA. <Plymouth Co.Deeds 31:118> ...24 Sept. 1737, Charles BRADFORD, labourer, for £150 sold to John BREWSTER, housewright...one third of lands...which my Honoured Father William BRADFORD died seized of...Witnesses: Joshua CUSHING, Cornelius DREW. Rec. 4 Oct. 1737.

Charles BRADFORD of Kingston MA to **Thomas ADAMS** of Kingston MA. <Plymouth Co.Deeds 32:138> ...18 July 1738, Charles BRADFORD, seafayring man, for £5 paid by Thomas ADAMS, mariner, over & above ninety pounds the said Adams paid to John BREWSTER, housewright of Kingston...whereas the said Thomas ADAMS bought of ye said Brewster one half part of my right & interest in that part of my estate that was my Father, William BRADFORD's, late of Kingston dec'd...lately divided into six shares by an order or warrant from the Judge of Probates...the third share fell to said Adams...Witnesses: Seth CHIPMAN, Samuel FOSTER. Rec. 8 Feb. 1738/9.

Samuel HARLOW of Plymouth MA to **Thomas ADAMS** of Kingston MA. <Plymouth Co.Deeds 40:128> ...25 Oct. 1749, Samuel HARLOW, mariner & wf Mercy for £70 sold to Thomas ADAMS, mariner...land in Kingston...the fourth lot in the first division of our Honoured Father William BRADFORD's estate. Witnesses: Jonathan SAMSON, Sarah HOLMES.

Edward SPARROW of Plymouth MA to **Thomas ADAMS** of Kingston MA. <Plymouth Co.Deeds 36:77> ...14 Nov. 1743, Edward SPARROW, mariner & wf Jerusha for £160 sold to Thomas ADAMS, clothier... all that our right title and interest in several lots of land which fell to the said Jerusha which was formerly her Honoured Father's William BRADFORD of Kingston dec'd...set off to Jerusha ...15 Dec. 1737.

Estate of **Edward SPARROW**, mariner of Plymouth MA. <Plymouth Co.PR 9:462> ...5 June 1745, administration granted to **Jerusha SPARROW**, widow.

Will of **Edward SPARROW** of Middleborough MA. <Plymouth Co.PR 48:353> ...28 Sept. 1802, mentions wf **Rhoda**, daughters: **Polly SPARROW** (under 18), **Jerusha LOVELL** wf of Joseph, **Susanna MILLER** wf of John, **Elizabeth WOOD** wf of Gorham, **Rhoda WOOD** wf of Alfred; six sons: **Edward SPARROW** (executor), **Philip SPARROW, Josiah SPARROW, William SPARROW, James SPARROW, Bradford SPARROW.** Witnesses: "Nehmiah" BENNET, James THOMAS, William PORTER. Pr. 21 Feb. 1817.

Josiah BRADFORD of Plymouth MA to **Thomas ADAMS** of Kingston MA. <Plymouth Co.Deeds 37:146>
...17 Apr. 1745, Josiah BRADFORD, cordwainer for Ł32.10s sells to Thomas ADAMS, mariner, my four acres of land...in Kingston...being in the first division of William BRADFORD's estate lately divided. Rec. 30 July 1745.

Charles BRADFORD et al to **Joshua WRIGHT, Joseph SAMSON** of Plymouth MA. <Plymouth Co.Deeds 82:40>
...30 Jan. 1797, **Josiah BRADFORD, Samuel BRADFORD, Charles BRADFORD, Zepheniah BRADFORD,** mariner; **Ruth BRADFORD** widow of William; **Hannah BRADFORD, Lois BRADFORD, Betsey BRADFORD,** spinsters, all of Plymouth and **Thomas PERKINS,** yeoman & wf **Mercy** of Halifax, for $50 sold to **Joshua WRIGHT** and **Joseph SAMSON,** yeomen of Plymouth...one undivided third part of land laid out to Josiah FINNEY, (see) proprietors' Second Book of Records page 281...for bounds thereof and to our Grandmother Elizabeth BRADFORD's deed to our father Josiah BRADFORD of Plymouth dec'd, dated 21 Dec. 1772.

MICRO #15 OF 15

Zephaniah HOLMES of Plymouth MA to **John ADAMS** of Kingston MA. <Plymouth Co.Deeds 33:74>
...27 Dec. 1739, Zephaniah HOLMES, cordwainer & wf Sarah, for Ł150 sold to John ADAMS, seafayring man...sundry tracts of land in Kingston being all the land that was allotted to the said Sarah in the Estate of her late Father William BRADFORD (son of William BRADFORD) late of Kingston dec'd.. which said share is always to be understood exclusive of what may be allotted to said Sarah after ye decease of Elizabeth BRADFORD the mother of ye said Sarah HOLMES who at present holds her thirds in said estate. Rec. 28 Dec. 1739.

FOOTNOTES

<1> p.72, The files contain a page of handwritten pencilled data concerning the inventory of Benjamin VERMAYE's estate, however much of it is illegible. In fact there are eight pages of data from the Essex Co.Deeds that, due to the handwriting, I am not attempting to transcribe as much of it would be guess work which would undoubtedly result in errors. Much of the data in question refers to Esther EASTWICK, Benjamin VERMAYES, John GEDNEY, John MARSH, John WILLIAMS and William BATH, most are of Salem between 1650-1700.
<2> p.73, In 1948 the Massachusetts Society of Mayflower Descendants received a copy of the original of this deed. It was given to them by Hamilton Vaughan BAIL of The Franklin Institute of the State of Pennsylvania. Mr. Bail states in his letter, "...it is of much more historical and genealogical interest than the ordinary deed." Mr. Bail is quite correct, which is why I have reprinted the deed in its entirety. A note following the transcription states the deed appears to be in the handwriting of William BASSITT.
<3> p.77, A letter dated 13 Jan. 1922 from the Town Clerk of Springfield VT states the first mention of Simeon BRADFORD^4 (Ephraim^3) in the town records is in a deed dated 15 July 1772. The letter also gives the following data: "The copies of the inscriptions on early burial stones show the following: Simeon BRADFORD, age 64, died 7 Oct. 1793; Thankful BRADFORD, his wife, died 1 Apr 1796". What is interesting is that both Bowman and MFIP, Bradford (1991) #103 use this death date for Simeon while ignoring the discrepency in the name of the wife. Both sources state Simeon's wife Phebe (WHITON) was alive when his estate was administered (as shown within, p.77). Has the Town Clerk made an error writing the name Thankful instead of Phebe? If it is not an error, who is this Simeon BRADFORD as he obviously could not be the same who left a widow, Phebe.
<4> p.77, The Town Clerk's letter mentioned above in <3> states the first mention of Simeon BRADFORD in the Springfield records is a deed dated 15 July 1772. These two deeds would indicate Simeon made the move from Kingston MA to Springfield VT between 1765-1772.
<5> p.79, The files show a discrepency in the identity of Lydia Holmes (BRADFORD) Barrows, the daughter of Luther BRADFORD. His probate records say she was the wife of Jacob BARROWS. The Mass.VR 419:568 say she died 9 June 1891, ae 78y3m21d, the wife of George H. BARROWS and the daughter of Luther BRADFORD & 1st wf Ruth HOLMES. This would place her birth at c1817 which presents another problem as her alledged mother, Ruth (HOLMES) died in 1815.
<6> p.82, This probate data is on a small piece of paper and does not specify exactly what the records are referring to.
<6a> p.82, Peabody BRADFORD had an illegitimate son who was not mentioned in the probate rcds. - Peabody BRADFORD, b. 15 Mar. 1758 by Lydia FREEMAN.
<7> p.87, From the wording in these records it is apparent that Capt. Samuel GILBERT "defected" to the British during the Revolution, sometime in the year 1775. He is called an absentee, with the first reference to his death 6 Sept. 1796 when his wife is called a widow. On 5 Aug. 1800 he is actually called deceased.
<8> p.89, A copy of the original will can be found in the files. As a matter of interest, the files also contain a transcript of his account in "Biographical Sketches of Loyalists of the American Revolution, by Lorenzo Sabine, 2 Vols. 1864. Boston, p.525-6. He appears to have been extremely active in the war and took great pleasure in "annoying the Whigs".
<9> p.91, The files contain 22 pages of the original probate records, with the inventory being extremely lengthy - James BRADFORD was obviously a man of means. These pages should be referred to in the files by descendants of this family who would find the data most interesting although the handwriting is often difficult to decipher. The records were filed in the district of Plainfield.

FOOTNOTES (cont-d)

<10> p.92, The files contain a page headed "Samuel Cole" with various references to probate records. At first glance one would think they all pertain to the same Samuel Cole, but upon a closer look they are probably references to three different men. The 1st has been transcribed within; the 2nd gives dates of 1724 <4:396>, 1730 <5:82>, 1727 <5:376> guardianship, and an agreement made 9 Jan. 1730/1 <6:77> between the following heirs, viz: Seth FULLER & wf Deborah (widow of Samuel COLE), Isaac WRIGHT & wf Mary, Robert HARLOW & wf Hannah, Elizabeth DUNBAR, John COLE, Edward COLE, Thomas COLE, Joseph COLE and Benjamin COLE. References to the 3rd are: 1812 <39:352,44:446, 447>, division, <45:68> division and <47:18>. Since this data is so sketchy it has not been included in the main body within.

==
==

WILLIAM BREWSTER

MICRO #1 OF 18

PLYMOUTH COUNTY PROBATE RECORDS:

1696	Wrestling BREWSTER	Duxbury	#2790, 1:253,254
1755	Nathaniel BREWSTER	Duxbury	#2772, 13:443,444
1767	Wrestling BREWSTER	Kingston	#2791, 19:417,418
1767	Joseph BREWSTER	Duxbury	#2753, 19:475,549;20:413;30:119,120,192
1770	John BREWSTER	Kingston	#2752, 20:296-7,393,409;21:111;27:494;29:1,362
1774	Lemuel BREWSTER	Kingston	#2764, 21:372;23:49;27:509;30:7,117-8,165
1780	Abigail BREWSTER	Kingston	#2730, 25:525;30:366,520;31:141
1791	Joseph BREWSTER	Duxbury	#2754
1794	Hosea BREWSTER	Kingston	#2745, 34:17;35:241;36:31

PLYMOUTH COUNTY PROBATE RECORDS, 1800-1850:

1801	Elisha BREWSTER	Kingston	will	#2739, 37:504,505
1801	Rebecca BREWSTER	Kingston	adm.	#2780, 37:525;38:64,235;43:373
1807	Joseph BREWSTER	Duxbury	adm.	#2755, 39:136;42:203,407,451,530;44:159
1808	Melzar BREWSTER et al	Duxbury	gdn.	#2770, 32:354,355,356;41:90
1810	Hosea BREWSTER	Kingston	gdn.	#2746, 41:21
1815	Thomas BREWSTER	Kingston	adm.	#2786, 46:122;48:21,22;50:566;53:74,76,80
1816	Wrestling BREWSTER	Kingston	adm.	#2792, 46:191;49:10,11
1818	Ellis BREWSTER	Plymouth	adm.	#2741, 46:299;49:603,605;50:121,123,343
1820	Elisha BREWSTER et al	Kingston	gdn.	#2740, 51:73
1822	William BREWSTER	Hanson	gdn.	#2788, 51:183;55:64;56:194,350;57:337;59:16
1825	William BREWSTER	Hanson	adm.	#2789, 52:333;55:342;59:6,7,189;60:226
1828	James D. BREWSTER et	Kingston	gdn.	#2750, 65:64,357;67:566;73:375;76:229-30; 369;84:16,18;90:30
1828	Martin BREWSTER Jr.	Kingston	adm.	#2767, 61:230;66:350;67:48,565;70:284
1831	Joshua BREWSTER	Duxbury	gdn.	#2757, 70:477;72:493;65:209;70:545;68:232; 72:493
1832	Hosea BREWSTER	Kingston	will	#2747, 72:26
1832	Joshua BREWSTER	Duxbury	gdn.	#2758, 71:108;72:549;68:340;74:182
1834	Job E. BREWSTER	Duxbury	adm.	#2751, 71:274;75:182;77:24,48,469,553
1840	Lydia BREWSTER et al	Duxbury	gdn.	#2766, 1:98**R**;2:414**O**;8:165**L**
1840	Stephen BREWSTER	Duxbury	will	#2785, 1:358**G**;82:111
1842	Aaron BREWSTER	Kingston	adm.	#2729, 11:31**B**
1842	Judith BREWSTER	Kingston	gdn.	#2763, 2:462**O**;6:291**U**;8:475,476**L**;84:403
1844	Spencer BREWSTER	Kingston	will	#2784, 1:270**G**;7:35**V**;86:43
1846	Joseph BREWSTER	Duxbury	adm.	#2756, 7:172**V**;11:475**B**;89:11,42,419
1848	America BREWSTER	Plymouth	will	#2731, 1:481**G**;90:6
1848	Persis BREWSTER	Kingston	adm.	#2775, 7:411**V**;12:29**C**;91:8,502
1850	Pelham BREWSTER	Kingston	adm.	#2774, 8:187**W**;12:345**C**;93:381,488;94:27,29, 392;95:140,242

Will of **Jonah BREWSTER**, yeoman of Windham CT. <CT Hist.Society, Thomas S. Weaver papers> ...15 May 1750, mentions wf **Joanna**; her father **Edward WALDON**; children: **Jonathan BREWSTER, Nathan BREWSTER, Ezekiel BREWSTER, Ann BREWSTER** and unborn child (named **Jonah BREWSTER** in probate rec.). Pr. 10 July 1750. Inventory 31 May 1766, total Ł3258.

Will of **William DURKEE** of Gloucester CT. <CT Hist.Society, Thomas S. Weaver papers> ...11 Sept. 1731, mentions wf **Rebecca**. (No further details.)

Will of **William DURKEE** of CT. <CT Hist.Society, Thomas S. Weaver papers> ...10 Jan. 1795, mentions **Rebecca ROBINSON,** daughters **Abigail HAMMOND** wf of Josiah, **Hannah FOSTER** wf of William Jr., chil of **Mary BREWSTER** dec'd, viz: **Mary, Royal & John BREWSTER.** Pr. 1 Mar.1795.

Will of **Elijah BREWSTER** of CT. <CT Hist.Society, Thomas S. Weaver papers> ...24 Apr. 1755, mentions brothers & sisters **James BREWSTER, Peleg BREWSTER, Hannah BARKER, Mary BINGHAM, Sarah HOLMES,** children of **Jonah BREWSTER** dec'd, **Jerusha RUDD; John BARKER.**

Amos DODGE to **Jonathan BREWSTER** of Lebanon CT. <CT Hist.Society, Thomas S. Weaver papers> ...26 July 1729, Amos DODGE sold to Jonathan BREWSTER 16 acres...being northerly part of my house lot west of meeting house in "W."...(Brewster quit claimed it back to Dodge.)

Will of **Jonathan BREWSTER** of Lebanon CT. <CT Hist.Society, Thomas S. Weaver papers> ...14 Mar. 1748, mentions children: **James BREWSTER** (eldest son), **Peleg BREWSTER, Jonah BREWSTER,**

Hannah BARKER, Mary BINGHAM wf of Jeremiah, **Jerusha RUDD** wf of Zebulon, **Sarah HOLMES, Elijah BREWSTER, Jonathan BREWSTER.** Pr. 29 Sept. 1754.

Will of **Christopher CHRISTOPHERS**, Esq. of New London CT. <New London CT PR #1203>
...21 Oct. 1775, mentions wife **Elizabeth**, my four children, viz: **Sarah, Joseph CHRISTOPHERS, Elizabeth, Allen CHRISTOPHERS.** Widow's letter dated 20 Nov. 1775. Estate insolvent.

Will of **Joshua RAYMOND** of New London CT. <New London CT PR #4300, 4301><1>
<#4300>...14 Feb. 1763, mentions wife **Sarah**, children: **Joshua RAYMOND, John RAYMOND, Edward RAYMOND, Christopher RAYMOND, Elizabeth HAZZARD, Mercy WILLIAMS**; grandsons **Daniel & Christopher RAYMOND.** Witnesses: James FITCH, William HILLHOUSE, David JEWETT. Pr. 13 Dec. 1763. Inventory sworn to 6 Feb. 1764 by William FRENCH, John BRADFORD, total £427.7.2. <#4301> Administration of estate of **Joshua & Elizabeth RAYMOND**, 21 Nov. 1771 by **Joshua RAYMOND.** Surety: William DOUGLAS. Inventory 17 Nov. 1771 of estate of **Joshua & Elizabeth RAYMOND** which Elizabeth was one of the heirs of **John CHRISTOPHERS** of said New London, dec'd, total: £43.17.6; additional £12 added 26 July 1773. Division of estate to heirs, viz: **Joshua RAYMOND** (eldest son), **John RAYMOND, Christopher RAYMOND, Edward RAYMOND, Elizabeth HAZZARD** (eldest dau), **Thomas WILLIAMS** in right of his wife **Mary/Mercy.**

Estate of **Thomas MANWARING.** <New London CT PR #3422>
Bond 13 Aug. 1776, **Lydia MANWARING**, admx. Inventory 11 June 1776. Account 17 June 1776, mentions seven unnamed children. Estate insolvent.

Will of **Christopher CHRISTOPHERS**, Esq. of New London CT. <New London CT PR #1202>
...30 Jan. 1728/9, mentions wife **Sarah**, children: **Christopher CHRISTOPHERS** (eldest son), **John CHRISTOPHERS, Mary CHRISTOPHERS, Sarah CHRISTOPHERS, Lucretia CHRISTOPHERS.** Pr. 5 Mar. 1728/9. Distribution 4 Oct. 1742 to heirs: sons **Christopher CHRISTOPHERS** (eldest son) and **John CHRISTOPHERS**; children of dau **Mary HAMLIN** dec'd, viz: **Christopher HAMLIN, Sarah HAMLIN, Esther HAMLIN**; daus **Sarah PRENTISS** wf of John and **Lucretia PALMER** wf of Edward. (Distribution by Jonathan STARR, Humphrey AVERY, Jeremiah CHAPMAN.)

Will of **Sarah CHRISTOPHERS**, widow of New London CT. <New London CT PR #1213>
...26 Jan. 1744/5, mentions sons **Christopher CHRISTOPHERS, John CHRISTOPHERS**, daus **Sarah PRENTISS** and **Lucretia PALMER**; grandchildren **Sarah HAMLIN, Esther HAMLIN, Christopher HAMLIN**, heirs of dau **Mary HAMLIN.** Pr. 30 Apr. 1745.

Will of **Richard CHRISTOPHERS** of New London CT. <New London CT PR #1212>
...15 Dec. 1735, mentions wife **Elizabeth**, eldest son **Richard CHRISTOPHERS**, second son **Joseph CHRISTOPHERS**, three daughters, viz: **Elizabeth, Mary, Sarah.** Pr. 16 Feb. 1735/6.

Will of **Richard CHRISTOPHERS** of New London CT. <New London CT PR #1211>
...13 July 1720, mentions wife **Grace**, children: **Christopher CHRISTOPHERS, Richard CHRISTOPHERS, Mary GRAY** widow of John, **Grace, Lydia, Ruth, Joanna, Lucretia** (when 14), **Lucy** (youngest dau). Codicil 7 Feb. 1721/2. Pr. 27 June 1726. Division 10 Nov. 1736 of real estate bequeathed to sons **Christopher & Richard**, now both dec'd.

Will of **John CHRISTOPHERS** of New London CT. <New London CT PR #1207>
...20 Feb. 1722/3, mentions sister **Esther MANWARING**; cousins **John, Mary, Sarah** (when 21) and **Christopher CHRISTOPHERS**, children of my cousin **Christopher CHRISTOPHERS**; sister **Elizabeth RAYMOND.** Executors: cousins **Christopher & Richard CHRISTOPHERS** of New London. Distribution 24 Dec. 1782 among heirs of **Mrs. Esther MANWARING** of her part of estate of **John CHRISTOPHER** to following heirs, viz: heirs of **Thomas MANWARING**, dec'd, eldest son; son **Adam MANWARING**; heirs of dau **Elizabeth CHRISTOPHERS**, dec'd; heirs of son **Peter MANWARING**, dec'd; son **Josiah MANWARING**; heirs of dau **Esther PLUMBLEY**, dec'd; heirs of son **John MANWARING**, dec'd; dau **Lucretia TEAGUES** wf of Jesse.

Guardianship of Children of **Richard CHRISTOPHERS** of New London CT. <New London CT PR #1204>
...30 Jan. 1738/9, Mr. Nathaniel GREEN of New London appointed guardian of **Mary** and **Elizabeth CHRISTOPHERS**, daughters of Mr. Richard CHRISTOPHERS, dec'd, in place of Mr. John PICKETT of New London.

Will of **Capt. Benjamin LATHROP** of Norwich CT. <Norwich CT PR #6589>
...11 Feb. 1774, mentions daughter in law, **Abigail**, dau of my late wife **Mary** (which Mary was my last wife); grandson **Walter LATHROP** son of my son **Benjamin LATHROP** dec'd; son **Cyprian LATHROP**; son **Arunah LATHROP**; dau **Lucy ROCKWELL** wf of Josiah; grandson **Benjamin LATHROP** son of **Arunah.** Son **Cyprian** named executor. Witnesses: Richard HIDE, Ebenezer LATHROP, Isaac JOHNSON. Pr. 4 July 1786. Bond 5 Sept. 1786 of Simeon LATHROP, admr., the executor being deceased. Distribution 25 Mar. 1789 to heirs of **Cyprian LATHROP, Lucy ROCKWELL** wf of Josiah, **Walter LATHROP** grandson, **Arunah LATHROP** and his son **Benjamin LATHROP.**

JONATHAN BREWSTER[2] (WILLIAM[1])

Stephen PAYNE of Lebanon CT to **Benjamin PAYNE** of Lebanon CT. <Lebanon CT Deeds 9:95>
...19 Apr. 1759, Stephen PAYNE for £187.10s sold to Benjamin PAYNE...two tracts of land containing fourteen acres...part of ye farm which my honoured Father Mr. Benjamin PAYNE late of Lebanon, dec'd died seised...which were set out to me in the division of the real estate of my said Father

...and also my fourth part of ye land which was given & conveyed by deed by my Grandfather **Mr. John PAYNE** late of said Lebanon dec'd to me with my Bretheren Benjamin, Dan & Seth, the whole of which land contains thirty three acres & half lying upon the rear of the farm whereon my Grandfather & Father last dwelt adjoining to Suscatomscot brook & land of Jonathan METCALFE...reserving only to and for my honoured Mother **Mrs. Mary PAYNE**, widow the use...Rec. 20 Apr. 1759.

Stephen PAYNE of Partridgfield CT to **Allen PAYNE** of Partridgfield CT. <Lebanon CT Deeds 14:489>
...27 May 1786, Stephen PAYN, yeoman & wf Rebecca, for ₤14 sold to Allen PAYN...land in Lebanon, formerly the land of Nathan BUSHNELL late of Lebanon dec'd, laid out to contain eight acres being the aforesaid Rebecca's part of said Nathan's real estate...Witnesses: Ebenezer PEIRCE, Ebenezer PAYN. Rec. 13 June 1786.

Will of **Benjamin PAYN/PAYNE** of Lebanon CT. <Windham Co.CT PR #2879>
...11 Jan. 1755, mentions wife **Mary**, to eldest son **Benjamin PAYNE** the house where he now lives; three sons under age, **Stephen PAYNE, Dan PAYNE, Seth PAYNE**; daughters **Mary, Lydia, Hannah, Sarah.** Witnesses: Benjamin SEABURY, Dan THROOPE, Joshua BARKER. Pr. 22 Jan. 1755. <u>Distribution</u> 22 Nov. 1756 of real estate to widow & four sons, land given them by their grandfather **John PAYNE.**

Will of **Jabez FITCH** of Norwich CT. <Norwich CT PR #3862>
...10 Aug. 1768, mentions wife **Anna**, sons **Elisha FITCH, Pelatiah FITCH**; daughters **Lurena RUDD**, wf of Samuel & **Cynthia FITCH**; son **Jabez FITCH**. Witnesses: Solomon ANDREWS, Roger HASKELL, Benjamin HASKELL. Pr. 10 May 1779.

Estate of **John CHRISTOPHERS** of New London CT. <CT State Library, #1207>
...1723...Will, distribution of estate...(No details given.)

Will of **John CLARK** of Saybrook CT. <CT State Library, #456>
...19 July 1796...to wife **Mary** clothing which she brought with her etc.; to eldest son **Paul CLARK** land where he now lives; son **Nathaniel CLARK**; dau **Hester PRATT**; granddaughters **Nabby CLARK, Elizabeth PRATT, Hester SPENCER**, the daughters of dau **Elizabeth SPENCER**; dau **Phebe RATHBONE.** Will was signed again 20 July 1796 as there was some question as to his competency. <u>Witnesses</u> sworn 11 Mar. 1801. <u>Inventory</u> 11 Nov. 1801. <u>2nd Inventory</u> 13 Apr. 1802.

<u>MICRO #2 OF 18</u>

Will of **John CHRISTOPHERS** of New London CT. <New London CT PR 3:49,50,51>
...1 Feb. 1702, at Barbadoes, mentions wife **Elizabeth**; brother **Richard CHRISTOPHERS**; son **John CHRISTOPHERS**; dau **Elizabeth CHRISTOPHERS**; to child wife now goes with. Wife & brother named executors. Friends: William DURY, Thomas JACKMAN, William HARRIS and Timothy MULFORD to sell all property in Barbadoes and send proceeds to executors in New London in my barkentine. Witnesses: Charles HILL, Benjamin SULLAVANT, Daniel RICHARDS. Pr. 12 Feb. 1702. <u>Inventory</u> 18 Aug. 1703 at New London, by George DENISON, Jonathan PRENTO, John PLUMBE, incl. land bought of John WICKWIRE; small piece of land originally Peter BRADLEY's, dec'd; meadow next to John LEWIS; land on Mill Cove between Adam PICKET & John ROGERS, with an old warehouse; 6 ton boat; farm called Pine Neck; all rights in Black Point, 170 acre upland & 18 acre meadow; total ₤1166.10.7. Sworn to 14 Nov. 1704 by **Mrs. Elizabeth CHRISTOPHERS**, widow. (Copy of original will in files.)

Will of **Thomas MANWARING** of Lyme CT. <CT State Library>
...15 Nov. 1769, mentions wife **Easther**; children: **Esther PLUMBE** wf of Nathaniel; **Lucretia TEAGUE** wf of Richard of New London; heirs of dec'd dau **Elizabeth CHRISTOHERS** wf of John late of New London now of Norwich; **Thomas MANWARING** of New London; **Peter MANWARING** of Lyme; **John MANWARING; Adam MANWARING; Josiah MANWARING.** Executors son **Peter MANWARING** and George DOW, Esq. of Lyme. Pr. 4 Feb. 1783. (Copy of original will in files.)

Estate of **Daniel WETHERELL** of New London CT. <"#5625">
...1719...will, inventory, bond...(No details given in files.)

<u>MICRO #3 OF 18</u>

Will of **John TURNER** of Scituate MA. <MD 5:41>
...4 Mar. 1695, mentions sons **Jonathan TURNER, Joseph TURNER, Ezekiel TURNER**; six grandchildren: **Isaac TURNER, John JAMES, Thomas PRINCE, Margaret TURNER, Alice PRINCE** and the eldest child of son **Ezekiel**; sons **John TURNER, Elisha TURNER, Amos TURNER**; daughters **Grace CHRISTOPHERS, Lydia, Mary, Ruth** and **Grace**; son **Benjamin TURNER**; wife **Mary.** Pr. 28 June 1697. Inventory 20 May 1697.

<u>PLYMOUTH COUNTY PROBATE to 1849</u>: (re: TURNER)

1688	Thomas	Scituate	will	#21453, 1:34,35	<PN&Q 5:19>
1689	Israel	Scituate	adm.	#21359, 1:40,41	<PN&Q 5:20>
1690	Lazarus	Scituate	adm.	#21405, 1:75	<MD 30:72>
1690	Japheth	Duxbury	adm.	#21373, 1:66,67	<PN&Q 5:117>
1694	Ephraim	Scituate	adm.	#21341, 1:150,180;2:36	
1694	Nathan	Scituate	adm.	#21420, 1:193:2:126,127	
1695	George	Bridgewater	adm.	#21345, 1:236	

PLYMOUTH COUNTY PROBATE to 1849, cont-d: (re:TURNER)

1697	John	Scituate	will	#21382, 1:266,269
1698	David	Scituate	will	#21320, 1:291,292
1700	Elisha	Scituate	will	#21334, 1:330,331 <MD 32:71>
1701	Eliab	Scituate	adm.	#21328, 1:334,335;3:448
1703	Nathan et al	Scituate	gdn.	#21421, 1:193;2:37,126,127
1710	Elisha et al	Scituate	gdn.	#21334, 3:41,42 <MD 32:77>
1710	Elizabeth	Scituate	will	#21336, 3:35-37 <MD 32:77>
1710	Japhet	Duxbury	adm.	#21374, 3:39,182
1712	Amasa	Scituate	adm.	#21293, 3:145,146
1712	Elnathan	Scituate	will	#21339, 3:187,188
1712	Japhet et al	Duxbury	gdn.	#21375, 3:183-185;4:169
1712	Lazarus et al	---	gdn.	#21406, 3:180,181
1717	Hannah	Pembroke	will	#21354, 4:68,69,70
1718	Charles	Scituate	adm.	#21309, 4:153,154,345;5:22,24,366
1719	Abiel et al	Scituate	gdn.	#21285, 4:204,205
1719	Abigail	Scituate	gdn.	#21288, 4:208,209;5:584
1719	John	Scituate	adm.	#21383, 4:203,208,209;5:585
1721	Abner	Scituate	will	#21291, 4:282,283
1721	Thomas	Scituate	will	#21454, 4:292,293,337;6:406
1722	Charles et al	Scituate	gdn.	#21310, 4:339,340
1723/4	Joseph	Scituate	adm.	#21394, 4:383
1724	Jonathan	Scituate	will	#21392, 4:450;5:12,14,39,81,88
1725	Eliab	Scituate	gdn.	#21329, 5:128
1728	John	Bridgewater	adm.	#21381, 5:411,584;7:388,389
1728	Joshua	Pembroke	will	#21400, 5:502,504,505
1730	Joshua	Pembroke	gdn.	#21401, 5:831
1733	Thomas	Rochester	adm.	#21455, 6:397,7:8,78,83,85,113,205,269,270,281, 14:280,466;15:292
1734	Benjamin	Scituate	will	#21301, 7:114,115,116
1736	Philip	Scituate	will	#21429, 7:209,210,211
1739	Amos	Scituate	will	#21294, 8:23,26;13:252
1743	Seth	Scituate	will	#21448, 9:156,157,280;13:115,116
1744	Abigail	Scituate	will	#21289, 9:415,417;10:267,268
1744	Elizabeth	Scituate	will	#21337, 9:420,421,422
1745	Abiezer et al	Scituate	gdn.	#21287, 10:272,273,274
1746	Amos	Scituate	gdn.	#21295, 10:407
1746	Hannah	Scituate	gdn.	#21350, 10:354,408;12:118
1747	George	Bridgewater	gdn.	#21346, 10:400,410
1747	William	Bridgewater	adm.	#21464, 10:400,12:359;11:374
1748	Benjamin	Scituate	will	#21302, 11:144,145,178;12:233
1749	Mary	Pembroke	will	#21412, 12:37,38
1751	Hannah	Scituate	adm.	#21351, 12:118,454
1752	Abiezer	Scituate	adm.	#21286, 12:455,473
1752	Richard	Scituate	will	#21436, 13:41,78,102,132-34;14:60
1753	Ruth	Scituate	will	#21438, 13:126,251
1754	John	Scituate	gdn.	#21384, 13:332
1759	Samuel	Scituate	will	#21442, 15:424,432,434;16:79
1759	William	Scituate	will	#21446, 15:134,246,247
1760	Elizabeth	Scituate	will	#21338, 16:103,104,105
1760	Vine	Scituate	adm.	#21461, 15:522;16:101,171
1760	Israel	Pembroke	will	#21364, 16:20,21,38;24:439,440;28:320
1761	Israel et al	Pembroke	gdn.	#21365, ---
1761	Simeon	Scituate	will	#21451, 16:160-162;20:18,19
1763	Joshua	Scituate	gdn.	#21397, 18:140
1764	Benjamin	Scituate	inv.	#21304, 19:152
1766	John Jr.	Scituate	gdn.	#21385, 18:186;19:361;20:326
1767	Caleb	Hanover	adm.	#21307, 17:190;20:20,82,148,286
1768	Hannah	Scituate	adm.	#21352, 20:33
1768	Benjamin	Scituate	adm.	#21303, 20:40
1769	David	Plymouth	will	#21322, 20:183,184
1769	Isaac	Hanover	gdn.	#21357, 20:298,324;21:177-179
1769	Israel	Scituate	will	#21360, 20:259,260;21:440
1770	Joseph	Duxbury	adm.	#21395, 20:397,459
1771	Benjamin	Pembroke	will	#21305, 20:544;21:69
1771	Hawkins	Scituate	adm.	#21356, 20:541;21:38
1772	Isaac	Hanover	adm.	#21358, 21:177,178
1772	Waitstill	Hanover	gdn.	#21462, 21:178,179
1773	Ezekiel	Hanover	will	#21343, 21:562,564,565
1775	David	Plymouth	adm.	#21323, 23:77;24:111;25:75;28:95;29:140;37:172-3
1776	James	Scituate	will	#21366, 24:202,203,204
1777	Samuel	Scituate	adm.	#21443, 23:118;25:75
1778	John	Scituate	will	#21386, 25:76-78;30:537;35:142
1779	Daniel	Pembroke	will	#21319, 25:347-349;28:252-255
1782	Charles	Scituate	will	#21311, 28:499,500

PLYMOUTH COUNTY PROBATE to 1849, cont-d: (re: TURNER)

1787	Abigail	Pembroke	will	#21290, 30:300,301;31:442
1792	Philip	Rochester	adm.	#21428, 27:388;33:56,57,450
1793	Elisha	Scituate	adm.	#21333, 27:422;33:197-201;35:22
1793	Philip	Scituate	will	#21430, 33:271,273,274,320;35:13,15,17,18
1793	Joshua et al	Scituate	gdn.	#21399, 26:265,318,319
1794	John	Pembroke	will	#21390, 33:556,557,558
1794	Ruth et al	Scituate	gdn.	#21439, 26:293
1794	Thomas	Pembroke	will	#21456, 33:561,563,564
1795	Joshua	Scituate	adm.	#21398, 34:55;35:339,430,493,531
1796	Nathaniel	Scituate	will	#21422, 35:480,482,551,552
1796	Jonathan	Hanover*	adm.	#21391, 34:81;35:552;36:9;38:190 (*or Pembroke)
1798	Abiel	Scituate	will	#21284, 36:456,457,458
1799	Ebenezer	Pembroke	gdn.	#21326, 37:127,171,172;32:365,38:169,188;53:140
1799	Israel	Scituate	gdn.	#21361, 32:366;37:134,135,314;48:380,381,382
1799	Jesse	Scituate	will	#21378, 37:73,75,166
1802	Israel	Scituate	adm.	#21362, 34:313;38:105;48:380,381
1802	Japhet	Pembroke	gdn.	#21371, 32:377;38:64,169;49:85
1803	James	Scituate	will	#21367, 38:480,481,482;40:62
1804	Charles	Pembroke	adm.	#21316, 34:384;40:384;43:249,252;44:310;47:176
1805	George	Pembroke	will	#21347, 40:150,151
1807	Samuel H.	Scituate	adm.	#21444, 39:114;42:69;43:426;47:210;48:508,512
1808	William	Marshfield	adm.	#21465, 39:168;42:413
1809	Thomas	Pembroke	adm.	#21457, 39:182;42:541;43:216;44:387-9,472;45:189
1810	Charles et al	Pembroke	gdn.	#21318, 41:35,118
1812	Charles	Pembroke	will	#21317, 44:153,154;39:456;44:278,468,475;45:188
1812	Nathaniel	Scituate	adm.	#21423, 39:372;44:418-9;45:90-2,94;49:375
1813	Joseph G.	Pembroke	gdn.	#21396, 41:159
1813	Nathaniel et al	Scituate	gdn.	#21421, 41:156
1816	Joshua	Pembroke	will	#21402, 48:4;49:65
1818	Plato	Plymouth	gdn.	#21431, 49:251,252,350;53:310
1820	Plato	Plymouth	adm.	#21432, 46:394;53:310
1821	Charles H.	Scituate	adm.	#21312, 52:82;54:194-5,336-7,416,520;56:172-174
1821	David	Scituate	adm.	#21321, 52:26;53:317,495;54:42,43;58:91
1821	John	Pembroke	will	#21389, 52:434;53:255-6,301-03;54:10,122,136
1821	Sally	Scituate	gdn.	#21440, 51:146;58:421,438
1822	Amos	Hanover	will	#21296, 54:393,393,510,511,512;55:2;56:317
1822	Perez	Scituate	adm.	#21425,52:179;55:98;56:449;57:283,285;58:290,323
1823	Elijah	Scituate	will	#21330, 55:124;57:6,9
1823	Job	Pembroke	adm.	#21380, 52:202;55:182;56:481;57:535,551;58:232; 59:384
1823	Jonathan	Scituate	adm.	#21393, 52:212;58:25,88,89
1823	Mercy	Scituate	will	#21418, 56:436,437
1823	Seth	Hanson	adm.	#21448, 52:221;55:126;57:159,181;58:166
1823	Perez et al	Scituate	gdn.	#21426, 51:213,214;58:336-39;58:337,340
1824	Seth et al	Hanson	gdn.	#21450, 51:247;58:339;69:267,344
1829	Thomas	Hanover	adm.	#21459, 61:313;67:459;68:19
1832	Jesse	Plymouth	adm.	#21376, 68:306;71:50;72:382;76:339
1832	Sarah	Pembroke	gdn.	#21447, 65:218;68:278;72:127,274;73:129;74:274, 381;77:332;78:351;80:223
1833	Mary	Scituate	will	#21414, 74:213;75:66
1834	Jesse H.	Plymouth	gdn.	#21377, 65:361;76:580;79:536
1835	James	Scituate	will	#21368, 77:70
1835	Lothrop	Plymouth	adm.	#21408, 71:332;73:163;75:236;77:384-5;78:42,43, 149,183,338,344
1836	Joshua D.	Hingham	adm.	#21404, 10**A**:40;75:397;79:75,514
1837	Joshua D.	Hingham	gdn.	#21403, 8**L**:37;79:515
1838	Charles et al	Scituate	gdn.	#21313, 8**L**:84
1839	Charles	Scituate	will	#21314, 1**G**:116;81:311
1843	Lemuel	Scituate	adm.	#21407, 11**B**:169;6**U**:493
1843	Samuel	Scituate	adm.	#21445, 6**U**:475;11**B**:208;86:84,552;87:129,191;95: 269,533
1844	Caleb	Bridge'ter	adm.	#21308, 6**U**:592;11**B**:277;86:537,539;87:106
1845	Hallet	Rochester	dower	#21349, 87:442
1845	Samuel et al	Scituate	gdn.	#21446, 1**R**:315,399;3**P**:493;9**M**:24;87:131;88:68;95: 268;96:253,254
1847	Samuel	Plymouth	adm.	#21441, 3**P**:74;7**V**:258;11**B**:533;89:414,563;90:325&9
1848	Elisha	Hull	adm.	#21332, 7**V**:376;11**B**:612;90:489,492
1849	Israel	Scituate	adm.	#21363, 7:471;12**C**:60;91:299,419,587
1849	John P.	Scituate	will	#21387, 2**H**:190;91:95

Will of **Amos TURNER** of Scituate MA. <Plymouth Co.R #21294>
<8:23>...13 Apr. 1739...wife **Hannah TURNER** shall have all the particulars of goods returned to her again which she brought with her in marriage according to the agreement betwixt us before marriage...also thirty pounds for a mourning suit to be paid to her by my Executors within one

month after my decease in bills of creditt of the old Tennor or Silver in proportion thereto one ounce of silver be reckoned equal to seven & twenty shillings of said bills, also I give her the Liberty of remaining in my now dwelling house for the space of one year next after my decease and all upon the condition that she release to my Executors any further claim or demand on my estate ...to my son **Ezeikel/Ezekiel TURNER** two hundred acres...where said Ezekiel now dwells being partly in Hanover and partly in Abbington...and also my cedar swamp in Hanover & my ninth part of the Saw Mill called Hatches Mill...also meadow in Scituate on south side of Rotten Marsh Creek by meadow of John CUSHING; grandson **Amos TURNER** (under 21); to son **Seth TURNER** thirty acres bordered by land of Deacon David JACOB, John CUSHING, Rotten Marsh Creek...also one half of pasture near Benjamin BRIGGS; daughters **Ann STOCKBRIDGE, Jane OTIS, Mary TURNER**; to daughter **Lydia TURNER**...my negro girl named Phillis; grand daughters (sisters of grandson Amos), **Priscilla TURNER, Jane TURNER, Ann TURNER** (all under 18);...my negro servant Primus should have Liberty to choose which of my said sons he pleases to live with. Sons Ezekiel & Seth named executors. Witnesses: David CLAP, Benjamin STOCKBRIDGE, Benjamin JAMES. <8:26,13:252> Probate/Bond 19 Apr. 1739. Surety: David CLAP of Scituate. Witnesses: Benjamin STOCKBRIDGE, Benjamin JAMES.

Amos TURNER Sr. of Scituate MA to **Amos TURNER Jr.** of Scituate MA. <Plymouth Co.Deeds 26:25>
...25 May 1730, Amos TURNER Sr., gentleman, for love etc. to son **Amos TURNER Jr.**, mariner, half acre where he has now dug a cellar. Rec. 16 Dec. 1730.

Guardianship of Child of **Amos TURNER Jr.** of Scituate. <Plymouth Co.PR 10:407>
...8 Aug. 1745, **Amos TURNER**, son of Amos TURNER Jr., mariner, dec'd, chooses his uncle **Dr. Benjamin STOCKBRIDGE** of Scituate his guardian. Witnesses: Mary CUSHING, William CUSHING.

BRISTOL COUNTY DEEDS:

6:233 - 23 Apr. 1710, Edward SHOVE of Taunton to mother Lydia WETHERELL, widow of Taunton.
7:67 1/2- May 1711, Lydia WETHERELL of Taunton to John PAUL of Taunton.
14:479 - 8 Apr. 1716, Lydia WETHERELL of Dighton to son in law Edward SHOVE of Dighton.
32:165 - 8 Feb. 1737, Thomas CLAP, clerk, of Taunton, & wf Mary to Dr. Joseph WITHERELL of Taunton, land in Taunton.
34:212 - 13 Jan. 1745, Thomas CLAPP, Esq. of Scituate, judgement against Dr. Joseph WITHERELL.
36:174 - 30 Aug. 1748, Thomas CLAP, Esq. of Scituate to Lydia WETHERELL of Taunton, widow of Dr. Joseph WETHERELL, land obtained by judgement.
37:312 - May 1750, Jabez LOTHROP of Norwich & wf Lydia who is sole executor of estate of Dr. Joseph WETHERELL of Taunton, granted power to sell land to pay debts.
37:317 - 22 June 1750, Jabez & Lydia LOTHROP to Nathaniel FALES of Bristol.
37:318 - 23 June 1750, Nathaniel FALES sells above land to Timothy FALES, Esq. of Taunton.
- 23 June 1750, Jabez & Lydia LOTHROP to Timothy FALES, Esq. of Taunton.

Estate of **Joseph WITHERELL** of Pembroke MA. <Plymouth Co.PR 25:334,543;27:24>
...1779...No details given in files.

Estate of **Dr. Joseph WETHERELL** of Taunton MA. <Bristol Co.PR>
<11:515>...16 June 1748, **Lydia WETHERLY/WETHERELL** admx. of husband's estate. <11:547> Inventory, 16 Aug. 1748. <12:1> Duplicate Inventory, 3 Aug. 1748. <12:2> Account of admx., **Lydia LOTHROP**, wf of Jabez of Norwich. <12:301> Widow's Thirds set out 3 Oct. 1749 to **Lydia LOTHROP**, admx. <12:322> Account of admx. 25 June 1750. <12:323> Estate insolvent. <130:122> 4 Apr. 1786, Guardianship of Joseph (and others) of Elijah WITHERELL of Norton.

Will of **Capt. James TURNER** of Scituate MA. <Plymouth Co.PR #21366>
<24:202>...2 Sept. 1775, mentions heirs of daughter **Desire CURTIS**; dau **Mehittable CHITENDEN**; woodland adjoining land of Judge CUSHING's; dau **Molly TURNER**; sons **James TURNER, Samuel TURNER** & son in law **Eli CURTIS** named executors. Witnesses: John COLMAN, Joseph COLMAN, Ensign OTIS, yeomen of Scituate. <original> Warrant to appraise, 5 Aug. 1776.

Heirs of **Capt. James TURNER** of Scituate MA. <Plymouth Co.Deeds 59:35>
...17 June 1777, heirs to the estates of **James TURNER** and **Samuel TURNER**, dec'd, viz: **James TURNER**, yeoman; **Mehitable CHITTENDEN** wf of Gideon; **Mary TURNER**, spinster; heirs of **Desire CURTIS** late wife of Eli, viz: **Eli CURTIS Jr., Abner CURTIS, Luther CURTIS, Desire CURTIS, Seth CURTIS, Asa CURTIS.** <60:66> 27 July 1778, **Eli CURTIS**, yeoman of Scituate on behalf of his six children, the heirs of **Desire CURTIS** and **Mary TURNER**, spinster, divide land received from **James TURNER.**

Will of **Seth TURNER**, gentleman of Scituate MA. <Plymouth Co.PR #21448>
<9:156>...3 Oct. 1743, mentions wf **Mehitable**; sisters **Jane OTIS, Anna STOCKBRIDGE, Mary TURNER, Lydia WITHERELL**; brother **Ezekiel TURNER**; cousin **Amos TURNER**, son of my brother **Amos TURNER**, dec'd <9:157> Pr. 14 Oct. 1743. <13:115> Account 23 Jan. 1748 by **Mehitable TURNER**, executrix. <13:116> Account 23 Jan. 1753 by **Mehitable COLE**, exx.

Amos TURNER to **Benjamin STOCKBRIDGE** of Scituate MA. <Plymouth Co.Deeds 43:205>
...8 Mar. 1756, Amos TURNER, blacksmith to Benjamin STOCKBRIDGE, Esq., land received by will of grandfather Amos TURNER, Esq. of Scituate.

Will of **Benjamin TURNER** of Scituate MA. <Plymouth Co.PR #21301>
<7:114>...10 May 1731, mentions wf **Elizabeth**; sons **John TURNER, Joseph TURNER, Hawkins TURNER,**

William TURNER, Benjamin TURNER; granddaughter **Grace DWELLY**, dau of my dau **Grace** dec'd; dau **Elizabeth BREWSTER**. Wife **Elizabeth** and son **William**, executors. Witnesses: John CUSHING Jr., Mary CUSHING, Deborah CUSHING. <7:115> Pr. 21 Feb. 1734. <7:116> Inventory.

Will of **Elizabeth TURNER**, widow of Scituate MA. <Plymouth Co.PR>
<9:420>...14 Jan. 1740, mentions sons **John TURNER, William TURNER**; dau **Elizabeth BREWSTER**; grandson **Joseph TURNER**; granddaughter **Grace DWELLY** alias TURNER; daus **Mercy & Lucy**, wives of my sons **Benjamin TURNER** and **Hawkins TURNER**. Sons **Benjamin** & **Hawkins** and John RUGGLES named executors. Witnesses: Nehemiah RANDALL, Gideon ROSE, Joseph BRUK(sp). <9:421> Pr. 8 Mar. 1744.

Will of **Benjamin TURNER**, caulker, of Scituate MA. <Plymouth Co.PR>
<11:144>...28 May 1748, mentions unnamed wife; youngest son **Peleg TURNER** (under 14); sons **Elisha TURNER** (under 21), **Benjamin TURNER** (under 21), **Joseph TURNER**; two unnamed daughters. Wife and Charles TURNER named executors. Witnesses: John RUGGLES, John JAMES Jr., Abigail TURNER. <11:145> Pr. 15 Oct. 1748, widow called **Mercy**. <11:178> Inventory 7 Dec. 1748, appraisers app'td., John TURNER, John JAMES, John RUGGLES; mentions lands in partnership with Charles TURNER, his bretheren in Hanover & elsewhere. <12:233> Account 2 May 1751 of **Mercy TURNER**, exx.

Estate of **Elisha TURNER** of Scituate MA. <Plymouth Co.PR #21333>
<27:422> Letter (mentions widow **Prudence**). <33:197> Warrant to Appraise. <33:198> Inventory, Estate Insolvent, Adm. Notice. <33:199> Adm. Account. <33:200> Warrant of Distribution. <33:201> Oath for Sale of Real Estate. <35:22> Bond to Secure Sale. (No details given in files.)

Elisha TURNER & Benjamin STETSON of Scituate to **Samuel STAPLES** of Hanover MA. <Plymouth Co.Deeds>
<57:89>...15 Feb. 1772, Elisha TURNER, Esq. and Benjamin STETSON, yeoman, for Ł6 sell to Samuel STAPLES half of seven and a half acres woodland in Hanover near the meeting house formerly laid out to Mr. Benjamin TURNER late of Scituate dec'd in third division of Scituate Common...Prudence TURNER and Mercy STETSON, wives, release dower.

Elisha TURNER of Scituate MA & **Joshua JACOB** of Scituate MA. <Plymouth Co.Deeds 58:120>
...4 Aug. 1773, Joshua JACOB, gentleman and Elisha TURNER, gentleman & wife Prudence, the dau of John JAMES...division of land.

Elisha TURNER of Scituate MA to **Lazarus BOWKER Jr.** of Scituate MA. <Plymouth Co.Deeds 59:181>
...15 Apr. 1777, Elisha TURNER, gentleman for Ł27 sells to Lazarus BOWKER Jr., yeoman, three acre salt meadow in Scituate; bounded by land of Col. Thomas CLAP, dec'd and Capt. Benjamin JAMES. Wife Prudence TURNER releases dower. Rec. 4 Nov. 1778.

Elisha TURNER of Scituate MA to **Elisha TURNER Jr.** of Scituate MA. <Plymouth Co.Deeds 71:54>
...12 Nov. 1788, Elisha TURNER, gentleman to Elisha TURNER Jr., yeoman, part of my homestead in Scituate. Wife Prudence releases dower. Witnesses: Joseph TURNER, Charles TURNER Jr. Ack. 12 Nov. 1788. Rec. 12 Apr. 1791.

Elisha TURNER of Scituate MA to **Lemuel JACOBS** of Scituate MA. <Plymouth Co.Deeds 72:184>
...16 Jan. 1792, Elisha TURNER, gentleman sells to Lemuel JACOBS, shipwright, three and a half acre pasture land, part of Elisha's homestead; bounded by land of Elisha TURNER Jr., Jesse TURNER, Rev. Charles TURNER. Rec. 11 Apr. 1792.

MICRO #4 OF 18

John HASCALL of Middleboro MA to **Elisha TURNER** of Scituate MA. <Plymouth Co.Deeds 14:239>
...25 Feb. 1719, John HASCALL, husbandman, for Ł3 sold to Elisha TURNER, housewright...all my right...in cedar swamp land which ye said Elisha TURNER now holds...in the sixth lot in ye great division of ye cedar swamp in the Majors Purchase...in Pembroke...as they are particularly set out to Elisha TURNER late of Scituate dec'd Father of ye first named Elisha TURNER...dated 21 Feb. 1699/1700 and since settled upon ye said Elisha TURNER ye son. Rec. 1 Mar. 1719.

Elisha TURNER of Scituate MA to: <Plymouth Co.Deeds 16:186>
...11 Apr. 1722, Elisha TURNER, house carpenter, for Ł800 sells to **Joseph STOCKBRIDGE, Abraham HOWLAND, Samuel DAWS, Isaac BARKER, Ebenezer BARKER, Elijah BISBEE, Elisha BISBEE, John BISBEE**, husbandmen, all of Pembroke and **Theodosia MORE**, husbandman of Bridgewater...six lots cedar swamp in Majors Purchase which fell to my Honoured Father Elisha TURNER, fifty six and three quarters acres; also three sixty acre lots of upland in said Purchase, 14th, 64th & 65th...in Pembroke. Rec. 2 May 1723.

Elisha TURNER of Scituate MA to **Benjamin TURNER** of Scituate MA. <Plymouth Co.Deeds 21:115>
...24 Oct. 1726, Elisha TURNER, mariner, for Ł150 sold to Benjamin TURNER, yeoman...seven acres in Scituate...was formerly ye homestead of my Honoured Father Elisha TURNER late of Scituate dec'd; bounded by land of John JAMES, Zebulon SILVESTER, Hatherly FOSTER, Joseph TURNER. Rec.17 Feb. 1726/7.

John & Elizabeth (TURNER) TURNER. <Plymouth Co.Deeds>
<12:20>...3 Mar. 1715, Elizabeth, dau of Elisha TURNER, sells part of her father's estate.
<29:146>...2 May 1734, John & Elizabeth TURNER, formerly of Sandwich...(no details).

John DILLINGHAM of Hanover MA to **Zebulon SILVESTER** of Scituate MA. <Plymouth Co.Deeds 30:185> ...7 July 1732, John DILLINGHAM, cordwainer, now of Hanover, formerly of Sandwich and wf Jael, for £115 did on 14 May 1716 convey unto Zebulon SILVESTER, house carpenter, 15 acres of upland, 2 acres of meadow lying in Scituate & was a part of the Estate of our Honoured Father **Elisha TURNER** of Scituate...and whereas the said deed was given...by us when said Jael was under the age of twenty one years...Witnesses: John CUSHING Jr., Elijah CUSHING. Ack. by John & Jael 11 Oct. 1732. Rec. 26 July 1736.

Will of **John DILLINGHAM** of Pembroke MA. <Plymouth Co.PR #6474>
<20:241>...10 Feb. 1769, mentions wf **Jael**, dau **Lydia RECCORD**; son **Elisha DILLINGHAM**; dau **Elizabeh SIMMONS**; dau **Jael PETERSON**; granddaughter **Jael DILLINGHAM** dau of **John DILLINGHAM**, dec'd, late of New York; dau **Mary STERTEVANT**; dau **Deborah HOWLAND**; son **Henry DILLINGHAM**; son **Jeremiah DILLINGHAM**; dau **Princess PETERSON**. Samuel GOOLD, sadler, of Pembroke, named executor. Pr. 1 May 1769. <20:289> Inventory. <20:333> Insolvency. <20:434> Claims.

Will of **Zebulon SYLVESTER**, yeoman of Scituate MA. <Plymouth Co.PR #20030>
<19:380>...26 Apr. 1766, mentions wife **Mary**; sons **Jacob SILVESTER, Nathaniel SILVESTER, Zebulon SILVESTER, Israel SILVESTER, Luke SILVESTER, Elisha SILVESTER**, daus **Mary SILVESTER, Olive GROCE, Martha PROUTY**; mentions lands bordered by Joshua JACOBS, Benjamin JACOBS. Wife **Mary** and son **Elisha** named excutors. Pr. 4 Aug. 1766. <19:489> Inventory taken 16 Dec. 1766 by Joshua JACOB, Isaac DAMAN, John BRIANT; real estate valued at £133.6s8d, total £209.9s7d, "an Indian girls time we apprize at nothing more than what is to be done for her when her time expires". Oath to inventory by executors 3 Apr. 1767. <21:354> Account of **Elisha SILVESTER**, executor, 16 Apr. 1774. Payments to: Dr. JACOB, Charles STOCKBRIDGE, James CUSHING, Abiel TURNER, constable, Joshua SIMMONS, John CARLOW, Benjamin PERRY, James OTIS, John BRYANT, Daniel DAMON, Isaac DAMMON, Isaac OTIS, Peleg SIMMONS, Joshua JACOB, Nathan CUSHING, Joseph COPELAND, Jacob SILVESTER, Benjamin BOWKER.

Guardianship of **Mary SILVESTER**, widow of Scituate MA. <Plymouth Co.PR #20005>
Petition 13 Nov. 1773...The Subscribers, children, rela tions & friends of **Mary SILVESTER**...that your Petitioners apprehend the said Mary to be a person non compos mentis & incapable of taking care of herself or her Estate, wherefore they pray that a guardian may be appointed her...Signed by Joseph JACOB, David JACOB, John JACOBS, Joshua JACOB, Israel SILVESTER, Elisha SILVESTER, Mary SILVESTER, Elisha JACOBS. On 30 Nov. 1773 the Selectmen of the Town of Scituate were instructed to investigate. On 2 Dec. 1773, the Selectmen: Barnabas LITTLE, Elisha JAMES and Joseph TOLMAN reported the said Mary SILVESTER to be a person non compos mentis. Bond 16 Apr. 1774, Elisha SILVESTER, yeoman of Scituate, appointed guardian. Sureties: Israel SILVESTER, James SILVESTER, yeomen of Scituate. Witnesses: Lucy DYRE, Abigail CUSHING.

Joseph & Elisha FOSTER to **Israel & Elisha SILVESTER** of Scituate. <Plymouth Co.Deeds 52:153> ...28 June 1765, Joseph FOSTER & Elisha FOSTER, gentleman of Scituate for £73.6.8. sold to Israel SILVESTER, housewright and Elisha SILVESTER, shipwright...several pieces of land in Scituate... bordered by land that Mr. James CUSHING sold to our honoured Father **Hatherly FOSTER**; land that was William TURNER's and land that was John JAMES & the Parsonage Land

---

Estate of **Israel SILVESTER** of Scituate MA. <Plymouth Co.PR #19973>
<39:342> Administration 31 Jan. 1812 by Peeks GROSS, shipwright; mentions widow **Sarah**, eldest male heir **Abel SILVESTER**. Order to Divide real estate among grandchildren: **Abel SILVESTER, Solon SILVESTER, Jotham SILVESTER, Levi DAMON, Harris DAMON.** <44:133> Inventory. <44:240> Dower. <44:241> Adm. notice. <44:420> Insolvency. <45:102> Claims. <45:285> Account & Division.

Will of **Elisha SYLVESTER**, yeoman of Scituate MA. <Plymouth Co.PR #19960>
<19:525>...29 June 1747, mentions wife **Eunice**, sons **Elisha SYLVESTER, James SYLVESTER** (minor). <19:526> Letter. Pr. 6 Dec. 1767. <29:89> Warrant & Dower, 4 & 11 Apr. 1781; mentions wife **Eunice** executrix, sons **Elisha SYLVESTER** (under 21), **James SYLVESTER** (under 14).

Estate of **Eunice SYLVESTER**, widow of Scituate MA. <Plymouth Co.PR #19964>
<27:247;30:179,333>...1787, adm., petition of grandchildren, bond. <30:353> Account 12 Apr. 1788 by Joshua JACOB, admr.; incl. paid to Benjamin BOWKER for boarding & nursing said Eunice.

Zebulon SYLVESTER of Scituate MA to **Nathaniel SYLVESTER** of Scituate MA. <Plymouth Co.Deeds 12:20> ...22 Feb. 1715/6, Zebulon SYLVESTER & wf Mary sell to Nathaniel SYLVESTER, clerk, land in Scituate set off to them by the dividers of the estate of their honored father **Elisha TURNER** of Scituate dec'd, as by his will appears.

Estate of **James SYLVESTER**, yeoman of Scituate MA. <Plymouth Co.PR 27:61>
...9 Feb. 1781, Joseph JACOB app'td admr. Dower set off 11 Apr. 1781 to **Joanna/Anna BOWKER**, late the widow of James SYLVESTER and now the wife of Benjamin BOWKER; mentions land this day set off to the widow **Eunice SYLVESTER.** <54:49> Division of Widow's Dower 15 June 1821 to **Eunice CLAPP**, widow, **Bethia NICHOLS**, heirs of **Meriam BRIGGS.**

Elisha SILVESTER of Scituate MA to **John TURNER** of Scituate MA. <Plymouth Co.Deeds 39:208> ...1 Feb. 1747, Elisha SILVESTER, yeoman & wf Eunice for £100, old tenor, sold to John TURNER, innholder...four and a half acres in Scituate at the southerly end of Hooppole Hill Cedar Swamp.. bounded by land of Joseph BENSON. Witnesses: Gideon STETSON, Martha SILVESTER. Rec. 23 Sept. 1748

Elisha SILVESTER of Scituate MA to **Joseph CUSHING Jr.** of Scituate MA. <Plymouth Co.Deeds 43:113> ...5 Apr. 1755, Elisha SILVESTER, yeoman & wf Eunice for Ł12 sell to Joseph CUSHING Jr., Esq... two ninths of real estate which Edward PROUTY, late of Scituate, yeoman, dec'd...and was set off to Elizabeth PROUTY his widow as dower...all our rights in said dower. Rec. 20 May 1755. <43:113> 8 Apr. 1755, **Samuel CURTIS** & wf Eleanor sell one ninth of same. 15 Apr. 1755, **Elisha PROUTY** & wf Martha sell one ninth of same.

Elisha SILVESTER of Scituate MA to **Timothy SYMMES** of Scituate MA. <Plymouth Co.Deeds 44:2> ...5 July 1756, Elisha SILVESTER, yeoman & wf Eunice for Ł9.7s sold to Timothy SYMMES, yeoman, three and a half acres in Scituate next to Symmes' home farm. Rec. 20 July 1756.

Samuel CURTIS of Scituate MA to **Elisha SILVESTER** of Scituate MA. <Plymouth Co.Deeds 48:100> ...18 Nov. 1757, Samuel CURTIS, shipwright & wf Eleanor for Ł4 sold to Elisha SILVESTER, yeoman, one quarter of 55th lot cedar swamp in Scituate, Hooppole Hill Swamp, two acres...part of the real estate of Edward PROUTE late of Scituate, yeoman, dec'd and was set off to Elisabeth PROUTE dec'd, one of the daughters of said Edward in the division of his real estate. Ack. by both 26 Dec. 1757. Rec. 6 Apr. 1763.

John EELLS of Scituate MA to **Israel & Elisha SILVESTER** of Scituate MA. <Plymouth Co.Deeds 35:142> ...10 Jan. 1742, John EELLS, tanner, for Ł110 sold to Israel SILVESTER, housewright and Elisha SILVESTER Jr., shipwright...thirteen acres in Scituate near dwelling house of Zebulon SILVESTER and land of John CURTIS. Witnesses: Peleg BRYANT, Caleb TORREY. Abiah EELLS, wf of John releases dower. Rec. 11 Jan. 1742.

Edmund GROSS of Scituate MA to **Elisha SILVESTER Jr.** of Scituate MA. <Plymouth Co.Deeds 52:153> ...23 Feb. 1746, Edmond GROOSE, cooper, for Ł300 sold to Elisha SILVESTER Jr., shipwright...five acres bounded by land of Thomas BRIANT, Esq. Witnesses: Caleb TORREY, Israel SILVESTER. Ack. 6 Apr. 1747 by Edmond GROSS & wf Alice who releases dower. Rec. 31 Oct. 1765.

Samuel RANDALL of Scituate MA to **Elisha SILVESTER Jr.** of Scituate MA. <Plymouth Co.Deeds 52:153> ...5 Feb. 1750, Samuel RANDALL, blacksmith for Ł53.6.8. sold to Elisha SILVESTER Jr., shipwright, twenty two acres in Scituate bounded by land belonging to heirs of Rev. Nathaniel EELLS, dec'd, land of Nathaniel CLAP, Esq. and Israel TURNER...at the same time Ruth RANDALL the widow of Capt. Nehemiah RANDALL dec'd, in token of her relinquishing her right in the premises has also signed the same. Witnesses: Nathaniel CLAP, Benjamin RANDALL Jr. Rec. 31 Oct. 1765.

Israel SILVESTER of Scituate MA to **Elisha SILVESTER** of Scituate MA. <Plymouth Co.Deeds 21:211> ...16 June 1713, Israel SILVESTER, husbandman gave to son Elisha SILVESTER, ten acres where he now dwells by 2d Herring Brook; two acres of meadow on east side of North River bought of Samuel MARSHALL of Boston; three acres near White Oak Plain laid out to Israel in 1706...to take possession after Israel's death. Witnesses: John CUSHING, Mary SILVESTER. Ack. 2 July 1713. Rec. 24 Apr. 1727.

Elisha & Zebulon SILVESTER of Scituate MA to **Joseph JACOB** of Scituate. <Plymouth Co.Deeds 33:41> ...13 Feb. 1735, Elisha SILVESTER and Zebulon SILVESTER, yeomen, for Ł28.6s8d sold to Joseph JACOB, yeoman...all that our two thirds of five acres of land...laid out in the right of Israel SILVESTER late of Scituate dec'd in the Second Division of Scituate Common being the 287th lot in Hanover at a place called Walnut Tree Hill. Witnesses: James CUSHING, Joshua JACOB. Rec. 18 Sept. 1739.

Elisha SILVESTER of Scituate MA to **William ESTES** of Hanover MA. <Plymouth Co.Deeds 43:58> ...30 Jan. 1755, Elisha SYLVESTER, yeoman for Ł2.13.4. sold to William ESTES, tanner, five acres in Hanover at Candlewood Plain...laid out to Israel Sylvester 27 Dec. 1698 by Jeremiah HATCH and Samuel CLAP, surveyors...and is the land where Margaret PETER now lives. Witnesses: David STOCKBRIDGE, Thomas TURNER. Rec. 10 Feb. 1755.

PLYMOUTH COUNTY DEEDS: (re: Elisha SILVESTER, grantor)

59:146 - 6 June 1778, Elisha SILVESTER & Lillis.
62:51 - 10/4th/ 1783, Elisha SILVESTER Jr., yeoman of Scituate to Joseph ROGERS of Marshfield, three acres where I live, part of land I bought of James & George TORREY.
70:216 - 9 Apr. 1782, Elisha SILVESTER Jr. & wf Abigail.
72:87 - 6 Dec. 1791, Elisha SILVESTER, yeoman, of Green, Lincoln co.
78:106 - 26 Apr. 1777, Elisha SILVESTER & Lillis, sell thirteen acres, all the land my father gave me by will; bounded by land of Benjamin JACOBS, Israel SILVESTER, Luke SILVESTER, Capt. JACOBS. Rec. 13 May 1797.
101:27 - , Elisha SILVESTER & Lillis to Thomas SILVESTER Jr.
101:28 - , Elisha SILVESTER & Lillis to Thomas SILVESTER.

No details given for following references: 26:103;27:149;28:201;33:41;39:208;40:206;43:58,113;44:2;50:172;60:181;69:249;80:78;89:29;108:113,185;109:72,73;109:199;119:21.

PLYMOUTH COUNTY DEEDS: (re: Elisha SILVESTER, grantee)

23:67 - 21 Jan. 1727, Thomas JENKINS, yeoman of Scituate to Barnabas BARKER, Elisha SILVESTER, Peter SILVESTER, yeomen of Scituate, 5 acres in 2nd division of estate

of Edward JENKINS deceased.
25:226 - 3 Feb. 1728, Silence SILVESTER receipts to brother Elisha SILVESTER, both of Scituate, as executor of will of father Israel SILVESTER, dec'd.
26:103 - 30 Mar. 1731, Timothy SYMMES, yeoman of Scituate allows Elisha SILVESTER right of way to Silvester's land on account of road being straightened by Town.
27:50 - 2 Feb. 1731, Nehemiah RANDALL to Elisha SILVESTER, yeomen of Scituate.
29:53 - 31 July 1734, Job OTIS, yeoman to Elisha SILVESTER, yeoman, both of Scituate, for Ŀ18, two acres in Scituate bounded by land of Silvester & Robert WOODWARD.
32:221 - 10 Apr. 1736, Robert WOODARD/WOODWARD Jr. to Elisha SILVESTER, yeomen of Scituate.
52:153 - 1746, Edmund GROSS to Elisha SILVESTER Jr., shipwright. Rec. 31 Oct. 1765.
52:153 - 1750, Samuel RANDALL to Elisha SILVESTER Jr., shipwright. Rec. 31 Oct. 1765.
52:153 - 1765, "FOSTERS" to Elisha SILVESTER, shipwright and Israel SILVESTER. " "
61:143 - 7 May 1781, "TORREYS" to Elisha SILVESTER Jr., yeoman of Scituate.
80:78 - 13 Mar. 1786, Elisha SILVESTER, shipwright and Israel SILVESTER, yeoman, divide land bought of Fosters.

Elisha SILVESTER of Scituate MA to **Timothy SYMMES** of Scituate MA. <Plymouth Co.Deeds 27:149>
...26 May 1731, Elisha SILVESTER, yeoman to Timothy SYMMES, yeoman...Ack. 15 June 1731.

Elisha SILVESTER of Scituate MA to **Thomas TURNER Jr.** of Scituate MA. <Plymouth Co.deeds 28:201>
...18 Dec. 1731, Elisha SILVESTER, yeoman to Thomas TURNER Jr., shipwright, land where Silvester now dwells...Ack. 2 Apr. 1733.

Elisha SILVESTER of Scituate to **Nathaniel BROOKS** of Scituate MA. <Plymouth Co.Deeds 40:206>
...25 June 1742, Elisha SILVESTER, yeoman to Nathaniel BROOKS, yeoman, one acre in Scituate joining Brooks' land.

MICRO #5 OF 18

Will of **Elisha SILVESTER**, yeoman of Scituate MA. <Plymouth Co.PR #19961>
<42:209>...17 July 1805, advanced in years, mentions wife **Lillis**; to son **Thomas SILVESTER**...a large silver spoon marked "Z.S. & E.S."; granddaughter **Mary Stockbridge CUSHING**, dau of my late dau **Lillis CUSHING; Daniel TORREY & Caleb TORREY Jr.**, sons of my late dau **Hannah TORREY**; son **Elisha SILVESTER**; daughters **Lurana TURNER** and **Chloe WARREN.** Real estate incl. homestead farm; pasture purchased of Elijah RANDALL; part of meetinghouse field purchased of Warren SILVESTER; two acres swamp land purchased of Caleb TORREY by deed dated 5 Dec. 1791; eight acres called Jordan Lot; six acres meadow purchased of Deacon John RUGGLES. Wife **Lillis** & Charles TURNER Jr., Esq. named executors. Witnesses: Thomas CUSHING, Hannah TURNER, Charles TURNER Jr. <42:312> Account of executors, 6 June 1808. Land had been sold to: Elnathan CUSHING, Warren SILVESTER, Laban SOUTHER, George LITTLE, Elisha HAYDEN, James CURTIS Jr. and Nathaniel CUSHING. Payments to: James SPARRELL, Warren SILVESTER, Edward DAMAN, Elisha ELMES, Lillis SILVESTER, Thomas CUSHING and Hannah TURNER; Thomas SILVESTER for funeral expenses, $11.17 and for measuring land, $2.00; legacies of $100.00 each paid to: **Elisha SILVESTER, Chloe WARREN, Lurana TURNER,** Elnathan CUSHING the guardian to **Mary S. CUSHING.** <42:210> Bond 7 Dec. 1807 by executors. Sureties: Silvanus CLAP, Thomas SILVESTER. Witnesses: Israel GERRY, Joshua MANN. <44:424> Warrant to divide land, 3 Nov. 1812, David STOCKBRIDGE, Esq. of Hanover, Thomas CUSHING, trader and Lazarus BOWKER, yeoman, both of Scituate, app'td appraisers. <44:424> Division of real estate, 30 Nov. 1812 by appraisers to following heirs: to **Lurana TURNER**, wf of Abiel, two acres bounded by land of Deacon Thomas CUSHING & Warren SILVESTER; to **Thomas SILVESTER** six acres bounded by land of George TORREY and Rev. Mr. DEAN's Meeting house; to **Chloe BISBE**, wf of Elisha, two and a half acres bounded by land of said Thomas CUSHING & Warren SILVESTER; to **Mary Stockbridge CUSHING** three pieces of land totalling about five acres, bounded by land of Seth TURNER, Meeting House, Elnathan CUSHING, Thomas SYLVESTER and James SPARREL.

Will of **Lillis SILVESTER**, widow of Scituate MA. <Plymouth Co.PR #19998>
<44:325>...10 June 1810, to my granddaughter **Mary Stockbridge CUSHING** all my estate of every name and nature whatsoever where ever it may be found...Elnathan CUSHING of Scituate ap'td executor. Witnesses: Thomas CUSHING, Christopher CUSHING, Warren SILVESTER. <44:326> Bond 7 Sept. 1812 by executor. Sureties: Christopher CUSHING, Esq. and Thomas CUSHING, trader, both of Scituate. <44:413> Warrant to appraise estate, 7 Sept. 1812, Christopher CUSHING, Esq., Thomas CUSHING, trader, Warren SILVESTER, yeoman, app'td. <44:413> Inventory taken 8 Oct. 1812 by appraisers; items incl. clock, $12.00; Bible, $2.00; gold necklace & rings, $6.00; total $161.66. <44:476> Account of executor 1 Mar. 1813. Payments to: Thomas CUSHING; Christopher STETSON for digging the grave, $2; Christopher CUSHING; Warren SILVESTER, Anson ROBBINS.

Elisha SILVESTER Jr. of Scituate MA to **Job TURNER** of Scituate MA. <Plymouth Co.Deeds 60:181>
...14 May 1781, Elisha SILVESTER Jr. & Hannah SILVESTER, for Ŀ34.6s8d silver money, sold to Job TURNER, yeoman...one half of five acre salt marsh or meadow in Scituate near Noah NICHOL's, bounded by Isaacher VINAL. Abigail SILVESTER, wf of Elisha, releases dower. Rec. 5 July 1781.

Elisha SILVESTER Jr. of Scituate MA to **Thomas RUGGLES** of Scituate MA. <Plymouth Co.Deeds 69:249>
...7 Mar. 1783, Elisha SILVESTER Jr., yeoman, for Ŀ10 sold to Thomas RUGGLES, yeoman...thirty acres in Scituate near the Rev. Mr. BARNE's Meeting house...being that part of the homestead farm of my Grandfather John RUGGLES, dec'd which he left me under the improvement of the widow Sarah CLAPP & gave to his grandchildren in his last will...and Abigail the wife of the said Elisha

SILVESTER doth hereby give up her right of dower. Witnesses: Elisha YOUNG, William TURNER.

==

Elisha SILVESTER of Scituate MA to **Thomas SILVESTER Jr.** of Scituate MA.<Plymouth Co.Deeds 101:27>
...1 Aug. 1787, Elisha SILVESTER, shipwright & wf Lillis, for £90 sold to Thomas SILVESTER Jr., shipwright...nine acres in Scituate...bounded by land of Caleb TORREY, said Elisha SILVESTER, Israel TURNER, Benjamin COLLAMORE. Lillis SILVESTER, wf of Elisha, releases dower. Witnesses: William TURNER, Benjamin STETSON. Rec. 17 Oct. 1804.

==

Elisha SILVESTER of Scituate MA to **Thomas SILVESTER** of Scituate MA. <Plymouth Co.Deeds 101:28>
...20 Apr. 1789, Elisha SILVESTER, shipwright & wf Lillis, for £12 sold to Thomas SILVESTER, yeoman...two acres in Scituate called dead swamp...bounded by land of Isaac TORREY. Witnesses: Lillis SILVESTER, Elijah TURNER. Ack. 4 May 1796 by Elisha & Lillis. Rec. 17 Oct. 1804.

==

Agreement between heirs of **Mary LOVELL** of Weymouth MA. <Plymouth Co.Deeds 50:172>
...2 Dec. 1754...An agreement between heirs of Mary LOVELL, viz: **Joshua LOVELL; Capt. Ebenezer HUNT** as representative for three of his children**, Samuel, Kezia & Ebenezer; Enoch HUNT; Nathaniel BAYLEY** & wf **Tamar; Joseph WEBB** & wf **Eleanor; Solomon LOVELL,** all the abovesaid of Weymouth in the County of Suffolk...and **John HOLLIS** & wf **Alithea; John HOLBROOK Jr.** & wf **Mary**, all of Braintree.. and **Micah HUNT, Isaac HERSEY & Gideon HERSEY** representatives of **Jonathan WHITE** & wf **Hannah**, said **HERSEY** of Abington; and **Elisha SYLVESTER** of Scituate as representative for his child **Urania...** concerning a division of land in Abington...which lands descended to us as heirs of **Mary LOVELL,** late of Weymouth, dec'd...bounded by lands of heirs of Elizabeth HUNT, dec'd, Capt. Daniel REED, Thomas ROGERS, dec'd, Samuel NASH, Adam CUSHING...seventy acres more or less...divided into six parts among subscribers. Witnesses: Ezra WHITMARSH, Daniel REED, Benjamin DYAR, Solomon LOVELL. Ack. by all 1 Jan. 1756. Rec. 2 Oct. 1765.

==

Estate of **Jacob SYLVESTER** of Hanover MA. <Plymouth Co.PR #19977>
<40:494> Will 16 May 1794, entire estate to wf **Mary.** Pr. 1 Sept. 1806, wife (who is blind) refuses to administer estate. <39:434> Letter. <40:494> Petition. <42:16> Adm. notice.

==

Estate of **Edmund GROSS** of Scituate MA. <Plymouth Co.PR #8743>
...1799...<34:1> Letter. <35:271> Warrant to appraise. <35:275> Inventory.

==

Estate of **Edmund GROSS Jr.** of Scituate MA. <Plymouth Co.PR #8742>
...1768...<20:44> Administration. <20:197> Inventory.

==

Will of **Ezekiel TURNER** of Groton CT. <Stonington CT PR #3319>
...3 June 1769, mentions wf **Borridel** and son **Ezekiel TURNER Jr.** (executors), son **Amos TURNER,** daughters **Prudence FOX** and **Eunice BROWN**;to granddaughter **Theody BROWN** the remaining quarter of my personal estate...and all the household goods which I lent to my daughter **Theody BROWN** and were returned to my house again from Stonington after her decease; grandson **Daniel BROWN** (under 21). Pr. 13 Mar. 1770. Inventory 13 Mar. 1770. <original> Receipt 1772, of **Amos & Eunis BROWN,** both of Preston. Witnesses: Jesse FOX, Rebekkah DENNISON. Receipt 11 Jan. 1773, of **Samuel & Prudence FOX** of Preston...from executor **Mrs. Borradill TURNER.** Witnesses: Ezra BENJAMIN, Jesse FOX. Receipt 19 July 1776, of **George DENISON 4th** & wf **Theody DENISON** of Stonington...from executor **Mrs. Borradil TURNER.** Witnesses: James MASON, Sarah MASON. (Copies of all originals in files.)

MICRO #6 OF 18

Will of **Prudence FOX** of New London CT. <New London CT PR>
...2 Mar. 1810; to sons **Jesse FOX, Ezekiel FOX, Elijah FOX** (executor)**, John FOX** - $1.00 each; to daughters **Thankfull RUSWELL/BUSWELL** and **Boradell PIERCE** wf of Thomas, rest of estate. Witnesses: John FELCH, N. ENSWORTH, David SMITH. Pr. 14 Apr. 1825, Elijah FOX, executor, living in Maine.

==

Heirs of **Samuel TURNER** of Stonington CT. <Stonington CT Deeds 20:7>
...24 Nov. 1755, **Moses PALMER** & wf **Prudence**, of Stonington, for £217 paid by our Elder brother, **Samuel TURNER** of Stonington...convey all our right to two thirds of the lands that our honoured father **Samuel TURNER** late of Stonington, died seized...**Prudence PALMER** being one of the said daughters of said **Samuel TURNER**...four acre farm, exclusive of mother **Rebecah TURNER**'s thirds. Witnesses: John PALMER, Amos CHESEBROUGH.

==

Will of **Benajah LEFFINGWELL** of Norwich CT. <Norwich CT PR #6846>
...2 May 1752, to wf **Joanna** the silver tankard that was Madam Levingston's and all lands until children come of age, viz: **Christopher LEFFINGWELL, Benajah LEFFINGWELL, Hezekiah LEFFINGWELL, Elisha LEFFINGWELL, Richard LEFFINGWELL, Mary LEFFINGWELL, Sarah LEFFINGWELL, Lucretia LEFFINGWELL.** Witnesses: Thomas LEFFINGWELL, Thomas MARSHALL, Daniel KELLEY. Pr. 14 June 1756. Inventory taken 20 July 1756 and sworn to 1 Sept. 1756 by Ebenezer LOTHROP, Thomas LEFFINGWELL, Samuel LEFFINGWELL 3rd; total £1414.

==

Will of **Dr. Guy PALMER** of New London CT. <New London CT PR #3914>
...21 Feb. 1757, mentions wf **Lucy,** unnamed five children (all under 18), brother **Edward PALMER,** friend James MUMFORD. Pr. 12 Apr. 1757. Inventory 28 Feb. 1758. Account 3 June 1767.
(Receipt 21 Feb. 1737/8 of **Guy PALMER** to his guardian John RICHARDS, estate from my father **Andrew PALMER** and grandmother **Mrs. Sarah PALMER.** Witnesses: Timothy GREEN, Bryan PALMER.)

==

Will of **Daniel DESHON** of New London CT. <New London CT PR #1723>
...11 Feb. 1772, old & weak...to wf **Ruth** entire estate; mentions eldest son **John DESHON** and other unnamed children. Pr. 12 Jan. 1782.

Will of **Jonathan DOUGLAS** of New London CT. <New London CT PR #1794>
...11 Sept. 1731...to wf **Lucy**, if with child, all estate she brought into marriage; mentions brother **Samuel DOUGLAS** and unnamed brothers & sisters. Witnesses: John COIT Jr., Daniel DESHON, Elizabeth LIVINGSTON. Pr. 23 July 1733. Inventory sworn to 3 Oct. 1733 by widow.

Grace COIT of New London CT to **Daniel COIT** of New London CT. <New London CT Deeds 19:272>
...31 May 1769, Grace COIT, dau of John COIT Jr. of New London, dec'd, for 48s sold to Daniel COIT...all rights in two shares of the Common and Undivided land in New London...which belonged to my Honoured Great Grandfather **Richard CHRISTOPHERS**, Esq. formerly of New London, dec'd. Witnesses: Richard LAW, Ann LAW. Ack. by Grace & Rec. 5 June 1769.

Estate of **John TURNER** of Scituate MA. <Plymouth Co.PR>
Settlement of estate, 16 Mar. 1719/20; sixteen acres appraised at Ł112...said lands cannot be divided among all the children without great predejice...therefore land is settled upon **John TURNER**, the eldest son...he having paid unto the other children their equal share, Ł13 ea., viz: **Richard TURNER, Abiel/Aibell TURNER, Abigail/Abigale BRIANT** wf of Samuel, **Margaret TURNER, Lydia/Ledia TURNER, Deborah TURNER.**

Will of **Joseph SYLVESTER** of Scituate MA. <Plymouth Co.PR>
<21:62>...2 May 1771, mentions sons **Lemuel SYLVESTER, Joseph SYLVESTER**, to dau **Deborah SYLVESTER** the loom & round table that was her sister **Ruth**'s, dau **Lydia SYLVESTER.** Pr. 14 Aug. 1771.

Estate of **Abigail TURNER** of Scituate MA. <Plymouth Co.PR 4:208,209;5:584>
...1719...(No details given in files.)

Will of **Abiel TURNER**, gentleman of Scituate MA. <Plymouth Co.PR>
<36:456>...25 Dec. 1787; to son **Abial TURNER** the whole of my wearing apparel including my silver knee buckels; to daus **Annah HATCH** and **Bethiah TOLMAN**, 12s each; to dau **Martha CLAPP** the one half of my pew in the Rev. William BARNES' meeting house, also 12s; to granddaughter **Elizabeth CUDWORTH**, 12s; to son **Roland TURNER** the remainder of estate; son Roland and friend Charles TURNER Jr., Esq. named executors. Witnesses: Jonathan HATCH, Thomas RUGGLES, Charles COLE. Pr. 3 Dec. 1798. <36:457-458>...Refusal of executors, bond, etc. (not specified in files).

Plymouth Co.Deeds referring to **Abiel TURNER:**
41:158;42:231;52:240;53:172,173;62:212;67:169;70:267;72:69,261;79:58;81:158;83:194. (no details)
Plymouth Co.Deeds referring to the surname **TURNER:**
26:176;30:90;50:97;55:43;56:211;59:9;63:57;64:73,251;66:266;73:239.

Elizabeth ROSE of Scituate MA to **Richard TURNER** of Scituate MA. <Plymouth Co.Deeds 24:201>
...18 Apr. 1727, Elizabeth ROSE, dau of Jeremiah ROSE of Scituate, dec'd, for Ł30 sold to Richard TURNER, wheelwright, four acres belonging to said Jeremiah. Witnesses: Gideon ROSE, Thomas ROSE. Rec. 15 Dec. 1729.

Samuel BRYANT of Scituate MA to **Richard TURNER** of Scituate MA. <Plymouth Co.Deeds 24:201>
...10 Dec. 1727, Samuel BRYANT, wheelwright, for Ł396 sold to Richard TURNER, wheelwright, forty four acres in Scituate. Ack. 25 Mar. 1729.

Samuel BRYANT of Scituate MA to **Richard TURNER** of Scituate MA. <Plymouth Co.Deeds 42:137>
...5 Sept. 1734, Samuel BRYANT, wheelwright to Richard TURNER, wheelwright. On 3rd Tues. Sept. 1753, witnesses swore to the signature of Samuel BRYANT, now dec'd.

Samuel BRYANT & wf **Mary** to **Timothy SYMMES**, 11 Mar. 1763 (no details). <Plymouth Co.Deeds 48:101>

Estate of **Richard TURNER** of Scituate MA. <Plymouth Co.PR>
...1752...(No details given in files.) <13:41,78,102,132-34;14:60>

Estate of **Amos PERRY**, shipwright of Scituate MA. <Plymouth Co.PR #15670>
<14:77>...5 July 1756, **Amos PERRY**, yeoman of Scituate app'td admr. <original> Bond 5 July 1756 of admr. Sureties: Jesse TURNER, yeoman of Scituate & Benjamin TURNER, gentleman of Hanover. Witnesses: Jonathan PETERSON, Edward WINSLOW. <14:406> Inventory 5 July 1756 by Jesse TURNER, Benjamin TURNER, Elisha BARKER; housing & lands valued at Ł181,6s8d, total Ł347.14s3d. <14:382> Insolvency declared by **Amos PERRY**, admr. on estate of his father **Amos PERRY**...<14:435> Dower set off 7 Nov. 1757 to widow **Ruth PERRY**, by Caleb TORREY, Jonah STETSON, Mathew STETSON, Jesse TURNER, John RUGGLES Jr., all of Scituate. <15:11> 19 Mar. 1757 Thomas STOCKBRIDGE & William SILVESTER, gentlemen of Scituate app'td to examine claims of creditors; sworn 7 Nov. 1757; claims total Ł264.15s3d. <15:13> Account of admr. 7 Aug. 1758, he to pay creditors 13s4d on the pound.

MICRO #7 OF 18

Estate of **Joseph TURNER** of Scituate MA. <Plymouth Co.PR #21394>
<4:383>...2 Mar. 1723/4 at Marshfield, Joseph STOCKBRIDGE of Pembroke app'td admr. on estate of

Father In Law Deacon Joseph TURNER, dec'd. (No further details.)

Estate of **William BARRELL** of Scituate MA. <Plymouth Co.PR #1070>
<1:48,49>...1689...(No details given in files.)

Estate of **William BARRELL,** blacksmith of Scituate MA. <Plymouth Co.PR #1071>
<13:58> Letter 4 Nov. 1752, **William BARRELL,** yeoman of Scituate app'td. admr. <13:101> Inventory 15 Nov. 1752. <13:111> Account 7 July 1753. <13:180> Dower set off 3 Dec. 1753 to widow Abigail. <13:428> Account 5 Feb. 1755.

Plymouth Co.Deeds referring to surname **BARRELL:**
7:293;8:19,25;16:178;17:150;24:34;28:98;39:88;40:245;46:107;47:16,69;48:234;51:75,171;55:43;56:79,93;64:85;66:133,140;67:61;73:248;76:126;80:204;81:227;89:31,233,267.

William BARRELL of Bridgewater MA to **Samuel CLAP.** <Plymouth Co.Deeds 42:239>
...13 Dec. 1753, William BARRELL, blacksmith, as admr. on estate of William BARRELL, yeoman of Scituate...to Samuel CLAP, eight acres in Scituate with parts of house & barn.

James BARRELL of Scituate MA to **Samuel CLAP.** <Plymouth Co.Deeds 42:239>
...17 May 1754, James BARRELL, yeoman to Samuel CLAP, all right in Cedar Swamp part of 66th lot; also all right in the thirds set off to **Abigail BARRELL** and all rights in house & barn that fell to me out of the estate of **William BARRELL,** dec'd.

William BARRELL of Bridgewater MA to **Joshua BARRELL** of Bridgewater MA. <Plymouth Co.Deeds 68:4>
...8 Sept. 1787, William BARRELL, yeoman & Sarah BARRELL, spinster wife to said William...to Joshua BARRELL, yeoman...

Joshua BARRELL of Bridgewater MA to **Josiah HILL Jr.** of Bridgewater MA. <Plymouth Co.Deeds 77:24>
...8 Sept. 1787, Joshua BARRELL, blacksmith to Josiah HILL Jr., yeoman...2nd lot...in Second Share towards Abington as they were divided by the heirs of the four sisters of Isaac ALDEN, late of Bridgewater, dec'd. Wife Olive BARRELL releases dower. Ack. by J.B. 19 Oct. 1787.

Joshua BARRELL to **Mark PHILLIPS Jr.** both of Bridgewater MA. <Plymouth Co.Deeds 78:261>
...2 Sept. 1795, Joshua BARRELL, gentleman to Mark PHILLIPS Jr., yeoman...Witness: William BARRELL 2nd. (No details given in files.)

Joshua BARRELL, gentleman of Bridgewater MA to **Elijah HAYWARD 3d.** <Plymouth Co.Deeds 82:172>
...7 Apr. 1797...agreement...(No details given in files.)

Joshua BARRELL to **James BARRELL,** both gentlemen of Bridgewater MA. <Plymouth Co.Deeds 90:248>
...26 June 1801...(No details given in files.) <Note: two deeds rec. 155:201 show Joshua BARRELL of Bridgewater, 18 May 1801 and of Turner ME, 24 June 1804.>

Estate of **William BARRELL,** yeoman of Scituate MA. <Plymouth Co.PR #1072>
<40:493> Will 18 Aug. 1806, mentions wife **Rebecca;** to son **William BARRELL** twenty acres on Simons Hill; daughters **Rebecca BARRELL, Bathsheba BARRELL, Betsey BARRELL, Lucinda BARRELL, Lucy BARRELL** and **Ruth BARRELL.** Pr. 1 Sept. 1806. <42:1> Warrant for Inventory, 1 Sept. 1806. <42:51> Account 2 Mar. 1807.

Estate of **Elisha JAMES,** mariner of Scituate MA. <Plymouth Co.PR 9:355>
...Letter/Bond 8 Sept. 1744, John JAMES app'td. admr., deceased died intestate.

Estate of **Benjamin JAMES,** yeoman of Scituate MA. <Plymouth Co.PR #11334>
<original>...25 Mar. 1797, **Benjamin JAMES, Nathaniel TURNER Jr., John JAMES Jr., Mercy JAMES, Polly JAMES** and **Elisha JAMES ye 3d,** children & heirs at law, petitioned the court to appoint Charles TURNER Jr. admr. <36:85> Warrant to appraise, 27 Mar. 1797; Augustus CLAPP, yeoman, Benjamin HOLMES, yeoman and James CLAPP, gentleman, all of Scituate were app'td. <36:85> Inventory taken 28 Mar. 1797; homestead & buildings, $1,120.00, outlands $1,900.00. <34:107> Letter/Bond 29 Mar. 1797, Charles TURNER Jr. of Scituate app'td admr. Sureties: Ephraim SPOONER, William JACKSON both of Plymouth. <36:112> Notice 29 Mar. 1797. <original> Bond 15 Apr. 1787 of admr. Sureties: Lemuel JACOB, shipwright and Job VINALL, yeoman. <36:206> Notice 13 Apr. 1797, that fifty acres of pasture and wood land in Scituate would be sold at public vendue at the house of Hawke CUSHING innholder in Scituate on the 15th day of May next. <36:207> Oath 15 May 1797 by Charles TURNER Jr. that he would exert his utmost endeavours to dispose of the estate to the greatest advantage of all persons interested therein. <36:347>...23 Nov. 1797, Charles TURNER Jr., Esq., James BRIGGS Jr., yeoman and James CLAP, gentleman, all of Scituate, were app'td to divide the real estate of Benjamin JAMES, dec'd...into six equal parts to the heirs, viz: **Benjamin JAMES, John JAMES, Elisha JAMES, Sarah TURNER** wf of Nathaniel Jr., **Mercy JAMES** and **Polly JAMES.**

Estate of **Samuel STOCKBRIDGE** of Scituate MA. <Plymouth Co.PR 15:39>
...will dated 6 Feb. 1755, aged & infirm; mentions wife **Lydia;** sister **Sarah PINCIN;** son **Samuel STOCKBRIDGE** (named executor); dau **Persis TOWER** wf of Daniel; dau **Abiel;** dau **Abigail TURNER** & her present children; children of dau **Lydia SOPER,** dec'd wife of Joseph; grandson **Joseph BENSON** (under 21). Codicil 27 June 1755 and 19 July 1758. Pr. 27 July 1758.

Estate of **Lydia STOCKBRIDGE**, widow of Scituate MA. <Plymouth Co.PR>
<19:445> Petition 9 Mar. 1767, for guardian for Lydia STOCKBRIDGE, widow of Samuel, between 80-90 years of age; 27 Mar. 1767 John BRIANT of Scituate app'td. Sureties: Samuel STOCKBRIDGE, Joseph BENSON. <20:48> 4 May 1768, Samuel STOCKBRIDGE app'td admr. on estate of Lydia STOCKBRIGE. Sureties: John BRYANT, John JOSSELYN. <20:110> Account 13 Aug. 1768 of John BRYANT, gdn. of Lydia. Paid to: Samuel STOCKBRIDGE, expense of lawsuit begun at his mother's request; heirs of Lydia SOPER; my wife's part of estate; Perces TOWER's part of estate. <20:218> Insolvency of estate. <40:219> Allowances paid to heirs of Lidia SOPER, dec'd; Persis TOWER; Abiel BRYANT.

Joshua BARRELL of Bridgewater MA to **Zachariah SHAW** of Bridgewater MA. <Plymouth Co.Deeds 155:201> ...18 May 1801, Joshua BARRELL, gentleman for $850.00 sold to Zachariah SHAW, yeoman...all my homestead farm except the ten acres I bought of Isaac ALDEN...bounded by land of Isaac ALLEN, William BARRELL...about twenty three acres. Wife Olive BARRELL releases dower. Witnesses: Nathan ALDEN Jr., Content BARRELL. Ack. 1 June 1802. Rec. 21 Nov. 1825.

MICRO #8 OF 18

Joshua BARRELL of Turner ME to **Zachariah SHAW** of Bridgewater MA. <Plymouth Co.Deeds 155:201> ...27 June 1804, Joshua BARRELL, blacksmith for $250.00 sold to Zachariah SHAW, yeoman...ten acres bounded by land of John TIRRILL Jr., Deacon ALDEN, William BARRELL's homestead, to land I sold the said Zachariah at first...Wife Olive BARRELL releases dower. Witnesses: John BISBEE, William L. VAUGHAN. Ack. at Portland ME 27 June 1804. Rec. 21 Nov. 1825.

Will of **Joseph PRINCE**, mariner of Boston MA. <Suffolk Co.PR #11708>
<53:79>...20 Jan. 1758, mentions Rev. Mr. Thomas PRINCE of Boston to make sale of my share in Mr. Jonathan LORING, dec'd, his real estate; to wf **Mary** all those lands lying in the County of Worcester which she conveyed to me by deed the third of Feb. 1757 before our intermarriage; my grandchildren, the children of my dau **Sarah PROVINCE**; dau **Sarah PROVINCE**; children **Joseph PRINCE, Isaac PRINCE, Caleb PRINCE, James PRINCE, Mary, Elizabeth & Abigail**; to daus **Elizabeth & Abigail**, all the wearing apparel which belonged to my former wife **Mary PRINCE**, dec'd; son in law **Joseph BALLARD** and dau **Mary BALLARD**, and good friend David JEFFRIES of Boston, app'td executors. Witnesses: Oxenbridge THACHER, Oliver WISWALL, Hannah GREENWOOD. <53:78> Pr. 27 Jan. 1758. <53:261> Inventory taken 6 & 7 Feb. 1758 by Peter OLIVER, John KNEELAND and Belcher NOYES. Joseph BALLARD and David JEFFRIES made oath to inventory 7 Apr. 1758; incl. house & land on Milk St., Boston, £213.6s8d; a negro man named Jack, £46,13s4d; a two mast boat, rigging sails, etc., £26.13s4d. <original> Account 5 Aug. 1768 of Joseph BALLARD one of ye executors shows payments amounting to £171.3s3d and receipts of £190.15s7d. <original> Account 2 Sept. 1768 of David JEFFRIES one of the executors shows receipts of £466 and payments of £457.14s3d; payments made throughout 1761 to the heirs (incl. dau **Elizabeth KIRKWOOD** and three children of **David PROVINCE**), their share in money "received for sufferers in the Fire" and "for loss in the Fire".

Eliza DEXTER of Albany NY to **Sarah LECAIN** of Boston MA. <Suffolk Co.Deeds 365:197> ...8 Feb. 1831, Eliza DEXTER, widow, for $1.00 quitclaimed to Sarah LECAIN, widow...a house and lot on the west side of Lynde St., Boston...bounded by land now or formerly belonging to: the widow of Bartholomew TROW, the Widow Agnes PRINCE, Adam THAXTER...being in front about twenty seven feet six inches, in rear about twenty seven feet and in depth about eighty feet and being the same house and lot of ground, of which John PROVINCE, formerly of Boston, died seized and which descended to the parties to these presents as his heirs at law. Witness: James DEXTER of Albany NY. Rec. 18 Jan. 1833.

Sarah LECAIN of Boston MA to **Thomas Lindall WINTHROP** of Boston MA. <Suffolk Co.Deeds 365:206> ...19 Jan. 1833, Sarah LECAIN, widow, for $1962.00 sold to Thomas Lindall WINTHROP...land with buildings on Lynde St., Boston...bounded easterly on said Street twenty seven feet six inches, northerly on land late of Isaac DICKMAN eighty feet, westerly on land late of John STANIFORD(sp) twenty seven feet and southerly on land late of Joseph WHITTEMORE eighty feet...being the same premises which said WHITTEMORE conveyed to my late father **John PROVINCE** by deed 26 Sept. 1760, recorded in Suffolk deeds 95:146...The said **John PROVINCE** died seized thereof forty years ago leaving a widow who died twenty two years ago and two only children and heirs, to whom the said premises descended, to wit, me the said **Sarah**, then the wife of **John LECAIN** and **Eliza** then the wife of **Samuel DEXTER**. And the said **Eliza** being now a widow, conveyed her share and interest therein to me by deed dated 8 Feb. 1831. Witnesses: E. Ritchie DORR, Jno Eliot THAYER. Rec. 19 Jan. 1833.

Guardianship of Children of **John PROVINCE** of Boston MA. <Suffolk Co.PR>
<57:192>...5 Sept. 1760, John PROVINCE, taylor, app'td guardian to his daus **Mary & Sarah PROVINCE** (under 14). <57:193>...5 Sept. 1760, he was app'td guardian to son **David PROVINCE** (under 14).

Will of **John PROVINCE**, taylor of Boston MA. <Suffolk Co.PR #20012>
<91:541>...25 May 1792, mentions wf **Sarah**; daus **Sarah LARAIN/LECAIN**, wf of John of Annapolis Royal in the Province of Nova Scotia, and **Elizabeth DEXTER**, wf of Samuel of Albany NY. Witnesses: Samuel W. HUNT, James RICHARDSON, David JACOBS. <91:540> Pr. 14 Aug. 1792, administration granted to **Sarah PROVINCE.**

Will of **Joseph GOOLD** of Hull MA. <Suffolk Co.PR #14752>
<69:191>...23 Sept. 1769, "being aged", mentions son **Samuel GOOLD**; dau **Jane LORING**, wf of Samuel; grandson **Joshua GOOLD** (under 21), only son of my son **Joshua GOOLD**, late of Hingham, dec'd; grand-

children, "the sons & daughters of my **Joseph GOOLD**", late of Georgetown, dec'd, viz: **Joseph GOOLD Mercy BATES, Hannah GOOLD, Mary GREENLEAF, Moses GOOLD, Anstis GOOLD, Stephen GOOLD**; sons **Caleb GOOLD** and **Elisha GOOLD** named executors. Pr. 3 July 1770.

Estate of **Francis LOUD**, housewright of Weymouth MA. <Suffolk Co.PR #15585>
<73:528> Eliot LOUD, admr., made oath to inventory (date?). <74:340> Account mentions widow and a Francis LOUD (date?). <73:601> Administration granted 18 Mar. 1774 to Ellet/Eliot LOUD, housewright of Weymouth.

Estate of **Jacob LOUD**, housewright of Weymouth MA. <Suffolk Co.PR #17145>
<79:131> Will dated 4 Oct. 1777, mentions wf **Mary**, sons **Jacob LOUD Jr., Esau LOUD, Eliphalet LOUD and Reuben LOUD** (minor). Three eldest sons named executors. <79:130> Pr. 3 Mar. 1780, adm. granted to three eldest sons. <79:489> 3 Mar. 1780, Nathaniel BAYLEY, Esq., Josiah COLSON and John VINTON were app'td to appraise estate. Inventory taken 13 Mar. 1780; incl. mansion house & barn adjoining fifty acres, eight acre Personage Lott; real estate totals Ŀ5852, total Ŀ9875.17s11d.
<82:170> Account of Esau LOUD, 4 Mar. 1783. Received of: Micah PORTER, John BOSON, Calvin WHITE, Micah TURNER Jr., Jonathan TORREY, Thomas POOL, Ebenezer JOY, Joseph VINING, Joseph POOL, Abner HOLBROOK, Eliphalet LOUD. Payments: Isaac BEALS, Silas HOLBROOK, Moses BEACKER, Widow Sarah HOLBROOK, Jeremiah WHITE, Ebenezer SHAW, Andrew ORCUTT, David WHITMORE, Ebenezer AGAR, Reuben LOUD.

Eliphalet LOUD of Weymouth MA to **Benjamin BEALE Jr.** of Dorchester MA. <Suffolk Co.Deeds 171:198>
...Dec. 1791, Eliphalet LOUD, gentleman for Ŀ41 sold to Benjamin BEALE Jr., Esq...a piece of salt marsh in Dorchester, about five and two thirds acre. Wife Anna releases dower. Ack. 15 dec. 1791.

Jacob & Esau LOUD of Weymouth MA to **Jonathan RANDALL** of Abington MA. <Suffolk Co.Deeds 161:205>
...1 Jan. 1787, Jacob LOUD & Esau LOUD, housewrights sold to Jonathan RANDALL...a piece of cedar swamp in Braintree containing four acres. Ack. 11 Apr. 1787.

SUFFOLK COUNTY DEEDS:

130:247 - 1779, Eliphalet LOUD from Jacob JOY.
130:248 - 1779, Eliphalet LOUD from John VINING et al.
125:237 - 1774, Esau LOUD from Isaac JOY.
168:182 - 1790, Esau LOUD from Daniel BLANCHARD Jr.
174:7 - 1792, Esau LOUD from Nicholas PHILLIPS.

Estate of **Esau LOUD** of Weymouth MA. <Norfolk Co.PR #11906>
...1807...<14:107> Guardian app'td. (bond filed, Samuel LOUD app'td. <43:138> Account allowed.

Estate of **Jacob LOUD** of Weymouth MA. <Norfolk Co.PR #11914>
<68:175,176> Letter/Bond 2 Sept. 1837, son **Jacob LOUD** app'td admr.; mentions widow **Ruth LOUD** and sons **Jacob LOUD, John W. LOUD** and **Samuel B. LOUD**. <68:417> Inventory approved 10 Dec. 1838 by **Ruth LOUD, John W. LOUD** and **Samuel B. LOUD**. <69:82> Account allowed. <69:83> Order of distribution 20 Jan. 1838.

Ruth LOUD, widow to **Jacob LOUD** et al. <Norfolk Co.Deeds 18:300>
...6 Feb. 1838, Ruth LOUD, widow sells all her right to real estate of her late husband to **Jacob LOUD, John W. LOUD** and **Samuel B. LOUD**. Rec. 20 Feb. 1838.

Jacob LOUD of Weymouth MA to **John W. LOUD** and **Samuel B. LOUD.** <Norfolk Co.Deeds 18:300>
...6 Feb. 1838, Jacob LOUD sells to John W. LOUD and Samuel B. LOUD, all right in land which belonged to our father Jacob LOUD, dec'd. Eliza T. LOUD releases dower. Rec. 20 Feb. 1838.

Estate of **Nehemiah JOY** of Weymouth MA. <Norfolk Co.PR #10825>
...1802...<8:576> Letter. <8:642> Inventory. <8:643> Notice. <9:380> Account allowed. <9:381> Order to distribute. <8:644> Order to sell personal estate. <9:377> Division of real estate, 1 Jan. 1803, to following heirs, viz: widow **Susanna, Benjamin JOY, Turner JOY, Lydia LOUD** wf of Jacob, **Caleb JOY, Jesse JOY, Nehemiah JOY, Sarah JOY, Olive JOY.**

Jacob LOUD of Pittston, Kennebec Co. to **Abner BLANCHARD** of Weymouth MA. <Norfolk Co.Deeds 18:122>
...11 July 1802, Jacob LOUD, yeoman, sold to Abner BLANCHARD, cedar swamp and upland in Weymouth.

Jacob LOUD of Pittston, Kennebec Co. to **Eliphalet LOUD** of Weymouth MA. <Norfolk Co.Deeds 18:207>
...1 Jan. 1803, Jacob LOUD, yeoman & Lydia LOUD, spinster, sold to Eliphalet LOUD...three pieces of land, being Lydia's share in the estate of **Nehemiah JOY**, dec'd. Rec. 26 Apr. 1803.

Jacob LOUD of Pittston, Kennebec Co. to **Jared WHITE** of Weymouth MA. <Norfolk Co.Deeds 12:212>
...29 Oct. 1800, Jacob LOUD, housewright sold to Jared WHITE, meadow & cedar swamp in Weymouth.

NORFOLK COUNTY DEEDS:

7:240 - 1797, Jacob LOUD & Esau LOUD from David THAYER.
7:241 - 1797, Jacob LOUD from Esau LOUD.
11:272 - 1800, Jacob LOUD & Eliphalet LOUD from Joseph PORTER.
15:95 - 1801, Jacob LOUD from R. THAYER et al.
23:14 - 1805, Jacob LOUD et al from E. BLANCHARD.

NORFOLK COUNTY DEEDS: (cont-d)

23:124 - 1805, Jacob LOUD et al from N. BLANCHARD.
25:154 - 1806, Jacob LOUD et al from Moses ORCUTT.
49:194 - 1814, Jacob LOUD from Asa WHITE 2d.
49:211 - 1814, Jacob LOUD from Peter NASH Jr.
49:212 - 1814, Jacob LOUD from Eliphalet LOUD.
49:213 - 1814, Jacob LOUD from Daniel SHAW.
63:4 - 1820, Jacob LOUD from Asa WHITE.
64:41 - 1821, Jacob LOUD from Thomas VINSON.
65:61 - 1821, Jacob LOUD from Samuel BAILEY.
74:136 - 1825, Jacob LOUD from S. PENNIMAN, adm.
74:137 - 1825, Jacob LOUD from Thomas VINSON.
75:132 - 1825, Jacob LOUD from David JOY.
75:132 - 1825, Jacob LOUD from Edward COBB.
81:149 - 1827, Jacob LOUD from Thomas VINSON.
81:150 - 1827, Jacob LOUD from Asa WEBB.
81:150 - ( ), Jacob LOUD et al from David JOY.

Jacob LOUD of Weymouth MA to **Esau LOUD.** <Norfolk Co.Deeds 7:242>
...11 Dec. 1788, Jacob LOUD, housewright to Esau LOUD, housewright, land in Weymouth bounded partly by swamp belonging to both. Rec. 26 Sept. 1797.

Jacob LOUD of Weymouth MA to **Isaac THAYER.** <Norfolk Co.Deeds 11:9>
...11 Feb. 1799, Jacob LOUD, yeoman to Isaac THAYER, land in Randolph bounded by land of said Jacob LOUD, Eliphalet LOUD and land of the heirs of Esau LOUD, dec'd. Rec. 26 June 1799.

Jacob LOUD of Pittston, Kennebec Co. to **Eliphalet LOUD** of Weymouth MA. <Norfolk Co.Deeds 18:11>
...9 June 1801, Jacob LOUD, housewright sold to Eliphalet LOUD, dwelling house & barn in Weymouth with other pieces of land, bounded partly by land of Jacob and land of heirs of Esau LOUD.

Jacob LOUD of Pittston, Kennebec Co. to **Eliphalet LOUD** of Weymouth MA. <Norfolk Co.Deeds 17:239>
...9 July 1802, Jacob LOUD, housewright sold to Eliphalet LOUD land partly in Weymouth & Randolph that said Jacob & Eliphalet bought together of Joseph PORTER of Randolph. Rec. 3 Dec. 1802.

Estate of **Esau LOUD** of Weymouth MA. <Norfolk Co.PR #11905>
...1798...<4:169> Bond, Huldah LOUD, Samuel BAYLEY, app'td admrs. <4:502> Inventory. <4:504> Notice. <7:584> Account allowed. <7:585> Order to distribute. <12:112> Dower to widow & assignment of real estate. <33:46> Agent appointed.

Estate of **Reuben LOUD** of Weymouth MA. <Norfolk Co.PR #11921>
...1796...<2:229> Bond, **Jacob, Esau & Eliphalet LOUD** app'td admrs. <3:23,4:461> Inventory. <4:506> Oath, bond for sale. <4:506> Account allowed. <5:5> Receipt of Commissioners. <5:51> Notice. <5:50-60> 2nd Account allowed. <4:518> Order to pay Commissioners.

Will of **William LOUD** of Weymouth MA. <Norfolk Co.PR #11934>
<18:296>...3 Nov. 1802, mentions wife **Lucy**, daughters **Polly WHITE, Lucy PENNIMAN, Neomy HOBART,** sons **David LOUD, William LOUD, Benjamin LOUD, Daniel LOUD.** Sons William & Daniel named executors. Witnesses: Nathaniel BAYLEY, John TIRRELL, Samuel BAYLEY. Pr. 14 Aug. 1810. <18:295> Bond, 14 Aug 1810, **William & Benjamin LOUD,** housewrights of Weymouth, admrs. Sureties: Samuel PENNIMAN, gentleman and Jonathan WILD, yeoman, both of Braintree. <18:480> Inventory taken 25 Aug. 1810 by Samuel BAYLEY, Esq., John VINSON Jr. and Samuel TORREY, all of Weymouth; incl. homestead farm in Weymouth containing four acres, $900.00; ten acres pasture, $300.00; half a pew in the body of the Meeting House, $60.00; half a pew in the gallery, $25.00; total $1636.85. <18:482> Order to sell personal estate, 13 Nov. 1810. <19:87> Oath of admrs. 1st Tues. Mar. 1811. <19:418> Account dated at Quincy 13 Aug. 1811. <20:252> Account 7 Jan. 1812. <21:505> Account 8 Dec. 1812. <57:126> Account 6 Mar. 1832, executors charge themselves with sundry articles of household furniture of which the widow of said deceased has had the use during her life agreably to the will of said dec'd amounting to as sold at auction, $49.35; paid Asa PENNIMAN for a legacy to his wife, $40; paid Jonathan WHITE, $40; paid Noami HOBART for a legacy, $40. <57:290> Order, 8 May 1832, bond of executors ordered to be put in suit, they having failed to perform conditions, on petition of Daniel LOUD, one of the devisees of William LOUD.

Will of **Jonathan WHITE**, gentleman of Weymouth MA. <Norfolk Co.PR #19891>
<97:107>...14 Dec. 1855, mentions wife **Mary**; granddaughters **Belinda CURTIS** widow of Joseph P., **Mary Ann CURTIS** wf of John, **Lydia SPEAR** wf of Samuel, **Emily TORREY,** all of Weymouth and children of my dec'd dau **Mary Ann TORREY** wf of Beriah; grandchildren **Lois SHAW** wf of John Jr., **Jonathan WHITE, Charles V. WHITE** and **Mary V. WHITE,** children of my dec'd son **Jonathan WHITE Jr.**; sons **George W. WHITE, Boylston A. WHITE, William L. WHITE** and dau **Lucy VINING,** widow of David. Henry A. TORREY of Weymouth app'td executor. Pr. 11 Apr. 1857. <97:698> Inventory 15 Apr. 1857. <101:382> Account allowed 16 Apr. 1859; incl. legacies paid to: **Lois SHAW,** 28 Dec. 1858; **Belinda CURTIS,** 17 Jan. 1859; **Mary A. CURTIS,** 17 Jan. 1859; **Lydia W. SPEAR,** 24 Jan. 1859; **George W. WHITE, Boylston A. WHITE, Lucy W. VINING, William L. WHITE.** <101:1086> Petition 30 Apr. 1859 of **George W. WHITE** that a certain piece of real estate be divided among himself and **Boylston A. WHITE, Lucy W. VINING** and Patrick WELCH holding under **William L. WHITE.** <101:1099> Division 14 May 1859.

Estate of **Thomas PRINCE**, mariner of Boston MA. <Plymouth Co.PR #16250>
<2:25> Bond, 27 Nov. 1703 of Israel SILVESTER, ship carpenter of Duxbury and **Ruth** his wife, late relect widdow of **Thomas PRINCE**, as admrs. Witnesses: Caleb THOMAS, Elizabeth CROADE. <2:31> Inventory 13 Dec. 1703 by Samuel SPRAGUE and Samuel BARTLETT; incl. cash, £315; £45 layd out in a sloop; one silver headed cane, £2; one walking staff, 5s; no real estate mentioned. <2:47> Account 7 July 1704 of **Ruth SILVESTER**, total £416.18.0. to be divided between widow and three sons, viz: **Thomas PRINCE** (eldest son), **Benjamin PRINCE** (2nd son) and **Job PRINCE. Samuell PRINCE,** uncle and guardian to said three children, consents to account & settlement. <original> Guardianship, 24 June 1704, **Samuel PRINCE** of Sandwich, uncle, was app'td gdn. of **Thomas, Benjamin & Job PRINCE,** all minors, two under 14. <original> Bond 25 June 1704, by **Samuel PRINCE,** merchant and Nathaniel WARREN of Plymouth. Witnesses: Nathaniel THOMAS Jr., Cornelius WALDO.<2:57> Receipt 7 July 1704 of **Samuel PRINCE,** guardian of his brother's children, is satisfied that the children have received from Isaac SILVESTER their portion, £184., of their father's estate. Witnesses: John ROBINSON, Mercy WISWALL.

PLYMOUTH COUNTY PROBATE, re: PRINCE ("all to 1881")

1703	Thomas	Boston	adm.	#16250,	2:25,31,47,57
1704	Thomas, Benjamin, Job	Boston	gdn.	#16251,	2:47
1722	Elizabeth	Rochester	adm.	#16235,	6:384
1730	Samuel	Rochester or Middleboro	will	#16245,	5:748,751,809
1731	Job	Kingston	adm.	#16237,	6:55,85,145-6,157;9:138
1733	Mercy	Middleboro	non comp	#16243,	7:307,308,338,339,375
1744	Christopher, James & Kimbal	Kingston	gdn.	#16234,	10:86
1755	Thomas	Duxbury	adm.	#16247,	13:378;14:207,492
1756	Mercy	Middleboro	adm.	#16242,	14:74
1757	Nathan	------	adm.	#16244,	15:91,92,93,94
1768	Thomas	Kingston	adm.	#16248,	20:17,28;25:328
1769	Isaac	Duxbury	adm.	#16236,	20:191
1783	Thomas	Kingston	will	#16249,	29:65,66
1814	Kimball	Kingston	will	#16239,	45:351,352,422,423
1824	John	Kingston	will	#16238,	58:237-8,295-6;62:15
1825	Levi, Betty, Thomas	Kingston	gdn.	#16241,	51:277;60:352
1852	Sylvester	Marshfield	adm.	#16246,	12C:388;94:74,137,526, 8W:242; 3P:228
1862	Levi S.	Kingston	will	#16240,	114:433;117:40

Estate of **Israel SILVESTER** of Duxbury MA. <Plymouth Co.PR #19975, #19976>
...1716/7...Widow **Ruth**, daus **Ruth, Grace.** <3:454>; <4:24> Inventory. <4:25> Division of real estate. <4:26> Division. <4:27> Guardianship.

Estate of **Ruth SILVESTER.** <Plymouth Co.PR #20019>
...1729...<5:588,626>. <6:145> Thomas PRINCE, admr. (mentions being sued by "brother Partridge")

Estate of **Israel SILVESTER** of Scituate MA. <Plymouth Co.PR #19970>
...1727...wf **Martha**...<5:253,255>

MICRO #9 OF 18

Estate of **Thomas PRINCE.** <Suffolk Co.PR #19444>
...1790...<89:119,127,152,189,633,635,639>. (No details.)

Estate of **Job PRINCE.** <Suffolk Co.PR #19540>
...1790...<89:486,604,630;90:623;91:163,281,283,339,355,444,448,462>. (No details.)

Estate of **Job PRINCE.** <Suffolk Co.PR #20807>
...1798...<96:249> Will. <96:40,96:276,381;102:128,129,152;98:347;99:307;106:595;111:55>

Will of **Thomas PRINCE** of Kingston MA. <Plymouth Co.PR #16249>
...14 Oct. 1783, mentions honored Mother **Lydia PRINCE** (executor); brother **James PRINCE;** sisters **Abigail STETSON, Thankful DREW, Lydia BEAL, Sylvia PRINCE.** Pr. 3d Mon. Nov. 1783. <MD 7:169>

Will of **Job DREW** of Halifax MA. <Plymouth Co.PR #6698>
...12 May 1832, mentions wf **Thankful;** children **Ezra DREW, Job DREW Jr., Fanny SAMPSON, Sophia THOMSON, Sukey FORD.**.direct that my body be buried in the Kingston burial ground where are buried several of my children. Thomas P. BEAL of Kingston named executor but declined. Pr. 4 June 1833.

Will of **Thankful D. DREW,** widow of Kingston MA. <Plymouth Co.PR #6740>
...20 Dec. 1833, mentions granddaughter **Sarah L. GRIFFIN,** dau of my son **Job DREW;** son **Ezra DREW;** dau **Fanny SAMPSON;** dau **Sophia THOMSON;** dau **Sukey FORD.** Sukey's husband, Elisha FORD named exr. Pr. 3d Mon. Jan. 1841.

Will of **Israel SILVESTER** of Duxbury MA. <Plymouth Co.PR #19974>
...8 Feb. 1771...aged...mentions wf **Abigail;**...to son **Joseph SILVESTER** my cane that was my Granfather's and three hundred pounds; to son **Israel SILVESTER** my farm...bought of William BREWSTER

both upland & meadow; to son **Zachariah SILVESTER** my old farm that was my fathers; dau **Abigail SILVESTER**. Sons Israel & Zachariah named executors. Witnesses: Joshua HALL, Thadeus PETERSON, Samson HOLMES. The will was not proved but on 2 Mar. 1789 the Judge of Probate ordered it to "lie on file till further directions". <27:262> Administration granted 3 Mar. 1788 to John SAMPSON, yeoman of Duxbury. <original> Bond 3 Mar. 1788 of admr. Sureties: Joseph SAMPSON, gent. and John FAUNCE, yeoman, both of Kingston. Witnesses: Seth CUSHING, Isaac LOTHROP.

PLYMOUTH COUNTY DEEDS:

42:73 - 21 July 1727, Josiah SNELL to Josiah SNELL Jr. Rec. 14 Apr. 1753.
42:66 - 10 Mar. 1753, Josiah SNELL to dau Abigail SILVESTER, of Duxbury.
45:258 - 11 Jan. 1759, Israel SILVESTER, shipwright & wf Abigail, of Duxbury, sell to John PORTER of Bridgewater, clerk, part of 11th Little Lot in Bridgewater. Ack. by both 28 Feb. 1760
69:249 - (   ) 1783, Elisha SILVESTER & wf Abigail.
(   ) - (   ) 1783, Martha SNELL & Sarah SNELL sell all their right in Northerly Division of 15th Lot in the West Shares in Bridgewater.

Estate of **Adam PICKETT** of New London CT. <New London CT PR #4128>
...Inventory taken 7 Nov. 1709 by Jonas GREEN & John PLUMB, total Ł327.6.6. Sworn to 8 Nov. 1709 by John PICKETT, admr. on estate of his brother Adam PICKETT. Citation to **Susanna PICKETT**, late wife of Adam, dated 8 Aug. 1706.

Will of **Benjamin SHAPLEY** of New London CT. <New London CT PR #4758>
...dated 5 July 1706, mentions wf **Mary**; son **Daniel SHAPLEY**; to grandsons **Benjamin & Joseph** land where son **Benjamin SHAPLEY** built his home; "all my children". Witnesses: John PLUMB, John RICHARDS, Christopher CHRISTOPHERS. Inventory sworn to 18 Sept. 1706 by widow **Mary SHAPLEY**, executrix who gives a list of the name and ages of the children, viz: **Ruth MORGAN**, 33; **Mary TRUMAN**, of age; **Anne AVERY**, of age; **Daniel SHAPLEY**, 17; **Jane SHAPLEY**, 12. Petition 23 Jan. 1738/9 of Joshua APPLETON & wf, Joseph FREEMAN and Daniel SHAPLEY.

Estate of **Benjamin SHAPLEY** of New London CT. <New London CT PR #4759>
...Bond 10 Feb. 1712 of **Daniel SHAPLEY**, admr. Sureties: Robert LATTEMORE, Joshua HEMPSTEAD. Inventory taken 11 Feb. 1713/4 by John EDGCAMBE(sp), C. CHRISTOPHERS, Solomon COIT. His children are listed as **Benjamin SHAPLEY**, 11 and **Joseph SHAPLEY**, 9. Account mentions coffin for widow. Receipt 9 Dec. 1723 by **Benjamin SHAPLEY** and Joshua APPLETON as guardian to **Joseph SHAPLEY**.

Will of **Daniel SHAPLEY** of New London CT. <New London CT PR #4761>
...dated 6 Jan. 1753, mentions wf **Abigail**; children **John SHAPLEY** (eldest son), **Daniel SHAPLEY, Joseph SHAPLEY, Benjamin SHAPLEY, Adam SHAPLEY, Mary, Abigail** and **Ruth.** Pr. 2 July 1753. Distribution of undivided estate, 27 July 1782 among following: Edward HALLAM(sp) who purchased **Abigail RICHARD**'s share, heirs of **John SHAPLEY**, heirs of **Adam SHAPLEY Jr.**, dec'd.

Guardianship of child of **Daniel SHAPLEY.** <New London CT PR #4756>
...4 June 1752, **Adam SHAPLEY,** son of Daniel, chose his brother **John SHAPLEY,** his guardian.

Will of **Deacon James MORGAN** of Groton CT. <New London CT PR #3733>
...dated 29 Mar. 1745, mentions unnamed wife, son **James MORGAN,** dau **Mary GALLUP,** heirs of dau **Anna OWEN,** dec'd. Codicil 6 Apr. 1748. Pr. 11 May 1748. Receipt 13 July 1750 of John OWEN, guardian to his children.

Will of **Capt. John MORGAN** of Groton CT. <New London CT PR #3736>
...dated 30 May 1744, to only son **John MORGAN,** land by deed from my honoured Father; two children of my dau **Ruth BREWSTER**, dec'd; my seven daughters, viz: **Mary, Sarah, Hannah, Rachel, Martha, Elizabeth, Jemima**; estate that came by wife **Ruth**, dec'd, by father in law Mr. **Benjamin SHAPLEY** or Mrs. **Mary SHAPLEY.** Witnesses: David WILLIAMS, Theophilus MORGAN, William WILLIAMS. Pr. 16 Mar. 1746/7. Receipts, 28 Mar. 1747, of: **Martha GEER**, widow, of Groton; **Moses FISH** & wf **Elizabeth**; **James MORGAN Jr.** & wf Mary of Groton; **Robert KENNEDY** & wf **Sarah** of Norwich; **Peter PLUMB** & wf **Hannah** of New London; **Thomas FISH** & wf **Jemima** of Groton; **Rachel MORGAN** of Groton.

Estate of **Capt. Samuel FOSDICK.** <New London CT PR #2041>
...Bond 9 Sept. 1701 of **Mercy FOSDICK**, admx. Surety: Moses NOYES(sp) of Lyme. Inventory sworn 17 Sept. 1702 by widow, total Ł581.10.00. Receipt 15 Sept. 1708 by **Mercy FOSDICK** of Ł18 from "my brother **Samuel FOSDICK** for share in my dec'd father's estate. Account 18 Feb. 1706/7, incl. care of his son **Samuel**, Ł16; widow's thirds; balance into 8 parts, there being 7 children. Distribution 16 May 1708 to: widow, **Samuel FOSDICK** (eldest son), **John FOSDICK** (2nd son), **Thomas FOSDICK** (3rd), **Mercy FOSDICK** (eldest dau), **Ruth FOSDICK** (2nd dau), **Ann FOSDICK** (3rd), **Mary FOSDICK** (youngest dau). Account 20 Sept. 1706 of John ARNOLD, incl. to keeping **John FOSDICK** from Dec. 1703 - 6 Dec. 1705; to keeping **Thomas FOSDICK** & **Mary FOSDICK** from 6 Dec. 1705 to this day.

Estate of **Ann MORGAN** of Groton CT. <New London CT PR #3718>
...Bond 22 June 1751 by Daniel RUFF of Groton, admr. Surety: Joseph TRUMAN. Inventory sworn 9 July 1751 of Widow **Ann MORGAN** by John AVERY and Nathan SMITH. Account 17 July 1753, incl. payment to mother, and to brother **James MORGAN** for gravestones, balance of Ł1052.4.3 to be divided. Receipts of: **Samuel & Mary DIBBELL**, Ł210.18.9, 28 June 1751; **Silvanus & Ann MINOR**, Ł214.9.8, 29 June 1751; **Jean RUFF** of Groton, Ł217.3.6, 12 Jan. 1753.

Will of **Deacon Thomas FOSDICK** of New London CT. <New London CT PR #2044>
...dated 10 Mar. 1762, mentions wf **Grace**; three oldest children, viz: **Thomas FOSDICK, Katharine, Sarah**; three youngest children, viz: **Clement FOSDICK, Samuel FOSDICK, Grace**, "when of age". Witnesses: Benjamin BEEBE, William FOLLETT, Hanna LAMPHEIR. Agreement 7 Nov. 1779 between **Grace FOX** wf of Ezekiel and late widow of **Thomas FOSDICK, Clement FOSDICK, Grace FOSDICK, Samuel FOSDICK.** On 12 Nov. 1791 **Samuel FOSDICK** was dec'd and dau Grace is called **Grace BEEBE.**

Will of **Moses NOYES**, Pastor of the Church of Christ at Lyme CT. <New London CT PR #3845>
...dated 19 Aug. 1719, mentions sons **Moses NOYES, John NOYES**, daus **Ruth WADSWORTH, Sarah MATHER.** Codicil 21 Aug. 1724. Pr. 21 Nov. 1729

Will of **John NOYES** of Lyme CT. <New London CT PR #3840>
...dated 20 July 1733, mentions wf **Mary**; to my child if Providence of God shall continue its life, if not, equally divided to **Moses NOYES Jr.** of Lyme, **Timothy MATHER Jr.** and **James WADSWORTH** of Durham, each of them grandchildren to my honoured father **Mr. Moses NOYES**, Rev. Pastor of Lyme, dec'd. Witnesses: Moses NOYES, Thomas WAIT, Benjamin BECKWITH. Inventory taken 17 Sept. 1733 by Samuel MARVIN, Joseph DEWOLF, total £3127.9.10. Sworn to by widow **Mary**, 18 Sept. 1733.

Will of **James WADSWORTH**, Esq. of Durham CT. <Middleton CT PR #3629>
...dated 22 Apr. 1776, advanced in years; to eldest son **James WADSWORTH** the sword which belonged to my father **James WADSWORTH**; grandson **James WADSWORTH**; dau **Ruth ATWATER**; youngest son **John Noyes WADSWORTH** and his three sons **John Noyes WADSWORTH Jr., William WADSWORTH, James WADSWORTH.** Witnesses: Elisha CRANE, Samuel CAM( ), Titus HOSMER. Pr. 13 Sept. 1777. Inventory sworn to 6 July 1778 by Daniel HALL, Samuel CAM( ), Stephen NORTON, total £5078.2.7.

Will of **Moses NOYES** of Lyme CT. <New London CT PR #3847>
...dated 13 Jan. 1786, mentions wf **Hannah**, children: **Calvin NOYES, Moses NOYES, Eliakim NOYES, Esther MINER** the widow of Elias and her three sons **Joseph MINER, Benjamin MINER, Selden MINER** (all under 21), **Hannah STODDARD** wf of Seth, **Mindwell NOYES, Elizabeth AVERY** wf of Abraham and **Eunice NOYES.** Pr. 6 Mar. 1786.

Estate of **Capt. Charles HILL Jr.** <New London CT PR #2614>
...Inventory taken 12 Nov. 1711 by Robert LATTEMORE, Joshua HEMPSTEAD, total L233.12.11. Sworn to by widow **Abigail HILL**, 13 Nov. 1711. Account 4 Apr. 1720. Division 5 Apr. 1720 to widow **Abigail**, only son **Charles HILL**, eldest dau **Hannah HILL**, youngest dau **Abigail HILL.** Receipts 4 Apr. 1720 to John HARRIS, Samuel FOX, Joshua HEMPSTEAD and **Jonathan HILL** as guardian to the three children of his brother **Charles HILL.**

Estate of **Jonathan HILL** of New London CT. <New London CT PR #2623>
...Bond 13 July 1725 of **Mary HILL**, admx. Sureties: Joseph TRUMAN, Christopher DARROW. Inventory taken by Christopher DARROW, John DIXSON, Daniel ROGERS, total £714.2.9. Sworn to by **Mary HILL**, admx. 13 Apr. 1726. Division 9 Jan. 1727/8, to widow, eldest son **Charles HILL**, eldest dau **Jane**, second dau **Mary**, second son **George HILL**, youngest son **John HILL**, youngest dau **Ruth.**

LOVE BREWSTER[2] (William[1])

MICRO #10 OF 18

Estate of **Nathaniel BREWSTER** of Duxbury MA. <Plymouth Co.PR 3:2:40>
...Court held at Plymouth 2 Nov. 1676...I **Benjamin BARTLETT** being with **Nathaniel BREWSTER** to visitt him being sick I advised him to settle matters relateing to his worldly estate; to prevent differences heerafter; and hee seemed to be very willing to attend the motion; and said that if it should please God to take mee away (after my Debts be payed) I will give all that I have to my wife; this land heer is none of mine, to dispose off; butt there is some att the falls that she shall have. **Benjamin BARTLETT** made oath to the above...last will & testament of **Nathaniel BREWSTER**, dec'd and that hee wrote the same about a fortnight after his death; And **Wrastling BREWSTER** the brother of said Nathaniel gave free consent and concurred with the said will. Inventory exhibited 2 Nov. 1676 on oath of **Wrastling BREWSTER**, no real estate mentioned. Appraisal of estate, 11 Oct. 1676 by William PAYBODY. <Plymouth Colony Court Orders 5:146> 1 Nov. 1676, administration granted to Robert VIXON of Eastham.

Will of **Joseph BREWSTER** of Duxbury MA. <Plymouth Co.PR #2753>
<19:475>...dated 10 Feb. 1767, mentions wf **Elizabeth**, son **Lemuel BREWSTER**, dau **Eunice WALKER.** Son in law **Timothy WALKER** named executor. Witnesses: Nathan BREWSTER, Job BREWSTER, Beriah DELANO, Wait WADSWORTH. Pr. 1 June 1767. <19:549> Inventory taken 14 Oct. 1767 by Israel SYLVESTER, Eliphalet BRADFORD, Wait WADSWORTH, incl. homestead farm, £533.6.8, two wood lots, total £883.3.3. <20:413> Account 6 Aug. 1770 of executor. Paid to: John SAMSON, Jedediah SIMONS, Nathan BREWSTER, Thomas CHANDLER, Gamaliel BRADFORD, Dr. LeBARON, Thomas WESTON, Job BREWSTER, Wait WADSWORTH, Robert (ST)ANFORD, Deborah WESTON, John HUNT, Ebenezer DELANO, Ebenezer BARTLETT, Elizabeth BREWSTER, Benjamin GOODWIN, Lemuel BREWSTER, Dr. WADSWORTH, Joshua LORING, Nathaniel GOODWIN, Carpus WHITE. <30:119> Warrant & Division 3 July 1786, by Calvin PARTRIDGE, Joseph SOUL, Ezekiel SOULE. Estate divided into three equal parts: two shares to the heirs of **Lemuel BREWSTER**, dec'd and one share to **Eunice WALKER** wf of Timothy of Wilmington. Division confirmed 4 Apr. 1787. <30:120> Account of executor 6 Apr. 1787, he charges himself with one third of what remained of ye personal estate set off to ye widow of the dec'd. <30:192> Account 4 July 1787 of executor. <original>

Oath 4 July 1787 of executor Timothy WALKER that in disposing of the estates lately belonging to **Lemuel BREWSTER** now dec'd and the estate of **Joseph BREWSTER** now dec'd, both of Duxbury, that he will use his best skill...

Estate of **Lemuel BREWSTER** of Kingston MA. <Plymouth Co.PR #2764>
<23:49> Bond/Letter 18 Apr. 1774, **Abigail BREWSTER**, widow, app'td. admx. Sureties: William SEVER, Samuel KENT. Witnesses: William SEVER Jr., Sally SEVER. <21:372> Inventory taken 25 Apr. 1774 by Charles FOSTER, Samuel KENT, Wrestling BREWSTER, sworn by widow 3 May 1774, total personal estate Ł28.9. <21:372> Account of admx. 3 May 1774. <original> Bond 3 July 1786, Timothy WALKER of Wilmington app'td admr. de bonis non in place of **Abigail BREWSTER**. Sureties: Calvin PARTRIDGE, Joseph SOUL. Witnesses: Mallatiah COBB, Isaac LOTHROP. <27:509> Letter of Adm., 3 July 1786, to Timothy WALKER, **Abigail BREWSTER** having deceased. <30:7> Insolvency 3 July 1786. <30:117> Inventory taken 5 July 1786 by Joseph SOUL, Calvin PARTRIDGE, Ezekiel SOULE; sworn by admr. 5 Apr. 1787, total Ł365.10.10. Commissioners app'td 3 July 1786, Calvin PARTRIDGE, Joseph SOUL. <30:118> List of claims 4 Apr. 1787: estate of Dr. John THOMAS dec'd, Isaac BREWSTER, Timothy WALKER (heaviest creditor), Nathan BRADFORD, Edward WINSLOW, Charles STOCKBRIDGE, Dr. Isaac WINSLOW, Isaac LeBARON, Dr. John WADSWORTH, Capt. Levi LORING, William SEVER. <30:118> Account 6 Apr. 1787 of Timothy WALKER, admr., who asks for allowance of legacy bequeathed me by **Joseph BREWSTER**...to be paid out of that part of his estate bequeathed to the said **Lemuel BREWSTER** as directed in said last will...and for the interest from 10 Feb. 1767 is 20 years and 2 months to this day. <30:165> Account of admr. 4 July 1787. Order to pay creditors 7 Aug. 1787.

Will of **Abigail BREWSTER**, widow of Kingston MA. <Plymouth Co.PR #2730>
<25:525>...dated 30 Feb. 1780, mentions children: **Elizabeth, Rebecca, Royal BREWSTER, Joseph BREWSTER, John BREWSTER**; friend William DREW (named executor) to be guardian of Rebecca & Royal. Witnesses: John ADAMS, Cornelius SAMPSON, Abner HOLMES. Pr. 3 July 1780. <30:366> Inventory taken 2 May 1783 and 2 Nov. 1780 by Nathaniel LITTLE, Cornelius SAMPSON, James DREW; sworn to by William DREW 23 May 1788, total Ł534.13.2. <30:520> Account of admr. 2 Mar. 1789. Paid to: Elisha BREWSTER, Cephas WADSWORTH, Joseph HOLMES, Deborah COOK, Daniel LORING, Seth DREW's wife, Nicholas DAVIS Jr., Dr. Isaac WINSLOW, account against Sarah BREWSTER, second account against Abigail BREWSTER, Cornelius SAMPSON's wife, Dr. WHITMAN's account against Sarah & Abigail BREWSTER, Peleg WADSWORTH, Thaddeus RANSOM, Dr. HARLOW, James COBB for digging grave for Sally, Jesse FULLER, Francis ADAMS, Nicholas DAVIS's wife, account schooling children, Jabez WASHBURN Jr., Nathan BRADFORD, Samuel STETSON, Seth COBB, Dr. FULLER, Jabez WASHBURN, Elisha WASHBURN, Mrs. KENT, balance due Isaac BREWSTER, Malletiah HOLMES' wife, to half the household furniture to Elizabeth and Rebecca. <31:141> Division 20 Apr. 1789, by John ADAMS Jr., Judah WASHBURN, Thomas BREWSTER, to following heirs: **Arial BREWSTER** ("known in his mother's will by the name of **Royal**), **Rebecca, Elizabeth, John BREWSTER, Joseph BREWSTER**. Sworn 5 Nov. 1789, confirmed 1 Mar. 1790.

Will of **Nathaniel BREWSTER** of Duxbury MA. <Plymouth Co.PR #2772>
<13:443>...dated 11 Feb. 1755, under decays of nature, mentions wf **Mary** (named executrix), eldest son **Samuel BREWSTER**, second son **William BREWSTER**, youngest son **Joseph BREWSTER**, daus **Marcy WOODCOCK** and **Ruth MORGAN**, 5 shillings to each. Witnesses: Samuel ALDEN, Ichabod WADSWORTH, John WADSWORTH. <13:444> Bond 7 Apr. 1755, of **Mary BREWSTER**. Sureties: Joseph BREWSTER Jr. of Duxbury and Elisha STETSON of Kingston. Witnesses: John BRADFORD, John LOTHROP.

Will of **Joseph BREWSTER** of Duxbury MA. <Plymouth Co.PR #2754>
...dated 1 June 1791, mentions wf **Jedidah**, children: **Ruth BREWSTER, Zadock BREWSTER, Joseph BREWSTER, Nathaniel BREWSTER, Freelove BREWSTER, Mary FREEMAN**; grandson **Derias BREWSTER**. Dau **Ruth** and grandson **Derias** named executors. Witnesses: Josiah SOULE, Araunah BREWSTER, Wait WADSWORTH.

Estate of **Wrestling BREWSTER**, carpenter of Duxbury MA. <Plymouth Co.PR #2790>
<1:253> Bond/Letter 2 Feb. 1696/7, **Mary BREWSTER**, widow, app'td admx. Sureties: Edward SOUTHWORTH and John SPRAGUE. Witnesses: Thomas PERREY, William PERREY. <1:254> Inventory taken 15 Jan. 1696/97 by Edward SOUTHWORTH, John SPRAGUE, total Ł150; sworn to by widow 2 Feb. 1696/7.

Heirs of **Wrestling BREWSTER**. <Plymouth Co.Deeds 10:2:244>
...3 Oct. 1707, Joseph HOLMES & wf Mary of Plymouth, Caleb STETSON & wf Sarah, Abigail BREWSTER, Hannah BREWSTER, Elizabeth BREWSTER, all of Duxbury, sons in law and daughters of Wrestling, to their brothers Wrestling BREWSTER & John BREWSTER. Ack. 15 Jan. 1713 by Joseph HOLMES & wf Mary, Caleb STETSON & wf Sarah, Abigail STETSON wf of Elisha, Elizabeth BRADFORD wf of Ephraim and Hannah ALDEN wf of Benjamin. Rec. 31 Mar. 1714. <MD 20:114>

Estate of **Elisha STETSON**, cordwainer of Kingston MA. <Plymouth Co.PR>
<13:412> 3 Mar. 1755, **Elisha STETSON**, cordwainer of Kingston, app'td admr. on estate of father. <15:97> Settlement 20 July 1756, mentions widow, only son **Elisha STETSON** and four daus, viz: **Sarah BRADFORD** wf of Robert, **Zerash BRADFORD** wf of Benjamin, heirs of **Hopestill SIMMONS** and **Eglah WASHBURN** wf of Ephraim. <15:97> Agreement & Receipt of heirs (date?), signed by Elisha STETSON, Robert BRADFORD, Ephraim WASHBURN, Benjamin BRADFORD and John SIMMONS.

Will of **Noah SIMMONS**, gentleman of Kingston MA. <Plymouth Co.PR>
<58:364>...dated 30 May 1824, mentions wife, son **William SIMMONS** (executor); son **John SIMMONS**; to Charles SIMMONS the land I bought of his father Hezekiah SIMMONS, dec'd, said Charles to pay $2 to each of the other children of said Hezekiah; son **Stevens SIMMONS**; children of son **James SIMMONS**; Sarah SIMMONS; daus **Silvester CLARK** and **Diana CHANDLER**; Mary SIMMONS & Henry SIMMONS, chil. of Peleg SIMMONS, dec'd; granddaughter **Elizabeth SNOW**; six children of son **Noah SIMMONS**, dec'd.

<58:365> Pr. 5 Oct. 1824. <58:383> Inventory sworn to 18 Oct. 1824, incl. 15 acres in Halifax and 20 acres in Kingston. <62:167> Order of Notice, 5 Oct. 1824. Oath, 13 Aug. 1827 by **William SIMMONS** that order was posted. <64:190> Account, 13 Aug. 1827.

Noah SIMMONS of Kingston to **Thomas W. & William PETERSON** of Duxboro MA. <Plymouth Co.Deeds> <73:23>...2 June 1792, Noah SIMMONS, gentleman for £18.19s sold to Thomas Whitemore PETERSON and William PETERSON, yeomen...twelve acres in Duxbury Noah bought from Mark KEEN who bought it from Robert CUSHMAN. Molley SIMMONS, wf of Noah, releases dower. Witnesses: Samuel SAMSON, Diana SIMMONS. Rec. 23 June 1792.

Noah SIMMONS of Kingston MA to **John SIMMONS** of Kingston MA. <Plymouth Co.Deeds 75:236> ...31 Dec. 1793, Noah SIMMONS, gentleman, for £10 sold to John SIMMONS, yeoman, nine acre farm Noah now lives on in Kingston, bounded by the Holmes' mill, the late dwelling house of Nathaniel RANDALL and the land of Col. Thomas LOTHROP...reserving the liberty of passing acrost said land in the winter season also the previledge of purchasing said land at any time that the said John shall be disposed to sell the same if I will give as much for it as any other person. Witnesses: Benjamin CROOKER, Elijah BISBE Jr. Rec. 18 Feb. 1794

John SIMMONS of Kingston MA to **Noah SIMMONS** of Kingston MA. <Plymouth Co.Deeds 100:249> ...23 Oct. 1795, John SIMMONS, mariner, for £12, sold to Noah SIMMONS, gentleman...nine acres in Kingston, bounded by said Simmons' dwelling house, Holmes' mill, dwelling house of Tilden HOLMES, land of Col. Thomas LOTHROP...with reserve of the house standing on said land & the liberty of taken down said house, carting of cartain across said land all that belongs to said house. Witnesses: Frances ADAMS Jr., Alice ADAMS. Ack. 27 Feb. 1796. Rec. 22 Mar. 1796.

Will of **John BREWSTER**, innholder of Kingston MA. <Plymouth Co.PR #2752> <20:296>...dated 24 June 1766, mentions wife **Rebecca**; dau **Rebecca SAMSON**, dec'd and her children **Elisha SAMSON & Rebecca SAMSON**; dau **Abigail BREWSTER** wf of Lemuel BREWSTER; dau **Sarah BREWSTER**. Witnesses: Wrestling BREWSTER Jr., Lidia FOSTER, John WADSWORTH. <20:297> Pr. 1 Jan. 1770 by widow **Rebecca BREWSTER**, executrix. <20:393> Inventory taken 18 May 1770 by John WADSWORTH, Robert BRADFORD, Samuel KENT. Sworn by widow **Rebecca**, 6 Aug. 1770, total £884.0.3. <20:409> Bond/Letter 7 Jan. 1771, Robert BRADFORD of Kingston app'td admr. in place of **Rebecca BREWSTER**, dec'd. Sureties: John ADAMS, John SAMSON. Witnesses: Jonah EDSON, John THOMAS. <21:111> Inventory taken 14 Jan. 1771 by Samuel FOSTER, Samuel KENT, John ADAMS. Sworn by Robert BRADFORD 15 May 1772, total £845.15.5. <27:494> Bond 6 Jan. 1783, William DREW, Esq. of Kingston, app'td admr. de bonis non with will annexed in place of Robert BRADFORD, dec'd. Sureties: Jed. HOLMES, Ebenezer WASHBURN. Witnesses: James LEACH, Isaac LOTHROP. Letter 6 Jan. 1783 to William DREW, whereas **John BREWSTER** late of said Kingston, yeoman, dec'd on the 24 June 1766. <29:1> Inventory taken 2 May 1783 by Nathaniel LITTLE, Cornelius SAMPSON. Sworn by William DREW 5 May 1783, total £470.13.4. <29:362> Account 5 Sept. 1785 of admr., who charges himself with balance due from estate of **Capt. Robert BRADFORD** late of Kingston, dec'd, £18.12.6. Paid to: Stetson BRADFORD, Elisha BRADFORD, Ebenezer DAWES Jr., Jabez WASHBURN, Peleg WADSWORTH, estate of Uriah WADSWORTH, Elisha BREWSTER's note, Thomas LORING Jr., Dr. Eleazer HARLOW, Mr. WILK's.

Joseph HOLMES Sr. to **Joseph HOLMES Jr.**, both of Plymouth MA. <Plymouth Co.Deeds 31:120> ...13 May 1723, Joseph HOLMES Sr. to son Joseph HOLMES Jr., land in Plymouth, reserving right for himself & wife Mary for life.

William BRADFORD of Plymouth to **Joseph HOLMES** of Marshfield MA. <Plymouth Co.Deeds 1:70> ...18 Mar. 1688/9, William BRADFORD, Esq. for love and good affection convey to my welbeloved friend & son in law Joseph HOLMES...my farme in Plimouth...thirty acres more or less. Witnesses; Samuel SPRAGUE, John FOSTER Jr. Ack. 16 Sept. 1689. Rec. 12 Nov. 1689.

Joseph HOLMES & John HOLMES to **Caleb STETSON** of Plymouth MA. <Plymouth Co.Deeds 9:376> ...17 Dec. 1712, Joseph HOLMES, weaver of Plymouth and son John HOLMES, weaver of Marshfield, for L120, sold to Caleb STETSON, shipwright...thirty acres given to Joseph in a deed bearing date of 18 Mar. 1688 by **Maj. William BRADFORD**, late of Plymouth, dec'd. Witnesses: John FAUNCE, John SPRAGUE, Josiah COTTON. Rec. 26 Feb. 1712/3.

Estate of **Keziah THOMAS**, widow of Kingston MA. <Plymouth Co.PR #20402> <27:258> 7 Jan. 1788, Isaiah THOMAS, gentleman of Kingston, app'td admr. and appraisers app'td. Inventory taken 2 Feb. 1788. Insolvency 4 Feb. 1788. List of Claims 4 Aug. 1788. Account of admr. 6 Sept. 1789.

Holmes THOMAS of Dixfield MA to **Hopestill BISBEE** of Rochester MA. <Plymouth Co.Deeds 100:57> ...25 Sept. 1804, Holmes THOMAS, Esq. & wf Susanna, for $48.86 quitclaim to Hopestill BISBEE... all our right to the estate of Nathaniel (omitted), late of Plimton, de'cd as bequeathed to the said Susanna by her honoured father, the said Nathaniel CHURCHELL. Rec. 26 Dec. 1804.

Estate of **Micah THOMAS**, mariner of Kingston MA. <Plymouth Co.PR #20426> <original> 7 Jan. 1788, Isaiah THOMAS, gentleman of Kingston, app'td admr. and appraisers app'td. <original> 4 Jan. 17(78) <error for 1788>...To the Honorable Joseph CUSHING Esq...my former hus. **Micah THOMAS** of Kingston was lost at sea in ye year 1775 and died siezed of a dwelling house and one acre of land - his Mother held ye improven dureing her life and she deceased last June and I pray your Honner would give ye administration unto Isaiah THOMAS as ye Estate is some in debt and must be settled according to law...allso pray that said THOMAS may have administration on ye est of my Mother in law **Keziah THOMAS**. Signed by **Lydia EVERSON.** <original> Inventory taken 2 Feb. 1788. Insolvency 4 Feb. 1788.

Estate of **Spencer THOMAS**, mariner of Plymouth MA. <Plymouth Co.PR #20476>
...16 May 1842, Joseph L. BEAL of Kingston, asked to be app'td administrator.

Jacob DINGLEY of Duxbury MA to **John DINGLEY** of Duxbury MA. <Plymouth Co.Deeds 93:61>
...8 Mar. 1799, Jacob DINGLEY for $1000.000 sells to son John DINGLEY...all my real estate lying in Duxbury and Marshfield...seventy acre homestead farm where Jacob lives excepting a one quarter acre piece with small dwelling house, rights in a saw mill and a piece of pasture and salt marsh. Althea DINGLEY also signs. Witnesses: Asa WATERMAN, (   ). Rec. 22 Apr. 1802.

Will of **Jacob DINGLEY** of Duxbury MA. <Plymouh Co.PR>
<21:260>...dated 10 June 1768, mentions wf **Mary**; son **Jacob DINGLEY Jr.**; dau **Mary COOK** wf of Sim-; eon; son **Joseph DINGLEY**; son **Abner DINGLEY** (executor); grandson **William DINGLEY**;...I give and bequeath to the inhabitants of Duxborough the priviledge to bury their dead in the burying place on my farm. Witnesses: Briggs THOMAS, David OLDHAM, Benjamin WHITE. Pr. 7 Jan. 1773 by son Abner.

MICRO #11 OF 18

Will of **Wrestling BREWSTER**, gentleman of Kingston MA. <Plymouth Co.PR #2791>
<19:417>...dated 23 Jan. 1765, under some decays of nature, mentions wf **Hannah**; eldest son **Wrestling BREWSTER**; second son **Isaac BREWSTER**; third son **Thomas BREWSTER**; youngest son **Elisha BREWSTER** (executor); dau **Mary BREWSTER.** <19:418> Pr. 2 Feb. 1767, **Elisha BREWSTER** app'td admr.

Wrestling BREWSTER et al to **Joseph LANGRELL** of Duxborough MA. <Plymouth Co.Deeds 24:51>
...8 Mar. 1729, **James THOMAS** of Duxborough, **Ebenezer THOMAS** of Norwich CT, **Wrestling BREWSTER** & wf Hannah of Kingston, for Ł8 sell to **Joseph LANGRELL,** weaver, three quarter of an acre salt meadow in Marshfield...near a place called ye Hither Point it being one half of ye meadow that was settled on our brother Peleg THOMAS, dec'd, bounded by meadow of John THOMAS of Marshfield which he bought of Ebenezer THOMAS and by meadow of Caleb SAMSON of Duxborough. Witnesses: Isaac PARTRIDGE, Ezekiel THOMAS. Rec. 18 Mar. 1728/9.

Estate of **Hosea BREWSTER,** mariner of Kingston MA. <Plymouth Co.PR #2745>
<34:17> Bond/Letter 14 Nov. 1794, **Rebecca BREWSTER,** widow, app'td admx. Sureties: Elnathan HOLMES Jr., Nathan REED. Witnesses: Thomas NICOLSON, Isaac LOTHROP. <35:241> Inventory taken by Seth DREW, Samuel STETSON, Seth COBB. Sworn by widow 23 Apr. 1795, incl. nine acres of pasture land which will revert to said estate after the decease of the father and mother of the deceased. <36:31> Account of admx. 2 Jan. 1797. Paid to: Capt. Jo. RIPLEY of Boston, Dr. Jabez FULLER, Dr. James THATCHER, Bildad WASHBURN, Amos COOK, Jno. FULLER, Amaziah GOODEN, Jno. Chamberlin. Cash due from James & Zenas DREW.

PATIENCE BREWSTER[2] (William[1])

Estate of **Nathaniel MAYO** of Eastham MA. <PCR 4:8>
...4 Mar. 1661, administration granted to widow **Hannah.** <MD 17:215> Will dated 19 Dec. 1661.

Heirs of **Nathaniel MAYO** of Eastham MA. <copy of original in files>
...26 Feb. 1678...Agreement between **Thomas MAYO, Nathaniel MAYO and Samuel MAYO** about lands left them by their father **Nathaniel MAYO,** incl. ten acres by the Cove where Thomas & Nathaniel now live; house lott in town; ten acre upland in Poche between Thomas ROGER's and land that was granted to John MAYO. Witnesses: Thomas PAINE Sr., Jonathan SPARROW. Ack. 7 Jan. 1679.

Estate of **Nathaniel YOUNG** of Eastham MA. <Barnstable Co.PR>
<3:3> 22 May 1706, **Mercy YOUNG,** widow, app'td admx. <3:16> Inventory taken 11 May 1706 by John SPARROW, Micajah SNOW. <3:50> Settlement 11 July 1707 to heirs: **Nathan YOUNG** (eldest son); to son **Elisha YOUNG** the house where he now dwells and has for some time; other unnamed children. <3:90> 27 Mar. 1710, **Mercy MAYO** of Eastham...Relict of Nathaniel MAYO of Eastham for...the goods or estate which was my first husband's Nathaniel YOUNG...that she brought into her 2nd marriage...mentions executors to last will of husband Nathaniel MAYO and a charge for keeping her two young children. She releases all claims on estate of husband Nathaniel MAYO.

Will of **Nathaniel MAYO** of Eastham MA. <Barnstable Co.PR>
<3:182>...dated 21 Nov. 1709, mentions wf **Mercy;** sons **Nathaniel MAYO, Elisha MAYO;** daus **Alice MAYO, Hannah MAYO;** brother **Samuel MAYO** & son **Nathaniel** named executors. Witnesses: Joseph DOANE, James MAKER, Thomas FREEMAN. <3:184> Inventory taken 7 Dec. 1709 by Samuel FREEMAN, Nathaniel FREEMAN, Joseph DOANE, incl. land adjoining Thomas MAYO's, small interest of upland & meadow at Little Billengsgate in partnership with Thomas MAYO & Samuel MAYO and land at Middleboro.

Estate of **Samuel MAYO** of Eastham MA. <Barnstable Co.PR 5:450>
...Will dated 9 Apr. 1734, mentions legacy to heirs of dau **Sarah HIGGINS,** dec'd wf of James HIGGINS. Pr. 15 Nov. 1738.

Will of **Samuel MAYO** of Eastham MA. <Barnstable Co.PR>
<5:450>...dated 9 Apr. 1734, mentions sons **Samuel MAYO** (executor), **Jonathan MAYO**; daus **Mercy COLE** wf of John, **Rebecca COLE** wf of Stephen; grandson **Thomas MAYO**; dau **Mary SMITH** wf of Ralph; heirs of daus **Hannah HOPKINS**, dec'd and **Sarah HIGGINS**, dec'd wf of James. Witnesses: James ROGERS Jr., Ebenezer COLE, Israel COLE. <5:451> Pr. 15 Nov. 1738. <5:452> Inventory taken 28 Nov. 1738 by Samuel KNOWLES, Nathaniel GOULD, Richard SPARROW. Presented 29 Aug. 1739 by executor. <5:454> Account 8 July 1741 of executor, paid according to will: Ralph SMITH, Stephen COLE, James HIGGINS, Judah HOPKINS, Jonathan MAYO. <5:455> Inventory taken 3 May 1739 by John FREEMAN, Nathaniel DOANE and Thomas FREEMAN of land left out of will. Presented 29 Aug. 1739 by executor. <5:455> Account 27 Nov. 1740, **Samuel MAYO** (eldest son) to take real estate and pay **Jonathan MAYO, Rebecca COLE, Mercy COLE, Mary SMITH,** heirs of **Hannah HOPKINS**, heirs of **Sarah HIGGINS.**

Will of **Thomas SMITH** of Middletown CT. <Middletown CT PR #3201>
...dated 7 Sept. 1759, mentions wf **Ruth;** sons **Thomas SMITH, Zoeth SMITH, Enoch SMITH, Jonathan SMITH;** daus **Mary SMITH, Mercy SMITH, Ellis SMITH.** Witnesses: Stephen STILES, Enoch SMITH, Ezra SMITH. Pr. 5 Nov. 1759. Inventory 4 Apr. 1760. Rcds. state he d. 19 Sept. 1759. <Copies of the original probate records are in the files.>

Will of **John COLE,** yeoman of Eastham MA. <Barnstable Co.PR>
<9:79>...dated 12 Oct. 1753, mentions wf **Marcy;** son **John COLE** (executor); dau **Rebecca COLE;** mentions land adjoining that of Richard SPARROW. Witnesses: Benjamin COLE, Apphia TWINING, Richard SPARROW. <9:80> Pr. 6 Nov. 1753, administration granted to **John COLE.** <9:81> Inventory taken 27 Nov. 1753 by Richard SPARROW, Jonathan HIGGINS Jr. and William TWINING, yeomen of Eastham, total Ł175.4s. Sworn to 4 Dec. 1753 by the executor.

Estate of **Thomas MAYO** of Eastham MA. <from original in poss. of Stanley W. SMITH, 1911>
...29 Apr. 1729, Joseph DOANE, Esq., John SPARROW and Israel COLE, yeomen of Eastham were app'td to appraise estate.

Heirs of **Israel MAYO** of Eastham MA. <original unrecorded deed - see MD 16:91>
...30 Oct. 1771, Nathaniel PAINE & wf Phebe of Sandisfield MA and Dr. Samuel KENWRICK & wf Esther of Harwich MA sell land in Harwich that was the "seisin" of our honoured Father Israel MAYO, dec'd and is one fourth part of the 16th lot, 2d division, Sipson's Purchase. Witnesses: Thomas ROGERS, Thomas PAINE.

MICRO #12 OF 18

Joseph AREY of Eastham MA to **Judah ROGERS** of Eastham MA. <Barnstable Co.Deeds 35:41>
...17 Apr. 1776, Joseph ARY, yeoman, for Ł93.6.8d sold to Judah ROGERS, yeoman...my homestead land, about five acres. Wife Hannah AREY releases dower. Witnesses: Thomas PAINE, James PAINE. Rec. 11 July 1776. <The deed was re-recorded 9 Dec. 1904 in 270:171>

Will of **Oliver AREY,** yeoman of Eastham MA. <Barnstable Co.PR 12:57>
...dated 22 Mar. 1760, mentions wf **Elizabeth;** sons **Oliver AREY Jr., Thomas AREY;** daus **Abigail AREY, Elizabeth AREY, Mary AREY, Jedidah AREY, Eunice AREY;** mentions land bought of Henry YOUNG, and Dr. KENWRICK. Wife and brother in law **Samuel PAINE** named executors. Pr. 6 May 1760.

Will of **Thomas AREY** of Orleans MA. <from certified copy made by Registrar of Probate, 1909>
...dated 14 Feb. 1816, Thomas AREY, yeoman, mentions wf **Rebecca;** to son **Joseph AREY** my homestead land together with my land at Nemecoik, my land over the river that I bought of Jabez SPARROW, my meadow on Sampson's island flatt, my meadow at the cartway and at the beach creek with my meadow at rock harbour together with all my wood land; to dau **Phebe AREY** a piece of wood land near John HURD's that I bought of Shubael MAYO together with a privilidge of living in my dwelling house as long as she lives a single life; to son **Joseph AREY** my oxen, horse, scow, cart, wheels and all my farming tackling and tools of husbandry and my salt works; daus **Phebe AREY, Rebecca SEABURY, Sukey HOPKINS, Mary YOUNG** (whom he also calls **Mary AREY**); granddaughter **Hannah AREY;** mentions a piece of woodland near the white rock so called and a piece of woodland at grassy neck, near Deacon Judah ROGER's that I bought of James YOUNG. Witnesses: Josiah SPARROW, Judah ROGERS, Joseph R. ATWOOD.

Passport of **Joseph AREY,** 1811. <original in possession of Henry AREY, Yarmouthport MA, 1909>
...24 Apr. 1811, #2345, I, Henry DEARBORN, Collector for the District of Boston and Charlestown, do hereby certify that Joseph AREY an American Seaman, aged Twenty six years, or thereabouts, of the Height of Six Feet---Dark Complexion, Brown Hair, Blue Eyes, a scar on the left thigh, has this day produced to me proof in the manner directed...that the said Joseph AREY is a citizen of the United States of America.

Estate of **Thomas GOULD** of Eastham MA. <Barnstable Co.PR>
<22:209> 1 Apr. 1785, Warren Austin KINWRICK of Wellfleet app'td guardian of **Solomon GOULD,** minor son of Thomas GOULD, dec'd. <25:641> 31 Mar. 1789, **Nathaniel GOULD** (minor above 14) chose Joseph DOANE, Esq. of Chatham as his guardian. Witness: Solomon FREEMAN. <25:642> 31 Mar. 1789, **PAIN GOULD** of Chatham (minor above 14) chose Joseph DOANE, Esq. of Chatham as his guardian. <24:415> 26 Aug. 1791, Isaac SPARROW, Esq., Eliakim HIGGINS and Simion KINGMAN all of Eastham app'td to appraise estate. <25:57> 26 Aug. 1791, James YOUNG of Eastham app'td admr. <25:437> Insolvency, 26 Aug. 1791. <27:192> 26 Aug. 1791, "the memorial & request of **Phebe GOULD** now **Phebe YOUNG** shows

that my late husband **Thomas GOULD** late of Eastham went a voyage to sea two years ago and the vessels nor any of the ships company being two hundred in number have not been heard of since, all hopes of their returning have long since been given up, no administration hath been taken of the Estate of Mr. GOULD, I have lately married with Mr. James YOUNG of said Eastham and do hereby resign my right to administer said estate and desire you would appoint my said husband YOUNG to administer and settle said estate. Signed by mark of **Phebe YOUNG.** Witness: Sally STURGIS. <28:41> Inventory taken 26 Sept. 1791 by Isaac SPARROW, Eliakim HIGGINS, Simeon HIGGINS; real estate, £65. 10.0., personal, £16.13.6. Approved 26 Oct. 1791. <25:858> Allowance 26 Oct. 1791 to **Phebe GOULD** now **Phebe YOUNG,** widow of Thomas GOULD. <28:351> Dower 11 Nov. 1791 set off to widow. <27:297,28: 103> Account 27 Mar. 1792 of James YOUNG, admr.

Will of **Nathaniel GOULD** of Orleans MA. <Barnstable Co.PR #1857>
<60:315>...dated 16 Nov. 1843, mentions wife; five sons, viz: **Jonathan GOULD, Nathaniel GOULD** (executor), **Joseph GOULD, Franklin GOULD** (executor), **Benjmain GOULD;** four daus, viz: **Sally, Nancy, Hannah, Mary**; mother **Mary GOULD.** Witnesses: Alexander KENRICK, Tabitha T. KENRICK, John (--). Witnesses sworn 9 Jan. 1844. Pr. 13 Feb. 1844. <63:377> Decree.

Nathaniel GOULD of Harwich to chil. of son **John GOULD.** <MD 16:225>
...29 Apr. 1755, Nathaniel GOULD to **Thomas GOULD, Richard GOULD, Abigail GOULD,** children of son John GOULD...orchard in Harwich. (15 Feb. 1772, Richard GOULD receipts to John GOULD for one quarter of said orchard.)

Estate of **Nathaniel GOULD** of Orleans MA. <Barnstable Co.PR #3504>
...8 Jan. 1856, **Hannah H. GOULD,** widow, declines administration and requests that John DOANE of Orleans be appointed. Bond signed by John DOANE, Joseph K. GOULD, Henry DOANE. Witnesses: Martha DOANE, Caroline D. KNOWLES.

Guardianship of Children of **Nathaniel GOULD** of Orleans MA. <Barnstable Co.PR #3503>
...23 Apr. 1856, **Joshua GOULD,** minor over 14, chose mother **Hannah K. GOULD** as guardian. <69:319> 9 Dec. 1856, **Hannah K. GOULD,** guardian of **Joshua GOULD, Nathaniel GOULD, Sarah GOULD, Nancy GOULD and Theresa GOULD,** minor children. Sureties: Joseph K. GOULD, Franklin GOULD.

Thomas MAYO of Eastham MA to **Jonathan SPARROW** of Eastham MA. <MD 16:9>
...18 May 1761, Thomas MAYO, yeoman sold to Jonathan SPARROW...half lot of meadow in Eastham on Pochey Flats...being half the lot of meadow granted by the town of Eastham in 1703 to Jonathan LINNEL and myself...the 19th lot in division of meadow made that year, is north east half of said lot...as per deed of division between John YATES of Harwich and myself 2 Aug. 1744. Elizabeth MAYO, wf of Thomas releases dower. Ack. by both 18 June 1761. Not recorded.

Town of Eastham to **Thomas MAYO** of Eastham MA. <Eastham Land Grants, 1659-1710, p.31>
Rec. 1 June 1700...granted by the Town of Eastham, to Thomas MAYO, son of John MAYO...a piece of land to sett a house on at the westerly end of his father's land in the nooke.

Thomas MAYO of Eastham MA to **Icchabod HIGGINS** of Eastham MA. <Barnstable Co.Deeds 5:72>
...20 Apr. 1704, Thomas MAYO (the son of John MAYO), for £6, sells to Icchabod HIGGINS...meadow in Eastham on Town flats, being the 13th lot, bounded by land of Thomas SMITH. Witnesses: Richard HIGGINS, Joshua HIGGINS. Rec. 22 May 1706.

MICRO #13 OF 18

Will of **Richard SPARROW,** yeoman of Eastham MA. <Barnstable Co.PR>
<17:200>...dated 28 Jan. 1774, mentions wf **Hannah**; to son **Isaac SPARROW,** all lands in Eastham & Harwich, my sixth part of the Grist Mill called the Stage Mill, my pew in the South meeting house in Eastham he allowing my daughter Hannah to set in it if she is so minded, my scow, cart, wheels with all my farming tackling, all my wearing apparrel; daus **Rebecca HOPKINS, Hannah HAMBLENTON**; granddaughter **Mercy MAYO.** Son Isaac named executor. Witnesses: Joseph COLE, Zaccheus HIGGINS, Joshua COLE. Pr. 28 June 1774. <17:202> Inventory taken 5 July 1774 by above witnesses, total £109.17.11. Sworn to by executor 12 July 1774. <17:252> Account of executor 11 Apr. 1775, incl. payment for gravestones.

Will of **Isaac SPARROW,** Esq. of Orleans MA. <Barnstable Co.PR>
<37:353>...dated 15 Mar. 1808, mentions wf **Rebecca**; two sons **Richard SPARROW, Josiah SPARROW** (named executors); children of dec'd daus **Sarah LINNEL & Mary MAYO**; daus **Rebecca AREY, Hannah KNOWLES, Elizabeth FREEMAN**; granddaughter **Anna SPARROW,** dau of dec'd son **Isaac SPARROW**; grandson **Isaac LINNEL**; granddaughter **Sally HIGGINS**; grandsons **Uriah MAYO, Thomas MAYO**; granddaughters **Sally ROGERS, Eunice FREEMAN, Polly MAYO, Cynthia MAYO**; mentions land he owns on Sampson's Island in partnership with Jabez SPARROW. Witnesses: Elkanah HOPKINS, Curtis HOPKINS, Asa HOPKINS. <32:228> Pr. 12 July 1808. <38:528> Inventory taken 7 Aug. 1808 by Edmund SNOW, Abner FREEMAN, Elkanah HOPKINS.

<"Sup. Ct. of Jud. (case FREEMAN and PERRY), #6397 (6), (9 papers)>
The Testimony of **John FFREEMAN** of Eastham, Esq. aged about 77 years, saith that whereas Maj. William BASSETT of Sandwich writt to me to give him the best Information that I could Respecting my brother Edmond FFREEMAN's Condition and Estate, I accordingly Gave him the best account I could in writing and whereas I am abused by it, and that it hath been said by my cousin Edmond FFREEMAN

or some of his family that it was a pack of lyes...Taken upon oath...3 July 1704 before Jonathan SPARROW, Justice of the Peace.

Estate of **Edmund FREEMAN** of Eastham MA. <MD 8:65,67>
...Administration, 25 Feb. 1717/8. Division, 12 Feb. 1718, mentions following children: **Isaac FREEMAN** (eldest son), **Ebenezer FREEMAN, Edmund FREEMAN, Ruth DOANE, Sarah HIGGINS, Mary HINCKLEY, Experience GROSS, Mercy COBB, Thankful SNOW, Elizabeth PEPPER, Hannah REMICK, Rachel FREEMAN.**

Will of **Sarah (Mayo) FREEMAN**, widow of Edmund above, of Harwich MA. <8:69,70>
...dated 26 Mar. 1736/7, mentions following children: **Ebenezer FREEMAN, Edmund FREEMAN, Thankful SNOW, Mary HINCKLEY,** four children of son **Isaac FREEMAN, Sarah HIGGINS, Mercy COBB, Hannah REMICK** and **Rachel GRAY.** Inventory, 5 Mar. 1745/6.

Estate of **Thomas GROSS** of Eastham MA. <Barnstable Co.PR>
<4:399>...14 Mar. 1727/8, David DOANE, yeoman of Eastham app'td admr. <4:408> Inventory taken Apr 1728 by Joseph MYRICK, Edward KNOWLES, Samuel FREEMAN Jr. Sworn to by admr. 24 Apr. 1728, total £566.13.11. Set out to widow, **Joan GROSS** for support of self & family, £40.6.0. <4:502-504> 18 Mar. 1729, **Sarah FREEMAN,** seamstress/spinstress, of Eastham, app'td guardian of **Sarah GROSS, Thomas GROSS** and **Freeman GROSS,** minor children of the dec'd. <3:682> Receipt of dower, 10 May 1731, of **"Jane" GROSS,** widow. Witnesses: Richard AREY, Hannah AREY.

Samuel HINKLEY of Brunswick ME to **Mehitable HINKLEY.** <Cumberland Co.ME Deeds 2:34>
...16 Mar. 1757, Samuel HINKLEY to Mehitable HINKLEY...the tract of land in Brunswick on which I now dwell...as soon as God shall be pleased to remove me and my dearly beloved wife Mary HINKLEY by death and not before. Rec. 15 Apr. 1762.

Samuel HINKLEY of Brunswick ME to **Daniel WEED.** <Cumberland Co.ME Deeds 4:5>
...11 Oct. 1759...land on Sibarcodigon(sp) Island. Ack. 23 Jan. 1760 by Deacon Samuel HINKLEY. Rec. 25 June 1764.

Samuel HINKLEY gives land for a meeting house in Brunswick ME...26 May 1759. Rec. 3 Aug. 1769. <Cumberland Co.ME Deeds 6:349>

KENNEBEC COUNTY MAINE DEEDS:

Shubael HINCKLEY: 1:410; 7:339,489 (1805, yeoman of Hall).
Thomas HINCKLEY : 3:368; 8:248; 16:148; 16:575; 18:37; 19:73; 21:250.

Estate of **Clark S. HINCKLEY.** <Kennebec Co.ME PR>
<original> Letter 17 Oct. 1814, Portland ME, of **Lydia BACON,** formerly a wife of Clark S. HINCKLEY who died at sea (the son of James HINKLEY whose widow has since died) had sold out his rights in his brother Nicholas HINCKLEY's estate..."the widow of Mrs. James HINCKLEY a Grandmother to my child has lately deceast".

Guardianship of Child of **Aaron HINKLEY,** mariner. <Kennebec Co.ME PR>
...18 July 1819, **Benjamin HINKLEY,** ae 20, son of Aaron, dec'd, chooses Tibbets HINKLEY, mariner of Hallowell, as his guardian. (No further details given in files.)

Guardianship of Child of **Enoch HINKLEY** of Freeman ME. <Kennebec Co.ME PR>
...5 July 1821, **Whiting Stevens HINKLEY** of Farmington ME, minor above 14, son of Enoch, chooses John CHURCH Jr., blacksmith of Farmington as his guardian. (No further details given in files.)

Will of **Frances Ellen LORD,** singlewoman of Wakefield MA. <Middlesex Co.PR #128,238>
<928:639>...dated (16) Aug. 1920, everything to sisters **Nathalie LORD** and **Agnes McCartney LORD.** <933:39> Bond, 29 Sept. 1920. <873:306> Bond. <932:239> Notice. <969:179> Inventory, no real estate, personal estate total $8329.46. (Note: The date of the will is questionable as elsewhere in the files her death date is given as 1 Aug. 1920. Frances E. Lord was the sister of Ernestine LORD, the mother of George E. BOWMAN, compiler of these Bowman Files.)

Will of **Nathalie LORD,** singlewoman of Wakefield MA. <Middlesex Co.PR #166,586>
<1103:647>...dated 3 Mar. 1923, mentions sister **Agnes McCartney LORD;** nephews & neices; **Austin RICE; Stephen EMERY;** half of estate to the American Bible Society, Astor Place, New York City. <1095:62> Inventory, 29 June 1923, total personal estate $5940.80. (See directly above.)

Will of **Agnes McCartney LORD,** singlewoman of Wakefield MA. <Middlesex Co.PR #203,463>
<1257:176>...dated 3 Mar. 1923 (same day as above sister), mentions sister **Nathalie LORD;** nephews & neices; **Austin RICE; Stephen EMERY;** half of estate to the American Bible Society, Astor Place, New York City. <1256:474> Inventory (no date), total personal estate $5081.25.

MICRO #14 OF 18

Estate of **Samuel HINCKLEY** of Georgetown ME. <Lincoln Co.ME PR, 1760-1800, p.34>
...18 June 1767, **Sarah HINCKLEY,** widow, app'td admx. Sureties: Edmund HINCKLEY, Abiel LOVEJOY. Inventory taken 1 July 1767 by George RODGERS, Joseph HARFORD, Matthew McKENNEY all of Georgetown

---

Estate of **James HINKLEY**, yeoman of Hallowell ME. <Kennebec Co.ME PR>
Petition 26 Feb. 1805, of **Mary HINKLEY**, widow, that her son be app'td admr. Bond 27 Feb. 1805 of **Thomas HINKLEY 2d**, gentleman, admr. Sureties: James HINKLEY, husbandman and Benjamin PRESCOTT, gentleman, all of Hallowell. Inventory taken 25 Mar. 1805 by Nathaniel PERLEY, Esq., Joseph SMITH, Esq., Isaac PILSBURY, gentleman, all of Hallowell; incl. nine acres land with buildings, $900.,four cows & six sheep, four green chairs, old gun, three axes, glass ware, iron ware, feather beds and bedding, an order on the Town of Hallowell $54.95, cash on hand $113.20, owed by Joshua WINGATE & Sons $9.77, note signed by LOWELL & SMITH $21.97, two pews in Hallowell meeting house $100.00; total $1347.89. Account of admr. 28 Jan. 1806. Account of admr. 28 Feb. 1809.

Clark HINKLEY of Hallowell ME to **Thomas HINKLEY** of Hallowell ME. <Kennebec Co.ME Deeds 16:148>
...5 Oct. 1809, Clark HINKLEY, mariner, to my brother Thomas HINKLEY, gentleman, all my right in estate of my late father James HINKLEY or to my late brother Nicholas HINKLEY, dec'd...to pews #73 & #78 in 1st Parish meeting house.

Edward AUSTIN of Dresden to **Thomas HINKLEY 2d.** <Kennebec Co.ME Deeds 16:577>
...28 Aug. 1811, Edward AUSTIN, joiner, & wf Mercy, to Thomas HINKLEY 2d, gentleman, Mercy's rights in estate of her father James HINKLEY.

Ebenezer HINKLEY of Hallowell ME to **Thomas HINCKLEY 2d** of Hallowell. <Kennebec Co.Deeds 16:575>
...28 Aug. 1811, Ebenezer HINKLEY, mariner & wf Tabitha, to Thomas HINCKLEY 2d, all rights in estate of my late father James HINKLEY and the share that I the said Ebenezer bought of my brother James HINKLEY, yeoman.

Mehitable HINKLEY of Hallowell ME to **Thomas HINKLEY 2d** of Hallowell. <Kennebec Co.Deeds 16:576>
...30 May 1812, Mehitable HINKLEY, maiden, to Thomas HINKLEY 2d, gentleman, her share in estate of her father James HINKLEY and her brother Nicholas HINKLEY.

Levi HINKLEY of Hallowell ME to **Thomas HINKLEY 2d.** <Kenenbec Co.ME Deeds 16:577>
...17 May 1813, Levi HINKLEY, mariner, to Thomas HINKLEY 2d, gentleman, his rights in estate of father James HINKLEY and brother Nicholas HINKLEY. Beulah HINKLEY signs.

Levi HINKLEY of Hallowell ME to **Thomas HINCKLEY 2d** of Hallowell ME. <Kennebec Co.ME Deeds 16:574>
...5 Apr. 1816, Levi HINKLEY & wf Beaulah, to Thomas HINCKLEY, gentleman, all rights in real estate of my late brother Nicholas HINKLEY dec'd.

Zenas BACKUS of Farmington ME to **Thomas HINKLEY 2d** of Hallowell ME. <Kennebec Co.ME Deeds 16:576>
...20 May 1816, Zenas BACKUS, gentleman, & wf Mehitable, to Thomas HINKLEY 2d, gentleman, all rights in real estate and two pews of Mehitable's late brother Nicholas HINKLEY.

LINCOLN COUNTY ME PROBATES, 1760-1800

p.18 - 31 Dec. 1764, James HINKLEY & Aaron HINKLEY, wit. will of Ben. THOMPSON of Georgetown.
p.88 - 1 Apr. 1778, Thomas HINKLEY of Hallowell, surety for admx. of estate of David HANCOCK.
p.123 - 27 July 1783, Thomas HINKLEY & James HINKLEY witnessed will of David CLARK of Hallowell.
- 17 Dec. 1783, Thomas HINKLEY of Hallowell, et al, took inv. of estate of David CLARK.
p.196 - 28 Apr. 1791, James HINKLEY of Hallowell took inv. of estate of Obed HUSSEY of Hallowell.

Will of **Lot HARDING**, yeoman of Truro MA. <Barnstable Co.PR 31:359, 32:119>>
<31:359>...dated 6 Aug. 1802, mentions son **Lot HARDING** (executor); seven daus, viz: **Tamar SNOW**, wf of Anthony SNOW; **Esther PAINE**, wf of Elkanah PAINE Jr.; **Hannah COLLINS**, wf of John COLLINS; **Huldah DYER**, widow; **Mercy LUMBARD**, wf of Cornelius LUMBARD; **Sarah HARDING; Martha HARDING.** To each daughter, $25.00, Sarah & Martha to have use of dwelling house while unmarried, son Lot to receive remainder. Witnesses: Silvanus SNOW, Solomon SNOW, Betsey SNOW. Pr. 7 Mar. 1803.

Will of **Thoms GREY** of Harwich MA. <Barnstable Co.PR 13:204>
...20 Sept. 1765, mentions wf **Rachel**; daus **Hannah GREY, Mary GREY**; dau **Elizabeth** (prob. marr.); son **Joshua GREY.** Pr. 12 Mar. 1766.

Will of **Joshua GRAY** of Harwich MA. <Barnstable Co.PR 35:81>
...dated 8 Oct. 1808, mentions wf **Mary**; nephews: **William PEEKS**(sp), **Thomas BANGS, Silvanus BANGS, Ebenezer BANGS Jr., Joshua BANGS**; sister **Mary GRAY.** <32:216> Pr. 10 Oct. 1809.

Will of **Benjamin HIGGINS**, yeoman of Eastham MA. <Barnstable Co.PR 12:153>
...dated 1 July 1760, mentions wf **Marcy** "liberty to carry off all the personal estate she brought with her when I married her"; sons **Thomas HIGGINS, Paul HIGGINS, Benjamin HIGGINS, Zaccheus HIGGINS** (executor), **Isaac HIGGINS, Freeman HIGGINS**; daus **Preseler/Priscilla SMITH, Sarah SMITH, Experience FOHY, Loes/Lois CURKEN**; grandchildren **Solomon YOUNG, Enos YOUNG, Sarah YOUNG, Elisabeth YOUNG, Henery/Henry YOUNG.** Witnesses: Richard SPARROW, Moses HIGGINS, Elnathan HIGGINS. Pr. 11 May 1761. <12:156> Inventory taken 27 Apr. 1762 by Richard SPARROW, Edmund FREEMAN, Moses HIGGINS Sworn to 11 May 1761 by **Zaccheus HIGGINS**, executor. <12:252> Inventory 17 Mar. 1762. Account Sworn to 16 Mar. 1762.

MICRO #15 OF 18

Will of **Benjamin HIGGINS**, yeoman of Eastham MA. <Barnstable Co.PR>
<20:9>..dated 17 Sept. 1777, mentions wf **Margaret**; daughter in law **Susanna SEARS**; sons **Edmund HIGGINS, Benjamin HIGGINS, Lot HIGGINS** (executor), **Elisha HIGGINS**; dau **Sarah HIGGINS**; grandchildren **Lones HIGGENS/HIGGINS, Experance/Experience HIGGENS/HIGGINS.** Pr. 15 Oct. 1777. <20:11> Inventory 28 Dec. 1777. <20:14> Division of real estate 28 Dec. 1777 (five equal shares).

Estate of **Benjamin HIGINS**, mariner of Orleans MA. <Barnstable Co.PR>
<38:60> Will dated 6 Dec. 1809, everything to wf **Dorcas** (executor). <32:307> Pr. 13 Oct. 1816. <45:134> Inventory & dower 31 Oct. 1825. <45:210> Inventory & dower 20 Mar. 1826. <45:464> Account 1 Nov. 1826.

CUMBERLAND COUNTY ME DEEDS:

<25:305> - 15 May 1781, Nathaniel KNIGHT, gentleman to Timothy HIGGINS, housewright of Gorham, land in Pearsontown.
<25:305> - 17 Apr. 1795, Joshua FREEMAN, yeoman of Portland to Timothy HIGGINS, yeoman/Standish.
<25:306> - July 1795, Enoch ISLEY (& wf Eliz.), trader of Portland to Timothy HIGGINS " " .
<35:170> - 7 Oct. 1800, Jonathan SAMPSON, yeoman of Standish to Timothy HIGGINS, yeoman/" " .
<116:283> - 6 Sept 1825, Timothy HIGGINS, yeoman of Standish to Prince HIGGINS, yeoman of Standish, land in Baldwin bought of Jonathan SANBORN 18 Aug. 1804. Ack. 6 Sept. 1805.
<116:285> - 6 Sept 1805, Timothy HIGGINS, yeoman of Standish to Ephraim HIGGINS of same. Ack."".

CUMBERLAND COUNTY ME DEEDS: (Re: Prince HIGGINS)

Index #14: <39:430;65:115;116:88,283;140:166;152:357;155:34;168:183;174:180;209:154,247;239:366; 284:114 (ment. Chesley HIGGINS, son of Prince, 18 Nov. 1857); 310:48>

Will of **John MAYO** of Harwich MA. <Barnstable Co.PR>
<4:277>...dated 3 Feb. 1723/4, mentions wf **Hannah**; to son **Samuel MAYO** all rights in Oyster Bay or Jericho on Long Island N.Y.; to son **John MAYO** "whose house has been burnt", half lot I bought of Thomas SNOW in Harwich, also my part of a lot I bought "of Old Mr. Stephen HOPKINS dec'd" in Harwich; to son **Joseph MAYO** land where his house now stands, also the third of the meadow I had of James COLE and John FREEMAN; daus **Hannah HOPKINS, Mercy HOPKINS, Rebeckah PAINE, Mary HOPKINS, Elisabeth MAYO.** Witnesses: Edward SNOW, Jonathan GODFREE, Philip SELEW. <4:279> Pr. 15 Feb. 1725/26. (Inventory - none indexed.)

Will of **Hannah MAYO**, widow of John, of Harwich MA. <Barnstable Co.PR>
<6:370>...dated 5 Jan. 1740, mentions sons **Samuel MAYO, John MAYO, Joseph MAYO** (executor); daus **Hannah HOPKINS, Mercy HOPKINS, Rebecca PAINE, Mary HOPKINS, Elizabeth NICKERSON.** Witnesses: John WING Jr., Samuel BANGS, Chillingsworth FOSTER. <6:373> Pr. 21 Mar. 1743. <6:374> Inventory taken 11 Apr. 1744 by Chillingsworth FOSTER, Nathaniel STONE Jr., John WING Jr. Sworn to 14 Apr. 1744 by **Joseph MAYO**, executor.

Joseph MAYO of Newbury MA to **John MAYO** of Hingham MA. <Barnstable Co.PR 4:389>
...8 July 1702, Indenture between Joseph MAYO, cordwinder and his brother John MAYO, cordwinder.. said Joseph, for a valuable sum of money, sold to John all his rights in land at Oyster Bay N.Y. Witnesses: Hopestill FOSTER, Richard HARRIS, John GYLES.

Estate of **Reuben MAYO** of Princeton, Minnesota. <Sherburne Co.MN PR>
Petition 23 Dec. 1911, of S.M. CROCKETT of Elk River, Minn., for the judicial determination of the descent of the real estate belonging to Reuben MAYO who died at Princeton, Minnesota the 13th day of May 1882 without leaving a last will...to the following heirs, children of dec'd, viz: **Emily A. McCLELLAN, Hannah M. TIBBETTS, Sarah T. THOMAS, Reuben M. MAYO, Mercy Ellen HEATH, Fannie HEATH, Viola WEDGEWOOD, Frederick G. MAYO** and grandchildren **Charles L. MAYO** & **Malon H. MAYO.**

MICRO #16 OF 18

Will of **Stephen HALL** of Norway ME. <Oxford Co.ME PR>
...dated 25 Dec. 1854, to dau. **Abbie W. HALL**, $300.000 when she becomes of lawful age; to wife **Sarah T. HALL**, notes of hand amounting to $1018.54 given by Isaiah STEVENS; wife and Jeremiah HACKER of Portland named executors. Witnesses: David NOYES, William NEEDHAM, William THORN. Bond 20 Mar. 1855 of executors. Sureties: William NEEDHAM, William HALL Jr., both of Norway ME. Account 3 Nov. 1857 of executors, total personal estate $1345.31. <3:135> Inventory taken by Francis W. WHITMAN, Henry PIKE, William THORN, presented by **Sarah T. HALL** 3rd Tues. Apr. 1855; incl. two cottage bed steads, one cross, one rocking chair, two childs' chairs, six common chairs one chamber sink, two mirrors, one portable desk, bed furniture, crockery, one dozen knives and forks, eleven spoons, tea pot, kettle, toilet table, three flat irons.

Estate of **Asa MAYO**, yeoman of Brewster MA. <Barnstable Co.PR>
<42:115> 19 Oct. 1824, David MAYO, blacksmith of Brewster app'td admr. <45:109> Inventory taken 16 Aug. 1825 by Joseph CROCKER, Josiah SEABURY, Elisha CROCKER. <39:128> Allowance to widow, **Sally**, 28 Mar. 1826. <45:217> Dower to widow 9 Mar. 1826, set off by Joseph CROCKER, Elisha CROCKER,

Josiah SEABURY. <45:218> Account 28 Mar. 1826 of David MAYO, admr.

Will of **Benjamin FREEMAN**, gentleman of Harwich MA. <Barnstable Co.PR>
<9:372>...dated 25 Nov. 1757, mentions wf **Temperance**; sons **Benjamin FREEMAN** (executor), **John FREEMAN**; my six daus, viz: **Desire PARKER, Rebecca PARKER, Temperance FOSTER, Sarah REMICK** (if she becomes a widow and so remains), **Fear SEARS, Mehetable FESSENDEN.** Witnesses: Joseph CLARK, Nathaniel CLARK, John SNOW. <9:373> Pr. 4 Apr. 1758.

Will of **Mary FREEMAN**, single woman of Harwich MA. <Barnstable Co.PR>
<26:548>...dated 29 Sept. 1787, mentions niece **Mary ATWOOD**, nephews **Barnabas ATWOOD, Watson FREEMAN** (executor).

John FREEMAN of Rochester MA to Estate of **John WATSON** of Plymouth MA. <Plymouth Co.Deeds 28:6>
...21 Feb. 1732/3, John FREEMAN, yeoman, mortgage of Ł197.17s5d to the administrators of estate of John WATSON, dec'd, viz: Nathaniel THOMAS, Esq., Isaac LOTHROP, Jr., gentleman and Priscilla LOTHROP. Discharged 18 Sept. 1747.

John FREEMAN of Rochester MA to **Simon HATHAWAY** of Rochester MA. <Plymouth Co.Deeds 36:71>
...17 Feb. 1742/3, John FREEMAN, yeoman to Simon HATHAWAY, husbandman...40 acres with house, formerly the homestead of Theophilus DOTY. Rec. 3 Nov. 1743.

John FREEMAN of Rochester MA to **Moses MENDALL** of Dartmouth MA. <Plymouth Co.Deeds 36:223>
...29 Sept. 1744, John FREEMAN, yeoman & wf Mercy, to Moses MENDALL, gentleman...homestead in Rochester which I bought of John BLACKMER (then Jr.) of Rochester by deeds of 22 Feb. 1725/6 and 1730...and meadow in Rochester I bought of Stephen BLACKMER now of Tiverton. Ack. 6 Sept. 1744 by John FREEMAN. Rec. 13 Oct. 1744.

John FREEMAN of Rochester MA to **James BOWDOIN.** <Plymouth Co.Deeds 37:99>
...11 Apr. 1745, mortgage to James BOWDOIN of house, land, iron works, etc. in Rochester. Released 1 Oct. 1747. Rec. 4 Apr. 1752.

John FREEMAN of Rochester to **Ithamar COOMBS** of Rochester MA. <Plymouth Co.Deeds 52:83>
...(no date), John FREEMAN, yeoman (ae 70) to Ithamar COOMBS, yeoman, one quarter of new fire in Iron Works on Sippecan Mill River, also right of stream and half of new coal house. Witnesses: Samuel WING, Timothy RUGGLES. Ack. 9 May 1748. Rec. 30 Oct. 1765.

John FREEMAN of Rochester MA to **Zaccheus HANDY** of Sandwich MA. <Plymouth Co.Deeds 39:84>
...27 Aug. 1747, John FREEMAN, yeoman & wf Mercy, for Ł1100 old tenor, sell to Zaccheus HANDY, carpenter...20 acre homestead; two thirds of grist mill on Sippecan Mill River; William NYES' 85 acre homestead bounded by John GOODSPEED's homestead, land formerly of John RANDALL sold to John BLACKMER and land of heirs of Peter BLACKMER...containing meadow Peter BLACKMER dec'd conveyed to son John BLACKMER who conveyed it to William NOYES; salt meadow in "Wareham once in Rochester" being part of meadow Peter BLACKMER bought of William CLARKE now in partnership with John COOMBS and others; 15 acres said John FREEMAN bought of John BLACKMER Jr. <see 30:196>; 14 acres near the mill which Constant MIRRICK sold to said John FREEMAN 18 Mar. 1733. Witnesses: Timothy RUGGLES, Mary RUGGLES. Rec. 29 Aug. 1747.

Estate of **Thomas ASHLEY** of Rochester MA. <Plymouth Co.PR #544>
<16:332> Inventory "Rochester 24:1762", widow **Mary ASHLEY** says "my husband promised my daughter **Elizabeth** a cow; **John ASHLEY** (second son) had loaned his father money; **Elkanah ASHLEY** (third son) had been promised a sheep & lamb. <16:466> Dower set off 15 Oct. 1762 to widow. <16:490> Account 6 July 1763 mentions son **Thomas ASHLEY.** <19:451> Refers to three suits in court. <17:81> Adm.

PLYMOUTH COUNTY DEEDS:

<36:97> - 10 Mar. 1741/2, Thomas ASHLEY of Rochester to Edmund SHERMAN et al, land in Rochester.
<47:217> - (   ) 1762, Thomas ASHLEY of Rochester from Joseph ASHLEY.
<53:53> - 18 July 1764, Estate of Thomas ASHLEY of Rochester to Nathaniel MORTON, land bought of his father, Joseph ASHLEY.
<53:105> - 18 July 1764, Est. of Thomas ASHLEY of Rochester to Joseph ASHLEY, part of land bought of his father Joseph ASHLEY.

Will of **Judah BERRY**, yeoman of Harwich MA. <Barnstable Co.PR>
<17:96>...dated 21 Nov. 1769, mentions two grandsons **Judah BERRY** and **Scotto BERRY** (sons of my dec'd son **Lemuel BERRY**) and their sisters **Mary, Rebecca, Mehitable, Sarah, Elizabeth, Lydia**; son **Theophilus BERRY** (executor); my five daus now living, viz: **Hannah HOPKINS, Mercy FULLER, Sarah HINCKLEY, Azuba CROSBY, Mary HOPKINS**, widow of Joseph; heirs of my two dec'd daus **Ruth HOPKINS, Experience BANGS.** Witnesses: Benjamin FREEMAN, Jonathan BERRY, Chillingsworth FOSTER. <17:97> Pr. 11 May 1773.

Will of **Nathaniel FREEMAN**, yeoman of Harwich MA. <Barnstable Co.PR>
<5:247>...dated 1 Aug. 1735, mentions wf **Mary**; sons **Prence FREEMAN** (executor), **Lemuel FREEMAN**; dau **Mary DOANE.** Witnesses: Benjamin FREEMAN, Jonathan BANGS, Temperance FREEMAN. Pr. 27 Aug. 1735 <5:248> Inventory taken 12 Sept. 1735 by Benjamin FREEMAN, Kenelm WINSLOW, Thacher FREEMAN. Sworn to by executor 22 Oct. 1735.

Will of **Eleazer CROSBY**, yeoman of Harwich MA. <Barnstable Co.PR> <9:441>...dated 23 Oct. 1759, mentions wf **Easter**; daus **Rebecca HOPKINS, Phebe CLARK, Sarah YEATS, Patience PAINE, Zerviah CROSBY**; granddaughter **Kezia BAKER**; sons **Eleazer CROSBY** (executor), **Isaac CROSBY, Prince CROSBY, Silvanus CROSBY.** Witnesses: Moses CROSBY, Eleazer COBB, John SNOW. Pr. 17 Dec. 1759. <12:81> Account of executor 7 May 1760. <12:396> Dower set off to widow, **Hester** 20 or 28 July 1760. <13:253> Account of executor 6 May 1766; incl. paid wages to **Silvanus CROSBY**, a minor, £12.10.0; paid widow two thirds of Silvanus' wages, £4.3.4.; paid **Zerviah CROSBY** her legacy, £9.12.1.

Will of **Eleazer CROSBY**, yeoman of Harwich MA. <Barnstable Co.PR 26:51> ...dated 24 Mar. 1784, mentions wf **Lydia**; daus **(Desire*) COBB, Rebeckah CROSBY, Lydia LAHA**; granddaughters **Lydia CROSBY, Anna CROSBY**, daus & heirs of son **Watson CROSBY**; son **Isaac CROSBY** (executor). Witnesses: Nathaniel CROSBY, Silvanus CROSBY, James PAINE. Pr. 6 Oct. 1784.
<Note: *Bowman questions whether Desire is meant to refer to his dau **Keziah CROSBY** who married Eleazer COBB. There is no dau Desire in the listing of Eleazer's children.>

Will of **Joseph CLARK** of Harwich MA. <Barnstable Co.PR 26:344> ...dated 21 May 1787, mentions wf **Phebe**; heirs of eldest **Mary LINCOLN**, dec'd; daus **Sarah BANGS, Phebe CROSBY**; grandson **Benjamin MYRICK**, son of youngest dau **Patience MYRICK**, dec'd; sons **Silvanus CLARK, Joseph CLARKE** (executors) and **Nathaniel CLARK.** Pr. 9 Oct. 1787.

Will of **Samuel KNOWLES**, yeoman of Eastham MA. <Barnstable Co.PR> <5:295>...dated 1 June 1732, to wf **Mercy** the estate set to her from the estate of her honoured father **Major John FREEMAN** at his decease; son **Amos KNOWLES**; daus **Ruth KNOWLES, Elizabeth KNOWLES**; son **Samuel KNOWLES** (executor); dau in law **Elizabeth KNOWLES**; sons **Richard KNOWLES, James KNOWLES**; "one Samuel COOKE in the coloney of Connecticut"; sons **Nathaniel KNOWLES, John KNOWLES, Cornelius KNOWLES**; granddaughter **Rebecca KNOWLES**; daus **Mary RICH, Rebecca WITHREL.** <5:296> Codicil 6 June 1737...legacy to dau in law **Elizabeth KNOWLES** revoked and given to children of my dec'd son **Nathaniel KNOWLES**, said Elizabeth not to receive it; mentions wife **Mary**. <5:297> Pr. 7 July 1737. <5:299> Account of what Maj. FREEMAN gave to his dau **Mary KNOWLES**, widow of said dec'd. Inventory taken 28 July 1737.

Will of **Mercy KNOWLES**, widow of Eastham MA. <Barnstable Co.PR> <8:87>...dated 5 Sept. 1739, mentions sons **Samuel KNOWLES** (executor), **Richard KNOWLES, John KNOWLES, Cornelius KNOWLES, Amos KNOWLES, James KNOWLES**; children of dec'd son **Nathaniel KNOWLES**; granddaughter **Rebecca**, dau of dec'd son **Nathaniel**; dau **Rebecca WITHRELL**; granddaughter **Ruth RICH**; granddaughter **Mercy GODFREE**; daus **Mercy RICH, Ruth AVERY.** <8:88> Pr. 17 Apr. 1745. <8:89> Inventory taken 22 Apr. 1745.

MICRO #17 OF 18

Will of **Edmund FREEMAN**, gentleman of Harwich MA. <Barnstable Co.PR> <8:1>...dated 18 Feb. 1745, mentions wf **Phebe**; sons **Watson FREEMAN, Joshua FREEMAN, Edmund FREEMAN.** Sons Watson & Edmund named executors. Witnesses: Nathaniel LINCOLN, Seth MERRICK, John SNOW. <8:3> Pr. 14 Mar. 1745. <8:4> Inventory taken 25 Mar. 1746, total real estate £5084. Sworn to 18 Apr. 1746 by executors.

Estate of **Phebe FREEMAN**, widow of Harwich MA. <Barnstable Co.PR> <7:126> Adm. 4 July 1749, **Watson FREEMAN**, gentleman of Harwich, admr. <8:285> Inventory taken 29 Mar. 1749 by William FREEMAN, John SNOW, Thacher FREEMAN. Sworn to 19 July 1749 by admr.

Will of **Mary FREEMAN**, widow of Harwich MA. <Barnstable Co.PR> <28:119>...dated 20 Feb. 1797, mentions sons **Seth FREEMAN** (executor), **Haskal FREEMAN**; dau **Phebe FOSTER**; granddaughter **Hannah SNOW**; grandson **Seth FREEMAN Jr.** <24:163> Pr. 29 Mar. 1797.

Will of **Hatsuld FREEMAN**, yeoman of Harwich MA. <Barnstable Co.PR> <17:101>..dated 13 May 1773, mentions wf **Abigail**; heirs of dau **Sarah FREEMAN**, dec'd; daus **Abigail CHILDS, Betty CHIPMAN, Mary PERRY, Jerusha CLARK**; sons **David FREEMAN, Jonathan FREEMAN.** Wife **Abigail** and Edmund FREEMAN named executors. Witnesses: Isaac FOSTER Jr., Edmund FREEMAN, Susanna FREEMAN. <17:102> Pr. 13 July 1773. <17:134> Inventory 7 Aug. 1773. <17:191> Account 11 Apr. 1774 by Edmund FREEMAN, executor. <15:161-5> Guardianship of grandchildren.

Estate of **Jonathan FREEMAN** of Harwich MA. <Barnstable Co.PR 3:488> ...27 May 1718, set out to **Mercy CUSHMAN**, wf of Isaac CUSHMAN, late widow of Jonathan FREEMAN... for her comfort and ye support of her children she had by said Freeman.

Will of **Joseph FREEMAN**, Esq. of Harwich MA. <Barnstable Co.PR> <9:228>...dated 10 Mar. 1756, mentions wife; grandaughter **Anna FREEMAN**; daus **Elizabeth PERRY, Lydia CLERK/CLARK, Rebecca HOPKINS**; son **Thacher FREEMAN** (executor). Witnesses: Watson FREEMAN, Nathaniel STONE, Esq., William FESSENDEN. Pr. 18 Mar. 1756.

MICRO #18 OF 18

Edmund FREEMAN Jr. of Sandwich MA to **Joseph BURGE.** <Plymouth Co.Deeds 5:379>
...29 Apr. 1674...in a fatherly affection unto my son in law Joseph BURGE & his wife, my daughter **Patience**...according to my promise att their marriage doe give freely...upland containing six acres in Sandwich...formerly in the possession of Mr. Edmond FFREEMAN Sr., bounded by land of Thomas BURGE Sr. and Joseph BURGE. Witnesses: Richard BOURNE, Thomas BURGE. Ack. 2 Mar. 1684/5 by Edmund FREEMAN with wf Margaret releasing dower.

==

Joseph & Patience BURGE of Sandwich MA. <Plymouth Co.Deeds>
<4:213>...30 May 1673...Ack. 2 June 1673 by both. <4:214>...14 Dec. 1677...Ack. 4 Mar. 1677 both.

==

Estate of **Edmund FREEMAN** of Sandwich MA. <Barnstable Co.PR>
<2:166>...5 Jan. 1703/4, Ezra PERRY, yeoman of Sandwich, son in law of said deceased was app'td. admr. <2:171> Inventory taken Mar. 1703/4 by Elisha BOURNE, Benjamin PERRY. Sworn to 21 Mar. 1703 by admr. <2:190> Distribution of estate 9 June 1705, to following heirs, children of dec'd, viz: **Edmond FREEMAN, Alice POPE** wf of Isaac, **Margaret FISH** wf of John, **Rachel LANNDERS** wf of John, **Patience BURG**, widow, **Rebekah PERRY** wf of Ezra; payment also made to Richard ALLEN of Sandwich.

FOOTNOTES

<1> p.98, The probate data on Joshua RAYMOND is confusing at first glance as his will mentions wife Sarah and the administration mentions wife Elizabeth. Elizabeth was his first wife who died in 1730 and it is her estate, which she inherited from her father, John CHRISTOPHERS, which is being divided. Sarah was Joshua's second wife.

==

==

PETER BROWN

MICRO #1 OF 5

MARY BROWN[2] (Peter[1])

PLYMOUTH COUNTY PROBATE, re: TINKHAM (1700-1800)

1709	Peter	Middleboro	adm.	#20895, 2:115;3:56,57
1713	Ephraim	Middleboro	adm.	#20841, 3:240;4:139 <MD 17:163>
1714	Ephraim	Middleboro	will	#20842, 3:358,359 <MD 17:162>
1717	Samuel	Middleboro	gdn.	#20902, 4:28
1718	Jeremiah	Middleboro	adm.	#20867, 4:139,146,217
1718	Ebenezer	Middleboro	will	#20828, 4:78-80 <MD 17:164>
1720	Jeremiah et al	Middleboro	gdn.	#20868, 4:343,344;5:404;7:385
1722	Elizabeth	Middleboro	gdn.	#20838, 4:324
1726	Ebenezer	Middleboro	adm.	#20829, 5:158,173
1726/7	Peter et al	Middleboro	gdn.	#20898, 5:227,228
1727	Ephraim et al	Middleboro	gdn.	#20843, 5:378
1730	John	Kingston	adm.	#20875, 5:745,785;10:205,206,207
1730	John et al	Kingston	gdn.	#20876, 5:820,822;7:454;8:11,12
1731	Hilkiah	Plymouth	will	#20855, 6:81,82,427,435 <MD 12:145>
1732	Isaac	Plymouth	will	#20863, 6:160 <MD 17:66>
1739	Ebenezer et al	Middleboro	gdn.	#20835, 8:38-41;9:53
1739	Shubael	Middleboro	will	#20911, 8:35,37,38
1740	Jacob	Middleboro	gdn.	#20865, 8:89
1745	Peter	Middleboro	adm.	#20896, 10:62,63;16:141
1745	Peter et al	Middleboro	gdn.	#20897, 10:95,97,98
1746	Hilkiah	Plymouth	adm.	#20856, 10:372,373;11:100,164,165;19:28,138
1747	Ebenezer et al	Plymouth	gdn.	#20836, 10:485,486;11:107,441;12:304
1747	Joanna et al	Middleboro	gdn.	#20869, 10:509,510;11:208,230
1747	Sarah	Plympton	gdn.	#20906, 11:76
1747	Samuel	Middleboro	adm.	#20903, 10:430,434;11:96,406,411
1748	John	Kingston	adm.	#20874, 11:117
1749	Mary	Middleboro	adm.	#20887, 11:97,186,274
1750	Seth	Middleboro	adm.	#20909, 11:521;12:229
1750	Seth et al	Middleboro	gdn.	#20910, 11:524;12:78,79
1750	Isaac	Halifax	adm.	#20864, 11:458;12:73;15:212,213,225
1752	Ebenezer	Boston	inv.	#20827, 12:431
1756	Peter	Middleboro	adm.	#20894, 14:184,245,378
1757	Keziah	Middleboro	gdn.	#20887, 14:229
1759	Joseph	Kingston	gdn.	#20878, 15:171
1760	Perez	Middleboro	will	#20893, 16:29,30
1763	Caleb	Plymouth	adm.	#20820, 17:152;19:300,301
1763	Elizabeth	Plymouth	adm.	#20839, 17:117;19:130
1765	Noah	Halifax	will	#20890, 19:242,243,376;20:122
1765	Seth	Middleboro	adm.	#20908, 17:150
1766	John	Middleboro	will	#20870, 19:370,372
1767	Joseph	Middleboro	will	#20879, 19:465,467;20:344
1767	Joseph et al	Middleboro	gdn.	#20880, 19:551;20:24;22:225
1770	Ephraim	Middleboro	adm.	#20844, 20:357,380;21:101,357,358
1773	Ephraim et al	Middleboro	gdn.	#20845, 22:11,12,13,149
1776	Amos	Middleboro	adm.	#20813, 23:105;24:167;28:391
1776	Amos et al	Middleboro	gdn.	#20814, 22:86,97,98
1776	Samuel	Middleboro	will	#20904, 24:107,108
1776	Shubael	Middleboro	adm.	#20912, 23:95;24:168
1780	Huldah	Middleboro	gdn.	#20857, 26:102
1780	Isaac	Middleboro	will	#20861, 25:455,457;27:483;30:469
1790	Jeremiah	Middleboro	will	#20866, 31:221,218;33:190
1793	John	Middleboro	will	#20871, 33:437,438,445;35:4
1796	Samuel	Middleboro	will	#20905, 35:505,506,554,566;36:357

PLYMOUTH COUNTY PROBATE, re: TINKHAM (1800-1850)

1802	Ebenezer	Middleboro	will	#20830, 37:547,549;38:357,358
1805	Ruth	Middleboro	will	#20901, 40:280,281,302,303
1807	Asa	Plymouth	gdn.	#20815, 32:311
1807	Ephraim	Halifax	gdn.	#20840, 32:352;42:298,531
1811	Abishai	Middleboro	will	#20809, 43:375;39:447;43:376,449;47:413
1814	Patience	Middleboro	will	#20892, 45:527,528,558;47:144,403
1816	Silas	Middleboro	will	#20913, 48:5,7,84
1818	Isaac	Middleboro	will	#20862, 49:294,296,586,589 58:136
1818	John 2nd	Middleboro	gdn.	#20872, 49:385;51:165,220;54:533;57:397,402;

PLYMOUTH COUNTY PROBATE, re: TINKHAM (1800-1850 con-d)

1820	Ebenezer	Middleboro	adm.	#20831, 46:405;52:467;53:54-5;55:337;59:408,409; 80:388
1820	Zebedee	Middleboro	adm.	#20919, 52:15;53:231-2,238-9,241;54:76,234,236; 66:209
1821	Asaph	Middleboro	gdn.	#20817, 51:115;53:298-9,498-9;54:79;57:36;58:279 60:117;64:493;66:66
1822	Charles	Rochester	will	#20824, 56:222,223;55:206 86:205
1823	Sylvanus	Middleboro	gdn.	#20914, 51:217;57:186,305-6,537;59:454;85:329;
1824	Cornelius	Middleboro	adm.	#20826, 52:260;58:101,102;59:168,198
1824	Ebenezer 2nd	Middleboro	adm.	#20832, 52:279;55:264;58:384,385
1825	Ebenezer 3rd	Middleboro	gdn.	#20833, 51:311
1829	John	Middleboro	will	#20873, 67:18,20,334;68:117,436
1829	Lucretia	Middleboro	will	#20886, 67:382,384;68:102
1832	Sarah	Halifax	will	#20907, 5:191**T**; 72:340
1835	Huldah	Middleboro	adm.	#20858, 71:334;75:246;77:447;78:412
1836	Elisha	Middleboro	will	#20837, 1:285**G**;75:350;78:187
1838	Chandler	Middleboro	adm.	#20823, 5:62**T**;10:177**A**;80:389
1838	George W.	Middleboro	adm.	#20847, 2:81**O**;10:213**A**;80:383,484;81:38,257,259, 597;85:217
1839	Hazael	Middleboro	adm.	#20853,2:114**O**;5:187**T**;81:339,401;82:21,162,85:241
1839	Mary	Middleboro	adm.	#20888, 6:14**U**;10:293**A**;81:566;82:371
1840	Levi 2nd	Middleboro	adm.	#20884, 2:215**O**;10:440**A**;83:121;85:82;90:166
1841	Charles	Rochester	will	#20825, 1:161**G**;6:263**U**;83:232;84:274;88:496;100: 412,414
1841	Levi F. et al	Middleboro	gdn.	#20885, 8:329**L**;9:149**M**;85:604;91:338
1842	Betsey	Middleboro	gdn.	#20818, 1:139,140**K**;2:51**S**;4:351;6:290**U**;8:477,478**L** 84:376;89:28,29;101:173;102:182
1842	Joseph	Halifax	will	#20877, 1:112**G**;6:259**U**;84:19
1842	Mary	Middleboro	gdn.	#20889, 8:276**L**;84:376
1847	Asa	Wareham	adm.	#20816, 7:316**V**;11:528**B**;90:109,110
1847	Priscilla A.	Middleboro	adm.	#20899, 11:470**B**;93:82
1848	Abraham	Rochester	adm.	#20810, 7:440**V**;12:18**C**;91:374,375
1848	Alanson H.	New Orleans	adm.	#20812, 3:141**P**;12:38**C**;91:336-7;92:75,274,332
1850	George H. et al	Middleboro	gdn.	#20848, 9:235**M**,460**M**
1850	Lavinia	Middleboro	adm.	#20884, 12:169**C**

PLYMOUTH COUNTY DEEDS:

<1:240> , Ephraim TINKHAM to Henry SAMSON.
<1:189> , Ephraim TINKHAM to James SHAW.
<3:111> 25 Mar. 1667, William SNOW & wf Rebecca to Ephraim TINKHAM.
<3:240> , Ephraim TINKHAM to Edward GRAY.
<3:249> 10 Aug. 1672, Ephraim TINKHAM & wf Mary of Plymouth to Francis WEST of Duxbury.
<3:323> 25 June 1674, Ephraim TINKHAM one of seven to sign agreement.
<4:256> , Ephraim TINKHAM to Edward GRAY.
<5:197> , Ephraim TINKHAM & wf Mary to John BROWNE.

Estate of **John TINKHAM** of Dartmouth MA. <Bristol Co.PR>
<9:314> 15 Jan. 1739, adm. granted to **John TINKHAM** of Dartmouth, son of dec'd. <9:481> Account 16 Sept. 1740 of admr. <9:386> Inventory 26 Feb. 1739/40.
(Note: The files contain a page titled "John TINKHAM" with 26 citations from the Bristol Co.Probate records with only five of these citations containing very faint pencilled data. Three have been given directly above, the additional two are: <28:476> Inventory 26 Feb. 1785. <35:20> Division 24 May 1794 of estate of John & Mary TINKHAM, of New Bedford, both dec'd. It is not clear how many "John TINKHAMS" these citations refer to, they do not appear to refer to one man. The remaining citations from the Bristol Co.PR are: <29:36> Dower. <29:40> Inventory. <35:7> Account. <46:11> Inventory. <46:365> Dower. <48:453> Account. <61:326> Adm. <61:341> Inventory. <62:26> Dower. <62:263> Account. <63:448> Account. <111:438> Notice. <120:26> Notice. <148:214> Adm. <150:430> Adm. <152:37> Adm. <166:72> Adm. <195:36> Inventory. <217:147> Account. <217:574> Account. <224:10> Allowance.)

BRISTOL COUNTY DEEDS: re: TINKHAM

<9:65> 6 July 1714, Ebenezer TINKHAM, John TOMSON, both of Middleboro to brother John TINKHAM of Dartmouth. <:70> Mary, wf of John TOMSON releases dower 19 Mar. 1715/6.
<7:418> 1712, Ephraim TINKHAM to John TINKHAM.
<7:455> 1712/3, Elkiah, Isaac & Peter TINKHAM to John TINKHAM.
<7:457> 1712/3, Elkiah TINKHAM to John TINKHAM.
<36:195> 1 Dec. 1746, Hezekiah TINKHAM of Swansea, son of John of Dartmouth, to Gamaliel HATHAWAY
<36:232> 1 Dec. 1746, Hezekiah TINKHAM of Swansea to Joseph SPOONER.
<36:236> 1 Dec. 1746, Hezekiah TINKHAM of Swansea to Nathaniel SPOONER.
<39:408> 4 Apr. 1747, Hezekiah TINKHAM of Swansea to William WOOD. Ack. 21 Mar. 1752.
<48:456> 5 Dec. 1746, Hezekiah TINKHAM of Swansea, son of John of Dartmouth & brother of Peter to Jabez JENNE. Ack. 25 Oct. 1765.

BRISTOL COUNTY DEEDS: re: TINKHAM (con-d)

<32:312>	1744,	Isaac TINKHAM to Ephraim LEONARD.
<4:226>	6 June 1695,	John TINKHAM to Thomas HATHAWAY.
<9:687>	14 Sept 1714,	John TINKHAM to Christopher GIFFORD.
<10:5>	14 Oct. 1715,	John TINKHAM to Benjamin CRANE.
<13:478>	13 Aug. 1714,	John TINKHAM to Joseph RUSSELL Jr.
<40:308>	20 June 1741,	John TINKHAM to George BADCOCK. <40:309 - 2 July 1750, G.B. sold>
<41:210>	25 Jan. 1737,	John TINKHAM to George ALLEN. Ack. 2 Oct. 1739 by John & wf Sarah. Witnessed by John TINKHAM Jr.
<49:234>	24 Jan. 1745,	John TINKHAM to Stephen TABER.
<66:40>	12 Sept 1749,	John TINKHAM to William KEMPTON. Sworn by witnesses 24 Jan. 1787, at which time the grantor is dec'd.
<62:269>	1784,	John TINKHAM Jr. et al, agreement to erect a mill.
<36:199>	1748,	Peter TINKHAM to Nathaniel BLACKWELL.
<39:349>	1753,	Peter TINKHAM to Bartholomew TABER.
<41:207>	1754,	Peter TINKHAM to Benjamin PIERCE.
<41:514>	1756,	Peter TINKHAM to Jacob HATHAWAY 2d.
<42:251>	1757,	Peter TINKHAM to Bartholomew WEST.
<42:384>	1757,	Peter TINKHAM to Isaiah ELDRIDGE.
<43:69>	1758,	Peter TINKHAM to Samuel KENNEY.
<44:516>	1761,	Peter TINKHAM to Jacob HATHAWAY.
<47:57>	1764,	Peter TINKHAM to Reuben DELANO.
<47:418>	1765,	Peter TINKHAM to Isaac DREW.
<47:567>	1765,	Peter TINKHAM to Thomas POPE Jr.
<48:454>	1765,	Peter TINKHAM to Jabez JENNE.
<53:384>	1771,	Sarah TINKHAM to Bartholomew WEST.

BRISTOL COUNTY DEEDS: re: TINKHAM (all grantees to 1795)

<1:365>	1694/5,	William BRADFORD Jr. to John TINKHAM et al.
<3:455>	29 Apr. 1675,	Constant SOUTHWORTH to Ephraim TINKHAM et al.
<9:70>	1717,	Mary TOMSON to John TINKHAM.
<62:268>	1784,	Jethro ALLEN to John TINKHAM Jr. et al.
<73:70>	1794,	Darius CHACE to Arthur TINKHAM.

Estate of **Ebenezer TINKHAM** of Boston MA. <Plymouth Co.PR #20827>
<12:431> Warrant & Inventory. (no further details in files)

Estate of **Ebenezer TINKHAM** of Middleboro MA. <Plymouth Co.PR #20829>
<5:158>...7 Nov. 1726, **Shuball/Shubael TINKHAM** of Middleborough app'td admr. on brother's estate. <original> Bond 7 Nov. 1726 of admr. Sureties: John BENNET, James SPROUT, both of Middleborough. Witnesses: Isaac CUSHMAN Jr., Ichabod KING. <5:193> Inventory taken 9 Dec. 1726 by Henry WOOD, John TINKHAM, John BENNETT; incl. homestead, £340; farm he bought of Jacob LOVELL, £80; 13th lot of land in ye little Lott mens Purchase, £16; halfe ye fifteenth lott in sd Purchase, £9; meadow in Winnauxit meadows about 2 acres, £36; halfe a lott of cedar swamp in ye six & twenty mens Purchase, £10. <original> Receipt 26 Apr. 1727, of **Hannah TINKHAM**, widow, for her thirds, £47.17sld. Witnesses: Ephraim WOOD, Robert BARROWS. <original> Receipt 9 June 1727 of **Elizabeth TINKHAM** for £15.18s9d, her share of her father's estate. Witnesses: Ephraim WOOD, Mary TINKHAM (mark). Receipt 9 June 1727 of **Mary TINKHAM** for £15.8s9d, her share of father's estate. Witnesses: Ephraim WOOD, Elizabeth TINKHAM (mark). Receipt 9 June 1727 of Ephraim WOOD as guardian for **Peter TINKHAM Precela/Priscilla TINKHAM** and **Patience TINKHAM**, for their share in their father's estate. Witnesses: Elizabeth TINKHAM & Mary TINKHAM (both by mark). <5:227,228> Guardianship 22 Mar. 1726/7, Ephraim WOOD of Middleborough was chosen guardian of **Peter TINKHAM** (betw 14-21) and appointed guardian of **Patience TINKHAM** and **Priscilla TINKHAM** (both under 14). Bonds 22 Mar. 1726/7. Surety: Thomas TOMSON. Witnesses: John TOMSON, Jacob TOMSON.

Guardianship of Child of **Ebenezer TINKHAM** of Middleboro MA. <Plymouth Co.PR #20838>
<4:324>...16 May 1722, **Ebenezer TINKHAM** app'd guardian of his daughter **Elisabeth TINKHAM**, minor betw 14-21, who chose her father.

Will of **Edmund WOOD** of Middleborough MA. <Plymouth Co.PR #23342>
<40:387>...dated 3 June 1791, mentions children: **Edmond WOOD Jr., Joshua WOOD 2d, Francis WOOD, Peter WOOD, Patience SMITH** wf of Lt. James and **Priscilla CHURCHILL** wf of Perez. Codicil 10 Apr. 1800. <40:388> Pr. 4 Feb. 1806.

John WOOD/WOODS of Bridgewater MA to **Heirs of Peter TINKHAM.** <Plymouth Co.Deeds 49:65>
...12 Feb. 1755, John WOOD, yeoman & wf Priscilla...quit claim to the heirs of Peter TINKHAM, now dec'd, all rights in land they formerly sold to Peter, said land formerly belonging to Ebenezer TINKHAM, dec'd..."and whereas we are informed the said deed is not upon record, but lost..." Witnesses: Josiah EDSON Jr, Josiah DUNBAR. Rec. 15 May 1764.

Estate of **Jeremiah TINKHAM** of Middleboro MA. <Plymouth Co.PR #20867>
<4:146>...17 July 1718, **Joanna TINKHAM,** widow, app'td admx. <4:139> Inventory 17 July 1718.. <4:217> Settlement 24 June 1720.

Guardianship of Children of **Jeremiah TINKHAM** of Middleboro MA. <Plymouth Co.PR #20868> <4:343,344;5:404> Letters re guardianship of **Joanna TINKHAM, Jeremiah TINKHAM** and **Ebenezer TINKHAM.** <7:385> "Acquital" by **Jeremiah TINKHAM,** 1737. (no further dates or details given in files)

Will of **Jeremiah TINKHAM** of Middleboro MA. <Plymouth Co.PR>
<31:218>...dated 2 June 1790, mentions wife **Naomi** & her father **John WARREN,** dec'd, of Middleboro; children: **Jeremiah TINKHAM, Elisha TINKHAM, Jesse TINKHAM, James TINKHAM, Abigail TINKHAM, Huldah TINKHAM, Anna WARREN** and **Ebenezer TINKHAM;** brother **Ebenezer TINKHAM;** grandson **Tiler TINKHAM.** <31:221> Pr. 5 July 1790. Warrant for Inventory 1 July 1790. <33:190> Account of executor.

Will of **Simeon CURTIS,** gentleman of Hanover MA. <Plymouth Co.PR>
<37:214>...dated 4 Mar. 1794, mentions wf **Lucy;** children: **Melzar CURTIS, James CURTIS, Simeon CURTIS, Barker CURTIS** and **Mary YOUNG;** granddaughter **Asenath STETSON;** grandson **Charles STETSON.** Witnesses: Joseph SOPER, Relief SOPER, Calvin CURTIS. Pr. 31 Mar. 1800.

PLYMOUTH COUNTY DEEDS:

<56:196> 6 Feb. 1772, Thomas MACOMBER Jr. to brother William MACOMBER.
<56:196> 4 Apr. 1772, Thomas MACOMBER to brother Onesimus MACOMBER.
<58:55> 25 Apr. 1774, Thomas MACOMBER, yeoman of Marshfield & wf Leah to brother Onesimus MACOM.
<60:34> ( ), Thomas MACOMBER Jr. & Prudence to William MACOMBER.
<62:42> 7 Apr. 1783, Thomas MACOMBER of Marshfield & wf Leah to Daniel LEWIS of Marshfield.
<74:28> 25 Dec. 1787, Thomas MACOMBER & brother Onesimus MACOMBER, both of Marshfield.
<105:3> 1 Dec. 1804, Ichabod MACOMBER of Randolph MA sells land in Bridgewater to Edwin HOWARD of Bridgewater.

Ichabod MACOMBER of Boston MA to **Zadock LEACH** of Bridgewater MA. <Plymouth Co.Deeds 155:226> ...4 Oct. 1823, Ichabod MACOMBER sells his rights in widow's thirds as set off from estate of Zacoc LEACH, dec'd, of Bridgewater, being an undivided right in said thirds. Wf Abigail releases her right of dower.

Ichabod MACOMBER et al of Boston MA to **George W. PERKINS** of Augusta ME.<Plymouth Co.Deeds 164:29> ...15 Feb. 1828, Ichabod MACOMBER & wf Abigail and Ezekiel (SAWIN)sp? & wf Martha, all of Boston, sell to George W. PERKINS, land at West Bridgewater.

Thomas MACOMBER of Bridgewater MA to **Perez SOUTHWORTH** of Bridgewater MA. <Plymouth Co.Deeds 92:2> ...16 Jan. 1801, Thomas MACOMBER & wf Prudence, for $166.66, sell to Perez SOUTHWORTH, land at Bridgewater. Witnesses: Ichabod MACOMBER, Isaac MACOMBER. (The same day Thomas & Prudence sold land in Bridgewater for $166.66 to Benjamin & Elizabeth CROSSWELL. <124:37>)

Thomas MACOMBER of Jay ME to **Thomas WHITE** of Bridgewater MA. <Plymouth Co.Deeds 92:257> ...26 May 1801, Thomas MACOMBER & wf Prudence, for $23.00, sell to Thomas WHITE land in Bridgewater. Witnesses: Joseph ALDEN, Winchester MACOMBER.

Guardianship of Children of **Shubael TINKHAM** of Middleboro MA. <Plymouth Co.PR #20835> <8:38-41;9:53>...1739, guardianship for **Ebenezer TINKHAM, Perez TINKHAM, Sarah TINKHAM, Priscilla TINKHAM** and **Joseph TINKHAM.** (no further details given in files)

Will of **Ephraim TINKHAM** of Middleboro MA. <Plymouth Co.PR>
<3:358>...dated 17 Sept. 1714, mentions wf **Esther,** named executrix; children: **John TINKHAM** (eldest son), **Isaac TINKHAM, Samuel TINKHAM, Martha SOUL, Mary TINKHAM** and **Ephraim TINKHAM,** dec'd. Pr. 3 Mar. 1714/5 <3:359> Inventory 22 Nov. 1714. <3:360> Oath to inventory, 19 Sept. 1715 by executrix.

Isaac TINKHAM et al of Middleboro MA to **John TINKHAM** of Middleboro MA. <Plymouth Co.Deeds 26:194> ...1 Mar. 1731/2, Isaac TINKHAM, Samuel TINKHAM, John SOULE & wf Martha, Henry WOOD & wf Mary, sell their rights in 100 acre lot where our Honoured Father Ephraim TINKHAM dwelt and was given to him by his son Ephraim TINKHAM, dec'd, of Middleborough. (See below.)

Will of **Ephraim TINKHAM** of Plymouth MA. <Plymouth Co.PR 4:222>
...dated 17 Jan. 1683. Pr. 5 June 1685. (no further details in files)

MICRO #2 OF 5

Will of **William CURTIS** of Pembroke MA. <Plymouth Co.PR 54:230>
...dated 18 Aug. 1818. Pr. 19 Nov. 1821. (No details given other than the mention of daughter **Lydia CROOKER.**)

Guardianship of Children of **Ephraim TINKHAM** of Middleboro MA. <Plymouth Co.PR #20843> <5:378>...2 Feb. 1727, **Ephraim TINKHAM** and **Moses TINKHAM,** age 14-21, choose James SOULE of Middleboro as their guardian.

Aaron SIMMONS to heirs of **Ephraim TINKHAM** of Middleboro MA. <Plymouth Co.Deeds 28:151> ...31 Aug. 1730, Aaron SIMMONS & wf Martha, in consideration of the yearly rents already due for the farm or homestead that was Ephraim TINKHAM's and given him by his father Ephraim TINKHAM, dec'd, of Middleboro, and also that upper meadow, so called in the 26 men's purchase, for the next seven years quit their claim unto the now heirs, namely **John TINKHAM, Isaac TINKHAM, Samuel TINKHAM, John SOULE** & wf **Martha, Henry WOOD** & wf **Mary** who quit their claim to rents.

Estate of **Seth TINKHAM** of Middleboro MA. <Plymouth Co.PR #20908>
<17:150>..31 Aug. 1765, adm. granted to **Amos TINKHAM**, laborer, of Middleboro. Sureties: Joseph TINKHAM, Esq., Israel TINKHAM, yeoman, both of Middleboro. Witnesses: Edward WINSLOW, Tho. TORREY

Will of **John TINKHAM**, yeoman of Middleboro MA. <Plymouth Co.PR #20870>
<19:370>...dated 13 Feb. 1766, mentions wf **Hannah**; to son **John TINKHAM** that tract of land whereon he now dwells which did formerly belong to **Governor PRINCE**; son **Abisha TINKHAM**; to **Amos TINKHAM** land bought of John VAUGHAN; dau **Esther VAUGHAN**; to daus **Hannah WESTON, Susannah COBB, Mary WESTON** and **Zilpah MILLER**, land formerly belonging to my brother **Seth TINKHAM**, dec'd, and land bought of Samuel BENNET; son **Amos** shall keep for his mother two cows both winter & summer, pay to her yearly one quarter part of the corn & grain, cyder & apples and flax together with one quarter part of whatever else is raised on said land (hay & grass excepted), and also find for her a horse to ride for her necessary riding, find her fire wood brought to the house & cut fit for the fire. Sons **John** & **Amos** named executors. Witnesses: Thomas TUPPER, Micah BRYANT, Joseph TINKHAM. <19:370> Pr. 23 May 1766.

Estate of **Ephraim TINKHAM** of Middleboro MA. <Plymouth Co.PR #20844>
<original> Petition 21 Nov. 1769 of **Sarah TINKHAM**, widow, that **Silas TINKHAM** be app'td admr. Witnesses: Joshua EDDY, Fear TINKHAM. <20:357> 28 Feb. 1770, administration granted to **Silas TINKHAM** of Middleboro. Sureties: Jacob SOULE, Daniel THOMAS, of Middleboro. <20:380> Inventory, 9 Mar. 1770. <21:357> Petition 21 Feb. 1774, of William SHAW, guardian of the children, with the consent of Adam WRIGHT & wf Sarah, who is the mother of the children, to sell land. (four children, the eldest a daughter, youngest a son age about four). Petition granted 8 Mar. 1774.

Guardianship of Children of **Ephraim TINKHAM** of Middleboro MA. <Plymouth Co.PR #20845>
...21 June 1773, **Sarah WRIGHT** requests that William SHAW of Middleboro be app'td guardian to her four children, viz: **Abigail TINKHAM** (above 14), **Sarah, Ephraim** and **Samuel TINKHAM** (all under 14).

Caleb LEACH et al to **Peter WOOD** of Middleborough MA. <Plymouth Co.Deeds 77:166>
...12 Apr. 1791, Caleb LEACH, Silver SMITH & wf Abigail, of Plymouth, Ephraim TINKUM/TINKHAM, husbandman and Samuel TINKUM/TINKHAM, Physician, both of Middleborough, for £12 sold to Peter WOOD, yeoman...all our right in a two & a quarter acre meadow in Plimton at a place called Winnotuxit...that our Honoured father Mr. Ephraim TINKUM/TINKHAM, dec'd, purchased of our Honoured Grandfather Mr. Samuel TINKUM/TINKHAM, dec'd, as by deed on record 53:57,58. Witnesses: Jesse HARLOW, Ephraim SPOONER. Rec. 21 Mar. 1795.

Ephraim SPOONER of Plymouth MA to **Caleb LEACH** of Halifax MA. <Plymouth Co.Deeds 67:276>
...2 May 1789, Ephraim SPOONER, Esq., for £100, sold to Caleb LEACH, watch maker...dwelling house and garden in Plymouth that I purchased of the estate of Mr. James SHURTLEFF, dec'd..bounded easterly by Main St., southerly by land of John BARTLETT, westerly by the road at the foot of the Burying Hill and northerly by the land of the heirs of Mr. John RUSSELL, dec'd, together with one half the well...the other half owned by said John BARTLETT. Wf Elizabeth SPOONER releases dower.

Caleb LEACH of Halifax MA to **Thomas DAVIS** of Plymouth MA. <Plymouth Co.Deeds 68:262>
..2 May 1789, Caleb LEACH, watch maker, for £70, mortgages to Thomas DAVIS, merchant, the house & garden bought the same day from Ephraim SPOONER (above). Rec. 9 Oct. 1789. Released 17 Sept 1798.

Estate of **Caleb TINKHAM** of Plymouth MA. <Plymouth Co.PR>
<17:152>...26 Oct. 1765, Joseph RIDER of Plymouth app'td admr. <19:300> Inventory 29 Oct. 1765. <19:301> Order to distribute among his five children, viz: **Mercy TINKHAM, Patience TINKHAM, Fear WATERMAN,** representatives of **Sarah SMITH** and **Nelle BRYANT.**

Guardianship of Child of **Ebenezer TINKAM/TINKHAM** of Plympton MA. <Plymouth Co.PR #20906>
<11:76>...21 Nov. 1747, William BONNEY, husbandman of Plympton, app'td guardian of **Sarah TINKHAM**, minor. Surety: Ebenezer TINKAM/TINKHAM, seafaringman of Plymouth. 23 Nov. 1747, **Sarah TINKUM**, minor, chose...my Uncle William BONNEY...to be my guardian in estate of my Grandfather William BONNEY, dec'd, of Plimton.

Estate of **Hilkiah TINKHAM**, mariner. <Plymouth Co.PR #20856>
...1746...<10:372,373;11:100,107,164,165;19:28,138;10:485,486;11:441;12:354>..no further details.

Estate of **Ebenezer TINKHAM.** <Plymouth Co.PR 11:441>
...Receipt of heirs, 1 Sept. 1750; received of **Elizabeth TINKHAM** "as she is guardian to Ebenezer TINKHAM"...full share of estate of Ebenezer TINKHAM. Signed by Benjamin EATON, Isaac TINKHAM, Ruth TINKHAM, Elizabeth SANDERS, Sarah TINKHAM, Hannah TINKHAM, Elizabeth TINKHAM as guardian to Lydia TINKHAM, Martha SYLVESTER and Zedekiah TINKHAM.

Guardianship of Children of **Hilkiah TINKHAM** of Plymouth MA. <Plymouth Co.PR #20836>
<10:485,486>...1747...**Ebenezer TINKHAM, Lydia TINKHAM, Ruth TINKHAM.** <11:107> Letter. <11:441> Receipt. <12:354> Account.

Estate of **Isaac TINKHAM** of Halifax MA. <Plymouth Co.PR #20864>
...1750...<11:458> Administration by son **Isaac.**. <12:73> Inventory. <15:212,213> Receipts. <15::225> Account. (No further data in files. A pencilled note states "Deacon Isaac d. 7 Apr. 1750.")

Will of **William CURTIS**, gentleman of Pembroke MA. <Plymouth Co.PR>
<54:230>...dated 19 Aug. 1818, mentions daus **Hannah, Polly TRASK, Lydia CROOKER**; sons **James CURTIS, Jacob CURTIS** and heirs of son **William CURTIS**, dec'd. Pr. 19 Nov. 1821. <54:342> Warrant to appraise; Inventory. <54:302> Notice of appointment. <58:51> Account of executor.

Estate of **William CURTIS**, yeoman of Duxbury MA. <Plymouth Co.PR>
...1811...<39:318> Letters of administration. <44:14> Warrant & Inventory. <44:15> Adm. notice. <44:15> Estate rendered insolvent. <44:297> Warrant & list of claims. <44:298> Warrant & dower to widow **Olive**, 11 Oct. 1811. <44:392> Oath, sale of real estate. <44:453> Bond to secure sales. <44:454> Notice for sale of real estate; Account of admr. <44:455> Warrant to distribute.

John GRAY of Plymouth MA to **Anna TINCOM/TINKHAM** of Plymouth MA. <Plymouth Co.Deeds 11:251>
...2 May 1716, John GRAY, yeoman to dau Anna TINCOM and son in law John TINCOM...land in Plymouth on which their house now stands bounded by land of Thomas HOWLAND. Witnesses: Thomas CROADE, Anne PALMER. Rec. same day.

John GRAY of Plymouth MA to **John TINKCOM/TINKHAM** of Plymouth MA. <Plymouth Co.Deeds 21:96>
...12 Feb. 1725/6, John GRAY for one shilling sells to John TINKCOM...one tract of land lying below the land which he now owns, viz: from high water mark & so downwards provided ye said Tinkcom make & keep a sufficient stone wall from the high water mark down to the lowermost round rock forever...Witnesses: Peter TOMSON, Giles RICKARD. Rec. 31 Jan. 1726.

Estate of **John TINKHAM** of Kingston MA. <Plymouth Co.PR>
<5:745>...31 July 1730, Samuel GRAY of Kingston, app'td admr. Sureties: Joseph MICHELL, Ebenezer FULLER. Witnesses: James WARREN, Mercy THOMAS. <5:785> Warrant to appraise, 31 July 1730, to Francis ADAMS, Joseph MITCHELL, Seth CHIPMAN, all of Kingston. <5:786> Inventory taken 23 Nov. 1730 by the three appraisers; incl. dwelling house, barn & land, £330; fish house by the waterside, £5; meadow at Barnstable, £15. <10:205> Appraisal of real estate, 2 Feb. 1745/6 by Joseph MITCHELL, John BREWSTER, John COOPER; incl. twelve acre homestead, at £35 per acre, £420; fifty five acre woodlot, at fifty shillings per acre, £135.15s; salt marsh at Barnstable, £37. <10:206> "The following account of Samuel GRAY his admn. on the Estate of John TINKHAM late of Kingston deceased is by Thomas BURTON & Patience GRAY the admrs. on the Estate of the said Samuel offered for allowance". Guardianship of Children: <5:820,7:454> **Edward TINKHAM**; <5:821,7:454> **John TINKHAM, Ephraim TINKHAM**; <5:822,8:11> **Joseph TINKHAM**; <5:822,8:12> **Anna TINKHAM.**

Edward TINKHAM of Kingston MA to **Benjamin LOTHROP** of Kingston MA. <Plymouth Co.Deeds 38:104>
...1 Aug. 1746, Edward TINKHAM, nailer, for £600 old tenor, sold to Benjamin LOTHROP, gentleman, the whole of the real estate that my Honoured Father **John TINKHAM** late of Kingston dec'd died seized of, said lands lying in Kingston and Barnstable...viz: the homestead of the said John TINKHAM containing about twelve acres bounded by land of John COOKE, dec'd, on the north side, Samuel GRAY late of Kingston, dec'd, on the south side, on the east by the bay or salt water, on the west by the countrey road that leads from Plymouth to Boston, reserving to the heirs of Capt. Joseph HOWLAND, dec'd and heirs of John GRAY, dec'd, a cart way of twenty four foot wide through said land...And also I sell...the fifty five acre wood lot that belonged to my Honoured father John TINKHAM, dec'd and Anne his wife, the same wood land which John GRAY, late of Plimouth, husbandman, dec'd...gave to John TINKHAM & Anna his wf as per deed dated 2 May 1716...Also a piece of salt marsh in Barnstable which the said John TINKHAM purchased of Ebenezer COBB Jr. late of Plymouth as per deed dated 11 Jan. 1720/1, Reference being had to said deed and to two Grants made & granted by the Town of Barnstable unto Barnabas LOTHROP, Esq. late of said Barnstable, deceased, one of which grants was made on 1 June 1668 and the other on 17 July 1669. Signed by Edward & Lydia TINKHAM. Witnesses: Edward WINSLOW, Enoch WARD. Rec. 29 Aug. 1746.

Edward TINKHAM of Kingston MA to **Benjamin PRIOR** of Duxborough MA. <Plymouth Co.Deeds 47:107>
...6 May 1761, Edward TINKHAM, nailer, for £53.6s8d, sold to Benjamin PRIOR, tanner...forty acres in Kingston bounded by land of: John "Mararthththling" Jr., Nathan WRIGHT, Joseph HOLMES. Signed by Edward & Lydia TINKHAM. Witnesses: Nathan WRIGHT, Judah HALL. Rec. 24 Nov. 1761.

Edward TINKHAM of New Yarmouth, N.S. to **Elisha BREWSTER** of Kingston MA.<Plymouth Co.Deeds 57:251>
...28 Nov. 1770, Edward TINKHAM of New Yarmouth in the County of Queen's County, In the Province of Hallifax in Nova Scotia, husbandman, for £200 sold to Elisha BREWSTER, trader...a certain farm in Kingston, being the whole of land I formerly bought of three certain men, viz: James LOW, Seth CHIPMAN and Michael SAMSON; all three lots containing about one hundred acres...together with a dwelling house, barn, orchard, wood & fencing, with a reserve for a cart way, agreeable to a reserve made by the said CHIPMAN in his deed. Witnesses: Ephraim BRADFORD, Elisha HALL. Rec. 12 Mar. 1774.

Ephraim TINKHAM of Middlebury MA to **John TINKHAM** of Dartmouth MA. <Bristol Co.Deeds 7:418>
...15 Apr. 1696, Ephraim TINKHAM, yeoman, for £14, sells to brother John TINKHAM, two parts of eight of one third of a share of land in Dartmouth. Witnesses: John ALLYN, Mary ALLYN. Rec. 29 Nov. 1712.

Peter TINKHAM et al to **John TINKHAM.** <Bristol Co.Deeds 7:455>
...16 June 1696, Peter TINKHAM of Middleboro, Elkiah TINKHAM of Plymouth and Isaac TINKHAM of Plymouth, for Ł21, sell all our rights & interest in two thirds of a whole share of land that was our Honoured Father **Ephraim TINKHAM**'s, late of Plimouth, dec'd, our two thirds being three parts of eight. Witnesses: James COLE, Eleazer RICKARD. Rec. 7 Jan. 1712/3

==========

Elkiah TINKHAM of Plymouth MA to **John TINKHAM** of Dartmouth MA. <Bristol Co.Deeds 7:457>
...6 Nov. 1689, Elkiah TINCOM/TINKHAM to brother John TINCOM/TINKHAM, all that land given to me by my father **Ephraim TINKHAM,** of Plimouth, dec'd, lying in Dartmouth, being the one third share. Witnesses: Thomas FAUNCE, Joan FAUNCE. Rec. 7 Jan. 1712/3

==========

Ebenezer TINKHAM & **John THOMSON** of Middleboro MA to **John TINKHAM.** <Bristol Co.Deeds 9:65>
...6 July 1714, Ebenezer TINKHAM and John THOMSON, for Ł90, sell to brother John TINKHAM, two eighths part of one third part of one whole share. 19 Mar. 1715/6 Mary TOMSON releases her right.

MICRO #3 OF 5

...13 Nov. 1694, **Maj. William BRADFORD** confirms grant to proprietors of Dartmouth, which includes Abraham TUCKER and John TINKHAM. <Bristol Co.Deeds 1:365>

==========

Dartmouth Proprietors... <Bristol Co.Deeds; New Bedford copy 1:11>
(no date)...Peter BROWN's share: Abraham TUCKER claims one third part of said share as appears by deed from said TUCKER's father to said TUCKER...date 7 Sept. 1686; John TINKCOM/TINKHAM claims for himself and his brothers two thirds of said share; Abraham TUCKER ( ) 40 acres by deed from Giles SLOCUM bearing date 16 Apr. 1701, 20 acres of said land sold to John TUCKER, said TUCKER ( ) acres by deed from James SAMSON.

==========

Estate of **John TINKCOM/TINKHAM**, yeoman of Dartmouth MA. <Bristol Co.PR>
<9:314>...15 Jan. 1739, adm. granted to **John TINKCOM/TINKHAM,** yeoman, of Dartmouth, son of the deceased. <9:386> Inventory 26 Feb. 1739/40, incl. 258 acre homestead on east side of Acushnet River, bounded on the north by heirs of Jonathan HATHAWAY, Ł2058; 8 acre meadow at foot of homestead, Ł200; 7 acres at Sconticut Neck, Ł30; 35 acres at Peaked Rock, Ł175; 25 acres at Peaked Rock, Ł125; 21 acres at Puranopit, Ł94; 52 acres & 65 acres eastward from Puranopi, Ł234, Ł227; 120 acres west of homestead, Ł360; undivided land, Ł100; 49 acres farm land east of Acushnet River, bounding north on Philip TABOR's homestead, Ł500; 10 acre meadow at Skipping Creek, Ł200; 3 acre meadow on Miery Neck, Ł60; one acre meadow on Newland's Neck, Ł21; two thirds share in Cedar Swamp, Ł150. <original> Division of real estate, 20 Apr. 1741 to the children, viz: **John TINKHAM** (eldest son), **Peter TINKHAM, Hezekiah TINKHAM, Mary TABOR, Martha TINKHAM.** <9:481> Account. Guardianship of Children: <9:364> 18 Mar. 1739, Henry SAMPSON, yeoman of Dartmouth, chosen guardian by **Hesekiah/Hezekiah TINKHAM** and **Martha TINKHAM** (both betw. 14-21). <9:365> 18 Mar. 1739 Joseph TABOR, yeoman of Dartmouth, chosen guardian by **Peter TINKHAM** (14-21). (Note: **Hezekiah TINKHAM** is also called **Elkiah TINKHAM** in these records.)

==========

Hezekiah TINKHAM of Swanzey MA to **Gamaliel HATHAWAY** of Dartmouth MA. <Bristol Co.Deeds 36:195>
...1 Dec. 1746, Hezekiah TINKHAM, laboror, for Ł39, sold to Gamaliel HATHAWAY, yeoman...a certain piece of salt meadow...at ye foot of the homestead that did belong to my father Mr. **John TINKHAM,** late of Dartmouth, dec'd and is since set off to my brother John TINKHAM. Witnesses: Jethro DELANO, Paul MANDALL. Rec. 6 May 1748.

==========

John TINKHAM of Dartmouth MA to **Stephen TABER** of Dartmouth MA. <Bristol Co.Deeds 49:234>
...24 Jan. 1745, John TINKHAM, yeoman, for Ł30, sold to Stephen TABER, yeoman...all that my right of ceder swamp in Dartmouth that doth belong to me in right of heirship by lineal decent from my honoured father **John PECKHAM** late of said Dartmouth, dec'd, it being two sixth parts of all ye ceder swamp my said father died seized off/of his right being then two thirds of one whole shear/share in ye sixteen acre division of Ceder Swamp in Dartmouth. Witnesses: Peter TINKHAM, Hezekiah TINKHAM. Rec. 30 Oct. 1765.

==========

BRISTOL COUNTY DEEDS (re: ELLIS)

<43:213>	1755,	Joseph ELLIS, late of Harwich, now of Dartmouth.
<43:435>	1757,	Joseph ELLIS, cordwainer, late of Harwich, now of Dartmouth.
<53:383>	10 Apr. 1759,	Joseph & Martha ELLIS, Martha's mother Sarah TINKHAM acknowledges.
<53:42>	1769,	Joseph & Martha ELLIS to son Seth ELLIS.
<55:66>	1770,	Joseph ELLIS to son Seth ELLIS.
<58:70>	30 Mar. 1777,	Joseph & Martha ELLIS.
<62:263>	6 Jan. 1783,	Joseph & Martha ELLIS, Seth ELLIS, Luke ELLIS, Elijah ELLIS.
<62:15>	21 Jan. 1783,	Joseph & Martha ELLIS to son John ELLIS.
<62:16>	21 Jan. 1783,	Joseph & Martha ELLIS to sons Elijah ELLIS, Luke ELLIS, John ELLIS.
<69:136>	26 Feb. 1790,	Seth ELLIS sells land; parents Joseph & Martha ELLIS consent.

(Additional citations pertaining to surname ELLIS (possibly Joseph & Martha), with no details given, viz: 36:17,233;39:349;40:135,232;42:426;43:214;46:215 (1763); 53:270,325 (1770),381 (1755) 382 (1759); 74:174;77:261;84:244;94:70;95:252;116:511;140:389. The files also state that the Bristol County Probate Records were checked for the following but no records were found, viz: Elizabeth ELLIS, Luke ELLIS, Joseph ELLIS, Elijah ELLIS.

Joseph ELLIS of Dartmouth MA to **John TABER Jr.** of Dartmouth MA. <Bristol Co.Deeds 43:213>
...17 Feb. 1755, Joseph ELLIS, cordwainer, & wf Martha, late of Harwich, now Inhabitant of Dartmouth, for Ł17, sold to John TABER Jr., mariner, land in Dartmouth.

Joseph ELLIS of Dartmouth MA to **Bartholomew WEST** of Dartmouth MA. <Bristol Co.Deeds 53:383>
...9 May 1758, Joseph ELLIS, cordwainer & wf Martha, for Ł14, sold to Bartholomew WEST, yeoman, seven and one half acres in Dartmouth...and **Sarah TINKOM/TINKHAM** ye mother of ye said Martha ELLIS...doth quit her right of dower. Ack. 10 Apr. 1759 by the three grantors.

Henry JENNE to **Luke ELLIS** & **Elijah ELLIS** of Dartmouth MA. <Bristol Co.Deeds 59:121>
...31 Jan. 1778, Henry JENNE sold to Luke ELLIS & Elijah ELLIS, labourers, the six acres in Dartmouth he had bought from Seth ELLIS. Rec. 1 Feb. 1779.

Joseph ELLIS et al of Dartmouth MA to **Richard DELANO** of Dartmouth MA. <Bristol Co.Deeds 62:263>
...6 Jan. 1783, Joseph ELLIS, yeoman & wf Martha, Seth ELLIS, yeoman, Luke ELLIS & Elijah ELLIS, labourers, for $200.00 sold to Richard DELANO, yeoman, sixty acres in Dartmouth.

Joseph ELLIS of Dartmouth MA to **Elijah ELLIS** of Dartmouth MA. <Bristol Co.Deeds 62:16>
...21 Jan. 1783, Joseph ELLIS, yeoman, for Ł60, sold to my son Elijah ELLIS, labourer, land in Dartmouth partly bounded by my son Seth ELLIS' land.

Joseph ELLIS of Dartmouth MA to **Luke ELLIS** of Dartmouth MA. <Bristol Co.Deeds 62:16>
...21 Jan. 1783, Joseph ELLIS, yeoman, & wf Martha, for Ł40, sold to my son Luke ELLIS...all the land that remains between my son John ELLIS & Samuel PROCTOR's land.

Seth ELLIS to **Luke ELLIS.** <Bristol Co.Deeds 72:356>
...9 Apr. 1785, Seth ELLIS sells to Luke ELLIS, cordwainer, nineteen and a half acres of land he bought from his father Joseph ELLIS. Rec. 8 Feb. 1794.

Division of land of **Joseph ELLIS** of New Bedford. <Bristol Co.Deeds 78:309>
...15 Apr. 1788, **Seth, Luke, John** and **Elijah ELLIS**, sons of Joseph, all of New Bedford, divide land bought from their father who signs by a mark. Witnesses: Samuel SPRAGUE, Martha ELLIS (wf of Joseph). Rec. 2 Nov. 1799. <78:310> 30 Sept. 1799, **Elijah ELLIS** sells his part of above with wf Elizabeth signing.

Seth ELLIS of New Bedford to **Samuel PROCTER** of New Bedford MA. <Bristol Co.Deeds 69:136>
...26 Feb. 1790, Seth ELLIS, yeoman, for Ł7.5s9d, sold to Samuel PROCTER, land in New Bedford... and Joseph ELLIS, yeoman of New Bedford, the father of the said Seth, and Martha his wife...doth surrender all his & her right...

Luke ELLIS of Fairhaven MA to **Abraham TINKHAM** of Rochester MA. <Bristol Co.Deeds 96:246>
...27 Dec. 1813, Luke ELLIS, cordwainer, for $200.00 sold to Abraham TINKHAM, yeoman, his homestead farm in Fairhaven.

Estate of **Seth ELLIS** of New Bedford. <Bristol Co.PR>
<47:231> Warrant for inventory, 1 May 1812, mentions nineteen and a half acres valued at $90.00. <150:523> Administration 5 May 1812, Manasseh KEMPTON, gentleman, of New Bedford, app'td admr. <47:249> Account 5 May 1812 of admr.; incl. bill of **Thankful ELLIS** which was paid by the town of New Bedford. <48:229> 2nd Account 4 May 1813; two lots, seven acres and twelve and a half acres sold to Thankful ELLIS. <48:242> Notice of sale, (no date), of two lots of land joining that of **Luke ELLIS**, being the only real estate of Seth ELLIS'; notices posted at house of Luke ELLIS and house of Thankful ELLIS which was "the place where Seth ELLIS last lived".

Estate of **Naomi ELLIS** of New Bedford MA. <Bristol Co.PR>
<original> Petition 15 Mar. 1864, "Caleb G. SHEPARD of New Bedford, friend, represents at the request of Sarah E. MAXIM, a sister of the alledged insane person that Naomi ELLIS...of New Bedford ...is an insane person" and prays that he or someone be app'td guardian...I Sarah E. MAXIM, widow of Nathan MAXIM, deceased, and next of kin of the said Naomi ELLIS and sister, unite in the above petition. <original> Petition 30 Mar. 1864, Caleb G. SHEPHERD represents that **Naomi ELLIS** died 29 Mar. 1864 and the only next of kin or heirs are: Joseph P. ELLIS, brother; Benjamin R. ELLIS, of Croghan NY, brother; Mary BENNETT wf of John, of Jamestown, Iowa, sister; Lavinia HAMMOND, widow, Philadelphia, Jefferson co. NY, sister; only children of deceased sister Eliza WASHBURN, viz: William WASHBURN & James WASHBURN of California and Charles WASHBURN of Mass.; Sarah E. MAXIM, widow, of New Bedford, sister; Harvey FARRINGTON & George B. FARRINGTON, Brooklyn NY, only suriving children of Deborah M. FARRINGTON, dec'd sister.
<106:111> Bond of admr., 20 May 1864 of Joseph P. ELLIS of Antwerp, Jefferson co., NY, on estate of Naomie ELLIS, dec'd. <166:569> 20 May 1864, Caleb G. SHEPARD, Joseph P. ELLIS and Sarah E. MAXIM each asked to be app'td admr. <106:112> 20 May 1864, Joseph P. ELLIS and Sarah MAXAM, brother & sister of dec'd, app'td admrs.. <120:253> Notice 1 June 1864 of Sarah MAXIM. <195:332> Appraisers app'td, 28 July 1864. <217:216> 1st Account of admrs, 19 Oct. 1864. <217:552> Final Account, 5 Jan. 1866 of Sarah E. MAXIM, admx. Interested parties: C.G. SHEPARD, attorney for Mrs. Lavinia HAMMOND; William G. WHITE, attorney for C.F. WASHBURN, James M. WASHBURN and William H. WASHBURN; William C. COFFIN as attorney for Benjamin R. ELLIS, Harry FARRINGTON/FARMINGTON and George B. FARRINGTON/FARMINGTON; Joseph ELLIS.

Samuel TINKHAM Jr. of Middleborough MA to **Shubael TINKHAM, Joseph BATE.** <Plymouth Co.Deeds 20:56> ...29 Sept. 1725, Samuel TINKHAM Jr. sells to Shubael TINKHAM and Joseph BATE, of Middleboro... meadow in Plimpton which...did formerly belong unto my Honoured Father **Peter TINKHAM** and my Uncle **Ebenezer TINKHAM.** (A division of land, 15 Feb. 1725, between Samuel TINKHAM Jr. and Seth TINKHAM states their father, Peter TINKHAM was dec'd. <Plymouth Co.Deeds 22:166>)

Guardianship of Child of **Peter TINKHAM** of Middlebury MA. <Plymouth Co.PR #20904>
<4:28> 19 Sept. 1717, John BENNIT Jr. of Middlebury was app'td guardian of **Samuel TINKHAM**, minor (14-21), son of Peter TINKHAM, dec'd. Bond 18 Sept. 1717, of guardian. Witnesses: Richard BARNFIELD, Thomas CROADE.

Estate of **Peter TINKHAM.** <Original, no source or date given; See entry below>
Petition of **Mercy TINKHAM**, widow. Honoured Collonel: I would humbly request that in the Settling of the Estate of my late husband: that your honour would be pleased to State the home Stead unto my Eldest Son: **Samuel**: together with the four acres of meadow at winatuxet meadows: and unto my youngest Son **Seth** the two hundred acre lots of the last division in 26 mens purchase with the meadow in the upper meadow and the lower meadow and that the Share of cedar Swamp may be Equally divided between them two: and that my Eldest daughter **Mercy** might have the whole share in the Sixteen shilling purchase and in assawamset neck: and that my youngest daughter **Joanna** might have the five and twenty acre lot at tomsons Bridges: and the whole share in the South purchase: So I Rest your honours humble servant **Mercy TINKHAM.** ("probably in handwriting of Jacob TOMSON")

Estate of **Peter TINKHAM** of Middleboro MA. <Plymouth Co.PR #20895> (See above)
<2:115> Inventory appraised 2 Mar. 1709/10, by Adam WRIGHT & Ebenezer TINKCOM/TINKHAM; total Ł182.7s6d. (See entry above for real estate.) Oath to inventory 10 Mar. 1709/10, by **Mercy TINCUM/TINKHAM**, admx. <unrecorded> Bond of admx. 10 Mar. 1709/10. Surety: Adam WRIGHT of Plympton. Witnesses: Joseph OTIS, Stephen BARNEBE. <unrecorded> Warrant 23 June 1710, Capt. Jacob TOMSON of Middlebury, Adam WRIGHT & Jonathan SHAW of Plimton, app'td to appraise the several percells of land. <3:56> Inventory taken 5 Sept. 1710 by the three appraisers; total Ł135. <3:57> Settlement of estate, 22 Sept. 1710, to children **Samuel TINKHAM, Seth TINKHAM, Mercy TINKHAM, Joanna TINKHAM** (as shown in above Petition).

Patience TINKHAM of Middleboro MA to **Peter TINKHAM** of Middleboro MA. <Plymouth Co.Deeds 42:202> ...16 Mar. 1743, Patience TINKHAM sells to brother Peter TINKHAM, one sixth of land of father, Ebenezer.

Amos TINKHAM of Middleborough MA to **Joseph BATES Jr.** of Middleborough. <Plymouth Co.Deeds 49:66> ...24 Apr. 1753, Amos TINKHAM, husbandman, & wf Sarah, for Ł13.6s8d, sold to Joseph BATES Jr., cordwinder...one fifth part of the land which our honoured Father **Peter TINKHAM** at his death had ...which fifth part became mine upon the decease of our said Father. Witnesses: Jerusha TINKHAM, Patience TINKHAM. Ack. 30 Oct. 1761 by Amos & Sarah. Rec. 15 May 1764.

Patience TINKHAM of Middleboro MA to **Joseph BATES Jr.** of Middleboro MA.<Plymouth Co.Deeds 42:203> ...5 May 1753, Patience TINKHAM sells to Joseph BATES Jr., cordwainer, one fifth of land of father Peter TINKHAM in Middleboro. Ack. 6 Nov. 1753.

Cornelius BENNETT of Middleboro MA to **Joseph BATES Jr.** of Middleboro MA.<Plymouth Co.Deeds 49:66> ...10 May 1756, Cornelius BENNETT, school master, (Ruth signs also), sells to Joseph BATES Jr., yeoman...

Samuel TINKHAM of Middleboro MA to **Joseph BATES Jr.** <Plymouth Co.Deeds 53:95>
...16 Feb. 1761, Samuel TINKHAM, yeoman, with wf Malatiah releasing dower, sells to Joseph BATES, Jr., cordwainer...

Peter TINKHAM Jr. of Middleboro MA to **Joseph BATES Jr.** of Middleboro MA.<Plymouth Co.Deeds 53:95> ...11 July 1764, Peter TINKHAM Jr., cordwainer, with wf Molly releasing dower, to Joseph BATES, Jr., cordwainer...

Joseph BATES Jr. of Middleboro MA to **Peter TINKHAM Jr.** of Middleboro MA.<Plymouth Co.Deeds 53:96> ...14 Mar. 1765, Joseph BATES Jr., cordwainer, with wf Eunice releasing dower, to Peter TINKHAM, Jr., cordwainer...

Patience TINKHAM of Plymouth MA to **Sarah TINKHAM.** <Plymouth Co.Deeds 88:125>
...22 July 1793, Patience TINKHAM, spinster, dau of Caleb TINKHAM, dec'd, sells to Sarah TINKHAM, dau of my brother Hilkiah TINKHAM...(also mentioned are two neices, Patience BRYANT, Lucy BRYANT, daus of Samuel BRYANT of Plymouth).

James RAYMENT of Middleborough MA to **Walter DRINKWATER** of Freetown MA. <Plymouth Co.Deeds 15:227> ...15 Sept. 1721, James RAYMENT & wf Mercy, for Ł8 sold to Walter DRINKWATER...one whole share of cedar swamp being one quarter part of the tenth lot of cedar swamp in ye purchase called the sixteen shilling purchase in Middleborough, which said share did originally belong unto ye right of our Honoured Grandfather **Ephraim TINKHAM,** dec'd, as may appear upon ye records. Witnesses: John BENNETT, Thomas NELSON. Ack. by James & Mercy 15 Sept. 1721. Rec. 26 Feb. 1721 (O.S.).

Joseph BATE of Middleborough MA to **Isaac TINKHAM** of Middleborough MA. <Plymouth Co.Deeds 25:220> ...9 Apr. 1729, Joseph BATE & wf Joanna, for Ł71.5s sold to Isaac TINKHAM...twenty five acres, the twenty second lot in six & twenty mens purchase in Middleborough...said lot did formerly belong unto the right of our Honoured Grandfather **Ephraim TINKHAM**, dec'd. Witnesses: Moses TINKHAM, Hannah PARLOW. Ack. by Joseph & Joanna 5 Nov. 1729. Rec. 25 Sept. 1730.

Jonathan REED of Middleboro MA to **Ebenezer TINKHAM** of Middleboro MA. <Plymouth Co.Deeds 47:50>
...9 May 1757, Jonathan REED & wf Joanna, for £6.13.4, sell to Ebenezer TINKHAM, four acres in Middleboro, being part of the 20th lot in the first allotment of one hundred acre lots in twenty sixth mens purchase and is part of homestead of our honoured Father **Samuel TINKHAM**, late of Middleboro, dec'd, bounded as per division deed dated 14 May 1750. (also under 47:50 - **Thomas TUPPER** to **Ebenezer TINKHAM**, blacksmith, of Middleboro...no details)

Samuel TINKHAM Jr. of Middleboro MA to **Ebenezer TINKHAM** of Middleboro. <Plymouth Co.Deeds 47:49>
...25 Sept. 1750, Samuel TINKHAM Jr. to Ebenezer TINKHAM, part of (above) lot received in same division of estate of father, Samuel TINKHAM, dec'd.

Mercy DONHAM of Middleboro MA to **Ebenezer TINKHAM** of Middleboro. <Plymouth Co.Deeds 47:49>
...25 Sept. 1750, Mercy DONHAM to Ebenezer TINKHAM, part of lot received in same division of estate of her father Samuel TINKHAM. (See above deed 47:50)

Samuel TINKHAM Jr. et al to **Ebenezer TINKHAM** of Middleboro MA. <Plymouth Co.Deeds 47:51>
...9 May 1757, Samuel TINKHAM Jr., **Gideon TINKHAM, Deborah TINKHAM, Jonathan REED** & wf Joanna, all of Middleboro, and **Joseph BESSE** & wf Mercy of Wareham, and **Keziah TINKHAM** of Bridgewater, sell to Ebenezer TINKHAM, a lot in twelve mens purchase...which lot of land our brother **Peter TINKHAM,** dec'd, bought of Polycarpus LORING. 31 Dec. 1759, **Jonathan AMES** & wf Keziah of Bridgewater, Keziah not having been of lawful age when she signed the preceding deed, being now of age and married to Jonathan AMES, she confirms the above deed.

Deborah TINKHAM of Middleboro MA to **Ebenezer TINKHAM** of Middleboro MA. <Plymouth Co.Deeds 47:52>
...1 Jan. 1760, Deborah TINKHAM to Ebenezer TINKHAM, land set off to her in division of estate... of my honoured Father **Samuel TINKHAM**, dec'd. (as above)

Estate of **Peter TINKHAM** of Middleboro MA. <Plymouth Co.PR #20894>
...17 Nov. 1756, **Samuel TINKHAM Jr.**, yeoman of Middleboro, admr. of estate of his brother, Peter TINKHAM, dec'd. Sureties: Gideon TINKHAM, yeoman of Middleboro and Polycarpus LORING, M.D. of Plympton.

Estate of **Seth TINKHAM** of Middleboro MA. <Plymouth Co.PR #20909>
...1750...<11:521> Adm. <12:229> Inventory. <#20910, 11:524;12:78-79> Guardianship of children, viz: **Seth TINKHAM, Joanna TINKHAM, Elizabeth TINKHAM, Marcy TINKHAM.** (no details in files)

PRISCILLA BROWN[2] (Peter[1])

Will of **William ALLEN** of Sandwich MA. <Barnstable Co.PR>
<2:210>...dated 17 Feb. 1697/8...being aged and under decayes of body...mentions wife **Priscilla**; entire estate to nephew **Daniel ALLEN** (executor) of Sandwich, son of my brother **George ALLEN**; Quakers to be allowed to hold meetings in the southerly end of house. Overseers: John WING, Zachariah JENKINS. Witnesses: Stephen SKEFFE, William BASSETT, James CLAGHORN. <2:229> Pr. 26 Oct. 1705. <2:211> Inventory 26 Oct. 1705, by William BASSETT, Ebenezer WING; total £374.13.6. (Inventory states that William ALLEN d. 1 Oct. 1705.) <Note: William ALLEN & Priscilla BROWN had no known issue.)

REBECCA BROWN[2] (Peter[1])

PLYMOUTH COUNTY DEEDS:

<3:111> 25 Mar. 1668, William SNOW & wf Rebecca to E. TINKHAM of Dartmouth MA.
<3:159> 15 Apr. 1669, William ALLIN of Sandwich MA to Henry TUCKER of Milton MA.
<4:83> 18 Apr. 1699, William SNOW Sr. to eldest son William SNOW, both of Bridgewater.
<4:83> 9 June 1701, William SNOW Sr. to eldest son William SNOW, both of Bridgewater.
<15:166> 1721, William SNOW to son William SNOW Jr.
<19:2> 1723, William SNOW to Jonathan WASHBURN Jr.
<19:164> 1725, William SNOW to William FENTON.
<20:117> , William SNOW to Francis WOOD.
<20:137> , William SNOW to Edward FOBE.
<20:220> , William SNOW to James SNOW et al.
<20:221> , William SNOW to Eleazer SNOW.

MICRO #4 OF 5

Will of **Benjamin SNOW**, husbandman of Bridgewater MA. <Plymouth Co.PR>
<9:83>...dated 12 Sept. 1738, mentions wf **Sarah**; sons **Ebenezer SNOW** (youngest son & executor),

Benjamin SNOW, Solomon SNOW; two daus **Rebecca CAMPBELL** & **Eliza CARVER**; grandson **Seth PRATT**, son of dau **Sarah**, dec'd. Witnesses: Josiah EDSON Jr., Nathan BASSET, John WASHBURNE, Jr. (all three testified 6 June 1743). <9:84> Pr. 6 June 1743. <9:117> Inventory 20 June 1743.

Will of **Seth PRATT**, gentleman of Bridgewater MA. <Plymouth Co.PR>
<35:448>...dated 29 Nov. 1794, mentions wf **Hannah**; sons **Nathaniel PRATT, Simeon PRATT, Sylvanus PRATT & Asa PRATT** (joint executors), **Joseph PRATT, Seth PRATT**; daus **Cloe CONANT**, wf of Jeremiah and **Joanna BESSEE**, widow; grandson **Marshall BESSEE** (under 21). Witnesses: Beza HAYWARD, Benjamin POPE, Azor HOWE. <35:449> Pr. 6 Jan. 1796. <35:509> Inventory.

PLYMOUTH COUNTY DEEDS: (re: Joseph SNOW)

<70:462>	,	Joseph SNOW from Josiah KEITH.
<19:175>	,	Joseph SNOW from Samuel EDSON Jr.
<21:70>	,	Joseph SNOW from John FIELD.
<21:199>	1726,	Joseph SNOW Jr. from John FIELD.
<24:95>	,	Joseph SNOW from Abial PACKARD.
<29:133>	,	Joseph SNOW Jr. from Samuel EDSON.
<31:152>	,	Joseph SNOW from Samuel POOL.
<33:162>	1723,	Joseph SNOW Jr. from Isaac SNOW.
<33:187>	21 Apr. 1728,	Joseph SNOW of Easton from Jacob ALLEN.
<33:199>	3 Dec. 1725,	Joseph SNOW Jr. from Joseph LATHROP.
<40:221>	11 Sept 1749,	Joseph SNOW & wf Elizabeth of Providence.
<42:259>	30 Mar. 1730,	Joseph SNOW of Easton to Joseph EDSON.
<44:184>	16 Jan. 1733/4,	Joseph SNOW of Providence to Peter HAYWARD. Rec. 1757.
<46:158>	31 Aug. 1753,	Joseph SNOW of Providence to Jonathan HAYWARD. Rec. 1760.
<50:236>	1762,	Joseph SNOW & Rachel of Dartmouth (re: land in Rochester).
<55:9>	1760,	Joseph SNOW, son of David.

(Additional reference numbers with no data, viz: 37:117; 48:112;56:111,249,250;58:63;59:238;61:139;75:43,66;76:78;77:120;81:214;82:107;91:205.)

Thomas HAYWARD of Bridgewater MA to **Joseph SNOW.** <Plymouth Co.Deeds 18:38>
...25 Jan. 1689/90, Thomas HAYWARD, for £14, sell to my kinsman Joseph SNOW...50 acres lying on the Plain between the Town & Matfield joyning to ye land of Joseph EDSON and William BASSETT; also ten acres of swamp lying between the Wolf Trap & Joseph BASSETT's land, which land I Thomas HAYWARD "being the true owner & right Proprietor thereof I do absolutely sell & really make over to the aforesaid Joseph SNOW"*...Witnesses: Joseph HAYWARD, John BOLTON. Ack. by Thomas HAYWARD 19 Feb. 1689. Rec. 17 June 1724. (*The following deed sheds light on the "possessive" wording:)

Joseph SNOW, Joseph SNOW Jr. and **Thomas HAYWARD et al.** <Plymouth Co.Deeds 19:129> (See above)
...1 Oct. 1724, Agreement between Joseph SNOW Sr. & Joseph SNOW Jr. of Bridgewater of the one part, and **Joseph EDSON, Samuel EDSON, Thomas HAYWARD, John LATHROP** and **Solomon JOHNSON**, all of Bridgewater, husbandmen, of the other part...whereas divers...controversies have been had...between the Parties, relating to the Head of Poison Plain & where the head of said Snow's lotts or tracts of land, on which they now dwell (which was formerly Capt. Hayward's) ought to be.

Joseph SNOW of Bridgewater MA to **Joseph SNOW** of Bridgewater MA. <Plymouth Co.Deeds 18:38>
...16 June 1718, Joseph SNOW to son Joseph SNOW...lands in Bridgewater, incl half of 50 acre homestead (bounded by Samuel EDSON's land); one half of ten acre swamp lying at Small Gain joyning Ensign JOHNSON's land. Witnesses: Joseph LATHROP, Samuel EDSON. Ack. 28 Feb. 1723/4. Rec. 17 June 1724.

Joseph SNOW of Bridgewater MA to **Daniel ALDEN** of Bridgewater MA. <Plymouth Co.Deeds 34:105>
...16 June 1729, Joseph SNOW, for £8, sells to Daniel ALDEN, yeoman, land in Bridgewater near a place called Buckhill Plain on the northerly side of Matfield River...consisting of one third part of a 20 acre lot. Witnesses: Joanna SNOW, David SNOW. Ack. 22 Sept. 1735. Rec. 25 Apr. 1741.

Joseph SNOW of Providence to **Caleb PHILLIPS** of Bridgewater MA. <Plymouth Co.Deeds 36:11>
...16 Mar. 1737/8, Deacon Joseph SNOW, yeoman, for £42.10s., sells to Caleb PHILLIPS, blacksmith ...four and a quarter acres of swampy or low land in Bridgewater and northwesterly from the dwelling house of said Caleb, bounded by land of Peter HAYWARD.

PLYMOUTH COUNTY DEEDS: (re: Samuel SNOW)

<51:206>	28 Apr. 1764,	Samuel SNOW to Silas WOOD.
<57:3>	11 Apr. 1772,	Samuel SNOW & wf Jedidah to William CUSHMAN.
<60:1>	8 Mar. 1769,	Samuel SNOW & wf Jedidah of Middleboro, both ack. 16 Oct. 1778.
<60:1>	6 Oct. 1778,	Samuel SNOW & wf Jedidah of Middleboro, heirs of Joseph BUMPAS, dec'd, of Middleboro, to our brother Joseph BUMPAS, son of said dec'd.
<61:46>	20 Dec. 1774,	Samuel SNOW of Middleboro to Ambrose SHAW of Plympton, land in Plympton. Ack. by Samuel 10 Jan. 1775.
<84:88>	22 Sept 1797,	Caleb BRIGGS of Rochester (as guardian to Rebecca, Samuel, Nathaniel, Hannah and Mary SNOW) to Nathan REED, land of Samuel SNOW, dec'd.
<96:46>	3 Jan. 1802,	Samuel SNOW of Rochester.
<106:24>	7 May 1806,	Samuel SNOW of Rochester.

PLYMOUTH COUNTY DEEDS (cont-): (re: Samuel SNOW)

<118:166> 2 Apr. 1812, Samuel SNOW of Rochester to Elijah WILLIS. (Also signed by Rhoda SNOW.)

(Additional reference numbers with no data, viz: 123:96;124:95;125:12;164:83;178:93;202:42;223:132;236:31;253:32;283:175.)

Josiah KEITH of Bridgewater MA to **Joseph SNOW Jr.** of Bridgewater MA. <Plymouth Co.Deeds 10:462> ...11 May 1714, Josiah KEITH, for £14.10s, sells to Joseph SNOW Jr...land laid out to the seven shears (shares?) on ye north easterly side of ye town ye said purchase right being origenally Mr. James KEITH's and lyeth in ye first shear...Witnesses: Nathaniel BRETT, Seth BRETT. Ack. & Rec. 28 Dec. 1714.

Joseph SNOW of Easton MA to **Thomas WADE** of Bridgewater MA. <Plymouth Co.Deeds 37:113> ...11 Mar. 1727/8, Joseph SNOW & wf Elizabeth, for £130, sell to Thomas WADE, two lots of land... the first lot on which the house stands, bounded by land that said Joseph SNOW sold to Samuel EDSON and land of Joseph SNOW Sr...the second lot bounded beginning at a maple tree which Capt. DYER and the other arbitrators made for a corner and the land of Samuel EDSON and Joseph SNOW Sr. ...according to the record of the agreement made by the arbitrators to the bound first mentioned. Witnesses: Thomas HAYWARD 3rd, Jacob ALLEN. Ack. by Joseph SNOW 10 Feb. 1740. Rec. 22 May 1745.

Joseph SNOW of Easton MA to **James SNOW** of Bridgewater MA. <Plymouth Co.Deeds 36:167> ...25 Dec. 1729, Joseph SNOW, for £30, sells to James SNOW, 30 acres in Bridgewater...one half of the fifth lot in that part of the first share which lyeth at Beaver Brook. Witnesses: David SNOW, Zacharias SNOW. Ack. 16 Apr. 1743. Rec. 15 May 1744.

Joseph SNOW of Easton MA to **Daniel ALDEN** of Bridgewater MA. <Plymouth Co.Deeds 34:105> ...1 Feb. 1731/2, Joseph SNOW, yeoman, for £15, sells to Daniel ALDEN, yeoman, ten acres of land already granted to the Snow's Purchase Right in the undivided land of Bridgewater (it being one third part of the last 20 acre grant and one third part of ye last 10 acre grant which was granted to the Snow's Purchase Right in said town). Witnesses: Mark LATHROP, James SNOW. Ack. 11 Sept. 1740. Rec. 25 Apr. 1741.

Joseph SNOW of Providence RI to **Abiah MANLY, Daniel MANLY** of Easton MA. <Bristol Co.Deeds 34:26> ...15 May 1744, Joseph SNOW, for £40, sells to Abiah MANLY & Daniel MANLY, yeomen, twelve acres in Taunton North Purchase. Ack. 25 Dec. 1744. <35:518> 11 Sept. 1749 Joseph sells land to Abiah for £1000, with wf Elizabeth consenting.

Joseph SNOW et al of Providence RI to **Daniel SNOW** of Bridgewater MA. <Bristol Co.Deeds 56:241> ...1 Apr. 1774, Joseph SNOW, Daniel SNOW, James SNOW, yeomen, for £9, sell to Daniel SNOW, gentleman, all their purchase rights in Taunton No. Purchase, in towns of Norton, Easton & Mansfield District...all which descended to us by heirship from our Father Joseph SNOW, late of Providence, dec'd. Ack. 8 Sept. 1774.

Will of **Joseph SNOW**, Esq. of Providence RI. <Providence RI PR #A396, W:6:71> ...12 Jan. 1765, mentions wf **Elizabeth;** to grandchildren (whom my oldest daughter **Elizabeth DEEN/DEAN** late of said Providence deceast left), namely **Sibble DEEN** and **Elizabeth DEEN,** each of them one house lot fronting to the rhoad that leads from Mr. SEVERS' to Pautuxet, adjoining to lot of John FIELD (when they come of age)...to three sons **Joseph SNOW, Daniel SNOW** and **James SNOW** (executor), remainder of estate in Rhode Island and Massachusetts Bay. Witnesses: Solomon SEARLE, Isaac CORY, William COMPTON. Pr. 7 Aug. 1773, oath by Isaac CORY and William COMPTON. Inventory 31 July 1773, by widow **Marcy SNOW**; incl. one table in the great room, one looking glass, nine chairs, one feather bed, one old bed & furniture upstairs, seven old chairs, six teaspoons, two large silver spoons, teapot and crockeryware, one desk and what is in it except securities, books in the kitchin, two cases drawers, brass kittle & scales, pewter in closet, sundrys in shoproom, two table mats, milk cow, old mare, twenty sheep; notes against James SHELDON, Ebenezer AMOS, Joseph SNOW 3d and Nathan BROWN; total £101.17.3., signed by Barzillia RICHMOND, Benoni PEARCE. <7C:4:347> Administration granted.

Estate of **James SNOW** of Providence RI. <Providence RI PR #A4147>
<P:2:208> Petition 28 Dec. 1812, of **Hannah SNOW**, widow, that her son **John SNOW** be app'td admr. Sureties: Stephen WARDWELL, Walter PAINE. <P:2:219> Inventory 8 Mar. 1813, total $200.31. <P:2:278> Insolvency 7 Mar. 1814 by admr., Walter PAINE & James HAMMOND app'td to appraise. <P:2:330> Claims presented 6 Mar. 1815, of $928.78. <P:2:331> Account 7 Mar. 1815 of admr., showing debts of $244.90, credits of $200.31. <P:2:332> Petition 13 Mar. 1815 of admr. for right to sell land. <P:2:338> 28 Mar. 1815, John SNOW's petition to Supreme Judicial Court having been approved, sale to be made under direction of Probate Court; said Probate Court decrees sale to be made 2d Tues. of May next at 11 o'clock a.m.; sale to be advertized three weeks in paper printed in town; 10% cash to be paid down, 45% in 30 days, 45% in 60 days from day of sale and he to give bond for £2000 with Stephen WARDWELL and Chester BLASHFIELD as sureties. <W:11:239> 20 Feb. 1813, Walter PAINE, James HAMMOND and John DUMWELL/DUNNWELL appraised the estate as follows: Bible & Psalm Book, $3; maple desk, $4.50; round maple dining table, $3; square maple dining table (three and a half feet), $3; looking glass, $6.25; six framed chairs, $3; 19 blue & green edged plates, $1.50; china fruit bowl, 2 sugar bowls, .50; 6 china cups & saucers, $1; 3 cream pots, .25; 6 silver tea spoons & 1 pr sugar tongs, $2; butter boat & 2 pickle plates, .10; 14 wine glasses & 3 glass salts, $1.34; 2 half pint tumblers & 1 pint decanter, .50; 2 small waiters & 1 plate, .25; 1

block tin tea pot, .33; 2 table cloths & 4 knapkins, $3; 9 cotton pillow cases, $3; 7 cotton & 1 linnen shirts, $8; 2 checked window curtains, .25; 1 pr bellows, 1 pr dogs, shovel & tongs,$1.25; 1 small maple table, .25; 2 patch work chair cushions, .50; 1 maple bedstead & cord, $1.25; 1 feather bed, under bed, 1 pr coton sheets, 1 bolster, 2 pillows, 2 blankets, 2 pillow cases & bedspread, $22; 1 armed chair and 7 kitchen chairs, $1.75; 1 old desk & old round maple table, $1.25; 2 leather fire buckets, 1 water bucket, 1 knife box, $2.25; 1 small mortar & pestle, coffee mill, .83; tin nurse lamp & qt jack, .37; 2 brass candlesticks & iron, .75; 5 knives, 4 forks and 6 pewter spoons, .50; broken looking glass, .25; cedar milk pail, 3 bowls, 6 cups & saucers, .62; qt mug, qt pitcher, coffee pot, tin pan, .92; 6 pewter platters, 5 plates, 1 porringer, qt pot, $3.75; small brass kettle, iron pot, tea kittle, $2.75; iron skillet, bake kittle, dish kittle, $1.15; pr iron hand irons, frying pan, $2.33; water dipper, new clothes chest, $1.75; clothes chest, warming pan, $1.50; oak bedstead, lead, 2 small boxes, $1; 2 feather beds, 1 under bed, 1 bowlster, 2 pillows, 2 sheets, 2 pillow cases, one blanket, 1 bed quilt, 1 cotton coverlet,$40; blue great coat, black broadcloth coat, $9; velvet jacket, breeches, $3; pr old boots, shoes and old high case drawers, $3; chest containing 43 tools incl. 3 hand saws, $15; other chest of old tools, 29 in number, incl. hatchet, log chain, cross cutt saw, $10; scythe, sneaths, machine to cut straw with, $2.50; accounts against **Daniel SNOW,** Valentine MARTIN; total $200.31. Oath to inventory 8 Mar. 1813 by **John SNOW,** admr. <Ac.1:345,346> Account 15 Mar. 1824, of **John SNOW,** admr; balance on hand, $3.36; 2 lots sold to Stephen WARDWELL, shop sold to J. SNOW, lot sold to W. PAINE. <W:11:239> Inventory of personal estate, (no date), contains a note signed by **James SNOW, Jr.,** dated 23 Oct. 1804 with interest, $34.87; amount against the estate of **Joseph SNOW,** dec'd, $134.48; amount against Joseph FIELD, $9. <original> List of claims, 6 Mar. 1815, incl. Dr. Pardon BOWEN's note against **Joseph SNOW,** dec'd, one half of which his father (and ours), **Deacon James SNOW,** agreed to pay, signed by **James SNOW, Stephen WARDWELL, Daniel SNOW, John SNOW.**

Will of **Daniel SNOW,** yeoman of Providence RI. <Providence RI PR #A1197>
<W:6:442>...(no date on will), mentions wf **Sarah** & brother **Joseph SNOW** (executors); son **Daniel SNOW;** daus **Elizabeth SNOW, Susanna SNOW, Lydia SNOW, Rebecca SNOW, Sarah SNOW;** executors given power to sell land to pay for education of daughters. Witnesses: Benoni PEARCE, James SNOW, Theodore FOSTER. <W:6:443> Pr. 6 Dec. 1784, adm. granted to **Mrs. Sarah SNOW,** widow and **Mr. Joseph SNOW,** clerk. <W:6:450> Inventory taken 1 Dec. 1784 by Benoni PEARCE and Barzillai RICHMOND.

Will of **John C. JENCKES** of Providence RI. <Providence RI PR 16:465>
...dated 18 July 1848, mentions wf **Fanny S. JENCKES;** to sons **Charles W. JENCKS** & **John J. JENCKS,** spoons formerly property of their grandmother; daus **Sarah J. JENCKS, Eliza SNOW, Amey Ann HALE;** granddaughter **Frances GASTON.** Executors - son **Charles** and Charles F. TILLING(HAST).

Josiah BYRAM, Arthur HARRIS to **Samuel & Eleazer RICKARD** of Plympton MA. <Plymouth Co.PR 8:17>
...17 May 1739, Josiah BYRAM & wf Hannah, Arthur HARRIS & wf Mehitable, all of Bridgewater MA, for £38, sell to Samuel RICKARD and Eleazer RICKARD, yeomen...all our rights in personal & real estate which our Honoured Father **Samuel RICKARD** died seized, also all our right in real estate given them by deed of gift from our said Father. Witnesses: John CUSHING, David BESSE.

Estate of **William SNOW** of Bridgewater MA. <Plymouth Co.PR #18729>
<5:160> Administration granted, 7 Nov. 1726, to son **James SNOW** of Bridgewater. <5:181> Inventory taken 11 Nov. 1726 by Jonathan HOWARD, John AMES, Edward HOWARD. <5:182> Agreement, 22 Nov. 1726, of **James SNOW, William SNOW, Eleazer SNOW** and **John SNOW,** all of Bridgewater...sons to **William SNOW,** dec'd...whereas ye said James, William, Eleazer and John, having bought of their two sisters, viz: **Bethiah HOWARD,** wf of Eisha and **Susannah ALGER,** wf of Israel, both of Bridgewater, all their right...in and unto ye estate of their Father...make a division of said land.

MICRO #5 OF 5

(This microfiche card contains 12 pages of BROWN data (no deeds, wills or probate) and 21 pages of CHILTON data which is repeated in the CHILTON Family microfiche.)

JAMES CHILTON

MICRO #1 OF 7

MARY CHILTON[2] (James[1])

Will of **John WINSLOW** of Boston MA. <MD 3:131>**<1>**
...dated 12 Mar. 1673, mentions wf **Mary**; son **John WINSLOW** (executor); grandson **William PAYNE,** son of my dau **Sarah MEDDLECOTT**; granddaughter **Parnell WINSLOW,** dau of my son **Isaac WINSLOW**; daus of my Daughter **LATHAM**; son **Benjamin WINSLOW** (under 21); son **Edward WINSLOW** and his children; granddaughter **Susanna LATHAM**; son **Edward GREY** and the children he had by my dau **Mary**; two children of my son **Joseph WINSLOW**; granddaughter **Mercy HARRIS**; kinsman **Josiah WINSLOW**, now Governor of New Plimoth; brother **Josiah WINSLOW**; kinswoman **Eleanor BAKER,** dau of my brother **Kenelm WINSLOW**; to Mr. PADDY's widow, five pounds as a token of my love; my Negro girle Jane (after she has served twenty yeares from the date hereof) shall be free, and that she shall serve my wife during her live/life and afer my wifes decease she shall be disposed of according to the discression of my overseers; friends Thomas BRATTLE, William TAILER and John WINSLEY named overseers. Pr. 21 May 1674. Inventory 27 Oct. 1674.

Will of **Mary WINSLOW,** widow of Boston MA. <MD 1:65>**<1>**
...dated 31 July 1676, mentions son **John WINSLOW**; grandson **William PAINE**; dau **Susanna LATHAM**; granddaughter **Ann GRAY**; Mrs. TAPPIN; Goodman CLEAR; **Mary & Sarah WINSLOW,** daus of son **Edward WINSLOW**; grandchildren **Parnell WINSLOW, Chilton LATHAM, Mercy HARRIS, Mary POLLARD, Susanna LATHAM, Mary WINSLOW** (dau of son **Joseph WINSLOW**); son **Samuel WINSLOW**; dau **Sarah MIDDLECOTT**; Thomas THACHER, pastor of third Church in Boston. William TAILOR, merchant of Boston named executor. Executor refused to serve, 1 May 1679. Inventory 29 July 1679.

Will of **Isaac WINDSLOW/WINSLOW** of Charlestown MA. <Middlesex Co.PR #18085>
<3:223>...dated 26 Aug. 1670 at Port Royal, Jamaica, mentions wf **Mary**; dau **Parnill/Parnell WINSLOW**...I give my part of the Katch Pellican to the child my wife went with all when I left her upon the twelve day of July in case it lives...Witnesses: John TURELL, Thomas BANFIELD. Sworn to by John TURELL, 29 Aug. 1670, Thomas BANFIELD, 30 Aug. 1670. Inventory taken 14 Dec. 1670 by John CUTLER, Aaron LUDKIN; **Mary WINSLOW,** widow, app'td admx. and swears to inventory "on behalf of herselfe & child; 12 3rd mth 1671, cash, clothes & chest from Jamaica were added.

SUFFOLK COUNTY DEEDS: (re: WINSLOW)

<24:218> 1709, Edward WINSLOW, goldsmith to Benjamin FITCH, land bought in 1702 of Hutchinson.
<26:27> 1711, Capt. Edward WINSLOW, goldsmith to Nathaniel GREEN et al.
<27:55> 1712, Edward WINSLOW et al to Jonathan DOWSE.
<26:172> ( ), Edward WINSLOW, goldsmith & wf Hannah to Jonathan DOWSE.
<27:6> ( ), Edward WINSLOW to Benjamin DAVIS.
<28:51> 1714, Edward WINSLOW and Samuel GOWEN, agreement re partition wall on King St.
<33:154> 1718, Edward WINSLOW, goldsmith to Capt. Samuel MOODY of Casco Bay.
<35:100> 1720, Edward WINSLOW, Esq. & wf Elizabeth to Thomas CLARKE.
<36:125> 1722, Edward WINSLOW, goldsmith, King St., et al, agreement.

<15:96> 3 Oct. 1678, Joseph WINSLOW & wf Sarah to his mother Mary WINSLOW and executors of his father's estate.
<16:247> 14 May 1690, Elizabeth WINSLOW, widow, dau of Capt. Edward HUTCHINSON, dec'd, et al - brothers & sisters of Edward WINSLOW, sell.
<25:11> 2 Mar. 1709, Elizabeth WINSLOW, widow, mentions father Edward HUTCHINSON, Gent. & only son Edward WINSLOW, goldsmith.
<36:125> ( ), Edward WINSLOW, goldsmith, et al.
<38:138> 16 Feb. 1724, Joshua WINSLOW & wf Elizabeth.
<39:199> 31 Mar. 1726, Joshua WINSLOW & wf Elizabeth, mortgage to Nathaniel HUBBARD.
<45:14> 12 Dec. 1730, John ALFORD, Esq. & wf Margaret, Joshua WINSLOW, merchant & wf Elizabeth, all of Boston, said Margaret & Elizabeth being only children & heirs of Thomas SAVAGE, merchant of Boston, dec'd.
<47:91> 20 Jan. 1732, Joshua WINSLOW & wf Elizabeth dau of Thomas & Margaret SAVAGE.
<53:180> 3 Sept 1735, Joshua WINSLOW & wf Elizabeth.

Estate of **Capt. Nathaniel WINSLOW,** mariner of Boston MA. <Suffolk Co.PR #13381>
<62:590> Bond 2 Dec. 1763, **Ruth WINSLOW,** widow of Boston, app'td admx. Sureties: Job PRINCE, mariner of Boston and Anthony THOMAS of Marshfield. Warrant to appraise, 2 Dec. 1763 to Job WHEELWRIGHT, Benjamin BARNARD(sp), Joseph WEBB, all of Boston. Inventory 16 Nov. 1764.

Guardianship of Children of **John Conrad WINSLOW,** labourer of Boston MA. <Suffolk Co.PR #13807-8>
Bonds 21 Mar. 1766 of John Christopher LEHR, baker as gdn of **John Conrad WINSLOW** (above 14) and **Sophia WINSLOW** (under 14), children of John Conrad WINSLOW ("apparently living, deceased is crossed out"). Sureties: Philip Godfrid KAST/CAST, physician and Peter CRAMMER, both of Boston.

Estate of **William HILTON.** <Middlesex Co.PR #8138>
Administration, 14 11th mth 1675, granted to **Mehetable HILTON,** on behalf of herself and children, and she took oath to the inventory. Inventory taken 23 Sept. 1675 by Aaron LUD( ) and Daniel EDMONDS; mentions mariner instruments.

Isaac ABRAHAMS to **Robert SCOTT** of Boston MA & **John COOKE** of Plymouth MA. <Suffolk Co.Deeds 1:138> ...18 Nov. 1648, Isaac ABRAHAMS sells a bark to Robert SCOTT, merchant and John COOKE, planter. Witnesses: John WINSLOW, William ASPNWALL.

William HARRIS et al of Boston MA to **Benjamin DAVIS** of Boston MA. <Suffolk Co.Deeds 27:6> ...19 July 1712, William HARRIS, merchant, Thomas FITCH, upholder, Edward WINSLOW, goldsmith & wf Elizabeth late Elizabeth PEMBERTON (which said William, Thomas & Elizabeth are three of the executors of the last Will and Testament of Benjamin PEMBERTON late of Boston, brewer, dec'd), Benjamin BRAME, brewer, of Boston & wf Mary (late PEMBERTON) of the one part...and Benjamin DAVIS, chairmaker, of the other part... <27:55>...21 Jan. 1712/3, William HARRIS, Thomas FITCH and Edward WINSLOW, goldsmith, of Boston & wf Elizabeth, relict of Benjamin PEMBERTON, brewer of Boston dec'd, three of the executors of will of said Benjamin...

Henry GIBBS of Salem MA to **Joshua CHEEVER** of Boston MA. <Suffolk Co.Deeds 73:196> ...2 May 1747, Henry GIBBS, gentleman and Joshua CHEEVER, Esq., "fcoffee in Trust" to Susanna WINSLOW, wf of Edward WINSLOW, Esq. of Boston, of the other part...said Henry GIBBS, for Ł215, sells to Joshua CHEEVER, as fcoffee etc., for the use of the said Susanna WINSLOW, a parcel of land or wharff with the warehouse hereon...at north end of Boston near Fish St. on the wharf formerly called Roby's Wharf...as the same was sett off to me in and by the division of the estate of my late mother, dec'd.

Will of **Isaac WINSLOW** of Halifax N.S.. <Suffolk Co.PR>
<84:644>...(no date)...I, Isaac WINSLOW now residing in Halifax Nova Scotia...being now just about to embark with my Family for New York...; mentions my wife's legacy from her brother; rest of estate to unnamed children and grandchild **George ERVING,** son of dau **Lucy WINSLOW** who married an Erving; nephews **Isaac WINSLOW Jr., Jonathan CLARKE** & **Isaac Winslow CLARKE,** named executors. <85:177> Bond 15 Apr. 1786 of **Isaac WINSLOW Sr.**, merchant of Boston, as executor...of **Isaac WINSLOW, Esq.**, late of Roxbury, dec'd. Sureties: Samuel WINSLOW, Isaac WINSLOW, merchants of Boston. <87:85> Inventory 18 Oct. 1787, of lands in Cumberland Co. <92:109> Bond 25 Feb. 1793 of Oliver SMITH, apothecary, of Boston, as admr. de b.n. Sureties: Samuel WINSLOW, gent., Samuel WALDO, merchant of Portland. <95:220> 16 May 1797, John LOWELL Jr., Esq. of Boston, admr. d.b.n.<97:699> Account 5 Mar. 1798. <100:318> Distribution 14 Feb. 1799 to heirs, viz: John WALL & wf Hannah; Elizabeth WINSLOW; George William ERVING; Thomas WINSLOW; Samuel WINSLOW; Sarah T. WALDO, wf of Samuel. ("son Isaac deceased" is crossed out & replaced with "Isaac an heir") Ack. 26 July 1802.

Will of **Joshua WINSLOW,** Esq. of Boston MA. <Suffolk Co.PR #14559, 68:305;77:523> <2>
...dated 29 Sept. 1769, mentions wf **Elizabeth;** sons **Isaac WINSLOW, Joshua WINSLOW, John WINSLOW, Edward WINSLOW** (eldest); son in law **John WINNIETT** & wife, she in poor health; my eleven children now living; dau **Martha,** incapable of managing her own affairs; grandson **John WINNIETT** (under 21); brother **Isaac WINSLOW, Esq.** Pr. 18 Oct. 1769. Inventory taken 6 Nov. 1778. Warrant to divide real estate, 22 Nov. 1786...whereas **Mary BARBER** died before her mother without issue, and **Susannah WINSLOW,** another child, had more advance than her whole share will amount to...ordered to divide among his other nine children or their legal representatives, viz: Widow & Children: Edward WINSLOW, clerk (out of state); widow **Margaret POLLARD** (present); legal representatives of **Hannah JEFFRIES; John WINNIETT Jr.** (absent); **Catherine MALBONE,** widow (out of state); **Martha WINSLOW,** incapable of managing her own affairs, **Isaac,** guardian (present); children of **Joshua WINSLOW** (out of state); legal representatives of **John WINSLOW** (no admr. app'td); **Isaac WINSLOW** (present).

Will of **John ALFORD** of Charlestown MA. <Charlestown by Wyman 1:16> <3>
...(no date, pre 30 Sept. 1761), mentions wife; brother **Benjamin ALFORD** of New London; sister **Joanna ALFORD;** sister **Sarah TYNG,** wf of Eleazer, and her children **James TYNG** and **J. Alford TYNG;** Sarah VRYLING and Elizabeth LOWELL, children of Mary VRYLING; Elizabeth SEWALL, grandmother of John A. MASON; nephew **Rev. Edward WINSLOW** of Stratford, son of Joshua & Elizabeth; children **Thomas ALFORD, Margaret ALFORD, Hannah** and **Mary;** nephew **Joshua WINSLOW;** Margaret POLLARD; Sampson STODDARD & wf Margaret of Chelmsford. Pr. 27 Oct. 1761.

Guardianship & Estate of **Martha WINSLOW,** single of Boston MA. <Suffolk Co.PR #18763>
<85:615> (1786?) **Isaac WINSLOW,** merchant of Boston, app'td guardian of Martha, non comp. <92:476> 1793, Certif. of Gdn. <92:514> Inventory. <105:533> Account. <94:260> 1796, Certif. Gdn. (non comp). <94:283> Inventory. <94:296> Certif. of Evid. perpet. <116:337> Account. <116:193,194> Assent of heirs, 22 July 1816, **Benjamin WINSLOW, Joshua WINSLOW, Elizabeth PICKERING, Mary WINSLOW** and **Edward WINSLOW,** heirs at law of **Martha WINSLOW,** late of Boston, dec'd...agree to settlement of her estate with **Isaac WINSLOW,** merchant of Boston. The above heirs interest each one seventh of a quarter...One quarter to **Katherine MALBONE,** signed & sworn at Newport 12 Aug. 1816; one quarter to **Joshua Loring WINSLOW,** signed at London, 7 Apr. 1818; three fifths of one quarter to **Marshall R. WILKINGS, Catherine Isabella WILKINGS, James WYATT, Mary WYATT** and **Isabella Katharine KING,** signed at New York, 7 Dec. 1816; two fifths of one quarter to **John WINSLOW** and **Elizabeth WINSLOW** of Fayetteville, N.C.

Benjamin WINSLOW et al of Boston MA to **Isaac WINSLOW** of Boston MA. <Suffolk Co.PR 254:272> ...22 July 1816, Benjamin WINSLOW, Mary WINSLOW, Joshua WINSLOW, Elizabeth PICKERING, all of Boston and Edward WINSLOW of Wilmington, North Carolina, for $460 "to each severally" sold to Isaac WINSLOW, merchant of Boston...all our right...as Heirs at Law of Martha WINSLOW, late of Boston, dec'd, in real estate incl. one half share or forty eighth part of the Long Wharf in Boston and one Store #37 & one undivided half of Store #49 on said Wharf...also a wooden tenement with land on Milk St. in Boston which was conveyed to Joshua WINSLOW by Joseph RUSSELL by James BOWDOIN and John TINKHAM...both said estates being set off to Martha WINSLOW as by act of division of her Father Joshua WINSLOW's real estate <Suffolk Co.PR 86:10>; also an undivided quarter of Store #32 on Union St., Boston, being formerly the estate of Margaret ALFORD & by her devised to the children of her sister Elizabeth WINSLOW, of which the said Martha WINSLOW was one. Signed by all five grantors incl Abigail Amory WINSLOW, wf of Benjamin. Rec. 25 Apr. 1817.

=====

Katherine MALBONE of Newport RI to **Isaac WINSLOW** of Boston MA. <Suffolk Co.Deeds 254:273> ...4 Sept. 1816, Katherine MALBONE, widow, for $5.00 sells to Isaac WINSLOW, merchant, her share in same property described above in 254:272. Rec. 25 Apr. 1817.

=====

Marshall R. WILKINGS et al of New York to **Isaac WINSLOW** of Boston MA. <Suffolk Co.Deeds 254:274> ...7 Dec. 1816, Marshall R. WILKINGS & wf Catharine in her right, James WYATT & wf Mary in her right and Isabella C. KING, for $600 to each severally paid by Isaac WINSLOW, merchant, in all $1800, sell to Isaac all their rights in same property described above in 254:272. Signed by Marshall WILKINGS, Katharine Isabella WILKINGS, James WYATT, Mary WYATT, Isabella Catharine KING. Ack. same day in New York City by all except James WYATT who ack. at Greenwich, Fairfield Co., 16 Dec. 1816. Rec. 25 Apr. 1817.

=====

John WINSLOW of Fayetteville, N.C. to **Isaac WINSLOW** of Boston MA. <Suffolk Co.Deeds 254:275> ...13 Nov. 1816, John WINSLOW, Esq. & wf Elizabeth, for $600 to each of us paid, sold to Isaac WINSLOW, merchant, all their rights in same property described above in 254:272. On 17 Mar. 1817, Caroline M. WINSLOW, wf of John WINSLOW, Esq. of Fayette Ville, for $5.00 paid by Isaac WINSLOW, relinquishes her right of dower in said estate. Rec. 25 Apr. 1817.

=====

Joshua Loring WINSLOW of Great Britain to **Isaac WINSLOW** of Boston MA. <Suffolk Co.Deeds 254:276> ...11 Jan. 1817, Joshua Loring WINSLOW, Esq. of Heairtree/Heavitree(sp), Great Britain, for Ł500, sold to Isaac WINSLOW, merchant, his share in property described above in 254:272. Ack. 11 Jan. 1817 at Marseilles. Rec. 25 Apr. 1817.

=====

Joshua WINSLOW of Boston MA to **Benjamin WINSLOW, George G. CHANNING.** <Suffolk Co.Deeds 262:73> ...8 Apr. 1819, Joshua WINSLOW, merchant, for $5000.00 sold to Benjamin WINSLOW and George G. CHANNING, merchants of Boston...a certain piece of land with the dwelling house thereon...at the westerly part of Boston...being the same premises which Joseph BAXTER Jr. conveyed to me 6 Sept. 1817. Ack. & Rec. 8 Apr. 1819.

=====

SUFFOLK COUNTY DEEDS:

<215:179> 1806, Joshua WINSLOW, estate, to Margaret POLLARD et al.
<249:188> 1815, Joshua WINSLOW, estate, to D. INGRAHAM, adm.
<256:93> 1817, Joshua WINSLOW to Joseph BAXTER Jr.
<260:141> 1818, Joshua WINSLOW to Sarah E. WALDO.
<278:42> 1822, Joshua WINSLOW et al to John BRAZIER.
<304:55> 1825, Joshua WINSLOW et al to Oliver BREWSTER.

=====

Guardianship of Children of **Joshua WINSLOW,** mariner of Boston MA. <Suffolk Co.PR #19517-8> <89:458> Certif. of Gdn., 1790, Isaac WINSLOW of Boston, gdn. to **Abigail WINSLOW** (over 14) and **Joshua WINSLOW** (under 14). <92:308-10> Account, 1790, **Mary WINSLOW,** admx. est. Isaac WINSLOW, dec'd swears to account. <92:286> Certif. of Gdn., 1793, James MORRILL, guardian to **Abigail** and **Joshua,** both above 14.

=====

Estate of **Capt. Joshua WINSLOW** of Boston MA. <Suffolk Co.PR #20308> ...1794...<93:282> Petition for administration by James MORRILL, William SHERBURNE and Abigail WINSLOW, guardians of his children. Certif. of Amos CROSBY, gent. of Boston, admr. <93:527> Perpet. <94:679> Commissioners Return. <94:322> Account. <94:680> Distribution to James MORRILL, John WINSLOW, Esq. and Thomas SHERBURNE for their debts against the estate.

MICRO #2 OF 7

Joshua WINSLOW et al to **Oliver BREWSTER** of Boston MA. <Suffolk Co.Deeds 304:55> ...16 Apr. 1792, Joshua WINSLOW, John Benjamin PAIBA & wf Mary Loring PAIBA in her own right, Elizabeth WINSLOW, John WINSLOW, Joshua WINSLOW, James WYATT & wf Mary in her own right, Charles HANDFIELD & wf Margaret Alferd HANDFIELD in her own right, Thomas Wright WRIGHT and wf Ann in her own right, Joseph KING & wf Isabella Catherine in her own right, Marshall Robert WILKINGS & wf Catherine Isabella in her own right, Elizabeth WINSLOW and Lucy WINSLOW, the grantors in two certain deed this day executed by us to Joseph WOODWARD of Boston, merchant, for 5 shillings to each of us in hand respectively paid, granted to Oliver BREWSTER, merchant of Boston...all & every the benefits of an exception reserved in the said deeds regarding said WOODWARD...not erecting any building on the lot conveyed by said deeds, within nine feet of Beacon St. so called & appointed said Oliver BREWSTER our attorney. Rec. 14 Sept. 1825.

=====

Estate of **Isaac WINSLOW**, distiller of Roxbury MA. <Suffolk Co.PR #20095>
<92:77> Pr. 12 Feb. 1793, **Mary WINSLOW**, widow, app'td admx. Bondsmen: Thomas AMORY Jr., merchant and Isaac WINSLOW, gentleman, both of Boston. <92:299> Inventory taken 9 Apr. 1793 by Edward DAVIS, Jacob ROWE and Richard W. COOPER. **Mary WINSLOW**, admx., made oath to inv. 4 May 1793; she was allowed £100 for her necessary support. <92:318> Order 12 Feb. 1793 for admx. to advertise her appointment in the "Adams Independent Chronicle" and he "Massachusetts Centinel"; 20 May 1793 Isaac WINSLOW testified that the notice had been posted. <92:401> List of Debts (not dated, but c18 June 1793), viz: Miss Elizabeth WINSLOW, balance of £118; Joshua Loring WINSLOW, balance of £13.11.5.; Mary Loring PAILA, £41.9.11.; Mrs. Catherine MALBONE, £450; Estate of Isaac WINSLOW, Esq., £1000; Estate of Joshua WINSLOW, Esq., £200; Estate of John WINSLOW Jr., £571.4.8.; heirs of Edward WINSLOW, £100; Abigail WINSLOW, minor, £30.13.1; Joshua WINSLOW, minor, £30.15.9; Estate of Margaret ALFORD, £100. Presented by Isaac WINSLOW in behalf of **Mary WINSLOW**, admx. <93:207> Account 10 Sept. 1794, sworn to 13 Jan. 1795 by admx. <94:269> 2nd Inventory 12 Apr. 1796, of admx.; mentions a law suit pending, instituted by Oliver SMITH. <95:354> 25 July 1797, **Mary WINSLOW** became bound with Isaac WINSLOW Jr. and Thomas WINSLOW, merchants of Boston, to perform orders of Court. <95:414> 3rd Inventory 13 Aug. 1797, presented by admx. 29 Aug. 1797; concerning 109 acre tract of land in Holliston, near Lovering's Mills, appraised at $430 and a three acre piece on the boundary line between Framingham & Southborough, $33. <99:89> 10 Feb. 1801, Isaac WINSLOW Jr., merchant of Boston, admitted admr. de bonis non on Estate of Isaac WINSLOW. Sureties: Thomas WINSLOW, Joshua BLANCHARD, merchants of Boston. <99:517> Account 29 Sept. 1801 by Thomas WINSLOW, admr. on estate of **Mary WINSLOW** who was admx. on estate of said Isaac; incl. advance paid on Bill of Exchange remitted to London for Mrs. Sparhawk's debt and paid Catherine MALBONE mortgage on Distill House. Oct. 1798, paid John LOWELL Jr., Esq., admr. on estate of Isaac WINSLOW, Esq. of Roxbury, being in full for demand of said Winslow's estate against the present John WINSLOW's. Sept. 1797, real estate sold at Public Vendue, viz: Distill house in Cole Lane to Isaac WINSLOW Jr., land in Holliston to Aaron EAMES, undivided 5th of building in Middle St. to Hopestill CAPEN; balance due upon settlement of admrs. account from estate of Joshua WINSLOW, Esq.

Estate of **Mary WINSLOW**, widow of Boston MA. <Suffolk Co.PR #21503>
<99:438> Pr. 11 Aug. 1801, son **Thomas WINSLOW**, merchant of Boston, app'td admr. Sureties: Isaac WINSLOW Jr. and Edward EDES Jr., both of Boston. <99:450,453> Certif., Inventory. <99:520> Account. <100:31> Distribution 8 Feb. 1802, the Court ordered **Thomas WINSLOW**, admr. on the estate of Mary WINSLOW deceased who was admx. on estate of Isaac WINSLOW, insolvent, to pay creditors 24.35 cents on the dollar. Creditors incl. Elizabeth WINSLOW; Joshua Loring WINSLOW; James MORRILL as guardian to Abigail WINSLOW & Joshua WINSLOW; Oliver SMITH, admr. de bonis non on estate of Isaac WINSLOW of Roxbury; John WINSLOW; heirs of Edward WINSLOW; James WINSLOW, one of heirs.

Isaac WINSLOW of Boston MA to **John BRAZER** of Boston MA. <Suffolk Co.Deeds 171:48>
...29 Apr. 1791, Isaac WINSLOW, merchant, for £1200, sold to John BRAZER, merchant...brick dwelling house in Boston, fronting northerly on the Street Dock Square (33'8"), westerly on Shrimpton's Lane (122'2"), southerly on house & land of heirs of Charles HANCOCK, dec'd (36'9"), easterly on land of heirs of Joseph JACKSON, dec'd. Wf Mary WINSLOW releases dower. Rec. 8 Nov. 1791.

Joshua WINSLOW et al of Boston MA to **John BRAZER** of Boston MA. <Suffolk Co.Deeds 278:42>
...20 July 1822, Isaac WINSLOW, John D. WINSLOW, Benjamin WINSLOW, Joshua WINSLOW, merchants, and Elizabeth PICKERING of Dorchester, for $178.57, paid to each of us respectively, sold to John BRAZER, Esq....all rights in land described in above deed <171:48>...from Isaac WINSLOW "since deceased". Margaret WINSLOW, wf of Isaac, releases dower. Ack. at Boston 20 July 1822 by Isaac, John D., Benjamin and Joshua WINSLOW. Ack. in Norfolk co. same day by Elizabeth PICKERING. Rec. 22 July 1822.

Estate of **William PICKERING** of Greenland N.H. <Suffolk Co.PR #42145>
...1859...<227:78> Petition for adm. <185:336> Order of notice. <227:78> Bond, Letter. <296:175> Inventory. <327:261> Evidence perpet. <158:15> Account. Records mention widow **Susan B. PICKERING** and children **Lucretia M. FRINK, Charles W. PICKERING.**

Will of **Thomas S. WINSLOW.** <Suffolk Co.PR #32129>
<137:181-2>...dated 16 June 1838, sister in law **Abigail WINSLOW** sole heir. Pr. 13 May 1839. <241:240> Petition for probate. <137:280> Citation. <137:283> Decree of Executor. <137:331> Petition for special administration, Order of notice. <137:304> Claim of appeal. <137:322-3> Bond, Letter. <276:187> Inventory. <321:23> Evidence perpet. <137:128> Petition for sale of personal estate. <137:203> Reasons of appeal. <137:268> Decree. <262:21> Bond, Letter.

Estate of **William H. PICKERING.** <Suffolk Co.PR #67593>
...1882...<546:531> Partition tenants in common.

Estate of **Mary HUDGENS**, widow. <Suffolk Co.PR #33138>
<217:43> Petition 19 Feb. 1842, by Arthur PICKERING, merchant of Boston, for administration. He was app'td 21 Mar. 1842 and gave bond with Isaac WINSLOW, merchant of Boston as surety. <141:161> Receipt 27 Mar. 1843 of **Augustus P. HUDGENS**, being the only heir at law and being of full age, acknowledges receipt of $356.31.

Will of **John WILLIAMS**, tanner of Roxbury MA. <Norfolk Co.PR I:97,151>
<1:97>...dated 17 Sept. 1793, mentions son **Stephen WILLIAMS**; daus **Mary SMITH**, widow, **Lucy STANDART, Sally ESTEY, Rebecca WILLIAMS**; grandson **John HOUGHTON**; sons **John WILLIAMS, Thomas WILLIAMS**

and **Ezekiel WILLIAMS**; sons **John & Stephen** named executors. Witnesses: John READ, John HAWES, William BOWMAN. Pr. 4 Mar. 1794. <I:151> Inventory 6 May 1794.

Richard WINSLOW of Boston MA to **Zachariah EDDY** of Swansea MA. <Bristol Co.Deeds 2:117>
...5 July 1697, Richard WINSLOW, for £100 silver, sold to Zachariah EDDY, land in Swansea.

Richard WINSLOW to **Hannah JOLLS** of Boston MA. <Bristol Co.Deeds 2:292>
...12 Oct. 1698, Richard WINSLOW, late of Boston, now of the Island of Nevis, marchant, gave power of attorney to his mother Hannah JOLLS, widow.

Hannah JOLLS of Boston to **Capt. Nathaniel WINSLOW** of Marshfield MA. <Bristol Co.Deeds 2:293>
...21 Dec. 1698, Hannah JOLLS, widow, attorney of Richard WINSLOW, late of Boston now of the Island of Nevis, marchant, the only son & heir of Samuel WINSLOW, sometime of Boston, marchant, deceased (first husband of the said Hannah), for £113...to the use of her said son Richard WINSLOW by Capt. Nathaniel WINSLOW. <The meaning is not quite clear.??>

Estate of **John TAYLOR**, clothier of Roxbury MA. <Suffolk Co.PR #5295>**<4>**
...1726...administration; mentions wf Lucy. <25:36,85,364;26:269;27:175> (no details given)

Estate of **John TAYLOR**, clerk of Milton MA. <Suffolk Co.PR #9463>**<4>**
...1750...mentions wf Dorothy, children **John, Anne, Nathaniel, William, Dorothy.** <43:364,365;44:83;45:501> (no details given)

Estate of **John TAYLOR.** <Suffolk Co.PR #11031>**<4>**
...1755, administration...<50:99,124,512,527,698;51:521,522;55:9> (no details given)

Guardianship of Children of **Nathaniel GREEN**, merchant, dec'd of Boston MA. <Suffolk Co.PR #7866>
<36:256> 27 Jan. 1742, Rufus GREEN, goldsmith of Boston, app'td gdn. of **Nathaniel GREEN,** minor aged about eleven years. 27 Jan. 1742, Benjamin GREEN, goldsmith of Boston, app'td gdn. of **John GREEN,** minor aged about six years. (also new series 22:239,357)

Nathaniel GREEN of Boston MA to **Samuel DENNING**(sp) of Boston MA. <Suffolk Co.Deeds 102:127>
...29 Sept. 1764, Nathaniel GREEN, mariner & wf Annapell, sell to Samuel DENNING/DERNING(sp)... one sixth of an antient messuage in Boston on the northwestern side of Main St. opposite to the old south meeting house.

Nathaniel GREEN of Boston MA to **John HANCOCK** of Boston MA. <Suffolk Co.Deeds 105:222>
...21 Sept. 1765, Nathaniel GREEN, mariner & wf Annapell, sell to John HANCOCK, Esq., land near Beacon Hill...late part of the estate of our honoured father John HENDERSON, dec'd.

Nathaniel GREENE of Boston MA to **Nathaniel GREENE Jr.** <Suffolk Co.Deeds 119:225>
...18 Mar. 1769, Nathaniel GREENE, mariner & wf Annaple, mortg. to Nathaniel GREEN Jr., merchant.

Will of **Capt. Nathaniel GREENE** of Boston MA. <Suffolk Co.PR #15362>
<72:482>...dated 13 Aug. 1772, wife **Annapell** (executor) to have whole estate. Witnesses: John STEDMAN, Nathaniel APPLETON, Rachel APPLETON. <72:481> Pr. 9 Apr. 1773. <72:576> <u>Inventory</u> 4 May 1773 and sworn to by executor.

John WINSLOW, mariner of Boston, son of Abigail PENHALLOW, wf of Samuel PENHALLOW of Portsmouth. <Suffolk Co.Deeds 39:250> (Deed dated 16 May 1726, no further details given; See below.)

Will of **John WINSLOW,** hatter of Boston MA. <Suffolk Co.PR>
<73:317>...dated 27 Sept. 1773, mentions wf **Elizabeth,** three children, viz: **John WINSLOW, Sarah** and **Elizabeth.** <73:316> Pr. 17 Dec. 1773. <73:453> Inventory presented 4 Mar. 1774.

<u>MICRO #3 OF 7</u>

Abigail PENHALLOW of Portsmouth N.H. to **Jonas CLARKE** of Boston MA. <Suffolk Co.Deeds 34:267>
...10 Dec. 1719, Abigail PENHALLOW, wf of Samuel PENHALLOW, Esq., widow & executrix of will "of Winslow" of Boston, sells to Jonas CLARKE, brazier...land on Spring Lane, being home & land that the said Winslow dec'd devised to his executrix; mentions "antenuptial" contract with present husband, dated 6 Sept. 1714. Rec. 10 Oct. 1720.

John WINSLOW et al of Boston MA to **Jonas CLARKE.** <Suffolk Co.Deeds 34:268>
...12 Oct. 1719, John WINSLOW, mariner and Alexander TODD, mariner of Boston & wf Elizabeth (which said John WINSLOW and Elizabeth TODD are the only children & heirs of John WINSLOW, formerly of Boston, mariner, dec'd) sell to Jonas CLARKE, all rights in land in above deed, 34:267. Ack. by all three 19 Sept. 1720. Rec. 10 Oct. 1720.

Capt. Nathaniel THOMAS et al of Plimouth Co. to **Caleb CHURCH** of Watertown MA. <Bristol Co.Deeds>
<3:149>...1687/8...Capt. Nathaniel THOMAS, Edward WANTON, Edward GRAY, Susanah GRAY, Nathaniel SOUTHWORTH & wf Desire, Seth ARNOLD & wf Elizabeth, Samuel LITTLE & wf Sarah, Ephraim COLE & wf Rebecah...for twenty shillings for every share (9 shares - 1 to each person or couple with Capt. Thomas having 2 shares), sell to Caleb CHURCH, land at a place called the Fall River, Bristol co. Witnesses: Benjamin CHURCH, Ephraim LITTLE, Edward SOUTHWORTH, John GRAY, Samuel HARLOW, Edward

GRAY, John JONES. Ack. 29 Dec. 1697 by Nathaniel THOMAS, Ephraim COLE, Edward GRAY and Samuel LITTLE. Ack. 14 Apr. 1711 by Sarah LITTLE. Rec. 10 July 1700.

==

Estate of **Edward GRAY** of Plymouth MA. <Plymouth Col.Deeds 5:180>[<5>] (See all below & nxt pg.) ...at March Court, 1682/3, **John GRAY**, eldest son of Edward GRAY and the rest of the children by theire substitutes or agents came before the Court for a settlement of the lands which theire father died seized of...**John GRAY** chose house & land where his father lived (contained in the two deeds of John COOKE and Francis COMBE given & delivered to his father), with those smale additions of land which were granted by the towne of Plymouth to his father, also two shares and a half of Punckaeest(sp) Land, being about 28 acres...mistris **Dorothy GRAY** to receive sixty pounds for the bringing up of the three youngest children of Edward GRAY. <5:210-11> 9 Mar. 1682/3, Ephraim MORTON Sr. and John TOMSON Sr. ordered by court to divide lands, incl. 16 acre meadow at Jones River bounded by meadows of Samuel FULLER, Francis COMBS and Steven BRYANT. <5:223> Inventory taken July - 24 Aug. 1681 by Ephraim MORTON, Joseph WARREN, Nathaniel THOMAS and William CROW, incl. books & spectacles, 11s; Indian youth called Robin; Indian gerle sicke of a consumption, £00.00.0; two oxen in Joseph VAUGHAN's lands; two oxen in SAVORY's land; 2 oxen in HARRIS's land; the colt in Samuell WOOD's posession; 2 oxen in John ANDREWS' land; the boate John MORTON goes in with all her tackling & furniture, £22; the boate Edward DOTEN goes in, £15; the boate John BRYANT goes in, £11; dwelling house & land bought of John COOKE, viz: 75 acres upland, 26 acres meadow, 4 acres at Jones River, 22 acres woods, £200; land bought of Francis COMBE, viz: 65 acres at Rockey Nooke, 50 acres at Jones River Meddow & 8 acres of meddow, £70; warehouse at Plymouth, £12; 2 acre meadow bought of Samuel DUNHAM, £2; 12 acre meadow at Winnatucksett, £10; 30 acres upland, 2 acre meadow bought of John HARMON at Moon Ponsett Pond, £4.10s.; 50 acres layed out to Mr. Gray at a necke made by moon ponsett pond, £3; 30 acres lying by HARMON's at Moonponsett, £1.10s; 34 acres upland, 6 acre meddow bought of John RICKARD & 34 acres upland of John ANDREWS' lying together att Lakenham, £25; 6 acre meddow at south meddow bought of Samuel WOOD, £4.10s; land that was Peter RIFFE's, £1.5s; two 25 acre lots at Winnatucksett River, £3; 200 acre uplands & 9 acre meddow att Pachague Necke on both sides of River, £40; 6th part of a tract of land in partnership with Leift. MORTON, Joseph WARREN, etc., £20; 36 acres att Taunton Path, £1.16s; 30 acres att Pokshee Pond, £2; two smale lotts containing 16 acres, £20; nine shares of land at Pocassett, £720 per share; 28 shares of land in Punckateest Necke, 30 shares without the necke which makes in all 29 shares and 9 thirtieth partes of a tract of land lying above Punkateest lands, £580; one share of land att Saconett excepting 30 acres, £100; land bought of HIGGINS att Saconett, £25; house & land lately bought of Thomas LETTICE was surrendered back to Lettice who returned the money which was divided among the widow & children of Edward Gray. <5:229> Inventory presented 24 Aug. 1681 by mistris **Dorethy GRAY**, widdow; after deducting desperate debts and £150.3s6d of Indian debts, total is £2741.5s.11d. At the same court is mentioned the division and settlement among the widow, children **John GRAY, Desire SOUTHWORTH** wf of Nathaniel, **Elizabeth ARNOLD** wf of Seth, **Sarah GRAY, Anna GRAY** and six youngest children, estate to be divided into twelve parts with eldest son John receiving his double portion. <5:301> 28 Jan. 1684, **Dorothy GRAY** agrees to pay the six younger children, viz: **Edward, Susana, Thomas, Rebeca, Lidia** and **Samuel GRAY**, or their guardian, Capt. Nathaniel THOMAS of Marshfield, the sums of £753,10s and £366.18s to be divided between them. Witnesses: William SHURTLEFFE, Jacob COOKE, Thomas CLARKE. Ack. same day before William BRADFORD, Deputy Governor.

==

Estate of **Edward GRAY** of Plymouth MA. <Plymouth Col.Deeds 5:287> ...28 Oct. 1684...Whereas Mr. Edward GRAY sometime before his death made sale of a certain tract of land lying in Shawamett & ingaged to pass a deed for ye same but being prevented by Death, **John GRAY** eldest son of ye sd Edward hath passed a Deed for ye same & for as much as ye said Edward GRAY lands have been divided amongst all his children & ye sd John haveing only a Double portion therof it was therefore mutually agreed between ye sd John GRAY & all ye other Children of ye sd Edward GRAY That if it should so happen that ye sd John GRAY or his heires should at any time here after be sued or otherwise molested for or by reason of ye sd Deed or any other matter for or concerning their sd fathers land whereby he may be put to damage charg or costs more then Double above what any of ye rest of ye children of ye said Edward GRAY shall be put unto that then they ye said children & their heirs shall respond & pay unto ye sd John GRAY or his heirs all such damage, costs or charges to be equally raised amongst them & this agreement was acknowledged by all ye said children that were then of age & by ye guardians of such as were within age before ye Court held at Plymouth. Rec. 30 Oct. 1684 by Nathaniel MORTON, Secretary. Receipt 30 Oct. 1684 of **Dorothy GRAY**, admx...received of **John GRAY** ye sum of £12.4s6d which he was to pay to my six children by their allottments of land. Witnesses: Nathaniel THOMAS, Stephen SKEFF.

==

Estate of **Edward GRAY** of Plymouth MA. <Plymouth Col.Court Orders>[<6>] <6:1:49> 7 July 1681, Mr. Nathaniel THOMAS, Leift. Ephraim MORTON, Mr. William CROW and Joseph WARREN app'td to take the inventory...and to give meeting to our honoured Govr. and Major BRADFORD. <6:1:50> 7 July 1681, Mistris **Dorithy GRAY** granted adm. <6:1:60> 28 Oct. 1681, depositions taken concerning exchanges of lands between **Edward GRAY**, dec'd and Walter HATCH. <6:1:61> 28 Oct. 1681...In reference to the dispose of the corne...the court have ordered that two thirds be disposed to the widdow and those children the said Mr. GRAY had by her; and the remaining third part to those children said Mr. GRAY had before hee married her. <6:1:65> 7 Mar. 1681/2, the widow is to keep £150 for the payment of debts and bringing up of children. <6:1:80> 31 Oct. 1682, Samuel SPRAGUE ordered to "give meeting to the propriators of Punckateest & Pocasett. <6:1:86> 6 Mar. 1682/3, mistrise **Dorethy GRAY** allowed £60 for the bringing up of the three youngest children. <6:2:3> 5 Mar. 1683/4, Order for admx. to appear. <6:2:14> 1 July 1684, Mrs. **Dorethy GRAY** graunted £30. <6:2:14> (1684), **Edward GRAY** and (Susanna) **GRAY**, son & dau, made choice of Capt. Nathaniel THOMAS as guardian.[<7>] **Thomas GRAY, Rebecka GRAY, Lyia/Lydia GRAY** and **Samuell GRAY** chose

Capt. Nathaniel THOMAS and Mistris **Dorethy GRAY** theire mother, to be theire gaurdians. <6:2:19> 28 Oct. 1684, Mistris **Dorethy GRAY** consented that the lands should be divided amongst his children before her dower was sett out to her. **Ann GRAY** chose John WALLEY as her guardian. <6:2:21> Account dated July 1684 presented by widow at the General Court held 5 Mar. 1684/5...I was busied every day about the concernes of the estate; in Generall I was faine to hier/hire an nurse for my younge child which cost mee for about four or five monthes time three shillings per weeke and her diett which come to five or six pound, and it is about three yeers time that I have bine thus concerned about the estate in Generall with Neglect to my owne particulare concerns and judge I may well Deserve att least fifty pound, whereof the Court allowes thirty pounds.<8>

John GRAY of Plymouth MA to **William SLADE** of Newport RI. <Plymouth Col.Deeds 5:154>
...12 Oct. 1682, John GRAY, in consideration of twenty pounds silver payed unto my father **Edward GRAY** of Plymouth, dec'd, by Thomas PURDAINE of Plymouth, and twenty one pounds silver payed by William SLADE...sell one whole share being the one and thirtieth part of lands called Weeckpimsett or Shawamett...on the west side of Taunton River in said Collonie of New Plymouth; which said lands were bought by **Edward GRAY**, dec'd, together with twenty nine other persons...in a deed dated 12 Nov. 1677...also the ninth lott containing forty five acres. Witnesses: Nathaniel THOMAS, Samuel SPRAGUE, Thomas PURDAINE. **Dorethy GRAY**, widdow of Edward, releases dower. Ack. 13 Oct 1682 before John ALDEN, Assistant.

Edward GRAY of Little Compton to **Samuel LITTLE** of Marshfield MA. <Plymouth Col.Deeds 5:448>
...29 June 1689, Edward GRAY, late of Plimouth, now residing at a place called Punkateast within the constablerick of Little Compton in the Colony of New Plimouth...in consideration of four small shares of land...in Sepowetneck & Punkateast...together with six pounds...paid by Samuel LITTLE & wf Sarah...confirm unto them two shares of land, each containing eleven acres...the 19th lott at Punkateast neck, bounded by lands of Daniel WILLCOCKS. Witnesses: Samuel SPRAGUE, Hannah SPRAGUE. Ack. 26 Dec. 1689 by Edw. Gray.

Will of **Lieut. Samuel LITTLE**, joiner of Bristol (RI). <Bristol Co.PR 2:196>
...dated 13 Jan. 1707, mentions wife **Sarah** (executrix), eldest son **Samuel LITTLE**, dau **Sarah BILLINGS** wf of Richard of Little Compton, granddaughter **Sarah BILLINGS Jr.**, youngest son **Edward LITTLE**, grandson **Richard BILLINGS Jr.**. <2:198> Inventory 4 Feb. 1707.

James LEBLOND of Boston MA to **William PABODIE Jr.** of Little Compton. <Bristol Co.Deeds 5:519>
...25 Nov. 1691, James LEBLOND, marchant, & wf Anne, for £10, sell to William PABODIE Jr., husbandman of the Town of Little Compton in ye County of Bristol in ye Collony of New Plimouth... land in Little Compton being the seventh lott amongst the lotts in that tract of land called the three quarters of a mile square containing ten acres more or less. Witnesses: Caleb CHURCH, Thomas GRAY. Rec. 17 May 1709.

Anne GRAY of Plimouth to **William SHIRTLIFF** of Plimouth. <Plymouth Col.Deeds 5:450>
...17 Feb. 1686, Anne GRAY, for twenty shillings in money to me in hand paid and alsoe for the sum of three pounds fourteene shillings in money already paid at Little Comton to Joseph CHURCH, Edward RICHMOND, David LAKE and others, late purchasers from the Indians the lands here under written...sell to William SHIRTLIFF...my two shares of lands in Little Compton lately purchased of Mamanuah the Indian Sachem by the abovesaid Church, Richmond & Lake and others by two deeds (see 5:451) for the use and to the behoofe of the proprietors of said Little Compton. Witnesses: Seth ARNOLD, Elizabeth ARNOLD. Ack. 24 May 1687 by Anne GRAY. Rec. 17 Apr. 1690. (<5:453> 3 June 1690, William SHIRTLIFF exchanges above & other lands with Nathaniel WARREN of Middleboro.)

James LEBLOND of Boston MA to **Thomas GRAY** of Plymouth MA. <Bristol Co.Deeds 6:259>
...29 Jan. 1691, James LEBLOND, marchant, & wf Anna, for £200, sell to Thomas GRAY...land on Seconet Neck in Little Compton, County of Bristol, which Anna received as her portion of the estate of her late father Edward GRAY of Plimoth...excepting what Anna formerly sold to Joseph CHURCH. Poscript: It is agreed & so intended in the within written grant that **Dorothy CLARKE** relect widow of **Edward GRAY** to have her thirds. Witnesses: Addington DAVENPORT, Mich PERRY. Rec.22 Sept. 1710.

Will of **James LEBLOND**, merchant of Boston MA. <Suffolk Co.PR #3515><9>
<18:185>...dated 17 Oct. 1700, mentions wf **Anne** to receive house etc. in Prison Lane; mentions unnamed children. Witnesses: Daniel POWNING, Joseph DOLBEAR, Eliezer MOODY. <21:474> Inventory taken 11 June 1719 by William PAYNE, Edward WINSLOW, Elisha COOKE Jr. 17 Sept 1719, executrix presents inventory of "James LEBLOND deceased Boston June 11th 1719". <22:63> Account 17 Sept. 1719, mentions debts paid by son **James LEBLOND**, approved 9 Jan. 1720. <22:220> 2nd Account of executrix, 28 Aug. 1721, to bringing up her children **Phillippa LEBLOND, Mary LEBLOND** and **Alexander LEBLOND** from 23 Oct. 1713 to 1 May last past which is 7 years; son **Gabriel LEBLOND** also mentioned.

Estate of **Ann LEBLOND**, widow of Boston MA. <Suffolk Co.PR #6016>
<28:245> Administration granted to son **James LEBLOND**, 30 Nov. 1730.

Estate of **Ichabod SOUTHWORTH**, gentleman of Middleboro MA. <Plymouth Co.PR>
<14:460> Adm. granted 29 Sept. 1757 to Rowland HAMMOND & Samuel SHAW, yeomen of Plympton.<15:255> Inventory taken 17 Oct. 1757, of estate of Capt. Ichabod SOUTHWORTH, sworn to 26 Apr. 1759. <15:387> Account of admrs. (Samuel SHAW now of Middleboro), 9 Nov. 1759. <15:591> Account of admrs. 29 Oct. 1760, mentions suit by or against Bathsheba SOUTHWORTH & Capt. SMITH.

Estate of **Mary HAMMOND** of Plympton MA. <Plymouth Co.PR 27:264>
...1788...William SHAW app'td. administrator. (No further details given.)

PLYMOUTH CO. DEEDS: (re: SHAW)

<51:136> 1762, Elijah SHAW, Samuel SHAW Jr. & Zachariah WESTON, division.
<52:185> 7 Feb. 1763, Elijah SHAW to William HARLOW, both of Middleboro, part of 79th lot in South Purchase which fell to me in division <above 51:136>.
<52:58> 14 Oct. 1765, Elijah SHAW, husbandman to Ichabod WOOD, both of Middleboro, part of 79th lot cedar swamp in South Purchase.
<50:219> 22 Oct. 1765, Elijah SHAW, husbandman to Samuel SHAW Jr., both of Middleboro, land bought of Nathaniel BRIGGS in 1763. Ack. 23 Oct. 1765.
<52:215> 3 Apr. 1766, Elijah SHAW, yeoman of Middleboro to Thomas FOSTER, blacksmith of Marshfield, house & land. Wife Phebe releases dower.
<55:79> 7 Mar. 1767, Elijah SHAW, yeoman of Middleboro to Job MACOMBER of same, part of his share in division of <51:136>.
<67:237> 11 Dec. 1788, Ichabod SHAW of Plymouth, Elijah SHAW of Taunton, William SHAW of Middleboro & Nathaniel WOOD Jr. of Woodstock VT to Peter HOAR of Middleboro... all that fell to us by our Aunt Mary HAMMOND, dec'd of Plympton.
<74:81> 16 Jan. 1793, Elijah SHAW & Isaac SHAW of Middleboro to Andrew LEACH of Boston, forge on Eel River. Wives Jemima & Deborah release dowers.
<85:7> 25 Aug. 1794, Elijah SHAW, laborer of Middleboro to Azel & David THOMAS, traders of same store & land on road to Plympton. Wf Deborah releases dower. Ack. in Plymouth co. 24 Apr. 1798 by Elijah.
<89:216> 23 Feb. 1798, Elijah SHAW, yeoman of Middleboro to Josiah CLARK, gentleman of same, half swamp bought of Noah FULLER.
<83:249> 23 May 1798, Ichabod SHAW, blacksmith of Plymouth to sons Ichabod Jr. & Southworth SHAW blacksmiths of Plymouth. Wife Priscilla releases dower.
<88:130> 1 Oct. 1799, Ichabod SHAW to son Ichabod SHAW Jr., Plymouth.
<87:263> 11 June 1800, Elijah SHAW, gentleman of Abington to Zebulon PANE Jr. cordwainer of same, land in Abington. Wife Hannah releases dower. Ack. 21 July 1800.
<93:70> 1 Mar. 1802, Elijah SHAW, yeoman of Middleboro to Crocker COBB of same, my hatter's shop. Wife Deborah signs. Ack. 12 Mar. 1802.
<137:115> 13 Jan 1807, Elijah SHAW, yeoman of Middleboro to Jacob & James SOULE of same, all rights in cedar swamp given me by William & Lydia SHAW, 20 Mar. 1806.
<112:214> 9 ( ) 1810, Elijah SHAW, yeoman of Middleboro. (Mar. or Apr.)
<130:155> 1810, Elijah SHAW of Middleboro.
<117:260> 1812, Elijah SHAW & wf Deborah of Middleboro.
<153:34> 1824, Elijah SHAW & wf Deborah of Middleboro et al
<169:145> 1830, Elijah SHAW & wf Deborah of Middleboro, right of Deborah from her mother, Hannah CLARK.
<226:233> 20 Apr 1847, Elijah SHAW & wf Susanna in her right, Ira SHAW & wf Fanny in her right, Lucy BRIGGS, widow of Samuel, all of Middleboro to Nathaniel SAMPSON of same, all their rights in homestead farm of Isaac SAMPSON, late of Middleboro, dec'd.

Will of **Nathaniel THOMAS**, yeoman of Plymouth MA. <Plymouth Co.PR #20436>
<80:261>...dated 8 May 1830, everything to wf **Jane**; mentions children. Pr. 2nd Mon. Aug. 1838.

Will of **Jane THOMAS**, widow of Plymouth MA. <Plymouth Co.PR #20359, F1:20>
<93:81>...dated 24 May 1843, dau **Harriet JONES** wf of Samuel to receive dwelling house & lot in Plymouth on the road to Carver; daus **Jane REED, Mary Ann CALLAWAY**; one quarter in trust for dau **Deborah MACOMBER**, wf of Elijah Jr., for her sole use, separate and independent of her husband. Witnesses: William THOMAS, Joshua B. THOMAS, J.N. STODDARD. Pr. 3rd Mon. Feb. 1851.

Enoch DRAKE et al to **Nathaniel C. LANMAN** of Plymouth MA. <Plymouth Co.Deeds 269:185>
...16 Oct. 1854, Enoch DRAKE of Middleboro & wf Jane in her right, **Elijah MACOMBER** of Rochester & wf Deborah in her right, **Mary Ann CALLOWAY** and **Harriet JONES**, widow of Plymouth...for $300 paid by Nathaniel C. LANMAN, sell a one acre lot in Plymouth bounded by land of Elias THOMAS, Joseph SEYMOUR & Andrew L. RUSSELL, on the road to Carver, being late the property of Nathaniel THOMAS of Plymouth, dec'd and devised by Jane THOMAS to the grantors in her last Will and Testament. Witness: George R. CALLIWAY. Ack. by Harriet JONES only same day.

Heirs of **Nathaniel THOMAS**. <Plymouth Co.Deeds 273:272>
...9 Jan. 1854, **Deborah MACOMBER, Mary A. CALLIWAY, Harriet JONES** and **Jane DRAKE**, for $100.00, sell to Joseph SEYMOUR, nailor of Plymouth...lot of land in Plymouth bounded as per deed from Israel HOYT to Nathaniel THOMAS 27 Apr. 1814. Witnesses: Elijah MACOMBER, Webster SEYMOUR. Rec. 13 May 1856.

Will of **Joseph RYDER**, yeoman of Plymouth MA. <Plymouth Co.PR 19:421,422>
...dated 21 Apr. 1764, aged, & under decays of nature, mentions daus **Jemima SAMSON, Philippa LORING**, child & heirs of dau **Hannah COOPER**, grandson **Southworth SAMSON**, son **Joseph RIDER** (executor). Pr. 2 Feb. 1767.

Joseph RIDER of Plimouth MA to **Joseph WANTON** of Tiverton. <Bristol Co.Deeds 18:183>
...4 July 1728, Joseph RIDER & wf Mary, for £30, sell to Joseph WANTON...all our rights in the

Twenty Seventh House Lott and the Share belonging to it in the Gore Lotts in Pocasset Lands in Tiverton...as it descended from our honoured mother **Desire SOUTHWORTH** dec'd. Witnesses: Joshua FREEMAN, Elkanah LEONARD. Rec. 8 July 1728

Edward SOUTHWORTH of Middleboro MA to **Joseph RIDER** of Plymouth MA. <Plymouth Co.Deeds 15:47>
...22 Sept. 1720, Edward SOUTHWORTH, for Ł68 already paid by my brother in law Joseph RIDER, sold 80 acre homestead in Middleboro...bounded by land of Nathaniel SOUTHWORTH.

Will of **Joseph RIDER** of Plymouth MA. <Plymouth Co.PR #17370, 25:316>
...dated 16 Mar. 1779, weak & infirm, mentions wf **Elizabeth**; son **Job RIDER** (executor); daus **Hannah BARNES, Mary LEONARD, Elizabeth DREW, Bathsheba CHURCHELL, Sarah RIDER**; daus **Desire & Phebe**; son **Nathaniel RIDER.** Witnesses: John COTTON, Jonathan DIMAN, Ebenezer NELSON. Pr. 7 July 1779, sworn to by Jonathan DIMAN & John COTTON, Esq. Bond 7 July 1779, of **Job RIDER** of Plymouth, **Nathaniel RIDER**, yeoman of Plymton and Andrew CROSWELL, goldsmith of Plymouth. Witnesses: Robert BROWN, Isaac LOTHROP.

Guardianship of Children of **Isaac HALL.** <Original owned by Miss Cora E. Pierce>
...4 Dec. 1799, Taunton...**Isaac HALL** late of Raynham, now resident in Westmoreland NH, app'td gdn of **Alfreda HALL, Philip HALL, Betsey HALL** and **Elishua HALL,** minor children of the said **Isaac HALL** and grandchildren of **Paul LEONARD,** late of Raynham, dec'd. Receipt 2 May 1814 of their shares, signed by **Alfreda SNOW** wf of Benjamin, **Philip HALL, Betsey HALL** and **Elihu HALL.**

MICRO #4 OF 7

PLYMOUTH CO. DEEDS (re: Joseph RIDER)

<10:1:629> - 8 Feb. 1713/4, Joseph RIDER of Marshfield, cordwainer, land at Two Mile.
<14:193> - 1 Aug. 1719, Joseph RIDER of Hull, mariner, house & land at Plymouth & Plympton.
<15:47> - 22 Sept 1720, Joseph RIDER of Plymouth.
<15:198> - 9 Oct. 1721, Joseph RIDER Jr. of Plymouth, cordwainer.

The following citations only are given with no details:

Grantee: 22:110;23:223;25:204;26:42;27:187;28:219;34:55;35:54;41:93;53:202;58:260;75:80;78:101; 80:7;81:77;96:102.
Grantor: 22:106;34:190;35:195;53:202;55:264;65:44;71:88;77:277;88:141;96:102.

Samuel RIDER et al to **Samuel WINSLOW** of Rochester MA. <Plymouth Co.Deeds 32:64>
...5 Sept. 1731, Philip VINCENT, Samuel RIDER & Theophilus CROSBY, yeomen of Yarmouth and Kenelm WINSLOW, yeoman of Harwich, sell to our uncle Samuel WINSLOW, yeoman, lands of our Grandfather **Kenelm WINSLOW** of Harwich, dec'd, who gave it by his will to his grandchildren **Mercy, Bethiah, Rebecca & John WING.** Signed by all four grantors as well as Mercy VINCENT, Rebecca RIDER and Thankful CROSBY.

Phillippe LORING of Barnstable MA to **Uriah SAMSON** of Middleboro MA. <Plymouth Co. Deeds 64:226>
...19 Apr. 1780, Phillippe LORING, spinster, sold land in Middleboro to Uriah SAMSON, gentleman. Witnesses: Daniel TYLOR, John HINCKLEY Jr. Rec. 31 Jan. 1786.

David LORING & wf Philippa, dau of Joseph RIDER...25 Dec. 1767. <Plymouth Co.Deeds 54:146>

Will of **Capt. Nathaniel SOUTHWORTH** of Middleboro MA. <Plymouth Co.PR #18938>
<14:318>...25 Dec. 1755, mentions son **Gideon SOUTHWORTH;** brother **Ichabod SOUTHWORTH;** son **Nathaniel SOUTHWORTH** (executor); my two grandchildren, the heirs of dec'd son **Samuel SOUTHWORTH;** to daus **Fear LEONARD** and **Hannah SPROUT** my twenty seven acres which I bought of Ebenezer BARROWS in the little Lott mens purchase. <14:320> Pr. 2 May 1757. <14:370> Inventory, 19 May 1757.

Will of **Seth ARNOLD,** yeoman of Duxbury MA. <Plymouth Co.PR 4:307-8>
...dated 11 Dec. 1715, mentions wf **Elizabeth;** sons **Edward ARNOLD, James ARNOLD, Benjamin ARNOLD;** two children of dec'd dau **Desire BARTLETT,** viz: **Sarah BARTLETT, Seth BARTLETT.** Witnesses: Samuel SEABURY, Israel SYLVESTER, Isaac BARKER. Sworn by Samuel SEABURY 11 Dec. 1721, by Isaac BARKER 31 Oct. 1721. Pr. 22 Dec. 1721.

Estate of **Samuel THOMAS** of Marshfield MA. <Plymouth Co.PR 4:254>
Inventory taken 30 Sept. 1720...Seth ARNOLD one of the appraisers.

Estate of **James THOMAS** of Duxbury MA. <Plymouth Co.PR 4:257>
Division of lands, 9 Mar. 1719/20, by Seth ARNOLD, John PARTRIDGE, Israel THOMAS and John ALDEN.

Capt. Seth ARNOLD of Duxborough MA to **Thomas FISH** of Duxborough MA. <Plymouth Co.Deeds 15:29>
...15 May 1719, Capt. Seth ARNOLD, for Ł350, sold to Thomas FISH, yeoman...all that my farm or tract of upland & meadow which I formerly bought of Samuel SAMSON lying at a place called Blue Fish River in Duxborough...bounded by land of Abraham SAMSON Sr., Robert BARKER, Benjamin ALDEN, said Thomas FISH, Ichabod SAMSON. Rec. 21 June 1720 at which time Seth ARNOLD ack. and wf Elizabeth releases dower.

Will of **Ezra ARNOLD**, yeoman of Duxbury MA. <Plymouth Co.PR 25:416>
...dated 1 Nov. 1779, mentions wf **Rebecca**; sons **Seth ARNOLD, Gamaliel ARNOLD**; dau **Lucy FREEMAN**, wf of Edmund; sons **William ARNOLD, Edward ARNOLD**. Pr. 6 Mar. 1780.

Will of **John GRAY** of Kingston MA. <Plymouth Co.PR #8693>
<6:191>...dated 23 Sept. 1728, mentions wf **Johanna**; son **Samuel GRAY** (executor); son in law **John TINKHAM**; daus **Mercy GRAY, Johanna FULLER, Anne TINCOM/Tinkham.** <6:192> Pr. 21 July 1732. <6:215> Warrant to appraise & witnesses sworn, 4 July 1732. <7:427> Inventory taken 7 Aug. 1732.

Estate of **Samuel GRAY** of Kingston MA. <Plymouth Co.PR 8:5,62,63,187;13:162;21:4>
<21:4> Division, 22 July 1771, of real estate that was set off to **Patience GRAY** as her thirds in the estate of her husband, Samuel GRAY, and to divide the same into five equal parts, viz: **John GRAY** (two shares), **Mary COOK** wf of Benjamin, **Samuel GRAY**, and to the heirs of **Wait GRAY**...heirs may hold their part in severalty after the decease of their said mother...also set off to **Samuel GRAY**, ten acre homestead farm, bounded by land of John GRAY, heirs of Thomas CUSHMAN, heirs of Ebenezer FULLER, Benjamin WARREN.

Will of **Richard MIDDLECOTT**, merchant of Boston MA. <Suffolk Co.PR #2883, 15:299,300,414;82:69,72>
<15:300>...dated 22 June 1700, mentions wf **Sarah** (executrix); to son **Edward MIDDLECOTT**, Ł20 besides lands I have settled upon him in Old England; dau **Mary GIBBS** wf of Henry; to daus **Sarah MIDDLECOTT** and **Jane MIDDLECOTT**, Ł500 each; son in law **William PAYNE**; loveing friends Col. Elisha HUTCHESON and Maj. John WALLEY to be overseers. Witnesses: John INDECOTT, Joseph HILLER, Joseph PROUT. Attached to will is a letter, dated 20 June 1704, signed by **Sarah MIDDLECOTT** stating that "by reason of my lameness I do desire & request to take the testimony" of the witnesses. Pr. 20 June 1704. <original> Inventory taken 23 Aug. 1704 by Joseph HILLER, John INDECOTT, incl. three dwelling houses (one in Wing's Lane), negro man & girl. Sworn by widow 23 Apr. 1705.

Estate of **Sarah MIDDLECOTT**, widow of Boston MA. <Suffolk Co.PR #5246>
<13:347;24:482> Adm. granted 12 May 1726, to children **Sarah BOUCHER, Elisha COOKE** & wf **Jane.** <27:33> Inventory, 23 Jan. 1728. <13:349> Objections to account, 18 Mar. 1727 and answer, 15 Apr. 1728. <13:350> Bond to appeal, 4 June 1728. <13:351> Reasons & decree, 24 Dec. 1728. <27:176> Account, 19 May 1729. <27:179> Division 26 May 1729, Ł293.16.5 to each, viz: **Sarah BOUCHER; Elisha COOKE** in right of his wf **Jane; William PAYNE**, Esq., double portion, Ł587.12.10; heirs of **Mary HAGGET**, dec'd; heirs of **Edward MIDDLECOTT**, dec'd.

Estate of **Tobias PAINE** of Boston MA. <Suffolk Co.PR 6:28>
...Nuncupative will, dated 11 Sept. 1669, directed to father in law **John WINSLOW**, viz:...What I have heere in money or Goods, what shall come in from any other place as debts & adventures, what is due from mee being first made good & moderate funerall expences discharged, I doe hereby fully & freely Give & bequeath unto youre daughter my wife & to our little sonne, to whose care, Charge & Education I leave him, enjoyning her in case shee marries againe that hee may not be abused or wronged but duly taken care for which I hope also you will mind if it happens during youre life.. **Mr. John WINSLOW** deposed, 21 Sept. 1669, that hee heard his late sonn in lawe Mr. Tobias PAINE on the 11th instant to declare it to bee his mind & last will that hee was of a sound disposing mind, hee departed this life the 12 instant. Adm. granted 21 Sept. 1669 to **Sarah PAINE** his relict in behalfe of her selfe & the sonne of the said Tobias & Sarah, **William PAINE**, to performe the imperfect will. <7:14> Inventory taken 26 Jan. 1669/70 by John WINSLOW, Thomas BRATTLE, William TAILER, Richard MIDDLECOTT; incl. Indian boy called William BRANDY; voyollin/violin, L1. Debts due from: Nicholas BYRAM, Adrian HYCKS of London, Robert LATHAM, Edward WANTON, Ephraim HUNT, Martin KREIGER(sp) of New Yorke, Capt. OLIVER, Nathaniel ADAMS, Thomas JENNERS, Capt. Robert MUNDEN, John WINSLEY, Edmund DOWNES, Joseph ROCK, William DARVALL, Robert GIBBS, Mrs. PEARSON, Deacon PARKS, Benjamin GIBBS, Job WINSLOW, John DRURY, William CROW, Goodwife BLAKE, Francis COMBS, Edward GRAY, Nathaniel WHITMORE, John LEONARD, Isaac HARRIS, Edward DOTY, Henry HOGGS/HOGES of London, Thomas PAYN of Breeman. Payments due to: Peter COSTON, Jeronimo MULLER, Thomas REVELL, Major James BEAK, Francis KEMPE, Abraham MAJOR, David Raphiell DEMERCADO, Robert NEWBALD, Thomas PHIPP, Mr. HELDEN & Mr. BROOCKS In Company, Adrian HICKS.

Will of **William PAYNE**, gentleman of Boston MA. <Suffolk Co.PR B:32:176-178;B:40:272>
...dated 25 Jan. 1733, mentions son **Tobias PAYNE**; dau **Mary SEWALL**; children of my late wife **Mary** who was the dau of **James TAYLOR**, Esq., dec'd...I give to my other children by **Margaret** my present wife, namely **Sarah, Anne, John, Margaret, Richard, Edward** and **Jane PAYNE** (youngest dau); debts left me by my honoured Father **Tobias PAYNE** at the time of his decease in the hands of my cousin Mr. **Thomas PAYNE** of E(m)de(n)?, merchant; mentions brick house on Cornhill St., Boston. Pr. 1 July 1735. <B:40:272> Receipt of heirs, 23 Sept. 1747...subducting out of our parts what we had received from our Grandfather TAYLOR's estate...acknowledge receipt from mother Mrs. **Margaret PAYNE**, signed by: **Mary SEWALL, Richard PAYNE, Edward PAYNE, John PAYNE, John COLEMAN, Sarah COLEMAN, Ann PAYNE, Margaret PHILLIPS, Jane PAYNE** and Kenelm WINSLOW as guardian to **Mary PAYNE**, only child of **Tobias PAYNE**, dec'd.

Estate of **Elisha COOKE** of Boston MA. <Suffolk Co.PR #7042>
...1737...<33:274> Will. <33:273> Pr. <34:241> Inventory. <62:513> Account. <62:519> Warrant for Division. <62:520> Division. (No further details in files.)

MICRO # 5 OF 7

Robert LATHAM to **Mitchell HAYWARD.** <Plymouth Co.Deeds 5:28>
...6 Mar. 1685, Robert LATHAM & wf Susanna to Mitchell HAYWARD. Ack. by Robert & Susanna 14 Nov. 1685. Rec. 17 May 1703.

Samuel LEONARD to **John LEONARD.** <Plymouth Col.Deeds 3:199>
...6 May 1671, Samuel LEONARD confirms deed of gift of father & mother to brother John LEONARD of land bounded by land of Elder BRETT, bought or exchanged with Robert LATHAM.

BRISTOL COUNTY DEEDS: (re: LATHAM) <"all on index">

<56:402> - 16 Oct. 1775, Nathan BAKER to James LATHAM.
<57:156> - 26 Mar. 1777, Seth DEAN et ux to Rebecca LATHAM et al.
<59:55> - 7 Dec. 1778, Zephaniah SIMMONS et ux to James LATHAM.
<59:56> - 7 Dec. 1778, John STEPHENS to James LATHAM.
<59:56> - 10 Dec. 1778, Zephaniah SIMMONS et al to James LATHAM.
<59:57> - 14 Dec. 1778, James LATHAM & wf Esther to John STEPHENS.
<61:465> - 23 May 1783, James LATHAM to John KING.

Josiah HAYWARD et al to **Nathaniel HAYWARD** of Bridgewater MA. <Plymouth Co.Deeds 33:184>
...3 Feb. 1734/5, **Josiah HAYWARD, Isaac HAYWARD, Joseph LATHAM** & wf Sarah, **Elisha DUNBAR** & wf Mercy, **David KINGMAN** & wf Mary, **Timothy HAYWARD, Elizabeth HAYWARD, Susanna HAYWARD, Bethiah HAYWARD**, all of Bridgewater to our brother **Nathaniel HAYWARD**...rights in certain land of deceased father **Nathaniel HAYWARD.**

Chilton LATHAM & wf Susanna, dau of John KINGMAN dec'd...11 May 1724 <Plymouth Co.Deeds 27:125>

James LATHAM of Bridgewater MA to **Anne WADE** of Bridgewater MA. <Plymouth Co.Deeds 13:107>
...16 Sept. 1717, James LATHAM conveys a gift to daughter Anne WADE and her husband Nicholas WADE ...refers to land "I have given to Nathaniel HARDEN out of ye same lot". Ack. 16 Oct. 1717.

James LATHAM of Bridgewater MA to **Nathaniel HARDING.** <Plymouth Co.Deeds 20:139>
...1720/1, James LATHAM conveys gift to son in law Nathaniel HARDEN/HARDING and daughter Susanna HARDING, his wife...refers to land given to son in law Nicholas WADE. Ack. 8 Feb. 1720/1.

Jerusha LATHAM, widow of Robert LATHAM of Bridgewater...2 Apr. 1791 <Plymouth Co.Deeds 71:73>

Thomas LATHAM of Bridgewater MA to **John HOLMAN** of Milton MA. <Plymouth Co.Deeds 22:228>
...11 Apr. 1728, Thomas LATHAM, yeoman, sold to John HOLMAN, gentleman...homestead in Bridgewater containing 80 acres...fourty acres of which homestead I bought of my Father **James LATHAM**...bounded by land of Joseph LATHAM and heirs of Thomas WHITMAN. Wife Deborah LATHAM releases dower. Rec. 30 Apr. 1728.

Will of **Nicholas WADE**, yeoman of Bridgewater MA. <Plymouth Co.PR 19:476>
...dated 20 Jan. 1767, mentions wf **Ann**; sons **Samuel WADE, Thomas WADE, John WADE, James WADE, Nicholas WADE, Amasa WADE,** dau **Mary MITCHELL**; son **Amasa** to receive two acres in Bridgewater that was formerly John BOLTON's. Pr. 22 May 1767. <19:493> Inventory taken 25 May 1767. <19:553> Division 13 Oct. 1767, of remainder of personal property to dau **Mary MITCHELL** and the widow.

Amasa WADE of Weymouth MA to **Nicholas WADE** of Bridgewater MA. <Plymouth Co.Deeds 60:35>
...7 Feb. 1772, Amasa WADE, housewright, for £2, sells to Nicholas WADE, yeoman, two acres in Bridgewater near land of heirs of John BOLTON. Ack. 20 Apr. 1779. Rec. 13 Nov. 1779.

Will of **Joseph LATHAM** of Bridgewater MA. <Plymouth Co.PR 15:78,79,253>
...dated 2 June 1758, mentions wf **Sarah**, eldest dau **Betty LATHAM**, dau **Sarah LATHAM**, four sons. <15:53> Inventory 19 Jan. 1759.

PLYMOUTH COUNTY DEEDS: (re: Thomas LATHAM)

<17:167> - 5 Feb. 1723/4, Thomas LATHAM to Josiah SEARS, homestead in Bridgewater.
<18:37> - 4 June 1724, Thomas LATHAM to Thomas AMES, land near Poor Meadow.
<18:55> - 25 June 1724, Thomas & Deborah LATHAM, of Bridgewater to Deacon Samuel SEABURY, land near Poor Meadow.
<20:189> - 29 Sept 1725, Thomas & Deborah LATHAM of Middleboro to Ezra CLAP, land in 26 Mens Purchase & his house thereon.
<20:214> - 2 Aug. 1726, Thomas & Deborah LATHAM of Bridgewater, mortgage.
<22:228> - 11 Apr. 1728, Thomas & Deborah LATHAM of Bridgewater, to John HOLMAN, his dwelling bot of his father James LATHAM.
<42:183> - 7 Nov. 1753, Thomas LATHAM of Bridgewater to dau Rhoda CONANT & her husband David CONANT of Bridgewater, one sixth of land on Kennebeck River.
<42:246> - 18 Apr. 1754, Thomas LATHAM, Nicholas & Ann WADE, to brother Joseph LATHAM of Bridgewater, all rights in estate of father James LATHAM, dec'd.
<45:186> - 2 Jan. 1759, Thomas LATHAM of Bridgewater to Joseph GANNETT Jr. of Bridgewater, land adjoining Latham's house.

PLYMOUTH COUNTY DEEDS: (re: Thomas LATHAM) cont-d

<63:168> - 22 Aug. 1785, William LATHAM & Thomas LATHAM to William SNELL.

PLYMOUTH COUNTY DEEDS: (re: Joseph LATHAM)

<2:26> - 28 Feb. 1688, Joseph LATHAM & wf Phebe to John THOMSON Sr., land my honoured father Robert LATHAM, dec'd, formerly bought. Rec. 1696.
<10:1:147> 12 Apr. 1690, Joseph LATHAM of Providence to James LATHAM of Bridgewater. Ack. 28 May 1694. Rec. 1713.
<10:1:149> 25 Aug. 1705, Joseph LATHAM of Providence to James LATHAM of Bridgewater. Ack. 2 May 1705. Rec. 1713.
<33:184> - , Joseph LATHAM to Nathaniel HAYWARD.
<41:154> - 30 Aug. 1738, Joseph LATHAM to John HOOPER.
<47:13> - 4 June 1742, Joseph LATHAM Jr. to Noah WASHBURN. Ack. 6 Apr. 1761.
<51:25> - 1 Jan. 1746, Joseph LATHAM to David KINGMAN, land in original right of Robert LATHAM in 8 mile grant. Ack. 7 July 1749. Rec. 1765.
<40:159> - 2 Dec. 1749, Joseph LATHAM & Robert LATHAM divide land they dwell on which did formerly belong to our Honoured Grandfather Robert LATHAM, dec'd.
<43:10> - 10 June 1752, Joseph LATHAM to son Joseph LATHAM.
<42:269> - 16 May 1754, Joseph LATHAM to son Thomas LATHAM.
<43:183> - 15 May 1754, Joseph LATHAM & wf Sarah to son Joseph LATHAM. Ack. 17 May 1754 by both.
<43:269> - 22 June 1757, Joseph LATHAM 3d to Shadrack KEENE.
<45:42> - 15 Feb. 1757, Joseph LATHAM to sons Nathaniel LATHAM and Seth LATHAM (youngest son). Ack. 2 June 1758 (date he made his will).
<47:14> - 10 Sept 1759, Joseph LATHAM Jr. to Noah WASHBURN. Ack. 29 Oct. 1761.
<49:80> - 11 Apr. 1761, Joseph LATHAM and Robert LATHAM to Reuben HALL.
<47:223> - 21 May 1761, Joseph LATHAM and Robert LATHAM & wf Bethiah to Joab WILLIS.
<48:266> - 19 Nov. 1762, Joseph LATHAM and Robert LATHAM & wf Bethiah to Jonathan WASHBURN.
<54:237> - 7 Aug. 1762, Joseph LATHAM Jr. to Amos WHITMAN. Ack. 13 Mar. 1769.
<55:3> - 18 May 1769, Joseph LATHAM Jr. to Shadrach KEEN.
<55:169> - 10 Mar. 1770, Joseph LATHAM Jr. & wf Mary to Israel HILL.
<56:11> - 26 Mar. 1771, Joseph LATHAM 2d/Jr. & wf Mary to Samuel THAXTER.
<57:264> - 9 Nov. 1773, Joseph LATHAM and Robert LATHAM & wf Bethiah to Ebenezer BURGESS.
<58:189> - 7 Nov. 1758, Joseph LATHAM Jr. & wf Mary to Sarah ALLEN. Ack. 1 Oct. 1759. Rec. 1775.

Estate of **Isaac HARRIS** of Bridgewater MA. <Plymouth Co.PR #9328>
...1706...<2:85> Adm. granted to sons in law Pelatiah SMITH and John KINGMAN; wf **Mary** is called sister of Peter DUNBAR; children **Benjamin** & **Martha HARRIS** under 7 years. <2:91> Inventory. <3:11> Warrant to appraise real estate. <3:12> Division of real estate. Account. <3:14> Receipts. <3:73> Receipts. The Account mentions the following children, viz: **Isaac HARRIS** (eldest living son), **Samuel HARRIS, Desire KINGMAN** wf of John, **Jane SMITH** wf of Pelatiah, **Susanna NULAND/NEWLAND, Mary, Mercy, Benjamin HARRIS, Martha.**

Isaac HARRIS of Bridgewater MA to **Eleazer WASHBURN** of Bridgewater MA. <Plymouth Co.Deeds 32:104>
...2 June 1736, Isaac HARRIS, for ₤350 bills of credit, sold to Eleazer WASHBURN...two twenty acre lots in Bridgewater butting on Satuckett River, land formerly belonging to Nathaniel AMES and David PERKINS.

Will of **Arthur HARRIS**. <Plymouth Co.PR #9322>
<12:141-3>...dated 27 Mar. 1750, mentions wf **Bethiah; Benjamin HARRIS** (eldest son); **Silas HARRIS** (2nd son); **William HARRIS & Caleb HARRIS** (youngest sons); **Luce HARRIS** (eldest dau); **Bethiah HARRIS** and **Mehitable HARRIS** (youngest daus).

Estate of **Isaac HARRIS** of Bridgewater MA. <Plymouth Co.PR #9329>
<7:434;8:193,196,198>...1738. <8:194> Division 20 May 1740 among heirs, viz: **Arthur HARRIS**, yeoman, **Abner HARRIS, John HOLMAN Jr.** & wf **Ann,** all of Bridgewater and **Jane JOHNSON** of Middletown CT

Will of **John KINGMAN** of Bridgewater MA.
...dated 1 Jan. 1744/5, mentions wf **Bethiah;** son **Ebenezer KINGMAN** (executor) to receive homestead sons **John KINGMAN, Josiah KINGMAN, David KINGMAN;** daus **Mary COPELAND, Deliverance ORCUTT, Abigail ALLEN; John ORCUTT** (under 21) and **Susanna ORCUTT** (under 18), children of dec'd dau **Desire ORCUTT;** son in law **John ORCUTT; Ebenezer ALLEN** (under 21) and **Bethiah ALLEN** (under 18) children of dec'd dau **Bethiah ALLEN;** son in law **James ALLEN.** Witnesses: Josiah/Joseph EDSON, Jesse EDSON, James EDSON. Pr. 3 Feb. 1755.

MICRO #6 OF 7

Estate of **Nathaniel P. HEWES**, auctioneer of Boston MA. <Suffolk Co.PR #24046, 188:254;203:21>
Bond/Letter 26 Oct. 1812, **Sally HEWES**, widow, app'td admx. Surety: David M. EATON, merchant.

Charles WILLIS of Boston MA and **Susanna C. HUNT.** <Suffolk Co.Deeds 354:248>
...16 Sept. 1831, agreement between Charles WILLIS, trader and Susanna C. HUNT re land adjoining house of Willis' deceased father on Sun Court St.

Charles WILLIS of Boston MA to **Charles WILLIS** of Boston MA. <Suffolk Co.Deeds 339:261,262,263> ...8 Sept. 1829, Charles WILLIS, sailmaker, to son Charles WILLIS, trader, house & land on Sun Court St. <:262> Charles WILLIS Jr. leases above to father for life. <:263> Charles WILLIS Jr. sells to Joseph R. NEWELL. (no details)

Charles WILLIS Jr. of Boston MA. <Suffolk Co.Deeds 262:110>
...5 Apr. 1819, Sheriff's sale to Charles WILLIS Jr., auctioneer, on account of judgement in favor of Larkin SNOW, wharfinger of Boston, against John ETHERIDGE.

Isaac COPELAND of Braintree MA to **Jonathan FRENCH** of Boston MA. <Suffolk Co.Deeds 96:138> ...18 Sept. 1760, Isaac COPELAND, husbandman, for £6, sold to Jonathan FRENCH, minor...two acre meadow in Braintree and is one quarter part of eight acres lately owned by Capt. Ebenezer THAYER of Braintree...now undivided, the other three quarters now belonging to Benjamin HAYDEN and Moses FRENCH Jr....bounded by land of Moses FRENCH Jr., Capt. John THAYER, Benjamin HAYDEN. Witnesses: Deliverance FRENCH, Moses FRENCH Jr. Ack. 14 June 1761. Rec. 18 June 1761.

Isaac COPELAND of Braintree to **Ebenezer THAYER Jr.** of Braintree MA. <Suffolk Co.Deed 108:70> ...21 Sept. 1764, Isaac COPELAND, yeoman, for £69.15s, sold to Ebenezer THAYER Jr., gentleman... one half of a certain parcel of land in Braintree...being part of the South Common...bounded by land of Jonathan HAYWARD, Thomas FRENCH, William FRENCH, Seth COPELAND, Samuel CURTIS...the whole containing sixty eight and one quarter acres. Witnesses: Richard FAXON Jr., Ebenezer THAYER 3d. Ack. 31 Oct. 1765 by Isaac COPELAND. Rec. 31 Oct. 1765.

Isaac COPELAND of Braintree MA to **Ebenezer THAYER Jr.** of Braintree MA. <Suffolk Co.Deeds 113:85> ...9 Apr. 1768, Isaac COPELAND, yeoman, & wf Lydia, for £112.13.4d, sold to Ebenezer THAYER Jr., Esq...twenty acres at Clay Swamp in Braintree with a dwelling house & barn...bounded by land of John VINTON, ALDRIDGE's farm, Capt. Richard FAXON...excepting one square acre now in the improvement of Lemuel THAYER, the land whereon his house now stands. Witnesses: John COPELAND, Ebenezer THAYER. Rec. 26 Aug. 1768.

Isaac COPELAND of Braintree MA to **John COPELAND** of Braintree MA. <Suffolk Co.Deeds 137:52> ...23 Mar. 1779, Isaac COPELAND, yeoman, for £69.15s, sold to son John COPELAND, labourer... thirty four and a quarter acres of the South Common land in Braintree...being the one moiety of a lot of land in said South Common...being in Common and Undivided with the other moiety belonging to Ebenezer THAYER Esq...bounded by land of Jonathan HAYWARD, Meshach PENNIMAN, Benjamin VEAZIE, Seth COPELAND, Samuel CURTIS, William HOBART, Benjamin CLEVERLY and Micah NEWCOMB. Wf Lydia COPELAND gives consent. Witnesses: Micah NEWCOMB, Henry FIELD. Ack. 6 Apr. 1779. Rec. 8 Feb. 1783.

Isaac COPELAND of Braintree MA to **Ebenezer THAYER** of Braintree MA. <Suffolk Co.Deeds 140:20> ...15 Sept. 1783, Isaac COPELAND, yeoman, for £156, sold to Ebenezer THAYER, Esq....nineteen acres in Braintree bounded by land of Mis^{s} HAYWARD, Jonathan HAYWARD, Daniel HAYWARD, Meschech PENNIMAN and Seth COPELAND. Wf Lydia COPELAND releases dower. Witnesses: Samuel Miller THAYER, Judah WILD. Ack. 6 Oct. 1783. Rec. 7 Oct. 1783.

Isaac COPELAND of Braintree MA to **Thomas NEWCOMB** of Braintree MA. <Suffolk Co.Deeds 147:84> ...1 Jan. 1785, Isaac COPELAND, yeoman, for £120, sold to Thomas NEWCOMB, gentleman...in the middle parish of Braintree...being all that part of the homestead of me said Isaac which I have not mortgaged to Ebenezer THAYER Esq....bounded by land of Jonathan ARNOLD, Gideon FRENCH, Seth COPELAND, road leading to Newcomb's Landing. Witnesses: Ebenezer VISEY, Samuel COPELAND. Ack. 31 Jan. 1785. Rec. 3 Feb. 1785.

SUFFOLK COUNTY DEEDS: (re: Isaac COPELAND)

<162:186> - 1788, Isaac COPELAND to Nathaniel HAYWARD, land in Braintree.
<162:187> - 1788, Isaac COPELAND to Elkanah COPELAND of Braintree, land & holdings in Braintree.
<163:166> - 1788, Isaac COPELAND to Ebenezer THAYER, land & buildings in Braintree.

Will of **Ruthy COPELAND**, single woman of Boston MA <Suffolk Co.PR #35174>
<145:59>...dated 10 Feb. 1847, mentions mother **Ruth COPELAND** of Quincy; sister **Eliza JACKSON**, wf of Francis of Boston; brother **Thomas COPELAND** of Boston; brother **Samuel COPELAND** of Quincy; **Francis JACKSON** of Boston in trust for sisters: **Nancy ADAMS**, wf of Hezekiah of Milton, **Polly BAXTER**, wf of Lewis, of Boston and **Nabby WELLINGTON**, wf of Jonathan, of Milton, without any interference or control on the part of their husbands; brother in law **Francis JACKSON** named executor. <145:60> Pr. 16 Aug. 1847. <145:105> Account of executor, 20 Sept. 1847; no real estate, cash totals $1279.25. Payments of legacies to above mentioned heirs, incl. sister **Sally BRIESLER**, wf of John, of Quincy. <263:255> Petition for probate. <243:158> Order of notice. <263:255> Bond & Letter. <284:188> Inventory.

Estate of **Samuel COPELAND**, husbandman of Braintree MA. <Suffolk Co.PR #8648>
<39:307> Letter of administration, 6 Jan. 1746, to **Mary COPELAND**, widow and Samuel COPELAND, tailor. <39:478> Inventory taken 4 Mar. 1746, sworn to by admrs. 31 Mar. 1747; mentions son **Isaac COPELAND**. <41:93> Account. <41:249> Dower. <41:447-8> Real estate appraised. <41:449> Settlement of real estate, 30 Aug. 1748, valued at £1000; lands could not be divided without great prejudice therefore lands were assigned to son **Samuel COPELAND**, he paying unto his brothers & sisters, viz: **Isaac COPELAND, Seth COPELAND, Mary DUNHAM, Desire HUBBART, Abigail KINGMAN, Hannah COPELAND, Bethiah COPELAND** and **Susanna COPELAND**, the sum of £66.13s.4d. each...and upon the death of their

mother, **Mary COPELAND**...the said **Samuel COPELAND** paying unto his said brothers & sisters...the further sum of £33.6s8d.

Guardianship of Children of **Samuel COPELAND**, dec'd of Braintree MA. <Suffolk Co.PR #8997,8768>
<#8768, 39:595> 29 May 1747, **Seth COPELAND**, minor above 16, chose mother **Mary COPELAND** as gdn.
<#8997, 41:140> 17 May 1748, **Bethiah COPELAND**, minor aged about 19, chose Uncle **Seth COPELAND** of Braintree, yeoman, as gdn.

Samuel COPELAND of Stoughton to **Recompense WADSWORTH** of Stoughton. <Suffolk Co.Deeds 107:147>
...24 Aug. 1765, Samuel COPELAND, cordwainer, sold to Recompense WADSWORTH, yeoman, ten acres of cedar swamp & upland in Stoughton, bounded by Indian land. Wf Mary COPELAND releases dower. Witneses: Elijah TILDEN, John WADSWORTH. Ack. by Samuel & Mary 29 Oct. 1765. Rec. 30 Oct. 1765.

Samuel COPELAND of Stoughton to **Thomas NEWCOMB** of Braintree MA. <Suffolk Co.Deeds 160:254>
...25 Feb. 1772, Samuel COPELAND, yeoman, sold to Thomas NEWCOMB, housewright...four and a half acres in Braintree, part upland, part salt marsh, bounded by land of John RUGGLES, Ebenezer NEWCOMB, said Thomas NEWCOMB and Ship Cove. Wf Mary COPELAND releases dower. Witnesses: Ebenezer MILLER, Samuel CLARK. Rec. 30 July 1787.

Samuel COPELAND of Stoughton to **Recompense WADSWORTH** of Stoughton. <Suffolk Co.Deeds 146:215>
...1 May 1775, Samuel COPELAND, cordwainer, for £74.13s4d, sold to Recompense WADSWORTH, yeoman, 40 acres in Stoughton with a dwelling house & barn, bounded by land of Recompense WADSWORTH, Dr. SPRAGUE, Christopher CAPEN. Wf Mary COPELAND consents. Witnesses: Ezra TILDEN, Jonathan DRAPER. Rec. 3 Jan. 1785.

Arthur & Abner HARRIS of Bridgewater MA to **John COOKE et al.** <Plymouth Co.Deeds 27:217>
...17 Nov. 1731, We Arthur HARRIS & Abner HARRIS, children of **Isaac HARRIS**, yeoman of Bridgewater & of Jane his late wife who is now deceased, for and in consideration of our parts of ye sum of £55 heretofore paid to our Honoured Father **Isaac HARRIS** by **John COOKE**, yeoman, **James COOK**, mariner, **Joseph COOKE**, mariner, **Robert CARVER**, mariner, all of Kingston and **Robert JOHNSON**, taylor, now of North Yarmouth...quit claim all rights in estate of our Uncle **Caleb COOKE Jr.** late of Plymouth, dec'd. Witnesses: Moses BISBEE, Coombs BARROWS. Ack. by both grantors 21 Mar. 1731/2. Rec. 21 Mar. 1732/3.

Isaac HARRIS of Bridgewater MA to **Abner HARRIS.** <Plymouth Co.Deeds 32:105>
...3 Oct. 1738, Isaac HARRIS, yeoman..in consideration of the paternal love & affection towards my son **Abner HARRIS** & for divers other good causes...have given unto the said **Abner HARRIS** and to the male heirs of his body lawfully begotten forever all that part of my homestead in Bridgewater ...whereon I now dwell, bounded by land of Noah WASHBURN, LATHAM and Satucket River...it being all the remaining part of my said homestead lying on the southerly side of said River excepting what I have already given to my son **Arthur HARRIS** by deed...(excepting & reserving only to myself ye possession & improvement of the premises during the time of my natural life)...to possess & enjoy the same immediately after my decease. Witnesses: Micah PRATT, Thomas CROADE. Ack. 3 Oct. 1738. Rec. 26 Oct. 1738.

Thomas SANDFORD of Mendon MA to **Pelatiah SMITH** of Bridgewater MA. <Suffolk Co.Deeds 29:247>
...11 July 1715, Thomas SANDFORD, for £300, sells to Pelatiah SMITH...mansion house on a farm formerly known by the name of Mr. RAWSON's farm, on the road between Medfield & Mendon.

Pelatiah SMITH of Bellingham to **Samuel SMITH** of Bellingham. <Suffolk Co.Deeds 37:185>[10]
...11 July 1722, Pelatiah SMITH, blacksmith, conveyed to son **Samuel SMITH**, blacksmith, as part of his portion...fifty acres of land in Bellingham being upland, meadow and swamp, being a part of my homestead...It is mutually agreed before signing and sealing that the before named Samuel SMITH shall in no wise make disposition of the premises during the life of his father the grantor Ack. 11 July 1722. Rec. 11 Mar. 1723.

Pelatiah SMITH of Bellingham to **James SMITH** of Bellingham. <Suffolk Co.Deeds 99:116>
...11 July 1722, Pelatiah SMITH, for £30, sold to James SMITH...all my right in land lying on the westerly part of the eight hundred acres being part of a farm commonly known by the name of ROSON /RAWSON's farm, also my right...in the fourth part of Iron mine or ore lying in partnership with the heirs of William HAYWARD, dec'd. Wf Jane SMITH releases dower. Ack. by Pelatiah & Jane, 11 July 1722. Rec. 16 Feb. 1762.

Samuel SMITH of Boston MA to **Samuel HINSDELL** of Medfield. <Suffolk Co.Deeds 38:102>[10]
...24 Oct. 1724, Samuel SMITH, blacksmith & wf Agnes, for £160, sold to Samuel HINSDELL, tanner.. fifty acres of land, upland, meadow and swamp in Bellingham...and being given & granted to the said Samuel SMITH by his Father Pelatiah SMITH as part of his portion & was part of the said Pelatiah SMITH's homestead. Ack. by Samuel & Agnes 26 Jan. 1724. Rec. 26 Jan. 1724.

Will of **Pelatiah SMITH**, blacksmith of Bellingham. <Suffolk Co.PR #5526>
<25:540>...dated 28 Apr. 1727, mentions wf **Jane** (executor); son **James SMITH** (executor). Pr. 1 Nov 1727. Administration granted to **Jane SMITH, James SMITH** renounced his executorship. <26:134> Inventory taken 1 Feb. 1727/8; incl 110 acres with buildings, £540; 50 acres disposed of by deed of gift to his son **Samuel SMITH**, £130. Sworn to by widow 15 Feb. 1727/8. <27:151> Account 14 Apr. 1729. <15:248> Petition, 29 Dec. 1729 of David LAWSON & Eliner his wife, formerly **Eliner SMITH**, that by an act providing for posthumus children she is entitled to a share in the estate of her

father Pelatiah SMITH.

John THAYER of Mendon MA to **Samuel SMITH** of Cambridge MA. <Suffolk Co.Deeds 45:204>
...13 June 1729, John THAYER & wf Ruhamah, sell to their brother **Samuel SMITH**, innholder, all their right in the estate of **Pelatiah SMITH**, blacksmith, late of Bellingham, dec'd father of the said Ruhamah THAYER & Samuel SMITH...Ack. 4 Dec. 1730. Rec. 13 Apr. 1731.

David LAWSON of Hingham MA to **Samuel SMITH** of Cambridge MA. <Suffolk Co.Deeds 45:204>
...9 Jan. 1729, David LAWSON & wf Elenor sell to their brother Samuel SMITH, innholder, all their right in estate of **Pelatiah SMITH**, father of Elenor & Samuel. Ack. 9 Jan. 1729.Rec. 13 Apr. 1731.

Thomas BURCH of Bellingham to **Samuel SMITH** of Cambridge MA. <Suffolk Co.Deeds 45:205>
...20 Jan. 1730, Thomas BURCH & wf Sarah, dau of **Pelatiah SMITH**, blacksmith of Bellingham, dec'd, sell to their brother Samuel SMITH, all their right in the estate of Pelatiah SMITH. Ack. 30 Jan. 1729/30 by Thomas BURCH. Ack. 19 Dec. 1730 by Sarah BURCH. Rec. 13 Apr. 1731.

Jane SMITH of Bellingham to **James SMITH** of Bellingham. <Suffolk Co.Deeds 70:51>
...12 Feb. 1730...Whereas **Pelatiah SMITH**, late of Bellingham, blacksmith, dec'd...leaving behind him nine children and the daughter of one other child who died in the lifetime of her said Father and without making any mention of any of his said children & grandchild in his last will...whereon or whereby giving them...a legacy so that by the province law the said children & said grandchildren are well entitled to all the real estate their said Father died seized of. Jane SMITH, spinster, one of the children of said **Pelatiah SMITH**, sells to her brother **James SMITH**, blacksmith, all her right in the real estate. Ack. by Jane 16 Nov. 1744. Rec. 7 May 1745.

Benjamin SMITH of Bellingham to **James & Robert SMITH.** <Suffolk Co.Deeds 70:52>
...14 Mar. 1737, Benjamin SMITH sells to brothers James SMITH and Robert SMITH, all his share in his father's estate. Ack. by Benjamin 16 Mar. 1737. Rec. 7 May 1745.

Benjamin SMITH et al to **Jonathan WINSHIP.** <Suffolk Co.Deeds 158:16>
...1 Jan. 1786, Benjamin SMITH & wf Lydia (& others not specified) sell to Jonathan WINSHIP, land in Bellingham bought of Seth & Samuel ARNOLD. (Laban BATES & wf Olive mentioned.)
(<176:72>...1793, Benjamin SMITH sold land to **Laban BATES**, no details.)

Will of **Robert SMITH.** <Suffolk Co.PR #18864>
<86:152>...dated 21 Feb. 1784, mentions wf **Margaret**; legacies to **Margaret FISHER** wf of Ebenezer of Woodstock, **Pelatiah SMITH** eldest son of Robert Smith Jr. of Bellingham and **Nancy WHITE** dau of Simeon dec'd. <86:152> Probate. <86:584> Inventory. <88:251> Account.

Robert SMITH of Bellingham to **Pelatiah SMITH** of Bellingham. <Suffolk Co.Deeds 97:140>
...12 Mar. 1754, Robert SMITH, gentleman, for £13 sold to Pelatiah SMITH, currer...three pieces of land in Bellingham, one piece 2 acres, one piece 5 acres, one piece 10 acres. Ack. 26 Apr. 1756. Rec. 11 Feb. 1762.

Estate of **Pelatiah SMITH**, gentleman of Bellingham. <Suffolk Co.PR #11386>
<51:776> Administration 17 Dec. 1756, granted to Robert SMITH, gentleman of Bellingham. <52:593> Inventory taken 3 Jan. 1757, incl. 41 acres with buildings, £124.18s8d. Ack. by admr. 18 Mar. 1757. <60:107> Account 8 Feb. 1762; incl.: 4 July 1755, lend money to his widow; paid Hannah PARTRIDGE for nursing his widow; "Feb." paid for five pr gloves for minister & bearers at the funeral of said Widow; "1756", board & cloathing ye deceased's son, 2 years & 8 months, untill he was 7 years old, the same for his daughter, almost 4 years & 8 months until she was near 7 years of age. <64:101> Account 8 Feb. 1765. <64:101> Distribution 1 Mar. 1765, of personal estate; £8.10s 5p, which by law belongs to his only son **Robert SMITH**, his other child **Margaret SMITH** having been advanced more than her single share of said estate.

Guardianship of Children of **Pelatiah SMITH** of Bellingham. <Suffolk Co.PR #12901-2>
<60:109> 12 Feb. 1762, Robert SMITH of Bellingham, gentleman, app'td gdn. to **Robert SMITH** and **Margaret SMITH**, minors under 14.

Guardianship of Children of **Robert SMITH**, dec'd of Bellingham. <Suffolk Co.PR #19991>
<91:478> 31 July 1792, Stephen METCALF, Esq. of Bellingham app'td gdn. of **Pelatiah SMITH**, minor above 14.

SUFFOLK COUNTY DEEDS: (re: Pelatiah SMITH)

<29:259> - 1715, Province of Mass. Bay, discharge of mortgage.
<77:280> - 1749, Oliver HAYWARD to Pelatiah SMITH, land in Bellingham.
<97:141> - 1762, Samuel WISWALL to Pelatiah SMITH.
<97:142> - 1762, John GOLDSBURG Jr. to Pelatiah SMITH.

NORFOLK COUNTY DEEDS: (re: Robert SMITH)

<11:47> - 1799, Aaron SMITH to Robert SMITH Jr.
<14:95> - 1801, R. RICHARDS et al admrs. to Robert SMITH.
<15:76> - 1801, Moses BACON to Robert SMITH.
<15:57> - 1801, Reuben RICHARDS to Robert SMITH.

MICRO #7 OF 7

Estate of **Robert SMITH.** <Suffolk Co.PR #24608>
...1815...<204:41> Bond. <189:256> Letter. <113:288> Inventory. <310:233> Evidence. <114:342> Account. (No further details.)

NORFOLK COUNTY DEEDS, 1793-1849: (re: Pelatiah SMITH) (all on index)

<6:214> - 1797, Pelatiah SMITH to William CLARK, land in Needham.
<7:257> - 1797, Pelatiah SMITH from Charles CHACE.
<14:79> - 1801, Pelatiah SMITH from Aaron SMITH.
<14:79> - 1801, Pelatiah SMITH from Jabez BARKER.
<15:25> - 1801, Pelatiah SMITH from Aaron SMITH.
<37:1> - 1810, Pelatiah SMITH to Aaron SMITH, all his interest in estate of Aaron SMITH.
<42:185> - 1812, Pelatiah SMITH to Nathan PENNIMAN, land in Bellingham.
<42:185> - 1812, Pelatiah SMITH from Nathan PENNIMAN.
<54:84> - 1817, Pelatiah SMITH to Jabez DAGGETT, land in Needham.
<65:123> - 1821, Pelatiah SMITH to Daniel MANN, land in South Needham.
<68:116> - 1823, Pelatiah SMITH to George FISHER et al, land in Needham.
<73:92> - 1824, Pelatiah SMITH to E.S. WILSON et al, land in Needham.
<75:77> - 1825, Pelatiah SMITH to J.A. TAFT, land in North Bellingham.
<97:179> - 1832, Pelatiah SMITH to E.C. GRANT, land in North Bellingham.
<111:90> - , Pelatiah SMITH to Zebina BULLARD.
<128:7> - 1840, Pelatiah SMITH to John BAKER 2d, land in Bellingham.
<140:256> - 1843, Pelatiah SMITH to Joseph ADAMS 2d, land in Bellingham.
<98:210> - 1847, Pelatiah SMITH to Henry HOWARD, discharge of mortgage.
<171:288> - 1847, Pelatiah SMITH to Henry HOWARD, land in Bellingham.
<177:171> - 1847, Pelatiah SMITH Jr. to Ruel ADAMS, administrator.

Estate of **Daniel COOK** of Bellingham MA. <Norfolk Co.PR #4367>
...1825...<46:295> Administration. <47:75> Inventory. <47:77> Notice. (No further details.)

Estate of **Daniel COOK** of Bellingham MA. <Norfolk Co.PR #4368>
...1852...<89:211,754;91:304;92:753;103:334,987,1119> (No details given.)

SUFFOLK COUNTY DEEDS: (re James SMITH)

<64:231> - 1742, James SMITH to John METCALF land in Bellingham.
<70:44> - 1745, James SMITH to Peter LUCE.
<70:53> - 1745, James SMITH to James BOWDOIN, land in Bellingham.
<70:59> - 1745, James SMITH to James BOWDOIN, mortgage.
<74:205> - 1747, James SMITH to Daniel PENNIMAN, land in Bellingham.
<86:204> - 1755, James SMITH to Joseph ROCKWOOD, Rawson's Farm in Bellingham.
<101:63> - 1763, James SMITH, est. to John CORBET, part of iron mine.

Estate of **Eunice SMITH.** <Suffolk Co.PR #70404>
...1883...Administration...(no details given.)

Guardianship of Children of **Matthew SMITH** of Bellingham MA. <Suffolk Co.PR #16197>
<76:39> 28 Mar. 1777, Jonathan WALES of Wrentham app'td gdn. of **Eunice SMITH** & **Lois SMITH**, minors over 14, daus of Matthew SMITH, blacksmith.

Estate of **Peletiah SMITH** of Bellingham MA. <Norfolk Co.PR #17006>
...1864...<112:93> Will proved. <112:93> Letter/Bond. <113:589> Inventory. <113:227> Account. <137:470> Notice. (No details given.)

Estate of **Peletiah SMITH** of Needham MA. <Norfolk Co.PR #17005>
...1825...<44:349> Letter/Bond. <45:21> Inventory. <45:39> Notice. <47:386> Account.

SUFFOLK COUNTY DEEDS: re Samuel SMITH

<14:105> - 1686, Samuel SMITH from estate of Henry SMITH.
<14:106> - 1686, Samuel SMITH from John SMITH, est. of Henry SMITH.
<15:54> - 1690, Samuel SMITH from Sampson SHEAFE, land in Boston.
<26:107> - 1711, Samuel SMITH from Elisha SMITH, land in Medfield.
<37:185> - 1723, Samuel SMITH from Pelatiah SMITH.
<39:236> - 1726, Samuel SMITH from William WEEKES et al, land in Medfield.
<45:43> - 1730, Samuel SMITH from Aaron SMITH, land in Needham.
<46:228> - , Samuel SMITH from Addington GARDNER, land in Brookline.

Robert SMITH of Bellingham MA to **Daniel PENNIMAN.** <Norfolk Co.Deeds 25:72>
...16 July 1784, Robert SMITH, gentleman, sells to Daniel PENNIMAN, one acre meadow on east side of Stall River in Bellingham. Ack. same day. Rec. 5 Mar. 1806.

Robert SMITH, estate to **Daniel PENNIMAN.** <Norfolk Co.Deeds 25:72>
...10 Apr. 1789, Margaret SMITH, widow & executor of estte of Robert SMITH, gentleman, dec'd, sells to Daniel PENNIMAN land in Bellingham.

Estate of **Robert SMITH Jr.**, trader of Bellingham MA. <Norfolk Co.PR #17020>
<1:86> 4 Feb. 1794, **Levina SMITH,** widow, app'td admx. Sureties: Abner COOK of Wrentham and Amos ELLIS of Bellingham. Appraisers app'td: Stephen METCALF, Esq., Amos ELLIS, yeoman and Benjamin BASS, yeoman, all of Bellingham. <1:134> 4 Feb. 1794, admx. represents the estate as insolvent. <1:136> Inventory taken 17 Mar. 1794 by appraisers, allowed 1 Apr. 1794; no real estate ment.; sworn to by admx. 29 Mar. 1794. <1:220> Order to post appointment 4 Feb. 1794; 18 Aug. 1794, admx made oath that notice had been posted. <1:248> Receipt 1 Apr. 1794, Stephen METCALF, Esq. and Amos ELLIS, yeoman, app'td to receive claims of creditors; list was presented 29 Sept. 1794, allowed 7 Oct. 1794. <1:247> Account of admx. 7 Oct. 1794, incl. to pay a person to go to Woodstock to inform his sister of his death. <1:249> Order to pay commissioners, 7 Oct. 1794; allowance of L14 made to **Levina SMITH,** widow, out of personal estate, it being insufficient to pay his debts.

Heirs of **Robert SMITH** to (   ), rec. 20 Dec. 1864. <Norfolk Co.Deeds 328:314>

Estate of **Julia B. SMITH** of Bellingham MA, 1877. <Norfolk Co.PR #16948>

Thomas BURCH of Bellingham MA to **Samuel SMITH** of Cambridge MA. <Suffolk Co.Deeds 45:205>
...13 Apr. 1731, Thomas BURCH, husbandman & wf Sarah, the dau of Pelatiah SMITH, blacksmith, late of Bellingham, dec'd, acknowledge receipt of Ł25 paid by Samuel SMITH, blacksmith.

FOOTNOTES

<1> p.140, The files contain only sketchy details of these two wills, but since they were mentioned I have added to the particulars, instead of leaving them "sketchy" as Bowman did.
<2> p.141, Additional citations are given for one or more Joshua WINSLOW(s), viz: Suffolk Co.PR #15777 (1775, adm.); #17242 (1780, adm.); #20308 (1794, adm.) and #21166 (1799, adm.)
<3> p.141, Wyman, Thomas B. The Genealogies and Estates of Charlestown. 2 vols. Boston, 1879.
<4> p.144, Additional citations are given for one or more John TAYLOR(s), viz: Suffolk Co.PR #4296, 21:687 (1720); #16816 (1779, adm.) and #17056 (1779, absentee).
<5> p.145, The files contain extensive probate & deed records pertaining to Edward Gray, before his death, he was one of the richest men in Plymouth Colony. I have included more detail than I normally would, on his estate & the lands he owned as it is interesting to see how much property this man amassed between his arrival in the Colony c1643 and his death in June 1681.
<6> p.145, The first citation in the listing is the following: "<6:1:44> At Court held at Plymouth the 1st Tues. Mar. 1680/1 upon the Petition of Mr. Nathaniel THOMAS, Capt. Benjamin CHURCH and Edward GRAY in the behalfe of themselves & partenor purchasers of the lands att Pocassett..." Thus, it is known that Edward GRAY was alive Mar. 1681 and deceased by 7 July 1681 (see within).
<7> p.145, The records give the daughter's name as Hannah, however Edward GRAY did not have a daughter named Hannah. Since all of the children under 21 are accounted for but one, this Hannah must refer to Susanna GRAY.
<8> p.145, Immediately after this entry on the same page is written "6:2:60,61, Divorce case", with no clue as to whose divorce it refers to.
<9> p.146, MF 2:38 states James' will was pr. 10 Nov. 1713, but wonders why the inventory is dated six years later in 1719. Bowman draws attention to the statement in the inventory "James LEBLOND deceased Boston June 11th 1719"- which he takes exception to as he also highlights the following date in the 2nd Account - "bringing up the children from 23 Oct. 1713" - which one would assume to mean that James died on or near this date. Bowman does not have the probate date of 10 Nov. 1713 and since all his probate sources match those in MF, it is not clear where MF got this date from, however, it does seem to fit. We are left with two options: 1/ James d. 23 Oct. 1713, will pr. 10 Nov. 1713, inv. 17 Sept. 1719 or 2/ James d. 11 June 1719, inv. 17 Sept. 1719 (assuming the sourceless pr. date of 1713 an error). The 2nd option, while it would take care of the six year gap in dates, is not feasible as widow Ann had been raising the children since 1713 and (according to MF) sons James & Peter mentioned their dec'd father in a 1718 deed. Therefore, the reference in the inventory to James dying 11 June 1719 must have been interpreted incorrectly and James most probably died on or near 23 Oct. 1713.
<10> p.153, It is unclear why, in the deed dated 11 July 1722, Pelatiah gives son Samuel this land on the condition he does not sell it until after Pelatiah's death, and yet in the deed dated 24 Oct. 1724, Samuel sells the land. Pelatiah SMITH did not die until 10 Sept. 1727.

FRANCIS COOKE

MICRO #1 OF 30

PLYMOUTH COUNTY PROBATE: (re: COOK)

Year	Name		Town	Reference
1722	Caleb		Plymouth	#4857, 4:324,326,328
1724	Caleb		Plymouth	#4858, 4:445;5:104,666
1724	Francis Jr.		Plympton	#4873, 4:426;5:111,582
1725	Ruth et al		Plympton	#4919, 5:52
1732	Nathaniel et al		Kingston	#4906, 6:161,162;8:343;9:30
1732	Robert		Kingston	#4911, 6:186,187,188;9:385
1736	Jane		Kingston	#4884, 7:194,195
1741	John		Kingston	#4887, 8:402,404,412
1743	Robert		Kingston	#4912, 9:166,167;9:224,514,515
1744	Robert		Kingston	#4913, 9:388;15:153,154
1744	John		Kingston	#4888, 9:427,451;10:432,433,487;13:107;39: 429;40:361,362;42:195
1744	Simeon		Plymouth	#4922, ---
1746	Francis		Kingston	#4874, 10:328,330,331
1747	Jacob		Kingston	#4883, 10:419,420,437
1752	Lydia et al		Kingston	#4897, 12:439,440
1753	Molly et al		Kingston	#4902, 13:32,33,60,61
1757	Barnabas		Marshfield	#4853, 14:417;15:32;16:108,188
1757	Caleb		Kingston	#4859, 14:220,275
1760	Hannah		Kingston	#4876, 15:594;16:54,55,56
1760	Nathaniel		Kingston	#4905, 15:460,498,504;16:6,19,41,42
1762	Amos et al		Kingston	#4851, 18:112,113,114;19:156,157;20:266
1762	Caleb		Kingston	#4860, 16:374,375,389;16:414;19:40
1770	Peleg		Kingston	#4908, 20:428,429
1776	Robert		Scituate	#4916, 22:199
1794	Zenas		Plympton	#4926, 34:10;35:156,210,342;36:28,29
1795	Zenas et al		Plympton	#4929, 32:26,27
1798	Isaac		Kingston	#4881, 32:127
1800	Benjamin		Kingston	#4855, 34:229;37:315,316,484;44:356
1815	Sylvanus	adm.	Kingston	#4924, 46:86;48:22,24,367,370,371
1816	Phebe	gdn.	Kingston	#4909, 41:250,306;48:38,393,431,457,458;53: 145,146
1819	John & Lucy	gdn.	Pembroke	#4889, 50:187
1819	Zenas	adm.	Plympton	#4927, 46:321
1827	Josiah	adm.	Plympton	#4890, 61:107;62:162;64:154,155,344,394,395 491
1828	Robert	adm.	Scituate	#4917, 68:279;71:39;72:49,50,396,498;73:388 74:84
1828	Sarah	will	Kingston	#4920, 62:303;66:47,48
1829	Benjamin et al,	gdn.	Kingston	#4856, 65:81;69:330
1831	Charles	adm.	Scituate	#4862, 68:280;70:579;71:19;72:275,277,565, 586;73:21
1832	Robert	adm.	Kingston	#4914, 61:242;62:322;66:564;69:71
1835	Zenas	will	Kingston	#4928, 77:178
1837	Joanna	will	Kingston	#4886, 10:486**A**;75:516;79:145,147;80:31
1837	Josiah & Lydia,	adm.	Kingston	#4891, 10:58**A**
1838	Patience	adm.	Kingston	#4907, 5:80**T**;10:150**A**;80:461,462
1839	Elkanah	adm.	Kingston	#4869, 6:23**U**;10:288**A**;82:14;83:21
1839	Fanny & Harriet,	gdn.	Scituate	#4872, 8:129**L**;75:409;79:111,351;80:116
1844	Robert	will	Kingston	#4915, 2:1**H**,319**O**;6:491**U**;86:60,187;88:41; 114:182,184
1845	Eli	will	Kingston	#4866, 10:544**A**;87:216,299;88:358,545
1845	Judith	will	Scituate	#4893, 2:52**H**;87:318
1847	Martin	will	Kingston	#4899, 2:135**H**;7:328**V**;89:425;90:196
1850	Maria A.	gdn.	Middleboro	#4898, 9:273**M**;11:150**N**;93:423;101:63;102:60

Jonathan DELANO of Dartmouth MA to **John COOKE** of Dartmouth MA. <Plymouth Co.Deeds 5:466>
...20 July 1694, Jonathan DELANO grants right of way to John COOKE...mentions land between lands of John COOKE & Thomas TABER, where they now dwell.

Francis COOKE to **Jacob COOKE.** <Plymouth Col.Deeds 1:307>
...9 Apr. 1650, Francis COOKE did com before the Gove^{r} and acknowledge y^{t} hee hath freely given & made over unto his sonne Jacob COOKE all his right title and enterest of & into a certaine tract of upland & meadow being estemated att an hundred acars bee it more or lesse; lying att the North River accordingly as it was graunted unto him the said Ffrancis COOKE as appeers by the record of the said graunt bearing Date the fift of October 1640. The said tract of upland & meadow with all

& singulare the apurtenances & privilidges therunto belonging to have & to hold to him the said Jacob COOKE his heaires & assignes for ever unto the only proper use & behoofe of him the said Jacob COOKE his heaires and assignes for ever.

Division of land of **Francis COOKE et al.** <Plymouth Col.Deeds 3:216>
...14 Oct. 1671, division of cedar swamp in the Majors Purchase near Mattakeesett alias Namassakeesett Ponds as it was done by John THOMPSON, John NELSON & Isaac HOWLAND. Owners of 5th lot: John TURNER, Benjamin BARTLETT, Francis WALKER, Francis COOKE, Thomas DOGGET.

Guardianship of Child of **Isaac COOK,** dec'd of Kingston. <Plymouth Co.PR #4881>
<32:127> Bond/Letter 5 Feb. 1798, Joseph EVERSON app'td gdn. of **Isaac COOK,** minor above 14. Witnesses: Philip BRYANT, Caleb HOWARD. Sureties: Thomas GANNETT, Caleb LORING.

PLYMOUTH COLONY DEEDS: (re COOKE)

<1:32>	-	, John COOKE exchanges land with Robert BARTLETT.
<1:74>	-	, John COOKE Jr. to George PARTRIDGE.
<1:186>	-	, Josias COOK to Gyles RICKARD.
<1:196>	-	, Josias COOK to Gyles RICKARD.
<1:246>	-	, John COOK, William PADDY, Ja^{s}. HUST, Deacons of Plymouth Church to Nathaniel MORTON
<1:307>	-	, Francis COOKE to Jacob COOK.
<1:307>	-	, Jacob COOKE to Moris TRUANT.
<1:327>	-	, John COOKE Jr. to Thomas TILDEN.
<1:350>	-	, John COOK, grant of land at Rockey Nook.
<2:35>	- 10 June 1646	, Francis COOK to son Jacob COOK. <2:1:35>
<2:68>	- 2 Aug. 1653	, John COOK Sr. to Thomas LETTICE. <2:1:68>
<2:163>	- 25 Dec. 1655	, Josias COOK to John RICKARD. <2:1:163>
<2:42>	- 25 3mth 1657	, Josiah COOKE to Thomas SHERIVE. <2:2:42>
<2:42>	- 9 July 1660	, Josiah COOKE, his meadow lot. <2:2:42>
<2:74>	- 14 Dec. 1661	, John COOK to John HOWLAND. <2:2:74>
<3:82>	- 9 Feb. 1663	, John COOKE to John HAYWOOD.
<3:64>	- 8 Mar. 1665	, John COOK, planter of Acushanett from Phillip, Sachem.
<3:69>	- 8 Mar. 1665	, John COOKE of Dartmouth from Phillip, Sachem. <6:69,70>
<3:168>	- 18 May 1665	, Jacob COOKE, husbandman to William MACOMBER.
<3;68>	- 25 Oct. 1665	, Josiah COOKE of Eastham from Simon & Pompono, Indians.
<3:73>	- 8 June 1666	, John COOKE to Wright & Mitchell.
<3:130>	- 7 June 1667	, John COOKE, yeoman to Edward GRAY.
<3:97>	- 5 Aug. 1667	, John COOKE, yeoman of Dartmouth from Henry WOOD, planter.
<3:295>	- June 1669	, John COOK, planter of Acushanett from Phillip, Sachem.
<3:194>	- 11 Aug. 1669	, Josiah COOKE, husbandman to John FREEMAN.
<3:163>	- 11 Aug. 1669	, Josias COOKE Sr., husbandman from John FREEMAN, gentleman of Eastham.
<3:191>	- 24 Mar. 1670	, John COOKE, yeoman of Dartmouth from Edward GRAY, yeoman.<also 5:12>
<3:248>	- 4 July 1672	, John COOKE, yeoman of Dartmouth exchanges land with Jacob COOK Sr., Plym.
<5:467>	- 21 May 1672	, John COOKE to son in law Thomas TABOR, mason of Dartmouth.
<3:298>	- 4 July 1672	, Jacob COOKE Sr., yeoman to John COOKE, yeoman of Dartmouth.
<3:339>	- 17 July 1673	, John COOKE, yeoman of Dartm. to Phillip TABOR, mason & wf Mary of Dartm.
<4:48>	- 7 May 1674	, John COOKE of Dartmouth from James SHAW, husbandman of Dartmouth.
<5:12>	- 26 June 1674	, John COOKE to son in law Arthur HATHAWAY.
<3:325>	- 10 July 1674	, John COOKE, yeoman of Dartmouth to Daniel WILCOX, yeoman of Dartmouth.
<3:322>	- 14 July 1674	, Jacob COOKE, his lands.
<4:108>	- 8 Mar. 1676	, Jacob COOKE of Plymouth...division of estate.
<5:114>	- 30 Apr. 1680	, John COOKE of Portsmouth RI to Thomas WARD of Newport RI.
<5:35>	- 30 May 1681	, Jacob COOKE to Samuel STURTEVANT & Isaac KING, all planters of Plymouth.
<6:67>	- 8 June 1681	, Caleb COOKE, yeoman of Plymouth to Wresling BREWSTER, carpenter, Duxbury.
<5:465>	- 7 July 1681	, John COOKE, yeoman of Dartmouth to Jonathan DILLENO, carpenter of Dartm.
<5:388>	- 28 Nov. 1683	, John COOKE of Dartmouth to Thomas TABOR, mason of Dartmouth.
<5:264>	- 2 June 1684	, Elisha COOKE, Esq. of Boston from Andrew WILLETT, merchant of Newport RI.
<6:44>	- 4 June 1686	, John COOKE, yeoman of Dartmouth to Arthur HATHAWAY of Dartmouth.
<6:70>	- 8 July 1686	, John COOKE of Dartmouth to Stephen WEST of Portsmouth RI.
<5:497>	- 27 July 1691	, John COOKE, yeoman of Little Compton to Samuel LITTLE of Marshfield.
<5:466>	- 6 Nov. 1691	, John COOKE, yeoman of Dartmouth to Jonathan DILLENO, carpenter of Dartm.
<3:339>	- 27 Feb. 1693	, John COOKE confirms to heirs of Phillip TABOR, dec'd.
<5:466>	- 20 July 1694	, John COOKE of Dartmouth from Jonathan DELANO of Dartmouth.

Estate of **Nathaniel COOK** of Norton MA. <Bristol Co.PR>
<147:220> Letter 21 Dec. 1778, John COOK, yeoman of Norton, app'td admr.
(Note: the following references pertain to one or more Nathaniel COOK, viz: <92:78,106> Administration & Inventory, 1849; <117:2,121:195> Notice of Appointment; <156:179> Adm. 1848; <162:192> Adm. bond. <169:293> Adm. <197:158> Inv. <210:360> Sale of land. <219:478,614> Account.)

Estate of **John COOK** of Freetown MA. <Bristol Co.PR>
<38:75> Inventory taken 4 Jan. 1801. <149:364> 3 Mar. 1801, **Marcy COOK,** widow, app'td admx. <38:82> Account 3 Mar. 1801 of admx., **Mary COOK**; incl. allowance for widow's housekeeping; <42:10> Inventory 11 Jan. 1806 of real estate of **John COOK** of Troy, **Mary COOK,** admx.; <42:266> Insolvency & Account; <42:456> Dower. <42:465> Account. <42:466> Distribution. <109:61> Notice. <168:253>

Administration. (Due to the way this data is arranged in the files and the inconsistencies, it is possible that the references refer to more than one John COOK. The following references refer to two or more **John COOK**, viz: <1:139,140>; <6:31,32> Will & Pr.; <8:502-504> Will, Pr., Inv.

Nathaniel HODGES of Norton MA to **Paul COOK** of Kingston MA. <Bristol Co.Deeds 35:205>
...29 Dec. 1747, Nathaniel HODGES & wf Hannah, sold to Paul COOK, mariner, 50 acres in Norton.

Gideon BASSET of Norton MA to **Paul COOK** of Kingston MA. <Bristol Co.Deeds 35:209>
...29 Dec. 1747, Gideon BASSET & wf Bathsheba, sold 52 acres & 28 acres with house to Paul COOK, mariner.

Thomas NYE, Avery PARKER of Dartmouth MA to **Paul COOK** of Dartmouth MA. <Bristol Co.Deeds 56:284>
...24 Sept. 1774, Thomas NYE and Avery PARKER, sell land in Dartmouth to Paul COOK, mariner.

BRISTOL COUNTY DEEDS: (re: COOKE)

<43:369> - 26 May 1759, Paul COOKE to son John COOK, both of Norton, house & land in Norton.
<44:215> - 21 Apr. 1760, Paul COOKE of Norton to Jerusha DAY, wf of Jonathan DAY of Wrentham, late widow of Hezekiah KING of Norton.
<46:458> - 22 Sept 1763, Paul COOKE to Eliphalet HODGES.
<70:258> - 6 Dec. 1791, Paul COOKE, mariner of New Bedford to Preserved FISH.
<71:195> - 12 Sept 1792, Paul COOKE to Ebenezer ALLEN. (dated 1781)

Estate of **Paul COOK Jr.**, mariner of New Bedford. <Bristol Co.PR 149:308>
...12 Feb. 1800, **Paul COOK,** yeoman, of New Bedford was app'td. admr. of estate of **Paul COOK Jr.**

HESTER COOKE^2 (Francis^1)

Heirs of **Richard WRIGHT** of Plimouth. <Plymouth Col.Deeds 7:65>
...13 July 1691...Whereas our honoured father Richard WRIGHT of Plimoth deceased did by his last will etc...**Ephraim TINKAM** & wf **Esther** of Middleboro and **Mary PRICE** of Plimoth, mentions their brother **Adam WRIGHT.**

PLYMOUTH COLONY DEEDS: (re WRIGHT)

<1:24> - 17 Nov. 1637, Richard WRIGHT, tailor of Plymouth to George RUSSELL, yeoman of Plymouth.
<1:36> - 24 Mar. 1637, Richard WRIGHT, tailor of Plymouth to William HILLER, carpenter.
<1:46> - 25 Aug. 1638, Richard WRIGHT from Peter MAYCOCK, 40 acres.
<2:192> - 16 June 1657, Nicholas WRIGHT, sometimes of Sandwich, to James SKIFFE of Sandwich. (A note in the margin says this deed was made divers yrs. before 1657.)
<3:73> - 8 June 1666, Wright & Mitchell from John COOKE.
<3:228> - 5 Dec. 1666, Richard WRIGHT, tailor of Plymouth from Abigail CLARKE, spinster of Plym.
<3:228> - 15 Mar. 1668, Richard WRIGHT, land laid out.
<3:166> - 9 May 1669, John WRIGHT, 2nd son of Richard, from Richard WRIGHT & wf Ester of Plym.
<3:234> - 1 Aug. 1672, Richard WRIGHT, tailor of Plymouth from Thomas MITCHELL, planter of Duxb.
<3:331> - 4 July 1672, Adam WRIGHT, blacksmith of Middleb. from George VAUGHAN, tailor of Middl.
<3:332> - 4 July 1672, Adam WRIGHT to Benjamin CHURCH of Duxbury.
<3:322> - 14 July 1674, Richard WRIGHT, HOWLAND, Jacob COOK, Edward GRAY, agreement.
<5:281> - 2 Feb. 1684, Jonathan WRIGHT of Flushing, Long Island, son & heir of Capt. George WRIGHT of Flushing, to John DOGGED of Rehoboth.

PLYMOUTH COUNTY PROBATES: (re WRIGHT)

1691	Richard	Plymouth	will	#23539, 1:101,102
1710	Thomas	Scitute	adm.	#23547, 3:28,29,205,243
1712	John	Scituate	adm.	#23522, 3:206,243
1712	Thomas	Marshfield	will	#23546, 3:169,221
1724	Adam	Plympton	will	#23497, 5:26,28 <MD 4:239>
1760	Martin	Plymouth	adm.	#23533, 15:514,485
1762	Nathan	Kingston	adm.	#23535, 16:331;17:74
1766	Isaac	Plympton	will	#23515, 19:345,346
1773	Edmond	Plympton	gdn.	#23510, 22:150
1773	Samuel	Plympton	will	#23542, 21:308,309,310,335
1774	Abigail	Marshfield	gdn.	#23496, 22:43,44,45,172
1774	John	Plympton	will	#23525, 21:617,619;24:460
1776	Adam	Plympton	adm.	#23498, 23:83;24:428;28:112-115
1776	John et al	Plympton	gdn.	#23526, 22:76,127,197,200
1792	Benjamin	Plympton	adm.	#23501, 27:392;33:54;35:214
1797	Isaac	Plympton	will	#23516, 36:31,33;37:182,183
1797	James	Plymouth	adm.	#23519, 34:132;36:327,395,408,409
1797	Winslow et al	Plympton	gdn.	#23551, 32:69
1801	James	Scituate	adm.	#23520, 34:279;37:445,491,492

PLYMOUTH COUNTY PROBATES cont-d: (re WRIGHT)

1804	Joseph	Plymouth	will	#23528, 40:94,95
1809	Sarah	Plympton	adm.	#23544, 39:201;43:77;53:59
1815	Samuel	Plympton	adm.	#23543, 46:93;48:80,81,83,84
1816	Ebenezer	Plympton	adm.	#23508, 46:146;48:48,120,123,541;49:261,262;66:4,154
1821	John	Plympton	adm.	#23523, 52:31;53:392-3;54:295;56:335 341;58:230,243;59:59,190-4;64:409,410
1821	Joseph	Plympton	gdn.	#23529, 51:130,195;53:542;56:400;76:447
1821	Lydia et al	Plympton	gdn.	#23531, 51:118
1829	Daniel	Marshfield	will	#23506, 67:448,450;68:78
1836	Billya	Plympton	will	#23503, 1:16**G**;75:396;78:448;79:37
1837	Levi	Plympton	gdn.	#23530, 5:18**T**;8:403,404**L**;80:147
1840	Jabez	Marshfield	will	#23518, 1:141**G**;6:103**U**;82:275,314;84:191
1842	Patience	Plympton	will	#23536, 6:338**U**;10:516**A**;84:5,613
1844	Caleb	Wareham	adm.	#23504, 6:551**U**;11:267**B**;86:294
1848	Ebenezer	Plympton	will	#23509, 2:158**H**;7:344**V**;90:215
1850	Barzillai E.	Plympton	will	#23500, 1:12**F**;3:175**P**;8:81**W**;92:413,487;96:333
1850	James W. et al	S.Scituate	gdn.	#23521, 1:336**R**,339**R**,393**R**;3:440**P**,444**P** 486**P**;9:264**M**;92:438;93:223;94:357
1850	Sarah	Plympton	will	#23545, 2:237**H**;8:167**W**;92:275

Richard WRIGHT of New Plimoth to **Georg RUSSELL** of New Plimoth. <Plymouth Col.Deeds 1:24>
...17 Nov. 1637, Richard WRIGHT, taylor, sells to Georg RUSSELL, yeoman, a lot at Oulbery Playne which he had bought of Mr. Alexander HIGGENS.

Richard WRIGHT to **William HILLER.** <Plymouth Col.Deeds 1:30>
...24 Mar. 1637/8, Richard WRIGHT acknowledged sale to William HILLER, carpenter, 5 acres granted to him at fishing poynt towards the Eele River. <1:48> 6 Nov. 1639 William HILLER sold this land to Mark MENDLOVE.

Moses WRIGHT of Plimton MA to **Joseph THOMAS** of Plimton MA. <Plymouth Co.Deeds 29:138>
...2 Apr. 1725, Moses WRIGHT, for £60, sold to Joseph THOMAS...all my iron oare or iron mine which I now hath lying & being within or upon the Neck between Winnatuxett River & Colchester Brook...in Plimton known by ye name of Donham Neck with liberty to dig & carry off the abovesd iron oare or iron mine which was given to me by my Honoured Father **Adam WRIGHT** by deed of gift under his hand & seal bearing date 9 September 1721. Witnesses: Isaac WRIGHT, Thomas PHILLIP. Ack. 29 Apr. 1734. Rec. 25 Feb. 1734.

Estate of **Martin WRIGHT,** seafaring man of Plymouth MA. <Plymouth Co.PR>
<15:514> 3 Mar. 1760, **Sarah WRIGHT** app'td admx. <15:485> Inventory & Account 24 Mar. 1760.

Guardianship of Children of **Isaac WRIGHT,** yeoman, dec'd of Plympton MA. <Plymouth Co.PR>
<32:69> 14 Jan. 1797, **Faith WRIGHT,** widow, app'td gdn. of **Winslow WRIGHT & Hannah WRIGHT,** minors above 14. Sureties: John DOTEN, Joseph SAMSON.

Estate of **Thomas RIGHT/WRIGHT** of Scituate MA. <Plymouth Co.PR>
<3:28> 22 Dec. 1710, **John RIGHT/WRIGHT** app'td admr. of father's estate. <3:29> Inventory taken 17 June 1710 by Samuel CLAP and Stephen CLAP. <3:205> 13 Feb. 1712/3, **Lidia RIGHT/WRIGHT,** widow of **John RIGHT/WRIGHT** of Scituate is app'td admx. in his place. <3:206> Inventory dated 13 Feb. 1712/13, **William TAYLOR,** father of Lidia, made oath to inventory. <3:243> Accounts 13 Aug. 1713, of both estates (Thomas & John) allowed; Lidia's children & Thomas' widow are mentioned.

Estate of **Thomas WRIGHT** of Marshfield MA. <Plymouth Co.PR>
<3:169> 29 Nov. 1712, Hannah GREEN of Cambridge, app'td admx., his nuncupative will stating he intended soon to have married her and gives her all his property. Inventory taken 8 Dec. 1712 by James FORD and Thomas FOSTER. 12 Dec. 1712, Hannah GREEN made oath to inventory.

Adam WRIGHT et al to **John TOMSON Jr.** of Middleboro. <Plymouth Co.Deeds 2:28>
...16 Mar. 1690/1, Adam WRIGHT & wf Sarah and **Richard WRIGHT,** his father, join in sale to John TOMSON Jr...all his title to land in Middleboro of which my honoured Great-grandfather **Ffrancis COOKE** deceased had a share to dispose amongst his children and he disposed of ye one half thereof unto my Honoured Ffather Richard WRIGHT & ye other half to John TOMSON Sr. and my ffather Richard WRIGHT gave his half share unto me. Witnesses: Elisha BRADFORD, Benjamin SOULE. Rec. 3 Aug. 1696.

Adam WRIGHT of Plymton to **John WRIGHT.** <Plymouth Co.Deeds 7:214>[<1>]
...21 Feb. 1707/8, Adam WRIGHT & wf Mehitable to son John WRIGHT, 50 acres formerly property of my Honoured Father Richard WRIGHT.

Adam WRIGHT to **Isaac WRIGHT.** <Plymouth Co.Deeds 13:119>
...13 Dec. 1709, Adam WRIGHT deeds to son Isaac WRIGHT, 90 acres. 28 Dec. 1720, wf Mehitable gave up her right of dower.

Estate of **Robert BARROW** of Plymouth MA. <Plymouth Co.PR 4:12>
...20 June 1717, we **George BARROW, Adam WRIGHT** & wf **Mahitable,** children of our honoured father Robert BARROW, have received of our mother in law **Lydia BARROW,** executrix to the last will & testament of our said Father, all our part & portion of our said father's estate. Witnesses: Thomas CROADE, Joseph THOMAS. Ack. 20 June 1717.

Richard WRIGHT of Plymouth to **John WRIGHT.** <Plymouth Col.Deeds 3:166>
...9 May 1669, Richard WRIGHT deeds to second son John WRIGHT, land received from town of Plymouth by record dated 16 Oct. 1659.

Will of **John WRIGHT**...about to go to war. <Plymouth Co.PR 3:1:177>
...7 Dec. 1675, mentions brothers **Isaac WRIGHT, Samuel WRIGHT,** father **Richard WRIGHT,** brother **Adam WRIGHT,** sisters **Esther & Mary.** Inventory 8 June 1676. Receipt 9 June 1676 of **Ester WRIGHT** and **Mary WRIGHT** to their brother **Adam WRIGHT.** Pr. 7 July 1676.

Will of **Isaac WRIGHT** of Plimton MA. <Plymouth Co.PR 19:345,346>
...dated 2 July 1760, mentions children **Joseph WRIGHT** (executor), **Isaac WRIGHT, Mary THOMSON** & her heirs, **Rachel WRIGHT** & her heirs. Witnesses: Benjamin WESTON, Hannah WESTON, Job WESTON.

Will of **Daniel PRATT** of Plympton MA. <Plymouth Co.PR 8:46>
...dated 30 Mar. 1739, mentions wf **Annis** (executrix), sons **Benjamin PRATT, James PRATT & Joshua PRATT** (both under 21), **Nathaniel PRATT, Jabez PRATT,** daus **Easter HOWARD** wf of John and **Sarah DONHAM** wf of Joshua. Pr. 18 May 1739.

Richard WRIGHT to son in law **W. SABINE,** 2 Dec. 1672. <Plymouth Col.Deeds 3:2:262>

PLYMOUTH COUNTY DEEDS: (re: DUNHAM)

<23:127> - 30 Aug. 1728, Joshua DUNHAM, shipwright, wf Sarah releases dower.
<27:144> - 21 Sept 1732, Joshua DUNHAM sells land, wf Sarah releases dower.
<31:40> - 1 Mar. 1736/7,Joshua DUNHAM, shipwright & wf Sarah of Plymouth sells his house.

MICRO #2 OF 30

Will of **Isaac WRIGHT** of Plymton MA. <Plymouth Co.PR 36:31,33>
...dated 20 Sept. 1796, mentions wf **Faith;** children **Billey WRIGHT & Isaac WRIGHT** (executors), **Chandler WRIGHT, Nathaniel WRIGHT, Caleb WRIGHT, Winslow WRIGHT, Molley, Hannah.** Witnesses: Elijah BISBE Jr., Asa SHERMAN, Joseph COBB. Pr. 12 Jan. 1797.

Will of **Joseph WRIGHT,** yeoman of Plymouth MA. <Plymouth Co.PR 40:94>
...dated 27 Feb. 1788, mentions wf **Sarah,** daus **Deborah CHURCHILL** (eldest dau) of Plimpton, **Mary SAMSON** wf of Sylvanus; sons **Joshua WRIGHT** and **Joseph WRIGHT** (who has disappeared). Witnesses: Josiah COTTON, Joseph ( ), William PEARSONS. Pr. 4 Sept. 1804.

Will of **John WRIGHT** of Plympton MA. <Plymouth Co.PR #23525>
<21:617>...dated 6 Aug. 1772, mentions children **John WRIGHT, Adam WRIGHT, Repentance WRIGHT, Sarah WRIGHT, Benjamin WRIGHT;** grandchildren **John HUNT, Judah HUNT, Mary HUNT.** Esteemed friends, Benjamin WESTON and Joseph WRIGHT, both of Plympton, named executors. Witnesses: Josiah CHANDLER, Joseph BENNETT, Zebedee CHANDLER. <21:619> Pr. 6 June 1774, Joseph WRIGHT the only surviving executor renounced executorship and **Adam WRIGHT** was app'td. Inventory. <24:460> 20 May 1776, Ebenezer THOMPSON, gentleman of Halifax, Seth CUSHING, Esq. & Isaac CHURCHILL Jr., yeoman, both of Plymton, app'td to divide real estate. Division 4 Aug. 1777 to **Repentance WRIGHT, Sarah WRIGHT, Benjamin WRIGHT** and heirs of **Adam WRIGHT,** dec'd.

Estate of **Sarah WRIGHT,** singlewoman of Plympton MA. <Plymouth Co.PR #23544>
<39:201> 24 May 1809, **John WRIGHT** of Plympton app'td admr. <43:77> Inventory 13 Nov. 1809, real estate valued at $619.00. <53:58> Division 14 July 1810 to heirs of **John WRIGHT,** heirs of **Esther HUNT** and heirs of **Adam WRIGHT.** <53:59> Division 3 July 1820, to heirs of **Adam WRIGHT** dec'd, heirs of **John WRIGHT** dec'd and heirs of **Esther HUNT** dec'd.

Estate of **Benjamin WRIGHT,** yeoman of Plympton MA. <Plymouth Co.PR #23501>
<27:392> 28 Apr. 1792, Gideon BRADFORD Jr., gentleman of Plymton, app'td admr. <33:54> 28 Apr. 1792, James CHURCHILL, gentleman, George SAMSON, yeoman and Sylvanus BARTLETT Jr., yeoman, all of Plympton, app'td to appraise estate. Inventory dated 23 May 1792; real estate valued at £81.6s. <35:214> Order to divide, 19 July 1794 to Elijah BISBEE Jr., Esq., James CHURCHILL, gentleman and George SAMSON, clothier, all of Plympton. Division 3 Feb. 1795 to following heirs, viz: **Repentance WRIGHT, Sarah WRIGHT,** heirs of **Esther HUNT,** heirs of **Adam WRIGHT** and children & heirs of **John WRIGHT.**

Estate of **Benjamin WRIGHT** to **Samuel WRIGHT** of Plimton MA. <Plymouth Co.Deeds 88:222>
...9 Sept. 1794, Gideon BRADFORD, gentleman of Plymton, for 13s sold to Samuel WRIGHT...I the

said Gideon as administrator to the estate of Benjamin WRIGHT...one sixth part of one half of the second share in the fifth Great Lot in the Last Division of Plymouth and Plimton Commons. Ack. 12 Sept. 1800. Rec. 13 Sept. 1800.

Estate of **John WRIGHT** of Chatham CT. <Middletown CT PR #3969>
...Adm. granted 3 Apr. 1780 to William WRIGHT of Chatham. Division 8 Apr. 1780, to following heirs, viz: **William WRIGHT, Ezekiel WRIGHT, Thomas SMITH** & wf **Urania.**
(Note: John WRIGHT, originally from Plympton MA went to CT sometime after 1741.)

Estate of **Adam WRIGHT** of Plympton MA. <Plymouth Co.PR>
<23:83> 4 Mar. 1776, **Joseph WRIGHT** app'td admr. <24:428> Inventory taken 1 Sept. 1777 by Zebedee CHANDLER, Seth CUSHING, Elijah BISBEE. <28:112> Dower set off to widow **Sarah WRIGHT,** 5 Oct. 1781, by Gideon BRADFORD, Esq., James CHURCHILL, gentleman and Jabish NEWLAND, yeoman, all of Plympton. <28:114> Decree 7 Jan. 1782, mentions following heirs, viz: **Sarah WRIGHT,** widow, **Levi WRIGHT** (eldest son), **Hester HOOPER** wf of Asa of Plympton, **Lydia THRASHER** wf of Daniel of Middleboro, **John WRIGHT** and **Benjamin WRIGHT.** <28:115> Account.

Benjamin WRIGHT of Barnstable MA to **Henry COBB** of Barnstable MA. <Barnstable Co.Deeds 4:195>
...5 May 1823, Benjamin WRIGHT, cordwainer, for $162.00, sells to Henry COBB, mariner...12 acres in the westery part of Barnstable bounded by land of Silas JONES, Deacon Joseph CROCKER, Samuel CROCKER. Wf Sarah WRIGHT releases dower. Witnesses: Nymphas MARSTON, Sylvanus N. LAWRENCE, Sophia WRIGHT. Ack. 5 May 1823. Rec. 7 May 1823.

John WRIGHT et al to **Benjamin WRIGHT** of Plymouth MA. <Plymouth Co.Deeds 39:131>
...20 Oct. 1795, Asa HOOPER, cooper & wf Easther, Levi WRIGHT, cordwainer and John WRIGHT, cooper all of Plimton, for ₤8 sold to Benjamin WRIGHT, silversmith...four fifth parts of half a lot of wood land near the Furnace called Larell & Company's Furnace in Carver, the other fifth part of said half lot is owned by said Benjamin, the whole lot is said to contain about one hundred acres and is the fourteenth share in the third Great Lot in the Last Division of the Commons between the Proprietors of Plymouth & Plimton drawn by John BARROWS as appears by the Proprietors records Book 2d page 105...it was bought by Mr. John WRIGHT and Mr. Nathaniel THOMAS, Esq. in the year 1723 and recorded in 1724 Book 18 Folio 18 and by said John WRIGHT given to his two sons Benjamin & Adam WRIGHT. Benjamin's half was sold some time past to Capt. Benjamin CROOKER, the other half being said Adam's descended to us his children the Givers of this deed, viz: four fifths to the said Adam's part...and we hereby warrant said four fifths of said half share, viz: said HOOPER & wife one share, said HOOPER one fifth part more that he bought of Daniel THRASHER & wf Lydia, which Lydia was also a daughter of said Adam WRIGHT, Levi WRIGHT one fifth and John WRIGHT one other fifth of said lot. Ack. 20 Oct. 1795 by John & Levi WRIGHT, Asa HOOPER. Ack. 8 Jan. 1796 by Esther HOOPER. Rec. 11 Jan. 1796.

Benjamin WRIGHT of Plymouth MA to **Rosseter COTTON** of Plymouth MA. <Plymouth Co.Deeds 79:21>
...29 Dec. 1795, Benjamin WRIGHT, clock maker, for $55.00 sold to Rosseter COTTON, Physician... one undivided half part of the fourteenth share in the third great lot & Last Division in Plymouth & Plimton Commons lying in Plymouth...said lot was laid out to John BARROWS & sold by him to Nathaniel THOMAS & by said Thomas to my grandfather John WRIGHT as by his deed of exchange dated December 7th 1723 & recorded Book 18 folio 18. Ack. & Rec. 29 Dec. 1795.

John GIFFORD et al to **Zephaniah EDDY** of Dartmouth MA. <Bristol Co.Deeds 66:406>
...24 May 1777, John GIFFORD, blacksmith of Little Compton, David GIFFORD son of Joseph GIFFORD late of Portsmouth dec'd now...of Tiverton...and Isaac GIFFORD, yeoman, Peleg GIFFORD, yeoman, Benjamin GIFFORD, Adam GIFFORD, yeoman, David GIFFORD, yeoman, Gideon GIFFORD, yeoman son of William GIFFORD dec'd, David GIFFORD 2d & wf Hannah, William WOOD & wf Alice...all of Dartmouth ...for ₤90, sell to Zephaniah EDDY, merchant, sixty acres in Dartmouth, bounded by land of Timothy RUSSELL, Joseph ALLEN and heirs of Henry GIDLEY. Witnesses: Benjamin RUSSELL Jr., Thomas SHEARMAN, Eliashib SMITH, Benjamin AKIN.

Estate of **Jeremiah GIFFORD** of Dartmouth MA. <Bristol Co.PR>
<22:21> Inventory taken 13 Mar. 1771 by Joseph AIKEN, Jabez BARKER(sp), Thomas SHEARMAN; personal estate, ₤44.16.1; real estate, ₤8. Oath of administrator, 19 Apr. 1771 (no name). <22:129> 27 Jan 1772, Jonathan SOWLE app'td admr. <146:193> 21 Jan. 1771, Jonathan SOWLE of Tiverton RI app'td admr.

Jeremiah GIFFORD of Dartmouth to **Benjamin & Isaac GIFFORD** of Dartmouth. <Bristol Co.Deeds 53:115>
...3 Mar. 1768, Jeremiah GIFFORD, yeoman...for love & gratitude which I have & do bare to my two sons Benjamin GIFFORD & Isaac GIFFORD, yeomen...three acres in Dartmouth, bounded by land of Robert KIRBEY, William WOOD, Enos GIFFORD. Witnesses: Richard KIRBY, Abner MERIHEW. 2nd Tues. June 1770, Richard KIRBEY made solemn oath that he was present & saw Jeremiah GIFFORD sign (GIFFORD is since deceased). Rec. 14 June 1770.

Benjamin GIFFORD Sr. of Dartmouth MA to **Ichabod GIFFORD** of Dartmouth. <Bristol Co.Deeds 77:140-1>
...19 Oct. 1781, Benjamin GIFFORD Sr., yeoman, for ₤90 silver money, sells to son Ichabod GIFFORD ...two pieces of land in Dartmouth...being part of ye land or farm that I have lately bought of Seth HUDDLESTON...one piece four acres, the other fifteen acres. Witnesses: Nathaniel SOWLE, Joshua TRIPP. Ack.. 24 Aug. 1797 by Benjamin GIFFORD. Rec. 18 Aug. 1798.

Benjamin GIFFORD of Dartmouth MA to **Ichabod GIFFORD** of Dartmouth MA. <Bristol Co.Deeds 77:141-2> ...16 Feb. 1782, Benjamin GIFFORD, yeoman, for £90 silver money, sells to son Ichabod GIFFORD... forty three acres in Dartmouth...part of that farm I lately bought of Seth HUTTLESTON...bounded on land I lately sold to son James GIFFORD and land of son William GIFFORD...reserving the right for son William to water his creatures at the Great Spring. Witnesses: Nathaniel SOWLE, Joseph BOZWORTH. Ack. by Benjamin GIFFORD 24 Aug. 1797. Rec. 18 Aug. 1798.

==========

Ichabod & James GIFFORD Jr. of Dartmouth to **William GIFFORD** of Dartmouth. <Bristol Co.Deeds> <77:142>...17 Aug. 1798, Ichabod GIFFORD and James GIFFORD Jr., yeomen, for $450.00, sell to William GIFFORD, yeoman...eighty three acres in Dartmouth...described by two several deeds of sale from Benjamin GIFFORD to Ichabod GIFFORD...bounded by land of James GIFFORD, Stephen CORNELL, James GIFFORD Jr...with all buidlings (except ye house that Jeremiah GIFFORD owns); mentions a lease that Benjamin GIFFORD holds. Also signed by Sarah GIFFORD. Witnesses: John SMITH, Jacob ANTHONY. Ack. 18 Aug. 1798 by James & Ichabod GIFFORD. Rec. 18 Aug. 1798.

==========

William GIFFORD of Westport RI to **Jeremiah BROWNELL** of Westport RI. <Tiverton Rcds.84:301> ...22 Oct. 1804, William GIFFORD, for $650.00 sells to Jeremiah BROWNELL, 98 acres, bounded by land of James GIFFORD, excepting a lease that Benjamin GIFFORD holds on part of said land as well as Gifford's wife's right of dower. Witnesses: William GIFFORD, Freelove GIFFORD. Ack. 22 Oct. 1804. Rec. 12 Dec. 1804.

==========

Will of **Adam GIFFORD** of Dartmouth MA. <Bristol Co.PR 26:6>
...dated 26 Sept. 1778, mentions wf **Anna**; son **William GIFFORD** (executor); grandson **Adam WING**, granddaughters **Anna WING & P( ) WING** (all under 21), the children of **Benjamin WING**; daus? (names too faint). Pr. 4 May 1779. (Note: handwriting is quite faint in files)

==========

Will of **Gideon GIFFORD** of Dartmouth MA. <Bristol Co.PR 17:6>
...dated 10 Dec. 1759, mentions wf **Elizabeth**; mother, and father **Jeremiah GIFFORD**; cousin **Joshua GIFFORD**; sister **Elizabeth SOULE**; sister **Margaret POTTER**(sp); sister in law **Elizabeth GIFFORD**, widow; sister **Sarah PARKS**; cousin (**Deborah**?) **CORNELL**, widow & her sisters; brothers **Adam GIFFORD**, **David GIFFORD**; cousins **Gideon GIFFORD & Hannah GIFFORD**, children of brother **William GIFFORD**, dec'd; **Essok**(sp) **WILHU/WILBOUR**'s son; brothers **John GIFFORD & Joseph GIFFORD** executors. Witnesses: John WERDEN(sp); Joshua BARKER. Pr. 14 Apr. 1760. Receipts 5 Mar. 1761. (Note: The files contain additional names & probate data however the faint handwriting is almost illegible.)

==========

Will of **Jonathan GIFFORD** of Dartmouth MA. <Bristol Co.PR 15:330>
...dated 30 Dec. 1756, mentions daus (**Debbe**?) **CORNELL, Dinah POTTER**; son **Jeremiah GIFFORD**; dau **Mary CASE**; **Timothy POTTER** of Dartmouth, son of my (deceased wife?); grandchild **Elizabeth CASE**. Pr. 3 May 1757. (Note: handwriting is quite faint in files)

==========

Estate of **William GIFFORD** of Dartmouth MA. <Bristol Co.Deeds 73:486>
...11 Nov. 1769...whereas William GIFFORD of Dartmouth died intestate and left his estate to his brother **David GIFFORD**, his widow **Elizabeth GIFFORD** and his son & dau, **Gideon GIFFORD** and **Hannah SHEPARD**, widow... (Note: On a small scrap of paper is written: Adm. estate of William GIFFORD of Dartmouth, 5 Nov. 175(4?), widow Elizabeth GIFFORD. <Bristol Co.PR 14:199>)

MICRO #3 OF 30

Benjamin GIFFORD to **Alice GIFFORD**, both of Dartmouth MA...4 Oct. 1768. Elizabeth GIFFORD signs. **Benjamin GIFFORD**, yeoman of Dartmouth MA...15 Sept. 1781. Alice GIFFORD signs. <Bristol Co.Deeds 65:581; 65:105> (No details given for either deed.)

==========

Estate of **Benjamin GIFFORD** of Dartmouth MA. <Taunton PR 43:261,514,535>
<43:535>...16 Dec. 1807, **William GIFFORD** app'td admr., fears insolvency. Bondsmen: Joseph HART, Abner GIFFORD; **Alice GIFFORD**, widow receives thirds; Jeremiah BROWNELL owns the other half of the homestead farm, about 100 acres. Appraisers app'td, 4 Jan. & 28 Apr. 1808, Abner GIFFORD, Jonathan PECKHAM and Charles PARKER. Inventory 4 Oct. 1808, sworn to by admr. Real Estate appraised, 30 Apr. 1808 by Lemuel MILK, Jonathan PECK, John MOSHER; incl. 100 acre homestead farm in Dartmouth (appraised at $20 an acre), widow to receive 20 acres as her dower. List of Claims, 7 Dec. 1808, incl. William GIFFORD, Stephen MOSHER, Jonathan PECKHAM, Job MILK, Humphrey KIRBY, Ruth BORDEN, Isaac HOWLAND, Abner GIFFORD, John GIFFORD, Jeremiah BROWNELL, Adam GIFFORD, Simeon P. WINSLOW; paid 20 cents on the dollar.

==========

Benjamin GIFFORD of Dartmouth MA to **Seth HUDDLESTONE**. <Bristol Co.Deeds 65:105>
...15 Sept. 1781, Benjamin GIFFORD, for 800 spanish milled dollars, sells to Seth HUDDLESTONE... 50 acre homestead farm in Dartmouth...where I now dwell...bounded by land of Daniel WHALING, Abiel GIFFORD, John DAVOL, Prince POTTER...together with a tract of cedar swamp. Witnesses: Champlain POTTER, Samuel SMITH. Wf Alice GIFFORD signs. Ack. by Benjamin GIFFORD 21 Oct. 1783. Rec. 28 Jan. 1786.

==========

Ichabod GIFFORD of Dartmouth MA to **Jonathan GIFFORD** of Dartmouth MA. <Bristol Co.Deeds 80:503> ...19 Aug. 1790, Ichabod GIFFORD, for £30, sells to Jonathan GIFFORD...land lying west of Commins Pond in Dartmouth, bounded by Gifford's land and land of Joseph SOWL/SOUL and Stephen GIFFORD. Witnesses: Stephen GIFFORD, Eunice SMITH. Ack. 13 Mar. 1801. Rec. 28 Dec. 1801.

==========

Ichabod GIFFORD of Dartmouth MA to **Matthew & Jonathan RUSSELL** of Westport.<Bristol Co.Deeds> <80:81>...29 May 1797, Ichabod GIFFORD, for $30.00, sells to Matthew RUSSELL and Jonathan RUSSELL ..eight acres of white pine swamp in Dartmouth...bounded by land of James GIFFORD, Jethro SOWLES, John TUCKER and said Ichabod GIFFORD. Witnesses: Sarah GIFFORD, John SMITH. Ack. 24 Aug. 1797. Rec. 22 Apr. 1801.

Benjamin GIFFORD of Dartmouth MA to **Jacob CHASE.** <Bristol Co.Deeds 55:144>
...1 May 1772, Benjamin GIFFORD, cordwainer, conveys to Jacob CHASE...a certain piece of salt meadow & sedge...lying in ye horse neck meadows against ye opening adjoyning to the beach...bounded by land of Isaac GIFFORD, William WOOD and the meadow that formerly belonged to Robert KIRBY. Witnesses: Ichabod GIFFORD, Amos CORNELL. Ack. 5 Nov. 1772. Rec. 17 Mar. 1773.

Benjamin GIFFORD of Dartmouth MA to **Abiel GIFFORD.** <Bristol Co.Deeds 65:581>
...4 Oct. 1768, Benjamin GIFFORD sells to Abiel GIFFORD, five acres in Dartmouth, bounded by land of Peleg GIFFORD, said Benjamin GIFFORD and said Abiel GIFFORD's homestead. Witnesses: Prince POTTER, Gideon GIFFORD. Elizabeth GIFFORD also signs. Ack. by Benjamin GIFFORD 5 Nov. 1772. Rec. 28 Jan. 1786.

Jeremiah GIFFORD of Dartmouth MA to **Benjamin GIFFORD** of Dartmouth MA. <Bristol Co.Deeds 41:194>
...16 Feb. 1752, Jeremiah GIFFORD, yeoman, for £100, sells to son Benjamin GIFFORD, labourer... all that part of my homestead (in Dartmouth)...lying to ye northward of that part of my said farm that I sold to my son Isaac GIFFORD and to ye westward of that part...I sold to my son Peleg GIFFORD. Witnesses: Samuel POTTER, George MOSHER. Ack. 23 or 28 Mar. 1752. Rec. 10 Sept. 1754.

Estate of **Nathan WRIGHT** of Kingston MA. <Plymouth Co.PR #23535>
<17:74> 7 Apr. 1762, **Hannah WRIGHT**, widow, app'td admx. Bondsmen: Job HALL, John ADAMS. <16:331> Inventory 29 July 1762, appraisers: Job HALL, Peter WEST, Judah HALL.

Hannah WRIGHT of Kingston MA to **David LUCAS** of Kingston MA. <Plymouth Co.Deeds 64:218>
...26 Jan. 1776, Hannah WRIGHT, for £5.10s6d, sells to David LUCAS, yeoman...six and one fifth acre in Kingston...part of land which was given me by my Father **William COOK.** Ack. 28 Mar. 1777. Rec. 30 Nov. 1785.

Will of **Samuel WRIGHT**, yeoman of Plympton MA. <Plymouth Co.PR 21:308>
...dated 14 Oct. 1772, mentions wf **Anna**; dau **Sarah HALL** of Kingston; son **Samuel WRIGHT** (executor) and son **Jacob WRIGHT**; children of son **Edmund WRIGHT**; grandchildren **Nathan WRIGHT, Edmund WRIGHT** & **Lydia HALL.** Witnesses: Gideon BRADFORD, Esq., Levi BRADFORD, Zebedee CHANDLER. Pr. 1 Feb. 1773.

JACOB COOKE^{2} (Francis^{1})

Jacob COOKE of Plymouth to **William MACOMBER** of Marshfield. <Plymouth Col.Deeds 3:168><2>
...18 May 1665, Jacob COOKE, husbandman, for £15, sells to William MACOMBER, son of William MACOMBER of Marshfield, one quarter share of land given by his deceased father Ffrancis COOKE, in Dartmouth. Ack. 20 Oct. 1666 by **Jacob & wf.**

John COOKE of Dartmouth with **Jacob COOKE Sr.** of Plymouth. <Plymouth Col.Deeds 3:248>
...4 July 1672, John COOKE, yeoman, exchanges with Jacob COOKE Sr., for one quarter of one share of upland & meadow in Dartmouth...which was formerly Ffrancis COOKE's of the Towne of New Plymouth deceased.

John DOTEN/DOUGHTY against the Estate of **Jacob COOKE.** <Plymouth C.O.V:141>
...7 July 1676, In reference unto the issueing of a difference between John DOTEN and the executors and overseers of the Last Will of Jacob COOKE deceased and the rest of the children concerned in that estate; touching five pounds demannded by the said DOUGHTEY comitted to the finall determination of this court; This court haveing heard and considered theire mutuall pleas; Doe order that the said John DOUGHTY shall have alowed unto him by the sonnes that enjoy the Lands of the said Jacob COOKE proportionable to theire respective partes by them enjoyed either two acres of the marsh lying together out of the six acrees lying att Joneses River; or forty shillings in Current New England money; and forty shillings more to him in Curent Country pay; out of the estate belonging to the sisters according to theire respective partes; and this to be a finall end of the said Difference.

Guardianship of Heirs of **Cephas WADSWORTH** of Kingston MA. <Plymouth Co.PR #4856>
<60:81> Bond/Letter 19 Jan. 1829, Elkanah COOK of Kingston app'td gdn. of **Benjamin, Zilpah & Peleg COOK**, minors above 14, and **Mary Gray COOK**, minor under 14, heirs at law to the estate of Cephas WADSWORTH. Sureties: Constant SAMSON & Henry COBB, of Kingston. Witness: William SPOONER. <original> Warrant to appraise, 9 Aug. 1830, to Pelham HOLMES, Zenas CUSHMAN of Plympton and Robert HOLMES of Kingston. <69:330> Inventory sworn 9 Aug. 1830...estate of minors, the lawful heirs of Cephas WADSWORTH of Kingston deceased, being a forty-ninth part each.

Estate of **Charles COOK**, mariner of Scituate MA. <Plymouth Co.PR #4862>
<71:19> Bond/Letter 29 Nov. 1831, **Clarissa COOK**, widow, app'td admx. Sureties: Peleg JENKINS & John BEAL of Scituate. <70:579> Insolvency 29 Nov. 1831. <72:275> Inventory taken 15 Mar. 1832 by

Asa LITCHFIELD, Theophilus CORTHELL, Stephen MOTT Jr., all of Scituate; incl. dwelling house & land, $750.00; part of two pews in Rev. Mr. JEWELL's meetinghouse, $20.00; personal estate totals $134.00; sworn to by admx. 5 June 1832. <68:280> Notice 29 Nov. 1831. <72:277> List of Claims, 4 Apr. 1832 by Asa LITCHFIELD & Stephen MOTT Jr., incl. Theophilus CORTHELL, Elijah PEIRCE, William STUDLEY, Amos TILDEN, Dr. Milton FULLER, GANNETT & BAILEY, Dexter VINAL, Ichabod COOK, John COOK, Stephen MOTT Jr., Thomas VINAL. <73:21> Petition of admx. to sell real estate, 5 June 1832. <72:586> Account of admx. allowed 27 Nov. 1832; received from Peleg JENKINS, $400.00 for sale of house & land; from John STUDLEY for pews, $8.00; from BEAL & JENKINS on settlement, $10.35; payments made to Stephen MOTT Jr., Asa LITCHFIELD, Theophilus CORTHELL, John B. TURNER, Ebenezer T. FOGG, Dexter MERRITT & William PEAKES for taxes, Sarah LITCHFIELD, J. FARMER. <72:565> Dower assigned to **Clarissa COOK**, $256.66; Commissioners: John B. TURNER, Asa LITCHFIELD, Stephen MOTT Jr. Accepted by Court, 3 Dec. 1832.

Will of **Eli COOK**, Esq. of Kingston MA. <Plymouth Co.PR #4866>
<87:216>...dated 21 Aug. 1834, mentions wf **Hannah**; namesake Eli Cook DREW, youngest son of Seth DREW; wife & Job W. DREW named executors. Codicil (no date) mentions wife & nephew Eli Cook DREW who is named executor in place of Job W. DREW. At the end of the will is the declination of **Hannah COOK** with the request that her brother Seth DREW be appointed admr. with will annexed during the minority of her co-executor (no date). <10:544> 3 June 1845, Bond of adm. with will annexed, of Seth DREW of Kingston, representing that Hannah COOK one of the Executors had declined and Eli C. DREW the other executor was a minor. Sureties: Gamaliel B. ADAMS, Samuel E. CUSHMAN, both of Kingston. Letter 1st Tues. June 1845, Eli COOK app'td admr. with will annexed. <87:299> Inventory taken 1 July 1845 by Nathaniel FAUNCE, Samuel E. CUSHMAN, Francis DREW; incl. homestead farm & buildings, $2000.00; Thatcher lot woodland, $188; Common lot, $60; Davis lot, $63; Cook lot, $202 Birch swamp, $250; Mill & Sever lot, $1600; Black grass meadow, Kingston, $500.00; Black grass meadow, Duxbury, $100; D. Bradford lot, pasture land, $250; half the Allen house & lot, $600; one quarter undivided meadow, $25; two shares in Baptist Meeting house & lot, $200; total: personal, $1837.44, real estate, $6038.00. <88:358> 1st Account of admr., 10 Aug. 1846, assented to by widow; Debts due from: Peter WINSOR, John CUSHING, Nahum BAILEY, Spencer CUSHMAN, Hannah COOK, Otis WATERMAN, Lydia FOSTER's est., Ira CHANDLER, Charles BARTLETT. Payments to: estate of Robert COOK, Seth WASHBURN, Justus HARLOW, Ezra PERKINS, P.L. NICHOLS, Alexander HOLMES, Charles C. FAUNCE, W.S. STETSON, Joseph CUSHMAN, Thomas C. HOLMES, Elkanah CUSHMAN, Nathaniel WASHBURN, Jedediah HOLMES, Nathaniel FAUNCE, Thomas P. BEAL, Ira COOK's note, Benjamin SAMPSON, Horace HOLMES Nathaniel CUSHMAN, Joseph S. BEAL, note of Charles BARTLETT. <88:515> 2nd Account of admr. 7 Dec. 1846, assented to by widow; Payments from: Hannah COOK, Josiah HOLMES note; Payments to: Thomas ADAMS, George BONNEY, Melzar WHITTEN, Hannah COOK, Joseph HOLMES.

Estate of **Elkanah COOK** of Kingston MA. <Plymouth Co.PR #4869>
<10:288> Petition/Bond 1 Oct. 1839, of Peleg BRADFORD of Kingston, representing that he has been requested to administer the estate by the heirs-at-law. Sureties: Benjamin COOK, Henry SOULE, both of Kingston. Letter 1 Oct. 1839, Peleg BRADFORD app'td admr. <82:14> Inventory dated 21 Oct. 1839, appraised by Spencer BRADFORD & Daniel RING of Kingston and Martin HAYWARD of Plympton.; total: real estate, $1880, personal, $334.59. <6:23> Notice 1 Oct. 1839. <83:21> Account of admr. 18 Jan. 1841; Received from: Seth DREW, Eunice COOK for tax & the heirs of this estate. Paid to: Joseph SAMPSON for tax on Patience COOK's estate in the hands of E. COOK, admr., Joseph HOLMES, Nathaniel THOMAS, Asaph HOLMES, Elkanah CUSHMAN, Jedidiah HOLMES, Daniel RING, Martin HAYWARD, Martin COOK for labor, P.L. NICHOLS, Ezra FULLER, George THOMPSON, David BEAL, Spencer BRADFORD, Christina COOK's bill for housework, heirs of Elizabeth STETSON from the estate of Patience COOK in the hand of Elkanah COOK, admr. on said Patience COOK's estate.

Guardianship of Children of **Henry COOK** of Scituate MA. <Plymouth Co.PR #4872>
<8:129L> Bond/Letter 5 Mar. 1839, **Fanny HOLMES** of Scituate, app'td gdn. of **Fanny COOK** and **Harriet COOK**, minor children of Henry COOK late of Scitute dec'd. Sureties: Elijah PEIRCE, Ammiel CURTIS, both of Scituate. <original> 5 Mar. 1839, subscribing minors over the age of fourteen years do hereby make choice of our mother **Fanny HOLMES** for our guardian. Signed by **Fanny & Harriet COOK.**

Will of **Joanna COOK**, widow of Kingston MA. <Plymouth Co.PR #4886>
<79:145>...dated 24 Dec. 1816, widow of **Zenas COOK** late of Plympton; mentions sisters **Hannah FAUNCE, Eleanor FAUNCE, Sarah FAUNCE & Lydia COOK** wf of Josiah; heirs of sister **Molly COOK** dec'd; brother **John FAUNCE,** Esq., dec'd; brothers **Eliezer FAUNCE** (executor) **& Elijah FAUNCE.** <10:486> Petition 15 May 1837 of Charles C. FAUNCE of Kingston representing **Joanna COOK** as a widow and that **Eliezer FAUNCE** the executor had deceased. Bond 15 May 1837, of Charles C. FAUNCE as admr. with will annexed. Sureties: Kilborn FAUNCE, Ira COOK, both of Kingston. <79:147> Inventory, warrant issued 10 Apr. 1837 to Josiah HOLMES, John GRAY, John FULLER 2d, all of Kingston; total: real estate, $858, personal, $143.80. <75:516> Notice 15 May 1837. <80:31> Account 14 Feb. 1838, allowed 19 Feb. 1838; received from Sarah FAUNCE and estate of Daniel BISBEE; payments to Sarah FAUNCE the amount of personal estate ($143.80), J. THURBER, John GRAY, Elkanah CUSHMAN, Dr. P.L. NICHOLS.

Receipt of **John & Lucy COOK** of Pembroke MA. <Plymouth Co.PR #4889>
<50:187> Receipt 10 May 1819 of **John COOK & Lucy COOK** to their late guardian Isaac SOPER, $23.42, it being in full for their share of the personal estate left them, with what they have heretofore received. Witnesses: Thomas BARREL.

Estate of **Josiah COOK**, yeoman of Kingston MA. <Plymouth Co.PR #4890>
<61:107> Bond/Letter 21 May 1827, Josiah COOK, bricklayer of Kingston, app'td admr. Sureties:

Daniel BISBEE, Tilden FAUNCE, both of Kingston. Witness: P.U. WARREN. <64:154,155> Warrant & Inventory dated 21 May 1827, sworn to 23 June 1827; appraisers John GRAY, Robert COOK Jr., Peleg BRADFORD, all of Kingston; incl. homesead farm & 46 acres, $1230.00; Crossmus Pasture by the Pond, 7 acres, $70.00; half pew in Congregational Meeting house, $10; cedar swamp at White oak arm in Hanson, one third undivided of 5 acres, $16.00; fresh meadow, one undivided third of six acres in Jone's Meadows in Plympton, $21; allowance to **Lydia COOK**, widow, $220.00. <62:162> Notice sworn to 16 July 1827. <62:394> Warrant for Dower to John GRAY, Robert COOK Jr., Peleg BRADFORD, all of Kingston to set off dower to **Lydia COOK**, widow; sworn to 27 Nov. 1827. <62:394> Assignment of Dower, 27 Nov. 1827, land adjoining Robert COOK's. <64:344> 1st Account 19 Nov. 1827, of admr.; Received from: estate of Stephen BRADFORD, Kilborn FAUNCE on account with Charles C. FAUNCE, estate of Daniel BISBEE; Paid to: Spencer CUSHMAN, John McLAUTHLIN, Elisha STETSON, Nathaniel FOSTER Jr., Dr. Paul L. NICHOLS, Tilden FAUNCE, Robert COOK Jr., Kilborn FAUNCE. <64:395> Petition to sell real estate 19 Nov. 1827, granted 17 Dec. 1827. <64:491> Adv. of Sale, 17 Dec. 1827, sworn 18 Feb. 1828; payment of debts, $490; one third of 5 acre lot of cedar swamp in Hanson; half a pew; Crossmus Pond pasture in Kingston and so much of the homestead of Josiah COOK as shall make up the aforesaid sum. <64:491> 2nd Account of admr., 18 Feb. 1828; Paid to: John McLAUTHLIN for tax; Zenas CUSHMAN for tax, John GRAY, appraiser; Nathaniel WASHBURN for surveying Robert COOK Jr. for appraising, Peleg BRADFORD for appraising; Received from: Capt. Ira COOK who bought the real estate mentioned above, balance of account from estate of Benjamin WATERMAN. <original> Admr.'s Private Account, Josiah COOK to Josiah COOK Jr., 16 Nov. 1827; Payments to: Seth PERKINS for work, Pelham BRADFORD, Ezra PERKINS, Levi FISH; Received from: Widow EVERSON, Joanna SIMMONS, widow, Hosea BREWSTER for plowing, etc.

Estate of **Lydia COOK**, widow of Kingston MA. <Plymouth Co.PR #4891>
<10:58> Petition/Bond 20 Feb. 1837, of **Josiah COOK**, eldest son, of Kingston. Sureties: James N. SEAVER, Kilborn FAUNCE, both of Kingston. <79:111> Warrant & Inventory 20 Feb. 1837, appraisers John GRAY, Lewis GRAY, Thomas BRADFORD; totals: personal, $129.64, real estate, $1030.00; incl. one undivided fifth part of 79 acres of pasture lying partly in Kingston & Plympton, $210; nine and a half acres woodland in Kingston adjoining heirs of James CUSHMAN, $275; one and three quarter acre of fresh meadow, $85; forty one acres of woodland in the Commons so called, $450; one third of five acres cedar swamp at Whiteoak arm in Hanson, $10. <75:409> Notice 20 Feb. 1837. <79:351> Warrant & Division of estate of **Josiah & Lydia COOK**, issued 10 Apr. 1837 to John GRAY, Lewis GRAY and Thomas BRADFORD, all of Kingston, to following heirs: **Olive WESTON**, wf of Noah of Plympton; **Josiah COOK**; **Lydia FAUNCE** wf of Tilden; **Molly COOK**; **Abigal BISBEE** wf of Daniel; **Daniel FAUNCE** of Maumee OH; **Nancy FAUNCE** wf of Kilborn; mentions land which was bounded and set off to **Lydia COOK** in the division of the estate of John FAUNCE, Esq., dec'd. <80:116> Account of admr., 9 Apr. 1838; shares of $21.60 each were paid to **Olive WESTON, Lydia FAUNCE, Abigail BISBEE, Nancy FAUNCE, Molly COOK** and **Josiah COOK.**

Will of **Judith COOK**, widow of Scituate MA. <Plymouth Co.PR #4893>
<87:318>...dated 14 June 1842, mentions son **William COOK** (executor), daus: **Deborah CORTHELL, Sally MERRITT, Anna DAMON, Judith VINAL, Emily STUDLEY, Caroline ELLMS**, sons **Tobias COOK** & **Israel COOK**; grandchildren: **Fanny COOK, Harriet COOK, Charles COOK, Clarissa COOK, Mercy COOK, Charles Henry COOK.** Witnesses: Francis THOMAS, Areilla DAMON, Gideon W. YOUNG. <2:52> Bond of **William COOK.** Sureties: Francis THOMAS, Caleb W. PROUTY, both of Scituate.

Guardianship of **Maria A. COOK** of Middleborough MA. <Plymouth Co.PR #4898>
<original> Citation 5 Nov. 1850, **Maria A. COOK** has no natural guardian, her mother **Mary Ann COOK** has deceased; that about six months before the birth of Maria the mother was divorced from her husband **Charles COOK**, now a resident of Boston. <9:273> Bond 2 Dec. 1850 of guardian Thomas M. CUSHMAN of Middleborough. Sureties: William S. SAVERY of Carver, Benjamin COBB of Plymouth. <93:423> Inventory 4 Nov. 1851 of gdn.; appraisers James R. SPROAT, George VAUGHAN, George WATERMAN, total of estate, $273.17. <101:63> Account of Jerusha W. CUSHMAN, executrix of will of Thomas M. CUSHMAN, gdn. allowed 3d Monday Feb. 1859. <11:150> Bond of Jerusha W. CUSHMAN of Carver, representing that **Maria A. COOK** of Carver, under 14, child of **Charles COOK**...Sureties: Benjamin COBB, Ebenezer COBB Jr., of Kingston. Witnesses: Henry SHERMAN, A.L. DREW; bond approved 21 Feb. 1859. <102:60> Inventory of Jerusha W. CUSHMAN, gdn., 17 Feb. 1860; appraisers W.L. SAVERY, Ezra VAUGHN and E.C. BLAKE; total of estate, $653.00.

Will of **Martin COOK** of Kingston MA. <Plymouth Co.PR #4899>
<2:135>...dated 23 Oct. 1847, mentions wf **Hannah** and **Martin COOK Jr.** (executor). Witnesses: Zenas BRYANT, Ezra FULLER, Oliver EVERSON. <21:135> Bond of executor, 2 Nov. 1847. Sureties: Zenas BRYANT of Plympton, Ezra FULLER of Kingston. <7:328> Notice 15 May 1848. <90:196> Inventory taken 27 Dec. 1847 by Zenas BRYANT, Ezra FULLER, Oliver EVERSON; totals: real estate, $2347.00, personal, $483.00.

Estate of **Patience COOK** of Kingston MA. <Plymouth Co.PR #4907>
<10:150> Petition & Bond 3d Mon. Jan. 1838, of **Elkanah COOK**, brother of dec'd. Sureties: Martin COOK, Benjamin COOK, both of Kingston. <original> Choice of Admr. 25 Mar. 1838, **Eunice COOK** makes choice of her brother **Elkanah COOK** as admr. on estate of **Patience COOK.** <80:461> Inventory 24 Aug. 1838; appraisers Spencer BRADFORD, Thomas BRADFORD, Daniel RING; totals: real estate, $1204, personal, $1348.56. <5:80> Notice 15 Jan. 1838. <80:462> Division of real estate, 22 Nov. 1838 by appraisers to following heirs, viz: **Elkanah COOK, Eunice COOK,** heirs of **Elizabeth STETSON**; mentions 3 acres in the White Oak wood lot set off in the division of Benjamin COOK's estate to **Patience COOK** (6 Oct. 1800) and land set off to **Mary GRAY** in the division of her father, Samuel

GRAY's estate. <80:462> Account 3 Dec. 1838, payments made to: Peleg BRADFORD, Elkanah CUSHMAN, P.L. NICHOLS, Asaph HOLMES, H. TRIBLE, Spencer BRADFORD, Thomas BRADFORD, Daniel RING, Oliver EVERSON.

Guardianship & Estate of **Phebe COOK** of Kingston MA. <Plymouth Co.PR #4909>
<48:38> Warrant 30 Apr. 1816, of **John COOK**, brother of **Phebe COOK**, singlewoman, that she is non compos and asks for appointment of guardian. <original> Bond 1 May 1816, **John COOK**, housewright of Kingston, app'td gdn. Sureties: George SAMPSON 2d, Isaac SAMPSON, both of Plymouth. <41:250> Letter of guardianship, 1 May 1816. <48:373> Warrant to appraise, 1 May 1816, by Martin PARRIS, John THOMAS, Robert COOK Jr., all of Kingston. <48:393> Inventory 26 Feb. 1817, incl. land assigned her in division of her father's estate near Elisha WASHBURN's; totals: real estate, $643.50, personal, $27.67. <48:393> Notice 1 May 1816. <48:431> Request of **John COOK** to be discharged as guardian. Decree 15 Apr. 1817, discharging him and appointing John THOMAS of Kingston as gdn. <original> Statement of Overseers of Poor of Kingston. <original> Citation on **John COOK** as gdn.,a complaint of his neglect to settle an account of his guardianship, 28 Apr. 1817. <48:458> Account of **John COOK**, gdn., 3 May 1817; Received from: Wiswall STETSON, James CUSHMAN, estate of Silvanus COOK, dec'd; Paid: Samuel BROWN, Elisha STETSON for boarding **Phebe COOK** from 17 Feb. to 18 Apr. <48:306> Letter. <48:457> Warrant to Appraise. <48:457> Inventory. <53:145> Petition.

Estate of **Robert COOK** of Kingston MA. <Plymouth Co.PR #4914>
<61:242> Letter/Bond 20 Oct. 1828 of Robert COOK & Eli COOK, of Kingston, admrs. Sureties: James N. SEVER of Kingston and William SAMPSON of Duxbury. <66:564> Inventory taken 24 Oct. 1828 by Joseph HOLMES, John GRAY, Thomas C. HOLMES, all of Kingston; incl. homestead farm, 66 acres, $3353.00; half pew in 1st Congregational Meeting house; pew #30 in Baptist Meeting house; totals: real estate, $6639.00, personal, $7573.39. <62:322> Notice 20 Oct. 1828. <69:71> Division of real estate, 28 Sept. 1829, to following heirs, viz: **Robert COOK, Eli COOK, Ira COOK, Levi COOK.**

Will of **Robert COOK** of Kingston MA. <Plymouth Co.PR #4915>
<86:60>...dated 25 Dec. 1843, mentions wf **Betsey** (executrix), children **Lydia PERKINS, Robert COOK Jr, Judith Almina CUSHMAN.** Witnesses: Jedediah HOLMES, Eli COOK, Eli C. DREW. <2:1> Bond of **Betsey COOK**, widow. Sureties: Eli COOK, Jedediah HOLMES, of Kingston. Witnesses: Josiah COOK, Ira COOK. <86:187> Inventory approved 2d Mon. Apr. 1844; incl. pews in Unitarian meeting house; appraisers app'td 19 Feb. 1844, Jedediah HOLMES, Josiah COOK, Ira COOK. <6:491U> Notice. <2:319O> Petition & Order for Sale of land by exx. by her attorney Eli COOK for payment of debts amounting to $1195.33. <88:41> Account 19 Jan. 1846 of **Betsey COOK.** <114:184> Petition, 2d Mon. Dec. 1863, for appointment of administrator de bonis non with will annexed by Ezra PERKINS of Kingston, stating that **Robert COOK** deceased in January 1845 leaving a widow **Betsey COOK** who has since died; mentions children **Lydia A. PERKINS** wf of Ezra, **Judith A. CUSHMAN** wf of Edwin, both of Kingston and **Robert COOK**, now residing in Kingston but whose right in the estate is now claimed by Alexander BRADFORD of Raynham by right of purchase. <114:84> Bond 14 Dec. 1863 of Ezra PERKINS. Sureties: Philander COBB & David G. ELDREDGE of Kingston. Witnesses: Abner P. CHILDS, Martin COBB.

Estate of **Robert COOK**, mariner of Scituate MA. <Plymouth Co.PR #4917>
<originals> Declination 29 Feb. 1832, of **Judith COOK**, widow as admx. Request of sons **Tobias COOK** and **Ichabod COOK** that their brother **William COOK** be app'td admr. <71:39> Bond/Letter 6 Mar. 1832, of **William COOK**, cooper, of Scituate as admr. Sureties: Perez LITCHFIELD, John TURNER, both of Scituate. <72:50> Insolvency 6 Mar. 1832. <72:49> Inventory taken 29 Feb. 1832 by William PEAKES, Joseph N. ELMS, Marshall LITCHFIELD; totals: real estate, $566.00, personal, $75.42. <68:279> Notice. <72:396> Assignment of Dower, 5 June 1832 to **Judith COOK**, widow. <72:498> List of claims, 6 Mar. 1832, William COOK, Daniel ELLMS, JOseph N. ELLMS, Simeon LITCHFIELD, Elijah PEIRCE. <73:388> Petition to sell real estate, 28 Aug. 1832. <74:84> Account of admr. allowed 5 Mar. 1833; Payments to: Daniel ELLMS, Simeon LITCHFIELD, Theophilus CORTHELL, Elijah PEIRCE, Marshall LITCHFIELD, Franklin JACOBS, Joseph N. ELLMS, Amos TILDEN, J. FARMER, Dr. Milton FULLER, William PEAKES, Lewis STUDLEY, John TURNER, William COOK.

Will of **Sarah COOK**, singlewoman of Kingston MA. <Plymouth Co.PR>
<66:48>...dated 14 Jan. 1828, mentions brother **Elkanah COOK** (executor) and sister **Patience COOK.** <66:48> Warrant of appraisal, 18 Feb. 1828, to James CUSHING, Seth CUSHING, Martin COOK, all of Kingston. <66:47> Letter/Bond 14 Apr. 1828 of **Elkanah COOK.** Sureties: Seth CUSHING of Kingston and Pelham HOLMES of Plympton. <66:48> Inventory taken 3 Jan. 1828 by above appraisers. <62:303> Notice 14 Apr. 1828, sworn by executor 17 Nov. 1828.

Estate of **Silvanus COOK** of Kingston MA. <Plymouth Co.PR #4924>
<46:86> Bond/Letter 16 Jan. 1815 of John COOK, housewright, app'td admr. <48:22> Warrant 16 Jan. 1815 to appraisers, John THOMAS, Esq., Pelham BREWSTER, yeoman and John GRAY, gentleman, all of Kingston. Inventory taken 5 Apr. 1816; incl. pew in Congregational Church; totals: real estate, $3916.00, personal, $252.59. <48:24> Notice 16 Jan. 1815. <48:367> Warrant 1 May 1816 to John THOMAS, Esq., Robert COOK Jr. and Martin PARRIS, all of Kingston, to divide estate to following children & heirs, viz: **Sally WARNER** wf of Abel, **John COOK, Phebe COOK, Sylvanus COOK, Nathaniel COOK, Lydia FOSTER** wf of Joseph, heirs of **Barstow COOK**; partition made 14 May 1816. <48:370> Account allowed 5 Mar. 1817; Paid to: Dr. P.L. NICHOLS, Ezra D. MORTON, Peleg TUPPER, David BEAL Jr., Ebenezer DREW, Benjamin DELANO; Received from: estate of Dr. Jabez FULLER. <48:371> Order of Distribution of balance of account, 12 Mar. 1817, $50.96; $7.28 each to above heirs.

MICRO #4 OF 30

Estate of **Zenas COOK** of Plympton MA. <Plymouth Co.PR #4927>
<46:321> Bond/Letter 1 Feb. 1819, of Zenas COOK, shipwright of Kingston, admr. Sureties: Eleazer FAUNCE, yeoman, Samuel BARKER, physician of Pembroke. Witnesses: Eleazer JOSSLYN, Merritt JENKINS

Will of **Zenas COOK** of Kingston MA. <Plymouth Co.PR #4928>
<77:178>...dated 10 Mar. 1835, mentions wf **Lucy**, son **Charles COOK**. Witnesses: P.L. NICHOLS, Martin COOK, Melzar ADAMS. Bond 13 Apr. 1835 of **Lucy COOK**, exx. Sureties: Martin COOK, Eleazer FAUNCE, both of Kingston. Witnesses: Horatio WASHBURN, John FULLER 2d.

PLYMOUTH COUNTY DEEDS: (re: COOKE)

<31:33> - 1728, Jacob COOKE of Kingston to son John COOKE of Kingston.
<32:20> - 1728, Jacob COOKE Jr. of Kingston to Benjamin ORCUTT, land in Abington.
<31:5> - 1736, Jacob COOKE of Abington, innholder.
<31:166> - 1737, Jacob COOKE Jr. of Kingston to Joshua CUSHING.
<32:20> - 1738, Jacob COOKE Jr. of Kingston to William COOKE, lands of Jacob COOKE Sr.
<31:213> - 1738, Jacob COOKE Jr., gentleman of Kingston, to Benjamin ORCUTT Jr., land at Abington
<32:59> - 1738, Jacob COOKE Jr., gentleman of Kingston, to William COOKE, house & lands, wife Rebecca signs.
<33:77> - 1739, Jacob COOKE Jr. of Kingston & wf Rebecca.
<34:187> - 1741, Jacob COOKE Jr., gentleman of Kingston, sells land in Bridgewater.
<35:63> - 1742, Jacob COOKE Jr., gentleman of Kingston, sells land in Abington.
<56:170> - 1771, Jacob COOKE of Mendon NJ.
<58:163> - 1771, Jacob COOKE of Mendon NJ, son of Jacob COOKE of Kingston dec'd, mentions land of William & Tabitha COOK.

Richard WRIGHT of Plymouth MA to **Caleb COOKE** of Plymouth MA. <Plymouth Co.Deeds 29:131>
...21 May 1688, Richard WRIGHT, for £14, sold to Caleb COOKE, all his interest in land at Rocky Nook...fifth part of...estate of Francis Cooke of Plymouth...& agreeable to the will of the said Francis COOKE was by mutual consent of all his children divided amongst them. Rec. 15 Feb. 1734/5

Robert JOHNSON of N. Yarmouth ME to **Joseph JOHNSON** of N. Yarmouth ME. <Cumberland Co.ME Deeds>
<1:263>...8 Apr. 1757, Robert JOHNSON, taylor, for pearental affection & good will and £4, convey to son Joseph JOHNSON, coaster...fifty acres...easterly half of lott number sixty one on Heresicket River. Witnesses: Jonas MASON, Mary MASON. Ack. by R. Johnson 25 Apr. 1758. Rec. 2 June 1761.

Joseph JOHNSON of N. Yarmouth ME to **John HAMILTON Jr.** of N. Yarmouth ME. <Cumberland Co.ME Deeds>
<4:250>...28 June 1762, Joseph JOHNSON, coaster, & wf Mary, for £4 sold to John HAMILTON Jr., joyner...three quarters of an acre in N. Yarmouth...being a part of the homestead of our Father Andrew RING late of N. Yarmouth dec'd, bounded by land of Susanna YORK (being a part of our homestead). Witnesses: Jonas MASON, Eleazer RING. Ack. by Joseph & Mary, 22 Jan. 1763. Rec. 16 Dec. 1765.

Mary JOHNSON, widow of N. Yarmouth ME to **Joseph JOHNSON** of Falmouth ME. <Cumberland Co.Deeds>
<8:217>...20 Aug. 1774, Mary JOHNSON, widow of Joseph JOHNSON, mariner, dec'd, for £20, sold to son Joseph JOHNSON, mariner...one half southeasterly half part of the hundred acre lot #51 on the west side of Royals River, in N. Yarmouth, containing twenty five acres...being a part of the estate of my late Honoured Father Andrew RING, dec'd, which was set off to me in the division of said estate. Witnesses: David MITCHELL, John LORING Jr. Ack. 20 Aug. 1774. Rec. 27 Aug. 1774.

Mary JOHNSON, widow of N. Yarmouth ME to **Joseph JOHNSON** of Falmouth ME. <Cumberland Co.Deeds>
<8:211>...22 Aug. 1774, Mary JOHNSON, widow of Joseph JOHNSON, dec'd, in consideration of love and good will and also twenty shillings, sells to son Joseph JOHNSON, mariner...(the other half of the above southeasterly half part of lot #51)...and is bounded as by the division of said lot between me and my brother Eleazer RING and by North Yarmouth Proprietors Records. Witnesses: David MITCHELL, Jotham MITCHELL. Ack. 22 Aug. 1774. Rec. 27 Aug. 1774.

Joseph JOHNSON of Falmouth ME to **James PRINCE** of same. <Cumberland Co.Deeds 8:451>
...4 Oct. 1774, Joseph JOHNSON, mariner, for £36.13s.4d., sold to James PRINCE, cordwainer...one half Lot #51 in the hundred acre division on the west side of Royal's River viz: the southeasterly part of said lot containing fifty acres. Wf Abigail and mother Mary JOHNSON sign. Witnesses: John GRAY, Andrew GRAY. Ack. by Joseph JOHNSON 17 Oct. 1774. Rec. 8 Mar. 1776.

Daniel JOHNSON et al of Portland ME to **Stillman BUXTON** of Falmouth ME. <Cumberland Co.Deeds>
<151:211>...25 Mar. 1837, Daniel JOHNSON, Elbridge JOHNSON of Raymond and Sarah JOHNSON, widow of Portland, for $17.00 sold to Stillman BUXTON...two sevenths parts of one eighth part in common & undivided of a certain piece of land in Falmouth...which is particularly described in the deed from William TITCOMB and others to said Buxton dated Nov. 28th 1836 and recorded, 147:240...said real estate which descended to Daniel & Elbridge from their late father Joshua JOHNSON dec'd... the said Sarah JOHNSON releases all her right to dower. Abigail JOHNSON, wf of Daniel signs. Witnesses: John L. MEGGUIER, Eunice SMALL. Ack. by Daniel, Elbridge & Sarah, 25 Mar. 1837. Rec. 26 Apr. 1837.

Sarah JOHNSON, widow of Portland ME to **Stillman BUXTON** of Falmouth ME. <Cumberland Co.Deeds> <153:61>...25 Apr. 1837, Sarah JOHNSON, as guardian of **Leonard JOHNSON, Ann B. JOHNSON, William R. JOHNSON, Andrew J. JOHNSON** and **Isabella JOHNSON**, minor heirs of **Joshua JOHNSON**, late of said Portland, dec'd, having obtained license from the Honorable judge of the Probate Court to sell and convey the real estate of the minors...on 25 Apr. 1837 sold at Public Vendue to Stillman BUXTON, yeoman of Falmouth, for $42.80...all rights in land in Falmouth being the same that was set off to Abigail JOHNSON now deceased formerly the wife of Joseph JOHNSON in the division of the estate of William BUCKNAM late of Falmouth dec'd, the legal shares of said minors in the right of their late father Joshua JOHNSON dec'd being five seventh parts of six acres and one fourth a part of said lot in common and undivided with the other heirs of said Abigail JOHNSON and Joshua JOHNSON, dec'd and partly owned by the said Stillman BUXTON. Witness: David QUINBY. Ack. & Rec. by Sarah JOHNSON 26 Apr. 1837.

==========

Estate of **Thomas DAVEE Jr.**, mariner of Plymouth MA. <Plymouth Co.PR #6094> <20:510> Bond 16 Apr. 1771, **Jane DAVEE**, widow, app'td admx. Sureties: Eleazer HOLMES & Ichabod HOLMES, yeomen of Plymouth. <#6078, 20:510> **Jane DAVEE** app'td gdn. of children **Deborah DAVEE** and **Thomas DAVEE**, 16 Apr. 1771.

==========

William DAVEE of Plymouth MA to **Jesse HARLOW** of Plymouth MA. <Plymouth Co.Deeds 76:107> ...20 Apr. 1790, William DAVEE, mariner & wf Lydia, sell to Jesse HARLOW, gentlemen, house & land in Plymouth bounded by land of heirs of Joseph RIDER, dec'd. Ack. 8 May 1790 by William. Rec. 9 Apr. 1794. (references with no data: <168:187; 199:98 (mortgage); 204:117; 205:91; 218:97>.)

==========

Ebenezer DAVIE et al to **Eleazer S. RAYMOND** of Plymouth MA. <Plymouth Co.Deeds 205:91> ...19 May 1841, Ebenezer DAVIE, mariner, Thomas TORREY, mariner & wf Lydia in her right, John DAVIE, mariner, William DAVIE, mariner, all of Plymouth & Oliver EDES & wf Susan in her right, of Braintree, for $357.15, sold to Eleazer S. RAYMOND, mariner...five undivided seventh parts of the westerly half of a dwelling house with the lot...on Sandwich St. in said Plymouth, bounded westerly by ERLAND's land, northerly by the town brook, easterly by Samuel HARLOW's half of said house & lot and southerly by said Sandwich St., being the same estate of which Ebenezer DAVIE dec'd died seized, and which he purchased of James ROBBINS by deed 90:177-8. Signed by all grantors. Mercy DAVIE wf of Ebenezer and Marcia DAVIE wf of William release their rights of dower. Ack. 23 June 1841 by Ebenezer DAVIE only. Rec. 25 June 1841.

==========

Will of **John DAVIE**, mariner of Plymouth MA. <Plymouth Co.PR #6083> <83:510>...dated 24 June 1841, mentions brother **Ebenezer DAVIE** & his family; brothers & sisters. Pr. 1st Mon. Dec. 1841.

==========

Will of **Paul COOK**, gentleman of Billerica MA. <Middlesex Co.PR #5028> <70:462>...dated 5 Dec. 1785, mentions eldest son **John COOK**; dau **Abigail PEARSON** wf of James; dau **Mercy KNAP** wf of Jonathan, provided she shall live to my decease; dau **Sarah LAWS** wf of Jonathan; grand daughter **Sarah JAY** (under 18); son **Sears COOK** (executor). Witnesses: Benjamin WALKER, Jonathan BEARD, Timothy WALKER. <originals> Citation 5 Dec. 1787, to heirs at law to appear. Bond 2 Apr. 1788 of **Sears COOK**, gentleman of Billerica, admr. Sureties: Timothy WALKER, Esq., Jonathan BEARD, gentleman, both of Wilmington. Witnesses: Amos COTTING, James WINTHROP. <70:463> Pr. 2 Apr 1788 by executor.

MICRO #5 OF 30

Will of **Jonathan KNAP** of Norton MA. <Bristol Co.PR> <32:442>...dated 6 June 1786, mentions wf **Mehitable**; oldest sons **Jonathan KNAP** and **Abiel KNAP**; oldest dau **Mehitable TITUS** wf of Ebenezer; two grand daughters **Paddy & Fanny**, daus of my dau **Bethiah**, dec'd; son **(Daniel?) KNAP** (name is faint).
(Note: several references are cited with no data, which appear to be all references to the name **Jonathan KNAP** on the index of the probate records, viz: <5:251> gdn.; <14:311,314> adm. & inv.; <15:288> account; <33:82> notice; <125:70> 14 Oct. 1755, **Abiah KNAP**, widow of Easton, gdn. of **Jonathan KNAP** (under 14), son of Jonathan late of Easton, dec'd.)

==========

Williams LAWS of Billerica MA to **John Steel TYLER** of Roxbury MA. <Middlesex Co.Deeds 92:469> ...1 Mar. 1783, William LAWS, yeoman, sold to John Steel TYLER, Esq., land in Billerica (some of it was bought of James LAWS in 1775). Wf Sarah LAWS signs. Rec. 4 June 1786. (Note: Bowman's note says this is the same land as sold by James LAWS to son William LAWS by deed of 86:31- see below)

==========

MIDDLESEX COUNTY DEEDS: (re LAWS)

<86:31> - 1 Mar. 1775, William LAWS, yeoman of Billerica from father James LAWS of same.
<86:30> - 3 Apr. 1776, William LAWS, yeoman of Billerica from Joseph SHED, yeoman of Billerica
<124:277> - 10 Mar. 1795, William LAWS, yeoman of Chelmsford & wf Sarah sell land, house, etc. to William BYAM, cordwainer of Chelmsford.
<134:408> - 21 Mar. 1796, William LAWS of Chelmsford from Gains PROCTOR, yeoman of Chelmsford.
<203:169> - 30 Nov. 1808, William LAWS, yeoman of Chelmsford to William BYAM.
<231:270> - 4 Sept 1819, William LAWS of Chelmsford to Amos BYAM.
<251:475> - 25 Dec. 1823, Sears Cook LAWS & wf Mary of Chelmsford to William LAWS 2d of Hillsboro NH, land in Westfield and Chelmsford lately owned by William LAWS late of Chelmsford, dec'd. Rec. 7 Jan. 1824.

MIDDLESEX COUNTY DEEDS (cont-d): (re LAWS)

<369:191> - 19 Dec. 1837, William LAWS, yeoman of Westfield from Madison LORING of Littleton.

(Note: additional references (with no data) to the surname LAWS as grantors are: 92:469; 252:249 (23 Feb. 1829); 252:474; 252:475; 253:382; 245:313,316,319,322,326; 256:416; 257:272; 259:313; 276:103; 266:490; 302:461.)

Will of **William LAWS**, yeoman of Chelmsford MA. <Middlesex Co.PR 146:457>
...dated 14 Aug. 1819, mentions dau **Abigail LAWS** wf of William of Sharon; to granddaughter **Judith LAWS**, six silver tea spoons for her names sake; grandchildren **Horatio CHAMBERLAIN** and **Martha CHAMBERLAIN**; sons **William LAWS Jr.** (executor) and **Sears Cook LAWS**. 4 Aug. 1823 the executor refuses to serve. Pr. 7 Oct. 1823, Joel ADAMS app'td admr.
(Bowman's Note: William LAWS Jr. went to Hillsboro NH, see deeds 252:474,475, there called William LAWS 2d - see p.169)

Will of **William TAY** of Woburn MA. <Middlesex Co.PR 60:237,240>
...dated 19 Feb. 1772, mentions wf **Abigail**; son **Samuel TAY**; son **Nathaniel TAY**, dec'd and his children **Nathaniel TAY, Ruth BLUNT** wf of David and **Lucy**; sons **William TAY, Isaiah TAY, John TAY, Joshua TAY, Benjamin TAY, Aaron TAY**; daus **Abigail GRAY** wf of Robert, **Elizabeth ABBOTT** wf of William and **Sarah EAMES** wf of Joshua.

MIDDLESEX COUNTY DEEDS: (re: Archelans TAY, grantor**)**

<180:422> - 20 Jan. 1809
<224:73> - 17 Dec. 1817
<228:220> - 2 Mar. 1819
<228:226> - 2 Mar. 1819
<272:480> - 14 Mar. 1827
<293:485> - 23 Jan. 1830
<317:27> - 15 Sept 1832
<338:561> - 24 Feb. 1835
<338:611> - 26 Feb. 1835

BRISTOL COUNTY PROBATE: (re John PECKHAM)

<26:405> Will of John PECKHAM of Dartmouth, dated 25 Nov. 1780.
<71:349> Will of John PECKHAM of New Bedford dated 22 Sept. 1818.
<4:159> Will of John PECKHAM (no details).

Jonathan LAWRENCE of Norton MA to **Silas COOK** of Kingston MA. <Bristol Co.Deeds 36:414>
...5 Dec. 1748, Jonathan LAWRENCE & wf Sarah, for Ł2420 old tenor, sold to Silas COOK, three pieces of land in Norton, totalling 105 acres. <36:415>...18 Feb. 1748/9, Jonathan LAWRENCE of Norton sells to Silas COOK of Kingston, land in Norton. Both deeds rec. 20 Feb. 1748/9.

Will of **Silas COOK,** yeoman of Norton MA. <Bristol Co.PR>
<12:392>...dated 12 June 1750, mentions wf **Elizabeth** (executrix), son **Joshua COOK** (under 21), daus **Sarah COOK, Elizabeth COOK, Deborah COOK** and **Unice COOK**; Whereas I was ordered by the last will of my honoured father to pay to my mother Ł10 per year while a widow, the said to be paid as long as due. <12:394> Pr. 19 Sept. 1750. <12:395> Inventory 30 July & 1 Aug. 1750, sworn to by exx. 19 Sept. 1750. <19:389> Order to appraise, 28 Oct. 1765, to John CRANE, Gideon TIFFANY, Samuel MOREY. Division 12 Mar. 1766 to children, viz: **Joshua COOK,** heirs of **Sarah HART,** dec'd; **Elisabeth LANE** wf of Samuel; **Deborah SHEPARDSON** wf of Zebediah; **Unice COOK.**

Estate of **George MOREY Jr.** of Norton MA. <Bristol Co.PR 36:514>
...26 Nov. 1773, Joshua COOKE, labourer of Norton & wf Mary have received of Samuel NEWCOMB, yeoman of Norton & wf Mary, who was guardian to the said Mary COOKE during her minority, Ł7.8s8d lawfull money in full of what the said Newcomb & Mary his wife received for her as Guardian out of the estate of her Father George MOREY Jr. Witnesses: Rachel NEWCOMB, David BURT.

Joshua COOK of Norton MA to **Samuel LANE** of Norton MA. <Bristol Co.Deeds 49:450>
...31 Oct. 1765, Joshua COOK, yeoman sells to Samuel LANE, innholder, one acre in Norton. Ack. 31 Oct. 1765. Rec. 8 May 1766.

Joshua COOK of Norton MA to **Samuel MOREY** of Norton MA. <Bristol Co.Deeds 52:411>
...7 Nov. 1769, Joshua COOK, yeoman sells to Samuel MOREY, yeoman...50 acres with house in Norton ...being all ye land that was set out to me out of my honnered father's estate late dec'd. Ack. 7 Nov. 1769. Rec. 22 Nov. 1769.

Will of **Zebadiah SHEPARDSON** of Rehoboth MA. <Bristol Co.PR 45:541>
...dated 16 Apr. 1810, to wf **Deborah** all except what is given to her daughters; eldest dau **Nancy COBB**, wf of Simeon; youngest dau **Elona ABELL** wf of Caleb; grandaughter **Elona HODGES**; son in law **Caleb ABELL** sole executor. Pr. 4 Sept. 1810.

Will of **Francis COOK** of Kingston MA. <Plymouth Co.PR 10:328>
...dated 28 Oct. 1732, mentions son **Caleb COOK** (executor); children of dec'd son **Robert COOK**; dau **Elizabeth COOK**; children of dec'd son **Francis COOK**; dau **Susanna STURTEVANT**; children of dau **Sarah COLE.** Codicil 15 May 1736. Pr. 18 Sept. 1746.

Will of **Caleb COOK** of Kingston MA. <Plymouth Co.PR #4860>
<16:374>...dated 13 May 1762, to wf **Hannah**, use & improvement of my homestead farm that was given me by my Honoured father **Francis COOK**; son **Caleb COOK**, dec'd; sons **Benjamin COOK** (executor), **Ephraim COOK**; daus **Hannah COOK, Rebecca COOK, Lidia COOK**; grandsons **Amos COOK** and **Bartlett COOK**, the sons of my son **Caleb**, dec'd. Witnesses: Ephraim WASHBURN, Francis ADAMS, Robert BRADFORD. <16:375> Pr. 5 Sept. 1762. <16:375> Inventory taken 14 Oct. 1762 by Robert BRADFORD, John BRADFORD, John WADSWORTH; incl. Ripley farm, six acres meadow at Jones River, 16th part of the Furnace; total Ł1377. Sworn to by exr. 1 Nov. 1762. <16:389> Division 24 Dec. 1762, one third each to **Benjamin COOK, Ephraim COOK, Amos & Bartlett COOK**, the latters share set off to Thomas ADAMS as guardian. <16:414> Account 27 Apr. 1763 of admr. <19:40> Account 2 June 1764 of admr., incl. legacies paid to: honoured mother, Ephraim, Hannah, Rebecca & Lidia Cook and Thomas ADAMS.

Estate of **Benjamin COOK** of Kingston MA. <Plymouth Co.PR #4855>
<34:229> Bond/Letter 10 Apr. 1800, Elkanah COOK app'td admr. Sureties: John ADAMS Jr., John THOMAS, Nathaniel LOTHROP, Isaac LOTHROP. <37:315> Warrant for appraisal 10 Apr. 1800. <37:316> Inventory taken 11 July 1800 by John GRAY, Josiah COOK, John FAUNCE; sworn by admr. 6 Oct. 1800; incl. Jones River meadow & upland; pine plain belonging to the Ripley farm (27 acres); Pine Plain land bought of Everson, 28 acres; two and one quarter acre cedar swamp in Halifax; totals: real estate, $2592.50, personal estate, $463.69. <37:484> Account of admr. 3 Aug. 1801; Received from: William CROMBE, Samuel STETSON, Isaiah THOMAS, Amos COOK, Jeremiah SAMPSON, Samuel S. STURTEVANT, Jedediah HOLMES, Benjamin WATERMAN,Joseph HOLMES, John BRADFORD, James BRADFORD, Seth CUSHING, Job/John FAUNCE, Zephaniah PERKINS, Elizabeth STETSON, Lettice EVERSON. Paid to: **Sarah COOK**, widow's allowance, Patience COOK, Severs FAUNCE, John ADAMS, Dr. Jabesh FULLER, Daniel PERKINS, Samuel EVERSON, Bildad WASHBURN, Amos COOK & boy, Lot EATON, Jedediah HOLMES Jr., John GRAY, Josiah COOK & John FAUNCE for appraising the estate, personal estate delivered to Elizabeth STETSON, Eunice COOK, Sarah COOK and Patience COOK. <37:316> Division by appraisers, 6 Oct. 1800, to the following heirs, viz: **Mary COOK**, widow; **Elizabeth STETSON** wf of Thomas; **Sarah COOK; Elkanah COOK; Lettice EVERSON** wf of Samuel; **Eunice COOK; Patience COOK.** <44:356> Division of Dower, 5 Oct. 1812 by John FAUNCE, Josiah COOK and Samuel S. STURTEVANT to above six heirs.

Estate of **Patience COOK** of Kingston MA. <Plymouth Co.PR #4907>
...15 Jan. 1838, **Elkanah COOK** of Kingston, brother of deceased, app'td admr. Estate was divided among **Elkanah COOK, Eunice COOK** and heirs of **Elizabeth STETSON.**

Estate of **Elkanah COOK** of Kingston MA. <Plymouth Co.PR #4869>
<10:288**A**> 1 Oct. 1839, Peleg BRADFORD of Kingston app'td admr. Sureties: Benjamin COOK, Henry SOULE, both of Kingston. Witness: J.H. LOUD. <6:23**U**> Notice of admr. 1 Oct. 1839. <original> Warrant to appraise to Spencer BRADFORD, Daniel RING, both of Kingston and Martin HAYWARD of Plympton. <82:14> Inventory taken by appraisers, 21 Oct. 1839; incl. homestead farm, 37 acres, $1200; 14 acres woodland, $380; 30 acres pasture land & swamp, $270; 7 acres fresh meadow in Jones River meadow, $30; totals: real estate, $1880, personal estate, $334.59; sworn to by admr. 3d Mon. Jan. 1840. <83:21> Account of admr. 18 Jan. 1841; Received from: Seth DREW, Eunice COOK and the heirs; Payments to: Joseph SAMPSON, to Joseph SAMPSON on Patience COOK's estate in the hands of E. COOK, admr., Joseph HOLMES, Nathaniel THOMAS, Asaph HOLMES, Elkanah CUSHMAN, Jedediah HOLMES, Daniel RING, Martin HAYWARD, Martin COOK, P.L. NICHOLS, Ezra FULLER, George THOMPSON, David BEAL, Spencer BRADFORD, Christina COOK, heirs of Elizabeth STETSON from the estate of Patience COOK in the hands of Elkanah COOK, admr. on said Patience COOK's estate.

Martin COOK et al to **Benjamin COOK** of Kingston MA. <Plymouth Co.Deeds 199:126>
...4 Nov. 1840, Martin COOK, Christiana COOK, Zilpah SOULE and Mary G. COOK of Kingston and Melinda VAUGHAN & Peleg COOK of Raynham, for $1611.43, sold to Benjamin COOK, mariner...homestead farm of Elkanah COOK dec'd, containing about 37 acres with 14 acres woodland in the pine plane... also 20 acres...which our Honoured father Elkanah COOK received from his sister, Patience COOK's, estate...bounded by land of Ezra FULLER, Francis R. SOULE, Spencer BRADFORD, Eunice COOK...also 7 acres in Jones River meadow, containing the two lots set off in the division of the estate of Benjmain COOK to Sarah COOK and Patience COOK. Ack. 4 Nov. 1840.

Benjamin COOK et al to **Frank H. HOLMES** of Kingston MA. <Plymouth Co.Deeds 256:164>
..28 Dec. 1853, Benjamin COOK, Mary COOK, Melinda VAUGHAN, Henry SOULE, Zilpah SOULE, Peleg COOK, Adaline COOK, Mary G. TURNER, Jane COOK, Martin COOK, Gustavus COREY, Susan COREY, David L. HARLOW, Lucy HARLOW, Charles ROBBINS, Clarinda ROBBINS, Hannah COOK, Edwin COOK, Sarah COOK, Henry COBB, Polly COBB...sold to Frank H. HOLMES, land in Kingston.

<256:183>...28 Dec. 1853, same grantors as above "all heirs of Eunice COOK" sell to Noah PRINCE of Kingston, three acres of land in Kingston.

<257:397>...28 Dec. 1853, same grantors as above sell land in Kingston to Capt. Ezra FULLER of Kingston.

Benjamin COOK et al to heirs of **Martin COOK**, dec'd. <Plymouth Co.Deeds 265:21>
..28 Dec. 1853, Benjamin COOK, Mary COOK, Melinda VAUGHAN, Henry SOULE, Zilpah SOULE, Peleg COOK, Adaline COOK, Mary G. TURNER, Henry COBB, Polly COBB...sell to the heirs of Martin COOK, viz: Jane COOK, Martin COOK, Gustavus COREY, Susan COREY, Charles ROBBINS, Clarinda ROBBINS, David L. HARLOW, Lucy HARLOW, Hannah COOK, Edwin COOK, Sarah COOK...land in Kingston.

Estate of **Caleb COOK** of Kingston MA. <Plymouth Co.PR #4859>
<14:220> Letter/Bond 28 Mar. 1757, **Sarah COOK,** widow and Thomas ADAMS app'td admrs. Sureties: Robert BRADFORD, Briggs ALDEN. Witnesses: Edward WINSLOW, John LOTHROP. <14:275> Inventory taken 23 May 1757 by Robert BRADFORD, Samuel RING, James EVERSON; sworn to by admrs. 3 June 1757; total personal estate, £150.

Guardianship of Children of **Caleb COOK** of Kingston MA <Plymouth Co.PR #4851>
<18:112,114> 7 Dec. 1762, Thomas ADAMS app'td gdn. of **Amos COOK** and **Bartlett COOK.** Sureties: Francis SHURTLEFF, Elisha BRADFORD. Witnesses: Edward WINSLOW, Edward WINSLOW Jr. <19:156> Petition 18 Oct. 1764, of Thomas ADAMS for license to sell certain real estate of his wards in order that they may pay off the legacies which their grand father **Caleb COOK** in his will directed them to pay. <19:157> Bond, 8 Feb. 1765, for sale of real estate, by Thomas ADAMS. Surety: Peabody BRADFORD. Witnesses: Edward WINSLOW, Edward WINSLOW Jr. <20:266> Bonds 23 Aug. 1769, Gershom COBB app'td gdn. of **Bartlett COOK** (above 14) and **Amos COOK** (under 14). Sureties: James COBB, Josiah HOLMES. Witnesses: Edward WINSLOW, Edward WINSLOW Jr.

Estate of **David LEACH,** yeoman of Bridgewater MA. <Plymouth Co.PR #12422>
<14:184> Letter/Bond 6 Dec. 1756, **Hannah LEACH,** widow, app'td admx. Sureties: James KEITH, yeoman of Bridgewater and Jabez CUSHMAN, yeoman of Middleboro. Witnesses: Nathaniel LITTLE, John LOTHROP <14:367> Inventory taken 10 Dec. 1757 by Amos KEITH, Thomas HAYWARD, James KEITH; incl. homestead farm, 35 acres & house; one sixteenth part of Titicutt Furnace; corn house on Thomas HAYWARD's land; one third part of Kingston furnace come by his first wife; notes against Robert LATHAM, Ephraim LEACH, Benjamin SHAW, Henry RICHMOND; his son **James LEACH**'s coat, jacket, etc...Oath by appraisers, 30 Apr. 1757, oath by admx. 18 May 1757. <14:369,457> Insolvency 18 May 1757, declared by widow; Ephraim KEITH & Jonathan WOOD app'td commissioners. List of Claims: John BARTLETT, Dr. John SHAW, Thomas PERKINS, Thomas PERKINS Jr., Francis PERKINS, Nathan MITCHELL, Amos KEITH, Thomas HAYWARD, Deacon TUCKER, Jabez CUSHMAN, Elijah CLAP, Silvanus BLOSSOM, Hannah CURTIS, widow, John WOOD, Caleb TOMSON, Joseph HALL Jr., Abiezer EDSON, Deacon Silvanus PRATT, Capt Samuel FOWLER, Elisha CROSMAN, John ADAMS, Job WILLIS, Elijah SNOW, Jabez CARPENTER, John HALL, Abel EDSON, James KEITH, Jonathan WOOD, Nathaniel HOOPER Jr., Woodword TUCKER, Ephraim KEITH, Micah PRATT Jr., Benjamin WASHBURN 3d, Margaret RATCHFORD, widow, Elijah EDSON, Capt. Benjamin WASHBURN, John SNELL, John WILLIS, Esq., Josiah DEAN, Josiah EDSON, Marcy LEACH, Daniel JOHNSON, Esq., Joseph WASHBURN Jr., Elizabeth LEACH, Ezra CLAP, Shadrack KEEN, Maj. John JOHNSON, Timothy FALES, Dr. Robert LISCOMB, Daniel KEITH, Col. James OTIS, James WARREN, Nathaniel SNELL, Joseph ANTHONY, John CANDON. Oath of commissioners, 5 Dec. 1757. Oath of Ephraim KEITH & James KEITH, 2 Dec. 1758. <14:458> Account of admx. allowed 5 Dec. 1757. <15:119> Account of **Hannah EDSON,** formerly **Hannah LEACH,** 26 Apr. 1759.

Heirs of **Samuel TILDEN** of Marshfield MA. <Plymouth Co.Deeds 34:113>
...16 Apr. 1741, whereas **Lydia COOK, Sarah HOLMES** and **Rebekah TILDEN** all of Kingston...the children of Samuel TILDEN...deceased bequeathed to said children land in Marshfield, 14 acres and land in Pembroke, 27 acres, we three with Ephraim HOLMES, husband of said Sarah...divide land. Witnesses: Gideon THOMAS, Francis ADAMS. Ack. 4 May 1741 by all.

Francis COOKE of Bridgewater MA. to **Charles COOKE** of Kingston MA. <Plymouth Co.Deeds 38:152>
...20 Jan. 1746/7, Francis COOKE, blacksmith, for £166 old tenour, sells to Charles COOK, housewright...land in Kingston, Halifax, Pembroke and Bridgewater...12 acres adjoining land of Nathaniel COOKE, heirs of Samuel BRADFORD and my brother Simeon COOKE...4 (or 5) acres meadow & upland bounded by land of William RIPLEY, Caleb COOKE and the road which was laid out in the divisions of my honoured Father Robert COOKE'S estate...also one sixth part of all the cedar swamp which belonged to the estate of my father deceased laying in Halifax, Pembroke and Bridgewater which belonged to me which my Grandfather **Francis COOKE** deceased gave to my Honoured Father **Robert COOKE** dec'd. Witnesses: Judah HALL Jr., John FAUNCE Jr. Ack. 21 Jan. 1746/7. Rec. 27 Feb. 1747.

John TURNER of Bridgewater MA to **Francis COOK** of Easton MA. <Plymouth Co.Deeds 75:85>
...23 Dec. 1754, John TURNER, blacksmith, for £42, sells to Francis COOK, blacksmith...land in Bridgewater at a place called West Shares being one half of a 50 acre division agreed upon by William HAYWARD of Easton and the said John TURNER. Witnesses: Ichabod BRYANT, Samuel PHILLIPS, Jr. Ack. 30 May 1757. Rec. 10 Apr. 1794.

MICRO #6 OF 30

Guardianship of Children of **Charles COOK** of Kingston MA. <Plymouth Co.PR #4897>
<12:439,440> Bond/Letter 6 Mar. 1752, Charles COOK app'td gdn. of his children **Lydia, Abigail, Josiah COOK;** mentions their mother **Hannah COOK,** dec'd. Surety: James SHURTLEFF. Witnesses: James BARNES, John LOTHROP.

Guardianship of Children of **Zenas COOK,** dec'd of Plympton MA. <Plymouth Co.PR #4929>
<32:26,27> Bond/Letter 2 Nov. 1795, Josiah COOK of Kingston app'td gdn. of **Zenas COOK** and **John COOK** (both under 14). Sureties: John FAUNCE, Eliezer FAUNCE. Witnesses: Samuel S. STURTEVANT, Jehiel WASHBURN. Bond/Letter 2 Nov. 1795, John FAUNCE of Kingston app'd gdn. of **Charles COOK** (under 14). Sureties: Josiah COOK, Eliezer FAUNCE. Witnesses: Samuel S. STURTEVANT, Jehiel WASHBURN.

Estate of **Zenas COOK** of Plympton MA. <Plymouth Co.PR #4926>
<original> Request 29 July 1794, of **Joanna COOK,** widow, that her brother **John FAUNCE** be app'td

admr. <34:10> Letter/Bond 13 Aug. 1794, John FAUNCE app'td admr. Sureties: Ebenezer WASHBURN, Robert COOK. Witnesses: Zaccheus FISH/IRISH(sp), Isaac LOTHROP. <35:156> Inventory 6 Oct. 1794 by appraisers, viz: Elijah BISBEE Jr., Zephaniah PERKINS, Elias CHURCHILL; sworn to by John FAUNCE, 6 Oct. 1796; incl. wearing apparel of the first wife of the deceased; totals: real estate, £237, personal estate, £353.7.4. <35:210> Notice 13 Aug. 1794. <35:342> Account of admr., 25 Nov. 1795, mentions wearing apparel of the first wife to go to the two oldest sons **Zenas COOK & John COOK;** Creditors: George COBB, John WRIGHT, Oliver PARKER, Noah WESTON, Elijah BISBE, Jabez CUSHMAN, Gideon SAMPSON, Libeus WASHBURN, John COOK, Isaac LOBDELL Jr., John FAUNCE, widow Susanna RIDER. <36:29> Notice of Sale 3 Feb. 1796 of admr.; farm to be sold situated within one mile of Plympton meeting house & on the road that leadeth to Caleb LORING's. <36:28> 2nd Account 2 Jan. 1797 of admr.; proceeds of real estate to Capt. Elias CHURCHELL, $991, to Joshua CHURCHILL, $201, and to Shadrach CHURCHILL, $40; Paid to: Joshua WRIGHT, Sarah COOK, Joshua CHURCHILL, Dr. Jabez FULLER, Caleb LORING, Josiah CHANDLER, Col. Seth CUSHING, Zenas BRYANT.

Estate of **Nathaniel COOK** of Kingston MA. <Plymouth Co.PR #4905>
<15:460> Letter/Bond 1 Mar. 1760, Ephraim COOK and **Mary COOK,** widow, app'td admrs. Surety: John FAUNCE. Witnesses: Isaac LOTHROP, Consider HOWLAND. <15:498> Insolvency 1 May 1760 by admrs. <15: 504> Inventory taken 21 Mar. 1760 by John WADSWORTH, Samuel RING, Benjamin COOK; incl. homestead farm and half part of the Tan House, total estate, £175.14.3. <16:6> Dower to widow 1 Dec. 1760 by commissioners Robert BRADFORD, John WADSWORTH, John GRAY; land bounded by land of Charles COOK and Caleb COOK. <16:19> List of Claims: Samuel BARTLETT, Joshua ADAMS, Dr. John SEVER, Ephraim COOK, Nathan PERKINS, Perez RICKARD, John ADAMS, Dr. Lazarus LeBARON, Thomas LORING, Levi LORING, Thomas CUSHMAN, Samuel DARLING, William SEVER, John FAUNCE, John EVERSON, Ezekiel CHANDLER, Joshua LORING, Ebenezer SHURTLEFF, John FULLER, John EVERSON Jr., Gershom COLE, John LAWSON, William RIPLEY Jr., William RAND Jr., Kimball PRINCE, Jonathan RING, Samuel RING, widow Sarah COOK, Jabez WASHBURN Jr., Deacon WASHBURN, Perez RANDALL, Caleb COOK, Simeon COOK, Seth EVERSON, William RIPLEY, widow Priscilla FULLER, Priscilla SAMSON, John JOHNSON, Isaac BREWSTER, Giles RICKARD, Peleg WADSWORTH, James EVERSON, Capt. John BRADFORD, David STURTEVANT, Wrestling BREWSTER Jr., Perez TILLSON, widow Mary HOLMES, Charles COOK, John BREWSTER, Dr. LORING, Ebenezer ROBINS, Josiah HOLMES, Francis COOK, "John FAUNCE as guardian Robert COOK", John FAUNCE for his wifes right of dower in her first husband's estate, Seth CUSHING JR., Elisha STETSON, Simeon SAMSON, Elisha BRADFORD, Ephraim WASHBURN, Ezekiel WASHBURN, Deborah EATON, Simeon WASHBURN, Dr. John WADSWORTH. <16:41> Account allowed 5 Mar. 1761, sworn to by admrs. <16:42> Order of Court to pay over to creditors the balance of the account, £89.17.6.

Estate of **Peleg COOK,** mariner of Kingston MA. <Plymouth Co.PR #4908>
<20:428> Bond 8 Nov. 1770, **Hannah COOK,** widow, app'td admx. Sureties: Samuel KENT of Kingston and John THOMAS of Plymouth. Witnesses: Edward WINSLOW, Sarah WINSLOW. <20:428> Inventory taken by Samuel KENT and Robert CUSHMAN; sworn to by admx. 18 Nov. 1770; no real estate, total estate, £164.8. <20:428> Insolvency 18 Nov. 1770, "estate greatly insolvent". <20:429> Account of admx., 18 Nov. 1770. <20:429> Certificate from Judge stating that no proceedings can be had regarding creditors as there is no estate.

Estate of **Robert COOK Jr.**of Kingston MA. <Plymouth Co.PR #4912>
<9:166> Request (no date) of **Hannah COOK,** widow, that her brother in law **Nathaniel COOK** be app'td admr. <9:167> Letter/Bond 7 Nov. 1743, Nathaniel COOK of Plympton app'td admr. Sureties: Gershom BRADFORD, Elijah BISBE. Witnesses: Joseph JOSSELYN, Edward WINSLOW. <9:224> Inventory taken 19 Nov. 1743 by Gershom BRADFORD, Francis ADAMS, Robert BRADFORD; mentions his right in real estate his father died seized of. <9:514> Account of admr. 9 July 1745; Creditors: John BREWSTER, Abigail HALER, Elijah BISBEE, Philip SAMSON, John WASHBURN, Nicholas SEVER, B. SAMSON, Jas. HALER Jabez WASHBURN, Jabez LEACH, Hopestill BISBEE, Ephraim SAMSON, Samuel RING, Charles COOK, Giles RICKARD, Richard EVERSON, Alexander HATTER, Jas. COBB, Thomas ADAMS, Dr. LORING, Job PRINCE, John FAUNCE, John BRADFORD, Abner HALL, Jonathan RING, John BRYANT, John EATON, Nathaniel WHITE, Nathaniel COOK.

Guardianship of Children of **Robert COOK** of Kingston MA. <Plymouth Co.PR #4913>
<9:388> Bond/Letter 24 Dec. 1744, **Nathaniel COOK** of Kingston app'td gdn. of **Robert COOK.** Surety: Robert BRADFORD. Witnesses: Ephraim EVERSON, Edward WINSLOW. <15:153> Request 8 May 1759, of **Robert COOK,** aged 15 years, that John FAUNCE of Kingston be app'td gdn. <15:154> Letter/Bond 4 June 1759, John FAUNCE app'td gdn. Surety: Benjamin SHURTLEFF. Witnesses: Jonathan CARY, Edward WINSLOW.

Heirs of **James STURTEVANT,** gentleman of Halifax MA. <Plymouth Co.Deeds 44:165>
...16 Apr. 1757, Division of estate; mentions wf **Susanna;** surviving children viz: **Francis STURTEVANT** of Bridgewater, **Caleb STURTEVANT & James STURTEVANT** of Halifax, **Peleg BRADFORD** & wf **Lydia** of Kingston, **Mary STURTEVANT & Sarah STURTEVANT** of Halifax. Ack. 23 May 1757 by **Lydia BRADFORD.**

Will of **Jacob COOK** of Kingston MA. <Plymouth Co.PR #4883>
<10:419>...dated 16 Oct. 1728, "being aged", mentions sons **William COOK, Jacob COOK, Josiah COOK, John COOK** (executor), daus **Damaris COOK, Lydia, Rebecca, Margaret.** Witnesses: Thomas CROADE, John WASHBURN, Rachel CROADE. Pr. 21 May 1747. <10:419> Bond/Letter 1 June 1747, **John COOK** of Kingston who was named as executor having died before the testator Jacob COOK, Benjamin SAMSON is app'td admr. Sureties: Abner HOLMES, Charles DYER. Witnesses: Edward WINSLOW, Hannah WINSLOW. <10:437> Inventory taken 13 June 1747 by Samuel FOSTER, Joseph MITCHELL, Robert BRADFORD; sworn to by admr 14 July 1747; total estate, £341.3.

John KINGMAN 2d to **Jacob COOKE Jr.** of Kingston MA. <Plymouth Co.Deeds 34:188>
...29 Oct. 1741, John KINGMAN 2d sold to Jacob COOKE Jr., gentleman, land in Abington in Old Men's Share, bounded by land of James NASH, said Jacob COOKE and Young Men's Shares.

Jacob COOKE Jr. of Kingston MA to **Asa COOKE** of Kingston MA. <Plymouth Co.Deeds 35:47>
...1 Apr. 1742, Jacob COOKE Jr., gentleman sold to Asa COOKE, blacksmith above land. Ack. 28 May 1747.

Jacob COOKE Jr. of Kingston MA to **Benjamin SAMSON** of Kingston MA. <Plymouth Co.Deeds 33:77>
...7 Jan. 1739, Jacob COOKE Jr. having sold to Benjamin SAMSON, 20 acres of my homestead lying near the Brook called Trout Brook the bounds whereof will more fully appear in the deed I have given to said Samson...whereas in said deed my wife hath not given up her right or dower...in sd land and whereas said Samson has bought of my Brother William COOKE 14 acres of land adjoyning to the said 20 acres that I sold to said Samson the said 14 acres was part of my Homestead or Farm which I sold to my said brother...now know ye that I Jacob COOKE Jr....& Rebekah COOKE my wife do acquit any right either of dower or otherways. Witnesses: Joshua CUSHING, Phebe COOKE. Ack. 7 Jan 1739 by Jacob & Rebekah. Rec. 9 Jan. 1739.

Estate of **John COOKE** of Kingston MA. <Plymouth Co.PR #4888>
<9:427> Letter 6 Mar. 1744, **Phebe COOKE**, widow, app'td admx. <9:452> Inventory, 20 Mar. 1744. <10:432> Account. <10:433> List of Claims. <10:487> Warrant & Dower. <13:107> Division (date?), mentions son **Silvanus COOK**, daus **Sarah KENT** wf of Samuel, **Lydia COOK, Margaret COOK, Molly COOK.** <39:429> Adm. de bonis non. <40:361> Warrant & Inventory. <40:363> Warrant & Dower. <42:195> Account.

Guardianship of Children of **John COOKE** of Kingston MA. <Plymouth Co.PR #4902>
<13:32,33,60,61> Bonds/Letters 12 Feb. 1753, Samuel KENT of Kingston app'td gdn. of **Molly COOK, Margaret COOK, Lydia COOK** (at her request) and **Silvanus COOK** (at his request). Surety: Thomas TORREY. Witnesses: Edward WINSLOW, Sarah WARREN.

Estate of **Phebe KENT** of Kingston MA. <Plymouth Co.PR #12044>
...1805...<39:1> **Sylvanus COOK** app'td admr. <40:250> Warrant & Inventory. <42:194> Account.

Jacob COOKE of Kingston MA to **Josiah COOKE** of Tolland CT. <Plymouth Co.Deeds 24:95>
...12 Oct. 1728, Jacob COOKE, deed of gift to son Josiah COOKE, part of Jacob's homestead in Kingston. <26:98>...14 Oct. 1728, Josiah COOKE of Tolland CT sells land at Kingston; mentions land of his brother William COOKE of Kingston.

Will of **John FAUNCE,** yeoman of Kingston MA. <Plymouth Co.PR>
<12:415>...dated 21 Oct. 1751, mentions sons **John FAUNCE** (executor) and **Benjamin FAUNCE** (minor); five daus **Judith WARSHBORN/WASHBURN, Lydia WARSHBURN/WASHBURN** (widow)**, Mary CURTIS, Mehitebal CUSHMAN** and **Rebekah REPLEY/RIPLEY;** three children of dau **Hannah COOK,** dec'd. Pr. 2 Dec. 1751. <12:411> Warrant & Inventory. <13:40> Warrant & Division of swamp.

Estate of **Lydia FAUNCE** of Kingston MA. <Plymouth Co.PR #7532>
...1742...<9:371> Warrant. (She is called "wife of John FAUNCE late of sd Kingston deceased"). Inventory. (She is called deceased wife of John FAUNCE.) <12:427> Account.

Will of **John FAUNCE** of Kingston MA. <Plymouth Co.PR #7524>
<20:165>...dated 11 Aug. 1768, he signed it 28 Nov. 1768, mentions wf **Hannah;** sons **John FAUNCE, Eliezer FAUNCE, Elijah FAUNCE;** son in law **Robert COOK;** daus **Hannah FAUNCE, Eleanor FAUNCE, Molly FAUNCE, Joanna FAUNCE, Sarah FAUNCE.** <20:166> Pr. 2 Jan. 1769. Inventory.

William COOKE of Kingston MA to **Hannah WRIGHT** of Kingston MA. <Plymouth Co.Deeds 31:114>
...12 July 1737, William COOKE, yeoman, for and in consideration of the love, good will & affection that I have & do bear unto my loving & dutifull daughter Hannah WRIGHT the wife of Nathan WRIGHT, cordwainer...twenty five and a half acres in Kingston...the southerly part of eighty acres of land that I formerly bought of my Brother John COOKE...bounded by land the aforesaid John COOKE formerly bought of his brother Josiah COOKE and is now sold to the said William COOKE. Witnesses: Robert SHATTUCK, John REVIS. Ack. & Rec. 26 Sept. 1737.

William COOKE of Kingston MA to **Nathan WRIGHT** of Kingston MA. <Plymouth Co.Deeds 31:115>
...12 July 1737, William COOKE, yeoman, for £100, sold to Nathan WRIGHT, cordwainer...land in Kingston that I formerly bought of my Brother John COOKE containing about 20 acres...bounded by land I gave to my daughter Hannah WRIGHT wife of the said Nathan; mentions land formerly bought of brother John COOKE. Witnesses: Robert SHATTUCK, John REVIS. Ack. & Rec. 26 Sept. 1737.

William COOKE of Kingston MA to **Lydia BASSETT** of Kingston MA. <Plymouth Co.Deeds 33:88>
...5 Jan. 1739/40, William COOKE, yeoman, for and in consideration of the love, good will & affection that I have for & bear unto my loving & dutifull daughter Lydia BASSETT the wife of Moses BASSETT, blacksmith...have given...30 acres in Kingston, the 146th Lot lying by Jones River Pond, bounded by land of Jonathan CROOKER and the said William COOKE...bounds of the lot are in the Records of the Town of Marshfield. Witnesses: Joshua CUSHING, Damaris COOKE. Ack. 7 Jan. 1739/40. Rec. 13 Feb. 1739/40.

William COOKE of Kingston MA to **Benjamin SAMSON** of Kingston MA. <Plymouth Co.Deeds 33:76> ...7 Jan. 1739/40, William COOKE, yeoman, for Ł283.15s, sold to Benjamin SAMSON, gentleman...14 acres in Kingston...beginning at the north east corner of the 20 acre lot which the said Samson bought of Jacob COOK Jr...bounded by land of John FAUNCE. Wf Tabitha COOKE releases dower. Witnesses: Joshua CUSHING, Damaris COOKE. Ack. by Wm. & Tabitha, 7 Jan. 1739/40. Rec. 9 Jan. 1740.

PLYMOUTH COUNTY DEEDS: (re: William COOKE, grantee - all to 1801)

<10:129> from Ichabod BARTLETT et al.
<10:209> from Ebenezer SHERMAN.
<10:207> from John WHITE.
<10:235> from Benjamin EATON.
<10:239> from John BRADFORD.
<10:242> from Eleazer JACKSON.
<10:18> from Charles LITTLE.
<10:70> from Isaac LITTLE.
<10:237> from Ebenezer WHITE.
<10:239> from John BRADFORD.
<10:240> from Gilbert WINSLOW et al.
<11:68> from Jacob COOK.
<11:219> from Benjamin PHILLIPS.
<11:3> from Job SIMMONS.
<11:42> from Samuel SEABURY.
<13:201> from Jacob COOKE.
<14:73> from Jacob COOKE.
<16:68> from Hezekiah BRADFORD.
<17:168> from Isaac LITTLE.
<18:127> from Elisha STETSON.
<23:54> from James SPRAGUE.
<25:24> from John ROGERS et al.
<26:218> from Joseph HATCH et al.
<29:190> William COOKE et al, division.
<29:80> from Elnathan FISH.
<29:188> from Zebulon WATERMAN.
<30:3> from John JONES et al.
<30:71> from "Ichabon" SAMSON.
<30:101> from Abner BARKER.
<30:178> from John COOK Jr.
<30:189> from Jonathan CROOKER.
<31:6> from Ichabod SAMSON.
<32:20> from Jacob COOK Jr.
<32:59> from Jacob COOK Jr.
<33:234> from Judah HALL et al.
<33:234> from son Elisha COOK (20 Nov. 1740).
<34:2> William COOK et al.
<86:251> from Gurdon AVERY, 1799 (Wm. of Tiverton).
<87:36> from Thomas BEALS, 1799 (Wm. of Boston).
<87:38> from Thomas BEALS, 1799 (Wm. of Boston).

PLYMOUTH COUNTY DEEDS: (re William COOKE, grantor - all to 1801)

<12:28> 1716, to Elnathan FISH.
<12:158> 1717, to Judah HALL.
<13:193> 1718, to Essex Trustees.
<13:202> 1719, to Essex Trustees.
<15:113> 1720, to Jacob COOKE.
<16:190> 1723, to Barnstable Commissioners.
<18:201> 1725, to John WATSON.
<21:194> 1726/7, to John ROGERS et al.
<22:218> 1727/8, to Isaac LITTLE.
<22:225> 1728, to Isaac LITTLE.
<22:124> 1727, to Isaac LITTLE.
<25:96> 1730, to Essex Co. Trustees.
<25:72> 1729/30, to John WATSON.
<27:4> 1731, to Ephraim HOLMES.
<27:80> 1732, to Joseph HOLMES Jr.
<28:68> 1733, to Judah HALL.
<29:81> 1734, to Elnathan FISH.
<28:68> 1733, to Judah HALL.
<29:81> 1734, to Elnathan FISH.
<29:190> 1735, William COOK, division.
<30:39> 1735, to Jonathan CROOKER.
<31:29> 1736/7, to William CHURCHILL.
<33:191> 13 June 1740, to son Elisha COOK.
<33:59> 1739, to Judah HALL et al.
<34:192> 1741, agreement with Samuel SEABURY.
<34:11> 1740, to Manufacturing Co.
<34:197> 1741, to Thomas THOMSON.
<34:157> 1741, to William TAYLOR.
<35:53> 5 Mar. 1724, to Isaac LITTLE.Rec.1742.
<35:216> 29 Dec. 1741, to Isaac BARKER & Thomas PAINE.
<35:217> 29 Dec. 1741, to BARKER & PAINE above.
<35:103> 1 Oct. 1742, to Samuel SEABURY.

Jacob COOKE Jr. of Kingston MA to **Benjamin ORCUTT Jr.** of Weymouth MA. <Plymouth Co.Deeds 31:213> ...26 Apr. 1738, Jacob COOKE Jr., gentleman, for Ł850, sold to Benjamin ORCUTT Jr., land in Abington, part of farm formerly owned by Thomas TIRRELL, dec'd. Witnesses: William COOKE, Ezra WHITMARSH Jr. Rec. 27 Apr. 1738.

Jacob COOKE Jr. to **Benjamin ORCUTT Jr.** of Weymouth MA. <Plymouth Co.PR 32:20> ...26 Apr. 1738, Jacob COOKE Jr., gentleman, for Ł250, sells to Benjamin ORCUTT Jr., two pieces of land in Abington & Bridgewater. Witnesses: William COOKE, Ezra WHITMARSH Jr. Ack. 27 Apr 1738.

MICRO #7 OF 30

Will of **Elisha COOK** of Harwich NJ. <Sussex Co.NJ PR 38:(4?)97> ...dated 25 Jan. 1799, mentions wf **Abigail** (a widow when they wed); son **Simeon COOK**, dec'd, his widow **Anna COOK** and their three minor children, **Alexander COOK, Elisha COOK, Rebecca COOK**; dau **Hannah HARAGMAN** & her children; son **Daniel COOK**; dau **Tabitha HUNT**; dau **Experience LANDON**, dec'd and her sons & daus; dau **Rebecca HOWELL**; son **Abner COOK**, dec'd and his sons & daus; dau **Phebe BUNDY**; dau **Lydia VOUGHT**; son **Levi COOK**; son **Elisha COOK**; son **James COOK**; dau **Mary EDWARD.** Friends George ARMSTRONG and William COOK, executors. Witnesses: Daniel CURLIS, David ALBERTSON, George CURLIS. Pr. 2 Nov. 1799.

Jacob COOKE of Mendon NJ to **Jabez WASHBURN** of Kingston MA. <Plymouth Co.Deeds 56:170> ...7 May 1771, Jacob COOKE, blacksmith, for two bonds of Ł45 each, sold to Jabez WASHBURN, housewright...88 acres in Kingston, bounded by land of John ADAMS and a stone wall where a certain deed begins which William COOKE gave in to the Land Bank Scheme bearing date 9 Sept. 1740 <34:11> It being the last tract in said deed and there being 11 acres taken by two executions, one for Esqr. SEVER, the other by Isaac LOTHROP of Plymouth which I do reserve to them and this said land is taken by execution for my honoured Father dec'd which I now have disposed of. Witnesses: John ADAMS, Melzar ADAMS. Ack. 9 May 1771 before William SEVER, Justice of the Peace. Rec. 21 Feb.1772

William COOKE of Kingston MA, mortgage to Manufacturing Co. <Plymouth Co.Deeds 34:11>
...9 Sept. 1740, William COOK, yeoman & wf Tabitha, for £200 manufactury bills...land in Kingston incl. part of his homestead, one hundred & thirty nine and a half acres; meadow, eleven and a half acres; fifteen acre parcel; seventy five acre parcel (see deeds dated 30 Nov. 1714 & 31 Mar. 1718) and part of the former homestead of brother Jacob COOKE, ninety nine and a half acres. Ack. 20 Nov. 1740 by Wm. & wf Tabitha. Rec. 20 Nov. 1740.

Moses BASSETT of Kingston MA to **Peter & Elisha WEST** of Kingston MA. <Plymouth Co.Deeds 38:178>
...21 Jan. 1746/7, Moses BASSETT, blacksmith & wf Lydia, for £120, sold to Peter WEST and Elisha WEST, yeomen...the one hundred and fourty sixth lot of upland in the division that formerly belonged to Marshfield Upper Lands lying and being in Kingston...together with all the housing and buildings that is erected or standing on the one hundred and fourty fifth lot adjoyning unto it. Witnesses: Judah HALL, Abner HALL. Ack. by Moses & wf Lydia 5 Feb. 1746. Rec. 17 Mar. 1746/7.

Will of **John RICKARD** of Plymouth MA. <Plymouth Co.PR #16907>
<3:138>...dated 20 Apr. 1711, mentions wf **Mary**; sons **John RICKARD** (eldest), **James RICKARD** (under 21); bequests to sons incl. 15 acres of land laid out to mee in Plymouth between Southmeadow path and Lakenham path with my said son's (John) 60 acre lott; my sloop; dwelling house with the old house adjoining; 45 acres being part of my 60 acre lott near West ponds in Plymouth adjoining to the land of Eleazer JACKSON together with my common right or interest in all ye common & undivided lands in Plymouth and Plymton; wharfe with all the lands thereto adjoining that I formerly purchased of Robert RANSOME dec'd with the housing both upon the wharfe & adjoining, only my will is that **John** have the cooper's shop & new wharehouse and **James** the old wharehouse; 8 acres lying between the first and second brooks in Plymouth; four daus **Mercy CUSHING, Mary RICKARD, Hester RICKARD** and **Elisabeth RICKARD**...to those that are marryed or of age within one year after my decease...In case my Negro man called Toby shall faithfully and diligently serve my said wife or any of mine or those that he may be disposed to or whose lott he may fall in the division of my moveable estate, that then he my said Negro at the expiration of ye term of tenn years from the date of these presents shall have and enjoy his freedom and not any longer be held and kept as a slave. Wf **Mary** and son **John**, executors. Witnesses: John DYER, John FOSTER, Ephraim LITTLE, Jr. who all made oath to will 20 June 1712. <3:141> Pr. 19 June 1712. <3:142> Inventory taken 4 June 1712 by John DYER, Thomas FAUNCE, John FOSTER; incl. a sloop, £90; Toby Negro man, £40. Debts: Mr. BALLENTINE; Mr. BURRIL for wine at Boston; grave stones & other funerall charges, £3.7s.8d; graving the slooper, 14s4d. **Mary RICKARD**, executrix made oath to inventory 20 June 1712.

JANE COOKE[2] (Francis[1])<3>

Affidavit of **Experience MITCHELL.** <no source>
...15 Feb. 1679, Experience MITCHELL being called to give evidence Testifieth and saith that goodman WILISE/WILLIS decon to the church of Bridgewater came to my house to make way for his sone to spake with my daughter but I denied him severall times: he told mee that if hee colld/could but spake with her of or on it wolld/would satisfie him: where upon through my wives and my daughters perswatione I gave way to it: The said WILISE asked mee what I had against his sone he was a stranger to me: I tolde him that his sone did not know what love was the Abovesaid WILISE asked me what the Reson was that I thought so: I told him that he was in leage with one: and cast his eye one/on another and lefte her that he was in leage with and came to her that he had cast his eye upon and do you thinke that this is love saide I: I named nobody: but hee said I know nothing of that: and he said my son is basely abused: and said I have been with them and given them good satisfation and there is nothing in it: and he said I have been with your son and daughter and have given them good satisfaction and thay are very wilin and free to it and I doe not questione if you wold here me that I shold give you good satisfaction two whereupon I praied him to forbere for I wold enter into no discorse with him no more I did not: and farther saith not. Witnesses: Mary MITCHELL, Mary SHAW.

Will of **Experience MITCHELL.** <MD 32:97>
...5 Dec. 1684, mentions wf **Mary**; son **Edward MITCHELL** of Bridgewater; son **John MITCHELL**; grandson **Experience MITCHELL**, son of son John; daus **Mary SHAW, Sarah HAWARD, Hannah HAWARD**; grandson **Thomas MITCHELL**; grandaughter **Mary MITCHELL.** Pr. 4 Sept. 1689. Inventory 14 May 1689.

Experience MITCHELL of Bridgewater to **Thomas CLARKE** of Plimouth. <Plymouth Col.Deeds 5:345>
...25 Feb. 1684, Experiance MICHELL, formerly of the town of Duxbury but now of the town of Bridgewater...old planter & one of the purchasers of the lands of said Plimouth Colony...for a certain competttent sum of currant...sells to Thomas CLARKE, one other of said purchasers...land bounded by Yarmouth, Namsscakett and Eastham...reserving one small lot of upland with som meadow layed out to me adjoyning or neer unto Mr. William BRADFORD's lott neer Bound Brooke...which sd lott I gave my son in law John WASHBOURN who sold it to sd BRADFORD...all which said tracts of land...are scittuate upon a neck of land for the most part called Cape Cod. Witnesses: John RICHMOND, Joseph HAYWARD, Edward MICHELL. Ack. 2 June 1685 by Edward MICHELL, attorney for his father Experience MICHELL

RECORDS OF THE TOWN OF DUXBURY, 1642-1770:

<p.23> - 10 Oct. 1670, Town gave to Experience MITCHELL, 50 acres on the south side of rocky plain near Namassakeesit.
<p.25> - 6 May 1672, Town gave Experience MITCHELL, 5 acres swampy meadow land, lying towards the head of Pudding brook, near Namassakeeset.
<p.27> - 26 May 1674, Mutual agreement between William PABODIE & Experience MITCHELL concerning bounds of land between them.

RECORDS OF THE TOWN OF PLYMOUTH:

<12:6> ( ), land granted to those who came over in the Anne in 1623, incl. Experience MITCHELL.
<12:18> 9 May 1631, Experience MITCHELL sold land to Samuel EDDY.
<12:109> ( ) , John HOLMES sells land to Experience MITCHELL of Duxbury. (betw. last of Feb. 1644 - 13 June 1645).
<1:47> 6 Jan. 1636, mentions land of Experience MITCHELL.
<1:57> 20 Mar. 1636/7, mentions land of Experience MITCHELL.
<1:71> ( ), mentions land of Experience MITCHELL.
<1:72,73> 1 Jan. 1637/8, mentions land of Experience MITCHELL
<1:90> 2 July 1638, land granted to Experience MITCHELL.
<1:95> 3 Sept 1638, mentions land of Experience MITCHELL.
<1:165> 2 Nov. 1640, land granted to Experience MITCHELL.
<12:151> 20 Mar. 1647, Samuel EDDY sells land to Experience MITCHELL of Duxbury.
<12:198> 20 Nov. 1650, William PABODIE of Duxbury sells land to Experience MITCHELL of Duxbury.
<4:27> 3 Oct. 1662, Experience MITCHELL nominated to be considered for land grant.
<4:94> 7 June 1665, Experience MITCHELL granted land for his children.
<4:185> 3 June 1668, Experience MITCHELL granted land.
<5:5> 29 Oct. 1668, Experience MITCHELL granted land.
<5:20> 1 June 1669, mentions land of Experience MITCHELL.
<5:26> 5 July 1669, mentions land of Experience MITCHELL.
<5:44> 5 July 1670, mentions land given to Thomas MITCHELL by Francis COOKE, dec'd.
<5:188> 7 Mar. 1675, Experience MITCHELL & Edward MITCHELL, app'td to care for the estate of Jacob MITCHELL, dec'd, as well as possible for his children.
<2:5> 8 May 1705, 20 acres granted to Jacob MITCHELL, bounded on the north by Jones River.
<2:210> 3 Oct. 1721, mentions land of Jacob MITCHELL.

Experience MITCHELL to **Thomas CLARKE.** <Eastham Land Grants 1659-1710, p.113>
...7 Mar. 1654, Experience MITCHELL, in considertion of a three year old heifer, sells to Thomas CLARKE...all interest in lands at Palmett and Namskkett...also two acres of meddow at Nanscakett. Witnesses: John HOARE, John MORTON. Ack. 30 Apr. 1655 by Experience MITCHELL who has received the heifer from CLARKE.

Acknowledgement of **Experience MITCHELL.** <poss. same source as above>
...29 July 1661...Memorandum, this bargayne contayning all the lands of the sayd Experience his part of purchase lying there except some lands and meddow lying betweene bound brooke and stony river which hee gave to John WASHBORNE/WASHBURN which the sayd John WASHBORNE sould to Mr. William BRADFORD: all other lands and meddowes except the same att Bound Brooke the sayd Experience hath sould and receved full satisfaction for att the hands of the sayd Thomas CLARKE and therefore doth ratify and confirme to him and his heires for ever all the abovesaid land not excepted. Witnesses: Richard TAYLOR, John PARSLEY.

PLYMOUTH COUNTY DEEDS: (re: John WASHBURN, grantor, no details given**)**

7:114,273; 10:336,466; 11:264,265; 12:13,126; 14:33,133,150,265,267,270; 15:55,134,166; 16:21,23, 26,61,130; 17:104,114; 18:27,157; 24:159; 27:43,69; 31:89; 36:159,160,174; 38:65,131; 39:27; 51: 226; 54:83; 62:22,24; 66:34.

<12:144> 22 Jan. 1706/7, John WASHBURN of Plymouth to Samuel BRADFORD, gentleman of Duxbury, land south of Jones River.

MICRO #8 OF 30

Will of **John WASHBURN Sr.** of Bridgewater. <Plymouth Col.PR; MD 15:298>
<1:84>...dated 30 Oct. 1686, mentions wf **Elizabeth**; brother **Phillip WASHBURN** to be taken care of by son **John WASHBURN**; sons **James WASHBURN, Thomas WASHBURN, Joseph WASHBURN, Samuel WASHBURN, Jonathan WASHBURN**; to son **Benjamin WASHBURN**, 50 acres which formerly was my father's lot; younger son **James WASHBURN** (minor); daus **Mary** and **Elizabeth** (& her husband); to dau **Jane**, 20 acres on easterly side of Satucket River adjoining lands of Samuel ALLEN; dau **Sarah** (minor); brother **Edward MITCHEL.** Pr. 8 June 1687. <1:86> Inventory taken 19 Nov. 1686 says he d. 12 Nov. 1686.

Will of **Edward MITCHELL** of Bridgewater MA. <Plymouth Co.PR #14060>
<38:3>...dated 10 Feb. 1787. Codicil dated 3 Mar. 1790. Pr. 1 Feb. 1802. (no details given)

PLYMOUTH COUNTY DEEDS: (re: John MITCHELL, grantee)

<62:201> - 25 Dec. 1771, Edward MITCHELL, gift to son John MITCHELL, yeomen of Bridgewater.

<62:204> - 8 Apr. 1774, William MITCHELL, cordwainer of Bridgewater to John MITCHELL of same.

<62:202> - 22 Dec. 1778, Edward MITCHELL Jr. & wf Jane to John MITCHELL, yeomen of Bridgewater.

<62:202> - 15 June 1779, Bradford MITCHELL, tanner, of Plantation No.5 in Hampshire Co. to John MITCHELL, yeoman of Bridgewater.

<60:60> - 3 Feb. 1780, John MITCHELL, yeoman of Bridgewater, one of purchasers of confiscated land of Josiah EDSON, Esq., late of Bridgewater, absentee.

<66:109> - 29 Apr. 1786, Seth MITCHELL to John MITCHELL, yeomen of Bridgewater.

<72:224> - 8 Mar. 1787, Elijah CHANDLER, housewright of Plymouth to John MITCHEL & Ezra MITCHELL labourers of Kingston.

<80:63> - 1 June 1789, Michael LOWDEN & wf Eunice to John MITCHELL & Ezra MITCHELL, all yeoman of Duxbury.

<77:118> - 4 May 1792, Seth MITCHELL Jr. to John MITCHELL, yeomen of Bridgewater.

<72:244> - 21 May 1792, John MITCHELL, yeoman of Bridgewater from several...

<77:163> - 10 Dec. 1793, John MITCHELL et al of Bridgewater.

<83:131> - 21 Sept 1793, John MITCHELL of Bridgewater et al.

<102:248>- 3 Dec. 1805, John MITCHEL of Bridgewater et al.

<110:54> - 27 Jan. 1809, John MITCHELL of Bridgewater et al.

RECORDS OF THE TOWN OF BRIDGEWATER: (re: Benjamin WASHBURN)

<1:104> - 10-12 Jan. 1686, Benjamin WASHBURN chose 10 acre lot.

<1:115> - 26 Mar. 1689/90, Benjamin WASHBURN owned 50 acres at Pole Hill; Serjt. WASHBURN and John WASHBURN owned land nearby.

<2:66> - 27 Sept 1717, mentions highway laid out near Titicut lands owned by Benjamin WASHBURN, Nehemiah WASHBURN, Joseph HAYWARD.

<2:196> - 28 Feb. 1736/7, Renewal of bounds between Two Mile Grant or Titicut Lands and Eight Mile Line which runs by land of Thomas HAYWARD and Benjamin WASHBURN.

<3:143> - 23 Feb. 1748, Benjamin WASHBURN and others give land for highway in Bridgewater, where highway crosses the land of Thomas HAYWARD 2d, David LEACH, sd Capt. Benjamin WASHBURN, William HOOPER, Amos KEITH, Daniel KEITH, Joseph HARVEY, Jonathan WOOD, Samuel KEITH, Nathaniel HOOPER, Capt. Nehemiah WASHBURN, dec'd.

Zadock LEONARD of Middleborough MA to **Benjamin WASHBURN** of Middleboro. <Plymouth Co.Deeds 95:176> ...3 Jan. 1799, Zadock LEONARD, yeoman, sells to Benjamin WASHBURN, yeoman...one half grist mill near my dwelling house, near land that Benjamin bought of Dr. Samuel SHAW & Elkanah LEONARD. Witnesses: Samuel DUNBAR, Samuel DUNBAR Jr., Salmon WASHBURN, David RICHMOND. Wf Cynthia LEONARD signs. Ack. 12 Mar. 1803. Rec. 26 Mar. 1803. <95:176> 12 Mar. 1803, Benjamin WASHBURN, mortgage from Zadock LEONARD. Witnesses: Daniel THRACHER, David RICHMOND. Rec. 26 Mar. 1803.

Simeon LEONARD of Middleborough to **Benjamin WASHBURN** of Middleboro. <Plymouth Co.Deeds 101:133> ..29 Apr. 1805, Simeon LEONARD, blacksmith, to Benjamin WASHBURN, yeoman...farm which Zadock LEONARD gave Benjamin mortgage deed of. Witnesses: Samuel WHITE, David RICHMOND. Rec. 29 July 1805.

Sears WASHBURN of Bridgewater MA to **Benjamin WASHBURN 2d et al** of Bridgewater.<Plymouth Co.Deeds> <16:247>...18 Apr. 1829, Sears WASHBURN, gentleman, to Benjamin WASHBURN 2d and Willard WASHBURN, yeomen...farm formerly owned by Alice WASHBURN, dec'd, bounded by land of Capt. Joseph HOOPER, Ruthers WASHBURN, widow Celia WHITMAN, Baschall BASSET. Witnesses: Benjamin POPE, Hannah POPE. Rec. 3 Aug. 1830.

Joshua WASHBURN of Bridgewater MA to **Benjamin WASHBURN** of Bridgewater.<Plymouth Co.Deeds 176:168> ...29 Jan. 1833, Joshua WASHBURN, yeoman, to Benjamin WASHBURN, laborer...part of farm of my father Joshua WASHBURN. Witnesses: Cornelius HOLMES Jr., Solomon ALDEN, Jr. Rec. 30 Mar. 1833.

Benjamin WASHBURN of Bridgewater to **Nehemiah WASHBURN** of Bridgewater. <Plymouth Co.Deeds 16:25> ...5 Sept. 1720, Benjamin WASHBURN, cordwainer to brother Nehemiah WASHBURN, yeoman...one half of a right in little cedar swamp by the great meadow that is all the right my father gave me in his will. Rec. 15 Mar. 1721.

Benjamin WASHBURN et al of Bridgewater to **John KEITH** of Bridgewater MA. <Plymouth Co.Deeds 19:90> ...30 Jan. 1722/3, Samuel WASHBURNE, Nehemiah WASHBURNE and Benjamin WASHBURNE, brethren, yeomen, sell to John KEITH, yeoman, three quarters of five acres of undivided land in Bridgewater. Witnesses: Ichabod ORCUT, Bethiah WASHBURN. Ack. by all three 21 Dec. 1724. Rec. 4 Aug. 1725.

Benjamin WASHBURN Jr. et al to **Nehemiah WASHBURN** of Bridgewater MA. <Plymouth Co.Deeds 23:101> ...8 July 1728, Samuel WASHBURN, Benjamin WASHBURN Jr. and John KEITH & wf Hannah, all of Bridgewater, to Nehemiah WASHBURN...land in Bridgewater...two lots in Tetaquot Purchase (37th & 41st) near the road from Joshua FOBES running to Great River...also 20 acre lot (19th lot in last 20 acre division) near Millstone Plain. Rec. 12 July 1728.

Benjamin WASHBURN Jr. et al to **Thomas HAYWARD 3d** of Bridgewater MA. <Plymouth Co.Deeds 24:215> ...24 Dec. 1724, Samuel WASHBURN, Nehemiah WASHBURN, Benjamin WASHBURN Jr., John KEITH & wf Hannah KEITH, all of Bridgewater, sell to Thomas HAYWARD 3d...tract of land near Beaver Brook, half a purchase right in Second Division. Rec. 17 Dec. 1729. Ack. by all 24 Dec. 1724.

==

Benjamin WASHBURN of Bridgewater MA to **Ephraim HAWARD** of Bridgewater. <Plymouth Co.Deeds 27:123> ...7 Feb. 1729/30...one half of 20 acre lot in Bridgewater, granted by Proprietors of Eight Mile Square of land in Bridgewater in 1724, together with 15 acres in sd Eight Mile Square, 10 acres of which is part of 20 acre grant granted by Proprietors in 1725/6 - 5 acres is part of 10 acre grant in 1717 not laid out. Witnesses: John AMES, Edward HAWARD. Ack. 17 May/Rec. 16 Aug.- 1732.

==

Benjamin WASHBURN Jr. of Bridgewater MA to **John FIELD** of Bridgewater. <Plymouth Co.Deeds 27:132> ...25 June 1729, Benjamin WASHBURN Jr., cordwainer, to John FIELD, gentleman...meadow land on south side of Town River of Bridgewater, 14th lot. Witnesses: Joshua WILLIS, Thomas HAYWARD 3d. Rec. 9 Sept. 1732.

==

Benjamin WASHBURN Jr. of Bridgewater MA to **John KEITH** of Bridgewater. <Plymouth Co.Deeds 134:143> ...10 Apr. 1730, Benjamin WASHBURN Jr., cordwainer, to John KEITH, husbandman...74 acres in Titicut Purchase in Bridgewater, between 32nd & 33rd lots of first division, running south to the river near KEITH's land. Ack. 20 Dec. 1737. Rec. 2 or 7 July 1741.

==

Benjamin WASHBURN of Bridgewater MA to **Thomas PERKINS** of Bridgewater. <Plymouth Co.Deeds 37:142> ...5 Nov. 1744, Benjamin WASHBURN, gentleman to Thomas PERKINS, yeoman...land in south part of Bridgewater, south end of 22nd lot of Titicut great lots beginning near Great River near PERKIN's land. Ack. 17 May 1745. Rec. 10 July 1745.

==

Benjamin WASHBURN of Bridgewater to **Thomas PERKINS Jr.** of Bridgewater. <Plymouth Co.Deeds 42:272> ...6 Oct. 1753, Benjamin WASHBURN, gentleman, to Thomas PERKINS Jr., blacksmith, land at Titicut. Ack. 3 June 1754. Rec. 7 Aug. 1754.

==

Benjamin WASHBURN Jr. et al to **Ebenezer BYRAM** of Bridgewater MA. <Plymouth Co.Deeds 42:238> ...17 Dec. 1739, Benjamin WASHBURN Jr., cordwainer & John KEITH, gentleman, both of Bridgewater to Ebenezer BYRAM, gentleman...one quarter of a purchase right of ye undivided lands in the Eight mile so called in Bridgewater which derived from Samuel WASHBURN late of Bridgewater, dec'd. Ack. 23 May 1753 by both. Rec. 21 May 1754.

==

Benjamin WASHBURN et al to **Thomas HAYWARD 4th & Jacob HAYWARD Jr.** <Plymouth Co.Deeds 44:20> ...5 Oct. 1741, Benjamin WASHBURN & wf Bethiah; Elizabeth HANMER wf of Wm. dec'd; Benjamin PRATT & wf Sarah; Martha WASHBURN wf of Benjamin dec'd; John ALDEN & wf Hannah; Gershom CONANT & wf Ann, all of Bridgewater and Eleazer KEITH & wf Keziah; William KEITH & wf Mary, all of Easton, to to Thomas HAYWARD 4th and Jacob HAYWARD Jr. of Bridgewater...43 acres being part of a 9 acre lot and a 40 acre lot, near land of Samuel EDSON and Joseph EDSON. Ack. by Keziah KEITH 5 June 1749. Ack. by Mary KEITH 2 Dec. 1752. Ack. by rest 5 Oct. 1741. Rec. 11 Sept. 1756.

==

Benjamin WASHBURN 3d of Bridgewater to **Benjamin LEACH Jr.** of Bridgewater. <Plymouth Co.Deeds> <42:81>...21 Apr. 1752, Benjamin WASHBURN 3d, housewright to Benjamin LEACH Jr., yeoman...land in south precinct. Witness: James HOPKINS. Ack. 31 Mar. 1753. Rec. 14 May 1753.

==

Heirs of **Henry KINGMAN** of Bridgewater MA. <Plymouth Co.Deeds 42:148> ...18 Nov. 1749, Benjamin PRATT & Sarah PRATT, Benjamin WASHBURN & Bethiah WASHBURN, Martha WASHBURN, Gershom CONANT & Anne CONANT, all of Bridgewater and Eliezer KEITH & Keziah KEITH, William KEITH & Mary KEITH, all of Easton, heirs of Henry KINGMAN, dec'd, for £4 received of Jonathan PACKARD, dec'd of Bridgewater, sell to his heirs...one quarter of a 20 acre lot (17th lot) in Bridgewater, laid out in 1723. Ack. 18 Nov. 1749 by the three Washburns. Rec. 9 Nov. 1753.

==

Benjamin WASHBURN 3d et al to **Edmund CURTIS** of Bridgewater MA. <Plymouth Co.Deeds 43:269> ...12 Mar. 1757, Benjamin WASHBURN 3d, yeoman, Joseph WASHBURN Jr., laborer & wf Mary, Martha WASHBURN Jr., spinster, all of Bridgewater to Edmund CURTIS, laborer...cedar swamp called poor meadow cedar swamp, partly in Halifax & Pembroke...derived from our grandfather Jonathan WASHBURN dec'd to our father Benjamin WASHBURN dec'd. Ack. by all 14 Mar. 1757. Rec. 7 May 1757.

==

Benjamin WASHBURN 3d of Bridgewater to **Nicholas WADE Jr.** of Bridgewater. <Plymouth Co.Deeds> <52:151>...12 June 1764, Benjamin WASHBURN 3d, yeoman to Nicholas WADE Jr., yeoman...4 acres undivided land in Eight Mile Limit in Bridgewater...to lay out on the 4th grant of the half purchase right made to sd Benjamin on 17 Apr. 1749 by the purchasers. Witnesses: Elijah HAYWARD, Peres FOBES. Ack. 29 Oct. 1764. Rec. 31 Oct. 1765.

==

Benjamin WASHBURN 3d of Bridgewater to **James WADE** of Bridgewater. <Plymouth Co.Deeds 52:151> ...12 June 1764, Benjamin WASHBURN 3d, yeoman to James WADE, yeoman...14 acres undivided land in Eight Mile in Bridgewater...to lay out on first, third and fifth grants of half purchase right made to Benjamin WASHBURN dec'd and since his decease made to Benjamin WASHBURN 3d. The first on 28 Jan. 1744/5. The third on 11 Apr. 1748. The fifth on 11 Feb. 1750 by the purchasers agreed upon. Witnesses: Elijah HAYWARD, Peres FOBES. Ack. 29 Oct. 1764. Rec. 31 Oct. 1765.

==

Benjamin WASHBURN of Bridgewater MA to **Amos HAYWARD** of Bridgewater. <Plymouth Co.Deeds 55:51> ...9 Dec. 1763, Benjamin WASHBURN to Amos HAYWARD, yeoman...twenty and a half acres land in south Bridgewater, part of homestead farm I last dwelt on...bounded by land I sold to Benjamin PERKINS, Thomas HAYWARD and my son Benjamin WASHBURN. Ack. 9 Dec. 1763. Rec. 25 Oct. 1769.

==

Benjamin WASHBURN of Bridgewater to **Kezia HARVEY** of Bridgewater. <Plymouth Co.Deeds 55:85> ...11 Jan. 1770, Benjamin WASHBURN, gentleman to Kezia HARVEY, widow...20 acres in south Bridgewater, near westerly range of 25th of Titiquot great lots of first division...bounded by homestead of Daniel KEITH. Wf Bethiah WASHBURN signs. Witnesses: Ezra WASHBURN, Ephraim KEITH. Ack. by both 10 Jan. 1770. Rec. 8 Feb. 1770.

Benjamin WASHBURN 3d of Bridgewater to **John HAYWARD** of Bridgewater. <Plymouth Co.Deeds 56:81> ...13 Feb. 1771, Benjamin WASHBURN 3d, housewright to John HAYWARD, yeoman...5 acres in south Bridgewater, which land I bought of my father Benjamin WASHBURN, near widow Kezia HARVEY's homestead. Mary WASHBURN, wf of Ben.3d, releases dower. Witnesses: Elias HAYWARD, Thomas PERKINS. Ack 20 May 1771. Rec. 30 May 1771.

Benjamin WASHBURN Jr. of Bridgewater to **John WATERMAN Jr.** of Halifax MA.<Plymouth Co.Deeds 59:65> ...6 May 1777, Benjamin WASHBURN Jr. & wf Desire to John WATERMAN Jr...land in Halifax formerly belonging to Isaac KING, fell to us from our father, late of Halifax dec'd...southeast of Benjamin CURTIS' 5 acre lot near land of sd WATERMAN. Witnesses: Cornelius WASHBURN 2d, Edward SEARES. Ack. 18 June 1777. Rec. 16 Sept. 1777.

Benjamin WASHBURN Jr. of Bridgewater to **Edward SEARS** of Halifax MA. <Plymouth Co.Deeds 62:165> ...6 May 1777, Benjamin WASHBURN Jr. & wf Desire to Edward SEARS, yeoman...land in Halifax, it being part of land which fell to us from our Father Edward SEARS late of Halifax dec'd...bounded by Benjamin CURTIS' 5 acre lot, land of John WATERMAN, land set off to Benjamin CURTIS' wife and land of sd SEARS. Witnesses: Cornelius WASHBURN 2d, John WATERMAN Jr. Ack. 18 June 1777. Rec. 23 Mar. 1784.

Benjamin WASHBURN 2d of Bridgewater MA to **Joseph POPE** of Bridgewater. <Plymouth Co.Deeds 79:70> ...9 Feb. 1779, Benjamin WASHBURN 2d, cooper & wf Desire to Joseph POPE, gentleman...land beginning at stake on Great Hill...bounded by land of Cornelius WASHBURN, Eliphalet CARY. Witnesses: Benjamin WILLIS Jr., Cornelius WASHBURN. Ack. 9 Feb. 1779. Rec. 23 Apr. 1796.

Benjamin WASHBURN 2d of Bridgewater MA to **Noah WHITMAN** of Bridgewater. <Plymouth Co.Deeds 62:66> ...19 Mar. 1783, Benjamin WASHBURN 2d, cooper to Noah WHITMAN, bricklayer...land in Bridgewater near land said Noah bought of Hezekiah HOOPER. Wf Desire WASHBURN releases dower. Witnesses: Nathan ALDEN, Sarah WASHBURN. Ack. 20 Mar. 1783. Rec. 6 May 1783.

Benjamin WASHBURN 2d of Bridgewater MA to **Noah WHITMAN** of Bridgewater. <Plymouth Co.Deeds 63:96> ...19 May 1783, Benjamin WASHBURN 2d, cooper, to Noah WHITMAN, bricklayer...land in Bridgewater adjoyning land I sold last March. Wf Desire WASHBURN releases dower. Witnesses: Benjamin CONANT, Nathan ALDEN Jr. Ack. Sept. 1784. Rec. 9 Sept. 1784.

Benjamin WASHBURN 2d of Bridgewater to **Oliver WASHBURN** of Bridgewater. <Plymouth Co.Deeds 64:64> ...3 Sept. 1784, Benjamin WASHBURN 2d, yeoman, to Oliver WASHBURN, cooper...one half of homestead where I now dwell containing 45 acres...bounded by homestead of Hezekiah HOOPER, land of Eliphalet CARY and Joseph POPE, and land Noah WHITMAN bought of me. Desire WASHBURN, wf of Benjamin, releases dower. Ack. 5 Apr. 1785. Rec. 11 May 1785.

Benjamin WASHBURN 2d & Oliver WASHBURN to **Noah WHITMAN** of Bridgewater. <Plymouth Co.Deeds 66:57> ...22 Mar. 1786, Benjamin WASHBURN 2d and Oliver WASHBURN, yeomen of Bridgewater to Noah WHITMAN, yeoman...land adjoining land sd Benjamin formerly sold to sd Noah WHITMAN. Desire WASHBURN, wf of Benjamin, releases dower. Ack. 7 Apr. 1786. Rec. 11 Apr. 1786.

Benjamin WASHBURN 2d & Oliver WASHBURN of Bridgewater MA. <Plymouth Co.Deeds 72:243> ...23 Mar. 1789, Benjamin WASHBURN 2d, yeoman and Oliver WASHBURN, yeoman...divide land, each owning half. Witness: Hezekiah HOOPER. Ack. by both 23 Mar. 1789. Rec. 23 May 1792.

Benjamin WASHBURN 2d of Bridgewater to **Oliver WASHBURN** of Bridgewater. <Plymouth Co.Deeds 72:243> ...26 Apr. 1792, Benjamin WASHBURN 2d, yeoman to Oliver WASHBURN, yeoman...land on west side of South Brook, being of my homestead where I now reside. Desire WASHBURN, wf of Benjamin, releases dower. Witnesses: Joseph HOOPER, Beza HAYWARD. Ack. 21 May 1792. Rec. 23 May 1792.

Benjamin SNOW Jr. of Bridgewater to **Benjamin WASHBURN Sr.** of Bridgewater. <Plymouth Co.Deeds> <32:51>...7 Mar. 1728/9, Benjamin SNOW Jr., cordwainer to Benjamin WASHBURN Sr., yeoman...land in Eight Mile Grant in Bridgewater on river next to Edward WASHBURN's. Ack. by Snow 5 Sept. 1737. Rec. 6 July 1738.

Agreement, **Benjamin WASHBURN et al.** <Plymouth Co.Deeds 38:181> ...10 Dec. 1744, Nehemiah WASHBURN, gentleman, Benjamin WASHBURN, gentleman, Thomas HAYWARD 3d, husbandman, Henry WASHBURN, husbandman, Ezra WASHBURN, cordwainer, all of Bridgewater and Israel WASHBURN, housewright of Raynham...agree to build forge on land of sd Nehemiah WASHBURN, near his dwelling in Bridgewater. Ack. by all 24 June 1746.

Jonathan WOODS of Bridgewater MA to **Benjamin WASHBURN** of Bridgewater. <Plymouth Co.Deeds 41:222> ...5 Apr. 1743, Jonathan WOODS, bricklayer, son of Francis, to Benjamin WASHBURN, housewright... house & land in south Bridgewater. Rec. 20 May 1752.

John KEITH of Bridgewater MA to **Benjamin WASHBURN Jr.** of Bridgewater. <Plymouth Co.Deeds 41:222> ...5 Apr. 1743, John KEITH, gentleman to Benjamin WASHBURN Jr., housewright...land in south Bridgewater. Rec. 20 May 1752.

John WOODS of Bridgewater MA to **Benjamin WASHBURN 3d** of Bridgewater. <Plymouth Co.Deeds 31:223> ...12 Dec. 1751, John WOODS, yeoman to Benjamin WASHBURN 3d, carpenter..land in south Bridgewater Rec. 20 May 1752.

Benjamin LEACH Jr. of Bridgewater MA to **Benjamin WASHBURN 3d** of Bridgewater. <Plymouth Co.Deeds> <41:223>...21 Apr. 1752, Benjamin LEACH Jr., yeoman to Benjamin WASHBURN 3d, housewright...land on south side of sd Washburn's. Rec. 20 May 1752.

Benjamin LEACH Jr. of Bridgewater MA to **Benjamin WASHBURN 3d** of Bridgewater. <Plymouth Co.Deeds> <42:83>...31 Mar. 1753, Benjamin LEACH Jr., yeoman to Benjamin WASHBURN 3d...land on south side of sd Washburn's homestead. Correction of deed of 21 Apr. 1752. Rec. 15 May 1753.

Benjamin WASHBURN of Bridgewater MA to **Benjamin WASHBURN Jr.** of Bridgewater. <Plymouth Co.Deeds> <42:103>...12 June 1753, Benjamin WASHBURN, gentleman, for £16 sells to Benjamin WASHBURN Jr., housewright...part of his homestead in south Bridgewater. Rec. 13 June 1753.

Benjamin LEACH Jr. of Bridgewater MA to **Benjamin WASHBURN 3d** of Bridgewater. <Plymouth Co.Deeds> <43:126>...25 Apr. 1755, Benjamin LEACH Jr., cooper to Benjamin WASHBURN 3d...part of Leach's homestead in south Bridgewater, next to land of sd Washburn and bounded by land of Elkanah RIC-. KARD. Wf Hannah LEACH releases dower. Rec. 24 May 1755.

Heirs of **Benjamin WASHBURN** of Bridgewater MA. <Plymouth Co.Deeds 48:68> ...22 Sept. 1755, Benjamin WASHBURN, of Bridgewater and Mary WASHBURN & Martha WASHBURN, spinsters, the children of Benjamin WASHBURN dec'd...Mary & Martha sell to brother Benjamin all rights in homestead and outlands of father. Witnesses: Josiah EDSON Jr., Cornelius WASHBURN. Rec. 17 Mar. 1763.

Jacob LEACH of Bridgewater MA to **Benjamin WASHBURN 2d** of Bridgewater. <Plymouth Co.Deeds 47:191> ...13 Apr. 1760, Jacob LEACH, husbandman to Benjamin WASHBURN 2d, housewright...land in south Bridgewater, north east of sd Washburn's land and bounded by land of Elkanah RICKARD...south end of land bought by sd Leach from his father, Josiah LEACH. Rec. 8 Apr. 1762.

Edward CURTIS of Hardwich MA to **Benjamin WASHBURN 3d** of Bridgewater. <Plymouth Co.Deeds 55:60> ...13 Nov. 1769, Edward CURTIS, yeoman to Benjamin WASHBURN 3d, yeoman...all right to certain lot of cedar swamp in poor meadow cedar swamp, lying partly in Halifax & Pembroke...which lot was derived from Jonathan WASHBURN dec'd to his son Benjamin dec'd which right sd Curtis purchased of said Benjamin WASHBURN 3d and Joseph WASHBURN then Jr. & wf Mary and Martha WASHBURN Jr. by deed 12 Mar. 1757. Rec. 5 Dec. 1769.

Benjamin WASHBURN Jr. of Bridgewater from **Solomon LEONARD** of Bridgewater. <Plymouth Co.Deeds> <64:23>...2 May 1774, Solomon LEONARD Jr., gentleman to Benjamin WASHBURN Jr., wheelwright...land adjoyning sd Washburn's. Wf Joanna LEONARD releases dower. Rec. 10 Mar. 1785.

James KEITH Jr. of Middleborough MA to **Benjamin WASHBURN** of Middleborough. <Plymouth Co.Deeds> <80:91>...20 Sept. 1777, James KEITH Jr. to Benjamin WASHBURN, yeoman...land in Middleborough near land of Levi HATHAWAY, Seth WILLIAMS and Jonathan WASHBURN. Wf Phebe KEITH releases dower. Ack. 26 Nov. 1779. Rec. 27 Mar. 1790.

Division of land between **Benjamin WASHBURN 2d** and **Oliver WASHBURN.** <Plymouth Co.Deeds 72:243> ...23 Mar. 1789, Benjamin WASHBURN 2d and Oliver WASHBURN, yeomen of Bridgewater...divide land owned jointly, containing dwelling house, barn and cooper shop...bounded by homestead of Lieut. Hezekiah HOOPER, river and south brook. Rec. 23 May 1792.

Robert GREEN of Middleborough MA to **Benjamin WASHBURN** of Middleborough. <Plymouth Co.Deeds 80:92> ...24 Oct. 1791, Robert GREEN, yeoman to Benjamin WASHBURN, yeoman...land & meadow in Middleboro bounded by land of Joseph JACKSON, John ALDEN, Silas WHITE and sd Green. Wf Lydia GREEN signs. Rec. 28 Oct. 1791.

Archelus LEONARD of Shutesbury MA to **Benjamin WASHBURN** of Middleborough.<Plymouth Co.Deeds 80:93> ...31 Oct. 1794, Archelus LEONARD, yeoman to Benjamin WASHBURN, yeoman...land in Middleboro in the third allotment in the Sixteen Shilling Purchase...half of sd Leonard's father's homestead, the fourth lot of division...bounded by land of Zadoc LEONARD. Wf Lydia LEONARD releases dower. Rec. 12 Apr. 1796.

Benjamin WASHBURN Jr. of Bridgewater to **Thomas HAYWARD 4th** of Bridgewater. <Plymouth Co.Deeds> <108:68>...2 Jan. 1739/40 Benjamin WASHBURN Jr., cordwainer to Thomas HAYWARD 4th, yeoman...land in Bridgewater...22nd lot in Titicut purchase. Witnesses: Solomon PERKINS, Ephraim LEONARD. Rec. 3 Feb. 1808.

Benjamin WASHBURN of Middleborough to **Nathan & Cyrus WASHBURN** of Middleboro. <Plymouth Co.Deeds> ...17 Apr. 1815, Benjamin WASHBURN, yeoman to Nathan WASHBURN and Cyrus WASHBURN, yeomen...land I bought of Robert GREEN bounded by Silas WHITE, Seth ALDEN, Cyrus WHITE. Witnesses: Jonathan WASH-

BURN, David RICHMOND. Ack. 17 Apr. 1815. Rec. 10 Feb. 1821.

PLYMOUTH COUNTY DEEDS: (re: Benjamin WASHBURN)

<145:113> - 20 Aug. 1821, Suit brought against Benjamin WASHBURN of Middleboro by Lois WASHBURN, singlewoman of Bridgewater.
<147:166> - Jan. 182-, Benjamin WASHBURN & Linus WASHBURN, adm. to James PADELFORD & Jarvis ROBINSON, yeomen of Raynham.
<147:166> - 21 Jan. 1823, Benjamin WASHBURN & Linus WASHBURN, adm. to John PADELFORD & Nathan THING, gentlemen of Taunton.
<147:167> - 21 Jan. 1823, Benjamin WASHBURN & Linus WASHBURN, yeomen of Middleborough, adm. to Israel HALL, yeoman of Raynham.
<151:60> - 21 Jan. 1823, Benjamin WASHBURN & Linus WASHBURN, yeomen of Middleborough, adm. to Orland/Orlando SHAW, Paul HATHAWAY, Zephaniah SHAW Jr. & Ebenezer SHAW.

Estate of **Benjamin WASHBURN**, yeoman of Middleborough MA. <Plymouth Co.Deeds 151:59>
...21 Jan. 1823, **Linus WASHBURN** and **Benjamin WASHBURN**, yeomen of Middleborough, administrators of estate of our father Benjamin WASHBURN, dec'd...to Paul HATHAWAY, Ebenezer SHAW, Orlando SHAW, all yeomen of Middleborough, Allice WASHBURN, widow of Benjamin dec'd releases dower. Witnesses: Seth EATON Jr., Seth RICHMOND Jr. Ack. by Linus & Benjamin 3 Feb. 1823. Rec. 7 Jan. 1824.

PLYMOUTH COUNTY DEEDS: (re: Benjamin WASHBURN, grantor**)**

(References only, no details given: 164:184; 167:28; 178:218; 180:136; 185:55,163,164; 189:162; 192:230; 196:131; 202:142; 205:56; 208:170; 213:219; 217:240; 204:261; 241:144; 245:250,256; 249:80,126.)

PLYMOUTH COUNTY DEEDS: (re: Huldah L. WASHBURN)

<131:157> - 11 July 1816, Huldah L. WASHBURN, singlewoman of Middleboro from Elias DUNBAR.
<215:38> - 10 July 1844, Huldah L. WASHBURN of Middleboro from Solomon L. HARLOW.
<253:17> - 3 Jan. 1845, Huldah L. WASHBURN, widow of Middleboro, dau of Bradford HARLOW.

PLYMOUTH COLONY DEEDS: (re: Experience MITCHELL)

<1:10> - 9 May 1631, Experience MITCHELL to Samuel EDDY.
<1:190> - ( ), Experience MITCHELL of Duxbury from John HOLMES.
<1:244> - 20 Mar. 1647, Experience MITCHELL of Duxbury from Samuel EDDY.
<1:313> - 1 July 1650, Experience MITCHELL to Andrew RING.
<1:331> - 20 Nov. 1650, Experience MITCHELL, planter of Duxbury to William PAYBODY of Duxbury.
<2:1:27> - ( ), Experience MITCHELL from Nathaniel MORTON.
<2:1:9> - ( ), Experience MITCHELL from Henry HOWLAND.
<2:1:51> - ( ), Experience MITCHELL, planter of Duxbury to Thomas WILLETT.
<2:1:123> - 29 Nov. 1653, Experience MITCHELL from William TUBBS.
<3:193> - 6 July 1671, Experience MITCHELL from the Court.
<3:160> - 7 July 1669, Experience MITCHELL of Duxbury from Tuspaquin & his son.
<3:73> - 8 June 1666, Thomas MITCHELL & WRIGHT from John COOKE.
<3:300> - 15 Nov. 1669, Thomas MICHELL surrenders to Experience MICHELL.
<3:300> - 15 Nov. 1669, Experience MICHELL, planter of Duxbury to Jacob MITCHELL.
<5:440> - 20 Oct. 1670, Experience MITCHELL, planter of Duxbury to son Edward MITCHELL.
<3:234> - 1 Aug. 1672, Thomas MICHELL, planter of Duxbury to Richard WRIGHT, tailor of Plym.
<6:40> - 3 Apr. 1682, John MITCHELL, weaver of Duxbury to John PARTRIDGE, planter of Duxbury.
<5:345> - 25 Feb. 1684, Experience MITCHELL, planter, formerly of Duxbury now of Bridgewater to Thomas CLARKE of Plymouth.
<5:346> - 2 July 1685, Experience MITCHELL of Bridgewater, letter of attorney to son Edward.

MICRO #9 OF 30

BRISTOL COUNTY DEEDS: (re: Joshua STEARNS/STERNS)

<61:120> - 3 Sept 1778, Joshua STERNS, yeoman of Mansfield sells land in Mansfield. Ack. 1782.
<67:76> - 19 Mar 1779, Joshua STERNS of Mansfield & Edward WHITE of Easton, sell land in Mansfield they bought 24 May 1777 <57:270>.
<74:348> - 22 Apr 1795, Joshua STERNS, yeoman of Mansfield sells land in Mansfield. Ack. 1796.

BRISTOL COUNTY DEEDS: (re: Benjamin HEWES)

<48:256> - 6 Feb. 1754, Benjamin HEWES, yeoman of Attleboro & wf Sarah sell 42 acres in Easton.
<43:99> - 11 May 1758, Benjamin HEWES, yeoman of Attleboro sells land in Attleboro.
<45:409> - 11 Feb. 1762, Benjamin HEWES, yeoman of Attleboro to Sarah SANFORD. Wf Eliz. signs.
<76:126> - 18 Mar. 1797, Benjamin HEWES, yeoman of Swansea NH & other heirs of Dr. Joseph HEWES of Providence.
<150:546>- 23 Aug. 1836, Benjamin HEWES, yeoman of Foxboro quit claims farm in Mansfield.

Benjamin HEWES of Norton MA. <Bristol Co.Deeds 35:336>
...23 Nov. 1748, Benjamin HEWES, husbandman & wf Sarah, sell land in Norton, bounded by land set

out to Joseph HART & wf Hannah of estate of their father Benjamin SEELEY (whose widow is alive.)

James WASHBURN Sr. of Bridgewater to **David PACKARD** of Bridgewater. <Plymouth Co.Deeds 38:166> ...25 Nov. 1723, James WASHBURN Sr., for £10 sold to David PACKARD...ten and a half acres undivided land of former divisions granted to the purchase right of the sd Washburn to be taken up within the four mile grant of Bridgewater. Witnesses: Thomas AMES, James FIELD. Rec. 4 Mar. 1746.

James & Gideon WASHBURN to **Cornelius WASHBURN** of Bridgewater MA. <Plymouth Co.Deeds 44:97> ...1 Sept. 1741, James WASHBURN and Gideon WASHBURN, yeomen of Bridgewater, for £29 sold to Cornelius WASHBURN, yeoman...three and a quarter acres in the Eight Mile grant in Bridgewater, bounded by land of sd Cornelius. Witnesses: Nathaniel WASHBURN, Abisha WASHBURN. Ack. 28 Nov. 1745 by James & Gideon. Rec. 17 May 1757.

James WASHBURN of Bridgewater MA to **Samuel DUNBAR** of Bridgewater MA. <Plymouth Co.Deeds 45:14> ...9 Mar. 1738, James WASHBURN, yeoman, for £15 sold to Samuel DUNBAR, yeoman...half a purchase right of undivided lands in the eight mile in Bridgewater being half of right which was originally John WASHBURN's incl. land granted but not laid out. Witnesses: Thomas LAWRENCE, Josiah EDSON Jr. Ack. 9 Mar. 1740/1. Rec. 24 Apr. 1758.

James WASHBURN of Bridgewater MA to **Ephraim FOBES** of Bridgewater MA. <Plymouth Co.Deeds 31:204> ...25 Feb. 1728/9, James WASHBURN, yeoman, for £12 sold to Ephraim FOBES, clothier...ten acres of the common or undivided land in the Eight Mile grant in Bridgewater to be taken up on the last division of twenty acres and on the purchase right of John WASHBURN Jr. dec'd. Witnesses: Daniel JOHNSON, Joseph JOHNSON. Ack. same day. Rec. 10 Mar. 1737.

James WASHBURN of Bridgewater MA to **Daniel ALDEN** of Bridgewater MA. <Plymouth Co.Deeds 34:104> ...15 Dec. 1722, James WASHBURN, yeoman, sold to Daniel ALDEN, yeoman...half acre meadow on south side of Town River against Deacon ALDEN's meadow. Witnesses: Benjamin ALLEN, Elizabeth ALLEN. Ack same day. Rec. 25 Apr. 1741.

James WASHBURN of Bridgewater MA to **John BOLTON** of Bridgewater MA. <Plymouth Co.Deeds 36:133> ...16 Jan. 1726/7, James WASHBURN, yeoman, for £5 sold to John BOLTON, yeoman...half lot of meadow at the Great Meadow nigh the Great Pond in west Bridgewater. Witnesses: Benjamin ALLEN, Elizabeth ALLEN. Ack. 27 Mar. 1730. Rec. 13 Mar. 1743.

James WASHBURN of Bridgewater MA to **Ebenezer LEACH** of Bridgewater MA. <Plymouth Co.Deeds 33:36> ...20 July 1733, James WASHBURN, husbandman, for £6 sold to Ebenezer LEACH...five acres in two lots. Witnesses: Josiah EDSON, Abiezer EDSON. Ack. 21 July 1733. Rec. 24 Aug. 1739.

James WASHBURN of Bridgewater MA to **Nathaniel WASHBURN** of Bridgewater. <Plymouth Co.Deeds 36:174> ...23 Feb. 1743, James WASHBURN, yeoman, for 20s sold to Nathaniel WASHBURN, husbandman...all my right in the cedar swamp commonly called Cutting Cove Swamp in Bridgewater...also my right in the cedar swamp called poor meadow swamp in the Major's Purchase. Witnesses: John WASHBURN, John WASHBURN Jr. Ack. 11 May 1744. Rec. 16 May 1744.

Estate of **Edward WASHBURN Jr.** of Middleboro MA. <Plymouth Co.PR #21952>
<17:180> Letter 25 Mar. 1767, Edward WASHBURN, yeoman of Middleboro, app'td admr. <19:523> Inventory taken 12 June 1767 by Thomas NELSON, Ezra CLARKE; sworn to by admr. 24 July 1767. <20:345> Account 17 May 1770; Paid to: Dr. Samuel PERRY, Dr. John SHAW, Ezra CLARK, Isaac PRATT, James STROWBRIDGE, John MONTGOMERY, Thomas NELSON, Henry STROWBRIDGE, Barnabas SAMSON, William CANADY, John NELSON, Dr. POWERS and necessaries allowed to the widow.

Guardianship of Children of **Edward WASHBURN Jr.** of Middleboro MA. <Plymouth Co.PR #21915>
<19:407-8> Letters/Bonds 10 Dec. 1766, Edward WASHBURN, yeoman of Middleboro app'td gdn. of **Abiel WASHBURN** and **Abigail WASHBURN**, minors. Sureties: Elkanah ELMES, Ebenezer WOOD Jr. Witnesses: Samuel SPRAGUE, Seth WILLIAMS Jr.

Estate of **Amos WASHBURN**, gentleman of Middleborough MA. <Plymouth Co.PR #21921>
<34:15> Letter/Bond 24 Oct. 1794, **James WASHBURN**, yeoman of Middleboro app'td admr. Sureties: Hugh MONTGOMERY, Uriah SAMSON, both of Middleboro. Witnesses: Abraham SHAW Jr., Amos WASHBURN. <original> Request 25 Oct. 1794, of **Prudence WASHBURN**, widow, that her oldest son **James WASHBURN** administer estate. <35:216> Inventory taken 20 Jan. 1795 by Hugh MONTGOMERY, Uriah SAMPSON, yeoman and Abraham SHAW Jr., all of Middleboro; incl. 145 acre homestead; 51 acre farm at Titicut; pew in the Rev. Mr. TURNER's Meeting House. Sworn to by admr. 12 Feb. 1795.

James WASHBURN of Middleboro against **Jedediah CASWELL** of Middleboro. <Plymouth Co.Deeds 78:127> ...4 June 1795, James WASHBURN, gentleman, as admr. of estate of Amos WASHBURN, gentleman of Middleboro...execution against Jedediah CASWELL, yeoman; appraisers app'td 19 June 1795; execution levied same date, James WASHBURN receipted for £2.17s3d in full. Rec. 4 July 1795.

James WASHBURN et al of Middleboro MA to **Gamaliel SAMSON et al.** <Plymouth Co.Deeds 89:104> ...26 Nov. 1799, James WASHBURN, Amos WASHBURN and Luther WASHBURN, yeomen, for $320 sold to Gamaliel SAMSON and Lazarus SAMSON, yeomen of Middleboro...15 acres in Middleboro with dwelling house...same land set off to sd James as admr. on estate of Amos WASHBURN by execution against Jedediah CASWELL. Witnesses: John NELSON, Ezra NELSON. Rec. 21 Nov. 1800.

Jedediah CASWELL of Shutesbury MA to **James WASHBURN** of Middleboro. <Plymouth Co.Deeds 78:121>
...30 June 1795, Jedediah CASWELL, laborer, for Ł35 quit claimed to James WASHBURN, gentleman, admr. of estate of Amos WASHBURN dec'd...all his right in 13 acres with dwelling in Middleboro. Witnesses: John POWERS, Joseph PERRY. Ack. 30 June 1795. Rec. 4 July 1795.

Estate of **General Abiel WASHBURN** of Middleboro MA. <Plymouth Co.PR #21910>
...1843...will...<1:254**G**; 6:446**U**; 85:377,523; 92:314> (no details given in files).

Will of **Edward WASHBURN** of Middleboro MA. <Plymouth Co.PR #21951>
<original>...dated 12 Dec. 1791, being in advanced years, mentions son **Amos WASHBURN**; grandson **Abial WASHBURN** (minor), granddaughter **Abigail DICKENS** wf of John Jr.; grandson **Edward WASHBURN**. Witnesses: Caleb TURNER, Moses CAIN Jr., Thomas CAIN. Will filed 9 Oct. 1793.

Estate of **Gideon WASHBURN**, yeoman of Bridgewater MA. <Plymouth Co.PR #21978>
<23:173> Letter/Bond 6 Oct. 1777, widow **Ruth WASHBURN** app'td admx. Sureties: David KINGMAN, gentleman of Bridgewater, Jonah WHITMAN of Plympton. Witnesses: Zebedee SPROAT, Joseph CUSHING. <28:173> Inventory, 6 Oct. 1777 appraisers app'td, viz: Hezekiah HOOPER, Jonah WHITMAN, Seth PRATT; personal estate only; 29 Nov. 1782, oath by Seth PRATT, Hezekiah HOOPER, Ebenezer WRIGHT; 2 Dec. 1782, oath by **Ruth RIPLEY**, formerly **Ruth WASHBURN**, admx. <28:174> Account 2 Dec. 1782 by admx.; incl. cash paid to Doctor for herself & children; to supporting a child from four and a half years to the age of seven years.

Heirs of **John WASHBURN** of Bridgewater MA. <Bristol Co.Deeds 4:83; MD 15:252>
...1 Apr. 1700, James WASHBURN, John WASHBURN, Thomas WASHBURN, Joseph WASHBURN, Samuel WASHBURN, Jonathan WASHBURN, Samuel KINGSLEY & wf Mary, widow Elizabeth SOLE, John AMES & wf Sarah, heirs of John WASHBURN...to John ROGERS.

James WASHBURN Jr. of Taunton MA to **John CAVENDER** of Middleboro MA. <Bristol Co.Deeds 33:301>
...4 Nov. 1740, James WASHBURN Jr., yeoman to John CAVENDER...20 acres in Taunton on which his dwelling house stands. Wf Elizabeth WASHBURN releases dower. Ack. 4 May 1741 by James. Rec. 10 Apr. 1745.

James WASHBURN of Bridgewater MA to **James WASHBURN.** <Plymouth Co.Deeds 18:140>
...25 Feb. 1722/3, James WASHBURN, yeoman, in consideration of love & goodwill, gives to son James WASHBURN...two lots of land lying in the southerly part of Bridgewater...fifty acres more or less. Witnesses: Benjamin ALLEN, Nathaniel CARVER. Ack. 4 Apr. 1723. Rec. 30 Dec. 1724.

John LENARD/LEONARD of Bridgewater MA to **James WASHBURN Jr.** of Bridgewater. <Plymouth Co.Deeds>
<26:112>...17 Oct. 1728, John LENARD, husbandman, for Ł200 sold to James WASHBURN Jr., husbandman ...30 acres in Bridgewater. Witnesses: John BENSON, Ephraim LENARD. Ack. 5 Apr. & Rec. 8 Apr.1731

Josiah LENARD/LEONARD of Bridgewater MA to **John LENARD/LEONARD.** <Plymouth Co.Deeds 26:216>
...23 June 1731, whereas Josiah LEONARD, husbandman, did give to his son John LENARD of Bridgewater a deed of a certain tract of land containing by estimation thirty acres...bearing date of 12 July 1727 which land the said John hath since conveyed by deed to James WASHBURN Jr. (A contraversy regarding bounds is settled.)

James WASHBURN Jr. of Bridgewater MA to **Zechariah WHITMAN** of Bridgewater. <Plymouth Co.Deeds>
<31:145>...7 Dec. 1737, James WASHBURN Jr., yeoman, for Ł270, sold to Zechariah WHITMAN...all my farm, about 30 acres, part of a lot of land about 100 acres, formerly of Josiah LEONARD of Bridgewater...8th lot in 1000 acre grant. Wf Elizabeth WASHBURN signs. Witnesses: Benjamin JOHNSON, Ebenezer WHITMAN. Ack. 7 Dec. 1737. Rec. 9 Dec. 1737.

Jonah WASHBURN of Middleboro MA to **Theophilus CROCKER** of Middleboro. <Plymouth Co.Deeds 50:77>
...19 Mar. 1764, Jonah WASHBURN, tanner, for Ł120, sold to Theophilus CROCKER, husbandman...20 acres with buildings in Titicut. Wf Huldah WASHBURN signs. Witnesses: Jabez VAUGHAN Jr., Reuben WASHBURN. Ack. 19 Mar. 1764 by Jonah. Rec. 19 Aug. 1765.

Jonah WASHBURN of Middleboro to **Benjamin PEMBERTON** of Roxbury MA. <Plymouth Co.Deeds 59:266>
...27 June 1781, Jonah WASHBURN, tanner, for 350 silver Spanish milled dollars, sold to Benjamin PEMBERTON...about 100 acres in the 26 Men's Purchase in Middleboro...being the whole I bought of Isaac TINKHAM 16 Jan. 1772...to be paid on or before 27 June 1782. Wf Huldah WASHBURN releases dower. Witnesses: John COTTON, John COTTON 3d. Ack. by Jonah 12 Sept. 1781. Rec. 12 Sept. 1781.

Jonah WASHBURN of Middleboro MA to **Rebecca SCOLLEY** of Middleboro. <Plymouth Co.Deeds 62:4>
...15 Nov. 1782, Jonah WASHBURN, tanner, for 350 Spanish milled dollars, sold to Rebecca SCOLLY.. land in 26 Men's Purchase, being all I bought of Isaac TINKHAM, 16 Jan. 1772 & rec 57:45. Wf Huldah WASHBURN signs. Witnesses: Abner WASHBURN, James SOULE 3d. Rec. 4 Feb. 1783.

Jonah WASHBURN of Middleboro MA to **Joshua EDDY** of Middleboro. <Plymouth Co.Deeds 68:98>
...15 Apr. 1786, Jonah WASHBURN, gentleman, for Ł900, sold to Joshua EDDY, Esq...all my lands and buildings in Middleborough in the 26 Men's Purchase that I bought of Moses LEONARD & Isaac TINKHAM, being about 300 acres. Wf Huldah WASHBURN signs. Witnesses: Solomon McFARLAND, William SHAW. Rec. 3 Oct. 1787.

Estate of **Moses WASHBURN**, yeoman of New Bedford. <Bristol Co.PR>
<45:215> 18 Oct. 1809, son **Lettice WASHBURN** of New Bedford asked that a guardian be app'td for Moses WASHBURN who is noncompos mentis. 1 Nov. 1809, James TABER, gentleman of New Bedford, ap'td gdn. <45:258> Inventory, 1809. <45:416> 1st Account, 1809. <46:19> Notice of Sale, 1810. <46:361> 2nd Account, 1811. <46:565> 3rd Account, 1811. <47:247> 4th Account, 1812. <48:234> 5th Account, 1813. <48:468> 6th Account, 1813. <48:240> Notice of Sale, 1813. <48:501> 7th Account & Account of administrator, 1813. <48:499> Inventory, 1813. <original> Petition 8 Oct. 1813, of **Lettice WASHBURN** that James TABER be app'td admr. of estate of **Moses WASHBURN** dec'd...it being too inconvenient for me to administer estate. <49:147> Account, 1814. <49:263> Division of real estate, 18 Mar. 1814 by Stephen HATHAWAY, Philip SPOONER, Joel PACKARD to following children: **Lettice WASHBURN** (eldest son), **Bezaliel WASHBURN** (second son), **Nehemiah WASHBURN** (third son), **Moses WASHBURN** (fourth son), **Israel WASHBURN** (fifth son), **Reliance RANDALL** (eldest dau), **Abigaile MARTHERS** (youngest dau).

Guardianship of **Moses WASHBURN**, non compos, of New Bedford. <Bristol Co.PR>
<49:276> Order, 29 Apr. 1814. <110:168> Letter/Bond 3 May 1814, Samuel PERRY app'td gdn. <49:500> Inventory taken 3 Sept. 1814 by Levi WALKER, Jirah SWIFT Jr., Loune(sp) SNOW; 21 acres wood land, $150., 5 acres cleared land, $105.

Moses WASHBURN of Taunton MA to **Nathaniel GILBERT** of Taunton. <Bristol Co.Deeds 37:348>
...28 Jan. 1750, Moses WASHBURN, husbandman sells to Nathaniel GILBERT...his homestead farm in Taunton...excepting one acre sold to son Moses WASHBURN. Wf Hannah WASHBURN releases dower. Ack. by both 28 July 1750. Rec. 29 July 1750.

Moses WASHBURN Sr. of Taunton MA to **Moses WASHBURN Jr.** of Taunton. <Bristol Co.Deeds 37:258>
...29 Mar. 1750, Moses WASHBURN Sr. sells to Moses WASHBURN Jr...one acre of land in his homestead in Taunton. Ack. & Rec. 26 Apr. 1750

Moses WASHBURN Jr. of Taunton MA to **Nathaniel GILBERT** of Taunton. <Bristol Co.Deeds 37:375>
...15 Sept. 1750, Moses WASHBURN Jr., blacksmith, to Nathaniel GILBERT...the acre in Taunton conveyed to him by his father Moses WASHBURN as rec. in 37:258. Ack. & Rec. 15 Sept. 1750.

Moses WASHBURN Jr. & Peter WASHBURN to **John EASTLAND.** <Bristol Co.Deeds 42:554>
...18 Feb. 1757, Moses WASHBURN Jr. & Peter WASHBURN, husbandmen of Dartmouth, sell to John EASTLAND...all their homestead in Dartmouth where they now dwell. Abigail wf of Peter and Sarah wf of Moses release their dowers. Ack. 19 Feb. 1757. Rec. 15 Dec. 1757.

Moses WASHBURN of Dartmouth MA to **Peter WASHBURN** of Dartmouth. <Bristol Co.Deeds 45:536>
...4 Mar. 1758, Moses WASHBURN, husbandman, for £2, sold to son Peter WASHBURN, laboror...ten acres in Dartmouth taken off northerly part of my homestead. Ack. 16 Apr. 1761. Rec. 11 June 1762

Peter WASHBURN of Dartmouth MA to **Bezaleel WASHBURN** of Dartmouth. <Bristol Co.Deeds 49:257>
...18 Dec. 1761, Peter WASHBURN sells the above tract of land. Wf Abigail WASHBURN signs. Ack. by Peter 18 Dec. 1761. Rec. 31 Oct. 1765.

Heirs of **Thomas POPE** to **Thomas PELL.** <Bristol Co.Deeds 47:236>
...1764, Moses WASHBURN & wf Sarah, Peter WASHBURN & wf Abigail, Susanna POPE widow of Benjamin ...and other heirs of Thomas POPE sell land in Dartmouth to Thomas PELL.

Moses WASHBURN of Dartmouth MA to **Bezaleel WASHBURN** of Dartmouth. <Bristol Co.Deeds 49:263>
...28 Oct. 1765, Moses WASHBURN, yeoman to son Bezaleel WASHBURN, laborer...half of homestead farm in Dartmouth incl. the part Bezaleel bought of his brother Peter WASHBURN. Ack. 29 Oct. 1765 Rec. 31 Oct. 1765.

Moses WASHBURN of Dartmouth MA to **Thomas WASHBURN** of Dartmouth. <Bristol Co.Deeds 49:267>
...26 Oct. 1765, Moses WASHBURN, yeoman to son Thomas WASHBURN, mariner...south half of homestead in Dartmouth. Ack. 29 Oct. 1765. Rec. 31 Oct. 1765.

Moses WASHBURN of New Bedford to **James CHASE** of Somerset. <Bristol Co.Deeds 71:185>
...1 Mar. 1772, Moses WASHBURN, yeoman to James CHASE, merchant...land in Dartmouth. Wf Sarah WASHBURN signs. Ack. 6 Sept. 1792. Rec. 12 Sept. 1792.

BRISTOL COUNTY DEEDS: (re: Moses WASHBURN)

<93:34> - 25 Sept. 1810, Moses WASHBURN, by guardian James TABER, to Lettice WASHBURN of New Bedford, land in New Bedford. Ack. 27 Sept. 1810. Rec. 9 Sept. 1811.
<93:35> - 25 Sept. 1810, Moses WASHBURN, by guardian, to Elnathan TABER of New Bedford, land in New Bedford. Ack. 27 Sept. 1810. Rec. 9 Sept. 1811.
<91:556> - 1810, Moses WASHBURN, by guardian, to Jabez TABER & Co.
<91:557> - 1810, Moses WASHBURN, by guardian, to Jabez TABER & Co.
<92:364> - 1811, Moses WASHBURN, by guardian, to Seth BUMPUS.
<92:518> - 1811, Moses WASHBURN, by guardian, to Worth POPE et al.
<94:325> - 1812, Moses WASHBURN, by guardian, to Alfred NYE, land in New Bedford.
<94:388> - 1812, Moses WASHBURN, by guardian, to Worth POPE et al, land in New Bedford.
<94:413> - 1812, Moses WASHBURN to William WHITE Jr.
<98:134> - 1815, Moses WASHBURN, by guardian, to Gideon WOOD.

BRISTOL COUNTY DEEDS, cont-d: (re: WASHBURN)

<100:114> - 1816, Moses WASHBURN, by admr., to Philip SPOONER.
<100:522> - 1816, Moses WASHBURN, by guardian, to Seth BUMPUS.
<101:271> - 1816, Moses WASHBURN to Joseph PEIRCE.
<110:415> - 1821, Moses WASHBURN, by guardian, to John TOBY.
<128:17> - 1829, Moses WASHBURN, by excon. to Inhabitants of New Bedford.
<134:80> - 1832, Moses WASHBURN, by admr., to John COGGESHALL
<120:282> - 1826, Lettice WASHBURN to Jabez TABER.
<122:254> - 1827, Lettice WASHBURN to John S. WASHBURN.

Lettice WASHBURN of Fairhaven MA to **Samuel T. BALL** of Fairhaven. <Bristol Co.Deeds 106:506> ...27 Apr. 1814, Lettice WASHBURN, yeoman, for $324, sold to Samuel T. BALL, mariner...two acres in Fairhaven with buildings. Wf Sarah WASHBURN releases dower. Ack. by Lettice 27 Apr. 1814. Rec. 15 Sept. 1819.

Lettice WASHBURN of Fairhaven MA to **Charles SPOONER** of New Bedford. <Bristol Co.Deeds 100:118> ...6 June 1816, Lettice WASHBURN, yeoman sells to Charles SPOONER...land in New Bedford being half the lot that Elnathan TABER bought of James TABER as appears by his deed to me of 19 Dec. 1810. Wf Sarah WASHBURN signs. Ack. 7 June 1816. Rec. 10 June 1816.

Will of **Joseph SPOONER** of Dartmouth MA. <"Spooner:66,83"> ...dated 3 Oct. 1770...Pr. 17 Feb. 1771. (no details given in files)

MICRO #10 OF 30

Will of **John WASHBURN**, gentleman of Bridgewater MA. <Plymouth Co.PR #22020> <10:318>...dated 3 Apr. 1746, mentions son **John WASHBURN**; to son **Nathaniel WASHBURN** part of cedar swamp bought of Ephraim LEONARD which was originally Samuel WASHBURN's, also my servant boy Edward CURTIS; to son **Robert WASHBURN** half of cedar swamp which Samuel WASHBURN gave to his son Samuel, also remainder of land sold to Abisha WASHBURN...said Robert not to come into possession for 20 years said land having been leased to Nathaniel WASHBURN for said term; son **Abisha WASHBURN**; daus **Jane, Content** and heirs of dau **Margaret HOLMES** dec'd. Witnesses: Jonathan PRATT, Eleazer CARVER Jr., Josiah EDSON Jr. <10:320> Pr. 8 July 1746. <10:282> Inventory 11 July 1746 by Josiah EDSON Jr., Eleazer CARVER, Moses ORCUTT. <12:79> Account Mar. 1749, Paid to: Jonathan CARVER, widow Hannah KINGMAN, Benjamin MAHURIN, Ebenezer KEITH, Ephraim LEACH, Jonathan SPRAGUE, David CONANT, Leiut. CARVER, Jonathan CHANDLER, Josiah EDSON Jr., Dr. WHITE, Esqr. SEVER, John FOBES, Thomas PERKINS, Cornelius WASHBURN.

Estate of **Nathaniel WASHBURN** of Bridgewater MA. <Plymouth Co.PR #22066> <11:386> Letter/Bond 2 Apr. 1750., widow **Mary WASHBURN** and John WASHBURN, yeoman, both of Bridgewater, admrs. Sureties: Josiah EDSON Jr., William LEACH, both of Bridgewater. Witnesses: Edward WINSLOW, James KEITH. <12:75> Inventory taken 2 Apr. 1750 by Josiah EDSON Jr., Ebenezer CARVER, Jonathan CHANDLER, who took oath 4 June 1750. <12:135> 1st Account sworn 5 Nov. 1750 by admrs.; Paid to: Dr. LeBARON, Isaac SWIFT, Nicholas SEVER, Esq., Robert WASHBURN, Joseph COWEN, Joseph PACKARD, Jos^{h} CONANT, Isaac POOLE, Pelatiah FINNEY, Samuel HAYWARD, Thomas TOMSON, John WASHBURN, John FIELD, Dr. PRATT, Dr. OTIS, Walter DOWNEY, Thomas PERKINS, Benjamin SNOW, Dr. WILLIS, Mr. SHAW, Abisha WASHBURN. Due from: Nathan & Mary MITCHELL, heirs of Rebekah HOMES. <15:20> Division of estate to widow and children, viz: widow **Mary WASHBURN**, now the wife of Eleazer CARY; eldest son **Abraham WASHBURN**; dau **Lucy MORTON** wf of Nathaniel; dau **Hannah WASHBURN**; son **Nathaniel WASHBURN** dec'd (minor & unmarried); division mentions Nathaniel's father John WASHBURN, dec'd. Oath to division sworn to 22 May 1758 by Josiah EDSON, Eleazer CARVER, Jonathan CHANDLER, Edward MITCHELL and on 1 June 1758 by Samuel KINSLEY. <16:457> Warrant to divide real estate, sworn to 22 Dec. 1762.

Guardianship of Children of **Nathaniel WASHBURN** of Bridgewater MA. <Plymouth Co.PR #22048> <14:219,255> Letters 7 Mar. 1757, 5 May 1757, June 1757, Jacob HAYWARD, yeoman of Bridgewater, app'td gdn. of the three children. <original> Bond 7 Mar. 1757 by Jacob HAYWARD, gdn. of **Abraham WASHBURN** and **Lucy WASHBURN**, minors above 14, and **Hannah WASHBURN**, minor under 14. Surety: Eleazer CARY of Bridgewater. Witnesses: Joseph BICKNELL, John LOTHROP. <original> Request 5 Mar. 1757 of **Mary CARY**, mother to **Hannah WASHBURN**, 11 years of age, desires Jacob HAYWARD to be app'td gdn.

Estate of Capt. **Abraham/Abram WASHBURN**, gentleman of Bridgewater MA. <Plymouth Co.PR #21916> <27:188> Letter/Bond 1 Aug. 1785, Benjamin WILLIS, Esq. and widow **Rebecca WASHBURN**, of Bridgewater, app'td admrs. Sureties: John MILLER, yeoman of Middleborough and Seth JOSSELYN, gentleman of Hanover. Witnesses: Noah BISBEE, Isaac LOTHROP. <29:478> Inventory taken 1 Aug. 1785 by Eliphalet CARY & Solomon LEONARD, gentlemen and Isaac LAZELL, trader, all of Bridgewater; incl. homestead; land at South Brook at Titiquit; cedar swamp in Pembroke; pew in South Meeting House; the reversion of **Mrs. Mary CARY**'s dower. Oath by appraisers 4 Jan. 1786; oath by Benjamin WILLIS, 6 Mar. 1786. <29:479> Insolvency, 6 Mar. 1786. <29:490> 6 Mar. 1786, John WASHBURN, Eliphalet CARY, gentleman and Eleazer CARY, yeoman, all of Bridgewater, app'td to set off dower to widow. Dower set off 10 Mar. 1786, incl. land adjoining John WASHBURN's; allowed 11 Apr. 1786. <30:34> Claims, 6 Mar. 1786, by Commissioners Eliphalet CARY and Solomon LEONARD; Due to: Isaac LAZELL, Nathan LAZELL, Cornelius HOLMES, Dr. Samuel SHAW, Joab WILLIS, Elijah STORRS, Seth KEITH, John WASHBURN, Moses LEONARD, widow Jane TOMSON, Nathan MITCHELL, Esq., Simeon AMES, Isaac JOHNSON Jr., Deacon

Seth PRATT, Capt. Elisha MITCHELL, Jireh SWIFT, Silvanus CONANT, William BLAKELEY, Capt. Solomon LEONARD, Maj. Eliphalet CAREY, Hezekiah HOOPER, Oliver ALDEN, Samuel KINSLEY, Sophia KINSLEY, Isaac LAZELL as gdn. of Josiah EDSON, Freeman WATERMAN, Dr. Nathaniel MORTON, Joseph AMES, Thomas MORTON, William WHITE, Benjamin HAYWARD, Benjamin WASHBURN, Elijah SNOW, widow Rebecca WASHBURN, Maj. James ALLEN, Noah WHITMAN, Abner PRATT, Isaac SWIFT, Calvin WHITE, Calvin WASHBURN, Robert KEITH Jr., Col. John COOK, David KINGMAN, Ezra KINGMAN, Joseph SHEPHERD, Tomson BAXTER, Seth PADDELFORD, Esq., John PORTER, Cuff ASHPORT, Elijah REED, Oliver PHELPS, Esq., Eleazer CARY, Benjamin SNELL, William SNELL, Ebenezer WHITMAN. Oath by Commissioners, 3 Nov. 1786. <30:36> Account of admrs. allowed 6 Nov. 1786; Debts due from: Nathan RICHARD, John SHAW, Elijah EATON, Moses LEONARD, Jireh SWIFT, James DUNHAM, Solomon PRATT, James PERKINS, Samuel WILLIS, Hezekiah HOOPER, Obadiah EDDY, James PERKINS, Jonathan WILLIS, John CONANT Jr., Dr. Eleazer CARVER, Joseph POPE; mentions supporting two children from the death of their father in July 1785 to Oct. 1786. <30:548> Division 26 Jan. 1789 by Nathan MITCHELL, Eliphalet CARY, gentleman and Solomon LEONARD, gentleman, all of Bridgewater, to following heirs, viz: **Nathaniel WASHBURN** (eldest son), **Chloe WASHBURN, Seth WASHBURN, Abram WASHBURN, Lucy WASHBURN.**

Guardianship of Children of **Abraham/Abram WASHBURN** of Bridgewater. <Plymouth Co.PR #21917> <original> Bond 1 Apr. 1788/89, of widow **Rebecca WASHBURN.** Sureties: Hezekiah HOOPER, Nathan MITCHELL, both of Bridgewater. Witnesss: Jehil BENSON, Isaac LOTHROP. <26:224> Letter 1 Apr. 1788/89 widow **Rebecca WASHBURN** app'td gdn. of **Seth WASHBURN, Abraham WASHBURN** and **Lucy WASHBURN,** minors under 14.

Estate of **Josiah WASHBURN** of Bridgewater MA. <Plymouth Co.PR #22029>
<7:11> Letter/Bond 24 May 1734, widow **Sarah WASHBURN** and Edward RICHMOND, husbandman of Taunton, app'td admrs. Sureties: John HACKET and Robert RANSOM, husbandmen of Middleborough. Witnesses: Thomas WETHRELL, Samuel SHURTLEFF.

PLYMOUTH COUNTY DEEDS: (re: JOHNSON)

<49:72> - 18 Mar. 1752, David JOHNSON, gentleman of Bridgewater to son Isaac JOHNSON of same.
<49:107> - 21 Feb. 1756, Isaac JOHNSON, gent. of Bridgewater to Daniel JOHNSON, Esq. of same. Wf Mary releases dower.
<50:48> - 28 Dec. 1762, Isaac JOHNSON, gent. of Bridgewater, grantor.
<52:232> - 21 Mar. 1726/7, Witnesses sworn 12 Oct. 1764, Isaac JOHNSON since dec'd to Elisha DUNBAR. Rec. 5 June 1766.
<63:92> - 23 Feb. 1784, Isaac JOHNSON, Esq. of Bridgewater & wf Mary to Daniel HARTWELL.
<66:1> - 3 Mar. 1784, Isaac JOHNSON, gentleman of Bridgewater to eldest son Thomas JOHNSON, gentleman of Bridgewater...reserves half use of house for life.
<66:217> - 7 Feb. 1787, Isaac JOHNSON Jr., yeoman of Bridgewater from Jesse HARLOW & wf Elizabeth of Plymouth.
<68:226> - 21 Jan. 1789, Isaac JOHNSON Jr. of Bridgewater to Joseph POPE of Bridgewater. Wf Molly JOHNSON signs. Rec. 12 Feb. 1789.
<69:17> - 27 Mar. 1789, Isaac JOHNSON Jr., yeoman of Bridgewater from "2 Lindsays & 4 Lindsays"
<74:89> - 1793, Isaac JOHNSON Jr. of Bridgewater by guardian.
<166:228> - 1821, Mary JOHNSON, single, of Kingston.
<149:93> - 23 Apr. 1823, Isaac JOHNSON & wf Mary of Bridgewater to Nahum JOHNSON.
<149:93> - 22 Apr. 1823, Isaac JOHNSON from Thomas JOHNSON.
<161:12> - 1827, Mary JOHNSON of Boston, executrix of Seth JOHNSON of E. Bridgewater.
<162:25> - 1827, Mary JOHNSON, dau of Joseph JOHNSON.
<166:150;168:76> 1829, Mary JOHNSON.
<167:119> - 1830, Mary JOHNSON et al.
<190:175> - 1838, Mary JOHNSON.
<232:246> - 1840, Mary JOHNSON of Boston, widow of Seth JOHNSON.

Additional references with no details are given as follows:
Isaac JOHNSON, grantor: <10:558; 13:63; 21:198; 25:74,128,173-176; 27:79; 28:112; 39:32; 48:109>.
Isaac JOHNSON, grantee: <6:90,93;10:350;12:153;22:92;25:116-7;42:265;44:1;45:13;47:166;48:12>.
Mary JOHNSON, both: <(all 1826)- 148:275;155:285;157:180; (1827)- 157:189>
(Bowman notes the above are all references to the names Isaac JOHNSON and Mary JOHNSON, to 1859, in the Plymouth County Deeds.)

Guardianship of **Isaac JOHNSON Jr.**, yeoman of Bridgewater MA. <Plymouth Co.Deeds #11493>
<31:295> 2 Oct. 1790, Nathan WILLIS, Seth PRATT, John WHITMAN Jr. and Jesse PERKINS, Selectmen of Bridgewater, petition for a guardian. <26:493> 1 Nov. 1790, Nathan WILLIS, Seth PRATT and Jesse PERKINS, gentlemen of Bridgewater, app'td gdn. of Isaac JOHNSON Jr...idleness & intemperance. <31:296> Inventory taken 29 Oct. 1790 by Joshua GILMORE of Easton, George LOTHROP and Israel ALGER of Bridgewater; totals: personal, £175.4.2., real estate, about 34 acres, £106. <31:455> Account of gdns. 2 Nov. 1791. <31:480> Account of gdns. 18 Feb. 1792. <31:506> Sale of real estate 15 Mar. 1792. <31:507> Sworn to 16 Mar. 1792. <33:85> Account of gdns. 2 July 1792; paid for support of his family and paid ye sd Isaac's father.

Will of **Joseph WASHBURN**, gentleman of Bridgewater MA. <Plymouth Co.PR #22027>
<19:423>...dated 11 Jan. 1765, mentions wf **Deliverance**, sons **Jeremiah WASHBURN, Joseph WASHBURN, Eliphalet WASHBURN, Silvanus WASHBURN** and **Eliab WASHBURN**, daus **Hannah PRATT** wf of Seth, **Joanna LEONARD** wf of Solomon, **Martha WASHBURN**. Witnesses: Josiah EDSON, Josiah WASHBURN, Josiah DUNBAR. <19:424> Pr. 2 Feb. 1767. <19:548> Inventory taken 24 Feb. 1767 by Ichabod ORCUTT, Josiah WASH-

BURN, Josiah DUNBAR who made oath 30 Mar. 1767; oath by executor **Jeremiah WASHBURN**, 13 Oct. 1767.

Estate of **Josiah WASHBURN**, yeoman of Bridgewater MA. <Plymouth Co.PR #22031>
<original> 4 Dec. 1789, **Elizabeth WASHBURN, widow**, signifies her utter aversion to administer the estate and says he left no brother and but one son living within this Commonwealth and requests that Benjamin WILLIS be appointed. <27:313> Letter 7 Dec. 1789, Benjamin WILLIS of Bridgewater appt'd admr. <original> Bond 7 Dec. 1789 by admr. Sureties: Ebenezer BENSON, tanner and Oliver ALLEN, yeoman of Bridgewater. Witnesses: Salmon WASHBURN, Isaac LOTHROP. <31:106> Inventory taken 7 Dec. 1789 by Nathaniel LITTLE, Solomon LEONARD and Jeremiah WASHBURN, all gent. of Bridgewater. Oath of appraisers, 31 Dec. 1789. Oath of admr., 4 Jan. 1790. <31:243> 4 Jan. 1790, Nathaniel LITTLE and Nathan LAZELL of Bridgewater app'td as Commissioners to examine following debts due: Thomas WASHBURN, Rev. John SHAW, Capt. Nathaniel LITTLE, Jacob PERKINS, Isaac LAZELL, Nathan LAZELL, William LORING, Elijah SNOW, Samuel KINSLEY, Jeremiah WASHBURN, Enoch PERKINS the admr. on estate of Thomas PERKINS, Solomon AMES, John CONANT Jr., Dr. Philip BRYANT, Nathan MITCHELL, Winslow HOOPER, Thomson BAXTER, Jonathan AMES, David TAYLOR, David HOOPER, Luther HOOPER the exr. of the will of Thomas HOOPER, Philip PADDLEFORD, Benjamin WILLIS, Solomon ALDEN, Casar AUGUSTUS, Jonathan BENSON, Lot CONANT, Azor HOW, Dr. Eleaser CARVER, Salmon WASHBURN and Bethuel WASHBURN. Allowed by oath of Commissioners, 18 Oct. 1790. <31:244> Account of admr., 18 Nov. 1790. <31:245> Account of admr., 14 Apr. 1791. <31:246> Claims allowed 26 Apr. 1791. <52:463> Letter 4 Jan. 1825, Seth WASHBURN app'td admr. d.b.n. in place of Benjamin WILLIS dec'd. <original> Bond 4 Jan. 1825 of admr. Sureties: Artemus HALE, merchant and Holmes SPRAGUE, cabinet maker, both of Bridgewater. Witnesses: S. RUSSELL, Calvin TILDEN. <58:544> Inventory taken 4 Jan. 1825 by Spencer LEONARD, Philander WOOD and Rufus WOOD, all of Bridgewater. Oath of appraisers 18 Feb. 1825. Oath of admr. 21 Feb. 1825. <58:545> Petition 4 Jan. 1825 for sale to pay debts. <58:547> License for sale, 21 Feb. 1825. <55:266> Notice of appointment. <59:502> Notice of sale to be held 28 Mar. 1825. <59:503> Account of admr. allowed 1 Nov. 1825.

Benjamin WILLIS of Bridgewater MA to **Cornelius HOLMES** of Bridgewater. <Plymouth Co.Deeds 82:24>
...9 Apr. 1795, Benjamin WILLIS, Esq., as administrator to estate of Josiah WASHBURN, yeoman, late of Bridgewater, dec'd, for £107.10s6d, sold to Cornelius HOLMES, cordwainer...by virtue of license to me granted by the Justices of the Court of Common Pleas...forty acres in south Bridgewater...also a small piece of land adjoining...also a garden spot with two thirds of the dwelling house. Witnesses: Ebenezer BENSON, Benjamin WILLIS Jr. Ack. 22 Apr. 1795. Rec. 12 Jan.1797.

Seth WASHBURN of Bridgewater MA to **CARVER, WASHBURN & Co.** <Plymouth Co.Deeds 157:55>
...30 Mar. 1825, Seth WASHBURN, admr. de bonis non to the estate of Josiah WASHBURN dec'd...by order of the Court of Probate...did on 28 Mar. 1825, for $50.00 sell three and three quarters acre of land in Pond meadow to...Eleazer CARVER Jr., Seth WASHBURN, Abram WASHBURN, Artemas HALE, Abram WASHBURN 2d, Nathaniel WASHBURN and Solomon WASHBURN Jr., all of Bridgewater doing business under the name of Carver, Washburn & Co. No Witnesses. Ack. 20 June 1825. Rec. 11 Apr. 1826.

Will of **William WASHBURN**, husbandman of Bridgewater MA. <Plymouth Co.PR #22117>
<14:362>...dated 11 Dec. 1749, mentions wf **Experience**, son **Ezekiel WASHBURN** (executor), dau **Abigail TRUELOVE**, son **William WASHBURN**, daus **Zipporah WASHBURN, Thankful KINSLEY.** Witnesses: Josiah WASHBURN Jr., Timothy PERKINS, Benjamin WILLIS Jr. Pr. 5 Apr. 1757. <14:407> Inventory taken 25 Mar. 1756 by John BENSON, Benjamin WILLIS Jr., Daniel SNELL who made oath 3 Apr. 1756; oath of executor 8 Apr. 1756.

Estate of **Ezekiel WASHBURN**, yeoman of Bridgwater MA. <Plymouth Co.PR #21968>
<original> Request 5 Apr. 1785 of widow **Naomi WASHBURN** that Anthony DIKE be app'td admr. <27:200> Letter/Bond 5 Apr. 1785 of Anthony DYKE, blacksmith. Sureties: Ephraim NOYES of Abington and widow **Naomi WASHBURN.** Witnesses: Jonathan PETERSON, Lurana RIDER. <29:419> Warrant for Inventory, 6 Apr. 1785 to William SHAW, yeoman and Samuel BRETT Jr., gent., both of Bridgewater and Ephraim NOYES of Abington; oath of appraisers, 20 Apr. 1785, oath of admr. 10 Dec. 1785. <29:420> Estate declared insolvent, Matthew KINGMAN of Bridgewater and Ephraim NOYES app'td Commissioners. 3 Dec. 1785, List of claims declared just and reasonable: John PETTINGAL, Simeon BRETT, Gideon LINCOLN, Jesse PERKINS, Ezra WARREN, James PERKINS, Moses CARY, Abia PACKARD, Ebenezer WARREN, Nathan WARREN, William JAMSON, Simeon ALDEN, William SHAW, William EDSON, Seth EDSON, Jos[a] PACKARD, Ebenezer EDSON, Ebenezer WARREN Jr., Phillip BYRANT, Nathan LEACH, Ephraim NOYES, Anthony DIKE, Abial HARRIS, William SHAW, Jr., Ichabod HOWARD, Oliver PACKARD, Ichabod EDSON, Simeon BRETT Jr., John ROBINSON, Samuel BRETT Jr., Seth KINGMAN, Josiah PACKARD, Samuel STAEL(sp), Jonathan BASS, Henry KINGMAN, Asa FORD, Isaac PACKARD. <19:421> Account allowed 20 Dec. 1785. <19:421> 1785, **William & Else FRENCH, Nathaniel & Betty PRATT** and **William Jr. & Deliverance SHAW,** quit claim to our honoured father's estate. <29:450> Dower assigned 10 Dec. 1785, William SHAW, yeoman & Ephraim NOYES of Abington & Samuel BRETT Jr. of Bridgewater app'td to view real estate Ezekiel WASHBURN died seized of (a part of which his deceased father died seized of and set off to his widow Experience WASHBURN her dower) and Secondly to set off to widow **Naomi WASHBURN** her thirds. <30:48> Account of admr. allowed 27 Nov. 1786. 3rd Account allowed 13 Jan. 1802. <37:20> Memorandum: Sale of dwellling house with 5 or 6 acres of land...3 July 1800.

Will of **David FORD Jr.**, mariner of Charlestown. <??? #8105>
...dated 13 Sept. 1746, being bound to sea...leaves everything to wife Mary. Witnesses: James TRUMBAL, T. TRUMBAL, Stephen BADGER Jr. Pr. 10 July 1758.

Heirs of **David NEWTON** of Marlboro MA. <Middlesex Co.Deeds 22:280>
...5 June 1723, Thankful NEWTON of Bridgewater and Lydia MORSE of Marlboro...only surviving heirs

of their father David NEWTON of Marlboro.

Estate of **Ebenezer WASHBURN** of Bridgewater MA. <Plymouth Co.PR #21948>
<5:356> Letter/Bond 3 Apr. 1728, of brother **Benjamin WASHBURN** of Bridgewater, admr. Sureties: Ebenezer BYRAM, Amos SNELL. Witnesses: Daniel HUDSON, John WINSLOW. <original> 3 Apr. 1728, Capt. John FIELD, Lieut. Ephraim HAYWARD and Jonathan HAYWARD app'td to appraise estate. Inventory taken 25 May 1728 by Ephraim HAWARD, John FIELD, Jonathan HAWARD Jr., of estate of **Ebenezer WASHBURN** who died October ye tenth 1727; incl. five acres near Amos SNELL's. Memorandum: the estate is settled upon **Benjamin WASHBURN** he haveing paid to his brothers and sisters their proportionable part thereof according to apprisement, viz: **Josiah WASHBORNE, Elizabeth BENSON** wf of John, **Cornelius WASHBORNE, Martha WASHBOURN** and **Joannah WASHBORNE.**
(Bowman's note: "brothers **Jonathan & Nathan** not mentioned in division!)

Estate of **Benjamin WASHBURN**, yeoman of Bridgewater MA. <Plymouth Co.PR #21925>
<8:261> Letter/Bond 3 Nov. 1740 of **Cornelius WASHBURN**, husbandman of Bridgewater, admr. Sureties: Jonathan CARY, gent. and Moses ORCUTT, yeoman, both of Bridgewater. Witnesses: Jno. MAGOUN, Isaac HATCH. <8:308> Inventory 21 Nov. 1740 by Jonathan CARY, Nathaniel CARVER, Jonathan CHANDLER, incl eighteen and a half acres lying between land of Cornelius WASHBURN and Isaac POOLE; bonds from Jeremiah ALLEN, Joseph ALLEN, Joseph PACKARD, Jonathan KINGMAN, Thomas CUSHING. Debts due from: William KEITH, Solomon LEACH, Ebenezer BATES, Mr. EDSON and Mr. SHAW; oath of appraisers 3 Apr. 1741, oath of admr. 17 Apr. 1741. <16:408> Account 27 Apr. 1763, debts paid to: Nicholas SEVER, Esq., Thomas CROUDE, Esq., William HOLMES, Enoch LEONARD, Jonathan WASHBURN, Jonathan PETERSON, Benjamin SAMSON, Jonathan CHANDLER, Ruban THOMSON, Zacheriah WASHBURN, Joseph PRATT, Edward MITCHELL, Daniel JOHNSON, Esq., William DAVENPORT, John KINGMAN, Josiah WASHBURN Jr., John WASHBURN, Hezekiah HOWARD, Lot CONANT Jr., William BRYANT, Bethiah HAYWARD, Ebenezer WHITMAN, Daniel HUDSON Lois DAVIS, Thomas LAWRENCE, Jno. KEITH, Elkanah LEONARD, Joseph HALL, Malatiah BOURN, widow of dec'd. <16:413> Acquital of heirs, 25 Apr. 1763, viz: widow **Martha WASHBURN, Joseph WASHBURN Jr.** & wf **Mary, Jonathan LEONARD** & wf **Martha, Benjamin WASHBURN 3d**, each received £44 from **Cornelius WASHBURN**, admr. and signed acquital. Witnesses: Josiah EDSON, David CARVER.

Benjamin WASHBURN of Bridgewater MA to **Isaac HARRIS** of Bridgewater.
...20 June 1717, Benjamin WASHBURN, yeoman, for £2 sold to Isaac HARRIS, yeoman...two eighth parts or one quarter part of the saw mill at Saquatuket in Bridgewater.
(From the original in the possession of Robert O. Harris, 1920's.)

Benjamin SNOW Jr. of Bridgewater MA to **Benjamin WASHBURN Sr.** of Bridgewater. <Plymouth Co.Deeds>
<32:51>...17 Mar. 1728/9, Benjamin SNOW Jr., cordwainer, for £106.10s, sold to Benjamin WASHBURN, Sr., yeoman...eighteen and a half acres in Bridgewter...bounded by land of Edward WASHBURN and the river. Witnesses: Ephraim LEONARD, William WASHBURN. Ack. 5 Sept. 1737. Rec. 6 July 1738.

Benjamin WASHBURN 3d of Bridgewater MA to **Nicholas WADE Jr.** of Bridgewater. <Plymouth Co.Deeds>
<52:151>...12 June 1764, Benjamin WASHBURN 3d, yeoman, for £1.1s4d, sold to Nicholas WADE Jr., yeoman...four acres undivided land within the Eight Mile (so called) in Bridgewater...to lay out on the fourth grant of the half purchase right that was made to Benjamin WASHBURN dec'd and was since made to me the said Benjamin WASHBURN 3d on the 17 Apr. 1749 by the Purchasers. Witnesses: Elijah HAYWARD, Peres FOBES. Ack. 29 Oct. 1764. Rec. 31 Oct. 1765.

Benjamin WASHBURN 3d of Bridgewater MA to **James WADE** of Bridgewater. <Plymouth Co.Deeds 52:151>
...12 June 1764, Benjamin WASHBURN 3d, yeoman, for £3.14s8d, sold to James WADE, yeoman...fourteen acres undivided land within the Eight Mile (so called) in Bridgewater...to lay out on the first third and fifth grants of the half purchase right that was made to Benjamin WASHBURN dec'd and was since his decease made to me the said Benjamin WASHBURN 3d, the first on 28 Jan. 1744/5, the third on 11 Apr. 1748 and the fifth on 11 Feb. 1750/1 by the Purchasers. Witnesses: Elijah HAYWARD, Peres FOBES. Ack. 29 Oct. 1764. Rec. 31 Oct. 1765.

Estate of **Benjamin WASHBURN**, yeoman of Bridgewater MA. <Plymouth Co.PR #21926>
<original> Request 7 Mar. 1796 of widow **Desire WASHBURN** that **Oliver WASHBURN** be app'td admr. <34:70> Letter/Bond 7 Mar. 1796, of **Oliver WASHBURN**, yeoman of Bridgewater, admr. Sureties: Hezekiah HOOPER & Oliver HAWARD of Bridgewater. Witnesses: William JAMESON, Noah NICHOLS. <35:535> Inventory taken 7 May 1796 by Hezekiah HOOPER, Eliphalet CARY, Peter CONANT. <35:536> 2nd Appraisal, 12 May 1796 by Simeon PRATT, William MITCHELL, Benjamin POPE who made oath 21 May 1796.<original> 2nd Bond 1 Aug. 1796 of admr. Sureties: James LEACH & Robert KEITH of Bridgewater. Witnesses: Joseph LORING, John FAUNCE. Memorandum 1 Aug. 1796, list of heirs: **Oliver WASHBURN** (eldest son), **Azel WASHBURN, Sarah HAYWARD** wf of Seth, **Lydia WASHBURN** since married to Samuel RYDER, **Sears WASHBURN, Polly WASHBURN, Huldah WASHBURN**...the estate is settled upon **Oliver** and he is authorized to deliver to widow **Desire WASHBURN**, $80.00 in furniture or goods. <36:241> Account of admr. allowed 2 Oct. 1797; Paid to: Lt. Winslow HOOPER, Lt. Hezekiah HOOPER, Maj. Isaac LAZELL, Maj. Nathan LAZELL, Dr. Eleazer CARVER, Seth HOWARD, Solomon AMES, Simeon AMES, Lt. Noah WHITMAN, Nathan MITCHELL, Beza HAYWARD, Jacob BENNET, Jas. BARNEY, Experience STORRS, Thomas WASHBURN, Peter CONANT, Benjamin HARRIS, William HARRIS, Cornelius HOLMES, Lt. Benjamin POPE, Dr. Nathan FOBES, Ebenezer THOMSON, Cornelius WASHBURN, Elijah STORRS, Edward MITCHELL, Jos. POPE, Capt. Jos. ALDEN, Nathan THOMSON, Ebenezer BENSON, Lt. Edward MITCHELL, Lt. Benjamin CONANT, Azariah HOWARD, Dr. Samuel SHAW. <36:242> Notice of appointment 7 Mar. 1796, oath by admr. 2 Oct. 1797. <36:243> 1 Aug. 1796, Hezekiah HOOPER, gent., Peter CONANT, Cornelius WASHBURN, all of Bridgewater, set off dower to widow **Desire WASHBURN**...privilege in easterly part of dwelling house and one acre land adjoining Cornelius WASHBURN. <36:547> Division of real estate, 8 Dec. 1800, to

Oliver WASHBURN, he to pay his six brothers & sisters (already cited), $7.73 each.

Benjamin WASHBURN Jr. of Bridgewater to **John WATERMAN Jr.** of Halifax MA.<Plymouth Co.Deeds 59:65> ...6 May 1777, Benjamin WASHBURN Jr. & wf Desire, for £6.19s, sold to John WATERMAN Jr...two acres in Halifax formerly belonging to Isaac KING...fell to us from our honoured Father late of Halifax dec'd...bounded by land of Benjamin CURTIS and sd John WATERMAN. Witnesses: Cornelius WASHBURN 2d, Edward SEARES. Ack. by both 18 June 1777. Rec. 16 Sept. 1777.

Benjamin WASHBURN Jr. of Bridgewater MA to **Edward SEARS** of Halifax MA. <Plymouth Co.Deeds 62:165> ...6 May 1777, Benjamin WASHBURN Jr. & wf Desire, for £55.11s8d, sold to Edward SEARS, yeoman... sixteen acres in Halifax...being part of the land that fell to us from our honoured Father Edward SEARS late of Halifax dec'd...bounded by land of Benjamin CURTIS, John WATERMAN, Benjamin CURTIS' wife and land of sd Edward SEARS. Witnesses: Cornelius WASHBURN 2d, John WATERMAN Jr. Ack. by Benjamin & Desire 18 June 1777. Rec. 23 Mar. 1784.

Benjamin WASHBURN 2d of Bridgewater MA to **Joseph POPE** of Bridgewater. <Plymouth Co.Deeds 79:70> ...9 Feb. 1779, Benjamin WASHBURN 2d, cooper & wf Desire, for £84, sold to Joseph POPE, gent... seven and one quarter acres bounded by land of Cornelius WASHBURN and Eliphalet CARY. Witnesses: Benjamin WILLIS Jr., Cornelius WASHBURN 2d. Ack. 9 Feb. 1779. Rec. 23 Apr. 1796.

Benjamin WASHBURN 2d of Bridgewater MA to **Noah WHITMAN** of Bridgewater. <Plymouth Co.Deeds 62:66> ...19 Mar. 1783, Benjamin WASHBURN 2d, cooper, for £34.13s, sold to Noah WHITMAN, bricklayer... ten and a half acres in Bridgewater...bounds of the land said Noah bought of Hezekiah HOOPER. Wf Desire WASHBURN releases dower. Witnesses: Nathan ALDEN Jr., Sarah WASHBURN. Ack. 20 Mar. 1783. Rec. 6 May 1783.

Benjamin WASHBURN 2d of Bridgewater MA to **Noah WHITMAN** of Bridgewater. <Plymouth Co.Deeds 63:96> ...19 May 1783, Benjamin WASHBURN 2d, cooper, for £9.15s4d, sold to Noah WHITMAN, bricklayer... land adjoining the land I sold last March. Wf Desire WASHBURN releases dower. Witnesses: Benjamin CONANT, Nathan ALDEN Jr. Ack. 8 Sept. 1784. Rec. 9 Sept. 1784.

Benjamin WASHBURN 2d of Bridgewater MA to **Oliver WASHBURN** of Bridgewater. <Plymouth Co.Deeds> <64:64>...3 Sept. 1784, Benjamin WASHBURN 2d, yeoman, for £150, sold to Oliver WASHBURN, cooper ...one half of homestead where I now dwell containing forty five acres...bounded by land of Hezekiah HOOPER, Noah WHITMAN (which he bought of me), Eliphalet CARY, Joseph POPE. Wf Desire WASHBURN releases dower. Witnesses: Hezekiah HOOPER, Winslow HOOPER. Ack. 5 Apr. 1785. Rec. 11 May 1785.

Benjamin 2d & Oliver WASHBURN of Bridgewater to **Noah WHITMAN.** <Plymouth Co.Deeds 66:57> ...22 Mar. 1786, Benjamin WASHBURN 2d and Oliver WASHBURN, yeomen, for £26, sold to Noah WHITMAN, yeoman of Bridgewater...seven and a half acres in Bridgewater...bounded by sd Washburn's dwelling house and adjoining land he formerly sold to Noah. Wf Desire WASHBURN releases dower. Witnesses: Peter CONANT, Joseph HOOPER. Ack. 7 Apr. 1786. Rec. 11 Apr. 1786.

Benjamin WASHBURN 2d and **Oliver WASHBURN** of Bridgewater. <Plymouth Co.Deeds 72:243> ...23 Mar. 1789, Benjamin WASHBURN 2d, yeoman and Oliver WASHBURN, yeoman...jointly owning 20 acres...bounded by land of Lt. Hezekiah HOOPER...divide land between them. Witnesses: Hezekiah HOOPER, (   ) WASHBURN. Rec. 23 May 1792.

Benjamin WASHBURN 2d of Bridgewater to **Oliver WASHBURN** of Bridgewater. <Plymouth Co.Deeds 72:243> ...26 Apr. 1792, Benjamin WASHBURN 2d, yeoman, for £32.12s, sold to Oliver WASHBURN, yeoman... five and one quarter acres on westerly side of South Brook being of my homestead where I now reside...mentions one half of homestead which he sold to Oliver. Wf Desire WASHBURN releases dower. Witnesses: Joseph HOOPER, Beza HAYWARD. Ack. 21 May 1792. Rec. 23 May 1792.

Will of **Cornelius WASHBURN,** yeoman of Bridgewater MA. <Plymouth Co.PR #21943> <25:258>...dated 11 Apr. 1774, being aged & infirm, mentions wf **Experience;** to son **Daniel WASHBURN** ten acres in south Bridgewater near dwelling house of Josiah WASHBURN 2d and adjoining land of Seth PRATT, Jonathan BENSON and Benjamin BENSON; to dau **Experience** 28 acres bought of William DAVENPORT; to dau **Joanna** 18 acres on which Daniel CONANT now liveth; to grandson **Cornelius WASHBURN,** homestead, reserving thirds to widow during her life. Witnesses: Benjamin WILLIS Jr., Jacob WASHBURN, Josiah WASHBURN. Pr. 5 Apr. 1779, **Daniel WASHBURN** app'td executor.<25:260> Inventory taken 5 Apr. 1779 by Benjamin WILLIS, Seth PRATT, Hezekiah HOOPER, gentlemen of Bridgewater, who made oath 20 May 1779, oath of executor, 7 June 1779.

Joseph WASHBURN and **Nicholas BYRAM Jr.** of Bridgewater MA. <Plymouth Co.Deeds 15:10> ...9 Sept. 1678, Joseph WASHBURN, with consent of father John WASHBURN, exchanges with Nicholas BYRAM Jr...meadow land in Bridgewater at Blacks Brook and bounded by meadow of John HAYWARD and Samuel ALLEN, which was George PARTRIDGE's...for meadow land in Bridgewater bounded by upland which was Samuel WADSWORTH's and land of Lawrence WILLIS. Witnesses: John WASHBURN, Nicholas BYRAM Sr., Samuel ALLEN, Sr., John CARY. Ack. by Joseph 14 Mar. 1683. Rec. 19 May 1720.

Joseph WASHBURN of Bridgewater MA to **Cornish,** negro of Duxborough. <Plymouth Co.Deeds 10:2:131> ...30 Aug. 1695, Joseph WASHBURN to Cornish...twenty acres in Bridgewater, west of Setucket pond being the 8th lot of Division, joyning 7th lot laid out for Thomas HAYWARD, gent. and 9th lot

Joseph WASHBOURNE of Bridgewater from **Timothy WADSWORTH** of Boston. <Plymouth Co.Deeds 4:16> ...13 July 1687, Joseph WASHBOURNE buys from Timothy WADSWORTH...20 acres in Bridgewater on easterly side of Satucket River...bounded on west and north by land of sd Joseph, south by Samuel ALLIN...also lot of meadow lying at mouth of Satucket pond bounded by land of sd Joseph and Robert LATHAM. Wf Susanna WADSWORTH signs. Ack. 13 July 1687. Rec. 2 May 1701.

Joseph WASHBURN of Bridgewater from **Lieut. John HAWARD** of Bridgewater. <Plymouth Co.Deeds 4:17> ...May 1692, Joseph WASHBURN, smith, buys from Lieut. John HAWARD...25 acres in Bridgewater on easterly side of Satucket River...bounded south east by land of LATHAM, north by land of Thomas WHITMAN, south by land of sd Joseph. Witnesses: James LATHAM, Samuel ALLIN Sr. Ack. by John 4 Sept. 1694. Rec. 3 May 1701.

Joseph & James WASHBURN of Bridgewater to **Thomas SNELL Sr.** of same. <Plymouth Co.Deeds 17:114> ...12 Apr. 1697, Joseph WASHBURN and James WASHBURN, sell to Thomas SNELL Sr...land in Bridgewater towards west side in a great swamp known as Cutting Cove, it being half of twenty acres of swamp and meadow land. Witnesses: James KEITH, John ALDEN, John WASHBURN. Ack. 30 Aug. 1705. Rec. 24 Jan. 1723.

Joseph WASHBURN of Bridgewater to **Thomas MITCHEL** of Bridgewater. <Plymouth Co.Deeds 7:187> ...13 Aug. 1705, Joseph WASHBURN sells to Thomas MITCHEL...land in Bridgewater bounded by lands of Thomas MITCHEL and lands bought of Samuel ALLYN Sr. Ack. 11 Feb. 1707. Rec. 16 Feb. 1707/8.

Joseph WASHBURN of Bridgewater to **Jonathan WASHBURN** of Bridgewater. <Plymouth Co.Deeds 10:1:528> ...13 Jan. 1706/7, Joseph WASHBURN to son Jonathan WASHBURN...land in Bridgewater on east side of Satucket River, northerly by Whitman's land...to a white oak stump which was an ancient bounds between father Latham's lot and Deacon Willis' lot. Witnesses: Ebenezer LEACH, Benjamin LEACH. Ack. 14 Jan. 1706/7. Rec. 12 Feb. 1713.

Joseph WASHBURN of Bridgewater from **James LATHAM** of Bridgewater. <Plymouth Co.Deeds 12:118> ...Joseph WASHBURN buys from James LATHAM...land in Bridgewater in Titticutt Purchase which was my father Latham's right in sd purchase...bounded by land of Thomas SNELL on west and Josiah EDSON on east...it being the 19th lot...also two small lots, one (10th lot) on path going to Titticutt between lots of Jno. LEONARD and Nathaniel WILLIS. Witnesses: Joseph HAYWARD, Timothy EDSON. Ack. 26 May 1708. Rec. 10 Apr. 1717.

Joseph WASHBURN Sr. of Bridgewater from **Francis CARY** of Bridgewater. <Plymouth Co.Deeds 12:119> ...7 Mar. 1714/5, Joseph WASHBURN Sr. buys from Francis CARY...one eight part of a right in 5th share of great cedar swamp commonly known as Poor Meadow Cedar Swamp in county of Plymouth. Ack. by Francis 27 June 1715. Rec. 10 Apr. 1717.

Joseph WASHBURN of Bridgewater to **Isaac LAZELL** of Plymouth. <Plymouth Co.Deeds 12:153> ...17 Apr. 1717, Joseph WASHBURN, blacksmith, sells to Isaac LAZELL, cordwainer...my homestead whereon I now dwell in Bridgewater, about forty acres...easterly side of Satucket River, bounded by land formerly belonging to Samuel ALLYN now William CONANT's. Witnesses: Samuel LOTHROP Jr., Thomas HAYWARD. Ack. 10 May 1717. Rec 11 May 1717. Wf Hannah WASHBURN releases dower 13 May 1717. <19:98>...14 June 1720, Joseph WASHBURN, of Plympton, formerly of Bridgewater, confirms above. Wf Hannah releases dower. Both ack. 1 July 1725.

Joseph WASHBURN of Bridgewater from **Susanna WILLIS** of Bridgewater. <Plymouth Co.Deeds 13:101> ..2 July 1717, Joseph WASHBURN, blacksmith, buys from Susanna WILLIS, widow...20 acres in Bridgewater on Satucket River...bounded on north by lands formerly belonging to George TURNER. Ack. 2 July 1717. Rec. 24 Sept. 1717.

Joseph WASHBURN of Bridgewater to **Joseph WASHBURN** of Bridgewater. <Plymouth Co.Deeds 24:61> ...2 July 1717, Joseph WASHBURN, blacksmith to son Joseph WASHBURN...land in east Bridgewater on east side of Satucket River...Ack. 2 July 1717. Rec. 9 Apr. 1729.

Joseph WASHBURN Sr. et al of Bridgewater to **Thomas HAYWARD Sr.** of same. <Plymouth Co.Deeds> <13:1:102>...3 Aug. 1717, Joseph WASHBURN Sr. and James WASHBURN to Thomas HAYWARD Sr...land in Four Mile grant of Bridgewater...in third of seven shares. Witnesses: Joseph HAYWARD Sr., Nathaniel BRETT. Ack. by both 16 Sept. 1717. Rec. 2 Oct. 1717.

Joseph WASHBURN Sr. of Bridgewater from **William CONANT** of Bridgewater. <Plymouth Co.Deeds 13:101> ...13 Aug. 1717, Joseph WASHBURN Sr. buys from William CONANT...land in Bridgewater on west side of Satucket River...on east side of WHITMAN's 20 acre lot lying against mouth of Black Brook. Witnesses: John FIELD, Thomas HAYWARD. Ack. by William 13 Aug. 1717. Rec. 24 Sept. 1717.

Joseph WASHBURN Sr. of Plimton MA to **Benjamin HAYWARD Sr.** of Bridgewater. <Plymouth Co.Deeds> <16:62>...25 June 1718, Joseph WASHBURN Sr. sells to Benjamin HAYWARD Sr...land in Bridgewater being north of land that was Cornish's running northerly to Indian land. Ack. 25 June 1718. Rec. 9 Jan. 1722. (See bottom of p.190 for reference to Cornish.)

Joseph WASHBURN of Plympton to **Jonathan WASHBURN** of Bridgewater. <Plymouth Co.Deeds 14:195> ...25 June 1718, Joseph WASHBURN, blacksmith to son Jonathan WASHBURN, yeoman...

Joseph WASHBURN of Plympton to **Joseph WASHBURN** of Bridgewater. <Plymouth Co.Deeds 14:256> ...27 Feb. 1719/20, Joseph WASHBURN, blacksmith, to son Joseph WASHBURN. Ack. 26 Mar. 1720. <14: 256>...1 Mar. 1719/20, Joseph WASHBURN Jr., yeoman, sells the above to Benjamin HAYWARD. Ack. by Joseph Jr. 7 Apr. 1720.

==

Joseph WASHBURN of Plimton to **Ebenezer WASHBURN** of Bridgewater. <Plymouth Co.Deeds 15:41> ...6 May 1720, Joseph WASHBURN to son Ebenezer WASHBURN...upland & meadow on east side of Satucket River and poor meadow river near Middleborough line...meadow was formerly Samuel WADSWORTH's. Ack. 6 May 1720. Rec. 1 Aug. 1720. (Bowman's Note: On 30 July 1720, Ebenezer sold this to Timothy WASHBURN, tanner of Bridgewater.)

==

Joseph WASHBURN of Plimton to **Jonathan WASHBURN** of Bridgewater. <Plymouth Co.Deeds 15:204> ...12 Aug. 1721, Joseph WASHBURN, blacksmith, to son Jonathan WASHBURN...all that land where my son Jonathan now dwelleth...bounded by land of Nicholas WHITMAN & heirs of Ebenezer WHITMAN dec'd ...east to stump that was bound between lands of Robert LATHAM & Deacon WILLIS. Wf Hannah releases dower. Ack. by both 12 Aug. 1721. Rec. 24 Nov. 1721.

==

Joseph WASHBURN of Plimton to **Samuel JACOB** of Bridgewater. <Plymouth Co.Deeds 16:53> ...11 Apr. 1722, Joseph WASHBURN to Samuel JACOB...all right in undivided land within the Four Mile grant in Bridgewater. Ack. 15 May 1722. Rec. 6 June 1722.

==

Joseph WASHBURN of Plimton to **David BOSWORTH Sr.** of Plimton. <Plymouth Co.Deeds 16:62> ...22 June 1722, Joseph WASHBURN to David BOSWORTH Sr....one eighth part of one share in the 5th lot of cedar swamp in Great Cedar Swamp, now in Pembroke, which said eighth part I bought of Francis CARY of Bridgewater. Ack. 20 June 1722.

==

Joseph WASHBURN of Plimton to **Miles WASHBURN** of Plimton. <Plymouth Co.Deeds 18:109> ...4 Aug. 1723, Joseph WASHBURN to loving son Miles WASHBURN...all my 20 acres of upland I bought of John BENSON in Plimton. Wf Hannah releases dower. Ack. 15 Oct. 1723. Rec. 17 Sept. 1724.

==

Joseph WASHBURN, blacksmith of Plympton buys land in Plympton, 18 May 1724. <Plym.Co.Deeds 18:37>

==

Joseph WASHBURN of Plimton to **Edward WASHBURN** of Plimton. <Plymouth Co.Deeds 20:213> ...11 Apr. 1726, Joseph WASHBURN, blacksmith sells to Edward WASHBURN, yeoman...upland & meadow in Plimton near land of Cornelius GIBBS which I bought of Capt. William SHURTLEFF...20 acres near house that John HUNT built being part of the land I bought of John BENSON Jr. Witnesses: Thomas WITHERELL, James SHURTLEFF. Ack. & Rec. 3 Aug. 1726.

==

Joseph WASHBURN of Plimton to **Miles WASHBURN** of Plimton. <Plymouth Co.Deeds 24:140> ...27 Mar. 1727, Joseph WASHBURN, blacksmith to Miles WASHBURN, blacksmith...upland & meadow in Plimton containing one quarter part of Wonquencow meadow in partnership with John WATSON of Plymouth and Edward WASHBURN of Plimpton, which was laid out to John BENSON of Rochester by virtue of deed from Thomas MARTIN, 27 Mar. 1712...and all meadow which I bought of John BENSON, 15 Apr. 1718 except what I have already dispensed of. Ack. 5 Mar. 1727/8. Rec. 4 Aug. 1729.

==

Joseph WASHBURN 3rd of Bridgewater from **Sarah AMES** of Bridgewater. <Plymouth Co.Deeds 27:62> ...5 Sept. 1730, Joseph WASHBURN 3rd buys from Sarah AMES...land in Bridgewater...second great lot of Titaquit Lots running on Four Mile Line. Witnesses: Edward HAWARD, Isaac KINGMAN. Ack. 5 Sept. 1730. Rec. 3 Apr. 1732.

==

Joseph WASHBURN of Bridgewater from **Josiah WASHBURN** of Bridgewater. <Plymouth Co.Deeds 27:62> ...25 Nov. 1731, Joseph WASHBURN, husbandman, from Josiah WASHBURN, husbandman...land in Bridgewater...near Four Mile Line south east of Nathaniel CONANT's land. Witnesses: Joseph LEACH, William WASHBURN. Ack. 3 Dec. 1731. Rec. 3 Apr. 1732.

==

Joseph WASHBURN of Bridgewater from **Josiah WASHBURN** of Bridgewater. <Plymouth Co.Deeds 34:81> ...3 Dec. 1731, Joseph WASHBURN Jr. from my father Josiah WASHBURN...land whereon I now dwell as by deed of sale 25 Nov. 1731, which deed & sum contained are so contrived that I have received my portion of my father's estate. Witnesses: Joseph LEACH, William WASHBURN. Ack. 3 Dec. 1731. Rec. 13 Apr. 1741.

==

Joseph WASHBURN Jr. of Bridgewater from **William WASHBURN** of Bridgewater.<Plymouth Co.Deeds 27:62> ...29 Dec. 1731, Joseph WASHBURN Jr., husbandman from William WASHBURN, husbandman...land in Bridgewater adjoining to land of sd Joseph. Witnesses: Joseph LEACH, Nehemiah CAMPBELL. Ack. 29 Dec. 1731. Rec. 3 Apr. 1732.

==

Joseph WASHBURN of Bridgewater to **John JOHNSON** of Bridgewater. <Plymouth Co.Deeds 27:79> ...21 Mar. 1731, Joseph WASHBURN, blacksmith to John JOHNSON, yeoman...land in Bridgewater on easterly side of Satucket River, that is to say, all my homestead...beginning where the two rivers meet running easterly by Mr. HOLMAN's land, southerly to Lazell's land. Ack. 21 Mar. 1732. Rec. 27 Apr. 1732.

==

Miles & Edward WASHBURN of Plympton. <Plymouth Co.Deeds 36:189> ...6 Sept. 1738, Miles WASHBURN and Edward WASHBURN sell...land bought 15 Apr. 1718 by our father Joseph WASHBURN dec'd.

==

Joseph WASHBURN of Bridgewater MA to **Robert LATHAM** of Bridgewater. <Plymouth Co.Deeds 35:86>
...11 Dec. 1738, Joseph WASHBURN & wf Hannah to Robert LATHAM...53 acres, it being my homestead. Ack. by both grantors 19 Mar. 1738/9. Rec. 17 Aug. 1742.

Joseph WASHBURN of Bridgewater MA from **Jonathan CARY** of Bridgewater. <Plymouth Co.Deeds 34:82>
...7 Jan. 1739, Joseph WASHBURN, yeoman from Jonathan CARY, gent...10 acres in south Bridgewater ...part of 16th great lots. Ack. 10 Jan. 1739. Rec. 13 Apr. 1741.

Joseph WASHBURN of Bridgewater MA from **Jonathan CARY** of Bridgewater. <Plymouth Co.Deeds 34:82>
...7 Jan. 1739, Joseph WASHBURN, yeoman, from Jonathan CARY, gent...4 acres in south Bridgewater ...at northerly ends of 5th & 6th lots in Division of Titaquit Great Lots. Ack. 10 Jan. 1739.

Miles WASHBURN and **George BARROWS**, division. <Plymouth Co.Deeds 48:147>
...21 Oct. 1741, Miles WASHBURN and George BARROWS...division of land Miles received from his father Joseph WASHBURN dec'd.

MICRO #11 OF 30

Cornelius GIBBS of Plimton MA to **Ephraim WASHBURN** of Plimton. <Plymouth Co.Deeds 23:112>
...17 May 1728, Cornelius GIBBS, husbandman, for £70, sold to Ephraim WASHBURN, blacksmith...all his lands in Plimton, 60 acres, being a lot formerly granted by town of Plymouth to Eleazer DONHAM of sd town at town meeting holden 12 Feb. 1705...also one quarter of cedar swamp in Plimton which formerly belonged to John HUNT, formerly of Plymouth...and one half of one fourth share common land which formerly belonged to John HUNT. Witnesses: Samuel SPRAGUE, Remember TUPPER. Rec. 9 Aug. 1728.

Estate of **Ephraim WASHBURN**, yeoman of Plimton MA. <Plymouth Co.PR #21965>
<13:487>...16 July 1755, William WASHBURN app'td admr. <original> Bond 16 July 1755 of admr. Sureties: Joshua BENSON, yeoman of Middleborough and John BISHOP, gent., of Wareham. Witnesses: Manasseh CLAP, John LOTHROP. <13:554> Inventory taken 25 Sept. 1755 by John BISHOP, Ebenezer BRIGGS, Joshua BENSON; oath of admr. 2 Oct. 1755. <14:512> Division 24 Apr. 1758 to following heirs, viz: widow **Mary WASHBURN**, sons: **William WASHBURN** (eldest son), **Stephen WASHBURN**, **Isaac WASHBURN**, **Japhet WASHBURN**, **John WASHBURN** and daus **Lydia NORRIS** wf of Samuel, **Elizabeth BENSON** wf of Consider, **Marcy WASHBURN**, **Phebe WASHBURN**, **Jemima WASHBURN**. The division of the estate was carried out by the following Commissioners, viz: Roland HAMMOND & Bartlett MURDOCK of Plimpton, Ebenezer BRIGGS of Wareham and Henry THOMAS & James LeBARON of Middleborough.

Guardianship of Child of **Ephraim WASHBURN** of Plympton MA. <Plymouth Co.PR #22009>
<original> Bond 4 Jan. 1765 of William WASHBURN, cooper of Plympton as guardian of **Japhet WASHBURN**, minor. Surety: Samuel BENSON, yeoman of Middleboro. Witnesses: Edward WINSLOW, Edward WINSLOW Jr.

William WASHBURN et al to **Asa HUNT** of Middleborough MA. <Plymouth Co.Deeds 69:144>
...9 Sept. 1784, William WASHBURN of Plympton, Consider BENSON, Elizabeth BENSON, David VAUGHAN, Phebe VAUGHAN and Mercy WASHBURN, all of Middleborough and Isaac WASHBURN of Rochester, for £39. 12s, sold to Asa HUNT...three acre fresh meadow in Plimton, being part of four acres which our father Ephraim WASHBURN dec'd bought of Nathaniel THOMAS, being the whole of that piece of fresh meadow set off to our mother Mary WASHBURN in the division of our said father's estate, excepting two elevenths which belongs to our brother John WASHBURN and the heirs of our late sister Jemima MANDELL/RANDELL(sp) dec'd. Witnesses: Noah FEARING, David BURGES. Ack. by all 29 Sept. 1784. Rec. 6 Aug. 1789.

John MATTHEWS of Rochester MA to **Japheth WASHBURN** of Rochester MA. <Plymouth Co.Deeds 58:170>
...8 Apr. 1773, John MATTHEWS conveys to Japheth WASHBURN, blacksmith...land in Rochester being a part of a parcel I bought of Capt. Edward WINSLOW of Rochester and contains by estimation three acres and three quarters.

Japheth WASHBURN of Rochester MA to **Hopestill BISBEE**. <Plymouth Co.Deeds 63:160>
...11 Feb. 1780, Japheth WASHBURN conveys to Hopestill BISBEE...all my homestead land that I now live upon and all the lands that I bought of the widow Judith O MAY of Middleboro and John MATTHEW of Rochester, being eighteen and three quarters acres...bounded by land of Caleb COMBS. Wf Priscilla WASHBURN releases dower. Witnesses: Caleb COMBS, Isaac THOMAS. Ack. 10 Mar. 1784. Rec. 7 July 1785.

Joshua RAYMOND of Middleborough MA to **Japheth WASHBURN** of Middleborough.<Plymouth Co.Deeds 69:19>
...3 Sept. 1783, Joshua RAYMOND conveys to Japheth WASHBURN, blacksmith...60 acres, being part of lots 51 and 52 in the South Purchase. Wf Grace RAYMOND signs.

Japheth WASHBURN of Middleborough MA to **Jonathan SHAW**. <Plymouth Co.Deeds 69:210>
...3 Mar. 178( ), Japheth WASHBURN, blacksmith, confirms unto Jonathan SHAW...60 acres in Middleborough, being lots 51 and 52 in the South Purchase. Wf Priscilla WASHBURN signs. Witnesses: Ichabod BENSON, Benajah LEONARD. Ack. 8 Apr. 1789. Rec. 4 June 1790.

Japheth WASHBURN of Middleborough MA to **Benoni LUCAS**. <Plymouth Co.Deeds 69:209>
...26 Mar. 1787, Japheth WASHBURN, blacksmith confirms to Benoni LUCAS...one acre fresh meadow in

Plympton on the Weweantick River...being the whole of my share of meadow set off to me in the division of my honored father, Ephraim WASHBURN's estate. Ack. 14 July 1787. Rec. 1790.

Japheth WASHBURN of Middleborough MA to **David VAUGHAN.** <Plymouth Co.Deeds 138:73>
...(?faint), Japheth WASHBURN conveys to David VAUGHAN...2 acres, being part of the homestead farm whereon William (?faint) late of Middleborough owned...Rec. 19 Mar. 1819

Japheth WASHBURN of Middleborough to **Foxwell THOMAS** of Middleborough. <Plymouth Co.Deeds 147:252>
...28 Jan. 1788, Japheth WASHBURN, blacksmith, for £28, sells to Foxwell THOMAS...(most of the pencilled writing is too faint to read)...mentions 125th and 141st lots in the South Purchase of Middleborough, said lots set off to John WASHBURN in the division of the estate of his father, Ephraim WASHBURN, dec'd of Plympton. Wf Priscilla WASHBURN signs. Ack. by Japheth 4 Jan. 1796. Rec. 13 May 1823.

Samuel NORRIS of Wareham MA to **Japhet WASHBURN** of Plimpton MA. <Plymouth Co.Deeds 58:96>
...7 Dec. 1773, Samuel NORRIS, yeoman & wf Lydia, for £14.2s8d, sell to Japhet WASHBURN, blacksmith...all our share of land in Plimpton that came to us by our honored Father Ephraim WASHBURN, late of Plimpton, dec'd. Witness: Isaac BOWLER Jr. Rec. 7 July 1774.

Samuel NORRIS of New Sandwich MA to **Samuel NORRIS Jr.** of Plymouth MA. <Plymouth Co.Deeds 77:129>
...30 Apr. 1794, Samuel NORRIS, yeoman, of New Sandwich without the bounds of any town but in the County of Lincoln and State of Massachusetts, do hereby constitute and appoint Samuel NORRIS Jr., yeoman...my lawful attorney to sell a tract of land in Wareham at White Island Pond...which I own in common with Jabez BESSEE of Wareham. Witnesses: Moses WING, Martha WING.

Melvin NORRIS of Wayne ME. <sworn affidavit>
...I, Melvin NORRIS, of Wayne, County of Kennebec and State of Maine, born Oct. 17, 1826, son of Ephraim NORRIS and Temperance (BILLINGTON) Norris and grandson of Josiah NORRIS and Militiah (SMITH) Norris, know that Jemima (NORRIS) Lane, the wife of Giddings LANE, of Leeds, ME (dec'd) to be a sister of my grandfather, Josiah NORRIS and that the said Josiah NORRIS and Jemima (NORRIS) Lane were the children of Samuel NORRIS and Lydia (WASHBURN) Norris, who came to Wayne, then New Sandwich, Maine, about the year 1785, from Wareham, Mass. Sworn to 25 Nov. 1897, by Melvin NORRIS, before B.F. BRADFORD, Notary Public.

Estate of **Rowland WASHBURN**, mariner of Wareham MA. <Plymouth Co.PR #22078>
<original> Citation 5 Aug. 1794, **Abigail STEVENS**, widow and Paul STEVENS, both of Wareham, cited to appear at Court to show cause why administration on the estate of Rowland WASHBURN should not be committed unto his father **William WASHBURN** of Carver. Citation served 6 Aug. 1794 by Elisha BURGESS, Constable of Wareham. <34:9> Letter/Bond 13 Aug. 1794, Rowland THACHER of Wareham, app'td admr. Sureties: John FEARING & Paul STEVENS, yeomen of Wareham. Witnesses: Nathan TOBEY, Timothy THACHER. <original> Citation 15 Apr. 1795, **William WASHBURN**, yeoman & wf Sarah, of Carver, Perez WASHBURN and Jemima WASHBURN, spinster, all of Carver, cited to appear at Court holden at Caleb LORING's, Innholder in Plympton, to answer complaint of Rowland THACHER for with holding goods belonging to the estate of Rowland WASHBURN. Citation served 17 Apr. 1795 by Benjamin WHITE Constable of Carver.

Guardianship of Child of **Rowland WASHBURN** of Wareham MA. <Plymouth Co.PR #22080>
<26:306> Letter/Bond 12 Aug. 1794, **Abigail STEVENS**, widow, of Wareham, app'td guardian of **Sally Stevens WASHBURN**, minor under 14. Sureties: David NYE, Esq. & Paul STEVENS of Wareham. Witnesses: Perez WASHBURN, Isaac LOTHROP. <36:238> Account 12 Oct. 1796 of guardian.

Estate of **Benjamin LEACH Jr.**, cooper/husbandman of Bridgewater MA. <Plymouth Co.PR #12415>
<14:67> Letter/Bond 3 May 1756, **Hannah LEACH**, widow, app'td admx. Sureties: James KEITH, blacksmith & William HOOPER, bricklayer, both of Bridgewater. Witnesses: Josiah EDSON Jr., Edward WINSLOW. <14:267> 21 July 1756, Josiah EDSON & Ephraim KEITH of Bridgewater app'td commissioners to examine claims of creditors.<14:268> List of claims: Nathaniel SNELL, John BRATTLES, Samuel EDSON Treat PERKINS, Maj. John JOHNSON, Silvanus BLOSSOM, James KEITH, Joseph LATHAM, Zepheniah KEITH, James KEITH. Oath by commissioners, 27 Nov. 1756. <14:398> Inventory taken 26 Apr. 1756 by Joseph WASHBURN, Amos KEITH, Israel WASHBURN who made oath 1 May 1756; oath of admx. 3 May 1756.<14:436> Insolvency 10 Oct. 1757, widow being left with a family of small children. <14:442> Account 10 Oct. 1757 of admx. Paid Dr. SHAW's bill.

Guardianship of Child of **Benjamin LEACH Jr.** of Bridgewater MA. <Plymouth Co.PR #12445>
<15:459>...4 Feb. 1760, **Jedediah LEACH**, minor above 14, made choice of Edward HAWARD Jr. as his guardian. Witnesses: Edward HAWARD, James HAWARD. <original> Bond of guardian. 3 Mar. 1760. Sureties: Edward HAWARD & Nathan HAWARD of Bridgewater. Witnesses: Jonathan HAWARD, William BROWN Jr.

Will of **Joseph LEACH**, yeoman of Bridgewater MA. <Plymouth Co.PR #12450>
<16:36>...dated 18 Mar. 1755, to wf **Anna**, improvement of real estate until son **Jephthah** comes of age; to son **Benjamin LEACH**, 100 acres bought of Selectman of Bridgewater adjoining 4 acres swamp land my Father gave me, half right in cedar swamps and saw mill; to son **Jephthah LEACH** whole of homestead and half right in cedar swamps and saw mill; to six daughters, viz: **Rhoda, Dinah, Orpha, Lois, Eunice** and **Cloe,** all the estate my father gave me in his last will. Witnesses: Thomas HOOPER, Zephaniah WILLIS, Bithiah WILLIS. Pr. 1 Dec. 1760, Israel WASHBURN of Raynham, exr. <16:201> Inventory taken by appraisers Joseph PHINNEY, Zephaniah WILLIS and William HOOPER who made oath 23 Jan. 1761, oath of admr. 3 Aug. 1761. <25:442> Assignment 22 Feb. 1779 by commis-

sioners, Ebenezer AMES, Thomas HOOPER, Joshua WHITE; one tenth of real estate set off to David ALDEN, admr. of estate of Isaiah LEACH, late of Bridgewater.

Estate of **Jephthah LEACH**, yeoman of Bridgewater MA. <Plymouth Co.PR #12446>
<original> Bond 7 Dec. 1779, of John SHAW of Raynham, admr. on estate of Jephthah LEACH, supposed to have been lost at sea. Sureties: Hezekiah HOOPER, gent. of Bridgewater and Benjamin RAMSDELL, labourer of Pembroke. Witness: Stephen RANDALL. <originals> Petition 7 Jan. 1780 of several of the heirs, representing that sd Jephthah hath for several years absented himself & praying that his only Brother, **Benjamin LEACH**, take charge of his property. Signed by widow **Annah LEACH**, Seth PACKARD Jr., William KEITH. On 1 Jan. 1780, Kenricke WILBER testified that while at Yorke in the first campaign, a man told him that he saw Jephthah LEACH in North Carolina not long before. Petition 30 Aug. 1783 of Caleb FOBES that James LEACH be app'td admr., signed by heirs: Edward FOBES David ALDEN and Seth PACKARD. Petition 10 Nov. 1783...Whereas your honour hath app'td Capt. John SHAW admr., sd Capt. SHAW doth agree with the other heirs that James LEACH be app'td, signed by: Capt. Jno. SHAW, John SHAW & Benjamin LEACH. <27:144> Letter/Bond 2 Feb. 1784, James LEACH, yeoman of Bridgewater app'td admr. Sureties: Hezekiah HOOPER, gent. and Eleazer CARY, yeoman, both of Bridgewater. Witnesses: William DREW, Andrew CROSWELL. <29:104> Warrant to appraise Inventory to Hezekiah HOOPER & James LEACH of Bridgewater and Joshua WHITE of Middleboro, who made oath 10 Nov. 1783; oath of admr. 1 Mar. 1784; dower set off to widow **Annah LEACH**. <29:210> Account 4 Oct. 1784 of admr. Debts: Benjamin LEACH, Edward FOBES, Seth PACKARD, James WALKER, William KEITH, David ALDEN, widow **Anna LEACH**.

Estate of **Isaiah LEACH** of Bridgewater MA. <Plymouth Co.PR #12441>
<23:182> Letter/Bond 7 Dec. 1778, David ALDEN, yeoman of Middleborough app'td admr. Sureties: Jeremiah WASHBURN & Simeon WOOD, yeomen of Bridgewater. Witnesses: Warren WESTON, Zephaniah WILLIS. <25:443> Inventory taken 18 Feb. 1779 by Thomas HOOPER, Elijah AMES, Daniel FOBES; incl. thirty acres given him by his Grandfather LEACH and fourteen acres which is his right in Benjamin LEACH's land; oath by appraisers 22 Feb. 1779, oath by admr. 6 Mar. 1780.

Will of **John FOBES** of Potsdanz(sp) NY. <no source>
...20 Nov. 1838, mentions present wife **Electa FOBES**...my wife by second marriage, she has children and so have I, at the time of our marriage she had both real & personal estate, it was mutually understood & agreed by us that my estate should be divided among my heirs & her estate among her heirs; eldest son **Peris FOBES**, second son **John FOBES Jr.**, eldest dau **Clarrissa POST**, daus **Almira SPENCER, Lucina BROCKINS, Abigail COOCK, Lucy WHEELER, Orpha GLINES.** Pr. 18 Mar 1842.

MICRO #12 OF 30

Jonathan LEACH of Bridgewater MA to **Nathan LEACH** of Bridgewater. <Plymouth Co.Deeds 55:184>
...7 Sept. 1770, Jonathan LEACH, yeoman, for Ł200 silver money, sold to Nathan LEACH, labourer... four pieces of land in Bridgewater...(first) is the north end of my house lands with my dwelling house & barn, 56 acres, bounded by land of Joseph BASSETT, Samuel PACKARD and land which was formerly Stephen LEACH's...(second) is half lot in Little Cedar Swamp...(third) lot in the Great Meadow between the Great Island and the Little Island and is in partnership with William LEACH & others...(fourth) is my third part of a lot of meadow and a fifth part of a purchase right of undivided land within the eight mile grant in Bridgewater. Wf Abigail LEACH signs. Witnesses: Josiah CROCKER, Joshua PACKARD 2d. Ack. by Jonathan 13 Sept.1770. Rec. 25 Sept. 1770.

Ezra WASHBURN et al, Agreement. <Plymouth Co.Deeds 38:181>
...10 Dec. 1744...Agreement to build & operate a furnace, between Nehemiah WASHBURN of Bridgewater, Isaac CHURCHILL, yeoman of Plympton, John BENSON, gent., Benjamin WASHBURN, gent., John BOLTON, yeoman, Benjamin PRATT, bricklayer, Thomas HAYWARD 3d, husbandman, David LEACH, husbandman, Amos KEITH, yeoman, Joseph PRATT, husbandman, Israel KEITH, husbandman, Jonathan CARVER, blacksmith, Samuel ANDREWS, shipwright, Joseph LEONARD Jr., yeoman, Henry WASHBURN, husbandman, Ezra WASHBURN, cordwainer...all of Bridgewater and Josiah DEAN & Israel WASHBURN of Raynham. Ack. 24 June 1746. (See below.)

Solomon LEACH of Bridgewater MA to **Ezra WASHBURN** of Bridgewater. <Plymouth Co.Deeds 38:82>
...6 Mar. 1745/6, Solomon LEACH, yeoman, for Ł85, sold to Ezra WASHBURN, cordwainer...15 acres in Middleborough near the bridge upon the River near land of Capt. Nehemiah WASHBURN, it being the south westerly part of the land I bought of James THOMAS at publick vendue. Ack. 18 Apr. 1746. Rec. 23 June 1746.

Ezra WASHBURN of Middleboro MA to **David LEACH** of Bridgewater MA. <Plymouth Co.Deeds 39:141>
...10 Jan. 1746, Ezra WASHBURN, cordwainer sells to David LEACH, yeoman...his interest in Titicut Furnace in Bridgewater. Ack. same day. (See above.)

Ezra WASHBURN of Middleboro MA to **Silvanus EATON** of Middleboro. <Plymouth Co.Deeds 63:72>
...13 July 1772, Ezra WASHBURN, cordwinder, for Ł66.13s4d, sold to Silvanus EATON, yeoman...my homestead farm in Middleboro, 18 acres, bounded by land of Josiah DEAN...the north & easterly line being according to a settlement I made with Ezekiel CURTIS 4 Mar. 1766. Wf Susanna WASHBURN signs. Witnesses: Joshua WHITE, Zebulon WHITE, Zadock LEACH. Ack. 11 Nov. 1772 by Ezra. Rec. 19 May 1774 or 1784 (original not clear).

Ichabod PACKARD of Oakham MA to **Ezra WASHBURN** of Oakham. <Worcester Co.Deeds 82:487>
...7 Oct. 1773, Ichabod PACKARD, yeoman, for Ł12, sold to Ezra WASHBURN, yeoman...10 acres in Oakham bounded by the mill road to ye County road that leads from Brookfield to old Rutland and land of Capt. BOTHWELL and sd WASHBURN. Witnesses: Daniel DELAND, Alexander BOTHWELL Jr. Ack. 11 Apr. 1780. Rec. 5 June 1780.

===

Nathan ABBOTT of Stafford CT to **Ezra WASHBURN** of Stafford CT. <Stafford CT Deeds 5:423>
...1 Oct. 1781, Nathan ABBOTT, for Ł130, sold to Ezra WASHBURN...40 acres in Stafford bounded by land of sd ABBOTT and Richard LAIRD Jr. Witnesses: Daniel ALDEN, Hannah ALDEN. Ack. 1 Oct. 1781 by Nathan. Rec. 9 Oct. 1782.

===

Nathan ABBOTT of Stafford CT to **Ezra WASHBURN** of Stafford CT. <Stafford CT Deeds 5:421>
...6 Mar. 1782, Nathan ABBOTT, for Ł18, sold to Ezra WASHBURN...60 acres in Stafford bounded by land of Richard LAIRD, Mr. TOWNSEND and sd ABBOTT. Witnesses: Abraham FULLER Jr., Daniel ABBOTT. Ack. 10 Oct. 1782 by Nathan. Rec. 9 Oct. 1782.

===

James DUNBAR of Oakham MA to **Benjamin DUNBAR** of Oakham MA. <Worcester Co.Deeds 81:474>
...28 May 1778, James DUNBAR, yeoman, for Ł250, sold to Benjamin DUNBAR, yeoman...57 acres in Oakham bounded by land of Capt. John CRAWFORD. Witnesses: Asa BRIGGS, Ezra WASHBURN Jr. Ack. & Rec. 29 June 1779.

===

Ezra WASHBURN of Oakham MA to **William BOTHWELL** of Oakham. <Worcester Co.Deeds 137:36>
...10 Apr. 1780, Ezra WASHBURN, yeoman, for Ł6000, sold to William BOTHWELL, yeoman...30 acres, the westerly part of the farm I now live on...bounded by land of sd BOTHWELL and CRAWFORD. Witnesses: Thomas HALE Jr., Ezra WASHBURN. Ack. 13 May 1784 by Ezra. Rec. 17 Apr. 1799.

===

Capt. Josiah CONVERSE of Stafford CT to **Ezra WASHBURN et al** of Oakham MA. <Stafford CT Deeds> <5:405>...5 Apr. 1782, Josiah CONVERSE, for Ł310, sold to Ezra WASHBURN and Benjamin DUNBAR of Oakham in the county of Worcester...100 acres with a dwelling house & barn in Stafford...and is the ninth and tenth lots on the east side of vilidge Street. Witnesses: William WASHBURN/WORSHBURN, Isaac PINNEY. Ack. by Josiah 5 Apr. 1782. Rec. 5 Apr. 1782.

===

Ezra & William WASHBURN of Oakham MA to **John BOTHWELL** of Oakham. <Worcester Co.Deeds 92:435>
...30 Mar. 1782, Ezra WASHBURN & William WASHBURN, yeomen, for Ł160, sold to John BOTHWELL, yeoman...48 acres in Oakham bounded by land of John CRAWFORD, William BOTHWELL and John BOTHWELL. Witnesses: William CRAWFORD, Ichabod PACKARD. Ack. 13 May 1784 by Ezra. Rec. 18 May 1784.

===

Nathan ABBOTT of Stafford CT to **Ezra WASHBURN** of Stafford. <Stafford CT Deeds 7:143>
...7 Apr. 1783, Nathan ABBOTT, for Ł42, sold to Ezra WASHBURN...20 acres in Stafford bounded by land of sd WASHBURN and John TOWNSEND. Witnesses: Philip SCOTT, Isaac FOOT. Ack. 7 Apr.1783. Rec. 10 Oct. 1793.

===

Estate of **Ezra WASHBURN Jr.** of Stafford CT. <Stafford CT PR>
<4:-->...15 May 1793, widow **Lucy WASHBURN/WORSHBURN**, app'td admx. Surety: Robert MOOR of Stafford. <4:--> 16 May 1793, Robert MOOR app'td gdn. of **Libeus WASHBURN**, minor of about 14 yrs. <4:66> Inventory, 15 May 1793, incl. 86 acres, Ł200; 1 cowe, Ł3.13.6.; 1 colt, Ł8; 1 black mare, Ł6.5.; 3 swine, Ł2.2.; (numerous listings for bedding, tools, household utensils). <4:165> Addition to Inventory incl. 40 weight of flax, 7 bushels rye, 3 bushels Indian corn, 1 bushel wheat, 40 weight pork, 30 bushels potatoes. Account 16 Dec. 1793, of admx. <4:204> 13 Nov. 1794, Joshua BLODGET, Robert MOOR & Daniel MEACHAM, all of Stafford, app'td to distribute estate to following heirs, viz: widow **Lucy WASHBURN, Keziah NASON** wf of William, **Lucy WOODWARD** wf of John, **Silas WASHBURN, Ezra WASHBURN, Libbeus WASHBURN, Simon WASHBURN, Peter WASHBURN, Andrew WASHBURN** and **Voadisa WASHBURN.** <4:--> 13 Nov. 1794, **Lucy WASHBURN** app'td gdn. of **Voadisa WASHBURN,** minor of about 8 yrs, **Andrew WASHBURN**, minor of about 10 yrs and **Peter WASHBURN**, minor of about 12 yrs. Surety: Alden BLODGET of Stafford. 13 Nov. 1794, Alden BLODGET app'td gdn. of **Simon WASHBURN,** minor of about 14 yrs. Surety: **Lucy WASHBURN.** Account 15 Nov. 1794, of admx. <4:--> Distribution 31 Aug. 1795 by Joshua BLODGET and Robert MORE. (Note: Some records have no page numbering.)

===

James PEARL of Stafford CT to **David NORRIS** of Stafford CT. <Stafford CT Deeds 8:363>
...8 Mar. 1796, James PEARL & wf Lucy, for Ł70, sold to David NORRIS...15 acres set out to Lucy in lieu of dower in the real estate of her former husband, Ezra WASHBURN. Witnesses: Rufus FISK, Sarah LILLIBRIDGE. Ack. 31 Oct. 1796 by James & Lucy. Rec. 30 Dec. 1800.

===

James PEARL of Hampton CT to **James PEARL** of E. Windsor CT. <Stafford CT Deeds 8:71>
...29 Nov. 1799, James PEARL, for $710.00, sold to James PEARL...two parcels containing 115 acres in Stafford. Witnesses: Richard PEARL, Philip PEARL. Ack. 5 Dec. 1799. Rec. 21 Feb. 1800.

===

John WOODWARD of Hancock VT to **David NORRIS** of Stafford CT. <Stafford CT Deeds 8:362>
...7 Mar. 1797, John WOODWARD & wf Lucy, for $150.00, sold to David NORRIS...all our rights in the farm lately belonging to Ezra WASHBURN Jr., late of Stafford, dec'd...which came to the said Lucy by heirship of her father's estate incl. her rights in the widow's thirds. Witnesses: John PHELPS, Jacob JOHNSON, Enoch EMERSON, Chadwick CHAFFE. Ack. 7 Mar. 1797 at Stafford by John, 27 Mar. 1797 at Rochester VT by Lucy. Rec. 30 Dec. 1800.

===

William NASON of Stafford CT to **Silas WASHBURN** of Stafford CT. <Stafford CT Deeds 7:491>
...22 Dec. 1794, William NASON & wf Kezia, for Ł12, sold to Silas WASHBURN...all our right in

land in Stafford...which was set off and distributed to us out of our Honoured Father's estate, Ezra WASHBURN Jr., late of Stafford, dec'd, incl. our right in the widow's thirds. Witnesses: Solomon MOULTON, Joseph HIXSON. Ack. 22 Dec. 1794 by William & Kezia. Rec. 22 Sept. 1795.

Robert MORE of Stafford CT to **David NORRIS** of Stafford. <Stafford CT Deeds 7:566>
...2 Apr. 1796, Robert MORE, for Ŀ36, received from David NORRIS, binds himself...whereas Libeas WASHBURN, a minor and son to Ezra WASHBURN Jr., late of Stafford dec'd, has this day sold all his right or share in his Father's estate together with his right in the widow's dower...that the sd Libeas WASHBURN, a minor, shall in a reasonable time after he arrives at the age of twenty one years shall well and truly execute a good warrantee deed togeather with an acquitance to his mother's thirds. Witnesses: Joseph RIDDLE, Daniel SAMSON. Ack. 2 Apr. 1796. Rec. 5 Apr. 1796.

Libeus WASHBURN of Stafford MA to **David NORRIS** of Stafford. <Stafford CT Deeds 8:325>
...24 Feb. 1800, Libeus WASHBURN, laborer, for $200.00, sold to David NORRIS...all rights in the farm lately belonging to Ezra WASHBURN Jr., late of Stafford dec'd...which came to sd Libeus by heir ship from his father's estate, incl. widow's dower. Witnesses: John PHELPS, David YOUNG. Ack 24 Feb. 1800 by Libeus. Rec. 30 Dec. 1800.

Silas WASHBURN of Stafford CT to **Cephas PERKINS** of Stafford. <Stafford CT Deeds 8:206>
...22 Sept. 1795, Silas WASHBURN, for Ŀ40, sold to Cephas PERKINS...all my right in two parcels of land in Stafford...which was set off and distributed to me and to William NASON & wf Kezia out of my Honoured Father's estate, Ezra WASHBURN Jr., late of Stafford dec'd, incl. widow's dower. Witnesses: Daniel MEACHAM, Jerusha MEACHAM. Ack. 22 Sept. 1795 by Silas.

Ezra WASHBURN of Rochester VT to **David NORRIS** of Stafford CT. <Stafford CT Deeds 8:249>
...21 Mar. 1797, Ezra WASHBURN, for $60.00, sold to David NORRIS...all rights in land in Stafford ...set off to me out of the estate of my Honoured Father Ezra WASHBURN Jr., late of Stafford dec'd, incl. widow's thirds. Witnesses: Joseph ALDEN, Daniel SAMSON. Ack. 21 Mar. 1797 by Ezra. Rec. 30 Dec. 1800.

Vodisa AUSTIN of Rochester VT to **Liba WASHBURN** of Pitsfield VT. <Stafford CT Deeds 8:488>
...18 Dec. 1802, Vodisa AUSTIN, for $50.00, sold to Liba WASHBURN...all rights in estate of my Honoured Father Ezra WASHBURN of Stafford CT, dec'd...In witness whereof with the free consent of my beloved husband I hereunto set my hand. Husband Phineas AUSTIN signs. Witnesses: Enoch EMERSON and Eunice EMERSON. Ack. 21 Dec. 1802 by Phineas & Vodisa. Rec. 15 Feb. 1803.

Liba WASHBURN of Pitsfield VT to **William WALBRIDGE** of Monson MA. <Stafford CT Deeds 9:203>
...14 Feb. 1803, Liba WASHBURN, husbandman, for $100.00, sold to William WALBRIDGE...all rights in estate of Honoured Father Ezra WASHBURN of Stafford, dec'd. Witnesses: Eliab ALDEN, Joseph ALDEN. Ack. 14 Feb. 1803 by Liba. Rec. 15 Feb. 1803.

Eliab & Joseph ALDEN of Stafford CT to **David NORRIS** of Stafford. <Stafford CT Deeds 7:619>
...2 Apr. 1796, Eliab ALDIN and Joseph ALDIN, for Ŀ40, quitclaimed to David NORRIS...all our rights in two tracts of land in Stafford which was set off & distributed to William & Kezia NASON and Silas WASHBURN out of the estate of Ezra WASHBURN Jr., late of Stafford dec'd, incl. widow's thirds...being the same parcels of land which we bought of Cephas PERKINS. Witnesses: Daniel SAMSON, Joseph RIDDLE. Ack. 2 Apr. 1796 by Eliab & Joseph. Rec. 5 Apr. 1746.

James KEITH to **Zadock LEACH.** <Plymouth Co.Deeds 53:106>
...25 Sept. 1762...land in Bridgewater MA.

Zadock LEACH of Bridgewater MA to **Giles LEACH** of Bridgewater. <Plymouth Co.Deeds 86:157>
...21 May 1774, Zadock LEACH, yeoman, sells to Giles LEACH, laborer...one half of land & house I bought of Daniel KEITH as admr. on estate of Joseph PERKINS dec'd of widow Martha PERKINS. Wf Susanna LEACH signs. Ack. 25 May 1785 by Zadock. Rec. 7 Aug. 1799.

Estate of **Zadock LEACH,** yeoman of Bridgewater MA. <Plymouth Co.PR #12480>
<30:416> Warrant 5 May 1788, Thomas HOOPER, gent., Solomon KEITH, gent. and Robert FOBES, yeoman, all of Bridgewater, app'td to appraise estate. Inventory taken 29 May 1788; 30 acres with buildings, Ŀ163.8s. Ack. by **Susanna LEACH,** admx., 1 Sept. 1788. <40:380> Warrant 18 Sept. 1805, Solomon ALDEN Jr., gent., Isaac WILBORE, yeoman, both of Bridgewater and Simon BACKUS, yeoman of Middleborough, were app'td to divide estate. Division 1 Oct. 1805, to widow **Susanna LEACH** and the remainder divided into eight equal parts, viz: **Susanna RICHMOND** wf of Edward, **Beza LEACH, Abraham LEACH, Zebedee LEACH, Parney EATON** wf of Apollos, **Rufus LEACH, Zadock LEACH** and **Ezekiel LEACH.**

Guardianship of Children of **Zadock LEACH** of Bridgewater MA. <Plymouth Co.PR #12481>
<26:220> Letter 1 Sept. 1788, **Susanna LEACH** app'td gdn. of **Rufus LEACH, Zadock LEACH** and **Ezekiel LEACH,** minors under 14. Bond 1 Sept. 1788 of **Susanna LEACH,** covers guardianship of **Abraham LEACH, Zebedee LEACH** & **Parnelee LEACH,** minors above 14, and **Rufus LEACH, Zadock LEACH** & **Ezekiel LEACH,** minors under 14.

Apollas EATON of Bridgewater MA to **Zadock LEACH.** <Plymouth Co.Deeds 124:85>
...12 May 1812, Apollas EATON & wf Parna, quit claim to Zadock LEACH...all their right in land in Bridgewater containing about four acres and the widow LEACH's thirds. Rec. 12 Apr. 1814.

Samuel DUNBAR Jr. of Taunton MA to **Zadock LEACH et al.** <Plymouth Co.Deeds 124:93>
...29 Mar. 1814, Samuel DUNBAR Jr. sells to Zadock LEACH et al...land in Bridgewater. Wf Abigail DUNBAR releases dower.

Simeon LEONARD by admx. to **Zadock LEACH.** <Plymouth Co.Deeds 154:117>
...25 June 1817, Phebe LEONARD, admx. of estate of Simeon LEONARD late of Raynham, sells to Zadock LEACH...land in Bridgewater. Ack. 25 June 1817. Rec. 10 Aug. 1825.

Edward RICHMOND of Taunton MA to **Zadock LEACH.** <Plymouth Co.Deeds 154:118>
...24 Apr. 1818, Edward RICHMOND & wf Susanna, quit claim to Zadock LEACH...all their right in estate of our late Father Zadock LEACH, dec'd. Ack. 16 Apr. 1825 by Edward & Susanna. Rec. 10 Aug. 1825.

Mary LEACH to **Zadock LEACH.** <Plymouth Co.Deeds 154:119>
...26 May 1823, Mary LEACH, widow of Abram LEACH, late of Bridgewater dec'd, quit claims to Zadock LEACH...all right to eight acres of land...which was set off to the late widow Susannah LEACH as her right of dower in her husband's, the late Zadock LEACH's, estate...and all personal estate left to the said Susannah LEACH at her decease. Ack. 26 May 1823. Rec. 10 Aug. 1825.

Zebedee LEACH of Bridgewater to **Zadock LEACH.** <Plymouth Co.Deeds 154:118>
...24 Apr. 1818, Zebedee LEACH quit claims to Zadock LEACH...all his right in land formerly belonging to my late Honoured Father Zadock LEACH dec'd...also land I bought of Samuel DUNBAR Jr. in company with the sd Zadock LEACH. Ack. 24 Apr. 1818. Rec. 10 Aug. 1825.

Ichabod MACOMBER of Boston MA to **Zadock LEACH** of Bridgewater MA. <Plymouth Co.Deeds 155:226>
...4 Oct. 1823, Ichabod MACOMBER, merchant, quit claims to Zadock LEACH, yeoman...all my right in the widow thirds as set off from the estate of Zadock LEACH, late of Bridgewater dec'd...it being an undivided right in said thirds. Wf Abigail MACOMBER releases dower. Ack. 4 Oct. 1823. Rec. 10 Aug. 1825.

Jacob WICKER of Leicester MA to **William WICKER** of Hardwick MA. <Worcester Co.Deeds 105:229>
...8 Sept. 1788, Jacob WICKER, yeoman, for Ł300, sold to William WICKER, yeoman...70 acres lying partly in Paxton & Leicester...it being the farm whereon I now live...bounded by land of Jonathan KNIGHT, Isaac CHOATE, Jabez GREEN Jr., Christopher WHEATON and Ezekiel BELLOWS...also 4 acres in Paxton bounded by land of Samuel BRIGHAM, David DAVIS, J. WARE and Ebenezer COGGSWELL...for particulars see my deeds whch I hold from David LYND, A. OLIVER and Ephraim AMSDAL. Witnesses: Seth WASHBURN, Sarah WASHBURN. Ack. & Rec. 10 Sept. 1788.

Estate of **Jacob WICKER** of Leicester MA. <Worcester Co.PR #65384>
<186:479> Bond 28 Mar. 1789 of **James WICKER**, innholder of Boston.. <119:263> Letter, 28 Mar. 1789. <22:232> Warrant to appraise, 28 Mar. 1789 to Jonathan KNIGHT, Ebenezer WHITMORE & Christopher WHEATING, all of Leicester; all 3 sworn 7 Apr. 1789. <466:450> Assent, 30 Mar. 1789...Sir this is to inform you that I refuse to administer on the estate of Jacob WICKER late of Leicester deceased and my oldest son also refuses on the account of his liveing at a distance therefore I should be glad if you would grant the administration to my son **James WICKER** of Paxton, this with respect from Leicester. Signed by **Abial WICKER.** <22:233> Inventory sworn 23 Apr. 1789, personal estate only. <616:239> Insolvency, 23 Apr. 1789. <22:358> Account of admr. Apr. 1790; paid Nathan SERJANT for coffin & bier, 8s; Abraham(sp) RUSSEL for Doctoring in the last sickness, 5s4d; Francis CHOTE for digging grave, 6s.

Abial WICKER et al to **Jonathan KNIGHT** of Leicester MA. <Worcester Co.Deeds 113:411>
...26 Oct. 1791, Abial WICKER & Joseph WICKER, of Leicester and William WICKER, yeoman of Hardwick, for Ł3, sold to Jonathan KNIGHT, yeoman...land in Paxton...bounded by our farm and land the sd Jonathan bought of Eber WHITMORE...sd Jonathan to have a privilege to pass with or without a team through our lands to his. Witnesses: Christopher WHETON, Seth WASHBURN. Ack. 27 Nov. 1791 by Joseph WICKER. Rec. 18 Feb. 1792.

William WICKER of Hardwick MA to **Joseph WICKER** of Leicester MA. <Worcester Co.Deeds 112:359>
...29 Jan. 1791, William WICKER, yeoman, for Ł200, sold to Joseph WICKER, labourer...73 acres partly in Paxton & Leicester...bounded by land of Jonathan KNIGHT, Deacon Isaac CHOATE, Jabez GREEN, Jr., Christopher WHEATING and Lt. Ezekiel BELLOWS...also 5 acre meadow in Paxton bounded by land of Ebenezer COGGSWELL, Samuel BRIGHAM, Deacon David DAVIS and Amos WARE. Susannah WICKER, wf of William, releases dower. Witnesses: Jonathan HOW, Edmund NEWTON. Ack. 31 Jan. 1791 by William. Rec. 6 Oct. 1791.

William WICKER of Harwick MA to **Benjamin RUGGLES 3d** of Hardwick. <Worcester Co.Deeds 125:630>
...18 May 1795, William WICKER, yeoman, for Ł6, sold to Benjamin RUGGLES 3d, yeoman...one acre at the southwest corner of the farm on which I now live...bounded by land of Lemuel GILBERT and sd RUGGLES. Wf Susanna WICKER signs. Ack. 2 Jan. 1796 by William. Rec. 5 Jan. 1796.

William WICKER of Hardwick MA to **John & Lemuel WICKER** of Hardwick. <Worcester Co.Deeds 192:400>
...20 Oct. 1812, William WICKER, yeoman, for $3000.00, sold to John WICKER and Lemuel WICKER... land in Hardwick...bounded by land of Benjamin PAIGE, Samuel COOLEY, RUGGLES and land owned by heirs of Moses FARBUSH.

WORCESTER COUNTY DEEDS: (re: WICKER)

<39:272> 1757, William WICKER to Jacob WICKER.
<72:236> 1774, William WICKER to David WICKER.
<87:116> 1782, Jacob WICKER to Luther WICKER.
<89:408> 1783, James WICKER to Asa STEARNS.
<93:315> 1785, William WICKER to Luther WICKER.
<101:283> 1787, William WICKER to Samuel WICKER.
<102:143> 1787, James WICKER to Timothy PAINE.
<105:229> 1788, Jacob WICKER to William WICKER
<107:19> 1789, Jacob WICKER to Abraham SMITH Jr.
<112:291> 1791, James WICKER to Timothy SPRAGUE.
<120:231> 1794, James WICKER to Ebenezer ESTABROOK Jr.
<192:401> 1815, William WICKER to Jonathan BILLINGS.
<192:403> 1814, William WICKER Jr. to Lemuel WICKER.
<193:245> 1814, Lemuel WICKER to William WICKER.
<192:573> 1815, Lemuel WICKER to Nathan PARK.
<195:233> 1815, Lemuel WICKER to Giles WARNER.
<195:542> 1815, Lemuel WICKER to Martin RUGGLES.
<264:115> 1828, Lemuel WICKER to Masa. BASSETT.

(The following references with year only are given for William WICKER, grantee, being all for that name betw. 1769-1839 in the records of Worcester Co.Deeds: <59:536> 1769; <60:357> 1769; <60:358> 1769; <78:348> 1777; <91:11> 1783; <115:582> 1792; <143:614> 1801; <143:611> 1801; <143:613> 1801; <192:404> 1814; <193:245> 1814; <197:400> 1815.)

Lemuel WICKER of Hardwick MA to **John GILBERT** of Hardwick. <Worcester Co.Deeds 197:387>
...5 Jan. 1815, Lemuel WICKER, blacksmith, for $180.00, sold to John GILBERT...13 acres in Hardwick...part of the farm formerly owned by Joseph WICKER...bounded by land of heirs of Moses FARBUSH and heirs of John PAIGE. Witnesses: Thomas WESTURN, William WICKER, Giles WARNER. Ack. 6 Jan 1815 by Lemuel. Rec. 4 July 1815.

Lemuel & William WICKER of Hardwick MA to **Jonathan BILLINGS** of same. <Worcester Co.Deeds 197:401>
...21 Jan. 1815, Lemuel WICKER and William WICKER, yeomen, for $140.00, sold to Jonathan BILLINGS ...13 acres in Hardwick...bounded by land of Lemuel NEWTON. Witnesses: Seth WILLIS, Mark HASKELL, Ezra RUGGLES, Samuel EASTMAN. Ack. 21 Jan. 1815 by Lemuel & William. Rec. 7 July 1815.

Estate of **Joseph WICKER** of Hardwick MA. <Worcester Co.PR #65385>
<185:38> Petition 18 Dec. 1795 by widow **Dorothy WICKER** and William WICKER, a principal creditor of Hardwick. <186:480> Bond 23 Dec. 1795, of Jonathan FLYNT of Hardwick, admr. Witness: Levina WICKER. <122:296> Letter, 23 Dec. 1795. <274:305> Notice, 23 Dec. 1795. <624:281> Warrant to appraise. <26:505> Inventory, 30 Dec. 1795. <401:525> Widow's allowance, 5 Jan. 1796.

WORCESTER CO. PROBATE: (re: WICKER)

1789	Jacob WICKER of Leicester	adm.	#65384
1795	Joseph WICKER of Hardwick	adm.	#65385
1803	David WICKER, of Paxton	adm.	#65381
1815	Samuel WICKER of Paxton	gdn.	#65386
1815	Samuel WICKER of Paxton	will	#65387
1851	David WICKER of Leicester	will	#65382
1853	George S. WICKER of Oxford	adoption	#65383

MICRO #13 OF 30

Heirs of **John WASHBURN** of Bridgewater MA to **John ROGERS** of Boston MA. <Bristol Co.Deeds 4:83>
...1 Apr. 1700, John WASHBURN, Thomas WASHBURN, Joseph WASHBURN, Samuel WASHBURN, Jonathan WASHBURN, James WASHBURN, Samuel KINGSLEY & wf Mary, Elizabeth SOLE, John AMES & wf Sarah, all of Bridgewater, heirs of John WASHBURN, dec'd, sell to John ROGERS, merchant of Boston...one share of land granted to John WASHBURN, as an Ancient Servant, at Saconet or elsewhere as may appear by the records of the Court of Plimouth bearing date June 1662. Ack. by all 15 Apr. 1702. Rec. 8 Mar 1702/3. (Bowman questions whether the name Elizabeth SOLE above should be Elizabeth SELE. The deed was also transcribed in MD 15:252>

Samuel KINGSLEY of Bridgwater MA to **James KEITH** of Bridgewater. <Bristol Co.Deeds 4:364>
...28 July 1702, Samuel KINGSLEY sells to James KEITH, minister of Bridgewater...land in Taunton North Purchase. Wf Mary KINGSLEY signs. Ack. by both 28 July 1702. Rec. 27 Jan.1704/5.

Estate of **Samuel KINSLEY/KINGSLEY** of Taunton North Purchase MA. <Bristol Co.PR>
<original> Bond 13 July 1714, son **Samuel KINSLEY** of Taunton N. Purchase, admr. <3:194> Inventory 19 Feb. 1713/4 (says he d. 17 Dec. 1713). <3:247> Account, 10 Nov. 1715. <4:44> Guardianship of 2 youngest daus. <4:141> Division 5 Oct. 1722, mentions widow (unnamed); eldest son **Samuel KINSLEY**; **Benjamin KINSLEY** (2nd & youngest son); **Hannah HAYWARD** (eldest dau); **Sarah HAYWARD** (2nd dau); **Mary WILLIS** (3rd dau); **Susanna KINSLEY** (4th dau); **Abigail KINSLEY** (5th dau) and **Bethiah KINSLEY** (6th).

Estate of **Benjamin KINGSLEY** of Easton MA. <Bristol Co.PR>
<17:202> Inventory, 4 July 1759. <23:605> Division, 1775, to following heirs, viz: widow **Priscilla KINGSLEY**; eldest son **Silas KINGSLEY**, dec'd; **Benjamin KINGSLEY** (2d son); **Zebadiah KINGSLEY** (3d son); **Abiel KINGSLEY** (4th son); dau **Martha LATHROP**, dec'd; dau **Hannah RIPLEY** wf of Robert. <23:609> Receipt.

BRISTOL COUNTY DEEDS: (re: KINSLEY)

<14:139> - 1716, Thomas & Mary WILLIS.
<15:476> - , William HAYWARD to Edward HAYWARD.
<15:541> - 26 Nov. 1723, Susanna KINSLEY of Bridgewater, dau of Samuel KINSLEY to Benjamin KINSLEY of North Purchase, mother's thirds. Ack. 27 Oct. 1724.
<15:542> - 30 Aug. 1723, Susanna KINSLEY, dau of Samuel KINSLEY to Benjamin KINSLEY, land belonging to Susanna from estate of Samuel KINSLEY. Ack. 27 Oct. 1724.
<35:509> - 15 Apr. 1728, Bethiah (KINSLEY) Brett.
<37:89> - 15 Apr. 1728, Bethiah (KINSLEY) Brett.
<35:510> - 26 Apr. 1728, Abigail KINSLEY of Easton, 5th dau of Samuel KINSLEY.
<37:82> - 4 Mar. 1733, Edward HAYWARD & wf Hannah to Benjamin KINSLEY.
<27:407> - 1733/4, Benjamin KINSLEY to Edward HAYWARD of Easton. Ack. 1738.
<28:305> - 1740, Samuel KINSLEY et al to "minister".
<35:226> - 1744/5, Benjamin KINSLEY & Edward HAYWARD sell land.
<35:365> - 1745/6, William HAYWARD & wf Abigail sell land.
<39:230> - 1752, Samuel KINSLEY and Benjamin KINSLEY, grantees.
<50:99> - 1765, Abigail HAYWARD, widow et al, division.
<54:141> - 1771, Benjamin KINSLEY from Samuel PACKARD 3d.
<54:559> - 1772, Edward HAYWARD et al, division.
<59:57> - 1778, Samuel KINSLEY & wf Hannah and Jonathan HOWARD, all of Bridgewater.
<64:470> - 1785, Samuel KINSLEY & wf Hannah and Jonathan HOWARD, grantors as above.

William HAYWARD of Bridgewater MA to **Israel ALGER.** <Bristol Co.Deeds 35:365>
..21 Mar. 1745/6, William HAYWARD & wf Abigail, sell to Israel ALGER...their homestead in Bridgewater & Easton...bounded by land of Benjamin KINSLEY. Ack. by both 22 Mar. 1745/6. Rec. 11 Mar 1746/7.

BRISTOL COUNTY DEEDS: (re: HAYWARD)

<4:215> - William HAYWARD to Edward BOSWORTH. Rec. 11 Oct. 1703.
<4:343> - William HAYWARD to Samuel KENT et al. Rec. 8 Dec. 1704.
<10:95> - William HAYWARD to William CHASE. Rec. 9 May 1716.
<10:149> - William HAYWARD to John REED. Rec. 25 June 1716.
<15:476> - William HAYWARD to Edward HAYWARD. Rec. 9 Sept. 1724.
<18:145> - William HAYWARD to Isaac LEONARD. Rec. 10 Apr. 1728.
<19:331> - William HAYWARD to Thomas MANLEY, Sr. Rec. 14 July 1730.
<45:195> - William HAYWARD to Edward HAYWARD. Rec. 21 Aug. 1761.
<45:196> - William HAYWARD to John HAYWARD. Rec. 21 Aug. 1761.
<45:196> - William HAYWARD to Edward HAYWARD. Rec. 21 Aug. 1761.
<45:494> - William HAYWARD to John HAYWARD. Rec. 19 Feb. 1762.
<45:495> - William HAYWARD to Jonathan HAYWARD. Rec. 19 May 1762.
<45:497> - William HAYWARD to Edward HAYWARD. Rec. 19 May 1762.
<47:108> - William HAYWARD to William THAYER. Rec. 23 Apr. 1764.
<50:99> - Abigail HAYWARD et al, division. Rec. 30 Sept. 1765.
<50:281> - Abigail HAYWARD to Abraham GASHET, Jr. Rec. 30 Oct. 1765.
<49:466> - William HAYWARD to Jonathan HAYWARD. Rec. 31 Oct. 1765.
<51:35> - Abigail HAYWARD to Abraham GUSHEE, Jr. Rec. 20 Nov. 1767.
<52:408> - Abigail HAYWARD to Elijah WILBORE. Rec. 18 Nov. 1769.
<54:426> - William HAYWARD to Lemuel WILLIS. Rec. 23 June 1772.
<59:443> - 31 Oct. 1772, Abigail HAYWARD, widow of Bridgewater to Ichabod RANDALL. Ack. 25 June 1774. Rec. 9 Nov. 1779.
<56:179> - May 1773, Abigail HAYWARD, widow of Bridgewater to Elisha DEAN. Ack. 25 June 1774. Rec. 14 July 1774.
<56:162> - 20 June 1774, Abigail HAYWARD, widow of Bridgewater, dau of Jonathan WILLIAMS of Taunton to Jonathan HAYWARD. Ack. 25 June, Rec. 8 July 1774.

BRISTOL COUNTY DEEDS: (re: Benjamin KINGSLEY, grantee, all to 1800)

<26:523> - 19 Mar. 1733, Benjamin KINGSLEY, blacksmith of Swansea from Stephen BOWEN. Ack. 20 June 1738. Rec. 9 Sept. 1741.
<33:122> - , Benjamin KINGSLEY from Jacob CHACE et ux. Rec. 15 Dec. 1744.
<33:120> - , Benjamin KINGSLEY from 1st Church Swansea.
<34:57> - , Benjamin KINGSLEY et al, petition. Rec. 16 Oct. 1745.
<35:509> - 15 Apr. 1728, Benjamin KINGSLEY from Bethiah KINSLEY. Rec. 14 Sept. 1749.
<35:510> - , Benjamin KINGSLEY from Abigail KINSLEY. Rec. 14 Sept. 1749.
<37:82> - 4 Mar. 1733, Benjamin KINGSLEY, yeoman of Easton from Edward HAYWARD & wf Hannah. Ack by Edward 17 July 1741, by Hannah 15 Jan. 1744. Rec. 15 Sept. 1749.
<37:83> - 26 Apr. 1728, Benjamin KINGSLEY of Easton from Abigail KINSLEY of Easton, land set off unto my honoured mother Mary KINSLEY late wf of Samuel. Ack. 17 July

BRISTOL COUNTY DEEDS, cont-d: (re: Benjamin KINGSLEY, grantee, all to 1800)

<37:84> - 23 Apr. 1736, Benjamin KINGSLEY from Thomas ALGER. Ack. 15 Aug. 1741. Rec. 14 Sep 1749

<37:89> - 15 Apr. 1728, Benjamin KINGSLEY from Bethiah KINSLEY, dau of Samuel, dec'd, her right in dower of mother Mary KINSLEY. Ack. 17 July 1741 by Bethiah BRETT, wf of William. Rec. 13 Sept. 1749.

<39:230> - , Benjamin KINGSLEY et al from George HALL & ux. Rec. 16 Dec. 1752.

<42:76> - , Benjamin KINGSLEY et al from Edward SLADE. Rec. 9 July 1756.

<49:35> - , Benjamin KINGSLEY from Matthew HAYWARD. Rec. 28 Oct. 1765.

<49:65> - , Benjamin KINGSLEY from Ephraim RANDALL et al. Rec. 28 Oct. 1765.

<50:509> - , Benjamin KINGSLEY from David KINGSLEY. Rec. 20 Aug. 1767.

<52:249> - , Benjamin KINGSLEY from John KINGSLEY Jr. Rec. 24 Aug. 1769.

<53:32> - , Benjamin KINGSLEY from Abiah MANLEY. Rec. 17 Apr. 1770.

<53:33> - , Benjamin KINGSLEY from David RANDALE. Rec. 17 Apr. 1770.

<54:141> - , Benjamin KINGSLEY from Samuel PACKARD 3d. Rec. 10 Oct. 1771.

<57:162> - , Benjamin KINGSLEY from estate of Silas KINGSLEY. Rec. 2 Apr. 1777.

<60:48> - , Benjamin KINGSLEY from Daniel WOOD. Rec. 22 Apr. 1780.

BRISTOL COUNTY DEEDS: (re: Benjamin KINGSLEY, grantor, all to 1800)

<15:618> - 17 Feb. 1724/5, Benjamin KINGSLEY of Norton to Samuel WALTERS. Ack. 2 Mar. 1725/6. Rec 2 Mar. 1725/6.

<20:213> - 30 Nov. ( ), Benjamin KINGSLEY, yeoman of Easton to Samuel WALTERS, land in 5th division in Taunton North Purchase. Ack. 9 Mar. 1729/30. Rec. 15 Sept. 1731.

<22:287> - 3 Jan. 1731/2, Benjamin KINGSLEY, yeoman of Easton to Thomas RANDALL Jr., 10 acres in Taunton North Purchase on original right of Richard BURT, dec'd. Ack. 9 Jan. 1734/5. Rec. 14 Jan. 1734/5.

<26:169> - 13 Mar. 1729, Benjamin KINGSLEY, yeoman of Easton to John WILLIAMS, land in Cranberry meadow pine swamp in Easton. Ack. 6 Mar. 1737/8. Rec. 14 June 1738.

<26:311> - 10 Jan. 1738, Benjamin KINGSLEY, yeoman of Easton to Edward HAYWARD, gent. of Easton, meadow in Easton adjoyning Hayward's. Ack. 12 Sept. 1739, rec. 14 Sept.

<26:312> - 3 Mar. 1729/30, Benjamin KINGSLEY, yeoman of Easton to Peter HAYWARD, yeoman of Bridgewater, 5 acres in Taunton North Purchase, original right of Richard BURT, dec'd. Ack. 1 June 1739. Rec. 13 Sept. 1739.

<27:407> - 6 Mar. 1733/4, Benjamin KINGSLEY, yeoman of Easton to Edward HAYWARD, land in Easton bounded by land which sd Hayward had by his wife. Ack. 10 Oct. 1738. Rec. 14 Mar. 1738/9.

<28:305> - 6 Feb. 1729/30, Benjamin KINGSLEY, Samuel KINSLEY, Josiah KEITH, Benjamin WILLIAMS, John WILLIAMS, John AUSTIN, William MANLEY, Thomas PRATT to Matthew SHORT, Pastor of Easton Church. Ack. by B.K.. 9 Mar. 1729/30. Rec. 18 Sept. 1740.

<34:57> - 10 Jan. 1744/5, Benjamin KINGSLEY et al, Petition. Ack. 13 Aug. 1745. Rec. 6 Oct 1745.

<34:158> - 13 Aug. 1745, Benjamin KINGSLEY, blacksmith of Swansea to James COLE. Ack. 13 Aug. 1745. Rec. 8 Feb. 1745/6.

<35:75> - 13 Aug. 1745, Benjamin KINGSLEY, blacksmith of Swansea to James MASON. Rec. 30 Oct '46

<35:226> - 25 Mar. 1744/5, Benjamin KINGSLEY and Edward HAYWARD, of Easton to Ephraim RANDALL, 9 acres in Cranberry Meadow Neck in Easton. Ack. by B.K. 25 Mar. 1745. Ack. by E.H. 15 Mar. 1747/8. Rec. 18 May 1748.

<36:504> - 17 Jan. 1745, Benjamin KINGSLEY, yeoman of Swansea & wf Sarah to Benjamin WEAVER. Ack. by B.K. 27 Mar. 1749. Rec. 11 May 1749.

<37:247> - 10 July 1749, Benjamin KINGSLEY of Easton to Israel ALGER. Ack. 30 Mar. 1750. Rec. 13 Apr. 1750.

<38:158> - , Benjamin KINGSLEY to Amos DAGGETT. Rec. 30 Sept. 1751.

<41:491> - , Benjamin KINGSLEY et al to Joseph MASON. Rec. 20 Jan. 1756.

<42:43> - , Benjamin KINGSLEY to Ebenezer PHILLIPS. Rec. 9 June 1756.

<44:226> - , Benjamin KINGSLEY to Peter WEAVER. Rec. 13 Mar. 1760.

<50:412> - , Benjamin KINGSLEY to Asa KINGSLEY. Rec. 6 May 1767.

<55:203> - , Benjamin KINGSLEY to Thomas MANLEY Jr. Rec. 11 Mar. 1773.

<55:240> - , Benjamin KINGSLEY to Joseph ALLEN 2d. Rec. 20 May 1773.

<56:519> - , Benjamin KINGSLEY to Abiel KINGSLEY. Rec. 21 July 1776.

<57:62> - , Benjamin KINGSLEY to John HOWARD. Rec. 16 Dec. 1776.

<60:48> - 15 Mar. 1780, Benjamin KINGSLEY, yeoman of Easton & wf Mary to Thomas WILLIS, land with grist mill which Seth MANLEY bought of John RANDALL, dec'd of Easton, 2 July 1762 <45:542>. Ack. 5 Apr. 1780. Rec. 22 Apr. 1780.

<66:562> - , Benjamin KINGSLEY & wf Anna to John BOWEN. Rec. 9 Mar. 1787.

<68:481> - , Benjamin KINGSLEY to Edmund ALGER. Rec. 20 Apr. 1790.

<73:220> - , Benjamin KINGSLEY to Elisha CHACE. Rec. 23 Oct. 1794.

BRISTOL COUNTY DEEDS: (re: Edward HAYWARD, grantor, all to 1795)

<15:484> - , Edward HAYWARD to Matthew SHORT. Rec. 14 July 1724.

<18:578> - , Edward HAYWARD to Matthew SHORT. Rec. 14 Oct. 1729.

<23:430> - , Edward HAYWARD to Josiah WINSLOW. Rec. 7 July 1735.

<26:446> - , Edward HAYWARD to Richard ELLIS. Rec. 22 Oct. 1740

<35:147> - 21 May 1744, Edward HAYWARD, gent. of Easton to Henry HAWARD. Ack/Rec 11 Mar. 1746/7.

BRISTOL COUNTY DEEDS, cont-d: (re: Edward HAYWARD, grantor, all to 1795)

<35:226> - 25 Mar. 1744/5, Edward HAYWARD & Benjamin KINSLEY, both of Easton sell to Ephraim RANDALL, nine acres in Cranberry Meadow Neck in Eaton. Ack. 15 Mar. 1747/48 by E.H. Rec. 11 May 1748.
<35:523> - 24 Oct. 1748, Edward HAYWARD, gent. of Easton to Matthew HAYWARD. Rec. 30 Oct. 1749.
<36:473> - , Edward HAYWARD to Caleb TRIPP. Rec. 5 Apr. 1749.
<37:82> - , Edward HAYWARD to Benjamin KINSLEY. Rec. 15 Sept. 1749.
<37:424> - , Edward HAYWARD to Hannah DEAN. Rec. 12 Sept. 1750.
<37:426> - , Edward HAYWARD to Hannah DEAN. Rec. 12 Sept. 1750.
<38:278> - , Edward HAYWARD to Matthew HAYWARD.
<40:145> - , Edward HAYWARD to Joseph BELCHER. Rec. 29 June 1753.
<44:289> - , Edward HAYWARD to Matthew HAYWARD. Rec. 25 June 1760.
<44:293> - , Edward HAYWARD to Hannah DEAN. Rec. 25 June 1760.
<45:50> - , Edward HAYWARD Sr. to Edward HAYWARD Jr. et al. Rec. 23 Mar. 1761.
<49:464> - , Edward HAYWARD to John HAYWARD. Rec. 31 Oct. 1765.
<50:212> - , Edward HAYWARD to William KEITH. Rec. 31 Oct. 1765.
<54:559> - , Edward HAYWARD et al, division. Rec. 14 Oct. 1772.
<61:3> - , Edward HAYWARD to Seth BAILEY. Rec. 5 June 1782.
<68:76> - , Edward HAYWARD et al to Adams BAILEY. Rec. 1 June 1789.
<68:198> - , Edward HAYWARD to Solomon LOTHROP. Rec. 17 Sept. 1789.
<68:408> - , Edward HAYWARD to Caleb DUNBAR. Rec. 10 Mar. 1790.
<72:450> - , Edward HAYWARD to Ephraim DRAKE. Rec. 4 Apr. 1794.

Estate of **Edward HAYWARD,** Esq. of Easton MA. <Bristol Co.PR>
<17:52> 30 June 1760, **Keziah HAYWARD,** widow and Mathew HAYWARD, gent., both of Easton, app'td admrs. <126:166> Guardianship, 1 July 1760, **Keziah HAYWARD,** widow, app'td gdn. of **Keziah HAYWARD,** minor under 14. <17:162> Inventory 9 July 1760. <17:168> Account of admrs., 15 Dec. 1760; due from Silence BONNEY, Zilpha WHITE, Nathan WHITE, David WHITE. <17:494> Warrant to appraise & divide, 10 Dec. 1760. Division 13 Apr. 1761 to following heirs: widow **Kezia HAYWARD;** dau **Hannah DEAN** wf of James; eldest son **Matthew HAYWARD;** sons **Edward HAYWARD, Joseph HAYWARD, Solomon HAYWARD;** dau **Kezia HAYWARD.** <19:281> Warrant to appraise & divide estate (which was omitted) among the children, the said widow having refused her dower. Division 25 Oct. 1765 to above six chil.

Thomas WILLIS of Bridgewater MA to **Samuel KINSLEY** of North Purchase. <Bristol Co.Deeds 14:139>
...28 Dec. 1716, Thomas WILLIS & wf Mary, having received of Samuel KINSLEY, admr. upon estate of Mary's father, Samuel KINSLEY late of North Purchase, dec'd, the full sum of fifteen pounds... quit claim their share. Witnesses: John AMES Jr., Experience WILLIS.

Josiah HAYWARD of Bridgewater MA to **Edward HAYWARD** of Easton MA. <Bristol Co.Deeds 24:81>
...7 Nov. 1733, Josiah HAYWARD & wf Sarah to Edward HAYWARD, gent., all rights in lands of Samuel KINGSLEY, late of Easton. Ack. by both same day.

BRISTOL COUNTY DEEDS: (re: Samuel KINGSLEY, grantor & grantee, all to 1800)

<2:363> - Samuel KINGSLEY from John BURT et al. Rec. 5 June 1699.
<3:145> - Samuel KINGSLEY to Jonathan KINGSLEY. Rec. 22 June 1700.
<4:83> - Samuel KINGSLEY, ux. et al to John ROGERS. Rec. 1 Apr. 1700.
<4:364> - Samuel KINGSLEY to James KEITH. Rec. 27 July 1704/5.
<24:106> - Samuel KINGSLEY to Joseph DRAKE Jr. Rec. 8 July 1735.
<28:305> - Samuel KINGSLEY et al to Matthew SHORT. Rec. 18 Sept. 1740.
<33:407> - Samuel KINGSLEY to Joseph PACKARD. Rec. 12 June 1745.
<36:118> - Samuel KINGSLEY to Ebenezer AMES. Rec. 27 May 1748.
<36:515> - Samuel KINGSLEY to Wetherell WHITTON. Rec. 15 Mar. 1748.
<39:230> - Samuel KINGSLEY et al from George HALL & ux. Rec. 16 Dec. 1752.
<41:179> - Samuel KINGSLEY to Nathan KINSLEY. Rec. 16 July 1754.
<46:490> - Samuel KINGSLEY from Pelatiah EASTY et al. Rec. 14 Oct. 1763.
<56:33> - Samuel KINGSLEY to Eleazer KEITH. Rec. 17 Mar. 1774.
<58:322> - Samuel KINGSLEY from Ebenezer BRUCE. Rec. 18 Aug. 1778.
<59:57> - Samuel KINGSLEY & ux. & al. to Elisha DEAN. Rec. 9 Dec. 1778.
<64:470> - Samuel KINGSLEY & ux. & al. Rec. 15 Sept. 1785.

Will of **Josiah HAYWARD,** husbandman of Bridgewater MA. <Plymouth Co.PR #9816>
<19:65>...dated 14 June 1759, mentions wf **Sarah,** children **Josiah HAYWARD, Nathan HAYWARD** (executor), **Sarah HAYWARD, Hannah HAYWARD.** Witnesses: Thomas MITCHELL, Nehemiah LATHAM, Arthur LATHAM. <19:66> Pr. 2 June 1764.

Josiah HAYWARD of Bridgewater MA to **Edward MITCHELL** of Bridgewater. <Plymouth Co.Deeds 47:266>
...12 Jan. 1758, Josiah HAYWARD, yeoman, for £20, sold to Edward MITCHELL, gent...10 acres in Bridgewater, on south side of road from my house to Packard's and adjoining sd Mitchell's land. Wf Sarah HAYWARD releases dower. Witnesses: Josiah EDSON Jr., Nathan HAYWARD. Ack. 12 Jan. 1758 by Josiah. Rec. 8 Sept. 1762.

Guardianship of Children of **Josiah HAYWARD,** yeoman of Bridgewater MA. <Plymouth Co.PR #9817>
<18:239,240> Letters 28 Aug. 1765, Josiah HAYWARD app'td gdn. of his daus **Lois & Sarah HAYWARD...** in right of their Grandfather **Thomas PERKINS** of Bridgewater, dec'd. <originals> Bonds 28 Aug.

1765, of Josiah HAYWARD, yeoman of Bridgewater and John FAUNCE of Kingston; guardianship of **Josiah HAYWARD, Lois HAYWARD** and **Sarah HAYWARD.**

References to **Otis HAYWARD** in Plymouth Co.Deeds: 137:222; 149:19,20; 227:185 (no data given).

Josiah HAYWARD to **Jabez MUXHAM et al** of Plympton. <Plymouth Co.Deeds 71:199>
...27 June 1783, Josiah HAYWARD, cordwainer & wf Dinah, for £13.10s in silver, sell to Jabez MUXHAM, John MUXHAM Jr. and Thomas MUXHAM, yeomen...our right in the estate of Edmund MUXHAM late of Plimpton dec'd and who was honoured father of the sd Dinah, our right being one ninth. Witnesses: Eliphalet HOWARD, Sarah HAYWARD. Ack. 8 Nov. 1784 by Josiah & Dinah. Rec. 20 June 1791.

Josiah HAYWARD et al of Bridgewater MA to **Nathaniel HAYWARD** of same. <Plymouth Co.Deeds 33:184>
...3 Feb. 1734/5, Josiah HAYWARD, Isaac HAYWARD, Joseph LATHAM & wf Sarah, Elisha DUNBAR & wf Mercy, David KINGMAN & wf Mary, Timothy HAYWARD, Elizabeth HAYWARD, Susanna HAYWARD and Bethiah HAYWARD to brother Nathaniel HAYWARD...rights in estate of our father Nathaniel HAYWARD who died 30 Sept. 1731.

Josiah HAYWARD of Bridgewater MA to **Nathan HAYWARD** of Bridgewater. <Plymouth Co.Deeds 39:98>
...24 Dec. 1747, Josiah HAYWARD to son Nathan HAYWARD, yeoman...45 acres in S. Bridgewater. Witnesses: Hezekiah HAYWARD, Josiah EDSON Jr. Ack. 31 Dec. 1747. Rec. 30 Mar. 1748.

Josiah HAYWARD of Bridgewater MA to **Reuben HALL** of Bridgewater. <Plymouth Co.Deeds 42:104>
...31 Dec. 1751, Josiah HAYWARD & wf Mary, for £10, sold to Reuben HALL, bricklayer...11 acres in S. Bridgewater, east from the dwelling house, bounded by the highway. Witnesses: Ebenezer PERKINS and Francis PERKINS. (Signed "Josiah HAYWARD Jr.") Ack. 6 Dec. 1752. Rec. 15 June 1753.

Josiah HAYWARD Jr. of Bridgewater MA to **Peres WATERMAN.** <Plymouth Co.Deeds 51:32>
...26 Oct. 1757, Josiah HAYWARD Jr., yeoman, for £2 sold to Peres WATERMAN, housewright...two acres near sd Peres' house near Middleborough road. Witnesses: Robert WATERMAN, Joseph PACKARD. Ack. 9 Dec. 1757. Rec. 11 Oct. 1765.

Josiah HAYWARD Jr. of Bridgewater MA to **Robert & Joseph LATHAM** of same.<Plymouth Co.Deeds 48:138>
...29 Nov. 1760, Josiah HAYWARD Jr., for £13.4s8d, sold to Robert LATHAM and Joseph LATHAM...6 acres, part of my homestead land whereon I now dwell. Wf Mary HAYWARD releases dower. Witnesses: Jacob TOMSON, Robert GILLMOR. Ack. 1 May 1761 by Josiah & Mary. Rec. 28 Apr. 1763.

Josiah HAYWARD of Bridgewater MA to **Nathan HAYWARD** of same. <Plymouth Co.Deeds 48:205>
...11 Feb. 1763, Josiah HAYWARD, yeoman, for £300, sold to Nathan HAYWARD, yeoman...my house & lands in the south precinct of Bridgewater containing about 30 acres...bounded by the river, Packard's Bridge and the lands of Nathan HAYWARD...also 10 acres bounded by Town river and lands of Hezekiah HAYWARD and Capt. MITCHELL. Witnesses: Edward MITCHELL, Edward MITCHELL Jr. Ack. 26 Mar. 1763. Rec. 10 May 1763.

Josiah HAYWARD Jr. of Bridgewater MA to **Robert & Joseph LATHAM** of same. <Plymouth Co.Deeds 48:84>
...22 Mar. 1763, Josiah HAYWARD Jr., for £40, sold to Robert LATHAM & Joseph LATHAM...13 acres in Bridgewater, part of my homestead whereon I now dwell...bounded by river and land of sd Lathams. Wf Mary HAYWARD releases dower. Witnesses: Jacob TOMSON, Ephraim HOLMES. Ack. 5 Apr. 1763 by Josiah. Rec. 5 Apr. 1763.

Josiah HAYWARD of Middleborough MA and **Joseph BESSE** of same. <Plymouth Co.Deeds 55:89>
...26 Dec. 1769, Josiah HAYWARD and Joseph BESSE, husbandmen, joint owners of land they bought of Nathaniel & Sarah ROGERS 9 Oct. 1766...divide land & iron ore. Witnesses: Nathaniel SHAW, Abraham PERKINS Jr. Ack. same day. Rec. 8 Feb. 1770.

Josiah HAYWARD of Middleboro MA to **Francis PERKINS & Robert LATHAM.** <Plymouth Co.Deeds 55:89>
...26 Dec. 1769, Josiah HAYWARD, yeoman, for £28, sold to Francis PERKINS and Robert LATHAM, gentlemen of Bridgewater...55 acres in 102nd lot, 4th division in South Purchase in Middleboro. Wit: nesses: Nathaniel SHAW, Abraham PERKINS Jr. Ack. same day. Rec. 8 Feb. 1770.

Robert LATHAM & Francis PERKINS to **Josiah HAYWARD** of Middleboro MA. <Plymouth Co.Deeds 59:249>
...26 Oct. 1773, Robert LATHAM, yeoman and Francis PERKINS, gent., for £28.7s7d, sold to Josiah HAYWARD, yeoman...land in Middleboro that we bought of sd Hayward, it being the homestead whereon he now dwells. Witnesses: Joseph LATHAM, Moses SIMMONS. Ack. 3 Nov. 1773. Rec. 1 June 1779.

Josiah HAYWARD of Middleboro MA to **Perez THOMAS** of same. <Plymouth Co.PR 59:249>
...12 Mar. 1779, Josiah HAYWARD, yeoman, for £100, sold to Perez THOMAS...20 acres in Middleboro, part of the lot I bought of Nathaniel ROGERS. Witnesses: David THOMAS, Deborah THOMAS. Ack. 31 May 1779. Rec. 1 June 1779.

PLYMOUTH COUNTY DEEDS: (re: Josiah HAYWARD)

<14:30> - 8 May 1718, Josiah HAYWARD, weaver of Bridgewater to uncle Benjamin HAYWARD, yeoman of Bridgewater. Ack. 8 May 1718.
<28:228> - 8 Jan. 1733/4, Josiah HAYWARD, yeoman of Bridgewater to Joseph HAYWARD, weaver of Bridgewater, land in Middleboro bought of John LOVEL.Ack. 8 Feb. 1733/4.

PLYMOUTH COUNTY DEEDS, cont-d: (re: Josiah HAYWARD)

<14:30> - 8 May 1718, Josiah HAYWARD, weaver of Bridgewater to uncle Benjamin HAYWARD, yeoman of Bridgewater. Ack. 8 May 1718.
<32:131> - 10 Oct. 1738, Josiah HAYWARD, yeoman of Bridgewater to son Josiah HAYWARD.
<71:199> - 1791, Josiah HAYWARD & wf Dinah.
<71:108> - 14 Oct. 1790, Josiah HAYWARD, yeoman of Middleboro to Nathan HAYWARD, yeoman of same, 10 acres bounded by land of Asaph CHURCHILL, Perez THOMAS, William SHAW, Joseph BESSEY. Ack. same day. Rec. 20 Nov. 1790.

Nathan HAYWARD of Bridgewater MA to **Phinehas HAYWARD** of same. <Plymouth Co.Deeds 71:127>
...14 Oct. 1790, Nathan HAYWARD, yeoman, for £6, paid by Phinehas HAYWARD, minor...quit claim all rights in 10 acres of woodland in Middleborough purchased of Josiah HAYWARD. Witnesses: Beza HAYWARD, Abigail HAYWARD. Ack. same day by Nathan. Rec. 20 Nov. 1791.

Josiah HAYWARD of Middleboro MA to **Cyrus HAYWARD** of Bridgewater MA. <Plymouth Co.Deeds 77:38>
...19 Nov. 1794, Josiah HAYWARD, yeoman to son Cyrus HAYWARD, nailor...17 acres in Middleboro, bounded by land of Perez THOMAS, Nellson CHURCHILL, Joseph BESSE and lands I formerly sold to my son Phineas HAYWARD...reserving to my self the improvement of the premises dureing my natural life. Witnesses: Phineas HAYWARD, Beza HAYWARD. Ack. same day. Rec. 27 Nov. 1794.

Cyrus HAYWARD of Boston MA to **Winslow HOOPER** of Bridgewater MA. <Plymouth Co.Deeds 100:97>
...4 Dec. 1800, Cyrus HAYWARD, yeoman, for $100.00, sell to Winslow HOOPER, gentleman...all my real estate in Middleboro, bounded by lands of Perez THOMAS, Nelson CHURCHILL, Joseph BESSE and land formerly owned by my father Josiah HAYWARD which he deeded to Phinehas HAYWARD...it being the whole of said land that my father, Josiah HAYWARD dec'd, deeded to me, about 17 acres. Ack. 5 Dec. 1804. Rec. 18 Apr. 1805.

MICRO #14 OF 30

Benjamin WASHBURN of Bridgewater MA to **Nehemiah WASHBURN** of same. <Plymouth Co.Deeds 16:25>
...5 Sept. 1720, Benjamin WASHBURNE, cordwainer, for £7, sold to brother Nehemiah WASHBURNE, yeoman...one half of a right in the little cedar swamp by the great meadow...that my Father gave to me in his last will. Witnesses: Benjamin ALLEN, Nathaniel BRETT. Ack. same day. Rec. 15 Mar. 1721

Benjamin WASHBURN et al of Bridgewater MA to **John KEITH** of same. <Plymouth Co.Deeds 19:90>
...30 Jan. 1722/3, Samuel WASHBURN, Nehemiah WASHBURN, Benjamin WASHBURN, brethren, yeomen, for £3.15s, sold to John KEITH...three quarters of five acres of undivided land in Bridgewater. Witnesses: Ichabod ORCUT, Bethiah WASHBURN. Ack. 21 Dec. 1724 by three grantors. Rec. 4 Aug. 1725.

Benjamin WASHBURN Jr. et al of Bridgewater to **Thomas HAYWARD** of same. <Plymouth Co.Deeds 24:215>
...24 Dec. 1724, Samuel WASHBURN, Nehemiah WASHBURN, Benjamin WASHBURN Jr., John KEITH & wf Hannah, for £20, sell to Thomas HAYWARD...land in Bridgewater lying neer Beaver Brook, namely half a purchase right in ye Second Division otherwise called the Second Share. Witnesses: Josiah EDSON Jr., Abraham STAPLES. Ack. same day by grantors. Rec. 17 Dec. 1729.

Benjamin WASHBURN Jr. of Bridgewater MA to **John FIELD** of same. <Plymouth Co.Deeds 27:132>
...25 June 1729, Benjamin WASHBURN Jr., cordwainer, for £15, sold to John FIELD, gent...meadow on southerly side of Town river in Bridgewater, being 14th lot. Witnesses: Joshua WILLIS, Thomas HAYWARD 3d. Ack. same day. Rec. 9 Sept. 1732.

Benjamin WASHBURN Jr. of Bridgewater MA to **John KEITH** of same. <Plymouth Co.Deeds 34:143>
...10 Apr. 1730, Benjamin WASHBURN Jr., cordwainer, for £250, sold to John KEITH, husbandman... 74 acres in land commonly called Teticut Purchase in Bridgewater, bounded by river and Keith's land. Witnesses: Nathaniel WOODWARD, Nathaniel WILLIS. Ack. 20 Dec. 1737. Rec. 2 or 7 July 1741.

Benjamin WASHBURN Jr. of Bridgewater MA to **Thomas HAYWARD** of same. <Plymouth Co.Deeds 108:68>
...2 Jan. 1739/40, Benjamin WASHBURN Jr., cordwainer, for £60, sold to Thomas HAYWARD, yeoman... 15 acres in north end of 22nd lot in land commonly called Titicut purchase. Witnesses: Solomon PERKINS, Ephraim LEONARD. Ack. 24 Mar. 1739/40. Rec. 3 Feb. 1808.

Jonathan WOODS of Bridgewater MA to **Benjamin WASHBURN** of same. <Plymouth Co.Deeds 41:222>
...5 Apr. 1743, Jonathan WOODS, bricklayer, for £300 bills of credit, sell to Benjamin WASHBURN, housewright...eight acres in south Bridgewater...on easterly side of the road of that parcell of land which my Father Francis WOOD bought of Enoch LEONARD...and also three quarters of an acre of land which my said Father laid out joining the sd eight acres..and also the dwelling house. Witnesses: Israel KEITH, James KEITH. Ack. 26 Apr. 1749. Rec. 20 May 1752.

John KEITH of Bridgewater MA to **Benjamin WASHBURN** of same. <Plymouth Co.Deeds 41:222>
...5 Apr. 1743, John KEITH, gent., for £300 sell to Benjamin WASHBURN Jr., housewright...26 acres in south Bridgewater...bounded by my fifty acre lot and land of Solomon LEONARD...also half acre bounded by land of Francis WOOD and land of some time Israel KEITH's...also half acre bounded by highway and land of Israel KEITH. Witnesses: Israel KEITH, James KEITH. Ack. 25 Apr. 1749. Rec. 20 May 1752.

Benjamin WASHBURN of Bridgewater MA to **Thomas PERKINS** of same. <Plymouth Co.Deeds 37:142> ...5 Nov. 1744, Benjamin WASHBURN, gent., for £21.5s, sold to Thomas PERKINS, yeoman...17 acres in south end of 22nd lot of Titticutt great lots. Witnesses: Abraham PERKINS, David JOHNSON Jr. Ack. 17 May 1745. Rec. 10 July 1745.

John WOODS of Bridgewater MA to **Benjamin WASHBURN 3d** of same. <Plymouth Co.Deeds 41:223> ...12 Dec. 1751, John WOODS, yeoman, for £7.14s8p, sell to Benjamin WASHBURN 3d, carpenter...land in south Bridgewater, being south east part of my home lands...bounded by land of sd Washburn and highway. Witnesses: John CONANT, Thomas PERKINS Jr. Ack. 29 Apr. 1752. Rec. 20 May 1752.

Benjamin LEACH Jr. of Bridgewater MA to **Benjamin WASHBURN 3d** of same. <Plymouth Co.Deeds 41:223> ...21 Apr. 1752, Benjamin LEACH Jr., yeoman, for £8, sold to Benjamin WASHBURN 3d, housewright... land in Bridgewater on south side of sd Washburn's land. Witnesses: James HOPKINS, Thomas PERKINS Jr. Ack. 29 Apr. 1752. Rec. 20 May 1752.

Benjamin WASHBURN of Bridgewater MA to **Amos HAYWARD** of same. <Plymouth Co.Deeds 55:51> ...9 Dec. 1763, Benjamin WASHBURN, for £56.13s4d, sold to Amos HAYWARD, yeoman...21 and a half acres in south Bridgewater, part of my homestead farm I last dwelt on in Bridgewater...bounded by land I sold to Benjamin PERKINS and Thomas HAYWARD, and the five acres I sold to my son Benjamin WASHBURN. Witnesses: Benjamin PERKINS, James KEITH. Ack. 9 Dec. 1763. Rec. 25 Oct. 1769.

Benjamin WASHBURN of Bridgewater MA to **Kezia HARVEY** of Bridgewater. <Plymouth Co.Deeds 55:85> ...11 Jan. 1770, Benjamin WASHBURN, gent., for £53.6s8d, sold to Kezia HARVEY, widow...20 acres in south Bridgewater...bounded by 25th lot of Titiquot and homestead of Daniel KEITH. Wf Bethiah WASHBURN releases dower. Witnesses: Ezra WASHBURN, Ephraim KEITH. Ack. 16 Jan. 1770 by Benjamin & Bethiah. Rec. 6 Feb. 1770.

Benjamin WASHBURN 3d of Bridgewater MA to **John HAYWARD** of same. <Plymouth Co.Deeds 56:81> ...13 Feb. 1771, Benjamin WASHBURN 3d, housewright, for £23.6s8d, sell to John HAYWARD, yeoman... 5 acres in south Bridgewater which land I bought of my Father Benjamin WASHBURN...bounded by home stead of widow Kezia HARVEY. Wf Mary WASHBURN releases dower. Witnesses: Eliab HAYWARD, Thomas PERKINS. Ack. 20 May 1771 by Benjamin. Rec. 30 May 1771.

Solomon LEONARD of Bridgewater MA to **Benjamin WASHBURN Jr.** of same. <Plymouth Co.Deeds 64:23> ...20 May 1774, Solomon LEONARD, gent., for £24.4s, sold to Benjamin WASHBURN Jr., wheelwright... eight and one quarter acres on southerly end of my homestead in south Bridgewater...bounded by land of Uriah RICKARD. Wf Joanna LEONARD releases dower. Witnesses: Luther KINSLEY, Jacob LEONARD Ack. 18 Jan. 1785. Rec. 10 Mar. 1785.

Benjamin WASHBURN of Bridgewater MA to **Joshua WASHBURN** of same. <Plymouth Co.Deeds 64:24> ...13 Jan. 1785, Benjamin WASHBURN, housewright, for £164, sold to Joshua WASHBURN, yeoman...41 acres in south Bridgewater...being a part of my homestead being the land 26 acres of which I bought of John KEITH 5 Apr. 1743 and the remaining 15 acres thereof I bought of Jacob LEACH 13 Apr. 1760. Witnesses: Benjamin WILLIS, Moses LEONARD. Ack. 14 Jan. 1785. Rec. 10 Mar. 1785.

Will of **Benjamin WASHBURN**, housewright of Bridgewater MA. <Plymouth Co.PR #21927> <44:347>...dated 14 Jan. 1785, mentions wf **Mary**; son **Asa WASHBURN**; to son **Joshua WASHBURN** (executor), lands bought from Jonathan WOODS, Benjamin LEACH Jr., John WOODS & Solomon LEONARD; son **Benjamin WASHBURN**; dau **Susanna HOOPER** wf of James; dau **Eunice RICHMOND** wf of Asa; dau **Mary WASHBURN, Olive WASHBURN, Kezia WASHBURN.** Witnesses: Benjamin WILLIS, Moses LEONARD, Benjamin WILLIS Jr. The will was "republished" Oct. 1809 in the presence of Daniel MITCHELL, Joseph AMES Jr. and Galen CONANT. <44:348> Pr. 5 Oct. 1812, presented by executor. Daniel MITCHELL, Esq. and Joseph AMES Jr., two of the witnesses made oath that they heard the said Testator declare & republish the said instrument to be his last will & testament & that he had signed the same in presence of Benjamin WILLIS, Esq., Moses LEONARD and Benjamin WILLIS Jr., the three witnesses thereto first subscribed who at the time of said republication were deceased.

Joshua WASHBURN of Bridgewater MA to **Hiram WENTWORTH** of same. <Plymouth Co.Deeds 202:275> ...16 June 1840, Joshua WASHBURN, yeoman, for $1800.00, sold to Hiram WENTWORTH, cordwainer...my homestead farm in Bridgewater, 15 acres...bounded by land of heirs of Joshua BATES and land of sd Wentworth and Cornelius HOLMES Jr. Wf Charity WASHBURN releases dower. Witnesses: Zephaniah A. BATES, Horace AMES. Ack. 17 June 1840 by Joshua. Rec.7 Oct.1840.

Hiram W. WENTWORTH et al to **Philo & James H. LEACH** of Bridgewater MA. <Plymouth Co.Deeds 505:283> ...27 Mar. 1884, Hiram W. WENTWORTH of New Bedford, Julia A. KEITH & Maggie WENTWORTH of Bridgewater, for $2083.32, sold to Philo LEACH and James H. LEACH...five undivided sixth parts of land with dwelling house and stable on easterly side of South St. in Bridgewater, containing 66 acres ...bounded by land of Parna LEACH, Betsey DUNBAR, Horace & Virgil AMES, land lately of Samuel W. BATES now owned by one LAPHAM and land formerly of Harry SNELL...being all the real estate which Hiram WENTWORTH late of Bridgewater died siezed, between Bedford and South Streets in Bridgewater ...the same conveyed to sd Hiram by four deeds, one from Joshua WASHBURN 16 June 1840 <202:275>, one from Cornelius HOLMES 10 Aug. 1844 <213:215>, one from Abram WASHBURN 4 Apr. 1838 <197:202> and one from Levi HALE 4 Aug. 1856 <276:67>...the sd Maggie owning three and the sd Hiram W. & Julia A. each one sixth as devisees under the will of the sd Hiram dec'd...the sd Maggie to have the right to occupy sd buildings until July 1st next without paying rent. Maggie WENTWORTH, widow and Phebe T. WENTWORTH, wf of sd Hiram W., release dowers. Witnesses: Hosea KINGMAN, Mrs.

Catherin W. SIGSWORTH, Carrie C. ELLIS, Ellen R. CONGDON. Ack. 27 Mar. 1884 by Hiram. Rec. 29 Mar. 1884.

Joshua WASHBURN by admr. to **Joshua WASHBURN** of Bridgewater MA. <Plymouth Co.Deeds 174:119> ...25 Dec. 1832, Cornelius HOLMES Jr., admr. on estate of Joshua WASHBURN, late of Bridgewater, dec'd...for payment of debts...to raise the sum of twelve hundred dollars, for $1187.47, sold to Joshua WASHBURN...22 acre homestead of dec'd in Bridgewater bounded on land owned by sd Washburn. Witnesses: Martin WENTWORTH, Artemas HALE. Ack. 31 Dec. 1832. Rec. 30 Mar. 1833.

Estate of **Israel WASHBURN** of Bridgewater MA. <Plymouth Co.PR #21999>
<original> 3 Feb. 1721/2, **Samuel WASHBURN, Nehemiah WASHBURN** and **Benjamin WASHBURN**, sons of **Samuel WASHBURN**, late of Bridgewater dec'd, that are now living, relinquish their right to administer the estate of their brother Israel WASHBURN and ask to have our well beloved friend Samuel SUMNER, who is uncle on the mother's side of the children of our sd deceased brother, app'td admr <original> Bond 2 Mar. 1721/2 of Samuel SUMNER of Taunton, admr. Sureties: Eleazer CARVER, Josiah EDSON Jr., both of Bridgewater. Witnesses: David PERKINS, Eleazer CARVER Jr. <4:320> Letter 27 Feb. 1721, Samuel SUMNER app'td admr. <4:363> Inventory taken 3 Mar. 1721/2 by David PERKINS, Eleazer CARVER and Josiah EDSON Jr.; Debts due from: Ebenezer PRATT, Eleazer CARVER, Nehemiah WASHBURN, Jonathan BLAKE. <5:565> Division of lands, 19 May 1729 by Ephraim HAWARD, John AMES, John WASHBURN and Ephraim FOBES. <original> 13 May 1729, John AMES, John WASHBURN and Nehemiah WASHBURN, all of Bridgewater, app'td to appraise lands. <5:567> Settlement 5 June 1729, to son **Israel WASHBURN**, lands adjoining John, James and Samuel WASHBURN in Bridgewater; to **Deborah RIPLEY** wf of John of Bridgewater; to dau **Sarah WASHBURN**. <5:758> Account of admr., 6 Mar. 1729/30; mother's wearing apparel appraised and given to daughter **Sarah**, one of the minors, and to daughter **Deborah**, now wife of John RIPLEY. Debts paid to: Ebenezer PRATT, Jonathan BLAKE, Jonathan CARY, Benjamin SUMNER, Eleazer CARVER Jr., Thomas LEONARD, Nehemiah WASHBURN, Samuel WASHBURN, Eleazer CARVER Sr., Nathaniel CARVER.

Guardianship of Children of **Israel WASHBURN** of Bridgewater MA. <Plymouth Co.PR #22000>
<4:321> Bond/Letter 7 May 1722, Seth SUMNER app'td gdn. of **Israel WASHBURN** (under 14) and **Seth WASHBURN**. Witnesses: Eleazer CARVER, John FULLARTON. <4:322> Bonds/Letters 7 May 1722, Eleazer CARVER app'td gdn. of **Deborah WASHBURN** and **Sarah WASHBURN** (both under 14). Witnesses: Seth SUMNER, John FULLARTON.

Estate of **Jason FOBES** of Bridgewater MA. <Plymouth Co.PR>
<39:218> Letter 7 Aug. 1809, Salmon FOBES app'td admr. <43:22> Committee to appraise, 7 Aug. 1809 Nathan MITCHELL, James ALGER 3d and Joseph BASSETT. <43:23> Inventory 14 Aug. 1809. <43:282> Account 1 Oct. 1810, of admr.

Estate of **Nehemiah WASHBURN**, gent. of Bridgewater MA. <Plymouth Co.PR #22068>
<11:209> Letter 24 Mar. 1748, Josiah DEAN of Raynham & Abiel HAWARD, Physician of Bridgewater, app'td admrs. Surety: David ALDEN. Witnesses: Edward WINSLOW, Isaac THOMAS. <12:518> Agreement & Division of real estate, 24 May 1751; incl. homestead and several small pieces of land in Abizer EDSON's possession; three and a half acres bought of Daniel HOWEL; twenty acres bought of James KEITH; twenty nine acres bought of Benjamin WHITE, Esq.; one third of thirty five acres which James THOMAS, Indian man, quitted his claim to, unto the heirs of Nehemiah WASHBURN, Israel WASHBURN and James BOIRE; twelve acres bought of sd Samuel THOMAS. Real estate divided into two equal parts to daus **Silence HAWARD** and **Jane/Jean DEAN**. Witnesses: John CUSHING, Josiah EDSON Jr. Oath of heirs, 16 May 1752.

Estate of **Eleazer WASHBURN** of Bridgewater MA. <Plymouth Co.PR #21955>
<17:72> Bond/Letter 5 Apr. 1762 of Ebenezer ALDEN, gent., admr. Sureties: Josiah EDSON, Esq. and Ebenezer KEITH, yeoman, both of Bridgewater. Witnesses: Amos FULLER, Edward WINSLOW. <16:300> Inventory taken 8 Apr. 1762 by Thomas WHITMAN, John ORCUTT, Nathan ALLEN; mentions "the household goods that Susannah carried away". <19:115> Account 8 Apr. 1764 of admr. Debts received of: Joseph BYRAM, William WASHBURN, Deacon SHAW, Jonathan ALDEN, Zachary WHITMAN, Samuel PRATT, Isaac PETERSON, Zachary SHAW. Paid to: Hugh ORR, Joseph GANNET, Noah WASHBURN, Lieut. KINGMAN & son, Thomas PARRISH, Simeon WHITMAN, Israel HILL, Joseph WESLEY, Elizabeth HAYWARD, Eliakim BRIGGS, John SHAW, Ebenezer WHITMAN, Samuel WHITMAN, Silas HARRIS, Nathaniel BRETT, Deborah HOUSE, Thomas SNELL Jr., Edward MITCHELL, Mary PICKNEY, Eliab FOBES, Joseph GANNET Jr., Ebenezer ALDEN, Dr. OTIS, John CARY, Matthew ALLEN, Thomas WHITMAN, Nehemiah LATHAM, Edward HAWARD (Town Treasurer), Mr. VINING, Joseph KEITH Jr., Nathan BEAL. Necessaries paid to widow and wearing apparel for children. <19:280> Warrant to divide 8 Oct. 1764. Division 10 Nov. 1764 by Capt. Edward MITCHELL, Ephraim CARY, John ORCUTT, to following heirs, viz: **Anna WASHBURN**, widow, **Eleazer WASHBURN, Susannah BYRAM, Asa WASHBURN, Anna WASHBURN, Levi WASHBURN, Oliver WASHBURN, Alden WASHBURN, Isaac WASHBURN**; confirmed 7 Oct. 1765. <19:550> Account 13 Oct. 1767 of admr.; received from: Dr. OTIS, Amos WHITMAN, Jos. RAMSDELL; paid: James ALLEN, Nathan BEAL, Ezekiel TURNER. <19:564> 1 Feb. 1768 widow **Annah WASHBURN** complains that the amount allowed her is insufficient.

Guardianship of Children of **Eleazer WASHBURN** of Bridgewater MA. <Plymouth Co.PR #21956>
<18:194-6> 4 Oct. 1764, **Asa, Anna** & **Eleazer WASHBURN** ask to have their mother, **Anna WASHBURN**, app'td gdn. <18:199-203> Letters 8 Oct. 1764, appointing **Anna WASHBURN**, widow, guardian of **Asa, Isaac, Alden, Oliver** and **Levi WASHBURN**. <originals> Bonds 8 Oct. 1764, of **Anna WASHBURN** as gdn. of the seven children (**Eleazer** & **Anna** over 14). Sureties: Ebenezer ALDEN, gent. of Bridgewater and Ebenezer WHITMARSH of Abington. Witnesses: Josiah EDSON, Daniel SNELL. <original> Request (no date) of **Anna WASHBURN**, being in poor health, for a new guardian for children. <20:184> Letters/

Bonds 6 Mar. 1769. Ephraim CARY, yeoman of Bridgewater app'td gdn. to **Oliver WASHBURN** and **Levi WASHBURN** (above 14). Sureties: Hugh ORR & Benjamin WHITMAN of Bridgewater. Witnesses: Ebenezer BAILEY & Edward WINSLOW Jr. Ephraim WHITMAN app'td gdn. of **Isaac WASHBURN** and **Alden WASHBURN** (under 14). Sureties: Hugh ORR & Ephraim CARY. Witnesses: Ebenezer BAILEY, Edward WINSLOW Jr.

Nathaniel THOMAS of Marshfield MA to **Abigail HEYFORD.** <Plymouth Co.Deeds 8:87>
...7 June 1710, Nathaniel THOMAS, gent., for Ł9, sold to Abigail HEYFORD, relict widdow of John HEYFORD late of & inhibitant on ye land called ye Majors Purchase, dec'd...half part of 38th lot in Major's Purchase...and wheron ye sd Abigail HEYFORD now dwelleth containing thirty acres. Witnesses: Japhet TURNER, Nathaniel THOMAS Jr. Ack. & Rec. 21 June 1710.

Thomas WASHBURN Sr. et al to **Edward HEYFORD et al.** <Plymouth Co.Deeds 13:136>
...7 Aug. 1717, Thomas WASHBURN Sr., yeoman & wf Abigail of Bridgewater, for ye love, good will & affection, to Edward HEYFORD, yeoman of Pembroke and Samuel HEIFORD, cordwainer of Duxboro...in equal shares, half the 38th lot in the upland in Major's Purchase now in Pembroke, containing 30 acres. Witnesses: Thomas WADE, Josiah EDSON Jr. Ack. 22 Aug. (---). Rec. 11 Jan. 1717/8.

Edward HEYFORD & John ROGERS of Pembroke MA to **Stephen BRYANT.** <Plymouth Co.Deeds 13:198>
...12 Jan. 1718/9, Edward HEYFORD and John ROGERS, sell to Stephen BRYANT...38th lot in Major's Purchase in Pembroke, 60 acres...the northwest half being Edward HEYFORD's. Ack. 12 Jan. 1718/9.

Daniel HAYFORD of Pembroke MA to **Isaac BARKER** of Pembroke. <Plymouth Co.Deeds 27:130>
...6 May 1729, Daniel HAYFORD, sells to Isaac BARKER...one fourteenth of half of 38th lot in Maj. Purchase, 30 acres. Witnesses: Thomas WOOD, Mary BARKER. Ack. 7 July 1730. Rec. 4 Sept. 1732.

Estate of **Thomas WESTON**, mariner of Plymouth MA. <Plymouth Co.PR #22448>
<9:74> Letter/Bond 19 May 1743, **Prudence WESTON**, widow, app'td admx. Sureties: David TURNER, ship wright, Samuel FOSTER, gent. Witnesses: Francis ADAMS Jr., Lemuel JACKSON. <9:100> Inventory taken 4 June 1743 by Samuel FOSTER, Josiah CARVER, David TURNER. <13:442> Account of admx. 7 Apr. 1755; Received of: Col. LOTHROP; Paid: Thomas HOLMES, John ATWOOD, James BOWDOIN, Isaac LeBARON, Nathaniel DONHAM, Abigail SNELL, Joseph SHURTLEFF, Eleazer ROGERS, Thomas SPOONER, Silvanus BRIMHALL, Thomas CUNNETT, Nathaniel GOODWIN, Robert BROWN, Dr. LeBARON, Melatiah LOTHROP, Isaac LITTLE, James HOVEY, Samuel BARTLETT, Benjamin LOTHROP.

Will of **Prudence WESTON**, widow of Plymouth MA. <Plymouth Co.PR #22434>
<19:363>...dated 26 Oct. 1765, mentions dau **Mary WESTON** wf of William WESTON of Plymouth; three grandchildren, chil. of son **Thomas WESTON**, dec'd; dau **Sarah WESTON** (alias BALL). Witnesses: Edward WINSLOW, Edward WINSLOW Jr., Asaph SOUL. Pr. 22 May 1766. <19:364> Bond 12 June 1766 by **Sarah WESTON** otherwise called **Sarah BALL**, spinster. Sureties: Thomas FOSTER, Jeremiah HOLMES, of Plymouth. Witnesses: Edward WINSLOW, Edward WINSLOW Jr.

MICRO #15 OF 31

Edward HAYWARD et al to **Mary AMES et al** of Bridgewater MA. <Middlesex Co.Deeds 24:429>
...6 Mar. 1723/4, Hannah HAYWARD, widow, Joseph HAYWARD 2d, Thomas HAYWARD 3d, Peter HAYWARD, all of Bridgewater and Edward HAYWARD of North Purchase, Bristol co., sell to Mary AMES wf of Thomas, Hannah BYRAM wf of Ebenezer and Abigail HAYWARD...interest in estate of Peter TOWN late of Cambridge, dec'd. Witnesses: Josiah BYRAM, Elisha ALLEN, Thomas HAYWARD, Ebenezer HAYWARD.

Will of **Joseph HAYWARD**, yeoman of Bridgewater MA. <Plymouth Co.PR 4:136>[4]
...dated 19 June 1718, mentions wf **Hannah**; eldest son **Joseph HAYWARD**; second son **Thomas HAYWARD**; third son **Edward HAYWARD**; youngest son **Peter HAYWARD**; to four daughters, viz: **Mary EAMES, Hannah BYRAM, Susannah HAYWARD** and **Abigail HAYWARD**, all my right & title in estate of Peter TOWN of Cambridge, dec'd; grandaughter **Alice ALGAR**, the only suriving dau of my oldest dau **Alice ALGAR**, deceased upon condition that she live with my wife her Grandmother til she arrive to eighteen years of age or til her Grandmother's decease but in case her father take her away before, then my will is... Pr. 17 July 1718. Inventory taken 16 July 1718; says he died 20 June 1718.

Estate of **Thomas HAYWARD**, yeoman of Bridgewater MA. <Plymouth Co.PR #9866>
<13:360> Letter/Bond 4 Nov. 1754, Edmond HAYWARD, yeoman of Bridgewater app'td admr. Sureties: John WILLIS, Esq. and Abia KEITH, yeoman, of Bridgewater. Witnesses: Samuel GOOLD, John LOTHROP. <13:395> Inventory taken 8 Nov. 1754 by Edward HAYWARD, Ebenezer HAYWARD and Nathaniel BRETT; real estate incl. 85 acre homestead, Ł285; 20 acres adjoyning Hurtlebury Plain, Ł44; 11 acres adjoyning homestead, Ł11; meadow with one acre of upland, Ł18. <14:4> Decree, 1755, mentions eldest son **Edmond HOWARD/HAYWARD**, son **Elijah HOWARD/HAYWARD**; daughters **Jane PEARCE** wf of Benjamin 3d of Bridgewater, **Hannah CHINA** wf of Oliver, **Bethia WILLIS** wf of Zepheniah and **Rebecca HOWARD/HAYWARD.** <14:495> Dower set off to widow **Bethiah HAYWARD** by Edward HAYWARD, Robert HAWARD, Samuel PACKARD 2d, Joseph AMES and Thomas PERKINS Jr. Sworn to 9 Dec. 1755. <19:533> Account of admr., 1767.

Estate of **Jacob MITCHELL** of Dartmouth MA. <Plymouth Co.PR 1:92>
Inventory of estate of Jacob MITCHEL late of Dartmouth who deceased in the year 1675; exhibited t the county court at Plimouth 17 Mar. 1690/91, on oath of son **Thomas MICHEL/MITCHELL.** <original> Bond 17 Mar. 1690/1 of **Edward MITCHELL** of Bridgewater and son **Thomas MITCHELL.** Surety: Edward FOBES of Bridgewater. Witnesses: John HAWARD, John KINGMAN, Samuel SPRAGUE.

PLYMOUTH COUNTY DEEDS: (re: Akerman PETTINGALE)

<75:143> - 12 Oct. 1738, Akerman PETTINGALE, ordered arrested for debt, the debtor having absconded or absented himself for some time before.
<41:87> - 10 Apr. 1750, Akerman PETTINGALE, cooper of Bridgewater to Inhabitants of W. Bridgewater, one acre next to minister's lot.
<42:102> - 24 Apr. 1753, Akerman PETTINGALE, yeoman of Bridgewater, land for ministry.
<112:18> - 12 Apr. 1808, Akerman PETTINGALE, yeoman of Bridgew. to Mary SMITH & Gilbert SNELL.
<109:95> - 30 July 1808, Akerman PETTINGALE, yeoman of Bridgewater to Simeon KEITH.
<108:248> - 14 Nov. 1808, Akerman PETTINGALE, yeoman of Bridgewater to Joseph SNELL.
<112:3> - 14 Nov. 1808, Akerman PETTINGALE, yeoman of Bridgewater to Ruel DUNBAR & Josiah DUNBAR of Bridgewater, land in Bridgewater.
<112:217> - 30 May 1810, Akerman PETTINGALE, yeoman of Bridgewater to Simeon KEITH.
<122:225> - 8 Mar. 1814, Akerman PETTINGALE, yeoman of Bridgewater to Oliver JACKSON.
<130:173> - 8 Apr. 1817, Akerman PETTINGALE, yeoman of Bridgewater to Silas PACKARD.
<135:228> - 17 Aug. 1818, Akerman PETTINGALE, yeoman of Bridgewater to Pardon KEITH.

Estate of **Akerman PETTINGALE**, laborer of N. Bridgewater MA. <Plymouth Co.PR #15833>
<71:230> Letter, 6 Apr. 1834. <75:105> Notice of app'tment. <76:137> Inventory. <77:202> Account. <81:143> Account.

Benjamin VICKERY of Bridgewater MA to **Josiah ALLEN** of same. <Plymouth Co.Deeds 42:133>
...26 Jan. 1743/4, Benjamin VICKERY sells to Josiah ALLEN...house and part of my lands in E. Bridgewater. Wf Mary VICKERY releases dower. Ack. 4 Aug. 1753 by both. Rec. 18 Sept. 1753.

Benjamin VICKERY of Bridgewater MA to **Joseph GANNETT.** <Plymouth Co.Deeds 45:186>
...27 Feb. 1758, Benjamin VICKERY, housewright, sells to Joseph GANNETT...nine acres in Bridgewater. Wf Mary VICKERY signs. Ack. 3 Apr. 1758 by both. Rec. 12 June 1759.

Benjamin VICKERY of Mendon MA to **John HAMNER** of Bridgewater MA. <Plymouth Co.Deeds 47:258>
...24 May 1762, Benjamin VICKERY, house carpenter, sells to John HAMNER, gent...nineteen and three quarter acres with house & barn in E. Bridgewater. Ack. 26 May 1762 by both & Rec 31 July.

PLYMOUTH COUNTY DEEDS: (re: John MITCHELL)

<73:243> - 1701, John MITCHELL & wf Mary.
<62:201> - 1772, Edward MITCHELL to son John MITCHELL of Bridgewater.
<62:202> - 1774, William MITCHELL to John MITCHELL of Bridgewater.
<62:202> - 1778, Edward MITCHELL Jr. to John MITCHELL of Bridgewater.
<62:202> - 1779, Bradford MITCHELL to John MITCHELL of Bridgewater.
<63:164> - 1783, John MITCHELL of Bridgewater.
<72:224> - , John MITCHELL & Ezra MITCHELL.
<75:74> - , John MITCHELL & wf Rizpah.

(References only with no data: 68:6; 83:144; 60:60; 66:109; 77:118,163; 83:131.)

Michael LOWDEN of Duxbury MA to **John & Ezra MITCHELL** of same. <Plymouth Co.Deeds 80:63>
...1 June 1789, Michael LOWDEN, yeoman, for £6, sold to John MITCHELL and Ezra MITCHELL, yeomen of Duxbury...all my right in a piece of salt marsh that Jonathan PETERSON of Duxbury gave to his son David PETERSON in his last will...about one acre on west side of Pine Point River in Duxbury. Wf Eunice LOWDEN releases dower. Witnesses: Seth CHANDLER, Michael LOWDEN Jr. Ack. 2 Apr. 1796 by Michael. Rec. 9 Apr. 1796.

Estate of **John HAYWARD** of Bridgewater MA. <Plymouth Co.PR #9806>
<3:14> Letter 21 Nov. 1710, son **Joseph HAYWARD** and son in law **Nathaniel BRETT** app'td admrs. Surety: Edward FOBES of Bridgewater. <original> Bond 7 Dec. 1710 of admrs. Witnesses: Isaac JOHNSON, John FIELD. <3:16> Inventory taken 30 Nov. 1710, by Edward FOBES, Isaac JOHNSON, John FIELD; numerous real estate holdings incl. 36 acres with housing, £150; 72 acres at Matfield, £200; 44 acres near Tettequot, £40; half a right in Taunton North purchase, £40; meadow near mouth of Cowweset River, £6. Sworn to by appraisers, 7 Dec. 1710. Inventory of personal estate, total £228.11s9d sworn to by **Sarah HEYWARD/HAYWARD**, widow. <original> Memorandum, debts due from: Elisabeth HAYWARD, Jonathan SPRAGUE, Nicholas WHITMAN, Ebenezer WHITMAN, Capt. FIELD, Ensign. MITCHEL, Mr. MURDOCH of Plymouth and Capt. AMES. <3:17> Settlement of estate, 12 Dec. 1710 to following heirs, viz: widow **Sarah HAYWARD**; eldest son **John HAYWARD**, dec'd and his two minor daughters **Susanna & Sary HAYWARD**; sons **Joseph HAYWARD** (2nd), **Thomas HAYWARD** (3rd), **Benony HAYWARD** (4th); daughters: **Sarah BRETT** wf of Nathaniel, **Mary EAMES** wf of William, **Susanna HAYWARD** wf of Thomas, **Elizabeth HAYWARD** and **Mercy HAYWARD.** <original> Account 23 Dec. 1723, of admrs.

Sarah HAYWARD, widow of Bridgewater to **Josiah HAYWARD** of same. <Plymouth Co.Deeds 19:31>
...12 May 1714, Sarah HAYWARD, widow of John HAYWARD, for £20.15s, sold to Josiah HAYWARD...land in Bridgewater between the Town River & Satuckett River, being the one half of a fifty acre lot laid out upon the purchase right of Elisha HAYWARD dec'd. Witnesses: William WASHBURN, John WILLIS. Ack. 30 Aug. 1716. Rec. 2 June 1725.

Sarah HAYWARD, widow of Bridgewater MA to **Jacob TOMSON** of Middleborough MA. <Plymouth Co.Deeds>
<12:194>...13 Apr. 1715, Sarah HAYWARD, dau of Experience MICHELL dec'd, for £8, sold to Jacob

TOMSON...my one quarter part of that whole share of land both divided & undivided which did originally belong unto my Honoured Father Experience MICHELL in ye Purchase called ye Sixteen Shilling Purchase in Assawamsett Neck...also my one quarter part which did originally belong unto my sd father in ye Purchase called ye South Purchase in Middleborough. Witnesses: Nathaniel BRETT, Benoni HAYWARD. Ack. 4 May 1715. Rec. 20 June 1717.

==

Petition of **Nathaniel & Sarah BRETT** of Bridgewater MA. <Book of Sessions 2:34,37>
...At his Majesties Court of General Sessions of the Peace...held at Plymouth...third Tuesday of December A.D.1731...Nathaniel BRETT of Bridgewater in the County of Plymouth and Sarah his wife one of the daughters of **John HAYWARD** late of Bridgewater deceased, shewing That the said deceased left **Sarah HAYWARD** his widow, and mother of said Sarah one of the complainants, and that for about twelve years last past they have wholly maintained her at their own cost and that for the space of about four years last she hath been bead-riden and is now about ninety years old during the whole time and now is incapable of maintaining her self, and that the Complainants have often requested **Joshua HAYWARD** and **Susanna** his wife of Bridgewater, **Josiah WINSLOW** and **Sarah** his wife of Easton, said said(sic) **Susanna** and **Sarah** being the only children of **John HAYWARD** deceased, and one of the sons of said Widow, **Joseph ALGER** and **Mary** his wife, **William AMES, Thomas CONANT** and **Martha** his wife, **Bethiah AMES** and **Hannah AMES** all of Bridgewater, **Jonathan NELSON** of Mendon and **Sarah** his wife, which said Mary, William, Martha, Bethiah, Hannah and Sarah are the children of **Mary AMES** deceased one of the daughters of said Widow and are Grand-children of said Widow; **Joseph HAYWARD, Thomas HAYWARD** and **Benoni HAYWARD** all of Bridgewater and sons of said Widow; and **Thomas HAYWARD** of said Bridgewater and **Susanna** his wife one of the daughters of said Widow; **Edmund RAWSON** of Uxbridge and **Elizabeth** his wife daughter of said Widow, and **John RAWSON** of Mendham who married with **"Mercy"** now deceased one of the daughters of said Widow in the behalf of said two children had by said **"Mary"** and are now minors, to do their proportionable part towards the maintenance of said Widow, but they utterly refused so to do. <p.38> Wherefore the Complainants pray that all the afore named Persons may be summoned to appear before this Court at the next Sessions to shew cause if any they have, why they do not do their proportion towards the said Widows maintainance for time past as well as time to come, and to be proceeded against as the law directs in such cases. Whereupon said Court ordered that the several Persons complained against be summoned to appear at the next term to shew cause if any they have, why they neglect to do their proportionable part toward the maintanance of said **Sarah HAYWARD** as set forth in the Petition.

MICRO #16 OF 30

Estate of **Benoni HAYWARD** of Bridgewater MA. <Plymouth Co.PR #9755>
<10:94> Letter 4 Mar. 1745, Samuel DUNBAR and Nathaniel BRETT, husbandmen of Bridgewater, app'td admrs. <original> Bond 4 Mar. 1744/5, of admrs. Sureties: Daniel HUDSON, Samuel EDSON, gentlemen of Bridgewater. Witnesses: Edward WINSLOW, Hannah WINSLOW. <10:151> Inventory taken 11 Mar. 1745 by Joseph EDSON, Josiah HAWARD, Shepard FISK; incl. homestead, L980; appraisers made oath to inventory 16 Mar. 1745, admrs. on 7 Apr. 1746. <10:152> Allowance 7 Apr. 1746 to widow **Hannah HOWARD/HAYWARD,** Ł50 out of personal estate for house keeping. <10:266> Dower set off to widow, 20 June 1746 by Joseph EDSON, Jona. HAWARD, Shepard FISK, David HAWARD, Josiah SNELL Jr. who made oath 24 June 1746.

==

Estate of **John HAYWARD Jr.** of Bridgewater MA. <Plymouth Co.PR #9805>
<2:58> Letter/Bond 21 June 1705 of widow **Susanah HOWARD/HAYWARD,** admx. Surety: Samuel EDSON. Witnesses: Job OTIS, Cornelius WALDO. <2:58> Guardianship, 21 June 1705, **Susanah HAYWARD,** widow, app'td gdn. of daughters **Susanah HAYWARD** and **Sarah HAYWARD** (both under 14). <original> Inventory taken 4 May 1705 by Nicholas BYRAM, John FIELD, Nathaniel BRETT; the only real estate is housing and land, Ł54; admx. made oath 22 June 1705. <2:58> Division of personal estate, to widow Ł15.6s 8d, to the two children, Ł30.13s4d.

==

Will of **Joseph HAYWARD** of Bridgewater MA. <Plymouth Co.PR #9814>
<14:498>...dated 6 July 1751, mentions wf **Mehetable,** daus **Hannah HAYWARD, Sarah/Sary HAYWARD, Mehetable EDSON, Jonna SNOW;** children of dec'd dau **Melatiah DUNBAR;** sons **Thomas HAYWARD** and **Benjamin HAYWARD** (executors); mentions land lying between the road that leads from Lieut. John JONES to Esqr. WILLIS'. Witnesses: Daniel JOHNSON, Josiah EDSON Jr., James JOHNSON. On 9 May 1758, Daniel JOHNSON and James JOHNSON made oath to will. <14:500> Letter 9 May 1758, **Thomas HAYWARD** and **Benjamin HAYWARD** app'td admrs. <original> Division 16 Apr. 1774, to daus **Hannah HAYWARD** and **Sarah HAYWARD,** in joint partnership with the estate of their brother **Benjamin HAYWARD** late of Bridgewater dec'd; oath to division made 6 June 1774 by Edward HAWARD, James ALGER, Jesse HAWARD.

==

Estate of **Benjamin HAYWARD** of Bridgewater MA.
<original> Warrant for Division 4 Apr. 1774, to Edward HAWARD, Isaac JOHNSON, Simeon BRETT. Division 16 May 1774, to eldest son **Joseph HAYWARD,** sons **Daniel HAYWARD, Benjamin HAYWARD, Cary HAYWARD,** daus **Sarah SNELL** wf of Isacher & **Mary HAYWARD;** mentions lands in partnership with Benjamin's sisters **Hannah HAYWARD & Sarah HAYWARD** and lands bounded by land of Francis CARY, Ephraim WILLIS, John BRETT, Widow BRETT, Edmund HAYWARD, Shepard FISK, James HAWARD, Joseph HAWARD, Jonathan HAWARD, Mr. JOHNSON, Terah WHITMAN, George PACKARD, Jabez FIELD, Silas DUNBAR.

==

Will of **Daniel MANLY,** yeoman of Bridgewater MA. <Plymouth Co.PR 38:536>
...dated 13 Dec. 1796, mentions wf **Sarah** and eldest son **Daniel MANLEY** (executors); 2nd son **Nathaniel MANLY;** daus **Olive HAYWARD** wf of Joseph and **Sarah MANLY** (minor); grandsons **Daniel MANLY** (son

of **Daniel MANLY Jr.**), **Hayward MANLY** (son of **Nathaniel MANLY**) and **Manly HAYWARD** (son of **Joseph HAYWARD**); to son in law **Joseph HAYWARD** fifty dollars...in consideration for a piece of ground of a suitable bigness for a burying ground in the place where my first wife was buried; fifty dollars...for the use or for to build a school house in the English school Rick wherein my habitation lies; real estate mentioned incl. ten acre woodland bought of Daniel DUNBAR adjoining land of Jacob DUNBAR & land in Taunton North Purchase which I had of my father, **Thomas MANLY** formerly living in Eastown. Witnesses: Jona. PACKARD 2d, Peres PACKARD, Isaacher SNELL Jr., Abigail SNELL. Pr. 3 Apr. 1804 by **Daniel MANLY/MANLEY**, exr., Peres PACKARD and Isaacher SNELL Jr.

Estate of **Manly HAYWARD**, yeoman of N. Bridgewater MA. <Plymouth Co.PR>
<52:416> Letter 6 Dec. 1825, Mark PERKINS of N. Bridgewater, appt'd admr. Sureties: Benjamin KINGMAN, Benjamin AMES. <60:89> 6 Dec.1825, Daniel MANLEY, Howard MANLEY, John TILDEN Jr., yeomen of N. Bridgewater, app'td to appraise estate. Inventory, real estate, $740, personal, $1352.46. <60:91> Allowance 3 Jan. 1826, to widow **Mary HAYWARD.** <63:78> 2nd Account of admr., 24 Apr. 1826; incl. payments to widow as guardian to two of her children and Salmon, guardian to a minor son. <63:79> 4 Apr. 1826, John TILDEN Jr., Howard MANLEY and Hayward MARSHALL Jr., all of N. Bridgewater, app'td to appraise estate of **Martha HAYWARD & Mary Ann HAYWARD,** minor daus, of whom the widow is guardian. Inventory 21 June 1826, incl. 37 acres at $20 per acre. <78:104> Warrant to appraise estate of Manly HAYWARD, to Jesse PERKINS, Galen MANLEY and Howard MANLEY, and to divide among three children, **Joseph HAYWARD, Martha HAYWARD & Mary Ann HAYWARD.** Division made to heirs, 21 Mar. 1836. <76:297> Inventory 30 June 1834, by John TILDEN Jr., Salmon MANLEY and Howard MANLEY of estate of **Martha & Mary Ann HAYWARD,** minor daus. <78:286> Account 1 July 1834, of Hayward MARSHALL Jr., gdn. to **Martha & Mary Ann HAYWARD;** incl. payments to Herman PACKARD, Jesse PERKINS. <79:270> Account 4 July 1837, of Hayward MARSHALL Jr.

Will of **Lyman DRAKE** of Sharon CT. <no source>
...dated 5 Oct. 1844, mentions wife **Mary Ann,** son **Manly DRAKE** (under 21), dau **Emily DRAKE** (under 21). John SELEE of Easton executor. Witnesses: George HOWARD, Charles STONE, Lois FRENCH.

Estate of **William AMES** of Bridgewater MA. <Plymouth Co.PR #459>
<3:171,249> Bond 19 Dec. 1712, of brother **Nathaniel AMES,** admr. <55:88,225> Settlement of estate 26 Jan. 1726, among following heirs, viz: son **William AMES,** daus **Mary ALGER** wf of Joseph, **Martha CONANT** wf of Thomas, **Bethiah AMES, Hannah AMES** and **Sarah AMES.**

Will of **Capt. Jacob HAZEN** of Norwich CT. <Norwich CT PR>
<8:360>...dated 16 June 1789, mentions wf **Mary,** children **Jacob, William, Philena, Lydia, Frederick, Celinda, Levinia** and **Jaben.** <8:413> Distribution 10 Nov. 1791 to following children, viz: **Jacob HAZEN, William HAZEN, Frederick HAZEN, Jaben HAZEN** (youngest son), **Philena BURNHAM** wf of James Jr., **Lydia CORWIN** wf of Hubbard and **Celinda BALDWIN** wf of Waterman.

Hubbard CORWIN of Tunbridge VT to **Frederick HAZEN.** <Norwich CT Deeds 30:382>
...28 Oct. 1797, Hubbard CORWIN & wf Lydia, sell to Frederick HAZEN...all our right in estate of our brother Jabin HAZEN of Norwich dec'd.

William BRETT to **Mary HAZEN** of Norwich CT. <Norwich CT Deeds 15:536>
...19 Mar. 1761, William BRETT, in consideration of ye love, good will and parental affection that I have and do bear towards my well beloved & dutiful daughter Mary HAZEN, wf of Jacob HAZEN.

NORWICH CT DEEDS: (re: William BRETT)

<9:518> - 8 July 1745, William BRETT from Joshua HUNTINGTON, land on Potapauge Hill.
<12:375> - 10 Apr. 1747, William BRETT to Ruth BINGHAM.
<13:206> - 6 Oct. 1757, William BRETT & wf Bethiah, mortgage to James BOWDOIN of Roxbury MA, land on Potapage Hill (save part disposed to Joseph BINGHAM).
<15:530> - 10 Dec. 1760, Release of above mortgage by James BOWDOIN.
<15:232> - 25 Apr. 1760, William BRETT sells to Jacob HAZEN, land on Potapauge Hill.
<16:510> - 9 Apr. 1761, William BRETT sells to son Ephraim BRETT of Norwich, land on Potapauge Hill with house & barn, adjoining Jacob HAZEN's.
<17:74> - , William BRETT to Abner LADD. Witnesses: Sarah BRETT, Sarah GIDDINGS.
<17:137> - , William BRETT to Jacob HAZEN, land bounded by land I conveyed to said Jacob HAZEN & wf Mary by deed of gift 19 Mar. 1761.
<17:197> - , William BRETT to son in law Nathaniel GIDDINGS Jr.
<22:186> - , William BRETT to Ephraim BRETT.

Will of **Thomas HAYWARD,** husbandman of Bridgewater MA. <Plymouth Co.PR #9865>
<8:367>...dated 18 July 1740, mentions wf **Bethia** (executrix); to son **Seth HAYWARD,** all my home farme with one yoke of oxen, two cows, eight sheep, one horse, husbandry tools, gunn, sword, ammunition; to dau **Alice CUSHMAN** & her son **Thomas CUSHMAN,** ten acres on north side of Great River below Richard JENNINGS; to daus **Bethia & Mary** land on ye southerly side of ye land that was formerly James BARRETT's; to dau **Phebe,** land which I bought of Japhet PRATT Jr. in Bridgewater. Witnesses: Richard DAVENPORT, Enoch LEONARD, Nathaniel HAYWARD who made oath 8 June 1741. <8:369> Letter/Bond 8 June 1741, **Bethia HAYWARD,** widow, app'td admx. Sureties: Jacob HAYWARD, Joseph PRATT, yeomen of Bridgewater. Witnesses: Arthur HARRIS, William LUNT.

MICRO #17 OF 30

Thomas MITCHELL to **Experience MITCHELL.** <Plymouth Co.Deeds 3:300>
...15 Nov. 1669, Thomas MITCHELL to father Experience MITCHELL. Ack. 6 6mth 1674. On same date, deed from Experience MITCHELL to son Jacob MITCHELL.

Thomas MITCHELL of Duxbury MA to **Richard WRIGHT** of Plymouth MA. <Plymouth Co.Deeds 3:234>
...1 Aug. 1662, Thomas MITCHELL, planter, for £6, sells to Richard WRIGHT, tailor...his part of a tract in Plymouth given him by his grandfather **Francis COOKE** of Plymouth, lying about Jones River meadow at a place called Cooke's Holes, 60 acres. <MD 3:104>

JOHN COOKE^{2} (Francis^{1})

PLYMOUTH COUNTY DEEDS: (re: COOKE)

<3:24> - 6 Nov. 1664, John WASHBURN Jr. sells to Gov. BRADFORD, land at Yarmouth given him by Experience MITCHELL.
<3:41> - 15 Nov. 1665, land laid out on west side of Nemassakett River, mentions Experience Mitchell's 8th lot.
<5:465> - 7 July 1681, John COOKE to Jonathan DELANO.
<5:388> - 28 Nov. 1683, John COOKE sells to Thomas TABER, mason of Dartmouth.
<6:70> - 8 July 1686, John COOKE sells to Stephen WEST of Portsmouth RI...Mackatan Island.
<5:466> - 6 Nov. 1691, John COOKE to Jonathan DELANO.
<5:491> - 27 July 1691, John & Ruth COOKE of Little Compton sell to Samuel LITTLE of Marshfield.

John COOKE to **Richard WRIGHT & Thomas MICHELL.** <Plymouth Co.Deeds 3:73>
...8 June 1666, John COOKE confirms to Richard WRIGHT & Thomas MICHELL...threescore acres of upland and meadow given by my father **Francis COOKE** unto the said Wright & Michell...which lyeth near Jones River meadow. Witnesses: John BOURNE, Nathaniel MORTON.

William MAKEPEACE of Freetown MA to **William DAVIS** of same. <Bristol Co.Deeds 7:141>
...31 Aug. 1688, William MAKEPEACE, husbandman, conveys to William DAVIS, husbandman & wf Mary... 100 acres in Freetown. "Abigail MAKEPEACE wife of William & Anna MAKEPEACE mother of William consent". Witness: John KNOWLMAN, Thomas MAKEPEACE, Elias WILLIAMS. Ack. 31 Aug. 1689 by Wm. MAKEPEACE. Rec. 25 Jan. 1711/12.

BRISTOL COUNTY DEEDS: (re: William DAVIS)

<15:160> - 1719/20, William DAVIS sold land he bought in 1688.
<18:107> - 1727/8, William DAVIS & William DAVIS Jr. to Ambrose BARNABY.
<40:279> - 1754, William DAVIS & wf Keziah to Ambrose BARNABY.
<41:164> - 1754, William DAVIS, mortgage to Nathan SIMMONS.

Petition of **John COOKE** of Dartmouth MA. <Mass.State Archives: Indian, 1639-1705, p.327>
...To his Excell^{y} Sr. Wm. Phips & the Honord Council for their Maties Province of ye Massachusetts Bay in New England. The Humble Petition of **John COOKE** of Dartmouth...in the County of Bristol in ye Province afores^{d} Humbly Sheweth

That your Petitioner one of the Antientest Inhabitants in this Province who arrived from England in the County of Plim^{o} Anno Dom 1620 with his Father who was one of the first Purchasers and Old Comers who layd out and expended a Considerable Estate in setling the first Plantation, and your Petitioner being much conversant with the Sachems Papamoe, Machacom, Achawannomet who had a considerable Tract of Land situate between Dartmouth & Sandwich the chief of them being Papamo was indebted to your Petitioner and by reason of the obligaion he had to and kindness he had for your Petitioner did often in his life time by word and deed and before his Death will the said land to your Petitioner and Mr. **William BRADFORD** and entrust them requiring & desiring our care of his Children But ye said Land is kept away from your Petitioner & the said Papamos Children who have had no benefit thereof altho they were very serviceable in the Late Indian Warr against our Enemies under ye Command of **Major CHURCH** and have received the Christian Faith and notwithstanding there was a Reserve or Exception of the said land when the rest about it was Surrendered as being Indian or English mens rights which hath administred Occasion of Offence to the Indians Some reflecting on your Peticoner as not being faithfull to his trust, which is ground of Trouble to your Aged Peticoner and if not Remedied desires that he may be satisfactorily discharged of his trust and he will then desist tho grieved that he cannot doe as he ought for them.

And Further May it please your Excell^{y} & the Honourble Councell your Peticoner did by Peticon obtaine of the General Court of Plimouth a Grant that if your Peticoner could find out any land undisposed of and not Granted to others he should be accommodated with the same as by reference to the said Grant bearing date July 1683 being had doth fully appeare Now so it is your Petitioner doth here by certify that there is a little Island called Little Island of 2 or 3 acres of land which lyes neer Dartmouth & the said Indians Land which if with some part of the same may be conferred on your Peticoner for the good of your Peticoner and his children. Read in Council, 6 Apr. 1693.

William & Benjamin WILCOX of Dartmouth to **Samuel WILCOX.** <Bristol Co.Deeds 59:227>
...28 Mar. 1769, William WILCOX & Benjamin WILCOX, laborers, to brother Samuel WILCOX...by our

honoured Father Jeremiah WILLCOX by his last will...Ack. 9 Oct. 1769. Rec. 5 May 1779.
(Note: three references to William WILCOX, grantor: 33:255 (1745), 34:400 (1746), 50:127 (1765).)

Capt. Benjamin WILCOX et al, divide land. <Bristol Co.Deeds 66:357>
...19 May 1787, Jesse CORNELL, Capt. Benjamin WILCOX and William WILCOX, yeomen of Dartmouth, divide land formerly of Jeremiah WILCOX, dec'd.

Estate of **Benjamin WILCOX** of Westport MA. <Bristol Co.PR 222:128>
Division of estate, 4 Nov. 1864, to following heirs, viz: **Henry T. WILCOX, Patience WILCOX** (double portion), **Jeremiah WILCOX, Thomas B. WILCOX, Sarah W. SEABURY** wf of Charles P., all of New Bedford and **Hodiah B. WILCOX** of Cranston RI.

Richard ALMY et al to **Jeremiah WILCOX et al.** <Bristol Co.Deeds 103:496>
...15 June 1816, Richard ALMY & wf Patience of Dartmouth and Christopher SLOCUM & wf Phebe of Chilmark, to Jeremiah WILCOX of Scipio(sp) NY, Benjamin WILCOX of Westport and Henry WILCOX of Dartmouth. Ack. by grantors 10 Jan. 1818.

Benjamin WILCOX et al to **Sylvia SISSON.** <Bristol Co.Deeds 103:111>
...8 Sept. 1817, Jeremiah WILCOX, of Soipio, Cayuga co. NY, Benjamin WILCOX and Henry WILCOX, the legal heirs of Benjamin WILCOX of Westport dec'd, sells to Sylvia SISSON, land mortgaged by her.

Benjamin WILCOX of Westport MA to **Jeremiah & Henry WILCOX** of NY. <Bristol Co.Deeds 118:298>
...3 Nov. 1825, Benjamin WILCOX, yeoman (son of Benjamin) & wf Patty, for $4000.00, mortgage to Jeremiah WILCOX and Henry WILCOX of Genoa(sp), Cayuga co., NY.

BRISTOL COUNTY DEEDS: (re: WILCOX)

<118:331> - 2 Nov. 1825, Jeremiah WILCOX & wf Ruth, Benjamin WILCOX & wf Patty...
<118:332> - 2 Nov. 1825, Jeremiah WILCOX & wf Ruth, Henry WILCOX & wf Hannah, sell to Benjamin WILCOX of Westford.

(Note: additional references to Benjamin WILCOX: 51:252 (1768); 66:357 (1787); 66:358 (1787); 71: 2 (1792).)

Will of **Samuel WILCOX** of Westport MA. <Bristol Co.PR #41:353>
...dated 12 Jan. 1804, mentions wf **Comfort**; sons **Samuel WILCOX, Humphrey WILCOX**; dau in law **Sarah WILCOX**; daus **Mary WHITE** wf of Theophilus, **Judith BRIGHTMAN** wf of Gardner and **Lydia BRIGHTMAN** wf of Ellis.

Daniel WILCOX/WILCOCKES of Portsmouth RI to **Edward LAY.** <no source>
...1 Aug. 1661, Daniel WILCOCKES, for £40, sold to Edward LAY of the island called the vineyard ...sixteen acres in Portsmouth...bounded by land of Capt. Richard MORRIS...excepting halfe a rod broad from the high way next the sea...above the grave of my deere buried wife. Witnesses: Philip TABOR, John ARBER.

Will of **Edward WILCOCKS/WILCOX**, husbandman of Tiverton RI. <Bristol Co.PR 3:433>
...dated 19 May 1718, mentions wf **Sarah**; sons **Josiah WILCOCKS. Ephraim WILCOCKS** (under 21), **William WILCOCKS** (under 21); dau **Freelove WILCOCKS**; brother Stephen **WILCOCKS** of Dartmouth; brother in law **John MANCHESTER** of Tiverton. Witnesses: Stephen MANCHESTER, Thomas MANCHESTER, Samuel SANFORD Pr. 2 June 1718. <3:434> Inventory taken 29 May 1718.

John EARL of South Kingstown RI to **Benjamin EARL** of Warwick RI. <Bristol Co.Deeds 23:519>
...9 June 1735, John EARL, yeoman, for £100, sold to brother Benjamin EARL, yeoman...all rights in Tiverton in the county of Bristol and province of the Massachusets Bay...and is known by the name of Pocasset...170 acres...bounded by land of Joseph WANTON and David DURFEY, the highway and Nannaquacok Pond...land that was given to our honoured mother Mary EARL and her children by the last will...of our grandfather Mr. Daniel WILCOCKS. Witnesses: John WICKES, Thomas MARKHAM. Ack. 9 June 1735. Rec. 17 June 1735.

Benjamin EARLE of Warwick RI to **William EARLE** of Providence RI. <Warwick RI Deeds 10:327>
...29 May 1770, Benjamin EARLE, yeoman, for three hundred Spanish Milled Dollars, sold to William EARLE, mariner...60 acres in Warwick...known by the name of the Four miles Township and in the Plain Land Division...bounded by land of Capt. Benjamin GREENE. Witnesses: Sarah GORTON, Robert RHODES. Ack. 30 May 1770. Rec. 18 July 1771.

Estate of **Capt. Benjamin EARLE**, yeoman. <Warwick RI PR 3:307>
Inventory taken 13 Sept. 1773, personal estate only.

William EARLE of Providence RI to **Benjamin GORTON** of Warwick RI. <Warwick RI Deeds 10:349>
...30 Sept. 1771, William EARLE, mariner, for three hundred Spanish Milled Dollars, sold to Benjamin GORTON, mariner...60 acres in Warwick...in that part thereof called...the Four Miles Township and in the Plain Land Division...bounded by land of Capt. Benjamin GREENE. Wf Mary EARLE releases dower. Witnesses: Samuel CHACE, Gershom CARPENTER. Ack. 26 Oct. 1771. Rec. 6 Jan. 1772.

Capt. Benjamin EARLE of Warwick RI to **Sarah GORTON** of Warwick RI. <Warwick RI Deeds 10:266>
...30 May 1770, Benjamin EARLE, yeoman, for and in consideration of the paternal love & affection

which I have...towards my daughter Sarah GORTON, wife of Capt. Benjamin GORTON, mariner, and also for the Care and trouble she hath for several years past been at not only attending upon her Mother but also upon me, as we stood in Need of Assistance through age and Infirmity of Body have given...unto her...my lot of land lying at Rockey Hill in Warwick which I bought of Joseph POTTER containing about thirteen acres and a half...bounded by land of Capt. Benjamin GORTON, John WARNER, Zebulon UTTER, Elder HOLDEN, John BUDLONG, Nathan BUDLONG...also eight acres of land lying in the Horse Neck Division in Warwick...together with my thatch bed...bounded by land of John BARTON, Esq., Capt. Anthony SNOW...also three lots of land lying in the first point in Warwick which I bought of John CARDER and a piece of land adjoining thereto I bought of the Town, the whole contains near about an acre and a half, bounded by land of Mrs. LEPPITT, John WARNER Jr. and son in law Capt. Benjamin GORTON. Witnesses: Jer. LIPPITT, Daniel BRAYTON. Ack. 31 May 1770 by Capt. Benjamin EARLE. Rec. 21 Dec. 1770.

Will of **William EARLE** of Providence RI. <Providence RI PR 9:442>
...dated 16 Mar. 1801, bequests to: eldest son **John EARLE** the dwelling house and lot of land whereon he now lives; grandsons **John Tillinghast EARLE** and **William EARLE**, sons of son **William EARLE**, dec'd; son **George EARLE**, lands bought of Joshua HACKER and Joseph WHIPPLE; son **Oliver EARLE**, the mansion house where I now dwell on the Main or Water St.; dau **SHELDON** wf of Capt. Charles SHELDON; grandchildren (unm.,under 21), **George Brown EARLE, Sarah Ann EARLE, Martha EARLE, Maria EARLE** and **Fanny EARLE**; grandchildren (unm., under 21), **William Earle TILLINGHAST, Joseph TILLINGHAST, Polly TILLINGHAST** and **Amy Ann TILLINGHAST**; sons **George & Oliver**, executors. Witnesses: George TILLINGHAST, Moses EDDY and Charles W. TILLINGHAST. Pr. 11 Feb. 1805. <9:514> Inventory taken by executors, no date.

Mary WILCOCKS/WILCOX of Dartmouth MA to **Jeremiah WILCOCKS** of Newport RI.<Bristol Co.Deeds 45:207>
...24 Sept. 1705, Mary WILCOCKS, dau of Samuel WILCOCKS late of Dartmouth, dec'd and Mary his wife, single woman, for ye goodwill and affection which I have and bare to my Loving Brother Jeremiah WILCOCKS, joyner...all my right...unto one eighth part of land in Dartmouth which was given by my Honoured Grandfather Daniel WILCOCKS late of Dartmouth dec'd to my youngest brother William WILCOCKS infant dec'd. Witnesses: William CARTER, John STEPHENS. Ack. 25 Sept. 1705. Rec. 8 Sept 1761.

MICRO #18 OF 30

Estate of **Benjamin WILLCOX/WILCOX**, yeoman of Dartmouth MA. <Bristol Co.PR>
<51:534> Inventory taken 9 Mar. 1816 by John WING, yeoman and Henry TUCKER, merchant, both of Dartmouth and William WHITE, Esq. of Westport; incl. live stock on the Wilbour farm, $861.50; hay, $302.00; cash & notes, $7271.97; property on the Allen farm and on the old homestead; total, $10,120.43. <original> Petition 11 Mar. 1816 of **Patience WILLCOX** that her son in law **Richard ALMY** be app'td admr., as she is too feeble and infirm. Signed by Patience WILLCOX, Patience WILLCOX, Benjamin WILLCOX, Christopher SLOCUM and Henry WILLCOX. Witnesses: William WHITE 2d, Henry TUCKER <151:242> 5 Apr. 1816, **Richard ALMY**, yeoman of Dartmouth app'td admr. <original> Bond 5 Apr. 1816 of admr. Sureties: Peleg ALMY, Resolved HOWLAND, yeomen of Dartmouth. Witnesses: Thomas COOK Jr., Arnold BLISS Jr. <110:332> Order, 5 Apr. 1816, to admr. to post his appointment in The New Bedford Mercury and in the town of Dartmouth; oath of admr. that notice had been posted, 7 May 1816. <54:492> Release 15 June 1816, **Patience WILLCOX**, widow, for & in consideration of being well and comfortably supported during my natural life by my children **Jeremiah WILCOX, Benjamin WILCOX, Henry WILCOX, Patience ALMY** wf of Richard and **Phebe SLOCUM** wf of Christopher...forever quit claim unto the said children...all manner of dower...which I have. Witnesses: Zebedee A. MACOMBER, Holder RUSSELL. <54:624> Receipt 15 June 1816 of above children to admr...for the whole amount of the personal estate...in a Division of said Estate this day made with all the heirs. Witnesses: Zebedee MACOMBER, Russell SHERMAN.

Will of **Jeremiah WILCOX**, yeoman of Dartmouth MA. <Bristol Co.PR>
<20:294>...dated 31 Dec. 1765...far advanced in years, mentions sons **Samuel WILCOX** and **Benjamin WILCOX**; children of dec'd dau **Mary**; real estate: homestead farm, ten acre salt meadow at Masquamscuset, salt meadow in the Hors Neck Segg Flats in the river, cedar swamp at Wattuppa. <20:296> Pr. 10 May 1768. <20:320> Inventory.
(Note: Additional references to the name **Jeremiah WILCOX** are given with no clue as to how many men of this name they pertain to: <120:509> Notice of sale; <121:18> Notice of appointment; <167:181> Adm. (1864); <183:575> Will; <189:13> Pr.; <195:504> Inventory; <214:303> Sale of land (1861); <217:540> Account; <221:30,359> "Homestead"; <222:53,392> Dower.

References to **Jeremiah WILCOX**, grantee, all to 1795. <Bristol Co.Deeds>
<1:123> 1696; <13:386> 1718; <28:239> 1740 (mortgage); <45:207> 1761; <51:473> 1768>

Will of **George SMITH** of Dartmouth MA. <Bristol Co.PR>
<75:361>...dated 3 Apr. 1835, mentions son **Holder SMITH**; children of son **Howland SMITH**; son **George SMITH Jr.** (executor); son **Moses SMITH**; dec'd dau **Rebecca L. HOWLAND**; dau **Abigail T. KIRBY**; dau **Mary S. MACOMBER**. Pr. 28 July 1835. <75:369> Inventory.

Daniel WILCOKS/WILCOX of Little Compton to **Jeremiah WILCOK/WILCOX.** <Bristol Co.Deeds 1:5>
...4 Oct. 1689, Daniel WILCOKS, for & in consideration of the naturall affection I bare unto my Grandson Jeremiah WILCOKS...doe hereby give one eighth part of a share of land in Dartmouth divided or undivided one hundred accers where the dwelling house now stands with one half of the

meadow lyeing at the Horse Neck, five acres...bounded by land of Nathaniel SOULE and Philip TABER Witnesses: Sarah WHITE, Zachariah ALLEN. Ack. by Daniel 11 May 1693. Rec. 6 July 1696.

BRISTOL COUNTY DEEDS: (re: **Henry WILCOX**, grantee (all to 1910) & grantee)

<72:498>	- 26 Apr. 1792,	Henry WILCOX, cordwainer of Dartmouth, buys land in Dartmouth.
<90:323>	- 30 June 1809,	Henry WILCOX, tanner of Dartmouth, buys land in Dartmouth.
<91:204>	- 22 Jan. 1810,	Henry WILCOX, tanner of Dartmouth, buys land in Dartmouth.
<94:65>	- 1 Apr. 1812,	Henry WILCOX, farmer of Dartmouth, buys land in Dartmouth.
<95:168>	- 15 Dec. 1812,	Henry WILCOX of Dartmouth, buys wood lot in Dartmouth.
<96:67>	- 22 June 1813,	Henry WILCOX, tanner of Dartmouth, buys land in Dartmouth.
<97:379>	- 2 Nov. 1814,	Henry WILCOX, mortgage.
<101:544>	- 15 Nov. 1816,	Henry WILCOX, yeoman et al, buy land.
<105:374>	- 18 May 1818,	Henry WILCOX et al, buy land.
<111:196>	- 10 Apr. 1818,	Henry WILCOX, yeoman of Dartmouth, buys land in Dartmouth.
<106:88>	- 8 May 1818,	Henry WILCOX, tanner of Dartmouth & wf Ruby, sell land.
<136:238>	- 24 Dec. 1820,	Henry WILCOX, yeoman of Westport buys land.
<114:413>	- 1824,	Henry WILCOX & wf Ruby of Dartmouth sell land.
<118:546>	- 1826,	Henry WILCOX & wf Ruby sell land.
<124:87>	- Dec. 1827,	Henry WILCOX, yeoman of Westport, buys by execution.
<126:113>	- 3 May 1828,	Henry WILCOX & wf Hannah, sell land got by execution.
<141:249>	- 10 Jan. 1834,	Henry WILCOX, yeoman of Westport, buys land & building on Middle St. in New Bedford.
<298:40>	- 1869,	Henry WILCOX to Samuel B. WILCOX, land in Fall River.

Jeremiah WILCOX et al to **Richard ALMY et al.** <Bristol Co."PR" 105:15> (PR=Deeds?)
...15 June 1816, Jeremiah WILCOX, yeoman of Scipio, Cayuga co., NY, Benjamin WILCOX, yeoman of Westport and Henry WILCOX, yeoman of Dartmouth, for $15,000.00, quit claim to Richard ALMY & wf Patience of Dartmouth and Christopher SLOCUM & wf Phebe of Chilmark...all our right to a farm in Dartmouth known by the name of the Wilbour farm, late owned by Benjamin WILCOX late of said Dartmouth dec'd...together with the salt marsh adjoining...together with the wood land that said Wilcox bought of Holder SLOCUM, Esq. Witnesses: Zebedee A. MACOMBER, Holder RUSSELL. Ack. by grantors 15 June 1816. Rec. 10 Mar. 1818.

Heirs of **Benjamin WILCOX** of Westport MA to **Silvia SISSON** of Westport. <Bristol Co."PR" 103:111>
...8 Sept. 1817, Jeremiah WILCOX of Scipio, Cayuga co., NY, Benjamin WILCOX and Henry WILCOX of Westport MA, for $526.09, paid to us the legal heirs of Benjamin WILCOX, sell to Silvia SISSON... the farm called the Burdick farm that the said Silvia mortgaged to the said Benjamin...35 acres in Westport bounded by land of Henry HOWLAND, Ichabod BROWNELL and heirs of George BROWNELL. Witnesses: Alden MACOMBER, Zebedee A. MACOMBER. Ack. by grantors 9 Sept. 1817. Rec. 11 Sept. 1817.

Heirs of **Benjamin WILCOX** of Westport MA. <Bristol Co.Deeds 110:503>
...16 Oct. 1821, Jeremiah WILCOX of Scipio, Cayuga co., NY, Benjamin WILCOX & Henry WILCOX of Westport MA, all legal heirs to the estate whereof Benjamin WILCOX late of Dartmouth dec'd died seized, made a division of the land or farm belonging to the said three, known as the George farm in Westport...bounded by land of Daniel GIFFORD, Benjamin TUCKER and Wilbour GIFFORD. Witnesses: Abner B. GIFFORD, Eliza P. GIFFORD. Ack. by grantors 17 Oct. 1821. Rec. 18 Oct. 1821.

Estate of **Henry WILCOX** of Dartmouth MA. <Bristol Co.PR>
<80:277> Adm. 2 Apr. 1839, Barrett BEARD, admr. <80:334> Inventory. <81:228> Account, 1840, mentions widow.
(Note: References to the name "Henry WILCOX, all on old index" are given with no data, viz: <115:14> Notice. <121:280> Notice. <122:13> Notice. <154:285> Adm. letter. <160:299> Bond. <168:501> Adm. <168:507> Adm. <188:620> Adm. d.b.n. 19 Dec. 1873. <197:12> Inventory. <197:262> Inventory. <197:262> Inventory. <220:151> Account.)

Will of **Samuel PERRY** of Sandwich MA. <Barnstable Co.PR>
<8:490>...dated 2 Aug. 1750...advanced in years, to dau **Mary**, hir choise of either of my feather beds with four pair of sheets, two coverlids & two blankets; to daus **Elisabeth, Deborah, Mary** and children of my dau **Mercy** dec'd, all my beds and bedding; to sons **Nathan PERRY** and **Ebenezer PERRY** (executors) the rest and residue of my personal estate. Witnesses: Stephen SKEFF, John BOURN and Thomas BOURN. Pr. 7 Sept. 1751. <9:167> Inventory taken 18 Sept. 1751 by Stephen SKIFF, John BOURN and Thomas BOURN, total L39.8s. Oath of executors 6 Dec. 1751.

Will of **Thomas BARLOW**, husbandman of Sandwich MA. <Barnstable Co.PR>
<13:339>...dated 27 Apr. 1768, mentions wf **Mehitable**; four daughters **Sarah BARLOW, Mary BARLOW** (under 21), **Elizabeth BARLOW, Mehetable BARLOW** (under 12); five sons **Levi BARLOW, Jesse BARLOW, Obed BARLOW, Nathan BARLOW, Moses BARLOW** (all under 21); brother in law **Simeon WING** and eldest son **Levi**, executors. Witnesses: Elijah PERRY, Seth BARLOW, Abraham WILLIAMS. <13:341> Pr. 11 May 1768. <13:342> Inventory, 13 June 1768. <13:476> Division of real estate, 1 June 1769, by Elijah PERRY, Nathaniel WING and Micah BLACKWELL, to five sons. <12:408> Account, 1769, "various references to law suits; many names". <12:410> Account 30 Nov. 1770 of **Levi BARLOW**, incl. payments to: Capt. Thomas BOURN for my Mother as she was guardian to her four daughters, Ł128; my Mother as guardian to my four sisters, Ł31.16.3.; household goods to Capt. Thomas BOURN as guardian to my three youngest brothers, Ł40.5.3.; **Jesse BARLOW** for his part of the household goods, Ł15.12.0.

Guardianship of Children of **Thomas BARLOW** of Sandwich MA. <Barnstable Co.PR>
<14:222-5> 29 Nov. 1768, **Mehitable BARLOW**, widow, app'td gdn. of minor daus **Sarah BARLOW, Mary BARLOW, Mehitable BARLOW** and **Elizabeth BARLOW.** <14:226-9> 29 Nov. 1768, Thomas BOURN, gent. of Sandwich app'td gdn. of minor sons of Thomas BARLOW, viz: **Moses BARLOW, Nathan BARLOW, Jesse BARLOW** and **Obed BARLOW.** <15:159> 12 May 1773, **Jesse BARLOW**, yeoman of Sandwich app'td gdn. of **Nathan BARLOW**, minor. <15:262> 27 Feb. 1777, **Jesse BARLOW** app'td gdn. of **Moses BARLOW**, aged 15.

Will of **Nathan BARLOW** of Sandwich MA. <Barnstable Co.PR>
<27:432>...dated 18 Sept. 1795, mentions wife **Betsey**; brother **Moses BARLOW**; nephew **Jesse BARLOW** (under 21), son of brother **Jesse BARLOW**, to receive one half of real estate; brother **Obed BARLOW**; sisters **Mary WITHERLY** wf of James and **Mehitable HAMMOND** wf of Nathan; neice **Mehitable WITHERLY** (under 18), dau of James WITHERLY; nephews **Moses BARLOW & Lewis BARLOW**, sons of brother **Moses BARLOW.** <24:157> Pr. 3 Nov. 1795. <28:35> Letter, de bon non. <18:163> Bond. <28:172> Inventory. <28:166> Will. <28:168> Letter. <28:170> Letter. <28:174> Affidavit. <28:175> Complaint. <28:181> Bond. <28:184> Account. <28:189> Executor resigns. <28:190> Bond. <28:504> Receipt of heirs.

Jesse BARLOW of Sandwich MA to **Nathan BARLOW** of Sandwich. <Barnstable Co.Deeds 1:267>
...30 Dec. 1789, Jesse BARLOW, yeoman, sells to Nathan BARLOW, yeoman...land at Pocasset bought of Obed BARLOW of Sandwich, 3 Oct. 1764...all of which fell to the said Obed in the division of his father's estate. Ack. 30 Dec. 1789.

Jesse BARLOW of Sandwich MA to **Nathan BARLOW** of Sandwich. <Barnstable Co.Deeds 1:268>
...15 Mar. 1794, Jesse BARLOW, yeoman & wf Sarah, sell to Nathan BARLOW, yeoman...land bounded by lot set to Moses BARLOW in the division of his father Thomas BARLOW's estate.

Jesse BARLOW of Sandwich MA. <Barnstable Co.Deeds 2:384>
...10 Aug. 1802, Jesse BARLOW, yeoman, sells land that was legacy from Uncle Nathan BARLOW.

Jesse BARLOW of Newport RI to **John FREEMAN** of Sandwich. <Barnstable Co.Deeds 2:385>
...11 Aug. 1809, Jesse BARLOW, yeoman, sells to John FREEMAN, Esq...part of a swamp surrounded by John's land and near land Obed BARLOW sold to Nathaniel BURGESS...also land between Silas WHITFORD and Nathaniel WING.

Jesse BARLOW, mariner, & wf Polly, 4 Mar. 1812. <Barnstable Co.Deeds 2:463>
Jesse BARLOW, mariner of Sandwich, Sheriff's sale, 7 June 1826. <Barnstable Co.Deeds 2:462>
Jesse BARLOW of Sandwich, deposition, 16 Jan. 1833. <Barnstable Co.Deeds 11:143>

MICRO #19 OF 30

Will of **Nathan PERRY**, yeoman of Sandwich MA. <Barnstable Co.PR>
<13:488>...dated 5 May 1769, mentions wf **Martha**; minor sons **Seth PERRY, Thomas PERRY, Ebenezer PERRY**; dau **Mary PERRY** (under 18); daus **Sarah WING, Anna COBB**; sons Seth & Thomas executors. <13:489> Pr. 29 Nov. 1769. <12:413> Inventory, 29 Dec. 1769.

Will of **Thomas TABER Jr.**, tanner of Dartmouth MA. <Bristol Co.PR>
<4:103-4>...dated 2 Aug. 1722, mentions wf **Rebecca**; three daus (under 23), **Priscilla TABER, Esther TABER, Mary TABER**; sons **Seth TABER** (under 14), **Jonathan TABER**; brother **Joseph TABER**; son Jonathan and brother Joseph, executors. Witnesses: Jonathan DELANO, Samuel SPOONER, Thomas KENNEY. Pr. 4 Sept. 1722. Inventory 3 Dec. 1722.

Estate of **Benjamin TABER**, cooper of New Bedford MA. <Bristol Co.PR>
<55:491> Warrant for inventory, 30 Apr. 1819; house & land in north Bedford, $575, personal estate, $124.77; insolvency, 4 May 1819. <55:520> 4 May 1819, **Desire TABER**, widow, app'td admx. <57:78> Account of admx., 16 May 1820. <57:92-3> Dower, 15 Oct. 1819. <110:738> Notice, 4 May 1819. <151:431> Letter, 4 May 1819.

John COOKE of Plymouth MA to **Philip TABER** of Dartmouth MA. <Bristol Co.Deeds 10:450>
...17 July 1673, John COOKE, yeoman, for & in consideration of the love & affection I beare unto my son in law Philip TABER, mason & his wife Mary, my daughter...fifty acres in Dartmouth. Witnesses: Thomas TABER, William PALMER. Ack. 17 July 1673 by John COOKE & wf Sarah. Rec. 8 May 1717 (Note: also recorded in Plymouth Col.Deeds 3:324 and printed in MD 10:45.)

Estate of **Eunice TABER** of Fairhaven MA. <Bristol Co.PR>
<76:61,62,68> Guardianship, 6 Nov. 1835, Alfred NYE app'td gdn. of Eunice TABER, non comp. (Note: The additional references with no dates appear to refer to the same Eunice TABER with the notation that they were all that were found on the index: <30:445; 78:20,458> Accounts. <113:561> Notice of appointment. <128:214;129:281,336;142:43> Letter of guardian. <204:126;206:74> Sale of land.

References to the name **Philip TABER.** <Bristol Co.PR>
<13:6,9,10> Will, 1749, probate, inventory. <26:259,262,579> Will, inventory. <27:471> Account. <27:473,474> Receipt. <63:472> Adm. <82:19> Adm. <82:107> Inventory. <83:84> Division. <112:131> Notice. <115:89> Notice. <130:26> Guardianship. <152:257> Adm. <154:421> Adm. <160:433> Bond.

Will of **John MACOMBER**, yeoman of Dartmouth MA. <Bristol Co.PR>
<4:232>...dated 7 Oct. 1723, mentions wf **Bethiah** (exx.); sons **Philip MACOMBER** (eldest), **Abiall MACOMBER, John MACOMBER, William MACOMBER** (all under 21); unborn child; daus **Marcy MACOMBER, Mary MACOMBER** (both under 18); mother **Mary MACOMBER**; sister **Elisabeth**; father **William MACOMBER**; brother **Phillip TABER** and friends William WOOD & Nathaniel SOLE, of Dartmouth, overseers. Witnesses: William MACOMBER, William WOOD, Jedediah WOOD, Nathaniel SOLE. <4:231> Pr. 4 Nov. 1723, **Bethiah MACOMBER** app'td admx. Sureties: William WOOD, Nathaniel SOULE. <4:238> Inventory taken 28 Oct. 1723 by William WOOD & Nathaniel SOULE of Dartmouth and Thomas CORY of Tiverton; total £422.1s. <5:53> Account 17 Nov. 1724 of exx. <5:54> Receipts.

Will of **Bethiah MACOMBER**, widow of Dartmouth MA. <Bristol Co.PR>
<26:280>...dated 11 Sept. 1776, mentions sons **Philip MACOMBER, William MACOMBER** (executor); dau **Mary MACOMBER**; son **Job MACOMBER**; dau **Marcy CLOSSON**. Witnesses: Philip TRIPP, Abner POTTER, Israel WOOD. Pr. 3 Oct. 1780 on oath of Philip TRIPP and Israel WOOD.

Will of **Abial MACOMBER**, yeoman of Dartmouth MA. <Bristol Co.PR>
<9:423>...dated 22 May 1740, mentions three youngest brothers **John MACOMBER, William MACOMBER, Job MACOMBER**; mother **Bethiah MACOMBER**; brother **Philip MACOMBER**; sisters **Mary MACOMBER, Mercy CLOSSON**; mentions father's will and land bought by my father of my Uncle **Ephraim MACOMBER**. Pr. 17 June 1740.

Will of **Philip MACOMBER**, yeoman of Westport MA. <Bristol Co.PR>
<38:152>..dated 17 Feb. 1798, mentions wf **Margaret/Margrate**; sons **John MACOMBER, Philip MACOMBER, Abiel MACOMBER, Noe MACOMBER, Archer MACOMBER, Constant MACOMBER**; two children of dec'd son **Zebedee MACOMBER**; son **Humphrey MACOMBER** (executor); grandson **Zebedee MACOMBER**; dau **Margrate/Margaret ALLEN** and granddaughter **Ester CASE**; granddaughter **Nancy MACOMBER** (now living with him); granddaughters **Almy MACOMBER, Judith MACOMBER**; my five youngest daughters that are now living, granddaughter **Esther CASE**'s mother is dead. Pr. 5 May 1801.

BRISTOL COUNTY DEEDS: (re: Benjamin TABER)

<18:448> - 11 Oct. 1728, William MANCHESTER of Tiverton to my sister Susanna TABER, widow of Dartmouth.

<19:470> - 1 Aug. 1729, Philip TABER, yeoman of Dartmouth to Susanna TABER, widow of Dartmouth, sister of William MANCHESTER.

(Note: Additional references with year only: 48:464 (1765); 52:247; 57:23 (1776); 56:419 (1775); 71:322 (1792).

Will of **Joseph MOSHER**, mason of Dartmouth MA. <Bristol Co.PR>
<14:194>...dated 15 Nov. 1743, mentions wf **Lydia**; sons **James MOSHER, Philip MOSHER, Jonathan MOSHER**; daus **Ruth TRIPP, Lydia DEVILE**; children of dec'd dau **Rebecca TRIPP**, viz: **Hannah TRIPP, Constant TRIPP, Rebecca TRIPP, Daniel TRIPP, Joseph TRIPP, Thomas TRIPP, Charles TRIPP**; **Rebecca MOSHER**, dau of dec'd son **Benjamin MOSHER**; sons **Philip, Jonathan, James**, executors. Witnesses: Robert WILLBOR, John DEVEL, Restcome SANFORD. <14:197> Pr. 7 May 1754.

Will of **Joseph MOSHER**, yeoman of Dartmouth MA. <Bristol Co.PR>
<19:405>...dated 16 May 1761, mentions wf **Mehitable.** (Will is not transcribed in files.) <19:407> Pr. 28 Apr. 1766. <19:444> Inventory, 25 Apr. 1766, sworn to 28 Apr. 1766 by **Joseph MOSHER**, exr.

Estate of **Joseph MOSHER**. <Bristol Co.PR>
<21:466> Inventory, 29 Dec. 1770, sworn to 31 Dec. 1770 by **Joanna MOSHER**, exx. <146:189> Pr.

BRISTOL COUNTY DEEDS: (re: Joseph MOSHER)

<9:35> - 7 July 1713, Joseph MOSHER, mason of Dartmouth to Jeremiah DAVOL, husbandman of Dartmouth, meadow in Dartmouth. Ack. 12 June 1714.

<9:457> - 19 Feb. 1710/1, Joseph MOSHER, mason of Dartmouth, to Eleazer SLOCUM, meadow which my father Hugh MOSHER gave to me.

<17:210> - 25 Jan. 1714/5, Heirs of Philip TABER, incl. Lydia MOSHER wf of Joseph, to brother Philip TABER.

<9:107> - Feb. 1715, Joseph MOSHER, mason of Dartmouth to John TRIPP.

<15:29> - 9 Sept 1718, Joseph MOSHER, mason of Dartmouth to James MOSHER, husbandman.

<13:25> - 29 Apr. 1719, Joseph MOSHER, mason of Dartmouth to Benjamin DAVIS, yeoman of same.

<15:605> - 30 Jan. 1723, Joseph MOSHER of Dartmouth to son Philip MOSHER of Dartmouth, 54 acres, part of homestead bounded by land of Benjamin DAVIS, Stephen PECCOM, Joseph MOSHER, Thomas WAITE.

<15:602> - 30 Jan. 1724, Joseph MOSHER of Dartmouth to son Joseph MOSHER of Dartmouth, 53 acres, part of homestead bounded by land of Jonathan MOSHER, Thomas CORY, Joseph MOSHER, James TRIPP.

<16:16> - 15 Jan. 1723, Joseph MOSHER of Dartmouth to son Jonathan MOSHER of same, 54 acres, part of homestead bounded by land of Philip MOSHER, Thomas CORY, Joseph MOSHER, James TRIPP, Benjamin WAIT.

<19:224> - 28 Nov. 1728, Joseph MOSHER Jr., husbandman of Dartmouth to Timothy GIFFORD, husbandman of Dartmouth, part of the antient homestead of my father Nicholas MOSHER. Ack. 4 Feb. 1729.

BRISTOL COUNTY DEEDS, cont-d: (re: Joseph MOSHER)

<27:525> - 19 Mar. 1729, Joseph MOSHER of Dartmouth to son James MOSHER of same, 41 acres.
<27:258> - 2 Apr. 1729, Joseph MOSHER, mason of Dartmouth, to William TRIPP, cooper of same, 7 acres, part of homestead bounded by land of Thomas CORY, Jonathan MOSHER
<27:158> - 2 Apr. 1729, Joseph MOSHER, mason of Dartmouth to dau Ruth TRIPP & her husband, William TRIPP, part of homestead.
<20:72> - 5 Apr. 1729, Joseph MOSHER, mason, to son Jonathan MOSHER, husbandman, 7 acres, part of homestead bounded by land of sd Jonathan, Thomas CORY, Joseph MOSHER, James TRIPP.
<27:169> - 16 May 1732, Joseph MOSHER, mason of Dartmouth to Thomas BORDEN, Joseph BORDEN and Samuel BORDEN, yeomen of Tiverton, cedar swamp at Cranberry Neck, Dart.
<28:151> - July 1733, Joseph MOSHER of Dartmouth to son Benjamin MOSHER of same, part of homestead bounded by son James MOSHER, John MOSHER, William CADMAN.
<32:120> - 8 Mar. 1734/5, Joseph MOSHER, yeoman of Dartmouth to Jonathan MOSHER of Dartmouth, part of homestead bounded by sd Jonathan, William TRIPP, James MOSHER and James TRIPP, dec'd.
<28:241> - 16 June 1739, Joseph MOSHER, yeoman of Dartmouth to Philip CORY, yeoman of Tiverton, salt meadow in Dartmouth.
<46:341> - 10 Apr. 1763, Joseph MOSHER, carpenter of Dartmouth to Solomon SOUTHWICK, merchant of Newport RI, all his homestead in Dartmouth. Wf Meribah MOSHER signs.
<55:331> - 9 Mar. 1769, Joseph MOSHER, carpenter of Dartmouth to Joseph SMITH and Thomas SMITH, yeomen of Dartmouth, 85 acres. Wf Joanna MOSHER signs.
<66:348> - 3 Dec. 1786, Joseph MOSHER, yeoman & wf Elizabeth of White Creek NY; David ALLEN, yeoman & wf Rhoda and Anna BRIGG, of Cambridge NY; Jeremiah BRIGG, yeoman & wf Anne of Queensbury NY; Catherine HOWLAND, widow of Abraham Jr. of Dartmouth MA, sell to David WILBOUR, mariner of Dartmouth, the late homestead farm of our Honoured Father Benjamin BRIGGS, dec'd.

Estate of **Benjamin MOSHER** of Dartmouth MA. <Bristol Co.PR>
<original> Bond 16 Mar. 1741, **Sarah MOSHER**, widow, admx. Sureties: Edward CORNELL, Timothy TRIPP. <original> Inventory 11 Jan. 1741/2, incl. house & land, £459.0.0., mason tools, £1.13s. <original> Account of exx. 1 May 1750.

BRISTOL COUNTY DEEDS: (re: Benjamin MOSHER, grantee)

<19:189> - 21 Nov. 1727, James KIRBY to Benjamin MOSHER Sr., gift of 3 acres.
<28:320> - 17 Mar. 1729/30, Henry TUCKER, yeoman of Dartmouth to Benjamin MOSHER of same, one acre where Benjamin's house now stands. Rec. 10 Sept. 1740.
<28:151> - 10 Mar. 1734/5, Jonathan MOSHER, yeoman of Dartmouth to Benjamin MOSHER of same, son of Joseph, land bounded by land of James MOSHER, William TRIPP.
<28:150> - 26 Feb. 1736/7, Jonathan MOSHER, mason of Dartmouth, for £100, to brother Benjamin MOSHER, mason of same, twelve acres adjoining Benjamin's land and on brother James MOSHER's land. Rec. 15 Mar. 1739.
<28:152> - 12 Feb. 1739/40, William TRIPP, cooper of Dartmouth to Benjamin MOSHER, mason of same, homestead in Dartmouth bounded by sd Benjamin & James MOSHER. Wf Ruth TRIPP releases dower. Rec. 15 Mar. 1739.
<34:343> - 23 Dec. 1741, Henry TUCKER, husbandman of Dartmouth to Benjamin MOSHER, cordwainer of same. Wf Phebe TUCKER signs. Rec. 25 Aug. 1746.
<34:344> - 18 Feb. 1744/5, Deborah WING, seamstress of Dartmouth to Benjamin MOSHER, cordwainer of same. Ack. 22 Nov. 1745. Rec. 25 Aug. 1746.
<43:538> - 22 Nov. 1748, Isaac SHEARMAN, yeoman of Dartmouth to Benjamin MOSHER, late of Dartmouth now of Chilmark, land in Dartmouth next to Ben.'s homestead.
<41:500> - 8 Feb. 1755, Benjamin WAIT, yeoman of Dartmouth to Benjamin MOSHER, son of Philip, of same, two acres in Dartmouth by Philip MOSHER's mills.
<43:180> - 24 Aug. 1758, Richard CRAW, cooper of Dartmouth to Benjamin MOSHER, cordwainer of same land in Dartmouth adjoining land Benjamin purchased from Richard, next to land of Timothy MAXFIELD. Rec. 31 Aug. 1758.
<45:273> - 3 Mar. 1759, Benjamin WAIT, carpenter of Dartmouth to Benjamin MOSHER, cooper of same land next to Benjamin's. Rec. 10 Sept. 1761.
<49:434> - Apr. 1766, Stephen MERIHEW, cooper of Dartmouth to Benjamin MOSHER 2d, cooper of same, (for self & brothers John MERIHEW & David MERIHEW), land bounded by William MOSHER and Joseph MOSHER. Rec. 28 Apr. 1766.
<71:480> - 25 Feb. 1792, Lemuel TOBEY, gent. of New Bedford to Benjamin MOSHER, cooper of same, house lot in New Bedford. Wf Eliza TOBEY releases dower.

BRISTOL COUNTY DEEDS: (re: Benjamin MOSHER, grantor).

<62:181> - 23 Jan. 1732/3, Benjamin MOSHER, cordwainer of Dartmouth to John HANDY, cordwainer of same, house & land from 19:189,28:230. Rec. 17 Dec. 1783.
<36:38> - 19 Aug. 1746, Benjamin MOSHER, cordwainer of Dartmouth to William HALLADAY, land adjoining the Wing land. Rec. 12 May 1748.
<43:179> - 6 Nov. 1752, Benjamin MOSHER, cordwainer of Dartmouth to Richard CRAW, cooper of same homestead near Town House lot, bounded by land of Timothy MAXFIELD, WING and land bought of Isaac SHERMAN. Rec. 31 Aug. 1758.

BRISTOL COUNTY DEEDS, cont-d: (re: Benjamin MOSHER, grantor)

<56:278> - 2 Dec. 1757, Benjamin MOSHER, cordwainer of Dartmouth to Joseph CASWELL, laborer of same, land in Dartmouth. Ack. 31 July 1761. Rec. 19 Oct. 1774.

<46:143> - 16 Feb. 1760, Benjamin MOSHER, cordwainer of Dartmouth to Timothy MAXFIELD, carpenter of Dartmouth, house & land adjoining that of both men. Ack. 31 July 1761 Rec. 14 Oct. 1762.

<52:110> - 16 Jan. 1763, Benjamin MOSHER, yeoman of Dartmouth, son of Daniel MOSHER dec'd, to Giles TRIPP, joiner of Dartmouth. Wf Dorcas MOSHER releases dower. Ack. 8 Sept. 1768 by Benjamin. Rec. 28 Apr. 1769.

<47:181> - 20 Feb. 1764, Benjamin MOSHER, cooper of Dartmouth to Jonathan DAVEL, yeoman of Dartmouth, part of homestead. Ack. 3 May 1764. Rec. 3 July 1764.

<52:124> - 3 Apr. 1766, Benjamin MOSHER, cooper of Dartmouth to William RIDER of Dartmouth. Wf Phebe MOSHER signs. Ack. 20 May 1767 by both. Rec. 2 May 1769.

<53:256> - 3 Mar. 1769, Benjamin MOSHER 2d, cooper of Dartmouth to William MOSHER, cooper of same, 75 acres bought of Stephen MERIHEW & brothers. Wf Phebe MOSHER releases dower. Ack. 6 Mar. 1769 by both. Rec. 16 Aug. 1769.

<71:253> - 28 Feb. 1792, Benjamin MOSHER, cooper of New Bedford to Zebedee McDANIEL, trader of same, south half of lot bought of Lemuel TOBEY on Water St. Wf Abigail MOSHER releases dower. Rec. 22 Oct. 1792.

Will of **Jonathan MOSHER**, yeoman of Dartmouth MA. <Bristol Co.PR>
<17:105>...dated 10 May 1760, mentions wf **Isabel**; sons **Job MOSHER, Wesson MOSHER**; daus **Rebecca, Isabel** ("evidently deceased")**, Elizabeth, Judah;** sons **Jonathan MOSHER, Joseph MOSHER**; wf & son **Wesson** executors. Witnesses: George MOSHER, William TRIPP Jr., Hannah MOSHER. <17:106> Pr. 4 Nov. 1760, **Wesson MOSHER** declines to serve. <17:106> Inventory taken 4 July 1760.

BRISTOL COUNTY DEEDS: (re: Philip MOSHER)

<15:603> - 7 Feb. 1724, Benjamin DAVOL to Philip MOSHER, cedar swamp in Cranberry Neck in Dartmouth. Witnesses: Hugh MOSHER, Benjamin DAVIS. Rec. 13 Jan. 1725/6.

<20:75> - 7 Mar. 1729/30, Philip MOSHER, cooper of Dartmouth, for Ł300, to Benjamin DAVIS, yeoman of same, 54 acres in Dartmouth bounded by land of sd Davis, Robert KIRBY, Jonathan MOSHER, George BROWNELL. Ack. 11 Mar. 1729/30.

<28:79> - 10 Mar. 1734/5, Jeremiah DEVOL, yeoman of Dartmouth, for Ł360, sells to Philip MOSHER, cooper of Dartmouth, land & salt meadow bought of Nicholas HOWLAND. Rec. 13 Dec. 1739.

<28:80> - May 1734, William SHERMAN, yeoman of Dartmouth, for Ł40, to Philip MOSHER, cooper of same, cedar swamp in 16 acre division Quanapog Great Swamp, bounded by land of Jeremiah DEVELL which was formerly Nicholas HOWLAND's. Ack. 29 Mar. 1735. Rec. 15 Dec. 1739.

<23:456> - 27 June 1734, Philip MOSHER, cooper of Dartmouth, for Ł13.6s8d, to Timothy MAXFIELD Jr., yeoman of same, part of cedar swamp bought of William SHERMAN. Ack. 29 Mar. 1735. Rec. 19 Aug. 1735.

<23:458> - 24 Jan. 1734/5, Philip MOSHER, cooper of Dartmouth, for Ł13.6s, to Joseph MOSHER, son of Nicholas, part of cedar swamp bought of William SHERMAN, bounded by land of Timothy MAXFIELD. Ack. 29 Mar. 1735.

<28:316> - 27 Aug. 1737, Philip MOSHER, cooper of Dartmouth & wf Abigail, for Ł182, to Daniel MOSHER, yeoman of same, salt meadow in Dartmouth bought of Jeremiah DEVEL, bounded by homesteads of James SHERMAN & Robert KIRBY and land of Aaron POTTER. Ack. 6 Sept. 1740. Rec. 10 Sept. 1740.

<71:217> - Aug. 1738, Philip MOSHER, cooper of Dartmouth, for Ł10, to Samuel BORDEN, yeoman of Tiverton, cedar swamp at Cranberry Neck, Dartmouth. Ack. 26 Aug. 1738. Rec. 14 Sept. 1792.

<47:163> - 29 Dec. 1740, Philip MOSHER, cooper of Dartmouth, for Ł27.10s, to Joseph MOSHER, son of Nicholas, 14 acre cedar swamp in Dartmouth bounded by land of Jona-. than RUSSELL. Ack. 30 Mar. 1741. Rec. 26 June 1764.

<42:90> - 5 Mar. 1747, Philip MOSHER, cooper of Dartmouth & wf Abigail, for Ł140, to William DEVOL, son of William of same, my homestead farm, bounded on land I sold to Daniel MOSHER and land of Henry POTTER, RUSSELL, Aaron POTTER, James. SHEARMAN, George MOSHER, John ALLEN, HOWLAND, Robert KIRBY. Ack. 30 Mar 1747 by Philip. Rec. 13 July 1756.

<56:362> - 31 Jan. 1759, Philip MOSHER, cooper of Dartmouth, for Ł20, to son Israel MOSHER, cordwainer of same, half of land bought of Joseph TUCKER, 25 acres, bounded by land of Jonathan MOSHER; the other half being sold to William GAGE. Ack. 24 Mar. 1760. Rec. 25 Apr. 1775.

<44:403> - 16 Feb. 1760, Philip MOSHER, cooper of Dartmouth, for Ł13.10s, to Jacob ANTHONY, grazier of same, 20 acres, being half of lot bought of Joseph TUCKER, bounded by land of William READ, Jonathan MOSHER, Israel MOSHER. Wf Elinor MOSHER signs. Ack. 24 Mar. 1760. Rec. 11 Sept. 1760.

MICRO #20 OF 30

Will of **Caleb MOSHER** of Charlotte, NY. <Dutchess Co.PR A:366>
...dated 8 Feb. 1786, mentions wf **Elizabeth**; daus **Martha PALMER, Abigail FINTEH, Elizabeth REY-**

NOLDS; sons **Tripp MOSHER, Philip MOSHER, Samuel MOSHER, Esek MOSHER, Israel MOSHER**; sons **Tripp** & **Esek**, executors. Pr. 31 Aug. 1793.

Will of **Samuel WILLBOR**, yeoman of Little Compton RI. <Newport Co.PR 1:124>
...dated 27 Feb. 1749/50, mentions wf **Elizabeth** (executrix); sons **Robert WILLBOR, Thomas WILLBOR, Abishai WILLBOR, Esek WILLBOR, Samuel WILLBOR, Ebenezer WILLBOR, David WILLBOR**; daus **Susanna TRIPP, Mary DAVEL, Elizabeth MOSHER, Martha WILLBOR, Ruth WILLBOR, Joanna WILLBOR**. Witnesses: Thomas PALMER, Israel STODDARD, Job BROWNELL.

Will of **Elizabeth WILBOUR**, widow of Little Compton RI. <Newport Co.PR 2:16>
...dated 26 Mar. 1764, mentions sons **Robert WILBOUR, Thomas WILBOUR, Abisha WILBOUR, Samuel WILBOUR, Esek WILBOUR, Ebenezer WILBOUR, David WILBOUR**; daus **Susannah TRIPP, Mercy DIVEL, Elizabeth MOSHER, Joanna WILBOUR** (for her trouble, time and care in tending me when weak & low of body); sons **Ebenezer** and **David**, executors. Witnesses: Enos GIFFORD Jr., Joseph GIFFORD, Nathaniel SEARLS

Will of **Israel MOSHER**, yeoman of Westport MA. <Bristol Co.PR>
<35:491>...dated 4 Jan. 1798, mentions wf **Sarah**; to son **Joseph MOSHER**, $1.00; to son **Maxson MOSHER** (executor), everything after death of mother. <35:492> Pr. 2 Oct. 1798. Inventory taken 22 Sept. 1798, total $250.00.

BRISTOL COUNTY DEEDS: (re: Maxson MOSHER)

<56:362> -	20 Feb. 1773,	Thomas REED of Dartmouth to Maxson MOSHER, laborer. Rec. 25 Apr. 1775.
<59:153> -	4 June 1776,	Maxson MOSHER to Jeremiah CHASE, land bought of Thomas REED. Rec. 1802.
<81:403> -	,	Maxson MOSHER to Ebenezer BAKER.
<84:315> -	20 Apr. 1802,	Humphrey RICKETSON & Sarah RICKETSON widow of John (by his will) to Maxson MOSHER, yeoman. Rec. 13 Dec. 1804.
<83:462> -	1804,	Maxson MOSHER to Timothy MACOMBER.
<84:316> -	1804,	Maxson MOSHER to Lemuel PARKER.
<94:150> -	6 June 1812,	Phebe RICKETSON, Sarah GRINNELL, Abigail RICKETSON (heirs of John RICKETSON) to Maxson MOSHER. Rec. 10 June 1812.
<103:81> -	1817,	Maxson MOSHER to Wesson BRIGGS.
<108:471> -	1820,	Maxson MOSHER to Eliphalet MACOMBER.
<108:477> -	1820,	Thomas WAINER to Maxson MOSHER.
<115:552> -	1824,	Maxson MOSHER to Joseph MOSHER.
<139:150> -	1833,	Maxson MOSHER to Matthew RUSSEL.
<150:508> -	1836,	Maxson MOSHER to Reuben MOSHER.
<150:510> -	1836,	Maxson MOSHER to Thomas HILL.

Will of **William TRIPP**, yeoman of Dartmouth MA. <Bristol Co.PR>
<21:497>...dated 21/25 Nov. 1770, mentions wf **Ruth**; sons **William TRIPP, Jonathan TRIPP, Elijah TRIPP** (all three executors); daus **Desire, Eddy SHERMAN, Martha ALLEN, Abigail MOSHER, Ruth ALLEN, Lydia TRIPP**. <21:498> Pr. 4/7 Jan. 1771. <21:499> Inventory 4 Jan. 1771.

BRISTOL COUNTY DEEDS: (re: William MOSHER)

<30:433> -	15 June 1741,	William MOSHER, yeoman of Dartmouth to John MOSHER of same.
<37:4> -	8 Sept 1748,	William MOSHER, yeoman of Dartmouth & Margaret, to Elizabeth DAVOL, spinster of same, homestead in Dartmouth.
<51:316> -	,	William MOSHER et al to Henry HOWLAND.

(Note: Additional ref. to William MOSHER with no data are given: 56:463,464; 57:48; 60:8,171.)

Will of **William MOSHER**. <Bristol Co.PR 27:557>
...dated 2 Aug. 1783, mentions wf **Hannah**. (no further details in files.)

Will of **William MOSHER**. <Bristol Co.PR>
<45:389>...dated 19 Jan. 1810. <45:391> Inventory. <46:358> Account. <109:363> Notice.
(Note: In brackets next to the date of the will is added "son of Michael & Judith, b. 1783" - however it is not clear if this is Bowman's own note, or a fact stated in the will.)

Will of **Philip TABER** of Dartmouth MA. <Bristol Co.PR>
<13:6>...dated 14 July 1749, mentions wf **Margaret**; sons **Philip TABER** (eldest son), **Jonathan TABER William TABER, John TABER, Josiah TABER**; daus **Martha SHEFFIELD, Comfort BOWERS, Mary HATHAWAY, Rebecca BOWERS, Margaret BOWERS**. <13:9> Pr. 5 Nov. 1751. <13:10> Inventory. <original> Receipts, 1781, 1782.

Will of **Margaret TABER**,widow of Swansea MA. <Bristol Co.PR>
<15:337>...dated 16 May 1755, mentions sons **Philip TABER, William TABER, Jonathan TABER, Josias TABER, John TABER**; daus **Martha SHEFFIELD, Comfort BOWERS, Mary HATHAWAY, Rebecca BOWERS, Margaret BOWERS**; granddaughter **Elizabeth BOWERS**. Son in law **Benjamin BOWERS**, executor. <15:338> Pr. 3 May 1757. <15:390> Inventory.

Will of **Benjamin BOWERS**, shipwright of Swanzey MA. <Taunton PR 23:511>
...dated 13 Sept. 1773; to wf **Comfort**, my great Bible and my Negro man named Barter and my Negro woman named Violet together with my round Table made of mahogany, six new framed chairs, two

framed chairs, two feather beds, two under beds, two bedsteads with cords, one set of curtains, one cotton coverlid, two wooling coverlids, six thick blankets, eight linnen sheets, two flannel blankets, four pillows, eight pillow cases, two boulsters, four bolster cases, all the kitchen chairs, one white table, twelve pewter plates, twelve blue and white earthen plates, twelve light square earthen plates, two iron pots, one brass kettle, a large looking glass, one case of draws, three pewter basins, six pewter porringers, one teapot and tea kittle, six china tea cups and saucers, six silver teaspoons, six large silver spoons, one case of knives and forks, one pair of andirons, one shovell, tongs and tramell, one frying pan, one warming pan, two heaters, driping pan, twelve towels, four table clouths, two powdering tubbs, one cheese tub, two milk pails, two iron kittles, one skillet, six milk pans, two trays, one churn, one kuler, one pair of bellows, one chafendish, one scimmer, one lining wheel and woolen wheel, two candlesticks, two muggs, one half of all my new home spun cloth I shall have by me at my decease...one yoke of oxen, two cows, ten sheep, three swine, all my fowls, one riding beast, with the shay wide saddle, bridle and pillion and one maple desk, one case of bottles...one hundred dollars...all which gifts herein given to **Comfort** my wife is in lieu of her thirds or dower...to grandson **William BOWERS**, son of my son **Philip BOWERS**, dec'd, part of my homestead bounded by land of Stephen MARVELL near Labour In Vain Creek...reserving a burying place of five rods square where the burying place now is for my relatives the Bowers and their heirs forever...to grandsons **Philip BOWERS** and **Benjamin BOWERS**, sons of my son **Philip** dec'd, all the land I bought of Jared BOURN...to my sd grandson **Benjamin BOWERS** and his sisters **Sarah BOWERS** and **Anna BOWERS**, to each a silver spoon marked with this motto **"B+C"**...to my son **Benjamin BOWERS** the farm I bought of Keabial CHASE...to dau **Elizabeth CLARK** one hundred dollars...to my dau **Comfort HUNTINGTON** one hundred dollars and my negro girl named Dinah who now resides with her...to my dau **Martha KING** one hundred dollars and my negro boy named Jack...to my daus **Anna BOWERS** and **Roby BOWERS**, a riding beast and one hundred dollars...to dau **Anna** my silver tankard and negro girl named Silvia...to dau **Roby** my negro boy named Newport, one young mare and fifty dollars...to my son **Jonathan BOWERS** all my homestead farm with a piece of land I lately bought of David CHASE, my mahogany desk and all my wearing apparel. Witnesses: Jared BOURN, Stephen MARSHAL, David PIERCE. Pr. 5 June 1775.

Will of **Comfort BOWERS**, widow of Swanzey MA. <Taunton PR 30:65>
...dated 5 Dec. 1782; to my two grandsons, the sons of my son **Philip BOWERS** dec'd, one silver dollar each and to their sister **Sarah BRAYTON** wf of John, I give two brass candle sticks and twelve eight square turtle shell plates...to my son **Benjamin BOWERS**, one feather bed, bolster and pillows...to my son **Jonathan BOWERS** one feather bed, bolster and pillows and all my living stock and that money which he was ordered to pay to me in his father's will and my riding chase...to my three grandsons, **Henry CLARK, Joseph HUNTINTON** and **Philip HUNTINTON** a silver dollar each...to **Comfort CLARK** my silver shoe buckles...to **Comfort KING** my gold sleave buttons...to my dau **Ann BOWERS** my gold beeds & locket and my silk damers gown and my black russel petticoat and my side sadle and my silver tea spoons and my new blue petticoat, one red undercoat, flowered serge petticoat and purple, blue and white calico gown and three large silver spoons and the other three large silver spoons I give to my son **Jonathan BOWERS**...to my dau **Ann BOWERS** my mahogany table and six framed chairs and my will is that my two daus **Ann BOWERS** and **Martha KING** shall have the one half of the remaining part of my wearing clothes and personal estate that is not given away already in this my will and my granddaughters **Comfort CLARK, Sary CLARK, Robe CLARK, Margaret CLARK, Anna CLARK** and **Rebecca CLARK**, the daus of my dau **Elizabeth** dec'd and my two granddaughters the daus of my dau **Comfort HUNTINTON** shall share the other half of sd wearing clothes and personal estate...my will is that my negro woman Vilet shall go out free at my decease; son **Jonathan**, executor. Witnesses: James CHACE, Jonathan BAKER, Russell MASON. Pr. 4 Nov. 1788.

Will of **Jonathan BOWERS**, yeoman of Somerset MA. <Bristol Co.PR 60:139>
...dated 18 Sept. 1821; to dau **Ruth BOWERS** half acre in Somerset near Labor And Vain Creek, formerly occupied for a yard in order for ship building, also my silver watch...to my two daus **Ruth BOWERS** and **Gertrude BOWERS** all my household furniture...to my four daus, **Ruth BOWERS, Hannah PIERCE** wf of Ebenezer, **Rhoby SLADE** wf of Mial and **Gertrude BOWERS** all my living stock except the swine and ten sheep together with my implements for farming...to my two daus **Ruth BOWERS** and **Gertrude BOWERS**, twenty bushels of corn, wood standing and all my swine, butter and cheese...to my two grandsons, the sons of **Mial SLADE, Jonathan Bowers SLADE** and **Benjamin Bowers SLADE**, ten sheep and all my wearing apparel...to dau **Ruth BOWERS** all my lands in Swanzey...to four daus and granddaughter **Ruth Bowers ROBINSON** dau of my dau **Deborah ROBINSON** dec'd, all the rest and residue of my estate; dau **Ruth BOWERS** and son in law **Mial SLADE**, executors. Witnesses: Daniel BRAYTON, John BUFFINTON, Job SLEAD.

Will of **Joseph SLEAD**, yeoman of Somerset MA. <Bristol Co.PR 36:448>
...dated 21 4mth 1797, mentions wf **Priscilla**; to son **Stephen SLEAD** the farm where he now lives, the land in Sommerset I purchased of Henry GIBBS' heirs and three acres in Swansey I purchased of Robert GIBBS; to son **Benjamin SLEAD** the lands where he now lives, land joining John SLEAD's, land where the tan works is, my salt meadow in Swanzey and five acres woodland I purchased of Robert GIBBS; to my four daus **Phebe CHASE, Esther HART, Hannah BOWDASH** and **Ruth BOWERS**, fifty silver dollars apiece and the household furniture; to my two sons **Stephen** and **Benjamin** all my lands in Freetown and land in Somerset that I purchased of the Chases; wf **Priscilla** and sons **Stephen** & **Benjamin**, executors. Witnesses: Ebenezer SLEAD, Benjamin SLEAD, Daniel BRAYTON.

Will of **Stephen WEST**. <Bristol Co.PR>
<21:43>...dated 3 Jan. 1763, mentions wf **Susanna**; sons **Samuel WEST, Stephen WEST, Bartholomew WEST**; daus **Almy WEST, Susanna WEST, Hannah HATHAWAY, Anne MOTT**; grandson **Stephen MOTT** (under 23); Kinsmen Thomas HATHAWAY, Bartholomew TABER; son in law **Jethro HATHAWAY.** <21:50> Pr. 31 July 1769.

<21:344-93> Inventory.

(Note: Several additional references to the name Stephen WEST are given with no dates, viz: 25: 578, (Releases, 1778, widow Hopestill WEST, dau Mary WEST); 83:23, (Inventory); 83:56, (Adm.); 83:57, (Allowance); 85:471, (Account); 85:479, (Notice of sale); 86:50, (Account); 115:250, (Appointment); <154:507, (Adm.); 160:518, (Bond); 176:392, (Citation); 209:412, (Sale of land).)

Will of **Bartholomew WEST**, yeoman of Dartmouth MA. <Bristol Co.PR>
<26:144>...dated 17 Oct. 1761, mentions wf...whereas I apprehend my said wife is big with child & near her time; sons **William WEST, Bartholomew WEST** (if they live to the age of 30); dau **Andrea WEST** (under 21); cousin **Bartholomew AKIN**; son **Edward WEST**; Society of People called Quakers; sister **Anne WEST**; Friends and cousins **Bartholomew TABER, Jethro HATHAWAY** and **Bartholomew WEST 2d** to be guardians of all his minor children; mentions land bought of Joseph ELLIS & wf Martha and land adjoining Daniel HUMMERTON/SUMMERTON; cousin **Jethro HATHAWAY**, executor. Witnesses: Thomas WEST, Robert EASTERBROOKS, Edward ELDREDGE, Stephen WEST. <original> Codicil 15 Apr. 1767, mentions sons **William, Bartholomew, Thomas, Edward**; dau **Andria COOK** wf of Job; cousin **Bartholomew AKIN** (under 21); gift to Quakers in Acushnet cancelled. Witnesses: Robert ESTERBROOK, Edward ELDREDGE, Bartholomew TABER. <26:151> Pr. 3 Oct. 1779; 4 Oct. 1779, **Jethro HATHAWAY** declines to serve as executor. <original> Bond 5 Oct. 1779 of Richard DELANO, admr. Sureties: Jethro HATHAWAY, Edward WEST, all yeomen of Dartmouth. Witnesses: Griffin BARNEY, B. WILLIAMS Jr. <original> Inventory taken 1 Nov. 1779 by Nathan DELANO, Jethro HATHAWAY and John PECKENS. <original> Order to appraise, 12 Apr. 1780 to Samuel SMITH, Jethro HATHAWAY and John WEST, freeholders. <26:318> Division 6 Nov. 1780, heirs: son **Bartholomew WEST** (dec'd before father), son **Thomas WEST** (dec'd after father), **Andria COOK** (eldest dau), **William WEST** (eldest son), **Edward WEST** (2nd son), **Mercy WEST** (youngest dau), **Anna WEST**, widow.

(Note: Additional references to the name Bartholomew WEST are given with no dates, viz: 47:242, (Inventory); 55:180, (Will, 23 Jan. 1817); 55:297, (Inventory); 60:334, (Account); 95:363, (Adm.) 96:58, (Inventory); 96:67, (Account); 109:520, 110:620, 117:283, (Notices of appointment); 150: 521, (Adm.); 156:461, (Adm.); 162:475, (Bond).)

Will of **John WEST** of New Bedford. <Bristol Co.PR>
<30:540>...dated 25 June 1789, mentions kinsman **Bartholomew TABER**; sister **Mary SISSON**; friends Stephen HATHAWAY, Peter FULLER to be Trustees; Anna GIBBS, dau of widow GIBBS of Rochester. <30: 542> Probate.

(Note: Additional references to the name John WEST are given without data, viz: 8:532, (Will & Pr., 1797); 9:1, (Inventory); 25:267, (Will, 1708); 25:270, (Pr.); 25:579, (Receipt); 31:45, (Inventory); 32:215, (Account); 34:354, (Account); 66:273, (Will); 107:89, (Selling of real estate); 126:26, (Letter).)

MICRO #21 OF 30

Will of **Stephen WEST** of Dartmouth MA. <Bristol Co.PR>
<21:43>...dated 3 Jan. 1763...being now in ye sixty eighth year of my age, mentions wf **Susannah**; sons **Samuel WEST, Stephen WEST, Bartholomew WEST**; daus **Hannah HATHAWAY, Almy WEST, Susannah WEST, Anne MOTT**; brother **John WEST**; Kinsmen Thomas HATHAWAY, Bartholomew TABER; son in law **Jethro HATHAWAY**; grandson **Stephen MOTT**. Witnesses: Jireh SWIFT, Thomas WEST, Philip CONNON, John McPHERSONE. <21:50> Pr. 31 July 1769 <21:344-93> Inventory of personal estate, taken 21 July 1769.

Jethro HATHAWAY of New Bedford to **Hepzibah DAVIS** of same. <Bristol Co.Deeds 71:24>
...20 June 1788, Jethro HATHAWAY, yeoman, for & in consideration of love & goodwill which I have & do bear to my daughter Hepzibah DAVIS, wf of Timothy, give to her...cedar swamp in New Bedford which formerly belonged to Joseph SAMPSON dec'd late of Dartmouth now of New Bedford which ye aforesaid Jethro bought of Peleg DELANO then of Dartmouth, containing three acres, bounded by land of Zacheus TOBEY & wf Ruhamah.

Guardianship of **Jethro HATHAWAY**, non comp. of New Bedford. <Bristol Co.PR 35:512>
...2 Oct. 1798, To the Selectmen of the Town of New Bedford...In compliance with the request of **Stephen HATHAWAY**, of New Bedford, son of **Jethro HATHAWAY**...the sd Jethro is so insane that he is incapable of taking care of himself & family and requesting that inquisition thereof be made & a guardian appointed...On the same day, Alden SPOONER and Joseph BENNET, major part of Selectmen of said New Bedford certified that by reason of old age & infirmity the sd Jethro is really insane. **Stephen HATHAWAY**, yeoman, appointed guardian. <36:187> 2 Oct. 1798, Peleg HUDDLESTONE, Jonathan KEMPTON and Lemuel WILLIAMS, Esq. were app'td to appraise the estate of **Jethro HATHAWAY**, a person non compos mentis. Inventory taken 20 Apr. 1799 incl. farm improved by Clark HATHAWAY, $1300.00; 20 acre cedar swamp, $200.00; one acre salt marsh, $45.00, total $1877.05.

Will of **James SISSON** of Dartmouth MA. <Bristol Co.PR 8:168>
..dated 15 June 1734, mentions sons **Richard SISSON, James SISSON, Jonathan SISSON, Thomas SISSON**; dau **Content** being dead her children to have one fifth part; daus **Mary, Sarah, Hannah, Rebeckah.** <8:167> Pr. 17 Dec. 1734. <8:180> Inventory.

(Note: Additional references are given for the name James SISSON, with no dates, viz: 35:265,272, (Will & Inv.); 41:521, (Will), 42:49, (Inv.), 43:15, (Account); 51:207,208, (Will & Pr.); 62:193, 221, (Adm. & Inv.), 63:221, (Account); 109:156, (Notice); 110:358, (Notice); 111:559, (Notice).)

Will of **Richard SISSON.** <Bristol Co.PR 10:506>
...dated 29 Sept. 1744, mentions wf **Mehitable,** many chil. (not named in files). Pr. 12 Nov. 1744.

Will of **Richard SISSON.** <Bristol Co.PR 31:14>
...dated 10 Jan. 1782, mentions children & grandchildren (not named in files).

Will of **Richard SISSON** of Swansea MA. <Bristol Co.PR 41:67>
...dated 27 Mar. 1799, mentions wf **Mary**; brother **George SISSON**; sisters **Sarah CHASE, Abigail HUDSON.**

Will of **James SISSON** of Westport MA. <Bristol Co.PR 35:265>
...dated 15 Aug. 1797, mentions children & grandchildren (not named in files).

Will of **James SISSON** of Swansea MA. <Bristol Co.PR 41:521>
...dated 10 July 1799, mentions brother **George SISSON,** late of Warren, dec'd.

Will of **James SISSON** of Portsmouth, now residing in Seekonk. <Bristol Co.PR 51:207>
...dated 23 Feb. 1815, mentions several children (not named in files).

Will of **Jonathan SISSON.** <Bristol Co.PR 14:364>
...dated 14 Mar. 1755, mentions brother in law **William WOOD**; many children (not named in files). <16:277> Receipts. <21:137> Division.

Will of **Jonathan SISSON** of Westport MA. <Bristol Co.PR 41:410>
...dated 21 Sept. 1804, mentions wf **Hannah**; many children (not named in files).

Will of **Stephen PECKHAM,** yeoman of Dartmouth MA. <Bristol Co.PR>
<18:345>...dated 19 Mar. 1757, mentions wf **Katurah**; son **Richard PECKHAM** (under 21); daus **Elizabeth PECKHAM** & **Eunice PECKHAM** (both under 21); sons **James PECKHAM** & **Stephen PECKHAM** (executor). <18:347> Pr. 3 July 1764. <18:423> Inventory, 26 June 1764. <19:105> Receipts. <22:534> Division.

(Note: Additional references to the name Stephen PECKHAM are given with no dates, viz: 4:317,318, 320, (Pr., Will & Inventory); 6:215,218,221, (Receipts, Account); 34:446,429, (Inv. & Will); 37: 423,434, (Notice & Receipt).)

Heirs of **James PECKHAM** of Little Compton. <Bristol Co.Deeds 8:68>
...25 Dec. 1712...We the Legal Representatives of the estate of James PECKHAM who dec'd 26 Feb. 1711/12...power of attorney to William PECKHAM, Philip PECKHAM, John TAYLOR, all of Newport. Signed by Elinor PECKHAM, Isaac PECKHAM, Deborah TAYLOR, Stephen PECKHAM "and others".

Stephen PECKHAM of Dartmouth MA to **Stephen PECKHAM Jr.** of same. <Bristol Co.Deeds 45:280>
...14 Feb 1757, Stephen PECKHAM, yeoman to son Stephen PECKHAM Jr., blacksmith...20 acres in Dartmouth, one quarter of my now homestead.

Stephen PECKHAM of Dartmouth MA to **Seth RUSSEL.** <Bristol Co.Deeds 54:267>
...14 Feb. 1770, Stephen PECKHAM, blacksmith to Seth RUSSEL, cooper...northerly half of homestead of my late father Stephen PECKHAM of Dartmouth; mentions spring given in my Grandfather's last will to John PECKHAM.

Stephen PECKHAM of Dartmouth MA to **Nathan PETTY** of Tiverton. <Bristol Co.Deeds 58:136>
...1 Oct. 1773, Stephen PECKHAM, blacksmith to Nathan PETTY, laborer...land in Dartmouth bought of William SOULE, 6 Dec. 1768. Wf Elizabeth PECKHAM signs.

Stephen PECKHAM, division of land. <Bristol Co.Deeds 63:540>
...6 Apr. 1774, Stephen PECKHAM et al, of Dartmouth, division of common land in Dartmouth near Naquechunck(sp) Bridge where Stephen's dwelling house now stands.

George CADMAN of Dartmouth MA to **William WOOD et al.** <Bristol Co.Deeds 63:318>
...19 July 1716, George CADMAN, yeoman sells to William WOOD, Stephen WILCOX, Henry TUCKER, Thomas TABER Jr. and Joseph TABER, husbandmen of Dartmouth...one and a half acres in Dartmouth, part of land where son in law William WHITE now lives. Rec. 1 Mar. 1785.

Will of **George CADMAN** of Dartmouth MA. <MD 22:2,5>
...dated 24 Nov. 1718, mentions wf **Hannah**; grandson **George WHITE** (under 20); dau **Elizabeth WHITE** wf of William; grandchildren **William WHITE, Roger WHITE, Christopher WHITE, Sarah WHITE, Elizabeth WHITE**; Alice ANTHONY, dau of John of RI. Pr. 6 Jan. 1718.

Will of **Hannah CADMAN** of Dartmouth MA. <MD 22:2>
...13 Feb. 1748/9...to dau **Elizabeth WHITE,** wf of William of Dartmouth, a silver Tankard; to grandson **William WHITE** my great Bible & my siler spoon marked "W.C."; to grandson **George WHITE** a spoon & gun which was his grandfather Cadman's and all my farming tools; granddaughter **Sarah BROWN,** wf of John of Tiverton; granddaughter **Hannah TABER,** wf of William of Dartmouth; great-granddaughters **Hannah SLOCUM** and **Mary SLOCUM,** daus of my granddaughter **Elizabeth SLOCUM**; grandchildren **Roger WHITE, Christopher WHITE, Oliver WHITE, Thomas WHITE, Susanna WHITE.** Pr. 2 May 1749.

Will of **William WHITE**, gent. of Dartmouth MA. <Bristol Co.PR 26:286>
...dated 6 Jan. 1768...very aged, mentions wf **Elizabeth** in her aged, weak & low condition; grandchildren, chil. of son **George WHITE**, dec'd, viz: **Israel, Peleg, William, Silvanus, Obed, Ruth, Sarah, Hannah, Mary, Unice**; daus **Sarah BROWN, Hannah TABER**; sons **Roger WHITE, Christopher WHITE**, to **Thomas WHITE** my silver Tankard; grandchildren, chil. of dau **Elizabeth SLOCUM**, dec'd; son **Oliver WHITE**; granddaughter **Phebe SMITH**; son **Abner WHITE**; dau **Susanna WHITE** executrix with grandson **Peleg**. Witnesses: William GIFFORD, Daniel HATHAWAY, Restcome SANFORD. Pr. 3 Oct. 1780.

Will of **Richard KERBEE/KIRBY** of Dartmouth MA. <Bristol Co.PR 3:658>
...dated 30 Jan. 1707/8. Witness: William WHITE who swore to will 4 Apr. 1720.

Robert BARKER of Newport to **William WHITE** of Dartmouth...May 1718. <Bristol Co.Deeds 12:397>

Will of **Christopher WHITE**, blacksmith of Little Compton RI. <"Tiverton Rcds.:267,268">
...dated 18 Dec. 1793, mentions wf **Sarah**; sons **Noah WHITE, Perigrin WHITE, Thomas WHITE**; daus **Sarah HILYARD/HILLIARD, Mary BAILEY, Elizabeth BROWN, Ruth MAYHEW**. Witnesses: Thomas TABER, Samuel TABER, Elisha BROWN. Pr. 5 Oct. 1795

Estate of **William WHITE**, blacksmith of Newport. <Newport PR, Town Council 16:111>
...4 Jan. 1770, Christopher WHITE, yeoman of Little Compton app'td admr. <16:112> Inventory, 2 Jan. 1770.

Will of **George WHITE**, yeoman of Dartmouth MA. <Bristol Co.PR>
<18:318>...dated 28 Dec. 1762, mentions wf **Deborah**; to son **Israel WHITE**, 1500 Spanish milled dollars; to son **Peleg WHITE** (executor), all my farm east of Acoxset River which I bought of Joseph HOLLEY late of Dartmouth; to son **William WHITE**, 50 Spanish milled dollars, cattle and 140 acres to be set off on west end of my homestead farm incl. that land called the Frenchman's place...my widow to possess it until sd William marries; to son **Silvanus WHITE** all land & housing I bought of Joseph BROWNELL late of Dartmouth...other lands when he marries; son **Obed WHITE**, unm.; daus **Ruth WILCOX, Hannah WING, Sarah WHITE, Mary WHITE, Eunice WHITE**; negro slaves Zip & Vilot to be free 25 Mar. 1766, with Zip receiving 10 acres of land. Witnesses: Moses HOAG, Lemuel SISSON, Beriah GODDARD. Pr. 29 Mar. 1764. <18:405> Inventory taken 18 Apr. 1764 by Ezekiel CORNELL(sp), William WHITE Jr., Peleg HUDDELSTONE. <19:270> Receipt 7 May 1764 of **Deborah WHITE**, widow to **Peleg WHITE**, exr. Witnesses: William DAVELL, Elisha RUSSELL. Receipt 7 May 1764 of **Culbut & Ruth WILCOX**. Witnesses: Thomas WILCOKS, Henry BRIGHTMAN. <19:271> Receipt 7 May 1764 of **William WHITE**. Witness: John SIMMONS. Receipt 29 Oct. 1764 of **Thomas WING & Hannah WING**. Witnesses: David WING. Receipt 5 July 1765 of widow **Deborah WHITE** as guardian of **Eunice WHITE** for her share. Witnesses: William DAVEL, Elisha RUSSELL. Receipt 12 Oct. 1765 of **Sarah WHITE**. Witness: John GIFFORD. Receipt 1 Aug. 1765 of **James & Mary SOUL**. Witness: Ruth WILLCOX, Sarah WHITE. Receipt 8 May 1764 of **Israel WHITE**. Witnesses: Benjamin TRIPP, Esek WOOD.

Will of **Deborah WHITE**, widow of Dartmouth MA. <Bristol Co.PR>
<19:438>...dated 15 Jan. 1766...to son **Israel WHITE** my riding beast and biggest pair of steers and the rents for 1765 of the farm he now lives on; to sons **Peleg WHITE, William WHITE, Silvanus WHITE**, one Spanish milled dollar each; to son **Obed WHITE** all my farming tools; personal effects to daus **Ruth WILCOX, Hannah WING, Mary SOULE, Sarah WHITE, Eunice WHITE**; to Deborah DAVENPORT & Deborah WILCOX, one silver spoon each; maid servant Violet. **William WHITE**, son of **William WHITE**, sole executor. Witnesses: Jonathan SOWLE, John MACUMBER, Lydia SISSON. Pr. 24 Nov. 1766.

Will of **William WHITE**, blacksmith of Dartmouth MA. <Bristol Co.PR>
<26:282>...dated 17 Feb. 1777, "son of **William WHITE** of Dartmouth"...to son **Jonathan WHITE** (executor), farm my honoured grandfather **George CADMAN** gave me after the decease of my honoured father and mother; daus **Hannah KIRBY** (eldest), **Elizabeth PECKHAM** (2nd), **Abigail WHITE** (youngest). Pr. 3 Oct. 1780. <26:293> Inventory taken 9 Sept. 1780, presented 3 Oct. 1780 by **Jonathan WHITE**.

Will of **John HATHAWAY Sr.** of Dartmouth MA. <Bristol Co.PR>
...dated 11 July 1732, sick & weak of body, mentions wf **Patience**; son **John HATHAWAY**; daus **Sarah CANNON, Joanna BLACKWELL, Mary DUGLAS**; son **Jonathan HATHAWAY**; dau **Hannah BOOMER**; sons **Richard HATHAWAY, Honiwell HATHAWAY, Abiah HATHAWAY, Benjamin HATHAWAY, James HATHAWAY, Ebenezer HATHAWAY Arthur HATHAWAY**; daus **Patience PECKHAM, Elizabeth HATHAWAY**. Wf **Patience** and son **Jonathan**, executors; mentions lands bounded by land of Stephen PECKHAM's Cove, John PECKHAM, William ALLEN and land bought of Benjamin CRANE. Witnesses: Richard PEARCE, Samuel PECKHAM, Stephen WEST.

MICRO #22 OF 30

Ebenezer HATHAWAY et al to **John McPERSON** of same. <Bristol Co.Deeds 56:420>
...17 May 1774, Ruth HATHAWAY widow of Ebenezer dec'd, Ebenezer HATHAWAY and Timothy HATHAWAY, sons of sd Ebenezer dec'd, sell to John McPERSON, trader...all their interest in land that John HATHAWAY, late of Dartmouth dec'd, gave his son Thomas HATHAWAY since dec'd without issue. Ack. 5 Jan. 1775. Rec. 28 Nov. 1775.

Ebenezer HATHAWAY of New Bedford to **Sylvester HOLMES** of same. <Bristol Co.Deeds 101:275>
...11 July 1815, Ebenezer HATHAWAY, mariner, sells to Sylvester HOLMES, clerk...land in New Bedford. Wf Hannah HATHAWAY signs. Rec. 10 Dec. 1816.

Ebenezer HATHAWAY of Wellington MA to **Nathaniel WHEELER** of same. <Bristol Co.Deeds 101:248>
...30 Sept. 1816, Ebenezer HATHAWAY, mariner sells to Nathaniel WHEELER, Esq., land & buildings in Wellington. Rec. 30 Nov. 1816.

Ebenezer HATHAWAY of New Bedford to **Thomas NASH** of same. <Bristol Co.Deeds 105:381>
...6 Nov. 1818, Ebenezer HATHAWAY, yeoman sells to Thomas NASH, land in New Bedford. Wf Hannah HATHAWAY releases dower. Ack. 29 Nov. 1818. Rec. 17 Dec. 1818.

Will of **Hunewell HATHAWAY**, yeoman of Dartmouth MA. <Bristol Co.PR>
<22:244>...dated 2 Mar. 1772, mentions wf **Mary**; sons **Obed HATHAWAY, James HATHAWAY, Richard HATHAWAY, Paul HATHAWAY**; grandsons **Worth BATES, William RUSSEL, Jonathan RUSSEL**; mentions land bought of Henry WRIGHTENTON. <22:149> Pr. 29 June 1772. <22:259> Inventory, 10 June 1772.

Richard & Paul HATHAWAY to **Jabez HATHAWAY** of New Bedford. <Bristol Co.Deeds 83:458>
...12 Apr. 1804, Richard HATHAWAY of New Bedford and Paul HATHAWAY of Dartmouth, yeomen, for $37.50, sold to Jabez HATHAWAY, trader...all our right & title in land in New Bedford...reference may be had to John HATHAWAY's will to Hunnewell HATHAWAY and from him to the sd Richard and Paul. Witnesses: Rodolphus H. WILLIAMS, Benjamin TABER 3d. Rec. 19 Apr. 1804.

Guardianship of Children of **Hunniwell HATHAWAY** & **Philip CANNON.** <Bristol Co.PR 128:228-34>
...25 Feb. 1771, Honeywell HATHAWAY, yeoman of Dartmouth, app'td gdn. of Paul HATHAWAY & Richard HATHAWAY (both over 14), sons of sd Honeywell and the following children of Philip CANNON, dec'd, viz: Philip CANNON & Sarah CANNON (over 14), Ruba CANNON & John CANNON (under 14) and Mary CANNON aged 14.

Estate of **Philip CANNON** of Dartmouth MA. <Bristol Co.PR 20:318>
Inventory taken 23 June 1768, widow **Mary CANNON**, admx.

Will of **Capt. William HATHAWAY** of Dartmouth MA. <Bristol Co.PR>
<19:236>...dated 17 Aug. 1765, mentions wf **Ruth** and unborn child, if child does not live, its portion to be given to all my brothers...after ye marriage or decease of my said wife.; father in law **Joseph BARKER** executor. Pr. 29 Oct. 1765. <21:616> Receipt 3 Apr. 1771 of **Hunewell HATHAWAY**, of the half part of the estate. Receipt 3 Jan. 1771 of **James HATHAWAY** and **Obed HATHAWAY** as ye fourth part.

Richard HATHAWAY of New Bedford to **William PECKHAM** of same. <Bristol Co.Deeds 85:37>
...24 Oct. 1802, Richard HATHAWAY, yeoman, for $164.00, sold to William PECKHAM, mariner...ten acres in New Bedford, bounded by land of William TALMAN. Wf Sarah HATHAWAY signs. Ack. by Richard 21 Feb. 1805. Rec. 10 May 1805.

Richard HATHAWAY of New Bedford to **Ebenezer HATHAWAY** of same. <Bristol Co.Deeds 85:333>
...16 Jan. 1805, Richard HATHAWAY, yeoman, for $775.00, sold to Ebenezer HATHAWAY, mariner...one half of the Thomas ROTCH farm, except ten acres which I sold William PECKHAM, about 100 acres, bounded by land of Isaiah PECKHAM, Benjamin SMITH, Ebenezer HATHAWAY, Richard HATHAWAY. Wf Sarah HATHAWAY signs. Ack. 21 Feb. 1805 by Richard. Rec. 23 Oct. 1805.

Will of **Richard HATHAWAY**, yeoman of New Bedford. <Bristol Co.PR>
<64:189>...dated 4 Mar. 1825...to wf **Sarah**...fifty dollars, the use & improvement (so long as she shall remain my Widow) of the Great room in the northeast corner of my now Dwelling house and the south part of said house, above & below, incl. cellar & garret so far, with the west closet in the northwest corner of said house & a privilege, what she may need to use, in the poarch & in the wood-house above and below, with a privilege to pass & repass through the kitchen & to the well and elsewhere as she may have occasion, also one good milch Cow, all the time the year round, & if by age or accident become unfit for her, then to be replaced with another, also eight pounds good sheep's wool a year & every year, also three geese & six dunghill fowls, and the use and improvement of the garden at the south of my dwelling house, also all my house-hold goods and indoors movables and my silver watch, I also give her yearly & every year, so long as she remains my widow, one barrel good flour, nine bushels Indian Corn, three bushels rye, one hundred pounds good beef, one hundred pounds good pork, cut up & salted for her use, twelve pounds tallow & twelve pounds hogs lard, twelve pounds good flax from the swingle, six cords good fire-wood cut suitable for her fire & put into the wood-house & should that quantity be insufficient for her use, as much more as she may need to be provided, I also give her six bushels good winter apples & as much summer fruit as she may need for her use...I also give her all the provision that may be laid in at my decease, incl. grain of all kinds, meat sauce, etc. and should she need at any time a Doctor or a nurse, or both, they are to be provided for her, all which, as are also all the foregoing supplies to be done at equal charges by my four sons...in lieu of her right of dower...to son **William HATHAWAY,** land bounded by land of Perry RUSSELL & Asa SMITH, also five acre cedar swamp, also one ox chain, one iron bar, one clevis & pin, one broad ax, one inch & quarter pod augar, eight crow feet for a sled, two large iron bolts for a draft, one pair handirons, two frows, and also my right in a hitchel now owned in common with Paul HATHAWAY...to son **Ebenezer HATHAWAY,** the farm I bought of Thomas ROTCH, my ox waggon, ox cart, horse waggon & harness, sled, yoake chains, one large log chain, one ox chain, one large iron bar & one small one, one large stone sledge & all my carpenters & coopers tools, one broad axe & one adze, two frows, one small ox harrow, one small horse harrow & gears, one sett cartwheel boxes & hub hoops which were taken from a pair wheels & two stone peckers...to son **Ezra HATHAWAY,** part of homestead bounded by Peckham brook and land of Paul HATHAWAY, also cedar swamp I bought of Abigail

WOOD, also my horse sleigh, one large ox harrows, two chains, one iron bar, hog-scalding trough, two augars, my half of one large crosscut saw owned in common with Paul HATHAWAY...to son **Weston HATHAWAY**, remainder of homestead, all my wearing apparel and my right in the destrict school-house, one iron bar, one ox chain & hand-cart...to dau **Sarah HATHAWAY**, privileges in my said dwelling house...my silver watch and clock and her choice of books...to granddaughter **Sarah HATHAWAY**, dau of son **Ezra**, one good feather bed...to dau **Lydia CONGDON** wf of William, a piece of land called the plain field, that I bought of Henry WRIGHTINGTON, containing about sixteen acres on the condition her husband **William CONGDON** pays to Samuel RODMAN the amount of a certain note and interest for which I am holden as endorser for the same, date not recollected, but when given was two hundred dollars... I hereby order my son **William HATHAWAY** (in consideration of the back rents of the farm on which he now lives and which I have herein given him) to pay Jane BATES the amount of a certain note and interest which I gave to her some years ago (and still remains unpaid); son **Ebenezer**, executor if living & at home, but if at sea, son **William** is executor. Witnesses: William TALLMAN, Francis TABER, Barnabas TABER. <original> Acknowledgement of heirs, 24 Sept. 1827, signed by **William HATHAWAY, Ezra HATHAWAY, Hannah HATHAWAY, Mercy Ann HATHAWAY, Sarah HATHAWAY, Lydia H. CONDON.** Pr. 2 Oct. 1827. <68:54> Inventory, 28 Oct. 1827. <69:393> Account, 3 May 1831. <112:299> Notice.

Estate of **Abigail HATHAWAY** of New Bedford MA. <Bristol Co.PR>
<92:269> Decree 4 July 1848, James BEETLE app'td admr. <162:213> Bond 4 July 1848, of admr. <92:338> Inventory taken 30 Aug. 1848 by Alexander HATHAWAY, Simeon N. WEST, Pardon B. POTTER; incl. two story house & lot, $1000.00. <210:482> Petition of James BEETLE to sell real estate to pay the debts; 4 Sept. 1849 he was ordered to notify all persons interested. <94:361> Notice of sale, 24 Oct. 1849, of dwelling house, buildings and about a quarter of an acre of land situated on road leading from New Bedford to Perry's Neck about two miles from the village of New Bedford and formerly known as the **Ezra HATHAWAY** house. <original> Bond 3 Oct. 1849 of admr. Surety: James M. LAWTON. <97:238> Account 1 Dec. 1851; proceeds of estate sold, $600.00. Payments to: George C. TEW as guardian of Mary E., George H., Sarah T., Henrietta M. and Helen L. TEW, $75.23; Isaac JENNINGS as guardian of Abby A., Caroline A., Isaac A., Latham T., William Henry, Lydia A. and Charles T. JENNINGS, $75.23; Benjamin KING as guardian of Adeline H. and Georgiana KING, $75.23; George W. HATHAWAY, $75.23; Hannah W. KING, $75.23; Ann A. HATHAWAY, $75.23; Sarah A. TEW,$75.23.

Guardianship of Children of **Benjamin KING** of New Bedford MA. <Bristol Co.PR>
<136:60, 140:171> 3 Oct. 1848, **Benjamin KING** app'td guardian of **Adeline H. KING** and **Georgiana KING**, minors under 14, children of the said Benjamin. <92:423> Decree.

Ezra HATHAWAY of New Bedford MA to **George WANTON** of Newport RI. <Newport Co.Deeds 2:258>
...18 Aug. 1809, Ezra HATHAWAY & wf Abigail, daughter and one of the heirs at law of John WANTON, Esq., late of Newport RI and Providence Plantation, dec'd, for $850.00, sell to George WANTON, merchant...all John WANTON's rights in land with dwelling house in Newport...by a certain Order of Partition made by the Superior Court...Sept. 1790 between the heirs at law of James WANTON & Patience WANTON, his widow...bounded by Thames St. and land of Jonathan MARSH, SANFORD and John SCOTT. Witnesses: Jno. R. SHEARMAN, Jonathan ALMY. Rec. 14 Dec. 1809.

Ezra HATHAWAY of New Bedford MA to **Isaac JENNINGS** of Dartmouth MA. <Bristol Co.Deeds 133:143>
...5 Nov. 1830, Ezra HATHAWAY, yeoman, for $783.00, sold to Isaac JENNINGS...land with a house in Dartmouth, on the north side of the old county road which passes from Acushnet village to Smiths mills, bounded by land of Paul HATHAWAY. Wf Abigail HATHAWAY releases dower. Rec. 12 Sept. 1831.

Ezra HATHAWAY of New Bedford MA to **Isaac JENNINGS** of Dartmouth MA. <Bristol Co.Deeds 140:192>
...23 Mar. 1832, Ezra HATHAWAY, for $1200.00, sells to Isaac JENNINGS, yeoman...30 acres in Dartmouth & New Bedford, bounded by land of Paul HATHAWAY. Wf Abigail HATHAWAY releases dower. Rec. 25 Oct. 1833.

Ezra HATHAWAY & George C. TEW of New Bedford MA. <Bristol Co.Deeds 151:257>
...10 Aug. 1836, a trust deed was executed between Ezra HATHAWAY and George C. TEW, coppersmith.. that the said Ezra HATHAWAY, in consideration of the covenant on the part of the said TEW hereinafter contained & of the love and affection which he bears to his wife, Abagail HATHAWAY, does hereby give...unto the said TEW...land situated in the said New Bedford on the road leading from the village to Allen's Mills, bounded by land of William ROTCH and Samuel RODMAN, containing fourteen and a half acres...during the life of the said Abagail...upon the following trusts and purposes...that the said TEW his heirs and assigns, shall take care of and manage the said premises and receive the rents & profits of the same and...pay over to the said Abagail for her seperated use...whatsoever rents...he or they may receive...during her natural life and after her death, the premises shall be held by TEW for the use of any children of Abigail & Ezra HATHAWAY then living, or the children of any deceased child. Rec. 12 Aug. 1836.

Ezra HATHAWAY of New Bedford MA to **Benjamin KING** of same. <Bristol Co.Deeds 150:257>
...18 Dec. 1835, Ezra HATHAWAY, yeoman, for $1200.00, sells to Benjamin KING, labourer...38 and one half acres partly in New Bedford and partly in Dartmouth...on the road leading from New Bedford village to Perrys neck, bounded by land of George W. HATHAWAY, Paul HATHAWAY and Isaac JENNINGS...it being the one half as set off to me of that farm recently owned in common by George W. HATHAWAY & myself excepting the right of dower which Sarah HATHAWAY may have to any part of said premises. Wf Abigail HATHAWAY releases dower. Rec. 20 June 1836.

BRISTOL COUNTY DEEDS: (re: Ezra HATHAWAY, all on index 1795-1840, none on 1840-66 index**)**

<96:68> - 1813, Ezra HATHAWAY & Abigail HATHAWAY & others (grantors).
<116:229> - 1824, Ezra HATHAWAY to Charles W. MORGAN.
<149:415> - 1836, Ezra HATHAWAY to William ROTCH Jr.
<150:378> - 26 July 1836, Ezra HATHAWAY, yeoman of New Bedford to Samuel RODMAN. Wf Abigail HATHAWAY releases dower. Rec. 15 Aug. 1836.
<152:147> - 26 July 1836, Ezra HATHAWAY, yeoman of New Bedford to Isaac CASE, housewright of same Wf Abigail HATHAWAY releases dower. Rec. 8 Dec. 1836.
<152:151> - 26 July 1836, Ezra HATHAWAY, yeoman of New Bedford to Daniel BORDEN. Wf Abigail HATHAWAY releases dower. Rec. 8 Dec. 1836.

Ezra HATHAWAY of New Bedford MA to **George WANTON** of Newport RI. <Bristol Co.Deeds 91:352>
...3 Mar. 1810, Ezra HATHAWAY, yeoman & wf Abigail, sell to George WANTON...land & house in New Bedford. Rec. 12 July 1810. (On 4 May 1810, George WANTON sells same back to sd Abigail HATHAWAY, <91:354>.)

Ezra HATHAWAY of New Bedford MA to **George W. HATHAWAY** of same. <Bristol Co.Deeds 138:280>
...23 Mar. 1832, Ezra HATHAWAY, for $1214.00, sold to George W. HATHAWAY...one undivided half part...75 acres in New Bedford, bounded by land of Paul HATHAWAY, land sold Isaac JENNINGS and land given sd Ezra by Richard HATHAWAY by will. Wf Abigail HATHAWAY releases dower.

Ezra HATHAWAY of New Bedford MA to **Gardner THOMAS** of Portsmouth RI. <Bristol Co.Deeds 151:370>
...22 Sept. 1836, Ezra HATHAWAY, yeoman, mortgages to Gardner THOMAS, yeoman...land & barn partly in New Bedford, partly in Dartmouth. Wf Abigail HATHAWAY releases dower. Rec. 24 Sept. 1836.

MICRO #23 OF 30

Guardianship of Children of **George Cornell TEW** of New Bedford. <Bristol Co.PR>
<<92:376> Decree, 1848. <136:157> 5 Sept. 1848, **George C. TEW** app'td gdn. of **Mary E. TEW** (above 14) of Spencer NY, **George Henry TEW** (above 14), **John L. TEW, Sarah T. TEW, Henrietta M. TEW** and **Helen L. TEW** all of sd New Bedford and all minors. <140:168> Bond 5 Sept. 1848. Sureties: Barjona D. TRIPP, James BEETLE.

Mercy Ann HATHAWAY of Northbridge MA to **Ezra HATHAWAY** of New Bedford MA.<Bristol Co.Deeds 135:43>
...18 July 1831, Mercy Ann HATHAWAY, widow and guardian to her five children, viz: Elizabeth B. HATHAWAY, Sarah Ann HATHAWAY, Nancy Eliny HATHAWAY, William HATHAWAY and Thomas S. HATHAWAY, minors under 21, for $2520.00, sells to Ezra HATHAWAY, yeoman of New Bedford...land in New Bedford bounded by land of Paul HATHAWAY and Ezra HATHAWAY. Rec. 10 Apr. 1832.

Barber PECKHAM of S. Kingstown RI to **Thomas PETER** of same. <S. Kingstown Deeds 8:422>
...1 Mar. 1791, Barber PECKHAM, yeoman, for £22.10s, sells to Thomas PETER, a mustee so called... 5 acres in S. Kingstown, bounded by land of Gardner William MUMFORD and sd PECKHAM. Wf Elizabeth PECKHAM releases dower. Witnesses: Silas HELME, Phillip BOSS. Rec. 13 Apr. 1791. Ack. 8 Mar 1791.

Thomas PETER of S. Kingstown RI to **Barber PECKHAM** of same. <S. Kingstown Deeds 9:87>
...21 Sept. 1795, Thomas PETER, mustee, for 25 silver dollars, sold to Barber PECKHAM, Esq...the same tract...I purchased 1 Mar. 1791. Wf Bridget PETER releases dower. Witnesses: Levi TOTTEN, J. HOGADORN(sp). Rec. 24 Dec. 1795.

Will of **Timothy PECKHAM** of S. Kingstown RI. <S. Kingstown RI PR>
<4:15>...dated 13 July 1821, mentions wf **Ruth** (executor); daus **Amy STANTON, Sally PECKHAM**; children of dec'd son **Barber PECKHAM**; sons **Timothy PECKHAM Jr., Stephen PECKHAM**; grandchildren, the chil. of **Patience LANGWORTHY** dec'd wf of Benjamin; grandchildren, the chil. of **Rachel REYNOLDS** dec'd wf of James; dau **Joanna SHELDEN** wf of Henry; dau **Ruth WHITEHORN** wf of Samuel; grandchildren chil. of dau **Lydia BENTLEY** dec'd wf of Ebenezer; dau **Mary ELDREDGE** wf of Thomas; dau **Susannah COTHRELL** wf of Samuel; dau **Waity LANGWORTHY** widow of Thomas; dau **Amy STANTON** wf of John C.; mentions all real estate purchased of Benjamin POTTER. Witnesses: Christopher CHAMPLIN, Samuel HELME, Weeden UNDERWOOD. <4:45> Pr. 14 Apr. 1823. <6:6> Inventory, 4 Mar. 1824, insolvent.

David COTTRELL of S. Kingstown RI to **Barber & Timothy PECKHAM** of same. <S. Kingstown RI Deeds>
<8:35>...7 Mar. 1785, David COTTRELL, yeoman, for $700.00, sold to Barber PECKHAM & Timothy PECKHAM 3d...as tenants in common, 112 acres in S. Kingstown...bounded on the Middle Stream of Mumford's Mill River and land of Gardner William MUMFORD, Samuel WHALEY, Thomas HOPKINS, Samuel HOPKINS. Wf Mary COTTRELL releases dower. Witnesses: Stephen BOYER, William CARD. Rec. 20 Aug. 1785.

Timothy PECKHAM 3d of Exeter RI to **Barber PECKHAM** of S. Kingstown RI. <S. Kingstown Deeds 8:184>
...22 Jan. 1787, Timothy PECKHAM 3d late of S. Kingstown, now residing at Exeter, for £105, sold to Barber PECKHAM, Esq...all his right...in 112 acres with dwelling house & blacksmith shop... bounded by...(same as above deed). Wf Freelove PECKHAM releases dower. Witnesses: Eber SHERMAN, Lucy COTTRELL. Rec. 26 Jan. 1787.

Elisha R. POTTER of S. Kingstown RI to **Barber PECKHAM** of same. <S. Kingstown RI Deeds 8:545>
...31 Aug. 1792, Elisha R. POTTER, Esq. & wf Mary, for £80, sold to Barber PECKHAM, Esq. alias yeoman...all their rights in land & buildings in S. Kingstown, 90 acres, in the possession of sd

PECKHAM...bounded by Middle Stream of River that leads to Mumford's Mills, land of Samuel WHALEY, Thomas HOPKINS, sd PECKHAM and land of Thomas PETER being a lot of land mortgaged by the late Stephen COTTRELL Jr. of S. Kingstown dec'd unto Joseph PERKINS late of sd S. Kingstown dec'd. Witnesses: John HAGADOIN, Adam HELME. Ack. by both 3 Sept. 1792. Rec. 25 Sept. 1792.

Barber PECKHAM of S. Kingstown RI to **David & Nathan KNIGHT** of Exeter RI. <S. Kingstown Deeds> <9:546>...13 Feb. 1800, Barber PECKHAM, Esq. leases to David & Nathan KNIGHT, gentlemen...the farm where I now live, 112 acres with dwelling house, barn, corn house, blacksmith shop, etc... bounded by highway to Mumford's Mill, Mill Pond and land of Samuel & George WHALEY, John HOPKINS, Samuel HOPKINS dec'd, Gardner William MUMFORD. Wf Sarah PECKHAM signs. Witnesses: Gardner William MUMFORD, James WHITCHOME, Jeremiah TEFFT. Rec. 17 Feb. 1800.

Barber PECKHAM of Freetown MA to **Joseph REYNOLDS** of S. Kingstown RI. <S. Kingstown Deeds 9:568> ...28 Apr. 1800, Barber PECKHAM, Esq., for $866.35, mortgaged to Joseph REYNOLDS, yeoman...112 acres in S. Kingstown...bounded by land of John HOPKINS, heirs of Samuel HOPKINS dec'd, Gardner Wm. MUMFORD, Samuel & George WHALEY; mortgage to be paid on or before 24 Aug. 1807. Witnesses: Samuel GARDINER, John HAGADOIN. Rec. 28 Apr. 1800. Endorsement on side of page: 28 Mar. 1801, mortgage discounted & paid by Joseph REYNOLDS. Witnesses: John L. BOSS Jr., James HELME.

Barber PECKHAM of Freetown MA to **Elisha R. POTTER** of S. Kingstown RI. <S. Kingstown Deeds 9:643> ...9 Jan. 1801, Barber PECKHAM, Esq., for $262.40, mortgaged to Elisha R. POTTER, Esq...112 acres in S. Kingstown...(same boundaries as above deed); mortgage to be paid on or before 1 July 1807. Witnesses: Samuel GARDNER, John L. BOSS Jr. Mortgage released 28 Mar. 1801. Rec. 2 Feb. 1801.

Barber PECKHAM of Freetown MA to **David & Nathan KNIGHT** of S. Kingston RI. <S. Kingstown Deeds> <9:650>...28 Mar. 1801, Barber PECKHAM, Esq., for $500.00, sold to David & Nathan KNIGHT, gentlemen...90 acre farm in S. Kingston bounded by land of Gardner William MUMFORD, Daniel GINNEDO, John HOPKINS, Samuel & George WHALEY. Witnesses: Samuel E. GARDINER, John L. BOSS Jr. Rec. 28 Mar 1801.

Barber PECKHAM of Freetown MA to **David & Nathan KNIGHT** of S. Kingston RI. <S. Kingstown Deeds> <9:651>...28 Mar. 1801, Barber PECKHAM, Esq., for $1098.00, mortgaged to David KNIGHT, yeoman and Nathan KNIGHT, Physician...20 acres with dwelling house...bounded on land this day sold by PECKHAM to sd KNIGHTS, highway to MUMFORD's Mill, mill pond. Warranty against everything except a lease by PECKHAM to sd KNIGHTS ending 25 Mar. 1807. Mortgage to be paid on or before 25 Mar. 1807 Witnesses: Samuel E. GARDINER, John L. BOSS Jr. Rec. 28 Mar. 1801.

Barber PECKHAM of Freetown MA to **Timothy PECKHAM** of S. Kingston RI. <S. Kingstown Deeds 10:23> ...1 Mar. 1802, Barber PECKHAM, Esq., for $1800.00, sold to Timothy PECKHAM, blacksmith...20 acres with dwelling house...subject to a lease to David & Nathan KNIGHT ending 28 Mar. 1807. Witnesses: J. HELME Jr., John T. NICHOLS. Rec. 1 Apr. 1802.

Benjamin PECKHAM of S. Kingstown RI to **John PECKHAM** of same. <S. Kingstown RI Deeds 6:41> ...4 Dec. 1758, Benjamin PECKHAM, yeoman...for ye love I have & do bare towards my loving son John PECKHAM, cordwainer, convey...10 acres in S. Kingstown...bounded by land of John POTTER. Witnesses: Benjamin PECKHAM Jr., George Hazard PECKHAM.

Benjamin PECKHAM of S. Kingstown RI to **Timothy PECKHAM** of same. <S. Kingstown RI Deeds 6:41> ...5 Dec. 1758, Benjamin PECKHAM, yeoman...in consideration of ye love...I have & do bare towards my loving son Timothy PECKHAM, husbandman, convey...12 acres in S. Kingstown bounded by land of John PECKHAM. Witnesses: Benjamin PECKHAM Jr., George Hazard PECKHAM.

Samuel ROGERS of S. Kingstown RI to **Timothy PECKHAM** of E. Greenwich RI. <S. Kingstown Deeds> <6:129>...1 Apr. 1761, Samuel ROGERS, yeoman, for Ł2500, sold to Timothy PECKHAM, yeoman...two tracts of land in S. Kingstown...the largest piece contains 26 acres bounded by land of Benjamin SHEARMAN, John SHELDEN...other lott consisting of 10 acres bounded by land of Jeremiah CRANDAL, Benjamin SHEARMAN and the Pettequamscut Line. Wf Lydia ROGERS releases dower. Witnesses: Benjamin BARBER, Jeremiah CRANDALL. Rec. 13 Apr. 1761.

Benjamin PECKHAM of S. Kingstown RI to **Timothy PECKHAM** of Jamestown RI. <S. Kingstown Deeds> <6:237>...22 Nov. 1762, Benjamin PECKHAM, yeoman, for Ł4000, sold to Timothy PECKHAM, yeoman, late of S. Kingstown...10 acres in S. Kingstown...bounded by land of Joseph CONGDON, Carder HAZARD in ye present tenure and occupation of Joseph SEGAR. Wf Mary PECKHAM releases dower. Witnesses: Hannah ADAMS, Jane NASH. Rec. 14 Jan. 1763.

Benjamin BARBER of Hopkinton RI to **Timothy PECKHAM** of S. Kingston RI. <S. Kingstown Deeds 6:396> ...31 Mar. 1767, Benjamin BARBER, yeoman, for Ł225, sold to Timothy PECKHAM, blacksmith...100 acres in S. Kingstown...bounded by land of Samuel BABCOCK, Benjamin SHEARMAN, Jeremiah CRANDAL. Wf Mary BARBER releases dower. Witnesses: Nathaniel PULMAN, Edward PERRY. Rec. 3 Apr. 1767

Caleb WESTCOT of S. Kingston RI to **Timothy PECKHAM Jr.** of same. <S. Kingstown Deeds 7:573> ...24 Feb. 1783, Caleb PECKHAM, housewright, for Ł180, sold to Timothy PECKHAM Jr., blacksmith... lot of land in S. Kingston on Little Rest Hill...one hundred and thirteen feet by seventy nine and one third feet...bounded by land of Joseph PERKINS, John WEEDEENS, Robert POTTER, Esq., the school house lot and Main Street...with two dwelling houses thereon and one stable. Witnesses: R. POTTER, George GARDNER. Rec. 26 Mar. 1784. (See next deed.)

Caleb WESTCOT of S. Kingston RI to **Ruth WESTCOT** of same. <S. Kingstown Deeds 7:574> ...27 Mar. 1784, Caleb WESTCOT sold to Ruth WESTCOT, spinster...all rights in previous deed. (<8:87>...13 Feb. 1786, Ruth WESTCOT, now residing in Newport RI, sold the land back to Timothy PECKHAM Jr.)

Will of **Benjamin PECKHAM**, yeoman of S. Kingstown RI. <S. Kingstown RI PR 5:169> ...dated 21 June 1761, mentions wf **Mary**...to son **Benjamin PECKHAM**, 5s, he having already had his portion...to son **Peleg PECKHAM**, one third of my farm with dwelling house which he now liveth... according to ye annexed plan made by Simeon PERRY, surveyor, 27 Mar. 1760...also all ye lands on ye Hills, so called, which I purchased of Daniel McCOONE dec'd...to son **Isaac PECKHAM** my Great Bible & Ł200...within two years next after my decease the one half of said sum to be paid by my son **Peleg** and the other half to be paid by my son **Timothy**...to son **John PECKHAM** one third part of ye farm I now live, incl. dwelling house & land I have already given him by deed, about 43 acres ...bounded by land of Daniel CARPENTER...also all my wearing apparel...to son **Timothy PECKHAM** my dwelling house & remaining third part of my homestead farm incl. land I have already given him by deed; farm to be divided among three sons...to sons **John & Timothy** all my lands in S. Kingstown which I purchased of Jonathan TURNER...to dau **Mary HOXSEY** my silver tankard now in her possession and Ł50...to be paid to her by my son **John**...to sister **Mercy KINYON**, Ł10 yearly; son **Peleg**, executor. Witnesses: Freeman PERRY, Jonathan HOLLEY, Elizabeth AUCH(UMTY)(sp). Pr. 17 Aug. 1762.

Will of **Benjamin PECKHAM**, yeoman of S. Kingstown RI. <S. Kingstown RI PR 9:262> ...7 Dec. 1790, mentions wf **Mary**; son **Peleg PECKHAM**; grandson **Benjamin PECKHAM**, son of dec'd son **George Hazard PECKHAM**; son **Josephus PECKHAM** (executor); brother **Peleg PECKHAM**; sons **William PECKHAM, John Pain PECKHAM**; dau **Mary PERRY** wf of Joshua; grandson **Benjamin ROBINSON** son of dau **Sarah ROBINSON**. Pr. 12 Mar. 1792.

Will of **Peleg PECKHAM**, yeoman of S. Kingstown RI. <S. Kingstown RI PR 9:343> ...31 Dec. 1788, mentions brother **John PECKHAM**; nephew **Henry PECKHAM** son of dec'd brother **Isaac PECKHAM**; clothes of dec'd wife to go to Caleb CARPENTER's three daughters, Elizabeth, Mary and Hannah; brother in law **Joseph HOXSIE** of Charlestown and nephew **William PECKHAM** son of brother **Benjamin PECKHAM**, executors. Pr. 11 Apr. 1796. Inv. 11 Apr. 1796.

Will of **Benjamin BARBER**, yeoman of Westerly, Washington Co. RI. <Westerly Town PR 7:171> ...6 Feb. 1792, mentions daus **Lydia ROGERS, Mary PECKHAM, Mercy ROGERS, Ruth KINYON**; granddau. **Johannah ROGERS**; son **Benjamin P. BARBER** (under 21); chil. of son **Nathan BARBER**; son **Nathan BARBER** to be guardian of son **Benjamin**; grandson **John BARBER** of Westerly, executor. Witnesses: James SHEFFIELD, Susanna PENDLETON, Prudence CLARKE. Pr. 26 Mar. 1792.

Estate of **Jonathan HATHAWAY** of Dartmouth MA. <Bristol Co.PR>
<6:79> 6 Mar. 1727/8, **Susannah HATHAWAY**, widow, app'td admx. Inventory taken 2 Dec. 1727 by Nathaniel BLACKSWELL, Elnathan POPE, Stephen WEST Jr.; total, Ł2291.15s. <6:91> Account of admx., 9 Apr. 1728. <6:159> Guardianship of children, **Jonathan HATHAWAY, Silas HATHAWAY, Elnathan HATHAWAY** (all under 14), granted to widow **Susannah HATHAWAY**. <12:578> Order to Divide, 18 Oct. 1728, to Isaac POPE Sr., William SPOONER, Stephen WEST, Henry SAMPSON and Nathaniel BLACK. <12:579> Division 14 Feb. 1729/30 between widow, **Gamaliel HATHAWAY** (eldest son), **Seth HATHAWAY, Jonathan HATHAWAY, Silas HATHAWAY, Elnathan HATHAWAY, Abigail HATHAWAY, Hannah HATHAWAY, Deborah HATHAWAY.**

Will of **Susanna HATHAWAY** of Dartmouth MA. <Bristol Co.PR>
<16:518>...dated 14 Jan. 1760, widow of Jonathan, mentions daus **Abigail SPOONER, Hannah HATHAWAY**; granddaughter **Anne HATHAWAY**; sons **Gamaliel HATHAWAY** (executor), **Seth HATHAWAY, Jonathan HATHAWAY, Elnathan HATHAWAY**; dau **Deborah SWIFT**; grandson **Micah HATHAWAY.** <16:519> Pr. 12 Mar. 1760.<16:520> Inventory, 19 Feb. 1760. <58:426> Adm. <59:251> Inventory. <59:273> Account.

Will of **Gamaliel HATHAWAY**, yeoman of New Bedford MA. <Bristol Co.PR 34:441> ...dated 3 June 1793, mentions sons **Obed HATHAWAY, Eleazer HATHAWAY, Micah HATHAWAY**; sister **Hannah** to have a room in the house; pew in meeting house to **Eleazer** and **Micah**, they allowing their sister **Anna DILLINGHAM** to set in it; housekeeper Francis DEMERANVILE. Pr. 2 Mar. 1797.

Will of **Benjamin DILLINGHAM**, mariner of Fairhaven MA. <Bristol Co.PR>
<63:451>...dated 25 June 1821, mentions wf **Freelove**; dau **Nabby HAWES**; granddaughter **Clarissa HAWES**; dau **Ester CRANDON**; sons **Paul DILLINGHAM, Benjamin DILLINGHAM, Lemuel DILLINGHAM**; daus **Anna HATHAWAY, Priscilla KEMPTON, Hannah TERRY**; sons **Edward DILLINGHAM, Asa DILLINGHAM.** Pr. 25 July 1826. <63:507> Inventory, 12 Aug. 1826. <83:160> Account. <112:135> Notice.

Will of **Anna HATHAWAY** of Fairhaven MA. <Bristol Co.PR 99:340> ...dated 1 May 1844, mentions children **John D. HATHAWAY, Shadrach HATHAWAY, Hannah WHITWELL, Bradford HATHAWAY, Paul D. HATHAWAY, Ann BURGESS.** Pr. 7 June 1853.

Estate of **Joseph HATHAWAY.** <Bristol Co.PR 54:491>
Insolvency, 5 May 1818, widow **Anna HATHAWAY** applies for a commission.

Will of **Micah HATHAWAY**, yeoman of New Bedford MA. <Bristol Co.PR>
<52:8>...dated 12 Feb. 1812, mentions sons **Thomas HATHAWAY** (executor), **Nathan HATHAWAY, Micah HATHAWAY**; my six single daughters; granddaughter **Lydia HATHAWAY** (under 18), dau of son **Obed HATHAWAY**; if in case my son **Obed HATHAWAY** should be yet alive and returne home then it is my will that the whole of my homested to the eastward of the highway be equely divided between my two

sons **Obed** and **Nathan**...and the leagacy given to my granddaughter be null and void; to my daughters all my personal estate...respect to be had to what those that are marred/married have received. <original> Order to appraise 29 Jan. 1816 to Stephen HATHAWAY, Jonathan KEMPTON, John TABER 2d, all of Fairhaven. <original> Adm. 7 May 1816 to **Thomas HATHAWAY.** Bond 7 May 1816 of admr. <original> Notice of admr. 29 Oct. 1816. <52:512> Inventory 29 Oct. 1816; real estate, $3030.00; total, $3844.34.

Estate of **Nathan HATHAWAY** of Fairhaven MA. <Bristol Co.PR>
<original> Petition 1 May 1827 of widow **Elizabeth HATHAWAY** to have Bartholomew TABER app'td admr. <65:105> Adm. 1 May 1827, Bartholomew TABER app'td admr. <65:207> Inventory sworn to 31 July 1827 by admr.; incl. dwelling house & land in Fairhaven, subject to the right of dower of Joseph TERREY's widow during her life, $500; 30 acres in Fairhaven, $1000; salt marsh at the head of the cove in Fairhaven, $120. <67:155> Account. <112:255> Notice. <152:326> Adm. <202:356> Sale of land. <133:426> Guardianship, 2 Oct. 1827, **Elizabeth HATHAWAY**, widow, app'td gdn. of **Phebe K. HATHAWAY** (over 14) and **Daniel K. HATHAWAY** (under 14).

BRISTOL COUNTY DEEDS: (re: HATHAWAY)

<101:299> - 1816, Nathan HATHAWAY, cordwainer of Fairhaven MA et al to Henry PIERCE, judgment against HATHAWAY and Drury TURNER.
<103:61> - , Nathan HATHAWAY, grantor.
<112:233> - 21 May 1821, Nathan HATHAWAY, tanner of Fairhaven MA to Enoch S. JENNEY, tanner of Fairhaven, land both bought of Bradford HOWLAND 14 Oct. 1815. Wf Betsey/Elizabeth HATHAWAY releases dower.
<114:269> - , Nathan HATHAWAY et al to Samuel HOWS, judgement.
<122:544> - , Estate of Nathan HATHAWAY by admr. to Royal HATHAWAY.
<126:117> - , Estate of Nathan HATHAWAY by admr. to Royal HATHAWAY.
<126:121> - , Royal HATHAWAY to Bartholomew TABER & Elizabeth HATHAWAY, annullment of above deed that errors might be corrected.
<130:521> - , Elizabeth HATHAWAY et al to Thomas BENNETT.
<133:13> - , Estate of Nathan HATHAWAY by admr. to Abner PEASE.
<142:146> - , Estate of Nathan HATHAWAY by admr. to Enoch S. JENNEY.
<142:148> - , Elizabeth HATHAWAY to Enoch S. JENNEY, one tenth part of land in Fairhaven that James KEMPTON, late of Fairhaven, dec'd, gave by will to his sons Samuel and Noah KEMPTON.

Will of **Obed HATHAWAY** of New Bedford MA. <Bristol Co.PR>
<42:110>...dated 15 Aug. 1805, mentions wf **Desire**...to dau **Hannah HATHAWAY**, part of homestead which was given me by my father **Gamaliel HATHAWAY**...to dau **Sarah SHEARMAN**, rest of estate...to four minor grandchildren, chil. of my dau **Elisabeth WASHBURN** dec'd, land purchased of John DILLINGHAM and Samuel BOWERMAN...to dau **Anna**, $100; dau **Hannah** app'td admx. <42:111> Pr. 6 May 1806.

Will of **James SISSON**, yeoman of Dartmouth MA. <Bristol Co.PR>
<8:168>...dated 15 June 1734, mentions sons **Richard SISSON, James SISSON, Jonathan SISSON** (executor), **Thomas SISSON**; daus **Sarah DAVIL, Rebeckah WEST**; grandaughter **Susanna SISSON**; chil. of dec'd dau **Content**; daus **Mary, Hannah.** Witnesses: David IRISH, William DAVEL Jr., Beriah GODDARD.<8:167> Bond of admr., 17 Dec. 1734. Sureties: Beriah GODDARD, William DAVEL, yeomen of Dartmouth. Witnesses: Stephen PAINE, Samuel GOFF. <8:180> Inventory taken 2 Dec. 1734, by George WHITE, William DAVEL Jr. and Beriah GODDARD; no real estate mentioned, total £172.18s.

MICRO #24 OF 30

Will of **Samuel HAMMOND** of Rochester MA. <Plymouth Co.PR 5:477>
...dated 12 July 1728, mentions wf **Mary**; son **Thomas HAMMOND**; brother **Nathan HAMMOND**; sons **Jedediah HAMMOND, John HAMMOND**; grandsons **Archelaus HAMMOND** and **Peter SPOONER**; dau **Maria CLARK**; sons **Samuel HAMMOND, Josiah HAMMOND, Barnabas HAMMOND, Seth HAMMOND**; grandaughter **Abigail**; grandaughters **Elizabeth SPOONER** (under 18) and **Rose SPOONER**; grandchildren **Jeduthun SPOONER, Benjamin SPOONER, John SPOONER, Thomas SPOONER, Hobbs SPOONER, Mary SPOONER**; dau **Jedidah.** Witnesses: Thomas CLARKE, Joshua COGGSHALL, Nathaniel DELANO. Pr. 20 Sept. 1728.

Will of **Thomas HATHAWAY**, glazier of Dartmouth MA. <Bristol Co.PR 29:76>
...dated 10 Jan. 1775, mentions the chil. of brother **Jethro HATHAWAY**, viz: **Stephen HATHAWAY, Clark HATHAWAY, Hepzibath DAVIS; Thomas MOTT** & **Adam MOTT**, sons of sister **Apphiah MOTT** dec'd (& her female heirs); **Thomas HATHAWAY**, third son of **Stephen HATHAWAY**; heirs of **Clark HATHAWAY; Jonathan KEMPTON** the youngest son (under 30 & unm.) of sister **Mary KEMPTON** dec'd; **Lois HATHAWAY** wf of **Clark HATHAWAY** & her brother **Benjamin AKENS**; wf **Lois; Nathaniel HATHAWAY**, son of brother **Antipas HATHAWAY; David KEMPTON** son of sister **Mary** dec'd; **Hepzibah WING** and **Lydia WING**, daus of sister **Hepzibah WING**; heirs of my two brothers & 4 sisters; brother in law **Bartholmew TABER** and Kinsman **Stephen HATHAWAY**, executors. Pr. 2 May 1787 by Stephen HATHAWAY.

BRISTOL COUNTY DEEDS: (re: Antipas HATHAWAY)

<20:221> - 27 Apr. 1731, Antipas HATHAWAY, glazer of Freetown & wf Patience to Benjamin DURFEE of Freetown, Patience as admx. of estate of Capt. Constant CHURCH & his late widow. Ack. 13 May 1731. Rec. 16 June 1731.

BRISTOL COUNTY DEEDS, cont-d: (re: Antipas HATHAWAY)

<21:448> - 12 Apr. 1732, Antipas HATHAWAY, glazer of Dartmouth & wf Patience, to Benjamin DURFEE, yeoman of Freetown, land in Freetown. Rec. 12 July 1733.
<28:51> - 28 July 1737, Antipas HATHAWAY, glazer of Dartmouth & wf Patience as admx. of estate of her former husband, Capt. Constant CHURCH, to Benjamin DURFEE, yeoman of Freetown, land in Freetown. Rec. 24 July 1739.
<27:283> - 1738, Antipas HATHAWAY from Thomas HATHAWAY.
<30:41> - 1739, Antipas HATHAWAY from William ASHLEY.
<31:109> - 27 Aug. 1742, Antipas HATHAWAY, yeoman of Dartmouth to Ebenezer CHADWICK, sea faring man of Falmouth, land in Dartmouth laid out to Thomas HATHAWAY on 15 Mar 1710/1 and 26 June 1713. Rec. 20 Sept. 1742.
<34:13> - 8 Feb. 1742/3, Antipas HATHAWAY, yeoman of Dartmouth to Moses MENDALL, land in Pocasset Purchase in Tiverton. Wf Patience HATHAWAY signs. Rec. 11 Sept. 1745.
<37:322> - 8 Jan. 1747, Antipas HATHAWAY, glazier of Newport to James WEEDEN, cordwainer of Tiverton, all his homestead in Dartmouth; mentions father Thomas HATHAWAY. Wf Patience HATHAWAY signs. Rec. 13 June 1750.
<57:289> - 24 Aug. 1752, Antipas HATHAWAY, glazier of Newport to Jethro HATHAWAY, yeoman of Dartmouth, land in Acushnet Village in Dart., part of homestead of Thomas HATHAWAY, dec'd. Rec. 12 June 1777.
<41:223> - 25 Aug. 1752, Antipas HATHAWAY, glazier of Newport to Jethro DELANO, gentleman of Dartmouth, land in Dartmouth bounded by land of my father Thomas HATHAWAY, dec'd. Rec. 27 Dec. 1754.
<42:360> - 1757, Antipas HATHAWAY from John WING Jr.
<49:124> - 30 May 1764, Antipas HATHAWAY, yeoman of Dartmouth to William SANFORD, yeoman of Dartmouth, northerly corner of homestead farm in Dart. Rec. 29 Oct. 1765.
<50:331> - 1767, Antipas HATHAWAY from Jonathan EASTON.
<51:535> - 17 Jan. 1769, Antipas HATHAWAY, glazier of Dartmouth, mortgage to William STORY, Esq. of Ipswich, house & land in Dartmouth; released 25 Nov. 1769. Rec. 18 Jan. 1769.
<52:407> - 1769, Antipas HATHAWAY from William STORY.
<81:423> - 4 Aug. 1800, Antipas HATHAWAY, mariner of New Bedford to Nathaniel STETSON, one quarter of land in New Bed. which my uncle Thomas HATHAWAY gave to me & my other brother & two sisters. Rec. 16 Sept. 1802.
<87:242> - 1807, Antipas HATHAWAY et al to Edward WING.
<92:150> - 1811, Antipas HATHAWAY et al to John SHERMAN.
<92:250> - 1811, Antipas HATHAWAY et al from John JENNE.
<118:340>- 1825, Antipas HATHAWAY, power of attorney, to Humphrey DAVIS.

John HULL of Dartmouth MA to **Nathaniel HATHAWAY** of same. <Bristol Co.Deeds 60:113>
...22 Aug. 1780, John HULL, mariner, sells to Nathaniel HATHAWAY, mariner...53 acres in Dartmouth with buildings.

Nathaniel HATHAWAY of Dartmouth MA to **Isaac LAWRENCE** of same. <Bristol Co.Deeds 60:238>
...5 Mar. 1781, Nathaniel HATHAWAY, mariner, sells to Isaac LAWRENCE...six acres in Dartmouth... I lately bought of John HULL. Rec. 14 Mar. 1781.

Estate of **Capt. Nathaniel HATHAWAY**, mariner of Dartmouth MA. <Bristol Co.PR>
<original> Warrant to appraise, 28 Sept. 1784, to Giles SLOCUM, Josiah WOOD, Clothier PEARCE. <33:130> Inventory taken 28 Sept. 1784; sworn to 1 Oct. 1784 & 7 Oct. 1794 by **Elizabeth HATHAWAY**, widow. <149:73> Bond 7 Oct. 1794, widow app'td admx. Sureties: John WING of Dartmouth & Richard KIRBY of Westport, yeomen. <40:447> Receipt, 1 Apr. 1803, of heirs **Noah GIFFORD, Resolved HOWLAND, Eliza HATHAWAY Jr.** and **Nathaniel HATHAWAY**, to **Elizabeth HATHAWAY**, widow, admx., for $568.28, being in full of the two thirds of the personal estate.

Clothier PEIRCE of Dartmouth MA to **Elizabeth HATHAWAY** of same. <Bristol Co.Deeds 91:465>
...28 May 1799, Clothier PEIRCE, yeoman, for $900.00, sells to dau Elizabeth HATHAWAY, widow... land bounded by heirs of Nathaniel HATHAWAY dec'd; mentions her sister Lydia PEIRCE. Rec. 11 Sept. 1800.

Nathaniel HATHAWAY et al to **Ebenezer HOLMES & John CLARK.** <Bristol Co.Deeds 84:28>
...4 Apr. 1801, Resolved HOWLAND, yeoman & wf Patience, Nathaniel HATHAWAY, Elisabeth HATHAWAY, spinster, all of Dartmouth and Noah GIFFORD, yeoman & wf Martha of Little Compton, sold to Ebenezer HOLMES, yeoman of Rochester & John CLARK, yeoman of New Bedford...one half of wood land formerly laid out to Thomas HATHAWAY & his heirs, bounded by land of John BROWNELL, Seth POPE... for particulars see division deed of sd HATHAWAY's lot between ye heirs of Nathaniel HATHAWAY dec'd and John BROWNELL. Rec. 4 Aug. 1804.

Nathaniel HATHAWAY of Nantucket to **Elizabeth HATHAWAY Jr.** of Dartmouth MA. <Bristol Co.Deeds>
<105:134>...23 Mar. 1809, Nathaniel HATHAWAY, sells to Elizabeth HATHAWAY Jr...all my right...in the homestead farm that Nathaniel HATHAWAY late of Dartmouth...died seized of, reference being had to the deed given by John HULL to Nathaniel HATHAWAY. Rec. 24 Apr. 1818.

Noah GIFFORD of Little Compton to **Howard POTTER** of Dartmouth MA. <Bristol Co.Deeds 105:135>
...6 Mar. 1813, Noah GIFFORD & wf Martha, sold to Howard POTTER, yeoman...all their right in the homestead farm that Nathaniel HATHAWAY of Dartmouth...died seized of, reference being had to the

deed given by John HULL of the...premises. Rec. 24 Apr. 1818.

Nathaniel HATHAWAY et al to **John BROWNELL** of New Bedford MA. <Bristol Co.Deeds 79:337>
...14 Dec. 1798, Resolved HOWLAND, yeoman & wf Patience, Nathaniel HATHAWAY, yeoman and Elisabeth HATHAWAY, Jr., singlewoman, all of Dartmouth and Noah GIFFORD, yeoman & wf Martha of Little Compton, for $135.00, sold to John BROWNELL, yeoman...one half of a salt meadow with two small knowls or islands being in the sd marsh...containing four acres...in Sconticut neck in New Bedford... being formerly laid out to Thomas HATHAWAY. Ack. 19 Nov. 1800 by grantors. Rec. 1 Dec. 1800.

Resolved HOWLAND of Little Compton to **Howard POTTER** of Dartmouth MA. <Bristol Co.Deeds 105:135>
...(no date), Resolved HOWLAND, yeoman, sold to Howard POTTER, yeoman...all his right in one fifth part of land in Dartmouth...which Nathaniel HATHAWAY dec'd bought of John HULL. Wf Patience HOWLAND signs. Ack. by both 4 Mar. 1813. Rec. 24 Apr. 1818.

Estate of **Nathaniel HATHAWAY**, yeoman of Berkeley MA. <Bristol Co.PR>
<46:412> Inventory, 1811. <47:333> Account, 2 June 1812, of **Anna HATHAWAY**, admx. <47:22> Insolvency, 1811. <48:28> Account, 4 Dec. 1812. <109:452> Notice, 6 Feb. 1811, of admx. <150:452> Letter 1811.

Estate of **Nathaniel HATHAWAY** of New Bedford MA. <Bristol Co.PR>
<83:56> Adm., 1841. <83:421> Inventory, 1841. <115:244> Notice of appointment, 1841. <154:501> Letter, 1841. <160:512> Bond, 1841.

Estate of **Elizabeth HATHAWAY**, single woman of Dartmouth MA. <Bristol Co.PR>
<17:18> Will, dated 8 July 1759. <17:19> Pr. 6 May 1760. <17:32> Inventory, 15 Apr. 1760.

BRISTOL COUNTY PROBATE: (re: Elizabeth HATHAWAY)

<74:232> - 1834, Guardianship of Elizabeth, dau of Isaac N. HATHAWAY, dec'd of Freetown MA.
<124:130> - , Guardianship of Elizabeth, dau of Ephraim HATHAWAY.
<128:337> - , Guardianship of Elizabeth, dau of Abiel HATHAWAY.
<128:395> - , Guardianship of Elizabeth, dau of John HATHAWAY.
<134:160> - , Guardianship of Elizabeth, dau of Isaac N. HATHAWAY.
<171:31> - 1876, Adm. of estate of Elizabeth HATHAWAY of Dighton.

BRISTOL COUNTY DEEDS: (re: Nathaniel HATHAWAY, all on index to 1840**)**

<80:121> - 1801, Nathaniel HATHAWAY to Isaiah WESTON.
<86:69> - 1806, Nathaniel HATHAWAY to Richard JOHNSON.
<94:488> - 1812, Est. of Nathaniel HATHAWAY of Berkeley to Thomas BURT.
<105:134> - 1818, Nathaniel HATHAWAY to Elizabeth HATHAWAY Jr.
<113:15> - 1823, Nathaniel HATHAWAY to George HATHAWAY.
<115:564> - 1824, Nathaniel HATHAWAY to Howard POTTER.
<115:565> - 1824, Nathaniel HATHAWAY from Howard POTTER.
<123:56> - 1827, Nathaniel HATHAWAY from Elkanah HATHAWAY.
<135:138> - 1832, Nathaniel HATHAWAY to Elizabeth POTTER.
<137:537> - 1833, Nathaniel HATHAWAY from David S. FLETCHER.
<140:508> - 1834, Nathaniel HATHAWAY from Simeon PRICE, trust deed.
<142:83> - 1834, Nathaniel HATHAWAY from William ROTCH Jr. et al.
<145:430> - 1835, Nathaniel HATHAWAY from Simeon PRICE.
<146:322> - 1835, Nathaniel HATHAWAY from Simeon PRICE.
<147:72> - 1835, Nathaniel HATHAWAY to Abraham RUSSELL 2d.
<150:131> - 1836, Nathaniel HATHAWAY from George HATHAWAY.

Elisabeth & Martha HATHAWAY of Dartmouth MA to **Cook HOWLAND** of same. <Bristol Co.Deeds 75:498>
...17 Apr. 1793, Elisabeth HATHAWAY, widow and dau Martha HATHAWAY, sell to Cook HOWLAND, wheelwright...four acres in Dartmouth bounded by land of Josiah WOOD, Clothier PIERCE. Ack. 23 Apr. 1793. Rec. 21 Apr. 1797.

Stephen HATHAWAY et al of New Bedford MA to **William TOBEY** of same. <Bristol Co.Deeds 113:485>
...27 June 1796, Stephen HATHAWAY, John Clark HATHAWAY, Timothy DAVIS & Hipsyby/Hepzibah DAVIS, for $200.00, sold to William TOBEY, husbandman...59 acre cedar swamp in New Bedford...being the north end of lot laid out to Thomas HATHAWAY by a place called Aaron's Cosway. Witnesses: Jonathan TOBEY, James DAVIS Jr. Rec. 8 Sept. 1823.

Stephen HATHAWAY et al of New Bedford MA to **Amos ELDRIDGE** of same. <Bristol Co.Deeds 90:28>[5]
...7 Jan. 1806, Hephziba/Hepzibah DAVIS, Stephen HATHAWAY and Clark HATHAWAY, for $131.00, sold to Amos ELDRIDGE...land & house in New Bedford...being the lot & house thereon conveyed by Salathiel ELDRIDGE to Jethro HATHAWAY...Signed by Stephen HATHAWAY, Hephziba DAVIS and Bartholomew AKIN, guardian. Witnesses: Humphry DAVIS, Robert COOK. Ack. 13 Mar. 1806 by Stephen, 1 Apr. 1806 by Bartholomew, 13 May 1809 by Hephziba. Rec. 15 May 1809.

Guardianship of **Jethro HATHAWAY**, non comp. of New Bedford MA. <Bristol Co.PR>
<35:512>...2 Oct. 1798, To the Selectmen of the Town of New Bedford...In compliance with the request of **Stephen HATHAWAY** of New Bedford and son of **Jethro HATHAWAY**, representing to me that the sd **Jethro** is so insane that he is incapable of taking care of himself & family and requesting

that inquisition thereof be made & a guardian appointed for the said **Jethro**...Alden SPOONER and Maj. Joseph BENNET, part of the Selectmen, certified that by reason of old age & infirmity the sd **Jethro** is "really insane". <36:187> 2 Oct. 1798, Peleg HUDDLESTONE, Jonathan KEMPTON and Lemuel WILLIAMS, Esq. were appointed to appraise the estate of **Jethro HATHAWAY**, a person non compos mentis. Inventory taken 20 Apr. 1799 and sworn to 7 May 1799 by **Stephen HATHAWAY**, gdn. of **Jethro**; incl. farm improved by Clark HATHAWAY, $1,300.000; 20 acre cedar swamp, $200.00 and one acre salt marsh, $45.00; total, $1,877.05.

==

Will of **Jethro HATHAWAY** of New Bedford MA. <Bristl Co.PR>
<40:123>...dated 16 Aug. 1798, to wf **Mary**, her choice of beds and one hundred & fifty dollars which I was to give her by a covenant made & signed by us both before mariage dated the seventh day of July 1792 to be considered as a sufficient consideration for her extra trouble (if any she hath had)...to dau **Hepsibah DAVIS**, salt meadow at a place called Skipping Creek, cedar swamp in Rochester near Wing HEADLEY's, all household furniture, one cow and my present riding mare...to son **Stephen HATHAWAY**, cedar swamp at Philips country neck, cedar swamp at northeast end of Nathaniel DELANO's swamp, cedar swamp at Squins country, house lot in the village called Oxford in New Bedford, land at Skonticut Neck adjoining salt meadow of John SHEARMAN of Rochester, land near the friend's meeting at the head of the river in New Bedford...a Bible in two folio volums, one half of wearing apparel, my clock which stands in his house & the iron crain which hangs in the chimney where he now lies, my gun with the apparatus, all my farming implements, my large cain which was my father's marked "T H", farming utensils & meanual tools which belong in partnership with Jonathan KEMPTON & myself...to my son **Clark HATHAWAY**, the use & improvement of that farm which I bought of John SHAW & where he now liveth & other half of lands given to son Stephen, one half of my printed books & also one new folio Bible, half of wearing apparel, the whole of my live stock (which is on the place where he now lives), my desk & book case, case of bottles, all my other walking cains and the whole balance of accounts on book between us; four grandchildren, chil. of son **Clark HATHAWAY** and his present wife, viz: **Antipas HATHAWAY, Eunice DAVIS, Benjamin HATHAWAY, Hannah HATHAWAY**; other half of printed books to be equally divided between son **Stephen** and dau **Hepsibah**; son **Stephen**, executor. <40:126> Letter/Bond 4 Oct. 1803, of **Stephen HATHAWAY**, yeoman, admr. Sureties: Alden SPOONER, Esq., Walter SPOONER 2d, both of New Bedford.

==

Will of **Thomas DAVIS** of Freetown MA. <Bristol Co.PR 27:333>
...dated 29 Oct. 1782, mentions 2nd wf **Deborah**; sons by 1st wf, **Thomas DAVIS, Benjamin DAVIS**; sons **Elisha DAVIS** and **Joseph DAVIS** (both under 21); daus **Rhoda HATHAWAY, Anna DAVIS, Hannah DAVIS**

==

Will of **Mary DAVIS** of Dartmouth MA. <Bristol Co.PR 30:254>
...dated 1 Feb. 1786, mentions sister **Tabitha GIFFORD** wf of James; legacies to chil. of Jacob CHASE, viz: Abner CHACE, Patience CHACE, Keziah CHACE.

==

Will of **Daniel DAVIS** of Rehoboth MA. <Bristol Co.PR>
<54:114,116,351>...dated 10 Apr. 1816, advanced in years, mentions wf **Patience** (executrix); nine chil. of dec'd dau **Patience LOUNDSBURY**, viz: **Nathan, John, Phineas, Daniel, Ina, Polly, Sally, Nancy, Abigail**; granddaughters **Polly DAVIS, Charlotte DAVIS**; great-grandson **William GIFFORD**, son of **Betsey GIFFORD**, dec'd; grandsons **John DAVIS, Daniel Nelson DAVIS**, sons of son **Daniel DAVIS**, dec'd; dau in law **Anna DAVIS**, widow of son **Daniel**.

==

Will of **Thomas DAVIS** of Freetown MA, 1756. <Bristol Co.PR 15:93>

==

Will of **Hannah DAVIS** of Westport MA. <Bristol Co.PR 90:241>
...dated 27 Aug. 1845, wf of George. (no details in files)

==

Estate of **Jethro DAVIS** of Fairhaven MA. <Bristol Co.PR>
<66:155> Warrant for inventory, 28 Feb. 1828. <66:181> 4 Mar. 1828, **Timothy DAVIS** of Wareham, eldest son, app'td admr., heirs at law having declined & recommended him. <69:403,70:67> Account of **Timothy DAVIS** as guardian to all the heirs at law.

==

Guardianship of **Clark HATHAWAY** of New Bedford MA. <Bristol Co.PR>
<34:389> 23 Feb. 1797, Selectmen of New Bedford ask that a guardian be app'td for reasons of "drinking & gaming". <34:390> Bartholomew AKIN app'td. (Additional references given are 35:245, 509 (insolvent), 510.)

==

BRISTOL COUNTY PROBATES: (re: Ruth TABER)

<122:557> - 1877, Ruth TABER. (no details in files)
<130:26> - , Ruth TABER, guardianship.
<187:183> - 25 May 1872, Will of Ruth TABER, widow of Fairhaven MA.
<191:352> - , Ruth TABER. (no details in files)
<198:544> - , Ruth TABER. (" ")

==

Timothy DAVIS of New Bedford MA to **Nicholas DAVIS**. <Bristol Co.Deeds 70:360>
...5 Jan. 1792, Timothy DAVIS, tanner, for £180, sold to son Nicholas DAVIS, tanner...all my homestead farm, incl. tan yard, on both sides of highway that leadeth from Bedford to Boston... bounded by land of Pardon COOK, Joseph COOK, Nicholas DAVIS Sr., Ebenezer ALLEN, Joseph SEVERENCE Witnesses: Paul COOK, John JENNE. Ack. & Rec. 24 Feb. 1792.

==

Hepzibah DAVIS, widow of New Bedford MA to **John JENNE** of same. <Bristol Co.Deeds 81:64>
...1802, Hepzibah DAVIS, seamster, widow of Timothy DAVIS, for $20.00 sold to John JENNE, housewright...three acre cedar swamp in New Bedford...which was conveyed to sd Hepzibah by deed from Jethro HATHAWAY, of New Bedford, minor...bounded by land of Zacheus TOBEY.

MICRO #25 OF 30

Will of **Stephen HATHAWAY** of Fairhaven MA. <Bristol Co.PR 63:72,130,239,519;64:209>
...dated 18 Aug. 1824, mentions wife; sons **Jethro HATHAWAY** (out of country) and **George HATHAWAY**; grandsons **Stephen HATHAWAY, William HATHAWAY, George S. HATHAWAY, Henry HATHAWAY, Humphrey HATHAWAY**; children of son **Humphrey HATHAWAY** dec'd; daus of son **Stephen HATHAWAY** dec'd; daus of son **George**; **Eliza**, wf of son **George**; daus **Hepzibah HOWLAND, Mary TABER, Hannah NYE, Rebecca DILLINGHAM, Abigail HOWLAND, Elizabeth SWIFT, Silvia NYE**; sons in law **Weston HOWLAND, Jireh SWIFT**. Pr. 7 Feb. 1826. Citation 6 Dec. 1825.

Will of **Abigail HATHAWAY** of Fairhaven MA. <Bristol Co.PR 70:202>
...dated 4 4mth 1830, mentions son **George S. HATHAWAY**; granddaughters **Hannah NYE, Alice H. HASKELL, Alice DELANO, Eliza HOWLAND, Elizabeth HIT( )H, Sarah R. HUTTLESTONE, Lydia Ann HATHAWAY, Sylvia NYE, Jr.**; a silver spoon each to **Hannah NYE Jr., Sylvia NYE, Lydia Ann HATHAWAY, Mary HATHAWAY, Sarah HATHAWAY, Susanna HATHAWAY & Hannah NYE** dau of **Gideon NYE**; seven daus, **Mary TABER, Hannah NYE, Rebecca DILLINGHAM, Abigail HOWLAND, Hepzibah HOWLAND, Elizabeth SWIFT, Sylvia NYE**; son in law **Gideon NYE**, executor. Heirs notified 22 Sept. 1831. Pr. 4 Oct. 1831.

Will of **Thomas KEMPTON**, yeoman of Dartmouth MA. <Bristol Co.PR>
<20:409>...dated 6 Jan. 1768...to wf **Phebe**, the goods she brought with her and a horse to ride to Little Compton to see her friends; sons **Thomas KEMPTON** (executor), **Ephraim KEMPTON, David KEMPTON** and **Jonathan KEMPTON**; daus **Esther BUTLER** wf of Benjamin and **Mary KEMPTON**. Witnesses: Ephraim KEMPTON, Manasseh KEMPTON, John GERRISH. <20:412> Pr. 27 Feb. 1769.

Estate of **Ephraim KEMPTON** of New Bedford MA. <Bristol Co.PR>
<41:1> Division 1 May 1804, to following heirs, viz: sons **Lemuel KEMPTON** (eldest son), **Obed KEMPTON, Elijah KEMPTON**; grandson **Thomas CUSHMAN**; daus **Wealthy MAXFIELD** wf of Timothy, **Silvia KEMPTON** and **Nancy KEMPTON**; granddaughters **Pamelia Willis KEMPTON, Abigail KEMPTON.** <41:455> Account 1 Oct 1805 of **Elijah KEMPTON**, admr. <40:429> Account 1 May 1804, of admr., mentions widow.

Estate of **Ephraim KEMPTON 3d.** <Bristol Co.PR>
<52:69> Division 3 Oct. 1815, to only heirs, viz: daus **Pamelia W. KEMPTON, Abigail W. KEMPTON.**
(Note: The following two records may or may not pertain to this Ephraim.)

Estate of **Capt. Ephraim KEMPTON Jr.**, mariner. <Bristol Co.PR>
<39:103,500> Accounts, 4 May 1802 & 3 May 1803 by Ephraim KEMPTON, admr.

Estate of **Ephraim KEMPTON 3d** of New Bedford MA. <Bristol Co.PR>
<36:3> Inventory 17 Dec. 1798, by Ephraim KEMPTON, admr. <36:189> 2d Inventory 3 May 1799 by admr <36:198> Appointment of Commissioners, 1 Jan. 1799. <36:199> Account 6 May 1800.

Estate of **Ephraim KEMPTON 2d** of New Bedford MA. <Bristol Co.PR>
<40:435> Appointment of Committee to divide estate, 7 Feb. 1804. Division 28 Apr. 1804 to following heirs, viz: widow, **David KEMPTON 2d** (eldest son), **Lydia FOSTER** wf of Peter, **Thomas KEMPTON 2d Mary KEMPTON, Ephraim KEMPTON, Elizabeth KEMPTON Jr**; approved 1 May 1804. <40:441> Order to set off dower to widow, **Elizabeth KEMPTON.** <40:443> Dower. <39:257> Inventory 5 Oct. 1802, of **David KEMPTON 2d**, admr. <39:521> Account, 4 Oct. 1803. <40:315> Account 7 Feb. 1804, of **David KEMPTON 2d**, admr. <40:431> 2d Account of **David KEMPTON 2d**, admr.

Joseph GIFFORD of Dartmouth MA to **Elizabeth KEMPTON** of New Bedford MA. <Bristol Co.Deeds 88:29>
...2 Oct. 1807, Joseph GIFFORD, yeoman, in consideration of love & affection, gives to daughter Elizabeth KEMPTON and son in law David KEMPTON...land in Dartmouth. Rec. 7 Oct. 1807.

Estate of **David KEMPTON 2d** of New Bedford MA. <Bristol Co.PR>
<69:91> 5 Oct. 1830, the widow asked for **Ephraim KEMPTON** of New Bedford to be app'td admr. as the heirs are all minors. <69:370> Inventory, 25 Oct. 1830.

BRISTOL COUNTY DEEDS: (re: David KEMPTON 2d)

<91:14> - 16 Feb. 1810, Division, David KEMPTON (no "2d" added).
<135:572> - 1832, David KEMPTON 2d, re estate.

(Note: The following references have no data: 84:80; 84:80,81,82;88:29;114:200;127:565.)

MARY COOKE[2] (Francis[1])

TOMSON WILLS: (in the Mayflower Descendant (MD))

Lt. John TOMSON <4:22;19:95>; John TOMSON <20:159>; Jacob TOMSON <24:167>; Abigail (WADSWORTH) Tomson <25:20>; Peter TOMSON, James TOMSON <22:135>; Thomas & Mary TOMSON <25:175>; Mercy TOMSON <19:135>; Peter TOMSON, Ebenezer TOMSON <25:56>.

PLYMOUTH COLONY DEEDS: (re: John TOMSON)

<1:--> - 3 Mar. 1645, John TOMPSON from Samuel EDDY.
<3:216> - 14 Oct. 1671, John THOMPSON, one of owners of share in cedar swamp in Majors Purchase.
<3:294> - 9 July 1672, John TOMSON of Barnstable from GRAY & BARTLETT.
<3:309> - 3 July 1673, John TOMSON of Barnst., Benjamin CHURCH of Duxbury from Tuspaquin & son.
<4:41> - 1 Nov. 1673, John TOMSON from Tuspaquin & other Indians.
<4:272> - 20 Apr. 1675, TOMSON & SOUTHWORTH, lands about Titicut.
<4:103> - 14 May 1675, TOMSON & SOUTHWORTH, from Tuspaquin.
<4:204> - 14 May 1675, TOMSON & SOUTHWORTH, from Tuspaquin.
<4:272> - 20 Apr. 1675, John TOMSON from two Indians.
<5:437> - 10 Mar. 1682/3, John TOMSON of Middlebury from William CLARKE & Barnabas LOTHROP.
<5:438> - 8 Mar. 1683/4, John TOMSON to Capt. John WILLIAMS of Scituate.

Estate of **Jacob TOMSON**, mariner of Marshfield MA. <Plymouth Co.PR>
<original> Bond 24 Apr. 1746, John CARLOO, app'td admr. Sureties: William HALL, Samuel DURANT. Witnesses: John BALL, Elizabeth KELSEY. <10:214> Letter 24 Apr. 1746, of admr., John CARLOO, leather dresser of Boston. <10:292> Inventory sworn 6 Oct. 1746 by appraisers Peleg FOORD, Nathaniel PHILLIPS & Adam HALL; incl. in cash of the Committee of War, received £26 and notes in the hands of Capt. Jno. LITTLE & Ephraim LITTLE; no real estate mentioned; total, £112.7.6.

PLYMOUTH COUNTY PROBATES, to 1800: (re: TOMSON/THOMPSON)

1696	John	#20588, 1:241,243,245 <MD 4:22;19:95>
1705	Rev. Edward	#20541, 2:61,62 (of Marshfield)
1725	John	#20089, 5:266,269 <MD 20:159>
1726	Jacob	#20571, 5:140,299,427,430 <MD 24:167>
1726	Mary et al	#20612, 5:230,231 <MD 24:167>
1726	Peter	#20624, 5:141,229;7:47 <MD 25:56>
1727	Ebenezer	#20536, 5:302,377;7:47 <MD 25:56>
1731	Peter	#20623, 6:9,91,92,95
1733	Shubael	#20642, 6:384,391;7:12,13,15,105,106
1733	Shubael et al	#20643, 6:401,403,408;7:45
1734	Shubael & Mary	#20644, 7:52,56,105,106
1734	Francis	#20549, 7:57,118,158
1739	James	#20581, 8:86,180,226,227 <MD 22:140>
1740	Isaac	#20562, 8:191,192,318
1742	Thomas	#20655, 9:22,95,201,202 <MD 25:175>
1743	Ebenezer & Zebadiah	#20540, 9:104,135
1744	Abigail	#20506, 9:411-3;31:256,295 <MD 25:20>
1744	Ephraim	#20546, 9:404,425;10:31,32,160
1745	Mary	#20608, 10:53,125,159,160
1746	Jacob	#20576, 10:214,292
1751	Jacob	#20577, 12:154,296,299;16:415
1756	Marcy	#2060-, 14:67,71,395 <MD 19:135>
1756	Thomas	#20651, 14:56,120,161,206
1757	John	#20585, 14:312,313,370
1760	Thomas	#20656, 15:479,481,500
1761	Mary	#20609, 16:146,359;17:18
1761	Nathaniel	#20620, 16:145,358,416;17:17
1762	Daniel & Ephraim	#20531, 18:106,109
1765	John	#20587, 17:154;19:520
1766	John	#20590, 19:382,384,385;20:203
1766	Sarah et al	#20640, 18:246-8;19:390;20:27,461
1769	Thomas	#20657, 20:266,309,487;21:170
1770	Martha	#20605, 20:360,451
1770	Shubael	#20641, 20:358,359;21:100
1770	Susanna	#20649, 20:359
1771	Thomas et al	#20658, 20:542,543
1771	Sarah	#20639, 20:456,485
1771	Lucy	#20600, 20:465
1773	Andrew	#20515, 21:570;23:16;28:227;45:155
1773	Beza	#20523, 21:602;23:15;24:192
1775	Rachel & Moses	#20630, 22:64,66;26:488;29:426
1775	Zebediah	#20663, 24:39,41,42;29:487
1776	Ebenezer	#20537, 24:104,105,106,192
1777	John	#20586, 23:158;24:252;25:257;29:305

PLYMOUTH COUNTY PROBATES, to 1800 (cont-d): (re: TOMSON/THOMPSON)

1779	Abel et al	#20504, 26:31,32,33
1779	Betty	#20522, 27:19;29:307,308
1779	Josiah	#20597, 25:280,281
1779	Nathan et al	#20619, 25:51-4;26:194,433;29:348,350
1781	Mary	#20610, 28:182,183,521 <MD 25:185>
1783	Isaac	#20566, 27:115;28:576;35:36,115,116,117
1787	Caleb	#20524, 30:100,102,109,290
1788	Joseph	#20592, 27:284;30:474,475;31:31,40,264
1789	Jacob	#20572, 27:294;31:15,16;33:86
1793	Reuben	#20631, 33:433,435,490;35:160;42:76
1794	Isaac et al	#20567, 26:303
1798	Francis	#20550, 36:473,476,568;37:145;42:144,145
1800	Irena	#20561, 34:214;37:13,16,17,18,19

PLYMOUTH COUNTY PROBATES, to 1850: (re: TOMSON/THOMPSON)

1806	Jacob	Middleboro	will	#20573, 40:395-7,408,479,533;42:302
1807	Amasa	Halifax	adm.	#20512, 39:130;42:196,197,378;43:447
1807	Thomas	Middleboro	adm.	#20650, 39:98;42:67,142,223,297,298
1809	Joseph	Halifax	adm.	#20593, 39:180;42:467;43:112;44:148
1809	Priscilla	Halfiax	gdn.	#20628, 32:345;41:105,148;47:440
1813	Ebenezer	Halifax	will	#20538, 45:133,134,244,245;46:427;47:141
1813	Reuben	Halifax	div.	#20632, 45:155
1815	Ezra Jr.	Halifax	adm.	#20548, 46:129;48:49
1816	William	Middleboro	will	#20660, 48:7,10,11,260
1818	Jacob	Halifax	adm.	#20578, 46:278;49:484;50:37,38,196,197;53:45,309 310;54:399
1818	Ebenezer 2d	Halifax	gdn.	#20539, 49:574,575;51:20;54:190
1818	Eliab	Halifax	adm.	#20543, 46:274;50:145;53:396,397
1820	Isaac	Middleboro	will	#20563, 50:463,464;53:63
1821	Ichabod	Halifax	will	#20559, 54:50,52-4,252;56:149,150;57:231,239,263 62:320
1822	Adam	Halifax	adm.	#20508, 52:122
1828	Josiah	Halifax	adm.	#20595, 61:215;62:280;66:259;76:304
1830	Asa	Hanson	will	#20519, 68:113;69:44,46,120,366
1831	Nathan	Halifax	will	#20618, 68:255;70:502,533;72:141;78:409
1833	Thomas	Pomfret CT	gdn.	#20653, 65:333;73:417,474;79:558
1834	Lucy	Middleboro	will	#20601, 75:184;76:556;77:37,375
1835	Jane & Ezra	Rochester	gdn.	#20584, 65:412
1835	Thomas	N. Bridgewater	will	#20652, 77:543
1835	Eliab	Halifax	adm.	#20544, 71:370;75:292;78:67
1835	Eliab Jr.	Halifax	adm.	#20545, 71:299;73:157;75:195;77:143,555;79:306; 83:277
1835	Isaac	Rochester	adm.	#20564, 71:325;77:227;78:457,458;79:465;80:409
1836	Hannah/al	Halifax	gdn.	#20555, 65:453,454;79:175,176;80:254,255;83:145; **O2**:376;**R1**:40
1838	Abigail W.	Middleboro	will	#20507, 1:73;80:86,165;**J5**:19;85:405
1838	Josiah	Halifax	will	#20596, **G1**:81;80:250;81:71,267;**T5**:125
1838	Thomas	Halifax	adm.	#20654, **A10**:146;80:87,441
1841	Hannah W.	Bridgewater	adm.	#20554, **A10**:434;83:296;**U6**:179;86:325
1842	Mercy F.	Middleboro	will	#20613, **G1**:198;84:204,246;**U6**:258;**O2**:232;85:128, 320,412,414
1843	William A.	Middleboro	gdn.	#20661, **L8**:342;86:209;**M9**:75;89:188;98:425
1843	Arad	Middleboro	will	#20518, **A10**:524;85:137,381,454;**U6**:413;86:210-2; **A10**:550;88:304;89:189;94:153;103:180; 104:140-1;158:315;210:102;209:291
1843	Deborah	Middleboro	will	#20533, **A10**:525,526;85:145,443;**U6**:411
1844	Nehemiah	Halifax	will	#20621, **G1**:276;86:79,173;**U6**:485;91:120;93:400
1844	Solomon	Middleboro	will	#20647, **G1**:425;86:149,167;**U6**:598;87:438;92:45; 93:141;95:417
1845	Martin	Middleboro	adm.	#20606, **B11**:323;87:314,324;**V7**:7;88:162;**P3**:15
1845	Jabez	Plympton	adm.	#20569, **B11**:311;**U6**:590;87:147;88:476
1847	Ichabod W.	Brighton IL	adm.	#20560, **B11**:542
1847	Hannah	Halifax	adm.	#20556, **B11**:509;89:457;**V7**:263;89:458;93:142
1848	Jacob	Middleboro	adm.	#20574, **C12**:12;92:164;**W8**:16
1848	Mary W.	Middleboro	adm.	#20611, **C12**:8;91:371;**V7**:433;91:373
1849	Reuben	Halifax	adm.	#20633, **C12**:78;91:334;**V7**:473;**P3**:125;92:312,313
1849	Jacob	Middleboro	adm.	#20575, **C12**:74;91:335,336;7:455
1849	Henry W.	N. Bridgewater	gdn.	#20558, **M9**:209;**P3**:416;**R1**:304;91:609
1850	Ezra	Rochester	adm.	#20547, **C12**:247;**W8**:148;93:220

Will of **Josiah THOMSON** of Abington. <Plymouth Co.PR>
<25:280>...23 Sept. 1777, mentions wf **Mary**, only son **Josiah THOMSON**, dau **Marcy THOMSON** (under 18)
Witnesses: Nathan SNOW, Jacob SNOW, John NOYES. <25:281> 3 May 1779, **Josiah THOMSON**, app'td admr.

Estate of **John THOMSON** of Hanover MA. <Plymouth Co.PR #20587>
<17:154> Letter/Bond 28 Oct. 1765, Ebenezer THOMSON of Hanover, app'td admr. Sureties: David STOCKBRIDGE, Ezekiel PALMER. Witnesses: Samuel BALDWIN, Edward WINSLOW. <19:520> Inventory taken 28 Oct. 1765 by Joseph TOLMAN, Anthony WATERMAN; personal estate only, incl. notes of Ebenezer STETSON & James SILVESTER; total £6.17.4. Sworn to 3 Aug. 1767 by Rev. Ebenezer TOMSON, admr.

Estate of **Joseph TOMSON** of Halifax MA. <Plymouth Co.PR #20592>
<27:284> Letter/Bond 3 Nov. 1788, of Benjamin PARRIS, admr. Sureties: Isaac TOMSON, Oliver ALDEN. Witnesses: Jonathan SMITH, Isaac LOTHROP. <30:474> Warrant & Inventory taken by Benjamin CUSHING, Ephraim TINKHAM, Abraham WHITEN Jr. Sworn to 1 Dec. 1788 by admr.; total, £90.8.6. <30:475> Insolvency 1 Dec. 1788. <31:31> Commissioners app'td 1 Dec. 1788, Benjamin CUSHING, Ephraim TINKHAM <31:31> List of Claims: heirs of Mrs. Ruth CROADE dec'd; Abraham WHITON, John FOREST, Moses INGLEE as exr. to will of Josiah HATHAWAY; Peter TOMSON; Ephraim TINKHAM; John LEACH; Timothy WOOD as admr. on his father's estate; John TILSON; heirs of Jonathan RIPLEY dec'd; Ebenezer TOMSON as exr. to will of Ichabod STANDISH; widow Jerusha TOMSON; James WADE; widow Mary FAUNCE; Daniel DUNBAR; Asa TOMSON; Benjamin HARRIS; heirs of Thomas HOOPER; Obadiah LYON; William DREW as admr. of estate of Thaddeus RANSOM; Ebenezer TOMSON as exr. to will of Zebadiah TOMSON; John BOSWORTH; Abraham WHITON Jr., Job CUSHMAN; allowed 7 Sept. 1789. <31:40> Account allowed 5 Oct. 1789, payments made to: Moses INGLEE, Freeman WATERMAN, Ebenezer TOMSON, Noah TOMSON, Ignatius LORING, Gideon SOULE, William TILSON, Zebediah TOMSON, John POOL. <31:264> Account of admr. allowed 6 Sept. 1790. <31:264> Certificate of oath respecting estate, 10 Nov. 1789.

Estate of **Mary THOMPSON** of Halifax MA, widow of Reuben. <Plymouth Co.PR #20609>
<17:18> Letter/Bond 6 Apr. 1761, Jacob TOMSON app'td admr. Sureties: Josiah HAYWARD, Robert GILLMORE. Witness: Nehemiah RIPLEY. <16:146> Inventory taken 21 Apr. 1761 by John TOMSON, Ebenezer TOMSON, Moses INGLEE; total personal estate, L12.19. <16:359> Account 13 Oct. 1762; Debts paid: Isaac OTIS; David KINGMAN; Thomas MANSFIELD; John TOMSON Jr.; Daniel DUNBAR; Deborah DELANO; Benjamin PRICE; James TOMSON; Robert LATHAM; Josiah STURTEVANT; Amasa TOMSON; Nathan TINKHAM; Thomas HAWARD Jr.; John BOSWORTH; Ebenezer TOMSON; Mary STANDISH; Martha TOMSON; Martha TOMSON Jr.; Josiah HATHAWAY; John TOMSON; Simeon HAYWARD; Nathaniel HAYWARD; Zebulon MAY. <original> Warrant for Division, 4 Oct. 1773, to Jacob TOMSON, Barnabas TOMSON & Ebenezer TOMSON, all of Halifax; one half set off to legal representatives of **Andrew TOMSON** dec'd, one quarter to **Deborah REED** wf of Micah and one quarter to **Lucy TOMSON** (minor). <original> Division 25 Oct. 1773.

MICRO #26 OF 30

Estate of **Mercy TOMSON**, spinster of Halifax MA. <Plymouth Co.PR #20604; MD 19:135>
<14:67> Letter/Bond 3 May 1756, Zebediah TOMSON of Halifax, app'td admr. Sureties: Moses STANDISH & Thomas FOSTER. Witnesses: Josiah MORTON Jr., Edward WINSLOW. <14:395> Inventory taken 13 May 1756 by Moses STANDISH, Robert WATERMAN, Noah CUSHING; total personal estate, L92.18. <14:71> Account 5 July 1756; Paid to: widow Martha SOUL, Peter TOMSON, David SIMONS, widow Mary TOMSON Sr., widow Mary TOMSON Jr., Thomas TOMSON Jr., Dr. LORING. <14:71> Distribution of £81.13.2, said dec'd leaving no surviving brothers or sisters the admr. is directed to pay out to the surviving children of several brothers & sisters as follows: to the children of **John, Jacob, Thomas & Peter TOMSON**, all dec'd & brothers of the sd **Mercy/Marcy**, £10.4.1. and also a like sum to the children of **Mary TABOUR, Esther REED, Elizabeth SWIFT** & **Lydia SOUL**, dec'd & sisters of the sd **Marcy**.

Will of **Joseph SWIFT**, yeoman of Sandwich MA. <Barnstable Co.PR>
<12:85>...dated 13 Jan. 1755, mentions wf **Rebecca**; sons **William SWIFT, Joshua SWIFT**; daus **Jane BARTLETT, Joanna GLOVER**; son **Thomas SWIFT** (executor). <12:86> Pr. 1 July 1760.

Estate of **Jonathan BEALE**, yeoman of Quincy MA. <Norfolk Co.PR #1449, 64:109>
Petition for distribution, by Benjamin BEALE, admr., of balance of $269.31, to children & heirs at law, viz: **William S. BEALE, Jonathan BEALE, Benjamin BEALE, Joseph S. BEALE, Maria A.P. BEALE** and **Cynthia A. BEALE**. Allowed 1st Tues. Sept. 1835.

Estate of **Otis SPEAR 2d** of Randolph MA. <Norfolk Co.PR #17240, 77:489>
Petition Aug. 1844, of widow **Eliza H. SPEAR**, to administer husband's estate on behalf of herself and four children. Surety: Alice HOLBROOK of Braintree. Petition allowed, 26 Oct. 1844.

Estate of **Otis SPEAR 2d** of Randolph MA. <Norfolk Co.PR #17234, 78:954>
Petition to sell real estate, of **Eliza H. SPEAR**, guardian to **Nancy E. SPEAR, Jannette B. SPEAR, George C. SPEAR** and **William B. SPEAR**, minor children...seized of real estate consisting of about fifteen acres of land on both sides of the Blue Hill Turnpike with a house and barn thereon in sd Randolph and six acres of wood land...value of $608.75...it would be for the benefit of the sd minors to have interest therein sold...the interest upon the money for which the same might be sold will be more than the income from sd estate...the only person interested in the estate of said minors as next of kin, presumptive heirs or otherwise is their mother, sd **Eliza H. SPEAR**.

Will of **Joshua SWIFT**, yeoman of Plymouth MA. <Plymouth Co.PR>
<24:253>...dated 9 Mar. 1776, mentions wf **Jane**; sons **John SWIFT** & **Joshua SWIFT**; daus **Lusanna SWIFT, Jonnah SWIFT, Marcy SWIFT** & **Rebecca SWIFT**; son **Joseph SWIFT**; daus **Abigail CORNISH** & **Jane RIDER**. Wf **Jane** & son **John**, executors. <24:254> Pr. 7 Apr. 1777. <24:433> Inventory, 25 Apr. 1777. <40:333> Account.

Will of **Samuel RYDER** of Plymouth MA. <Plymouth Co.PR>
<38:514-5>...dated 26 Dec. 1803, mentions wf **Jane**; sons **George RIDER, Samuel RIDER, Ezekiel RIDER**; daus **Lucy RIDER, Sarah B. RIDER**; grandson **Caleb BATTLES**. Pr. 7 Feb. 1804. <40:87> Account.

PLYMOUTH COUNTY DEEDS: (re: Thomas SWIFT)

<46:68> - 28 Dec. 1757, Thomas SWIFT, yeoman of Plymouth to son Phineas SWIFT, yeoman of same, land in Plymouth & Sandwich where Phineas lives. Rec. 29 Apr. 1760.
<46:99> - 9 Oct. 1759, Thomas SWIFT, yeoman of Plymouth to son Lemuel SWIFT, yeoman of same, land in Plymouth & Sandwich where Thomas lives. Rec. 31 May 1760.
<49:33> - 12 Feb. 1763, Thomas SWIFT, yeoman of Plymouth to son Phineas SWIFT, yeoman of same.
<54:29> - 12 Feb. 1763, Thomas SWIFT, yeoman of Plymouth to Samuel GIBBS Jr., yeoman of Sandwich
<56:179> - 6 Jan. 1769, Thomas SWIFT Jr., yeoman of Rochester & wf Rebecca to Ichabod BILLINGTON of Middleboro.

(Note: The remaining references are without data, viz: 28:119;31:14,201;38:196;41:50;44:239;44:245;71:43;91:55.)

Will of **Thomas SWIFT**, yeoman of Rochester MA. <Plymouth Co.PR #19934>
<35:255>...dated 4 Dec. 1793, mentions wf **Rebecca**; sons **James SWIFT** (executor), **Thomas SWIFT** & **Joseph SWIFT**; four daus **Lucy, Marabah, Mary** & **Rebeccah.** <35:257> Pr. 21 May 1795.

MICRO #27 OF 30

Estate of **Benjamin CORNISH** of Plymouth MA. <Plymouth Co.PR #5022>
<27:64> Bond 11 Apr. 1782 of John CORNISH of Plymouth, admr. Sureties: Benjamin CORNISH of Plymouth and J. GIBBS of Sandwich.

Will of **Nehemiah SAVERY** of Plymouth MA. <Plymouth Co.PR #17724>
...dated 18 May 1877, mentions son **Nehemiah Lewis SAVERY**; daus **Sarah S. THOMPSON, Esther S. BARTLETT, Irene F. PETERSON.** Witnesses: Mary D. STEPHENS, Winsor T. SAVERY, Elmira F. SAVERY.

Estate of **William SWIFT,** yeoman of Falmouth MA. <Barnstable Co.PR>
<7:190> 13 Oct. 1750, widow **Lydia SWIFT** app'td admx. <8:426> Inventory taken 10 Nov. 1750; sworn to by admx. 26 Nov. 1750.

Will of **Mary ALLEN**, widow of Bridgewater MA. <Plymouth Co.PR>
<15:267>...dated 1 Oct. 1751, mentions sons **Nathaniel/Nathan ALLEN, William ALLEN**; daus **Ester EDSON** wf of James, **Betty ALLEN**; children of son **Micah ALLEN** dec'd, viz: **Micah ALLEN, Mary ALLEN, Joseph ALLEN, Daniel ALLEN**; **Josiah ALLEN**, son of son **Josiah ALLEN** dec'd; **Nicholas BYRAM**, son of **Japhet** & **Sarah BYRAM**. Pr. 2 Apr. 1759.

Will of **Micah ALLEN**, husbandman of Bridgewater MA. <Plymouth Co.PR #311>
<9:437>...dated 11 Dec. 1744, mentions wf **Hannah** (executrix); three sons **Micah ALLEN, Joseph ALLEN** & **Daniel ALLEN**; only dau **Mary**; mentions land bought of brother **Nathan ALLEN.** <9:439> Pr. 1 Apr. 1745. <9:481> Inventory taken 5 Apr. 1745, house & lands, £150; sworn to by exx. 3 June 1745

Will of **Micah ALLEN** of Mansfield MA. <Bristol Co.PR 61:95,107,144,160>
<61:95>...dated 26 Mar. 1822...far advanced in years; mentions wf **Catharine**; dau **Catharine COBB** wf of John; son **Micah ALLEN; Polly COBB** wf of Capt. David; son **Elijah ALLEN**; dau **Nancy FRANCIS** wf of Peleg; **Fanny COPELAND** wf of Amasa; sons **Oliver ALLEN, Otis ALLEN**; dau **Cloe LANE** wf of George.. to each one dollar only, they having had heretofore their several shares out of my estate; to three sons of my son **Oliver**, viz: **Erastus Wendell ALLEN, James Oliver ALLEN, Benjamin Guild ALLEN** ...all the rest & residue of my estate. Son **Oliver**, executor. Witnesses sworn 4 Nov. 1823. <originals> 4 Nov. 1823, **Oliver ALDEN** declines to administer and **Otis ALLEN** app'td. Inventory taken 13 Nov. 1823; real estate, $1211.00, total, $1869.82. Sworn to 2 Dec. 1823. Petition of admr. to sell real estate, 2 Dec. 1823, signed by **Catherine ALLEN, Catherine COBB, Micah ALLEN, Mary COBB, Elijah ALLEN, Nancy FRANCIS, Fanny A. COPELAND, Oliver ALLEN, Chloe A. LANE.** Account, 2 Dec. 1823 of admr. 2d Account of admr. 5 July 1825; incl. legacies to children, $9.00 and necessaries to **Oliver ALLEN** for taking care of the widow in her last sickness.

Micah ALLEN of Mansfield MA to **Micah ALLEN Jr.** of same. <Bristol Co.Deeds 82:334>
...16 Apr. 1802, Micah ALLEN, gent. to Micah ALLEN, yeoman...part of house & land in Mansfield. Catharine ALLEN signs also. Rec. 21 Apr. 1803.

Otis ALLEN to **Daniel FISHER.** <Bristol Co.Deeds 114:447>
...27 Jan. 1824, Otis ALLEN, as admr. of estate of Micah ALLEN of Mansfield, sells land to Daniel FISHER to pay debts.

BRISTOL COUNTY DEEDS: (re: Micah ALLEN)

<56:506> - 30 Mar. 1776, Micah ALLEN, gent. of Stoughton from Moses KNAPP Jr., land in Mansfield.
<56:507> - 19 June 1776, Micah ALLEN, gent. of Mansfield to Lemuel FISHER, land in Mansfield.
<65:235> - 23 Apr. 1777, Micah ALLEN, housewright of Mansf. to Lemuel FISHER, land in Mansfield.
<60:495> - 3 Apr. 1782, Micah ALLEN, gent. of Mansf. to Daniel PRATT. Wf Catharine ALLEN signs.

Micah ALLEN et al to **Benjamin WHITMAN.** <Plymouth Co.Deeds 85:179>
...9 Oct. 1761, Nathan ALLEN & wf Rebecca, Micah ALLEN & Betty ALLEN sell to Benjamin WHITMAN... mentions land of Jonah & Josiah ALLEN.

Micah ALLEN of Middleboro MA to **Isaac PERKINS** of Bridgewater MA. <Plymouth Co.Deeds 49:32>
...Feb. 1764, Micah ALLEN, Physician, for £156.13.4., sold to Isaac PERKINS, husbandman...18 acres with house...the farm where I now live in Middleboro, parish of Titicut. Wf Hannah ALLEN releases dower. Ack. 18 Feb. 1764 by Micah. Rec. 4 Apr. 1764.

Micah ALLEN of Stoughton MA to **Joseph ALLEN** of Bridgewater MA. <Plymouth Co.Deeds 50:132>
...5 Feb. 1765, Micah ALLEN, carpenter, sells to Joseph ALLEN...twenty & three quarters acres in Bridgewater...being part of Thomas PHILLIP's farm...bounded by my father PHILLIP's 50 acre lot. Katherine ALLEN signs.

Will of **John REED** of Abington MA. <Plymouth Co.PR #16619>
<original>...dated 20 Mar. 1733, mentions wf **Mary** (executor); children: **James REED** (under 21, 2nd son) **John REED** (eldest son), **Joseph REED, Ezekiel REED, Peter REED, Squire REED, Samuel REED, Mary REED.** Witnesses: NIcholas PORTER, Jacob REED. <8:73> Letter/Bond 16 May 1739, of **James READ, Jr.**, admr. <8:214> Account 2 June 1740. <8:55,151> Inventory. <8:234> Decree. <original> Settlement of estate, 12 July 1740, to the widow & eight children.

PLYMOUTH COUNTY DEEDS: (re: FORD)

<45:53>	-	, Adam FORD from Jeremiah SIMMONS et al.
<45:265>	-	, Adam FORD from John FORD.
<46:154>	-	, Adam FORD from Josiah KEEN.
<47:54>	- 1761,	Adam FORD of Plympton to John FORD Jr.
<49:7>	- 1764,	Adam FORD of Pembroke to John CHUBBUCK.
<59:21>	- 1777,	Adam FORD of Pembroke to John FORD.
<65:205>	- 1786,	Adam FORD of Pembroke to Asaph TRACY Jr.
<56:205>	- 10 May 1771,	Luke FORD, yeoman of Abington, sells to Daniel SHAW, yeoman of same, 14 acres in Abington. Ack. 14 Apr., Rec. 16 Apr., 1772.
<59:230>	- 10 May 1776,	Luke FORD, yeoman of Abington, sells land.
<64:189>	- 1 Feb. 1785,	Luke FORD, yeoman of Abington, sells to Edward BASS of Bridgewater, 72 acres in Abington. Wf Hannah FORD releases dower.
<72:7>	- 9 Mar. 1789,	Luke FORD, yeoman of Cunnington MA sells to Ebenezer KINGMAN of Abington land in Abington & Bridgewater. Wf Hannah FORD releases dower.

Estate of **James REED**, yeoman of Abington MA. <Plymouth Co.PR #16603>
<13:141> Letter 5 Nov. 1753, Samuel POOL Jr., app'td admr. <13:465> Inventory taken 1 Dec. 1753, sworn to by admr. 5 May 1755. <14:9> Account 1 Dec. 1755; incl. paid to guardian of **Mathew & Silas REED** and necessaries to widow. <19:305> Division of real estate of **James REED Jr.** ordered, 4 Mar. 1764, to widow and **Hezekiah REED, Jeremiah REED, Joseph REED & Naomi REED.** <14:308> 1 Apr. 1765..."**James REED** & **James REED Jr.** both of Abington, held land in Abington & Bridgewater called Mitchell's lot, half now belonging to heirs of **James REED Jr.** and half by will of **James REED Sr.** belongs to his four daus, viz: **Tabitha REED, Experience REED, Huldah REED & Molly REED**". Division of estate made 1 May 1765 to the widow, **Ruth PORTER**, wf of Samuel, and children **Hezekiah, Jeremiah, Joseph & Naomi.** <18:218,220> Guardianship of children, 4 Mar. 1765, Ebenezer BISBE, yeoman of Abington app'td gdn. of **Naomi & Joseph REED.**

Will of **Joseph REED,** yeoman of Bridgewater MA. <Plymouth Co.PR #16633>
<24:306>...dated 1 Sept. 1776, mentions brother **Hezekiah REED** and his children (all minors); brother **Jeremiah REED** (executor); sister **Naomi.** Witnesses: Anthony DIKE, Isaac OTIS. <24:307> Bond 7 Apr. 1777. <25:121> Account. <original> Inventory, 5 May 1777.

Estate of **Hezekiah REED,** yeoman of Abington MA. <Plymouth Co.PR #16589>
<27:290> Letter 21 Mar. 1789, Isaac TIRRELL Jr., yeoman of Abington, app'td admr. <30:530> Warrant to take inventory, 16 Mar. 1789; inventory taken 21 Mar. 1789 (states **Hezekiah** d. 1 Mar. 1789). <30:531> Insolvency. <31:126> Claims. <31:127> Dower to widow **Deborah REED,** 21 Oct. 1789. <31:128,129> Accounts, 1790. <31:129> Warrant to distribute, 1790. <31:430> Account, 1792. <33:42> Order, 13 Mar. 1792, for view of part of real estate of **James REED,** yeoman of Abington, dec'd which was set off to **Ruth REED** his widow & you are to set off to **Deborah REED,** widow of **Hezekiah,** her thirds therein. <53:319> Petition to sell real estate, 1821. <54:381> Advertisement of sale, 1822. <54:381> Account.

Estate of **Isaac REED** of E. Bridgewater MA. <Plymouth Co.PR #16598>
<108:502> Appraisers app'td, 12 June 1871, to take inventory. <110:445> Account. <113:104> Petition for dower, 4th Mon. Sept. 1871, of widow **Sarah W. REED.** <116:245> Petition to sell real estate. <122:482> Petition/Letter/Bond, 12 June 1871, William P. CORTHELL of Abington, app'td admr. <128:35> Petition. <130:70> Acount. <137:47> Notice of appointment.

MICRO #28 OF 30

Will of **James REED**, husbandman/yeoman of Abington MA. <Plymouth Co.PR #16604>
<16:378>...dated 5 May 1758, mentions wf **Abigail** (with child); sons **Solomon REED, Adam REED, Stephen REED, Abel REED**; daus **Tabitha, Experience, Huldah, Molly**; brother **Daniel REED** & wf **Abigail**, executors. <16:379> Letter 5 Sept. 1762 of exrs. <16:380> Inventory, Sept. 1762. <19:308> Warrant & Division, 1 Apr. 1765, one fifth to children: **Solomon, Adam, Stephen, Abel & James.** <19:313> Warrant & Division, 6 May 1765, **Tabitha & Experience REED** and Daniel REED as guardian of **Huldah & Molly REED**, apply for division of real estate.

Guardianship of Children of **James REED** of Abington MA. <Plymouth Co.PR #16605>
<18:213,214,221-24> Bonds, 1 Apr. 1765, of Daniel REED Jr. as guardian of children of **James REED**, dec'd, viz: **Abel, Huldah, Molly, Adam, Stephen & James.** Bond 4 Mar. 1765, of Ebenezer BISBE, as guardian of **Jeremiah REED**, above 14. (Note: Bowman questions whether **Jeremiah** belongs here.)

Will of **Abigail REED**, widow of Abington MA. <Plymouth Co.PR #16537>
<42:245>...dated 21 May 1807, mentions son **James REED**; daus **Tabitha LINCOLN, Experience REED.** Philip PRATT, executor. <42:246> Pr. 1 Feb. 1808.

Will of **Huldah REED**, spinster of Abington MA. <Plymouth Co.PR #16592>
<31:338>...dated 16 Oct. 1790, mentions brothers **Adam REED, Stephen REED**; wf of brother **James REED**; sisters **Tabitha & Experience; Susanna & Abigail** (under 18), daus of brother **James REED**; my Honoured mother; **Abel REED**, son of brother **James**; sister **Tabitha**'s son **David**; Sarah TORREY, dau of Dr. TORREY of Weymouth; **Molly GURNEY**, dau of dec'd brother **Solomon REED**; brother **Silas REED**, executor. <31:339> Pr. 1 Mar. 1791. <31:340> Inventory ordered 1 Mar. 1791; incl. thirteen and a half acres wood land.; sworn to by exr. 8 Mar. 1791.

Elisha STETSON of Kingston MA to **Moses INGLEE** of same. <Plymouth Co.Deeds 83:17>
...21 Dec. 1797, Elisha STETSON, cordwainer, sells to Moses INGLEE, mariner...dwelling house in Kingston. (Note: additional references to Moses INGLEE with no data, viz: 38:270;42:245;44:164; 45:52;65:252.)

Estate of **Isaac TOMSON** of Halifax MA. <Plymouth Co.PR #20566>
<27:115> Letter/Bond 3 Mar. 1783, Adam TOMSON app'td admr. Sureties: William SHAW, Silas TINKHAM. Witnesses: James COWING, Ephraim SPOONER. <28:576> Inventory taken 11 Mar. 1783 by Moses INGLEE, Jesse STURTEVANT, Jacob SOULE; real estate, £75.10.0.; total, £288.4.0. <35:36> Account of admr., 8 Apr. 1794. Receipts from: Nathaniel RIDER, Jacob SOULE, John LEACH, Jesse STURTEVANT, Judah HALL, Nathan TINKHAM. Paid to: Moses INGLEE, Gideon SAMPSON, Noah BISBEE, George SAMPSON, Jonathan PARKER, Nathan PERKINS, Richard BOSWORTH, Caleb LAPHAM, Jabez NULAND, Ichabod TOMSON, Dr. HUTCHINS, David CHURCH, Jonathan CURTIS, Silas DUNHAM. <35:115> Account of admr., 7 July 1794; Paid to: the widow, **Huldah TOMSON**, her dower; **Huldah TOMSON** as guardian to the children, viz: **Isaac TOMSON, Olive TOMSON, Abigail TOMSON, Jacob TOMSON**; the eldest son, **Jabez TOMSON.** <35:116> Assignment of Dower, 7 July 1794, to widow **Huldah TOMSON**, by Isaac TOMSON, John WATERMAN, Jacob SOULE; incl. that part of the home farm given to the heirs of sd dec'd by Deacon Barnabas TOMSON, father of the dec'd. <35:117> Division, 7 July 1794, to the above named five children.

Guardianship of Children of **Isaac TOMSON** of Halifax MA. <Plymouth Co.PR #20567>
<26:303> Letter/Bond, 5 May 1794, **Huldah TOMSON** app'td gdn. of her children, **Isaac, Olive & Abigail** (above 14) and **Jacob** (under 14). Sureties: Adam TOMSON, Ezekiel CHANDLER. Witnesses: Caleb LORING, Isaac LOTHROP.

Estate of **Jabez THOMPSON.** <Plymouth Co.PR>
...10 Oct. 1846, the following heirs approve the account, viz: **Zadock THOMPSON**, attorney for **Ichabod W. THOMSON, Simeon THOMPSON, Samuel V. THOMPSON, Josiah THOMSON, Arioch THOMSON, Otis THOMPSON.** Account of admr., 3 Nov. 1846, payments to: **Zadock THOMPSON**, $74.82; **Otis THOMPSON**, $74.82; **Samuel V. THOMPSON**, $149.64; **Josiah THOMPSON**, $74.82; **Simeon THOMPSON**, $74.82.

Will of **Caleb TOMSON** of Middleborough MA. <Plymouth Co.PR #20524>
<30:100>...dated 28 Dec. 1785, mentions wf **Abigail**; sons **William TOMSON** (executor), **Nathaniel TOMSON, Caleb TOMSON**; daus **Molly TINKHAM** wf of Peter, **Hannah TOMSON, Abigail TOMSON** wf of John, **Silve THOMAS, Sarah MILLER** dec'd wf of David; grandson **Frederick MILLER.** Witnesses: Jacob TOMSON Jr., Abigail WESTON 3d, William SHAW. <30:109> Inventory taken by John SOULE, Jacob TOMSON, Jacob MILLER; sworn to 2 & 4 Apr. 1787 by exr.; total, £236.4.0., no real estate. <30:290> Account of exr. 2 Apr. 1788; "persons named": Job THOMAS, John LEACH, Noah CUSHMAN, Frances TOMSON, William DREW, Andrew LEACH, Ebenezer WOOD, John SOULE, Caleb TINKHAM, Noah THOMAS, Nehemiah BESSEE, Zebediah TOMSON, Capt. Jacob TOMSON, Jacob MILLER, William BENNETT, Abigail WASHBURN, Abner WOOD, Lydia CUSHMAN, Silve THOMAS wf of Elias.

Estate of **Jacob TOMSON** of Middleborough MA. <Plymouth Co.PR #20572>
<27:294> Letter/Bond, 4 May 1789, Jacob TOMSON app'td admr. Sureties: Zadock LEONARD, David KINGMAN. Witnesses: Abiezer ALGER, Isaac LOTHROP. <31:15> Inventory taken 8 May 1789 by John SOUL, Jacob MILLER, Oliver HOLMES; total, £11.0.5., no real estate. <31:16> Account, 1 June 1789. <33:86> 2nd Account, 2 July 1792 of admr.; only creditor is Ebenezer WOOD.

Estate of **Nehemiah BENNETT** of Middleboro MA. <Plymouth Co.PR 21:236>
...6 July 1771, William SHAW, Nathaniel WOOD & Ephraim WOOD, yeomen of Middleboro, app'td to div-

ide estate amongst widow & children, viz: dower to widow **Mercy BENNETT, Jacob BENNETT** (eldest son), **Abigail WESTON** wf of David, **William BENNETT, Martha DARLING** wf of Nathan and heirs of **Hannah SAVERY** dec'd wf of Thomas.

==

Estate of **Peter TOMSON** of Middleborough MA. <Plymouth Co.PR #20624>
<5:141> Letter/Bond 23 June 1726, **John TOMSON** of Plympton and **Ephraim TOMSON** of Middleborough, brothers of dec'd, app'td admrs. Surety: Jacob TOMSON. Witnesses: Mary LITTLE, Sarah LITTLE. <5: 229> Inventory taken 16 Dec. 1726 by Peter TOMSON & James SOUL of Middleboro and David BOSWORTH of Plympton; incl. land in 16 Shilling Purchase; 40 acres at home; meadow at Winatuckut; cedar swamp. <7:47> Settlement, 18 June 1728, of the estate of **Peter TOMSON** & **Ebenezer TOMSON** (that deceased without issue), the sons of **John TOMSON** of Middleboro, dec'd, among their brothers & sisters, viz: to **John TOMSON,** the eldest brother, the 39th lot in the 2d Allotment in the 16 Shilling Purchase that belonged to his brother **Ebenezer TOMSON;** to **Ephraim TOMSON** the 48th lot; **Shubael TOMSON; Thomas TOMSON; Francis TOMSON; Jacob TOMSON; Mary TOMSON,** eldest sister; **Martha TOMSON** and **Sarah TOMSON.** Witnesses: Jacob TOMSON, Ichabod STANDISH.

==

Estate of **Ebenezer TOMSON** of Middleborough MA. <Plymouth Co.PR #20536>
<5:302> Letter/Bond 22 Mar. 1726/7, brother **John TOMSON** of Plympton app'td admr. Sureties: Thomas TOMSON, Jacob TOMSON. Witnesses: Cornelius BRIGGS, Thomas READ. <5:377> Inventory taken 1 May 1728 by Peter TOMSON, Thomas TOMSON, Jacob TOMSON; total, £183.11.5. <7:47> Account 18 June 1728; Debts due from: Thomas SHURTLEFF, Ebenezer FULLER, Samuel TINKHAM, James STURTEVANT, Ichabod STANDISH, Shubael TOMSON, Francis TOMSON, Benjamin WASHBURN; Debts due to: Thomas, John, Ephraim, Peter and Jacob TOMSON. <7:47> Settlement of estate of **Peter & Ebenezer TOMSON** (dec'd without issue), the sons of **John TOMSON** of Middleboro, among their brothers & sisters, viz: **John TOMSON** (eldest brother), **Ephraim TOMSON, Shubael TOMSON, Thomas TOMSON, Francis TOMSON, Jacob TOMSON, Martha TOMSON, Sarah TOMSON, Mary TOMSON** (eldest sister). Division, 18 June 1728.

==

Estate of **Francis TOMSON** of Halifax MA. <Plymouth Co.PR #20549>
<7:57> Letter/Bond 7 Oct. 1734, John TOMSON of Halifax app'td admr. Sureties: Thomas TOMSON, James WARREN. Witnesses: Josiah COTTON, John WINSLOW. <7:118> Inventory taken 18 Nov. 1734 by Thomas TOMSON, David BOSWORTH of Halifax and Jacob TOMSON of Middleboro; mentions land that was his brother **Peter TOMSON'**s which he bought of Ichabod STANDISH. <7:158> Division 17 Oct. 1735 by Thomas TOMSON, David BOSWORTH, Barnabas TOMSON of Halifax and Jacob TOMSON & James SOULE of Middleboro, to following brothers & sisters, viz: **Mary TOMSON, Martha TOMSON, Sarah TOMSON, Ephraim TOMSON, Jacob TOMSON, Isaac, John & Thomas TOMSON** the children of dec'd brother **Shubael TOMSON, John TOMSON, Thomas TOMSON.** <7:158> Account 2 Oct. 1735, one creditor, Ebenezer FULLER.

==

Will of **Sarah TOMSON** of Halifax MA. <Plymouth Co.PR #20639>
<20:456>...dated 1 July 1760, mentions sister **Martha TOMSON;** dec'd brother **Thomas TOMSON;** children of dec'd brother **Jacob TOMSON;** sons of dec'd brother **Thomas TOMSON,** viz: **Peter TOMSON Jr.** (executor), **Nathan TOMSON, Francis TOMSON** & **James TOMSON.** Witnesses: Jacob TOMSON, William TORREY, Jacob TOMSON Jr. <20:456> Letter 7 Jan. 1771, **Peter TOMSON Jr.** app'td admr. <20:485> Inventory taken 15 Jan. 1771 by Ebenezer TOMSON, Moses INGLEE, Hosea DUNBAR; total, £135.13.0.

==

Will of **Martha TOMSON** of Halifax MA. <Plymouth Co.PR #20605>
<20:360>...dated 1 July 1760, mentions sister **Sarah TOMSON,** dec'd brother **Thomas TOMSON;** children of dec'd brother **Jacob TOMSON;** children of dec'd brother **Thomas TOMSON,** viz: **Peter TOMSON Jr.** (executor), **Nathan TOMSON, Francis TOMSON** & **James TOMSON.** Witnesses: Jacob TOMSON, William TORREY & Jacob TOMSON Jr. <20:360> Letter 16 May 1770, **Peter TOMSON Jr.** app'td admr. <20:451> Inventory taken 15 Jan. 1770 by Ebenezer TOMSON, Moses INGLEE, Hosea DUNBAR; total, £139.18.2.

==

Estate of **Mary TOMSON,** spinster of Halifax MA. <Plymouth Co.PR #20608>
<10:53> Letter/Bond 3 Dec. 1745, Jacob TOMSON app'td admr. Sureties: Thomas TOMSON, John TOMSON. Witnesses: George KING, Ezekiel TURNER. <10:125> Inventory taken 10 Feb. 1745 by Jacob TOMSON, Thomas CRODE & Ruben TOMSON. <10:160> Agreement, between surviving brothers & sisters of **Ephraim TOMSON** & **Mary TOMSON** late of Halifax & the legal representatives of **Shubal TOMSON** dec'd (who was also their brother) which (by agreement with Joseph WORKES & Joanna his wife) accrues to us. Division 15 May 1746 to following: **John TOMSON, Sr.** (to receive one quarter part of meadow given to **Ephraim TOMSON** by his father's will); **Thomas TOMSON; John TOMSON** of Middleboro & **Thomas TOMSON** of Bridgewater, the sons of **Shubal TOMSON; Martha TOMSON; Sarah TOMSON; Francis TOMSON,** decd; **Jacob TOMSON.** Witnesses: Jno. CUSHING, Ichabod STANDISH.

==

Estate of **Ephraim TOMSON** of Halifax MA. <Plymouth Co.PR #20546>
<9:404> Letter/Bond 6 Dec. 1744, Benjamin WESTON app'td admr. Sureties: Gamaliel BRADFORD, Samuel WOOD. Witnesses: J. SKINNER, Jacob PEABODY. <9:425> Inventory taken 5 Mar. 1744 by Noah CUSHING, John FULLER, Moses CUSHMAN; total, £2028.6.2. <10:31> Account 6 Dec. 1745; Creditors: Ebenezer FULLER, Obadiah EDDY, William COOMER, Thomas MURDOCK, Jabez SOULE, Nathan FULLER, Thomas TOMSON Jr., Jacob TOMSON Jr., Thomas TOMSON. <10:32> Receipt 6 Dec. 1745 from Joseph WORKS of Ashford & wf **Joanna,** late widow of **Ephraim TOMSON.** <10:160> Agreement between surviving brothers & sisters of **Ephraim TOMSON** & **Mary TOMSON** and the legal representatives of brother **Shubal TOMSON** dec'd, viz: **John TOMSON Sr.; Thomas TOMSON** of Halifax; **John TOMSON** of Middleboro & **Thomas TOMSON** of Bridgewater, the sons of **Shubal** dec'd; **Martha TOMSON; Sarah TOMSON; Francis TOMSON** dec'd; to **Jacob TOMSON,** land that fell to **Ephraim** from Francis TOMSON. Division 15 May 1746. Witnesses: Jno. CUSHING, Ichabod STANDISH.

==

Will of **Jacob TOMSON** of Halifax MA. <Plymouth Co.PR #20577>
<12:296>...dated 5 Jan. 1750, mentions wf **Mary**; sons (under 21), **Jacob TOMSON, Ebenezer TOMSON, Nathaniel TOMSON, Ephraim TOMSON, Daniel TOMSON**; mentions lands formerly belonging to brother **Francis TOMSON.** Witnesses: Jacob TOMSON, John TOMSON 3d, Peter TOMSON Jr. <12:299> Letter 1 July 1751, widow **Mary TOMSON** app'td admx. <12:154> Inventory taken 23 Mar. 1750 by Barnabas TOMSON, Jno. TOMSON, Nathaniel HAYWARD Jr.; total, Ł467.3.10. <16:415> Division 27 Oct. 1762 by John TOMSON, Nehemiah BENNET, Moses ENGLY/INGLEE; to sons **Jacob TOMSON** (eldest), **Ebenezer TOMSON,** heirs of dec'd son **Nathaniel TOMSON,** one third each.

Guardianship of Children of **Jacob TOMSON** of Halifax MA. <Plymouth Co.PR #20531>
<18:106> Bond/Letter 15 Oct. 1762, Ebenezer TOMSON app'td gdn. of **Daniel TOMSON.** Surety: John TOMSON. Witnesses: Edward WINSLOW, James HAWARD. <18:109> Bond/Letter 15 Oct. 1762, Ebenezer TOMSON app'td gdn. of **Ephraim TOMSON.** Surety: John TOMSON. Witnesses: Edward WINSLOW, James HAWARD.

Estate of **Nathaniel TOMSON** of Halifax MA. <Plymouth Co.PR #20620>
<17:17> Letter/Bond 6 Apr. 1761, Jacob TOMSON of Halifax, app'td admr. Sureties: Josiah HAYWARD, Jr., Robert GILLMORE. Witness: Nehemiah RIPLEY. <16:146> Inventory taken 21 Apr. 1761 by John TOMSOM, Ebenezer TOMSON, Moses INGLEE; total, Ł79.21.9. <16:358> Account 13 Oct. 1762; Paid to: Thomas CROADE, Esq., Israel HILL. <16:416> Warrant for Division, 16 Oct. 1762 to Nehemiah BENNET, John TOMSON, Moses INGLEE; divided into four equal parts to the following heirs, viz: **Jacob, Ebenezer, Ephraim & Daniel TOMSON**; mentions cedar swamp given to him by his honoured father dec'd in his last will.

Will of **John TOMSON** of Halifax MA. <Plymouth Co.PR #20585>
<14:312>...dated 11 May 1757, mentions wf **Elizabeth**; son **John TOMSON**; daus **Lydia TOMSON, Elizabeth FULLER**; mentions land that fell unto me in the settlement of the estate of my brother **Francis TOMSON** dec'd. Witnesses: Jacob TOMSON, Moses INGLEE, Ephraim SOULE. <14:313> Letter 5 July 1757, widow **Elizabeth TOMSON** and son **John TOMSON** app'td exrs. <14:370> Inventory taken 2 July 1757 by Barnabas TOMSON, Robert WATERMAN, Noah CUSHING, of estate of **John TOMSON Sr.**.

Estate of **John TOMSON 2d** of Halifax MA. <Plymouth Co.PR #20586>
<original> Request 1 Mar. 1777, of widow **Betty TOMSON,** asking for the appointment of Jacob SOULE as admr. She states that she has six children, the eldest daughter about 16. <23:158> Letter/Bond 7 Apr. 1777, Jacob SOULE app'td admr. Sureties: Noah TOMSON, Ephraim TILLSON. Witnesses: Israel VINAL Jr., Joseph CUSHING. <24:252> Inventory taken 26 Mar. 1777 by Ebenezer TOMSON, Moses INGLEE & Noah TOMSON; total, Ł472.13.0. <25:257> Account 5 Apr. 1779; Paid to: Jonathan FULLER, Samuel ADAMS, Isaac TOMSON, Freeman WATERMAN, William PERREY, Mary FULLER, Thomas DREW, Chipman FULLER, James BOSWORTH, Nathan PERKINS, Richard BOSWORTH, Daniel WILLIS, Asenath FULLER, Sarah BOSWORTH, Jacob CHIPMAN, Martha FULLER, Nathan TINKHAM, Joseph PERREY, Barnabas TOMSON, Abiah SAMPSON, Gideon SOULE, John SHAW, Samuel FULLER, Huldah FULLER, John FULLER. Debts due from: Timothy RIPLEY, Benjamin CORTIS, Josiah RIPLEY, Freeman WATERMAN. <29:305> Division 6 June 1785, by Ebenezer TOMSON, John WATERMAN Jr., Noah TOMSON, to the remaining children & heirs of the dec'd, viz: **Thaddeus TOMSON** (eldest son), **Susannah TOMSON, Nathan TOMSON, Zacheus TOMSON, Elizabeth TOMSON, Stephen TOMSON.**

Estate of **Betty TOMSON,** widow of Halifax MA. <Plymouth Co.PR #20522>
<original> Request 3 May 1779, of father **Ebenezer FULLER,** stating that dec'd left no heirs capable of settling the small estate & asks for the appointment of Jacob SOULE. <27:19> Letter/Bond, 3 May 1779, Jacob SOUL app'td admr. <29:307> Inventory taken 13 May 1779 by Moses INGLEE, Ephraim FULLER, Noah TOMSON; total, Ł341. <29:308> Account 6 June 1785; Paid to: Isaac TOMSON, John LEACH, Dr. Jonathan FULLER, Joseph WATERMAN, Dr. Isaac OTIS, Lydia FULLER, Gideon SOULE, Thomas STURTEVANT, Freeman WATERMAN, Martha FULLER, Dr. Ephraim WALES, Chipman FULLER, William PERREY, Ephraim FULLER, Ephraim SOUL, Noah TOMSON.

Guardianship of Children of **John TOMSON 2d** of Halifax MA. <Plymouth Co.PR #20619>
Bonds/Letters, 5 Apr. 1779, Freeman WATERMAN app'td gdn. of **Stephen TOMSON,** age 5 <26:51>; **Zacheus TOMSON,** age 11 <26:52>; **Nathan TOMSON,** age 13 <26:53>; **Elizabeth TOMSON,** age 9 <26:54>; and **Thaddeus TOMSON** & **Susannah TOMSON,** above 14. <original> Bond 4 July 1785, Jacob SOULE app'td gdn. of **Nathan, Zacheus** & **Elizabeth TOMSON,** above 14; <26:194> and **Stephen,** under 14. Sureties: Freeman WATERMAN & Thomas STURTEVANT. Witnesses: Gideon SOULE, Ignatius LORING. <26:433> Nomination, 4 July 1785, of Jacob SOULE, gdn., by **Nathan, Zacheus** & **Elizabeth.** Witnesses: Susanna TOMSON, Ebenezer PORTER. <29:348> Account 4 July 1785 of Freeman WATERMAN, gdn. who resigns, **Susanna** & **Thaddeus** being of age. <original> Statement 30 Mar. 1779, of **Ebenezer FULLER,** grandfather of sd children, stating that **John TOMSON 2d** died leaving a widow & six children. On back of statement: **Susannah TOMSON,** 17, **Thaddeus TOMSON,** 15, **Nathan TOMSON,** 13, **Zacheus TOMSON,** 11, **Elizabeth TOMSON** 9 and **Stephen TOMSON,** 5.

Estate of **Shubael TOMSON** of Middleborough MA. <Plymouth Co.PR #20642>
<6:384> Letter/Bond 7 Aug. 1733, Susannah TOMSON & Francis TOMSON, app'td admrs. Sureties: Josiah THOMAS, John TOMSON. Witnesses: Edward WINSLOW, Mercy GOLDTHWAIT. <6:391> Inventory taken 18 Sept 1733 by John BENNET, Jabez VAUGHAN, Jacob TOMPSON; mentions real estate in 26 Men's Purchase, 16 Shilling Purchase & Major's Purchase. <7:12> Account 5 Nov. 1733; Debts due: (incl. desperate & contrary): William COMBES, John SOULE, William MORSE, Samuel WATERMAN, John COX, Edmund WESTON, Ebenezer FINNEY, Thomas KING, Joseph THOMAS, James COBB, Simon LAZELL, Noah THOMAS, Mary HOLMES, Ebenezer REDDING, Nathan HOWLAND, William HASKELL, Richard DIKINS, Jabez WOOD, Nathaniel ALLEN, Lydia HACKETT, Eleaser PRATT Jr., Japheth TURNER, Lydia LORING, John WILLIS, Thomas PALMER, Mary

THOMSON, Thomas THOMSON, Barnabas THOMSON, John THOMSON, Jacob THOMSON, Jacob THOMSON Jr., Francis MILLER, Francis THOMSON, Joseph BATE, Ephraim WOOD, Robert BROWN, Jabez VAUGHAN, Mrs. JACKSON, John MURDOCK, John BENNETT, Lazarus LeBARON, Joseph WILLIAMS, Elizabeth LEWES, Samuel BARTLETT, Thomas NELSON, Peter THACHER, Jonathan FULLER, William CHURCHILL. <7:13,15> Warrant to divide, 5 Nov. 1733, to John BENNET, Jabesh VAUGHAN, Jacob TOMSON, James SOULE, Thomas TOMSON; estate set off to the widow **Susanna** and children **Mary TOMSON, Thomas TOMSON, John TOMSON, Shubael TOMSON, Isaac TOMSON** (eldest son). <7:106> Division as above, the estate of the deceased children **Shubael** & **Mary** was divided into three equal parts. <7:105> Division of Dower, 23 Dec. 1734, divided into four equal parts & also the real & personal estate of **Shubael** & **Mary TOMSON**, dec'd children, set off to **Isaac TOMSON** (eldest son), **John TOMSON, Thomas TOMSON.**

=====================================

Guardianship of Children of **Shubael TOMSON** of Middleborough MA. <Plymouth Co.PR #20643>
<6:408> Letters/Bonds 5 Nov. 1733, Edmond WESTON app'td gdn. of **Shubael, Isaac** & **Mary TOMSON**, all minors between 14-21. Surety: John COB. Witnesses: Francis TOMSON, John DOUGLAS. <6:401> Letter/Bond 5 Nov. 1733, Francis TOMSON app'td gdn. of **Thomas TOMSON**, minor under 14. Surety: John COB. Witnesses: Edmond WESTON, John DOUGLAS. <6:403> Letter/Bond 5 Nov. 1733, John COB app'td gdn. of **John TOMSON**, minor under 21. Surety: Edmond WESTON. Witnesses: Francis TOMSON, John DOUGLAS. <7:45> Letter/Bond 5 Aug. 1734, Jacob TOMSON app'td gdn. of **Thomas TOMSON**, minor under 14. Surety: John TOMSON. Witnesses: John COB, Edward WINSLOW.

=====================================

Estates of **Shubal TOMSON** & **Mary TOMSON** of Middleborough MA. <Plymouth Co.PR #20644>
<7:52> Letter/Bond 5 Aug. 1734, Thomas TOMSON app'td admr. on estate of **Shubael & Mary TOMSON**, deceased children of **Shubal TOMSON**. Sureties: John TOMSON, Jacob TOMSON, Edmond WESTON. Witneses: John COB, Edward WINSLOW. <7:56> Inventory taken 19 Sept. 1734 by John BENNET, Jacob TOMSON, Jabez VAUGAN; incl. real estate in 26 Men's Purchase. <7:56> Account 4 Oct. 1734. <7:105> Division 23 Dec. 1734, of estate of **Susanna TOMSON**, widow of **Shubael** and the estates of children **Shubael & Mary TOMSON**; estate of children divided into three parts among the three suriving children of **Shubael**. <7:106> Settlement 6 Jan. 1734, to the three surviving children, viz: **Isaac TOMSON** (eldest son), **John TOMSON** and **Thomas TOMSON.**

==

Estate of **Isaac TOMSON** of Middleborough MA. <Plymouth Co.PR #20562>
<8:191> Letter/Bond 20 May 1740, John TOMSON app'td admr. Sureties: Ebenezer REDING, Nathaniel HAYWARD/HOWARD. Witnesses: Daniel JOHNSON, James SHURTLEFF. <8:192> Inventory taken 31 May 1740 by John BENNET, Jabez VAUGHAN, of Middleboro and Thomas THOMSON & Barnabas THOMSON of Halifax; estate set off to the brothers of the dec'd, **John THOMSON** and **Thomas THOMSON.**

==

Will of **John TOMSON** of Middleborough MA. <Plymouth Co.PR #20590>
<19:382>...dated 12 May 1766, mentions wf **Sarah**; children **Shubal TOMSON** (executor), **Isaac TOMSON, John TOMSON, Ezra TOMSON, Susanna THOMAS, Lidia TOMSON, Sarah TOMSON, Fear TOMSON, Priscilla TOMSON** and **Mary TOMSON** (youngest dau under 7 years). Witnesses: Daniel VAUGHN, Joseph TINKHAM, Jabez VAUGHN. <19:384> Pr. 4 Aug. 1766, **Shubal TOMSON** app'td admr. <19:385> Inventory taken 10 July 1766 by Isaac TINKHAM, Daniel VAUGHN, Joseph TINKHAM; incl. Pachade farm, farm bought of Nelson FINNEY and one quarter of sawmill. <20:203> Account 17 May 1769; Debts paid: Stephen POWERS, Samuel RAYMOND, Abner WOOD, Ebenezer SPROAT, John BENT, Jonah WASHBURN, Moses READING, Gideon WHITE, Joseph TINKHAM, Jabez VAUGHN, Daniel VAUGHN, Hushai THOMAS, DAVIS & HARLOW, Isaac TINKHAM, Mercy COBB, Charles ELLIS, Francis TOMSON, Josiah WOOD, widow Mary THOMAS, Samuel SMITH, Jacob TOMSON Jr., Micah BRYANT, Zachariah PADDOCK, Samuel BENSON, Elijah CLAP, Jonathan TILSON, Joseph FAUNCE, Nathaniel BILLINGTON, John TINKHAM, Ezra ALLEN, Jacob TOMSON, Moses EDDY, Abial LEACH, Estate of widow SOUL, John HOLMES, Abner BARROW, Nehemiah BRYANT, Nehemiah LATHAM, Reuben TOMSON, John MORTON, Amos TINKHAM, Isaac OTIS, Benjamin TUCKER Jr.

=====================================

Guardianship of Children of **John TOMSON** of Middleborough MA. <Plymouth Co.PR #20640>
<18:246> Letter/Bond 2 July 1766, Moses EDDY app'td gdn. of **Fear TOMSON.** Sureties: Moses REDDING, Francis TOMSON. Witnesses: Joseph TINKHAM, Edward WINSLOW Jr. <18:248> Letter/Bond 2 July 1766, Shubael TOMSON app'td gdn. of **Sarah TOMSON.** Sureties: Moses EDDY, Francis TOMSON. Witnesses: Joseph TINKHAM, Edward WINSLOW Jr. <18:247> Letter/Bond 2 July 1766, widow **Sarah TOMSON** app'td gdn. of **Mary TOMSON.** Sureties: Moses REDDING, Moses EDDY. Witnesses: Joseph TINKHAM, Edward WINSLOW, Jr. <18:248> Statement/Bond 2 July 1766, Moses REDDING app'td gdn. of **Priscilla TOMSON.** Sureties: Francis TOMSON, Shubael TOMSON. Witnesses: Joseph TINKHAM, Edward WINSLOW Jr. <19:390> Bond 2 July 1766, Shubael TOMSON appt'd gdn. of **Lidia TOMSON.** Sureties: Moses EDDY, Francis TOMSON. Witnesses: Joseph TINKHAM, Edward WINSLOW Jr. <19:390> Bond 2 July 1766, Francis TOMSON app'td gdn. of **Ezra TOMSON** (above 14). Sureties: Shubael TOMSON, Moses REDDING. Witnesses: Joseph TINKHAM, Edward WINSLOW Jr. <20:27> Bond 22 Mar. 1768, Joshua WHITE app'td gdn. of **Mary TOMSON.** Sureties: Samuel RAYMOND, Shubael TOMSON. Witnesses: Edward WINSLOW, Edward WINSLOW Jr. <20:461> Bond 30 Oct. 1770, James COBB app'td gdn. of **Sarah TOMSON.** Surety: Joseph CUSHMAN. Witnesses: Pelham WINSLOW, Edward WINSLOW. <original> Request 18 Mar. 1768, for a new guardian for "my grandchild **Mary TOMSON** daughter to the widow **Sarah TOMSON**, she being non comp mentis, she living in Middleboro". Signed by: George BRYANT, John BRYANT Jr., Ephraim BRYANT.

==

Will of **Shubael TOMSON** of Middleborough MA. <Plymouth Co.PR #20641>
<20:358>...dated 20 Jan. 1770, mentions wf **Ruth**; mother **Sarah TOMSON**; son **Shubael TOMSON** (under 7); dau **Susanna TOMSON** (under 9); brother **Isaac TOMSON**, executor. Witnessses: Francis TOMSON, Jacob SOULE, William SHAW. <20:359> Pr. 6 Mar. 1770. <20:359> Inventory taken 17 Mar. 1770 by Isaac TINKHAM, James COBB, Francis TOMSON; total £324.17.6. <21:100> Account 1 June 1772; Paid: to the guardian for the surviving child; the executor also prays allowance for the doctor's bill & for getting the medicines for the deceased's son that died after his father, also for getting

gravestones for the child.

Guardianship of Child of **Shubael TOMSON** of Middleborough MA. <Plymouth Co.PR #20649>
<20:359> Bond 17 May 1770, Jacob SOULE of Middleboro app'td gdn. of **Susanna TOMSON** (under 14). Sureties: Ebenezer COX, Isaac TOMSON. Witnesses: Benjamin SHURTLEFF, Edward WINSLOW.

MICRO #29 OF 30

Estate of **Thomas TOMSON**, cordwainer of Bridgewater MA. <Plymouth Co.PR #20651>
<14:56> Letter/Bond 5 Apr. 1756, Josiah EDSON Jr. app'td admr. Sureties: Benjamin WILLIS Jr., Josiah WASHBURN. Witnesses: Thomas AMES, Thomas WILLIS Jr. <14:161> Inventory taken 8 Apr. 1756 by Samuel KINSLEY, Joseph WASHBURN, Jonathan CHANDLER; total L98.8.2. <14:120> Account 22 July 1756; mentions the widow. <19:206> Account 21 May 1765; Paid to: Simeon HAYWARD, Eleazer CARVER, Esq. SEVER, Solomon PRATT, Abisha WILLIS, Francis STURTEVANT, John FIELD, Moses INGLY, Amos HAYWARD, Jacob TOMSON, Jabez EATON, Seth MITCHELL, David ALDEN, Nathaniel BOLTON, Noah WISWALL, William SNOW Jr., Thomas MITCHELL, Seth HAYWARD.

Will of **Thomas TOMSON** of Halifax MA. <Plymouth Co.PR #20656>
<15:479>...dated 7 July 1759, mentions wf **Martha**; sons **Peter TOMSON, Nathan TOMSON, Francis TOMSON, James TOMSON**. Witnesses: Jacob TOMSON, Nathan TOMSON, Jacob TOMSON Jr. <15:481> Pr. 7 Apr. 1760, widow **Martha TOMSON** and sons **Peter & Francis TOMSON**, app'td exrs. <15:500> Inventory taken 23 Apr. 1760 by Joseph BOZWORTH, Ebenezer TOMSON, Moses INGLEE; total Ł848.

Will of **Francis THOMSON** of Middleborough MA. <Plymouth Co.PR #20550>
<36:473>...dated 20 Nov. 1798, mentions wf **Mary**; sons **Elias THOMSON, Thomas THOMSON** & **Ruel THOMSON**; daus **Zilpah CUSHMAN** wf of Noah, **Cynthia COX** wf of John & **Molley THOMSON**; mentions land bought of Levi & Jane WOOD and Israel & Abigail THOMSON. Witnesses: Jonathan HARLOW, Lemuel HARLOW, Isaac THOMPSON. <36:476> Letter/Bond 31 Dec. 1798, **Thomas THOMSON** app'td admr. Sureties: Isaac THOMSON, Jonathan HARLOW. Witnesses: Z. BARTLETT, Isaac LOTHROP. <36:568> Inventory taken by Isaac THOMSON, Jonathan HARLOW, Jabez VAUGHAN; sworn to 10 Apr. 1799 by **Thomas THOMSON**. <37:145> Account 12 Nov. 1799; Received from: Nathaniel THOMSON; Paid to: Isaac THOMSON, Eleazer HARLOW, John SAWYER, Daniel TUCKER, Elijah SHAW, Enoch THOMAS 2d, William CROMBEE, Susanna COBB, John BENNET, Thomas FOSTER, Isaac THOMSON for grave stones for dec'd & a child of dec'd who died before its father. <42:144,145> Dower set off 5 Aug. 1807 to widow **Mary THOMSON**; the son **Thomas** died prior to this date.

Heirs of **Thomas TABER**. <Bristol Co.Deeds 41:6>
...3 June 1752, Caleb BLACKWELL, blacksmith & wf Bethiah of Rochester, Ebenezer TABER, cordwainer & wf Abigail of Tiverton and Mary MORTON widow of Manasseh of Dartmouth, sold to Bartholomew TABER, cooper of Dartmouth...three twelfths of lands of our Honoured father Thomas TABER, late of Dartmouth, dec'd. Ack. 28 Aug. 1752 by Ebenezer & Abigail; 24 Apr. 1753 by Caleb & Bethiah; 6 July 1753 by Mary MORTON.

Will of **Jacob TABER**, yeoman of Dartmouth MA. <Bristol Co.PR>
<22:470>...dated 4 Jan. 1763...to **Sarah** my loving wife ye use & improvement of my Great room and Chamber above it; with ye two closets oppening into said rooms; with ye use & improvement of ye little inclosure where my well is; with ye priveledge of passing & repassing to and from each and every part above mentioned; together with ye use of six of my apple trees she to take her choice yearly in my orchard when ye fruit is on ye trees; all ye above mentioned priveledgs I give to my sd wife during ye time she remains my widdow......likewise...the one half of all my indoor moveables (except my cask & tubs I keep grain in)...All ye above sd gifts...together with what I shall order to be paid and performed for her yearly...is in lue of her right of dower in my estate...To my son **Stephen TABER**...all my right in land which was laid out formerly to my Father at a place called Arons Causey; together with my lot of ceder swamp lying nere sd Causey; together with my cedar swamp at a place called Squins Country...to my son **Bartholomew TABER**...all that part of my homstead lying to ye west of ye way that leads from Thomas NYE's to Elnathan POPE's... also the wood lot which I bought of William MICHEL; together with one fether bed, to be that which he commonly lodges upon, with ye common winter furniture to the same belonging; together with all my live stock...farming utencials...all my cask & tubs...he paying & performing to and for his mother my wife yearly as hereafter mentioned...That is to say: 5 pounds lawfull money, 12 boshels of good Indian corn & 3 boshels of rye, one quarter of good beaf to be the hinder quarter with the kidney tallow there belonging and to be in wate/weight not less than ninty pounds, one swine when fatted and well drest not less than 140 pounds, 14 pounds of sheeps woll, 10 coard of good wood at ye door of a suteable length for her chimney provided she wants it for her own fire, two good cows and a riding beast with good keeping for all both winter and summer... And pay to my daughters **Jerusha** and **Lois** each the sum of five pounds ten shillings...And five pounds ten shillings to the children of my daughter **Eunice** dec'd...To my son **Jacob TABER**...land lying on the westerly side of that called Hathaway's Ceder Swamp; land nere Deep Brook which sd brook runs into Accoshanut River; cedar swamp at a place called The old Tarkill way which runs across Hemlock Island; together with the use & improvement of that row of apple trees on the westerly side of the wall...for the space of seven years...Son **Bartholomew**, executor. Witnesses: Stephen NYE, Zerviah WOOD, Stephen WEST. Pr. 28 June 1773. <23:87> Inventory taken 27 Nov. 1773 by Stephen NYE, Zerviah WOOD and Richard DELANO; total, Ł141.8.11.

Estate of **Jacob TABER**, mariner of Fairhaven MA, 1816. <Bristol Co.PR>
<52:33> Inventory. <110:408> Notice. <151:245> Pr. <159:32> Bond.

Stephen TABER of Dartmouth MA to **Bartholomew AKIN** of same. <Bristol Co.Deeds 59:151>
...4 Apr. 1777, Stephen TABER, yeoman, for Ł60, sold to Betholomew AKIN, house carpenter...all my right & title in that part of the late homstead of my father Jacob TABER late of Dartmouth dec'd ...bounded by land of Thomas NYE, Zevviah WOOD...being one third part there of now lying in common & undivided with my brothers Bertholomew TABER and Jacob TABER. Witnesses: Sarah McPHERSON, Benjamin AKIN. Ack. 9 Feb. 1778. Rec. 26 Feb. 1779.

Jacob TABER of Dartmouth MA to **Bartholomew AKIN** of same. <Bristol Co.Deeds 65:78>
...24 Apr. 1780, Jacob TABER, sadlar, for 250 Spanish silver milled dollars, sold to Bartholomew AKIN, house carpenter...all the part of the late homested of my Honoured Father Jacob TABER late of Dartmouth dec'd which he gave me in & by his last will...it being one third part...lying in common & undivided with the sd Bartholomew AKIN and Bartholomew TABER. Witnesses: Elnathan TABER, Bartholomew TABER. Ack. 24 Apr. 1780. Rec. 26 Jan. 1786.

Heirs of **Jacob TABER** of Dartmouth MA. <Bristol Co.Deeds 74:476>
...3 Apr. 1795, Indenture between Bartholomew AKIN, house carpenter of New Bedford and Bartholomew TABER, yeoman of New Bedford...whereas the sd AKIN & TABER do stand seized in equal halves of all the land that Jacob TABER died seized of between ye way that goes between sd parties dwelling houses & Noah ALLAN's land in part & part on ye way which land the said Jacob TABER gave to his three surviving sons, Stephen TABER, Jacob TABER and the sd Bartholomew TABER to be equally divided amongst them...the sd Bartholomew AKIN bought the sd Stephen's right and one of ye sd Jacob's right...and the sd Bartholomew the other half of ye sd Jacob's right altho the sd Bartholomew AKIN took ye deed of ye sd Jacob TABER for ye whole of his right and ye sd parties soon after ye date of sd deed taken of ye sd Jacob TABER, did mutually agree ...to an equal division of ye above sd land...AKIN received his half of twenty seven acres, TABER received thirty seven acres. Witnesses: John TABER, Susanna TABER. Ack. 1 Apr. 1796. Rec. 21 Apr. 1796.

Estate of **Bartholomew TABER** of New Bedford MA. <Bristol Co.PR>
<40:400> Will. <41:12> <u>Inventory</u> taken 1 Oct. 1804 by Richard DELANO, Samuel KINNEY, Peter FULLER incl. 90 acre homestead farm, $7000.00; land in the village of Oxford adjoining house lot of Benjamin SISSON, $34.00; house lot in Oxford in common with John MacPHERSON adjoining lot of the Widow BABCOCK, $42.00; one quarter of wharf in Oxford, $75.00; lott in common with John MacPHERSON adjoining lots of Stephen HATHAWAY & Thomas NYE; 40 acre wood lot adjoining homestead farm of Samuel KINNEY, $1600.00; 5 acre wood lot adjoining Obed NYE & Jire SWIFT, $100.00; 4 acres adjoining Daniel SUMMERTON's, $80.00. Sworn to by John TABER, executor, 2 Oct. 1804.

(Note: Additional references pertaining to the name **Bartholomew TABER** are given, but it is unclear if they relate to the above, viz: <105:263> Adm. <119:822> Notice. <158:902> Letter. <165:165> Bond. <194:98> Inventory. <217:43> Account. <222:148,155,480> Petition.

Bartholomew TABER of Dartmouth MA to **Jonathan TOBEY** of same. <Bristol Co.Deeds 50:104>
...July 1753, Bartholomew TABER, cooper, for Ł4, sold to Jonathan TOBEY...nine acres in Dartmouth ...on ye neck near to Arons Cassey way...being part of that lot of land that was laid out to my Grandfather Thomas TABER late of Dartmouth dec'd...bounded by land sd Jonathan bought of Phillip TABER of Middletown, late of Dartmouth, land of Benjamin HATHAWAY and land of some of the heirs of sd Thomas TABER. Witnesses: Benjamin HATHAWAY, Samuel PERRY. Ack. 21 Feb. 1754. Rec. 31 Oct. 1765.

Bartholomew TABER of Dartmouth to **Joseph ELLIS** of same. <Bristol Co.Deeds 58:70>
...29 Apr. 1777, Bartholomew TABER, yeoman, sells to Joseph ELLIS...all rights in 11 acres that brother John TABER, dec'd of Dartmouth, died seized of...being that percell of land that ye sd John TABER held by two certain deeds of sale from ye sd Joseph ELLIS & Martha ELLIS dated 2 June 1756 & 31 Jan. 1759.

<u>BRISTOL COUNTY DEEDS</u>: (re: Bartholomew TABER)

<39:349> - , Bartholomew TABER from Joseph & Martha ELLIS.
<39:349> - , Bartholomew TABER from Peter TINKHAM.
<48:454> - , Bartholomew TABER, grantor.
<63:37> - 1753, Bartholomew TABER from Jabez JENNE.
<72:243> - 1792, Bartholomew TABER from Samuel MENDELL.
<74:171> - 1795, Bartholomew TABER to Jethro BABCOCK, house & land in Oxford.
<74:475> - 1795, Bartholomew TABER and John MacPHERSON of Albany NY, from Elnathan ELDRIDGE, land in Oxford.
<74:477> - 1796, Bartholomew TABER to Bartholomew AKIN.
<75:139> - 1796, Bartholomew TABER to Benjamin SISSON, land in Oxford & New Bedford.
<80:46> - 1801, Bartholomew TABER to Daniel NYE, land in Oxford.
<84:535> - , Bartholomew TABER, hatter of New Bedford & Jacob TABER, from brother John TABER (2d or Jr.), yeoman of New Bedford, son of Bartholomew.
<93:32> - 1811, Bartholomew TABER to John HOWLAND 3d.

(Note: Additional references with no data, viz: <u>Grantor</u>: 48:454;97:48;103:17;122:544;126:117;133:

BRISTOL COUNTY DEEDS, cont-d: (re: Bartholomew TABER)

13;134:303;134:531;138:330;142:146. Grantee: 52:247;74:476;79:545;111:204;117:120;118:55;126:121; 128:519;89:49-55.)

Estate of **John TABER.** <Bristol Co.PR>
<6:39> Will. <6:40> Inventory. <6:221> Account. (no further details in files)

Estate of **John TABER** of Dartmouth MA. <Bristol Co.PR>
<16:61> Adm. 25 May 1758, widow **Mary TABER** app'td admx. <19:18> Inventory. <19:26> Account, mentions child born after father's decease. <20:409> Account of **Mary TABER**, guardian of minor son **John TABER.** <20:426> Division between **Jonathan TABER** & heirs of **John TABER.** <20:427> Division between **John TABER** (minor son) and **Meribah.** <26:219> Account 1780, "no inventory of sd minor's other estate being taken, nothing ever to be found".

Estate of **John TABER** of Fairhaven MA. <Bristol Co.PR>
<53:127> Inventory. <54:90> Account, 1817. <54:472> Account. <54:458> Inventory. <54:461> Account <54:489> Commissioners' report. <54:491> Distribution. <54:492> Notice of sale.

Will of **John TABER.** <Bristol Co.PR>
<91:292>...dated 17 Mar. 1847. <110:506> Notice. <116:402> Notice. <126:33;127:277> Guardian letters. (no further details in files)

Estate of **John TABER.** <Bristol Co.PR>
<147:222;151:308,380> Adm. <159:76,162> Bond. <174:195> Bond. <177:3> Citation.

Will of **Amaziah TABER,** cloather of New Bedford MA. <Bristol Co.PR>
<45:245>...dated 14 Oct. 1809...to dau **Thankful WOOD,** all my indore movabels excepting my desk and one olde chest in the small beadroome at the head of the stares and all my wearing apparel... to granson **Thomas WOOD** all my real estate of every description and all my live stock, farming tooles and my desk and the old chest at the head of the stares with all that the sd chest containes and what ever money remaines after paying my just debts...in case he should die without a lawfull hire/heir then...the real estate descends to my granson **Amaziah Taber WOOD,** his brother; nephew **James TABER** app'td executor. Witnesses: Elisha CUSHMAN, Jabez TABER, Stephen WEST 2d. <original> Bond 18 Dec. 1809, **James TABER** app'td admr. <45:251> Inventory taken 18 Dec. 1809 by Elisha CUSHMAN, John R. DAVIS, Samuel TABER, all of New Bedford; incl. homestead farm, $2250.00; 16 acres at the Long plain, $444.50; salt marsh, $200.00; cedar swamp in Freetown, $150.00. <46:350> Account 7 May 1811; Paid to: **Gideon WOOD** for his wife **Thankfull,** $233.50; **Thomas WOOD,** $311.38.

BRISTOL COUNTY DEEDS: (re: Joseph TABER)

<2:207> - 5 Jan. 1696/7, Joseph TABER of Tiverton sells land at Tiverton.
<2:41> - 22 May 1697, Joseph TABER & wf Hannah of Tiverton sell land at Tiverton.
<6:216> - 19 June 1707, Joseph TABER of Tiverton to Philip TABER of Dartmouth, land at Tiverton.
<8:232> - 6 Mar. 1712, Joseph TABER, mason of Tiverton, to Philip TABER, cordwainer of Tiverton, land at Tiverton. Witnesses: Joseph TILLINGHAST, Ebenezer TABER.
<10:688>- 1 Feb. 1713/4, Joseph TABER, mason of Tiverton, to Ebenezer TABER, cordwainer of same, land at Tiverton. Witnesses: Joseph TILLINGHAST, Philip TABER.
<19:268>- 24 Feb. 1729/30, Joseph TABER, mason of Tiverton, to Ebenezer TABER, cordwainer of same land at Tiverton.

Will of **Joseph TABER,** yeoman of Dartmouth MA. <Bristol Co.PR>
<13:289>...dated 20 Dec. 1748...to **Lydia,** my dearly beloved wife ye use & improvement of my eastermost fire roome with ye two bed rooms adjoyning...two feather beds with ye furniture to each belonging, one iron pot, one kittle, one skillit, one joynt stool, one chist, one platter, four plaits, two basons, one warming pan, one meat tub, one washing tub, one large can, one pale, one bed pan, one great chear and two small ones, one side saddle, one crane, one pair of handirons, one slice & tonges, together with so many apples out of my orchard as she shall stand in need of for her own use; all ye particulars above mentioned to be for ye use of my said wife during ye time she remains my widow & does not remove from ye above said house roome to make elsewhere her home by carrying away said household goods...to my son **Benjamin TABER**...all my land and meadow being part of my homsted...together with all my salt marsh meadow upon ye island called Round Island, together with ye one third part of...cedar swamp at ye place called ye old Tarrkill way together with one half a cow and one third part of all my sheep...one eighth part of my orchard during ye term of seven years...he providing for his mother my wife one half ye milk of one cow and one third part of ten cord of wood at ye door...one third part of suteable souse for her meat, one third part of eight boshel of Indian corn, one third part of four boshel of rye, one third part of twelve pound of woll, one third part of six pound of flax, one third part of eighty pound of pork, one third part of forty pound of beef, one third part of one pair of new shoes, one third part of ten pound of tallow, one third part of two gallons of mollasses, one third part of one peck and half of salt...and perform the same yearly year by year and every year seasoneably during ye time she remains my widdow...And paying to his four sisters, viz: **Sarah MERITHEW, Elenor CRAPO, Elizabeth BROWNEL** and **Abigail BENNIT,** ye sum of seven pounds ten shillings each...within one year next after my decease...to my grandson **Antipas TABER** ye only surviveing son of my son **Amos TABER** dec'd, all that part of my homstead lying to ye eastward and northward...together with one third part of my lot of cedar swamp at Tarrkill way...he paying to his

two sisters, my granddaughters, **Hannah BENNIT** and **Rebeckah TABER** ye sum of twenty pounds each good bills of credet old tenure to be of eaqual value as said bills now are when he shall arive to ye age of twenty one years...To my son **Joseph TABER**...all ye remaining part of my homsted... one third part of ceder swamp at old Tarrkill way...one third part of all my sheep and one half a cow...he providing for his mother my wife...To my son **Peter TABER**...all my land lying between Accoshanut River and ye Country Road adjoyning to that land I conveyed to my son **Thomas TABER**, deceased, by deed...also one half of my salt meadow at ye hed/head of ye cove below Elnathan POPE's homsted together with all that my lot of ceder swamp at Rockway, together with ye use of one eighth part of my orchard...for seven years...he providing for his mother my wife...To my son **William TABER**...land near John SPOONER's ceder swamp...half my meadow...ceder swamp at Sacakaweams Pond...one quarter part of ye grist mill...all lands in Dartmouth...he providing for his mother my wife....and paying to my three daughters...ye sum of ten pounds...within three years next after my decease...; mentions lands on Coshanut River adjoining homestead of Christopher TURNER and ten acres disposed of to Nathan SPOONER which did belong to son **John TABER**, dec'd; son **Benjamin TABER**, executor. Witnesses: James CUSHMAN, Amaziah TABER, Stephen WEST. <13:293> Pr. & Inventory. <14:86> Account. <14:89> Account.

Will of **Joseph TABER**, yeoman of New Bedford MA. <Bristol Co.PR>
<34:92>...dated 6 Oct. 1795, mentions wf **Elizabeth**; youngest son **Nathaniel TABER** (under 21); eldest son **Archelins**(sp) **TABER**; sons **Elnathan TABER, Lewis TABER, Sanford TABER, Peleg TABER.**

Will of **Joseph TABER**, tailor of Pawtucket MA. <Bristol Co.PR>
<86:479>...dated 18 Apr. 1838. (no further details in files)

Will of **Benjamin TABER**, yeoman of Dartmouth MA. <Bristol Co.PR>
<27:87>...dated 1 9mth 1774, mentions wife; five sons **Joseph TABER** (executor), **Benjamin TABER, John TABER, Jeduthan TABER, Seth TABER**; three daus **Elizabeth TABER, Mary HAMMOND, Rebecca SEVERENCE.** Witnesses: Lewis TABER, Gideon DELANO, Bartholomew TABER. Pr. 7 May 1782.

Estate of **Benjamin TABER** of New Bedford MA. <Bristol Co.PR>
<56:447> Pr. 7 Mar. 1820, William TALLMAN of New Bedford, app'td admr. <56:460> Inventory taken 8 Mar. 1820; incl. house & land where he last dwelt, $1600.00; land on Prospect St., $2500.00; personal estate, $229.59. <56:465> Account, 10 Mar. 1820. <151:483> Letter, 7 Mar. 1820. <201:100> 10 Mar. 1820, personal estate insufficient to pay debts, therefore land to be sold. <59:439> 2nd Account 30 July 1822, of admr.; by order of court, land sold to Francis TABER for $1780.00; all land east of Water St. sold to Benjamin TABER for $2500.00; Paid to heirs, $56.18 each, viz: **Barnabas TABER, Francis TABER, Caleb & Susanna CONGDON, Daniel TABER.**

MICRO #30 OF 30

Will of **Joseph TABER** of Dartmouth MA. <Bristol Co.PR>
<22:220>...dated 25 Jan. 1772, mentions wf **Mary**; to son **William TABER**...homestead farm at Skipping Creek...he to provide for...my mother in law **Lydia TABER** yearly what I was ordered in my father's will; daus **Elisabeth TABER, Jemima TABER, Rubee BRIGHTMAN, Hannah ELDREDGE**; son **William**, executor. Witnesses: Joseph TABER 2d, Robert BENNIT Jr., Bartholomew TABER.

Will of **Mary TABER** widow of Joseph, of Dartmouth MA. <Bristol Co.PR>
...dated 3 5mth 1785, mentions daus **Elizabeth HART, Jemima TABER**; son **William TABER** (executor); daus **Hannah ELDREDGE, Rube BRIGHTMAN**; son in law **Edward ELDREDGE.** Witnesses: Judah SAMSON, Thomas SEVERENCE, Joseph TABER.

Estate of **Peter TOMSON** of Plympton MA. <Plymouth Co.PR #20625>
<6:9> Letter/Bond 29 Apr. 1731, **James TOMSON**, son of dec'd, app'td admr. Sureties: David BOSWORTH of Plympton & Jacob TOMSON of Middleboro. Witnesses: Barnabas SHURTLEFF, Edward WINSLOW. <6:91> Inventory taken 23 Sept. 1731 by Thomas TOMSON, David BOSWORTH, Jacob TOMSON; total £1509.14.4. <6:92> Division 23 Sept. 1731, to following heirs: widow **Sarah TOMSON**; eldest son **Peter TOMSON**; sons **James TOMSON, Joseph TOMSON**; dau **Sarah BOSWORTH** wf of Nehemiah, all of Plympton. <6:95> Release 23 Sept. 1731, of all demands by widow. Witnesses: Jacob TOMSON, Francis TOMSON.

Estate of **James TOMSON** of Halifax MA. <Plymouth Co.PR #20581>
<8:86> Letter/Bond 20/27 Dec. 1739, Joseph TOMSON app'td admr. Sureties: Thomas CROADE, James BARR/BARC. Witnesses: James WARREN, Benjamin WHITE. <8:180> Warrant 20 Dec. 1739. <8:226> Inventory taken 28 Apr. 1740 by Jacob TOMSON of Middleboro, Thomas TOMSON & Barnabas TOMSON of Halifax total, L869.1.2. <8:227> Agreement of heirs, 7 July 1740, brothers **Peter TOMSON** & **Joseph TOMSON** and sister **Sarah BOSWORTH** wf of Nehemiah, all of Halifax.

Estate of **Thomas TOMSON** of Halifax MA. <Plymouth Co.PR #20655>
<original> Bond 12 Jan. 1742, widow **Mary TOMSON** and Ruben TOMSON, both of Halifax, app'td admrs. Sureties: John MURDOCK, Ebenezer MORTON. Witnesses: Peres TILLSON, Edward WINSLOW. <9:22> Letter 29 Sept. 1742. <9:95> Inventory taken 13 July 1743 by Thomas CROADE, Ebenezer MORTON, Jacob TOMSON; total, £9878.11.1. <9:201> Warrant for appraisal, 12 Jan. 1742. <9:202> Warrant for division 13 July 1743. <9:202> Division 18 Dec. 1743 among following heirs, viz: widow **Mary TOMSON**; eldest son **Ruben TOMSON**; sons **Ebenezer TOMSON, Zebadiah TOMSON, Thomas TOMSON, Amasa TOMSON**; dau **Mary WATERMAN** wf of Sámuel.

Guardianship of Children of **Thomas TOMSON** of Halifax MA. <Plymouth Co.PR #20540> <9:104> Request 14 July 1743, of **Zebadiah TOMSON**, minor son, for appointment of his mother, **Mary TOMSON**, as guardian. Surety: Ebenezer MORTON. Witnesses: John WHITMAN, Peres TILSON. <original> Bond 14 July 1743, **Mary TOMSON** app'td gdn. of **Zebadiah.** <9:104> Letter/Bond 14 July 1743, **Mary TOMSON** app'td gdn. of **Ebenezer TOMSON**, minor son. Surety: Ebenezer MORTON. Witnesses: John WHITMAN, Peres TILLSON. <9:135> Request 14 July 1743, of **Ebenezer TOMSON** that his mother be app'td gdn. Witnesses: Reuben TOMSON, Amasa TOMSON.

Will of **Mary TOMSON**, widow of Thomas, of Halifax MA. <Plymouth Co.PR #20610> <28:182>...dated 1 May 1756, mentions sons **Reuben TOMSON, Thomas TOMSON, Amasa TOMSON, Ebenezer TOMSON** (executor), **Zebadiah TOMSON**; dau **Mary WATERMAN**, dec'd. Witnesses: Jno. COTTON, Hannah COTTON, Lucy DYRE. <28:183> Pr. 4 July 1781, **Ebenezer TOMSON** app'td admr. <28:521> Inventory taken 7 July 1781 by Moses INGLEE, Judah WOOD, Jacob TOMSON; total, ₤40.11.3.

Will of **Reuben TOMSON**, yeoman of Halifax MA. <Plymouth Co.PR #20631> <33:433>...dated 28 Nov. 1788, mentions wf **Sarah**; eldest dau **Deborah REED** wf of Abiah; daus **Lucy DREW** wf of Thomas & **Joanna TOMSON**; grandchildren **Reuben TOMSON, Abel TOMSON, Abigail NOICE** wf of Nehemiah, the children of my son **Andrew TOMSON** dec'd; **Judeth TOMSON**, widow of my son **Andrew.** <33:435> Letter/Bond 8 Oct. 1793, Isaac THOMSON app'td admr. Sureties: Thomas SPROAT, James TINKHAM. Witnesses: Joseph BUMP, Isaac LOTHROP. <33:490> Inventory taken 31 Oct. 1793 by Moses INGLEE, John WATERMAN, Zebadiah TOMSON; total, ₤1124.9.9. <35:160> Account 8 Oct. 1794; Paid to: Reuben TOMSON, Abel TOMSON, Ebenezer TOMSON 2d, Ignatius LORING, Ephraim TINKHAM, John TILSON, heirs of Andrew TOMSON dec'd, William WATERMAN, Joanna MORTON (dau of dec'd), & "others". <42:76> Warrant for division, 6 Oct. 1806, to Samuel S. STURTEVANT, Zebediah TOMSON & Timothy WOOD; estate set off to the widow **Sarah TOMSON, Lucy DREW,** heirs of **Andrew TOMSON, Joanna MORTON** wf of Nathaniel, heirs of **Deborah REED**, late of Abington dec'd. Division allowed 7 Apr. 1807. <45:155> Dower assigned 1 Nov. 1813 to **Judith TOMSON**, widow of **Andrew TOMSON**, according to the will of **Reuben**, by Nathaniel MORTON, Obadiah LYON & Zebadiah THOMSON.

Guardianship of Child of **Reuben TOMSON** of Halifax MA. <Plymouth Co.PR #20600> <20:465> Bond 4 Feb. 1771, **Reuben TOMSON** of Halifax app'td gdn. of his daughter **Lucy TOMSON**, minor above 15. Surety: Micah REED. Witnesses: David STOCKBRIDGE, Edward WINSLOW.

Estate of **Andrew TOMSON** of Halifax MA. <Plymouth Co.PR #20515> <23:16> Letter/Bond 5 July 1773, **Judith TOMSON**, widow, app'td admr. Sureties: John NOYES of Abington & Ephraim SOULE of Plimton. Witnesses: Briggs ALDEN, Edward WINSLOW. <21:570> Inventory taken 11 Sept. 1773 by Barnabas TOMSON, Ebenezer TOMSON, Jacob TOMSON; total, L222.1.9. <28:227> Account 26 Nov. 1781; Debts due from: William DREW, Jesse DUNBAR, Francis PERKINS, Deborah TORREY, Lemuel STURTEVANT, Jacob CHAPMAN, Samuel STURTEVANT, Cushing MITCHELL, Jesse STURTEVANT, Edmund SEARS Jr., Edward PACKARD; Debts paid to: Judah WOOD, Deborah TORREY, Gideon SOUL, John ADAMS, Ebenezer THOMSON Jr., Huldah FULLER, Tabitha PORTER, Rebecca FAXON, Isaiah FORREST, Jacob TOMSON, Barnabas TOMSON, Elisha FAXON. <45:155> Division 1 Nov. 1813, of estate of **Reuben TOMSON** to grandchildren, the children of son **Andrew TOMSON,** dec'd, viz: **Reuben TOMSON, Abel TOMSON** and **Abigail NOYES** wf of Nehemiah; one third set off to **Judith TOMSON,** widow of **Andrew,** land adjoining that set off to **Joanna MORTON** and **Lucy DREW.**

Guardianship of Children of **Andrew TOMSON** of Halifax MA. <Plymouth Co.PR #20504> <original> Request 2 Feb. 1779, of **Judith TOMSON** that James HERSEY be app'td gdn. of her children Letter/Bond 2 Feb. 1779, James HERSEY app'td gdn. of **Abigail TOMSON,** aged 13 <26:31>; **Abel TOMSON** aged 8 <26:32>; **Ruben TOMSON,** aged 10 <26:33>. Sureties: Eliab NOYES, William CHAPMAN. Witnesses: Elijah GILBERT, Ruth CUSHING.

Estate of **Thomas TOMSON** of Halifax MA. <Plymouth Co.PR #20657> <20:266> Bond 4 Oct. 1769, Ebenezer TOMSON of Halifax, app'td admr. Sureties: Moses INGLEE, Zadock BOSWORTH. Witnesses: Edward WINSLOW, Sarah WINSLOW. <20:309> Inventory taken 7 Dec. 1769 by Moses INGLEE, Jacob TOMSON, Hosea DUNBAR; total, ₤503.5.8. <20:487> Account 21 May 1771; Paid to: Jacob TOMSON Sr., Noah CUSHING, Mary STANDISH, Nathan TINKHAM, Amasa TOMSON, Submit HARLOW, Ichabod STANDISH, Jacob TOMSON Jr., Hosea DUNBAR, Barnabas TOMSON, Moses INGLEE, Judah WOOD, Abner KINGMAN, Zadock TOMSON, Robert FOSTER, Adam PORTER, George KEITH, David HATCH, Thomas CRODE, Isaac OTIS, Nathan PERKINS, Zebediah TOMSON, Abijah WOOD, Peter TOMSON Jr., Andrew TOMSON, Peter TOMSON Sr., John WATERMAN, Lemuel STURTEVANT, Mary LORING, Ignatius LORING, Micah ALLEN, Samuel PERRY, Josiah STURTEVANT Jr., Asa TOMSON. <21:170> Warrant to divide, 22 May 1771 to Zebedee CHANDLER, Moses INGLEE & Jacob TOMSON. Division 3 Aug. 1772, to following heirs: widow **Mary TOMSON**, children: **Asa TOMSON** (eldest son), **Mary TOMSON, Sarah TOMSON, Beza TOMSON, Loring TOMSON, Caleb TOMSON, Lois TOMSON, Seth TOMSON, Thomas TOMSON.**

Guardianship of Children of **Thomas TOMSON** of Halifax MA. <Plymouth Co.PR #20658> <20:542>...22 May 1771, **Mary TOMSON,** widow, app'td gdn. of **Loring TOMSON** & **Mary TOMSON** (above 14), **Caleb TOMSON** & **Beza TOMSON** (under 14), <20:543> **Sarah TOMSON** & **Thomas TOMSON** (under 14); <20:543> Caleb TOMSON app'td gdn. of **Lois TOMSON** & **Seth TOMSON** (under 14). Sureties & Witnesses: Ignatius LORING, Edward WINSLOW, Caleb TOMSON, Asa TOMSON, Joshua WHITE.

Estate of **Beza TOMSON** of Halifax MA. <Plymouth Co.PR #20523> <23:15> Letter/Bond 3 May 1773, Ignatius LORING app'td admr. Sureties: Caleb TOMSON, Joseph ALDEN Witnesses: Nathan CUSHING, Edward WINSLOW. <21:602> Inventory taken 17 June 1773 by Jacob TOMSON, Moses INGLEE, Daniel DUNBAR; total, ₤28.18.8. <24:192> Account 4 Mar. 1776, of admr., incl. paid

Mary TOMSON for boarding & clothing Abezer TOMSON one year; Asa TOMSON for funeral charges & for gravestones.

Will of **Zebediah TOMSON** of Halifax MA. <Plymouth Co.PR #20663>
<24:39>...dated 3 Aug. 1773, mentions sons **Thomas TOMSON** (under 21), **Zebadiah TOMSON, Moses TOMSON**; daus **Rebecca WOODS, Zerviah FULLER, Marcy TOMSON, Rachel TOMSON**; brother **Ebenezer TOMSON**, executor. Witnesses: Hosea DUNBAR, Jacob TOMSON, Zechariah EDDY Jr. <24:41> Letter 6 Nov. 1775, **Ebenezer TOMSON**, app'td admr. <24:42> Inventory taken 14 Nov. 1775 by Moses INGLEE, Jacob TOMSON, Judah WOOD; total, £748.4.0. <29:487> Division 6 Feb. 1786, by John WATERMAN Jr., Samuel S. STURTEVANT, Isaac WATERMAN; mentions land the dec'd bought of Blaney PHILLIPS, being the 3rd share in the 3rd Great lot in Majors Purchase which is to be divided among the four daughters, **Rebecca WOOD, "Mary" PARRIS, Rachel TOMSON & Zerviah FULLER.**

Guardianship of Children of **Zebediah TOMSON** of Halifax MA. <Plymouth Co.PR #20630>
<22:60,64> Letters/Bonds 4 Dec. 1775, Ephraim FULLER of Halifax app'td gdn. of **Rachel TOMSON** (age 12) **Moses TOMSON** (under 14). Sureties: Ebenezer TOMSON, Ephraim FULLER. Witnesses: Israel VINAL Jr., J. CUSHING. <26:488> Bond 3 Oct. 1785, Benjamin PARRIS of Halifax app'td gdn. of **Rachel TOMSOM** (above 14). Sureties: Zebadiah TOMSON, Samuel S. STURTEVANT. Witnesses: Elijah BISBE Jr., Isaac LOTHROP. <original> Citation 5 Sept. 1785 by Benjamin PARRIS to Ephraim FULLER, gdn. of **Rachel**, complaining that no account had been rendered to the great prejudice of the sd **Rachel**. <29:426> Account 5 Dec. 1785, Ephraim FULLER, gdn. of **Rachel**, received a legacy paid by **Thomas TOMSON**, also "to her grandmother's estate".

FOOTNOTES

<1> p.160, Adam WRIGHT[3] married 1st Sarah SOULE, 2nd Mehitable BARROW. In an attempt to find out when Sarah was last mentioned and Mehitable first mentioned, Bowman has cited several deeds with no data as follows, viz: <7:264> 15 June 1694, no wf ment.; <3:36> 1698, no wf ment.; <7:214> 21 Feb. 1707/8, 1st ment. of Mehitable (cited within). Two later deeds do not mention a wife, viz: <6:205> 19 May 1707 and <7:300> 1 Mar. 1707/8.
<2> p.164, Jacob COOKE's first wife was Damaris HOPKINS, dau of Mayflower passenger Stephen HOPKINS. MF5G (Hopkins) 6:13 states Damaris died after Jan. 1665/6 (the birth of her last child) and pre Nov. 1669 (Jacob's remarriage). This deed cited within narrows down this span - Damaris apparently survived the birth of her child Ruth in Jan. 1665/6 and died between 20 Oct. 1666 (this deed) and Nov. 1669.
<3> p.176, Transcribing records which deal with the family of Experience MITCHELL & Jane COOKE is difficult when contraversy exists surrounding the actual number of children Jane had. In my last book, **Mayflower Births & Deaths**, (2 Vols., 1992) it was necessary to change line of descent for a great many generations to show descent not from Jane COOKE but her husband Experience & his second wife Mary. Since this present volume does not indicate lines of descent, the reader should be aware that many of the records listed under Jane's sub-heading in the text may refer to the descendants of her husband and not herself.

As descendants of this family must find this issue extremely puzzling, as I myself do, I thought we might both benefit from a short discussion of the facts and the arguments put forth in the various genealogical publications over the years.

Facts: Gov. Bradford's account of the Mayflower passengers, written in Mar. 1651 <MD 1:161> states Francis Cooke had three children still living (son John is accounted for seperately). It is known that of his children, Jacob, Hester & Mary were living. Therefore, Jane must have been deceased by Mar. 1651. He also states that Francis has "seene his childrens, children, have children". The only one of his grandchildren to have children was Jane's daughter Elizabeth, who married in 1645 John Washburn. To have married this early, she must have been born by 1629, therefore Experience & Jane were probably married c1628 (certainly not earlier as Jane was single in the 1627 Cattle Division). Thru land deeds <Plymouth Co.Deeds 3:234; MD 3:104>, Thomas MITCHELL (b. c1631) has been proven to be a grandson of Francis Cooke & shared in the division of his estate; therefore, both Elizabeth & Thomas are accepted as children of Jane. The next child, Mary, was married in 1652, which places her birth at sometime before 1635; researchers suggest she could have been Jane's daughter. There is now a span of at least 6 years before the birth of Sarah, c1641 (ae 90 in 1731). A span of time such as this usually indicates stillborn or infant deaths, or a re-marriage. The remaining Mitchell children were Jacob, b. "perhaps" c1643; Edward, b. "perhaps" c1645; John, b. "probably" after 1650 (m. 1675) and Hannah, b. after 1657 (last child b.1702). With the exception to the reference to Elizabeth MITCHELL, Bradford did not mention the number of children Experience & Jane had.

Bowman states: "In the edition of Governor Bradford's History of Plimouth Plantation published by the Massachusetts Historical Society in 1912, it is stated <Vol.2, p.408> that Francis COOKE's daughter Jane married about 1628, Experience MITCHELL and died without issue. This error appeared first, I believe, in William T. DAVIS's Ancient Landmarks published in 1883, but the error was corrected in the appendix of the second edition published in 1899...in years of study of the original records I have not seen an item which seemed to indicate that Experience MITCHELL's second wife Mary was the mother of any of his children."

Around the same time (1936) appeared an article in TAG 12:193-99, "Gaining Experience - A Problem In The Mitchell Family, by Merton T. Goodrich. This article discusses the problem in identifying Thomas MITCHELL of Block Island, not with the identification of Experience & Jane's children as one might suspect from the title. In it, Mr. Goodrich lists the eight children of Experience as "his children all by his first wife".

In 1973, "Comments On The Two Wives Of Experience Mitchell Of Plymouth, Mass." appeared in the NEHGR 127:94-95, written by John B. Threlfall. He states that Thomas & Elizabeth and perhaps Mary were the only children of Jane. The only explanation given for the remaining children is "not one of the later children bore a Cooke name...except perhaps Jacob".

In 1983, "Some Descendants of Francis Cooke, Mayflower Passenger" appeared in MQ 49:130-34, written by Barbara L. Merrick. The only discussion of the remaining Mitchell children is that of Hannah who married Joseph Hayward and had children as late as 1702, therefore she must have been born after 1652 when Jane was deceased. It further states that Bradford "did not mention the Mitchell "encrease" with an exact number because he may have been uncertain just how many children Jane (Cooke) Mitchell had borne prior to her death".

About the same time as the above article, came "Not All The Children Of Experience Mitchell Are Mayflower Descendants" by Robert S. Wakefield, F.A.S.G., published in TAG 59:28-31. He states, "The fact that Bradford forgot to include Jane's children in the count suggests she had been dead some time". He goes on to state that the strongest evidence that Jane had few children is in the fact that only son Thomas shared in the division of Francis Cooke's estate, and although daughter Elizabeth was not included, she had been married for over 20 years and had probably been provided for during Francis' lifetime. Mr. Wakefield concedes that Mary could have been Jane's daughter, while Hannah clearly was not.

In 1986, came "Francis Cooke of the Mayflower: Four Generations", by Ralph V. Wood, Jr. Mr. Wood reiterates that Thomas & Elizabeth are Jane's daughters and Hannah is not, and states only that "there is uncertainty as to the identity of the mother for some of the Mitchell children".

In 1987, "Mayflower Families In Progress: Francis Cooke of the Mayflower And His Descendants for Four Generations", by Robert S.Wakefield and Ralph V. Wood, Jr., repeats the statements in the above work by Mr. Wood.

Thus, the uncertainty began in 1651 with Gov. Bradford who recorded the five grandchildren of Francis Cooke by his other children, but did not include the number of Jane's children. His reference to Francis Cooke having three children still living, tells us Jane is deceased by 1651. The fact that Hannah Mitchell must have been born after 1651 and therefore could not have been Jane's daughter, starts the wheels turning - if one child wasn't Jane's then she was obviously not the mother of all of Experience's children - how many more have been wrongly attributed to her? Of course, we can also say, how many children have been wrongly taken away from Jane? With the exception of Hannah, there is no evidence to suggest that Jane was not the mother of Mary, Sarah, Jacob, Edward & John. However, it must also be said that there is just not enough evidence to prove she was. Without her date of death, or the date of Experience's remarriage to his 2nd wife Mary, we may never know if some of her children have been wrongly disinherited of their Cooke ancestry.

<4> p.207, Joseph's granddaughter, Alice ALGAR/ALGER, was born Patience ALGER, 20 Sept. 1713 <MD 15:47>, but was renamed Aice after the death of her mother Alice (Hayward) ALGER, 30 Jan. 1715/6 <MD 15:47>.

<5> p.231, See p.232 for an explanation of the guardian.

==

==

EDWARD DOTY/DOTEN

MICRO #1 OF 6

John ROUSE of Marshfield MA. <Plymouth Co.Deeds 7:35>
...6 Mar. 1705/6...John ROUSE, aged 62 years and upwards Testifieth and Saith that between 30 and forty years agoe I did often frequent ye gurnet & stage point and ye Gurnet Meadoe etc. and to the best of my judgment all along ye south west side of ye stage point between sd point & ye Gurnet creek did not grow so much salt grass or sedge in a year as would make one cook of hey.

John ROUSE of Marshfield MA to **Abraham HOWLAND** of Duxborough MA. <Plymouth Co.Deeds 33:151>
...16 Apr. 1694, John ROUSE, shoemaker with consent of wf Elizabeth, for and in consideration of the good will & affection we bear to Abraham HOWLAND late of Duxborough...who hath for divers years performed good and faithfull service to us and is also under engagement yet to continue the like service to us both or either of us if our lives and his life also be continued until the third day of April 1696 come & be complete...give to him half share of upland in Sippican which John received in exchange from William PAYBODY of Little Compton. Rec. 17 June 1740.

Samuel HOWLAND of Freetown MA to **Abraham HOWLAND.** <Plymouth Co.Deeds 33:151>
...30 Dec. 1698, Samuel HOWLAND, yeoman, for love & affection, give to son Abraham HOWLAND half of the 14th lot of meadow at Mattapoisett in Rochester. Rec. 17 June 1740.

John ROUSE of Marshfield MA to **Abraham HOWLAND** of same. <Plymouth Co.Deeds 33:151>
...3 May 1705, John ROUSE, cordwainer, for £5 sells to Abraham HOWLAND, husbandman...all his meadow in Rochester and all rights to future division. Wf Elizabeth ROUSE releases dower. Rec. 17 June 1740.

PLYMOUTH COUNTY PROBATE: (re: DOTY/DOTEN)

1689	Edward	Plymouth		#6619, 1:53,251 <MD 5:216>
1695	Samuel et al	Plymouth		#6630, 1:118,208
1701	John	Plymouth		#6623, 1:341,342,343 <MD 6:78>
1701	Martha et al	Plymouth		#6626, 1:139;3:30,265;4:258
1721	Thomas	Cape Cod		#6631, 4:316
1721	Thomas	Cape Cod		#6632, 4:286
1724	Isaac	Plymouth		#6621, 4:398,449,456;5:87;6:143;7:183,186
1730	Jabez et al	Plymouth		#6586, 5:677,678 <MD 25:164>
1730	Mary et al	Plymouth		#6599, 5:677,679,680 <MD 25:164>
1734	Joseph	Rochester		#6624
1738	Neviah(sp)	Plymouth		#6602, 7:455;8:65 <MD 25:164>
1740	Samuel	Plymouth		#6629, 8:189,270
1740	Isaac	Wareham		#6622, 8:188
1747	Jacob	Plymouth		#6587, 10:401,449,450;12:463;13:98
1747	John	Plympton		#6593, 10:452,453,472,473;11:73,287 <MD 20:27>
1749	John	Plympton		#6594, 11:185;12:102,103,242
1749	Hannah et al	Plymp or Plym		#6584, 11:113;12:460,465
1750	Nathaniel	Plympton		#6600, 11:371
1754	Elisha	Plymouth		#6577, 13:312,314,371 <MD 19:176>
1754	Hannah	Plymouth		#6581, 13:292 <MD 20:30>
1759	Barnabas	Rochester		#6618, 15:190,191
1763	Samuel Jr.	Plymouth		#6606, 16:516;17:107;19:16
1765	Edward	Plympton		#6573, 17:142;19:200,258,340
1770	Isaac	Plymouth		#6585, 20:367;39:188,443
1771	Josiah	Plymouth		#6597, 20:483
1776	Edward Jr.	Rochester		#6620, 23:107;24:330,332;28:442
1785	Jacob	Kingston		#6588, 27:189;29:389;30:7,8
1786	James	Plymouth		#6589, 30:10,11,324-6;34:382;40:61-2;53:419
1786	Ebenezer	Plympton		#6572, 27:219;30:123,124;31:133;35:356
1787	Edward	Plympton		#6574, 26:464
1797	James Jr.	Plymouth		#6590, 34:95
1797	John	Plymouth		#6595, 32:78
1799	Hannah	Plymouth		#6582, 34:202;37:137,258
1801	Nathaniel	Plymouth	adm.	#6601, 34:272;38:291
1802	Stephen	Plymouth	adm.	#6610, 34:334;40:70;53:420
1804	Susanna	Plymouth	gdn.	#6614, 32:245
1805	Abigail	Plymouth	adm.	#6569
1805	Edward	Plymouth	adm.	#6575, 39:29;42:250;44:258,439;48:44
1805	Hannah	Kingston	adm.	#6583, 34:395;42:327
1808	Deborah & Mary	Plym/Carver	gdn.	#6571, 32:331;41:303;50:482,505;59:4
1813	William	Plymouth	will	#6615, 45:125,126,129
1817	James	Plymouth	will	#6591, 49:25,226,227

PLYMOUTH COUNTY PROBATES, cont-d: (re: DOTY/DOTEN)

1819	Edward	Plymouth	gdn.	#6576, 50:94;51:32;54:164;57:513;58:537;60:484; 64:447;67:216
1820	Nathaniel	Wareham	adm.	#6627, 46:416;53:136,137,164,343-5;56:55,57
1826	Nathaniel et al	Wareham	gdn.	#6628, 51:327;60:132
1828	Elisha	Plymouth	adm.	#6578, 61:207;62:271;66:156,292,417;67:107
1831	Stephen	Plymouth	will	#6611, 65:177;70:111;72:365,366;77:113
1850	Samuel 2d	Plymouth	adm.	#6607, 3:231**P**;8:103**W**;12:258**C**;93:41;94:128;94:559 & 561
1850	Joseph	Rochester	adm.	#6625, 12:201**C**

Estate of **Edward DOTEN** of Plymouth MA. <Plymouth Co.PR #6575>
<39:29> Letter/Bond 2 Nov. 1805, Ebenezer DOTEN of Carver, app'td admr. Sureties: Samuel LUCAS, Jr. & Benjamin RANSOM of Carver. Witnesses: Lucy LOTHROP, Isaac LOTHROP. <42:250> Notice of appointment, 10 Apr. 1806 & 1 Jan. 1807. <42:250> Inventory taken 17 May 1806 by Nehemiah COBB, Esq Samuel LUCAS, Benjamin RANSOM, all of Carver. <44:258> Dower assigned 2 Apr. 1812, by Samuel LUCAS, Benjamin RANSOM, Joshua COLE, to late widow, **Deborah COBB**, now wf of Nathan COBB 2d; mentions land bounded by land of Ebenezer DOTEN, HAMMOND, Isaac SHERMAN & Doten's Meadows. <44:439> Account 1 Jan. 1813 of admr.; Paid to: Dr. THATCHER, Dr. HAYWARD, Levi WHITING. <48:448> Division 21 Apr. 1817, to children **Deborah Cobb DOTTEN** and **Polly/Marah Edward DOTEN**; mentions land bounded by Spring hill swamp & Doten's meadow and land of Rufus SHERMAN, Ebenezer DOTEN, John SHERMAN, Benjamin RANSOM, Isaac SHERMAN.

Guardianship of Children of **Edward DOTEN**, yeoman of Plymouth MA. <Plymouth Co.PR #6571>
<32:331> Letter/Bond 20 Jan. 1808, widow **Deborah DOTEN** of Carver, app'td gdn. of **Deborah DOTEN** & **Mary DOTEN**, both under 14. Sureties: Ebenezer DOTEN, yeoman & Joshua COLE, gent., both of Carver. Witnesses: Marcy DOTEN, Zilpah LUCAS. <original> Certificate of choice 12 Apr. 1817, **Deborah Cobb DOTEN** makes choice of her father in law <step-father>, **Nathan COBB**, to be her guardian. Bond 12 Apr. 1817 of **Nathan COBB**, housewright of Carver, as guardian of **Deborah Cobb DOTEN** (above 14) and **Polly Edward(s) DOTEN** (under 14). Sureties: Nehemiah COBB, Thomas COBB, both of Carver. Witnesses: Frederick COBB, Melissa COBB. <41:303> Letter of gdn. 12 Apr. 1817. <50:482> Account 15 Jan. 1820 of **Nathan COBB**, gdn. of **Deborah C. DOTEN** since **Deborah C. BARROWS**. <50:505> Notice of sale 21 May 1817, of **Deborah's** share in father's estate. <59:47> Account 19 Feb. 1825, of gdn. of **Mary E. DOTEN.**

Estate of **Hannah DOTEN**, spinster of Kingston MA. <Plymouth Co.PR #6583>
<34:395> Letter/Bond 16 Mar. 1805, Ebenezer DOTEN, yeoman of Carver, app'td admr. Sureties: Benjamin RANSOM & Calvin HOWLAND of Carver. <42:327> Notice 16 Mar. 1805. <original> Inventory taken 25 Mar. 1805 by Seth COBB, John GRAY, John FULLER, all of Kingston; total personal estate, $184.

Estate of **Stephen DOTEN**, yeoman of Plymouth MA. <Plymouth Co.PR #6610>
<34:334> Letter/Bond 29 Nov. 1802, Stephen DOTEN, gent. of Plymouth, app'td admr. Sureties: John DOTEN & Stephen DOTEN Jr., both of Plymouth. Witnesses: Silvanus FINNEY, Rebeckah MORTON. <original> Warrant & Inventory, 29 Nov. 1802, appraisers app'td, viz: Abner BARTLETT, Esq., Silvanus FINNEY, Solomon FINNEY, all of Plymouth; real estate incl. 80 acres improved land & 100 acres woodland, $944.00; personal estate incl. pew in Mr. HOVEY's meeting house. <40:70> Dower assigned 7 May 1804 to widow **Jane DOTEN**, by Abner BARTLETT, Esq., Thomas MORTON Jr., Sylvanus FINNEY, all of Plymouth; mentions land abutted by land of Elkanah FINNEY, Deacon BLACKMER, HOLMES, Paul DOTEN and pew in Monument Ponds meeting house. <53:420> Account 21 May 1821, of admr.; mentions cash due from Ephraim SPOONER and James DOTEN.

Estate of **Nathaniel DOTEN**, yeoman of Plymouth MA. <Plymouth Co.PR #6601>
<34:272> Letter/Bond 13 Apr. 1801, Nathaniel DOTEN, mariner of Plymouth, app'td admr. Sureties: Ichabod HOLMES Jr., trader & Samuel BURBANK, taylor, both of Plymouth. Witnesses: Frederick HARVEY, John Boies THOMAS. <original> Warrant & Inventory 13 Apr. 1801, appraisers Ichabod HOLMES Jr Solomon CHURCHILL, Benjamin WARREN, all of Plymouth; total real estate, Ł150; total estate, Ł179. <original> Insolvency, 10 Apr. 180(-), by **Nathaniel DOTEN**, admr. on his father's estate. <39:291> Dower & Partition, 31 Jan. 1803, of the estate from that of John RIDER & Mercy DOTEN, widow of dec'd, the share of the dec'd being five sevenths part of the house & lot in Plymouth, where he last dwelt, sd land abutted by land of William STEPHEN, Ebenezer RIDER and land lately of Lothrop TURNER's wf.

Guardianship of Child of **James DOTEN Jr.**, yeoman of Plymouth MA. <Plymouth Co.PR #6614>
<32:245> Letter/Bond 12 Oct. 1804, Joshua TORREY, cordwainer of Plymouth, app'td gdn. Sureties: Benjamin WARREN, gent., Josiah DIMAN, yeoman, both of Plymouth. Witness: Job COBB Jr.

Estate of **Abigail DOTEN**, spinster of Plymouth MA. <Plymouth Co.PR #6569>
<34:395> Letter/Bond 25 Mar. 1805, William DOTEN, mariner of Plymouth, app'td admr. Sureties: Barnabas CHURCHILL, trader & Jonathan TUFTS, yeoman, both of Plymouth.

Will of **William DOTEN**, yeoman of Plymouth MA. <Plymouth Co.PR #6615>
<45:125>...dated 29 Sept. 1813, mentions grandchildren **Martha CHURCHILL, Betsey Bartlett CHURCHILL**, to receive $10.00 each; to dau **Mary DOTEN**, half of remainder, the other half to the remainder of our children, viz: mine & my late wife's children; James SPOONER, executor. <45:126> Bond 18 Oct. 1813, of James SPOONER, trader of Plymouth. Sureties: Thomas SPOONER, Barnabas OTIS, both

of Plymouth. <45:129> Inventory, 18 Oct. 1813, Barnabas OTIS & Thomas SPOONER app'td to appraise; incl. half of dwelling house on High or Thatcher St., $750.00 and one quarter ticket #2378 P.B. Lottery. <45:129> Notice of appointment of James SPOONER executor, 20 Oct. 1813.

Guardianship of **Edward DOTEN**, sailmaker of Plymouth MA. <Plymouth Co.PR #6576>
<50:94> Complaint 1 Mar. 1819, of Selectmen of Plymouth, that **Edward DOTEN**...by excessive drinking etc., asks for appointment of a guardian...adjudged a spendthrift 15 Mar. 1819. <51:32> Bond/Letter 15 Mar. 1819, Nathan HAYWARD, Esq. of Plymouth app'td gdn. Sureties: Henry WARREN, William S. RUSSELL. Witnesses: James T. HAYWARD, Richard WARREN. <54:164> Account 31 Dec. 1821, of Nathaniel HAYWARD as gdn. of **Edward DOTEN**, a United States Pensioner. <57:513> Account, 31 Dec. 1823. <58:537> Account, 1 Jan. 1825. <60:484> Account, 1 July 1826. <64:447> Account, 1 Jan. 1828. <67:216> Account Jan. 1829, of Nathan HAYWARD, gdn. of **Edward DOTEN**, deceased; mentions sundries furnished to widow.

Estate of **Nathaniel DOTY**, housewright of Wareham MA. <Plymouth Co.PR #6627>
<46:416> Letter/Bond 19 June 1820, widow **Olive DOTY** app'td admx. Sureties: Jeduthan DOTY, cordwainer of Wareham & John H. BRADFORD, inn holder of Plymouth. <53:136> Warrant to appraise, 19 June 1820, to Ichabod LEONARD, Eliphalet BUMPUS & Samuel ELLIS, all of Wareham. <53:137> Insolvency 18 Sept. 1820. <53:344> Appointment, 18 Sept. 1820, of Commissioners, Ichabod LEONARD & Peter SMITH. <53:136> Inventory taken 14 Sept. 1820 by Ichabod LEONARD, Eliphalet BUMPUS & Samuel ELLIS; real estate totals $1750.00. <53:137> Allowance to widow, 18 Sept. 1820. <53:164> Order of notice of **Olive DOTY**'s appointment, 8 Nov. 1820. <53:343> Petition to sell real estate granted 3 Apr. 1821 to widow, she having "notified all persons interested as directed, they being my children & minors". <53:345> List of Claims 15 Mar. 1821: Peter SMITH, David FEARING's estate; William FEARING, Hallet SWIFT, Ezra & Hallet SWIFT, Josiah BOURNE, Timothy CROCKER, David SWIFT, Eliphalet BUMPUS, Dr. Peter MACKIE, Curtis TOBEY, Jeduthan DOTY, Benjamin FEARING, Rowland LEONARD, Isaac CUSHMAN, Thomas & William SAVERY, Capt. Asa SWIFT, Col. Bartlett MURDOCK, Hercules WESTON, Obed BOWLS; total $1442.12. <53:344> License to sell real estate granted to admx. 16 Apr. 1821. <56:55> Warrant 16 Apr. 1821, to Benjamin FEARING, Esq., Peter SMITH & Ichabod LEONARD, freeholders of Wareham, to assign dower to widow. <original> Bond 16 Apr. 1821, of widow, to secure sale. Sureties: Benjamin FEARING of Wareham & Henry HOLLIS of Plymouth. <56:57> Account 21 May 1822. <56:56> Dower assigned 15 May 1821. <original> Notice of sale by admx., 11 Sept. 1821. Witness: Rosina DOTY.

Guardianship of Children of **Nathaniel DOTY**, housewright of Wareham MA. <Plymouth Co.PR #6628>
<original> Choice of guardian, 17 Feb. 1826, **Nathaniel DOTY** & **Cyrus DOTY**, minors above 14, made choice of Jeduthan DOTY, cordwainer of Wareham. <51:327> Letter/Bond 20 Feb. 1826 of Jeduthan DOTY, gdn. of **Nathaniel DOTY** & **Cyrus DOTY** (above 14) and **Calvin DOTY, Bethiah DOTY & Parnam DOTY** (under 14). Sureties: Peter SMITH, Timothy SAVERY, both of Wareham. <60:132> Order to sell personal estate of children, 20 Feb. 1826.

Estate of **Elisha DOTEN**, yeoman of Plymouth MA. <Plymouth Co.PR #6578>
<original> Refusal, 16 June 1828, of **Jan/Jane DOTEN**, to administer her husband's estate; requests Andrew MACKIE be app'td. <61:207> Letter/Bond 16 June 1828, Andrew MACKIE, Physician of Plymouth appointed admr. Sureties: Rosseter COTTON, John THOMAS, both of Plymouth. <66:156> Insolvency, 16 June 1828. <67:107> List of debts, 16 Mar. 1827: William HOLMES, Crosby LUCE, Ezra SWIFT, Sally WARREN, John S. HAYWARD, William M. JACKSON, William W. MORTON, John PIERCE Jr., Andrew MACKIE, Susan TORREY, Ann COBB, Henry MORTON, William SWIFT, Zacheus BARTLETT. <62:271> Order of notice of admr., 16 June 1828. <66:292> Inventory taken 16 June 1828 by Ezra FINNEY, Belcher MANTER & William BURGESS, all of Plymouth; total estate, $372.30. <66:417> Petition to sell real estate, 15 Dec. 1828. <67:107> Account 16 Mar. 1829, of admr.; Paid to: James MORTON Jr., Benjamin DREW, L. BROWN, A. DANFORTH, A. MACKIE & Jane DOTEN; Received from: A. DANFORTH, William MANTER.

Estate of **Samuel DOTEN 2d**, housewright of Plymouth MA. <Plymouth Co.PR #6607>
<original> Request, 28 Nov. 1850, of widow **Sally B. DOTEN** & heirs at law **Edward DOTEN & Hannah THRASHER**, that Timothy GORDON of Plymouth be app'td admr. <12:258> Bond/Letter 2 Dec. 1850, Timothy GORDON app'td admr. Sureties: J.H. LOUD, William R. SEVER. <93:41> Inventory taken 2 Dec. 1850 by Eleazer S. BARTLETT, Winslow DREW & Comer WESTON Jr.; total real estate, $200.00; total personal estate, $207.92. <8:103> Notice. <94:128> Insolvency, 2d Mon. Apr. 1852. <3:231> Petition to sell real estate, granted 14 Sept. 1852. <94:559> List of Claims: S. & T.B. SHERMAN, George SIMMONS Jr., John BATTLES, John WASHBURN, SAVERY & MORTON, Nathan T. HOSKINS, William B. TRIBBLE, Timothy GORDON. <94:561> Account of admr. 1st Mon. Dec. 1852; incl. sums received for rent from Mrs. HARVEY, William B. TRIBBLE, L.S.B. BARROWS and F.W. RAY; cash received from John CHURCHILL for deceased's right of redemption in real estate; Paid to: Edward ROBBINS, Winslow DREW, James THURBER and the widow.

Estate of **Joseph DOTY** of Rochester MA. <Plymouth Co.PR #6625>
<12:201> Petition, 8 May 1850, of Elias S. CHASE of Rochester, that he is requested by the heirs at law to administer estate. Letter/Bond of admr. 8 May 1850. Sureties: William P. MENDELL, Theophilus KING, both of Rochester.

Will of **Stephen DOTEN** of Plymouth MA. <Plymouth Co.PR #6611>
<70:111>...dated 23 Apr. 1830, mentions wf **Abigail**; daus **Mary DOTEN, Esther DOTEN**; sons **Joseph DOTY, Stephen DOTEN**; grandson **James Isdell CLARK**; son **Paul DOTEN**; grandchildren **Samuel W. LEWIS, Jesse J.H. LEWIS & Marcia LEWIS**. Witnesses: William B. THOMAS, Roland E. COTTON, Rosseter COTTON. <original> Bond 16 May 1831, of **Stephen DOTEN**, yeoman, admr. Sureties: William W. MORTON, Stephen

DOTEN Jr., all of Plymouth. <65:177> Notice 16 May 1831, **Stephen DOTEN**, executor. <72:365> Inventory taken by Lemuel LEACH, Elkanah FINNEY & Ichabod MORTON, all of Plymouth; total real estate, $3230.00; total personal estate, $201.40; sworn to 13 Aug. 1832 by exr. <72:366> Account 13 Aug. 1832; Received from: Nathan HOWLAND, Ichabod HOWLAND, Thomas MANTER, Caleb FINNEY; Paid to: Caleb BATTLES, Jeroboam SWIFT, Amasa CLARK, Nathaniel HOLMES, A. DANFORTH, L. BROWN, N. HARLOW, Nathan WHITING, I. MORTON, E. MORTON. <77:133> 2d Account of exr., 13 Apr. 1835.

Estate of **Hannah DOTEN**, spinster of Plymouth MA. <Plymouth Co.PR #6582>
<34:202> Letter/Bond 23 Oct. 1799, Nathaniel SMITH of Bowdoin, Lincoln co., app'd admr. Sureties: Stephen SAMPSON, Ephraim SPOONER. Witnesses: Isaac LOTHROP, Nathaniel LOTHROP. <37:137> Inventory taken 31 Oct. 1799 by Stephen SAMPSON, Benjamin DREW & Ephraim SPOONER; incl. 71 acres wood land in Freetown; total $616.50. <37:137> Account 5 June 1800 of admr.; Received from: Elkanah WATSON.

DESIRE DOTY[2] (Edward[1])

Will of **Desire STANDISH** of Marshfield MA. <MD 12:48>
...dated 30 July 1723, mentions sons **William SHERMAN** (eldest son), **Ebenezer SHERMAN, Israel HOLMES, John HOLMES, Thomas STANDISH, Ichabod STANDISH**; daus **Hannah RING, Experience STANDISH, Desire WESTON**; granddaughter **Desire WORMWALL.**

Will of **Ebenezer SHERMAN**, laborer of Marshfield MA. <Plymouth Co.PR>
<15:263>...dated 10 Jan. 1759...to **Ebenezer SHERMAN** (2d son), homestead farm & salt meadow in Marshfield bought from Thomas BOURN...to **Elisha SHERMAN** (youngest son), 23 acres in Marshfield bought from Joseph PHILLIPS...to **William SHERMAN** (eldest son), one acre salt meadow...sons **Robert SHERMAN, John SHERMAN**...to daughters **Rachel JOYCE, Elisabeth WITHERELL, Abigail CARVER & Barshaba WALKER**, Ł6.13s4d to be paid by son **Ebenezer** within twelve months...to wf **Barshaba** one of my best cowes and one third part of my moveables; sons **William & Elisha**, executors. Witnesses: Aaron SOULE, John HOLMES, Lem FORD. <15:264> Objections to probate, 14 Feb. 1759. <15:265> Pr. 31 Mar. 1759. <15:125> Inventory taken 6 Apr. 1759 by Kenelm BAKER, Israel HATCH, Nehemiah THOMAS; total, Ł3182.6.2. old tenor. <15:149> Dower set off 11 Apr. 1759 to widow. <15:576> Account, 13 Aug. 1760. <16:491> Division 26 May 1760 of salt marsh at Green Harbor by **William, Ebenezer, Robert John & Elisha SHERMAN**. Ack. by all five, 9 Feb. 1761.

Will of **Elisha SHERMAN**, yeoman of Marshfield MA. <Plymouth Co.PR>
<36:71>...dated 5 Jan. 1797...to wf **Lydia**, half of personal & real estate...to son **Abiel SHERMAN**, the farm & buildings where I now live & the farm & buildings where he now lives; wood lots bought of William ROGERS, Jedediah EAMES & Seth EWELL; 6 acres salt marsh adjoining Little's Island; 3 acre salt marsh adjoining land of Capt. William THOMAS; pew in Rev. Elijah LEONARD's meeting house...to son **Ebenezer SHERMAN**, the farm & buildings, wood land & salt marsh that I bought of Thomas EAMES; 2 acre salt marsh in Bourne's Cove...to grandson **Alanson CARVER**, the farm & buildings bought of Zephaniah DECROW & Jeremiah HATCH; 6 acre salt marsh adjoining land of William MACOMBER; 3 acre salt marsh bought of Isaac BISBE; 1 acre cedar swamp adjoining highway from Pembroke to Bridgewater; pew in Baptist meeting house, he paying what remains not paid towards said pew...my sd grandson pay unto **Zibe CARVER, Israel CARVER Jr., Elisha CARVER & Lydia CARVER**, one dollar to each of them out of what I have given to him. Witnesses: Thomas JOYCE, Amos JONES, William MACOMBER. <36:72> Pr. 6 Mar. 1797.

Will of **Ebenezer SHERMAN**, yeoman of Marshfield MA. <Plymouth Co.PR>
<77:130>...dated 13 June 1828, mentions sons **Aaron SHERMAN, Elisha SHERMAN, Ebenezer SHERMAN, Jr.** daus **Sarah PALMER** wf of Elijah, **Lydia SHERMAN, Mary HATCH** widow of Jonathan Jr., **Betsey Winslow DAMON** wf of Lincoln and **Bulah DAMON** wf of Amos. <77:131> Pr. 13 Apr. 1835. <77:138> Inventory taken 6 Apr. 1835.

Estate of **Josiah WORMALL**, yeoman of Duxbury MA. <Plymouth Co.PR #23493>
<7:449> Letter/Bond 3 Nov. 1738, widow **Grace WORMALL** app'td admx. Sureties: John CHANDLER, yeoman & Jethro SPRAGUE, taylor, both of Duxbury. Witnesses: John BISBE, Caleb OLDHAM. <7:449> Inventory taken 6 Nov. 1738 by George PARTRIDGE, Philip DILANO, Samuel SPRAGUE; homestead, Ł260 and wood lot, Ł40. <8:3> 14 Nov. 1738, best bed & furniture set off to widow. <8:238> Account 7 Apr. 1740; Paid to: John SAMSON, Ichabod WORMAL, Samuel WORMAL, Sarah ROGERS, Ebenezer BARTLETT, Ebenezer WORMAL, Joseph BREWSTER, Dr. LEBARON, Nathaniel DUNHAM, Jonathan DELANOE, John PRIOR, Benjamin PRIOR Jr., John WADSWORTH Jr., William BREWSTER, Amaziah DELANOE, Samuel WESTON, Zerviah CHANDLER, Col. WINSLOW, Mr. COTTON, Benjamin PETERSON, Ichabod WADSWORTH, Joshua DELANOE, Joshua BREWSTER, Jethro SPRAGUE, Priscilla STANDISH, Miles STANDISH, Dr. Eleazer HARLOW, Joshua SOUL, Moses SOUL, John CRANDON, George PARTRIDGE, Isaac KEEN Jr., Francis ADAMS, Isaac LOTHROP Jr., Elisha DOTY Jr., Joshua LORING, Joshua DELANOE and Samuel SPRAGUE as Town Trustees, "a sheet for ye burial Patience OLDHAM", Jethro SPRAGUE, Isaac LITTLE of Plymouth; total, Ł139.9s3d; Due from: Samuel TILDEN; total personal estate, Ł170.19s2d. <8:239> Dower to widow, 7 July 1740, by Edward ARNOLD, Benjamin ALDEN, Joseph BREWSTER, John SAMSON & Nathaniel LORING.

Will of **William SHERMAN** of Marshfield MA. <Plymouth Co.PR #18199>
<8:172>...dated 30 Nov. 1739, mentions dau **Sarah HALL** wf of Adam; children of my dau **Thankful POLDEN** dec'd, viz: **John POLDEN** (under 21) & **Mary POLDEN** (under 18); daus **Mary SHERMAN, Abigail SHERMAN**. Witnesses: Samuel SHARMAN/SHERMAN, Garshom SHERMAN, Arthur HOWLAND. <8:174> Pr. 7 Apr.

1740. <8:351> Inventory, 17 Apr. 1740.

Adam HALL et al of Marshfield MA to **Cornelius WHITE Jr.** <Plymouth Co.Deeds 36:144>
...28 Mar. 1744, Adam & Sarah HALL and Mary SHERMAN & Abigail SHERMAN, spinsters, sell seven eighths of an acre to Cornelius WHITE Jr. Ack. same day.

Adam & Sarah HALL of Marshfield MA and **Mary & Abigail SHERMAN** of same. <Plymouth Co.Deeds 54:74>
...19 Apr. 1754, An agreement between Adam HALL, yeoman & wf Sarah of the one part and Mary SHERMAN & Abigail SHERMAN, spinsters, of the other part...whereas we...are owners...of a certain farm or tract of land and salt meadow in Marshfield that came to us by our honoured Father Mr. William SHERMAN late of Marshfield, dec'd...we have agreed to divide the same...Ack. 1758.

Mary & Abigail SHERMAN of Marshfield MA to **Nathaniel PHILLIPS** of same. <Plymouth Co.Deeds 45:30>
...26 May 1758, Mary SHERMAN & Abigail SHERMAN, spinsters, sell to Nathaniel PHILLIPS, gent... eleven acres of upland in Marshfield bounded by land of Samuel SHERMAN, Cornelius WHITE & Adam HALL. Ack. same day.

Mary & Abigail SHERMAN of Marshfield MA to **Ignatius SHERMAN** of same. <Plymouth Co.Deeds 50:32>
...30 May 1765, Mary SHEARMAN/SHERMAN & Abigail SHEARMAN/SHERMAN, spinsters, sell to Ignatius SHEARMAN/SHERMAN, yeoman...one quarter & half quarter of land bounded by land of Ignatius TOMSON, M. & A. SHERMAN and Lieut. HALL's watering place. Ack. same day.

Mary & Abigail SHERMAN of Marshfield MA and **Mary PHILLIPS** of same. <Plymouth Co.Deeds 64:268>
...11 Jan. 1782, Judgement against Mary SHERMAN & Abigail SHERMAN, spinsters, in favor of Mary PHILLIPS, widow.

PLYMOUTH COUNTY DEEDS: (re: SHERMAN)

<21:26> - 15 Oct. 1724, Samuel SHERMAN & wf Mary of Marshfield...all rights in Father Nathan WILLIAMSON's estate.
<50:236> - 19 May 1761, William SHERMAN & wf Mary of Rochester sell to John MARSHALL of same.
<58:199> - 1775, Abigail & Mary SHERMAN, division.
<64:268> - 1782, Abigail & Mary SHERMAN ("evidently daus of William").
<75:216> - 1787, Mary SHERMAN, widow of William of Rochester, confirms deed of 1749.

EDWARD DOTY[2] (Edward[1])

Estate of **Edward DOTY** of Plimoth MA. <Plymouth Co.PR #6630>
Bond 3 Aug. 1695, of Thomas FAUNCE & John DOTY, as guardians of the orphan children of Edward DOTEY. Witnesses: Samuel DOTY, Benjamin & Mercy ( ).

MICRO #2 OF 6

James WARREN et al to **David BOSWORTH** of Plimouth MA. <Plymouth Co.Deeds 4:32>
...26 Sept. 1698, James WARREN & wf Sarah and Mary DOTEY, all of Plimouth and Tobias OAKMAN & wf Elizabeth of Marshfield, for £30 sold to David BOSWORTH...50 acres of upland together with three acres of meadow at Monponset...which sd land was formerly granted to our Honoured Father Edward DOTEY late of Plimouth dec'd, by the Inhabitants of the Town of Plimouth at a Town meeting...on the 30th of Jan. 1667 as per Town record...and since upon the division of our sd Father's estate is allotted unto us above mentioned by agreement upon court record. Witnesses: Samuel BRADFORD, Thomas FAUNCE. Ack. 20 May 1699 by Tobias & Elizabeth & witnessed by Abraham HOLMES & Deborah CUSHING. Ack. 28 Aug. 1699 by James & Sarah and Mary DOTEY. Rec. 4 June 1701.

Estate of **Edward OAKMAN** of Marshfield MA. <Plymouth Co.PR #14825>
<27:369> Pr. 1791. <31:453> Inventory. <33:333> Appraisal of real estate. <33:334> Decree. <35:436> Account of admr.

Will of **Elisha FORD** of Marshfield MA. <Plymouth Co.PR #7895>
<15:84>...dated 4 Oct. 1758, mentions wf **Elizabeth**; sons **Lemuel FORD, Elisha FORD, Isaac FORD**; daus **Patience SPRAGUE, Bethiah TURNER, Zerviah HOWLAND, Priscilla FOORD/FORD, Tabitha FOORD/FORD**. <15:85> Pr. 11 Dec. 1758. <15:276> Inventory, 11 Jan. 1759. <16:66> Account, 17 Mar. 1761.

Estate of **Thomas FOSTER** of Marshfield MA. <Plymouth Co.PR #8065>
<14:483> Letter/Bond 3 Apr. 1758, Thomas FOSTER, blacksmith, app'td admr. Sureties: Abijah WHITE, Esq., Adam HALL, yeoman, both of Marshfield. Witnesses: William CUSHING, John LOTHROP. <15:34> Inventory taken 4 Apr. 1758 by James SPRAGUE, Arthur HOWLAND; no real estate mentioned; total, £30.2s8d; oath of admr. 20 May 1758.

Estate of **Jedediah EAMES** of Marshfield MA. <Plymouth Co.PR>
<7:409> 15 May 1738, widow **Mary EAMES** app'td admx. Sureties: Tobias OAKMAN, Edward OAKMAN, mariner, both of Marshfield. Witnesses: Samuel PALMER, Mary WINSLOW. <7:410> Inventory taken 23 May 1738 by Nathaniel EAMES, John CARVER & Jonathan TILDEN <9:291> Division, 1 May 1744 by Thomas

MACOMBER, Nathaniel EAMES, John CARVER, John TILDEN & Timothy ROGERS all of Marshfield, to the widow **Mary SHAREMAN/SHERMAN** now the wife of Robert SHAREMAN/SHERMAN; only son **Jedediah EAMES** and daus **Jane EWELL, Mary STUTSON/STETSON** wf of Joseph and **Penelope EAMES.** <9:289> 1 May 1744, Tobias OAKMAN, yeoman of Marshfield, app'td gdn. of **Penelope EAMES**, minor. Surety: Robert SHAREMAN/SHERMAN. Witnesses: Nathaniel EAMES, Elisha SHARMAN/SHERMAN. <9:290> 1 May 1744, **Jedediah EAMES**, minor, chooses grandfather **Tobias OAKMAN** as gdn.

Estate of **Samuel OAKMAN**, mariner of Marshfield MA. <Plymouth Co.PR #14837>
<8:87> 15 Jan. 1739, widow **Elizabeth OAKMAN** app'td admx. Sureties: Tobias OAKMAN & Edward OAKMAN, boatmen of Marshfield. Witnesses: Samuel TILDEN, Lydia WHITE. <8:126> Inventory taken 28 Jan. 1739/40 by Samuel HATCH, Israel HATCH Jr. & John JONES; sworn to by admx. 29 Jan. 1739/40. <9:296> Account 5 May 1744 of admx. <9:297> Account allowed 31 May 1744; incl. mourning clothes for the children. <11:516> Division 16 Sept. 1748 among the children, viz: **Samuel OAKMAN**, eldest son and **Tobias OAKMAN.** <11:517> Receipt 1 Nov. 1748 of Israel HATCH, gdn. to **Samuel.** <14:465> 29 Apr. 1757, **Tobias OAKMAN** discharges his brother **Samuel OAKMAN**, having received his share, Ł520.

Guardianship of Child of **Samuel OAKMAN**, mariner of Marshfield MA. <Plymouth Co.PR #14840>
Bond 14 Sept. 1748, Israel HATCH, yeoman of Scituate app'td gdn. of **Tobias OAKMAN**, minor. Surety: Samuel OAKMAN. Witnesses: Elisabeth OAKMAN, Lydia WHITE.

Will of **Samuel OAKMAN**, Esq. of Marshfield MA. <Plymouth Co.PR #14838>
...dated 20 Sept. 1784, mentions wf **Deborah**; son **Melzar Turner OAKMAN**; daus **Deborah HATCH** wf of John & **Eunice RUGGLES**; two oldest grandchildren **William TURNER** & **John HATCH**; grandsons **Samuel Oakman HATCH** & **Warren HATCH**; dau **Mercy TURNER.** Witnesses: Charles TURNER, William TURNER, David JOYCE. Warrant for appraisal, 25 July 1791. Inventory taken 17 Aug. 1795; total Ł1633.9.2. Warrant, 16 Mar. 1797, for dividing part devised to heirs of **Melzar Turner OAKMAN** to the following: **Persis OAKMAN, Polly OAKMAN, Rachel OAKMAN, Betsey OAKMAN & Xoa OAKMAN.** <33:51> Account. <36:113> Division of real estate.

Estate of **Deborah OAKMAN** of Marshfield MA. <Plymouth Co.PR #14822, 34:53;35:336-8>
<35:358> Division 5 Sept. 1796 to following heirs, viz: Joseph ROGERS as exr. to the will of **Melzar Turner OAKMAN** dec'd; **Deborah HATCH** wf of John; **Mercy TURNER** wf of Israel; **Eunice RUGGLES** wf of Thomas; heirs of **Elizabeth TURNER** dec'd wf of William.

Tobias OAKMAN of Marshfield MA to **Constant Fobes OAKMAN** of same. <Plymouth Co.Deeds 71:74>
...7 Mar. 1792, Tobias OAKMAN, yeoman, for Ł300 sells to son Constant Fobes OAKMAN, housewright ...all his real estate in Marshfield & his live stock & farming tools and one feather bed...Priviledge in dwelling house reserved for use of daughter Hope OAKMAN. Witnesses: Job TURNER, John TURNER.

Will of **Thomas MORTON**, yeoman of Plymouth MA. <Plymouth Co.PR; MD 27:135>
<11:69>...dated 26 Aug. 1741, mentions wf **Martha**; grandchildren **Bathshuah MORTON & Martha MORTON**, daus of my son **Thomas MORTON** dec'd; sons **Lemuel MORTON & Nathaniel MORTON**; two grandchildren, the daus of my dau **Lydia BARTLETT** dec'd (both under 18); daus **Sarah BARTLETT & Mary NELSON.** Wf & sons **Lemuel & Nathaniel**, executors. Witnesses: Samuel BARTLETT, Nathaniel SHURTLEFF, Noah BRADFORD. <11:70> Pr. 12 Sept. 1748, **Lemuel MORTON** app'td admr., **Nathaniel MORTON** "the other surviving executor" declining to serve. <11:71> Inventory sworn to 1 Nov. 1748.

Will of **Lemuel MORTON.** <no source>
...1779, mentions brother **Nathaniel MORTON**; nephew **Lemuel MORTON Jr.**, "he taking good care of his parents"; neice **Mary MORTON** wf of Thomas; sister **Sarah BARTLETT**; **Bathsheba RICKARD & Martha MORTON**, the two daus of my brother **Thomas MORTON** dec'd; children of my sister **Mary NELSON**; **Mercy MORTON**, the dau of my brother **Nathaniel MORTON**; nephews **Joseph BARTLETT Jr. & Thomas BARTLETT**; **Nathaniel MORTON Jr.** & nephew **Lemuel MORTON Jr.**, executors.

JOHN DOTY[2] (Edward[1])

MICRO #3 OF 6

Estate of **Samuel DOTEY**, mariner of Plymouth MA. <Plymouth Co.PR #6606>
<17:107> Letter/Bond 20 July 1763, Nathaniel DOTEY/DOTEN of Plymouth app'td admr. Sureties: James DOTEN & Ephraim SPOONER. Witnesses: Edward WINSLOW, Lewis BARTLETT. <16:516> Inventory of estate of **Samuel DOTEN Jr.**, taken Oct. 1763; total, Ł22.10.13; sworn to by admr. 28 Oct. 1763. <19:16> Receipt 1763, **Hannah HOLMES & Joanna FISH** "received of **Nathaniel DOTEN** as he is administrator on the estate of **Samuel DOTEN** as he is administrator on the estate of **Samuel DOTEN Jr.**", our share ...and **Elizabeth DOTEY** "received from my brother **Nathaniel DOTEN.**

John DOTEN of Plympton to **Isaac WRIGHT.** <Plymouth Co.Deeds 103:5>
...21 Mar. 1799, John DOTEN sells to Isaac WRIGHT...land he bought of heirs of Isaac WRIGHT, deceased. Wf Molley/Polly DOTEN releases dower.

Stephen DOTEN of Plymouth to **John DOTEN.** <Plymouth Co.Deeds 99:194>
...13 June 1803, Stephen DOTEN, yeoman, as admr. of his father, Stephen DOTEN, yeoman dec'd, sells to John DOTEN at public sale...all the homestead farm, reserving to the widow her right of

dower. Ack. 26 Mar. 1804

John DOTEN of Plymouth MA to **Paul DOTEN.** <Plymouth Co.Deeds 98:175>
...2 May 1804, John & Polly DOTEN, sell to Paul DOTEN...part of land bought of Stephen DOTEN, 13 June 1804 (1803?).

John DOTEN & Paul DOTEN of Plymouth MA to **Stephen DOTEN.** <Plymouth Co.Deeds 98:175>
...14 June 1804, John & Polly DOTEN and Paul DOTEN, mortgage to Stephen DOTEN...the homestead farm bought of said Stephen, as admr., on 13 June 1803. Ack. 26 May 1804. Rec. 29 May 1804. Discharged 26 Mar. 1817.

John & Polly DOTEN and Stephen & Hannah DOTEN of Plymouth MA. <Plymouth Co.Deeds 107:255>
...7 Sept. 1808, John DOTEN & wf Polly and Stephen DOTEN Jr. & wf Hannah...sell land that was given to Polly & Hannah in will of their father Isaac WRIGHT of Plympton dec'd. Ack. 23 Sep 1809.

Stephen DOTEN et al to **William DAVIS.** <Plymouth Co.Deeds 129:186>
...29 Mar. 1817, Stephen DOTEN & wf Abigail, Consider CLARK, mariner & wf Sarah, Charles HOWLAND, mariner & wf Deborah, sell to William DAVIS...land in Plymouth formerly owned by Thomas CLARK and set off by his will as follows: one third to Consider CLARK, one third to Deborah CLARK and one third to Abigail CLARK who was then the widow of the sd Thomas CLARK. Ack. 14 Apr. 1817.

PLYMOUTH COUNTY DEEDS: (re: DOTEN)

<112:149> - , John & Sally DOTEN. (son of James)
<115:16> - 24 Jan. 1811, John & Sally DOTEN, formerly of Plymouth, now of New Grantum(sp) NH.
<129:157> - 1815, Stephen & John DOTEN (sons of Stephen & grandsons of Stephen).
<130:133> - 27 Mar. 1817, John DOTEN, yeoman & wf Molly, of Plymouth.
<134:191> - 27 Mar. 1817, John DOTEN, yeoman & wf Molly, of Plymouth, house & land in Plymouth.

Estate of **James DOTEN Jr.**, shoreman of Plymouth MA. <Plymouth Co.PR #6590>
<original> Request 13 Jan. 1797, of widow **Sarah DOTEN** that **John DOTEN** be app'td admr. <34:95> Letter/Bond 13 Jan. 1797, **John DOTEN,** trader of Plymouth, app'td admr. Sureties: Solomon INGLEE, Joseph HOLMES. Witnesses: George HOLMES, Isaac LOTHROP. <original> Inventory taken 9 Oct. 1798, by Thomas MATTHEWS, Nathaniel THOMAS & Daniel (or David) BACON; total, $289.53.

Estate of **Dr. Joshua MORSE** of Rochester MA. <Plymouth Co.PR 15:413>
Bond 5 Jan. 1760, Nathaniel RUGGLES, gent. of Rochester, app'td admr. Sureties: Hezekiah FORD of Abington and Benjamin CLAP of Rochester.

Estate of **Isaac DOTY** of Plymouth MA. <Plymouth Co.PR #6621>
<4:398> Letter/Bond 30 Apr. 1724, widow **Martha DOTY** app'td admx. Sureties: John FAUNCE Sr. and Thomas FAUNCE Jr. Witnesses: Timothy WHITE, David SHURTLEFF. <4:449> Inventory taken 16 July 1724 by Isaac LOTHROP, John DYER & Thomas HOLMES; real estate incl. house & barn with 132 acres, share in south meadows in Plympton and 120 acres in Plymouth. <4:456> Warrant for appraisal, 30 Apr. 1724. <5:87> Account of admx. 26 July 1725; charges herself with expense of a journey to Barnstable & Marshfield. <6:143> Division of personal estate, 14 Apr. 1730, among widow **Martha DOTEN, Isaac DOTEN, Elizabeth DOTEN, Jane DOTEN, Rebecca DOTEN, Neviah DOTEN, Jabez DOTEN, Ichabod DOTEN** and **Mary DOTEN.** <7:183> Division of real estate, 15 Mar. 1735/6 to: widow **Martha DOTEN, Isaac DOTEN** (eldest son); dau **Elizabeth STUDLEY** wf of John of Hanover; **Jane PALMER** wf of John Jr. of Scituate; dau **Rebecca DOTEN;** sons **Neviah/Neriah DOTEN, Jabez DOTEN, Ichabod DOTEN;** dau **Mary DOTEN** <7:186> Account allowed 29 Mar. 1736.

Guardianship of Children of **Isaac DOTY/DOTEN** of Plymouth MA. <Plymouth Co.PR #6599>
<original> Bonds 14 Apr. 1730, **Martha DOTEN** app'td gdn. of her children. Surety: Thomas HOLMES. Witnesses: Israel LOTHROP, John DYER. <5:677>...dau **Rebecka DOTEN** (betw 14-21); <6:679>...son **Ichabod DOTEN** (under 14); <6:680>...dau **Mary DOTEN** (under 14).

Guardianship of Children of **Isaac DOTY/DOTEN** of Plymouth MA. <Plymouth Co.PR #6586>
<5:678> Letter/Bond 14 Apr. 1730, John DYER app'td gdn. of **Jabez DOTEN** (betw 14-21). Surety: Isaac LOTHROP. Witnesses: Thomas HOLMES, Isaac DOTEN. <5:677> Letter/Bond 14 Apr. 1730, Isaac LOTHROP app'td gdn. of **Neviah/Neriah DOTEN** (under 21). Surety: John DYER. Witnesses: Thomas HOLMES, Isaac DOTEN.

Heirs of **Ichabod DOTEN** of Plymouth MA. <Plymouth Co.Deeds 46:141>
...7 May 1751, Isaac DOTEN, mariner of Plymouth, John STUDLEY, cordwainer of Hanover & wf Elisabeth, Lemuel BARTLETT & wf Mary of Plymouth, Rebekah WARREN, widow of Plymouth, Silvanus BARTLETT trader of Plymouth and Jabez DOTEN, joyner of New York City...divided eleven and a half acres of wood land which was the estate of Ichabod DOTEN dec'd...bounded by land of Joseph RIDER Jr., the estate of Nathaniel HOLMES dec'd, Thomas HOLMES and land that was late in possession of Mrs. Martha DOTEN dec'd...also fifteen and a half acres wood land bounded by land of Josiah RIDER, Joseph RIDER, Thomas FOSTER and estate of Nathaniel JACKSON. Witnesses: Thomas FOSTER, Joseph BARTLETT Jr., David STOCKBRIDGE, "RAMSDELL", Chandler ROBBINS & Benjamin WARREN. Ack. 7 May 1751 by Isaac DOTEN, Lemuel & Mary BARTLETT, Rebecca WARREN & Silvanus BARTLETT. Ack. 23 Nov. 1751 by John & Elizabeth STUDLEY. Ack. 26 Aug. 1760 by Jabez DOTEN.

Isaac DOTEN et al to **Lemuel BARTLETT** of Plymouth MA. <Plymouth Co.Deeds 40:146>
...19 Aug. 1749, Isaac DOTEN, mariner, Jabez DOTEN, joyner, of New York City, John PALMER Jr. of Scituate & wf Jane, John STUDLEY, cordwainer & wf Elizabeth of Hanover and Rebekah WARREN, widow, simstress of Plymouth, for Ł14.11s7d, sold to Lemuel BARTLETT, fisherman...five sixth parts of two acres in Plimouth bounded partly by land belonging to Mary the wife of the sd Lemuel. Witnesses: Joseph BARTLETT Jr., Lemuel JACKSON, Elijah CUSHING & Sarah STUDLEY. Ack. 19 Aug. 1749 by Isaac DOTEN, Jabez DOTEN, John & Jane PALMER, Rebecca WARREN. Ack. 31 Aug. 1749 by John & Elizabeth STUDLEY. Rec. 19 Dec. 1749.

Isaac DOTEN et al to **Isaac TINKHAM** of Halifax MA. <Plymouth Co.Deeds 40:125>
...1 Sept. 1749, Isaac DOTEN, mariner, Lemuel BARTLETT, fisherman & wf Mary, Rebecca WARREN, semstress, all of Plymouth and John STUDLY, cordwainer & wf Elizabeth of Hanover and John PALMER Jr. trader & wf Jane of Scituate and Jabez DOTEN, joyner of New York City, for Ł162.10s, sold to Isaac TINKHAM, yeoman...45 acres upland in Middleborough...which sd land was the estate of our Honoured Grandfather Elder Thomas FAUNCE late of Plymouth dec'd. Ack. 4 Sept. 1749 by John STUDLEY & wf, John PALMER Jr. & wf and Jabez DOTEN. Ack. 11 Sept. 1749 by John PALMER in behalf of Isaac DOTEN, Mary BARTLETT and Rebecca WARREN. Ack. 25 Sept. 1749 by Lemuel BARTLETT. Rec. 28 Sept. 1749.
(The same day, same source, all the above sold to **John TOMSON**, cooper of Middleborough, for Ł25, 8 acres fresh meadow in Middleborough in the six & twenty Men's Purchase...which was the estate of our Honoured Grandfather Elder Thomas FAUNCE...All ack. the same as above deed.)

John PALMER Jr. of Scituate MA to **Silvanus BARTLETT & Joseph FULGHAM.** <Plymouth Co.Deeds 41:25>
...21 Sept. 1750, John PALMER Jr., trader & wf Jane, for Ł11.13s4d, sold to Silvanus BARTLETT, trader and Joseph FULGHAM, mariner, both of Plimouth...one sixth part of a wood lot in Plimouth ...which in the division of the estate of our Honoured Father Mr. Isaac DOTEN dec'd was assigned to our brother Ichabod DOTEN now dec'd...and also all our estate & interest in that part of the wood land which belonged to the sd Ichabod that was in the settlement of our sd Father's estate assigned as dower to our Honoured Mother Mrs. Martha DOTEN dec'd...the one moiety to the sd Silvanus...and the other moiety to the sd Joseph. Witnesses: Ephraim COBB, Barnabas CHURCHELL Jr. Ack. 22 Sept. 1750 by both grantors. Rec. 5 Dec. 1750. Endorsement: On 27 Oct. 1750, Joseph FULGHAM sold his half to Silvanus BARTLETT for L5.16.8d. Witnesses: Samuel CLARKE, Ephraim SPOONER.

Lemuel & Mary BARTLETT of Plymouth to **Lemuel JACKSON** of same. <Plymouth Co.Deeds 41:231>
...14 May 1752, Lemuel BARTLETT, seafaring man & wf Mary, for Ł40 sold to Lemuel JACKSON, shoreman...four acres in Plymouth, north of town, east of Kings Road or High Way...being one half that was settled on ye sd Mary in ye settlement of ye estate of our Honoured Father Mr. Isaac DOTEN dec'd and ye other half thereof was belonging to ye heirs of our Brother Ichabod DOTEN dec'd, five sixth parts thereof the sd Lemuel bought of Isaac DOTEN & others as may appear by their deed dated 19 Aug. 1749...bounded by land that was Hilkiah TINKCOM's late of Plymouth dec'd now the land of Samuel NELSON & land of sd JACKSON. Witnesses: Samuel BARTLETT, Seth BARNES Jr., Rebecca WARREN. Ack. 14 May 1752 by Lemuel, 2 June 1752 by wf Mary. Rec. 9 June 1752.

Neriah/Neviah DOTEN of Plymouth MA to **Joshua DREW** of same. <Plymouth Co.Deeds 31:141>
...28 Nov. 1737, Neriah/Neviah DOTEN, cordwainer, sold to Joshua DREW, shipwright...9 acres in Plymouth received in the division of my father's estate, on the road to Kingston. Ack. same day. Rec. 29 Nov. 1737.

Neriah DOTEN of Plymouth MA to **Isaac DOTEN** of same. <Plymouth Co.Deeds 31:142>
...26 Nov. 1737, Neriah DOTEN, cordwainer, to brother Isaac DOTEN, mariner...his share of mother's thirds & other estate from father's division. Ack. same day. Rec. 1 Dec. 1737.

Will of **Isaac DOTEN**, mariner of Plymouth MA. <Plymouth Co.PR #6585>
<20:367>...dated 6 May 1770, mentions wf **Mary** (executrix), daus **Hope CARVER** (dec'd), **Mary WHITMAN**; wf **Mary** to receive the improvement of the estate for her support & for bringing up of the younger children, **Hope & Mary** having already received their share. Witnesses: Mary BARTLETT, Lazarus LeBARON, Thomas FOSTER. <20:367> Letter 16 May 1770, **Mary DOTEN** app'td exx. <39:188> Letter /Bond 5 Apr. 1809, William DOTEN & Job COBB Jr., app'td admrs. Sureties: Salisbury JACKSON, Ezekiel MORTON. Witnesses: Jno. B. THOMAS, Isaac M. SHERMAN. <39:443> Letter 5 Apr. 1809, above adminstrators app'td de bonis non with will annexed; **Mary DOTEN** the exx. having dec'd.

Will of **James DOTEN**, housewright of Plymouth MA. <Plymouth Co.PR #6591>
<49:25>...dated 10 June 1817, mentions wf **Elizabeth**; children **Hope, James, Isaac, John, Elizabeth, Daniel** (executor), **Mary, Thomas, Lucy, Lois, Elenor.** Witnesses: Solomon CHURCHILL, Thomas DREW, Joel PERKINS. <original> Bond of **Daniel DOTEN**, housewright of Plymouth, exr. Sureties: Job RIDER Jr., Daniel RIDER, both of Plymouth. <49:25> Pr. 30 Sept. 1817. <49:226> Order of notice, 5 Mar. 1818. <49:226> Inventory taken 30 Aug. 1817 by William WHITE, Micah FOSTER Jr., Joseph TORREY Jr., all of Pembroke; no real estate; personal estate total, $84.78. <49:227> Account of exr. 5 Mar. 1818.

Guardianship of Child of **Thomas DOTEN**, mariner of Plymouth MA. <Plymouth Co.PR #6595>
<32:78> Letter/Bond 28 Mar. 1797, Lemuel DOTEN of Plymouth app'td gdn. of **John DOTEN**, under 14. Sureties: William HOLMES, Joseph THOMAS. Witnesses: Robert BARKER, Isaac LOTHROP.

MICRO #4 OF 6

Estate of **Jacob DOTY** of Plympton/Plymouth MA. <Plymouth Co.PR #6587>
<10:401> Letter/Bond 26 June 1747, widow **Deborah DOTY** & Joseph RICKARD, both of Plympton, app'td admrs. Sureties: Jabez PRATT, John RICKARD, both of Plympton & Joseph BENT of Middleboro. Witnesses: Edward WINSLOW, Thomas SPOONER Jr. <10:449> Inventory taken 7 July 1747 by Benjamin FULLER, Elisha WYTON, Thomas PRATT; incl. homestead building & meadow at Swan hold, Ł350; total, Ł474.13.6. <10:450> Account 17 July 1747 of Joseph RICKARD, admr.; Debts due from: Col. LOTHROP, John CRANDON, Samuel BARTLETT, Samuel LUCAS, Jno. LUCAS, William LUCAS, Elisha WHITON, Matthew LEMOTE, Francis ADAMS, Eleazer RICKARD, Eleazer ROBENS/ROBBINS. <12:463> Account 27 Apr. 1752 of Joseph RICKARD, admr.; Paid to: **Deborah DOTEN**, Jonathan TILSON, Thomas PRATT, Silvanus BARTLETT, James HOVEY, Ebenezer ROBENS/ROBBINS, Joseph BRIDGHAM, George BARROWS, Silvanus BRIMHALL, William SHURTLEFF, Thomas HOLMES, Edward DOTEN, Isaac LOTHROP's estate. <13:98> Division Feb. 1753 among following heirs, viz: widow **Deborah DOTEN; Solomon DOTEN** (eldest son); dau **Hannah FULLER**, wf of Seth Jr.; dau **Jemima DOTEN**; son **Zephaniah DOTEN**; dau **Sarah DOTEN**; son **Jacob DOTEN.**

Guardianship of Children of **Jacob DOTY/DOTEN** of Plympton/Plymouth MA. <Plymouth Co.PR #6584>
<11:113> Bond/Nomination 12 Apr. 1749, Elisha WYTON of Plympton app'td gdn. of **Hannah DOTEN**, minor above 14). Surety: Abel CROCKER. Witnesses: Benjamin FULLER, Edward WINSLOW, Silvanus DONHAM, James RICKARD. <original> Bonds 30 Mar. 1752, William LUCAS of Plymouth app'td gdn. of **Jemimah DOTEN & Jacob DOTEN.** Surety: Joseph RICKARD. Witnesses: Susannah NORCUT, John LOTHROP. <12:460> Letters/Bonds 30 Mar. 1752, Joseph RICKARD of Middleboro app'td gdn. of **Sarah DOTEN & Zepheniah DOTEN.** Surety: William LUCAS. Witnesses: Susannah NORCUT, John LOTHROP. <12:465> Nomination 3 Apr 1752 of William LUCAS as gdn., by **Jemima DOTEN & Jacob DOTEN.** Witnesses: Joseph BRIDGHAM, Abigail BRIDGHAM.

Estate of **Jacob DOTEN** of Kingston MA. <Plymouth Co.PR #6588>
<27:189> Letter/Bond 30 Aug. 1785, widow **Sarah DOTEN** app'td admx. Sureties: John COBB, Seth COBB. Witnesses: Isaac LOTHROP, Joshua THOMAS. <29:389> Inventory taken 28 Sept. 1785 by Ebenezer NELSON, Ebenezer DOTEN, John COBB; personal estate, Ł40.13.8.; real estate, Ł33. <original> List of Debts: Ebenezer COBB, John COBB, Joanna COBB, Mercy COBB, John LUCAS, Silas MORTON, Ebenezer DOTEN, John ADAMS, Ephraim PRATT, Bildad WASHBURN, Nathan PERKANS/PERKINS, Patience TINKHAM, Seth COBB, Zadock BARROW, widow Patience DUNHAM; sworn to by admx. 5 July 1786. <30:7> Warrant for dower, 17 Apr. 1786. <30:8> Dower assigned, 1 May 1786 by John GRAY, John COBB, Caleb DOTEN, to widow **Sarah DOTEN**, land in Plympton that Jacob bought of widow Joanna DOTEN, John DOTEN and others.

Will of **John DOTEN Jr.** of Plympton MA. <Plymouth Co.PR #6594>
<12:102>...dated 19 Jan. 1748, mentions wf **Lydia**; sons **Edward DOTEN, Ebenezer DOTEN**; dau **Elizabeth FULLER**; son **Nathaniel DOTEN**; Ebenezer SPOONER, executor. Witnesses: William LUCAS, Elisha WYTON, Rebecca ROBINS. <12:103> Letter 3 Apr. 1749, Ebenezer SPOONER of Plymouth app'td exr. <11:185> Inventory taken 7 Apr. 1749 by Abel CROCKER, Benjamin FULLER, Elisha WHITON; incl. homestead Ł848; total estate, Ł2135.17.2. <12:242> Division 12 July 1751, by Abel CROCKER, John COLE Jr., Samuel LUCAS; dower set off to widow **Lydia DOTEN**, part of Dotey's meadow in Plymouth which was "old Mr. John DOTEN's", also a lot in sd meadow which deceased bought of Mary DOTEN; 1st share set off to **Edward DOTEN**, land on the way that goes from Anna SNAPET's to Wenham all but what the widow Hannah DOTEN now improves; 2nd share set off to **Ebenezer DOTEN**; 3rd share set off to **Nathaniel DOTEN.**

Guardianship of Child of **John DOTEN** of Plympton MA. <Plymouth Co.PR #6600>
<11:371> Nomination/Bond 7 Aug. 1750, Benjamin FULLER of Plympton app'td gdn. of **Nathaniel DOTEN.** Surety: Edward DOTEN of Plympton. Witnesses: Edward WINSLOW, Hannah WINSLOW, John COLE Jr., Samuel LUCAS.

Estate of **Ebenezer DOTEN** of Plympton MA. <Plymouth Co.PR #6572>
<27:219> Letter/Bond 2 Dec. 1786, **Caleb DOTEN** app'td admr. Sureties: William WESTON, Thomas MATTHEW. Witnesses: Isaac LOTHROP, Nathaniel LOTHROP. <30:123> Inventory taken by Isaac JACKSON, John DONHAM, Samuel LUCAS 3d; total, Ł618.13.6.; incl. 12 acres at Doten's meadows now in the hands of Capt. Cornelius DONHAM & Ebenezer DOTEN; sworn to 11 Apr. 1787 by admr. <30:124> Division 11 Apr. 1787 by Isaac JACKSON, John DONHAM & Samuel LUCAS Jr. to the following heirs, viz: widow **Mary DOTEN**; eldest son **Caleb DOTEN** of Plymouth; dau **Elizabeth WOOD** wf of David Jr.; son **Amaziah DOTEN** of Lee; son **Ebenezer DOTEN**; dau **Sarah TILSON** wf of Jonathan; dau **Phebe HARLOW** wf of James of Crydon; dau **Lydia SHERMAN** wf of John Jr.; son **Edward DOTEN.** <31:133> Account of admr., 1 Feb. 1790; Creditors: Stephen SAMSON, Abner BARROW, Ebenezer DOTY, Barnabas COBB, Lemuel SAVERY, Ichabod CHURCHILL, Gideon BRADFORD Jr., John LUCAS, Samuel LUCAS, James THACHER, Jonathan FULLER, Eleazer RICKARD, Benjamin RIDER, Lot EATON, Ebenezer DEANE, Barnabas COBB for Elizabeth ROBBIN's tax, Jno ADAMS, Eleazer HOLMES, Caleb DOTY, Dr. LeBARON and Eleazer ROBBINS. <35:356> 2nd Warrant for appraisal, 2 Oct. 1795...whereas that part of the real estate whereof **Ebenezer DOTEN** late of sd Carver dec'd died seized which was assigned to his widow who is also dec'd. <35:356> Inventory taken 17 Nov. 1795, incl. 12 acre homestead, 4 acre swamp, 14 acres at Bell's hole, three and a third acres at Doten's meadows, half of house, one third of barn. <original> Security Bond 26 Nov 1795, **Ebenezer DOTEN & Edward DOTEN** shall cause to be paid to their brothers and sisters as follows: **Caleb DOTEN** the eldest, **Amaziah DOTEN, Elizabeth WOOD, Phebe HARLOW, Sarah TILSON, Lydia SHERMAN.** Sureties: Eleazer ROBBINS, Benjamin RANSOM Jr. Witnesses Lemuel COLE 2d, Benjamin PRATT.

Guardianship of Child of **Ebenezer DOTEN** of Plympton MA. <Plymouth Co.PR #6574>
<26:464> Bond/Nomination 21 Apr. 1787, **Mary DOTEN** app'td gdn. of **Edward DOTEN** (above 14). Sureties: Caleb DOTEY, Ebenezer DOTEN. Witnesses: James HARLOW, Edward DOTEN, David WOOD Jr., Eleazer ROBBINS.

Estate of **Edward DOTEN** of Plympton MA. <Plymouth Co.PR #6573>
<17:142> Bond 27 Apr. 1765, Elisha WHITTON of Plympton app'td admr. <19:200> Inventory taken by Samuel LUCAS, Zebedee CHANDLER, Lemuel CROOKER; sworn to 4 May 1765 by appraisers, 11 May 1765 by admr.; total estate, £76. <19:258> Dower assigned to widow **Joannah DOTEN**, land set off near the land which Ebenezer DOTEN bought of **Edward DOTEN** dec'd and to the woodlot set off to the widow Hannah DOTEN dec'd; allowed Oct. 1765. <19:340> List of Claims: Joseph LUCAS, Nathaniel COB Jr., Elisha WHITTEN, Issacher FULLER, Samuel BARTLETT, James HOVEY, widow Lydia DOTEN, Jonathan TILSON Lemuel CROOKER, Silvanus DONHAM, Ephraim SPOONER, Elisha WHITTEN Jr., Ebenezer DOTEN, Nathaniel ATWOOD, Jedediah WHITON, Dr. William THOMAS, Edward STEPHENS, Dr. Lazarus LeBARON, Deborah RANSOM Ebenezer CHURCHELL, Azariah WHITON, Zadock BARROWS, Mary CROCKER, Timothy COBB, Benjamin DREW, to Elisha WHITON what he stands engaged to pay to James HOVEY, Esq. for sd DOTEN, Samuel BARROWS, William LUCAS; sworn to 31 Oct. 1765 by commissioners Samuel LUCAS & Jonathan TILLSON.

Estate of **Josiah DOTEN**, mariner of Plymouth MA. <Plymouth Co.PR #6597>
<20:483> Bond 22 Feb. 1771, widow **Deborah DOTEN** app'td admx. Sureties: Thomas SAVERY, John NELSON Witness: Edward WINSLOW. <20:483> Inventory taken 22 Feb. 1771 by Thomas SAVERY, John NELSON; total, L6.8.8. <20:483> Insolvency 22 Feb. 1771, by admx. <20:483> Account of admx. 22 Feb. 1771.

Estate of **Samuel DOTY**, mariner of Plymouth MA. <Plymouth Co.PR #6629>
<8:189> Letter/Bond 20 May 1740, Silas WEST app'td admr. Sureties: Thomas FOSTER, Joshua DREW, both of Plymouth. Witnesses: Thomas WETHERELL Jr., Charles DYRE. <8:270> Inventory 20 May 1740 by John ATWOOD, Thomas HOLMES, Thomas FOSTER; real estate, £150, total, £247.1.6.; sworn to 20 Sept. 1740 by Silas WEST.

JOSEPH DOTY^2 (Edward^1)

Estate of **Edward DOTY Jr.** of Rochester MA. <Plymouth Co.PR #6620>
<23:107> Letter/Bond 1 July 1776, John DOTY app'td admr. Sureties: Timothy RUGGLES, John BRADFORD Witnesses: Judah DELANO, Joseph CUSHING. <24:330> Inventory taken 29 Aug. 1776 by John BURGES, Consider KING, Ebenezer PARKER Jr.; incl. homestead farm & mills, £187.01.4, total, £222.10.6. <24:332> Dower assigned 24 May 1777 to widow **Hannah DOTY**, by Barzillai HAMMOND, Isaac SNOW, Ebenezer PARKER Jr. <24:330> List of Debts, 2 June 1777: Col. Elisha TOBEY, Edward HAMMOND, James FOSTER Jr., Richard BOSWORTH, Elnathan HASKELL, John BURGES Jr., Walter SPOONER, Abishai SHERMAN, Charles CHURCH, Joshua & Joseph BRIGGS, Samuel SPRAGUE, Henry BISHOP, Dr. John PITCHER, Edward MORSE, Joseph BASSET, David WING, Hathaway RANDAL, Isaac SNOW, Consider KING, Bangs BURGES, Nicholas SNOW, Widow BAKER, Abner BAKER, Thomas HORSKINS, Benjamin INGERSOL, Nathaniel SPRAGUE, Nehemiah RANDALL, Mark SNOW, John BURGESS, Samuel RIDER, John DOTY, Stephen WING, Ephraim GRIFFITH, William BASSETT. <original> Complaint of heirs, 2 Sept. 1782, against John DOTY for neglecting to settle estate, signed by: **Huldah DOTY, Azubah DOTY, Jerahmeel DOTY, Theadoras DOTY, Elihu DOTY & Deliverance DOTY.** <original> Appointment of Referees: Ebenezer TOMSON, Joshua WHITE & Moses INGLEE, who met at the house of Samuel RIDER in Rochester 19 Nov. 1782 to receive evidence. <28:442> Account of admr. allowed 2 Dec. 1782.

Joseph DOTY of Rochester MA to **John WHITE** of same. <Plymouth Co.Deeds 25:120>
...7 June 1700, Joseph DOTY, yeoman, for £10 sells to John WHITE...40 acres sea lot in Rochester, numbered 10...by me purchased of Samuel HATCH my brother being made over to him by his Father HATCH & did belong to Mr. Thomas HINCKLEY in the first Purchase of sd Rochester Lands. Ack. 25 Oct. 1700. Rec. 15 May 1730.
(26 Sept. 1700, John WHITE sold the above to Jacob BUMPAS. Rec. 15 May 1730. <25:121>)

Estate of **Joseph DOTY** of Rochester MA. <Plymouth Co.PR #6624>
...18 Sept. 1734...To the Ho^d Isaac WINSLOW, Esq., Judge of the Probate of Wills & Impowerd to grant administration etc. for the County of Plymouth. The Humble Petition of **Sarah DOTY** widow and relict of **Joseph DOTY** late of Rochester deceased Humbly sheweth: That wheras my sd decased Husband In his lifetime by Reason of old age & adverse Providences was Reduced to such Circumstances as to be obliged to live with & be supported In A measure by his son **Joseph DOTY** & Dyed there & so all the moveables we had was In our sd sons House and since My sd Husbands Death I Cannot Comfortably Dwell with him but might live with more Comfort with my own son **Joseph EDWARDS** Could I obtain such Beding & other necessary household stuff as My Husband & I had at his Decease which he my sd son In Law **Joseph DOTY** withholds (as I apprehend) very Unjustly from me, knowing I am through my own Poverty unable to take administration etc. your Petitioner therefore Humbly prayes you will take my Case Into your wise Consideration and offer me such Releife In the Premises as In your Great wisdom may appear best and your Petitioner as in Duty Bound shall Ever Pray: signed by the mark of **Sarah DOTY.**

Estate of **Barnabas DOTY** of Rochester MA. <Plymouth Co.PR #6618>
<original> Bond 21 May 1759, Barzillai HAMMOND & wf Sarah HAMMOND of Rochester app'd admrs. Sureties: Archelaus HAMMOND, Josiah HAMMOND, both of Rochester. Witnesses: Benjamin ALLEN, Marcy HAM-

MOND. <15:190> Inventory taken 29 June 1759 by Samuel WING, Benjamin ALLEN, Nathan NYE; total, £11.9.4., no real estate. <15:191> Account of Barzillai HAMMOND & wf **Sarah** on the estate of her former husband **Barnabas DOTY,** allowed 6 Aug. 1759. <15:191> Insolvency 6 Aug. 1759, Judge decrees that there is no estate to settle.

Estate of **Isaac DOTY,** mariner of Wareham MA. <Plymouth Co.PR #6622>
<8:188> Letter/Bond 8 May 1740, widow **Elizabeth DOTY** app'td admx. Sureties: William BLACKMER, John BLACKMER. Witnesses: Thomas WITHERELL, Ebenezer DOGGETT.

MARY DOTY[2] (Edward[1])

Will of **Samuel HATCH Sr.,** yeoman of Scituate MA. <Plymouth Co.PR 7:143;MD 7:29>
...dated 13 June 1728, mentions sons **Samuel HATCH & Isaac HATCH** (executor); dau **Desire HATCH;** grandsons **Isaac HATCH & Josiah HATCH,** sons of son **Isaac HATCH;** daus **Hannah TINKHAM, Elizabeth BONNEY & Desire HATCH;** grandchildren **Ebenezer & Sarah,** chil, of son **Ebenezer HATCH,** dec'd; grandchildren **Edmund, Jabez, Josiah, Desire, Zerviah & Mercy,** chil. of son **Josiah HATCH** dec'd; sons **Elisha HATCH & Ezekiel HATCH.** Witnesses: John CUSHING Jr., Deborah WHETEN, Susanna MOREY. Pr. 7 July 1735. Inventory taken 9 July 1735.

Will of **Ebenezer HATCH,** yeoman of Pembroke MA. <Plymouth Co.PR #9490>
<4:419>...dated 7 Jan. 1724, mentions wf **Abigill/Abigail,** son **Ebenezer HATCH** (under 21) and dau **Sary/Sarah HATCH** (under 18); wife **Abigail** and brother **Samuel HATCH,** executors. Witnesses: David MAGOON, Marcy OLDHAM, Elisha BISBE. <4:418> Pr. 4 May 1724. <4:420> Inventory taken 21 Apr. 1724 by Joseph STOCKBRIDGE, Gershom STETSON and Elias (---); incl. homeland, buildings & cedar swamp, £1500 and a horse stable. <original> 7 Aug. 1732, **Samuel HATCH,** exr. adds to inventory.

Isaiah HATCH & Joseph SNOW to **Zadock STURTEVANT** of Rochester MA. <Plymouth Co.Deeds 61:139>
...21 Sept. 1773, Isaiah HATCH, yeoman of Harwich & Joseph SNOW, yeoman of Rochester, for £24 sold to Zadock STURTEVANT, blacksmith...9 acres in Rochester bounded by the late Ezekiel HATCH's land. Ack. same day by Joseph, 2 Oct. 1773 by Isaiah.

Stephen PERRY & Isaiah HATCH of Rochester MA to **Zadock STURTEVANT** of same. <Plymouth Co.Deeds>
<61:139>...18 Feb. 1773, Stephen PERRY & Isaiah HATCH, yeomen, for £6 sold to Zadock STURTEVANT, blacksmith...5 acres in Rochester. Ack. same day. Rec. 7 Sept. 1782.

PLYMOUTH COUNTY DEEDS: (re: Isaiah HATCH)

<46:2>	- 27 Aug. 1759,	Isaiah HATCH & Lemuel CHURCH, division.
<50:237>	- 7 Jan. 1763,	Isaiah HATCH & James DEXTER to Seth JENNEY.
<48:137>	- 15 Apr. 1763,	Isaiah HATCH & James DEXTER, division.
<49:175>	- 19 May 1764,	Isaiah HATCH, husbandman of Rochester to Charles STURTEVANT.
<56:250>	- 1 Apr. 1766,	Isaiah HATCH & Anthony SHERMAN, of Rochester to Joseph SNOW of same.
<54:86>	- 9 Mar. 1768,	Isaiah/Isaac HATCH & Stephen PERRY to John CLARK.
<58:127>	- 14 May 1770,	Isaiah HATCH, yeoman of Rochester to Isaac VINCENT of Dartmouth.
<58:176>	- 6 Oct. 1770,	Isaiah HATCH of Rochester to Zebeth COWING. Rec. 8 June 1775.
<56:84>	- 26 Apr. 1771,	Isaiah HATCH, yeoman of Rochester to James DEXTER of same.
<56:150>	- 10 July 1771,	Isaiah HATCH & Stephen PERRY against Silas RANDALL, land in Rochester.
<59:101	- 27 June 1771,	Isaiah HATCH & Stephen PERRY, yeomen of Rochester to Silas RANDALL of same, land in Rochester. Rec. 9 Mar. 1778.
<57:106>	- 5 Jan. 1773,	Isaiah HATCH, yeoman of Rochester to Jonathan CHURCH of same.
<57:106>	- 4 Feb. 1773,	Isaiah HATCH, yeoman of Rochester to James DEXTER of same, land in Rochester. Joanna HATCH signs.
<60:88>	- 24 Feb. 1773,	Isaiah HATCH, yeoman of Rochester to John MARSHALL of same, land in Rochester. Rec. 5 July 1780.
<58:176>	- 18 Feb. 1773,	Isaiah HATCH & Stephen PERRY of Rochester to John SIMMONS, land in Roch.
<89:150>	- 27 Feb. 1773,	Isaiah HATCH to Luce HATCH, 12 acres in Rochester. Joanna HATCH signs. Rec. 23 Dec. 1800.

MICRO #5 OF 6

Will of **Israel TURNER,** Esq. of Pembroke MA. <"from original will">
...dated 23 Aug. 1760...to son **Jonathan TURNER,** 140 acres at westerly end of my farm in Pembroke I bought of the Guardians to the Indians...one pare of oxen...and one cow...to son **Israel TURNER** the farm whereon I now dwell and is the farm I purchased of the widow Bethiah BARKER...excepting and reserving to my wellbeloved wife **Abigail TURNER** the easterly end of the front part of my sd house that is to say the lower roome chamber and garret over it together with a priviledge in the ketchen seller and oven...also the use & improvement of one third part of all my real estate... also my read horse and rideing chere and one cow...so long as she shall remain my widow...to son **Israel TURNER** my clock, he paying my executrix £6.13s4d for the use of my heirs...to my two sons **Daniel TURNER & Elisha TURNER** my farm I bought of Caleb BARKER...also my part of the grist mill ...also five acers of land I bought of Isaac HATCH which joyns to ye farm I bought of Caleb BARKER...to dau **Elisabeth BARKER,** £20...to dau **Christiany TURNER,** £40...my executrix shall sell...my

farm in Scituate I purchased of Joshua OLDHAM and also what I bought of Benjamin TURNER as admr. to ye estate of John GORHAM and also my part of an iron mill in Kingston (called) Holms Iron Mill and also my part of the Iron oar in Jones River Pond and also one sixth part of a sawmill standing on Pine Brooke and also one quarter of a Schooner called good intent of which Isaac PHILLIPS is the present master and also my Sloope standing on the stocks and also my Negro woman Zilpha & my negro Boy Dick and my Negro Garl Dina; wf **Abigail**, executrix. Witnesses: Joseph CUSHING, Ruth RANDALL, John TURNER. Pr. 3 Nov. 1760.

Estate of **Jonathan TURNER** of Hanover/Pembroke MA. <Plymouth Co.PR #21391>
...1796...<34:81;35:552;36:9;38:190> (no details given).

Elisha TURNER of Pembroke MA to **Israel TURNER** of same. <Plymouth Co.Deeds 62:100>
...19 Mar. 1783, Elisha TURNER, yeoman, for £259.6s8d sold to Israel TURNER, yeoman...that part of the farm lying in Pembroke that my Father Israel TURNER late of Pembroke Esq. dec'd gave me in his last will...and which is divided between me & my Brother Daniel TURNER late of Pembroke dec'd as by sd division now on the Probate records will fully appear. Wf Sarah TURNER releases dower.

Elisha TURNER of Pembroke & **Rebecca KEEN** of same. <Plymouth Co.Deeds 64:42>
...28 Mar. 1783, Elisha TURNER, mariner & wf Sarah, and Rebecca KEEN, spinster...as owners of the homestead farm on which our Father Josiah KEEN late of sd Pembroke Esq. dec'd dwelled...in equal halves or shares, about 175 acres on both sides of highway from Plymouth to Pembroke mill called Matakeset mill..divide the land. Ack. 9 May 1783.

Elisha TURNER et al of Pembroke to **Robert McLAUTHLEN** of Kingston MA. <Plymouth Co.Deeds 70:207>
...9 Aug. 1790, Elisha TURNER, yeoman & wf Sarah, Rebecca KEEN, seamstress and Isaac KEEN & Joseph KEEN, yeomen, for £36 sold to Robert McLAUTHLEN, yeoman...all rights in 4 acres in Pembroke that John KEEN dec'd sold in 1749 to Isaac KEEN dec'd.

Elisha TURNER of Pembroke MA to **Joshua THOMAS** of Plymouth MA. <Plymouth Co.Deeds 66:8>
...19 Mar. 1785, Elisha TURNER, Esq., power of attorney to Joshua THOMAS, Esq...to sell land in Pembroke to settle accounts regarding estate of Josiah KEEN, Esq. late of Pembroke dec'd. Rec. 13 Apr. 1786.

Joshua THOMAS et al to **Jonathan BONNEY & Oliver BONNEY** of Pembroke MA. <Plymouth Co.Deeds 66:87>
...1 Apr. 1786, Joshua THOMAS, Esq., as attorney of Elisha TURNER, gent. & wf Sarah & Rebecca KEEN, single woman of Pembroke, for £158.7s4d sold to Jonathan BONNEY & Oliver BONNEY, yeomen... 117 acres in Pembroke, same formerly belonged to Isaac SOULE dec'd called the SOULE place or farm ...sold to pay debts of estate of Josiah KEEN, Esq. late of Pembroke. Rec. 13 Apr. 1786.

Will of **Isaac HATCH**, yeoman of Pembroke MA. <Plymouth Co.PR #9506>
<15:446>...dated 11 Dec. 1756, mentions wf **Penelope**; to son **Isaac HATCH**, the farm I bought of Joseph DWELLE which sd farm sd DWELLE bought of Robert BARKER and lyes in Pembroke excepting what part...I have sold to Israel TURNER...also one half of my ceder swamp in the Little Ceder Swamp in Pembrook lying near Samuel WITHERELL's; to sons **Seth HATCH** and **Josiah HATCH**, the farm I bought of Isaac BARKER which was formerly Josiah HOLMES' and also a peice of meadow adjoyning to the same which I bought of Capt. Nehemiah CUSHING all lying in sd Pembroke, my minde and will is that my son **Seth** shall have the new dwelling house in which he now lives standing on the land aforesd and that my son **Josiah** shall have the old house & barn...also in equal halves a peice of meadow I bought of Benjamin BARSTOW lying in Scituate containing five acres...also ten acres of meadow which I bought of Joseph JOSSELYN and Thomas JOSSELYN...I also give my son **Seth** the other half of my ceder swamp; to son **Samuel HATCH**...the farm on which I now dwell...containing the lands which I purchased of my Father **Samuel HATCH** dec'd, Isaac BARKER & Joshua OLDHAM, all lying in Pembroke ...also my gun which was formerly my Father's...also one half of wareing apparrell; to my son **Josiah HATCH** the one half of my wareing apparrell...my Negro Boy named James; farming tools to be divided among **Seth, Samuel** and **Josiah** who also share the pew in Pembrook meeting house with daus **Penelope, Lydia & Sarah** (who each receive £100); to dau **Mary HATCH** wf of Israel Jr., £100, deducting therefrom what she hath already received...It is my minde and will that my son **Seth** should provide house room in his house and fier wood for my daughter **Penellope** dureing the time she shall continue unmarried...son **Samuel** to do the same for daughters **Lydia & Sarah**; son **Seth**, executor. Witnesses: Betty TURNER, Christiana TURNER, Israel TURNER. <15:447> Pr. 3 Dec. 1759, **Seth HATCH** app'td admr. <15:430> Inventory taken (no date) by David STOCKBRIDGE, Esq., Israel TURNER and Aaron SIMONS; incl. "his purse", £24.10s11d; cattle, horses, sheep & swine, £110.8s; negro boy, £40; share of the sloop Dolphin, £128.1s; cash due on sundry notes of hands, £333.11s4d; pew in Pembroke meeting house, £13.6s8d; real estate, £1887.13s4d; total, £2744.1s9d. <16:526> Account 5 Dec. 1763, of **Seth HATCH**, admr., shares paid to the following heirs: **Samuel HATCH**, £80. 10s8d; **Josiah HATCH**, £83.17s6d; **Job CLAP**, £173.19s; **Lydia PHILLIPS**, £172.4s5d; **Mary HATCH**, £171. 15s9d; **Sarah HATCH**, £176.17s7d; to mother **Penelope HATCH**, £43.16s8d; my own shear in sd personal estate, £73.18s; Paid to: Christiane TURNER, Caleb TURNER, Jeremiah DILLINGHAM, Capt. Josiah CUSHING, Israel HATCH Jr., Israel HATCH, John TURNER, Samuel OAKMAN, Deacon JOSSLYEN, Seth BRYANT, Isaac GOOSE, Seth JACOB (constable), David STANDISH (collector), Rodah WING, Dr. James OTIS, Cornelius COOK; mourning clothes for mother, £10.9s; pare of grave stones, £1.18s; Josiah's negro boy, £40; pew in meeting house, £13.6s8d.

Estate of **Penelope HATCH**, widow of Pembroke MA. <Plymouth Co.PR #9585>
<23:78> Letter/Bond 1 Jan. 1776, John TURNER, Esq. of Pembroke app'td admr. Sureties: Seth HATCH, Seth BRIGGS, both of Pembroke. Witnesses: Comfort BATES, J. CUSHING. <24:72> Inventory taken 4

Jan. 1776 by Aaron SOUL and Seth BRIGGS; incl. notes of hand, £181.; gould necklass, buttons, ring & silver spoons, £6.13s; total, £247.1s2d; oath of appraisers, 1 Apr. 1776.

Will of **Isaac HATCH** of Pembroke MA. <Plymouth Co.PR #9507>
<37:189>...dated 15 Apr. 1799, mentions wf **Sarah**; unnamed children of son **Walter HATCH**; sons **Fisher HATCH, Jabez HATCH, Harris HATCH, Isaac HATCH**; grandson **Clift HATCH**, son of son **Clift HATCH** dec'd; daus **Lydia LITTLE, Sarah WINSLOW**; unnamed son of dau **Judith TURNER** dec'd; to daughter in law **Rachel CUSHING** all the moveable estate I had with her mother at our marriage; sons **Harris & Isaac**, executors. Witnesses: Seth HATCH, Simeon JONES Jr., Josiah SMITH. <37:188> Pr. 6 Jan. 1800. <37:190;38:94> (no details given).

PLYMOUTH COUNTY PROBATE: (re: HATCH)

1758	Josiah	Pembroke	adm.	#9546, 15:49,98,389,469,564;16:29,42,43,44
1759	Josiah	Pembroke	will	#9506, 15:430,446,447;16:526
1763	Josiah	Pembroke	adm.	#9545, 16:545-549;17:118
1765	Lydia	Scitute	adm.	#9598, 17:149;20:104,116
1776	Samuel	Pembroke	adm.	#9589, 12:111;24:140;29:78
1791	Sarah	Marshfield	will	#9598, 33:279
1799	Seth	Pembroke	will	#9601, 37:118,120,166,167
1831	Josiah	Pembroke	adm.	#9544, 61:429;70:448;72:226
1832	Abigail	Pembroke	adm.	#9462, 68:274;71:31;72:226,274

Estate of **Josiah HATCH** of Rochester MA. <Plymouth Co.PR #9542>
<3:341> Letter/Bond 30 Mar. 1715 of widow **Desire HATCH**. <4:398> Adm. d.b.n. <3:342> Inventory taken 22 Mar. 1715 by Peter BLACKMER & John HAMMOND; incl. house & lands, £130; half saw mill, £40; sworn to 30 Mar. 1715 by widow **Desire HATCH**. <5:56> Account.

Will of **Samuel HATCH**, yeoman of Scituate MA. <Plymouth Co.PR 19:425>
...dated 23 Oct. 1766...to wife **Mary** all the estate she brought to me when I married her; grandsons **John MITCHEL, Job MITCHEL, Samuel JONES, Amos JONES & Ezekiel JONES**; daus **Lydia MITCHEL & Ruth JONES**; grandaughters **Elizabeth MITCHEL & Betty JONES**; kinsman Benjamin HATCH Jr. of Scituate executor. Witnesses: James RANDALL, Elizeus TAYLOR, John TURNER. Pr. 2 Feb. 1767.

Estate of **John MITCHELL**, labourer of Scituate MA. <Plymouth Co.PR #14083>
<originl> Petition (no date)...of widow **Lydia MITCHEL** that son **John MITCHEL** be app'td admr. <27:45> Letter/Bond 16 Oct. 1779, **John MITCHEL** yeoman of Scituate, app'td admr. Sureties: Job MITCHEL yeoman of Scituate & Elizeus TAYLOR, yeoman of Pembroke. Witnesses: Ruth CUSHING Jr., Elizabeth CUSHING. <25:408> Warrant to appraise, 16 Oct. 1779, to Elizeus TAYLOR of Pembroke and Joshua LAPHAM & Samuel JONES, yeomen of Scituate. <25:409> Inventory taken 29 Oct. 1779 by Elizeus TAYLOR & Benjamin HATCH Jr.; sworn to by admr. 4 Dec. 1779. <25:409> Insolvency presented by **John MITCHEL**, shipwright of Scituate. <28:468> Warrant 1 Apr. 1780, to John TURNER Jr., gent. and Daniel BAKER, yeoman, both of Pembroke, to examine claims of creditors. List of Claims: Anthony Eastes HATCH, Dr. Isaac WINSLOW, estate of Josiah KEEN, Esq.; sworn to 8 Oct. 1782 by TURNER & BAKER. <28:134> Account 10 Dec. 1781, of admr.; incl. paid funeral charges of father & mother; to taking care of my mother 9 weeks in her last sickness & providing wood & other necessaries.

MICRO #6 OF 6

Estate of **John MITCHELL Jr.**, mariner of Marshfield MA. <Plymouth Co.PR #14082>
Bond 1 Jan. 1770, Joseph KENT, yeoman of Marshfield, as admr.

THOMAS DOTY[2] (Edward[1])

<Plymouth Town Records, printed 1:99>...18 May 1668...Liberty was graunted by the Towne unto **Edward DOTEY, Thomas DOTEY** and **Thomas HEWES** to sett up a stage for fishing att Clarke's Island. <Plymouth Town Records, printed 1:116>...13 Dec. 1670...An acree and an halfe of and is graunted by the Towne unto **Thomas DOTEN** lying in Alcarmus feild to sett a house on.

PLYMOUTH COLONY DEEDS: (re: DOTY/DOTEN)

<3:98> - 17 Jan. 1667, John & Thomas DOTY, sons of Edward DOTY dec'd.
<3:391> - Mar. 1678, John WATERMAN of Marshfield to Thomas DOTEN.
<4:226> - 1678, Thoms DOTEN of Plymouth to James COLE Sr., land bought of John WATERMAN.

Henry CHURCHILL of Plympton MA to **Thomas DOTY** of Cape Cod. <Plymouth Co.Deeds 11:160>
...8 July 1714, Henry CHURCHILL, laborer, for love & good will unto my dutifull son in law Thomas DOTY, cooper...all lands in Plympton, Plymouth and Sepican alias Rochester...after my decease & the decease of my wife Mary. Witnesses: Barnabas LOTHROP, Thomas PAINE Jr. Rec. 3 Mar. 1714/5.

Mary CHURCHELL of Cape Cod to **Thomas DOTY** of Cape Cod. <Plymouth Co.Deeds 16:10>
...6 Mar. 1721/2, Mary CHURCHELL of Cape Cod, late of Rochester, widow of Henry CHURCHILL of Plimton...for love good will...towards my grandson Thomas DOTY...convey to him one quarter of a share in the 16 Shilling Purchase. Witnesses: John DYER, Beriah SMITH.

Mary CHURCHELL of Rochester MA to **John WHITE Jr.** of same. <Plymouth Co.Deeds 19:152>
...11 Oct. 1725, Mary CHURCHELL, widow of Henry CHURCHELL who was also widow of Thomas DOTY of Plymouth, for £100 sells to John WHITE Jr...

Will of **Thomas DOTY** of Truro, Cape Cod. <Plymouth Co.PR #6631>
<4:45>...dated 9 May 1721, mentions wf **Mercy;** Joseph ABBIT the child that now lives with me, £20 when he is twenty one; son **Thomas DOTEY,** he maintaining his Grandmother **Mary CHURCHILL;** Joseph HATCH & Christopher STOUT, both of Cape Cod, executors. Witnesses: Samuel MARSHALL Jr., Thomas BINNEY, Samuel TYLEY Jr. 8 Feb. 1721/2, Christopher STOUT renounced his power of executorship. <4:46> Oath 16 Feb. 1721/2 of Thomas BINNEY, 9 Mar. 1721/2 of Samuel MARSHALL Jr. Pr. 9 Mar. 1721/2. <4:47> Allowance to widow, 16 Apr. 1722...ye sd deceased leveing but one son of about nineteen years of age and of good discretion & his Guardian Joseph HATCH both consenting. <4:47> 16 Apr. 1722, Joseph HATCH of Cape Cod chosen guardian by **Thomas DOTY,** minor about nineteen years <4:48> Inventory taken 16 Feb. 1721/2 by Hezekiah DOANE, Beriah SMITH & George STOUT; incl. dwelling houses, £180; cooper's shop & warehouse; boat; schooner & rigging; half a whale boat; pew in meeting house. <4:49> Inventory sworn to 16 Apr. 1722 by widow **Mercy DOTY** and Joseph HATCH, exr. <4:49,316> Inventory taken 3 Mar. 1721/2 by John DYER, John FOSTER & Beriah SMITH; incl. old dwelling & land between land of Return WAITE & James RICKARD's land in Plymouth, £50; land in Plymouth below Cole's Hill, 30 ft. water front with cooper's shop, £16; house & land at Wellingsley, £60; 6 acres between land of Samuel HARLOW & John FAUNCE, £8; five tracts of land between land of Thomas HARLOW & Jonathan MORY, £80; 30 acres above Josiah FINNEY's land & near Warren's Wells, £30; share of cedar swamp in 9th lot, £15; pew in gallery in meeting house in S. Precinct of Plymouth, £2. Oath to inventory, 8 Mar. 1721/2 by Joseph HATCH, executor.

Guardianship of Child of **Thomas DOTY/DOTEN** of Truro, Cape Cod. <Plymouth Co.PR #6632>
<original> Bond 24 Dec. 1720, of Thomas HARLOW of Plymouth...stands bound for the use of **Thomas DOTEN** the son of **Thomas DOTEN** of Cape Cod alias Truro in ye County of Barnstable who is a minor ...the above bounded Thomas HARLOW upon whom is settled all the lands belonging to his sister Mary HARLOW late of Plymouth dec'd...shall cause to be paid unto **Thomas DOTEN Jr.** £3.11.5, it being his proportionable part. Witnesses: Thomas CROADE, Nathan CLARKE. <4:286> Letter/Bond 13 June 1721, Thomas HARLOW app'td gdn. of **Thomas DOTY,** son of **Thomas DOTY & Elizabeth** his late wife (late sister of sd Thomas HARLOW) dec'd, a minor under 21. Surety: Stephen CHURCHILL. Witnesses: Thomas CROADE, Josiah CORNISH.

Estate of **Mary HARLOW** of Plymouth MA. <Plymouth Co.PR>
<4:232> 11 July 1720, **Thomas HARLOW,** husbandman of Plymouth, app'td amr. on sister's estate. Surety: Francis ADAMS, clothier. Witnesses: John CHURCHELL, Thomas CROADE. <4:250> Warrant to appraise, 30 Aug. 1720 to Capt. Benjamin WARREN, Deacon Thomas CLARKE & Ebenezer HOLMES, all of Plymouth. Inventory taken 16 Nov. 1720, sworn to 23 Dec. 1720. <4:251> Division 24 Dec. 1720, in equal shares to **Thomas HARLOW, William HARLOW, Robert HARLOW, Isaac HARLOW, Thomas DOTY** the son of **Elisabeth** (late wife of **Thomas DOTY**) dec'd, **Lydia CHURCHELL** wf of Barnabas and **Rebeckah HARLOW**

Amasa TURNER of Duxbury MA to **Nicholas & Lemuel DREW** of Plymouth MA. <Plymouth Co.Deeds 28:67>
...21 Aug. 1733, Amasa TURNER, cordwainer, sells to Nicholas DREW, shipwright & Lemuel DREW, mariner...all rights in estate of mother in law Elizabeth DELANO dec'd, former wife of Dr. Benoni DELANO, that she received from estate of her parents John & Hannah DREW. Witnesses: Samuel DREW, John WINSLOW.

Estate of **Capt. Lemuel DREW,** mariner of Plymouth MA. <Plymouth Co.PR #6710>
<original> Petition 12 June 1738, of **John RIDER...**I married Lemuel DREWE's eldes daughter and his father hath deseased and he having no child of age I understand that it lays with me to adminester...but I being a seafairing man I cannot attend to it and so decline it & desire that my Unkel Jonathan BARNES administer. Witness: Seth DREW. <7:417> Letter/Bond 15 June 1738, Jonathan BARNES cordwainer, app'td admr. Sureties: John BARNES, yeoman & Lemuel BARNES, shoreman, both of Plymouth. <7:433> Inventory taken July 1738 by Stephen CHURCHELL, William DUNHAM & Thomas FOSTER; incl silver watch & chain, £10.10s; homested, £430; 12 acre wood lot, £48; houselot adjoining Capt. ESDAEL's house lot, £25; cedar swamp, £15; total, £694.9.7.; sworn to 28 Sept. 1738 by admr. & appraisers. <11:1> Account 12 Apr. 1748 of admr. <11:4> Division of real estate, 13 Apr. 1748, by Thomas HOLMES, Eleazer HOLMES, Joseph BARTLETT, Consider HOWLAND & James HOVEY to children of dec'd, viz: **Lemuel DREW, James DREW, William DREW, Mary RIDER** wf of Jno. and **Sarah SAMSON** wf of Jonathan; sworn to 8 June 1748. Guardianships: <7:435> 29 Sept. 1738, John BARNES of Plymouth app'td gdn. of **Lemuel DREW** (under 14). <originals> 17 Apr. 1741, John BARNES app'td gdn. of **Sarah DREW, James DREW & William DREW.** <9:381> 5 June 1744, **James DREW** chose Nathaniel BARTLETT, husbandman of Plymouth as gdn. in right of my mother **Hannah DREW** late of Plymouth dec'd. <9:382> 5 June 1744 same for **Sarah DREW,** 16 Jan. 1744 same for **Lemuel DREW.** <9:383> 16 Jan. 1744 same for **William DREW.** <13:373> Account of gdn. 3 Jan. 1755, on behalf of minors; incl. paid their Grandmother **Ann BARNES** two payments as her right of dower in the sd minors' estate.

Estate of **Seth DREW,** shipwright of Plymouth MA. <Plymouth Co.PR #6731>
<original> Bond 10 Mar. 1740, of Jonathan BARNES, cordwainer of Plymouth, admr. Sureties: Ansell

LOTHROP, mariner & Gershom HOLMES, cordwainr, both of Plymouth. <10:236> Inventory taken 11 May 1741 by Stephen CHURCHELL, John HARLOW & Thomas FOSTER; personal estate total, £64.14s. <10:301> Account 27 Dec. 1746, of admr.

Heirs of **William DREW**, mariner of Plymouth MA. <Plymouth Co.Deeds 44:244>
...11 Mar. 1758...Whereas William DREW...was seized of a certain house lot containing about half an acre lying at the easterly corner of the homestead that Capt. Lemuel DREW (father of sd William) dyed seized of...& other lands...so that his brothers Lemuel DREW & James DREW and his sister Mary RIDER are his heirs and the sd heirs having agreed to make partition of the premises among themselves.

FRANCIS EATON

MICRO #1 OF 4

PLYMOUTH COUNTY PROBATE: (re: EATON)

Year	Name	Town	Type	Reference
1690	William			#7067, 1:82,83 <MD 12:227>
1719	Marcy	Plymouth		#7054, 4:179
1724	Samuel	Middleboro		#7059, 4:391;4:403,404,454 <MD 12:227>
1738	Elisha	Plympton		#7043, 8:10,68,69;8:88,128;9:409,410
1745	Benjamin	Kingston		#7036, 10:70,73,120,431;11:10,21,160
1746	Seth et al	Kingston		#7062, 10:250,251;13:229;14:229;18:163;20:337
1749	Francis	Middleboro		#7045, 11:250,326;14:2
1750	John	Kingston		#7052, 11:451;12:457;13:368,454
1751	Benjamin	Kingston		#7037, 12:284,327,394,495,409,467;14:260
1755	Benjamin et al	Middleboro		#7038, 13:556,557,567,568;15:18,19
1755	John	Halifax	gdn.	#7051, 13:406
1759	David	Kingston		#7041,15:304,313,402;16:121;21:443;43:229;48:322
1769	Consider et al	Kingston		#7039, 20:184,433-36;20:434
1795	Noah	Plympton	gdn.	#7055, 26:504;35:229
1799	Oliver	Middleboro		#7057, 34:197;36:540,542,543,545
1805	Jabez	Plympton	adm.	#7049, 39:24;40:287
1812	Job	Kingston	adm.	#7050, 39:339;44:175;48:322
1812	Olive	Middleboro	gdn.	#7056, 41:101
1820	Samuel	Middleboro	will	#7060, 50:501;53:91
1827	Freedom	Halifax	adm.	#7046, 61:137;62:223;64:295,420,479,480;66:74,75 171,186
1831	Elijah	Middleboro	will	#7042, 68:257;70:116,229;74;6
1832	Arabella	W.Bridgewater	adm.	#7034, 68:366;71:93;74:114,132,406
1833	Israel	Middleboro	will	#7048, 73:72,309;74:136;77:468
1834	Cyrus	Middleboro	gdn.	#7040, 65:382;73:447;77:46,486
1834	Solomon	Middleboro	will	#7065, 76:110,166;77:58,205
1840	Alfred	Middleboro	will	#7032, 2:163**O**; 6:108**U**;10:509**A**;82:311,366;83:308
1849	Abby et al	Middleboro	gdn.	#7030, 1:291**R**; 3:408**P**;9:195**M**;92:159
1849	Alden	Middleboro	adm.	#7031, 12:87;91:180
1849	Apollos	Middleboro	adm.	#7033, 7:568**V**;12:81**C**;91:181
1849	Harriet A.	Middleboro	gdn.	#7047, 9:213**M**;11:83**N**;92:392;99:473;100:306;102: 180;104:538;106:22
1849	Seth	Middleboro	will	#7061, 2:210**H**;8:19**W**;91:438,441;92:328

Estate of **Francis EATON**, carpenter of Plymouth. <Plymouth Colony Records (PCR) 1:19>
...25 Nov. 1633, It was ordered that whereas Frances EATON...dyed undebted for more than the estate of the said Francis would make good, insomuch as **Christian**, his late wife, durst not administer, it was ordered that Mr. Thomas PRENCE & Mr. John DONE/DOANE in the behalfe of the Court, should enter upon the estate according to the inventory brought in upon oath the day of (-----) that the creditors might have so far as the estate will make good & the widow be freed & acquitted from any claim or demands of all or any his creditors whatsoever.

PLYMOUTH COLONY RECORDS (PCR):

<1:8> - 8 Jan. 1632/3, Francis EATON acknowledges sale of his dwelling house to Kenelm & Josias WINSLOW for £26.

<1:24> - 22 Jan. 1633/4, Josias WYNSLOW hath sold unto Kenelm WYNSLOW his share of dwelling bought of Frances EATON.

<1:70> - 4 Dec. 1637, ...landing lying at end of Mr. William BREWSTER's & Francis EATON's lotts graunted unto Captaine Miles STANDISH.

<2:79> - 7 Jan. 1644/5, Samuel EATON deposed that his meaning was to confirm the acre of land Mr William BREWSTER bought of his mother, unto Love BREWSTER; see the great book where it is entered one against another at large.

<2:117> - 1 June 1647, Mr. ALDEN & John WASHBORNE ordered to view the bounds betwixt the lands of Capt. STANDISH & Francis EATON & sett them at rights.

<2:135> - 4 Oct. 1648, Boundary dispute between Love BREWSTER & Samuell EATON to be reported on by Mr. ALLDIN, Henery SAMPSON & Phillip DELANOY.

<2:147> - 29 Oct. 1649, Mr. ALDEN, Phillip DELANOY & Henery SAMPSON to measure Samuell EATON's land at the uper end & report.

<4:95> - 7 June 1665, Benjamin EATON granted one share in that tract of land comonly called the Major's Purchase, who are to have 30 acrees appece out of the best of it.

<5:129> - 20 Mar. 1667, By order from the honored Court of this colonie, have measured unto Thomas SAVORY and Benjamine EATON sixty acres of upland in the land called the Major's Purchase near Namassakett, which land att the eastward end thereof joyneth unto the land of Sacariah EEDY/Zachariah EDDY..Signed by William CROW, William NELSON.

PLYMOUTH COLONY RECORDS (PCR), cont-d:

<5:293> - 27 Oct. 1685, Thomas EATON, one of those complained against by William WOOD et al, for occupying in common lands in Dartmouth. Action was non-suited.
<12:16> - 25 June 1631, Francis EATON to Edward WYNSLOW, 4 acres of land lying in the north field for a cow calf.
<12:16> - 30 Dec. 1631, Francis EATON & William BREWSTER...twenty acres lying at a place called Nothingelse, also 12 acres at same place.
<12:18> - , Experience MICHELL to Samuell EDDY. Witness: Frances EATON.
<12:48> - , Francis BILLINGTON & wf Christian sell to Jonathan & Love BREWSTER...her thirds of estate of Francis EATON, her former husband.
<12:99> - Jan. 1644, Agreement concerning a water spring on an acre of land & statement of confirmation of title from Samuel EATON to Love BREWSTER.
<12:100> - Apr. 1644, Samuel EATON, eldest son & heire apparent unto sd Francis EATON, aged 24 yrs and upwards, confirms title to William BREWSTER in property bought of Christian, late wf of Francis EATON but now wf of Francis BILLINGTON.
<12:144>- 10 Mar. 1646, Samuel EATON to Love BREWSTER, ack. by wf Elizabeth EATON.
<12:205> - , Sarah BREWSTER, widow of Love BREWSTER, confirms sale of 3 acres of meadow in Duxburo to Samuel EATON.

==========

Will of **William EATON.** <Plymouth Co.PR>
...dated July 1690...being cald forth to go against the ffrench I give one cow and calf to my father and mother. Elkanah CUSHMAN & wf Martha made oath 18 Mar. 1690/1. Inventory presented 18 Mar. 1690/1 by Benjamin EATON, father of sd William.

BENJAMIN EATON^2 (Francis^1)

PLYMOUTH COLONY DEEDS: (re: EATON)

<2:1:165> - 18 Dec. 1655, Edward GRAY sells house & land at Plymouth to Benjamin EATON, he to take possession in Sept. 1656.
<2:2:13> - 2 Nov. 1658, Benjamin EATON sells above to Stephen BRYANT of Plymouth.
<3:57> - 30 Mar. 1666, Samuel EATON of Middleboro, deed of gift to brother Benjamin EATON & wf of Plymouth & to their heirs, land at Dartmouth.
<3:130> - 6 Feb. 1668, Benjamin EATON & wf Sarah sell to Zachariah EDDY, their rights in the Major's Purchase.
<5:368> - 29 Oct. 1685, Benjamin EATON & wf Sarah of Plymouth & son Benjamin EATON Jr. late of Plymouth, sell to John HATHAWAY, land in Dartmouth given them in 1666 by Samuel EATON (above).

==========

Will of **Benjamin EATON**, housewright of Kingston MA. <Plymouth Co.PR #7036>
<10:70>...dated 3/23 Apr. 1745; mentions son **William EATON**, to receive 70 acres of homestead in Kingston & 2 acres meadow in Plimpton..."I look upon my son **William** non compos mentis"; sons **Benjamin EATON, David EATON, Francis EATON, Elisha EATON, John EATON**; unnamed children of my dau **Sarah CUSHMAN**; daus **Mary SOULE, Elizabeth STURTEVANT**; grandchild **Phebe BRYANT**;...to **Mercy & Hannah** of late paid them their portion and there remains due of **Micah BRYANT**'s portion, £15.10s and to **Jesse BRYANT**, £25.16s; son **Benjamin**, executor. Witnesses: William RIPLEY, John EVERSON, Francis ADAMS who made oath 20 Dec. 1745. <10:73> Pr. 20 Dec. 1745. <10:120> Inventory taken 21 Jan. 1745 by Gershom BRADFORD, Samuel FOSTER & Samuel RING; incl. land bought of Samuel BRADFORD. <10:431> Additional Inventory taken 18 May 1747 by Benjamin SAMSON, John BREWSTER & James EVERSON, all of Kingston. <11:21> Account of **Benjamin EATON**, exr.; Debts to: William RIPLEY, TYLER & WINSLOW, Jno. BREWSTER, Giles RICKARD, Deacon PERKINS, Judah HALL; Paid to: Francis ADAMS, Nicholas SEVER, Nathaniel BRYANT, Solomon CUSHMAN, Benjamin CUSHMAN Jr., to the widow, David CHURCHEL, Thomas ADAMS, John LORING, Benjamin CUSHMAN, Joshua CUSHING, Jno. BREWSTER, Solomon LEACH, Zachariah SOUL, Judeth WASHBURN, Jacob TOMSON, Cornelius STURTEVANT and mourning for the widow; Legacies paid to: chil. of **Sarah CUSHMAN; Mary SOUL, Elizabeth STURTEVANT, Phebe BRYANT, Micah BRYANT, Jesse BRYANT.** <11:160> Division 15 June 1748 by Jacob TOMSON of Middleboro, Josiah PERKINS, James HARLOW, George BRYANT & Nathaniel FULLER, to the following heirs, viz: son **David EATON**; son **Rev. Elisha EATON**; heirs of **Hannah BRYANT** dec'd wf of Benjamin, viz: **Michel BRYANT & Mercy LEACH** wf of Nehemiah; son **John EATON**; son **Benjamin EATON.** The part belonging to dau **Mary SOUL** wf of Zachariah, son **Francis EATON** dec'd, dau **Elizabeth STURTEVANT** wf of Cornelius, dau **Sarah CUSHMAN** dec'd wf of Benjamin and heirs of **Hannah BRYANT** dec'd wf of Benjamin dec'd, having been sold to Capt. John LORING of Plympton.
(Note: Refer to the files for the lengthy records.)

==========

PLYMOUTH COUNTY DEEDS: (re: Andrew BEARCE, grantor)

<48:208> - 1740, Andrew BEARCE & wf Margaret.
<58:117> - 1774, Andrew BEARCE & Shubael BEARSE.
<66:213> - 1784, Andrew BEARCE of Halifax MA.
<74:174> - 1791, Andrew BEARCE of Halifax MA.
<79:192> - 4 Feb. 1796, Andrew BEARCE, yeoman of Halifax & wf Mary sell 10 a. to Benjamin BRIGGS.

==========

Estate of **Andrew BEARCE** of Halifax MA. <Plymouth Co.PR #1750>
<34:366> Letter. <38:322> Warrant & Inventory. <38:423> Warrant & List of claims. <40:60> Account

---

PLYMOUTH COUNTY DEEDS: (re: John LORING)

<31:119> - 8 Sept 1738, John LORING from Benjamin EATON Jr., cordwainer, 3 acres.
<37:184> - 25 Oct. 1745, John LORING from Thomas PAINE, eleven and a half acres.
<38:48> - 20 Apr. 1746, John LORING from Benjamin EATON, cordwainer of Kingston, 3 acres.
<38:266> - 28 May 1747, John LORING from Jesse BRYANT of Middleboro, "one sixth of one ninth".
<38:267> - 2 July 1747, John LORING from David & Hannah CURTIS of Halifax, " ".
(Note: the following references have no data, viz: 39:155;41:167,156;42:91;55:209.)

PLYMOUTH COUNTY DEEDS: (re: Benjamin EATON, grantor)

<1:146> - 1691/2, Benjamin EATON to Caleb WILLIAMSON.
<3:233> - 17 Dec. 1700, Benjamin EATON Sr. & Benjamin EATON Jr., of Plympton to John GRAY.
<10:1:500>- 23 Jan. 1703, Benjamin EATON to William CHURCHILL. Rec. 1713.
<5::242> - 7 Mar. 1704, Benjamin EATON Sr. of Plymouth to John STURTEVANT, land given him by Francis BILLINGTON.
<10:1:61> - 4 Apr. 1704, Benjamin EATON Jr., carpenter of Plymouth to Samuel & John STURTEVANT.
<9:39> - 1711, Benjamin EATON to Joseph SILVESTER.
<9:291> - 1712, Benjamin EATON to John EVERSON.
<10:2:235>- 1713/4, Benjamin EATON to William COOK.
<10:2:243>- 29 Mar. 1714, Benjamin EATON gift to son Jabez EATON.
<10:2:301>- 1714, Benjamin EATON to Thomas SHURTLEFF.
<12:41> - 1716, Benjamin EATON to Richard COOPER.
<15:82> - 1720, Benjamin EATON to Nathaniel THOMAS.
<16:124> - 1722, Benjamin EATON & John EVERSON, division.
<17:124> - 1723/4, Benjamin EATON, Samuel BRADFORD et al, agreement.
<18:35> - 1724, Benjamin EATON to Eleazer RING.
<20:121> - 1726, Benjamin EATON to John EVERSON.
<23:192> - 18 Dec. 1728, Benjamin EATON Sr. gift to son Benjamin EATON Jr., both of Kingston.
<23:192> - 18 Dec. 1728, Benjamin EATON Sr. gift to son Francis EATON, both of Kingston.

PLYMOUTH COUNTY DEEDS: (re: Benjamin EATON, grantee)

<3:38> - 20 June 1687, Benjamin EATON Jr., late of Plymouth from Samuel & Rebecca WOOD of Middl.
<3:38> - 17 Apr. 1693, Benjamin EATON Jr. of Plymouth from Town of Plymouth.
<3:40> - 13 Apr. 1694, Benjamin EATON Jr. of Plymouth from Caleb COOKE.
<3:236> - 13 Aug. 1692, Benjamin EATON Jr. of Plymouth from Caleb COOKE of Plymouth.
<3:237> - 12 July 1692, Benjamin EATON Jr. of Plymouth from John BRADFORD of Plymouth.
<3:138> - 2 May 1698, Benjamin EATON Jr. of Plymouth from Stephen BRYANT Jr. of Plymouth.

(Note: the following references have no data, viz: 10:25,26;11:28,134;14:227;16:124;17:124;23:171 172,192;24:221;29:84,87,190;39:176;53:192.)

Guardianship of **Noah EATON**, labourer of Plympton MA. <Plymouth Co.PR #7055>
<35:229> Representation 21 Mar. 1795...The Major part of the Selectmen of Plymton represent that **Noah EATON** does by excessive intemperence and idleness expose himself & family to suffering circumstances...and pray that such procedure may be had thereon as the law has provided. Signed by Gideon BRADFORD & George SAMPSON. <original> Citation 21 Mar. 1795 to **Noah EATON** to appear at Court to be holden at Caleb LORING's, Innholder in Plymton, to show cause why a guardian should not be appointed. (To be served by Joel ELLIS, Constable of Plimton.) <26:504> Letter/Bond 21 Mar 1795, Gideon BRADFORD & George SAMPSON app'td gdns. Sureties: William RIPLEY 2d of Plymton & Ephraim SPOONER of Plymouth. Witnesses: Levi BRYANT, Isaac LOTHROP.

Estate of **Benjamin EATON**, cordwainer of Kingston MA. <Plymouth Co.PR #7037>
<12:327> Letter/Bond 25 June 1751, Robert WATERMAN, yeoman of Halifax. Sureties: Consider HOWLAND innholder & Nathaniel SHURTLEFF, both of Plymouth. Witnesses: Abraham HAMMATT, Edward WINSLOW. <12:394> Account 7 Oct. 1751; Paid to: James EVERSON, Samuel KING, Samuel FOSTER, Nathaniel COOK, James STURTEFENT/STURTEVANT, Esq. SEVER, Ebenezer COALE/COLE, Cornelius STURTEVANT, Dr. LORING, necessaries to widow. <12:395> Receipt 7 Oct. 1751 of **Marcy EATON**, to admr. Robert WATERMAN, for Ł20.1.9. for necessaries. <12:409> Account 13 Nov. 1751 of admr.; Paid to: Dr. LORING, Dr. HARLOW Dr. LEBARON, John FAUCE/FAUNCE, Samuel RING, Nathaniel TOREY, Ebenezer LEACH, Capt. JACKSON. <12: 467> Decree 3 Jan. 1752, to sell real estate to pay debts. <original> Bond of admr. 14 Feb. 1752. Surety: Samuel SEABURY of Duxbury. Witnesses: Hannah WINSLOW, John LOTHROP. <12:468> Account 5 Apr. 1752; land sold to: David EATON, Ebenezer COLE, Nathaniel BRYANT, Ebenezer BRIGGS, Capt. CUSHING, Austin BARIE, Jonathan RIPLEY, John TILSON & William STURTEVANT; Paid to: Ephraim & John EVERSON, Allerton CUSHMAN, David EATON, Josiah PERKINS, Thomas CUSHMAN, David STURTEVANT, Hanna SOULE, David DARLING, Francis STURTEVANT, Nathaniel DUNHAM, James BARIE, Moses WRIGHT, Ephraim TILLSON, Lemuel STURTEVANT, Isaac TINKHAM, Ebenezer TOMSON, John THOMAS, Noah STURTEVANT, Isaac LITTLE, John WRIGHT. <14;260> Warrant for dower & division, 7 Mar. 1757, to widow **Mary EATON** & heirs. Division 26 Apr. 1757 by Samuel SHAW, Robert WATERMAN, John BRADFORD, Nathaniel COOKE & Zebede CHANDLER to following heirs, viz: the widow, her thirds plus one fifth of the share of her son **Thaddeus EATON** dec'd; eldest son **Noah EATON; Seth EATON; James EATON; Benjamin EATON.**

Guardianship of Children of **Benjamin EATON**, yeoman of Kingston MA. <Plymouth Co.PR #7062> <10:250> Letters/Bonds 6 Oct. 1746, **Benjamin EATON** app'td gdn. of his sons **Noah & Seth EATON.** Surety: Joseph HOLMES of Kingston. Witnesses: David STOCKBRIDGE, Edward WINSLOW. <13:229> Letter/Bond 8 Apr. 1754 of Jonathan TILLSON, blacksmith of Plympton, app'td gdn. of **James EATON.** Surety: Cornelius STURTEVANT of Plimpton. Witnesses: Isaac PARTRIDGE, John LOTHROP. <original> Letter 27 Apr. 1754, **Seth EATON** constitutes Cornelius STURTEVANT his gdn. Witnesses: Samuel JACKSON & John LOTHROP. Bond 8 Apr. 1754, of Cornelius STURTEVANT as gdn. of **Seth & Noah EATON.** Surety: Jonathan TILLSON of Plympton. Witnesses: Isaac PARTRIDGE, John LOTHROP. <14:229> Letter/Bond 14 Apr. 1757, **Mary EATON**, widow of Kingston, app'td gdn. of **Benjamin EATON.** Sureties: Nathaniel COOKE, Cornelius STURTEVANT. Witnesses: Elkanah WATSON, John LOTHROP. <18:163> 13 Sept. 1763, **Benjamin EATON** makes choice of Seth CUSHING of Plympton as his gdn. Witnesses: Edward WINSLOW, Joshua CUSHING. Bond 13 Sept. 1763, of Seth CUSHING, gdn. Sureties: James EVERSON, Rufus RIPLEY, both of Kingston. Witnesses: Edward WINSLOW, Joshua LORING. <20:337> 5 Mar. 1770, **Benjamin EATON** of Plymout releases Seth CUSHING of Plymton as gdn. Witnesses: Pelham WINSLOW, Simeon SAMSON.

Estate of **David EATON**, yeoman of Kingston MA <Plymouth Co.PR #7041> <15:304> Letter/Bond 8 Sept. 1759, widow **Deborah EATON** app'td admx. Sureties: John FAUNCE of Kingston & Seth CUSHING Jr. of Plimpton. Witnesses: Benjamin SMITH, Edward WINSLOW. <15:304> Inventory taken 11 Oct. 1759 by Gideon BRADFORD & Seth CUSHING Jr. of Plimton and Benjamin COOK of Kingston; mentions real estate in Kingston, Plimton & Pembroke. <16:121> Account, Paid to: Dr. HILL, heirs of Benjamin EATON dec'd, Ebenezer COLE, Benjamin WESTON, Nathan PERKINS, Deacon Robert WATERMAN, William SEVER, William RAND, Samuel FOSTER, Gershom COB, Thomas LORING, Kimbal PRINCE, Seth EVERSON, Thomas LORING Jr., Jonathan RING, Seth CUSHING, Ignatius LORING; oath by admx. 9 June 1761. <21:443> Division 13 Apr. 1771, by Zebede CHANDLER & Ephraim BRIANT of Plimton and Benjamin COOK of Kingston, to widow & children, viz: widow **Deborah EATON, Lot EATON, Jabez EATON, Job EATON, Consider EATON, Joshua EATON, Eunice EATON.** <43:229> Division 7 May 1810 by Samuel Stafford STURTEVANT of Halifax and Josiah COOK & Jeremiah SAMPSON of Kingston, to divide the real estate assigned to **Deborah EATON**, widow, into seven equal shares, viz: eldest son **Lot EATON** (2 shares); **Jabez EATON; Job EATON;** heirs of **Consider EATON**, dec'd, **Joshua EATON**, dec'd & **Eunice COOK** dec'd wf of Amos. "Lot, Jabez, Job and the heirs of Eunice Cook, are the only remaining heirs of Consider & Joshua dec'd. <48:322> Division of real estate of **Job EATON**, late of Kingston dec'd and also the widow's thirds, assigned to the following heirs of **Eunice COOK** dec'd, viz: **Lydia COOK** now **Lydia BRADFORD** wf of Thomas, **Deborah COOK, Eunice COOK & David Eaton COOK.** The division was made by John GRAY, Jeremiah SAMPSON & Seth CUSHING & allowed 6 Jan. 1817.

Guardianship of Children of **David EATON**, yeoman of Kingston MA. <Plymouth Co.PR #7039> <20:184> Letter/Bond 14 Mar. 1769, Ebenezer FULLER of Halifax app'td gdn. of **Job EATON**, minor under 14. Surety: Simeon STURTEVANT. Witnesses: Edward WINSLOW, Edward WINSLOW Jr. <20:433> Letter 27 Dec. 1770, Seth CUSHING of Plimton app'td gdn. of **Consider EATON**, minor above 14. <20:433,436> Letters/Bonds 27 Dec. 1770, widow **Deborah FULLER** makes choice of Seth CUSHING as gdn. of **Joshua EATON & Eunice EATON**, both under 14. Sureties: Samuel BRYANT of Plimton & Benjamin EATON of Plymouth. Witnesses: Penelope WINSLOW, Edward WINSLOW Jr.

MICRO #2 OF 4

Estate of **Francis EATON**, husbandman of Middleboro MA. <Plymouth Co.PR #7045> <11:326> Letter/Bond 11 July 1749, widow **Lydia EATON** app'td admx. Sureties: John MILLER & Benjamin EATON of Kingston. Witnesses: Edward WINSLOW, Isaac THOMAS. <11:250> Inventory taken 25 July 1749 by Ezra CLAP, Seth TINKHAM & William HOOPER. <14:2> Account of admx. allowed 19 Nov. 1755; Paid to: Stephen CHURCHILL, Dr. HOWARD, William REED, Jacob BARDIN, Jonathan CARVER, Dr. WILLIS, Elijah CLAP, John REED, Benjamin WHITE, David EATON, Jonathan WOOD, Samuel CONTON, John FORD, Benjamin HAYFORD, Widow WETHRELL, Benjamin WHITE, Joseph LATHROP, Jabez CUSHMAN, Dr. PRATT, James LINSEY, Edward WESTON, Jo. BARDIN, Dr. OTIS, Benjamin SHAW, William BRITT, Samuel ANDREWS, Henry RICHMOND, Widow HALL, Lieut. BRETT, Dr. LeBARON, necessaries set off to the widow.

Guardianship of Children of **Francis EATON**, husbandman of Middleboro MA. <Plymouth Co.PR #7038> <13:556-7> Letters 3 Nov. 1755, Azariah THRASHER of Middleboro, app'td gdn. of **Susanna EATON & Benjamin EATON.** <13:567-8> Letters 3 Nov. 1755, Azariah THRASHER chosen gdn. by **Mary EATON, Elijah EATON & John EATON**, all above 14. Witnesses: David ALDEN Jr., Silvanus EATON. <original> Bonds 3 Nov. 1755 of Azariah THRASHER, as gdn. of the above 5 children. Surety: William HOOPER, bricklayer of Bridgewater. Witnesses: Jabez EATON, John LOTHROP. <15:18,19> Letters 7 Aug. 1758, David ALDEN of Middleboro chosen gdn. by **Elijah, Susanna, Benjamin & Mary EATON.** Witnesses: Ephraim KEITH, Abiezer EDSON. <original> Bonds 3 July 1758 of David ALDEN ad gdn. of the above 4 children, all above 14. Surety: Jacob HAYWARD of Bridgewater. Witnesses: Nathaniel STETSON, Edward WINSLOW.

Will of **Elijah EATON** of Middleborough MA. <Plymouth Co.PR #7042> <70:116>...dated 31 Oct. 1825, mentions son **Barzillai EATON**; daus **Lucretia PERKINS, Mersena EATON & Bethana LEONARD**; son **Zebina EATON**; dau **Salona FOBES; Salona EATON & Elijah EATON**, the chil of **Daniel EATON** who married my dau; **Sarah KEITH** wf of John & **Elijah E. PERKINS**, chil of **Azel PERKINS** who married my dau; to Rev. Philip COLBY, all my right to the Proprietor's house in this Parish; Elijah E. PERKINS, trader and Luke REED, yeoman, executors. Witnesses: George PICKENS Jr., Harriot S. SMITH, Sarah Ann SPROAT. <original> Bond 11 Apr. 1831 of exrs. Sureties: Samuel MILLER & Azel PERKINS, yeomen of Middleboro. Witness: J.H. LOUD. <70:229> Inventory taken 2 Mar. 1831 by Simon BACKUS, Azel PERKINS, Daniel ALDEN, all of Middleboro; incl. homestead farm, $1900.00.

<68:257> Notice of appointment, sworn by Elijah E. PERKINS, 3 Apr. 1832. <74:6> Account 18 Feb. 1833 of exrs., mentions payment to Salona E. WHITE.

Joseph EATON of Middleborough MA to **Micah ALLEN Jr.** <Plymouth Co.Deeds 48:204>
...7 Apr. 1760, Joseph EATON, for £84 sold to Micah ALLEN Jr....land in Middleboro, part of estate of my Father Francis EATON dec'd and is set off to me as my double share. Wf Hannah EATON releases dower. Ack. 26 Apr. 1760 by Joseph. Rec. 2 Aug. 1763.

Joseph EATON of Middleborough MA to **David ALDEN** of same. <Plymouth Co.Deeds
...8 Apr. 1760, Joseph EATON, yeoman & wf Hannah, for £59.15s sold to David ALDEN...our whole right in the estate of our Father, Barnabas CROSMAN dec'd of Middleboro & Mother Hannah CROSMAN dec'd...partly bounded by land set off to Joseph ALDEN & Theophilus CROSMAN from mother's thirds. Witnesses: Job ALDEN, John EATON. Ack. 26 Apr. 1760. Rec. 10 Apr. 1794.

PLYMOUTH COUNTY DEEDS: (re: EATON)

<58:116> - 5 May 1762, Joseph EATON from James KEITH, land at Titicut.
< > - 5 July 1764, Joseph EATON from Jonathan KING, land at Titicut.
<67:80> - 20 Mar. 1784, Joseph EATON, yeoman & wf Hannah of Middleboro to Joseph HATHAWAY of same, land J.E. bought in Middleboro. Rec. 22 June 1786.

Joel EATON et al to **Alfred EATON** of Middleboro MA. <Plymouth Co.Deeds 140:194>
...29 Nov. 1819, Joel EATON, yeoman; John SHAW & wf Polly in her right, of Foxborough; and Abigail SHAW of Paris ME, heirs at law of Joseph EATON late of Middleborough dec'd, for $30.00 sold to Alfred EATON, yeoman...three quarters of an acre in Middleborough, lying in Titicut...being the same land Jonathan KING sold to Joseph EATON by a deed dated 5 July 1764 and rec. 58:116. Ack same day by John & Polly; 26 Apr. 1820 by Joel. Rec. 3 June 1820.

Abner SHAW of Middleboro MA to **John SHAW Jr.** of same. <Plymouth Co.Deeds 97:19>
...8 Mar. 1791, Abner SHAW, cordwainer, for £90 sold to John SHAW Jr., yeoman...all my interest in real estate of Benjamin HACKET dec'd, late of Middleboro, that I bought of sd HACKET and the other heirs.

PLYMOUTH COUNTY DEEDS: (re: SHAW, HACKET)

<97:18> - 14 Oct. 1780, Mercy HACKET, spinster of Middleboro, dau of Benjamin HACKET dec'd of same, to John HACKET.
<97:18> - 14 Sept 1782, John HACKET of Westmoreland NH to Abner SHAW, yeoman of Middleboro, all interest in estate of father Benjamin HACKET dec'd of Middleboro.
<97:18> - 18 Oct. 1782, Sarah HACKET, spinster of Middleboro, dau of Benjamin HACKET dec'd to Abner SHAW.
<97:19> - 21 Mar. 1789, Asahel HACKET, blacksmith of Dighton, son of Benjamin HACKET dec'd to Abner SHAW.
<101:80> - 1805, John & Abigail SHAW of Carver & others sell land.
<131:189> - 1805, John & Abigail SHAW of Carver & others sell land.
<134:28> - 4 Mar. 1818, Abigail SHAW, widow of George, of Middleboro to John SHAW Esq. of same, land George bought of his father Joseph SHAW.
<157:128> - 1821, Samuel SHAW Esq. & wf Abigail of Carver sell land.
<159:230> - 16 Oct. 1826, Abigail SHAW, widow of Paris ME to Alfred EATON, yeoman of Middleboro.. land in Middleboro...inheritance from my late father Joseph EATON dec'd
<162:25> - 1828, Children & grandchildren of Isaac RICKARD dec'd (Abigail SHAW ment.).
<227:215> - 1847, Abigail SHAW, dau of Joshua SHAW.

Estate of **Polly SHAW** of Norton MA. <Bristol Co.PR>
<103:213;158:383> 2 June 1857, **Marshall SHAW** of Mansfield app'td admr. <164:263> Bond. <119:72> Notice. <192:543> Inventory, personal estate only, total $424.23. <103:213> Account 1 June 1858 signed by heirs **Marshall SHAW, John SHAW & Mary S. HAWES**; Estate distributed to following heirs, viz: $5.40 ea to: **Mary S. HAWES, Joel S. SHAW, John S. SHAW, Zephemiah S. CROSSMAN, Eliza J. WETH(ERELLsp)**; $10.80 ea to: **Fanny RING, John SHAW, Hannah C. (SAMSONsp), Leander/Lucinda WHITE, Keziah E. ALDEN, Marshall DEAN**; $9.54 ea to: **Abigail J. LINCOLN, Nancy DREW, Simeon LINCOLN.**

Estate of **Benjamin BRYANT** of Plympton MA. <Plymouth Co.PR>
<4:396> Adm./Bond 19 May 1724, Benjamin EATON of Plympton app'td admr. Sureties: Frances COOK of Plimpton & Jacob TOMSON of Middleborough. Witnesses: John ROBINSON, Nathaniel THOMAS. <4:428> Warrant to appraise, 19 May 1724, to Jacob TOMPSON, Esq. of Middleborough, Capt. Caleb LOREING of Plimpton & Jacob MITCHELL of Plimoth. <5:179> Account of admr. 23 May 1724; Paid to: Nathaniel THOMAS, Esq., Jonathan BRYANT on account of his father on a bond, Andrew RING, Samuel FOSTER, widow Sarah LITTLE, Capt. Caleb LORING, Constable BEIRCE, Samuel CUSHMAN, Israel BRADFORD, David BRADFORD for rates, Samuel SPRAGUE, my son Benjamin EATON, Benjamin CUSHMAN, Samuel BRYANT, John SPRAGUE, John EVERSON Jr., widow Mary RIPLEY, Jonathan BRYANT for his father, Elizabeth CUSHMAN, John FULLER's wife for tayloring, John EVERSON, Jacob COOKE, Thomas TOMSON, William BREWSTER, Thomas CROADE, Mrs. Sarah LITTLE, Jonathan BRYANT, William COOMER, Jonathan BRYANT in part for keeping his father; cloathing ye children fit to put out, £2.11s; Ignatius CUSHING for making a coffin, 7s; Jacob MITCHELL; Capt. Benjamin WARREN, coroner; Elisha STETSON, John MURDOCH, Isaac BARKER, Col. WINSLOW, Capt. Jacob TOMSON, Dr. PALMER, John GRAY, Ebenezer EATON, Benjamin SAMSON, Isaac THOMAS, Joseph STETSON, Madam Sarah WARREN, Major Isaac LOTHROP, widow Hannah BRADFORD,

Jno. WATSON, Esq.; boards & nails to make ye coffin, 7s.; total paid, Ł135.2s7d. <4:428> Inventory taken 9 June 1724 by Caleb LORING, Jacob TOMSON & Jacob MICHELL; incl. homestead & meadow on Barrow's brook, Ł430; one share of cedar swamp in 33d lot, Ł10; half share cedar swamp in 36th lot, Ł3. <6:73> Account 21 Sept. 1731 of admr.; payments incl. towards the keeping ye Old Mr. BRYANT, L21.12s. <6:80> Account allowed 28 Sept. 1731; shows further payments to Jonathan BRYANT for keeping his father, Joseph HOLMES Jr., Samuel BRYANT Jr., Jonathan ALDEN, heirs of Joseph FINNEY, Samuel BRYANT for keeping his father, Mr. COTTON for writing a petition to ye Superior Court and Col. WINSLOW. Received: for rent, Ł60; for a pew, Ł1.13s6d; Deacon WASHBURN, Seth CHIPMAN. <original> Bond 24 Dec. 1733 of Benjamin EATON, housewright of Plimton, admr., to sell real estate to pay debts. Surety: John MURDOCH of Plymouth. Witnesses: Joseph BYRAM, Nathaniel CUSHMAN. <Plymouth Co.Deeds 27:223>...23 Feb. 1732/3, Benjamin EATON, yeoman of Kingston...being licensed...to sell & dispose of ye real estate of **Benjamin BRYANT**...sold to William RIPLEY of Kingston...all that tract of land, homestead etc. Witnesses: William CHURCHELL, John BELL.

Guardianship of Children of **Benjamin BRYANT** of Plympton MA. <Plymouth Co.PR #3177>
<original> Bonds 30 Apr. 1725, of Benjamin EATON of Plimpton, as gdn. of **Hannah BRIANT, Jerusha BRIANT, Jesse BRIANT, Mercy BRIANT, Micah BRIANT & Phebe BRIANT**, all under 14. Surety: Thomas WETHRELL. Witnesses: James WARREN, John COWING. <12:418> Receipt 22 Dec. 1733 of **David SEARS**, millwright of Plimton & wf **Phebe**, for Ł53, for their share of estate. Witnesses: Joseph WATERMAN, Lemuel STERTEVANT. <12:417> Receipt 2 Aug. 1735, of **David CURTIS**, husbandman of Halifax & wf **Hannah**, for Ł59.7s, for their share. Witnesses: Benjamin CURTIS, John ROBINSON Jr. <12:418> Receipt 6 July 1736 of **Nehemiah LEACH** of Plimton & wf **Marcy**, for Ł62, for their share. <8:31> Bond May 1739, Benjamin CUSHMAN, yeoman of Plympton app'td gdn. of **Jesse BRYANT**. Witnesses: Benjamin WESTON, George HOLMES. <12:419> Receipt 24 Jan. 1742 of **Micah BRYANT**, housewright of Middleborough, to my Grandfather **Benjamin EATON**, my guardian, for Ł160.3s6d, his share. Receipt 20 Aug. 1744 of **Jesse BRYANT**, to my Grandfather **Benjamin EATON**, for Ł92.3s1d, his share. <12:418> Receipt 18 Apr. 1746 of **Solomon LEACH**, husbandman of Bridgewater, on behalf of his dec'd wife **Jerusha LEACH**, for Ł76, for their share. Witnesses: Ezra WASHBURN, Giles RICKARD.

Jesse BRYANT of Middleboro MA to **John LORING**. <Plymouth Co.Deeds 38:266>
...28 May 1747, Jesse BRYANT sells to John LORING...one sixth of one ninth part of land...late the estate of Benjamin EATON of Kingston.

David CORTIS/CURTIS of Halifax MA to **John LORING**. <Plymouth Co.Deeds 38:267>
...2 July 1747, David CORTIS & wf Hannah sell to John LORING...one sixth of one ninth of land in Kingston late the estate of Benjamin EATON late of Kingston dec'd.

PLYMOUTH COUNTY DEEDS: (re: David SEARS)

<35:91> - 29 May 1743, David SEARS, millwright of Middleboro, judgement against Samuel THATCHER
<37:48> - 5 Dec. 1743, David SEARS, millwright of Middle. to Ebenezer MORTON of Middleboro.
<43:12> - 24 July 1754, Samuel WARREN of Middleboro, judgement against David SEARS of same.
<44:192> - 21 May 1756, David SEARS, millwright of Middleboro to John LEACH of same.
<44:272> - 1 May 1758, David SEARS, millwright of Middle. & wf Phebe sell to Thomas WOOD of same, land in Titicut bought of James KEITH & Jonathan WOOD.
<48:177> - 30 Nov. 1762, David SEARS, gent. of Middleboro to Jonah WASHBURN, land in Middleboro.
<67:121> - 12 Feb. 1785, David PECKHAM, admr. of Judah SEARS Jr. & David SEARS, late of Rochester dec'd, sells land in Rochester.

Estate of **John EATON**, non compos mentis, of Kingston MA. <Plymouth Co.PR #7052>
<11:451> Letter/Bond 9 June 1750, Benjamin CUSHMAN Jr., husbandman of Plimton, app'td gdn. Sureties: Zachariah SOULE & Timothy RIPLEY of Plimton. Witnesses: Edward WINSLOW, Ebenezer DOGGETT. <12:457> Inventory taken 22 July 1751 by Francis ADAMS of Kingston, Benjamin WESTON & Josiah PERKINS of Plimton; total real estate, Ł128.6.8. <13:368> Account allowed 2 Dec. 1754; Paid to: John EVERSON, John ADAMS, Zachariah SOUL, Seth EVERSON, Ephraim EVERSON, Ebenezer COBB, Robert WATERMAN, James OTIS, Mary SOULE, Timothy RIPLEY, David EATON, Col. BRADFORD, Josiah PERKINS, Benjamin WESTON. <13:454> Account of gdn. 6 Apr. 1755.

Estate of **John EATON**, non compos mentis, of Kingston MA. <Plymouth Co.PR #7051>
<13:406> Letter 6 Feb. 1755, Ebenezer FULLER Jr., yeoman of Halifax, app'td gdn...sd John EATON is and for a long time has been a person non compos mentis & whose person & estate has been under the direction of a guardian, sd guardian having settled his accounts and desiring no further concerns as guardian. <original> Bond 6 Feb. 1755 of gdn. Sureties: Austin BEARSE of Halifax and Timothy RIPLEY of Plimton. Witnesses: John LOTHROP, Hannah DYER.

Will of **Elisha EATON**, yeoman of Plympton MA. <Plymouth Co.PR #7043>
<original>...dated 3 Nov. 1737, wf **Elizabeth** to receive all personal & real estate in Plimton and N. Yarmouth. Witnesses: John CUSHMAN, James CUSHMAN, Nathaniel FULLER. <original> Letter 3 July 1738 of **Elizabeth EATON**, informing the judge of probate that there will be little or nothing left after paying her husband's debts and declines as executrix and prays for an allowance. <8:10> Letter/Bond 12 Mar. 1738, Nathaniel FULLER, yeoman of Plympton, app'td admr. Sureties: Joseph LUCAS & Samuel SHAW, yeomen of Plympton. Witnesses: Nehemiah BENNETT, Francis MILLER. <8:68> Inventory taken 13 Apr. 1739 by John FULLER of Kingston, James HARLOW & Elisha WHITON, yeomen of Plympton; three and a half acres upland & meadow at N. Yarmouth; widow's allowance, Ł16. <8:88> Receipt 11 Apr. 1740 of widow. <8:128> Account 23 May 1740 of admr.; Debts due to: Lemuel WHITE, Stephen JONES, John FAUNCE, Samuel BARTLETT, Isaac POPE dec'd, John ROSSE, Samuel BAKER, Jeduthan

ROBINS, Deacon LUCAS, Joseph RICKARD, Eleazer RING, Dr. BRIDGMAN, Nathaniel FULLER. <9:409> Insolvency 9 June 1744 by commissioners George SAMSON & Benjamin WESTON, both of Plympton. <9:409> Account of admr.; all real estate sold; Paid to: James HOVEY, Samuel BAKER, Lemuel WHITE, Edward WINSLOW. <9:410> Account examined by commissioners 4 Jan. 1744.

Guardianship of Child of **Ebenezer EATON** of Plymouth MA. <Plymouth Co.PR #7054>
<4:179> 15 May 1719, Ephraim LITTLE of Plymouth app'td gdn. of **Mercy EATON**, under 14. Witnesses: John RICKARD, Thomas CROADE.

SAMUEL EATON[2] (Francis[1])

Heirs of **Samuel EATON** of Middleborough MA to **Nathaniel BARDEN** of same. <Plymouth Co.Deeds 30:81>
...24 Feb. 1727, Barnabas EATON of Middleborough, William CANEDY & wf Elizabeth of Taunton... which sd Barnabas & Elizabeth are the only children & heirs of Samuel EATON dec'd, for £23, quitclaim to Nathaniel BARDEN...all our right...into the third part of two lots of land in the first division of lands in the Little Lotmens Purchase in Middleborough...being our whole right...by vertue of a deed from sd Nathaniel BARDEN to the sd Samuel EATON dated 26 May 1722 upon record. Witnesses: Elkanah LEONARD, Japheth TURNER, Edward ARNOLD. Ack. by grantors 18 Mar. 1727/8. Rec. 21 Jan. 1735.

<Plymouth Co.Deeds 3:244>...3 Aug. 1698, **Samuel EAIGHTON/EATON** of Middleboro sells to Jacob TOMSON. Ack. 21 Oct. 1700.

MICRO #3 OF 4

Will of **William CANEDY**, gent. of Taunton MA. <Bristol Co.PR>
<23:268>...dated 26 Jan. 1773...to wf **Elisabeth**, the use & improvement of one third part of all my lands, orchards, meadows, dwelling houses, barns and out houses excepting one part or half of the new end of the house, barn and land which my son **Barnabas** now occupys...also the disposal of all my negroe servants excepting my negroe man named Laban and my negroe man named Ammon which I have disposed to my two sons **William & Barnabas**...all my moveable estate both in doors and out of doors excepting my wearing apparrel, sword and gun which I give to my two sons as afforesaid...to my son **William CANEDY**, one half of my wearing apparrel beside several parcels of land that I have already given him by a deed of gift bearing date 16 Mar. 1763...to son **Barnabas CANEDY**, one half of my apparrel besides several parcels of land that I have already given him by a deed of gift bearing date 14 Mar. 1763...to my dau **Mercy WILLIAMS**, six shillings, besides a deed of gift of lands bearing date 10 Feb. 1763...to my dau **Hannah PEIRCE**, six shillings...deed of gift, 11 Dec. 1772...to my dau **Thankfull MACOMBER**, six shillings...deed of gift 11 Dec. 1772...to my dau **Fear PERKINS**, six shillings...deed of gift 11 Dec. 1772; sons **William & Barnabas**, executors. Witnesses: Josiah MACOMBER, Elijah MACOMBER, Abiel MACOMBER. <23:270> Pr. 18 July 1774, **William CANEDY & Barnabas CANEDY**, app'td admrs. <23:531> Inventory taken 23 Sept. 1774 by Josiah MACOMBER, Elijah MACOMBER & Josiah KING; incl. negro woman named Ninn, £38; negro garl named Dinah, £19; negro boy named Dan, £3; Due from: Isaac PEIRCE, William CANEDY, David & Jonathan CASWELL, Barnabas CANEDY, Henry HASKENS, Joseph BARDEN, William CANEDY Jr., Zachariah PADDLEFORD. <original> Division 10 Apr. 1778 by Gideon WILLIAMS, Abiel MACOMBER.

Heirs of **William CANEDY.** <Bristol Co.Deeds 117:23>
...1 Oct. 1801, David PERKINS Jr., yeoman of Rochester, Barney PERKINS, yeoman of New Bedford and Thomas CAIN & wf Hannah of Taunton...which we the sd David, Barney & Hannah are the children & heirs of Fear PERKINS dec'd...whereas the Hon. William CANADY, Edq. dec'd, gave to our Honoured Mother the sd Fear dec'd...twenty nine acres...in Taunton...which sd lands we divide. Witnesses: David PERKINS, Godfrey ROBINSON. Rec. 6 Jan. 1825.

David PERKINS of Taunton MA to his Children. <Bristol Co.Deeds 80:336>
...2 Oct. 1801, David PERKINS, blacksmith, in consideration of $20.00 paid by my three belovid sons & one daughter, that is, David, Barnabas, William & Hannah...convey title of 29 acres conveyed by William CANADY, Esq. to Fear PERKINS, my dec'd wife. Witnesses: Joanna READ, Godfrey ROBINSON. Rec. 3 Oct. 1801.

PLYMOUTH COUNTY DEEDS: (re: William CANEDY, grantor)

<57:69> - 1773, to William CANEDY Jr.
<57:71> - 1773, to Barnabas CANEDY.
<74:218> - , Executor to Robert HOAR.
<99:249> - 1804, to William CANEDY Jr.
<99:184> - 1804, to Noble CANEDY.
<110:43> - 1809, to Charity HINDS.
<114:40> - , to Barsheba HOWLAND.
<156:189> - , to John W. CANEDY.

(Additional references to William CANEDY, grantor: 60:101;101:223;115:202;176:18,158;185:259; 200:110,112;269:7.)

Estate of **Barnabas S. PERKINS** of New Bedford MA. <Bristol Co.PR>
<181:31> Will, 1855. <173:387> Bond 5 Feb. 1856. <181:29> Pr., wf **Matilda D. PERKINS**, exx. <109:396> Account of **Matilda D. PERKINS**, 1856. <178:210> Citation. <192:366> Division.

Barnabas PERKINS of New Bedford MA to **Benjamin FAY** of Taunton MA. <Bristol Co.Deeds 80:398>
...1 Oct. 1801, Barnabas PERKINS, yeoman sells to Benjamin FAY...share of his dec'd mother's estate in Taunton.

David PERKINS of Rochester MA to **James WASHBURN** of Middleboro MA. <Bristol Co.Deeds 80:462>
...23 Nov. 1801, David PERKINS, yeoman, sells to James WASHBURN, gent...share of mother's estate in Taunton. Witnesses: Luther WASHBURN, Joshua WASHBURN. Rec. 9 Dec. 1801.

David PERKINS of Freetown MA to **John HATHAWAY 2d** of same. <Bristol Co.Deeds 84:48>
...6 Aug. 1804, David PERKINS, mariner & wf Lois, sell to John HATHAWAY 2d...Lois' one seventh right in estate of her father Lot HATHAWAY.

Will of **William CANEDY** of Middleboro MA. <Plymouth Co.PR #3540>
<40:43>...dated 17 Mar. 1804, mentions wf **Charity**; sons **William CANEDY** (executor), **Noble CANEDY**; daus **Charity HINDS, Bathsheba HOWLAND**; grandsons **William CANEDY, Alexander CANEDY.** <40:44> Pr. 11 Apr. 1804.

Will of **William CANEDY** of Middleboro MA. <Plymouth Co.PR #3539>
<79:483>...dated 28 Sept. 1836, mentions dau **Elizabeth E. CLARK** wf of Noah; dau **Jane ASHLEY** wf of William; dau **Mary B. CANEDY**; grandaughter **Hannah WINSLOW** dau of **Asa T. WINSLOW**; son **William H. CANEDY**; dau **Lucy H. HOAR** wf of Stephen; sons **Alexander CANEDY, Zebulon L. CANEDY, John W. CANEDY** (executor). Pr. Nov. 1837. <original> Petition for division, 1855, mentions **Olive CANEDY** as gdn. of **Salmon S. CANEDY**, minor child of **Zebulon L. CANEDY** dec'd; **William CANEDY & Elkanah W. CANEDY** the chil "of age" of **Zebulon L.; Sarah V. CANEDY** who has care of **Susan S. CANEDY, Jane A. CANEDY & Sarah O. CANEDY** the minor chil of **Alexander CANEDY** dec'd; **Charity L. CANEDY & Alexander CANEDY** the "of age" chil of **Alexander; William JENNEY** & wf **Mary** who is the dau of **Zebulon L. CANEDY** and **Elizabeth C. CANEDY** the child of **Alexander CANEDY.**
(References with no data: <10:491**A**;80:354,384;97:131>.)

Estate of **Zebulon L. CANEDY** of Middleboro MA. <Plymouth Co.PR #3542>
Bond, 1840, Widow **Olive CANEDY**, app'td admx. Inventory 18 Mar. 1840. Account May 1848. Division 1863, mentions following heirs: **Salmon S. CANEDY** of Lexington Mich.; **Betsey W. PERKINS** wf of Thomas P.W. of Rochester; **Elkanah W. CANEDY** of Lakeville; **William CANEDY** of Lakeville; **Mary B. JENNEY** wf of William T. of Lexington, Mich. (Additional references with no details, viz: 10:339**A**; 82:154;84:243;90:140;104:322,466;113:315. References to **Zebulon L. CANEDY** in the Plymouth Co. Deeds (no data given), viz: 136:4;167:238;175:125;178:166;196:197;199:2;265:110.)

Guardianship of Children of **Zebulon L. CANEDY** of Middleboro MA. <Plymouth Co.PR #3541>
<8:211**L**> 18 Jan. 1841, **Olive CANEDY** app'td gdn. of **William CANEDY** (over 14 who chose his mother), **Betsey W. CANEDY, Elkanah W. CANEDY, Mary B. CANEDY & Salmon S. CANEDY** (under 14). Sureties: Hopestill BISBEE, John W. CANEDY.

Estate of **Robert CROSMAN Sr.** of Taunton MA. <Bristol Co.PR>
<1:72> 7 Dec. 1687, Marriage settlement between Robert CROSMAN, carpenter and **Martha EATON**, widow of Bristol. <1:73> Inventory taken 24 Nov. 1692, mentions goods to the widow before marriage. The widow **Martha CROSMAN** is too aged & infirm to go to Bristol so took oath to the division at Taunton 23 Jan. 1692/3.

Martha CROSMAN to **Thomas SAWYER** of Marshfield MA. <Plymouth Co.Deeds 1:288>
...4 Oct. 1694...Martha CROSMAN dau of Francis BILLINGTON late of Middleborough dec'd...whereas my father did by deed of gift...bearing date 3 Jan. 1663 give grant & confirm unto my then husband Samuel EATON and my self...half of that his lot of land lying on ye northerly side of Namasket River within the Township of Middleborough together with land to set our house upon...and after ye decease of us to our daughter Sarah now ye wife of Phillip BUMPUS. Phillip & Sarah have sold this land to Thomas SAWYER, Martha releases all claims. Witnesses: Isaac LITTLE, Jael BRADFORD. Rec. 11 Oct. 1694.

RACHEL EATON[2] (Francis[1])

PLYMOUTH COUNTY DEEDS:

<2:16> - 1658, Samuel JENNEY to Joseph RAMSDEN.
<3:86> - 21 June 1667, Joseph RAMSDEN & wf Mary of Lakenham sell to Giles RICKARD Sr. of Plymth.
<3:329>- 2 Feb. 1673, Joseph RAMSDEN of Lakenham gift of house & land to eldest son Daniel RAMSDEN. Rec. by order of Court, 4 June 1674.

EDWARD FULLER

MICRO #1 OF 1

Will of **Consider FULLER**, housewright of Kingston MA. <Plymouth Co.PR #8204> <67:287>...dated 20 Apr. 1829, $5.00 ea to the following children, viz: eldest son **Ezra FULLER**; eldest dau **Betsey DRAKE** wf of Linus; dau **Joanna BASSETT** wf of Ichabod; dau **Sally BIRD** wf of Elijah; sons **John FULLER, Nathan FULLER, Daniel W. FULLER & Samuel FULLER**; dau **Hannah FULLER**; rest & residue of estate to son **Smith FULLER &** youngest son **Waldo Ames FULLER**, they to support my wife **Hannah.** Witnesses: Josiah HOLMES, Jehiel WASHBURN, Samuel SOULE. <original> 15 Sept. 1829 widow **Hannah FULLER** declines & asks that Eli COOK be app'td admr. <61:475> Letter/Bond 21 Sept. 1829, Eli COOK of Kingston app'td admr. as Josiah HOLMES, executor, declines. Sureties: Thomas C. HOLMES of Kingston & Isaiah ALDEN of Duxbury. <67:555> Inventory taken 1 Oct. 1829 by Jehiel WASHBURN, Thomas C. HOLMES, Isaiah HOLMES, all of Kingston, total real estate, $875.00. <69:84> Insolvency 15 Feb. 1830. <69:351> List of Debts 14 Aug. 1830; Claimants: Daniel WESTON, Stephen DREW, John FULLER 2d, Timothy FRENCH, Josiah HOLMES, Samuel SOULE, Levi FISH, George STETSON, Paul L. NICHOLS, Harvey FULLER, Nathan FULLER, Martin HOLMES, Jehiel WASHBURN, Ezra FULLER, Jonah WILLIS, Jedidiah HOLMES. <69:349> Petition to sell real estate for $190.00, 7 Sept. 1830; sons **Ezra & Smith FULLER** assent to sale 30 Aug. 1830. <70:231> Division of real estate, 15 Nov. 1830 by Nathaniel HOLMES, Thomas C. HOLMES & John FULLER 2d to the two children named as devisees in sd will, viz: **Smith FULLER & Waldo Ames FULLER**, each to receive part of homestead farm; division confirmed 11 Apr. 1831.

==

Guardianship of Child of **Consider FULLER**, housewright of Kingston MA. <Plymouth Co.PR #8299> <65:124> Letter/Bond 15 Feb. 1830, of Ezra FULLER, gdn. of **Waldo Ames FULLER**, under 14. Suretie: Eli COOK of Kingston & Joseph P. BOSWORTH of Duxbury. <72:22> Inventory taken 4 Apr. 1831 by Nathaniel HOLMES, Thomas C. HOLMES & John FULLER 2d, of estate of **Waldo Ames FULLER**, incl. northerly part of homestead farm his father died seized of; sworn by gdn. 21 May 1832.

==

Will of **Susannah FULLER**, widow, seamster of Pembroke MA. <Plymouth Co.PR #8293> <29:27>...dated 14 June 1783, mentions son in law **Jairius BISBE** (executor), daus **Susanah BISBE & Abigail SMITH**; grandson **Isaac BISBE**, son of dau **Susanah**; to the grandchildren of my dau **Abigail SMITH** the sum of twenty pounds. Witnesses: Seth FORD, Naby EMES, Elisha FOORD. <29:28> Letter 9 Aug. 1783, **Jairius BISBEY** app'td exr. <29:28> Inventory taken 11 Aug. 1783 by Lot KEEN, William HOWLAND & Elisha FORD; real estate, £104.2.7.; total, £137.11.7.; sworn to by exr. 12 Aug. 1783.

==

Jairius BISBEE of Pembroke MA to **Isaac KEEN Jr.** of same. <Plymouth Co.Deeds 43:190> ...29 May 1754, Jairius BISBEE to Isaac KEEN Jr...mentions land of Susanna WADSWORTH of Pembroke then widow of Isaac WADSWORTH of Pembroke & now wife of Isaac FULLER of Pembroke.

==

PLYMOUTH COUNTY PROBATE, to 1800: (re: FULLER)

1695	Samuel	Middleboro	#8280, 1:223,246
1695	Isaac	Middleboro	#8229, 1:224
1709	John	Middleboro	#8248, 2:113,114,117;3:196
1712	Jabez	Middleboro	#8231, 3:128,129,130,131;7:108
1712	Mercy et al	Middleboro	#8268, 3:132,133,134
1714	Samuel	Middleboro	#8281, 3:332,348
1720	Abiel	Plympton	#8186, 4:230,268;5:242
1726	Elkanah	Plympton	#8216, 5:162
1727	Isaac	Middleboro	#8230, 5:358,393,583
1728	Samuel	Plympton	#8283, 5:407,620
1729	Jabez	Middleboro	#8232, 5:499,500,501
1748	Lydia et al	Plympton	#8263, 11:89,91
1750	Nathaniel	Plympton	#8275, 12:6,107,108
1756	Seth Jr.	Plympton	#8289, 14:74,85,160
1757	Jabez	Kingston	#8233, 14:238
1758	Samuel	Plympton	#8284, 14:478,521;15:5
1760	James	Kingston	#8235, 16:25
1761	Nathan	Halifax	#8271, 16:60,61,62
1766	Abigail	Halifax	#8187, 19:389,391
1766	John	Halifax	#8244, 17:158;19:406,458
1770	Ebenezer Jr.	Halifax	#8210, 20:311,375;21:72,148
1771	Ezra	Kingston	#8222, 21:20,21,53;28:531
1771	Priscilla et al	Halifax	#8278, 20:512;21:68,74
1772	Ebenezer	Kingston	#8209, 21:192
1778	John	Kingston	#8239, 25:96,97,152
1783	Susannah	Pembroke	#8293, 29:27,28
1786	Ebenezer	Halifax	#8211, 30:45,47,112

PLYMOUTH COUNTY PROBATE, to 1800, cont-d: (re: FULLER)

1791	William	Middleboro		#8303, 32:7
1796	Chipman	Halifax		#8203, 34:91;36:87,88,312;40:119,120

PLYMOUTH COUNTY PROBATE, to 1850: (re: FULLER)

1802	Jonathan	Middleboro	adm.	#8252, 34:314;38:127,128,129
1803	Lydia	Middleboro	adm.	#8261, 34:372
1804	Nathan et al	Halifax	gdn.	#8274, 32:243
1807	Zephaniah Jr.	Kingston	adm.	#8306, 39:109;42:68
1809	John	Middleboro	adm.	#8249, 39:199;43:87,437
1810	Silvia et al	Middleboro	gdn.	#8291, 41:17
1811	Thomas	Halifax	adm.	#8297, 39:279;43:401,451,452;47:197
1812	Lydia	Halifax	adm.	#8262, 39:458;44:260,261,358,363
1812	Wheelock	Halifax	gdn.	#8302, 41:107;44:146,147,188,256
1813	Sophia & Sally	Kingston	gdn.	#8292, 41:161
1813	Ephraim	Halifax	adm.	#8218, 39:402
1813	Jabez	Kingston	adm.	#8234, 29:414;45:65,347
1814	Hannah	Halifax	adm.	#8226, 46:84;47:138,139;48:536
1816	Cyrus	Halifax	adm.	#8206, 46:145;48:153,154;53:228
1816	Zephaniah	Kingston	adm.	#8307, 46:136;47:475,476
1820	Josiah	Kingston	will	#8253, 53:10,146
1821	Consider	Kingston	will	#8204, 61:287,555;69:84,349,351;70:231
1827	John	Kingston	gdn.	#8240
1828	John	Kingston	adm.	#8241, 61:247;62:321;66:568;67:97,98;69:156
1830	Samuel & Hannah	Kingston	gdn.	#8286, 65:137,138;69:148,149
1830	Waldo A.	Kingston	gdn.	#8299, 65:124;72:221
1832	Nathan	Kingston	adm.	#8270, 71:30;72:7,51;68:260;72:220
1835	John B.	Middleboro	adm.	#8250, 71:331;77:385;73:473;75:235;78:234;83:123
1836	Benjamin	Halifax	adm.	#8195, 71:394;78:45,46
1836	Sarah	W.Bridgewater	adm.	#8287, 10:46**A**;75:478;79:67;80:75
1838	George	Kingston	adm.	#8225, 5:101**T**;10:224**A**;81:17;83:54
1839	Benjamin	Kingston	will	#8196, 1:127**G**;6:24**U**;81:597;82:17;83:51
1839	Lucy	Middleboro	will	#8259, 1:137**G**;6:156**U**;10:581**A**;82:36
1839	Philemon	Plympton	adm.	#8277, 5:85**Y**;10:235**A**;81:67,190;82:120
1840	John et al	Middleboro	gdn.	#8251, 8:179**L**,180**L**;83:253,254
1843	Samuel	Middleboro	adm.	#8282, 6:415**U**;11:166**B**;85:318,319;86:239
1843	Samuel	Halifax	will	#8285, 1:238**G**;6:389**U**;85:164,241;86:468
1844	Eliza P. et al	Middleboro	gdn.	#8215, 2:491**O**;8:368**L**;86:324,526
1844	Ephraim	Halifax	adm.	#8219,1:173**R**;2:293**O**;6:461**U**;11:223**B**;86:69,132,467
1844	William H.	Halifax	gdn.	#8304, 8:367**L**;9:165**M**;87:160;90:150,399;87:160; 110:508
1845	Josiah	Duxbury	adm.	#8255, 7:28**V**;11:326**B**;87:482
1846	Sarah T.	Halifax	gdn.	#8288, 9:82**M**;89:170
1846	Thomas	Halifax	adm.	#8298, 7:229**V**;11:391**B**;88:53;89:52;90:254
1847	Eliza C.	Plympton	gdn.	#8213, 9:124**M**
1847	Ephraim	Plympton	adm.	#8220, 3:90**P**;7:286**V**;11:548**B**;89:532;90:255;91:16, 481,483
1847	Miranda	Halifax	will	#8269, 7:230**V**;10:556**A**;89:281,290;90:143,252
1849	Darius A.	Duxbury	adm.	#8208, 8:6**W**;12:90**C**;91:505;92:125,126,511
1849	Ebenezer	Halifax	will	#8212, 6:492**U**;10:537**A**;86:145,200,232,349
1849	Lucy	Kingston	adm.	#8260, 7:554**V**;12:146**C**;92:110;95:98,110
1850	Barzillai	Hanson	adm.	#8194, 8:55**W**;12:179**C**;92:239,240

SAMUEL FULLER^2 (Edward^1)<1>

John & Hannah FULLER et al to **Nehemiah BENNETT.** <Plymouth Co.Deeds 39:83>
...2 Feb. 1747, Hannah FULLER & husband John of Halifax, Elizabeth ROBIN of Middleboro and David THOMAS of Windham CT sell to Nehemiah BENNETT...Hannah & Elizabeth, daus of David THOMAS dec'd & David THOMAS, grantor, grandson of David THOMAS dec'd.

John & Hannah FULLER of Halifax MA to **Samuel ROBBINS** of Middleboro MA. <Plymouth Co.Deeds 44:200>
...16 May 1752, John & Hannah FULLER sell to Samuel ROBBINS...their rights to land of their father David THOMAS of Middleborough dec'd.

John & Hannah FULLER of Halifax MA to **Samuel THOMAS Jr.** of Middleboro. <Plymouth Co.Deeds 50:144>
...5 Feb. 1753, John & Hannah FULLER sell to Samuel THOMAS Jr...land which formerly belonged to David THOMAS of Middleboro dec'd.

Jabez FULLER of Middleboro MA to **David WESTON.** <Plymouth Co.Deeds 48:114>
...2 Oct. 1762, Jabez FULLER, husbandman, sells to David WESTON...land Jabez bought of Samuel PRATT Jr. in 1742. Wf Hannah FULLER signs.

Jabez FULLER of Middleboro MA to **James WOOD** of Bridgewater MA. <Plymouth Co.Deeds 54:212>
...22 Mar. 1769, Jabez FULLER, husbandman, sells to James WOOD, husbandman...my homestead whereon I now dwell in sd Middleborough...and is the lot of land I bought of Seth RICHMOND 13 Apr. 1765.

MATTHEW FULLER^{2} (Edward^{1})<2>

Estate of **Jabez FULLER** of Middleborough MA. <Plymouth Co.PR #8231>
<3:128> Letter/Bond 20 June 1712, widow **Mary FULLER** app'td admx. Surety: Samuel FULLER. Witnesses: Nathaniel THOMAS Jr., Thomas CROA(DE). <3:129> Inventory taken 15 Sept. 1711 by Jacob TOMSON Thomas NELSON & Samuel BARROWS; personal estate, £102.16.2., incl. washed leather, £1.1s; knife & fork, 2 rasors, lance, tooth drawers, candlestick, 10s; tanned leather £7.18s; shoemaker's tools, seats & lasts & shoes in the shop, £3.2s8d; about four yeare time in an Indian boy, £4; real estate, £94. On back of inventory are the names & ages of the children, viz: **Samuel FULLER,** full age; **Jonathan FULLER; Mercy FULLER,** 15; **Mary FULLER,** 13; **Lois FULLER,** 8; **Ebenezer FULLER,** 4. <3:130> Appraisal of real estate 20 June 1712. <3:131> Division 20 June 1712 among the widow and above 6 children. <7:108> Receipt 11 May 1721 to **Mary FULLER,** admx. from **Jabez & Mercy WOOD** of our part of the estate that was our honoured father's & our brother's **Samuel FULLER** dec'd. Witnesses: Jonathan FULLER, Samuel BENNETT

Guardianship of Children of **Jabez FULLER** of Middleborough MA. <Plymouth Co.PR #8268>
<original> Bonds 20 June 1712 of widow **Mary FULLER,** app'td gdn. of children **Mary,** about 13; **Lois,** under 9; **Ebenezer,** under 5 and chosen gdn. by **Mercy,** under 21. Letters 20 June 1712 of gdnship. of **Ebenezer** <3:132>; **Marcy/Mercy & Mary** <3:133> and **Lois** <3:134>

Estate of **Samuel FULLER** of Middleborough MA. <Plymouth Co.PR #8281>
<3:332> Letter/Bond 4 Mar. 1714/5, **Jonathan FULLER,** next brother of dec'd, app'td admr. Surety: Isaac TINKCOM. Witnesses: Elizabeth THOMAS, Thomas CROADE. <3:348> Inventory taken 20 June 1715 by Jacob TOMSON, Thomas NELSON & John BENNET Sr.; incl. his two thirds of the housing & land of the homestead which was his father's, £59.6.8.; a debt due the estate to be paid to his mother. <3:348> Settlement (no date); the dec'd died intestate without wife or child...the sum of six pounds due from the estate of their father **Jabez FULLER** paid since his decease by his widow towards the maintenance of **Joseph HALLET** the sd widow's father & now to be paid by the sd **Jonathan** to his sd mother; the sum of £29.5.2. divided into six equal parts, viz: to the mother & her five children, viz: **Ebenezer, Mercy, Mary, Lois & Jonathan.**

Will of **Mathias FULLER** of Barnstable MA. <Barnstable Co.PR 2:49>
...dated 7 Aug. 1696, at Boston...being designed for and upon ye country's cervice against the French and Indian enemies and not knowing how God shall dispose of me...to brother **Timothy FULLER** of Haddam, the land that was given them by their grandfather **Matthew FULLER** late of Barnstable dec'd; mentions mother and brothers & sisters; brother **Timothy,** executor. Witnesses: (--)ick MANNING, Joseph HINCKLEY, John WATSON. Pr. 22 May 1697.

Will of **Leift. Samuel FULLER.** <Plymouth Co.PR 3:179>
<3:179>...dated 2 Aug. 1675...the son of **Captaine Matthew FULLER**...being now goeing from home... mentions wf **Mary;** eldest son **Thomas FULLER** (under 21); sons **Jabez FULLER, Timothy FULLER, Matthias FULLER;** daus **Abigail & Anne;** wf **Mary** with friends Elder John CHIPMAN & Thomas HUCKENS, executors. Witnesses: Thomas HINCKLEY (who made oath 7 June 1676) & Mary HINCKLEY (who made oath 3 5mth 1676. On 8 June 1676, widow **Mary FULLER** is said to be with child, "beyond the expectation of her sd husband when he made his will". On 2 June 1680, John CHIPMAN renounced his executorship. <3:180> Inventory taken by Edward PERREY, Nathaniel FITCHRANDALL, William THROOPE; sworn to by widow **Mary,** 3 June 1676; livestock & various household items incl. 3 brasse kettles, 3 skillets & warming pan, £2; 2 iron kettles & pott, 20s; frying pan, 2s; pewter, 20s; spoones, 3s; earthen things, 2s6d; chaires, chests & a box; wheeles, cardes & a smoothing iron; pistolls, holsters; flax, sickle, sythe, 18s; sissers & combe, 12d; cotton, woole & yarn, 10s; sugar & spice, 4s; nailes, 10s; bookes, 6s; cart wheeles, boxes & hoopes, 54s; howes & axes; corne on the ground; wages due for service hee did for the country.

FOOTNOTES

<1> p.274, Matthew FULLER^{2} is shown in the files as being Matthew FULLER^{1}; also, the files for this Matthew and Samuel FULLER^{2} are inter-mixed, therefore if you were to refer to the microfiche the data would not be in the order found here. I have added the sub-heading for Matthew^{2} and arranged the data accordingly.
<2> p.275, See above.

SAMUEL FULLER

MICRO #1 OF 3

PLYMOUTH COUNTY DEEDS: (re: Mercy FULLER)

<10:2:259> - 28 Apr. 1711, Mercy WARREN, widow of John, of Middleboro, to Samuel WARREN, land where he lived. Ack. 2 Mar. 1713/4.
<43:150> - 18 Feb. 1711/2, Mercy FULLER, widow of John, grantee. Rec. 1755.
<30:183> - 22 Dec. 1735, Jabez FULLER of Kingston & wf Mercy, the dau of John GRAY dec'd.
<49:59> - 27 Apr. 1764, Mercy FULLER, widow of Kingston, to son Jabez FULLER of same, land given her by her father John GRAY dec'd of Kingston in 1728.
<56:14> - 24 Jan. 1771, Jabez FULLER, mariner, with mother Mercy FULLER, widow, of Kingston. Wf Ruth FULLER signs.
<80:31> - 4 Aug. 1789, Mercy FULLER, widow of Kingston, letter of attorney to Barnabas FULLER of same, re: land of Robert CUSHMAN. Ack. by Mercy 19 Mar. 1796.

(Note: the following references concerning **Mercy FULLER** have no data, viz: 24:193,199;25:64,90; 29:82;35:51;39:174;41:21;45:105;50:248;56:13.)

Guardianship of Child of **William FULLER** of Middleborough MA. <Plymouth Co.PR #8303>
<32;7> Letter/Bond 6 June 1791, Jireh SWIFT of Bridgewater app'td gdn. of **William FULLER**, above 14. Sureties: Zebedee SPROUT, Nehemiah BENNET. Witnesses: Caleb LORING, Isaac LOTHROP.

Estate of **Seth FULLER Jr.** of Plympton MA. <Plymouth Co.PR #8289>
<14:74> Letter/Bond 18 July 1756, widow **Hannah FULLER** app'td admx. Sureties: Silvanus DONHAM, Eleazer CROCKER, both of Plympton. Witnesses: Edward WINSLOW, Hannah WINSLOW. <14:160> Inventory taken --- 21 1756, by Elisha WITON, Silvanus DONHAM, Azariah WITON; no real estate, total estate, £17. <14:160> Insolvency. <14:85> Account sworn by admx. 27 July 1756.

SAMUEL FULLER[2] (Samuel[1])

16 Shilling Purchase, re: **Samuel FULLER.** <no source>
<p.17>...20 Nov. 1706, 2nd allotment 38th lot, 20 acres...in the right of Mr. Samuel FULLER now claimed: one third each by the following, viz: Samuel EATON, Jonathan MORSE Jr. & Jacob TOMSON.
<p.33>...16 Dec. 1706, Allotment of cedar swamp, 9th lot...in the right of Mr. Samuel FULLER, now claimed: one third each by: Samuel EATON, Jonathan MORSE, James WOOD.

PLYMOUTH COUNTY DEEDS: (re: John FULLER, grantor:**)**

<3:249> - 1700, to Jacob TOMSON.
<4:160> - 1702, to Thomas PALMER.
<7:222> - 1707, to Rodolphus ELMES.
<12;93> - 1716, et al to Experience BENT.
<16:10> - 1721/2, to John THOMAS Jr.
<35:104> - 1742, et al to John HOLMES.
<36:122> - 1743/4, et al, division.
<39:83> - 1747, et al to Nehemiah BENNETT.
<43:151> - 1755, et al, division.
<44:33> - 1756, by exr. to Silvanus DREW
<44:200> - 1757, et al to Samuel ROBBINS
<45:116> - to Zadock BOSWORTH.
<50:144> - et al to Samuel THOMAS Jr.
<52:131> - to Benjamin FAUNCE.
<56:177> - to Samuel JACKSON.
<56:228> - by exon. to Ebenezer ROBBINS.
<57:78> - et al to Ebenezer ROBBINS.
<59:250> - to James COLLINS.
<67:41> - to Joseph WRIGHT.
<83:156> - to Noah FULLER.

Plymouth Co.Deeds, re: **Mary FULLER**, grantor: 24:193,199;25:64,90;29:82;35:51;39:174;41:21;45:105; 50:248. (no data given)

Estate of **James WOOD** of Middleboro MA. <Plymouth Co.PR 5:406,470,579;7:126>
Settlement of estate, 15 Mar. 1736...cannot be divided without great prejudice, prized at £90, the whole being in Middleboro is settled upon **Jonathan WOOD** the eldest son, he paying shares to the other children, £15.10s ea, viz: **Benjamin WOOD** of Middleboro, chil of **Barnabas WOOD** late of Middleboro dec'd, **Abell WOOD, Ichabod WOOD** of Rehoboth, **Lydia HOLMES** wf of George of Plimoth and **James WOOD** who has already received his part so receives nothing.

PLYMOUTH COUNTY DEEDS:

<54:16> - 10 Mar. 1765, Lydia HOLMES of Plymouth, widow of George to George HOLMES, cordwinder of Plymouth, her dower rights. Ack. 8 Jan.1768.

PLYMOUTH COUNTY DEEDS, cont-d:

57:150 - 1773, George & Anna HOLMES et al; heirs of Rebecca RICH, wf of Walter.

Guardianship of Children of **Barnabas WOOD**, dec'd of Middleboro MA. <Plymouth Co.PR>
<7:231,232> Bonds 5 Oct. 1736, Joseph LUCAS app'td gdn. of **Experience WOOD, Lydia WOOD & Rebecca WOOD**, all under 14.

PLYMOUTH COUNTY DEEDS: (re: WOOD)

<31:101> - 22 Apr. 1737, Jonathan WOOD, yeoman of Middleboro to Lemuel ROBBINS of Plympton.
<31:101> - 29 Aug. 1737, Same as above, division.
<47:167> - 13 Jan. 1759, Jonathan WOOD, yeoman of Bridgewater, for £24 sold to son Jedediah WOOD, cordwinder of same. Wf Persis WOOD signs. Ack. 14 Oct. 1761. Rec. 1762.
<47:167> - 15 Oct. 1761, Jonathan WOOD, yeoman of Bridgewater, gives to son James WOOD of same... part of homestead in Bridgewater bounded by land given to son Jedediah WOOD. Ack. 17 Oct. 1761 by Jonathan. Rec. 16 Mar. 1762.
<47:168> - 15 Oct. 1761, Jonathan WOOD, yeoman of Bridgewater gives to son Jedediah WOOD part of homestead. Ack. 17 Oct. 1761.
<55:160> - 5 Feb. 1770, James WOOD, laborer of Middleboro, for £53.6.8. sold to Noah PHINNEY of Bridgewater, laborer...31 acre homestead I now live on. Wf Achsa WOOD signs. Witnesses: Joseph PHINNEY, Hannah RICHMOND, Theophilus CROCKER.
<56:86> - 3 June 1771, James WOOD, yeoman of Plymouth buys land.
<55:264> - 13 Feb. 1772, James WOOD, yeoman of Plymouth to Phineas SWIFT, house & land in Plymouth near the cliffs.
<59:190> - 11 Dec. 1778, Jonathan WOODS of Middleboro to Abiel WOOD, merchant of Pownalboro, Lincoln co., ME...share of land set off to Perez TINKHAM in division of homestead farm of Joseph TINKHAM Esq., dec'd of Middleboro. Wf Keziah WOODS signs. Witnesses: John TINKHAM, Isaiah WASHBURN.

Will of **Experience COOPER**, widow of Kingston MA. <Plymouth Co.PR #4945>
...dated 30 June 1813, mentions dec'd husband **Thomas COOPER**; sisters **Lydia CLARKE, Sarah LANMAN, Elizabeth BARTLETT, Mary LANMAN**; nieces **Rebecca BARTLETT & Judith GRAY**; nieces **Sarah BREWSTER & Nancy BREWSTER**; niece **Nancy LOUDEN**; **Joshua Holmes LOUDEN**, son of my sd niece **Nancy**; dec'd brother **Joshua HOLMES**; brother **George HOLMES**; niece **Susanna/Susan BARTLETT**; half sister **Rebecca AUSTIN**; niece **Experience BREWSTER**; brothers **Richard HOLMES, Barnabas HOLMES**. Pr. 30 Dec. 1813. The will is not transcribed in the files except for the following: To my brother **George HOLMES**...one hundred and fifty dollars a year for the term of four years.

Estate of **Joshua HOLMES**, yeoman of Kingston MA. <Plymouth Co.PR #10481>
<39:408> Letter/Bond 7 May 1813, **Richard HOLMES**, yeoman of Plymouth app'td admr. Sureties: **Barnabas HOLMES Jr.**, yeoman & **Richard HOLMES 3d**, trader, both of Plymouth. Witnesses: Isaac LeBARON & Beza HAYWARD. <45:66> Inventory taken 2 Aug. 1813 by John FAUNCE Esq. & Elijah FAUNCE, yeoman, both of Kingston and Jabez WESTON, cooper of Plympton; incl. homestead, $1900.00; two acres fresh meadow by Capt. COOKE, $75.00; four acres at Jones river meadow, $45.00; four acre wood land near BRYANT land, $60.00; seventeen acres bought of PORTER, $250.00; fifteen acres bought of Job EATON $275.00. <50:488> Notice of sale of real estate, 10 Feb. 1814 by admr. <50:489> Division 17 Jan. 1820 by admr. to following heirs, viz: heirs of **George HOLMES** dec'd; heirs of **Bethiah CHURCHILL**, dec'd; **Lydia CLARK** wf of Benjamin; **Joshua H. LOWDEN**, a devisee in the last will of **Experience COOPER**, dec'd; **Sarah LANDMAN**, widow; **Barnabas HOLMES Jr.**; **Elizabeth BARTLETT** wf of Caleb; **Mary LANDMAN** wf of Peter; **Rebecca AUSTIN**, widow and **Richard HOLMES**, admr., to each the sum of $121.80.

Estate of **Barnabas HOLMES** of Plymouth MA. <Plymouth Co.PR #10327>
<10:80**A**;75:413;79:148,149;80:135;82:26> (no details given in files).

Estate of **George HOLMES** of Plymouth MA. <Plymouth Co.PR #10411>
...1823...<52:193;55:175;57:477,511> (no details given in files).

Will of **Richard HOLMES** of Plymouth MA. <Plymouth Co.PR #10555>
<53:168>...dated 19 Oct. 1820, mentions dau **Abigail LEONARD** wf of William; sons **Richard HOLMES 3d & Thomas Cooper HOLMES**, executors; under age children of dec'd dau **Polly BRADFORD** wf of Thomas; daus **Experience BREWSTER** wf of Spencer, **Nancy/Anna LOWDEN** wf of Isaac, widow **Elizabeth CARVER, Sarah HOLMES & Jane HOLMES**. Pr. 20 Nov. 1820. <53:370,373> Division. <53:362> Inventory. <53:482> Order. <56:32> Account. (Plymouth Co.Deeds 149:240, 19 Nov. 1822, all the above heirs sold land & half of house in Plymouth to Zaccheus BARNES.)

PLYMOUTH COUNTY DEEDS: (re: Eleazer LEWIS)

<48:271> - 21 Feb. 1765, Eleazer LEWIS, cordwainer of Middleboro sells all right in house where he now dwells.
<48:110> - 1 May 1758, Eleazer LEWIS...
<50:76> - 30 Sept 1761, Eleazer LEWIS, cordwainer & wf Mary of Middleboro...
<55:156> - 16 May 1770, Eleazer LEWIS of Bridgewater...

Eleazer LEWIS of Middleboro MA to **Jonathan MORSS Jr.** of same. <Plymouth Co.Deeds 8:83>
...11 Oct. 1703, Eleazer & Hannah LEWES, for £3.2s sold to Jonathan MORSS Jr...one third part of

land in Sixteen Shilling purchase in Middleboro...which share did formerly belong unto our honoured Father Mr. Samuel FULLER dec'd. Witnesses: Jacob TOMSON, Thomas NELSON. Ack. 11 June 1707 by Eleazer & Hannah. Rec. 24 June 1710.

Estate of **Eleazer LEWIS** of Middleborough MA. <Plymouth Co.PR>
<5:352> 3 Feb. 1727, **Edward LEWIS** of Middleboro app'td admr. on his father's estate. <6:24> Inventory taken 5 Mar. 1727 by John BENNET & Peter BENNET; incl. homestead & lands, Ł150 and 45 acres in S. Purchase, Ł10; sworn to by admr. 7 Mar. 1728/9. Settlement 12 May 1731, real estate cannot be divided therefore estate settled on eldest son **Edward LEWIS**, he to pay Ł16.13.4. to the following heirs, viz: **Susanna LEWIS** of Middleboro; **Hannah SNELL** wf of Thomas of Bridgewater; **Elizabeth LEWIS** of Middleboro; **Shubael LEWIS** of Plympton; **Kezia LEWIS** of Middleboro; **Samuel LEWIS** of Plympton and **Mary LEWIS** of Middleboro. Receipt 21 May 1731 of Samuel TINKHAM as guardian of **Keziah, Samuel & Mary LEWIS**, to **Edward LEWIS**, admr. & Henry WOOD.

Estate of **Isaac FULLER** of Middleborough MA. <Plymouth Co.PR #8230>
<5:358> Letter/Bond 16 Nov. 1727, widow **Mary FULLER** app'td admx. Sureties: Isaac WRIGHT, Benjamin WESTON, both of Plympton. Witnesses: John COB, John FULLER. <5:393> Inventory taken 2 Feb. 1727/8 by James SOUL, Ebenezer FULLER, Isaac TINKHAM, all of Middleboro; incl. homestead, Ł200; halfe of 24th lott of cedar swamp & meadow on Winatuxet River in Twenty Six mens purchase, Ł46; share in his own right in purchase called South Purchase, 10s. <5:583> 3 May 1728, necesary utensells set out to widow **Mary FULLER**, Ł21.11s5d.

Isaac FULLER of Middleboro MA to **Elkana PEMBROOK** of Boston MA. <Plymouth Co.Deeds 5:86>
...13 Aug. 1703, Isaac FULLER, for 30s sells to Elkana PEMBROOK, shopkeeper...one and a half strip of land whereon now stands the dwelling house of John HASCAL Jr. Witnesses: John ALLYN, Thomas PALMER & John HASCALL.

Isaac FULLER of Plymouth MA to **Thomas NELSON** of Middleboro MA. <Plymouth Co.Deeds 9:130>
...6 May 1707, Isaac FULLER, for Ł8 sells to Thomas NELSON...his 20 acre lot on westerly side of Upper Meadow in 26 Men's Purchase, lot #4. Witnesses: John BENNET, Elnathan WOOD.

Isaac FULLER of Plymouth to **Ephraim WOOD** of Middleboro MA. <Plymouth Co.Deeds 11:235>
...7 Nov. 1707, Isaac FULLER, for Ł38 sells to Ephraim WOOD...dwelling house where he lately lived in Middleboro with the 20 acres the house stands on which did formerly belong to my father Samuel FULLER dec'd. Witnesses: Jacob TOMSON, Abigail TOMSON. Ack. 20 May 1712. Rec. Mar. 1716.

Isaac FULLER of Plympton MA to **John HASCALL** of Middleboro MA. <Plymouth Co.Deeds 15:196>
...26 Dec. 1712, Isaac FULLER, for Ł7 sells to John HASCALL...12 acres formerly belonging to my father Samuel FULLER dec'd, lying between land of sd HASCALL & William NELSON in 26 Mens Purchase excepting the part formerly sold to Elkanah PEMBROOKE. Witnesses: Jacob TOMSON, Jacob TOMSON Jr. Ack. 25 Nov. 1717. Rec. 2 Oct. 1721.

Isaac FULLER of Plympton MA to **James SMITH** of Middleboro MA. <Plymouth Co.Deeds 19:179>
...30 Mar. 1714, Isaac FULLER for Ł10 sells to James SMITH...two lots, 45 acres each in South Purchase, in third division. Witnesses: Ebenezer FULLER, John FULLER. Rec. 22 Dec. 1725.

Isaac FULLER & Ichabod CUSHMAN, of Middleboro MA. <Plymouth Co.Deeds 22:111>
...18 Mar. 1724/5...bounds between the two...Witnesses: Jedediah THOMAS, Jonathan SMITH. Rec. 17 Nov. 1727.

Mary FULLER of Middleboro MA to **James SMITH** of same. <Plymouth Co.Deeds 24:193>
...28 Aug. 1729, Mary FULLER, widow & admx. of Dr. Isaac FULLER of Middleboro, by authority of Court as personal estate insufficient to pay debts, sells for Ł10, to James SMITH...half of 24th lot of cedar swamp in Little Cedar Swamp in 26 Mens Purchase. Witnesses: Isaac WRIGHT, Francis MILLER. Ack. 11 Nov. 1729. Rec. 28 Nov. 1729.

Mary FULLER of Middleboro MA to **Joseph BATES** of same. <Plymouth Co.Deeds 25:64>
...11 Oct. 1729, Mary FULLER, by authority of court, for Ł18 sells to Joseph BATES...half of 12th lot in upper meadow in 26 Mens Purchase, containing about five and a half acres formerly belonging to Samuel FULLER. Witnesses: Ichabod KING, Moses TINKHAM. Rec. 6 Mar. 1729/30.

Mary FULLER of Middleboro MA to **Dr. Thomas PALMER** of same. <Plymouth Co.Deeds 25:90>
...11 Nov. 1729, Mary FULLER, widow & admx. of Dr. Isaac FULLER, by authority of court, for Ł3. 10s, sold at auction to Dr. Thomas PALMER...one acre in 31st of 100 acre lots in last allotment of 26 Mens Purchase. Witnesses: Joseph BATES, Francis MILLER.

Estate of **Dr. Jonathan FULLER** of Middleboro MA. <Plymouth Co.PR #8252>
<original> Request 24 Apr. 1802 of widow **Lucy FULLER**, that her brother **Joshua EDDY** be app'td admr <34:314> Letter/Bond 24 Apr. 1802, **Joshua EDDY** app'td admr. Sureties: William SHAW, Joshua EDDY Jr., trader, both of Middleboro. Witnesses: Jonathan St(---), Nathaniel EDDY. <38:127> Inventory taken by Isaac THOMSON, Ebenezer COX & Thomas BENNETT who were app'td 24 Apr. 1802; personal estate only, $253.61. <38:127> Insolvency 16 Aug. 1802. <38:127> List of Claims 19 Mar. 1805 by commissioners Isaac THOMSON & Thomas BENNETT; Creditors: Thomas WESTON, Levi PIERCE, James SOULE 2d, Nathan DARLING, Col. Abiel WASHBURN, Thomas SPROAT, estate of Moses LEONARD, William CORNISH, Dr. Thomas STURTEVANT & son, Elijah SHAW, Capt. Joshua EDDY & son, Nathaniel VAUGHAN, Asaph BISBEE, Southworth ELLIS, Nathaniel CLARK of Boston, John BENNETT, estate of Jacob BENNETT. <38:129>

Account of admr. 7 June 1805; Received from: Joseph RANSOM, Job DONHAM, David WOOD, Eli SHAW; Paid to: widow, her thirds & dower.

MICRO #2 OF 3

Estate of **Jabez FULLER**, Physician of Kingston MA. <Plymouth Co.PR #8234>
<original> Request 10 June 1813, of widow **Lucy FULLER**, that her son in law **Capt. Silas TOBEY** be app'td admr. <39:414> Letter/Bond 10 June 1813, **Silas TOBEY**, mariner of Kingston app'td admr. Sureties: Samuel LORING of Duxbury & George THOMAS of Kingston. <45:65> Inventory taken 10 June 1813 by John FAUNCE & Nathaniel THOMAS of Kingston and Samuel LORING of Duxbury; real estate, $2210.00; personal estate, $1492.31. <45:347> Warrant for assignment of dower to **Lucy FULLER**, 20 Oct. 1813 by John FAUNCE, Nathaniel THOMAS & John GRAY, all of Kingston. <45:347> Division 13 Apr. 1814 to widow and following heirs, viz: daus **Lucy FULLER, Betsey TOBEY** wf of Silas, **Sophia FULLER & Sally FULLER.**

Guardianship of Children of **Jabez FULLER**, Physician of Kingston MA. <Plymouth Co.PR #8292>
<41:161> Letter/Bond of **Lucy FULLER**, widow of Kingston as gdn. of **Sophia FULLER**, above 14 & **Sally FULLER**, under 14. Sureties: Silas TOBEY of Kingston and John B. THOMAS of Plymouth.

Estate of **Lucy FULLER**, widow of Kingston MA. <Plymouth Co.PR #8260>
<12:146> Petition 21 Nov. 1849 of **Edward S. TOBEY** of Boston to be app'td admr. Letter/Bond 27 Nov 1849, **Edward S. TOBEY** app'td admr. Sureties: Phineas SPRAGUE, Henry WINSOR, both of Boston. Witnesses: George S. WHEELWRIGHT, Charles M. CUSHMAN. <7:554> Notice 27 Nov. 1849. <92:110> Inventory taken 13 Dec. 1849 by Jas. N. SEVER, Joseph F. WADSWORTH, Nathaniel FAUNCE; personal estate, $3470.68; real estate, $1423.69 <95:98> Account of admr., 10 Jan. 1853; payment & transfer of stock to following heirs, viz: **Lucy DAVIS** wf of Timothy of Kingston, $412.77; **Betsey SPRAGUE** wf of Phineas of Boston, $302.77; **Sally BARKER** wf of Ebenezer of Charlestown, $412.77 and **Sophia FULLER** of Kingston, $412.77 who also received $800.00 for extra services rendered to her mother.

Estate of **John FULLER** of Middleborough MA. <Plymouth Co.PR #8248>
<2:113> Letter/Bond 10 Mar. 1709/10, widow **Marcy FULLER** app'td admx. Surety: Samuel FULLER. Witnesses: Nathaniel THOMAS Jr., Thomas FISH. <2:113> Inventory taken 23 Feb. 1709/10 by James SOOL/SOUL, Samuel EDDY. <2:114> Account of admx. (not dated), mentions Nathaniel THOMAS, Mr. MURDO, Richard GODFREY, John KING, Capt. TOMSON, James BARNABAS. <original> Inventory taken 8 June 1710 by James SOOL/SOUL, Samuel EDDY & Isaac FULLER; incl. farm on Nemasket river, £60; homestead, £180. <2:117> Inventory of real estate taken 18 Dec. 1710 by James SOUL, John BENNETT Jr. & Thomas NELSON. <3:196> Settlement 19 Sept. 1712 to following heirs, viz: **Ebenezer FULLER & John FULLER** to have all lands, saving their mother's third, and shall pay £10 to each of the other children when they come of age or marry, viz: **Samuel FULLER, Jabez FULLER, Elizabeth FULLER, Joanna FULLER, Mary FULLER, Marcy FULLER & Lidia FULLER.**

John FULLER et al to **Experience BENT** of Plymouth MA. <Plymouth Co.Deeds 12:93>
...30 Apr. 1714, Isaac FULLER of Plympton, Ebenezer FULLER & John FULLER of Middleboro, for £1.7s 6d, sell to Experience BENT...twelve and a half acres being one quarter of 50 acres...on east side of Whetstone Vineyard Brook in 26 Mens Purchase...formerly belonged to John FULLER & Isaac FULLER. Witnesses: Adam WRIGHT, Jacob TOMSON. Rec. 12 Jan. 1716.

Estate of **Jabez FULLER** of Middleborough MA. <Plymouth Co.PR #8232>
<5:499> Letter/Bond 30 Apr. 1729, brother **Ebenezer FULLER** of Middleboro app'td admr. Sureties: Samuel SAMPSON, Jonathan SAMSON. Witnesses: John WINSLOW, Isaac LITTLE Jr. <5:500> Inventory taken 23 May 1729 by James SOUL, Nathan WESTON & George SAMPSON Jr.; sworn to by admr. 23 May 1729; no real estate. <5:500> Warrant for appraisal, 30 Apr. 1729. <5:501> Dower set off to widow **Priscilla FULLER**, 23 May 1729, £25.6.6.

Estate of **John FULLER** of Halifax MA. <Plymouth Co.PR #8244>
<17:158> Letter/Bond 6 May 1766, Ephraim FULLER app'td admr. Sureties: Isaac TINKHAM, Charles ELLIS. Witnesses: Josiah EDSON, Edward WINSLOW. <19:406> Inventory taken 29 May 1766 by Josiah STURTEVANT Jr., Ebenezer TOMSON & Moses INGLEE; sworn to by admr. 7 July 1766; incl. homestead farm, £253.6.8. and land in Middleboro which belonged to the first wife of the dec'd; total real estate, £339.6.8. <19:458> Division 6 Oct. 1766 by Nathaniel WOOD, Jacob BENNET & Judah WOOD to following heirs, viz: widow **Lidia FULLER**; half of remainder to daus **Hannah FULLER & Barsheba ELLIS** wf of Charles; other half to grandchildren **Ephraim FULLER, Thomas FULLER & Abigail FULLER.**

Guardianship of Child of **John FULLER** of Halifax MA. <Plymouth Co.PR #8187>
<19:389,391> Bond 4 Aug. 1766, Joseph WATERMAN app'td gdn. of **Abigail FULLER**, under 14, minor dau of **John FULLER Jr.**. Surety: Joseph TINKHAM. Witnesses: Zechariah PADDOCK, Shubael TOMSON. <19:391> Nomination 8 Sept. 1766 by **Abigail FULLER** of Joseph WATERMAN as gdn. Witnesses: Joseph WATERMAN Jr., Joanna WATERMAN Jr.

Estate of **Samuel FULLER** of Plympton MA. <Plymouth Co.PR #8283>
<5:407> Bond 20 Dec. 1728, Letter 21 Dec. 1728, brother **Nathaniel FULLER** app'td admr. Sureties: Joseph THOMAS, Eleazer JACKSON. Witnesses: John HARLOW, Mary WINSLOW. <original> Inventory taken 25 Dec. 1728 by James WITON, James HARLOW & John BELL; total, £3.7.6; no real estate. <5:620> Account of admr. 5 Jan. 1729; estate insolvent.

Guardianship of Child of **James FULLER** of Plympton MA. <Plymouth Co.PR #8216>
<5:162> Letter 17 Jan. 1726, Bond 16 Jan. 1726, **James FULLER** app'td gdn. to his son **Elkanah FULLER**, under 14. Surety: Samuel FULLER. Witnesses: John BARTLETT, Samuel (blank).

Estate of **Samuel FULLER** of Plympton MA. <Plymouth Co.PR #8284>
<14:478> Letter/Bond 9 May 1758, widow **Anna FULLER** app'td admx. Sureties: Benjamin WESTON, John FULLER. Witnesses: Edward WINSLOW, Hannah DYER. <14:521;15:5> Inventory taken 10 May 1758 by John FULLER, James HARLOW & Amos FULLER; total, £98.4.1.; sworn to by admx. 9 May 1758.
(Note: The files contain two references (with no data) to **Anna FULLER** as admx. in the Plymouth Co.Deeds, viz: <45:133> 11 Sept. 1758 and <45:239> 2 Oct. 1759.

Will of **Ebenezer FULLER**, cordwainer of Kingston MA. <Plymouth Co.PR #8209>
<21:192>...dated 29 (--) 1755, mentions wf **Joanna**; sons **Josiah FULLER** (executor) **& Ebenezer FULLER**; daus **Rebeccah, Lois & Eunice.** Witnesses: John ADAMS, Nathan PERKINS & Francis ADAMS. Pr. 1 Dec. 1772, **Josiah FULLER** app'td exr.

Ebenezer FULLER of Kingston MA to **Josiah FULLER** of same. <Plymouth Co.Deeds 56:245>
...11 July 1772, Ebenezer FULLER, mariner to Josiah FULLER, yeoman...three shares in 30 acre wood lot, being three sixteenths parts of the whole given by John GRAY dec'd of Kingston to his daughter Joanna FULLER...also all that part of the homestead belonging to the estate of my honoured Father Ebenezer FULLER late of Kingston dec'd which he gave me in his last will. Witnesses: John GRAY, Samuel GRAY.

Will of **Josiah FULLER** yeoman of Kingston MA. <Plymouth Co.PR 53:10>
...dated 15 Sept. 1814...to wf **Elizabeth,** all estate for life; to son **John Holmes FULLER,** $100.00 & a bed in one year; to son **Josiah FULLER,** $20.00 in one year; to son **Ephraim FULLER** (executor), rest of estate after wife's death Pr. 3 July 1820.

Guardianship of **John FULLER** of Kingston MA. <Plymouth Co.PR #8240>
<originals> Petition (not dated) of James FULLER, Eleazer R. FULLER & Ephraim PATY representing that Mr. John FULLER, seignor, on account of age, infirmity & debility has been for years past of settling & adjusting his business in proper order...recommend the appointment of Capt. John GRAY. Citation issued 19 Feb. 1827. Bond was not completed nor executed.

Estate of **John FULLER** of Kingston MA. <Plymouth Co.PR #8241>
<61:247> Letter/Bond 17 Nov. 1828, John GRAY of Kingston app'td admr. Sureties: James FULLER, Eleazer R. FULLER, both of Kingston. <62:321> Notice, 15 Dec. 1828. <66:568> Inventory filed 26 Dec. 1828, by appraisers Lewis GRAY, Pelham BREWSTER, Spencer BREWSTER; incl. homestead farm with half a dwelling house & shop, estimated at 30 acres; 12 acres woodland in Kingston adjoining Elisha STETSON's; total real estate, $928.00; total personal estate, $38.75. <67:97> Insolvency 16 Feb. 1829. <67:8> Petition to sell real estate by admr. 13 Apr. 1829. <69:156> Account of admr. 9 Apr. 1830; Paid to: James FULLER, Lewis GRAY, Elisha STETSON, Bildad WASHBURN, Dr. Andrew MACKIE, Dr. Paul L. NICHOLS, Thomas WASHBURN, John FULLER, Ezra D. MORTON, Eleazer R. FULLER, Eli COOK, Melzar WHITTEN, Ephraim PATEY, Thomas C. HOLMES, Spencer BREWSTER, Pelham BREWSTER; Received from: Thaddeus CHURCHILL.

Estate of **Jabez FULLER** of Kingston MA. <Plymouth Co.PR #8233>
<14:238> Letter/Bond 26 May 1757, widow **Marcy FULLER** app'td admx. Sureties: Hezekiah RIPLEY, John GRAY. Witnesses: Thomas S. HOWLAND, John (----).

Estate of **James FULLER** of Kingston MA. <Plymouth Co.PR #8235>
<original> Bond 13 Dec. 1760, of mother **Mercy FULLER,** widow, admx. Sureties: Josiah FULLER of Kingston & Ebenezer ROBBINS of Plymouth. Witnesses: Edward WINSLOW, Penelope WINSLOW. <16:25> Letter 17 Dec. 1760, **Mercy FULLER** app'td admx.

Will of **Ebenezer FULLER** of Halifax MA. <Plymouth Co.PR #8211>
<30:45>...dated 12 July 1785...to grandson **Chipman FULLER**...besides what I formerly gave to his father **Ebenezer FULLER** dec'd my half of the five & twenty acres of land which we bought of Samuel FULLER; grandaughters **Lydia FULLER, Priscilla FULLER, Lois FULLER;** to grandaughters **Asenath KIMLINS & Susanah WOOD**...besides what I gave their father **Nathan FULLER** a piece of land adjoining land which John TOMSON gave to his dau Elizabeth FULLER; grandson **Jeams/James BOSWORTH;** dau **Elizabeth TOMSON;** grandson **Thaddeus TOMSON;** grandaughter **Elizabeth TOMSON.** Witnesses: Ephraim BRIGGS, Ephraim FULLER & Jacob SOULE. <30:47> Letter/Bond 4 Dec. 1786, James BOSWORTH of Halifax app'td admr. Sureties: Jacob SOULE, Ephraim FULLER. Witnesses: Isaac LOTHROP, Thomas MORTON. <30:112> Inventory taken 19 Feb. 1787 by Moses INGLEE, Noah TOMSON & Ephraim FULLER; total real estate, £96.8; total estate, £104.14; sworn to by admr. 4 Apr. 1787.

Ebenezer FULLER of Halifax MA to **Betty TOMSON** of same. <Plymouth Co.Deeds 57:111>
...23 Mar. 1772, Ebenezer FULLER gives to dau Betty TOMSON...one quarter part of cedar swamp in Middleborough in 26 Mens Purchase. Witnesses: James BOZWORTH, Eli BOZWORTH. Ack. 6 Apr. 1773. Rec. 21 Apr. 1773.

Samuel FULLER of Halifax MA to **Ebenezer FULLER** of same. <Plymouth Co.Deeds 50:246>
...22 Oct. 1765, Samuel FULLER, yeoman, for £7 sold to Ebenezer FULLER, yeoman...three acres in Middleboro bounded by land of Dr. STURTEVANT. Wf Elizabeth FULLER signs. Witnesses: John TOMSON Jr., James BOZWORTH. Ack. 24 Oct. 1765 by grantors. Rec. 26 Oct. 1765.

Heirs of **Ebenezer FULLER Jr.** <Plymouth Co.Deeds 59:60>
...4 Mar. 1774, John WATERMAN as admr.; dau Ruth LEACH wf of Elijah; Timothy RIPLEY gdn. of Chipman FULLER & Priscilla FULLER, minors and Thomas CUSHMAN as gdn. of Eunice FULLER & Lydia FULLER, minors...re-convey land.

PLYMOUTH COUNTY DEEDS: (re: FULLER)

<24:131> - 16 Aug. 1728, Samuel FULLER, yeoman of Plympton gives to son Ebenezer FULLER of Kingston, half of 100 acre lot near Wenhenquay.

<50:246> - 2 Feb. 1752/3, Samuel & Elizabeth FULLER of Halifax sell to Ebenezer FULLER Sr. and Ebenezer FULLER Jr. of Halifax.

<50:248> - 16 Aug. 1757, Ebenezer FULLER Sr. & wf Elizabeth to son Ebenezer FULLER Jr.

<86:143> - 25 Sept 1769, Ebenezer & Elizabeth FULLER of Halifax to Thomas FULLER of Pembroke.

<84:183> - 26 Aug. 1786, Chipman FULLER, Thankful FULLER, Lydia FULLER, Priscilla FULLER, all of Halifax & Eunice FULLER of Worthington MA, for £30 sell to Samuel BROWN of Halifax, 15 acres in Halifax.

PLYMOUTH COUNTY DEEDS: (re: Ebenezer FULLER, grantor, all to 1801)

<12:93> - 1716, Ebenezer FULLER et al to Experience BENT.

<14:174> - 1719, Ebenezer FULLER to John THOMSON Jr.

<18:224> - 1725, Ebenezer FULLER et al, division.

<39:174> - 1748, Ebenezer FULLER to James SMITH.

<40:126> - 1749, Ebenezer FULLER & Ebenezer FULLER Jr., division.

<40:199> - 1749, Ebenezer FULLER to Barnabas TOMSON.

<43:151> - 1755, Ebenezer FULLER et al, division.

<44:76> - 1757, Ebenezer FULLER Jr. to Benjamin CUSHMAN Jr.

<46:62> - 1760, Ebenezer FULLER to Thomas WELD.

<50:43> - 1765, Exon., Samuel RIDER's estate.

<50:247> - 1765, Ebenezer FULLER Sr. to Ebenezer FULLER Jr. (also 50:248)

<52:46> - 1765, Ebenezer FULLER Jr. to Elkanah CUSHMAN.

<52:226> - 1766, Ebenezer FULLER to Lemuel THOMAS et al.

<53:57> - 1765, Ebenezer FULLER Sr. & Ebenezer FULLER Jr. to Samuel TINKHAM.

<56:82> - 16 Jan. 1771, Ebenezer FULLER to grandson James BOZWORTH, mentions brother John FULLER deceased.

<56:245> - 1772, Ebenezer FULLER to Josiah FULLER.

<57:111> - 1773, Ebenezer FULLER to Betty THOMSON.

<57:111> - 23 Mar. 1772, Ebenezer FULLER of Halifax to grandson James BOZWORTH of same.

<59:33> - 1777, Ebenezer FULLER to Elijah LEACH.

<59:60> - 1777, Heirs of Ebenezer FULLER Jr. to Benjamin CARTER.

<86:143> - 25 Sept. 1769, Ebenezer & Elizabeth FULLER of Halifax to Thomas FULLER of Pembroke, 2 acres in Halifax on Winnetuxet river. Rec. 27 June 1799.

<63:18> - 1783, Elizabeth FULLER to Isaac THOMSON.

PLYMOUTH COUNTY DEEDS: (re: Ebenezer FULLER, grantee, all to 1801)

<43:151> - 19 Dec. 1720, Ebenezer & John FULLER of Middleboro, sons of John dec'd, division; mentions uncle Isaac FULLER.

<18:224> - 1724, Ebenezer FULLER et al, settlement of bounds.

<20:35,36> , Ebenezer FULLER from John GRAY.

<28:131> - 16 Aug. 1728, Ebenezer FULLER from father Samuel FULLER, yeoman of Plympton.

<33:175> - 9 Jan. 1734/5, Ebenezer FULLER, yeoman of Halifax from Reliance FULLER of Middleboro, part of home of her fatner Isaac FULLER.

<35:51> - 1 June 1735, Ebenezer FULLER, highest bidder on land in Middleboro, from Mary FULLER, admx., widow of Dr. Isaac FULLER of Middleboro.

<39:179> - , Ebenezer Jr. from Joel EDDY.

<50:247> - 10 Jan. 1745/6, Ebenezer FULLER Jr. of Halifax from Samuel WOOD Jr.

<50:246> - 18 Apr. 1746, Ebenezer FULLER Sr. of Halifax from Eleazer PRATT Jr. of Middleboro. Rec 26 Oct. 1765.

<40:57> - 15 June 1747, Ebenezer FULLER Jr. of Halifax from Abigail EDDY (mother of Joel).

<50:247> - 24 May 1748, Ebenezer FULLER Sr. & Ebenezer FULLER Jr. of Halifax from James SMITH.

<40:126> - 18 Sept 1749, Ebenezer FULLER Jr. & Ebenezer FULLER, of Halifax division of land in Plympton with John & Hannah TINKHAM.

<40:127> - 3 Oct. 1749, Ebenezer FULLER Sr. of Halifax from Eleazer PRATT Jr.

<43:52> - 1 Nov. 1752, Ebenezer FULLER Jr. of Halifax from Benjamin CUSHMAN Jr.

<50:246> - 2 Feb. 1752/3, Ebenezer FULLER Sr. & Ebenezer FULLER Jr., of Halifax from Samuel & Elizabeth FULLER of same, land in Middleboro formerly belonging to Dr. Isaac FULLER of Middleboro dec'd. Ack. 24 Oct. 1765.

<50:249> - 29 June 1757, Ebenezer FULLER Jr., yeoman of Halifax from Samuel FULLER, son of Isaac FULLER dec'd of Middleboro. Wf Elizabeth FULLER signs. Rec 26 Oct. 1765.

<50:248> - 16 Aug. 1757, Ebenezer FULLER Jr. from father Ebenezer FULLER Sr. & wf Elizabeth of Halifax, part of house, land E.F. Jr. bought of Samuel FULLER.

<50:248> - 27 Feb. 1762, Ebenezer FULLER Jr. from Mary FULLER, widow of Nathan of Halifax.

<56:245> - 1762, Ebenezer FULLER from Rebecca FULLER, spinster of Kingston.

<50:246> - 22 Oct. 1765, Ebenezer FULLER, yeoman of Halifax from Samuel & Elizabeth FULLER of Halifax, land in Plympton & Middleboro. Rec. 26 Oct. 1765.

PLYMOUTH COUNTY DEEDS, cont-d: (re: Ebenezer FULLER, grantee, all to 1801**)**

<50:248> - 22 Oct. 1765, Ebenezer FULLER Jr. of Halifax from Ebenezer FULLER Sr. & wf Elizabeth.
<50:247> - 23 Oct. 1765, Ebenezer FULLER & Ebenezer FULLER Jr., division of land lately bought of James SMITH of Middleboro.
<50:43> - , Exon. from S. RIDER.
<55:5> - , Ebenezer FULLER Jr. from Benjamin CARTER.

Estate of **Ebenezer FULLER** of Kingston MA. <Plymouth Co.PR #8209>
...1772...<21:192> Will & Pr. (no details given).

Estate of **Ebenezer FULLER Jr.** of Halifax MA. <Plymouth Co.PR #8210>
<20:312> Letter/Bond 12 Feb. 1770, John WATERMAN of Halifax app'td admr. Sureties: Jesse STURTEVANT, Asa BEARES. Witnesses: Edward WINSLOW, Nicholas DREW Jr. <20:375> Inventory taken 24 Apr. 1770 by Timothy RIPLEY, Samuel SMITH & Noah CUSHING; sworn to by admr., 17 May 1770; total real estate, £378.13.4; total estate, £496.5.6. <21:72> Account of admr. 3 Feb. 1772; Paid to: Joseph BOSWORTH, John BOSWORTH; to binding out John TAYLOR; Eli BOSWORTH, Daniel DUNBAR, Elisha BRADFORD Nathan PERKINS, William SEVER, Elijah LEACH, David HATCH, Josiah STURTEVANT, Andrew THOMSON, Asa THOMSON, Lemuel STURTEVANT, James WARREN, Judah WOOD, Dr. Stephen POWERS, Thomas CROADE, Ignatius LORING, Josiah WATERMAN, Moses INGLEE, CROMBIE, Josiah RIPLEY, Sarah BOSWORTH Jr., Jonathan PARKER Jr., Micah ALLEN, Gideon BRADFORD, GOODWIN, John TOMSON, Ebenezer TOMSON, Joel ELLIS, Benjamin WRIGHT, Adam WRIGHT, Benjamin CUSHMAN, James BOSWORTH, Reuben TOMSON, Timothy RUGGLES, Silas STURTEVANT, Zebediah SAMSON; to widow **Deborah FULLER** for necessaries; to Thomas CUSHMAN & Timothy RIPLEY, guardians of the children; to Elijah LEACH Jr. for his wife's part. <21:148> Division 6 July 1772 by Samuel SMITH, Elijah BISBEE & Isaac CHURCHILL 3d, to the following heirs, viz: to widow **Deborah FULLER**, part of the 15 acre lot near the widow Mary FULLER's house & adjoining Ephraim FULLER's; to the only son **Chipman FULLER**, land between sd estate & Ebenezer FULLER's which they purchased of Samuel FULLER of Halifax; to dau **Ruth LEACH** wf of Elijah, part of 40 acre lot, partly in Plimpton & partly in Middleboro which was formerly Dr. Isaac FULLER's; daus **Lydia FULLER, Priscilla FULLER & Eunice FULLER.**

Guardianship of Children of **Ebenezer FULLER Jr.** of Halifax MA. <Plymouth Co.PR #8278>
<original> Request 4 Apr. 1771 of **Ebenezer FULLER** that Timothy RIPLEY be app'td gdn. "for my little grand daughter **Priscilla FULLER**", under 14. <20:512> Bond 10 Apr. 1771, Timothy RIPLEY of Plympton app'td. Sureties: Ebenezer TOMSON, Timothy RIPLEY Jr. Witnesses: Briggs ALDEN, Edward WINSLOW. <21:68> Bonds 7 Oct. 1771, Thomas CUSHMAN of Plympton app'td gdn. of **Eunice FULLER**, under 14 and **Lydia FULLER**, above 14. Sureties: Nathan COBB, Samuel BRADFORD. Witnesses: Josiah EDSON, Edward WINSLOW. <original> Request 4 Jan. 1771 of **Chipman FULLER**, above 14, that Timothy RIPLEY be app'td his gdn. <21:74> Letter/Bond 3 Feb. 1772, Timothy RIPLEY app'td. Sureties: Thomas CUSHMAN, John BRADFORD. Witnesses: James CUSHING, Elisha JACOBS. <original> Letter 10 Apr. 1771, Timothy RIPLEY app'td gdn. of **Priscilla FULLER.**

Will of **Lydia FULLER**, single woman of Halifax MA. <Plymouth Co.PR #8262>
<44:260>...dated 15 Feb. 1812, mentions Ebenezer FULLER, Nathan FULLER, Ruth SOULE, Lydia RIPLEY, Priscilla BOZWORTH, Nancy FULLER, Priscilla RIPLEY wf of Ezekiel, Saba RIPLEY, Priscilla RIPLEY dau of Ezekiel, Thankful FULLER; Noah BOZWORTH, executor. Witnesses: Nathaniel MORTON, Joseph BOSWORTH & Lydia TOMSON. <39:458> Letter/Bond 6 July 1812, Ebenezer FULLER app'td admr. with will annexed, Noah BOSWORTH having refused. Sureties: Timothy WOOD, Joseph BOSWORTH, both of Halifax. <44:358> Inventory taken 26 Aug. 1812 by Timothy WOOD, Jacob SOULE & Isaac THOMSON, all of Halifax; total estate, $397.26. <44:363> Order of notice, sworn to by admr. 3 Nov. 1812.

Joel PERKINS of Woodstock VT to **Ezekiel RIPLEY** of Plimton MA. <Plymouth Co.Deeds 85:46>
...22 Dec. 1796, Joel PERKINS & wf Eunice, for £10.10s sold to Ezekiel RIPLEY, yeoman...all rights in a ceder swamp in Middleboro...that our honoured father Mr. Ebenezer FULLER bought of Mr. Samuel FULLER 22 Oct. 1765. Witnesses: Solomon THOMAS, Elisha PERKINS. Rec. 3 July 1798.

Estate of **Chipman FULLER** of Halifax MA. <Plymouth Co.PR #8203>
<34:91> Letter/Bond 7 Nov. 1796, widow **Thankful FULLER** app'td admx. Sureties: William SHAW, James BOSWORTH. Witnesses: Isaac LOTHROP, Thomas GANNETT. <36:87> Warrant for appraisal 7 Nov. 1796 to William SHAW, John WATERMAN & Samuel LUCAS. <36:88> Inventory taken 15 Nov. 1796 by appraisers; total real estate, $746.00; total estate, $1259.06; sworn to by admx. 4 Apr. 1797. <37:312> Account of admx. 6 Oct. 1800; Due from: Timothy RIPLEY, Isaac BONNEY, Richard BOSWORTH; Paid to: Dr. Jabez FULLER, Dr. Nathaniel MORTON, Sala BOSWORTH, Isaac & Josiah TOMSON, George SAMSON, Ephraim TINKHAM, Isaac WRIGHT, Josiah PERKINS, Arthur CHANDLER, Asa TOMSON, Elijah SHAW, James SOULE Joshua WOOD, Nathan TOMSON, Deborah FULLER, John WATERMAN, Samuel LUCAS, William SHAW, Nathan TOMSON and John ADAMS for "Contanental Tax". <40:119> Warrant for division, 1 Oct. 1804, to John WATERMAN, Adam TOMSON & Jacob SOULE. <40:120> Inventory confirmed 23 Nov. 1804; to following heirs, viz: widow **Thankful FULLER**, dau **Ruth FULLER**, sons **Ebenezer FULLER, Nathan FULLER**, daus **Priscilla FULLER, Nancy FULLER**; mentions lands adjoining that of James BOSWORTH, Lady FULLER, Deborah FULLER, Winnatuxet meadows & includes land formerly owned by Dr. Isaac FULLER.

Guardianship of Children of **Chipman FULLER** of Halifax MA. <Plymouth Co.PR #8274>
<32:243> Letter/Bond 1 Oct. 1804, widow **Thankful FULLER** app'td gdn. of **Nathan & Priscilla FULLER**, above 14 and **Nancy FULLER**, under 14. Sureties: Jacob SOULE of Halifax & Ebenezer WRIGHT Jr. of Plympton. Witness: Thomas GANNETT.

MICRO #3 OF 3

Will of **Ebenezer FULLER**, yeoman/gent. of Halifax MA. <Plymouth Co.PR #8212>
<86:145>...dated 30 Apr. 1840, mentions wf **Abigail**; to daus **Luirah**(sp) **N. GAMMON** wf of Calvin & **Rebecca FULLER** wf of Ephraim, $100.00 each to be paid by son **Ebenezer FULLER Jr.** when he arrives at the age of 21; Dexter C. THOMPSON, executor. Witnesses: Thomas POPE, Calvin STURTEVANT & Harriet THOMSON. <10:537> Petition for admr. with will annexed by Ebenezer FULLER, 1st Tues. Apr. 1844. Letter/Bond 2 Apr. 1844, Ebenezer FULLER app'td admr. as Dexter C. THOMPSON declines. Sureties: Isaac FULLER, Dexter C. THOMPSON, both of Halifax. <86:200> Inventory taken 3d Mon. May 1844 by Dexter C. THOMSON, Nathan FULLER & Isaac FULLER; total real estate, $2725.00; total estate, $3090.00. <6:492> Notice. <86:232> Waiver of provisions of the will by the widow **Abigail FULLER**, 28 May 1844, claims dower & prays for an allowance out of personal estate. <86:349> Dower assigned, 13 June 1844, to widow by Jabez P. THOMPSON & Zadock THOMPSON of Halifax and Samuel THOMPSON of Middleboro; real estate is appraised at $2400.00 of which one third, $800.00, is assigned to her along with the westerly half of dwelling house as first built, also one third of celler, one third of barn, one third of pew #9 in Mr. HOWLAND's meeting house, fresh meadow on Winatuxett River known as Cobb meadow, 6 acre pasture land and wood land adjoining Jacob SOULE's.

Will of **Nathan FULLER**, cordwainer of Halifax MA. <Plymouth Co.PR #8271>
<16:60>...dated 12 Nov. 1760, mentions wf **Mary**, eldest son **Noah FULLER** (under 21), daus **Hannah FULLER, Lucy FULLER, Asenath FULLER,** son **Thomas FULLER,** dau **Susanah FULLER.** Witnesses: Ebenezer FULLER Jr., Lydia TOMSON & Moses INGLEE. <16:61,62> Letter/Bond 6 Apr. 1761, widow **Mary FULLER,** app'td exx. Sureties: Ebenezer FULLER Jr. & Moses INGLEE of Halifax. Witnesses: Jonathan FULLER, Edward WINSLOW.

Will of **John FULLER**, yeoman of Kingston MA. <Plymouth Co.PR #8239>
<25:96>...dated 31 Dec. 1761 "at beginning, 22 Mar. 1764 at end!", mentions sons **Issachar FULLER, Ezra FULLER, Consider FULLER, Eleazer FULLER,** daus **Deborah PRINCE, Susanna DINGLEY, Hannah BISBE;** son **Issachar** and son in law **Kimball PRINCE,** executors. Witnesses: Ebenezer WASHBURNE, Eleazer RICKARD Jr. & John FAUNCE. <25:97> Pr. 5 Oct. 1778. <25:152> Inventory taken 9 Oct. 1778 of estate of **Deacon John FULLER;** total real estate, Ł910.13.4; total estate, Ł1221.17.10.

Will of **Ezra FULLER** of Kingston MA. <Plymouth Co.PR #8222>
<21:20>...dated 20 Mar. 1771, mentions wf **Elizabeth** and children (all under 21), viz: **Samuel FULLER, Consider FULLER, James FULLER, Susanna FULLER, Molly FULLER;** Ebenezer WASHBURN named as gdn. of the three youngest, **Consider, James & Molly;** Robert COOK named as gdn. to **Samuel & Susanna;** wf **Elizabeth** and Robert COOK, executors. Witnesses: Kimbal PRINCE, Consider FULLER & Simeon HOLMES. <21:21> Letter 5 Aug. 1771, **Elizabeth FULLER** & Robert COOK app'td exrs. <21:53> Inventory taken 13 Aug. 1771 by Benjamin COOK, Josiah HOLMES & Ebenezer WASHBURN; total real estate, Ł100; total estate, Ł171.10.2; sworn to by exrs. 7 Oct. 1771. <28:531> Account 6 Jan. 1783, of Robert COOK, surviving executor; List: Josiah HOLMES, Charles COOK, Eleazer RING, Samuel RIPLEY, to the widow Mary LORING, Simeon HOLMES, Thomas LORING, Jabez WASHBURN, Cornelius SAMPSON, Ebenezer DREW, Gershom COBB, Susanna HOLMES, Sarah HALL, Francis RING, Robert COOK, John ADAMS, Kimball PRINCE, Josiah WEST, Abner RICKARD, Josiah HOLMES, Benjamin COOK, Francis HOLMES, Josiah HOLMES Jr., William SEVER, Job DREW, Dr. John THOMAS, Dr. William THOMAS, Dr. Stephen POWERS.

Isaac & Noah FULLER of Middleboro MA to **Benjamin SHURTLEFF** of Carver MA. <Plymouth Co.Deeds>
<286:148>...20 Feb. 1792, Isaac FULLER & Noah FULLER, for Ł15 sell to Benjamin SHURTLEFF...land in Carver that they bought of Benjamin BARNES. Wives sign, Lydia & Sarah FULLER. Ack. by Isaac 4 Oct. 1794. Rec. 19 Mar. 1858.

Isaac FULLER of Middleboro MA to **Isaac RYDER** of same. <Plymouth Co.Deeds 81:259>
...24 Nov. 1796, Isaac FULLER, for $1333.00 sells to Isaac RYDER...land in Middleboro...formerly part of the home farm of James PALMER dec'd...also half part of PALMER's sawmill. Wf Lydia FULLER releases dower. Ack. by both 1 Mar. 1797.

Isaac FULLER of Rochester MA to **Earl CLAP** of same. <Plymouth Co.Deeds 83:96>
...7 Apr. 1798, Isaac FULLER, yeoman, for $1700.00 mortgages to Earl CLAP...all lands in Rochester bought of sd CLAP.

<Plymouth Co.Deeds>...**Isaac & Lydia FULLER** of Rochester: <95:8> 24 Aug. 1801; <99:158> 18 May 1803, sell woodland in Rochester to Gideon BARSTOW(sp). References with no data: 241:101;102:11; 121:164.

Estate of **Issacher FULLER.** <?-- "Docket #8230, 105:480 (Norfolk co.?>
Petition (date?) of **Tilson FULLER** to be app'td admr. on estate of **Issacher FULLER** who died at Hingham, 11 Feb. 1866, leaving will with exrs. **Matilda N. FULLER & Thomas B. FULLER** who decline to serve; only heirs & next of kin, viz: wf **Matilda N. FULLER** of Hingham, son **Thomas B. FULLER** of Boston, dau **Eliza N. GRAVES** wf of James of Weymouth, son **Tilson FULLER** of Hingham, son **Charles M. FULLER** of Boston and son **Joshua T. FULLER** of Boston.

PLYMOUTH COUNTY DEEDS: (re: Issacher FULLER)

<49:44> - 27 Mar. 1764, Issacher FULLER buys land in Plimpton & Middleboro.
<58:188> - 27 Sept 1775, Issacher FULLER & wife.
<79:259> - 23 Dec. 1789, Issacher FULLER.

PLYMOUTH COUNTY DEEDS, cont-d: (re: Issacher FULLER)

<80:261> - 18 Mar. 1794, Issachar FULLER, yeoman & wf Lucy of Carver sell to John LUCAS of same. Ack. 7 May 1795 by Issachar.

(Note: the following references to **Issacher FULLER** are given with no data, viz: 47:264;48:167;50:225;52:254;63:13;71:81:245;81:245. The following are references to **Isaac FULLER**, viz: 39:99;41:118;59:31;71:44;77:64;81:259;83:96.)

Will of **Nathaniel FULLER**, mason of Plympton MA. <Plymouth Co.PR #8275>
<12:107>...dated 16 Mar. 1749, mentions wf **Martha**, eldest son **Amos FULLER** (executor), daus **Sarah STURTEVANT, Ruth COBB**, son **Barnabas FULLER**, grandson **William FULLER**, grandaughter **Lydia FULLER** dau of son **Nathaniel FULLER** dec'd. Witnesses: James HARLOW, Elkanah CUSHMAN & Josiah PERKINS. <12:108> Letter 7 May 1750, **Amos FULLER** app'td exr. <12:6> Inventory taken 13 June 1750 by Josiah PERKINS, Isaac BONNEY & Samuel LUCAS; sworn by "Thomas FULLER", exr., 12 July 1750; incl. homestead farm, £202.13.4.; meadow at Doten's meadow; cedar swamp in Doten's Cedar Swamp; land east of Jones River meadow.

Guardianship of Children of **Nathaniel FULLER** of Plympton MA. <Plymouth Co.PR #8263>
<11:89,91> Letters/Bonds 9 Apr. 1748, Amos FULLER of Plympton app'td gdn. of **Lydia FULLER & William FULLER**. Surety: Joseph PARRY. Witnesses: Edward WINSLOW, Hannah WINSLOW.

Estate of **Philemon FULLER** of Plympton MA. <Plymouth Co.PR #8277>
<10:235> Petition/Bond 21 Jan. 1839, of eldest son **Charles FULLER** of Plympton. Sureties: John BARTLETT 3d of Plymouth & Stafford STURTEVANT of Halifax. <81:67> Warrant for inventory, 21 Jan. 1839 to Martin HAYWARD, William PERKINS & Jonathan PARKER, all of Plympton. <5:85> Notice of appointment, 25 Feb. 1839, of **Charles FULLER**, admr. <81:190> Division by appraisers; $4449.98 to be divided among the following seven heirs, viz: **Charles FULLER, Harvey FULLER, Bildad FULLER, Amos FULLER, Philemon FULLER, Warren FULLER & Sarah STANDISH**; signed 4 Apr. 1839 by six sons & widow **Mercy FULLER**. <82:120> Account of admr., 13 Apr. 1840.

STEPHEN HOPKINS

MICRO #1 OF 18

PLYMOUTH COLONY DEEDS: (re: HOPKINS)

<1:20> - 17 July 1637, Stephen HOPKINS, gent. to George BEARE.

<1:58> - 30 Nov. 1638, Stephen HOPKINS, gent. to Josias COOKE.

<1:148> - 8 June 1642, Stephen HOPKINS, gent. from William CHASE.

<1:182> - 28 Oct. 1644, Gyles HOPKINS & Caleb HOPKINS, to each other.

<2:1:171> - 9 May 1642, Gyles HOPKINS, planter of Yarmouth to Andrew HALLET Jr. planter of same

<2:1:196> - 10 Oct. 1657, Elizabeth HOPKINS to Jacob COOKE, planter of Plymouth.

<4:252> - 21 Aug. 1672, Gyles HOPKINS, planter of Eastham from Indians.

==========

Edward GRAY of Plymouth to **John COTTON** of Plymouth. <Plymouth Col.Deeds 3:166>
...19 May 1670, Edward GRAY, merchant, for £5 sold to Mr. John COTTON...two homsteeds or garden plotes...in Plymouth...in the great street on the northsyde of the sd street...now in the...occupation of Nathaniel MORTON and Thomas LETTICE...the one of them the homsteed of Mr. Steven HOPKINS deceased.

==========

Gyles HOPKINS of Eastham to **John WING** of Yarmouth. <Plymouth Col.Deeds 3:1:91>
...9 Nov. 1666, Gyles HOPKINS, planter, sells to John WING, husbandman...lands of Stephen HOPKINS dec'd, heired by his son Caleb HOPKINS dec'd. Witnesses: Josias COOKE, John FREEMAN, Stephen HOPKINS.

CONSTANCE HOPKINS^2 (Stephen^1)

PLYMOUTH COL.DEEDS: (re: SNOW)

<3:148> - 25 Mar. 1669, Nicholas SNOW witnessed deed of Richard HIGGINS.

<3:192> - 10 June 1669, Mark SNOW witnessed deed of Alice BRADFORD Sr. to John DOANE.

<3:201> - 12 Jan. 1671, mentions land of Nicholas SNOW.

<3:267> - , Mark SNOW, witness.

<3:276> - , Nicholas SNOW et al, purchasers of Nauset.

<3:279> - , Mark SNOW, witness.

<3:334> - , Nicholas SNOW, witness.

==========

Estate of **Lt. Jabez SNOW** of Eastham MA. <Barnstable Co.PR>
<1:39> Inventory taken 20 Apr. 1691, presented 22 Apr.1691 by widow **Elizabeth SNOW.** <1:113> Settlement 8 Apr. 1695 to the heirs, viz: widow, eldest son **Jabez SNOW**, 2d son **Edward SNOW**, 3rd son **Thomas SNOW** and six daughters (unnamed).

==========

Estate of **Marcy COOK**, widow of Eastham MA. <Barnstable Co.PR>
<10:105> 29 June 1762, Silvanus SNOW, yeoman of Eastham, app'td admr. <12:288> Inventory of personal estate; one of appraisers, Richard COOK.

==========

Will of **Edward SNOW**, yeoman of Harwich MA. <Barnstable Co.PR>
<9:382>...dated 8 Apr. 1754...under the decays of old age, mentions sons **Jabez SNOW & Joseph SNOW** (executor); seven grandchildren, heirs of son **Nathaniel SNOW** dec'd; four grandchildren, heirs of dau **Martha BAKER** dec'd; grandson **Edward SNOW.** Witnesses: Nathaniel MERRICK, Mehitable SNOW (d. pre probate) & John SNOW. <9:383> Pr. 20 Sept. 1758. <9:384> Inventory taken 29 Sept. 1758; sworn to 21 Mar. 1759 by exr.

==========

Estate of **Joseph SNOW**, yeoman of Harwich MA. <Barnstable Co.PR>
<10:88> 7 May 1761, John SNOW, gent. of Harwich, app'td admr. <11:208-11> 1 July 1762, Isaac FOSTER , blacksmith of Harwich, app'td gdn. of **Silvanus SNOW, Desire SNOW, Sarah SNOW & Mercy SNOW.** <12:222> Inventory 7 July 1761. <12:346> Account July 1761, mentions the widow and what is reserved for **Martha BAKER's** heirs which is her due. <14:4> 5 Apr. 1763, John SNOW, gent. of Harwich, app'td gdn. of **Edward SNOW.** <14:165> 12 Aug. 1766, Enos SNOW, yeoman of Harwich, app'td gdn. of **Edward SNOW.** <13:65> Settlement 18 Apr. 1764 to following children, viz: eldest son **Joseph SNOW, Silvanus SNOW** (minor), **Nathan SNOW, Isaac SNOW, Edward SNOW, Martha FOSTER** wf of Ebenezer, **Sarah SNOW, Hannah SNOW, Mercy SNOW, Desire SNOW & Mary SNOW.**

==========

Estate of **Thomas SNOW Jr.** of Harwich. <Barnstable Co.PR>
<5:53> 28 July 1732, Nathaniel FREEMAN of Harwich, app'td admr. <5:83> Inventory taken 1 Aug. 1732, "property shown to appraisers by father of deceased".

==========

Will of **Joseph SNOW** of Harwich MA. <Barnstable Co.PR 27:363>
...dated 25 Jan. 1793, mentions wf **Priscilla,** children **Zoheth SNOW** (executor), **Silvanus SNOW, Joseph SNOW, David SNOW, Jonathan SNOW, Priscilla & Mary**; grandson **Martin.** Pr. 28 Oct. 1793.

Estate of **Nathaniel SNOW,** yeoman of Harwich MA. <Barnstable Co.PR>
<7:179> 9 May 1750, widow **Thankful SNOW** app'td admx. <8:361> Inventory taken 3 Aug. 1750 by Jonathan LINCOLN, John SNOW & Nathan FOSTER. <11:186,187> 6 Jan. 1762, Joseph SEARS of Harwich app'td gdn. of **Elizabeth SNOW & Reuben SNOW,** minors. <11:237,238> 1 Mar. 1763, Thomas SNOW Jr. of Harwich app'td gdn. of **Elizabeth SNOW & Reuben SNOW,** minors. <12:251> Dower set off 10 Apr. 1762 to widow **Thankful SNOW.** <12:252> Division 10 Apr. 1762 among heirs, viz: **Edward SNOW, Thomas SNOW, Seth SNOW, Nathaniel SNOW, Patience HOPKINS, Elisabeth/Betty SNOW & Reuben SNOW.** <13:286> Account 18 Mar. 1767 of **Thomas SNOW Jr.,** gdn. of **Reuben SNOW** (mentions brother **Edward**). <14:183> 10 Mar. 1767, Nathaniel SNOW, yeoman of Harwich, app'td gdn. of **Reuben SNOW.**

Estate of **Seth SNOW,** yeoman of Harwich MA. <Barnstable Co.PR>
<10:130>...15 Feb. 1764, widow **Azubah SNOW** app'td admx. <13:43> Inventory taken 14 Feb. 1764. <13:74> Account of admx. 11 Dec. 1764. <14:49> 18 Apr. 1764, **Azubah SNOW** app'td gdn. of **Sarah SNOW,** minor. <13:282> Account 10 Mar. 1767 of **Silvanus CROSBY & Azubah,** his wife as admx.

Estate of **Edward SNOW,** yeoman of Harwich MA. <Barnstable Co.PR>
<10:109> 7 Dec. 1762, **Seth SNOW,** yeoman of Harwich app'td admr. <10:133> 16 Feb. 1764, **Thomas SNOW Jr.,** yeoman of Harwich app'td admr. de bonis non...**Seth SNOW** brother of **Edward** died before he completed settlement. <13:78> Inventory taken 21 Feb. 1764; incl. a whale voiage unsettled, £15.6.8. <13:281> Account of admr. 13 Jan. 1767.

Estate of **Dr. Reuben SNOW** of Harwich MA. <Barnstable Co.PR>
<25:134> 1 Feb. 1796, **Reuben SNOW** app'td admr. <24:204> Settlement 2 Apr. 1801, to following heirs, viz: sons **Reuben SNOW & John SNOW** of Harwich; dau **Patience CLARKE** wf of Perez of Westmins-VT; dau **Betsey WINSLOW** wf of Isaac of Harwich; dau **Rhoda SNOW** of Harwich; dau **Patty SNOW** of Harwich; son **Nathaniel SNOW** of Harwich; dau **Sally SNOW** of Harwich; dau **Reliance SNOW** of Harwich; son **Obed SNOW** of Harwich.

Will of **Jabez SNOW,** yeoman of Eastham MA. <Barnstable Co.PR>
<8:457>...dated 11 Oct. 1743, mentions wf **Elizabeth;** sons **Jabez SNOW** (executor), **Silvanus SNOW, Samuel SNOW;** daus **Elizabeth KNOWLES, Tabitha MAYO, Phebe SMITH.** Pr. 23 Jan. 1750. No inventory.

Will of **Capt. Jabez SNOW,** gent./yeoman of Eastham MA. <Barnstable Co.PR 12:151,152,177-9;17:59>
...dated 31 July 1760...arrived to declining age...mentions wf **Elizabeth;** sons **Jabez SNOW** (executor), **Joshua SNOW, Edward SNOW;** daus **Eunice HERTING/HORTON, Elizabeth SNOW, Hannah SNOW.** Pr. 17 Mar. 1761. Inventory taken 24 Mar. 1761.

Estate of **Silvanus SNOW** of Eastham MA. <Barnstable Co.PR>
<12:524> 7 Apr. 1772, **Edward SNOW,** yeoman of Eastham app'td admr. <12:520> Inventory taken 15 Apr 1772. <12:523> Dower to widow. <12:524> Division 11 Aug. 1772 among widow **Deborah SNOW** and children, viz: **Edward SNOW, Collier SNOW, Silvanus SNOW, Heman SNOW, Hannah SNOW, Mary DEAN** wf of William, **Tabitha HOLBROOK** wf of Isaiah. <15:111,112> 5 May 1772, **Edward SNOW** app'td gdn. of **Silvanus SNOW & Heman SNOW,** minors. <15:157> 13 Apr. 1773, Barnabas FREEMAN, gent., app'td gdn. of **Hannah SNOW,** minor. <17:193> Account of admr. 12 Mar. 1774. <19:138> 25 Apr. 1786, **Collier SNOW,** yeoman of Eastham app'td admr. d.b.n., the former admr. being removed out of the state. <24:198> Settlement 10 Oct. 1786, to children (widow dec'd): **Collier SNOW,** eldest son **Edward SNOW** of Penobscot, **Mary DEAN/DOANE** of Eastham, **Tabitha HATCH** wf of George of Wellfleet and **Hannah RICH** wf of Elisha of Wellfleet. <26:209> Division of real estate, 8 May 1786. <26:210> Account of admr. 10 Oct. 1786.

MICRO #2 OF 18

Heirs of **Benjamin COLLINGS.** <from originals owned 1908 by Mrs. Susan J. DYER of Provincetown MA>
...Truro 12 Mar. 1759, Receipt of **Robert & Leady RICH** from...brother **Benjamin COLLINGS,** executor to will of our Honoured deceased father namely Mr. **Benjamin COLLINGS,** the sum of four pounds money a legacy willed unto us by our sd father. Witnesses: Bathier GROOES, Richard COLLINGS Jr.
...Truro 17 Apr. 1759, Receipt of **Amasa & Mary SNOW** from...brother **Benjamin COLLINGS...**same as above. Witnesses: Levi SMITH, James SNOW.
...Truro 26 Apr. 1766, we **Amasa SNOW** & wf **Mary** of Truro...in consideration of a deed of sale from **Benjamin COLLINGS,** gent., **Jonathan COLLINGS,** yeoman and **Benjamin ATKINS,** mariner & wf **Ruth...** quit claim all rights...of our sd father's will on account of a certain previledge our sd father gave us for cuting fire wood during the life of the sd **Mary.** Witnesses: Joseph SNOW, B. PAINE. (None of the above were recorded.)

Will of **Benjamin SNOW** of Orrington, Hancock co., ME. <Penobscot Co.PR>
<1:97>...dated 25 Dec. 1807, mentions wf **Elizabeth/Betsy** and children, viz: **Amasa SNOW, Cyprian SNOW, Benjamin SNOW, Elizabeth SEVERANCE, Deliverance SMITH;** son **Joseph SNOW** (executor). Pr. 7 Dec. 1818.

Will of **Ambrose SNOW** of Truro MA. <Barnstable Co.PR 26:360>
...dated 12 Dec. 1787, mentions wf **Hannah** and children, viz: **Joshua SNOW, Richard SNOW** (dec'd),

Josiah SNOW, Hannah AVERY (wf of John), **Elizabeth SNOW** wf of David; grandchild **Hannah** dau of **Richard**; wf **Hannah**, executor.

Guardianship of Children of **Ambrose SNOW** of Truro MA. <Barnstable Co.PR 15:33-35>
18 Jan. 1770, **Ambrose SNOW** app'td gdn. of his children **Barnabas SNOW & Hannah SNOW**, the grandchildren of **Barnabas PAINE** of Truro.

Will of **Elisha SNOW** of Truro MA. <Barnstable Co.PR 37:412>
...(no date), mentions wf **Keziah** (executor), 1st wf **Hannah** and children, viz: **Elisha SNOW, John SNOW, Paul SNOW, Jesse SNOW, Sarah, Samuel SNOW** (dec'd). Pr. 28 Oct. 1802.

MICRO #3 OF 18

Will of **Larkin SNOW** of Boston MA. <no source>
...dated 30 Jan. 1846, estate to wf **Nancy** for life, then to the five children, viz: **Ephraim L. SNOW, Margaret Ann STETSON, George M. SNOW, Henry A. SNOW, Mary B. HORTON.** Petition for probate, 4 Apr. 1846, signed by the children & heirs at law, viz: **Ephraim L. SNOW, Emmeline SNOW, Lemuel STETSON, Margaret Ann STETSON, George M. SNOW, Francis M. SNOW, Henry A. SNOW, Sarah A. SNOW, William R. HORTON, Mary B. HORTON.**

Nathaniel P. Hewes WILLIS of Boston MA to **Larkin SNOW** of same. <Suffolk Co.Deeds 481:74>
...19 Mar. 1842, Nathaniel P. Hewes WILLIS, trader & wf Lydia sell to Larkin SNOW, gent...land on Sun Court St. he bought of Joseph R. NEWELL 18 Mar. 1836 <419:59>.

James WASHBURN of Boston MA to **Larkin & Ephraim SNOW** of same. <Suffolk Co.Deeds 240:295>
...12 Sept. 1812, James WASHBURN, shipwright, mortgages to Ephraim SNOW & Larkin SNOW, woodwharfingers. Discharged 20 Sept. 1825.

Will of **Joseph SNOW**, yeoman of Eastham MA. <Barnstable Co.PR>
<4:101>...dated 23 Nov. 1717, mentions wf **Mary**; grandsons **Nathaniel SNOW & Joseph SNOW**; sons **Benjamin SNOW, Stephen SNOW, James SNOW** (executor), **Josiah SNOW**; daus **Sarah YOUNG, Lidia LINCOLN, Ruth BROWN, Rebekah SNOW**; grandaughter **Rebekah HAMBLETON.** <4:102> Pr. 30 Jan. 1722/3, the executor **James SNOW** having died before his father, the widow **Mary** & son **Josiah** app'td admrs. Inventory taken 1 Feb. 1722/3.

Estate of **James SNOW** of Eastham MA. <Barnstable Co.PR>
<4:25> 16 Jan. 1721/2, **Stephen SNOW**, yeoman of Eastham, app'td admr. <4:38> Inventory taken 13 Feb. 1721/2, mentions land owned in common with Nathaniel SNOW.

Will of **Benjamin SNOW**, yeoman of Eastham MA. <Barnstable Co.PR>
<8:458>...dated 1 Feb. 1747/8...arived to old age...mentions wf **Thankful**; sons **Thomas SNOW, James SNOW** (executor), **Seth SNOW**; grandson **Nathan SNOW** son of **Benjamin SNOW** dec'd; daus **Bety HATCH, Mary PEPPER, Susanna SMITH, Rebecca SNOW, Jane SNOW, Thankful PITTS**; grandaughters, chil. of **Benjamin SNOW** dec'd, viz: **Ruth SNOW, Martha HIGGINS, Kezia SNOW.** Pr. 13 Mar. 1750. <9:159> Inventory taken 28 Mar. 1751.

Will of **Nathan SNOW** of Harwich MA. <Barnstable Co.PR 26:538>
...dated 1 May 1788, mentions wf **Lydia** (executrix) and children **Molly, Moses SNOW, Reliance, Nathan SNOW, Seth SNOW.** Pr. 17 Oct. 1788.

Estate of **Joseph SNOW** of Eastham MA. <Barnstable Co.PR>
<3:1> May 1706, widow **Sarah SNOW** app'td admx. <3:10> Inventory taken 4 Feb. 1705/6.

Estate of **George BROWN**, yeoman of Wellfleet MA. <Barnstable Co.PR 17:92>
Settlement 9 Mar. 1773, to following children, viz: eldest son **Samuel BROWN** of Wellfleet; **George BROWN, Mary KNOWLES, Phebe BROWN, Zilpa BROWN, Priscilla BROWN, Theodore BROWN.**

Estate of **George BROWN** of Eastham MA to **William MIRICK & John DOANE Jr.**
...10 Mar. 1784, Benjamin CLARK, yeoman of Eastham, admr. on insolvent estate of George BROWN... sold to William MIRICK and John DOANE Jr., yeomen of Eastham...they being the highest bidders of £27.18s...60 acres in Eastham in a place cald/called great neck...bounded by land sd CLARK bought of David RICH and land of Hatsel NICORSON/NICKERSON...except two and a half acres belonging to Jemima MAGNER. Witnesses: Edward KNOWLES, Sarah DOANE. Ack. 11 May 1794. (Not recorded, the above is from the original in the possession of Miss Helen CLARK of Eastham in 1908.)

John MULFORD of Eastham MA to **George BROWN Jr.** of same. <Barnstable Co.Deeds 23:220>
...4 May 1754, John MULFORD, yeoman, for £45 sold to George BROWN Jr., yeoman...dwelling house & barn in Eastham...meadow, sedge ground & upland. Witnesses: Jemima MULFORD, David RICH. Rec. 11 May 1754. Re-recorded 17 Nov. 1898 in 236:39-41.

Estate of **Benjamin YOUNG**, yeoman of Eastham MA. <Barnstable Co.PR>
<5:257> 17 Oct. 1734, son **John YOUNG**, husbandman of Eastham app'td admr. <5:234> Inventory taken 5 Nov. 1734. <5:461> Receipt of heirs, 6 Apr. 1742...excepting our rights to our Honoured Mother **Sarah YOUNG** for her thirds...each having received from brother **John YOUNG**, £26: **Daniel YOUNG, Joseph YOUNG, Benjamin YOUNG, Moses & Thankfull WILEY, Thomas & Sarah SNOW Jr., Mary YOUNG**, all

of Eastham. (Reference is also given to New York Gen.Rcd. 35:260.)

Estate of **Stephen SNOW**, yeoman of Eastham MA. <Barnstable Co.PR>
<10:216> 8 Aug. 1769, **Stephen SNOW**, yeoman of Eastham app'td admr. <13:461> Inventory taken 2 Oct 1769 by Silas SNOW, Isaiah HIGGINS & James SNOW; dwelling house & barn & land to the north end of the brook, £97.3s; land to south of brook, £52; personal estate, £30.8s3d. <17:94> Inventory taken by Silvanus (---), Joseph PEPPER & Isaiah HOLBROOK; house & land on north of brook called first brook, £60; land on south side of brook, £40.13s4d. Account 13 Apr. 1773 of admr.; Paid to: the widow for necessaries, £15.2s; Robert SNOW; costs of maintaining the widow more than her goods amounted to, £6.15s1d. <17:95> Settlement 13 Apr. 1773 to following children, viz: **Stephen SNOW & Robert SNOW**, yeomen of Eastham; **Margaret LOVERIN**, widow; **Lydia MOTT**; heirs of **Elkins SNOW** dec'd; **Ruth SMITH, Mercy SMITH, Sarah SMITH,** heirs of **Jane SMITH** dec'd.

Estate of **Reuben SNOW**, laborer of Eastham MA. <Barnstable Co.PR 10:106>
...6 July 1762, Stephen SNOW, yeoman of Eastham, app'td admr.

Estate of **John SNOW**, yeoman of Eastham MA. <Barnstable Co.PR>
<10:137> 20 Mar. 1764, Stephen SNOW, yeoman of Eastham app'td admr. <13:41> Inventory taken 26 Mar. 1764; mentions estate he had of his father. <13:42> Dower set off, 14 May 1764, to widow **Phebe SNOW.** <13:539> 10 Jan. 1770, widow **Phebe SNOW**'s thirds set off; mentions land of widow Margaret SNOW. <13:557> Account 14 Apr. 1767 of Stephen SNOW Jr., admr.; incl. to father **Stephen SNOW**, L15.15.

Estate of **Elkins SNOW**, mariner of Eastham MA. <Barnstable Co.PR>
<7:75> 10 Aug. 1748, William WALKER, yeoman of Eastham, app'td admr. <8:137> 10 Aug. 1748, appraisers app'td. <8:138> Inventory taken 28 Aug. 1748 by Samuel DOANE, Josiah SNOW & Jonathan DOANE, all of Eastham. Dower set off 1 Aug. 1749 to widow **Susannah SNOW.** <8:139> Insolvency 8 Sept. 1748; mentions claims of Stephen SNOW & John SNOW. <8:140> Account of admr. 3 Oct. 1749.

Will of **Mark SNOW** of Eastham MA. <Barnstable Co.PR; MD 18:199>
<1:111>...dated 23 Nov. 1694, mentions wf **Jane** (executor); sons **Nicholas SNOW, Thomas SNOW, Prince SNOW;** grandchild **Jonathan SNOW.** <1:110> 16 Jan. 1694/5, widow **Jane SNOW**, admx. <1:112> Inventory taken 9 Jan. 1694/5.

Will of **Jane SNOW**, widow of Harwich MA. <Barnstable Co.PR>
<3:271>...dated 21 Dec. 1703, mentions sons **Nicholas SNOW, Thomas SNOW, Prince SNOW;** to **Anne ATWOOD**, a pewter wine cup; grandchildren **Jane NICKERSON, Jane SNOW;** daus **Mercy & Sarah**; brother **Jonathan SPARROW** & son **Nicholas**, executors. Witnesses: Mercy SPARROW, Martha COBB. <3:272> Pr. 2 July 1712, **Jonathan SPARROW**, dec'd. Inventory taken 28 June 1712. <3:274> Account (no date) calls her of Eastham & mentions providing house room for her from 26 Oct. to latter end of May following.

MICRO #4 OF 18

Will of **Deacon Seth NICKERSON** of Provincetown MA. <Barnstable Co.PR>
<31:14>...dated 25 Dec. 1799; $1.00 ea to sons **Nathan NICKERSON, Ebenezer NICKERSON, Enos NICKERSON;** $20.00 ea to daus **Elizabeth SMITH** wf of Edmund and **Hannah NICKERSON** wf of Nehemiah Jr.; $1. ea to the two children of dau **Mary NICKERSON** dec'd; $20.00 ea to daus by 2nd wf, viz: **Jemima COLLINS** wf of Richard, **Jane NICKERSON & Thankful NICKERSON;** after decease of wife **Isabel**, estate to go to four youngest sons, viz: **Seth NICKERSON, John NICKERSON, Jesse NICKERSON, Eldridge NICKERSON;** wf **Isabel**, executrix. Witnesses: Samuel WATERMAN, Daniel SMALLEY, Joseph NICKERSON (WATERMAN & NICKERSON were sworn 15 Oct. 1801). <32:19> Pr. 15 "Jan." 1801 (Oct.?). <37:297> Inventory taken 18 Nov. 1801; incl. one quarter of schooner John; one half of schooner Susannah; sworn to by admx. 18 Mar. 1802. <37:271> Account 18 Mar. 1802 of admx.; incl. legacies paid to: **Eunice COLLINS**, $20.00; **Edmund SMITH**, $20.00; **Hannah NICKERSON**, $20.00; **Emina COLLINS**, $20.00. <22:279> 18 Mar. 1802, **Isabel NICKERSON** app'td gdn. of **Seth, Jesse, John & Eldridge NICKERSON.** <25:730-1> 18 Mar. 1802, **Thankful & Jenny NICKERSON**, over 14, choose their mother **Isabel** as gdn.

Heirs of **Nicholas SNOW** of Rochester MA to **Jonathan SNOW** of same.. <Plymouth Co.Deeds 48:112>
...22 Feb. 1758, Joseph SNOW, husbandman of Rochester & Charles BROWNELL & wf Hannah of Tiverton RI, which Joseph & Hannah were children of the late Prince SNOW & grandchildren of Nicholas SNOW late of Rochester dec'd and legatees in sd Nicholas SNOW's last will, for £7.2s.8d, sell to Jonathan SNOW, yeoman...all their share in estate of sd Nicholas. Witnesses: Joseph PALMER, Dominicus HOVEY, Restcome SANFORD & Smiton HART. Ack. 5 May 1758 by Joseph SNOW, 1 Oct. 1761 by Charles & Hannah. Rec. 6 Apr. 1763.

Will of **Lieut. Nicholas SNOW** of Rochester MA. <Plymouth Co.PR 13:304>
...dated 25 June 1751...advanced age...mentions granddaughter **Phebe BURGE**, infant dau of dau **Phebe BURGE** dec'd; eldest son **Jonathan SNOW; Joshua SNOW & Marcy SNOW**, chil. of dec'd son **Joshua SNOW; Joseph SNOW, Mary SNOW & Hannah SNOW**, chil. of son **Prince SNOW**; daus **Thankfull BURGE, Sarah HAMMOND**; to son **Prince SNOW** 1 shilling lawful money...and the reason I give him no more is his leaving me & his family as he did; sons **Jonathan & Nathaniel**, executors. Witnesses: Samuel RIDER Jr., Mary HOLMES & Noah SPRAGUE. Pr. 17 July 1754. Inventory taken 29 May 1754.

Will of **Prince SNOW**, gent. of Harwich MA. <Barnstable Co.PR 6:227>
...dated 13 Jan. 1740, mentions wf **Hannah** & land she received in Mansfield CT from her father; brother **Nicholas SNOW**; grandchildren **Hannah SNOW, Mark SNOW, Prence SNOW, Mary SNOW**; sons **Jabez SNOW** (executor) **& Jonathan SNOW.** Pr. 20 July 1742.

Will of **Hannah SNOW**, widow of Harwich MA. <Barnstable Co.PR>
<8:485>...dated 19 Oct. 1751...well striken in years, to dau **Mary BURGE**, pewter platter marked "S:S:M"; grandaughter **Hannah SNOW** dau of son **Samuel SNOW** dec'd; grandson **Prince SNOW**; grandaughter **Mary SNOW** dau of son **Prince SNOW** dec'd; sons **Jabez SNOW & Jonathan SNOW.** Pr. 19 Dec. 1751.
<8:505> Inventory taken 14 Jan. 1751.

Will of **Deacon John LEWES/LEWIS**, yeoman of Barnstable MA. <Barnstable Co.PR>
<5:323>...dated 5 Aug. 1736, mentions wf **Elizabeth**; sons **James LEWIS & Shubael LEWIS** (executors); sons **Edward LEWIS, John LEWIS & Gershom LEWIS**, have already had part of their portion; dau **Elizabeth SNOW & Thankful LEWIS.** Pr. 25 Apr. 1739 <5:457> Receipt 22 June 1741 to exrs. from **Gershom LEWIS**; 13 Feb. 1741 of **Jabez SNOW & Elizabeth SNOW.**

Estate of **Prince SNOW Jr.**, mariner of Harwich MA. <Barnstable Co.PR>
<5:458> Inventory taken 13 Sept.1740; presented by Jabez SNOW one of admrs.; sworn to 13 May 1741 by **Jane SNOW** one of admrs. <5:459> 13 May 1741, allowance to widow **Jane SNOW**, she having two small children, one posthumous. Account of admrs. 13 May 1741; mentions only son **Prince SNOW** & only dau **Mercy.** <6:187-8> 22 Oct. 1742, Jabez SNOW of Harwich app'td gdn. of **Prince SNOW**, ae about 5 yrs and **Mary SNOW**, ae about 2 yrs. <7:438-9> 9 Dec. 1756, Samuel COLLINGS of Chatham app'td gdn. of **Mary SNOW & Prince SNOW.** <9:264> Account 9 Dec. 1756, of Jabez SNOW as gdn. of **Prince & Mary SNOW.**

Estate of **Samuel SNOW** of Harwich MA. <Barnstable Co.PR>
<4:569> 21 Oct. 1730, **Prince SNOW** of Harwich app'td admr. <4:570> Inventory taken 28 Oct. 1730. <5:46> 24 Nov. 1730, **Prince SNOW** app'td gdn. of his grandaughter **Hannah SNOW**, dau of his dec'd son **Samuel SNOW.** <6:187> 22 Oct. 1742, **Hannah SNOW** ae about twelve & a half years, of Barnstable chooses father in law **Shoble/Shubael LEWIS** of Barnstable as gdn. <6:163> 22 Oct. 1742, Jabez SNOW, exr. of his father Prince SNOW's estate renders account of latter's guardianship of Hannah.

Estate of **Thomas SNOW** of Harwich MA. <Barnstable Co.PR 19:15;20:178,186-9,191,193,194>
...adm. 3 Apr. 1779; distribution 9 Feb. 1779; mentions widow **Rachel SNOW** and following children, viz: eldest son **Samuel SNOW** of Marblehead; dau **Ruth HIGGINS** wf of Jethro; heirs of dec'd sons: **Thomas SNOW, Silas SNOW & Isaac SNOW**; dau **Priscilla WHILDEN** wf of Elisha of Yarmouth.

Estate of **Aaron SNOW**, mariner of Harwich MA. <Barnstable Co.PR>
<6:152> 15 Mar. 1741, Matthew GAGE, yeoman of Yarmouth app'td admr. <6:162> Inventory taken 1 Apr 1741. <6:163> Account of admr. 14 July 1742.

Estate of **Abraham COAN Sr.** of Truro MA. <Barnstable Co.PR>
<36:370> 19 Mar. 1817, Francis SMALL of Wellfeet app'td admr. <41:280> Inventory taken 21 Apr. 1817 by Silvanus NYE, Jesse KNOWLES & James SMALL; incl. 28 acre homestead, $258.40; 5 acres in Truro, $10.00; three quarters of a pew in Rev. J. DAMON's meeting house, $45.00; total personal estate, $82.35; total estate, $395.75. <40:43> Account of admr. 15 Oct. 1818; receipts from sales of personal & real estate, $324.51 and payments of $146.51, left a balance of $178.00. Paid to: S. NYE; Jesse PAINE for making a coffin, $2.67; Dr. AYRES, $4.95; J. SMALL; Allen HINCKLEY, Esq.; J. LOMBARD, Esq.; Isaiah SNOW; cash paid for rum at vendue, $2.45; N. FREEMAN. <40:70> 15 Oct. 1818, Joshua SMALL of Truro was app'td gdn. of the children of **Samuel COAN** dec'd, the children of **Hannah LOMBARD** (wf of Israel Jr.) dec'd, the children of **John COAN** dec'd and the children of **Abraham COAN** dec'd. <41:295> Distribution 15 Oct. 1818; the remaining balance of $178.00 to be distributed to the following heirs, viz: **Elisha D. COAN** of Maine; **Joanna SMALL** wf of Francis; **Benjamin COAN** of Wrentham; **Christian SNOW** wf of Isaiah of Maine; **Joanna ATKINS** wf of James L. of Truro; **Rebecca MILLS** wf of Stephen of Truro; **Polly STEVENS** wf of John of Truro; **Nabby STEVENS** wf of Thomas of Truro; children of **Hannah LOMBARD** late wf of Isaac/Israel Jr. of Truro; children of **Samuel COAN**; children of **John COAN** of Liverpool, Eng.

Estate of **Israel LOMBARD** of Truro MA. <Barnstable Co.PR>
<42:36> 8 Nov. 1821, **Elizabeth LOMBARD** of Truro app'td admx. <43:346> Inventory. <39:106> Widow's allowance. <43:350> Dower. <43:423> Account. <45:19> Account. <40:159,160> Guardianships.

MICRO #5 OF 18

Estate of **Abraham COAN** of Truro MA. <Barnstable Co.PR>
<36:358> 12 Nov. 1816, Silvanus NYE of Truro app'td admr. <41:3> Account 20 Mar. 1817 of admr.; Paid to: Mr. LEWIS, Judge DAVIS, Nathaniel FREEMAN, Esq., Dr. AYRES $0.25; credit wages received, $175.00. <41:5> Distribution 20 Mar. 1817 of the balance of $150.05 to the following heirs, viz: mother **Betsy COAN**, sister **Betsy COAN**, brothers **Samuel COAN, Benjamin COAN**; sisters **Emma COAN, Hannah COAN, Mary COAN, Christian COAN**; brothers **Paul COAN & John COAN.**

Estate of **Shubael COAN** of Truro MA. <Barnstable Co.PR>
<25:220> 17 Oct. 1800, **Deliverance COAN** app'td admx. <22:254> 17 Oct. 1800, **Deliverance COAN** was app'td gdn. of **Joanna COAN, Rebecca COAN, Mary COAN & Nabby COAN**, minor daus of dec'd. <30:382>

Inventory taken 14 Mar. 1801 by Israel LOMBARD, Samuel ATKINS & Levi STEVENS; incl. 9 acre brush land near land of Isaac SMALL's, $24.75; two acre woodland near land of Fulk DYER's, $7.00; 7 acres adjoining the dwelling house, $28.00; one barn, $10.00; dwelling house, $280.00; pew in the meeting house, $130.00; total real estate, $479.75; total personal estate, $110.66. <30:382> Account of admx. 20 Mar. 1801, by her attorney Silvanus SNOW, Esq. <30:383> Dower set off 20 Mar. 1801 to widow by Israel LOMBARD, Samuel ATKINS & Levi STEVENS. <31:191> Final Account of admx. 15 Oct. 1801; the four daughters receive their shares.

***

Deliverance COAN of Truro MA to **Israel LOMBARD Jr.** of same. <Barnstable Co.Deeds 56:130>
...13 Dec. 1801, Deliverance COAN, widow & admx. to estate of Shubael COAN, mariner, dec'd, for $65.00 sold to Israel LOMBARD Jr., mariner...one half of a certain pew in the meeting house of Publick worship in sd Truro sd pew adjoining the maine or great alley on the west the womans seats on the north the pew of Francis SMALL and others on the east by the pew of John GROSS on the south. Witnesses: Jonathan COLLINS, Benjamin COAN. Ack. 1 Jan. 1802. Rec. 6 Jan. 1802.

***

Thomas PAINE of Eastham MA to **Thomas PAINE** of same. <Barnstable Co.Deeds 2:8>
...14 Feb. 1683/4, Thomas PAINE of the towne of Eastham in the jurisdiction of Plymouth in America, gives to son Thomas PAINE...two acre meadow in Eastham at a place called great blackfish creeke at great Billingsgate...bounded by land of Edward BANGS. Witnesses: Nicholas PAINE, James PAINE. Ack. same day by Thomas & wf Mary. Rec. 15 July 1695.

***

Mary PAINE of Wellfleet MA to **Noah YOUNG** of same. <Barnstable Co.Deeds 2:281>
...5 June 1817, Mary PAINE, widow woman, for $60.00 sold to Noah YOUNG, mariner...land in Wellfleet begining at the south west corner of the dwelling house that was the sd Mary's late father John SWEAT dec'd. Witnesses: William COLE, Sally YOUNG. Ack. same day.

***

John BAKER et al of Waldo co. ME to **Noah YOUNG** of Wellfleet MA. <Barnstable Co.Deeds>
...12 Apr. 1841, John BAKER, Elizabeth PHILLIPS, Rebecca COLE, Zebiah SHERMAN & Enoch HOLBROOK, sell to Noah YOUNG, mariner...land in Wellfleet that was set off to the heirs of John SWEAT.

***

Estate of **Noah YOUNG** of Wellfleet MA. <Barnstable Co.PR #4819>
...1863...mentions wf **Emina** and children **Noah YOUNG, Barnabas YOUNG** and **Sarah P. HINCKLEY** wf of Sylvester, all three of Wellfleet.

***

BARNSTABLE COUNTY DEEDS:

<18:275> - 1823, Heirs of Barnabas PAINE to Barnabas PAINE.
<31:124> - 1842, Doane RICH & wf Sarah the dau of Barnabas PAINE.
<43:59> - 1842, Doane RICH & wf Sarah et al, the heirs of Barnabas PAINE.
<17:114> - 3 Jan. 1833, Stephen YOUNG, yeoman of Wellfleet to Noah YOUNG, mariner of same. Wf Mercy YOUNG releases dower.
<20:173> - 28 Apr. 1835, Same names as above deed.

(The remaining references contain no data, they may refer to Barnabas PAINE: 27:229,357;31:418; 34:49;38:181;43:474 (1848);50:115;53:189;61:130 (1855);89:73;14:6;91:487 (1867).)

***

Will of **Samuel PAINE,** husbandman of Truro MA. <Barnstable Co.PR>
<23:243>...dated 19 Jan. 1784, mentions wf **Mary** (executrix); to Rosanna SMITH that I have brought from a child, one quarter of estate; brother **Nathaniel PAINE;** heirs of sister **Elizabeth SPARROW,** dec'd; sister **Bennet CROSBY;** sister **"GREEN".** <23:244> Pr. 4 May 1784.

***

Will of **Samuel PAINE,** yeoman of Truro MA. <Barnstable Co.PR 53:151>
...dated 19 Dec. 1831, mentions unnamed wife, sons **Benjamin PAINE, Barzillai PAINE;** grandson **Samuel Paine REMICK** son of **Isaac & Azubah REMICK;** my five children (unnamed). Pr. 29 Mar. 1832.

***

BARNSTABLE COUNTY PROBATE: (re: PAINE)

1706	Thomas	Eastham	will	3:360,361,362
1713	Joseph	Harwich	adm.	3:112,113;4:396
1713	Samuel	Eastham	adm.	3:114,115;4:72
1721	Thomas	Truro	will	4:7,9,10
1729	James	Barnstable	adm.	4:478;5:105
1732	John	Eastham	will	5:13,15,41,47
1733	Nicholas	Eastham	will	5:174,175,184
1734	Ebenezer	Eastham		5:166,172
1734	Bethiah	Barnstable	will	3:700,701;5:183,184;6:257,259
1745	Thomas	Truro	adm.	5:392;6:406;7:19
1746	William	Eastham		7:31;8:124,125,126,127,128
1749	Hugh	Truro		7:129;8:328
1752	Jonathan	Truro	will	8:534,537;9:267,268
1755	Theophilus	Eastham		7:394,399,400,401,402,403,404,405;9:352
1759	Thomas	Truro		9:492,493;10:30
1762	Isaac	Eastham		10:113
1762	Jonathan	Eastham	will	11:200-205;12:240,241;13:27,31,32
1762	Ebenezer	Chatham	will	12:300,301
1764	Moses	Truro	will	13:71,72,99

BARNSTABLE COUNTY PROBATE, cont-d: (re: PAINE)

1766	Ebenezer	Chatham		10:166;13:249,365;14:132,133,134,135,136
1768	Barnabas	Truro		10:201;12:416,419;13:383;15:32-43
1769	Mary	Truro		10:212;12:416;13:495
1771	Joseph	Harwich	will	12:437,438,452;17:254
1774	Elkanah	Truro	will	17:194,195,223
1779	Nathaniel	Eastham		11:39,43,60;16:153;21:116,132,133
1780	Joseph	Chatham	will	21:68,70
1784	Samuel	Eastham	will	23:243,244
1784	Seth et al	Eastham	gdn.	22:29,30,31,32,33
1785	Daniel	Truro	will	26:5,64
1787	Samuel	Wellfleet		25:2
1789	Solomon	Truro	adm.	24:200;25:32;27:125,126,127
1789	Richard	Truro	adm.	24:199,358;25:33;27:122,123,124
1805	Eleazer	Barnstable	adm.	19:160;22:328;31:416,439;33:280
1807	Thomas	Eastham		19:241;22:529-30;25:89;33:132,155,293,297,298
1807	James	Barnstable	will	32:193;33:30
1808	Thomas	Wellfleet	will	32:241;33:56,323;35:14,151
1809	Maria & Henrietta	Cambridgeport		22:406;43:53
1814	Isaac	Eastham		36:165
1816	Nathaniel	Harwich		32:210,213;36:360;39:36
1818	Mary	Barnstable		36:394
1820	Isaac	Harwich	non comp	40:149;43:27

Will of **Elisha PAINE** of Canterbury CT. <Windham CT PR>
<2:127>...dated 15 Jan. 1729/30...God haveing gracously blessed me with many children...to unnamed wife besides her thirds, the new orchard & pasture bounded by land of Josiah CLEAVELAND & Solomon PAIN and twenty acres bought of John PIKE bounded by land of Thomas BROWN, Solomon PAIN and the Quenebaug River...to youngest son **John PAINE**, house & barn, which land is bounded by Quenebaug River, blackwels brook and land of Jonathan HIDS/HIDES, Josiah CLEAVELAND, sons **Abraham & Solomon PAIN**, land bought of Major FITCH and my oald farm....son **John** also to pay his mother yearly 5 bushels Indian corn, 2 bushels rye, 1 bushel wheat, 12 lbs. flax...I have given to my eldest son **Abraham PAIN** a good setlement of land by deed...my othar two sons, viz: **Elisha PAIN** and **Solomon PAIN** haveing their setlements by deeds as also my four daughters, viz: **Abigall, Rebecca, Mary & Dorcas**...to my daughter **Hanah PAIN**, 100 acres of land abuting southarly on land I sould to Benjamin BAULDWIN/BALDWIN...which she by deed now hath...to my youngest daughter **Constance PAIN** 100 acres northward from the 200 acres caled Whits lott...bounded by 100 acres given to dau **Rebeccah CLEVELAND**, land sold to Necolas/Nicholas WILLIAMS & land of John BROWN...which she now hath by deed...remaining estate to be divided among the four sons & six daughters; sons **Abraham PAIN, Elisha PAIN, Solomon PAIN & John PAIN**, executors. Witnesses: Joshua PAIN, William DERBY & Edward SPAULDING. Pr. 17 Feb. 1735/6. <2:258> Inventory taken 19 Feb. 1735/6 by Joshua PAINE, Deliverance PROWN/BROWN; incl. one doz. plate butons & a silver clasp, Ł1.10s; money seals & brass weights, 6s; mesuring chain & oald compas, 9s; putar platter, 12s; lignomvite mortar, 4s; knot bowl, 4s; knot dish, 1s; great glass botle, 3s6d; one silver spoon, Ł1.10s; iron bound chest, 8s; floward glas cup, 2s6d; wine glas, 2s; an othar wine glas, 2s; books, Ł2.8s2d. Due the estate, notes from: David ADAMS Jr., dated 14 Jan. 1735/6, Ł6; Joshua PAIN, dated 2 May 1729, Ł24.10s; John PAINE, dated 9 Aug. 1734, Ł12.10s.

Estate of **Nathaniel FREEMAN** of Barnstable MA. <Barnstable Co.PR>
<4:423> Letter 22 May 1728, James PAINE & Mrs. Mary FREEMAN app'td admrs. <4:438> Widow's allowance. <4:443> Inventory. <4:493> Adm. discharged.

Will of **Deacon Samuel FREEMAN** of Eastham MA. <Barnstable Co.PR>
<8:483>...dated 28 Jan. 1750/1, mentions wf **Mary**, sons **James FREEMAN** (executor) & **Barnabas FREEMAN** and seven daus, viz: **Mary FREEMAN, Priscilla FREEMAN, Abigail FREEMAN, Elizabeth SNOW, Alice BROWN, Rebecca WALKER, Hannah FREEMAN.** Witnesses: Willard KNOWLES, Samuel SMITH Jr., Nathaniel ATWOOD. <8:484> Pr. 2 July 1751. <8:485> Inventory taken 15 July 1751; sworn to by exr. 17 July 1751. <9:161> Account 7 Apr. 1752.

BARNSTABLE COUNTY PROBATE: (re: Samuel FREEMAN)

1713	Samuel	Eastham	adm.	3:108,135,426
1732	Samuel	Harwich	gdn.	5:51
1742	Samuel	Eastham	will	6:269,270,275,278,278,312
1751	Samuel	Eastham	will	8:483,484,485;9:161
1813	Samuel	Brewster	adm.	36:142;22:471
1837	Samuel	Eastham	will	58:295;60:30
1829/30	Samuel	Sandwich	adm.	39:75;42:387;47:534;48:52;50:82,90;52:219

BARNSTABLE COUNTY DEEDS: (re: Samuel FREEMAN)

<1:62> - 30 Sept 1789, Samuel FREEMAN of Eastham to Elkanah HIGGINS.
<2:72> - 1795, Samuel FREEMAN, division.
<3:191> - 1797, Samuel FREEMAN et al to Peter NYE.

BARNSTABLE COUNTY DEEDS, cont-d: (re: Samuel FREEMAN)

<1:477> - 24 Aug. 1800, Samuel FREEMAN to Branch DILLINGHAM.
<2:497> - 1800, Samuel FREEMAN to Stephen BASSETT.
<2:139> - 1800, Samuel FREEMAN et al to John DILLINGHAM Jr.
<2:549> - 1800, Samuel FREEMAN to James FREEMAN.
<2:419> - 1808, Samuel FREEMAN to Thomas FREEMAN.
<1:412> - 26 Sept 1809, Samuel FREEMAN of Eastham to Richard SPARROW.
<1:413> - 6 Oct. 1810, Samuel FREEMAN of Eastham to Richard SPARROW.
<1:405> - 21 Feb. 1812, Samuel FREEMAN of Eastham to Richard SPARROW.
<1:191> - 1813, "Samuel FESSENDEN not FREEMAN".
<2;107> - 1814, Smuel FREEMAN et al to David SNOW.
<1:410> - 20 Aug. 1815, Samuel FREEMAN of Eastham to Richard SPARROW.
<1:335> - 26 June 1816, Samuel FREEMAN of Eastham to Barnabas F. KNOWLES.
<1:398> - 27 Dec. 1816, Samuel FREEMAN of Eastham to Joseph LINKHORNEW.
<1:401> - 2 Apr. 1816, Samuel FREEMAN et al (Selectmen) to Thomas CROSBY.
<1:121> - 1822, Samuel FREEMAN et al to Lewis HOWES.
<1:121> - 1822, Samuel FREEMAN Jr. et al to Lewis HOWES.
<1:25> - 7 Feb. 1822, Samuel FREEMAN by admr. to George CLARK et al.

Estate of **Joshua KNOWLES** of Truro MA. <Barnstable Co.PR>
<16:154;19:25> Letters. <10:76> Inventory. <10:161> Widow's allowance. <10:164>Insolvency. <21:235> Receipt. <14:85> Dower. <10:62> Account. <21:213,228> Account. <23:11> Account. <23:16> Inventory. <23:12> Settlement. <18:77-82> Guardianships. <22:141> Guardianships.

MICRO #6 OF 18

Will of **Deacon Paul CROWELL** of Chatham MA. <Barnstable Co.PR>
<33:83>...dated 26 Feb. 1801 at beginning, 4 Apr. 1801 at end...mentions wf **Mehitable** & children viz: sons **Thomas CROWELL, Joseph CROWELL, Hallett CROWELL, Ezra CROWELL, Paul CROWELL** and daus **Reliance HOPKINS, Patience RIDER, Betsey SMITH**; grandchildren **Betsy KNOWLES, Paul SEARS & Betsey SEARS.** <32:237> Pr. 13 Dec. 1808. <33:314> Inventory taken 23 Dec. 1808. <35:71> Dower. <35:246> Account. (Barnstable Co.Deeds 1:73, 5 May 1809, mentions Ezra CROWELL, exr. of this estate.)

Paul CROWELL of Southamton NY to **Ezra CROWELL** of Chatham MA. <Barnstable Co.Deeds 2:309>
...25 Sept. 1809, Paul CROWELL, mariner to Ezra CROWELL...all rights received by will of father Paul CROWELL of Chatham. Wf Olive CROWELL releases dower.

Paul CROWELL & Reuben RYDER of Chatham MA to **Jonathan CROWELL** of same.<Barnstable Co.Deeds 2:180>
...21 Mar. 1783, Paul CROWELL & wf Mehitable and Reuben RYDER & wf Keziah, to Jonathan CROWELL, gent...land in Chatham. Ack. same day.

Will of **Israel COLE** of Barnstable & Eastham MA. <Barnstable Co.PR 4:204>
...dated 21 Jan. 1723/4, mentions son **Israel COLE** and grandchildren **Israel HIGGENS, Theoder HIGGENS, Jacob HIGGENS & Samuel HIGGENS.** Pr. 23 July 1724. Inventory taken 23 & 27 July 1724.

Benjamin ACKLY of Hartland CT to **Israel HIGGINS** of Chatham CT. <Chatham CT Deeds 2:232>
...5 June 1770, Benjamin ACKLY/ACKLEY & wf Hannah, quit claim to Israel HIGGINS...all their right in the lands of Israel COLE of Eastham dec'd. Witnesses: Nathan BECKWITH, Nehemiah ANDREWS. Ack. same day. Rec. 24 Nov. 1770.

Israel COLE et al of Eastham MA to **Jonathan SPARROW et al.** <MD 15:207>
...18 Feb. 1750, Israel COLE, Silvanus COLE, Benjamin COLE & Rufus COLE, yeomen, to Jonathan SPARROW, Joseph SPARROW, John SPARROW & Jabez SPARROW...our half part of a lot of land excepting what was taken "off there from for" David TOBEY, in Harwich, 7th Shares Purchase, 7th lot, 1st division. Ack. 20 Feb. 1750. Not recorded.

Will of **Israel COLE,** yeoman of Eastham MA. <Barnstable Co.PR>
<8:46>...dated 23 July 1746, to wf **Emary**, her thirds and two oxen, mair, two cows, ten sheep and all the swine, corn...excepting what my sons have planted, also my negro man Bacary...if my sd wife should dye before Bacary...he shall be taken care of by my five sons...I give unto Bacary all the things which are now called his for his to the end...to my three natural sons **Ebenezer COLE, Israel COLE & Silvanus COLE** all that my several lotts...of land whereon their housing stand...sons **Benjamin COLE & Rufus COLE,** land where my dwelling house now stands...to dau **Hannah SNOW**...land near Great Neck which I bought of Israel HIGGINS...to daus **Emery COLE & Dorcas BURGIS** all lands in Truro...also to three daus, Indian servant Tom TRIP; son **Ebenezer,** executor. Witnesses: Jonathan LINNEL, James ROGERS Jr. & Thomas ROGERS. Pr. 9 Sept. 1747. <8:49> 9 Sept. 1747, Nathaniel MAYO, Richard SPARROW & Jonathan LINNELL, yeomen of Eastham, app'td appraisers. <8:50> Inventory taken 13 Oct. 1747 by appraisers; incl. Indian boy, Ł50; homestead, Ł780; land at the great hill, Ł60; land at Great Neck, Ł60; cedar swamp, Ł130; meadow, Ł180; land at Truro, Ł100. <8:54> Account of exr. 7 July 1748.

Will of **Seth ALLEN,**yeoman of Harwich MA. <Barnstable Co.PR #1088>
<60:66>...dated 14 Aug. 1822, mentions wf **Anne**; sons **Matthew ALLEN, James ALLEN**; grandson **Mulford ALLEN**; daus **Hannah SMITH, Noamy PERRY, Elizabeth WEEKS, Sally ELDREDGE, Mercy BAKER, Anna HOWES,**

Huldah HOWES; grandaughter **Amela ALLEN** sister of **Mulford**; grandson **Francis SMALL**, under 21; son **James**, executor. <48:496> Notice of adm. 22 Jan. 1838; notice of app'tment 13 Feb. 1838. <originals> Inventory taken 23 Jan. 1838 by Nathan UNDERWOOD Jr., Esq., Isaiah DOANE & Marshall UNDERWOOD, all of Harwich; total real estate, $1588.00; total personal estate, $187.74. Bond 13 Feb. 1838 of exr. **James ALLEN**. Sureties: Obed BROOKS, Esq. & Ebenezer SMITH, yeoman, both of Harwich. <64:59> Dower set off, 7 Mar. 1838, to widow **Sally ALLEN**. <original> 13 Mar. 1838, allowance of $62.50 made to widow **Sally ALLEN**.

Will of **Thomas PAINE** of Truro MA. <MD 28:160-66>
...dated 6 Apr. 1720, mentions wf **Elizabeth**, sons **Thomas PAINE, Jonathan PAINE, Elkanah PAINE, Moses PAINE, Joshua PAINE, Barnabas PAINE** (under 21) and daus **Hannah BINNEY, Abigal WHITE, Phebe PAINE, Lidia HICKLY/HINCKLEY**. Pr. 4 July 1721. Inventory taken 14 July 1721.

Heirs of **Elisha PAIN** of Middletown CT. <Middletown CT Deeds 22:121>
...10 Nov. 1769, Freeman HIGGINS & wf Thankful of Eastham; Prince SNOW, mariner & wf Reliance of Barnstable; Marcy HIGGINS, widow of Truro and Mary KING of Boston, the legal heirs of Elisha PAIN dec'd...appoint Titus HOSMER of Middletown their attorney to sell two acres in Middletown that Elisha PAIN bought of Hopestill CRUTTENDEN 5 July 1751. Witnesses: David ATWOOD, Heman SNOW. Ack. 18 Jan. 1770 by Freeman, Thankful, Prince & Reliance; 23 Dec. 1769 by Marcy. Rec. 25 June 1770. On 11 June 1770, Titus HOSMER sold the above land to James HOPKINS of Middletown.

MICRO #7 OF 18

Will of **John COLE Sr.**, yeoman of Eastham MA. <Barnstable Co.PR>
<4:224>...dated 12 Aug. 1717...to eldest son **John COLE Jr.**, lands in Truro and land in Eastham purchased of Joseph YOUNG...to son **Joseph COLE** the homestead; daus **Ruth, Hephzebath, Hannah, Mary & Sarah**; former servant Samuel KING; sons **John & Joseph**, executors. Witnesses: Israel COLE Jr., Samuel FREEMAN Jr. & Nathaniel FREEMAN. <4:226> Pr. 13 Jan. 1724/5. <4:226> Inventory taken 15 Jan. 1724/5 by Nicholas SNOW, Jonathan LINNEL & Israel COLE; incl. old gun & sword, 8s; total estate, Ł1015.3s11d.

Will of **Hannah COLE** of Eastham MA. <Barnstable Co.PR 5:59>
...dated 5 Feb. 1725/6, mentions two sisters **Mary COLE & Sarah COLE** (executors); cozen **Hannah TWINING**. Witnesses: Ebenezer COLE, Thomas HINKLEY, Israel COLE. Pr. 18 Mar. 1729.

Will of **John COLE**, yeoman of Eastham MA. <Barnstable Co.PR>
<8:39>...dated 30 July 1743...to wf **Sarah**, all the money & moveable estate she brought with her when I married her and also all that is due to her from her former husband's estate that she hath not yet received...priviledges in dwelling house, use & improvement of one third of lands incl. land at Potchy Island, land in Seventeen Shares Purchase in Harwich, woodland in Smith's Purchase bought of Samuel KNOWLS & Nathaniel FREEMAN, Esq...also six sheep, one cow, one swine, one half of grain growing in my fields, all my firewood at the door...to heirs of dec'd son **Jonathan COLE**, meadow at Pochey Flatts which was formerly Joseph YOUNG's and part of a money lott at Town Flatts ...to sons **Joshua COLE & Joseph COLE** lands incl. lot at Rock Harbour, wood lot bought of Micaiah SNOW at first Brook and land in Eastham...also my great iron kettle cranes & trammells, part of my scow Little Boat Cart wheels & timber for cart...and all other tools...belonging to the management of husbandry work...and horse & working oxen...to sons **James COLE & Moses COLE** lands in Truro...that was my former wife's...to grandson **Jonathan COLE** one half of dwelling house where he now lives...near Ebenezer HIGGINS that was formerly Stephen SNOW's; grandchildren **Nathaniel COLE & Jesse COLE** & their mother **Hope COLE** widow of dec'd son **Jonathan**; granddaughters **Hope COLE, Dorcas COLE, Mercy COLE**; daus **Mercy SNOW, Phebe WICKAM, Thankful SNOW**; mentions dec'd father **John COLE**; wood lot on the road that goes to Isaac HIGGINS' near Benjamin HIGGINS Jr. shall be sold by my executors if need be; son **Joshua**, executor. Witnesses: Joseph DOANE, Richard SPARROW & John SPARROW. <8:43> Pr. 19 Jan. 1746, **Joshua COLE** app'td admr. <8:45> Inventory taken 21 Feb. 1746/7 by Stephen SPARROW, Richard SPARROW & Jonathan HIGGINS Jr., all of Eastham. <8:45> Account of admr. 8 Apr. 1747; incl. fourty eight ounces & fourteen peny weight silver, Ł97.8s; total personal estate, Ł695.13s10d; Paid to: Nathaniel SPARROW, Chillingsworth FOSTER, Henry YOUNG, Joshua HIGGINS, Mary LEWIS, Mercy PAIN, David YOUNG, Richard PAIN, Stephen SPARROW, Judah YOUNG, William TWINING, John COLE, Richard SPARROW, Mr. OTIS.

Will of **Joseph COLE**, yeoman of Eastham MA. <Barnstable Co.PR>
<27:436>...dated 12 July 1790, mentions wf **Mary**; dau **Kezia HARDING**; son in law **Joshua CROSBY**, executor; son **James COLE**...for many years been deprived of his reason; to grandsons **Nathaniel HARDING, John HARDING & Seth HARDING**...the house & land once their father's & is the house where dau **Keziah** now lives in Eastham; daus **Mary AREY, Phebe GOULD**; grandaughters **Deborah LINNEL & Rebeca CROSBY**; grandsons **James GOULD, Solomon GOULD, Joseph CROSBY, Joshua CROSBY & Abiel CROSBY**. Witnesses: Solomon FREEMAN, Seth FOSTER & Solomon FREEMAN Jr. Codicil 20 Sept. 1794, gives share of dec'd dau **Keziah HARDING** to grandchildren **Nathaniel HARDING & Sally HARDING**. <24:154> Pr. 5 Nov. 1794, 1 Apr. 1795, **Joshua CROSBY** app'td admr. <30:81> Inventory taken 18 Nov. 1794 by Isaac SPARROW, Jonathan TWINING & Joshua COLE; incl. pew in meeting house, Ł9; total estate, Ł402.7s3d. <34:89> Account 20 Oct. 1800 of admr.; legacies paid to the daus as per will, Ł112.11s3d; to **Sally HARDING**, Ł3 and to **Oliver AREY**, Ł3; Paid to: Nathaniel FREEMAN Jr., Simeon KINGMAN, Keziah HARDING, Stephen ROGERS, widow Abigail YOUNG, Joshua HOPKINS, Dr. SEABURY, Eleazer ATWOOD, Jonathan TWINING, Solomon GOULD, Reuben RICH, James GOULD, Oliver AREY, Azubah YOUNG, Timothy DOANE,

Isaac SPARROW, Sarah MAYO, Richard SPARROW, Ebenezer YOUNG, Heman SNOW, Joseph HURD, Ebenezer HIGGINS, Mr. BASCOM.

Will of **Joseph COLE**, yeoman of Eastham MA. <Barnstable Co.PR>
<13:195>...dated 25 Feb. 1764...being arrived to old age...I having no wife to provide for shall proceed as followeth...to sons **Gershom COLE & Joseph COLE** all lands in Eastham & Harwich...farming tools & wearing apparel...to son **Joseph** my dwelling house; daus **Ruth DOANE & Elisabeth COLE**; chil. of my dau **Sarah COLE** dec'd, viz: **Nathan COLE, Sarah COLE, Lydia COLE, Joshua COLE, Markus COLE & Rachel COLE**; dau **Mercy MAYO**; heirs of dau **Patience ROGERS** shall have no more of my estate than that they have already had; son **Gershom**, executor. Witnesses: Richard SPARROW, Jonathan LINNELL & Joseph COLE Jr. <13:196> Pr. 12 Mar. 1766, **Gershom COLE** app'td admr. <13:196> Inventory taken Mar. 1766; sworn to by admr. 16 Apr. 1766. <13:248> Account of admr. 11 Nov. 1766.

Joseph COLE of Eastham MA to **Gershom & Joseph COLE** of same. <MD 16:9>
...18 Apr. 1764, Joseph COLE, yeoman to sons Gershom COLE & Joseph COLE...all land in Eastham & Harwich. Ack. 25 Apr. 1764. Rec. 26 Feb. 1764.

Gershom & Joseph COLE of Eastham, division. <MD 16:11>
...29 Jan. 1768, Gershom COLE & Joseph COLE, yeomen, sons of Joseph COLE dec'd of Eastham, divide land at Eastham & Harwich; "long description", bounded by lands of Israel COLE, Joseph COLE Jr., BANGS, Jonathan MAYO, Amos KNOWLES, Jonathan LINNEL, Rock Harbour, Samuel MAYO, Clift Pond, Sipsons Purchase, Joshua COLE, Joseph COLE, Quason's Purchase, Gershom COLE, John COLE, Richard SPARROW, Little Beach. Mary wf of Gershom & Sarah wf of Joseph consent. Ack. 8 Feb. 1768 by both. Rec. 15 Feb. 1768.

Will of **Joseph COLE Jr.**, yeoman of Eastham MA. <Barnstable Co.PR>
<30:22>...dated 26 Jan. 1794, mentions wf **Anna**; three sons **Reuben COLE, Abiel COLE** (executor) & **Jesse COLE**; daus **Mary SNOW & Sarah SNOW**; grandsons **Joseph COLE & Edward COLE**; grandchildren **Rachel SHAW, Elizabeth COLE, Phebe COLE, Eunice COLE, Huldah COLE, Henry COLE, Abiel COLE**; son **Henry COLE**. Witnesses: Isaac SPARROW, Richard SPARROW, Josiah SPARROW. <34:82> Pr. 30 Oct. 1800, **Abiel COLE** app'td admr. <31:239> Inventory taken 20 Nov. 1800 by Isaac SPARROW, Prince ROGERS & Richard SPARROW; incl. dwelling house, $160.00; barn, $8.00; corn house, $4.00; homestead land, $390.00; sworn to by admr. 3 Nov. 1801. <31:237> Account of admr. 3 Oct. 1801; Paid to: Benjamin BANGS, Hannah SMITH, Edmund LINEL, Timothy BASCOM, David FOSTER, Josiah LINEL, Prince ROGERS, Isaac SPARROW, Richard SPARROW, David SNOW, Judge DAVIS, Nathaniel FREEMAN, Lettice COLE, Thomas ROGERS, Richard SNOW & Peter WALKER.

Will of **Jonathan TWINING**, yeoman of Orleans MA. <Barnstable Co.PR>
<37:31>...dated 6 Aug. 1812, mentions wf **Sarah**, sons **Barnabas TWINING** (executor), **Nathan TWINING**; dau **Mercy TWINING**; grandchildren **Tabitha ROGERS, Miriam CALKINS, Solomon HIGGINS.** <32:257> Pr. 12 Jan. 1813, **Barnabas TWINING** app'td admr. <25:919> Widow's allowance. <37:57> Account. <37:114> Inventory.

Will of **William TWINING**, yeoman of Eastham MA. <Barnstable Co.PR>
...dated 9 Mar. 1769...infirm of body...mentions wf **Apphia**, sons **Thomas TWINING, Elijah TWINING & Thomas TWINING**; grandaughter **Apphia ROGERS**, minor & unm.; son **Thomas**, executor. Witnesses: Joseph COLE, Jonathan TWINING & Isaac SPARROW.

MICRO #8 OF 18

Will of **Stephen SNOW** of Eastham MA. <Barnstable Co.PR>
<3:18>...dated 2 Apr. 1697, mentions unnamed wife...what was hers before marriage; sons **Micajah SNOW** (executor) **& Ebenezer SNOW**; dau **Mehitable**; father **Nicholas SNOW.** Pr. 10 Jan. 1705/6. <3:19> Inventory taken 20 Dec. 1705. <3:17> Receipt 21 May 1706, of widow **Mary SNOW, Ebenezer SNOW, John KING, William COLE, John SMITH & Mehitable SNOW,** all of us or our wives children of ye dec'd..to **Micajah SNOW**, exr., for their share.

Will of **John KING** of Harwich MA. <Barnstable Co.PR>
<9:20>...dated 18 Nov. 1752, mentions unnamed wife; heirs of son **John KING**; heirs of dau **Joanna COLE**; grandson **Stephen KING**; son **Ebenezer KING**; dau **Bathshua RIDER**; heirs of son **Samuel KING**; son **Rodger KING.** Witnesses: Phillip SLEW, Nathaniel STONE Jr., Isabel TAYLOR. <9:22> Pr. 1 May 1753. <9:23> Inventory taken 16 May 1753.

BARNSTABLE COUNTY PROBATE: (re: KING)

1718	Stephen	Harwich	adm.	3:451,4:387
1733	Samuel	Harwich	adm.	5:166,167,240
1753	Isaac	Harwich	gdns.	7:177,178,305,306
1753	John	Harwich	will	9:20,22,23,44;14:176
1766	Samuel	Harwich	adm.	10:176;13:250,251;14:178,219;18:68
1766	Thomas	Harwich	gdn.	14:156
1768	Roger	Harwich	will	13:246,247,248,414,551;14:213,214,215
1769	Stephen	Wellfleet	adm.	10:209;13:430,450,451
1794	Thomas	Harwich	will	24:136;27:412

Will of **Heman KING** of Southeast, Dutchess co. NY. <Dutchess co.NY PR D:65>
...dated 28 Mar. 1805...being infirm & weak in body...mentions wf **Elizabeth**; daus **Phebe & Rhoda**; heirs of dec'd son **Ebenezer KING**; son **Stephen KING**; daus **Alice, Mercy & Elizabeth**; grandson **Jedutha KING**, minor son of son **Jedutha KING**; son **Heman KING**, executor. Witnesses: Talmon SANFORD, Berma HARKIN & Abram MEAD. (Note: **Heman** also written as **Herman**.) Pr. 1 May 1812.

Will of **Stephen KING** of Wilton, Saratoga co. NY. <Saratoga co.NY PR 8:163>
...dated 3 Oct. 1827, mentions wf **Elizabeth**; sons **Henry H. KING, Jerome B. KING, Horace KING & James D. KING**; daus **Isabella HARRIS, Hannah LEWIS, Sophia DUNHAM, Altha ARNOLD & Sally FONDA**; grandson **James LEWIS**, minor; sons **Henry & Jerome**, executors. Witnesses: Dudley EMERSON, Cyrus PERRY, Cornelius PERRY. Pr. 22 Sept. 1828.

Estate of **Ebenezer SNOW**, yeoman of Eastham MA. <Barnstable Co.PR>
<4:263> Inventory taken 2 July 1725. <4:264> 22 Sept. 1725, widow **Hopestill SNOW** app'td admx. <4:257> 23 Sept. 1725, widow **Hopestill SNOW & Thomas SNOW** app'td gdns. of: **Hopestill SNOW**, <4:259> **Hannah SNOW**, <4:260> **Elisha SNOW**, <4:260> **Henry SNOW**, ae about 18, <4:261> **Aaron SNOW**, ae about 13, <4:261> **Bathsheba**, <4:262> **Thankfull**, ae about 10, <4:262> **Samuel SNOW**, ae about 15. <4:264> Allowance to widow, 23 Sept. 1725, ₤60 for support of self & numerous small children. <8:61> Division of real estate, 4 Mar. 1737/8 between widow & children.

Estate of **Henry SNOW** of Middletown CT. <Middletown CT PR #3209>
Inventory taken 19 Oct. 1752 by Robert YOUNG & Ebenezer DARTE; total, ₤735. Account 3 Dec. 1753 of widow **Rebecca SNOW** & Daniel BRAYMEND(sp). Distribution 12 Mar. 1759 to following heirs, viz: widow **Rebecca SNOW** alias **Rebecca GATES**, eldest son **Samuel SNOW**, 2d son **Ebenezer SNOW**, 3d son **Thomas SNOW**, eldest dau **Elizabeth SNOW** and dau **Rebecca SNOW**.

Estate of **Edmund SNOW**. <Saybrook CT PR 3:361>
Distribution 1797, mentions **Rhoda SNOW**, exx., sons **Freeman SNOW, Aaron SNOW, Edmund SNOW, Ebenezer SNOW**; daus **Lilly, Rhoda, Sarah & Rebecca**.

FRANKLIN COUNTY MA PROBATE: (re: SNOW, all 1812-1900**)**

Year	Name	Place	Type	No.
	Arthur L.	Colrain	minor	#10511
1886	Asaph W.	Colrain	adm.	#9370
1899	Barnabas	Greenfield	will	#12677
	Beatrice M.	Colrain	minor	#10511
	Benjamin F.	Heath	minor	#4525
1891	Charles R.	Colrain	adm.	#10511
	Clarence A.	Colrain	minor	#10511
1856	Edward H.	Bernardston	adm.	#4522
1834	Elisha	Bernardston	adm.	#4524
1865	Gardner M.	Shelburne	adm.	#4523
	George D.	Bernardston	minor	#4522
	George Dutton	Bernardston	adopt.	#5774
	Hugh B.	Colrain	minor	#10511
1828	Jacob	Heath	adm.	#4525
1890	Jane P.	Colrain	adm.	#10180
1884	Julia A.	New Salem	adm.	#8787
	Mercy	Heath	minor	#4525
186-	Mercy	St. Louis MO	adm.	#4526
1889	Newell	Greenfield	will	#10021
	Olive	Heath	minor	#4525
182-	Prince	Bernardston	will	#4527
	Ralph J.	Colrain	minor	#10511
	Rodney S.	Heath	minor	#4525
1865	Sally & Sarah (insane)	Hawley	will	#4528
1892	Sarah H.	Greenfield	adm.	#10723
1865	Sybil	Greenfield	will	#4529
1858	Thomas	Bernardston	will	#4530
	William W.	Heath	minor	#4525
1872	Zephaniah	Ohio	adm.	#4531

HAMPSHIRE COUNTY ABSTRACTS IN FRANKLIN COUNTY DEEDS: (re: SNOW, all to 1786**)**

<13:377;3:15> - 9 Oct. 1773, Jonathan SNOW of Hardwick from Simeon HAZELTIME of same, 50 acres in Conway.
<14:516;3:78> - 9 June 1777, Ebenezer SNOW of Sunderland to Samuel BUTTERICK of Lunenburg, land in Montagne.
<20:440;3:356> - 30 May 1783, Jonathan SNOW of Conway from Elijah BILLINGS of same, 10 acres.
<21:523;4:15> - 24 May 1784, Barnice SNOW of Whately from Benjamin RENNELLS of Ashfield, 50 acres in Ashfield.
<23:219;4:123> - 4 Nov. 1784, Brenice SNOW of Whately from Benjamin RENNILS of Ashfield, 100 acres in Ashfield.
(Note: original numbering is first, followed by the "copy" number.)

John BLACK of Barre MA to **Moses SNOW** of Conway, Hampshire co. MA. <Franklin Co.Deeds 2:404>
...12 Sept. 1787, John BLACK, gent., for Ł184 sold to Moses SNOW, gent...71 acres in Conway bounded by land of Widow GALLOWAY and Capt. LOOK. Witnesses: Percival HALL, Samuel WARE Jr. Ack. same day. Rec. 3 Mar. 1788.

Moses SNOW of Conway, Hampshire co. MA to **David LUCE** of same. <Franklin Co.Deeds 5:423>
...8 Sept. 1788, Moses SNOW, gent., for Ł30.16s sold to David LUCE, yeoman...14 acres in Conway, part of Lot #100, bounded by land of Widow GALLOWAY. Thankful SNOW signs. Witnesses: David FIELD 2d, Noah LOOK. Ack. 31 Jan. 1792 by Moses & Thankful. Rec. 2 Apr. 1793.

Moses SNOW of Conway, Hampshire co. MA to **John BOND** of same. <Franklin Co.Deeds 5:432>
...28 Apr. 1790, Moses SNOW, gent., for Ł20 sold to John BOND, yeoman...8 acres in Conway on north side of road leading by David LUCE's house. Thankful SNOW signs. Witnesses: Joel RICE, Jonas BOND, Consider BOND. Ack. 10 Mar. 1792. Rec. 2 Apr. 1793.

Moses SNOW of Conway, Hampshire co. MA to **John & David FIELD** of same. <Franklin Co.Deeds 5:130>
...22 Sept. 1791, Moses SNOW, gent., for Ł4 sold to John FIELD & David FIELD, yeomen...two rods in Conway, Lot #99, bounded by land of Noah LOOK and sd FIELDS. Witnesses: Daniel MANTER, John LOOK. Ack. 9 Mar. 1792. Rec. 2 Mar. 1792.

Moses SNOW of Conway, Hampshire co. MA to **Lebbeus CHILDS** of same. <Franklin Co.Deeds 5:51>
...3 Nov. 1791, Moses SNOW, gent., for Ł167 sold to Lebbeus CHILDS, yeoman...53 acres in Conway, part of Lots #99 & #100, beginning on east side of County rode leading from Conway Meeting house to Northampton, bounded by land of John LOOK. Thankful SNOW signs. Witnesses: David FIELD 2d, Noah LOOK, Samuel WARE Jr. Ack. 5 "Oct." 1791 by Moses. Rec. 5 Nov. 1791.

Estate of **Elisha SNOW,** yeoman of Harwich MA. <Barnstable Co.PR>
<10:234> 11 Dec. 1770, widow **Abigail SNOW** app'td admx. <12:425> Inventory taken 7 Mar. 1771, by Gershom HALL, James COVELL & John ALLYN; real estate: land in reversion, Ł2; small part of cedar swamp, Ł1.6s8d; meadow, Ł8; homestead land & boggs, Ł41.6s8d. <15:142> 9 Mar. 1773, widow **Abigail SNOW** app'td gdn. of **Samuel SNOW, Aaron SNOW, James SNOW, Edward SNOW & Eunice SNOW.** <17:85> Account 10 Nov. 1772 of **Abigail & Elisha SNOW;** Paid to: Edward KNOWLES, Ammiel WEEKS, Nathaniel DOWNS, Widow BANGS, Dr. FESSENDEN, Ebenezer BROADBROOKS, John SIDMORE, Temperence HOWES, Kenelm WINSLOW, Gershom HALL, Seth HALL, Nathaniel ROBINS, Dr. HERCEY, Osborn SNOW, Elisha SNOW, Thomas NICKERSON, James COVEL, Joshua ELLIS, John ALLEN, Samuel ELLIS, Isaac ELDREDGE, Nathaniel DOANE, John BROADBROOKS. <17:86> Dower 6 Jan. 1773, one third of real estate set off to widow; Inventory of real estate, 6 Jan. 1773; 17 acre homestead bounded by land of Samuel NICKERSON, Mary DOANE, Nathaniel SNOW & ALLIN, Ł22.13s4d; also 8 acres land & bogs bounded by land of Gershom HALL, Ł8; share in cedar swamp, one acre, Ł1.6s; ten acres woodland lying in Grey's Neck, Ł4; 2 acre salt meadow bounded by land of Barier BROADBROOK, Chace's Swamp & Gershom HALL, Ł7.10s. <17:87> Account 9 Mar. 1773 of admx.; Settlement 9 Mar. 1773 mentions son **Elisha SNOW,** yeoman of Yarmouth, he to pay the eldest son **Nathaniel SNOW** and the other brothers & sisters. <17:244> 13 Mar. 1775, one third of lands set off to widow. <17:245> Account 3 Apr. 1775 of **Elisha SNOW** of Harwich, in settling part of real estate of his father.

"S.W.SMITH DEEDS, No.9": (re: Elisha SNOW)

<9:102>- 3 Apr. 1775, Elisha SNOW of Harwich to Osborn SNOW, land settled this day on me by the Probate Judge.
<9:93> - 27 Nov. 1794, Doane SNOW of Ellington CT, grandson of Elisha SNOW, to Osborne SNOW.
<9:103>- 9 Jan. 1810, Agreement between Silvanus CHASE, Elisha SNOW, gdn. of Reuben SNOW minor, Elisha SNOW Jr., David SNOW & Osborn SNOW.

Elisha SNOW et al of Harwich MA to **Osborn SNOW** of same. <"S.W. Smith coll. (Apr. 1921)">
...7 (--) 1772, Elisha SNOW, Abigail SNOW, Nathaniel SNOW & Hannah SNOW...severly promise and oblige our selves to give our Brother Osbron/Osborn SNOW a quit claime dead/deed of that peace of land that lyeth to the westard of the swamp between the two ways between Daniel DOAN's and the widow DONE/DOAN's house on the fourfitture of the sum of fourteen pounds sixteen shillings. Witnesses: Edward KNOWLES, Elisha DOANE. Not ack. or rec.

Elisha SNOW et al of Harwich MA to **Osborn SNOW** of same. <Barnstable Co.Deeds 34:161>
...Mar. 1772, Abigail SNOW, Nathaniel SNOW, Elisha SNOW, Hannah SNOW & Thomas SNOW, for 10s quit claim to Osborn SNOW, yeoman...all rights to one acre in Harwich bounded by dwelling house of sd Osborn and land of Daniel DOANE. Witnesses: Silvanus CHASE, Daniel DOANE. Ack. 13 Feb. 1773 by Nathaniel, 13 Apr. 1772 by rest. Rec. 13 Mar. 1773. ("It has not been re-recorded since the fire" Source also: S.W. Smith coll. 9:99.)

Osborn SNOW of Harwich MA to **Elisha SNOW et al** of same. <"S.W. Smith coll. 9:94>
...16 Mar. 1782, Osborn SNOW, yeoman gave a bond of Ł100 silver money to Elisha SNOW, Thomas SNOW 3d yeoman, Aaron SNOW, Eunice SNOW & James SNOW, yeomen...the condition...is such that if the above bounden Osborn/Orsborn SNOW doth suport his Honoured Mother Abigail SNOW during her natural life & pay all her just debts & funaral charge...then the above obligation to be void. Witnesses: Thankfull BANGS, Kenelm WINSLOW. Not ack. or rec.

Elisha SNOW et al of Harwich MA to **Osborn SNOW** of same. <Barnstable Co.Deeds 48:49>
...20 Mar. 1782, Elisha SNOW, Thomas SNOW 3d, Aaron SNOW, Eunice SNOW & James SNOW, in considera-

tion of our Honored mother Abigail SNOW being honorablely suported during her natural life & her just debts paid by our Brother Orsborn SNOW & we the subscribers saved from any costs arising thereby we...quit claime to any right...we have to any estate either real or personal that is now in the improvement of our sd mother we do hereby convey the same to our sd Brother Orsborn SNOW. Witnesses: Elisha DOANE, Joseph NYE. Ack. 10 Apr. 1782. Rec. 22 Dec. 1794. ("It has not been re-recorded since the fire". Source also: S.W. Smith coll. 9:95.)

Edward SNOW of Harwich MA to **Osborn SNOW** of same. <Barnstable Co.Deeds 43:118>
...5 Nov. 1790, Edward SNOW, yeoman for £2 sold to Osbron/Osborn SNOW, yeoman...all rights in real estate the sd Osborn now improves or posseses. Witnesses: Daniel DOANE, Elisha SNOW. Rec. 23 Nov. 1790. ("It has not been re-recorded since the fire. Source also: S.W. Smith coll.9:92.)

Lot BAKER Jr. of Ellington CT to **Osborn SNOW** of Harwich MA. <Barnstable Co.Deeds 47:165>
...30 Sept. 1794, Lot BAKER Jr., yeoman & wf Hannah, for £6 quit claim to Osbron/Osborn SNOW, yeoman...all rights in real estate of father Elisha SNOW dec'd that was set off to his widow Abigail SNOW dec'd, in Harwich. Witnesses: Ebenezer SNOW, Doane SNOW. Rec. 22 Dec. 1794. (Note: "It has not been re-recorded since the fire." Source also: S.W. Smith coll.9:100)

MICRO #9 OF 18

Estate of **Elisha SNOW**, yeoman of Harwich MA. <Barnstable Co.PR>
<42:211> 14 Mar. 1826, Thomas SNOW, yeoman of Harwich app'td admr. <45:225> Inventory taken 21 Mar. 1826 by Nathan NICKERSON, Nathaniel DOANE & Elisha SNOW; total personal estate, $400.90; total real estate, $1798.00 incl. the following: homestead, $150.00; barn, $70.00; 20 acres east of the road, $183.00; out buildings, $20.00; three acre woodland adjoining James CHASE, $75.00; salt meadow joining the Oyster Creek, $80.00; meadow near Pine Island, $175.00; cleared land & swamp joining the Widow DOANE, $100.00; 22 acre woodland in the Neck, $600.00; six acres D. NICKERSON's lot so called, $150.00; half a pew in the Parish Meeting House, $20.00. <47:119> Account 31 Mar. 1828 of admr.; payments received from Knowles SNOW & Ebenezer SNOW; personal estate divided among the following heirs, viz: **Knowles SNOW, Elisha SNOW, Thomas SNOW, Ebenezer SNOW,** the widows of **Levi SNOW & Isaiah SNOW, James CHASE, Laban SNOW, Nathan BAKER & Priscilla SNOW,** all being adults.

Estate of **Levi SNOW**, mariner of Harwich MA. <Barnstable Co.PR>
<42:204> 14 Feb. 1826, widow **Asenath SNOW & Seth BROOKS**, mariner, both of Harwich, app'td admrs. <40:254> 27 Mar. 1826, widow **Asenatha SNOW** app'td gdn. of **Laurann SNOW, Sukey SNOW, Eliza SNOW, Chester SNOW, Sewall F. SNOW, Clementina SNOW & Levi E. SNOW.** <47:63> Inventory taken 25 Sept. 1826 by Thomas SNOW, Obed BROOKS & Ebenezer BROOKS Jr.; incl. 20 homestead, $570.00; 7 acre woodland near Thomas ELLIS, $80.00; two acre scrub land near M. BASSET, $14.00; cedar swamp near Gershom HALL, $34.00; cedar swamp near Jonathan BURGES, $75.00; meadow at Andrew's river, $140.00; cleared land & swamp north of Meeting House, $30.00; scrub land near Joseph PHILLIPS, $30.00; total personal estate, $763.00 incl. a watch, $15.00 and one sixteenth of the sloop Boston Packet at $125.00. <39:144> 26 Mar. 1827, $500.00 was allowed for the widow.

Will of **Thomas SNOW**, yeoman of Eastham MA. <Barnstable Co.PR>
<13:200>...dated 7 May 1765, mentions wf **Abigail**; son **Elnathan SNOW** (executor); daus **Abigail PAINE** wf of Isaac**, Susanah SNOW & Ruth SNOW.** Witnesses: Moses HIGGINS, Jesse SNOW & David SNOW. Pr. 12 Mar. 1766. <13:201> Inventory taken 20 Mar. 1766. <13:219> Account, 16 Apr. 1766.

Heirs of **Thomas SNOW** of Eastham now Orleans MA. <Barnstable Co.Deeds 1:254>
...3 Oct. 1799, Elnathan SNOW & Prince ROGERS of Orleans, Isaac PAINE, yeoman of Eastham and Joseph MAYO of Eden, yeomen...owning several peices of land and meadow lying in Eastham, Orleans and Harwich that came to us by our father Thomas SNOW dec'd...divide sd land. Phebe SNOW, Abigail PAINE, Susanna ROGERS & Ruth MAYO also sign. Ack. 9 Oct. 1800 by Edmund SNOW attorney to Ruth MAYO; Ack. 3 Oct. 1799 by rest. Rec. 3 Nov. 1801.

Will of **Micajah SNOW**, yeoman of Eastham MA. <Barnstable Co.PR 9 :147-150>
...dated 25 Dec. 1753, mentions son **John SNOW**; grandsons **Jonathan SNOW, Moses SNOW & Heman SNOW**; sons **Jesse SNOW, David SNOW** (executor) **& Micajah SNOW**; daus **Phebe PAINE, Marcy SEARS & Ruth AREY.** Pr. 23 July 1754. Inventory taken 4 Sept. 1754.

Edmund SNOW of Eastham MA to **Philip YOUNG** of same. <Barnstable Co.Deeds, Orleans 1:283>
...5 Feb. 1792, Edmund SNOW, yeoman & wf Mary, for £20 sell to Philip YOUNG, yeoman...seven eighths of a field by Town Cove (& other land) that was his mother Lois SNOW's that came to her from her father Lt. Edmund FREEMAN.

Will of **John SNOW**, gent. of Harwich MA <Barnstable Co.PR>
<13:206>...dated 13 Feb. 1766, mentions wf **Elizabeth;** grandson **Edward SNOW** heir of dec'd dau **Phebe SNOW;** heirs of dec'd dau **Hannah HOUSE;** dau **Abigail WING;** son **Jonathan SNOW, John SNOW, Enos SNOW** (executor)**, Gideon SNOW, Eli SNOW, William SNOW & David SNOW.** <13:207> Pr. 8 Mar. 1766. <13:207> Inventory. <12:466,470> Accounts.

Prince SNOW of Orleans MA to **Joseph HURD** of same. <Barnstable Co.Deeds, Orleans 1:300>
...29 Sept. 1798, Prince SNOW, yeoman, for $118.83 sold to Joseph HURD, yeoman...ten acres and is the field on which my Honoured Father Micajah SNOW late of Orleans deceast dwelt...bounded by

land of widow Phebe FREEMAN, Eleazer FREEMAN, Simeon KINGMAN and land lately of the ATWOODS. Witnesses: Kezia HARDING, Simeon KINGMAN. Ack. same day. Rec. 6 Oct. 1798, 52:32.

Will of **Stephen SNOW Jr.**, yeoman of Eastham MA. <Barnstable Co.PR>
<8:481>...dated 26 Oct. 1751, mentions wf **Marah**; sons **Moses SNOW & Heman SNOW**; brother **David SNOW** of Eastham, executor. Pr. 3 Mar. 1752. <8:520> Inventory taken 7 Mar. 1752.

Will of **Heman SNOW** of Orleans MA. <Barnstable Co.PR 38:348-349>
...dated 16 Oct. 1819, mentions wf **Jedidah**; son **Heman SNOW**; dau **Sally SNOW**; sons **Gideon Smith SNOW** (executor), **Aiathar/Abiathar SNOW & Robert SNOW**; daus **Molly TWINING, Thankful GLOSSIN, Jedidah GLOSSIN & Abigail KENRICK**; mentions half a house & orchard owned with William C. KENRICK. Pr. 22 Mar. 1820.

DEBORAH HOPKINS^2 (Stephen^1)

PLYMOUTH COUNTY PROBATE: (re: RING)

1692/3	Andrew	Plymouth	will	#16947, 1:163,164
1730	William	Plymouth	adm.	#16956, 5:704,744,745
1731	William	Plymouth	will	#16957, 6:34,35
1735	Eleazer	Plymouth	will	#16948, 7:112,132,486
1749	Eleazer	Kingston	will	#16949, 12:176,177
1768	Samuel	Kingston	will	#16953, 20:79,80
1820	Francis	Kingston	will	#16950, 53:154,156,242

PLYMOUTH COLONY RECORDS (PCR) (printed): (re: Andrew RING)

<12:64> - 26 Oct. 1640, For given consideration, Matthew FULLER sells to Andrew RINGE his garden place at Plymouth and six acres of land at the New Field.
<1:166> - 2 Nov. 1640, Andrew RING granted 5 acres at South Meadows toward Aggawam & Colebrook Meadows.
<2:25> - 16 Sept 1641, Andrew RING granted enlargement at the west end of his garden.
<2:48> - 17 Oct. 1642, Andrew RING granted four acres of upland adjoining his property.
<12:113>- 24 Sept 1645, Edward & Amy HOLMAN sell to William BROWNE, land next to Andrew RING's property at New Field.
<12:189>- 1 July 1650, Andrew & Deborah RINGE of Plymouth sell property at Duxbury to Experience MITCHELL.
<4:19> - 3 June 1662, Andrew RING granted land by the court.
<4:152> - 5 June 1667, Andrew RING granted land lying at end of his land at Namassakett.
<6:104> - 8 Mar. 1682/3, One of the children of Francis COMBE left to Andrew RINGE & Lettice RINGE his wife, whoe is grandmother thereunto.

<Plymouth Col.Deeds 2:2:31> **Andrew RING**, planter & wf Deborah of Plymouth sell land to William CLARKE, planter of Duxbury.

Joseph YORK of Falmouth MA to **James & Adams MERRILL** of same. <Cumberland Co.Deeds 2:142>
...16 Jan. 1760, Joseph YORK, yeoman & wf Susannah, for £23.6s3d sell to James MERRILL & Adams MERRILL, yeomen...an equal quarter part...of the one hundred acre lott in N. Yarmouth numbered nine in the one hundred acre division. Witnesses: James MASON, Mary MASON, Benjamin YORK, Ichabod CLARK. Ack. same day. Rec. 24 July 1762.

Susannah YORK, widow of Falmouth MA to **Thomas DRINKWATER** of N. Yarmouth MA. <Cumberland Co.Deeds>
<2:118>...7 June 1762, Susannah YORK, for £46.10s sells to Thomas DRINKWATER, husbandman...seven and three quarters acres in N. Yarmouth...being part of the homestead of my late Hon'd Father Andrew RING late of N. Yarmouth dec'd that fell to my share in the division of sd homestead. Witnesses: Jonas MASON, David BARKER. Ack. same day. Rec. 22 June 1762.

PLYMOUTH COUNTY DEEDS: (re: CLAGHORN, all to 1859)

References only: Grantee: 14:44;28:228;30:175;44:62;56:261;58:198;61:144;62:185;91:156;145:247;147:99;245:163;279:55. Grantor: 14:210;37:96;49:222;56:261;58:198;59:79;61:144;80:32;87:273;110:99;171:85;186:21;279:55.

Estate of **Lemuel CLAGHORN** of Wareham MA. <Plymouth Co.PR #4118>
...1743...<9:99> Pr. <9:136> Inventory. <9:137;15:294> Accounts. <9:138> Widow's allowance.

Estate of **James CLAGHORN** of Rochester MA. <Plymouth Co.Pr #4117>
...1723...<4:348> Pr. <4:368> Inventory.

Estate of **Hanable HANDY** of Rochester MA. <Plymouth Co.PR #9096>
<13:262> 3 June 1754, Benjamin HAMMON app'td admr. <13:522> Inventory taken 21 June 1746, mentions eldest dau **Elizabeth HANDY**; additional inventory in 1754, eldest dau **Elizabeth CLAGHORN** wf

of Joseph. <14:87> Account 21 July 1756 mentions payment of shares to the widow & following children, viz: **Seth HANDY** (eldest son), **Elizabeth, Nathan HANDY & Hannah.**

MICRO #10 OF 18

Will of Francis RING of Kingston MA. <Plymouth Co.PR 53:154>
...dated 28 Nov. 1806, mentions wf **Mary**; youngest sons **Daniel RING & Samuel RING** (minors); son **Rufus RING** (executor); daus **Mary SOUL, Lucy RING, Ruth RING & Susanna RING**; grandsons **Joseph RING & Andrew RING**, minors and their sisters **Elizabeth RING & Rebecca RING.** Pr. 16 Oct. 1820.

Rufus RING of Kingston MA to **Daniel & Samuel RING** of same. <Plymouth Co.Deeds 151:95>
...13 Apr. 1818, Rufus RING, yeoman, for $1100.00 sells to Daniel RING & Samuel RING, yeomen... land in Kingston...I bought of my Father...as per deed of...Francis RING to Rufus RING...bounded by land of father Francis RING. Wf Fanny RING releases dower.

Estate of **Rufus RING** of Mansfield MA to **Fanny RING** of same. <Plymouth Co.Deeds 253:58>
...8 Jan. 1853, Samuel A. RING, admr. of esatate of Rufus RING...sold at auction to Fanny RING, meadow in Kingston on Jones River which Rufus bought of Thomas STETSON.

Estate of **William MAYO** of Eastham MA. <Barnstable Co.PR 1:55>
Inventory taken 16 Oct. 1691 by John DOANE, Joseph SNOW; incl. three acres upland & house, £12 and a cradle. Inventory taken 16 Apr. 1692 of the wearing clothes of the wife of the dec'd who died a short time after her husband; sworn to 21 Apr. 1692 by John MAYO. Rec. 23 Apr. 1692.

Heirs of **Andrew RING** to **Eleazer RING** of Plimton MA. <Barnstable Co.Deeds 13:249>
...4 Jan. 1717/8, Samuel TUCKER & wf Hannah of Chatham and Thankful MAYO of Eastham, the daus of Elizabeth MAYO dec'd of Eastham, sell to their uncle Eleazer RING...their land in Middleboro in the 16 Shilling Purchase that they received by the will of their Grandfather Andrew RING.

Heirs of **John MORTON**. <Plymouth Co.Deeds 6:185>
...21 Feb. 1725/6, Thomas TOMSON & wf Mary; Jonathan INGLEE & wf Deborah; Joanna VAUGHAN, widow, all of Middleboro; John MURDOCK & wf Phebe of Plymouth and John HODGES & wf Hannah of Norton, children of John MORTON dec'd, sell land in Middleboro. <31:194> On 21 Feb. 1725/6, the same grantors sold land to James SHAW. Rec. 8 Mar. 1737.

Will of **John MORTON** of Middleboro MA. <Plymouth Co.PR #14303>
<4:76>...dated 17 Jan. 1717/8, mentions wf **Mary**, five daus **Johanah, Phebe, Mary, Hannah & Deborah** and son **Ebenezer MORTON.** Pr. 1 May 1 718. <4:131> Inventory taken 22 May 1718, mentions John died 20 Mar. 1718.

Estate of **Capt. Ebenezer MORTON** of Middleboro MA. <Plymouth Co.PR #14254>
...1750...<11:356> Pr. <12:3,214> Inventory. <12:187> Division. <#14325, 12:45-47> Guardianship of children **Lucy MORTON, Sarah MORTON, Nathaniel MORTON & Seth MORTON.**

Eleazer MORTON of Stephenton NY **et al** to **Ichabod MORTON Jr.** of Middleboro MA. <Plymouth Co.Deeds>
<79:185>...29 Oct. 1795, Eleazer MORTON of Stephenton & Elisha MORTON of Schodack, yeomen, both of the County of Rawsley, New York and Sarah BARROWS widow of John BARROWS, gent. dec'd of Middleboro, Ichabod CUSHMAN, husbandman & wf Molley, John MORTON, yeoman, Elizabeth MORTON, spinster, Nathaniel MORTON, shop joiner and Mordica MORTON, shop joiner, all of Middleboro, for $323.00 sell to our brother Ichabod MORTON Jr., yeoman...rights in real estate that fell to our honoured Mother Deborah MORTON late of Middleborough in the division of the real estate of her honoured father Ebenezer MORTON late of Middleborough dec'd. Witnesses: Ichabod MORTON, Isaac THOMSON. Ack same day by all except Nathaniel. Rec. 17 May 1796.

Hannah RING of Plymouth MA to **Caleb SHERMAN** of same. <Plymouth Co.Deeds 32:111>
...7 Nov. 1738, Hannah RING, widow of William, deed of gift to son in law Caleb SHERMAN, cooper, who married her daughter Deborah, dec'd. On the same date an agreement was made with Caleb for her maintenance.

Hannah RING of Plymouth MA to Children of **Elizabeth PEARCE** of Sandwich MA. <Plymouth Co.Deeds>
<32:185>...12 Apr. 1739, Hannah RING, widow of William, deed of gift to Elizabeth PEARCE & all the other children of dau Elizabeth PEARCE wf of Joseph PEARCE of Sandwich...certain land rec'd by will of Hannah's son Eleazer RING dec'd.

Will of **William RING**, husbandman of Plymouth MA. <Plymouth Co.PR #16957>
<6:34>...dated 16 June 1730, mentions wf **Hannah,** son **Eleazer RING** (executor) and daus **Elizabeth PEARCE, Deborah RING.** Witnesses: Robert COOKE, Gershom BRADFORD, Francis ADAMS. <6:35> Witnesses sworn 21 May 1731, Pr. 22 May 1731. (Also incl. is the following with no source: **Hannah RING** of Plymouth, relict of **William RING**...have received of Haviland TORREY, executor of the Last will & testament of my son **Eliazer RING** the sum of £230.6s9d out of the movable estate of sd Eleazer. Dated 1 Feb. 1741. Witnesses: Eleazer RING & (sp)Beniam JENNINGS.

GILES HOPKINS^2 (Stephen^1)

BARNSTABLE COUNTY PROBATE: (re: HOPKINS)

1728	Caleb	Truro		4:433.440
1733	Stephen	Harwich	will	5:112,114
1738	Joshua	Eastham	will	5:372;6:26,28,29,30,31
1739	John	Harwich		5:346,347,348
1741	Caleb	Truro		6:57,118,119
1741	Elisha		will	6:207,209,210,356,257,409,410,411
1748	Judah	Harwich	will	8:354,356,357
1749	Samuel	Harwich	will	8:336,338
1752	Nathaniel	Truro	will	7:248,249,250;9:46,47,48,49;12:97
1754	Thomas	Truro	will	9:138,140,141,461-64;11:50-52;12:94
1760	John	Truro		10:49;11:139;12:80,184
1761	Thomas	Truro	will	12:164,166,251,351
1762	Judah	Harwich		10:107;12:318,395;13:160;14:2,3,5
1762	Samuel	Harwich	will	12:279,280;14:166,167
1766	Moses	Harwich		10:178;13:417
1766	Nathaniel	Harwich	will	13:246,247
1767	Reuben	Harwich	will	13:289,290;36:93;37:510,514,515
1771	Joseph	Harwich	will	12:439,440,453
1776	Edmund & Scotto	Harwich	gdn.	15:250,254
1780	Joshua	Eastham	will	11:36,54,56
1790	Elkanah	Harwich		25:39,286,650,651,761;27:178-80,183,184
1795	Hugh	Truro		25:115,429,857;28:52,106
1800	Edward	Harwich		25:194;30:18
1800	Constant	Truro		25:222;30:325,367,381;34:8
1800	Prince	Harwich	will	30:32;32:1
1807	John	Harwich		19:213;25:897;31:436;33:102
1812	Rowland	Harwich		22:500;36:85,92;37:509
1812	Reuben	Harwich		36:93;37:510,514,515
1813	Freeman	Brewster		-----
1814	Jonathan	Brewster		-----

==========

Gyles HOPKINS of Eastham to **John WING** of Yarmouth. <Plymouth Col.Deeds 3:91>
...9 Nov. 1666, Gyles HOPKINS, planter sells to John WING...mentions brother Caleb HOPKINS "now also deceased". Witnesses: John FREEMAN, Stephen HOPKINS. (Also, <4:252> 21 Aug. 1672, Gyles HOPKINS et al bought land.)

==========

Will of **Nathaniel HOPKINS**, yeoman of Truro MA. <Barnstable Co.PR>
<9:46>...dated 9 May 1752, mentions wf **Sarah**; three sons **Isaac HOPKINS, John HOPKINS & Elisha HOPKINS**; six daus **Mary SMITH, Sarah SMALLEY, Lydia BRAGDIN, Phebe HOPKINS, Elisabeth HOPKINS & Priscilla HOPKINS**. Witnesses: Barnabas PAINE, Benjamin COLLINGS Jr. & Benjamin LOMBARD. Pr. 23 June 1752. <9:48> Inventory taken 26 June 1752 by Benjamin COLLINGS, Barnabas PAINE & Benjamin COLLINGS Jr.; incl. the buildings, £6; the orchard, £9.6s8d; land & meadow on south side of Pamet River, £123.6s8d; land on north side, £120.10s8d; sworn to 30 June 1752 by **Isaac HOPKINS**, exr.

MICRO #11 OF 18

Guardianship of Children of **Samuel HOPKINS** of Harwich MA. <Barnstable Co.PR>
<14:166,167> 11 Nov. 1766, Reuben RIDER app'td gdn. of **James HOPKINS & Mercy HOPKINS**, children of Samuel HOPKINS, dec'd.

==========

BARNSTABLE COUNTY DEEDS (re-recorded) to 1827: (re: HOPKINS)

<Harwich, 3:122> - 1795, Barzillai HOPKINS to Gamaliel CHASE.
<Dennis, 3:30> - 1796, Abigail HOPKINS et al to Samuel CHASE.
<Truro, 1:128> - 1802, Caleb HOPKINS et al (Selectmen) to Theophilus NEWCOMB.
<Wellfleet, 1:285> - 1814, Benjamin HOPKINS to Giles HOPKINS.

==========

Will of **William MEYRICK/MYRICK**, yeoman of Harwich MA. <Barnstable Co.PR>
<5:33>...dated 5 May 1723, mentions wf **Elizabeth**...to sons **Benjamin MYRICK & Nathaniel MYRICK**, lots of land bought of Annanias WING, Thomas SNOW and Nathaniel DOANE...to **Benjamin**, two acres out of the great parcel of meadow at Billingsgate with the remaining divided among sons **Benjamin, Nathaniel, Stephen & Joshua**...to sons **Benjamin, Nathaniel & Stephen**, two parcels of meadow lying at ye boat meadow and Rock harbour meadow in Eastham...to son **John MYRICK**, meadow at Billinsgate commonly called Beriah's meadow...to son **Nathaniel MYRICK**, land had of Major FREEMAN lying between the pond & sea in Harwich he my sd son acquitting all claims to my lands I give to my son **Joshua MYRICK** by vertue of any right or claim in or to any lands that I received title to from my father in law **Giles HOPKINS**...also to **Nathaniel**, two acres of land that I had of Thomas SNOW near the Whale house...to son **Stephen MYRICK** & his wife **Deborah**, land where they now live, being about thirty acres...to sons **Stephen & Joshua**, land being in the Sheep pond neck called a twenty acre

lott as also one half part of the land I had of Nathaniel DOANE...also half of a twenty acre lott I had of Mr. John FREEMAN lying on ye easterly side ye way that goes to Chathamnear the great Long pond...to the children of my deceased daughter **Rebeckah SPARROW** tenn pounds...to dau **Ruth SEARS**, tenn pounds...to daughters in law **Mercy WITHEREL & Rachel HUGENS**, twenty shillings each; sons **Benjamin & Nathaniel**, executors. Witnesses: Joseph DOANE, Mary DOANE & Phebe DOANE. Codicil 29 Aug. 1729...the great parcel of meadow at Billinsgate, bequeathed to sons **Benjamin, Nathaniel, Stephen & Joshua** has since been sold to Benjamin SWET for £100 as per bond dated 1 Oct. 1728, therefore the £100 is bequeathed to the four sons. Witnesses: Joseph DOANE, Desire DOANE & Lydia DOANE. Pr. 29 Nov.1732 on oath of Joseph DOANE & Phebe DOANE, that they with Mary DOANE now deceased, witnessed the will and on oath of the witnesses of the codicil. <5:35> Inventory taken 8 Jan. 1732/3 by Joseph DOANE, Jonathan LINCOLN & Joshua FREEMAN; incl. homestead land, £140; old dwelling house, £40; land where **Stephen MYRICK** lived by will given to sd **Stephen**'s wife, £260; meadow at Rock Harbour, £35; land in Smith's purchase, £12; note of hand of Jonathan BANGS, 38s; the goods the widow **Elizabeth** brought with her to sd deceased's and obtained since...all at ye house of **Stephen MYRICK** dec'd; personal property at Jabez SNOW's; sworn to 17 Jan. 1732/3 by exrs

---

Estate of **Samuel MYRICK** of Truro MA. <Barnstable Co.PR 3:153>
6 Apr. 1714, father **William MYRICK**, yeoman of Harwich, app'td admr.

Will of **Benjamin MYRICK**, yeoman of Harwich MA. <Barnstable Co.PR 8:357-360>
...dated 13 Aug. 1743...to wf **Rachel**, all that estate she brought with hir to me and...twenty pounds out of my estate according to the sd agreement which wee made & committed to wrighting before marrage...to son **John MYRICK**...that dwelling house he now dwells in...to sons **Nathaniel MYRICK & Benjamin MYRICK**, the dwelling house I now live in and my barn...to all three sons, all lands in Harwich & Yarmouth...excepting my fresh meadow at Namskaket which I give to my son **Nathaniel**...in consideration of the full value thereof I have receied of him in cash...to son **Benjamin**, all my wearing appearell...to daus **Abigail MAYO** wf of Joseph **& Rebecca BAKER**, £7 each; son **Nathaniel** & son in law **Joseph MAYO**, executors. Witnesses: Nathan FOSTER, Seth SEARS & Nathaniel FOSTER. Presented for probate, 20 May 1749. <8:359> Pr. 24 May 1749, **Nathaniel MYRICK** of Harwich app'td admr. <8:359> 21 May 1749, Nathaniel STONE Jr., Esq., John SNOW & Nathan FOSTER, all of Harwich and sufficient freeholders, app'td to take inventory. Inventory taken 5 June 1749; incl. homestead, £275 and meadow & woodland, £110; total, £590; sworn to 4 July 1749 by admr.

Will of **John MYRICK**, yeoman of Truro MA. <Barnstable Co.PR>
<9:24>...dated 13 Mar. 1750, bequests to wf **Hannah** and friend Paul KNOWLS of Truro (executor). Witnesses: Abner PAINE, Jonah GROSS & Benjamin GROSS. <9:25> Pr. 6 Oct. 1753; sworn to by witnesses & executor. Inventory taken 16 Nov. 1753 by John RICH, Ambrose DYER & Abner PAINE; total personal estate, £52.11s4d; total real estate, £98.9s4d.; sworn to 4 Dec. 1753 by exr.

Estate of **Joshua MYRICK**, cordwainer of Harwich MA. <Barnstable Co.PR>
<5:479> Inventory taken 25 Apr. 1740 by Chillingsworth FOSTER, Joseph MAYO & Thomas WINSLOW; incl homestead, £600; his right in Nameskeket flats, £5; his right in Satucket flats, £10; his right in Quoivet Meadow in Yarmouth, £50; land he bought of CHIPMAN, £45; land he had of Nathaniel CLEARK/CLARKE, £8; land he bought of Stephen MYRICK, £20; land in the Sheep Pond Neck, £98; land on west side of Chatham Rhoad, £30; land he bought of Elisha DOANE, £19; total estate, £1900.3s9d sworn to 30 Apr. 1740 by **Lydia MYRICK**, admx. <5:481> Account, 12 Mar. 1745. <5:482> Dower, 1 Apr. 1746. <5:483> Appraisal of real estate, 18 Mar. 1745. <6:474-476> Guardianship, 18 Apr. 1746 of the children, viz: **Lydia MYRICK, Barnabas MYRICK, Hannah MYRICK, Mary MYRICK & Bezaleel MYRICK.**

Will of **Capt. Nathaniel MERRICK**, yeoman of Harwich MA. <Barnstable Co.PR>
<6:345>...dated 18 Oct. 1743, mentions wf **Elce/Alice**; to sons **Constant MERRICK & Benjamin MERRICK** lands in Harwich & Yarmouth; to grandson **William MERRICK** son to my son **William MERRICK** dec'd, £25 two years after my decease; to grandson **Gideon MERRICK** son to my son **William** dec'd, a pair of large silver shoebuckles marked "GM"; to dau **Sarah MERRICK**, £10, one feather bed & suitable furniture to it and the looking glass and one pair of gould buttons markt "GM"; remainder of personal estate divided amongst the six daus, viz: **Hannah SNOW, Mercy KING, Ruth HINKLEY, Priscilla COB, Elce/Alice RUGGLES & Sarah MERRICK**; son in law **John SNOW** and trusty friend Deacon Joseph MAYO, executors. Witnesses: Nathaniel MERRICK Jr., Thomas MAYO & Chillingsworth FOSTER. Pr. 14 Dec. 1743 on the oath of the three witnesses. <6:348-9> Inventory taken 24 Dec. 1743 by Joseph FREEMAN Esq., Chillingsworth FOSTER, blacksmith and Nathaniel HOPKINS, blacksmith, all of Harwich; incl. a pair of silver buckels, 16s6d; gold buttons, £1.2s6d; pair of specticles, 1s3d; homestead, £75; meadow in Yarmouth, £15; land by FREEMAN's, £10; land by Nathaniel SNOW's, £18.15s; four pieces wood land, £41.17s; total estate, £252.13s9d; sworn to 27 Dec. 1743 by exrs. <8:325> Account 7 June 1748 of **John SNOW**, exr.; Payments to: Joshua FREEMAN, John WING, Col. Edmund FREEMAN, Edward SNOW, John MERRICK, Constable FOSTER, Capt. David GORHAM, David HOPKINS, Isaac FOSTER, Benjamin THACHER, Heman STONE, David BANGS, Jonathan LINCOLN, Dr. BANGS, Rebecca HOPKINS, Joseph FREEMAN, Esq., Nathaniel STONE, Edward BANGS, Joseph HOPKINS Jr., Thomas HINKLEY, Judah HOPKINS Jr., Deacon FOSTER, Dr. KENWRICK, Nathaniel MERRICK, Joseph WING, Deacon MAYO, Joshua HINKLEY, Thomas MERRICK, Constable TOBY, Peleg MAKER; paid for grave stones, £4. Additional Account 6 Sept. 1748, mentions "one note prised due from Joshua MERRICK that I can git nothing for, £4.10s".

Estate of **Gideon MERRICK**, mariner of Harwich MA. <Barnstable Co.PR 6:106>
...13 Jan. 1740, father **Nathaniel MERRICK**, yeoman of Harwich, app'td admr.

Estate of **Stephen MERRICK** of Harwich MA. <Barnstable Co.PR>
<3:647> 18 Apr. 1732, widow **Deborah MERRICK** app'td admx. <3:649> Inventory taken 26 May 1732 by

Chillingsworth FOSTER, Joseph MAYO & Samuel CROSBY; sworn to 26 July 1732 by widow; total estate, £128.2s7d.

Thomas Coverly VERNON to **Caleb HOPKINS** of Boston MA. <Suffolk Deeds 166:193>
...12 Aug. 1789, Thomas Coverly VERNON to Caleb HOPKINS, merchant...land bounded on land of Caleb HOPKINS which was left to his wife Jane HOPKINS by her father Fortesque VERNON dec'd.

Aaron HINCKLEY, Esq. of Brunswick ME to **Caleb HOPKINS** of Boston MA. <Cumberland Co.ME Deeds> <8:490>...22 Apr. 1771, Aaron HINCKLEY, Esq., gent...whereas the General Court granted to Capt. Joseph SYLVESTER & Co. a township called Sylvester Canada, now found to be in New Hampshire, therefore the General Court on 18 June 1768 granted to James WARREN, Esq. et al another township to be laid out west side of Androscoggin River in Cumberland Co., for £8 sells to Caleb HOPKINS, merchant...one sixty fourth of sd township it being in right of one Lazarus TURNER one of the first grantees. Witnesses: William SYLVESTER, Mary HINCKLEY.

Caleb HOPKINS of Boston MA to **Ichabod BONNEY** of Pembroke MA. <Cumberland Co.ME 19:123>
...20 June 1783, Caleb HOPKINS, merchant, for £180, sells to Ichabod BONNEY, gent...lot #77 in Sylvester, Cumberland Co., which lot with others were drawn in right of Lazarus TURNER dec'd. Wf Mary HOPKINS releases dower. Witnesses: John ADAMS, Hannah WATTS. Ack. same day. Rec. 30 May 1792

Capt. Caleb HOPKINS of Boston MA to **Samuel PUMPELLY** of Turner ME. <Cumberland Co.ME Deeds 22:131>
...14 Oct. 1794, Caleb HOPKINS, merchant & wf Mary, for £43.10s, sell to Samuel PUMPELLY, yeoman ...the 69th lot in Turner, about 125 acres. Witnesses: John LORING, Mehitable HOPKINS. Ack. 15 Oct. 1794 by Capt. Caleb HOPKINS. Rec. 3 Feb. 1795.

Will of **Caleb HOPKINS**, merchant of Boston MA. <Suffolk Co.PR 90:668-9,827>
...dated 11 Aug. 1788...to wf **Mary** (executrix), everything for life; to dau **Jane HOPKINS**, everything after death of wife; wf **Mary** & friend Jonathan HOMER, clerk of Newton, to be gdns. of **Jane**. Pr. 8 Oct. 1799. Bond 8 Oct. 1799 of **Mary HOPKINS** & Isaac RAND 3d, M.D., on estate of Caleb HOPKINS, "intestate". Sureties: Michael HOPKINS, mariner & David WEST. Warrant for Inventory 8 Oct. 1799, sworn to 26 Nov. 1799; incl. land in north Boston; house & land on Orange Tree St. & Cambridge St.; 100 acres at Harpswell; lots #77 & #175 in Turner Town and pew #100 in Mr. STILLMAN's meeting house. Account 8 Dec. 1801, one third of estate to widow **Mary HOPKINS**, two thirds to **Isaac RAND 3d**.

Will of **Mary HOPKINS**, widow of Boston MA. <Suffolk Co.PR 121:121>
...dated 26 Aug. 1820, mentions neice **Miss Mehitable HOPKINS**; grandsons **Isaac H. RAND & Caleb H. RAND**; Caleb Hopkins SNOW & Mary Hopkins SNOW, chil. of Prince SNOW Jr.; Rev. Jonathan HOMER of Newton, executor. Witnesses: Charles P. CURTIS, Joseph KIDDER & Joseph CARR. Codicil 2 Aug. 1822. Pr. 17 Feb. 1823.

Estate of **Constant HOPKINS** of Truro MA. <Barnstable Co.PR>
<25:222> 17 Oct. 1800, **Constant HOPKINS** of Truro, app'td admr. <34:8> Inventory taken 24 Oct. 1800 by Levi STEVENS, Elkanah PAINE & Jane AVERY; incl. ten acres near Barzillai SMITH's, $16.66; home land, $25.00; dwelling house, $40.00; barn, $18.00; land at Moon Pond, $6.00; land at Eastern Harbor, $20.00; salt meadow, $25.00; salt meadow near Hopkins Will, $40.00; salt meadow at Cedar Islands, $42.00; meadow at Little Harbour, $80.00; woodland at the Cape, $20.00. <30:325> Account 4 Nov. 1800 of admr. <30:381> Account 19 Mar. 1801 of admr.; total estate, $377.99. <30:367> Settlement 19 Mar. 1801, to following children, viz: **Constant HOPKINS** of Truro; **Jonathan HOPKINS** of Provincetown; **Richard HOPKINS** of Boston; widow & heirs of **Caleb HOPKINS** of Boston; **Phebe WHITNEY** wf of Asa of Gorham ME; **Mary RICH** wf of Barzillai of Penobscot River; **Hannah HOPKINS, Betsy HOPKINS & Mercy PAINE** wf of Henry, all of Provincetown.

MICRO #12 OF 18

Will of **Caleb HOPKINS**, mariner of Boston MA. <Suffolk Co.PR #19829>
<90:669>...dated 15 Oct. 1791...to wf **Bethiah** all personal estate while my widow...after to be equally divided between my heirs; wf **Bethiah** and brother **Michael HOPKINS**, executors. Witnesses: Jedidiah PARKER, Barzilla SMITH Jr. & John JENKS. <90:669> Letter/Bond 1 Nov. 1991, **Bethiah HOPKINS & Michael HOPKINS**, mariner, app'td admrs. of estate of **Caleb HOPKINS Jr.** Sureties: Caleb HOPKINS, Esq. & Jedediah PARKER, gent., both of Boston. <90:827> Inventory of estate of **Capt. Caleb HOPKINS Jr.**, taken 26 Dec. 1791; mentions mansion house & land in Ship St., £265.

Estate of **Michael HOPKINS Jr.**, mariner & minor, of Boston MA. <Suffolk Co.PR #24768>
<113:115> 28 Oct. 1815, **David GREEN & Bethiah GREEN** decline to administer on the estate of our son **Michael HOPKINS Jr.**, we request your Honor to appoint **Michael HOPKINS**, mariner of Boston, as admr. <190:57> Letter/Bond 30 Oct. 1815, **Michael HOPKINS** app'td admr. Sureties: **David GREEN**, wharfinger & Prince SNOW, trader, both of Boston. <311:19> 20 Oct. 1815, admr. makes oath he posted notices. <113:543> Inventory taken 4 Nov. 1815 by F. GREEN, Joseph AUSTIN & Prince SNOW Jr consisting of half a dwelling house in Ship St., Boston, $1283.00; sworn to 27 Nov. 1815 by admr. <114:63> Account 22 Jan. 1816 of admr. List of debts 22 Jan. 1816, balance of **David & Bethiah GREEN**'s bill, $795.62. <346:110> Bond 28 Mar. 1816 of admr. **Michael HOPKINS**, merchant, to sell real estate. Sureties: **David GREEN**, wharfinger & Barzillai HOLMES, merchant, both of Boston. <114:223,284> Oath 3 Apr. 1816 of admr.; to advertise sale, at auction, of enough real estate as

shall produce $900.00 to pay debts. 13 May 1816, **David GREEN** made oath that he had posted above notice in Boston, Charlestown & Cambridge, 30 days before date of sale.

Estate of **Michael HOPKINS Jr.**, mariner of Boston MA. <Suffolk Co.Deeds 251:155>
...17 May 1816, Michael HOPKINS of Boston, admr. of estate, by order of the court, 4th Tues. Nov. 1815 to sell enough real estate to pay $900.00, for $800.00 sold to Bethiah GREEN, wf of David GREEN, trader of Boston...land in north Boston on Ship St...reserving to the occupants of the sd adjoining tenement now or late of sd Caleb HOPKINS an uninterrupted passage way at all time through the yard...and to the Welland Pump standing on sd premises. Witnesses: Isaac F. COFFIN, John HEARD Jr. Same day, David GREEN gives his consent. Witnesses: Daniel E. POWERS, Michael HOPKINS. Rec. 18 May 1816.

Caleb HOPKINS of Boston MA to **Bethiah GREENE** of Boston MA. <Suffolk Co.Deeds 234:18>
...27 May 1809, Caleb HOPKINS...in consideration of the duty & affection which I justly owe to my dear & honoured Mother Mrs. Bethiah GREENE now the wife of Mr. David GREENE, wharfinger and also in consideration of fifty dollars...quit claim rights in land in north Boston with a privilege in common to the passageway...reserving to myself and to the occupants of my adjoining tenement uninterrupted passage way through the yard...and to the well and pump...the sd premises béing part of the estate of my late honoured father Capt. Caleb HOPKINS dec'd and the part thereof hereby released & quitclaimed being the part in which my sd honoured Mother and the fmaily now reside. Witnesses: John L. GARDNER, Robert GARDNER. Ack. same day by Caleb. Rec. 12 Sept. 1810.

Caleb HOPKINS of Boston MA to **Josiah MIXER & Ebenezer CRAFTS.** <Suffolk Co.Deeds 234:17>
...12 Aug. 1810, Caleb HOPKINS, mariner, for $500.00 sold to Josiah MIXER, merchant of Cambridge and Ebenezer CRAFTS, Esq. of Roxbury...land & tenement in north Boston, fronting 27'6" on Ship St., 104' in depth with a way lying in common on the northerly side 5'6" wide and running 48'... bounded by land of heirs of Philip BASS(sp) dec'd, Salutation Alley, land formerly of Nicholas RASHBY but now of Alexander DAVISON, land formerly of William HOUGH but now of William DYAR and Joseph DYAR's heirs...it being the same which was conveyed to my father by Benjamin DOLBEARE as by his deed recorded with Suffolk deeds libro 154...excepting nevertheless so much of sd Estate as was conveyed to Robert ALLCOCK by my sd father, And part of the sd Estate being subject to the life estate of my mother therein as by my deed of gift to her will appeare. Witnesses: L. RICHARDSON, William AYLWIN. Ack. & Rec. 12 Sept. 1810.

SUFFOLK COUNTY DEEDS: (re: Caleb HOPKINS & others, with location of real estate in Boston**)**

<98:118> - 29 July 1762, Caleb HOPKINS, mariner from David JENKINS, Love Lane and a street, formerly Thornton's pasture, in Boston.
<101:201> - 31 Mar. 1764, Caleb HOPKINS from Katherine KERR, lane from Hanover St. & Mill Pond.
<103:109> - 22 Jan. 1765, Caleb HOPKINS from William HOSKINS, land from Hanover St. & Mill Pond.
<138:87> - 25 Apr. 1783, Caleb HOPKINS to William HARRIS.
<145:283> - 15 Nov. 1784, Caleb HOPKINS to Michael HOPKINS, Love Lane & St. formerly Thornton's.
<148:93> - 19 Apr. 1785, Caleb HOPKINS from William HARRIS, mortgage.
<154:5> - 1 Dec. 1785, Capt. Caleb HOPKINS of Malden, from Benjamin DOLBEARE, Ship St. way & Salutation Alley.
<154:7> - 2 Dec. 1785, Caleb HOPKINS & wf Bethiah of Malden, to Benjamin DOLBEAR, mortgage to above. Discharged 26 May 1786.
<153:230> - 1787, Mary HOPKINS, widow et al
<163:164> - 10 Sept 1788, Caleb HOPKINS from Samuel DASHWOOD, Marlborough St. incl. passageway.
<163:165> - 11 Sept 1788, Caleb HOPKINS, merchant of Boston & wf Mary to Ann DASHWOOD, Marlborough St. incl. passageway.
<166:193> - 26 Aug. 1789, Caleb HOPKINS from Thomas C. VERNON, north part of Boston.
<175:19> - 13 Feb. 1793, Caleb HOPKINS to Robert ALLCOCK, Salutation Alley.
<178:46> - 10 Jan. 1794, Michael HOPKINS & wf Joanna sell real estate on Love Lane.
<179:196> - 5 Jan. 1795, John DUGGAN & wf Mary to Daniel ENGLISH. (Same day English sold it back to Duggan.)
<184:4> - 4 Aug. 1796, Caleb HOPKINS, gent. from William TUDOR, Hanover St. & highway leading to Sudbury St.
<189:107> - 7 Feb. 1798, Caleb HOPKINS from Peter SIGOURNEY et al, Back St. & passageway.
<189:108> - 7 Feb. 1798, Caleb HOPKINS & wf Mary to Peter SIGOURNEY, Back St. & passageway.
<189:157> - 8 Mar. 1798, Michael HOPKINS, grantee.
<193:163> - 10 Dec. 1799, Mary HOPKINS, widow of Boston from David WOOD.
<195:86> - 1800, Michael HOPKINS & wf Joanna sell land.
<519:263> - 1844, Caleb HOPKINS of Catskill, exr. of will of Mehitable HOPKINS, singlewoman late of Catskill.
(Note: On another page, written very "roughly" are some of the above, with different dates. I have used the dates from the "neatly" written list.)

MIDDLESEX COUNTY DEEDS: (re: Caleb HOPKINS)

<352:424> - 24 Nov. 1835, Caleb HOPKINS, chaisemaker of Charlestown.
<352:425> - 24 Nov. 1835, Caleb HOPKINS, chaisemaker of Charlestown, "mortgages back".
<367:539> - 1 Dec. 1837, Caleb HOPKINS from Richard ROBINS, the land below.
<367:537> - 1 Dec. 1837, Caleb HOPKINS, trader & wf Elizabeth Augusta, Charlestown mortg. land.
<361:12> - 19 Jan. 1837, Caleb HOPKINS, trader of Charlestown.
<369:280> - 17 Jan. 1838, Caleb HOPKINS & wf Elizabeth Augusta, mortgage.

MIDDLESEX COUNTY DEEDS, cont-d: (re: Caleb HOPKINS)

<369:451> - Oct. 1837, Caleb HOPKINS of Charlestown.
<371:148> - 7 Feb. 1838, Caleb HOPKINS, carpenter & wf Elizabeth Augusta sell land bought 1 Dec. 1837 from Richard ROBINS.

SUFFOLK COUNTY PROBATE: (re: HOPKINS)

1784	Alexander	will	#18210	1884	Charles	will	#70856
1872	Alexander	will	#52315	1888	Charles F.	adm.	#80491
1885	Annie C.	adm.	#73796	1887	Daniel	adm.	#78700
1827	Barnabas	adm.	#28173	1825	Elizabeth	will	#27614
1708	Benjamin	adm.	#3127	1868	Elizabeth A.	adm.	#48568
1791	Caleb	will	#19829	1890	Elizabeth P.	will	#86267
1799	Caleb	will	#21112	1786	Enoch	adm.	#18730
1835	Charles	gdn.	#31097	1875	Fred E.	gdn.	#57090
1875	George F.	gdn.	#57090	1883	Lucy R.	adm.	#70444
1890	George F.	adm.	#84560	1684	Margaret	caveat	#1328
1867	Harry E.	gdn.	#48010	1719	Martyn	adm.	#4141
1854	Henrietta	will	#39152	1823	Mary	will	#26883
1891	Hilliard	adm.	#86865	1815	Michael	adm.	#24768
1860	Huldah	will	#42854	1848	Parthenia	adm.	#35819
1882	Isabella H.	adm.	#53156	1841	Sarah	adm.	#32924
1832	John	adm.	#20946	1864	Sterling A.	adm.	#45530
1835	John	gdn.	#31098	1873	Terrence	will	#53993
1874	John	adm.	#55298	1878	Theophilus	will	#61236
1883	John	adm.	#70519	1792	Thomas	adm.	#19960
1856	Jonathan	adm.	$40758	1821	Thomas	will	#26491
1819	Joseph H.	adm.	#25997	1827	Thomas R.	adm.	#28247
1701	Julian	adm.	#2678	1852	Warren	adm.	#38120
1893	LeRoy D.	adop.	#94530	1827	Zoraida	gdn.	#28450
1875	Lucy B.	adm.	#57089				

Mrs. Mary BRAZIER to **Samuel ADAMS.** <original receipt>
...Boston, 6 Nov. 1821, to tuition her son William B. DUGGAN at $100 per year, $91.50; to fuel 5 months at 25 cents per week, $5.25.; total paid to Samuel ADAMS, $96.75. (Note: Directly under this is the following: "5 May 1827, Tufts letter to Dr. William DUGGAN hiring him as teacher West School District of Medford".)

Will of **Nathaniel HOPKINS**, yeoman of Truro MA. <Barnstable Co.PR>
<9:46>...dated 9 May 1752, mentions wf **Sarah**; sons **Isaac HOPKINS** (executor), **John HOPKINS & Elisha HOPKINS**; daus **Mary SMITH, Sarah SMALLEY, Lydia BRAGDIN, Phebe HOPKINS, Elizabeth HOPKINS & Priscilla HOPKINS**. Pr. 23 June 1752. Inventory taken 26 June 1752. <7:248> Guardianship of chil., 6 July 1752, **Priscilla, Elizabeth, Elisha & John** chose brother **Isaac HOPKINS** as gdn. <12:97> Division, 8 Aug. 1760 by Benjamin COLLINS, Jonathan COLLINS, Anthony SNOW, of real estate of **Isaac HOPKINS, John HOPKINS**, dec'd and **Elisha HOPKINS**, all of Truro.

Estate of **John HOPKINS**, yeoman of Truro MA. <Barnstable Co.PR>
<10:49> 11 Feb. 1760, Stephen SNOW Jr., yeoman of Eastham, app'td admr. <11:139> Guardianship, 18 Mar. 1761, Stephen SNOW of Harwich app'td gdn. of **John HOPKINS**, son of dec'd. <12:80> Inventory taken 18 Feb. 1760; mentions widow and two sisters of dec'd. <12:184> Account of admr., Stephen SNOW of Eastham, 18 Mar. 1761.

Will of **Thomas HOPKINS**, yeoman of Truro MA. <Barnstable Co.PR>
<9:138>...dated 3 Jan. 1754, mentions wf **Deborah**; sons **Samuel HOPKINS & Thomas HOPKINS** (executors); youngest child **Jeremiah HOPKINS**; sons **Michael HOPKINS, Caleb HOPKINS**; daus **Hannah HOPKINS, Rebecca HOPKINS, Apphia HOPKINS, Deborah HOPKINS, Mary HOPKINS & Sarah HOPKINS**. Pr. 5 Feb. 1754. Inventory taken 11 Feb. 1754. <11:50,52> Guardianship 11 July 1759, Constant HOPKINS of Truro app'd gdn. of **Sarah**; Ambrose DYER of Truro app'td gdn. of **Mary**; Ephriam LUMBARD of Truro app'td gdn. of **Caleb**. <9:461> Division 13 Feb. 1760 by Barnabas PAINE, Thomas LUMBARD, James LUMBARD, Anthony SNOW & Joshua FREEMAN; division of meadows with Ambrose DYER, Constant HOPKINS & others holding meadows in common with the heirs of **Thomas HOPKINS** dec'd, viz: one third each to: heirs of **Thomas HOPKINS**; to Ambrose DYER and to Constant HOPKINS. <9:464> Division of real estate, 27 Mar. 1760 to following children: eldest son **Thomas HOPKINS**, 2d son **Samuel HOPKINS**, youngest son **Caleb HOPKINS**, eldest dau **Hannah LEWIS** wf of John of Billingsgate, 2d dau **Rebecca COVIL** wf of Philip of Billingsgate, 3d dau **Apphia HOPKINS**, 4th dau **Deborah HOPKINS**, 5th dau **Mary HOPKINS**, youngest dau **Sarah HOPKINS**.

MICRO #13 OF 18

Will of **Samuel HOPKINS** of Truro MA. <Barnstable Co.PR 53:258>
...dated 12 Oct. 1818...to granddaughters **Sally (Hopkins) BACON & Peggy (Hopkins) BACON** of Boston $20.00...to grandsons **Michael HOPKINS** (executor) & **Samuel HOPKINS**, remainder of estate. Pr. 31 Oct. 1833.

Will of **Thomas HOPKINS**, yeoman of Truro MA. <Barnstable Co.PR 12:164>
...dated 25 June 1761, mentions wf **Keturah** (executrix); eldest daus **Keturah HOPKINS & Sarah Doane HOPKINS** and youngest dau **Thankful HOPKINS** (all under 18); brother **Samuel HOPKINS**; mentions land bought of my brother **John LEWIS** & wf **Hannah** of Eastham. Pr. 1 Sept.1761. Inventory 17 Nov. 1761.

Estate of **Barnabas COOK**, mariner of Marshfield MA. <Plymouth Co.PR #4853>
<14:417> Letter/Bond 18 Nov. 1757, widow **Mercy COOK** & Isaac PHILLIPS app'td admrs. Sureties: Benjamin WHITE, Nathaniel PHILLIPS. Witnesses: Seth BRYANT, David PHILLIPS. <15:32> Inventory taken 23 Nov. 1757 by Abijah WHITE, Nathaniel PHILLIPS & Benjamin WHITE; total personal estate, Ł107; no real estate. <16:108> List of Creditors 1 Sept. 1760: Silvanus SNOW, Josiah KEEN, Samuel LINCOLN, Abijah WHITE, Seth BRYANT, John THOMAS, Dr. HARLOW. <16:188> Account of admrs. 11 Aug. 1761 incl. "porke & bread used by the widdow & children". <16:188> Order to pay creditors the balance of Ł23.15.2 in the admrs' hands.

Estate of **Marcy COOK**, widow of Eastham MA. <Barnstable Co.PR>
<10:105> 29 June 1762, Silvanus SNOW of Eastham app'td admr. <12:288> Inventory of personal estate only. (Richard COOK one of the appraisers.)

Will of **Moses GODFREY**, yeoman of Chatham MA. <Barnstable Co.PR>
<6:306>...dated Feb. 1741/2, mentions wf **Deborah**; sons **Samuel GODFREY** (executor), **Moses GODFREY, David GODFREY, George GODFREY, Benjamin GODFREY, Joshua GODFREY & Richard GODFREY; Caleb, Jonathan & Rebecca**, chil. of dec'd son **Jonathan GODFREY**; dau **Desire RIDER** wf of Nathaniel; dau **Mary NICKERSON** wf of Caleb; to **Deborah BASSET** wf of Thomas with what she hath alredy had; dau **Elizabeth BEARSE** wf of Benjamin. Witnesses: Ann SEARS, Hannah BUCK, Samuel STEWART. <6:307> Pr. 21 May 1743 (one witness ack. 16 May 1743). <6:333> Appraisers app'td 22 May 1743, Inventory completed 8 Aug. 1743. <6:328> Guardianship 14 Sept. 1743, **Benjamin BEARSE**, blacksmith of Chatham, app'td gdn of his children, the grandchildren of **Moses GODFREY**, dec'd, viz: **Jonathan BEARSE** (about 10), **Moses BEARSE** (about 8), **Elizabeth BEARSE** (about 6), **George BEARSE** (about 4) and **Benjamin BEARSE** (about 2). <8:283> Account of exr. mentions his mother's appearell which was inventored, who died after hir husband's decease.

Will of **George GODFREY**, yeoman of Chatham MA. <Barnstable Co.PR>
<13:386>...dated 22 Feb. 1768, mentions wf **Jane**; sons **Richard GODFREY, Benjamin GODFREY, George GODFREY** (executor), **James GODFREY & Jonathan GODFREY**; daus **Marcy BERSS/BEARSE, Martha GODFREY, Sarah GODFREY & Molley GODFREY**; grandchildren **Knowles GODFREY & Mercy GODFREY**, chil of dec'd son **Knowles GODFREY**. Witnesses: Joseph DOANE, Benjamin SHATTUCK, Thomas HAMILTON Jr. <13:387> Pr. 26 Dec. 1768. <4:236> Guardianship 26 Dec. 1768, **George GODFREY**, yeoman of Chatham app'td gdn. of **Jonathan & Molly GODFREY**, chil. of dec'd. <13:393> Inventory taken 7 Jan. 1769. <13:422> Account of **George GODFREY** as admr. on estate of **Knowles GODFREY** as presented by **George GODFREY** exr. of will of first named **George GODFREY** dec'd. <13:550> Inventory taken 13 Oct. 1770 de bonis non, the executor, **George GODFREY** now dec'd. <13:552> 11 Oct. 1770, **Benjamin GODFREY** app'td admr. d.b.n.

Estate of **Knowles GODFREY**, fisherman/seafaring man of Chatham MA. <Barnstable Co.PR>
<10:155> 11 Mar. 1766, **George GODFREY**, yeoman of Chatham app'td admr. <13:226> Inventory taken 26 Mar. 1766. <14:115,116> Guardianship 11 Mar. 1766, **George GODFREY** app'td gdn. of **Knowles GODFREY & Mercy GODFREY**, chil. of dec'd.

MICRO #14 OF 18

James COOK et al to **Barzillai HIGGINS** of Provincetown MA. <Barnstable Co.Deeds "folio 110">
...16 Oct. 1826, James COOK, Isaac COOK, David BROWN, James SPARKS, Deliverance HILL, Thomas RIDLEY, heirs of John COOK, heirs of Josiah COOK and Isaiah AITKINS, all of Provincetown, mariners, for $300.00 sell to Barzillai HIGGINS, mariner...a dwelling house in Provincetown bounded by land of David BROWN & Benjamin RIDER. Witnesses: Thomas HILLYARD, Lewis L. SMITH. Rec. 8 Jan. 1827.

Will of **Solomon COOK** of Provincetown MA. <Barnstable Co.PR>
<40:197>..dated 9 Feb. 1809, mentions wf **Katherine**; sons **Paran Cowell COOK** (eldest son, executor) **Solomon COOK & Joshua COOK**; dau **Rebecca KILBURN** wf of David of Buckstown, Hancock co.; grandchildren, **Polly AREY, Thomas KILBURN & David KILBURN**, chil. of dau **"Betsy" KILBURN** wf of sd David. <40:234> Inventory. <41:62> Letter. <38:462> Dower & division. <38:460> Account. <43:107,163> Settlement.

Will of **Paran Cowel COOK** of Provincetown MA. <Barnstable Co.PR 48:409;56:177,212>
...dated 17 Sept. 1834...to wf **Hannah**, all estate; son **Newcomb COOKE** (executor); to chil. of my two dec'd daus **Seviah HOLMES & Betsey SOPER**, but one share of my property (after my wife's death) between the two families...to eldest dau **Hannah YOUNG &** dau **Salome DYER**, widow, my pew #20 in the Methodist meetinghouse in this town. Witnesses: Stephen HILLYARD, Philip COOK 2d, John E. RISLEY, Newcomb COOK & Thomas COOK. Codicil 14 Oct. 1834 (same bequest of pew). Will presented 2d Tues. Dec. 1834. Pr. 23 Apr. 1835.

Heirs of **Paran Cowel COOK**, mariner of Provincetown MA. <Barnstable Co.Deeds 27:429>
...27 Apr. 1837, Newcomb COOK, Thomas COOK, Salome DYER widow, Isaiah YOUNG, Elisha YOUNG Jr., John YOUNG, Reuben YOUNG, Henry YOUNG, Elisha YOUNG as gdn. for Saviah H. YOUNG minor dau of Elisha YOUNG & Hannah YOUNG his late wife dec'd, Robert SOPER, John SWIFT & wf Betsey C. SWIFT, Samuel SOPER gdn. for Lucy H. SOPER & Samuel T. SOPER chil. of Samuel SOPER & Betsey SOPER his dec'd

wf, all of Provincetown and Naoman B. HOLMES and Elisha HOLMES, gdn. for Saviah HOLMES dau of Elisha HOLMES & Saviah HOLMES his dec'd wf of Quincy...all heirs at law of Paron C. COOK, dec'd, for $2000.00 sold to Lydia STULL dau of George STULL and who now lives with Obed WYER, all of Provincetown...land in Provincetown bounded by the county road and land of Joshua COOK, Thomas COOK, Isaiah YOUNG, heirs of Benjamin DYER dec'd...to the northwest corner of the dwelling house formerly occupied by sd Paron C. COOK...also a tract of land with a store thereon, situated on the south of the aforesd premises...bounded by the sea shore and land of the heirs of sd Benjamin DYER...the sd Lydia STULL...shall forever allow Thomas COOK & Isaiah YOUNG, their heirs...the privilege of a landing at the sea shore...also a pass way acrost sd premises as described in their deed from the aforesd Paron C. COOK. Witnesses: Asa ATKINS, John ATKINS, Asa S. BOWLEY & Lemuel BRACKETT. Ack. 23 May 1837, Norfolk co. by Elisha HOLMES. Ack. by rest (except Naoman B. HOLMES) 27 Apr. 1837. Rec. 7 Apr. 1842.

Heirs of **Elisha HOLMES** of Provincetown MA to **Ebenezer HOLWAY** of same. <Barnstable Co.Deeds 34:30> ...26 Feb. 1844, Naoman/Naaman B. HOLMES, James BRADFORD & wf Saviah C. BRADFORD, all of Quincy, heirs at law of Elisha HOLMES dec'd, for $80.00 sold to Ebenezer HOLWAY, carpenter...land in Proincetown bounded by land occupied by Reuben GOODSPEED and land of the heirs of sd Elisha HOLMES.. 57'x 79'x 55'x 61'. Sibel HOLMES wf of sd Elisha and Sylva HOLMES wf of sd Naoman, release dowers Witnesses: Benjamin RICHARDS, John BELCHER Jr. Ack. Norfolk co., same day. Rec. 6 May 1844. (Note: three deeds are cited for these same grantors with no details, viz: <34:465;37:142> 5 Nov. 1844 and <37:331> 4 Apr. 1844.)

BARNSTABLE COUNTY DEEDS: (re: Paran C. COOK)

<5:219> - 19 Nov. 1831, Paran C. COOK, mariner of Provincetown & wf Hannah to Thomas COOK, mariner of same. Ack. same day.
<10:198> - 3 May 1832, Paran C. COOK, yeoman of Provincetown & wf Hannah to Rufus CONANT, merchant of same. Ack. same day.
<12:132> - 30 Mar. 1833, Paran C. COOK, gent. of Provincetown & wf Hannah to Isaiah YOUNG, mariner of same. Ack. 5 Apr. 1833 by Paran.
<15:130> - 22 Dec. 1832, Newcomb COOK (for Paran C. COOK) et al sell land.

James FITCH of Plainfield CT to **Maziah HARDING & Richard COOK** of Eastham MA.<Plainfield CT Deeds> <1:1>...27 Jan. 1701/2, James FITCH sells to Maziah HARDING & Richard COOK...1000 acres in Plainfield. Witnesses: Elisha PAINE, Samuel KNOWLES. Ack. same day in Barnstable Co. Rec. 1 Apr. 1702.

Richard COOK of Eastham MA to **Elisha PAINE** of same. <Plainfield CT Deeds 1:2> ...12 Mar. 1701/2, Richard COOK, husbandman, sells to Elisha PAINE...500 acres in Plainfield being half of 1000 acres he had bought of Maj. James FITCH of Plainfield in partnership with Maziah HARDING by deed of 27 Jan. 1701/2. Witnesses: Thomas MULFFORD, Jonathan HIGGINS. Ack. same day in Barnstable Co. Rec. 4 Aug. 1702.

Heirs of **Jedediah SMITH** of Eastham MA. <original, owned 1905 by George A. SMITH of Dorchester> ...6 June 1818, Nehemiah SMITH, Davis SMITH & Dean SMITH, mariners of Eastham, and Philip COOK & wf Anna, Richard ATKINS, mariner & wf Polly and Nabby SMITH, of Provincetown, quitclaim to Richard SMITH, mariner...all the real estate that was set off to our mother Jedediah SMITH late of Eastham dec'd...also one third of dwelling house she occupied in Eastham bounded...by land of (Na)thaniel NICKERSON & Silvanus SMITH...and is the land our grandfather Simeon SMITH's dwelling house formerly stood on...also cedar swamp bounded by land of Silvanus SMITH, Nathaniel NICKERSON ...also one third of dwelling house that formerly belonged to her husband Nehemiah SMITH...also one third of cleared land and orchard. Witnesses: Samuel FREEMAN, Isaac HOPKINS. Rec. 23 Jan. 1833 at Barnstable Co.Deeds, 9:102.

Josiah MYRICK of Eastham MA to **Deacon Elisha SMITH** of same. <original, owned 1905 by G. SMITH> ...2 Dec. 1790, Josiah MYRICK, yeoman sells to Deacon Elisha SMITH...my share woodland on Higgins Neck so called which came to me by my father Josiah MYRICK late of Eastham dec'd, adjoining my brothers William & Joseph MYRICK's woodland. Witnesses: John DOANE, Nehemiah SMITH. Not rec.

Will of **John TAYLOR**, cordwinder of Eastham MA. <Barnstable Co.PR 12:94-96> ...dated 3 Feb. 1747, mentions unnamed wife; sons **John TAYLOR** (executor) **& Edward TAYLOR**; grandsons **Solomon LEWIS & John LEWIS**; dau **Mary LEWIS** who lives with him; daus **Anne TAYLOR & Abigail TAYLOR**; mentions wood lot he bought of his Father HOPKINS in the 17th Lot Purchase. Witnesses: Joshua HOPKINS, Jonathan HIGGINS Jr. & Enos KNOWLES. Pr. 5 Aug. 1760, all three witnesses made oath. Inventory taken 27 Aug. 1760 & sworn to by exr.

MICRO #15 OF 18

Will of **Elisha HOPKINS**, yeoman of Chatham MA. <Barnstable Co.PR> <6:207>...dated 29 Jan. 1741/2, mentions wf **Experience**; sons **John HOPKINS, Elisha HOPKINS & Bazillah HOPKINS**; daus **Elizabeth GODFREE** wf of Benjamin, **Mary HOPKINS & Experience HOPKINS**; wf & son **John**, executors. Pr. 8 Mar. 1741/2. Inventory presented 10 May 1742 by exrs. <6:356> Guardianship 28 Dec. 1743, **Joshua HOPKINS**, yeoman of Eastham, app'td gdn. of **Experience & Barzilla**; <6:357> same day **Elisha HOPKINS** chooses his uncle **Joshua HOPKINS** as his gdn. <6:409> Account 13 May 1745 of **Experience OSBOURN** (formerly **Experience HOPKINS**) & **John HOPKINS**, exrs.; incl. "keeping & clothing my mother 10 mths." <6:411> 2nd Account 9 Oct. 1745.

Will of **Joshua HOPKINS**, yeoman of Eastham MA. <Barnstable Co.PR 11:36,54,56> ...dated 15 Nov. 1775, mentions dau in law **Rebecca HOPKINS**, widow of dec'd son **Joshua HOPKINS**; dau **Priscilla HOPKINS**; negro woman Bess; grandsons **Joshua HOPKINS** of Eastham (executor), **John HOPKINS, Elkanah HOPKINS, Elisha HOPKINS & Curtis HOPKINS**; grandaughters **Lydia HIGGINS, Rebecca HOPKINS, Mary KINNEY, Mary HOPKINS & Abigail HOPKINS.** Pr. 11 Apr. 1780. Inventory 12 Apr. 1780.

Estate of **Dean SMITH**, yeoman of Chatham MA. <Barnstable Co.PR> <4:506,566> 18 Mar. 1729, Samuel SMITH, yeoman & Hester SMITH, spinster, both of Chatham, app'td admrs. <4:567> Inventory taken 21 Apr.1730 by Thomas DOANE, John COLLEN & Thomas NICKERSON Jr.; incl. houslot & medow att town, Ŀ200; land joining to Melit GODFRY's in Chatham with rite at the beach, Ŀ360; wood lot in Chatham, Ŀ8; part of wood lot in Harwich, Ŀ8.10s & meadow, Ŀ14. <4:568> Dower set off 23 Apr. 1731 to widow...being left with four small children to bring up.

Estate of **Asaph SMITH** of Harwich MA. <Barnstable Co.PR> <7:241> 23 June 1752, Lot GRAY of Harwich app'td admr. <9:501> Receipt of heirs, 21 Mar. 1763, **Eleazer CROSBY, Easter CROSBY, Dean SMITH & Heman SMITH** have received of Lot GRAY.

Estate of **Dean SMITH** of Harwich MA. <Barnstable Co.PR> <10:69> 27 Sept. 1760, Jonathan LINNELL, yeoman of Harwich, app'td admr. <12:109> Inventory taken 7 Sept. 1760. <11:163-67> Guardianship 20 June 1761, Jonathan LINNELL app'td gdn. of minor chil. of dec'd, **Martha SMITH & Edward SMITH** & Thomas KENDRICK, yeoman of Harwich app'td gdn. of **Asaph SMITH, Easter SMITH & Rachel SMITH.** <12:210> Dower set off, 29 July 1761, to the widow **Mrs. Rachel LINNEL.** <13:464> Division 3 May 1769, among the remaining children, viz: **Asaph SMITH, Edward SMITH, Martha SMITH, Esther SPARROW & Rachel SMITH.**

Will of **John SMITH**, carpenter of Eastham MA. <Barnstable Co.PR 13:288> ...23 Oct. 1766, mentions wf **Lydia SMITH**; sons **Reuben SMITH, Benjamin SMITH**; daus **Elizabeth ROGERS, Mehitable BAKER, Rhoda NICORSEN/NICKERSON**; son **Thomas SMITH**; wife & son **Reuben**, executors. Witnesses: Benjamin HIGGINS, Giddeon(sp) SMITH, Nathaniel SNOW. Pr. 14 Apr. 1767.

Solomon HIGGINS of Orleans MA to **Azariah SNOW** of same. <Barnstable Co.Deeds 41:331> ...2 Feb. 1847, Solomon HIGGINS, mariner, for $96.00, sold to Azariah SNOW, yeoman...all the real estate which Thomas ROGERS of New Orleans conveyed to me 15 Jan. 1847...consisting of a house, cleared land, peat swamp, meadow and wood land, partly in Orleans & partly in Brewster. Wf Olive S. HIGGINS releases dower. Ack. same day by Solomon. Rec. 9 Mar. 1847.

Will of **Seth SMITH**, yeoman of Chatham MA. <Barnstable Co.PR> <26:253>...dated 23 Mar. 1787...to son **Hugh SMITH**...all my estate...to son **Seth SMITH**, Ŀ18 in two years, also my blue coat & black jacket & my silver shoebuckles; children of dec'd dau **Mary NICKERSON**; dau **Elizabeth MAYO** wf of Moses; grandchild **Abigail SNOW** wf of Aaron; dau **Zillah PAINE** wf of Miller; son **Hugh**, executor. Witnesses: John EMERY Jr., Seth HARDING, Isaac SMITH. <24:11> Pr. 2 May 1787, on testimony of EMERY & HARDING.

Will of **Eldredge SMITH**, mariner of Provincetown MA. <Barnstable Co.PR #2547> ...dated 5 Mar. 1839, mentions wf **Experience**; daus **Maria ATWOOD** wf of Nathaniel, **Mary H. SMITH**; sons **Jonathan E. SMITH, Heman M. SMITH, Robert E. SMITH, Eldredge F. SMITH**; son in law **Nathaniel ATWOOD**, executor. Petition of heirs, 24 Oct. 1849 that **Nathaniel ATWOOD** be app'td admr.; signed by the six above mentioned children with **Mary H. SMITH** now **Mary H. NICKERSON** wf of **Timothy E. NICKERSON.** Pr. 2 Nov. 1849.

Estate of **Stephen SMITH**, yeoman of Chatham MA. <Barnstable Co.PR> <10:156> 11 Mar. 1766, son **George SMITH**, yeoman of Chatham, app'td admr. <13:225> Inventory taken 18 Mar. 1766 by Nathan BASSET, Samuel COLLINS, Paul CROWELL; incl. dwelling house & other buildings, Ŀ53.12; wood lot, 54 acres, Ŀ54; meadow & upland att the muddy cove & meadow at Strong Island, Ŀ30.13s4d; 15 acre homestead lot plus 23 acres west of sd lot, Ŀ53.6s8d; total estate, Ŀ283.12s5d. <14:146-7> Guardianship 6 May 1766, **George SMITH** app'td gdn. of **James SMITH & Phebe SMITH**, minor chil. of dec'd.

Will of **Capt. Elijah SMITH**, yeoman of Barnstable MA <Barnstable Co.PR> <38:7>...dated 15 July 1801, mentions wf **Mary**; sons **Solomon SMITH** (executor), **James SMITH, David SMITH & Reuben SMITH**; daus **Hannah ELDRIDGE** wf of Stephen, **Susanna TAYLOR** wf of James, to the children of dau **Lettes KNAP**, viz: $30 to **Gilbert KNAP**, $1 apiece to the rest; daus **Elizabeth HOWES** wf of Enoch, **Molly HOWES** wf of Benjamin and **Sarah HOWES** wf of Isaac. Witnesses: Asa CROCKER John GORHAM & Henry GORHAM. <32:30> Pr. 14 Dec. 1801. <31:41> Inventory taken 11 Jan. 1803. <25:708> Guardianship 14 Dec. 1802, son **Reuben SMITH** chose **Isaac HOWES**, mariner of Barnstable, as gdn

---

MICRO #16 OF 18

Estate of **James SMITH**, yeoman of Barnstable MA. <Barnstable Co.PR> <42:550> 8 Jan. 1833, **James SMITH**, yeoman of Barnstable app'td admr. <52:481> Inventory, 10 Jan. 1833 ("much land", no details given). <39:202> Allowance, 12 Feb. 1834, to widow, $400.00. <52:541> Account, 18 Apr. 1834. <56:75> Dower, 24 May 1834 to widow **Susannah SMITH**; "Polly SMITH owned one quarter of pew & sd dec'd three quarters". <56:78> Division 24 May 1834, to children, viz: **James SMITH, Stephen SMITH, Rebecca SCUDDER** wf of Edward, all three heirs now of age; and to the four minor heirs, viz: **Bethiah SMITH, Susan Davis SMITH, Mary Ann SMITH & George Lewis SMITH.** <56:74> Final Account, 13 Feb. 1835.

==========

Will of **Thomas HAMILTON**, gent. of Chatham MA. <Barnstable Co.PR>
<17:18>...dated 9 Apr. 1772, mentions wf **Rebecca**; daus **Lydia HAMILTON, Mary SAUNDERS, Rebecca SMITH, Jane SMITH, Zurviah SMITH & Dalilah COLEMAN**; sons **Thomas HAMILTON & Nathaniel HAMILTON...** if dau **Lydia** should be incapable of labor my two sons shall bear their equal share of her support while they are able, so she shall not become a Town charge; both sons, executors. Witnesses: Thomas HAMILTON Jr., Richard SEARS, James NICKERSON. Pr. 12 May 1772 by **Nathaniel HAMILTON & Thomas HAMILTON Jr.**, exrs. <17:20> Inventory taken 2 June 1772 by Paul SEARS, Thomas HAMILTON, Richard SEARS; incl. meadow at Great Beach, Ł24; meadow at Little Beach, Ł21; land north & east of barn, Ł140; half the dwelling house, Ł6; Benjamin BASSETT's time till he is 21, Ł5.6.8d.

==========

Guardianship of Children of **Mary SMITH**, dec'd widow of Eastham MA. <Barnstable Co.PR; MD 15:177>
<6:28> 22 June 1741, Joseph SMITH, cordwainer of Eastham, app'td gdn. of **Mary HICKMAN**...with full power to take into custody such part & portion of estate as accrues to her in right of her Grandfather **Joshua HOPKINS** late of Eastham dec'd; <6:29> same for **Bashua SMITH**, <6:30> **Samuel SMITH** and <6:31> **Huldah SMITH.**

==========

Will of **Samuel SMITH**, Esq. of Wellfleet MA. <Barnstable Co.PR 13:367-8>
...dated 18 Apr. 1768, mentions wf **Sarah**...also what houshold goods she brought into my estate before the death of her Honoured Father; heirs of dec'd son **Zoheth SMITH**, viz: **Zoheth SMITH, Richard SMITH, Elizabeth SMITH, Samuel SMITH & Ruth SMITH**; heirs of dec'd dau **Bathsheba ATWOOD**, viz: **Abigail ATWOOD, Martha ATWOOD, John ATWOOD, William ATWOOD, Bathsheba ATWOOD, Thankful ATWOOD, Anna ATWOOD & Zoheth ATWOOD**; heirs of dec'd dau **Martha RICH**, viz: **Martha RICH & Abigail YOUNG**; daus **Abigail ELDREDGE** wf of Jesse & **Susanna ATWOOD**; son **Joseph SMITH.** Pr. 11 Oct. 1768.

==========

Guardianship of Children of **Zoheth SMITH** of Eastham MA. <Barnstable Co.PR>
...29 June 1748, **Zoheth SMITH**, gent., is app'td gdn. of his children, the grandchildren of Deacon **John RICH** of Eastham dec'd, they to receive such part & portion of estate as accrues in right of sd Grandfather...<7:63> App'td gdn. of **Zoheth SMITH**; <7:64> **Richard SMITH** and <7:65> **Samuel SMITH**

==========

Heirs of **Seth HOPKINS**, mariner of Wellfleet MA. <Barnstable Co. Deeds 84:82>
...20 Feb. 1793, **Elizabeth HOPKINS**, spinster widow of **Seth HOPKINS**, together with **Benjamin HOPKINS, Solomon HOPKINS & Theophilus HOPKINS**, mariners of Wellfleet and **Hannah HOLBROOK, Sarah RICH Elizabeth MURRY, Rachel BAKER & Deliverance ATWOOD** spinster, all of Wellfleet, being the widow & children of sd **Seth HOPKINS** dec'd, quit claim to **Giles HOPKINS**, son of dec'd...all rights to two thirds of the homestead estate that was our Father **Seth HOPKINS'** which he purchased of Jonas CAHOON & Samuel SMITH, Esq....for the sum of Ł34.7s to be paid in the following manner...he to pay all debts of the dec'd with any remaining money to be divided among the sd children with **Giles** himself receiving one share...the other third together with several other pieces of land as yet undivided is reserved by us for the use & comfortable support of our Honored mother the widow **Elizabeth HOPKINS**...two thirds of eighteen acres being twelve acres...to the sd **Giles.** Signed by **Elizabeth HOPKINS, Benjamin HOPKINS, Jermimiah HOPKINS, Solomon HOPKINS, Hannah HOPKINS, David HOLBROOK, Elizabeth MURRY, Theophilus HOPKINS, Thankful HOPKINS, David BAKER Jr., Rachel BAKER, Freeman ATWOOD, Deliverance ATWOOD, Isaac RICH & Sarah RICH.** Witnesses: Samuel WATERMAN, Joseph HIGGINS. Ack. 9 Sept. 1794 by **Freeman ATWOOD**; 12 July 1794 by **Benjamin & Solomon HOPKINS** and 22 Jan. 1794, by rest. Rec. 20 Nov. 1794. (Source is also recorded as Wellfleet Rec. 1:283.)

==========

Will of **Joseph HOPKINS**, yeoman of Harwich MA. <Barnstable Co.PR 12:439>
...dated 5 Mar. 1771, mentions sons **Isaac HOPKINS, Prince HOPKINS, Jonathan HOPKINS**; dau in law **Mary HOPKINS** widow of dec'd son **Joseph HOPKINS**; daus **Mary FOSTER** wf of Thomas & **Elizabeth ROWLEY**; grandaughters **Phebe MERRICK & Huldah MERRICK**, daus of dec'd dau **Hannah MERRICK**; son **Nathan HOPKINS.** Pr. 9 May 1771. <13:453> Inventory taken 13 Aug. 1771.

==========

Guardianship of Grandchildren of **Deacon Edmund FREEMAN** of Harwich MA. <Barnstable Co.PR>
<15:250> 9 July 1776, **Jonathan HOPKINS** of Harwich app'td gdn. of his son **Edmund HOPKINS**, grandson of Deacon Edmund FREEMAN dec'd; <15:254> 9 July 1776, **Mary FREEMAN** of Harwich app'td gdn. of **Scotto HOPKINS**, grandson of sd Deacon.

MICRO #17 OF 18

Will of **Judah HOPKINS**, yeoman of Harwich MA. <Barnstable Co.PR 8:354; MD 15:117>
...dated 20 Jan. 1747...to wf **Hannah**, half of land...to dau **Rebecca HOPKINS**, half of land...to dau **Hannah**, a feather bed...to son **Judah HOPKINS** (executor), land near his son **Judah**'s dwelling house; grandson **Jonah/Josiah HOPKINS**; sons **Silvanus HOPKINS, Stephen HOPKINS**; daus **Martha/Mercy LEWIS, Martha PADDOCK.** Pr. 7 Mar. 1748. Inventory 12 Mar. 1748.

==========

Estate of **John HOPKINS** of Harwich MA. <Barnstable Co.PR 5:346>
Inventory taken 19 Mar. 1738/9; sworn to 26 Apr. 1739 by Joseph CROSBY, admr. Account (no date), mentions allowance to widow **Mehitable HOPKINS.** 27 Feb. 1739, Joseph CROSBY, admr., represents the estate is insolvent. 30 July 1740, creditors allowed 2s10d3p on the pound.

==========

Estate of **Judah HOPKINS**, yeoman of Harwich MA. <Barnstable Co.PR>
<10:107> 6 July 1762, Elisha CLARK, yeoman of Harwich, app'td admr. <12:318> Inventory taken 29

July 1762. <12:395> Division of real estate, 12 Mar. 1763, mentions widow's thirds. <13:60> Account of admr., 30 Oct. 1765. <14:2> Guardianship, 4 May 1763, Nathaniel MIRICK, yeoman of Harwich app'td gdn. of **Tabitha HOPKINS & John HOPKINS**; 9 May 1763, Nathaniel MIRICK of "Eastham" is app'td gdn. of **Mercy HOPKINS**.

Will of **Timothy LEWIS** of Sunderland/Manchester VT. <no source>
...dated 1 May 1813, mentions daus **Martha LEWIS, Rebecca LEWIS**; sons **Isaac LEWIS, Timothy LEWIS**; daus **Sarah CENTER, Adnah CLARK, Elizabeth TRYALL, Mary DAVIS**; son **John LEWIS**. Pr. 6/8 Jul 1818.

BARNSTABLE COUNTY PROBATE: (re: MAKER)

1725	James	Harwich	4:220-223	1787	Benjamin Jr.	Harwich	25:7,361;26:306-7, 523,546
1763	David	Eastham	10:127;13:36				
1781	Benjamin	Harwich	19:51;21:143-4,197	1820	James	Harwich	36:471
				1831	Bortin	Harwich	42:463

Will of **Nathaniel HOPKINS**, yeoman of Harwich MA. <Barnstable Co.PR 13:246>
...dated 25 Mar. 1765...in an advanced age; mentions wf **Mercy**; daus **Elizabeth CROSBY, Mercy WHITE** sons **Nathaniel HOPKINS, David HOPKINS, Reuben HOPKINS, Theophilus HOPKINS** (executor); grandchildren **James & Mercy**, chil of dec'd son **Samuel HOPKINS**. Pr. 21 Oct. 1766.

Will of **Reuben HOPKINS**, yeoman of Harwich MA. <Barnstable Co.PR 13:289>
...dated 20 Mar. 1767, mentions wf **Elizabeth** (executrix); son **Rowland HOPKINS**; daus **Lucy & Lydia**; dec'd father **Nathaniel HOPKINS**. Pr. 13 Apr. 1767.

Will of **Samuel HOPKINS** of Harwich MA. <Barnstable Co.PR>
<12:279>...dated 25 Feb. 1761...everything to wf **Mehitable** unless she marries. Pr. 16 Mar. 1762. <14:166,167> Guardianship, 11 Nov. 1766, Reuben RIDER of Chatham app'td gdn. of **James HOPKINS & Mercy HOPKINS**, chil. of dec'd.

Estate of **Moses HOPKINS**, yeoman of Harwich MA. <Barnstable Co.PR>
<10:178> 21 Oct. 1766, widow **Hannah HOPKINS**, app'td admx. <13:417> Inventory taken 20 Nov. 1766 by Chillingsworth FOSTER, Edmund FREEMAN & Theophilus BERRY. Account 11 Apr. 1768 of admx.; Debts to: Benjamin BANGS, Nathaniel STONE, Esq., John SEYMORE, Silvanus CROSBY, Moses MAYO, George WATSON, Nathan MAYO, Ichabod SEABURY, Nathaniel SNOW, Theophilus HOPKINS, David BANGS, Nathan HOPKINS, Nathaniel CROSBY, Lemuel BERRY, Thomas KENWRICK, Jonathan SNOW, Samuel WING, Rebecca SEARS, Enos SNOW, Moses HOPKINS, Benjamin SMALL, Dr. William FESSENDEN, Dr. Thomas SMITH.

Will of **Stephen HOPKINS**, yeoman of Harwich MA. <Barnstable Co.PR 5:112>
...dated 9 Jan. 1732/3, mentions wf **Sarah**; daus **Hannah HOPKINS, Sarah COBB, Rebecca HIGGINS, Thankful LINNELL, Mary SNOW, Phebe BANGS**; sons **Thomas HOPKINS & Ebenezer HOPKINS**, executors. Witnesses: Joseph DOANE, Rebecca PAINE, Desire DOANE who ack. 18 Apr. 1733. Pr. 20 Apr. 1733.

Will of **Jonathan HIGGINS**, yeoman of Eastham MA. <Barnstable Co.PR>
<27:324>...dated 23 May 1791...being advanced in years; mentions grandaughters **Rebecca TAYLOR** (unm.) **& Abigail YOUNG**; great-grandaughters **Rebecca SEARS & Kate SEARS** (both unm.); grandsons **Edward TAYLOR & Benjamin TAYLOR** (executor). <24:103> Pr. 27 Mar. 1792.

Will of **William HOPKINS**, yeoman of Shelter Island NY. <original>
...dated 28 Apr. 1710, mentions son **William HOPKINS**; dau **Hannah HOPKINS**; son **Ephraim HOPKINS**; wf **Rebekah** (executrix); my eight children (unnamed) as they come and be of age. Witnesses: Mary BROWN, John KNOWLINGE, Sarah PAYNE. Pr. 2 Oct. 1718. ("An old bond & deed of gift held now (1920) by S.E.HOPKINS shows that on 4 Apr. 1718, **William HOPKINS Sr.** promised his son **William HOPKINS Jr.** 250 pounds of money on condition that **William Jr.** should make no other claim on the estate as an heir." Witnessed by: John MANEWY(sp), William PAIN, John KNOWLINGE. <In 1920, the original copy of this will (& bond) was in the possession of S.E. HOPKINS, Miller Place, Long Island, NY.>

MICRO #18 OF 18

Will of **Richard WHITEHEAD** of Windsor CT. <NEHGR 44:387>
...dated 23 Apr. 1645, mentions dau in law **Mary LEWIS**. Pr. 26 June 1645 in England.

JOHN HOWLAND

MICRO #1 OF 18

PLYMOUTH COUNTY PROBATE, to 1800: (re: HOWLAND)

1670	Henry	Duxbury		#10918
1672	John	Plymouth		#10932
1692	Joseph	Duxbury		#10939, 1:142,168
1703	Joseph	Plymouth		#10940, 2:43,44,45
1713	Prince	Marshfield		#10955, 3:266,267,464;7:91,92
1713	Prince et al	Marshfield		#10956, 3:267,268,269
1723	Israel Jr.	Middleboro		#10922, 4:388,407
1724	Isaac	Middleboro		#10923, 4:408,409;5:6
1724	Jeremiah et al	Middleboro		#10930, 4:444;7:136,137
1727	Arthur	Marshfield		#10901, 5:389,390,391
1727/8	Elizabeth	Middleboro		#10913, 5:391,392
1729	Seth	Middleboro		#10970, 5:603,640;6:147,148,150 <MD 21:179>
1737	Thomas	Pembroke		#10971, 7:363,369,370;8:181,182
1739	Thomas	Plymouth		#10972, 8:135,139,313,314,316,317;34:338
1745	John	Middleboro		#10934, 9:455
1747	Abraham	Pembroke		#10898, 10:468,470,471
1749	Arthur	Marshfield		#10902, 11:369,371;12:163
1753	Samuel	Pembroke		#10963, 13:59,76;19:431,432
1759	Consider	Plymouth		#10910,15:304,419,421;16:250;19:227-8,375;27:484
1759	Nathan	Middleboro	gdn.	#10949, 15:192
1768	John	Plymouth		#10933, 20:6
1774	Rouse	Pembroke		#10959, 21:628;23:59
1780	Thomas S.	Plymouth		#10973, 27:42
1784	William	Pembroke		#10977, 29:115,116,148,149
1787	Isaac	Middleboro		#10924, 27:253;30:275
1790	Jeremiah	Middleboro		#10929, 27:315;31:107;33:439,440
1793	Patience	Plymouth		#10959, 27:433
1796	Samuel	Plymouth		#10965, 32:45,123;37:229
1797	Arthur	Marshfield		#10903, 34:119;36:143,144,146,147,148
1798	Samuel	Pembroke		#10964, 34:154;36:316;37:235,249
1799	Caleb	Plymouth		#34:194;37:134,267,268

PLYMOUTH COUNTY PROBATE, 1800-1850: (re: HOWLAND)

1802	Jerusha	Marshfield	adm.	#10931, 34:330
1804	John	Carver	will	#10935, 40:134,135,136
1818	Arthur	Marshfield	adm.	#10904, 46:286;49:591,593;50:172,486,565
1818	Jacob	Plymouth	adm.	#10928, 46:344;50:311,312
1818	Sarah P.	Marshfield	gdn.	#10969, 41:380;50:471;79:101
1819	Warren	Pembroke	adm.	#10975, 46:353;50:333;53:355-6;54:278;66:191
1821	Robert	Pembroke	adm.	#10958, 52:50;53:504
1822	Joseph	Hanson	will	#10941, 56:27,30,519;55:108;57:73,74,75,76
1823	Samuel et al	Hanson	gdn.	#10968, 51:207
1825	Samuel	Scipio NY	adm.	#10966, 52:378;55:318;59:275,276,325,504
1826	Ichabod	N.Bridgewater	"	#10920, 61:67;62:130;63:440,441,442
1827	Henry	Plymouth	adm.	#10919, 61:158;62:294;67:503
1828	Charles	Hanson	gdn.	#10908, 65:50;69:82
1828	Jonathan	Hanson	adm.	#10937, 61:231;62:296;66:332,335
1828	Lydia et al	Hanson	gdn.	#10946, 65:44
1829	Ruth	Pembroke	gdn.	#10961, 65:95;67:500,501;68:3;69:25;73:60,146; 78:132;80:6
1832	Isaac	Plymouth	adm.	#10925, 68:345;71:98;74:19,20
1838	Ruth	Pembroke	adm.	#10962, 2:61**O**;10:151**A**;75:515;80:32,223,344,346
1842	Zerujah	Hanson	will	#10979, 10:520**A**;84:234
1846	Ichabod	Plymouth	adm.	#10921, 1:238**R**;3:44**P**;7:173**V**;11:466**B**;89:21;93:43
1846	Lewis	Hanson	adm.	#10944, 3:38**P**;11:424**B**;88:230-1,368,566;89:258
1846	Warren	Hanson	will	#10976, 2:70**H**;7:135**V**;88:171,173,434;118:568;157: 455;187:347;188:403;193:231;194:584;198:114,485 200:519;202:120
1847	Ethan	Hanson	adm.	#10914, 3:77**P**;7:243**V**;11:522**B**;89:335-6;90:44,204
1848	Deborah C.	Plymouth	gdn.	#10911, 9:166**M**
1849	Celia S.	Pembroke	gdn.	#10907, 9:181**M**;91:217

BARNSTABLE COUNTY PROBATE: (re: HOWLAND, "all to 1837")

1737	Shubael	Barnstable	will	5:370
1738	John	Barnstable	will	5:326,327
1741	Zaccheus	Barnstable	div.	6:48,288
1747	John	Barnstable	will	7:59-62;8:167,168
1751	Isaac	Barnstable	will	8:499-501
1759	Mercy	Barnstable	will	9:417
1765	Jabez	Barnstable	will	13:83,84,137;14:85;17:272;20:45,46
1805	Lemuel	Sandwich	adm.	19:159;35:450,451,453,497,509
1812	Jonathan	Sandwich	adm.	35:548;36:128;37:2
1813	Levina	Sandwich	gdn.	22:469 (non comp)
1814	Joshua	Yarmouth	adm.	36:167;38:475;39:13,57,59
1820	Job P.	Barnstable	adm.	36:464;40:132;43:521,522
1833	James N.	Barnstable	adm.	42:585;48:319;50:216;53:324;56:286
1837	Ansell	Barnstable	will	58:23;60:81;62:38;63:221

Estate of **Thomas HOWLAND** of Pembroke MA. <Plymouth Co.PR #10971>
<7:363> Letter/Bond 2 Jan. 1737, Nehemiah CUSHING of Pembroke app'td admr. Sureties: Ebenezer BARKER, Kenelm WINSLOW. Witnesses: Edward & Mary WINSLOW. <7:369> Warrant for appraisal, 2 Jan. 1737. <7:370> Inventory taken 25 Jan. 1737 by Ebenezer BARKER, Robert BARKER, Samuel JACOBS; no real estate. Widow's allowance, 31 Jan. 1737, to **Mary HOWLAND.** <original> Insolvency 28 Feb. 1737 <8:181> Extension of time for proof of claims, 8 Feb. 1739. <original> Citation 28 Feb. 1737 "and runs to the following - for embezzlement", viz: widow **Mary HOWLAND**, son **Ebenezer HOWLAND** of Pembroke, son **William HOWLAND** of Marshfield, dau **Mrs. Robert BARKER** of Hanover and dau **Mercy HOWLAND** <8:182> Account of admr. 4 Feb. 1739; List of Debts, 8 Aug. 1739: Malitiah BOURN, Esq., Capt. Josiah CARVER, William WITHERELL, John BISHOP, Jabez WHITTAMORE, Oliver EARL, Eliezer FREEMAN, Richard MAYO, Capt. John KNOWLS.

Estate of **Caleb HOWLAND** of Plymouth MA. <Plymouth Co.PR #10905>
<34:194> Letter/Bond 16 July 1799, widow **Mary HOWLAND** of Plymouth & John GRAY of Kingston, app'd admrs. Sureties: Ichabod SHAW & Benjamin ROBBINS of Plymouth. Witnesses: Ephraim EVERSON, Isaac LOTHROP. <37:134> Inventory taken 11 Oct. 1799 by John COBB, Benjamin ROBBINS, Job COBB; total estate, $192.69. <37:268> Account of admrs. 7 July 1800; received of Capt. William STURTEVANT, $11.54; paid to Dr. Zaccheus BARTLETT, $13.17. <37:267> Insolvency 7 July 1800, of admrs. <37: 268> Notice of app'tment of admrs., 7 July 1800. <37:268> Decree, Court finds there is no estate after the allowance of account, therefore no further proceedings can be had.

Guardianship of Children of **Issachar HOWLAND,** dec'd of Plymouth. <Plymouth Co.PR #10965>
<32:45> Letter/Bond 8 June 1796, Caleb HOWLAND app'td gdn. of **Samuel HOPKINS** (under 14), son of **Issachar HOWLAND,** seafaring man, dec'd. Sureties: Ephraim SPOONER & Barnabas HEDGE Jr., both of Plymouth. Witnesses: Nathaniel LOTHROP, Isaac LOTHROP. <32:123> Letter/Bond 18 July 1799, James THACHER app'td gdn. of **Samuel HOWLAND** (under 14). Sureties: N. HAYWARD & William GOODWIN both of Plymouth. Witnesses: Zacheus BARTLETT Jr., Isaac LOTHROP. <37:229> Account, 28 Apr. 1800, of Caleb HOWLAND, dec'd gdn. of **Samuel HOWLAND,** exhibited by the admrs. of **Caleb HOWLAND's** estate, **Mary HOWLAND** and John GRAY; they charge themselves as follows: "by sd ward's dividend in the estate of his grandfather **Joseph MITCHELL** dec'd, by a legacy bequeathed his father in the will of Isaac OLDHAM dec'd, $10.00...to clothing, boarding and schooling sd minor 6 years is 312 wks, $15.12.

Estate of **Patience HOWLAND,** widow of Plymouth MA. <Plymouth Co.PR #10959>
<27:433> Letter/Bond 2 May 1793, Benjamin RIDER app'td admr. Sureties: Josiah COTTON & Elnathan HOLMES Jr. of Plymouth. Witnesses: Priscilla L. BUM, Isaac LOTHROP. <original> Citation 1 Mar. 1792 to Benjamin RIDER Jr...Ephraim SPOONER, Esq. complains that no adm. has been taken out on above estate, Ephraim being a large creditor to sd estate...You are therefore cited to appear and show cause why Ephraim SPOONER should not be app'td admr.

Estate of **Thomas Southworth HOWLAND** of Plymouth MA. <Plymouth Co.PR #10973>
<27:42> Letter/Bond 5 May 1780, Elkanah WATSON, Joshua THOMAS & Consider HOWLAND, all of Plymouth app'td admrs. Sureties: William THOMAS, Isaac LeBARON. Witnesses: Isaac & Nathaniel LOTHROP.

Estate of **John HOWLAND,** mariner of Plymuth MA. <Plymuth Co.PR #10933>
<20:6> Appointment/Bond 1 Jan. 1768, widow **Patience HOWLAND** app'td admx. Sureties: Ephraim SPOONER, Benjamin DREW. Witnesses: Nathaniel COOPER, Edward WINSLOW Jr.

Estate of **John HOWLAND** of Middleboro MA. <Plymuth Co.PR #10934>
<9:455> Letter/Bond 21 May 1745, widow **Mercy,** alias **Peggy HOWLAND,** Indian woman, app'td admx. Sureties: Peter THACHER & Samuel THACHER of Middleboro. Witnesses: Otis LITTLE, Edward WINSLOW.

Will of **Abraham HOWLAND** of Pembroke MA. <Plymouth Co.PR #10898>
<10:468>...dated 15 June 1747, mentions wf **Ann**; sons **Rouse HOWLAND, Abraham HOWLAND, Samuel HOWLAND, Joseph HOWLAND**...to have a living in my dwelling house, **Benjamin HOWLAND**; daus **Sarah DAWES, Elizabeth BONNEY;** grandchildren **Mary MITCHELL, Jonathan MITCHELL, Howland BEALS.** Witnesses: Nehemiah CUSHING, D. LEWIS, Elizabeth LEWIS. <10:470> Pr. 3 Aug. 1747. <10:471> Bond 3 Aug. 1747, widow **Ann HOWLAND** app'td exx.

Estate of **Samuel HOWLAND** of Pembroke MA. <Plymouth Co.PR #10964>
<34:154> Letter/Bond 31 Mar. 1798, Warren HOWLAND app'td admr. Sureties: Robert HOLMES of Kingston & William WHITE of Pembroke. Witnesses: Ebenezer BONNEY, Isaac LOTHROP. <36:316> Inventory taken 19 Mar. 1798 by Robert HOLMES, Isaac B. BARKER, Levi EVERSON; total real estate, $1620.00; total estate, $2027.89. <37:249> Dower set off, 2 June 1800, to widow **Sarah HOWLAND**...thirty acres, by Isaac Bowen BARKER, Ebenezer BONNEY & Robert HOLMES. <37:235> Account of admr. 21 May 1800; Paid to: Margaret COLE, Levi EVERSON, Nathaniel THOMAS, Micah FOSTER Jr., Nathaniel JONES, Gershom RAMSDELL, Oliver WHITTEN, Samuel RAMSDELL, Bailey HALL, Nathan STEVENS, William DELANO, Josiah CUSHING, William FORD, Gideon Thomas WHITE, Noah BONNEY, Ebenezer BONNEY, John THOMAS, Robert SALMOND, Isaac BEALS, Isaac B. BARKER, Robert HOLMES and "to my note of hand to Ruth HOWLAND for a debt due her $79.50 to one year's interest paid her on sd note".

Will of **William HOWLAND** of Pembroke MA. <Plymouth Co.PR #10977>
<29:115>...dated 3 Mar. 1772...being grown into years...mentions wf **Mercy**, son **William HOWLAND** (executor) and dau **Rebekah KEEN**. Witnesses: Robert BARKER, Gideon BARKER, Robert BARKER Jr. <29:116> Pr. 17 Mar. 1784. <29:148> Warrant for appraisal, 17 Mar. 1784. <29:149> Inventory taken 21 5mth 1784 by Joseph ROGERS, James ROGERS, John BAILEY Jr.; total estate, £364.4.10; incl. notes of hand against James THOMAS & R. HOWLAND; sworn by exr. 3 June 1784.

Estate of **Rouse HOWLAND** of Pembroke MA. <Plymouth Co.PR #10959>
<23:59> Letter/Bond 4 July 1774, Perez HOWLAND app'td admr. Sureties: Increase ROBINSON & Samuel HOWLAND of Pembroke. Witnesses: David KINGMAN, Edward WINSLOW Jr. <21:628> Inventory taken 4 July 1774 by Josiah CUSHING, Increase ROBINSON, Samuel HOWLAND; no real estate inventoried; total estate, £31.2.9.

Estate of **Samuel HOWLAND** of Pembroke MA. <Plymouth Co.PR #10963>
<13:59> Letter/Bond 7 May 1753, Josiah CUSHING app'td admr. Sureties: Edward THOMAS & Daniel HAYFORD of Pembroke. Witnesses: John TOMSON, John LOTHROP. <13:76> Inventory taken 7 May 1753 by Ichabod BONNEY, Daniel HAYFORD, Edward THOMAS; incl. farm & buildings, £253.6.8.; total estate, £329.6.10. <19:431> Division 2 Dec. 1766 by Isaac OLDHAM, Josiah CUSHING, Samuel GOOLD to the widow **Sarah HOWLAND** and children, viz: **Zebulon HOWLAND** (eldest son), **Caleb HOWLAND, Ruth HOWLAND, Samuel HOWLAND, Ichabod HOWLAND, Abigail HOWLAND.** <19:432> Account of admr. 11 Dec. 1766, mentions necessaries set off to the widow.

PLYMOUTH COLONY DEEDS: (re: HOWLAND)

<1:60>	- 26 Dec. 1638,	John HOWLAND from William HOLMES.
<1:62>	- 2 Feb. 1638,	John HOWLAND from John JENNEY.
<1:62>	- 2 Feb. 1638,	John HOWLAND to John JENNEY.
<1:93>	- 2 Apr. 1640,	John HOWLAND to William KEMP, Duxbury.
<1:99>	- 27 July 1640,	Henry HOWLAND of Duxbury from William REYNOLDS.
<1:213>	- 17 Mar. 1645,	John HOWLAND & others to Edmond FREEMAN.
<1:222>	- (no date) ,	John HOWLAND from Joseph ROGERS.
<1:245>	- 20 Jan. 1647,	Arthur HOWLAND, planter of Marshfield from FREEMAN, gent. of Sandwich & PADDY, merchant of Plymouth.
<1:269>	- 8 Mar. 1648,	John HOWLAND of Plymouth from Gov. William BRADFORD.
<1:269>	- 8 Mar. 1648,	John HOWLAND to John GORHAM.
<1:303>	- 14 Mar. 1649,	John HOWLAND & wf Elizabeth to George PARTRIDGE, tailor of Duxbury.
<1:303>	- 7 Mar. 1649,	John HOWLAND to Elizabeth HICKS, wf of Ephraim HICKS, dec'd.

DESIRE HOWLAND[2] (John[1])

BARNSTABLE COUNTY PROBATE: (re: GORHAM)

1707	James	Barnstable	will	3:256,259,674 <MD 13:51>
1715	Isaac & Hezekiah	Yarmouth	adm.	3:196,275
1717	Col. John	Barnstable	will	3:389,391,392 <MD 13:52>
1718	James	Barnstable	will	3:497,498,499
1726	Joseph	Yarmouth	will	4:309,311
1729	John	Yarmouth	will	4:559,560,561
1733	Mary	Barnstable	will	5:110,111 <MD 13:54>
1733	Joseph,	Barnstable	gdn.	5:141 (non comp) & 12:113 (1760)
1739	Sarah	Yarmouth	will	5:377,378
1742	James	Barnstable	will	6:222,223,260,277
1743	Stephen	Barnstable	will	6:343,345
1744	Jonathan	Barnstable	adm.	6:369
1746	Shubael Jr.	Barnstable		8:5,6,134,136,137
1746	William	Barnstable		7:2;8:215
1746	Daniel	Barnstable	will	8:6,7,9,261
1748	Shubael Jr.	Barnstable	adm.	7:123
1749	Shubael	Barnstable	will	7:181;8:265-7;9:501,502 (non comp)

BARNSTABLE COUNTY PROBATE, cont-d: (re: GORHAM)

1753	Isaac	Barnstable	will	7:181;8:265,266,267;9:501,502
1762	Job	Barnstable	will	12:309,310

EDGARTOWN, DUKES COUNTY DEEDS: (re: HAWES)

<2:350> - 3 Mar. 1709, Benjamin HAWES from Samuel SMITH.
<3:372> - 24 Oct. 1718, Benjamin HAWES, gent. of Edgartown app'td commissioner for the county for profagating the Gospel.
<3:369> - 27 July 1719, Benjamin HAWES as arbitrator in land division.
<4:180> - 10 Apr. 1723, Dorcas HAWES, widow of Benjamin.
<6:272> - 14 Jan. 1737, Samuel HAWES of Dartmouth.
<6:326> - 15 May 1738, Samuel HAWES of Dartmouth to Benjamin HAWES.
<8:564> - 6 Oct. 1743, Samuel HAWES & wf Elizabeth of Dartmouth.
<7:523> - 23 Sept 1746, Shubael HAWES of Newport.
<9:606> - 22 Sept 1748, Benjamin HAWES & wf Sarah of Boston.

Will of **Benjamin HAWS/HAWES**, Esq. of Edgartown MA. <Dukes Co.PR>
<1:137>...dated 15 Oct. 1722, mentions wf **Dorcus**...if the unborn child lives she to have Ł5 per annum till it is 6 yrs old for bringing it up...to eldest son **Benjamin HAWES** my silver headed cane and seal ring...to eldest dau **Experience HAWES** my great Bible which was my Mothers...to sons **Benjamin HAWES & Samuel HAWES**...all housing & home lot...& my eleventh part of Chappaquaddick... not to be sold out of the name of the Hawses forever...to sons **Benjamin & Samuel & unborn child** if it be a son all the rest of lands & meadows in Edgartown & on Chappaquiddick & elsewhere..to daus **Experience HAWES & Jedidah HAWES** & the **unborn child** the privilege in the northern chamber & garret in my house & a privilege in the cellar for beer & in the kitchen to wash, brew & bake while they remain single...wf **Dorcas** (executrix) to have sole use of whole estate for bringing up children until the sons reach 21 and the daus 18, provided she remains my widow; friends Benjamin SMITH, Thomas SMITH & Benjamin PEASE, overseers. Witnesses: Daniel GREENLEAF, Shubael GORHAM, Ebenezer HAWES, Desire HAWES. Pr. 28 Nov. 1722. <1:148> Inventory taken 1 Nov. 1723 by Thomas DOGGETT, Thomas HARLOCK; incl. desperate debt, William WHITE et al, 40s; Debts due from estate: Capt. Joseph HAWS/HAWES, Jean LITTLE, Samuel STURGES, Mr. WEALDING; total estate, Ł913.9.2.<2:74> Adm. de bonis non, granted to Benjamin SMITH, Esq. of Edgartown, **Mrs. Dorcas HAWES**, widow & exx. having also deceased. Inventory of remainder taken 14 Feb. 1731/2 by Benjamin PEASE & Daniel DUNHAM; incl. due from Shubael CLAGHORN for ye Indian lad, Ł9.

Dorcas HAWES of Edgartown MA to **Jacob SECKNONT**. <Dukes Co.Deeds 4:180>
...10 Apr. 1723, Indenture between Dorcas HAWES, widow & exx. of will of Benjamin HAWES, Esq. and Jacob SECKNONT in regard to Island of Chappaquiddick.

Samuel SMITH of Edgartown MA to **Benjamin HAWES** of same. <Dukes Co.Deeds 2:350>
...(worn) 1708/9, Samuel SMITH, yeoman, for Ł30 sells to Benjamin HAWES, choardwayner...land & dwelling house in Edgartown, being part of a house lot late in tennure of William WEEKES late of Edgartown dec'd, bounded by house lot late of Thomas BAYER dec'd and east by side of hill near the harbor. Witnesses: Matthew MAYHEW, Enock/Enoch COFFIN. Ack. 3 Mar. 1708/9.

Lieut. John WORTH of Edgartown MA to **Benjamin HAWES** of same. <Dukes Co.Deeds 3:80>
...20 Aug. 1714, John WORTH for Ł20 sells to Benjamin HAWES, lawyer...part of a house lot in Edgartown late in tenure of William WEEKES dec'd, bounded by house lot late of Thomas BAYES dec'd ...excepting what is excepted in a deed I had of Capt. BUTLER dated 13 Aug. 1709. Witnesses: Nicholas BUTLER, Peter RAY. Ack. 10 Sept. 1714 by John & Ann WORTH, & Rec.

Thomas BUTLER of Chilmark MA to **Benjamin HAWES** of Edgartown MA. <Dukes Co.Deeds 3:331>
...5 July 1718, Thomas BUTLER, mariner, for a valuable sum of money, sells to Benjamin HAWES, lawyer...his rights in land at Edgartown bounded by land formerly of Capt. BAYES, west on harbour and land of sd HAWES...being below the bank joining the foot path mentioned in my deeds heretofore & reserved there in my deed to Lieut. John WORTH that sd HAWES has since bought. Witnesses: Mary WORTH, Mary DAGGETT. Ack. 8 July 1718. Rec. 6 July 1718.

Samuel HAWS/HAWES of Dartmouth MA to **Enoch COFFIN** of Edgartown MA. <Dukes Co.Deeds 6:272>
...14 June 1737, Samuel HAWES, house carpenter, for Ł13.6s8d, sells to Enoch COFFIN, Esq...one sixth of a share of meadow & common in Chappaquiddick in Edgartown which derived to me from my honoured father Benjamin HAWES late of Edgartown dec'd by his last will. Witnesses: Simeon BUTLER & Israel SWIFT. Ack. 15 June 1737. Rec. 1 July 1737.

Samuel HAUS/HAWES of Dartmouth MA to **Benjamin HAUS/HAWES** of Edgartown MA. <Dukes Co.Deeds 6:326>
...15 May 1738, Samuel HAWES, house carpenter & wf Elizabeth, for Ł50 sell to brother Benjamin HAWES, mariner...half part of a dwelling in Edgartown near the harbor...which formerly belonged to our Honoured father Benjamin HAWS/HAWES, Esq. dec'd...to be equally divided between my brother and myself...also one fourth part of two pews in the meeting house in Edgartown formerly owned by our dec'd father and John NORTON dec'd...which half part of sd pews was equally given to my sd brother & myself by our Father. Witnesses: Mary SMITH, Jedidah SMITH. Ack. 19 May 1738 by Samuel & Elizabeth and Rec.

Samuel HAWS/HAWES of Dartmouth MA to **John SUMNER** of Edgartown MA. <Dukes Co.Deeds 8:564> ...6 Oct. 1743, Samuel HAWES, housewright & wf Elizabeth, for Ł11.5s, sell to John SUMNER, gent.. five rights on Chappaquiddick, i.e. one fifth part of ye eight part of ye grass & herbage that doth or ever shall grow on sd Island as it is now improved, i.e. from ye 20th Oct. untill the 25th Mar. yearely...which rights were received from father Benjamin HAWS, late of Edgartown, dec'd which he bought of Jacob SEICKNONETT, Indian Sachem of sd Island. Witnesses: Susanna MENDAL & Isaac SPOONER. Ack. 19 Oct. 1743 by Samuel & Elizabeth. Rec. 22 Feb. 1758.

Shobal HAWS/HAWES of Newport RI to **Enoch COFFIN** of Edgartown MA. <Dukes Co.Deeds 7:523> ...23 Sept. 1746, Shobal HAWES, cordwainer, for Ł16 sells to Enoch COFFIN, Esq...one sixth part of the whole & compleat shear of meadow & comon on Chappaquiddick, received from my father Benjamin HAWS of Edgartown by his will. Witnesses: Thomas WEST, Enoch COFFIN Jr. Ack. same day. Rec. 28 Oct. 1746.

Benjamin HAWES of Boston MA to **Eleazer FLAGG** of same. <Dukes Co.Deeds 9:606> ...22 Sept. 1748, Benjamin HAWES, mariner & wf Sarah, mortgage to Eleazer FLAGG, innholder...all his rights in Chappaquiddick & all other rights in the estate of his father Benjamin HAWES dec'd, for loan of Ł75. Witnesses: Thomas PEMBERTON, Richard CODMAN. Ack. same day by Benjamin & Sarah. Rec. 27 Aug. 1768.

Samuel & Shubal HAWS/HAWES of Dartmouth MA to **Ephraim PEASE et al** of Edgartown. <Dukes Co.Deeds> <9:525>...14 Sept. 1765, Samuel HAWES, carpenter & Shubal HAWES, husbandman, for Ł25.10s sell to Ephraim PEASE, mariner and Abraham PREBLE, mariner...three acres in Edgartown bounded by land of John HARPER, John BUTLER, David NORTON, heirs of Joseph BUTLER dec'd and the harbor...which was the house lot of Benjamin HAWS, Esq. of Edgartown dec'd and from him descended to us. Witnesses: John NORTON, John PEASE Jr. Ack. same day. Rec. 22 Mar. 1766.

EDGARTOWN, DUKES COUNTY DEEDS: (re: CLAGHORN)

<8:213> - 15 Nov. 1752, Elisha AMOS, Indian of Gay head.
<8:296> - 15 June 1753, Mary BRYANT, seamstress of Plymouth to Shubael CLAGHORN Jr., mariner of Chilmark, land in Chilmark.
<8:297> - 31 Jan. 1754, Matthew CLARK & wf Grace of Chilmark to Shubal CLAGHORN, mariner of same land adjoining Shubal's.
<8:356> - 30 Dec. 1754, Joseph COOMES, Indian to Shubael CLAGHORN, mariner of Chilimark.
<8:472> - 1 Aug. 1757, Shubal CLAGHORN, mariner of Chilmark, power of atty. to Dr. Matthew MAYHEW of same.
<8:557> - 3 Mar. 1758, Samuel COSHOMON, Indian to Shubal CLAGHORN, mariner of Chilmark.

(Note: Additional citations with no data: 8:363;13:365,366;14:234;15:77,106,215,363.)

Joseph HILLMAN of Chilmark MA to **Shubal CLAGHORN Jr.** of same. <Dukes Co.Deeds> ...17 June 1751, Joseph HILLMAN, husbandman & wf Kesiah, for Ł20.13s4d, sell to Shubal CLAGHORN, Jr., mariner...land in Chilmark. Witnesses: John ALLEN, Samuel HILLMAN.

Micajah MAYHEW et al to **Shubal CLAGHORN** of Chilmark MA. <Dukes Co.Deeds 8:368> ...27 Dec. 1752, Micajah MAYHEW, gent.; Fortunatus MAYHEW, gent., Sarah GOULD, seamstress; William WINPANNEY, tailor & wf Hannah; Solomon DAGGETT, laborer & wf Jean; Matthew CLARK, laborer, all of Chilmark and Isaac COTTLE, laborer & wf Mary of Tisbury; Beriah TILTON of Chilmark as atty for Thomas MAYHEW, dealer of Plymouth...for Ł11 sell to Shubal CLAGHORN, mariner...all their rights in land in Chilmark bounded by lands of Joseph HILLMAN, Nathaniel CLARK and the Kiphigon Lots and the Roaring Brook. Witnesses: Edward FOSTER, Pain MAYHEW. Rec. 28 Oct. 1755.

Fortunatus MAYHEW of Chilmark MA to **Matthew MAYHEW** of Nantucket. <Dukes Co.Deeds 8:456> ...29 Feb. 1752, Fortunatus MAYHEW, gent., sells to Matthew MAYHEW, carpenter of Sherborn/Sherbon, Nantucket...all rights in lease of lands in Edgartown...from my brother Micajah MAYHEW of Chilmark.

Thomas SMITH of Tisbury MA to **Experience CLAGHORN** of Chilmark MA. <Dukes Co.Deeds> ...8 Jan. 1755, Thomas SMITH, yeoman, for Ł40 sells to Experience CLAGHORN, widow...twenty acres at Fann(sp) Neck in Edgartown bounded by Squash Meadow or Pond, Tristram COFFIN's line, Holmes hole harbor and down the neck. Wf Elizabeth SMITH signs. Witnesses: Israel BUTLER, Nathan SMITH. Rec. 22 June 1758. (<8:575>...22 June 1758, **Experience**, seamstress, sells above for Ł20 to Ebenezer SMITH Jr., housewright of Edgartown. Witnesses: William JERNIGAN, Enoch COFFIN Jr.

Pain MAYHEW et al of Chilmark MA, division. <Dukes Co.Deeds 8:455> ...24 Dec. 1757, Pain MAYHEW, Esq.; Beriah TILTON, clothier & wf Mary; William BASSETT, blacksmith & wf Anne; Anne MAYHEW, seamstress; William CLARK Jr., laborer; Bethiah COOES, seamstress; William CLARK, yeoman as atty. for Thankful CLARK and Shubal CLAGHORN, mariner, all of Chilmark, holding jointly 250 acres bounded by Roaring Brook and land of sd Shubael & Joseph HILLMAN...land is divided...for convenience of purchasing the planting rights of the natives...to Shubal the west end being ten acres, less than half...the remainder to belong to the others.

Estate of **Ebenezer HAWES** of Yarmouth MA. <Barnstable Co.PR>
<4:400> 14 Mar. 1727/8, widow **Sarah HAWES** app'td admx. <5:145> Dower & Division 16 Jan. 1733 to

the widow and six children, viz: **John HAWES** (eldest son), **Ebenezer HAWES, Isaac HAWES, Benjamin HAWES, Bays HAWES, Jacob HAWES, Desire HAWES & Ruth HAWES.** <6:140> Division 11 Feb. 1741, of real estate of widow **Sarah HAWES** (being dec'd) to following chil.: **John HAWES, Isaac HAWES, Benjamin HAWES, Bayes HAWES, Desire HEDGE, Ruth THACHER** and chil. of **Ebenezer HAWES** dec'd.

Will of **Sarah HAWES**, widow of Yarmouth MA. <Barnstable Co.PR>
<6:114>...dated 29 Dec. 1741, mentions son **John HAWES**; daus **Desire HEDGE & Ruth THACHER**; chil. of son **Ebenezer HAWES**; son **Isaac HAWES; Benjamin HAWES**, son of son **Benjamin HAWES**; son **Bayes HAWES.** <6:115> Pr. 11 Feb. 1741. <6:117> Inventory, 17 Feb. 1741. <6:364> Account. <6:494> Receipts.

Will of **Capt. Thomas DAGGETT**, gent. of Edgartown MA. <Dukes Co.PR>
<2:14>...dated 8 July 1726...being sick & weak of body...mentions wf **Elizabeth**...to chil. of dec' son **Samuel DAGGETT**, half that land at Edgartown Harbour that was my father's homestead; sons **Thomas DAGGETT, Timothy DAGGETT & Benjamin DAGGETT** (executors); daus **Hannah, Elizabeth, Thankful, Mary, Jemima & Desire.** Witnesses: Israel BUTLER, David BUTLER, Daniel BUTLER. <2:15> Pr. 4 Oct. 1726, three sons app'td admrs.. <2:117> Inventory taken 31 Mar. 1727, by Samuel SMITH, Benjamin PEASE, Benjamin SMITH; incl. housing & lands, Ł340; lands at Monequoy, Ł400; lands at town or harbour, 250; lands at Chappaquiddick & Cape Poage, Ł240; lands at Sachacontakkett & Nothomis, Ł63; saddle pillion & bridle, Ł3.10s; boate & three oars, Ł1; sword & cane, Ł2; guns, Ł4; books, Ł4; puter/pewter & looking glasses & bellows, Ł8.19s.

Will of **Elizabeth DAGGETT**, gentlewoman of Edgartown MA. <Dukes Co.PR>
<2:79>...dated 25 Dec. 1732...being very sick in body...to son **Benjamin DAGGETT**, my horse, andirons & pott, all debts due me, gridiron & tongs & four chears two of a sort...to dau **Thankfull DAGGETT**, my best suit of cloaths, viz gown & peticoat...to dau **Mary NORTON** my callaminco gown & my red curtains...to dau **Jemimah BUTLER**, my silk crape suit of cloaths...to dau in law **Mary DAGGETT**, my silk scarfe...to sons **Timothy DAGGETT** (executor), **Thomas DAGGETT & Benjamin**, all tools, guns, oxen; daus **Hannah, Elizabeth & Thankfull**; grandsons **Samuel DAGGETT, Seth DAGGETT, Solomon DAGGETT, Silvanus DAGGETT**; grandaughters **Betty alias Elizabeth DAGGETT, Lydia NORTON.** Witnesses: Benjamin SMITH, John BASSETT, Jedidah SMITH. <2:80> Pr. 21 Jan. 1732/3.

Estate of **Nicholas BUTLER** of Edgartown MA. <Dukes Co.Deeds 1:313>
Inventory incl. one common & half with house, Ł80; 35 pounds of pewter; silver boule, Ł3.7s; brass candlestick, 2s; two iron potts, Ł2.10s.
(Note: This handwritten page is numbered "2", there is no sign of page "1" which probably has a date & additional data.)

John BUTLER Jr. of Edgartown MA to **Malachi BUTLER** of same. <Dukes Co.Deeds 5:439>
...27 Apr. 1728, John BUTLER Jr., yeoman, for Ł187.10s sells to Malachi BUTLER, yeoman...land near the swiming place, bounded by harbor and lands of sd Malachi. Ack. 6 Nov. 1734 by Elizabeth BUTLER wf of John.

John BUTLER Jr. of Edgartown MA to **Thomas SNOW** of same. <Dukes Co.Deeds 6:133>
...24 May 1736, John BUTLER Jr., yeoman & wf Elizabeth, sell to Thomas SNOW, mariner...land & half a house in Edgartown.

John BUTLER of Tisbury MA to **Timothy DAGGETT** of Edgartown MA. <Dukes Co.Deeds 6:386>
...17 Mar. 1739/40, John BUTLER, yeoman, for Ł30 sells to Timothy DAGGETT, gent. & gdn. of Sarah WORTH & Dorcas WORTH, minor daus of John WORTH, Esq. & wf Dorcas, both of Edgartown dec'd...one share in 3rd division of the Old Purchase in Edgartown commonly called the Plain Division. Elizabeth BUTLER signs. Witnesses: John WORTH, Elizabeth VINSON. Ack. 25 Mar. 1740 by John & Rec. (<15:177>...6 Sept. 1790, Dorcas WORTH, seamstress of Edgartown sells her share to John WORTH.)

John BUTLER of Tisbury MA to **Priscilla SNOW** of Edgartown MA. <Dukes Co.Deeds 8:19>
...5 Sept. 1748, John BUTLER, yeoman, deed of gift to sister Prissila/Priscilla SNOW, widow... land in Edgartown.

MICRO #2 OF 18

John BUTLER of Tisbury MA to **John BUTLER Jr.** of same. <Dukes Co.Deeds 8:375>
...May 1750, John BUTLER, yeoman, for Ł500 sells to John BUTLER Jr...land in Edgartown & Tisbury, also the house he (Sr.) now lives in, after his death. Witnesses: John SUMNER, Jane BUTLER. Rec. 29 Apr. 1754.

<Dukes Co.Deeds 8:82>...17 May 1750, **John BUTLER** of Tisbury MA sells to sister **Jane BUTLER**, seamstress of Tisbury...land at Edgartown. Wf Elizabeth BUTLER signs.
<Dukes Co.Deeds 8:260>...8 Oct. 1753, **John BUTLER**, yeoman of Tisbury MA to **Samuel OSBORN**, housewright of Edgartown MA and **Phebe COFFIN** wf of Abner COFFIN, mariner of Edgartown...
<Dukes Co.Deeds 8:293>...9 Oct. 173, **John BUTLER**, yeoman of Tisbury MA, for Ł14.13.4. sells to son **John BUTLER Jr.**, yeoman of Tisbury...

John BUTLER of Tisbury MA to **John BUTLER Jr. et al.** <Dukes Co.Deeds 8:374>
...6 Feb. 1754, John BUTLER, yeoman, for Ł100 sells to John BUTLER Jr., Phebe COFFIN wf of Abner, Keziah OSBORN wf of Samuel and Abigail BUTLER, all of Dukes co...certain lands & personal property, not to take effect until the death of John BUTLER & wf Elizabeth...Keziah to receive half

share in Penny Wise Division, also half of one sixteenth in New Purchase & all rails at OSBORNS house in Edgartown and part of pew in gallery in meeting house in Edgartown.

Abigail BUTLER of Tisbury MA to **Bayes NORTON** of Edgartown MA. <Dukes Co.Deeds 12:108>
...21 Feb. 1754, Abigail BUTLER, spinster to Bayes NORTON, yeoman...certain lands derived to me from my Honoured Father John BUTLER of Tisbury.

Samuel OSBORN of Tisbury MA to **William JERNIGAN** of Edgartown MA. <Dukes Co.Deeds 8:488>
...28 Apr. 1755, Samuel OSBORN, carpenter, for £18 sells to William JERNIGAN, carpenter...the two ninths of land that did belong to my father Samuel OSBORN late of Edgartown dec'd where his dwelling house now standeth...also two ninths of sd house. (<9:15>..."23 June 1759, Matthew BUTLER & wf Elizabeth, one ninth lands lately of Samuel OSBORN, dec'd father unto Elizabeth.")

Keziah PEASE of Edgartown MA to **William JERNIGAN** of same. <Dukes Co.Deeds 15:157>
...10 Oct. 1768, Keziah PEASE, widow, for £6 sells to William JERNIGAN, carpenter...all her rights in lands now belonging unto me whether divided or to be divided...in Edgartown. On 8 Mar. 1769, Peter RIPLEY & Jethro DUNHAM appeared before the Court of General Sessions of the Peace & made oath they saw Keziah PEASE sign above deed. Rec. 12 Mar. 1806.

Phebe COFFIN of Sherborn, Nantucket to **William JERNIGAN** of Edgartown MA. <Dukes Co.Deeds 11:489>
...21 Nov. 1783, Phebe COFFIN, widow, for £9 sells to William JERNIGAN, yeoman...all her rights in all lands in Edgartown...which derived to me by my Honoured Father John BUTLER dec'd and my sister Jane BUTLER dec'd. Ack. same day. Rec. 27 Jan. 1784.

Estate of **Samuel OSBORN**, carpenter of Edgartown MA. <Dukes Co.PR>
<4:19> 9 Mar. 1754, widow **Keziah OSBORN**, seamstress, app'td admx. <4:21> Inventory taken 27 Sept 1754 by John NORTON, Timothy DAGGETT, Matthew NORTON; incl. dwelling house, wood lot & windmill.

Estate of **Matthew PEASE**, cordwainer of Edgartown MA. <Dukes Co.PR>
<4:36> 2 Aug. 1756, widow **Keziah PEASE** app'td admx. <4:39> Inventory taken 10 Sept. 1756 by John SUMNER, Matthew NORTON, Timothy DAGETT.

Estate of **Matthew NORTON.** <Dukes Co.PR #368>
...1779...<6:159> Will. <6:161> Pr. <7:37> Receipts.

Will of **Timothy DAGGETT**, gent. of Edgartown MA. <Dukes Co.PR #359>
<6:137>...dated 6 Mar. 1775, mentions wf **Mary; Nathan DAGGETT** son of **Seth DAGGETT** of Tisbury; brother **Benjamin DAGGETT; Elijah DAGGETT** (under 21) son of **Elijah DAGGETT** of Nantucket dec'd; **Kathrine DAGGETT** dau of brother **Benjamin DAGGETT; Seth DAGGETT** (aforesd) **& Isaac DAGGETT** of Tisbury; to brothers **Benjamin & Thomas DAGGETT**, land received from my grandmother; **Brotherton DAGGETT; Ebenezer DAGGETT; Andrew BUTLER** (under 21) son of **Shobal BUTLER; Timothy DAGGETT** (under 21) son of **Silvanus DAGGETT** of Tisbury dec'd; **Thankful PADDOCK** wf of Seth of Nantucket; kinsman **Thomas COOKE** of Edgartown, executor. <6:140> Codicil 19 May 1775. <6:139> Pr. 29 Nov. 1775. <6:142> Inventory taken 5 Mar. 1776.

Joseph HAWES et al to **Cornelius BENNETT** of Middleborough MA. <Plymouth Co.Deeds 29:121>
...27 Sept. 1734, Joseph HAWES, gent.; Thomas HAWES, cordwainer; Joseph HAWES Jr., cordwainer; David HAWES, labourer & Prence HAWES, mariner, all of Yarmouth, Edmund HAWES, cooper; David PARKER, yeoman & wf Mary; Ebenezer GORHAM, joyner & wf Temperance; Thomas ANNABLE, husbandman & wf Thankfull, all of Barnstable and Jonathan SEARS & wf Elizabeth of Harwich...sold to Cornelius BENNETT, physician...all ye right of Mary the late wife of the aforementioned Joseph HAWES...in lands of Gov. PRENCE at Middleboro & Bridgewater. Rec. 30 Jan. 1734.

Estate of **Nathaniel BACON**, gent./innholder of Barnstable MA. <Barnstable Co.PR>
<8:268> Order for distribution, 17 Mar. 1749, on application of Augustin BEARSE, gdn. of **Lemuel BACON, Benjamin BACON & Jabez BACON**, minor chil. of dec'd, for distribution of real estate not set off to **Thankful BERSE**, late widow of sd dec'd as her dower; mentions will of dec'd (which Bowman notes is not in the records) giving legacies to sons **John, Lemuel, Benjamin & Jabez**; estate is now divided among the three sons & heirs of son **John BACON** dec'd. Guardianship of chil., 15 Nov. 1744, Augustin BEARSE of Barnstable app'td gdn. of: <6:392> **Lemuel BACON**, ae about 13; <6:393> **Banjamin BACON**, ae about 11 and <6:393> **Jabez BACON**, ae about 7; <7:227> 7 Aug. 1751, **Benjamin BACON** chooses Ebenezer PARKER, yeoman of Barnstable as gdn.

Will of **John BACON Jr.** of Barnstable MA. <Barnstable Co.PR>
<8:153>...dated 14 June 1744; leaves one third of estate to brother **Daniel BACON** and two thirds to sister **Mercy BACON**; mentions real estate received from dec'd father. <8:154> Pr. 8 Mar. 1746.

Estate of **Jabez BACON**, mariner of Barnstable MA. <Barnstable Co.PR>
<7:470> 5 Apr. 1757, Edward BACON, yeoman of Barnstable, app'td admr. <9:397> Inventory taken 29 Apr. 1757. Account 4 July 1758, mentions the dec'd is entitled to one quarter of his father's estate. <9:398> Distribution 5 July 1758 to the following brothers & sisters, viz: **Daniel BACON, Benjamin BACON, Lemuel BACON, Levi BEARSE, Mercy HALLETT, Hannah DUNHAM, Jane LUMBERT & Sarah BEARSE.** <9:399> Receipt 28 Nov. 1758, of **Hannah DUNHAM** wf of David of Boston. Witnesses: Benjamin BACON, Thankful BACON.

Estate of **John BACON**, sadler of Barnstable MA. <Barnstable Co.PR>
<6:403> 9 Oct. 1745, widow **Elisabeth BACON** app'td admx. <8:403> Inventory taken 13 Oct. 1745 by Ebenezer LEWIS, Esq., Nathaniel BAKER & Robert DAVIS, all freeholders of Barnstable; incl. smiths shop tools & iron, £20; sadlers tools, leather saddletrees nails etc., £7.10s; total real estate, £960; total estate, £1251.25s; sworn to 20 Dec. 1745 by admx. <8:404> Account 1 July 1746 of admx incl. funeral charges, viz: coffin gloves, £7.1s6d and grave stones, £4.15s; Paid to: John STURGIS, Col. BOURN, Deacon DAVIS, Capt. LOTHROP, Capt. HINCKLEY, Nathaniel BAKER, Dr. HERSY, Thomas ALLIN, Benjamin TAYLOR; MORTON's children, £30; Edward HOWIE, James OTIS, Esq., Mrs. BACON, £100; nessaries for housekeeping allowed to the widow, £156.10s. <8:405> Dower set off 16 June 1746, by Ebenezer LEWIS, Robert DAVIS, Nathaniel BAKER, Samuel BACON & Edward BACON, all freeholders of Barnstable, to the widow **Elisabeth BACON** as follows: westerly half of the dwelling house with the west part of the sellar...the north bedroom in the Chamber Alley togather with joynt previledge with the heirs in the Alleys in the middle of the House and also two acres of land...beginning from the middle of the back doar of sd house...bounded by land of Edward BACON & Ebenezer BACON ...till it comes to the house with the shop thereon standing...and also one acre...bounded by land of Edward BACON & Judah BACON...also one sixth part of the grist mill at Blishes Bridge... also woodlot lying in the first division...one half the meadow at Sandy Neck as it lyeth in partnership with others. <8:406> Account 9 Mar. 1750 of admx.; incl. received for land sold at vandue by special order of court to pay debts, from Jonathan BACON, Deacon Robert DAVIS & Ebenezer PARKER, £57.14.8d.

Will of **Mary BACON**, spinster of Barnstable MA. <Barnstable Co.PR>
<13:523>...dated 4 Dec. 1764...to my dear and tender Mother for her better support in her old age and also to enable her to pay my funeral charges etc., all my real estate...in Barnstable...and all personal estate; sisters **Desire BACON & Mary BACON**; mother **Elizabeth BACON**, exx. Witnesses: Adino HINCKLEY, Jabez HINCKLEY & Edward BACON. Pr. 8 May 1770, by exx.; sworn to by Jabez HINCKLEY & Edward BACON, Esq.

Will of **Desire BACON**, spinster of Barnstable MA. <Barnstable Co.PR>
<35:313>...dated 18 Mar. 1811...to my brother **Isaac BACON**, $1.00...to my sister **Elizabeth DIMOCK** widow of Thomas one of my poorest beds without any covering...to my sister **Mary DAVIS** widow of Joseph...all my real and freehold estate; John DAVIS Jr. & Abner DAVIS, exrs. Witnesses: John GORHAM, Nathaniel GORHAM & Hannah DAVIS. <32:282> Pr. 9 Apr. 1811 by exrs.

Will of **John BACON**, Esq. of Barnstable MA. <Barnstable Co.PR>
<5:1>...dated 2 Dec. 1730...to sons **Nathaniel BACON, John BACON, Solomon BACON & Judah BACON**... all my husbandry utensils...and all my quick stock & hay; mentions prenuptual agreement dated 27 Sept. 1726 with wife **Sarah**; negroe Dinah to be sold after wife's decease and proceeds to be used to buy bibles for his grandchildren;...and the sd calash shall be returned unto my sd wife's daughters...to son **John BACON**...upland & meadow at Strawberry Hill adjoyining to Joseph DAVIS...and my cane...to son **Nathaniel BACON**...lands he doth hold by deed...where his home doth stand...bounded by Samuel DIMMOCK's meadow...and land lying between the Cobbs Lane & lands belonging unto the heirs of Samuel BACON dec'd...and my best hatt & wigg...to dau **Desire GREEN**...land adjoyning... land that my son **GREEN** doth hold by deed where his house doth stand...to dau **Hannah MORTON** my great Bible...and one third of all my houshold goods & wares; grandaughter **Mary MORTON** and male heirs of dau **Hannah**; to son **Solomon BACON**...lands & meadows...and my law book...to son **Judah BACON**...my dwelling house I now live in...and lands bounded by land of Solomon OTIS, Gershom COBB & heirs of Samuel BACON dec'd...meadow by the grist mill in partnership with some of the heirs of Jeremiah BACON dec'd...to grandaughter **Mary BACON** dau of dec'd son **Isaac BACON**, 20s to buy her a bible...to sd son **Isaac**'s heir or heirs if his wife have another child...son **Solomon BACON** if he have no other house to live in shall have full liberty to live in my dwelling house on my abovesd farm at Strawberry Hill with his own family...my son **Judah BACON** shall procure a good gentle beast for my wife to have to go in her calash to carry herself when & where she will in the town of Barnstable and if she desire it to carry her self once in a year to Plymouth;...if what corn & meat the sd BACON hath be not enough to support the sd Warrens family for the space of four months after sd BACON's decease and to the value of £25 more which the sd BACON doth give her to procure a mourning suit, then what it doth fall short of it shall be made up by his sons which he doth give his part of the grist mill unto...; sons **Nathaniel & John**, executors. Witnesses: George LEWIS, Elizabeth CASE, Mary LEWIS. Witneses sworn, 2 Sept. 1731. Pr. 8 Oct. 1731. <5:6> Inventory taken 23 Sept. 1731 by Ebenezer LEWIS, James COBB, Nathaniel BAKER; incl. Great Bible, £1.5s; housing lands & meadow, £2646. <6:390> Account, 15 Nov. 1744, of **John BACON**, exr.; payments made to James OTIS, Esq. & Coll. BOURN.
(Note: The files contain a very lengthy transcription of the will which, due to the many details, is a little confusing, i.e., the passage written in the third tense regarding the Warrens which must refer to his 2nd wf Sarah (Doty)(Warren) Bacon & her Warren children.)

MICRO #3 OF 18

Will of **Thomas LOTHROP**, yeoman of Barnstable MA. <Barnstable Co.PR>
<9:300>...dated 24 May 1751, mentions daus **Rebecca LOTHROP, Mehitable DAVIS, Mary TAYLOR, Lydia BACON & Elizabeth BARTLETT**; dec'd son **Thomas LOTHROP**; grandson **Thomas LOTHROP** (under 21) son of dec'd son **Thomas**; heirs (under 21) of sons **Ansel LOTHROP & James LOTHROP**, dec'd; son **Seth LOTHROP** executor. Codicil 15 Mar. 1755 mentions all five daus. <9:301> Pr. 3 Aug. 1757.

Will of **David TURNER**, boat builder of Plymouth MA. <Plymouth Co.PR #21322>
<20:183>...dated 4 June 1766, mentions **Ruth TURNER** (under 18), dau of nephew **David TURNER**, shipwright of Plymouth who is to have remainder of estate. <20:183-4> Letter/Bond 6 Feb. 1769.

Estate of **David TURNER Jr.**, shipwright of Plymouth MA. <Plymouth Co.PR #21323>
<23:77> Letter, 1775, David LOTHROP app'td admr. <24:111> Inventory. <25:75> Account, 12 Aug. 1778. <28:95> Dower set off 20 Apr. 1781 to widow **Deborah SAMPSON,** now the wife of Stephen SAMPSON of Plymouth. <29:140> Account. <37:173> Decree on dower, 11 May 1803, mentions the widow who is then deceased and the following children, viz: eldest son **Lothrop TURNER,** 2d son **David TURNER, Ruth FOSTER** wf of Jacob, **Deborah CURTIS** widow of Zacheus, **Rebecca RUSSELL** wf of Jonathan, **Hannah HARLOW** wf of Jesse Jr., **Molly JOHNSON** wf of Richard and **Lucy BARTLETT** wf of Peabody.

Will of **James GORHAM,** yeoman of Barnstable MA. <Barnstable Co.PR 6:222,223,260,277>
...dated 19 Mar. 1738...entire estate to brother **Hezekiah GORHAM,** yeoman of Barnstable who is named executor. Pr. 26 Oct. 1742. Inventory taken 16 Feb. 1742; sworn to 19 Feb. 1742 by **Hezekiah**

Will of **James GORHAM** of Barnstable MA. <Barnstable Co.PR>
<3:497>...dated 30 Sept. 1717...my just debts & funerall charges be paid by the sale on one acre and one quarter of my land bounding upon my uncle **Shubal**'s land in the comon feild with one fifth part of a lott of land at the south sea known by the name of skunk lott...to wf **Mary** one third part of my household stuff within doors, my Indian Girl Jemima, my best bed & furniture, two cows, two yearlings with ye advantage one fatted red stear, two swine, two shoats and corn to fat them, one brass citle, the use & improvement of my house & land till my three sons hereafter named come of age she bringing up sd children togather with my daughter **Thankfull** and lastly I give to my wife aforesd forty bushels Indian corn & five bushels of rye...to my three sons **Isaac GORHAM, Hezekiah GORHAM & James GORHAM** all my lands & meadows...they paying unto my daughter **Thankfull GORHAM** the sum of twenty four pounds; wf **Mary,** Thomas JOYCE of Yarmouth and Joseph DAVIS of Barnstable, executors. Witnesses: Shubal GORHAM, Joseph DIMMOCK & James McSPARRON. Pr. 26 Jan. 1718 (O.S.), 6 Feb. 1719 (N.S.). <3:499> Inventory taken 20 Oct. 1718 by Peter THACHER & John MILLER; incl. 3 Indian servants, £50; total real estate, £400; sworn to 5 Nov. 1718 by widow

---

Will of **James GORHAM** of Pitt Co., NC. <original in poss. of Wm. E. ENNIS, Bowling Green VA, 1902>
...dated 24 Dec. 1804...being but in a low state of health...to wf **Sarah,** all the negroes and other property and the increase of the negroes I had by her in write of marriage to her...also the use of the plantation...I lend to my beloved wife so long as she remains a widow Simon, Phil, John & China and if she should marry it is my will that Simon be free and the rest return to be divided among my children...my sd wife cut what cypress she may want with her own hands for shingles over the River and also with the children should she keep them which is my desire. It is my will & desire that all my negroes be equally divided among my children in manner & form following that is after my decease there be a division among them, and those belonging to them under age to be hired out for there benifits and to receive them as they come of age. All my lands over the River it is my will be hired out for the benifit of all my children, when the youngest comes of age it is my will that all the lands be sold and the money divided among all my children...if the death of my mother in Barnstable Massichusetts that my executors sell my property there and apply the money to the use of my children...In the before mentioned bequests I do not include my son **Edward GORHAM,** but I give & bequeath unto him the sum of five pounds in addition to what my executors shall think sufficient to support him in a manner they think best annually...In addition to the above will I give & bequeath unto my wf **Sarah** a negro girl named Lucy. I lend to my wf **Sarah** a negro man Jess during her widowhood. I give & bequeath unto my daughter **Penelope GORHAM** a negro girl, China. Witnesses: John DIXON, Jas. D. McLURE Jr. Pr. Feb. 1805. Filed 23 Aug. 1841, at the Court of Pleas & Quarter Sessions, Greenville, Pitt Co., North Carolina.

Will of **Lt. John FULLER** of Barnstable MA. <Barnstable Co.PR>
<5:30>...(not dated)...the quarter of a lott of meadow which I own with Benjamin JONES & Timothy NYE and my meadow calld the Triangle Stack yeilding about three loads of hay lying by the Eel Creek bridge and my six acres of wood lott...to be sold towards the paying my debts...wife **Thankfull**; to son **John FULLER**...all my land calld ye point being in two pastures twenty acres, also that lott of meadow calld the Eel Creek Lott, my dwelling house & barn & the land extending back to Benjamin JONES' land...to son **Nathaniel FULLER**...my land calld the neck & all other my upland on Scoton Neck...also meadow adjoyning his land...in consideration of which several bequests... they shall pay to my daughters as followeth...**John** shall pay unto my dau **Bethiah** fifty pounds at her marriage or arrival to twenty & five years and also unto my dau **Mary** the like sum...my son **Nathaniel** shall pay unto my dau **Hannah** tenn pounds in one year...and pay unto my dau **Thankfull** fifty pounds at her marriage or age of twenty five years; brother in law **John GORHAM** & wf **Thankfull,** executors. Witnesses: Mehitable BLOSSOM, Silvanus BOURN & Mary JONES. <5:32> Inventory taken 25 Jan. 1732/3 by Joseph SMITH, Benjamin BODFISH & Benjamin FULLER; incl. Indian boy & girl valued at £20 for both; total real estate, £2250; sworn to 8 Feb. 1732/3 by exrs. <5:339> Receipt 17 Nov. 1737 of **Seth LOTHROP** & wf **Mary** once **Mary FULLER,** of our brother **John FULLER,** £50 in full of a legacy devised to the sd **Mary.** <5:340> Receipt 4 Apr. 1740 of **Joseph BURSLEY Jr.** & wf **Bethiah** late **Bethiah FULLER** of our brother **John FULLER,** fourty shillings money being with what the sd **Bethiah** hath heretofore received the full sum of fifty pound. <12:533> Receipt 24 July 1771 of **Hannah SMITH** of my brother **Nathaniel FULLER,** £3.14s3d, in full for a legacy.

Estate of **Matthias SMITH,** gent. of Barnstable MA. <Barnstable Co.PR>
<10:202> 21 Oct. 1768, Matthias SMITH, yeoman of Barnstable app'td admr. <13:381> Inventory taken

28 Oct. 1768. <13:433> Dower set off, 3 Apr. 1769, to widow **Hannah SMITH**, by Nathan BASSETT, John CROCKER & Matthias FULLER. Account 5 May 1769 of **Matthias SMITH**, admr., son of dec'd.

MICRO #4 OF 18

Will of **John GORHAM**, Esq. of Barnstable MA. <Barnstable Co.PR>
<13:490>...dated 4 Nov. 1762, mentions wf **Prudence**; sons **Benjamin GORHAM** (executor) **& Nathaniel GORHAM**; to daus **Thankfull, Mary, Abigail & Rachel**, Ł3 over and above what I have already given them; dau **Prudence GORHAM**; grandaughter **Thankful ANNABLE**; grandsons **John GORHAM, Daniel GORHAM & Joseph GORHAM** (the latter being under 21); unnamed daus of son **Joseph GORHAM**, dec'd. Codicil 21 Oct. 1765, states dau **Abigail GORHAM** has died leaving a dau **Sarah GORHAM** (under 18). Codicil 12 Jan. 1767, states dau **Prudence** has since married. Codicil 3 Nov. 1768 states dau **Mary CLAP** has died leaving a dau **Prudence CLAP**. <13:492> Pr. 19 Oct. 1769. <13:512> Inventory, 27 Oct. 1769.

Will of **Joseph HINCKLEY**, gent. of Barnstable MA. <Barnstable Co.PR>
<9:6>...dated 11 Sept. 1751, mentions sons **John HINCKLEY & Isaac HINCKLEY** who has been at Harvard daus **Mercy BOURN & Mary DAVIS**; brother **Isaac HINCKLEY**; unnamed children of dec'd dau **Thankful**; grandaughters **Mary BOURN & Mehitable DILLINGHAM** (under 21 & unm.); grandson **Joseph DAVIS**; dec'd son **Samuel HINCKLEY**. <9:8> Pr. 7 Aug. 1753.

Estate of **Shubael GORHAM Jr.** of Barnstable MA. <Barnstable Co.PR>
<7:1>...16 Aug. 1746, James LOVELL Jr., gent. of Barnstable app'td admr. <8:5> Inventory taken 17 Nov. 1746 by David CROCKER, Esq., Deacon Robert DAVIS & Lieut. John HINKLEY, all of Barnstable; incl. land in the comon field & meadow, Ł1500; place called Fuller's Pasture, Ł315; a 10 piece of land at Leach Pond, Ł40; place called Lewis' Farm, Ł150; 4 lotts of salt meadow at Gray beach, Ł160; woodland, Ł200; an old negro slave called Limus, Ł40; total estate, Ł2844.18s6d. <8:6> Petition 14 Jan. 1746 of widow **Mary GORHAM**, to be allowed housekeeping utensils to the value of Ł100. <8:133> Insolvency, 11 Dec. 1746, represented by admr.; David CROCKER & Deacon DAVIS ordered to examine claims of creditors; 5 July 1748, an extension of time was granted. <8:134> List of Creditors, 31 Oct. 1748: Maj. Joseph THACHER, Benjamin HATCH, Nathaniel GORHAM, Maj. John OTIS, Henry ATKINS, merchant, Col. John GORHAM of Boston, Joseph GORHAM of Annapolis, Col. James OTIS, "Col. Otis JAMES exr. to his father", John HOWLAND of Tiverton, Capt. Joseph HINKLEY, Lieut. John HINKLEY, Samuel HALLET, Joseph MAGGS, Col. Edward WINSLOW, Noah DAVIS, Col. BOURN, John FULLER, David PHINEY, Samuel GOODSPEED, Thomas HINKLEY, John GORHAM, Esq., Ebenezer GOODSPEED Jr., James GOODSPEED, Samuel HALLET, Thomas PHINEY Jr., John BURSLEY, William MIRICK, David LORING Jr., Gideon HATHAWAY, Thomas STURGIS, Joseph HOWES, Nathaniel BAKER, Samuel DIER, Thomas BRYANT, Esq., Thomas DOANE, Thomas WINSLOW, Esq., Ezra BOURN, Esq., Moses MENDAL, John TRAIL, merchant, Seth HALLET, Daniel UPDIKE, Esq., Isaac CHAPMAN, John HUNT, merchant of Boston, John OKILLEY by Ezekiel BURGIS, Elisha COB, Dr. Abner HENRY, Benjamin HIGGINS, Samuel DOANE, Capt. Moses PEARSON, Eleazer OKILLEY, Jonathan BACON, James DAVIS, Nathaniel BACON's heirs or estate, Josiah DENNIS, Timothy HALLET, Ebenezer CROWELL, Joseph CROWELL, Edward GRAY of Boston, John WINTHROP, Andrew HALLET, Capt. Edward BANGS, Thomas HALLET, Ebenezer HALLET, Thomas DEAN, John HALLET, Esq., David HALLET, John LEWIS, James KNOWLS, Capt. Richard KNOWLS, Judith BARNARD, William DOWNES, Joseph BACON, Nathaniel BACON's estate, John OKILLEY, Job DAVIS, Edward STURGIS' estate, Tho. THACHER's estate, Jno. PHILLIPS, merchant of Boston, Dr. Charles CHAUNCY, Jno. SAVELL of Boston, Jonathan LEWIS' estate, Samuel STURGIS, Esq., David GORHAM, James LOVELL Jr. and Shubael GORHAM. <8:136> Order, 8 Feb. 1749, to James LOVELL Jr., admr., to pay widow **Mary GORHAM**, Ł60. Account 9 Feb. 1749 of admr.; incl. payments for freight of his things from Boston, a journey to Boston to settle with ye committee about his wages and a journey to York Records about his eastern land. <8:137> 9 Feb. 1749, admr. was ordered by the court to pay the creditors one shilling & six pence on the pound.

Estate of **Shubael GORHAM Jr.**, mariner of Barnstable MA. <Barnstable Co.PR>
<7:123> 7 June 1748, David GORHAM, Esq. of Barnstable app'td admr.

Will of **Joseph GORHAM** of Yarmouth MA. <Barnstable Co.PR>
<4:309>...dated 27 July 1723, mentions wf **Sarah**; sons **Josiah GORHAM & Joseph GORHAM**; dau **Desire BAXTER**; grandchild **Sarah SEARS**, dau of dec'd dau **Sarah HOWES** and her other three children, **Thomas HOWES, Ebenezer HOWES & Elizabeth HOWES**; wf **Sarah** & son **Josiah**, executors. Witnesses: Peter THACHER, Thankfull THACHER, Ann LOTHROPE. <4:311> Pr. 20 July 1726.

Will of **Josiah GORHAM** of Yarmouth MA. <Barnstable Co.PR>
<17:248>...dated 17 Jan. 1772...advanced in age; mentions son **David GORHAM**; dau **Rebecca BROWN**; grandson **Josiah GORHAM** (minor); sons **Samuel GORHAM** (executor), **Hezekiah GORHAM & Stephen GORHAM**; wf **Marcy**. Witnesses: Judah THACHER, Stephen HALLET, Thomas HOWES/HAWES. <17:249> Pr. 15 Apr. 1775 <17:270;21:84> Inventory. <21:90;14:22> Account. <14:21> License.

Heirs of **William HEDGE** of Bristol to **Jabez HOWLAND Jr.** of same. <Bristol Co.Deeds 6:320>
...11 Mar. 1709/10, Robert FOWLER, mariner of Boston & wf Sarah, Samuel GOREHAM, mariner of Newport & wf Elizabeth, which sd Sarah and Elizabeth are the only surviving children of William HEDGE, mariner, dec'd, sold to Jabez HOWLAND Jr., blacksmith...house & land in Bristol.

Will of **John THACHER** of Yarmouth MA. <Barnstable Co.PR>
<3:295>...dated 25 Apr. 1713, mentions wf **Lydia**; son **Peter THACHER**; son **John THACHER** to receive the gold ring with the seal that was my father's; male heirs of dec'd son **Josiah THACHER**; minor

sons **Judah THACHER, Joseph THACHER, Benjamin THACHER & Thomas THACHER**; daus **Rebecca STURGIS & Bethiah PAINE**; unnamed children of dec'd dau **Elizabeth HATCH**; mentions four youngest daughters are by his present wife **Lydia**; daus **Lydia FREEMAN & Mary GORHAM**; to ye two drummers of Yarmouth if they beat at my funeral, 5s apeice...thou I had much rather be decently buryed without any military cerimony. <3:298>Pr. 19 June 1713. <3:299> Inventory 1 July 1713.

Will of **Joseph DENISON**, yeoman of Stonington CT. <New London CT PR #1705>
...dated 16 Feb. 1724/5, mentions wf **Prudence**; eldest son **Joseph DENISON** (under 21); sons **Amos DENISON & Nathan DENISON**; daus **Prudence, Boradal, Joanna, Elizabeth, Thankful & Anna**; brother* **Joseph MINOR**, overseer. Witnesses: George DENISON, James CHIPMAN, Amos HALLAN(sp). Pr. 23 Mar. 1724/5. Inventory taken 26 June 1725 by Stephen RICHARDSON & John WILLIAMS; total estate, L2437. 13.8. (*brother in law)

Will of **Joseph DENISON**, Esq. of Stonington CT. <Stonington CT PR #1112>
...dated 12 Mar. 1794, mentions wf **Elizabeth**, what she brought with her from New London; sons **Peleg DENISON & Amos DENISON**; daus **Content WILLIAMS & Bridget MASON**. Pr. 3 Mar. 1795. Receipt 31 Aug. 1795 by **John WILLIAMS 3d** & wf **Content**.

Will of **John WILLIAMS** of Stonington CT. <New London CT PR #5749>
...dated 26 July 1760, mentions wf **Prudence**, what she brought with her; sons **John WILLIAMS, William WILLIAMS, Thomas WILLIAMS, Robert WILLIAMS, George WILLIAMS & Edward WILLIAMS**; daus **Desire CHESEBOROUGH, Thankful DENISON & Mercy WHEELER; Eunice WILLIAMS** wf of son **George**. Codicil 26 Aug. 1761, mentions son **Robert WILLIAMS**, dec'd, his widow **Rebecca** and children, **Robert, Abigail, Mary & Rebecca**; "brother **Benajah WILLIAMS**, housing & food for 7 years".

Will of **Daniel ELDREDGE**, husbandman of Groton CT. <New London CT PR #1892>
...dated 6 Oct. 1748, mentions honoured mother **Abigail DENISON**; wf **Sarah**; eldest son **Daniel ELDREDGE** when 21; 2d son **John ELDREDGE**; youngest son **Amos ELDREDGE**; only dau **Abigail**; wf **Sarah** & Hubbard BURROWS, executors. Pr. 28 Oct. 1748. Receipt 10 Feb. 1764, of **John ELDREDGE** from my honored mother **Mrs. Sarah AUSTING** of Sheffield. Receipt 9 Nov. 1761 of **Daniel ELDREDGE**, from Hubbard BURROWS & **Mrs. Sarah AUSTIN**. Receipt 30 May 1769 of **Amos ELDREDGE** from **Mrs. Sarah AUSTIN** wf of Capt. Nathaniel AUSTIN of Sheffield. Receipt 9 Jan. 1767 of **Jonathan PELL** & wf **Abigail** of Sheffield.

Will of **Shubael GORHAM/GORUM**, yeoman of Barnstable MA. <Barnstable Co.PR>
<8:265>...dated 23 Sept. 1748, mentions son **George GORHAM** and daus **Abigail, Lydia, Hannah, Theodate, Desire, Ruth & Deborah**; trusty friend Deacon John HINKLEY of Barnstable, executor. <7:181> On 8 July 1749, James LOVELL Jr., gent. of Barnstable was app'td gdn. of **Shubal GORHAM** who is adjudged by the Inquisition of the Selectmen of the sd town to be a person non compos.

MICRO #5 OF 18

Will of **James LOVELL**, gent. of Barnstable MA. <Barnstable Co.PR>
<12:158>...dated 2 May 1755, mentions wf **Abigail**; daus **Ruth CLERK, Abigail GORHAM, Desire CHAPMAN Susanna LOVELL, Deborah GORHAM, Lydia LOVELL** (under 21), **Puella LOVELL** (under 21) and **Anna LOVELL** (under 21); sons **Daniel LOVELL, James LOVELL & Shoball LOVELL**. Codicil in Feb. 1760, dau **Abigail** now dec'd leaving minor children. <12:174> Pr. 1 June 1761.

Will of **Daniel LOVELL**, yeoman of Barnstable MA. <Barnstable Co.PR>
<26:77>...dated 30 July 1785, mentions wf **Sarah**; son **Daniel LOVELL**; a meadow which brother **James** and I own; sons **Christopher LOVELL, Nehemiah LOVELL, Gorham LOVELL & Shubael LOVELL**; eldest dau **Desire LOVELL**; youngest dau **Sarah LOVELL**; 2d dau **Abigail FREEMAN**. <26:79> Pr. 17 Oct. 1785.

Nunccupative Will of **Edward STURGIS Jr.** of Yarmouth MA. <Plymouth Col.Wills 4:1:26>
...15 Nov. 1678...The last words that **Edward STURGIS Jr.** spake was, that concerning settleing his estate; was that I give to my wife one third of my estate, and the other two thirds to my children onely to my son **Joseph STURGIS** to have twenty pounds more then the reste; and to Mr. THORNTON I give twenty one shillings, and to Joseph GORUM I give five pounds in silver; and to my daughter I give my silver Tanker; as to say my daughter **Desire** as a token of my love. Witnesses: John SUNDERLAND, Joseph GORRUM, **Elizabeth STURGIS** the widow; sworn to 3 June 1679 by John SUNDERLAND & **Elizabeth STURGIS**. Inventory taken 24 May 1679 by Jeremiah HOWES, Joseph RYDER & John GORUM; incl. one halfe of the farme bought of Mr. WALLEY & corne on the ground, Ł65; land att Mathakeesett, Ł10; dwelling house, land & barn, Ł80; third parte of a catch abroad, Ł80; quarter parte of a catch with Goodman HUCKENS, Ł25; silver bowle a gift formerly to his eldest dau **Desire**; halfe parte of a sayne, Ł3.10s; a negro boy; total estate, Ł970.4s6d. <Court Orders 6:23>...2 Mar 1679/80...this court doth order that **Temperance BAXTER** the relict of **Edward STURGIS** shall have the third parte of sd estate and the other two partes therof to be devided amongst the children in equall & alike proportions onely the eldest son to have twenty pounds; to be aded to his parte and the negroe to be aded to the womans parte towards the bringing up of the children and incase that **Thomas BAXTER** & his wife will give cecuritie to the court for the childrens estate they shall have the improvement therof unto the children come of age; Mr. HINCKLEY, Mr. Barnabas LAYTHORP & Mr. MILLER app'td to divide estate. <Plymouth Col.Deeds 4:372>...28 Oct. 1680, In order to the better settlement of the estate...and prevention of wast of the sd estate & discord & discomfort between the admrs. and parties concerned this court orders that the admrs. give in a true

accompt of the debts due...reasonable allowance to **Thomas BAXTER** and **Temperance** his wife for the bringing up the children of the sd **Edward STURGIS.** (A committee of Deputy Gov. Thomas HINCKLEY, Assistant John FREEMAN and Barnabas LAYTHORPE & John THACHER, was app'td to settle the estate.)

BARNSTABLE COUNTY PROBATE: (re: BAXTER)

1713	Thomas	Yarmouth		3:303,305,306;4:358,503
1714	Temperance	Yarmouth		3:200,202,252,257
1741	Shobael	Yarmouth	will	6:40,42
1746	Elizabeth	Yarmouth	will	8:23,24,25,26
1749	Lemuel	Yarmouth	gdn.	7:168
1755	Malachi	Yarmouth	adm./gdn.	7:352,377-384;9:330,331
1783	Richard	Yarmouth	will	23:93,95
1795	Richard	Barnstable		---

Will of **John THACHER**, Esq. of Barnstable MA. <Barnstable Co.PR>
<13:17>...dated 27 May 1763...to dau **Abigail HALLET** over & beside what I have already given her, six shillings per year for five years...to the children of dau **Fear LEWIS** dec'd as followeth: to **Elisabeth PENFIELD**, six shillings within the year of my decease and the like sum to each of the others as they arrive to the age of twenty one years...to the children of my grandaughter **Mary LOTHROP** dec'd, six shillings to each of them as they arrive to twenty one...to son **Rowland THACHER**, four pounds to be paid him twenty shillings per year...to the children of my grandson **Lot THACHER** dec'd, six shillings to each as they arrive to twenty one...to my grandaughter in law **Martha THACHER**, six shillings per year while she is **Lot**'s widow...remainder of estate to son **John THACHER Jr.**, executor. Witnesses: Peter THACHER, Elisabeth DIMOCK, Lydia GORHAM. Pr. 20 Apr. 1764 on oath of witnesses Peter THACHER and Lydia BACON (once Lydia GORHAM).

Estate of **Edward STURGIS**, gent. of Yarmouth MA. <Barnstable Co.PR>
<5:490> Settlement 11 Apr. 1745, one third of real estate was endowered on widow for life & cannot be readily divided without prejudice ...only son **Edward STURGIS** takes the whole & pays his sisters & their legal representatives, viz: **Heman STONE**, gdn. of chil. of **Temperance STONE** (a sister), **Abigail STURGIS, Jerusha HOWES, Mary GORHAM & Mehitable HINCKLEY.** <5:491> Receipt same day of **Abigail STURGIS, Samuel & Jerusha HOWES, Benjamin & Mary GORHAM, Ebenezer Jr. & Mehitable HINCKLEY.**

Will of **Mehitable STURGIS**, innholder, widow of Yarmouth MA. <Barnstable Co.PR>
<6:494>...dated 26 Dec. 1744, mentions son **Edward STURGIS**, dau **Abigail STURGIS**, grandaughter **Mehitable STONE**, daus **Jerusha HOWES, Mary GORHAM & Mehitable HINKLEY**, dec'd dau **Temperance STONE;** brother **Jonathan HALLET** & son in law **Samuel HOWES**, executors. <6:495> Pr. 13 Feb. 1744. <6:496> Inventory taken 20 Feb. 1744/5. Guardianship 7 Mar. 1744, **Heman STONE**, seafaring man of Harwich, app'td gdn. of his children, the grandchildren of **Mehitable STURGIS** dec'd, viz: <6:399> **Nathaniel STONE,** <6:400> **Edward STONE & Keziah STONE,** <6:401> **Mehitable STONE,** <6:402> **Temperance STONE,** <6:403> **Reliance STONE.** <12:401> Account of exrs., 26 Apr. 1757.

Will of **Ebenezer HINCKLEY**, yeoman of Barnstable MA. <Barnstable Co.PR>
<10:83>...dated 23 July 1779, mentions daus **Sarah LORING, Temperance PHINNEY, Mehitable LEWIS, Mary HINCKLEY** (under 18) and son **Ebenezer HINCKLEY.** <10:86> Pr. 11 July 1780. <18:111> Guardianship, 5 Mar. 1781, Timothy PHINNEY of Barnstable app'td gdn. of **Mary HINCKLEY.** <11:212> Petition, 9 Mar. 1781, for appraisers. <21:109> Inventory taken 19 July 1781. <21:152> Inventory, 13 Mar. 1781, of estate given to dau **Mary.**

Will of **Capt. John HOLMES** of Stonington CT. <original>
...dated 1 Mar. 1783, mentions wf **Hannah;** sons **John HOLMES, Jeremiah HOLMES, Jabez HOLMES, Silas HOLMES;** daus **Temperance ANDRIS, Abigail STERRY, Mary BROWN, Eunice MINER, Lucretia PRENTISS, Lucy HOLMES.** Inventory taken 2 Sept. 1783. (Note: The original will is in the files, however it did not film well and cannot be read.)

Estate of **Roger STERRY**, Esq. of Preston CT. <Norwich CT PR #10291>
Bond 5 May 1780, of admrs. **Abigail STERRY** and **Daniel KIMBALL.** Distribution, 4 May 1781 widow **Abigail STERRY** and children, viz: **Roger STERRY,** eldest dau **Mary KIMBALL** wf of Daniel, **Mehitable STERRY,** eldest son **Consider STERRY, John STERRY** and 2d dau **Abigail STERRY.**

MICRO #6 OF 18

Estate of **James STURGIS** of Yarmouth MA. <Barnstable Co.PR>
<3:441> 3 Feb. 1717/8, widow **Rebecka STURGIS** app'td admx. <4:42> Settlement 22 Feb. 1721/2, on the widow, now **Rebecka LEWIS** and children, viz: eldest daus **Hannah MATTHEWS & Bethiah FREEMAN, Thankful HALLET, Elizabeth STURGIS & James STURGIS** (minor). <4:231> Settlement, 18 Feb. 1724/5, of estate of minor son **James STURGIS**, by his gdn. Ebenezer LEWIS of Barnstable.

Will of **Samuel STURGIS** of Yarmouth MA. <Barnstable Co.PR>
<5:283>...dated 29 June 1736...advanced in years & under indisposion of body...to son **John STURGIS** my sealed gold ring...to my son **Prince STURGIS**...land lying between Joseph HAWES' & Ebenezer HALLET's land in Yarmouth which I bought of Isaac HAVEN and...meadow I bought of Seth TAYLER lying in ye Loan Tree Furlong so called...and meadow bought of John TAYLER...and cedar swamp by

Baxters Brook...and wood lot in ye second division #4 lying at prospect Hill and...woodlot lying in ye first division that I bought of Seth TAYLOR, all in Yarmouth...also three thousand pounds.. and whereas I have given by deed to my son **Samuel STURGIS** ye one half of all of my piece of land & meadow lying in ye Prime field at a place called crows Bridge...bounded by heirs of William HEDGE, WHEALDEN & others...the remaining half...unto my son **Thomas STURGIS**...to sons **Samuel & Thomas**...my homestead dwelling house & lands & woodlots in Yarmouth...to my dau **Hannah QUINCY** all those goods & moneys she hath already received of me and also...one thousand pounds...to son **Samuel** my ivory headed cain...to my son **Thomas** my gold buckle & silver tancker...to my son **Prince** a silver tanker to be of the same weight with **Thomas'**...to Rev. Mr. Thomas SMITH our present minister, Ł80...I give & grant ye sum of two hundred pounds unto the poor of the Town of Yarmouth; three eldest sons, **John, Samuel & Thomas**, executors. Witnesses: Benjamin THACHER, Elisaha/Elisha WHELDEN & John THACHER. Pr. 17 Feb. 1736/7.

Estate of **Peter LEWIS**, shipwright of Barnstable MA. <Barnstable Co.PR>
<25:90> 27 Apr. 1793, Timothy PHINNEY of Barnstable app'td admr. <25:860> Allowance, 25 Aug. 1793, to widow **Mehitable LEWIS**, Ł30.15s for necessaries. <28:56> Inventory taken 29 Apr. 1793. <30:434> Account, 11 Nov. 1794, of admr.; incl. paid **Thacher LEWIS** for a legacy due from **Peter LEWIS** as exr. to his brother **John LEWIS**; to a hat for the son of the dec'd. <25:89> 20 Aug. 1793, Timothy PHINNEY app'td admr. on estate of **Mehitable LEWIS**. <30:126> Inventory taken 7 Oct. 1793.

Will of **Richard BAXTER** of Yarmouth MA. <Barnstable Co.PR>
<23:93>...dated 25 June 1781...to wf **Mary**, real estate & all the houshold stuff she brought with her at the time of our marriage; dau **Thankful HALLET**; to dau **Desire TAYLOR**, $55.00 & use of chamber in my now dwelling house during her natural life; dau **Jene BRAGG**; grandsons **Thomas BAXTER, Warren BAXTER & Shobael BAXTER** (all under 21); sons **Richard BAXTER & Prince BAXTER**. <23:95> Pr. 10 Nov. 1783.

Will of **Capt. Thomas BAXTER**, mariner of Barnstable MA. <Barnstable Co.PR>
<31:162>...dated 25 Apr. 1806, mentions wf **Lydia**; mother **Mary EWER**; brothers **Warren BAXTER, Shubal BAXTER & Seth EWER** (youngest brother); wf **Lydia & Warren BAXTER**, executors. Witnesses: Jesse LEWIS, Silvanus EWER, Samuel DEWEY. <32:134> Pr. 10 June 1806. <31:440> Account, 8 Sept. 1807. <31:454> Inventory taken 13 June 1806; "considerable estate" incl. goods in store.

Will of **Deacon Joseph HALLETT**, yeoman of Barnstable MA. <Barnstable Co.PR>
<33:339>...dated 5 Aug. 1808...to wf **Thankful**, the improvement of the whole estate...to eldest dau **Jane BAKER**, the improvement of my best chamber, after mother's decease, so long as she remains a widow...to 2d dau **Mary SMITH**, $15.00...to 3d dau **Hannah LEWIS**, $15.00...to 4th dau **Desire SHEPHERD**, four acres woodland adjoining Richard LEWIS & others...to sons **Joseph HALLETT & Richard HALLETT**, all cleared land lying to the northward of the road, leading from Baxter's Mill to the Baptist Meeting house in Barnstable...excepting half an acre adjoining sd **Richard**'s dwelling house which I give unto him...grandson **Hiram BAKER** shall support his mother **Jane BAKER** so long as she remains a widow; sons **Joseph & Richard** and grandson **Hiram**, executors. Witnesses: Gorham LOVELL, Richard LEWIS, Benjamin FURNAL(sp). <32:158> Pr. 11 Apr. 1809. <35:387> Inventory taken 15 June 1809. <35:389> Account 26 Sept. 1809.

Will of **Jonathan LEWIS** of Kelso twp., Dearborn Co., Indiana. <Dearborn Co.Ind. PR 2:198>
...date 26 Jan. 1844...directs his executors to sell all his real estate; to granddaughter **Angeline YAGER** (unm.) one good bed & bedding with such other of my house hold furniture as may be convenient for her to keep house with & $100.00, all of which I consider her just due for services rendered me...son **John W. LEWIS** to keep possession of the farm I now occupy for ony year... children of my dau **Asenath** by **Joseph H. SMITH** and my grandchildren **Adelia LANGDON, Isaac LENISON William YAGER & Julia Ann YAGER** and the heirs of my son **Watson LEWIS** be allowed...one dollar each and no more...remainder of estate divided among children, viz: **Clement LEWIS, Redman LEWIS, William LEWIS, Richard LEWIS, John W. LEWIS, Freborn LEWIS, Laura RAWLING, Hannah DAVIS**...the chil. of dau **Sophia YAGER**, viz: **Volney YAGER, Angeline M. YAGER & Edwin YAGER** be allowed that part which the sd daughter(s) would have been alowed if living; son **John** and friend William RAWLING app'td exrs. Witnesses: Zedekiah BONHAM, William DONLON. Pr. 1 Oct. 1845.

BARNSTABLE COUNTY DEEDS: (re: Richard BAXTER, all grantors to 1845**)**

<4:31> - 1 Jan. 1789, Richard BAXTER, gent. of Yarmouth & wf Patience to Gershom CROWELL.
<3:187> - 19 Mar. 1790, Richard BAXTER, gent. of Yarmouth to Jonathan HALLETT of same.
<4:88> - 19 Mar. 1790, Richard BAXTER, gent. of Yarmouth & wf Patience.
<4:26> - 24 Dec. 1793, Richard BAXTER, gent. of Yarmouth & wf Patience.

MICRO #7 OF 18

HANNAH HOWLAND[2] (John[1])

PLYMOUTH COUNTY DEEDS: (re: David BOSWORTH, grantee**)**

<4:32> - 26 Sept. 1698, D.B. of Plymouth from James & Sarah WARREN, Mary DOTY, of Plymouth and Tobias & Elizabeth OAKMAN of Marshfield...land in Plymouth granted to father Edward DOTY.

PLYMOUTH COUNTY DEEDS, cont-d: (re: David BOSWORTH, grantee)

<7:260> - 7 Aug. 1701, D.B. of Plymouth from Francis CURTIS of same...land near Monponsett Pond Ack. 5 Mar. 1705/6.
<7:261> - 5 Mar. 1705/6, D.B. of Plymouth from Joseph KING of same...land in Plymouth.
<10:374> - 17 Mar. 1705/6, D.B. of Plymouth from Eleazer CUSHMAN of same. Ack. 9 Mar. 1708.
<11:268> - 4 Nov. 1714, D.B. of Plympton from Jonathan BRYANT of Plymouth...land in Plympton. Ack. 7 Feb. 1714/5.
<11:269> - 30 Mar. 1714/5, D.B. of Plympton from Robert WATERMAN & John WATERMAN Jr. of Plympton ...land in Plympton. Ack. by Watermans with consent of John WATERMAN Sr.
<11:268> - 23 Dec. 1714, D.B. of Plympton from Samuel STURTEVANT Jr. of same. Ack. 21 Dec. 1714.
<11:270> - 9 May 1716, D.B. of Plympton from Thomas THOMSON of Middleboro...land in Plympton.

<14:26> from John CURTIS, <16:62> from Joseph WASHBURN, <19:5> from James BRYANT, <19:6> from Josiah STURTEVANT et al, <24:181> David BOSWORTH Jr. from Francis CURTIS.

<26:208> - 23 Sept 1731, D.B. of Plympton from Thomas TOMSON of Middleboro...land in Plympton.
<45:112> - 10 Apr. 1758, David & Nehemiah BOSWORTH of Rochester from their parents Nehemiah & Sarah BOSWORTH of Halifax "& Susanna & Sarah BOSWORTH of Halifax from Nehemiah & Sarah"...land in Middleboro.
<45:13> - , D.B. from Nehemiah BOSWORTH.
<66:273> - 5 Mar. 1787, D.B. of Halifax from Jesse STURTEVANT of same, gdn. to Lemuel STURTEVANT n.c.m...land in Halifax. Ack. 23 Oct. 1787.
<68:171> - , D.B. from Joseph LAZELL.
<70:94> - 3 July 1790, D.B., yeoman of Halifax from Benjamin CURTIS, yeoman of same.
<71:241> - 31 Dec. 1790, D.B. from Thomas STURTEVANT.
<173:105>- , D.B. from John LEACH Jr.

PLYMOUTH COUNTY DEEDS: (re: David BOSWORTH, grantor, all on index)

<19:20> - 11 Jan. 1724/5, D.B. Sr., John BRYANT Jr. & James BRYANT, all of Plympton to Mark PERKINS, blacksmith of same...land for a shop.
<24:182> - 17 Oct. 1729, D.B. Jr. of Plympton to Ichabod CUSHMAN of Middleboro...land in Middleb.
<26:190> - 30 Sept 1729, D.B. Sr. of Plympton to Francis PUMMERY of Hanover...land in Plympton where David BOZWORTH Jr. now dwelleth.
<26:208> - 23 Sept 1731, D.B. of Plympton to Thomas THOMSON Sr. of Middleboro...land in Plympton.
<26:211> - 23 Sept 1731, D.B. of Plympton to son Jonathan BOSWORTH of same...land in Plympton incl. part of homestead land with some reservation to wf Patience.
<37:58> - 7 July 1708, D.B. of Plympton to Samuel LUCAS of Plymouth...land in Plympton bought from James WARREN et al. Ack. 14 July 1744.
<66:273> - 23 Oct. 1787, D.B., yeoman of Halifax to John WATERMAN Jr. of same...land in Halifax bought of Lemuel STURTEVANT.
<70:227> - 27 Jan. 1791, D.B., yeoman of Halifax to Daniel BRYANT of Watertown & Perez BRYANT of Boston, tanners...part of land bought of Benjamin CURTIS.
<71:50> - 7 Mar. 1791, D.B., yeoman of Halifax to John BOSWORTH Jr. of same...land in Halifax bought of Benjamin CURTIS with priviledges in house. Ack. 14 Mar. 1791.

==========

Joseph LOOMIS of Lebanon CT to **David BOZWORTH** of Lebanon CT. <Lebanon CT Dees 4:482> ...27 Apr. 1733, Joseph LOOMISSE/LOOMIS, for Ł220 sold to David BOZWORTH, now residing in Lebanon ...23 acres...at the uper end of ye Town street in Lebanon...half lott that was originally Capt. John AVERY's and that which my Honored father Joseph LOOMISS/LOOMIS purchesed of Henery WOODWARD ...bounded by land of Zachariah LOOMISSE and land laid out in the fifth division in the five mile square of land. Witnesses: Joseph FOWLER, John WOODWARD. Ack. same day. Rec. 17 July 1733.

==========

David BOZWORTH of Lenox MA to **Ichabod BOZWORTH** of Lebanon CT. <Lebanon CT Deeds 15:43> ...12 Aug. 1788, David BOZWORTH, for Ł100 sold to Ichabod BOZWORTH...all rights in land in Lebanon ...which I hold by mortgage on a conditional deed from the sd Ichabod dated 8 Apr. 1786... 1786...bounded by highway that leads from Lebanon to Colchester and land of Isaiah LOOMIS and WELLES. Witnesses: Elkanah TISDALE, Ephraim HILL. Ack. same day by David. Rec. 16 Aug. 1788.

==========

<Killingly CT Deeds 3:115>...31 May 1731, **David BOSWORTH** bought 60 acres in Killingly; <3:163>... 28 Oct. 1732, sold the above; <8:-->...Mar. 1746, **David BOSWORTH,** late of Lebanon, lately of Norwich, now of Brimfield...sold land in Killingly. <Springfield MA Deeds 10:74>...11 Aug. 1743, **David BOSWORTH** of Norwich CT bought land in Brimfield, Rec. 30 Aug. 1753; <10:76>...6 May 1746, of Brimfield, sold the above.

==========

References to **BOZWORTH** deeds (grantors) in Lebanon CT Deeds: 5:126;6:79,480;7:106;12:49,287,527; 13:197,300,311;14:395,459,500;15:37,43.

==========

LEBANON CT DEEDS: (re: BOZWORTH, grantees)

<5:42> - 30 Nov. 1733, Gershom HINKLEY, yeoman of Lebanon to son in law Nathaniel BOZWORTH, carpenter of same.
<6:356> - 24 June 1743, Gershom CLARKE of Lebanon to David BOZWORTH of same.
<6:474> - 8 Apr. 1745, Eliphalet CLARK, blacksmith of Lebanon to David BOZWORTH of same.

LEBANON CT DEEDS, cont-d: (re: BOZWORTH, grantees)

<12:371> - 28 May 1772, Samuel GAY of Lebanon to David BOZWORTH Jr. of same...part of land distributed to heirs of Samuel GAY of Lebanon.
<12:397> - 28 May 1772, Benjamin WOOD of Lebanon to Joseph LOOMIS Jr. & Ichabod BOZWORTH of Lebanon...land in Goshen.
<14:460> - 21 June 1773, Joshua CHAPPEL of Lebanon to my only dau Abigail, now the wife of Ichabod BOZWORTH of same.
<12:372> - 1 Feb. 1774, Seth ROSE of Lebanon to David BOZWORTH Jr. of same...land adjacent land D.B. bought of Samuel GAY.
<12:284> - 28 Apr. 1774, Stephen & Mary LEE of Lebanon to David BOZWORTH Jr. of same.
<12:285> - 28 Apr. 1774, James & Lucy BAILEY, Samuel & Abigail BAILEY & Samuel GAY to David BOZWORTH, all of Lebanon.
<12:373> - 23 Sept 1774, Daniel STRONG, son of Stephen, of Lebanon to David BOZWORTH Jr. of same.
<13:24> - 13 Apr. 1778, Asel GAY of Lebanon to David BOZWORTH Jr. of same.
<14:499> - 3 Dec. 1782, Joshua CHAPPEL to Ichabod BOZWORTH of Lebanon...J.C. mentions grandson Brewster CHAPPEL.
<14:394> - 12 June 1784, Elizabeth CHAPPEL of Lebanon to Ichabod BOZWORTH of same.
<14:500> - 8 Apr. 1786, Ichabod BOZWORTH of Lebanon to David BOZWORTH of Spencer Town NY.
<14:530> - 15 Dec. 1787, "attachment" on Ichabod BOZWORTH of Lebanon.
<15:312> - 11 Aug. 1788, Lieut. Ichabod BOSWORTH of Lebanon to William WILLIAMS Jr. of same.

Will of **Zadock BOSWORTH** of Montgomery MA. <Hampshire Co.PR>
...dated 4 July 1810, mentions wf **Joanna**; to son **Zadok BOZWORTH Jr.**, $60.00; to son **Joshua BOZWORTH,** $4.00; $10.00 ea to daus **Rebekah BARRET, Hannah BRANT, Charlotte MOOR & Priscilla KING;** remainder of estate to son **Raymond BOZWORTH;** Daniel BARRET/BARRETT, executor. Witnesses: Oliver KELLOGG, James WHEELER Jr., Abner MOREY Jr. Pr. 17 July 1810.

PLYMOUTH COUNTY DEEDS: (re: David RIPLEY)

<63:161> - 28 Apr. 1780, David RIPLEY, yeoman of Plympton & wf Jane to Ebenezer CUSHMAN et al. Ack. 29 Apr. 1780 by David. Rec. 22 July 1785.
<60:180> - 16 June 1780, David RIPLEY, yeoman of Plympton & wf Jane to Shadrach STANDISH. Ack. 3 July 1781 by David. Rec. 4 July 1781.
<60:176> - 8 Feb. 1781, David RIPLEY, yeoman of Plympton & wf Jane to Dependence STURTEVANT. Ack 22 June 1781 by David. Rec. 2 July 1781.
<60:172> - 2 July 1781, David RIPLEY, yeoman of Plympton to Jabez WESTON, yeoman of Pelham NH... farm in Halifax & woodland lately bought of Jonathan HOLMES 3d of Kingston, 69 acres in all. Rec. 4 July 1781.
<100:49> - 2 July 1804, David RIPLEY, trader of Greenfield to chil. of Nehemiah RIPLEY of Hingham dec'd, viz: Nehemiah RIPLEY, Jerome RIPLEY, Esq. of Greenfield, John RIPLEY, trader of Boston, Peter RIPLEY, currier of Boston & Thomas RIPLEY.
<113:27> - 1809, David RIPLEY Jr., mortgage to Barnabas HEDGE Jr. of Plympton...land he bought of Billey WRIGHT.
<114:233> - 1810, David RIPLEY of Plympton, mortgage to Barnabas HEDGE Jr...land bought of William STURTEVANT.
<115:190> - 1811, David RIPLEY & wf Hannah to Winslow DEAN.
<119:267> - 1813, David RIPLEY & wf Hannah to Barnabas HEDGE Jr.
<122:75 - 1813, David RIPLEY Jr. & wf Hannah to Barnabas HEDGE Jr.
<125:143> - 1813, David RIPLEY, mariner of Plymouth to Richard HOLMES 3d.
<126:47> - 1815, David RIPLEY, mariner of Plympton & wf Hannah to Philemon FULLER.
<130:124> - 1817, David RIPLEY, mariner of Plympton & wf Hannah to Sarah DEAN.

References to **Jonathan JENKS** in Bristol Co.Deeds: 31:284,293;37:82;40:250;41:176,177,374;42:56; 46:250,267;56:213;62:41,42;71:169,559.

Providence RI Deeds: <2:374>...9 Nov. 1714, **Jonathan JENKS** to uncle William JENKS of Providence. <2:446>...Jonathan JENKS to Benjamin SOULE of Plympton.

Peter THACHER Jr. of Attleboro MA to **Jonathan JENKS,** Esq. **et al.** <Bristol Co.Deeds 62:41>
...4 Apr. 1783, Peter THACHER Jr., yeoman & wf Nanna, for £340 sell to Samuel SLACK, yeoman of Attleboro, Eliphalet SLACK, gent. of Rehoboth & Jonathan JENKS, Esq. of N. Providence...land in Attleboro. <62:42>...4 Apr. 1783, Jonathan JENKS sells his share of above for 6,000 continental dollars received in Dec. 1779, to Samuel SLACK, yeoman of Attleboro. Ack. 2 Sept. 1783.

MICRO #8 OF 18

Will of **Thomas BARNS**, yeoman of Barrington RI. <Barrington RI PR 1:27>
...dated 8 May 1787...to heirs of dec'd son **Levi BARNES,** viz: **Hannah DROWN** wf of Jonathan, **John BARNES, Jerusha KENT** wf of Joseph, **Mary BARNES, James BARNES & Ruth BARNES**...seven acres in Barrington...bounded by...land I once gave by deed to their sd Father...and land of Joseph VIALL and Josiah HUMPHRY; to grandaughter **Althea BARNES** dau of dec'd son **Peleg BARNES,** 50 silver spanish milled dollars; to dau **Ruth GREEN** wf of Richard, 80 silver spanish milled dollars, one good cow and household furniture; to son **Samuel BARNES** (executor) remainder of estate incl. farming uten-

sils, stock, lambs & tackling. Witnesses: Daniel KINNICUTT, Daniel Vasiel KINNICUTT, Thomas TOWNSEND Jr. Pr. 19 July 1800.

Hannah DROWN of Barrington RI to **John BARNES** of same. <Barrington RI Deeds 2:7>
...3 Aug. 1784, Hannah DROWN, wf of Jonathan J. DROWN & dau of Levi BARNES dec'd, for £4 sells to John BARNES, yeoman...all rights in real estate of sd Levi BARNES lying in Barrington and Rehoboth. Witnesses: Daniel DROWN, Solomon TOWNSEND.

Will of **Jeremiah SCOTT** of Cumberland. <Cumberland PR 6:425>
...dated 11 Aug. 1790, at Barrington, mentions wf **Rebeckah**; sons **Stephen SCOTT, Jeremiah SCOTT** (executor), **Charles SCOTT, Nathaniel SCOTT**; daus **Sarah OLNEY** wf of Coggeshall, **Rebeckah RAY** wf of Daniel, **Rachel DROWN** wf of Benjamin, **Betty SHORT** wf of John, **Joanna ALLEN** wf of Benjamin. Witnesses: Solomon TOWNSEND, Samuel ALLEN Jr., Samuel ALLEN. Pr. 25 Apr. 1795.

Estate of **John BOZWORTH** of Barrington. <Bristol Co.PR>
<3:714> Inventory taken 10 Nov. 1719 by John DEVOTION, Samuel HILLS & James BROWN; total real estate, £400; total estate, £602.14s.<3:713> Bond 6 Aug. 1721, widow **Elizabeth BOZWORTH** app'td admx. Sureties: John DEVOTION, schoolmaster & John FINNEY, yeoman, both of Swansea. Witnesses: Edward ADAMS, Elizabeth PRINCE. <4:314> Account 14 June 1724, of admx.; Paid to: John CARPENTER, Jonathan KINSLEY, Elisha MAY, John SALISBURY, Joseph BROWN, Josiah CARPENTER, John HUNT, Richard HARDING, David THURSTON, William COLE, Joseph ALLEN, Ebenezer MARTIN, Philip SHORT, John SHOREY, Dr. William WOOD; for suite of clothes to Samuel TUGED being his fredom clothes; for the lying in with an imposthumus child after the death of ye father, £6; Samuel HILL, John WHITTAKER, Joseph KENT, Nathaniel INKS, Hannah WEST, Thomas WOOD, Jabez BROWN. <4:460> Guardianship, 15 Dec. 1724, Peter HUNT of Rehoboth app'td gdn. of **John BOSWORTH & Lydia BOSWORTH**, minor chil. of dec'd. <5:135> Warrant to divide, 16 Feb. 1724/5, to Peter HUNT, Samuel HILL, Joseph PECK, Robert WHEATEN & James BOWEN. <original> Division 2 Mar. 1724/5 to the widow and following children, viz: eldest son **Nathaniel BOZWORTH** to receive four acres of the home lot...where formerly old Mr. BOZWORTH's house stood, bounded by land of James THOMAS; 2d son **John BOZWORTH**; 3d son **David BOZWORTH**; 4th son **Oliver BOZWORTH**; eldest dau **Elizabeth THOMAS** wf of John; 2d dau **Mary BOZWORTH**; 3d dau **Anna BOZWORTH**; 4th dau **Lydia BOZWORTH**; the late widow (viz) the wife of James THURBUR.

Heirs of **Nathaniel TOOGOOD** of Swansey MA to **John TOOGOOD** of Barrington. <Bristol Co.Deeds 23:399>
...5 Nov. 1733, Samuel TOOGOOD, cordwainer of Swansey; Elisabeth THURBER wf of James THURBER, husbandman of Rehoboth; Mary BARNEY, widow of Barrington; John FINNEY, husbandman of Swansey & wf Anne and Samuel GOOF/GOFF, husbandman of Rehoboth & wf Rachel...sell to John TOOGOOD, boatman... all rights in the estate of our father Nathaniel TOOGOOD dec'd. Ack. 7 Nov. 1733 by Elizabeth THURBER; 6 Feb. 1734 by John & Ann FINNEY; 14 Apr. 1735 by Samuel & Rachel GOFF; 15 May 1735 by Mary BARNEY & Samuel TOOGOOD. Rec. 17 June 1735.

George POTTER et al of Providence to **Calvin BULLOCK** of Rehoboth. <Bristol Co.Deeds 70:202>
...19 Sept. 1791, George POTTER, Nancy POTTER, Samuel THURBER & Elizabeth THURBER sell to Calvin BULLOCK...land set off to Ruth WHITAKER in the division of Ruth BURR's land.

Estate of **James THURBER**, Esq. of Rehoboth MA. <Bristol Co.PR>
<34:188> Guardianship, 23 Nov. 1795 Samuel THURBER & Benjamin THURBER request the Selectman to examine & report; 25 Nov. 1795, Selectmen report that **James THURBER** is insane; 28 June 1796, Philip MILLER of Rehoboth app'td gdn. <34:175> Inventory taken 2 July 1796.
(Note: The following references appear to refer to the same man: <35:91> Account. <35:315> Guardian discharged. <41:547> Inventory. <41:558> Account. <42:77> Account. <42:396> Division. <43:17> Account. <109:155> Notice of appointment. <150:123> Adm.

BRISTOL COUNTY DEEDS: (re: THURBER)

<16:74> - 31 Dec. 1716, James THURBER to William HAMMOND.
<18:481> - 9 Apr. 1722, James THURBER to Edward THURBER.
<18:472> - 9 Apr. 1722, James THURBER to Samuel THURBER.
<16:250> - Jan. 1723/4, James THURBER to Samuel THURBER.
<15:425> - 1724, James THURBER to Jonathan THURBER.

Samuel BULLOCK of Rehoboth MA to **David ALLEN** of same. <Bristol Co.Deeds 40:325>
...14 Oct. 1735, Samuel BULLOCK Jr., husbandman & wf Annah, for £30 sell to David ALLEN, yeoman ...5 acres in Rehoboth bounded by land of James THOMAS and sd ALLEN's land which he purchased of Lydia BOZWORTH...being part of land set off to Annah BOZWORTH in the division of the estate of her father John BOZWORTH dec'd. Witnesses: Joseph ALLEN Jr., Stephen PECK. Ack. 9 Mar. 1754 by Samuel & Anna. Rec. 12 Mar. 1754.

Lydia BOZWORTH of Barrington to **David ALLEN** of Rehoboth MA. <Bristol Co.Deeds 41:100>
...19 Mar. 1734/5, Lydia BOZWORTH, spinster, for £22 sold to David ALLEN, yeoman...four and a half acres, partly in Rehoboth & Barrington, bounded by land of Thomas WALY, James THOMAS and land that was divided to "Annh" BOZWORTH. Ack. 17 Oct. 1747. Rec. 5 Feb. 1754.

Samuel BULLOCK of Rehoboth MA to **Preserved BRAYTON** of Swansea MA. <Bristol Co.Deeds 21:88>
...10 Dec. 1731, Samuel BULLOCK, housewright & wf Anna and James BOWEN, wheelwright of Rehoboth & wf Elizabeth, sell to Preserved BRAYTON, yeoman...a farm in Rehoboth...of late belonging to

Jonathan NELSON. Ack. 12 Jan. 1731 by Samuel & James. Rec. 12 Jan. 1731/2

Samuel BULLOCK Jr. of Rehoboth MA to **James THOMAS** of Barrington. <Bristol Co.Deeds 27:183> ...(---) 1737, Samuel BULLOCK Jr., yeoman & wf Annah, for 40s sold to James THOMAS, yeoman...all rights in a piece of land in Rehoboth that Nicholas TANNER, formerly of Swansey dec'd had of Jonathan BOSWORTH formerly of Swansey upon an exchange now in the possession of sd James THOMAS bounded by land of David ALLEN & sd THOMAS. Witnesses: Seth BULLOCK, Jonathan DIMAN. Ack. 23 Dec. 1737 by Samuel & Anna. Rec. 25 July 1738.

David BOSWORTH of Lebanon CT to **Richard THOMAS** of Swanzey MA. <Bristol Co.Deeds 33:289> ...13 Jan. 1740/41, David BOSWORTH, son of John BOSWORTH of Barrington dec'd, quit claims to his brother in law Richard THOMAS, shipwright...all rights in mother Elizabeth THURBER's thirds of estate of father John BOZWORTH of Barrington dec'd. Witnesses: Jabez REDE, Daniel LUTHER. Ack. 12 Jan. 1742 by David. Rec. 21 Mar. 1744/5.

Nathaniel BOZWORTH of Middletown CT to **Richard THOMAS** of Barrington. <Bristol Co.Deeds 33:289> ...2 Oct. 1741, Nathaniel BOZWORTH, housewright for Ŀ100 sells to Richard THOMAS, shipwright... five acres in Barrington...bounded by mother's thirds in estate of father John BOSWORTH and land of James THOMAS...with dwelling house & barn...my share in my sd father's real estate. Witnesses: Abigail BRADFORD, Abigail BRADFORD Jr. Ack. same day by Nathaniel. Rec. 21 Mar. 1744/5.

Daniel BROWN of Hampshire co. MA to **Nathaniel BOSWORTH** of Middletown CT. <Berkshire Co.Deeds> <4:151>...14 July 1757, Daniel BROWN of Number three, Hampshire co., for Ŀ30 sells to Nathaniel BOSWORTH...80 acres in Number three, in the 16th lot in the third division. Witnesses: Nicholas AYERAULT, Elisha WILLIAMS. Ack. same day by Daniel. Rec. 24 Oct. 1765.

Estate of **Jonathan BOZWORTH** of Rehoboth MA. <Bristol Co.PR>
<original> Petition (no date) of widow **Sarah BOZWORTH**, that she is old and very uncapable of administering the estate, desires her son **Amos BOZWORTH** be app'td. <16:240> 3 Apr. 1759, son **Amos BOZWORTH**, yeoman of Rehoboth app'td admr. <original> Bond of admr., 3 Apr. 1759. Sureties: Samuel BULLOCK, Daniel BULLOCK, yeomen of Rehoboth. Witnesses: Noah SABIN Jr., Samuel FRENCH. <16:240> Inventory taken 23 Feb. 1759 by Benjamin KINGSLEY, blacksmith of Swanzey, Ephraim HIX and Daniel BULLOCK; homestead, Ŀ63 and a five acre lott, Ŀ12; total estate, Ŀ122.19d. <16:541> Account 1 Apr 1760 of admr.; incl. provisions for his ancient mother, the widow of the dec'd; Paid to: John WHEELER for "docktrain" him in his sickness, John HIX, John MILLERD, John MASON, "Squier" WHEELER Jr., Capt. Thomas PECK, Ichabod BOZWORTH, Walter HAIL, Amos BOZWORTH, Elihu MASON, Jonathan KINGSLEY, Daniel BULLOCK, Jotham CEARPENTER/CARPENTER.

References to the name **Ichabod BOSWORTH** in Bristol Co.PR, viz: <24:31> Will, 10 Aug. 1775. <24:33> Inventory. <24:232> Account. <57:105> Will. <84:386> Inventory. <84:401> Adm. <85:471> Account. <115:437> Notice. <155:82> Adm. <161:82> Bond. <228:441> Inventory. <229:46> Adm. <230:543> Account. <230:582> Sale of land.

BRISTOL COUNTY DEEDS: (re: BOSWORTH)

<83:252> - 17 Feb. 1785, Peleg BOSWORTH to William HORBEN. Rec. 29 Dec. 1803.
<94:330> - , Peleg BOSWORTH of Bristol RI, son of Benjamin, to Daniel BOSWORTH. Rec. 16 Sept. 1812.
<112:175> - , Peleg BOSWORTH of Rehoboth & wf Levina to Stephen BOSWORTH. Rec. 31 May 1823.
<127:65> - 2 June 1829, Peleg BOSWORTH 2d, son of Peleg Jr. late of Rehoboth dec'd, sells to Susanna BOSWORTH, widow of Rehoboth, all his rights in father's estate.
<134:38> - 23 Nov. 1831, Lloyd BOSWORTH as gdn. of Peleg BOSWORTH, non comp, sells to Smith BOSWORTH, land of Peleg's, being the same that Ichabod BOSWORTH bought.
<141:82> - 12 Nov. 1833, Lloyd BOSWORTH sells land of Peleg, subject to right of dower of Levina wf of Peleg.

Estate of **Peleg BOSWORTH** of Rehoboth MA. <Bristol Co.PR>
<67:277> 2 June 1829, widow **Susanna BOSWORTH** app'td admx. <67:509> Inventory taken 19 June 1829. <69:323> Guardianship, 5 Apr. 1831, Lloyd BOSWORTH app'td gdn. of **Peleg BOSWORTH & Stephen BOSWORTH**, non compos mentis, of Rehoboth. <70:8> Inventory. <70:81> Account, 1831, of Lloyd BOSWORTH as gdn. <71:241> 2d Account, 5 June 1832, of Lloyd BOSWORTH, gdn. of **Peleg BOSWORTH**, non compos; signed by the heirs, **Susannah BOSWORTH**, guardian, for **Smith BOSWORTH, Aneliza BOSWORTH, Henry A. BOSWORTH, George S. BOSWORTH, Edwin E. BOSWORTH** and signed by **Smith BOSWORTH, Susan R. MORRIS, William P. MORRIS, Electa A. REMINGTON, Susanna BOSWORTH, Mary B. MASON & John H. MASON 2d.** <71:338> Notice of Sale. <72:501> Account. <72:13> Notice of sale. <73:411> Account. <74:157,431> Notice of sale. <original> 3rd Account, 5 Oct. 1832, signed by heirs, viz: **Peleg BOSWORTH 2d, Susanna BOSWORTH** as guardian to above named five; **Susan R. MORRIS, William P. MORRIS, Mary B. MASON, John H. MASON 2d** and **Smith BOSWORTH**; signed 24 Oct. 1832 by **Electa A. REMINGTON.** <74:266,424> 5th Account, 7 Feb. 1834, signed by heirs, viz: **John H. MASON 2d, Peleg BOSWORTH 2d, William P. MORRIS, Susan R. MORRIS, Elisha PADELFORD, Electa Ann R. PADELFORD, Smith BOSWORTH, Smith B. ROUND, Smith BOSWORTH** and **Susanna BOSWORTH** as gdn. for **Aneliza W.C. BOSWORTH, HENRY A. Lonzo BOSWORTH, George S. BOSWORTH & Edwin R. BOSWORTH.** (Note: The following references also appear to belong to this Peleg, viz: 112:499;113:23;142:14;152:507;202:170,208,292;205:26.)

Guardianship of Children of **Peleg BOSWORTH Jr.** of Rehoboth MA. <Bristol Co.PR 133:522>
...2 June 1829, widow **Susannah BOSWORTH** app'td gdn. of the children of **Peleg BOSWORTH Jr.** dec'd, viz: **Smith BOSWORTH** (over 14), **Ann Eliza Winsor BOSWORTH, Henry Alonzo BOSWORTH, George Smith BOSWORTH** and **Edwin Ruthven BOSWORTH**, all under 14.

MICRO #9 OF 18

HOPE HOWLAND[2] (John[1])

BARNSTABLE COUNTY PROBATE: (re: CHIPMAN)

1713	Ruth	Sandwich	will	3:258,260
1723	Samuel	Barnstable	will	4:125,126
1745	Sarah	Barnstable	will	6:433,434,436
1753	Samuel	Barnstable	will	9:28,30,31
1758	John	Sandwich	will	9:371,372
1759	Barnabas	Barnstable	will	9:442,443
1770	Timothy	Barnstable	will	13:529,530;12:407;17:152;27:403
1771	Perez	Eastham	adm.	12:469,539;15:133-5;16:12;18:8-10
1795	William	Wellfleet	adm.	24:211;25:112,668;28:44,104,217,389; 33:151
1800	William	Wellfleet	adm.	22:266;25:229;30:358,421;31:193,231

...1 June 1649, **Edward FITZRANDOLPH** of Barnstable to **John CHIPMAN.** <Plymouth Col.Deeds 1:299>

Heirs of **Joseph GALLISON**, shoreman of Marblehead MA. <original owned by Wm. H. GALLISON, 1908>
...12 Apr. 1757, Mary GIRDLER, widow, John GRIST, tinkerman & wf Elizabeth and Henery CODMAN & wf Sarah, all of Marblehead and coheirs of Joseph GALLISON, dec'd, for Ł100 sell to John GALLISON, gent. of Marblehead, coheir with us & executor of estate...all our right in the personal estate of Joseph GALLISON. Witnesses: Nicholas BROUGHTON, Benjamin MARSTON.

Will of **Hosea JOYCE**, yeoman of Yarmouth MA. <Barnstable Co.PR 3:346,349>
...dated 24 Jan. 1711/12, mentions wf **Elizabeth**, sons **John JOYCE, Samuel JOYCE, Thomas JOYCE & Hosea JOYCE**; daus **Martha GODFREE, Dorcas HOWSE/HOWES, Mary GORHAM, Lydia HOWES, Mehitable & Dorothy.** Witnesses: Daniel GREENLEAF, Elisha TAYLOR, Shubal TAYLOR. Inventory taken 15 Feb. 1711/12; housings, land & meadow, Ł600; total estate, Ł800.3.

Estate of **Samuel JOYCE**, yeoman of Yarmouth MA. <Barnstable Co.PR 6:43,62,280,490;8:306>
Adm. 18 Sept. 1741. Inventory 28 Sept. 1741; no wife or children.

Will of **Thomas JOYCE**, yeoman of Yarmouth MA. <Barnstable Co.PR>
<8:149>...dated 3 Oct. 1737, mentions wf **Mercy** (executrix); daus (under 18), **Elizabeth JOYCE, Mercy JOYCE, Mary JOYCE, Dorcas JOYCE & Sarah JOYCE**; only son **Jeremy JOYCE.** Pr. 12 May 1743. <8:150> Inventory taken 28 May 1744.

Estate of **Thomas HUCKINS**, yeoman of Barnstable MA. <Barnstable C.PR>
<3:159> 15 Oct. 1714, son **John HUCKINS** app'td admr. <3:162> Inventory taken 5 Oct. 1714 by John LEWIS, John BAKER & Ebenezer PHINNEY; incl. one bible which the widow **Sarah HUCKINS** claims, 5s. <3:164> 5 Nov.1714, widow's thirds of real estate set off by John BAKER, John LEWIS, David LORING. <3:161> Settlement 11 Dec. 1714, to following children, viz: **John HUCKINS, Thomas HUCKINS, Samuel HUCKINS, Hope HAMBLEN** wf of Benjamin & **Hannah HUCKINS.** <4:99> 7 Feb. 1722/3, **Mary HUCKENS**, executrix of estate of her husband **John HUCKINS**, late of Barnstable dec'd, who was admr. on estate of his father **Thomas HUCKINS**, made her account with respect to her administration of estate of sd Thomas and is discharged as regards this estate.

Will of **John HUCKINS** of Barnstable MA. <Barnstable Co.PR>
<4:18>...dated 20 July 1721, mentions wf **Mary** (executrix); sister **Hope CHILDS**; Rev. Jonathan RUSSELL; nephew **John HUCKENS** (under 21) & his elder brother **Thomas HUCKENS**; the three chil. of sister **Hope**, the son to have half; brother **Thomas HUCKINS.** <4:18> Pr. 5 Sept. 1721. <4:19> Inventory taken 12 Sept.1721. <4:170> Account 20 Mar. 1723/4, of admx., **Mary DAVIS** former widow.

Estate of **Thomas NELSON** of MIddleboro MA. <Plymouth Co.PR #14584>
<13:457> Letter/Bond 5 May 1755, son **Thomas NELSON** app'td admr. Sureties: Uriah SAMSON, yeoman of Middleborough & Joseph HOUSE, husbandman of Hanover. Witnesses: Edward WINSLOW, William CUSHING. <13:525> Inventory taken 27 May 1755, by Uriah SAMSON, John MACOMBER & Joseph PHINNEY; no real estate mentioned; incl. apparell & books, Ł7.13.4.; arms, 18s; money notes & book debts, Ł97.2.1. beds, beding, rye, wheat, leather & skins, husbandry & carpentry tools, livestock; total estate, Ł202.11s; sworn to 2 June 1755 by appraisers, 14 Aug. 1755 by admr.

PLYMOUTH COUNTY DEEDS: (re: Thomas NELSON)

<38:126> - 1 Apr. 1745, Thomas NELSON of Middleboro gift to son Thomas NELSON Jr. of same.
<38:126> - 10 Nov. 1746, Thomas NELSON of Middle. gift to son Thomas NELSON Jr. Ack. same day by Thomas & Hope NELSON.

PLYMOUTH COUNTY DEEDS, cont-d: (re: Thomas NELSON)

<38:127> - 10 Nov. 1746, Thomas NELSON of Middleboro, gift to sons Thomas NELSON Jr. & William NELSON Jr. of Middleboro; mentions his dec'd father William NELSON. Ack. by Thomas & wf Hope.
<38:129> - 10 Nov. 1746, Thomas NELSON of Middleboro, gift to grandaughters, Abiah NELSON, Charity NELSON & Hope NELSON of same, chil. of dec'd son John NELSON.

Thomas NELSON of Middleboro MA to **Hannah WOOD et al.** <Plymouth Co.Deeds 38:128>
...10 Nov. 1746, Thomas NELSON...in consideration of the love & good affection which I bear unto my five daus, viz: Hannah WOOD wf of Jabez, Lois THOMAS wf of Jedediah, Ruth THOMAS wf of Henry, all of Middleboro and Elizabeth COLE wf of Benjamin & Sarah COLE, widow, both of Swanzey...two shares in the South Purchase in Middleboro...the share which did belong unto the original right of my Honoured Father William NELSON dec'd and also that share therein which did originally belong unto my own right...also 73rd lot in third allotment in the Sixteen Shilling Purchase...the original right of my Honoured Father. Witnesses: Barnabas SAMSON, William HOLLOWAY. Rec. 13 Nov. ...<38:245>...15 June 1747, the above daughters divide the land as follows: Jabez & Hannah WOOD to have the land in the South Purchase near Beaver Dam bounded on land of George SHAW & Nehemiah BENNETT; Jedediah & Lois THOMAS to have land in the South Purchase between CLARKE's & LITTLE's lots; Henry & Ruth THOMAS to have land in South Purchase bounded by land formerly belonging to Elder FAUNCE near sd Henry THOMAS' dwelling house; Benjamin & Elizabeth COLE to have land in South Purchase bounded by homestead farm of Benoni SHAW; Sarah COLE, widow to have land in Sixteen Shilling Purchase; Jedediah & Lois THOMAS to have remaining part of the two shares in South Purchase. Witnesses: Thomas NELSON, William HOLLOWAY, Sarah KINGSLEY, Benjamin KINGSLEY. Ack. 2 July 1747, Warren RI, by Benjamin & Elizabeth COLE and Sarah COLE. Ack. 30 July 1747, Middleborough, by others. Rec. 1 Aug. 1747.

MICRO #10 OF 18

Benjamin COLE of Swanzey MA to **Jedediah THOMAS** of Middleboro MA. <Plymouth Co.Deeds 39:204>
...16 June 1747, Benjamin COLE & wf Elizabeth, for £14 sell to Jedediah THOMAS...land in Plimton which is part of the land our father Thomas NELSON gave to his five daughters. Witnesses: Thomas NELSON Jr., William NELSON Jr. Ack. 29 Mar. 1748, Warren RI, by Benjamin.

Will of **Cyrus COLE** of Providence RI. <Providence PR 12:258>
...5 Jan. 1817, mentions unnamed wife (executrix); three eldest chil. **Jeremiah COLE, Mary Ann & Susan**; three youngest chil. **Samuel COLE, Elizabeth, Andrew COLE**. Pr. 3 Feb. 1817.

Will of **Benjamin COLE** of Swanzey MA. <Taunton PR 11:578>
...dated 22 Jan. 1744, mentions wf **Hannah**; sons **Andrew COLE** (executor), **Jonathan COLE, Benjamin COLE, Israel COLE, Ebenezer COLE;** daus **Hopestill BUTTERWORTH** wf of Joseph, **Hannah ORMSBE** wf of Joseph. Witnesses: Peres BRADFORD, Daniel SALSBURY, Barnard COLE. Pr. 4 Oct. 1748.

TAUNTON DEEDS: (re: Benjamin COLE)

<33:318> - 28 Feb. 1740/1, Benjamin COLE, yeoman of Swanzey to son Jonathan COLE of same, land at Rehoboth. Witnesses: Perez BRADFORD, Benjamin COLE.
<33:318> - 18 June 1742, Benjamin COLE to Jonathan COLE of Rehoboth, land in Rehoboth.
<34:1> - 3 Aug. 1745, Benjamin COLE Jr., yeoman of Swanzey to Thomas PECK of same.
<33:447> - 8 Aug. 1745, Benjamin COLE Jr., yeoman of Swanzey sells meadow to 1st Baptist Church.
<37:20> - 22 Jan. 1746, Benjamin COLE, yeoman to Israel COLE, weaver of Rehoboth, land inherited in Swanzey.
<39:161> - 7 Feb. 1748/9, Benjamin COLE of Swanzey to Samuel BOWEN, his homestead.
<41:251> - 31 Jan. 1755, Benjamin COLE & wf Hannah to Daniel HARDING, both of Swanzey.
<41:255> - 18 Mar. 1755, Benjamin COLE Sr. to Eleazer HARDING, house carpenter of Providence, home & land.
<44:115> - 1760, Benjamin COLE & wf Desire of Dartmouth...
<51:353> - 1768, Benjamin COLE of Swanzey & wf Hannah, late widow of Job/John LUTHER.

PROVIDENCE RI DEEDS: (re: Andrew COLE)

<19:79> - 3 Feb. 1770, Benjamin HARDING, house carpenter & wf Hannah, of Providence to Andrew COLE, house carpenter of same, land on Main St.
<19:503> - 16 Nov. 1784, Hannah HARDING, widow of Benjamin to Andrew COLE, housewright of Woodstock, her rights in a lease by COLE to HARDING dated 3 Feb. 1770.
<21:341> - 25 Jan. 1786, Thomas WRIGHT to Andrew COLE, housewright of Prov., land on Transit St.

Will of **Andrew COLE**, housewright of Providence. <Providence PR 7:170>
...dated 25 Dec. 1787, mentions wf **Lillis** (executor) and sons **Joseph COLE & Cyrus COLE**. Inventory total, L130.10.

Guardianship of Children of **Benjamin COLE**. <Warren, Bristol Co.RI, record not specified>
...6 Feb. 1758, "**Benjamin COLE & Andrew COLE, Elizabeth COLE & Lillice COLE**, chil. of the sd **Benjamin**", request that Joseph BUTTERWORTH be app'td gdn. of **Andrew, Elizabeth & Lillice.**

Heirs of **Elkanah LEONARD** of Middleborough MA. <Plymouth Co.Deeds 37:20>
...6 Sept. 1727, Joseph LEONARD, John NELSON & wf Abiah, all of Middleboro...which sd Joseph & Abiah are two of the children and coheirs of Elkanah LEONARD, gent., dec'd, for Ł70 sold to our brother Elkanah LEONARD, attorney at law of Middleboro...all our right...two full seventh parts of one third part of the farm, orchard, dwelling house, barn, forge, dam, saw mill...which was set off unto our mother Mrs. Charity PERKINS who was ye relict widow of our sd Father during her life as her right of dower...in the homestead or farm of land whereon our sd Fatherlast dwelt... together also with all our right...all the iron mine or iron ore given to our sd Father by our Grandfather Maj. Thomas LEONARD Esq. in his last will...excepting & reserving to our sd Mother ye improvement of sd premises that belongeth to her during her sd life. Witnesses: Ebenezer RICHMOND Jr., Simeon LEONARD. Ack. 16 June 1740 by Abiah NELSON & witnessed by Thomas NELSON & James FRANKLING. Ack. 12 Nov. 1744 by Joseph LEONARD & Abiah HASKALL (who was lately Abiah NELSON). Rec. 13 Nov. 1744.

John NELSON of Middleborough MA to **Thomas NELSON** of same. <Plymouth Co.Deeds 27:213>
...29 Dec. 1730, John NELSON & wf Abiah, for Ł36 sold to Thomas NELSON our father...20 acres upon the Neck called Assawamsett Neck in Middleborough...26th lot on sd Neck and did belong to Benjamin BARTLETT dec'd...and also one half lot of land containing 30 acres...upon the Neck...the 4th lot in sd Neck & did originally belong unto the right of David THOMAS. Witnesses: Joseph LEONARD, Thomas NELSON Jr. Ack. 22 Apr. 1731 by grantors. Rec. 14 Mar. 1732.

Thomas NELSON of Middleborough MA to **Abiah NELSON et al.** <Plymouth Co.Deeds 38:129>
...10 Nov. 1746, Thomas NELSON...in consideratin of the love & good affection which I bear unto my three granddaughters, viz: Abiah NELSON, Charity NELSON & Hope NELSON, all of Middleborough, children of my son John NELSON dec'd, give to them...three lots on Assawamsett Neck in Middleboro ...13th lot in the original right of Francis COOMBES, 58th lot in the original right of John EDDY and the 59th lot in the original right of John WINSLOW Jr...also two acres...being one third part of an Island called by the Indians Anuxanan...in Quitteques Pond (the whole Island containing by estimation six acres). Witnesses: Barnabas SAMSON, William HOLLOWAY. Ack. same day by Thomas. Rec 13 Nov. 1746.

Seth HASKELL et al to **Jedidiah BEALS** of Middleboro MA. <Plymouth Co.Deeds 48:3>
...30 Aug. 1757, Seth HASKELL & wf Abiah of Rochester, Charity NELSON, Jacob BENNETT & wf Hope of Middleboro, for Ł45.18s, sold to Jedidiah BEALS...48 acres in two lots, #58 & #59, in the Sixteen Shilling Purchase in Middleboro called Assawamset Neck...in the original right of John EDDY & John WINSLOW Jr....and also one third part of an Island in Quitticus East Pond near the aforesaid lots, sd Island was called by the Indians Aunuxaunun. Witnesses: Mark HASKELL, Samuel HASKELL. Ack. 20 May 1761 by all grantors. Rec. 8 Sept. 1762.

Abiah HASKELL et al to **Roger HASKELL et al.** <Plymouth Co.Deeds 85:230>
...17 Dec. 1791, Abiah HASKELL of Rochester, George LEONARD & wf Charity of Middleboro and Jacob BENNET & wf Hope of Middleboro, for Ł100 sold to our brothers Roger HASKELL, Elisha HASKELL & Zebulon HASKELL, all of Middleboro...all rights in certain lots of land which our Honoured Mother Abiah HASKELL late of Middleboro dec'd, died seized lying in Assawampsett Neck...also two Islands which our sd dec'd Mother died seized of known by the name of the Great Island & the Little Island...each of which lye near about the Town Line between sd Middleborough & Rochester...in the East Quitiquos Pond. Witnesses: Nehemiah BENNET, John BENNET, Nathaniel SPRAGUE & Ruth SERMON/ SHERMON. Ack. 29 Dec. 1791 by Abiah; 25 Sept. 1792 by Jacob & Hope; 12 Feb. 1797 by George & Charity. Rec. 22 May 1799.

Estate of **John NELSON** of Middleboro MA. <Plymouth Co.PR #14561>
<original>...12 Mar. 1732, widow **Abiah NELSON** requests her father in law **Thomas NELSON** be app'td admr. <6:294> Letter/Bond 14 Mar. 1732, **Thomas NELSON,** yeoman of Middleboro, app'td admr. Sureties: Samuel NELSON & Thomas FAUNCE 2d, yeomen of Plymouth. Witnesses: Joshua CUSHING, Josiah COTTON. <6:363> Inventory, 14 Mar. 1732/3, Capt. Ichabod SOUTHWORTH, Jonathan FINNEY & Benjamin BOOTH Jr., all of Middleboro, app'td to appraise estate. "An Inventory of ye Real & Personal Estate of **John NELSON** of Middleborough who deceased July the sixth Anno Domini 1732" (no date); incl. quarter of a forge, Ł90; Indian servant boy, Ł25; sworn to 21 Sept. 1733 by admr. <8:123> Account 18 Sept. 1739 of admr.; Due from: Edward HACKETT, Ł4.1s2d and income of the forge to 12 Sept. 1739, Ł54.17s9d; Paid to: Jedediah WOOD, ROUNSFULL, Elkanah LEONARD, Thomas RAMSDELL, Joseph COBB, Samuel BARTLETT, John MURDOCH, Ebenezer HATHAWAY, Joseph LEONARD, John FINNY, Dr. PALMER; the Indian servant had died in Mar. 1738/9. <3:347> Receipt, 16 June 1740 of widow **Abiah NELSON,** to the admr. for her share of Ł286...saveing seven pound upon a bond by Phillip BUTLER who as yet cannot be found. Witnesses: Elkanah LEONARD, James FRANKLING. <7:141,142> Guardianship 24 May 1735, widow **Abiah NELSON** app'td gdn. of her children, viz: **Abiah NELSON, Charity NELSON & Hope NELSON,** all under 14.

Zebulon HASKELL of Rochester MA to **Benjamin PICKENS** of same. <Plymouth Co.Deeds 80:276>
...24 Mar. 1786, Zebulon HASKELL, yeoman, for Ł60 sold to Benjamin PICKENS, cordwainer, late of Middleborough now dwelling in Rochester...all rights in real estate conveyed to me by my Honoured father Seth HASKELL of Rochester dec'd in his last will & testament & also all the right in sd real estate which I have purchased of my brothers & sisters...for the particular bounds of the land, reference being had to the deed of sd land given to my father by his father Mark HASKELL of sd Rochester dec'd...reserving the right of improvement to my honoured Mother Abiah HASKELL. Witnesses: Samuel NELSON, Charity NELSON. Ack. 28 Dec. 1786 by Zebulon. Rec. 25 Oct. 1796.

Will of **Mark HASKELL** of Middleboro MA. <Plymouth Co.PR #9424, 29:376,378,379>
...dated 10 or 20 Feb. 1770...to wf **Abiah**, one half of all lands while a widow, one horse, two cows & ten sheep...to eldest son **Nathaniel HASKELL**, £48...to 2d son **Samuel HASKELL**, 6s...to 3d son **Micah HASKELL**, all rights in the farm where the Rev. Mr. Thomas WEST lives...also cedar swamp in Rochester which I hold by deed from my honoured Father **Roger HASKELL** dec'd...also £28...to 4th son **Roger HASKELL**, my homstead farm. Pr. 6 Sept. 1785.
(Note: The transcription of this will does not appear to have been completed, the writing stops midway in a sentence on the 2nd page. On the first page, in the upper corner, Bowman has written in pencil the names of six sons, viz: 5th **Elisha HASKELL**, 6th **Zebulon HASKELL**.)

Will of **Seth HASKELL** of Rochester MA. <Plymouth Co.PR #9431>
<20:306>...dated 12 Oct. 1769, mentions wf **Abiah** (executrix) and children: **Charity, Job HASKELL, Zebulon HASKELL, Mary, Seth HASKELL, Lydia, Hannah, Leonard HASKELL, Abiah & Joanna.** Pr. 17 Nov. 1769. <20:307> Inventory taken 9 Nov. 1769.
(Note: This will is not transcribed, the names of the children only are listed, therefore the reference to a "?child unborn" may be Bowman's.)

Will of **Abiah HASKELL**, widow of Middleboro MA. <Plymouth Co.PR 38:324,325,362,461;40:531>
...dated 28 Feb. 1803, mentons sons **Job HASKELL, Zebulon HASKELL**; daus **Lydia HAMMOND** wf of Benjamin, **Abiah PICKENS** wf of Benjamin; dec'd dau **Charity NELSON** wf of Samuel and her chil. viz: **Mercy NELSON, Sally NELSON, William NELSON, Hipsibah NELSON & Abiah NELSON**; dec'd dau **Mary SOUTHWORTH** wf of Gideon and her chil., viz: **Seth SOUTHWORTH, Thomas SOUTHWORTH, William SOUTHWORTH & Hannah SOUTHWORTH**; dec'd son **Seth HASKELL** and his children **Polly HASKELL & Thomas Allen HASKELL**; dau **Hannah SOUTHWORTH** wf of Nathaniel. Pr. 5 May 1803.

Hunnewell HASKELL et al of Craig, IND to **Thomas SHAW** of Rochester MA. <Plymouth Co.Deeds 157:128>
...1823...Hunnewell HASKELL, Betsy FREEMAN & Amelia HASKELL (and Hunnewell & Amelia for the heirs of Roxellana DEAN), Nabby LAWSON, Eveline FREEMAN, Lucy FREEMAN & Job FREEMAN, all of Craig Township, county of Switzerland, State of Indiana, for $50.00 sell to Thomas SHAW...land and marsh in Mattapoisett Neck formerly owned by Job HASKELL & his wf Elizabeth.

PLYMOUTH COUNTY DEEDS: (re: HASKELL)

<59:50> - 3 June 1777, Job HASKELL, cordwainer of Rochester. Wf Elizabeth signs.
<59:63> - 30 June 1777, Barzillai HAMMOND, yeoman & wf Sarah to Job HASKELL, cordwainer of same, mentions land of Antipas HAMMOND.
<84:164> - 10 Oct. 1793, Deborah HASKELL & "Joa"/Job HASKELL of Rochester and Nathaniel SOUTHWORTH & Hannah SOUTHWORTH of Middleboro to Benjamin PICKENS of Rochester ...land rec'd by will of their father Seth HASKELL.

(Note: References only with no data, viz: 64:248;67:58;78:140;90:125.)

Will of **Thomas CHIPMAN** of Salisbury CT. <Litchfield CT PR #1432>
...dated 31 July 1752, mentions wf **Abigail** and children: **Thomas CHIPMAN, John CHIPMAN** & his wf, **Samuel CHIPMAN, Jonathan CHIPMAN, Sarah BIRD & Amos CHIPMAN.** Pr. 2 Sept. 1753 or 8 Apr. 1754.

Estate of **John CHIPMAN** of Salisbury CT. <Litchfield CT PR #1431>
...7 Nov. 1754, **Sarah CHIPMAN** app'td admx. Distribution to heirs (no date), viz: widow, **Thomas CHIPMAN, Mary CHIPMAN, Sarah VAN DUSER**(sp), **Abigail PAINTERS**(sp) **& John CHIPMAN.**

Will of **Daniel ELDRIDGE** of Groton CT. <Stonington CT PR #1210>
...dated 1 Sept. 1789, mentions wf **Betsey** and children: **Daniel ELDRIDGE, Salley AVERY, Lucy ELDRIDGE, Betsey ELDRIDGE & Nancy ELDRIDGE.** Pr. 6 Oct. 1789. Receipt 25 June 1790 of **Samuel & Sally**.* Receipt 7 Apr. 1795 of **Nancy.** Receipt 12 Sept.1793 of **Joseph & Betsey COTTON.** Receipt 27 Feb. 1794 of **Elijah & Lucy PORTER.** (* Samuel & Sally AVERY)

Will of **Capt. Daniel ELDREDGE** of Groton CT. <New London CT PR #1891>
...dated 5 Mar. 1736/7, mentions wf **Abigail** and children: **Daniel ELDREDGE, Charles ELDREDGE, Abigail PACKER** wf of Ichabod, **Zeruiah PACKER** wf of James, **Sarah ELDREDGE & Barshebe ELDREDGE.** Pr. 10 May 1737. Petition 21 Jan. 1745/6 of **Thomas CHESTER** & wf **Sarah** one the the daus. Division of land 27 Jan. 1745/6 to the above four daus.

Estate of **Isaac FITCH** of Lebanon CT. <Windham CT PR #1369>
Bond 15 Nov. 1791, Ebenezer CROWELL app'td admr. Estate insolvent.

Will of **Ruth THOMAS**, widow of Middleboro MA. <Plymouth Co.PR 20:538>
...dated 18 June 1770, mentions youngest sons **Elijah THOMAS & Enoch THOMAS**; sons **Barzillai THOMAS & Moses THOMAS**; grandchildren **Ebenezer HACKET & Henry HACKET**, the chil of **Ebenezer HACKET.** Witnesses: Jacob BENNET, Hope BENNET, Hope THOMAS. Pr. 22 May 1771. Inventory taken 29 Mar. 1771.

Will of **Amos NELSON**, yeoman of Middleboro MA. <Plymouth Co.PR #14541>
<35:452>...dated 1 Sept. 1795, mentions sons **Isaac NELSON, Amos NELSON Jr.**; daus **Hannah BRIGGS, Mary NELSON**; brother **Ebenezer NELSON.** Witnesses: Ebenezer NELSON, Samuel PICKENS, Nehemiah BENNET
<35:454> Letter/Bond 15 Jan. 1796, of Isaac NELSON, yeoman, admr. Sureties: Ebenezer NELSON, clerk & Samuel PICKENS, yeoman, all of Middleboro.

Will of **Ebenezer BRIGGS.** <Plymouth Co.PR #2836, 93:179>
...dated Oct. 1844, mentions children: **Ebenezer BRIGGS, Catharine BRIGGS, Daniel BRIGGS, Samuel BRIGGS & Polly N. THOMAS.** Codicil (no date given) states sons **Samuel & Daniel** are dec'd. Pr. May 1851.

Will of **Samuel BASSETT**, gent. of Chilmark MA. <Dukes Co.PR 6:41>
...dated 18 Mar. 1762...being far advanced in years...mentions wf **Martha**; to dau **Sarah NORTON** wf of Petter/Peter, land in Chillmark bounded by land of Zachariah MAYHEW, Matthew MAYHEW, Esq., Beriah TILTON, William BASSETT, Nathaniel BASSETT, William STEWARD and lands now in the improvement of Sarah COTTLE and Shobal SMITH...containing 43 acres; son **Cornelius BASSETT** (executor). Witnesses: Samuel HUNT, Shubael BUTLER, Jno. TILLTON, David HILLMAN. Witnes. sworn, 19 Dec. 1770.

Will of **John CHIPMAN** of Newport RI. <Newport Town Council, 1756-1760>
<p.11>...dated 17 Oct. 1749, mentons sons **James CHIPMAN, Handley CHIPMAN, John CHIPMAN**; dau **Lydia SWIFT**; grandchildren **Isaac SMITH & Mary SMITH**; dau in law **Mary CHIPMAN** & her son **William CHIPMAN**; children, **Perces, Bethia & Deborah**; **Perces CHIPMAN** son of son **James**; dec'd dau **Rebecca MOORE** (her husband & children living); son **Handley** & son in law **David MOORE**, executors. <p.9> Pr. 2 Feb. 1756. <p.12> Rec. 3 Feb. 1756. <p.16> Inventory 1 Mar. 1756, total Ł1976.

BARNSTABLE COUNTY PROBATE: (re: Samuel SMITH)

1768	Samuel	Wellfleet	will	13:367,368
1768	Samuel	Harwich	will	13:369
1794	Samuel	Wellfleet	will	24:341;27:284,373;28:27,47,93,157,206,313,314,369
1802	Samuel	Orleans	adm.	25:285
1817	Samuel	Barnstable	will	40:119,131;41:21;43:512,513

Will of **Joseph BLAKE**, Esq. of Billerica MA. <Middlesex Co.PR #1843>
...dated 11 Sept. 1813, mentions wf **Huldah** and children: **Francis BLAKE, Charles BLAKE, George BLAKE, John Welland BLAKE, Joshua BLAKE, Sophia RICE & Harriet MILLS**; unnamed chil. of son in law **Watson FREEMAN** dec'd; son **George BLAKE**, Esq. of Boston & Josiah CROSBY Jr., Esq., executors. Petition 14 Nov. 1820 of widow **Huldah BLAKE**, for her dower...and that **George BLAKE** of Boston and the chil. of **John W. BLAKE** late of Brattleboro VT dec'd and the chil of **Francis BLAKE**, Esq. late of Worcester dec'd and **Charles BLAKE** and **Joshua BLAKE** and the chil. of **Sophia RICE** late wf of **Nathan RICE** have...neglected to assign to her, her reasonable dower. Petition 10 Nov. 1887, Francis M. BOUTWELL of Groton CT asks to be app'td admr. on the will of **Joseph BLAKE**...duly proved on 25 Aug. 1818 and **George BLAKE** app'td exr...has since dec'd without having fully executed sd will; adm. granted 15 Nov. 1887.

MICRO #11 OF 18

Estate of **William CHIPMAN** of Wellfleet MA. <Barnstable Co.PR>
<25:112> 8 Apr. 1795, widow **Betty CHIPMAN** app'td admx. <25:869> 27 Oct. 1795, allowance paid to widow. <25:668> Guardianship 29 Apr. 1795, **David CHIPMAN, Martha CHIPMAN & Ebenezer CHIPMAN** choose their mother **Betty CHIPMAN** as their gdn. <28:44> Inventory taken 27 Apr. 1795. <28:104> Account 29 Mar. 1796, of admx. <28:217> Division 21 Mar. 1796, to widow and following children, viz: **Mercy RICH** wf of John, **Mary PEPPER** wf of Isaac, **William CHIPMAN, John CHIPMAN, Samuel M. CHIPMAN, David CHIPMAN, Martha CHIPMAN & Ebenezer CHIPMAN.** <28:389> Account 27 Oct. 1795 of admx. <33:151> 14 June 1808, the widow being now dec'd, her thirds to be divided. <24:211> Division, 12 July 1808, widow's thirds assigned to **John CHIPMAN**, mariner of Boston, he to pay $79.55 to each of his brothers & sisters, viz: **Samuel Mayo CHIPMAN** of Wellfleet, **David CHIPMAN** of Wellfleet, **Ebenezer CHIPMAN** of Wellfleet, **Mary RICH** wf of John, **Mercy PEPPER** wf of Isaac of Hardwick, **Martha HINKLEY** wf of Moses of Wellfleet and **Betsey CHIPMAN** of Wellfleet, the dau of **William CHIPMAN** of Wellfleet dec'd who was a brother.

Estate of **Jabez SARGENT** of Maldon MA. <Middlesex Co.PR #19881>
<8:335> 11 Jan. 1693/4, brothers **Joseph SERGEANT & John SERGEANT**, app'td admrs. <8:370> Inventory taken 20 Dec. 1693; no real estate. <8:616> Account, 14 Jan.1694/5. <8:617> Division 4 Feb. 1694/95, the estate being Ł66.19s, to be equally divided between **Joseph & John SERGEANT** and **Seth & Deborah TOBY** the chil. of **Nathan & Mary TOBY**, only brothers & sister of **Jabez SERGEANT** dec'd in the whole blood.

Daniel CROCKER of Yarmouth N.S. to **Joseph COBB** of Plympton MA. <Plymouth Co.Deeds 66:239,240>
<66:239>...14 Aug. 1784, Daniel CROCKER appoints son Heman CROCKER of Plympton his attorney. <66:240>...2 Feb. 1787, Heman CROCKER, attorney for Daniel CROCKER, sells to Joseph COBB...one fifth share of homestead of Eleazer CROCKER late of Plympton.

Estate of **Eleazer CROCKER**, yeoman of Plympton MA. <Plymouth Co.PR>
<29:294-6> Order for division, 7 Mar. 1785. Division 2 May 1785, to widow **Hannah CROCKER** and following heirs, viz: eldest brother **Daniel CROCKER**, youngest brother **Joseph CROCKER, Rebecca DUNHAM** wf of Sylvanus, **Mary SAVORY** wf of Thomas and **Sarah PERRY** wf of Elijah.

Estate of **Jacob CHIPMAN** of Halifax MA. <Plymouth Co.PR 25:526>
Division 3 July 1780, to widow **Anna** and following children, viz: **George CHIPMAN, Lucy, Content,**

Lydia, Joseph CHIPMAN, Jacob CHIPMAN (eldest son). Guardianship, 1778 for all children except George.

ESSEX COUNTY PROBATE: (re: CHIPMAN)

1761	Capt. Samuel	Salem	adm.	#5319
1768	John	Marblehead	adm.	#5313
1775	Rev. John	Beverly	will	#5314
1791	Anstice, widow	Salem	adm.	#5310
1803	Mary, widow	Salem	adm.	#5318
1804	Eleazer M., mariner	Salem	adm.	#5311
1808	Thomas Jr., trader	Salem	adm.	#5320
1814	Thomas, mariner	Newburyport	adm.	#5321
1817	Elizabeth, widow	Beverly	non comp	#5312
1817	John H. & Maria	Beverly	gdns.	#5316
1817	Joseph	Beverly	adm.	#5317
1820	John, cabinet maker	Salem	adm.	#5315
1822	Capt. Thomas, trader	Salem	will	#5322

John HOLMES of Plimton MA to **Jacob CHIPMAN** of Barnstable MA. <Plymouth Co.Deeds 21:92> ...7 Jan. 1726/7, John HOLMES for Ł800, sells to Jacob CHIPMAN, husbandman...the farm tenement whereon I now dwell in Plimton...about 200 acres upland meadow & swampy land.

Will of **Jacob CHIPMAN**, husbandman of Halifax MA. <Plymouth Co.PR> <8:468>...dated 17 Sept. 1740...bound on an expedition against the Spaniards in the West Indies.. what is due him from his first wife's estate to be given to his two eldest daughters **Sary & Abigail** when they reach 18; wf **Bethiah** to have income of whole estate till son **Jacob CHIPMAN** is 20 yrs. old, then he to pay the nine daughters Ł15 ea, viz: **Sary, Abigail, Lucretia, Lydia, Ann, Bethia, Priscilla, Hannah & Mary**; wf **Bethiah** & brother **Seth CHIPMAN**, executors. <11:77> Guardianship, 4 Apr. 1748, **Jacob CHIPMAN** chose Robert WATERMAN of Halifax as his gdn.

MICRO #12 OF 18

ISAAC HOWLAND[2] (John[1])

Heirs of **Isaac HOWLAND Jr.** of Middleboro to **Elkanah LEONARD** of same. <Plymouth Co.Deeds 40:134> ...6 July 1738, Isaac HOWLAND, Jeremiah HOWLAND & Joseph HOWLAND, all of Middleboro, only sons & heirs of Isaac Jr. dec'd and grandsons of Isaac HOWLAND late of Middleboro dec'd, for Ł45 sell to Elkanah LEONARD, Esq...30 acres in Assawamsett Neck in Middleboro, being the 11th lot in the right of Isaac HOWLAND. Rec. 30 Oct. 1749.

Heirs of **Isaac HOWLAND Jr.** of Middleboro. <Plymouth Co.Deeds 35:139> ...17 Mar. 1739, Isaac HOWLAND, Jeremiah HOWLAND & Joseph HOWLAND, all of Middleboro, divide land left by their father Isaac HOWLAND Jr. dec'd & formerly of their grandfather Isaac, left to him by their father Isaac who died first...mentions being nephews & coheirs of uncle Seth HOWLAND of Middleboro. Witnesses: Isaac BENNET, John MILLER. Rec. 3 Jan. 1742.

Joseph HOWLAND of Middleboro to **Cornelius BENNETT** of Newport RI. <Plymouth Co.Deeds 35:150> ...31 Dec. 1742, Joseph HOWLAND sells to Cornelius BENNET...land in Middleboro. Witnesses: Elkanah LEONARD, Benjamin WHITE. Ack. same day.

Isaac & Jeremiah HOWLAND of Middleboro MA to **Isaac PEIRCE Jr. & John HOWLAND.** <Plymouth Co.Deeds> <46:168>...1 Apr. 1756, Isaac HOWLAND & Jeremiah HOWLAND, sell to Isaac PEIRCE Jr. & John HOWLAND ...all their interest in the 154th lot in 3rd allotment in Sixteen Shilling Purchase in Middleboro...in original right of Isaac HOWLAND. Witnesses: William THRASHER, Thomas NELSON. Rec. 3 Nov 1760

Joseph HOWLAND of N. Yarmouth MA to **Isaac PEIRCE Jr. & John HOWLAND.** <Plymouth Co.Deeds 46:168> ...4 Nov. 1756, Joseph HOWLAND, for Ł3 sells to Isaac PEIRCE Jr. & John HOWLAND, both of Middleboro...all his interest in the 154th lot in 3rd allotment in Sixteen Shilling Purchase in Middleboro...in original right of Isaac HOWLAND. Witnesses: John BARROWS, William CUSHMAN. Rec. 3 Nov. 1760.

Joseph HOWLAND of N. Yarmouth MA to **Elkanah LEONARD** of Middleboro MA. <Plymouth Co.Deeds 47:247> ...5 Nov. 1756, Joseph HOWLAND, housewright, for Ł15 sells to Elkanah LEONARD...one third of lands in Assawamset Neck in Middleboro...30 acres...the 11th lot in the right of Isaac HOWLAND. Witnesses: Jeremiah HOWLAND, Zebulon LEONARD. Rec. 7 July 1762.

Estate of **Isaac HOWLAND Jr.** of Middleboro MA. <Plymouth Co.PR #10922> <4:388> Letter/Bond 6 Mar. 1723/4, widow **Sarah HOWLAND** app'td admx. Sureties: Nathaniel SOUTHWORTH & Nathaniel THOMAS of Middleboro. <4:407> Inventory taken 13 Mar. 1723/4 by Jonathan COB, Peter BENNET, Nathaniel SOUTHWORTH; total real estate, Ł158; sworn to 1 June 1724 by admx.

Guardianship of Children of **Isaac HOWLAND Jr.**, dec'd of Middleboro MA. <Plymouth Co.PR #10930> <4:444> Appointment/Bonds 19 June 1724, of **Jeremiah THOMAS** as gdn. of his grandsons **Jeremiah HOWLAND, Isaac HOWLAND & Joseph HOWLAND**, all under 14, the sons of **Isaac HOWLAND Jr.** dec'd. Surety: Samuel RANSOM. Witnesses: Thomas WETHERELL, Marcy KEEN. <7:136,137> Letters/Bonds 21 May 1735, Samuel WOOD app'td gdn. of **Jeremiah, Isaac & Joseph HOWLAND**, all under 21. Surety: Joseph BENNETT Jr. Witnesses: Josiah COTTON, Jno. CUSHING Jr.

Estate of **Isaac HOWLAND**, labourer of Middleboro MA. <Plymouth Co.PR #10924> <27:253> Letter/Bond 5 Nov. 1787, Nehemiah BENNET app'td admr. Sureties: Zebulon LEONARD, Rufus RICHMOND, all of Middleboro. Witnesses: Aaron NORTON, Isaac LOTHROP. <30:275> Inventory taken 13 Nov. 1787 by Josiah VAUGHAN, George VAUGHAN, Jacob WOOD; total personal estate, Ł191.16.9; sworn to 7 Jan. 1788 by admr.

Estate of **Jeremiah HOWLAND** of Middleboro MA. <Plymouth Co.PR #10929> <27:315> Letter/Bond 4 Jan. 1790, Roger CLARK app'td admr. Sureties: Zebulon CUSHMAN, Nehemiah BENNET, all of Middleboro. Witnesses: Benjamin WHITMAN, Isaac LOTHROP. <31:107> Inventory taken 1 or 26 Dec. 1789 by John MILLER 3d, George VAUGHAN, Silvanus TILLSON; total personal estate, Ł238. 6.7.; total real estate, Ł730.4.7., incl. meadow on Winatuxet River, rights in the Pond iron ore and small scraps of land in the 16 Shilling & South Purchase; sworn to 4 Jan. 1790 by admr. <33: 439> Account of admr., 8 Oct. 1793; Received from Nehemiah BENNET which was due the dec'd as heir to the estate of **Isaac HOWLAND** dec'd and from Benjamin STROBRIDG/STROWBRIDGE; Paid to: Charity HOWLAND, Dr. John SAMSON, Lucy LEACH, Amos FULLER, Josiah CARVER, Gideon SAMSON, Joel ELLIS, Robert WATERMAN, Bez(e)a SOULE, Seth MILLER, Peleg THOMAS, John SMITH 3d, Andrew LEACH, Isaiah CUSHMAN, Israel WOOD, Elkanah BENNET, Dr. Thomas STURTEVANT, Samuel PERRY, Abraham THOMAS, Ruth SAMSON, John WESTON, Jacob THOMAS, Silvanus TILLSON, Judith WASGATE, George SIMMONS, Ephraim THOMAS, Elias MILLER & George VAUGHAN. <33:440> Division 3 June 1791, by Zebedee SPROUT, Simeon DOGGETT & George VAUGHAN, of homestead of dec'd lying in a place called Wapponocket adjoining to Anawamset & Pockshire Ponds and fresh meadow in Plimton & adjoining Winatuxet River which formerly belonged to **Isaac HOWLAND**, grandfather of dec'd; divided among the following children, viz: **Thankful SIMMONS** wf of George; **Betsy MILLER** wf of Jedediah; **Jeremiah BENNET**, only child of dec'd dau **Sarah BENNET** wf of Nehemiah; **Charity HOWLAND** and **Susanna CLARK** wf of Roger.

Guardianship of Child of **Seth HOWLAND**, dec'd of Middleboro MA. <Plymouth Co.PR #10949> <15:192> Bond/Appointment 3 Apr. 1759, James COLE of Middleboro app'td gdn. of **Nathan HOWLAND** (who chose him). Surety: David SIMMONS. Witnesses: Edward & Hannah WINSLOW, Daniel VAUGHAN, Jabez VAUGHAN Jr.

Thomas COLE of Middleboro MA to **Archippus COLE** of same. <Plymouth Co.Deeds 52:128> ...25 Jan. 1762, Thomas COLE to brother Archippus COLE...north east end of 14th lot in 3rd Allotment in Little Lot Men's Purchase. Rec. 1765.

PLYMOUTH COUNTY DEEDS: (re: David THOMAS)

<79:272> - 31 Dec. 1770, D.T. & wf Deborah of Middleboro to brother Silvanus THOMAS of same, sons of William THOMAS of same. Ack. 9 Aug. 1771 by both. Rec. 8 Oct. 1796.

<60:90> - 5 Mar. 1779, D.T., yeoman of Middleboro, for Ł75 sold to Benjamin THOMAS, yeoman of same, one acre meadow in Wood's purchase. Deborah THOMAS signs.

<67:207> - 8 Mar. 1779, D.T., yeoman of Middleboro to Benjamin THOMAS Jr., yeoman of same, one acre meadow in Wood's Purchase. Rebecca THOMAS signs. Rec. 9 Oct. 1788.

<60:228> - 1781, D.T. of Marshfield.

<62:138> - 1783, D.T. of Marshfield.

<62:218> - 28 July 1783, D.T. Jr. & wf Rebecca and Levi THOMAS & wf Hannah, of Middleboro, to Andrew COLE. (Signed David THOMAS 2d.)

<72:215> - 5 Nov. 1787, D.T., gent. of Middleboro, sells land bought of his brother John THOMAS. Wf Deborah THOMAS releases dower. Ack. 8 July 1790, Plymouth Co., by D. T. Rec. 23 May 1792.

<82:288> - 5 Feb. 1791, D.T., gent. & wf Deborah of Middleboro to Isaac TINKHAM of same. Ack. 9 Feb. 1791 by Capt. D.T. Rec. 20 Oct. 1797.

<72:166> - 15 Nov. 1791, D.T. of Woodstock VT, admr. of est. of Eliphalet THOMAS late of Middleboro, sells to Thomas STURTEVANT. Rec 12 Apr. 1792. <also 73:131,79:255>

(Note: References to David THOMAS with no data, viz: 52:32,163,164;60:84;63:56.)

David THOMAS of Middleboro MA to **Levi THOMAS** of same. <Plymouth Co.Deeds 99:68> ...23 Nov. 1790, David THOMAS, gent. to Levi THOMAS...the homestead where I now live near Sawmill Brook...and land I sold to Benjamin THOMAS & Benjamin THOMAS Jr. reserving Saw Mill Dam. Wf Elizabeth THOMAS releases dower. Ack. 22 Jan.1791. Rec. 7 Feb. 1791.

Will of **Capt. Peter BENNET** of Middleboro MA. <Plymouth Co.PR #1844> <11:382>...dated 5 Oct. 1749...to son **Isaac BENNET**...my one seventh and one quarter of one seventh of the 200 acres formerly laid out to Gov. PRENCE being what I bought of Col. Shubael GORHAM dec'd...also land bought of Nathan HOWLAND which is part of the homestead of my brother **Seth HOWLAND** dec'd which fell to sd Nathan HOWLAND in the division of **Seth HOWLAND**'s estate; grandsons **John BENNET & Samuel BENNET**, sons of my dec'd son **Joseph BENNET**; minor grandchildren **Peter BENNET Anna BENNET & Jael BENNET**, chil. of dec'd son **Peter BENNET**; granddaughters **Priscilla BENNET & Susanna BENNET**, daus of dec'd son **Nathan BENNET** & his widow **Jemima BENNET**; daus **Elizabeth DARLING**

Susanna DREW, Priscilla MILLER; grandson **Abiezer EDSON**, son of dec'd dau **Jael EDSON**; dau **Deborah THACHER**. <11:385> Pr. 6 Nov. 1749. <11:316> Inventory taken 20 Nov. 1749; total real estate, Ł5085; total personal estate, Ł1013.17.

Estate of **Priscilla BENNET**, widow of Middleboro MA. <Plymouth Co.PR #1847>
<11:317> 1 Jan. 1749, admr. app'td. <11:318> Inventory taken 27 Dec. 1749 of estate of **Mrs. Priscilla BENNET**, late wife of **Capt. Peter BENNET** late of Middleboro dec'd; total, Ł650.

Estate of **Isaac BENNET** of Middleboro MA. <Plymouth Co.PR #1806>
<13:470> Letter/Pr. <13:548> Inventory. <14:120> Bond for sale of real estate. <14:265> Division, 26 Men's Purchase. <14:412> Account. <19:441> Division 9 July 1760 to following heirs, viz: widow **Mary BENNET**; 1st son **Isaac BENNET**; 2d son **Joseph BENNET**; 3d son **Nathan BENNET**; 4th son **Jedediah BENNET**; only dau **Mary BENNET**.

Nathan BENNETT of Middleborough MA to **John MILLER** of same. <Plymouth Co.Deeds 49:256>
...16 Jan. 1764, Nathan BENNETT, labourer, sold to John MILLER, yeoman...all his right in the thirds & right of dower in the real estate of my honoured Father Isaac BENNETT late of Middleboro dec'd which was set off to my honoured mother Mary BENNETT widow. Witnesses: Seth MILLER, John HOLMES. Ack. 2 Apr. 1765. Rec. 11 Apr. 1765.

Matthias ELLIS et al of Middleborough MA to **John MILLER** of same. <Plymouth Co.Deeds 49:257>
...26 Sept. 1763, Matthias ELLIS & wf Lucia and John MORTON & wf Elizabeth, for Ł12.13s4d sold to John MILLER, yeoman...all rights in first allotment in Twelve Men's Purchase in Middleborough... and is part of the land given to the children of Nathan BENNETT as may appear by the will of our Grandfather Capt. Peter BENNETT...and land in the second allotment...as was given to the children and grandchildren of our honoured Grandfather dec'd. Ack. same day by John & Elizabeth; 16 Nov. 1763 by Matthias & Lucia. Rec. 11 Apr. 1765.

John & Peter BENNETT of Middleborough MA to **John MILLER** of same. <Plymouth Co.Deeds 49:255>
...17 Aug. 1757, John BENNET, tanner and Peter BENNETT, labourer, sold to John MILLER, yeoman... all our right in land in Middleboro...given to the children of Nathan BENNETT dec'd by our Grandfather Capt. Peter BENNETT dec'd...and they dying in their immature age...also our right in the 21st lot in the 2nd allotment in the Twelve Men's Purchase which was our honoured Grandfather's. Witnesses: Zechariah WESTON Jr., Nathan BENNETT. Ack. 26 Dec. 1757. Rec. 11 Apr. 1765.

Estate of **Samuel BENNETT**, labourer of Middleboro MA. <Plymouth Co.PR #1849>
<original> Petition 29 Jan. 1779, of Edmond WOOD, Abner KINGMAN, Thomas NELSON & Amos NELSON, the Select men of Middleboro...request Isaac TOMSON be app'td admr. <23:223> Letter/Bond 1 Feb. 1779, Isaac TOMSON of Middleboro app'td admr. Sureties: William TOMSON, William CUSHMAN. Witnesses: David KINGMAN, J. LOTHROP. <25:217> Inventory taken 29 Mar. 1779 by Edmund WOOD, John MILLER 3d, Zackariah WESTON, all yeomen of Middleboro; total personal estate, Ł44.18s4d; no real estate; sworn to 5 Apr. 1779 by admr. <original> Petition 1 Feb. 1779 of admr., that estate is insolvent and requests that Ebenezer TINKHAM & John COBB be app'td to examine claims. <25:265> Account 4 Oct. 1779, of admr.; Claims allowed to: Dr. Thomas STURTEVANT, Ł17.18s, Samuel THOMAS, Ł3 and Elnathan HASKELL, 3s; admr. ordered to pay creditors at the rate of 16s8d, one and one twentieth farthing, on a pound.

Samuel BENNETT Jr. of Middleborough MA to **Samuel THACHER** of same. <Plymouth Co.Deeds 49:148>
...20 Sept. 1757, Samuel BENNETT Jr., cordwinder, sold to Samuel THACHER...land in Middleboro... given me as an heir of my honoured Father Lieut. Joseph BENNETT of Middleborough...by my Grandfather Capt. Peter BENNETT of same...also one quarter of a share in lands given by my Grandfather to my uncle Nathan BENNETT & his heirs. Ack. 2 Jan. 1758. Rec. 15 Mar. 1764.

Samuel BENNETT of Middleborough MA to **John MILLER** of same. <Plymouth Co.Deeds 49:256>
...6 Mar. 1765, Samuel BENNETT, cordwinder & wf Anna, for Ł5 sold to John MILLER, yeoman...all rights in land in the 11th & 12th lots in the first allotment of 100 acre lots in the Twelve Men's Purchase in Middleboro given to the children of Nathan BENNETT by their Grandfather Capt. Peter BENNETT dec'd. Witnesses: Thomas VAUGHAN, Seth MILLER. Ack. 2 Apr. 1765 by both. Rec. 11 Apr. 1765.

PLYMOUTH COUNTY DEEDS: (re: Samuel BENNETT, grantor**)**

<44:227> - 1758, S.B. to Ebenezer SPROUT.
<46:229> - 1761, S.B. to Ebenezer WOOD.
<51:205> - 1765, S.B. to Samuel BENNETT Jr.
<52:49> - 1765, S.B. to Elias MILLER.
<55:1> - 1769, S.B. to dau Ruth SNOW.
<56:226>- 1772, S.B. b Zachariah WHITMAN admr. to Job RANDALL.

Anne BENNETT of Middleborough MA to **Cornelius BENNET** of same. <Plymouth Co.Deeds 50:65>
...2 Sept. 1763, Anne BENNET, singlewoman, sold to Cornelius BENNET...land in Middleboro...one third part of a share which did belong to Peter BENNET Jr. dec'd, about one acre...and a third part of an acre, special reference being had to the Records Surveys & Settlement of this lot among the heirs of Capt. Peter BENNET dec'd. Witnesses: Agnes TINKHAM, Shubael TINKHAM. Ack. 23 Jan. 1764. Rec. 17 July 1765.

Peter BENNETT of Middleboro MA to **John MILLER** of same. <Plymouth Co.Deeds 49:256>
...25 Feb. 1761, Peter BENNETT, yeoman sold to John MILLER, yeoman...all rights in the home farm

of my honoured Grandfather Capt. Peter BENNETT of Middleborough...as conveyed to me by deed from Isaac BENNETT son of Isaac son of sd Peter...7 May 1757...also one quarter part of a grist mill given me in the last will of my sd Grandfather. Wf Lydia BENNETT releases dower. Witnesses: Joseph LOVELL, John MILLER 3d. Ack. 2 Apr. 1765 by Peter. Rec. 11 Apr. 1765.

Paul PRATT of Middleboro MA to **Ichabod WOOD** of same. <Plymouth Co.Deeds 52:59>
...26 Oct. 1765, Paul PRATT & wf Jael, for £8.13s4d sold to Ichabod WOOD...15 acres in Middleboro in the Prince's & Coombe's Purchase...bounded by land of John HARLOW, Moses WOOD, sd Ichabod WOOD and heirs of Robert BARROWS...and is all our right of land given to the sd Jael PRATT by the last will of her Grandfather Capt. Peter BENNETT. Witnesses: Zebulon LEONARD, Shubael TINKHAM. Ack. 29 Oct. 1765 by both grantors.

Paul PRATT of Dartmouth MA to **Seth & Jedediah MILLER** of Middleboro MA. <Plymouth Co.Deeds 70:3>
...12 Jan. 1771, Paul PRATT, labourer & wf Jael, for £6.13s8d sold to Seth MILLER & Jedediah MILLER...all rights in 90 acre lot that Capt. Peter BENNETT dec'd gave to the heirs of Nathan BENNETT dec'd which is in the first allotment in the Twelve Men's Purchase in Middleboro, about four acres or the third of a share. Witnesses: Peter BENNETT, Noah PRATT. Ack. 13 Feb. 1790 by both grantors. Rec. 18 Feb. 1790.

Paul PRATT of Middleborough MA to **Aaron SNOW** of same. <Plymouth Co.Deeds 82:226>
...19 Aug. 1796, Paul PRATT, yeoman for $400.00 sold to Aaron SNOW, yeoman...about eighteen acres in 26 Men's Purchase in Middleboro and contains all of that part of lands given to me by the last will of my honoured father Eleazer PRATT late of Middleboro dec'd, that lyeth northeasterly of the highway that crosseth sd lands. Wf Jael PRATT releases dower. Witnesses: Luther REDDING, Enoch THOMAS. Ack. same day. Rec. 14 Sept. 1797.

Paul PRATT of Middleborough MA to **Enoch THOMAS 2d** of same. <Plymouth Co.Deeds 85:110>
...19 Aug. 1796, Paul PRATT, yeoman for $800.00 sold to Enoch THOMAS 2d, gent...50 acres in the 26 Men's Purchase in Middleborough and contains all that part of lands given me by the last will of my honoured father Eleazer PRATT late of Middleborough dec'd that lyeth southwesterly of the highway that crosseth sd lands. Wf Jael PRATT releases dower. Witnesses: Luther REDDING, Aaron SNOW. Ack. same day. Rec. 25 Mar. 1799.

Paul PRATT of Middleborough MA to **Noah CUSHMAN** of same. <Plymouth Co.Deeds 93:2>
...12 May 1796, Paul PRATT, yeoman for $90.00 sold to Noah CUSHMAN, yeoman...three sixteenths part of a saw mill in Middleborough on Nemaskett River, southwardly side thereof at the end of the dam...formerly owned by Judge OLIVER. Wf Jael PRATT releases dower. Witnesses: Nathaniel RUSSEL, Hannah SNOW. Ack. 8 Aug. 1796 by Paul. Rec. 13 Apr. 1802.

Benaiah PRATT of Farmington MA to **Silvanus WARREN** of Middleborough MA.<Plymouth Co.Deeds 151:231>
...15 Sept. 1810, Benaiah PRATT, clerk & wf Louisa, for $483.66 sold to Silvanus WARREN, yeoman.. all of our undivided fifth part of the two thirds of all real estate...that our Honoured father Silvanus WARREN late of Middleborough, gent. dec'd, died seized...our other fifth part...we leave for our Honoured Step mother Sarah WARREN, widow of our sd father. Witnesses: Nehemiah COBB 2d, Louis COBB. Ack. 17 Sept. 1810 by both grantors. Rec. 7 Oct. 1824.

Benaiah PRATT Jr. of Farmington ME to **Abial WASHBURN** of Middleborough MA. <Plymouth Co.Deeds> <155:235>...16 Sept. 1825, Benaiah PRATT Jr., for $15.48 sold to Abial WASHBURN, Esq...all rights ...in real estate in Middleborough which was assigned and set off to & improved by the widow Sarah WARREN late of Middleborough dec'd as her thirds or dower of estate of her husband Silvanus WARREN dec'd...being one seventh of one fifth...which I the sd Benajah hold by inheritance from my mother Louisa PRATT dec'd the late wife of Benaiah PRATT who inherited the same from her late father Silvanus WARREN. Witnesses: Philander WASHBURN, George WASHBURN. Rec. 18 Oct. 1825.

Will of **Deacon Ephraim WOOD** of Middleboro MA. <Plymouth Co.PR 9:269>
...dated 20 May 1738, mentions wf **Patience**; sons **Josiah WOOD, Samuel WOOD, Ephraim WOOD & Manassa WOOD** (under 12); dau **Rebecca BARTLETT;** to dau **Barsheba WOOD** at the age of eighteen or day of marriage, £40, a handsom wedding suit & a good bed & furniture; **Ephraim Jr. & Rebecca** must confirm father's sale of estate of their uncle **Seth HOWLAND.** Witnesses: Samuel BARROWS, Samuel WOOD, Elkanah LEONARD. <9:270> Pr. 12 July 1744, Ephraim WOOD app'td admr. <9:349> Inventory taken 31 July 1744 by Deacon Samuel BARROW, Capt. Nathaniel SOUTHWORTH, John BENNET; incl. house & barn with one acre, £440; 13 acres adjoining Mr. THACHER's, £150; blacksmith shop, £30; total estate, £999.13s. <14:237> Account 1 Mar. 1757 of admr.; Paid to: Josiah WOOD, Samuel WOOD, Ebenezer REDING, Deacon Samuel WOOD, John REDING, Ebenezer RAYMENT, Ichabod WOOD, Seth HOWLAND, C. HOWLAND, Bathsheba WOOD, Ephraim DONHAM, S. BARTLETT, Esq., Josiah FREEMAN, Benjamin SOUL, Samuel PALMER, Isaac BENNETT, William READING, Nathaniel WOOD, William READ, William THOMAS, Israel THOMAS, Moses STURTEVANT, Josiah COTTON Esq., James WARREN Esq., John COBB, Samuel THACHER, Ann WHITAURE, Robert BARROWS, Josiah CUSHMAN, John READING, Samuel WARREN Jr., Thomas TUPPER, Jeremiah THOMAS, Abraham BROWN, Noah THOMAS, Mr. THACHER, Jacob THOMSON, Gershom SAMSON, John DARLING, Elisha VAUGHAN, Nathaniel SOUTHWORTH, David CHURCHILL, Dr. MORSS, Timothy FULLER, Elkanah LEONARD Esq., Ichabod TUPPER, Peter OLIVER Esq., James SMITH, George WATSON Esq., Rodolphus ELMES Jr., Capt. Josiah MORTON, Ebenezer SPROUT, Benjamin WESTON, William COOMER, John CAVENDER, Josiah LEONARD, Benjamin WHITE Jr., Nathan THOMAS, Dr. LUNT, Thomas FOSTER Esq., John MURDOCH Esq., John HOLBROOKE, John HOWLAND, Robert BARTLETT, Josiah EDSON Esq., Lemuel MORTON, Philip WHITAMORE, Simeon TOTMAN, Deacon BARROW, John PALMER, Rodolphus ELMERS, Elias MILLER, John MILLER, Dr. LeBARON, Consider HOWLAND, estate of Thomas MORTON dec'd, Hannah DYER.

MICRO #13 OF 18

References to the surname **BARTLETT** in Plymouth County Deeds:49:87,139,166;56:127;59:179;60:84;61:151,154;67:1,17,115,142,146,205,218.

Estate of **Josiah WOOD,** blacksmith of Middleboro MA. <Plymouth Co.PR #23389, 20:148,206>
...13 Dec. 1768, widow **Mary WOOD** app'td admx. Sureties: Josiah WOOD, blacksmith & Ephraim WOOD, labourer, all of Middleboro. Witnesses: Zechariah PAD( ), Edward WINSLOW. Estate insolvent.

Josiah WOOD of Middleborough MA to **Josiah WOOD Jr.** of same. <Plymouth Co.Deeds 54:89>
...13 Apr. 1768, Josiah WOOD, blacksmith & wf Mary sell to Josiah WOOD Jr., blacksmith...land which was bought of Isaac BENNETT, 31 May 1756.

Josiah WOOD of Middleborough MA to **Shubael TINKHAM** of same. <Plymouth Co.Deeds 55:14>
...22 May 1769, Josiah WOOD, blacksmith, for £40 sold to Shubael TINKHAM, yeoman...30 acre meadow Wf Salome WOOD releases dower. Rec. 21 June 1769.

Josiah WOOD of Middleborough MA to **Shubael TINKHAM** of same. <Plymouth Co.Deeds 55:14>
...15 June 1769, Josiah WOOD, blacksmith, for £26.6s3d sells to Shubael TINKHAM, yeoman...my half of the dwelling house wherein I now live being the same that was my honored Father's Josiah WOOD late of Middleborough dec'd...and also my blacksmith shop. Rec. 28 June 1769.

JABEZ HOWLAND^2 (John^1)

Will of **Simon DAVIS**, gent. of Bristol MA. <Bristol Co.PR>
<8:414>...(no date given), mentions wf **Bethiah** & her son Nicholas BRAGG; sons **Nicholas DAVIS, Simon DAVIS**; Sarah NORTON, Shubael NORTON, Ann NEWTON, Henry & Elizabeth BRAGG, Frances THROOP widow of Rev. Amos of Woodstock; grandson **George BRADLEY** at Newport. <8:413> Pr. <8:427> Inventory. <8:441> Release. <10:219> Agreement. <10:221> Division. <10:277> Account. <original> Petition...requesting that **Bethiah DAVIS**, widow, aquit herself of suspicion of having embezzled money and goods of the personal estate.
(Note: The will is not transcribed, only the above is written with no dates and very little accompanying data. The relationship of some of those mentioned in the will is not specified.)

Estate of **Nicholas BRAGG**, mariner of Bristol MA. <Bristol Co.PR>
<7:387> 2 Aug. 1732, brother **Henry BRAGG** of Bristol, app'td admr. <7:412> Claims, 25 Sept. 1732. <7:421> Inventory taken 25 Apr.1732, incl. dwelling house & lands, L700. <7:423> Account. <7:471> Dower set off, 23 Nov. 1732, to widow **Bethiah BRAGG.** <8:42> Account. <8:51> Claims.

Estate of **Joseph HOWLAND** of Bristol MA. <Bristol Co.PR>
<9:3> Inventory taken 22 Sept. 1737; no real estate; mentions his brother **Samuel HOWLAND,** admr.

(Note: The following are all the references to the name **Joseph HOWLAND** on the index of the Bristol Co.PR: <42:440> Will. <80:456> Will. <81:147> Inventory. <81:473> Account. <83:47> Account. <83:52> Notice of Sale. <96:373> Account. <105:289> Adm. <115:146-67> Notice. <121:366> Notice. <133:278> Letter. <158:918> Adm. <165:177> Bond. <169:132> Adm. <172:106> Bond. <197:104> Inventory. <208:107> Bond. <209:358> Sale of land. <219:540> Account.)

Estate of **Josiah HOWLAND.** <Bristol Co.PR, "all on index">
<3:453> Inventory. <6:223> Account. (no further data given)

JOHN HOWLAND^2 (John^1)

Will of **Joseph CROCKER**, gent. of Barnstable MA. <Barnstable Co.PR>
<6:154>...dated 27 Apr. 1741, mentions wf **Anne;** son **Benjamin CROCKER** (executor); dec'd brother **Nathaniel CROCKER;** to dau **Prudence GORHAM** and her son **Joseph GORHAM,** the farm where I now dwell; to each of my grand children, £10 as they come of age, the males at 21, the females at 18, excepting **Joseph GORHAM,** he having had real estate. <6:157> Pr. 11 Feb. 1741. <6:159> Inventory taken 10 Mar. 1741. <8:219> Account.

Will of **John BURSLEY** of Barnstable MA. <Barnstable Co.PR>
<4:326>...dated 18 July 1726, mentions wf **Elizabeth;** sons **Joseph BURSLEY** ("shall be kind to his mother in law"), **John BURSLEY, Jabez BURSLEY** (who lives with him); daus **Mary, Joanna, Abigail, Elizabeth & Temperance** ("being weakly...& her mother in law"); sons **John & Joseph,** executors. <4:329> Pr. 30 Aug. 1726. <4:330> Inventory taken 27 Aug. 1726. <4:347> Allowance to widow. <4:576> Receipt 10 Feb. 1729/30, signed by: **Joseph & Mary SMITH, Nathan & Joanna CROCKER, Nathan & Abigail BODFISH, Elizabeth CROCKER & Temperance BURSLEY.**

Will of **Jabez BURSLEY** of Barnstable MA. <Barnstable Co.PR>
<5:76>...dated 5 Jan. 1731, mentions wf **Hannah;** to son **Barnabas BURSLEY,** one & a half acres next

to my brother **Joseph BURSLEY**'s land; son **John BURSLEY**; daus **Elizabeth, Abigail, Hannah, Joanna & Mary**; son **Benjamin BURSLEY**; my late dec'd Father; son **Benjamin** & brother **John BURSLEY**, executors. Witnesses sworn, 26 Jan. 1731. <5:78> Pr. 30 Aug. 1732. <5:79> Inventory. <6:256> Account.

==========

Estate of **John BURSLEY**, yeoman of Barnstable MA. <Barnstable Co.PR>
<7:86> 5 Apr. 1748, Benjamin LOTHROP, yeoman of Barnstable, app'td admr. <23:215> Settlement 6 July 1784...To John SMITH, gent. of Sandwich, Ansel HOWLAND, gent. & John BURSLEY of Barnstable.. Whereas **Experience LOTHROP**, wf of **Benjamin LOTHROP**, late of Barnstable dec'd, died in the life time of her sd husband seized & possessed of a considerable real estate in sd Barnstable & sd Sandwich which fell to her as sole heir to **John BURSLEY** late of Barnstable dec'd intestate and her sd husband having since dec'd, also, the sd **Experience LOTHROP** having died intestate her whole estate descended to her three children, viz: **Joseph LOTHROP, Benjamin LOTHROP & Mary LOTHROP** (the latter of whom married with Nathan FOSTER of Barnstable), in the following proportion... to **Benjamin** one half, to **Joseph & Mary** each a quarter, and the sd **Joseph** afterwards dying also in his minority, unmarried, his quarter part of sd estate descended by law equally to sd **Benjamin** and **Mary** wf of sd Nathan by which according to law the sd Nathan's wf **Mary** became seized in fee in her life time of three eighth parts of all sd estate which the sd **Experience** died seized...and the sd **Mary**...having since died also intestate having first had issue by the sd husband...the sd Nathan being desirous & making application to enjoy & improve his wife's portion...

==========

Will of **Benjamin LOTHROP**, yeoman of Barnstable MA. <Barnstable Co.PR>
<9:3>...dated 9 Nov. 1752, mentions sons **Benjamin LOTHROP** (to receive all real estate) & **Joseph LOTHROP**; dau **Mary LOTHROP**; trusty friends William CROCKER & his brother Benjamin CROCKER, executors. Witnesses: Benjamin BURSLEY, David SMITH, David CROCKER. <9:4> Pr. 6 Feb. 1753. <9:5> Inventory taken 6 Mar. 1753. <7:312,313> Guardianship 6 Mar. 1753, **Abigail LOTHROP**, spinster, app'td gdn. of **Joseph LOTHROP & Benjamin LOTHROP.** <7:460> Guardianship 5 July 1757, Nathan FOSTER, barber of Barnstable app'td gdn. of **Benjamin LOTHROP.** <9:399> Account 4 July 1758. <11:193> Account 9 Jan. 1781, of Nathan FOSTER, gdn. of **Benjamin LOTHROP**, non comp since 1753, who's Aunt **Abigail LOTHROP** was gdn. for a time; mention's **Benjamin**'s share of estate of his brother **Joseph LOTHROP.**

==========

Estate of **Joseph LOTHROP**, minor of Barnstable MA. <Barnstable Co.PR>
<7:458> 5 July 1757, Nathan FOSTER, yeoman of Barnstable app'td admr. on estate of **Joseph LOTHROP,** dec'd son of **Benjamin LOTHROP.** <11:189> Account & Inventory 9 Jan. 1780, of Nathan FOSTER, admr. incl. live stock pretended to be given in Abigail LOTHROP's will to Benjamin LOTHROP and my first wife; my first wife's part of the estate, £78.13.4; many articles sold at auction.

==========

Will of **Abigail LOTHROP**, single woman of Barnstable MA. <Barnstable Co.PR>
<9:286>...dated 18 May 1757, to brother **Samuel LOTHROP** & his children, marsh that was my **Aunt Experience's**; to my kinsman **Joseph LOTHROP**, half of what I own of **Uncle Nathaniel**'s woodlot; sister **Mary DAVIS**; kinsmen **Nathan FOSTER, Benjamin LOTHROP, David LOTHROP**; Isaac JONES and kinsman **Joseph LOTHROP**, executors. <9:287> Pr. 18 June 1757. <9:287> Inventory taken 20 June 1757. <12:176> Account.

==========

Estate of **Benjamin LOTHROP**, non comp. <Barnstable Co.PR>
<13:139> Guardianship, 1765. <11:193> Inventory & Account. <23:85> Account, 1782, says he died 24 Jan. 1782. <23:63> Inventory. <23:86> Account.

MICRO #14 OF 18

Will of **Nathan FOSTER** of Barnstable MA. <Barnstable Co.PR>
<32:19>...dated 19 Oct. 1814...to dau **Mercy CROCKER**, widow of Ephraim, two thirds of my real estate incl. dwelling house that I bought of Ebenezer NYE, Melatiah NYE & Lucretia STURGES, lying in Barnstable...see deed dated 19 Jan. 1793...also salt meadow at Bass Creek I bought of Shearjashub BOURNE...to son **Nathan FOSTER**, one third of the above named real estate...$1.00 each to heirs of dec'd chil. **James FOSTER, Thomas FOSTER & Mary CROCKER**...to son **John FOSTER**, $1.00...to dau **Elizabeth FOSTER**, half of household furniture; dau **Mercy**, executrix

==========

Will of **Joseph BURSLEY**, yeoman of Barnstable MA. <Barnstable Co.PR>
<8:292>...dated 14 June 1750, mentions son **Joseph BURSLEY** (executor) and dau **Mercy BURSLEY.** <8:293> Pr. 5 July 1750. <8:294> Inventory taken 5 Sept. 1750.

==========

Will of **Joseph BURSLEY** of Barnstable MA. <Barnstable Co.PR>
<20:353>...dated 25 Sept. 1778, mentions wf **Bethiah**; dau **Abigail BURSLEY**; son **John BURSLEY**; daus **Bethiah JENKINS, Sarah NYE.** <20:355> Pr. 8 Jan. 1779. <20:356> Inventory taken 18 Jan. 1779. <10:"half"> Receipts, 12 Jan. 1779 of **Joseph JENKINS, Peleg NYE, Abigail BURSLEY**; 27 Jan. 1779 of **Abigail BURSLEY**; 27 Jan. 1779 of **Bethiah BURSLEY** to son **John BURSLEY**, exr.

==========

Estate of **John BURSLEY Jr.**, mariner of Barnstable MA. <Barnstable Co.PR>
<10:188> 11 Aug. 1767, John BURSLEY, yeoman of Sandwich, app'td admr.

==========

Will of **Jeremiah THOMAS** of Middleboro MA. <Plymouth Co.PR>
<7:267>...dated 29 Sept. 1735, mentions wf **Mary**; sons **Jeremiah THOMAS, Jedediah THOMAS**; daus **Sary WOOD, Elizabeth THOMSON, Mary BLUSH, Lydia HACKETT, Thankfull COBB, Bethiah CHIPMAN, Priscilla THOMAS**; son **Ebenezer THOMAS**, executor. Witnesses: Henry WOOD, Nathaniel HOLMES, Samuel THOMAS. Pr. 7 Feb. 1736.

Estate of **Jeremiah THOMAS** of Middleboro MA. <Plymouth Co.PR #20362>
<16:507,17:105,19:28>...1763...

References to the name **George HACKETT** in Plymouth County Deeds: 14:31,147,148;20:144;31:192;43:225;45:177;53:51;60:193;70:229;72:246;85:91;91:42.

Estate of **George HACKETT** of Middleboro MA. <Plymouth Co.PR>
<6:220>...1732, adm. <6:223> Inventory.

Gideon HACKET of Middleboro MA to **Philip LEONARD** of same. <Plymouth Co.Deeds 43:225>
...31 Mar. 1756, Gideon HACKET, husbandman for Ŀ80 sold to Philip LEONARD, bloomer...four fifths of five lots in Little Lot Men's Purchase in Middleboro, #40,41,42,43,44 in 3rd allotment, being 93 acres...sd four fifths contains 74 and two fifths acres...which sd five lots did formerly belong unto my Honoured Father George HACKET dec'd, always reserving unto my Honoured Mother Lydia HACKET the improvement of her dower or thirds. Wf Betty HACKET releases dower. Rec. 30 Apr. 1756.

MICRO #15 OF 18

JOSEPH HOWLAND[2] (John[1])

James COLE of Plymouth MA to **Ephraim COLE et al.** <Plymouth Co.Deeds 5:229>
...28 Jan. 1702/3, James COLE, for love & affection, conveys to his children Ephraim COLE, Elisha & Hannah BRADFORD, Nathaniel & Martha HOWLAND and Thomas & Joanna HOWLAND...

Estate of **Isaac HAMBLEN/HAMLIN** of Barnstable MA. <Barnstable Co.PR>
<3:87> 8 Feb. 1709/10, widow **Elizabeth HAMBLEN** and brother **Joseph HAMBLEN,** app'td admrs. <4:180> Settlement of real estate, 15 Feb. 1723/4; the former widow **Elizabeth CANNON** having resigned her right of dower in sd lands, the real estate is settled on the eldest son **Eleazer HAMLIN,** he to pay his brother **Joseph HAMLIN** and sister **Elizabeth.**

Lot CROWELL of Yarmouth MA to **Silas BAKER** of same. <Barnstable Co.Deeds 44:149>
...15 Mar. 1791, Lot CROWELL, gent., for Ŀ12 sold to Silas BAKER, mariner...10 acres of woodland & clear land in one piece in Yarmouth...on Parker's Neck. Wf Hannah CROWELL releases dower. Rec. 16 Dec. 1791.

Will of **Lot CROWELL** of Yarmouth MA. <Barnstable Co.PR>
<33:340>...dated 5 July 1808, mentions wf **Hannah;** $1.00 each to sons **Heman CROWELL, Mathewes CROWELL, Willard CROWELL;** daus **Asenah H. CROWELL, Hannah CROWELL;** $1.00 each to three eldest daus **Elizabeth HALLET, Mercy DOANE, Sarah BAKER;** remainder of estate to sons **Allen Bangs CROWELL, Seth CROWELL;** wf **Hannah,** executrix. Witnesses: Elisha DOANE, Jonathan KILLEY, Anna HOMER(sp). <32:153> Pr. 29 Mar. 1809. <37:106> Inventory taken 29 Apr. 1809. <37:191> Account.

Hannah CROWELL of Yarmouth MA to **Silas BAKER Jr. & Elisha BAKER.** <Barnstable Co.Deeds 4:156>
...19 Dec. 1811, Hannah CROWELL, widow, exx. of will of Lot CROWELL dec'd, by order of court to pay expenses, sells to Silas BAKER Jr. & Elisha BAKER, both of Yarmouth...land in Parker's Neck. Ack. 3 Jan. 1812 by Hannah. On 23 Mar. 1812, Elisha sold to Silas all his right in above.

PLYMOUTH COUNTY DEEDS: (re: James RICKARD)

<17:34> - 4 Sept 1723, James RICKARD, cooper of Plymouth to Deacon John WOOD, yeoman of same.
<18:139> - 10 Nov. 1724, James RICKARD, cooper of Plymouth to Samuel BARTLETT, half of wharf next to my brother John's cooper shop. Wf Hannah RICKARD releases dower.
<18:139> - 1 Dec. 1724, James RICKARD, cooper of Plymouth to Samuel BARTLETT, land granted by Town of Plymouth to my father John RICKARD dec'd.
<18:174> - 23 Feb. 1724/5, James RICKARD, cooper of Plymouth to John BARNES Jr., land at south east corner of lot of Thomas DOTY dec'd.
<113:57> - 2 Aug. 1731, James RICKARD, cooper of Plymouth, to John WATSON, Esq., land received by will of father John RICKARD dec'd.

Will of **Joseph JENKINS.** <Barnstable Co.PR 5:233>
...dated 25 Jan. 1733 (he does not give his place of residence)...to wf **Lidia,** all my moveable estate within doors to wit all my housel stuff togeather with my west room in my dwelling house next the ground & the bed room with half the leanto & half the seller room from top to bottom with two cows out of my live stock with a beast to ride whan she wants & to be maintained out of my farme winter & sumer: eight bushels of Indian corn, two of rye, two of wheete, eighty pound of pork & eighty pound of beef, twenty pound of flax from the swingle & fifteen pound of sheeps wool with fire wood for one fire cut & drawed to ye door & then cut fit to burn in ye chimne...to dau **Abigail HINCKLEY,** Ŀ10...to dau **Lidia CROCKER,** Ŀ25...to dau **Prudence BAKER,** 10s...to dau **Hannah JENKINS,** Ŀ60...to my two sons **Joseph JENKINS & Benjamin JENKINS** all my houseing & lands...in Barnstable; both sons executors. Witnesses: Joseph LATHROP, Ebenezer JENKINS, Jacob LEAVITT, William BASSETT 3d. Pr. 8 Nov. 1734.

Will of **Samuel CROCKER** of Barnstable MA. <Barnstable Co.PR #5022>
...dated 15 July 1859...to son **Samuel CROCKER,** $1.00...to son **Warren P. CROCKER,** $50.00...to daus

Lucy J. PARKER wf of Daniel, **Hodiah J. WRIGHT** wf of Asa, **Emeline HOWLAND** wf of Thomas and **Abbie P. JONES** wf of Henry, the whole amount due on a note of hand given by Freeman PERCIVAL...to dau **Maria P. CROCKER**, a home & support out of my estate...to son **Joseph CROCKER** (executor) remainder of estate. Witnesses: S.C. HOWLAND, William HOWLAND, Adelia F. HOWLAND. Pr. 15 May 1866.

Will of **Prince HINCKLEY** of Barnstable MA. <Barnstable Co.PR #1861>
<60:324>...dated 18 Feb. 1822, mentions wf **Eunice** and children, viz: **Reliance, Allen HINCKLEY, Lydia, Prince HINCKLEY, Oliver HINCKLEY, Watson HINCKLEY, Robert HINCKLEY, Anna, Louisa, Seth HINCKLEY, Eunice & Sophia.** Witnesses: Gorham LOVELL, Asa JONES Sr., Andrew GARRETT. Pr. 13 Feb. 1844. <61:597> Account. <original> 20 May 1845, **Prince HINCKLEY**, exr., received of **Seth G. HINCKLEY** as exr. of the will of the widow of said testator.

Will of **Eunice HINCKLEY** of Barnstable MA. <Barnstable Co.PR #1976>
<60:377>...dated 21 Sept. 1844, mentions son **Allen HINCKLEY**; dau **Lydia FISH** wf of Reuben, **Louisa BOURNE** wf of Edward, **Eunice WEST** wf of Thomas, dau **Sophia CROCKER** wf of Bridgham; sons **Oliver HINCKLEY, Robert HINCKLEY, Prince HINCKLEY, Watson HINCKLEY**; dau **Anna HINCKLEY**; son **Seth G. HINCKLEY**, executor. Witnesses: Lothrop DAVIS, Thomas P. LEWIS, Leander JONES. Pr. 20 May 1845.

Will of **Silvanus HINCKLEY**, yeoman of Barnstable MA. <Barnstable Co.PR>
<28:252>...dated 20 May 1799, mentions wf **Sarah**; to dau **Elizabeth HINCKLEY** (after the decease of my wife), half of furniture & $100.00, bedroom in west end on lower floor and one quarter of small pew in Meeting house in Phinney's neighborhood so called in Barnstable...to grandson **Jabez ALLEN**, two acre woodland in Barnstable I bought of Benjamin LOMBARD of Barnstable bounded by land of Jesse CROSBY and heirs of Lemuel BARNES, also $30.00 when 21...to sons **Silvanus HINCKLEY Jr., Prince HINCKLEY & Levi HINCKLEY**, remainder of estate...reserving to my son **Levi** liberty to take off his shop from the east end of my house he repairing any breach that may be made in the house when sd shop is removed; son **Silvanus**, executor. Witnesses: Oakes SHAW, Joseph LOMBARD, David SCUDDER. <34:223> Pr.

PLYMOUTH COUNTY DEEDS: (re: HOWLAND)

<6:246> - 2 Aug. 1704, Elizabeth HOWLAND, widow of Plymouth to James SOULE of Middleboro, two acres meadow being one sixth of 12th lot formerly of Mr. BRADFORD at Winnatuxet.

<6:137> - 25 Jan. 1706/7, Thomas HOWLAND, Joanna HOWLAND, Nathaniel HOWLAND, Martha HOWLAND... mentions father James COLE and brother Ephraim COLE.

<12:146> - , Nathan/Nathaniel HOWLAND of Middleboro to father Isaac HOWLAND Sr.

(References without data, viz: 23:116, 44:160 (Elizabeth HOWLAND); 14:101,105 (Nathaniel HOWLAND) and 26:163 (Thomas HOWLAND).)

MICRO #16 OF 18

PLYMOUTH COUNTY PROBATE: (re: CONANT)

<3:672> - 15 Nov. 1723, Bond of Jonathan LOVEL to pay Deborah CONET/CONANT. Receipt, Feb. 1730, of Deborah for her share of her father, Lot CONANT's, estate. Witnesses: Hannah CONANT, Joseph LOVEL.

<6:368> - 23 May 1744, Caleb CONANT of Truro app'td admr. on estate of his son Joshua CONANT, late of Truro, mariner.

<10:54> - 14 Mar. 1760, Joshua ATKINS, gent. of Truro app'td admr. on estate of John CONANT, late of Truro, laborer.

Will of **John CONANT**, yeoman of Marblehead MA. <Essex Co.PR #6158>
...dated 6 Oct. 1737...being aged and infirm...my friends & kinsmen Deacon William DODGE & Jonathan CONANT, both of Beverly, executors...couzen **John CONANT Jr.**, weaver of Beverly...I give to my several kindred following the several sums following in bills of credit, viz: Deacon William DODGE, Ł50; Jonathan CONANT of Beverly, Ł50; Sarah TROW wf of George, Ł50; Martha PURKINS/PERKINS wf of Luke, Ł20; William CONANT, Ł20; Roger CONANT, Ł50; Ebenezer CONANT son of sd Roger, Ł20; Daniel CONANT, Ł20; Joshua DODGE, Ł20; Lott CONANT, Ł10; widow Mary KIMBOL, Ł10; Rebecca RAYMENT wf of Nathaniel, Ł10; Caleb CONANT of Barnstable Co., Ł20; John CONANT of Barnstable Co., Ł20; Joshua CONANT son of sd Caleb, Ł50 and to each of the children of Caleb CONANT, late of Mansfield in Connecticot Colony, dec'd, Ł10. Pr. 24 Apr. 1738. <original> Receipt 28 May 1744...Caleb CONANT, admr. of the goods, chattels, rights & credits of Joshua CONANT late of Truro, mariner have this day received of Jonathan CONANT of Marblehead, one of the executors of the testament of John CONANT dec'd, fifty pounds in old tenor bills of credit, being a legacy given by the sd John CONANT to the sd Joshua CONANT by his last will. Witness: Nathan BOWEN. <original> Receipt 11 Apr. 1744, of Caleb CONANT to Jonathan CONANT, having received fifteen pounds, which with five pounds formerly received is in full sattisfaction of a legacy of twenty pounds. <original> Receipt 28 Jan. 1743/44, of John CONANT for his twenty pound legacy.

Thomas HOWLAND of Plymouth MA to **Thomas HOWLAND Jr.** of same. <Plymouth Co.Deeds 29:104>
...4 Dec. 1734, Thomas HOWLAND, gent., for Ł150 sold to Thomas HOWLAND Jr., cordwainer...half part of land in Plymouth, the whole of which contains two acres...bounded on land of Nicholas DREW, George LITTLE, Col. LOTHROP, Timothy MORTON and Salt Water or Bay...excepting & reserving

to my Self ye benefit of improving ye sd Premises...during ye term of my natural life and...fencing & paying tax for ye same. Witnesses: John WINSLOW, Zaccheus HAMBLEN. Rec. 21 Dec. 1734.

Thomas HOWLAND of Plymouth MA to **Thomas HOWLAND Jr.** of same. <Plymouth Co.Deeds 29:104>
...4 Dec. 1734, Thomas HOWLAND, gent., for the good will & natural affection which I...bear towards my son Thomas HOWLAND Jr., cordwainer...grant unto him...land in Plymouth on Main St. leading to Kingston & beginning at the north westerly corner bounds of William HARLOW's land & from thence to extend northerly as the Street runs fifty & five foot and...back...eighty foot. Witnesses: John WINSLOW, Zaccheus HAMBLEN. Ack. & Rec. 21 Dec. 1734.

PLYMOUTH COUNTY DEEDS: (re: Thomas HOWLAND, grantor)

<2:76> - 1697, T.H. to Samuel LUCAS
<7:31> - 1705/7, T.H. to Jonathan BRYANT.
<6:137> - 1706/7, T.H. et al to Ephraim COLE.
<7:119> - 1706/7, T.H. et al to Ephraim COLE.
<8:17> - 1708, T.H. to Benjamin SOULE.
<8:58> - 1708, T.H. to Benjamin SOULE.
<8:120> - 1708, T.H. et al to Joseph BUMPAS Sr.
<9:98> - 1711, T.H. to Thomas SNELL.
<9:207> - 1712, T.H. to Joshua CUSHING.
<9:322> - 1712, T.H. et al to George SAMPSON.
<9:372> - 1712, T.H. to Ephraim LITTLE.
<9:405> - 1713, T.H. to Thomas PHILLIPS.
<9:406> - 1713, T.H. to Thomas PHILLIPS.
<10:1:169> 1713, T.H. to Ignatius CUSHING.
<10:2:2> - 1713, T.H. to Thomas LITTLE.
<10:2:233> 1714, T.H. to William HARLOW
<10:2:396> 1714, T.H. to Job CUSHMAN.
<11:69> - 1714, T.H. to James WARREN et al.
<12:62> - 1716, T.H. to Nicholas DREW.
<12:59> - 1716, T.H. to John GIBBS.
<12:140> - 1717, T.H. to John TINKHAM.
<13:168> - 1718, T.H. to James HOWLAND.
<14:94> - 1718, T.H. to Ebenezer DUNHAM.
<14:248> - 1719, T.H. et al to Isaac BARKER.
<15:104> - 1720, T.H. et al to Samuel CURTIS.
<15:137> - 1721, T.H. to Samuel CORNISH Jr.
<15:132> - 1721, T.H. to Ephraim COLE Sr.
<15:226> - 1722, T.H. et al to Benjamin CUSHMAN.
<16:71> - 1722, T.H. to Consider HOWLAND.
<16:139> - 1723, T.H. to John BARNES.
<16:194> - 1723, T.H. to Consider HOWLAND.
<17:19> - 1723, T.H. to Abial SHURTLEFF.
<17:29> - 1723, T.H. et al to John WATSON.
<17:20> - 1723, T.H. to James SHURTLEFF.
<17:83> - 1723, T.H. et al to Isaac BARKER.
<18:173> - 1725, T.H. to Thomas JACKSON.
<18:181> - 1724, T.H. to Israel JACKSON.
<19:42> - 1725, T.H. to John COLE.
<20:43> - 1726, T.H. to Nicholas DREW.
<21:95> - 1726, T.H. et al to Ephraim Cole/al.

<21:103> - 1726, Thomas HOWLAND, carpenter of Marshfield to Samuel BAKER.
<21:107> - 3 Feb. 1726/7, Thomas HOWLAND, gent. of Plymouth to John SPARHAWK, land in Plymouth.
<22:93> - 21 Sept 1727, Thomas HOWLAND of Plymouth to Edward TILSON, land in Plymouth.
<22:174> - 20 Feb. 1727, Thomas HOWLAND, gent. of Plymouth to Thomas HOLMES, part of homestead in Plymouth. Wf Joanna HOWLAND releases dower.
<23:116> - 6 Aug. 1728, Thomas HOWLAND, gent. gives land for a street to be called Howland's St.
<23:117> - 6 Aug. 1728, Thomas HOWLAND, yeoman of Plymouth to Lemuel DREW, house lot in Plymouth
<23:124> - 16 Aug. 1728, Thomas HOWLAND, gent. of Plymouth to Isaac LOTHROP, land in Plymouth.
<23:123> - 21 Aug. 1728, Thomas HOWLAND, gent. of Plymuth to John ATWOOD, land in Plymouth.
<23:173> - 8 Aug. 1728, Thomas HOWLAND, gent. of Plymouth to Ebenezer CURTIS, land in Plymouth.
<23:131> - 10 Sept 1728, Thomas HOWLAND, gent. of Plymouth to Joseph LEWIN, land in Plymouth.
<24:58> - 31 Mar. 1729, Thomas HOWLAND, gent. of Plymouth to Thomas SPOONER, land in Plymouth. Wf Joanna HOWLAND releases dower.
<24:25> - 12 Feb. 1728/9, Thomas HOWLAND, gent. of Plymouth to Thomas SPOONER, land in Plymouth. Wf Joanna HOWLAND releases dower.
<24:110> - 23 May 1728, Thomas HOWLAND, gent. of Plymouth to Thomas BARKER of Pembroke, land in Plymouth. Rec. 23 May 1729.
<25:36> - 25 Feb. 1729, Thomas HOWLAND, gent. of Plymouth to Thomas HOLMES, land in Duxbury.
<28:146> - 29 Dec. 1729, Thomas HOWLAND, gent. of Plymouth to Timothy MORTON, land in Plymouth. Rec. 22 Feb. 1733.
<25:49> - 3 Mar. 1729/30, Thomas HOWLAND, gent. of Plymouth to Thomas SPOONER, land in Plymouth Wf Joanna releases dower.
<28:80> - 27 May 1730, Thomas HOWLAND of Marshfield to Benjamin KEEN of Pembroke, land in Pembroke. Rec. 29 Sept. 1733.
<26:163> - 14 June 1731, Thomas HOWLAND, yeoman to Benjamin LOTHROP, hatter of Plymouth.
<28:121> - 21 Jan. 1733/4, Thomas HOWLAND, gent. of Plymouth to David TURNER, part of homestead in Plymouth. Rec. same day.
<28:121> - 21 Jan. 1733/4, Thomas HOWLAND, gent. of Plymouth to Noah SAMPSON, part of homestead in Plymouth.
<29:215> - 13 June 1735, Thomas HOWLAND, gent. of Plymouth to James HOVEY, land in Plymouth.
<30:111> - 1735, Thomas HOWLAND of Marshfield to Joseph BARSTOW.
<30:139> - 1736, Thomas HOWLAND of Marshfield to sons John & William HOWLAND.
<31:68> - 1737, Thomas HOWLAND of Marshfield to Jonathan DAWES.
<32:148> - 1738, Thomas HOWLAND, gent. of Plymouth to Robert FINNEY.
<36:183> - 1744, Thomas HOWLAND to Samuel KING Jr.
<41:206> - Rec.1752, Thomas HOWLAND to Timothy TAYLOR. (dated 1731)
<44:162> - 1757, Thomas HOWLAND of Tiverton RI to James OTIS, land in Bridgewater.
<65:22> - Rec.1785, Thomas HOWLAND to Isaac LITTLE of Pembroke. (dated 12 July 1731)
<73:100> - 15 Aug. 1792, Heirs of Thomas HOWLAND to William H. JACKSON.

PLYMOUTH COUNTY DEEDS: (re: Joseph HOWLAND, grantor)

<1:277> - 1694, J.H. to John GRAY.
<2:27> - 1696, J.H. to John THOMPSON

PLYMOUTH COUNTY DEEDS, cont-d: (re: Joseph HOWLAND, grantor)

<2:76> - 1697, J.H. to Thomas HOWLAND.
<2:65> - 1697, J.H., atty. to Richard COOPER.
<3:164> - 1699, J.H. to Elkanah CUSHMAN.
<4:62> - 1701, J.H. to John BRADFORD.
<4:116> - 1702, J.H. to John STURTEVANT.
<9:322> - 1712, J.H. et al to George SAMPSON.
<10:552>- 1713, J.H. to Nathaniel SOUTHWORTH.
<12:42> - 1716, J.H. to Nehemiah STURTEVANT.
<35:139> - 1742, J.H. et al, division.
<35:150> - 1742, J.H. to Cornelius BENNETT.
<36:208> - 1744, J.H. to John PRATT.
<38:65> - 1746, J.H. to Ebenezer MORTON.
<40:134> - 1749, J.H. et al to Elkanah LEONARD.
<46:168> - 1760, J.H. to Isaac PEIRCE Jr. et al.
<47:247> - 1762, J.H. to Elkanah LEONARD.

Estate of **Consider HOWLAND** of Plymouth MA. <Plymouth Co.PR #10910>
<15:304> Letter/Bond 14 Sept. 1759, son **Thomas Southworth HOWLAND** of Plymouth app'td admr. Sureties: Elkanah WATSON, John CHURCHILL, both of Plymouth. Witnesses: Edward WINSLOW, Nathaniel LEONARD. <15:419> Inventory taken Dec. 1759 by William THOMAS, Ebenezer SPOONER, Elkanah WATSON; total real estate, £588; total estate, £689.16.7; sworn to 7 Jan. 1760 by admr. <15:421> Insolvency 14 Jan. 1760. <16:250> List of Claims, 29 Aug. 1761: John WINSLOW, James HOVEY, Perez TILLSON, Stephen SAMSON, Wrestling BREWSTER, Timothy BURBANK, John LOTHROP, Benjamin LOTHROP Jr.'s estate, Samuel GOULD, Joseph JOSSELYN, Joseph MORTON, Jonathan MORTON, Daniel DIMAN, Nathaniel DUNHAM Jr, Elijah McFARLING, Nathaniel COB Jr., Benjamin MORTON, Nathaniel HARLOW Jr., Nathaniel BRADFORD's estate, Ebenezer SPOONER, John WETHERELL, Benjamin ROBINS, Joel ELLIS, Benjamin CASELY, Sylvanus BRAMHALL, Ichabod SHAW, Job MORTON, John GODDARD, Samuel BARTLETT, Jedediah SAMSON, Nathaniel LITTLE, Thomas LANMAN, John COTTON, Caleb SHERMAN, widow Margaret KEEN, Jonathan KING, Lazarus LeBARON Sr., Nathaniel ATWOOD Jr., Benjamin ELDREDGE, John SHAW, Ebenezer ROBINS, Nathaniel LEONARD, Job & Silas MORTON, Maletiah LOTHROP, Ichabod WADSWORTH, Ebenezer HOLMES, Samuel JACKSON, Solomon HEWIT, Nathaniel GOODWIN, Thomas CLAPP, Job BAILEY, Ansel LOTHROP estate, Joseph GIFFORD, Josiah MORTON 3d, John TINKHAM, Micah SYLVESTER, Joseph TROWANT, Richard ADAMS, Samuel N. NELSON, Zacheus CURTIS, Thomas JACKSON, Josiah STURTEVANT, Benjamin BARNES' estate, Benjamin HOLMES Jr., Harry HOWLAND, Abigail HOWLAND, Samuel DREW, Snow WINSLOW, widow Experience MILLER, Adam BAILEY, Charles MITCHELL, Coll. Isaac LOTHROP's estate, Joseph SHURTLEFF, Sylvanus COB, John PINKERTON, Jabez HOWLAND, Nathaniel BOYLSTON, James HOWLAND, Ebenezer HATCH, Rebecca WITHERELL's estate, George WATSON, John MURDOCK, James MURDOCK, Jonathan BARTLETT, Prince BARKER, Nathaniel COB, James NICOLNSON(sp), John BARTLETT, Andrew TOMSON, Nathaniel TORREY, Joshua LORING, Levi LORING, Col. James WARREN estate, Maj. WARREN, Capt. Theophilus COTTON, Thomas SPOONER Jr., Jona. DIMAN, Foster DIMAN, John WATERMAN, Thomas DAVIS, WATSON & MAYHEW, Lemuel BARNES, Robert BROWN, Peleg BRIANT, WINSLOW & WHITE, Rev. Shearjashub BOURNE, Thomas SAVERY Jr., Edward WINSLOW; Stephen & William GREENLEAF attorneys to Nathaniel FAILS; Nathaniel LORING, Josiah RIDER, Cornelius BENNET, John CHURCHILL, Ebenezer RANSOM, Joseph TRASK, Capt. Gideon WHITE, Capt. Nathan DELANO, Thomas WITHERELL Jr. estate, Thomas FOSTER, Kenelm WINSLOW, Robert ODIOM, John PRINCE, Col. James OTIS, Adam & Benjamin WRIGHT, Dr. Benjamin STOCKBRIDGE, Joseph HAMBLIN, Samuel WHITE, James CAHOON, James THOMAS, Elisha WHITING Jr., Hannah THOMAS now ye wf of Capt. Nehemiah CUSHING, Samuel DONHAM Jr., Thomas CRANDON, Joseph TUCKER, Capt. Nathan DELANO on account of his wife, Thomas Southworth HOWLAND, Dr. William THOMAS, Capt. Abraham HAMMETT, Thomas FOSTER Jr. <19:227> Account 3 June 1765 of admr., mentions necessaries to the widow. <19:375> Dower, 4 June 1760, to widow **Ruth HOWLAND,** half the house & lot on Howland St. in Plymouth which was Lazarus SAMSON's. <27:484> Letter/Bond 5 May 1780, Elkanah WATSON, Joshua THOMAS & Consider HOWLAND app'td admrs. de bonis non, the former admr., **Thomas Southworth HOWLAND** having dec'd. Sureties: William THOMAS, Isaac LeBARON. Witnesses: Isaac LOTHROP, Nathaniel LOTHROP. <original> Warrant, 3 Mar. 1779, to Jonathan DIMAN, Thomas JACKSON & Isaac SYMMES to appraise real estate set off to widow **Ruth HOWLAND.** <original> Bond 22 Nov. 1780 of Edward WINSLOW...Whereas the Hon. Joseph CUSHING, Esq...hath commenced a suit against Elkanah WATSON, the only surviving bondsman to **Thomas Southworth HOWLAND** who was the admr...Witnesses: T. LOTHROP, Sarah WINSLOW.

Estate of **Capt. Benjamin LOTHROP** of Kingston MA. <Plymouth Co.PR #13226>
<27:251> Letter/Bond 1 Oct. 1787, Josiah THACHER of Kingston & Williams BARKER of Scituate, gentlemen, ap'td admrs. Sureties: Seth COBB, yeoman & Hezekiah RIPLEY, gent., of Kingston. Witnesses: Edward HOWARD, Asa KEITH. <30:240> Warrant 1 Oct. 1787 to John GRAY, Esq., Seth COBB & Hezekiah RIPLEY, all of Kingston, to appraise estate. Inventory taken 2 & 3 Oct. 1787; total real estate, £719.2s6d; sworn to 4 Oct. 1787 by admrs. <30:241> Dower 8 Oct. 1787, to widow **Mary LOTHROP.**

Will of **John LOTHROP**, gent. of Plymouth MA. <Plymouth Co.PR #13237>
<16:163>...dated 26 Mar. 1761; mentions honoured father **Capt. Benjamin LOTHROP** of Kingston; cousen **Mary HOWLAND;** cussen **Thomas Southworth HOWLAND;** remainder of estate to be divided between Aunts, **Hannah WINSLOW** wf of Edward, Esq. and **Joannah WHITE** wf of Capt. Gideon WHITE; Gideon & Joanna WHITE, executors. Witnesses: Eliphalet BRADFORD, Samuel COLE, Ephraim SPOONER. <16:164> Pr. 3 Aug. 1761. <16:177> Inventory taken 29 July 1761; incl. house & land and many books; sworn to 3 Aug. 1761 by admrs. <19:232> List of claims, 7 Mar. 1765. <19:554> Account 21 Nov. 1767, of admrs.; incl. house rent from 2 Nov. 1761 to 12 May 1767 when sold; John LOTHROP & Benjamin LOTHROP Jr.'s proportion in the claims against Consider HOWLAND's estate.

Estate of **Capt. William DYRE**, mariner of Plymouth MA. <Plymouth Co.PR #6998>
<8:294> Letter 6 Mar. 1740, widow **Hannah DYRE** app'td admx. <8:461> Inventory taken on or about the first day of May 1741. <8:462> Allowance 14 July 1742, to widow. <8:536> Warrant for dower, 30 Aug. 1742. <8:517> Dower set off to widow, 25 Sept. 1742. <9:161> List of claims, 20 Sept. 1743. <9:161> Account of Edward & Hannah WINSLOW, admrs.

LYDIA HOWLAND[2] (John[1])

Estate of **Joseph KENT** of Swansea MA. <Bristol Co.PR>
<2:99> Inventory taken 5 Sept. 1704. <2:99> Guardianship 18 Sept. 1704, Deacon Samuel NEWMAN, app'td gdn. of **Susanna KENT,** minor dau of dec'd. <2:101> Division 15 Sept. 1704 to widow **Susanna KENT,** eldest son **Joseph KENT,** sons **Samuel KENT, Joshua KENT** and dau **Susanna KENT** by gdn.

Will of **Joseph KENT** of Rehoboth MA. <Bristol Co.PR>
<8:217>...dated 12 Mar. 1734/5...to wf **Mary** the ten pounds due by contracte and over and above I give to her L20 in movabels...the ten pounds paid fifty shillings yearly...to son **Joseph KENT,** the house in which he now dwells, all lands in Watchamoket neck, three acers of meadow on Mile Brook adjoyning to Isaac PERRIN's meadow, ten acers of land att ye north end of my homstead, five acers of meadow att ye south end which I bought of John MASON, a quarter parte of my salte meadow below Bowens Brigge/Bridge joyning to Peter HUNT's meadow, quarter parte of cedar swamp att Squanemaconk, twenty acers on ye east side of sd Squanamaconk and twenty pound right in Commonage in Rehoboth, he paying to my daughters twenty pounds each, viz: **Lidia BOSWORTH, Dorethea NEWMAN, Susanna BOWEN, Mary KENT**...to son **John KENT**...all ye lands where he now lives...which I have already given him by deed...also forty acers adjoyning to ye homstead that I bought of Samuel MASON and twenty acers lying near ye house that was Joseph TITUS', quarter parte of salte marsh & cedar swamp and ten pounds right in Commonage...to dau **Mary KENT,** Ł100, twenty pounds therof to be paid her by my son **Joseph**...to son **Hezekiah KENT**...the house where he now dwells and halfe my barne & corne cribb...he paying to his sister **Mary** eighty pounds...to son **James KENT**...my own dwelling house with half ye barne & corne cribb...he paying to my beloved wife **Mary** ye forty pounds above mentioned...to sons **Hezekiah & James**...all my lands in Rehoboth and elswhere not otherways disposed of; sons **Joseph & Hezekiah,** executors. Witnesses: Jonathan CHAFFEE, John LINDLY, David TURNER; CHAFFEE & TURNER made oath to the will, 15 Apr. 1735. <8:224> Inventory taken 7 Apr. 1735 by Edward GLOVER, Jonathan CHAFFE, Ezekiel READ; total real estate, Ł2748; total estate, Ł3278.1s9d. <original> Bond 15 Apr. 1735 of exrs. Sureties: Jonathan CHAFFEE, yeoman & David TURNER, clerk, both of Rehoboth. Witnesses: Stephen PAINE, Samuel TOOGOOD. <8:320> Receipt 12 Mar. 1735/6, of **Mary KENT,** spinster of Rehoboth to her brothers for her legacy of Ł100. Witnesses: Samuel HILLS, John LINDLEY. Receipt 10 June 1735 of **Joseph & Lidia BOSWORTH, Noah & Dorothey NEWMAN** and **Peter & Susannah BOWEN,** all of Rehoboth, to brother **Joseph KENT,** one of the exrs., for their legacies. <8:321> Receipt 5 June 1735, of widow **Mary KENT** to **Joseph KENT** for her legacy of...thirty pounds in money & moveables & ten pounds in fulfilment of ye promise by contract by me made with my sd late husband before marriage. Witnesses: Daniel CARPENTER, John LINDLEY. <8:319> Account, sworn to 16 Mar. 1735 by the two exrs.; Paid to: Ezekiel CARPENTER for funeral charges, Ł10.16s; Jonathan PAINE for funeral charges, Ł3.12s; Mr. TURNER; Thomas LINDLEY; **Lidia BOSWORTH,** a legacy, Ł20; **Dorothey NEWMAN,** a legacy, Ł20; **Susanah BOWEN,** a legacy, Ł20; **Mary KENT,** a legacy, Ł100.

Heirs of **Nathaniel CARPENTER** of Attleboro MA. <Bristol Co.Deeds>
<32:317>...10 July 1741, Ezekiel CARPENTER, Ezra CARPENTER, John KENT & wf Rachel, children of Nathaniel CARPENTER, sell to our brother Daniel CARPENTER of Attleboro...
<49:468>...22 Oct. 1742, John KENT & wf Rachel of Rehoboth sell swamp...which our Honoured father Nathaniel CARPENTER purchased of his brothers namely Noah CARPENTER & Obadiah CARPENTER.

MICRO #17 OF 18

Depostions of **Jabez BROWN & Samuel BROWN** of Rehoboth MA. <Bristol Co.Deeds 36:71>
...12 May 1747, Jabez BROWN of that part of Rehoboth that was Barrington, being in the eightieth year of his age...testifies in regard to lines of land sureyed 60 years earlier by Capt. John BROWN, dec'd, father of Daniel BROWN of Rehoboth...12 May 1747, Samuel BROWN now in the seventy first year of his age, son of Capt. John BROWN and brother of Daniel BROWN, testified...

Jabez BROWN of Swansea MA to **Ebenezer TIFFANY** of same. <Bristol Co.Deeds 5:352>
...30 Mar. 1708, Jabez BROWN, yeoman & wf Jane, for Ł23 sell to Ebenezer TIFFANY, yeoman...four acre salt meadow at Moshassuck Neck in Swansea.

Will of **Jabez BROWN** of Barrington/Rehoboth. <Bristol Co.PR 11:281,292,360;12:475;16:91,94>
<11:281>...dated 11 Apr. 1746...being aged...to wf **Abijah,** the use & improvement of half of dwelling house & homestead in Barrington containing about forty acres...to son **John BROWN,** my dwelling house and orchard...bounded by land where son **Hezekiah** lives...to dau **Jane BOSWORTH** wf of Nathaniel, Ł10...to my son **Oliver BROWN**'s two daughters, viz: **Rebecca BROWN & Ann BROWN,** 5s each when they arrive at 18...to the two children of my dau **Rebeccah PECK,** viz: **Jerush PECK & Winchester PECK,** 5s each when they arrive at 18...to sons **Hezekiah BROWN & John BROWN** all the rest of my land in Barrington; son **John** app'td executor and...shall take good care & provide sutably for my dau **Elizabeth** all things necessary during her naturall life & give her a decent buriall. Witnesses: Samuel HOWLAND, Daniel BROWN, Sarah BROWN. <11:292> Pr. 7 July 1747, **John BROWN** app'td admr. <11:360> Inventory taken 24 Oct. 1747 by Daniel CARPENTER, Benjamin BROWN, Joseph WHETON; incl. gun, sword & ammunition, Ł10; total personal estate, Ł335.8; total real estate, Ł850. <original> Petition 4 Sept. 1750 by **Hezekiah BROWN** for division of lands left to himself & brother **John BROWN** which had not yet been carried out. Citation 4 Sept. 1750 to widow **Abijah BROWN & John BROWN** of Rehoboth, to appear 2 Oct. 1750 at the house of Capt. Thomas COBB, innholder in Taunton to show why an order for division should not be granted. <12:475> Division 8 Nov. 1750, by Aaron KINGSLEY, Ezekiel READ, Nathaniel VIALL, Peleg RICHMOND & Joseph WHETEN; to

the widow, twelve and a half acres bounded by land of **Hezekiah BROWN, John BROWN** and Benjamin VIAL, dec'd, valued at £54; to **Hezekiah BROWN**, eight acres, bounded as above, valued at £27; to. **John BROWN**, nine acres, bounded as above, valued at £27. Petition 4 Dec. 1750 of **John BROWN**, that his part in sd division includes about three acres which belongs to Daniel BROWN.

Estate of **Abijah BROWN**, widow of Rehoboth MA. <Bristol Co.PR 8:306;20:516,552>
<20:552> Inventory taken 5 Apr. 1766 by Capt. Daniel HUNT, Thomas BROWN, Samuel VIAL, all of Rehoboth; total estate, £21.1s6d. <146:139> Bond 21 Apr. 1765, of **John BROWN**, yeoman, admr. Sureties: Daniel HUNT & James CLAY, gentlemen. Witnesses: Nicholas BAYLIES, George LEONARD Jr. <20:516> Account of admr. 30 Jan. 1769; incl. for finding her the use of a cow & keeping hur the tarim of 18 years, £36; for 180 bushels of grain for 18 yrs, £18; for cuting wood at the dore & making fiers for hur 18 yrs at 12s per year, £10.16; for the use of about twelve acres of land for 18 yrs., £43.4s; Payments to: Dr. Ephraim BOWEN, Dr. HASE, Col. Thomas BOWEN, Col. LEONARD, Capt. HUNT, Thomas BROWN and Samuel VIAL.

Guardianship of **Hezekiah BROWN**, non compos, of Rehoboth MA. <Bristol Co.PR>
<originals> Petition 30 June 1755 of Selectmen of Rehoboth for appointment of gdn. Bond 5 Aug. 1755, of Jabez BROWN, cooper of Warren RI as gdn. Sureties: Daniel HUNT & Benjamin BROWN, gent. of Rehoboth. Inventory taken 15 Aug. 1755 by Daniel CARPENTER, Esq., Capt. Benjamin BROWN and Capt. Daniel HUNT; total £200.

Estate of **Hezekiah BROWN** of Rehoboth MA. <Bristol Co.PR>
<15:450> 5 Apr. 1757, Jabez BROWN, cooper of Rehoboth app'td admr. Bond 1 Aug. 1758 of Benjamin VIAL, yeoman of Rehoboth, as admr. de bonis non. <original> Division 15 Sept. 1759...dec'd left seven children which would have made eight shares, but two, viz: **Hezekiah BROWN & Solomon BROWN** have since died without issue and one died since but left heirs; estate divided among the following: eldest son **Asa BROWN**, heirs of 2d son **Jabez BROWN**, 3d son **William BROWN**, 4th son **Nathaniel BROWN** and dau **Keziah VIAL** wf of Benjamin. <16:89> Account (no date given) of **Molly BROWN**, admx. on estate of Jabez BROWN late of Warren RI dec'd who was gdn. of **Hezekiah BROWN** who was non comp...the whole time my father was at my house was one year one month two weeks and a day.

Will of **Joshua BICKNALL.** <Warren RI Town Council Rcds.>
<1:84>...dated 23 Jan. 1749/50, mentions wf **Abigail** (executrix) and children: **Joshua BICKNALL, Olive BICKNALL, Molly BICKNALL, Hannah PADDLEFORD** wf of Jonathan. Pr. 2 Mar. 1752. <1:86> Guardianship 2 Mar. 1752, Ebenezer ADAMS of Warren app'td gdn. of **Molly BICKNALL**, above 14 yrs; Peter BICKNALL app'td gdn. of **Olive BICKNALL**, above 14 yrs. <1:92> Guardianship 4 Dec. 1752, Jabez BROWN, mariner of Warren & wf Molly discharge Ebenezer ADAMS as gdn. of **Molly.**

Estate of **Jabez BROWN**, mariner of Warren RI. <Warren RI Town Council Rcds.>
<1:160> 5 June 1758, widow **Molly BROWN** app'td admx. <1:162> Inventory taken 31 May 1758.

Nathaniel BROWN of New Medford CT to **Benjamin VIALL** of Rehoboth MA. <Bristol Co.Deeds 50:52>
...1 Nov. 1760, Nathaniel BROWN, blacksmith, for £35 sells to Benjamin VIALL, yeoman...eight acres that his father late of Rehoboth died seized of & was set off to Nathaniel...bounded by the widow **Habijah BROWN**'s thirds and brother **William BROWN**'s rights...reserving the buring place on sister Keziah, wf of sd Benjamin.

Elizabeth BROWN of Swansea MA to **Thomas DEXTER** of Barrington. <Warren RI Deeds 1:349>
...4 Nov. 1728, Elizabeth BROWN, widow & admx. of James BROWN dec'd, sells to Thomas DEXTER...the part allotted to Rachel DEHANE one of the daus of Samuel LOW dec'd, on the south side of the sd widow's third part. Witnesses: Joseph BROWN, Benjamin BROWN. Rec. 30 Mar. 1758.

Elizabeth BROWN of Barrington to **Michall BROWN** of same. <Bristol Co.Deeds 31:133>
...31 July 1742, Elizabeth BROWN, widow, for £100 sold to son Michall BROWN, taylor...100 acres in Attleborough...that was set off & divided to me in ye division & settlement of ye real estate of my honoured father Richard BOWEN late of Rehoboth dec'd. Rec. 22 Nov. 1742.

Josiah HUMPHRY Jr. to **James BROWN** of Barrington. <Warren RI Deeds 1:13>
...21 Dec. 1744, Josiah HUMPHRY Jr. & wf Abijah one of the daus of James BROWN late of Barrington dec'd, sell to their brother James BROWN...all their rights in the thirds of Elizabeth BROWN, widow of sd James BROWN dec'd. Witnesses: William PEARSE, Lydia PEARSE. Rec. 15 Apr. 1747.

Estate of **Elizabeth BROWN**, widow of Warren RI. <Warren RI Town Council Rcds.>
<1:173> 6 Aug. 1759, son **James BROWN**, Esq. of Warren app'td admr. <1:176> Inventory taken 6 Aug. 1759, mentions bonds due from Maj. HUMPHREY, £67.6.9 and Mr. PEARSE, £40.9.3. <1:210> Account 2 Mar. 1761 of admr.; Paid to: John ADAMS, £90; Josiah HUMPHREY, £88; Enoch HUNT, £88; William PEIRCE, £88; Mary ALLEN, £88; James BROWN, £88; Enock HUNT, £50; Josiah HUMPHREY, £40 and William PEIRCE, £9.12.

Estate of **James BROWN** of Barrington. <Bristol Co.PR>
<5:107> Inventory of estate of **James BROWN**...deceased 21 Feb. 1724, was taken 8 May 1725 by Samuel BROWN, Thomas DEXTER & Mathew ALLEN; total real estate, £1310; total estate, £1770.18s2d. <5:46> Pr. 25 Mar. 1725, widow **Elizabeth BROWN**, app'td admx. <7:509> Guardianship 22 Feb. 1732/3, Benjamin BROWN of Rehoboth app'td gdn. of **James BROWN**, minor son of dec'd, above 14. <8:305> Account 16 Dec. 1735 of admx. <8:307> Guardianship 16 Dec. 1735, widow **Elizabeth BROWN** app'td gdn. of son **Micah BROWN**, minor son of dec'd, above 14.

Division of estate of **James BROWN** of Barrington. <Bristol Co.PR 8:331>
...15 Jan. 1735/6, real estate was divided among the widow and following children, viz: eldest son **James BROWN,** eldest dau **Elizabeth ADAMS,** 2d dau **Abijah BROWN,** 3d dau **Liddy BROWN,** youngest son **Michael BROWN.** Signed by Richard HARDING, Robert JOLLS, Thomas THROOPE, Benjamin BOSWORTH, Jonathan PECK.

John ADAMS et al of Barrington to **James BROWN** of same. <Bristol Co.Deeds 31:168>
...7 Jan. 1742/3, John ADAMS & wf Elizabeth, Josiah HUMPHRY Jr. & wf Abijah and Michel BROWN, for £52.10s sell to our brother James BROWN...three sixths or one half part of upland & meadow at a place called Nait in the township of Barrington...about five acres & a half...which was given by James BROWN, grandfather of above named James, in his last will, to his son James BROWN late of Barrington dec'd...for & use of his wife Margaret BROWN during her natural life. Witnesses: Samuel HOWLAND, Samuel HUMPHREY Jr. Rec. 19 Jan. 1742/3.

Will of **Enoch HUNT,** yeoman of Rehoboth MA. <Bristol Co.PR>
<3:92>...dated 28 Nov. 1711, mentions grandson **Enoch HUNT** to have house that was his father's; grandaughter **Mary HUNT**; dau **Rebecca** (minor); sons **Nathaniel HUNT & Stephen HUNT.** <3:93> Inventory taken 3 Apr. 1712.

Estate of **Enoch HUNT** of Taunton MA. <Bristol Co.PR>
<37:398> Inventory taken 25 Aug. 1800. <38:135> 26 Aug. 1800, **Jael HUNT** app'td admx. <38:236> Account 2 June 1801. <38:501> Account 15 Jan. 1802. <38:238> Dower set off, 13 May 1801, to widow **Jael HUNT.** <38:486> Division 5 Jan. 1802, to following children, viz: eldest son **Enoch HUNT; Stephen HUNT;** eldest dau **Lavinia WOODWARD;** 2d dau **Dorinda COBB; Lucinda PITCHER;** youngest dau **Lydia HUNT.** <38:512> Notice of sale, 1 July 1801. <149:338> Letter.

Will of **Micah BROWN,** tailor of Warren RI. <Warren RI Town Council Rcds.>
<1:12>...dated 4 Jan. 1747/8...to Mother, income of £300 for life...to kinsman **Enoch REMINGTON,** all wearing apparell...to kinswoman **Jael SABIN,** £50 when she is 21...to friend Mrs. Elizabeth KINNICUTT, £250...brother **James BROWN,** executor...sisters **Abijah HUMPHREY & Lydia PEIRCE.** Pr. 1 Feb. 1747/8. <1:13> Inventory taken 3 Feb. 1747/8. <1:51> Account 20 Mar. 1748/9 of **James BROWN,** exr.; Received from: Charles BROWN, £14; widow BOSWORTH, £1.5.; Thomas MEDBURY, £2; Jeremiah BROWN, £3.2; Paid to: Jonas HUMPHREY; Deacon Josiah HUMPHREY; Lydia BOSWORTH, £30.18; Enock REMINGTON, £94; Elizabeth KINNICUT, £250; William PEARSE, £238.16; Josiah HUMPHREY, £238.16.

Micah BROWN of Barrington to **James BROWN** of same. <Bristol Co.Deeds 31:133>
...31 July 1742, Micah BROWN, taylor, for £50 sold to brother James BROWN, yeoman...land in Barrington...that was my honoured father's James BROWN late of Barrington dec'd & in ye division...of his real estate was set off & divided to me being part of ye homstead. Rec. 22 Nov. 1742.

Micah BROWN of Barrington to **Timothy FREEMAN & Abraham COMINGS.** <Bristol Co.Deeds 36:36>
...29 Feb. 1742, Micah BROWN, taylor, for £330 sold to Timothy FREEMAN & Abraham COMINGS, refineers of Attleborough...100 acres of upland & swamp in Attleborough...being ye land that was laid out to John TITUS Sr....reserving a way...for Thomas BOWEN, Esq. of Rehoboth or his heirs to pass to & from his land. Ack. 29 Jan. 1742/3 by Micah. Rec. 19 May 1748.

Damaris PECK of Rehoboth MA to **Micah BROWN.** <Bristol Co.Deeds 33:57>
...10 May 1743, Damaris PECK, widow, sold to Micah BROWN...land she purchased of Amos HAMMON.

Micah BROWN of Barrington to **James BROWN** of same. <Bristol Co.Deeds 34:260>
...24 Mar. 1745/6, Micah BROWN, taylor...one of ye sons of James BROWN late of Barrington dec'd, for L75 sold to brother James BROWN, yeoman...all rights...to that part of real estate of ye sd James BROWN dec'd which was set of or divided to his widow Elisabeth BROWN for her thirds. Ack. 12 Apr. 1746 at Providence. Rec. 9 May 1746.

Will of **Avis WATSON** of Barrington RI. <Barrington PR 1:107>
...4 Feb. 1804, mentions sons **Samuel WATSON** (executor), **Matthew WATSON & John WATSON;** mentions 10 acres...being the same that I hold by will from my honoured Father dec'd.

MICRO #18 OF 18

Estate of **Rebecca BROWN** of Rehoboth MA. <Bristol Co.PR>
<11:595> Inventory taken 16 Sept. 1748; total real estate, L400. <12:358> Account of Richard BULLOCK, admr., of Warren; sister **Anne,** sole heir.

Estate of **Rebecca BROWN** of Seekonk. <Bristol Co.PR>
<73:257> Adm., 1833. <73:272> Inventory. <73:291,494> Accounts. <73:448;113:299> Notices.

References to the name **Rebecca BROWN** in Bristol Co.PR: <10:266> 1742, gdn. of Rebecca, dau of Oliver BROWN. <129:248> 1777, gdn. of Rebecca, dau of Noah BROWN. <153:314> Adm. <176:314>Citation. <202:316> Sale of land.

William TRIPP of Rehoboth MA to **Isaac BROWN** of same. <Bristol Co.Deeds 59:366>
...4 Jan. 1775, William TRIPP, yeoman & wf Jerusha the dau of William BROWN, dec'd of Rehoboth, sold to Isaac BROWN, yeoman...her share of thirds of widow Rebecca BROWN dec'd; mentions land

Amos BROWN bought of heirs of Bethiah WALKER and heirs of Elizabeth BISHOP.

Will of **Daniel BISHOP** of Attleboro MA. <Bristol Co.PR>
<11:390>...dated 27 July 1747, mentions minor children, viz: **Daniel BISHOP, Comfort BISHOP, Timothy BISHOP, Jeremiah BISHOP, Jemima BISHOP & Bethiah BISHOP**; brother **Joseph BISHOP**, gent. of Attleboro; friends Obadiah FULLER of Attleboro & Amos BROWN of Rehoboth. <11:391> Pr. 5 Jan. 1747. <11:487> Inventory taken 7 Jan. 1747/8. <14:317;16:229> Accounts. <18:311> Receipt 7 June 1762, of **Daniel BISHOP** of Rehoboth, **Abraham WALKER**, hus. of **Jemima** and **Timothy BISHOP** by his gdn. Nathaniel BISHOP, to Amos BROWN.

Guardianship of Child of **Benjamin BRIGGS** of Rehoboth MA. <Bristol Co.PR 127:51>
...9 Feb. 1762, **Benjamin BRIGGS Jr.**, blacksmith of Taunton app'td gdn. of **Bethiah BRIGGS**, under 14, dau of **Benjamin BRIGGS** of Rehoboth & wf **Bethiah** dec'd who was dau of **Daniel BISHOP** of Attleboro, dec'd.

William BROWN 3d et al to **Amos BROWN** of Rehoboth MA. <Bristol Co.Deeds 59:223>
...9 Nov. 1774, William BROWN 3d, shipwright of Falmouth ME, Ezra BROWN & Amos BROWN, yeomen and Lydia BROWN, spinster, all of Windham ME, sell to Amos BROWN, blacksmith...eight acres set off to heirs of Ezra BROWN out of estate of William BROWN, dec'd of Rehoboth. Rec. 21 Apr. 1779.

Dorothy BROWN et al of Rehoboth MA to **Amos BROWN** of same. <Bristol Co.Deeds 59:217>
...25 Mar. 1773, widow Dorothy BROWN, Sarah BROWN, William ARMINTON, cordwainer & wf Lucy, sell to Amos BROWN, blacksmith...two fifths of land laid out to Lt. James BROWN's heirs, being 3 acres

---

Heirs of **William BROWN**. <Bristol Co.Deeds>
<37:520>...7 Sept. 1743, Ezra BROWN, husbandman and Jerusha BROWN, single woman, of Rehoboth, sell to Amos BROWN of same...all rights in land of Anna BROWN, 4th dau of William BROWN. Ack. 24 Sept. 1743 by both. <37:521>...7 Sept. 1743, Ezra BROWN sells to Amos BROWN, my share of my father William BROWN's real estate. <37:521>...7 Sept. 1743, Jerusha BROWN, single woman sells to Amos BROWN, my share of real estate of my father William BROWN. <37:523>...18 Mar. 1745/6, Daniel BISHOP & wf Elizabeth of Attleboro sell to Amos BROWN, rights in real estate of Anna BROWN dec'd, 4th daughter.

Estate of **Noah BROWN** of Attleboro MA. <Bristol Co.PR>
<147:128> 6 May 1776, son **Noah BROWN**, yeoman, app'td admr. <24:274> Inventory taken 26 May 1776. <28:23> Account 3 Mar. 1784, of admr., mentions the widow.

Guardianship of Children of **Noah BROWN**, dec'd of Attleboro MA. <Bristol Co.PR>
<129:246-51> 28 Apr. 1777, **Noah BROWN**, yeoman of Attleboro, app'td gdn. of chil. of **Noah BROWN**, dec'd, viz: **Hannah BROWN, Bethiah BROWN, Stephen BROWN, John BROWN** and **James BROWN**, all under 14. Sureties: Thomas FRENCH & Elisha WILMARTH, yeomen of Attleboro. Witnesses: George LEONARD Jr. & Experience LEONARD.

BRISTOL COUNTY DEEDS: (re: Noah BROWN, grantor)

<38:21> - 7 Dec. 1748, Amos BROWN, yeoman of Rehoboth to brother Noah BROWN, husbandman of Rehoboth. Ack. 27 Mar. 1749. Rec. 13 Mar. 1750.
<38:21> - 7 Dec. 1748, Abiah CARPENTER of Rehoboth to Noah BROWN of same.
<41:55> - 29 Aug. 1752, Jonathan WILLMOUTH, husbandman of Attleboro to Noah BROWN of Rehoboth, land in Attleboro.
<65:2> - 17 Apr. 1784, N.B., yeoman of Attleboro sells 10 acres in Attleboro. Wf Judith signs.
<70:388> - 17 Apr. 1784, N.B. as admr. of father Noah BROWN's estate sells to his mother, the widow Deborah BROWN of Attleboro. Rec. 12 Mar. 1792.
<70:389> - 4 May 1784, N.B. of Attleboro to widow Deborah BROWN, her widow's thirds. Rec. " .
<83:140> - 3 May 1784, N.B. as admr. of father Noah BROWN dec'd, sells to Josiah CARPENTER of same...not to take possession until death of widow Deborah BROWN.

(References only, no data: 37:527,529;39:248;40:225,296;48:140;59:220,367;65:1;69:546.)

RICHARD MORE

MICRO #1 OF 2

James HYNDES of Salem to **Richard MOORE/MORE.** <Essex Co.Deeds 1:7>
...15 3mth 1650, James HYNDES, cooper sells to Richard MOORE...dwelling house on the south river side with three quarters of an acre thereto adjoyning and tenn acres of upland in the south field as by a writing dated the 3d day of October last.

John HOME/HORNE(sp) of Salem to **Richard MOORE/MORE** of same. <Essex Co.Deeds 2:82A>
...3 7mth 1655, John HOME/HORNE sold to Richard MOORE...dwelling house & one acre in Salem... bounded by land of Mr. DOWNING, sd HOME/HORNE, Thomas RIX and sd MOORE.

Henry BARTHOLOMEW of Salem to **Richard MORE** of same. <Essex Co.Deeds 2:82A>
...11 July 1664, Henry BARTHOLOMEW sells to Richard MORE...dwelling house & about one acre next to house & land of George KEISER and sd MORE.

Robert STARR to **Capt. Richard MORE & Philip CROMWELL.** <Essex Co.Deeds 3:139>
...18 Mar. 1671/2, Robert STARR gave to Capt. Richard MORE & Philip CROMWELL, as guardians of my three children, viz: Robert, Richard & Susanna...the house & land I received of my father in law Richard HOLLINGSWORTH as a portion with my wife.

Capt. Richard MORE Sr. of Salem MA to **Samuel DUTCH** of same. <Essex Co.Deeds 6:123>
...4 June 1684, Richard MORE Sr. sells to Samuel DUTCH, mariner, in consideration of his marriage with my dau Susanna his now wife and to his heirs by Susanna...one quarter acre in Salem where Samuel's house now stands...bounded by land of sd Richard. Ack. 6 June 1684 by R.M.& Rec. 10 June

---

Richard MORE Sr. to **John HIGGINSON Jr..** <Essex Co.Deeds 8:9>
...29 Oct. 1687, Richard MORE Sr., mariner sells to John HIGGINSON Jr...land bounded by my garden orchard & wharf and wharf & flats of Samuel DUTCH. Ack. 28 Nov. 1687. Rec. 14 Jan. 1687/8.

Capt. Richard MORE of Salem MA to **Philip CROMWELL** of same. <Essex Co.Deeds 8:15>
...17 Dec. 1687, Capt. Richard MORE, mariner, mortgaged to Philip CROMWELL...with priviledge of both wharf & well. Ack. same day. Rec. 18 Jan. 1687/8

Richard MORE Sr. of Salem MA to **William BROWNE** of same. <Essex Co.Deeds 8:85>
...14 May 1688, Richard MORE Sr., mariner to William BROWNE, Esq. & William BROWNE...all my homestead in Salem...bounded by land of son Richard MORE...except a small piece mortgaged to Philip CROMWELL. Ack. same day. Rec. 15 May 1688.

Richard MORE Sr. & Jr. of Salem MA to **Peter OSGOOD** of same. <Essex Co.Deeds 8:93>
...5 July 1688, Richard MORE Sr. & Richard MORE Jr., mariners, sell to Peter OSGOOD, tanner... part of their land in Salem...with a free privilidge of ye sd Richard MORE Sr. to his wharfe upon all occasions. Ack. same day. Rec. 14 Aug. 1688.

Richard MORE of Lynn MA to **John MORE** of same. <Essex Co.Deeds 10:138>
...12 Nov. 1688, Richard MORE, husbandman, to son John MORE...land next to sd John's. Witnesses: Thomas MORE "et al". Rec. 6 Mar. 1694/5.

Heirs of **Richard MOORE/MORE** of Lynn MA. <Essex Co.Deeds 20:178>
...27 Sept. 1707, Richard MOORE, only surviving son of John MOORE of Lynn dec'd, Ephraim MOORE of Boston, eldest son of Samuel MOORE of Lynn dec'd...the grandsons of Richard MOORE of Lynn dec'd ...divide land.

Richard MOWER/MORE of Lynn MA to **Ebenezer HAWKS** of same. <Essex Co.Deeds 26:89>
...27 Oct. 1707, Richard MOWER, husbandman sells to Ebenezer HAWKS. Wf Thankful MOWER/MORE releases dower; widow Susanna MOWER/MORE quit claims her rights. Ack. same day by all.

ESSEX COUNTY DEEDS: (re: Richard MORE)

<3:303> - 30 Aug. 1673, Richard MORE, mariner & wf Christian of Salem sell their rights as purchaser at Swansea to Samuel SHRIMPTON of Boston. Ack. 20 Oct. 1673.
<4:46> - 1 Dec. 1673, Release of mortgage by Capt. Richard MORE.
<4:114> - 10 June 1675, Richard MORE to Caleb MORE et al.
<7:132> - 4 July 1687, Capt. Richard MORE to son Richard MORE of Salem.
<8:95> - 10 July 1688, Richard MORE to son Richard MORE.
<9:18> - 1 May 1690, Richard MORE Jr. & wf Sarah of Salem, sell.
<8:150> - 10 May 1690, Capt. Richard MORE to Philip CROMWELL, slaughterer of same. Rec. 11 May.

ESSEX COUNTY DEEDS, cont-d: (re: Richard MORE)

<9:17> - 27 Nov. 1690, John OSGOOD Sr., yeoman of Andover to son Peter OSGOOD, tanner of Salem. Witnesses: Richard MORE Jr., Thomas MOULD.
<38:89> - 27 Oct. 1707, Richard MOWER/MORE & wf Thankful of Lynn.
<50:222> - 10 Jan. 1707/8, Richard MOWER/MORE & wf Thankful of Lynn sell; widow Susanna releases.
<54:23> - 7 May 1708, Richard MOWER & wf Thankful of Lynn sell.
<50:220> - 3 Aug. 1708, Richard MOWER/MORE of Lynn sells.
<43:163> - 4 Aug. 1712, Richard MOWER/MORE of Lynn sells.
<38:85> - 2 Apr. 1713, Richard MOWER/MORE of Lynn sells.
<20:188> - 21 Jan. 1716, Richard MOORE/MORE, husbandman of Lynn as admr. of Nathaniel BEADLE of Salem dec'd, sells.
<52:189> - 21 Jan. 1729/30, Richard MOWER/MORE, innholder of Lynn sells.
<78:236> - 20 Feb. 1730, Richard MOWER/MORE, innholder of Lynn sells.
<80:42> - 23 Nov. 1735, Richard MOWER/MORE, innholder of Lynn sells.
<79:204> - 9 Sept 1740, Richard MOWER/MORE, gent. & wf Thankful of Lynn sell.

(Note: References only with no data, viz: 1:69;3:5,27,101,107,127,174;82:7;83:66;83:261,317;88:58;97:240;98:41,233;100:113,279;101:9;103:8,52;104:136,156;106:69;112:76;115:133;122:186;125:240)

Deposition of **Richard MOORE.** <Essex Co.Court Files 49:75>
...1 Apr. 1690, Richard MOORE, aged aboute 78 yeares saith that beinge...a retainer and a labourer in the service of my father in law Richard HOLLINGWORTH Sr. aboute fivety six yearss agoe...

Deposition of **Capt. Richard MOARE/MORE Sr.** of Salem MA. <Essex Co.Court Files 49:76>
...12 July 1690, Capt. Richard MOARE Sr. aiged aboute 78 yeares and Elizabeth GRIGS aiged aboute 64 yeares: Both Testified and Say: that Richard HOLLINGSWORTH Sr: formery of Salem in the County of Essex in New England Shipwright, Deceased had a parcell of Land of Aboute two acres: Neare the point of Rocks, soe called on the Neck of Land in the Townseship of Salem in the County Aforesaid And part of the Said Land is Now fenced in: and the whole of the sd: Land is Bounded as followeth Easterly partly with the Towne Comon and partly with A strip of Land of Aboute a quarter of an Acre now fenced In: which was formerly the Towne Comon Southerly, with a parcell of Land.

Deposition of **Capt. Richard MOORE & Henry SKERRY.** <Essex Co.Court Files 49:74>
...29 Sept. 1690, Capt. Richard MOORE, aged about 78 and Henry SKERRY, aged about 89 yeares...

Deposition of **Capt. Richard MORE Sr.** of Salem MA. <Essex Co.Court Files 49:138>
...25 9mth 1690, Capt. Richard MORE Sr. of Salem, aged about 78 years this deponant doth testifie and say that my Father in law Richard HOLLINSWORTH Sr. of Salem desesed did give unto Richard HOLLINSWORTH his younger son...the widdow my mother in law Relect of sd Hollinsworth....

Estate of **Richard HOLLINGSWORTH Sr.** of Salem MA. <Suffolk Co.Court Files 41:5,8,9>
...27 Oct. 1696, writ attachment, £300 against Philip ENGLISH, merchant of Salem, to answer at Salem 2d Tues. of Nov. 1696 the appeal of Richard READ, shoreman of Marblehead. (At the Court of Common Pleas, last Tues. Mar. 1695/6, appeared Philip ENGLISH & wf Mary who was admx. of estate of Richard HOLLINGSWORTH Sr.) The appeal of Richard READ states...that Richard HOLLINGSWORTH Sr. did not dye seized of the lands in controversy, is evident by the testimonyes of **Capt. Richard MORE** and Mr. William BEALE, for it was give (by) the intestate to his son Richard who in the life time of his father entred upon the same, cutt downe timber & was possessed thereof until he sold it to the appell^{t} on 27 Apr. 1674. Testimony had been given 25 Nov.1690 by William BEALE, ae 64 of Marblehead and 31 Dec. 1695 by John NORMAN, ae 57.

Richard HUTTON of Wenham MA. <Essex Co.Deeds 30:109>
...25 Mar. 1695, Richard HUTTON & wf Susanna...sell land in Wenham. Witnesses: Thomas FISK, Henry MORE, John BEARC. Ack. 31 Dec. 1695 by Richard. <20:22>...14 May 1707, Richard HUTTON & wf Susannah...sell land in Wenham. Ack. 20 May 1707 (Richard being blind).

Richard MOORE/MORE of Duxbury to **Abraham BLUSH.** <Plymouth Col.Rec. 12:22>
...1 Nov. 1637, Richard MOORE, yeoman sells to Abraham BLUSH...house & all land at Duxbury.

SALEM TOWN RECORDS: (re: MOORE)

<9:63> - 25 10mth 1637, Richard MOORE is Rec. Inhabitant and is granted halfe an acre on the neck
<9:92> - 20 9mth 1639, Graunted to (Richard crossed out) "William" MOORE, halfe acre for a fisher lott near about winter harbour.
<9:119>- 8 5mth 1642, Granted to Richard MORE, halfe acre joyned to his house as a fisherman.

John SAFFIN against **Richard MORE** of Salem MA. <Plymouth Col.Deeds 3:194>
...Gov. Prence...Mr. John SAFFIN arrested Mr. Richard MORE of Salem for defamation because MORE had reported that SAFFINS's actions in Virginia were scandalous. Suit was to have been tried 27 Oct. 1657 at Boston but arbitration agreed on & decision was rendered 23 Oct. 1657, MORE to apologize & do so no more. William PADDY, James COLLINS, Josias WINSLOW & John WINSLOW, arbitrators.

Natives of New Plimouth to **Richard MORE et al.** <Bristol Co.Deeds 3:416>
...2 Apr. 1659...Know all men by these presents that We Ursamequin, Wamsutta, Tattapnum, natives inhabitting & lieing within the Government of Newplimouth in New England in Americah have...sold

...unto Capt. James CUDWORTH, Josiah WINSLOW, Constant SOUTHWORTH, John BARNES, John TESDALE/TISDALE, Humphery TURNER, Walter HATCH, Samuel HOUSE, Samuel JACKSON, John DAMON, Mr. Timothy HATHERLY, Timothy FFOSTER, Thomas SOUTHWORTH, George WATSON, Richard MOORE, Edmond CHANDLER, Samuel NASH, Henry HOWLAND, Mr. Ralph PATRIDGE/PARTRIDGE, Love BREWSTER, William PAYBODIE, Christopher WADSWORTH, Kenelme WINSLOW, Thomas BOURN and John WATERMAN the sonne of Robert WATERMAN...all the tract of upland & meadow lyeing on the easterly side of Taunton River...begining...southerly with the River called the ffalls or Quequechand...extending northerly...to Staceyes Creeke...into ye woods...four miles...including all meadows, neckes or islands lying & being betwixt Assonate Necke & the ffalls (Except the land that Tabasacason hath in present use)...and all the meadow on the westerly side of Taunton River...to the head of weypoyset River...in & for the consideration of twenty coates, two ruggs, two iron potts, two kettles and one little kettle, eight pair of showes, six pair of stockins, one dozen of howes, one dozen of hachets, two yard of broad cloth and a debt sattisfyed to John BARNES which was due from Wamsitta unto John BARNES before the 24th of December 1657 all being unto us in hand payd. Witnesses: Thomas COOKE, Jonathan BRIGS, John SASSAMON. Rec. 16 July 1702.

Estate of **Sampson MORE** of Boston MA. <Suffolk Co.PR #3114, 16:457,481;17:229>
...17 July 1708, widow **Elizabeth MORE** app'td admx.

SUFFOLK COUNTY PROBATE: (re: MOORE/MORE)

1667 - Gawen MOORE, adm. <#447,5:51,126>
1670 - Joseph MOORE, mariner of Boston, adm.; inv. by Hannah MOORE, mentions debts in Virginia. <#526,7:19>
1680 - John MORE of Mendham, will. <#1132,12:344>
1683 - John MOORE, shipwright of Boston, widow Mary, d. Virginia, adm. 15 Jan. <#1263,9:104>
1693 - John MOORE, adm. <#2046,13:196,563>
1707 - Francis MOORE (betw 14-20), son of John MOORE, brewer of Boston, chooses Amos MERRETT as his guardian, 29 Apr. 1707. <#3033,16:275>
1713 - Sarah MOORE, adm. <#3461,18:94>
1716 - Samuel MOORE, will; Ⱡ5 to brother in law John BURNET of Windham CT, remainder to 1st Meeting House & South Meeting House. <#3787,19:200,201,273;20:187,232>
1727 - Ann MOORE, adm. <#5456,25:377,466,467;26:370,371,372>
1735 - John MOORE, adm. <#6728,32:147>
1740 - Samuel MOORE, will. <#7400,34:566,567>
1744 - William MOORE, will. <#8166, 37:335,336>
1746 - James MOORE, adm. <#5537,39:94>
1759 - Thomas MOORE, adm. <#12204,56:19>
1761 - William MOORE, will. <#12689, 58:403,404;59:52;65:3,4,541>
1763 - Richard MOORE, adm. <#13212,62:3,256>

Will of **Richard MORE/MOWER** of Lynn MA.
...19 Nov. 1688...sick & weak...to my beloved wife...she renouncing all other right to my estate either by bargain or contract at or before marriage...by me done...also her right of third in my estate as the law directeth...during her natural life I give her five pounds per annum to be paid ...as followeth twenty bushels of good sound marchantable Indian corn and two good loads of good hay to be dilivered to her or to her order at Salem...yearly...and likewise all that rent at the town of Ipswich...which did formerly belong to her and also...my mare and three cows and ten sheep if they shall be alive at my decease and all that household stuff that she brought with her ...But if it shall please God that my sd wife shall first depart this life before myself then I give her & to be at her disposal the sum of ten pounds in pay that is in Indian corn at three shillings per bushel...and all household stuff...and all the rent at Ipswich...unto my son **Thomas MOOR** if he shall be now alive and demand the same, the sum of five shillings...unto my son **John MOOR** two thirds of all my lands...unto my son **Samuel MORE** the other third of all my lands...unto my grandchild **Hannah CHILLS** the sum of fifty shillings...unto son **John MOOR**'s children and son **Samuel MOOR**'s children, three sheep...unto son **John** the half of my orchard...at Clay Holl...for the term of fiveteen years & then it is to return to my son **Samuel**...son **John**, executor. Witnesses: Jno. DIVAN, John BURRILL Jr., Moses HUDSON. (He signed "Richard MOWER".)

MICRO #2 OF 2

SUSANNA MORE[2] (Richard[1])

Estate of **Samuel DUTCH**, mariner of Salem MA. <Essex Co.PR #8420>
Bond 19 Mar. 1693/4 of widow **Susanna DUTCH**. Sureties: Simon WILLARD of Salem & Richard HUTTON of Wenham. Witnesses: Richard MORE, Stephen SEWALL. Receipts: to **Richard & Susanna HUTTON** of Wenham from: John CONANT of Marblehead, 1 Dec. 1696; Timothy LINDALL, 7 Dec. 1696; Philip ENGLISH, 8 Dec. 1696; Benjamin BROWNE for Mrs. BAYLEY, William BROWNE, 9 Dec. 1696; Nathaniel BEADLE, 10 Dec. 1696; Benjamin MARSTON, 1 Feb. 1697; John CROMWELL, 9 Feb. 1696/7. Receipt 15 Dec. 1696, Robert FITZHUGH of Boston receipts for Hannah MAN to Joseph FOULLER son in law of Richard HUTTON the now husband of the relict of **Samuel DUTCH**. <305:128> Inventory taken by Elizur KESAR, Simon WILLARD; sworn to 19 Mar. 1693/4 by **Susanna DUTCH**; mentions quarter acre at the northermost corner of **Capt. MORE**'s orchard. <305:129> 3 Dec. 1694, **Susan/Susanna HUTTON**, admx. asks that a committee be app'td to receive claims as estate is insolvent. 1 Oct. 1689, note of **Samuel DUTCH** to Nathaniel BOWMAN for 35s silver or Ⱡ3.10s country pay. Witnesses: Benjamin LOTHROP, Stephen

CHESTER. 1 Oct. 1695, Nathaniel BOWMAN assigned to Mr. John BUTTOLPH of Salem. Witnesses: Nathaniel FOOT, Francis WHITMORE; Ack. 6 May 1696 by Nathaniel BOWMAN. 10 Dec. 1696, John BUTTOLPH receipts to Richard HUTTON. <305:129> Account 6 Jan. 1695/6 of **Susannah DUTCH** alias **HUTTON**; mentions bringing up one child two and a half years; sworn to 3 Feb. 1695/6 by admx. <#8426,305:131> 3 Feb. 1695/6, Richard HUTTON app'td gdn. of **Susannah DUTCH**, minor about 12 yrs.

Richard HUTTON of Wenham MA to **Richard FOWLER & Hutton GOLDSMITH.** <Essex Co.Deeds 18:219>
...5 Apr. 1706, Richard HUTTON, gift to two grandsons Richard FOWLER and Hutton GOLDSMITH...40 acres in Wenham after his death...5 acres of it resered for the improvement of wf Susanna.

Richard HUTTON of Wenham MA to **William ROGERS** of same. <Essex Co.Deeds 20:22>
...14 May 1707, Richard HUTTON, yeoman & wf Susanna sell to William ROGERS, weaver...land at Ipswich. Ack. 20 May 1707...& whereas ye sd Richard HUTTON is now blind I read ye deed...signed by Stephen SEWAL, J.P.

Depositions of **Richard HUTTON** of Wenham MA. <Essex Co.Deeds>
<21:168>...31 Mar. 1710...that he had lived in Wenham about 60 yrs. <22:70>...31 Mar. 1710...that he came to Wenham in 1649.

Estate of **Richard HUTTON** of Wenham MA. <Essex Co.PR #14445>
<311:116,220> 22 Apr. 1714, son in law **Joseph FOWLER** of Wenham app'td admr. in right of his wf **Elizabeth**, eldest dau of dec'd.

ESSEX COUNTY DEEDS: (re: HUTTON)

<7:54> - 12 Dec. 1678, Richard HUTTON, aged 57 yeares.
<11:228> - 28 Dec. 1681, William KNOWLTON to his father Richard HUTTON of Wenham.
<30:109> - 25 Mar. 1695, Richard HUTTON, husbandman & wf Susanna of Wenham to John LEVERETT, husbandman of same. Ack. 31 Dec. 1695. Rec. 30 Mar. 1715.
<15:262> - 3 May 1698, Richard & Susanna HUTTON of Wenham, for £4 sell to John BROWN of same... land near their dwelling house. Ack. 20 Mar. 1698/9.
<16:156> - 29 Mar. 1704, William & Lydia KNOWLTON and Richard HUTTON to Rice KNOWLTON.

(Note: References only to the name **HUTTON**, viz: grantees: <2:412> 1660. <4:206> 24 July 1678, deposition. <9:9> 1691. <9:223> 1693. <13:254> 1699, deposition; grantors: <4:81;10:21;18:125,128,219;19:170;30:109;44:233>.)

Estate of **Samuel DUTCH Sr.**, mariner of Ipswich MA. <Essex Co.PR #8421>
...1711...<310:333> Adm. <310:361> Inventory. <310:499> Account & Division. <311:77> Appraisal. <311:83> Account after dth of widow. <312:432> Quitclaim. <312:433> Receipts. <312:434> Settlement. <313:453,537> Accounts.

Estate of **Samuel DUTCH Jr.**, coaster of Ipswich MA. <Essex Co.PR #8422>
...1719...<313:30> Adm. <313:70> Receipt. <313:728> Inventory & Claims. <313:729> Account. <313:730> Distribution.

Estate of **Samuel DUTCH** of Ipswich MA. <Essex Co.PR #8423>
...1753...<331:298> Adm. <332:283> Inventory. <336:423> Account. <344:133> Sale of real estate. <#8424, 336:519> Guardianship of children, viz: **John, Mary, Mehitable, Samuel.**

Estate of **Samuel DUTCH**, yeoman of Danvers MA. <Essex Co.PR #8425>
...1811...<380:361> Adm. <380:508> Inventory. <382:213> Account.

Estate of **Osmond DUTCH.** <Essex Co.PR #8418>
<304:151> 6 July 1685, **Samuel DUTCH & Hezekiah DUTCH** consent to sale by their mother **Grace DUTCH** of Gloucester, of land for her needs. Witnesses: Israel (worn) and Richard MORE Jr.

Heirs of **Ozmond DUTCH** to **Epes SARGENT** of Glocester. <Essex Co.Deeds 54:213>
...23 July 1730, John LEGRO, taylor & wf Martha of Salem, Mary ASHTON, widow of Marblehead, sd Martha & Mary being the children of Hezekiah DUTCH who was son of Ozmund DUTCH late of Glocester dec'd, Benjamin KNOWLTON, weaver of Ipswich & wf Susanna the only dau of Samuel DUTCH son of sd Ozmond and Benjamin STUDLEY, shipwright of Ipswich & wf Elizabeth the dau of Benjamin & granddaughter of Robert who was also son of the sd Ozmond dec'd...for five shillings sold to Epes SARGENT, Esq...three sixth parts of about four acres in Glocester...bounded by land of Peter DOLIVER William CARD & Jonathan INGERSOLL...being part of the homested of the sd Ozmund DUTCH. Witnesses: John HIGGINSON, John CABOT Jr. Ack. 23 July 1730 by all grantors. Rec. same day.

Benjamin KNOWLTON of Ipswich MA to **John WHITE** of Glocester MA. <Essex Co.Deeds 61:24>
...20 July 1730, Benjamin KNOWLTON, weaver & wf Susannah late Susannah DUTCH dau of Samuel DUTCH of Salem dec'd & one of the heirs to Ozmond DUTCH late of Glocester dec'd...whereas John WHITE, cordwainer is in possession of a small peice of land containing about twenty & five poles... bounded by Common land used as a highway and land of Epes SARGENT, Esq....which land sd WHITE purchased of Capt. William CARD...be it known that we...claiming a right & proper title to a part of sd land as one of the heirs of our Grandfather Ozmund DUTCH dec'd, for £3.11s.5d, quitt claim all that our right. Witnesses: Benjamin STUDLEY, Aaron POTTER. Ack. 15 Mar. 1731/2 by Susanna.

Benjamin KNOLTON/KNOWLTON of Ipswich MA to **Mathew HOOKER** of same. <Essex Co.Deeds 111:182> ...27 July 1762, Benjamin KNOLTON, yeoman, for £16 sold to Mathew HOOKER...meadow in Ipswich being part of the farm known by the name of Saltonstall Farm containing five acres...bounded by land of Nathaniel POLAND, Solomon SMITH, Joseph POLAND, Charles TUTTLE & Nathaniel POTTER...reserving to the proprietors of sd farm to pass & repass over the same. Wf Susannah KNOWLTON releases dower. Witnesses: John HUBBARD, Richard DODGE Jr. Ack. 18 Aug. 1762 by grantors. Rec. 27 Aug. 1763.

Will of **Benjamin KNOWLTON Sr.**, yeoman of Ipswich MA. <Essex Co.PR #16055>
<342:7>...dated 5 Aug. 1759...to wf **Susanna** the use of one half of my dwelling house, viz the easterly part from the top to ye bottom, with a part in the cellar & the liberty of the well during her natural life...also for her own...all the house hold goods...also £8 annualy...six cords of good wood yearly...a good cow winter & summer and...a pig...also my sd executor shall take good care that she be carried to Meeting whensoever she is able...to my daus **Susanna DODGE** and **Elizabeth BROWN** I give £33.6s8d apeice...remainder to son **Benjamin KNOLTON** (executor)...only my clock which I give to my wife's use. Witnesses: Samuel WIGGLESWORTH, Anne DANE, Esther DANE. Pr. 17 Dec. 1764 on the testimony of Rev. Samuel WIGGLESWORTH and Mrs. Anna DEAN. <342:49> Inventory taken 4 Feb. 1765 by John HUBBARD, Nathaniel KNOWLTON & Israel DANE; incl. silver cup, £2; negro man servant, £50; 70 acre homestead, £429.6s8d; total estate, £680.16s4d; sworn to 19 Feb. 1765 by exr.

ESSEX COUNTY DEEDS: (re: Benjamin KNOWLTON, grantor, all to 1799)

<28:94> - 1715, B.K. to Thomas BOARMAN Jr.
<36:278> - 1720, B.K. to John DEANE et al.
<57:130> - 1730, B.K. to John KNOWLTON.
<54:213> - 1730, B.K. et al to Epes SARGENT.
<79:71> - 24 Oct. 1722, B.K. to Joseph DAY.
<61:24> - 1732, B.K. et ux to John WHITE.
<61:237>- 1732, B.K. et al to Jacob STOREY.
<81:241>- 4 Feb 1731, B.K. to Ebenezer PARSONS.

<108:202> - 26 July 1758, B.K. to Jacob SMITH.
<111:182> - 27 July 1762, B.K. to Mathew HOOKER. Wf Susanna KNOWLTON signs.
<124:131> - 31 Mar. 1763, B.K. Jr. & wf Abigail to William CLEEVES.
<146:100> - 16 Dec. 1785, B.K. estate to William DODGE. Rec. 30 Mar. 1786.
<162:5> - 14 July 1785, B.K. estate to Francis BURNHAM Jr. Rec. 27 Sept. 1796.
<162:274> - 15 June 1785, B.K. estate to Malachi KNOWLTON. Rec. 22 Nov. 1797.

ESSEX COUNTY DEEDS: (re: Benjamin KNOWLTON, grantee, all to 1799)

<8:124> - 1688, B.K. from Nathaniel KNOWLTON.
<25:271> - 1714, B.K. from John KNOWLTON.
<26:250> - 1713, B.K. from John KNOWLTON.
<43:210> - 1723, B.K. from Jonathan COGSWELL.
<77:176> - 1740, B.K. from Samuel KNOWLTON.
<79:176> - 1740, B.K. from Joseph DAY
<153:35> - 1791, B.K. from Nehemiah DODGE.
<43:211> - 1723, B.K. from John KNOWLTON et ux.
<43:211> - 1724, B.K. from John KNOWLTON et ux.
<49:133> - 1726, B.K. from Michael FARLEY.
<56:148> - 1729, B.K. from Samuel APPLETON.
<79:177> - 1740, B.K. from Philip FOWLER.
<106:172>- 1758, B.K. from David DODGE et ux.

<100:92> - 25 May 1711, B.K., husbandman of Ipswich from John STAMFORD & wf Margaret. Rec. 1754.
<100:94> - 25 May 1711, B.K. from Jonathan WADE. Rec. 8 June 1754.
<77:160> - 10 Jan. 1732, B.K. from Thomas BERRY, attorney.
<100:92> - 7 May 1733, B.K., weaver of Ipswich from Andrew BURLEY & wf Lydia. Rec. 8 June 1754.

Estate of **Benjamin KNOWLTON** of Ipswich MA. <Essex Co.PR #16056>
<original> Petition 6 Apr. 1781, to appoint Richard DODGE, admr., signed by heirs, viz: **Abigail KNOWLTON, Ezra KNOWLTON, Nehemiah KNOWLTON, Edmond KNOWLTON, Moses KNOWLTON, Malachi KNOWLTON & Nathaniel POLAND Jr.** <358:230> List of heirs, 1786, children of dec'd, viz: **Ephraim, Moses, Ezra, Malachi, Nehemiah, Abigail, Benjamin, Hepzibah, Hannah, Esther**; chil. of dec'd dau **Susanna POLAND** wf of Nathaniel Jr., viz: **Nehemiah POLAND**, ae 17, **Susanna POLAND**, ae 14, **Benjamin POLAND**, ae 13 & **Esther POLAND**, ae 11; **Edmund, Annis & Betty KNOWLTON.** <361:29> Division of widow's dower, 2 Aug. 1790 to the above mentioned children & heirs with Hepzibah called **Hepsibah CUMMINGS.**
(Note: The following references are given with no data, viz: 354:389,409;355:207,334,335;356:493 (Account); 357:369,370,400;358:231-33.)

Guardianship of Children of **Benjamin KNOWLTON** of Ipswich MA. <Essex Co.PR #16045>
<354:411;360:485;364:81>...7 May 1781, widow **Abigail KNOWLTON**, gdn. of **Abigail KNOWLTON**, ae 17; **Benjamin KNOWLTON**, ae 15; **Hannah KNOWLTON**, ae 14; **Esther KNOWLTON**, ae 12; **Annis KNOWLTON**, ae 10 and **Betty/Elizabeth KNOWLTON**, ae 7. Bond 8 June 1790, of Col. Robert DODGE as gdn. of **Annis KNOWLTON**, ae 19 and **Elizabeth KNOWLTON**, ae 17. Surety: Malachi KNOWLTON. Receipts, 16 Dec. 1790, of **Abigail, Benjamin & Hannah KNOWLTON** to widow **Abigail KNOWLTON**, their gdn. during their minority.* Receipt 19 Mar. 1795, of **Annis & Elisabeth KNOWLTON** to Col. Robert DODGE, their gdn. during their minority. Witness: Malachi KNOLTON/KNOWLTON.
(* As widow **Abigail KNOWLTON** died in May 1790, it is not clear why the wording is "to" her.)

Estate of **Abigail KNOWLTON**, widow of Ipswich MA. <Essex Co.PR #16046>
<360:507;361:31;362:302;364:81> Bond 5 July 1790, Malachi KNOWLTON, yeoman of Ipswich, app'td admr. Sureties: Richard DODGE & John DODGE, gentlemen of Wenham. Account 7 July 1795; incl. paid to Daniel RUST & Esther RUST, £33.8s.

Ezra KNOWLTON of Ipswich MA to **Malachi KNOWLTON** of same. <Essex Co.Deeds 163:11>
...17 Apr. 1786, Ezra KNOWLTON, fisherman, for £4 sold to Malachi KNOWLTON, yeoman...three quarter acre upland & meadow land in Ipswich in the Hamlet parish formerly belonging to my father Benjamin KNOWLTON. Wf Abigail KNOWLTON releases dower. Witnesses: Moses KNOWLTON, John T. DODGE. Ack. same day. Rec. 29 Nov. 1797.

Will of **Nathaniel DANE** of Ipswich MA. <Essex Co.PR #7121, 337:229,231,526>
<337:229>...dated 26 May 1760, mentions wf **Esther** and children, viz: **Israel DANE, Nathaniel DANE, Edward DANE, Nehemiah DANE, Elizabeth, Mary, Anna, Abigail & Esther.**

Will of **Nathaniel DANE** of Ipswich MA. <Essex Co.PR 358:215>
...dated 20 Nov. 1769, mentions eldest son **Nathaniel DANE,** minor son **Nehemiah DANE,** daus **Anna DANE, Mary DANE & Tabitha**; brother **Israel DANE,** executor.

Estate of **Esther DANE** of Ipswich MA, 1770. <Essex Co.PR #7085, 346:396,464>
Estate of **Israel DANE** of Ipswich MA, 1776. <Essex Co.PR #7096, 351:570;352:142>
Estate of **Israel DANE** of Hamilton MA, 1795. <Essex Co.PR #7097, 363:488;364:78;366:348>

ESSEX COUNTY DEEDS:

<61:237> - 8 Nov. 1721, Rice & Mary KNOWLTON of Wenham & Benjamin & Susanna KNOWLTON of Ipswich to Jacob STOREY, marsh in Chebacco. Ack. 6 Nov. 1722 by four grantors.
<79:171> - 24 Oct. 1722, Benjamin KNOWLTON of Ipswich to Joseph DAY, land in Hamlet. Wf Susanna KNOWLTON signs. Ack. 10 Nov. 1722 by grantors.
<81:241> - 4 Feb. 1731, Benjamin STUDLEY, shipwright, & wf Elizabeth and Benjamin KNOWLTON, yeoman & wf Susanna, all of Ipswich to Ebenezer PARSONS of Gloucester, land at Gloucester in common right of Osmund DUTCH.
<202:220> - 23 May 1812, Malachi KNOWLTON, yeoman of Hamilton to Jacob TOWNS, 4 acres in Hamilton. Wf Abigail KNOWLTON releases dower.

Will of **John KNOWLTON Sr.**, housewright of Ipswich MA. <Essex Co.PR #16078>
<316:349>...dated 29 Feb. 1713/14, mentions sons **John KNOWLTON** (eldest son), **Rice KNOWLTON, Benjamin KNOWLTON** (& his wf), **Thomas KNOWLTON** (& his wf), **Timothy KNOWLTON**; daus **Abigail GIDDINGS, Miriam KNOWLTON, Hannah POTTER** wf of Nathaniel, **Bethiah WOODEN, Susanna CORNING, Elizabeth CORNING** and heirs of dec'd dau **Mary PATCH**; four eldest sons, executors. <318:16> Pr. 24 Aug. 1728. <316:130> Committee to divide real estate. <316:130> Inventory. <316:131> Account 11 Nov. 1728, of estate of John KNOWLTON who dec'd 14 Aug. 1728; incl. funeral charges with mother's mourning cloathes, £27.3s and debt due to Timothy KNOWLTON, £3. <316:133> Receipt 10 Oct. 1728 of widow **Susanna KNOWLTON** to son **John KNOWLTON** for a morning sute. <319:350> Receipt 30 Oct. 1728 of widow to son **John**, executor, for fifty shillings.

John KNOWLTON Sr. of Ipswich MA to **John KNOWLTON** of Manchester MA. <Essex Co.Deeds 27:50>
...26 May 1714, John KNOWLTON Sr., housewright, for £100 sold to son John KNOWLTON, gent...my now dwelling house...and about fifty acres of upland & meadow...bounded by land of Thomas KNOWLTON, Samuel POLAND, Thomas PATCH, William DODGE...also a comonage in the undivided comon land in Ipswich...also two parcels of salt marsh bought of Richard LEE...in Chebacco marsh. Wf Susanna KNOWLTON signs. Witnesses: Nicholas WEBSTER, Joseph DAY. Ack. 29 June 1714 by grantors & Rec 9 Aug.

Will of **Nathan BROWN,** yeoman of Ipswich MA. <Essex Co.PR 363:235-7>
...dated 15 Nov. 1787, mentions wf **Elizabeth** and children, viz: **Susanna BROWN, Jeremiah BROWN, John BROWN, Hannah BOARDMAN, Nathan BROWN, Abraham BROWN**; granddaughter **Christian GIDDINGS.** On 29 May 1794, **Jeremiah BROWN,** one of the executors, declines because of distance. Pr. 2 June 1794.

Will of **Nathan BROWN** of Salem MA. <Essex Co.PR 359:219>
...dated 13 Nov. 1783, mentions wf **Rebecca** & her children; mother **Rebecca BROWN.** Pr. 1 Oct. 1787.

Estate of **Isaac GIDDINGS** of Middleton MA. <Essex Co.PR #10837>
<369:145> Bond 30 Mar. 1802, of Zaccheus GIDDINGS, admr. <370:325> Inventory taken 10 Apr. 1802; no real estate. <374:238> Account 2 Sept. 1806, presented by Hannah GIDDINGS, admx.

ESSEX COUNTY DEEDS: (re: Josiah DODGE, grantor, all to 1799**)**

<22:223> (1710), <28:228> (1714), <62:272> (1734) - Josiah DODGE of Ipswich.
<81:34> - 10 June 1738, J.D. of Wenham to Richard GOLDSMITH.
<81:35> - 1 Aug. 1738, Sarah DODGE, widow of Thomas to Richard GOLDSMITH.
<91:135> - 18 Jan. 1742, J.D. of Wenham & wf Prudence to William DODGE of Ipswich.
<120:67;124:54,57,59> - 1765, J.D. of Wenham & wf Prudence.
<162:269> - 1797, J.D. of Amherst NH et ux Eleanor, dau of Benjamin EDWARDS dec'd of Wenham, sell to Abraham EDWARDS of Wenham, all right in thirds of B.E.'s estate.

DEGORY PRIEST

MICRO #1 OF 3

MARY PRIEST[2] (Degory[1])

Land Grant to **Phineas PRATT** of Charlestown. <Rec. of Mass., Vol.4, Part 2, p.56 (1661-1674)> ...7 May 1662...In answer to the petition of Phineas PRAT of Charls Toune, who presented to this Court with a narrative of the streights & hardshipes that the first planters of this colony under went in their endeavors to plant themselves at Plimouth, & since whereof he was one, the Court judgeth it meet to graunt him three hundred acres of land where it is to be had, not hindering a plantation...<p.154-5>...Layd out to Phineas PRATT of Charls Toune, three hundred acres of land (more or less) in the wilderness, on the east of Meremack River neere the upper end of Nacooke Brooke, on the south east of it: it begins at a great sare pine standing anent the midle of Nacooke Pond & joyneth to the line of five hundred acres of land lately granted to the toune of Billirrikey...1 June 1665.

Will of **Phineas PRATT** of Charlestown. <Middlesex Co.PR #17922>
<5:412>...dated 8 Jan. 1677. Pr. 15 June 1680. <17:117> 25 Nov. 1723, Henry FAREWELL, Thomas BLANCHARD & Joseph BLANCHARD appraised the above three hundred acres at Ł135; mentions Daniel FLETCHER, admr. of estate.

Will of **Aaron PRATT**, yeoman of Hingham MA. <Suffolk Co.PR #6701>
<32:383>...dated 1 June 1730, mentions wf **Sarah**...to son **Benjamin PRAT**, fourteen acres & dwelling house...to eldest son **Henry PRAT**, Ł20...to son **Aaron PRAT**, Ł20...which sd sum...I had intended to have given to my dafter/daughter **Sarah WEBB** dec'd...he haveing purchesed her right in my estate in her life time...to daus **Elizabeth, Mercy ORCUT, Hannah** and **Abigail PRATT**, Ł35 each; mentions land lying near Hezekiah TOWERS land; remainder of estate to eight sons **Henry PRATT, Daniel PRATT, Aaron PRATT, Jonathan PRATT, John PRATT, Moses PRATT, Phenies/Phineas PRATT & Nathaniel PRATT**; sons **Henry & Aaron**, executors. Witnesses: Joshua BATE, Thomas ORCUTT Jr., Ebenezer MOTT. <32:383> Pr. 9 Mar. 1735, **Henry PRATT & Aaron PRATT**, app'td admrs. <32:448> <u>Inventory</u> taken 29 Apr. 1736 by Joshua BATES, John JACOB, Benjamin LINCOLN; incl. home lands, Ł1200; land in the 2nd part of the 3rd division, Ł120 and land in the 2nd division, Ł45; total estate, Ł1484.17s; sworn to 25 May 1736 by admrs.

Estate of **Henry PRATT**, blacksmith of Newton MA. <Middlesex Co.PR #12729>
Pr. 26 Nov. 1750. <46:394> <u>Division</u> of real estate, 2 Sept. 1752; thirds to widow **Hannah**, remainder to eldest son **Oliver PRATT**, admr. and son **Lemuel PRATT**, blacksmith, they paying to their brothers & sisters, viz: heirs of **Zebediah PRATT**, dec'd **& Henry PRATT Jr.**, dec'd, **Ebenezer PRATT, Silas PRATT, Moses PRATT**, husbandman of Newton, **Hannah WOOD, Sarah WHEATEN** wf of James, **Sibil BADCOCK** wf of Samuel and **Mercy BIGELOW** wf of Joseph. <u>Division</u> of widow's thirds, 31 Mar. 1767, by Capt. Abner FULLER of Newton, Capt. Eleazer KINGSBURY(sp) & Josiah UPHAM, both of Needham, to the following children, viz: heirs of eldest son **Oliver PRATT** dec'd; **Lemuel PRATT**; heirs of **Zebediah PRATT; Hannah HAVEN; Sarah WHEATON**; heirs of **Sybil BADCOCK** dec'd; **Ebenezer PRATT; Silas PRATT; Moses PRATT**; heirs of **Henry PRATT Jr.** dec'd and heirs of **Mercy BIGELOW** dec'd.

Estate of **Dr. Henry PRATT**, physician of Medway MA. <Suffolk Co.PR #8269>
...27 Aug. 1745, widow **Sarah PRATT** app'td admx. <u>Inventory</u> taken 25 Sept. 1745. <u>Account</u> 28 June 1748 of admx.; mentions allowance to the widow for support of herself and two young children. <#9035> <u>Guardianship</u> 28 June 1748, widow **Sarah PRATT** of Newton app'td gdn. of **Henry PRATT**, ae about two yrs. <#12730> <u>Guardianship</u> 4 Apr. 1760, **Bulah PRATT**, in her 17th yr, chose Capt. Joseph PERRY of Sherburn as her gdn...7 Apr. 1760, **Henry PRATT**, in his 15th yr, chose Amariah FULLER of Newton as his gdn.

Will of **Jonathan FULLER**, gent. of Newton MA. <Middlesex Co.PR #6107>
...dated 26 Sept. 1759, mentions wf **Sarah** and among his children, dau **Sarah LEARNED** and her eldest son **Henry PRATT**. 5 Dec. 1764, **Edward & Sarah LEONARD** gave consent to probate. Witness: Henry PRATT. Pr. 18 Dec. 1764.

Estate of **Joshua MURDOCK** of Newton MA. <Middlesex Co.PR #11192>
<u>Receipt</u> 26 June 1798 of the heirs to Samuel MURDOCK; among the heirs is **Henry PRAT/PRATT** in behalf of wf **Elizabeth.** <u>Warrant</u> 7 Oct. 1797, for widow's dower.

Will of **Edward LEARNED** of Sturbridge MA. <Worcester Co.PR #A36620>
...dated 7 June 1791...wf **Sarah** and brother **Henry PRATT**, executors.

Henry PRATT of Sturbridge MA to **Freeman PRATT** of same. <Worcester Co.Deeds 138:237;139:48>
...(no date given)...Henry PRATT, yeoman & wf Elizabeth sell to Freeman PRATT...all their real estate with agreement for the use of a part of it during their lifetimes, then Freeman to pay $100.00 to each of the heirs and give Henry & Elizabeth a decent burial.

Estate of **Henry PRATT** of Sturbridge MA. <Worcester Co.PR #A47667>
...17 Oct. 1801, Elizabeth PRATT petitions for letter of administration.

Joseph LUDLAM & John PRATT of Hogg Island NY. <Oyster Bay NY Deeds B:390>
...6 Dec. 1697, an exchange of meadow on Hogg Island by and between Joseph LUDLAM and John PRATT both of Hogg Island within the township of Oysterbay in Queens county on ye Island of Nassaw in ye colony of Newyorke. Witnesses: Job WRIGHT, Anthony WRIGHT, John TOWNSEND.

Will of **Joseph PRATT** of Charlestown MA. <Middlesex Co.PR #17902>
<13:197>...dated 23 July 1712, mentions wf **Dorcas** and son **Joshua PRATT** (executor). Witnesses: James LOWDEN, Benjamin PHILLIPS, James AUSTIN. Pr. 26 Jan. 1712/3. <13:159> Inventory taken 17 Jan. 1712/3 by Joseph PHIPPS, William KETTELL, Joseph WHITTEMORE; dwelling house, £32; sworn to 26 Jan. 1712/3 by exr.

John SWAN Sr. of Cambridge MA to **Mercy SWAN** of same. <Middlesex Co.Deeds 13:186>
...15 Jan. 1701/2, John SWAN Sr., yeoman for...the love...I do bare unto my loveing daughter Mercy SWAN, she not only being my youngest daughter, but hath lived with me in the time of my old age and hath been a great comfort to me and her aged mother...have given her...half part of all the three acre home stead in Cambridge...bounded by land of Edward WINSHIP & Gershom CUTTER that was Thomas HALL's...immediately after ye decease of me...and Mary my now married wife...divided between her ye sd Mercy SWAN and my son Ebenezer SWAN at her demand. Witnesses: Henry GARDENER, Isaac WALKER, James CONVERS. Ack. 23 Jan. 1701/2. Rec. 4 Apr. 1702.

MIDDLESEX COUNTY DEEDS: **(re: John SWAN,** grantor)

<9:235> - 20 June 1684, John SWAN & wf Mary. Ack. 19 Mar. 1684/5.
<13:586> - 21 Apr. 1696, J.S., yeoman of Woburn & wf Sarah, mortg. to John EMERSON. Disch. 1714.
<14:501> - 23 Apr. 1708, Gershom SWAN & wf Sarah to son John SWAN.
<24:369> - 25 Mar. 1719/20, J.S. of Cambridge & Ebenezer SWAN of Dorchester to Joseph BOWMAN, land in Lexington. Ack. 25 Mar. 1720 by both. Rec. 3 May 1725.

Ebenezer SWAN & Mercy PERRY of Cambridge to **William SWAN & James PERRY.** <Middlesex Co.Deeds>
<41:333>...11 July 1737, Ebenezer SWAN & widow Mercy PERRY convey to William SWAN, husbandman of Cambridge and James PERRY, chairmaker of Charlestown...one ninth part of land in Nottingham containing three hundred acres...which was granted by the Great & General Court to Phinehas PRATT late of Charlestown.

John SWAN of Cambridge MA to **Ebenezer SWAN** of same. <Middlesex Co.Deeds 12:122>
...20 July 1697, John SWAN, husbandman, for £8 sold to son Ebenezer SWAN...two acre meadow...in that meadow comonly called by ye name of Reedy Meadow in Cambridge...bounded by meadow of John FFRANCIS, land of Amos MARRET and Cooks farm. Witnesses: William JOHNSON, John BALDWIN. Ack. 2 Dec. 1697. Rec. 20 Jan. 1697/8.

John SWAN of Cambridge MA to **Ebenezer SWAN** of same. <Middlesex Co.Deeds 12:122>
...29 Nov. 1697, John SWAN, husbandman sold to son Ebenezer SWAN...half part of tenement in Cambridge...in that part called...Menotomy Row...the whole consisting of four acres with dwelling house...after ye death of my selfe & wife...bounded by land of Edward WINSHIP & Gershom CUTTER. Witnesses: William JOHNSON, Timothy GOODIN, Benjamin SIMONDS. Ack. 2 Dec. 1697. Rec. 20 Jan 1698.

John SWAN Sr. of Cambridge MA to **John SWAN Jr.** of Woburn MA. <Middlesex Co.Deeds 12:538>
...27 June 1700, John SWAN Sr., yeoman, for £12 sold to John SWAN Jr., husbandman...20 acres in Cambridge part upland & part swamp...bounded by land of Samuel ANDREWS & Samuel GOOKIN...also two acre meadow at a place called Reedy Medow...bounded by land of Ebenezer SWAN, Samuel COOK & sd John Sr....also two acres bounded by land of Phillip RUSSELL & the Cook's land. Wf Mary consents. Witnesses: Sara WINSHIP, Margaret ADDAMS, James CONVERS. Ack. & Rec. 8 Aug. 1700.

John SWAN Sr. of Cambridge MA to **Ebenezer SWAN** of same. <Middlesex Co.Deeds 14:124>
...23 Dec. 1703, John SWAN Sr., husbandman, for £6 sold to son Ebenezer SWAN, husbandman...two acres in Charlestowne...in a place comonly called...Menotomy field...bounded by land of William RUSSELL & Gershom CUTTER...after my decease. Witnesses: Jonathan BUTTERFIELD, Abraham HILL, Abraham WATSON. Ack. same day. Rec. 4 Oct. 1706.

Ebenezer & James PERRY of Cambridge MA to **James DIX** of Watertown MA. <Middlesex Co.Deeds 37:737>
...25 Mar. 1736, Ebenezer PERRY, cordwainer and James PERRY, chairmaker, for £40 sold to James DIX, husbandman...two parcels of land in Watertown...being two fifth parts of said pieces...the first being three acres orchard land bounded by land of Jonas BOND, Capt. HENDERSON, Henry SPRING and Thomas BOND...the other...on a hill commonly called Mackrill hill...bounded by land of George LAWRANCE, Nathaniel BRIGHT, John BEIRCE and land late of George LAWRANCE Sr. Witnesses: Edward MANNING, Samuel ANDREW. Ack. same day. Rec. 21 Mar. 1736.

Mercy PERRY of Cambridge MA to **Jonathan GATES** of same. <Middlesex Co.Deeds 27:448>
...(not dated)...Mercy PERRY, widow & admx. to the estate of Jonathan PERRY late of Cambridge dec'd, for £33 sold to Jonathan GATES, husbandman...eight acres of wood land...on Cambridge Rocks bounded by land of Samuel GIBSON, Thomas ANDREWS, Enos SAWTELL, Edmund GOFFE and Jason RUSSELL. Witnesses: Isaac WATSON, Daniel GOOKIN. Ack. & Rec. 19 Apr. 1728.

Mercy PERRY of Cambridge MA to **Ebenezer PERRY** of same. <Middlesex Co.Deeds 30:336>
...1 Mar. 1730, Mercy PERRY, widow & admx. of estate of John PERRY, husbandman, late of Cambridge dec'd, for Ł48.5s sold to Ebenezer PERRY, cordwainer...by virtue of the power...to her given...by the Superiour Court of Judicature...last Tuesday in July 1727...four & a half acre meadow in Cambridge...being the southwesterly part of the homestead of the sd dec'd...bounded by land of Rev. Mr. John WHITING & Abraham HILL and the other part of sd homestead.. Witnesses: John LAWRANCE, Ruth BOWMAN. Rec. 6 Mar 1730.

Mercy PERRY of Cambridge MA to **James PERRY** of Charlestown MA. <Middlesex Co.Deeds 44:187>
...22 Apr. 1741, Mercy PERRY, widow, for Ł100 sold to James PERRY, cheir-maker...four & a half acres in Cambridge being the southwesterly part of the homestead of John PERRY dec'd...bounded by land of Rev. Mr. ROGERS of Littleton late the land of the Rev. Mr. John WHITING of Concord, Abram HILL and the other part of sd homestead...the sd Mercy PERRY is to have the use & improvement of sd land during her naturall life. Witnesses: Marcy PERRY, Abner HARRIS. Ack. 19 July 1742. Rec. 3 Aug. 1743.

Ephraim FROST et al to **James PERRY** of Cambridge MA. <Middlesex Co.Deeds 136:349>
...5 Mar. 1800, Ephraim FROST in the right of his wife, William HILL, Mary HILL, Jonathan PERRY, John PERRY, John TUFTS, Elizabeth TUFTS, John ADAMS, Joseph PERRY and Samuel WHITTEMORE 3d, for $450.00 sold to James PERRY, yeoman...all our right...to that part of the real estate of our Father and Grandfather James PERRY late of Cambridge dec'd that was set off to his widow as her dower of thirds. Ack. same day by E. FROST, W. HILL, J. & E. TUFTS, S. WHITTEMORE 3d and the PERRYS. Ack. 25 Aug. 1800 by J. ADAMS. Rec. 25 Aug. 1800.

Estate of **James PERRY** of Cambridge MA. <Middlesex Co.PR #17187>
<52:340> 2 July 1771, widow **Lydia PERRY** and James PERRY, husbandman, app'td admrs. Bond 2 July 1771 of admrs. Sureties: Richard CLARK, yeoman of Watertown and James TUFTS, yeoman of Medford. Witnesses: Ebenezer STEDMAN, William KNEELAND. <52:449> Inventory taken 24 Sept. 1771 by Samuel LIVERMORE, Esq., Joseph WELLINGTON, Richard CLARK. <53:324 Warrant, 11 Sept. 1771, for assessment of dower, to Samuel LIVERMORE, Esq. of Waltham, Joseph WELLINGTON of Cambridge & Richard CLARK of Watertown, as commissioners. <53:326> Report, 28 Sept. 1771, of commissioners; homestead containing twenty one & one quarter acres, bounded by land of Rev. Mr. Daniel ROGERS, Capt. Ephraim FROST, Abraham HILL and heirs of Zachariah HILL dec'd, Ł141.13s4d; dwelling house on homestead land, Ł33.6s8d; the barn, Ł20; pasture bounded with lands of Joseph WILLINGTON/WELLINGTON, Josiah SHATTUCK, Samuel BOWMAN, John HASTINGS and sd HILL heirs, Ł94; four and a half acre rock swamp bounded with lands of Joseph WELLINGTON, William BOWMAN, Rev. Nathaniel APPLETON and Ebenezer PRENTICE, Ł16.4s; one and three quarter acre salt marsh in Medford bounded by land of Stephen HALL, William HALL and Medford River, Ł20. Dower set off to widow; dau **Lydia FROST** has already been advanced her portion, Ł194.8s, in her father's lifetime; dau **Marcy HILL**'s portion, Ł186.3d; remaining two thirds to be settled upon eldest son **James PERRY,** he paying to his brothers & sisters. <53:329> Settlement 8 Oct. 1771, two thirds of real estate settled upon **James PERRY,** he paying to his brothers & sisters their shares, viz: **John PERRY, Jonathan PERRY, Joseph PERRY, Benjamin PERRY, Ruth & Elizabeth,** Ł21.1s9d each. <53:320> Account 4 Aug. 1772.

MICRO #2 OF 3

Estate of **James TUFT** of Medford MA. <Middlesex Co.PR #22937>
<51:13> Letter/Bond 20 June 1769, James TUFT, brickmaker of Medford, app'td admr. Sureties: Joshua SIMONDS, yeoman & John LEATHE, cordwainer, of Medford. Witnesses: Abraham A( )DEN, William KNEELAND. <51:23> Inventory taken 3 July 1769 by Dr. Simon TUFTS, Joshua SIMONDS, Nathan TUFTS, all of Medford; total real estate, Ł812; total estate, Ł929.16s1d. <53:279> Warrant for distribution, 5 Dec. 1769, to Dr. Simon TUFTS, Joshua SIMONDS, Nathan TUFTS, Ebenezer BROOKS Jr., James WYMAN, all of Medford. <53:280> Report of commissioners, 18 Apr. 1770; estate divided & set off to eldest son **James TUFTS,** 2d son **Gersham TUFTS,** 3d son **Ebenezer TUFTS,** 4th son **Jonathan TUFTS,** 5th son **Isaac TUFTS,** dau **Hannah TUFTS** wf of Samuel and dau **Ruth BINFORD** wf of Thomas; daus **Lydia & Elizabeth** having already received their portions. <53:286> Decree for settlement, 13 Apr. 1772; distribution of estate allowed; mentions heirs of dec'd dau **Elizabeth.**

Will of **Josiah MIXER** of Waltham MA. <Middlesex Co.PR #15309>
<71:297>...dated 10 Sept. 1788...to wf **Lydia,** Ł20 to be paid her by my executors at her removeal from my house agreeable to the bargain & contract we entered into previous to our marriage; sons **Samuel MIXER, Josiah MIXER, Daniel MIXER;** daus **Mary BUDGES, Anna BARTLET;** chil. of dec'd daus **Sarah VILES & Perces PERRY;** daus **Eunice BIGELOW, Lois LIVERMORE, Lydia WELLINGTON;** son **Elijah MIXER.** <71:298> Pr. 15 Nov. 1788. <71:373> Inventory taken 8 Nov. 1788. (No data for the following references, viz: 72:248,523;73:20,272,292,295.)

MIDDLESEX COUNTY PROBATE: (re: TUFTS)

1733, James TUFTS of Charlestown, adm., #22933.
1756, James TUFTS of Medford, adm., #22935.
1769, James TUFTS of Medford, adm., #22937.
1787, James TUFTS of Medford, adm., #22939.
1810, James TUFTS of Medford, will, #22940.
1817, John TUFTS of W. Cambridge, adm., (widow Rebecca), #22955.
1824, John TUFTS of Medford, gdn., #23014.
1838, John TUFTS of W. Cambridge, adm., (widow Lucy A.), #22956.

Estate of **James TUFTS** of Medford MA. <Middlesex Co.PR #22939>
...mentions widow **Tabitha**, eldest son **James TUFTS**, 2d son **Daniel TUFTS** and daus **Elizabeth GATES**, **Mary COLLINS** and **Abigail TUFTS**. (The files do not specify which of the following records the heirs are listed in.) <195:126> Pr. <69:371> Inventory, 15 Mar. 1787. <69:463> Warrant for dower. <69:464> Report 5 Apr. 1787. <69:467> Decree for settlement, 5 Apr. 1787. <69:453> Account 6 Apr. 1787. <101:329> Warrant for distribution. <101:330> Report, 1 Sept. 1806. <101:328,331> Decrees. <115:96> Petition. <115:97> Decree.

Estate of **Abigail TUFTS** of Charlestown MA. <Middlesex Co.PR #43345>
<232:71> Bond...1848 (or 1898?), of husband **William A. TUFTS** of Somerville, admr.

PLYMOUTH COUNTY DEEDS: (re: Samuel PRATT, of Middleboro, grantor, all to 1801**)**

<4:120> - 23 Dec. 1698, S.P. to Thomas TOMSON of same, my whole share in two thirds of South Purchase, 33rd & 153rd lots. Ack. 21 Oct. 1700.
<9:56> - 15 May 17--, S.P. to Rodolphus ELMES of same, land in 4th lot 2d division, Little Men's Purchase in Middleboro. Rec. 11 July 1711.
<14:197> - Dec. 1713, S.P., husbandman to Elnathan WOOD of same, land in Pochade Purchase.
<11:157> - 6 May 1715, S.P. to Samuel PRINCE of Rochester, land in South Purchase, 33rd lot, 2nd division. Ack. 18 Oct. 1715.
<19:45> - 16 Apr. 1716, S.P. and Jacob TOMSON, exchange land. Ack. 24 May 1725. Rec. 5 June 1725
<12:60> - 21 Sept 1716, S.P. to John WATSON, 45 acres in South Purchase & land lately bought of Capt. Jacob TOMSON. Ack. same day.
<14:25> - 16 Oct. 1716, S.P. to Ichabod NYE of same, 36 acres in 16 Shilling Purchase. Ack. 1718
<14:148> - 7 Feb. 1717/8, S.P. to George HACKET of same, 17 acres in Little Lot Men's Purchase, 43rd lot. Ack. 2 Mar. 1718/9.
<14:163> - 1718, S.P. to Samuel EATON of same, 31 acres in Little Lot Men's Purchase, 38th lot, fell to me in right of Nathaniel MORTON. Ack. 2 Mar. 1718/9.
<14:225> - 13 Dec. 1718, S.P. to John CAVENDER of Bridgewater, land in Little Lot Men's Purchase, 4th lot. Ack. 17 Dec. 1719.
<15:106> - 20 Jan. 1720, S.P., yeoman & wf Hannah to Andrew MANSFIELD, yeoman of Lynn, lots in Little Lot Men's Purchase where I now dwell.
<22:160> - 12 Jan. 1724/5, S.P., Sr. to John MILLER of same, land in Little Lot Men's Purchase.
<24:92> - 18 Aug. 1724, S.P., Sr. to son John PRATT of same, lot in 16 Shilling Purchase formerly of Capt. Benjamin WARREN, & other lands. Rec. 15 May 1729.
<36:209> - 7 Oct. 1729, S.P., Sr. to son John PRATT of same, land in Middleboro. Rec 24 Aug 1744
<29:135> - 9 June 1732, S.P. to Elkanah RICKARD of same, lot in 16 Shilling Purchase bought of Proprietors of Pachade Purchase.
<28:193> - 24 Apr. 1734, S.P. to Benjamin DEXTER Jr., yeoman of Rochester, land in Rochester.
<36:114> - 18 Nov. 1743, S.P.3d & wf Wibrey to Caleb THOMSON of same; mentions our honoured father Joseph BUMPUS late of Middleboro dec'd. Rec. 16 Feb. 1743/4.
<36:32> - 16 May 1743, S.P. of Bridgewater to Capt. Jonathan BUSS of same., 75 acres in Bridgewater. Rec. 13 July 1743.
<38:83> - 28 June 1743, S.P., Jr. to father Samuel PRATT Sr. Rec. 26 June 1746.
<37:163> - 21 Aug. 1745, S.P. & wf Jerusha to John MURDOCK; re: estate of Josiah CONANT.
<41:272> - 18 Nov. 1745, S.P., yeoman & wf Jerusha to Benjamin WHITE Jr. of same, land of Josiah CONANT, set off to widow Elizabeth CONANT & one seventh to her dau Jerusha. Rec. 28 Sept. 1752.

<48:113> - S.P., Jr. to Jabez FULLER.
<50:221> - S.P. to Benjamin WHITE.
<53:112> - S.P. to Samuel PRATT Jr.
<54:31> - S.P. to Silas WOOD.
<56:181> - S.P., exr. to John CAVENDER.
<56:243> - S.P. to Nathaniel GOODWIN.
<58:243> - S.P. to Levi WOOD.
<59:34> - S.P. to Samuel PRATT Jr.
<60:12> - S.P., Jr. to Winslow CLIFT.
<60:91> - S.P., Jr. to Joseph ALLEN.
<73:47> - S.P. to Nathaniel BUMPUS et al.
<73:74> - S.P. to Joseph PRATT.
<75:76> - S.P. to Ebenezer PRATT.

Will of **Samuel PRATT Sr.** of Middleboro MA. <Plymouth Co.PR #16197>
<9:511>...dated 27 June 1745, mentions sons **Samuel PRATT** (eldest) **& Phineas PRATT** (executors); chil. of dec'd son **John PRATT**; daus **Sarah BARROWS & Mary WASHBURN.** Witnesses: John TINKHAM, Barnabas EATON & Benjamin WHITE (who made oath 10 July 1745); <9:513> Pr. 10 July 1745. <10:16> Inventory taken 19 July 1745 by Samuel WARREN, Elnathan WOOD, Nathaniel SOUTHWORTH; incl. home farm £840; land at Titicut meadows, £24; pew in the old meeting house, £6; total estate, £1157.18s; sworn to 18 Sept. 1745 by **Phineas PRATT**, exr.

Phinehas PRATT et al to **David ALDEN** of Middleboro MA. <Plymouth Co.Deeds 38:231>
...5 Sept. 1746, Phinehas PRATT, Ebenezer BARROW & wf Sarah, Elizabeth PRATT widow of John, Jabez FULLER & Nathan PRATT, all of Middleboro and Nathaniel WASHBURN & wf Mary of Bridgewater, quit claim to David ALDEN...all rights in a half lot in the Pachade Purchase...sd lot was conveyed to Samuel PRATT late of Middleboro dec'd our Honoured Father, and Lieut. Thomas KNOWLTON of Middleboro and by them equally divided...the sd half lot was sold by Samuel PRATT dec'd to the sd David ALDEN for L14 in 1741. Ack. 11 Sept. 1746 by all grantors.

Will of **John PRATT** of Middleboro MA. <Plymouth Co.PR #16133>
<9:86>...dated 18 Apr. 1743, mentions wf **Elizabeth,** minor sons **John PRATT** (eldest) **& Jedediah PRATT** and daus **Hannah PRATT** (eldest, under 21), **Kezia PRATT** (2nd, under 18) **& Sarah PRATT** (under

18); wf **Elizabeth** and brother **Israel TURNER** of Pembroke, executors. <9:88> Pr. 6 June 1743. <9:114> Inventory taken 27 June 1743.

Guardianship of Children of **John PRATT** of Middleboro MA. <Plymouth Co.PR #16134>
<9:188-91> 14 July 1743, widow **Elizabeth PRATT** app'td gdn. of her children, viz: **John PRATT, Sarah PRATT, Hannah PRATT, Jedediah PRATT & Keziah PRATT.**

Will of **Samuel PRATT** of Middleboro MA. <Plymouth Co.PR #16198>
<10:117>...dated 30 July 1745, mentions wf **Jerusha;** sons **Nathan PRATT** (executor) **& Samuel PRATT** (under 21); dau **Betty PRATT;** dau **Thankful PRATT** (under 21). Witnesses: Jabez FULLER, Phineas PRATT, Nathaniel SOUTHWORTH. <10:119> Pr. 6 Mar. 1745. <10:162> Inventory, 12 Mar. 1745/6; sworn to 13 May 1746 by exr.

Samuel PRATT of Middleborough MA to **Benjamin WHITE Jr.** of same. <Plymouth Co.Deeds 41:272>
...18 Nov. 1745, Samuel PRATT, yeoman sells to Benjamin WHITE Jr...seventh part of twelve acres in Middleboro...which did formerly belong to Josiah CONANT late of Middleboro dec'd and sd lot was set off to the widow Elizabeth CONANT...and the reversion...as to her daughter Jerusha PRATT now the wife of Samuel PRATT above named. Ack. 19 Nov. 1745 by Samuel.

PLYMOUTH COUNTY DEEDS: (re: Jerusha PRATT)

<37:163> - 21 Aug. 1745, Jerusha PRATT et al to John MURDOCK.
<45:113> - , Jerusha PRATT to Benjamin WHITE.
<53:113> - , Jerusha PRATT to Nathan PRATT et al.

SARAH PRIEST[2] (Degory[1])

Will of **Daniel COOMES** of Scituate MA. <Plymouth Col.Rec. 4:68>
...dated 1 Jan. 1683, mentions children **James COOMES, Mary & Susanna;** Timothy & Abigail WHITE, chil. of loving friend Timothy WHITE of Scituate (executor). Pr. 1 Mar. 1683.

Francis COMBE of Plymouth to **Edward GRAY.** <Plymouth Col.Deeds 3:234>
...31 Dec. 1668, Francis COMBE sells to Edward GRAY...house & land & all his rights in land granted by the town of Plymouth on 30 Dec. 1641 to my father John COMBE.

Francis COMBE of Middleboro to **Benjamin CHURCH** of Duxbury. <Plymouth Col.Deeds 48:176>
...4 July 1672, Francis COMBE sells to Benjamin CHURCH...land in Middleboro granted by Court on 5 June 1666 and laid out by Thomas PRENCE on 28 Feb. 1667/8. ("had previously sold 40 acres to John WOOD")

Estate of **Francis COMBS** of Middleboro. <Plymouth Co.Deeds 9:101>
Division 15 May 1711, mentions following heirs, viz: widow **Mary WOOD; Ralph JONES** & wf **Deborah; Frances COMBS; Samuel BARROWS** & wf **Mercy; John MILLER** & wf **Lydia; Ebenezer BENNETT** & wf **Ruth.**
<11:164> Division, 2 Feb. 1712, of land not before distributed, to **Samuel & Mercy BARROWS, John Jr. & Lydia MILLER, Ebenezer & Ruth BENNETT** and **Nathan & Frances HOWLAND.**

Estate of **Francis COMBE.** <Plymouth Col.Rec. 6:112>
...6 Mar. 1682/3, John THOMPSON, William CROW & John BARKER, app'td admrs. In July 1683, they were released and John RICHMOND of Taunton & Mrs. Mary COMBE were app'td. (6:141...1 July 1684, Mrs. Mary COMBE was licensed to keep an ordinary at Middleboro.)

MICRO #3 OF 3

Estate of **John MILLER** of Middleborough MA. <Plymouth Co.PR>
<5:323> 16 Nov. 1727, **Lydia MILLER & Francis MILLER,** app'td admrs. <5:592> Division, 24 Oct. 1729, of real estate appraised at £1268, to the widow **Lydia MILLER** and following children, viz: **Francis MILLER, John MILLER, David MILLER & Elias MILLER.**

Will of **Peter BENNETT** of Middleborough MA. <Plymouth Co.PR 11:382>
...dated 5 Oct. 1749, mentions dau **Priscilla MILLER**..(no further details given). Pr. 6 Nov. 1749.

Francis MILLER of Middleboro MA to **Ebenezer SPROUT.** <Plymouth Co.Deeds 35:211>
...10 Aug. 1738, Francis MILLER & wf Experience to our son Ebenezer SPROUT...land Experience MILLER (alias Experience SPROUT) bought of James SOULE.

Experience MILLER of Middleboro MA to **John MILLER et al** of same. <Plymouth Co.Deeds 39:97>
...19 Sept. 1747, Experience MILLER, widow of Francis, for £50 cash and £5 annually for life, sold to John MILLER, David MILLER & Elias MILLER...all right to real & personal estate of Francis MILLER dec'd.

Will of **John MILLER 2d,** gent. of Middleborough MA. <Plymouth Co.PR #14024>
<42:292>...dated 7 June 1794...to wf **Zilpah,** one third of all lands, one half of gristmill and

dwelling house...half of indoor movables, 2 cows, 6 sheep...and also the privilege of a horse to ride at any time...during her widowhood...to son **John MILLER 3d**...all real estate, live stock & outdoor movables...one good cow and two sheep each to daus **Hannah SHAW** wf of Abraham, **Lydia WOOD** wf of Jacob & **Zilpah PORTER** wf of James...one cow, two sheep & Ł15 in ware & furniture for housekeeping to daus **Priscilla MILLER, Susanna MILLER & Minerva MILLER**; mentions estate due him from estate of his father **John MILLER** dec'd and land which fell to his wife as heir to her father **John TINKHAM** dec'd; son **John**, executor. Witnesses: Seth MILLER, Nehemiah BENNET, Joseph MILLER. <42:293> Bond 13 Apr. 1808 of **John MILLER 3d**, gent., admr. Sureties: Nemiah/Nehimah BENNET, Esq. of Middleboro and Benjamin ELLIS, Esq. of Carver. <42:517> Inventory taken 26 May 1808; incl. right in dec'd father's estate, $100.00; sworn to 3 June 1809 by exr.

Estate of **John MILLER** of Middleborough MA. <Plymouth Co.PR #14023, 34:38;37:482;48:99>
Warrant 19 Feb. 1805 to **John MILLER, Seth MILLER, Peter MILLER, Mary MILLER, Priscilla ALDEN** wf of Nathan and **Lucy MILLER**, all of Middleboro...whereas **Jedediah MILLER** as admr...

Silvanus BARROWS of Windham CT to **Samuel RIDER** of Plymouth MA. <Plymouth Co.Deeds 43:221>
...26 Dec. 1755, Silvanus BARROWS, felt maker, for Ł240 sold to Samuel RIDER, labourer...30 acres in Middleborough...where I the sd Silvanus lately dwelt...bounded by the Namasket River and land of Isaac BENNET and William PRATT (sometimes of sd Middleborough afterwards of Carolina)...also wood land in Middleborough which I sometime since purchased of Cornelius BENNETT...bounded by land of Zechariah WESTON, PRENCE's & COOMBE's Purchase...together with one quarter part of a saw mill I have in Middleborough lying in partnership with Ignatius ELMES & David MILLER. Wf Ruth BARROWS consents. Witnesses: Nathaniel WALES, Josiah WOOD. Ack. 16 Jan. 1756 by Silvanus & Ruth. Rec. 22 Apr. 1756.

Seth SUMNER of Taunton MA to **Israel DEAN 3d** of same. <Bristol Co.Deeds 36:48>
...28 June 1742, Seth SUMNER & wf Elizabeth, for Ł68.10S, sold to Israel DEAN 3d...land in Taunton at a place called Cottley...bounded by land of Israel DEAN, Ebenezer DEAN, John WILLIAMS, Edward COBB and Benjamin SHAW...containing eighteen and three quarters acres...also five acres. Witnesses: Ebenezer SUMNER, John SUMNER. Ack. 28 June 1742 by grantors. Rec. 18 May 1748.

Ichabod DEAN of Taunton MA to **Israel DEAN 3d** of same. <Bristol Co.Deeds 36:47>
...9 Dec. 1743, Ichabod DEAN, for Ł11, sold to Israel DEAN 3d...one half of a certain tract in Taunton...two and a half acres...bounded by land of John WILLIAMS, sd Israel DEAN, Nicholas STEPHENS...also two and a half acres on the ten acre division in the common & undivided land in Taunton. Witnesses: Israel DEAN, Josiah DEAN. Ack. same day. Rec. 18 May 1748.

Will of **Israel DEAN 2d**, yeoman of Taunton MA. <Bristol Co.PR>
<25:85>...dated 23 Sept. 1765, mentions unnamed wife, son **Gidion DEAN**, daus **Abiah & Mary**; brother **Noah DEAN**, executor. Witnesses: Josiah DEAN, Joel DEAN, Benjamin DEAN Jr. <25:86> Pr. 30 Sept. 1777 (& sworn to by Benjamin DEAN Jr.). Bond 30 Sept. 1777, of widow **Hannah DEAN**, admx. (**Noah DEAN**, exr. declines 19 Sept. 1777.) Sureties: Benjamin DEAN, gent. and Job DEAN, yeoman, both of Taunton. Witnesses: Leon CRANE, George LEONARD. <original> Inventory taken 19 Nov. 1779 by Benjamin DEAN, Noah DEAN & Job DEAN; 70 acre homestead at Ł60 per acre, Ł4200. <original> Guardianship, 30 Nov. 1779, widow **Hannah DEAN** app'td gdn. of **Israel DEAN** (under 14). Sureties: Benjamin DEAN Jr., Abiel MACOMBER. Witnesses: Gideon DEAN, Job DEAN.

Gideon DEAN to **Philip DEAN.** <Bristol Co.Deeds 61:243>
...3 Jan. 1783, Gideon DEAN sells to Philip DEAN...land in Taunton. Hannah DEAN acquits her "life improvement" in same.

Joshua CASWELL of Middleborough MA to **Gideon DEANE** of Taunton MA. <Plymouth Co.Deeds 64:44>
...4 Mar. 1783, Joshua CASWELL, yeoman, for Ł120 sold to Gideon DEANE, yeoman...my whole farm where I now dwell containing 47 acres...in Middleborough. Zilpah CASWELL signs. Witnesses: Joshua HASKINS/HOSKINS, Jeremiah JONES Jr. Ack. 10 Mar. 1783 by Joshua. Rec. 26 Mar. 1785.

Gideon DEANE of Middleborough MA to **Israel DEANE** of Taunton MA. <Plymouth Co.Deeds 64:44>
...24 Feb. 1785, Gideon DEANE, yeoman, for Ł120 sold to Israel DEANE, yeoman...my whole farm containing 47 acres...in Middleborough...bounded by land of Jedediah CASWELL, David CASWELL & Ebenezer BARROWS. Witnesses: Priscilla CUSHMAN, Ebenezer BARROWS Jr. Ack. 2 Mar. 1785 by Gideon. Rec. 26 Mar. 1785.

Gideon DEAN late of Middleboro MA to **Joshua CASWELL.** <Bristol Co.Deeds 65:233>
...17 Jan. 1786, Gideon DEAN, laborer...land sold for debt due Joshua CASWELL as follows, viz: land in Taunton...beginning at a rock on ye east side of ye highway leading from Benjamin DEAN's to Abiel MACOMBER's and is a corner of land set off to Israel DEAN from ye estate of his father ...bounded by land of sd Israel and Phillip DEAN...containing sixteen acres...now in ye possession of widow Hannah DEAN...as her dower in her sd husband's estate...the reversion thereof is ye property of ye sd Gideon. (<66:335>...in 1787 Joshua CASWELL sells the above to Israel DEAN with Philip DEAN releasing all rights.)

Gideon DEAN et al to **John ROUNDY 3d** of Marblehead MA. <Essex Co.Deeds 181:44>
...16 Aug. 1806, William HAMMOND, yeoman & wf Susanna of Eastport, Washington Co. MA and Gideon DEAN, fisherman & wf Mary of Deer Island, Charlotte Co., New Brunswick, for $25.00 sold to John ROUNDY 3d, housewright...all rights in...land & rocks on Brimblecomes hill (so called) in sd Marblehead whereon late stood an old dwelling house, the estate of Roger VICKERY, dec'd...bounded

by highway over sd hill and land of Nathaniel BRIMBLECOME and the PEDRICKS heirs; sale is made on behalf of the grantors by their attorney Edward HAMMOND. Witnesses: Nathan BOWEN, Sally M. BOWEN. Ack. same day by grantors. Rec. 10 Feb. 1807.

William HAMMOND et al, power of attorney to **Edward HAMMOND.** <Essex Co.Deeds 181:44>
...1 May 1806, William HAMMOND, yeoman & wf Susanna of Eastport MA and Gideon DEAN, fisherman & Wf Mary of Deer Island, N.B....appoint Edward HAMMOND, mariner of Marblehead...our true & lawful attorney for the purposes following...Whereas Roger VICKERY, mariner of Marblehead dec'd and father of the sd Susanna & Mary, in his life time was seized & posessed of a certain tract or parcel of land...in Marblehead...whereby a certain part of sd land descended to the sd Susanna & Mary... have hereby authorized our sd attorney...to sell sd land. Witnesses: John C. TODD, Jonathan D. WESTON. Ack. same day. Rec. 10 Feb. 1807.

Estate of **Capt. John BARROWS** of Taunton MA. <Bristol Co.PR>
<28:41> Inventory taken 6 July 1784; incl. bible & other books, 6s; 50 acres with dwelling house & small barn, £200; sworn to same day by **Sarah BARROWS**, admx. <130:76> Guardianship 6 July 1784, widow **Sarah BARROWS** app'td gdn. of **Micah BARROWS, Deborah BARROWS, Elisha BARROWS, Lucy BARROWS & Mercy BARROWS**, all under 14. <28:223> Account 2 Nov. 1784, of admx. ("<32:323> 19 Mar. 1793, insolvent estate, apparently another John BARROWS.")

BRISTOL COUNTY DEEDS: (re: BARROWS)

<59:10> - 16 Mar. 1774, John BARROWS (son of Ebenezer) & wf Sarah, grantors. Rec. 25 Apr. 1777.
<60:174> - 1781, John BARROWS of Attleboro to youngest sons William & Fillbrook BARROWS.
<65:568> - 2 June 1785, Sarah BARROWS, spinster & admx. of est. of Capt. John BARROWS of Taunton
<65:87> - 1786, John BARROWS of Attleboro, grantor.
<78:57> - 25 Mar. 1794, Joshua WOOD, yeoman & wf Mary of Middleboro to Micah BARROWS of Taunton.

(References to **John BARROWS**, grantor: <39:251> 1753; <45:12>; <48:129> 1765; <48:131> 1765; <49:307> 1765; <50:28>; <55:396> 1773; **Micah BARROWS**, grantor: <72:413> 1794.)

Micah BARROWS of Taunton MA to **Abner ELMS** of same. <Bristol Co.Deeds 73:38>
...14 Mar. 1794, Micah BARROWS, yeoman, for £135 sold to Abner ELMS, hatter...26 acres in Taunton ...bounded by land of Dr. SAMPSON and Col. HALL...with dwelling house. Witnesses: Alexander RICHMOND, James WILLIAMS, Jeremiah JONES, Ransom CASWELL. Rec. 26 May 1794.

Heirs of **Capt. John BARROWS** of Taunton MA. <Bristol Co.Deeds 89:328>
...18 Feb. 1795, Deborah NELSON wf of Elias, Elisha BARROWS, Lucy BARROWS & Mercy BARROWS, chil. of Capt. John BARROWS dec'd...whereas Micah BARROWS son & heir of sd John...has sold land & dwelling house which...belonged to our father...unto Abner ELMS...whereas the sd Micah BARROWS has paid to us our equal share...we acquit...all our rights. Ack. 19 Feb. 1807 by Lucy PULLEN wf of Capt. Jonathan; 7 Mar. 1808 by Mercy CUMMINGS wf of John; 29 June 1808 by Elisha BARROWS; 19 Aug. 1808 by Elias & Deborah NELSON. Rec. 10 Jan. 1809.

Will of **Ebenezer BENNETT**, yeoman of Middleboro MA. <Plymouth Co.PR 12:100>
...dated 8 Dec. 1750, mentions son **Cornelius BENNETT** (executor) & dau **Sarah ELMES**. Pr. 4 Feb.1751

Estate of **Dr. Cornelius BENNETT** of Middleboro MA. <Plymouth Co.PR #1795>
<17:159> Letter 22 May 1766, widow **Ruth BENNETT** app'td admx. <19:369> Inventory taken 4 Apr. 1766 <20:25> Distribution, 13 June 1767, to widow **Ruth** and following chil., viz: dau **Theodate,** son **Silvanus BENNETT**, eldest son **William BENNETT**, daus **Sally & Christiana**, sons **Batchelor BENNETT &** son **Ebenezer Livy BENNETT**. <20:109> Account of admx. <33:229> Dower divided, 3 Nov. 1792 to children: **William BENNETT, Ebenezer Levy BENNETT, Christiana RUSSELL** wf of Samuel, **Bathchelor BENNETT Sally WOOD** wf of Ebenezer**, Theodate MILLER** wf of Elias and **Sylvanus BENNETT.**

Estate of **Ruth BENNETT** of Middleboro MA. <Plymouth Co.PR #1848>
...1792...<33:184,185,228,229>. (no details given)

Dr. Cornelius BENNETT of Middleboro MA to **Josiah WOOD** of same. <Plymouth Co.Deeds 30:160>
...6 Nov. 1735, Dr. Cornelius BENNETT, for £360 sells to Josiah WOOD, blacksmith...land in Middleboro lying on both sides of the Country Road from Middleboro Old Meeting House to Rochester & on the northerly side of the Fall brook on which Capt. Peter BENNETT's mills now stand, which parcel is part of the 200 acres formerly granted by the General Court to Gov. Thomas PRENCE...excepting & reserving one twentieth belonging to Prence HOWES and one seventh & one quarter of one seventh belonging to Capt. Peter BENNETT...also two sevenths and one half of one seventh of 100 acres formerly granted to sd Gov. PRENCE...also 60 acres or two thirds of the 64th & 137th lots in South Purchase in Middleboro, also in Gov. PRENCE's right. Ack. 15 Mar. 1735. Rec. 22 May 1736.

Joseph HOWLAND of Middleboro MA to **Dr. Cornelius BENNETT** of Newport RI.<Plymouth Co.Deeds 35:150>
...31 Dec. 1742, Joseph HOWLAND, husbandman for £200 sold to Dr. Cornelius BENNETT...7th lot in 1st allotment of Little Lot Men's Purchase in Middleboro...23 acres...bounded by land of John WINSLOW, late Nathan BASSETT's and the land of Capt. Peter BENNETT which he claims in right of his wife. Rec. 25 Jan. 1742.

THOMAS ROGERS

MICRO #1 OF 10

PLYMOUTH COUNTY PROBATE, to 1800: (re: ROGERS)

1692	John	Duxbury	#17172, 1:145
1696	John Jr.	Duxbury	#17173, 1:248,249
1707	Moses	Marshfield	#17185, 3:60,61
1716	Joseph	Pembroke	#17177, 3:441,442,443
1718	Abigail	Pembroke	#17139, 4:107,108,142
1718	John	Marshfield	#17174, 4:130,131,135,226;5:413,414;6:74
1718	Thomas	Pembroke	#17219, 4:92,93
1728	Timothy	Marshfield	#17224, 5:481,482
1738	John	Scituate	#17171, 7:425,426
1742	Elisha	Marshfield	#17157, 9:34,160;14:371
1745	Thomas	Marshfield	#17220, 10:129,130,131
1747	Benjamin	Kingston	#17147, 10:522;11:159,292
1747	Samuel	Marshfield	#17207, 10:517,519
1756	Thomas Jr.	Plymouth	#17217, 14:82,83,84
1760	Joseph	Marshfield	#17178, 16:32,84,290;17:7;19:130-142
1760	Samuel	Plymouth	#17204, 15:436,499,567
1761	Samuel	Marshfield	#17208, 16:237,249
1762	John	Marshfield	#17175, 16:332,346,490;17:76;19:80
1763	Timothy	Marshfield	#17225, 16:543,544;19:7,191
1764	William	Marshfield	#17227, 19:70,71
1781	Ebenezer	Rochester	#17153, 27:77;28:416,417,418,419,439,440
1791	Asenath et al		#17146, 26:246

PLYMOUTH COUNTY PROBATE, 1800-1850: (re: ROGERS)

1802	Amos	Marshfield	will	#17142, 38:161,162,130;39:448;40:138,268;43:214, 434,435
1802	Polly & Rachel	Marshfield	gdn.	#17195, 32:198
1804	Thomas	Plymouth	adm.	#17218, 34:379
1805	Peleg Jr.	Marshfield	adm.	#17192, 39:40;40:4,5,6,335
1812	Israel	Marshfield	adm.	#17167, 39:343;44:235,545,546;45:97
1814	Thomas	Marshfield	will	#17221, 45:206,207,308
1816	Howland	Marshfield	adm.	#17163, 46:196;48:432,433;49:133,134,135
1816	Joseph	Marshfield	will	#17179, 47:459,460;157:400
1816	Zacheus Jr.	Marshfield	adm.	#17231, 46:181;48:289,290,292
1817	Zacheus	Marshfield	will	#17230, 49:55,136
1818	Libni	Rochester	adm.	#17181, 46:285;49:397,399;50:260,382-3,385-6,407
1825	Naomi	Marshfield	adm.	#17188, 52:391;59:385-6;60:267,399;62:27
1828	Charles R.	Marshfield	adm.	#17152, 61:175;62:254;66:134,135
1831	Elizabeth	Marshfield	will	#17159, 70:90,102
1832	Elisha	Marshfield	adm.	#17158, 68:330;71:87;72:524
1832	Prince	Marshfield	will	#17196, 71:460;72:240;73:378;75:225
1832	Samuel	Marshfield	adm.	#17209, 71:86;72:520
1833	Caleb	Hanover	adm.	#17150, 71:162;74:168,340;76:61,63,82
1835	Stephen	Marshfield	will	#17213, 75:305;77:501;157:399
1836	Stephen R.	Marshfield	gdn.	#17214, 8:15**L**
1837	Sarah	Hanover	will	#17210, 1:57**G**;79:435
1838	Samuel	E.Bridgewater	will	#17206, 1:82**G**;5:57**T**;80:257,354;81:593
1841	Ebenezer	Rochester	will	#17154, 6:266**U**;11:383**G**;83:434
1844	Bethiah	Marshfield	adm.	#17149, 11:240**B**
1844	William	Plymouth	will	#17228, 86:383
---	Timothy	Marshfield	adm.	#17226, 7:8**V**;11:342**B**;87:295;90:101
1846	Benjamin	Pembroke	will	#17148, 2:78**H**;7:113**V**;88:288,330;90:53
1848	Arthur F. et al	Marshfield	gdn.	#17144, 2:574**O**;9:140**M**
1850	Rebecca M.	Rochester	adm.	#17199, 12:156**C**;92:23

Estate of **Samuel ROGERS**, fisherman of Plymouth MA. <Plymouth Co.PR #17204>
<15:436> Letter/Bond 1 Feb. 1760, widow **Hannah ROGERS** app'td admx. Sureties: Thomas ROGERS, Walter RICH. Witnesses: Matthew CUSHING, Edward WINSLOW. <15:567> Inventory taken 18 Apr. 1760 by Lemuel BARTLETT, Amaziah CHURCHILL; no real estate; total personal estate, £14.16.4. <15:499> Account of admx. 30 Apr. 1760; assets, £22.3.11, disbursements, £22.3.11.

Estate of **Thomas ROGERS Jr.**, fisherman of Plymouth MA. <Plymouth Co.PR #17217>
<14:82> Letter/Bond 24 July 1756, widow **Elizabeth ROGERS** app'td admx. Sureties: Thomas MORTON,

Timothy BURBANK Jr. Witnesses: Daniel JOHNSON, John LOTHROP. <14:84> Inventory taken 26 July 1756 by Samuel DONHAM, Benjamin BARTLETT, Thomas FAUNCE; total estate, Ł8.9. <14:84> Insolvency. <14: 83> Account of admx., 27 July 1756.

Estate of **Ebenezer ROGERS**, mariner of Rochester MA. <Plymouth Co.PR #17153>
<27:77> Letter/Bond 5 Nov. 1781, Stephen WING of Rochester ap'td admr. Sureties: Matthew HILLMAN, Benjamin HAMMOND. Witnesses: Philip TURNER, David HILLER, Job HASKELL, Anne WING. Request 4 Nov. 1781 of the widow **Abigail ROGERS** that Capt. Stephen WING be app'td admr., as her husband...the beginning of last summer on a voyage at sea was lost. <28:416> Inventory of estate of **Ebenezer ROGERS** who deceased on the 9th day of April last, taken 17 Nov. 1781 by Enoch HAMMOND, Timothy HAMMOND, Benjamin HAMMOND; real estate, Ł300; total estate, Ł393.13. Estate rendered insolvent, 3 Dec. 1781. <28:417> List of Claims, 27 June 1782: John ALDEN, Ichabod MORTON, Enoch HAMMOND, Joshua DELANO, Samuel HATCH, George CLARK, Rev. Lemuel LeBARON, Elisha STEVENS, Surviah ROGERS, Ebenezer ALLEN, Tanhem MEAD, Gideon BARSTOW, Amittai BARLOW, Ebenezer CANNON, Dr. John PITCHER, David DUNHAM, Sylvanus GIBBS, Elihu SHERMAN, Caleb DEXTER, Joseph HAMMOND, Aaron MORTON, John HOLMES, William WHITTENDON, John DOTY, Jonathan TRIPP, William THOMSON, John HAMMOND, Matthew HELMONS, Joseph CALLENDAR, Hopestill BISBEE. <28:419,439> Accounts of admr., 4 Sept. 1782 & 8 Sept. 1784. <28:440> Distribution to creditors, 14 Sept. 1784.

JOHN ROGERS[2] (Thomas[1])

Heirs of **Silvester RICHMOND**, Esq. to **Hannah BRADFORD** of Duxbury MA. <Bristol Co.Deeds 34:43>
...5 May 1733, Nathaniel SEARLE, weaver of Little Compton & wf Sarah one of the daus of John ROGERS, Esq., late of Barrington and the following children of Silvester RICHMOND, dec'd viz: William RICHMOND, gent. of Little Compton; Silvester RICHMOND, gent. of Dighton; Peleg RICHMOND, yeoman of Barrington; Peres RICHMOND, yeoman of Little Compton; Ichabod RICHMOND, physition of Dighton; Rogers RICHMOND of Little Compton; Elizabeth FISHER wf of Nathaniel, clerk of Dighton; Ruth ATWOOD wf of Ephraim of Dighton; Sarah HEATH wf of Peleg, clerk of Barrington and Mary RICHMOND of Little Compton...to Hannah BRADFORD, widow, dau & heir of sd John ROGERS...land in Little Compton, Taunton & Kingston.

Hannah BRADFORD of Duxbury MA to **Peres BRADFORD** of Milton MA. <Bristol Co.Deeds 34:45>
...16 July 1733, Hannah BRADFORD, widow to son Peres BRADFORD, gent...land of my honoured father John ROGERS, late of Barrington dec'd. Witnesses: Sarah S(---), Mercy WARREN.

Estate of **James PHILLIPS** of Taunton MA. <Bristol Co.(?PR) 2:352>
...13 June 1695, John RICHMOND, admr.; mentions heir apparent **James PHILLIPS** & his bretheren and portion due **Sarah WILBUR** wf of Samuel. <3:398> 8 Sept. 1693, **Seth PHILLIPS** of Taunton, being of full age to receive his portion of father's estate.

BRISTOL COUNTY DEEDS: (re: John RICHMOND)

<14:200>- 27 Sept 1675, John RICHMOND & wf Abigail of Taunton.
<5:5> - 17 Mar. 1680/81, John RICHMOND of Taunton to eldest dau Mary GODFREY wf of Richard Jr. of same. Wf Abigail RICHMOND consents.
<5:4> - 26 Oct. 1686, John RICHMOND & wf Abigail of Taunton to Richard GODFREY. Ack. 1687.
<5:482> - 13 Mar. 1689, John RICHMOND & wf Abigail of Taunton.
<12:505>- 4 Apr. 1692, Richard GODFREY & wf Mary of Taunton & brother John GODFREY & wf Martha of Barnstable.
<17:512>- 1 June 1702, John RICHMOND of Little Compton. Ack. 26 Nov. 1705.
<9:277> - 28 Dec. 1702, John RICHMOND of Taunton to son John RICHMOND Jr.
<5:7> - 5 June 1703, John RICHMOND of Taunton to Richard GODFREE.
<5:28> - 22 Mar. 1704/5, John RICHMOND & wf Elizabeth of Little Compton.

Estate of **Thomas RICHMOND** of Taunton MA. <Bristol Co.PR>
<2:146> Inventory taken 19 Dec. 1705 of estate of Thomas RICHMOND who dyed 14th of sd month; taken by Benjamin CRANE, Abrahm HATHWAY, Peter WALKER; mentions his sister **Mary GODFREE** and money due from Joseph RICHMOND of Taunton. Pr. 4 Feb. 1705 by father **John RICHMOND** and **Richard GODFREE,** admrs. <2:174> Account 6 Mar. 1706 of admr.; **John RICHMOND** mentions his sons **Ebenezer RICHMOND, Joseph RICHMOND, Samuel RICHMOND, Edward RICHMOND & John RICHMOND** and his sons in law **Richard GODFREE & James WALKER.** <2:175> Division 6 Mar. 1706, to heirs, viz: to **Mary GODFREE** wf of Richard of Taunton and **Susanah REED** wf of James of Middlebury...being all of the whole blood...all real estate, to father **John RICHMOND** all personal estate. (Father **John** appealed this ruling; apparently he had sometime before deeded seventy acres to son **Thomas** and now expected it to be returned to him. According to the deed below, it was.)

John RICHMOND Sr. of Taunton MA to **Edward & Ebenezer RICHMOND.** <Bristol Co.Deeds 5:49>
...6 Dec. "1705/6", John RICHMOND Sr., for...love & affection which I bear unto my sons Edward RICHMOND of Taunton and Ebenezer RICHMOND of Plimouth...seventy acres in Taunton...which was layd out upon the right of me sd John and which my son Thomas RICHMOND late of Taunton dec'd did...for sometime live on...together with two acres in Taunton adjoining land lately layde out to William PHILIPS. Witnesses: Abel BURT, Uriah LEONARD. Ack. 7 Feb. 1705 by John. Rec. 31 May 1706.

James REED of Middlebury MA to **Edward RICHMOND** of Taunton MA. <Bristol Co.Deeds 5:47>
...20 Dec. 1705, James REED & wf Susannah to Edward RICHMOND...all our right in...dwelling house, homestead, moveables, stock & all other estate of our brother Thomas RICHMOND dec'd. Witnesses: Peter WALKER, Abel BURT. Ack. 19 Apr. 1706 by James. Rec. 30 May 1706.

Richard GODFREE of Taunton MA to **John GODFREE** of same. <Bristol Co.Deeds 17:508>
...14 Dec. 1722, Richard GODFREE & wf Mary to son John GODFREE...all our interest in estate of our brother Thomas RICHMOND late of Taunton dec'd...being our half part. Witnesss: Richard GODFREE Jr., Sary ANNER. Ack. 25 Dec. 1722 by grantors. Rec. 10 Oct. 1727.

Deposition of **John RICHMOND** of Taunton MA. <Bristol Co.Deeds 2:32>
...6 Jan. 1696/7, John RICHMOND aged about sixty seven years testifyeth & saith...the year 1639 I very well remember that then when we came first to Taunton which was in 1639 as abovesaid, then Mr. John GILBERT had a house...John HATHWAY aged about 67 years also testified.

References to **Caleb COWING** in Plymouth Co.Deeds: 22:75;31:163;32:132;34:72;40:197.
References to **James COWING** in Plymouth Co.Deeds: 59:174;61:160;62:61,275,276;64:268.

Estate of **Caleb COWING** of Rochester MA. <Plymouth Co.PR #5114>
Petition 30 June 1777, of David WING & Jabez COTTLE, the Selectmen of Rochester...Whereas **Anne COWING** of Rochester, widow, is verry aged & indigent: and hath a right of dower in a considerable estate lying in sd Rochester, which is withheld from her...

Guardianship of **Anna COWING**, widow of Rochester MA. <Plymouth Co.PR #5112>
Petition 10 Feb. 1783, of **James COWING** of Rochester...Whereas the widdow **Anne COWING** mother of him the sd **James** is by reason of advanced age and troubles incident thereto become non compos mentis these therefore are to pray your Honour to grant to him the sd **James** letters of guardianship.

Estate of **John RICHMOND** of Taunton MA. <Bristol Co.PR>
<17:45>...dated 16 Oct. 1739, mentions brother **Edward RICHMOND**; sons **Stephen RICHMOND, John RICHMOND**; dau **Mary.** <17:46> Pr. 24 June 1760.

Will of **Stephen RICHMOND** of Taunton MA. <Bristol Co.PR>
<39:34>...dated 8 Jan. 1801, mentions wf **Silence**; son **Stephen RICHMOND** & his daus **Katharine, Silence & Sarah**; sons **Abiel RICHMOND, Asa RICHMOND, Noah RICHMOND**; daus **Silence CASWELL** wf of Joseph, **Weltha CASWELL** wf of John and **Anna ROBINSON** wf of Ebenezer. <39:35> Pr. 29 Mar. 1802. <40:347> Inventory.

Will of **Abiel RICHMOND**, yeoman of Taunton MA. <Bristol Co.PR>
<60:467>...dated 14 Mar. 1822, to eldest son **Abiel RICHMOND**, $2.00; to son **Allen RICHMOND**, $30; to son **Thomas RICHMOND**, $10.00; to daus **Joanna STAPLES & Silence FOREST**, $2.00 ea; dau **Deborah RICHMOND**; son **Marcus RICHMOND.** Witnesses: David RICHMOND, Bathsheba RICHMOND, Mercy SAMPSON. <60:345> Offered for probate, 6 May 1823; Pr. 5 Aug. 1823.

Will of **Joseph RICHMOND** of Taunton MA. <Bristol Co.PR 12:495-7>
...dated 2/22 Dec. 1750, mentions unnamed wife; children: **Seth RICHMOND, Joseph RICHMOND, Sarah DEAN, Hannah RICHMOND, Peres RICHMOND & Welthy RICHMOND.** Pr. 5 Feb. 1750 (1750/51).

Will of **William REED.** <Bristol Co.PR>
<8:139>...dated 31 Mar. 1725, mentions wf **Marah** and minor children: **William REED, John REED & Mary REED.** <8:138> Pr. 16 July 1734. <8:140> Inventory.

Christopher RICHMOND of Middleborough MA to **Stephen LEONARD** of Taunton MA. <Bristol Co.Deeds>
<10:396>...28 Dec. 1716, Christopher RICHMOND & wf Phebe, for £6.10s sold to Stephen LEONARD... one share in Dead Swamp in Taunton which is one seventeenth of Dead Swamp Propriety...that fell to Phebe WILLIAMS alias Phebe RICHMOND...being the 15th lot. Ack. 21 Jan. 1716/7 by both.

Christopher RICHMOND of Middleborough MA to **Richard WILLIAMS** of Taunton MA. <Bristol Co.Deeds>
<13:80>...27 Apr. 1719, Christopher RICHMOND & wf Phebe, for £14 sold to Richard WILLIAMS...six acres in Taunton. Ack. 22 June 1719 by Phebe, 22 Sept. 1719 by Christopher.

Eliakim RICHMOND of Middleborough MA to **John CAVENDER** of Taunton MA. <Plymouth Co.Deeds 47:92>
...4 Oct. 1752, Eliakim RICHMOND, husbandman, for £50 sold to John CAVENDER, nailer...land in Middleboro...being my homestead...containing fifteen acres...bounded by land of John RICHMOND & Elkanah LEONARD, Esq...being the land I bought of Elkanah LEONARD by a deed bearing date 15 Apr. 1747. Wf Sarah RICHMOND releases dower. Witnesses: Ephraim DEAN, Israel DEAN, Jacob TOMSON, John HACKETT. Ack. 30 Oct. 1752 by Eliakim. Rec. 13 Oct. 1761.

Jesse JENCKES of Smithfield RI to **Eliakim RICHMOND** of E.Hoosuck MA. <Berkshire Co.Deeds 10:531>
...12 June 1773, Jesse JENCKES sold to Eliakim RICHMOND...100 acres, the northerly part of Lot #4 in the Proprietor's First Division. <22:352>...11 Sept. 1777, Eliakim sold the above land to **Caleb HILL** of Swansea. Wf Sarah signs.

Mathew LYON of Wallingford VT to **Eliakim RICHMOND** of E. Hoosuck MA. <Wallingford VT Deeds 1:45>
...25 Dec. 1777, Mathew LYON sold to Eliakim RICHMOND...ten acres with house & barn in Walling-

ford VT. <2:172>...16 Aug. 1791, Eliakim gave this land (except one and one third acres previously sold) to son **George RICHMOND.** <2:173>...17 Aug. 1791, George RICHMOND leased this land to his parents, Eliakim & Sarah RICHMOND (where they were dwelling) for their natural lives. <4:236>... 27 Jan. 1808, Eliakim & Sarah RICHMOND of Wallingford VT quitclaimed to **Samuel TOWNSEND**...the farm Eliakim now lives on, which he sold to George RICHMOND and which George leased to Eliakim & Sarah for their natural lives.

Estate of **Benjamin RHOADES** of Wallingford VT. <Rutland Co.VT #128>
...20 Mar. 1792, widow **Judith RHOADES** app'td admx. Surety: Eliakim RICHMOND of Wallingford.

Estate of **Samuel RICHMOND** of Taunton MA. <Bristol Co.PR>
<8:375>...dated 11 June 1736, mentions wf **Elizabeth;** sons **Thomas RICHMOND, Silas RICHMOND, Oliver RICHMOND, Samuel RICHMOND;** daus **Hannah BOOTH, Lydia THOMAS, Mehitable HORTON;** cousin **Joseph RICHMOND.** Pr. 20 July 1736. <8:488> Inventory.

Estate of **Paul LEONARD,** yeoman of Raynham MA. <Bristol Co.PR>
<35:317> Petition, 22 Jan. 1798, for guardian of **Paul LEONARD,** non comp., by his son **Benjamin LEONARD;** 5 Mar. 1798, gdn. app'td. <35:342> Inventory, 13 Mar. 1798, of estate of **Paul LEONARD,** non comp. <35:350> Account of gdns. 1798. <36:80> Inventory 5 Mar. 1799 of estate of **Paul LEONARD** dec'd, by **Mary LEONARD,** admx. <37:19> Division, 21 Jan. 1800, of real estate by Godfrey ROBINSON, Thomas DEAN & George WILLIAMS, (who appraised it at $1920.00) each share worth $240.00, to the following heirs, viz: to **Benjamin LEONARD,** eight & a half acres with the old barn, valued at $240; to **Samuel LEONARD,** six acres and nine & a quarter acres; to **Paul LEONARD,** one & a half acre with part of the dwelling house; to **Walter LEONARD,** eight acres; to **Eliab LEONARD,** eight acres; to **Olive PERKINS** wf of Isaac, eight acres; to heirs of **Mary HALL,** eight acres; to **Elizabeth WILBUR** wf of Daniel, eight acres.
<The following references are not detailed, viz: 36:89,165;37:10,17;49:290;50:432;51:304; 55:392, 566;110:260;130:456;149:260;151:90>

MICRO #2 OF 10

All references to the name **Anna WILLIAMS** in Bristol Co.PR.
<43:333> Inventory. <43:367> Division, 1808. <60:569> Citation. <61:54> Will. <111:373> Notice of Appointment. <150:262> Adm.

Anna WILLIAMS of Taunton MA to **Benjamin TERRY** of same. <Plymouth Co.Deeds 22:53>
...24 July 1710, Anna WILLIAMS, widow of Samuel WILLIAMS dec'd, for £5 sold to son Benjamin TERRY ...all rights in land in Middleboro...which were given to me by the last will of my Honoured Father John ROGERS of Duxboro dec'd...according to...an agreement...signed by me sd Anna WILLIAMS, my sister Elizabeth WILLIAMS, John TISDELL and Joseph RICHMOND which bears date 5 Oct. 1709 that is to say one half part of the fourty acre lot laid out on the right of sd John ROGERS in Middleborough near Elkanah LEONARD's and one half part of all lands...at Assawamsett Neck...also a quarter part of the twenty & three quarter acres in the Beach Woods...also quarter part of undivided lands on the 16 Shilling Purchase. Witnesses: Samuel DANFORTH, Mary HACKETT. Ack. 11 Sept. 1710. Rec. 18 July 1727.

Will of **Samuel WILLIAMS** of Taunton MA. <Bristol Co.PR 1:199-200>
...dated 6 Aug. 1697, mentions eldest son **Seth WILLIAMS** (executor), minor son **Daniel WILLIAMS,** daus **Sarah DEAN, Mary ANDROS & Hannah BUN;** wife has liberty to live with my son **Seth** for 12 mths Pr. 9 Oct. 1697. Inventory taken 31 Aug. 1697.

Estate of **Simeon TISDALE.** <Bristol Co.PR>
<17:621> Adm., widow **Phebe.** <19:238> Inventory. <19:263> Account. <19:335> Division. <127:74> Gdn

---

References in Plymouth Co.Deeds to **TISDALE,** viz: <30:165,216> Abigail. <35:160> Ebenezer & James. <10:34> Joshua. <39:145,248> James. <55:55>...4 Feb. 1769, John TISDALE & wf Sarah the dau of John REED of Middleboro.

John TISDALE & Anna WILLIAMS to **Jonathan BRIGGS.** <Bristol Co.Deeds 3:259>
...13 Sept. 1700, John TISDALE of Taunton, the onely sonne of John TISDALE dec'd and his mother Anna WILLIAMS, sell to Jonathan BRIGGS...

Estate of **Anna WILLIAMS,** widow. <Bristol Co.Deeds 27:27>
Division of dower, 29 June 1737, to the following heirs, viz: one half to son **Thomas TERRY,** the other half to son **Benjamin TERRY,** grandson **John TERRY,** blacksmith and great-great grandaughter **Remember TERRY** only dau of **Silas & Sarah TERRY** (Sarah TERRY who is now Sarah DAVIS).

Will of **Thomas TERRY** of Freetown MA. <Bristol Co.PR>
<original>...dated 10 Aug. 1691...aged about 60 years...mentions minor sons **Thomas TERRY** (eldest son), **John TERRY & Benjamin TERRY** and wife **Ana;** Oath to the above will, 30 Oct. 1691 by Joseph FRENCH, aged about 52 and Samuel BLAKE, aged about 40. <6:275> Agreement, 8 June 1704, to divide real estate, between widow **Anna WILLIAMS** for herself & minor son **Benjamin** and sons **Thomas & John.**

Will of **William MACKPEICE/MAKEPEACE** of Taunton MA. <Bristol Co.PR>
<8:480>...dated 16 Nov. 1736, mentions sons **Seth MAKEPEACE, William MAKEPEACE, Thomas MAKEPEACE;**

daus **Annah, Mary, Susanah, Lidia, Deborah, Remember & Priscilla (MAKEPEACE)**; daus **Lydia & Susannah**, exx. Witnesses: Seth WILLIAMS, Mercy MASON, Stephen MACOMBER. <8:479> Pr. 21 June 1737, **Lydia WITHERIL** wf of Simeon and **Susannah GODFREY** wf of Joseph, of Norton, app'td admx. <8:481> Inventory taken 5 Jan. 1736/7.

Estate of **William MAKEPEACE** of Norton MA. <Bristol Co.PR>
<9:442> 19 Aug. 1740, widow **Experience MAKEPEACE** app'td admx. <9:461> Inventory taken 1 July 1740. <10:249> 15 Feb. 1742/3, brother **Seth MAKEPEACE** app'td admr., the widow being dec'd. <10:267> Guardianship, 19 Apr. 1743, **Seth MAKEPEACE** app'td gdn. of **George MAKEPEACE, William MAKEPEACE & Abigail MAKEPEACE**, all under 14. <10:275> Inventory taken 19 Apr. 1743. <12:23> Guardianship, 14 July 1749, Simeon WITHEREL of Norton app'td gdn. of **Peter MAKEPEACE & George MAKEPEACE**, over 14 and **William MAKEPEACE**, under 14. <12:276> Account 19 May 1750, of **Mary MAKEPEACE**, widow & admx. of **Seth MAKEPEACE**, on estate of **William MAKEPEACE.**

Estate of **William MAKEPEACE** of Taunton MA. <Bristol Co.PR>
<27:626> Inventory, 1783. <49:303,327;50:348,381;110:146;144:463;148:150;151:93, no details>

Will of **Capt. Gershom WILLIAMS**, gent. of Dighton MA. <Bristol Co.PR>
<24:10>...dated 9 Sept. 1775, mentions wf **Abigail**; sons **Jonathan WILLIAMS** (youngest), **Gershom WILLIAMS** (eldest), **David WILLIAMS, George WILLIAMS, Lemuel WILLIAMS, John WILLIAMS, Simeon WILLIAMS**; daus **Abigail BRIGGS** wf of John, **Hannah HOLLEWAY** wf of William Jr. and **Ruth WILLIAMS**; mentions fifty acres purchased of Ephraim TALBOT on 25 Apr. 1763, eleven acres purchased of Mary BRIGGS on 17 Nov. 1768 and the remainder of four lots which were sold to sons **David & George**, , being about one hundred & thirty acres, all to be equally divided among sons **Gershom, Lemuel & John**...with the five acres I purchased of Hannah LEONARD & Elijah LEONARD which sd Hannah before her inter marriage with sd Elijah was Hannah PITTS. Witnesses: Experience POOL, Josiah TALBOT, Nathaniel HAYFORD, George GODFREY. <24:12> Pr. 17 Nov. 1775. <24:386> Warrant, 25 Nov. 1776, for widow's dower; mentions sixty four acres formerly belonging to Capt. Henry PITTS & Ephraim TALBUT. <26:463> Report 25 Jan. 1779. <26:360> Division, 6 Feb. 1781, of real estate by George GODFREY, Esq., David WHITMARSH & Elijah WALKER. <26:436,464> Accounts, 6 Feb. 1781, 14 June 1781.

BRISTOL COUNTY DEEDS: (re: John WILLIAMS)

<60:163> - 7 Oct. 1777, J.W. of Dighton from Lemuel WILLIAMS, yeoman of same, son of Gershom. Wf Abigail signs. Ack. by Lemuel 12 Apr. 1780. Rec. 21 Dec. 1780.
<60:163> - 26 Aug. 1778, J.W., cordwainer of Dighton from Jonathan WILLIAMS of same, all rights in estate of Gershom WILLIAMS of Dighton dec'd. Wf Phebe signs. Ack. 12 Apr. 1780. Rec. 21 Dec. 1780.
<60:164> - 12 Dec. 1778, J.W. of Dighton from Jonathan WILLIAMS. Ack. 12 Apr. & Rec. 21 Dec 1780.
<60:164> - 12 Apr. 1780, J.W., cordwainer of Dighton from brother George WILLIAMS, yeoman of same all rights in estate of brother Gershom WILLIAMS of Dighton dec'd.
<60:164> - 20 Dec. 1780, J.W., cordwainer of Dighton sells land. Wf Anstress WILLIAMS signs.

Estate of **David WILLIAMS** of Fall River/Wellington/Dighton MA <Bristol Co.PR>
<52:179> 2 Apr. 1816, Simeon WILLIAMS, Ephraim GOODING & Nathaniel WALKER, app'td to appraise estate. Inventory taken 24 May 1816; incl. homestead farm, $2000.00 and note of George WILLIAMS, $91.13; sworn to 4 June 1816 by Gershom WILLIAMS, admr. <54:360> Order for division, 10 Apr. 1817 <54:361> Division 19 Apr. 1817, to the six children, viz: **Nancy WILLIAMS, Lydia WILLIAMS, David WILLIAMS, Gershom WILLIAMS, Bathsheba GOFF & Eleanor LAKE.**

Will of **Stephen WEBSTER**, yeoman of Berkley MA. <Bristol Co.PR 27:253>
...dated 25 June 1782...chil. of dec'd dau **Lois WILLIAMS.** Pr. 26 Nov. 1782. (The files do not contain a complete abstract of the will.)

John TERRY of Freetown MA to **Jonathan DAVIS** of same. <Bristol Co.Deeds 26:71>
...23 Mar. 1735, John TERRY, blacksmith & wf Lydia who was the dau of Immanuel WILLIAMS late of Taunton, yeoman, dec'd, for Ł80 sold to Jonathan DAVIS, husbandman...thirty nine acres in Taunton being our share in the homestead of our sd Father Immanuel WILLIAMS dec'd. Witnesses: Thomas TERRY, John WILLIAMS. Ack. 25 Mar. 1735/6 by grantors. Rec. 15 June 1737.

Will of **John TERRY**, yeoman of Freetown MA. <Bristol Co.PR>
<24:233>...dated 18 Feb. 1774, mentions wf **Lydia**; to eldest son **Zephiniah TERRY**, 6s, he having had his portion by deed of gift dated 14 Feb. 1774; son **Ebenezer TERRY** to pay dau **Rachel CRANE** wf of John of Norton, Ł6; son **Silas TERRY** to provide firewood for his sister **Lydia TERRY** and pay Ł6 to dau **Hannah PAINE** wf of Job; to son **Job TERRY**, homestead farm, one half of salt meadow & Thatch Flats at Bryants Neck and upland there joining land of Solomon TERRY & Philip HATHEWAY, he paying dau **Welthe JONES** wf of Thomas, Ł6; son **Job**, executor. Witnesses: Abiel TERRY, Abiel TERRY Jr., Solomon TERRY. <24:234> Pr. 2 Sept. 1776, **Job TERRY** app'td admr.

Guardianship of **Lydia TERRY**, single woman, non comp of Freetown MA. <Bristol Co.PR>
<41:188> Guardianship, 1805, Peter NICHOLS app'td gdn. <42:5> Inventory, 1806. <46:200> Account, 1811.

Estate of **John TERRY Jr.**, mariner of Freetown MA <Bristol Co.PR>
<146:164> Adm., 1770. <21:509> Inventory, 1770. <21:593> Account.

Will of **John TERRY** of Fall River MA. <Bristol Co.PR>
<183:117>...dated 1854, wf **Priscilla**...<188:63> Pr. 1862. <195:246> Inventory taken 1862. <217:449> Account, 1865.

Estate of **John TERRY** of New Bedford MA. <Bristol Co.PR>
<101:18> Adm., 1854. <101:384> Account, 1855. <157:499> Adm. <163:468> Bond, 1854.

Will of **Abner WINSLOW** of Freetown MA. <Bristol Co.PR 39:475>
...dated 25 Nov. 1800, mentions unnamed wife, sons **Philip WINSLOW & John WINSLOW** (executors); daus **Rebecca TERRY, Martha JONES & Hannah WINSLOW**; minor grandson **Abner JONES**. Pr. 3 May 1803.

Will of **Job TERRY** of Little Compton. <Bristol Co.PR>
<183:17>...dated 9 Apr. 1861, mentions dau **Amy DAVENPORT** wf of Alonzo of New Bedford; dau **Abby EVANS** wf of Thomas & their children; son **David TERRY** (executor) to have the Job TERRY farm in Freetown, Abner WINSLOW farm and Bryant's Neck lot, all in Freetown, after his death to go to his children **Job TERRY & David TERRY**; Henry H. FISH & Leander BORDEN, of Fall River named as Trustees of Bank & Railway stock. (Note: In the following records, 1861-1880, (which are not detailed), Job is called "of" New Bedford, Little Compton & Freetown, viz: <107:272,274;112:466;119:788;152:489;179:243;188:11,646;195:219,469;217:55,409,551;218:502,517>. The following references may also pertain to this **Job TERRY**, they refer to Trustees' Accounts between 1866-1879, of the estate of **Job TERRY** of Freetown, viz:218:303,462, 536,553,590;219:9,30;220:446,564.)

BRISTOL COUNTY DEEDS: (re: Job TERRY)

<77:108> - J.T. to Ebenezer TERRY
<77:167> - J.T. to Jonathan DAVIS Jr.
<105:542> - J.T., Jr. to Amos BORDEN
<110:178> - J.T. to Thomas BLETHENS
<112:179> - J.T., Jr. to John CHASE.
<113:70> - Job & John TERRY, partition.

<110:115> - 1821, Job TERRY, yeoman of Troy to Hezekiah WILSON of same, land in Troy. Wf Rebecca TERRY releases dower.
<116:15> - 11 May 1823, Job TERRY Jr, mariner of Troy, John STRANGE, Betsey CHASE, John STRANGE Jr. and Abner SMITH, divide land.
<117:288> - , Job TERRY Jr. et al to William ASHLEY.
<125:472> - 21 Apr. 1825, Job TERRY 2d, yeoman of Troy to Lydia TERRY of same, half the farm I now live in, given to him & brother Charles Mason TERRY by their father Ack. 7 Feb. 1826. Rec. 4 Apr. 1829.
<121:152> - 8 Sept 1826, Job TERRY Jr. of Troy & William ASHLEY, yeoman of Troy, divide land.
<121:154> - 3 Mar. 1827, Job TERRY, yeoman of Freetown, divides land.
<139:390> - 19 Mar. 1827, Job TERRY, yeoman of Freetown to Job MILLARD, yeoman of Dartmouth, land in Dartmouth. Wf Rebecca releases dower. Rec. 3 Sept. 1833.
<138:163> - 26 Mar. 1827, Job TERRY, yeoman of Freetown to William ASHLEY. Wf Rebecca releases dower. Ack. 17 Mar. 1833. Rec. 18 Mar. 1833.
<121:463> - 27 Apr. 1827, Job TERRY Jr., mariner to Job PEIRCE. Wf Ruth TERRY releases dower.
<123:416> - 25 Mar. 1828, Job TERRY, yeoman of Freetown to Rusell HATHAWAY. Wf Rebecca TERRY releases dower. Ack. 2 Apr. 1828. Rec. 22 Apr. 1828.
<123:486> - 3 May 1828, Job TERRY to grandson Job T. WILSON. Rec. 6 May 1828.
<125:475> - 10 Dec. 1828, Job TERRY 2d, yeoman of Troy and Lydia TERRY, single woman of same.
<128:344> - , Job TERRY Jr. to Gilbert W. SNELL.
<159:457> - 22 Apr. 1829, Job TERRY, gent. of Freetown to Isaac RICHMOND of same. Wf Ruth signs. Ack. same day. Rec. 14 June 1839.
<129:404> - 11 Aug. 1830, Job TERRY, yeoman of Freetown to Job TERRY Jr., mariner of Troy. Wf Rebecca signs. Ack. 14 Aug. 1830. Rec. 18 Aug. 1830.
<131:224> - 11 Aug. 1830, Job TERRY Jr., mariner of Troy mortgage to Job & Rebecca TERRY of Freetown. Ack. 18 Aug. 1830. Rec. 20 Apr. 1831.
<131:364> - 11 Aug. 1830, Job TERRY Jr., mariner of Troy bond to Job & Rebecca TERRY of Freetown, to pay them $100 a year as long as they live, also half of their house.
<132:425> - 1830, Elizabeth TERRY, admx. of Job TERRY 2d to Lemuel READ, part of land which Charles M. TERRY gave to his brother Job TERRY, 16 Mar. 1824.

<144:232> - 3 Oct. 1833, Job TERRY Jr., mariner of Troy to William ASHLEY of same. Wf Ruth releases dower. Rec. 15 Oct. 1834.
<197:506> - 19 Dec. 1833, Job TERRY Jr. of Freetown & William ASHLEY, yeoman of Troy, sell to Job T. WILSON, yeoman of Troy, land in Troy. Ruth TERRY & Jane ASHLEY release dowers. Ack. 31 Dec. 1833. Rec. 12 Sept. 1850.
<145:415> - 3 Sept 1834, Job TERRY of Freetown to Job T. WILSON of Fall River, for $20, the land conveyed in deed of 3 May 1828. Rec. 23 Apr. 1835.
<152:264> - 17 Nov. 1836, Job TERRY Jr., mariner of Freetown to William ASHLEY, trader of Fall River, land in Steepbrook at Fall River. Wf Ruth releases dower. Ack. same day. Rec. 13 Jan. 1837.

Estate of **Job TERRY 2d** of Troy MA. <Bristol Co.PR>
<67:122> Adm. 10 Apr. 1829, widow **Elizabeth TERRY**, admx. <67:381> Inventory taken 28 July 1829. <67:409> Insolvency 28 July 1829. <65:550> Report, 1830. <68:373> Citation. <70:66> Account of admx., 1831. <202:458> Sale of land.

Hezekiah WILSON & David TERRY to **Job TERRY Jr.** of Troy MA. <Bristol Co.Deeds 103:471>
...7 Jan. 1816, Hezekiah WILSON, merchant of Troy and David TERRY, merchant of Freetown for $900 sold to Job TERRY Jr., mariner...land in Troy...which we bought of Edmund HATHAWAY. Wealthy WILSON signs. Ack. 27 Jan. 1816 by grantors. Rec. 31 Jan. 1818.

==

Job TERRY of Freetown MA to **Job Terry WILSON** of Troy MA. <Bristol Co.Deeds 123:486>
...3 May 1828, Job TERRY, yeoman, in consideration of the love, good will & affection that I have for my grandson Job Terry WILSON son of Hezekiah WILSON, convey...two and a half acre salt marsh in Dighton...bounded by land of Job SLADE, Ebenezer TALBOT, William RICHMOND and Levi PEARCE... excepting the right of improvement and profits of the same to me during my natural life. Ack. same day. Rec. 6 May 1828.

==

Will of **John TISDAL/TISDALE** of Taunton MA. <Bristol Co.PR>
<6:66>...dated 6 Jan. 1727/8, mentions wf **Abigail,** eldest son **John TISDAL,** 2d son **Abraham TISDAL** & 3d son **Israel TISDAL** (both under 21), sons **Ephraim TISDAL & Jedediah TISDAL;** daus **Deborah TISDAL, Abigail TISDAL & Anna TISDAL.** <6:120> Pr. 5 Feb. 1727/8.

==

Will of **Benjamin TERRY** of Freetown MA. <Bristol Co.PR>
<22:456>...dated 28 June 1768, mentions wf **Margaret;** sons (in order of age) **Robert TERRY** (mentions the estate received of Robert's grandfather SPUR), **Benjamin TERRY, John TERRY, George TERRY** of Swansea, **William TERRY & Solomon TERRY** (executor); daus (in order of age) **Mary WARREN, Johanna GIBBS, Lydia WINSLOW, Phebe DAGGETT, Margaret LEWING, Meriam TISDALE, Sarah WINSLOW & Dinah TERRY.** Witnesses: Abiel TERRY, Richard WINSLOW Jr., John CRANE. <22:459> Pr. 29 Mar. 1773.

==

Heirs of **Nathaniel HOLLOWAY** of Middleboro MA. <Plymouth Co.Deeds 26:52>
...16 Feb. 1729...Deliverance HOLLOWAY, Nathaniel HOLLOWAY, Nathan HOLLOWAY, Samuel HOLLOWAY, Sarah HOLLOWAY, all of Middleboro and Benjamin TERRY & wf Margaret of Freetown...the widow & children of Nathaniel HOLLOWAY dec'd.

==

PLYMOUTH COUNTY DEEDS: (re: TERRY)

<39:64> - 3 Dec. 1747, Benjamin TERRY & wf Margaret of Freetown.
<39:65> - 24 Dec. 1747, Benjamin TERRY & wf Joanna of Dartmouth.
<42:169> - 11 May 1749, Benjamin TERRY of Freetown to son John TERRY of Dartmouth.
<47:273> - 30 Aug. 1755, Benjamin TERRY, yeoman & wf Margaret of Freetown.
<55:226> - 1776, John TERRY & wf Joanna to son in law Samuel SAMSON of Rochester.

(Note: The following are references only, to grantors, viz: **Abiel TERRY,** 57:198;71:248. **Benjamin TERRY,** 42:169;47:273;59:213. **George TERRY,** 48:196;52:106;61:71. **John TERRY,** 43:40;60:16.

==

BRISTOL COUNTY DEEDS: (re: TERRY)

<39:437> - 13 Mar. 1734/5, Benjamin TERRY & wf Margaret; heirs of Nathaniel HOLLOWAY.
<52:397> - 15 Mar. 1765, Benjamin TERRY & wf Joanna of Dartmouth to Stephen RUSSELL of same.
<52:554> - 23 Oct. 1769, Benjamin TERRY & wf Joanna of Dartmouth to Elnathan POPE of same, half of land Stephen POPE bought of Isaac POPE in 1711.
<56:531> - 1 Nov. 1774, Benjamin TERRY & wf Joanna of Dartmouth to Seth SPOONER Jr.
<109:204> - 20 July 1819, Thomas TERRY of Fairhaven.
<110:509> - 10 Sept 1821, Thomas TERRY of Fairhaven.
<112:98> - 18 Oct. 1822, Thomas TERRY of Fairhaven; mentions heirs of Benjamin TERRY dec'd.
<121:336> - , Elias TERRY as admr. of estate of Thomas TERRY.

(Note: References to **Benjamin TERRY,** grantor, iz: 4:404,406 (1705); 5:472 (1709); 26:25 (1736); 27:27,30,34 (1737); 36:346 (1748).

==

Estate of **Benjamin TERRY** of Fairhaven MA. <Bristol Co.PR>
<54:88> Inventory, 26 Sept. 1817 appraisers app'td. <54:473> Account, 5 May 1818. <56:201> Account, 5 Oct. 1819. <56:209> Dower, 29 Sept. 1718, to widow **Mary TERRY.**

==

Will of **Thomas TERRY** of Freetown MA. <Bristol Co.PR>
<15:380>...dated 5 May 1748, mentions wf **Abigail;** son **Thomas TERRY...**not of sound understanding ...and is incapable to provide for himself; son **Abiel TERRY** to be gdn. of brother; dau **Lydia JONES.** <15:381> Pr. 15 June 1757. <original> Bond 4 Oct. 1757, of **Abiel TERRY,** Esq. of Freetown, admr. Sureties: James WILLIAMS, Esq. of Taunton and Thomas GILBERT, Esq. of Berkley.

MICRO #3 OF 10

Estate of **Thomas TERRY** of Fairhaven MA to **Mason TABER** of same. <Bristol Co.Deeds 121:301>
...25 Oct. 1826, Elias TERRY, admr...licensed to make sale of the real estate of sd dec'd, for $71.00 sells to Mason TABER...salt marsh in Fairhaven at Sconticut neck near Winsegakuset...being the same lot...that was conveyed by deed by Benjamin TERRY & Joanna TERRY, 18 Mar. 1781 to the sd Thomas TERRY. Witnesses: Joseph TRIPP, Levi JENNY. Rec. 26 Apr. 1827.

==

Benjamin TERRY formerly of Dartmouth MA to **Thomas TERRY** of same. <Bristol Co.Deeds 66:374>
...18 Mar. 1781, Benjamin TERRY, yeoman & wf Joanna, for the love...confirm unto our son Thomas

TERRY...land in Dartmouth...our homestead farm where we formerly lived...bounded by land of Prince TABER, Maj. CLAP, Joshua SHEARMAN, Chillingsworth FOSTER & Jeremiah BENNET...also all the salt marsh that was set of for our share in the last division in Sconticut Neck lying nigh to a Pond known by the name of Winsegauset in sd neck. Witnesses: Newman PERKINS, John PERKINS. Ack. 2 May 1781 by both grantors at Exeter RI. Rec. 10 Nov. 1787.

Benjamin TERRY formerly of Dartmouth MA to **Benjamin TERRY.** <Bristol Co.Deeds 67:204>
...20 Mar. 1781, Benjamin TERRY, yeoman & wf Joanna, for love...confirm unto our son **Benjamin TERRY**...part of homested farm in Dartmouth where we formerly lived...bounded by land of son Thomas TERRY which we gave him, Hix JENNE dec'd, John BENNET and Maj. CLAP. Witnesses: Newman PERKINS, John PERKINS. Ack. 2 May 1781, Exeter RI by grantors. Rec. 13 Aug. 1788.

Benjamin TERRY of Exetor RI to **Lamuel PERRY** of Dartmouth MA. <Bristol Co.Deeds 65:135>
...19 Aug. 1785, Benjamin TERRY, gent. & Joanna, for £15 sell to Lamuel PERRY, yeoman...three acres in Dartmouth...a peice of my former homestead farm...bounded by sd Lamuel's homestead. Witnesses: Samuel GORTON, Benjamin GORTON. Ack. 28 Oct. 1785 by both in RI. Rec. 30 Jan. 1786.

Benjamin TERRY of Exeter RI to **Samuel SPRAGUE** of Dartmouth MA. <Bristol Co.Deeds 65:533>
...19 June 1786, Benjamin TERRY, gent. for three hundred & thirty seven Spanish mil'd silver dollars, sell to Samuel SPRAGUE, Esq...twenty two and three quarters acres in Dartmouth...a parcel of what was formerly my homsted farm...bounded by wood land now owned by Silas SWEET and homestead farm of Robert BENNET. Wf Joanna TERRY releases dower. Witnesses: Jonathan DEAN, Mary DEAN. Ack. 19 June 1786 by grantors in RI. Rec. 13 Sept. 1786.

Benjamin TERRY of Exeter RI to **Elnathan TERRY.** <Bristol Co.Deeds 66:375>
...24 Nov. 1786, Benjamin TERRY, gent. & wf Joanna, in consideration of love & affection which we bare to our son Elnathan TERRY...give...23 acres in Dartmouth...also four acre salt meadow...on east side of Sconticut Neck...bounded by land of Hannah VINCENT and Collins' Meadow...and is the same meadow that fell to the sd Joanna as her portion out of her father's estate...together with a 10 acre wood lot. Witnesses: Stephen REYNOLDS, William HIAMS. Ack. 3 Mar 1787 by Benjamin. Rec. 10 Nov. 1787.

Will of **Thomas TERRY** of Freetown MA <Bristol Co.PR>
<original>...dated 10 Aug. 1691...aged 60 yeres or therabouts...eldest son **Thomas TERRY**; mentions an affidavit dated 3 Oct. 1691. <6:275> Agreement 8 June 1704, widow **Anna WILLIAMS** and three sons.

Estate of **Thomas TERRY** of Fairhaven MA. <Bristol Co.PR>
<62:66> Adm., 5 Oct. 1824, son **Seth TERRY** declines adm., Elias TERRY app'td admr. <62:64> Insolvency. <62:331> Inventory taken 2 Nov. 1824; total real estate, $2239.33; sworn to 3 May 1825 by admr. <62:346> Report. <62:457> Citation. <62:553> Account 5 Apr. 1825 and agreement of heirs, viz: **Cynthia PIERCE, Deborah OMEY, Mary Ann BATES, Betsey CASWELL,** Julius MAYHEW as gdn. of **Hannah N. TERRY & Priscilla D. TERRY.** (Note: The following references also appear to belong to this **Thomas TERRY:** <111:519,152:86> 5 Oct. 1824, Elias TERRY app'td admr. <63:462> 2nd Account 25 July 1826 of admr. <201:456> Petition of admr, 25 July 1826, to sell real estate. <65:105> Citation, 1st Tues. May 1827.

Estate of **Thomas TERRY Jr.** of Fairhaven MA. <Bristol Co.PR 110:229, 151:105>
...7 Oct. 1814, **Thomas TERRY,** yeoman of Fairhaven app'td admr.; sworn to 9 May 1815.

Estate of **Benjamin TERRY** of Freetown MA. <Bristol Co.PR>
<22:456>...dated 28 June 1768, wf **Margaret.** <22:459> Pr. 29 Mar. 1773.

References to the name **Benjamin TERRY** in Bristol Co.PR, viz: 54:88,473;56:201,209;74:433;75:81; 78:344;79:13,144,147,148,284,299,303;110:568;113:447;130:232;132:423;138:132;151:340;153:408;159: 119;168:537;209:164.

Estate of **Nathaniel WILLIAMS** of Taunton MA. <Bristol Co.PR 1:223>
Division 25 July 1698, by Thomas LEONARD, James LEONARD, Henry HODGES, John RICHMOND Sr. & Thomas WILLIAMS, all of Taunton, among the following heirs, viz: widow **Elizabeth WILLIAMS,** admx., eldest son **John WILLIAMS,** admr., 2d son **Nathaniel WILLIAMS** and only dau **Elizabeth WILLIAMS.**

Will of **John MACCOMBER/MACOMBER,** yeoman of Taunton MA. <Bristol Co.PR 11:426-28>
...dated 28 Dec. 1742...labouring under Indisposition of Body and in the advanced years of my age ...to wf **Lydia,** one third of all personal estate & moveables...to son **Nathaniel MACCOMBER,** one third of land in 16 Shilling Purchase in Middleboro...to son **Josiah MACCOMBER,** one third of lands in Middleboro...to son **John MACCOMBER Jr.,** one third of land in 16 Shilling Purchase...also one third of all other lands and confirms deeds of gift to each of the above three sons dated 1 Jan. 1732...to son **James MACCOMBER,** £100 bills of credit old tenor this day paid, also £80.15s lawfull money or £35 bills of credit old tenor, accounting silver at 26s8d per oz...to son **Elijah MACCOMBER** the whole of homestead lands...to son **Joseph MACCOMBER,** £100 bills of credit old tenor accounting silver at 26s8d per oz or £25 lawful money...when sd **Joseph** is 21 with interest at 6% ...to dau **Elizabeth ROWNSEVIL** wf of William, 50s lawfull money...to dau **Abia MACCOMBER,** £12.10s lawful money, also one third of indoor moveables...to dau **Anna MACCOMBER,** £12 when 18 or at marriage, also 50s to be paid at age 19, also one third of indoor moveables...son **Elijah** to pay all

debts & legacies; son **Nathaniel**, executor. Witnesses: William HOLLOWAY, Benjamin PAUL, James WILLIAM. Pr. 5 Apr. 1748. Inventory taken 2 Dec. 1747 (per record) or 25 Dec. 1747 (per original).

Will of **Nathaniel WILLIAMS**. <Bristol Co.PR 23:508,509>...dated 24 May 1775. Pr.

Estate of **Nathaniel WILLIAMS** of New Bedford MA. <Bristol Co.PR>
<46:338;109:488;150:470> Warrant for inventory, 25 Apr. 1811. Notice. Adm. <46:380> Insolvency, 7 May 1811, represented by Job EDDY, adm. <49:242,271>...

Estate of **Nathaniel WILLIAMS**, Esq. of Dighton MA. <Bristol Co.PR>
<61:182>...2 Dec. 182(3)?, widow **Lydia WILLIAMS** refuses adm., Seth WILLIAMS app'td admr. <61:179> Insolvency represented by admr. <61:560> Report. (records are duplicated in 111:408;152:27)

Will of **Nathaniel WILLIAMS**, Esq. of Taunton MA. <Bristol Co.PR>
<67:410>...dated 2 June 1827, mentions wf **Lusilda** and children **John WILLIAMS, Cassender WILLIAMS, Nathaniel H. WILLIAMS, Simeon WILLIAMS, Polly COPELAND, Charlotte DEAN, Lusilda WILLIAMS, Susanna WILLIAMS & Amella**(sp) **WILLIAMS.** Pr. 4 Aug. 1829. <68:105> Inventory, 4 Aug. 1829. (records duplicated in 112:513)

Estate of **William ROUNSEVELL** of Freetown MA. <Bristol Co.PR>
<13:381>...2 May 1753, William ASHLEY, yeoman of Freetown and his wife **Elizabeth ASHLEY** widow of dec'd, app'td admrs. <14:81-3> Inventory taken 30 Apr. 1754 by William PALMER, David EASTEE, John BARDEEN; incl. part of saw mill; additional inventory taken 7 May 1754. <19:354> Dower & appraisal of real estate, 19 Oct. 1765 by John PAUL, John CRANE, Benajah BABBITT, all of Bristol; one third set off to widow **Elizabeth ROUNSEVELL.** <19:354> Division 30 Oct. 1765 to the children, viz: eldest son, **William ROUNSEVELL, Joseph ROUNSEVELL,** only dau **Elizabeth PEIRCE** and **Levi ROUNSEVELL**; to widow **Elizabeth ASHLEY**, her thirds, also dower in the house where sd William ASHLEY now dwells also one tenth of sawmill as mentioned in the first return of ye division of **Phillip ROUNSEVELL**'s estate; mentions land set off to son **Levi** in...ye other division in his Grandfather's real estate <21:345> Receipt 29 Oct. 1765...we the subscribers being Grand children to our honoured Grandfather **Philip ROUNSEVELL** late of Freetown dec'd intestate, haveing recevd of our unkle **John ROUNSVELL** of sd Freetown, gent., admr.

Will of **James MACOMBER**, yeoman of Berkley MA. <Bristol Co.PR>
<40:395>...dated 16 Jan. 1797...being arrived to more than seventy years of age...wf **Rachel**...to son **Elijah MACOMBER**, three acres in Cotley in Taunton which I purchased of Joseph WILLIAMS and one quarter acre in Cotley bounded by land of Nathan MACOMBER and Joseph HALL...also three acres in Cotley bounded by land of Benjamin WILLIAMS, Richard GODFREY, Nathaniel STAPLE, Isaac WILLIAMS and the ten acres bought of Henry MACOMBER...also all rights in Bare Swamp lots except what I purchased of George MACOMBER...to son **Josiah MACOMBER**, half a twenty acre lot which he now lives, the other half I have heretofore conveyed to him by deed...also half of ten acres in Cotley I purchased of Henry MACOMBER...also half of wearing apparel...also one third of two and a half acres wood land in Berkley bounded by land of George SANFORD, Ebenezer PAULL and the ten acre lot I purchased of MIRECK...to son **Venis MACOMBER**, two and a quarter acre wood land in Taunton bounded by land of Abiel MACOMBER, George WILLIAMS 2d and Nathaniel STAPLE...also one half of ten acre wood land in Taunton I purchased of Henry MACOMBER...also one third of two and a half acres in Berkley bounded by land of George SANFORD, Ebenezer PAULL and land I bought of MIRECK...also half of wearing apparel and all farming tools...to dau **Sinthe MACOMBER** wf of Stephen Jr., half of ten acres in Berkley bounded by land of Ebenezer PAULL, George SANFORD and land I bought of Samuel MIRECK...to dau **Meram BRIGGS** wf of Ezra all she received at time of marriage and $1.00...to dau **Elinor SANFORD** wf of Joseph, half of the ten acres in Berkley and one third of the two and a half acre wood land in Berkley...to sons **Josiah & Venis** all horses, cattle, sheep & swine except the two cows given to wf **Rachel**; son **Venis**, executor. Witnesses: Lemuel WILLIAMS, Josiah MACOMBER, Abiel MACOMBER. <40:396> Pr. 6 Apr. 1804. <40:399> 11 Jan. 1804, Abiel MACOMBER, Lemuel WILLIAMS, John BRIGGS app'td to appraise. <40:400> Inventory taken 24 Jan. 1804. <42:360> Order, 25 Mar. 1806, for dower to be set off to widow **Rachel MACOMBER.** Division 13 May 1806, mentions **Eleanor SANFORD** wf of Capt. SANFORD, **Lintha MACOMBER** wf of Stephen, "and others".

Estate of **Deacon John MACOMBER** of Middleborough MA. <Plymouth Co.PR #13475>
<23:60> Pr. <24:5> Inventory taken 16 Feb. 1775. <24:327> Warrant & Division, 19 May 1777, to following children, viz: eldest son **John MACOMBER, Cyrus MACOMBER, Enoch MACOMBER, Elizabeth MACOMBER, Mary MACOMBER, Samuel MACOMBER,** all minors, and **Abiah REED** wf of Benjamin. <24:328> Account Apr. 1777. <22:46-49,167,168,173,174> Guardianship, 1775, for children **John, Cyrus, Enoch, Elizabeth, Mary & Samuel.**

Luke ELLIS & Daniel WESTON to **Samuel PICKENS** of Middleborough MA. <Plymouth Co.Deeds 111:181>
...21 Jan. 1805, Luke ELLIS & wf Elizabeth of New Bedford and Daniel WESTON & wf Mary of Middleborough, for $50.00 sold to Samuel PICKENS, yeoman...all rights in Long Pond Lot...which our Father Deacon John MACOMBER died seized. Witnesses: Daniel DUNBAR, John ATWOOD, Enoch MACUMBER. Ack. 14 Aug. 1809 by Luke, 16 Sept. 1805 by Daniel Rec. 25 Nov. 1809.

Will of **Joseph GOODING**, yeoman of Dighton MA. <Bristol Co.PR 51:327>
...dated 15 Jan. 1806, mentions wf **Rebecca** and children, viz: **Josiah GOODING, John GOODING, Joseph GOODING** (executor), **Henry GOODING & Alanson GOODING** (both under 21), **Deborah STANDISH, Elizabeth PERRY & Rebecca REED.** Pr. 8 Mar. 1816 (dec'd is called late of Wellington).

Guardianship of Children of **John WILLIAMS,** dec'd of Taunton MA. <Bristol Co.PR>
<7:85>...21 Oct. 1730, Nathan HODGES of Norton app'td gdn. of **Timothy WILLIAMS,** above 14. 30 Oct. 1730, widow **Hannah WILLIAMS** app'td gdn. of **Simeon WILLIAMS,** under 14.

Timothy WILLIAMS of Easton MA to **Simeon WILLIAMS** of Taunton MA. <Bristol Co.Deeds 37:183>
...1 Feb. 1748, Timothy WILLIAMS, cordwainer, for Ŀ400 sells to Simeon WILLIAMS...one third of all the land which was my brother Nathaniel WILLIAMS' late of Taunton dec'd, which was given me in his last will...excepting what we had in reversion namely, his mother's thirds. Wf Elizabeth WILLIAMS releases dower. Witnesses: Silas WILLIAMS, Mary CRANE. Ack. 24 Feb.1749 by Timothy.

Will of **Nathaniel WILLIAMS** of Taunton MA. <Bristol Co.PR>
<11:330>...dated 22 May 1745...to wf **Sarah**...all the goods & personal estate she brought to me at time of our inter marriage & one brass kittle bought since marriage...new end of the dwelling house we now live in with the half acre of land...as the same was set to me in the division of my honoured father's estate...also fifty pounds accounting coined silver at 30s per oz....also two hundred pounds accounting coined silver at 30s per oz.; sister **Experience HODGES** wf of Nathan of Norton; mentions land bought of Nicholas WHITE; brothers **Silas WILLIAMS, Timothy WILLIAMS & Simeon WILLIAMS,** executors. <11:332> Pr. 6 Oct. 1747.

Heirs of **Deacon Simeon WILLIAMS** of Taunton MA. <Bristol Co.Deeds 74:213>
...7 Aug. 1795, Simeon WILLIAMS, clerk of Weymouth, Job KING, gent. & wf Ziporah of Taunton, Joseph HODGES, yeoman & wf Luranna of Norton, James DEAN, gent. & wf Hannah of Taunton, Elijah GUSHEE, gent. of Raynham in behalf of Williams GUSHEE an infant, James HART Jr., yeoman & wf Cyntha of Taunton...being owners of certain tracts of lands & swamps in Taunton, Easton and Raynham, which lands were given & bequeathed by ye last will...of Deacon Simeon WILLIAMS late of sd Taunton dec'd, have made partition and division of sd premises into six parts.

Will of **Deacon Simeon WILLIAMS,** gent. of Taunton MA. <Bristol Co.PR>
<33:116>...dated 15 May 1787, mentions wf **Weightstill/Waitstill;** eldest son **Simeon WILLIAMS;** son **Nathaniel WILLIAMS;** daus **Ziporah KING, Luranah HODGES, Hannah DEAN, Jemima WILLIAMS, Cynthia WILLIAMS;** chil of dec'd dau **Experience HODGES,** viz: **Abiel HODGES, Experience HODGES, Weightstill/ Waitstill HODGES;** wife and son **Nathaniel,** executors. Codicil 14 Aug. 1789. Pr. 29 Sept. 1794. <33:182> Inventory taken 24 Dec. 1794. <33:417> Account 1 Sept. 1795; incl. funeral charges of two gallons of rum, Ŀ2.50s and wine & sugar, Ŀ3.33s.

References to the name **Simeon WILLIAMS** in Bristol Co.PR, viz: <91:196> Will, 1847-48. <116:343> Notice, 1845-49. <130:447> Guardianship, 1798, of Simeon, son of Joseph WILLIAMS. <174:189> Bond, 1836-51. <176:289> Citation, 1838-51.

Will of **Nathaniel WILLIAMS** of Taunton MA. <Bristol Co.PR 5:350>
...dated 23 Aug. 1726, mentions wf **Lydia** (executrix); sons **Edmund WILLIAMS, Nathaniel WILLIAMS;** daus **Lydia, Bethiah, Judeth & Elisebeth.** Witnesses: Ebenezer CAMPBIL/CAMPBEL, Ebenezer WILLIAMS, Hannah WILLIAMS. Pr. 21 Feb. 1726. Inventory taken 16 Dec. 1726; mentions 32 acres at Cotley and land at Stony/Storry Weir, Long Plain, Rock Plain and Tan hill.

Heirs of **Nathaniel WILLIAMS** of Taunton MA. <Bristol Co.Deeds 37:248>
...2 Mar. 1748, **Edmund WILLIAMS & Nathaniel WILLIAMS** of Raynham divide between themselves the land in Raynham which was their sister **Judith WILLIAMS'** lott in ye division of **Nathaniel WILLIAMS** dec'd's estate to and among his children which **Judith** is since dec'd. Ack. & Rec. 19 Apr. 1750.

Henry PITTS Jr. of Dighton MA to **Edmond & Nathaniel WILLIAMS** of Raynham MA. <Bristol Co.Deeds>
<36:415>...29 Dec. 1748, Henry PITTS Jr., for Ŀ12.10s sold to Edmond WILLIAMS & Nathaniel WILLIAMS...dureing my natural life...26 acres in Raynham lying between and on Rock plain and Tareall plain...bounded by land of sd Edmond & Nathaniel, Capt. Ebenezer ROBBINSON and Thomas LEONARD Witnesses: Elijah DEAN, Jairus BISBEE. Ack. same day. Rec. 20 Feb. 1748 (O.S.).

BRISTOL COUNTY DEEDS: (re: Ichabod KEITH)

<25:213> - 1736/7, Ichabod KEITH & wf Lydia to Edmund WILLIAMS.
<25:416> - 1737, Ichabod KEITH to John WILLIAMS.
<35:211> - 1748, Ichabod KEITH & ux & al to Israel DEAN Jr.
<37:156> - 1749, Ichabod KEITH & ux & al to Nathaniel STAPLE Jr.

Will of **Edmund WILLIAMS,** yeoman of Raynham MA. <Bristol Co.PR>
<34:308>...dated 9 June 1791, mentions wf **Abiah** (agreement made with her 6 May 1790 is confirmed) sons **Nathan WILLIAMS & Stephen WILLIAMS;** daus **Huldah WILLIAMS & Phebe LEONARD;** grandson **Silas BURT;** son **Noah WILLIAMS;** grandson **Silas WILLIAMS;** minor chil. of dec'd son **Edmund WILLIAMS,** viz: **Susanna WILLIAMS & Nancy WILLIAMS;** dau **Lydia SHAW;** grandson **David SHAW;** dau **Sarah PADELFORD;** son **Jason WILLIAMS.** Pr. 3 Jan. 1797. <34:378> Inventory.

Estate of **Edmund WILLIAMS Jr.** of Raynham MA. <Bristol Co.PR>
<147:95>...18 Sept. 1775, widow **Susanna WILLIAMS** app'td admx. <24:227> Inventory, 1775, of admx. <129:94> Guardianship, 18 Sept. 1775, widow **Susanna WILLIAMS** app'td gdn. of **Edmund WILLIAMS,** under 14. <94:364;136:231;140:242> Guardianship. <30:87> Account. <30:110> Dower. <30:107> Division (no date), to widow **Susanna,** only son **Silas WILLIAMS** and daus **Susanna & Nancy WILLIAMS.**

All References to the name **Ebenezer WILLIAMS** in Bristol Co.PR: <6:95,96> Will & Pr.; <23:597,598> Will & Pr.; <24:12> Inv.; <27:193,627,487> Accounts & Division; <28:497,498> Will & Pr.; <29:38> Inv.; <43:369> Division; <44:406> Notice of sale; <97:302,452> Will, 1850; <99:103> Division; <101:215> Allowance; <119:293> Notice; <174:272,175:17> Bonds; <177:101,179:10> Citations; <182:53,54> Will & Pr.; <222:131,369> Partition.

Will of **Jonathan PADDLEFORD** of Taunton MA. <Bristol Co.PR>
<76:51>...dated 7 Jan. 1828, mentions wf **Huldah**; $1.00 to be divided among the children of dec'd dau **Anna WILLIAMS**, viz: **Harrison WILLIAMS, Ebenezer WILLIAMS, Joseph WILLIAMS, Sarah WILLIAMS & Nathan WILLIAMS**; $6.00 to be divided among the children of dec'd dau **Lydia CARPENTER**, viz: **Mary Ann CARPENTER, Thornton CARPENTER, Dan CARPENTER, Samuel S. CARPENTER & Lucy CARPENTER**; dau **Sarah PADDLEFORD**; dau **Betsey PADDLEFORD** wf of Capt. John PADDLEFORD (executor). <76:69> Pr. 6 Nov. 1835 Capt. John PADDLEFORD refuses adm., Godfrey ROBINSON app'td admr. <76:109> Inventory taken 12 Nov 1835. <76:124> Insolvency, 8 Jan. 1836. <76:472> Report.

MICRO #4 OF 10

Will of **Ebenezer WILLIAMS** of Berkley MA. <Bristol Co.PR 182:53>
...dated 28 June 1858, mentions wf **Caroline** & children, viz: **E. Jerome WILLIAMS, Ann C. WILLIAMS & Sarah E. WILLIAMS**...if she survives testator; son executor. Witnesses: Joseph WILBAR, Thomas E. DEAN, Sally H. DEAN. Pr. 31 Aug. 1858.

Nathaniel WILLIAMS of Raynham MA to **Phillip ARTHERTON** of Norton MA. <Bristol Co.Deeds 40:124>
...5 Dec. 1746, Nathaniel WILLIAMS, husbandman & wf Mary one of daus of Joshua ARTHERTON late of Norton dec'd, for Ł110 sold to Phillip ARTHERTON...thirteen acres in Norton bounded by land of our brother Joshua ARTHERTON...being land set off to us in division of father's estate...our mother Elisabeth ARTHERTON to have a third part of ye income. Witnesses: Edmund WILLIAMS, Mary CRANE Ack. 5 Jan. 1753 by Nathaniel, 7 June 1753 by Mary. Rec.7 June 1753.

Philip KING Jr. of Raynham MA to **Nathaniel WILLIAMS** of same. <Bristol Co.Deeds 47:426>
...27 Feb. 1765, Philip KING Jr., gent., for Ł100.8s sold to Nathaniel WILLIAMS, yeoman...28 acres in Raynham...which I purchased of my honoured father Capt. Phillip KING...bounded by land of Seth DEAN, Benjamin KING and Benjamin HALL. Witnesses: Edmund WILLIAMS JR., Jason WILLIAMS. Ack. 25 Mar. 1765 by Philip. Rec. 29 Mar. 1765.

Benjamin HALL of Raynham MA to **Nathaniel WILLIAMS** of same. <Bristol Co.Deeds 47:557>
...11 Apr. 1765, Benjamin HALL, yeoman for Ł13.8s8d sold to Nathaniel WILLIAMS, yeoman...six acres in Raynham...bounded by land of Edmond WILLIAMS & sd Nathaniel. Wf Phebe HALL releases dower. Witnesses: Edmund WILLIAMS, Edmund WILLIAMS Jr. Ack. 4 July 1765 by Benjamin. Rec. 4 July 1765.

Benjamin HALL of Raynham MA to **Nathaniel WILLIAMS** of same. <Bristol Co.Deeds 50:9>
...5 May 1766, Benjamin HALL, yeoman, for Ł10 sold to Nathaniel WILLIAMS, yeoman...four acres in Raynham...bounded by land of sd Nathaniel. Witnesses: Edmund WILLIAMS Jr., Jason WILLIAMS. Ack. & Rec. 21 June 1766

Benjamin HALL of Raynham MA to **Nathaniel WILLIAMS** of same. <Bristol Co.Deeds 51:82>
...25 Sept. 1766, Benjamin HALL, yeoman, for Ł15.16s sold to Nathaniel WILLIAMS, yeoman...six acres in Raynham...bounded by land of sd Nathaniel. Witnesses: Edmund WILLIAMS Jr., Jason WILLIAMS. Ack. & Rec. 16 Feb. 1768.

John WILLIAMS of Raynham MA to **Nathaniel WILLIAMS** of same. <Bristol Co.Deeds 61:470>
...15 Mar. 1776, John WILLIAMS, schoolmaster, for Ł173 sold to brother Nathaniel WILLIAMS, yeoman ...44 acres in Raynham...bounded by land of Benjamin HALL, Seth DEAN, Thomas DEAN, Seth WILLIAMS, Edmund WILLIAMS & Lieut. Benjamin KING...sd land was purchased by my honoured father WILLIAMS of Ensign Phillip KING & Benjamin HALL. Witnesses: Edmund WILLIAMS, Lydia CONSTOCK. Ack. 23 May 1783 by John. Rec. 24 May 1783.

John WILLIAMS et al, of Raynham MA, division. <Bristol Co.Deeds 74:310>
...14 Nov. 1794, Isaac HALL, John HALL & wf Huldah, John WILLIAMS & wf Silence and Seth HALL, all yeoman...being now ye legal owners...of all the lands that were set off to Hannah HALL the late widow of Phillip HALL late of Raynham dec'd as her right of dower...divide the two pieces of land Ack. 8 Apr. 1795 by all. Rec. 5 Feb. 1796.

John WILLIAMS of Raynham MA to **Samuel JONES** of same. <Bristol Co.Deeds 95:181>
...20 Oct. 1810, John WILLIAMS, yeoman, for $300.00 sold to Samuel JONES, yeoman...eleven acres in Raynham bounded by land of Amos HALL, Josiah DEAN & Lewis HALL...also nine acres bounded by land of Josiah DEAN & widow Prudence JONES...also eight and a half acres bounded by land of widow Sarah ELLIS, Samuel JONES & Josiah DEAN. Witnesses: Elisha GILMORE Jr., William A. LEONARD. Ack. 19 Apr. 1811 by John & wf Silence. Rec. 11 Mar. 1813.

Silence WILLIAMS of Raynham MA to **George WILLIAMS & John HART.** <Bristol Co.Deeds 103:149>
...27 Sept. 1817, Silence WILLIAMS, widow of John of Taunton, sells to George WILLIAMS of Middleboro & John HART of Taunton, both yeoman...all rights in husband's estate. Ack. & Rec. same day.

BRISTOL COUNTY DEEDS:

<69:276> - 11 Mar. 1788, Seth WILLIAMS to Job DEAN, yeomen of Raynham, two & a half acres in Taunton Great Cedar Swamp. Ack. 9 May 1789. Rec. 18 Feb. 1791.
<69:274> - 2 Feb. 1791, Seth WILLIAMS, yeoman to George WILLIAMS, both of Raynham, homestead in Raynham. Wf Mary releases dower. Ack. 15 Feb. 1791.
<69:274> - 2 Feb. 1791, Seth WILLIAMS, yeoman to Joseph COLE, both of Raynham, land in Taunton. Wf Mary releases dower. Ack. 15 Feb. 1791.
<73:236> - 5 Feb. 1793, John WILLIAMS, son of Silas WILLIAMS.
<93:214> - 6 Aug. 1810, Samuel JONES of Raynham, admr. of est. of Samuel JONES Jr., sells land.
<97:419> - 30 Apr. 1814, Samuel JONES & wf Polly of Raynham sell swamp.
<118:197> - 1825, Execution against Samuel JONES of Raynham.

Estate of **Philip HALL** of Raynham MA. <Bristol Co.PR>
<146:29> Adm., 1764, Jonathan HALL app'td admr. <21:53> Inventory taken 1 May 1764. <127:230> Guardianship, 1764, Jonathan HALL app'td gdn. of **Philip HALL,** above 14. <131:36> Guardianship. <21:2> Division, 1764, among widow **Hannah HALL** & children, viz: eldest dau **Huldah,** 2d dau **Phebe,** son **Isaac HALL,** dau **Hannah,** eldest son **Elijah HALL,** 2d son **Philip HALL,** dau **Silence** & son **Joshua.** <27:423> Account, 1783.

Seth WILLIAMS et al to **David DEAN** of Taunton MA. <Bristol Co.Deeds 76:249>
...1 Jan. 1795, Seth WILLIAMS, Esq., George WILLIAMS, Esq., Ebenezer CASWELL, gent., all of Taunton, Abraham WHITE, esq. of Norton and John STAPLE, clerk of Canterbury CT, sell to David DEAN, yeoman...the 10th Great Lot in Burnt Ground Cedar Swamp in Taunton...the 1st share which was laid out in original right of William PHILLIPS. Seth owned one ninth, George & Ebenezer owned one sixth, Abraham owned two ninths and John owned three ninths. Witnesses: Joseph WILLIAMS, James WILLIAMS, Seth SMITH, Hannah TERRY(sp), Lydia WILLIAMS, Samuel WHITE, Alfred WILLIAMS & Mason WILLIAMS. Ack. 19 Oct. 1797 by John STAPLE, 4 Dec. 1797 by Maj. Seth WILLIAMS. Rec. 4 Dec. 1797.

Mary MEADS of Brookline MA to **John ROGERS** of Swanzey MA. <Suffolk Co.Deeds 26:178>
...3 June 1712, Mary MEADS, widow, eldest sister to Sarah STRANGE late of Boston, widow, dec'd, sells to brother in law John ROGERS, gent...the house & land in Boston belonging to Sarah STRANGE which was assigned to Mary by the probate courts, 2 June 1712...bounded by land of the late Josiah COBHAM dec'd and heirs of Simon LYNDE dec'd...which granted premises are more particularly described in and by a certain indenture from the sd Josiah COBHAM & wf Mary to John STRANGE dec'd & the sd Sarah his wife, dated 11 Feb. 1687/8 on record may appear. Witnesses: Thomas GILBERT, James BENNET, Sarah KNIGHT. Ack. same day by Mary & Rec.

Estate of **John ROGERS.** <Bristol Co.PR>
<7:404> Adm. <7:434> Inventory. <7:583> Complaint, 11 July 1733. <8:50> Affidavit of widow, 25 Sept. 1733. <9:363> Probate of widow, **Marah,** 19 Feb. 1739. (Also mentioned are originals dated 1732-33 which include petitions, personal inventory, bond, complaints & summons; under "widow **Marah**" is listed petitions, bond, complaint & citations for 1739, however none are expanded on.)

Abigail HANNIFORD of Boston MA to **John ROGERS** of Bristol MA. <Suffolk Co.Deeds 18:183>
...20 Aug. 1695, John SOAMES, cooper of Boston as Trustee to Abigail HANNIFORD, widow & sole executrix to the last will of her late husband John HANNIFORD dec'd and heretofore wife of George DELL of Boston...long since also dec'd...at a court held 29 May 1695, John SOAMES was empowered to sell the estate of George DELL and with the proceeds...shall maintain & keep the sd Abigail dureing her natural life...after Abigail's death, any money remaining to be paid...to the dau of the sd John HANNIFORD (who are only living of the children of the sd George DELL & John HANNIFORD ...the sd John SOAMES as Trustee, for £150 sold to John ROGERS...the aforementioned house & land ...at the northerly end of the Towne of Boston consisting of a double tenement yard & garden... bounded by Forestreet leading from the Great Drawbridge downe towards Charlestowne Ferry where it measureth in breadth forty five foot three inches, northeasterly by land of John FOSTER Esq. & Abigail his wf (formerly Abigail KELLOND) where it measureth in length sixty six foot three inches...southwesterly by land in the tenure & occupacon of Robert SMITH, where it measureth in length eight one foot. Witnesses: Daniel BALLARD, Abiah PAIGE, Eliezer MOODY Sr. Ack. same day. Rec. 14 June 1698.

SUFFOLK COUNTY DEEDS: (re: John ROGERS)

<18:239> - 13 Oct. 1697, John ROGERS, gent., late of Bristol, now of Boston, grantee.
<14:433> - 2 Aug. 1701, John ROGERS, mortgage.
<21:378> - 3 Sept 1703, John ROGERS, gent. formerly of Boston, now of Duxbury, grantee.
<23:25> - 3 June 1706, John ROGERS, gent. of Boston & wf Marah to John JENKINS, mariner of same house & land in north Boston, formerly Abigail HANNIFORD's.
<26:175> - 17 June 1706, John ROGERS, gent. of Boston, grantee.
<26:16> - 1 June 1711, John ROGERS, grantor.

(Note: The following are references without data to **John ROGERS**, viz: Grantor: 21:130;22:236,238; 29:215;30:109;52:196;59:155;83:105;87:46;95:197,198;105:155;115:170. Grantee: 8:256,422;9:143;33:164;47:109;83:151,152,163.)

BRISTOL COUNTY DEEDS: (re: John ROGERS)

<1:247> - 27 Oct. 1681, John ROGERS of Mount Hope Neck to four daus & son John ROGERS.
<1:100> - 15 Feb. 1688, John ROGERS & wf Hannah of Bristol to Timothy ROGERS, clerk of same.
<2:14> - 18 July 1694, John ROGERS from James & Ruth BENNET.
<4:84> - 29 Aug. 1694, John ROGERS from Silvester & Elizabeth RICHMOND.
<1:354> - 8 Apr. 1696, John ROGERS, yeoman of Bristol to dau Hannah BRADFORD & hus. Samuel.
<2:112> - 8 Apr. 1696, John ROGERS from Samuel & Hannah BRADFORD.
<1:373> - 16 Apr. 1696, John ROGERS, yeoman & wf Marah of Bristol to dau Sarah SEARLE & hus. Nathaniel.
<1:377> - 16 Apr. 1696, John ROGERS from Nathaniel & Sarah SEARLE.
<2:122> - 2 July 1697, John ROGERS, gent. of Boston to George WEBB of Little Compton (L.C.).
<2:224> - 21 June 1697, John ROGERS, yeoman late of Bristol, sells dwelling house there.
<2:250> - 3 Nov. 1697, John ROGERS, late of Bristol now of Boston, from James PAUL, mortgage; disolved 10 Sept. 1713.
<33:190> - 29 May 1701, John ROGERS, merchant of Boston, to son in law Silvester RICHMOND of Little Compton. Ack. same day. Rec. 20 Feb. 1744/5.
<4:85> - 19 Feb. 1702/3, John ROGERS of Duxbury from son in law Samuel BRADFORD.
<15:122> - 4 Jan. 1708, John ROGERS, gent. of Taunton from Nathaniel WILLIAMS, part of land given to grandson Nathaniel SEARLE Jr. <15:123>.
<6:66> - 14 May 1708, John ROGERS of Taunton, deposition made at Boston re: land in Freetown.
<15:123> - 4 Nov. 1723, John ROGERS, Esq. of Swansea to grandson Nathaniel SEARLE Jr. of L.C.
<51:158> - 23 June 1733, Division of lands. Rec. 15 Apr. 1768.

(Note: The following are references only to **John ROGERS**, viz: Grantor: <3:108,225,454;5:179;8:302;9:75,499,528;10:3;13:230,231;14:215;16:69,434. Grantee: 3:12,49,102,455;4:83,477;5:76,397,398;6:189,245,247;12:210,327;16:106,111;33:225;72:157.)

Heirs of **John ROGERS**, Esq., dec'd. <Bristol Co.Deeds 34:43>
...25 May 1733, Nathaniel SEARLE & wf Sarah the dau of John ROGERS dec'd and the children of Silvester RICHMOND by 1st wife Elizabeth dec'd, viz: William RICHMOND, gent. of Little Compton; Silvester RICHMOND, gent. of Dighton; Peleg RICHMOND, yeoman of Barrington; Peres RICHMOND, yeoman of Barrington; Dr. Ichabod RICHMOND of Dighton; Rogers RICHMOND of Little Compton; Rev. Nathaniel FISHER & wf Elizabeth of Dighton; Ephraim ATWOOD & wf Ruth of Dighton; Rev. Peleg HEATH & wf Sarah of Barrington & Mary RICHMOND of Little Compton...to Hannah BRADFORD dau of John ROGERS dec'd...their rights as heirs to land in Little Compton, Swansea, Bridgewater, Boston & Kingston. Rec. 26 Sept. 1745. (<21:406>...same day Hannah BRADFORD, widow and Nathaniel & Sarah SEARLE to all the above. Rec. 28 May 1733. <21:407>...same day Silvester RICHMOND, Esq. conveys to the above his rights in estate of John ROGERS.)

Heirs of **John ROGERS**, dec'd. <Bristol Co.Deeds 51:158>
...23 June 1733, division of lands. Ack. 5 July 1733 by Nathaniel & Elizabeth FISHER, Ephraim & Ruth ATWOOD, Sylvester RICHMOND & Ichabod RICHMOND. Ack. 6 Sept. 1750 by Peleg RICHMOND. Ack. 13 Dec. 1750 by Peres RICHMOND. Ack. 25 May 1761 by Roger(s) RICHMOND. Ack. 2 June 1761 by Mary RICHMOND. (A note reads: not ack. by William RICHMOND, Peleg & Sarah HEATH.)

Mary BELCHER of Boston MA to **John ROGERS** of Duxbury MA. <Suffolk Co.Deeds 21:378>
...3 Sept. 1703, Mary BELCHER wf of Gill BELCHER, mariner...by vertue & authority of a letter of attorney from her sd husband bearing date 26 Oct. 1702, for £133.4s current silver money of New England, sold to John ROGERS, gent., late of Boston now dwelling at Duxbury...tenement, wharfe & warehouse with the land...at the south end of Boston...bounded westerly with the Street leading to Roxbury there measuring ninety nine foot, southerly by a lane leading to the water side there measureing sixty foot, northerly by a certain creek there measureing sixty foot, easterly by the sea or saltwater there measureing seventy one foot...together with the fflatts to the sd land...downe as far as low water mark...provided...that if the above named Gill BELCHER, his attorney, exrs., admrs...shall..pay...unto the sd John ROGERS, £141,3s9d current silver money in new England or pieces of eight of Mexico Sevil or pillar coine at six shillings piece weighing full 17d weight on or before 4 Sept. 1704, then this present deed of sale...to be utterly void. Witnesses: John MARION Jr., Abigail DAVIS Jr. Ack. & Rec. same day. Mary BELCHER gave receipt for £133.4s to John ROGERS. (See below)

John ROGERS to **Deborah MAN** of Boston MA. <Suffolk Co.Deeds 26:16>
...1 June 1711, "Endorsed on an Original Deed from Mary BELCHER to John ROGERS bearing date 3 Sept. 1703"...John ROGERS, for £153.9s9d lawful money according to Act of Parliament, sold to Deborah MAN, widow...this present within written deed of mortgage & all the messuage or tenement, wharffe & warehouse with the land...in Boston, together with the Flatts adjoyning down to low water mark. Witnesses: Joseph BELKNAP Jr., Samuel TYLEY Jr. On 1 June 1711, John ROGERS was in receipt of £153.9s9d from Deborah MAN. Ack. same day.

Will of **Sylvester RICHMOND** of Dartmouth MA. <Bristol Co.PR>
<14:236>...dated 29 Dec. 1752, mentions wf **Deborah**; sons **Perez RICHMOND, William RICHMOND, Sylvester RICHMOND, Peleg RICHMOND, Ichabod RICHMOND, Rogers RICHMOND**; daus **Elizabeth, Ruth & Mary**; grandaughter **Mary PAINE**, dau of dec'd dau **Sarah**; grandson **Gamaliel RICHMOND** son of son **Peleg**; grandson **Silvester RICHMOND** son of son **Silvester**; grandson **Joshua RICHMOND** son of son **Perez**; grandson **Silvester RICHMOND** son of son **William**; grandson **Richmond LORING** son of dau **Mary**. <14:

241> Pr. 3 Dec. 1754. <16:336,337,338,339> Receipts.

Estate of **Sylvester RICHMOND** of Dighton MA. <Bristol Co.PR>
...1784...<28:207,210;35:180,200,201>

Estate of **Col. Sylvester RICHMOND** of Dighton MA. <Bristol Co.PR>
<36:1> Inventory, 1798. <36:467> Account, 1799. <36:486> Notice. <36:533-39> Dower & Division, 1798, to widow **Abigail** and children, viz: eldest son **Joseph RICHMOND**, 2d son **Sylvester RICHMOND**, 3d son **Samuel RICHMOND**, eldest dau **Betsey**, 2d dau **Sally**, 3d dau **Nancy**, daus **Sukey RICHMOND**, **Polly RICHMOND** & youngest dau **Abigail RICHMOND**. <38:411;42:204,230;148:143;149:200,147>

JOSEPH ROGERS[2] (Thomas[1])

BARNSTABLE COUNTY PROBATE: (re: ROGERS)

1696	Joseph	Eastham		2:21,22
1704	Thomas	Eastham		2:167,169,195
1714	John	Eastham	will	3:160,168
1739	John	Harwich		5:344;9:355
1742	Judah	Eastham	will	5:313;6:224
1751	James	Eastham	will	8:496,497,498;9:163
1757	Joseph	Eastham	will	9:302,303,304
1759	James	Eastham	will	9:433;14:200,201
1759	Ensign	Harwich		10:19;11:89,90;12:44,45
1760	Elkanah	Eastham		10:51;11:72,73,74,75,76,77;12:49,50,57
1760	Eleazer	Harwich	will	12:37,38,39
1760	Henry et al	Harwich		11:92,93
1761	Joseph	Harwich		9:498;10:79;11:142-4;12:220,451;13:363;14:239
1765	Isaac	Eastham	non comp	13:111,161,219
1767	Isaac	Eastham		10:187;13:315,316,318,319
1769	Martha	Harwich	will	13:462,522
1770	Crisp	Harwich	will	13:530,531,541;14:239
1773	Judah	Eastham	will	15:160;17:102,104,137,138,139
1775	Ann M.	Sandwich	will	17:275,320
1777	Mary	Eastham		15:275
1779	Thomas	Eastham	will	20:318,319
1783	Crisp	Eastham	will	22:173;23:89,90,238;25:645-7;27:111-114
1784	Eleazer	Eastham		14:199;19:108;22:71;23:299,359/61,364;26:416,455
1795	Moses	Harwich	will	24:146;27:439;30:250
1800	Moses	Harwich		22:253;25:223;30:326,342,344;34:73
1804	David	Eastham		25:315;43:450
1807	Levi	Orleans		19:218;33:110,111;35:168,169
1810	Freeman	Dennis		22:414,467;25:905;35:228;36:1;40:198;43:574
1810	James	Dennis	will	32:183;35:85
1816	Thomas	Orleans	will	32:142,227,355;38:537;40:7,101
1823	Prince	Orleans		39:93,105;42:65;44:--
1826	Ensign	Dennis		39:133;40:247;42:205;45:223,224;47:57-59
1826	Foster	Orleans		39:144;42:243;47:60,116,136;50:24;52:65
1828	Dean	Brewster	will	41:233;42:343;47:259,475;48:230
1829	Josiah	Harwich	gdn.	39:240;42:355;52:130;53:178
1834	Jonathan	Orleans	will	48:379;53:516;56:128
1837	Daniel Jr.	Brewster		48:473;54:136;57:33;61:292;62:57
1837	Bethiah et al		gdn.	46:324;56:473;59:45;61:293

Joseph HIGGINS Sr. of Eastham MA to **Jonathan Jr. & Elisha HIGGINS** of same. <S.W.Smith Coll.,1921>
<9:11>...28 May 1711, Joseph HIGGINS Sr., for Ł8 sold to Jonathan HIGGINS Jr. & Elisha HIGGINS... all that my one third part of that parcell of land lying at the barly neck in Eastham given to our deceased mother Elizabeth HIGGINS by our deceased Grandffather Leut. Joseph ROGERS the whole being eight acres more or les buted & bounded as may apeer by the origenall Grant there of with my one third part of all swamp & medow ground there to belonging as also my one third part of a small adition of land granted by the Town of Eastham. Witnesses: John MULFORD, Benjamin MYERICK. Ack. same day. Not Rec.

Joseph HIGGINS Jr. of Eastham MA to **Jonathan HIGGINS Jr.** of same. <S.W.Smith Coll., 1921>
...9 June 1714, Joseph HIGGINS Jr., marener, for Ł2.10s sold to Jonathan HIGGINS Jr., yeoman... six acres in Eastham...westerly side of the barly neck both upland & seder swamp...also all the right to my brother Beriah HIGGINS...which I bought of him...which our Honoured great Grandfather Lieut. Joseph ROGERS gave to our Honoured Grand Mother HIGGINS in his last will. Witnesses: William DYER, Joseph DOANE Jr. Ack. same day. Rec. 16 Mar. 1730/1 in Barnstable Co.Deeds 15:87.

Joseph HIGGINS Sr. of Eastham MA to **Samuel HIGGINS Jr. & Joshua TREAT.** <S.W.Smith Coll.,1921>
...26 May 1720, Joseph HIGGINS Sr., yeoman, for Ł19 sold to Samuel HIGGINS Jr., yeoman & Joshua TREAT, joyner, both of Eastham...four acres in Eastham...at Pochey Beach between the old ship and

the inermost point of sd Beach and is all that my lot or shear of medow or sedge ground, that in the Division there of fell to me for my low shear lot. Witnesses: Joseph DOANE, Joseph DOANE Jr. Ack. same day. Rec. 12 Sept. 1720 in Barnstable Co.Deeds 10:286.

MICRO #5 OF 10

Will of **James YOUNG**, yeoman of Truro MA. <Barnstable Co.PR 8:420>
...dated 2 June 1750, mentions wf **Mary**; son **Samuel YOUNG**; daus **Phebe ATWOOD** wf of Nathaniel, **Sarah COWELL** wf of Joshua, **Mary NEWCOMB** wf of Robert, **Lydia RICH** wf of John, **Hannah BUEL** wf of Reuben & **Elizabeth SMALLEY** wf of Francis; son **James YOUNG**, executor. Pr. 26 June 1750.

Crisp ROGERS et al of Eastham MA to **Judah ROGERS** of same.
...1 Apr. 1773, Crisp ROGERS & wf Deborah, Ebenezer HARDING & wf Apphia and Josiah ROGERS, for £4 5s4d sell to Judah ROGERS...our parsal of lands lying and ajoyning to the land that is John YATS/ YATES' being the lot that was set of for the sisters...bounded by land of Crisp ROGERS, Judah ROGERS & John YATES...eight acres. Witnesses: John GOULD, Joshua GOULD, Reuben MYRICK. Ack. 17 Mar. 1777 by Crisp, Ebenezer & Josiah. Not Rec.

Will of **James ROGERS**, yeoman of Eastham MA. <Barnstable Co.PR 8:496-98,9:163>
...dated 5 Mar. 1749, mentions wf **Susanna**; dau **Abigail YOUNG** (the use of part of house); son **Isaac ROGERS**; dau **Mary DAVIS**; granddaughter **Susanna ROGERS** (under 21); grandsons **Thomas ROGERS, James ROGERS & Isaac DAVIS**; sons **James ROGERS, Thomas ROGERS.** Pr. & Inventory ordered 1 Oct. 1751

Will of **Jonathan ROGERS** of Orleans MA. <Barnstable Co.PR>
<53:516>...dated 23 Feb. 1832, mentions wf **Hannah**; sons **Jonathan ROGERS Jr., Timothy ROGERS**; dau **Sally WARD** wf of Benjamin; silver headed cane to son **Jonathan**, executor. Witnesses: Gideon S. SNOW, Abner MAYO Jr., Rebecca G. HIGGINS. Pr. 29 Oct. 1834. <48:379> Affidavit. <56:128> Inventory taken 24 Dec. 1834; incl. house & one & a half acres.

Will of **Timothy ROGERS**, housewright of Orleans MA. <Barnstable Co.PR>
<81:225>...dated 15 Nov. 1852, mentions wf **Reliance** and children, viz: **Timothy ROGERS Jr., Albert C. ROGERS, Jerusha F. COLE, Reliance C. FREEMAN, Elkanah C. ROGERS** (executor), **Olive ROGERS & Ansel H. ROGERS.** Witnesses: Blossom ROGERS, Nathaniel ROBBINS, John DOANE. Notice 14 Mar. 1853. Pr. 3d Wed. Apr. 1853 & 17 May 1853. <83:187> Bond. <82:110>.

Albert C. ROGERS of Boston MA to **Alexander C. ROGERS** of Orleans MA. <Barnstable Co.Deeds 224:244>
...18 Sept. 1885, Albert C. ROGERS & wf Julia A.F. ROGERS in her own right, for $1.00 sold to Alexander C. ROGERS...piece of swamp at a place called Namacoit in Orleans...bounded by land of Levi ROGERS, Joseph W. ROGERS & Eli S. HIGGINS...also three fourths of an acre swamp in same place bounded by land of Lot HIGGINS, Eveline MAYO & Franklin GOULD. Witness: John KENDRICK. Ack. same day by Julia. Rec. 7 July 1896.

Albert C. ROGERS of Boston MA to **Albert H. ROGERS** of Medford MA. <Barnstable Co.Deeds 170:549>
...18 Aug. 1886, Albert C. ROGERS & wf Julia A.F. ROGERS in her own right, for $1.00 sold to Albert H. ROGERS, clerk...woodland in Brewster to the south of Ralph's Pond containing two & a half acres...bounded by what was Abner ROGERS' lot, woodland formerly of Godfrey SPARROWS and what was formerly Joseph AREY's. Witness: John KENDRICK. Ack. 19 Aug. 1886 by Julia. Rec. 13 Apr. 1887.

Joseph AREY of Eastham MA to **Judah ROGERS** of same. <Barnstable Co.Deeds 35:41>
...17 Apr. 1776, Joseph AREY, yeoman, for £93.6s8d sold to Judah ROGERS, yeoman...homestead land that I have not yet dispose of whareon my barn now stands...and all land & meadow owned in northerly part of Pochet Island in partnership with Joshua HIGGINS & William HIGGINS, about five acres Witnesses: Thomas PAINE, James PAINE. Ack. same day by Joseph & Hannah AREY. Rec. 1 July 1776.

Will of **Eleazer ROGERS**, yeoman of Harwich MA. <Barnstable Co.PR>
<12:37>...dated 20 Apr.1759, mentions wf **Martha**; sons **Moses ROGERS, Eleazer ROGERS**; heirs of dec'd son **Henry ROGERS**, viz: **Jesse ROGERS, Henry ROGERS & Ameriah ROGERS**; heirs of dec'd son **Insign ROGERS**, viz: **Thomas ROGERS & Insign ROGERS**; daus **Elizabeth BASSET, Marcy FULLER & Martha CHASE**; wf **Martha** & son **Moses**, executors. Witnesses: Isaac FREEMAN Jr., Mary FREEMAN, Thomas FREEMAN. <12:38> Pr. 6 May 1760. <12:39> Inventory, 16 May 1760; Division of real estate, 22 May 1760

Will of **Moses ROGERS**, yeoman of Harwich MA. <Barnstable Co.PR>
<27:439>...dated 23 May 1791, mentions wf **Elizabeth**; to my little grandson **James KENWRICK** son to my dau **Mercy ROGERS**, one acre upland; sons **Abner ROGERS, John ROGERS, Moses ROGERS, Aaron ROGERS, Daniel ROGERS, Mulford ROGERS, Enos ROGERS & Ruben ROGERS**; dau **Mary ROGERS**; my five daus **Martha CAHOON, Betty KENWRICK, Elizabeth SMALL & Mercy ROGERS**; sons **John & Mulford**, executors. Witnesses: Simeon BEARS, Patience NICKERSON, Nathan BASSETT. <24:146> Pr. 7 Apr. 1795. <30:250> Inventory taken 15 Apr. 1795; total real estate, £409.

Ephraim BAYLEY of Holden MA to **Abner ROGERS** of Harwich MA. <Worcester Co.Deeds 83:138>
...27 Sept. 1779, Ephraim BAYLEY, taylor, for £800 sold to Abner ROGERS...fifty acres in Holden ...that I purchased of my Honoured Mother 20 July 1778. Sophia BAYLEY consents. Rec. 26 Jan. 1780

Abner ROGERS et al of Holden MA to **Jonathan NICHOLS.** <Worcester Co.Deeds 110:434>
...1 Mar. 1791, Abner ROGERS, yeoman & wf Doly, David NICHOLS, William NICHOLS, Levi NICHOLS,

Thaddeus NICHOLS and Betty NICHOLS, spinster, sold to Jonathan NICHOLS, miller...all rights in grist mill & saw mill in Holden...owned by our honoured Father William NICHOLS late of Holden dec'd. Ack. 2 Mar. 1791 by all. Rec. 4 Mar. 1791. <110:435>...1 Mar. 1791, all the above sell to Thaddeus NICHOLS...rights to 112 acres in Holden owned by dec'd father William NICHOLS...sd Thaddeus to have the privilege of turning the water from the Mill pond. Ack. & Rec. as above. Miriam NICHOLS widow of William, for Ł100 paid by her above children, releases her rights in 112 acres.

WORCESTER COUNTY DEEDS: (re: ROGERS)

<128:77> - 1796, Abner ROGERS from Stephen H. BINNEY.
<128:519> - 1796, Abner ROGERS from Holden Inhabitants.
<276:22> - 1830, Moses ROGERS to Nathan ROGERS.
<305:556> - 1835, Abner ROGERS from Moses CROSBY.
<334:78> - 1838, Abner ROGERS to Nathan ROGERS.
<23:25> - 1838, Abner ROGERS et al to Judah ROGERS.
<21:205> - 1839, Abner ROGERS et al to Judah ROGERS.

MICRO #6 OF 10

Estate of **John ROGERS**, yeoman of Harwich MA. <Barnstable Co.PR>
<5:344> Inventory exhibited 5 Apr. 1739, taken by Kenelm WINSLOW, Nathaniel GOOLD, Stephen COLE; incl. sword; silver bowed spectacles; ten acres grain in the ground; wearing apparrell of his dec'd son who died sence ye father; dwelling house, barn & 20 or 22 acres upland adjoining; 50 acres upland between ye sd homestead & Ebenezer ROGERS' house; 20 acres woodland between Judah ROGERS & Ebenezer ROGERS; 10 acres woodland near KENWICK's; meadows at Strong Island & Sampsons Island; one eighth of cedar swamp by YATES; one fourth cedar swamp in Eleazer ROGERS' hand; half a lott at Yarmouth; Indian girl. <9:355> Receipt 26 Sept. 1758, Samuel TRACEY of Norwich by virtue of Power of Attorney executed by **Levi BUMPUS** of Norwich, grandson to **John ROGERS** dec'd, have received of **Joseph ROGERS**, yeoman of Yarmouth and gdn. to the sd **Levi**, seven pounds ten shillings & eleaven pence as **Levi**'s share. Witnesses: David GORHAM, Benjamin GORHAM.

Estate of **Benjamin ROGERS** of Kingston MA. <Plymouth Co.PR #17147>
<10:522> Letter/Bond 3 Feb. 1747, John BREWSTER of Kingston app'td admr. Sureties: Judah HALL, Wrastling BREWSTER. Witnesses: Joseph HOLMES, Job HALL. <11:292> Petition (no date), of widow **Phebe ROGERS**, representing that her husband died leaving her with six small children & asks for an allowance; petition granted. <11:159> Inventory taken 23 Feb. 1747 by Job HALL, Joseph HOLMES, Josiah WATERMAN; total real estate, Ł550; total estate, Ł746.7.

PLYMOUTH COUNTY DEEDS: (re: Benjamin ROGERS)

<25:24> - , Benjamin & John ROGERS to William COOKE.
<28:179> - 26 Mar. 1733/4, B.R., labourer of Plymouth mortgages to Isaac LOTHROP, land in Kingston that he bought of Jonathan BRYANT on 29 Dec. 1729; mortgage released 29 Nov. 1760 on payment of principal & interest by John BREWSTER, admr. Ack. same day. Rec. 9 pr. 1734.
<46:205> - 29 Nov. 1760, John BREWSTER admr. sells the above to Wrestling BREWSTER. Ack. 2 Feb. 1761. Rec. 13 Feb. 1761.
<90:155> - 28 Jan. 1801, Benjamin ROGERS, shipwright of Marshfield & wf Rachel, to John THOMAS, land in Marshfield he bought of Amos ROGERS. Rec. 16 May 1801.
<90:217> - 19 May 1801, Benjamin ROGERS, shipwright of Marshfield & Samuel JONES to Mercy RANDALL, widow of Pembroke, meadow in Pembroke. Rec. 23 June 1801.
<105:5> - 11 Mar. 1806, Benjamin ROGERS, yeoman of Marshfield to Thomas ROGERS 4th, shipwright of same, land in Marshfield. Wf Rachel releases dower. Rec. 16 Oct 1806.

<119:16> - 1812, B.R. to Samuel HATCH.
<125:206> - 1815, B.R. et al to Charles JONES.
<134:89> - 1818, B.R., grantor.
<147:168> - 1823, B.R. to Asa LAPHAM.
<151:165> - 1824, B.R. to Elias MAGOUN.
<177:15> - 1832, B.R. to George LEONARD.
<182:205> - 1834, B.R. to Phillips EVERSON.
<216:210> - 1846, B.R. to Joel HATCH.
<216:213> - 1846, B.R. to Israel HATCH.

Will of **Benjamin ROGERS**, yeoman of Pembroke MA. <Plymouth Co.PR #17148>
<88:288>...dated 14 Mar. 1846, mentions wf **Rachel**; $1.00 to the following children & heirs with balance of estate to wife, viz: sons **Benjamin ROGERS Jr., Aloin ROGERS**; chil. of dec'd dau **Rachel HATCH**; son **Harvey ROGERS**; chil. of dec'd son **Prince ROGERS**; dau **Mary CHURCH**. <2:78H,7:113V> Pr. June 1846, John FORD app'td exr. <88:330> Inventory taken 19 June 1846; total real estate, $2965. <90:53> Account.

Will of **Joseph ROGERS** of Marshfield MA. <Plymouth Co.PR #17179>
<47:459>...dated 25 Oct. 1815, mentions wf **Elizabeth**; son **Abraham ROGERS**; five daus **Mary KIRBY, Anna WING, Esther DILLINGHAM, Sarah GIFFORD, Edy LITTLE**; dau **Elizabeth ROGERS**; son **Stephen ROGERS** <47:460> Pr. 5 Feb. 1816. <157:400> Petition adm. d.b.n.; Bond & Letter.

Eliphalet NICKERSON & Ruth MAYO of Eastham MA to **Judah ROGERS** of same. <Barnstable Co.Deeds>
<45:174>...23 Aug. 1784, Eliphalet NICKERSON, yeoman & Ruth MAYO, for Ł4.8s sell to Judah ROGERS,

yeoman...land in Eastham, being part of the land that came to us by our mother Prissilar/Priscilla NICKERSON of Harwich decest that was formerly Mr. John ROGERS of Harwich desed/dec'd...bounded by land of Reuben NICKERSON & sd Judah ROGERS...six acres. Witnesses: Solomon FREEMAN, Desire FREEMAN. Ack. same day. Rec. 3 Apr. 1793.

Eliphalet NICKERSON of Eastham MA to **Judah ROGERS** of same. <Barnstable Co.Deeds 45:174>
...23 Sept. 1784, Eliphalet NICKERSON, yeoman, for Ł42.10s sold to Judah ROGERS, yeoman...land lying to the eastward of my honored father Ruben NICKERSON's homestead land...eight & a quarter acres, bounded by land of sd Judah...also piece of fresh meadow to southward of the main creek between sd Judah's & sd creek. Witnesses: Solomon FREEMAN, Solomon FREEMAN Jr. Ack. same day. Rec 3 Apr. 1793.

Eliphalet NICKERSON of Orrington MA/ME to Judah ROGERS & Jonathan KENDRICK Jr.
...26 Apr. 1792, Eliphalet NICKERSON of Orrington, Hancock Co., Mass. <now Maine>, yeoman, for L4 10s sold to Judah ROGERS & Jonathan KENDRICK Jr., yeomen of Eastham...all his lot in Eastham... nine acres, bounded by land of sd Judah. Witnesses: Simeon FOWLER, George GARDNER. Ack. 23 June 1792, Hancock Co. by Eliphalet. Not Rec.

Guardianship of Child of **Joseph ROGERS**, dec'd of Harwich MA. <Barnstable Co.PR>
...17 Mar. 1760, **Crisp ROGERS**, yeoman of Harwich app'td gdn. of **Apphia ROGERS**, minor dau of dec'd

---

Estate of **Joseph ROGERS**, mariner of Harwich MA. <Barnstable Co.PR>
Division of real estate, 3 Dec. 1770, by Solomon PEPPER, Isaac SPARROW, Thomas TWINING; one third set off to the widow **Abigail ELDREDGE**...she to receive land in Chatham bounded by land of Richard SPARROW & widow Elizabeth ROGERS.

Will of **Ebenezer HARDING** of Tolland MA. <Hampden Co.PR>
...26 Dec. 1827...weak in body...mentions wf **Apphia**, her thirds; to grandsons **William MINER, Timothy MINER & Thomas MINER Jr.**, $50.00 ea. when they reach 22; remainder of estate to son **Timothy HARDING**. Witnesses: Roger HARRISON, Harley MOORE, Lucina HARRISON.

Estate of **Elkanah ROGERS**, yeoman of Eastham MA. <Barnstable Co.PR>
<10:51>...4 Mar. 1760, widow **Mercy ROGERS** app'td admx. <11:72> Guardianship, 4 Mar. 1760, **Crisp ROGERS**, yeoman of Eastham app'td gdn. of **Elkanah ROGERS**, <11:73-77> widow **Mercy ROGERS** app'td gdn. of **Martha ROGERS, Elkanah ROGERS, Joshua ROGERS, Ebenezer ROGERS & Relyance ROGERS.** <12:49> Inventory taken 20 Mar. 1760 by Richard SPARROW, Josiah SEARS, Seth KNOWLES; incl. homestead, Ł55.6s8d; middle, upper, lower & east fields, Ł98.15s; Rock Harbour land, Ł15; ceder swamp, Ł8; wood land, Ł38.10s; Rock Harbour meadow, Ł13.6s8d; meadow at the flats, Ł21. <12:50> Division of real estate, 26 Mar. 1760, by Richard SPARROW, Seth KNOWLES, Josiah SEARS, Thomas FREEMAN & William TWINNEY, among **Crisp ROGERS**, his share in partnership with the estate of the dec'd, the widow **Marcy/Mercy ROGERS** and children; viz: to **Crisp ROGERS**, wood land in Harwich bounded by land of Moses ROGERS, land purchased of Nathaniel DOAN agent to the Quakers, land bought of Prince SNOW, land of Thomas KENWRICK, the Sipsons Range and the Indian land...also land laid out to Joseph ROGERS & Nathan YOUNG, both dec'd, bounded by land of Solomon KENWRICK...also meadow in Eastham at a place called the Boat Meadow bounded by Twinnings Meadow, Sparrows flatt and Jonathan MAYO's meadow...also meadow at Broad Creek bounded by Desire DOANE's meadow...also one third part of a meadow by Broad Creek in partnership with Richard SPARROW & others...also one sixteenth part of the meadow at Strong Island except six acres...also one eighth part of cedar swamp...also one sixteenth part of ceder swamp by Moses ROGERS' and in sd division Daniel COLE's part...to widow **Mercy ROGERS**, lands incl. one third of homestead bounded by land that was Henry YOUNG's and Stephen SPARROW's...also the westerly end of the house beginning at the middle of the fore door through ye middle of the chimney to the middle of the back window from top to bottom...and to the following children, viz: eldest son **Nathaniel ROGERS**, 2d son **Josiah ROGERS**, son **Ebenezer ROGERS**, 4th son **Joshua ROGERS**, youngest son **Elkanah ROGERS**, eldest dau **Reliance ROGERS**, youngest dau **Martha ROGERS.** <12:57> Account 31 Mar. 1760, of admx.; Paid to: Dr. BREED, Dr. FESSENDEN, Dr. SMITH, Thankful SNOW, Nathaniel CROSBY, Willard KNOWLES, Rebecca SMITH, Cornelius KNOWLES, Mary LEWIS, Joseph CROCKER, Sarah COLE, Nathaniel FREEMAN, Zaccheus HIGGINS, Seth KNOWLES, Samuel KNOWLES, Jonathan COBB, Isaac FOSTER, Crisp ROGERS, Richard PAINE, Kenelm WINSLOW Jr.; necessaries to the widow having small children, Ł20.

Estate of **Ebenezer BURGIS**, yeoman of Yarmouth MA. <Barnstable Co.PR>
<6:408>...10 Apr.1745, widow **Mercy BURGIS** app'td admx. <8:300> Inventory taken 7 May 1745 by Ralph CHAPMAN, Joseph CROSBY, Daniel HALL; incl. homestead, Ł200. <8:301> Account 18 July 1745 of admx.; the estate was indebted to: John DILLINGHAM Jr., Mr. DENNIS, Paul RIDER, Mathew GAGE, Timothy ROBBINS, Thomas WINSLOW, Benjamin THACHER, John OKILLEY, Dr. Samuel HOWES, Ebenezer SEARS, David BURGIS, Joseph PADDOCK, Dr. HERCY, Nathaniel STONE, Samuel HOWES, Daniel SEARS, Christopher CROWELL, Isaac CHAPMAN, Mr. SMITH, Theophilus CROSBY, Deborah KENWICK, Ebenezer HALL, Joseph HALL Samuel SEARS, Ralph CHIPMAN, Daniel HALL, John ELDRED, BASSET, GODFREE; necessaries to the widow to support her self & family, Ł45.

MICRO #7 OF 10

Will of **Jonathan GODFREY**, yeoman of Chatham MA. <Barnstable Co.PR>
<13:114>...dated 7 Mar. 1765...to wf **Mercy**, the improvement of one half of estate...to son **Thomas GODFREY**, the half lot of land in Chatham that lays in partnership with Thomas & Joshua ATKINS,

also my best coat & waist-coat & breches...to son **Thomas GODFREY**, heirs of son **Jeptha GODFREY**, dec'd and daus **Hannah ROGERS, Mercy ROGERS, Ruth MYRICK, Lydia SMITH, Mehitable HAMILTON & Anna FREEMAN** and heirs of dec'd dau **Berbary/Barbara YOUNG**, to be equally divided among them the whole of my lands; son **Thomas** & dau **Mehitable** to share pew or mansion seat; son **Thomas** and son in law **Nathaniel HAMILTON**, executors. Witnesses: Nehemiah HARDING, Thomas HARDING, Thomas HAMILTON Jr. <13:125> Inventory taken 20 May 1765 by Samuel TAYLOR, John HAWES, James COVELL; incl. pew in Chatham Meetinghouse, £4; homestead, £100; wood land, £5.6s8d; meadow & marsh land, £10.13s4d. <12:479> Account 6 May 1766 of **Thomas GODFREY**, exr.; Paid to: James COVELL, Richard GOULD, Samuel TAYLOR, Joshua GREY, John HAWES, John SEARS, Jerusha GODFREY, Nathan BASSET, Constable HAWES, Samuel HINCKLEY, Jeremiah ELDREDGE, James KNOWLES, Nathaniel STONE, Esq., Reuben RIDER, Nehemiah DOANE, David GORHAM.

MAYFLOWER DESCENDANT: (re: John YEATS/YATES)

<15:190> - 12 May 1705, Will of Thomas PAINE of Eastham, names three eldest chil. of dau Mary COLE wf of Israel, viz: James ROGERS, Mary COLE, Abigail YEATS.
<8:156> - 27 June 1705, ...land bounded by John YATES in Harwich.
<16:218> - 4 June 1717, John YATES of Harwich bought land in Harwich in Namacoik Neck from Isaac LARRAME Jr., Indian of Harwich.
<16:220> - 9 Dec. 1731, Joseph ROGERS of Eastham sold land in Harwich at Namacoick Neck to Nathaniel GOULD, yeoman, Abigail YATES & Mary MAKER, widows, of Harwich.
<15:205> - 2 Aug. 1744, Thomas MAYO of Eastham & John YEATS, yeoman of Harwich, divide 19th lot at Pochey Flats. Ack. same day.
<9:239> - 27/29 May 1747, Jonathan KENWICK, Crisp ROGERS, Elkanah ROGERS & John YATES, on behalf of the heirs of John YATES dec'd, yeomen of Harwich and Amos KNOWLES & Elkanah ROGERS, yeomen of Eastham...
<19:84> - 13 July 1751, Dr. Jonathan KENWRICK of Harwich sold land in Harwich bounded by J.YATES
<16:9> - 18 May 1761, Thomas & Elizabeth MAYO of Eastham sold his half of land divided with John YATES on 2 Aug. 1744. Witness: Asa MAYO.
<17:174> - 16 Apr. 1762, John YEATS/YATES of Harwich sells to Paul HIGGINS of same.
<18:99> - 3 May 1774, John YATES of Eastham sold land at Namacoit.
<18:100> - 11 June 1779, John YATES of Eastham sells 7 acres. Abigail YATES signs. Ack. 3 Jan. 1781 by John.
<19:87> - 14 Dec. 1781, John HIGGINS & wf Sarah of Eastham sell to Thomas AREY of same, land at Namecoyck, being that parcel that came to Asa MAYO's chil. by their Grandfather John YATES dec'd.
<19:87> - 19 Mar. 1782, John GOULD & wf Apphia of Eastham to Thomas ARY of same, two acres at Namecoyk Neck bounded on ranges of Jonathan KENWICK, Jonathan MAYO and land that was Asa MAYO's.

John YATES Jr. to **John GOULD.** <original, in poss. of Isaiah LINNELL of S. Orleans MA, 1910> ...20 Mar. 1782, John YATES Jr., for 6s sold to John GOULD...my part of a seder swamp in Eastham in a neck of land called Naimeacoik itt being one eighth of a fifth of sd swamp which was laid out in the devision to Marcy YATES of Eastham.

Will of **Judah ROGERS** of Eastham MA. <Barnstable Co.PR>
<5:313>...dated 28 Mar. 1738/9, mentions children, viz: **Judah ROGERS, Hannah ROGERS, Mary COLE & Patience MAYO**; father **John ROGERS**; brother **Elezar/Eleazer ROGERS**; son in law **Gershom COLE**; mentions land held by his father's will. Pr. 8 Nov. 1739. <6:224> Inventory presented 29 Apr. 1742.

Will of **John PHINNEY Sr.**, weaver of Barnstable MA. <Barnstable Co.PR>
<3:595>...dated 19 Apr. 1718, mentions unnamed wife and children, viz: **Mary EASTLAND, Mercy CROCKER, Reliance MORTON, John PHINNEY** (executor), **Joseph PHINNEY, Thomas PHINNEY, Ebenezer PHINNEY, Samuel PHINNEY, Benjamin PHINNEY & Jonathan PHINNEY.** Witnesses: Moody RUSSELL, Martha RUSSELL, James PAINE. <3:596> Pr. 18 June 1719. <3:597> Inventory taken 9 Mar. 1718/9; total estate, L116.14.0.

Will of **Benjamin PHINNEY**, yeoman of Barnstable MA. <Barnstable Co.PR>
<9:389>...dated 24 Mar. 1758, mentions wf **Elizabeth** and children, viz: **Seth PHINNEY** (executor), **Temperance FULLER & Melatiah;** to Lusannah DIMOCK, 20s (no relationship stated); to my five grandsons descending of **Barnabas PHINNEY & Zaccheus PHINNEY**, viz: **Ichabod PHINNEY, Benjamin PHINNEY, Timothy PHINNEY, Barnabas PHINNEY & Zaccheus PHINNEY.** <9:390> Pr. 2 Oct. 1758. Inventory taken 19 July 1758.

Estate of **Barnabas PHINNEY**, yeoman of Barnstable MA. <Barnstable Co.PR>
<7;57>...12 Jan. 1747, Benjamin PHINNEY, yeoman of Barnstable. <7:67> Guardianship 3 Apr. 1748, Samuel CHURCHEL of Plymouth app'td gdn. of **Ichabod PHINNEY**, minor son. <8:211> Inventory taken 26 Jan. 1747.

Estate of **Zaccheus PHINNEY.** <Barnstable Co.PR>
<7:216>...27 Mar. 1751, Seth HAMLIN, gent. and widow **Susanna PHINNEY**, both of Barnstable, app'td admrs. <8:512> Inventory taken 1 Apr. 1751 by Barnabas CHIPMAN, Isaac FULLER, Jedediah JONES, all of Barnstable. <9:171> Account of admrs., 1 May 1753.

Will of **Ebenezer PHINNEY**, yeoman of Barnstable MA. <Barnstable Co.PR>
<9:122>...dated 26 Nov. 1754, mentions children: **Samuel PHINNEY & Ebenezer PHINNEY** (executors),

Mary DAVIS, David PHINNEY, Mehitable HIGGINS & Rebecca DAVIS; grandaughter **Lydia PHINNEY.** <9:123> Pr. 10 Jan. 1755.

Will of **John DAVIS** of Falmouth MA. <Barnstable Co.PR 4:507> ...dated 10 Jan. 1728, mentions Susannah PHINNEY, formerly LINNEL, the wf of Ebenezer PHINNEY of Barnstable. ("long will, many legatees" - however the will is not transcribed)

Will of **David PHINNEY,** yeoman of Barnstable MA. <Barnstable Co.PR> <27:294>...dated 1 July 1789, mentions wf **Mary;** to grandson **David LEWIS** two third parts of my pine or salt meadow lying at Sandy Neck that I bought of my honored father **Ebenezer PHINNEY** dec'd by one deed dated 2 Feb. 1750...grandson **Peter LEWIS** to have the other third; dau **Sarah GORHAM.** <24:111> Pr. 10 Dec. 1793.
(Note: Written in pencil under the above are: "dau **Mary TAYLOR;** three grandchildren, viz: **Seth TAYLOR, Elizabeth Phinney TAYLOR & Susanna TAYLOR**", however it is not clear if these names were included in the will.)

Will of **Deacon John PHINNEY,** yeoman of Barnstable MA. <Barnstable Co.PR> <6:510>...dated 29 Nov. 1735, mentions wf **Sarah** & son **Jabez PHINNEY** (executors); sons **John PHINNEY, Thomas PHINNEY;** five daus **Elisabeth, Hannah, Sarah, Patience & Martha**...reconing what each one hath already had. <6:511> Pr. 15 Jan. 1746. <6:513> Inventory taken 11 Feb. 1746/7.

MICRO #8 OF 10

Will of **Roger GOODSPEED,** yeoman of Barnstable MA. <Barnstable Co.PR> <27:51>...dated 13 Dec. 1781, mentions wf **Hannah;** sons **Isaac GOODSPEED & Joseph GOODSPEED Jr.** (executors); grandson **Thomas GOODSPEED;** grandaughter **Puella GOODSPEED;** to dau **Elisabeth WINSLOW,** all my wife's wearing apparel after my wife's death. Witnesses: Solomon BODFISH Jr., Benjamin LOMBARD, Rebecca ADAMS. <24:100> Pr. 18 Apr. 1791.

Will of **Jabez PHINNEY,** yeoman of Barnstable MA. <Barnstable Co.PR> <17:472>...dated 20 May 1771, mentions wf **Jane** and children, viz: **Joseph PHINNEY & John PHINNEY** (executors), **Mary PHINNEY, Anna SHAW & Hannah CROSBY.** <17:474> Pr. 24 Dec. 1776. <17:475> Appraisers app'td, 13 Dec. 1776. <17:476> Inventory taken 6 Mar. 1777.

Will of **Eleazer NICHOLS** of Freetown MA. <Bristol Co.PR> <41:541>...dated 27 Sept. 1805, mentions unnamed wife (executrix), son **John NICHOLS,** apprentice Joseph SEARS and "my dear children" (unnamed). Pr. 5 Nov. 1805, by **Elizabeth NICHOLS,** exx. <42:6> Inventory taken 1 Feb. 1806; sworn to 6 Feb. 1806 by exx. <42:455> Account 3 Feb. 1807, by exx. <109:82> Order to post notice, 4 Feb. 1806.

Will of **Elizabeth DURFEE** of Freetown MA. <Bristol Co.PR 100:201; Durfee Fam.(1902) 1:248,250> ...dated 3 Mar. 1852...being of great age...to son **William NICHOLS,** $1.00; to grandson **Eleazer NICHOLS,** $1.00; remainder of estate to dau **Chloe HILLS/HILL** wf of David; son in law **David HILLS,** executor. Witnesses: E.P. HATHEWAY, Nicholas HATHEWAY, John N. HILL. Pr. 3 Jan. 1854.
(Note: Elizabeth (Holmes)(Nichols) DURFEE was the widow of Eleazer NICHOLS (above) and Col. Joseph DURFEE whose will was dated 17 Apr. 1834, Fall River.)

Will of **Chloe HILL,** widow of Freetown MA. <Bristol Co.PR> ...dated 8 May 1860...being feeble in body...to dau **Elizabeth NICHOLS,** the westerly side of the house...also land bounded by land of Hermon PEIRCE & Howland PEIRCE...to son **Henry L. HILL** & dau **Clarissa E. MALONY,** $5.00 each...to sons **John N. HILL & David B. HILL,** all other property; son **David,** executor. Witnesses: Margaret NICHOLS, Guilford HATHAWAY, Thomas G. NICHOLS.

John NICHOLS et al to **Joseph DURFEE,** all of Freetown MA. <Bristol Co.Deeds 109:380> ...4 Nov. 1820, John NICHOLS, William NICHOLS, Abigail DEAN and Chloe HILL wf of David, for $240 sold to Joseph DURFEE, Esq...all our rights in land & buildings (as per 106:37). Rec. 25 Apr 1821

Guardianship of **Thomas PHINNEY,** non comp, of Barnstable MA. <Barnstable Co.PR> <21:249> Petition 13 Apr. 1783...We the subscribers Relatives & Friends to **Thomas PHINNEY,** yeoman are of the opinion that the sd Thomas is lunatick and...incapable of taking care of his person, family & estate & that it is necessary a Guardian should be appointed. Signed by: Eleazer SCUDDER Jacob LEWIS, James LUMBARD, Lemuel LUMBARD, Hercules HODGES & Lemuel BEARSE. On 22 Apr. 1783, the Selectmen of Barnstable, Isaac HINCKLEY & Joseph DAVIS, were directed to investigate; they agreed a guardian was necessary. <22:16> On 12 May 1783, Lemuel BEARS, yeoman of Barnstable was app'td gdn. <22:49> Inventory taken 13 June 1783 by Lemuel LUMBARD, Eleazer SCUDDER & Jacob LEWIS; total real estate, ₤391.3s4d; total estate, ₤432.6s4d.

Will of **Thomas PHINNEY,** yeoman of Barnstable MA. <Barnstable Co.PR> <23:439>...dated 24 Apr. 1780...being far advanced in years...to wf **Reliance** in lieu of her dower the use & improvment of all my estate...to daus **Lydia HODGE & Sarah HINKLEY** and the chil. of my late dau **Patience BEARSE**...the five eight parts of my peice of meadow...in Barnstable with the same proportion of the beach adjoining the whole lying to the southard of the River that runs from Clay Hill towards Plain Hill...also all personal estate...to son **Isaac PHINEY/PHINNEY**...one half part of the remainder of all my real estate...reserving to my other children & grandchildren the whole of the cranberries that may from time to time grow on my beach...also one half of my wearing apparel he the sd **Isaac** to pay my grandaughter **Lydia HODGE** ten Spanish milled dollars.. to my two grandsons **Solomon PHINEY & Paul PHINEY**...the remainder of my real estate...half of my wearing apparel...they paying to their sister **Jenny** ten Spanish milled Dollars at her arrial at the age of eighteen...they also paying to my grandaughter **Lydia HODGE** five dollars like money... to my grandaughter **Lydia HODGE** one cow...in lieu of the twenty Spanish milled dollars ordered to be paid by my son **Isaac** and my two grandsons **Solomon & Paul** and notwithstanding what is above written my will is that instead of their paying the same to the sd **Lydia** they shall...pay the abovesaid sum...to my grandson **Prince HINCKLEY**...in two months after my wife's decease; son in law **Silvanus HINCKLEY**, executor. Witnesses: Edward BACON, Jacob LEWIS, Benjamin LUMBARD. <23:442> Codicil 28 Oct. 1780, adding as executors son **Isaac PHINEY** & grandson **Nymphas HINCKLEY**. Pr. 19 July 1784, son **Isaac PHINEY** app'td admr., the others having refused on 12 July. <23:443-46> Agreement of heirs, 17 July 1784, between **Isaac PHINNEY** of Granville, Annapolis co., N.S. the only surviving son and Eleazer SCUDDER of Barnstable, attorney to **Solomon PHINNEY & James HATHEWAY** of Barnstable on behalf of **Paul PHINNEY & Jane PHINEY**, the sd **Solomon, Paul & Jane** being the children of **Eli PHINNEY** the eldest son of sd dec'd on the one part...and **Silvanus HINCKLEY** & wf Sarah, **Harculas HODGERS/Hercules HODGES** & wf Lydia for themselves & their dau **Lydia**, **Prince HINCKLEY** for himself and **Lemuel BEARSE Jr.** on behalf of **Isaac, James, Lemuel Jr. & Abigail BEARSE** the children of **Patience BEARSE** of Barnstable on the other part...are all fully persuaded that the ad **Thomas PHINNEY** at the time of making and signing the sd paper (will) was not of such sound mind and memory as to be able to dispose of his estate...and untill the day of his death was so impared in his understanding as to make it necessary to appoint a Guardian...whereof great expence has been incured and the personal estate much diminished...Witnesses: Jacob LEWIS, Davis LOMBARD. <23:446> Inventory taken 20 July 1784 by Joseph PHINNEY, Jacob LEWISS & John PHINNEY, of Barnstable; total real estate, Ł391,3s4d; total estate, Ł422.7s10d. <23:447-8> Division of real estate 2 Aug. 1784, to son **Isaac PHINNEY**, part of dec'd's homested bounded by land of Solomon HAMBLIN and land Prince HINCKLEY lately bought of the sd dec'd, (reserving to **Solomon & Paul PHINNEY** the other half); also land & meadow at the Hill bounded by land of Lemuel BEARSE, Jesse LEWISS, Lemuel LUMBART and the Chequaquit River; also one eighth beach meadow; also woodland, part of the 2d Division of the late common lands in Barnstable bounded by woodland of Lot GAGE, Samuel SCUDDER and lott the sd dec'd lately gave to his dau **Lydia HODGERS/HODGES**; also woodland bounded by land of Solomon HAMBLIN, Harculas HODGERS/Hercules HODGES, Prince HINCKLEY & heirs of Joseph LUMBART...to **Solomon PHINNEY & Paul PHINNEY** the grandchildren of sd dec'd, part of homested bounded by land of Joseph & John PHINNEY and heirs of **Eli PHINNEY**; also land & meadow called Chequaquit meadow bounded by land of **Lemuel BEARSE** & Jacob LEWISS; also two eighths part of the Beach meadow; also woodland, part of the 3d Division of the sd Commons bounded by woodland of Lot GAGE, Eleazer SCUDDER, heirs of John LINNEL and the way leading from Joseph PHINNEY's to Highanus/Hyannis...to **Sarah HINCKLY, Lydia HODGERS/HODGES** and the chil of **Patience BEARSE** dec'd, five eights of the beach meadow with five eights of the beach adjoining.

Heirs of **Paul PHINNEY** dec'd of Barnstable MA to **Benjamin LEWIS.** <Barnstable Co.Deeds 21:238> ...10 Jan. 1839, Susan BAXTER, Thomas WILLIAMS & Lydia WILLIAMS of Providence RI, Enoch P. BEARSE & Charlotte BEARSE of New Bedford, Harvey HAMLIN & wf Lois, Leander JONES & wf Deborah and Prince HATHAWAY, of Barnstable, for $300.00 sold to Benjamin LEWIS, yeoman of same...all the right, title & interest which we are entitled as heirs to the personal & real estate of Paul PHINNEY dec'd. Witnesses: Samuel ASHLEY, Resolved W. CADY, James MUNROE, Thomas H. JONES, Zeno SCUDDER.

Solomon PHINNEY of Barnstable MA to **Benjamin HATHAWAY** of same. <Barnstable Co.Deeds 1:291> ...23 June 1808, Solomon PHINNEY & wf Anna the dau of Samuel LINNEL, for $17.50 quit claim to Benjamin HATHAWAY, yeoman...our quarter part of salt meadow in Barnstable...in common & undivided with Davis CROCKER who owns one half.

References to the name **HODGES** in Barnstable Co.Deeds, viz: 2:184 (1802); 1:133 (1803); 1:122 (1806); 1:182 (1818); 4:270 (1818); 2:162 (1819); 3:65 (1828); 27:280 (1841); 32:196 (1843).

George CABOT of Beverly MA to **Asa JENKINS & Lemuel SNOW** of Barnstable. <Barnstable Co.Deeds 1:21> ...6 Sept. 1791, George CABOT, Esq., for Ł36 sold to Asa JENKINS & Lemuel SNOW, yeomen...six acre salt meadow & upland in Barnstable near Childs' dock...bounded by estate of Col. James OTIS dec'd and meadow of Abner & Goodspeed JONES and land I sold this day to Hezekiah MERCHENT. Wf Elizabeth CABOT releases dower. Witnesses: I. LOWELL, Jonathan JACKSON. Rec. 13 Sept. 1791.

Abner JONES of Barnstable MA to **Lemuel SNOW & Asa JENKINS** of same. <Barnstable Co.Deeds 1:24> ...26 Apr. 1790, Abner JONES, yeoman, for Ł4.10s sold to Lemuel SNOW & Asa JENKINS, yeomen...one eight part of a dock, upland & meadow adjoining with a true use of a cart way through gates & bars from the County road to sd dock along the land formally Robert PARKER's now in possession of the Town of Barnstable...was formally Hamlin's but now is called Child's dock and in common & undivided with James OTIS, Esq. heirs & others...containing three acres...bounded by land of Hezekiah MERCHANT, sd Lemuel SNOW & Asa JENKINS. Wf Anna JONES releases dower. Witnesses: Seth CARSLEY, Jared FULLER. Ack. "20 Feb. 1800". Rec. 1 Jan. 1791 in 33:62.

Lemuel SNOW of Barnstable MA to **Abigail CROCKER** of same. <Barnstable Co.Deeds 3:174;73:247> ...17 Aug. 1813, Lemuel SNOW, for $190.00 sold to Abigail CROCKER...21 acre wood land bounded by the old Meeting-way and land of William CROCKER, Joseph BLISH, Jabez HOWLAND, Almon GOODSPEED, Prince HINCKLEY & Joseph BLISH Jr. Witnesses: Jonas WHITMAN, Christopher LOVELL. Ack. 18 Aug. 1814. Rec. 17 Sept. 1814.

Lemuel SNOW of Barnstable MA to **Reuben FISH** of same. <Barnstable Co.Deeds 4:197;73:243> ...28 July 1814, Lemuel SNOW, yeoman, for $20.00 sold to Reuben FISH, yeoman...one quarter of 12 acre meadow in Barnstable...bounded by land of Joseph PARKER, Ebenezer CROCKER and heirs of Shubal HAMBLEN & Simeon JENKINS. Wf Lydia SNOW releases dower. Witnesses: Jabez HOWLAND, Daniel PARKER. Ack. 21 July 1814. Rec. 7 Sept. 1814.

Lemuel SNOW of Barnstable MA to **David PARKER** of same. <Barnstable Co.Deeds 4:215;73:141> ...9 Feb. 1814, Lemuel SNOW, yeoman, for $1500.00 sold to David PARKER, yeoman...all my homestead lands, partly cleared & partly woodland, in Barnstable on each side the Country road called Falmouth road & contains 60 acres...with my dwelling house...which I purchased of Joseph HOWLAND, David HOWLAND, Jonathan HOWLAND & Rachel JENKINS as per their several deeds...reserving to my self...until the last day of September next liberty to take off the corn that shall grow on the land the ensuing season & if by reason of sickness or other casualty I shall be hindred from removing my family I reserve the use of the buildings & a privilege to cut fire wood until the first of May 1815. Witnesses: David SCUDDER, Joseph PARKER. Ack. same day. Rec. 26 Mar. 1814.

Silas BLISH of Barnstable MA to **Lemuel SNOW** of same. <Barnstable Co.Deeds 4:257> ...21 Mar. 1791, Silas BLISH, yeoman, for £9.12s sold to Lemuel SNOW, yeoman...one half of salt meadow in Barnstable lying in common & undivided with Elisha BLISH who owns the other half...the whole piece contains a sufficient quantity of meadow to cut nine tons of hay yearly...bounded by land of Ebenezer BLISH, Deacon Ebenezer HAMBLEN, Joseph BLISH & Silvanus HINCKLEY...also one half of an Island of thatch ground...reserving to Jane Ewer widow of John EWER...the use & improvement of half...the same meadow I bought of Hezekiah MARCHANT Jr. & Jonathan EWER. Witnesses: Ebenezer BACON, Peter WHILDEN. Wf Chloe BLISH releases dower. Ack. & Rec. 21 Mar. 1791.

Elisha BLISH of Barnstable MA to **Lemuel SNOW** of same. <Barnstable Co.Deeds 4:252;44:202> ...1 Sept. 1791, Elisha BLISH, yeoman, for £11 sold to Lemuel SNOW, yeoman...one half of eight acre salt meadow in Barnstable...in common & undivided with the sd Lemuel who owns the other half ...bounded northerly by the Harbour and land of Ebenezer BLISH, Deacon Ebenezer HAMBLEN, Joseph BLISH & Silvanus HINCKLEY...also one half of an Island of Thatch ground...being in common with the sd Lemuel...reserving to Jane EWER widow of John EWER late of Barnstable dec'd, the use & improvement of half...and is the same meadow I bought of Hezekiah MARCHANT & Jonathan EWER. Wf Rebeckah BLISH releases dower. Witnesses: David HAMBLEN, Reliance HAMBLEN. Ack. 30 Mar. 1792 by Elisha. Rec. 30 Mar. 1792.

Solomon HINCKLEY of Barnstable MA to **Lemuel SNOW** of same. <Barnstable Co.Deeds 4:218;47:207> ...3 Apr. 1795, Solomon HINCKLEY, yeoman, for £8.19s5d sold to Lemuel SNOW, yeoman...three & a half acre wood land in Barnstable adjoining sd Lemuel's land...bounded by land of Robinson T. HINCKLEY & John HINCKLEY. Wf Mercy HINCKLEY releases dower. Witnesses: Robinson T. HINCKLEY, Ebenezer BACON. Ack. same day. Rec. 6 Apr. 1795.

Joseph PARKER of Barnstable MA to **Lemuel SNOW** of same. <Barnstable Co.Deeds 5:105;66:20> ...18 Mar. 1809, Joseph PARKER, yeoman, for $125.00 sold to Lemuel SNOW, yeoman...three & a half acres in Barnstable in a place called the Timber-land...bounded by land of Asa NYE, Capt. John CROCKER & Daniel PARKER. Wf Mehitable PARKER releases dower. Witnesses: Joseph SNOW, Hercules SNOW. Ack. 8 May 1809 by Joseph. Rec. 26 May 1809.

Isaac HODGES of Barnstable MA to **Isaac BEARSE et al** of same. <Barnstable Co.Deeds 1:133> ...26 Apr. 1802, Isaac HODGES, gent., for $1282.00 sold to Isaac BEARSE, James BEARSE & Lemuel BEARSE, yeomen...land in Barnstable incl. dwelling house & homestead lands. Wf Lydia HODGES releases dower.

Hercules HODGES & Isaac HODGES of Barnstable MA to **Isaac BEARSE et al.** <Barnstable Co.Deeds> <2:184;57:213>...26 Apr. 1802, Harcules HODGES, mariner & Isaac HODGES, gent., for $60.00 sold to Isaac BEARSE, James BEARSE & Lemuel BEARSE, all of Barnstable...two acres in Barnstable...bounded by road leading from Phinneys lane and land of Thomas LEWIS, sd BEARSES and Prince LUMBARD. Wives Lydia HODGES & Lydia HODGES release dowers. Witnesses: David SCUDDER, Moses STURGIS. Ack. same day by grantors.

Isaac HODGES of Barnstable MA to **Isaac EWER** of Nantucket. <Barnstable Co.Deeds 1:182> ...26 Feb. 1818, Isaac HODGES, gent., for $1500.00 sold to Isaac EWER, housewright...a certain piece of land all that I purchased of Peter CAMMET, five acres more or less with the dwelling house thereon that I now live in...

Isaac HODGES of Barnstable MA to **Benjamin F. CROCKER** of same. <Barnstable Co.Deeds 4:270;78:167> ...20 June 1818, Isaac HODGES, ship carpenter, for $250.00 sold to Benjamin F. CROCKER...one half of salt works standing on south side of Barnstable and are the same that we bought of Capt. Nehemiah LOVELL. Wf Lydia HEDGE/HODGES releases dower. Witnesses: Josiah SAMPSON, Lucy HODGES. Ack. 24 June 1818 by Isaac & Lucy. Rec. 27 June 1818.

Isaac HODGES & Benjamin HADAWAY of Barnstable MA to **Eli HINCKLEY** of same. <Barnstable Co.Deeds> <2:162;79:232>...28 June 1819, Isaac HODGES & Benjamin HADAWAY, gentlemen, for $13.00 sold to Eli HINCKLEY, cordwainer...two pieces of cedar swamp in Barnstable...bounded by land of David CHAISE, Abner HINCKLEY & others, Silvanus HINCKLEY, Benjamin KILLEY, Levi KILLEY and Elisha BLISH. Witnesses: Lydia HODGES, Silvanus HINCKLEY, Benjamin F. HADAWAY, Mary Ann HADAWAY. Ack. 13 July 1819 by Benjamin. Rec. 23 Aug. 1819.

Isaac HODGES et al of Barnstable MA to **Theophilus L. ADAMS** of same. <Barnstable Co.Deeds 3:65> ...8 Mar. 1828, Isaac & Hannah HODGES, Hercules & Esther HODGES (mariners) and Sarah PARKER, for $50.50 sold to Theophilus L. ADAMS, mariner...nine acre woodland in Barnstable bounded by land of Isaac CROCKER, Chipman HINCKLEY, Abner HINCKLEY, Ezra LOVELL and Isham Meeting Road. (Isaac signed "Isaac HODGES Jr.") Witnesses: Benjamin HALLET, Parsis WAIT, Urial ADAMS. Ack. same day by all grantors. Rec. 7 May 1828.

Heirs of **Jehiel PARKER** of Barnstable MA to **Wilson CROSBY** of same. <Barnstable Co.Deeds 35:151> ...12 Feb. 1829, Isaac HODGES, mariner for myself & all the heirs to the estate of Jehiel PARKER of Barnstable dec'd, for $400.00 sold to Wilson CROSBY, mariner...Signed by Isaac HODGES & Hercules HODGES with Sarah CROSBY, Esther HODGES, Hanah HODGES & Sarah PARKER releasing dowers. Witnesses: Benjamin HALLETT, James LOVELL. Ack. same day by Isaac. Rec. 26 Feb. 1845.

Isaac HODGES of Barnstable MA to **Samuel A. WILEY** of same. <Barnstable Co.Deeds 27:280> ...29 Dec. 1834, Isaac HODGES, mariner, for $400.00 sold to Samuel A. WILEY, mariner...all right ...to a certain piece of land...that Isaac EWER hath deeded to Isaac HODGES Jr. & Samuel A. WILEY with the dwelling house thereon that the sd Samuel A. WILEY now lives on...Reference may be had to Peter CAMMET's deed to Isaac HODGES Sr. for the bounds of sd land. Wf Hannah HODGES releases dower. Witnesses: Benjamin HALLETT, Jacob P. CROSBY. Ack. 18 Feb. 1835 by Isaac. Rec 29 Dec 1841.

Isaac HODGES et al to **Ephraim RICHARDSON** of Barnstable MA. <Barnstable Co.Deeds 32:196> ...20 July 1842, Francis WEST of Saybrook CT, Isaac HODGES & Cornelius LOVELL of Barnstable and our wives, for $40.00 sold to Ephraim RICHARDSON...one quarter part of salt & fresh meadow in Centreville lying in common & undivided with Edward LEWIS & George HINCKLEY and being the same which was the property of Jehiel PARKER dec'd...for bounds reference to be had to the deed of Levi & Paul PHINNEY to Jehiel PARKER & others dated 19 Feb. 1801 & Rec. 5:18. Signed by Francis WEST, Esther P. WEST, Cornelius LOVELL, Sarah P. LOVELL, Isaac HODGES, Hannah HODGES. Witnesses: Jacob P.CROSBY, Malvina CROSBY. Ack. 25 July 1842. Rec. 13 June 1843.

MICRO #9 OF 10

BARNSTABLE COUNTY DEEDS (Town cop.): (re: Nymphas HINCKLEY, Isaac HODGES)

<5:143> - 2 Jan. 1792, Nymphas HINCKLEY & Hezkeiah MARCHANT to Joseph BLISH, land at Sconknet which formerly belonged to Nathaniel HINCKLEY & Benjamin JENKINS dec'd, bounded by land of Lemuel SNOW, William CROCKER, sd BLISH and the heirs of Jabez HOWLAND dec'd.
<1:122> - 12 Mar. 1806, Samuel SCUDDER, Silvanus HINCKLEY, Lot SCUDDER, Nymphas HINCKLEY, Isaac HODGES, gent. and Levi HINCKLEY, all of Barnstable sell to Lewis CROSBY, three quarters at Chequaquet Beach, undivided with heirs of Samuel BEARSE dec'd who own the other quarter.
<3:150> - 12 Mar. 1821, Nymphas HINCKLEY, grantor. Wf Chloe HINCKLEY releases dower.
<4:48> - 5 Aug. 1822, Nymphas HINCKLEY, grantor. Wf Chloe HINCKLEY releases dower.
<4:99> - 19 Aug. 1823, Nymphas HINCKLEY & wf Chloe and Ebenezer PARKER & wf Abigail, grantors.

<4:98> - 8 Jan. 1796, Levi HINCKLEY & Isaac HODGES buy land.
<2:277> - 16 June 1807, Isaac HODGES et al buy land.
<4:271> - 16 June 1807, Isaac HODGES, gent. & Benjamin Fuller CROCKER, housewright, bought 12 acres in Barnstable by the salt water or cock a choise Bay or Harbour.

Nymphas HINCKLEY to **Lot HINCKLEY.** <Barnstable Co.Deeds 18:26> ...17 June 1824, Nymphas HINCKLEY, yeoman & wf Chloe to son Lot HINCKLEY, mariner...one quarter of dwelling house I now live in...also half of meadow on Oyster Island in Barnstable bought of Silvanus EWER of Nantucket.

References to the name **Isaac HODGES** in Barnstable Co.Deeds: <25:445> 1835; <25:446> 1837; <28:318-20> 1842; <35:81>1842.

Will of **Joseph PHINNEY** of Plympton MA. <Plymouth Co.PR>
<5:278>...dated 27 June 1726, mentions wf **Esther** and children, viz: **John PHINNEY, Joseph PHINNEY, Pelatiah PHINNEY, Alice HAMBLIN, Mary HAMBLIN, Mercy PHINNEY, Patience PHINNEY.** Witnesses: Samuel BRIANT, Isaac WATERMAN, Samuel BRYANT Jr. Appraisers app'td & witnesses ack., 15 July 1726. Pr. 22 July 1726. <5:169-70> Guardianship of children, 23 Sept. 1726, Samuel WEST of Kingston app'td gdn. of **Patience PHINNEY** (under 14) and chosen gdn. by **Joseph, Pelatiah & Mercy PHINNEY** (14-21).

Will of **Gershom PHINNEY**, cooper of Harwich MA. <Barnstable Co.PR>
<12:303>...dated 4 Dec. 1761, mentions wf **Rebecca** and children, viz: **Isaac PHINNEY, Gershom PHINNEY** (executor), **Lazarus PHINNEY, James PHINNEY, Seth PHINNEY, Thankful TAYLOR, Rebecca BANGS, Temperance PHINNEY, Mehitable PHINNEY & Rhoda PHINNEY.** <12:304> Pr. 7 Sept. 1762. <12:317> Inventory taken 3 Oct. 1762.

PLYMOUTH COUNTY DEEDS: (re: Eleazer ROGERS)

<3:186> - 25 Jan. 1699/1700, Eleazer ROGERS to George MORTON.
<14:159> - 24 Apr. 1719, Eleazer ROGERS, innholder & wf Ruhamah sell land.

PLYMOUTH COUNTY DEEDS, cont-d: (re: Eleazer ROGERS)

<17:48> - 16 Oct. 1723, Eleazer ROGERS, innholder & wf Ruhamah confirm deed 3:186.
<19:104> - 17 Aug. 1725, Eleazer ROGERS, seafaring man, & wf Ruhamah confirm deed of 15 Mar 1699.
<21:96> - 17 Aug. 1726, Eleazer ROGERS & wf Ruhamah & George MORTON, division of land.
<24:148> - 9 June 1729, Eleazer ROGERS & wf Ruhamah sell land in Middleboro. Ack. 15 Aug. 1729.

(Note: References only, viz: 2:50,53;3:174,175,257;7:335,345;8:108;10:81,406;14:261;15:87;16:86; 17:48;19:104;21:208;24:148.)

Eleazer ROGERS of Plimouth MA to **George MORTON** of same. <Plymouth Co.Deeds 3:186>
...25 Jan. 1699/1700, Eleazer ROGERS, for Ł20 currant silver money of New England, sold to George MORTON...my whole right...of land lying in that tract of land purchased by Major Josiah WINSLOW & Edward GRAY of William son of Tispequin, lying on ye easterly side of Assawamset Pond in...Middleborough...sixth lott...also all my whole interest of undivided land...in sd purchase. Witnesses: Abiel SHURTLEFF, Samuel STURTEVANT, Thomas FAUNCE. Ack. 6 Mar. 1699/1700 by Eleazer & wf Ruhamah. Rec. 19 Mar. 1699/1700.

Eleazer ROGERS of Plymouth MA to **Jabesh EDDY** of Plimton MA. <Plymouth Co.Deeds 14:229>
...19 Jan. 1719, Eleazer ROGERS & wf Ruhamah, for Ł12 sold to Jabesh EDDY...cedar swamp which is the 2nd lot in the 10th great lot of South Meadow Cedar Swamp in Plimton. Witnesses: Josiah COTTON, George HOLMES. Ack. & Rec. same day.

Estate of **Samuel TOTMAN**, husbandman/bricklayer of Plymouth MA. <Plymouth Co.PR>
<11:329> Letter/Bond 16 Feb. 1749, widow **Experience TOTMAN** app'td admx. Sureties: John HARLOW & Isaac MORTON, coopers of Plymouth. <12:33> Inventory taken 21 Mar. 1749/50; no real estate. <12:34> Allowance to widow, 2 Apr. 1750.

PLYMOUTH COUNTY DEEDS: (re: TOTMAN, grantors 1685-1801)

<52:259> - Ebenezer TOTMAN to John TURNER
<53:92> - Joanna TOTMAN, admx. to Josiah CHURCHILL.
<14:93> - Stephen TOTMAN to Thomas HOWLAND.
<59:199> - Joshua TOTMAN & wf Elizabeth of Plympton to Jabez CHURCHILL (1 Jan. 1779).
<72:99> - Stephen TOTMAN to Abijah BROWN.
<76:108>- Stephen TOTMAN to David KENT.
<39:46> - Simeon TOTMAN to Jeremiah GRIDLEY.
<56:22> - Simeon TOTMAN to James LITTLEJOHN.

(re: TOTMAN, grantees)

<52:258> - Ebenezer TOTMAN from Daniel COIT.
<76:102> - Hannah TOTMAN from Isaac DAMAN.
<60:105> - John TOTMAN from Ozras WHITTEN.
<54:215> - Joshua TOTMAN from David SHAW.
<59:181> - Joshua TOTMAN from Nathaniel ATWOOD.
<59:181> - Joshua TOTMAN from Hezekiah COLE.
<56:22> - Simeon TOTMAN from Benajah PRATT.
<67:235>- Stephen TOTMAN from David KENT.
<76:102>- Stephen TOTMAN from Isaac DAMAN.
<80:87> - Stephen TOTMAN from Robert NORTHEY
<87:114>- Stephen TOTMAN Jr from Samuel BARSTOW.

Estate of **Willis CHUBBUCK**, mariner of Wareham MA. <Plymouth Co.PR #3929, 46:387;50:507-509>
<46:387>...3 Jan. 1820, Lot CHUBBUCK, yeoman of Plymouth app'td admr. <originals> Insolvency 29 Feb. 1820. Allowance to widow, Mar. 1820. Inventory taken 14 Jan. 1820.

Willis CHUBBUCK of Wareham MA to **William FEARING** of same. <Plymouth Co.Deeds 140:217>
...14 Mar. 1819, Willis CHUBBUCK, yeoman to William FEARING, merchant...land & buildings on Long Neck, sd land bought of Joseph SWIFT 28 Feb. 1816. Witnesses: Lot CHUBBUCK, Israel FEARING. Ack. 15 Mar. 1819. Rec. 8 Apr. 1819.

PLYMOUTH COUNTY DEEDS: (re: Willis CHUBBUCK)

<105:159> - 1807, Division.
<132:195> - 27 Apr. 1816, Willis CHUBBUCK, mariner of Sandwich to Israel FEARING Jr., gent. of Wareham, mortgage. Released 22 Mar. 1819.
<226:12> - 26 July 1847, Willis CHUBBUCK & wf Esther and Thomas CHUBBUCK & wf Betsey to the Cape Cod R.R. Ack. same day.
<255:13> - 1 Oct. 1847, Willis B. CHUBBUCK to Thomas CHUBBUCK, both master mariners of Wareham, half of wood land Willis bought of Stephen WRIGHT 9 July 1839 & rec. in 211:235. Ack. same day. Rec. 29 July 1853.
<255:14> - 23 Jan. 1845, Willis B. CHUBBUCK to Thomas CHUBBUCK, as above.

MICRO #10 OF 10

Will of **Maziah HARDING.** <Barnstable Co.PR 5:180>
...dated Apr. 1734, mentions children **John HARDING, Nathan HARDING, Cornelius HARDING** (under 21), **Elizabeth FISH, Hannah FISH, Phebe ROGERS**; grandchildren **Mary CLARK & Elizabeth CLARK**, daus of dau **Mary CLARK**; grandchildren **Thomas HARDING & James HARDING** sons of son **James HARDING.**

Will of **Ebenezer HARDING** of Chatham MA. <Barnstable Co.PR #1670>
...dated 31 July 1801; Pr. 13 Oct. 1801; Inventory 13 Oct. 1801; 42 acres, Ł168 and 30 acres,

£112.10s; total estate, £442.12.4. Account. Distribution. (no further details)

==

Will of **Huldah HARDING**, widow of Chatham MA. <Barnstable Co.PR #1671>
...dated 15 Dec. 1808, mentions eldest son **George HARDING**, 2d son **Ebenezer HARDING**, 3d son **Amos HARDING**, 4th son **Asael HARDING**, heirs of eldest dec'd dau **Anna MATTHEWS**, 2d dau **Huldah HUDSON**, 3d dau **Elizabeth HOMLES/HOLMES**, 4th dau **Lydia GOFF**, 5th dau **Jemima HARDING** (executrix), 6th dau **Martha ACKLEY**; $1.00 to each, remainder to dau **Jemima**. Pr. 29 Mar. 1819 by exx.

HENRY SAMSON/SAMPSON

MICRO #1 OF 7

PLYMOUTH COLONY RECORDS:

<12:4> - , Land granted to Henerie SAMSON at north side of town.
<12:16> - 25 June 1631, Henry SAMPSON due one acre of land.
<1:72> - 1 Jan. 1637/8, Lands of Henery SAMPSON.
<1:120> - 1 Apr. 1639, Abraham SAMPSON requests land.
<1:144> - 6 Apr. 1640, Land granted to Henery SAMPSON.
<1:145> - 6 Apr. 1640, Land of Abraham SAMPSON.
<1:154> - 1 June 1640, Land granted to Abraham SAMPSON.
<1:159> - 3 Aug. 1640, Abraham SAMPSON requests land.
<1:165> - 2 Nov. 1640, Land granted to Henery SAMPSON.
<2:119> - 26 Oct. 1647, Land sold to Henery SAMPSON.
<12:146>- 27 Oct. 1647, Ephraim & Mary TINKHAM to Henry SAMPSON.
<4:18> - 3 June 1662, Abraham SAMPSON & others allowed to look for land they wish granted them.
<4:94> - 7 June 1665, Henery SAMPSON granted land.
<4:160> - 2 July 1667, Henery SAMPSON, "land for his children".

PLYMOUTH COLONY DEEDS:

<3:193> - SAMSON, MITCHELL & LITTLE, grant.
<3:240> - Henry SAMSON from Ephraim TINKHAM.
<3:237> - Henry SAMSON to Edward GRAY.
<3:160> - Henry SAMSON from Tuspaquin.
<3:193> - Henry SAMSON from the court.
<4:188> - Henry SAMSON to Hannah HOLMES.
<5:207> - Henry SAMSON to Seth POPE.
<5:292> - Henry SAMSON to Joseph RUSSELL (18 Dec 1684.) Ack. 19 Dec. 1684.

(daughter) SAMSON^2 (Henry^1)

Samuel & Ebenezer RICHMOND of Middleboro MA to **John HANMER** of Rochester. <Plymouth Co.Deeds> <10:2:75>...10 Mar. 1700/01, Samuel RICHMOND & Ebenezer RICHMOND sell to John HANMER of Rochester alias Sipican...two lots in the South Purchase in Middleboro, #89 and #104, 90 acres. Witnesses: James READ, Susanna READ. Ack. 8 Sept. 1711. Rec. 8 Sept. 1711.

John HANMER of Middleboro MA to **Samuel WHITE Jr.** of Rochester. <Plymouth Co.Deeds 10:2:93> ...29 Sept. 1702, John HANMER, for £9 sells to Samuel WHITE Jr., above two lots. Witnesses: Samuel HAMON, Isaac HOLMES, Peter BLACKMORE. Ack. & Rec. 8 Sept. 1711.

John HANMER of Taunton MA to **Job RANDALL** of Scituate MA. <Plymouth Co.Deeds 5:140> ...22 Feb. 1703, John HANMER, eldest son of John HANMER late of Rochester dec'd who was eldest son of John HANMER late of Scituate dec'd, conveys to Job RANDALL...all his rights in any lands in Scituate as heir of his father or grandfather. Witnesses: Deborah CUSHING, Agatha BRYANT. Ack. same day. Rec. 1 Mar. 1703/4.

John WADSWORTH of Duxbury MA to **John HANMORE** of Plymouth MA. <Plymouth Co.Deeds 11:62> ...26 Nov. 1713, John WADSWORTH, for £70 sells to John HANMORE...76 acres in Bridgewater on easterly side of Pore meadow River, laid out in three divisions, which land the sd WADSWORTH bought of Elisha WADSWORTH of Duxbury, 25 Feb. 1707/8 & rec. 7:219,220...also half a lot of meadow on west side of Pore meadow river bought of Thomas WASHBURNE of Bridgewater, 26 Dec. 1711 & rec. 9:199. Witnesses: Benjamin PRIOR, Isaac WADSWORTH. Ack. 2 Mar. 1714. Rec. 3 Mar. 1714/5.

John HANMORE of Bridgewater MA to **John WADSWORTH** of Duxbury MA. <Plymouth Co.Deeds 11:151> ...3 Mar. 1714/5, John HANMORE mortgages the above to John WADSWORTH, mariner for £70, payable 1 Oct. 1724 at 6%...land is described as near the line of the Major's Purchase & bounds on meadow of John WHITMAN & James CARY and is the farm John HANMORE now lives on. Witnesses: Nathaniel HOWLAND, Joseph STURTEVANT. Rec. 29 Dec. 1715. Discharged 10 Apr. 1719. <13:210>...10 Apr. 1719, John HANMER of Bridgewater mortgaged the above land to Essex Co. Commissioners for £100. Wf Mary HANMER consents. Discharged 17 Apr. 1723.

John HANDMER/HANMER of Bridgewater MA to **Israel HATCH** of Scituate MA. <Plymouth Co.Deeds 16:155> ...16 June 1722, John HANDMER, wheelwright, for £114 sells to Israel HATCH, yeoman...sixty eight and one quarter acre of the land bought of John WADSWORTH 26 Nov. 1713, subject to the mortgage to Essex Co. Commissioners. Ack. 16 July 1722. Rec. 5 Mar. 1722.

CALEB SAMSON^2 (Henry^1)

Ephraim THOMAS of Little Compton to **Caleb SAMSON** of Duxbury MA. <Plymouth Co.Deeds 39:78> ...21 Feb. 1699, Ephraim THOMAS, for £5 sells to Caleb SAMSON...one seventh of half of parcel of marsh meadow in Marshfield, being about 40 acres...which John THOMAS dec'd and William CARVER purchased of Isaac WINSLOW. Rec. 3 Mar. 1747.

James & Stephen SAMPSON to **Caleb SAMPSON** of Duxbury MA. <Bristol Co.Deeds 12:24> ...22 Jan. 1711/12, James SAMPSON of Dartmouth and Stephen SAMPSON of Duxbury deed to their brother Caleb SAMPSON...60 acres in undivided lands of Dartmouth. Witnesses: Seth ARNOLD, Hazadiah DELANO. Rec. 17 Apr. 1718.

Josiah HOLMES et al of Pembroke MA to **Caleb SAMSON** of Duxbury MA. <Plymouth Co.Deeds 39:182> ...13 May 1713, Josiah HOLMES, John HOLMES & William HOLMES, for £18 sold to Caleb SAMSON...three fifths of 7th lot of salt meadow in 2nd Division of Commons in Duxbury...bounded by little Wood Island River. Rec. 25 Aug. 1748.

Caleb SAMSON of Duxbury MA to **Thomas TRACY** of Marshfield MA. <Bristol Co.Deeds 18:309> ...26 June 1725, Caleb SAMSON, for £200 sells to Thomas TRACY...my two lotts...in Dartmouth... given to me by my two brothers James SAMSON and Stephen SAMSON dec'd...sd land was laid out by Benjamin CRANE, surveyor & recorded. Witnesses: Arthur HOWLAND Jr., Abigail HOWLAND. Ack. 28 June 1725. Rec. 20 Nov. 1728. <Plymouth Co.Deeds 37:4>...26 June 1725, Thomas TRACY, for £220 sold to Caleb SAMSON land he bought of Andrew ALDEN 2 Feb. 1722. Rec. 20 Sept. 1744.

PLYMOUTH COUNTY DEEDS:

<36:13> - 7 Jan. 1741/2, Caleb SAMSON Sr. of Duxbury to Caleb SAMSON Jr. of same.
<36:162> - 7 May 1744, Caleb SAMSON of Duxbury, for £132 sells to Mary SAMSON, widow of Joshua of Duxbury.
<37:5> - 9 July 1744, Caleb SAMSON to son Caleb SAMSON.

Estate of **Caleb SAMSON**, husbandman of Duxbury MA. <Plymouth Co.PR #17467>
<11:466> Letter/Bond 5 Nov. 1750, widow **Mehitable SAMSON** app'td admx. Sureties: Robert SAMSON, innholder of Duxburough & Richard LOWDIN, yeoman of Pembroke. Witnesses: Edward WINSLOW, John CHANDLER 3d. <12:235> Inventory taken 3 June 1751 by Samuel ALDEN, Blany PHILLIPS, Ichabod SAMPSON; total personal estate, £66.18.2.; total real estate, £122.2.8.

Guardianship of Child of **Caleb SAMSON** of Duxbury MA. <Plymouth Co.PR #17600>
<11:415> Letter/Bond 5 Nov. 1750, **Micah SAMSON** chooses Robert SAMSON, innholder of Duxbury, his guardian. Sureties: Josiah HATCH, seafaring man of Pembroke. Witnesses: Edward WINSLOW, John CHANDLER 3d.

Abner FORD et al to **Paul SAMSON** of Duxbury MA. <Plymouth Co.Deeds 45:152> ...5 May 1758, Abner FORD, coaster, Bethiah FORD, weaver of Marshfield and Michael SAMSON, cordwainer of Abington to Paul SAMSON, housewright...all rights in real estate of our father Caleb SAMSON dec'd and our brother Martin SAMSON who died a minor. Ack. same day by Abner & Bethiah. Ack. 16 May 1758 by Michael. Rec. 11 Apr.1759.

Micah/Michael SAMSON et al of Abington MA to **Jacob DYER** of same. <Plymouth Co.Deeds 49:98> ...1 Mar. 1760, Micah SAMSON & wf Hannah and Noah GURNEY & wf Ruth, for £5.15s sell to Jacob DYER housewright...two acres in Abington...bounded by land of Christopher DYER & Deacon Samuel POOLL. Witnesses: David LOVELL, Jonathan HEARSEY, Jonathan HEARSEY, Joseph POOL. Ack. 30 Sept. 1762 by all four grantors. Rec. 4 July 1764.

Michael SAMSON of Abington MA to **Ephraim WHITMAN** of same. <Plymouth Co.Deeds 87:161> ...21 Nov. 1793, Michael SAMSON, yeoman, for £300 sells to Ephraim WHITMAN, gent...35 acres in Abington...bounded by land of Jacob DYER, Joseph POOL, Aaron HOBART, Esq., Lt. John GURNEY...also one and a half acre meadow in Bridgewater known by the name of Snells meadow...bounded by land of Jacob WHITMARSH, Rachell BATES, Benjamin BATES & Samuel PORTER. Witnesses: Eliphaz CURTIS, Jacob DYER Jr. Ack. 28 Nov. 1793 by Michael & wf Deborah. Rec. 26 May 1800.

Michael SAMSON of Bridgewater MA to **John KING** of Abington. <Plymouth Co.Deeds 101:253> ...10 Sept. 1805, Michael SAMSON, yeoman & wf Deborah, spinster, for $1500 sell to John KING, trader...50 acres in Bridgewater...bounded by land of Roland HOWARD & Nehemiah HOWARD. Witnesses: John POOL, John KING Jr. Ack. same day by Michael. Rec. 28 Sept. 1805. <105:193>...7 Mar. 1807, John & Hannah KING sell same back to Michael SAMSON for same amount. <105:194>...7 Apr. 1807, Michael & Deborah SAMSON resell above to David HEARSEY Jr. for $1680.00

Michael SAMSON Jr. of Leeds MA to **Michael SAMSON** of Bridgewater MA. <Plymouth Co.Deeds 105:211> ...29 Aug. 1806, Michael SAMSON Jr., yeoman, for $50.00 sells to Michael SAMSON, yeoman...all rights in real estate...that my Honoured father Michael SAMSON formerly of Abington & my mother Hannah formerly owned in the town of Abington which estate my father...sold to Ephraim WHITMAN of Abington after the decease of my mother. Witnesses: John KING, Samuel NORTON. Ack. same day. Rec. 14 Apr. 1807.

Estate of **Gideon SAMPSON** of Pembroke MA. <Plymouth Co.PR #17521>
...1814...<45:467;46:59;47:43,44,139,268,269> (no details given)

Will of **Paul SAMPSON** of Marshfield MA. <Plymouth Co.PR 43:463>
...dated 25 Feb. 1806...to unnamed wife, half of estate while his widow; to six sons **Luther SAMPSON, Caleb SAMPSON, Chandler SAMPSON, Calvin SAMPSON, Proctor SAMPSON & Martin SAMPSON,** the other half of estate, whole at mother's decease; to four daus **Silvia TURNER, Olive FOORD, Martha BOURN & Esther MAGOON,** $50.00 each and additional $25.00 at wife's decease; to wife, children & grandchildren, two pews in the meeting burying yard & right in a stable; son **Chandler,** executor. Witnesses: Luke WADSWORTH, Thomas BOURN, Ichabod WADSWORTH. Pr. 3 June 1811.

Will of **David SAMSON,** yeoman of Duxbury MA. <Plymouth Co.PR #17490>
<21:164>...dated 26 Mar. 1767, mentions wf **Mary**; to eldest son **Charles SAMSON** one half of lands in Duxborough...excepting fifteen acres of land at the southeast corner of my farm which I give to my son **David SAMSON** who is labouring under bodily weakness & indisposition...to sons **Ebenezer SAMSON & Jonathan SAMSON,** £6.13s4d each; to son **Chaphen SAMSON** the other half of lands; to son **David SAMSON**...liberty to live in my house; to daus **Lidia BOZWORTH** wf of Nathaniel, **Mary LITTLE** wf of John, **Mercy HUTCHINSON** wf of Timothy, **Elizabeth PENEO/PINEO** wf of Peter & **Eleanor FARNUM** wf of Joseph, remainder of movable estate; son **Chaphen,** executor. Witnesses: William THOMAS, Nathaniel THOMAS, Nehemiah THOMAS. <21:165> Pr. 17 June 1772, **Chaphen SAMSON** app'td admr. <21:165> Inventory taken 18 June 1772 by Samuel BAKER, Thomas WATERMAN, Nehemiah THOMAS; total real estate, £316.13s4d. <21:287> Insolvency, 28 Dec. 1772; commissioners app'td to examine claims. <21:370> List of Claims, 28 Dec. 1773, by Ebenezer FISH & Benjamin WHITE; Creditors: Charles SAMSON, **Chapin SAMSON** dec'd, Samuel BAKER, Thomas BAKER, Anthony THOMAS, Ebenezer FISH, William THOMAS of Duxboro, Edward WINSLOW, Jonathan SAMPSON, Ebenezer SAMSON, Jacob DINGLEY, Abner DINGLEY, Joshua LORING, James SOUTHWORTH, Nehemiah THOMAS, James THOMAS, Benjamin WHITE, Joseph THOMAS, Elisha FOORD, Jethro TAYLOR, Charles BAKER, Samuel HOLMES, Joseph DELANO, Amos FORD, Tabitha SILVESTER, Aaron SOUL, Barsheba BARTLETT, Saul SAMSON, David CARVER, Mary BOYCE, Abigail BOZWORTH; total claims, £296.2s5d. <original> Bond 9 Feb. 1774, **Charles SAMSON,** mariner of Duxbury, app'td admr. de bonis non. Sureties: Ebenezer FISH, yeoman of Duxbury & Benjamin WHITE, yeoman of Marshfield. Witnesses: Samuel BALDWIN, William CUSHING. <21:609> Inventory taken 19 Mar. 1774 by Ebenezer FISH & Jedediah SIMONS, yeomen of Duxborough and Benjamin WHITE, yeoman of Marshfield; total real estate, £304; total personal estate, £25.11s9d. <21:396-7> Dower to widow, 19 May 1774; mentions land bounded by Samuel BAKER & Capt. Anthony THOMAS; salt meadow in Duxborough bounded by land of Ichabod DELANO, Abner SAMSON, Joseph BREWSTER & Samuel ALDEN. <21:371> Account 5 Sept. 1774 of admr., **Charles SAMSON;** Payments had been made to: Paul SAMSON for a coffin, 6s8d; Esq. WINSLOW, Ebenezer FISH, Benjamin WHITE, Joseph DELANO, Jedediah SIMMONS, Chaphin SAMSON's account for setling estate, £2.19s6d; personal estate set off to widow, £25.11s11d. He charges himself as follows: with what the two thirds of the real estate sold for, viz: seven acres at 42s8d per acre; two thirds of barn & orchard, £14.18s8d; fifteen & a half acre woodland, £31; fifteen & a half acre woodland, £43.8s; twenty two acre pasture with the old house, £45.9s4d; two & three quarter acre salt marsh, £16.10s. The balance of £109.6s to be paid to the creditors at the rate of six shillings seven pence on the pound. <27:530> On 4 Apr. 1792, Elijah BAKER, yeoman of Duxbury, app'td admr. (Both **Chaphin & Charles SAMSON** having died before completion of the administration.) <original> Bond 4 Apr. 1792 of admr. Sureties: Israel PERRY & David STOCKBRIDGE, gent. of Hanover Witnesses: Charles TURNER Jr., Eli CURTIS. <31:457> Oath of admr., 28 Apr.1792; Notice of sale, 9 June 1792 & 13 July 1792, of remaining real estate. <31:458> Account 13 July 1792; Creditors: Charles SAMPSON, Chapin SAMPSON dec'd, Samuel BAKER, Thomas BAKER, Anthony THOMAS, Ebenezer FISH, William THOMAS of Duxbury, Edward WINSLOW, Jonathan SAMPSON, Ebenezer SAMPSON, Jacob DINGLEY, Abner DINGLEY, Joshua LORING, James SOUTHWORTH, Nehemiah THOMAS, James THOMAS, Benjamin WHITE, Joseph THOMAS, Elisha FORD, Jethro TAYLOR, Charles BAKER, Samuel HOLMES, Joseph DELANO, Amos FORD, Tabitha SYLVESTER, Aaron SOULE, Barsheba BARTLETT, Saul SAMPSON, David CARVER, Mary BOYCE, Abigail BOZWORTH.

Estate of **Capt. Chapin SAMSON,** yeoman/mariner of Duxbury MA. <Plymouth Co.PR #17471>
<23:45> Letter/Bond 3 Jan. 1774, Anthony THOMAS, yeoman of Marshfield, app'td admr. Sureties: Jeremiah HALL, physician of Pembroke & Melatiah DILLINGHAM, blacksmith of Hanover. Witnesses: William CUSHING, Edward WINSLOW Jr. <21:392> Warrant 9 Nov. 1773. <21:585> Inventory taken 27 Dec. 1773 by Nehemiah THOMAS, Benjamin WHITE & Thomas DINGLEY of Marshfield; total estate, £478 18s2d. <21:392> Division 6 June 1774, by Briggs ALDEN of Duxbury, Nehemiah THOMAS & Thomas WATERMAN of Marshfield; 160 acres in Duxbury, formerly the farm of James THOMAS, which Anthony THOMAS holds in common with the heirs of Chapin SAMSON. <24:193> Account of admr., 15 Apr. 1776; Received from: Job PRINCE and estate of David SAMSON; Paid to: John REED, Samuel GORDON, Benjamin LORING, INGLESBY, Thomas WALDO, Deborah SIMONS, Judah THOMAS, Briggs THOMAS, Joshua HALL, Abraham PETERSON, Amos FORD, Joshua SOUTHWORTH, Thomas FISH, Sena FOORD, Elizabeth WESTON, Paul SAMSON, Samuel SMITH, Samuel HOLMES, Lydia SIMONS, Edward WINSLOW, Tobias WHITE, Luther WHITE, Jacob DINGLEY, Lydia WHITTEMORE, Rebecca THOMAS, Isaac PARTRIDGE, Abia DELANO, Benjamin WHITE, Job CROCKER, John CHANDLER, John SAMSON, Charles STOCKBRIDGE, Dr. WINSLOW, SIMMONS, Rebecca CHANDLER, Cordas WALKER, Thomas WATERMAN, Asa WATERMAN, Capt. HINKLY, Joseph HENDERSON, Bernard TUELS, Mr. BAXTER, Widow HATCH, Hannah WHITE, William THOMAS, Elija FOAR, Deacon THOMAS, Job GOODEN, Levi LORING, William CLIFT, John THOMAS, Anthony THOMAS, Jethro TALER, Isaac KEEN.

Guardianship of Children of **Capt. Chapin SAMSON** of Duxbury MA. <Plymouth Co.PR #17472>
<22:35-39> Letters/Bonds, 30 Nov. 1774, widow **Betty SAMSON** app'td gdn. of **Chapin SAMSON, Job SAMSON, Briggs SAMSON, Judith Clift SAMSON & Elizabeth SAMSON,** all under 14. Sureties: William CLIFT & Joseph CLIFT of Marshfield. Witnesses: Robert CUSHING, Lucy DYER.

MICRO #2 OF 7

Estate of **Melzar SAMPSON**, mariner of Duxbury MA. <Plymouth Co.PR #17593>
<27:233> Letter/Bond 7 Feb. 1787, widow **Sarah SAMSON** and William KENT, mariner, of Marshfield, app'td admrs. Sureties: Benjamin WHITE & Gideon HARLOW of Duxbury. Witnesses: Adam FISH, William CLAP. <30:94> Inventory taken 14 Feb. 1787.

Estate of **Capt. Charles SAMPSON**, gent. of Waldoborough ME. <Lincoln Co.ME PR>
<10:306> On 21 Mar. 1804, Joshua HEAD, Esq., William H. THOMPSON, trader and William SPROUL, merchant, all of Waldoborough, app'td to appraise estate. Inventory sworn to 11 Jan. 1805 by **Elizabeth SAMPSON**, admx.; incl. one third of the schooner "Independence", $1200.00; five eights of schooner "Sally", $958.32; one coat of arms, $2.00; farm in Waldoboro, $3200.00; farm in Medumcook, $800.00; four acre salt marsh in Thomaston, $120.00; Promissory notes from: Thomas STARRET, Story THOMPSON, John BUTLER, Henry EWELL, Jehiel SIMMONS, James SIMMONS, Job SIMMONS, Samuel PAYSON, Andrew JACOBS, Stephen PEABODY, Thomas SIMMONS, Abel FISH, Joshua BRADFORD, Adam TEALL, John PAINE, Charles SAMPSON Jr.; total estate, $8962.92. <11:165> Account 10 Jan. 1806, of admx.; payments incl.: Port Royal for digging grave, $3.75; Waterman THOMAS as surveyor, $1.00; gravestone, $9.00; total payments, $1302.36.

Will of **Elizabeth SAMSON**, widow of Thomaston ME. <Lincoln Co.ME PR>
<40:122>...dated 21 Sept. 1831...to son **Daniel SAMSON** of Waldoboro, all house hold furniture & utensils, stock of cows & sheep...remainder of estate to Oliver FALES, Esq. of Thomaston in trust for dau **Sarah Dingley HASKELL** for her sole and seperate use and benefit during her coverture; Oliver FALES, executor. Witnesses: Hezekiah PRINCE Jr., Charles LORING, William I. FARLEY. Pr. 15 May 1834. <40:326> Inventory taken 6 Nov. 1834 by Halsey HEALEY, Hezekiah PRINCE Jr., William I. FARLEY; incl. land near Shepard ROBBINS, $30.00; land & buildings near LORING's Store, $600.00; pew in Cong. Meeting house, $60.00; total estate, $724.00.

LINCOLN COUNTY ME DEEDS: (re: Charles SAMPSON)

<8:173> - 16 Sept 1771, Charles SAMPSON, mariner of Broadbay, buys land next to his own.
<8:223> - 7 Oct. 1771, Charles SAMPSON Jr., mariner of Broad bay, buys land there.
<16:251> - 24 Oct. 1783, Charles SAMPSON, gent. of Waldoboro, buys land at Stage Cove next to his
<18:39> - 26 Nov. 1784, Charles SAMSON, gent. of Waldoboro, buys land on Penobscot River.
<32:13> - 8 Apr. 1794, Charles SAMSON, gent. of Waldoboro, buys land from Joshua & Abiah COLLAMORE.

(References only to the name **Charles SAMPSON**: 35:44;37:54;38:241;46:202;47:87;50:75;51:49.)

Jonathan ROBBINS of Broad Bay ME to **Charles SAMSON & Abijah WATERMAN.** <Lincoln Co.ME Deeds 7:206>
...3 Apr. 1770, Jonathan ROBBINS, yeoman, for Ł51.6s8d sold to Charles SAMPSON, mariner & Abijah WATERMAN, yeoman, both of Broad Bay...90 acres in Broad Bay...being part of Lot #28...bounded by Robbins' Cove and land of Samuel SWEETLAND, heirs of Brig. Samuel WALDO, Esq., dec'd and Jane ROBBINS. Witnesses: Ezra PITCHER, Jeremiah BATTELS. Ack. same day. Rec. 5 June 1770.

Samuel WALDO et al to **Charles SAMSON Jr.** <Lincoln Co.ME Deeds 8:66>
...12 Apr. 1770, Samuel WALDO, Esq. & Francis WALDO, Esq. of Falmouth, Cumberland Co., sons & coheirs of the late Brigadier General Samuel WALDO dec'd intestate, Isaac WINSLOW, Esq. of Roxbury and Thomas FLUCKER, Esq. of Boston & wf Hannah the dau & coheir of sd Brigadier Samuel WALDO... for Ł16 sold to Charles SAMSON Jr...100 acres at Broad Bay in the County of LIncoln...being lot #2 now in the occupation of Henry FENNER...bounded by land of Abijah WATERMAN & John DAVID...reserving to us...all the marble & lime stone & all the quarries & ledges...being part of the real estate that descended to his sd sons & daughter & to Lucy WINSLOW formerly Lucy WALDO now dec'd. Ack. 5 July 1770 by Thomas & Hannah. Rec. 30 Jan. 1771.

Thomas MURPHEE of Pownalborough ME to **Charles SAMPSON** of Broad Bay ME. <Lincoln Co.ME Deeds>
<8:116>...25 Feb. 1771, Thomas MURPHEE, mariner, for Ł13.6s8d sold to Charles SAMPSON, mariner... 25 acres, being one quarter part of Lot #3 adjoining sd Samson's in Broadbay. Wf Priscilla MURPHEE consents. Witnesses: Abijah WATERMAN, Joshua MORTON. Ack. 12 June 1771 by Thomas MURPHEY Jr. & Rec. same day.

Frederick SEECHRIST of Broadbay ME to **Charles SAMSON** of same. <Lincoln Co.ME Deeds 8:116>
...25 Feb. 1771, Phedrec SECRETS/Frederick SEECHRIST, yeoman & wf Mary, for Ł13.6s8d sold to Charles SAMSON, mariner...25 acres being one quarter part of Lot #3 adjoining sd Samson's. Witnesses: Abijah WATERMAN, Joshua MORTON. Ack. 28 Mar. 1771 by grantors. Rec. 12 June 1771.

Abraham LOCKE of Cambridge MA to **Charles SAMPSON** of Waldoborough ME. <Lincoln Co.ME Deeds 12:253>
...27 Jan. 1778, Abraham LOCKE, yeoman, for Ł10 sold to Charles SAMPSON, mariner...two & a half acre salt marsh in Thomaston lying in Wesaweskeeg Marsh...bounded by the great Creek and land of Oliver ROBINS. Wf Hannah LOCKE signs. Witnesses: Waterman THOMAS, Mary FARNSWORTH, Francis LOCK Jr. Ack. 2 Feb. 1778 by Abraham. Rec. 1 June 1778.

Abraham LOCKE of Cambridge MA to **Charles SAMPSON** of Waldoborough ME. <Lincoln Co.ME Deeds 12:254>
...27 Jan. 1778, Abraham LOCKE, yeoman, for Ł550 sold to Charles SAMPSON, mariner...ninety six & three quarter acres in Warren ME, being Lot #6 on eastern side of St. George's River with house & barn...bounded by land of Capt. Thomas STARRET. Wf Hannah LOCKE signs. Witnesses: Waterman THOMAS

Mary FARNSWORTH, Francis LOCKE Jr. Ack. 2 Feb. 1778 by Abraham. Rec. 1 June 1778.

Thomas STARRET of Warren ME to **Charles SAMSON Jr.** of Waldoborough ME. <Lincoln Co.ME Deeds 13:65> ...9 Jan. 1779, Thomas STARRET, gent., for £5 sold to Charles SAMSON Jr., gent...three & one quarter acres in Warren...bounded by their lands. Wf Rebecca STARRET releases dower. Witnesses: Waterman THOMAS, Mary STARRET. Ack. same day by both. Rec. 18 Jan. 1779.

Nathaniel PITCHER of Waldoborough ME to **Charles SAMPSON Jr.** of same. <Lincoln Co.ME Deeds 19:136> ...18 Apr. 1786, Nathaniel PITCHER, yeoman & wf Experience, for £6 sold to Charles SAMPSON Jr., gent...one half of fresh meadow known by the name of Jaddacanaus Meadow...lying on Goose River Brook about two miles east of Sweedland Cove on Medomock River. Witness: Waterman THOMAS. Ack. same day by all.

John TUCK of Warren ME to **Charles SAMSON** of Waldoborough ME. <Lincoln Co.ME Deeds 21:21> ...10 May 1787, John TUCK, yeoman, for £9 sold to Charles SAMSON, gent...land in Warren. Rec. 9 June 1787.

Nathaniel BARTLETT of Medumcook ME to **Charles SAMSON** of Waldoborough ME. <Lincoln Co.ME Deeds> <29:8>...13 July 1792, Nathaniel BARTLETT, yeoman, for £30 sold to Charles SAMSON, gent...50 acres in Medumcook...bounded by land of Joshua BRADFORD. Witnesses: John HAUPT, Thomas McGUYER. Ack. same day. Rec. 2 Aug. 1792.

James SOUTHWORTH of Duxborough MA to **Charles SAMSON Jr.** of Waldoborough ME. <Lincoln Co.ME Deeds> <35:44>...9 June 1795, James SOUTHWORTH, shipwright, for £150 sold to Charles SAMSON Jr., mariner ...land at Waldoborough.

Charles SAMPSON Jr. of Waldoborough ME to **Chapin SAMPSON** of same. <Lincoln Co.ME Deeds 37:54> ...15 Mar. 1796, Charles SAMPSON Jr., mariner, for £150 sold to Chapin SAMPSON, gent...

Charles SAMSON Jr. of Waldoboro ME to **George STORER.** <Lincoln Co.ME Deeds 53:251> ...24 Jan. 1804, Charles SAMSON Jr., mariner, sells to George STORER...land on Broad Bay River. Wf Sarah SAMSON releases dower. Ack. 2 Apr. 1804.

Charles SAMSON of Waldoborough ME to **John LABE.** <Lincoln Co.ME Deeds 72:117> ...3 May 1805, Charles SAMSON, yeoman & wf Sally, sell to John LABE...land in Waldoborough.

Charles SAMSON et al to **Joseph COMBS** of Thomaston ME. <Lincoln Co.ME Deeds 66:231> ...12 Aug. 1806, Charles SAMSON, gent. of Waldoborough as agent for Lucy TROUANT wf of Church TROUANT of Marshfield MA and Daniel SAMSON, yeoman of Waldoborough, for $60.00 sold to Joseph COMBS, yeoman...one half of marsh in Thomaston...bounded by the great Creek and land of Oliver ROBINS...being all the salt marsh which Charles SAMSON bought of Abraham LOCK, which the grantors hold in common with Elizabeth SAMSON & Sally D. SAMSON. Witness: Susan FARLEY. Rec. 1 Mar. 1808.

Charles SAMSON of Waldoborough ME to **Loren SIDES et al.** <Lincoln Co.ME Deeds 64:182> ...7 Apr. 1809, Charles SAMSON, gent. sells to Loren SIDES et al...Lot #9 on east side of Broad Bay River. Wf Sally SAMSON releases dower. <83:188>...3 July 1813, Charles SAMPSON, gent. of Waldoborough & wf Sally sell land in Waldoborough.

Will of **Caroline T. SAMPSON** of Waldoboro ME. <Lincoln Co.ME PR> <original>...dated 2 Sept. 1904, mentions following children, viz: **Alfred B. SAMPSON** of Thomaston ME, **Laura S. COONEY** wf of John of Brooklyn NY, **Frank SAMPSON** of Worcester MA, **Emily H. ELDRIDGE** wf of Herbert H. of Gardiner ME, **Mary Elizabeth TURNER** wf of Levi of Portland ME and **Isabel S. PARSONS** wf of Lincoln W. of New Harbor ME; granddaughter & adopted child, **Grace Caroline SAMPSON.** Pr. 13 Mar. 1906.

Oliver FALES of Thomaston ME to **Sarah D. HASKELL** of same. <Lincoln Co.ME East.Dist.Rcds. 2:463> ...30 May 1838, Oliver FALES, merchant & named executor & trustee in the last will...of Mrs. Elizabeth SAMPSON late of Thomaston dec'd, in discharge of sd trust, for $1.00 to me paid by Sarah D. HASKELL, inkeeper...quitclaimed to her land in Thomaston, also a pew in the new Congregational Meeting house in Thomaston & numbered sixty two. Ack. same day. Rec. 10 June 1838.

Sarah D. HASKELL of Thomaston ME to **Washington ROBBINS** of same. <Lincoln Co.ME East.Dist.5:183> ...22 Apr. 1841, Sarah D. HASKELL sold to Washington ROBBINS...land in Thomaston...being the same purchased of Charles CLELAND as per his deed dated 1 May 1838...also land called the Marsh lot being the same I received of my father Charles SAMPSON, being about 3 acres. Rec. 15 July 1841. <12:194>...24 July 1847, Sarah D. HASKELL quit claimed to George A. STARR, land in Thomaston.

Ebenezer SAMSON et al of Plymouth MA to **Oliver KEMPTON** of same. <Plymouth Co.Deeds 88:113> ...Apr. 1799, Ebenezer SAMSON, yeoman; Ephraim BARTLETT, mariner & wf Elizabeth; Bennet SIMMONS, laborer & wf Sarah; Richard COOPER, gent. & wf Hannah; Lydia EDWARDS, widow; George SAMSON, bricklayer; Mary COVINGTON, widow; Deborah WRIGHT, widow; Lemuel BRADFORD Jr.; Thomas BRADFORD, housewright; Mary BRADFORD, spinster; Hannah CHURCHILL, widow; Zephaniah BARTLETT, mariner & wf Elizabeth and Lemuel BRADFORD Sr., gent...for $120.00 release to Oliver KEMPTON, mariner...all their right to part of the dwelling that William HARLOW Sr. of Plymouth owned & where he died, which was set off to Mrs. Hannah SAMSON dec'd who was wf of Ebenezer SAMSON & dau of Wm. HARLOW.

Bennet SIMMONS of Plymouth MA to **Ebenezer SAMSON** of same. <Plymouth Co.Deeds 68:217>
...23 June 1788, Bennet SIMMONS, fisherman, for Ŀ16 releases to Ebenezer SAMSON, yeoman...all rights in a dwelling house & garden in Plymouth...which was set off to Sally SIMMONS my wife as her dower in the estate of John COOPER late of sd Plymouth dec'd.

==========

References to the name **Ebenezer SAMSON**, grantor (to 1801) in Plymouth Co.Deeds: 52:166;56:178;57:27;58:218;63:30;65:172;66:268;77:76;82:247;88:164.

==========

Ebenezer SAMSON et al of Plymouth MA to **Rosseter COTTON** of same. <Plymouth Co.Deeds 98:184>
...29 Dec. 1803, Ebenezer SAMSON, yeoman; George SAMSON, bricklayer; Mary COVENTON, widow; Richard COOPER, gent. & wf Hannah; Lydia EDWARDS, widow; Elizabeth BARTLETT, widow; Sarah SIMMONS, widow; Thomas BRADFORD; Ephraim HOLMES & wf Polly and Susanna SAMSON, widow of Ebenezer Jr., for $12.00 sold to Rosseter COTTON, Esq...five acre woodland & cedar swamp...being the land & swamp which was assigned to Hannah SAMSON wf of sd Ebenezer and mother of the others above named...in Harlow's Swamp...and was formerly the sd Hannah's father's William HARLOW, reference to the division of sd land among sd William HARLOW's children for the bounds, sd land joins John COTTON's heirs' land. Also signed by Polly BRADFORD, Eleanor BRADFORD & Hannah SOUTHWICK.

==========

Heirs of **Ebenezer SAMSON** of Plymouth MA to **Sarah KEMPTON** of same. <Plymouth Co.Deeds 121:24>
...17 July 1811, Susanna SAMSON widow of Ebenezer dec'd; Hannah FAUNCE and John FAUNCE, mariner; Olive GRIFFIN, widow; Susanna SAMPSON 2d and Ebenezer SAMSON, children of sd Ebenezer SAMSON dec'd, for $13.00 sold to Sarah KEMPTON widow of Oliver...all our right...unto that part of a dwelling house that William HARLOW Jr. late of Plymouth dec'd owned and where he died & which was sett off to our Grandmother Hannah SAMSON late of Plymouth dec'd, it being the front room & chamber over it, all the celler, a privilege in the yard & privilege in the well, sd house standing near the house of John PERREY & near sd Sally KEMPTON's house. Ack. 22 July 1811 & Rec. 10 Aug.

==========

PLYMOUTH COUNTY DEEDS: (re: SAMSON)

<34:116> - 8 May 1733, David SAMSON, for Ŀ30 sells land to Joshua SAMSON. Rec. 20 May 1741.
<34:116> - 10 Feb. 1734/5, Samuel & Ruth RING and Isaac PARTRIDGE & wf Grace, for Ŀ14 sell land to Joshua SAMSON. Rec. 20 May 1741.
<34:117> - 22 Nov. 1739, Samuel BREWSTER to Joshua SAMSON. Rec. 20 May 1741.
<42:41> - 22 Feb. 1753, Mary SAMSON of Duxbury, widow of Joshua, for Ŀ29 sells to son Anthony SAMSON of same, 20 acres, 55th lot in 1st division.
<46:45> - 23 Mar. 1756, Abraham & Mary SAMSON to Philip CHANDLER & Anthony SAMSON.

==========

Caleb SAMSON of Duxborough MA to **Mary SAMSON** of same. <Plymouth Co.Deeds 36:162>
...7 May 1744, Caleb SAMSON, yeoman, for Ŀ29 sold to Mary SAMSON, widow of Joshua...farm in Duxborough...which Joshua SAMSON died seized of...one half of one lot and half of the common lands which formerly belonged to the Township of Duxborough and Pembroke, viz: The 55th and half the 56th lot which were laid out in the year 1710 in the first Division of Common Lands in Duxborough & is that part of my land which was set off to the sd Joshua SAMSON...by a deed of division between the sd Joshua SAMSON & Caleb SAMSON Jr. bearing date 5 July 1738 & Recorded in the Second Parchment Book of the Records of Duxborough 21:22. Witnesses: Joshua CHANDLER, Robert SAMSON. Ack same day by Caleb. Rec. same day.

==========

Estate of **Joshua SAMPSON**, yeoman of Duxbury MA. <Plymouth Co.PR #17580>
<8:464> Letter/Bond 17 Sept. 1741, widow **Mary SAMSON** app'td admx. Sureties: Samuel ALDEN & Philip CHANDLER of Duxbury. Witnesses: Samuel SEABURY, Edward WINSLOW. <8:488> Inventory taken 17 Sept. 1741 by Samuel ALDEN, Philip CHANDLER, Samuel SEABURY; incl. notes of Jno. WADSWORTH & Samuel SEABURY and bond of Israel SILVESTER. <13:77> Account 2 Apr. 1753, of admx.; Paid to: Benjamin LORING, Joshua CHANDLER, Samuel SEABURY, Philip CHANDLER, Thomas PHILLIPS, Thomas PHILLIPS, Jr., John THOMAS, Benjamin BRYANT Jr., Ebenezer HARLOW, Benjamin SAMSON, George PARTRIDGE, Joshua SOUL, Cornelius DREW.

==========

Guardianship of Children of **Joshua SAMPSON** of Duxbury MA. <Plymouth Co.PR #17447>
<8:445>...27 Jan. 1741, **Amos SAMSON** of Duxbury, minor above 14, chooses Samuel SEABURY as his gdn. Witnesses: George PARTRIDGE, Abiell FULLER. <original> Bond 17 Mar. 1741, of Samuel SEABURY as gdn. Surety: Joshua SOULE of Duxbury. Witnesses: Benjamin HANKS, Edward WINSLOW. <9:181> 3 Feb. 1743, **Anthony SAMSON** of Plymouth, minor son, chooses Samuel ALDEN of Duxbury as his gdn. Witnesses: Edward WINSLOW, Hannah WINSLOW.

DORCAS SAMSON[2] (Henry[1])

MICRO #3 OF 7

Will of **Thomas BONNEY**, husbandman of Duxbury MA. <Plymouth Co.PR #2280>
<7:156>...dated 9 July 1735...aged & in daily expectation of dissolution by reason of many infirmities...to dau **Elisabeth NORCUTT** now the wife of Ephraim, half of his farm & dwelling...to grandchildren, the children of dau **Mercy** (now the wife of John CURTIS) which she had by her late husband Nathaniel DELANOE of Duxbury dec'd, the other half, viz: one third to grandson **Nathaniel DELANO** and two thirds to his four sisters **Mercy, Lydia, Zerviah & Mary**...I give my gun to my grandson **Nathaniel DELANOE**...to my granddaughter **Mercy DELANOE** if she shall be married within twelve months after my decease one feather bed...to dau **Elisabeth** my biggest Bible & one feather

bed, warming pan & largest iron pot, my trammels & other untensils belonging to ye chimney...to son in law **Ephraim NORCUT**...half of all ye hay, grain, apples; friend Thomas PRINCE of Duxborough executor. Witnesses: Elisha BREWSTER, Bethiah PRIOR, John WADSWORTH who all made oath 19 Aug. 1735. Pr. 22 Aug. 1735. <7:169> Inventory taken by John ALDEN, Israel SILVESTER, John WADSWORTH, all of Duxbury; incl. bonds due from Christopher WADSWORTH & Ichabod SAMSON; total real estate, £600. <11:374> Warrant to divide real estate, 4 Sept. 1749, to Samuel SEABURY, Samuel WESTON, George PARTRIDGE, Ebenezer BARTLETT & John WADSWORTH Jr., all of Duxborough; to following heirs, viz: to Israel SILVESTER, guardian to **Mary DELANOE**, a person non compos mentis, one share of homestead farm bounded by land of William BREWSTER & Rev. Samuel VEAZIE and one half of fourteen acre woodland in Duxborough; to **Nathaniel DELANOE** his share; to Rev. Samuel VEAZIE and Benjamin PRIOR, as assignees or legal representatives of **Mercy PRIOR** wf of John, **Lydia DELANOE** wf of Ebenezer and **Zerviah BRIGGS** wf of Joshua, their parts which were their shares.

Estate of **Mary DELANO**, non comp. <Plymouth Co.PR #6298>
..."1747?"...<10:453,354,503,504;11:372;19:458;20:146,290> (no details given)

PLYMOUTH COUNTY DEEDS: (re: BONNEY)

<5:62>	- 1702,	John BONNEY to Edward WANTON.
<6:109>	- 1703,	William BONNEY & Daniel RAMSDEN to Benjamin SOULE of Plymouth.
<14:4>	- 15 June 1708,	William BONNEY of Plympton to brother James BONNEY of Dartmouth.
<8:41>	- 1709,	William BONNEY.
<9:199>	- 1712,	James BONNEY et al.
<10:323>	- 1713,	William BONNEY.
<10:576>	- 1713/4,	William BONNEY.
<10:278>	- 1714,	Joseph BONNEY, James BONNEY et al.
<11:244>	- ,	John BONNEY.
<12:7>	- 10 Jan. 1715,	Thomas BONNEY Sr., yeoman of Duxbury.
<12:84>	- 4 Apr. 1715,	Joseph BONNEY & James BONNEY , yeomen of Pembroke.
<14:125>	- 1716,	Thomas BONNEY.
<15:214>	- 1721,	Thomas BONNEY.
<16:184>	- 1723,	James BONNEY.
<17:168>	- 3 Mar. 1723/4,	John BONNEY of Pembroke, son of Thomas BONNEY dec'd of Duxbury. Witnesses: Perez BONNEY, Ichabod BONNEY.
<17:170>	- 4 Mar. 1723,	John BONNEY Sr.
<17:21>	- 1723,	James BONNEY.
<17:210>	- 4 Mar. 1723/4,	John BONNEY Sr. of Pembroke.
<17:220>	- 1724,	Ichabod BONNEY to Elisha BONNEY.
<18:189>	- 17 July 1724,	Desire BONNEY, widow of James BONNEY of Pembroke to son James BONNEY, her rights to land of her Grandfather Francis BILLINGTON.
<19:4>	- ,	James & Desire BONNEY to Thomas PALMER, their right to seven eights of land of our Grandfather Francis BILLINGTON.
<20:39>	- 1725,	John BONNEY & James BONNEY to Mary THOMAS.

Estate of **Ebenezer BONNEY**, fisherman of Duxbury MA. <Plymouth Co.PR #2236>
<3:202> Letter/Bond 29 Dec. 1712, father **Thomas BONNEY Sr.** of Duxbury app'td admr. Witnesses: Elizabeth THOMAS, Elizabeth OTIS. <3:203> Inventory taken 21 Feb. 1712/3 by Israel SILVESTER & Philip DELANO; incl. his comon right of upland and meadow, £17; a gun, £2.15s; his part of the whale boat & craft, £5.17s4d; his part of a whale, £23.1s5d; Account 17 Mar. 1712/3 of admr., estate is settled on the father.

Zerviah DELANO of Duxbury MA to **Samuel VEAZIE** of same. <Plymouth Co.Deeds 35:21>
...12 Mar. 1741/2, Zerviah DELANO, spinster, sells to Samuel VEAZIE, clerk...one sixteenth of one half of farm in Duxbury where her grandfather Thomas BONNEY dec'd dwelt at the time of his death ...this half fell to the children of her mother Mrs. Mercy CURTIS by her first husband Nathaniel DELANOE of Duxbury. Witnesses: John PRIOR, Bethiah PRIOR.

John PRIOR & Lydia WORMAL of Duxbury MA to **Benjamin PRIOR Jr.** of same. <Plymouth Co.Deeds 36:16>
...30 June 1740, John PRIOR, husbandman & wf Mercy and Lydia WORMAL, relict of Ichabod WORMAL, sell to Benjamin PRIOR Jr...two sixths of 8th lot in 2nd Division of Commons of Duxbury & Pembroke laid out in 1713.

Guardianship of Children of **Nathaniel DELANO** of Duxborough MA. <Plymouth Co.PR #6310>
<7:168> Bond 21 Jan. 1735, John PRIOR, husbandman of Duxborough app'td gdn. of **Lydia DELANO** (14-21) who chose him. Surety: Samuel ALDEN, yeoman of Duxborough. Witnesses: Sarah WINSLOW, Mary WINSLOW. <7:171> Bond 21 Jan. 1735, Samuel ALDEN app'td gdn. of **Nathaniel DELANO** and **Mary DELANO** (both under 14). <10:10> Letter/Bond 20 Aug. 1745, Ebenezer DELANO, labourer of Duxborough app'td gdn. of **Nathaniel DELANO.** Surety: John PRIOR. Witnesses: Margret WADSWORTH, James WARREN Jr. <10:100> 28 Sept. 1745, **Nathaniel DELANO,** minor, chose Ebenezer DELANO, mariner of Duxborough as his gdn. Witnesses: Jonathan DELANO, David DELANO.

ELIZABETH SAMSON^2 (Henry^1)

Robert SPROUT of Middleboro MA to **Mercy OLDHAM et al.** <Plymouth Co.Deeds 10:2:28> ...6 June 1712, Robert SPROUT, for £5 sold to Mercy OLDHAM wf of Thomas, Anna RICHMOND wf of Ebenezer and Hannah KEEN wf of Ephraim...all my whole eighty acres in ye sought/south purchase together with my lot in Assawompsett and also two & one quarter acres which lyeth on a brook that cometh out of Elders Pond and eight acres lying upon Spring brook and my thirty acres of upland upon ye last division lying near Spring brook with three quarters of a share of cedar swamp and half a whole share of ye undevided in ye Sixteen Shilling purchase. Witnesses: Josiah KEEN, Mary SPROUT who made oath 3d Tues. Dec. 1712. Rec. 17 Dec. 1712.

Thomas KEEN et al to **Thomas NELSON** of Middleboro MA. <Plymouth Co.Deeds 12:32> ...16 June 1713, Thomas OLDHAM & wf Mercy of Scituate, Ephraim KEEN & wf Hannah of Pembroke and Ebenezer RICHMOND & wf Anna of MIddleborough, for £12 sold to Thomas NELSON...25 acres, lot #23 at Assawamsett Neck in Middleborough...which did formerly belong unto our Honoured Father Robert SPROUT dec'd. Witnesses: David WOOD Jr., David BRYANT, Ichabod NYE, Elizabeth NYE. Ack. 6 Nov. 1714 by Thomas OLDHAM, 20 June 1716 by Anna RICHMOND and 16 June 1713 by other grantors. Rec. 17 July 1716.

James SPROUT & Ebenezer RICHMOND of Middleboro to **William STRAWBRIDGE** of same.<Plymouth Co.Deeds> <25:50>...1 Apr. 1729, James SPROUT, yeoman and Ebenezer RICHMOND, yeoman & wf Anne/Anna, for £9.6s sold to William STRAWBRIDGE, husbandman...interest in the 127th lot in the third allotment in the Sixteen Shilling Purchase in Middleborough and was laid out in ye right of Our Honoured Father Robert SPROUT...37 acres...one quarter belonging to James SPROUT and one sixth belonging to Ebenezer & Anna RICHMOND...also interest in one fifth part of the 130th lot...which was left undrawn in sd third allotment & drawed in ye fourth allotment...one quarter belonging to James SPROUT and one quarter to Ebenezer & Anna. Witnesses: Robert RICHMOND, James STRAWBRIDGE. Ack. 14 Apr. 1729 by all grantors. Rec. 4 Mar. 1729 O.S. (15 Mar. 1730 N.S.).

Anna RICHMOND of Middleborough MA to **John PARRIS & Isaac PEIRCE Jr.** of same. <Plymouth Co.Deeds> <33:122>...13 Dec. 1738, Anna RICHMOND, widow of Ebenezer RICHMOND dec'd, for £10 sold to John PARRIS and Isaac PEIRCE Jr...one sixth part of lot #122 in the third allotment in the Sixteen Shilling Purchase in Middleborough...about 40 acres...and was laid out unto the original right of Robert SPROUT. Witnesses: Thomas NELSON Jr., Timothy TILSON. Ack. 7 Dec. 1739. Rec. 22 Apr. 1740.

Will of **Thomas HOLMES** of Middleborough MA. <Plymouth Co.PR> <6:425>...dated 8 Sept. 1733...to wf **Mary**, that part of land that fell to me which was my brother **Benjamin HOLMES'** and that piece of meadow that I bought of James COBB...to dau **Experience HOLMES** my homestead and also that piece of land that I bought of David MILLER; wf **Mary**, executrix. Witnesses: Ebenezer FINNEY, Jane FINNEY, James COB. Pr. 20 Dec. 1733. <6:444> Inventory taken 27 Feb 1733/4 by John BENNETT, James SOUL, Francis MILLER; incl. 40 acre homestead, £400; land bought of David MILLER, £50; land bought of Benjamin HOLMES, £50; 10 acre meadow in the Upper Meadow, £40; will sworn to 15 Mar. 1733/4 by exx. <7:136> Guardianship, 21 May 1735, Joseph BENNETT Jr., yeoman of Middleboro app'td gdn. of **Experience HOLMES,** minor under 14.

Will of **Col. Ebenezer SPROUT**, Esq. of Middleboro MA. <Plymouth Co.PR #19134> <29:474>...dated 4 Aug. 1785, mentions wf **Bathsheba** and the following children, viz: **Ebenezer SPROUT, Earl SPROUT, Thomas SPROUT** (executor), **James SPROUT, Samuel SPROUT, Mary TORREY** wf of William, **Bathsheba KEITH** wf of Cyrus. Pr. 6 Mar. 1786. Inventory taken 6 Mar. 1786.

Ephraim KEEN of Middleborough MA to **William STRAWBRIDGE** of same. <Plymouth Co.Deeds 28:29> ...23 Sept. 1729, Ephraim KEEN, husbandman, for £7.9s sold to William STRAWBRIDGE, husbandman... one quarter of one fifth part of Lot #130 in the third allotment of the Sixteen Shilling Purchase in Middleboro but drawn for in the fourth allotment...also one third part of one half of Lot #127 in the third allotment...laid out & recorded to the right of Robert SPROUT. Witnesses: Ralph FEALLOR, James STRAWBRIDGE. Ack. 29 Oct. 1731. Rec. 25 June 1733. (<28:29>...12 Feb. 1730/1, Ephraim PRAY of Dighton to William STRAWBRIDGE...land laid out in right of Robert SPROUT.)

Ephraim KEEN Jr. of Swanzey MA to **John PARRIS & Isaac PAINE Jr.** <Plymouth Co.Deeds 33:122> ...23 Jan. 1738, Ephraim KEEN Jr., late of Freetown, but now of Swanzey, for £10 sold to John PARRIS and Isaac PAINE Jr., both of Middleborough...one sixth part of Lot #122 in the third allotment of the Sixteen Shilling Purchase in Middleborough...about 40 acres...laid out unto the original right of Robert SPROUT. Witnesses: John BOOTH, Josiah HOLLOWAY. Ack. 4 Mar. 1738/9. Rec. 22 Apr. 1740.

PLYMOUTH COUNTY DEEDS: (re: Rachel SPROUT)

<25:170> - 1730, Rachel SPROUT, wf of James SPROUT & widow of John DWELLY to grandson Simeon KEEN
<25:190> - 1730, Rachel SPROUT, (as above ") to son Joseph DWELLEY.
<25:209> - 1730, Rachel SPROUT, (as above ") to son John DWELLEY.
<25:210> - 1730, Rachel SPROUT, (as above ") to son Abner DWELLEY.
<25:219> - 1730, Rachel SPROUT, (as above ") to Rachel TURNER wf of Caleb of Scituate.
<27:136> - 1730, Rachel SPROUT, (as above ") to dau Mary DWELLEY.
<28:53> - 1730, Rachel SPROUT, (as above ") to son Jedediah DWELLEY.

PLYMOUTH COUNTY DEEDS, cont-d: (re: Rachel SPROUT)

<32:202> - 1730, Rachel SPROUT, wf of James SPROUT & widow of John DWELLY to youngest dau Mercy DWELLEY.
<27:147> - 1732, Rachel SPROUT (as above ") to son Joseph DWELLEY.
<28:54> - 9 Sept 1732, Rachel SPROUT, spinner of Middleboro to son Jedediah DWELLEY of Scituate.
<25:20> - 1 June 1726, Caleb TORREY, yeoman of Scituate to Rachel DWELLEY, widow of same.
<162:166>- 6 Jan. 1828, Sarah DWELLE & Rachel DWELLE of Scituate to Joseph COLMAN, one acre with house all three live in.

Estate of **Rachel SPROUT** of Middleboro MA. <Plymouth Co.PR #19142>
<7:416> Letter 31 May 1738, **Joseph DWELLEY** of Pembroke app'td admr. of estate of mother **Rachel SPROUT** late wife of James SPROUT. <7:436> Inventory taken 5 June 1738; incl. half pew in Scituate meeting house, Ł10. <9:38> Account 12 Mar. 1741, of admr.

MICRO #4 OF 7

Estate of **Lemuel DWELLY**, shipwright of Scituate MA. <Plymouth Co.PR>
<8:255> Letter 11 Oct. 1740, John DWELLY, yeoman of Scituate app'td admr. <8:254> Inventory taken 1 Nov. 1740 by Nehemiah RANDALL, Robert BARKER, John JAMES Jr.; incl. bonds & notes from John CLARKE, Joseph DWELLY, William FOBES, Caleb TURNER, Stephen CLAPP, Coombs BARROW & Zoath SPOONER. <9:275> Account 11 Mar. 1741 of admr. <9:277> Warrant to divide real estate, 21 Mar. 1742. <9:278> Division 1 Apr. 1743, among following heirs, viz: **John DWELLY, Rachel TURNER, Thankful FOBES** heirs of **Jedediah DWELLY**, heirs of **Deborah KEEN**, heirs of **Abner DWELLY, Mary BARROW, Joseph DWELLY** and **Mercy LINCOLN.**

James SPROUT of Middleborough MA to **Nathaniel SPROUT** of same. <Plymouth Co.Deeds 39:198>
...10 Sept. 1748, James SPROUT, husbandman, for Ł26 sold to son Nathaniel SPROUT...one quarter part of 7th lot...of the Sonet River Cedar Swamp which share was in the original right of Robert SPROUT...about two acres...part of the Sixteen Shilling Purchase. Witnesses: Benjamin DURFEY, Benjamin WHITE. Ack. same day. Rec. 21 Sept. 1748.

James SPROUT of Middleborough MA to **Nathaniel SPROUT** of same. <Plymouth Co.Deeds 56:5>
...13 Sept. 1748, James SPROUT, husbandman, for Ł100 sold to Nathaniel SPROUT, labourer...all the undivided land that is not now sold in the Sixteen Shilling Purchase in Middleborough...the whole share of Pond Ore. Witnesses: John SAMSON, Ebenezer SOTHARD. Ack. 14 Sept. 1748. Rec 4 July 1770.

Nathaniel SPROUT of Hardwick MA to **James STROBRIDGE Jr.** of Middleboro. <Plymouth Co.Deeds 55:188>
...16 Jan. 1766, Nathaniel SPROUT, husbandman, for Ł4.16s sold to James STROBRIDGE Jr., husbandman...one share of the Iron ore in mine call Pond ore in the Sixteen Shilling Purchase in Middleborough. Witnesses: Silas PRATT, John MONTGOMERY. Ack. 26 Sept. 1770. Rec. 4 Oct. 1770.

Nathanial SPROUT of Hardwick MA to **Robert SPROUT** of Middleborough. <Plymouth Co.Deeds 56:201>
...15 Apr. 1772, Nathaniel SPROUT, husbandman, for 5s sold to Robert SPROUT, gent...all my right in the undivided land in the Sixteen shililng Purchase in Middleborough...and I do also acquite the sd Robert SPROUT & his heirs of all claim and demand for the Pond Ore he has drawn out of Assawamset Pond in sd Middleborough upon my Father's right in years preceeding this date. Witnesses: John COTTON, Sophia COTTON. Ack. & Rec. 15 Apr. 1772.

Andrew WHITE of Dudley MA to **Nathaniel SPROUT** of Middleborough MA. <Worcester Co.Deeds 30:23>
...16 Sept. 1748, Andrew WHITE, cordwainer of Dudley, for Ł300 sold to Nathaniel SPROUT, husbandman...100 acres in Hardwick...Lot #8 by plan in 2nd Range...bounded by 1000 acres owned by Mr. RUGGLES et al and land of Mr. HASKEL, Col. DUDLEY and AMMIDOWN. Rec. 11 July 1750.

Nathaniel SPROUT of Hardwick MA to **Ebenezer LAWRENCE** of same. <Worcester Co.Deeds 32:2>
...9 Apr. 1752, Nathaniel SPROUT, husbandman, for Ł20 sold to Ebenezer LAWRENCE, husbandman...30 acres in Lot #8 in Hardwick, west of Ware River. Esther SPROUT signs. Ack. 23 Apr. 1752 by both. Rec. 14 Aug. 1752.

Nathaniel SPROUT of Hardwick MA to **Nathaniel SPROUT** of same. <Worcester Co.Deeds 66:506>
...30 Mar. 1772, Nathaniel SPROUT, husbandman, for Ł100 sold to son Nathaniel SPROUT, husbandman ...50 acres in Hardwick. Ack. 9 July 1772. Rec. 11 July 1772.

Nathaniel SPROUT Jr. of Hardwick MA to **Nathaniel SPROUT** of same. <Worcester Co.Deeds 82:86>
...15 Apr. 1774, Nathaniel SPROUT Jr., yeoman, for Ł400 sold to Nathaniel SPROUT, yeoman...120 acres & my dwelling house. Ack. same day. Rec. 2 June 1779.

Nathaniel SPROUT Jr. of Hardwick MA to **Robert SPROUT** of same. <Worcester Co.Deeds 84:2>
...19 Apr. 1779, Nathaniel SPROUT Jr., yeoman, for Ł900 sold to brother Robert SPROUT, husbandman ...100 acres in Hardwick. Ack. 9 July 1779 by Nathaniel. Rec. 16 Oct. 1780.

Nathaniel SPROUT Sr. of Hardwick MA to **Nathaniel SPROUT Jr.** of same. <Worcester Co.Deeds 82:339>
...3 Dec. 1779, Nathaniel SPROUT Sr., yeoman, for Ł400 sold to Nathaniel SPROUT Jr., yeoman...120 acres...where I now dwell in Hardwick...bounded by land of Robert SPROUT et al. Wf Esther SPROUT

releases dower. Witnesses: Susanna MANDELL, Paul MANDELL, Samuel SPROUT, Nathan SPROUT. Ack. same day. Rec. 18 Dec. 1779.

Nathaniel SPROUT Jr. of Hardwick MA to **Samuel HOPKINS** of same. <Worcester Co.Deeds 86:340>
...28 Mar. 1782, Nathaniel SPROUT Jr., husbandman, for £50 sold to Samuel HOPKINS, husbandman... twenty two & a half acres in Hardwick. Aznbah SPROUT signs. Witnesses: Samuel SPROUT, Lemuel SPROUT. Ack. 21 May 1782 by Nathaniel. Rec. 22 May 1782. (Same day Samuel HOPKINS sold land to Nathaniel SPROUT Jr.)

Nathaniel SPROUT VS **Nathaniel SPROUT Jr.** <Worcester Co.Deeds 135:216>
...13 Dec. 1798...Whereas Nathaniel SPROUT, yeoman of Hardwick by Court of Common Pleas holden at Worcester...on monday next preceding the first tuesday of December instant moved Judgement against Nathaniel SPROUT Jr., yeoman, for $851.94 damages and $11.01 costs of suit...whereof execution remains to be done...If not enough goods to satisfy...We command you to take the body of the sd SPROUT Jr. & him commit unto our Gaol in Worcester...& hold him there until judgment & fees are paid...or that he be discharged by the sd SPROUT the creditor. On 29 Dec. 1798, Annas NEWCOMB, Earle FLAGG & Lemuel WHEELER appraised fifty five & a half acres in Hardwick bounded by land of Robert SPROUT, Isaac CUMMINGS, Nathan SPROUT, Edward CLARK, Nehemiah HAYWARD and BANGS. Nathaniel SPROUT has...taken the right of equity of redeeming the sd land charged in mortgage by Nathaniel SPROUT Jr. the debtor to the Union Bank for $303.00...equity is worth $881.42. Witness: Nathan SPROUT. Rec. 24 Mar. 1799.

<u>WORCESTER COUNTY DEEDS</u>: (re: Nathaniel SPROUT)

<30:127> - 1750, Nathaniel SPROUT to Walter HASTINGS.
<29:554> - 1752, Nathaniel SPROUT to James ROBINSON.
<66:507> - 6 Dec. 1756, Nathaniel SPROUT, husbandman bought land at auction. Rec. 11 July 1772.
<82:312> - 1772, Nathaniel SPROUT from Prudence FAY.
<73:187> - 1774, Nathaniel SPROUT Jr. from Joseph TIDD.
<114:643> - 1792, Nathaniel SPROUT Jr. to Union Bank.
<123:423> - 1795, Nathaniel SPROUT Jr. from Ebenezer CURTIS.
<133:493> - 1798, Nathaniel SPROUT Jr. to Robert SPROUT.
<134:405> - 1798, Nathaniel SPROUT to David PAIGE.
<135:218> - 1799, Nathaniel SPROUT Jr. to Nathan SPROUT, execution.
<136:203> - 1799, Nathaniel SPROUT to Uriah DOANE.
<136:63> - 1799, Nathaniel SPROUT Jr. to Isaac CUMMINGS.
<136:204> - 1799, Nathaniel SPROUT Jr. from Edward SMITH.
<136:206> - 1799, Nathaniel SPROUT Jr. from Ephraim CLEVELAND Jr.
<136:207> - 1799, Nathaniel SPROUT Jr. from Silas COBB.
<139:5,6> - 1799, Nathaniel SPROUT to Isaac CUMMINGS.

Will of **Ebenezer SPROUT**, yeoman of Greenwich MA. <Hampshire Co.PR 34:53>
...dated 12 Apr. 1820...to wf **Miriam**, an honourable maintenance of all the necessaries of life... to eldest dau **Relief SPROUT**, $100.00 and a convenient room in my dwelling house while single...to eldest son **Ebenezer SPROUT**, $2.00...to 2d dau **Miriam SPROUT**, $90.00 and a convenient room in my dwelling house while single...to 2d son **Ezra SPROUT**, one half of home farm and the whole of my lot on the plain and one half of building conveniences, upon condition of his paying one half of the legacies...to 3d son **David SPROUT** one half of my home farm and one half of building conveniences upon condition of his paying one half of my legacies...to 4th son **Charles SPROUT**, $2.00... to 5th son **Hosea SPROUT**, $100.00...to 3d dau **Salome SPROUT**, $80.00...to brother **Samuel SPROUT**, necessaries for living while...a resident in my house; sons **Ezra & David**, executors. Witnesses: Joseph BLODGET, Eunice NASH, Vesta WHITCOMB. Pr. 8 Oct. 1822.

Will of **Ezra SPROUT** of Greenwich MA. <Hampshire Co.PR>
...dated 15 May 1856...to sons **Brigham D. SPROUT & Elmer M. SPROUT**, $300.00 each...equal to what I have done for my other sons...to daus **Amanda M. POWERS, Aurelia D. FISK, Emeline M. GROSS** and **Luthera S. FISK**, $12.50 each...to wf **Dency**, $1000.00 together with all household furniture and wearing apparel...in lieu of dower; son **Alfred L. SPROUT**, executor. Witnesses: Samuel HALE, Cyrus POWERS, Hannah POWERS. <u>Codicil</u> 16 May 1856...estate to be equally divided among sons **Alfred L. SPROUT, Bradford E. SPROUT, Brigham D. SPROUT** and **Elmer M. SPROUT**. Witnesses: Samuel HALE, Hannah POWERS, Lavina POWERS. Pr. 12 Aug. 1856.

Robert SPROUT of Middleboro MA to **Zebedee SPROUT** of same. <Plymouth Co.Deeds 79:27>
...28 Aug. 1778, Robert SPROUT, gent., to son **Zebedee SPROUT**, laborer...land given me by my father in law Nathaniel SOUTHWORTH 2 Sept. 1746. Ack. same day. Rec. 5 Jan. 1796.

Jedediah CASWELL of Middleborough MA to **Mercy SPROUT**, spinster of same.<Plymouth Co.Deeds 75:231>
...18 May 1793...20 acres with house in Middleboro and other land not specified.

Mercy SPROUT of Middleborough MA to **David CASWELL** of same. <Plymouth Co.Deeds 91:243>
...4 Apr. 1795, Mercy SPROUT, wf of Robert SPROUT, gent., to David CASWELL, yeoman...land she bought of Jedediah CASWELL 18 May 1793 & rec. 75:231. Witnesses: Eleanor TILSON, Zebedee SPROUT. Ack. 14 June 1797. (References only, to **Mercy SPROUT**: 62:129;79:26;84:132.)

Will of **Robert SPROUT**, gent. of Middleboro MA. <Plymouth Co.PR #19145>
<36:293>...dated 30 May 1797...advanced in age...mentions contract made with present wife before

our marriage and what she brought with her; everything else to son **Zebedee SPROUT**; wf **Mercy**, executrix. <36:294> Pr. 5 Feb. 1798 by exx. <36:397> Inventory taken 9 Feb. 1798. <36:424> Notice. <36:582> Insolvency, 1 June 1798. <37:341> Account 28 Oct. 1800 by exx.

Estate of **Robert SPROUT Jr.**, yeoman of Middleboro MA. <Plymouth Co.PR #19144>
<original> Petition, 29 Nov. 1782, of widow **Hannah SPROUT**, says he died last April in Continental Service leaving three small children. <27:106> Letter 2 Dec. 1782, Zebedee SPROUT, yeoman of Middleboro app'td admr. <29:20,21,127> "Insolvency?". <33:26> Dower set off to widow **Hannah SPROUT**, 19 Feb. 1787. <original> Letter 12 Sept. 1787, calls **Zebedee SPROUT** brother of dec'd. <33:29> Creditors' claims allowed, 23 Apr. 1793.

Thomas OLDHAM of Scituate MA to **Nehemiah BENNETT** of Middleborough MA. <Plymouth Co.Deeds 19:153>
...6 Sept. 1725, Thomas OLDHAM & wf Mercy, for Ł15 sold to Nehemiah BENNETT...our one third part of that whole share of land which did originally belong unto the right of our Honoured Grandfather Henry SAMPSON...in South Purchase. Witnesses: Joshua MORSS, Thomas LATHAM. Rec. 21 Oct. 1725.

Heirs of **Mercy OLDHAM** of Scituate MA. <Plymouth Co.Deeds 37:178>
...8 Oct. 1728, Joshua OLDHAM, Thomas OLDHAM Jr. and Caleb OLDHAM, husbandmen of Scituate...quit our claim unto a certain tract or tracts of land or lands given by our Honourable Mother to her seven daughters by will upon her Death Bed. Witnesses: Joseph BENNETT, Thankfull BENNETT, Elisha CORNISH, Hopestill BISBEE. Ack. 3 Nov. 1738 by Joshua & Caleb. Rec. 25 Oct. 1745.

Heirs of **Mercy OLDHAM** of Scituate MA to **John BISBEE** of Pembroke MA. <Plymouth Co.Deeds 37:178>
...28 Feb. 1742, John DAMMAN, cooper & wf Elizabeth of Pembroke; Nathaniel EAMES, yeoman & wf Abigail of Marshfield; Samuel TILDEN, yeoman & wf Desire of Marshfield and Anthony EAMES, yeoman & wf Grace of Marshfield...for Ł20 sold to John BISBEE, yeoman...all rights in lands in Middleborough...of our Honoured Mother Mercy OLDHAM. Witnesses: Thomas TRACY, Silvanus EAMES. Ack. same day by all except the DAMMANS; Ack. 4 Oct. 1743 by DAMMANS. Rec. 25 Oct. 1745.

Will of **Thomas OLDHAM**, yeoman of Scituate MA. <Plymouth Co.PR #14876>
<7:121>...dated 21 Feb. 1733...being aged and weak...to son **Joshua OLDHAM**, five shillings which is (with what I have given him allready) a sufficient portion for him...to son **Thomas OLDHAM**, all that part of my farm whereon I now dwell on the west side of the high way...bounded by meadow that was Thomas STETSON's and meadow of Michall WANTON...also three acres of sd farm on east side ...bounded by land of Samuel LAPHAM...also twelve acres at the head of HIXE's lott...also one half of cedar swamp in Hanover and one half of personal estate...to son **Caleb OLDHAM**, remainder of farm...other half of ceder swamp and other half of personal estate...to dau **Mercy**, Ł10...to daus **Mary, Elizabeth, Abigal, Ann, Desire** and **Grace**, Ł5 each...thay haveing allready received part of their portions; sons **Caleb & Thomas**, executors. Witnesses: Samuel SILVESTER, Josiah EAMES and Caleb TORREY who made oath 24 Jan. 1734. <7:122> Letter 26 Feb. 1734, **Caleb OLDHAM & Thomas OLDHAM**, app'td admrs. <original> Bond 24 Jan. 1734, of exrs. Sureties: John SILVESTER & Joshua SILVESTER, husbandmen of Marshfield. Witnesses: Caleb TORREY, Samuel MARSHALL.

Estate of **Thomas OLDHAM** of Scituate MA. <Plymouth Co.PR #14877>
<7:149,155,167,295,447,448;10:168>...non-cupative will, bond 1735, bond 1738, inventory...

Guardianship of Children of **Thomas OLDHAM** of Scituate MA. <Plymouth Co.PR #14878>
<7:150,449;9:369;12:355>...1 Aug. 1735, **Josiah WORMALL** app'td gdn. of his grandson **Thomas OLDHAM**, and grandaughter **Patience OLDHAM**, both minors under 14. On 3 Nov. 1738, Samuel TILDEN Jr. app'td gdn. of **Thomas OLDHAM**, under 14. On 1 Oct. 1744, Samuel TILDEN app'td gdn. of **Thomas**. Surety: Joshua OLDHAM.

Will of **Samuel TILDEN**, yeoman of Marshfield MA. <Plymouth Co.PR #20753>
<21:605>...dated 6 Apr. 1757...to wf **Desire** the income of land bought of Ebenezer JONES, land bught of Thomas BRYANT called Mill Pasture and income of one third of the farm...to son **Samuel TILDEN**, the other two thirds and his clock, farming tools, desk, cane, guns, swords, pistols, one bed & furniture, wearing apparel and pew...to daus **Mercy MACOMBER, Ruth EELLS & Sarah JAMES**, remainder of personal estate after death of their mother. Pr. 31 Mar. 1774. Inventory taken 5 Apr. 1774.

Anthony EAMES of Marshfield MA to **Ruth EAMES** of same. <Plymouth Co.Deeds 63:21>
...24 Nov. 1773, Anthony EAMES, yeoman, in consideration of the natural love & affection which I have & bear to my daughter Ruth EAMES, widow and also the sum of five shillings...confirm unto her...all the right...which I have or can claim...in all the lands...by the last will of Lemuel EAMES dec'd late husband of sd Ruth, bearing date 22 Nov. 1766. Witnesses: Sarah PORTER, Phebe TILDEN. Ack. 21 Jan. 1774. Rec. 5 Feb. 1784.

HANNAH SAMSON[2] (Henry[1])

MICRO #5 OF 7

Henry SAMPSON of Duxbury to **Hannah HOLMES**. <Plymouth Co.Deeds 4:188>
...22 May 1675, Henry SAMPSON, planter, for love & naturall affection to dau Hannah HOLMES wf of Josiah...40 acres at Robinson Creek granted him by the town of Duxbury...bounded by land of Robert BARKER Sr. and Robert SPROUT of Scituate. Ack. 14 May 1677.

JAMES SAMSON[2] (Henry[1])

Samuel WAIT of Portsmouth RI to **William BOVINGTON**(sp) of same. <original, G.A. Moriarty Jr. 1912> ...13 Mar. 1692/3, Samuel WAIT, for Ł50 sells to William BOVINGTON...16 acres at Little Silver... bounded by land of sd BOVINGTON, also two acres bounded by land of Daniel FISH. Witnesses: (Benjamin) GREENE, Jeremiah FONE, Jeremiah WELLS, John FONES. Ack. 31 Mar. 1693 by Samuel & Rec. 1:355. On 12 Oct. 1694, James & Hannah SAMSON of Dartmouth gave their consent...to our son Samuel WAIT to make sufficient sale of that house & land which was formerly Thomas WAIT's dec'd. (Note: Bowman questions the first name "Thomas".)

James SAMSON Jr. of Dartmouth MA to **Abraham TUCKER** of same. <"New Bedford copy" 2:135> ...8 Dec. 1712, James SAMSON Jr. sells to Abraham TUCKER...nine acres taken up in Dartmouth and to be part of the eight hundred acres division already agreed on to be layed out..in the undivided land. Witnesses: Elizabeth TUCKER, Benjamin CRANE.

Giles SLOCUM of Portsmouth RI to **Abraham TUCKER** of Dartmouth MA. <"New Bedford copy" 2:142> ...16 Apr. 1701, Giles SLOCUM sells to Abraham TUCKER...40 acres bounded by Poneganset harbour and land of widow RUSSELL and Matthew ALLEN...also four & a half acre meadow.

Will of **Joseph SAMSON**, yeoman of New Bedford MA. <Bristol Co.PR>
<44:112>...dated 29 Dec. 1803...to wf **Marcy** the improvment of one third of real estate & indoor moveables during her life...two cows, six sheep, one swine...the improvment of ye room we usually live in below, the square chamber above it, two bedrooms in the chamber over the north room, the butery & cellar under her keeping room and so much of the garret as she may need, with the long entery in the chamber & closeroom...also half the barn and corn house...to son **Edward SAMSON** the other two thirds of real estate...to six grand daughters, viz: **Sarah GIFFORD, Mary GURNEY, Rhoda ROUNSEVILL, Marcy HATSET, Keturah BENNET & Jean SAMSON** to receive estate given to wife after her death...son **Edward** take care that sufficient fuel be provided for his sd mother & cut at the door ...all due attention & kindness be rendred to his sd mother at all times & in all cases wherein she may stand in need; son **Edward** and **John HATSET**, husband of grandaughter **Marcy**, executors. Witnesses: Isaac VINCENT, Thomas SEVERENCE, Thomas TERRY, Samuel SPRAGUE. <original> Petition 14 July 1808 of **Edward SAMSON**, who declines to serve as executor & asks that **John ATSETT** be app'td sole executor. Witnesses: Nathan WILLCOX, Annie SAMSON. <44:114> Letter/Bond 14 July 1808, **John ATSATT**, blockmaker, app'td admr. Sureties: Samuel SPRAGUE, Esq. & Thomas TERRY, yeoman, both of New Bedford. Witness: John G. DEANE. <44:298> Warrant to appraise, 14 July 1808, to Samuel SPRAGUE, Esq., Paul COOK, Jonathan POPE. <44:299> Inventory taken 25 July 1808 by appraisers; incl. homestead farm east of road, $3066.00; dwelling house, $666.00; corn house, $16.00; homestead farm west of road, $3143.00; small seder swamp, $34.00; seder swamp in Freetown, $40.00; total estate, $7144.45. <44:480> Account 7 Mar. 1809, of admr. <45:59> Order, 2d Mon. Mar. 1809, to **John ATSATT**, admr., to sell so much of real estate as would bring $450.00 for payment of debts. <45:71> Notice of sale, 20 Apr. 1809, admr. made oath that he had posted notices at George ATWOOD's in Taunton, SAMSON's Inkeeper in Middleborough, Jonathan POPE's in New Bedford and in the Old Colony Gazette in New Bedford, for the sale of part of homestead, small pine swamp, pew in Baptist meeting house in Long Plain, one ox cart, one log chain, two draught chains, one iron bar and one yoke of oxen. <44:571> Warrant, 20 Apr. 1809, to Alden SPOONER, Esq., Gideon WOOD & Amos BRALEY to set off dower to widow; Dower set off to widow **Marcy SAMSON**, 24 Apr. 1809. <45:157> 2d Account, 3 Oct. 1809, of admr.; Paid to: Samuel SPRAGUE, Esq., Jonathan POPE, Edward BENNETT, William SKIFF, Nathan WILLCOX, Shubael HAMMETT, Humphrey HATHAWAY, Amos BRALEY, George BRALEY, Abner VINCENT, James TABER, Edward SAMSON, Jacob BENNETT, John JENNE, John HAWES, Esq., Alden SPOONER, Esq., Gideon WOOD, William ROTCH, Samuel PERRY, Esq., Stephen HATHAWAY, William KEMPTON.

Estate of **Joseph SAMPSON.** <Bristol Co.PR>
<9:162> Adm. & Inventory, 20 Mar. 1738/9, by widow **Sarah SAMPSON.** <11:238> Account. <11:246> Guardianship. <11:393> Division, 5 May 1747, to following children, viz: **Joseph SAMPSON, Ruhama SAMPSON, Sarah SAMPSON & Lois GRAY.**

Guardianship of **Joseph SAMPSON,** non comp, of New Bedford MA. <Bristol Co.PR>
<42:94>...gdn. app'td 4 Mar. 1806. <42:120> Inventory. <42:342,552,542> Account, Notice, 1806.

Guardianship & Estate of **Edward SAMPSON** of New Bedford/Fairhaven MA. <Bristol Co.PR>
<31:438>...25 Feb. 1792, gdn. app'td for **Edward SAMPSON,** non comp. <31:439> Inventory. <36:216> ...1797, gdn. discharged as Edward is "restored to reason". <52:12> On 26 Apr. 1816, Humphrey DAVIS, Joseph BENNET & Richard DELANO, all of Fairhaven, app'td to appraise estate of **Edward SAMPSON,** dec'd of Fairhaven. Inventory taken 4 May 1816; incl. pew in Baptist Meeting in Long Plain, $23.34; no real estate mentioned. <151:257;159:3> Letter/Bond 8 May 1816, John ATSATT, yeoman of Fairhaven app'td admr. Sureties: James TABER, Esq. & Bartholomew AKIN, yeoman, both of Fairhaven. Witnesses: Henry STODDARD, Francis BAYLIES. <110:393> Notice, 8 May 1816. <52:524> Account of admr., 29 Oct. 1816; payments to Jethro DAVIS "for the deceaseds Mother's coffin" and widow's allowance of $200.00. <53:421> 2d Account of admr., 6 May 1817; payments to Allerton CUSHMAN, Abner VINCENT and a pair of grave stones.

Estate of **John ATSATT** of Mattapoisett MA. <Plymouth Co.PR>
<originals> Petition 19 May 1860, to have John T. ATSATT app'td admr., signed by: **Laura ATSATT, Edward S. ATSATT, Sarah A. LeBARON & Mary H. PURRINGTON.** Last Account 9 May 1864, by John T. AT-

SATT, admr.; The undersigned, being all the parties interested, request the account be allowed, viz: **Edward S. ATSATT, Mary H. PURRINGTON, Sarah A. LeBARON, James LeBARON & Isaiah PURRINGTON.** Dower assigned, 30 Oct. 1860, to widow **Laura ATSATT.**

Edward SAMPSON of Fairhaven MA to **Joseph SAMSON.** <Bristol Co.Deeds 99:262>
...27 Jan. 1815, Edward SAMPSON, yeoman, sold to son Joseph SAMSON...part of the homestead farm bequeathed to me by my Honoured Father Joseph SAMSON dec'd in his last will and being all the residue...of the land which I possess excepting what I this day conveyed to my son in law John ATSATT by deed of sale...in case he my sd son Joseph should decease before me or my wife his Mother that the sd premises shall revert to me. Witnesses: Humphrey DAVIS, Samuel TABER. Ack. 28 Jan. 1815 by Edward. Rec. 30 Jan. 1816.

Edward SAMPSON of Fairhaven MA to **John ATSATT** of same. <Bristol Co.Deeds 99:261>
...27 Jan. 1815, Edward SAMPSON, yeoman, for $800.00 sold to John ATSATT...part of the homestead farm bequeathed to me by my Honoured Father Joseph SAMPSON dec'd in his last will. Sarah SAMSON signs. Ack. 28 Jan. 1815 by Edward. Rec. 30 Jan. 1816.

John ATSATT of Fairhaven MA to **Edward SAMPSON.** <Bristol Co.Deeds 99:262>
...27 Jan. 1815, John ATSATT...let unto my father in law Edward SAMPSON & his wife Sarah my Mother all the land & buildings thereon that I hold be deed of sale bearing even date with these presents...during their natural lives. Witnesses: Humphrey DAVIS, Samuel TABER. Rec. 30 Jan.1816.

Ebenezer & Katharine BENNETT of Plainfield VT. <Bristol Co.Deeds 105:2>
...19 Aug. 1815, Ebenezer & Katharine BENNETT...are seized in fee simple of land in Fairhaven MA ...it being the whole of the tract of land willed to me the sd Ebenezer by my father Edward BENNETT...and all the tract willed to me the sd Katharine by my Grandfather Joseph SAMPSON dec'd, appoint Jacob BENNETT of Fairhaven, attorney. Signed: Edward & "Caty" BENNETT.

John ATSATT et al, division. <Bristol Co.Deeds 99:560>
...16 Apr. 1816, John ATSATT, gent. & wf Mercy of Fairhaven; widow Sarah GIFFORD of Fairhaven and Ebenezer BENNETT & wf Keturah of Ohio (by their attorney Jacob BENNETT of Fairhaven)...divided land in Fairhaven...opposite the Baptist meeting house, in the long plain...for a more particular description referance may be had to our honoured Grandfather Joseph SAMPSON's last will & testament by which sd premises came to us. Rec. 27 Apr. 1816.

BRISTOL COUNTY DEEDS:

<83:472> - 1804, Sarah SAMPSON et al to John HATSETT.
<99:261> - 1816, Edward SAMPSON to John HATSETT.
<100:503> - , Ebenezer BENNETT & Edward BENNETT et al, division.
<105:3> - 1818, Ebenezer & Caty BENNETT et al to Humphrey DAVIS.
<105:71> - 1818, Katharine SAMPSON et al to Apollos PADDELFORD et al.
<107:450> - 1820, Sarah SAMPSON et al to Cornelius HOWLAND.
<110:558> - 1822, Guardian of Rhoda ROUNSEVILLE to Abijah REED.
<128:85> - 1829, Ebenezer & Caty BENNETT et al to John ATSATT.
<130:296> - 1830, Sarah SAMPSON to John ATSATT.
<130:298> - 1830, Sarah GIFFORD to Humphrey DAVIS Jr.
<135:39> - 1832, Guardian of Rhoda ROUNSEVILLE to John WHITE et al.
<140:-51> - 1834, Guardian of Rhoda ROUNSEVILLE to Mary SPRAGUE.

BRISTOL COUNTY DEEDS: (re: John ATSATT, grantor 1795-1840, all on index)

<78:35> - 1799, to Daniel BENNETT.
<80:47> - 1801, to Caleb JENNE.
<90:119> - 1809, Exr., to Amos BRAYLEY et al.
<90:449> - 1809, to John S. HASKELL.
<94:416> - 1812, Exr., to Jacob BENNETT.
<94:418> - 1812, Exr., to Jacob BENNETT et al.
<94:522> - 1812, Exr., to Aaron DAVIS.
<99:262> - 1816, to Edward SAMPSON & wf.
<99:560> - 1816, & Mercy et al, division.
<105:3> - 1818, et al to Humphrey DAVIS.
<105:75> - 1818, to Bartholomew AIKEN.
<106:283> - 1819, Exr., to Nathaniel SEARS.
<107:450> - 1820, et al to Cornelius HOWLAND.
<110:105> - 1821, to James RANDALL.
<116:541> - 1825, to Cornelius HOWLAND.
<119:405> - 1826, to Humphrey DAVIS Jr.
<128:84> - 1829, to Humphrey DAVIS Jr.
<130:297> - 1830, to Humphrey DAVIS Jr.
<132:534> - 1831, & Mercy to Joseph BATES.

Amos NELSON of New Bedford MA to **John ATSATT** of Rochester MA. <Bristol Co.Deeds 99:246>
...10 Jan. 1811, Amos NELSON & wf Jane, for $150.00 sell to John ATSATT, gent...all our right & title which was given unto us by our Honoured Grandfather Joseph SAMPSON in has last will & testament, reference being had to the division of our sd Grandfather's estate. Rec. 10 Jan. 1816. <99:247>...28 July 1812, **Oliver GURNEY** & wf Mary of Freetown, for $200.00 sold the same to John.

William ROUNSEVELLE of Freetown MA to **John ATSATT** of Fairhaven MA. <Bristol Co.Deeds 100:268>
...6 Apr. 1816, William ROUNSEVELLE & wf Rhoda sell to John ATSATT...all our right & title in the homestead farm & buildings that was given to me Rhoda ROUNSEVELLE in the last will & testament of my Honored Grandfather Joseph SAMSON...on the Long Plain in Fairhaven. Rec. 10 July 1816.

Ebenezer BENNETT & John RIGHT of Harmony OH to **John ATSATT** of Bristol Co. MA <Bristol Co.Deeds>
<128:85>...22 Aug. 1829, Ebenezer BENNETT & wf Caty and John RIGHT & wf Jane, for $500.00 sold to

John ATSATT...all the right...we may have as heirs...of Joseph SAMSON late of Fairhaven...to all the lands that sd Joseph SAMSON may have had. Witnesses: John WHITELEY, Edward S. BENNETT. Ack. 22 Aug. 1829 in Clark Co., Ohio by all grantors. Rec. 21 Oct. 1829.

James SAMSON of Dartmouth MA to **Samuel HAMMOND.** <Bristol Co.Deeds 10:706>
...27 Dec. 1712, James SAMSON, for natural affection & love...conveys to son in law Samuel HAMMOND...40 acres in Dartmouth.

Samuel HAMMOND Jr. of Rochester MA to **Samuel HAMMOND** of same. <Bristol Co.Deeds 21:232>
...24 Aug. 1725, Samuel HAMMOND Jr., for other lands received from father Samuel HAMMOND, conveys to him...40 acres in Dartmouth.

MICRO #6 OF 7

STEPHEN SAMSON^{2} (Henry^{1})

Benjamin SAMSON & John SAMSON to **Edmund FREEMAN** of Harwich MA. <Plymouth Co.Deeds 16:415>
...22 Mar. 1725/6, Benjamin SAMSON, dealer of Plymouth and John SAMSON, yeoman of Duxbury, for £340 sell to Edmund FREEMAN, gent...half of all lands in Dartmouth of their father Stephen SAMSON late of Duxbury dec'd...one half of one third of a share excepting what their father had sold to Caleb SAMSON of Duxbury and Lettice JENNEY & James SAMSON of Dartmouth. Witnesses: Joseph THOMAS, Thomas CROADE. Ack. same day.

BRISTOL COUNTY DEEDS: (pre 1795)

<25:285> - John PLUMLY & wf Dorcas et al to Benjamin SAMSON.
<25:288> - John PLUMLY & wf Dorcas et al to Benjamin SAMSON.
<25:288> - Robert TYLER & wf Hannah et ux et al to Benjamin SAMSON.

Heirs of **Stephen SAMSON** to **John WADSWORTH** of Duxborough MA. <Plymouth Co.Deeds 12:88>
...27 Oct. 1716, Samuel THARE/THAYER 3d & wf Mary, Hannah SAMSON and Elizabeth SAMSON...daughters of Stephen SAMSON of Duxborough dec'd, for £26 sold to John WADSWORTH, coaster...43 acres in Majors Purchase in Pembroke...81st lot in 2nd & last division of Commons belonging to ye towns of Duxborough & Pembroke which were laid out in 1713...which did formerly belong to our Honoured Father Stephen SAMSON dec'd. Witnesses: Benjamin SAMSON, John SAMSON. Ack. 29 Oct. 1716 by grantors. Rec. 19 Dec. 1716.

Heirs of **Stephen SAMSON** to **Benjamin SAMSON** of Plymouth MA. <Plymouth Co.Deeds 18:89>
...12 Mar. 1723/4, Elizabeth SAMSON, widow, relict of Stephen SAMSON late of Duxborough dec'd, John SAMSON of Duxborough and Robert TYLER & wf Hannah, Samuel THAYER & wf Mary, Jonathan THAYER & wf Elizabeth, John PLUMLY & wf Dorcas and Abigail SAMSON, all of Mendon, for £50 sold to Benjamin SAMSON, coaster...one twelfth part of the lands of Stephen SAMSON dec'd. Witnesses: Josiah CHAPIN, Philip AMMIDOWN, George BRUCE, Jonathan THAYER, Elizabeth THAYER. Ack. 12 Mar. 1724 by the TYLERS, Plumlys & Abigail SAMSON; Ack. 13 Mar. 1724 by the THAYERS. Rec. 8 Sept. 1724.

BRISTOL COUNTY DEEDS: (re: THAYER)

<8:166> - 1713, Jonathan THAYER to Benjamin NEWLAND.
<10:425> - 1717, Jonathan THAYER (on behalf of self, wife & child) to Benjamin ALLEN.
<18:112> - 1727, Jonathan THAYER et al to Thomas LINCOLN 4th.
<18:416> - 1728, Jonathan THAYER et al to Morgan COBB 2d.
<22:193> - 1734, Jonathan THAYER et ux to Josiah WINSLOW.
<41:408> - 1736, Jonathan THAYER to John RANDALL et ux.
<27:297> - 1736/7, Jonathan THAYER to Richard WILLIAMS Jr.
<25:287> - 1737, Samuel THAYER 3d & wf Mary et ux to Benjamin SAMSON et al.
<25:288> - 1737, Jonathan THAYER & wf Elizabeth et ux et al to Benjamin SAMSON.
<27:285> - 1738, Jonathan THAYER et ux to John WHITMAN Jr.
<27:347> - 1738, Jonathan THAYER to Samuel CLARKE et al.
<28:359> - 1740, Jonathan THAYER to Eliphalet LEONARD.
<28:403> - 1740, Jonathan THAYER to William LEE et al.
<37:485> - 1736, Jonathan THAYER et ux to Josiah WINSLOW.
<42:185> - 1757, Jonathan THAYER to George GODFREY.
<43:367> - 1759, Jonathan THAYER to John THAYER.
<44:42> - 1759, Jonathan THAYER 1st to Jonathan THAYER 2d.
<44:196> - 1760, Jonathan THAYER et ux et al to Israel RANDELL.
<45:560> - 1762, Jonathan THAYER to George GODFREY.
<46:287> - 1763, Jonathan THAYER to George GODFREY.
<56:423> - 1775, Jonathan THAYER to Abijah LINCOLN.
<60:54> - 1780, Jonathan THAYER et al, division.
<60:54> - 1780, Jonathan THAYER estate, division.
<72:360> - 1794, Jonathan THAYER et al.

Benjamin SAMSON et al to **William MACUMBER** of Dartmouth MA. <Bristol Co.Deeds 15:26>
...28 May 1722, Benjamin SAMSON, mariner of Plimouth, John SAMSON, yoeman of Duxborough & Dorcas SAMSON, for £26 sold to William MACUMBER, yeoman...two acre meadow or sedge flatt in Dartmouth on

the great flatt in the westermost arm of Agoxset River...bounded by land of Isaac POPE, Capt. TABOR and Samuel HIX...Benjamin SAMSON owns seven twelfs, John SAMSON four twelfs and Dorcas SAMSON one twelf. Witnesses: Samuel FOSTER, John WASHBURN. Ack. same day by Benjamin and Dorcas; 29 May 1722 by John. Rec. 8 June 1723.

Estate of **Cornelius SAMPSON**, gent. of Kingston MA. <Plymouth Co.PR #17485>
<original> Request, 16 Apr. 1796 of widow **Desire SAMPSON** (aged), that Joseph SAMPSON be app'td admr. <34:75> Letter/Bond, 21 Apr. 1796, Joseph SAMPSON of Kingston app'td admr. Sureties: Thomas JACKSON, yeoman of Plymouth and Josiah SAMPSON of Barnstable. Witnesses: Crocker SAMPSON, Isaac LOTHROP. <36:96> Inventory taken 15 June 1796 by Jedediah HOLMES & John FAUNCE of Kingston and Samuel LORING of Duxbury; incl. lands in Kingston & Duxbury and half a pew in Kingston Meeting house, the other half belonging to heirs of Benjamin SAMPSON dec'd. <36:94> Inventory taken 21 June 1796 by David PARKER, Joseph CROCKER Jr., Benjamin PERCIVAL, all of Sandwich; incl. lands in Barnstable. <36:97> Division of real estate, 3 Mar. 1797, by Jedediah HOLMES, John FAUNCE, Samuel LORING to following heirs, viz: **Crocker SAMPSON, Joseph SAMPSON, Josiah SAMPSON, Anne SAMPSON, Lucy JACKSON** wf of Thomas and **Desire SAMPSON Jr.**, with the widow consenting. <36:104> Account 4 Apr. 1797, of admr.; items incl. balance due from estate of Benjamin SAMPSON and money paid 1 May 1794 for purchase of land of Micah SAMPSON; Paid to: John FAUNCE, Jedediah HOLMES, Joshua BREWSTER of Duxbury, William SEVER, Capt. Samuel LORING, Col. GRAY, Dr. WHITMAN, Bildad WASHBURN, Eliezer HARLOW. (The following clearly does not belong with the probate records but has been included) <28:261> Division 15 Feb. 1781, Thomas FOORD, Thomas DINGLEY & Asa WATERMAN, all of Marshfield, divide homestead owned by Kenelm WINSLOW late of Marshfield dec'd and Cornelius SAMPSON, trader of Kingston...half to heirs of Kenelm, half to Cornelius.

Josiah SAMPSON of Barnstable MA to **Simeon JENKINS et al.** <Barnstable Co.Deeds 2:62>
...10 Oct. 17(0)7, Josiah SAMPSON, gent. sells to Simeon JENKINS, Prince JENKINS & Brayley JENKINS, housewrights...pew formerly belonging to Benjamin CROCKER of Barnstable dec'd. Ack. 17 Oct. 1797. Rec. 1797.

Will of **Benjamin SAMSON**, merchant of Kingston MA. <Plymouth Co.PR #17457>
<14:523-6>...dated 20 Feb. 1750/51, mentions wf **Rebecca**; minor grandson **Micah SAMPSON**; eldest living son **Cornelius SAMPSON**(executor); son **Benjamin SAMPSON**; dau **Deborah VEAZIE** wf of Rev. Samuel...if my sd grandson **Micah** should dwell or settle in Kingston my two sons **Cornelius & Benjamin**...shall be obliged to keep him...along with their own for the space of twelve years upon free cost. Witnesses: Lemuell KENT, Sarah CHIPMAN, John WADSWORTH. <15:103> Receipts to exr., **Cornelius SAMPSON**: On 14 Mar. 1759, from **Benjamin SAMPSON** for his share. Witnesses: Seth CHIPMAN Jr., Wrestling BREWSTER Jr. On 9 Jan. 1759, from **Samuel VEAZIE**, for 133 shillings 8 pence, deducting what my late wife **Deborah VEAZIE** received of her Father in her lifetime...In behalf of the children of my late wife, viz: **John VEAZIE, Samuel VEAZIE, Deborah VEAZIE & Rebecca VEAZIE.** Witnesses: William BREWSTER Jr., William SEVER. <15:233> Bond 14 Mar. 1759 of **Cornelius SAMSON** of Kingston, as admr., to pay **Micah SAMSON**, grandson to dec'd, the sum of Ł133.6.8. when he reaches 21. Surety: John SEVER, physician of Kingston. Witnesses: Seth CHIPMAN Jr., James DREW. <16:324> Receipt 24 Feb. 1762, of **Micah SAMSON** to **Cornelius SAMSON**, admr., for his share. Witnesses: Wrestling BREWSTER Jr., Seth TUPPER.

Will of **Rebecca SAMSON** of Kingston MA. <Plymouth Co.PR #17631>
<20:226>...dated 6 Jan. 1769, mentions son **Cornelius SAMSON** (executor) & his wife Desire; son **Benjamin SAMSON** & wf Deborah; grandchildren **Micha SAMSON, John VEAZIE, Samuel VEAZIE, Deborah VEAZIE & Rebecca VEAZIE.** Witnesses: Samuel KENT, Silvanus COOK, Lydia CUSHING. Pr. 15 May 1769. <20:265> Inventory taken by Samuel KENT, William DREW, Silvanus COOK; incl. an obligation on Zadock THOMAS & Isaac CHANDLER; total estate, Ł157.14s5d; sworn to 15 Aug. 1769 by admr. <20:481> Receipt 26 June 1770 of **Samuel VEAZIE** for his children's legacies. Witnesses: William DREW, Rebecca SAMSON. Receipt 24 Jan. 1771 by **Benjamin SAMSON.** Witnesses: Joseph SAMPSON, Josiah SAMSON. On 24 May 1770, of **Micha SAMSON** for his share.

Will of **Benjamin SAMSON**, yeoman of Kingston MA. <Plymouth Co.PR #17459>
<25:196>...dated 4 Nov. 1778, mentions wf **Esther** (executrix) and children, viz: **Benjamin SAMPSON, Croade SAMPSON, Micah SAMPSON, Deborah SAMPSON & Priscilla SAMPSON.** Witnesses: Joseph SAMPSON, Isaac COOK, John FAUNCE. Pr. 1 Mar. 1779. <25:452> Inventory taken 22 Feb. 1780 by John GRAY, Elisha BREWSTER, John FAUNCE.; incl. real estate in Kingston & Duxbury. <28:155> Division 16 Apr. 1781, real estate divided between **Esther SAMPSON** and **Benjamin, Croade & Micah SAMPSON; Deborah SAMPSON** to have privilege of living in dwelling house. <27:495> Letter/Bond 3 Mar. 1783, John FAUNCE, yeoman of Kingston, app'td admr., **Esther SAMPSON** having deceased. Sureties: Benjamin SAMSON & Jedediah HOLMES of Kingston. <28:574> Inventory taken 8 Mar. 1783 by John ADAMS, John GRAY & Elisha BREWSTER, all of Kingston; incl. bonds & notes of Lucy BOURN, Wrestling BREWSTER & James EVERSON. <29:225> Warrant for division, 2 Dec. 1783, to Elisha BREWSTER, John GRAY & John ADAMS of Kingston, to divide real estate set off to widow **Esther SAMPSON.** Division 3 Jan. 1784, to the three sons. <29:308> Warrant 1 Mar. 1784, to James DREW, John ADAMS, Cephas WADSWORTH, all of Kingston, to appraise estate set off to **Deborah & Priscilla SAMPSON.** <29:352> Account of admr., 1 Aug. 1785; Paid to: Jonas WHITMAN, Elisha BREWSTER, Jabez WASHBURN, Cephas WADSWORTH, Job DREW, Col. John GRAY, Col. Briggs ALDEN, John ADAMS, Sylvanus COOKE, Isaac WINSLOW, Hannah THOMAS, estate of John THOMAS, Nathaniel GILBERT, James COBB. <35:542> 2d Account 1 Aug. 1796; Paid to: Joseph DAWES, Capt. Joshua LORING, estate of Jabez WASHBURN Jr., Samuel DREW, Cornelius SAMPSON, Deborah SAMPSON, Capt. Robert FOSTER, Capt. Judah WASHBURN

Guardianship of Children of **Benjamin SAMSON** of Kingston MA. <Plymouth Co.PR #17460>
<22:219> Letter/Bond 3 May 1779, **Benjamin SAMSON,** above 14, made choice of Joseph SAMSON as his gdn. Sureties: Bildad ARNOLD of Duxbury, Samuel SAMPSON of Kingston. Witnesses: David KINGMAN, Isaac LOTHROP. <26:90> Letters/Bonds 6 Mar. 1780, widow **Esther SAMPSON** app'td gdn. of **Micah SAMPSON,** aged 6 and **Priscilla SAMPSON,** aged 3. Sureties: Seth CUSHING of Plympton, Noah SIMMONS of Kingston. Witnesses: Nathaniel BARNEY, Jedediah HOLMES. <26:360> Letter/Bond 2 Oct. 1780, **Croad SAMSON** makes choice of Nicholas DAVIS Jr., cordwainer of Kingston as his gdn. Sureties: Daniel BONNEY & Ephraim BRYANT of Plymton. Witnesses: Isaac COOK, Elnathan HOLMES Jr., Benjmain THOMAS, Jacob BENNET.

Will of **Esther SAMSON,** widow of Kingston MA. <Plymouth Co.PR #17510>
<28:481>...dated 10 May 1782, mentions son **Micah SAMPSON** and dau **Priscilla SAMPSON;** friend Cornelius SAMPSON app'td exr. & gdn. of the two children. Witnesses: Samuel STETSON, Abner HOLMES, Joseph SAMPSON. Pr. 7 Oct. 1782. <30:116> Inventory taken 24 Feb. 1785 by John FAUNCE, Jedediah HOLMES & Samuel STETSON; sworn to 4 Apr. 1787 exr.

Estate of **Benjamin SAMSON,** yeoman of Kingston MA. <Plymouth Co.PR #17458>
<original> Request 8 Apr. 1794, of widow **Priscilla SAMSON** that John FAUNCE of Kingston be app'td admr. <27:476> Letter/Bond 8 Apr. 1794, John FAUNCE app'td admr. Sureties: John BRADFORD of Plymton & Levi BRADFORD of Kingston. Witnesses: James LEACH, Joshua BRAYTON. <35:134> Inventory taken 13 Aug. 1794 by Joseph SAMPSON, Nicholas DAVIS Jr., Samuel STETSON. <35:209> Notice, sworn to 2 Feb 1795 by admr. <35:441> Account of admr., 4 Jan. 1796; Paid to: Zach. BARTLETT, Amos COOKE, Col. Jotham LORING, Elisha STETSON Jr., David BEAL, James CUSHMAN, Abner HOLMES, Silvanus COOK, Dr. Isaac WINSLOW, Elkanah WASHBURN, William SEVER, Esq., James THATCHER, Benjamin COOK, Samuel STETSON, Robert COOKE. <36:92> Notice of sale of real estate, 13 Apr.1796. <36:92> 2d Account of admr., 4 Apr. 1797; incl. 20 acres sold to Nicholas DAVIS Jr. & Abner HOLMES; Paid to: Seth EVERSON, William CHURCHILL, Amos COOK, John FULLER, Job DREW, John ADAMS, Judah WASHBURN, Samuel SAMPSON, Jabez FULLER, William COBB, John COOK, Jacob FISH, Cornelius SAMPSON, Col. Joseph SAMPSON, Bildad WASHBURN, Nicholas DAVIS Jr., John HOLMES, Jonathan HOLMES Jr., Col. John GRAY, Samuel STETSON; to the balance due to me on my second account of Father's estate; to what I supply the family as per account. <36:92> Dower set off, 3 Apr. 1797, to widow **Priscilla SAMPSON.** <46:437> Letter/Bond, 23 May 1815, Isaac SAMPSON, trader of Plymouth app'td admr. de bonis non, John FAUNCE having dec'd. Sureties: George SAMPSON 3d, trader & John GOODING, gent., both of Plymouth. Witnesses: Ebenezer SPOONER, Beza HAYWARD.

Guardianship of Children of **Benjamin SAMSON** of Kingston MA. <Plymouth Co.PR #17551>
<32:49> Letter/Bond 10 Aug. 1796, John FAUNCE, yeoman of Kingston app'td gdn. of **Priscilla SAMPSON,** minor above 14. Sureties: Robert HOLMES & Bildad WASHBURN of Kingston. Witnesses: Isaac LOTHROP, Nathan LUCAS. <32:60> Letter/Bond, 16 Nov. 1796, of John FAUNCE as gdn. of **James SAMPSON, Isaac SAMPSON, George SAMPSON & Deborah SAMPSON,** all minors under 14. Sureties: Joseph SAMPSON of Kingston & Elijah BISBEE Jr. of Plympton. Witnesses: Nathaniel LOTHROP, Isaac LOTHROP.

Will of **Deborah SAMSON,** spinster of Kingston MA. <Plymouth Co.PR #17491>
<30:497>...dated 7 Nov. 1788, mentions brothers **Croad SAMSON, Micah SAMSON;** sister **Priscilla SAMSON;** brother **Benjamin SAMSON** (executor); Lydia DAWS. Witnesses: Zephaniah WILLIS, Samuel STETSON, Cephas WADSWORTH. <30:498-9> Bond 5 Jan. 1789, of Benjamin SAMSON, exr. Sureties: Samuel STETSON, cordwainer & Cephas WADSWORTH, housewright, both of Kingston. Witnesses: Thomas GANETT, Issac LOTHROP.

Estate of **Micah SAMPSON,** trader of Kingston MA. <Plymouth Co.PR #17598>
<8:271> Letter/Bond 25 Nov. 1740, widow **Deborah SAMPSON** and Benjamin SAMPSON, gent. of Kingston, app'td admrs. Sureties: Samuel FOSTER, gent. & Joshua CUSHING, blacksmith of Kingston. Witnesses: Edward WINSLOW, Elisha BISBE. <8:281> Inventory taken 5 Dec. 1740 by Thomas CROADE, Esq. of Halifax, Samuel FOSTER, gent. of Kingston and Joshua LORING, gent. of Duxborough; incl. three sixteenths of the schooner "Union", Ł60; Ł100 paid towards the purchase of the house & land whereon he dwelt, which his father bought of Thomas CROADE, Esq. but gave no deed to him; shopp goods incl. salt, mollasses, iron & lumber, Ł912.9s6d; warehouse, Ł80; total estate, Ł1651.8s6d. <9:365> 24 Sept. 1744, widow **Deborah SAMPSON,** for Ł286.11s8d in household goods, etc. releases dower; mentions bringing up **Micah SAMPSON,** son of dec'd. <13:504> Account, 7 Mar. 1755, of Benjamin SAMSON & **Deborah GOULD** (late Deborah SAMSON), admrs.; Paid to: Josiah CUSHMAN, Stephen CHURCHILL, Thomas CROADE, Isaac CHURCHILL, Ebenezer FULLER, David STERTEVANT, Jonathan SMITH, Nicholas SEVER, Joshua SOUL, Thomas ADAMS, Daniel INDIAN, John ADAMS, S. GARDNER, John BISHOP, Ebenezer RICKARD, Thomas CUSHMAN, Francis COOK, Samuel GARRISH, Jonathan CUSHING, George HOLMES, Theophilus CUSHING, John HYNDS, Theophilus HANCOCK, Joseph BLAKE, Joseph SHERBUN, Capt. DEERING, S. BRADFORD, Jacob BRIGGS, Edward QUINCY, Charles COFFIN, E. RICKARD Jr., R. CUSHMAN Jr., B. LORING, D. TURNER, Isaac WINSLOW, D. DARLING, R. WATTS, Till RIPLEY, Norton QUINCY, Mrs. GARDNER, OLIVER & Co., W. BAKER, W. TAYLOR, Mrs. HYNDS, William LOW, S. BRADFORD, John BRADFORD, John SCOLLEY, George BRYANT, Joseph BALCHER, Jacob TOMSON, N. BONNEY, Widow SAMSON, Joseph HARRIS, S. LAZELL, Phillip CHANDLER, John SHAW, Joseph BARTLETT, D. HENCHMAN, Mary BLAIR, James TOMPSON, R. BROWN, Elisha BARSTOW, N. GLOVER, T. COTTON, N. WADE, Dr. STOCKBRIDGE, Jonathan SMITH Jr.; also sundrys paid to the widdow for support of the family from the Intestate's death to Oct. 1744, about four years.

Guardianship of Children of **Micah SAMSON** of Kingston. <Plymouth Co.PR #17599>
<9:365> Letter/Bond 1 Oct. 1744, Benjamin SAMPSON, gent. of Kingston app'td gdn. of **Micha SAMPSON** Surety: Israel TURNER, innholder of Pembroke. Witnesses: Daniel PACKARD, Edward WINSLOW. <13:431>

Letter/Bond, 1 Apr. 1755, **Micha SAMSON,** minor above 14, chose "father in law" <step-father> Jacob GOULD, yeoman of Weymouth, as his gdn. Witnesses: Joseph GOULD, Jr., Mary THAYER, Mathew REED and Mary REED. <13:507> Account, 7 Mar. 1755, of **Benjamin SAMSON** as gdn. of his grandson **Micha SAMSON**; item: to keep sd **Micha** from 4 years old till he was seven, saving about half the time when he was with his mother.

Will of **Jonathan THAYER,** physician of Bellingham MA. <Suffolk Co.PR #8751> <original>...dated 31 Mar. 1747...to wf **Elizabeth,** £12.10s, black riding mare and one cow...to son **Curnelues/Cornelius THAYER,** over & above what I have allready given him, twelve acres...near Bellingham meeting house and bounding on his land and land that Jonathan DRAPER bought of Jonathan MILL...also all land lying on the plain or common field...to son **Ezra THAYER,** remainder of land bounded by land of Jonathan THOMPSON, on both sides of the road leading from sd meating house to Wrentham excepting my lott or right of land that lyeth in the Pine Swamp near Isaac THAYER's...the hole of my land that lyeth beteen the land that Dockter GARNER took from me by a execution...also one half of land in Mendon at the north purchis...to son **Micah THAYER**...all land between the land that Dockter GARNER took from me...and the land belonging to John JONES and...15 acres on sd road...and half of land in Mendon...three sons to have the lott in the Pine Swamp... to daus **Sarah THAYER & Hopstill THAYER,** £15...to dau **Elizabeth THAYER,** £20 to be paid to her guardian when she comes to be 14 years of age; wf **Elizabeth,** executrix. Witnesses: John JONES, Jonathan BOZWORTH, David THAYER Jr. (Endorsed on back: will filed 28 Apr. 1748; 2 first witnesses sworn not of sound mind; executor renounced & claimed her dower.) <original> Letter dated 9 May 1747 of David THAYER Jr...concerning Dockter THAYER will which I rit for him and signed as a witness. <original> Letter dated 11 May 1747 of dau **Sarah THAYER**...that I am twenty two years of age and am not in good state of health...my honoured Father left a will which I desire may not be proved for the reason that I apprehend my Father was not of sound mind & memory enough to dispose of his estate by will & I therefore desire your Honour to order the settlement of his estate according to law. Witnesses: Caleb PHILLIPS Jr., John METCALF. <39:574> Letter/Bond, 12 May 1747, widow **Elizabeth THAYER** and Cornelius THAYER, husbandman, both of Bellingham, app'td admrs. Sureties: John JONES, yeoman & John METCALF, gent., of Bellingham. Witnesses: John HOLBROOK Jr., John PAYNE. <39:572> Letter/Bond, 12 May 1747, widow **Elizabeth THAYER** app'td gdn. of **Elizabeth THAYER,** minor aged about six years. <39:570> Letter/Bond, 12 May 1747, **Ezra THAYER,** minor above 14 chose John JONES as his gdn. <39:569> Letter/Bond 12 May 1747, **Hopestill THAYER,** minor aged about 16 chose John JONES as her gdn. <40:335> Inventory taken 17 May 1747 by Ebenezer THAYER, Caleb PHILLIPS Jr., John METCALF.; incl. wearing apparel of his son **Jonathan THAYER** lately dec'd in his minority, £5.9s; silver watch, £30; physition's & astroligy books & instruments, £20.12s; phisical drugs, medicines, etc., valued by John CORBIT and David JONES, Practioners in Physick, £77. 6s1d; Cornelius THAYER received of his father on portion account, £150; real estate incl. a lese from Chileaf BEMISS for 90 acres in Government of New York which may be worth £100.; <41:221> Additional Inventory taken 20 May 1748 by Ebenezer THAYER, John METCALF, Caleb PHILLIPS Jr. <41: 222> Account, 8 June 1748; Paid to: Joseph CHILSON, KNEELAND & GREEN for advertisements, Caleb PHILLIPS, Isaac THAYER, Cornelius THAYER, Justice BLAKE, Samuel RAWSON, Joseph HOLBROOK, Dr. WHEAT, John JONES, John ALDIS; a journey to New York to get in debts, £4; a journey to Newton to pay Dr. WHEAT, £1. <original> Division of real estate, 15 Nov. 1755, among widow **Elizabeth THAYER** and the six children or their legal representatives; portion of **Cornelius THAYER** to be settled on: **Ezra THAYER, Micah THAYER, Sarah WIGHT, Hopestill DAMAN & Elizabeth NELSON.**

Estate of **Elijah SAMPSON** of Duxbury MA. <Plymouth Co.PR #17504> ...1805...<39:8;40:219,410>...(no details given).

MICRO #7 OF 7

Will of **Samuel THAYER** of Mendon MA. <Worcester Co.PR #A:58793> <8:425>...dated 17 Oct. 1761; mentions wf **Mary**; to dau **Abigail PARTRIDGE,** one new Bible; to son **Samuel THAYER,** £136s8d and one cow or £2.13s; to the four surviving children of dau **Zilphah HOLBROOK,** dec'd, £16s8d divided between them at age 21; to dau **Thankfull HOLBROOK** one two yr old heiffer; to grandaughter **Olive FARNUM,** one new Bible at age 18; to dau **Susanna THAYER** one half of indoor moveables & houshold stuff at decease of wife, also £5.6s8d at the time of her marriage; to son **Stephen THAYER** (executor), the whole of my land lying at the Round Meadow in Mendon containing ten acres, twenty acres at Wigwam Hill in Mendon, three acres at Dam Swamp in Mendon, three acres in the old field so called which was given to me by my honoured father **Thomas THAYER** dec'd and all right to ceder swamp in Mendon...also all my husbandry tools, cattle, out door moveables...and my cane...he to pay all legacies...also to take prudent care and provide for and sufficiently maintain my beloved daughter **Mary THAYER** in sickness & health...the sd **Mary** to be under the care & inspection of Leit. John FRENCH, gent. of Mendon; to grandaughter **Fern THAYER,** £213s4d and one two yr old heiffer when she reaches 18...provided she shall live with my son **Stephen.** Witnesses: William THAYER Jr., William THAYER, Edward RAWSON. Pr. 20 Aug. 1764.

GEORGE SOULE

MICRO #1 OF 11

BRISTOL COUNTY PROBATE: (re: SOULE)

(The following list is comprised of ten pages of lists which have been written in a format totally unlike that of similiar lists in the files. They have been compiled alphabetically by first name and appear to be comprised of all references found in the index to each given name not to each person with said given name. For example, under Henry are 17 entries and judging by the dates, the data could pertain to as many as five Henry SOULES; similiar lists in the files would have separated the entries under the Henry they pertained to. Although the following would be more useful if it was organized by person rather than by name, an attempt to do this would most certainly result in errors of placement, therefore it is printed here as it appears. The date given is the "Date of Vol.")

Alice : 1858-59, Account <104:130>; 1857-64, Notice <119:149>; 1849-58, Bond <173:433>; 1851-61, Citation <178:249>; 1856-58, Probate <181:353>; 1856-58, Will <181:354>; 1854-58, Inventory <192:464>.

Benjamin : 1802-03, Will <39:474>; 1802-03, Receipts <39:527>; 1841-42, Will <83:12>; 1796-1804, Notice <108:58>; 1840-45, Notice <115:195>; 1836-49, Bond <172:186>.

Caroline : 1810-21, Guardianship <132:223>.

Charles H. : 1871-78, Notice <122:3>; 1871-74, Adm. <169:574>.

David : 1781-83, Will <27:8>, Probate <27:10>, Division <37:261>, Inv. <27:575>; 1800-01, Will <37:152>, Inv. & Pr. <37:154>; 1860-61, Adm. <105:51>; 1859-61, Bond <165:69>.

Deborah : 1699-1710, Will & Inv. <2:275>; 1710-21, Account <3:20>.

Ebenezer V.: 1810-21, Gdn. <132:233>; 1814, Inv. <49:410>, Insolvency <49:420>, Account <50:132>, Report <50:139>; 1816, Acc't <52:47>; 1820, Notice <110:209>; 1813-23, Adm. <151:99>

Edward G. : 1861-75, Notice of sale <120:647>; 1865-71, Notice <121:261>; 1867-71, Adm. <168:423>; 1866-80, Inv. <196:266>; 1861-77, Insolvency <199:569>; 1861, Sale of land, <214:401>; 1870-76, Account <219:300>; 1862-81, Allowance <224:125>.

Eleanor : 1821-32, Guardianship <133:205>

Elizabeth : 1861-75, Notice <120:248>; 1861-64, Adm. <166:557>; 1861-66, Inv. <195:323>, Account <217:506>; 1862-74, Notice of sale <106:259>.

Emeline T. : 1834, Guardianship <74:401>; 1832-36, Guardianship <134:189>.

Esther H. : 1834, Gdn. <74:401>; 1832-36, Gdn. <134:189>; 1876-78, Adm. <171:150>.

Frederic A.: 1834, Guardianship. <74:401>; 1832-36, Gdn. <134:189>.

George : 1699-1710, Will <2:93>, Inv. <2:94>; 1710-21, Receipts <3:585>, Petition <3:586>, Appeal <3:599>; 1871-78, Notice <122:579>; 1844-78, Will <187:315>; 1878-79, Probate <226:208>.

George L. : 1834, Guardianship. <74:401>; 1832-36, Gdn. <134:189>.

Gideon : 1852, Adm. <97:394>, Inv. <98:253>; 1848-53, Notice <117:557>; 1851-54, Adm. <157:129>; 1851-55, Bond <163:125>.

Hannah H. : 1875-80, Sale of land <215:429>; 1878-79, Inv. <227:295>, Gdn. <227:231>.

Henry : 1769-71, Receipt <21:26>; 1804-06, Inv. <41:260>; 1834, Adm. <74:84>; 1834-35, Inv. <75:86>, Account <75:530>, Dower <75:180>, Notice of sale <75:541>; 1846-47, Adm. <90:502>; 1847-48, Inv. <91:169>; 1830-36, Notice <113:426>; 1840-49, Notice <116:281>; 1798-1810, Gdn. <131:306>; 1803-12, Adm. <150:82>; 1830-36, Adm. <153:363>; 1846-51, Adm. <156:73>, Bond <162:76>; 1834-36, Sale of land <205:62>.

Hilliard W.: 1810-21, Guardianship <132:223>

Isaac : 1785-92, Inv. <31:300>; 1780-93, Adm. <148:390>.

Jacob : 1745-49, Will <11:451>, Probate <11:453>, Inv. <11:457>; 1824-25, Will <62:431>, Inv. <62:441>, Account <62:545>; 1825-29, Account <63:300>; 1820-25, Notice <111:642>; 1818-27, Sale of land <201:540>.

James : 1794-96, Will <33:129>.

Jethro : 1797-99, Inv. <35:150>; 1802-03, Gdn. discharged <39:533>; 1806-07, Account <42:131> 1781-98, Gdn. <130:426>; 1854-61, Gdn. <131:141>; 1793-1803, Adm. <149:198>.

John : 1771-73, Will <22:5>, Probate <22:6>, Inv. <22:48>.

John A. : 1845, Gdn. <88:184>; 1836-46, Gdn. <135:515>, Bond <139:526>.

John H. : 1838, Inv. <79:241>, Account <79:250>, Adm. <79:260>, Allowance <79:261>; 1836-39, Notice <114:167>; 1836-42, Adm. <154:227>, Bond <160:235>.

Jonathan : 1767-69, Inv. <20:479>; 1769-71, Receipt <21:26>; 1771-73, Declination <22:470>; 1779-81, Will <26:156>, Probate <26:158>; 1763-72, Adm. <146:136>.

Jonee : 1860-61, Account <105:428>; 1857-64, Notice <119:751>; 1857-61, Bond <175:229>; 1851-61, Citation <179:218>; 1858-62, Probate <182:907>, Will <182:908>.

Joseph : 1792-94, Will <32:186>; 1821-32, Gdn. <133:205>.

Joseph E. : 1845, Adm. <88:184>, Inv. <88:316>, Notice of sale <88:331>; 1842-46, Adm. <155:420> Bond <161:423>; 1844-51, Sale of land <210:126>; 1836-55, Bond <208:4>

Laurinda : 1810-21, Guardianship <132:223>

Lydia : 1876-78, Adm. <171:52>; 1875-80, Inv. <198:139>.

BRISTOL COUNTY PROBATE, cont-d: (re: SOULE)

Martha	: 1806-07, Will <42:102>, Probate & Inv. <42:103>.
Mary	: 1771-73, Will <22:99>, Probate <22:101>, Inv. <22:102>; 1821-32, Gdn. <133:205>.
Mary E.	: 1845, Gdn. <88:184>; 1836-46, Gdn. <135:515>, Bond <139:526>; 1798-1810, Letter <131:306>.
Mary J.	: 1798-1810, Gdn. <131:306>.
Matthew	: 1862-74, Notice of sale <106:259>; 1861-75, Notice of sale <120:578>; 1865-71, Notice <121:77>; 1864-67, Adm. <167:316>; 1861-66, Inv. <195:591>; 1861, Sale of land <214:78>; 1866-74, Account <218:144>; 1862-81, Allowance <224:71>.
Nathan	: 1733-37, Will & Pr. <8:416>, Inv. <8:418>.
Nathaniel	: 1699-1710, Account <2:47>, Division <2:56>; 1765-69, Will, <19:417>, Pr. <19:420>, Inv. <19:457>; 1769-71, Receipt <21:26>, Will <21:77>, Pr. <21:81, Inv. <21:115>; 1804-06, Inv. <41:255>; 1806-07, Division <42:218>; 1847-48, Adm. <91:72>; 1804-12, Notice <109:49>; 1810-21, Gdn. <132:223>; 1861-67, Gdn. <143:489>; 1803-12, Adm. <150:103>; 1846-57, Adm. <156:98>, Bond <162:101>; 1861-66, Inv. <195:446>; 1866-74, Account <218:451>.
Oliver	: 1871-74, Adm. <169:332>.
Peleg	: 1825-29, Adm. <63:312>, Inv. <63:394>, Insolvency <63:401>; 1821-23, Account <65:269>, Report <65:284>, Disbribution <65:300>; 1825-31, Notice <112:78>; 1823-30, Adm. <152:233>.
Phebe	: 1812-13, Adm. <152:233>.
Phebe V.	: 1798-1810, Gdn. <131:306>.
Polly	: 1823-30, Notice <48:242>.
Resolved	: 1865-71, Notice <121:222>; 1871-74, Adm. <169:439>.
Robert P.	: 1856-57, Adm. <103:336>; 1854-61, adm. <158:448>; 1855-59, Bond <164:322>.
Ruhame	: 1747-51, Guardianship <12:569>.
Russell	: 1871-78, Notice <122:15>; 1871-84, Adm. <169:575>; 1870-76, Inv. <197:256>, Account <219:442>.
Ruth A.	: 1861-64, Adm. <166:156>.
Sarah	: 1781-98, Guardianship <130:31>.
Stephen	: 1788-89, Will <30:140>, Pr. <30:142>, Inv. <30:143>.
Susan	: 1821-32, Guardianship <133:205>.
Tillinghurst	: 1864-69, Will <184:488>; 1866, Pr. <189:175>.
Wesson	: 1769-71, Receipt <21:27>; 1824-25, Will <62:428>; 1820-25, Notice <111:629>.
William	: 1721-23, Adm. <4:181>, Agreement <4:180>, Inv. <4:182>, Receipt <4:335>, Account 4:337>; 1733-37, Inv. <8:297>; 1825-29, Adm. <63:312>, Inv. <63:458>, Account <63:513>; 1826-27, Account <64:306>; 1821-23, Dower <65:97>, Insolvency <65:103>, Account <65:276>, Report <65:303>, Distribution <65:304>; 1827-28, Citation <66:113>; 1852, Adm. <97:342>, Inv. <97:380>; 1852-53, Insolvency <99:499>; 1853-54, Report <100:428>, Account <100:565>;1855-56, Distribution <102:305>; 1825-31, Notice <112:82>; 1848-53, Notice <117:442>; 1823-30, Adm. <152:231>; 1851-54, Adm. <157:123>; 1851-55, Bond <163:121>; 1851-61, Citation <178:395>; 1821-34, Sale of land <202:368>; 1787-88, Account <8:298>.
William H.	: 1804, Guardianship <74:401>; 1832-36, Gdn. <134:189>.

PLYMOUTH COUNTY PROBATE, to 1800: (re: SOULE)

1690/1	Zechariah	Duxbury	#18890, 1:87
1707	John	Duxbury	#18810, 2:87,91
1729	Benjamin	Plympton	#18760, 5:617,619,632,655,741;6:96-99,374;12:481
1729/30	Ebenezer	Plympton	#18771, 5:657
1734	John	Duxbury	#18811, 7:135,141,203,275
1736	Samuel/Lydia	Duxbury	#18868, 7:275-276
1740	Sarah	Plympton	#18869, 8:175,202,237;11:278
1743	John	Middleboro	#18813, 9:84,85,138
1744	Jacob	Middleboro	#18799, 9:352,405;10:299;13:68
1744	James	Middleboro	#18805, 9:341,343,391;10:243-5;13:73
1746	Jacob et al	Middleboro	#18800, 10:249-50,294-5;11:487-9;14:30;16:74
1747	Rebecca	Middleboro	#18861, 10:435-6,490
1748	Abigail	Scituate	#18751, 11:130
1748	Moses	Duxbury	#18845, 11:125,176,505;12:411
1750	Gideon	Duxbury/Pembroke	#18786, 11:359;12:162,274,357,496;13:269
1750	Jacob	Middleboro	#18798, 11:486;12:203;244;14:85
1750	John	Middleboro	#18814, 11:522;12:194,241,470
1751	Benjamin	Plympton	#18761, 12:195,216,483;15:6
1751	Jabez	Halifax	#18794, 12:382,435;15:44
1751	John	Middleboro	#18815, 12:279,15:15
1751	Zachariah	Plympton	#18887, 12:181,183;16:531
1752	Priscilla/al	Plympton	#18860, 12:437,440
1758	Lois	Plympton	#18829, 15:38
1758	Martha	Middleboro	#18836, 15:29,30,224
1759	James	Plympton	#18803, 15:102,530,549;16:525;16:520
1759	Rebecca	Middleboro	#18862, 15:280,281
1760	Zachariah	Plympton	#18888, 15:422,473;19:19
1761	Jacob/Mercy	Halifax	#18802, 18:44,49

PLYMOUTH COUNTY PROBATE, to 1800 cont-d: (re: SOULE)

1763	Joseph	Duxbury	#18819, 16:483,484,534;19:353,354
1764	Josiah	Duxbury	#18825, 19:56,57
1767	Joshua	Duxbury	#18822, 20:73,74,146,211;21:7;36:313
1768	Abigail et al	Duxbury	#18752, 20:138
1768	Jabez et al	Plympton	#18795, 20:53
1768	Samuel	Duxbury	#18867, 20:44,84,137;40:376-7;57:490,491
1773	Mary	Plympton/Middle.	#18837, 21:329,352;23:12
1776	Isaac	Pembroke	#18791, 23:92;24:187,188,189;25:123
1778	Abisha	Duxbury	#18753, 25:123,124
1778	Micah	Duxbury	#18842, 25:124,125;28:377,378
1778	William	Middleboro	#18885, 23:189;25:127;28:547;38:77
1783	Aaron	Pembroke	#18748, 27:132;28:538,539
1783	Rebecca	Pembroke	#18863, 27:137;28:555,558
1783	William et al	Middleboro	#18886, 26:172,173,174,401
1792	Gideon	Halifax	#18787, 27:403;33:214;35:562
1793	Esther	Middleboro	#18777, 33:374,375,432
1792	John	Pembroke	#18812, 26:496,501;33:149,262,327,394;508,567; 35:108,321,528
1793	Orphan	Marshfield	#18853, 27:421;33:307,362,502;35:307;39:438;42: 330,331,334,357
1794	James	Duxbury	#18807, 34:20;35:216;37:203;42:245
1800	Joseph	Duxbury	#18820, 37:254-5,270-1,356,486;42:243

PLYMOUTH COUNTY PROBATE, 1800-1850: (re: SOULE)

1803	Joshua	Duxbury	adm.	#18823, 34:377;38:506;40:446
1804	Zachariah	Plympton	adm.	#18889, 34:384;40:200,201
1805	Joseph	Duxbury	adm.	#18821, 39:3;40:211
1806	Josiah	Duxbury	adm.	#18826, 39:89;42:25,295
1807	Josiah et al	Duxbury	gdn.	#18827, 32:322,323;41:248
1809	Ephraim	Plympton	gdn.	#18776, 41:1;43:227,228,281;48:171
1811	Nathaniel	Duxbury	adm.	#18850, 39:321;44:28,29,35,502
1816	John	Middleboro	adm.	#18816, 46:154;48:119,120,390,391
1817	Nathaniel 2d	Duxbury	adm.	#18851, 46:211;48:425,426,477;49:11,21,74,151, 152,173;73:117;77:192
1820	William	Middleboro	adm.	#18884, 52:53;53:250,502;54:105,106,135,196,287, 369;56:22,23,24
1822	Mary T.	Duxbury	gdn.	#18839, 51:181;56:469;83:487
1822	Micah	Duxbury	adm.	#18843, 52:172;55:142;56:340;57:215-6,253
1822	Otis	Duxbury	adm.	#18854, 52:94;54:405,406,407;56:109,198
1823	Jacob	Middleboro	will	#18797, 55:160;57:308,311,402
1824	Jacob	Halifax	adm.	#18801, 52:302;58:379,380,392;59:191,192
1827	Elijah	Hartford ME	adm.	#18773, 61:102;62:166;64:168,169
1827	Jabez	Halifax	will	#18793, 62:173;63:317;64:246
1828	James	Middleboro	adm.	#18806, 61:204;62:298;66:407;67:571;72:461;79: 254
1832	Simeon	Duxbury	will	#18872, 68:347;72:122,215,217;76:182;113:33 105:526
1833	Alfred	Middleboro	adm.	#18757, 71:150;73:58,317;74:396;76:155-6,176
1833	Richard et al	Duxbury	gdn.	#18864, 65:303;86:381,383
1833	Samuel	Kingston	adm.	#18865, 71:157;74:333;75:98;76:130,195
1834	Marcia	Kingston	gdn.	#18834, 65:354;76:373
1835	Micah A.	Duxbury	gdn.	#18844, 65:461;73:144;78:182
1835	Thomas	Duxbury	adm.	#18878, 71:286;75:199;77:142;78:35
1835	Elijah	Duxbury	adm.	#18774, 71:311;75:238;77:406;79:123
1836	Betsey M.	Halifax	gdn.	#18763, 1:9**R**,30**R**;2:346**O**,368**O**;8:25**L**;78:391;80: 167,168,478
1836	George	Halifax	will	#18784, 73:325;78:82,110,204,205;80:37
1837	Mary	Carver	will	#18838, 1:52**G**;75:469;79:332,334;80:271
1840	Daniel	Plympton	will	#18769, 1:357**G**;6:80**U**;82:105
1842	Aaron	Plympton	gdn.	#18749, 11:38**N**;84:56
1842	Lois	Abington	adm.	#18830, 6:381**U**;11:58**B**;84:213;85:137
1843	Simeon	Duxbury	adm.	#18873, 11:212**B**;86:42
1844	Ezekiel	Duxbury	will	#18778, 1:443**G**,463**G**;86:58
1844	Susannah C.	Plympton	adm.	#18877, 11:271**B**;87:347
1845	Priscilla	Duxbury	adm.	#18858, 11:380**B**;88:147;89:149
1845	Simeon	Duxbury	gdn.	#18874, 9:41**M**
1847	Thomas B.	Middleboro	gdn.	#18879, 9:101**M**,189**M**;90:410;91:205
1848	Marcia	Halifax	will	#18835, 1:484**G**;7:467**V**;90:129
1850	Isaac 2d	Middleboro	adm.	#18792, 7:561**V**;12:167**C**;92:52,122,195;93:51;94:46

Mary SHERMAN of Rochester MA to **Susanna OLIVER** of same. <Plymouth Co.Deeds 75:216>
...11 Apr. 1787, Mary SHERMAN, widow of William, to Susanna OLIVER, single woman...all her right in legacy from will of father, as in deed by husband Peter OLIVER dated 3 July 1749.

Estate of **William SOULE** of Tiverton. <Britol Co.PR>
<originals> Bond 28 Oct. 1734, widow **Rachel SOULE**, app'td admx. Inventory taken 29 Oct. 1734. Account, 18 Nov. 1735 of admx. <8:297,298>...

BRISTOL COUNTY DEEDS, 1686-1795: (re: SOULE, grantors)

<19:285> - 15 Apr. 1730, Benjamin SOULE to Samuel HULL.
<23:59> - 2 Mar. 1733/34, Benjamin SOULE to Joseph HOLLEY.
<23:334> - 18 Mar. 1734/35, Benjamin SOULE to Holder SLOCUM.
<32:135> - 27 Sept 1743, Cornelius SOULE to Ann WEST.
<60:398> - 27 Dec. 1781, David SOULE to Nicholas HOWLAND.
<42:49> - 8 June 1756, Deborah SOULE to William SHERMAN.
<52:513> - 23 Feb. 1770, Edward SOULE et al to George CHASE.
<59:286> - 1 June 1779, Edward SOULE et al to Samuel BAKER.
<66:384> - 20 Nov. 1787, Edward SOULE to David BAKER.
<19:157> - 13 Jan. 1729/30, George SOULE to Benjamin SOULE.
<27:214> - 13 Sept 1738, George SOULE et al to John WILBORE.
<30:117> - 11 June 1741, George SOULE to Nathaniel PARKER.
<30:404> - 19 Mar. 1741/2, George SOULE to Edward CORNELL.
<34:213> - 14 Mar. 1745/6, George SOULE to John SOULE.
<45:275> - 10 July 1761, George SOULE to John LAWTON.
<64:515> - 21 Dec. 1785, George SOULE to Nicholas HOWLAND.
<72:159> - 12 Sept 1793, Henry SOULE Jr. to James SOULE.
<68:196> - 17 Sept 1789, Isaac SOULE to Paul CUFFE.
<7:22> - 3 July 1711, Jacob SOULE et al, division.
<9:96> - 17 Mar. 1714/5, Jacob SOULE to Jeremiah DAVOL.
<19:230> - 21 Apr. 1730, Jacob SOULE to Robert GIFFORD.
<23:223> - 24 Sept 1734, Jacob SOULE to Nathan SOULE.
<36:359> - 21 Dec. 1748, Jacob SOULE to Nathaniel SOWLE.
<61:16> - 11 June 1782, James SOULE to Silvanus SISSON.
<65:52> - 11 Jan. 1786, James SOULE to Zephaniah EDDY.
<60:125> - 10 Oct. 1780, James SOULE 2d to David SOULE.
<30:397> - 19 Mar. 1741/2, John SOULE to William HIX.
<43:170> - 13 June 1758, John SOULE to Job DAVIS.
<27:214> - 13 Sept 1738, Jonathan SOULE et al to John WILBORE.
<28:93> - 7 Jan. 1739, Jonathan SOULE to Benjamin WAIT.
<39:81> - 26 June 1752, Jonathan SOULE to John DRYER.
<39:89> - 9 June 1752, Jonathan SOULE to Christopher GIFFORD.
<40:219> - 9 Nov. 1753, Jonathan SOULE to Elisha MASON.
<41:539> - 17 Mar. 1756, Jonathan SOULE to David JONSON Jr.
<48:21> - 5 Aug. 1765, Jonathan SOULE to James SOWLE.
<51:109> - 7 Jan. 1768, Jonathan SOULE to James PECKHAM.
<52:253> - 28 Aug. 1769, Jonathan SOULE to Joseph SOWLE.
<60:126> - 10 Oct. 1780, Jonathan SOULE to David SOWLE.
<66:459> - 7 Jan. 1788, Jonathan SOULE to Benjamin DAVIS.
<66:585> - 12 Mar. 1788, Jonathan SOULE to Preserved TRIPP.
<63:27> - 7 Sept 1784, Jonathan SOULE Jr. to John MACOMBER.
<62:253> - 9 Mar. 1784, Jonathan SOULE Sr. to Joshua CORNELL.
<19:138> - 13 Jan. 1729/30, Joseph SOULE to Benjamin SOULE.
<19:573> - 21 June 1731, Joseph SOULE to William HIX.
<33:270> - 13 Mar. 1744/5, Joseph SOULE to Philip TABER.
<56:6> - 28 Feb. 1774, Joseph SOULE to Edward WING Sr.
<56:167> - 5 June 1774, Joseph SOULE, exr. to Richard SMITH & al.
<70:202> - 19 Oct. 1791, Lydia SOULE et al to George LAWTON.
<71:458> - 18 Mar. 1793, Lydia SOULE et al to Humphrey HOWLAND et al.
<65:588> - 1 Feb. 1786, Meribah SOULE to Lemuel SISSON et al.
<7:22> - 3 July 1711, Nathan SOULE et al, division.
<23:252> - 10 July 1734, Nathan SOULE to Jonathan WOOD.
<6:128> - 24 Feb.1709, Nathaniel SOULE to Eleazer SLOCUM.
<7:22> - 3 July 1711, Nathaniel SOULE et al, division.
<8:374> - 23 June 1714, Nathaniel SOULE to William WOOD.
<12:328> - 30 Dec. 1718, Nathaniel SOULE to William SOULE.
<12:466> - 1 May 1719, Nathaniel SOULE to Robert KERBIE.
<13:253> - 8 July 1720, Nathaniel SOULE to William WOOD.
<14:176> - 6 Mar. 1721/2, Nathaniel SOULE to Benjamin WAIT.
<14:66> - 21 Aug. 1721, Nathaniel SOULE to Benjamin TRIPP.
<15:208> - 28 Jan. 1723, Nathaniel SOULE to William HART.
<23:177> - 10 July 1734, Nathaniel SOULE to BenjamiN CHASE.
<23:269> - 15 Jan. 1734/5, Nathaniel SOULE to Bethiah MACOMBER.
<30:259> - 12 Sept. 1741, Nathaniel SOULE to Holder SLOCUM.
<36:485> - 2 May 1749, Nathaniel SOULE to Jacob SOULE.
<37:25> - 14 June 1749, Nathaniel SOULE to William DAVOL.
<39:86> - 9 June 1752, Nathaniel SOULE to Jonathan SOULE.
<39:273> - 6 Feb. 1753, Nathaniel SOULE to Daniel SUMMERTON.
<47:58> - 13 Mar. 1764, Nathaniel SOULE to Wesson SOULE.
<43:354> - 2 May 1759, Ruhamah SOULE ux Wesson to John HATHAWAY.

BRISTOL COUNTY DEEDS, 1685-1795, cont-d: (re: **SOULE**, grantors)

<43:479> - 29 June 1759, Ruhamah SOULE ux Weston to William GIFFORD.
<44:386> - 9 Sept 1760, Ruhamah SOULE ux Wesson to Ichabod EDDY.
<33:272> - 13 Mar. 1744/5, Samuel SOULE to Philip TABER.
<33:273> - 13 Mar. 1744/5, Samuel SOULE to Philip TABER.
<42:50> - 8 June 1756, Samuel SOULE to William SHERMAN.
<6:44> - 19 Oct. 1709, Sarah SOULE to Nathan SOULE.
<9:252> - 12 May 1715, Sarah SOULE ux Sylvanus to Trustees of Mass. Bay Prov.
<10:588> - 9 May 1717, Sarah SOULE ux Sylvanus to Commissioners of Mass. Bay Prov.
<39:133> - 16 Sept 1752, Stephen SOULE to Ichabod EDDY.
<48:45> - 20 Aug. 1765, Stephen SOULE to Joseph SOULE.
<5:342> - 27 Apr. 1708, Sylvanus SOULE to Peleg SLOCUM.
<7:22> - 3 July 1711, Sylvanus SOULE et al, division.
<9:252> - 12 May 1715, Sylvanus SOULE et ux to Trustees of Mass. Bay Prov.
<10:588> - 9 May 1717, Sylvanus SOULE et ux to Commissioners of Mass. Bay Prov.
<15:68> - 18 Jan. 1722/3, Sylvanus SOULE to Joseph CHACE Jr.
<21:533> - 8 Jan. 1733/4, Sylvanus SOULE to Stephen GIFFORD.
<23:125> - 22 May 1734, Sylvanus SOULE to estate of William HUTCHINSON.
<25:57> - 17 May 1736, Sylvanus SOULE to Nathaniel SOULE.
<25:410> - 11 Oct. 1737, Sylvanus SOULE to Samuel HILL.
<27:337> - 16 Jan. 1735, Sylvanus SOULE to Nathaniel POTTER.
<31:188> - 21 Feb. 1742/3, Sylvanus SOULE to Nathaniel SOULE et al.
<37:65> - 28 Aug. 1749, Timothy SOULE to Ichabod EDDY.
<43:354> - 2 May 1759, Wesson SOULE et ux to Jonathan HATHAWAY.
<44:386> - 9 Sept 1760, Wesson SOULE et ux to Ichabod EDDY.
<58:94> - 1 Dec. 1771, Wesson SOULE to Zephaniah JONES.
<43:479> - 29 June 1759, Weston SOULE et ux to William GIFFORD.
<5:442> - 5 Nov. 1708, William SOULE et al to Benjamin HOWLAND et al.
<7:22> - 3 July 1711, William SOULE to Peleg SLOCUM.
<9:37> - 18 Feb. 1714, William SOULE to Jeremiah DAVOL.
<9:456> - 19 Aug. 1715, William SOULE to Eleazer SLOCUM.
<9:458> - 26 Aug. 1715, William SOULE to Eleazer SLOCUM.
<12:248> - 11 Oct. 1718, William SOULE to Jeremiah DAVOL.
<12:449> - 22 Apr. 1719, William SOULE to Thomas HATHAWAY.
<13:2> - 10 Sept 1719, William SOULE to Benjamin ALLEN et al.
<13:82> - 9 July 1723, William SOULE to Benjamin SOULE.
<16:392> - 29 Mar. 1725/6, William SOULE to Jeremiah DAVOL.
<17:390> - 18 May 1727, William SOULE to Nathaniel SOULE.
<17:498> - 11 Oct. 1727, William SOULE to Thomas MACOMBER.
<18:283> - 17 Sept 1728, William SOULE to William WOOD.
<19:269> - 3 Mar. 1729/30, William SOULE to Ebenezer ALLEN.
<19:339> - 14 Apr. 1730, William SOULE to Job BRIGGS.
<23:193> - 17 Aug. 1733, William SOULE to Samuel SANFORD.
<23:200> - 11 Sept 1734, William SOULE to Thomas MACOMBER.
<23:578> - 10 Sept 1735, William SOULE to Samuel HART.
<25:390> - 26 Sept 1737, William SOULE.
<26:232> - 13 Mar. 1738/9, William SOULE to John GIFFORD.
<27:276> - 16 Sept 1738, William SOULE to Nathaniel TOMPKINS.
<28:63> - 7 Aug. 1739, William SOULE to John PIERCE.
<30:424> - 25 Mar. 1741/2, William SOULE to Thomas MOSHER.
<34:91> - 29 Oct. 1745, William SOULE to Philip TABER.
<34:92> - 29 Oct. 1745, William SOULE to Philip TABER.
<51:50> - 12 Jan. 1768, William SOULE to Samuel BORDEN 2d.
<51:51> - 15 Jan. 1768, William SOULE et al to Benjamin SLOCUM.
<51:63> - 20 Jan. 1768, William SOULE to Benjamin SLOCUM.
<51:110> - 7 Jan. 1768, William SOULE to Stephen PECKHAM.
<51:113> - 7 Jan. 1768, William SOULE to George WOOD.
<54:528> - 12 Oct. 1772, William SOULE to Joseph SLEAD et al.
<15:14> - 9 Nov. 1723, William SOULE Sr. to William SOULE Jr.

BRISTOL COUNTY DEEDS: (re: **SOULE**, grantees)

<15:82> - 9 July 1723, Benjamin SOULE from William SOULE.
<19:138> - 13 Jan. 1729/30, Benjamin SOULE from Joseph SOULE.
<19:156> - 13 Jan. 1729/30, Benjamin SOULE from Samuel HOWLAND et ux.
<19:157> - 13 Jan. 1729/30, Benjamin SOULE from George SOULE.
<19:158> - 13 Jan. 1729/30, Benjamin SOULE from Jonathan RICKETSON.
<23:24> - 12 Oct. 1733, Benjamin SOULE from William RICKETSON.
<23:59> - 3 Sept 1733, Benjamin SOULE from Joseph HOLLEY.
<71:429> - 5 Mar. 1793, Charles SOULE et al from Abraham ALLEN.
<30:128> - 13 Mar. 1740, Cornelius SOULE from Philip TAILER et ux.
<30:130> - 13 Mar. 1740, Cornelius SOULE from Thomas MANCHESTER.
<58:40> - 9 Sept 1777, David SOULE from John SMITH.
<60:125> - 10 Oct. 1780, David SOULE from James SOWLE 2d.
<60:126> - 10 Oct. 1780, David SOULE from Jonathan SOWLE.

BRISTOL COUNTY DEEDS, cont-d: (re: SOULE, grantees**)**

<69:332> - 10 Mar. 1791, David SOULE from Gershom SMITH.
<58:181> - 23 Mar. 1778, Henry SOULE Jr. from Lemuel BAYLEY.
<7:22> - 5 July 1711, Jacob SOULE et al, division.
<20:119> - 14 July 1731, Jacob SOULE from William CADMAN.
<31:188> - 21 Feb. 1742/3, Jacob SOULE et al from Silvanus SOULE.
<36:485> - 2 May 1749, Jacob SOULE from Nathaniel SOULE.
<48:21> - 5 Aug. 1765 James SOULE from Jonathan SOWLE.
<72:159> - 12 Sept 1793, James SOULE from Henry SOWLE Jr.
<34:213> - 14 Mar. 1745/6, John SOULE from George SOULE.
<30:170> - 30 June 1741, Jonathan SOULE from Thomas SAYER.
<39:83> - 9 June 1752, Jonathan SOULE from Daniel WOOD.
<39:86> - 9 June 1752, Jonathan SOULE from Nathaniel SOULE.
<41:538> - 17 Mar. 1756, Jonathan SOULE from Nathan COBB.
<43:290> - 12 Dec. 1758, Jonathan SOULE from William DAVOL.
<48:22> - 5 Aug. 1765, Jonathan SOULE from Samuel HOWLAND Jr.
<56:254> - 13 Sept 1774, Jonathan SOULE from Stoton POTTER.
<56:254> - 13 Sept 1774, Jonathan SOULE from Samuel HOWLAND.
<56:256> - 13 Sept 1774, Jonathan SOULE et al from Nathaniel STODDARD.
<56:256> - 13 Sept 1774, Jonathan SOULE from Champlain POTTER.
<57:90> - 23 Jan. 1777, Jonathan SOULE from Benjamin GRINNELL.
<65:210> - 1 Feb. 1786, Jonathan SOULE et al from Constant MACOMBER et al.
<67:84> - 29 Apr. 1788, Jonathan SOULE, excn. from Benjamin RUSSELL.
<53:534> - 11 June 1771, Jonathan SOULE Jr. from Judah CHASE.
<57:91> - 23 Jan. 1777, Jonathan SOULE Sr. from John WOOD.
<18:390> - 20 Feb. 1728/9, Joseph SOULE from Jeremiah DAVOL.
<48:45> - 20 Aug. 1765, Joseph SOULE from Stephen SOULE.
<52:233> - 28 Aug. 1769, Joseph SOULE from Jonathan SOWLE.
<55:444> - 19 Nov. 1773, Joseph SOULE from Robert BENTLY.
<70:197> - 22 Oct. 1791, Joseph SOULE from Thomas GIDLEY.
<71:214> - 13 Sept 1792, Lemuel SOULE from Jeremiah WAIT.
<6:44> - 19 Oct. 1709, Nathan SOULE from Sarah SOULE.
<7:22> - 5 July 1711, Nathan SOULE et al, division.
<14:235> - 7 May 1722, Nathan SOULE from Joshua COGGESHALL et ux.
<23:214> - 24 Sept 1734, Nathan SOULE from Mary DEVOL.
<23:215> - 24 Sept 1734, Nathan SOULE from Benjamin CHASE.
<23:219> - 24 Sept 1734, Nathan SOULE from Samuel WILLIS.
<23:219> - 24 Sept 1734, Nathan SOULE from James TRIPP Jr.
<23:220> - 24 Sept 1734, Nathan SOULE from Benjamin DAVOL.
<23:221> - 24 Sept 1734, Nathan SOULE from John HATHAWAY.
<23:223> - 24 Sept 1734, Nathan SOULE from Jacob SOULE.
<6:104> - 2 Feb. 1709, Nathaniel SOULE et al from Zachariah ALLEN.
<7:22> - 5 July 1711, Nathaniel SOULE et al, division.
<9:693> - 3 Jan. 1715, Nathaniel SOULE from Daniel WOOD.
<10:33> - 16 Mar. 1715/6, Nathaniel SOULE from William WOOD.
<10:35> - 16 Mar. 1715/6, Nathaniel SOULE from Nicholas LAPHAM.
<10:36> - 16 Mar. 1715/6, Nathaniel SOULE from Robert KERBEE.
<10:37> - 16 Mar. 1715/6, Nathaniel SOULE from Benjamin TRIPP.
<15:5> - 6 May 1723, , Nathaniel SOULE from Benjamin TRIPP.
<15:6> - 6 May 1723, Nathaniel SOULE from James AKIN.
<15:7> - 6 May 1723, Nathaniel SOULE from Ralph EARLE.
<15:147> - 13 Sept 1723, Nathaniel SOULE from George CADMAN.
<17:390> - 18 May 1727, Nathaniel SOULE from William SOULE.
<17:391> - 18 May 1727, Nathaniel SOULE from John DENNIS.
<21:431> - 11 July 1733, Nathaniel SOULE from John RUSSELL Jr.
<25:57> - 17 May 1736, Nathaniel SOULE from Sylvanus SOULE.
<25:474> - 14 Dec. 1737, Nathaniel SOULE from Jeremiah MACOMBER.
<28:378> - 25 Oct. 1740, Nathaniel SOULE from Stephen WILBORE.
<31:188> - 21 Feb. 1742/3, Nathaniel SOULE et al from Sylvanus SOWLE.
<36:359> - 21 Dec. 1748, Nathaniel SOULE from Jacob SOWLE.
<37:236> - 23 Mar. 1749, Nathaniel SOULE from William POTTER.
<43:282> - 13 Jan. 1759, Nathaniel SOULE from Christopher GIFFORD Jr.
<70:393> - 13 Mar. 1792, Nathaniel SOULE from Benjamin CORNELL.
<6:86> - 2 Jan. 1709, Sylvanus SOULE from William SLADE.
<7:22> - 5 July 1711, Sylvanus SOULE et al, division.
<9:227> - 19 May 1715, Sylvanus SOULE from William SLADE.
<13:376> - 1 Jan. 1719/20, Sylvanus SOULE from Morris TUCKER.
<19:240> - 21 Apr. 1730, Sylvanus SOULE from Hannah TALMAN et al.
<19:241> - 21 Apr. 1730, Sylvanus SOULE from estate Ephraim THOMAS et al.
<19:242> - 21 Apr. 1730, Sylvanus SOULE from estate Constant CHURCH.
<19:243> - 21 Apr. 1730, Sylvanus SOULE from William SPOONER.
<47:58> - 13 Mar. 1764, Wesson SOULE from Nathaniel SOULE.
<54:354> - 27 Apr. 1772, Wesson SOULE from Robert CROSSMAN.
<47:232> - 13 Sept 1764, Weston SOULE from Christopher GIFFORD.
<57:249> - 24 May 1777, Weston SOULE excon. from Thomas GILBERT.

BRISTOL COUNTY DEEDS, cont-d: (re: SOULE, grantees)

<5:441> - 4 Nov. 1708, William SOULE et al from Peleg SLOCUMB.
<5:461> - 27 Jan. 1708, William SOULE from William BROWNELL et ux.
<7:22> - 5 July 1711, William SOULE et al, division.
<12:338> - 30 Dec. 1718, William SOULE from Nathaniel SOULE.
<12:339> - 30 Dec. 1718, William SOULE from Eleazer SLOCUMB.
<12:346> - 2 Jan. 1718, William SOULE from Jeremiah DAVOL.
<12:347> - 2 Jan. 1718, William SOULE from Eleazer SLOCUMB.
<12:348> - 2 Jan. 1718, William SOULE from Peleg SLOCUMB.
<12:404> - 11 Mar. 1718/9, William SOULE et al from Benjamin ALLEN et al.
<12:405> - 11 Mar. 1718/9, William SOULE from Daniel ALLEN.
<12:407> - 11 Mar. 1718/9, William SOULE from Richard RUNDELLS et ux.
<14:234> - 7 May 1722, William SOULE from Joshua COGGESHALL et ux.
<17:211> - 30 Jan. 1726/7, William SOULE from John WILLCOX.
<17:212> - 30 Jan. 1726/7, William SOULE from Samuel CRANDALL.
<18:389> - 20 Feb. 1728/9, William SOULE from Philip TABER.
<18:492> - 3 June 1729, William SOULE from Richard SISSON et ux.
<18:395> - 20 Feb. 1728/9, William SOULE from Thomas MACOMBER.
<18:391> - 20 Feb. 1728/9, William SOULE from Jabez WILLCOX.
<19:191> - 28 Mar. 1730, William SOULE from Job BRIGGS.
<20:129> - 14 Aug. 1731, William SOULE from Thomas MACOMBER.
<48:518> - 26 Oct. 1765, William SOULE from Benjamin SLOCUM.
<51:46> - 12 Jan. 1768, William SOULE from Philip TABER et al.
<71:;429>- 5 Mar. 1793, William SOULE et al from Abraham ALLEN.
<73:484> - 21 Apr. 1795, William SOULE from estate Elihu AKIN.
<15:14> - 9 Nov. 1723, William SOULE Jr. from William SOULE Sr.

PLYMOUTH COUNTY DEEDS: (re: SOULE)

<54:139> - 1768, Micah SOULE, Hannah SOULE & Rebecca SOULE, spinsters to Nathaniel SOULE, all of Duxbury.
<84:115> - 1792, Simeon & Jane SOULE.
<68:204> - 1783, Orphan SOULE, widow of Aaron of Pembroke.

(References only to **SOULE**: 10:219,223;26:194;28:151;39:155;41:10,173;44:127;46:137;55:48;61:133, 138;64:254;68:82;76:215.)

PLYMOUTH COLONY DEEDS: (re: SOULE)

<12:4> - 1623, George SOULE granted one acre on south side of brook toward the bay.
<1:41> - 14 Mar. 1636, George SOWLE & Manasseh KEMPTON granted hay ground against the fence of sd George & against fence of Thomas LITTLE.
<1:56> - 20 Mar. 1636, George SOWLE granted hay ground where he gott hey the last yeare.
<1:45> - 6 Oct. 1636, Land occupied by George SOWLE granted to William BRADFORD.
<1:69> - 4 Dec. 1637, Garden place on Duxbury side by Samuel NASH's granted to George SOULE, to lye to his ground at Powder Point.
<1:83> - 7 May 1638, One acre granted to George SOULE, at the watering place; also two acres of Stony Marsh at Powder Point.
<1:72> - 13 July 1639, George SOULE sells to Robert HICKS, two acres at the watering place on the south side of Plymouth. <also 12:45>
<1:165> - 2 Nov. 1640, Land at Green's Harbor granted to George SOULE.
<3:110> - 20 Dec. 1667, George SOULE to Phillip BILL.
<3:134> - 4 May 1658, Five acres of meadow land granted to George SOULE.
<4:19> - 3 June 1662, George SOULE granted share in Majors Purchase.
<3:21> - 3 June 1662, George SOULE granted 21st lot near Namassakett.
<3:123> - 17 July 1668, George SOULE to son George SOULE.
<3:126> - 23 July 1668, George SOULE to dau Elizabeth WALKER wf of Francis.
<3:153> - 26 Jan. 1668/9, George SOULE to dau Patience HASKELL wf of John.
<3:245> - 22 Jan. 1668/9, George SOULE to Nathaniel SOULE.
<3:216> - 14 Oct. 1671, John SOULE & Francis WALKER, owners of a share in cedar swamp in Majors Purchase near Namassakeesett Ponds.
<3:244> - 30 July 1672, George SOULE & Mary SOULE to John PETERSON.
<4:43> - 30 Dec. 1674, John & Rebecca SOULE from father in law Moses SIMMONS.
<4:11> - 23 Mar. 1674/5, George & Mary SOULE to John PETERSON.
<4:155> - 20 Feb. 1675/6, George SOULE from John & Mary PETERSON. Ack. 24 Feb. 1675.
<4:50> - 24 Feb. 1675/6, George & Mary SOULE to John PETERSON.

ELIZABETH SOULE[2] (George[1])

PLYMOUTH COUNTY DEEDS: (re: WALKER)

<1:16> - 27 Mar. 1672, Francis WALKER to John WADSWORTH.
<9:189> - 9 Apr. 1702, Isaac WALKER, formerly of Woodbridge NJ now of Little Compton, land in

PLYMOUTH COUNTY DEEDS, cont-d: (re: WALKER)

<6:126> - 13 Mar. 1704/5, Isaac WALKER, yeoman of Swansea to Benjamin SOULE of Plymouth, half of 100 acres in Middleboro in partnership with John HASCALL.
<6:129> - 28 May 1705, Isaac WALKER of Swansea to Benjamin SOULE, land in Middleboro, formerly belonging to my honoured father Frances WALKER.
<12:17> - 31 May 1705, Isaac WALKER of Swansea..land in Middleboro formerly belonging to Francis WALKER & John HASKELL.
<25:169>- 9 June 1730, Isaac WALKER, blacksmith & wf Bethiah of Marshfield, her part in land of her father John NORTHEY.

GEORGE SOULE[2] (George[1])

MICRO #2 OF 11

All references to the name **William BROWNELL** in Bristol Co.PR:
<3:230> Will, dated 16 Nov. 1714, wf **Sarah.** <3:231> Inventory. <3:298> Account. <14:500> Adm. <14:505> Inventory. <15:513> Account. <17:585> Dower. <17:593> Account. <19:475> Account. <19:521> Division. <19:566> Receipt. <125:84;126:69;127:404> Letters of Guardianship.

Estate of **Joseph DEVOL/DEVIL** of Dartmouth MA. <Bristol Co.PR>
<5:323>...14 Nov. 1726, widow **Mary DEVOL** app'td admx. <5:326> Inventory taken 14 Nov. 1726 by Jeremiah DEVOL/DEVIL, George BROWNEL, William SOULE, all of Dartmouth. <6:249> Account of admx. 17 June 1729.

Estate of **Joseph DEVOL** of Dartmouth MA. <Bristol Co.PR>
<5:323> Letter/Bond 14 Nov. 1726, widow **Mary DEVOL** app'td admx. <original> Oath of appraisers, 11 Nov. 1726. <5:326> Inventory taken 17 Nov. 1726; no real estate. <6:249> Account.

Will of **Benjamin DAVOL,** yeoman of Westport MA. <Bristol Co.PR>
<39:155>...dated 28 May 1802, mentions wf **Sarah;** sons **Benjamin DAVOL, Reuben DAVOL;** dau **Judith DAVOL;** granddaughter **Zilphia DAVOL** to live with her grandmother and Aunt **Judith** until she is 21; sons **Abner DAVOL** (executor), **Jeremiah DAVOL, George DAVOL;** granddaughter **Deborah POTTER,** under 21 Witnesses: Henry HOWLAND, Prince HOWLAND, John MOSHER. Codicil 4 June 1802. Pr. 6 July 1802. Appraisers app'td, 2 July 1802. <39:158> Inventory. <40:164> Account.

Will of **Benjamin DEVIL/DEVOL** of ?. <"8:194">
...dated 16 Dec. 1734, mentions wf **Anne** (executrix) & children, viz: **Peter DEVOL** & his children, **John DEVOL** (under 21), **Sarah MOSHER, Elizabeth DEVOL, Rebecca BROWNEL, Frelove DEVOL, Anne DEVOL** & **Mary DEVOL.** Pr. 10 Feb. 1734 <1734/35>.

BRISTOL COUNTY DEEDS: (re: Benjamin DAVOL, all grantors to 1795**)**

<9:38> 1714; <15:603> 7 Feb. 1724; <21:415> 6 Mar. 1732/3. <22:131> 6 Mar. 1732/3.
<23:220> - 9 July 1731, Benjamin DAVOL & wf Ann.
<43:222> - 9 Oct. 1742, Benjamin DAVOL of Tiverton, sells land received from grandfather Jonathan DAVOL of Dartmouth dec'd.
<51:215> - 18 Apr. 1767, Benjamin DAVOL of Dartmouth.
<60:417> - 20 Aug. 1781, Benjamin DAVOL, yeoman of Dartmouth sells twelve & a half acres in Dartmouth. Sarah DEVELL/DAVOL signs.
<62:435> - 13 Feb. 1776, Benjamin DAVOL, yeoman & wf Sarah of Dartmouth sell one quarter of grist mill in Dartmouth formerly of Benjamin WAIT. Rec. 9 June 1784.
<65:213> - 31 Mar. 1785, Benjamin DAVOL/DAVEL, yeoman & wf Sarah of Dartmouth. Rec. 1 Feb. 1786.
<65:298> - 11 Mar. 1786, Benjamin DAVOL/DEVEL, yeoman & wf Sarah of Dartmouth sell house & land in Dartmouth. Ack. at Tiverton RI 13 Mar. 1786 by Benjamin.
<72:79> - 11 June 1793, Benjamin DAVOL & Joshua MACOMBER, agreement about boundaries. Ack. same day at Tiverton RI.

All references to the name **Benjamin DAVOL** in Bristol Co.PR to 1881:
<8:188> Pr. <8:194> Will. <8:196> Inv. <10:149> Account. <39:155> Will. <39:158> Inv. <40:164> Account. <65:204> Will. <80:277> Adm. <80:327> Inv. <80:369> Allowance. <80:474> Account. <112:266> Notice. <114:241> Notice. <154:284> Adm. <160:301> Bond.

Will of **Benjamin DEVEL/DAVOL** of Westport MA. <Bristol Co.PR 65:204>
...dated 22 June 1825, mentions wf **Sarah** & her dec'd sister Abigail; son **Peter DAVOL;** daus **Meribah DAVOL, Patience DAVIS;** grandchildren **Benjamin DAVOL, David Smith DAVOL** (under 21)**, Samuel Brown DAVOL, Susanna DAVOL, Clarissa DAVOL;** son **John DAVOL.**

References to the name **Joseph DAVOL** in Bristol Co.PR, all on old index:
<5:323> Adm., 1726. <5:326> Inventory. <6:249> Account. <27:203> Will.

Estate of **Edith HOWLAND** of New Bedford MA. <Bristol Co.PR 93:161>
...dated 27 Nov. 1847, mentions son **Joseph R. HOWLAND,** dau **Elizabeth WOOD** wf of Charles L.

Will of **Nathan SOULE**, yeoman of Dartmouth MA. <Bristol Co.PR>
<8:416>...dated 15 Nov. 1735...to wf **Mary**, my great mare that she commonly rideth on all so my side saddle & bridel...and improvement of estate; to eldest son **John SOULE**, one half of homsted land or farm that I now live on...bounded by the river and land of MACOMBER and Nathaniel SOULE ...with all my medow, upland or beach lying in the horsneck...and meadow lying on the bush flat in Acoxet River...to youngest son **Timothy SOULE**, half of homsted...bounded by river and land of MACOMBER, Jacob SOULE and Edward HOWARD....also marsh meadow lying on the great flat in Acoxet River, part of which was bought of John HATHAWAY...to son **George SOULE**, lands that I hold in the right of my Honoured father **George SOULE** late of Dartmouth dec'd...also cedar swamp which I bought of Benjamin DEVOL of Dartmouth dec'd, also rest of meadow on the great flat...part of it being the meadow that I bought of Benjamin CHASE...to son **Cornelius SOULE**...land bought of Jacob SOULE & James TRIPP of Dartmouth...ceder swomp which I clame & hold in the right of my honoured father **George SOULE**...to son **John SOULE** my cheas bords in the garrat & five hogsheds & two snagwood tubs...to dau **Content** one good feather bed and one third of household goods...to dau **Mary** one feather bed and one third of household goods...to son **John** one bed ticken filled with turkey feathers, husbandrey utentials, carpenter & cupper/cooper tools...to sons **Cornelius & Timothy**, one fether bed a peace...to son **Timothy** my loom...to son **Cornelius** Ł30...remainder of estate to son **John** (executor) who is named guardian to dau **Mary**. Witnesses: Gabriel HIX, Stephen WILLBOUR, Ichabod BROWNELL; HIX and BROWNELL made oath 19 Oct. 1736. <original> Appraisers sworn, 13 Oct. 1736. <8:418> Inventory taken 15 Oct. 1736 by Phillip TABER, Nathaniel SOULE, Gabriel HIX; Debts due from: John BLACKAMORE, John SOULE, Cornelius SOULE, Timothy SOULE, Rebecca KIRBY, Ichabod BROWNELL; total real estate, Ł3600; total personal estate, Ł804.4s6d. <original> Bond 19 Oct. 1736, of **John SOULE**, tanner, admr. Sureties: Phillip TABER, Gabriel HIX, yeomen of Dartmouth. Witnesses: Stephen PAINE, Samuel BORDEN. <8:416> Pr. 20 Oct. 1736.

Will of **Mary SOWLE/SOULE**, widow of Dartmouth MA. <Bristol Co.PR>
<22:99>...dated 7 Jan. 1772, widow of Nathan...to grandson, otherwise called my great-grandson, **Nathan DAVIS** son of **Job DAVIS**, Ł3, my great cubbord & live stock...to son **George SOULE**, my chafingdish, brass scimmer & couch with furniture...to son **Cornelius SOULE**, my two brass ladles & to his wife Sarah, my dueroy gound...grandson **Joseph SOULE**, son of son **Timothy SOULE** dec'd; grandson **Abner SOULE**, son of son **Cornelius**...to grandaughter **Ellefell TABER** dau of son **Cornelius**, my side saddle & dyeaper table cloath...grandaughters **Margret DAVEL, Content SHELDEN**...to granddaughters **Alice SOULE & Anne SOULE**, daus of son **George**, twelve of my best puter plates...to grandson **Joseph DAVIS** (under 21), son of dec'd dau **Mary DAVIS**, remainder of estate; son in law **Joseph DAVIS** and Christopher GIFFORD, executors. Witnesses: Benjamin SOWLE, James SOWLE, Joseph SOWLE. <22:105> 13 Jan. 1772, Christopher GIFFORD declines to serve. <22:101> Pr. 27 Jan. 1772; **Joseph DAVIS** app'td admr. <22: 102> Inventory taken 16 Jan. 1772, by James SOWLE, Joseph SOWLE, John WOOD (who were app'td 14 Jan. 1772.), all of Dartmouth; incl. two silver spoons marked "M S" , 24s; one pair of spectacles & case, 9d; one great cubbord, 18s; one large Bible, 7s6d; Notes due from: Peter WEAVER, Nathaniel POTTER, estate of John SOWLE, Job DAVIS, Thomas DAVIS, John LAWTON, Timothy MACOMBER, Stephen WILCOKS, James SOWLE.

Will of **John SOULE**, yeoman of Dartmouth MA. <Bristol Co.PR>
<22:5>...dated 9 Nov. 1768 (signed 10 Nov.)...to dau **Anne DAVIS**, improvement of homsted farm together with salt medow until grandson **John DAVIS** reaches 21...also to **John**, one half of salt meadow in horsneck, one half of right in bush flat and half of cedar swamp; grandsons **Nathan DAVIS & Job DAVIS**; dau **Reliance DAVIS**, wf of Stephen; to Aunt **Sarah TIBBITS**, my great chamber to live in dureing her natural life; to son in law **Job DAVIS** (executor), other half of salt meadow, cedar swamp & bush flat. Witnesses: Job ALMY Jr., Walter CORNELL, Isaac WOOD. <original> Oath 23 Sept. 1771, of Christopher GIFFORD regarding inventory. <22:48> Inventory taken 28 Sept. 1771 by James SOWLE, Christopher GIFFORD, Joseph SOWLE; total estate, Ł118.6s3d; sworn to 9 Oct. 1771 by exr. <original> Petition 7 Oct. 1771, of widow **Meribah SOULE**, that she was not mentioned in will & asks for her thirds as per law. <22:6> Pr. 9 Oct. 1771.

Job DAVIS of Dartmouth MA to **Lemuel SISSON & George TIBBETS** of same. <Bristol Co.Deeds 65:587> ...29 June 1772, Job DAVIS, yeoman to Lemuel SISSON and George TIBBETS, yeomen...land given to me by John SOWLE late of Dartmouth dec'd, in his will. Wf Anne DAVIS releases dower and Meribah SOWLE, widow of John SOLE/SOWLE late of Dartmouth dec'd, releases dower. Ack. same day by Job. Rec. 1 Feb. 1786.

All references to the name **TIBBITTS**, grantors & grantees to 1795, in Bristol Co.Deeds: 42:17;65: 208,209,587,588;68:543;71:505,557;72:151,152.

BRISTOL COUNTY DEEDS: (re: Nathan SOULE)

<6:44> - 18 May 1708, Sarah SOULE of Dartmouth to Nathan SOULE of same, rights in land of John SOULE, son of our father George SOULE.

<23:219> - 21 Sept 1714, Nathan SOULE of Dartmouth from Samuel WILLIS. Rec. 24 Sept. 1734.

<14:235> - 8 Apr. 1720, Nathan SOULE from Joshua & Mary COGGESHALL of Dartmouth, rights in land of our grandfather George SOULE of Dartmouth dec'd.

<23:215> - 21 Oct. 1721, Nathan SOULE, yeoman of Dartmouth from Benjamin CHASE. Rec. 24 Sept 1734

<23:221> - 30 July 1722, Nathan SOULE, yeoman of Dartmouth from John HATHAWAY, weaver of same. Ack. 2 May 1724. Rec. 24 Sept. 1734.

<23:219> - 21 Apr. 1729, Nathan SOULE of Dartmouth from James TRIPP Jr., weaver. Rec. Sept. 1734.

<23:232> - 10 June 1731, Nathan SOULE of Dartmouth to Jonathan WOOD son of William of same. Ack. 2 May 1732 at Little Compton. Rec. 29 Oct. 1734.

BRISTOL COUNTY DEEDS, cont-d: (re: Nathan SOULE)

<23:220> - 9 July 1731, Nathan SOULE from Benjamin DAVEL, both yeomen of Dartmouth. Wf Ann DAVEL releases dower. Ack. 6 Mar. 1732/3. REc. 24 Sept. 1734.
<23:214> - 10 May 1732, Nathan SOULE, yeoman of Dartmouth from sister Mary DAVELL, widow of Joseph of same. Ack. 6 Mar. 1732/3. Rec. 24 Sept. 1734.

Will of **Mary DAVIS.** <Bristol Co.PR 30:254>
...dated 1786, mentions sister **Tabitha GIFFORD** wf of James; Abner CHACE, Patience CHACE & Keziah CHACE, the children of Jacob CHACE; friend Jacob CHACE, executor.

Estate of **William SOULE**, yeoman of Dartmouth MA. <Bristol Co.PR>
<4:180> On 25 Apr. 1723, Jonathan DEAVILL/DAVOLL, Benjamin WILBORE, Philip ALLEN, all of Dartmouth, app'td to appraise estate. <4:182> Inventory taken 25 Apr. 1723; incl. 12 acre salt marsh, £120; land near the house of Benjamin DAVIS in Acoakset villig in Dartmouth, £200; 36 acres in Aponaganset vilige near the quakers meeting house in Dartmouth, £70; two acres seader swamp, £20; three acres of beach lying in the horsneck in Dartmouth, £6; home stid house & land, £440; total estate, £1193.7s6d; sworn to 6 May 1723 by sons of dec'd, **William SOULE & George SOULE.** <4:180> On 6 May 1723, widow **Hannah SOLE/SOULE** refused to administer estate and asked that her sons be app'td and that they should be guardians to her orphaned minor children. <4:181> Letter/Bond 6 May 1723, **William SOULE,** weaver **& George SOULE,** blacksmith, app'td admrs. Sureties: Nathaniel SOULE & John MACOMBER, husbandmen of Dartmouth. Witnesses: Nathaniel PAINE Jr., Stephen PAINE. <original> Receipt 10 Oct. 1723, of Sarah WILCOCKS. <4:336> Receipts 14 Oct. 1723 of Philip TABER & Joseph RUSSELL Jr.; 13 Jan. 1723/4, of Samuel WILLIS; 9 May 1724 of John AKIN & Philip TABER; 11 May 1724 of Seth POPE. <4:335> Receipts 3 Aug. 1724 of Joseph TILLINGHAST Jr. (on behalf of his father); 4 Aug. 1724 of Nathan SOULE. <4:337> Account 10 Apr. 1723, of admrs., Received from: Benjamin SOULE, William COREY, Richard KERBEE; Paid to: Thomas MACOMBER, Capt. Samuel WILLIS, Seth POPE, Esq., Joseph RUSSELL, Philip TABER, Lieut. Daniel WOOD, Thomas MOUCHER, James TRIPP, Benjamin WILLBORE, Jacob SOULE, Job MILK, brother Samuel SOULE, William WOOD Jr., Jedediah WOOD, Peleg SLOCUM, Nathaniel SOULE, Marchant WILLIS, Eleazer SLOCUM, Philip ALLEN, Joseph TILLENHAST, Sarah SOULE, George SOULE for smith work, John RUSSELL, our unkle Nathan SOLE for money which was borowed by our father in his life time, William SOULE, George SOULE. <original> Division of real estate, 26 Mar. 1725 by John AKIN, Richard BORDEN, Deliverance SMITH, Daniel WOOD & John RUSSELL; to the widow **Hannah SOULE,** her thirds; eldest son **William SOLE/SOULE** and 3d son **Benjamin SOLE/SOULE** haveing been advansed by gifts in their father's lifetime make no demand; to 2d son **George SOLE/SOULE,** one ninth of the homesteed farm, one ninth of the salt marsh meadow lying near Allens pond, one ninth of tract of land on both sides of the river that runs by the meeting house in Ponogancet village, one ninth of land in Accoxet village near homesteed of Benjamin DAVIS, one ninth of ceder swamp in Dartmouth adjoyning to John RUSSEL's lott; one ninth each to 4th son **Joseph SOLE/SOULE,** 5th son **Samuel SOLE/SOULE,** 6th son **Jonathan SOLE/SOULE,** eldest dau **Hannah HOLLEY** wf of Joseph, 2d dau **Mary PAGE** wf of William, 3d dau **Sarah HOWLAND** wf of Samuel dau **Allis SOLE/SOULE** & youngest dau **Deborah SOLE/SOULE;** division sworn to and allowed 18 May 1725

References to the name **William SOULE** in Bristol Co.PR: 8:297,298 (1734);63:312,458,513;64:306;65:97,103,276,303,304;66:113;97:342,380;99:499;100:428,565;102:305.

References to the name **William SOULE** in Bristol Co.Deeds, all to 1795; Grantee: 5:441,461;7:22;12:338,339,346,347,348,404,405,407;14:234;15:14;17:211,212;18:389,391,395,492;19:191;20:129;48:518;51:46;71:429;73:484. Grantor: 5:442;7:22;8:591;9:37,456,458;12:248,449;13:2;15:14,82;16:392;17:390,498;18:283;19:269,339;23:193,200,518;25:390;26:252;27:276;28:63;30:424,425;34:91,92;51:50,51,63,110,113;54:528. (<13:2> - 10 Sept. 1719, William SOULE, yeoman of Dartmouth & Ralph ALLEN, weaver of Newport RI, sell land.)

Heirs of **Josiah ALLEN** of Dartmouth MA to **Ralph ALLEN & William SOULE.** <Bristol Co.Deeds>
<12:404>...23 Oct. 1718, Benjamin ALLEN & Reuben ALLEN, of Cicle Co. MD, sold to our brother Ralph ALLEN, weaver of Newport RI and William SOULE, yeoman of Dartmouth...all our right in the estate of our brother Josiah ALLEN late of Dartmouth dec'd. Ack. 28 Oct. 1718 "by both" in Chester co. PA. Rec. 11 Mar. 1719. <12:407>...4 Nov. 1718, Richard RUNDLLS, carpenter of Shrewsbury NJ & wf Hannah, sold to brother Ralph ALLEN and William SOULE, their share. Ack. same day in Monmouth Co. NJ. <12:405>...10 Nov. 1718, Daniel ALLEN of Cicle Co. MD sold to brother Ralph ALLEN & William SOULE, his share. Ack. 4 Nov. 1718 in Monmouth Co. NJ. Rec. 11 Mar. 1718/19.

Will of **Richard SISSON** of Dartmouth MA. <Bristol Co.PR>
...dated 10 Jan. 1782, mentions sons **Philip SISSON, Benjamin SISSON, Joseph SISSON;** dau **Alice SANFORD;** grandson **Robert SISSON** son of son **Philip;** grandchildren **Rhode, Robert, Elizabeth & Peleg** (no surnames). Pr. 5 Oct. 1790.

MICRO #3 OF 11

William SOULE of Dartmouth MA to **William SOULE** of same. <Bristol Co.Deeds 15:14>
...6 Oct. 1722, William SOUL, yeoman for love, etc., coneys to son William SOULE, weaver...all that tract or parcell of land which I have where my sd son William's dwelling house now standeth in Dartmouth...also other land.

Estate of **William SOLE/SOULE** of Dartmouth MA/Tiverton . <Bristol Co.PR>
<original> Bond 28 Oct. 1734, widow **Rachel SOLE** app'td admx. Sureties: Benjamin CHASE, Benjamin ALLEN. <8:297> Inventory taken 28/29 Oct. 1734 at Tiverton; incl. one acre cedar swamp, Ł10; two acres in Tiverton, Ł8; six acres in Dartmouth, Ł18; total estate, Ł332.12.9.; sworn to 18 Nov. 1835 by admx. <8:298> Account 18 Nov. 1735, of admx.

Estate of **John BENNETT** of Dartmouth MA. <Bristol Co.PR>
<original> Warrant to appraise, 27 Nov. 1769, to Isaac VINCENT, Nicolas DAVIS, Joseph TABER Jr., all yeomen & freeholders of Dartmouth. <146:156> Letter/Bond 29 Nov. 1769, Walter SPOONER, yeoman of Dartmouth app'td admr. Sureties: Robert BENNET, yeoman of Dartmouth & Elijah WITHEREL, yeoman of Norton. Witnesses: George LEONARD Jr., Marcy WETHERELL. <21:114> Inventory taken 28 Nov. 1769 by Isaac VINCENT, Nicolas DAVIS, Joseph TABER Jr.; incl. silverheaded sword, 30s; total real estate, Ł1266.13s4d; total estate, Ł1407.6s5d. <original> Warrant, 8 Oct. 1770, to set off dower to widow (no record that it was carried out). <22:209> Warrant, 21 Jan. 1771, to Bartholemew TABER, Jethro HATHEWAY, Isaac VINCENT, all sufficient freeholders, app'td to divide real estate among the children. <original> Division 28 Mar. 1771, of real estate consisting of 205 acres valued at Ł771.15s, to the following, viz: to **Mary BENNITT**, one ninth, plus one seventh of one ninth which is the share of brother **Job BENNITT** who dec'd since their father's decease; the same to: eldest son **Gideon BENNITT, Robert BENNITT, Aulden BENNITT, Joseph BENNITT, Thomas BENNITT & John BENNITT**

Guardianship of Children of **John BENNETT** of Dartmouth MA. <Bristol Co.PR>
<128:152,153> 29 Nov. 1769, Robert BENNET, yeoman of Dartmouth app'td gdn. of **Mary BENNET & Joseph BENNET**, both under 14. <128:162,163> 25 Dec. 1769, Robert BENNET chosen gdn. by **Alden BENNET & Job BENNET.**

Alden BENNET of Charlotte NY to **Ignatious DILLINGHAM** of Dartmouth MA. <Bristol Co.Deeds 58:16>
...29 Aug. 1776, Alden BENNET of Charlotte Precint in Dutchess County NY, for Ł174.8s sold to Ignatious DILLINGHAM, yeoman...about 28 or 29 acres in Dartmouth...that fell to sd Alden by his father John BENNET...bounded by land of sd Ignatious, Joseph BENNETT & Nathaniel SEARS. Elisabeth BENNETT signs. Witnesses: "William BENNETT", Silas DEVEL/DAVOL Jr., "William BENNETT", Peter COOLY. Ack. 2 Sept. 1776, Sharon CT by Alden. Rec. 20 Aug. 1777.

JOHN SOULE[2] (George[1])

Will of **Lt. Samuel NASH** of Duxbury. <Plymouth Col.Wills 4:2:112>
...dated 2 June 1681...being grown weake of body through old age & expecting ere long to depart this life...to dau **Martha CLARKE** (executrix), my dwelling house, orchard, out houseing, meadows & improved upland...to the chil. of dec'd grandson **Samuel SAMSON**, viz: **Samuel SAMSON & Ichabod SAMSON**, all lands after decease of dau....remainder of estate to dau **Martha** and grand daughters **Elizabeth DILLONO/DELANO & Mary HOWLAND**; friends John SOULE & Thomas DILLONO/DELANO, overseers. Witnesses: Nathaniel THOMAS, Deborah THOMAS. <6:1:3>...5 Mar. 1683/4...whereas Leiftenant **Samuel NASH** of Duxberry being aged and not in a capassety to lie and keep house of himselfe; hath therfore put his estate into the hands of **William CLARKE** of Duxburrow, that therby hee may have a comfortable livelyhood, as alsoe to certify the sume & totall of his moveable estate; and it is as followeth: one great bed & beding, Ł5; another bed & beding, Ł2;iron ware, Ł1.10s; pewter & brasse, Ł1.1.4.; one chern/churn, 2s; wooden & earthen vessells, 5s; cubberd & tubb, 5s; table tubbs & chairs, Ł1.5s; chist, linnine & curtaines, Ł2.3.; belace, glasse & other thinges, 5s; one cow & swine, Ł2.15; corn, 11s3d; pitchforke, 1s; money, 4s; total 17.18.3. The prissors were John SOULE & Phillip LEONARD being chosen by William CLARKE and approved by Leift. NASH, written by Thomas DELANOE this 18th of 4th month <June>, also one gun, 12s; one prospective glass, one pestle & morter and the disposing of his house & land during his lifetime. This Court doth allow the abovewritten accoumpt to be the reall due of **Martha CLARKE** the wife of **William CLARKE** of Duxburrow in compensation of her paines & care in lookeing to her father **Samuell NASH** late dec'd.

Samuel NASH of Duxburrow to **Samuel & Ichabod SAMPSON.** <Plymouth Col.Deeds 5:179>
...20 Sept. 1682, Samuel NASH, for & in consideration of the naturall affection; which I did beare to the dec'd Samuell SAMPSON my grandson...and haveing formerly promised unto the above sd Samuell SAMPSON in his life time; to give to him all my right & title, unto all my land in Duxburrow...I therefore now give...unto Samuell SAMPSON & Ichabod SAMPSON, sonnes of the above sd Samuell...my dwelling house with barne...as a pure & lawfull estate of inheritance. Witnesses: Thomas DELANO, Abigail ALDEN. Ack. 20 7mth <Sept.> 1682 by Samuel NASH.

Abraham SAMPSON Sr. of Duxburrow to **Samuel SAMPSON.** <Plymouth Col.Deeds 5:178>
...31 Aug. 1678, Abraham SAMPSON, for & in consideration of the naturall afection that I did beare to my son Samuel SAMPSON...have given & promised to give unto the aforsd Samuel that tract of land which I did receive with the daughter of Leift. Samuel NASH, the mother of the aforsd Samuel, which land is lying att a place called blewffish river...bounded by land of Leift. NASH, mill river & the Glade...this land I say I have formerly given; but legall conveyance not being made, whilest the aforsd Samuel was serviveing, by any deed in writing; I now therfore...give unto the heires of the abovesd Samuel SAMPSON...to be holden by them from the day of my death...as a pure & lawfull estate of inheritance. Witnesses: John SOULE, William SOUTHWORTH. Ack. 16 Sept. 1678 by Abraham.

Estate of **Zachariah SOULE.** <Plymouth Co.PR 1:87>
Inventory taken 16 Mar. 1690/91 by Edward SOUTHWORTH & Samuel DILANO/DELANO; one mare, £2; one chest & cloathing, £3;ffethers & old cloath, 15s; severals more, 17s; one gun, £1; part of a whale boat & craught, £1; other items received from Boston, £1.2.6s; total estate, £9.14.6, besides his wages due for the Canadian Expedition. Adm. granted to father **John SOUL/SOULE** who made oath same day. <#18890> Bond 17 Mar. 1690/91, of **John SOULE.** Witnesses: Thomas DELANO, Samuel SPRAGUE.

PLYMOUTH COUNTY DEEDS: (re: SOULE)

<12:155> - 31 July 1695, John SOULE to son Aaron SOULE, both of Duxbury.
<12:155> - 1 Aug. 1712, Josiah BARKER of Pembroke, Josiah SOULE & Ichabod WADSWORTH of Duxbury to Aaron SOULE of Pembroke.
<12:155> - 27 July 1713, Experience SIMMONS of Pembroke, widow of John SIMMONS of Duxbury to Aaron SOULE of Pembroke.
<12:156> - 22 Mar. 1713/4, Stephen SAMSON of Duxbury to Aaron SOULE of Pembroke.
<12:156> - 6 Mar. 1713/4, John PEARSE of Pembroke to Aaron SOULE of Pembroke.
<12:156> - 1 Mar. 1715/6, Thomas LORING, Benjamin SAMSON & John SAMSON of Duxbury to Aaron SOULE

Estate of **Aaron SOUL/SOULE** of Pembroke MA. <Plymouth Co.PR #18748>
<original> Request, 27 Jan.1783, of widow **Orphan SOUL,** being advanced in years declines to adm. estate. <27:132> Letter/Bond 4 Feb. 1783, **John SOUL,** yeoman of Pembroke, app'td admr. Sureties: Robert BARKER & John TURNER Jr. of Pembroke and Thomas CHURCH of Scituate. Witnesses: Joseph CUSHING Jr., Elizabeth CUSHING. <28:538> Inventory taken 13 Feb. 1783 by John TURNER & Robert BARKER of Pembroke and Joseph BRYANT of Marshfield. <28:539> Division, 14 Mar. 1783, of real estate to the following children, viz: only son **John SOUL** and daus **Rebeccah SOUL, Huldah CHURCH** wf of Thomas, **Lydia DWELLE** wf of Jedediah and **Leonice BREWSTER** wf of Isaac; mentions lands in Bridgewater, Pembroke, Scituate & Marshfield and 19th lot of cedar swamp that the dec'd had of his father by a deed of gift 11 June 1741.

Estate of **Rebecca SOUL,** singlewoman of Pembroke MA. <Plymouth Co.PR #18863>
<27:137> Letter/Bond 22 Mar. 1783, **John SOUL,** yeoman of Pembroke, app'td admr. Sureties: Robert BARKER of Pembroke & Thomas CHURCH of Scituate. Witnesses: D. STOCKBRIDGE Jr., Abiatha ALLDEN Jr. <28:555> Inventory taken 24 Mar. 1783 by John TURNER, Robert BARKER, Joshua BRYANT. <28:558> Division 2 Apr. 1783 between only brother **John SOUL** and sisters **Leonice BREWSTER** wf of Isaac, **Huldah CHURCH** wf of Thomas and **Lydia DWELLE** wf of Jedediah.

Aaron SOULE of Pembroke MA to **Freedom CHAMBERLAIN** of same. <Plymouth Co.Deeds 43:249>
...23 Mar. 1752, Aaron SOULE, yeoman, for & in consideration of the love, etc. which I have & do bear towards my well beloved son in law Freedom CHAMBERLAIN, yeoman & my dau Mary CHAMBERLAIN, give...salt meadow in Marshfield & meadow I bought of Thomas TRACY of Pembroke 23 Mar. 1752 with Aaron SOULE Jr. & Daniel LEWIS Jr. Rec. 21 June 1756.

Freedom CHAMBERLAIN of Pembroke MA to **Job CHAMBERLAIN** of Bridgewater. <Plymouth Co.Deeds 57:197>
...25 Nov. 1772, Freedom CHAMBERLIN, yeoman, for £16.16s sold to son Job CHAMBERLIN, cordwainer ...three & a half acres in Bridgewater being the half of the land bought of Matthew GANNETT of Bridgewater 10 June 1756...bounded by land of John PRIOR. Witnesses: Ichabod BONNEY Jr., David STOCKBRIDGE. Ack. same day. Rec. 2 Nov. 1773. <57:197>...same day he sells the other half to son Nathaniel CHAMBERLIN, blacksmith of Bridgewater.

Nathaniel CHAMBERLAIN et al to **Joseph HOLMES** of Kingston MA. <Plymouth Co.Deeds 64:134>
...22 Oct. 1781, Nathaniel CHAMBERLEN, Benjamin CHAMBERLEN, Job CHAMBERLEN & John CHAMBERLEN, yeomen of Bridgewater and Freedom CHAMBERLEN, gent. of Pembroke, for 151 spanish milled dollars, sold to Joseph HOLMES, yeoman...one half of the 154th lot in the Second Division of the Commons of upland that belonged to the Township of Duxborough & Pembroke & was drawn by our honoured Grandfather Nathaniel CHAMBERLIN of Pembroke. Witnesses: Perez RANDALL, Noah SIMMONS. Ack. same day. Rec. 30 July 1785.

Will of **Mark PHILLIPS** of E. Bridgewater MA. <Plymouth Co.PR>
<original>...dated 9 June 1846, mentions wf **Celia**; daus **Lucinda HUDSON, Nabby PHILLIPS** & her son **Lot PHILLIPS, Phebe PORTER, Celia WASHBURN**; sons **Nathan PHILLIPS, Wadsworth PHILLIPS.** Letter from heirs, 23 Apr. 1851. Pr. 1st Tues. May 1851.

Estate of **Job CHAMBERLAIN** of Bridgewater MA. <Plymouth Co.PR #3716>
<27:263> Letter. <30:364> Inventory. <35:149> Appraisal of real estate. <42:197> Dower. <35:150> Decree, 24 Sept. 1794, mentions widow **Rachel CHAMBERLAIN** and the following children, viz: eldest son **Thomas CHAMBERLAIN,** 2d son **Isaac CHAMBERLAIN, Elizabeth SIMMONS** wf of Jospeh, **Rachel PACKARD** wf of Ichabod, **Celia PHILLIPS** wf of Mark Jr. and **Zerviah CUSHING** wf of Daniel.

Job CHAMBERLIN of Bridgewater MA to **John BONNEY** of Pembroke MA. <Plymouth Co.Deeds 51:223>
...21 Feb. 1765, Job CHAMBERLIN & wf Rachel, for £28.17s11d, sold to John BONNEY, blacksmith... homestead farm on which John BONNEY, father of Rachel, late of Pembroke did live...being one half of one third which sd BONNEY did give to Job & Rachel by his last will...also a piece of cedar swamp in Pembroke being part of the 2d lot which fell to us by the above mentioned will. Witnesses: Seth SNELL, Jabesh COLE. Ack. 25 Oct. 1765 by grantors. Rec. 29 Oct. 1765.

Will of **Nathaniel CHAMBERLIN**, yeoman of Bridgewater MA. <Plymouth Co.PR #3728>
...dated 1 Sept.1784...to **Deliverance** my true & beloved wife all the goods & estate she brot with her to me...and the improvement of one half of estate...to son **Joseph CHAMBERLIN** the other half.. wearing apparel to four sons...to children **Nathaniel CHAMBERLIN, Sarah, Ruth, Mary, Lydia, Benjamin CHAMBERLIN & Josiah CHAMBERLIN,** mother's half of estate at her re-marriage or decease.... and my will is that the sum or sums at which either of the above named children are charged in my Book, sd sums to be added to the above sd half of my estate and then to be equally devided betwext them. Witnesses: Simeon WHITMAN, Job CHAMBERLIN, William SNELL, Polycarpus SNELL. Pr. 12 Apr. 1814. <References cited but not specified: 45:334,335;47:255;48:268-272>
(Note: The book Nathaniel mentions is his Account Book; in May 1911 it was in the possession of Mercer V. TILLSON of South Hanson MA. The entries begin on 20 June 1743 in Pembroke and give the dates of deaths and/or births for himself, both wives and his children. Also included are accounts of portions he has given his children in his lifetime, viz: June 1766 to son **Nathaniel**; 20 Nov. 1770 to dau **Sary PRAT**; July 1774 to dau **Ruth RACORDS/RECORD**; July 1774 to dau **Mary WHIT/WHITE**; Mar. 1780 to dau **Lydia PRATT**.)

Aaron SOULE of Pembroke MA to **Rachel MAGOON** of same. <Plymouth Co.Deeds 51:156>
...24 Apr. 1741, Aaron SOUL, yeoman, in consideration of the love, etc. I have & do bare towards my loving & dutifull daughter Rachell MAGOON, give...40 acres in Pembroke, part of 2d and Last Division of the Commons...laid out 1713 and is the 127th lot...bounded by land which was Josiah HOLMES' and land of Robert BARKER. Witnesses: Lydia SOUL, Aaron SOUL Jr. Ack. 23 Mar. 1752 by Aaron. Rec. 24 Oct. 1765.

Will of **David MAGOUN**, yeoman of Plympton MA. <Plymouth Co.PR 30:176>
...22 Mar. 1782...being advanced in age, mentions unnamed wife; sons **Thomas MAGOUN, James MAGOUN, Abner MAGOUN, Aaron MAGOUN, Isaac MAGOUN**; to dau **Hannah STANDISH**, the two acres wheron she now dwells; grand daughters **Rebecca MAN, Betty NASH**; daus **Mary DWELLE, Rachel CHANDLER**; sons **James & Aaron**, executors. Witnesses: John TURNER, Job TURNER, Sarah TURNER. Pr. 7 June 1787.

MICRO #4 OF 11

Estate of **Benjamin SOULE**, yeoman of Plympton MA. <Plymouth Co.PR #18761>
<12:195> Letter 3 Sept. 1751, widow **Hannah SOLE** app'td admx. <12:216> Inventory taken 6 June 1751 by Polycarpus LORING, Zebedee CHANDLER, Benjamin WESTON; mentions Indian man John PEGE and Indian woman Betty PETTER. <12:483> Warrant, 2 Mar. 1752, to Rowland HAMMOND, Samuel WRIGHT, Jabez NEWLAND, Gideon BRADFORD & Zebede CHANDLER, to divide estate among following heirs, viz: widow **Hannah SOULE,** eldest & only son **Benjamin SOULE** and eldest dau **Abigail SOULE,** 2d dau **Hannah SOULE** & youngest dau **Priscilla SOULE**; oath of appraisers, 17 July 1752. <15:6> Account of widow **Hannah LITTLE**, admx., allowed 7 Aug. 1758; Paid to: George WATSON, Nathan HOWARD, Alerton CUSHMAN, Roland HAMMOND, Joseph PERRY, Elijah BISBEE, Timothy VIPLY, Joseph RIGHT, Thomas CROADE, Mercy CUSHMAN, Gideon SAMSON, Benjamin CUSHMAN, Perez TILLSON, Ebenezer SOUL, John LORING, Samuel WRIGHT, Mehitable BONNEY, Jabez NULAN/NEWLAND, Nehemiah CUSHING, Robert BROWN, John PEAGUE, Thomas FOSTER Bradford FREEMAN, Isaac BONNEY, Samuel BARTLETT, George SAMSON, Benjamin WESTON, Edward SEARS, David WESTON, David CHURCHILL, Lydia SAMSON, Zachariah WHITMAN, Benjamin SAMSON, Nathaniel BRIANT Thomas TORRY, Josiah PERKINS, Samuel CLARKE, John BRADFORD, Benjamin FULLER.

Guardianship of Children of **Benjamin SOULE** of Plympton MA. <Plymouth Co.PR #18860>
<12:437> Letters/Bonds 2 Mar. 1752, widow **Hannah SOULE** app'td gdn. of **Hannah & Priscilla SOULE.** Sureties: Zebedee CHANDLER, housewright & Zachariah PADDOCK, cordwainer, both of Plympton. Witnesses: Nathan HAYWARD, Edward WINSLOW. <12:440> Letter 7 Mar. 1752, Bond 6 Mar. 1752, **Abigail SOULE** chooses Polycarpus LORING of Plimpton as her gdn. Sureties: Consider HOWLAND, innholder & Benjamin SOULE, labourer. Witnesses: Edward WINSLOW, John LOTHORP.

Estate of **Aaron SOULE,** yeoman of Plympton MA. <Plymouth Co.PR #18749>
<11:38B> Petition 21 Feb. 1842, by son **Charles SOULE** of Plympton to be app'td admr., the widow having declined. Letter/Bond 21 Feb. 1842, **Charles SOULE** app'td admr. Sureties: Chipman PORTER & Ebenezer WOOD of Halifax. Witness: J.H. LOUD. <86:56> Inventory taken 16 Feb. 1842 by Jonathan PARKER, Joseph SHERMAN & Elijah BISBEE, all of Plympton.

Will of **George SAMSON** of Plympton MA. <Plymouth Co.PR #17518>
<21:607>...dated 27 Aug. 1773; mentions wf **Hannah** and children, viz: **Gideon SAMSON, Zebedial SAMSON, Deborah BISBEY, Hannah PERKINS, Rebecca KILLEY, Elizabeth CUSHMAN**; mentions mills standing on the Wenetuxset River; son **Zebedial**, executor. Witnesses: Thomas LORING Jr., Joseph SAMSON, Zebedee CHANDLER. <original> 4 Apr. 1774, **Zebdiel/Zebedial SAMSON** declines to administer. <original> Bond 18 May 1774, of **Gideon SAMSON**, yeoman of Plimton as admr. Sureties: Elisha BISBEE, yeoman of Plimton & William WESTON, merchant of Plymouth. Witnesses: Thomas FOSTER, Josiah STURTEVANT. <21:609> Inventory taken 16 June 1774 by Jabez NEWLAND, Francis SHURTLEFF, Thomas WATERMAN; sworn to 4 July 1774 by admr.

Will of **Gideon SAMSON Sr.**, yeoman of Plympton MA. <Plymouth Co.PR #17520>
<35:193>...dated 8 Oct. 1794...labouring under the infirmitys of old age; mentions wf **Rebeckah**; kinswomen **Hannah PERKINS, Rebeckah KILLEY, Elizabeth CUSHMAN**; my young kinswoman **Abigail CUSHMAN** the dau of **Joseph CUSHMAN** of Duxborough; trusty friend & relitive, **Joseph CUSHMAN**, executor. Witnesses: Arthur CHANDLER, Mercy CHANDLER, John WADSWORTH. (Note on will: 8 Jan. 1795, Gideon BRADFORD, by Jabez Newland CUSHMAN, claimed an appeal from ye above decree.) <original> Bond 9 Dec.

1794, of **Joseph CUSHMAN** of Duxbury, executor. Sureties: Joseph Soule CUSHMAN of Duxbury & Joshua PERKINS of Carver. Witnesses: Isaac LOTHROP, Noah BISBEE. <35:198> Order of notice, sworn to by exr., 5 Jan.1795. <38:394> Account 7 Sept. 1803 by exr.; Paid to: Jabez N. CUSHMAN, Joanna DUNHAM, Bildad WASHBURN for grave stones, Oliver PARKER, Thomas GANNET, Nehemiah COBB, Sylvanus BARTLETT, Arthur CHANDLER, E. BISBE (town treasurer), Ebenezer DEAN Jr. for himself & his father, Joseph Soul CUSHMAN, Zenas BRYANT for a tax, Dr. WADSWORTH, George SAMPSON, Joel ELLIS, Isaac WRIGHT, Josiah PERKINS, Benjamin BRYANT, Joshua LORING, Elijah BISBE, Isaac WRIGHT Sr. and to cash paid for balance due from ye dec'd to Capt. BRADFORD's children being the deceased's wards.

Estate of **Capt. Joshua PERKINS** of Carver MA. <Plymouth Co.PR #15607, 34:141;36:320>
Petition, 24 Nov. 1797, of **Gideon PERKINS**...I have a right by law to take the administration on estate of dec'd father **Joshua PARKINGS/PERKINS**...but it is inconvened...that my brother **Luke PARKINGS/PERKINS** may be app'td. Letter 25 Nov. 1797, **Luke PERKINS** of Carver app'td admr. Inventory taken 12 Mar. 1798; total real estate, $251.00; total estate, $884.81; sworn to by admr. 31 Mar.

Gideon PERKINS et al to John SHAW & Elisha MURDOCK of Carver MA. <Plymouth Co.Deeds 186:126> ...10 Sept. 1797 or 1799, Gideon PERKINS, Andrew BARROWS & wf Sarah, Deborah MURDOCK, Peleg SAVERY & wf Hannah, Betty PERKINS, Drusilla WARD, Luke PERKINS and Sampson PERKINS, all of Carver and Joshua PERKINS of Middleborough, for $300.00 sold to John SHAW, Esq. and Elisha MURDOCK, gent...one acre in south meadow cedar swamp in Carver...and is a lot that Capt. Joshua PERKINS bought of Capt. George HAMMOND. Ack. 16 Sept. 1799. <186:126>...10 Sept. 1799, the above grantors for $3.00 sell to John SHAW, Esq. & wf Abigail...one quarter and one twenty fourth of 3d share in 2d division in 10th great lot in south meadow cedar swamp in Carver.

Estate of **Betsey PERKINS** of Carver MA. <Plymouth Co.PR #15538>
<original> Division, 1821, $5.78 each to following heirs, viz: **Luke PERKINS, Martha MURDOCK, Sarah BARROWS, Deborah MURDOCK, Abigail SHAW, Asa BAMSON, Sampson PERKINS, Gideon PERKINS**; balance of $11.39 due to **Joshua PERKINS & Peleg SAVERY.**

PLYMOUTH COUNTY DEEDS: (re: John C. PERKINS)

<182:221> - 4 Mar. 1835, John C. PERKINS, yeoman of Middleboro sells land in Middleboro.
<182:225> - 5 Mar. 1835, John C. PERKINS sells land in Carver, bounded on swamp of Luke PERKINS, bought of my father Gideon PERKINS.
<245:38> - 1851, John C. PERKINS & wf Matilda.
<254:287> - 9 June 1851, John C. PERKINS, yeoman of Middleboro to Syene COBB & her heirs, one acre & house in Middleboro. Ack. 11 June 1851.
<257:161> - 12 Jan. 1850, John C. PERKINS & wf Matilda sell land in Middleboro.
<276:182> - 3 Nov. 1856, John C. PERKINS & wf Matilda sell land in Middleboro.
<287:74> - 15 Apr. 1858, John C. PERKINS of Middleboro sells land.
(References only: 151:168;216:68;219:162;263:130.)

Estate of **Gideon PERKINS** of Middleboro MA. <Plymouth Co.PR #15571>
<61:254;66:449;67:420;68:13>...Bond 17 Nov. 1828, of Seth EATON, Esq., admr. Inventory taken 29 Nov. 1828; no real estate; total personal estate, $75.41.

Estate of **Zabdiel SAMSON** of Plympton MA. <Plymouth Co.PR #17685>
<23:143> Letter/Bond 4 Nov. 1776, widow **Abiah SAMSON** app'td admx. Sureties: Gideon BRADFORD, Timothy RIPLEY, both of Plympton. Witnesses: Barnabas LITTLE, Joseph CUSHING. <24:252> Inventory taken 11 Feb. 1777, by Gideon BRADFORD, Eleazer CROCKER, William RIPLEY Jr. who made oath 7 Apr. 1777. <25:72> Account of admx., 3 Aug. 1778; Paid to: George WATSON, Nathan PERKINS, Ebenezer DEAN, Elijah BISBEE, Nathaniel CHURCHILL, Job CUSHMAN, Joseph SAMSON, Freeman ELLIS, Gideon BRADFORD, Ebenezer SOUL, Joseph SOUL, Timothy RIPLEY and to the widow for provisions spent in the family. <25:381> Division 3 July 1780, by James CHURCHILL, Ebenezer SOUL, Timothy RIPLEY, all of Plympton, to widow **Abiah SAMPSON** and following children, viz: eldest son **George SAMPSON, Sarah BENT** wf of William, 2d son **William SAMPSON,** 3d son **Gideon SAMPSON Jr.**, 2d dau **Abigail BRADFORD** wf of Gideon Jr., 3d dau **Hannah SAMPSON,** 4th son **Philemon SAMPSON,** 5th son **Issachar SAMPSON.** <38:153> Warrant to divide dower, 4 Mar. 1801, John BRADFORD, Isaac BONNEY, Ebenezer SOULE, all of Plympton, app'td to divide real estate set off as dower to **Abia SAMPSON.** Division of dower, 25 Dec. 1801, to **George SAMPSON,** heirs of **William SAMPSON** dec'd, **Gideon SAMPSON, Abigal BRADFORD, Hannah COOPER** wf of Richard Jr., **Philemon SAMPSON, Issachar SAMPSON & Sarah BENT.**

Guardianship of Children of **Zabdiel SAMSON** of Plympton MA. <Plymouth Co.PR #17528>
<26:92> Letter 6 Mar. 1780, **George SAMPSON,** clothier of Plympton app'td gdn. of **Issachar SAMPSON,** aged 12. <26:344,346> Letters/Bonds 6 Mar. 1780, **George SAMPSON** chosen gdn. by **Philemon SAMPSON, Gideon SAMPSON, Hannah SAMPSON,** all above 14. Sureties: Gideon BRADFORD Jr. & William SAMPSON of Plimpton. Witnesses: Ezra WESTON, I. LOTHROP. <29:234,235> Account, 7 Feb. 1785, of **George SAMPSON Jr.** as gdn. to **Hannah.** Receipt 7 Reb. 1785, of **Gideon SAMSON Jr.** to gdn., discharging him from all demands. Witness: Philemon SAMSON.

Will of **Zachariah SOULE,** yeoman of Plympton MA. <Plymouth Co.PR #18887>
<12:181>...dated 30 Apr.1751, mentions wf **Mary** and following children, viz: **Jabez SOULE & Zachariah SOULE** (eldest sons), **Ephraim SOULE, James SOULE, Mary SOULE, Sarah TINKHAM, Hannah SOULE, Eunice SOULE, Lois SOULE**; wf & son **Zachariah,** executors. Witnesses: Jonathan PARKER, Jabez NEWLAND, Beriah BONNEY. Pr. 3 June 1751. <16:531> Bond 7 Nov. 1763, of **Mary SOULE,** exx. & residuary legatee. Sureties: Ephraim SOULE, yeoman of Plimton and Austin BEARCE, cordwainer of Halifax.

Witnesses: Edward WINSLOW, Ephraim SPOONER.

Estate of **Mary SOUL**, widow of Plympton/Middleboro MA. <Plymouth Co.PR #18837> <23:12> Letter/Bond 5 July 1773, Ephraim SOULE, yeoman of Plimton, app'td admr. Sureties: John NOYES of Abington & Nathan TINKHAM of Halifax. Witnesses: Thomas BANISTER, Edward WINSLOW Jr. <21:329> Inventory taken 12 July 1773 by James COBB, Francis THOMSON, Isaac THOMSON. <21:352> Account of admr., allowed 4 July 1774.

Estate of **James SOUL** of Plympton MA. <Plymouth Co.PR #18803> <15:102> Letter/Bond 7 Mar. 1759, brother **Zachariah SOULE**, yeoman of Plimton, app'td admr. Sureties: Joel ELLIS, James HARLOW, both of Plimton. Witnesses: Edward WINSLOW, Hannah WINSLOW. <15:530> Letter/Bond 7 June 1760, **Ephraim SOULE**, husbandman of Plimton, app'td adm. d.b.n., the former admr. having dec'd. Sureties: Ebenezer SOULE, Elijah BISBEE. Witnesses: Edward WINSLOW, Consider HOWLAND. <15:549> Inventory taken 23 June 1760 by Ebenezer SOULE, Zebedee CHANDLER, Elijah BISBEE. <16:525> Division of estate, 6 June 1761, by Robert WATERMAN, Elijah BISBE, Zebedee CHANDLER, to following heirs <brothers & sisters>, viz: **Ephraim SOULE, Mary, Hannah, Eunice, Sarah, Lois** <spelled Lewis> and heirs of **Jabez SOULE & Zachariah SOULE.** <16:520> Account of admr. allowed 7 Nov. 1763; incl. payment to Mary SOULE, widow <mother>.

MICRO #5 OF 11

Will of **Daniel SOULE**, yeoman/gent. of Plympton MA. <Plymouth Co.#18769> <82:105>...dated 27 Apr. 1837, mentions wf **Lucy** & son in law **James BOSWORTH**. Witnesses: Jonathan PARKER, Ichabod W. THOMPSON, Seth SHURTLIFF. <1:357**G**> Letter/Bond 13 Apr. 1840, James BOSWORTH, exr. Sureties: Jonathan PARKER of Plympton & Seth SHRUTLEFF of Carver. Witness: William THOMAS. <6:80**U**> Notice of appointment allowed 10 Aug. 1840.

Estate of **Jabez SOULE** of Halifax MA. <Plymouth Co.PR #18794> <12:382> Letter/Bond 7 Oct. 1751, widow **Abigail SOULE** app'td admx. Sureties: Nehemiah BENNETT of Middleboro & Woodbridge BROWN, yeoman of Abington. Witnesses: Robert LATHAM, Edward WINSLOW. <12:435> Inventory taken 16 Oct. 1751, by Ebenezer FULLER Jr., Moses STANDISH, Timothy RIPLEY; house, land & cattle house, £113.6.8; total estate, £174.17.10. <15:44> Account, 10 Oct. 1758, of admx.; incl. to bringing up two small children for seven years, £23.8.2; Paid to: Barnabas TOMSON, Polycarpus LORING, Timothy RIPLEY, Thomas CROADE, Ebenezer SOUL, Mary SOUL, John SHAW, WARREN & GOODWIN, Dr. LeBARON, Jonathan DIAMOND, Nehemiah BOSWORTH, Nathan TINKHAM, James RASHFORD, Benjamin WESTON, Hopestill BISBEE, Jeremiah KELLEY, David CHURCHILL.

Guardianship of Children of **Jabez SOULE** of Halifax MA. <Plymouth Co.PR #18802> <18:44> Letter/Bond 28 Oct. 1761, Jacob BENNET, yeoman of Middleborough app'td gdn. of **Mercy SOULE**. Surety: Jabez THOMAS of Middleboro. Witness: Gideon WHITE. <18:49> Letter/Bond 31 Mar. 1761, **Jacob SOULE** chooses Jacob BENNET as his gdn. Surety: Jabez THOMAS. Witnesses: Gideon WHITE, Edward WINSLOW.

Will of **Marcia SOULE**, singlewoman of Halifax MA. <Plymouth Co.PR #18835> <90:129>...dated 17 Aug. 1847, mentions brother **Jabez SOULE** and sisters **Sally STURTEVANT & Nabby SOULE**. Witnesses: Joseph S. WATERMAN, Jane P. WATERMAN, Elizabeth B. HAYWARD. <1:484**G**> Letter/Bond 4 Apr. 1848, **Abigail/Nabby SOULE**, exx. Sureties: Jabez SOULE, Joseph S. WATERMAN, both of Halifax. Witness: J.H. LOUD. <7:467**V**> Notice of appointment posted, oath of exx. 2 June 1849.

Estate of **Jacob SOULE**, yeoman of Halifax MA. <Plymouth Co.PR #18801> <52:302> Letter/Bond 20 Sept. 1824, Jonathan PARKER, Esq. of Plympton app'td admr. Sureties: Oliver PARKER, gent. & Barnabas PHINNEY, yeoman, both of Plympton. Witnesses: William S. RUSSELL, William T. MAYO. <58:379,380> Inventory taken 2 Oct. 1824 by Oliver PARKER of Plympton and Isaac THOMPSON & Nathan FULLER, yeomen of Halifax. <58:292> Sale of real estate, 18 Oct 1824, to pay debts. <59:191> List of claims, 29 Mar. 1825: Hannah WOOD, Dr. Nathaniel MORTON, Adam THOMPSON, Zadock THOMPSON, Josiah THOMPSON, Ruth BOSWORTH, Jacob THOMPSON, Nathaniel & W.S. EDDY, Abigail SOULE. <59:192> Account of admr., 2 May 1825; Paid to: Nathaniel & Cyrus MORTON, Susanna THOMPSON, Joseph BOSWORTH, Nathan PERKINS, John STURTEVANT, Jacob PARKER, Abigail SOULE and personal property to the widow.

Estate of **Zachariah SOULE** of husbandman of Plympton MA. <Plymouth Co.PR #18888> <15:422> Letter/Bond 26 Jan. 1760, George BRIANT, gent. of Plimton app'td admr. Sureties: Zebedee CHANDLER, Thomas LORING. Witnesses: Edward WINSLOW, John LOTHROP. <15:473> Inventory taken 27 Mar 1760, by Gideon BRADFORD, David CHURCHILL, Timothy RIPLEY; homestead farm, £200. <19:19> Account of admr. 24 Apr. 1764; Paid to: James LITTLEJOHN, widow **Mary SOULE**, Daniel DIMAN, Samuel SMITH, Elijah BISBE, Zebedee CHANDLER, Silvanus BRAMHALL, Nathaniel GOODWIN, James WRIGHT, Ephraim SOULE, Jonathan PARKER, Nathaniel TORREY, Edward SEARS, Moses INGLE, James WARREN, Amasa TOMSON, Nathaniel CHURCHILL, William RAND, Policarpus LORING, Thomas CROADE, Edward WINSLOW.

Guardianship of Children of **Zachariah SOULE** of Plympton MA. <Plymouth Co.PR #18795> <20:53> Letters/Bonds 18 May 1768, Timothy RIPLEY of Plimpton app'td gdn. of **Jabez SOUL** (above 14) and **Abigail SOUL & Sarah SOUL** (under 14). Sureties: George BRYANT, Nathaniel BONNEY, both of Plimton. Witnesses: Sarah WINSLOW, Edward WINSLOW Jr.

Jabez SOULE, Abigail LORING, Sarah SOULE, division. <Plymouth Co.Deeds 64:254>
...20 Mar. 1777, Jabez SOULE & Abigail LORING wf of Ignatius Jr., of Plympton and Sarah SOULE of Halifax...owners of real estate that our Honoured Father Zachariah SOULE late of sd Plimpton dec'd died seized of and also of an acre and a half of land that fell to us by our Honoured Grandmother Mary SOULE dec'd...to Jabez SOULE, eldest son...one half of sd lands, bounded by meddow now owned by Silvanus BARTLETT...also one half of the house...to Abigail LORING & Sarah SOULE ...one quarter of above. Witnesses: Ephraim SOULE, Jonathan CHURCHELL Jr. Ack. 9 Apr. 1777 by all Rec. 31 Jan. 1786.

==

Will of **Jabez SOULE,** yeoman of Halifax MA. <Plymouth Co.PR #18793>
<63:317>...dated 11 Oct. 1824...being weak in body...to son **Zachariah SOULE,** $1.00 which with the expense of his education & other charges is his full share...to son **George SOULE** & daus **Nabby SOULE & Marcia SOULE,** all household furniture...to daus **Nabby & Marcia**...$150.00 each...and use of portion of house...to daus **Sally STURTEVANT, Lucy CHURCH & Betsey SOULE,** $20.00 each...to grandson **George Thomas SOULE,** $50.00 at age 21...and if he continues...to live in my family until he is sixteen years of age...he shall be furnished with decent cloathing suitable to go to a trade...to son **Jabez SOULE Jr.,** farming & mechanic tools...remainder of estate to sons **George & Jabez Jr.,** executors. Witnesses: Obadiah LYON, Abel RICHMOND, Jane P. WATERMAN. <original> Bond 19 Feb. 1827, of exrs. Sureties: Obadiah LYON, Esq. & Abel RICHMOND, clerk, both of Halifax. Witness: J.H. LOUD. <62:173> Notice, 13 Aug. 1827. <64:246> Division of real estate, 19 Aug. 1827, to **George SOULE & Jabez SOULE,** in common.

==

Will of **George SOULE** of Halifax MA. <Plymouth Co.PR #18784>
<78:82>...dated 4 Nov. 1835, mentions wf **Mary,** dau **Betsey Morton SOULE** (under 21), brother **Jabez SOULE** and "sisters"; Jabez P. THOMPSON, executor & guardian of **Betsey.** Witnesses: Elbridge G. MORTON, Louisa R. MORTON, Joanna MORTON Jr. <original> 15 Feb. 1836, widow **Mary SOULE** certifies that Jabez P. THOMPSON has given her notice that he should present the will. <original> Bond 1 Mar. 1836 of Jabez P. THOMPSON, exr. Sureties: Peleg JENKINS, Samuel A. TURNER, both of Scituate Witness: J.H. LOUD. <78:110> Waiver, 4 Apr. 1836 the widow waives the provision made for her in her husband's will and claims her dower. <78:204> Inventory taken 8 Mar. 1836 by Stafford STURTEVANT, Cyrus RICHMOND, Dexter C. THOMSON; total real estate, $1560.00, personal estate, $315.46. <78:205> Dower assigned, 15 Apr. 1836, to widow **Mary SOULE** by John SAVERY, Esq. of Carver and Dexter C. THOMPSON, Esq. & Stafford STURTEVANT, yeoman of Halifax. <73:325> Notice of appointment of admr. posted in Halfiax & published in Old Colony Memorial. <80:37> Account 17 Feb. 1838, of admr.; Paid to: widow **Mary SOULE,** John SAVERY, Zadock THOMPSON, George WATERMAN, Dexter C. THOMPSON, Elbridge G. MORTON, Thomas HOLMES, Cyrus MORTON, Caleb POOL, Ebenezer WOOD, Cyrus FULLER, Abisha WOOD, Nathaniel SYLVESTER, Nathaniel MORTON, John ATWOOD, Abigail SOULE, A. DANFORTH, J.S. WATERMAN, Simeon CHANDLER Jr.

===

Guardianship of Child of **George SOULE** of Halifax MA. <Plymouth Co.PR #18763>
<78:391> Inventory taken 30 Sept. 1836, by Cyrus RICHMOND & Dexter C. THOMPSON of Halifax; homestead farm & outlands and right in widow's thirds. <8:25L> Decree/Bond/Letter 4 Oct. 1836, Jabez P. THOMPSON of Halifax app'td gdn. of **Betsy Morton SOULE,** under 14. Sureties: Samuel THOMPSON of Middleboro & Jonathan PARKER of Plympton. <2:346O> Petition/Decree, 4 Oct. 1836 to sell real estate of **Betsy Morton SOULE,** sd minor being only four years of age. <1:9B> Bond to secure sale, 1 Nov. 1836, by gdn. <80:168> Notice, 1 Nov. 1836, of sale of real estate in Halifax incl. swamp on Hemlock Island near Melvin CROOKER. <80:36> 1st Account of gdn., 17 Feb. 1838; Paid to: Benjamin ATWOOD, Lysander HOWARD, Josiah THOMPSON, Mary SOULE, Seth MILLER for widow Mary SOULE, C.A. HACK. <2:368O> Petition, 3d Mon. Jan. 1838, to sell real estate in Carver...whereof **Mary SOULE** late of sd Carver dec'd & mother of sd minor died seized. <1:30R> Bond to secure sale, 19 Feb. 1838 by gdn. Sureties: Jonathan PARKER of Plimpton & Charles C. FAUNCE of Kingston. Witness: J.H. LOUD. <8:167> Notice, 19 Feb. 1838, of sale of residence of widow **Mary SOULE** dec'd, near house of Lewis PRATT, Esq. in Carver. <80:478> 2d Account of gdn., 1 Dec. 1838; Received from: Benjamin ATWOOD and wearing apparel of **Mary SOULE** dec'd; Paid to: John STURTEVANT, Abel RICHMOND Jr., Jabez SOULE, Benjamin ATWOOD, J. THURBER.

===

Will of **Mary SOULE,** widow of Carver MA. <Plymouth Co.PR #18838>
<79:332>...dated 10 June 1837, mentions dau **Betsey Morton SOULE;** Betsey RANSLOW, the girl that lives with me; brother **Benjamin ATWOOD** & wf; half brother **Elijah;** "father, brothers, sisters" (not named in files). Witnesses: John SAVERY, Lydia ATWOOD, Mercy BARROWS. <1:52G> Warrant to appraise, 4 July 1837, to John SAVERY, James WRIGHT, Salmon ATWOOD, all of Carver. <79:334> Inventory taken 6 July 1837; incl. notes against Benjamin ELLIS & Co., John SAVERY, William SAVERY. <1:52G> Letter/ Bond 14 Aug. 1837, **Benjamin ATWOOD** app'td admr. Sureties: John ATWOOD of Carver & Lothrop THOMAS of Middleboro. Witness: J.H. LOUD. <75:469> Notice, 16 Sept. 1837. <80:271> Account, 10 Aug. 1838 of admr.; Received from: Jabez P. THOMPSON, William S. SAVERY, Albert SHURTLEFF, John SAVERY, Benjamin ELLIS & Co.; Paid to: Jacob H. LOUD, William BARROWS, Mercy BARROWS, Patience WRIGHT, Ebenezer T. SOULE, Cyrus FULLER (taxes), Egatha WRIGHT, Tilson PRATT, John VAILER, Lavina HARLOW, Stafford STURTEVANT, Charles BARROWS, Job MORTON, Albert SHURTLEFF, Lucy SHURTLEFF, William Hutson SOULE Jr., Isaac BARROWS, William S. SAVERY & Co., Salmon ATWOOD, James SAVERY, James WRIGHT, John ATWOOD, Abijah LUCAS Jr., Lydia ATWOOD, Deborah ATWOOD, Salmon ATWOOD, Arad THOMPSON, John SAVERY, Huet MACFARLING, Betsey RANSLO.

==

Will of **Rebecca SOULE** of Middleboro MA. <Plymouth Co.PR #18861>
<10:435>...dated 20 Mar. 1746, mentions cousins **James FAUNCE & Joseph FAUNCE** and their mother, **Martha FAUNCE;** dec'd father **James SOULE;** cousin **Nathan FAUNCE** (under 21); cousins **Isaac SOULE, Jacob SOULE, William SOULE,** the sons of my brother **Jacob SOULE** deceased; cousins **Lydia SOULE,**

Judah FAUNCE, Lydia FAUNCE. Witnesss: Samuel TINKHAM, Jacob TOMSON, Elizabeth DREW. Pr. 14 July 1747, **James FAUNCE,** labourer of Middleboro, exr. <10:490> Inventory taken 3 Sept. 1747 by Samuel TINKHAM, Jacob TOMSON, Benjamin WESTON; sworn to 16 Sept. 1747 by exr.

Estate of **Jacob SOULE** of Middleborough MA. <Plymouth Co.PR #18799>
<9:352> Letter/Bond 20 Sept. 1744, widow **Mary SOULE** app'td admx. Sureties: Jonathan SMITH, Nehemiah BENNET, both of Middleboro. Witnesses: Benjamin WESTON, Edward WINSLOW. <9:405> Inventory taken 18 Dec. 1744 by Jonathan SMITH, Jonathan BENNET, Jacob TOMSON; mentions land bought of James FORD Jr. & wf Elizabeth of Marshfield. <10:299> Account of admx., 18 Sept. 1746; Received of: Joseph FAUNCE, Samuel HAMPTON, Samuel FULLER, Gershom SAMSON, estate of Father SOULE dec'd. <13:68> Division 18 July 1753, by Jacob TOMSON, Jonathan SMITH, Nehemiah BENNET, Benjamin WESTON, Jonathan TILLSON, yeomen of Plymouth to following children, viz: **Isaac SOULE** (eldest son), **Jacob SOULE, William SOULE & Lydia SOULE.**

Guardianship of Children of **Jacob SOULE** of Middleborough MA. <Plymouth Co.PR #18800>
<10:249> Letters/Bonds 18 Sept.1746, widow **Mary SOULE** app'td gdn. of **William & Jacob SOULE.** <10:294> Letters 18 Sept. 1746, widow **Mary SOULE** app'td gdn of **Lydia & Isaac SOULE.** <11:487> Letters/Bonds 26 Feb. 1750, Samuel SHAW of Plympton, chosen gdn. by **Jacob & Isaac SOULE** and app'td gdn. of **William & Lydia SOULE.** Sureties: Joseph MORTON Jr., cordwainer & David DAVIS, mariner of Plympton. Witnesses: Edward WINSLOW, John LOTHROP. <14:30> Letter/Bond 24 Feb. 1756, James SMITH, yeoman of Middleboro app'td gdn. of **William SOULE.** Surety: Samuel SMITH of Middleboro. Witnesses: Edward WINSLOW, John LOTHROP. <16:74> Receipt 30 Sept. 1760, to James SMITH by **William SOULE,** now of full age.

Estate of **Jacob SOULE,** yeoman of Middleborough MA. <Plymouth Co.PR #18798>
<11:486> Letter/Bond 26 Feb. 1750, Samuel SHAW, yeoman of Plympton app'td admr. Sureties: Joseph MORTON, cordwainer & David DAVIS, mariner, both of Plymouth. Witnesses: Edward WINSLOW, John LOTHROP. <12:203> Inventory taken 28 Feb. 1750, by Jonathan SMITH, Nehemiah BENNETT, Samuel TINKHAM; homestead that was his father's and meadow & swamp given him by his father. <14:85> Account, 2 Aug. 1756; Paid to: Nehemiah BENNETT, James PALMER, Jabez THOMAS, William THOMAS, WARREN & GOODWIN, Isaac BENNETT, Edmond WOOD, Jonathan TILLSON, James WRIGHT, Benjamin WESTON, Zachariah SOUL, Judah FAUNCE, Lydia FAUNCE, James FAUNCE, Joseph FAUNCE Jr., Ebenezer SPROUGHT/SPROAT, William CHURCHILL, David CHURCHILL, Joseph WILLIAMS, Samuel TINKHAM, Jonathan SMITH, Edmond WOOD, Jacob TOMSON, David SIMMONS, Dr. LORING, Patience McFUN, Joseph BATES, Jonathan SHURTLEFF.

William SHAW of Middleborough MA to **Elijah SHAW** of same. <Plymouth Co.Deeds 104:148>
...20 Mar. 1806, William SHAW, gent. & wf Lydia, for love & affection...to our nephew Elijah SHAW yeoman, convey...one and a quarter acre ceder swamp in 26th lot in Little Ceder Swamp in the 26 Men's Purchase in Middleborough referring to a deed dated 26 June 1749...given to me the sd Lydia and my Brothers namely Isaac SOUL, Jacob SOUL & William SOUL by Samuel FULLER in consequence of his the sd Samuel cutting ceder and white pine timber by mistake on swamp belonging to (us). Witnesses: James SOUL, Isaac THOMSON. Ack. same day. Rec. 12 Aug. 1806.

Will of **Jacob SOULE,** yeoman of Middleborough MA. <Plymouth Co.PR #18797>
<57:308>...dated 2 Dec. 1812, mentions dau **Sarah SOULE;** son **Isaac SOULE;** to dau **Mary SOULE,** fresh meadow purchased of Caleb THOMPSON; to dau **Phebe THOMPSON** wf of Isaac of Halifax, fresh meadow in Winatuxet meadow purchased of Capt. William SHAW; to dau **Faith FULLER** wf of Nathan of Halifax, fresh meadow in Winatuxet meadow purchased of Isaac WESTON; son **Elijah SOULE;** son **Joseph SOULE** and his son **Jacob SOULE; Jacob SOULE** son of son **Isaac;** son **Beza SOULE;** son **Isaac,** executor. Witnesses: Thomas SOULE, Ezra SOULE, Isaac THOMSON. <57:311> Letter/Bond 15 Sept. 1823, **Isaac SOULE** app'td admr. Sureties: Samuel THOMPSON, gent. & Ezra SOULE, yeoman, of Middleboro. Witnesses: Beza HAYWARD, William S. RUSSELL. <57:402> Inventory taken 9 Oct. 1823 by Samuel THOMPSON & Thomas SOULE of Middleboro and Noah BOSWORTH, yeoman of Halifax. <55:160> Notice, sworn to by exr. 4 Nov. 1823.

Estate of **William SOULE,** tanner of Middleboro MA. <Plymouth Co.PR #18885>
<23:189> Letter/Bond 6 July 1778, widow **Sarah SOULE** app'td admx. Sureties: Jacob SOULE & William SHAW of Middleboro. Witnesses: Ignatius LORING, Stephen DOTEY Jr. <25:127> Inventory taken 21 July 1778, by Samuel SMITH, Isaac SOULE, Jacob SOULE. <38:77> Division 7 Apr. 1783, by Jacob BENNET, Isaac TOMSON, Joshua EDDY; thirds to widow **Sarah SOULE;** real estate which fell to sd dec'd by the division of estate of his honoured father **Jacob SOULE** dec'd, to: daus **Hulda, Remember, Asenath** & son **James SOULE;** four acre cedar swamp which fell to sd dec'd by will of his Aunt **Rebecca SOULE** dec'd, to: dau **Lydia** and sons **Ansel SOULE & William SOULE;** division allowed 11 Apr. 1802 <28:547> Account of admx., 3 Mar. 1783; Received from: William BENNETT, John SHAW, Freeman WATERMAN, Daniel FANCE/FAUNCE, Perez THOMAS, Capt. John BRIDGHAM, Thomas WATERMAN, Samuel LUCAS, Timothy RIPLEY, Joseph WRIGHT; Paid to: Stephen ELLIS, Capt. William STURTEVANT, John COBB, Isaac NYE, Elisha COX, Dr. Thomas STURTEVANT, Beza SOULE, John RAYMOND, Ebenezer ELLIS, Gideon BRADFORD, Nathan TINKHAM, Capt. Nathaniel WILDER, Jabez NEWLAND, Brig. Nathaniel GOODWIN, Dr. Jonathan FULLER, Ebenezer WRIGHT, Daniel HOWLAND, Noah CUSHMAN, Nathaniel FOSTER, John CHAMBERLIN, William WATSON, William SHAW, Nathan PERKINS, Elizabeth COBB, Nathan DARLING, Samuel EDDY, Dr. Josiah RIPLEY, James McFARLING.

Guardianship of Children of **William SOULE** of Middleboro MA. <Plymouth Co.PR #18886>
<126:172> Letters/Bonds 3 Mar. 1783, widow **Sarah SOULE** app'td gdn. of **Remember SOULE,** about 10 & **Huldah SOULE,** about 8. Sureties: William SHAW & Silas TINKHAM, of Middleboro. Witnesses: William MORISON, Ephraim SPOONER. <26:173> Letters 3 Mar.1783, Silas TINKHAM of Middleboro app'td gdn. of

Anson SOULE, about 13. <original> Bonds 3 Mar. 1783 of Silas TINKHAM as gdn. of **Anson SOULE & William Shaw SOULE**. Sureties: William SHAW & James SOULE 3d of Middleboro. Witnesses: Ephraim SPOONER, Cornelius SMITH, Adam TOMSON. <26:401> 3 Mar. 1783, **William SOULE**, about 15, chose Silas TINKHAM as gdn.

PLYMOUTH COUNTY DEEDS: (re: James FAUNCE)

<42:154> - 29 Oct. 1747, James FAUNCE & Joseph FAUNCE Jr., of Middleboro divide land received by will of Aunt Rebecca SOULE of Middleboro.

<40:233> - 7 Dec. 1748, James FAUNCE, husbandman of Middleboro to Joel ELLIS, husbandman of Plympton, land received by will of Aunt Rebecca SOULE of Middleboro. Wf Abigail FAUNCE signs.

<52:89> - 14 July 1755, James FAUNCE, yeoman of Middleboro, sells land in Middleboro & Plympton. Wf Abigail FAUNCE releases dower.

<45:96> - 13 June 1757, James FAUNCE, yeoman of Middleboro to John LOVELL, house & land in Wareham. Ack. 14 June 1757 at Rochester.

Will of **John SOULE Sr.**, yeoman of Middleboro MA. <Plymouth Co.PR #18813
<9:84>...dated 1 Mar. 1743, mentions wf **Martha** & following children, viz: **John SOULE** (executor), **James SOULE, Martha TOMSON, Sarah SNOW, Esther SOULE, Mary SAMSON, Rebecca SOULE, Rachel SOULE.** Witnesses: Samuel TINKHAM, Daniel VAUGHN, Isaac TINKHAM Jr. <9:85> Pr. 6 June 1743. <9:138> Inventory taken 19 Sept. 1743, by Jacob TOMSON, Capt. Jabez VAUGHN, Samuel TINKHAM, all of Middleboro; sworn to 22 Sept. 1743 by **John SOULE**, exr.

Will of **Martha SOUL/SOULE Sr.** of Middleboro MA. <Plymouth Co.PR #18836>
<15:29>...dated 19 Nov. 1751, mentions heirs of son **John SOULE**, son **James SOULE**, heirs of dec'd dau **Sarah SNOW** and daus **Easter/Esther SOULE, Rebecca SOULE, Martha TOMSON, Mary SAMSON, Rachel VAUGHAN**; daus **Easter & Rebecca**, executrices. Witnesses: Samuel TINKHAM, David SIMONS, Nelson FINNEY. <15: 30> Pr. 2 May 1758, Isaac TINKHAM of Middleboro app'td admr., the daughters having declined. <original> Bond 1 May 1758 of Isaac TINKHAM, admr. Sureties: Samuel TINKHAM, David SIMONS. Witnesses: Edward WINSLOW, William CUSHING. <15:224> Inventory taken 19 May 1758 by Daniel VAUGHAN, William CUSHMAN, James COBB. <15:224> Account of admr., 6 Aug.1759; Paid to: Dr. Isaac OTIS, Ester/Esther & Rebecca SOULE, Dr. Josiah STURTEVANT, Thomas TOMSON, Obadiah SAMSON, Ebenezer VAUGHAN.

Will of **Rebecca SOULE** of Middleboro MA. <Plymouth Co.PR #18862; MD 19:139>
<15:280>...dated 23 Sept. 1758, mentions sister **Esther SOUL**; brother **James SOUL**; sisters **Martha TOMSON, Mary SAMSON, Rachel VAUGHAN**; chil. of dec'd sister **Sarah SNOW**; cossen/cousin **John SOULE** (under 21). Witnesses: John HOLMES, Johanna HOLMES, Joseph TINKCOM. Pr. 26 Apr. 1759.

Will of **Esther SOUL**, spinster of Middleboro MA. <Plymouth Co.PR #18777>
<33:374>...dated 16 Oct. 1792, mentions neice **Esther BRYANT** wf of Isaac; nephew **Nathan TOMSON** & other heirs at law; nephew **John SOULE** of Middleboro. Witnesses: Thomas BENNET, Priscilla BARROWS, Isaac THOMSON. <original> Bond 11 June 1793, of **John SOULE**, exr. Sureties: Nathaniel THOMSON, Thomas BENNET. Witnesses: Nathaniel LOTHROP, Priscilla BURR. <33:432> Inventory taken 29 June 1793 by Nathaniel THOMSON, William THOMSON, Thomas BENNETT; sworn to 7 Oct. 1793 by exr.

Estate of **John SOUL**, yeoman of Middleboro MA. <Plymouth Co.PR #18814>
<11:522> Letter/Bond 12 Mar. 1750, Abiel LEACH of Middleboro, app'td admr. Sureties: Robert WATERMAN of Halifax and Thomas WHITMAN of Bridgewater. Witnesses: Ebenezer FULLER Jr., Edward WINSLOW. <12:191> Inventory taken 16 May 1751 by Ephraim WOOD, William CUSHMAN, Daniel VAUGHN. <12:470> Account of admr., 5 Apr. 1752; Paid to: Elizabeth SOULE, Martha SOUL, Samuel SNOW, Thomas TOMSON, Isaac TINKHAM, Daniel VAUGHN, Thomas CROADE, William CUSHMAN, Ephraim HOLMES, Ephraim WOOD, Nathan WARREN, Dr. LORING.

Guardianship of Child of **John SOUL** of Middleboro MA. <Plymouth Co.PR #18815>
<12:279> Letter/Bond 10 July 1751, widow **Mary SOUL** app'td gdn. of **John SOUL.** Surety: Abiel LEACH. Witnesses: Caleb BENSON, Edward WINSLOW. <15:15> Account, 23 June 1758, of **Mary WOOD** wf of Ephraim, gdn. and mother of sd minor; incl. "seven years diet, etc. for the sd minor from his birth which was on 9 May 1751 (O.S.) to 20 May 1758.

Estate of **Obadiah SAMSON**, yeoman of Middleborough MA. <Plymouth Co.PR #17612>
<17:157> Letter/Bond 3 Mar. 1766, John SAMSON app'td admr. Sureties: John SHAW of Plimton and Joseph LUCAS of Plymouth. Witnesses: Edward WINSLOW, Penelope WINSLOW. <19:343> Inventory taken 4 Apr. 1766; incl. homestead, meadow at Rocky Meadow and cedar & spruce swamp at Mehen()ehet. <20:537> Account 22 May 1771; Paid to: Benjamin HARLOW, Jonathan TILSON, Nathaniel COB Jr., Nathaniel COB, Consider CHASE, Consider COB, David SHAW, Esther SOUL, Jonah WASHBURNE, Ebenezer PRATT.

Guardianship of Child of **Obadiah SAMSON,** yeoman of Middleboro MA. <Plymouth Co.PR #17509>
<19:405> Letter/Bond 18 Apr. 1766, Issachar FULLER app'td gdn. of **Esther SAMSON,** above 14.Surety: Samuel JACKSON, shoreman of Plymouth. Witnesses: Edward WINSLOW, Edward WINSLOW Jr.

Estate of **James SOULE,** laborer of Middleboro MA. <Plymouth Co.PR #18806>
<61:204> Letter/Bond 16 June 1828, Solomon ALDEN Jr., gent. of Bridgewater app'td admr. Sureties: John SOULE, yeoman of Bridgewater and Jacob MILLER, gent. of Middleborough. Witness: J.H. LOUD. <66:407> Inventory taken 24 June 1828, by Rufus WOOD, Cornelius HOLMES Jr., Lewis T. ALDEN, all

Bridgewater; on 4 Nov. 1828, the admr. was ordered to sell personal estate. <62:298> Notice, 4 Nov. 1828. <67:571> 1st Account 6 Oct. 1829, of admr.; Received from: Andrew TUCKER; Paid to: Holmes SPRAGUE, Philander WASHBURN & Co., Zenas CUSHMAN, Joseph BUMP, George THOMPSON, Edward THOMAS, Isaac STEVENS, John SOULE, Calvin MURDOCK, Rufus WOOD, Cornelius HOLMES, Lewis T. ALDEN, Austin PACKARD, Artemas HALE, Jacob MILLER as one of the heirs, Elias MILLER for himself & Sewall LONGFELLOW, John SOULE, James SOULE, Nathan P. SOULE, Mary SOULE. <72:461> 2d Account, 6 Nov. 1832; Received from: James SOULE on account of Sampson WASHBURN; Paid to: Samuel CLARK, Joseph WHITTEN, Isaac JACKSON, William REED, Cyrus SOULE, James SOULE, Mary RIPLEY, Jacob MILLER, Nathan P. SOULE. <79:254> 3d Account of admr., 4 July 1837; Paid to: Samuel CLARK, Isaac JACKSON attorney for William REED/READ, Cyrus SOULE, Isaac STEVENS, Welcome YOUNG attorney for Lewis KEITH, Joseph CHAMBERLIN, Joseph JACKSON; Heirs at law: **Rebecca WASHBURN** wf of Sampson, **Cyrus SOULE, John SOULE, Nathan SOULE, James SOULE, Mary SOULE, Sarah MILLER, Deborah WHITTEN** wf of Joseph, **Sarah CLARK** wf of Samuel, **Elias MILLER, Jacob MILLER, Saba MILLER, Betsey MILLER.** <original> Petition 2d Tues. Oct. 1829 of **Nathan SOULE** of E. Bridgewater, one of heirs. <original> Petition 19 Oct. 1829, of **Sampson WASHBURN** of E. Bridgewater, that his wife **Rebecca** is one of heirs.

MICRO #6 OF 11

Will of **Joseph SOULE**, yeoman of Duxbury MA. <Plymouth Co.PR #18819>
<16:483>...dated 16 Jan. 1755...by reason of old age...mentions grandchildren, the heirs of dec'd dau **Mary CUSHMAN** wf of Joshua; grandson **Joseph CUSHMAN** son of Joshua; dec'd dau **Alethea CUSHMAN**, wf of Allerton & chil.; daus **Hannah SOULE & Rebecca SOULE**; friend John WADSWORTH. Witnesses: Uriah WADSWORTH, Mary WADSWORTH, John WADSWORTH. Pr. 1 Aug. 1763, John WADSWORTH, **Hannah SOULE & Rebecca SOULE**, app'td admrs. <16:534> Inventory taken 12 Sept. 1763 by Gamaliel BRADFORD, Abner WESTON, Wait WADSWORTH; incl. cedar swamp in Pembroke great swamp in partnership with brothers **Josiah & Joshua SOULE.** <19:353> Account 22 May 1766, of admrs.; Paid to: Nathaniel Ray THOMAS, Capt. Wait WADSWORTH, Dr. Lazarus LeBARON, Dr. John SEVER, Joseph SOUL, George USSEL, Jacob PETERSON, Benjamin PETERSON, Jonathan PETERSON, John THOMAS, Elnathan WESTON, Ezekiel SOUL, Abisha SOUL, Isaac PARTRIDGE, Daniel FISHER, Jedediah BOURN, Jonathan SOUL, Warren WESTON, Benjamin PRIOR Jr., Joshua SOUL, Elisha FORD, Cyrus SIMMONS, Joshua SIMMONS, William COOMER, Thomas WESTON, Aaron SOUL, Gamaliel BRADFORD Jr., Jacob DINGLEY, Solomon LEVITT, Ezekiel CHANDLER, Samuel WINDSOR, Abner SAMSON, Deacon PHILLIPS, John WADSWORTH, Uriah WADSWORTH, Coll. BRADFORD, Abner WESTON, Wait WADSWORTH. <19:354> Release, 23 May 1766, of all demands of John WADSWORTH, executor, from **Hannah & Rebecca SOUL.** <19:354> Receipt 10 Apr. 1765, of **Allerton CUSHMAN**, for legacy given to the children of my mother **Alethea CUSHMAN** dec'd.

Will of **Joshua SOULE**, yeoman of Duxbury MA. <Plymouth Co.PR #18822>
<20:73>...dated 8 May 1767, mentions son **Ezekiel SOULE**; to son **Joseph SOULE**, land & islands at N. Yarmouth; son **Nathan SOULE**; grandson **Samuel SOULE**; dau **Zurviah SAMSON** wf of Ebenezer; dau **Abigail DREW** wf of Perez; dau **Sarah BISBEE** wf of Aaron; granddaughter **Lidia SIMMONS** wf of Jedediah. Witnesses: Joseph CUSHMAN, Elizabeth CUSHMAN, Judah DELANO. <20:74> Bond 24 Oct. 1767, of **Samuel SOULE**, exr. Sureties: Joseph SOUL & Ezra WESTON of Duxbury. Witnesses: Samuel BALDWIN, A. BURBANK Letter/Bond 19 May 1768, **Joseph SOULE**, yeoman of Duxbury app'td admr. with will annexed, **Samuel SOULE** having dec'd. Sureties: Eliphas PRIOR, Benjamin PRIOR. Witnesses: Sarah WINSLOW, Edward WINSLOW Jr. <20:146> Report, 23 Oct. 1767, of following commissioners: Gamaliel BRADFORD, Ebenezer FISH, Peleg WADSWORTH, Nathaniel SIMMONS, Judah DELANO, Thomas WESTON. <20:211> Inventory taken 24 June 1769, by Ebenezer FISH, Isaac PARTRIDGE, Judah DELANO. <20:211> Account of admr., 1 May 1769; Paid to: Nathan SOUL, Silvanus DREW, Ebenezer SAMSON, Jedediah SIMMONS, James HOVEY, Aaron BISBEE, Judah DELANO, Ebenezer SOUL, William COOMER. <21:7> Account of admr., 5 Aug. 1771; Paid to: Nathan SOUL, Silvanus DREW, Zerviah SAMSON, Jedediah SIMMONS, James HOVEY, Aaron BISBEE, Judah DELANO, Ebenezer SOUL, William COOMER, Joshua LORING, Joseph CUSHMAN. <36:313> Division 7 Oct. 1777, by Briggs ALDEN, Micha SOUL, Peleg WADSWORTH, all of Duxbury, of the lands owned by **Nathan SOUL** and the heirs of **Samuel SOUL,** late of Duxbury, dec'd; half to **Nathan,** half to the heirs of **Samuel.**

Ezekiel SOULE of Woolwich MA to **Ezra WESTON** of Duxbury MA. <Plymouth Co.Deeds 59:49>
...12 Mar. 1776, Ezekiel SOULE, gent. & wf Hannah, for £16 sell to Ezra WESTON, shipwright...two acres of salt meadow in Duxbury...being one fifth part of 19th lot in Duxborough's great salt marshes...together with land in Major's Purchase Ceder Swamp...that my honoured Father Joshua SOULE gave me in his last will...Ack. 30 Mar. 1776 by Ezra, 17 May by Hannah. Rec. 5 July 1777.

References to the name **Ezekiel SOULE** in Plymouth Co.Deeds: 36:103;40:201;48:107;78:136;91:40; 48: 32,221,241;49:234;52:36,255;54:44;59:49;92:8. (Accompanying note: "When did he go to Maine?")

Estate of **John SOULE** of Duxbury MA. <Plymouth Co.PR #18811>
<7:141> Letter/Bond 24 Feb. 1734, widow **Mabell SOULE** & Joshua SOULE, yeoman, app'td admrs. Surety: Thomas WATERMAN, husbandman of Marshfield. Witnesses: Sarah WINSLOW, Mary WINSLOW. <7:135> Inventory taken 27 Feb. 1734/5 by Coll. John ALDEN, Dr. Benjamin DELLANO, Samuel WESTON, all of Duxbury; sworn to, 15 Jan. 1735, by admrs. **Mabell SOUL** & Joshua SOULE. <7:203> Account 9 Sept. 1735; Debts due to: Capt. SEABURY, Barnabas SEABURY, Zche. CHANDLER, Benjmain PRINCE, Benjamin PETERSON, Cornelius SOULE, "to myself before ye news of death ye widow", Benjamin RANKIN, John THOMAS, Abraham BLUSH, "ye widow lying in Bill", John OSBORN, Joshua BREWSTER, Col. ALDEN, Dr. DELANO, Samuel WESTON, Thomas TYLER, Isaac PARTRIDGE, Isaac PETERSON, Rebekah WESTON, Joshua DELANO, Robert DAVIE, William BREWSTER, Thomas TYLER, Ebenezer DREW, Ebenezer SAMSON; Received from: Deacon SOUTHWORTH, Capt. W( )AI, R. CLARK, James RUSSELL, Abner BROWN, Jabez CLARK, Joseph

CHANDLER, Jacob BROWN, Sergt. ROUSE, Capt. RING, Samuel TOLMAN, Perez DREW. <7:275> Settlement, 15 Mar. 1736, of personal estate to: widow **Mabell KEMPTON** now the wf of Samuel Jr. of Plymouth, son **Samuel SOULE** and dau **Lydia SOULE.**

Guardianship of Children of **John SOULE** of Duxbury MA. <Plymouth Co.PR #18868>
<7:275,276> Letters/Bonds 23 Feb. 1736, Joshua SOULE of Duxbury app'td gdn. of **Samuel & Lydia SOULE** (under 14). Surety: Edward WINSLOW of Marshfield. Witnesses: John FRESIR, Hopestill OLIVER.

Estate of **Samuel SOUL**, mariner of Duxbury MA. <Plymouth Co.PR #18867>
<20:44> Letter/Bond 4 Apr. 1768, widow **Mehitable SOUL** app'td admx. Sureties: Briggs ALDEN & George PARTRIDGE, both of Duxbury. Witnesses: Edward HAWARD Jr., Edward WINSLOW Jr. <20:137> Inventory taken 15 June 1768 by Ebenezer FISH, Isaac PARTRIDGE, Judah DELANO. <21:84> Account of admx, 2 Mar. 1772; Paid to: Dr. HARLOW, Joseph SOUL, Perez DREW, Jedediah SIMMONS, Oliver KEMPTON, Levi LORING, Alexander ROBINSON, James SOUL, John THOMAS, John CUSHMAN, Benjamin PRIOR, William COOMER William THOMAS, Caleb OLDHAM, James GLASS, Eloch FREEMAN. <40:376> Dower assigned, 7 Oct. 1777, to widow **Mehitable WESTON** now wf of Ichabod of Duxbury. <40:377> Division, 30 Dec. 1777, by Briggs ALDEN, Micha SOUL, Peleg WADSWORTH to following children, viz: **Abigail PETERSON** wf of Reuben, **Silva/Silvia SOUL, Ellis/Alice SOUL, Lydia SOUL.** <57:490> Division of Dower, 30 June 1823 by Isaiah ALDEN, yeoman, Judah ALDEN & Peleg WESTON, all of Duxbury, to following children, viz: **Abigail PETERSON, Silvia PETERSON, Alice HATCH** and heirs of **Lydia BARTOW.**

Guardianship of Children of **Samuel SOUL** of Duxbury MA. <Plymouth Co.PR #18752>
<20:138> Letters/Bonds 1 Aug. 1768, widow **Mehitable SOUL** app'td gdn. of **Abigail, Alice, Lidia & Sylvia SOUL,** all under 14. Sureties: Isaac PARTRIDGE & Jedediah SIMMONS of Duxbury. Witnesses: Samuel BALDWIN, Edward WINSLOW Jr.

Will of **Ezekiel SOULE,** yeoman of Duxbury MA. <Plymouth Co.PR #18778>
<86:58>...dated 19 June 1837, mentions son **Charles SOULE**; dau **Clenthea/Clynthia SOULE**; chil. of dec'd sons **George SOULE & Otis SOULE,** viz: **George M. SOULE, Laura A. SOULE, James SOULE, Nicholas B. SOULE, Mary T. SOULE**; son **Marshall SOULE.** Witnesses: Seth SPRAGUE Jr., Daniel H. WATSON, Melzar BREWSTER. <original> Notice ordered published in the Old Colony Memorial 3rd Mon. Jan. 1844. <1:443G> Letter/Bond, 19 Feb. 1844, by **Marchal/Marshall SOULE,** exr. Sureties: Charles SOULE & Seth SPRAGUE Jr. of Duxbury. Witnesses: James CURTIS, Clenthea SOULE. <1:463G> Letter/Bond, 12 Apr. 1847, by **Marshall SOULE & Charles SOULE,** exrs. Surety: Seth SPRAGUE Jr. Witnesses: James CURTIS, Julian CURTIS.

Estate of **Capt. Otis SOULE,** mariner of Duxbury MA. <Plymouth Co.PR #18854>
<original> Consent, 31 Dec. 1821, of widow **Salumith W. SOULE,** that adm. be granted to her father, **Sylvanus SAMPSON** of Duxbury. <52:94> Letter/Bond 1 Jan. 1822, Sylvanus SAMPSON, merchant, app'td admr. Sureties: Zachariah EDDY of Middleboro, Nathan HAYWARD of Plymouth. Witnesses: Jacob HERSEY & Benjamin PARKER. <54:405> Inventory taken 26 Jan. 1822, by Ezra W. SAMPSON, Esq., Erastus BARTLETT, physician & Joshua HALL, mariner, all of Duxbury. <54:407> Order, 8 Apr. 1822, to sell real estate. <56:109> Additional Inventory taken Sept. 1822. <56:198> Account of admr., 19 Aug. 1822; incl. note against Ezekiel SOUL; paid John AV(ES) & Co. of Boston; paid funeral expenses of little daughter **Salumith SOULE.** <original> 19 Oct. 1822, widow **Salumith W. SOULE** requests that her father **Sylvanus SAMPSON** be app'td gdn. of her surviving child, **Mary T. SOUL.**

Guardianship of Child of **Capt. Otis SOULE** of Duxbury MA. <Plymouth Co.PR #18839>
<51:181> Letter/Bond 21 Oct. 1822, **Sylvanus SAMPSON,** merchant of Duxbury, app'td gdn. of **Mary Townsend SOULE,** under 14. Sureties: Perez H. SAMPSON, mariner of Duxbury & George W. VIRGIN, merchant of Plymouth. Witnesses: Oliver WHITTEN, Jacob BEARCE. <56:469> Inventory taken 3 Mar. 1823, by Ezra W. SAMPSON, Esq., Erastus BARTLETT, physician & Andrew SAMPSON Jr., yeoman, all of Duxbury; incl. notes of Sylvanus SAMPSON, Ezekiel SOULE. <83:487> Account to 22 Feb. 1840 of gdn.; **Mary T. SOULE** assents to account, 26 Nov. 1841.

Estate of **James SOUL,** mariner of Duxbury MA. <Plymouth Co.PR #18807>
<34:20> Letter/Bond 20/30 Oct. 1794, Joseph SOULE & Ezekiel SOULE, both of Duxbury, app'td admrs. Sureties: Samuel LORING & Samuel CHANDLER, both of Duxbury. <35:216> Warrant to take inventory, 22 Oct. 1794, to Samuel LORING, Samuel CHANDLER & Dura WADSWORTH, all of Duxbury who made oath 11 Feb. 1795. <37:203> Account of admrs., 17 Mar. 1800; Paid to: William MENIELL, Joseph RIPLEY, Thomas STETSON, John CUSHING, Job SAMSON, Winslow THOMAS, Joseph HUET, Benjamin CRANDON, Samuel CHANDLER, Samuel LORING, Joshua CUSHMAN, Wait WADSWORTH, Judah ALDEN, Eden WADSWORTH, John CLARK, Ezekiel CHANDLER, Zadock BRADFORD, John SAMSON, Joseph BARSTER, Silvanus SAMSON, Benjamin BOSWORTH, Isaac WINSLOW, Lot STETSON, Ebenezer ADAMS, Isaac DREW, Edward READ, Joshua THOMAS, Dr. Zachariah BARTLETT, Isaac DELANO, Arthur HOWLAND, Ezra WESTON, Samuel DREW, Joshua WINSOR, Isaiah ALDEN, Elijah SAMSON Jr., Andrew NEWELL, John CODMAN, Ira WADSWORTH, Nathaniel SAMSON, Joshua BREWSTER, Stephen RUSSEL, Jotham LORING, Nathaniel HODGES. <42:245> 2d Account of Ezekiel SOULE, admr., 9 Jan.1808; Paid to: Stephen RUSSEL; widow **Abigail SOUL,** settlement in full and chil.: **Joshua SOUL, Joseph SOUL, Abigail, James SOUL & Richard SOUL.**

Estate of **Joshua SOULE,** mariner of Duxbury MA. <Plymouth Co.PR #18823>
<original> Declination, 8 Dec. 1803, of widow **Rebecca SOULE** to serve as admx. and requests the appointment of Samuel LORING as admr. <34:377> Letter/Bond 10 Dec. 1803, Samuel LORING, gent., app'td admr. Sureties: Abijah FREEMAN, housewright & Peleg GULLIFER Jr., caulker, both of Duxbury Witnesses: Lucy LOTHROP, Isaac LOTHROP. <38:507> Warrant for inventory, 10 Dec. 1803, to Levi LORING, gent., Studley SAMPSON & Isaac DELANO, yeoman, all of Duxbury; total real estate, $316.00

total personal estate, $758.93; sworn to by admr., 22 May 1806. <40:446> Account 2 May 1806, of admr.; Received from: Capt. Daniel HALL, Deacon David TILDEN of Boston for wages due on a voyage with Capt. Jedidiah SOUTHWORTH, Samuel CHANDLER, Capt. E. WADSWORTH; Paid to: Isaac DELANO, Asa CHANDLER, Levi LORING Jr., Martin WINSOR, James SOULE, Stephen DREW, Samuel CHANDLER, Thomas CHANDLER, widow Rebecca SOULE and to the widow **Abigail SOULE, Joseph, James & Richard SOULE,** in books & other articles.

Estate of **Priscilla SOULE** of Duxbury MA. <Plymouth Co.PR #18858>
<11:380B> Petition, 29 Nov. 1845, of **Samuel SOULE** by **Lucy SOULE** (Samuel SOULE being of Sumner, Oxford Co. ME)...petitioner is a son of sd dec'd, and the eldest son of sd dec'd having neglected to take administration, your petitioner prays that Seth SPRAGUE Jr. may be appointed; petition granted. Bond, 1 Dec. 1845, of Seth SPRAGUE Jr., as admr. Sureties: George P. RICHARDSON & Thomas PETERSON of Duxbury. <88:147> Inventory taken 10 Dec. 1845 by George P. RICHARDSON, Charles SOULE & Sylvanus SAMPSON Jr.; incl. one fifth of one half of homestead, piece of wood land and one piece of salt meadow formerly belonging to Elijah SOULE dec'd; personal estate incl. note of hand signed by P.& S. SPRAGUE & Co. payable to Priscilla & William SOULE (the balance due being $1118.00, one half belonging to Priscilla) and note of hand by Samuel SOULE payable to William SOULE (the balance due being $241.60, one half belonging to Priscilla). <89:149> Account 12 Apr. 1847, of admr.; Received from: P.& S. SPRAGUE & Co., Samuel SOULE, William SOULE; Paid to: Thomas SOULE and to the heirs, as follows: **William SOULE, Thomas SOULE, William SOULE** the share of **Stephen SOULE** by assignment of deed, **Samuel SOULE** by hand of **Lucy SOULE** his attorney. On 20 July 1846, **William SOULE, Stephen SOULE, Thomas SOULE** and **Lucy SOULE** attorney to **Samuel SOULE,** having received the amounts stated in the account, $163.50 each, declared themselves satisfied.

Estate of **Capt. Elijah SOULE,** mariner of Duxbury MA. <Plymouth Co.PR #18774>
<original> Declination, 23 Apr. 1835, of mother **Priscilla SOULE** and brothers **William SOULE, Stephen SOULE & Samuel SOULE,** to adm. estate & request that Seth SPRAGUE Jr. be app'td. <71:311> Letter/Bond 18 May 1835, Seth SPRAGUE Jr., Esq. of Duxbury app'td admr. Sureties: Ralph PARTRIDGE & Avery RICHARDS, both of Duxbury. Witness: J.H. LOUD. <77:406> Inventory taken 30 May 1835 by George P. RICHARDSON, Charles SOULE & Sylvanus SAMPSON Jr., all of Duxbury. <75:238> Notice. <79:123> Account of admr., 7 Apr. 1837; Received from: John BROWN & Co., J. FOSTER; Paid to: Samuel SOULE, Priscilla SOULE, William SOULE, Stephen SOULE, Thomas SOULE - each "800" and to Gershom BRADFORD, P. BOSWORTH, SAMPSON & ALDEN. Receipt, 11 Mar. 1837, of heirs, viz: **Priscilla SOULE, William SOULE, Samuel SOULE, Thomas SOULE, Stephen SOULE.**

Will of **Simeon SOUL** of Duxbury MA. <Plymouth Co.PR #18872>
<72:122>...dated 20 Mar. 1829, mentions present wf **Asenath;** all real estate divided between sons **Nathan SOUL** (executor), **Thomas SOUL, Simeon SOUL, Henry SOULE, Charles SOUL;** granddaughter **Jane OAKMAN.** <72:215,217;68:347>...Pr. 9 Apr. 1832. Inventory, 9 Apr. 1832. <76:182> Division of real estate & pew in Cong. Church. <113:339;105:526>...

Estate of **Josiah SOULE** of Duxbury MA. <Plymouth Co.PR #18826>
<39:89;42:25,295>...1806, widow **Alice.**

Estate of **Thomas SOULE** of Duxbury MA. <Plymouth Co.PR #18878>
<71:286> Pr. 1835, Simeon SOULE, admr. <75:199> Notice. <77:142> Inventory. <78:35> Account.

Will of **Abisha SOUL,** yeoman of Duxbury MA. <Plymouth Co.PR #18753>
<25:123>...dated 1 Oct. 1777, mentions wf **Abigail** (executrix) and the following children, viz: **John SOUL, Abigail SOUL, Nathaniel SOUL, Abisha SOUL, Ellathear HALL** wf of Joshua, **Dusbury WADSWORTH** wf of Sinaca and **Mary SOUL.** Witnesses: Judah DELANO, Thaddeus PETERSON, Judah DELANO Jr. Pr. 7 Dec. 1778.

Jonathan SOUL of Duxboro MA to **Consider SIMMONS** of same. <Plymouth Co.Deeds 54:111>
...2 July 1768, Jonathan SOUL, yeoman, conveys the following to nephew Consider SIMMONS, in return for Consider to...provide for me & maintain me in a decent & christian like manner agreeable to a man in my circumstances...during the term of my natural life...all lands received from will of father Josiah SOUL of Duxborough dec'd dated 5 Nov. 1762...and is the one half part of the homestead whereon the sd Josiah last dwelt, one quarter of the meadow and share of cedar swamp. Witnesses: John WINSLOW, Polly LITTLE. Ack. same day. Rec. 6 July 1768.

Jonathan SOULE of Waterville, Kennebeck Co. <Plymouth Co.Deeds 107:112>
...28 Sept. 1807, Jonathan SOULE, yeoman...seized in fee of the one undivided full third part of a certain piece of salt marsh land in Dubury...being a part of the estate of my father Micah SOULE late of Duxbury dec'd & by him devised to me...appoint Asa SOUL, yeoman of Waterville, attorney...to sell & dispose of the land. Witnesses: George CLARKE, Timothy BOUTELLE. Ack. same day Rec. 15 Dec. 1807.

Jonathan & Asa SOULE of Waterville to **Charles DREW** of Duxbury MA. <Plymouth Co.Deeds 107:121>
...26 Oct. 1807, Jonathan SOULE & Asa SOULE, yeomen, tenants in common of one acre of salt meadow in Duxbury marshes & two acres meadow, belonging to the heirs of Josiah SOULE* late of Duxbury, yeoman dec'd...for $60.00 sold the above to Charles DREW, ship carpenter...reference may be had to a deed of the same dated with these presents given by Alice SOULE to the sd Charles DREW. Witnesses: Noah SIMMONS, Thomas HUNT. Rec. 5 Nov. 1807. <*rcds. mistakenly say Joshua SOULE>

PLYMOUTH COUNTY DEEDS: (re: SOULE)

<126:1> - 1815, Micah SOULE, yeoman & Lucy SOULE of Duxbury, Abigail & Nancy SOULE, singlewomen of Duxbury.
<127:220> - 1815, James SOULE & Thomas SOULE of Middleboro buy land in Marshfield.
<130:277> - 1817, Micah & Lucy SOULE of Duxbury to Levi WESTON Jr., land which fell to him in division of father's real estate.
<168:184> - 28 Jan. 1830, Daniel SAVORY & wf Huldah of Middleboro to Thomas SOULE & Francis ATWOOD of Middleboro, land in 26 Men's Purchase set off to Huldah in division of father, William SOULE's estate.
<181:156> - 18 Sept 1832, Hiram OAKMAN & wf Jane S. OAKMAN of Marshfield to Nathan SOULE, Thomas SOULE, Simeon SOULE & Henry SOULE, land bounded by Levi WESTON, Isaiah ALDEN, Sylvanus SAMPSON, Peleg WESTON. Witnesses: Constant OAKMAN, Joseph CLIFT.
<180:135> - 26 Oct. 1832, Nathan SOULE, blockmaker, Thomas SOULE & Simeon SOULE, master mariners and Henry SOULE, yeoman, all of Duxbury, sons of Simeon, divide land.
<221:127> - 1846, Lucy SOULE, widow of Duxbury to Micah A. SOULE of same, land received from estate of her father Samuel ALDEN dec'd.

Estate of **Lois SOULE**, widow of Abington MA. <Plymouth Co.PR #18830>
<11:58**B**> Warrant to appraise, 7 May 1842, to Harvey TORREY, Nathan BEAL & Micah POOL, all of Abington. <84:213> Inventory taken 9 May 1842. <11:58**B**> Petition 16 May 1842, eldest son **William F. SOULE** requests to be app'td admr. Letter/Bond 16 May 1842, **William F. SOULE** of Duxbury, app'td admr. Sureties: Daniel CHURCHILL & Harvey WESTON of Plymouth. Witness: George RIDER. <85:137> Account of admr., 15 May 1843; incl. bills of Nathan SOUTHWORTH for board & nursing, Dr. E. THAXTER and Dr. A CHAPIN(sp); Paid to: heirs, viz: **William F. SOULE, Thomas H. SOULE, Nathan SOUTHWORTH, Stephen D. SOULE.**

MICRO #7 OF 11

Estate of **Josiah SOULE**, yeoman of Duxbury MA. <Plymouth Co.PR #18826>
<39:89> Letter/Bond 29 Oct. 1806, widow **Alice SOULE** app'td admx. Sureties: Malachi DELANO & Jeptha DELANO, yeomen of Duxbury. Witnesses: Lucy LOTHROP, Isaac LOTHROP. <42:25> Inventory taken 22 Jan. 1807 by Malachi DELANO, Noah SIMMONS & Thomas SAMPSON, all of Duxbury. <42:295> 2d Account of admx., **Alice HATCH**, allowed 6 Apr. 1808; Paid to: William PETERSON "and 13 others"; Due to: Seth SPRAGUE, Peleg WESTON.

Guardianship of Children of **Josiah SOULE** of Duxbury MA. <Plymouth Co.PR #18827>
<32:322> Letter/Bond 8 June 1807, widow **Alice SOULE** app'td gdn. of **Lydia SOULE & Abigail SOULE**, above 14 and **Sylvia SOULE, Josiah SOULE & Abishai SOULE**, under 14. Sureties: Malachi DELANO, yeoman of Duxbury & Lemuel SIMMONS, cordwainer of Plymouth. Witnesses: William KEENE, Isaac LOTHROP. <32:323> Letter/Bond 26 June 1807, Judah ALDEN, Esq. of Duxbury app'td gdn. of **Asa SOULE**, above 14. Sureties: Thomas HUNT & James SOUTHWORTH Sr., yeomen of Duxbury. Witnesses: Lucia S. SMITH, Welthea ALDEN. <41:248> Letter/Bond 8 Apr. 1816, Benjamin ALDEN, gent. of Duxbury, app'td gdn. of **Josiah SOULE**, above 14 and **Abishai SOULE**, under 14. Sureties: Isaiah ALDEN & Benjamin ALDEN Jr. of Duxbury. Witnesses: Martha ALDEN, Ruth ALDEN.

Estate of **Josiah SOULE** of Duxbury MA to **Charles DREW** of same. <Plymouth Co.Deeds 107:120>
...26 Oct. 1807, widow Alice SOULE, admx. of estate, for $120.00 sells to Charles DREW, ship carpenter...two acres of salt meadow in Duxbury marsh near wood island...being two thirds of the meadow that lay in common & undivided between the dec'd & Jonathan SOULE & Asa SOULE...bounded by land of Consider SIMMONS, widow SOULE and ALDEN. Witnesses: Judah ALDEN, John ALDEN Jr. Ack. 7 Nov. 1807. Rec. 15 Dec. 1807.

Estate of **Micah SOULE**, mariner of Duxbury MA. <Plymouth Co.PR #18843>
<52:172> Letter/Bond 5 Nov. 1822, widow **Lucy SOULE** app'td admx. Sureties: Samuel A. FRAZAR, Esq. & Samuel SOULE, mariner of Duxbury. Witness: Amherst A. FRAZAR. <57:216> Inventory taken 17 July 1823 by Samuel A. FRAZAR, Esq., Isaiah ALDEN & Reuben DELANO, yeomen of Duxbury. <56:340> Insolvency 16 Dec. 1822. <57:215> Inventory taken 28 Nov. 1822 by Thomas B. WATERS, Nathaniel H. EMMONS, Thomas WINSOR; mentions the Sloop "Tangent". <55:142> Notice of appointment in Columbian Centinal (Boston newspaper) and Old Colony Memorial. <57:253> Allowance to widow, 11 Aug. 1823. <57:253> Account 11 Aug. 1823, to boarding the family of four from 3 Sept. 1822 to 11 Aug. 1823, at 75 cents per week, $135.00

Guardianship of Children of **Micah SOULE** of Duxbury MA. <Plymouth Co.PR #18844>
<original> 10 Nov. 1835, **Micah A. SOULE,** above 14, choses Benjamin ALDEN as gdn. <65:461> Letter/Bond 7 Dec. 1835, Benjamin ALDEN, yeoman of Duxbury, app'td gdn. Sureties: Ichabod ALDEN of Duxbury & Joel PETERSON of Pembroke. Witness: J.H. LOUD. <73:144> Petition to sell real estate, 7 Dec. 1835. <78:182> Inventory taken 7 Jan. 1836, by Ichabod ALDEN, Wadsworth CHANDLER, Wadsworth CHANDLER Jr.; incl. one undivided share in the thirds of the late widow **Alice HATCH** dec'd; sworn to 16 May 1836 by gdn.

Estate of **Nathaniel SOULE**, yeoman of Duxbury MA. <Plymouth Co.PR #18850>
<39:321> Letter/Bond 16 Oct. 1811, Thomas Whittemore PETERSON, yeoman of Duxbury, app'td admr.

Sureties: Arannah FORD of Marshfield & Barnabas HOLMES, yeoman of Plymouth. Witnesses: Joshua B. THOMAS, Charles H. WARREN. <44:28> Inventory taken 26 Oct. 1811 by Isaiah ALDEN & William PETERSON of Duxbury and James FORD, yeoman of Pembroke; incl. note against Levi WESTON. <44:29> Notice. <44:35> Dower set off, 16 Nov. 1811, to widow **Abigail SOULE**, her thirds in real estate which is bounded by land of Luther PETERSON and house lot of Nathaniel SOULE Jr. <44:502> Account of admr., 14 Apr. 1813; real estate sold to Ezra WESTON, Joseph WHITE & Nathaniel SAMPSON; Paid to: Alathea SOUL, Mary SOUL, Samuel A. FRAZER, Nathaniel SAMPSON, Martin SIMMONS, Weston SIMMONS, Dr. Isaac PAINE, William PETERSON, Jabez PETERSON, Benjamin ALDEN, Kilborn WHITMAN, Joseph WHITE, Elisha DELANO, Adam FISH, Judah ALDEN, James FORD, Nathaniel SIMMONS, Jesse SIMMONS, Isaiah ALDEN Peleg WESTON, Reuben PETERSON Jr., William POLEN for gravestones, Joel PETERSON and $100.00 each to the children of the dec'd, viz: **Nathaniel SOULE, Andrew SOULE, Lydia SAMPSON, Mary SOULE & Alathea SOULE.** <44:502> Sale of real estate, 17 Feb. 1812 at public auction, the dwelling house of the widow **Abigail SOULE**; sworn to 14 Apr. 1813 by admr.

Estate of **Nathaniel SOULE Jr.**, mariner of Duxbury MA. <Plymouth Co.PR #18851>
<original> Declination, 14 Mar. 1817, of widow **Polly SOULE** to administer estate and requests her brother **Ralph PARTRIDGE** be app'td. <46:211> Letter/Bond 15 Mar. 1817, Ralph PARTRIDGE, schoolmaster of Duxbury, app'td admr. Sureties: John ALDEN Jr., Jacob WESTON. Witness: Judah ALDEN. <48:425> Inventory taken 7 Apr. 1817, by Wadsworth CHANDLER, Jesse SIMMONS & Thomas W. PETERSON, all of Duxbury. <48:426> Insolvency 9 Apr. 1817. <48:426> Notice. <48:477> Dower set off, 2 May 1817, to widow **Polly SOULE**, by Wadsworth CHANDLER & Jesse SIMMONS, yeomen of Duxbury and Nathaniel HOLMES, yeoman of Kingston, her thirds in real estate which is bounded by land of Luther PETERSON, widow Abigail SOULE & Isaac DINGLEY. <49:2> License to sell real estate, 15 Aug. 1817. <49:11> Oath of admr. <49:74,75> List of claims, 13 Oct. 1817: Rufus HATHAWAY, Alden THOMAS, Jesse SIMMONS, widow Abigail SOUL, Elisha DELANO, Benjamin ALDEN, Ichabod DELANO, Joel PETERSON, William LORING, Judah ALDEN, David CUSHMAN, Asa SAMPSON, Ezra WESTON & son, Elezer HARLOW, L. & J. HARLOW, Ebenezer FISH, Thomas W. PETERSON, ELijah PETERSON, Packard PETERSON, Aaron SIMMONS, Weston SIMMONS, Seth SPRAGUE, WESTON & HOOPER, Benjamin CUSHMAN, Charles SIMMONS, Whittemore SIMMONS, Judah PETERSON, Daniel CHANDLER, Mary SOUL. <49:151> Account of admr., 11 Dec. 1817; Paid to: Wadsworth CHANDLER, Jesse SIMMONS, Thomas W. PETERSON, Nathaniel HOLMES, Ichabod ALDEN for surveying, M. SMITH for tax, Ichabod DELANO, Joshua BREWSTER, allowance to widow. <49:173> Notice of sale, 21 Aug. 1817, at the house of the widow **Polly SOUL** in Duxbury, the whole real estate except the widow's dower. <73:117> Petition to sell real estate, 25 Nov. 1834. <77:192> Affidavit of sale, 21 Mar. 1835, to be sold at the residence of Alethea SOULE in Duxbury, one quarter of the real estate late the dower of the widow. Account of admr., 18 May 1835; real estate, being one undivided fourth of the dower of the widow, sold to Mathew LANE.

Estate of **Barnabas PERRY** of Pembroke MA. <Plymouth Co.PR>
<13:41> Pr. 7 May 1753, Benjamin TURNER, gent. of Pembroke app'td admr. <13:78> Inventory taken 29 May 1753 by Capt. Benjamin TURNER. <13:158> Dower set off, 5 Nov. 1753, to widow **Alice PERRY.** <13:410> Claims allowed, 1754.

Amos SAMSON of Duxborough MA to **Peleg SPRAGUE** of same. <Plymouth Co.Deeds 42:69>
...10 Apr. 1753, Amos SAMSON, yeoman sells to Peleg SPRAGUE, house carpenter...my share...in two pieces of salt meadow in Duxborough...at Common Island and one piece lying on Carswell Marshes, all which was my father's sd meadow.

Guardianship of Children of **Ziba HUNT**, dec'd of Duxbury MA. <Plymouth Co.PR #11110>
<original> Letter/Bond 16 Dec. 1822, Sylvia HOLMES, widow, chosen gdn. by **Ziba HUNT, Henry HUNT & Mary L. HUNT**, above 14. Sureties: Studley SAMPSON, gent. and Lot HUNT, mariner, all of Duxbury.

Estate of **Gideon SOULE**, non comp of Duxbury/Pembroke MA. <Plymouth Co.PR #18786>
<11:359> Letter 6 June 1750, John HUNT, coaster of Duxbury, app'td gdn. <original> Bond 7 June 1750 of gdn. Surety: Gamaliel BRADFORD of Duxbury. Witnesses: Samuel SEABURY, Consider HOWLAND. <12:162> Account of gdn., Feb. 1750; Paid to: Esq. BRADFORD, Ezra ARNOLD. <12:274> Inventory taken 12 July 1751 by Gamaliel BRADFORD, George PARTRIDGE, Samuel SEABURY. <12:357> Account of gdn., 19 July 1751. <12:496> Account of gdn., 4 May 1752. <13:269> Account of gdn., 20 May 1754.

Estate of **Gideon SOUL**, yeoman of Halifax MA. <Plymouth Co.PR #18787>
<27:403> Letter/Bond 1 Oct. 1792, widow **Ruth SOULE** of Halifax app'td admx. Sureties: Moses INGLEE & Adam TOMSON of Halifax. Witnesses: Caleb LORING, Isaac LOTHROP. <33:214> Notice, sworn to by admx., 5 Nov. 1792. <33:214> Inventory taken 23 Oct. 1792 by Moses INGLEE, Adam TOMSON, Ichabod TOMSON. <35:562> Account of admx., 3 Oct. 1796; Paid to: Judah WOOD, William WATERMAN, William SOULE, Zenas BRYANT, Thomas DAVIS, Josiah TOMSON, Ephraim TINKHAM, John TILSON, Nathaniel MORTON, Asaph SOULE, Dr. James THACHER, Isaac WATERMAN, Ebenezer TOMSON, George SAMSON, Ephraim SPOONER.

Guardianship of Child of **Ichabod SOUL**, dec'd of Scituate MA. <Plymouth Co.PR #18751>
<11:130> Letter/Bond 28 Jan. 1748, John TURNER, blacksmith of Scituate app'td gdn. of **Abigail SOULE.** Surety: Melzar TURNER, blacksmith of Scituate. Witnesses: Benjamin BRYANT, Joseph STETSON.

Estate of **Isaac SOUL** of Pembroke MA. <Plymouth Co.PR #18791>
<original> Request 11 May 1776, of son **Moses SOUL** to nephew **Abraham JOSSELYN Jr.** of Pembroke, to administer estate. <23:92> Letter/Bond 3 June 1776, Abraham JOSSELYN Jr., yeoman, app'td admr. Sureties: Increase ROBINSON, William COX. Witnesses: Daniel NOYCE, Joseph CUSHING. <24:188> Insolency. <24:189> List of claims, 7 Apr. 1777, by Alexander SOPER, David TILDEN, Blaney PHILLIPS:

Thomas HOBBARTS, Noah PERRY, James CLARK, Samuel PERRY, Abigail SOUL, Deborah CLARK, James CLARK Jr., Maletiah DILLINGHAM, Reuben CLARK, Joseph CUSHING, Josiah KEEN, Bette RAMSDALL. <24:187> Inventory taken 21 June 1776 by Nathaniel CUSHING, James HATCH, Increase ROBINSON; incl. notes of Bildad SOULE, Reuben CARVER, Samuel WITHERELL. <24:189> Account 17 June 1777; paid Major TILDEN, Dr. CHILD, Nehemiah RAMSDEL, Deacon ROBINSON. <25:123> Account of admr.; paid Gamaliel BATES, Dr. HALL, Reuben CLARK; orchard sold to Robert BARKER; received from William EELLS, Nathaniel CLARKE. <original> Receipts: 10 Mar. 1777 of Daniel CHILD; 11 Apr. 1777 of Alexander SOPER; 16 Apr. 1777 of Nathaniel CUSHING; (no date) of Blany PHILLIPS & David TILDEN.

LETTER: To **Mr. Abraham JOSSELYN Jr.** in Pembrock/Pembroke, these with care.
Camp at Boston may the 11, 1776.

Dear Sir: I imbrace this oppertunity to inform you that I am through the goodness of a mercyfull God in Perfect Helth as my Prayers are these may find you and your beloved Family. Sir you are acquainted with the Surcumstance of my Fathers Esteat and that it must be settlead soon and I am hear ingaged and cant have time to doo it. I Should be Verry Glad if you would undertake to administer on the Esteat and Settle it. I have wrote to your unkle Isaac but the Surcumstance of his family is Such that He cant leave them to be gone so long and I find it will give such Satisfaction to your aunts that I Should you had Better Undertake it is a plenty time For money that things will fetch a good price at a Vandue. Sir I will give you up all the power that I have and nobody Shall take any advantage of you.

Sir I Should Wright more but I am in hast Desireing an Intrust In your Prayers I Subscribe my Self your tender affectionate Uncle.

(Signed) **Moses SOULE**

NB - Give my Love to your Father and mother and all Friends.

(Endorsed) Moses SOULS Request that Abraham JOSSELYN Jr. might administer on his fathers Estate.

PLYMOUTH COUNTY DEEDS: (re: Isaac SOULE)

<91:14> - 1778, Abraham JOSSELYN Jr. as admr. to estate of Isaac SOULE.
<56:87> - 27 Aug. 1764, Isaac SOULE to Bildad SOULE. Witnesss: Moses SOULE Sr., Isaac SOULE Jr.

References only to the name **Isaac SOULE**, viz: <55:123> 1770; <53:34> 1765; <53:163> 1767; <53:226> 1767; <54:87> 1768; <41:29>; <55:143> 1770; <56:231>; 59:41,42; <53:156> 1729,1736,1738; <53:157> 1736,1739,1741,1754,1767.

Estate of **Abraham JOSSELYN** of Pembroke MA. <Plymouth Co.PR 25:109>
Division, 8 Sept. 1778, to widow **Mary** and following children, viz: eldest son **Abraham JOSSELYN, Mary COX** wf of William Jr., **Elizabeth COX** wf of Seth, **Dorothy CLARK** wf of Reuben, **Eleazer JOSSELYN, Abigail, Lydia,Celia, Tamar, Isaac JOSSELYN.**

William COX Jr. of Chatham NH to **Nathan SPRAGUE** of Pembroke MA. <Plymouth Co.Deeds 85:26>
...20 Nov. 1797, William COX Jr., yeoman, by power of attorney from father & mother, sells to Nathan SPRAGUE...all rights of father & mother, William & Mary COX...being one eleventh part of all thirds set off to widow Mary JOSSELYN of Berry, Co. of Worcester dec'd, being in Pembroke.

Will of **John COB Sr.** of Middleboro MA. <Plymouth Co.PR #4546>
<5:528>...dated 29 May 1727, wf **Rachel**; son **John COB** & his two sons **Gershom COB & John COB**; to son **James COB**, the dwelling house where he now lives; three daus **Martha SIMONS, Patience TINKHAM, Rachel STANDISH**; my three yoak of oxen now in the possesion of John COB, James COB & Moses STANDISH be & remain to as their own proper estate. Witnesses: John BENNET, Jonathan FULLER, Shubael TOMSON. Codicil dated 28 Sept. 1727...Whereas it has pleased Almighty God to call to his Mercy the other day, my dear wife mentioned within. Witnesses: Joseph BENNETT, Shubael TOMSON, Ebenezer COBB Jr. <original> Pr. 16 Nov. 1727. <original> Inventory taken by John BENNET, James SOUL, John SOUL; total estate, £1534.14.11.

Estate of **Aaron SIMMONS** of Middleboro MA. <Plymouth Co.PR>
...only son **David SIMMONS**; only surviving daus, **Patience SIMMONS, Jane FINNEY, Abigail FINNEY**; heirs of dec'd dau **Martha FINNEY** wf of Nelson. <14:33> Adm., 1 Mar. 1756. <15:103> Inventory taken 7 Mar. 1756.

Estate of **Edmund WESTON** of Plympton MA. <Plymouth Co.PR #22374; MD 24:19
<5:318> Letter/Bond, 7 Nov. 1727, son Benjamin WESTON/WESTERN app'td admr. Sureties: Thomas DARLING of Middleboro, Phillip DELLANO of Duxbury. Witnesses: Thomas SOUTHWORTH, Cornelius SOUL. <5:349> Inventory taken 7 Nov. 1727 by James SOUL & Samuel SAMPSON of Middleboro and George SAMPSON Jr. of Plimpton. <5:350> Division of real estate, 6 Nov. 1727, between widow **Rebeckah** and following children: to **Nathan WESTON,** land in Plympton the dec'd bought of Moses SOUL & cedar swamp in South meadow; to **Zachariah WESTON,** land at Donham's Neck in Plympton formerly owned by John DONHAM Sr.; to **John WESTON,** one half of homestead in Plympton & part of meadow; to **Edmund WESTON,** land in Plympton the dec'd bought of James SOUL & part of meadow; to **Benjamin WESTON,** one half of homestead, 45 acres in Middleboro and two acres of meadow bought of Benjamin SOUL; to **Rebeckah DARLING** wf of Thomas, lot in South Purchase, Middleboro laid out to John SOUL. Witnesses: George SAMPSON Jr., John PERKINS.

Estate of **Benjamin WESTON**, yeoman of Plympton MA. <Plymouth Co.PR #22347>
<original> Request, 10 May 1773 of widow **Mercy/Marcy WESTON** that her son **Job WESTON** be app'td admr. of her husband who died 5 May 1773. <23:17> Letter/Bond 11 May 1773, **Job WESTON**, yeoman of Plimpton app'td admr. Sureties: William WESTON & Samuel JACKSON of Plymouth. Witnesses: Edward WINSLOW, Penelope WINSLOW. <21:304> Inventory taken 4 June 1773 by Timothy RIPLEY, Jabez NEWLAND & Zebdiel SAMSON; incl. homestead & fresh meadow, wood lot, cedar swamp, one quarter of grist mill & fulling mill. <21:304> Dower 22 May 1773, Timothy RIPLEY, Zebedee CHANDLER & Seth CUSHING all of Plympton app'td to set off one third of real estate to widow; they made oath 28 June 1773. <24:222> Account (no date), Paid to: Benjamin CUSHMAN, Abner HALL, Isaac LeBARON, William WESTON, James BISHOP, Gideon BRADFORD, Dr. Nathaniel LOTHROP, Timothy RIPLEY, Timothy RIPLEY Jr., Major Seth CUSHING, Joseph BRYANT, Thomas LORING Jr., Zadoc WESTON, Louis WESTON, Jabez NEWLAND, Josiah CHANDLER, Zabdiel SAMSON, Zebedee CHANDLER, Nathan PERKINS, Dr. Ebenezer DEAN, widow Mercy WESTON <24:223> Division of real estate; warrant dated 7 Oct. 1776, confirmed 2 Nov. 1776, to following children, viz: **Joshua WESTON** (eldest son), **William WESTON, Zadock WESTON, Hannah DEAN** wf of Joel of Ashford and **Job WESTON.** <original> Division of dower set off to widow **Mercy WESTON,** 14 Mar. 1796, to following children, viz: heirs of **Joshua WESTON**, dec'd, **William WESTON, Zadock WESTON, Hannah DEAN** and heirs of **Job WESTON**; sworn to 15 Mar. by Seth CUSHING & Zephaniah PERKINS and 14 Apr. 1796 by Nehemiah COBB.

==========

Estate of **Mercy WESTON**, widow of Plympton MA. <Plymouth Co.PR #22417>
<27:468> Letter/Bond 1 Mar. 1794, Isaiah CUSHMAN, yeoman of Plympton, app'td admr. Sureties: Benjamin DREW of Plymouth & Sylvanus BARTLETT Jr. of Plympton. Witnesses: Jesse CHURCHILL, Isaac LOTHROP. <35:32> Inventory taken 8 Apr. 1794 by James CHURCHILL, Ebenezer SOULE, Elias CHURCHILL, all of Plymton; sworn to by admr. 8 Apr. 1794.

==========

Estate of **Lieut. Job WESTON**, gent. of Plympton MA. <Plymouth Co.PR #22401>
<original> Request (no date) of widow **Hannah WESTON** that Elijah BISBEE Jr. be app'td admr. <27:141> Letter/Bond 6 Oct. 1783, Elijah BISBEE Jr. of Plympton app'td admr. Sureties: Thomas GANNETT & Joseph BRADFORD, Physician, both of Plymton. Witnesses: Samuel CLARK, Isaac LOTHROP. <29:126> Inventory taken 3 Apr. 1784 by Jabez NEWLAND, Ebenezer SOULE & Joel ELLIS, all of Plympton; incl. homestead farm & 20 acre woodland; sworn to by admr. 7 Apr. 1784.

==========

Estate of **Coomer WESTON**, mariner of Plymouth MA. <Plymouth Co.PR #22359>
<34:64> Letter/Bond 11 Feb. 1796, widow **Patty WESTON** app'td admx. Sureties: William WESTON & Jabez DOTEN, mariner, both of Plymouth. Witnesses: Mary WESTON, Mary MASON. <35:467> Inventory taken 13 Feb.1796 by Ephraim SPOONER, Josiah FINNEY, Rosseter COTTON; incl. homestead & garden bought of Dr. COTTON; sworn to by admx. 27 Feb. 1796. <35:547> Notice, sworn to 28 Aug. 1796 by William WESTON.

==========

Guardianship of Children of **Coomer WESTON** of Plymouth MA. <Plymouth Co.PR #22360>
<32:138> Letter/Bond 13 Jan. 1800, widow **Patty WESTON** app'td gdn. of **Coomer WESTON,** above 14 and **Isaac WESTON & Thomas WESTON,** under 14. Sureties: William WESTON & Freeman BARTLETT of Plymouth. Witnesses: Mary WESTON, Coomer WESTON.

MICRO #8 OF 11

Estate of **Edmund WESTON,** yeoman of Middleboro MA. <Plymouth Co.PR #22372>
<23:18> Letter/Bond 7 June 1773, James WESTON of Middleboro app'td admr. Sureties: Elijah CLAP of Middleboro & Job WESTON of Plimpton. Witnesses: Elnathan FISH, Edward WINSLOW Jr.

==========

Will of **Edmund WESTON** of Middleboro MA. <Plymouth Co.PR #22373>
<45:336>...dated 8 Sept. 1813. <45:337> Pr. 13 Apr. 1814. <45:407> Inventory taken 20 May 1814. <47:258> Oath for sale of real estate, 25 Apr. 1815. <48:29> Account, 2 Apr. 1816.

==========

Estate of **Nathan WESTON,** yeoman of Plympton MA. <Plymouth Co.PR #22418>
<13:365> Letter/Bond 21 Nov. 1754, Nathan WESTON, labourer of Plympton app'td admr. Sureties: Joel ELLIS, labourer of Plymton & Consider HOWLAND of Plymouth. Witnesses: Edward WINSLOW, John LOTHROP. <13:397> Inventory taken 23 Jan. 1755 by Josiah PERKINS, Joel ELLIS, Jabez NEWLAND; incl part of his real estate given by deeds to his sons **Nathan WESTON, Isaac WESTON & Jacob WESTON.** <14:62> Account of admr., 5 Apr. 1756; Paid to: Jonathan SMITH, Jabez NULAND/NEWLAND, Thomas LORING, George SAMSON, Joseph WILLIAMS, Joel ELLIS, James WRIGHT, Joseph WRIGHT, Joseph PERRY, David WESTON, Philomon SAMSON, Timothy RIPLEY, Polycarpus LORING, Gideon BRADFORD, Jediah SAMSON, Benjamin WESTON, Lydia PERRY, Ebenezer SOUL, Lazarus LeBARON, John WADSWORTH, Josiah PERKINS, Nathaniel PRATT, Josiah LEONARD, Zacheus BLOSOM, Samuel BARTLETT, Nathan WESTON, Winslow WHITE, widow **Desire WESTON**; due to Jacob WESTON, Edmond WRIGHT and a mourning suit for the widow.

==========

Estate of **Jacob WESTON,** of Plympton MA. <Plymouth Co.PR #22398>
<15:524> Letter/Bond 10 June 1760, Nathan WESTON of Plimton app'td admr. Sureties: Joel ELLIS & Elijah BISBEE of Plimton. Witnesses: Kenelm WINSLOW, Edward WINSLOW. <16:25> Inventory taken 2 Oct. 1760 by Joel ELLIS, Elijah BISBEE & Zebedee CHANDLER, all of Plimton; incl. cedar swamp, meadow & land at N. Yarmouth. <19:271> Release 9 Nov. 1761, of **Edmund WRIGHT** & wf **Desire** of Newbury MA, to Nathan WESTON, admr., for their interest in estate of their brother **Jacob WESTON.** Witnesses: Cornelius HESTER, Ebenezer SOUL Jr. <19:272> Release 11 Oct. 1765, of **Isaac WESTON,** yeoman of Plimton to Nathan WESTON, admr., for his interest in personal estate and third part of real estate. Witnesses: Job WESTON, Benjamin WESTON. <19:273> Division of real estate, 25 Mar.

1765, by Jabez NEWLAND, George HAMMOND & John SHAW Jr., all of Plimton, to brothers & sister of dec'd, viz: **Nathan WESTON, Isaac WESTON & Desire WRIGHT**; reserving to **Desire WESTON**, mother of dec'd, her share; among the real estate divided is an interest in N. Yarmouth that Elisha EATON of N. Yarmouth died seized; division confirmed 14 Oct. 1765.

Estate of **Hannah DARLING** of Middleboro MA. <Plymouth Co.PR #6050>
...(no date given) <61:216> Pr. <62 :334> Notice. <66:473> Inventory. <67:487> Account.

William WASHBURN of Stafford MA to **Zenas DARLING** of Oakham MA. <Worcester Co.Deeds 114:26>
...7 Nov. 1789, William WASHBURN, husbandman & wf Lurana, spinster, for £6 sold to Zenas DARLING, yeoman...all our right title & claim to the farm house & lands which our Honoured Father Thomas DARLING late of sd Oakham dec'd was seized & possessed of...sd farm lying in Oakham...containing 51 acres...bounded west of County Road leading from Brookfield to Rutland and land of Daniel BOLTON...also land on east side of road...Witnesses: George RICHARDSON, Dinah RICHARDSON. Ack. 9 Nov 1789 by grantors. Rec. 12 Mar. 1792.

Will of **Benjamin DARLING**, gent. of Middleboro MA. <Plymouth Co.PR #6042>
<42:350>...dated 10 July 1802, mentions wf **Hannah**; son **Daniel DARLING**; dau **Sally**; to son **John DARLING**, all the money I have paid for him to Noah THOMAS; to son **Joseph DARLING**, land in Woodstock VT; to **Benjamin DARLING & John DARLING**, sons of son **John**, half a cow each; my six daus, viz: **Zillah COX** wf of Ebenezer, **Selah COX** wf of Daniel, **Lydia TORREY** wf of Caleb (& her chil.), **Susanna DARLING, Rebecca DARLING, Sally DARLING**; wf **Hannah** & son **Daniel**, executors. <42:349> Pr. 5 Apr. 1808.

Stephen RICHARDSON et al of Pembroke MA to **Joseph SAMSON** of Plympton. <Plymouth Co.Deeds 61:80>
...10 Aug. 1779, Stephen RICHARDSON & wf Mary and Benjamin DARLING, blacksmith to Joseph SAMSON, yeoman...one fifth of lot in Plympton which their grandfather Benjamin SAMSON of Plympton died seized of and which he bought of James RICKARD in 1756. Ack. 24 Aug. 1779.

Benjamin DARLING of Middleboro MA to **Daniel DARLING** of same. <Plymouth Co.Deeds 90:265>
...18 Feb. 1800, Benjamin DARLING, gent. to Daniel DARLING, yeoman...lands in Middleboro incl. land bought with son Daniel DARLING, reserving use of half for self & wf Hannah. Wf Hannah DARLING signs. Ack. 14 Apr. 1801, by Benjamin.

Heirs of **Joseph HARRIS** of Middleboro MA. <Plymouth Co.Deeds 58:96>
...9 July 1772, Division of lands among heirs of Joseph HARRIS, dec'd, viz: to Benjamin DARLING & wf Hannah, half of lot; to John CLARK & wf Susa, half of lot; to Ezra HARRIS, homestead, all of Middleboro. Ack. 23 May 1774 by John, Susa & Ezra, 6 June by Benjamin & Hannah.

Samuel DARLING of Duxbury MA to **John DARLING** of same. <Plymouth Co.Deeds 72:32>
...9 June 1790, Samuel DARLING, yeoman to John DARLING, yeoman. Wf Priscilla releases dower. Witnesses: David DARLING, Mercy DARLING. Ack. 10 July 1790.

Will of **Zachariah WESTON**, yeoman of Middleboro MA. <Plymouth Co.PR #22462>
<19:35>...dated 27 Sept. 1763, wf **Mehitable**, executrix. Witnesses: Simeon DOGGETT, John COBB, Joseph TINKHAM. Pr. 24 Apr. 1764.

Estate of **Zachariah WESTON**, yeoman of Middleboro MA. <Plymouth Co.PR #22461>
<27:478> Letter/Bond, 5 May 1794, widow **Sarah WESTON** app'td admx. Sureties: Daniel WESTON of Middleboro & Hezekiah HOOPER of Bridgewater. Witnesses: James WASHBURN, Jonathan NASH. <35:157> Inventory taken 20 June 1794, by Nehemiah BENNETT, Joshua EDDY, Israel WOOD; incl. homestead; ten acres called Israel THOMAS' land at Nemaskett River; fresh meadow at Nemaskett River; 79th lot in cedar swamp in South Purchase; land bought of Lemuel THOMAS; land in 8 men's Purchase called Oliver & Spooner land; former homestead of Manasseh WOOD; 10 acres in lot #161 in Sixteen Shilling Purchase. <35:376> Dower assigned, 31 Oct. 1794, to widow. <35:376> Division, 1 Apr. 1795, to following children of dec'd, viz: **Zachariah WESTON, Daniel WESTON, Isaiah WESTON, Rebecca RYDER** wf of Elisha, **Rachel THOMAS** wf of Elisha, **Hannah THOMAS** wf of Levi, **Sarah PERKINS** wf of Ebenezer; sworn to 3 Nov. 1795 by the three appraisers of inventory. <35:380> Account of admx., 3 Nov. 1795 Received from: Peter TINKHAM, Israel THOMAS, Lewis WESTON; Paid to: Micah BRYANT, Melzer TRIBOU, Isaac THOMSON, Bezer SOULE, Dr. Thomas STURTEVANT, Thomas WOOD, Joseph VAUGHAN, Elisha RYDER, Josiah CARVER, Ichabod WOOD, Andrew WOOD, Abraham THOMAS, Abiel WASHBURN, Hannah Francis COBB, Sylvanus TILSON, Joseph S. HUNT, Cyrus KEITH, Ebenezer WOOD, William PORTER & Co., Rev. Perez FOBES, Elisha THOMAS, Andrew COBB, Nathaniel SHAW, Abner BOURNE, Joseph HARLOW, Patience DUNHAM, Lewis COBB, William WESTON, Jonathan FULLER, Thomas BURBANK, Thomas BENNETT, Thomas FOSTER, Nicholas WOOD, James PORTER, Nehemiah BENNETT, Daniel WESTON. <34:339> Letter/Bond 24 Feb. 1796, **Zachariah WESTON** app'td admx. d.b.n., **Sarah WESTON** having dec'd. Sureties: David VAUGHAN of Middleboro & Caleb LEACH, watchmaker of Plymouth. Witnesses: Nathaniel LOTHROP, Isaac LOTHROP. <35:496> Inventory taken 4 Apr. 1796 by David VAUGHAN, Ezra HARLOW & Israel WOOD, all of Middleboro; sworn to 5 Apr. 1796 by admr. <36:1> Division of dower, 29 Nov. 1796, by Nehemiah COBB, David VAUGHAN, Israel WOOD, to following children, viz: **Rebecca RYDER** wf of Elisha, **Rachel THOMAS** wf of Elisha, **Hannah THOMAS** wf of Levi, **Zachariah WESTON, Sarah PERKINS** wf of Ebenezer, **Daniel WESTON, Isaiah WESTON.**

Estate of **Sarah WESTON**, widow of Middleborough MA. <Plymouth Co.PR #22443>
<34:66> Letter/Bond 25 Feb. 1796, Nicholas WOOD, yeoman of Middleboro app'td admr. Sureties: Nehemiah BENNET & Stephen GIBBS of Middleboro. Witnesses: Abraham HAMMATT, Isaac LOTHROP. <35:567>

Notice. <36:62> Inventory taken 4 Mar. 1796 by Joseph KEITH, Nehemiah BENNET & John CARVER, all of Middleboro; personal estate only. <36:63> Insolvency 17 Feb. 1797. <38:433> Account of admr., 8 Nov. 1803; Received from: Daniel WESTON, Solomon INGLEY/INGLEE by way of Zachariah WESTON for other property which was in the hands of Zachariah; Paid to: Nathan ALDEN, expense in settling with Daniel WESTON; Silvanus TILSON, Isaiah WESTON, Joshua EDDY, Dr. William BAILEY, Japheth LeBARON, Israel WOOD, Andrew MACKIE, William PORTER & Co., Patience DUNHAM, Elisha RIDER

MARY SOULE[2] (George[1])

PLYMOUTH COUNTY PROBATES: (re: PETERSON)

1690	John	Duxbury		#15781, 1:62
1720	John	Duxbury		#15782, 4:232,234,235
1741	Isaac	Duxbury		#15774, 8:450,463;9:42,519
1745	Jonathan	Pembroke		#15783, 9:509,511,513
1747	Mary & Orphan	Duxbury		#15804, 9:422,423;11:243
1751	Joseph	Duxbury		#15787, 12:86,226,517;46:450;49:562,563
1761	David	Duxbury		#15748, 16:45,46
1765	Jonathan	Duxbury		#15785, 12:265;19:214,216,217,218,497
1765	Jonathan et al	Duxbury		#15786, 18:228,231,232,233;19:496;21:199,217
1769	Benjamin Jr.	Duxbury		#15740, 20:218,249
1784	Jacob	Duxbury		#15777, 29:219,220,270,271
1785	Isaac	Scituate		#15775, 27:202;29:387,388
1795	Reuben	Duxbury		#15813, 34:57,459,512,514
1803	Lewis	Duxbury	adm.	#15792, 34:375;38:501;40:174,204,476
1805	Ichabod	Duxbury	adm.	#15773, 39:31
1806	Elizabeth	Duxbury	adm.	#15754, 39:238
1811	Nehemiah	Duxbury	adm.	#15807, 39:290;43:431;44:189,190;45:376,377
1814	Jonathan	Duxbury	adm.	#15784, 45:342,343;46:29
1818	Lydia	Duxbury	gdn.	#15796, 41:364;49:320,321,382,402,442,464;50:290
1820	Elijah	Duxbury	adm.	#15750, 46:398;50:600;53:316
1820	George	Duxbury	adm.	#15761, 52:17;53:524;54:77
1823	Luther	Duxbury	adm.	#15795; 52:219;57:134,157,217,393,395,499,500; 57:501,502,538;86:485
1825	Thaddeus	Duxbury	adm.	#15822, 52:386;60:353
1827	George	Duxbury	adm.	#15762, 61:89;62:133;63:378,479,480-2;64:345,415
1830	Lydia	Duxbury	will	#15797, 69:493
1835	Edwin et al	Duxbury	sale	#15749, 73:452
1836	George et al	Duxbury	gdn.	#15765, 65:437;73:478;78:177
1836	Joshua	Duxbury	will	#15788, 71:465;75:312;78:159,173
1836	Rebecca	Duxbury	gdn.	#15812, 8:373,374L;79:546;83:373
1838	Marshall	Duxbury	adm.	#15799, 2:79O;5:14T;10:161A;80:75,120,210,384; 81:64;103:38,50
1839	Thomas W.	Duxbury	adm.	#15824, 2:123O;6:22U;10:321A;82:6,33;83:318,322
1841	William	Duxbury	adm.	#15828, 2:179O;6:167U;10:445A;83:267;84:385
1843	Caleb	Duxbury	adm.	#15744, 6:505U;11:191B;85:537;86:489
1843	Marshall A.	Duxbury	Gdn.	#15800, 8:351L
1843	Priscilla	Duxbury	adm.	#15811, 6:521U;11:155B;85:219
1843	Packard	Duxbury	adm.	#15809, 6:535U;11:207B,266B;85:577;86:385,425, 489;87:258
1843	Sarah J. et al	Duxbury	gdn.	#15819, 8:337L
1845	Abigail	Duxbury	will	#15738, 2:36H;7:57V;87:207,296
1845	Reuben	Duxbury	will	#15814, 2:35H;7:53V;87:208,295,465
1846	Betsey	Plymouth	adm.	#15741, 3:25P;7:123V;11:422B;88:379,579;89:238, 385
1846	Charles	Plymouth	adm.	#15745, 3:26P;7:86V;11:389B;88:50,144,393,448; 89:26,27
1846	Jane	Duxbury	adm.	#15778, 7:197V;11:464B;89:149,256
1846	Judah	Duxbury	will	#15789, 3:35P;10:552A;88:377,444;89:240,278
1847	Frederick	Duxbury	will	#15758, 2:117H;89:138,140;90:13
1847	Mary J.	Duxbury	gdn.	#15801, 9:99M;89:179

PLYMOUTH COLONY DEEDS:

<3:244> - 30 July 1672, John PETERSON from George & Mary SOULE.
<4:155> - 20 Feb. 1675, John PETERSON & wf Mary to George SOULE.
<4:2> - 23 Mar. 1674/5, John PETERSON from George & Mary SOULE.
<4:50> - 24 Feb. 1675, John PETERSON from George & Mary SOULE.

Will of **John PETERSON**, tailor of Duxbury MA. <Plymouth Co.PR 4:232>
...dated 29 Apr. 1718...of old age, mentions wf **Mary** and following children, viz: **Joseph PETERSON** (eldest son), **Jonathan PETERSON, David PETERSON, Isaac PETERSON, Martha PETERSON, Mary SOULE** wf

of Joseph, **Rebecca WESTON** wf of John; son **Benjamin**, executor. Witnesses: Joshua SOULE, Penelope SAMSON, John WADSWORTH. <4:234> Pr. 1 Aug. 1720. <4:235> Inventory of personal estate taken 16 Mar. 1719/20, by John WADSWORTH, Joshua SOUL; incl. bookes, £3.2.; beding, bedsted & furniture, £21.5.; one cow, £4; chairs & cradle, £1; work tubbs, 12s; iron potts, frying pan, driping pan, £1.19; tramell & pot hooks; pair of iron doggs & tongs, £1; pewter, £1.16.;glass bottles & earthen ware; one cart rope & canoo, £1.7.; pair of taylors shears & goose, 8s; one cow, £4; ten sheep, £5.; sworn to 26 Mar. 1720 by admr.

Estate of **John PETERSON** of Duxborough. <Plymouth Co.Deeds #15781, 1:62; PN&Q 5:115> Inventory taken 29 Mar. 1690, by Thomas DILLANO, Joseph HOWLAND; incl. one horse, £2.5.; one mare, £2.5.; bed & bedding, £6.10.; staff, belt, a skin & wearing cloaths, £4.5.; chest & cace glass bottles & viall & powder hornes, 18s; two guns, £2; brydle, stirrup irons & tobacco, 10s; hoggsheads & barrils, 10s; two iron potts & a paile, £1.6.; his parts in whale boats, £8; money in father's hands, £5.6.1.; jarr of oyle, 2s; debts due estate, £10.10.10.; sworn to 1 Apr. 1690, by brother **Joseph PETERSON.** Letter/Bond 1 Apr. 1690, brother **Joseph PETERSON** of Duxbury app'td admr. Surety: John SIMONS of Duxbury. Witnesses: William BRADFORD, John CUSHING.

Will of **David PETERSON** of Duxbury MA. <Plymouth Co.PR #15748>
<16:45>...dated 7 July 1760, mentions sister **Rebecca WESTON;** Hannah SOULE, Rebecca SOULE, Priscilla WESTON wf of Eliphas, Faith DREW wf of Samuel; kinsman **Jonathan PETERSON;** Jael PETERSON, John PETERSON, Jonathan PETERSON Jr., Turner PETERSON; to kinsman **David PETERSON** son of **Jonathan** above, cedar swamp in Pembroke. Witnesses: Thomas WESTON, Peres HOWLAND, Elnathan WESTON. <16:46> Pr. 2 Mar. 1761, **Jonathan PETERSON,** yeoman of Duxbury, app'td admr.

Will of **Jacob PETERSON** of Duxbury MA. <Plymouth Co.PR #15777>
<29:219>...dated 10 Mar. 1778, mentions grandson **Benjamin PETERSON;** grandaughters **Sarah SMITH** wf of Benjamin & **Hannah PETERSON;** son in law **Benjamin SMITH,** executor. Witnesses: George PARTRIDGE, Judah HUNT, Deborah HUNT. <original> Bond 6 Dec. 1784, of **Benjamin SMITH,** cordwainer, exr. Sureties: Gamaliel BRADFORD & Judah HUNT, mariner of Duxbury. Witnesses: Noah SIMMONS, Isaac LOTHROP. <29:270> Inventory taken 5 Mar. 1785, by Gamaliel BRADFORD, Israel SILVESTER Jr. & John SAMSON, all of Duxbury; personal estate only. <original> Complaint 26 June 1792, of **Benjamin PETERSON** against **Benjamin SMITH,** exr., for neglecting to settle his account.

Estate of **Isaac PETERSON,** yeoman of Duxbury MA. <Plymouth Co.PR #15774>
<8:450> Letter/Bond 27 Jan. 1741, Eliphas WESTON of Duxbury app'td admr. Sureties: Joshua DELANO, Ezekiel SOULE. Witnesses: Joseph BRIDGHAM, Edward WINSLOW. <8:463> Inventory taken 26 Feb. 1741/42 by Joshua SOUL, Pelatiah WEST & Samuel WESTON, all of Duxbury. <9:42> Account of admr., 12 Jan 1742; Paid to: David PETERSON, Dr. BULFINCH, Richard ADAMS, Nathaniel DUNHAM, Ezekiel SOULE, John THOMAS, Jonathan PETERSON, William BREWSTER, Joseph DELLANO, Jedediah BOURNE, Dr. HARLOW, Jacob DINGLEY, Benjamin PRYER, Benjamin SAMSON, Joseph RUSSELL, Joshua DELANO, Rebecca WESTON, Joseph SIMMONS, Joshua SOULE, Timothy HAYWARD, Samuel WESTON, Joshua CUSHMAN, Nathaniel SOULE, Jonathan SOULE, Moses SOUL, Abisha SOUL, Pelatiah WEST, Amariah DELLANO, Eliphas WESTON, Jonathan SPRAGUE, necessarys to the widow and corn & meat for the family. <9:519> Division of real estate, 4 Apr. 1744, by Joshua SOULE, George PARTRIDGE, Robert STANDFORD & Joshua DELANO, all of Duxbury and Nathaniel LORING of Pembroke; to widow **Mary PETERSON,** her thirds; homeland divided among three children, viz: **Joel PETERSON, Faith, Priscilla** and grandaughters **Mary PETERSON & Orphan PETERSON,** daus of son **Daniel PETERSON.**

Guardianship of Children of **Daniel PETERSON,** late of Duxbury MA. <Plymouth Co.PR #15804>
<9:422> Letters/Bonds 6 Mar. 1744, Eliphas WESTON of Duxbury app'td gdn. of **Orphan PETERSON & Mary PETERSON.** Surety: Joshua DELANO of Duxbury. Witnesses: Edward WINSLOW, Barnabas TOMSON. <11:243> Account 7 Aug. 1749, of widow **Deborah PETERSON** & Eliphas WESTON, guardians; incl. to necessarys & tendance when I lay in with my last child; to the nursing & tendance of my oldest child five full years and youngest child seven full years.

Will of **Jonathan PETERSON,** yeoman/Practitioner of Pembroke MA. <Plymouth Co.PR #15783>
<9:409>..dated 20 Feb. 1744/5...wf **Lydia;** bequests to children being besides that already given to them; to eldest son **John PETERSON,** £60; to sons **Jonathan PETERSON & Ruben PETERSON** (executors) £1; to dau **Hopestill DELANO,** yoke of oxen & 5 sheep; to dau **Lydia SOUL,** cow & 5 sheep; all land in Pembroke to three sons, reserving to Anna NORRES/NORRIS who now keeps my house to have use of the new room for four years; if either son sells his share of land it must be to brothers. Witnesses: Thomas PARRIS, Samuel HILL, Josiah CUSHING; Pr. 24 May 1745. <9:514> Inventory taken 1 June 1745, by Elisha BISBEE, Josiah CUSHING, Joshua BEARCE, all of Pembroke; incl. three & a half acre English meadow, £100; house & land, £700; personal estate incl. drugs, vials & glasses, £288.5.8.; sworn to 3 June 1745 by exrs.

Will of **Jonathan PETERSON,** yeoman of Duxbury MA. <Plymouth Co.PR #15785>
<19:216>...dated 30 Apr. 1765, mentions wf **Jael;** sons **John PETERSON** (eldest son), **Jonathan PETERSON, David PETERSON, Turner PETERSON;** dau **Lurania PETERSON;** unborn child; Judah DELANO & John PETERSON, executors. Witnesses: Ezra ARNOLD, Caleb OLDHAM, Amaziah DELANO. <19:216> Pr. 24 May 1765. <19:214> Inventory taken 31 May 1765; incl. farm in the wood called the upper farm & Oldham farm joining to it; farm bought of the SPRAGUES; homestead bought of Joshua DELANO; half a cedar swamp in Pembroke. <19:217> Division of real estate, 3 June 1765, by Aaron SOUL, Esq. of Pembroke and Ezra ARNOLD & Peleg WADSWORTH of Duxbury, to widow **Jael PETERSON,** the homestead farm; to **John PETERSON,** half of SPRAGUE farm; to **Turner PETERSON,** half of SPRAGUE farm & half of OLDHAM farm;

to **David PETERSON**, half of Oldham farm and half of cedar swamp in Pembroke bought of Mercy WADSWORTH, the other half given to sd David by will of his great uncle **David PETERSON.** <19:497> Account of exrs., 4 Aug. 1767; Received from: Thomas CROADE, Benjamin SOUTHWORTH, Thomas HUNT, Nehemiah PETERSON, Judah DELANO and earnings from the Sloop "Industry"; Paid to: William CURTIS, Ichabod SIMMONS, Amaziah DELANO, Elijah PETERSON, John SAMSON, Henry MUNROE, Perez HOWLAND, William THOMAS, Thomas DAMMON, Job CROOKER, Zebdiel WESTON, Nathaniel SIMMONS, Sylvanus DREW, Briggs ALDEN, Levi LORING, Gamaliel BRADFORD Jr., Elijah TOWER, Abner DINGLEY, Benjamin PRIOR, David PETERSON, Nathaniel LORING, Mary WESTON, Thomas WESTON, Ezekiel SOUL, Dr. Benjamin STOCKBRIDGE, John THOMAS, Eleazer HARLOW, Ruth DELANO, Lucy THOMAS, George UFFEALDS, James HOVEY, Samuel TAYLOR, Aaron SOUL, Rebecca SOUL, Elisha FORD, Ebenezer SOUL, William WESTON, William RAND. <12:265> ...15 Mar. 1750, The subscribers being desired by Jonathan PETERSON & Capt. Hezekiah RIPLEY to appraise the Schooner "Molly", Richard ADAMS, Master; Signed by John OTIS, Malachy SALTER Jr., Job PRINCE.

==========

Guardianship of Children of **Jonathan PETERSON** of Duxbury MA. <Plymouth Co.PR #15786>
<18:228> Letter/Bond 21 May 1765, Levi LORING, yeoman of Duxbury app'td gdn. of **Jonathan PETERSON** above 14, being chosen by sd minor. Sureties: Judah DELANO & Ezra ARNOLD of Duxbury. <18:231> Letter/Bond 21 May 1765, Judah DELANO, yeoman of Duxbury, app'td gdn. of **John PETERSON,** above 14, being chosen by sd minor. Sureties: Aaron SOUL of Duxbury & Ezra ARNOLD of Pembroke. Letter/Bond 21 May 1765, widow **Jael PETERSON** app'td gdn. of **Lurania PETERSON.** Sureties: Briggs ALDEN & Ezra ARNOLD of Duxbury. <18:232> Letters/Bonds 21 May 1765, Judah DELANO app'td gdn. of **David & Turner PETERSON.** Witnesses to all bonds: Edward WINSLOW, Edward WINSLOW Jr. <19:496> Account, 5 Aug. 1767, of Judah DELANO, as gdn. of **David PETERSON;** incl. paid Nathaniel SAMSON & Jedediah SIMMONS for rates. <21:199> Letter/Bonds 7 Dec. 1772, widow **Jael PETERSON** app'td gdn. of **David PETERSON,** above 14 and **Turner PETERSON,** under 14. Sureties: Jonathan PETERSON of Duxbury & Joshua DILLINGHAM, blacksmith of Hanover. Witnesses: William CUSHING, Edward WINSLOW Jr. <21:217> Account, 4 Jan. 1773, of Judah DELANO, gdn. of **Turner PETERSON.**

==========

Estate of **Reuben PETERSON** of Duxbury MA. <Plymouth Co.PR #15813>
<34:57> Letter/Bond 5 Dec. 1795, Elijah PETERSON, yeoman of Duxbury, app'td admr. Sureties: Nehemiah PETERSON & Thaddeus PETERSON of Duxbury. Witnesses: William WATSON, Isaac LOTHROP.<original> Consent, 19 Dec. 1795, of widow **Elizabeth PETERSON** to appointment of admr. <35:459> Inventory taken 21 Dec. 1795, by Peres CHANDLER, Samuel CHANDLER & Isaiah ALDEN of Duxbury; incl. homestead farm, Keen Brook lot, Great pine lot, saw mill lot, Hammok meadow, Rocky point meadow. <35:512> Dower allowed, 25 May 1796, to widow **Elizabeth PETERSON.** <35:514> Notice. <35:514> Account of admr., 25 May 1796; Received of: William LORING, Nathaniel LORING, Nathaniel THOMAS, Luther WHITE; Paid to: Thomas PETERSON, William PETERSON, Perez CHANDLER, Samuel CHANDLER, James FORD, Nathaniel WILLIAMSON, William HOWLAND, Isaiah ALDEN, Nathaniel SAMSON, James WESTON, Judah PETERSON, Nathaniel JENNINGS, Col. C. PARTRIDGE as Vendue master, Timothy WILLIAMSON, Samuel PETERSON, Robert WILLIS, Dr. Isaac WINSLOW, Consider SIMMONS, Abner DINGLEY, Reuben DELANO for digging grave, James DINGLEY.

==========

PLYMOUTH COUNTY DEEDS: (re: Joseph PETERSON, grantor**)**

<18:5> - 1706/7, "widow of John DOTY".
<33:198> - 1739, Joseph PETERSON & son Joseph, homestead, etc.
<47:80> - 1742, Joseph PETERSON as next male heir of Isaac PETERSON son of John, releases to Isaac's daughters, Priscilla, Jael & Faith.
<38:125> - 1746, Joseph PETERSON Jr. of Duxbury to Isaac SIMMONS Jr. of same.

(References only to the name **Joseph PETERSON,** grantor: <11:73> 1715; <12:59> 1715; <15:91> 1716; <33:106> 1739; <87:16> 1799.)

MICRO #9 OF 11

Estate of **Joseph PETERSON,** yeoman of Duxbury MA. <Plymouth Co.PR>
<12:86> Letter/Bond 1 Apr. 1751, Kenelm BAKER, yeoman of Marshfield app'td admr. Sureties: Ebenezer FISH & Jonathan PETERSON of Duxbury. Witnesses: David JOHNSON, Caleb TURNER. <12:226> Inventory taken by Thomas FORD, Isaac SIMONS, John BAKER; sworn to by admr. 3 June 1751. <12:517> Account of admr., 10 July 1752; Paid to: Jabez WHITTAMORE, Thomas FORD, Aaron SOULE, James SPRAGUE, William SOUTHWORTH, Susannah WHITE, Dr. HARLOW, Seth HACK, John THOMAS, Joseph BOYCE, Samuel BAKER, Elenor BAKER, Ruben CARVER, James SPRAGUE 3d, Joseph BARTLETT, J. SAMSON, Isaac SIMONS, Josiah WALKER, William MACKFARLAND, Nehemiah THOMAS, Barnabas FORD, Thomas LAPHAM, Robert HOWLAND, Thomas WESTON, Amaziah DELANO, William CORBET, Nathaniel WINSLOW, Levi KEEN and necessaries set off to the widow and provisions for the family.

==========

Estate of **Joseph PETERSON** of Duxbury MA. <Plymouth Co.PR #15787>
<original> Bond 19 Oct. 1818 of Zenas DELANO as admr. de bonis non. Sureties: Isaiah ALDEN & Benjamin ALDEN of Duxbury. Witnesses: Mercy ALDEN, Ruth ALDEN. (Note on bond calls **Zenas DELANO** a grandson of dec'd, the son of **Sarah DELANO** dec'd.) <46:450> Letter 16 Nov. 1818, **Zenas DELANO,** blacksmith of Duxbury app'td admr. d.b.n. <49:562> Inventory taken 19 Oct. 1808 by Isaiah ALDEN, James SIMMONS, Gideon HARLOW; mentions dower of the dec'd widow **Lydia PETERSON** and 20 acres of land with small dwelling house appraised at Ł181. <49:563> Division, 16 Nov. 1818, estate settled upon **Zenas DELANO** one of heirs, he to pay other heirs, viz: heirs of **Susanna EWELL, Mary WESTON,**

Abraham PETERSON & Joseph PETERSON, all dec'd and to **Lydia PETERSON**.. <49:320> Petition 21 May 1818 for guardianship for **Lydia PETERSON**, singlewoman, non compos.

NATHANIEL SOULE[2] (George[1])

Will of **Jacob SOULE**, yeoman of Dartmouth MA. <Bristol Co.PR>
<11:451>...dated 12 Aug. 1747...to son **Stephen SOULE**, west end of my homestead farm whare I now dwell...bounded by land of Ichabod EDDEY and ALLEN...also salt medow lying at bush flat, all waring apiril, best bead/bed & bead stead, two blankits, one sheet, best civerled, next to begest pot & grate cittel/kettle, loome & tacklin...to son **Joseph SOULE**, south side of my sd farm... bounded by land of Robert TRIP...and salt meadow; sons **Nathaniel SOULE, Benjamin SOULE**; daus **Elizabeth TRIP, Rosamond POTTER**; grandchildren **Phebe WAIT, Jeremiah WAIT**; son **Joseph**, executor. <11:453> Pr. 3 May 1748. <11:457> Inventory taken 2 Mar. 1747/8.
(Note: The will is partially transcribed in the files but it was not completed.)

Will of **Nathaniel SOULE** (son of Jacob, dec'd) of Dartmouth MA. <Bristol Co.PR>
<21:77>...dated 1763. <21:81> Pr. 25 Dec. 1769. <21:115> Inventory.

Will of **Capt. Nathaniel SOULE** of Dartmouth MA. <Bristol Co.PR>
<19:417>...dated 12 Mar. 1764...to youngest son **Wessen SOULE**, house & land I bought of Stephen WILBORE, land bought of Christopher GIFFORD and one & a half acre salt meadow lying in ye horsneck, all in Dartmouth...to son **Henry SOULE**, one half of homsted...that I bought of Zachariah ALLEN, at **Henry's** decease land to go to his wf **Barbrey** and at her decease to go to grandson **Nathaniel SOULE** and then to his male heir...& so to continue in that line from my sd grandson untill three generations be expired but if my sd grandson **Nathaniel** should happen to dye & leave no lawfull living heir then it shall go to my grandson **Henry SOULE** and unto his male heir in like manner...to son **James SOULE** (& his wf **Mary**), remainder of homstid farm...and his heirs for...male or female...untill three generations from him be expired; grandson **Henry SOUL**; grandson **James SOWLE**, son of son **Wesson**...to son **Wesson**, ye hye cubbard, ye beed/bed which his mother my wife brought with her when I married her, a great iron kittle/kettle all which is in his possesion all ready ...to son **Jonathan SOULE**, land laid out at Quanipauge in Dartmouth; sons **Henry & James**, executors Witnesses: John SOWLE, Job DAVIS, Eliger POTTER. <original> Warrant to appraise, 26 May 1766 to John SOUL, Job ALMY Jr., gent. & Benjamin SOUL, yeoman, all of Dartmouth. <19:457> Inventory taken 2 June 1766 by appraisers; total estate, £105.5s9d. <original> Petition, 18 June 1766, of **Henry SOWLE**...as I live at a considerable distance from my sd brother, I decline serveing, therefore request you to grant adm. wholy to him. <19:420> Pr. 30 July 1766, **James SOULE** appt'd admr. <21:26> Receipt, 1 Sept. 1767, of **Henry SOULE** to brother **James SOWLE**, exr., for his share. Witnesses: Thomas SPOONER, Ruth SOWLE. Receipt, 18 Feb. 1769, of **Jonathan SOWLE**, to brother **James SOWLE**, exr., for his share. Witnesses: Joseph SOWLE, Elisabeth NOLES.

Estate of **Nathaniel SOULE** of Westport MA. <Bristol Co.PR>
...1805...<41:255> Inventory presented 25 Apr. 1805. <42:218> Appraisal to divide real estate, 5 Nov. 1805, by Christopher CORNELL & William ALMY; to widow **Abigail SOULE**, one third, dower was $2100.00 and to the following children, viz: **Ebenezer B. SOULE** (eldest son), **John H. SOULE, Rebecca BRIGHTMAN, Henry SOULE, Polly SOULE, Phebe SOULE.** <109:49> Notice, 1805.

Estate of **Nathaniel SOULE.** <Bristol Co.PR>
...1847...<91:72> Adm. <132:223;143:489> Guardianship. <150:103> Adm. <156:98> Bond. <195:446> Inventory. <218:451,532> Account.

George SOULE to son **Nathaniel SOULE.** <Plymouth Col.Deeds 3:245>
...20 Jan. 1658...half of purchase lands at Coaksett, Cushanett & Ponigansett.

Estate of **Henry SOULE** of Westport MA. <Bristol Co.PR 41:260,261>
Inventory ordered, 2 Oct. 1804, presented 7 May 1805.

Estate of **Henry SOULE** of Fairhaven MA. <Bristol Co.PR 74:84>
Declination of widow **Ester SOULE** to administer estate; 6 May 1834, Joseph BATES app'td.

Estate of **Jonathan SOULE**, mariner of Freetown MA. <Bristol Co.PR>
<20:478> Inventory taken 25 Feb. 1769, by Ambrose BARNABY, Nathan SIMMONS, Joshua HATHAWAY; no real estate mentioned. <146:136> 27 Feb. 1769, widow **Molly SOUL** and Benjamin CLAVELAND, yeoman of Freetown, app'td admrs.

Will of **Jonathan SOULE** of Dartmouth MA. <Bristol Co.PR 26:156,158>
...dated 2 10mth 1779, mentions wf **Lydia** and following children, viz: **Joseph SOULE, Jonathan SOULE, David SOULE, James SOULE, Susanna RUSSELL, Thankful SOULE, Mary TRIPP, Jethro SOULE.** Pr. 2 Nov. 1779.

BRISTOL COUNTY DEEDS: (re: Jonathan SOULE, grantor**)**

<27:214> - 1738, et al to John WILBORE
<28:93> - 1739, to Benjamin WAIT.
<39:81> - 1752, to John DYER.
<39:89> - 1752, to Christopher GIFFORD.

BRISTOL COUNTY DEEDS, cont-d: (re: Jonathan SOULE, grantor**)**

<40:219> - 1753, to Elisha MASON.
<41:539> - 1756, to David JONSON Jr.
<48:21> - 1765, to James SOULE.
<51:109> - 1768, to Stephen PICKHAM.
<52:253> - 1769, to Joseph SOULE.
<60:126> - 1780, to David SOULE
<66:459> - 1788, to Benjamin DAVIS.
<66:585> - 1788, to Preserved TRIPP.
<63:27> - 1784, to John MACOMBER.
<62:253> - 1784, to Joshua CORNELL.

PATIENCE SOULE[2] (George[1])

John HASCALL Sr. & Jr. of Middleboro MA to **Jacob TOMSON** of same. <Plymouth Co.Deeds 16:91> ...6 Feb. 1699/1700, John HASCALL Sr. and John HASCALL Jr., for £3 sold to Jacob TOMSON...our one half of that whole share of upland which did formerly belong to George SOULE dec'd...in Majors Purchase in Plymouth, lots #3 & #33. Witnesses: Isaac FULLER, William HASCALL. Ack. 12 June 1707 by John Jr. Ack. 1st Tues. Mar. 1718 by William HASCALL & 3rd Tues. June 1722 by Isaac FULLER. Rec. 19 Sept. 1722.

William HASCALL of Middleboro MA receipts to **John HASCALL.** <Plymouth Co.Deeds 11:77> ...9 Sept. 1709, William HASCALL has received from brother John HASCALL his share of estate of father John HASCALL dec'd...25 acres of land. Witnesses: Jacob TOMSON, John TOMSON Jr. Ack. 2 Feb. 1712/3 by William. Rec. 12 July 1715.

John HASCALL of Middleboro MA to **Benjamin SOULE** of Plymton. <Plymouth Co.Deeds 11:33> ...22 Sept. 1709, John HASCALL, for £6 sold to Benjamin SOUL...one half of land containing 100 acres...28th lot in last division of the 26 Men's Purchase in Middleboro...formerly laid out in ye right of my honoured father John HASCALL dec'd & Francis WALKER. Witnesses: Joseph PHINNEY, Job OTIS. Rec. 10 May 1714.

Thomas DRINKWATER of Taunton MA receipts to **John HASCALL** of Middleboro. <Plymouth Co.Deed 11:77> ...10 Sept.1711, Thomas DRINKWATER & wf Elizabeth have received from John HASCALL...her full share in estate of father John HASCALL of Middleboro dec'd...and quit claim unto sd John any claim she might have. Witnesses: John EDDY, Ebenezer EDDY. Rec. 12 July 1715.

Thomas PAIN of Freetown MA receipt to **John HASCALL** of Middleboro. <Plymouth Co.Deeds 11:78> ...6 Aug. 1712, Thomas PAIN & wf Susannah have received from brother John HASCALL...£5, our part & portion of ye estate of our honoured father John HASCALL dec'd. Witnesses: John WETHRELL, William DAVIS, Jeremiah WETHRELL. Ack. same day by grantors. Rec. 12 July 1715.

Josiah HASKALL receipts to **John HASCALL** of Middleboro MA. <Plymouth Co.Deeds 11:194> ...22 Feb. 1716, Josiah HASKALL has received from brother John HASCALL...his right in estate of Father John HASCALL of Middleborough. Witnesses: Peter THACHER, Samuel PRATT. Rec. 25 Feb. 1715/6

John HASCALL of Middleborough MA to **Jonathan BRYANT** of Pembroke. <Plymouth Co.Deeds 21:72> ...4 Oct. 1718, John HASCALL, for £4.10s sold to Jonathan BRYANT...two share of land which fell by lot unto me in the last division in the South Purchase in Middleborough 10 June 1718. The one of the sd shares being the sixt part of the 76th lot and did belong unto the original right of my Honoured Father John HASCALL Sr. and the other share being the eighth part of the 77th lot and did belong unto the original right of my Uncle Francis WALKER & my self. Witnesses: Francis BARKER, Isaac BARKER. Ack. 12 Mar. 1725/6, by John at Killingsly CT. Rec. 27 Dec. 1726.

John HASKALL of Middleboro MA & **Samuel CUTLER** of Woodstock MA. <Plymouth Co.Deeds 15:225> ...29 Sept. 1721, John HASKALL & Samuel CUTLER, husbandmen...agree to exchange land...John & wf Mary convey to Samuel their 100 acre homestead in Middleboro...being ye one half of the hundred acre lot given by his Grandfather SOULE to his Father & Mother with some addition to it, also lands sd HASCALL bought of Isaac FULLER, Ichabod KING and the TOMSONS, all joyning together and bounded by land of Mr. THACHER & Mr. NELSON, land of Joseph BATE which he bought of sd HASKALL and the old hundred acre lot formerly belonging to Philip DELANO...in return Samuel conveys to John...500 acres in Killingsley CT...surveyed & laid out by Joseph LEVINS, Jabez ALLYN and surveyor Thomas KIMBERLY...bounded by land laid out to Gov. SALTONSTALL & "one" THOMPSON. Witnesses: Jacob TOMSON, Samuel THOMAS. Rec. 14 Feb. 1721/2.

PLYMOUTH COUNTY DEEDS: (re: HASKELL/HASCALL)

<10:385> - 1 Feb. 1699/1700, John HASCALL Jr. of Middleboro from John EDDY of Taunton.
<9:330> - 8 Mar. 1710/1, John HASCALL from David THOMAS of Middleboro.
<11:194> - 15 Feb. 1715/6, Henry BRIGHTMAN renews deed to John HASCALL.
<15:197> - , John HASKELL from Ichabod KING.
<15:225> - , John HASKELL from Stephen BORDEN(sp).
<15:225> - , John HASKELL from John KING.

(Note: References only to the surnames **NELSON, HASKELL** in Plymouth Co.Deeds: 62:15,20;80:276;85:230,231;87:122;90:188;91:200,203.)

Heirs of **Thomas DRINKWATER.** <Plymouth Co.Deeds>
<26:12> 18 June 1729, dau **Elizabeth DRINKWATER** of Freetown, one ninth to John DRINKWATER of N. Yarmouth. <26:13> 10 Nov. 1730, Joseph DRINKWATER of N. Yarmouth, one ninth to Samuel EDDY Jr. of Middleboro. <27:114> 25 Apr. 1732, Samuel DRINKWATER of Dighton, one ninth to John DRINKWATER of N. Yarmouth. <27:115> 25 Apr. 1732, John DRINKWATER of N. Yarmouth sells the one ninth to Samuel EDDY Jr. <30:24> 10 Dec. 1734, Patience DRINKWATER of Swansea, one ninth to Samuel EDDY Jr. <16:41> 1 Aug. 1721, Walter DRINKWATER of Freetown, one ninth to James RAYMENT. <17:30> 17 Nov. 1722, William DRINKWATER of Newport, one ninth to James RAYMENT. <17:30> 12 June 1723, George DRINKWATER of Freetown, one ninth to James RAYMENT. <21:35> 19 Mar. 1724, John DRINKWATER of Freetown, one ninth to James RAYMENT. <24:147> 20 June 1729, John DRINKWATER of N. Yarmouth, one ninth to Samuel EDDY Jr.

Will of **Squire HASKELL** of Killingley CT. <original in files>
...dated 9 May 1774, mentions wf **Elizabeth**; heirs of dau **Sarah**; son **Jonathan HASKELL**; daus **Mary & Susannah**; heirs of dau **Unes/Eunice**; sons **Squire HASKELL, Jeremiah HASKELL, Samuel HASKELL & David HASKELL.** Witnesses sworn 8 July 1774. Pr. 2 Aug. 1774.

MICRO #10 OF 11

Estate of **Thomas PAINE** of Norton MA. <Bristol Co.PR>
<16:346> Adm. & Inventory, 1759. <16:395> Account.

Will of **Thomas PAINE,** husbandman of Freetown MA. <Bristol Co.PR>
<16:420>...dated 27 Oct. 1752, mentions wf **Annable**; four sons **Ralph PAIN, Job PAIN, Charles PAIN, Peter PAIN**; four daus **Mary FARROW, Betty WINSLOW, Patince WINSLOW, Thankfull PAIN**; son **Job**, executor. Witnesses: William CANEDY, George WINSLOW, Ambrose BARNABY; sworn to by CANEDY & BARNABY, 6 Nov. 1759. <16:422> Pr. 6 Nov. 1759, **Job PAIN**, exr. <16:435> Inventory taken 8 Nov. 1759, by Capt. Amberos/Ambrose BARNEBE, David EVANS Jr., Thomas HATHAWAY, all of Freetown; no real estate mentioned; total estate, L42.19s9d; sworn to by exr., 15 Nov. 1759.

BRISTOL COUNTY DEEDS: (re: Thomas PAINE, grantor)

<18:410> - 6 Feb. 1728/9, Thomas PAINE of Freetown to John MARSHALL of same.
<25:217> - 8 Sept 1735, Thomas PAINE, yeoman to John MARSHALL, shipwright, both of Freetown.
<35:55> - 8 Feb. 1744/5, Thomas PAINE, merchant of Boston to George LEONARD of Norton.
<37:314> - 18 Jan. 1745/6, Thomas PAINE to David EVANS, yeomen of Freetown. Wf Anible PAINE releases dower. Rec. 19 June 1750.
<37:315> - 1 Mar. 1732/5, Thomas PAINE to David EVANS, yeomen of Freetown. Wf Anible consents.
<39:31> - 12 May 1739, Thomas PAINE, yeoman to Philip HATHAWAY, mariner, both of Freetown. Wf Anible releases dower. Ack. 29 Apr. 1752 by both. Rec. 13 May 1752.
<41:93> - 5 Mar. 1745/6, Thomas PAINE, yeoman of Freetown to Ralph PAINE, shipwright of same.
<41:180> - 1754, Thomas PAINE to Benjamin PETTINGILL.
<41:302> - 1755, Thomas PAINE to Solomon BATES.
<58:188> - 1778, Thomas PAINE to Benjamin WELLMAN.
<73:309> - 1794, Thomas PAINE et ux et al to Ebenezer DAGGETT.
<73:566> - 1794, Thomas PAINE et ux et al to Otis CAPRON.

Thomas PAINE of Freetown MA to **Ralph PAINE** of same. <Bristol Co.Deeds 30:381>
...27 May 1740, Thomas PAINE, yeoman sells to Ralph PAINE, shipwright...land in Freetown. Wf Annable PAINE releases dower. Ack. 7 July 1740 by both. Rec. 1741/2.

Thomas PAINE of Freetown MA to **Ralph PAINE** of same. <Bristol Co.Deeds 41:93>
...14 Jan. 1754, Thomas PAINE, yeoman sells to Ralph PAINE, shipwright...southerly half of homestead in Freetown. Ack. 4 Feb. 1754. Rec. 2 Feb. 1754.

Thomas PAINE of Freetown MA to **Job PAINE** of same. <Bristol Co.Deeds 43:555>
...14 Jan. 1754, Thomas PAINE, yeoman sells to Job PAINE, ship carpenter...northerly half of homestead in Freetown. Ack. 23 Apr. 1759. Rec. 1 Nov. 1759.

Lydia WARE of Dighton MA to **Job PAINE** of Freetown. <Bristol Co.Deeds 48:198>
...10 Oct. 1764, Lydia WARE, widow & executrix of William WARE, dec'd, for payment of debts, sells to Job PAINE, shipwright...land in Dighton. Ack. 20 Oct. 1764.

BRISTOL COUNTY DEEDS: (re: Job PAINE, grantor)

<52:244> - 20 June 1769, Job PAINE, shipwright of Freetown to Samuel BARNABY, yeoman of same, land in Dighton, formerly part of estate of Dr. William WARE. Wf Hannah releases dower.
<67:79> - 1 Nov. 1787, Job PAINE of Freetown to George SHOVE. Wf Hannah releases dower.
<68:277> - 17 Nov. 1789, Job PAINE, shipwright of Freetown, debtor to Nicholas HATHAWAY.
<68:278> - 17 Nov. 1789, Job PAINE, shipwright of Freetown, debtor to Philip HATHAWAY Jr.
<69:14> - 8 June 1790, Job PAINE, shipwright of Freetown to Lydia TERRY, spinster of same, land in Freetown bounded by land set off to Philip HATHAWAY be execution.
<79:1> - 1 Dec. 1784, Job PAINE & wf Hannah et al, as heirs of Silas TERRY dec'd, confirm sale of land by Silas TERRY to Ebenezer & Job TERRY. Rec. 16 Apr. 1800.

BRISTOL COUNTY DEEDS, cont-d: (re: Job PAINE, grantor)

<103:385> - 21 Nov. 1817, Job PAINE, shipwright of Freetown to Ebenezer PIERCE, Esq. of same, the land in Freetown morgaged by Silas PAINE.
<104:354> - 29 July 1818, Job PAINE, shipwright of Freetown to John T. LAWTON & George G. LAWTON, land in Freetown. Wf Betsy releases dower.
<107:383> - 1820, Job PAINE to Ezra DEAN.
<108:48> - 1820, Job PAINE to Olive HATHAWAY.
<108:51> - 1820, Job PAINE to Lydia DEAN.
<108:54> - , Job PAINE to Elkanah DAGGETT.
<108:176> - , Job PAINE to David EVANS.
<108:192> - , Job PAINE to John NICHOLS et al.

Will of **Job PAYNE**, shipwright of Freetown MA. <Bristol Co.PR 38:35>
...dated 29 Dec. 1800...to sons **Silas PAYNE & Job PAYNE** (executors), the homestead farm; to daus **Susanna PAYNE & Hannah PAYNE**, priviledge of living in the house while single and all indoor movables; to daus **Bety PIERCE & Lydia DAILY**, $1.00 each. Witnesses: Warden PAYNE, Job WINSLOW, Molbon HATHAWAY. <original> Letter/Bond 3 Feb. 1801, **Job PAYNE & Silas PAYNE** app'td admrs. Sureties: Malbon HATHAWAY & Warden PAYNE, shipwrights of Freetown. Witnesses: James HATHAWAY, Olive PAINE.

BRISTOL COUNTY DEEDS: (re: Silas PAINE, grantor)

<86:488> - 10 Oct. 1806, Silas PAINE, shipwright of Freetown to Job PAINE, shipwright & Seth CHASE, mariner of Freetown. Ack. & Rec. 10 Oct. 1806.
<87:475> - 14 Sept 1807, Silas PAINE to Job PAINE, shipwrights of Freetown, mortgage.
<88:232> - 11 Jan. 1808, Silas PAINE to Job PAINE, shipwrights of Freetown, mortgage.
<88:347> - 11 Mar. 1808, Silas PAINE, shipwright of Freetown to Hampton PEIRCE, caulker of same, half of house & land in Freetown. Wf Chloe releases dower.

SUSANNA SOULE[2] (George[1])

Clement WEST of N. Kingstown RI to **Benjamin MORY.** <N. Kingstown RI Deeds 5A:220>
...(not dated), Clement WEST, for one hundred (worn), sold to Benjamin MORY...67 acres in N. Kingstown...bounded by land laid out to Daniel BLY & John A(worn) and land of Joseph NORTHUP & J. CARD. Witnesses: Benjamin BENTLY, Christopher PHILLIPS. Rec. June 1724.

Will of **Francis WAST/WEST** of N. Kingstown RI. <N. Kingstown RI PR, ("badly worn")>
<6:160>...dated (worn), mentions two eldest sons **Peter WAST** (under twenty --) **& ( )**; wf **Sarah**; eldest daus **Susannah WAST, Sarah WAST & Mary WAST** (all under 18). <6:162> Oath, 13 Oct. 172(4) of witnesses to the will, viz: Samuel FONES, John FON(ES & Marg)aret FONES. Pr. 10 Nov. 1724. <6:163> Inventory taken 27 Oct. 1724, by William SPENCER, John VAUGHAN, Samuel CASEY. <6:164> Letter (10 Nov. 1724), widow **Sarah WAST** app'td admx. <6:165> Release (no date) of eldest son **Peter WAST** ...of his right in two pe(rcels of la)nd which his father dyed intestate of unt(o his b)rothers (viz): **Francis & Thomas WAST** & theire heires provide(d he ha)ve what his father has given him in his li(fetime).

Estate of **James CARD.** <N. Kingstown RI PR 1-5:52>
...Mar. 1704/5, widow **Martha CARD** app'td admx.

Rhode Island Agents to **Martha CARD et al.** <N. Kingstown RI Deeds 1:56>
...3 June 1709, Agents of the Colony of Rhode Island sold certain vacant lands in the Narraganset Country to several Inhabitants of Kingstown, incl. Martha CARD.

Jeremiah FONES of James Town RI to **Clement WEST** of Kingstown RI. <N. Kingstown RI Deeds 4:218>
..."1720/21", Jeremiah FONES & wf Martha, for £11 sold to Clement WEST...69 acres in Kingstown... bounded by land of Daniel BLY, sd FONES, Joseph NORTHUP & John AUSTIN. Witnesses: (Rober)t HALL, (Abigai)l HALL.

Jeremiah FONES of James TOWN RI to **James CARD** of same. <N. Kingstown RI Deeds 4:219>
...17 Jan. 1720/21, Jeremiah FONES & wf Martha...in consideration of the Great Love and Affection which we do bare unto our Son James CARD have given...69 acres in Kingstown...bounded by land of Clement WEST & NORTHUP. Witnesses: Robert HALL, Abigail HALL. Rec. ( ) Jan. 1720/1.

NORTH KINGSTOWN RI DEEDS:

<3:318> - , Jeremiah FONES from John FONES.
<5A:236> - 18 Nov. 1724, Jeremiah FONES & wf Martha to Peleg CARD. Martha signs 25 Nov. 1724.
<5A:26> - , Jeremiah FONES from John ALLEN.
<5B:180> - 1727, Jeremiah FONES, yeoman to son Joseph FONES, mariner of N. Kingstown.
<7B:190> - 1734/5, James CARD & wf Barbara to Samuel RATHBONE.

Will of **Jeremiah FONES** of N. Kingstown RI. <N. Kingstown RI PR>
<8:156>...dated 12 Dec. 1727, mentions (worn) FONES, the dau of son (worn), when she comes to the

age of 18; to son **Joseph FONES**, homstead which has already been given by deed of gift, also two silver spoons; to son **John FONES**, Ł5 and (worn) silver spoons; to grandson **John DAVIS** son of dec'd dau **Margaret DAVIS**...my grate two eared silver (cupp) when he comes to the age of 21; to son **Daniel FONES**, all lands to the westward of my dwelling house...bounded by land of William CHADSEY, when he reaches 21; to sons **Samuel FONES & Thomas FONES**, remaining part of my land to the eastward of the Pine Swamp River, bounded by land of Mr. BRIMLEY and (worn)es ELDRED. Witnesses: Francis WILLETT, William SPENCER, Job TRIPP; sworn to 13 July 1747 by WILLETT & SPENCER, 10 Aug. 1747 by TRIPP. <8:160> Inventory taken 2 & 4 (worn); incl. silver spoons, cupp. <8:162> Letter 13 July 1747, widow **Martha FONES** app'td exx.

NORTH KINGSTOWN RI DEEDS: (re: BARBER)

<1:44> - 16 Feb. 1709/10, Moses BARBER & wf Susanna to son William BARBER.
<1:98> - , Moses BARBER & wf Susanna to son Moses BARBER Jr. ("14th yr Maj. reign"). Rec. Nov. 1705 <1715?>.
<1:153> - , John BARBER to Moses BARBER.
<2:47> - , John BARBER from Beriah BROWN.
<2:131> - , Moses BARBER from Pettequamscut Purchasers.
<3:211> - , John BARBER to Samuel BOONE.
<5A:85> - 1722, Moses BARBER & wf Susanna to son Samuel BARBER, reserving for life.
<5A:224>- , William BARBER to Stephen WILCOX.
<5A:40> - , William BARBER from William HERRINGTON.
<9A:43> - 1740, Benjamin BARBER from Samuel STURTEVANT.

MYLES STANDISH

ALEXANDER STANDISH^2 (Myles^1)

MICRO #1 OF 4

Hannah GUSHE of Raynham MA to **Samuel GUSHEE.** <Bristol Co.Deeds 65:200>
...26 Jan. 1785, Hannah GUSHE, widow of Abraham, for £12 sold to son Samuel GUSHEE...21 acres in Raynham...bounded by road that leads to Bridgewater and land of Capt. SOPER and Elijah GUSHEE... together with all rights in the Island in Nepenicket Pond in Bridgewater...also right in cedar swamps in Raynham, Taunton or Bridgewater, it being in the whole a landed estate decended to me from my Honoured father Seth STAPLES late of Taunton dec'd. Witnesses: Elijah GUSHEE, Israel WASHBURN. Rec. 31 Jan. 1786.

BRISTOL COUNTY DEEDS: (re: GUSHEE)

<66:172> - 28 Nov. 1771, Abraham GUSHEE Jr.. Ack. Mar. 1787 by witness after Abraham's death.
<75:183> - 20 Oct. 1796, Abraham GUSHEE to Almond GUSHEE, rights in estate of father Abraham.
<80:8> - 1796, Almond GUSHEE of Raynham, grantor. Solomon SNOW also signs.
<82:367> - 1796, Almond GUSHEE of Raynham, grantor.
<88:216> - 1796, Almond GUSHEE, grantor. Ack. 1797.
<89:148> - 19 Feb. 1796, Almond GUSHEE of Raynham, grantor. Ack. 5 Oct. 1803.

(References only to the surname **GUSHEE**: <53:60> 18 May 1770. <54:420> 11 June 1772. <56:365> 14 Mar. 1781. <61:189> 15 Nov. 1782. <62:27> 20 Aug. 1783. <65:197> 31 Jan. 1786.
References only to the name **Almond GUSHEE**, grantor: <75:227> 17 Nov. 1796. <75:292> 7 Jan. 1797. <76:357> 22 Jan.1798. <76:358> 22 Jan. 1798. <77:23> 28 Apr. 1798. <78:196> 10 Sept. 1799. <153:367> 1837. <162:447;179:24,26,421,425,428,430,433,436;180:358>

Will of **David GUSHEE**of Dighton MA. <Bristol Co.PR>
<24:211>...dated 18 June 1770; mentions wf **Sarah** and children viz: **May GUSHEE, Joseph GUSHEE, David GUSHEE.** <24:212> Pr. 18 Dec. 1775.

Will of **Elijah GUSHEE,** gent. of Raynham MA. <Bristol Co.PR>
<75:71>...dated 31 Mar. 1819, mentions wf **Phebe** and children, viz: **Elijah GUSHEE, Williams GUSHEE Jairns GUSHEE, Sally WILLIAMS, Jemima GUSHEE, Julia Ann GUSHEE.** Pr. 10 Apr. 1835. <75:80> Inv. <75:266> Dower to widow.

Will of **Elijah GUSHEE** of Raynham MA. <Bristol Co.PR>
<94:130>...dated 30 May 1849, mentions wf **Mehala**; mother living; two daus **Sarah K. WILBUR, Martha W. HOBART**; two sons **William A. GUSHEE, Edwin GUSHEE.** <173:8> Pr.

Estate of **Abraham GUSHEE** of Raynham MA. <Bristol Co.PR>
<94:4> Inventory. <95:38> Account. <96:243> Surety discharged. <91:497> Guardianship, 7 Mar. 1848 **Elizabeth D. GUSHEE** app'td gdn. of **Samuel GUSHEE & Laura A. GUSHEE.** <102:239;104:211> Accounts.

BRISTOL COUNTY DEEDS: (re GUSHEE, "all on old index")

Abbie - Adm. <171:134>.
Abraham - Inv. <24:153>; Will <27:528>; Account <28:44>; 1847: Adm., Inv., Account, etc. <91:340,465;94:23;96:243;116:393;156:137,527;162:140,539>; Gdn. <129:115;130:79>.
Almond - Account <28:46>; Gdn. <130:79>; (not on index) <129:114>.
Artemas D. - Gdn. <133:69>.
Cruse - Gdn. <130:62>.
Edmund - Gdn. <129:114>.
Edward - Gdn. <133:69>.
Julia A. - Will <226:446>; Notice <227:508>; Pr. <228:212>.
Laura A. - Gdn. <91:497>; Inv. <94:4>; Account <95:38>; Surety <96:243>; Account <102:239>; Account <104:211>; Gdn. <136:118,309;140:127,324>; Sale of land <206:494>; Bond <208:286,293>; Account <217:310,401>.
Lois D. - Adoption <225:192>.
Mary - Inv. <49:87>; Insolvency <49:197>; Report <49:520>; Account <50:125,324>; Notice <110:101>; Adm. <151:57>.
Molly - Gdn. <130:62>.
Rachel - Adm. <166:95>; Inv. <195:48>; Account <217:210>.
Samuel - Will <81:493>; Notice <115:183>; Gdn. <136:118,309;140:127,324;144:599>; Bond <172:150;174:75>; Citation <176:126>; Inv. <197:577>; Sale of land <206:494;215:252>; Bond <208:286,293>; Accounts <217:310,401;220:598>.
Seth - Notice <121:440>; Gdn. <130:62>; Will <183:529>; Pr. <188:388>; Inv. <195:383>; Account <217:513>

BRISTOL COUNTY PROBATE, cont-d: (re: GUSHEE)

Susanna	- Adm. <91:280>; Adm. <156:129>; Bond <162:132>.
William	- Gdn. <130:354>

Will of **Williams GUSHEE** of Raynham MA. <Bristol Co.PR>
<95:453>...dated 7 Aug. 1850, mentions wf **Martha**, sons **OLIVER W. GUSHEE, Frederic W. GUSHEE.** (the dec'd "apparently brother of **Elijah & Jairns GUSHEE**"). <174:241> Pr. 5 Nov. 1850.

BRISTOL COUNTY PROBATE: (re: GATCHELL/GASHETT)

Henry	- Will <9:59>; Pr. <9:58>; Inventory <9:132>.
John	- Will & Pr. <6:372>; Inv. <6:378>; Adm. <7:242>; Account <7:244>; Resig. <7:252>; Inv. <7:278>; Account <10:96>.
Mary	- Will <9:75>; Pr. <9:74>; Inv. <9:77>; Account <9:257,270>; Receipt <9:259>; Gdn. <8:90>.
Simeon	- Gdn. <127:347>.
Susanna	- Gdn. <8:90>.
Thomas	- Will <9:131>; Pr. <9:130>; Inv. <9:133>; Account <9:258>.

Almond GUSHE of Barretston MA to **Elijah GUSHE** of Raynham MA. <Bristol Co.Deeds 81:562>
...7 Mar. 1801, Almond GUSHE, yeoman of Barretston, Lincoln co., for $110.00 sold to Elijah GUSHE gent...five acre cedar swamp in Titicut Swamp...bounded by land of Amos HALL and land formerly of John KING. Nancy GUSHE signs. Witnesses: Abraham SOULE, Elijah GUSHE. Ack. 10 Mar. 1801 at Raynham by Almond. Rec. 7 Dec. 1802.

Will of **Elijah GUSHEE**, gent. of Raynham MA. <Bristol Co.PR>
<75:71>...dated 31 Mar. 1819, mentions wf **Phebe**; sons **Elijah GUSHE & Williams GUSHE**; son **Jairus GUSHE** (under 21); daus **Sally WILLIAMS, Jemima GUSHE, Julia Ann GUSHE** (minor). Pr. 10 Apr. 1835. <75:80> Inventory. <75:266> Dower.

Will of **Elijah GUSHEE** of Raynham MA. <Bristol Co.PR>
<94:130>...dated 1849. <173:8> Bond.

BRISTOL COUNTY DEEDS: (re: Samuel JONES, all on index to 1840**)**

<52:536> -	1770,	Samuel JONES from John GARNER.
<53:52> -	1770,	Samuel JONES from father Timothy JONES.
<66:172> -	28 Nov. 1771,	Samuel JONES from Abraham GUSHEE Jr., half of land Abraham bought of Jonathan HAYWARD; both men yeomen of Raynham.
<77:368> -	23 Feb. 1796,	Samuel JONES from Ruth GUSHEE & Seth GUSHEE of Raynham, land there.
<79:305> -	1800,	Samuel JONES Jr. from Robert BRETTUN.
<79:306> -	1800,	Samuel JONES Jr. from Simeon WILBOR.
<83:327> -	1804,	Samuel JONES Jr. from W.H. BRETTUN.
<93:214> -	6 Aug. 1810,	Samuel JONES as admr. of Samuel JONES to Samuel GUSHEE Jr. of Raynham.
<93:215> -	1811,	Samuel JONES from Samuel GUSHEE Jr.
<93:215> -	1811,	Samuel JONES from Tisdale GODFREY et al.
<97:419> -	30 Apr. 1814,	Samuel JONES, yeoman to Ellis HALL. Polly JONES signs.
<118:197>-	1825,	Samuel JONES et al to Zephaniah LEONARD.

Tisdale GODFREY et al of Easton MA to **Samuel JONES** of Raynham MA. <Bristol Co.Deeds 93:215>
...26 Dec.1810, Tisdale GODFREY, gent. & wf Sally and Barnard DEAN, yeoman of Norton & wf Patty, for $600.00 quit claim to Samuel JONES, yeoman, rights of Sally & Patty...in real & personal estate whereof our father Samuel JONES late of Raynham dec'd intestate died the owner, excepting the widow's dower or thirds. Witnesses: George WHEATON, Daniel WHEATON. Rec. 11 Dec. 1811.

Estate of **Samuel JONES.** <Bristol Co.PR>
<44:441> Warrent for inv., 31 Oct. 1808. Inventory taken 12 Jan. 1809; sworn to by **Samuel JONES,** admr. <45:65> Dower set off, 10 Apr. 1809, to widow **Prudence JONES.** <45:115,349> Accounts 2 Sept. 1809 & 3 Apr. 1810, of admr. <46:174> Notice of sale, 14 June 1810, by admr.

References to the name **Samuel JONES** in Bristol Co.PR: Adm. <76:286>; Adm. <80:482>; Account <81:472>; Will <101:321>; Notice <109:249>; Notice <115:2>; Notice <118:356>; Adm. <150:306>; Adm. <154:317>; Adm. <160:334>; Bond <174:453>; Adm. <18:72>; Inv. <18:232>.

Will of **John GILMORE.** <Bristol Co.PR 57:436>
...dated 19 Dec. 1804, among those mentioned is dau **Hannah GUSHE.** Codicil 3 Jan. 1805 & 10 Dec. 1806. Pr. 2 Jan. 1821. (will is not transcribed)

Will of **Samuel GUSHEE** of Raynham MA. <Bristol Co.PR 81:493>
...dated 3 June 1837, mentions wf **Rachel**; chil. of dec'd son **Samuel GUSHEE Jr.**; chil. of dec'd dau **Hannah WILLIAMS** wf of Enoch; son **Abraham GUSHEE** (executor). Pr. 7 Aug. 1840.

Estate of **Rachel GUSHEE,** widow of Raynham MA. <Bristol Co.PR>
Petition, 4 Dec. 1861, states that **Samuel GUSHEE & Laura A. GUSHEE,** minor grandchildren, both under the guardianship of **Elizabeth D. GUSHEE** of Raynham, are the only next of kin to dec'd.

("Papers" re: **Samuel GUSHEE*** & **Laura A. GUSHEE**, minors, say they were chil. of **Abraham GUSHEE** & under 14 on 10 Jan.1851. *"became insane, mother & sister app'td gdn.") The two owned, or were heirs of undivided two thirds of undivided half of: homestead, $924.00; Mason Hall & upper pasture, $300.00; further woods lot, $56.00; 11 acres swamp (in 3 pieces), $66.00; H.B. KING farm, $200.00; Tucker Swamp, $41.00 and Hall place, $318.00.

Will of **Joseph DEAN** of Taunton MA. <Bristol Co.PR 80:106>
...dated 15 Dec. 1837, mentions wf **Anna** and children, viz: **Joseph DEAN, Artemas DEAN** of Cornwall NY, **George Washington DEAN, Anna WILLIAMS** wf of Abiathar; to grandchildren, viz: **Artemas Dean GUSHEE & Edward GUSHEE,** chil. of dec'd dau **Kezia GUSHEE,** one quarter of Job STAPLES farm.

Guardianship of Children of **Samuel GUSHEE Jr.** of Taunton MA. <Bristol Co.PR>
<133:69> Letter/Bond 7 May 1822, Paddock DEAN, yeoman of Taunton app'td gdn. of **Artemas Dean GUSHEE & Edward GUSHEE,** under 14; chil. of **Samuel GUSHEE Jr.** dec'd and heirs at law of **Hannah GUSHEE** late of Raynham dec'd. Sureties: Joseph DEAN & Joseph DEAN Jr., yeomen of Taunton. Witnesses: George W. DEAN, Lois DEAN.

Will of **Oliver SOPER.** <Bristol Co.PR 58:329;111:123> (no details given)

Will of **Oliver SOPER.** <Bristol Co.PR>
<101:419>...dated 1851. <102:78> Dower, 1855. <118:345> Notice, 1855. <173:332> Bond, 1855. <178:166> Citation, 1855. <192:158> Inventory, 1854-1858.

Daniel WILD et al of Taunton MA to **Seth & Elijah GUSHEE** of Raynham MA. <Bristol Co.Deeds 59:31>
...5 Nov. 1778, Daniel WILD, gent. & his infant children, Rhoda & Samuel WILD; John WILD, husbandman; Anna WILD & Rachel WILD, spinsters and Amos MARTIN, yeoman & wf Sarah of Norton, for Ł112 sell to Seth GUSHEE, laborer & Elijah GUSHEE, husbandman...land in Raynham according to bounds agreed upon 5 Oct. 1778 by the heirs of Deacon Seth STAPLES late of Taunton dec'd, being all of the real estate that came to sd Daniel WILD & heirs by vertue his intermarige with Sarah STAPLES his late wife & now dec'd which sd Sarah was one of ye daughters of Seth STAPLES late of sd Taunton. Witnesses: Welthey GODFREY, George GODFREY.

Estate of **Daniel WILDE** of Taunton MA. <Bristol Co.PR>
<originals> Warrant 4 Sept. 1792, to appraise. Bond 4 Sept. 1792, of **Anna WILDE**, admx. Sureties: Josiah CROCKER & Ebenezer WILLIAMS of Taunton. <32:142> Inventory taken 21 Sept. 1792, by Isaac TUBBS, John REED, James TISDALE; sworn to 1 Jan. 1792/3 by admx. <32:145> Division of real estate 24 Sept. 1792; to widow **Anna WILDE** and children, viz: **Samuel WILDE, Sarah MARTIN, Rhoda SANFORD, Samuel Sumner WILDE, Rebecca FARRINGTON, John WILDE, Anna WHITE, Molley WILDE, Rachel WILDE** and youngest dau **Selina WILDE.** <32:363> Account of admx., 5 Nov. 1793. <35:25> Division, 28 June 1797 of widow's dower, she being dec'd; mentions **Samuel WILDE** having bought out seven shares, viz: of **Anna, Sarah, Rhoda, Molly, Rebecca, Selina & Sumner** and John BURT having bought out two shares.

Will of **Anna WILDE** of Taunton MA. <Bristol Co.PR>
<original>...dated 8 Sept. 1794...to dau **Selina WILDE,** $100.00; to son **Samuel Sumner WILDE,** 20s; remainder to two daus **Rebecca Mason FARRINGTON & Selina WILDE;** Daniel FARRINGTON, executor. Witnesses: Rufus GODFREY, Wealthy GODFREY, James TISDALE. Will filed by exr. 15 Oct. 1794. Bond 4 Nov. 1794, of Daniel FARRINGTON, exr. Sureties: Nathaniel DEAN, gent. & Rufus TOBEY, yeoman, all of Taunton.

Will of **Amos MARTIN,** gent. of Rehoboth MA. <Bristol Co.PR 95:101>
...dated 9 Sept. 1848, mentions children, viz: **Thomas C. MARTIN** & wf **Rosamond, Daniel MARTIN, Joel MARTIN, Anna THOMAS**wf of Heman, **Sarah FREEMAN** wf of Nathaniel and chil. of dec'd son **Leonard MARTIN;** son **Thomas,** executor. Pr. 7 May 1850.

Heirs of **Daniel WILD** of Taunton MA to **Samuel WILD 3d** of Taunton. <Bristol Co.Deeds 72:342>
...15 Apr. 1793, Amos MARTIN, husbandman of Norton & wf Sarah who is one of the daughters of Daniel WILD, dec'd, for Ł15.9s sell to Samuel WILD 3d, yeoman...land in Taunton, according to division of real estate of sd Daniel WILD set off to Amos & Sarah. Rec. 29 Jan. 1794. <72:342>...13 Apr. 1793, Royal SANFORD, yeoman of Bristol RI & wf Rhoda who is dau of Daniel WILD dec'd...as above.

Daniel WILD of Taunton MA to **John THAYER & John THAYER Jr.** of same. <Bristol Co.Deeds 71:121>
...25 May 1792, Daniel WILD, gent. & wf Anne sell to John THAYER & John THAYER Jr...land in north Taunton...part of farm lately owned by Deacon Samuel SUMNER dec'd. Ack. 21 June 1792 & Rec. 6 Aug

---

Will of **Job WHITE** of Mansfield MA. <Bristol Co.PR>
<24:16>...dated 26 Sept. 1775, mentions children, viz: **Job WHITE, Lemuel WHITE** (to have Ł66.13s4d out of real estate more than any other son), **John WHITE, Elijah WHITE, Rachel WHITE** (under 18), **Lusannah WHITE** (under 18, to receive all the indoor moveables my late wife her mother brought to me when she came to live with me); to Asa WILLIAMS, a cow for the right had in a yoke of oxen; to Mrs. Meletiah WARE, Ł2 to buy mourning; George WHEETEN, Esq. & son **Job**, executors. <24:17> Pr. 23 Oct. 1775. <24:22> Inventory taken 13 Nov. 1775 ("long"). <25:19.533> Account, paid to **Lemuel WHITE** for debt due the heirs of Deacon Seth STAPLES. <129:169> Guardianship, 13 Nov. 1775, **Rachel WHITE,** above 14, chose Isaac DEAN of Marshfield.

Estate of **Abiel WILLIAMS** of Taunton MA. <Bristol Co.PR>
<147:223> Letter, 1779, Abiel WILLIAMS, gent. of Raynham app'td admr.

Guardianship of Children of **Macy WILLIAMS** of Raynham MA. <Bristol Co.PR>
<132:182>...8 Apr. 1814, **Macy WILLIAMS** app'td gdn. of his children, the grandchildren of **George WILLIAMS** late of Raynham, dec'd, viz: **Sarah WILLIAMS & Philo WILLIAMS** (over 14) and **Mary Ann WILLIAMS, Almira Barker WILLIAMS, Christopher Macy WILLIAMS, Abiel WILLIAMS & John Staples WILLIAMS**, all under 14.

Will of **Abiel WILLIAMS** of Raynham MA. <Bristol Co.PR 68:311>
...dated 3 Aug. 1825...to son **Macy WILLIAMS**, land where he now lives; to heirs of dec'd dau **Hannah ROBINSON**, one sixth of certain land; to dau **Mary BYRAM** wf of William, one sixth; to dau **Anna HOWARD** wf of Eliakim, one sixth; to dau **Zeruiah DEAN** wf of Enos, one sixth; to dau **Abiah BASSETT** wf of William, one sixth; to son **Abiel WILLIAMS** & grandson **Philo WILLIAMS**, land in Taunton opposite Capt. John WILLIAMS; the four sons of son **Jonathan WILLIAMS**. Pr. 9 Apr. 1830.

Heirs of **Deacon Abiel WILLIAMS** of Raynham MA. <Bristol Co.Deeds>
All the following heirs sold their one sixth shares to **Philo WILLIAMS**, viz: <177:93>...22 Nov. 1830, heirs of **Hannah ROBINSON** sold seven eighths of their one sixth, **Zeruiah DEAN & Abiah BASSETT** sold their shares. <177:103>...9 Oct. 1830, **Mary BYRAM & Anna HOWARD** sold their shares. <130:489>...21 Feb. 1831, grandson **Jonathan WILLIAMS** sold his share to James LEONARD who <177:104> sold it to **Philo WILLIAMS**, 2 Mar. 1831. <158:372;159:171>...22 May & 4 Apr. 1839, **Macy WILLIAMS** sold to **Philo WILLIAMS.**

Guardianship of **Mercy BASSETT.** <Bristol Co.PR>
<60:501> Guardian app'td. <60:557> Inventory. <61:351> Account. <61:357> Guardian discharged, 5 Mar. 1824, as she is cured. <11:333> Notice. <131:166> Gdn.

Guardianship of **Abiel WILLIAMS,** non comp. <Bristol Co.PR>
<82:147> **Philo WILLIAMS** app'td gdn., 1840. <86:408> Account, 1844. <99:50> Inventory, 1843. <99:56> Notice of sale, 1843. <99:96> Account, 1853. <209:562> Sale of land. <99:121> Guardian discharged, 1853. <132:182;139:258>

Joseph BASSETT 2d et al to **Jonathan WILLIAMS** of Raynham MA. <Bristol Co.Deeds>
<155:66>...6 Apr. 1831, Joseph BASSETT 2d, yeoman of Bridgewater & wf Hannah, Eli WILLIAMS, yeoman of Middleboro, Silas PICKENS Jr., yeoman of Middleboro & wf Sally L. and Eliab WILLIAMS, Esq. of Swansea, sold to Jonathan WILLIAMS, yeoman...rights in land of Capt. Jonathan WILLIAMS of Raynham dec'd which sd Capt. Jonathan bought of George ANDREWS, David LEONARD, Ezra LEONARD, John KING & Job DEAN...also all rights sd Eli & Eliab have by will of Abiel WILLIAMS.

Will of **Hannah ROBINSON**, widow of Attleboro MA. <Bristol Co.PR 66:327>
...dated 12 July 1827. Pr. 1 July 1828.
(Note: The following references may pertain to this **Hannah ROBINSON**, viz: Receipt <53:652>. Inv. <65:334>. Account <67:319>. Notice <112:395>. Guardianship <131:348;132:510>.

References to the name **Joseph BASSETT** in Bristol Co.PR, viz: Inv. <24:229>. Account <27:402>. Account <27:522>. Division <27:404> Division, 1780 <27:521>. Guardianship <129:158>. Adm. <147:135>

BRISTOL COUNTY DEEDS: (re: Joseph BASSETT 2d, grantee**)**

<85:274> from Job SHELLEY; <130:359> from George BASSETT. <130:360> from Enos DEAN et al. <135:20> from gdn. of Elizabeth D. ROBINSON. <135:21> from Abiel ROBINSON et al.

<122:8> - 10 May 1800, Joseph BASSETT 2d from Robert BRITTUN, land bought of Ebenezer ROBINSON, 26 May 1787.
<174:293> - 30 Oct. 1817, Joseph BASSETT 2d from George BASSETT.
<174:305> - 21 Apr. 1821, Joseph BASSETT 2d from George BASSETT.

MICRO #2 OF 4

Estate of **John STANDISH** of Halifax MA. <Plymouth Co.PR #19163>
<27:221> Letter/Bond 4 Dec. 1786, Joshua LORING app'td admr. Sureties: John SOUL, Solomon HAYWARD Witnesses: Stephen PADDOCK, Isaac LOTHROP. <30:115> Inventory taken 5 Feb. 1787 by Moses INGLEE, John WATERMAN Jr., Ephraim SOUL; total real estate, £393.6s; total estate, £744.16.9. <30:159> Insolvency, 2 July 1787. <30:281> List of Creditors: John FAUNCE, John CHAMBERLIN, Elijah FAUNCE, Jabez HALL, Dr. Nathaniel MORTON, Isaac THAYER, estate of Capt. Thomas DAVIS, Eliezer FAUNCE, Philemon FULLER, James SOULE, Thomas & William DAVIS, Isaiah FORRIST, Dr. Thomas STURTEVANT, Capt Francis SHIRTLEFF, Cornelius DUNHAM, James DREW, Eliphalet BISBEE, Gideon SOULE, Nicholas DAVIS Jr., Capt. William HOLMES, Dr. Jonas WHITMAN, Capt. Joseph BARTLETT, Josiah CHANDLER, Jonathan PARKER, Freeman WATERMAN, Lt. Josiah TOMSON, Jacob SOULE, Lt. Samuel S. STURTEVANT, Nathan TINKHAM, David BOSWORTH, Henry WARREN, Eliezer WATERMAN, Capt. Jesse STURTEVANT, Jabez WATERMAN, John BOZWORTH, Theophilus CUSHING, Joshua PALMER Jr., Sole BOZWORTH, Ephraim SOULE, Simeon STURTEVANT, Thomas FULLER, Zach. & Noah WHITMAN, Capt. John WATERMAN Jr., Zadock WESTON, Rev. Ephraim BRIGGS, Asaph BISBE, Zenas BRYANT, Isaac WATERMAN, Lydia PARKER, Obadiah LYON, estate of Isaac TOMSON,

Zenas COOK, Adam TOMSON, Zebadiah TOMSON, Moses TOMSON, Ichabod ATWOOD, Benjamin SHURTLEFF, John TILSON Jr., Ichabod SHAW, William GOODEN, Capt. Ebenezer WASHBURN, Solomon INGLEE, Thomas JACKSON Joshua THOMAS, Stephen ELLIS, Nathaniel JACKSON, John LEACH, William WATERMAN, John LEACH Jr., Ephriam TILSON, Dr. Rosittor COTTON, Judah DELANO, Hosea BUISTER, Robert BROWN, Ephraim SPOONER, John KEMPTON, William PORTER, Joanna WINSLOW, Consider PRATT, Jael WHITE, Jabez SOUL, Samuel TINKHAM, Joshua LORING, Caleb STURTEVANT, Amos FULLER, Peleg WADSWORTH, Reuben TOMSON, Samuel JACKSON, Elizabeth BARTLETT, Thomas WITHERELL, Joseph HATCH, Silvanus LEACH, Silvanus HARLOW, John DUNHAM, Capt. Joshua EDDY, Dr. William CROMBIE. <30:291> Account, 2 Apr. 1788, of Joshua LORING, admr. <30:357> Warrant to set off dower, 2 Apr. 1788, by James CHURCHILL, Noah CUSHING, Ephraim SOULE, to widow **Rebecca STANDISH**, viz: land adjoining Gideon & Ephraim SOULE and eight & a half acres woodland in Plympton called common meadow land; confirmed 5 May 1788. <31:35> Order of General Court regarding the validity of sale of real estate made by Joshua LORING; approved 3 June 1789. <31:35> Account of admr., 7 Sept. 1789, for sale of land; incl. dwelling house & land to Elisha FAXON, land & part of a Furnace to Ignatius LORING, upland & cedar swamp to Gideon SOULE & John FAUNCE, meadow & cedar swamp to John CHAMBERLIN and piece of meadow to John WATERMAN. <31:36> Insolvency & Order for distribution, 7 Sept. 1789. <33:66> 3d Account of admr., 2 July 1792, who charges himself with the reversion of the widow **Rebecca STANDISH's** thirds sold to sundry persons. <33:66> Distribution of balance of account to creditors, 10 July 1792. <original> Complaint 23 May 1793, of John FAUNCE et al, creditors & citation issued to Joshua LORING charging neglect in paying creditors.

PLYMOUTH COUNTY PROBATE: (re: STANDISH)

1702	Alexander	Duxbury		#19152, 1:362,364;2:29
1732	Desire	Duxbury		#19155, 6:177,178,180
1739	Miles	Duxbury		#19172, 8:107,110,162;10:157
1740	Penelope	Duxbury		#19177, 8:215,216,242
1747	Ebenezer Jr.	Plympton		#19156, 11:35,275,276,390,391
1769	Moses	Halifax		#19175, 20:289,346,388,389
1770	Zachariah	Plympton		#19188, 20:355,451;21:218;42:22
1772	Ichabod	Halifax		#19158, 21:136,137
1780	Isaiah et al	Plympton		#19161, 26:115,116,117,364,365
1780	Thomas Jr.	Pembroke		#19181, 25:509;27:52;28:93,228,229
1780	Zachariah	Plympton		#19189, 25:485,486,487,542;28:118,121
1786	John	Halifax		#19163, 27:221;30:115,159,281,357;31:35-6;33:66
1795	David	Hanover		#19154, 35:285,286
1803	Hannah	Hanover	will	#19157, 38:391,392,393
1805	Miles	Pembroke	adm.	#19173, 39:38;40:426;42:242;43:173,279;45:344; 50:118
1805	Miles et al	Pembroke	gdn.	#19174, 32:275;41:182;49:160
1816	Isaiah	Rochester	adm.	#19159, 46:166;48:246,247;49:113
1816	Isaiah et al	Rochester	gdn.	#19160, 41:280;50:411,412
1818	Phebe	Halifax	will	#19178, 49:198,267,268,486
1826	John C.	Middleboro	adm.	#19164, 60:308,338;61:26;62:23;63:115,208-9,261, 466,467;64:89
1829	William	Pembroke	will	#19183, 62:335;66:412
1833	Nathaniel	Middleboro	adm.	#19176, 71:153;76:24,25,40,79;76:576
1837	Jonathan	Middleboro	will	#19165, 1:297**G**;5:23**T**;79:45
1838	Miles B.	Middleboro	gdn.	#19169, 8:94**L**
1841	William Jr.	Duxbury	gdn.	#19186, 1:47,48**K**,473**R**;2:449**O**;3:525**P**;6:182**U**;8: 465,466**L**;83:333;93:134;96:195;98:40
1842	Job	Pembroke	adm.	#19162, 6:302**U**;11:76**B**;84:461;87:271
1849	Miles B.	Middleboro	adm.	#19170, 7:552**V**;12:130**C**;93:29,435;93:333
1849	Miles T.	Middleboro	gdn.	#19171, 1:314**R**;3:422**P**;9:218**M**;92:435;97:427;132: 116

Estate of **Fillemon/Philemon SAMSON**, yeoman of Plympton MA. <Plymouth Co.PR #17626>
<14:168> Letter/Bond 1 Nov. 1756, Moses STANDISH of Halifax app'td admr. Sureties: Jabez NEWLAND & Stephen TILLSON of Plympton. Witnesses: Bartlett MURDOCK, John LOTHROP. <14:377> Inventory taken 4 Dec. 1756 by James HARLOW, Jabez NEWLAND, Gideon SAMSON; homestead, meadow & swamp, L119. 6.8.; sworn to by admr. 2 May 1757. <16:325> Division of real estate, 21 June 1762 by Deacon Samuel LUCAS, Jabez NEWLAND, James HARLOW, all of Plimton, to widow **Rachel FULLER** now wf of Amos and to the following chil., viz: **Newland SAMSON, Sarah SAMSON, Lydia SAMSON, Benjamin SAMSON, Jeremiah SAMSON, Moses SAMSON.** <43:405> Inventory, 8 Jan. 1811, Judah WASHBURN, John PRINCE, Oliver CHURCHILL, all of Kingston, app'td to appraise real estate that was set off to widow **Rachel SAMPSON** as her dower; 4 Feb. 1811, real estate appraised at $53.00. On 23 Apr. 1811, estate set off to **Jeremiah SAMSON**, yeoman of Kingston, the only son now living, he paying to the other heirs, viz: heirs of **Newland SAMPSON** dec'd, **Moses SAMPSON** dec'd and **Benjamin SAMPSON** dec'd and to **Lydia HOLMES** wf of Francis. Bond 2 Apr. 1811, of **Jeremiah SAMPSON.** Sureties: John FAUNCE of Kingston & Oliver CHURCHILL of Plympton. Witnesses: Lot WHITMARSH, Robert COOK Jr.

Guardianship of Children of **Philemon SAMSON** of Plympton MA. <Plymouth Co.PR #17602>
<18:81,83,85> Letters/Bonds 27 Apr. 1762, Amos FULLER of Plimton app'td gdn. of **Lydia SAMSON, Benjamin SAMSON, Jeremiah SAMSON** and chosen gdn. by **Newland SAMSON & Sarah SAMSON** (over 14). Surety: Moses STANDISH of Plimton. Witnesses: Thomas TORREY, Edward WINSLOW. <18:77> Letter/Bond 27 Apr. 1762, Moses STANDISH, husbandman, app'td gdn. of **Moses SAMSON.** <20:256> Letter/Bond 19

Aug. 1769, Jabez NEWLAND, yeoman of Plimton app'td gdn. of **Moses SAMSON** (over 14). Surety: James COBB, yeoman of Kingston. Witnesses: Edward MORSE, Jonathan MORSE Jr.

Estate of **Sarah SAMSON**, spinster of Plympton MA. <Plymouth Co.PR #17649>
<27:391> Letter/Bond 13 Apr. 1792, Jeremiah SAMSON of Kingston app'td admr. Sureties: Ebenezer WASHBURN of Kingston & Caleb LEACH, watchmaker of Plymouth. Witnesses: Nathaniel LOTHROP, Isaac LOTHROP. <33:61> Inventory taken 14 May 1792 by John FAUNCE, Josiah COOK, Francis RING, all of Kingston. <31:61> Notice. <33:174> Account of admr., 8 Oct. 1792; Received from: Deborah SAMPSON, Luke PERKINS, Beza SOUL, Elkanah CUSHMAN, Samuel BRADFORD, Asaph SOULE, Benjamin SAMPSON; Paid to: Dr. Jonas WHITMAN, Dr. Jabez FULLER, Dr. Ebenezer DEAN, James COBB, Isaiah THOMAS, Bildad WASHBURN, Jeremiah SAMSON, Filemon FULLER, Isaiah CUSHMAN, Ebenezer WASHBURN, Moses SIMMONS. <37:433> Account of admr., 7 Apr. 1801; Paid to: Isaiah CUSHMAN and the following heirs, viz: **Rachel FULLER, Lydia HOLMES, Philemon FULLER, Amos FULLER, Gamaliel HATCH, Benjamin SAMPSON.**

Estate of **Zachariah STANDISH** of Plympton MA. <Plymouth Co.PR #19188>
<original> Request, 23 Apr. 1770, of widow **Abigail STANDISH** & son **Zachariah STANDISH**, for the appointment of Josiah STURTEVANT as admr. <20:355> Josiah STURTEVANT Jr. of Halifax app'td admr. <original> Bond 2 May 1770, of admr. Sureties: John THOMAS, Nelson FINNEY. Witnesses: Edward WINSLOW, Edward WINSLOW Jr. <20:451> Inventory taken 8 May 1770 by Moses INGLEE, John WATERMAN, Seth BRYANT; total real estate, £4; total estate, £95.8.3. <21:218> Account of admr., 4 Jan. 1773 <42:22> Warrant to divide cedar swamp in Halifax, 3 Dec. 1805, by Elijah BISBEE, Isaac CHURCHILL, John WATERMAN; divided into six parts & set off to following heirs, viz: heirs of **Ebenezer STANDISH** dec'd (two shares), heirs of **Hannah CUSHMAN** dec'd, heirs of **Sarah CUSHMAN** dec'd, heirs of **Abigail WRIGHT** dec'd & heirs of **Zachariah STANDISH** dec'd. <42:22> Division confirmed 5 Jan. 1807.

Will of **Zachariah STANDISH** of Plympton MA. <Plymouth Co.PR #19189>
<25:485>...dated 7 Feb. 1780, mentions wf **Olive** and following chil., viz: **Zachariah STANDISH, Isaiah STANDISH** (under 21), **Peleg STANDISH, Oliver STANDISH, Rebecca STANDISH, Sarah STANDISH.** Witnesses: John STANDISH, Nathaniel RIDER, Jabez SOULE. <25:486> Pr. 3 Apr. 1780, **Olive STANDISH** & John WATERMAN Jr. app'td exrs.; **Olive** declines. <25:487> Inventory taken 19 Apr. 1780 by Moses INGLEE, John STANDISH, Jabez SOULE; total real estate, £266.6.8.; total estate, £346.3.; sworn to 3 June 1780 by exr. <25:542> Warrant, 7 Aug. 1780, to set off dower to widow **Olive.** <28:118> Division of estate, by Jacob BENNETT, Jesse STURTEVANT, Jabez SOULE, exclusive of the widow's dower, among the following heirs, viz: **Zachariah, Isaiah, Peleg, Rebecca, Sarah** and to the heirs of **Oliver** dec'd, viz: mother **Olive** and above named brothers & sisters. <original> List of debts, 4 Oct. 1780, viz: Ichabod PARKER, David CHURCHIL, Mary LORING, Wooderd LATHAM, Isaac BRUSTER/BREWSTER, Dr. CHILD, Levi BRADFORD, John HAPPEN, Jacob SOUL, Nathaniel CROADE, Jaben NEWLAND, Nathan PARKINS/PERKINS, Dr. DEAN, William SEVER, Caleb LORING, Josiah WATERMAN, Thomas SAMSON, Josiah CUSHMAN, Job CUSHMAN, John WATERMAN, Gideon SOUL, Moses INGLEE, Benjamin CURTIS, Jaben SOUL, Nathaniel RIDER, Ebenezer WHITMAN, Fremon WATERMAN, John BOSWORTH, Judah WOOD, Dr. BRYANT, Josiah WEST, Shadrak STANDISH, widow **Olive STANDISH;** Receipts: James CHURCHIL, Jonathan PARKER, Daniel CHILD. <28:121> Account of exr., 1 Apr. 1782; Paid to: Ephraim SPOONER, William CROMBIE, Ebenezer SOULE, Sylvanus BARTLETT, Gideon SAMSON, Jonathan PARKER, Ignatius LORING, Peleg WADSWORTH, Thomas DAVIS, Barnabas TOMSON, Benjamin CUSHMAN, John SHERMAN, Jabez SOUL as one of the 12th class, Nathaniel LITTLE, Sarah BAGNAL, heirs of old **Zachariah STANDISH,** William WHITE, Lydia CHURCHELL, James BOSWORTH, William SHAW, Asaph SOUL, Jonathan LEONARD, Nathaniel CHURCHILL, Lydia STURTEVANT, Abner RIPLEY, James DREW, John COTTON, Oakes ANGIER, Nathaniel CROADE, John KEMPTON, Silas STURTEVANT, Ephraim WATERMAN, Ephraim SOULE, Jonathan NYE, Nathan ORCUTT, John HOOPER, John BRADFORD, Ebenezer DEAN, Zephaniah PERKINS, Caleb LORING, Richard BOSWORTH, Ebenezer WASHBURN, Jacob BENNETT, Jesse STURTEVANT.

Guardianship of Children of **Zachary/Zachariah STANDISH** of Plympton MA. <Plymouth Co.PR #19161>
<original> Bonds, 5 June 1780, Abner WOOD of Middleboro app'td gdn. of **Isaiah & Zachariah STANDISH**, above 14. Sureties: Joshua WHITE, Ephraim SOULE. Witnesses: Seth CUSHING, Isaac LOTHROP. <26:364,365> Power of guardianship given Abner WOOD by request of **Isaiah & Zackary STANDISH.** Witnesses: Ephraim FULLER, Zerviah FULLER, Adam TOMSON, Lydia HOLMES. <26:115-17> Letters/Bonds 5 Mar. 1781, widow **Olive STANDISH** app'td gdn. of **Peleg, Sarah & Rebecca STANDISH,** all under 14. Sureties: John WATERMAN Jr., Gideon SOULE. Witnesses: Seth CUSHING, Isaac LOTHROP.

Samuel DILANO/DELANO of Duxbury MA to **Capt. Nathaniel THOMAS** of Marshfield. <Plymouth Co.Deeds>
<"p.32">...19 May 1687, Samuel DILANO, for 35s sold to Capt. Nathaniel THOMAS...one half part of a share of land which is the 35th part of a tract in Plymouth, Duxbury & Bridgewater and other lands & was purchased from the Indian Sachem Josias Chickatabutt by Maj. WINSLOW...half of the share of William PONTUS. Witnesses: John SOULE, Caleb SAMPSON. Ack. (8?) May 1687. Rec. 19 July 1687.

Heirs of **Samuel DELANOE** of Duxbury MA. <Plymouth Co.PR 5:425>
...28 Sept. 1728, Agreement between heirs of our Honoured Father **Samuel DELANOE,** viz: Hazadiah DELANOE, Jessee/Jesice DELANOE, Samuel DELANOE Jr., Benjamin SIMMONS, Priscilla SIMMONS, Benjamin SOUTHWORTH, Rebecca SOUTHWORTH, Joshua SIMMONS, Sarah SIMMONS, Jane DELANOE & Mary DELANOE, all of Duxbury and Joseph CHANDLER of Pembroke.

Estate of **Samuel DELANO** of Duxbury MA. <Plymouth Co.PR #6318>
<5:424> Inventory taken 9 Aug. 1728 by Edward ARNOLD, Benjamin ALDEN, Thomas FISH; total real estate, the farm, £130; total estate, £246.17s; Debts to: Joshua SOUL, William BREWSTER, John DINGLEY, Isaac WALKER, Dr. DELINO/DELANO, Miles STANDISH, Benjamin PRIER, Nathan THOMAS,

Jedediah BOURN, Ezra ARNOLD, Jesse DELINO, Benjamin SIMONS, Joshua SIMONS, Jane DELINO, Thomas FISH, Constant SOUTHWORTH, Samuel ALDEN, John THOMAS and the Town of Duxbury; Debts due from: Benjamin SOUTHWORTH, Joseph CHANDLER; sworn to 24 Oct. 1728 by Edward ARNOLD & Benjamin ALDEN and on 28 Nov. 1728 by Thomas FISH & **Hasadiah DELLANO**, admr. <5:425> Agreement of heirs, 28 Sept. 1728. <See p.438>. <5:399> Letter/Bond 30 Sept. 1728, son **Hasadiah DELLANO** of Duxboro app'td admr Surety: Edward ARNOLD of Duxbury. Witnesses: Sarah WINSLOW, Elizabeth ROSE.

Petition of **Joseph CHANDLER.** <Duxbury Rcds.Prop.2d Div.:26; printed:285>
...1 Mar. 1747, Joseph CHANDLER petitioned the court for more common land...Whereas my Honoured Father Benjamin CHANDLER late of Duxborough...dec'd, dyed seized of a considerable real estate in ye Town of Duxborough & after his death, to wit, on ye third Tuesday of March A.D.1691/2 the County Court then holden at Plymouth Settled ye whole of ye real estate aforesd upon ye four sons which my sd Father left behind him, two fifth parts to ye eldest of ye sd sons & one fifth part to each of ye other sins...& by virtue of sd settlement I became seised of one fifth part of ye sd inheritance & ye freehold there of was acutally in me & continued so until ye 30th of Jan. A.D.1709.

Joseph CHANDLER of Duxbury MA & **Robert SAMSON** of same. <Plymouth Co.Deeds 40:47>
...4 Apr.1749, Joseph CHANDLER, yeoman & Robert SAMSON...divide 93rd lot in 2d Division of uplands of Duxbury & Pembroke.

Joseph CHANDLER of Duxbury MA to **Samuel TAYLOR** of Marshfield. <Plymouth Co.Deeds 39:88>
...Feb. 1747, Joseph CHANDLER, housewright sold to Samuel TAYLOR, housewright...lots #27 & #20 containing 40 acres each and part of 16th lot in 1st Division in Pembroke, laid out in 1710. Ack. 16 Feb. 1747.

Joseph CHANDLER of Cornwall CT to **John CHANDLER** of Duxbury MA. <Plymouth Co.Deeds 41:248>
...15 July 17151, Joseph CHANDLER conveys to son John CHANDLER...half of 39th lot in 2d Division of Commons in Duxbury & Pembroke, laid out in 1713...sd half formerly bought of Abraham PEIRCE & rec. 39:152. Ack. 16 July 1751 in Plymouth.

Guardianship of Children of **Joseph CHANDLER** of Pembroke MA. <Plymouth Co.PR #3747>
<5:415.416> Letters/Bonds 2 Dec. 1728, **Joseph CHANDLER** app'td gdn. of his chil., viz: **Benjamin CHANDLER, John CHANDLER, Simeon CHANDLER**, all under 14. Surety: Benjamin SOUTHWORTH of Duxbury. Witnesses: Josias SIMONS, Jesse DELANO.

Will of **John CHANDLER**, yeoman of Duxborough MA. <Plymouth Co.PR #3776>
<25:555>...dated 7 June 1780...to son **Abil/Abel CHANDLER**, all my real estate obliging him to find my dafter/daughter **Candace CHANDLER** a fire room in the house & fire wood at the dore for a fier sumer & winter allso to keep a cow sumner & winter for her so long as she shall live unmarried & I give to my dafter **Candace** a bed & beding for sd bed I allso Give to her one Cow I Give to my son **Abil** my teem & all my farming utentiels & one bed & beding & one Cow abliging him to pay all my debts & funeral charges & all the Rest of my Estate not here in yet Disposed of I Give to my Son **Abil** & my three dafters, viz: **Rebeck/Rebecca OLDHAM** wf of David, **Candice CHANDLER & Elizabeth OLDHAM** wf of John. Witnesses: Jacob WESTON, Abigail FREEMAN, Judah DELANO. <25:556> Receipt, 1 Aug. 1780, signed by above heirs, incl. husbands of daus. <25:555> Pr. 6 Nov. 1780, on oath of Jacob WESTON & Judah DELANO. <original> Bond 6 Nov. 1780, of **Abel CHANDLER**, exr. Witnesses: E. BRIGGS, Japheth LeBARRON.

PLYMOUTH COUNTY DEEDS: (re: Abel CHANDLER)

<62:52> - 21 June 1782, Abel CHANDLER, yeoman of Duxbury to Peleg GULLIFER, half the 39th lot in 2d Division of Commons of Duxbury & Pembroke.

<87:133> - 15 July 1797, Abel CHANDLER, yeoman of Duxbury to Asa WESTON, part of farm he now lives on, side of Duck Hill Rd. & wharf. Wf Sarah releases dower.

<89.236> - 1 Apr. 1801, Abel CHANDLER, yeoman of Duxbury to Joel WALKER of Marshfield, farm where he now lives on Plymouth Rd near Duck Hill River...also Thomas CHANDLER's salt marsh reserving way for Zebdial WESTON, Thomas CHANDLER & Asa CHANDLER. Wf Sarah releases dower.

<89:245> - 10 Apr. 1801, Abel CHANDLER, yeoman of Duxbury to Peleg WESTON of same, land on No.W. side road from No.W. Schoolhouse to the meeting house. Wf Sarah releases

<101:227>- 10 Apr. 1801, Abel CHANDLER, yeoman of Duxbury, for love etc., to John OLDHAM, shipwright of same., common land in Duxbury on Pools Path. Wf Sarah releases Witness: Sally CHANDLER Jr.

Estate of **Samuel DELANO** of Duxbury MA. <Plymouth Co.PR>
<6:265> Pr. 11 Dec. 1732, **Joshua DELANO** of Duxbury app'td admr. <6:2> Inventory taken 26 Dec. 1732 by John ALDEN, Pelatiah WEST, Samuel WESTON. <6:322> 19 Mar. 1732/3, Inventory sworn to by admr. <7:7> Account of admr., 17 Apr. 17(34).

Will of **Samuel DELLANO** of Duxbury MA. <Plymouth Co.PR>
<8:93>...dated 9 June 1739, mentions wf **Elisabeth** and following chil., viz: **Elisha DELLANO, Prince DELLANO, Ichabod DELLANO, Ruth DELLANO, Betty DELLANO, Abigail DELLANO**; brother in law **John BONNEY Jr.** of Pembroke, executor. Witnesses: Caleb SAMSON Jr., Micah SOUL, John WADSWORTH. <8:95> 2 July 1739, Lt. James THOMAS, Joseph DELANO, Samuel WESTON, app'td to appraise.

PLYMOUTH COUNTY DEEDS: (re: DELANO)

<1:32> - 19 May 1687, Samuel DELANO.
<1:312> - 1693/4, Samuel DELANO.
<7:85> - 1 Jan. 1693/4, Samuel DELANO & wf Elizabeth.
<16:138> - 1719, John DELANO to son John DELANO
<15:199> - 1721, John DELANO to Thomas & Joshua DELANO.
<29:28> - 1731, Hazadiah DELANO & Jesse DELANO to their mother.

(References only to the surname **DELANO**, viz: 7:215,217;8:118;10:167;12:84,86,217; 14:182, 259;15: 91,220;16:77,94,96.)

Samuel DELANO 2D of Duxborough MA to **John & William BARNES** of Plymouth.<Plymouth Co.Deeds 17:217> ...1724...Samuel DELANOE, yeoman, for £12 sold to John BARNES & William BARNES, yeomen...lot in a beach in Duxborough...

Thomas DELANO Sr. et al of Duxboro MA to **Isaac PEIRCE** of same. <Plymouth Co.Deeds 7:349> ...2 Apr. 1711, Thomas DILLENOE Sr. & Samuel DILLENO Jr. son of Phillip DILLENO dec'd, for £12 sold to Isaac PEIRCE...20 acres in the Sixteen Shilling Purchase in Middleboro...33rd lot in last division. Witnesses: Abraham SAMSON, Lorah SAMSON. Ack. same day. Rec. 16 Apr. 1711.

Will of **Phebe STANDISH**, singlewoman/spinster of Halifax MA. <Plymouth Co.PR #19178> <49:198>...dated 21 Oct. 1808...one quarter of real estate lying in Halifax & Bridgewater & one quarter of personal estate each to Lydia HOBART wf of Isaac, Gamaliel HATCH, Jabez HATCH and to the three chil. of Ichabod HATCH dec'd, viz: Nathan HATCH, David HATCH & Mary BRADFORD wf of Calvin Jr.; Isaac HOBART, executor. Witnesses: Josiah TOMSON, Howland HOLMES, Jabez Prior THOMSON. <49:198> Letter/Bond 9 Feb. 1818, Isaac HOBART, yeoman of Pembroke app'td exr. Sureties: Jabez P. THOMSON, gent. & Howland HOLMES, yeoman, both of Halifax. Witnesses: Beza HAYWARD, John S. HAYWARD. <49:268> Order to post notice, 9 Feb. 1818. <49:267> Inventory taken 17 Feb. 1818 by Lot WHITMARSH, Jabez P. THOMSON, Nathaniel COLLAMORE; incl. homestead farm, $1500.00; one half of a wall pew in the Gallery in the Rev. Mr. RICHMOND's Meeting house in Halifax, $2.00; total personal estate, $275.81. <49:486> Account of exr., 5 Oct. 1818; Payments: 3 Jan. 1818 to the funeral charges, $5.00; digging the grave & setting up the grave stones, $1.50; pair of grave stones, $11.00; coffin, $2.25; Paid to: LORING, Nathaniel MORTON, Azar HOW, Moley PRATT, Howland HOLMES, Jabez P. THOMSON, Isaac HOBART Jr., John POOL, Sears WASHBURN, Esq. LYON; Received from: Maj. MITCHELL, Col. BARSTOW.

Heirs of **Phebe STANDISH** of Halifax MA to **Nahum WASHBURN** of same. <Plymouth Co.Deeds 157:93> ...20 Mar. 1819, Isaac HOBART, yeoman of Pembroke & wf Lydia in her right, Calvin BRADFORD, yeoman of Plympton & wf Mercy in her right and Gamaliel HATCH, Jabish HATCH & David HATCH all yeomen of Tanmouth NH and Nathan HATCH, yeoman of Gifford NH, for $1100.00 sold to Nahum WASHBURN, yeoman...60 acres partly in Halifax & Bridgewater...being the homestead farm of Phebe STANDISH, single woman dec'd, it was given us by her last will...bounded by land of Ezra THOMPSON and land lately owned by Maj. Nathaniel THOMPSON. Also signed by Priscilla HATCH wf of Gamaliel, Molley HATCH wf of Jabish, Sukey HATCH wf of David & Phebe HATCH wf of Nathan. Ack. 29 Mar. 1819, Stafford CT by Gamaliel, Jabish/Jabez & David HATCH and witnessed by John M. PAGE & Abigail J. ORR. Ack. 3 Apr. 1819 Stafford NH by Nathan HATCH and witnessed by John EVANS & Barnard MORRILL. Ack. 17 Apr. 1819 at Pembroke by Isaac & Lydia HOBART and Calvin & Mary/Mercy BRADFORD and witnessed by Luther BRADFORD, Daniel WRIGHT, Thomas HOBART, Melinda BONNEY, Nathaniel ELLIS & Abigail SAUNDERS. Rec. 3 May 1826.

MICRO #3 OF 4

Isaac HOBART of Hanson MA to **Isaac HOBART Jr.** of same. <Plymouth Co.Deeds 159:184> ...14 Mar. 1827, Isaac HOBART, yeoman, sells to Isaac HOBART Jr., yeoman, for $2000.00 paid and $800.00 to be paid to David Hatch HOBART...Isaac Jr. to support Isaac Sr. & wf Lydia for life...

Will of **Abraham SAMSON**, yeoman of Duxbury MA. <Plymouth Co.PR #17434> <originals>...dated 22 May 1764, mentions wf **Mary** and following chil., viz: **Abraham SAMSON, Stephen SAMSON, Henry SAMSON, Hannah HOLMES, Rebeckah BLACKMORE, Penelopy SAMSON**; grandaughter **Rhoda CHANDLER** wf of Thomas; grandchildren, chil. of dec'd dau **Ruth DELANO** wf of Amaziah; Jonathan PETERSON, executor. Witnesses: Caleb OLDHAM, Silvanus DREW, Jonathan PETERSON. Codicil 30 May 1765...Whereas the above named Jonathan PETERSON being dec'st I appoint Joseph SOUL executor. Witnesses: Jonathan PETERSON, Joseph SOUL. Warrant for Inventory 8 Mar. 1776, to Ebenezer DELANO, Eliphas PRIOR & John SAMSON, all of Duxbury; incl. homestead farm, £173.6.8; blue river meadow, £30; Pine Hill meadow, £13.6.8.; sworn to by appraisers & admr. 11 Aug. 1777.

Will of **Henry SAMSON**, mariner of Duxbury MA. <Plymouth Co.PR #17531> <30:247>...dated 26 Apr. 1768...all estate to wf **Joanna**. Witnesses: Salumith WADSWORTH, Sarah WADSWORTH, John WADSWORTH. 1 Sept. 1787, John WADSWORTH swore to will. <27:513> Letter/Bond 1 Nov 1787, widow **Joanna SAMSON** app'td admx. Sureties: Silvanus DREW, shipwright of Duxbury & Stephen SAMSON of Plymouth. Witnesses: Andrew CROSWELL, Isaac LOTHROP. <30:249> Inventory taken 1 Aug. 1787, by Jepthah DELANO, Ezra WESTON & Silvanus DREW. <30:249> Insolvency. <30:357> List of Claims, 3 May 1788: Dr. Isaac WINSLOW, Dr. Eleazer HARLOW, Mrs. Abigail SAMSON for nursing in last sickness, Joseph CUSHMAN, John SAMSON, Jonathan PETERSON, Elias CHURCHEL, Gideon BRADFORD,

Jacob WESTON, Simeon SOUL, Joseph WESTON, Levi LORING, Samuel LORING, Asa WATERMAN, Freeman ELLIS, William SHAW, Melzar LORING, George SAMSON, Ezra SAMSON, Elijah BISBY, David CARVER, Aaron BISBY, William SAMSON, Gamaliel BRADFORD, Stephen SAMSON.

Will of **Ebenezer SAMSON**, yeoman of Duxbury MA. <Plymouth Co.PR #17499>
<25:198>...dated 23 May 1771, mentions wf **Zeruiah** and following chil., viz: **Nathan SAMSON, Rachel SAMSON, Joanna SAMSON, Abigial SAMSON, Eunice SAMSON, Hannah SAMSON.** Witnesses: Nathaniel SPRAGUE Daniel LORING, Silvanus DREW. Pr. 1 Mar. 1779, son **Nathan** exr. <25:199> Warrant for Inventory, 1 Mar. 1779, to Warren WESTON, Cornelius DELANO & Simeon SOULE of Dubury; incl. home farm, Ł1000; salt meadow, Ł750; wood lot, Ł250; sworn to 27 July 1779 by appraisers & 2 Aug. 1779 by exr.

Will of **Andrew SAMSON**, yeoman of Duxbury MA. <Plymouth Co.PR>
<30:40>...dated 5 Nov. 1785, mentons wf **Abigail** and following chil., viz: eldest son **Samuel SAMSON**, eldest dau **Jedidah, Andrew SAMSON, Abigail, William SAMSON** (executor). <30:41> Pr. 4 Dec. 1786. <original> Letter dated 21 Dec.1786, from widow **Abigail SAMSON** to the Judge stating her disapproval of her husband's will.

Will of **Nathaniel SAMSON**, yeoman of Duxbury MA. <Plymouth Co.PR #17607>
<11:378>...dated 15 May 1749, mentions wf **Keturah** and following chil., viz: **Robert SAMSON** (eldest surviving son); chil. of dec'd eldest son **Noah SAMSON; Abner SAMSON, Anna SAMSON, Fear SIMONS, Keturah CULLIFER.** Witnesses: Mary WADSWORTH, Elizabeth ALDEN, John WADSWORTH Jr. <11:380> Pr. 6 Nov. 1750, **Abner SAMSON,** husbandman of Duxborough app'td exr. <11:533> Inventory taken 30 Nov. 1749 by Joseph DELANO, Samuel SEABURY, Isaac PARTRIDGE; incl. homestead farm, salt meadow at beach & salt meadow at Gottaam. <13:67> Account of exr. 2 Apr.1753; Paid to: Dr. HARLOW, Benjamin SAMSON, Samuel SEABURY, Dr. John WADSWORTH, Robert SAMSON, Thomas GULEFOR, Nathaniel SAMSON, Isaac RUSSELL, Peleg SPRAGUE, Thomas CHANDLER, Ebenezer SAMSON, Joshua LORING, Isaac PARTRIDGE, Abraham SAMSON, Elizabeth ALDEN, John STETSON, John HUNT, Joseph DELANO, Samuel ALLEN, Jacob DINGLEY, Samuel WESTON, Stephen SAMSON, Benjamin LORING, Uriah WADSWORTH, John CHANDLER, David DELANO and William CARVER.

Will of **Nathaniel SAMPSON**, yeoman of Duxbury MA. <Plymouth Co.PR #17608>
<30:491>...dated 22 Apr. 1788...to wf **Mary** all estate during her life; to **Abner SAMSON** & his sister **Mary HUNT**, the chil. of **Abner SAMSON** dec'd, one third after widow's decease; to the heirs of brother **Robert SAMSON** & sister **Fear SIMMONS**, both dec'd, one third after widow's decease; the remaining third to be divided among the following, viz: **Thomas GULLEFER** son of sister **Caturah/Keturah GULLEFER** and **Anne, Keturah & Thomas SAMSON** the chil. of sister **Anne SAMSON**...and the other part that remains I give to my brother **Abner SAMSON**'s children that he had by his last wife; Gideon HARLOW of Duxbury, executor. Witnesses: John HANKS, Joseph PEARCE, Ichabod DELANO. <original> Bond 24 Nov. 1788 of exr. Sureties: John HANKS & Ichabod DELANO of Duxbury. Witnesses: John TURNER Jr., Israel PERRY. <30:492> Inventory sworn to 12 Dec. 1788 by exr. <33:160> Account of exr., 4 Sept.1792; Paid to: Abner DINGLEY, Dr. Eleazer HARLOW, Jed. HOLMES, David CARVER, Isaac SAMSON, Jesse HARLOW, Seve CHANDLER, John HANKS, Dr. Isaac WINSLOW, Emanuel FREEMAN, William SAMSON, Jonathan PETERSON, Jacob DINGLEY, Ezekiel CHANDLER, Reuben DELANO, Micah WESTON, Peleg GULLIFER, Mark KEEN, Ichabod DELANO, Daniel PETTINGAL, Capt. Adam FISH, James WESTON, William SIMMONS, William LORING.

Will of **Robert SAMSON**, yeoman of Duxbury MA. <Plymouth Co.PR #17638>
<24:43>...dated 24 Jan. 1775, mentions wf **Alice** and following chil., viz: **Noah SAMSON, Peres SAMSON, Alice SAMSON, Levi SAMSON, Consider SAMSON, Edeth SAMSON, Robert SAMSON.** Witnesses: Peres RANDALL, Anthony SAMSON, Sarah SAMSON. Pr. 4 Dec. 1775, **Noah SAMSON,** exr. <24:60> Inventory taken 5 Feb. 1776 by Perez HOWLAND, Ebenezer CHANDLER, Perez CHANDLER, all of Duxbury; sworn to 4 Mar. 1776 by appraisers & exr.

Estate of **Peres SAMPSON** of Duxbury MA. <Plymouth Co.PR #17621>
<6:424> Letter/Bond 17 Dec. 1733, father **Nathaniel SAMSON** of Duxbury app'td admr. Sureties: Edward ARNOLD of Duxbury & John FULLERTON of Marshfield. Witnesses: James GARDNER, John BARKER. <6:425> Inventory taken 9 Jan. 1733/4 by Edward ARNOLD, John ALDEN, Samuel WESTON, all of Duxbury; sworn to 11 Jan. 1733/4 by appraisers & admr.

Will of **Abner SAMSON**, yeoman of Duxbury MA. <Plymouth Co.PR #17431>
<25:483>...dated 11 Feb. 1780, mentions wf **Deborah** and following chil., viz: **Abner SAMSON** (eldest son), **Isaac SAMSON, Nathaniel SAMSON, Aaron SAMSON, Mary HUNT, Sarah SAMSON, Deborah SPRAGUE, Luce/Lucy SAMSON, Luna SAMSON, Welthea SAMSON.** Witnesses: C. PARTRIDGE, Thomas CHANDLER, Oliver SAMSON. <25:484> Pr. 3 Apr. 1780, widow **Deborah SAMSON** & Capt. Calvin PARTRIDGE, app'td admrs. <25:485> Inventory taken by Peres HOWLAND, Thomas CHANDLER, John HANKS; sworn to by appraisers & Calvin PARTRIDGE, 5 June 1780.

Guardianship of Children of **Abner SAMSON** of Duxbury MA. <Plymouth Co.PR #17423>
<26:94-96> Letters/Bonds 3 Apr. 1780, widow **Deborah SAMPSON** app'td gdn. of **Aaron, Nathaniel & Wealthy SAMPSON,** all under 14. Sureties: Calvin PARTRIDGE & Thomas CHANDLER of Duxbury. Witnesses: Isaac TOMSON, Zenas CUSHMAN. <26:351> Letter/Bond 3 Apr. 1780, **Luna SAMPSON,** above 14, choses mother **Deborah SAMPSON** her gdn. Witnesses: C. PARTRIDGE, Luse/Lucy SAMSON.

Estate of **Noah SAMPSON,** mariner of Plymouth MA. <Plymouth Co.PR #17611>
<original> Bond 13 July 1742, of widow **Jemima SAMSON,** as admx. Sureties: Nathaniel JACKSON, Joseph RYDER, both of Plymouth. Witness: Edward WINSLOW.

Estate of **Josiah SAMPSON** of Plympton MA. <Plymouth Co.PR #17581>
<5:663> Letter/Bond 9 Apr. 1730, brother **Ephraim SAMPSON** of Plympton app'td admr. Sureties: Peleg SAMPSON & Benjamin CUSHMAN of Plympton. Witnesses: Thomas BURTON, James FORD Jr. <5:737-8> Inventory taken 2 July 1730 by Samuel SAMPSON of Middleoboro and Benjamin CUSHMAN & Benjamin WESTON of Plympton; mentions: Isaac SAMSON, John DREW Jr., Daniel PRATT, Jonathan SAMSON, Peleg SAMSON, Ephraim SAMSON, Benjamin SAMSON, Barnabas SAMSON, David DILLENO, Thomas STACK, John ANDRES, Elisha CURTIS. <7:67-69> Receipts, 20 Mar. 1733/4, to admr.: of **Jonathan SAMSON**, husbandman of Plympton, for £6, his share; of **Isaac SAMSON**, husbandman of Plympton, for £12, his share; of **Peleg SAMSON**, nailer of Plympton, for £18.2.8., his share; of **Lydia SAMSON Jr.** & **Priscilla FULLER**, widow, both of Plympton for a lot of land in Plympton formerly laid out to our father **Isaac SAMSON** and after his decease settled on **Josiah SAMSON** late of Plympton; of **Barnabas SAMSON**, cordwainer of Plympton, for £18, his share; of widow **Lydia SAMSON** of Plympton, for £2.12s for her share. <Receipts of the brothers & sisters are also recorded in Plymouth Co.Deeds 29:43,44.>

Will of **Barnabas SAMSON**, yeoman of Middleboro MA. <Plymouth Co.PR #17451>
<12:131>...dated 4 May 1749, mentions wf **Experience** and eldest son **Barnabas SAMSON**...my estate... I give to my sd wife during her being my widow for the bringing up my children. Witnesses: Benjamin RUGGLES, Joseph PADDOCK, Steven MACOMORE/MULTMORE; sworn to 5 Nov. 1750 by PADDOCK & MULTMORE Pr. 6 Nov. 1750, widow **Experience SAMSON**, exx.

PLYMOUTH COUNTY DEEDS: (re: Ephraim SAMSON)

<22:135> - 11 Sept 1727, Ephraim SPOONER, cordwainer of Plympton from Isaac CUSHMAN Jr. of same.
<24:66> - 2 Apr. 1729, Ephraim SPOONER of Plympton from Samuel CUSHMAN of same.
<29:44> - 21 Mar. 1733/4, Ephraim SPOONER, cordwainer from Mercy CUSHMAN, widow of Plympton, for £2.10s, land next to that bought by Ephraim from various others.
<39:151> - 27 Oct. 1747, Ephraim SPOONER, cordwainer of Plympton to David WESTON, homestead in Plympton. Wf Abigail releases dower. Witness: Abigail SAMSON 3d.
<50:100> - 22 Dec. 1747, Ephraim SPOONER, cordwainer of Plympton from Nathaniel WOOD of Middleboro, land where Francis MORRO lived & died. Ack. 10 May 1755. Rec. 1765
<57:153> - 25 Jan. 1773, Ephraim SPOONER, cordwainer of Middleboro. Wf Abigail signs.
<60:84> - 3 May 1771, Ephraim SPOONER, cordwainer of Middleboro. Wf Abigail releases dower. Ack. 4 Feb. 1780 by Ephraim. Rec. 20 June 1780.

Estate of **Rebecca SHEPHERD**, widow of Plymouth MA. <Plymouth Co.PR 11:104,158>
Adm., 25 Mar. 1749, Joseph FULGHAM, mariner of Plymouth, app'td admr. Inv. taken 28 Mar. 1748/9

Will of **Isaac SAMSON**, yeoman of Middleboro MA. <Plymouth Co.PR #17541>
<12:342>...dated 23 Feb. 1748, mentions wf **Elizabeth** and following chil., viz: **Uriah SAMSON, John SAMSON** (to support his aged Grandmother during her life), **Isaac SAMSON, Jacob SAMSON, Sarah, Elizabeth, Margrett, Lydia, Anna, Hannah, Phebe**; son **John**, executor. Witnesses: Nathaniel SAMSON, Joseph PADDOCK, Barnabas SAMSON, Stephen MACOMBER. <11:355> Letter/Bond 7 May 1750, **Uriah SAMSON**, husbandman of Middleborough app'td admr. c.t.a., Whereas **Isaac SAMSON** app'td his son **John SAMSON** of Middleborough sole executor of sd will...but the executor aforenamed having been absent for a considerable time past & supposed to be dead. Sureties: Joseph PADDOCK & Nathaniel SAMSON of Middleborough. Witnesses: Caleb TURNER, Edward WINSLOW. <12:70> Inventory taken 10 May 1750 by Nathaniel SOUTHWORTH, Thomas NELSON Jr., Mark HASKALL; sworn to 21 May 1750 by appraisers, 4 June 1750 by admr. <12:280> Josiah EDSON Jr. of Bridgewater and Joseph PADDOCK & Thomas NELSON of Middleboro, app'td to settle a difference between **Elizabeth RICHMOND** wf of Edward and **Uriah SAMSON**, for labor done on lands of **Isaac SAMSON** after his death till **Elizabeth**'s right of dower was set off; settlement made 17 June 1751. <12:358> Account of admr., 12 July 1751; Paid to: Joseph TUCKER, Thomas COLLIER, Joseph ALLEN, Daniel RUSSELL, Edward SEARS, William READ, Thomas TORREY, Elias MILLER, Ebenezer SOUTHWORTH, Jacob SHERMAN, Nathaniel SAMSON, John SHAW, Edward WESTON, Josiah WOOD, Nicholas SEVER, Mark HASKEL, John BRADFORD, Micah PRATT, Benjamin RUGGLES, John HOLBROOK, David MILLER, Thomas CROSBEE, Isaac SAMSON, James HOVEY, Elkanah LEONARD, Joseph PADDOCK; charge in arbitration with **Mr. RICHMOND, Mrs. RICHMOND** late wife of dec'd her legacy; Debts yet unpaid to: Joseph TUCKER, Sarah ROUSE, James OTIS, John BRADFORD, Thomas NELSON, Joseph JOSSELYN, George WILLIAMSON, Ephraim SAMSON; Legacies yet unpaid to: heirs, **Isaac, Jacob, Sarah, Elizabeth, Margarett, Lydia, Ann, Hannah & Phebe SAMSON.** <21:210> On 7 May 1772, William SEVER, Josiah EDSON & Capt. Joseph CUSHING app'td to settle controversies in settlement of account of adm. on estate of **Isaac SAMSON** of Middleborough dec'd, also the account on estate of **John SAMSON** of Middleborough dec'd, also account of guardianship for **Peter SAMSON**, son of sd **John SAMSON**; settlement dated 27 Oct. 1772 & allowed 7 Dec. 1772.

Guardianship of Children of **Isaac SAMSON** of Middleboro MA. <Plymouth Co.PR #17547>
<12:535-36> Letters/Bonds 18 Oct. 1752, Edward RICHMOND, gent. of Taunton app'td gdn. of **Phebe SAMSON & Jacob SAMSON**. Surety: Seth RICHMOND, yeoman of Taunton. Witnesses: John LOTHROP, Hannah WINSLOW.

PLYMOUTH COUNTY DEEDS: (re: Isaac SAMSON, grantor**)**

<132:98> - 5 July 1791, Division between heirs of Uriah SAMSON.
<78:16> - 20 Mar. 1795, Isaac & Abigail SAMSON to Nathaniel & Aaron SAMPSON, land Isaac had from father Abner SAMSON of Duxbury.
<89:262> - 21 May 1801, Isaac SAMSON et al, heirs of Nathaniel SAMSON of Duxbury.
<89:265> - 21 May 1801, Isaac SAMSON et al, heirs of Nathaniel SAMSON of Duxbury.

PLYMOUTH COUNTY DEEDS, cont-d: (re: Isaac SAMSON, grantor)

<87:20> - 3 Apr. 1797, Isaac, James, George & Deborah SAMSON, minor chil. of Benjamin SAMSON of Plymouth, by John FAUNCE, gdn. (also <116:231>)
<103:230> - 4 Nov. 1800, Isaac & Uriah SAMSON of Middleborough. Serena & Delia SAMSON sign.
<93:62> - 21 May 1801, Isaac SAMSON et al, heirs of Nathaniel SAMSON of Duxbury.
<92:24> - 14 Jan. 1802, Isaac SAMSON et al, heirs of Nathaniel SAMSON of Duxbury.
<100:175> - 28 Apr. 1803, Isaac, James, George & Deborah SAMSON, minor chil. of Benjamin SAMSON of Plymouth by John FAUNCE, gdn.
<115:146> - 17 Dec. 1810, Isaac, James, George & Deborah SAMSON, minor chil. of Benjamin SAMSON of Plymouth by John FAUNCE, gdn.
<138:128> - 24 Mar. 1819, Isaac SAMSON et al, heirs of Benjamin SAMSON of Plymouth.
<172:223> - 28 May 1831, Isaac SAMSON, mortgage to Anselm RICHARDS. Discharged 19 Jan. 1834, by Elizabeth SAMSON, admx.
<181:3> - 10 Feb. 1834, Elizabeth SAMSON, admx. on estate of Isaac SAMSON of Plymouth dec'd, sells his interest in land & house which was formerly homestead of Benjamin SAMSON dec'd.
<222:107> - 11 Mar. 1835, Isaac SAMSON of Middleboro to son Nathaniel SAMSON.

Will of **Uriah SAMSON**, yeoman of Middleborough MA. <Plymouth Co.PR #17677>
<31:187>...dated 9 July 1789, mentions wf **Anna** (the use of my riding shay at any time she shall see cause to visit any of her daughters) and the following chil., viz: **Mary SAMSON, Phebe SAMSON, Ezra SAMSON, John SAMSON** (the dwelling house which I hold by deed under the hand & seal of Experience SAMSON), **Uriah SAMSON, Elias SAMSON, Isaac SAMSON, Daniel SAMSON, Sarah KING** wf of Capt. Josiah, **Hannah REED** wf of John and **Anna MONTGOMERY** wf of Hugh. Witnesses: Nehemiah BENNET, Seth HOAR, Jonathan CASWELL Jr. <original> Bond 7 June 1790, of **Uriah SAMSON & Isaac SAMSON,** exrs. Sureties: Nehemiah BENNETT of Middleborough & Henry BISHOP of Rochester. Witnesses: Isaac TIRRELL Jr., Isaac LOTHROP. <31:269> Inventory taken 7 Sept. 1790, by Nehemiah BENNET & John NELSON; sworn to 4 Oct. 1790 by appraisers & exrs.

Guardianship of Children of **Uriah SAMSON** of Middleborough MA. <Plymouth Co.PR #17504>
<32:3> Letters/Bonds 7 Mar. 1791, **Elias SAMSON,** above 14, chooses Hugh MONTGOMERY, yeoman of Middleborough as his gdn. Sureties: Isaac SAMSON of Middleboro, Joseph KING of Taunton. Witnesses: Benjamin WHITMAN, Isaac LOTHROP. <original> Bond 7 Mar. 1791, **Daniel SAMSON,** above 14, chooses Josiah KING of Taunton, as his gdn.

Guardianship of **Daniel SAMSON,** an intemperate, of Middleboro MA. <Plymouth Co.PR #17488>
<original> Complaint 19 Dec. 1795, by **Anna SAMSON, John SAMSON, Uriah SAMSON, Isaac SAMSON** and Josiah KING, requesting that Hugh MONTGOMERY be app'td gdn. <35:439> Request 29 Dec. 1795, of Nehemiah BENNET, Zephaniah SHAW & Hugh MONTGOMERY, Selectmen of Middleboro, that a gdn. be app'td <32:357> Letter/Bond 4 Jan. 1796, Hugh MONTGOMERY app'td gdn. Sureties: John SAMSON, physician & Uriah SAMSON, yeoman of Middleboro. Witnesses: Isaac SAMSON, Hiram NELSON. <35:498> Inventory taken 10 Mar. 1796 by John NELSON, Nehemiah BENNET & William STROBRIDGE 2d; incl. twenty two & a quarter acres set off to him in division of the homestead of his dec'd father as also 42 acres woodland, one fourth part of his father's dwelling house and three eighths of the new barn.

Jacob SAMSON of Middleborough MA to **Isaac WOOD** of same. <Plymouth Co.Deeds 59:158>
...1 Mar. 1768, Jacob SAMSON, husbandman, for Ł146.13s4d sold to Isaac WOOD, cordwainer...twenty six & a half acres in Middleborough...being all my homestead farm on which I now dwell. On 4 Mar. 1768, wf **Ellis/Alice SAMSON** releases dower. Ack. 7 Mar. 1769 by Jacob. Rec. 21 July 1778.

Estate of **John SAMSON,** husbandman of Middleborough MA. <Plymouth Co.PR #17563>
<11:364> Letter/Bond 5 June 1750, brother **Uriah SAMSON,** husbandman of Middleborough app'td admr. Sureties: Thomas TORREY & Isaac THOMAS, merchants of Plymouth. Witnesses: Edward WINSLOW, Hannah WINSLOW. <12:11> Inventory taken 10 June 1750 by Nathaniel SOUTHWORTH, Thomas NELSON Jr. & Mark HASKALL.

Guardianship of Child of **John SAMSON** of Middleborough MA. <Plymouth Co.PR #17622>
<11:373> Letter/Bond 12 July 1750, Uriah SAMSON, yeoman of Middleboro app'td gdn. of **Peter SAMSON** Surety: Thomas NELSON Jr. of Middleboro. Witnesses: Peter OLIVER, Edward WINSLOW. <21:210> Receipt 29 Oct. 1772, of **Peter SAMSON,** tanner of Swanzey, for five shillings received of Uriah SAMSON, as admr. on estate of grandfather **Isaac SAMSON** & father **John SAMSON,** both dec'd. Witnesses: Joseph CUSHING, Josiah EDSON.

Estate of **Jonathan SAMSON,** husbandman of Plympton MA. <Plymouth Co.PR #17568>
<14:482> Letter/Bond 9 Mar. 1758, Joseph PERRY, husbandman of Plimpton app'td admr. Sureties: Josiah CUSHMAN & Nathaniel BRYANT of Plimton. Witnesses: Gideon WHITE, Edward WINSLOW. <14:526> Inventory taken by Josiah PERKINS, John BRADFORD; incl. meadow in Winnetuxett & cedar swamp in Colchester. <15:122> Division, 24 Apr. 1759 by Josiah PERKINS, Rowland HAMMOND, Timothy RIPLEY, Ebenezer SOULE & Jabez NEWLAND, all of Plimton, to widow **Joanna SAMSON** and following chil., viz: **Jonathan SAMSON, Mary, Joanna, Priscilla PERRY** wf of Jonathan, **Abigail & Bethiah.**

Jonathan & Deborah SAMSON of Plympton MA. <Plymouth Co.Deeds 46:55>
...23 Feb. 1758, Jonathan SAMSON & wf Deborah sell all his rights to estate of dec'd father, also all lands given to his mother by his Grandfather LUCAS.

Will of **Joseph SAMSON** of Plympton MA. <Plymouth Co.PR #17576>
<25:229>...dated 10 Jan. 1794, mentions wf **Bethiah;** son **Peleg SAMSON;** grandson **Joseph Samson WATERMAN;** daus **Phebe RIPLEY** wf of Samuel and **Lucy WATERMAN** wf of Isaac; friend Elijah BISBE Jr. & son **Peleg,** executors. Witnesses: Thomas SAMPSON, John BISBE, John WRIGHT. <original> Bond 7 Apr. 1795 of exrs. Sureties: Thomas SAMSON of Plympton & Nehemiah COBB of Carver. Witnesses: Levi BRYANT, Ebenezer BRIGGS 2d. <35:323> Notice, sworn to 5 Oct. 1795 by exrs. <35:323> Inventory taken 5 Oct. 1795 by Thomas SAMSON & James CHURCHILL of Plympton.

Will of **Capt. Simeon SAMSON** of Plympton MA. <Plymouth Co.PR #17653>
<31:26>...dated 14 Mar. 1787, mentions wf **Deborah** and following chil., viz: **Lydia Cushing GOODWIN, Deborah SAMSON, Mercy SAMSON, Marie SAMSON, George Washington SAMSON.** Witnesses: Isaac LOTHROP, Stephen SAMSON, Joshua THOMAS. <original> Bond 3 Aug. 1789, of widow **Deborah SAMSON,** exx. Sureties: Seth CUSHING & John JOHNSON of Kingston. Witnesses: Stephen SAMSON, Isaac LOTHROP. <35:574> Inventory taken 17 Sept. 1789 by Kimbell PRINCE, Seth CUSHING; sworn to 28 Oct. 1796 by exx. & appraisers (John JOHNSON the other appraiser being dec'd.) <35:575> Account of exx., 28 Oct. 1796; Paid to: Dr. James THACHER, Judah WASHBURN, John FAUNCE, Joseph HOLMES, Lemuel DREW, Samuel DARLING, Job EATON, Lydia HOLMES, Perez BRADFORD, Elnathan HOLMES, Simeon STURTEVANT Jr., Mercy RUSIL/RUSSELL, William RIPLEY Jr., Silas MORTON, Seth CUSHING, Francis RING, Silvanus HARLOW, Robert BROWN, William LeBARON, Oliver CUSHMAN, Joanna WINSLOW, Steven SAMSON, Joel ELLIS, Ephraim SPOONER, Nathaniel LOTHROP, Nathan PERKINS, Ezra SAMSON, Jeremiah SAMSON admr. to Sarah SAMSON, Barnabas HEDG(E), Lydia C. GOODWIN, Benjamin WHITMAN, Lydia BRADFORD, Zebdiel BISBEY, Deborah SAMSON. <36:62> Account of exx., 17 Feb. 1797; Paid to: William GOODWIN, William CROMBY, George SAMSON, Benjamin DREW, Col. WATSON, John DAVIS, Seth CUSHING Jr., Kimbal PRINCE, John JOHNSON, Capt. Judah WASHBURN.

Guardianship of Child of **Capt. Simeon SAMSON** of Plympton MA. <Plymouth Co.PR #17517>
<32:70> Letter/Bond 15-17 Sept. 1796, **George Washington SAMSON,** above 14, chooses Zachariah CUSHMAN as his gdn. Sureties: Asa SHERMAN of Plympton & William GOODWIN, merchant of Plymouth. Witnesses: Nathaniel BRADFORD, Isaac LOTHROP.

MICRO #4 OF 4

Estate of **Desire JENNEY 2d,** single woman of Dartmouth MA. <Bristol Co.PR>
<127:36> Guardianship 6 Oct. 1761 of **Desire JENNE,** above 14, dau of **Caleb JENNE** dec'd of Dartmouth. <17:620> Pr. 4 May 1762, Hezekiah WINSLOW, gent. of Dartmouth, app'td admr. <18:36> Inventory taken 4 Dec. 1761 of estate of **Desire JENNEY 2d,** under 21. <18:527> Account of Hezekiah WINSLOW, guardian to **Desire JENNEY 2d** during her life & admr. after her decease.

Abner WESTON of Duxborough MA to **Micah & James WESTON** of same. <Plymouth Co.Deeds 66:202>
...2 Aug. 1786, Abner WESTON, yeoman for £40 sold to Micah WESTON & James WESTON, seamen...the whole of my farm whereon I now dwell lying in Duxborough...except a bed room in the north west corner of my house which I give unto my daughter Hannah WESTON...two thirds to Micah and one third to James. Witnesses: James TOWER, John WESTON. Ack. 2d Tues. Jan. 1787 by witnesses. Rec. 12 Jan. 1787.

James WESTON of Duxbury MA to **John WESTON** of same. <Plymouth Co.Deeds 106:176>
...3 June 1795, James WESTON, yeoman, for £20 sold to John WESTON, mariner...one third of the farm of the late Abner WESTON of Duxbury dec'd...being 10 acres in Duxbury. Witnesses: Deborah SPRAGUE, Benjamin SMITH. Ack. 16 June 1797 by James WESTON. Rec. 20 Mar. 1806.

Micah WESTON of Duxbury MA to **John WESTON** of same. <Plymouth Co.Deeds 106:176>
...22 Apr. 1794, Micah WESTON, inholder or mariner, for £10 sold to son John WESTON, mariner... one acre lying all around my dwelling house with a priveledge of the well the house he repaired at his own expense. Bethiah WESTON signs. Witnesses: Nathaniel HOLMES, Bethiah WESTON 2d. Ack. 30 May 1795. Rec. 20 Mar. 1806.

Micah WESTON of Duxborough MA to **James WESTON** of same. <Plymouth Co.Deeds 120:65>
...17 Mar. 1813, Micah WESTON, gent., for $150.00 sold to son James WESTON, miller...land in Duxborough...bounded by land of Enoch FREEMAN, Isaac SAMSON, John DELANO & John WESTON. Bethiah WESTON signs. Witnesses: Sarah WESTON, Otis WESTON. Ack. 26 Mar. 1813 by Micah & Rec. same day.

Micah WESTON of Duxbury MA to **Seth SPRAGUE** of same. <Plymouth Co.Deeds 120:132>
...13 Apr. 1813, Micah WESTON, yeoman & wf Bethiah, for $118.00 sold to Seth SPRAGUE, Esq...eleven acres in Duxbury...bounded by land of the estate of John WESTON and land of Enoch FREEMAN. Witnesses: Isaiah ALDEN, Peleg SPRAGUE. Ack. 30 Apr. 1813 by Micah. Rec. 4 May 1813.

Guardianship of **Rebecca PETERSON,** widow, insane, of Duxbury MA. <Plymouth Co.PR>
<81:373> Application for gdn., 1 Nov. 1836. <81:374> 5 Dec. 1836, **Daniel PETERSON** of Duxbury app'td gdn. <79:546> Account of gdn., 4 Dec. 1837; mentions trip to Boston to get pension; 6 yrs pension from 4 Mar. 1831 to 4 Mar. 1837, $480.00 and 6 mths pension from 4 Mar. 1837 to 4 Sept. 1837, $40.00. <83:372> Account of gdn., 6 Aug. 1841; U.S. Pension from 4 Mar. 1831 to 4 Mar. 1841, $800.00; balance on hand, $386.00; half balance paid to Joseph WADSWORTH & remainder is due to me (gdn.) as heir. (Note: The pension in question is that of her husband, **Joseph PETERSON,** who served in the Revolutionary War between 1775 until his death in 1777. <Claim W.File #21940>.)

Thomas STANDISH of Pembroke MA to **Thomas STANDISH Jr.** of same. <Plymouth Co.Deeds 40:236>
...10 May 1750, Thomas STANDISH, yeoman, for £66 sold to Thomas STANDISH Jr., labourer...one half of the farm on which I now dwell in Pembroke...and is the 50th lot of the fourty acre lots of land that belonged to the First Division of the Common Lands in Duxborough and was laid out in 1710...bounded by land of John RUSSEL, the brook by TUBBS' and up Herring Brook. Witnesses: Daniel LEWIS Jr., Sarah LEWIS. Ack. 10 May 1750 by Thomas STANDISH. Rec. 25 June 1750.

Thomas STANDISH of Pembroke MA to **William STANDISH** of same. <Plymouth Co.Deeds 58:73>
...16 June 1773, Thomas STANDISH, yeoman, for £66 sold to son William STANDISH, yeoman...20 acres in Pembroke...being the one half part of the 50th lot in the First Division of the Commons of upland which belonged to Duxborough & Pembroke and it being the one half part of the farm whereon I now do dwell...bounded by land of John RUSSELL, the brook by TUBBS' and up Herring Brook...excepting the dwelling house that sd William now dwells in, for that house the sd William is altogether the proper owner of. Witnesses: Josiah KEEN, John STETSON. Ack. 13 June 1774 by Thomas. Rec. 17 June 1774.

Will of **David STANDISH**, yeoman of Hanover MA. <Plymouth Co.PR 35:285>
...26 Oct. 1793, mentions wf **Hannah**; four daus **Olive JOSSELYN, Hannah STANDISH, Priscilla JOSSELYN, Mary STANDISH**; sons **Lemuel STANDISH, James STANDISH**; to son **David STANDISH**, executor, all real estate. Witnesses: Andrew BRADFORD, Cynthia BRADFORD, Polly BRADFORD. Pr. 6 July 1795.

Will of **Hannah STANDISH**, widow of Hanover MA. <Plymouth Co.PR 38:391>
...dated 19 Oct. 1801, mentions following chil., viz: **Hannah STANDISH & Polly STANDISH** (exx), **Lemuel STANDISH, James STANDISH, Olive JOSSELYN** wf of Stockbridge (now living separate from her husband), **Priscilla JOSSELYN** wf of Seth, **David STANDISH.** Witnesses: Reuben CURTIS, Consider CURTIS, William TORREY. Pr. 5 Sept. 1803.

Estate of **Thomas STANDISH Jr.** of Pembroke MA. <Plymouth Co.PR #19181>
<original> Request of heirs, 24 Nov. 1779...being owners of a certain tract of land lying in Pembroke which was the homestead of **Thomas STANDISH** but half sold to his son **Thomas STANDISH Jr.** who dies leaving a widow **Else/Alice** and three children, viz: **Amos STANDISH** (eldest son), **Hadley STANDISH** & **Betty Bisbe STANDISH. Thomas Sr.** conveyed the other half to his son **William STANDISH.** Signed by **William STANDISH, Else/Alice STANDISH, Amos STANDISH & Hadley STANDISH.** (Hadley being a minor but if he lives until Feb. next he will arrive to lawfull age.) <27:52> Letter/Bond 1 May 1780, Asaph TRACY app'td admr. Sureties: Josiah THOMAS, Abel BAKER. Witnesses: Asaph TRACY Jr., Jacob TRACY. <25:509> Inventory taken 27 May 1780, by John TURNER, Josiah THOMAS, Isaac JENNINGS; twenty two & one quarter acres of land with half an old dwelling house, half barn & orchard, £2640; sworn to 30 May 1780 by admr. <original> Insolvency. <28:93> List of Claims, 28 Mar. 1781; Creditors: Dr. John WADSWORTH and admrs. of estate of Joshua CARVER late of Marshfield & Abisha STETSON dec'd. <28:93> Account of admr., 6 Apr. 1781. <28:228> Division, 6 Nov. 1781, by John TURNER, Samuel GOOLD, Isaac JENNINGS; land held in common by **William STANDISH** & heirs of **Thomas STANDISH Jr.** formerly belonging to **Thomas STANDISH Sr.**; 45 acres in Duxbury; half of real estate set off to **William STANDISH** and the other half to the chil. of **Thomas STANDISH Jr.**, viz: **Amos STANDISH, Hadley STANDISH & Betty Bisbee STANDISH.** <28:299> Dower set off 20 Nov. 1781, to widow **Else/Alice STANDISH**, 10 acres adjoining **William STANDISH**'s lot being one third of 27 acres.

Estate of **Elisha BISBEE** of Pembroke MA. <Plymouth Co.PR #2032>
...1756...<14:79> Letter. <14:367> Inventory. <14:283> Account. <15:112> Dower. <15:533> Claims. <15:533> Account. <15:534> Distribution.

Will of **William STANDISH** of Pembroke MA. <Plymouth Co.PR #19183>
<66:412>...dated 14 May 1820...being advanced in age; mentions wf **Molly** and following chil., viz: **William STANDISH, Nabby COOK,** chil. of **Miles STANDISH** dec'd, **Job STANDISH** (executor). Witnesses: John TURNER, Daniel KEENE, Job TURNER. <original> Bond 19 Jan. 1829 of **Job STANDISH,** exr. Sureties: Daniel KEEN & John COX of Pembroke. Witness: William SPOONER. <62:335> Notice, sworn to 16 Feb. 1829 by exr.

William STANDISH Jr. et al, division. <Plymouth Co.Deeds 121:276>
...16 Oct. 1811, William STANDISH Jr., bricklayer of Pembroke & wf Ruth in her right and Asa KEEN, yeoman of Pembroke & wf Abigail in her right, divide land they hold in common which James BARSTOW late of Duxbury...gave to his daughters Abigail & Ruth. Ack. 16 Oct. 1811. Rec. 14 Jan. 1814.

PLYMOUTH COUNTY DEEDS: (re: William STANDISH, grantor**)**

<102:111> - 1805, William STANDISH, mortgage to Comfort BATES.
<169:10> - 8 Jan. 1830, William STANDISH, bricklayer of Pembroke to William STANDISH Jr., bricklayer of Duxbury, land in Duxbury. Witnesses: Lucy B. STANDISH, Abby STANDISH. Ack. 16 Feb. 1830. Rec. 17 Feb. 1830.
<180:285> - 18 June 1833, William STANDISH, bricklayer of Pembroke, bond to son William STANDISH Jr., to give him the land Sr. bought that day from Jr.
<177:70> - 19 June 1833, William STANDISH Jr. to father William STANDISH the same land bought 8 Jan. 1830. Wf Huldah releases dower.
<178:275> - 1 Dec. 1834, William STANDISH Jr. to Benjamin STANDISH. Rec. 4 Dec. 1834.
<205:154> - 17 Aug. 1841, William STANDISH, mason of Pembroke & wf Ruth to Benjamin BARSTOW.

PLYMOUTH COUNTY DEEDS,cont-d: (re: William STANDISH, grantor)

<237:75> - 1 Dec. 1834, William STANDISH Jr., bricklayer of Duxbury to Benjamin STANDISH, bricklayer of Pembroke. Wf Huldah signs. Rec. 3 Apr. 1850.
<206:132> - 3 Jan. 1842, William STANDISH Jr. (by gdn, a spendthrift) & wf Huldah of Duxbury to Benjamin STANDISH, bricklayer of Pembroke.

Estate of **William STANDISH** of Pembroke MA <Plymouth Co.PR #19184>
<12:403C> Petition, 5 Apr. 1852, **Ruth B. STANDISH, Benjamin STANDISH & E.O. STANDISH,** widow & chil. of dec'd, decline administration & request that **George B. STANDISH** of Duxbury be app'td. <12:403C> Bond. <94:150> Inventory. <95:112> Dower. <95:141> Distribution (no date given), to following heirs, iz: **George B. STANDISH, Benjamin STANDISH, Abby S. JOSSELYN, Lucy P. TURNER, Elizabeth O. STANDISH, Mary SAWIN,** Benjamin ALDEN as gdn. of **William STANDISH,** Ira GERRY as gdn. of **Miles STANDISH, Ruth SAMSON.**

Guardianship of **William STANDISH Jr.,** bricklayer of Duxbury MA. <Plymouth Co.PR #19186>
...June 1841, Joshua BREWSTER app'td gdn. of **William STANDISH Jr.,** insane, spendthrift; 17 May 1852, Joshua resigns and Benjamin ALDEN is app'td. Inventory taken Jan. 1856; one ninth of the homestead farm of the late **William STANDISH** of Pembroke.

JOSIAH STANDISH[2] (Myles[1])

Alexander & Josiah STANDISH. <Plymouth Co.PR 1:225>
...29 June 1682, Alexander STANDISH & Josiah STANDISH witnessed the will of George PARTRIDGE of Duxbury. On 16 Oct. 1695, Alexander made oath to the will and testified that he then saw his brother Josiah, now dec'd, subscribe with him as a witness also.

John RUSSELL of Dartmouth MA to **Edward GRAY** of Plymouth MA. <Plymouth Col.Deeds 3:73>
...16 Sept. 1664, John RUSSELL, planter to Edward GRAY. Witnesses: Sarah STANDISH, Francis BILLINGTON. Ack. same day.

Josiah STANDISH, yeoman of Duxbury. <Plymouth Col.Deeds 5:194>
...7 June 1670...Josiah STANDISH & wf Sarah...land on Manomet River. Ack. 4 July 1670 by both.

NORWICH CT DEEDS: (re: STANDISH)

<1:114> - 5 Feb. 1686, John PARKS to Capt. Josiah STANDISH now in Norwich.
<2B:733> - 9 Apr. 1714, Josiah STANDISH, carpenter of Preston to Nathaniel RICHARDS of same, part of land my father Josiah STANDISH bought of John PARK/PARKS.
<3B:790> - 19 Mar. 1723, Samuel STANDISH of Preston to John FORD. Witnesses: Joseph GATES, Josiah STANDISH Jr.

Estate of **Miles STANDISH** of Preston CT. <New London CT PR>
<3:79>...9 Apr. 1728, **Elizabeth STANDISH** app'td admx. <3:82> Inventory sworn to 7 May 1728 by admx. <3:88>...8 May 1729, admx. to sell land.

James CARY/CERY of Bridgewater MA to **James DEAN.** <original owned by H.D.FORBES, Apr. 1914>
...Taunton, 23 July 1689...Then Received of James CARY of Bridgewater for the use of **Josiah STANDISH** of New Preston a bed & bolster & case, 3 napkins, 2 spoons, 2 sheets, a rug, a blacket, 3 trays, a tin pan porrenger & cup & platter, a cushing & peece of curtaine, 5 yds of linnen cloth, a kitle & skilet, all these to be deliver at Stoningtown the danger of the sees excepte(d) I say received by mee as witnes my hand. Signed by James DEAN.

RICHARD WARREN

MICRO #1 OF 32

ABIGAIL WARREN[2] (Richard[1])

PLYMOUTH COLONY RECORDS:

<1:83> - 7 May 1638, Anthony SNOW desireth a pcell of land, about three acres, lying on the north side of Mr. DONE/DOANE's lands, towards the Fresh Lake.
<1:93> - 7 Aug. 1638, Nicholas SNOW desireth 5 or 6 acrees of land lying on the north side the lands graunted lately to Mr. ATWOOD...same day Anthony SNOW desireth 3.
<1:166> - 2 Nov. 1640, Several persons are granted land in South Meadows towards Aggawam, Colebrook Meadows...5 acres to Anthony SNOW.
<2:30> - 31 Dec. 1641, John SMALEY & Anthony SNOW granted 5 acres at Cole Brooke Meadow.
<3:131> - 2 Mar. 1657, Request of Jobe HAWKINS of Boston, for to enjoy the lands of Major William HOLMES att the North River...Josias WINSLOW Sr. & Anthony SNOW to prise the same.
<3:134> - 4 May 1658, Kenelme WINSLOW, Anthony SNOW & Timothy WILLIAMSON requested to lay out 5 acres granted to George SOULE.
<3:138> - 1 June 1658, Gorge/George SOULE, Constant SOUTHWORTH & Phillip DELANOE app'td by Court to sett range betwixt Mr. BOURNE's & Anthony SNOW's lands att Marshfield.
<4:8> - 4 Mar. 1661, Major Josias WINSLOW, Captaine William BRADFORD & Anthony SNOW are deputed by the Court to settle bounds between the lands graunted to Duxborrow men, bearing date August the last, 1640, and a tract of land graunted to Scittuate men bearing date in November following.
<4:20> - 3 June 1662, In reference unto a former graunt to sundry ancient freemen of the towne of Taunton...the Major, Captain SOUTHWORTH & Captaine BRADFORD are app'td by the Court to purchase the same of the Indians in the halfe of those heerafter named provided that which shalbee purchased shall not be prejudiciall to the Indians...Anthony SNOW (only one named here).
<4:67> - 8 June 1664, Anthony SNOW, Ensigne Mark EAMES, Joseph WARREN, Richard WRIGHT, William HARLOW, Nathaniel MORTON, Ephraim MORTON, William PAYBODY, John DUNHAM, Jr. & John ROGERS have libertie to looke out land for accomodations.
<4:104> - 1 Aug. 1665, The Major WINSLOW, Anthony SNOW, John BOURNE & William PAYBODY are app'td by the Court to rectify a difference & controversy between Moses SIMONS & Samuel CHANDLER in reference unto the bounds of theire lands in Duxburrow. <4:120>...1 May 1666, viewed lands.
<5:222> - 6 Mar. 1676/7, The order & destribution of this collonies parte of the contribution made by divers Christians in Ireland for the releiffe of such as are impoverished, destressed, and in nessesitie by the late Indian warr, was as it respects this collonie, proportioned as followeth: Ŀ2 to Anthony SNOW of Marshfield (only one named here).

Anthony SNOW to **John JENKINS/JENKYNE.** <Plymouth Col.Rec. 12:65>
...24 Dec. 1640, Anthony SNOW, for Ŀ16.10s sterling to be paid by John JENKINS, sell...all that his house & eight acres of land lying at Hobbs hole on the south side of Willingsly Brooke.

Anthony SNOW to **Thomas DUNHAM.** <Plymouth Col.Rec. 12:112>
...25 Aug. 1645, Anthony SNOW, for Ŀ6.18s to be paid by Thomas DUNHAM, sell...all that his house & eight acres.

Thomas PRENCE of Nauset/Nawset to **Richard CHURCH & Anthony SNOW.** <Plymouth Col.Rec. 12:176>
...13 July 1649, Thomas PRENCE, gent. of the towne of Nawset in the Coliny of New Plymouth in New England in america, for Ŀ45 sterling, sold to Richard CHURCH, carpenter of Nauset and Anthony SNOW, feltmaker of Marshfield...upland & marsh meadow at greens harbor alias Marshfield...betwixt Mr. BURNE/BOURNE's and a little creeke...towards Mr. BUCHLE's and 40 acres upland on other side of sd creeke...as is expressed in the record of the graunt of the sd lands unto Thomas PRENCE, 5 Feb. 1647. <12:197>...22 Oct. 1650, Richard CHURCH sold his share to John DINGLEY.

MARSHFIELD "OLD COPY" ("pig skin binding"):

<p.20> - 24 Oct. 1664, Lt. Peregrine WHITE & Anthony SNOW to lay out land for John THOMAS Sr.
<p.24> - 26 June 1665, Anthony SNOW, with William PABODIE of Duxbury laid out land to John ROUSE Sr. (also 12 July & 19 July).
<p.106> - 8 Jan. 1671/2, Town grants 60 acres to Joseph WATERMAN.

<no source>...25 June 1666, At a Town meeting...**Anthony SNOW** gave half an acre to the Town of Marshfield for a Burying Place on northerly side of highway near meeting house & next to land of WILLIAMSON. ...21 Sept. 1668, **Anthony SNOW** granted 60 acres in division between Duxbury & Marshfield if Duxbury agrees. Anthony surrenders his rights in land on which the meeting house stands.

References to **Nicholas SNOW**, grantor, in Plymouth Colony Deeds: <1:38> to Samuel EDDY; <1:220> to Thomas MORTON & Nathaniel MORTON; <3:335> to Peter WORDEN. **Mark SNOW**, grantor: <5:255> to Samuel SMITH.

References to **Nicholas SNOW**, grantor, in Plymouth County Deeds: <35:4> Settlement of bounds with John WINSLOW; <37:67> to Nathaniel SNOW; <37:143> to Isaac SNOW; <38:54> to Jonathan SNOW; <40:39> to Nathaniel SNOW; <41:177> to John WINSLOW et al; <50:40> to Barzillai HAMMOND; <68:164> to Daniel VAUGHAN; <71:219> to Benjamin DEXTER Jr.; <77:35> to Solomon HALL.

References to **Mark SNOW**, grantor, in Plymouth County Deeds: <28:180> wife of, to Jeremiah HOUSE; <59:255> to Paul GREEN; <60:227> to Lemuel LeBARON; <62:276> Settlement of bounds; <63:107> to Ebenezer WHITE; <66:276> to Ebenezer MORSE; <68:15> to John MILLARD; <71:171> to John BURGESS; <72:40> to Thomas TOBEY; <74:25> to Nathaniel SPRAGUE; <82:10> to Heman HIGGINS; <83:237> to James FOSTER Jr.; <91:199> Division.

Will of **Michael FORD** of Marshfield MA. <Plymouth Co.PR>
<5:498>...dated 12 June 1719, mentions wf **Bethiah**, sons **William FORD, James FORD, Thomas FORD, Ephraim FORD & Elisha FORD** and daus **Bathsheba, Mehitable, Mercy**; to son **William**, two acres fresh meadow at South River and my part of sawmill; to sons **Ephraim & Elisha**, farm where I now dwell, a gun each and husbandry tools and improvement of pasture at grist mill; sons **William & James**, executors. Witnesses: Seth ARNOLD, Edward ARNOLD, Jonathan ALDEN. <5:499> Pr. 16 May 1729, sons **William & James** app'td admrs. <5:484> Inventory taken 27 May 1729 by Edward ARNOLD, Fras. BARKER, Samuel JACOB; incl. salt marsh at beach, £500; fresh meadow at South River, £28; homestead, £1200 half of mill & pasture, £180; walking kane, 8s; ceder swamp, £20.16s.

Will of **James FORD** of Marshfield MA. <Plymouth Co.PR #7914>
<7:146>...dated 1 Feb. 1734, mentions wf **Hannah**, sons **James FORD, Michael FORD, Barnabas FORD** and daus **Abigail JOYCE, Hannah BAKER**; sons **Michael & Barnabas**, executors. Witnesses: James SPRAGUE, William HOWLAND, Arthur HOWLAND. <7:147> Pr. 15 July 1735. <7:148> Inventory taken 30 July 1735; sworn to same day by exrs.; incl. meadow at beach in Marshfield, £120; meadow in Duxbury, £90; woodlot in Duxbury, £50 and cedar swamp, £5.

References to the name **James FORD**, grantor, all to 1801, Plymouth Co.Deeds: <10:2:59> 1712, Marshfield; <12:159> 1717, Duxbury; <21:183> 1726, Jr. of Middleboro; <24:72> 1729, Marshfield. <25:183> 1730, Duxbury & Marshfield; <26:142> 1731, Marshfield; <27:211> 1732, Marshfield; <42:249> 1754, Duxbury; <68:93> 1788, Duxbury & Pembroke; <76:107> 1794, division. <84:49> 1798, Pembroke.
References to the name **James FORD**, grantee: <9:210,211;14:111;20:173;25:183;27:211;76:107;84:119.
References to the name **Barnabas FORD**: <30:4;34:31;40:144;42:249;46:258;56:192;57:197>.

Will of **John JOYCE**, yeoman of Marshfield MA. <Plymouth Co.PR #11723>
<16:377>...dated 17 July 1762, mentions wf **Abigail** and following chil., viz: **Ebenezer JOYCE** (executor), **John JOYCE, Abigail JOYCE, Abiah LAPHAM, Nathaniel JOYCE, Thomas JOYCE**. <16:378> Pr. 6 Dec. 1762. <16:445> Inventory taken 13 Dec. 1762; total real estate, £612; total, £724.2.11.

Estate of **Ebenezer JOYCE** of Marshfield MA. <Plymouth Co.PR>
...1776...<23:110> Letter. <24:205> Inv. <25:59> Account. <28:80> Division. <26:34-37> Guardianship of chil., viz: **Stephen, Asa, Alathea, Abiah JOYCE.**

Will of **Michael FORD** of Marshfield MA. <Plymouth Co.PR #7945>
<19:64>...dated 3 May 1764...to wf **Orphan**, use of all estate for five years from 20 Feb. 1764, to bring up children, also one eighth of sloop "Betty" which I own with Elisha FORD; children, viz: **Seth FORD** (executor), **Waterman FORD, Sarah FORD, Lucy FORD, Lydia FORD, Elizabeth FORD, Hannah FORD, Ann FORD.** <19:65> Pr. 2 June 1764. <19:108> Inventory taken 6 Aug. 1764. <20:254> Account, 24 July 1769.

Estate of **Orphan SOUL**, widow of Marshfield MA. <Plymouth Co.PR #18853>
<27:421> Letter/Bond 4 Mar. 1793, **Seth FORD**, yeoman of Marshfield app'td admr. Sureties: Elisha FORD & Arunah FORD of Marshfield. Witnesses: Benjamin WHITMAN, Isaac LOTHROP. <33:502> Notice. <33:362> Inventory taken 27 May 1793 by Asa WATERMAN, Daniel LEWIS, Elisha FORD. <35:307> Division 4 Sept. 1794, among following heirs, viz: **Seth FORD, Waterman FORD, Lucy FORD, Michael FORD,** heirs of **Elizabeth KEITH** dec'd wf of George, **Hannah KEEN** wf of Hezekiah and **Anna FORD** wf of Marlborough. Division 5 June 1795, of undivided land owned between the **Orphan SOUL** dec'd and the heirs of Pabody LITTLE late of Marshfield. <39:438> Letter/Bond 21 Dec. 1807, Chandler SAMSON, yeoman of Marshfield app'td admr. d.b.n., **Seth FORD** being dec'd. Sureties: Jesse CHURCHILL of Plymouth & Arthur HOWLAND of Marshfield. Witnesses: William SIMMONS, Isaac GOODWIN. <42:330> Inventory taken 4 Jan. 1808 by Arthur HOWLAND, Elisha FORD, Araunah FORD. <42:331> Notice. <42:331, 434> Account of admr., allowed 2 Jan. 1809; Paid to: Arthur HOWLAND, Elisha FORD, Araunah FORD, William WHITE, Bourne THOMAS, John PETERSON, Bildad WASHBURN, Samuel WILLIAMSON, Asa WATERMAN, Daniel LEWIS, Charles TURNER Jr., Jarie BISBEE, Isaac WINSLOW, Benjamin TOLMAN, Hannah FORD, George KEITH, Perez DREW. <43:357> Account of admr., allowed 3 Sept. 1810; Paid to: Lucy FORD,

heirs of **Elizabeth KEITH, Waterman FORD, Michael FORD, Marlborough FORD** & wf **Anna**, their shares; Due: **Hannah KEEN**; Paid: John JOYCE, Elisha FORD; charges himself with the estate of **Seth FORD** dec'd; Received of: **David & Calvin KEITH** on execution by Nahum MITCHELL; Land sold to: Calvin SAMSON, James KEITH, Rachel & Lucy FORD, Jabez HATCH, Joshua LORING, Consider & Frances FORD, Luther WHITE, Gideon WHITE, Lot PHILLIPS; Paid to: Dr. Isaac PAINE, Arthur HOWLAND, Elisha FORD, Arunah FORD, Luke WADSWORTH, Charles SPRAGUE, Luther SPRAGUE, Elisha PHILLIPS, Joseph CLIFT Jr., **Bethany FORD** widow of dec'd, Asa CHANDLER, Zabdiel BRADFORD, Nathaniel THOMAS, Hezekiah KEEN.

Estate of **Thomas BRANCH**, cordwainer of Plymouth MA. <Plymouth Co.PR #2680>
<6:129> Letter/Bond 14 Feb. 1731, widow **Lydia BRANCH** app'td admx. Sureties: John FAUNCE, glazier & Elisha BARROW, cordwainer, of Plymouth. <6:282> Warrant to appraise. <6:227> Inventory taken 10 May 1732 by Haviland TORREY, Stephen CHURCHELL, Thomas SPOONER, all of Plymouth; incl. house & home lott, Ł200; shop & land, Ł80; land att (--) Rock & frame, Ł60; land called Sherriffs hill, Ł110; land att Bonums & Daniels Neck, Ł200; soard/sword & belt, 12s; spoon mold, 6s; shomakers tools & lasts, Ł2.9s3d; pew in meeting house, Ł12; sworn to 28 Sept. 1732 by admx. & appraisers. <10:1> Warrant, 20 Sept. 1745, to Deacon John WOOD/ATWOOD, Timothy MORTON, Deacon Thomas FOSTER, James HOVEY & Caleb SHERMAN, all of Plymouth, having already set off dower to widow are now directed to divided remaining estate among the following chil., viz: **John BRANCH, Lydia SHURTLIFF** wf of Nathaniel, **Mercy BRANCH, Thankfull BRANCH & Experience BRANCH.** <10:4> Account.

Guardianship of Children of **Thomas BRANCH** of Plymouth MA. <Plymouth Co.PR #2674>
<9:536-38>...20 Sept. 1745...**Experience, Thankful & John BRANCH.**

Estate of **Lydia BRANCH**, widow of Plymouth MA. <Plymouth Co.PR #2677>
<13:23> Pr. 17 Nov. 1752, Nathaniel SHURTLEFF, tailor of Plymouth, app'td admr. <13:100> Inventory taken 29 Nov. 1752; only real estate is land in Bonums Neck, Ł20. <13:100> Account of admr., 2 Apr. 1753; received a debt due from **Thomas BRANCH,** a minor, Ł11.9.4. <13:155> 2d Account, 24 Nov. 1753. <13:169> Division 7 Dec. 1753, to following chil., viz: **Lydia SHURTLEFF** wf of Nathaniel, **Mary CHURCHELL** wf of Ebenezer, **Experience SHERMAN** wf of Samuel and **Thomas HOWARD** the only child of **Thankfull HOWARD** dec'd.

MICRO #2 OF 32

Estate of **Josiah SNOW** of Marshfield MA. <Plymouth Co.PR #18699>
<1:152> Letter/Bond 3 Jan. 1692/3, widow **Rebeckah SNOW** app'td admx. Sureties: William CARVER of Marshfield & Francis BARKER of Duxborow. Witnesses: Nathaniel WINSLOW, Samuel SPRAGUE Jr. <1:151> Inventory sworn to 3 Jan.1692/3 by admx.; upland & meadow, Ł150. <original> Account of admx., 3 Nov. 1693; Paid to: William THOMAS, William CARVER, Nathaniel WINSLOW Jr. <1:189> Settlement, 3 Nov. 1693, by William BRADFORD, Judge of Probate at Scituate; the sum of Ł183.4s10d to be divided as follows: Ł12 to each of the eight children when they reach 18 and the remainder to the widow as her thirds and to enable her to bring up the little children of sd dec'd. <3:112> Guardianship 5 Feb. 1711/12, William CARVER chosen gdn. by **Abia SNOW.** Surety: Samuel BAKER of Marshfield. Witness: William ASHCOMB.

Estate of **Rebeckah SAWYER** of Marshfield MA. <Plymouth Co.PR #17750>
<3:64> Letter/Bond 4 May 1711, sons in law **Nathaniel WINSLOW & Joseph WATERMAN** app'td admrs. Surety: John SPRAGUE of Duxbury. Witness: Elizabeth THOMAS. <3:79> Inventory taken 4 May 1711, of the estate of **Rebeckah SAWYER,** late wife of **John SAWYER,** by William CARVER & Joseph TAYLER; sworn to 22 June 1711 by admrs. <3:72> Receipt 20 June 1711, of **Gilbert WINSLOW, Samuel BAKER & John SPRAGUE,** to the admrs. of the estate of our late Mother, in full share for our part.

Heirs of **Josiah SNOW** of Marshfield MA. <Plymouth Co.Deeds 10:1:375>
...10 May 1712, Nathaniel WINSLOW & wf Lydia, Gilbert WINSLOW & wf Marcy, Samuel BAKER & wf Sarah Joseph WATERMAN & wf Lusanna, John SPRAGUE & wf Bethia and William CARVER as guardian of Abiah SNOW...being the proprietors of all that tract of land & meadows which did formerly belong unto Anthony SNOW dec'd...and the sd John SPRAGUE having lately sold unto Samuel THOMAS of Marshfield a certain part of his right in the aforesd land & meadows by deed 1 Jan. 1711/2...divide sd land.

Samuel BAKER of Marshfield MA to **Nathaniel WINSLOW** of Swanzy MA. <Plymouth Co.Deeds 10:1:372>
...9 May 1712, Samuel BAKER & wf Sarah, for Ł89 sold to Nathaniel WINSLOW...land in Marshfield, being ye sixth part of ye upland of that farm...formerly the land of Anthony SNOW of Marshfield dec'd as also a sixth part of that parcel of land granted (by the Town of Marshfield) to the heirs of Josiah SNOW dec'd...also our right in a certain Island called Bourns Island together with the like interest in trees, timber & wood standing...with a sixth part of all the houses, barns, fences & orchards. Ack. 10 May 1712.

Gilbert WINSLOW & Joseph WATERMAN to **Nathaniel WINSLOW.** <Plymouth Co.Deeds 10:1:378>
...15 May 1712, Gilbert WINSLOW & wf Mercy and Joseph WATERMAN & wf Lusanna, of Marshfield, for Ł310 sold to Nathaniel WINSLOW of Swanzey...land in Marshfield <described above in 10:1:372>... bounded by land of Samuel THOMAS, Israel THOMAS, heirs of Joseph WATERMAN & Thomas BOURNE dec'd, John DINGLEY, John KEEN, Nathan WILLIAMSON...also our whole right...in two acres of meadow...that was given to our Father Josiah SNOW dec'd by Nicholas or Mark SNOW of Eastham near Turkey Point. Witnesses: Seth ARNOLD, Arthur HOWLAND Jr. Ack. 8 Aug. 1712 by grantors. <10:1:381>...29 Oct. 1712, **Abiah SNOW,** dau of Josias SNOW & grand daughter of Anthony SNOW, sold her interest in the above, for Ł155 to **Nathaniel WINSLOW Jr.** Witnesses: William CARVER, James OTIS. Ack. 29 Oct. 1712

by Abiah. Ack. 26 Oct. 1713 by Abiah SNOW being now of full age. <10:1:383>...16 Jan. 1712/13, **John & Bethiah SPRAGUE,** for £80, sold to **Nathaniel WINSLOW Jr.** their share in farm of Grandfather Anthony SNOW dec'd. Ack. 16 Jan. 1712/13.

Estate of **Nathaniel WINSLOW** of Marshfield MA. <Plymouth Co.PR #23210>
...1736...<7:180> Letter. <7:199> Inventory, Account. <7:293> Settlement.

Estate of **Samuel BAKER** of Marshfield MA. <Plymouth Co.PR #820>
<4:291> Letter/Bond 16 Jan. 1721, Gilbert WINSLOW & Samuel BAKER app'td admrs. Sureties: William FOORD/FORD & John JONES of Marshfield. Witnesses: Francis BARKER, John CHAMBERLIN. <4:315> Inventory taken 23 Jan. 1721/2 by John JONES, John KENT & Thomas FORD; incl. homesteed, £440; salt meadow, £52; fresh meadow, £48; lot he bought of BONNEY, £10.10s; lot he bought of BARKER, £30; lot he bought of WEST, £20; lot he drew himself, £16; lot he bought of GARNOR, £30; 5 acres on South River, £30; right in 2 lots at Pembroke, £36; his & her apparel, £21.12s; one sloop, £128; one drum & sticks, £2.15s; for druming, £7.10s; total real estate, £712.19s; sworn to 5 Mar. 1721/2 by admrs. & appraisers. <5:41> Account of admrs., 8 Mar. 1724; incl. receipt of £30 for 3 years rent of ye farm. <5:42> Settlement of real estate, 1 Mar. 1724/5 to the following chil., viz: to **Samuel BAKER** (eldest son), five acres on South River in Marshfield which the dec'd purchased of the Town of Marshfield, one half of 30 acre homestead (he to pay the rest of the children, £46.8s8d as he receives more than his share); to **Josiah BAKER,** one quarter of homestead (he to pay brother **Joshua** £8.4s4d as he receives more than his share); to **Joshua BAKER** the land in Marshfield the dec'd purchased of James GARDNER and the dec'd's right in two lots in Pembroke; to **Elisha BAKER** the seven acre fresh meadow in Marshfield above the bridge on Snows Creek and the lands the dec'd bought of Thomas BONNEY and Josiah BARKER dec'd in Duxborough; to **Nathaniel BAKER** four acre salt meadow on South River, land the dec'd bought of Samuel WEST in Duxborough and the share in Duxborough the dec'd purchased of Isaac BARKER of Pembroke; to **Sarah BAKER** one quarter of homestead (she to pay her brother **Joshua** £8.4s4d before 1 Apr. 1730 as she receives more than her share.) <5:44> Settlement of personal estate, 9 Mar. 1724/5; £120.2d to be divided among the above named five children, viz: £17.2s10d each. Guardianship of Children: <4:301-303> 13 Feb. 1721, **Josiah BAKER** (14-21) chose Gilbert WINSLOW as his gdn.; same day Gilbert WINSLOW was app'td gdn. of **Joshua BAKER & Samuel BAKER,** both under 14 and William FORD was app'td gdn. of **Elisha BAKER & Sarah BAKER,** both under 14. Witnesses: John LITTLE, John TILDEN. <5:19> 18 Sept. 1724, **Joshua BAKER** (14-21) chose Gilbert WINSLOW as gdn. Surety: Edward ARNOLD of Duxbury. Witnesses: James FORD Jr., Elizabeth WINSLOW. <original> 12 Oct. 1730, Nehemiah CUSHING was app'td gdn. of **Joshua BAKER.** Surety: Gilbert WINSLOW. Witnesses: Mercy THOMAS, Rebeckah WETHERELL. <6:119> 4 Jan. 1731, Samuel THOMAS of Marshfield app'td gdn. of **Nathaniel BAKER,** under 14. Surety: John FULLARTON, husbandman of Marshfield. Witnesses: Edward WINSLOW, Mercy THOMAS.

PLYMOUTH COUNTY PROBATE: (re: BAKER)

1753	Joshua	Pembroke		#795, 13:57,77
1760	Nathaniel	Pembroke	adm.	#815, 15:521,567,572;16:366,367,368
1793	Samuel	Duxbury	will	#824, 33:498,559

Will of **Thomas WEST,** yeoman of Dartmouth MA. <Bristol Co.PR>
<21:442>...dated 20 Sept. 1770, mentions wf **Hannah** and following chil., viz: **Mary POPE, Patience HUDSON, Hannah WEST & Abigail WEST** (both under 21), **Thomas WEST** (under 21), **Paul WEST;** wf **Hannah** & neighbor Jireh SWIFT Jr., executors. Witnesses: Samuel HAMMOND, Silas SWIFT, Christopher HAMMOND. <21:444> Pr. 31 Dec. 1770. <21:445> Inventory taken 11 Dec. 1770, by Hezekiah WINSLOW, Joseph KEMPTON & Nathaniel SPOONER of Dartmouth; menions a great Bible & a small one. <original> Order to divide real estate, 7 Aug. 1780, by Jethro HATHAWAY, Samuel SMITH & John WEST.

Will of **Capt. Luen POPE,** gent. of New Braintree MA. <Worcester Co.PR #A47352, 28:561>
...dated 7 Mar. 1799, mentions wf **Mary;** to sons **Luen POPE** (under 21) and **Thomas POPE,** east part of farm bounded by land of Lemuel KENADA & Edward HULSON and half of meadow on Winnimiset Brook; to son **Thomas** a pair of 2 yr old steers; to son **West POPE,** £18; to daus **Rebeckah KENNADA, Anna BARNABY & Hannah NYE,** $30.00 each; to daus **Polly POPE & Betsy POPE,** one bed & bedding & $60.00 each when they reach 21 or marry; to son **Asa POPE** (executor), remainder of estate. Witnesses: John FISHER, Stephen FAY, Abijah BIGELOW.

Will of **Joseph WATERMAN** of Marshfield MA. <Plymouth Co.PR #22163>
<3:33>...dated 6 Aug. 1709, mentions wf **Sarah** and following chil., viz: **Joseph WATERMAN, Anthony WATERMAN, Sarah HEWETT, Elizabeth BARTLETT** dec'd, **Abigail WINSLOW, Bethiah & Lydia; Joseph RYDER** my sister's son; Mary OKESMAN. <3:34> Pr. 12 Mar. 1710. <3:37> Inventory.

Will of **Kenelm WINSLOW,** Esq. of Marshfield MA. <Plymouth Co.PR #23202>
<14:293-5>...dated 5 Jan. 1749, mentions wf **Ann** and following chil., viz: **Kenelm WINSLOW & Joseph WINSLOW** (executors), **Sarah SMITH** & her dau **Mary PAIN** (under 18), **Abigail LEWIS, Faith TAYLOR;** grandson **Nathaniel WINSLOW** son of dec'd son **Nathaniel WINSLOW.** Witnesses: Samuel HILL, John THOMAS, Thomas WATERMAN. Pr. 19 July 1757, **Kenelm WINSLOW** of Marshfield & **Joseph WINSLOW** of Boston, exrs. <14:441> Dower requested, 11 Aug. 1757, by widow. Inventory taken by Jonathan PETERSON, Thomas WATERMAN, Thomas FORD Jr.; sworn to be exrs., 11 Aug. 1757. <14:516> Dower assigned by John JAMES Jr. of Scituate, Benjamin TURNER & Israel TURNER of Pembroke, Nehemiah THOMAS of Marshfield & Ebenezer FISH of Duxborough who swore to assignment, 1 May 1758. <16:126> Account of exrs., 4 Dec. 1760; Paid to: Nicholas WEBSTER, William HOWLAND, Widow TEWELS, John DINGLEY Jr.,

Nathaniel WINSLOW, Isaiah WALKER, John WINSLOW, Gamaliel BRADFORD, Josiah FOSTER, Dr. John THOMAS, Israel HATCH, Simeon JONES, Joshua CUSHMAN, Joshua LORING, Josiah WINSLOW, Barnabas TEWELS, Anthony THOMAS, Joseph SOULE, Thomas FOSTER, Ebenezer DAMMON, Thomas DINGLEY, Edward WINSLOW, Deacon Thomas WATERMAN, Jonathan PETERSON, Thomas FORD Jr., Michael FORD, Jacob DINGLEY, Dr. HARLOW, William SHERMAN, **Mrs. Ann WINSLOW; William TAYLOR, Isaiah LEWIS, Samuel SMITH & Jonathan HILLARD** towards their wives' legacies; Robert HOWLAND. <16:170> Receipt 24 Mar. 1761, by **Jonathan HILLARD** for legacy given in mill to **Mary HILLARD**, grand daughter to dec'd. Witnesses: Elizabeth WHITEMORE, Hannah CLAP. Receipt 3 Dec. 1760, by **Isaiah LEWIS, Samuel SMITH, William TAILOR/TAYLOR & Nathaniel WINSLOW**, for legacies given in will to **Sarah SMITH, Abigail LEWIS, Faith TAYLOR** and **Nathaniel WINSLOW.** Witnesses: Jno. CUSHING, John TURNER.

Estate of **Anthony WATERMAN** of Marshfield MA. <Plymouth Co.PR #22124>
<3:353> Inventory taken 19 May 1715 by Isaac WINSLOW & Joseph WATERMAN; Debts due from: Gilbert WINSLOW, John THOMAS, Thomas HOWLAND, Samuel WEST, Gershom BRADFORD, Edward ARNOLD, Nehemiah CUSHING, Joshua TURNER, Joseph PERRY, John BISHOP, Cornelius BRIGGS, "Jeffrey Indian"; Due to: Abiah SNOW, Mrs. WATERMAN, Joseph TAYLOR and the TRAYCES of Conecticut; incl. half the farm his father lived on as it was divided by his sd father between his brother Joseph & him excepting his mothers thirds during her life; one half of land his father purchased of Jacob DINGLEY; one half of a lot by Joseph TAYLOR's; six acres near Walter JOYCE; 18 acres between the road that leads to Pembroke and the road that leads to John ROGERS; one half of two lots in the lower division of lands lately laid out by the proprieters of Marshfield in partnership with his brother Joseph & two lots in the upper division; one half of two lots in Pembroke in partnership with brother Joseph; one eight part of a share in cedar swamp; 70 acres in Norwich CT; inventory sworn to 12 July 1715 by widow **Elizabeth WATERMAN.** <3:353> Letter/Bond 31 June 1715, widow **Elizabeth WATERMAN** app'td admx. Surety: Seth ARNOLD, Esq. of Duxbury. Witnesses: Elizabeth DELANO, Mary OAKMAN. <6:114> Division of real estate, 3 June 1731 by Capt. Francis BARKER of Pembroke, Caleb TORRY of Scituate, Thomas FOORD, Thomas TRACY & Samuel THOMAS of Marshfield. Settlement 5 Jan. 1731, to children, viz: **Thomas WATERMAN** (eldest son), **Joseph WATERMAN, Zebulon WATERMAN & Orphan WATERMAN.**

Guardianship of Children of **Anthony WATERMAN** of Marshfield MA. <Plymouth Co.PR #22186>
<4:22,23> Letter/Bond 17 July 1717, widow **Elisabeth WATERMAN** app'td gdn. of **Zebulon WATERMAN, Orphan WATERMAN, Thomas WATERMAN & Joseph WATERMAN**, all under 14. Surety: Edward ARNOLD. Witnesses: Elizabeth WADE, Abigail THOMAS. <original> The files contain a letter, dated 22 Mar. 1722, from **Jonathan ALDEN** who was the second husband of Anthony's widow, Elizabeth WATERMAN:

Colenol winslow honered Sir...Consarning the difucoltyes that I have ben and am under tho not so bad as it were I understand that James ARNOLD has ben down at your hos & desiers your honer to put in nu gardens <new guardians> & has ben down at my hous when I was not at home unbeknown to me & had perswaded my wife to give up her garden ship <guardianship> & I ascedentialy heard of it by a frend that he told it to I wold desier you Sir not to take any more notes of thar talk for she is of (---) agin & ses she thinks she shal not do it. Sir they have ben doing things unbeknown to me & so conterary to me I think a porpos to make deferanc betwen us two. Sir I desier you in al love as I have found you a faithful frend hether to & hope shal never find you no other I wold desier of your honer not to put in gardiens <guardians> til the Childeren are old anough to chus them gardiens for Sir I wil tel you if you do I am under the gratest hardship that can be for if the childerens gardiens take ther part of the farm into thar hands we shal have but a sixt part of the farm to pay mother **WATERMAN** her rent with & ourselfs to live on wich if it be so ordered we are totolly ruined as to this world if not for another it wil make such diferanc amongst us & I heard by the by that thay had ordered it for your self to be down the next week & thay know that I should be gone at the week to the Swamp & shal not be at home.

Sir I desier you Sir I desier you <sic> to let me know if you design to do any thing about it for if it be so ordered we must pul up stacks & be gon now we are just setteled ye wich wil ruin us.

Sir I think it best to rest the mater if you pleas from your humble Sarvent to command.

Jonathan ALDEN

Will of **Thomas WATERMAN** of Marshfield MA. <Plymouth Co.PR #22200>
<21:642>...dated 12 Feb. 1766, mentions wf **Abigail** and following chil., viz: **Thomas WATERMAN Jr., Anthony WATERMAN, Joseph WATERMAN, Nathaniel WATERMAN, Abijah WATERMAN, Asa WATERMAN, John WATERMAN, Anna HEWET.** <21:643> Pr. 17 Nov. 1774. <21:643> Inventory.

Will of **Abigail WATERMAN**, widow of Marshfield MA. <Plymouth Co.PR #22121>
<35:479>...dated 4 Jan. 1775, mentions following chil., viz: **Thomas WATERMAN, Joseph WATERMAN, Anthony WATERMAN, Abijah WATERMAN, Nathaniel WATERMAN, Anna HEWIT** wf of Joseph, **Asa WATERMAN, John WATERMAN.** <35:480> Pr. 7 Mar. 1796.

MICRO #3 OF 32

Estate of **Anthony WATERMAN**, gent. of Scituate MA. <Plymouth Co.PR>
Inventory taken 2 Dec. 1799. <36:555> Division, 1 Dec. 1800 to following chil., viz: **Samuel WATERMAN, Nathaniel WATERMAN, Anthony WATERMAN, Foster WATERMAN, Jotham WATERMAN, Deborah WATERMAN, Thomas WATERMAN.**

Estate of **Joseph WATERMAN** of Marshfield MA. <Plymouth Co.PR #22164>
<3:390> Letter 17 Jan. 1715, widow **Luce Anna WATERMAN** app'td admx. <3:390> Inventory taken 11 Jan 1715; mentions 299 acres at Norwich. <3:391> Lands. <7:88> Warrant & Division. <7:89> Settlement

(no date given), mentions daus **Abigail MAGOON** wf of John Jr. and **Abiah EELLS** wf of John, the only children of **Joseph WATERMAN.**

Estate of **John EELLS**, cordwainer of Scituate MA. <Plymouth Co.PR #7181>
<17:3> Letter/Bond 17 Nov. 1760, **Waterman EELLS**, shipwright of Middletown CT app'td admr.; Sureties: North ELLIS, yeoman of Scituate & Simeon TUBBS, mariner of Pembroke. <16:40> Inventory taken 17 Nov. 1760, of personal estate. <16:40> Account of admr., 21 Nov. 1760; mentions wages received of Province Treasurer, £10.3.9.

ANNA WARREN[2] (Richard[1])

PLYMOUTH COUNTY PROBATE: (re: LITTLE)

1699	Isaac	Marshfield		#13039, 1:314,315,316;3:283
1712	Thomas	Plymouth		#13078, 3:189,243,389;5:46,47,48
1712	Thomas et al	Plymouth		#13079, 3:189,190,191,192,219
1715	Nathaniel	Marshfield		#13065, 3:339,419
1719	Ephraim	Marshfield		#13033, 4:113,115 <MD 19:158>
1724	Charles	Plymouth/Kingston		#13025, 4:422;5:1,59,232;6:324,326;7:17
1724	Rev. Ephraim	Plymouth		#13032, 4:432,433
1725	Lemuel	Edgartown		#13052, 5:93
1727	Bethia	Kingston		#13055, 5:355
1736	Mayhew	Plymouth		#13062, 7:268,295
1748	Mary	Chilmark		#13060, 10:529
1755	Isaac	Plympton		#13040, 13:510;14:205,206,508
1755	Mary	Plymouth		#13059, 13:509
1756	Lucy	Kingston		#13056, 14:307,308,309
1758	Isaac	Pembroke		#13040, 14:530,533,534;15:466;16:182
1758	Lemuel et al	Pembroke		#13054, 15:1
1760	Sarah	Plymouth		#13073, 15:514,538,539;16:119,120
1763	George	Plympton		#13036, 16:537;17:109;19:89
1767	John	Marshfield		#13049, 19:461,464;20:292
1772	Constant	Marshfield		#13027, 21:196,197
1774	Isaac	Pembroke		#13042, 21:628;23:56;24:363-7,372
1779	Abigail et al	Pembroke		#13020, 26:71,72,73
1779	David	Scituate		#13029, 25:299,300,301
1779	Mercy	Pembroke		#13063, 25:296,298
1789	Barnabas	Scituate		#13024, 31:98,100,370,508
1793	Luther et al	Marshfield		#13058, 26:282
1793	Peabody	Marshfield		#13066, 27:439;33:417,418,550,564;35:140,141
1799	Lemuel	Marshfield		#13053, 36:484,486,510;37:33
1800	Sarah	Marshfield		#13074, 34:263;37:416,417;38:31
1803	James	Scituate	adm.	#13045, 34:376;40:25,27,28,490,491;10**A**:450
1803	Penelope	Marshfield	will	#13067, 38:405,406;42:236
1804	James et al	Scituate	gdn.	#13047, 32:227;43,109,136
1808	Ephraim	Marshfield	adm.	#13034, 39:171;42:507;43:74,75,76
1809	Ephraim	Marshfield	gdn.	#13035, 32:400;41:56;42:520,521;43:327,328,494; 44:133;51:323;55:380;60:134,147-9,355; 63:303,323;66:184,348;67:581
1809	George	Marshfield	will	#13037, 43:7,8,132,272,434;61:486
1809	Polly et al	Marshfield	gdn.	#13068, 41:2,5,286;48:331
1810	James	Scituate	adm.	#13046, 39:230;43:268,269;44:137
1810	Rachel W.	Marshfield	adm.	#13070, 39:243;43:215,435
1811	George	Scituate	adm.	#13038, 39:305;43:526;44:135,237;45:10,389;48:91 373
1815	Amos R.	Marshfield	adm.	#13021, 46:117;47:509,512
1815	Thomas	Marshfield	will	#13076, 47:98,99,100
1821	Charles	Pembroke	will	#13026, 54:14,178,180,181,366,367,417;56:18,59, 60,553
1821	Constant	Marshfield	adm.	#13028, 52:55;53:499;54:127,128
1826	Anna	Marshfield	gdn.	#13022, 51:322;55:384;60:133,145-7;63:304,324; 66:185,347;67:581;69:8;70:253,428
1826	Priscilla et al	Marshfield	gdn.	#13069, 51:318;60:430;66:145,146;72:285
1835	John	Marshfield	will	#13050, 73:141;75:214;77:29,31;78:13
1835	Mary	Pembroke	adm.	#13061, 71:293
1836	Elizabeth et al	Marshfield	gdn.	#13031, 8**C**:13;79:283
1838	Rachel	Marshfield	will	#13071, 1**G**:328;80:332
1842	Luther	Marshfield	will	#13057, 1**G**:199;6**U**:278;84:189,308,575;86:47
1842	Thomas	Marshfield	adm.	#13077, 6**C**:350;11**B**:116;85:33,514;87:34
1844	William H.	Marshfield	gdn.	#13080, 8**C**:511,512;87:335
1846	Isaac	Pembroke	will	#13043, 1**G**:450;7**V**:156;88:232

Isaac LITTLE & Ephraim LITTLE of Marshfield MA. <Plymouth Col.Rcds. 7:189>
...4 Mar. 1673, Isacke LITTLE & Ephraim LITTLE of Marshfield, complained against Leift. Peregrine WHITE, John DINGLEY and William FOORD/FORD Jr....for that...being assembled together since the twenty first day of December last past, did wrongfully enter into and upon the land of the sd Isacke & Epharim LITTLE, vis: a certain pcell of land formerly graunted unto John WATERMAN and purchased of him by Thomas LITTLE, deceased, father to the sd Isacke & Ephraim LITTLE, lying betwixt the land of John PHILLIPS and Joseph ROES and divers others as my appeer upon record, and marked divers trees, upon pretence of laying out land to the sd John PHILLIPS & Joseph ROES.

PLYMOUTH COLONY DEEDS: (re: LITTLE)

<5:423> - 21 May 1683, Ephraim LITTLE from John MENDALL.
<5:422> - 26 May 1684, Ephraim LITTLE from Peregrine WHITE.
<5:426> - 29 Dec. 1686, Ephraim LITTLE from David EAMES.
<5:419> - 30 Dec. 1686, Ephraim LITTLE to John CARVER.
<5:420> - 30 Dec. 1686, Ephraim LITTLE from John CARVER.
<5:507> - 7 June 1697, Ephraim LITTLE from Thomas PAINE.
<3:310> - 3 July 1673, Isaac LITTLE from John HASKALL.
<3:293> - 4 July 1673, Isaac LITTLE from Constant SOUTHWORTH.
<5:502> - 20 Jan. 1677, Isaac LITTLE from Jonathan JACKSON.
<5:503> - 17 Apr. 1683, Isaac LITTLE from James CLARK.
<5:504> - 7 July 1686, Isaac LITTLE from Matthew BOOMER.
<5:471> - 3 June 1692, Isaac LITTLE from William STEAD.
<5:475> - 3 Apr. 1693, Isaac LITTLE to Mark HASKELL.
<5:505> - 27 Mar. 1695, Isaac LITTLE from Robert BENNETT.
<5:506> - 4 July 1697, Isaac LITTLE from Richard WINSLOW.
<4:341> - 22 Dec. 1679, Samuel LITTLE from Crow MILLER.
<5:448> - 29 June 1689, Samuel LITTLE from Edward GRAY.
<5:477> - 15 Jan. 1689, Samuel LITTLE to John GRAY.
<5:449> - 1 Oct. 1689, Samuel LITTLE from John COLE.
<5:462> - 6 July 1691, Samuel LITTLE from John WILLIAMS.
<5:497> - 27 July 1691, Samuel LITTLE from John COOKE.
<5:498> - 1 Feb. 1694, Samuel LITTLE from Nathaniel THOMAS
<2:2> - 2 Aug. 1652, Thomas LITTLE to Richard FAXON.
<6:45> - 10 Jan. 1664, Thomas LITTLE from John WATERMAN.
<3:76> - 2 Nov. 1666, Thomas LITTLE from Humphrey DAVENPORT.
<3:110> - 2 May 1668, Thomas LITTLE from Humphrey DAVENPORT.
<3:110> - 13 May 1668, Thomas LITTLE from Josiah WINSLOW.
<3:160> - 7 July 1669, Thomas LITTLE from Tuspaquin.
<3:193> - 6 July 1671, Thomas LITTLE from General Court.
<3:311> - 4 July 1673, Thomas LITTLE from Constant SOUTHWORTH.
<6:29> - 20 Sept 1673, Thomas LITTLE from Thomas TILDEN.
<5:240> - 4 Dec. 1682, LITTLE, WARREN, CLARK, etc. buy Agawan.

Will of **Josiah KEEN**, yeoman of Pembroke MA. <Plymouth Co.PR 6:272-274>
...dated 2 Feb. 1728...to wf **Lydia**, a living in my present dwelling which I reserved in the deed I gave to son **Isaac**, also the use of residue of moveables while my widow...if she marries to have only Ł20; 4s each to sons **Benjamin KEEN, Josiah KEEN, Nathaniel KEEN, Samuel KEEN, Isaac KEEN & Hezekiah KEEN** (who have all had deeds); to dau **Eleanor THOMAS** wf of Joseph, Ł4 out of moveables; to grandchild **Mary BREWSTER**, 20s out of moveables; residue at wife's death or marriage to be divided among four daus or their heirs, viz: chil. of **Abigail DREW, Eleanor THOMAS,** chil. of **Lydia PARTRIDGE** and **Bethiah WEST.** Witnesses: Elisha BISBEE, Aaron SOULE Jr., Aaron SOULE. Witnesses sworn 23,25,26 Dec. 1732. Pr. 10 Jan. 1732. Inventory taken 5 Jan. 1732.

PLYMOUTH COUNTY DEEDS: (re: KEEN)

<30:62> - 1730, Benjamin KEEN & wf Deborah the dau of Robert BARKER.
<38:208> - 1746, Division of Estate of Benjamin KEEN to chil.: Benjamin KEEN, Deborah KEEN, Abigail KEEN, Luceanna KEEN.
<51:155> - 1762, re: Deborah KEEN.
<59:264> - 9 May 1771, Deborah KEEN, tayloress of Pembroke to Prince HOWLAND of Duxbury, her part of land of her dec'd father Benjamin KEEN.
<87:187> - 23 Feb. 1797, Deborah KEEN, singlewoman of Scituate et al.

Will of **Josiah WEST** of Kingston MA. <Plymouth Co.PR>
...dated 23 Feb. 1792...to my well beloved wife **Elizabeth,** the use & improvement of the easterly half of my dwelling house dureing the time that she remains my widow allso the incum of all my improved land allso fire wood nesesary for her fire halled to the door allso my cows & swine allso six pounds of sheeps wool per year allso the use of all the indoor moveables with all my provitions, but in case of her moveing then she is to have nothing but a bed & furniture...to nephew **Joshua HOLMES** the westerly half of dwelling house and all real estate...my grate Bible when my wife leaves it and my books and securities for cash...to neice **Elizabeth WRIGHT** wf of Levi, all my indore moveables when my wife has done with them at her deceas or marrage...to **Josiah WRIGHT,** eldest son of Levi, all my wareing apparrel & fire arms & Ł30; nephew **Joshua HOLMES,** executor. Witnesses: Zenas BRYANT, James CUSHING, Seth CUSHING.

Will of **Elizabeth DURFEY** of Plymouth MA. <Plymouth Co.PR>
<42:354>...dated 7 June 1802...wife of **Richard DURFEY**, seafareingman of Plymouth...to son **Richard DURFEY Jr.** all my intrest right & title in the dwelling house where I live in Plymouth & also all my intrest in the land adjoyning being what fell to me in the division of the Estate of my late Mother Mrs. **Rebecca RICH** (formerly **Rebecca MORTON**) late of Plymouth dec'd...he my sd son not to come into possession of sd part of a house & land untill the decease of my sd husband **Richard DURFEY Sr.**; son **Richard** to pay five Spanish milled dollars to each daughter, viz: **Betty WRIGHT** wf of Levi, **Rebecca BILLINGTON** wf of Isaac and **Bethiah BAGNALL** wf of Capt. Richard...In consequence of my haveing given each of my sd daughters considerable when they marryd I give them no more; sn **Richard**, executor. Witnesses: Ephraim SPOONER, Ebenezer SPOONER, Sally SPOONER. On 2 Jan. 1808, **Richard DURFEY Sr.** consents to will of his dec'd wife. <42:355> Pr. 2 Jan. 1808; sworn to by exr. & witnesses, Ephraim & Ebenezer SPOONER.

Will of **Isaac KEEN**, yeoman of Pembroke MA. <Plymouth Co.PR>
<30:98>...dated 30 Apr. 1784...being advanced in age...to wf **Abigail** the use...of the whole of my dwilling house & one half of my homsted farm whereon I now dwell & the use of three quarters of my salt meadow in Marshfield with liberty to cut her firewood on any part of my lands & also the use of my quarter part of my saw mill in Duxbury...use & improvement of personal estate so long as she shall remain my widow excepting one feather bed & furniture which I give to my daughter **Patience BROW**, I also give to my sd wife all ye personal estate that she brought to me at our marriage...to four sons **Simeon KEEN, Lemuel KEEN, Isaac KEEN & Lot KEEN** all real estate in Pembroke, Duxbury & Marshfield...to three daus **Deborah KEEN, Eleanor CUSHMAN & Patience BROW** all personal estate after my wifes marriag or death...sons **Simeon, Isaac & Lot** to pay 30s to son **Lemuel**...son **Lot** shall pay to son **Lemuel** for the buildings that **Lemuel** built on my land...if any of my chilldren shall make any demands on my Estate after my Death unless it shall be in notes of hand (that I have given them) the gifts in this will to them ...be null & void; sons **Simeon & Lot** executors. Witnesses: Isaac BISBE, Kenelm WINSLOW, John TURNER. <30:99> Pr. 26 Mar. 1787. <original> Warrant, 24 Mar. 1787, to John TURNER, Esq., William HOWLAND & John SOUL, all of Pembroke, to appraise estate. <30:100> Inventory taken 27 Mar. 1787 by appraisers; incl. farming tools; live stock; coopers tools & old lumber, Ł6.6.; homsted farm, Ł300; one quarter of saw mill & land adjoining, Ł300; salt meadow, Ł52.10.; personal estate given to widow by will, Ł13.5.; sworn to 28 Mar. 1787 by exrs. <original> Bond 4 Apr. 1787, of **Simeon & Lot KEEN**, exrs. Sureties: John TURNER, John TURNER Jr. Witnesses: Deborah TURNER, Sarah TURNER. <original> List of debts: Dr. STOCKBRIDGE, Elisha FORD, Simeon KEEN, Adam FORD, Kenelm WINSLOW, Comfort BATES, Paul SAMSON, William LEWIS, Dr. WINSLOW, JOseph PHILLIPS, Benjamin EAMES, Isaiah WALKER, Robert BARKER, Charles BAKER, Desire Barker KENT, Simeon MACKFARLEN, Benjamin BESTER, William TORREY, Abner DINGLEY, Edward STEVENS, Nathaniel PHILLIPS, Seth HATCH, Mark KEEN, Col. HALL, Joshua DILLINGHAM; sworn to 29 Oct. 1787, by exrs. <30:245> Account of exrs., 29 Oct. 1787. <30:367> Warrant 5 Apr. 1787 to John TURNER, Esq., William HOWLAND, yeoman, both of Pembroke & Luke WADSWORTH of Marshfield to set off dower; one half of homestead bounded by that part of homestead which the dec'd bought of Jairus BISBE and high way which leads by John SOUL's...also the salt meadow lying in South River Marsh in Marshfield...and we assign to the sd widow her fire wood...also the use of one quarter part of the saw mill in Duxborough; approved 30 May 1788. <30:535> Account of exrs., 17 Mar. 1789 Received Ł192.9.6. incl. land & stable sold by order of Court; Payments to: **Simeon**, on notes of hand, Ł17.11.7.2.; Kenelm WINSLOW, Dr. Benjamin STOCKBRIDGE, Dr. Isaac WINSLOW, Abner DINGLEE, Elisha FORD, Desire Barker KENT, William LEWIS, Adam FORD, John TURNER, Eq., William HOWLAND, Luke WADSWORTH, Edward STEVENS, Joseph PHILLIPS, Jeremiah PHILLIPS, John ROGERS Jr., Benjamin EMES, Nathaniel PHILLIPS, Benjamin WHITE, Mark KEEN, **Lemuel KEEN** a legacy as given in ye will Ł1.10., Simeon McFARLAND, Isaiah WALKER, Charles BAKER, Daniel LEWIS, Gideon HARLOW, Lemuel FORD, Bethiah THOMAS, Robert CUSHMAN, Robert BARKER, David CROOKER, Isaac BISBE, Paul SAMSON, Gideon HARLOW, Dr. Jeremiah HALL, William TORREY, Benjamin BARSTOW, Joshua DILLINGHAM, Adam FORD, Comfort BATES, Consider HOWLAND, Asher KEEN, Seth HATCH, Jacob BARSTOW, Jonathan PETERSON, Gideon Thomas WHITE.

Will of **George PARTRIDGE**, housewright of Duxbury MA. <Plymouth Co.PR #15326>
<20:56>...dated 14 May 1764; mentions wf **Hannah**; to eldest son **Samuel PARTRIDGE**, farm known by the name of the Wiswal place laying in Duxborough and is all that part of the purchase that I made of Peleg WISWALL of Boston that layeth to the southward of the home farm of Jacob PETERSON...to son **James PARTRIDGE**, five pounds & wearing apparel, together with what he hath already received of the estate of my uncle **James PARTRIDGE** that was given to me, I consented he should take the deed in his own name...to dau **Mable COOMER** wf of William, three pounds, together with what she hath already had...to dau **Sarah PARTRIDGE** wf of John, three pounds...to grandchildren **Ziba HUNT & Sarah HUNT**, six pounds...to grandson **Partridge RICHERSON/RICHARDSON**, five pounds & one bed & furniture...to youngest son **George PARTRIDGE**, my home farm; pew in meeting house in Duxborough; wood lot being the first lot in the last division of Duxborough Comons lying near Island creek pond; right in 11th lot in sd division; two pieces of salt marsh adjacent to Sprague's neck, near six acres, purchased of James PARTRIDGE dec'd; island of marsh known as Soul's island laying northward of Powder-point in Duxborough and remainder of estate; son **George**, executor. Witnesses: Elijah TOWER, Joshua STANFORD, Jonathan PETERSON. <20:57> Letter/Bond 4 Apr. 1768, **George PARTRIDGE**, gent. app'td admr. Sureties: Briggs ALDEN, Esq., Joshua STANFORD, gent. Witnesses: John BRADFORD, Edward WINSLOW Jr.

Estate of **Samuel KEEN**, yeoman of Pembroke MA. <Plymouth Co.PR #11815>
<13:175> Letter/Bond, 1 Jan. 1754, widow **Margaret KEEN** & **Abel KEEN**, tailor, both of Pembroke, app'td admrs. Sureties: Isaac KEEN Jr. & John TURNER, yeomen of Pembroke. <13:176> Inventory taken 4 Jan. 1754 by John TURNER, Ichabod BONNEY & Edward THOMAS; incl. farm & half pew in 1st Precinct meeting house, Ŀ308.13.4. <13:520> Account of exrs., 11 July 1755. <13:535> Order to divide real estate, 29 July 1755, by Daniel LEWIS, Esq., Israel TURNER, Ichabod BONNEY, Aaron SOUL Jr. & John TURNER, all of Pembroke; to widow **Margaret KEEN** and following chil., viz: **William KEEN** (eldest son), **Levi KEEN, Abel KEEN, Grace, Samuel KEEN, Isaiah KEEN, Ruth, Asher KEEN, Moses KEEN & Judah KEEN.**

Will of **Judah KEEN**, housewright of Pembroke MA. <Plymouth Co.PR #11795>
<19:327>...dated 11 July 1765...to mother **Margaret LEAVIT**, note of hand against John LEAVIT for Ŀ22.13.4. dated 20 May 1765; to sister **Ruth LEAVIT** note of hand against brother **Asher KEEN** for Ŀ1.6. dated 30 Aug. 1762; to brother **Asher KEEN**, wearing apparel; to brother **Moses KEEN**, remainder of estate; uncle **Isaac KEEN**, executor. Witnesses: Priscilla TAYLOR, Mercy HATCH, John TURNER. <17:154> Letter/Bond, 28 Oct. 1765, **Isaac KEEN** of Pembroke having renounced the executorship, John TURNER, yeoman of Pembroke was app'td admr. Sureties: John WADSWORTH, gent. of Duxbury & Seth HATCH, yeoman of Pembroke. <20:437> Inventory taken 7 Jan. 1771, by Aaron SOULE, Seth HATCH & Samuel GOOLD

John & Mary TURNER of Pembroke MA against Estate of **Ephraim LITTLE.** <Court of Common Pleas>
<original>...4 Nov. 1809...John TURNER & wf Mary against John LITTLE, admr. of estate of Ephraim LITTLE of Marshfield dec'd...whereas Ephraim LITTLE...on the 29 Aug. 1805 then in full life but since deceased, for value received then & there promised Mary TURNER...to pay her...the sum of fifty dollars to be paid at his the sd Ephraim's decease, out of his estate...the sd Ephraim has long since deceased...John LITTLE in his capacity as administrator has never yet paid the plaintiffs sd sum but neglects & refuses so to do...to the damage of the sd John & Mary (as they say) the sum of one hundred & fifty dollars. On 6 Nov. 1809, the courts attached two acres of salt meadow lying in the North River Marsh in Marshfield, bounded by land of Elisha ROGERS, widow Elsa HATCH, Isaac ROGERS, Samuel TROUANT & Church Clift TROUANT. And the sd John LITTLE...says his intestate never promised in manner & form as the sd John & Mary TURNER have set forth in their declaration. <original> 6 Apr. 1810, William MACUMBER, gent. of Marshfield, Briggs HATCH, gent. of Pembroke & Joanna WHITE, widow of George, were summoned to give evidence on 2nd Tues. Apr. at the Court held in Plymouth. (On the back is a statement by William MACOMBER, "I have travelled 40 miles & attend 3 days".)
<Plymouth Co.Deeds 113:208>...17 Apr. 1810...John TURNER & wf Mary...on the second Tuesday of Apr. 1810 recovered judgement against the estate of Ephraim LITTLE late of Marshfield...deceased under the administration of John LITTLE of Marshfield...for $18.37 damage and $25.57 costs of suit ...execution remains to be done. On 10 May 1810, Luther LITTLE, Joseph CLIFT Jr. & Jedediah LITTLE were sworn to appraise such real estate as should...satisfy this execution; one acre salt meadow in Marshfield bounded by land of Samuel TROWANT & Elisha ROGERS, valued at $59.22 was seized for the creditors. (Although two acres were "attached" on 6 Nov. 1809, only one acre was settled on the TURNERS; see the following deed pertaining to the estate of John TURNER.)

(The following proves that John & Mary TURNER did indeed have a claim on the estate of Ephraim LITTLE; across the top is written: Court of Common Pleas, Plymouth Co., Files:
...Pembroke, 29 Aug. 1805, For value rec'd I promis to pay to my Daughter Mary TURNER fifty dollars to be paid at my Decease out of my Estate. Signed by Ephraim LITTLE. Witnesses: Lucy VINAL, Patience Little VINAL.

Estate of **John TURNER**, Esq. of Pembroke MA to **Ann TURNER** of same. <Plymouth Co.Deeds 144:149>
...3 May 1821, Seth WHITMAN, yeoman of Pembroke, admr. on estate...by an order of the Probate Court...at Plymouth...on the 3d Mon. of March last past was licensed...to sell...so much of the real estate...for the payment of his debts...as would amount to $2500.00...did on the 30 Apr. last past...sell at public vendue the following...for $36.94 to Ann TURNER, tailoress...one half pew in the Congregationelst Meeting house in Pembroke on the lower floor and owned in common with Job TURNER, the widow Mary TURNER having a life estate in the same; also about one acre of salt marsh lying in Marshfield in the North river marsh, reference being had to the extension of an execution in favour of John TURNER and wife, against the Estate of Ephraim LITTLE dec'd...also the reversion of seven acres ow wood land...bounded by land of Job TURNER & Robert G. McFARLAND. the widow Mary TURNER having a life Estate in last described piece of land. Witnesses: Nathaniel SMITH, Edward SMITH. Ack. 12 May 1821. Rec. 13 Aug. 1821.

Guardianship of Children of **Anna GRAY.** <Plymouth Co.PR 4:53>
...31 Mar. 1718, David LITTLE of Scituate chosen gdn. by **Anna GRAY & Rebeckah GRAY** (14-21), daughters of his sister Anna GRAY dec'd.

Will of **Capt. Thomas GRAY**, yeoman of Little Compton. <Bristol Co.PR 4:19,25;3:731,732>
<4:19>...dated 21 Sept. 1721, mentions wf **Phebe**; sons **Thomas GRAY & Edward GRAY** (executors); dau **Anna RICHMOND**; dau **Rebecca GRAY** (under 24); grandchildren **Barzeller/Barzillai RICHMOND, Mary GRAY & Austes GRAY**; kinsman Nathaniel GIBBS son of Warren GIBBS. Codicil 21 Oct. 1721. <4:25> Inventory taken 7 Nov. 1721; mentions two houselots in Plymouth, Ŀ40. Pr. 23 Nov. 1721.

Will of **Dr. Thomas GRAY** of Little Compton. <Bristol Co.PR 4:196-7,199;6:139; MD 21:156>
<4:196>...8 July 1723, mentions mother in law **Phebe GRAY**; brother **Edward GRAY** & his son **Thomas**

GRAY (under 21); sister **Anna RICHMOND** wf of William; sister **Rebecca PABODIE** wf of John. Inventory taken 17 July 1723; sworn to 5 Aug. 1723 by brother **Edward GRAY.** Pr. 1 Aug. 1723.

PLYMOUTH COUNTY DEEDS: (re: David LITTLE, grantor, all to 1801)

<9:414> - 1713, to David TILDEN.
<10:245> - 1712/3, to Job OTIS.
<11:81> - , to Benjamin PEIRCE.
<12:167> - , to Thomas FISH.
<22:51> - , to Benjamin BALCH.
<24:55> - 1726, to Job OTIS.
<26:93> - 1730, to Joseph BAILEY.
<28:85> - 1733, to John HOLBROOK.
<29:40> - 1734, to Joseph WADE.
<32:134> - , to Elisha PEIRCE.
<36:67> - 1743, Jr. to Abial TURNER.
<37:115> - 1745, Jr. to Jonathan JACKSON.
<40:34> - , to Samuel HOLBROOK.
<42:239> - 1754, to Ambrose COLE.
<43:111> - 1755, Jr. to Joseph OTIS.
<45:162> - 1759, to Joshua RIPLEY.
<47:157> - 1758, Jr. to David DAMON.
<47:157> - 1763, to John McLAUTHLIN.
<53:30> - , to Zaccheus FISH.
<54:235> - 1769, to Samuel LITCHFIELD.
<55:121> - 1770, Jr. to James MERRITT.
<56:120> - 1771, (gdn.) to Thomas LITCHFIELD.
<56:260> - 1773, (gdn.) to Eleazer LITCHFIELD.
<57:93> - , (gdn.) to John DAMAN.
<57:124> - , (gdn.) to Eli CURTIS.
<61:114> - , to John COHMAN/COLEMAN.
<62:29> - 1783, to Nathaniel WATERMAN.
<63:56> - 1784, to Joshua DAMON.
<64:145> - , to Jonathan HOLMES Jr.
<68:45> - 1788, to Joseph OTIS.
<70:43> - , (admr.) to Snow STETSON.
<71:190> - , to James BRIGGS 3d.
<34:140> - 20 Dec. 1740, to son David LITTLE Jr. Witnesses: Mary CUDWORTH, Mercy LITTLE.

David LITTLE Jr. of Scituate MA to **Joseph OTIS** of same. <Plymouth Co.Deeds 43:111>
...28 Dec. 1752, David LITTLE Jr., for Ł32 sold to Joseph OTIS, gent...four acre salt marsh in Scituate. Witnesses: Anna HEARSEY, David LITTLE. Ack. 13 Nov. 1754 before David LITTLE, J.P. Rec. 20 May 1755.

David LITTLE & Samuel SEABURY to **Joshua RIPLEY** of Kingston MA. <Plymouth Co.Deeds 45:162>
...8 Aug. 1758, David LITTLE, Esq. of Scituate and Samuel SEABURY, yeoman of Duxborough, for Ł15 sold to Joshua RIPLEY, cooper...three quarters of a piece of land in Kingston, three acres. Witnesses: Oliver SEABURY, Wiswall SEABURY. Ack. 17 Aug. 1758 by grantors.

David LITTLE et al to **Zaccheus FISH** of Pembroke MA. <Plymouth Co.Deeds 53:30>
...8 Jan. 1762, David LITTLE, Esq. of Scituate, Job OTIS, yeoman of Scituate and Samuel SEABURY, yeoman of Duxborough, for Ł14.18s8d sold to Zaccheus FISH, yeoman...31 acres in Pembroke...126th lot in Marshfield upper lands...excepting certain reserves made in a deed from Charles LITTLE to William COOKE of this land with other lots dated 21 Mar. 1711 and rec. 10:18...we also reserve four acres which sd COOK sold or exchanged with Elnathan FISH for land in Kingston. Witnesses: Barnabas LITTLE, Mercy OTIS, Paul SEABURY, Wiswall SEABURY. Ack. 16 June 1762 by David, 17 June by Job and 11 Jan. "1762" by Samuel. Rec. 29 Oct. 1765.

David LITTLE of Scituate MA to **Joseph OTIS** of same. <Plymouth Co.Deeds 68:45>
...1 Mar. 1788, David LITTLE, gent., for Ł6 sold to Joseph OTIS, gent...two and one quarter acre salt meadow in Scituate...adjoining the beach that leads from the second clift to the third. Wf Deborah LITTLE releases dower. Witnesses: Israel VINAL Jr., John OTIS. Ack. 1 Apr. 1788 by grantor & wf. Rec. 2 Apr. 1788.

Will of **Rev. Ephraim LITTLE** of Colchester CT. <Colchester CT PR 5:384>
...dated 24 May 1787, mentions following chil., viz: **Ephraim LITTLE, Deodat LITTLE, Elizabeth COLMAN, Content HASTINGS, Mabel BILLINGS, Lucretia CHAMBERLIN, Molly DICKINSON, Faith PARSONS, Sophia RANSOME, Justin LITTLE.** Pr. 3 July 1787.

Will of **Joseph OTIS** of Scituate MA. <Plymouth Co.PR #14977>
<31:95>...dated 15 Mar. 1773, mentions wf **Mercy** and following chil., viz: **Molly OTIS** (under 18), **Joseph OTIS, John OTIS, Barnabas OTIS, Mercy WATERMAN**; brother in law **Barnabas LITTLE** & wf **Mercy** of Scituate, executors. <31:97> Executors decline. <31:97> Letter/Bond 20 & 21 Oct. 1788. <31:97> Inventory taken Nov. 1789. <31:310> Insolvency. <33:163> List of claims. <33:163;35:72> Accounts.

Estate of **Mercy OTIS** of Scituate MA. <Plymouth Co.PR #14990>
<original> Declination, 19 Aug. 1805, of unnamed eldest son to administer estate and defers to his brother **Barnabas OTIS.** <47:318> Letter/Bond 26 Aug. 1815, **Barnabas OTIS**, gent. of Plymouth app'td admr. Sureties: Rosseter COTTON, Esq. & John GOODING, gent. of Plymouth. <47:317> Inventory taken 4 Sept. 1815. <48:205> Account of admr., 30 Sept. 1816.

Will of **John LITTLE**, Esq. of Marshfield MA. <Plymouth Co.PR 19:461; MD 19:165-76>
...dated 14 Jan. 1764, mentions wf **Constant** and following chil., viz: **Fobes LITTLE, John LITTLE, William LITTLE, Anna WHITE** (to receive 43rd lot in first division in Marshfield, about 25 acres and negro woman Phillis), **Ruth OAKMAN, Ephraim LITTLE, Thomas LITTLE, Lemuel LITTLE**; granddaughter **Alice LITTLE**; sons **Ephraim, Thomas & Lemuel**, executors. Witnesses: Elisha PHILLIPS, Francis CROOKER, Nathaniel PHILLIPS. Pr. 6 Mar. 1767.

Will of **Constant LITTLE**, widow of Marshfield MA. <Plymouth Co.PR 21:196; MD 19:165-76>
...dated 18 Nov. 1767, mentions following chil., viz: **Fobes LITTLE, John LITTLE, Ephraim LITTLE, Thomas LITTLE, William LITTLE, Lemuel LITTLE, Anna WHITE** & hus Abijah, **Ruth OAKMAN** & hus Tobias;

son in laws, **Abijah WHITE & Tobias OAKMAN**, executors. Witnesses: David LAPHAM, Thomas SYLVESTER, Samuel OAKMAN. Pr. 6 Aug. 1772.

Estate of **Ephraim LITTLE**, gent. of Marshfield MA. <Plymouth Co.PR #13034>
<39:171> Letter/Bond 5 Dec. 1808, **John LITTLE**, yeoman of Marshfield app'td admr. Sureties: Charles HATCH, Constant LITTLE. <42:507> Inventory. <43:74> Claims. <43:75> Account. <43:76> Distribution of estate.

Estate of **Capt. Joshua VINAL**, mariner of Marshfield MA. <Plymouth Co.PR #21624>
<original> Petition 13 Nov. 1793, of widow **Lucy VINAL** declines to administer and requests that John TURNER Jr. be app'td. <27:454> Letter/Bond 20 Nov. 1793, John TURNER Jr., Esq. of Pembroke app'td admr. <33:493,494> Appraisers app'td. <35:132> Insolvency 2 Dec. 1793. <35:133> Delivered to widow **Lucy VINAL**, Ł29. <35:134> Notice.

Will of **Lucy VINAL**, widow of Marshfield MA. <Plymouth Co.PR #21627>
<40:233>...dated 6 May 1805...to sons **Joshua VINAL & Seth VINAL**, $2.00 each; to dau **Lucy VINAL**, two thirds of remainder & to dau **Patience VINAL**, one third of remainder; friend William MACOMBER, executor. Pr. 3 June 1805. <40:331> Inventory taken 22 June 1805. <40:311> Notice. <40:469> Account of exr., 2 June 1806.

Estate of **Capt. Joshua VINAL** of Marshfield MA to **Jedediah EWELL**. <Plymouth Co.Deeds 79:130>
...20 Oct. 1794, John TURNER, Esq. of Pembroke, as admr...by order of the Court...for Ł20.9s6d sold to Jedediah EWELL, yeoman of Marshfield...three acre salt meadow in Marshfield...bounded... beginning at the north east corner of that part of the Island that belongith to Elisha FOORD called Tilden Island...he being the highest bidder at a legal vandue. Widow Lucy VINAL releases dower. Witnesses: William MACUMBER, Joseph TILDEN, Charles FOORD, John TURNER. Ack. 29 Oct. 1744 by John TURNER. Rec. 4 May 1796.

Estate of **Capt. Joshua VINAL** of Marshfield MA to **Isaac ROGERS & Charles FOORD**.<Plymouth Co.Deeds>
<78:132>...20 Oct. 1794, John TURNER, Esq. of Pembroke, as admr...by order of the Court...for Ł5.7s sold to Isaac ROGERS, shipwright & Charles FOORD, yeoman, both of Marshfield...one acre pasture land in Marshfield...near the Rev. Elijah LEONARD's Meeting House...bounded by land of sd ROGERS & FOORD...they being the highest bidders. Widow Lucy VINAL releases dower. Witnesses: William MACOMBER, Joseph TILDEN, Jedediah EWELL, John TURNER. Ack. 29 Oct. 1794 by John TURNER. Rec. 15 Aug. 1795.

Seth VINAL et al to **Lydia SIMMONS** of Marshfield MA. <Plymouth Co.Deeds 178:252>
...15 Nov. 1834, Seth VINAL, shipwright of Scituate, Calvin CORTHELL, blacksmith of Hanover & wf Patience and Isaac ROGERS, yeoman of Marshfield & wf Lucy, for $75.00 sold to Lydia SIMMONS, widow...all our right...to two thirds of a dwelling house and about fifty three rods of land... in Marshfield...being all that part...that was released...to Hannah VINAL of Marshfield dec'd in a division deed between sd Hannah and Seth VINAL dated 4 May 1821. Hannah wf of Seth releases dower. Rec. 1 Dec. 1834.

Lucy VINAL et al to **Luther ROGERS** of Marshfield MA. <Plymouth Co.Deeds 109:62>
...(2) May 1808, Lucy VINAL, taylores & Joshua VINAL, housewright, both of Marshfield and Calvin CORTHELL, blacksmith & wf Patience Little CORTHELL, seamstres of Hanover, for Ł239.25. sold to Luther ROGERS, housewright...three quarters of our undivided shares in the pasture land lying in sd Marshfield that Capt. Joshua VINAL dec'd bought of the widow Mary PHILLIPS...except one acre that John TURNER, Esq., admr. on the estate of the sd Joshua VINAL dec'd debts...bounded by the highway that leads by the North Meeting house in Marshfield...southward of the place that the School House formerly stood...containing about six and two thirds acres. Witnesses: Wales TILDEN, Nabby BARSTOW. Ack. 2 May 1808 by grantors. Rec. 30 May 1808.

Estate of **Peabody LITTLE**, mariner of Marshfield MA. <Plymouth Co.PR #13066>
<original> Request 12 Aug. 1793, of father **Ephraim LITTLE**...being far advanced in life...that kinsman **Capt. James LITTLE** be app'td admr. and gdn. to his son's two children, **Nancy & Charles LITTLE**. <27:439> Letter/Bond 14 Aug. 1793, **James LITTLE** of Marshfield app'td admr. Sureties: Elisha FORD, James CLAPP. Witnesses: Nathaniel LOTHROP, Isaac LOTHROP. <33:417> Inventory taken 22 Aug. 1793, by Ephraim LITTLE, Sylvanus WHITE, Asa THOMAS; total estate, Ł39.0.7. <33:417> Insolvency. <33:418> Notice. <33:550> Appointment, 2 Sept. 1793, of commissioners, Sylvanus WHITE, Asa THOMAS. <33:551> List of claims, 27 Feb. 1794: Dr. Isaac WINSLOW, Dr. Charles STOCKBRIDGE, Jacob BARSTOW, James LITTLE, Sally GOODNO, Consider HOWLAND, Asa THOMAS, Benjamin STOCKBRIDGE, Abigail KEEN, Nathaniel CLIFT, John JOYCE. <33:564> Account of admr., 3 Mar. 1794. <35:140> Account of admr., 1 Sept. 1794. <35:141> Notice, 24 May 1794, for sale of real estate. <35:141> Notice of sale, 19 Apr. 1794.

Guardianship of Children of **Peabody LITTLE** of Marshfield MA. <Plymouth Co.PR #13064>
<26:276> Letter/Bond 2 Sept. 1793, James LITTLE of Marshfield app'td gdn. of **Nancy LITTLE & Charles LITTLE** (under 14). Sureties: Sylvanus WHITE, Asa THOMAS. Witnesses: Nathaniel HOWE, Isaac LOTHROP. <36:417> Account of gdn., 3 Sept. 1798; incl. half a note of hand given by Benjamin KEEN & Daniel WHITE for the wards fourteenth part of William KEEN's estate dated 6 Jan. 1798. <32:144> Letter/Bond 1 Sept. 1800, Daniel WHITE of Marshfield app'td gdn. of **Charles LITTLE** (above 14). Sureties: Ephraim LITTLE, Sylvanus WHITE. Witnesses: Charles TURNER Jr., James LITTLE. <37:483> Account of gdn., 2 July 1801; incl. received of Benjamin KEEN, admr. to estate of widow Lydia KEEN. <38:187> Account of gdn., 25 Oct. 1802; incl. cash pd to B. DELANO for boarding & lodging.

MICRO #5 OF 32

Fobes LITTLE to **Kenelm BAKER** of Marshfield MA. <Plymouth Co.Deeds 29:88>
...27 Apr. 1734, Fobes LITTLE & wf Sarah, for £155 sold to Kenelm BAKER...five acres of upland & three and three quarters of swamp adjoining land of sd Kenelm...and also part of ye house which James SPRAGUE of Marshfield now dwells in, viz: ye southerly great Chamber...ye north easterly Chamber in ye Leantoe over ye Bed room & the Liberty & Priviledge of ye southerly part of ye cellar from the summer & ye westerly Bay in the Barn & the Priviledge of Water in the Well...all which...is part of the house & land that Samuel BAKER of Marshfield, Father of ye sd Sarah, died seized of which...was set off to Sarah. Witnesses: John LITTLE, Anna LITTLE. Ack. same day by grantors. Rec. 28 Nov. 1734.

Will of **Lemuel LITTLE**, gent. of Marshfield MA. <Plymouth Co.PR #13053>
<36:484>...dated 5 Jan. 1796, mentions wf **Penelope** and following chil., viz: sons **Lemuel LITTLE, George LITTLE** (to receive Stevens Island), **James LITTLE, Luther LITTLE, Jedediah LITTLE & William Fobes LITTLE** (dec'd) and daus **Jane LITTLE, Olive OAKMAN, Polly ROGERS** (widow), **Persis PRATT**; grandchildren **Calvin LEWIS Jr. & Penelope LEWIS**, chil. of dec'd dau **Penelope LEWIS**; sons **Luther & Jedediah**, executors. Witnesses: John WHITE, Noah HATCH, Sylvanus WHITE. <36:486> Letter/Bond 8 Jan. 1799, **Luther & Jedediah LITTLE** app'td admrs. Sureties: John WHITE, Sylvanus WHITE. Witnesses: James LITTLE, Isaac LOTHROP. <36:510> Inventory taken 2 Mar. 1799, by Isaac WINSLOW, John WHITE, Daniel LEWIS; total real estate, L2873. <37:33> Notice, 21 May 1799.

Estate of **James LITTLE**, gent. of Scituate MA. <Plymouth Co.PR #13055>
<34:376> Letter 5 Dec. 1803, widow **Lydia LITTLE** and Charles TURNER Jr. of Scituate, app'td admrs. <40:25> Inventory taken 16 Dec. 1803; total $16,011.32. <40:491> Division, 12 Aug. 1806, of real estate; mentions the widow, daus **Lucy OTIS** wf of Ensign Jr. & **Lydia Young LITTLE** and son **James LITTLE.** (also 40:27,28,490,491;10A:450)

Guardianship of Children of **Luther LITTLE** of Marshfield MA. <Plymouth Co.PR #13058>
<26:282> Letter/Bond 31 Oct. 1793, **Luther LITTLE** app'td gdn. of his children, **Luther & Susanna LITTLE**, both under 14; mentions any estate that accrues to them in right of their mother **Susanna LITTLE** dec'd. Sureties: James LITTLE, William WHITE. Witnesses: Sylvanus WHITE, Elizabeth CLAP.

Will of **Thomas LITTLE**, yeoman of Marshfield MA. <Plymouth Co.PR>
<47:98>...dated 16 Mar. 1809, mentions wf **Lucy** (& antenuptial agreement); granddaughter **Abigail Little ROGERS**; dau **Abigail TILDEN**; son **Thomas LITTLE** (executor) and his sons **William Henry LITTLE & Thomas LITTLE**; to sons **Doty LITTLE & Otis LITTLE**, all real estate in Marshfield; daus **Ruth WATERMAN & Betsey TROUANT**; grandchildren **Joseph BRYANT & Sarah BRYANT.** <47:99> Pr. 11 Mar. 1815. <47:100> Appraisers app'td, 2 Jan. 1815.

Doty LITTLE of Castine ME to **Otis LITTLE** of same. <Plymouth Co.Deeds 155:229>
...29 May 1824, Doty LITTLE, gent., for $267.72 sold to Otis LITTLE, Esq...all right in certain real estate in Marshfield...being the same which was devised to me & the sd Otis by the late Thomas LITTLE of Marshfield in and by his last will. Signed by Doty LITTLE with wife "Hannah Briggs" releasing dower. Witness: William ABBOT. Ack. 29 May 1824 by Doty. Rec. 12 Sept. 1825.

Otis LITTLE of Castine ME to **Charles HATCH Jr. & Tilden AMES.** <Plymouth Co.Deeds 161:255>
...19 Sept. 1825, Otis LITTLE, Esq., for $175.00 sold to Charles HATCH Jr., Esq. & Tilden AMES, housewright, both of Marshfield...forty three and a half acres in Marshfield...bounded by land of Jedidiah LITTLE & Luther LITTLE being the same that was given & bequeathed to me & Doty LITTLE by the last will & testament of Thomas LITTLE late of Marshfield. Wf Dorothy LITTLE releases dower. Witnesses: Mary A. GAY, Ebenezer GAY. Ack. 20 Sept. 1825. Rec. 22 Nov. 1827.

Job OTIS Sr. & Jr. of Scituate MA to **Abigail HALLIBURTON** of Boston MA. <Plymouth Co.Deeds 38:138>
...14 Nov. 1746, Job OTIS Sr. & Job OTIS Jr., yeomen, for love & affection, convey to Abigail HALLIBURTON, widow, dau of sd Job Sr...one fifth of land in Hanover & Abington bought by Job Sr. on 18 Jan. 1721 and one fifth of land bought of Joseph STOCKBRIDGE on 4 July 1744. Mercy OTIS wf of Job Sr. & Prince OTIS wf of Job Jr, release dowers. Ack. 25 Nov. 1746. Rec. 16 Dec. 1746.

Job OTIS Jr. of Scituate MA to **Abigail HALLIBURTON et al.** <Plymouth Co.Deeds 39:273>
...30 Mar. 1749, Job OTIS Jr., gent. to Abigail HALLIBURTON, widow of Boston, Benjamin STOCKBRIDGE, physician of Scituate, Priscilla OTIS, spinster of Scituate and Mordecai ELLIS, cordwainer of Hanover & wf Sarah. <40:253>...1 Nov. 1749, all the above with Joseph RAMSDEN of Bridgewater divided land in Hanover & Abington. <40:260>...1 May 1750, Abigail HALLIBURTON sold her share of above to Mordecai ELLIS.

Will of **Mordecai ELLIS**, yeoman of Hanover MA. <Plymouth Co.PR #7265>
<43:261>...dated 22 June 1803...to son **Mordecai ELLIS Jr.**, half a silver tankard, the other half to grandsons **Spooner ELLIS & Thomas ELLIS**, sons of son **Clark ELLIS**; to son **Nathaniel ELLIS** the great bible & clock; son **Otis ELLIS** incapable of caring for himself & to be supported by **Nathaniel**; daus **Elizabeth RAMSDELL** wf of Joseph, **Rebecca BAILEY** wf of George & **Priscilla LITTLE** wf of John; **John ELLIS & Anna ELLIS**, chil. of dec'd son **David ELLIS.** <43:263> Pr. 3 Sept. 1810.

Will of **Job AVERY** of Truro MA. <Barnstable Co.PR>
<23:473>...dated 28 Oct. 1784. <23:475> Pr. 14 Apr. 1785. <26:56,59,62> Inv., Account, Dower.

Estate of **Stephen TILDEN** of Scituate MA. <Plymouth Co.PR #20757>
<3:104> Letter/Bond 7 Mar. 1711/12, son **Ephraim TILDEN** app'td admr. Surety: John SUTTON of Scituate. Witnesses: William BASSETT, Nathaniel THOMAS Jr. "Note that this letter of administration is rejected". <3:143> Letter/Bond 4 Apr. 1712, son **Joseph TILDEN** app'td admr. Surety: Ephraim TILDEN. Witnesses: Elizabeth THOMAS, Anne THOMAS

PLYMOUTH COUNTY DEEDS: (re: Stephen TILDEN, grantor, all to 1801**)**

<3:62> - 3 Aug. 1698, heirs of Stephen TILDEN.
<5:71> - 26 Mar. 1701, Stephen TILDEN Jr., worsted comber of Scituate & wf Mary.
<5:134> - 1704, Stephen TILDEN, husbandman of Scituate.
<5:136> - 25 Mar. 1704, Stephen TILDEN Jr. & wf Mary of Scituate.
<14:140> - 2 Mar. 1705/6, Stephen TILDEN Jr. of Scituate to Samuel STODDER, house & land at Brushy Hill in Scituate.
<7:343> - 14 Dec. 1710, Stephen TILDEN of Scituate to son Joseph TILDEN of Marshfield.
<9:50> - 14 Dec. 1710, Stephen TILDEN, husbandman of Scituate to son David TILDEN of same, David to support father.
<9:52> - 1710, Stephen TILDEN of Scituate to dau Ruth TILDEN wf of Nathaniel Jr.

Estate of **Stephen TILDEN** of Stoughton CT. <Suffolk Co.PR #13904>
<65:347> Letter 29 Aug. 1766, widow **Abigail TILDEN** app'td admx. <68:309> Inventory taken 3 Dec. 1766. <68:309> Account of admx., 20 Oct. 1769. <93:288,289> Dower assigned 25 Mar. 1794 to the widow **Abigail HOLMES,** of Sharon, now the wife of Lemuel HOLMES; remainder of estate divided into four parts. <original> Receipt 15 Apr. 1794 of **Peter & Rebecca DICKENMAN** and **Eleazer & Jerusha CLAP,** to **Stephen TILDEN** the only surviving son.

MICRO #6 OF 32

Will of **Ebenezer TILDEN** of Windham CT. <Windham Co.CT PR>
<6:522>...dated 11 June 1759...to son **Joseph TILDEN**...the halfe part of the farm on which I now live, this with the other halfe which I have given him by deed...also 22 acres bought of Jonathan LYMAN lying by John BREWSTER's...also husbandry tools & stock of cattel...to dau **Mary BLISS** wf of Azariah...12 acres bought of Isaac BAILEY adjoyning to land of sd son in law Azariah...also all beds, bedding, bedcloaths, linnen, pewter, brass vessells, iron potts, kittles, skillets, my best chist & half my books...also £85; son **Joseph,** executor. Witnesses: Solomon WILLIAMS, Mary WILLIAMS, Thomas WILLIAMS. <6:524> Pr. 7 May 1764, Rev. Solomon WILLIAMS & other witnesses swore. <original> Inventory taken 28 May 1764 by Jonathan CLARK & Ezekiel LOOMIS; Lyman lott, £77; home lott, £325; Baily Lott, £36; total estate, £685.3s5d. <7:62> Receipt 11 Sept. 1764 at Lebanon... of **Azariah & Mary BLISS** to brother **Joseph TILDEN,** exr., for their share of father's estate. Witnesses: Joseph WISE Jr., Sarah CLOSSON.

Plymouth Co.Deeds: <18:66>...4 Nov. 1720, **Ebenezer TILDEN,** weaver of Marshfield & wf Mary sell. <23:84>...5 May 1727, **Ebenezer TILDEN,** yeoman of Marshfield sells land.

LEBANON CT DEEDS: (re: Ebenezer TILDEN, all to 1788**)**

<2:537> - 1716, Ebenezer TILDEN from Nathaniel GOVE.
<4:143> - Jan. 1728/9, Ebenezer TILDEN of Lebanon from Proprietors.
<4:157> - Jan. 1728/9, Ebenezer TILDEN of Lebanon to Proprietors.
<4:424> - 1731, Ebenezer TILDEN to Benjamin SPRAGUE. (5:296 - from Benjamin, 1730)
<4:442> - 1732, Ebenezer TILDEN to Jedediah STRONG. (4:423 - from Jedediah, 1732)
<6:26> - 1738, Ebenezer TILDEN from Isaac BAILEY.
<7:332> - 1750, Ebenezer TILDEN to Joseph TILDEN.
<8:113> - 1752, Ebenezer TILDEN from Jonathan LYMAN.

Nathaniel GOVE of Lebanon CT to **Ebenezer TILDEN** of Scituate MA. <Lebanon CT Deeds 2:537>
...18 May 1716, Nathaniel GOVE, for £95 sold to Ebenezer TILDEN...100 acres in Lebanon...GOVE bought of William BREWSTER of Lebanon...bounded by land given to Benjamin BREWSTER. Witnesses: William WATTLE, Stephen TILDEN. Ack. & Rec. 18 May 1716.

Lebanon CT Deeds: (re: **Azariah BLISS,** all to 1784); <10:294> 1764, grantor. <10:457> 1750/1, grantor. <10:421> 1765, grantee.

Estate of **James THOMAS** of Duxborough MA. <Plymouth Co.PR>
<4:54>...25 Apr. 1718, adm. granted to widow **Mary THOMAS.** <4:256> Division of real estate to sons & the moveables to daughters **Mary & Hannah**; meadow in Marshfield next to Caleb SAMSON to son **Peleg THOMAS.**

John THOMAS et al to **James THOMAS** of Duxborough MA. <Plymouth Co.Deeds 28:19>
...10 Nov. 1732, John THOMAS, Ezekiel THOMAS, Joseph LANGRELL & wf Mary, all of Lebanon CT, Ebenezer THOMAS of Norwich CT and Wrestling BREWSTER & wf Hannah of Kingston MA, for £10 sold to brother James THOMAS...our whole right...in salt meadow in Marshfield...sd meadow was lately in ye possession of Deacon John FOSTER & Sarah his wife late of Marshfield dec'd & now in partnership between Daniel THOMAS, Israel THOMAS, John THOMAS & our selves. Witnesses: Ebenezer WAIT,

Amos RANDALL, Israel BRADFORD, Joshua CUSHING. Ack. 20 Apr. 1733 by Wrestling & Hannah, 5 Dec. 1732 by other grantors. Rec. 25 May 1733.

Elisha LITCHFIELD of Scituate MA to **Ruth LITCHFIELD et al.** <Plymouth Co.Deeds 56:196>
...20 Aug. 1771, Elisha LITCHFIELD, yeoman, for £380 sold to Ruth LITCHFIELD & Mary BAILEY, spinsters, Benjamin JACOB & Benjamin BAILEY, yeomen, all of Scituate and Ruth DWELLE wf of Lemuel of Topsham...all right in 95 acres in Scituate bounded by land of Daniel JENKINS, Pickels CUSHING & sd Elisha. Ack. 21 Aug. 1771. Rec. 15 Apr. 1772. <56:197>...same day all the above, for £212 sold to Elisha, 53 acres in Scituate with barn & corn house. Rec. 15 Apr. 1772.

Estate of **James LITCHFIELD** of Scituate MA. <Plymouth Co.PR>
<7:157> Letter 27 Oct. 17735, father **Nicholas LITCHFIELD** of Scituate app'td admr.
(References are given for wills of **Nicholas LITCHFIELD**, viz: <12:174> 1750; <25:440> 1780.)

Will of **Benjamin BAILEY** of Scituate MA. <Plymouth Co.PR #671>
<20:410>...dated 30 Apr. 1770, mentions wf **Patience** and following chil., viz: **Benjamin BAILEY** (unm.), **Jerusha CLAP, Ruth DWELLING, Mary BAILEY, Desire BAILEY, Roland BAILEY, Thankful BAILEY, Patience BAILEY.** Pr. 15 Sept. 1770. <20:411> Inventory taken 4 Oct. 1770; mentions apparel that belonged to his second wife. (References are given with no details, in Plymouth Co.Deeds, viz: <57:10>...4 Apr. 1772, **Benjamin BAILEY** to Thomas LITCHFIELD; <57:11>...18 June 1772, widow **Patience BAILEY** to Joseph BAILEY.)

Lemuel DWELLE of Braintree MA to **Thomas LITCHFIELD** of Scituate MA. <Plymouth Co.Deeds 57:10>
...2 Mar. 1772, Lemuel DWELLE, shipwright & wf Ruth, for £60 sold to Thomas LICHFIELD, yeoman of Scituate...19 acres of upland...being all our right...in 95 acres lying in common & undivided with Ruth LITCHFIELD, Benjamin BAILEY, Mary BAILEY & Eleazer LICHFIELD...bounded by land of John GARRETT, Daniel JENKINS, Pickels CUSHING & Elisha LICHFIELD...also all our right...in the Town Cedar Swamp in Scituate. Witnesses: William PENNIMAN, Jacob FRIEZE. Rec. 7 Oct. 1772.

Estate of **Lemuel DWELLE**, shipwright of Braintree MA. <Suffolk Co.PR #15952>
<75:153> Letter/Bond 3 June 1776, widow **Ruth DWELLE** app'td admx. Sureties: John VINTON, blacksmith of Braintree and Jeremiah BATTLE of Cohasset. <77:165> Inventory taken 25 June 1776 by James PENNIMAN, Thomas WHITE, Thomas VINTON; one acre with house & barn, £128; total £165.5. <77:166> Account of admx., 19 June 1778. <78:633> Dower set off to widow, 22 June 1778; allowed 31 Mar. 1779.

Guardianship of Children of **Lemuel DWELLE** of Braintree MA. <Suffolk Co.PR #16599,16600>
<77:664> 19 June 1778, widow **Ruth DWELLE** app'td gdn. of **Lemuel DWELLE & John DWELLE,** both under 14. Meshack PENNIMAN, yeoman of Braintree became bound with the sd Ruth for the faithful discharge of the sd trust.

Estate of **Lemuel DWELLE** to **Lemuel CLARKE** of Braintree MA. <Suffolk Co.Deeds 140:177>
...19 Apr. 1783, Meshech PENNIMAN, yeoman of Braintree & wf Ruth admx. to the estate of Lemuel DWELLE dec'd and gdn. to Lemuel & John DWELLE, minors...for £78 sold to Lemuel CLARKE, gent... half an acre with dwelling house. Ack. 5 May 1783 by Ruth, 17 May by Meshech. Rec 13 Dec. 1783.
<175:274>...21 Apr. 1783 they sold the other half. Ack. 20 May 1783 by Ruth.

SUFFOLK COUNTY DEEDS: (re: DWELLE)

<116:163> - 7 Mar. 1770, Lemuel DWELLE to John ADAMS, mortgage.
<140:177> - 13 Dec. 1783, John DWELLE et al estate.
<175:274> - 13 May 1793, John DWELLE et al estate.

MICRO #7 OF 32

Will of **Stephen TILDEN** of Lebanon CT. <Windham CT PR 1:261>
...8 May 1725, mentions wf **Mary**, son **Stephen TILDEN**, daus **Hannah TILDEN, Mary POWELL** and grandson **Joshua TILDEN**. Pr. 27 June 1728.

PLYMOUTH COUNTY DEEDS: (re: Bethiah LITTLE)

<4:36> - 26 Feb. 1700/01, Bethiah LITTLE, widow of Isaac, of Marshfield & eldest son Thomas LITTLE to Isaac HOWLAND.
<10:2:111> 27 Mar. 1705, Bethiah LITTLE, widow of Isaac, of Marshfield, in behalf of son Lemuel LITTLE, sells to Ellis DOTY, land in Rochester.
<18:165> - , Bethiah LITTLE to Abigail LITTLE et al.
<5:160> - , Bethiah LITTLE from Nathaniel WARREN.
<6:99> - , Bethiah LITTLE from Robert BARKER.

Mary LITTLE of Plymouth MA to **Joseph PEAS** of Edgartown MA. <Plymouth Co.Deeds 6:281>
...18 Mar. 1756, Mary LITTLE, seamstress to Joseph PEAS, mariner...her rights in lots formerly of Richard SARSON, Esq., dec'd, then of Mrs. Mehitable LATHROP dec'd & now of Mary LITTLE's.

John ARBUTHNOT et al to **Isaac LITTLE** of Marshfield MA. <Plymouth Co.Deeds 28:194>
...26 Sept. 1721, John ARBUTHNOT & wf Abigail of Boston and Thomas BARKER & wf Bethiah of Pemb-

roke, sold to Isaac LITTLE...our one fourth part of...several tracts...in Marshfield & Pembroke ...of late the estate of William THOMAS late of Marshfield...given to us by our Honoured Mother Bethiah LITTLE dec'd which did come to her from her sd brother William THOMAS dec'd. Ack. 13 Jan. 1726/7 by John & Abigail.

John ARBUTHNOT et al to Isaac LITTLE. <Plymouth Co.Deeds 28:195>
...14 May 1722, John ARBUTHNOT & wf Abigail and Thomas BARKER & wf Bethiah, sold to Isaac LITTLE ...our two sixteenth parts of ye furnace in Pembroke. Ack. 18 Apr. 1728 by Thomas & Bethiah.

Thomas BARKER of Pembroke MA to **John ARBUTHNOT** of Boston. <Plymouth Co.Deeds 28:33>
...28 June 1733...land & dwelling house in Pembroke. <36.137>...4 Nov. 1743, John sells this land to Bethiah BARKER, widow of Pembroke. Wf Abigail releases dower. <39:15>...20 June 1747, John (merchant of Boston) & wf Abigail sell land in Pembroke to Joshua BARKER of Boston.

Abigail ARBUTHNOT of Boston to **Gideon HACKETT** of Middleboro MA. <Plymouth Co.Deeds 45:177>
...20 Jan. 1757, Abigail ARBUTHNOT, widow of John, for £26.13s4d sold to Gideon HACKETT, laborer ...99th lot in South Purchase in Middleboro, containing 45 acres...in the right of my Father Isaac LITTLE, Esq., late of Marshfield dec'd. Witnesses: Benjamin GOTT, Mary SPEAKMAN. Ack. same day. Rec. 23 May 1759.

Estate of **Nathaniel LITTLE** of Marshfield MA. <Plymouth Co.PR #13065>
<3:339> Letter/Bond 25 June 1715, brother **William LITTLE** of Plymouth app'td admr. Surety: Isaac LITTLE of Marshfield. Witnesses: Joseph OTIS, Thomas CROADE. <3:419> Inventory sworn to 21 June 1716 by admr.; Debts due from: Preserved BRAYTON for his half of ye farm sold, £495; sloop Prosperous; sundry persons in Caroli <Carolina>; sundry persons in Antegua; Lemuel LITTLE, Richard BILLINGS, Thomas DOGGETT, Thomas WHITE, Eleazer WHITE, Cornel BRIGGS, Thomas BARKER, Ebenezer BARKER, Nathaniel MATSON, Thomas DONGAN; half the sloop Prosperous valued at £40; Debts due to: Francis WAINWRIGHT, Isaac LITTLE, Charles LITTLE, Abigail LITTLE, Thomas LITTLE estate, Mr. BURROUGHS at Boston, Benjamin JOHNS, Samuel BARRETT; a shoemaker; S. TYLEE, Cornelius WHITE, John SMITH, John STANFORD, Mr. BATTLESBY, Richard DRAPER, Mr. HATCH, Mother LITTLE, sundry persons in Carolina, sickness expences, funeral charges, William LITTLE, Thomas SELBY, William THOMAS, Zabdiel BOYLSTONE.

Estate of **Capt. Charles LITTLE** of Plymouth MA. <Plymouth Co.PR #13025>
<4:422> Letter/Bond 20 June 1724, widow **Sarah LITTLE** app'td admx. Sureties: James WARREN of Plymouth & Isaac LITTLE of Marshfield. Witnesses: John JONES, Benjamin PRINCE. <5:1> Inventory taken 26 June 1724 by Thomas BARKER, Elisha WADSWORTH, Thomas CROADE; incl. land in Plymouth, Pembroke, Rochester, Plympton, Muscongus & Middleboro; lands in Plymouth, £1285; total estate, £5803.1.5.; sworn to 18 Sept. 1724 by admx. <5:232> Account of admx. (not dated); Debts due from: Jona. WALDO, Mrs. Susannah JACOBS, Joseph BRIDGHAM, Henry DEERING, George CAMMELL, Mr. BULLFINCH, Mr. PLANCHER, James BOWDOIN, BOYLES, JACKSON, KNEELAND, HENCHMAN, Capt. FAREWEATHER, FITCH, BOYLSTON, WARNER, STODDARD, Samuel BRADFORD, Mrs. Sarah WARREN, Kenelm WINSLOW, Coll. BROWN, George BRYANT, Ebenezer SAMPSON, Thomas FISH, Paul DUDLEY. <6:324> Warrant for division, 28 Mar. 1732, by Edward ARNOLD, Wrastling BREWSTER, James WARREN, Nathaniel THOMAS Jr., John WINSLOW; to set off estate to the widow, **Sarah SEVER** now ye wife of Nicholas SEVER, Esq. of Kingston and also to set off to sd Sarah that part of her child's estate that dec'd after the father. <6:326> Division 26 Mar. 1733, to the widow and daus **Bethiah LITTLE & Lucy LITTLE.** <7:17> Division of personal estate, 24 May 1734; admx. has in hand, £2383.7.1., her thirds deducted there remains £1588.18.1; widow's part of the child's estate, £176.10.11, leaving for the two surviving children, £1412.7.2., viz: **Bethiah TYLER** wf of Thomas of Boston and **Lucie LITTLE.**

Guardianship of Child of **Capt. Charles LITTLE** of Plymouth MA. <Plymouth Co.PR #13055>
<5:355> Letter/Bond 3 Feb. 1727, widow **Sarah LITTLE** app'td gdn. of **Bethiah LITTLE,** under 14. Surety: James WARREN of Plymouth. Witnesses: Isaac LITTLE, Joseph STACEY.

Will of **Lucy LITTLE,** spinster of Kingston MA. <Plymouth Co.PR #13056>
<14:307>...dated 23 Sept. 1756...mentions **Bethiah TYLER** wf of Thomas of Boston...my only & beloved sister. Witnesses: Benjamin STOCKBRIDGE, Mary WARREN, Briggett O. NASH. <14:308> Letter 29 Mar 1757, **Bethiah TYLER** app'td admx. <14:309> Bond 5 Oct. 1757, of **Bethiah TYLER,** admx. Sureties: Thomas TYLER, James WARREN Jr., John LOTHROP. Witness: William THOMAS. <14:307> Affidavit 29 Mar. 1757, of Benjamin STOCKBRIDGE who attended the dec'd in her last sickness testifies that he believed her sane when the will was executed.

Will of **Isaac LITTLE,** Esq. of Pembroke MA. <Plymouth Co.PR #13041>
<14:530>...dated 15 Aug. 1751, mentions wf **Abigail** (exx.) and following chil., viz: **Mercy LITTLE** (under 18), **Otis LITTLE, Nathaniel LITTLE, Mary WINSLOW, Isaac LITTLE, Lemuel LITTLE;** mentions lands in York County, Dartmouth, Marshfield, N. Yarmouth & Plymouth. Witnesses: Benjamin LINCOLN, Joseph THAXTER, George LANE. Codicil 21 Jan. 1758. <14:533> Pr. 3 Apr. 1758, widow **Abigail LITTLE** app'td admx. <14:534> Inventory taken 18 May 1758 by Samuel JACOB, Benjamin TURNER, John FORD; total estate, £1483.14.2. <15:466> Bond to pay debts, 3 Mar. 1760, signed by **Abigail LITTLE** & Isaac LITTLE. Witnesses: John FAUNCE, Edward WINSLOW. <16:182> Bond to pay debts, 7 Sept. 1761, signed by same. Witnesses: Caleb TURNER, Edward WINSLOW.

Guardianship of Children of **Isaac LITTLE,** Esq. of Pembroke MA. <Plymouth Co.PR #13054>
<15:1> Letters/Bonds 3 Apr. 1758, widow **Abigail LITTLE** app'td gdn. of **Lemuel & Mercy LITTLE.**

Will of **Mercy LITTLE**, seamstress of Pembroke MA. <Plymouth Co.PR #13063>
<25:296>...dated 1 May 1779, mentions unnamed mother; neice **Mary THOMAS** dau of brother **Isaac THOMAS** dec'd; dec'd brother **Isaac LITTLE**, his widow **Lydia LITTLE** and his chil., viz: **Isaac LITTLE, Charles LITTLE, Otis LITTLE, Abigail LITTLE, Anna LITTLE, Judith LITTLE**; brother **Lemuel LITTLE**; Samuel GOOLD, executor. Witnesses: Deborah JOSSELYN, Benjamin BARKER, Isaiah JOSSELYN. <25:298> Pr. 3 June 1779, Samuel GOOLD of Pembroke app'td admr. <25:298> Inventory taken by Josiah SMITH, Josiah THOMAS, Wait FORD; total real estate, £145; total estate, £1141.17.4; sworn to by admr. 6 July 1779.

Estate of **Isaac LITTLE** of Pembroke MA. <Plymouth Co.PR #13042>
<23:56> Letter/Bond 3 May 1774, Asaph TRACY of Pembroke app'td admr. Sureties: Isaac HATCH, Daniel HATCH, Daniel MANLEY. Witnesses: Samuel BALDWIN, Lucy DYER. <21:628> Inventory taken 16 May 1774 by John TURNER, Prince BARKER, Samuel GOOLD; total real estate, £225.13.4.; total estate, £286.16.2. <24:364> Insolvency. <24:364> List of claims: Josiah THOMAS, Seth RANDALL, Samuel JENINGS, James COX, Dr. Jeremiah HALL, Adam FORD, Joseph MAGOUN, John MAGOUN, William WATSON, widow Mary LORING, widow Rebecca DAVIS, Philip TURNER, Thomas DAVIS, Lydia PRINCE, Prince BARKER, Isaac HATCH, Aaron SOULE, John STETSON, William WESTON, Isaac TUBBS, John JORDIN, Joshua PARKER/BARKER of Hingham, Nathan STEVENS, Jonathan TURNER, Seth FORD, Josiah KEEN, Thomas JOSSELYN, Jacob BARSTOW, Edward THOMAS, Seth HATCH, Joseph JOSSELYN, Capt. Nathaniel LITTLE, Ichabod THOMAS, Mrs. Abigail LITTLE, Nathaniel CHAMBERLIN, Seth JACOB. <24:363> Warrant to set off dower, 26 Nov 1776. <24:366> Account of admr., 7 Oct. 1776. <24:365> Dower set off 5 May 1777, to widow **Lydia LITTLE**; five acres woodland in Pembroke & five acres in Marshfield. <24:367> Account of admr., 7 July 1777. <24:372> Order to pay over balance in hands of admr., to creditors, £37.11.2.

Guardianship of Children of **Isaac LITTLE** of Pembroke MA. <Plymouth Co.PR #13020>
<26:71-73> Letters/Bonds 17 July 1779, Robert BARKER of Pembroke app'td gdn. of **Abigail LITTLE,** aged 12, **Anna LITTLE,** aged 13 **& Judah LITTLE,** aged 11 (girl). Lemuel BONNEY of Pembroke app'td gdn. of **Otis LITTLE, Charles LITTLE & Isaac LITTLE,** all above 14. Surety: Joshua BARSTOW. Witnesses. Ruth CUSHING Jr., Thankful OTIS.

References to **Nathaniel LITTLE** & wf **Keziah** in Plymouth Co.Deeds: <58:128> 1774, of Bridgewater; <70:80> 1782, of Kingston; <64:3> land of father Isaac LITTLE; <64:30> 1785; <64:45> 1785; <64:46> 1785; <66:75> of Bridgewater, 1786, land of John ATWOOD, father of Keziah; <77:234> 1795, of Bridgewater.

References to the name **Nathaniel LITTLE**, grantor (all to 1801), in Plymouth Co.Deeds:: 10:318, 394;38:49;42:127;43:130;46:249;47:33,86,110;49:252;54:79;55:36;57:96; 58:49,128; 61:56; 62:272; 64:3,30,45,46,67,148,191;66:75;69:123;70:80;73:101;77:234.

BRISTOL COUNTY DEEDS: (re: Nathaniel LITTLE)

<41:71> - 4 Jan. 1754, Peleg SLOCUM & wf Elizabeth of Dartmouth to Nathaniel LITTLE, ferryman of Tiverton, house & land in Dartmouth. Rec. 14 Jan. 1754.
<40:262> - 29 Jan. 1754, Nathaniel LITTLE, ferryman of Tiverton to Peleg SLOCUM. Wf Lydia releases dower.

References to the surname **LITTLE** (grantees, all to 1795), in Bristol Co.Deeds: 2:187,204;3:25, 197,281,376;4:49,210,271,347,349,350,482;5:85,92,209,254;7:56,465;8:356;9:440;10:511;12:16;13:39; 14:432;15:238;18:53,318;23:342;25:156;26:66,286;28:223;30:52,132;31:165,222;33:27;34:326;43:408; 63:510;66:471;73:397.

Nathaniel LITTLE Jr. of Bridgewater MA to **Melzar ADAMS** of Kingston MA. <Plymouth Co.Deeds 73:101>
...12 Sept. 1792, Nathaniel LITTLE Jr., gent. & wf Pamela, for £66 sell to Melzar ADAMS, gent... one & three quarter acre upland and seven eighth part of an acre of salt meadow...in Duxbury... being the homestead land that fell to us in the division of the real estate of Peabody BRADFORD late of Duxbury dec'd.

Nathaniel LITTLE of Kingston MA to **Barker LITTLE et al.** <Plymouth Co.Deeds 64:67>
...1785, Nathaniel LITTLE sells to Barker LITTLE of Dartmouth, Adams BAILEY of Scituate & Luther BAILEY of Hanover...land in Marshfield which was set off to Lydia LITTLE wf of Nathaniel, by the division of the estate of her father Isaac BARKER of Pembroke. <same source>...1785, Barker LITTLE sells to Adams & Luther BAILEY his share of the above.

George CORNELL of Dartmouth MA to **Barker LITTLE** of same. <Bristol Co.Deeds 63:510>
...3 7mth 1782, George CORNELL, yeoman, for £60 sold to Barker LITTLE, sadler...ten acres in Dartmouth...bounded by sd George's homestead farm and land of George MACOMBER & Stephen WOOD. Wf Mary signs. Witnesses: Henry HOWLAND, Jacob CHACE. Ack. 16 Nov. 1782 by George & Mary. Rec. 24 Jan. 1785.

Barker LITTLE of Dartmouth MA to **Seth CORNELL** of same. <Bristol Co.Deeds 63:512>
...12 Feb. 1784, Barker LITTLE, sadler, for $190 sold to Seth CORNELL, yeoman...ten acres in Dartmouth...bounded by land of sd Barker, George BROWNELL, George MACOMBER & Stephen WOOD. Wf Elizabeth signs. Witnesses: George BERDICK, Henry HOWLAND. Ack. 21 Jan. 1785 by Barker & Rec. 24 Jan.

Ichabod BROWNELL of Dartmouth MA to **Barker LITTLE** of same. <Bristol Co.Deeds 66:471>
...26 July 1784, Ichabod BROWNELL, taylor, sold to Barker LITTLE, sadler...ten acres in Dartmouth

Wf Delilah signs. Ack. 29 July 1784 by Ichabod. Rec. 30 Jan. 1788.

Barker LITTLE of Dartmouth MA to **Pardon DAVOL** of same. <Bristol Co.Deeds 66:473>
...7 June 1787, Barker LITTLE, sadler, sold to Pardon DAVEL/DAVOL, "saler"...10 acres in Dartmouth. (same bounds as land in previous deed 66:471). Elizabeth LITTLE signs. Ack. 8 June 1787 by Barker. Rec. 30 Jan. 1788.

Estate of **Barker LITTLE** of Dartmouth MA. <Bristol Co.PR>
<89:340;155:518;161:522> Letter/Bond 5 May 1846, Isaac FRANCIS app'td admr. <89:462> Inventory taken 4 Aug. 1846; no real estate. <92:286> Account 1 Aug. 1848. <116:159> Notice.

Will of **Esek LITTLE** of Dartmouth MA. <Bristol Co.PR>
<237:317>...dated 16 Apr. 1800, mentions wf **Ruth H.**, son **Edward A. LITTLE** and daus **Lucy GIFFORD, Sarah A. SEARS, Eliza J. BAKER.** Pr. 5 Oct. 1883. <234:61>...4 Aug. 1882, **Edward A. LITTLE**, eldest child, was app'td admr. of estate of **Ruth H. LITTLE** dec'd.

Estate of **Alexander P. SLADE** of Somerset MA. <Bristol Co.PR>
<69:123;153:38> Letter/Bond 8 Oct. 1830, widow **Ruth H. SLADE** app'td admx. Sureties: Ephraim MACOMBER, yeoman of Dartmouth & Anselm BASSETT, Esq. of Westport. <69:196> Inventory taken 26 Nov. 1830; no real estate. <69:204> Account 7 Dec. 1830. <112:627> Notice.

References to the name **Alexander P. SLADE** in Bristol Co.Deeds: (Grantor) 113:104;114:417;122:487; 124:293,390,415;125:223;127:408,431,436,437,499;128:96;129:398. (Grantee) 122:464,465,519;123:27; 124:326,403,417;127:430;130:82.

Will of **Keziah LITTLE** of Belpre OHIO. <no source>
...dated 3 Sept. 1811, mentions three daus **Lydia CRAIN, Christian TISDALL, Lucy COTTON** and the following grandchildren: **Theophilus COTTON, Lucy COTTON, Joshua COTTON, John COTTON, Welthy LITTLE, Charles LITTLE, Henry LITTLE, Lewis LITTLE, Nathaniel LITTLE, George LITTLE, Robert BRADFORD Samuel BRADFORD, Otis BRADFORD, George NASHE, Betsy SEALL, Morris SEALL, Sally DIER**; Col. Israel PUTNAM of Belpre, executor. Pr. Apr. 1814.

MICRO #8 OF 32

Will of **Lemuel LITTLE** of Edgartown MA. <Plymouth Co.PR #13052 & Dukes Co.PR 1:144,145>
<original>...dated 19 Feb. 1722/23, mentions wf **Jane** and daus **Abigail LITTLE & Sarson LITTLE**; wf **Jane** & brother **Isaac LITTLE** of Marshfield, executors. Witnesses: John NORTON, Peter RAY, Thomas CATHCART. <original> Letter 13 May 1723, **Isaac LITTLE** & **Jane LITTLE**, app'td exrs. <5:93> Inventory taken 3 Aug. 1724 by John BRIGGS, Edward WINSLOW, John WHITE; mentions house & land near Weweantit River and land at Crommicett, Charles Neck, Pine Islands, Great Neck, Muddy Brook, all in Rochester and land in Middleboro; total real estate, Ł1160.16.

Estate of **Dr. Thomas LITTLE** of Plymouth MA. <Plymouth Co.PR #13078>
<3:189> Letter/Bond 6 Jan. 1712, widow **Mary LITTLE** app'td admx. Surety: William CLARK Jr. Witnesses: Ephraim LITTLE, Thomas CROADE. <3:243> Inventory taken 20 May 1713 by Ephraim LITTLE, Joshua MORSS, William CLARK Jr.; total real estate, Ł1085.15; total estate, Ł1333.13.9. <3:389> Account of admx., 21 June 1716. <3:389> Division of personal estate, 21 June 1716, between the widow and following chil., viz: **Thomas LITTLE** (eldest son), **Isaac LITTLE** (2d son), **Mehew/Mayhew LITTLE** (3d son), **George LITTLE, Mary LITTLE.** <5:46> Inventory of real estate taken 4 Aug. 1724 by Isaac LOTHROP, John DYER, Thomas HOLMES; total real estate, Ł688.10; incl. land at Clam Puding Pond, South Purchase in Middleboro, Spring Brook & South Meadows in Plympton and 50 acres in Pembroke. <5:47> Warrant to divide. <5:48> Division 7 Sept. 1724, by Isaac LOTHROP, Nicholas DREW, Thomas HOLMES; to the widow **Mary BRYANT** and above children, except dau **Mary** as she already had a share set off to her at Martha's Vineyard. (Plymouth Co.Deeds 42:273...20 Nov. 1753, **Mary BRIANT**, gentlewoman of Plymouth, gives all real & personal estate in Plymouth to dau **Mary LITTLE** of Plymouth.

Guardianship of Children of **Dr. Thomas LITTLE** of Plymouth MA. <Plymouth Co.PR #13079>
<3:189-192> Letters/Bonds 6 Jan. 1712, **Mary LITTLE** app'td gdn. of her children **Isaac, Mary, Mahew, George & Thomas LITTLE**, all under 14. Surety: William CLARK Jr., Witnesses: Ephraim LITTLE, Thomas CROADE.

Estate of **Mayhew LITTLE**, mariner of Plymouth MA. <Plymouth Co.PR #13062>
<7:268> Letter/Bond 10 Mar. 1736, mother **Mary BRIANT** app'td admx. Sureties: Thomas HOWLAND, Jacob TAYLOR. Witnesses: Josiah COTTON, John CUSHING. <7:295> Inventory taken 4 May 1737, by Josiah CARVER, Thomas HOLMES, Samuel NELSON; one fifth part of two acres in Plymouth adjoining Nathaniel JACKSON; house lot in Plymouth, Ł200; land adjoining Mr. PULSIFER dec'd house to Mrs. BRYANT's house; half of 45 acre lot in Middleboro South Purchase; one fifth part of two 45 acre lots in Middleboro South Purchase, being lots #91 & #92; total estate (real estate only), Ł378.8.; sworn to 4 May 1737 by admx.

Will of **Mary LITTLE** of Plymouth MA. <Plymouth Co.PR #13059>
<13:509>...dated 24 Feb. 1755, mentions cousins **George LITTLE, Molley LITTLE, Sarah LITTLE**; George LITTLE, executor. Witnesses: Jonathan DIMAN, Joseph LeBARON, John GODDARD. <13:509> Letter 17 July 1755, George LITTLE, mariner of Plymouth app'td admr.

Thomas SMITH of Eastham MA to **Dr. Thomas LITTLE** of Plymouth. <Plainfield CT Deeds 1:48> ...1 Jan. 1709/10 & 5 Jan. 1710/11...no details. Ack. 6 Jan. 1710. Rec. 30 Sept. 1713. (Also rec. New London CT Deeds 2:113,114, on 25 June 1713.)

Will of **Isaac LITTLE** of Plympton MA. <Plymouth Co.PR #13040>
<13:510>...dated 27 May 1755, mentions wf **Hannah**, dau **Sarah LITTLE**, son **George LITTLE** (executor). Witnesses: Thomas MAYHEW, Benjamin SOULE, James HOVEY. Letter 17 July 1755, **George LITTLE**, mariner of Plymouth app'td exr. <14:205> List of claims, 29 Dec. 1756: Polycarpus LORING, John LITTLE, Esq., Marcy LITTLE's estate, Nathaniel BRADFORD, Zebedee CHANDLER, Robert BROWN, Mr. WARREN, Mr. GOODWIN, Sarah COBB, James SHURTLEFF, Joseph PERRY, James LANMAN, Gideon SAMPSON, Josiah RIDER, George LITTLE, John TORREY, Nathaniel LITTLE, John FINNEY, Timothy BURBANK, Daniel DIMAN, Joseph WRIGHT, James HOVEY, Stephen SAMSON, Kenelm BAKER, Nathaniel COBB, Isaac LOTHROP, Mr. DOTEY, Mr. TILLSON, Samuel CLARK, Samuel BARTLETT, Isaac LOTHROP Jr. his estate, Josiah CARVER's estate, WINSLOW & WHITE, Edward WINSLOW, Esq., TORREY & THOMAS. <14:206> Inventory taken 20 Nov. 1756, by John BARTLETT, James SHURTLEFF, Zaccheus CURTIS; incl. half of house & land, £27.6.8.; half a pine lot at Middleboro, being 45 acres in South Purchase; total estate, £33.12.5. <14:508> Account of exr., 20 Feb. 1758; by what I received of Mr. THOMPSON being what I sold him the indian boy for more than he was mortgaged at £2.13.4.

Estate of **George LITTLE**, mariner of Plympton MA. <Plymouth Co.PR #13036>
<17:109> Letter/Bond 24 Aug. 1763, Joseph WRIGHT of Plimton app'td admr. Sureties: Elkanah CUSHMAN, James HARLOW. Witnesses: Edward WINSLOW, Sarah WINSLOW. <16:537> Inventory taken 30 Nov. 1763 by James BONNEY, Zebedee CHANDLER, James HARLOW; total estate not exceeding £75. <16:537> Insolvency 5 Apr. (1763?). <19:89> List of claims, 5 June 1764: Thomas SAMSON, Josiah CUSHMAN, James HOVEY, Ephraim SPOONER, Jonathan PARKER Jr., Edward SEARS, Isaiah CUSHMAN, Abner BISBE, Joseph WRIGHT, Edward WINSLOW, Simeon BONNEY, Thomas MAYHEW, Robert BROWN, Hopestill BISBE, Zebede CHANDLER, Hannah LITTLE, Benjamin SOULE, James HARLOW, Abner HARLOW, William BONNEY, Ebenezer SOULE, Dr. Policarpus LORING. <19:89> Account of admr., 6 Aug. 1764; paid Capt. GOULD for charges in his last sickness & funeral charges, £3.5.8.; paid province rates for the years 1762 & 1763, 9s9d; paid Noah EATON to discharge the mortgage, £19.17.3.; necessarys to the widow, £27.14.7.

Guardianship of Child of **Thomas LITTLE** of Chilmark MA. <Plymouth Co.PR #13060>
<original> Bond 13 Apr. 1748, **Isaac LITTLE**, sadler of Plymouth, app'td gdn. of **Mary LITTLE** dau of Thomas LITTLE. Surety: Consider HOWLAND. Witness: Edward WINSLOW. <10:529> Letter, 15 Apr. 1748, **Mary LITTLE** chooses her uncle **Isaac LITTLE** to be her gdn. of property that may come to her from her father's estate. Witnesses: Nathaniel BOSWORTH, Benjamin LOTHROP Jr.

Will of **Anthony EAMES** of Marshfield MA. <Plymouth Co.PR>
<5:624>...dated 8 June 1726...being aged...to son **Anthony EAMES**, my dweling house...and all that part of my land where on I dwell...on the south side...and that part of my land that lieth on the north side of sd brook...to my three daughters **Mercy PHILIP/PHILIPS, Jerusha SAWER/SAWYER & Mary PHILIPS** ...to son **Anthony**, ten acre salt marsh...dau **Mercy** to have negrow woman named Sarah...dau **Mary** to have negrow girl named Pegge; sons in law **Joseph PHILIPS & Thomas SAWYER**, executors. Witnesses: John STETSON, Samuel ROGERS (Jr.), John JONES (Jr.); sworn to 22 Sept. 1729 by STETSON & ROGERS and 9 Dec. 1729 by JONES. Pr. 5 Jan. 1729(/30). <5:635> Inventory taken 14 Oct. 1729 by John LITTLE, John KENT, Nathaniel EAMES; incl. home sted, £900; meadow, £390; land on north side of the Brook, £220; 30 acre lot, £150; 23rd lot, £50; old neigro woman, £20; neigro girl about 14 yrs old, £85; sworn to 5 Jan. 1729 by **Joseph PHILLIPS**, exr. and on 27 Feb. 1729 by **Thomas SAWYER**, exr. <6:119> Account of exrs., 22 Sept. 1729, presented 9 Sept. 1731, "persons mentioned": Jedediah EAMES, Dr. OTIS, John CARVER, Samuel DOGGETT, Israel HATCH, Joseph SILVESTER, Caleb TILDEN, William FORD, Bathsheba FORD, Nathniel EAMES, Anthony EAMES, Thomas SAWYER, Joseph PHILLIPS, John DECROW, Dr. LORING, Esq. COTTON, Israel HATCH Jr., Capt. Francis BARKER, John ROGERS, William CLIFT, Samuel SILVESTER, Capt. Thomas BARKER, John DAMON. <6:120> Agreement, 22 Sept. 1729, of the following children as heirs, viz: **Anthony EAMES, Joseph PHILLIPS** & wf **Mercy, Thomas PHILLIPS** & wf **Mary**, all of Marshfield and **Thomas SAWYER Jr.** & wf **Jerusha** of Hingham...Whereas the sd **Anthony EAMES**...not having made any provision in sd will for his widow who being a person under distraction of mind...sd **Anthony EAMES** doth hereby farther oblige himself...to provide for & to support the sd widow. Witnesses: John STETSON, Samuel ROGERS, John WINSLOW, James WARREN, James FORD Jr., Mary POLAND. Ack. 4 May 1730 by **Anthony EAMES, Joseph PHILLIPS** & **Thomas SAWYER**; 8 Sept. 1731 by **Mercy PHILLIPS, Mary PHILLIPS** & **Jerusha SAWYER**; 22 Jan. 1731 by **Thomas PHILLIPS.**

Anthony EAMES of Marshfield MA to **Anthony EAMES.** <Plymouth Co.Deeds 29:141>
...25 Mar. 1728, Anthony EAMES gives to son Anthony EAMES...small tract of land in Marshfield being a part of 35th lot in 2d Division of Common Right lands in sd town...all that part of sd lot which I have not disposed of already. Witnesses: Nathaniel EAMES, Abigail EAMES. Ack. 3 Apr. 1728. Rec. 3 or 4 Mar. 1734.

Anthony EAMES 3d of Marshfield MA to **Samuel DOGGETT** of same. <Plymouth Co.Deeds 29:142>
...6 Jan. 1734, Anthony EAMES, boatman, for £20 sold to Samuel DOGGETT, yeoman...all my right... in the 35th lot in the 2d Division of Marshfield Commons...excepting fourteen acres which sd DOGGETT bought of Daniel MacLUCAS. Witnesses: John CUSHING Jr., Mary CUSHING. Ack. 13 Jan.1734. Rec. 3 or 4 Mar. 1734.

Anthony EAMES 3d of Marshfield MA to **Jonathan TILDEN** of same. <Plymouth Co.Deeds 32:82>
...7 May 1737, Anthony EAMES 3d, yeoman, for £1110 sold to Jonathan TILDEN, mariner...the farm & tract of land whereon I now dwell, being 50 acres...bounded by land of sd TILDEN, Jedediah EAMES,

Caleb & Joshua TILDEN & Nathaniel EAMES...also 16 acres wood land bounded by TILDEN's land and land of Capt. LITTLE & Jedediah EAMES...also 14 acre salt marsh bounded by meadows of Nathaniel EAMES, Joseph EAMES, Jedediah EAMES & Joseph PHILLIPS...all lying in Marshfield. Wf Anna releases dower. Witnesses: Samuel CLIFT, Josiah HOLMES. Rec. 19 Sept. 1738.

PLYMOUTH COUNTY DEEDS: (re: SAWYER)

<7:148> - 8 Mar. 1704/5, John SAWYER, wheelwright of Marshfield to Dr. Thomas LITTLE of Plymouth land in Marshfield.
<13:100> - 15 Apr. 1717, Mary SAYER/SAWYER wf of Thomas, John JORDAINE, carpenter and Mary JOURDAIN, spinster, all of Hingham, sell land in Plympton.
<45:56> - 5 Mar. 1729, Thomas SAWYER Jr., carpenter of Hing., to John PORTER, land in Abington.
<46:209> - 5 Mar. 1729, Thomas SAWYER Jr. of Hingham to Samuel BURRELL, land in Abington.
<26:228> - 5 Aug. 1730, Thomas SAWYER & wf Jerusha of Hingham sold to Joseph PHILLIPS of Marshfield, our share of land our father Anthony EAMES of Marshfield dec'd gave to his three daus, Mercy PHILLIPS, Jerusha SAWYER & Mary PHILLIPS.

Thomas PHILLIPS of Bridgewater MA to Children. <in poss. of Arthur PHILLIPS, Fall River MA, 1911> <original> Three receipts on one paper, dated 20 Aug. 1762...Received then of my Honoured father Thomas PHILLIPS of Bridgewater a piece of land containing about 13 acres which I thankfully accept off as my full portion & part out of his estate...Signed Lydia CARY...Received then of our Honoured father Thomas PHILLIPS of sd town a piece of land by way of swop with our Brother Mark PHILLIPS which we thankfully accept...Signed by Benjamin TAYLER & Abiah TAYLER...Received then of my Honoured father Thomas PHILLIPS of sd town a piece of land containing about 13 acres which I thankfully accept...Signed Deborah PHILLIPS. Witnesses: Benjamin TAYLER, John ORCUTT, Mark PHILLIPS. (Endorsed on back: The Discharge from Lydia, Abiah, Deborah to their father.)

William SHERMAN of Marshfield MA to **Anthony EAMES 2d** of same. <Plymouth Co.Deeds 31:174> ...22 May 1721, William SHERMAN, for Ł10 sold to Anthony EAMES 2d...my 13th lot of land in Marshfield being in the 2d Division...about 20 acres...bounded by Duxborough Line, Mattakeesit Way, Parting of the Ways and the way that leads to Samuel GARDNER's. Witnesses: Jonathan ALDEN, Thomas FOSTER. Rec. 14 Feb. 1737.

Will of **Joseph PHILLIPS** of Marshfield MA. <Plymouth Co.PR>
<19:509>...dated 5 Sept. 1765, mentions wf **Mercy**, daus **Jerusha HATCH, Mercy HATCH**, chil. of dec'd dau **Agatha HATCH** and son **Elisha PHILLIPS.** <19:510> Pr. 15 July 1767. <20:207> Petition for division, 1 Mar. 1769, by **Benjamin HATCH & Benjamin HATCH Jr.** in behalf of themselves & their wives **Jerusha & Mercy** and in behalf of the heirs of **Agatha HATCH.**

Estate of **Jonathan HATCH**, yeomano of Scituate MA. <Plymouth Co.PR 25:325>
...(not dated, Bowman guesses 1775)...Whereas it has been represented & made appear to me that the real estate of Jonathan HATCH dec'd...being appraised at the sum of Ł790...as by the inventory of his estate duly exhibited into the Probate Office of the County appears, cannot be divided to and among all his children & heirs, without great prejudice to or spoiling the whole, which children & heirs are: **Elisha HATCH, Jonathan HATCH, Mark HATCH, Zacheus HATCH, Phillips HATCH, Prince HATCH, James HATCH, Frederick HATCH, Briggs HATCH, Lucy JOYCE, Egarthy CROOKER, Jerusha CROOKER, Thankful JONES, Lydia PERKINS & Rachel HATCH...**

Estate of **Benjamin HATCH**, yeoman of Marshfield MA. <Plymouth Co.PR>
<originals> Request 28 Jan. 1796, of **Thomas ROGERS Jr.** & **Matthew TOWER**, that Joseph ROGERS be app'td admr. of their father in law's estate. On 1 Feb. 1796, Joseph ROGERS, yeoman of Marshfield was app'td admr. Memorandum of the children & heirs, viz: **Submit ROGERS** wf of Thomas Jr., **Jane HALL** wf or widow of Luke, **Naomi HATCH, Joseph HATCH, Jerusha TOWER** wf of Matthew.

Will of **John JONES Sr**, cooper of Marshfield MA. <Plymouth Co.PR 4:264>
...dated 21 May 1720, mentions following (all "cousins"), viz: **Ephraim JONES, Anna STURTEVANT & Sarah PETERSON**, chil. of dec'd brother **Joseph JONES** of Hingham; **Benjamin JONES & Thomas JONES**, chil. of dec'd brother **Benjamin JONES** of Hingham; **Joanna COLMAN; Joseph JONES** (exr.), **John JONES** (exr.) **& Thomas JONES**, sons of **Joseph JONES**. Witnesses: John CUSHING, Benjamin TURNER, Benjamin TURNER Jr., Hawkins TURNER. Pr. 5 Oct. 1720.

Will of **Ephraim JONES**, cordwainer of Hingham MA. <Suffolk Co.PR #8740>
<39:615>...dated 3 Mar. 1742, mentions wf **Margeret**; to couzin **Ephraim JONES Jr.** who now lives with me...all my dwelling house...and lands; both are named executors. Witnesses: Israel LAZALL, Cornelius NYE, Jeremiah SPRAGUE Jr. <39:614> Pr. 30 Apr. 1747. <44:349> Inventory taken 17 Sept. 1750 by James FEARING, Jeremiah SPRAGUE Jr., Hawkes FEARING; total real estate, Ł293.6s8d.; sworn to 13 Nov. 1750 by **Ephraim JONES** surviving exr.

Joseph PETERSON of Duxbury MA to **Isaac DOTY** of Plymouth MA. <Plymouth Co.Deeds 18:5>
...2 Jan. 1706/7, Joseph PETERSON, yeoman & wf Sarah, for Ł11 sold to Isaac DOTY, yeoman...all that our right...in ye housing, lands & meadows of her ye sd Sarah's late husband John DOTY of Plymouth dec'd.

Ephraim STURDIVANT of N. Yarmouth vs. **John STURDIVANT** of same. <Old Times N. Yarmouth ME:424>
...Mar. 1807, Cumberland Co. Court of Common Pleas...pleas of ejectment for 29 acres of land, being sd John's homestead set off to him from homestead of his late father Ephraim STURDIANT.

PLYMOUTH COUNTY DEEDS: (re: STURTEVANT)

<31:142> - 1737, David STURTEVANT, cordwainer of Kingston buys land.
<83:176> - 1796, David STURTEVANT of Wareham buys land.
<83:177> - 1796, David STURTEVANT & wf Betsey of Wareham, sell land.
<83:177> - 1798, David STURTEVANT of Wareham buys land.
<85:216> - 1798, Ephraim STURTEVANT, trader of Bridgewater sells land there.
<93:134> - 1802, Ephraim STURTEVANT of Bridgewater sells land.
<94:253> - 1803, Ephraim STURTEVANT & wf Abigail of Bridgewater sell land. (also 94:264)

(References only: **David STURTEVANT**, viz: 18:204;19:103;28:138;183:95;190:58; **Ephraim STURTEVANT:** 95:156 (1802); 107:162 (1808); 130:188 (1817); 135:97 (1817); 153:220 (1825); **STURTEVANT:** 103:172 (1808); 99:37 (1804); 103:115 (1806); 105:136 (1807); 163:226 (Jane); 165:191; 170:163; 176:16.

PLYMOUTH COUNTY PROBATE: (re: David STURTEVANT)

- 28 June 1765, David STURTEVANT, Esq. of Kingston app'td admr. of estate of David STURTEVANT Jr. mariner of Kingston. <17:148>
- 1771, Estate of David STURTEVANT. <20:486,540; 21:16 (Division), 285>
- 1806, Estate of David STURTEVANT. <39:55;40:425>

Estate of **Bezaliel PALMER** of Scituate MA. <Plymouth Co.PR #15224>
<11:101,134;12:443,453,456>...Bond 7 Nov. 1748, of widow **Anne PALMER**, admx. Sureties: John PALMER Jr., trader of Scituate & Amos SYLVESTER Jr. of Hanover.

Will of **Ann PALMER**, widow of Scituate MA. <Plymouth Co.PR #15219>
<13:426>...dated 15 Nov. 1754, mentions children **Bezeliel PALMER, Hulda LINCOLN, Benjamin PALMER, Priscilla PALMER, Ann JOSSELYN**; grand daughter **Hulda LINCOLN** (under 18); son **Bezeliel**, executor. Witnesses: Joseph COPELAND, Elizabeth COPELAND, Caleb TORREY. <13:427> Pr. 3 Mar. 1755. <13:453> Inventory taken 12 Mar. 1755 by David BRYANT, Joseph COPELAND, James BARKER; total estate, Ł311. 5s7d; sworn to 7 Apr. 1755 by exr.

PLYMOUTH COUNTY DEEDS: (re: PALMER)

<53:109> - 17 Apr. 1755, Bezeleel & Sarah PALMER et al, re: land of grandfather Rev. Nathaniel EELLS.
<43:206> - 29 Nov. 1755, Nathaniel PALMER, shipwright of Scituate sells 15 acres there. Wf Rachel releases dower.
<46:88> - 2 Dec. 1755, Henry JOSSELYN, yeoman of Pembroke to Nathaniel PALMER, shipwright of Scituate, land in Hanover.
<43:206> - 17 Feb. 1755, Joshua LINCOLN, yeoman of Scituate to Nathaniel PALMER, shipwright of same, 15 acres at Scituate. Wf Huldah releases dower.
<45:76> - 19 Mar. 1757, Nathaniel PALMER of Hanover sells land there he bought of Henry JOSSELYN of Pembroke.

MICRO #9 OF 32

Will of **Bezaliel PALMER**, shipwright of Scituate MA. <Plymouth Co.PR #15223>
<14:332>...dated 29 Sept. 1756...to my wife during her widowhood and no longer all my real & personall estate and after that to my onely daughter **Huldah** to her own proper use...& dispose at her will...onley one acre of meadow...near the Brook comonly called Palmers Brook and at the head of a lott I formerly bout of Mr. John PALMER in sd Scituate I Give & Bequeath to my Brother **Nathaniel PALMER**, And in case my Daughter's decease I Give & Bequeath all my whole Estate...to my two Brothers **Nathaniel & Benjamin PALMER.** Witnesses: Abel KEEN, Jeremiah ROGERS, Hezekiah HOLMES. <14:333> Pr. 7 Mar. 1757. <14:380> Inventory. <15:110> Account. <20:160> Guardianship, 2 Jan. 1769, Robert Lenthal EELS, blacksmith of Hanover app'td gdn. of **Huldah PALMER** (over 14) & **Sarah PALMER** (under 14).
(Note: Although his will mentions his "onley dau Huldah", dau Sarah was bpt. 17 Apr. 1757 as the dau of the Widow PALMER; an earlier dau named Sarah was bpt. 15 July 1753 but obviously d.y. <Scituate VR>.)

Will of **John JONES** of Marshfield MA. <Plymouth Co.PR #11574>
<24:9>...dated 3 June 1775, mentions wf **Grace** and daus **Jemima THOMAS & Ruth BAKER;** Asa THOMAS & John BAKER of Marshfield, executors. Witnesses: James OTIS, Zipporah CURTIS, Jonathan TOWER. <24:10> Inventory. <24:10> Insolvency. <24:11> Dower. <24:431> List of claims. <28:399> Account.

Ebenezer JONES et al to **Elisha JONES** of Marshfield MA. <Plymouth Co.Deeds 46:34>
...8 May 1750, Ebenezer JONES, yeoman of Pembroke, John JONES, yeoman of Scituate, William JONES, yeoman of Marshfield, Joseph STETSON Jr., yeoman of Pembroke & wf Abigail, for Ł29.6s8p sell to Elisha JONES, mariner...four fifths of the dwelling house & barn standing on the farm on which our late Brother Amos JONES of Marshfield dec'd dwelt...and in the division...his estate was set off to us...viz: one fifth each to Ebenezer, John, William & Abigail. Witnesses: Joseph JOSSELYN, David STOCKBRIDGE, Israel HATCH, Daniel LEWIS Jr. Ack. 24 Sept. 1750 by John JONES, 8 May 1750 by others. Rec. 24 Mar. 1760.

Estate of **Joseph JONES** of Marshfield MA. <Plymouth Co.PR 5:543>
Division 30 May 1729, to widow **Sarah JONES** and following chil., viz: **Amos JONES, Ebenezer JONES** (eldest son), **William JONES, John JONES, Abigail STETSON** wf of Joseph of Pembroke, **Elisha JONES;** each to receive seven or eight acres of the farm which is bounded by land of OAKMAN, Ebenezer JONES & Amos JONES.

Estate of **John JONES**, mariner of Scituate MA. <Plymouth Co.PR #11579>
<17:153> Letter/Bond 28 Oct. 1765, Seth HATCH, yeoman of Pembroke app'td admr. Sureties: Aaron SOUL & John TURNER of Pembroke. Witnesses: Jonathan PRATT, Edward WINSLOW. <19:522> Inventory taken 18 Nov. 1765 by John TURNER, Benjamin HATCH Jr., Samuel OAKMAN; incl. 4th part of the sloop "Polly", £100; pew in meeting house, north precinct in Marshfield, £2.13s4d; real estate, £170; sworn to 6 Mar. 1767 by admr. & appraisers.

Heirs of **John JONES** to **Samuel OAKMAN** of Marshfield MA. <Plymouth Co.Deeds 56:194>
...20 Mar. 1771, Samuel JONES, Amos JONES, Ezekiel JONES, Jonathan HATCH Jr. & Betty HATCH, all of Scituate, for £168.4s sold to Samuel OAKMAN...23 acres in Marshfield...the real estate that belonged to our late honoured Father John JONES dec'd that was in sd Marshfield...bounded by land of Samuel TILDEN & sd Samuel OAKMAN. Ruth JONES & Abigail JONES wf of Amos, release dowers. Witnesses: Nathan CUSHING, Job MITCHELL. Ack. 20 Mar. 1771 by all grantors. Rec. 15 Apr. 1772.

Amos JONES of Scituate MA to **Samuel JONES** of same. <Plymouth Co.Deeds 69:167>
...15 Mar. 1773, Amos JONES, mariner, for £82.13s4p sold to Samuel JONES, mariner...all my right ...in one third of all the lands that was given to three brothers of us by our Grandfather Samuel HATCH of Scituate dec'd in his last will...being as yet undivided containing...19 acres...bounded by land of Abner CROOKER, Job MITCHELL & Samuel HATCH. Witnesses: Joseph LAPHAM, Ezekiel JONES Abigail, wf of Amos signs. Ack. 14 Mar. 1789 by Amos JONES & 15 Apr. 1789 by wf Abigail. Rec. 29 Oct. 1789.

Ezekiel JONES of Marshfield MA to **Samuel JONES** of same. <Plymouth Co.Deeds 75:68>
...10 Mar. 1794, Ezekiel JONES, yeoman, for £7.10s sold to Samuel JONES, mariner...five acre upland in Marshfield...bounded by Samuel JONES' orchard and land of Job MITCHEL & Samuel HATCH. Witnesses: Samuel JONES Jr., Rachel JONES. Ack. 14 Mar. 1794 by Ezekiel. Rec. 15 Mar. 1794.

Samuel JONES of Marshfield MA to **Benjamin ROGERS** of same. <Plymouth Co.Deeds 104:58>
...19 May 1801, Samuel JONES, shipwright, for £524 sold to Benjamin ROGERS, shipwright...farm in Marshfield...that Samuel JONES late of Marshfield dec'd died seized the one half of sd farm contains about 25 acres reference being had to Amos JONES deed to Samuel JONES dated 1773 also one other division deed made by Samuel JONES, Amos JONES, Ezekiel JONES, John MITCHELL & Job MITCHELL dated 24 Mar. 1767...also two acre salt marsh in Marshfield in North river marsh reference being had to Ezekiel JONES deed to Samuel JONES for the bounds dated 13 Mar. 1789...also three eighths of a pew in the second parish in Marshfield...of which Elijah LEONARD is Minister, on the lower floor of sd house adjoining the pew of George LITTLE & heirs of John TILDEN dec'd. Witnesses: Constant F. OAKMAN, John TURNER. Ack. same day by Samuel. Rec. 22 May 1806.

Samuel HATCH of Scituate MA to **Benjamin ROGERS** of Pembroke MA. <Plymouth Co.Deeds 119:17>
...7 Apr. 1812, Samuel HATCH, yeoman for $4300.00 sold to Benjamin ROGERS, shipwright...160 acres of upland & meadow partly in Pembroke & Marshfield...and is the whole of that homested farm lying at that place which my father Samuel HATCH dec'd owned & occupied...reserving a right for David CHURCH to pass & repass over sd land to his meadow...lying near Jobs Landing...bounded by land lately owned by Ephraim RANDALL dec'd and land of Briggs HATCH & Gershom EWELL...reserving out of sd premises that spot of land which is now a burying place to be used for that purpose for me & all my friends & relatives at pleasure. Samuel's mother Mary HATCH releases dower. Witnesses: Thomas MACOMBER, Hayward PEIRCE. Rec. 14 Apr. 1812.

Estate of **Samuel JONES**, mariner of Marshfield MA. <Plymouth Co.PR #11599>
<4:265> Letter/Bond, 2 Mar. 1801, Samuel JONES, shipwright & Constant Fobes OAKMAN, housewright, both of Marshfield, app'td admrs. Sureties: Joseph TILDEN, Amos HATCH. Witnesses: Lemuel H. SYLVESTER & (   ) LITCHFIELD. <37:431> Notice. <37:431> Inventory taken 5 Mar. 1801 by Amos HATCH, clothier, Nathaniel WATERMAN, tanner & Anthony Eames HATCH, yeoman, all of Marshfield; total real estate, £275; sworn to 6 Apr. 1801 by appraisers & 7 Apr. 1801 by admrs.

Ezekiel JONES of Marshfield MA to **Samuel JONES** of same. <Plymouth Co.Deeds 69:167>
...30 Mar. 1789, Ezekiel JONES, yeoman, for £12 sold to Samuel JONES, mariner...two acre salt meadow in Marshfield...bounded by meadow of Charles HATCH and Branch creek. Wf Huldah JONES releases dower. Ack. 18 Apr. 1789 by grantors. Rec. 29 Oct. 1789.

John JONES et al to **Joseph JONES** of Marshfield MA. <Plymouth Co.Deeds 24:109>
...9 May 1722, John JONES, yeoman of Marshfield, Gershom COLYARE of Hull & Thomas JONES of Hingham, for £450 sold to Joseph JONES, yeoman...our three fourth part...of housing & land...in Marshfield...that our Uncle John JONES late of Marshfield dec'd died seized of...bounded by land of Job RANDALL & land formerly of Elisha BISBEE...whole tract contains 40 acres. Witnesses: Adam CUSHING, Hannah THAXTER. Rec. 22 May 1729.

MICRO #10 OF 32

Edward LITTLE of Bristol RI to **Ephraim TISDALE** of Freetown MA. <Bristol RI Deeds 1:47>
...19 Mar. 1746/7, Edward LITTLE, yeoman, for ₤4200 sold to Ephraim TISDALE, yeoman...176 acres in Bristol...bounded by land of Francis BORLAND, William MUNRO, Nathaniel MUNRO, William COGGESHALL...reserving to the sd MUNROS a priviledge to pass from the farm to the salt water. Wf Mary releases dower. Witnesses: George CHASE, Thomas THROOPE Jr. Ack. 20 Mar. 1746/7 by Ephraim & wf.

Edward LITTLE of New Haven CT, power of attorney. <Bristol RI Deeds 3:354>
...10 Nov. 1772, Edward LITTLE...have constituted...my trusty & loving friend Nathaniel FALES, Esq. of Bristol RI my true & lawfull attorney...to sue for & recover any debts...as also for the recovery of any house or lands to me belonging in the Colony of Rhode Island. Witnesses: John CHANDLER, Joshua CHANDLER. Ack. 10 Oct. 1772 by Edward. Rec. 6 July 1774.

Edward LITTLE of New Haven CT to **Nathaniel FALES** of Bristol RI. <Bristol RI Deeds 3:354>
...10 Nov. 1772, Edward LITTLE, for ₤100 sold to Nathaniel FALES, Esq...two peices of land in Bristol, one peice...fronting with Hope Street the other peice being two acres near or by High Street which two peices...are the same that was given & bequeathed to me by the last will & testament of my Honoured Father dec'd. Witnesses: John CHANDLER, Joshua CHANDLER. Rec. 5 July 1774.

Nathaniel FALES Jr. VS **Nathaniel FALES,** both of Bristol. <Bristol Co./RI Deeds 3:355>
...9 July 1774, writ citing that on 1st Mon. July 1774, case of Nathaniel FALES Jr., yeoman vs. Nathaniel FALES, Esq., about two pieces of land in Bristol...Nathaniel Esq. "got it" from Edward LITTLE, yeoman of New Haven, who "got it" from William WHITE, who "got it" from Hugh HUNT; Edward LITTLE appeared in court, William WHITE defaulted; land adjudged to Nathaniel FALES Jr.

Estate of **Capt. Samuel LITTLE** of Bristol RI. <Bristol RI PR>
<1:190> Account 7 Apr. 1755, of Joshua BAILEY, admr. d.b.n.; incl. ₤690 received on 16 Jan. 1745/46 for 30 acres sold to Capt. Thomas LAWTON and ₤230 received 27 May 1746 for 10 acres sold to same. <1:317> Account allowed.

Guardianship of Child of **Margaret LITTLE** of Bristol RI. <Bristol RI PR>
<1:118,332>...6 July 1752, **Mary LITTLE,** above 14, chose her mother **Margaret LITTLE** as her gdn.

ELIZABETH WARREN[2] (Richard[1])

Richard CHURCH Sr. to **Robert BARTLETT.** <Plymouth Col.Deeds 1:271 (original)>
...9 Apr. 1649...all his right in house & land at Eel River. Wf Elizabeth consents.
(The price appears to be ₤25, paid by Bartlett as follows: a red ox called Mouse, ₤8.10s; in commodities at Mr. PADDIES, ₤6 and remainder last of Sept. next year in cattle or corn or merchant's pay.)

PLYMOUTH COUNTY PROBATE: (re: CHURCH)

1689	Nathaniel	Scituate	adm.	#3972, 1:50,51;3:20;4:31
1703	Richard	Scituate	gdn.	#3975
1703	Richard	Scituate	adm.	#3976, 2:26,27
1707	Joseph	Plymouth	adm.	#3956, 2:86;3:121
1712	Sarah	Plymouth	gdn.	#3982, 3:114;4:387
1729	Charles	Freetown	adm.	#3937, 5:464
1753	Nathaniel	Scituate	adm.	#3973, 13:59,136;14:62,63
1756	Elizabeth et al	Scituate	gdn.	#3949, 14:48,49
1772	Lemuel	Rochester	adm.	#3958, 21:142;29:369;30:229
1773	Charles	Scituate	adm.	#3938, 21:242,243,277,320;23:2
1776	Lemuel	Rochester	adm.	#3959, 23:115;24:344;29:369
1776	Richard Jr.	Rochester	will	#3977, 24:275,277,279
1777	Hannah et al	Hanover	gdn.	#3950
1777	Timothy	Hanoer	adm.	#3986, 23:167;24:354,355
1778	Nathaniel	Scituate	adm.	#3974, 25:145,469;27:1;28:251
1779	Mary	Scituate	gdn.	#3966, 36:328
1779	Mehitable et al	Scituate	gdn.	#3969, 26:48,49,50,329,330
1784	Ebenezer et al	Rochester	gdn.	#3948, 26:187,431,432
1792	Thomas	Scituate	adm.	#3985, 33:233,234
1802	Huldah	Kingston	will	#3951, 38:144,145,209,210,361
1815	Constant	Pembroke	adm.	#3940, 46:119;47:321;506
1816	Ebenezer	Rochester	adm.	#3947, 46:169;48:146;49:551,552
1816	Jonathan	Rochester	will	#3954, 46:441;48:141,142,143;49:103
1816	Nabby et al	Rochester	gdn.	#3971, 41:265,277
1816	Richard et al	Rochester	gdn.	#3979, 41:279
1821	William	Scituate	will	#3988, 52:446;53:289,290;54:42,375
1822	Jael	Scituate	adm.	#3952, 54:104,272,352;56:405
1826	David F.	Pembroke	adm.	#3943, 60:540-2;61:40;62:47;63:240;69:153
1828	Timothy	Hanover	will	#3987, 62:317;66:150

PLYMOUTH COUNTY PROBATE, cont-d: (re: CHURCH)

1829	Lemuel	Scituate	will	#3957, 67:139;68:24
1831	Lewis et al	Pembroke	gdn.	#3962, 65:194;70:302
1831	Lucy H.	Fairhaven	gdn.	#3963, 65:200
1832	Bethiah	Rochester	will	#3935, 72;191
1839	David	Marshfield	will	#3944, **1G**:117;81:302,304;82:125
1840	Betsey	Marshfield	will	#3936, **1G**:355;82:39
1841	Jonathan	Rochester	will	#3955, **1G**:181;**6U**:268;83:435,437;84:521
1842	Lemuel et al	Rochester	gdn.	#3960, **8C**:289;84:522
1842	Sarah	Rochester	will	#3983, **6U**:436;**10A**:522;84:520;85:496
1843	Earl	Rochester	will	#3946, **1G**:410;**6U**:435;85:260
1848	David et al	Marshfield	gdn.	#3945, 4:271;**9M**:134

Edward CHURCH et al to **Jonathan WOOD** of Stow. <Middlesex Co.Deeds 73:396>
...15 Jan. 1770, Edward CHURCH, gent. of Boston & Caleb WILD, trader of Mendon sell to Jonathan WOOD...one quarter acre with potash house at Stow. <109:464>...19 July 1799...execution against Edward CHURCH, merchant of Boston.

References to the surname **CHURCH** in Middlesex Co.Deeds: 30:183;33:328;37:73,133,703;39:42,210, 708;40:200;44:287;56:306;66:103,104.

Estate of **Peter DUNBAR** of Bridgewater MA. <Plymouth Co.PR #6801>
Inventory taken 6 May 1720 by Josiah EDSON, Esq., Capt. John FIELD, Isaac JOHNSON, all of Bridgewater (appraisers were app'td 5 Oct. 1719)...states **Peter DUNBAR** dec'd intestate 23 Apr. 1719. Division of estate, 20 May 1725, by Josiah EDSON, Ephraim HAWARD, John KINGMAN, Isaac JOHNSON & John FIELD to widow **Sarah DUNBAR** and following chil., viz: **James DUNBAR** (eldest son), **Elisha DUNBAR** (2d son), **Peter DUNBAR** (3d son), **Samuel DUNBAR** (4th son), **John DUNBAR** (5th son), **David DUNBAR** (6th son), **Abigail FOBES, Sarah ALGER.** <4:231> 4 July 1720, son **James DUNBAR** of Middleboro app'td admr. <5:72,73> Guardianship 20 May 1725, **Peter DUNBAR** of Bridgewater chosen gdn. by his brother **John DUNBAR** (over 14) and app'td gdn. of brother **David DUNBAR** (under 14).

References to the name **Peter DUNBAR**, grantor to 1801, in Plymouth Co.Deeds: <9:2> 1711. <12:58> 1716. <17:69> 1723. <22:148> 1727/8. <24:216> 1729. <57:164> 1773. <86:121> 1799. <165:--->.
References to the name **Peter DUNBAR** in Suffolk Co.PR (all to 1894): #9766 (1751, adm.); #52026 (1871, adm.); #52220 (1871, adm.).

Estate of **David DUNBAR**, yeoman of Bridgewater MA. <Plymouth Co.PR>
<28:195> Inventory of personal estate taken 14 Aug. 1781 by Adams BAILEY, Theophilus HOWARD, Jonathan BURR; total, Ł74.17.0. <28:286> Dower set off 5 Dec. 1781, by Adams BAILEY, Elijah SNELL & Jonathan BURR to the widow **Mercy FANN** now the wife of John FANN. <30:317> Division 21 Apr. 1784, of remaining two thirds to sons **Abel DUNBAR, Sylvester DUNBAR & Walter DUNBAR.**

Will of **Elisha DUNBAR** of Bridgewater MA. <Plymouth Co.PR 21:588>
...dated 9 Oct. 1772, mentions wf **Mercy** and following chil., viz: **Abigail GILMORE** wf of Andrew, **Jacob DUNBAR, Elisha DUNBAR, Seth DUNBAR, Peter DUNBAR, Silas DUNBAR** (executor). Pr. 6 Dec. 1773.

Estate of **Peter DUNBAR**, housewright of Hingham MA. <Suffolk Co.PR #9766>
<45:138> Letter 4 June 1751. <44:183> Inventory taken 19 June 1751; land & buildings at home, Ł313.6s8d; land at Scituate, Ł2.13s4d; land at the eastward, Ł86.13s4d. <47:276> Account 9 Dec. 1752. <49:17,18> Warrant to set off dower, 13 Dec. 1752 to widow **Hannah DUNBAR** by Benjamin LINCOLN, Esq., Samuel GARDNER Jr., David GARDNER, Peter JACOB Jr., Enoch WITEN, all of Hingham. <49:18> Dower approved, 1 Feb. 1754.

MICRO #11 OF 32

Will of **Jeremiah BASSETT** of Taunton MA. <Bristol Co.PR>
<186:17>...dated 27 Mar. 1867, mentions wf **Lydia**; dau **Betsey Lavinia BASSETT**; son **Albert M. BASSETT** (executor); children & grandchildren: **Lydia TAYLOR, Jeremiah BASSETT, George A. BASSETT, Orin L. BASSETT, Albert M. BASSETT, Sarah J. STANTON** and chil of son **Andrew R. BASSETT.** <190:290> Pr. 21 Feb. 1873. <197:427> Appraisers app'td 21 Feb. 1873. <122:348> Notice. <224:171> Petition 17 Apr. 1874, of widow **Lydia BASSETT.** <219:210> Account 3d Fri. Feb. 1876. <223:538,546> Order for division, 1 Aug. 1879. <223:179> Petition for division of real estate, 8 Nov. 1878.

Will of **Lois BASSETT/Lois FIELD** of Taunton MA. <Bristol Co.PR>
<95:365>...dated 25 Dec. 1844, mentions niece **Rachel BASSETT** dau of **Ichabod BASSETT**; nephews & niece **Abner F. BASSETT, Ellen L. BASSETT & Eugene P. BASSETT**, chil of **Abner BASSETT**; brother **Ichabod BASSETT** (executor); brother **David BASSETT.** Witnesses: Joseph WALBAR(sp), Abner BASSETT, Linus BASSETT. Pr. 3 Sept. 1850, disallowed. <177:68> Citation 2 July 1850...Whereas...will...of **Lois BASSETT** otherwise **Lois FIELD** late of Taunton...dec'd. <101:91> Division, 10 June 1853, of estate of **Lois FIELD** to **Jeremiah BASSETT, David BASSETT, Ichabod BASSETT, George D. BOYCE** in right of **Abner BASSETT** all of Taunton and **Eddy LINCOLN** of Norton. (References only to the name **Lois FIELD:** 95:282;97:150,336;98:259,289,453;99:321;105:26;117:256;156:445;162:461;178:379,535; 211:56.)

Estate of **Abner BASSETT** of Fall River MA. <Bristol Co.PR>
<101:446;158:64;163:528> Letter/Bond 6 Mar. 1855, **Zilpha BASSETT** app'td admx. Sureties: Benjamin F. WINSLOW, Joseph G. CHACE. <119:735> Notice. <192:265> Inventory taken 6 Nov. 1855. <102:448> Account of admx., 16 June 1856.

BRISTOL COUNTY DEEDS: (re: Jeremiah BASSETT)

<12:308> - 12 May 1718, J.B. of Norton sells land.
<18:228> - 9 Mar. 1722, J.B. of Norton sells land.
<28:299> - 24 June 1723, J.B. of Norton sells land.
<38:293> - 15 Feb. 1745/6, J.B. of Taunton to Jonathan KNAP, land in Norton.
<34:355> - 5 Sept 1746, J.B., yeoman of Taunton from Nathaniel & Susanna WHITE, land by will of grandfather Robert CROSMAN.
<35:573> - 25 Apr. 1747, J.B., yeoman of Taunton to son Jeremiah BASSETT Jr., husbandman of same, land in Norton & Taunton.
<41:155> - 31 July 1747, J.B. Jr. of Taunton sells land in Norton bought of Nathaniel & Susanna WHITE of Easton, she the grandaughter of Robert CROSMAN.
<41:155> - 7 Sept 1748, J.B., yeoman of Taunton confirms deed to son Jeremiah BASSETT.
<39:112> - 22 Feb.1749/50, J.B. 2d, husbandman of Taunton to George MOREY (land in 35:573).
<47:207> - 13 Dec. 1763, J.B., yeoman of Taunton to sons Daniel & Samuel BASSETT of same.
<47:452> - 11 Mar. 1765, J.B. Jr., yeoman of Taunton from Huldah WOODWARD widow of Peter of Taunton & Peter WOODWARD, exr. of same.
<64:193> - 25 Oct. 1784, J.B. Jr., yeoman of Taunton & wf Hannah, sold one quarter of land on which widow Rachel THAYER lives.
<71:386> - 31 Jan. 1792, J.B. Jr., yeoman of Taunton & wf Hannah sell land in Raynham.
<72:366> - 2 Mar. 1793, J.B. Jr., yeoman of Taunton & wf Hannah.
<105:60> - 29 Oct. 1810, J.B. & wf Hannah.
<102:186>- 7 May 1816, J.B. to daus Mary, Rachel & Lois BASSETT, reserv. to wf Hannah for life.
<102:187>- 7 May 1816, J.B. of Taunton to sons Samuel, Stephen, Jeremiah Jr., Ichabod, David & Abner BASSETT, all of Taunton.
<155:265>- 22 Mar. 1822, J.B. & wf Lydia to Abner BASSETT.
<118:257>- 28 Apr. 1824, J.B. & wf Lydia, Ichabod BASSETT & wf Joanna, et al sell land.

(References only to the name **Jeremiah BASSETT**: 65:158,159,160;76:319;89:489;100:153;121:432;130:486;133:51.)

BRISTOL COUNTY DEEDS: (re: Abner BASSETT)

<153:275> - 27 Mar. 1837, A.B., trader of Fall River & wf Zilpha, sell land in Taunton & Norton.
<153:426> - 15 May 1837, A.B. to trustees to pay debts.
<156:138> - 12 Dec. 1837, A.B. of Taunton to Lois BASSETT of same, all right in undivided seventh of land in Taunton given by my father Jeremiah BASSETT to my sisters Rachel, Mary & Lois BASSETT. Ack. 31 Mar. 1838.

(References only to the name **Abner BASSETT**: 133:505;145:459;155:66.)

Heirs of **Benjamin CHURCH**, Esq. of Little Compton. <Bristol Co.Deeds 18:84>
...11 Nov. 1727, Benjamin CHURCH, gent. of Newport and George WANTON, merchant of Newport & wf Abigail...Whereas Benjamin CHURCH of Little Compton dec'd did by his deed of gift bearing date 27 Mar. 1702...give unto his son Edward CHURCH, mariner of Bristol...a certain tenement...in Bristol ...and whereas the sd Edward CHURCH afterwards dyed intestate whereby all his right & interest therein descended unto the sd Benjamin CHURCH and Abigail the now wife of the sd George WANTON, son & dau of the sd Edward CHURCH now know ye that we the sd...(grantors)...for Ł2860 sell sd tenement of 190 & a half acres to William WANTON the younger, mariner of Newport. Ack. 1 Feb. 1727(/28) by grantors.

Heirs of **Edward CHURCH**, mariner of Bristol. <Bristol Co.Deeds 18:85>
...13 Nov. 1727, Martha CHURCH, of Newport, widow of Edward CHURCH...to Benjamin CHURCH and Abigail CHURCH now wf of George WANTON of Newport, son & dau of me the sd Martha.

Heirs of **Benjamin CHURCH**, Esq. <Bristol Co.Deeds 25:101>
Petition, Boston, 19 Nov. 1735 of Charles CHURCH of Bristol...that Thomas CHURCH, Esq. & your petitioner had a grant of 500 acres of land made to them & the rest of the heirs & legall representatives of our Honoured Father Benjamin CHURCH, Esq. dec'd...which was confirmed on the 13 June last as may appear by the records...and Constant CHURCH one of the chil. of the sd Benjamin CHURCH dyed & hath left severall chilldren which are all minors & have hitherto neglected or refused to have Guardians appointed them that so they might joyn in applying to the Judges of the Superior Court of Judicature for an order for a Divsion of the sd 500 acres of land & your Petitioner applyed to the Judges of the Superior Court for an order for a Division but could not get one by reason of their not having any Guardians appointed them & it being a great Damage to your Petitioner & the other heirs to let it ly undivided...30 Dec. 1735 order for division. <25:102> ...5 Apr. 1736...Whereas Grant was made 13 June 1735, Jathniel PECK, Daniel CARPENTER, James REDAWAY, John WILLMOUTH & Edward GLOVER app'td to make division. <25:103>...Division 19 Apr. 1736, 1st share to Charles CHURCH, Esq. being the part he purchased of his brother Thomas CHURCH, Esq., adjoyning the 600 acre plot allowed by General Court to sd Thomas & Charles CHURCH; 2d share to Charles CHURCH, Esq., his own share; 3d share to Charles CHURCH, Esq., being part he purchased of

Benjamin CHURCH and George & Abigail WANTON, heirs of Edward CHURCH dec'd; 5th share to heirs & legal representatives of Constant CHURCH dec'd who was one of the heirs of sd Benjamin CHURCH dec'd. Rec. 21 May 1736 in probate rcds. 8:361,362. Rec. 7 Aug. 1736 in deeds.

PLYMOUTH COLONY DEEDS: (re: CHURCH).

<3:170> - 2 Feb. 1662, Thomas LINCOLN Sr. of Taunton to Richard CHURCH, carpenter of Hingham, his interest, being one whole share, in iron works in Taunton. On 8 June 1670, Joseph CHURCH, exr. assigned it to brother Caleb CHURCH.
<3:171> - 8 June 1670, Caleb CHURCH of Dedham sells the above to Capt. M. FULLER of Barnstable.
<3:206> - 31 Jan. 1662, Elizabeth PHILLIPS, widow of William, & son James PHILLIPS sell one share of iron works in Taunton to Thomas & Richard CHURCH. On 8 Dec. 1670, Joseph CHURCH, exr. makes offer to Benjamin CHURCH. On 9 Mar. 1670/1, Benjamin CHURCH sells to George WATSON of Plymouth.
<3:198> - 20 Dec. 1671, Benjamin & Alice CHURCH to Thomas LYNDE of Boston, land on Taunton River.

Power of Attorney from **Benjamin CHURCH** of Duxbury MA. <Old Norfolk Co.Recds;Essex 8:129>
...3 Dec. 1670, Benjamin CHURCH app'td friends Samuel DALTON & Nathaniel BATCHELLER, both of Hampton NH, attornies to sell his house & land at Hampton, lately in possession of Joseph MERRY.

Thomas JOY of Boston to **Richard CHURCH** of Charlestown. <Suffolk Co.Deeds 2:77>
...24 Jan. 1653, Thomas JOY, carpenter & wf Joane to Richard CHURCH, carpenter...half of land & mills at Town's Cove in Hingham. <2:83>...same day Thomas JOY leases to Richard CHURCH half of land & mills...

Samuel VAUGHN of Newport RI to **Benjamin CHURCH** of same. <Newport RI Deeds 6:421>
...21 Apr. 1797, Samuel VAUGHN, trader & wf Mary, for $600.00 sell to Benjamin CHURCH, cordwainer ...land, house & stable in Newport...bounded by land of Benjamin HAMMETT & James HONEYMAN dec'd.

Susanna CHURCH et al of Exeter RI to **Anna SHAW** of same. <Newport RI Deeds 5:222>
...24 Oct. 1793, Susanna CHURCH, widow; Sisson NICHOLS, yeoman & wf Marcy of Stephentown NY; Stephen SHAW, yeoman of Providence and Sarah SHAW, singlewoman of Exeter...children & some of the heirs at law of Anthony SHAW of Exeter dec'd, for £120 silver sold to Anna SHAW, widow of sd Anthony, & the relinquishment of her dower rights...sell one half of certain lands at Newport.

Samuel B. PHILLIPS et al to **Benjamin JAMES** of Newport. <Newport RI Deeds 15:329>
...18 Aug. 1826, Samuel B. PHILLIPS, Benjamin CHURCH & wf Elizabeth and Catharine PHILLIPS sell to Benjamin JAMES, mariner...land on the Hill on the street leading to Redwood Library. Mary PHILLIPS of N. Stonington CT, wf of sd Samuel, releases dower.

Martha CHURCH of Newport to **Abigail WANTON** of same. <Newport RI Town Rcds.:279> <?3:279>
...16 Mar. 1749/50, Martha CHURCH, widow, deeds to dau Abigail WANTON, wf of George, the following: one feather bed & furniture, one looking glass, 12 leather chairs, one silver tankard & 3 silver spoons all marked " F c M" (or E c M), all brass & pewterware; £1210 in bills of Public credit old tenor due from Col. John GARDNER & Ephraim HARRIS by bond and £300 due from sd George WANTON by note. Rec. 30 Apr. 1750.

NEWPORT RI DEEDS: (re: CHURCH)

<3:66; 14:453> - 1785, Isaac CHURCH from Joseph CLARKE, General Treasurer.
<21:453> - , George B. CHURCH from James JOHNSON, guardian.
<21:454> - , George B. CHURCH from Charles CHURCH, trustee.

Benjamin CHURCH of Providence RI to **John MUMFORD** of same. <Newport RI Deeds 5:17>
...1 Jan. 1779, Benjamin CHURCH, yeoman late of Newport, but now of Providence, & wf Bathsheba, for $30000(?) sell to John MUMFORD, merchant...130 acre farm in Newport with mansion...bounded by land of John Coggeshall ALMY, land late of Jahleel BRENTON Esq. but now of Charles WICKHAM and east & south by the sea. <5:18>...4 Jan. 1779, John & Austis MUMFORD sell same land back to Ben.

Benjamin CHURCH of Newport RI to **William GYLES** of same. <Newport RI Deeds 2:232>
...6 July 1784, Benjamin CHURCH, merchant/yeoman & wf Bathsheba sell to William GYLES...land on Thames St., 35'x 70'...bounded by land of John Coggeshall ALMY & land late of Joseph GLADDING(sp) dec'd. Ack. 23 July 1784 "by both".

Thomas HOWLAND Jr. of Newport RI to **Benjamin CHURCH** of same. <Newport RI Deeds 4:353>
...2 Nov. 1790, Thomas HOWLAND Jr., shopkeeper & Mary HOWLAND, for 950 Spanish Milled Dollars sell to Benjamin CHURCH, shopkeeper...house & land in Newport...bounded 53' on land of Miller FROST dec'd, 20' on land of Samuel CARR dec'd, 53' on land of Caleb CARR dec'd and 24' on Thames St.

John CARR of Newport RI to **Benjamin CHURCH** of same. <Newport RI Deeds 4:433>
...14 Oct. 1791, John CARR, gent. for £30.12s sells to Benjamin CHURCH, shopkeeper...land 18'10" by 78'6"...bounded by land of sd John & Benjamin, William LANGLY, widow Elizabeth THURSTON & land of Trinity Church.

Estate of **Benjamin CHURCH**, taylor of Newport RI. <Newport RI PR 2:216>
...13 Jan. 1792, adm. granted to widow **Elisabeth CHURCH.**

Will of **Isaac CHURCH**, shopkeeper of Newport RI. <Newport RI PR 2:136>
...dated 9 Sept. 1789, mentions wf **Hannah**; mother **Elisabeth CHURCH**; sister **Elisabeth CHURCH**; daus **Abigail & Mary**; all real estate to **Rebecca CHURCH**, dau of brother **Silas CHURCH** if daus die without issue; wf **Hannah** & Edward DAVIS, executors. Pr. 1 Feb. 1790.

Will of **Hannah CHURCH**, widow of Newport RI. <Newport RI PR>
<4:464>...dated 5 Jan. 1792, mentions daus **Abigail & Mary**; mother **Hannah POOL**; late husband's sister **Elizabeth CHURCH** & John GREENE, exrs. <4:463> Inventory taken 10 Oct. 1807. <4:437> Adm. 5 Oct. 1807, Joseph L. BAKER admr. for personal estate. Pr. 2 Nov. 1807.

Benjamin ELLERY of Newport RI to **Benjamin CHURCH** of same. <Newport RI Deeds 5:207>
...30 Sept. 1793, Benjamin ELLERY, gent., for 60 Spanish milled dollars sells to Benjamin CHURCH, shopkeeper...land 85'x 61'...bounded by street and land of Latham THURSTON, Samuel OXX, George MARTIN & John LANDERS.

Benjamin CHURCH of Newport RI to **Anthony WILBOUR** of Little Compton. <Newport RI Deeds 6:555>
...21 Nov. 1797, Benjamin CHURCH, yeoman, for 8000 Spanish Milled Dollars, sells to Anthony WILBOUR...140 acre farm in Newport...bounded east & south by the sea and by land of Thomas G. HAZARD, Esq. and by land of Robert CROOKE formerly belonging to Jahleel BRENTON, Esq. dec'd & lately to Capt. Charles WICKHAM dec'd. <6:556>...22 Nov. 1797, Anthony WILBOUR mortgages above to Benjamin CHURCH for 4000 Spanish Milled Dollars. On 7 July 1800, Jabez DENISON & wf Patience, Sarah CHURCH & Bathsheba CHURCH, surviving executors of Benjamin CHURCH, discharge the above.

Heirs of **Thomas COGGESHALL** of Newport RI. <Newport RI Deeds 7:341>
...31 July 1798, Mary STILES, widow of Newport; Nicholas P. TILLINGHAST late of Newport now of Washington Co. PA; Jabez DENISON, gent. & wf Patience and Sarah CHURCH, spinster, of Newport... Whereas Thomas COGGESHALL, merchant, late of Newport on 19 May 1756 made a will & by codicil 1 Mar. 1762 (pr. 3 May 1762) gave legacies to Mary STILES by name of his grandaughter Mary CRANSTON, to grandaughter Sarah ALMY dau of Benjamin ALMY who married Nicholas P. TILLINGHAST & hath since died, to grandchildren Patience CHURCH since married to Jabez DENISON and Sarah CHURCH... Patience & Sarah being daus of her dau Bathsheba CHURCH...sd legacies to be paid by his dau Bathsheba CHURCH & his grandson John Coggeshall ALMY...Therefore Mary STILES & others as above, receipt to Bathsheba CHURCH and John Coggeshall ALMY.

Will of **Capt. Benjamin CHURCH**, yeoman of Newport RI. <Newport RI PR 3:109>
...dated 11 May 1798...advanced in age...mentions daus **Patience & Sarah** and the will of their grandfather **Thomas COGGESHALL** dec'd; son **Thomas Coggeshall Cranston CHURCH**; dau **Bathsheba.** Pr. 1 Oct. 1798, names children **Patience DENNISON, Sarah CHURCH, Bathsheba CHURCH, Thomas C.C. CHURCH** <4:50> Account 4 Mar. 1803, mentions children **Patience, Sarah & Bathsheba** and **Deborah CHURCH** the widow of **Thomas C.C. CHURCH** dec'd.

Mary LANDERS et al of Newport RI to **Benjamin CHURCH** of same. <Newport RI Deeds 8:74>
...21 Jan. 1801, Mary LANDERS, widow of John, cordwainer dec'd; Edward LANDERS, mariner; Mary THURSTON wf of Samuel; Elizabeth LANDERS, spinster, all of Newport, children & heirs of John LANDERS dec'd, for $115.00 sell to Benjamin CHURCH, shopkeeper...land bounded 51' on a street, 60' on land of grantors, 51' on land of Samuel OX Jr. and 60' on land of grantee.

Benjamin CHURCH of Newport RI to **James PERRY** of same. <Newport RI Deeds 9:733>
...4 Nov. 1806, Benjamin CHURCH, merchant, for $3500.00 sells to James PERRY, merchant...two lots in Newport, one with dwelling...1st lot bounded 53' on land of William LANGLEY, 20' on the other lot sold, 53' on land of Samuel C. CARR and 24' on Thames St...2nd lot 18'10" x 78'6" and bounded by land of William LANGLEY, Elizabeth THURSTON, John YEOMANS & John CARR.

Benjamin TAYER to **Benjamin CHURCH** of Newport RI. <Newport RI Deeds 10:87,88>
...14 Apr. 1807, Benjamin CHURCH, merchant buys land of Benjamin TAYER, admr. on estate of John TAYER...he immediately re-conveys it.

Benjamin CHURCH of Holland MA to **Richard SMITH Jr.** of Bristol. <Newport RI Deeds 11:137>
...1 June 1809, Benjamin CHURCH, merchant, late of Newport but now of Holland MA, for $52.00 assigns to Richard SMITH Jr...one half of mortgage. (This deed refers to the following: <9:384>... 8 May 1805, Samuel CARR, ferryman of Newport, exr. of will of Samuel CARR, yeoman of Jamestown, for $104.00 assigns morgage. <9:383>...24 Jan. 1755, Peter TROBY(sp), sailmaker of Newport for £284.15s morgages land at Newport to Samuel CARR, ferryman of Newport.

Benjamin CHURCH of Holland MA to **Joseph MARTIN** of Newport RI. <Newport RI Deeds 15:234>
...16 May 1825, Benjamin CHURCH & wf Elizabeth, for $140.00 sell to Joseph MARTIN...land bought of Benjamin ELLERY 30 Sept.1793 and of widow Mary LANDERS & others 21 Jan. 1801.

Martha CHURCH to **Nicholas BRAGG** of Bristol. <Bristol Co.Deeds 34:7>
...22 Apr. 1743, Martha CHURCH confirms deed from her son Benjamin CHURCH now of Boston to Nicholas BRAGG of land in Bristol bounded by Charles St. and land of heirs of Longhlom McINTOSH. Witnesses: Benjamin CHURCH, Patience HOWLAND. Rec. 5 Sept. 1743.

Martha CHURCH of Newport RI to **Christopher TEMPLE** of Dunstable MA. <Middlesex Co.Deeds 37:133> ...11 May 1733, Martha CHURCH, widow, for Ł212 sells to Christopher TEMPLE, yeoman...two lots in Dunstable at Natticook Brook or Brenton's Farm...one lot, the 13th, contains 98 acres & was laid out by the right of Jahleel BRENTON, Esq. late of Newport dec'd...second lot, the 14th, contains 114 acres and was laid out to the right of me the sd Martha...sd lots bounded by land of SANFORD, CANLEY, Thomas BARRETT, Town Commons & Merrimac River. Witnesses: Barnabas TAYLOR, George WANTON, Benjamin CHURCH. Rec. 17 Dec. 1735.

Martha CHURCH of Newport RI to **Nathan KENDAL et al** of Chelmsford MA. <Middlesex Co.Deeds 37:73> ...4 Mar. 1735, Martha CHURCH, widow, for Ł914.10s sold to Nathan KENDAL, tailor & John HARVELL, housewright...Lot #14 in Litchfield MA...excepting one & a half acres given to Town of Litchfield on which to build a Meeting House. Witnesses: Benjamin CHURCH, Joseph FOX. On 4 Mar. 1735, above grantees mortgage, for Ł814.10s, the same property. <39:42>...1 Apr. 1736, Martha CHURCH, for Ł520, sells to Jacob KENDALL, yeoman of Bedford MA, lot #13 in Litchfield.

Samuel VIAL of Bristol MA to **Benjamin CHURCH** of same. <Bristol Co.Deeds 18:143> ...17 Apr. 1728, Samuel VIAL, Esq., for love, etc. towards my loving son & dau Benjamin CHURCH, gent. now of Bristol & wf Elisabeth have given...31 acres in Bristol. Witnesses: N. BLAGROVE, Timothy INGRAHAM. Ack. & Rec. same 17 Apr. 1728.

Benjamin CHURCH of Newport RI to **Samuel CHURCH & Martha CHURCH.** <Bristol Co.Deeds 27:419> ...13 Apr. 1739, Benjamin CHURCH, gent., for love, etc...which I have & do bear toward my children Samuel & Martha CHURCH, minors...give & grant...land in Bristol...bounded on land of my honoured Father in Law Samuel VIALL, Esq. Witnesses: Eleazer REYNOLDS, Nathaniel REYNOLDS.

SUFFOLK COUNTY DEEDS: (re: Benjamin CHURCH)

<55:141> - 14 Nov. 1747, Benjamin & Hannah CHURCH of Newport sell to Samuel FOSTER of Boston, land in Boston.
<59:5> - 24 Nov. 1738, Indenture betw. Benjamin CHURCH, gent. of Newport & wf Hannah as dau & heir at law of Giles DYER late of Boston of one part & Thomas WALLIS, blacksmith of Boston of the other part.
<59:174> - 1740, Thomas WALLIS to Benjamin & Hannah CHURCH.

MICRO #12 OF 32

Guardianship of Children of **Giles WELD**, gent., dec'd of Boston MA. <Suffolk Co.PR #23313,23314> <107:102>...13 Mar. 1809, **Benjamin WELD**, gent. of Boston app'td gdn. of **Giles WELD & Hermione WELD**, both above 14. <also 386:40>

Guardianship of Children of **Ebenezer T. ANDREWS** of Boston MA. <Suffolk Co.PR #23328,23329> <379:65,66>...(no date given)...**Ebenezer T. ANDREWS**, bookseller, app'td gdn. of **Isaiah T. ANDREWS & William ANDREWS Jr.** (above 14), sons of sd **Ebenezer**...in right of their Grandfather **Edward WELD** dec'd.

Estate of **Edward WELD**, gent. of Boston MA. <Suffolk Co.PR #23302> <187:132;107:78> Letter/Bond 27 Feb. 1809, Benjamin WELD, gent. & Ebenezer T. ANDREWS, bookseller both of Boston, app'td admrs. Sureties: William ANDREWS & Ebenezer LARKIN, booksellers of Boston. <107:106> Inventory of personal estate taken 9 Mar. 1809 by Nathaniel GREENOUGH, Thomas CLARK & Masa WILLIS. <107:162> Inventory of real estate; house & land on passage way leading from Newbury St., $2500.00; house & land in Newbury St., corner of Pond St., $5500.00; house & land at 6 Marlborough St., $11,000.00; house & land in Hatters Square, $3000.00; house & land in Margarets Lane $2200.00; house & land in Ship St., $2200.00; sworn to 17 Apr. 1809 by admrs. <107:183> Order to divide, 17 Apr. 1809, by Shubael BELL, William ANDREWS & Samuel PERKINS,all of Boston, to his six chil. or their representatives, viz: **Benjamin WELD; Hannah WELD; Mary THOMAS** wf of Isaiah Jr.; to chil. of dec'd son **Giles WELD**, viz: **Giles WELD & Hermione WELD**, minors and **Harriot WYETT & Hannah HARDY; Elizabeth ANDREWS** wf of Ebenezer T. of Boston; chil. of dec'd dau **Herminone ANDREWS**, viz: **Isaiah T. ANDREWS & William ANDREWS**, minors (the two chil. are called the chil. of "Thomas Turell ANDREWS & Herminone ANDREWS dec'd late wife of sd Ebenezer T. ANDREWS"); division allowed 24 Apr. 1809. <109:440> Account 15 Aug. 1811; payements to the above heirs incl. "Ebenezer T. ANDREWS for the proportion of his wife Elizabeth ANDREWS and also the proportion of the two children of his former wife, to whom he is guardian".

Will of **Hannah WELD**, singlewoman of Boston MA. <Suffolk Co.PR #33383> <140:155>...dated 10 Apr. 1840, mentions nephews **Isaiah THOMAS & Benjamin F. THOMAS**; Mary ANDREWS & Mrs. Mary DEAN, nieces of brother in law Ebenezer T. ANDREWS; **Eliza CHENA & Lucretia WYATT**, daus of niece **Harriet WYATT**; Hannah E. BREED (under 18), dau of Aaron BREED; **Emily Jane ANDREWS** dau of nephew **William T. ANDREWS**; one fifth of estate to the heirs of my late brother **Benjamin WELD**, being his children by his last wife; one fifth to heirs of dec'd brother **Giles WELD**; one fifth to heirs of dec'd sister **Mary THOMAS**; one fifth to sister **Elizabeth ANDREWS** wf of Ebenezer T.; one fifth to **William T. ANDREWS** the surviving child of dec'd sister **Hermione ANDREWS**; nephew **William T. ANDREWS**, executor. Codicil 9 May 1842...gives the fifth part bequeathed to heirs of brother **Benjamin** to...my dear nieces **Caroline WELD & Emeline WELD**...excepting $250 which shall be paid from that fifth part to each of the two daus of my late nephew **Charles WELD** the son of my sd brother **Benjamin** if they shall be living. Codicil 9 May 1842. <262:196> Petition for Probate. <140:157> Pr. 17 Oct. 1842. <262:196> Letter/Bond. <243:1> Notice. <279:220> Inventory. <143:99> Account.

Will of **John SAMPSON** of Bristol. <Bristol Co.PR>
<8:177>...dated 9 Dec. 1728, mentions wf **Elizabeth** and minor children **John SAMPSON & Mary SAMPSON**
<8:176> Letter 17 Jan. 1735, widow **Elizabeth SAMPSON** app'td admx.

Thomas CHURCH & Paul UNIS/UNICE to Samuel & Peleg SHEARMAN. <Bristol Co.Deeds 21:267>
...20 July 1732, Thomas CHURCH, Esq. of Little Compton and Paul UNIS, mariner & wf Alce/Alice of Bristol, for Ł600 sold to Samuel SHEARMAN & Peleg SHEARMAN of Tiverton...one half of the sixth great lott of land in the first Division of Pocasset Purchase in Tiverton...bounded by the Bay and land of Benjamin DURFEE. Witnesses: Timothy FALES, Samuel HOWLAND. Rec. 14 Sept. 1732.

Thomas CHURCH of Little Compton MA to **Alice UNICE** of Bristol. <Bristol RI Deeds 1:12>
...12 July 1737, Thomas CHURCH, Esq., for the naturall love & affection...unto my dutifull dau Alice UNICE, widow, in part of her portion as also for divers other good causes...give...land in Bristol...one peace containing half an acre...bounded by Thames St., Queen St., the sea to the ship channel & land belonging to the heirs of the late John WILKINS dec'd...the other peice is one common lott...#24...containing four acres...bounded by land belonging to the heirs of the late Jabez HOWLAND dec'd. Witnesses: N. BLAGROVE, Mary CHANDLER. Rec. 11 July 1747.

Alice UUNIS/UNICE of Bristol to Estate of **Nathaniel BLAGROVE** of same. <Bristol Co.Deeds 33:439>
...25 June 1745, Alice UUNIS, widow...Whereas ye honourable Nathaniel BLAGROVE, Esq. dec'd in his last will...did give..to ye sd Alice Ł100...upon condition or provided she gave a good & sufficient release...of all her right...of all that one seventh part of ye house & land...wherein ye sd Nathaniel BLAGROVE dwelt...for Ł120...to me in hand paid by Joseph GREENHILL, merchant, Mary EMERSON, widow & Jonathan WOODBURY, Esq., all of Bristol...executors of ye last will...release all rights...to ye one seventh part of ye house & land...and one seventh part of two common lotts so called belonging thereto which was sold by my honoured Father Thomas CHURCH to ye sd Nathaniel Witnesses: Joshua INGRAHAM. Samuel HOWLAND. Rec. 31 July 1745.

Alice UNIS/UNICE of Bristol RI to **Ephraim TISDALE** of same. <Bristol Co.Deeds 42:433>
...12 Aug. 1747, Alice UNIS, widow, for Ł416 sold to Ephraim TISDALE, yeoman...9th lot in Freetown...by ye name of the Quanipaug Lott...400 acres...bounded on Dartmouth line and land belonging to the heirs of Thomas BORDEN lately dec'd. Witnesses: Martha CHURCH, William COGGESHALL Jr. Ack. 30 Mar. 1756. Rec. 3 Oct. 1757.

Alice UUNIS/UNICE of Bristol to **John USHER** of same. <Bristol RI Deeds 1:121>
...12 Sept. 1750, Alice UUNIS, widow, for Ł80 bills of credit, sold to John USHER, clerk...one four acre lot in Bristol...bounded by land of sd John. Witnesses: Phebe SMITH, Rachel MANCHESTER. Ack. 25 Sept. 1750 by Alice. Rec. 8 Nov. 1750.

Will of **Nathaniel BLAGROVE**, Esq. of Bristol. <Bristol Co.PR>
<10:432>...dated 30 Dec. 1742...that the remaines of my first wife with the remaines of her former Husband Capt. Nathan HAYMAN to be taken up and enclosed in one coffin suitable and buryed either in my Grave with a tombstone over the same...to dau inlaw **Grace OTIS**, Ł200; to grandson in law **John OTIS**, Ł100; to grand daughter in law Mrs. **Alice UUNICE**, Ł100; to grandson in law **William BRATTLE**, Esq. & his wife, Ł5 each to buy a gold ring; to son in law **John OTIS**, Esq., Ł5 for a ring; to Rev. John BURT, pastor of Bristol Church, Ł20; niece **Mary EMERSON**; nephew **Joseph GREENHILL**; sister Mrs. **Mary CHANDLER**, widow (former husband JACKSON); niece **Sarah ROSSEY/ROFFEY**. <10:431> Pr. 23 Aug. 1744. <10:517> Inventory taken Dec. 1744.

Will of **Benjamin NORRIS** of Bristol RI. <Bristol RI PR 5:121>
...dated 15 Aug. 1848, mentions wf **Mary**; $5.00 each to the following: sons **Hezekiah NORRIS, John NORRIS, Benjamin NORRIS**; daus **Hannah HALL, Rebecca CHURCH**; chil. of dec'd son **William E. NORRIS**; chil. of dec'd dau **Mary BURR**; remainder of estate to dau **Ann NORRIS.** Pr. 3 Dec. 1855.

Estate of **Caleb CHURCH** of Watertown MA. <Middlesex Co.PR #4449> (lengthy!!)
<16:420> Letter/Bond 20 July 1722, Deacon John COOLEDGE, cooper of Watertown app'td admr. Surety: Isaac CHURCH, husbandman of Watertown. Witnesses: Alice McDANIEL, Francis FOXCROFT Jr. <16:459> Inventory taken 26 June 1722 by Samuel STEARNS, John COOLLIDG, Ebenezer WELLINGTON; house & barne with seven acres, Ł105; seven acres called Weights lot, Ł88; 10 acres on Charles river called Durty Green, Ł45; part of iron works in Newtowne, Ł80; land in south Boston joyning land of Mr. LORING, Ł10; total estate, Ł453.2s. <originals> Receipts to the admr. from: 12 Oct. 1722, **Isaac CHURCH** for a cow valued at Ł3.15s; 15 Nov. 1722, John MADDOCKS, atty. of Mrs. **Ruth INGERSOLE** for Ł3.14s for mourning ("as the other children had"); 17 Nov. 1722, Jonathan REMINGTON for Ł3.14s; 22 Nov. 1722, William BOND for 11s; 3 Jan. 1722/3, **Joshua WARREN Jr.** for 13s; 5 Jan. 1722/3, Martha BRECK for Ł8; 17 May 1723, Jonathan COOLLIDG for Ł1.3s.; 18 May 1723, Nathaniel LAMSON for Ł1.12s; 18 May 1723, Martha BRECK for Ł5.5s; 20 May 1723, George CUTTING for 6s; 21 May 1723, John ORMS for 5s. <original> Citation 17 May 1723, to the children of **Caleb CHURCH**, to appear at the exhibition of the admr.'s account on 22 May 1723...note on the back states the following appeared: **Isaac CHURCH**, only son, **Rebecca** & her husband **Joshua WARREN, John MADDOCK** eldest son & atty for his mother **Ruth** now wf of **Thomas INGERSOLE.** <16:517> 24 May 1723, Deacon John COOLEDGE was discharged as admr. <17:10> Letter/Bond 30 Aug. 1723, son **Isaac CHURCH** of Watertown app'td admr. Sureties: Lt.Coll. Edmund GOFFE, Esq. of Cambridge, Samuel BARNARD, housewright of Water-

town. Witnesses: Alice McDANIEL, Francis FOXCROFT Jr., Esq. <16:537> Order, 24 Oct. 1723. <16: 549> Receipt 23 Mar. 1723/4 of **Isaac CHURCH**, admr. de bonis non, to F. FOXCROFT the Judge of Probate for a bond of Jonathan GREEN of Newton. <original> On 16 Nov. 1724 **Mathew BOOMER** of Freetown appoints son **Joshua BOOMER** as his attorney to sue for his mother's rights in estate of her father **Caleb CHURCH.** Witnesses: William HOSKINS, James EDMISTER. <original> Agreement of heirs, 24 Nov. 1724, **Joshua WARRIN/WARREN, Joshua BOOMER** as attorney to his father, **John MADDOCK** as attorney to his mother **Ruth INGERSOLE** and **Rebekah WARREN**...being the persons intrested in ye Estate of our honoured father **Caleb CHURCH**...have agreed that **Rebekah** his daughter & **Joshua WARRIN** his son in law do administer upon his estate that is unadministered. <17:196> On 2 Dec. 1724, adm. is granted to son in law **Joshua WARREN,** housewright of Watertown (by the consent of the two daughters' attorneys) and his former admr. de bonis non, **Isaac CHURCH** (absconded) is hereby dismissed. Bond 2 Dec. 1724 of admr. Surety: Joseph HARRINGTON, husbandman of Watertown. Witnesses: Elizabeth NICHOLS, Francis FOXCROFT Jr. <17:438> Account of admr., 18 Apr. 1726. <17:439> Settlement 18 Apr. 1726, among following chil., viz: **Isaac CHURCH, Hannah BOOMER** wf of Matthew, **Ruth INGERSOLE** wf of Thomas and **Rebecca WARREN** wf of Joshua. <18:209> Account of admr., 12 Sept. 1728. <original> Claim July 1723, of **Isaac CHURCH** for Ⱡ59.14s1d, for work done by him & by his son **Caleb** and by his wife...on 21 Nov. 1717 I came to dwell with my father and I did his work with in dors on till 3 Feb. 1722.
(Note: The following two items, a deed & a letter are also with the probate records; they, along with some of the above probate data are found at the beginning of micro #13.)

==

Caleb CHURCH of Watertown MA to **Andrew BELCHER et al.**
...30 Mar. 1715, Caleb CHURCH, millwright & wf Rebekah, for Ⱡ80 mortgaged to Andrew BELCHER, Addington DAVENPORT, Thomas HUTCHINSON, Esq., John WHITE & Edward HUTCHINSON, gent., Trustees... six acres mowing land in Watertown...bounded by land of Simon TAYNTER, Ebenezer WOLLINGTON and Daniel BOND...also twelve acre pasture land in Watertown. Witnesses: Jonas BOND, Daniel BOND. Ack. 1 Apr. 1715 by Caleb & Rebekah. Rec. 1 Apr. 1715 at Charlestown in Book 17 (or 170):260. On the following dates, Caleb paid four pounds interest: 22 Aug. 1716, 17 Apr. 1717, 13 May 1719, 24 Feb. 1719/20, 11 May 1720. On 17 Apr. 1723, Addington DAVENPORT, Thomas HUTCHINSON & Edward HUTCHINSON receipted to John COOLLIDG, admr., for Ⱡ92.3s6d, viz: Ⱡ80 principal & Ⱡ123s6p interest, which is in full for the redemption of the within mortgaged premises & the mort. was discharged.

==

Springfield MA, 6 Oct. 1722

Loving Son,

I have here sent you a leter of attourney to act in the Right of the Estate of My father CHURCH's which Right that belongs to me I desire you to make the best Advantage of for Me in selling of as the Rest of My Brothers and sisters do. Which I hope in the best of your Discretion you will do to my advantage: I have Received no letter or a count of things from you since a letter by Mr. GAMAGE therefore send Me a compt of Matters by Mr. MARSHALL the Bearer hereof who will return in about Week. Leave this Letter as you send to me at Mr. Haris' and any other Letters from my Children And what money you make of the Estate of mine to improve till further order as your own: I have here Inclosed a letter to your sister Elizabeth GOODWIN Respecting my daughter Abigail which is that she be taken care of to be sent to Boston to some good place to be brought up in and the charge at my cost with what she can ern of her labor.

I desire you Would send Me some Garden seeds for there is none here. And now with my Cordial love to you your wife & yours And the Rest of my Relations And all my neighbours & friends together with my Husbands your affectionate Mother **Ruth INGERSOLE.**

David INGERSOLE & his wife Give their Love to your self And all other friends.

To **John MADDOCKS** att Watertown. Leave this at Mr. Harises by Watertown mill. Pr. Patrick MARSHAL.

MICRO #13 OF 32

Will of **Caleb BOOMER,** carpenter of Freetown MA. <Bristol Co.PR>
...dated 14 Mar. 1774...to wf **Sarah**, the north end of house above & below, one fourth part of one acre of land where the Garden now is, one cow & ten sheep, one hundred weight of beef & two hundred of pork, fifteen bushels of Indian corn & five bushels of rye yearly, six cords of wood yearly & all indore moveables & household goods...to son **Martin BOOMER** all land from the wall westward of house to Wattupper Pond...to son **Joshua BOOMER**, land known as Mingo field (already given by deed)...to son **Mathew BOOMER,** two lots in Tiverton & Dartmouth containing 80 acres...to son **Daniel BOOMER,** all land to westward of house, 140 acres in Tiverton & Dartmouth adjoining land of James WARRING and all my rights in estate of my son **Caleb BOOMER** dec'd...to dau **Johanna BOOMER,** Ⱡ20 and a priviledge in the house...to dau **Sarah WEST**'s two children, 20s when they arrive to lawfull age...to grand daughter **Elizabeth BOOMER,** one bed & furniture, one chest of drawers, two puter platters and Ⱡ5; son **Martin** (executor)...to keep the house in repair at all times. Witnesses: Henry BRIGHTMAN, Gideon BUTTS, Amos LEWIS. Pr. 5 Oct. 1790, **Martin BOOMER** app'td exr. Sureties: Jonathan READ, gent. & Harvey SIMMONS, yeoman, of Freetown. Inventory completed 23 June 1792 by Simeon BORDEN, Jonathan READ, Benjamin DURFEE.

==

Estate of **Martin BOOMER** of Fall River MA.
Division of real estate, 31 May 1803, by Charles DURFEE, Simeon BORDEN, Abiel MACOMBER...said estate bounded by land of James BOOMER, Thomas FREELOVE & heirs of Robert TERRY...containing 59 acres...(mentions a burying place on the land where sd Martin is buried); to widow **Sarah BOOMER**

and following heirs, viz: **James BOOMER, Ruth ELSBREE** wf of Ephraim, **Nathaniel BOOMER, Martin BOOMER, Nathan BOOMER, Jemima BOOMER, Polly BENNETT** wf of Sweet, **Charles BOOMER, William BOOMER, Henry BOOMER, Abraham BOOMER.** On 7 Feb. 1804, the widow **Sarah BOOMER** & the heirs that were of age, agreed to the division, viz: **James BOOMER, Martin BOOMER, Joseph BOOMER, Ephraim ELSBREE, Nathaniel BOOMER, Sweet BENNET.** (The widow is mentioned as being the gdn. of four minor children)

Estate of **Lydia SMITH**, widow of Marlboro MA.<Middlesex Co.PR #20709>
<195:85> Letter 13 Apr. 1786, Nathaniel SMITH, yeoman of Marborough app'td admr. <68:475> Account of admr., 13 Apr. 1786. <68:474> Inventory taken 11 Feb. 1786. <68:476> Receipt, 11 Feb. 1786, of the seven children; signed by: **Nathan SMITH, Nathan SMITH** in behalf of heirs of **David SMITH** dec'd, **Lydia CRANSON, Abigail STOW, Stephen STOW, Mary STOW, Peter STOW, Jane KNIGHT, "Amasiaht" KNIGHT, Anna WINCHESTER, Caleb WINCHESTER.**

Will of **Joshua WARREN**, yeoman of Waltham MA. <Middlesex Co.PR #23789>
...dated 23 Oct. 1752, mentions wf **Rebecca**; sons **Phinehas WARREN, Joshua WARREN** (double portion), **Nathaniel WARREN, Daniel WARREN**; daus **Rebecca HETHWAY/HATHAWAY, Mary TUCKER, Elizabeth GIBBINS, Abigail HOW, Hannah RICE, Prudence HARDY**; great-grandson **William SIBBLE** son of dec'd grandaughter **Rebecca SIBBLE**; grandsons **Thomas SOUTHWORTH & Stephen SOUTHWORTH**, sons of dec'd dau **Lydia SOUTHWORTH**; chil. of dec'd dau **Susanna FLAGG.** Pr. 16 June 1760. (The following may refer to probate records of this **Joshua WARREN**: #23879, 23:164,167;29:379 (15 Feb. 1762, accounts).)

Estate of **Jedediah HOW**, yeoman of New Braintree MA. <Worcester Co.PR #31735>
Bond 22 Sept. 1761, of son **Jedediah HOW** of Brookfield. Order to divide, 17 Feb. 1762, land in Brookfield & New Braintree. Division of real estate, 13 Apr. 1763; to sons **Jedediah HOW, Elijah HOW, Silas HOW & Jonah HOW**; provided that **Jedediah** pay brothers **Solomon HOW**, Ł57.10s & **Silas HOW**, Ł21.5s and sister **Dorothy**, Ł40.52 and **Elijah** pays sisters **Abigail GOULD**, Ł57.10s & **Dorothy**, Ł11. 5s and brother **Jonas/Jonah HOW.** Guardianship, 15 Oct. 1761, **Jedediah HOW**, husbandman app'td gdn. of **Solomon HOW**, aged about 10 yrs; 11 Mar. 1765, **Solomon HOW**, aged 14 the 14 Sept. 1764, chose Adam HOLMS/HOLMES, gent. of New Braintree as his gdn.

Estate of **Solomon HOWE** of New Salem MA. <Greenfield MA PR #2554>
Petition Feb. 1836, of widow **Catherine HOWE** to have William WHITAKER of New Salem app'td admr; he was app'td 9 Feb. 1836. Estate was declared insolvent; personal estate only amounting to $26.77 was settled on the widow who states she is of advanced years & of scanty means.

MICRO #14 OF 32

Will of **Daniel WARREN**, yeoman of Westboro MA. <Worcester Co.PR #62114>
<27:140>...dated 9 Oct. 1790, mentions son in law **Simeon BELLOWS** who married my dau **Rebecca** & their children; chil. of dec'd dau **Hannah BAKER** wf of Ezra, viz: **Nahum BAKER** (eldest son) and minor chil. **Mary BAKER, Joseph BAKER, Abigail BAKER, Hannah BAKER & Solomon BAKER**; Simeon BELLOWS executor. Witnesses: George BRIGHAM, Ashbel Samuel BRIGHAM, Jon WARD. <27:142> Pr. 1 Nov. 1796. <206:32> Assent to will, 31 Oct. 1796, widow **Martha WARREN** and grandaughters **Mary & Abigail BAKER**

James HAWS of Westboro MA to **Thaddeus WARREN** of same. <Worcester Co.Deeds 79:352>
...26 May 1767...three & one quarter acres in Westboro. Rec. 2 July 1778.

Samuel BARNES et al to **Phinehas WARREN.** <Middlesex Co.Deeds 87:231>
...15 Jan. 1781, Samuel BARNES mariner of Wrentham, Josiah WARREN, gent. of Cambridge & William WARREN, gent. of Watertown...to our aged Father & Mother Phinehas & Grace WARREN. Rec. 13 Aug. 1784.

Samuel BARNES of Waltham MA to **Samuel BARNES Jr.** of same. <Middlesex Co.Deeds 109:362>
...24 Dec. 1798, Samuel BARNES, mariner...by judgement...to Samuel BARNES Jr., cabinet maker... for debt...8 acres partly in Waltham & Watertown...one appraiser chosen by the wife of the within named Samuel BARNES the debtor, by reason of the sd BARNES being out of the Commonwealth. (<101:396>...8 Jan. 1790, Samuel BARNES, mariner of Waltham & wf Grace had mortaged this land to N. BEMIS, gent. of Watertown. <17:121>...1 Apr. 1807, Samuel BARNES, cabinet maker of Waltham to Grace BARNES, widow of same...8 acres partly in Waltham & Watertown, reserving barn on land to Phineas BARNES. <208:398>...31 Mar. 1814, Grace BARNES, widow mortages this land to C. EVERETT. <271:279>...23 Oct. 1826, Grace BARNES, widow of Waltham mortages this land to Thomas BARNES, yeoman of same.)

Phineas BARNES of Waltham MA to **Grace BARNES** of same. <Middlesex Co.Deeds 203:422>
...1 Dec. 1806, Phineas BARNES, yeoman, for love & affection...to my beloved mother Grace BARNES, widow...let...one undivided third part of the farm on which I now live...with one half of the dwelling house & improvement of one third of the barn...during the term of her...life or while she shall remain the widow of my late father Samuel BARNES...paying therefor the rate of one cent ...each and every year. Witnesses: Nathaniel HARRINGTON, Lydia HARRINGTON. Rec. 9 Mar. 1813.

Heirs of **Elizabeth RAND.** <Middlesex Co.Deeds 217:186>
...23 Mar. 1816, Benjamin RAND, yeoman of Weston; John RAND, yeoman of Weston; sd John RAND as guardian for minors Daniel RAND, Abigail RAND, Isaiah W. RAND & Nathan RAND and Abigail STONE; John DEAN, trader of Cambridge; Andrew BARNES, gent. of Newton & wf Sarah in her right; Josiah MIXER, trader of Cambridge & wf Mary in her right; Josiah NORCROSS, yeoman of Boylston & wf Sarah

in her right; Josiah HEMMENWAY, painter of Framingham & wf Nancy in her right; Nathan RAND, painter of Framingham and Nancy DEAN, singlewoman of Cambridge...petition for a division of land & buildings in Weston...being the same lands & tenements formerly assigned to Elizabeth RAND late of sd Weston dec'd for her dower. The shares are as follows: Benjamin RAND four ninths; John RAND two ninths; Daniel, Abigail, Isaiah & Nathan RAND, one quarter of one ninth each; Abigail STONE, John DEAN, Andrew & Sarah BARNES and Josiah & Mary MIXER, one fifth of one ninth each; Josiah & Sarah NORCROSS, Josiah & Nancy HEMMENWAY and Nathan RAND, one third of one ninth each. <217:188> Land was divided 10 Apr. 1816. Rec. 11 Jan. 1817.

Andrew BARNES of Newton MA to **John DEAN** of Cambridge MA. <Middlesex Co.Deeds 217:186> ...31 May 1816, Andrew BARNES, yeoman & wf Sarah, for $20.00 sold to John DEAN, trader...all our right...in land in Weston...of Elizabeth RAND of Weston dec'd widow of Thomas RAND dec'd...as came to the sd Sarah by descent...set off to her in April now last past. Witnesses: Nancy W. MITCHELL, Ebenezer CHENY. Ack. & Rec. same day.

MICRO #15 OF 32

Joseph CHURCH to **Daniel CUSHING Sr.** of Hingham. <Plymouth Col.Rcds. 11:169> ...21 Jan. 1678, Joseph CHURCH, late of Hingham, son in law of John TUCKER dec'd by marriage with Mary TUCKER, deeds to Daniel CUSHING Sr., yeoman...his share of the proportion of Mary his wife in sd John TUCKER's lot of Conihasset meadow in Hingham. <11:232>...26 May 1679, Joseph CHURCH carpenter, late of Hingham & wf Mary deed lots in Hingham once belonging to Joseph's father Richard CHURCH...to pastor of church in Hingham, John (?poss. NORTON).

Will of **Samuel GREY** of Little Compton. <Bristol Co.PR>
<3:88>...dated 20 Mar. 1712, mentions wf **Deborah** & brother **Thomas GREY** (executors) and following chil., viz: **Samuel GREY** (eldest son), **Simeon GREY & Ignatious GREY** (youngest sons), **Dorothy & Lydia**; brother **John CHURCH**. Witnesses: Edward GRAY, Jonathan HEAD, Richard BILLINGS. Pr. 7 Apr. 1712. Inventory taken 2 Apr. 1712; sworn to 7 Apr. 1712 by **Deborah GREY & Capt. Thomas GREY**, exrs <3:167,170> Account of exrs., 3 Nov. 1713 (**Deborah GREY** now **Deborah THROOPE**).

Will of **Jonathan BLACKMAN** of Little Compton. <Bristol Co.PR 3:313>
...dated 4 Oct. 1716, mentions unnamed wife, unborn child, unnamed child (poss. a dau), Uncle **John CHURCH**, to Mother while she lives, Ł12 yearly; mother & uncle, exrs. Adm. Bond (not dated & not executed), signed by John CHURCH, Thomas GRAY, William PABODIE (blank left for **Leah BLACKMAN** to sign.) Witnesses: Samuel LITTLE, E. BRENTON. Inventory taken 2 Nov. 1716; states **Jonathan** died 8 Oct. 1716; sworn to by **Leah BLACKMAN & John CHURCH**.

Will of **Capt. Samuel TISDALE**, gent. of Freetown MA. <Bristol Co.PR>
<21:62>...dated 31 Aug. 1765, mentions wf **Mary**; son **Samuel TISDALE** to have privilege to live in house for life & be provided for by executors; to dau **Mary NICHOLS** the eastermost end of my dwelling house above & below; to dau **Sarah TISDALE** the west end of the house after death of father & mother; dau **Rebeckah PORTER**; Benjamin PORTER; daus **Mary & Sarah**, executors. <21:64> Pr. 28 Oct. 1769. <26:159> Order to divide, 5 Jan. 1779, between **Mary NICHOLS & Sarah TISDALE**; mentions portion set off to the widow. <33:335-37> Guardianships. <37:54> Inventory. <37:56,309> Accounts. <38:539> Notice of sale. <40:318> Account.

Estate of **Mary TISDALE**, widow of Freetown MA. <Bristol Co.PR>
<148:153> Petition 3 May 1783, of **Benjamin PORTER** & wf **Rebecca** of Freetown for admr. to be app'td on estate of her mother who died "some time in March last. <original> Bond 3 June 1783, of William READ, yeoman of Freetown, admr. Sureties: Benjamin PORTER, yeoman of Freetown & Job HATHEWAY yeoman of Taunton. <27:587> Inventory taken 4 Nov. 1783; no real estate. (The files give a reference of 6:355 for a will of a **Mary TISDALE** but her identity is not given.)

Guardianship of Children of **Ephraim TISDALE** of Freetown & Dighton MA. <Bristol Co.PR>
<125:23>...1755..."Martha of Dighton" gdn. to **Mary TISDALE** dau of Ephraim of Dighton. <127:241>.. 1764...gdn. app'td for **Mary TISDALE** dau of Ephraim of Freetown. (These two entries may refer to two Ephraim TISDALES.)

Estate of **Eleazer NICHOLS**, blacksmith of Freetown MA. <Bristol Co.PR>
<13:494> Letter/Bond 6 Nov. 1753, brother William NICHOLS, mariner of Freetown app'td admr. Sureties: Samuel TISDALE, gent. & David CUDWORTH, yeoman of Freetown. <17:35> Inventory taken 14 May 1754; sworn to 6 May 1760 by exr. <original> Petition 24 May 1756, of widow **Mary NICHOLS** who complains that the admr. has not settled his account. <17:43> Account of admr. 3 June 1760; no real estate; necessaries to the widow.

Estate of **Eleazer NICHOLS**. <Bristol Co.PR>
...1805...<41:541> Will. <42:6> Inventory. <42:455> Account. <109:82> Notice. (Guardianship letter dated 1829 <133:498>, may or may not pertain to this estate.)

Will of **Mary NICHOLS** of Freetown MA. <Bristol Co.PR 34:201>
...dated 4 Aug. 1796, mentions sisters **Tryphena NICHOLS, Lydia NICHOLS, Joanna DEAN** wf of Benjamin Jr. and sister in law, the wf of brother **Eleazer NICHOLS**; Benjamin DEAN Jr., executor.

References to the name **Mary NICHOLS** in Bristol Co.PR: <126:173> 1760, gdn. of Mary dau of Aaron NICHOLS. <131:368> Gdn. 1788-1810. <186:214> Will, 1872-76. <190:416> Pr. <197:294> Inventory. <220:68> Account.

BRISTOL COUNTY DEEDS: (re: NICHOLS)

<77:162> - 8 Apr. 1793, Mary NICHOLS, widow of Freetown to Walter NICHOLS, yeoman of Freetown, half a dwelling house & blacksmith shop and her share of land set off to Sarah TISDALE dec'd. Witnesses: Moses NICHOLS, Eleazer NICHOLS.

<78:77> - 8 May 1799, Mary NICHOLS, widow & Walter NICHOLS, yeoman, both of Providence...land given to sd Mary & Sarah TISDALE by will of Samuel TISDALE.

<79:91> - 30 May 1800, Mary NICHOLS, widow & Walter NICHOLS, yeoman, both of Providence.

<81:528> - 13 Nov. 1802, Eleazer NICHOLS, blacksmith of Freetown sells all his right (one sixty fourth part) in land of dec'd uncle Edward NICHOLS of Berkley. Elliathe NICHOLS signs.

<106:37> - 5 Jan. 1819, Elizabeth NICHOLS, widow of Freetown to Joseph DURFEE, Esq. of Tiverton, all her right to land on Water St. in Freetown, bounded by land of Capt. John NICHOLS, heirs of Isaac BURBANK & estate of Joseph PADDOCK.

Will of **Joseph CHURCH** ... Co.PR>
<3:21,249> ... **ace**; sons **Nathaniel CHURCH, Caleb CHURCH** (under
21); ... n **Joseph CHURCH** (under 23); sons **Richard CHURCH**
& Isr ... **, Deborah, Elizabeth**; wf and son **Nathaniel**, executor ... tory taken 27 Dec. 1715; states he died 19 Dec.
1715. ... her **Nathaniel CHURCH**, exr. <8:358> Receipt
1735, ...

Will of ...
<8:464>. ... **CHURCH, Caleb CHURCH, Richard CHURCH**; grand-
son **Jose** ... **ael CHURCH**; daus **Sarah CHURCH, Deborah**
BRIGGS, ... > Pr. 19 Apr. 1737. <8:465> Inventory taken
29 Mar. 1 ...

References ... 44:444;45:49,290,291,298,501;46:250;76:
106;81:139 ... ;176:116.

Estate of ...
<3:227> Adm ... 231> Inventory taken 26 July 1748; sworn
to by admr. ... **Caleb.** <4:49> Account.

Will of **John** ...
...dated 23 ... xecutor); daus **Mary BAILEY** wf of Thomas & **Dorothy** ... ndaughters, the minor chil. of dau
Hannah PECK. ... oseph SOUTHWORTH. Pr. 18 Mar. 1739/
40. Inventory ...

Joseph WOOD of ... Co.Deeds 54:385>
...27 Mar. 1772 ... ther William WOOD, cordwainer...
land in Dartmou ... lliam TABER late of Dartmouth dec'd
Witnesses: Phili ... eph & Mary. <56:127>...17 June
1773, Joseph WOO ... land to Nathaniel TRIPP. Ack. 31
Aug. 1773 by Jos ...

William WOOD of L ... o.Deeds 20:146>
...29 May 1732, Wi ... ...north part of an orchard formerly belonging to ... ,32.

Will of **John WOOD** ... Bristol Co.PR 38:494>
...dated 23 Sept. 1 ... being infirm in body; to sons **Joseph WOOD & Benjamin WOOD**, $1.00 each; to son in law **Daniel HOWLAND**, all estate "he paying what is resonable worth"; to five daus **Abigail WILBUR, Meribeth MAXFIELD, Sarah HOWLAND, Eunice HOWLAND & Thiza STAFFORD**, all estate; sons in law **Daniel HOWLAND & Tilly STAFFORD**, executors. Witnesses: Holder SLOCUM, Micall RUSSELL, Ruben MOSHER. Pr. 2 Feb. 1802.

PLYMOUTH COUNTY DEEDS: (re: Charles CHURCH)

<7:47> - 19 Jan. 1704/5, Joseph WHETSON of Scituate (eldest son of John dec'd), Joseph PARKER & wf Mercy, Abigail & Bathsheba WHETSON/WHESTON, sell to Lieut. Charles CHURCH of Scituate, five eighths...

<7:156> - , Charles CHURCH...

<9:181> - 3 Jan. 1711/12, Nathaniel JACKSON to Capt. Charles CHURCH.

<9:181> - 8 Feb. 1711/12, Francis BILLINGTON, mariner of Plymouth to Capt. Charles CHURCH, gent of same.

<12:162> - 18 Apr. 1717, Hannah WHETSTONE, singlewoman of Barnstable to Charles CHURCH, gent. of Plymouth, all her rights in land in Scituate, formerly land of John WHETSTONE near mill of Charles STOCKBRIDGE.

PLYMOUTH COUNTY DEEDS, cont-d: (re: Charles CHURCH)

<13:113> - 4 Nov. 1717, Widow Sarah CHURCH of Plymouth sells to son Charles CHURCH of same, one third of lands & cornmill which belonged to her husband Nathaniel CHURCH dec'd of Scituate.

<14:30> - 16 May 1718, Settlement of bounds between Capt. Charles CHURCH & James BARNABY as gdn of the dau of Joseph CHURCH dec'd, both of Plymouth of the one part and John WATSON of Plymouth on the other part.

<13:172> - 16 June 1718, Charles CHURCH, cordwainer/miller & wf Mary of Plymouth sell to John DOANE & wf Hannah of Eastham, gristmill, etc. (mortgage). <17:188> 17 Jan. 1723/4, mortgage released by representatives of Charles CHURCH decd

---

PLYMOUTH COUNTY PROBATE: (re: CHURCH)

1689	Nathaniel	Scituate		#3972, 1:50,51;3:20;4:31
1703	Richard	Scituate	gdn.	#3975
1703	Richard	Scituate		#3976, 2:26,27
1707	Joseph	Plymouth		2:86;3:121
1712	Sarah	Plymouth	gdn.	#3982, 3:114;4:387
1729	Charles	Freetown		5:464
1753	Nathaniel	Scituate		#3973, 13:59,136;14:62,63
1756	Elizabeth & Sylvia	Scituate	gdn.	14:48,49

PLYMOUTH COUNTY DEEDS: (re: Richard CHURCH)

<18:168> - 9 Mar. 1723, Nathaniel CHURCH of Scituate (son of Nathaniel) to Richard CHURCH (grandson of Nathaniel).

<20:2> - 1 Jan. 1724, Richard CHURCH, housewright of Scituate, to Ebenezer STETSON. Witnesses: Nathaniel CHURCH Jr., Jerusha CHURCH.

<24:101> - 10 Feb. 1724/5, Richard CHURCH, carpenter of Scituate to Nathaniel CHURCH Jr., carpenter of same, land south of Nathaniel CHURCH Sr., being part of land divided by them 9 Mar. 1723.

<20:9> - 23 Dec. 1725, Richard CHURCH, housewright of Rochester to Caleb TORREY of Scituate, two thirds of the share granted to successor of Nathaniel CHURCH dec'd.

<20:141> - 17 Apr. 1725, Division between Richard CHURCH, house carpenter of Scituate & Nathaniel CHURCH, boatsman of same. (mentions Nathaniel CHURCH dec'd, the grandfather of Richard & father of Nathaniel)

<20:142> - 17 Apr. 1725, Richard CHURCH of Scituate, grantor; mentions uncle Nathaniel CHURCH.

<20:150> - 21 Mar. 1725/26, Richard CHURCH, carpenter of Rochester, grantor.

<21:191> - 1 Aug. 1726, Richard CHURCH, carpenter of Rochester to Jonathan STURTEVANT of Plymouth, part of land in Rochester Gore bought of John MUMFORD.

<22:109> - 17 July 1727, Richard CHURCH, carpenter of Rochester to John SHEARMAN of same.

<34:72> - 20 Sept 1727, Richard CHURCH, carpenter of Rochester, grantor.

<37:172> - Sept 1729, Richard CHURCH, carpenter of Rochester sells land on Dartmouth line.

<26:37> - 23 Nov. 1730, Richard CHURCH, housewright of Rochester, grantor.

<27:129> - 29 Aug. 1732, Richard CHURCH, carpenter of Rochester, sells land bought of John COWING 24 Jan. 1726/7.

<32:21> - 11 Mar. 1733, Richard CHURCH, carpenter of Rochester, grantor.(refers to above deed)

<31:19> - 28 June 1736, Richard CHURCH, carpenter of Rochester, sells 2 lots near dwelling.

<34:25> - 9 Sept 1740, Richard CHURCH, housewright of Rochester & wf Anna, mortgage to Commiss.

<44:235> - 31 May 1757, Richard CHURCH, carpenter of Rochester to son Lemuel CHURCH, carpenter, 50 acres bought of Israel COWING 27 June 1745.

<46:180> - 2 Feb. 1760, Richard CHURCH, carpenter of Rochester to Richard CHURCH Jr., shop joiner, part of homestead on Dartmouth line, reserving to self & wife firewood for life. Ack. 9 Feb. 1760 by Richard & wf Anne.

<49:83> - 12 May 1760, Richard CHURCH, carpenter of Rochester to son Lemuel CHURCH of same.

<49:52> - 23 Feb. 1762, Richard CHURCH, housewright of Rochester to Ebenezer CLAP, his dwelling house; mentions land sold to Robert WHITCOMB.

<50:34> - 5 May 1764, Richard CHURCH Jr., house carpenter of Rochester, grantor.

<49:240> - 9 Mar. 1765, Richard CHURCH Jr., house carpenter of Rochester, grantor.

<49:241> - 9 Mar. 1765, Richard CHURCH Jr., house carpenter of Rochester, grantor.

Nathaniel HARLOW Sr. of Plympton MA to children. <Plymouth Co.Deeds>
<14:79>...7 Apr. 1718, Nathaniel HARLOW Sr. to dau Abigail COOKE wf of Robert of Plymouth...reserving improvement for life to self & wife. <15:40>...8 July 1717...to eldest son Nathaniel HARLOW Jr. of Plympton. <15:41>...4 Apr. 1718...to eldest son Nathaniel HARLOW Jr.

Estate of **Nathaniel HARLOW** of Plympton MA. <Plymouth Co.PR #9276>
<4:317> Letter/Bond 6 Mar. 1721/22, widow **Abigail HARLOW** app'td admx. Sureties: Benoni LUCAS & Isaac CUSHMAN Jr. of Plympton. Witnesses: Nathaniel THOMAS, Josiah RICKARD. <4:318> Warrant, 21 Dec. 1721, to take inventory by Benoni LUCAS, Isaac CUSHMAN, Josiah RICKARD, all of Plympton. Inventory taken 6 Mar. 1721/22 by above three. <4:340> Agreement 6 Mar. 1721/22 of widow **Abigail HARLOW** and children: **Nathaniel HARLOW, James HARLOW** and **Abigail COOK** wf of Robert. Witnesses: Isaac CUSHMAN Jr., David BOSWORTH.

Estate of **Capt. Charles CHURCH** of Freetown MA. <Bristol Co.PR>
<5:403> Inventory taken 27 Mar. 1727. <6:68> Insolvency, 20 Feb. 1727/8. <6:350> Claims, Nov. 1729. <5:464,465> On 19 Apr. 1729, John BATT, Joseph LUCAS & Jeduthun ROBINS, all of Plimpton appraised all the real estate, which consisted of 30 acres in Plimpton near Dotens Ceder Swamp, £34. <6:344> Account of widow **Mary CHURCH**, admx., 18 Nov. 1729.

Estate of **Capt. Charles CHURCH** of Freetown MA. <Bristol Co.PR>
<13:18>...1762, widow **Frances CHURCH** & son **Charles CHURCH** app'td admrs. <18:57> Inventory. <19:35> Account. <20:91> Account, 1767. <20:291> Division, 1767.

Estate of **Charles CHURCH** of New Bedford MA. <Bristol Co.PR>
<32:251> Inventory taken 1793; sworn to by widow **Elizabeth CHURCH**. <41:423> Inventory. <42:141> Insolvency. <42:340> Account.

Estate of **Charles CHURCH** of New Bedford MA. <Bristl Co.PR>
<42:491> Account. <42:365> Dower, 1806, to widow **Keturah CHURCH**. <42:492> Disbtribution.

Guardianship of Children of **Constant CHURCH** of Bristol. <Bristol Co.PR 11:3>
...(no date given)...minor children, viz: **Mary, Charles & Peter CHURCH.**

Estate of **Nathaniel CHURCH**, yeoman of Scituate MA. <Plymouth Co.PR #3973>
<13:59> Letter 7 May 1753, eldest son **Nathaniel CHURCH** app'td admr. <13:136> Inventory taken 7 May 1753. <14:62> Account of admr., 24 Mar. 1756. <14:63> Settlement, 25 Mar. 1756; real estate settled on eldest son **Nathaniel CHURCH**, he to pay his brothers & sisters £29.2.8. each, viz: **Caleb CHURCH**, heirs of **Joseph CHURCH, Abigail TURNER** wf of William, widow **Judith CLIFT, Deborah FISH** wf of Ebenezer & **Mary SAMSON** wf of Charles. <14:48,49> Guardianship, 24 Mar. 1756, Ebenezer FISH, yeoman of Duxbury app'td gdn. of **Elizabeth CHURCH & Sylvia CHURCH**, daus of **Joseph CHURCH**, mariner of Scituate dec'd.

Estate of **William CLIFT**, yeoman of Marshfield MA. <Plymouth Co.PR #445>
<11:456> Letter. <12:8> Inventory. <20:66> Decree, 9 Dec. 1761, mentions the widow and following chil., viz: **William CLIFT** (eldest son), **Joseph CLIFT, Church CLIFT, Lydia, Sarah, Betty & Rhoda** and chil. of dec'd son **Nathaniel CLIFT.**

Will of **Samuel TROUANT** of Marshfield MA. <Plymouth Co.PR #21213>
<50:370>...dated 17 Sept. 1818, mentions wf **Rhoda**, son **Church Clift TROUANT** and daus **Huldah HATCH** wf of Joel & unnamed dau. <50:371,434> Pr. 6 Sept. 1819.

MICRO #16 OF 32

Estate of **Nathaniel CHURCH** of Scituate MA. <Plymouth Co.PR 25:469>
Division of real estate, 4 Apr. 1779, by William TURNER, Esq., Elisha TOLMAN, yeoman & William BRIGGS, yeoman, all of Scituate; to the widow and following chil., viz: **Thomas CHURCH** (eldest son), **Constant CHURCH, Lemuel CHURCH, William CHURCH**, chil. of **Nathaniel CHURCH** dec'd, **Charles CHURCH, Lydia PALMER** wf of Ezekiel of Hanover, **Abigail BRIGGS** wf of Seth of Pembroke, **Sarah LOTHROP** wf of Josiah of Bridgewater, **Jerusha BRIGGS** widow of Cornelius of Scituate and **Mary CHURCH** (youngest dau).

Nathaniel CHURCH of Scituate MA t **Charles & Lemuel CHURCH** of same. <Plymouth Co.Deeds 53:197>
...3 Apr. 1765, Nathaniel CHURCH, yeoman to Charles CHURCH & Lemuel CHURCH, mariners...land in Scituate...near the place where my Father Nathaniel CHURCH's dwelling house formerly stood...all the frame of my old house they wish to use.

Estate of **Charles CHURCH** of Scituate to **Lemuel CHURCH** of same. <Plymouth Co.Deeds 64:1>
...23 Dec. 1773, Thomas STOCKBRIDGE of Scituate, as admr., sells to Lemuel CHURCH, yeoman...one half of land, re: deed 53:197.

Will of **Lydia PALMER** widow of Scituate MA. <Plymouth Co.PR #15242>
<44:217>...dated 22 Mar. 1812, to dau **Lydia NASH**, all personal estate; to sons **Simeon NASH, Oliver NASH, Abel NASH, Thomas NASH, Samuel NASH** and the chil. of son **Church NASH** dec'd & dau **Deborah PARSONS** dec'd, all real estate; brother **Lemuel CHURCH**, executor. Witnesses: David STOCKBRIDGE, Nathaniel STEVENS, Huldah LEAVITT. <44:218> 1 June 1812, **Lemuel CHURCH** declines to admr. <39:457> Letter/Bond 1 June 1812, David STOCKBRIDGE, Esq. of Hanover app'td admr. Sureties: Elisha FOSTER, Samuel CURTIS.

Will of **Ezekiel PALMER**, yeoman of Hanover MA. <Plymouth Co.PR #15228>
<30:423>...dated 13 Mar. 1786...being far advanced in life; to wf **Lydia**, £53.6s8d together with all household goods; 5s together with one quarter of estate each to the following chil.: chil. of dec'd son **Thomas PALMER**; dau **Betty**; chil. of dec'd dau **Sarah**; dau **Hannah**; Jonathan PRATT, shipwright of Hanover, executor. Witnesses: Isaac PARSONS, Samuel NASH, Jerusha NASH. <30:425> Letter /Bond 6 Aug. 1788, Jonathan PRATT app'td admr. Sureties: Seth BRIGGS of Pembroke & Samuel NASH of Hanover. <30:490> Warrant to appraise, 6 July 1788. Inventory taken 20 Aug. 1788; total estate, £145.3.3.3.

Estate of **Simeon NASH**, shipwright of Scituate MA. <Plymouth Co.PR #14524>
<17:136> Letter/Bond 6 Dec. 1764, widow **Lydia NASH** app'td admx. Sureties: Elisha TOLMAN, housewright of Scituate & Ezekiel PALMER, yeoman of Hanover. <9:172> Inventory taken 6 Dec 1764 by Elisha TOLMAN, Ezekiel PALMER, Samuel EELLS; no real estate; total personal estate, Ł8.18.4. <19:173> On 7 Dec. 1764 the admx. reports the estate is greatly insolvent.

***

Abel NASH of Scituate MA to **David STOCKBRIDGE** of Hanover. <Plymouth Co.Deeds 75:204>
...15 Sept. 1794, Abel NASH, shipwright, for Ł110 sold to David STOCKBRIDGE, yeoman...six & a half acres with dwelling house & barn in Scituate...in which I now dwell & is the same land which I on 17 Dec. 1781 purchased of Nathaniel CHURCH...bounded partly by land of the widow Lydia PALMER. Wf Susanna releases dower. Rec. 4 Oct. 1794.

***

Estate of **Church NASH** of Waldoborough ME. <Lincoln Co.ME PR>
<6:104> Letter/Bond 10 Dec. 1795, widow **Eve NASH** app'td admx. Sureties: Joseph SIMMONS of Waldoborough & Benjamin PALMER of Bristol. <7:143> Inventory taken 16 Dec. 1795 by Thomas JOHNSTON & Benjamin PALMER of Bristol & Joseph SIMMONS; total, $2750.88. <8:99> Account of admx. 17 Sept. 1798. <9:192,247> Guardianship 17 Sept. 1798, **Eve NASH** app'td gdn. of **Lydia NASH, Jane NASH & Oliver NASH** and chosen gdn. by **Church NASH & Samuel NASH.**

***

Estate of **Lydia NASH,** singlewoman of Scituate MA. <Plymouth Co.PR #14502>
<original> Petition 13 Dec. 1816 of brother **Simeon NASH** that David STOCKBRIDGE by app'td admr. <46:197> Letter/Bond 17 Dec. 1816, David STOCKBRIDGE, Esq. of Hanover app'td admr. Sureties: Alden BRIGGS of Pembroke, Ephraim SPOONER. <48:355,356> Inventory taken 24 Dec. 1816 by Horatio CUSHING, Esq. of Hanover, Alden BRIGGS, gent. of Pembroke & Lemuel CHURCH, yeoman of Scituate; no real estate mentioned; fodder in the barn, $8.00; wood at the door, $2.50; bucket & well rope, $1.00; total $242.25. <49:26> Account of admr., 1 Sept. 1817; personal estate sold at auction; paid $18.00 for gravestones & setting them up. Distribution of $201.88 to brothers & sisters, viz: **Simeon NASH, Oliver NASH, Samuel NASH, Abel NASH,** heirs of **Church NASH** dec'd, heirs of **Deborah PARSONS** dec'd, **Betsey NASH** wf of **Thomas NASH** a brother residing out of the U.S.

***

Heirs of **Lydia PALMER** to **Cornelius B. CHURCH** of Scituate MA. <Plymouth Co.Deeds 141:149>
...12 May 1817, Oliver NASH of Bristol, Abel NASH Jr. of Waldoborough ME & wf Polly in her right, Samuel NASH & Church NASH of Nobleborough, Thomas OSYER of Bristol & wf Lydia in her right, Oliver NASH of Waldoborough, Jacob OVERLOOK of Nobleborough & wf Jane in her right, Abel NASH of Waldoborough, all in the County of Lincoln, Obadiah WHITMAN & wf Susannah in her right, Lydia CAMPBELL widow, Samuel FESSENDEN & wf Deborah in her right, Solomon Hewett CHANDLER, George Washington CHANDLER & Sally CHANDLER all of New Cloucester, County of Cumberland MA...for $333.32 sold to Cornelius B. CHURCH...three sevenths & sixteen eighteenths of one seventh of about thirteen & one quarter acres with dwelling house & barn in Scituate...bounded by land of John SYLVESTER, Lemuel CHURCH & Gad LEAVITT...also one acre meadow in Scituate being the same meadow formerly owned by Lydia PALMER of Scituate dec'd and lately possessed by Lydia NASH of Scituate dec'd ...bounded by land of John SYLVESTER, Thomas CHURCH, Lemuel CHURCH...being all the real estate in Scituate devised to us...by our dec'd relative Lydia PALMER & which we hold in common & undivided with the other devisers of the sd Lydia PALMER. Witnesses: Robert CURTIS, Elijah HAYWARD. Ack. same day. Rec. 8 Sept. 1820. <149:151>...20 June 1817, Samuel NASH, yeoman of Holden, Worcester Co., for $85.72 sold to Cornelius B. CHURCH, mariner of Scituate...one seventh of the real estate of Lydia PALMER of Scituate dec'd, received by her will & is undivided. Rec. 8 Sept. 1820.

***

Estate of **Richard CHURCH** of Scituate MA. <Plymouth Co.PR #3976>
<originals> Bond of widow **Hannah CHURCH,** admx. Surety: William BARSTOW of Scituate. Inventory taken 2 Dec. 1703 by Samuel STETSON, William BARSTOW; sworn to 23 Dec. 1703. <#3975> Guardianship <original> Bond 17 June 1703, William BARSTOW app'td gdn. of **Richard CHURCH,** infant son of dec'd.

***

Heirs of **Richard CHURCH** of Scituate MA. <Plymouth Co.Deeds 21:172>
...9 Feb. 1721, Ezekiel HATCH & wf Ruth of Rochester and Josiah STURTEVANT & wf Hannah of Plymouth, for Ł180 received from Richard CHURCH, housewright of Scituate...release all their right to the real estate...which was our Grandfather Nathaniel CHURCH's of Scituate dec'd...in Scituate & elsewhere which was set out to the children of our Father Richard CHURCH of Scituate dec'd. Witnesses: Consider HOWLAND, Joshua YOUNG, Elisha HATCH,John COURBY. Ack. 18 Oct. 1723 by Josiah & Hannah, 10 Mar. 1725/6 by Ezekiel & Ruth.

***

Estate of **Lemuel CHURCH,** house carpenter of Rochester MA. <Plymouth Co.PR>
<21:142> Letter/Bond 15 Apr. 1772, widow **Bethiah CHURCH** app'td amx. Sureties: Ebenezer CLAP, Joel ELLIS. Inventory taken 17 Apr. 1772 by Seth DEXTER, Joel ELLIS, Earl CLAP; incl. turner's tools, blacksmith tools; one eighth of a vessel, Ł38; total real estate, Ł466.13.4. <29:369> Account of admx., 6 Sept. 1785; payments to Richard CHURCH, Lemuel CHURCH Jr., Charles CHURCH. <30:229> Division of real estate to widow **Bethiah CHURCH** and following heirs, viz: **Lemuel CHURCH Jr.** dec'd, **John CHURCH, Jonathan CHURCH, Ebenezer CHURCH, Mary ALLEN, Hannah VINSON, Abigail CHURCH, Bethiah CHURCH Jr., Earl CHURCH.** <30:232> 7 Nov. 1785, division sworn to; 2 Oct. 1787, division approved.

***

Will of **Bethiah CHURCH,** widow of Rochester MA. <Plymouth Co.PR 72:191>
...dated 14 Jan. 1821...to grandchildren **Joseph W. CHURCH & William H. CHURCH,** the land I hold by deed from my son **John CHURCH** dec'd...to **Benjamin F. CHURCH, Walter S. CHURCH & George W. CHURCH,** two shares in lot known by the stony noll & all cedar swamp I have purchased since my husband's death...to granddaughters **Abigail H. CHURCH & Sally CHURCH,** one feather bed & furniture; remainder of personal estate to son **Earl CHURCH,** executor. Pr. 2 May 1832.

Will of **Jonathan CHURCH**, yeoman of Rochester MA. <Plymouth Co.PR 48:141>
...dated 13 Apr. 1816, mentions wf **Sally** and following chil., viz: **Betsey HOWARD** wf of Charles, **Mary CHURCH, Lemuel CHURCH, Nathan CHURCH, Albert CHURCH, Jonathan CHURCH, Richard CHURCH**; son **Nathan**, executor. Pr. 19 July 1816; son declines & widow is app'td. Inventory ordered 2 May 1816.

Will of **Sarah CHURCH**, widow of Rochester MA. <Plymouth Co.PR 84:520>
...dated 18 Aug.1825, mentions following chil., viz: **Lemuel CHURCH, Nathan CHURCH, Richard CHURCH, Albert CHURCH, Jonathan CHURCH** (executor), **Elizabeth HOWARD** wf of Charles, **Mary LUMBARD** wf of Charles. Pr. 2 Nov. 1842.

Will of **Josiah STURTEVANT** of Halifax MA. <Plymouth Co.PR #19761>
<21:600>...dated 7 June 1768, mentions unnamed wife...to son **Josiah STURTEVANT**, 12 acres on Hemlock Island...to son **Charles STURTEVANT**, 10 acres on Hemlock Island...to sons **Dependence STURTEVANT & Samuel Stafford STURTEVANT**, 18 acres on Hemlock Island...to sons **Josiah, Charles, Church & William**, 4 lots at Miscongus containing 200 acres, also 60 acres at Jones River Pond...to sons **Josiah & Dependence**, all land & meadow above the dam on south side of Monponset Meadow Brook...to sons **Church STURTEVANT & William STURTEVANT**, rest of the 60 acre lot on Hemlock Island...to son **Church**, land joining cedar swamp & Austin BEARSE's land...to son **Samuel Stafford**, remainder of estate reserving to wife one third during widowhood...**William** to pay to **Zadock**, Ł4 and to granddaughter **Clare**, Ł4 when she is 18...**Samuel Stafford** to pay to dau **Hannah COTTEN**, Ł4...**Dependence** to pay to dau **Lucy HAMMON**, Ł4...**Church** to pay to dau **TILSON**, Ł4; son **Samuel Stafford**, executor. Witnesses: Ephraim BRIGGS, Nathaniel WATERMAN, Seth WATERMAN. <21:601> Letter 7 Mar. 1774, **Samuel Stafford STURTEVANT** app'td admr. <21:602> Bond 15 Aug. 1774, of admr. Sureties: Josiah COTTON, gent. of Plymouth & **Dependence STURTEVANT**, yeoman of Plympton. Witnesses: Penelope WINSLOW, Edward WINSLOW Jr.

Samuel SHERMAN of Rochester MA to **Richard CHURCH et al** of same. <Plymouth Co.Deeds 42:62>
...23 Mar. 1752, Samuel SHERMAN sells to Richard CHURCH & his sons Richard & Lemuel CHURCH... half of cedar & spruce swamp.

Will of **Richard CHURCH Jr.**, yeoman of Rochester MA. <Plymouth Co.PR #3977>
<original>...dated 1 May 1776, mentions one third of 40 acre lot bought of Ezra CLARK which my dwelling house stands...one third of 10 acre lot on east side of Mattapoiset River which was part of Joseph LOVELL's farm...to son **Charles CHURCH**, lot of land containing between 30-40 acres lying on ye southwest corner of my homestead, joining on Dartmouth Line, being ye lot on which my Father lately lived...provided my sd son **Charles** should die in ye Campaign in which he is now engaged & not return home again...to dau **Lois BENNET**, one third of the above mentioned 10 acre lot ...to youngest dau **Sarah CHURCH**, two thirds of house lot while unmarried...if my Father survives me he should have my wearing apparel; wife & Deacon Seth DEXTER, executors. Pr. 3 June 1776, Timothy RUGGLES app'td admr.

BRISTOL COUNTY DEEDS: (re: James BURROUGHS)

<1:97> - 29 Sept 1688, Benjamin CHURCH sells to James & Sarah BURROUGHS.
<1:251> - 30 July 1694, James & Anne BURROUGHS, he a tailor of Bristol, sell the land bought of Benjamin CHURCH back to him.
<1:341> - 13 Oct. 1694, James BURROUGHS, tailor of Bristol sells to John BIRGE, tailor of same, 150th part of 600 acres. Ack. 30 July 1695.

JOSEPH WARREN[2] (Richard[1])

Will of **Capt. Benjamin WARREN**, gent./yeoman of Plymouth MA. <Plymouth Co.PR #21858>
<10:301>...dated 8 May 1745...aged...mentions wf **Esther** and following chil., viz: **Nathaniel WARREN, Priscilla WARREN, Patience WARREN, Mercy WARREN, Benjamin WARREN** dec'd who left a son **Benjamin, Abigail RIDER** widow of Joseph, **Hannah FAUNCE** wf of Eleazer. Witnesses: Thomas FAUNCE Jr., James FAUNCE, Josiah MORTON. <10:303> Letter 8 July 1746, **Nathaniel WARREN**, yeoman of Plymouth, app'td admr. <10:304> Inventory taken Aug. 1746 by James WARREN, Solomon SILVESTER; total estate, Ł3231.11.4. <16:297> Dower set off to widow, 7 May 1762 by Benjamin CORNISH, Jeremiah HOWES, John BLACKMER.

MICRO #17 OF 32

Estate of **Joseph RIDER** of Plymouth MA. <Plymouth Co.PR>
<7:336> Letter 24 Sept. 1737, widow **Abigail RIDER** app'td admx. of estate of **Joseph RIDER "Jr."**. <7:379> Inventory taken 26 Dec. 1737. <10:175> Division, 14 Mar. 1745, to widow **Abigail** and following chil., viz: **William RIDER** (eldest son), **Joseph RIDER, Benjamin RIDER & Abigail.** <9:516> Account of admx., 22 May 1745.

Ebenezer DUNHAM of Mansfield CT to **Joseph RIDER Jr.** of Plymouth MA. <Plymouth Co.Deeds 15:198>
...9 Oct. 1721, Ebenezer DONHAM, blacksmith, for Ł105 sold to Joseph RIDER Jr., cordwainer...my dwelling house & shop & land...in the Town of Plymouth being about sixty feet front & seventy feet back...bounded by land in the occupation of James BARNABY and land of Nathaniel JACKSON,

Thomas SPOONER and the high way...being that house & land where I last dwelt in Plymouth with my shop standing by it. Witnesses: John TAYLOR, Francis ADAMS. Ack. 9 Oct. 1721. Rec. 14 Oct. 1721.

Joseph RIDER Jr. of Plymouth MA to **Seth JOYCE** of Marshfield. <Plymouth Co.Deeds 22:106>
...22 May 1727, Joseph RIDER Jr., seafayring man, for Ł190 sold to Seth JOYCE, husbandman...100 acres in Marshfield...50 acres of which I bought of Samuel GARDNER...8 Feb. 1713/14...and 50 acres given to me by ye last will & testament of Joseph WATERMAN of Marshfield dec'd...also one fourth part of the flatts in Greens Harbour that was in partnership between the sd Joseph WATERMAN & Kenelm WINSLOW which was given me also by ye sd will. Witnesses: Francis ADAMS, Thomas ADAMS. Ack. 27 Oct. 1727 by Joseph. Rec. 27 Oct. 1727.

Thomas SPOONER of Plymouth MA to **Joseph RIDER** of Newport. <Plymouth Co.Deeds 41:93>
...19 Mar. 1750, Thomas SPOONER, gent. sells to Joseph RIDER, housewright...two acres bought of Mrs. Abigail RIDER of Plymouth and bought by her from John HARLOW of Plymouth on 11 June 1741.

PLYMOUTH COUNTY DEEDS:

<78:101> - 1791, Joseph RIDER, housewright of Plymouth, buys land.
<83:270> - 1798, Martha RYDER, Jacob ALBERTSON & wf Lydia.
<84:224> - 1798, Martha RYDER, Jacob ALBERTSON & wf Lydia.

(The following references only may pertain to **Joseph RIDER**: 96:102, 10:629, 53:202.)

Estate of **Benjamin WARREN Jr.**, mariner of Plymouth MA. <Plymouth Co.PR #21859>
<8:177> Letter/Bond 26 Apr. 1740, widow **Rebecca WARREN** app'td admx. Sureties: Thomas WARREN, Isaac DOTEN. Witnesses: Elizabeth WITHERELL, Lucy DYER. <8:274> Inventory taken 28 May 1740, by Stephen CHURCHILL, Thomas SPOONER, Thomas FOSTER; incl. notes & bonds against Nathaniel WARREN, Josiah MORTON Jr., Edmund MORTON, Jonathan BARNES, Jonathan BARTLETT, Isaac DOTEN, John WINSLOW, Esq., Consider HOWLAND; personal estate only, total Ł278.2.9. <10:108> Account 24 Mar. 1745; Debts due from: Ebenezer COFFIN, Joseph WARREN, Thomas WITHERELL, Thomas HOWLAND, John FAUNCE, Capt. WATSON, Charles SAMPSON, Jona. BARTLETT, Josiah MORTON, Consider HOWLAND, Edmond MORTON, Ebenezer TINKHAM.

Will of **Sylvanus BRAMHALL** of Plymouth MA. <Plymouth Co.PR>
<25:210>...dated 19 Apr. 1778 at Lincoln MA...no details given. 1st Codicil (not dated), mentions his obligation to maintain the widow Elizabeth TOMPSON & orders wf **Mercy** to do it out of effects made over by sd Tompson. 2nd Codicil 19 Dec. 1778. <25:211> Pr. 5 Apr. 1779. <25:493> Inventory. <28:406> Division. <35:67> Account. <35:72> Order for distribution; Appeal. <36:426> Division of dower, 13 Sept. 1798, widow **Mercy** dec'd.

Seth HARLOW et al to John SHAW Jr. & George HAMMOND. <Plymouth Co.Deeds 55:264>
...23 Dec. 1769, Seth HARLOW, housewright & admr. to estate of Deacon Nathaniel WARREN of Plymouth dec'd; Silvanus BRAMHALL, cloathier & wf Mercy; Priscilla WARREN & Patience WARREN, spinsters; Benjamin WARREN, trader; Benjamin MORTON, mason & wf Hannah; Peleg FAUNCE, cordwainer & wf Mary; Amos DONHAM, cooper & wf Abigail; Josiah JOHNSON, blacksmith, in behalf of & as guardian to his two chil. Patience & Eleazer who are minors; Josiah JOHNSON Jr., blacksmith; William RYDER & Benjamin RYDER 3d, cordwainers; Lemuel HOLMES & wf Abigail...all of Plymouth...and Joseph RYDER, housewright of Newport RI, for Ł24 sold to John SHAW Jr. and George HAMMOND, yeomen of Plimpton ...the sixth share in the 17th Great Lot of Cedar Swamp...at South Meadows in Plimpton originally belonging to Capt. Benjamin WARREN of Plymouth...as rec. in the first Book of Proprietors of Plymouth p.255...Seth HARLOW as admr. sells two eighths, the following each sell one eighth: Silvanus BRAMHALL & wf, Priscilla WARREN, Patience WARREN, Benjamin WARREN, heirs of Hannah FAUNCE dec'd & Abigail RIDER dec'd. Esther WARREN, widow of Capt. Benjamin WARREN releases dower. Witnesses: John COTTON, Ichabod THOMAS, Paul DOTEN, Solomon ATWOOD, Mary COTTON. Ack. 27 Feb. 1770 by Benjamin & Hannah MORTON and Lemuel & Abigail HOLMES; 4 July 1772 by Joseph RIDER; 22/23 Dec. 1769 by rest. Rec. 3 Dec. 1771.

Estate of **Nathaniel WARREN**, gent. of Plymouth MA. <Plymouth Co.PR #21897>
<17:188> Letter 1 June 1767, Seth HARLOW app'td admr. <19:521> Inventory taken 4 June 1767 by John FINNEY, Benjamin CORNISH, Joseph WARREN; total estate, Ł749.1.4. <20:23> Petition of the children, that the small estate be settled on the widow and asks that enough real estate sold to pay debts; allowed 19 Jan. 1768. <20:24> Bond 1 Mar. 1768 for sale. Sureties: Ephraim SPOONER, Richard COOPER. Witnesses: Penelope WINSLOW, Edward WINSLOW Jr. <21:154> Warrant to divide, 22 June 1772, by Silvanus BARTLETT, John BLACKMER & Stephen DOTY of Plymouth; to the widow **Sarah WARREN** and the following heirs: **Abigail & Ruth WARREN** (minors), **Hannah LEONARD** wf of Philip, **Sarah HARLOW** wf of Seth and **Susannah HARLOW** wf of Ezra. <21:158> Account 7 July 1772; cash received from land sold to George HAMMOND, John BLACKMER, Philip LEONARD; Paid to: Seth WASHBURN, Thomas MORTON, Thomas LANMAN, Stephen SAMSON, Charles STOCKBRIDGE, William THOMAS, Josiah CHURCHILL, Daniel DIMAN, William WATSON, Benjamin RIDER, Jonathan DIMAN, Nathaniel BARTLETT, Thomas Southworth HOWLAND, Josiah MORTON, John ADAMS, Jonathan BISHOP, Pelham WINSLOW, Gershom HOLMES, Ebenezer SOUL, John BARTLETT, John CHURCHILL, John COTTON, Jeremiah HOLMES, John COTTON, Benjamin WARREN, Elizabeth BARTLETT, Thomas FOSTER, Samuel EDDY, Capt. WATSON, John FINNEY Jr., Samuel ELLIS, Nathaniel GOODWIN, Coll. WARREN, Ezekiel MORTON, Ebenezer DONHAM, William SARGEANT, Zacheus CURTIS, Ebenezer BARTLETT, Thomas TORREY, Nathaniel FOSTER, Patience WARREN, Priscilla WARREN, William WARREN, Joshua SWIFT, Ezekiel MORTON, Jeremiah HOWES, Silvanus BRAMHALL,

Timothy BOURNE, Benjamin CORNISH, Zacheus BARTLETT, Amaziah CHURCHILL, Peleg FAUNCE, Ebenezer CHURCHILL, William RIDER, Seth HARLOW, Edward WINSLOW, Esq., William MORTON, Gideon WHITE, Samuel PEARSE, Silvanus BARTLETT, John BLACKMER, Lemuel MORTON, Thomas TORREY, Stephen DOTY, Consider HOWLAND.

Guardianship of Children of **Nathaniel WARREN** of Plymouth MA. <Plymouth Co.PR #21853>
<21:139> Bonds 11 Apr. 1772, widow **Sarah WARREN** app'td gdn. of **Abigail WARREN & Ruth WARREN.** Sureties: Josiah MORTON, Jeremiah HOLMES. Witnesses: Edward WINSLOW, Sarah WINSLOW.

Nathaniel WARREN et al of Plymouth MA to **Ichabod MORTON** of same. <Plymouth Co.Deeds 79:139>
...22 Aug. 1758, Nathaniel WARREN, gent. & wf Sarah, Seth LUCE, housewright & wf Hannah and Ezekiel MORTON, yeoman & wf Abigail, for divers good causes & Ł3 sold to our brother Ichabod MORTON, yeoman...all rights in land in Plymouth...which our Honoured Mother Susanna MORTON by her deed... dated 18 Aug. 1758...sold to the sd Ichabod...also all our right...in real estate of which our Honoured father Capt. Ephraim MORTON dec'd dyed seized. Witnesses: Samuel BARTLETT, John PATY. Ack. 23 Aug. 1758 by all grantors. Rec. 17 May 1796.

Will of **Josiah FINNEY** of Plymouth MA. <Plymouth Co.PR; MD 20:97>
<original>...dated 2 Jan.1723, mentions sons **Robert FINNEY, Josiah FINNEY, John FINNEY & Joshua FINNEY** and daus **Elizabeth BRADFORD, Priscilla MARSHALL & Phebe FINNEY.** Pr. 2 Jan. 1726. Inventory taken 5 Jan. 1726/7.

Will of **Ephraim FINNEY**, master mariner of Plymouth MA. <Plymouth Co.PR 104:28>
...dated 23 May 1853, mentions son **Ephraim FINNEY** and daus **Harriet GARDNER** wf of Grenville, **Phebe DAVEE** wf of Johnson & **Susan SHAW** wf of James N.; house & lot in trust with Elkanah FINNEY Jr. for son Ephraim & children.

Josiah FINNEY of Plymouth MA to **Thomas JACKSON Jr.** of same. <Plymouth Co.Deeds 81:120>
...29 Sept. 1796, Josiah FINNEY, mariner, for Ł1.4s sold to Thomas JACKSON Jr., trader...all my right in salt meadow in Plymouth or Duxbury...on Salt house Beach near the Gurnet Creek being my whole right to a piece of meadow assigned my wife Else FINNEY in the division of the estate of my father Lemuel BARNES dec'd & grandfather William BARNES dec'd. Ack. & Rec. same day.

Daniel FINNEY et al of Plymouth MA to **Thomas JACKSON Jr.** of same. <Plymouth Co.Deeds 88:164>
...19 Mar. 1800, Daniel FINNEY, Ebenezer SAMSON & wf Susanna, Nathaniel SILVESTER & wf Else and Joseph HOLMES, all mariners, the sd Joseph being guardian of his dau Polly HOLMES, for $41.50 sold to Thomas JACKSON Jr., merchant...all rights in salt meadow in Plymouth adjoining the Gurnet Creek which was assigned to Else FINNEY wf of Josiah FINNEY both dec'd who was father & mother of sd Daniel, Susanna & Else and grandfather & grandmother of sd Polly...what we hereby sell is four sixths parts of all the salt meadow on both sides of sd Creek as assigned to sd Else FINNEY in the division of the real estate of her father Lemuel BARNES dec'd...the other two sixths of sd meadow sd Thomas purchased of our father Josiah FINNEY dec'd which decended to him from his two daughters Olive & Sally...also we sell four sixth parts of two acres of wood land on the north side of Lont pond & bounded by land of Charles JACKSON...the other two sixths now belongs to sd Thomas. Ack. 20 Mar. 1800 by Joseph HOLMES & Daniel FINNEY; 16 Apr. 1800 by Nathaniel SILVESTER, Ebenezer SAMSON, Susanna SAMSON & Else/Alsey SILVESTER. Rec. 16 Apr.1800.

Daniel FINNEY of Plymouth MA to **Isaac BARNES** of same. <Plymouth Co.Deeds 77:136>
...27 Jan. 1795, Daniel FINNEY, mariner, for Ł6 sold to Isaac BARNES, yeoman...all right in two pieces of land in Plymouth...being one sixth part of the same...which descended to me from my Mother Elles FINNEY late of Plymouth dec'd and was her Grandfather William BARNES' land and was assigned to her in the division of his estate...containing in the whole six acres...bounded by land of Thomas JACKSON, Esq. & William BARTLETT...also my share in...land lying near the sea shore below Training Green containing three quarters of an acre which was assigned my sd Mother in the division of sd William BARNES' estate lying in Plymouth, referance to sd division for the bounds of all the above said land & to the deeds which my sisters Olive, Susanna & Alice with their husbands gave to sd Isaac BARNES recorded in 77:76. Witnesses: Joshua THOMAS, Rosseter COTTON. Ack. & Rec. 27 Jan. 1795.

Estate of **Daniel GODDARD.** <Plymouth Co.PR #8590>
<12:108**C**> Petition for adm., Bond. <91:506> Inventory. <7:496**V**> Notice. <110:31> Account.

Estate of **Joseph WARREN** of Plymouth MA. <Plymouth Co.PR #21881>
<1:258> Letter/Bond 10 Mar. 1696/7, widow **Mehitable WARREN** app'td admx. Surety: William CLARK. Witnesses: Nathaniel MORTON, ( ) LeBARON. <original> Inventory of personal estate taken 27 Jan. 1696 by Thomas FAUNCE, Nathaniel THOMAS, William SHURTLEFF; total, Ł97.13.7. <original> Account of admx., 1709; to keeping my son **Joseph WARREN** from two till nine years old; to keeping my daughter **Presilla/Priscilla WARREN** from half a year old. <3:403.404> Inventory of real estate taken 20 June 1716 by Benjamin WARREN, Ebenezer HOLMES, Francis ADAMS; 50 acres lying by Sandwich where his widow now dwells. Division of real estate, 21 June 1716 between the two children **Joseph & Priscilla**, subject to widow's thirds. <original> Receipt 8 Mar. 1715/6, of son **Joseph WARREN** who receives his whole share of estate from Francis ADAMS his gdn. Witnesses: Peter BLACKMER, Thomas CROADE. Account of admx. (no date); Creditors: Josiah PHINNEY, John COTTON, Nathaniel THOMAS, William SHURTLEFF, William CLARK, John FEARING, Benjamin WARREN, Mr. MURDO, Richard COOPER, Mr. LOTHROP, Samuel CORNISH, Bennony (YOWU?), William BLACKMER, John COB, Nathaniel MORTON,

Ephraim MORTON, Anna WILDER, Dr. LeBARRON, Josiah PHINNEY, Elder FAUNCE; Total inventory, Ł97.13s 7d less debts paid, Ł37.3s11d, left Ł60.9s8d of which the widow's third was Ł20.3.2d, the son's share, Ł40.6s6d and the daughters' shares, Ł26.17s10d; the estate was credited with 7 years rent of the lands, Ł42; rent of lands at Namaskett, Ł1.4s; 2 years rent while in the executrixes hand, Ł9. (This appears to be the account of 1709.)

Guardianship of Children of **Joseph WARREN** of Plymouth MA. <Plymouth Co.PR #21886>
<2:66> Letter/Bond 21 Sept. 1705, Maj. John BRADFORD, uncle in law to sd minor, app'td gdn. of **Joseph WARREN**, under 14. Surety: Benjamin WARREN. Witnesses: James WARREN, Cornelius WALDO. <2: 116> Letter/Bond 30 Mar. 1709, Francis ADAMS of Plymouth app'td gdn. of **Joseph WARREN**, above 14. Surety: John FOSTER. Witnesses: Nathaniel THOMAS Jr., Nathaniel OTIS. <3:27> Letter/Bond 30 Mar. 1709, John FOSTER of Plymouth app'td gdn. of **Priscilla WARREN**, under 14. Surety: Francis ADAMS. Witnesses: Nathaniel THOMAS Jr., Nathaniel OTIS. <3:400> Release, 8 Mar. 1715/6, of **Joseph WARREN** to his gdn., Francis ADAMS. Witnesses: Peter BLACKMER, Thomas CROADE.

Will of **Joseph WARREN**, yeoman of Plymouth MA. <Plymouth Co.PR #21882>
<14:125>...dated 24 June 1754, mentions wf **Alletheah/Alathea** and following chil., viz: **Joseph WARREN** (eldest son), **William WARREN, Elizabeth NELLSON/NELSON, Mary SHEPPARD, Priscilla DREW;** grandson **William MORTON** (under 21); mentions lands in Plimouth, Wareham, Middleboro, Freetown. Witnesses: Josiah MORTON Jr., Seth MORTON, Thomas FOSTER. <14:129> Letter 3 May 1756, son **Joseph WARREN** app'td exr. <14:156> Inventory taken 12 May 1756 by Josiah MORTON, Joseph BARTLETT, Joshua SWIFT; total real estate, Ł1865.12.7.

Estate of **Joseph WARREN**, yeoman of Plymouth MA. <Plymouth Co.PR #21883>
<original> Bond 6 Sept. 1770, widow **Mercy WARREN** app'td admx. Sureties: James HOVEY, Ephraim SPOONER. Witnesses: Edward WINSLOW, Sarah WINSLOW. <original> Bond 10 Jan. 1771, **William WARREN** app'td admr. Sureties: Jeremiah HOLMES, Seth MORTON. Witnesses: Edward WINSLOW, William TRENHOLM. <20:455> Appointment 10 Jan. 1771, of **William WARREN** as admr., "on the 6th of Sept. 1770, adm. was granted to **Mercy WARREN** who soon after died". <20:477> Inventory taken 18 Jan. 1771 by Thomas FOSTER, Jeremiah HOLMES, Seth MORTON; mentions land near Eel River in Plimouth; total real estate, Ł1336.13.4. <21:326> Account 6 Sept. 1773; Paid to: Robert ROBERTS, William MORTON, Samuel N. NELSON, George WATSON, Mercy STEPHENS, William FISH, Jonathan CHURCHILL, Joseph MORTON, Cornelius WHITE, Eleazer STEPHENS, Elisha BISBY, Caleb ATWOOD, Seth LUCE, James WARREN, William WINSLOW, Ephraim LUCE, William Hall JACKSON, Eleazer BARTLETT, Dr. LeBARON Jr., Ezekiel MORTON, Joseph BARROW, Thomas TORREY, Ebenezer & Patience HOLMES, Nehemiah BRYANT, Seth MORTON, Josiah MORTON, Thomas JACKSON, Pelham WINSLOW, David BESSE, Thomas S. HOWLAND, Susannah MORTON, exrs. of Nathaniel GOODWIN, Ebenezer SILVESTER, Cornelius JONES, Ebenezer HARLOW, John DUNHAM, Caleb ATWOOD, Robert FINNEY, John WITHEREL, John RUSSEL, Jeremiah HOWES, John THOMAS, Frances ADAMS, Deacon BARTLETT, John BISHOP, Mercy HEDGE, Esq. COTTON, David SEARS; to cloathing delivered ye guardian Sylvanus BARTLETT to cloath the son **Joseph WARREN**; John BRIDGHAM, Silvanus BRAMHALL, Isaac BURBANK, Joshua BLACKWELL, Seth WASHBURN, Stephen SAMSON, Bartlett LeBARON, Dr. LeBARON, Samuel JACKSON, Thomas FOSTER, Dr. THOMAS, Seth HARLOW, Ebenezer BARTLETT, Thomas SPOONER, William WATSON, Ephraim SPOONER, John ADAMS, Dr. LOTHROP, Thomas S. HOWLAND, John WINSLOW, Benjamin RIDER, Priscilla WARREN, Thomas LANMAN. <28:477> Account allowed 3 Oct. 1782; Claims paid: Lemuel DREW, Sylvanus BRAMHALL, James CLARKE, Benjamin RIDER, Nehemiah ALLEN, Elkanah CUSHMAN, Benjamin MORTON, Jeremiah HOLMES, Isaac BURBANK.

Guardianship of Child of **Joseph WARREN** of Plymouth MA. <Plymouth Co.PR #21884>
<20:478> Letter/Bond 8 Feb. 1771, Silvanus BARTLETT app'td gdn. of **Joseph WARREN**, under 14. Surety: Ephraim SPOONER. Witnesses: Edward WINSLOW, Edward WINSLOW Jr. <31:75> Account 29 Oct. 1789; received from creditors: Deacon DIMAN, Stephen DOTEN Jr.; claims paid: John COTTON, William WESTON Jr., James WARREN, Esq., William CROMBIE, Seth MORTON; paid Deacon DIMAN towards your board; Solomon HOLMES. <31:242> Receipt 8 Apr. 1791 of Sylvanus BARTLETT for Ł40.3.1. from **Joseph WARREN** "in full for ye ballance due to me on my account of guardianship against ye sd Warren as settled with ye Judge of Probate, 29 Oct. 1789."

Guardianship of Child of **Joseph WARREN** of Plymouth MA. <Plymouth Co.PR #21885>
<26:339> Letter/Bond 9 Oct. 1779, Jonathan DIMAN of Plymouth app'td gdn. of **Joseph WARREN**, above 14, being chosen by sd minor. Sureties: William THOMAS, Daniel DIMAN. Witnesses: Isaac LOTHROP, Nathaniel LOTHROP.

Estate of **William WARREN**, yeoman of Plymouth MA. <Plymouth Co.PR #21907>
<37:459> Letter/Bond 14 Nov. 1793, Joseph Warren NELSON & Caleb MORTON app'td admrs. Sureties: Samuel N. NELSON, Thaddeus FAUNCE. Witnesses: Job RIDER, Priscilla NELSON. <33:510> Insolvency. <33:528> Inventory taken 28 Nov. 1793 by Ezekiel MORTON Jr., Thomas MORTON Jr., Ichabod MORTON; incl. 25 acres wood land owned with Mrs. ROE & Stephen DOTEN Jr., Ł10; 56 acres at Island Pond and one eighth part of a forge; total real estate, Ł343.2.8. <36:165> List of claims, 1 July 1794; Creditors: Dr. James THATCHER, Benjamin DREW, Dr. Lazarus LeBARON, Stephen SAMSON, Silvanus FINNEY, Elijah CHANDLER, Thomas BARTLETT Jr., Daniel HUNT, John HUNT, William MORTON 3d, Nathaniel HOLMES, Mason JOHNSON, Samuel JACKSON, estate of James HOVEY, Moses NICOLS, Caleb MORTON, Joseph Warren NELSON, Ezekiel MORTON, Bartholomew LeBARON, Capt. S.N. NELSON, Seth HARLOW, John COTTON, Joshua THOMAS, Nathaniel CLARK, Lemuel DREW of Liverpool N.S., Dr. Isaac WINSLOW, Nathaniel LEWIS, Dr. Nathaniel LOTHROP. <36:166> Dower set off, 3 Apr. 1794 to widow **Betty/Elizabeth WARREN**; one half of dwelling house & land near Eel River. <36:167> Account 28 Jan. 1799 of surviving exr., Joseph W. NELSON.

Estate of **Elizabeth WARREN**, widow of Plymouth MA. <Plymouth Co.PR #21865>
<34:204> Letter/Bond 30 Nov. 1799, Elkanah CUSHMAN, hair dresser of Boston app'td admr. Sureties: Isaac LeBARON, William LeBARON. Witnesses: Joseph CROSWELL, Isaac LOTHROP. <37:310> Inventory taken 2 Dec. 1799 by Ezekiel MORTON, Isaac LeBARON, Thomas MORTON Jr.; no real estate; total personal estate, $98.24. <37:311> Account 11 Sept. 1800; names the following: William CLARK, John CLARK, Samuel RYDER, Nathaniel RIPLEY, Thomas MORTON Jr., Lemuel DREW Jr., Andrew HOLMES, THACHER & HAYWARD, Ichabod MORTON, Elnathan HOLMES Jr., Mrs. COWEL, George BRAMHALL, Ebenezer LUCE, Caleb FINNEY, William HOLMES Jr., Sally BRAMHALL, Jeremiah HOLMES, Ezekiel MORTON, Isaac LeBARON, Silvanus BARTLETT, William LeBARON.

MICRO #18 OF 32

Will of **Capt. Levi LUCAS**, mariner of Plymouth MA. <Plymouth Co.PR #13357>
<45:375>...dated 14 Mar. 1814...I give all my personal estate to my kind & dutifull wife for the convenience & accommodation of our family, she paying my debts, if they do not exceed fifty dollars, for which I make other provision if they do exceed that sum...also I give my sd wife **Betsy** the whole use & improvement of all my real estate for the maintainance of herself and her children & mine so long as she shall remain my widow & keep it in reasonable repair. But if she marry again it is my will that then sd real estate decend & be distributed by law, as if I had made no will...if my debts shall exceed fifty dollars, they shall be discharged by sale of some part of my real estate; wf **Betsy**, executrix. Witnesses: James KENDALL, Zacheus BARTLETT, Ansel HOLMES Jr. <45:376> Letter/Bond 23 May 1814, widow **Betsey LUCAS** app'td exx. Sureties: Zaccheus BARTLETT, Esq & Ansel HOLMES Jr., mariner, both of Plymouth. Witnesses: Joshua THOMAS, Isaac LeBARON, Beza HAYWARD. <original> Petition 17 Mar. 1823, of son **Isaac J. LUCAS**, that no inventory or account had been presented by the exx. <original> Citation 17 Apr. 1823 to **Jeremiah MAYHEW** & wf **Betsey** the exx., to settle the estate. <57:223> Account of exx, **Betsey MAYHEW**, formerly the widow, 16 Apr. 1823; incl. $800.00 received by sale of house of dec'd.

Guardianship of Children of **Capt. Levi LUCAS** of Plymouth MA. <Plymouth Co.PR #13358>
<41:205> Letter/Bond 15 Mar. 1815, Benjamin DREW Jr., gent. of Plymouth app'td gdn. of **Isaac LUCAS**, above 14. Sureties: Lewis GOODWIN & William BRADFORD, mariners of Plymouth. <41:212> Letter/Bond 3 June 1815, Benjamin DREW Jr. app'td gdn. of **Levi LUCAS**, above 14. Sureties: Lewis GOODWIN & Joseph LUCAS, mariners of Plymouth. <41:219> Letter/Bond 12 July 1815, Barnabas OTIS, yeoman of Plymouth app'td gdn. of **Allen LUCAS**, above 14. Sureties: Benjamin DREW Jr., Joseph LUCAS.

PLYMOUTH COUNTY DEEDS: (re: LUCAS)

<146:186> - 1825, Allen LUCAS to George PERKINS Jr.
<207:191> - 10 Feb. 1843, Levi LUCAS of E. Bridgewater to Isaac J. LUCAS of Plymouth, his share in real estate as one of heirs of Lydia COTTON, widow of Plymouth dec'd
<214:169> - 1845, Allen LUCAS of New Bedford, Dolly LUCAS et al, heirs of Lydia COTTON late of Plymouth, sell to Isaac J. LUCAS of Plymouth.
<260:151> - 1854, Levi LUCAS et al, Trustees of 1st Univ. Church in E. Bridgewater.
<272:143> - 1856, Levi LUCAS of Bridgewater, grantor.
<286:120> - 8 Mar. 1858, Allen LUCAS of New Bedford to Louisa R. LUCAS of E. Bridgewater, land in E. Bridgewater. Wf Deborah releases dower. Rec. 11 Mar. 1858.

Will of **Abijah LUCAS** of Carver MA. <Plymouth Co.PR #13314>
<80:466>...dated 18 Apr. 1831...have divided principal part in life among my children, viz: **Hosea LUCAS, Abijah LUCAS, Harvey LUCAS, Martin L. LUCAS, Rebecca SEARS, Polly COBB, Abigail LUCAS,** therefore they get nothing personal; to wife **Ruth**, half the improvement of the farm; wf exx. <1:336G> Bond 3 Dec. 1838, of widow **Ruth LUCAS**, exx.

Abijah LUCAS of Carver MA to **Hosea LUCAS** of same. <Plymouth Co.Deeds 111:202>
...4 Jan. 1810, Abijah LUCAS, yeoman, for $420.00 sold to Hosea LUCAS, yeoman...14 acre house lot, house & meadow...except Zilpah LUCAS has a right to live in the house and to git apples to eat out of the orchard. Wf Mary releases dower. Witnesses: Edmund SEARS, Rebecca SEARS. Rec. 6 Jan. 1810.

PLYMOUTH COUNTY DEEDS: (re: Abijah LUCAS)

<110:273> - 1810, Abijah LUCAS et al, division.
<134.115> - 25 May 1818, Abijah LUCAS, gent. of Carver to son Hosea LUCAS, yeoman of same.
<152:249> - 1818, Abijah LUCAS to Edmund SEARS.
<134:262> - 1819, Abijah LUCAS to Abijah LUCAS Jr.

MARY WARREN[2] (Richard[1])

Robert BARTLETT of Plymouth to **John ALMY** of Portsmouth RI. <Plymouth Col.Deeds 3:328>
...8 Mar. 1668, Robert BARTLETT, cooper, for Ł3 sells to John ALMY, merchant...his interest in the 24th lot at "Punck.".

Robert BARTLETT of Plymouth to **Thomas BURGE Jr.** of Newport RI. <Plymouth Col.Deeds 5:118>
...17 Feb. 1670, Robert BARTLETT, cooper, for Ł50 silver money sells to Thomas BURGE Jr...half his share of land at Acushena in Dartmouth, also one half of a share at Pascamansucke(sp) in Dartmouth, reserving one third part of the last named share...which sd severall shares of land are a parte of the Purchasers land, my selfe being one of the sd Purchasers.

Robert BARTLETT of Plymouth to **James BARNABY** of same. <Plymouth Col.Deeds 3:297>
...14 July 1670, Robert BARTLETT, wine cooper to son in law James BARNABY, cordwinder & dau Lydia BARNABY his wf...20 acres on southerly side of Eel River...which was sometimes the lot of Richard CHURCH Sr. dec'd and by mee purchased of the sd, my brother in law, Richard CHURCH...also four acre upland meadow called Sandwich meadow.

Estate of **Thomas BARTLETT**, minor. <Plymouth Co.PR>
<51:250> 1824. <65:467;73:148;77:560> 1835. <79:85> 1837, gdn. <80:454> 1838.

PLYMOUTH COUNTY PROBATE: (re: BARTLETT)

1697	Benjamin	Duxbury		#1236, 1:113,114,115,135
1697/8	Ebenezer	Duxbury		#1259, 1:288
1703	Joseph	Plymouth		#1321, 2:20,52;3:262,264
1704	Joseph et al	Plymouth		#1322, 2:46,68,83;3:300;4:152
1711	Joseph	Plymouth		#1315, 3:105,106,173,175,178
1713	Samuel	Duxbury		#1368, 3:255,291-294,296
1714	Elnathan	Plymouth		#1265, 3:334,349,350
1714	Elizabeth et al	Duxbury		#1262, 3:298,299,300
1716	Ichabod	Duxbury		#1293, 3:456;4:50,51,52
1717	Nathaniel et al	Duxbury	gdn.	#1354, 3:457,458,459,460,461
1717	William	Duxbury		#1396, 4:1
1718	Benjamin	Plymouth		#1239, 4:146,174,175;6:394
1718	Robert	Plymouth		#1364, 4:90,91,175,205,441
1720	Robert et al	Plymouth	gdn.	#1365, 4:220,222
1724	James	Plymouth		#1297, 4:446;5:83,173
1726	Joseph et al	Plymouth	gdn.	#1324,
1727	Benjamin	Duxbury		#1237, 5:354,569,570
1727	Hannah & Elnathan	Plymouth	gdn.	#1284, 5:237
1732	Nathaniel	Duxbury		#1353, 6:264,265,321,377;7:110
1741	Elnathan	S.Plymouth		#1266, 8:364,366,401
1751	Samuel	Plymouth		#1371, 12:71,455
1755	Benjamin Jr.	Plymouth		#1241, 13:469,521,522;14:242,243
1756	Joseph	Plymouth		#1316, 14:121,124,125
1760	Joseph Jr.	Plymouth		#1317
1760	Benjamin	Plymouth		#1240, 15:512;16:11;19:83
1764	Thomas	Plymouth		#1389, 19:131,134,268
1769	Samuel	Plymouth		#1372, 20:204,250;27:535;33:532;35:291;36:398
1773	Charles	Plymouth		#1244, 22:151
1773	John	Plymouth		#1302, 21:232,234;27:524;31:456,459
1776	Nathaniel	Plymouth		#1348, 23:82;24:109;29:483;35:202,204
1780	Samuel	Plymouth		#1373, 25:491-93;27:501;29:154;31:236,319,356
1782	Jonathan	Plymouth	gdn.	#1310, 26:387
1782	Thankful	Plymouth		#1387, 28:278,279;48:114
1783	Joseph	Plymouth		#1318, 29:59,61
1783	Joseph	Kingston		#1313, 27:125;28:408,409,410,411;29:315
1783	Jonathan	Plymouth		#1311, 27:113;33:317
1785	Samuel et al	Plymouth	gdn.	#1374, 26:189,426
1788	Joseph	Kingston		#1314, 27:286;30:515;31:93;33:433;35:123,124
1790	John Jr.	Plymouth		#1306, 27:335;31:306,308,461;33:516;35:92
1792	Charles	Plymouth		#1245, 27:393;33:85,427
1792	Lemuel	Plymouth		#1328, 27:411;33:426;36:22
1793	Jonathan	Plymouth		#1312, 27:428,539;33:315,316,528,529,562
1794	Lysander et al	Kingston	gdn.	#1340, 26:291
1793	Elizabeth	Plymouth		#1261, 27:437;33:530,531;35:292;44:184
1798	Caleb	Plymouth		#1243, 34:169;37:32,489
1798	Lois & Sarah	Plymouth	gdn.	#1333, 32:98
1800	Ephraim Jr.	Plymouth		#1267, 34:258
1802	Nathaniel	Plymouth	adm.	#1349, 34:362
1804	George	Plymouth	adm.	#1278, 34:386
1805	Margaret	Plymouth	adm.	#1341, 39:34
1807	Joshua	Plymouth	adm.	#1325, 39:214
1808	James	Plymouth	adm.	#1298, 39:150;42:328;43:61,62;115:177;116:34;108:80;117:24;118:42
1809	Andrew	Plymouth	adm.	#1227, 39:175;42:475-6,510;43:242;45:492;63:176
1811	Mary	Plymouth	will	#1342, 43:365,366,374
1811	Sylvanus	Plymouth	adm.	#1385, 39:329;44:70,71,179,395;48:158,160;44:184
1812	Hannah	Plymouth	gdn.	#1281, 41:106;44:183,184
1813	Abner	Plymouth	adm.	#1222, 45:180,181,317,432,514;46:6;48:474

PLYMOUTH COUNTY PROBATE, cont-d: (re: BARTLETT)

1814	Francis et ali	Plymouth	gdn.	#1270, 41:177
1814	John Jr.	Kingston	adm.	#1301, 46:21
1814	John	Plymouth	will	#1303, 45:362,363,517,518
1815	Dorothy	Plymouth	adm.	#1258, 46:113;47:272
1816	Dolly & Polly	Plymouth	gdn.	#1257, 41:247;48:29
1816	Isaac	Kingston	adm.	#1296, 46:198;48:402;57:184,535;63:258;64:421
1816	William	Plymouth	adm.	#1397, 46:151;48:116,117,332,547;49:49;80:518
1817	Sylvanus et ali	Plymouth	gdn.	#1386, 41:317
1818	Uriah	Kingston	will	#1393, 49:381,382,406;53:97,139
1819	Peleg	Kingston	adm.	#1359, 46:314;50:163-4;53:94-5,97,140,181-2;54:309,380,486
1822	Joseph T.et al	Plymouth	gdn.	#1323, 51:150,152;54:309,310
1822	Solomon	Plymouth	adm.	#1381, 52:117
1824	Francis D.et al	Kingston	gdn.	#1271, 51:230;64:422
1824	Thomas	Plymouth	gdn.	#1390, 51:250;65:467;73:148;77:560;79:85;80:454
1824	Thomas M.	Plymouth	adm.	#1391, 52:281;55:225;58:295
1825	Lemuel	Plymouth	adm.	#1329, 52:389;59:351,352,479
1825	Melatiah	Plymouth	adm.	#1345, 52:407;59:541;60:187;62:30;63:184;67:84
1826	Ansel	Plymouth	adm.	#1232, 61:14;63:177;67:442
1826	Lydia	Plymouth	adm.	#1338, 61:41;62:120;63:147,423
1827	Bradford	Rochester	will	#1242, 64:290
1827	Henry 2d	Plymouth	adm.	#1290, 61:84
1832	Oren	Plymouth	gdn.	, 65:255;84:612
1833	Ephraim 2d	Plymouth	adm.	#1268, 71:127;74:20,182,477;76:356
1833	John E.	Plymouth	adm.	#1307, 71:129;74:56
1833	Lewis et ali	Plymouth	sale	#1332, 73:420;74:559 (of real estate)
1835	Amasa	Plymouth	will	#1225, 77:101;75:196
1835	Joseph	Plymouth	adm.	#1319, 71:284;73:127;77:87
1835	Joseph	Plymouth	will	#1320, 71:463;75:274;77:127,180,183;78:317,522,544;82:18,19
1835	Stephen	Plymouth	adm.	#1382, 71:307;73:139;77:187,188,412;78:324
1836	Edward et al	Plymouth	gdn.	#1260, 65:452;73:482
1836	Zacheus	Plymouth	will	#1403, 78:10;101:385
1838	Lucia W.	Plymouth	gdn.	#1334, 8:101**L**;80:522
1838	Paran et al	Plymouth	gdn.	#1357, 1:65**R**;2:372**O**;8:83**L**
1838	William 3d	Plymouth	adm.	#1398, 10:162**A**;80:121,491,520
1839	Asa	Wareham	adm.	#1234, 5:151**T**;10:262**A**;81:208,587-8;82:173
1839	Asa et ali	Wareham	gdn.	#1235, 1:277**R**;3:396**P**;8:161**L**;82:95,178;91:277
1840	John	Plymouth	gdn.	#1304, 8:162**L**
1842	James	Middleboro	adm.	#1300, 11:33**B**;84:81,196
1843	Daniel W. et al	Hingham	gdn.	#1254, 1:180**R**;2:500**O**;8:339**L**
1843	Samuel	Plymouth	gdn.	#1370, 8:312**L**
1844	Cynthia	Plymouth	will	#1251, 6:566**U**;10:533**A**;86:13,573
1844	Elkanah	Plymouth	adm.	#1263, 11:227**B**;88:14,44
1844	Hannah	Plymouth	gdn.	#1282, 6:528**U**;8:505,506**L**;98:171
1845	James	Plymouth	adm.	#1299, 7:34**V**;11:349**B**;90:531
1845	Thankful	Plymouth	will	#1388, 2:49**H**;87:357;88:37
1846	Frank et al	Plymouth	gdn.	#1272, 9:60,182**M**;88:48;91:315;97:147
1847	Charles	Plymouth	gdn	#1246, 3:48**P**;7:205**V**;8:539,540**L**;89:143
1847	Hosea	Plymouth	adm.	#1292, 3:84**P**;7:395**V**;11:566**B**;90:533
1847	Rufus	Plymouth	adm.	#1366, 3:51**P**;7:196**V**;11:476**B**;89:142;90:29
1847	Susan	Plymouth	will	#1384, 2:125**H**;7:279**V**;89:223,517,518
1848	Freeman	Plymouth	adm.	#1276, 7:317**V**;11:574**B**;90:80;91:40
1848	Harriet W.	Plymouth	adm.	#1286, 7:417**V**;11:618**B**;90:530
1848	Rebecca	Plymouth	gdn.	#1361, 1:11**K**;1:459,540**R**;3:539**P**;4:283**Q**;96:369
1849	Mary	Plymouth	adm.	#1343, 7:530**V**;12:79**C**;91:314;95:164;98:168
1849	Sarah T.	Plymouth	adm.	#1377, 7:514**V**;12:113**C**;91:422
1849/50	Charles	Westbrook ME	will	#1248, 92:321
1850	Flavel	Plymouth	adm.	#1269, 8:43**W**;12:157**C**;92:369

Thomas BARTLETT of Plymouth to **Joseph & Thomas BARTLETT** of same. <Plymouth Co.Deeds 49:166> ...10 Sept. 1764, Thomas BARTLETT, yeoman, for & in consideration of the love affection & good will I bear to my two nephews Joseph the son of Joseph BARTLETT & Thomas the son of Ebenezer BARTLETT...Witnesses: Thomas FOSTER, Ebenezer BARTLETT. Ack. same day.

PLYMOUTH COUNTY DEEDS: (re: BARTLETT)

<62:17> - 25 Mar. 1783, Thomas BARTLETT, yeoman of Plymouth, son of Ebenezer BARTLETT dec'd, sells land received of father on 20 Mar. 1782.

<62:55> - 10 Apr. 1783, Thomas BARTLETT, cordwainer & Joseph BARTLETT Jr., shoreman, both of Plymouth, sell to Cornelius DUNHAM, land on south side of land sold same day to Silvanus BARTLETT, yeoman of Plymouth <62:56>.

<62:56> - 14 Apr. 1783, Silvanus BARTLETT, yeoman of Plymouth sells land received from father Joseph BARTLETT of Plymouth dec'd.

PLYMOUTH COUNTY DEEDS, cont-d: (re: BARTLETT)

<62:274> - 31 Oct. 1783, Joseph & Thomas BARTLETT, yeomen of Plymouth sell pew in upper meeting house that was their uncle's, Thomas BARTLETT. Molly wf of Joseph signs.
<62:273> - 4 Nov. 1783, Joseph & Thomas BARTLETT, yeomen of Plymouth sell rights in lands given them by will of their uncle Lemuel MORTON dec'd, being part of homestead of Thomas MORTON dec'd. Mary wf of Joseph releases dower.
<62:226> - 27 July 1784, Thomas BARTLETT, cordwainer of Plymouth sells land given him by will of his uncle Thomas BARTLETT of Plymouth dec'd.
<62:274> - 13 Dec. 1784, Joseph & Thomas BARTLETT, yeomen of Plymouth sell land given them by will of uncle Lemuel MORTON. Mary wf of Joseph releases dower.
<65:128> - 9 Feb. 1786, Thomas BARTLETT & Thomas BARTLETT Jr., yeomen of Plymouth sell to Thomas SAVERY, housewright of Plympton. Sarah wf of Thomas Jr. releases dower.
<76:41> - 8 Mar. 1786, Thomas BARTLETT Jr., yeoman of Plymouth sells part of homestead of Thomas BARTLETT dec'd near Double Brook. Wf Sarah releases dower.
<65:182> - 24 Apr. 1786, Joseph BARTLETT, gent. & Thomas BARTLETT, cordwainer, both of Plymouth sell house & land set off by execution to Deacon Joseph BARTLETT dec'd & the sd Joseph & Thomas from Ephraim BARTLETT, saving rights of dower of Elizabeth, widow of sd Ephraim. Mary wf of Joseph releases dower.
<66:179> - 22 July 1786, Execution against Joseph BARTLETT, son of Deacon Joseph BARTLETT dec'd.
<69:224> - 5 Nov. 1789, Execution against Sylvanus BARTLETT, laborer of Plympton.
<69:202> - 6 June 1789, Ex. against Joseph & Thomas BARTLETT "eerswill" Joseph BARTLETT dec'd.
<68:130> - 30 June 1788, Silvanus BARTLETT & wf Martha sell land bought of Samuel BARTLETT, Esq. on 3 May 1762.
<68:263> - 3 Oct. 1789, Joseph & Thomas BARTLETT, shoremen, for Ŀ40 sell to Joseph BARTLETT, gent. of Woburn, rights in real estate of their father Joseph BARTLETT late of Plymouth dec'd.
<67:227> - 24 Apr. 1788, Silvanus BARTLETT & wf Martha.
<69:232> - 24 Apr. 1788, Sylvanus BARTLETT, yeoman & Zaccheus BARTLETT, gent. of Plymouth; division of land bequeathed by late Joseph BARTLETT to his sd son Sylvanus.
<69:133> - 7 Apr. 1789, Execution against Joseph BARTLETT, gent. & Thomas BARTLETT, cordwainer, heirs of Joseph BARTLETT dec'd.
<69:233> - Apr. 1789, Sylvanus BARTLETT, yeoman of Plympton & wf Sarah to father Silvanus BARTLETT, yeoman of Plymouth.
<69:96> - 6 June 1789, Execution against Joseph & Thomas BARTLETT, heirs of Deacon Joseph BARTLETT dec'd.
<69:225> - 16 Nov. 1789, Execution against Sylvanus BARTLETT, yeoman against Joseph BARTLETT, gent. & Thomas BARTLETT, cordwainer, all of Plymouth, exrs. to will of Joseph BARTLETT, gent. late of Plymouth dec'd.
<69:234> - 3 Feb. 1790, Execution against estate of Joseph BARTLETT dec'd; Joseph & Thomas BARTLETT admrs., took land bought by sd Joseph dec'd of Jonathan BARNES on 30 Dec. 1734.
<75:252> - June 1791, Joseph & Thomas BARTLETT, yeoman of Plymouth sell undivided half of land which their uncle Thomas BARTLETT & Joseph WARREN bought of Samuel BARTLETT, Esq. on 13 Jan. 1741 & rec. 34:217. Polly wf of Joseph releases.
<83:185> - 20 Dec. 1793, Silvanus BARTLETT, yeoman & wf Martha and Mary TORREY, spinster, both of Plymouth to Jesse BARTLETT, tanner of Plymouth, one eighth acre formerly belonging to Deacon Haviland TORREY. Rec. 11 Nov. 1795.
<76:75> - 20 Dec. 1793, Joseph BARTLETT, yeoman & Thomas BARTLETT, cordwainer, both of Plymouth, sold land taken by execution 10 Jan. 1771 by their father from Zacheus CHURCHILL grandson of Stephen CHURCHILL.
<75:141> - 1 Apr. 1794, Thomas BARTLETT Jr., yeoman of Plymouth sells part of homestead given him by his uncle Thomas BARTLETT dec'd on Double Brook. Wf Sarah signs.
<77:71> - 28 June 1794, George WATSON, Esq. & Silvanus BARTLETT, yeoman of Plymouth, sold land they had purchased together.
<77:143> - 25 Aug. 1794, Thomas BARTLETT Jr., yeoman of Plymouth & wf Sarah, sold his dwelling house & barn & rights in land at Eel River near Double Brook.
<83:185> - 1797, Silvanus BARTLETT, yeoman to son Jesse BARTLETT, tanner. Wf Martha signs
<85:240> - 25 May 1799, Silvanus BARTLETT, yeoman of Plymouth to dau Sophia DREW wf of Benjamin Jr., cordwainer of Plymouth. Witnesses: Rosseter COTTON, Martha BARTLETT
<85:251> - 31 Aug. 1799, Silvanus BARTLETT, yeoman of Plymouth to dau Martha BARTLETT, single woman of same, for life reserving rights for himself & his now married wife for their lives.

(References only to the surname **BARTLETT**: 66:174;66:175,176,177,178,180;67:16;68:161,162;70:12, 102;71:240;72:277;73:213,236;74:162;80:25)

PLYMOUTH COLONY DEEDS: (re: BARTLETT)

<4:2:281> - 21 Jan. 1678, Benjamin BARTLETT Sr. of Duxbury to Seth POPE. Wf Sissillia consents.
<4:2:284> - 4 Aug. 1679, Sarah WARREN, widow of Nathaniel (mentions his mother Elizabeth WARREN) to Joseph BARTLETT.
<4:2:364> - 7 July 1680, Joseph BARTLETT to Seth POPE, land at Dartmouth.

Robert STANDFORD/STANFORD of Plimouth MA to **Hugh COLE Jr.** of Swanzey. <Bristol Co.Deeds>
...30 Aug. 1697, Robert STANDFORD, yeoman & wf Rebecca, for Ŀ7 sold to Hugh COLE Jr., yeoman...

my two lotts of land at a place commonly called Mattapoyset on the westerly side of Taunton River or Titticutt River...known by the name of Bartletts lotts the 9th & 13th...given to me...by her brother Benjamin BARTLET Jr. son & heire to Benjamin BARTLET Sr....bounded by 8th lot of Joseph CHANDLER, 10th lot of John TISDALE, 12th lot of John HOWLAND and 14th lot of John COGGESHALL. Witnesses: Henry CHURCHILL, John COLE, John GRAY. Ack. 2 Sept. 1697 by grantors & Rec. 14 Sept.

Estate of **William BARTLET** of Duxbury MA. <Plymouth Co.PR #1396>
<4:1> Inventory taken 12 Jan. 1716/7 by James PARTRIDGE & John WADSWORTH; incl. lands & meadows, L65; dwelling house, ₤80; sworn to 26 Apr. 1717 by admx. <4:1> Letter 26 Apr. 1717, widow **Sarah BARTLET** app'td admx.

Estate of **Ebenezer BARTLET** of Duxborough MA. <Plymouth Co.PR #1259>
<1:288> Letter/Bond 22 Mar.1697/8, widow **Hannah BARTLETT** app'td admx. Sureties: Samuel BARTLET of Duxbury & John BRYANT Sr. of Plymouth. Witnesses: John TRASIE/TRACY & John SPRAGUE. <1:288> Inventory taken 1 Mar. 1698 by Samuel BARTLET, William BREWSTER, John SPRAGUE; incl. houses, lands & meadows, ₤100; half a shallop with one half a new mainsail, ₤50; 6s owed the estate by Jacob SHANTOM.

Ebenezer BARTLETT of Duxbury MA to **Thomas DELANO Jr.** of same. <Plymouth Co.Deeds 14:37>
...11 July 1717, Ebenezer BARTLETT, yeoman sells to Thomas DELANO Jr., blacksmith...one half of farm on which sd DELANO dwells, all land which belonged to my brother Nathaniel BARTLETT of sd Duxbury late dec'd. <14:51>...8 Aug. 1717 Ebenezer sells to Thomas, one half part of sd farm.

Thomas DELANO Jr. of Duxbury MA to **Ebenezer BARTLETT.** <Plymouth Co.Deeds 18:75>
...18 Feb. 1719/20, Thomas DELANO Jr., blacksmith & wf Hannah sell to Ebenezer BARTLETT...one half of that farm of land in sd Dubury whereon ye sd Thomas DELANO & Hannah his wife now dwell ...which was formerly ye farm of Ebenezer BARTLETT late of Duxbury dec'd. <18:74>...18 Aug. 1724, Thomas sold the other half to Ebenezer.

MICRO #19 OF 32

Estate of **Capt. Joseph BARTLETT**, mariner of Kingston MA. <Plymouth Co.PR #1313>
<originals> Request 14 June 1783, that the eldest son **Joseph BARTLETT** be app'td admr. Bond 24 June 1783 of **Joseph BARTLETT**, mariner as admr. Sureties: Peleg WADSWORTH & Ephraim SPOONER of Plymouth. Witnesses: William THOMAS, Zacheus HARLOW. <27:125> Letter 25 June 1773, **Joseph BARTLETT** app'td admr. <28:408> Inventory taken 30 June 1783 by John DREW, Benjamin COOKE & John GRAY, all of Kingston; incl. dwelling house & land; land on way leading toward Bridgewater; land purchased of John SIMMONS; sworn to 4 July 1783 by appraiser & 7 July by admr. <28:409> Dower 2 Aug. 1783, widow **Sarah BARTLETT** quits claim to her dower to the chil. of her husband, viz: **Joseph BARTLETT** (eldest son), **Uriah BARTLETT** (2d son), **John BARTLETT** (3d son) & **Dorothy DREW** (eldest dau) wf of William, all of Kingston and **Elizabeth FOSTER** (youngest dau) & wf of Robert of Lunenburg Nova Scotia. Witness: Jabez FULLER. <28:410> 1st Account 7 Apr. 1784; Paid to: exx. of estate of John THOMAS, William DREW, Wrestling BREWSTER, Uriah BARTLETT, Abijah DREW, Jershom COBB, Job DREW, James DREW, Mercy WASHBURN; admr. of estate of Thaddeus RANSOM; John ADAMS, Sylvanus COOK, Jabez WASHBURN, Judah WASHBURN, Col. BRADFORD, Charles FOSTER. 2nd Account 3 May 1784; Paid to: the widow to purchase her thirds of the real estate, John BARTLETT, Dr. Jabez FULLER, Francis ADAMS. <28:411> Division 4 June 1784 by John ADAMS, John GRAY & Benjamin COOK, all of Kingston; divided into six equal parts to the five children (the eldest receiving double). <29:315> 3d Account of admr., 1 Aug. 1785; Paid to: Bildad ARNOLD, Amos COOK, Joseph HOLMES, Mary MITCHELL, Elisha BREWSTER.

Estate of **Uriah BARTLETT** of Kingston MA. <Plymouth Co.PR #1393>
...1818...<49:381,382,406;53:97,139> (no details given)

Estate of **Capt. Joseph BARTLETT**, mariner of Kingstn MA. <Plymouth Co.PR #1314>
<27:286> Letter/Bond 1 Dec. 1788, Seth DREW, gent. of Kingston app'td admr. Sureties: John FAUNCE yeoman of Kingston & Thomas GANNET, gent. of Plymton. Witnesses: Timothy HAYWARD, I. LOTHROP. <30:515> Inventory taken 29 Jan. 1789 by William DREW, John ADAMS & Isaac BREWSTER, all of Kingston; 28 acres with house & barn; sworn to 28 Feb. 1789 by appraisers & 2 Mar. 1789 by admr. <31:93> 1st Account 7 Dec. 1789; Due from: Uriah BARTLETT, James CUSHMAN, John BARTLETT, Benjamin JEPSON of Boston, estate of John STANDISH dec'd; Paid to: Jedediah HOLMES, Josiah COOK, Samuel STETSON, John WASHBURN, John ADAMS Jr., Rev. WILLIS, Ebenezer DREW, Isaiah THOMAS, Clement DREW. <33:433> 2nd Account of admr., 7 Oct. 1793; to first dividing John STANDISH's estate; received of Benjamin A. JEPSON of Boston; cash advanced to widow **Lurana BARTLETT;** funeral charges of **Ichabod BARTLETT**, one of the heirs; paid taxes to Seth SPRAGUE of Duxbury, Samuel CHANDLER, Jacob FISH of Kingston for 1789, James CUSHMAN for 1790, Amos COOK for 1791; paid Bill VOSE of Boston for wharfage; paid Seth CUSHING, Josiah WEST, John PADDOCK and allowance to widow for support of her son **Charles** in his infancy. <35:123> Dower assigned 29 Jan. 1794, by John GRAY, John ADAMS Jr. & Zenas DREW, to widow **Lurania/Lurana BARTLETT.** <35:124> Warrant to divide real estate, 29 Jan. 1794, among following chil., viz: **Joseph BARTLETT** (eldest son), **Seth BARTLETT, Lysander BARTLETT, Charles BARTLETT, Lurania & Sarah.**

Will of **Josiah BARTLETT** of Lebanon CT. <no source>
...dated 14 Jan. 1748/9, mentions wf **Mercy** & following chil., viz: **Ichabod BARTLETT** (to have L50 more than Nathaniel & Charles), **Nathaniel BARTLETT, Chandler BARTLETT** (under 21), **John BARTLETT**

(under 21, apprenticed), **Betty** (apparently married), **Mercy BARTLETT & Molly BARTLETT** (both under 18). Witnesses sworn 1 Apr. 1782. Pr. 1 Apr. 1782. Inventory 6 Apr. 1782. Receipts of heirs: 8 Apr. 1782 of **John BARTLETT**; 10 Apr. 1782 of **Peleg & Molly THOMAS** and **Patrick & Mercy BUTLER.**

References to the name **Chandler BARTLETT**, grantee in Lebanon CT Deeds: 15:124-129.

Will of **Patrick BUTLER** of Lebanon CT. <Windham CT PR 16:197>
...dated 3 Aug. 1813, mentions wf **Marcy/Mercy** and the following chil., viz: **Patrick BUTLER** (now in a declining state), **John BUTLER** ($1.00) and three youngest chil. **Molly, James & Henrietta** Wf **Mercy** & John GILES, executors. Witnesses: John SHAPLEY, Delight BARTLETT, Hannah SHAPLEY. Letter/Bond 6 Sept. 1813, John GILES app'td admr. Witnesses: Lucy RIPLEY, Henry F. DEWEY. (widow **Mercy BUTLER** declines, 29 Sept. 1813). Inventory taken 21 Sept. 1813; total, $1151.75.

LEBANON CT DEEDS: (re: BUTLER, grantors)

<2:530> - 1715, Peter BUTLER & wf Mary.
<5:391> - 1736, Malachi BUTLER.
<6:54> - 1739, Malachi BUTLER.
<6:128> - 1739, Malachi BUTLER.
<6:182> - 1740, Malachi BUTLER.
<8:13> - 1751/2, Malachi BUTLER.
<8:81> - 1753, Malachi BUTLER.
<20:439> - 1811, Patrick BUTLER to Charles WILLIAMS, land in Exeter Society.
<21:250> - 1811, Patrick BUTLER to John SHAPLEY, land near my house in Exeter Society, being part of land bought of Jared HINCKLEY.

(re: BUTLER, grantees**)**

<1:95> - 1713, James BUTLER.
<2:456> - 1714, Peter BUTLER.
<5:104> - 1734/5, Malachi BUTLER.
<5:246> - 1735/6, Malachi BUTLER.
<6:163> - 1739, Malachi BUTLER.
<8:12> - 1751/2, Malachi BUTLER.
<8:80> - 1753, Malachi BUTLER.
<12:518> - 1778, Patrick BUTLER from Jared HINCKLEY.
<15:384> - 1778, Patrick B. from James WEBSTER.

Capt. Josiah BARTLET of Lebanon CT to **Patrick BUTLER** of same. <Lebanon CT Deeds 10:447>
...20 June 1765, Capt. Josiah BARTLET, for love, good will, etc...unto my son Patrick BUTLER... do give...peice of land lying in Lebanon in the Parish of Goshen & is a part of the farm on which I now dwell...containing in the whole about one acre. Witnesses: Ebenezer BACKUS Jr., Jonathan TRUMBLE. Rec. 31 Oct. 1765. <15:125>...6 Feb. 1778, Patrick sold the above to Chandler BARTLETT. Witnesses: Jared HINCKLEY, Jonathan WEST. Rec. 25 June 1791.

Patrick BUTLER of Lebanon CT to **Ichabod BARTLETT** of same. <Lebanon CT Deeds 17:230>
...28 June 1798, Patrick BUTLER, for $35.31 sold to Ichabod BARTLETT...land in Lebanon, Goshen Society containing by estimation ninety nine rods together with a dwelling house...bounded by land now belonging to me and land of Chandler BARTLETT. Witnesses: Peleg THOMAS, Philip HARRIS. Ack. same day. Rec. 30 June 1798.

Mercy & Patrick BUTLER to **Simon ABELL Jr.** <Lebanon CT Deeds 22:160>
...7 Mar. 1816, Mercy BUTLER & Patrick BUTLER lease to Simon ABEL Jr...the dwelling house in which they now live, with the lands theretoo, containing about 35 acres...togather with a small wood lot lying in the limits of Colchester for the Term of five years next following the first day of April 1816, all which term of five years he is to improve sd let & leased premises, according to the rules of good Husbandry. He is permited to cut timber only for making & repairing the fences...and cut fire wood for the use of one fire only dureing sd term of five years; and to keep sd dwelling house in repaire; and in consideration...he the sd Simon on his part doth hereby agree to pay the following rents for the first year $35.00, for the four last years $40.00 the year...NB the quantity of fire wood above mentioned is hereby limited to ten loads or half cords a year. Witness: Peleg THOMAS. Rec. 16 Sept. 1816.

Harriot BUTLER et al of Hartford CT to **John BUTLER** of same. <E. Hartford CT Deeds 10:551>
...20 Apr. 1813, Harriot BUTLER, Sarah BUTLER & Frances BUTLER, for $2213.15 sold to John BUTLER ...land in E. Hartford...bounded by land of Joseph PITKIN, Timothy PITKIN & Daniel HALL...together with the paper mill & grist mill. Witnesses: Jonathan BULL, John BEACH. Ack. 22 Apr. 1813 by grantors. Rec. 10 May 1813.

Miles BEACH of Hartford CT to **John BUTLER** of same. <E. Hartford CT Deeds 10:580>
...7 Feb. 1814, Miles BEACH, for $2500.00 sold to John BUTLER...32 acres in E. Hartford...bounded by land of Elisha PITKIN, Esq. and J. KEENY...together with a dwelling house, paper mill and a grist mill. Witnesses: Chaney BARNARD, Jonathan BULL. Rec. 8 Feb. 1814.

Elizabeth BUTLER of Hartford CT to **John BUTLER** of same. <E. Hartford CT Deeds 12:13>
...1 Mar. 1814, Elizabeth BUTLER, for $771.05 sold to John BUTLER...land in E. Hartford...bounded by land of Joseph PITKIN, Timothy PITKIN and Daniel HALL...together with a paper mill & grist mill. Witnesses: Jonathan BULL, Charles BULL. Rec. 14 Mar. 1814.

Mervin KEENEY of Manchester CT to **John BUTLER** of Hartford CT. <Manchester CT Deeds 3:104>
...16 Nov. 1830, Mervin KEENEY, for $400.00 sold to John BUTLER...five acres in Manchester... bounded by land of the late Aaron BUCKLAND dec'd & the sd John BUTLER...and is the whole of the

property that was owned & in the occupancy of my late father George KEENEY at his decease. Witnesses: Benjamin WOLCOTT, Thomas SKINNER. Rec. 17 Nov. 1830.

CT Missionary Society to **John BUTLER** of Hartford CT. <Manchester CT Deeds 2:194>
...6 Feb. 1832, The Connecticut Missionary Society, for $1360.00 sold to John BUTLER...13 acres in the parish of Orford in East Hartford...being the same property which was mortgaged to the sd society by Daniel BUTLER by deed dated 24 May 1808 (9:185)...bounded by land of Elisha PITKINS, Esq....together with a dwelling house, paper mill & gristmill. Signed by A. KINGSBURY, Treasurer for the Society. Witnesses: Isaac SPENCER Jr., Samuel DODD. Rec. 17 Feb. 1832.

Benjamin LYMAN of Manchester CT to **John BUTLER** of Hartford CT. <Manchester CT Deed 3:415>
...17 July 1835, Benjamin LYMAN, for $619.00 sold to John BUTLER...one & one quarter acres in Manchester...with the dwelling house thereon being land lying southeasterly from sd BUTLER's paper mills. Witnesses: William W. GOODWIN, Francis PARSONS. Rec. 25 July 1835.

MICRO #20 OF 32

Estate of **Samuel BARTLETT** of Duxbury MA. <Plymouth Co.PR>
<3:255> Letter/Bond 9 Dec. 1713, widow **Hannah BARTLETT** app'td admx. Surety: William BREWSTER. Witnesses: Joseph TAYLOR, William ASHCOMB. <original> Inventory of moveables, 15 Jan. 1713/4, by Edward SOUTHWORTH, John WADSWORTH & Israel SILVESTER; sworn to 1 Mar. 1713/4 by admx. <3:293> Appraisal of real estate 15 Jan. 1713/4; farm where sd BARTLETT dwelt at the time of his decease; that part of sd farm which did formerly belong to William PAYBODIE now dec'd; that part of sd farm with the houseing which sd BARTLETT purchased of the Rev. John ROBINSON of Duxbury; meadow at the Salt house beach; 40 acre lott of land which belongeth to the first Division of the Commons in Duxbury & Pembroke; whole right in the Second & Last Division in sd Commons. <3:293-5> Distribution 1 Mar. 1713/4, of real estate, among following chil., viz: **Benjamin BARTLETT** (eldest son), **Joseph BARTLETT, Samuel BARTLETT & Ichabod BARTLETT**; mentions meadow & farm near Captain's Hill in Duxbury and land adjoining Deacon BREWSTER and Thomas BONNEY; ack. 19 Apr. 1714 by Edward SOUTHWORTH, William BREWSTER, Thomas BONY/BONNEY, Israel SILVESTER, John WADSWORTH. <3:296> Division of personal estate, 20 Apr. 1714, among the widow **Hannah BARTLETT** and following chil., viz: **Benjamin, Joseph, Samuel, Ichabod, Hannah, Elizabeth, Lydia & Sarah.** <3:298-300> Guardianship, 19 Apr. 1714, widow **Hannah BARTLETT** is app'td gdn. of **Ichabod BARTLETT & Elizabeth BARTLETT** (under 21) and **Sarah BARTLETT & Lydia BARTLETT** (under 14). Witnesses: Israel SILVESTER, Nathaniel THOMAS

Estate of **Benjamin BARTLETT** of Duxbury MA. <Plymouth Co.PR #1237>
<5:354> Letter/Bond 6 Feb. 1727, brother **Samuel BARTLETT** app'td admr. Sureties: Joseph BARTLETT & Samuel FISHER of Duxbury. Witnesses: Thomas BURTON, Elizabeth WINSLOW. <5:569> Inventory taken 28 Feb. 1727 by John PARTRIDGE, Benjamin ALDEN & Nathaniel BREWSTER, all of Duxbury; personal estate only.

Estate of **Samuel BARTLETT**, gent. of Plymouth MA. <Plymouth Co.PR #1371>
<12:71> Letter/Bond 27 Apr. 1751, son **Samuel BARTLETT**, fisherman of Plymouth, app'td admr. Sureties: Thomas FOSTER, Esq. & Job MORTON, cooper, both of Plymouth. Witnesses: Hannah WINSLOW, John LOTHROP. <12:455> Inventory taken 2 May 1751, by Thomas FOSTER, Samuel DENHAM/DONHAM, Joseph BARTLETT Jr.; incl. homestead & buildings; one sixth of saw mill in Plymouth; 17 acre wood lot; 10 acre wood lot.

Will of **Samuel BARTLETT**, yeoman of Plymouth MA. <Plymouth Co.PR #1373>
<25:491>...dated 5 Apr. 1780, the improvement of all estate to wife **Elizabeth** until youngest child then living shall arrive at the age of 14, then to be equally divided among the children except £20 to be deducted from shares of daus **Mary FINNEY & Elizabeth CHURCHILL**; Nathaniel MORTON Jr., executor. Witnesses: James DOTEN, Rebecca MORTON, Thaddeus CHURCHILL. <25:493> Inventory taken 24 Nov. 1780 by James DOTEN, Joseph BARTLETT Jr., Lemuel MORTON; incl. homestead and 17 acre wood lot at South Pond. <27:501> Letter/Bond 20 May 1784, Amasiah CHURCHILL Jr. & Joseph BARTLETT Jr., mariners of Plymouth, app'td admrs. in place of Nathaniel MORTON Jr. dec'd. Sureties: Thomas WETHRELL, Innholder & Samuel JACKSON Jr., both of Plymouth. Witnesses: Nathaniel LOTHROP, Isaac LOTHROP. <original> List of debts, 7 Oct. 1784: Eleazer HOLMES, Joseph BARTLETT, George WATSON, Barnabas CHURCHILL, Andrew CROSWELL, James DOTEN, DAVIS & SPOONER, James THATCHER, Stephen DOTEN, John TORREY, William TRENHOLM, Joseph ROBBINS, Stephen MARCY, Joseph CROSWELL, William THOMAS, Eleazer STEPHENS, William WATSON, Richard HOLMES, Dr. COTTON, Richard BAGNEL, Jeremiah HOLMES, Dr. N. LOTHROP, Lemuel MORTON, John GODDARD, William LeBARON, Rev. ROBBINS; provisions & clothing for the children from Sept. 1783 to Oct. 1784. <25:154> Inventory taken 21 May 1784 by Eleazer STEPHENS, Ichabod HOLMES, James DOTEN. <31:236> Account, 2 Aug. 1790, of Joseph BARTLETT Jr., only surviving admr.; received from sale of land: land at Little town sold to Ansel BARTLETT, land adjoining homestead sold to William DAVIS, wood lot sold to Isaac BARNES; Paid to: George WATSON, Cornelius HOLMES, Rev. Chandler ROBBINS, James DOTEN, Eleazer HOLMES, Eleazer STEPHENS, John GODDARD, Stephen CHURCHILL, Lemuel MORTON, William LeBARON, Rosseter COTTON, Joseph CROSWELL, Lemuel SAVORY, Andrew CROSWELL, Richard & William HOLMES, Dr. William THOMAS, William DAVIS for balance due Nathaniel MORTON Jr., Stephen DOTEN, Dr. MARCY, Sylvanus BARTLETT, William WATSON, Thomas & W. DAVIS, Dr. James THACHER, Jeremiah HOLMES, John COTTON, Ichabod SHAW, Seth HARLOW; supplies for family. <31:319> Division sworn to 10 Jan. 1791 by John GRAY, Sylvanus BARTLETT, Andrew CROSWELL, among the following chil., viz: **Joseph BARTLETT, Alexander BARTLETT, Samuel BARTLETT, Cornelius BARTLETT, Stephen BARTLETT, Freeman BARTLETT, Nathaniel BARTLETT, Elizabeth CHURCHILL** (widow) **& Mary FINNEY** (one ninth part of each of the shares of **William BART-**

LETT & John BARTLETT, both dec'd, added to each). <31:356> 2d Account of admr., 15 Apr. 1791; paid to Jesse CHURCHILL.

Estate of **Anthony SPRAGUE** of Attleboro MA. <Bristol Co.PR>
<original> Warrant to appraise, 12 May 1729, to Noah CARPENTER, Elisha PECK, Israel WHIPPLE. <6:239> Inventory taken 14 May 1729, by above three; housing & land and half a share of Commons in Attleborough, Ł600. <6:234> Letter/Bond 20 May 1729, son **Anthony SPRAGUE** app'td admr. Sureties: Elisha PECK & Israel WHIPPLE, husbandmen of Attleborough. Witnesses: Stephen PAINE, Jonathan RUSSELL. <6:380> Account of admr., 17 Mar. 1729/30; Received from: John LOVET, Nathaniel SHELDON, Caleb HALL, Jabez GOLD, John WILKENSON, Daniel JENKES Jr.; Paid to: Dr. WOOD, Dr. SWETEN, William TURPEN, Phillip TILLINGHAST, Col. Joseph WHIPPLE, Jonathan SPRAGUE, James WHIPPLE, Daniel JENKES, Mehitabel THURSTON for nursing, Mehitabel SPRAGUE for nursing, Keziah HAWKINS for nursing, Thomas SANDERS for diggen the grave, Daniel JENKES Jr., Thomas COMBSTOCK, William WHIPPLE, Jonathan SPRAGUE, Banfield CAPRON, Joseph WHEATHERHEAD, Elisha PECK, Justice LEONARD, Noah CARPENTER, Joseph BAGLEY, Israel WHIPPLE, Dr. Richard BOWEN. <original> Petition 25 May 1730, of **Richard HARRIS Jr. & John WHITMAN** of Providence, who married with two of the daughters of the dec'd, for the appointment of six men to make a division of sd estate among the children. <7:189> Division 24 May 1731, by Capt. John FOSTER, Noah CARPENTER, Henry TOLMAN, Daniel PERHAM/PERIN & Ebenezer TILER, all of Bristol Co. to following heirs, viz: to eldest son **Anthony SPRAGUE**, the house & four acres adjoining, bounded by Patucket River, together with half a share in Commonage in all future divisions, together with what his Father advanced him by deed of gift is his two shares; to dau **Sarah WHITMAN**, land on the northerly end of the farm next to Daniel JENCK's land and a road that leadeth over Martains Wading place and nine acres of land more to lay out due to sd estate on the last division; to daus **Elizabeth WHIPPLES, Mary WHIPPLES & Phebe SPRAGUE**, land south of their sister **Sarah**'s, across ye farm to John WILKESON's & Mercy JENCKES' land; to dau **Lydia HARRIS**, the southerly side of the farm from her sister **Phebe**'s; to dau **Mercy JENCKES**, two pieces containing 59 acres, the first piece bounded by land her father gave brother **Anthony** & land of sd WILKESON, Mr. WATERMAN, Mr. BUCKLEN and Joseph WEATHERHEAD and the second piece contains eight acres & is bounded by land of John WILKESON and formerly the heirs of Thomas MAN.

Anthony SPRAGUE fo Smithfield to **William BOLLAN et al** of Boston MA. <Bristol Co.Deeds 24:23>
...2 Apr. 1735, Anthony SPRAGUE, husbandman, for Ł1000 sold to Amos WOOD, merchant, Henry LAUGHTON, shopkeeper & William BOLLIN, gent...two lotts in Attleborough...or in Smithfield...the first lott being the sd Anthony's homestead containing 110 acres...bounded on land of Jonathan SPRAGUE Jr., John WILKINSON, William WHIPPLE and Pautucket River...the other lott called Grassy Hill... 109 acres...bounded by land of Daniel JENKS. Wf Ann SPRAGUE signs. Witnesses: Jonathan SPRAGUE Jr., Hezekiah SPRAGUE. Rec. 9 June 1735. <24:25>...same day Anthony sold to the above, for 40s, one half part of a propriety share in the Common & Undivided land in Attleborough.

Mary WHIPPLE of Attleborough to **Jemima MILLER et al.** <Bristol Co.Deeds 82:273>
...20 Aug. 1801, Mary WHIPPLE, widow, for love, good will, etc. towards my well beloved daughter Jemima MILLER wf of my beloved son in law Josiah MILLER, yeoman of Cumberland RI and Ruth WALCOT wf of my beloved son in law Moses WALCOT Jr., yeoman of Attleborough...and in consideration for ye provision they have made for me in my Advanced Age & money expended in my Service, have given ...all my personal estate...except ye use of my wareing apparel which I reserve for my own use so long as I shall need them. Witnesses: John RICHARDSON, John RICHARDSON Jr., David COTTING. Ack. 24 Oct. 1801 by Mary WHIPPLE. Rec. 20 June 1803.

Estate of **John SPRAGUE**, gent. of Boston MA. <Suffolk Co.PR #32305>
<216:159> Petition 21 Oct. 1839, of brother **Joseph SPRAGUE**, tailor of Boston, for admininstration on estate of his brother who died 29 Sept. last. <216:159> Letter/Bond. <137:224> Petition. <276:255> Inventory. <321:89> Evidence perpet. <138:250> 1st Account.

MICRO #21 OF 32

Estate of **Josiah SPRAGUE**, yeoman of Hingham MA. <Suffolk Co.PR #12336>
<56:400> Letter/Bond 17 Apr. 1760, of son **Josiah SPRAGUE**, yeoman of Hingham. Sureties: Benjamin LINCOLN, Esq. & Joshua HEARSEY, gent., both of Hingham. <57:84> Inventory taken 25 Apr. 1760 by James FEARING, Thomas JONES & Hawkes FEARING; house & barn & 87 acres, Ł470.3s4d; total estate, Ł651.12s9d. <57:169> Division agreed on 14 June 1760, by children, viz: **Josiah SPRAGUE, Benjamin SPRAGUE, Isaac SPRAGUE, Ephraim SPRAGUE, Daniel SPRAGUE, Elisha SPRAGUE & Hannah SPRAGUE**, all of Hingham, as follows: to eldest son **Josiah SPRAGUE**, one half of the dwelling house & barn, orchard fresh meadow & upland, bounded by land of Elisha CUSHING, Ephraim SPRAGUE, Daniel SPRAGUE, Jeremiah SPRAGUE, Jacob CUSHING, Esq., Hezekiah CUSHING & Matthew SPRAGUE, also two acres in the 2nd part of the Third Division bounded by land of Isaac SPRAGUE, also one half of six acres in Scituate, also Ł4.10s9p, two cowes, one year old creture, all the corn, butter & chees & the improvement of the estate; to **Elisha SPRAGUE** one fourth part of the house & barn & lands above mentioned, also one three years old creture; to **Hannah SPRAGUE**, one quarter part of above, also one two year old creture; to **Benjamin SPRAGUE**, land adjoyning to his dwelling house, bounded by land of Elisha CUSHING & Matthew SPRAGUE, also six and one quarter acres in the Third Division bounded by land of Matthew SPRAGUE, Ephraim SPRAGUE, Jacob CUSHING, Esq. & land formerly Jeremiah SPRAGUE's, also one ox; to **Isaac SPRAGUE**, three & a half acre fresh meadow called Briery meadow bounded by land of Hawke FEARING, Solomon CUSHING & Hezekiah CUSHING, also eleven acres in 2nd part of the 3rd Division bounded by land of Thomas ANDREWS & Daniel LASELL; also one cow; to **Ephraim SPRAGUE**, seven & one quarter acres in the Third Division bounded by land of Jacob CUSHING, Esq., land of

Daniel & Jonathan LASSELL, Benjamin SPRAGUE, Daniel SPRAGUE, Elisha LEAVITT and land formerly of Jeremiah SPRAGUE dec'd, also a one & a half acre fresh meadow bounded by meadow of Daniel SPRAGUE and one swine, one year old creture one calf; to **Daniel SPRAGUE,** ten acres in the second part of the 3rd Division, bounded by land of Daniel LASSELL, Hezekiah CUSHING, Jeremiah SPRAGUE's heirs, & Thomas ANDREWS and also three acres at Joys pasture and one ox. Witnesses: Peter RIPLEY, Hawkes FEARING. Ack. 12 Aug. 1760 by **Benjamin, Ephraim & Hannah SPRAGUE** and 22 Aug. 1760 by **Josiah, Isaac, Daniel & Elisha SPRAGUE.** <57:89> Account of admr., 4 July 1760; Paid to: John WILDER, Dr. HEARSEY, Benjamin THAXTER, Elisha LEAVITT, Isaac LANE, Hezekiah LEAVITT, Samuel STOCKBRIDGE, Jacob CUSHING, Esq., Israel LASSELL.

==========

Will of **Josiah SPRAGUE,** yeoman of Hingham MA. <Suffolk Co.PR #16610>
<77:172>...dated 1 Sept. 1766...to sister **Hannah SPRAGUE,** $2.00 a year...to brother **Daniel SPRAGUE,** two bushals of Indian corn a year...to brother **Benjamin SPRAGUE** & his heirs, all my land on the outheast of his house lot & south of the cart way which goeth from his house to the land of Matthew SPRAGUE...to brother **Elisha SPRAGUE** & his heirs, my house & barn with the land they stand on with all the remainder of my land in the third division, also all my land lying in Scituate, also all the moveable goods & live stock; brother **Elisha,** executor. Witnesses: Hawkes FEARING, Jacob LEAVITT, Hawkes FEARING Jr. On 26 June 1778, Jacob LEAVITT & Hawkes FEARING Jr. made oath that they together with Hawkes FEARING (now absent) witnessed the will. <77:171> Pr. 26 June 1778, **Elisha SPRAGUE** app'td admr. <77:205> Inventory taken 29 June 1778 by James FEARING, Thomas JONES & Hawkes FEARING, all of Hingham; half a dwelling house, £50; half a barn, £20; three & one quarter acres of meadow & orchard adjoining sd buildings, £100; three & one half acres on the way to Matthew SPRAGUE, £90; two acres at a place caled ye Gutters, £60; four acres south east of ye Gutters, £60; four & one half acres part in Hingham & part in Scituate, £54; total, £695; sworn to 2 Oct. 1778 by exr.

==========

Will of **Elisha SPRAGUE,** yeoman of Hingham MA. <Suffolk Co.PR #18892>
<86:250>...dated 28 Dec. 1786...to sister **Hannah SPRAGUE,** my interest in the piece of land called the Gutteras on the southerly side of land belonging to Seth STODDER & adjoining thereto, with the pasture on the easterly end of it...to nephew **Benjamin SPRAGUE Jr.** (executor), all the residue & remainder of estate. Witnesses: Charles CUSHING, Thomas JONES Jr., Shubael FEARING. On 1 May 1787, Charles CUSHING & Shubael FEARING made oath that they, together with Thomas JONES Jr. (now absent), witnessed the will. <86:249> Letter/Bond 1 May 1787, **Benjamin SPRAGUE** app'td admr. Sureties: Charles CUSHING, Esq. & Shubael FEARING, yeoman, all of Hingham. Witnesses: Jacob COOPER, James WHITE. <86:355> Inventory taken 28 May 1787 by Coll. Charles CUSHING, Thomas JONES & Shubael FEARING; three quarters of the house & land south of the way, £30; three quarters of the orchard, £9; three quarters of the barn & upland adjoining, £12; four & one half acre fresh meadow, £36; 14 acres pasture, £54,16s3d; two & three quarter acres tillage & mowing land, £24.17s6d; total, £228.14s; sworn to 3 July 1787 by exr.

==========

Will of **Isaac SPRAGUE** of Hingham MA. <Suffolk Co.PR #19413>
<88:724>...1789...mentions sons **Isaac SPRAGUE, Amos SPRAGUE, Moses SPRAGUE, David SPRAGUE** and daus **Leah JONES** wf of Benjamin, **Bethiah JOY** wf of Benjamin, **Tamar LINCOLN** wf of Joshua, **Rebecca HEARSEY** wf of Isaiah and **Rachel SPRAGUE.** <88:723> Pr. <88:726> Certificate of Executorship. <89:148> Inventory. <89:668> Evidence perpet.

==========

Estate of **Samuel BARTLETT.** <"Plymouth Co.PR?" #1372>
...1769...<20:204,250;27:535;33:532;35:291;36:398> (no details given)

==========

PLYMOUTH COUNTY DEEDS: (re: HOLMES)

<68:85> - 14 Apr. 1788, Bartlett & Lucy HOLMES of Plymouth sells to Abner BARTLETT, land in 2d Parish in Plymouth. Witness: Bartlett HOLMES Jr.
<72:149> - 15 Dec. 1791, Bartlett HOLMES Jr. sells land.
<88:159> - , Bartlett HOLMES Jr. sells land.
<90:182> - 3 Feb. 1801, Bartlett HOLMES of Plymouth mortgages to son John HOLMES. On 5 Dec. 1811 mortgage is released to Josiah CORNISH, admr. to Bartlett's estate.

==========

Estate of **Benjamin BARTLETT** of Plymouth MA. <Plymouth Co.PR>
<4:146> Letter/Bond 18 July 1718, widow **Sarah BARTLETT** app'td admx. Surety: John BARNES of Plymouth. Witnesses: Peleg WISWALL, Thomas CROADE. <4:174> Inventory taken 27 May 1718 by Abiel SHURTLEFF, John BARNES & Capt. Benjamin WARREN of Plymouth; 20 & 60 acres at Little Meadow; eight acres at Beaver Dam; homestead; land at Agawam; cedar swamp; 132 acres in last division. <4:175> Account of admx., 30 Apr.1719; mentions bringing up the children; List of debts: Joseph BARSTOW, John MURDOCK, Maj. Isaac LOTHROP, Mrs. Elizabeth BARNES, John BARNES, Josiah STURTEVANT, John CHURCHEL, Elder Thomas FAUNCE, Josiah MORTON, Nathaniel THOMAS, John WATSON, Thomas WETHEREL, Deacon John FOSTER, Francis ADAMS, Job CUSHMAN, Ephraim LITTLE, Ephraim WOOD, Widow THOMAS as admx. to estate of James THOMAS, Abigail CLARK, Samuel CLARK, Ebenezer DUNHAM, William BARNES. <original> Dower set off, 6 Apr. 1726, to widow **Sarah STURTEVANT** now the wife of John STURTEVANT Jr. of Plymouth, by Capt. Benjamin WARREN, Josiah MORTON, Thomas HARLOW, Benjamin RYDER, Joseph BARTLETT. <6:394> Settlement of lands, 27 June 1733, to the widow, **Sarah S. STURTEVANT** and following chil., viz: **Nathaniel BARTLETT** (eldest son), **Benjamin BARTLETT, Joseph BARTLETT, Jonathan BARTLETT, Hannah BARTLETT & Sarah BARTLETT.** (Plymouth Co.Deeds 24:59...25 Mar. 1729, John STURTEVANT Jr. of Plymouth & wf Sarah, relict & admx. of estate of Benjamin BARTLETT...)

==========

Guardianship of Children of **Benjamin BARTLETT** of Plymouth MA. <Plymouth Co.PR #1324>
<originals> Bonds 5 Apr. 1726, John BARNES of Plymouth app'td gdn. of **Benjamin, Joseph & Hannah BARTLETT** (all under 21) and **Mary BARTLETT** (under 14). Isaac LOTHROP app'td gdn. of **Sarah BARTLETT** (under 14). Witnesses: John STURTEVANT, Jonathan BARTLETT.

Benjamin BARTLETT of Duxborough MA to **Israel CLARK** of Plymouth MA. <Plymouth Co.Deeds 46:24>
...23 July 1755, Benjamin BARTLETT, cooper, for £16 sold to Israel CLARK, husbandman...eight acres in the Second Precinct in Plymouth...bounded by land of Josiah CLARK adjoining to Beaver Dam Brook & land of John BLACKMER...sd land fell to me in the Division of the Estate that my honoured Father Benjamin BARTLETT dyed seized of...Hannah BARTLETT wf of sd Benjamin consents. Witnesses: James HOLMES, Lemuel BARNES. Rec. 28 Feb. 1760.

References to the name **Benjamin BARTLETT** in Plymouth Co.Deeds: 40:164 (1749); 41:16;42:41,204;43:76,213;46:24,26 (1754),46;48:117;49:9,197;53:223.

Benjamin BARTLETT of Plymouth MA to **Benjamin BARTLETT** of Kingston MA. <Plymouth Co.Deeds 40:164>
...10 Feb. 1749, Benjamin BARTLETT, cooper, for £56.15s sold to Benjamin BARTLETT, cooper...part of a dwelling house in Kingston...which on 1 Jan. 1744 was sett off to me to satisfie an execution I then had against one Joshua BRADFORD late of sd Kingston, it being the front chamber & closetts adjoyning the whole garrett the front stairs & a priveledg of passing & repassing in the front entry of the sd house. Ack. & Rec. same day.

Benjamin BARTLETT of Kingston MA to **Elisha BRADFORD** of same. <Plymouth Co.Deeds 40:164>
...10 Feb. 1749, Benjamin BARTLETT, cooper, for £87.3s mortgaged to Elisha BRADFORD, cooper... dwelling house & garden spott where on I now dwell in Kingston & is the same house & land which was formerly Joshua BRADFORD's. (The mortgage was for one year.) Witnesses: Benjamin BARTLETT, James HOVEY. Rec. same day. On 19 Feb. 1753, the mortgage was discharged by Elisha BRADFORD. Witnesses: Samuel FOSTER, Hezekiah RIPLEY. Rec. 26 Feb. 1753.

Israel SILVESTER of Duxborough MA to **Benjamin BARTLETT** of same. <Plymouth Co.Deeds 46:26>
...14 Nov. 1754, Israel SILVESTER, shipwright, for £4.13s4d sold to Benjamin BARTLETT, cooper, late of Kingston but now resident in Duxborough...one & a half acres in Duxborough...the northwesterly corner of the farm whereon I now do dwell...bounded by land of the heirs of Christopher WADSWORTH dec'd. Witnesses: Jacob PETERSON, Joseph SILVESTER. Ack. 29 Feb. 1760 by Israel. Rec. 1 Mar. 1760.

Estate of **Jonathan BARTLETT**, yeoman of Plymouth MA. <Plymouth Co.PR #1311>
<27:113> Letter/Bond 17 Mar. 1783, William BARTLETT 3d, yeoman of Plymouth, app'td admr. Sureties: Lothrop CLARK & John BARTLETT of Plymouth. Witness: Ephraim SPOONER. <33:317> Inventory taken 10 Apr. 1783, by John BARTLETT, Zacheus BARTLETT & Joseph SYLVESTER, all of Plymouth; 6 or 7 acre pasture; sworn to 18 Mar. 1793 by admr. & appraiser John BARTLETT and 8 Apr. 1793 by other two appraisers.

Guardianship of Child of **Jonathan BARTLETT**, yeoman of Plymouth. <Plymouth Co.PR #1310>
<26:387>...26 Feb. 1782, **Jonathan BARTLETT**, above 14, chose Stephen DOTEN Jr., yeoman of Plymouth as his gdn. Witnesses: Seth HOLMES, Levi PATEE. Sureties: Stephen DOTEN & Seth MORTON, yeomen of Plymouth. Witnesses: James DOTEN 3d, Charles (---).

Will of **Thankful BARTLETT**, widow of Plymouth MA. <Plymouth Co.PR #1387>
<28:278>...dated 9 Feb. 1782...being stricken in years...to eldest son **James BARTLETT**, one third of estate...remaining two thirds to children **William BARTLETT, Lucy & Thankful** & grandson **Jonathan**; sons **James & William**, executors. Witnesses: John BLACKMER, Andrew BARTLETT, Branch BLACKMER. <28:279> Pr. 10 Apr.1782, sons **James & William**, executors. <48:115> Division approved, 29 June 1816, by Ichabod MORTON, John BLACKMER & Gideon HOLBROOK, all of Plymouth, among following chil., viz: heirs of **James BARTLETT**, heirs of **Lucy HOLMES, Thankful BARTLETT** and heirs of **William BARTLETT** for his share & his brother **Jonathan**'s share he bought.

Estate of **James BARTLETT** of Plymouth MA. <Plymouth Co.PR #1298>
...1808...<39:150> Letter. <42:328> Inventory. <43:61> Insolvency, Claims, Account. <115:177> Petition adm.d.b.n., Letter & Bond. <116:34> License to sell. <117:24> Notice. <108:80> Inventory. <118:42> Sale of real estate.

Jonathan BARTLETT of Plymouth MA to **William BARTLETT 3d** of same. <Plymouth Co.Deeds 102:123>
...5 June 1792, Jonathan BARTLETT, mariner, for £36 sold to William BARTLETT 3d, yeoman...all my interest right & title to the real estate which my grandmother Thankful BARTLETT late of Plymouth dec'd gave me in her last will. Witnesses: Isaac LeBARON, William LeBARON. Ack. 1 Apr. 1793. Rec. 1 Apr. 1804.

Estate of **William BARTLETT** of Plymouth MA. <Plymouth Co.PR #1397>
<46:151> Pr. <48:116> Inventory. <48:117> Dower, Insolvency. <48:332> List of Claims. <48:547> Admr. <49:49> Account of John CORNISH Jr., admr., 22 Sept. 1817; Paid to: Gideon HOLBROOK & John BLACKMER as appraisers on sd dec'd's estate, assignment of dower to widow & for dividing **Thankful BARTLETT**'s estate; Ichabod MORTON; probate fees for this estate & for division of **Thankful BARTLETT**'s estate. <80:518> Division, 14 Nov. 1838, of widow's dower...and **William BARTLETT 3d** now dec'd being entitled to one sixth part of the reversion of sd dower as heir at law of his father & to two other sixth parts by purchase of the rights of **Lucy CLARK & Polly DOTEN**, two other heirs

of sd dec'd, we have assigned to the heir at law of sd **William BARTLETT 3d** dec'd, one half part f sd reverson, viz: a lot of land at Monomet Ponds.

PLYMOUTH COUNTY DEEDS: (re: Lothrop HOLMES)

<70:251> - 8 Apr. 1786, Lothrop HOLMES, yeoman of Halifax to Thomas JOHNSON et al, 3 or 4 acres of land in Plymouth which he bought of Joseph SILVESTER on 20 June 1767. Wf Mary releases dower.
<69:233> - 1790, Lothrop HOLMES et al to Seth HOLMES.
<77:101> - 14 Mar. 1794, Lothrop HOLMES, yeoman of Halifax to Rosseter COTTON, sells land in Plymouth that he bought of Silvanus BARTLETT.
<85:40> - 8 July 1794, Lothrop HOLMES of Halifax to Oliver BRADFORD, land in Jones River meadow
<89:65> - 9 Apr. 1798, Lothrop HOLMES, yeoman of Halifax to Nathaniel HOLMES 3d, the whole of my homestead lands. Wf Mary releases dower.

PLYMOUTH COUNTY DEEDS: (re: Jonathan BARTLETT)

<37:25> - 1744, Jonathan BARTLETT to John HOLMES.
<37:103> - 1745, Jonathan & Thankful BARTLETT to John BARNES.
<37:181> - 1745, Jonathan & Thankful BARTLETT to Stephen CHURCHILL.
<40:54> - 1749, Jonathan & Thankful BARTLETT to Phebe HOLMES.
<56:231> - 25 Apr. 1771, Jonathan BARTLETT, yeoman of Plymouth to Zaccheus BARNES. Wf Thankful releases dower. Rec. 27 June 1772.
<56:269> - 18 July 1776, Jonathan BARTLETT to Zaccheus BARNES.
<64:157> - 29 Aug. 1785, Jonathan BARTLETT, mariner of Plymouth to Mercy DREW, two fifths of a house & lot in Plymouth which he bought of William & Mary FREEMAN. Wf Lydia releases dower.
<65:141> - 29 Aug. 1785, Jonathan BARTLETT, mariner of Plymouth mortgage to William DAVIS, three fifths of house & lot in Plymouth which he bought of William & Mary FREEMAN. Wf Lydia releases dower. Mortgage discharged 23 Mar. 1795 and premises reconveyed to admr. of Jonathan's estate.
<74:162> - 30 May 1793, William BARTLETT 3d as admr. to estate of Jonathan BARTLETT, yeoman, dec'd to Seth HOLMES Jr., seven & three quarter acres in Plymouth.
<78:48> - 23 Mar. 1795, A. CROSWELL as admr. to estate of Jonathan BARTLETT, mariner of Plymouth dec'd to William ROGERS, three fifths of house & lot in Plymouth where dec'd lived.

Will of **Thankful BARTLETT**, singlewoman of Plymouth MA. <Plymouth Co.PR #1388>
<87:257>...dated 20 June 1845, mentions **George W. BARTLETT** son of sister **Sarah BARTLETT**; nieces & nephews, viz: **Lucia W. BARTLETT, Catharine HOLMES, Deborah PIERCE, Eliza HAMMOND, Peter W. DOTEN, Lemuel DOTEN, Betsey DOTEN**; sisters **Henrittee BLACKMER** wf of Ezra H. and **Lucy CLARK** wf of Israel. <2:49H> Pr. 2d Mon. Aug. 1845. <88:37> Inventory.

Estate of **Jonathan BARTLETT**, mariner of Plymouth MA. <Plymouth Co.PR #1312>
<27:428> Letter/Bond 28 Mar. 1793, widow **Lydia BARTLETT** app'td admx. Sureties: William DAVIS, merchant & Eleazer HOLMES Jr., gent., both of Plymouth. Witnesses: Nathaniel LOTHROP, Isaac LOTHROP, Rosseter COTTON. <33:315> Inventory taken 5 Apr. 1793 by William DAVIS, Rosseter COTTON & Eleazer HOLMES Jr.; three fifths of a dwelling house & lot of which the widow Mary DREW owns two fifths; sd Jonathan's interest is under a mortgage to William DAVIS. <33:316> Account of admx., 9 Apr. 1793. <33:315> Insolvency. <27:539> Letter/Bond 11 Jan. 1794, Andrew CROSWELL app'td admr. d.b.n. as **Lydia BARTLETT** has dec'd. Sureties: William GOODWIN, merchant & Ephraim SPOONER, both of Plymouth. Witnesses: William BARTLETT Jr., Lewis WESTON. <33:528> Inventory taken 18 Jan. 1794 by Ephraim SPOONER, Joseph CROSWELL, William GOODWIN; three fifths of a dwelling house (which was the estate of Capt. Sylvanus COBB dec'd). <33:529> Insolvency declared 16 Jan. 1794 by admr. <35:563> List of Claims, allowed 28 Sept. 1796: Benjamin DREW, Lemuel DREW, Thomas & William DAVIS, William DAVIS, Andrew CROSWELL, Joanna WINSLOW, Hannah WHITE, George WATSON, Henry WARREN, Samuel VAUGHN, Dr. William THOMAS, Nathan REED, Mercy DREW, Samuel JACKSON.

Estate of **Joseph BARTLETT Jr.**, cordwainer of Plymouth MA. <Plymouth Co.PR #1317>
<original> Bond 22 Nov. 1760 by widow **Jane BARTLETT** as admx. Sureties: Job MORTON, cooper & Benjamin BARTLETT Jr., yeoman, both of Plymouth. Witnesses: Edward WINSLOW, Consider HOWLAND.

Estate of **Capt. Nathaniel BARTLETT** of Plymouth MA. <Plymouth Co.PR #1348>
<23:82> Letter/Bond 4 Mar. 1776, Andrew BARTLETT, yeoman of Plymouth app'td admr. Sureties: Nathaniel BARTLETT, William RIDER & Amos RIDER, all of Plymouth. Witnesses: Aaron HOBART, Joseph CUSHING. <24:109> Inventory taken 4 May 1776 by Silvanus BARTLETT, John BLACKMER, James CLARK; homestead, lot on the beach and one in ye Pond. <original> List of debts, July 1783 by James DOTEN, attorney, Paid to: Benjamin ELLIS, William MORTON, Phillip LEONARD, Benjamin CORNISH, James HOLMES, Capt. Zach. BARTLETT, Jonathan HARLOW Jr., Stephen DOTEN Jr., John FREEMAN, Dr. LeBARON, Robert BROWN, Ebenezer BARTLETT, Timothy BOURNE, Thomas DAVIS, Ansel HARLOW, Ellis HOLMES, Benjamin DREW, Stephen SAMSON, Jonathan SAMSON, Benjamin MORTON, William HARLOW, estate of Jonathan BARTLETT, Joseph BARTLETT, Sarah COBB, Deacon Jonathan DIMON. <29:483> Dower set off 1 Nov. 1785 by Stephen DOTEN, Branch BLACKMER & James CLARK, all of Plymouth to widow **Rebecca BARTLETT**. <35:204> Notice of sale of homestead farm at Monument Pond; sworn to 7 & 8 Jan. 1795 by Andrew BARTLETT & Andrew CROSWELL. <35:202> Account 7 & 8 Jan. 1795; Paid to: Ezra HOLMES, Benjamin DREW,

Jeremiah HOWES, Dr. THOMAS, Thomas SPOONER, Stephen ELLIS, Dr. WADSWORTH, John COTTON, Seth BARNES, Sarah COBB, William BARTLETT, Timothy BROWN, Benjamin CHURCHILL, Benjamin ELLIS, William MORTON, William WATSON, Isaac LOTHROP, Bartlett HOLMES, Dr. COTTON, Jonathan SAMPSON, James CLARK, Dr. PERRY, Elkanah HOLMES, Philip LEONARD, Benjamin CORNISH, James HOLMES, Capt. Zaccheus BARTLETT, Benjamin MORTON, John FREEMAN, Lazarus LeBARON, Robert BROWN, Ebenezer BARTLETT, Thomas DAVIS, Ansel HARLOW, Joshua THOMAS, James DOTEN, Elisha POPE, William TRENHOLM, Edward WINSLOW, George WATSON, James WARREN, Azariah THRASHER, Solomon HOLMES, heirs of William HARLOW, John BARTLETT, Stephen DOTY, Ebenezer RAYMOND, Sylvanus BARTLETT, James DOTEN; Received from: Branch BLACKMER, Abial ELLIS, Ansell HARLOW, James BARTLETT. <original> Division (no date) by Thomas MORTON Jr. & Ichabod MORTON Jr. to following heirs, viz: **Andrew BARTLETT, John BARTLETT, Nathaniel BARTLETT**; chil. of **Ansel HARLOW**; widow **Susanna CHURCHILL**, chil. of **William BARTLETT** and the chil. of **Abigail HOLMES** dec'd, wf of Solomon, viz: **Nathaniel HOLMES, Abigail NELSON & Solomon HOLMES.**

MICRO #22 OF 32

Estate of **Elnathan BARTLET** of Plymouth MA. <Plymouth Co.PR #1265, 3:334,349,350>
<original> Letter/Bond 3 Mar. 1714/5, widow **Hannah BARTLET** app'td admx. Surety: Joseph SILVESTER. Witnesses: John BARNES, Thomas CROADE. <original> Inventory taken 26 Mar. 1715 by Ensign Benjamin WARREN, Thomas CLARKE Jr. & Josiah MORTON, all of Plymouth; incl. homestead & housing; meadow at Beaver dam Brooke; four score acres at island ponde; meadow at grait dam & long dam near Benjamin WARREN's; 18 acres by Humphrey TURNER's & Joseph BARTLETT's children. <3:349> Inventory of personal estate, 26 Mar. 1715; sworn to 30 Mar. 1715 by widow.

Guardianship of Children of **Elnathan BARTLET** of Plymouth MA. <Plymouth Co.PR #1284>
<5:237> Letters/Bonds 12 May 1727, Benjamin RIDER of Plymouth app'td gdn. of **Elnathan BARTLETT & Hannah BARTLETT**, both betw. 14-21. Surety: Thomas CLARK of Plymouth. Witnesses: David BATES, Abigail BATES.

Will of **Elnathan BARTLETT**, cooper of Plymouth MA. <Plymouth Co.PR #1266>
<8:364>...dated 30 Aug. 1736...to brother **George NICHOLAS**, 60 acre homestead at Manomet Pond...to sister **Sarah NICHOLAS**, 80 acres adjoining Long ( ), land at Island ( ) and my right in township of Hingham; father in law **Rue NICHOLAS**, executor. Witnesses: Richard COLE, Peter ANDREWAT, Langlen FALLON; sworn to 12 June 1739 by Richard COLE. Presented for probate by Thomas FOSTER, attorney for the executor; sd will was made in Richmond County N.Y. where the dec'd resided some few days and fell sick and soon after died. Pr. 2 June 1741, **Rue NICHOLAS** app'td admr. <8:401> Inventory taken 3 June 1741 by Thomas HARLOW, Samuel CORNISH & Josiah CLARKE, all of Plymouth; house & 50 acres; right in Little Meadow; 60 acre wood lot; right in Harbour pond; sworn to 3 Aug 1741 by exr.

Will of **Joseph & Hannah SYLVESTER** of Plymouth MA. <Plymouth Co.PR 13:205,206,249,366>
...1 Nov. 1734, joint will...to the children of dec'd son **Joseph SILVESTER**, one fifth of estate; four fifths to daughters **Hannah HOLMES, Mary RIDER, Thankful RIDER & Content HOLMES**; son **Solomon SYLVESTER** and Eleazer HOLMES, executors. Pr. 4 Mar. 1754. Inventory taken 14 Mar. 1754.

Samuel RIDER of Middleboro MA to **James HOLMES & Joseph SILVESTER** of Plymouth. <Plymouth Co.Deeds>
<43:269>...25 Apr. 1757, Samuel RIDER, yeoman & wf Mary, for £105 sold to James HOLMES, yeoman & Joseph SILVESTER...all our right...unto all the real estate of our honoured Father Joseph SILVESTER late of Plymouth dec'd...in Plymouth. Witnesses: John BARROWS, Benajah PRATT. Ack. same day. Rec. 17 June 1757.

James HOLMES & Joseph SILVESTER of Plymouth MA. <Plymouth Co.Deeds 47:35>
...23 Apr. 1761, Whereas we...James HOLMES, yeoman & Joseph SILVESTER, mariner...hold by deed of purchase from Samuel RIDER & wf Mary, her interest & estate in the real estate which was her Father's Joseph SILVESTER dec'd lying at Monument Ponds in Plymouth...we are apprehensive that we hold the sd purchased estate as joynt tenants and not as tenants in common, contrary to our design in the sd purchase. For preventing therefore the sd deeds operating as Joynt Tenancy and that we may hold the sd estate as Tenants in common...each quit claims his share to the other. Witnesses: Nathaniel LITTLE, James HOVEY. Ack. 22 July 1761 by both & Rec.

Estate of **Joseph SILVESTER Jr.** <Plymouth Co.PR #19990>
<4:424>...17 June 1724, widow **Mercy SILVESTER** app'td admx. <5:86,87>...

Estate of **Ebenezer RIDER**, fisherman of Plymouth MA. <Plymouth Co.PR #17341>
<11:493>...25 Apr. 1750, John ELMES, yeoman of Scituate app'td admr. <12:273>...25 Feb. 1750, appraisers app'td. Inventory taken 13 Mar. 1750; sworn to 11 July 1751 by **Thankful RIDER**, admx. <19:454> Account of admx., 19 May 1767.

Estate of **James HOLMES.** <Plymouth Co.PR #10442,#10404>
<17:156>...28 Feb. 1766, widow **Content HOLMES** & Solomon HOLMES, mariner, app'td admrs. <18:244, 245> Guardianship of children, 12 Mar. 1766, **Ezra HOLMES & Caleb HOLMES** choose Stephen DOTY as gdn. <19:342> Inventory taken 12 Mar. 1766. <19:467> Division ordered 18 Mar. 1767, to divide lands between the widow & heirs and Seth HOLMES.

Estate of **Eleazer HOLMES**, gent. of Plymouth MA. <Plymouth Co.Deeds 77:77>
Division of estate, 1 May 1758, which had been set off as dower to the widow **Hannah HOLMES**, now dec'd, between the following chil., viz: **Eleazer HOLMES, Lemuel HOLMES, Ichabod HOLMES, Joshua HOLMES, Lydia CHURCHILL** wf of Barnabas Jr. and **Elizabeth BRADFORD** wf of John. <77:69>...18 June 1794, Elizabeth BRADFORD of Plympton, widow of John, sold to Eleazer HOLMES Jr. & Ichabod HOLMES, both of Plymouth, land rec'd in division.

Will of **Ichabod HOLMES**, yeoman of Plymouth MA. <Plymouth Co.PR #10431>
...dated 15 Oct. 1813...to three sons **Ellis HOLMES, Chandler HOLMES & Samuel HOLMES**, land...near my dwelling house in sd Plymouth to the northward of the land of Benjamin BARNES until it comes to the Lane leading from the Country road down into the Sea, Reserving the lane leading thro my land, as it is now fenced, And also reserveing two house lotts, to contain about a quarter of an acre each, To the Southward of my son **Ellis'** dwelling house...to be sold...for the purpose of paying my just debts...to dau **Esther SHAW** wf of Ichabod Jr., two lots of wood land, one lot containing about six acres is about a mile from my house adjoyning to the land of Barnabas HEDGE Jr. Esq. The other lott containing about five acres which I bought of Lemuel MORTON is about a mile & a half from my house. These lands I give to my sd dau by reason that I did not give her any household goods when she was Marryd as I did to all my other daughters and also for her Peculier Attention to her mother when she was sick and for her Attendance on me since...to three sons, the fishyard, the fish houses and all trucks & other articals used in drawing up and cureing fish.

<Plymouth Co.Deeds 28:143>...23 Jan. 1733, **Edward STEVENS**, mariner of Plymouth & wf Mercy who is one of the daughters of Elisha HOLMES of Plymouth & Sarah his wife now dec'd.

Guardianship of Child of **Abner SILVESTER** of Plymouth MA. <Plymouth Co.PR #20011>
<13:261>...28 May 1754, **Abner SILVESTER**, fisherman, app'td gdn. of son **Nathaniel SILVESTER**; mentions estate of Nathaniel's dec'd mother, **Jedidah SILVESTER.**

Will of **Nathaniel SILVESTER** of Hanover MA. <Plymouth Co.PR #20012>
...1781...<28:58> Will & Codicil. <28:60> Pr. <28:122> Inventory. <28:124> Division.

Guardianship of Children of **Solomon CHURCHILL** of Plymouth MA. <Plymouth Co.PR #4112>
<41:145> Bond 12 Apr. 1813, of **Solomon CHURCHILL**, yeoman as gdn. of his children, viz: **William CHURCHILL** (above 14) & **Elizabeth CHURCHILL** (under 14), the great-grandchildren of **Silvanus BARTLETT**, yeoman of Plymouth dec'd. Sureties: Francis BARTLETT, yeoman & Nathan REED, trader, both of Plymouth. Witnesses: Beza HAYWARD, Beza HAYWARD Jr.
<Plymouth Co.Deeds 125:127> Petition 2d Mon. Apr. 1813, of **Solomon CHURCHILL** as gdn. of above two children, to sell two fourth parts in one undivided moiety of a wood lot, containing about 30 acres & also a piece of tillage land in Plymouth...he is impowered to sell the land for their support. On 23 Jan. 1813, **Solomon CHURCHILL Jr. & Mendal CHURCHILL** appoint **Solomon CHURCHILL** attorney, to execute a good & sufficient deed of a certain piece of wood land which fell to us as part of our Mothers share of estate of **Sylvanus BARTLETT** dec'd. Both Rec. 20 May 1813.

Estate of **Joseph SYLVESTER**, yeoman of Halifax MA. <Plymouth Co.PR #19988>
<34:225> Letter/Bond 2 Apr. 1800, Reuben SYLVESTER, yeoman of Halifax app'td admr. Sureties: Samuel S. STURTEVANT, Thomas WETHRELL. <37:266,267,429,430>...

Will of **Reuben SYLVESTER** of Halifax MA. <Plymouth Co.PR>
...dated 6 July 1848...to dau **Mercy SYLVESTER**, $150.00 & the use of the west chamber in my house while she continues unmarried, which I think with $50.00 I gave her in the Savings bank at Plymouth and what I have paid her yearly will be just & right...to daus **Almyra DEWING & Susanna GOOGINS**(sp), $100.00 ea.; to the American Missionary Society, $25.00; household furniture to three daus; remainder of estate to only son **Joseph SYLVESTER** (executor) incl. one bed & bed clothes and the desk that was his grandfather's. Witnesses: Zenas BRYANT, James M. HARRUB(sp), Judith BRYANT.

Estate of **Joseph BARTLETT Jr.** of Plymouth MA. <Plymouth Co.PR #1321,1322>
<2:20> Letter 18 June 1703, widow **Lydia BARTLETT** app'd admx. <2:52> Inventory taken 21 Apr. 1703; total estate, £654.3.2. <2:20> Settlement 20 Dec. 1705, to widow & five chil., viz: **Joseph BARTLETT** (eldest son), **Samuel BARTLETT, Benjamin BARTLETT, Lydia BARTLETT & Sarah BARTLETT.** <2:46> 4 June 1704, **Lydia BARTLETT** app'td gdn. of the five children, all under 14. <2:68> 8 Mar. 1705/6, Ephraim LITTLE of Plymouth app'td gdn. of **Joseph, Samuel & Lydia**, all under 14 and <2:83> on 20 Dec. 1706 he is app'td gdn. of **Benjamin & Sarah**, both under 14. <3:262> Appraisal of lands, 3 Nov 1713 by James WARREN, Esq., Ensign Benjamin WARREN & Capt. Charles CHURCH. <3:264> Settlement 18 Dec. 1713, among the five children, reserving dower to their mother who is now the wife of **Joseph HOLMES Jr.** of Plymouth. <3:300> Receipt 18 June 1714, of **Joseph BARTLETT** to gdn. Ephraim LITTLE for his share in father's estate. <4:152> Receipt 17 Nov. 1718, of **Samuel BARTLETT**, trader of Plymouth, to gdn. Ephraim LITTLE, for his share.

Estate of **Benjamin BARTLETT**, cooper of Plymouth MA. <Plymouth Co.PR #1240>
<15:512> Letter/Bond 2 May 1760, Solomon BARTLETT, labourer of Plymouth app'td admr. Sureties: Samuel BARTLETT & Josiah CHURCHILL of Plymouth. Witnesses: Edward WINSLOW, Consider HOWLAND. <16:11> Inventory taken 16 May 1760 by John HARLOW, Ebenezer SPOONER, Ebenezer SAMSON; incl. one quarter of schooner "Shildrake"; house & land and a woodlot; sworn to 7 Nov. 1760 by admr. <19:83> Dower set off 24 Dec. 1762, to widow **Abigail BARTLETT**, by James HOVEY, Ebenezer SPOONER and Ebenezer SAMSON; the use of part of Mansion house & part of garden,northeasterly by Training

Green, also three & one third acre woodland on the way to Cook's Pond; sworn to by the three, 26 Apr. 1764.

Estate of **Benjamin BARTLETT Jr.**, mariner of Plymouth MA. <Plymouth Co.PR #1241>
<13:469> Letter/Bond 4 June 1755, widow **Jane BARTLETT** app'td admx. Sureties: Benjamin BARTLETT & John HARLOW, coopers of Plymouth. Witnesses: Edward WINSLOW, Lydia BARNES. <13:521> Inventory taken 18 June 1755 by John HARLOW, Jonathan BARTLETT, Elias TRASK; personal estate only; estate insolvent. <14:242> List of claims: 16 July 1756, examined by John TORREY & Thomas SPOONER; Creditors: Samuel BARTLETT Jr., Thomas FOSTER, Benjamin BARTLETT, Silvanus BARTLETT, Thomas DAVIS, Deacon Joseph BARTLETT, Joshua SWIFT, Stephen DOTY, Jonathan SAMSON, William BROWN. <14:243> Account of admx., 24 July 1756; distribution among creditors 2 June 1757.

Will of **Capt. Joseph BARTLETT**, gent. of Plymouth MA. <Plymouth Co.PR #1316>
<14:121>...dated 4 Sept. (1756?)...to wf **Elizabeth**, use of part of house & negro girl named Violet...to son **Silvanus BARTLETT**, the Warren Lott at Monumnet Ponds in Plymouth which I purchased of my brother **Benjamin BARTLETT**, Elnathan BARTLETT & Phebe BARNES, at several times; two thirds of Point Pasture, Sedge Ground near Beef Hill & cedar swamp in Plympton which I purchased of John CARVER; also half lot bought of Isaac & Sarah LITTLE near Sacrifice Brook in Plymouth...to son **Zacheus BARTLETT** the homestead; one third of Point Pasture; meadow next the sea at Monument Ponds; woodlot at Daniells Kills; woodland near homestead; cedar swamp in South Meadow & one purchased of Samuel MORTON; daus **Jerusha CROSSWELL** wf of Joseph, **Lydia PARKER** wf of Jonathan and **Elizabeth RIDER** wf of Benjamin RYDER Jr. Witnesses: James CURTIS, John COBB, James HOVEY. Pr. 3 July (1756?). <14:125> Bond 19 Aug. 1756 of sons **Silvanus & Zacheus BARTLETT** as exrs. Sureties: Elkanah WATSON, John LOTHROP. Witnesses: Melatiah LOTHROP, Benjamin LOTHROP Jr. (Note: Bowman questions the dates as Joseph died 13 July 1756.)

Estate of **Silvanus BARTLETT**, yeoman of Plymouth MA. <Plymouth Co.PR>
Warrant, 17 Feb. 1812, to Richard HOLMES & Ichabod MORTON, yeomen of Plymouth and Isaac WRIGHT, gent. of Plympton, to divide estate into nine equal parts and set off to the following chil. & heirs, viz: **Silvanus BARTLETT, Abner BARTLETT**, Esq., **Francis BARTLETT, Joseph BARTLETT**, Esq., **Jesse BARTLETT, Martha BARTLETT, Sophia DREW** wf of Benjamin Jr., the heirs of **Mary BARTLETT** dec'd and heirs of **Betsey BARTLETT** dec'd. <44:184> 3 Apr. 1812, Jesse BARTLETT & William DOTEN, yeomen and Frederick BARTLETT, physician, all of Plymouth were app'td to view the estate set off to the heirs of dau **Elizabeth BARTLETT** dec'd and set it off to her children & heirs, viz: heirs of **Elizabeth CHURCHILL** dec'd, **Jerusha HOLMES** wf of Nathaniel, **Hannah BARTLETT** (non comp), **Thomas BARTLETT** of Vermont, **Daniel BARTLETT & Deborah BARTLETT.**

Estate of **Capt. Zaccheus BARTLETT**, gent. of Plymouth MA. <Plymouth Co.PR>
<34:231> Pr. 7 Apr. 1800. <37:426> Inventory taken 21 June 1800. <42:361> Warrant, 12 Apr. 1802, to divide real estate among following chil., viz: **Joseph BARTLETT** (eldest son), **Zacheus BARTLETT, George BARTLETT, Isaac BARTLETT, Melatiah BARTLETT, Phebe PERRY, Elizabeth NYE, Mary MAYO/MAYHEW**; sworn to 12 Oct. 1811 by Ichabod MORTON, one of the dividers. <42:364> Division, 8 June 1808, of widow's dower among the following chil., viz: **Joseph BARTLETT, Isaac BARTLETT, Dr. Zacheus BARTLETT**, heirs of **George BARTLETT, Melatiah BARTLETT, Elizabeth NYE, Phebe PERRY & Mary MAYHEW.**

Thomas GOODWIN to **Nathaniel GOODWIN.** <Plymouth Co.Deeds 71:252>
...25 Jan. 1790, Thomas GOODWIN, taylor, quit claims to Nathaniel GOODWIN...all right to my mother Lydia GOODWIN's thirds in my Father's, Nathaniel GOODWIN, merchant, late of Plymouth dec'd, estate. Desire GOODWIN signs.

MICRO #23 OF 32

Samuel BARTLETT et al to **Thomas JACKSON Jr. & William JACKSON.** <Plymouth Co.Deeds 80:61>
...28 Aug. 1795, Samuel BARTLETT, merchant of Wells ME, Peleg WADSWORTH, Esq. of Portland ME & wf Elizabeth and Isaiah DOAN, gent. of Boston & wf Hannah, for Ł144 sold to Thomas JACKSON Jr. and William JACKSON, merchants of Plymouth...four undivided fifth parts of one third part...descended to us from our honoured father Samuel BARTLETT, Esq. late of Plymouth dec'd.

Estate of **Samuel BARTLETT** of Plymouth MA. <Plymouth Co.PR #1372>
<20:204> Letter/Bond 10 Apr. 1769, widow **Elizabeth BARTLETT** app'td admx. Sureties: Ephraim SPOONER, merchant & Thomas WETHRELL, trader, both of Plymouth. Witnesses: Edward WINSLOW, Edward WINSLOW Jr. <20:250> Inventory taken 27 June 1769 by John TORREY, Ezra ALLEN, Ephraim SPOONER; incl. dwelling house, store & garden; wharf & warehouse; 15 acre wood lot at Cooks Pond; 30 acres wood land north of Triangle Pond; three quarters of grist mill & half a wood lot at Middleborough; one quarter saw mill at Rocky Meadow in Middleborough; share in 7th great lot in last division of common lands at Plymouth & Plimton; seven acre wood land near duck plain; sworn to same day by admx. <27:535> Letter/Bond 10 July 1793, Thomas WETHRELL, innholder of Plymouth, app'td admr. d. b.n. Sureties: Ephraim SPOONER of Plymouth & Peleg WADSWORTH of Cumberland. Witnesses: Priscilla BURR, Isaac LOTHROP. <33:532> Inventory taken 10 Jan. 1794 by Ephraim SPOONER, Andrew CROSWELL, Nathaniel GOODWIN; incl. one third of a wharf with LOTHROP; 105 acre wood land at College Pond; 15 acres near Agawam. <35:291> 1st Account beginning 2 Dec. 1793, allowed 8 July 1795; Received from: Joseph THOMAS for rent of Store & Wharf; I. HARLOW, E. BARROWS, estate of Dr. Lazarus LeBARON, estate of Robert BROWN, Silvanus BRIMHALL, Eleazer RICKARD, William COBB, S. CHURCHILL, A. CROSWELL, S. SHERMAN, William T. JACKSON, James PRINCE, I. TRASK, J. TERRY, Jordan HIGNESS, S. MERCY, S. JACKSON, William NELSON, Ebenezer COBB, widow Temperence ROBBINS, B. WHITING (tax col-

lector; Judge SULLIVAN's fee, Lemuel SAVORY, Isaac LeBARON (town tax), William WATSON, Bartlett LeBARON, Stephen SAMPSON, Thomas & William JACKSON, Ephraim SPOONER, Thomas TORRY, Peleg WADSWORTH, Samuel BARTLETT, Dr. Samuel SAVAGE, Lemuel BRADFORD, Nathaniel HARLOW, S. BARTLETT, Eliza BARTLETT. <36:398> Account of admr., 14 June 1798; Collected of: Cornelius MORREY, Dr. William THOMAS, Lemuel COBB, Thomas JACKSON, William JACKSON, Capt. Joseph THOMAS, Isaac LOTHROP; Paid to: estate of Thomas DAVIS dec'd & Thomas & William DAVIS, Mrs. Sukey BAGART, Peleg WADSWORTH, Isaiah DOANE, Samuel BARTLETT; Uncollected notes: Samuel COBB Jr., Silas DUNHAM, Benjamin RANSOM, John EDWARDS, Benjamin LUCAS, Lemuel COBB, Nathaniel BURGESS.

Estate of **Elizabeth BARTLETT**, widow of Plymouth MA. <Plymouth Co.PR #1261>
<27:437> Letter/Bond 10 July 1793, Thomas WETHRELL, innholder of Plymouth, app'td admr. Sureties: Ephraim SPOONER of Plymouth & Peleg WADSWORTH of Portland, Cumberland Co. Witnesses: Priscilla BURR, Isaac LOTHROP. <33:530> Inventory taken 13 July 1793 by Ephraim SPOONER, Andrew CROSWELL, Nathaniel GOODWIN; personal estate only; sworn to 23 Oct. 1793 by SPOONER & CROSWELL, 10 Jan. 1794 by GOODWIN. <35:292> Account of admr., 8 July 1795; received balance of Stephen CHURCHILL's account; Paid to: William MOREY, William LUCAS, John MAY, Ebenezer LUCE, Jesse CHURCHILL, Nathaniel GOODWIN, Cornelius COBB, Peleg WADSWORTH, Samuel BARTLETT, Isaiah DOANE, Isaac BARTLETT.

Joseph SWIFT of Plymouth MA to **Joseph BARTLETT** of same. <Plymouth Co.Deeds 31:150>
...21 Dec. 1737, Joseph SWIFT, blacksmith & wf Sarah to Joseph BARTLETT, yeoman...their rights in one acre meadow east of Eel River...bounded by land of Capt. John DYER & Josiah CLARKE and near foot of Beef Hill in Plymouth. Ack. same day.

Sarah SWIFT of Plymouth MA to **Thomas DAVIS.** <Plymouth Co.Deeds 48:239>
...24 Oct. 1763, Sarah SWIFT, widow to Thomas DAVIS...dwelling house & lot in Plymouth...which I bought of Lazarus LeBARON & Samuel BARTLETT, admrs. of estate of my first husband Francis LeBARON by deed 14 Nov. 1773 <28:89>. Ack. & Rec. 24 Nov. 1763.

Sarah LeBARRON/LeBARON of Plymouth MA to **Lazarus LeBARRON** of same. <Plymouth Co.Deeds 29:37>
...10 Sept. 1734, Sarah LeBARRON, spinstress, for Ł300 sold to Lazarus LeBARON, physician...all my right...in several lots...and is one half...of my Honoured Father Joseph BARTLETT dec'd's estate as my fully appear by the settlement of my sd Fathers estate dated 15 Dec. 1713...that is to say, my one half of a 30 acre lot of land laid out with my sd Father's, ten acres he bought of ye Town laying near the land that was formerly John WANNOO's & bounded towards the west with the land that was Nathaniel WARREN's Sr. formerly of Plymouth dec'd; also one half of ye land called Tarrows Field being about 16 acres; also one half the land between Tarrows field & the Whale hole being about 48 acres; also one half the 20 acre lot & 60 acre lot laying near Little's Meadow; also half my sd Father's share laying in sd Littles Meadow above the Damm; also one half of my sd Father's part of Littles Meadow lying below the Dam given to him my sd Father by his Father and also one half of my sd Father's share of land being ye 14th lot in the 10th lot laid out in the Common Lands. Witnesses: Samuel BARTLETT, Samuel THACHER. Ack. 14 Sept. & Rec. 16 Sept. 1734.

Estate of **John BARNES** of Plymouth MA. <Plymouth Co.PR #1007>
<10:194> Order for distribution, 14 Jan. 1744, by Capt. Josiah MORTON, Benjamin RIDER, James HOVEY, Consider HOWLAND & John HARLOW, all of Plymouth, to children & their legal representatives viz: **John BARNES** (eldest son), **Seth BARNES, Jonathan BARNES**; heirs of **Hannah DREW**, viz: **Mary RIDER, Lamuel/Samuel DREW, William DREW; Mary WAITE, Thankful BARTLETT, Elizabeth CURTIS, Lydia BARNES.** <11:2> Division, 13 Apr. 1748, by Thomas HOLMES, Eleazer HOLMES, Joseph BARTLETT, Consider HOWLAND & James HOVEY of real estate which descended to the legal representatives of **Hannah DREW,** late wf of **Lemuel DREW,** mariner of Plymouth dec'd, in right of sd **Hannah** from **John BARNES** & wf **Mary,** dec'd, viz: **Lemuel DREW** (eldest surviving son), **James DREW, William DREW, Mary RIDER** wf of John, **Sarah SAMSON** wf of Jonathan. <9:271> Letter. <9:389> Quit claim of dower. <9:501> Inv. <10:315> Account.

Lemuel DREW of Liverpool N.S. to **James DREW** of Plymouth MA. <Plymouth Co.Deeds 56:264>
...29 Oct. 1773, Lemuel DREW, cooper, for Ł266.13s4d sold to brother James DREW, cooper...house lot or garden spot in Plymouth...with the dwelling house...sd lot being 50' front and 86' deep, being the same which formerly belonged to Silas WEST now dec'd and which was seized by his creditors...and by them sold to me as appears by a deed 10 Feb. 1752 and rec. 41:166. Wf Mary releases dower. Ack. & Rec. 30 Oct. 1773.

Lemuel DREW of Liverpool N.S. to **James DREW** of Plymouth MA. <Plymouth Co.Deeds 56:264>
...30 Oct. 1773, Lemuel DREW, cooper, for Ł106,13s4d sold to brother James DREW, cooper...three pieces of land in Plymouth...first is a house lot set off to me in the Division of our Father's Estate...second piece is a 12 acre wood lot...which our Father purchased of John HARLOW & which wa set off to me in the same division...last piece is a 16 acre wood lot...set off to me in the Division of our Brother William DREW's Estate and lays between Billington's Sea and loud Pond. Ack. & Rec. 30 Oct. 1773.

Estate of **Lemuel DREW.** <Plymouth Co.PR>
<original> Petition 12 June 1738, of **John RIDER,** who married **Lemuel DREW**'s eldest dau, that "my unkel" Jonathan BARNES be app'td admr. <11:4> Division 13 Apr. 1748, of real & personal estate among the following chil., viz: **Lemuel DREW, James DREW, William DREW, Mary RIDER** wf of John & **Sarah SAMSON** wf of Jonathan.

Estate of **Mary BARNES.** <Plymouth Co.PR #1033>
...1824...<52:324> Ezra PHINNEY app'td admr. <59:111> Inventory ("mentions land at Obery, see deed 124:110"). <55:291;59:110>...("no heirs mentioned").

Heirs of **Corbin BARNES** to **Ansel HOLMES Jr.** of Plymouth MA. <Plymouth Co.Deeds 151:253>
...20 Nov. 1810, Mary BARNES, widow of Corbin BARNES dec'd of Plymouth; Charlotte & Rebecca BARNES, spinsters; Eleazer HOLMES, housewright; Silvester HOLMES, clerk & wf Esther in her right; Polly HOLMES, seamstress; Levi LUCAS, mariner & wf Betsey in her right; Alden LUCAS, mariner & wf Deborah in her right and Abigail KEEN, widow, all of Plymouth...sell to Ansel HOLMES Jr....land in Plymouth. Ack. 25 Jan. 1825 by Alden & Deborah LUCAS, Charlotte BARNES, Rebecca BARNES, Betsey MAYHEW, Polly BARNES, Abigail CARVER. Rec. 25 Jan. 1825.

Heirs of **Corbin BARNES** to **Joseph WHITTING** of Plymouth MA. <Plymouth Co.Deeds 124:110>
...1 Dec. 1812, Mary BARNES widow of Corbin BARNES dec'd of Plymouth; Charlotte BARNES; Rebecca BARNES; Eleazer HOLMES, housewright & wf Polly; Levi LUCAS, mariner & wf Betsey; Ansel HOLMES Jr. mariner & wf Patty; Alden LUCAS, mariner & wf Deborah and Abigail KEEN, widow, all of Plymouth and Silvester HOLMES, clerk & wf Esther of Bristol Co., the children & grandchildren of sd Corbin BARNES...for $10.00 sold to Joseph WHITTING, yeoman...pasture land in Plymouth at Obry, containing one & a quarter acre...which sd land was assigned to sd Corbin BARNES dec'd in the division of his father John BARNES' estate & to us from sd Corbin. (Levi LUCAS and Silvester & Esther HOLMES did not sign. Rec. 10 July 1814.

Estate of **Eleazer CHURCHILL** of Plymouth MA. <Plymouth Co.PR #4016>
...1754...<13:364> Letter. <13:408> Inventory. (no details given)

George BARTLETT et al. <123:214 - Plymouth Co.Deeds?>
...11 Sept. 1814, George BARTLETT, salemaker and his children John BARTLETT, Mercy BARTLETT & Hannah BARTLETT, and James BARTLETT, mariner & son of Ephraim BARTLETT, all of Plymouth, sell land laid out to Samuel HARLOW & by him given by will our Grandfather & great-grandfather William HARLOW...in division of William HARLOW's estate; one tenth was set off to Sarah wf of Eleazer CHURCHILL...this land descends to us from sd Sarah CHURCHILL & our uncle James CHURCHILL...the mother of George BARTLETT's children being one of sd Sarah's daughters & the mother of sd James BARTLETT being another of sd Sarah's daughters.

Will of **John BARTLETT**, innholder of Plymouth MA. <Plymouth Co.PR #1302>
<21:232>...dated 14 Nov. 1772...being advanced in years; to wf **Sarah**, privilege in home during widowhood; to sons **John BARTLETT & Charles BARTLETT**, the home place; son **Charles** will not arrive at the age of 21 until the year 1780; to son **George BARTLETT**, half house lot & buildings & four acres at Ell River which was purchased by my brother **Joseph BARTLETT** & myself; daus: **Abigail BARTLETT, Sarah FAUNCE, Hannah DOTEN, Jerusha PECKHAM, Maria BABB.** Witnesses: John RUSSELL, Thomas WETHRELL, Edward WINSLOW Jr. Pr. 1 Mar. 1773, son **John BARTLETT**, exr. <21:234> Inventory taken 5 Mar. 1773 by Thomas FOSTER, Thomas MATTHEW, Edward WINSLOW Jr.; incl. Violet, a negro woman, Alexander a negro boy aged 8 & Jem aged 6; dwelling house & land; 21 acres wood lot; 10 acre wood lot bought of Thomas FAUNCE; salt meadow at Saquish; half a dwelling; house & land at Ell river in partnership with Deacon Joseph BARTLETT; sworn to 27 Mar. 1773 by appraisers & 4 May 1773 by exr. <27:524> Letter/Bond 4 Jan. 1791, widow Dorothy BARTLETT app'td admx. d.b.n. as her husband, John BARTLETT the executor is dec'd. Sureties: Joshua THOMAS & Thomas MATTHEW, yeoman, both of Plymouth. Witnesses: Isaac LOTHROP, Ephraim SPOONER. <31:456> Account of admx., 29 Oct. 1791; Received from: Ichabod HOLMES, John SAVERY, Samuel BARTLETT, Ebenezer WING, Jeremiah COLLINGS, Japhet ALLEN, Josiah CARVER, Benoni NICHOLSON for the servant by James, Thomas MAYHEW Jr., Nauman HOLBROOK for negro boy Alexander; for 10 acres sold to Isaac SYMMES 17 June 1777; for salt meadow sold to Stephen SAMPSON; Thomas DAVIS; the watch etc. returned by the **widow** at her 2nd marriage; provisions used by the widow, 2 children & servants; Paid to: Lemuel THOMAS, Thomas MORTON, Benjamin WARREN, DAVIS & HARLOW, Benjamin RYDER, William RIDER, Thomas LORING, Stephen DOTEN, Ephraim COBB, LANMAN & TUFTS, Joshua BLACKWELL, Nathaniel LOTHROP, Robert BROWN Jr., Bildad ARNOLD, Bartlett LeBARON, Peleg WADSWORTH, William COYE, Gideon BRADFORD, James DREW, widow Sarah BARTLETT, Elijah SNOW, Mrs. Mercy HEDGE, John CHAMBERLIN, Zacheus PADDOCK, Joshua PERKINS, Jonathan TILLSON, William Hall JACKSON; Legacies bequeathed to: **George BARTLETT**, wf of **Thomas FAUNCE**, wf of **Stephen DOTEN**, wf of **George PECKHAM, Abigail BARTLETT** & wf of **Richard BABB**; Debts paid to: Isaac LOTHROP, Ephraim SPOONER, Consider CHASE, Barnabas COBB, Jonathan TILLSON, Dr. William THOMAS, Capt. Benjamin CHURCHILL. <31:459> Division 29 Sept. 1791; sons **John BARTLETT & Charles BARTLETT** having dec'd, homestead & lands divided between their heirs.

George BARTLETT of Plymouth MA to **Samuel RYDER** of same. <Plymouth Co.Deeds 78:104>
...6 June 1795, George BARTLETT, sail maker, sells to Samuel RYDER, mariner...two acres at Eel River...given me by will of my father John BARTLETT dec'd and is undivided with two acres of land lately of Deacon Joseph BARTLETT dec'd now Samuel RYDER Jr.'s. Wf Sally releases dower.
(The following references only are on this page & may refer to George BARTLETT: 105:137;123:214; 139:255;179:261.)

Estate of **George BARTLETT** of Plymouth MA. <Plymouth Co.PR #1278>
<34:386>...1804, admr. app'td. (no details given)

Estate of **Charles BARTLETT**, mariner. <Plymouth Co.PR #1245>
<27:393> Letter/Bond 30 Apr. 1792, Andrew CROSWELL, gent. of Plymouth, app'td admr. Sureties: Thomas WETHRELL, innholder & James THACHER, Physician, of Plymouth. Witnesses: Turner STETSON,

Nathaniel BURGISS. <original> Inventory taken 4 June 1792 by Ephraim SPOONER, Joseph CROSWELL, Thomas WETHRELL; half a dwelling house that was given him & his brother **John BARTLETT** by their dec'd father. <33:427> Oath of admr., 11 Sept. 1793, re: sale of real estate & reversion of widow's dower.

Guardianship of Child of **John BARTLETT** of Plymouth MA. <Plymouth Co.PR #1244>
<22:151> Letter 21 Aug. 1773, **Charles BARTLETT**, minor above 14, son of **John BARTLETT**, late of Plymouth, innholder, named Thomas MATTHEW, merchant of Plymouth as his gdn. Witnesses: Sarah WINSLOW, Edward WINSLOW Jr. <original> Bond 24 Aug. 1773 of gdn. Sureties: Edward WINSLOW Jr., gent. & John WATSON, gent., both of Plymouth. Witnesses: Pelham WINSLOW, Bartlett LeBARON.

Estate of **John BARTLETT Jr.**, innholder of Plymouth MA. <Plymouth Co.PR #1306>
<27:335> Letter/Bond 25 Oct. 1790, widow **Dorothy BARTLETT** app'td admx. Sureties: Joshua THOMAS & Thomas MATHEW of Plymouth. Witnesses: Isaac LOTHROP, Ephraim SPOONER. <31:306> Inventory taken Oct. 1790 by Ephraim SPOONER, Joshua THOMAS, Thomas MATHEW; half the house & lot and 10 acre wood land near John NELSON. <31:308> 4 Jan. 1791, admx. represents the estate is insolvent. <31:461> Dower assigned to widow **Dorothy BARTLETT**; incl. one third part of her husband's interest in the estate of his brother **Charles BARTLETT**, dec'd; sworn to 29 Oct. 1791 by Sylvanus BARTLETT, Ephraim SPOONER, Joshua THOMAS. <31:461> Account 29 Oct. 1791; Paid to: James THASHER/THACHER, Consider CHASE (taxes), Ebenezer LAW (sexton), Lemuel SAVORY, Andrew CROSWELL, Dr. Isaac WINSLOW and allowance to widow for support of family. <33:516> List of claims, 25 Dec. 1793 by Ephraim SPOONER & Andrew CROSWELL, Due to: William BARTLETT Jr., Isaac LeBARON, John WATSON, William LeBARON; Zacheus SOUL on note due Ebenezer LOBDEL; Eleazer HOLMES Jr., Dr. William THOMAS; estate of Capt. Thomas DAVIS; Mrs. Mercy HEDGE, widow; DINIAN & THOMAS, Nathaniel GOODWIN, William WATSON, Isaac SYMMS, John SHAW of Carver, Thomas MORTON, Josiah THOMAS, Jesse CHURCHILL, William JACKSON, David BACON, Joseph TRASK, Timothy GOODWIN, Samuel JACKSON Jr., Sylvanus BARTLETT; Benjamin BARTLETT as admr. on estate of Thomas HOLMES; Nathaniel SPRAGUE, Stephen SAMSON, Benjamin DREW, Samuel JACKSON, Isaac LOTHROP, George WATSON; estate of Charles BARTLETT dec'd; John DAVIS; estate of Sylvanus BRAMHALL; Osborn MORTON, Elnathan HOLMES Jr., WATSON & SPOONER, John DAVIS; estate of Elisha DOAN; Isaac LOTHROP, Dr. Nathaniel LOTHROP. <35:92> 2d Account of admx., 2 Apr. 1796; incl. to debts paid due from estate of **John BARTLETT Sr.** dec'd; claims allowed. <original> Debts due from estate of **John BARTLETT Sr.** dec'd, for which the real estate of **John BARTLETT Jr.** dec'd was holden to pay; legacy to **George BARTLETT**; Isaac LOTHROP, Ephraim SPOONER, Dr. THOMAS, Crispus SHAW Jr., Delano COBB, Barnabas COBB, Joseph TRASK and estate of Sylvanus BRAMHALL.

Will of **Joseph BARTLETT** of Plymouth MA. <Plymouth Co.PR #1318>
<29:59>...dated 11 Oct. 1782; to wf **Sarah**, use of all estate, half of personal estate if she marries; to son **Joseph BARTLETT**, half of Mr. Henry's Annotations Books and pew in Mr. ROBBINS meeting house; son **Thomas BARTLETT** to give my son **Joseph** half of lands given to him by his Uncle **Thomas BARTLETT** dec'd and half his interest in 30 acre wood lot I bought of Ebenezer BARTLETT at Ell River; daus **Sarah BARTLETT & Martha JACKSON** wf of Nathaniel; to grandson **John BARTLETT**, half of pine lot of 40 acres at Billington Sea which I bought of the heirs of Nathaniel DUNHAM; to grandchildren **William HOSEA & Hannah HOSEA**, chil. of dau **Hannah** dec'd, one sixteenth part of my estate when they arrive at the age of 21. Witnesses: Isaac LOTHROP, Abrim HAMMATT, Thaddeus CHURCHILL. <29:61> Pr. 11 Oct. 1783, sons **Joseph & Thomas**, app'td admrs.

Estate of **Lemuel BARTLETT**, shoreman of Plymouth MA. <Plymouth Co.PR #1328>
<27:411> Letter/Bond 15 Dec. 1792, William BARTLETT Jr., yeoman of Plymouth, app'td admr. Sureties: Ephraim SPOONER & Lewis WESTON, goldsmith, of Plymouth. Witnesses: Nathaniel LOTHROP, Isaac LOTHROP. <33:426> Inventory taken 20 June 1793 by Sylvanus BARTLETT, Andrew CROSWELL, Thaddeus CHURCHILL; lot below Deacon BARTLETT's late dwelling house containing three quarters of an acre; dwelling house of the dec'd; six acre pasture; eight acre wood land; sworn to 7 Sept. 1793 by admrs. <36:22> Dower assigned to widow **Mary BARTLETT** by Sylvanus BARTLETT, Willard SEARS, Silvanus HARLOW; sworn to & confirmed 9 Dec. 1796.

Lemuel BARTLETT of Plymouth MA to **John & Joseph BARTLETT** of same. <Plymouth Co.Deeds 35:1,2>
...10 June 1741, Lemuel BARTLETT, tailor, sells to John BARTLETT, seafaring man...land at Wellingsly set off to sd Lemuel in division of estate of our Honoured Father Robert BARTLETT dec'd. <35:2>...10 June 1741, Lemuel BARTLETT sells to Joseph BARTLETT, shoreman...land set off to sd Lemuel in settlement of estate of our Honoured Father Robert BARTLETT dec'd.

Heirs of **Elder Thomas FAUNCE** of Plymouth to **John TOMSON** of Middleborough. <Plymouth Co.Deeds>
<40:125>...1 Sept. 1749, Isaac DOTEN, mariner, Lemuel BARTLETT, fisherman & wf Mary & Rebecca WARREN, simstress, all of Plymouth and John STUDLEY, cordwainer & wf Elizabeth of Hanover, John PALMER Jr., trader & wf Jane of Scituate and Jabez DOTEN, joyner of the City of New York in America...for Ŀ25 sold to John TOMSON, cooper...eight acre fresh meadow in Middleborough in the lower meadow in the 26 Mens Purchase which sd eight acres were heretofore the estate of our Honoured Grandfather, Elder Thomas FAUNCE, late of Plymouth dec'd.

Lemuel BARTLETT of Plymouth MA to **William BARTLETT 2d** of same. <Plymouth Co.Deeds 67:155>
...8 Apr. 1785, Lemuel BARTLETT, yeoman, for Ŀ100 sold to William BARTLETT 2d, trader and also in consideration of the love & affection I bear to the sd William BARTLETT and in consideration that the sd William pays my honest & just debts and furnishes me & my wife with decent & necessary support during our natural lives...convey to him...all the real estate I am now seized of lying in Plymouth or elsewhere. Witnesses: William WATSON, Joshua THOMAS. Rec. 27 June 1787.

William BARTLETT of Plymouth MA to **Lemuel BARTLETT** of Yarmouth N.S. <Plymouth Co.Deeds 67:268> ...10 Apr. 1789, William BARTLETT...in consideration of Ł42 due to my brother Lemuel BARTLETT on a note of hand bearing date 1 Apr. 1780 for Ł27.3s with interest, from my father Lemuel BARTLETT I do...convey...to sd Lemuel BARTLETT...six acre pasture...being the whole that my father Lemuel BARTLETT purchased of Jonathan MORTON by deed 11 May 1752...also a seven acre wood lot at Gravelly Hill in Plymouth...being part of the share set of to my father in the division of my Grandfather Robert BARTLETT dec'd (which parcels of land my father Lemuel BARTLETT conveyed to me in a deed for the purpose of paying his just debts) to the sd Lemuel BARTLETT. Witnesses: Timothy GOODWIN, Ephraim SPOONER. Rec. same day.

Guardianship of **Hannah BARTLETT**, non comp. <Plymouth Co.PR>
<44:182> Petition 10 Mar. 1812, of Benjamin DREW Jr. & Frederick BARTLETT, that **Hannah BARTLETT**, single woman of Plymouth and dau of **Thomas & Elizabeth BARTLETT** late of Plymouth dec'd, is non compos & incapable to take care of herself...request a guardian be app'td. <44:183> 13 Mar. 1812, Solomon CHURCHILL app'td gdn. <44:183> Inventory taken 13 Apr. 1812 by Beza HAYWARD, Benjamin DREW Jr. & Frederick BARTLETT; her right in the real estate of Silvanus BARTLETT dec'd, $221.17.

MICRO #24 OF 32

Will of **Elisha HOLMES**, yeoman of Plymouth MA. <Plymouth Co.PR #10380>
<13:183>...dated 21 Mar. 1745, mentions wf **Susanna** and eight children (now) liveing, viz: **Elisha HOLMES, Joseph HOLMES, Jabez HOLMES,** chil. of dec'd son **Elnathan HOLMES, John HOLMES, Marcy STEVENS** wf of Edward, **Elizabeth MORTON** wf of Elkanah, **Sarah BLACKMER** wf of John, **Rebecca CROSSWELL** wf of Andrew; friend Nathaniel BARTLETT, executor. <13:184> Pr. 3 Dec. 1753. <13:185> Inventory taken 1 Jan. 1754. <13:243> Division. <13:394> Account.

Heirs of **Sarah HOLMES** of Plymouth MA. <Plymouth Co.Deeds 27:26>
...21 Feb. 1731/2, Elisha HOLMES Jr., Joseph HOLMES, Jabesh HOLMES, Elnathan HOLMES, John HOLMES, Mercy STEVENS wf of Edward, Elizabeth MORTON wf of Elkanah and Sarah HOLMES, all being the children of Elisha HOLMES of Plymouth...divide lands...descended to us by our Honoured Mother Sarah HOLMES dec'd.

John BARNES of Plymouth MA and **Elisha HOLMES Sr. et al.** <Plymouth Co.Deeds 19:154>
...12 Oct. 1725, Indenture between John BARNES, yeoman & wf Mary on ye one part...and Elisha HOLMES Sr., yeoman, Elisha HOLMES Jr., Joseph HOLMES, Jabez HOLMES, Mercy SILVESTER, Elkanah MORTON & wf Elizabeth, Elnathan HOLMES, John HOLMES & wf Sarah, all of Plymouth on the other part... whereas several pieces & parcells of land & meadow lying & being at Monument Ponds or thereabouts in Plymouth, viz: some land at ye Mill Pond & Warren's Lot so called & some land or meadow at the Whale Hole & between Tarrows Field & SILVESTER's land at Shifting Cove Point & at ye Burch Swamp, belong to ye sd John BARNES & wf Mary, & to ye sd Elisha HOLMES Sr. during his life in ye right of Sarah his late wife now dec'd & after the decease of ye sd Elisha HOLMES Sr. to ye sd Elisha HOLMES Jr., Joseph HOLMES, Jabez HOLMES, Mercy SILVESTER, Elizabeth MORTON wf of Elkanah, Elnathan HOLMES, John HOLMES & Sarah HOLMES, children of Elisha HOLMES Sr. & his sd wife Sarah dec'd which land & meadow they hold together in common & undivided.

Will of **John BLACKMER**, yeoman of Plymouth MA. <Plymouth Co.PR #2096>
<35:169>...dated 30 Jan. 1776, to daus **Sarah, Susanna, Betty & Experience,** all the land at Monument Ponds I purchased of Jabez & Elnathan HOLMES (except woodlot) and all the land that belonged to my late wife at her decease, their brother's part as well as their own; to son **Branch BLACKMER** remainder of estate provided he gives a quit claim to his four sisters of his rights in his mother's estate; son **Branch**, executor. Witnesses: John COTTON, Mary COTTON, Rosseter COTTON. Sworn to 7 Oct. 1794 by Rosseter COTTON, the other two witnesses being dead. <35:170> Bond 20 Oct. 1794 of **Branch BLACKMER**, gent., exr. Sureties: Ephraim SPOONER and Stephen MARCY, Physician, of Plymouth. Witnesses: Jonathan HILL, Isaac LOTHROP. <35:206> Notice, sworn to by exr. 10 Jan. 1795.

John DILLINGHAM Jr. et al to **Deacon Branch BLACKMER** of Plymouth. <Plymouth Co.Deeds 77:263>
...22 Apr. 1795, John DILLINGHAM Jr. of Sandwich, Joseph SILVESTER of Plymouth & Jonathan HARLOW, of Halifax, all yeomen, for Ł168.15s sold to Deacon Branch BLACKMER, yeoman...land in Plymouth at a place called Homeses Point at Monument Ponds which was given to our wifes by their Honoured father's last will, Deacon John BLACKMER of Plymouth dec'd...also Susannah the wf of Joseph SILVESTER, Sarah the wf of John DILLINGHAM and Betsey wf of Jonathan HARLOW quits their whole right of & in the above premises. Signed by all except Betsey HARLOW. No witnesses. Ack. same day by all grantors except Betsey HARLOW. Rec. June 1795.

Joseph BRAMHALL of Merideth NY to **Deacon Branch BLACKMER** of Plymouth. <Plymouth Co.Deeds 107:40>
...18 Sept. 1805, Joseph BRAMHALL, yeoman & wf Experience of Merideth, Delaware Co. NY, for $186.00 sold to Deacon Branch BLACKMER, yeoman...land in Plymouth at Monument Ponds at a place called Holmes' Point, viz: all my right title & interest in sd peice of land which was given to my wife Experience by my honoured Father John BLACKMER late of Plymouth dec'd by his last will. Witnesses: Abner BARTLETT, Frances BARTLETT. Ack. same day by grantors in Plymouth Co. Rec. 8 Oct. 1805.

Estate of **Nathaniel BARNES** of Plymouth MA. <Plymouth Co.PR #1040>
...1781...<27:70;28:236,237;29:27>...(no details given).

MICRO #25 OF 32

Will of **Deacon Elisha HOLMES**, yeoman of Plymouth MA. <Plymouth Co.PR #10381>
<25:314>...dated 19 May 1779, mentions wf **Mary**; all real estate to three surviving sons, viz: **Elisha HOLMES, Bartlet HOLMES & Ellis HOLMES**; £10 each to three surviving daus, viz: **Sarah, Betty & Mary**; £10 each to the following: heirs of dec'd son **Samuel HOLMES**, heirs of dec'd son **Nathaniel HOLMES**, heirs of dec'd dau **Susannah** and heirs of dec'd dau **Jerusha**; three sons, executors. Witnesses: Ivory HOVEY, John BLACKMER, Sarah BLACKMER. <25:314> Letter 7 July 1779. <25:388> Inventory taken 20 July 1779.

Estate of **William BARNES** of Plymouth MA. <Plymouth Co.PR #1049>
<15:49> Letter/Bond 12 Feb. 1760, widow **Mercy BARNES** app'td admx. Sureties: Matthew LEMOTE, sailmaker & Charles CHURCHILL, sailmaker, both of Plymouth. Witnesses: Edward WINSLOW, Consider HOWLAND.

Estate of **James BARTLETT** of Plymouth MA. <MD 21:131>
...Adm. 3 Aug. 1724. Inventory taken 10 Feb. 1724/5. The following heirs are mentioned, viz: mother **Sarah BARTLETT** and brothers & sisters, viz: **Thomas BARTLETT, John BARTLETT, Joseph BARTLETT, Ebenezer BARTLETT, Robert BARTLETT, Lemuel BARTLETT, Hannah CHURCHEL** wf of Eleazer, **Sarah FINNEY** wf of John and **Elizabeth BARTLETT.**

Will of **Thomas BARTLETT** of Plymouth MA. <MD 21:167>
...dated 1 Apr. 1758, mentions wf **Abigail**; dec'd father **Robert BARTLETT**; brother **Ebenezer BARTLETT**, his wf **Abigail** and their sons **Thomas BARTLETT & Ebenezer BARTLETT**; brother **Joseph BARTLETT** & his son **Thomas BARTLETT**; chil. of brother **John BARTLETT** incl. his son **John BARTLETT**; chil. of brother **Robert BARTLETT**; chil. of brother **Lemuel BARTLETT** incl. his son **Lemuel BARTLETT**; chil. of sister **Elizabeth SEARS**, viz: **Thomas SEARS, Willard SEARS & Chloe SEARS**; Sarah FAUNCE wf of Thomas of Plymouth. Pr. 5 Nov. 1764. Inventory taken 15 Jan. 1765.

Thomas BARTLETT Jr. of Plymouth MA to **Rosseter COTTON** of same. <Plymouth Co.Deeds 73:236;72:277>
...3 Apr. 1792, Thomas BARTLETT Jr., yeoman sold to Rosseter COTTON, Physician...my right in certain land of my grandfather Robert BARTLETT late of Plymouth dec'd, being whole of my Father Ebenezer BARTLETT's share & whole of my uncle Thomas BARTLETT's share he gave me by will. Witness: Joanna COTTON.

James & Stephen BARNABE to **Ephraim MORTON.** <Plymouth Co.Deeds 2:12>
...4 Mar. 1695/6...mentions grandfather Robert BARTLETT.

Estate of **James BARNABY.** <Plymouth Col.PR 3:2:98>
Inventory taken 30 Oct. 1677 by Joseph BARTLETT, Thomas FAUNCE, William CLARK. <Plymouth Col.Rec. 5:247> Settlement of estate, 30 Oct. 1677, widow **Lydia BARNABY** to have all movables on condition, as she is to marry **John NELSON** of Plymouth late of Middleboro, if they will bring up the two children of **James BARNABY** till they are 14 & then pay them £6 apiece, then **Lydia** has movables & **John NELSON** the lands till the children come of age; her two brothers **Benjamin BARTLETT & Joseph BARTLETT**, overseers. <5:249> Guardianship, last Tues. Oct. 1684, **James BARNABY** chose father in law **John NELSON** as gdn.

Thomas FAUNCE to **Samuel NELSON.** <Plymouth Co.Deeds 32:220>
...On 26 Feb. 1738, Thomas FAUNCE having sold & wf Lydia not releasing, she does so now. Witnesses: Ruth DOTY, Ruth KEMPTON.

James FAUNCE et al to **Henry THOMAS** of Middleboro MA. <Plymouth Co.Deeds 50:81>
...10 Mar. 1761, James FAUNCE of Plimpton and Thomas FAUNCE, Peleg FAUNCE and Paul DOTY & wf Ruth all of Plymouth, for £5.6s8d sold to Henry THOMAS...all our right...in the fifth lot in the South Purchase in Middleborough...being four fifths of one sixth part of sd 45 acre lot. Ack. 23 Mar. 1761 by Ruth, 30 Mar. 1761 by James, Thomas & Peleg. Rec. 23 Aug. 1765.

Estate of **Thomas FAUNCE**, husbandman of Plymouth MA. <Plymouth Co.PR #7551>
<11:209> Letter 16 June 1749, son **James FAUNCE**, laborer of Plymouth, app'td admr. <11:272> Inventory taken 3 Jan. 1749; incl. homestead, £1800; 4 acre share in cedar swamp, £50; some things of his daughter **Ruth RIDER**'s & some things of **Jabez**'s. <11:345> Account of admr., 16 Feb. 1749; mentions sister **Ruth RIDER.** <11 :347> Settlement 6 Mar. 1749, all land to son **James FAUNCE,** he paying remaining siblings, viz: **Thomas FAUNCE, Peleg FAUNCE, Ruth DOTEN** wf of Paul, labourer of Plymouth and **Lydia FAUNCE.** <11:351> Account of admr., 31 Mar. 1750; **James FAUNCE**'s double portion is £148.8., remaining children's share, £74.40 each.

James FAUNCE of Plympton MA to **Shadrach STANDISH.** <Plymouth Co.Deeds 55:236>
...30 Jan. 1771, James FAUNCE, husbandman to Shadrach STANDISH...land & house in Plympton where I now dwell...also 20 acre lot I bought of George STURTEVANT that he bought of Nehemiah STURTEVANT. Joanna FAUNCE signs.

James FAUNCE of Halifax MA to **William PERRY** of same. <Plymouth Co.Deeds 59:1>
...12 Mar. 1777, James FAUNCE, yeoman to William PERRY, housewright...four acre fresh meadow in Halifax at Bearce's Meadow. Ack. 17 Mar. 1777.

James FAUNCE of Plimouth MA to **Josiah MORTON** of same. <Plymouth Co.Deeds 40:258>
...13 Mar. 1749, James FAUNCE, labourer, for Ł2400 sold to Josiah MORTON, gent...all the homestead that my Father died seized of...at the Ele/Eel River...also all that share or lot of cedar swamp which my Honoured Father Thomas FAUNCE bought of Stephen BARNABY 12 Oct. 1749...which estate ...on the 6 Mar. 1749 was assigned & settled on the sd James. Wf Sarah releases dower. Ack. same day. Rec. 17 Aug. 1750.

James FAUNCE of Plimpton to **Josiah CHURCHEL/CHURCHILL** of Plimouth. <Plymouth Co.Deeds 41:225>
...2 Sept. 1751, James FAUNCE, yeoman, for Ł43 sold to Josiah CHURCHEL, cordwainer...marsh & meadow at Ele/Eel River in Plymouth...bounded by land of Nathaniel WARREN & Capt. Josiah MORTON... being the same meadow & marsh which the late Rev. Elder Thomas FAUNCE dec'd by his last will... gave to my Honoured Mother Mrs. Lydia FAUNCE dec'd and in ye settlement of her Estate was settled upon me. Wf Sarah releases dower. Witnesses: James HOVEY, Lydia HOVEY. Ack. same day by James. Rec. 27 May 1752.

Estate of **James FAUNCE**, yeoman of Halifax MA. <Plymouth Co.PR #7515>
<27:99> Letter 5 Aug. 1782, **James FAUNCE,** mason of Sandwich, app'td admr. <28:453> Inventory taken 2 Sept. 1782 by Ignatius LORING, Esq. of Plympton and Thomas FULLER & William STURTEVANT of Halifax; homestead, Ł200; woodland adjoining Bridgewater, Ł15; four acre meadow, Ł13.6.8. <28:454> Account of admr., 3 Mar. 1783; paid widow **Mary FAUNCE** for necessaris, Ł20; provisions for the family. <28:455> 2d Inventory taken 12 Mar. 1783; homestead, Ł170.16s; wood lott, Ł19.4.; piece of meadow, Ł12. Division of real estate, 25 Mar. 1783; all real estate settled on 2d son **James FAUNCE,** he paying the remaining children, viz: **Nathaniel FAUNCE** (eldest son), **Sarah FAUNCE, Barnaby FAUNCE, William FAUNCE & Lucy FAUNCE.**

James FAUNCE of Sandwich MA to **Lothrop HOLMES** of Plymouth. <Plymouth Co.Deeds 52:89;55:236>
...26 Mar. 1783, James FAUNCE, mason, for Ł213.6s8d silver money sells to Lothrop HOLMES...all the land of his Father James FAUNCE of Halifax which the latter bought of Jonathan RIPLEY by deed of 14 Sept. 1772 (57:2)...also land bought by father of Caleb LORING 8 Aug. 1777 (59:62). Wf Thankful releases dower. Ack. 26 Mar. 1783 by both.

Estate of **James FAUNCE**, yeoman of Sandwich MA. <Barnstable Co.PR>
<44:volume burnt>...will burnt. Witnesses: Nathan NYE Jr., Obed B. NYE, Charles NYE. <41:161> Letter 12 July 1825, William FAUNCE app'td admr.

BARNSTABLE COUNTY DEEDS, through 1874: (re: FAUNCE, Sandwich)

<1:165> 1790, James FAUNCE from Eliab FISH of Fairfield ME.
<2:270> 1797, James FAUNCE, mason from Jonathan FISH Jr., admr. of Seth FISH.
<2:271> 1797, James FAUNCE, mason from Zenas NYE.
<2:272> 1799, James FAUNCE, bricklayer from Nathaniel FREEMAN et al.
<2:273> 1802, James FAUNCE from Nathan TOBEY et al, right in Joshua TOBEY.
<15:92> 1835, James FAUNCE from William H. COBB.
<19:42> 1835, James FAUNCE from William FAUNCE.
<45:411> 1849, James H. FAUNCE from Braddock R. CHILDS.
<47:562> 1851, James H. FAUNCE from John BARKER.
<52:324> 1852, James H. FAUNCE from John BARKER.
<53:63> 1852, James H. FAUNCE from Benjamin CHIPMAN.
<61:518> 1856, James H. FAUNCE from William HEFFERMAN.
<61:519> 1856, James H. FAUNCE from William HEFFERMAN.
<64:146> 1857, James H. FAUNCE from Charles SHULTS (also 64:429).

<19:38> 1835, James FAUNCE to William H. COBB.
<19:277> 1836, James FAUNCE to William H. FESSENDEN.
<19:42> 1835, William FAUNCE to James FAUNCE.
<49:160> 1852, James H. FAUNCE to Benjamin CHIPMAN.
<49:177> 1856, James H. FAUNCE to John BARKER.
<61:517> 1856, James H. FAUNCE & wf Polly to William HEFFERMAN.
<62:307> 1856, James H. FAUNCE to John A. SMITH.
<63:127> 1857, James H. FAUNCE to Charles SHULTS.
<75:491> 1864, James H. FAUNCE et al to Isaiah HATCH.
<75:494> 1864, James H. FAUNCE et al to John BASSETT.
<87:214> 1865, James H. FAUNCE et al to William HEFFERMAN.
<93:259> 1867, James H. FAUNCE et al to James W. CROCKER.
<95:433> 1870, James H. FAUNCE et al to William HEFFERMAN.
<107:295> 1872, James H. FAUNCE et al to William H.F. BURBANK.

Will of **Samuel NELLSON/NELSON** of Plimouth MA. <Plymouth Co.PR #14575>
<14:468>...dated 17 June 1754, mentions youngest son **Ebenezer NELSON;** 2d son **Samuel Nichols NELSON** & his son **Samuel NELSON;** eldest son **John NELSON** & his son **Lemuel Morton NELSON;** grandaughter **Sarah COBB;** wf **Sarah;** daus **Hannah DYER, Sarah SHURTLEFF, Bathsheba HOLMES;** son **Ebenezer** & son in law **Abner HOLMES,** executors. Witnesses: Mary WADSWORTH, Mary WADSWORTH Jr., John WADSWORTH. <14:475> Pr. 3 Apr. 1758. <15:136> Inventory taken 28 Apr. 1759 by Josiah MORTON, Theophilus COTTON, Joshua SWIFT; sworn to by exrs. 20 June 1759. <19:177> Petition of **John NELSON** to sell real estate to pay father's debts & support widow, his eldest son **Lemuel Morton NELSON** having died in

the lifetime of **Samuel**, the testator; granted 20 Jan. 1764. <19:186> Bond 13 Mar. 1765, of **John NELSON** & Lemuel MORTON. Witnesses: Edward WINSLOW, Sarah WINSLOW.

Elnathan HOLMES et al to **Elnathan HOLMES Jr.** of Plymouth MA. <Plymouth Co.Deeds 81:78> ...12 Oct. 1796, Elnathan HOLMES & wf Barshaba, Patience HOLMES, Lydia EVERSON, Joanna BURBANK & Joseph BURBANK, all of Plymouth & Kingston & Abner HOLMES, housewright of Kingston, for $11.33 sold to Elnathan HOLMES Jr., cordwainer...all our right & interest in the 10th share in the 2nd Division of the 8th great Lot & Last Division of Plymouth & Plimton Commons...sd lot was laid out to our grandfather Samuel NELLSON and one quarter of the same was given by him to our Mother who was his daughter by his will...also we hereby sell our Right to our grandfather George MORTON's out land being our Right to the land above Ealriver laid out to him called the Darling Lot which contains in the whole 45 acres...also our right to an 80 acre lot laid out to him at half way ponds Brook, referance to sd proprietors first Book Page 186 for bounds...also our right to his share in the 5th Great Lot of the Last Division of the Commons...excepting the right of Joanna BURBANK in the Lot laid out to Samuel NELLSON which she has sold to Rosseter COTTON. Signed & ack same day by Bathsheba HOLMES, Patience HOLMES, Lydia EVERSON, Joanna BURBANK/BURBANKS. Witnesses: Josiah COTTON, Rosseter COTTON. Rec. same day.

Guardianship of Children of **Lt. John WETHERELL** of Scituate MA. <Plymouth Co.PR 1:308> ...23 July 1700, **Jonathan MOREY** of Plymouth, father in law of **Thomas & Joshua WETHERELL**, sons of **Lt. John WETHERELL**, is chosen their gdn.

Will of **Jonathan MORY/MOREY** of Plymouth MA. <Plymouth Co.PR> <2:133>...dated 24 Feb. 1699/1700, mentions wf **Hannah** (executrix), son **John MORY**, dau **Hannah BUMPAS**, son **Jonathan MOREY**. Witnesses: Joseph BARTLET, Joseph HOLMES, William BASSETT. Pr. 16 June 1708 on oath of William BASSETT & Joseph HOLMES. <4:219> Receipt 12 May 1720, of **John & Hannah BUMPAS** of Rochester, to mother **Hannah**, exx. Witnesses: Thomas WITHERELL, Thomas CROADE.

Jonathan MORY/MOREY Sr. of Plymouth MA to **Jonathan MORY/MOREY** of same. <Plymouth Co.Deeds 5:45> ...17 July 1691, Jonathan MOREY Sr., for half a share of lands in Rochester, both divided & undivided...which is already secured & by deed confirmed unto me by ny natural son Jonathan MORY, sold unto him...halfe of all my lands in Plymouth...upland & meadoe...both of my tenement that I now dwell on & all other lands whatsoever...after ye decease of me ye sd Jonathan MORY & Mary my wife. Witnesses: Ephraim LITTLE, William BASSETT. Ack. 25 July 1704. Rec. 2 Feb. 1704.

William MOREY & Josiah MOREY of Plymouth MA. <Plymouth Co.PR #14170> ...1837...<32:326;41:293> Letters. (guardianships?)

Will of **John BUMP** of Wareham MA. <Plymouth Co.PR> <16:338>...dated 11 Sept. 1749...to wf **Jean**, one half of my dwelling house, viz: that end which we now live in...but if she shall encline (after my decease) to go and live with her children... to son **Jonathan BUMP**, one acre fresh meadow adjoining Plimo line on the northwest side of Weweantick river and allso that 20 acres which he hath laid out in the undivided on which he now dwells ...to son **John BUMP**, my dwelling house & barn & land...also meadow on east side of the river, also salt meadow on south side of Agawam river which I bought of Nathaniel CHUBBUCK, also one half of meaodw & upland in Woouknoco neck bounded by land of Edward BUMPS & Isaac BUMP...to son **Samuel** remaining part of homestead adjoining to SHEARMAN's land & meadows...to dau **Hannah BUMP**, ₤5...to dau **Sarah WHITE**, 5s; to dau **Mary ELLIS**, ₤10; to dau **Lydia KING**, ₤5; son **John**, executor. Witnesses: Ebenezer BENSON, Abigail THATCHER, Rowland THATCHER. Letter/Bond 2 Aug. 1762, **John BUMP**, exr Surety: Rowland THATCHER. (Ebenezer BENSON also swears to will same day.)

George WHITE, yeoman of Wareham to **Isaac LOTHROP & John BISHOP.** <Plymouth Co.Deeds 39:58> ...19 Dec. 1747...land he bought in 1739. Rec. 29 Dec. 1747.

George WHITE, yeoman of Sharon CT to **Jeremiah BUMP Jr.** of Wareham MA. <Plymouth Co.Deeds 53:166> ...12 Oct. 1765...land in Wareham. Ack. 2 June 1766 by George. Rec. 19 May 1767.

MICRO #26 OF 32

Will of **George WHITE**, gent. of Sharon CT. <Litchfield Co.PR 7:75> ...dated 20 June 1787...weak in body...to heirs of eldest son **John WHITE** dec'd, 20s...to son **Archelus WHITE**, 10s...to dau **Mary GOODRICH**, ₤10...to son **George WHITE** (executor), remainder of estate. Witnesses: Daniel ELUSE(sp), Beaane BOLAND, David BOLAND Jr. Codicil dated 20 Feb. 1788; to Hannah WHITE wf of Nathaniel, my iron pot; to Sarah HUNTER wf of Nathaniel, my low chest and to my two daughters **Mary GOODRICH & Elener STRONG** all my household furniture...to **Josiah STRONG** one suit of black broadcloth close/clothes...all the estate that which my two daughters **Mary & Elenor** shall receive...may not be taken by attachment or execution for their husbands' debts. Witnesses: Hannah WHITE, Elenor STRONG, Ashbel GOODRICH.

PLYMOUTH COUNTY PROBATE: (re: John BUMP, all on index**)**

1715	John	Rochester	will	#3273, 3:411,413,414
1762	John	Wareham	will	#3272, 16:338,339,340
1764	John	Wareham	will	#3274, 19:135,136,333
1813	John	Carver	gdn.	#3275, 41:157

PLYMOUTH COUNTY PROBATE, cont-d: (re: John BUMP, all on index)

1822	John	Wareham	adm.	#3271, 52:127;54:428
1875	John	Carver	adm.	#3276, 129:391;130:231;146:109

Will of **John BUMPUS Sr.** of Rochester MA. <Plymouth Co.PR #3273>
...dated 10 July 1710, mentions wf **Sarah** and following chil., viz: **John BUMPUS, James BUMPUS & Isaac BUMPUS** (all married), **Mary BENSON, Sarah PERRY, Job BUMPUS** (married), **Jeremiah BUMPUS, Edward BUMPUS.** Pr. 7 Mar. 1715/6. Inventory taken 7 Jan. 1715/6.

PLYMOUTH COUNTY DEEDS: (re: MOREY)

<91:179> - 1 Oct. 1787, Isaac BOWLES, Jr., shipwright of Wareham (wf Anna signs) to William & Elisha MOREY, seamen of Wareham.
<102:91> - 4 Oct. 1796, Ward SWIFT, gent. of Sandwich to Benjamin MOREY Jr. of Wareham, Elisha MOREY of Plymouth & William MOREY of Plymouth, all yeomen. Ack. 4 Jan. 1797. Rec. 12 Mar. 1805.
<101:209> - 23 Mar. 1804, Elisha MOREY, yeoman of Sandwich (wf Bathsheba signs) to William MOREY of Plymouth, all his real estate in Plymouth & Wareham. Rec. 5 Nov 1805
<101:209> - 23 Mar. 1804, Benjamin MOREY to William MOREY, yeomen of Plymouth. Rec. 5 Nov. 1805.
<147:37> - 25 Feb. 1822, Rev. Josiah STURTEVANT & wf Lucy of Barnstable; Ellis MOREY & wf Rebecca of Nantucket.

Heirs of **Job BOURNE** of Sandwich MA. <Barnstable Co.PR 3:198>
Receipt 13 Sept. 1714, of **Jonathan MOREY,** yeoman of Plymouth & wf **Hannah,** dau of Job BOURNE late of Sandwich dec'd, for Ł50 received of our mother in law Mrs. **Ruhamah HERSEY** of Sandwich & our Bretheren **Timothy BOURNE, Eliezer BOURNE & Hezekiah BOURNE** of Sandwich, for share of estate of our Deceased Father Job BOURNE. Witnesses: William BASSETT, Daniel PARKER. Ack. same day by both.

Will of **Jonathan MOREY,** yeoman of Plymouth MA. <Plymouth Co.PR #14163>
<6:347>...dated 1 Sept. 1732, mentions wf **Hannah**; to eldest son **Benjamin MOREY,** land near Wonconguo at Plymouth, 10th lot 2d division of Plymouth & Plympton; to son **Jonathan MOREY,** four acres south of (testator's) dwelling house; to dau **Mariah SWIFT,** 20s (has already given her Ł20); to dau **Thankfull SWIFT,** 20s (has already given her Ł20); to dau **Reliance,** Ł20; movable estate divided between wf **Hannah,** dau **Reliance** & son **Joseph MOREY**; to the two children of Maria TROWBRIDGE dec'd, viz: Mary & Maria, Ł10, I haveing heretofore paid to their Father John TROWBRIDGE, Ł37 in their mothers life time; to son **Joseph MOREY,** all real estate in Plymouth not already bequeathed; if he dies without issue, to be divided among the other children; to sons **Benjamin, Jonathan & Joseph,** all right in Providence RI, in ye right of my Grandfather & Father dec'd; wf **Hannah,** executrix. Witnesses: Nathaniel SHURTLEFF, Samuel BARTLETT, Francis ADAMS Jr. <6:348> Pr. 26 Apr. 1733; will sworn to by Samuel BARTLETT & Nathaniel SHURTLEFF; **Hanah MOREY** app'td admx. <6:390> Inventory taken 25 May 1733 by Stephen CHURCHILL, John BARTLETT, Ebenezer WING; incl. the old house & lot, Ł30; one acre in partnership with William ELLAS/ELLIS, Ł12; old orchard, Ł45; meadow & upland above the old orchard, Ł35; land soweast of ELLAS/ELLIS house he latley bought of MOREY, Ł12.10s; three acre feald near black ground, Ł16; 120 acres, Ł90; land in partnership with the Indans, 1000 ackers, Ł37.10s; sworn to 20 Sept. 1733 by Ebenezer WING & John BARTLETT and 25 Sept 1733 by Stephen CHURCHILL.

Estate of **Benjamin MOREY** of Plymouth MA. <Plymouth Co.PR #14151>
<9:219> Letter/Bond 3 Apr. 1744, Josiah SWIFT, yeoman of Sandwich, app'td admr. Sureties: Returne WAITE, tayler & James SHURTLEFF, cordwainer, both of Plymouth. Witnesses: Enoch WARD, Benjamin STEVENS. <9:288> Inventory taken 15 Apr. 1744 by Josiah MORTON, Joseph BARTLETT & John BLACKMER; dwelling house & homestead, Ł290; 20 acres at Herring Pond, Ł80; meadow at Sandwich, Ł80; land in the woods, Ł1; total estate, Ł800.16.. <10:365> Account of admr., 6 Mar. 1746; total personal estate, Ł349.16, minus payments of Ł209.11.6, left Ł140.4.6. <10:376> Letter/Bond 6 Mar. 1746, widow **Thankful MOREY** app'td gdn. of **John MOREY,** minor. <original> Bonds 6 Mar. 1746, widow is app'td gdn. of **Elijah MOREY & Cornelius MOREY,** minors.

Thankful MOREY et al of Plymouth MA to **James SWIFT** of Sandwich. <Plymouth Co.Deeds 41:59>
...23 Feb. 1750, Thankful MOREY, spinster, Benjamin MOREY, John MOREY, Cornelius MOREY & Elijah MOREY, yeomen, for Ł14 sold to James SWIFT, yeoman...land & dwelling house...wherein we now dwell ...bounded by Plymouth Road and land of William ROBIN...reserving to us our heirs & assigns the liberty of using the well on sd land and of passage to and from the same. Witnesses: Ebenezer HARLOW, Elisha TUPPER. Ack. 28 Feb. 1750/1 by all grantors. Rec. 16 Mar. 1750/1.

Benjamin MOREY et al to **Cornelius MOREY** of Plymouth MA. <Plymouth Co.Deeds 44:238>
...26 Oct. 1753, Benjamin MOREY, John MOREY, Elijah MOREY, Ebenezer HARLOW & wf Moriah & Thankful MOREY, all of Plymouth and Josiah SWIFT Jr. & wf Mary of Sandwich, for Ł40 sold to Cornelius MOREY, yeoman...land & swampy grounds in Plymouth...near to the dwelling house of Thomas SWIFT, which lands Benjamin MOREY late of sd Plymouth dec'd died seized of...bounded by land of Thomas SWIFT, the Sea, the Countrey Road leading from Sandwich to Plymouth and lands of William ROBIN... incl. the dwelling house...also another piece of land on south westerly side of sd Road...also land lying by the Herring Pond in Plymouth not far off from the aforesaid land...bounded by lands of Jabez WICKETT & William ROBIN. Witnesses: Thomas SWIFT, Jabez TUPPER, Abigail SWIFT, Samuel TUPPER. Ack. 31 Oct. 1753 by Benjamin MOREY, John MOREY, Josiah & Mary SWIFT and Jerusha MOREY

released dower. Ack. 28 Jan. 1756 by Elijah MOREY, Ebenezer & Moriah HARLOW and Thankful MOREY. Rec. 28 Feb. 1758.

Will of **Cornelius MOREY**, yeoman of Plymouth MA. <Plymouth Co.PR #14153>
<38:339>...dated 21 Mar. 1803, mentions wf **Jerusha**; eldest sons **Elijah MOREY & Cornelius MOREY** (both under age), youngest sons **William MOREY & Josiah MOREY** and daus **Sarah & Jerusha.** <38:340> Pr. 7 June 1803. <44:186> Dower. <44:187> Division.

<u>PLYMOUTH COUNTY DEEDS</u>: (re: Elijah MOREY, all to 1859)

<49:120> - 7 Apr. 1763, John CORNISH, yeoman of Plymouth to Elijah MOREY, husbandman of Plymouth land bounded by Cornelius MOREY. Rec. 14 July 1764.
<49:146> - 16 July 1764, Elijah MOREY to Sylvanus BARTLETT, land bought in 49:120. Wf Rebecca releases dower. Ack. 27 Aug. 1764. Rec. 1 Oct. 1764.
<97:27> - 16 June 1803, Robert HOLMES to Elijah MOREY, yeomen of Plymouth, land at Ponds.
<112:8> - 3 May 1809, Elkanah HOLMES & Elijah MOREY, yeomen of Plymouth to Josiah CORNISH.
<176:52> - 22 Oct. 1832, Elijah MOREY & wf Grace dau of Josiah & Abigail CORNISH. Jerusha MOREY releases dower.
<179:144>- 13 Jan. 1834, Elijah MOREY & wf Grace, grantor.
<180:214>- 27 Apr. 1835, Elijah MOREY, mariner of Plymouth & wf Grace to Elijah MOREY Jr., mariner of same, reserving for self & wf for life.

(References only: 101:87,189,191,202 (1805); 106:17 (1807); 122:18;123:60,70 (1813); 179:175 (1833); 182:72 (1835); 196:49 (1838); 214:239 (1845); 214:239 (1845).)

Will of **Josiah SWIFT**, yeoman of Wareham MA. <Plymouth Co.PR #19903>
<28:253>...dated 12 Mar. 1787, mentions wf **Mary**; estate to be divided among three sons **Jesse SWIFT, Elisha SWIFT & Benjamin SWIFT**; to dau **Mary ELLIS** wf of Stephen, ₤3; to daus **Hannah BENSON** wf of Joseph and **Mercy GIBBS** widow of Seth, ₤5 each; son **Jesse**, executor. Witnesses: Joseph STURTEVANT, Reward STURTEVANT, Jonathan GIBBS. On 12 Feb. 1803, all three sons decline to administer. Pr. 18 Feb. 1803, Josiah SWIFT app'td admr. <u>Inventory</u> taken 3 Mar. 1803. <u>Account</u> of admr., 3 Mar. 1803.

Will of **Elisha SWIFT** of Wareham MA. <Plymouth Co.PR #19867>
<38:519>...dated 25 Jan. 1804, mentions wf **Martha**; real estate to eldest sons **Samuel SWIFT & Asa SWIFT** (executors); $50.00 to eldest dau **Mary SWIFT**; dau **Martha SWIFT**; son **Elisha SWIFT**, under 14. Witnesses: Noble EVERETT, Josiah SWIFT, Jesse SWIFT Jr. Witnesses sworn, 5 Mar. 1804. <38:520> Letter; Executor declines. <40:59> Inventory. <40:60> Notice. <40:154> Account.

Will of **Elisha SWIFT** of Wareham MA. <Plymouth Co.PR>
<140:314>...dated 30 May 1871, to wf **Zerviah,** $500.00; chil. of dau **Betsey C. NICKERSON;** sons **Alexander SWIFT, Asa C. SWIFT, Thomas C. SWIFT** (executor) **& Andrew J. SWIFT.** <124:453> <u>Petition</u> 23 Oct. 1871, for probate by exr., signed by sons (all of Wareham except Thomas of Sandwich) and grandchildren, viz: **Lucy GODFREY** wf of Bina of Plymouth, **Cranston NICKERSON, Lorenzo NICKERSON, Emma ELLIS** wf of Puma of Dennis and **Arietta CAHOON** wf of Joshua of Cambridge. <124:453> Letter. <109:410> Inventory. (Bowman notes he left a wife named Sophia.)

<u>PLYMOUTH COUNTY DEEDS</u>: (re: MOREY)

<25:218> - , Jonathan MOREY from Malatiah BOURNE.
<28:161> - 22 Feb. 1733, Joseph MOREY, yeoman of Plymouth & William ELLIS, innholder of same, exchange land. Refers to deed of Benjamin MOREY of 1731.
<38:121> - 1746, Joseph MOREY from Seth SWIFT.
<38:121> - 1746, Joseph MOREY to William ELLIS.
<38:122> - 1746, Joseph MOREY to Seth SWIFT.
<38:122> - 13 Oct. 1746, Joseph MOREY to Thomas SWIFT. Wf Mary releases dower.
<41:59> - 1750/1, Elijah MOREY to James SWIFT.
<130:46> - 24 Oct. 1816, John BLACKWELL, mariner of Wareham & wf Hannah to Asa MOREY & Joseph MOREY, mariners of Plymouth.
<131:46> - 24 Oct. 1816, Asa MOREY & Joseph MOREY to John BLACKWELL.
<140:222> - 3 June 1820, Asa MOREY & Joseph MOREY, husbandmen of Nantucket to John BLACKWELL. Clarissa MOREY & Rebecca MOREY sign.

(References only: 44:238; 49:146; 53:154.)

Estate of **Sergt. William HARLOW.** <Plymouth Co.PR; MD 12:193>
<1:104> <u>Settlement</u> 18 Sept. 1691, mentions widow, seven daughters and sons **Samuel HARLOW, William HARLOW, Nathaniel HARLOW, Benjamin HARLOW.** <1:105> Pr. 3d Tues. Sept. 1691, widow **Mary HARLOW** app'td admr.

Estate of **William HARLOW.** <Plymouth Co.PR>
<3:107> <u>Letter</u> 5 Mar. 1711/2, widow **Lydia HARLOW** app'td admx. <3:135> <u>Division</u> 21 June 1712, among the widow **Lydia HARLOW**; grandson **Thomas DOTEN** only son of dec'd dau **Elizabeth;** eldest son **Thomas HARLOW**; sons **William HARLOW, Robert HARLOW & Isaac HARLOW**; daus **Mary, Elizabeth & Rebecca.**

Estate of **Lydia HARLOW**, widow. <Plymouth Co.PR>
<4:231> Letter 11 July 1720, son **Thomas HARLOW**, husbandman of Plymouth app'td admr. <4:250> Division 24 Dec. 1720, among surviving chil., viz: **Thomas HARLOW, William HARLOW, Robert HARLOW Isaac HARLOW, Lydia CHURCHILL** wf of Barnabas, **Rebecca HARLOW** and **Thomas DOTY Jr.** son of dec'd dau **Elizabeth** wf of Thomas.

Estate of **Thomas HARLOW.** <Plymouth Co.PR>
<10:238> Letter 3 Dec. 1746, widow **Jedidah HARLOW** & **Thomas HARLOW**, husbandman, app'td admrs. <10:309> Petition 6 Jan. 1746, of chil. & heirs, viz: Joseph BARTLETT as gdn. for **Nathaniel & Jedidah HARLOW; Thomas HARLOW, Jonathan HARLOW, Eleazer HARLOW & Lydia HARLOW.**

Will of **Jonathan HARLOW** of Plymouth MA. <Plymouth Co.PR #9239>
<30:26>...dated 28 Mar. 1786, mentions wf **Sarah,** sons **Ansel HARLOW & Jonathan HARLOW** and daus **Sarah, Jedidah, Lucy, Polly & Clarisy.** Letter/Bond 3 Oct. 1786, **Ansel HARLOW** of Plymouth & **Jonathan HARLOW** of Halifax. <Plymouth Co.Deeds 109:145>...20 Mar. 1789, division between Ansel HARLOW of Plymouth, Jonathan HARLOW, yeoman of Halifax, Isaac BARNES & wf Lucy, Jedidah BARNES widow of Lemuel and Mary/Polly & Clarissa HARLOW, all of Plymouth, chil. of Jonathan HARLOW dec'd.

Will of **Jonathan HARLOW** of Middleborough MA. <Plymouth Co.PR>
<77:455>...dated 27 Dec. 1830, mentions wf **Betsey;** daus **Mercy** and **Betsey WOOD** wf of Eliab; dec'd sons **Jonathan HARLOW & Eleazer HARLOW;** son **Stephen HARLOW;** remainder of estate to following sons & their heirs, viz: **Lewis HARLOW, John HARLOW, Lemuel HARLOW, Ivory HARLOW & Branch HARLOW.** Witnesses: Bradford HARLOW, Levi WOOD, Temperance WOOD. Pr. 6 Nov. 1832. <77:328> Division 27 Apr. 1835, to following heirs, viz: **John HARLOW,** heirs of **Lewis HARLOW; Lemuel HARLOW,** heirs of **Ivory HARLOW,** heirs of **Stephen HARLOW; Branch HARLOW.** On 2 Dec. 1833, **Branch HARLOW** of Middleboro app'd admr. of **Betsey HARLOW,** widow.

Estate of **Lewis & Hannah HARLOW.** <Plymouth Co.PR>
<66:309> Request 8 Jan. 1807, of widow **Hannah HARLOW** that Capt. John PATY be app'td admr. Dower set off, 13 July 1830, to the widow; sworn to 9 Aug. 1830. <12:31> Letter/Bond 4 Dec. 1848, Charles GOODWIN app'td admr. of estate of **Hannah HARLOW** of Plymouth. Sureties: Benjamin BRAMHALL, Benjamin B. GOODING.

Lemuel HARLOW et al to **Branch HARLOW** of MIddleborough MA. <Plymouth Co.Deeds 182:134>
...29 Sept. 1834, Lemuel HARLOW of Duxbury, Charles GOODWIN & wf Hannah, Lewis HARLOW, Jabez HARLOW & wf Betsey, Otis HARLOW, Isaac BARNES & wf Lucy and John HARLOW, convey to Branch HARLOW... two undivided sixth parts of real estate which Jonathan HARLOW late of Middleboro died seized.

PLYMOUTH COUNTY PROBATE: (re: HARLOW)

1691	William	Plymouth	adm.	#9305, 1:104,105
1692	Mary	Plymouth		#9268, 1:180
1711	William	Plymouth	adm.	#9306, 3:107,108,134,135
1712	Lydia et al	Plymouth	gdn.	#9267, 3:137,157,158;4:285,286
1720	Lydia	Plymouth	adm.	#9266, 4:231,249,250
1720	Mary	Plymouth	adm.	#9269, 4:232,250,251
1721	Nathaniel	Plympton	adm.	#9276, 4:317,318,340
1724	Isaac	Plymouth	adm.	#9219, 4:445;5:92
1728	Lemuel et al	Plymouth	gdn.	#9257, 5:406,838;7:269
1728	Samuel	Plymouth	will	#9288, 5:512,513,515
1738	Eleazer	Duxbury	gdn.	#9193, 7:428
1746	Nathaniel et al	Plymouth	gdn.	#9280, 10:293,353
1746	Thomas	Plymouth	adm.	#9302, 10:238,309,331,332
1748	Eleazer	Plymouth	adm.	#9192, 10:474,504
1749	Lemuel	Middleboro	adm.	#9258, 15:89,398;16:1
1749	William	Bridgewater	adm.	#9310, 11:481;12:13
1752	William	Plymouth	adm.	#9307, 12:196,248;16:164;21:106
1755	Amaziah	Plymouth	adm.	#9174, 13:470;16:262
1757	James	Plympton	will	#9255, 15:282,283
1759	Lemuel et al	Middleboro	gdn.	#9259, 15:396,398
1762	Amaziah et al	Plymouth	gdn.	#9175, 18:68,69
1767	Samuel	Plymouth	will	#9289, 19:511,512;20:139;21:152;27:511;35:306
1767	Samuel et al	Plymouth	gdn.	#9290, 19:494,498,508,512
1773	Jabez	Plymouth	adm.	#9233, 21:270,390,391,392;23:4
1779	Benjamin	Middleboro	will	#9179, 25:386,387,534
1781	William Jr.	Middleboro	adm.	#9311, 27:57;28:78,165,166,167,168
1786	Jonathan	Plymouth	will	#9239, 30:26,27
1793	William	Middleboro	will	#9312, 33:254,256,532,533
1795	George	Plymouth	adm.	#9209, 34:48
1795	Nathaniel	Plympton	will	#9277, 35:331,332
1796	Barnabas	Plympton	will	#9178, 35:538,575;37:433
1797	Ephraim	Middleboro	adm.	#9199, 34:140;36:372;37:29,30,31
1797	Ephraim et al	Plym/Midd.	gdn.	#9200, 32:95,333;42:284
1797	James	Plymouth	gdn.	#9226, 32:79
1799	Josiah	Middleboro	will	#9246, 34:348;36:482,483,571,572;37:374
1799	Lemuel	Plymouth	adm.	#9256, 34:179;36:517,518,529,531

PLYMOUTH COUNTY PROBATE, cont-d: (re: HARLOW)

1800	Sylvanus	Plymouth	adm.	#9297, 34:226;37:355
1802	Seth	Plymouth	will	#9293, 38:169,171;58:95,138,139
1804	Amaziah	Plymouth	adm.	#9172, 34:378
1806	Amaziah	Plymouth	adm.	#9173, 39:87
1806	Isaac 2d	Bridgewater	will	#9220, 40:394
1807	Lewis	Plymouth	adm.	#9261, 39:100;44:151,152;69:309
1808	Ezra	Middleboro	adm.	#9204, 39:368;42:544;44:339,340,341,342
1809	Jerusha et al	Plymouth	gdn.	#9229, 41:4
1809	Jesse	Plymouth	will	#9230, 43:26,27,80,177,179,198,301,478,481,523; 59:109;66:475
1810	William	Plymouth	gdn.	#9308, 41:19
1811	Jesse	Plymouth	adm.	#9231, 39:282;43:366
1811	Gideon	Duxbury	adm.	#9211, 39:301;43:487
1812	Eleazer	Duxbury	adm.	#9194, 39:369;44:360
1814	John	Middleboro	will	#9234, 45:436,437;47:26,27
1816	Benjamin	Plymouth	adm.	#9181, 46:188;48:210,211;49:354;50:388
1816	Levi Jr.	Plympton	adm.	#9260, 46:147;48:122,123;49:73,77,81
1821	Benjamin et al	Plymouth	gdn.	#9182, 51:126;74:548
1822	Pelham	Plympton	adm.	#9282, 52:152;56:187,373,374;60:96
1824	Jonathan	Duxbury	adm.	#9240, 52:252;55:296;59:178;60:118,119,120,299
1824	Sarah	Plymouth	adm.	#9291, 52:312;55:373;60:121
1827	Isaac	Midd/Bridge	will	#9221, 64:53,54;68:37;69:121;70:110,174
1827	Nathaniel	Plympton	adm.	#9278, 61:114;64:183,488;68:194;70:430
1828	Sarah	Plymouth	will	#9292, 66:386;67:52,103,212,339;62:328
1829	Ellis	Plymouth	adm.	#9197, 61:265
1831	Nathaniel	Plympton	adm.	#9279, 61:416;70:216;74:560
1831	Patience	Plympton	adm.	#9281, 61:425;70:362,557;68:206;72:39,407;73: 366,389
1832	Ansel	Plymouth	adm.	#9177, 71:120
1832	James	Plymouth	gdn.	#9227, 65:249;72:290;78:130
1832	Lot	Plymouth	adm.	#9264, 71:67
1832	Thomas P.	Plymouth	gdn.	#9303, 65:213;72:7;83:195
1833	Betsey	Middleboro	adm.	#9185, 71:206
1833	Jonathan	Middleboro	will	#9241, 72:455;73:78;74:474;75:58;77:328
1834	Henry	Plymouth	adm.	#9216, 71:253;75:179;77:4;82:136;92:9
1834	William R.	Plymouth	gdn.	#9309, 1**R**:16,23;2**O**:361,465;73:421,440
1835	Mercy	Plymouth	gdn.	#9272, 65:388;73:115;161;77:11,47;79:336
1837	Reuben	Plymouth	adm.	#9285, 10**A**:101;75:449;79:344,345;80:142,144
1839	Ezra	Plymouth	adm.	#10**A**:237;5**T**:180;81:180,181,187
1839	John	Plymouth	adm.	#9236, 5**T**:179;10**A**:239;81:434
1839	Susannah	Plymouth	adm.	#9296, 5**T**:176;10**A**:238;81:181,187
1840	Huldah H.	Plymouth	gdn.	#9217, 1**R**:108;2**O**:420;8:185
1840	John et al	Plymouth	gdn.	#9238, 1**R**:106;2**O**:422;8:194
1840	Nancy	Plymouth	will	#9273, 1**G**:360;82:122
1841	Ephraim	Carver	adm.	#9201, 6**U**:292;10**A**:422,438;83:155;84:407
1841	Ezra	Plymouth	adm.	#9207, 6**U**:256;10**A**:419;83:423;84:40,206,209
1842	Alvin et al	Carver	gdn.	#9171, 1**R**:138;2**O**:453,474;8:273;84:410
1844	Jesse	Plymouth	adm.	#9232, 11:468
1845	Joseph	Plymouth	will	#9244, 87:353
1846	Benjamin 2d	Carver	adm.	#9180, 1**R**:226;3**P**:28;7**V**:146;11**B**:443;88:464;89:385
1847	James	Plymouth	adm.	#9228, 7**V**:208;11**B**:485;89:178;90:43
1847	Sylvanus	Halifax	will	#9299, 1**H**:131;7**V**:341;89:392;90:257
1847	Zenas	Middleboro	will	#9315, 1**G**:469;89:290
1848	Hannah	Plymouth	adm.	#9213, 12**C**:31
1850	Samuel	Plymouth	will	#9287, 1**G**:512;92:10

Will of **Samuel HARLOW** of Plymouth MA. <Plymouth Co.PR 5:512,513,515>
...dated 17 Feb. 1724/5, mentions wf **Hannah**; sons **John HARLOW, William HARLOW, Samuel HARLOW**; minor chil. of dec'd son **Eleazer HARLOW**, viz: **Eliphaz HARLOW, Lemuel HARLOW, Eleazer HARLOW**; dau **Rebecca TABOR**; daus of dec'd son **Eleazer**, viz: **Elizabeth HARLOW, Patience HARLOW**; daus **Hannah HARLOW, Priscilla HARLOW**; wf & son **John**, executors. Witnesses sworn 17 Nov. 1727 & 2 Feb. 1727. Pr. 3 June 1728. Inventory taken 27 Feb. 1727/8.

Estate of **James LEONARD** of Taunton MA to **Eliphaz HARLOW**. <Bristol Co.Deeds 54:423>
...23 June 1772, Capt. Eliphalet LEONARD, gent. of Easton, as admr. on estate of James LEONARD, gent., sells to Eliphaz HARLOW, innkeeper of Taunton, he having been highest bidder at auction 22 June 1772 for £9.1s...the whole of lot #10 in Pine Swamp purchased by James LEONARD from John CRANE (39:86)...nine acres more or less. Witnesses: James WILLIAM. James WILLIAM Jr.

Estate of **Eliphaz HARLOW** of Taunton MA. <Bristol Co.PR>
<148:295> <u>Letter</u> 1 Jan. 1788, widow **Phebe HARLOW**, app'td admx. <29:549> Inventory taken 4 Jan. 1788. <30:204;32:316> Account.

Noah BRIGGS of Taunton MA to **Eliphaz HARLOW** of Rehoboth MA. <Bristol Co.Deeds 35:467> ...7 Mar. 1748, Noah BRIGGS, blacksmith, sells to Eliphaz HARLOW, joyner...dwelling house & one quarter acre & a blacksmiths shop in Taunton...bounded by rhoad that leads from Nathaniel LINKONS/LINCOLN's to Capt. Edmond ANDREWS' and by land of sd ANDREWS...together with another peice of land...opesite to ye afforesd dwelling house with a barn...20 acres...bounded by road that leads from Stephen ANDREWS' to Benjamin LINKON/LINCOLN's, land of sd Stephen ANDREWS and Three mile River...togather with about six acrees & a half in Taunton...bounded by fail Brook, land now owned by James ANDREWS, land of Isaac LINKON/LINCOLN and road that leads from Benjamin LINKON/LINCOLN's to sd Isaac's...togather with about fourteen & a half acres in Taunton...near Long plain and near the Rock called the smooking Rock...bounded by ye highway that was Landons a long by ye now dwelling house of James ANDREWS to Segueganset River & land of Daniel LINKON/LINCOLN & Edmond ANDREWS. Witnesses: Seth WILLIAMS 2d, Samuel WHITE, Nathaniel KNAP. Wf Elisabeth releases dower. Rec. 10 July 1749. <35:521>...1 Mar. 1748, Eliphaz HARLOW, joiner of Rehoboth & wf Hopestill sell to James SABIN...land with dwelling house. Rec. 21 Oct. 1749.

MICRO #27 OF 32

Guardianship of **Eliphaz HARLOW.** <Plymouth Co.Deeds>
<5:406,838>...21 Dec. 1728, guardian app'td for Eliphaz HARLOW (betw. 14-21) of Plymouth. <7:269> ...12 Mar. 1736/7, Eliphas HARLOW, housewright of Norton, now of full age & discharges to Thomas SPOONER of Plymouth.

Eliphaz HARLOW of Dighton MA to **Ephraim HOLMES** of Kingston. <Plymouth Co.Deeds 33:175> ...28 July 1740, Eliphaz HARLOW, joiner, for Ł16.13s4d sells to Ephraim HOLMES, yeoman...all his part of 157th lot in the 2nd Division of Commons in Duxbury & Pembroke & is one third part...settled on me as part of my portion or share in my Honoured Grandfather Benoni DELANO's estate. Witnesses: John HARLOW, Isaac LeBARON. Ack. same day. Rec. 30 Aug. 1740.

Eliphaz HARLOW of Taunton MA from **James SABIN** of Rehoboth. <Bristol Co.Deeds 38:181> ...31 May 1751, Whereas Eliphaz HARLOW, joyner...recovered judgment against James SABIN, yeoman, for Ł31.12s9d and Ł3.2d cost of suit...Where of Execution remains to be done; We Command you there fore that of ye Goods Chattles or Lands of ye sd James...you Cause to be paid...unto ye sd Eliphaz...the afforesd sums with 1s4d more for this Writt;..."Rehoboth ye 18th 1751", Daniel CARPENTER, Esq., chosen by Eliphaz HARLOW ye Creditor, Milles SHOREY chosen by ye wife of James SABIN ye Debtor...Samuel READ chosen by Seth WILLIAMS ye Sheriff all freeholders in ye County of Bristol...to make a just & true apprisement & valuation of so much of ye Real Estate of James SABIN as to answare this Excution;...18 Oct. 1751, appraisal of...part of ye home stead lands of James SABIN...containing nine acres in Rehoboth...bounded by lands of Samuel READ & Daniel PERRIN ...also sixteen & a half acre wood land in Rehoboth...bounded by land of Samuel READ & Daniel PERRIN...value at Ł37.9s11d;...18 Oct. 1851, Seth WILLIAMS, Deputy Sheriff, Delivered ye Quiet & peacable posesion of sd two peices of Land...to ye sd Eliphaz HARLOW ye Creditor, who Accepted ye same in full satisfaction. Rec. 26 Oct. 1751.

Benjamin LINKON/LINCOLN of Taunton MA to **Eliphaz HARLOW** of same. <Bristol Co.Deeds 42:158> ...30 Dec. 1756, Benjamin LINKON, yeoman, son of Thomas LINKON of Taunton dec'd, for Ł26.15s6d, sold to Eliphaz HARLOW, yeoman...eleven acres in Taunton...bounded by mill River, land my son George sold of late to Capt. James ANDREWS and near Isaac LINKON's dwelling house. Wf Mary releases dower. Witnesses: Nathaniel WHITE, James WILLIAMS. Ack. & Rec. same day.

Estate of **James LEONARD** of Taunton MA to **Eliphaz HARLOW** of same. <Bristol Co.Deeds 54:423> ...23 June 1772, Eliphalet LEONARD, gent. of Easton (admr. of estate of James LEONARD, gent. late of Taunton dec'd),...at publick vendue on ye 22 June 1772 at ye house of Eliphas HARLOW, innholder in Taunton, made sale of a certain lot of Swamp in ye Great pine Swamp in ye old Township of Taunton to Eliphas HARLOW for Ł9.1s...being ye 10 lot & is ye same lot that ye sd James dec'd purchased of John CRANE as per deed 39:86...nine acres. Witnesses: James WILLIAMS Jr., James WILLIAMS. Ack. & Rec. same day.

Eliphaz HARLOW of Taunton MA to **Rufus LINCOLN** of same. <Bristol Co.Deeds 62:196> ...5 Jan. 1784, Eliphaz HARLOW, yeoman, for 116 silver milled dollars, sells to Rufus LINCOLN, Esq...fourteen & a half acres in Taunton...bounded by road from Fredrick BAYLIES to James CODDINGS and land of heirs of Daniel LINCOLN and land of William BURT. Wf Phebe releases dower. Witnesses: John CARPENTER, James WILLIAMS. Ack. & Rec. same day.

Eliphaz HARLOW of Taunton MA to **John READ Jr.** of same. <Bristol Co.Deeds 62:341> ...17 Mar. 1784, Eliphaz HARLOW yeoman, for Ł95 silver money, sells to John READ Jr., blacksmith ...20 acres in Taunton...bounded by road from Capt. John READ's to Three Mill/Mile River, thence down the river to Capt. READ's land...being same land bought by Eliphaz of Noah BRIGGS 7 Mar. 1748. Wf Phebe releases dower. 1748. Witnesses: George GODFREY, Robert CALDWELL. Ack. same day by both. Rec. 22 Apr. 1784.

Eliphaz HARLOW of Taunton MA to **William BURT** of same. <Bristol Co.Deeds 63:528> ...13 Jan. 1785, Eliphaz HARLOW, innholder, for Ł36 sells to William BURT, yeoman...eleven acres in Taunton...bounded on Mill River and land of sd BURT, Col. George LEONARD and highway to Dighton. Wf Phebe releases dower. Witnesses: Seth PADELFORD, Levi HARLOW. Rec. 5 Feb. 1785.

Eliphaz HARLOW of Taunton MA to **Simeon & Joseph TISDALE** of same. <Bristol Co.Deeds 66:142>
...28 Feb. 1787, Eliphaz HARLOW, yeoman, for £33 sells to Simeon TISDALE & Joseph TISDALE, merchants...a shop or store near his dwelling house & fronting the Green and adjoining a shop now owned by the grantees, which was formerly Dr. William McKINSTRY's...the building being 14' wide on the front and about 23' the other way, with the privilege of using the land between the same & the road leading thereby. Wf Phebe consents. Witnesses: James WILLIAMS, Sally HARLOW. Ack. 3 Mar. 1787 by both. Rec. 7 Apr. 1787.

Eliphaz HARLOW of Taunton MA to **Sally HARLOW** of same. <Bristol Co.Deeds 66:370>
...27 Oct. 1787, Eliphaz HARLOW, yeoman, for love & affection, conveys to dau Sally HARLOW, spinster...easterly part of my dwelling house on the southeast side of the Green...viz: to ye middle of the (front) entryway by a line to run from ye middle of the front door through the middle of ye chimney & so ye same course through ye kitchen till it comes to ye southeasterly part of my land together with ye celler under sd part of sd house, with ye chamber & garret over ye same, with a prevelidge to pass & repass up & down stares...Witnesses: Job GODFREY, James WILLIAMS. Ack. same day. Rec. 3 Nov. 1787.

Phebe HARLOW of Taunton MA to **George WILLIAMS** of same. <Bristol Co.Deeds 68:365>
...2d Tues. Sept. 1789, widow Phebe HARLOW, admx. on estate of Eliphaz HARLOW dec'd, granted authority to sell real estate to pay debts of £80...12 Jan. 1790, Phebe HARLOW sold at auction, for £50 to George WILLIAMS, Esq...westerly part of the sd dec'd's late dwelling house & land in Taunton...bounded by land of John PORTER & heirs of Simeon TISDALE dec'd, Taunton Green and part of ye house & land conveyed by deed from sd dec'd to Sally HARLOW...reserving...right of dower... which belongs to me as widow of the sd Eliphaz dec'd. <68:366>...28 Jan. 1790, George WILLIAMS, for £50 sold the above back to Phebe. Witnesses: Sally HARLOW, Seth PADELFORD. Ack. 2 Feb. 1790 by George. Rec. 4 Feb. 1790. <68:366>...2 Feb. 1790, Phebe sold the above to Thomas WETHERBY, baker of Taunton, for £90. Witnesses: George WILLIAMS, Seth PADELFORD. Rec. 3 Feb. 1790.

Sally HARLOW of Taunton MA to **Thomas WETHERBY** of same. <Bristol Co.Deeds 68:367>
...2 Feb. 1790, Sally HARLOW, single woman & spinster, for £90 sold to Thomas WETHERBY, baker ... dwelling house & land in Taunton...bounded by Taunton Green, land of heirs of Simeon TISDALE and by the half sold by Phebe HARLOW, admx. of Eliphaz HARLOW dec'd to George WILLIAMS, Esq...and is ye same which my late father sd Eliphas conveyed to me by deed. Witnesses: George WILLIAMS, Seth PADELFORD. Rec. 3 Feb. 1790. On 2 Feb. 1790, Phebe HARLOW, widow of Taunton, for 6s paid by Thomas WETHERBY, releases her right of dower.

Phebe HARLOW of Taunton MA to **Simeon TISDALE et al.** <Bristol Co.Deeds 70:538>
...14 Oct. 1791, Phebe HARLOW, widow, for £6, releases to Simeon TISDALE & Joseph TISDALE, traders, Samuel FALES, Esq. & David CARVER, gent., all of Taunton...her right of dower in...estate of Simeon TISDALE late of Taunton dec'd...bounded on Mill River, Taunton Green and land of Mary MOREY, John PORTER, Thomas WETHERBY & James TISDALE...so much...as grantees may need for erecting a Slitting Mill, Mill Dam & pond, dikes...and also for a road from the Green to the mill when built...also her dower rights in the Mill River...and also leased for £12 per annum during her life the improvement of the residue of sd lot. Witnesses: Phebe GULLIVER, James WILLIAMS. Ack. & Rec. same day. <71:388>...9 Jan. 1793, Phebe HARLOW re-leases at the rate of £18 per annum to the above and to James TISDALE of Boston. (The last mention of Phebe in the files is in Bristol Co.PR 49:521...7 Oct. 1814, "(Estate of?) Phebe HARLOW, widow of Taunton, insolvent.")

Estate of **Simeon TISDALE** of Taunton MA. <Bristol Co.PR>
<17:621> Pr. 17 Mar. 1762, widow **Phebe TISDALE** app'td admx. <19:238> Inventory taken 11 June 1762 by George GODFREY, Elnathan WALKER, Israel TISDALE; mentions note from Eliphaz HARLOW dated 27 Oct. 1761 for £48.9.7. <19:263> Account, 28 Oct. 1765, of admx. **Phebe HARLOW** late **Phebe TISDALE**; incl. receipts from James WILLIAMS, Esq. as gdn. of **Simeon TISDALE, Joseph TISDALE, James TISDALE & Abigail TISDALE,** minor chil. of dec'd; receipts from Capt. George WILLIAMS gdn. of **Phebe TISDALE,** minor child; charges for lying in after death of husband, the child died in about one year. <19:335-9> Division of real estate, 31 Oct. 1765 to the widow and above named five children.

Will of **Benjamin HARLOW,** shoemaker of Middleboro MA. <Plymouth Co.PR 25:386,387,534>
...15 May 1779, wf **Elizabeth** and daus **Kesiah ATWOOD & Phebe SHURTLIFF.** Pr. 1 Nov.1779.

References to the name **Benjamin HARLOW** in Plymouth Co.Deeds: 4:5,89;21:215;22:28,60;24:104;39:33, 34,59;41:50;45:135;49:69;52:212,213;53:263;56:183,184;67:265.)

PLYMOUTH COUNTY DEEDS: (re: Thomas HARLOW)

<10:366>	- 1713, T.H. to Benjamin WARREN.	<43:96>	- 1755, T.H. & Jonathan HARLOW, bounds
<17:97>	- 1723/4, T.H. to Elisha HOLMES.	<86:11>	- 1798, T.H. et al to Ellis MENDALL.
<42:12>	- 1752, T.H. et al to Jonathan HARLOW.	<83:178>	- , T.H. et al from Ellis MENDALL.
<43:95>	- 1755, T.H., petition to General Court.	<43:96>	- , T.H. & Jonathan LITTLE, bounds
<43:98>	- 1755, T.H. to Elijah PACKARD.	<8:59>	- , T.H. et al, agreement.
<43:99>	- 1755, T.H. to Elijah PACKARD.		

Estate of **Capt. Richard COBB** of Taunton MA. <Bristol Co.PR>
<22:434> Inventory taken 18 Jan. 1773; mentions pew in Church of St. Thomas. <24:41,81,182;47: 196;147:21>...

Estate of **Lewis HARLOW** of Plymouth MA. <Plymouth Co.PR #9261>
<39:100> Letter, 1807. <44:151> Inventory. <44:152> Account, 1812. <69:309> Dower assigned to widow **Hannah HARLOW,** 1830.

All references to the name **Lewis HARLOW** in Plymouth Co.Deeds, 1685-1801: <87:190> from Thomas JACKSON Jr.; <91:182> from Nathaniel HARLOW.

Estate of **Levi HARLOW Jr.** of Plympton MA. <Plymouth Co.PR #9260>
...1816...<46:147> Letter. <48:122> Inventory. <48:123> Dower. <48:122> Insolvency. <49:73> List of Claims. <49:77> Account, Distribution. <49:81> Sale of real estate. (Records mention widow **Rebecca HARLOW.**)

Reuben KNAP of Taunton MA to **Levi HARLOW** of same. <Bristol Co.Deeds 55:197>
...13 Nov. 1771, Reuben KNAP, yeoman, for £180 sold to Levi HARLOW,laborer...52 acres in Taunton ...bounded by land of Elisha CODDING, Ephraim KNAP, Job STACEY and land latly belonging to William AUSTEN Jr. & Samuel AUSTEN dec'd...reference being had to a deed of mortgage I gave to Nicholas BAYLES dated 13 Apr. 1771 & rec. 53:470 and other deed of mortgage dated 8 Sept. 1768 & rec. 47:213 given to sd BAYLES...reserving ye right of improvement of ye one third part...to my mother Sarah KNAP. Wf Mary releases dower. Witnesses: James WILLIAMS Jr., James WILLIAMS, Daniel KNAP, Ebenezer KNAP. Rec. 21 Apr. 1773.

Levi HARLOW of Taunton MA to **Reuben KNAP** of same. <Bristol Co.Deeds 54:343>
...13 Nov. 1771, Levi HARLOW, laboror, for £90, mortgaged to Reuben KNAP, yeoman...52 acres in Taunton...bounded & discribed as appears by a deed from sd Reuben KNAP to me of this days date and what is hereby conveyed is ye whole of ye lands...conveyed to me by ye deed afforesd...only reserving ye right of improvement of one third part of ye primises to ye widow Sarah KNAP during her natural life. Witnesses: James WILLIAMS, James WILLIAMS Jr. Ack. & Rec. same day. On 21 Apr. 1773, Reuben KNAP receipted on the margin for principal & interest & discharged mortgage.

Levi HARLOW of Taunton MA to **Reuben KNAP** of same. <Bristol Co.Deeds 55:198>
...22 Feb. 1772, Levi HARLOW, yeoman, for £1.10s sold to Reuben KNAP, laborer...one quarter of an acre in Taunton...being a part of ye land I lately sold sd HARLOW joyning upon AUSTEN's land lying round ye house my Honoured Mother lives in, sd lot to lie square & contains sd House. Witnesses: Esther BAKER, Aaron KNAP. Ack. & Rec. 21 Apr. 1773.

Levi HARLOW of Rehoboth MA to **William THAYER** of Taunton MA. <Bristol Co.Deeds 55:198>
...21 Apr. 1773, Levi HARLOW, yeoman, late of Taunton but now resident in Rehoboth, for £97.13s, mortgaged to William THAYER, gent...52 acres in Taunton...ye same land...I...purchased of one Reuben KNAP by deed dated 13 Nov. 1771...save only one quarter of an acree of land with a small dwelling house & conveyed to Sarah KNAP. (Two notes, one for £51.4s6d for one year and one for £46.11s for eight mths.) Witnesses: Nathaniel BRIGGS Jr., Rufus COBB. Ack. & Rec. 21 Apr. 1773. Mortgage discharged 18 Mar. 1783 by Mary THAYER, exx. to the estate of William THAYER dec'd, sd notes having been paid in William's lifetime.

Levi HARLOW of Taunton MA to **Cornelius WHITE Jr.** of same. <Bristol Co.Deeds 61:394>
...18 Mar. 1783, Levi HARLOW, yeoman, for 800 Spanish Milled Silver Dollars, sold to Cornelius WHITE Jr., husbandman...52 acres with my dwelling house...bounded by land of Gideon HIX, Ephraim KNAP, John HOSKINS, Job STACY, Oliver PECK and land formerly belonging to ye AUSTENS and is the whole that I purchased of Reuben KNAP by deed dated 13 Nov. 1771...togather with the Road that I purchased of Richard COBB at ye easterly end of sd Farm. Wf Silance releases dower. Witnesses: James WILLIAMS Jr., James WILLIAMS. Ack. same day by Levi. Rec. 22 Mar. 1783.

Reuben KNAP of Westfield MA to **Nathaniel KNAP** of Taunton MA. <Bristol Co.Deeds 66:184>
...3 Jan. 1785, Reuben KNAP, laborer, for £20 sells to Nathaniel KNAP, cordwainer...the one quarter acre & house bought of Levi HARLOW...now bounded by Cornelius WHITE Jr. Witnesses: Moses SMITH, George GODFREY. Ack. 5 Jan.1785. Rec. 17 May 1787.

Estate of **Lemuel HARLOW,** cordwainer of Middleborough MA. <Plymouth Co.PR #9258>
<15:89> Letter 1 Jan. (   ), widow **Joanna HARLOW** app'td admx. <original> Bond 1 Jan. 1759, of admx. Sureties: Zachariah PADDOCK, cordwainer of Middleborough & Gideon BRADFORD, yeoman of Plympton. Witnesses: Benjamin WESTON, Edward WINSLOW. <15:398> Inventory taken 27 Apr.1759, by Daniel VAUGHAN, James COBB, Zachariah PADDOCK; personal estate only, total £61.4s9d; sworn to 12 Sept. 1759 by appraisers, 22 Oct. 1759 by admx. <16:1> Account of admx., 3 Nov. 1760; incl. cloathing the children, £1.10s8d.

Guardianship of Children of **Lemuel HARLOW** of Middleborough MA. <Plymouth Co.PR #9259>
<15:396,398> Letters/Bonds 22 Oct.1759, widow **Joanna HARLOW** chosen gdn. by **Lemuel HARLOW & Thomas HARLOW.** Sureties: Ebenezer SPOONER & Thomas FOSTER Jr., gent. of Plymouth. Witnesses: Edward WINSLOW, Hannah DYER.

PLYMOUTH COUNTY DEEDS, 1802-1859: (re: Levi HARLOW, grantor) <none on 1685-1801 index>

<100:176> - L.H. to Lewis PRATT.
<117:80> - L.H. to Levi HARLOW Jr.
<122:88> - L.H. to Nathaniel HARLOW.
<122:231> - L.H. et al to Benjamin WARD 2d.
<122:262> - L.H. to Hezekiah COLE.
<123:175> - L.H. to Isaac BARTLETT.
<124:190> - L.H. to Ezra D. MORTON.
<124:191> - L.H. to George RUSSELL.

PLYMOUTH COUNTY DEEDS, 1802-1859, cont-d: (re: Levi HARLOW, grantor)

<124:253> - L.H. to Ebenezer DEANE.
<124:254> - L.H. to Isaac WRIGHT et al.
<135:224> - L.H. to Ellis WRIGHT et al.
<151:225> - L.H. Jr. by adm. to Nathaniel HARLOW 2d.

PLYMOUTH COUNTY DEEDS, 1802-1850: (re: Levi HARLOW, grantee) <none on 1685-1801 index>

<100:214> - 1804, L.H. from Nathaniel HARLOW.
<114:203> - 1810, L.H. Jr. from John STANDISH.
<117:80> - 1811, L.H. Jr. from Levi HARLOW.
<122:231> - 1810, L.H. Jr. from Nathaniel HARLOW.
<122:233> - 1812, L.H.Jr. from Hopestill BISBEE
<136:18> - 1818, L.H.Jr. from Nathaniel HARLOW
<160:61> - 1827, L.H. from Consider CHASE.

Levi HARLOW of Plympton MA to **Hezekiah COLE** of Carver. <Plymouth Co.Deeds 122:262>
...23 Feb. 1815, Levi HARLOW, yeoman sells to Hezkeiah COLE, gent...part of cedar swamp in Carver ...descended to me by heirship from my father Nathaniel HARLOW dec'd. Rec. same day.

Nathaniel HARLOW of Plympton MA to **Levi HARLOW Jr.** of same. <Plymouth Co.Deeds 122:231>
...2 Apr. 1810, Nathaniel HARLOW sells to Levi HARLOW Jr...cedar swamp in Carver bequeathed to sd Nathaniel by his father Nathaniel HARLOW late of Plympton dec'd. Rec. 28 Nov. 1814.

PLYMOUTH COUNTY DEEDS: (re: Lemuel HARLOW)

<98:12> - 1799, L.H. to Barnabas HOLMES 3d.
<96:211> - 1803, L.H. to Jonathan BASSETT.
<182:134> - 1834, L.H. to Branch HARLOW.
<190:74> - 1838, L.H. to John DELANO.
<194:174> - 1839, L.H.Jr. to Warren WHITING.
<205:88> - 1841, L.H. to Henry BROOKS.
<205:250> - 1841, L.H. to Joseph BREWSTER.
<205:114> - 1841, L.H. to A.T.HARLOW et al.
<236:260> - 1850, L.H.Jr. to Hannah BRADFORD.
<266:238> - 1855, L.H. to Oliver LEONARD.

<96:211> - , L.H. from William HARLOW.
<100:65> - 1804, L.H. from Benjamin PRIOR Jr.
<147:86> - 1822, L.H. from Joseph PRIOR.
<147:86> - 1822, L.H. from Sylvanus WESTON.
<147:87> - 1822, L.H. from Robert WADSWORTH.
<171:106> - 1831, L.H. from Lydia PEIRCE et al.
<171:107> - 1831, L.H. from Joseph BREWSTER.
<172:71> - 1831, L.H. from Otis BAKER et al.
<172:72> - 1831, L.H. from John THOMAS.
<172:193> - 1831, L.H. from Jonathan HARLOW/adm
<189:63> - 1836, L.H.Jr. from Thomas RANDALL.
<207:67> - 1842, L.H. from Nancy PRIOR et al.
<213:247> - 1844, L.H. from Jesse CHANDLER.
<220:263> - 1846, L.H.Jr. from Arad T. HARLOW.
<221:234> - 1846, L.H.Jr. from Olive WADSWORTH.
<251:172> - 1853, L.H. from Arad T. HARLOW.

Lemuel HARLOW of Plymouth MA to **Ephraim HOLMES** of Kingston. <Plymouth Co.Deeds 33:118>
...17 Apr. 1740, Lemuel HARLOW, seafaring man, sells to Ephraim HOLMES, yeoman...my one third part of the 157th lot in 2nd Division of Commons of Duxborough & Pembroke...which was settled on me as a part of my portion or share in my Honoured Grandfather Benoni DELANO's estate. Ack. same day. Rec. 18 Apr. 1740.

Estate of **Lemuel HARLOW** of Plymouth MA to **James CLARKE** of same. <Plymouth Co.Deeds 88:150>
...14 May 1800, Phebe HARLOW, widow of Lemuel HARLOW, yeoman, dec'd and admx., sells to James CLARKE...land in Plymouth...being part of land sd Lemuel bought of William HARLOW. Rec. 21 May.

Will of **Lewis HARLOW** of Bridgewater MA. <Plymouth Co.PR #9262>
...1859...<101:440> Will. <3:143J> Bond. <102:86> Inventory. <103:229> Account.

Estate of **Joanna HARLOW**, widow of Middleborough MA. <Plymouth Co.PR #9233>
<14:229E> Letter 30 Oct. 1860, Ichabod F. ATWOOD of Middleborough app'td admr., at the request of the heirs. <102:457> Inventory. <10:303Y> Notice. <103:303> Account.

Estate of **Lemuel HARLOW** of Plymouth MA. <Plymouth Co.PR #9256>
...1799...<34:179> Letter, **Phebe HARLOW** app'td exx. <36:517> Inventory. <36:518> Insolvency. <36:529> List of claims. <36:531> Account & Distribution.

Will of **Lemuel HARLOW** of Duxbury MA. <Plymouth Co.PR #9254>
...1852...<94:573> Will (Lemuel HARLOW, exr.). <2:340H> Bond. <95:72,436> Inventory & Account.

Will of **Lemuel HARLOW** of Scituate MA. <Plymouth Co.PR #9255>
...1864...<104:558> Will (Eliza Jane HARLOW, exx.). <114:223> Letter & Bond. <109:87> Inventory.

PLYMOUTH COUNTY PROBATE: (re: Thomas HARLOW of Plymouth**)**

<#9302> - 1746, Jedidah HARLOW, admx.
<#9303> - 1832, Thomas PATY, gdn. to Thomas P. HARLOW.
<#9304> - 1874, Thomas HARLOW & Hiram CLARK, admrs.

MICRO #28 OF 32

Estate of **William HARLOW** of Plymouth MA. <Plymouth Co.PR>
<16:164> Division of estate, 10 Nov. 1758, to the widow **Mercy** and following chil., viz: **Benjamin HARLOW** (eldest son), **William HARLOW** (2d son), **Samuel HARLOW** (3d son), **Seth HARLOW** (youngest son),

Sarah CHURCHILL (eldest dau), **Hannah SAMSON** (2d dau), **Marcy HOLMES** (3d dau), **Rebekah RANSOM** (youngest dau). <21:106> Division of widow's dower, 10 Apr. 1772, to the following chil., viz: **Benjamin HARLOW**, **Sarah CHURCHILL** wf of Eleazer, **William HARLOW**, **Hannah SAMSON** wf of Ebenezer, **Mercy HOLMES** wf of Silvanus, **Phebe STEVENS** wf of Edward, chil. of **Samuel HARLOW** dec'd, **Rebekah RANSOM** wf of Ebenezer, **Seth HARLOW.**

<Plymouth Co.Deeds 74:237>...29 Apr. 1793...**Zephaniah HARLOW**, execution against **Solomon INGLEE**, blacksmith of Plymouth. (66:245 - Zephaniah, grantee)

Zephaniah HARLOW et al. <Plymouth Co.Deeds 85:75>
...28 Aug. 1793, Peleg FAUNCE, cordwainer & wf Mary and Zephaniah HARLOW & wf Patience...sd Mary being dau of Eleazer FAUNCE dec'd & wf "Hannah" & sd Patience being grandaughter to sd Eleazer & "Patience" FAUNCE, all of Plymouth...and Benjamin MORTON Jr., bricklayer of Plymouth who bought his mother Hannah MORTON's right 4 Jan. 1794...mentions grandfather Benjamin WARREN's will.

Zephaniah HARLOW of Plymouth MA to **Robert DAVIE Jr.** of same. <Plymouth Co.Deeds 76:238>
...14 Oct. 1794, Zephaniah HARLOW, mariner & wf Patience, to Robert DAVIE Jr., mariner...two thirds acre on road to Wellingsley Brook...bought of Josiah JOHNSON 16 May 1787 & Joseph BRIMHALL 23 Sept. 1790 & rec. 70:134. Ack. same day by both. (70:134 - Zephaniah grantee)

Zephaniah HARLOW of Plymouth MA to **Jotham LORING** of Duxbury. <Plymouth Co.Deeds 78:180>
...3 Jan. 1794, Zephaniah HARLOW, mariner to Jotham LORING, Esq...nine/one hundred & twenty eighth of forge on Town Brook in Plymouth with dam, 5 buildings & land...same set off to me by execution from Solomon INGLEE. Rec. 17 Mar. 1795.

Zephaniah HARLOW of Plymouth MA to **Nathaniel GOODWIN** of same. <Plymouth Co.Deeds 78:96>
...13 Apr. 1795, Zephaniah HARLOW, mariner to Nathaniel GOODWIN, Esq...house & half acre lot which sd Zephaniah bought of Solomon INGLEE 17 Dec. 1791 & rec 72:51. (72:51 - Zephaniah grantee)

Zephaniah HARLOW et al to **Lemuel BARTLETT** of Plymouth MA. <Plymouth Co.Deeds 165:197>
...18 May 1796, Benjamin RIDER, Jacob ALBERTSON, gent. & wf Lydia, widow Abigail HOLMES, Benjamin MORTON, brick layer, Zephaniah HARLOW, mariner & wf Patience, widow Mary FAUNCE, widow Mercy BRAMHALL, Thomas WITHERELL, gent., Abner BARTLETT, Esq., Eleazer HOLMES Jr., gent., all of Plymouth, for $40.00 sold to Lemuel BARTLETT, mariner...land given by Benjamin WARREN by will to his daughters. (Zephaniah did not sign; wf Patience signed & ack. 1 June 1796.)

Estate of **William HARLOW** of Plymouth MA. <Plymouth Co.PR #9306>
<3:107> Letter 7 Mar. 1711/12, widow **Lidia HARLOW** app'td admx. <3:108> Inventory taken 28 Feb. 1711/2, by Thomas FAUNCE, Benjamin WARREN, Isaac CUSHMAN; incl. 12 pounds of linnen & woolen yarn which in our judgement is needfull to bee left for shirting for ye children. <3:134> Appraisers app'td 28 Mar. 1712, viz: Ensign Benjamin WARREN, Deacon Thomas CLARKE & Ebenezer HOLMES, all of Plymouth; lands in Plymouth, Middlebury, Woponock(sp), Miller's Neck. <3:135> Division 21 June 1712, to widow **Lydia** and following chil., viz: **Thomas HARLOW** (eldest son), **William HARLOW** (2d son), **Robert HARLOW** (3d son), **Isaac HARLOW** (4th son); **Thomas DOTEN**, son of eldest dau, **Elizabeth** dec'd; **Mary** (2d dau), **Lydia** (3d dau), **Rebecca** (youngest dau). <3:137> 21 June 1712, widow **Lydia HARLOW** app'td gdn. of **Robert & Lydia HARLOW.** <5:92> Agreement 29 Apr. 1725, between brothers & sisters of **Isaac HARLOW**, viz: **Thomas HARLOW, William HARLOW, Thomas DOTY** son of **Elizabeth** (eldest sister); **Robert HARLOW, Barnabas CHURCHILL, Lydia CHURCHILL, Rebecca HARLOW.**

Guardianship of Children of **William HARLOW** of Plymouth MA. <Plymouth Co.PR #9267>
<3:137> Letters, 21 June 1712, widow **Lidia HARLOW** app'td gdn. of **Robert HARLOW & Lydia HARLOW.** <3:157,158> Letters/Bonds 19 Sept. 1712, widow is app'td gdn. of **Isaac HARLOW & Rebecca HARLOW**, both under 14. Surety: Thomas HARLOW of Plymouth. Witnesses: John SUTTON, Thomas CROADE. <originals> Bonds 24 Dec. 1720, by **Thomas HARLOW** to pay £3.11s5d each to **Robert HARLOW**, house carpenter of Plymouth, **William HARLOW**, cordwainer of Plympton, **Isaac HARLOW** and **Rebeckah HARLOW**, all chil. of William dec'd. Witnesses: Thomas CROADE, Nathan CLARKE. <4:285> Letters/Bonds 13 June 1721, **Thomas HARLOW** of Plymouth app'td gdn. of brother **Isaac HARLOW** & sister **Rebecca HARLOW.** Surety: Stephen CHURCHILL, cooper of Plymouth. Witnesses: Thomas CROADE, Josiah CORNISH.

Estate of **Lydia HARLOW**, widow of Plymouth MA. <Plymouth Co.PR #9266>
<4:231> Letter/Bond 11 July 1720, son **Thomas HARLOW**, husbandman of Plymouth, app'td admr. Surety: Francis ADAMS, clothier of Plymouth. Witnesses: John CHURCHILL, Thomas CROADE. <4:249> Warrant 30 Aug. 1720, to appraise, to Capt. Benjamin WARREN, Deacon Thomas CLARK & Ebenezer HOLMES, all of Plymouth. <4:249> Inventory taken 16 Nov. 1720; personal estate only; sworn to 23 Dec. 1720 by admr. & appraisers. <4:250> Division 24 Dec. 1720, among her surviving chil., viz: **Thomas HARLOW, William HARLOW, Robert HARLOW, Isaac HARLOW; Thomas DOTEN Jr.** son of dec'd dau **Elizabeth DOTY** wf of Thomas; **Lydia CHURCHILL** wf of Barnabas and **Rebecca HARLOW.**

Estate of **Mary HARLOW** of Plymouth MA. <Plymouth Co.PR #9269>
<4:232> Letter/Bond 11 July 1720, brother **Thomas HARLOW**, husbandman of Plymouth, app'td admr. Surety: Francis ADAMS, clothier of Plymouth. Witnesses: John CHURCHILL, Thomas CROADE. <4:250> Inventory taken 16 Nov. 1720 by Capt. Benjamin WARREN, Deacon Thomas CLARKE & Ebenezer HOLMES of Plymouth. <4:251> Division 24 Dec. 1720, to following heirs, (brothers & sisters), viz: **Thomas HARLOW, William HARLOW, Robert HARLOW, Isaac HARLOW, Thomas DOTY** son of **Elizabeth DOTY** dec'd wf of Thomas, **Lydia CHURCHILL** wf of Barnabas and **Rebecca HARLOW.**

Estate of **Isaac HARLOW**, cordwainer of Plymouth MA. <Plymouth Co.PR #9219>
<originals> Letter/Bond 30 Apr. 1724, brother**Thomas HARLOW**, husbandman of Plymouth, app'td admr. Sureties: Robert HARLOW & Simon LAZELL of Plymouth. Witnesses: John ATWOOD, Thomas BURTON. <4:445> Inventory taken 4 May 1724, by Thomas MORTON, Stephen CHURCHILL & Francis ADAMS; incl. 48 acres in 12 Mens Purchase in Middleborough; six acres in the New Meadows in Plimpton. <5:92> Agreement 29 Apr.1725, between the brothers & sisters, viz: **Thomas HARLOW** (eldest brother), **William HARLOW; Thomas DOTY** only child of dec'd eldest sister **Elizabeth DOTY, Lydia CHURCHILL** wf of Barnabas, **Rebecca HARLOW, Robert HARLOW.** Witnesses: Timothy MORTON, Francis ADAMS, Barnabas CHURCHILL, Simion LAZELL, Francis ADAMS.

Estate of **William KING**, mariner of Plymouth MA. <Plymouth Co.PR>
<34:97> Letter 31 Jan. 1797, widow **Susanna KING** app'td admx. Sureties: Benjamin COOPER, Joseph COOPER. <36:81> Inventory taken 20 Feb. 1797, by Simion VALLER(sp), Lemuel HARLOW, Cornelius MOREY; total $64.80. <36:82> Account of admx., 14 Mar. 1797; to Thomas & William DAVIS, rec'd for what the dec'd's wages fell short of paying ye expences of his last sickness at Jamaica, $19.90.

Estate of **John RIDER** of Plymouth MA. <Plymouth Co.PR #17358>
...1735...<7:165> Letter. <7:175> Inventory. <7:288> Division. <8:305> Widow's allowance. <3:304> Account. <7:186,187> 11 Mar. 1735/6, Thomas SPOONER of Plymouth chosen gdn. by **Charles RIDER** (14-21) and app'td gdn. of **Jerusha RIDER & Rebecca RIDER** (both under 14). <9:439,451> 20 Dec. 1744, **Rebecca RIDER**, spinster, being now of the age of 18, discharges her gdn.; **Jerusha RIDER**, spinster releases her gdn., having received bond of Samuel BARTLETT, Esq. & her brothers **Ebenezer RIDER & John RIDER.**

PLYMOUTH COUNTY DEEDS: (re: John RIDER)

<1:359>	- 1692/3, J.R. from Samuel HARLOW.	<43:198>	- 1755, J.R. to Josiah CHURCHILL.
<9:60>	- 1702, J.R. from Thomas DOTY.	<45:143>	- 1759, J.R. to Eleazer HOLMES et al.
<5:227>	- 1703, J.R. to James WARREN.	<45:143>	- 1759, J.R. to Charles RIDER.
<6:76>	- 1705, J.R. to Thomas TOMSON.	<45:144>	- 1759, J.R. to James HOVEY.
<9:245>	- 1712, J.R. to James WARREN.	<53:128>	- , J.R. from John BREWSTER.
<10:139>	- , Division of land.	<58:1>	- 1773, J.R. to Ebenezer RIDER.
<14:83>	- 1718, J.R. to John BARNES.	<58:85>	- 1773, J.R. to John WINSLOW.
<16:164>	- , J.R. from Ebenezer DUNHAM Jr.	<72:18>	- 1791, J.R. to William DREW.

<58:135> - 1772, J.R. & wf Sarah of Rochester, son of Samuel RIDER of same, dec'd to Samuel TRIPP
<66:270> - 1781, J.R. (" same as above ") to William DREW.

PLYMOUTH TOWN RECORDS (printed): (re: John RIDER)

<1:268> - 10 Apr. 1699, John RIDER GRANTED 40 feet of land to run up from his barn towards the highway then to run square of against his house for his convenience of building.
<1:276> - 13 May 1700, Town meeting granted land to Elisha HOLMES & Manasses MORTON along the road above John RIDER's land.
<1:278> - 2 Apr. 1700, Land granted to John RIDER, bounded by his house & his other land.

Estate of **William FOSTER**, blacksmith of Plymouth MA. <Plymouth Co.PR #8074,8075>
<7:188> Letter 23 Apr. 1736, Thomas FOSTER, blacksmith of Plymouth, app'td admr. <7:251> Inventory. <7:187,188> 11 Mar. 1735/6, Thomas FOSTER app'td gdn. of **William FOSTER, Joseph FOSTER & Mary FOSTER**, all under 14.

Estate of **Samuel RYDER** of Middleboro MA. <Plymouth Co.PR #17397>
<17:64> 1 Mar. 1762, Samuel RIDER & Joseph PORTER, app'td admrs. <16:375> Inventory taken 30 Mar. 1762; land in Wareham & Plympton. <19:347> Account of Joseph PORTER, 22 May 1766; mentions widow.

Heirs of **Samuel RIDER** to **Consider BARDEN** of Middleborough MA. <Plymouth Co.Deeds 55:221>
...22 Nov. 1770, Nathaniel WASHBURN, mariner & wf Mary, Ebenezer RIDER, mariner & wf Sarah, Josiah BRADFORD, mariner & wf Hannah and Archippus FULLER, wheelwright & wf Mariah, all of Plymouth, as heirs of Samuel RIDER late of Middleborough dec'd, for £4.16s sold to Consider BARDEN, husbandman...four ninths of wood land in Middleborough...descending to us from our sd Father Samuel RIDER dec'd containing about twenty one & a half acres...excepting eleven acres which has been heretofore sold to Ebenezer THOMAS Jr...bounded by land of John LEONARD Jr. which is called the Purchase Line and land of Ichabod BARDEN, land Cornelius BENNET formerly sold to Zechariah WESTON ...bounded as the same is set forth in a deed from Silvanus BARROWS to sd Samuel RIDER dated 26 Dec. 1755 and rec. 43:221. Signed by all grantors. Witnesses: John COTTON, Mary COTTON. Ack. by all grantors 19 Jan. 1771. Rec. 19 Jan. 1771.

MICRO #29 OF 32

Heirs of **Samuel RIDER** to **John BARDEN** of Middleborough MA. <Plymouth Co.Deeds 56:65>
...2 Jan. 1771, Samuel RIDER of Bolton, Hartford Co., Joseph PORTER & Martha PORTER and William FULLER & Deborah FULLER of Middleborough, for £5.6s8d sold to John BARDEN...four ninth parts of twenty one & a half acres in Middleborough...(see above deed for bounds). Witnesses: Ebenezer WOOD, Sally WOOD. Ack. 2 Feb. 1771 by William, Martha & Deborah (witnessed by Ichabod BARDEN,

Rodulphus BARDEN); ack. 15 Apr. 1771 by Samuel. Rec. 15 Apr. 1771.

NATHANIEL WARREN[2] (Richard[1])

Jabez WARREN of Plimouth to **John GIBBS** of same. <Plymouth Co.Deeds 1:278>
...19 Sept. 1694, Jabez WARREN/Jabiz WARRIN, yeoman, for Ł45 currant silver money, sold to John GIBBS...my whole share of land both upland, swamps & meadow land divided & undivided in Middleborough...excepting a 20 acre lott which my mother Sarah WARREN sold unto John HOLMES Jr. of Middleborough, which sd share of land was formerly the land of John ADAMS and bought by my father Nathaniel WARREN dec'd...which sd land was granted by ye Court on the account of ye first Borne in this Colony and being one of the 26 lots so called containing sevenscore & five acres of upland and eight & a quarter acres of meadow...the house lott being 25 acres is the first lott lotted for lying upon Bridgewater River. Witnesses: John SUTTON, Nathaniel CLARKE. Rec. 3 Oct.

PLYMOUTH COUNTY DEEDS: (re: WARREN)

<3:16> - 5 Dec. 1662, Nathaniel WARREN to Richard KERBEY. Witnesses: Joseph CHURCH, Jonathan MOREY.
<3:21> - , Re: lands on Pochade Neck near Namassakett, 5th lot Nathaniel WARREN.
<3:41> - 15 Nov. 1665, Land laid out at Namassakett River, Joseph WARREN, 15th lot and William HARLOW, 20th lot.
<3:59> - 2 July 1666, John BARNES to George BONUM. Witness: William HARLOW.
<3:213>- 29 Apr. 1672, Sarah WARREN, widow of Nathaniel, to Ralph ALLIN of Sandwich, her half share at Dartmouth. Joseph WARREN, overseer, consents.
<1:91> - 8 Mar. 1685, Sarah WARREN, widow of Nathaniel, to son Nathaniel WARREN.
<1:92> - 9 Jan. 1689/90, Sarah WARREN, widow of Nathaniel, to son Nathaniel WARREN.
<1:202> to James WARREN. <1:238> to Richard WARREN. <2:99> to John HOLMES. <3:251> to John TOMSON

Will of **Nathaniel WARREN** of Plymouth MA. <Plymouth Co.PR #21896>
<2:140>...dated 28 Oct. 1707, mentions wf **Phebe** and the following kindred & relations, viz: Warren GIBBS; **James WARREN & Sarah WARREN** chil. of brother **James**; Sarah GIBBS alias CUSHMAN, wf of Isaac Jr.; Alice BLACKWELL alias SPOONER, wf of William of Dartmouth; Mercy LUMBARD alias BURGES, wf of Ebenezer of Agawam; **James WARREN** son of dec'd brother **Richard WARREN**; Desire BLACKWELL alias GENNINGS/JENNINGS, wf of Lettice of Dartmouth. <2:141> Letter 3 Feb. 1707, widow **Phebe WARREN** app'td exx. <2:142> Inventory taken 14 Dec. 1707; no real estate; sworn to 24 June 1709 by exx. **Phebe GRAY.**

Will of **Thomas GIBBS Sr.**, husbandman of Sandwich MA. <Barnstable Co.PR>
<5:24>...dated 23 June 1725, mentions sons **Thomas GIBBS** (executor), **Cornelius GIBBS & Warren GIBBS**; sons **Ebenezer GIBBS & Jabez GIBBS**, beyond the sea; dau **Abigail**; chil. of daus **Bethiah & Sarah.** Witnesses: M. BOURN, Samuel JENNINGS, Bathshua NEWCOMB. Witnesses sworn 12 Jan. 1732. Pr. 28 Mar. 1733. Inventory taken 23 Jan. 1732; total, Ł75.3.0.; sworn to by exr. 5 Feb. 1732/3. <5:149> Receipts 9 May 1733 of **Warren GIBBS** to brother **Thomas** and from **Phebe SPOONER** to uncle **Thomas** for legacy from her grandfather **Thomas** for her brother **Nathaniel CUSHMAN** & herself.

Will of **Jirah SWIFT** of Wareham MA. <Plymouth Co.PR 11:241-3, 335>
...dated 29 Mar. 1744, mentions wf **Mary**, sons **Jabez SWIFT, Zephaniah SWIFT, Nathaniel SWIFT, William SWIFT, Jirah SWIFT, Job SWIFT, Silas SWIFT, Isaac SWIFT**; daus **Alice CROKER/CROCKER, Susanna ISHAM, Abigail HAMMOND**; grandchildren: **Abigail HAMMOND**; and **Abigail SWIFT & Jirah SWIFT** chil. of son **Jabez**; Catherine CURBY; son **Rowland SWIFT**, executor. Pr. 1 May 1749.

Honnewell HAMMOND et al. <Plymouth Co.Deeds 64:248>
...7 Apr. 1778, Honnewell HAMMOND, Joseph HAMMOND, Benjamin HAMMOND, yeomen and Job HASKELL, cordwainer & wf Elizabeth, all of Rochester...being Proprietors conjointly in a tract of land & meadow, swamp, etc. left us in the last will...of our Honoured Father dec'd, and which we have a right in by virtue of Heirship to the Estate of our Brother Jirah HAMMOND dec'd...

Will of **Roland SWIFT** of Lebanon CT. <Windham CT PR>
<13:411>...dated 18 Apr. 1785...to wf **Mary**, the use & reading of the works of Mr. John FLAVEL during her natural life & also for her dower, such a part or proportion of my real & personal estate as the laws of this State in such cases has made & provided...to son **Barzillai** the works of Mr. John FLAVEL after his Mothers decease...to dau **Abigail** 5s...to son **Roland SWIFT**, the house & barn & thirty five & a quarter acres of land I lately purchased of Ebenezer CHEVER (where the sd Roland now lives) to use & improve during his natural life and then I give & desire sd Estate to his oldest son that shall survive him...to son **Zepheniah**, my sword...to dau **Mary**, Ł30...to son **William SWIFT**, the whole of my real & personal estate...to dau **Thankful**, Ł30 and also household goods & furniture, equivalent to what has been given to either of her sisters in household furniture, when she shall arrive at the age of 21 or be married...to three sons, one half of the Stock...to three daus, household goods...to son in law **Lothrop DAVIS**, the improvement of a Farm I lately purchased of Chipman SWIFT, containing 100 acres lying in Wilmington VT...untill his son **Roland DAVIS** shall arrive at 21 and then I give & devise sd Farm to sd grandson...to son **Roland**, the whole of my wearing apparel. Witnesses: Jonathan GOODWIN Jr., William GOODWIN, Dan BEAUMONT.

Pr. 9 Mar. 1795, by William SWIFT Jr., exr. Witnesses: Jonathan GOODWIN, William GOODWIN. <13: 430> Inventory taken 11 Apr. 1795, by Andrew HIBBARD, James MASON

Will of **Zephaniah SWIFT** of Windham CT. <Windham CT PR 18:18,20,213>
<18:18>..dated 24 Aug. 1823...to wf **Lucretia** during her life the use & ocupation of the house in which I now live subject to the disposition hereafter made and of my home farm incl. the land at Chesnut hill and the land adjoining the House I purchased of Andrew EDGERTON, the House I purchased of Daniel BUCK near where I now live and the land I bought of Eleazer RIPLEY & wife, and I give to her forever all the household furniture, my horse & best chaise, all the Stock on the farm (the use of which I have given to her)...and also two hundred dollars...to my son **Henry SWIFT**, the right & priveledge of living in the house where I now live, and the right & priveledge of the Chamber over the Kitchen to occupy during his life; to be supported in the manner hereafter provided and I also give him three hundred dollars...to my son **George SWIFT**, my law Library ...to my children **Edward SWIFT, Lucretia SWIFT** the wf of **Rufus P. SPALDING, Emely SWIFT, Lucian SWIFT & Julia SWIFT**, all my estate both real & personal. (This transcription does not appear to have been completed by Bowman.)

Will of **William SWIFT** of Sandwich MA. <Barnstable Co.PR 8:344,346,347>
...dated 2 Oct. 1748, mentions wf **Abigail**...to eldest daus **Ann & Keziah**, all my household goods & untensills which I had & enjoyed while my former wife **Keziah** lived with me, to be equally divided when of age or married; minor daus **Abigail SWIFT & Mary SWIFT**; brother **Roland SWIFT**. Witnesses sworn 20 Dec. 1748. Pr. 29 May 1749. Inventory taken 21 Dec. 1748.

Guardianship of Children of **William SWIFT** of Sandwich MA. <"Plymouth" Co.PR #19853>
<9:237> Letters 11 Apr. 1744, **William SWIFT**, yeoman, app'td gdn. of his minor daus **Keziah & Ann SWIFT**, in right of their mother.

Will of **William & Deborah HILLIARD** of Little Compton. <Bristol Co.PR>
<3:186>...dated 15 Dec. 1713, "mentions among others" wf **Deborah** and dau **Abigail HILLIARD**. <3: 380> Receipt 28 May 1716, of **Warren & Abigail GIBBS** to mother **Deborah HILLIARD**. <3:385> Will of **Deborah HILLIARD**, dated 3 Jan. 1717, dau **Abigail GIBBS** wf of Warren is mentioned. Pr. 3 Mar. 1718

Will of **Thomas GRAY**. <Austin's Gen.Dict.RI:85>
...dated 21 Sept. 1721, gives 3 sheep & 3 lambs to kinsman **Nathaniel GIBBS** son of Warren. Pr. 23 Nov. 1721.

Estate of **William GREEN**, yeoman of Barnstable MA. <Barnstable Co.PR>
<7:412> Letter 16 Mar. 1756, **Warren GREEN**, blacksmith of Middletown CT app'td admr. <9:332> Inventory taken 17 Mar. 1756 by Solomon OTIS, Robert DAVIS, Silvanus COBB; Account 17 Mar. 1756, mentions the widow. <12:387> Settlement 27 Mar. 1756 to following chil., viz: **Warren GREEN** (eldest son), **William GREEN, John GREEN, James GREEN, Desire HINCKLEY, Sarah BARKER** and the minor chil. of **Mary BARKER** dec'd, viz: **Mercy, Joshua, Lucy, Content, Bersheba & Zipporah BARKER.**

Estate of **John NEAL**, mariner of Scituate MA. <Plymouth Co.PR>
<7:149> Letter 3 Aug. 1735, father **Joseph NEAL** of Scituate app'td admr. <7:181> Inventory. <7: 183> 16 Mar. 1735/6, necessaries set off to widow **Mary NEAL**. <7:297> Insolvency, 17 Mar. 1735/6. <7:409,413> Claims. ("nothing to indicate any children")

William SHATTUCK of Ashfield MA to **Warren GREEN Jr.** of Chatham CT. <Hampden Co.Deeds 16:524>
...28 Apr. 1779, William SHATTUCK, for £3000 sells to Warren GREEN Jr., yeoman...80 acres in Ashfield, part of 100 acre lot #56 in 2d Division...bounded by land of John (ARMES?), David COBB & John KARR. <16:525>...24 May 1779, Warren GREEN Jr. of Ashfield sells to Samuel STOCKING of Chatham CT, 16 acres of the above.

Warren GREEN of Ashfield MA to **Ephraim WILLIAMS** of same. <Franklin Co.MA Deeds 8:243>
<8:243>...16 Dec. 1793, Warren GREEN, for divers good causes & £6, quitclaims to Ephraim WILLIAMS ...all rights in 20 acres of Lot #35 in 4th Division in Ashfield. Ack. 7 Apr. 1794.

Warren GREEN of Ashfield MA to **Thomas RANNEY** of Chatham CT. <Franklin Co.Deeds 7:630>
...14 Jan. 1794, Warren GREEN, gent., sells to Thomas RANNEY...sixty three & one half acres in Lot #56 in 2d Division...also south half of 12 acres deeded to Samuel STOCKING by Aaron HOW 24 Dec. 1792, to contain six acres, except half the house & land. Lucy GREEN signs.

Warren GREEN of Ashfield mA to **Mary RANNEY** of Chatham CT. <Franklin Co.Deeds 7:631>
...14 Jan. 1794, Warren GREEN, husbandman sells to Mary RANNEY wf of Thomas...20 acres at west end of Lot #56 in 2d Division with half the sequestered land adjoining also one half the house standing on sd lot & half acre where the house stands. Lucy GREEN signs. Ack. 10 Mar. 1794 by Warren.

Will of **Barnabas BARKER**, yeoman of Scituate MA. <Plymouth Co.PR 16:425>
...dated 4 Nov. 1757, mentions the following 16 chil., viz: married son **Barnabas BARKER** (executor), **Thomas BARKER, John BARKER, David BARKER, Joshua BARKER, Sarah NEAL, Hannah BRIGGS, Desire BELL, Lydia BARKER, Mercy BARKER, Lucy BARKER, Mercy BARKER, Content BARKER, Barsheba BARKER, Zipporah BARKER, Mary BARKER, Abigail BELL.** Pr. 21 Apr. 1763.

Stephen HOSMER et al. <Franklin Co.MA Deeds 343:311>
...23 Apr. 1880, Stephen HOSMER of Gailand, Warren Co. PA, et al...all next of kin of Elijah HOSMER of Montague, sell...

Seth CHURCH of Ashfield MA to **Anne BEMENT** of same. <Franklin Co.Deeds 179:405>
...22 Nov. 1852, Seth CHURCH, for $150.00 sold to Anne BEMENT...the Ashford Place in Ashfield on road from Cong. Meeting house to Abel WILLIAMS...also bounded by land of Perez BARMS/BARNS...containing one quarter acre. Wf Sally releases dower. Rec. 13 Sept. 1853.

Oliver WARNER of Ashfield MA to **Anne BEMENT.** <Franklin Co.Deeds 202:110>
...10 Apr. 1856, Oliver WARNER, for $125.00, mortgaged to Anne BEMENT...one quarter acre in Ashfield on road from George STOCKING's to Oliver HALLS'...bounded by land of Percis BARMS/BARNS(?). Discharged 30 Jan. 1860 by Anne BEMENT & Chester BEMENT. <222:455>...10 Apr. 1856, sold above to Oliver WARNER.

MICRO #30 OF 32

Will of **Capt. James WARREN** of Plymouth MA. <Plymouth Co.PR #21874>
<3:360>...dated 28 Jan. 1711/12, mentions wf **Sarah**; only son **James WARREN** (under 21) "& nephew of **Nathaniel WARREN** dec'd. <3:361> Letter 23 June 1715. <3:362> Inventory taken 20 July 1715 by William BASSETT, Isaac LOTHROP; total real estate, Ł2869. A memoranda (latest date being 1764) names the following daus, viz: **Sarah, Alice, Patience, Hope, Mercy, Mary & Elizabeth**; "**Hope, Mercy & Elizabeth** died intestate". The memoranda also mentions "N. GOODWIN in right of Bethiah TYLER and J. WARREN heirs half Ann WARREN's right"; also "Lucy LITTLE gave by will dated 30 Sept. 1756 & presented for probate 5 Oct. of the same year, all her estate to her sister Bethiah TYLER. <21:302> Division of cedar swamp, 20 Mar. 1773, by Samuel LUCAS, George HAMMOND & John SHAW Jr., all of Plympton; **Hope, Mercy & Betty/Elizabeth** dec'd; **Mary** had sold her right to brother **James** who had also died leaving a son **James** who shared in the division with **Sarah SEVER** wf of William, **Alice FORD** dec'd and **Bethiah TYLER**, legal representative of **Sarah** one of the daus.

Estate of **Elizabeth WARREN**, seamstress of Plymouth MA. <Plymouth Co.PR #21864>
<11:75> Letter/Bond 5 Oct. 1747, Nicholas SEVER, Esq. app'td admr. Surety: Edward WINSLOW. Witnesses: William SEVER, Lucy LITTLE. <11:99> Inventory taken 28 June 1748 by Samuel NELSON, Consider HOWLAND, Thomas DOTY; incl. one sixth part of several lots, mostly cedar swamp, one lot at Turkey swamp in Plympton & one lot at Cross Monument; total real estate, Ł69.19.8; total estate, Ł328.6.2. <11:68> Account 24 Mar. 1748; mentions Mrs. Mary WARREN, Coll. WARREN & Esq. BARTLETT; remains in the admrs.' hands which divided into six parts is to a share Ł33.1.2. (Note: **Elizabeth** is called "Mrs.", however she was a single woman.)

Estate of **Mercy WARREN**, simstress of Plymouth MA. <Plymouth Co.PR #21893>
<11:74> Letter/Bond 5 Oct. 1747, Nicholas SEVER, Esq. app'td admr. Surety: Edward WINSLOW. Witnesses: William SEVER, Lucy LITTLE. <11:98> Inventory taken 28 June 1748 by Samuel NELSON, Consider HOWLAND, Thomas DOTY; (same lands as sister Elizabeth above); total real estate, Ł69.17.6; total estate, Ł368.2.6. <11:68> Account 24 Mar. 1748; mentions Deacon BREWSTER, Mrs. Mary WARREN, Coll. WARREN, Dr. LeBARON, Esq. BARTLETT; "Ł61.16.8 to a share being 6 parts". (Mercy is called "Mrs.", however she was single; this estate is almost identical to her sister's above.)

Estate of **Mary WARREN**, spinster of Plymouth MA. <Plymouth Co.PR #21891>
<34:56> Letter/Bond 30 Nov. 1795, widow Bethiah DYER app'td admr. Sureties: John COTTON, Josiah COTTON. Witnesses: Nathaniel LOTHROP, Isaac LOTHROP. <35:365> Inventory taken 2 Dec. 1795 by Abraham HAMMETT, John COTTON; no real estate. <35:365> Insolvency, 2 Dec. 1795. <35:366> List of Claims, 2 Dec. 1795: Bethiah DYER, Abigail HOLMES, Daniel DIMAN. <35:366> Account 31 Oct. 1796. <35:367> Distribution, 9 Nov. 1796, to the above three creditors, viz: to Abigail HOLMES for board 26 weeks, Ł8.13.4.; to Bethiah DYER for 273 weeks board at 20 cents per week, 4 weeks housing/nursing(?) in 1791 at $1.00 per week and 13 weeks boarding the nurse(?) last sickness.

Will of **James WARREN** of Plymouth MA. <Plymouth Co.PR #21875>
<14:298>...dated 31 May 1757...to son **James WARREN Jr.**, all the real estate that my honoured father in his will gave to me lying in Plymouth; daus **Ann WARREN & Sarah SEVER.** Witnesses: Consider HOWLAND, James HOVEY, John COBB. <14:300> Letter 19 July 1757, son **James WARREN** app'td exr. <15:275> Inventory taken 1 Sept. 1757 by Josiah MORTON, James HOVEY, Ebenezer SPOONER; mentions lands in Plimton & Rochester and half the stock on the farm held in partnership with Mr. DOTEN; total estate, Ł3314.1.8. <16:439> Account 1 Nov. 1762; Received from: Mr. WINSLOW, BURBANK, Thomas FOSTER Jr., Samuel JACKSON, John GOVERN Esq., John CHURCHILL, Mr. BACON, David GORAM, James HOVEY, Josiah WHITEMORE, Caleb TURNER, Jabez COBB, WATSON & MAYHEW, Benjamin LOTHROP, Joshua BENSON, Mr. LITTLE, Z. PADDOCK, J. FAUNCE, Joseph MORTON, Benjamin JOHNSON, Samuel BURGIS, Lemuel CHURCH, John MILLER, John KNOWLTON, Ephraim THOMAS, Joseph BLACKAMORE, Jeremiah THOMAS, Eleazer PRATT, Coombs BARROW, Richard DAVENPORT, Edward DOTY, Isaac PETERSON, Elkanah LEONARD Jr. & Son; Paid to: RICHES, Benjamin GOODWIN, Capt. NICHOLSON, Benjamin MORTON, Nathaniel Ray THOMAS, John BARTLETT, John MAY, Molly FISHER, John WINSLOW, Mr. TYLER, Thomas NORINGTON, Thomas TORREY, Dr. HOVEY, Nathaniel SHURTLEFF, Nathaniel COBB, John STURTEVANT, Joseph RIDER Jr., Thomas DINGLEY, Joshua LORING, Timothy BURBANK, Jonathan DIMAN, Zaccheus CURTIS, Dr. STOCKBRIDGE, James LANMAN, Dr. SEVER, Coll. WATSON, Nathaniel DUNHAM, James HOWARD, Caleb (---), Josiah CARVER, Noah SPRAGUE John MAY, Dr. LEBARON, Daniel DIMAN, Charles BELLAVOO, Mr. COTTON, Edward WINSLOW, Stephen SAMPSON, Capt. DELINO, Consider HOWLAND, Capt. WHITE, Michal BARN, John FULLERTON, Isaac KING,

Walter RICH, Nathaniel COBB Jr., Ebenezer NELSON, Mr. TILSON, William RICHARD, widow Hannah DIER, Dr. THOMAS, William LOTHROP for ballance of his grandfather & uncle's accounts, Abiel SHURTLEFF, Madam BACON, Robert BROWN, Job & Silas MORTON, James BOWDOWIN, John WATERMAN, Salvanis/Sylvanus BRIMHALL, Mr. TILER, Deacon FOSTER, Mercy WARREN, Patience COBB adm. on her husband's estate, Nicholas SEVER & Son, Coll. OTIS, WARREN & GOODWIN.

Will of **James WARREN**, Esq. of Plymouth MA. <Plymouth Co.PR #21876>
<42:419>...dated 8 June 1792, mentions wf **Mercy** and sons **Henry WARREN, James WARREN, George WARREN.** <42:420> Pr. 28 Dec. 1808. <46:432> Adm. de bonis non.

Will of **Jonathan DELANO** of Dartmouth MA. <Bristol Co.PR; MD 23:148>
<3:707>...dated 17 Dec. 1720 (not transcribed in files). <3:710> Inventory.

References to the name **Jonathan DELANO** in Bristol Co.PR, viz: <34:483> Inv. <34:484> Account. <20:277> Will. <20:279> Pr. <20:282> Inv. <21:165> Account. <42:341> Account. <128:245> Guardianship of son **Nathaniel DELANO**, 29 Apr. 1771. <129:410> Guardianship of son **Jonathan DELANO**, 11 Feb 1779. <149:175> Adm., 1797.

Estate of **John MAY**, yeoman of Plymouth MA. <Plymouth Co.PR #13737>
<20:285> Letter 24 Jan. 1770, Thomas WETHERELL, innholder of Plymouth, app'td admr. <20:440> Inventory taken 17 Oct. 1770; incl. land bought of Samuel SHAW and 15th lot in South Meadow cedar swamp. <21:209> Account 2 Nov. 1772. <21:398> Division 7 Dec. 1773 to following chil., viz: **John MAY** (eldest son), **Anna WETHERELL** wf of Thomas, **Bathsheba LOTHROP** wf of David, **Sarah MAY.** (#13736, 11:94...6 June 1748, Petition of relatives of **John MAY**, yeoman, of Plymouth non comp.)

Heirs of **John MAY** to **James SPOONER** of Plymouth MA. <Plymouth Co.Deeds 136:63>
...28 Sept. 1818, John MAY of Canaan NH and Thomas JACKSON Jr. & wf Sarah, William NELSON & wf Bathsheba all of Plymouth and Anna May BARTLETT of Portsmouth NH, heirs of John MAY dec'd, for $43.43 sold to James SPOONER, merchant...all our right...unto the third share in the 16th great lot in South Meadow Cedar Swamp in Carver...which decended to us by heirship from our father & Grandfather John MAY late of Plymouth dec'd which he purchased of Samuel SHAW by a deed dated 18 May 1748 & rec. 39:138...being about six acres...also we convey three quarter parts of the second share in the 15th great lot of cedar swamp in sd South meadow cedar swamp...containing three acres...which decended to us from sd John MAY...adjoining Rockey neck...which sd John purchased of Lemuel HOLMES by a deed dated 12 Mar. 1756 & rec. 43:255. Witnesses: Nathaniel SPOONER, Rosseter COTTON. Ack. same day. Rec. 2 Oct. 1818.

MICRO #31 OF 32

PLYMOUTH COUNTY DEEDS: (re: VALLER)

<28:216> - 25 Dec. 1733, John VALLER, husbandman & wf Mary sell land given Mary by her father John MAY 19 Nov. 1733, which sd MAY bought of William ELLIS, Gideon ELLIS & Benjamin CORNISH...at Ship Pond. Ack. 22 May 1734 by both.
<40:55> - 31 May 1749, John MAY Sr., yeoman of Plymouth to son John MAY Jr., wheelwright of same and dau Mary VALLER wf of John, husbandman of same. Same day John & Mary VALLER sold theirs to brother John MAY Jr.
<40:55> - 31 May 1749, John MAY Jr. & wf Bathsheba to sister Mary VALLER wf of John.
<46:185> - May 1758, John MAY admr. to estate of John VALLER, husbandman of Plymouth, sells.
<46:231> - 20 Jan. 1761, John MAY admr. as above sells to Sarah VALLER, spinstress of Plymouth.
<64:15> - 26 Nov. 1776, Mary VALLER, widow & spinster of Plymouth, to son Simeon VALLER, yeoman of same, half of salt marsh I bought of my brother John MAY Jr. of Plymouth dec'd...other half she sold same day to son Silas VALLER <69:54>.
<67:228> - 17 July 1788, Silas VALLER to brother Simeon VALLER, yeomen of Plymouth, right in land their father John VALLER bought of John WETHERHEAD. Wf Mary consents.
<69:233> - 21 May 1789, Simeon VALLER for self & wf Ruth the dau of Zacheus HOLMES of Plymouth dec'd, with others, sell rights in estate of Honoured Parents James & Content HOLMES dec'd of Plymouth.

(References only, viz: 72:56;74:15;77:202,203.)

Will of **John WARREN**, yeoman of Middleboro MA. <Plymouth Co.PR #21878>
<20:59>...dated 21 Jan. 1768, mentions wf **Ann**, sons **James WARREN, Nathaniel WARREN, Nehemiah WARREN** and daus **Naomi TINKHAM** wf of Jeremiah of Middleboro & **Ann DICKERSON** wf of Joseph; grandson **Elisha TINKHAM**; to the three chil. of **John WARREN** dec'd, viz: **Richard, John & Naomi**, £8 when they reach 21. Witnesses: Gershom RICHMOND, Eleazer RICHMOND, Samuel THATCHER. <20:60> Letter/Bond 4 Apr. 1768, **Elisha TINKHAM** app'td admr. Sureties: Gershom RICHMOND, Eleazer RICHMOND. Witnesses: Edward HAYWARD Jr., Edward WINSLOW Jr.

Will of **Anna WARREN**, widow of Middleborough MA. <Plymouth Co.PR #21855>
<20:321>...dated 21 Aug. 1769, mentions **Silva REED** dau of **Peter REED** dec'd; **Martha INGLEE** & her youngest dau **Waitstill**; brother **William REED** & his son **Jonathan REED**; to **William REED**, grandson of brother **William**, half the debt that is due on a note of hand from Deacon Edward RICHMOND of Taunton; to **Timothy INGLEE** a note that I have upon Lieut. Philip LEONARD; **Elisha TINKHAM**, residuary legatee & executor. Witnesses: Gershom RICHMOND, Eleazer RICHMOND, Benjamin WHITE. <20:322>

Letter 5 Feb. 1770, **Elisha TINKHAM**, app'td exr. <20:377> Inventory taken 23 Feb. 1770 by Benjamin WHITE, Joseph LEONARD, Joseph PHINNEY; total real estate, Ł15.4.; total estate Ł134.11.1.; sworn to 26 Feb. 1770 by appraisers.

PLYMOUTH COUNTY DEEDS: (re: Samuel WARREN)

<9:271> - 1701, James WARREN to Samuel WARREN. <MD 21:79>
<9:317> - 2 Aug. 1707, Samuel WARREN of Middleboro from Thomas PALMER of same.
<10:2:258>- 1711, John WARREN to Samuel WARREN. <MD 21:79>
<10:2:259>-28 Apr. 1711, Samuel WARREN from Mercy FULLER widow of John of Middleboro.
<10:2:261>- 1711, Samuel WARREN from David & Hope TORREY. <MD 21:80>
<11:240> - , Samuel WARREN from John & Anne MAY. <MD 21:80>
<13:149> - , Samuel WARREN from Joanna BUMPAS. <MD 14:256>
<14:104> - 13 Nov. 1718, Samuel WARREN & Abraham BARDEN of Middleboro divide land formerly of William BARDEN.

PLYMOUTH COUNTY DEEDS: (re: Silvanus WARREN)

<81:112> - 14 Oct. 1782, S.W., gent. of Middleboro, grantor. Sarah WARREN wf of Benjamin releases dower.
<79:195> - 13 Sept 1786, S.W., gent of Middleboro, son of Benjamin, grantor.
<129:168> - 4 Dec. 1816, S.W., gent., Benjamin WARREN, Andrew WARREN, yeomen of Middleboro to Ebenezer WILLIS. Huldah WARREN signs.
<129:249> - 12 Aug. 1817, Silvanus WARREN, yeoman of Middleboro, mortgage to Beza TUCKER, one undivided fifth of two thirds of lands of father Silvanus WARREN of Midd. dec'd, grandfather Benjamin WARREN.
<129:241> - 15 Oct. 1817, S.W., Benjamin WARREN & Andrew WARREN, yeomen of Middleboro, sons of late Sylvanus WARREN of Middleboro dec'd, mort. to Beza TUCKER releas.
<140:27> - 16 Aug. 1819, S.W. & Andrew WARREN, yeomen of Middleboro, execution for debt.
<140:30> - 16 Aug. 1819, S.W., Benjamin WARREN & Andrew WARREN, execution for debt.
<172:46> - 18 Apr. 1831, S.W. & wf Mercy of Middleboro, sell land bought by Mercy 29 Nov. 1823.

<61:159> - 20 Oct. 1770, S.W., husbandman of Middleboro from Joseph WARREN, housewright of same. Wf Mercy and mother Mercy HOWARD, widow sign. Rec. 26 Nov. 1782.
<61:159> - 9 Feb. 1782, S.W., yeoman of Middleboro from father Benjamin WARREN, yeoman of Plymouth. Wf Jedidah releases dower.
<97:108> - 2 Nov. 1789, S.W. of Middleboro from Caleb SIMMONS. Rec. 19 Aug. 1803.
<97:108> - 30 Oct. 1800, S.W., gent. of Middleboro from Thomson BAXTER.
<108:247> - 3 Sept 1804, S.W., gent of Middleboro from Robert CUSHMAN & wf Lucia of Middle.
<106:11> - 8 Oct. 1805, S.W., Daniel WESTON & John ATWOOD, yeomen of Middleboro from Robert CUSHMAN, gent. of Rutland VT.
<151:231> - 15 Sept 1810, S.W. of Middleboro from Benaiah PRATT & wf Louisa of Farmington ME.
<121:184> - 21 June 1813, S.W., Benjamin WARREN & Andrew WARREN from Daniel WESTON & John ATWOOD of Middleboro, their half of land bought with S.W. dec'd. (106:11)
<296:213> - 12 Feb. 1859, S.W. of Middleboro from Silvanus HINCKLEY & wf Sally of same.

David & Abigail WESTON of Middleboro MA to children. <Plymouth Co.Deeds 63:20>
...26 Aug. 1783, David & Abigail WESTON, for love & affection deed...to four of our children, viz: Jacob SOULE of Halifax, Mercy CUSHMAN wf of Noah of Middleboro, Susanna WARREN wf of Zenas and Abigail WESTON of Middleboro, Lots #106,107 & 108 in South Purchase in MIddleboro. Witnesses: Zech PADDOCK, James SPROUT. Rec. 1 Nov. 1783.

Zenas WARREN et al of Hartland VT to **Jacob SOULE** of Halifax MA. <Plymouth Co.Deeds 69:254>
...8 Nov. 1786, Zenas WARREN, yeoman and Susanna WARREN, spinster of same, for 5s sell to Jacob SOULE, gent...one quarter part of lots 106,107 & 108 in the South Purchase in Middleboro. Witnesses: Lucy WARREN, Elias WELD. Rec. 4 Feb. 1790.

Guardianship of Child of **Cornelius WARREN** dec'd of Middleborough MA. <Plymouth Co.PR #21860>
<original> Bond 6 June 1757, Elijah CLAPP of Middleborough app'td gdn. of **Benjamin WARREN.** Sureties: Jacob HAYWARD, James KEITH. Witnesses: Daniel WILLIS, Edward WINSLOW.

Estate of **Josiah WARREN,** husbandman of Middleborough MA. <Plymouth Co.PR #21888>
<15:515> Letter/Bond 2 June 1760, Micha BRYANT app'td admr. Sureties: Elijah CLAP, Ebenezer BISBE Witnesses: William TIRRELL(sp), Edward WINSLOW. <16:398> Inventory taken 2 June 1760 by Nathaniel BUMP, Edmund WESTON Jr., Joseph WARREN; no real estate; total personal estate, Ł11.17.9. <16:452> Account 4 Apr. 1763; allowance to widow, Ł7.17.9. <16:452> Insolvency.

Nathan WARREN of Middleboro MA to **Nathan WARREN Jr.** of same. <Plymouth Co.Deeds 62:21>
...24 Mar. 1781, Nathan WARREN, blacksmith to son Nathan WARREN Jr...land received by deed from his father Samuel WARREN late of Middleboro, by deed dated 8 Mar. 1745...also land bought of his brother Benjamin WARREN of Middleboro, by deed dated 5 Feb. 1749. Wf Rachel releases dower. "Nathan lost his sight before signing." Witnesses: Silvanus WARREN, Zenas WARREN. Rec. 28 Mar 1783...same day Nathan WARREN Jr. mortgages the land to Silvanus WARREN, gent. of Middleboro wh has become bondsman for sd Nathan on agreement to take care of Nathan Sr. & wf for their lives. Ack. 28 Mar. 1783. Rec. 27 Mar. 1783.

Will of **Sarah REED,** widow of Middleboro MA. <Plymouth Co.PR, filed with #16704>
...dated 27 Apr. 1779, mentions dau **Elizabeth REED,** the other children having already received their parts. Witnesses: Benjamin REED, Abiah REED. Citation 17 Sept. 1783, to following heirs, viz: **Sarah HOARS/HOAR** wf of Robert, heirs of **Priscilla PEARCE** wf of Abraham and all other heirs at law ...whereas the will of sd dec'd has been presented for probate, you are...cited to appear ...at the dwelling house of Caleb LORING, Inholder in Plymton on Monday the 6 Oct. next.

PLYMOUTH COUNTY DEEDS: (re: Robert HOAR)

<52:107> - 13 Oct. 1759, Deacon William HOAR & Robert HOAR, miller, from John BOOTH & Priscilla HOSKINS wf of Henry. Wf Lydia BOOTH signs & mother of John BOOTH releases rights.
<52:107> - 19 Mar. 1765, Mary SMITH, widow, Robert HOAR, miller et al.
<52:108> - 7 June 1765, 28 Oct. 1765, Robert HOAR.
<72:206> - 1776, Robert HOAR, yeoman of Middleboro & wf Rachel to son Peter HOAR, laborer of same; mentions land lately sold to son Samuel HOAR. Rec. 4 May 1792.
<74:218> - 12 Nov. 1776, Robert HOAR of Middleboro from estate of Barnabas CANEDY.
<74:219> - 14 Feb. 1777, Robert HOAR Jr. of Middleb. from Daniel RENNELS/REYNOLDS son of Ephraim dec'd.
<59:217> - 9 Feb. 1778, Robert HOAR Jr. sells two tracts bought in 1775 & 1777. Wf Sarah reles.
<74:219> - 18 Apr. 1778, Robert HOAR of Middleboro & wf Rachel to Robert HOAR Jr. of same; mentions land lately sold to Peter HOAR.
<74:220> - 7 July 1780, Robert HOAR, yeoman to son Robert HOAR Jr., both of Middleboro.
<75:145> - 11 July 1780, Robert HOAR to son Peter HOAR. Rec. Aug. 1793, Robert dec'd.
<75:146> - 11 July 1780, Robert HOAR to son John HOAR. Rec. Aug. 1793. " ".
<69:206> - 24 Feb. 1785, Robert HOAR of Middleboro.
<74:221> - 21 Mar. 1786, Peter HOAR, gent of Middleboro & wf Marcy to Robert HOAR.

Will of **Lettice JENNEY/JENNE,** yeoman of Dartmouth MA. <Bristol Co.PR>
<8:85>...dated 24 Jan. 1731/2...to eldest son **Cornelius JENNE** all that part of my home steed whare he now liveth...on the east side of nasktucket Brook...also three acre meadow...that I bought of Stephen SAMSON...the 26 Nov 1701...he paying to my wife...ten pounds...to son **Ignatius JENNE**...part of my home steed whare he now liveth...to son **Caleb JENNE**...part of my home steed whare my now dwelling hous now standeth...excepting one acre...by Nathaniel DELENO's...together with meadow, two nobs of sedgg lying in Nashtucket Crick...he paying my wife fifteen pounds...to son **Samuel JENNE,** all my land that lyeth to the north of that land that I have given to my son **Cornales** and to the east ward of the above sd Brook...to son **Nathaniel JENNE,** 51 acres...bounded by Ceader swamp commonly called Spooner's Ceader Swamp, together with once acre lying to the west ward of Nashtucket Brook...by Nathaniel DELENO's...also my ceader swamp; daus of son **Caleb**; son in law **Jeduthan SPOONER**; daus **Sarah SPOONER** wf of Samson, **Reliance POPE** wf of Thomas, **Mary WEST** wf of Thomas and **Elizabeth & Parnell**, both under 21; grandaughter **Ruth SPOONER** (under 10); wf **Desire**, executrix. Witnesses: Samuel HAMMOND, Abraham RUSSELL, Benjamin HAMMOND. Petition 26 Jan. 1733 of **Simpson SPOONER.** Adm. Bond 19 Mar. 1733/4, wf declines, **Cornelius JENNE** app'td admr. Inventory taken 25 Mar. 1733/4.

Nathaniel BLACKWELL to Heirs of **Lettis JENNE.** <Bristol Co.Deeds 42:153>
...10 June 1755...for & in Consideration that Lettis JENNE late of sd Dartmouth dec'd did in his life time unwitingly build his house partly on my Land now for ye Regard That I have to ye widow and fatherles Children have Given & Granted...unto ye heirs of ye sd Lettis JENNE...a certain peice of Land...in Dartmouth aforesd where on ye sd House Stands. Witnesses: Nathaniel SPOONER, John ROBINS. Ack. 16 Dec. 1755. Rec. 16 Dec. 1756.

Will of **Joseph SPOONER,** yeoman of Dartmouth MA. <Bristol Co.PR>
<21:505>...dated 23 Oct. 1770, mentions following chil., viz: **Simson SPOONER** (under 22), **Ruth SPOONER, Lucy SPOONER, Zoath SPOONER, Caleb SPOONER** (under 22), **Lois SPOONER, Mercy SPOONER;** friend Seth POPE, executor. <21:7> Bond 5 Feb. 1771, of Wesson TALLMAN, admr., Seth POPE having refused. <21:26> Inventory taken 17 Feb. 1771. <23:40> Account 26 Apr. 1773. Guardianships 28 Jan. 1771, Wesson TALLMAN, yeoman of Dartmouth chosen gdn. by following chil. (over 14), viz: **Simson** <128:222>, **Caleb** <128:223>, **Ruth** <128:224>, **Lois** <128:225>. On 26 Apr. 1773, Samuel SPOONER Jr. app'td gdn. of **Mercy** (under 14) <128:419> and chosen gdn. by **Lusanna** (over 14) <128:420>. On 26 Apr. 1773, Wesson TALLMAN app'td gdn. of **Zoeth** <128:416>. ON 16 DEC. 1778, Nathaniel SPOONER, yeoman of Dartmouth chosen gdn. by **Zoeth** (above 14) <129:375>.

Estate of **Caleb JENNE/JENNEY** of Dartmouth MA. <Bristol Co.PR>
<17:559> Inventory taken 23 Sept. 1761 by Seth POPE, Stephen WEST, Benjamin BLOSSOM; no real estate mentioned; first wife's wearing apparrel valued at £3.2s8d. <17:523> Adm., 6 Oct. 1761, widow **Silence JENNEY**, admx. <9:210> Account of admx., 1 Oct. 1765. <127:34> Guardianship, Letter/Bond 6 Oct. 1761, Seth POPE, gent. of Dartmouth chosen gdn. by **Patience JENNE,** above 14.Sureties: Hezekiah WINSLOW, gent. of Dartmouth & Samuel FRENCH, gent. of Berkley. <127:171> 4 Oct. 1763, **Silence JENNEY** chosen gdn. by **Caleb JENNEY,** over 14.

Will of **Silence JENNEY,** widow of Dartmouth MA. <Bristol Co.PR 24:190>
...dated 12 Mar. 1776, mentions following chil., viz: **Abel HOUSE, John HOUSE, Caleb JENNE, Sarah ROBBINS, Susanna BADCOCK, Elizabeth HORKSEY, Patience TABER**; grandaughters **Silence BADCOCK, Marcy HAMMOND**; son in law **Jeduthan TABER,** executor. Pr. 14 or 24 June 1776.

Estate of **Caleb JENNEY.** <Bristol Co.PR>
...1861...<119:754> Notice. <120:430> Sale. <175:228> Bond. <182:883,884> Pr. & Will. <194:202> Inv. <214:5> Sale of land. <217:118> Account.

BRISTOL COUNTY DEEDS: (re: Caleb JENNEY)

<81:454> - 28 Aug. 1802, C.J., mason of New Bedford to Lemuel TRIPP, land in N.B. Wf Elisabeth JENNE signs. Rec. 20 Sept. 1802.
<82:451> - 4 Apr. 1803, C.J. Jr., bricklayer to Gideon RANDALL. Wf Elizabeth JENNE signs.
<86:65> - 1806, C.J. Jr. to Nathaniel HATHAWAY.
<86:330> - 1806, C.J. Jr., grantor.
<87:106> - 1807, C.J., grantor.
<75:45> - 1797, C.J. Jr. from Benjamin SISSON.
<80:47> - 1801, C.J. from John ATSATT.
<83:187> - 1803, C.J. from Joseph RUSSELL.
<84:483> - 1805, C.J. et al from Loring TABER.
<87:109> - 1807, C.J. from Abraham RUSSELL.
<92:359> - 1811, C.J. et al from Jeduthan TABER.
<93:213> - 1811, C.J. Jr. from Henry JENNEY.
<93:213> - 1811, Jr. from Elkanah MITCHELL est.
<94:166> - , C.J., grantee.
<104:539>- 1818, C.J. from Caleb JENNEY.
<114:33> - 1823, C.J. Jr., grantee.
<102:109>- 2 Sept 1815, Caleb JENNE Jr., mason of New Bedford from Job OTIS. Rec. 26 Mar. 1817.
<102:107>- 13 Oct. 1815, Caleb JENNE Jr., cordwainer of New Bedford from Russell DAVIS.
<102:108>- 17 Mar. 1817, Caleb JENNE Jr., cordwainer of Middleboro from Jeduthan TABER, carpenter

---

Will of **Cornelius JENNE** of Dartmouth MA. <Bristol Co.PR 23:365,369,371>
...dated 3 Sept. 1771, mentions wf **Eleanor** (to receive whole of estate she brought to me) and following chil., viz: **Jethro JENNE, Levi JENNE, Benjamin JENNE, Cornelius JENNE, Timothy JENNE, Jahazel JENNE, Henry JENNE** (executor), **Jabez JENNE, Jean, Jemima, Deborah, Esther, Hannah, Rebecca.** Witnesses: Caleb JENNE, Nathaniel DELANO, Barzillai HAMMOND. Pr. 7 Nov. 1774 & Inv. 3 Nov.

Estate of **Cornelius JENNE Jr.** of Dartmouth MA. <Bristol Co.PR>
<23:375> Inventory taken 25 Oct. 1774, by Seth POPE, Lemuel POPE & Richard DELANO; sworn to 7 Nov. 1774 by **Elizabeth JENNE,** admx. <25:285> Account of admx., 7 Oct. 1778.

Estate of **Cornelius JENNE** of Fairhaven MA. <Bristol Co.PR 47:489>
Inventory taken 4 May 1812, by Jacob TABER 2d, Bartholomew TABER & Benjamin SISSON of Fairhaven; one third of dwelling house; sworn to 6 Oct. 1812 by **Ruth JENNE,** admx.

MICRO #32 OF 32

Will of **Levi JENNE,** merchant of New Bedford MA. <Bristol Co.PR>
<42:308>...dated 10 Sept. 1806...to wf **Mary** (executrix), use of all real & personal estate while his widow to bring up the children that are under age & for her own support...at her death to be equally divided between the living children & the heirs of dec'd children, reference being had to what the older children have already had. <42:309> Pr. "28" Oct. 1806. <42:309> Inventory taken 24 Oct. 1806; house at Fairhaven; half of house occupied by son **Levi JENNEY;** personal estate owned equally with son **Levi** under firm of **Levi JENNEY & Son;** sworn to same day by exx. <44:236> Account, 4 Oct. 1808, of **Levi JENNEY,** admr. on estate of **Mary JENNEY,** admx. of **Levi JENNEY.** <45:166> Division 22 June 1809, of estate after death of widow **Mary JENNEY** to following chil., viz: **Levi JENNEY** (eldest son), **Bathsheba WHITE,** dec'd, **Mary KEMPTON** (2d dau), **Stephen JENNEY, Ansel JENNEY, Sally JENNEY, Bernard JENNEY, Joseph JENNEY, Betsey JENNEY, Isaac JENNEY.**

Estate of **Reuben MASON** of New Bedford MA. <Bristol Co.PR>
...1806...<41:574> Receipts. <42:418> Inventory taken 29 Nov. 1806 (Warrant, 13 Nov.). <42:424> Insolvency. <43:146> Account, 1807. <48:237> Account, 4 May 1813. <131:360> Guardianship, 10 Dec. 1806 of **Mary & Reuben MASON.** <150:193> Adm. 10 Dec. 1806, Joseph WHELDEN, mariner of New Bedford, app'td admr. <44:566> Division 2 May 1809, to following chil., viz: **Richard MASON** (eldest son), **Ruth WHELDEN** wf of Joseph, **Parnal SMITH** wf of Consider, **Reuben MASON, Charles MASON, Mary MASON;** and grandchildren: **Betsey Mason TALLMAN** dau of **Timothy TALLMAN** and **Job COOK & Hannah COOK,** chil. of **Thomas COOK Jr.**

Will of **Joseph WHELDON** of Fairhaven MA. <Bristol Co.PR>
<101:366>...dated 29 Feb. 1853, mentions wf **Roby** and following chil., viz: to **Ruth, Thankful, Susan, Sally & George WHELDON,** the sum of $1.00; to son **Joseph WHELDEN** (executor), remainder of land, etc. <173:324> Adm.Bond, 6 Feb. 1855. <118:386> Notice. <178:161> Citation. <192:200> Inv.

Estate of **Ruth WHITE** of New Bedford MA. <Bristol Co.PR>
<original> Petition 17 Sept. 1879, for appointment of Richard W. HATHAWAY as admr. on estate of **Ruth WHITE** who died 1 Sept. 1879; only heirs are seven daus, viz: **Evelyn C. LAWTON** wf of Joseph M., **BETSEY J. SWIFT** wf of Robert, **Abby F. CORNELL, Mary G. JENNINGS** wf of Lewis S., **Susan W. JENNINGS** wf of B.R., all of New Bedford, **Ruth R. ESLEECK** of Holyoke MA & **Sarah H. RUSSELL** wf of Timothy H. of Dartmouth. <228:2> Adm., 3 Oct. 1879.

Will of **John BLACKWELL.** <Barnstable Co.PR 6:101>...dated 10 Apr. 1734, wf **Lydia,** dau **Lydia BLACKWELL.** Pr. 6 Jan. 1741. <6:331> Inventory taken 1 Feb. 1741; sworn to 7 Apr. 1742 by wf.

WILLIAM WHITE

MICRO #1 OF 7

PLYMOUTH COUNTY PROBATE: (re: WHITE)

1664	Gowan			#22555
1688	Sylvanus	Scituate		#22617, 1:20
1704	Peregrine	Marshfield		#22605, 2:48,49,50
1704	Timothy	Scituate		#22623, 2:53,54
1709	Malatiah	Rochester		#22592, 2:104,112;3:198,199,380
1709	Malatiah et ali	Rochester		#22593
1711	Joseph	Scituate		#22582, 3:101
1722	Joseph	Scituate		#22583, 4:335,337;5:586
1724	Benjamin	Marshfield		#22511, 4:423;5:67,68,120;8:387
1724	Daniel	Marshfield		#22533, 4:446,447,448
1728	Richard	Plymouth		#22608, 5:474,475
1737	Elkanah	Marshfield		#22544, 7:395
1740	Sarah	Middleboro		#22611, 8:262
1742	Sylvanus	Marshfield		#22618, 9:32,43
1746	John Jr.	Marshfield		#22577, 10:276,281;13:268
1746	John et ali	Marshfield		#22578, 10:277,278,279,289;13:332
1748	John	Rochester		#22571, 11:153,154
1751	Micah	Abington		#22599, 12:239,316
1753	John	Marshfield		#22576, 13:149,150,151,195
1756	Jacob	Abington		#22563, 14:28,364,374
1756	Timothy	Scituate		#22624, 14:239,350,352,358,359;15:68
1756	Cornelius	Marshfield		#22526, 14:190,193,402
1757	David	Eastown		#22538, 14:279
1757	Jacob et al	Abington		#22564, 14:274,275
1761	Daniel	Middleboro		#22535, 16:111,267;17:19
1765	Micah et al	Weymouth		#22600, 18:105,106
1766	Joseph	Marshfield		##22581, 17:182;19:490;20:295
1768	Hannah	Marshfield		#22557, 20:51,52,53
1773	Timothy	Scituate		#22625, 21:311,394;23:19,49
1774	Timothy Jr.	Scituate		#22626, 21:604;23:48;27:506;29:260,261;31:182
1774	Benjamin	Middleboro		#22515, 23:53;24:70,348
1776	Andrew et al	Middleboro		#22505, 22:69,70,71;22:202,203
1776	Hannah	Marshfield		#22558, 24:135,136,137
1776	Paul	Marshfield		#22603, 24:195,197
1779	Gideon	Plymouth		#22553, 25:304,305;28:16,17,304,328,333,336;31:108-9;39:454;44:147,242,243
1780	Resolved	Rochester		#22606, 25:553;27:48;33:110,111,112
1781	Sybilline	Marshfield		#22616, 28:151,152
1785	Paul	Marshfield		#22604, 29:83,84;30:82,303;33:265;37:383;38:160
1786	Benjamin	Hanover		#22512, 29:469,470;33:491;36:525
1786	Daniel	Marshfield		#22534, 29:438,440,449;33:359
1786	Samuel	Marshfield		#22610, 27:534;29:513-4;33:358-9,381;35:486,542;36:5,156,186
1792	Andrew	Middleboro		#22504, 27:404;33:171,172;35:58
1792	Hannah	Marshfield		#22559, 31:500,502-3;33:69,150,287;35:261;36:190
1794	Jeremiah	Abington		#22567, 35:128,129,141
1795	Micah	Bridgewater		#22597, 34:27;35:245,415,417-20;45:560
1797	Nabby et ali	Bridgewater		#22602, 32:92
1799	Malatiah	Rochester		#22591, 34:178;36:514,515
1803	Joseph	Scituate	adm.	#225-4, 34:376;40:14,15
1805	Micah	Bridgewater	adm.	#22598, 39:7;40:258,504
1809	Jeremiah	Abington	will	#22568, 42:463;43:100,261,341-2,344,510;44:411;45:42,43,191,204,423,424
1810	Friend	Pembroke	adm.	#22551, 39:268;43:283;44:22
1810	Friend et al	Pembroke	gdn.	#22552, 41:52
1811	Joanna	Plymouth	will	#22569, 43:446,447
1812	Sylvanus	Marshfield	will	#22619, 44:116,117,417;45:81,448,449,459;46:429;48:260
1813	Lucy	Bridgewater	adm.	#22588, 39:398;45:118,255,559;47:120
1816	Luther	Marshfield	will	#22589, 48:233,403;50:213,221,288,289
1817	William	Marshfield	gdn.	#22628, 41:326;49:65,66,132,133,245
1818	William	Marshfield	adm.	#22629, 46:261;49:327-8;50:63-4,78,80,172,215-7
1819	Benjamin	Marshfield	adm.	#22510, 46:372;50:547-8,576;53:146,223-4,267;54:555,556,557;79:442,443

PLYMOUTH COUNTY PROBATE, cont-d: (re: WHITE)

1819	Thomas F.	Marshfield	gdn.	#22620, 51:36
1821	Benjamin	Carver	will	#22514, 53:450-1,495-6;54:367-8;56:176;57,98,100
1822	Joel	Halifax	will	#22570, 55:63;56:123,125-6,198-9;58:259;72:32
1822	Samuel	Middleboro	adm.	#22609, 52:109;54:420-22;56:177-9;57:411
1824	Joseph	Scituate	gdn.	#22585, 51:246
1824	Timothy	Scituate	adm.	#22622, 52:272;55:228;58:220-1,342;59:381
1826	Martin	Bridgewater	adm.	#22595, 61:73;63:133,523-4;64:46
1827	Lemuel	Wareham	adm.	#22587, 61:112,201;64:108-9,349,350,392-3;66:84, 234,235,465,466
1828	Gideon C.	Plymouth	adm.	#22554, 61:191;62:245;66:109,234;67:499
1830	Cyrus	Middleboro	will	#22531, 69:57;77:104
1835	Benjamin	Middleboro	gdn.	#22516, 8:53;65:397;75:481;77:108;78:212-3;79: 166,483;81:405,414
1835	John	Bridgewater	will	#22572, 75:194;77:71
1835	Silas	Middleboro	Will	#22612, 75:251;77:34,473;78:214
1836	Gideon T.	Pembroke	will	#22555, 75:314;78:151,166,168-9;79:128,130;80: 144;81:220;82:140;83:208-9,369;84:211; 85:218;86:200;87:347;89:276;90:214;91: 235;92:275;93:233;94:223;95:282;96:259; 3**P**:503;13**D**:66.
1837	Lydia	Marshfield	will	#22590, 1**G**:41;5**T**:36;79:236,238;80:204
1838	Anna	Wareham	adm.	#22506, 5**T**:126;10**A**:180;81:273,286
1838	Anna	Marshfield	gdn.	#22508, 8**L**:413,414;80:364;85:391
1838	Thomas	Bridgewater	adm.	#22621, 5**T**:107;10**A**:223;81:162;82:317
1839	Benjamin	Hanover	will	#22518, 1**G**:351;6**U**:29;81:477
1839	Gilman Jr.	Rochester	adm.	#22556, 10**A**:285
1841	Cornelius	Hanover	will	#22527, 1**G**:380;6**U**:199;83:271,272
1841	Ezra S.	Plymton	adm.	#22549, 2**O**:213;6**U**:173;10**A**:432;83:146
1843	John A.	Marshfield	gdn.	#22574, 8**L**:483;85:213;132:157
1843	Joseph	Duxbury	adm.	#22579, 2**O**:294;6**U**:468;11**B**:195;85:475;86:404
1843	Elizabeth C.	Plymouth	adm.	#22543, 11**B**:217
1843	William H.	Bridgewater	adm.	#22631, 11**B**:206
1844	Almira et al	Duxbury	gdn.	#22502, 1**R**:166;2**O**:488;8**L**:354;87:16
1846	Alvin	Rochester	adm.	#22503, 1**R**:278,302;3**P**:54,127;7**V**:148;11**B**:437;88: 498;100:481
1846	Briggs	Duxbury	will	#22520, 2**H**:85;7**V**:200;88:456,594;89:333
1847	Asa	Bridgewater	will	#22509, 2**H**:105;7**V**:206;89:66,107
1848	John	Hanson	adm.	#22573, 7**V**:357;11**B**:583;90:113,385
1849	Benjamin	Middleboro	adm.	#22517, 8**W**:13;12**C**:126;92:168,411
1849	Cyrus	Rochester	adm.	#22532, 8**W**:147;12**C**:55;91:123,172;93:221,405
1849	Mary B. et al	Rochester	gdn.	#22596, 9**M**:227;11**N**:122;100:308;101:343,500,511
1849	Sybil	Rochester	will	#22614, 2**H**:207;8**W**:1;91:354,556;92:316

Philip WHITE of Beverly MA & **William FERRINGTON** of Lynn. <Middlesex MA Deeds 15:480>
...7 Apr. 1711, Philip WHITE, housewright & William FERRINGTON Jr., cordwainer, sell to Ephraim M( )ER(sp) (WHEELER?) of New Town...land, house & barn in New Town. Witnesses: William FERINGTON, Thomas FOXCROFT.

Philip WHITE of New Town to **Eliezer MOODY** of Dedham MA. <Middlesex MA Deeds 16:363>
...22 Aug. 1713, Philip WHITE, carpenter, for Ł100 mortgages to Eliezer MOODY...land in New Town, mentions Ephraim WHEELER(sp). Wf Deborah WHITE signs. Witnesses: Andrew WHITE, Humphrey THOMAS.

William FARRINGTON Jr. of Lynn MA to **Philip WHITE** of New Town. <Middlesex Co.Deeds 17:164>
...12 Mar. 1712/3, William FARRINGTON Jr. sells to Philip WHITE, carpenter...half part of land & barn...the whole was purchased by sd Philip & myself of Ephraim WHEELER(sp)...on highway from Cambridge to Dedham. Witnesses: John BURRILL, Anna BURRILL.

Philip WHITE of New Town to **Andrew WHITE.** <Middlesex Co.Deeds 20:619>
...28 Mar. 1722, Philip WHITE, yeoman & wf Deborah to son Andrew WHITE...land on which sd Andrew has erected a dwelling home.

PLYMOUTH COLONY DEEDS: (re: WHITE)

<2:1:145> - Gowin WHITE to Joseph TILDEN, mortgage.
<2:1:178> - WHITE & BASSETT, division.
<2:1:5> - Peregrine WHITE from William BASSETT.
<2:1:177> - WHITE & BASSETT from William BASSETT.
<2:1:5> - Gowin WHITE from William RICHARDS.
<2:2:53> - Gowin WHITE to William RANDALL.
<2:2:114> - Peregrine WHITE to Manasseh KEMPTON.
<3:3> - Resolved WHITE to William HILLS.
<3:12> - Gowin WHITE to John OTIS.
<3:87> - Peregrine WHITE, bounds.
<3:215> - Peregrine WHITE to Thomas DOGGETT.
<3:204> - William WHITE, son of Resolved, to John HOWLAND, 1671.
<3:296> - Resolved WHITE to John ROGERS.
<3:203> - William WHITE from John HOWLAND.
<4:130> - Resolved WHITE to Humphry JOHNSON.
<4:229> - Samuel WHITE to Benjamin CHURCH 1671
<4:419> - Nicholas WHITE from David ADAMS.
<5:82> - Peregrine WHITE to Symon LYNDE.
<5:423> - Peregrine WHITE to Ephraim LITTLE.
<5:474> - Timothy WHITE to Joseph THORNE.
<5:126> - Gowin WHITE to Thomas ENSIGN.

PLYMOUTH COLONY DEEDS, cont-d: (re: WHITE)

<5:472> - Timothy WHITE from Samuel BACON.
<6:25> - Peregrine WHITE to Thomas DAGGETT.
<6:83> - Peregrine WHITE to Daniel WHITE.
<6:112> - Nicholas WHITE to James BELL.
<6:114> - Peregrine WHITE et al.
<4:246> - Samuel WHITE from Josias WINSLOW 1667.

PLYMOUTH COUNTY DEEDS: (re: William WHITE)

<1:38> - 1687, William WHITE of Marshfield, son of Resolved, grantor.
<63:113> - 20 Aug. 1778, William WHITE of Marshfield, grantor.
<62:243> - 26 May 1784, Silvanus WHITE, William WHITE, yeomen, Sarah WHITE & Susanna WHITE, singlewomen, all of Marshfield & Ezra EDSON, yeoman & wf Anna of Bridgewater, chil. of Abijah WHITE, Esq. dec'd of Marshfield.
<78:262> - 26 Nov. 1793, Silvanus WHITE, William WHITE; Luther LITTLE as gdn. of his chil. Luther & Susanna; Ezra EDSON & wf Anna, Nathan WILLIS & wf Sarah, the chil. of Abijah WHITE.
<82:155> - , William WHITE, grantor.
<83:200> - , William WHITE, grantor.
<86:266> - 15 Mar. 1800, William WHITE & wf Hannah of Pembroke.
<87:22> - 5 Oct. 1799, William WHITE of Marshfield as gdn. of Thomas BAKER, minor.

PLYMOUTH COUNTY DEEDS: (re: Ebenezer WHITE, grantor)

<10:2:237> -6 Feb. 1712/3, E.W. of Marshfield to William COOK.
<15:39> - 26 June 1718, E.W. of Marshfield to John ROGERS Jr.
<16:95> - 9 June 1722, E.W. et al of Marshfield to Jacob TOMSON.
<16:187> - 13 Apr. 1723, E.W. et al of Marshfield to James SPRAGUE.
<38:252> - 24 July 1747, E.W., clerk of Danbury et al to Comfort STARR.
<40:44> - 22 Aug. 1748, E.W., clerk of Danbury to Ezekiel REED.
<40:207> - 18 May 1747, E.W., clerk of Danbury et al to Joseph GURNEY.
<42:43> - 18 Dec. 1749, E.W., laborer of Rochester to Thomas WHITE of same.
<45:61> - 13 May 1749, E.W. of Danbury to Thomas PRATT, land in Abington.
<50:53> - 5 Dec. 1764, E.W., yeomen of Rochester to James BLANKINSHIP, land in Rochester.
<52:76> - 1 Mar. 1764, E.W., yeoman of Rochester to Edward WINSLOW.
<53:169> - 16 Feb. 1767, E.W., yeoman of Rochester to David NYE, land in Rochester.
<53:169> - 16 Feb. 1767, E.W., yeoman of Rochester to Silvanus MENDALL, land in Rochester.
<54:35> - 16 Apr. 1767, E.W., yeoman of Rochester to Isaac SNOW, land in Rochester.
<54:67> - 29 Dec. 1767, E.W., yeoman of Rochester to Mark HASKELL, land in Rochester.
<55:198> - 17 Apr. 1767, E.W., yeoman of Rochester to Samuel SNOW, land in Rochester.
<57:160> - 8 Jan. 1768, E.W., yeoman of Rochester to John GOODSPEED, land in Rochester.
<57:36> - 19 Apr. 1771, E.W., yeoman of Rochester to Resolved WHITE, mariner of Rochester.
<67:119> - 29 Mar. 1780, E.W., yeoman of Middleboro to John RICKARD, land in Middleboro.
<63:51> - 26 Nov. 1783, E.W., yeoman of Middleboro to Silas WHITE, land in Middleboro.
<72:198> - 22 Mar. 1784, E.W., yeoman of Middleboro to Eliab ALDEN, land in Middleboro.

PLYMOUTH COUNTY DEEDS: (re: WHITE, grantors)

<30:160> - Anna et al to Barnabas EATON.
<37:125> - Anna et al to John MURDOCK.
<30:170> - Anna to Jeremiah GRIDLEY.
<53:97> - Anna to Joshua WHITE.
<62:243> - Anna et al, division.
<75:250> - Anna to Richard ESTES.
<88:251> - Anna to Calvin CURTIS.
<42:195> - Abijah to Paul WHITE.
<46:33> - Abijah to John STEVENS.
<48:162> - Abijah to Cornelius WHITE.
<49:121> - Abijah to John JOYCE.
<54:92> - Abijah exon. to Jesse WHITE.
<62:243> - Abijah, heirs of, division.
<76:276> - Abijah, agents to Ephraim LITTLE.
<63:50> - Andrew to Ebenezer WHITE.
<67:65> - Abigail to Edmund BOWKER.
<67:177> - Abigail to Lydia STOCKBRIDGE.
<67:190> - Abigail to John BOWKER.
<70:124> - Abigail to Stephen BOWKER et al
<72:58> - Abigail & Elizabeth, division.
<73:179> - Abigail & Daniel.
<73:188> - Abigail to John BOWKER.
<79:94> - Abigail to Temperance WHITE.
<78:270> - Alexander to Thomas CHANDLER et al.
<10:490> - Benjamin to Cornelius WHITE.
<29:41> - Benjamin to Samuel LYON.
<30:160> - Benjamin et al to Barnabas EATON.
<33:67> - Benjamin to Samuel THATCHER.
<34:66> - Benjamin to Manufacturing Co.
<36:83> - Benjamin to Benjamin HAYFORD.
<36:204> - Benjamin to Jeremiah GRIDLEY.
<37:36> - Benjamin to James WARREN.
<37:125> - Benjamin et al to John MURDOCK.
<39:124> - Benjamin to Phineas PRATT.
<39:142> - Benjamin to Nehemiah WASHBURN.
<39:256> - Benjamin to Jeremiah GRIDLEY et al.
<39:260> - Benjamin Jr. to Nathaniel PRATT.
<41:272> - Benjamin to Benjamin WHITE Jr.
<42:105> - Benjamin to Joshua WHITE.
<44:200> - Benjamin to Adam HALL Jr.
<44:220> - Benjamin to John ALDEN.
<46:49> - Benjamin et al to Elisha FORD Jr.
<47:194> - Benjamin to Simeon TURNER.
<48:89> - Benjamin to John HOUSE.
<48:90> - Benjamin to John HOUSE.
<51:89> - Benjamin to Benjamin WARREN.
<51:19> - Benjamin to Paul WHITE.
<52:73> - Benjamin to Daniel FISHER.
<53:113> - Benjamin Jr. to Samuel PRATT.
<54:58> - Benjamin to Seth BARNES.
<60:166> - Benjamin et al to Zephaniah DECROW.
<62:178> - Benjamin to Elisha FORD.
<66:54> - Benjamin to Cornelius WHITE.
<67:118> - Benjamin Jr. to Henry RICKARD.
<68:147> - Benjamin et al to Roland HAMMOND Jr.
<74:9> - Benjamin to Israel TURNER.
<84:216> - Benjamin et al to Elisha MURDOCK.
<85:109> - Benjamin to A. HOBART Jr.

PLYMOUTH COUNTY DEEDS, cont-d: (re: WHITE, grantors)

<85:206> - Benjamin et al to John MURDOCK et al.
<86:44> - Benjamin to Joseph VAUGHAN.
<88:254> - Benjamin & Mercy, division.
<89:38> - Benjamin to Silas WHITE.
<91:9> - Benjamin to Benjamin WHITE Jr.
<91:44> - Benjamin et al to Seth BARROWS.
<73:251> - Betty et al to Barnabas DUNBAR.
<100:74> - Betty et al to Daniel RIPLEY,1798.
<91:3> - Betsey to Timothy WHITE.
<11:69> - Cornelius to John WHITE.
<11:167> - Cornelius et al to Samuel THOMAS.
<11:242> - Cornelius to Ebenezer WHITE.
<16:92> - Cornelius to Jacob TOMSON.
<16:157> - Cornelius to Ephraim NORCUTT.
<23:147> - Cornelius & Hannah, division.
<32:87> - Cornelius to Benjamin RANDALL.
<32:101> - Cornelius to Israel TURNER.
<33:232> - Cornelius et al to Joshua RANDALL.
<36:82> - Cornelius with J. LITTLE, division.
<42:184> - Cornelius Jr. with A. HALL, bounds.
<42:93> - Cornelius to Caleb BEAL.
<55:77> - Cornelius to William CHURCHILL.
<55:164> - Cornelius to John HYLAND.
<58:160> - Cornelius et al to William STURTEVANT.
<58:234> - Cornelius to Samuel JACKSON.
<65:66> - Cornelius to Lucy WHITE.
<65:76> - Cornelius to Peleg WHITE.
<68:256> - Cornelius to Lucy PHILLIPS.
<70:265> - Cornelius to Lucy PHILLIPS.
<71:43> - Cornelius to Nathaniel PHILLIPS.
<73:125> - Cornelius to David TORREY.
<5:198> - Daniel to Joseph WHITE.
<6:220> - Daniel to John WHITE.
<7:123> - Daniel to Cornelius WHITE.
<7:139> - Daniel to John WHITE.
<7:144> - Daniel to John WHITE.
<8:163> - Daniel et al to Benjamin WHITE et al.
<66:11> - Daniel, re: Elkanah CROSMAN.
<78:210> - Daniel by exr. to Caleb BAILEY.
<78:282> - Daniel by exr. to Chandler SAMSON.
<81:29> - Daniel to Edmund BOWKER et al.
<81:242> - Daniel, admr., to Benjamin HATCH Jr.
<82:6> - Daniel to Luther LITTLE.
<82:36> - Daniel et al, division.
<82:79> - Daniel, admr., to Luke HALL.
<83:27> - Daniel to James WHITE.
<84:249> - Daniel to Christopher CUSHING.
<86:29> - Daniel et al to James LITTLE.
<90:254> - Daniel to Luther LITTLE.
<91:86> - Daniel to Benjamin HATCH.
<91:269> - Daniel to Jedediah LITTLE.
<9:73> - Elizabeth et al, division.
<42:89> - Elizabeth to Samuel CLAPP.
<72:58> - Elizabeth et al, division.
<10:237> - Ebenezer to William COOK.
<15:39> - Ebenezer to John ROGERS Jr.
<16:95> - Ebenezer et al to Jacob TOMSON.
<16:187> - Ebenezer to James SPRAGUE.
<38:252> - Ebenezer to Comfort STARR.
<40:44> - Ebenezer to Ezekiel REED.
<40:207> - Ebenezer et al to Joseph GURNEY.
<42:43> - Ebenezer to Thomas WHITE.
<45:61> - Ebenezer to Thomas PRATT.
<50:53> - Ebenezer to James BLANKINSHIP.
<52:76> - Ebenezer to Edward WINSLOW.
<53:169> - Ebenezer to David NYE.
<53:169> - Ebenezer to Silvanus MENDALL.
<54:35> - Ebenezer to Isaac SNOW.
<54:67> - Ebenezer to Mark HASKELL.
<55:198> - Ebenezer to Samuel SNOW.
<57:36> - Ebenezer to Resolved WHITE.
<57:160> - Ebenezer to John GOODSPEED.
<63:51> - Ebenezer to Silas WHITE.
<66:134> - Ebenezer to William WHITE.
<67:119> - Ebenezer to John RICKARD.
<72:198> - Ebenezer to Eliab ALDEN
<45:167> - Elisha to Benjamin CLARK.
<56:246> - Ezekiel et al to Francis BARKER.
<39:57> - George to Ebenezer PERRY Jr.
<39:58> - George to Isaac LOTHROP et al.
<53:166> - George to Jeremiah BUMPUS Jr.
<44:82> - Gideon by exon. to Jonathan HOLMES.
<45:228> - Gideon et al, division.
<45:213> - Gideon to Jonathan HOLMES.
<45:228> - Gideon et al, settlement of bounds.
<48:25> - Gideon to Elisha BRYANT.
<49:62> - Gideon to Elisha BRYANT.
<53:187> - Gideon by exon. to Ebenezer SPOONER
<53:216> - Gideon by exon. to Josiah CHURCHILL
<54:82> - Gideon, exr. to George WATSON et al
<54:141> - Gideon to Ephraim SPOONER.
<54:215> - Gideon to Samuel JACKSON.
<58:150> - Gideon to Cornelius WHITE.
<61:34> - Gideon et al to Thomas HOBART.
<69:237> - Gideon by exr., to Hannah WHITE.
<70:214> - Gideon by exr., to Hannah WHITE.
<71:14> - Gideon T. to Josiah THOMAS.
<75:80> - Gideon by admr., to Joseph RIDER.
<77:237> - Gideon T. to Isaac MAGOUN.
<89:102> - Gideon et al to MANN & CUSHING.
<16:187> - Hannah et al to James SPRAGUE.
<23:147> - Hannah et al, division.
<32:87> - Hannah et al to Benjamin RANDALL.
<33:232> - Hannah et al to Joshua RANDALL.
<44:232> - Hannah et al to Isaac HERSEY et al.
<50:256> - Hannah et al to Abner WRIGHT.
<60:166> - Hannah et al to Zephaniah DECROW.
<70:214> - Hannah to Joanna WHITE.
<82:93> - Hannah et al to Henry WARREN.
<41:228> - Hezekiah to Samuel WINSLOW.
<3:207> - Joseph to Stephen TILDEN.
<5:53> - Joseph to James CUSHING.
<5:218> - Joseph to Timothy WHITE.
<6:235> - Joseph to Thomas BUCK.
<7:49> - Joseph to Joseph RANDALL Jr.
<7:269> - Joseph to Samuel TURNER.
<8:14> - Joseph to John WHITE.
<9:375> - Joseph to Timothy WHITE.
<10:359> - Joseph et al, division.
<11:92> - Joseph et al to Job OTIS.
<10:367> - Joseph to Amos TURNER.
<10:382> - Joseph to John ROGERS Jr.
<10:443> - Joseph to Jonathan WALDO.
<12:204> - Joseph to James CUSHING.
<12:29> - Joseph to Charles JOSSELYN.
<39:161> - Joseph to Abijah WHITE.
<45:36> - Joseph to Daniel NOYES.
<46:39> - Joseph et al to Ebenezer WHITE.
<79:172> - Joseph to Jabez PRIOR et al.
<89:100> - Joseph, admr., to Isaac DELANO.
<89:197> - Joseph, admr., to Ezekiel GLASS.
<90:147> - Joseph, admr., to Nathaniel DELANO.
<6:219> - John to Joseph WHITE.
<8:163> - John et al to Benjamin WHITE et al.
<9:153> - John et al to Samuel PRINCE.
<10:5> - John to Thomas FORD.
<10:207> - John to William CLARK.
<10:518> - John to Isaac HOLMES.
<10:638> - John to Samuel PRINCE.
<11:237> - John to William STEVENS.
<11:39> - John to Joseph LEAVITT.
<11:237> - John to William STEVENS.
<11:89> - John to Samuel SPRAGUE.
<12:175> - John to Stephen ANDREWS.
<12:169> - John to Benjamin HAMMOND.
<13:206> - John et al to Essex Trustees.
<14:257> - John to Charles LITTLE.
<14:169> - John to John WING.

PLYMOUTH COUNTY DEEDS, cont-d: (re: WHITE, grantors)

<14:272> - John et al to Samuel SHERMAN.
<15:48> - John to Commr.Plym.Co.
<16:60> - John to Gilbert WINSLOW.
<16:134> - John to Boston Trustees.
<19:38> - John to William WHITRIDGE.
<19:152> - John Jr. to Lemuel DREW.
<19:43> - John to Samuel PRINCE.
<19:125> - John Sr. to John WHITE Jr.
<21:84> - John to Cornelius WHITE.
<23:109> - John et al to John HASKELL.
<25:121> - John to Jacob BUMPUS.
<26:120> - John to Joel ELLIS.
<26:197> - John to Joshua EASTY.
<26:198> - John, deposition.
<26:132> - John to Samuel WHITE.
<26:163> - John et al, evidence.
<27:72> - John Sr. to John WHITE Jr.
<28:130> - John to Leonard VASSALL.
<30:199> - John to Job LORING.
<30:208> - John to John WHITE Jr.
<30:209> - John to David NYE.
<31:206> - John to David NYE.
<31:207> - John to David NYE.
<32:58> - John to Noah SPRAGUE.
<32:103> - John to Edward WINSLOW Jr.
<32:124> - John to James FOSTER.
<32:171> - John to Edward MORSE.
<33:66> - John Jr. to Abijah WHITE.
<34:83> - John to Abijah WHITE.
<35:224> - John to Jeremiah DEVEL.
<35:6> - John to Silvanus WHITE et al.
<36:89> - John to Abijah WHITE.
<37:43> - John Jr. to Joshua BENSON.
<37:182> - John to Samuel PRINCE.
<37:162> - John to Caleb BLACKWELL.
<38:240> - John to Abijah WHITE.
<38:240> - John to Jesse WHITE.
<38:239> - John to Church of England Society.
<39:168> - John to Timothy RUGGLES.
<43:192> - John to Abner WRIGHT.
<50:256> - John et al to Abner WRIGHT.
<51:57> - John to William RANDALL.
<52:81> - John to Ebenezer WHITE.
<60:48> - John to Ebenezer WHITE.
<77:45> - John to Nathan NYE Jr.
<83:27> - John to James WHITE.
<32:173> - Judith to Abel CUSHING.

PLYMOUTH COUNTY DEEDS: (re: WHITE, grantees)

<35:97> - Abigail from William REED.
<72:58> - Abigail et al, division.
<33:66> - Abijah from John WHITE Jr.
<34:83> - Abijah from John WHITE.
<35:191> - Abijah from Otis LITTLE.
<36:89> - Abijah from John WHITE.
<37:18> - Abijah from Ebenezer DOGGETT et al.
<38:10> - Abijah from Sarah DOGGETT.
<38:10> - Abijah from Ebenezer DOGGETT.
<38:240> - Abijah from John WHITE.
<39:161> - Abijah from Joseph WHITE.
<62:243> - Abijah, heirs, division.
<75:225> - Abraham from Job WITHERELL.
<53:97> - Anne from Josiah DEAN.
<67:231> - Anne from Thomas JOSSELYN.
<8:163> - Benjamin et al from Daniel WHITE.
<9:392> - Benjamin from Ralph NORCUTT.
<20:157> - Benjamin from Timothy RUGGLES.
<22:53> - Benjamin from Hannah BICKNELL.
<23:23> - Benjamin from Ebenezer HALL.
<25:205> - Benjamin from Elizabeth CHAFFEE.
<26:217> - Benjamin from Japheth BICKNELL.
<30:149> - Benjamin from Mary BICKNELL.
<30:162> - Benjamin from Hugh MEHURIN.
<30:141> - Benjamin et al from Moses STURTEVANT.
<30:149> - Benjamin from Elias MILLER.
<30:206> - Benjamin et al, agreement.
<31:179> - Benjamin from John SALTER.
<32:67> - Benjamin et al from Peleg SAMSON.
<35:93> - Benjamin from Benjamin HAYFORD.
<37:122> - Benjamin from James WARREN.
<38:226> - Benjamin from Job AUHAUTON et al.
<44:272> - Benjamin Jr. from Benjamin WHITE.
<41:272> - Benjamin Jr. from Samuel PRATT et al.
<41:273> - Benjamin Jr. from Henry RICKARD.
<41:257> - Benjamin Jr. from Peter RAYMOND.
<42:105> - Benjamin Jr. from William LYON.
<45:113> - Benjamin from Prudence WESTON.
<45:113> - Benjamin from Jerusha PRATT.
<45:114> - Benjamin from John KNOWLTON et al.
<48:122> - Benjamin from John TORREY.
<48:122> - Benjamin from James SILVESTER.
<50:220> - Benjamin from Jacob GREEN.
<50:221> - Benjamin from Samuel PRATT.
<50:221> - Benjamin from John MURDOCK.
<56:175> - Benjamin, atty., from Thomas HUTCHINSON Jr.
<60:163> - Benjamin from Simmons BARROWS.
<61:166> - Benjamin Jr. from State of Mass.
<62:214> - Benjamin Jr. from Gideon HARLOW.
<63:85> - Benjamin et al from Nathaniel JACKSON
<71:128> - Benjamin from Phinehas PRATT et al.
<74:207> - Benjamin et al from John THOMAS.
<76:141> - Benjamin et al from Joshua EDDY.
<84:11> - Benjamin from Daniel PETERSON et al.
<88:254> - Benjamin et al, division.
<89:120> - Benjamin from Silas WHITE.
<89:254> - Benjamin from Daniel PETERSON et al.
<91:9> - Benjamin Jr. from Stephen TORREY Jr.
<91:9> - Benjamin Jr. from Benjamin WHITE.
<3:47> - Barnard from John HASCALL.
<24:226> - Catharine from Cornelius HOLMES.
<26:54> - Catharine from John WATERMAN.
<27:57> - Catharine from John WESTON.
<33:22> - Katharine from John ROBINSON.
<7:123> - Cornelius from Daniel WHITE.
<9:180> - Cornelius from John ROGERS.
<10:489> - Cornelius from Nathan WILLIAMSON.
<10:490> - Cornelius from Benjamin WHITE.
<12:10> - Cornelius from Jeremiah BURROUGHS.
<14:238> - Cornelius from Ephraim NORCUTT.
<16:5> - Cornelius from William MACOMBER et al
<16:91> - Cornelius from William MACOMBER et al
<17:139> - Cornelius from Thomas WHITE.
<20:3> - Cornelius from Richard CHILES.
<20:147> - Cornelius from Ephraim NORCUTT.
<21:84> - Cornelius from John WHITE.
<21:85> - Cornelius from Samuel STETSON Jr.
<21:85> - Cornelius from Benjamin PHILLIPS Jr.
<21:188> - Cornelius et al from Ephraim NORCUTT.
<21:48> - Cornelius from Richard CHILES.
<22:137> - Cornelius et al from Isaac LITTLE.
<23:146> - Cornelius from William BARSTOW et al.
<23:147> - Cornelius from Nathan SPRAGUE et al.
<23:225> - Cornelius from William SHERMAN.
<23:147> - Cornelius & Hannah, division.
<24:127> - Cornelius from John BARKER.
<25:112> - Cornelius from Edward BRISCO.
<25:43> - Cornelius from Thomas DOGGETT.
<27:184> - Cornelius from Thomas DOGGETT.
<28:113> - Cornelius from Ebenezer CURTIS.
<30:190> - Cornelius from John HILAND.
<30:70> - Cornelius from John EELLS et al.
<30:69> - Cornelius from Elizabeth FISH.

PLYMOUTH COUNTY DEEDS, cont-d: (re: WHITE, grantees)

<32:189> - Cornelius Jr. from Thomas EAMES.
<34:93> - Cornelius from Thomas DOGGET et al.
<34:94> - Cornelius from Issac LITTLE.
<34:212> - Cornelius from Ebenezer DOGGETT et al.
<36:2> - Cornelius from James HATCH.
<36:144> - Cornelius Jr. from Adam HALL et al.
<36:82> - Cornelius et al, division.
<38:77> - Cornelius from Joshua RANDALL.
<41:33> - Cornelius from Prince BARKER.
<42:238> - Cornelius Jr. from John STEVENS et al.
<42:184> - Cornelius et al, settlement.
<43:138> - Cornelius from Isaac PHILLIPS et al.
<46:243> - Cornelius from Anthony WATERMAN.
<48:162> - Cornelius from Abijah WHITE.
<51:20> - Cornelius from Thomas FOSTER.
<57:51> - Cornelius from Nathaniel FORD.
<57:181> - Cornelius from Thomas PHILLIPS.
<58:150> - Cornelius from Gideon WHITE.
<66:54> - Cornelius from Benjamin WHITE.
<43:266> - Daniel from Edward OAKMAN.
<47:210> - Daniel from John SHAW.
<73:179> - Daniel from Abigail WHITE.
<81:243> - Daniel from Temperance WHITE et al.
<82:36> - Daniel et al, division.
<83:241> - Daniel from Benjamin HATCH Jr.
<84:142> - Daniel from Benjamin SHAW Jr.
<86:30> - Daniel from James LITTLE.
<8:163> - Ebenezer et al from Daniel WHITE.
<11:242> - Ebenezer from John DOGGETT.
<21:133> - Ebenezer from Thomas SNELL.
<38:28> - Ebenezer from Jeremiah DEVIL.
<39:180> - Ebenezer from Comfort STARR.
<46:38> - Ebenezer from Malatiah WHITE et al.
<46:38> - Ebenezer from Ebenezer PARKER.
<46:40> - Ebenezer from Ebenezer PARKER.
<46:40> - Ebenezer from John HEDGE.
<46:41> - Ebenezer from Barnabas HEDGE.
<52:79> - Ebenezer from David NYE.
<52:80> - Ebenezer from James BLANKINSHIP.
<52:81> - Ebenezer from John WHITE.
<53:145> - Ebenezer from James BLANKINSHIP.
<54:191> - Ebenezer from Malatiah WHITE.
<55:229> - Ebenezer from Cornelius CLARK et al.
<60:48> - Ebenezer from John WHITE.
<60:48> - Ebenezer from John BROWN et al.
<63:50> - Ebenezer et al from Thomas KNOWLTON.
<63:50> - Ebenezer from Bethiah KNOWLTON.
<63:50> - Ebenezer from Silas WHITE.
<63:50> - Ebenezer from Andrew WHITE.
<63:51> - Ebenezer from State of Mass.
<63:107> - Ebenezer from Mark SNOW.
<66:134> - Ebenezer from Thomas ELLIS et al.
<74:93> - Ebenezer et al from Joshua CROCKER.

Will of **Daniel WHITE** of Marshfield MA. <Plymouth Co.PR #22533>
<4:447>...dated 25 May 1721...aged & infirm...mentions wf **Hannah** and children, viz: **John WHITE, Joseph WHITE, Thomas WHITE, Cornelius WHITE** (executor), **Benjamin WHITE, Eleazer WHITE, Ebenezer WHITE.** Witnesses: Josiah THOMAS, Ebenezer HOWLAND, Arthur HOWLAND Jr. <4:446> 8 May 1724, John BARKER, Arthur HOWLAND Jr. & Peleg FOORD(sp), all of Marshfield, were app'td to appraise personal estate. <4:448> Letter 8 June 1724, **Cornelius WHITE** app'td admr. <4:448> Inventory taken 15 June 1724 by above three appraisers; no real estate; sworn to 6 Aug. 1724 by admr.

PLYMOUTH COUNTY DEEDS: (re: Daniel WHITE, grantor)

<5:198> - 15 Feb. 1701/2, to Joseph WHITE.
<7:144> - 5 Oct. 1704, to John WHITE.
<7:139> - 10 Dec. 1706, to John WHITE.
<7:123> - 24 Feb. 1706/7, to Cornelius WHITE.
<6:220> - 21 Feb. 1708/9, to John WHITE.
<8:163> - 18 Jan. 1710/11, to Ben. & Eben. WHITE

Will of **John WHITE,** yeoman of Rochester MA. <Plymouth Co.PR>
<11:153>...dated 29 June 1748, mentions wf **Martha** and children, viz: **Silvanus WHITE, Mary, Thomas WHITE, Justice WHITE, Elizabeth & Deborah;** grandson **Nathaniel**, son of dau **Jedidah**; sons **Justice & Silvanus**, executors. Witnesses: Elisha BARREN(sp), Timothy RUGGLES, Thomas RUGGLES. <11:154> Pr. 9 Nov. 1748.

BARNSTABLE COUNTY DEEDS: (re: WHITE, grantors) <all on index 1703-1827>

<3:553> - 1786, Daniel et al to Barnabas ELDRIDGE.
<3:434> - 1791, Daniel et al to Samuel FARRIS.
<2:337> - 1792, Daniel et al to Samuel GRAY.
<3:433> - 1792, Daniel et al to Samuel FARRIS.
<2:528> - 1795, Daniel et al to Winthrop SEARS.
<2:354> - 1796, Daniel et al to Abraham BAKER.
<3:251> - 1812, Daniel et al to Alden GRAY.
<3:209> - 1813, Daniel et al to Edmund ELDRIDGE.
<3:217> - 1813, Daniel et al to Edmund ELDRIDGE
<3:89> - 1814, Isaac et al to Richard SEARS.
<3:212> - 1814, Isaac et al to Edmund ELDRIDGE.
<2:219> - 1816, Isaac et al to Benjamin TRIP.
<2:357> - 1817, Isaac et al to Abraham BAKER.
<4:43> - 1821, Isaac et al to Isaac BASSETT.
<2:335> - 1803, Joseph to Lydia GRAY.
<2:177> - 1822, Joseph to Prentiss WHITE.

References to the name **Ruth WHITE** in Bristol Co.PR:
<30:319> Will. <31:233> Inv. <31:241> Account. <32:376> Receipt. <119:44> Notice, 1857. <174:494> Bond. <178:275> Citation. <181:443> Pr. <181:444> Will. <228:2> Adm., 1879.

PEREGRINE WHITE[2] (William[1])

Will of **William NORCUTT Sr.** of Marshfield MA. <Plymouth Co.PR 1:178>
...dated 6 Dec. 1692. Witnesses: Peregrine WHITE Sr., Mercy WHITE, Daniel WHITE. Inventory taken 22 Sept. 1693.

PLYMOUTH COLONY DEEDS: (re: Peregrine WHITE)

<6:25> - 1664, Peregrine WHITE & wf Sarah of Marshfield to Thomas DOGGETT.
<3:21> - , Grant of land to Lieut. Peregrine WHITE et al.
<3:44> - 1665, Wampatucke to Peregrine WHITE.
<3:87> - 1667, Bounds of land, between Peregrine WHITE & Josias WAMPATUCKE.
<3:216> - 1671, Division of land by Lieut. WHITE et al.
<5:82> - 1677, Peregrine WHITE to Simon LYNDE. Wf Sarah resigns her right.
<4:348> - 1679, Peregrine WHITE witnesses deed of Josiah WINSLOW et al to Lieut. Joseph LAYTHORP.
<5:422> - 1684, Lieut. Peregrine WHITE to Ephraim LITTLE.
<6:32> - 1 Apr. 1686, Peregrine WHITE witnesses deed of Justus EAMES to John DOGGETT, of Marshf.
<6:114> - 6 Apr. 1686, Peregrine WHITE, Thomas DAGGETT, William FORD, Justus EAMES, John FOSTER, Samuel SPRAGUE, Samuel SHERMAN, John DAGGETT.

Estate of **Benjamin WHITE** of Marshfield MA. <Plymouth Co.PR #22511>
<4:423> Letter/Bond 7 July 1724, widow **Faith WHITE** app'td admx. Surety: Tobias OAKMAN of Marshfield. Witnesses: Elizabeth WINSLOW, Elizabeth ROSE. <5:120,57> Inventory taken 16 July 1724 by John BARKER, James SPRAGUE & Peleg FOORD; housing & lands, Ŀ170; iron work in the sloops, Ŀ41.3s 7d; total real estate, Ŀ170; sworn to by **Faith WHITE**, 24 Dec. 1724. <5:68> List of claims: Samuel OAKMAN, William STEPHENS, "Eshietiur" WINSLOW, Gilbert WINSLOW, Abigail STEPHENS, Capt. WHITE, Peleg FORD, Dr. OTIS, widow JONSON, Jeremiah CROOKER, John WHITE; to ye Corinal for his work; John LITTLE, Thomas HOWLAND, Benjamin PHILIPS Jr., Josiah THOMAS, Samuel DOGGET, estate of Ebenezer HATCH, Capt. TURNER, Capt. LITTLE. <8:387> Account of admx., **Faith FOSTER**, 17 June 1741; requests allowance for certain debts & for support of the children; Paid to: Dr. OTIS, Dr. DELLANO, Tobias OAKMAN, Joseph JOSLYN, William STEPHENS, Isachar WINSLOW, Gilbert WINSLOW, John WHITE; charge of my lying in with my son **Benjamin** born after the sd dec'd and providing all things necessary for sd child 6 years; providing for **Jedediah** 3 years and for **Lydia** 1 year.

MICRO #2 OF 7

Will of **Cornelius WHITE** of Marshfield MA. <Plymouth Co.PR #22526; MD 20:61>
<14:190>...dated 16 Apr. 1754, mentions wf **Hannah** and following chil., viz: **Lemuel WHITE, Cornelius WHITE, Paul WHITE, Joanna PHILLIPS** wf of Nathaniel, **Daniel WHITE, Gideon WHITE, Benjamin WHITE**; brother **John WHITE**; minor grandson **Cornelius WHITE.** Witnesses: Thomas CLAP, Ezekiel YOUNG, John THOMPSON. <14:193> Letter 23 Mar. 1756, son **Daniel WHITE,** Innholder of Marshfield, app'td exr. <14:402> Inventory taken 29 Mar. 1756 by Ensign OTIS, Thomas WATERMAN, Nehemiah THOMAS; mentions land in Marshfield, Hanover & Scituate; total real estate, Ŀ2709.6.8; total estate, Ŀ3175. 6.6.; sworn to 30 Mar. 1756 by exr.

Will of **Hannah WHITE,** widow of Marshfield MA. <Plymouth Co.PR #22557; MD 20:61>
<20:51>...dated 10 Sept. 1767...aged...mentions children: **Lemuel WHITE, Cornelius WHITE, Paul WHITE, Joanna PHILLIPS** wf of Nathaniel, **Daniel WHITE, Gideon WHITE & Benjamin WHITE**; grandchildren: **Lucy YOUNG** wf of Ezekiel, **Alice WHITE** dau of **Cornelius, Hannah WHITE** dau of **Paul, Joanna TURNER** wf of Thomas, **Abigail WHITE** dau of **Daniel, Hannah WHITE** dau of **Gideon** and **Hannah WHITE** dau of **Benjamin**; sons **Lemuel & Cornelius** & son in law **Nathaniel PHILLIPS,** executors. Witnesses: Adam HALL, Jeremiah PHILLIPS, Elisha PHILLIPS. <20:52> Pr. 2 Mar. 1768. <20:53> Inventory taken 3 Mar. 1768 by Elisha PHILLIPS, Ephraim LITTLE, Abner WRIGHT; no real estate; total personal estate, Ŀ213.11.2.; sworn to 4 Mar. 1768 by exrs.

Will of **Benjamin WHITE** of Hanover MA. <Plymouth Co.PR #22512>
<29:469>...dated 28 Dec. 1785, mentions wf **Hannah** and children **Hannah CROOKER** & her children, **Robert WHITE, Benjamin WHITE, Cornelius WHITE.** Witnesses: John TURNER, Joseph BATES, Benjamin BATES. <original> Bond 8 Mar. 1786, of **Cornelius WHITE,** exr. Sureties: Joseph BATES & Benjamin BATES of Hanover. Witnesses: Elizabeth CUSHING, Deborah CUSHING. <29:469> Letter 9 Mar. 1786, **Cornelius WHITE** app'td exr. <29:470> Inventory taken 9 Mar. 1786 by Seth BATES, George BAILEY, William STOCKBRIDGE; total estate, Ŀ336.6.6., incl. land & buildings given by deed of gift to the three sons, Ŀ311.5. <36:525> Receipt, 9 Mar. 1786, of **Hannah WHITE** to **Cornelius WHITE** for personal property given her in will. <33:491> Account of exr., 28 Nov. 1793; Paid to: Dr. HOBART, Anthony WATERMAN, James OTIS, Calvin CURTIS, Benjamin STETSON, Seth STETSON, Stephen BAILY, Daniel CROOKER as gdn., Samuel STETSON, James LEWIS, Gideon STUDLEY, widow Mary PHILLIPS, John COTTON Esq., Cornelius WHITE, Robert L. EELLS, Benjamin WHITE, Robert WHITE.

Will of **Daniel CROOKER,** yeoman of Pembroke MA. <Plymouth Co.PR #5249>
<49:220>...dated 13 June 1816...to eldest son **Ensign CROOKER,** $5.00; to youngest son **Daniel CROOKER Jr.,** $5.00; to dau **Nabby CHAMBERLIN** wf of Josiah, $5.00; to heirs of dau **Betty STURTEVANT** who was the wf of Barzillai, $1.00; to dau **Lydia CROOKER,** $5.00; to heirs of dau **Hannah ESTES** who was the wf of Matthew, $1.00; to dau **Mary BRYANT** wf of Nathaniel, $1.00; to dau **Matilda STUDLEY** wf of Walter, $1.00; to dau **Sarah GARDNER** wf of David, $1.00; $1.00 each to daus **Judith CROOKER, Joanna CROOKER, Deborah CROOKER & Ezsa CROOKER**; remainder of estate to the four sons of son **Daniel,** viz: **Daniel Studley CROOKER, Calvin CROOKER, Luther Harlow CROOKER & Amos Harden CROOKER**; son **Daniel,** executor. <49:221> Letter 10 Mar. 1818. <49:263> Inventory taken 27 Mar. 1818; total real estate, $300; total personal estate, $237.50. <49:264> Widow's allowance. <49:265> License to sell. <49:304> Dower to widow, **Hannah CROOKER,** 13 June 1818.

Will of **Daniel WHITE**, gent. of Marshfield MA. <Plymouth Co.PR 29:438>
...dated 6 Sept. 1785, mentions wf **Abigail**; 5s each to following chil., viz: **Daniel WHITE, Abigail SOUL, Lydia WHITE, Cate LEWIS, Urania WHITE**; to son **Samuel WHITE**, all land in Scituate received from his father by will; dau **Temperance WHITE**; mentions estate **Capt. Samuel TURNER** of Scituate gave to his dau **Abigail**, my wf; son **Samuel** & son in law **James LEWIS**, executors. Witnesses: William WHITE, James LITTLE, Nathaniel PHILLIPS. <29:440> Letter/Bond 21 Jan. 1786, **Samuel WHITE & James LEWIS**, app'td exrs. Sureties: Daniel LEWIS & Simeon KEEN of Marshfield. Witnesses: William WHITE, Simeon KEEN Jr. <29:449> Inventory taken 21 Jan. 1786; incl. 100 acres at Scituate owned by the widow; total estate, L906.9.10; sworn to 21 Jan. 1786 by **James LEWIS**, the other exr. being sick. <33:359> Notice 1 June 1793, **Daniel WHITE**, admr. on estate of **Daniel WHITE & Samuel WHITE.**

Daniel WHITE of Marshfield MA to **Jedediah LITTLE.** <Plymouth Co.Deeds 91:269>
...25 Dec. 1801, Daniel WHITE, mariner, to Jedediah LITTLE...land given him by his mother Abigail WHITE 3 Nov. 1792. Wf Margaret releases dower.

Will of **James LEWIS** of Marshfield MA. <Plymouth Co.PR #12729>
<33:328>...dated 23 Mar. 1793...entire estate to minor sons **James LEWIS, Daniel White LEWIS & Samuel White LEWIS**; brother(s) Daniel WHITE & Sylvanus WHITE, executors. <33:329> Pr. 6 May 1793. <33:359,360;35:174;36:83,467;37:63>...Guardianship, 6 May 1793.

Daniel WHITE & Silvanus WHITE to **James LITTLE** of Scituate MA. <Plymouth Co.Deeds 86:29>
...1 Dec. 1798, Daniel WHITE, mariner & Silvanus WHITE, gent., both of Marshfield, guardians of James LEWIS, Daniel White LEWIS & Samuel White LEWIS, sell to James LITTLE....land in Scituate sd minors received by will of Samuel WHITE dec'd as heirs of their mother Cate LEWIS dec'd.

Will of **Samuel WHITE** of Marshfield MA. <Plymouth Co.PR #22610>
<29:513>...dated 11 Mar. 1786, mentions mother **Abigail WHITE** and following brothers & sisters, viz: **Lydia WHITE, Urana WHITE, Temperance WHITE, Daniel WHITE** of Nova Scotia, **Katy LEWIS, Abigail SOUL**; sister **Lydia WHITE** and Capt. James LEWIS, executors. Witnesses: Isaac WINSLOW, Hannah WHITE & Peleg WHITE. <29:514> Pr. 8 Apr.1786. <29:514> Inventory taken 22 Apr.1786 by Daniel LEWIS, William WHITE & Simeon KEEN; incl. land at South & North River and gondola & ferry boat; total estate, Ł474.2.0. <original> Complaint of **Daniel WHITE**, brother of dec'd and others, stating that 7 years have elapsed since the the appointment of James LEWIS & Lydia WHITE and the estate has not been settled, that the executors by reason of bodily indisposition are incapable. <27:534> Letter/Bond 2 Apr. 1793, **Daniel WHITE**, mariner of Marshfield, app'td admr. de bonis non with will annexed. Sureties: Sylvanus WHITE, James LITTLE. Witnesses: Elizabeth CLAPP, Temperance CLAPP. <33:359> Notice, 1 June 1793, of appointment of **Daniel WHITE**, admr. on estate of **Daniel WHITE & Samuel WHITE**, both of Marshfield. <33:358> Inventory taken 3 June 1793, by Daniel LEWIS, Sylvanus WHITE, William WHITE; total real estate, Ł432.10. <33:381> Account of admr., 24 June 1793; Paid to: Samuel OAKMAN, Joseph TILDEN, Robert CUSHMAN, Asaph SOULE, Daniel LEWIS, John ROGERS, Sarah CLAP in full of her note against Daniel WHITE dec'd, Elijah FORD, Isaac BARKER, Paul WHITE for his note against sd dec'd, John & Abigail SOUL's receipt in full for sd Abigail's legacy, Amos ROGERS, Daniel LEWIS, John WHITE, Snow STETSON, Asa WATERMAN. <original> Citation, 21 Oct. 1793 to widow **Abigail WHITE** and **Lydia, Uraniah/Urana & Temperance WHITE**, single women, all of Marshfield, on complaint of **Daniel WHITE**, admr., that they are with holding Ł30 that belongs to the estate. <35:486> 2d Account, 29 Mar. 1796, of admr.; Creditors: John WHITE, Benjamin WHITMAN, James LITTLE, Sylvanus WHITE, Joshua YOUNG. <original> Citation 19 May 1796, to **Temperance WHITE**, spinster & **Urania HOWARD** wf of Luther of Bridgewater, complaint of embezzlement against the estate brought by **Daniel WHITE**, admr. <35:542> 3d Account of admr., 4 Aug. 1796. <36:5> Advertisement, 5 Sept. 1796, of sale of part of real estate; 10 acres meadow & upland joining Sylvanus WHITE's land. <36:156> Division 3 Apr. 1797, by Luke WADSWORTH, Joseph ROGERS & Elisha PHILLIPS, allowed 17 May 1797; the Farm at Whites Ferry in Marshfield was set off to **Daniel WHITE Temperance WHITE, Urania HAYWARD,** heirs of **Katy LEWIS** dec'd and heirs of **Lydia WHITE** dec'd. <36:186> 4th Account of admr., 11 July 1797; Paid to: Abigail WHITE; Sylvanus WHITE as gdn. to James LEWIS' heirs; Luther & Urana HAYWARD; Temperance WHITE for nursing my mother in her last sickness; heirs to Lydia WHITE one of ye exrs. to Samuel WHITE's will.

Lydia WHITE of Marshfield MA to **Urania & Temperance WHITE** of Marshfield. <Plymouth Co.Deeds>
<75:18>...16 Oct. 1790, Lydia WHITE to sisters Urania WHITE & Temperance WHITE...all rights to land from will of father Daniel WHITE, dec'd...and all right to land from will of brother Samuel WHITE dec'd...deed not to be recorded until my decease. Ack. 23 Oct. 1790. Rec. 26 Nov. 1793.

Luther HAYWARD et al to **Daniel WHITE** of Marshfield MA. <Plymouth Co.Deeds 81:243>
...30 May 1797, Luther HAYWARD, yeoman & wf Urana of Bridgewater and Temperance WHITE, seamster of Bridgewater but late of Marshfield, for $370.00 sold to Daniel WHITE, yeoman...three shares in farm at Whites Ferry, of Samuel WHITE of Marshfield dec'd, set off to sd Urana, Temperance and Lydia WHITE. Ack. same day by Luther & Temperance; 14 June 1797 by Urana.

Will of **Gideon WHITE** of Plymouth MA. <Plymouth Co.PR #22553>
<25:304>...dated 1 May 1766, mentions wf **Joanna** and following chil., viz: **Cornelius WHITE, Gideon WHITE, Joanna WHITE, Hannah WHITE, Mary WHITE, Elizabeth WHITE**; wf **Joanna** & son **Cornelius**, executors. Witnesses: Benjamin STOCKBRIDGE, William THOMAS, Edward WINSLOW. <25:305> Pr. 7 June 1779, **Joanna WHITE** app'td exr. <28:16> Inventory taken 1 Feb. 1780, by John WATSON & Isaac LeBARON; incl. land at Deep Water & Billington Sea; total estate, Ł25,348.15. <28:17> Insolvency. <28:328> Dower set off, 12 Apr. 1782, to widow, by Sylvanus BARTLETT, Samuel COLE, William LeBARON. <28:

333> List of Claims, presented 10 Oct. 1783 by Joshua THOMAS & Thomas DAVIS Jr., viz: estate of William RAND, George WATSON, John ROWE, estate of Melatiah BOURNE, Mr. LEE, Mr. JONES, George HATFIELD, Daniel WALDO, John GOODWIN, Ephraim SPOONER, Capt. Thomas DAVIS, estate of Thomas MAYHEW, Jonathan DIMAN, Capt. Barnabas HEDGE, DAVIS & SPOONER, estate of Nathaniel GOODWIN, estate of David TURNER, Benjamin DREW, Dr. Benjamin STOCKBRIDGE, Stephen SAMPSON, Ichabod SHAW, Samuel JACKSON, John LEVERETT, Jeremiah HOLMES, Thomas LEVERETT, Isaac LeBARON, John WATSON, Amos ROGERS Adams BAILEY, estate of James HOVEY, William HARLOW Jr., Jonathan TUFTS, Elijah DAMAN, James DREW estate of Dr. Lazarus LeBARON, Isaac LOTHROP, Priscilla HOBART, Capt. Elkanah WATSON. <28:334> Account of admx., 10 Oct. 1783. <28:336> Order, 30 Oct. 1783, to pay creditors. <31:108> Petition 29 Dec. 1789, of admx., for license to sell land. <original> Advertisement of sale, 7 Jan. 1790, part of the reversion of the widow's dower. <31:109> Oath of sale, 15 Feb. 1790 of admx. <44:242> 2d Account of admx., **Joanna WHITE,** 13 July 1790. <original> Letter/Bond 27 Feb. 1812, **Hannah WHITE,** single woman, app'td admx. de bonis non, **Joanna WHITE** having died & **Cornelius WHITE** the eldest son & joint executor being out of the Commonwealth also since dec'd. Sureties: William DAVIS & William DAVIS Jr. of Plymouth. Witnesses: Nathaniel W. DAVIS, Joseph DAVIS. <44:147> Inventory taken 27 Feb. 1812 by William DAVIS, Jonathan TUFTS & Beza HAYWARD; two acres of meadow in Plymouth by the Rope Walk being a part of the widow's dower, unsold; total estate, $300. <44:242> Advertisement of sale, 18 Apr. 1812. <44:243> Account of **Hannah WHITE,** admx., 25 May 1812.

Will of **Paul WHITE** of Marshfield MA. <Plymouth Co.PR #22603>
<24:195>...dated 6 Sept. 1768...aged...mentions wf **Elizabeth** and following chil., viz: **Paul WHITE Christopher WHITE, Peregrine WHITE, Experience CLAPP, Hannah WHITE;** sons **Paul & Christopher,** executors. Witnesses: Ignatius SHERMAN, Daniel WHITE Jr., Elisha PHILLIPS. Ignatius SHERMAN, swore to will, 1 July 1776. <24:197> Pr. 2 Sept. 1776, **Paul WHITE** app'td exr., **Christopher WHITE** being absent. <24:197> Inventory taken 2 Sept. 1776 by Daniel WHITE, Ignatius SHERMAN, William LEWIS; incl. six negroes; total real estate, Ł788; total estate, Ł1019.14.7.

Will of **Hannah WHITE,** spinster of Marshfield MA. <Plymouth Co.PR #22559>
<31:500>...dated 7 Oct. 1791, mentions mother **Elizabeth WHITE;** chil. of dec'd brother **Paul WHITE,** viz: **Edward WHITE & Elizabeth WHITE** (under 16); chil. of dec'd brother **Christopher WHITE,** viz: **Joseph WHITE & Christopher WHITE** (both under 20); to brother **Peregrine WHITE,** 10 lbs. of the legacy given to me in the will of my Honoured father **Paul WHITE** dec'd; sister **Experience CLAP,** divorced wife of Samuel; chil. of **Samuel CLAP,** viz: **Samuel CLAP Jr., Elizabeth CLAP, Temperance CLAP, Sarah CLAP;** sister **Experience** & friend Sylvanus WHITE, executors. Witnesses: William WHITE, Luther LITTLE, Joseph PHILLIPS. <31:502> Letter/Bond 14 Mar. 1792, Sylvanus WHITE app'td admr. (**Experience** being incapable). Sureties: William WHITE & Joseph PHILLIPS of Marshfield. Witnesses: Joseph VAUGHAN, Isaac LOTHROP. <31:503> Insolvency, 14 Mar. 1792. <33:69> Inventory taken 27 Apr. 1792 by William WHITE, Joseph PHILLIPS, Elisha PHILLIPS; total estate, Ł384.7.6. <33:150> Notice, 4 May 1792, to creditors to present claims. <33:287> List of Claims: Peregrine WHITE his demand for cash & notes of hand delivered **Hannah WHITE** as co-executrix with him to the last will of **Paul WHITE Jr.** late of Marshfield dec'd; balance due William WHITE on a book account. <35:261> Account of admr., 23 May 1795; Paid to: Peregrine WHITE, Ł358.0.6.; Elizabeth WHITE, Elizabeth CLAP, Temperance CLAP & Experience CLAP as per will; William WHITE, Joseph PHILLIPS, Elisha PHILLIPS, Caleb BAILEY, Daniel LEWIS, Sylvanus CLAP. <36:190> Account of admr., 1 July 1797; mentions Elisha PHILLIPS, Isaac BARKER; heirs of Ezra EDSON; Joseph PHILLIPS, Caleb BAILEY; cash received of William MACUMBER agent to Peregrine WHITE being for a legacy due from Christopher WHITE one of the heirs of Paul WHITE dec'd.

Will of **Paul WHITE,** mariner of Marshfield MA. <Plymouth Co.PR #22604>
<29:83>...dated 28 Sept. 1779, mentions wf **Susanna; Joseph & Christopher WHITE** the heirs of dec'd brother **Christopher WHITE;** Ł200 to heirs of sister **Experience CLAP;** brother **Peregrine WHITE** & sister **Hannah WHITE,** executors. Witnesses: Nathan GODLEY, John GODLEY, Thomas GODLEY. <original> Letter of foreign executorship, 5 July 1782, at Kinston, North Carolina. <original> Deposition 21 May 1785 of Nathaniel PHILLIPS & William WHITE, both of Marshfield, that they were intimately acquainted with **Paul WHITE** dec'd, the son of **Paul WHITE** also dec'd. <29:84> Pr. 21 May 1785, **Peregrine WHITE & Hannah WHITE,** exrs. <30:81> Inventory taken 3 Aug. 1786 by Simeon KEEN, William MACOMBER, Joseph PHILLIPS; total estate, Ł923.13.7.; sworn to same day by **Peregrine WHITE.** <30:82> Insolvency. <30:303> Warrant. <33:265> Account, 1 Mar. 1793, of **Peregrine WHITE** (**Hannah WHITE** having died); incl. expense of journey to & from North Carolina to prove will, Ł9.18.; expense in settling with Capt. John BAILEY; paid Esq. OAKMAN & Obediah WETHRELL. <37:383> Account of admr., 13 Jan. 1801; incl. improvement of land bought of Dr. Isaac WINSLOW; paid cost of Courts with Nathan WILLIS & wf in an action brought on me by them for the recovery of her legacy in Paul's will; paid Sylvanus WHITE, exr. of will of **Hannah WHITE** dec'd; paid Elizabeth & Temperance CLAP two legacies; Samuel CLAP one legacy; Nathan WILLIAMSON his account; paid Sylvanus WHITE, exr. of Hannah WHITE, one third part of the legacy given her by her father in his will, should have been paid by the heirs of Christopher WHITE dec'd; pd John THOMAS; Edward WHITE agent for **Susanna WHITE,** the sum set off to her from estate of **Paul WHITE;** William MACOMBER for his time & expenses in negotiating my business as exr. from 29 Mar. 1793 to 21 Dec. 1800; pd Sylvanus WHITE exr of **Hannah WHITE** one third of legacy given her by her father which should have been paid by **Paul WHITE** dec'd; to my time & expense from St. Johns to Marshfield three times on business, Ł172; to expences in keeping Coll. John BAILEY in Goal; pd Dr. Isaac WINSLOW. <38:160> Division 19 June 1802, by William MACOMBER, Sylvanus WHITE & Benjamin HATCH; set off to dau **Elizabeth WHITE,** 21 acres in Hanover the dec'd bought of John BAILEY, also wood lot in Marshfield, also $280 out of the personal estate to make the sd Elizabeth's share equal to the other moiety of sd dec'd's real estate which could not be divided without damaging the whole.
(Excerpts from two letters are included with the probate records as follows:)

Letter dated 12 Mar. 1780, from **Paul WHITE** to his brother **Capt. Peregrine WHITE** of Marshfield stating he was a great distance from home and it would be difficult moving his family back; another to his mother **Mrs. Elizabeth WHITE** dated 28 July 1782, Buofort County, stating that he had written many letters to Peregrine "(conclude you must have heard from me) but never have had answer which gives me uneasyness fearing things are not well with the family. Poor Christopher & I have some chatting(sp) Little Boys hear should be glad you could see...have expected the War at an end before this day and wait for nothing else to return to my native land...Give my love to sister CLAP & Hannah". Lastly, a letter dated 21 May 1785 from Joseph CUSHING to Isaac LOTHROP states, "**Mr. Peregrine WHITE** waits on you with his brother **Paul WHITE**'s will...he is going to Carolina you must let him have the Will after you have recorded it."

Estate of **Joseph WHITE**, mariner of Marshfield MA. <Plymouth Co.PR #22581>
<17:182> Letter/Bond 20 Oct. 1766, widow **Temperance WHITE** app'td admx. Sureties: Nathaniel CLAP & Israel TURNER of Scituate. Witnesses: Mary CLAP, Abigail CLAP. <19:490> Inventory taken 24 Feb. 1767 by Abijah WHITE, Israel TURNER & Daniel WHITE; incl. one quarter part of the sloop, **Paul WHITE**, master; total personal estate, Ł228. <20:295> Account of admx., **Temperance GORHAM** (late WHITE), 18 Nov. 1769; mentions Melatiah BOURNE, Esq. and balance received of **Paul WHITE.**

John DOGGETT of Marshfield MA to **Hannah WHITE** of same. <Plymouth Co.Deeds 11:243>
...25 Jan. 1714/15, John DOGGETT gives to dau Hannah WHITE...19 Mar. 1715/6, John DOGGET sells to Ebenezer & Hannah WHITE...

Guardianship of Child of **Eleazer WHITE** dec'd of Marshfield MA. <Plymouth Co.PR #22544>
<7:395> Letter 14 Apr. 1737, John WHITE app'td gdn. of **Elkanah WHITE**, betw. 14-21.

Will of **John WHITE** of Marshfield MA. <Plymouth Co.PR #22576>
<13:149>...dated 6 Oct. 1747...being aged...mentions unnamed wife; daus **Hannah WHITE, Sarah PHILLIPS**; dec'd son **John WHITE** and his chil., viz: **John, Susanna, Hannah, James & Andrew WHITE**; sons **Abijah WHITE & Jesse WHITE**, executors. Witnesses: Nathaniel PHILLIPS, Samuel KENT, Simeon CHANDLER, Mary WRIGHT. <13:150> Pr. 5 Nov. 1753. <13:151> Bond 5 Nov. 1753, **Abijah WHITE** of Marshfield app'td exr., **Jesse WHITE** being absent. <13:195> Inventory taken 4 Feb. 1754, by Adam HALL, Nathaniel PHILLIPS, Benjamin WHITE; no real estate; total personal estate, Ł92.17.5.

Will of **Hannah WHITE**, singlewoman of Marshfield MA. <Plymouth Co.PR #22558>
<24:135>...dated 14 July 1775, mentions brother **Abijah WHITE**; sisters **Sarah PHILLIPS, Anna WHITE** wf of Abijah; Silvanus WHITE, Abijah WHITE Jr., William WHITE, Sybelene WHITE; chil. of **Abijah WHITE**, viz: **Anna WHITE, Priscilla WHITE, Sarah WHITE, Susanna WHITE**; Christiana LEWIS wf of William; brother **Abijah**, executor. Witnesses: Ignatius SHERMAN, Elizabeth WHITE, James LEWIS. <24:136> Letter/Bond 6 May 1776, widow **Anna WHITE** app'td admx. with will annexed, the exr. named in the will having died. Sureties: Nathaniel FOORD & Ignatius SHERMAN of Marshfield. Witnesses: Samuel THACHER, Joseph CUSHING. <24:137> Inventory taken 25 May 1776, by James LEWIS, Nathaniel FOORD, Ignatius SHERMAN; total estate, Ł100.6.5.; sworn to by admx., 3 June 1776.

Estate of **Sylvanus WHITE** of Marshfield MA. <Plymouth Co.PR #22618>
<9:32> Letter 7 Feb. 1742, John WHITE of Marshfield, app'td admr. <9:43> Inventory taken 7 Feb. 1742, by Isaac WALKER, Stephen ROGERS, James SPRAGUE Jr.; no real estate; total personal estate, Ł140.15; sworn to by appraisers who state it was shown to them by **John WHITE**, father of dec'd.

MICRO #3 OF 7

Will of **Sibelene/Sybilline WHITE**, mariner of Marshfield MA. <Plymouth Co.PR #22616>
<28:151>...dated 1 May 1770, mentions mother **Catharina WHITE** and sister **Christiana WHITE** (executrix). Witnesses: John JOYCE, John LITTLE, Abijah WHITE Jr. <28:152> Letter/Bond 28 June 1781, **Christiana LEWIS**, wf of William, app'td admx. Sureties: William LEWIS, Daniel LEWIS, John JOYCE, all of Marshfield. Witnesses: Cardis WALKER, Rebekah PETERSON.

Estate of **John WHITE Jr.** of Marshfield MA. <Plymouth Co.PR #22577>
<10:281> Letter/Bond 4 Aug. 1746, Abijah WHITE app'td admr. Sureties: John WHITE of Marshfield & Amos SILVESTER Jr. of Hanover. Witnesses: David JOHNSON, William DWELLE. <13:268> Account of admr 10 May 1754; Paid to: William WHEELER, Thomas FOSTER, Anthony SHERMAN, Nathaniel CHURCH, Cornelius WHITE Jr., Aaron SOULE, Samuel WILLIAMSON, BRIDGES & BURNS notes, Paul WHITE, DAGGETTS, Adam HALL, Dr. STOCKBRIDGE, Isaac WALKER Jr., Elizabeth TILDEN, Coll. WARREN, Edward WINSLOW, Benjamin EAMES, Capt. PHILLIPS, Snow WINSLOW, James SPRAGUE, John ROGERS, Amos SILVESTER, Capt. FOORD, Kenelm BAKER, Micah FOORD, Timothy TAYLOR, Hezekiah KEEN, TUCKER & HOLMES, Capt. DOGGETT, Ebenzer EAMES, Jane BURNS, William HOWLAND, Isaac WALKER, Nathaniel PHILLIPS, John WHITE gdn., John LITTLE, Cornelius WHITE, Joshua LAPHAM, Dr. HARLOW.

Guardianship of Children of **John WHITE Jr.** of Marshfield MA. <Plymouth Co.PR #22578>
...12 Aug. 1746...<10:277> **John WHITE**, minor, choses his grandfather **Nathan SPRAGUE** of Marshfield as his gdn. and **Nathan SPRAGUE** is app'td gdn. of **Susanna WHITE** <10:277>; **James WHITE** <10:278>; **Hannah WHITE** <10:279>; John WHITE is app'td gdn. of **Andrew WHITE & Nathan WHITE** <10:280>. <13:332> Letter/Bond 10 May 1754, Nathaniel PHILLIPS is app'td gdn. of **Andrew WHITE.** Surety: Abigail WHITE. Witnesses: William CUSHING, Lydia KEEN.

John WHITE of Pembroke MA to **Abner WRIGHT** of Marshfield. <Plymouth Co.Deeds 43:192>
...28 July 1755, John WHITE, blacksmith, for Ł53.6s sells to Abner WRIGHT, cordwainer...all right to land in Marshfield my father John WHITE died seized...two sevenths of the whole tract and one fifth of one sixth of the whole tract. (same bounds as deed below)

John WHITE et al of Marshfield MA to **Abner WRIGHT** of Marshfield. <Plymouth Co.Deeds 50:256>
...29 Dec. 1761, John WHITE, blacksmith, Stephen FULLERTON, chair maker & wf Susanna of Boston, James WHITE, shipwright of Weymouth and Hannah WHITE, spinster of Pembroke, for Ł160 sold to Abner WRIGHT, cordwainer...all rights in land of our honoured father John WHITE Jr. late of Marshfield...bounded by highway from Whites' Ferry and land of Nehemiah THOMAS, John SHERMAN, William FORD, Nehemiah THOMAS & land in possession of Susanna WHITE, Ruth WITHERELL & Joanna COOPER.

Abner WRIGHT of Marshfield MA to **Jabez WRIGHT** of same. <Plymouth Co.Deeds 66:8>
...11 Mar. 1786, Abner WRIGHT, cordwainer, for Ł149 sells to Jabez WRIGHT, cordwainer...30 acres, part of my homestead...bounded by ferry road, road to Pembroke and land of Nathaniel WINSLOW dec'd and Jesse LAPHAM.

Abner WRIGHT of Marshfield MA to **Jabez WRIGHT** of same. <Plymouth Co.Deeds 67:97>
...27 Oct. 1787, Abner WRIGHT, cordwainer, for Ł9 sells to Jabez WRIGHT, cordwainer...six acres being all the remainder of my farm...bounded by Pembroke Rd. and land of William FORD dec'd and Jesse LAPHAM.

Will of **Deacon Thomas DINGLEY** of Marshfield MA. <Plymouth Co.PR #6507>
<40:512>...dated 12 Aug. 1806, mentions wf **Anna**; to son **Thomas DINGLEY**, one half of lands south of Greens harbor river in Marshfield after decease or widowhood of wf...to son **James DINGLEY**, the whole of my homestead or farm on which I now live and all my Beach meadow, about ten acres and all my woodland that I bought of the heirs of Deacon Nehemiah THOMAS and also one half of lands lying south of Greens harbor river...all household good & farming utensils...after decease or widowhood of wf...to daus **Sarah THOMAS & Hannah LORING**, one cow and $150.00 each...to grandson **John Thomas DINGLEY**, $260.00 at the age of 21...to dau in law **Elisabeth DINGLEY**, $10.00...remainder of estate to sons **Thomas & James** (executors). Witnesses: Luke WADSWORTH, John BOURN, Consider FORD. <40:513> Letter/Bond 14 Oct. 1806, **Thomas DINGLEY & James DINGLEY**, gent., app'td exrs. Sureties: Consider FORD & John BOURNE, yeomen of Marshfield. Witnesses: Nathaniel & Isaac LOTHROP.

Will of **Peregrine WHITE**, yeoman of Yarmouth MA. <Barnstable Co.PR>
<53:320>...dated 14 Oct. 1833, mentions eldest sons **Peregrine WHITE Jr.** (executor), **Alfred WHITE, William WHITE**; youngest sons **Nelson WHITE, Rufus WHITE, Henry WHITE** (all under 21); mentions lands of Isaac WHITE. Pr. 2d Tues Jan. 1834. <48:392> Letter 14 Jan. 1834. <original> Inventory taken 1 Mar. 1834 by Joseph WHITE et al. <46:237> 11 Feb. 1834, **Peregrine WHITE Jr.** app'td gdn. of **Nelson, Rufus & Henry WHITE.** <56:64> Inventory taken 11 Aug. 1834, by Joseph WHITE et al, of estates of the minor sons.

Will of **Peregrine WHITE**, blacksmith of Boston MA. <Suffolk Co.PR #5547>
<26:47>...dated 27 Oct. 1727...sick & weak of body...entire estate to wf **Mary**, executrix. Witnesses: Joseph CALLENDER, Isaac DICKMAN, Joseph MARION; sworn to 18 Dec. 1727 by CALLENDER & DICKMAN <26:47> Letter, 18 Dec. 1727, widow **Mary WHITE** app'td exx. <14:271> Bond 13 Mar. 1727, of **Mary WHITE.** Sureties: Joseph CALLENDER, pipe maker & Daniel DUPEE, blacksmith, both of Boston. Witnesses: Joseph SAVELL, John BOYDELL.

Joshua GEE of Boston MA to **Peregrine WHITE** of Weymouth MA. <Suffolk Co.Deeds 17:327>
...28 Apr. 1696, Joshua GEE, shipwright & wf Elizabeth, for Ł30 sold to Peregrine WHITE, blacksmith...land in Boston...on highway leading from the lower end of Blackhorse towards the Northernmost water mill...bounded by land of David CAPP in the present occupation of William CAPP. Witnesses: David NORTON, Eliezer MOODY Sr. Ack. same day. Rec. 10 Dec. 1696. <17:336>...26 Dec. 1696, Peregrine sells the above for Ł40 to Richard CHEEVER, cordwainer of Boston.

Joshua GEE of Boston MA to **Peregrine WHITE** of same. <Suffolk Co.Deeds 19:48>
...11 Sept. 1697, Joshua GEE, shipwright, for Ł20 sells to Peregrine WHITE, blacksmith...land in Boston...bounded on front by highway leading from the lower end of Blackhorse land towards the Northernmost water mills and land of sd Pergrine. Wf Elizabeth GEE signs. Witnesses: Joseph SNOW (sp), Nathaniel ADAMS. Rec. 16 Jan. 1698.

Peregrine WHITE of Boston, mortgages to **Richard CHEEVER** of same. <Suffolk Co.Deeds 18:26>
...16 Nov. 1697, Peregrine WHITE, blacksmith, bound & obliged unto Richard CHEEVER, cordwainer... in the full & just sum of Ł120...my new house & all the land...at the northerly end of the towne of Boston...bounded by highway leading from lower end of Blackhorse lane towards the Northernmost Water mill and land of David CAPP in the present occupation of William CAPP and land of Joshua GEE, shipwright of Boston...at the front 58', in the rear 57' and in depth 50'...together with the smiths shop. Terms: Peregrine to pay Ł3.12s by 25 Dec. 1698, Ł63.12s by 25 Dec. 1699. Witnesses: Stephen MINOTT, Caleb RAY, Joseph WEBB. Rec. 16 Dec. 1697. On 20 Jan. 1699, Richard CHEEVER ack. payment of mortgage which was discharged...mentions mortgaged premises of Thomas NEWTON, admr. of estate of Barnard WHITE.

Peregrine WHITE of Boston MA to **Jacob TURNER** of Weymouth. <Suffolk Co.Deeds 29:56>
...30 Aug. 1698, Peregrine WHITE, for Ł43 sold to Jacob TURNER...20 acres in the upper division of Common Lotts in Weymouth, being part of ten lotts, viz: William HOLBROOK's #60, John BLAKES'

Sarah HUNT's #63, Thomas BAILEY's #62, Mr. GILLAMS's #64, Andrew FORD's #65, George FRYE's #66, Widow STAPLES' #67, Giles LEACH/LEE()CH's #68, James SMITH's #69...bounded by Carpenters Rocks so called all but part of two lotts. Witnesses: Nathaniel SALE, Thomas KINGMAN. Ack. 7 Jan. 1714/5 by Peregrine. Rec. ( ) Jan. 1714/5.

Thomas JACKSON & Adam WINTHROP of Boston MA to **Joshua GEE** of same. <Suffolk Co.Deeds 20:441> ...19 Nov. 1700, Thomas JACKSON, merchant and Adam WINTHROP, merchant & son & exr. to will of father Adam WINTHROP, merchant of Boston dec'd, for Ŀ24.7s sold to Joshua GEE, shipwright...all that parcell of land lying at the northerly end of the towne of Boston...bounded by the street or highway leading from Black Horse Lane to centre (worn) and land of sd Joshua and land formerly belonging to Peregrine WHITE, blacksmith of Boston but lately delivered upon execution to Bernard WHITE now in the occupation of Thomas NEWTON...all with premises being heretofore the estate of the sd Peregrine...lately in due form of law delivered upon execution by Samuel GOOKIN, Sheriff for the county...unto the sd Adam WINTHROP ye father and sd Thomas JACKSON to satisfied a debt of Ŀ23.17s (incl. sheriffs fees) due from the sd WHITE by the sd execution. Rec. 25 Nov. 1701.

Joshua GEE to **Andrew SIGOURNEY.** <Suffolk Co.Deeds 33:86>
...10 Oct. 1716, Joshua GEE to Andrew SIGOURNEY...(no details). Endorsed 14 Apr. 1718 by Peregrine WHITE, blacksmith of Boston & wf Mary, for Ŀ6 paid by Andrew SIGOURNEY, quit claim all rights in the within granted land. Ack. 17 May 1718. Rec. 29 Aug. 1718.

John STAMFORD of Boston MA to **Peregrine WHITE** of same. <Suffolk Co.Deeds 36:89>
...13 Oct. 1721, John STAMFORD, tayler & wf Sarah, for Ŀ43.15s sold to Peregrine WHITE, blacksmith...land in Boston bounded northeasterly on our other land there measuring 110', northwesterly on a Lane of 24' wide by us lately laid out for a highway measuring on the lane thirty two & a half feet, southwesterly on our other land there measuring 100' and southeasterly on our Barn land there measuring eighteen & a half feet. Witnesses: Joseph RICKS, Ephraim CRAFT(sp). Ack. 3 Aug. 1722 by John & Sarah.

Estate of **Thomas YOUNG** of Scituate MA. <Plymouth Co.PR #23589>
<6:323> Letter 19 Mar. 1732, sons **George YOUNG & Thomas YOUNG** of Scituate app'td admrs. <6:330, 331> Inventory taken 2 Apr. 1733 by Samuel TURNER, Moses SIMONS, John WHITE; incl. twenty nine & a half acres with house, Ŀ468; pasture on ye third clift containing twenty acres & quarter at eleven pound ten an acre, Ŀ232.17s6d; fresh marsh joying to sd Clift five acres & three quarters at Ŀ18 per acre, Ŀ103.10s; eight acre salt marsh at ye Beach at Ŀ17 per acre, Ŀ136.162; three acre salt marsh at Dammins Creek at Ŀ17 per acre, Ŀ58.8s; four acre cedar swamp in Burnt Plain Swmap, Ŀ10; four acre swamp & half acre upland near land of Thomas HATCH, Ŀ15; one share of upland in the Third Division of Scituate Common, two & a half acres, Ŀ1.10s. <7:368> Receipts 23 Jan. 1737, of **Joseph YOUNG & Joshua YOUNG** to brothers **George & Thomas** for their full fifth parts of personal estate. Witnesses: James TURNER, Alexander DAYLE. <7:368> Account of admrs., 6 Feb. 1737; Paid to: Benjamin PHILLIPS Jr., Hannah SHERMAN, Mercy SHERMAN, John POLAND, Cornelius WHITE Joseph TILDEN Jr., Thomas YOUNG, Joseph YOUNG, John COLMAN, Mercy STOCKBRIDGE, Samuel STODDER, Dr OTIS, Benjamin TURNER, Ambrose COLE Jr., Thomas JENKINS, Timothy WHITE, Ensign OTIS, Benjamin HOUSE, Joseph CLAP, Israel CHITTENDEN, Joseph TILDEN, Bathsheba WADE, Capt. Samuel TURNER, Israel NICHOLS, Ebenezer DAMEN, Stephen VINALL, Josiah LECHFIELD.

Heirs of **Thomas YOUNG** of Scituate MA. <Plymouth Co.Deeds 28:22>
...11 May 1733, Joshua YOUNG, sadler of Scituate to Joseph YOUNG, yeoman of same...one fifth of lands of dec'd father Thomas...11 May 1733, Thomas YOUNG, housewright of Scituate to George YOUNG, yeoman of same...one fifth of land of dec'd father Thomas. <28:12>...14 May 1733, George YOUNG & Joseph YOUNG, yeomen of Scituate, sons of Thomas...division; George owns three fifths of father's real estate, Joseph two fifths.

PLYMOUTH COUNTY DEEDS: (re: YOUNG)

<30:204> - 21 Mar. 1728, Thomas YOUNG, yeomen of Scituate to George YOUNG, currier of same. Witnesses sworn Sept. 1736, Thomas YOUNG being dec'd.
<46:256> - 1761, George & Mary YOUNG et al, heirs of Sarah STOCKBRIDGE of Hanover dec'd.
<53:25> - 1765, Thomas & Hannah YOUNG to Ezekiel YOUNG.
<57:52> - 1773, Thomas YOUNG to Ezekiel YOUNG.

MICRO #4 OF 7

References to the name **Elisha YOUNG** in Plymouth Co.Deeds: 69:249,250;78:214;79:2;80:246;81:157; 117:236,237;118:211.

Estate of **James YOUNG**, mariner of Scituate MA. <Plymouth Co.PR 16:96,188,189;17:2>
<17:2> Letter 28 Nov. 1760, widow **Mehitable YOUNG** app'td admx. <16:188> Warrant 16 Dec. 1760.

Estate of **Ezekiel YOUNG**, yeoman of Scituate MA. <Plymouth Co.PR>
<original> Petition (no date), that Elisha JAMES of Scituate be app'td admr. Signed by **Lusanna YOUNG, Joseph YOUNG** (absent), **Lydia GANNETT, Christopher YOUNG, Stephen F. YOUNG, Ebenezer Scot YOUNG, John PROUTY.** <original> Inventory taken 11 Apr. 1814; half acre farm with house, barn & shop, $1240.00; seven acre cedar swamp & woodland, $87.00; total personal estate, $313.82. <45: 474> Division of real estate, 5 Sept. 1814, among the following children, viz: **Joseph YOUNG,**

Gideon YOUNG, Christopher YOUNG, Ebenezer Scot YOUNG, Stephen Fullington YOUNG, Lydia GANNETT & Joanna White PROUTY. <60:409> Division of dower, 1 May 1826, of widow **Lusanna YOUNG** to the following chil., viz: **Joseph YOUNG, Gideon YOUNG, Christopher YOUNG, Ebenezer Scot YOUNG, Stephen Fullerton YOUNG** ("or whoever may claim by or under him"), chil. & heirs of **Lydia GANNETT** dec'd (Lydia LITTLE is written in the original with LITTLE crossed out & GANNETT added) and **Joanna White PROUTY.**

Estate of **Lusanna YOUNG**, widow of Scituate MA. <Plymouth Co.PR>
<52:414> Letter/Bond 6 Dec. 1825, son **Gideon YOUNG**, yeoman of Scituate, app'td admr. Sureties: Charles TURNER, Esq. of Charlestown and Noble E. JENKINS, trader of Scituate. <60:408> Warrant to divide real estate (same heirs as <60:409> division of dower above). <60:6,7> Inventory. <60:49> Order to sell personal estate. <60:407> Account. <60:411> Division.

PLYMOUTH COUNTY DEEDS: (re: Joseph YOUNG)

<101:151> - , J.Y. to Cyrus DUNBAR.
<109:94> - 6 Mar. 1805, J.Y., mariner of Scituate to Joseph NASH Jr., land bought of Joseph NASH Jr. <97:123>.
<120:124> - 10 Mar. 1813, Ezekiel YOUNG, yeoman of Scituate & wf Lusanny to Ichabod R. JACOBS.
<131:191> - 25 Oct. 1816, J.Y., yeoman of Thomaston ME to Lusanna YOUNG, widow of Scituate, part of land set off to sd J.Y. as one of heirs of Ezekiel YOUNG dec'd.
<159:27> - 12 June 1826, J.Y. of Thomaston ME, Ebenezer YOUNG et al to Augustus COLE. Polly YOUNG signs (wf of one of the YOUNGS).
<168:177> - 14 Oct. 1829, J.Y., mariner of Wareham & wf Mary and Zaccheus YOUNG, shipwright & wf Temperance to William FEARING, land in Wareham.
<179:117> - 14 Dec. 1833, J.Y. & wf Lydia of Scituate to John S. VINAL.
<195:242> - 5 Apr. 1837, J.Y. & wf Mary of Wareham et al to Abram WASHBURN 2d, land of Nehemiah LEONARD dec'd of Bridgewater.

RESOLVED WHITE[2] (William[1])

Resolved WHITE of Salem MA to **Josiah WHITE** of same. <Essex Co.Deeds 4:177>
...6 Jan. 1677, Resolved WHITE & wf Abigail, exx. to will of William LORD dec'd, for love, etc. to son Josiah WHITE...<5:101>...30 Dec. 1680, Josiah WHITE & wf Remember sold this land back to father Resolved WHITE.

Will of **Abigail WHITE** of Salem MA. <Essex Co.Quart.Court Rec.8:361,362>
...dated 26 Apr. 1682...mentions last will of her former husband **William LORD** and her present husband **Resolved WHITE.** (will is not transcribed) Pr. June court 1682 (June court began 29 June.)

BRISTOL COUNTY DEEDS: (re: WHITE, grantees)

<7:347> - 1 Oct. 1712, Thomas WHITE from Thomas HARVEY.
<36:405> - 8 Feb. 1748, Thomas WHITE et al from Ephraim KIMTON et ali.
<39:264> - 15 Jan. 1753, Thomas WHITE of Freetown from Job ALMY.
<39:264> - 30 Jan. 1753, Thomas WHITE of Freetown from Joseph RUSSELL.
<39:353> - 20 Apr. 1753, Thomas WHITE of Taunton from James LEONARD Sr.
<39:354> - 20 Apr. 1753, Thomas WHITE of Taunton from sister Sarah WHITE of same, 40 acres rec'd from will of grandfather Nicholas WHITE.
<40:111> - 18 May 1753, Thomas WHITE of Taunton, from Jacob HARVEY et ux.
<40:112> - 18 May 1753, Thomas WHITE of Taunton from Seth LEONARD & wf Dorcas the dau of Nicholas WHITE dec'd.
<39:450> - 10 July 1753, Thomas WHITE Jr. from Samuel MENDALL.
<40:357> - 15 Apr. 1754, Thomas WHITE of Taunton from Meshech WILBORE.
<41:408> - 29 July 1755, Thomas WHITE of Taunton from William HODGES.
<41:409> - 29 July 1755, Thomas WHITE of Taunton from Ebenezer EDDY.
<41:409> - 29 July 1755, Thomas WHITE of Taunton from Nathaniel KNAP.
<41:410> - 29 July 1755, Thomas WHITE of Taunton from Nicholas WHITE.
<44:14> - 12 Nov. 1759, Thomas WHITE of Taunton from Propiretors of Taunton.
<44:47> - 10 Dec. 1759, Thomas WHITE of Taunton by agt. from estate of William SMITH.
<46:100> - 16 Sept 1762, Thomas WHITE of Taunton from Daniel GRIFFETH.
<50:258> - 30 Oct. 1765, Thomas WHITE of Taunton from Abraham WHITE.
<50:258> - 10 Dec. 1766, Thomas WHITE of Taunton from Thomas WHITE Sr.
<51:23> - 28 Nov. 1767, Thomas WHITE of Taunton from estate of Zerviah PITTS.
<54:317> - 11 Mar. 1772, Thomas WHITE of Taunton.
<62:17> - 18 Aug. 1783(rec.), Thomas WHITE of Taunton of John WHITE.
<66:126> - 12 Mar. 1787, Thomas WHITE 2d of Taunton from Abiel COLE.

<2:25> - 29 Mar. 1653, William WHITE et al from Ossamequin et al.
<10:383> - 9 Apr. 1717, William WHITE et al from Joseph WHITE Sr.
<12:397> - 26 Feb. 1718/9, William WHITE of Dartmouth from Robert BARKER
<28:437> - 3 Feb. 1740, William WHITE, blacksmith of Dartmouth, from Edward RICHMOND, one acre with house in Little Compton.

BRISTOL COUNTY DEEDS, cont-d: (re: WHITE, grantees**)**

<32:86> - 14 Sept 1743, William WHITE, labourer of Rochester from Jonathan BUTTS et al, land in Dartmouth on Tiverton line.
<34:465> - 10 Dec. 1746, William WHITE, husbandman of Tiverton from Jonathan NEGUS.
<36:401> - 8 Feb. 1748, William WHITE from Richard PIERCE.
<37:498> - 5 Feb. 1750, William WHITE Jr., blacksmith of Dartmouth from James TRIPP.
<47:189> - 12 June 1764, William WHITE from George WHITE.
<48:124> - 23 Sept 1765, William WHITE Jr., yeoman of Dartmouth from Edward (?faint).
<48:132> - 23 Sept 1765, William WHITE Jr., blacksmith of Dartmouth from Joseph (?POTTS).
<48:414> - 23 Oct. 1765, William WHITE from William BORDEN.
<48:415> - 23 Oct. 1765, William WHITE from Seth SPOONER.
<48:416> - 23 Oct. 1765, William WHITE from Ebenezer (KEEN? - too faint)
<51:413> - 26 Oct. 1768, William WHITE 3d of Dartmouth, son of George dec'd from John LAWTON.
<51:496> - 19 Dec. 1768, William WHITE from William BROWN
<59:387> - 27 Sept 1779, William WHITE et ali from Ebenezer WHITE.
<60:180> - 7 Feb. 1781, William WHITE from Richard GIFFORD.
<62:171> - 16 Dec. 1783, William WHITE of Dartmouth from Jonathan CLARK.
<62:172> - 16 Dec. 1783, William WHITE, yeoman of Dartmouth from Benjamin RUSSELL.
<62:172> - 16 Dec. 1783, William WHITE, yeoman of Dartmouth from Benjamin SPOONER 2d.
<62:173> - 16 Dec. 1783, William WHITE, yeoman of Dartmouth from Zurell HASKELL.
<62:173> - 16 Dec. 1783(rec.), William WHITE 3d of Dartmouth from Benjamin AKIN. (dated 1777)
<62:174> - 16 Dec. 1783, William WHITE, yeoman of Dartmouth from William LeBARON.
<62:229> - 20 Feb. 1784, William WHITE, Jr., blacksmith of Dartmouth from Micah PAR( ).
<64:519> - 21 Dec. 1785, William WHITE Jr., yeoman of Dartmouth from Joseph WING.
<67:399> - 21 Jan. 1789, William WHITE et ali, partition.
<67:410> - 5 Feb. 1789, William WHITE from Timothy FULLER.
<68:515> - 1 Oct. 1789, William WHITE from William PARKER(sp).
<68:496> - 24 May 1790, William WHITE Jr., blacksmith of New Bedford from Isaac (?TORRY).
<69:43> - 12 July 1790, William WHITE et al, division.
<72:402> - 11 Mar. 1794, William WHITE from Anthony BOOTH.
<72:402> - 11 Mar. 1794(rec.), William WHITE, yeoman of Dartmouth from Ebenezer WILLIS.(1773)
<72:403> - 11 Mar. 1794(rec.), William WHITE, yeoman of New Bedford from (?Jabez TABER).(1792)
<73:496> - 21 Apr. 1795, William WHITE of Dartmouth from (faint).
<73:497> - 21 Apr. 1795, William WHITE, yeoman of Westport from E( ) POTTS(sp).

<26:381> - 1737, William WHITE to Ebenezer WHITE, both of Norton.
<36:74> - 1740, "Taunton WHITES".
<36:54> - 1742-4, Hannah, Experience & Martha WHITE, daus of Rev. Ebenezer of Attleboro to Ebenezer WHITE of same.
<41:504> - 1756, Samuel WHITE of Berkley.
<43:77> - 1758, Samuel WHITE, Esq. & Nathaniel WHITE of Taunton.
<45:337> - 1761, Samuel WHITE, Esq. of Taunton.
<59:387> - 1779, Ebenezer WHITE of Mansfield to sons William, Jedediah & Ephraim WHITE 2d.
<59:385> - 1779, William WHITE, Jedediah WHITE & Ephraim WHITE 2d.
<67:142> - 1788, Ephraim WHITE of Mansfield to daus Ruth & Mary WHITE of same.
<70:308> - 1790, Samuel WHITE & wf Sarah of Mansfield.
<70:455> - 1791, "Mansfield WHITES".

Will of **John WHITE** of Dighton MA. <Bristol Co.PR 13:300>
...dated 10 Oct. 1753, mentions wf **Elizabeth;** grandsons **John WHITE & Peter WHITE,** sons of son **John WHITE;** dau **Sarah PAULL;** son in law **Samuel PAULL/POOL;** dau in law **Hannah SHAW,** widow of son **Peter WHITE.**

Will of **Samuel WHITE,** yeoman of Danvers MA. <Essex Co.PR 367:391>
...dated 4 Jan. 1799, mentions children **Joseph WHITE, Samuel WHITE, Mehitable PRESTON, Lydia KNIGHT, Anna WHITE, John WHITE** (executor). <371:524> Receipt 17 July 1802, of **Samuel WHITE;** 11 May 1802 of **Nehemiah & Lydia KNIGHT.** <367:541> 1 Sept. 1800, **John WHITE** of Danvers app'td gdn. to **Anna WHITE,** singlewoman of Danvers, non compos mentis. <371:523> Account 26 June 1804 of **John WHITE** as gdn. <372:419> Account 28 Mar. 1805 of gdn.
(The files contain the following notation: "There was another **Samuel WHITE** of Danvers, a mariner, belonging, I think, to the Rowley tribe".)

Will of **Thomas DIXEY** of Marblehead MA. <Suffolk Co.PR #1482>
...(no date given), mentions wf **Mary,** sons **John DIXEY & Samuel DIXEY** and daus **Mary HOLMAN, Abigail SMITH, Remember WHITE, Hannah BOWIN.** Pr. 31 Aug. 1686.

Josiah WHITE et al. <Essex Co.Deeds 16:148>
...16 Nov. 1704, Agreement between Henry WILKINS, Benjamin WILKINS, John WILKINS & Thomas BAYLEY of the one part, all of Salem and Josiah WHITE of the other part, of Boxford.

Will of **Josiah WHITE Sr.** of Boxford MA. <Essex Co.PR 310:244>
...dated 3 Mar. 1710, mentions wf **Remember,** sons **Josiah WHITE, Joseph WHITE, Samuel WHITE** and daus **Sarah WHITE & Hannah WHITE.** Pr. 5 June 1710.

ESSEX COUNTY DEEDS: (re: WHITE)

<18:78> - 28 Mar. 1692, Thomas WHITE Sr., planter of Marblehead & wf Remember.
<20:99> - 27 Oct. 1702, Josiah WHITE, carpenter of Salem to Richard WATERS, cooper of same.
<20:29> - 8 May 1707, Thomas WHITE Sr., planter of Marblehead & wf Remember.
<20:20> - 13 May 1707, Josiah WHITE Sr. of Boxford.
<21:57> - 5 May 1709, Testimony of John DIXEY of Marblehead, aged about 53, Remember WHITE and Elizabeth HARROD.
<32:23> - 11 May 1716, Joseph WHITE, joyner of Salem to John FULLER of Salem, land in Boxford.
<33:173> - 14 Apr. 1718, Joseph WHITE & Samuel WHITE, husbandmen of Salem; Samuel sells his half to John (FULLER?).
<45:174> - 20 July 1720, Joseph WHITE, joyner of Salem; Remember WHITE of Salem, relict of Josiah WHITE late of Salem & mother of within Joseph.
<37:162> - 1 Aug. 1720, Josiah WHITE, yeoman of Salem, mortg. to Israel RICHARDS of same.
<39:121> - 1 Aug. 1720, Samuel WHITE, wheelmaker of Salem to John WILKINS. Dinah WHITE signs.
<51:97> - 18 Nov. 1720, Samuel WHITE, wheelmaker of Salem, & wf Dinah to Dr. Daniel FELCH, land in Boxford.
<49:269> - 19 Nov. 1725, Josiah WHITE now of Sutton, formerly of Salem, to Israel RICHARDS by the hand of Daniel WILKINS Sr. of Salem.
<62:144> - 13 June 1729, Samuel WHITE, wheelwright of Salem to Joseph BUXTON(sp) of same, one right in the Common Land of Salem with my wife.
<81:27> - 21 Aug. 1740, Josiah WHITE of Wenham & wf Sarah to brother John WHITE of same.
<93:254> - 3 Apr. 1749, Josiah WHITE & John WHITE of Wenham to Samuel GO(TT?).
<105:276> - 16 Mar. 1759, Josiah WHITE of Wenham to sons Thomas WHITE & Haffield WHITE of same.

***

Joseph WHITE of Salem to **Daniel FELCH** of Ridding. <Essex Co.Deeds 38:79>
...29 July 1720, Joseph WHITE, joyner to Daniel FELCH...lands in Salem & Boxford...privilege reserved by John PUTNAM dec'd who sold part of this homestead unto William WAY from whom we derive our right. Ack. 20 May 1721 by Remember WHITE; 21 June 1721 by Beatrix WHITE wf of Joseph.

***

Heirs of **Thomas REED** of Salem to **Isaac REED**. <Essex Co.Deeds 75:178>
...23 Dec. 1713, Samuel STACEY, husbandman of Salem & wf Elizabeth and Remember WHITE, widow & joint admr. with son Joseph WHITE on estate of dec'd husband Josiah WHITE...sd Elizabeth & Remember the daus of Thomas REED dec'd...to our brother Isaac REED. Witness: Josiah WHITE.

***

Heirs of **Thomas WHITE** late of Marblehead MA. <Essex Co.Deeds 37:2 (34:2?)>
...(no date given, nor details)...Thomas WHITE, shareman, Benjamin WHITE, fisherman, Samuel WHITE fisherman, Henry GRANT, fisherman & wf Mary, Jeremiah READ, fisherman & wf Abigail and John WHITE, all of Marblehead and Edward NARRICE(sp) & wf Remember of Salem...chil. of Thomas WHITE.

***

Will of **Josiah WHITE**, yeoman of Sutton MA. <Worcester Co.PR #A64368>
...dated 26 Aug. 1761...being farr advanced in age...to son **Caleb WHITE**, all land, stock of cattle, tools, feather bed and the chest that was his Grand Father TAYLOR's...to dau **Mary WHITE**, one feather bed...remainder equally divided between **Caleb & Mary**...they to take care of and comfortably maintain both in sickness & health my son **Josiah WHITE 3d**; **Josiah WHITE Jr.**, yeoman of Sutton, executor. Witnesses: Elishu SIBLEY, Joshua MARSH, John FRY. Filed, 13 Aug. 1764, Pr. 27 Aug. 1764. Inventory taken 30 Aug. 1764 by Benjamin WOODBERY(sp), yeoman, Henry KING, gent. and Tarrant PUTNAM, gent. Account of exr., 31 Oct. 1765. <#A64369> Petition 19 Nov. 1787 of **Thomas PARKER** of Sutton, now the husband of the sd **Mary**, has done considerable more than his share in supporting **Josiah WHITE 3d** (a person non compos mentis), that the sd **Caleb WHITE** has disposed of his estate given him in sd will and has removed out of the State; he asks for a guardian to be app'td; 10 Dec. 1787, David HARWOOD app'td gdn. of **Josiah WHITE 3d.**

***

Guardianship of Child of **Josiah WHITE** of Sutton MA. <Worcester Co.PR #A64217>
...18 Aug. 1764, **Caleb WHITE** of Sutton, minor, seventeen years old last July has made choice of Elder Benjamin MARSH of Sutton to be his gdn. Sureties: Benjamin MARSH & Josiah WHITE, yeomen of Sutton. <#A64218>...26 June 1781, **Caleb WHITE** appears to be non compos mentis...his father died before he came of age and gave him considerable estate and obliged him in his will to support an elder brother.

***

Estate of **Joseph WHITE**, husbandman of Sutton MA. <Worcester Co.PR #A64354>
Letter/Bond, 20 Dec. 1750, of sons **Joseph & Josiah WHITE**, admrs.; widow **Sarah WHITE** & the eldest son **Jonathan WHITE** gave their consent to the appointment of the admrs. Inventory taken 27 Dec. 1750 by Cornelius PUTNAM, gent. and Isaac NICHOLS & Torrant PUTNAM, yeomen, all of Sutton. Account of admrs., 15 May 1752; Paid to: Josiah WHITE Jr., Perez (RICE?), Simeon CHAMBERLAIN, Tarrant PUTNAM, Thomas NICHOLS, Ben jamin MARSS, Hezekiah MERRIM(sp), Thomas LOVEL, Constable DWIGHT Jephthah(sp) PUTNAM, Isaac NICHOLS, Ebenezer LITTLE, (Freegrace MARBLE?), Elishu PUTNAM, John BURDON, Cornelius PUTNAM, Daniel K( )RNY, Robert ( )ITTS, Henry ( ), Robert BURNET, Rebecca ( ), Dr. GREEN, Josiah WHITE, Lydia SINGLETON(sp), Esq. GODDARD, Nathaniel WAIT, Benjamin MARSH, John NICHOLS, Thomas ( ), John CHANDLER(sp). Account of admrs., 27 July 1753; pd Lucy WHIPPLE. Order to divide 15 May 1752, by Benjamin MARSH, Cornelius PUTNAM, John FRY, Elishu RICH, Tarrant PUTNAM, to the following chil., viz: **Jonathan WHITE, Joseph WHITE, Josiah WHITE, John WHITE, Mary WHITE, Abigail CHURCH** wf of Jonathan and **Sarah BROWN** wf of Ebenezer. Settlement 27 July 1753, real estate is settled on son **Josiah WHITE**, husbandman of Sutton he to pay **Jonathan WHITE**, the eldest son and the other brothers & sisters. <#A64331> 27 Aug. 1750, son **John WHITE**, non comp; 26 Mar. 1756, Benjamin WOODBURY, gdn.

Will of **Peter WHITE** of Uxbridge MA. <Worcester Co.PR #A64459>
...dated 18 Apr. 1782, mentions wf **Jemima;** sons **Joseph WHITE, Peter WHITE, Nathan WHITE**; dau **Jemima CH(   )** wf of Joseph; grandchildren **Elizabeth CH(   ) & Bezaleel WHITE.**

Estate of **Capt. Josiah WHITE** of Spencer MA. <Worcester Co.PR #64371>
Division of real estate, 2 May 1811, to the following, viz: **Ebenezer MASON, Ebenezer MASON Jr., Abigail PARIN** wf of Augustine and **Judith RICHARDSON** wf of Benjamin.

Zacheus BEBEE of Marlow NH to **Caleb WHITE** of Sutton MA. <Cheshire Co.NH Deeds 38:454>
...31 Oct. 1786, Zacheus BEBEE, yeoman, for £60 sold to Caleb WHITE, yeoman...52 acres in Marlow ...bounded by MATHER's hundred acre lot. Witnesses: Joseph BROWN, Silas MACK, Benjamin BROWN. Ack 4 Nov. 1786 by Zacheus. Rec. 15 Nov. 1786.

MICRO #5 OF 7

Caleb WHITE of Sutton MA to **Micah THAYER** of same. <Worcester Co.Deeds 101:266>
...2 Jan. 1787, Caleb WHITE, for £210 silver money sold to Micah THAYER, yeoman...sixty & three quarter acres in Sutton...bounded by land of Richard DAVENPORT, Daniel STONE, BOWER, Rev. Dr. HALL, Phinies BARTLETT, Capt. Samuel SIBLEY. Witnesses: Peter MARSH, Andrew MARSH, Rebekah WHITE. Ack. same day by Caleb. Rec. 4 Jan. 1787 "at 38 minutes past two O clock A.M."

Caleb WHITE of Marlow NH to **John BINGHAM.** <Cheshire Co.Deeds 25:41>
...7 July 1795, Caleb WHITE, yeoman, for £18 sold to John BINGHAM, yeoman...four acres in Marlow ...bounded by sd BINGHAM's land. Witnesses: Nathaniel EVENS, Silas MACK. Rec. 8 July 1795.

Caleb WHITE of Marlow NH to **Lemuel MILLER** of same. <Cheshire Co.Deeds 40:44>
...28 May 1798, Caleb WHITE, yeoman for $10.00 sold to Lemuel MILLER, gent...land in Marlow, bounded by sd MILLER's land. Witnesses: Silas MACK, John MACK. Rec. 5 May 1802.

Caleb WHITE of Marlow NH to **Jeremiah BARRETT** of same. <Cheshire Co.Deeds 42:221>
...5 Mar. 1802, Caleb WHITE, yeoman, for $67.00 sold to Jeremiah BARRETT...land in Marlow...bounded by land of Lemuel MILLER & John BINGHAM...also ten acres bounded by land of sd WHITE, Eleazer MILLER & Lemuel MILLER. Witnesses: Asa MACK, Silas MACK. Rec. 6 Sept. 1803.

Caleb WHITE of Marlow NH to **John BINGHAM** of same. <Cheshire Co.Deeds 47:67>
...6 May 1802, Caleb WHITE, yeoman, for $42.00 sold to John BINGHAM...land in Marlow...bounded by land of sd BINGHAM & land he bo't of sd WHITE. Witnesses: Jacob SHAW, Silas MACK. Rec. 2 Mar 1805

Caleb WHITE of Marlow NH to **John BINGHAM** of same. <Cheshire Co.Deeds 47:67>
...28 Feb. 1805, Caleb WHITE, for $31.00 sold to John BINGHAM...land in Marlow...bounded by land of Eleazer BECKWITH and land sd BINGHAM bought of sd WHITE. Witnesses: William MACK, Silas MACK. Rec. 2 Mar. 1805.

PLYMOUTH COUNTY DEEDS: (re: WHITE)

<7:243> - , Samuel WHITE, grantor.
<10:2:462>- 12 Feb. 1696/7, Samuel WHITE of Rochester to Shearjashub BOURNE. Rec. 20 Jan 1714/5.
<14:272>- 1719, John & Susanna WHITE to Samuel SHERMAN (Susanna's father).
<17:152>- , Samuel WHITE to Malatiah WHITE (he to Kenelm WINSLOW).
<26:132>- , Samuel WHITE to Samuel WHITE Jr.
<33:190>- , Samuel WHITE to Peter CRAPO.
<46:38> - 14 Mar. 1753, Benjamin CROCKER & wf Abigail of Rochester to Malatiah WHITE & Joseph WHITE of same, all the land set off to sd Abigail in settlement of estate of her father John JENKINS dec'd of Rochester.
<46:39> - 18 Oct. 1757, Malatiah WHITE & Joseph WHITE of Rochester sell the above to Ebenezer WHITE of Rochester.
<46:39> - 25 Nov. 1757, Ebenezer & Thankful PARKER of Rochester to Ebenezer WHITE of same.
<46:40> - 1 Mar. 1759, Ebenezer & Thankful PARKER of Rochester to Ebenezer WHITE of same, land bounded partly by land of John WHITE.
<46:40> - 11 Mar. 1760, John HEDGE of Yarmouth to Ebenezer WHITE of Rochester, land formerly belonging to his dec'd father John HEDGE.
<46:41> - 2 Apr. 1760, Barnabas & Mercy HEDGE of Plymouth to Ebenezer WHITE of Rochester, land formerly belonging to his dec'd father John HEDGE.

(References only: 11:192;12:208;14:40,68,168;34:4,5.)

Will of **John WHITE**, yeoman of Rochester MA. <Plymouth Co.PR #22571>
<11:153>...dated 29 June 1748, mentions wf **Martha** and following chil., viz: **Silvanus WHITE, Mary, Thomas WHITE, Justice WHITE, Elizabeth, Deborah, Jedidah** & her son **Nathaniel**. Witnesses: Elisha BARROW, Timothy RUGGLES, Thomas RUGGLES. <11:154> Pr. 9 Nov. 1748, sons **Justice WHITE & Silvanus WHITE** app'td exrs.

John WHITE Sr. of Rochester MA to **John WHITE Jr.** of same. <Plymouth Co.Deeds 19:125>
...10 Sept. 1725, John WHITE Sr., for love & good will, etc. to son John WHITE Jr., husbandman... part of the third woods lot so called in Rochester...bounded by land of Samuel ARNOLD & dwelling

house of Joseph CLARKE. Witnesses: Timothy RUGGLES, Mary RUGGLES. Ack. & Rec. 21 Sept. 1725.

John WHITE of Rochester MA to **John WHITE Jr.** of same. <Plymouth Co.Deeds 30:208>
...27 Sept. 1736, John WHITE, yeoman, for £20 sold to son John WHITE Jr., yeoman...part of my homestead, bounded by land of Joseph CLARKE & homestead where John Jr. now dwells. <30:208>... same day, John WHITE, for £40 sells to son John WHITE Jr., seven acres upland, part of his homestead...bounded by John Jr.'s homestead and land of Josiah HOLMES & Joseph CLARKE. Witnesses: Ebenezer LOVELL, Samuel CLARKE. Rec. 6 Oct. 1736.

John WHITE Sr. of Rochester MA to **David NYE** of Sandwich. <Plymouth Co.Deeds 31:206>
...29 Sept. 1736, John WHITE Sr., for £30 quitclaims to David NYE, hatter...all rights in housing & lands in Rochester...which Jeremiah LEAVITT formerly of sd Rochester sold by his deed dated 12 Mar. 1716/7 & rec. 13:137 to my son John WHITE and he has quitted his claim to the same to me the sd John WHITE as by his quit claim dated 28 Sept. 1736. Witnesses: Cornelius BRIGGS, Timothy RUGGLES. <31:206>...same day, John WHITE, for £10 quitclaims to David NYE, all rights in 10 acres he mortgaged to the Trustees of Plymouth Co. Both deeds ack. 6 Sept. 1737 & Rec. 10 Mar. 1737/8.

John WHITE of Rochester MA to **David NYE** of Sandwich. <Plymouth Co.Deeds 30:209>
...29 Sept. 1736, John WHITE, yeoman, for £600 sells to David NYE, hatter...mansion house & lands in Rochester containing WHITE's dwelling house & homestead, the land containing the third & fourth woods lots in Rochester...excepting what WHITE has already sold to son John WHITE out of the 3d lot and about three acres more disposed of to sd son which there is no deed given...bounded by land of Joseph CLARK, an old cart path that formerly led from sd WHITE's house to Capt. HOLMES' and also excepting ye house of Joshua MORSS which his wife now liveth in with three acres of land...between John WHITE Jr. his land & ye Indian Hills planted...also excepting the land mortgaged to the Province Trustees for Plymouth Co. Witnesses: Cornelius BRIGGS, Timothy RUGGLES. Ack. 5 Oct. 1736. Rec. 6 Oct. 1736. <31:63>...27 Sept. 1736, wf Martha WHITE releases dower.

Joshua MORSS of Rochester MA to **David NYE** of same. <Plymouth Co.Deeds 31:206>
...5 Jan. 1737, Joshua MORSS & wf Elizabeth, for £20 sell to David NYE, hatter...three acres with dwelling house in Rochester they now live in & which they built...being on the Country or Town Road leading to Sniptuit...bounded by land of sd David and land of John WHITE Jr. Witnesses: John WHITE, Timothy RUGGLES. Ack. 10 Feb. 1737. Rec. 10 Mar. 1737.

John WHITE of Rochester MA to **David NYE** of same. <Plymouth Co.Deeds 31:207>
...5 Jan. 1737, John WHITE, yeoman & wf Martha, for £100 sell to David NYE, hatter...dwelling house & land in Rochester that Joshua MORSS now lives in with three acres...being that parcell I reserved out of my homestead which I theretofore sold to sd NYE. Witnesses: Joshua MORSE, Timothy RUGGLES. Ack. 10 Feb. 1737 by Martha, 22 Feb. 1737 by John. Rec. 10 Mar. 1737.

John WHITE of Rochester MA to **Samuel WHITE** of same. <Plymouth Co.Deeds 26:132>
...4 Jan. 1703/4, John WHITE & wf Martha, for £5 sell to brother Samuel WHITE...20 acres in Rochester...bounded by Snipatuit Pond and land of LOTHROPS & TOMSONS. Witnesses: Samuel WINSLOW, Experience HOLMES, Peter BLACKMER. Ack. 12 Apr. 1731 by John. Rec. 29 Apr. 1731.

John WHITE of Rochester MA to **Job LORING** of same. <Plymouth Co.Deeds 30:199>
...22 Mar. 1714/5, John WHITE, for £22 sells to Job LORING...20 acres in Rochester...bounded by meeting house to Stephen ANDREWS' dwelling house and fourth lot in the woods being originally Samuel WHITE's lot at the first. Witnesses: Stephen ANDREWS, Timothy RUGGLES. Rec. 21 Sept. 1736.

John WHITE of Rochester to Essex Commissioners. <Plymouth Co.Deeds 13:206>
...10 Apr. 1719, John WHITE, yeoman & wf Martha, for £100 mortgage to Essex Commissioners...their two lots in Rochester lying in the South Purchase...48 acres in 1st lot, 45 acres in 2d lot...Endorsed 17 June 1719 as not accepted by the Commissioners & therefore discharged.

William BROWN of Bristol to **Stephen BURTON** of same. <Bristol Co.Deeds 1:95>
...1 Feb. 1685/6, William BROWN, husbandman, sells to Stephen BURTON, merchant, for £10 and the further consideration that sd BROWN & wf Anna shall enjoy sd premises during their lives...ten acres in Bristol bounded by the Countrey Road and land of John WHITE and John CORPS.

Stephen BURTON to **NathanielBYFIELD.** <Bristol Co.Deeds 1:101>
...10 Jan. 1689/90, Stephen BURTON & wf Elizabeth sell to Nathaniel BYFIELD...certain lands incl. above 10 acres late in possession of William BROWN dec'd...bounded by land of Samuel COBBETT, John CORPS and land of James LLOYD late in possession of John WHITE dec'd.

Elijah HATCH of Freetown MA to **John WHITE** of same. <Bristol Co.Deeds 49:13>
...12 Mar. 1764...no details. Wf Kezia HATCH signs. Witnesses: Hope WHITE, Peregrine WHITE. Ack. 19 Mar. 1764. Rec. 28 Oct. 1765.

Justus & Silvanus WHITE of Rochester MA to **Edward WINSLOW** of same. <Plymouth Co.Deeds 44:9>
...6 June 1753, Justus WHITE & Silvanus WHITE, yeomen, for £80 sold to Edward WINSLOW, Esq... a certain mansion house & farm in Rochester containing one third of the dwelling house that was our honoured Father John WHITE's late of Rochester dec'd being a third of the great house so called which Esq. Samuel PRINCE built, with the homestead containing the substance of the 16th Wood's Lot so called with other lands joyning it, all fenced, which is all the homestead lands our Honoured Father bought of Peter CRAPO of Rochester as by his deed dated 22 Nov. 1736, except 10

acres sold to Edward MORSS with one third of sd dwelling house & 5 acres, also three quarters of an acre sold to Timothy RUGGLES joining the brook called Muddy Brook. 7 June 1753, Jean WHITE wf of Justus, releases dower; 13 Sept. 1753, Anna WHITE, wf of Silvanus, releases dower. Rec. 21 July 1756.

Ebenezer WHITE of Rochester MA to **Thomas WHITE** of same. <Plymouth Co.Deeds 42:43>
...18 Dec. 1749, Ebenezer WHITE, laborer, for Ł500 sells to Thomas WHITE, laborer...upland, salt marsh & meadowish ground in Rochester at the great neck...containing all my half part of all the land which we the sd Ebenezer & Thomas bought of & hold by a deed from Jeremiah DEVOL of Rochester dated 9 Jan. 1745. Witnesses: Thomas JENKINS, Malatiah WHITE. Rec. 1 Mar. 1753.

Thomas WHITE of Rochester MA to **Butler WING** of Wareham. <Plymouth Co.Deeds 42:43>
...12 Feb. 1753, Thomas WHITE, mariner, for Ł251, sells to Butler WING, yeoman...farm consisting of upland, meadow & meadowish ground in Rochester at the Great Neck, containing a whole seven acre lot of salt marsh, being the 13th lot & was formerly owned by Samuel HATCH...the upland being part of that laid out to Elisha & Ezekiel HATCH for 29 acres...together with that piece of upland which the late John WHITE of Rochester bought of John WINSLOW by deed of 8 Apr. 1723 and by sd WHITE sold to Jeremiah DEVOL by deed of 28 Mar. 1740 and sd DEVOL sold to sd Thomas WHITE & Ebenezer WHITE...also that land sd John WHITE bought of Jeremiah GRIFFETH of Rochester by deed of 8 Dec. 1731 and sd WHITE sold to Jeremiah DEVOL by deed of 28 Mar. 1740...the whole containing all the land sd Jeremiah DEVOL sold to sd Thomas WHITE & his brother Ebenezer WHITE 9 Jan. 1745 and sd Ebeneze sold his part to sd Thomas. Witnesses: Thomas PALMER, Timothy RUGGLES. Rec. 1 Mar 1753

Samuel LEWIS of Tisbury MA to **Samuel MANTER Jr.** of same. <Dukes Co.Deeds 10:25>
...25 Mar. 1772, Samuel LEWIS, blacksmith, for Ł53.6s8d, sold to Samuel MANTER Jr., gent...dwelling house & land in Tisbury...standing between the dwelling house of Samuel MANTER and the river Wf Deborah LEWIS releases dower. Witnesses: James ATHEARN, Benjamin BURGE. Rec. 28 Mar. 1772.

PLYMOUTH COUNTY DEEDS: (re: Samuel LEWIS)

<16:145> - 1 Feb. 1723, Samuel LEWIS, yeoman of Falmouth from Benjamin WEEKS of Plymouth, house & land at Agawam, also land & marsh on Martha's Vineyard.
<33:39> - 25 Jan. 1738, Samuel LEWIS, blacksmith of Rochester from Ithamar COOMBES, bloomer of same, house & land in Rochester.
<33:33> - 9 Apr. 1739, Samuel LEWIS, blacksmith of Rochester, grantor.

MICRO #6 OF 7

Will of **Timothy LUCE Jr.**, merchant of Tisbury MA. <Dukes Co.PR 14:17>
...dated 9 Jan 1830, all estate to wf **Jane**, she...to have the care & education of my two children **Maria A. LUCE & Jirah LUCE**; wf, executrix. Witnesses: E.A.SMITH, William ANDREWS, Leroy M. YALE. Pr. 8 Sept. 1830.

John WHITE of Freetown MA to **Thomas WEST & Jesse LUCE.** <Bristol Co.Deeds 57:214>
...25 Mar. 1777, John WHITE, laborer & wf Mercy, for Ł266.13s4d, sold to Thomas WEST & Jesse LUCE, mariners...one quarter of 15th lot of upland in Freetown...also 12 acres bought of William BORDEN in Freetown on east side of Boton Cedar Swamp...also half of a gore of land in Pocassett Purchase formerly in Tiverton now in Freetown...being part of that cedar swamp lot that belonged to Job ALMY, Esq., joining a lot that Thomas WHITE sold to sd grantees.

Will of **Joseph CLARK**, yeoman of Rochester MA. <Plymouth Co.PR>
...dated 11 Jan. 1771, mentions wf **Mercy** and following chil., viz: **Josiah CLARK & Isaac CLARK** (eldest sons), **Thankful, Lydia & Elizabeth** ("when the youngest of my sd daus shall come to be 18 yrs of age"), **Joseph CLARK** ("who is inform and not likely ever to be able to get his own living") brother **Nathaniel CLARK** of Rochester, executor. Witnesses: John SMITH, Robert CLARK, Thomas WEST. Pr. 4 Oct. 1773.

Will of **Weston ALLEN** of Rochester MA. <Plymouth Co.PR 43:219>
...dated 23 Mar. 1809...to wf **Thankful**, the best room in my dwelling house, one bead & furniture, firewood for one fire delivered at the door & cut up in suitable length to burnt in the room she may live in, one cow to be kept summer & winter & to give milk during the whole time, ten bushels of corn & five bushels of rye yearly, 100 pounds of beef, 70 pounds of pork, four gallons of molasses, twelve pounds of sugar, two pounds of tea or coffy, three bushels of potatoes, two bushels of turnips, six pounds of sheeps wool, twelve pounds of flax, also six common chairs, a table & a desk or chist of draws...to be provided yearly as long as she remains my widow...to dau **Ruth ALLEN**, $2.00...to dau **Unice BATES**, $2.00...to son **Joseph ALLEN**, $10.00...to dau **Catherine ALLEN**, $20.00...to son **John ALLEN**, $30.00...to son **Ruben ALLEN**, my dwelling house, all lands & meadows & half the house **Ruth ALLEN** now lives in...to dau **Lydia ALLEN**, $20.00...to dau **Thankfull ALLEN**, $20.00...my two youngest sons **Weston ALLEN & Andrew Mackie ALLEN** should be put out to some propper trade by my son **Ruben** & if they are not put to any propper trade, I give & bequeath to them $20.00 each...to son **Ruben**, all personal estate. Witnesses: Harper DELANO, Andrew MACKIE, Benjamin FEARING; DELANO & FEARING sworn 21 June 1810. Pr. 21 June 1810.

Thomas WHITE of Freetown MA to **Thomas WEST & Jeffrey LUCE** of Tisbury. <Bristol Co.Deeds 57:213>

...24 Mar. 1777, Thomas WHITE, yeoman & wf Elizabeth, for £488.5s sold to Thomas WEST, mariner & Jeffrey/Jessey LUCE, mariner...13th lot of upland and one quarter of the 8th lot of cedar swamp that is called Pocasset Purchase in Freetown which is my homestead farm ...also land I bought of Joseph TABER...bounded by country road from Dartmouth to Freetown and house of David BRAYLEY... fourth in number in 20 acres set off to me in the division of my Grandfather's estate. Witnesses: Ruth WHITE, Aaron WHITE, John WHITE. Ack. 11 Apr. 1777. Rec. 28 Apr. 1777.

Thomas WHITE 2d & Benjamin LAWRENCE of Freetown MA to **Jethro HATHAWAY.** <Bristol Co.Deeds 57:289>
...5 Nov. 1771, Thomas WHITE 2d & Benjamin LAWRENCE, yeomen, to Jethro HATHAWAY of Dartmouth... cedar swamp in Acushnet Great Cedar Swamp...part of that formerly belonging to Nathaniel DELANO of Dartmouth dec'd.

All References to the name **Thomas WHITE** in Bristol Co.PR: <7:207> Guardianship. <36:406,410> Will & Pr. <62:426> Adm. <62:566> Inv. <63:447> Account. <111:628> Notice. <152:148> Adm.

Will of **Thomas WHITE,** husbandman of Freetown MA. <Bristol Co.PR>
<36:406>...dated 3 June 1799, mentions wf **Ruth**; sons **Marchant WHITE, Thomas WHITE Jr.**; dau **Ruth WHITE**; brother **William WHITE**; chil. of dec'd dau **Mary HILLMAN**, wf of Seth, viz: **Ruth HILLMAN, Susanna HILLMAN, Seth HILLMAN, Thomas HILLMAN, Marchant HILLMAN, Abigail HILLMAN**; dau **Love TOBEY**, wf of Jonathan; chil. of dec'd dau **Elizabeth ASHLEY**, viz: **Abraham ASHLEY, Williams ASHLEY, Mary ASHLEY**; mentions Indian lot bought of William PALMER & Thomas WEST; lot west of Bolton Cedar Swamp bought of Thomas DEMORANVILLE & lot adjoining bought of brother **William WHITE**; swampy land in New Bedford bought with Benjamin LAWRENCE from William HOAR. Witnesses: Benjamin LAWRENCE, John LAWRENCE, Nathaniel MORTON Jr. <36:410> Letter/Bond 1 Oct. 1799, **Marchant WHITE & Thomas WHITE**, yeomen, app'td admrs. Sureties: Nathaniel MORTON Jr., Esq. & John LAWRENCE, yeoman, of Freetown. Witnesses: Francis BAYLIES, Jireh WILLIS.

Jonathan TOBEY of Dartmouth MA to **John WHITE** of Freetown. <Bristol Co.Deeds 49:36>
...8 Feb. 1753, Jonathan TOBEY & wf Elizabeth, sell to John WHITE, laborer...20 acres in Dartm.

Will of **Jonathan TOBEY,** yeoman of New Bedford MA.<Bristol Co.PR 52:497>
...2 Nov. 1811, to unnamed wife, two cows, all sheep, household goods & real estate to posses dureing the time she shall remain my widow and such goods as she brought with her...with the following exceptions, I reserve my wearing apparel to my son **Leonard**, also one bed with suitable furniture to the use of my sons so long as any one of them shall continue single & make a home to my house, and after I give it to my son **Abishua**; $100.00 each to sons **John TOBEY, Silas TOBEY, Marchant TOBEY, William TOBEY & Cornelius TOBEY**; $200.00 each to sons **Leonard TOBEY & Abishua TOBEY**...the said legacies to be paid by my son **Jonathan** in the following manner after one year after my decease he shall pay fifty dollars a year, beginning at the oldest son so continue to pay the oldest off first, untill he has paid the whole of the above...to daus **Sarah & Love**, all household goods after my wife to be eaqually divided between them, after **Love** has been as well fitted for house keeping out of the same, as **Sarah** was when she went to house keeping...son **Jonathan** shall educate or cause my sons **Cornelius, Leonard & Abishua** to be learned to read, write & cypher, so far as is suitable for children to be put out to a trade and then provide some usefull trade for them after they have become of a suitable age...remainder of estate to son **Jonathan** (executor). Witnesses: James HOLMES, Jabez TABER, Joseph WHITE; sworn to 29 Oct. 1816 by TABER & WHITE, James HOLMES having since dec'd. <original> Letter/Bond 29 Oct. 1816, **Jonathan TOBEY** app'td admr. Sureties: Jabez TABER & Joseph WHITE, yeomen of Fairhaven. Witnesses: James TABER, Francis BAYLIES.

Will of **William WHITE** of New Bedford MA. <Bristol Co.PR 54:65>
...10 Mar. 1795...being far advanced in years, mentions wf **Mercy**; to son **Joseph WHITE** (executor), swamp in Freetown bought of Zueil HASKELL; to son **William WHITE,** swamp in Freetown bought of Anthony BOOTH; to son **Samuel WHITE,** swamp bought of William LeBARON; to son **Ebenezer WHITE,** swamp bought of William LeBARON; to dau **Anna TABER,** swamp in Dartmouth bought of Benjamin AKIN; to dau **Mercy WHITE,** swamp bought of Jabez TABER. Pr. 7 Oct. 1817 (he is also called late of Fairhaven).

Resolved WHITE of Rochester MA to **John BASSETT** of same. <Plymouth Co.Deeds 117:265>
...7 Oct. 1812, Resolved WHITE, for $135.00 sold to John BASSETT, trader...a certain dwelling house & lot in Rochester at Sippican Harbour near the wharf, the sixth lot, being the same house & lot that Justice WHITE lives on & improves...reference may be had to a general plan of the lots for bounds. Witnesses: John R. PREBLE, Nathaniel RUGGLES. Rec. 17 Nov. 1812.

Resolved WHITE of Rochester MA to **Enoch Sears JENNEY & Nathan HATHAWAY.** <Plymouth Co.Deeds>
<127:161>...12 Oct. 1813, Resolved WHITE, mariner, for $132.00 sold to Enoch Sears JENNEY & Nathan HATHAWAY, shoemakers of Fairhaven...land & dwelling house in Rochester at Sippecan harbour, being the sixth lot in number agreeable to a general plan of the Village...the same lot on which Capt. Justus WHITE now lives on & improves...being the same lot which I purchast of John BASSETT by deed 12 Oct. 1813. Witnesses: Edward DILLINGHAM, William LeBARON. Rec. 5 Sept. 1815.

Resolved WHITE of Wareham MA to **Curtis TOBEY** of same. <Plymouth Co.Deeds 126:113>
...30 Sept. 1815, Resolved WHITE, mariner, for $109.00 sold to Curtis TOBEY, gent...dwelling house & land in Rochester where Justus WHITE now lives...at Scipercan Harbour...6th lot...which lot of land I hold by deed from John BASSETT & Roland LUCE...also pew #13 on the lower floor in meeting house in 4th parish of Rochester. Witnesses: Eliza FEARING, John FEARING. Rec. 2 Oct 1815

Willard SHEPHARD et al of Plainfield VT to **Daniel VAUGHAN** of Rochester MA. <Plymouth Co.Deeds> <95:263>...19 July 1802, Willard SHEPHARD, yeoman & wf Betsey and Jane WHITE, single woman, for $33.00 sold to Daniel VAUGHAN, yeoman...all our reversionary right in land in Rochester...which was set of to our Mother the present wife of the sd Daniel as her dower or thirds in the estate of our Late father her first husband Rowland WHITE late of Rochester dec'd. Witnesses: Lydia KINNEY, Bradford KINNEY. Ack. 8 Sept. 1802 by all 3 grantors. Rec. 16 June 1803.

Estate of **Resolved WHITE** of Rochester MA. <Plymouth Co.PR #22606>
<original>...5 Aug. 1780, Sir, I would informe your Honour of the Death of my Husband **Resolved WHITE** who was Lost at Sea on ye 25 day of March Last and the Surcimstance of my famely has ben such that I could not send before I Pray your Honer would apoynt **Melatiah WHITE** as admr. to my husband's estate, Signed **Charity WHITE.** <27:48> Letter/Bond 7 Aug. 1780, **Melatiah WHITE,** yeoman of Rochester, app'td admr. Sureties: Phillip TURNER & Joel ELLIS, yeomen of Rochester. Witnesses: Ephraim SPOONER, Caleb LORING. <25:553> Inventory taken 7 Sept. 1780, by Thomas WHITRIDGE, Seth BLACKWELL & Seth DEXTER of Rochester, "inventory is taken as in our judgement the several articles would vend the year 1774"; total real estate, Ł186; total estate, Ł260.19.2.; sworn to 2 Oct. 1780 by admr. <original> Memorandum (not dated), lists the heirs, viz: widow **Charity VAUGHAN** and chil., **Thaddeus WHITE, Jonathan WHITE, Elisabeth WHITE, Jane WHITE.** <33:111,112> Dower 23 Dec. 1793, by George Bonum NYE, Mark SNOW & Thomas WHITTERIDGE, all of Rochester, to the widow **Charity VAUGHAN,** now wf of Daniel. <original> Bond 31 Dec. 1793, of **Thaddeus WHITE** to pay his brother & sisters (above named) their shares.

Ephraim KIMTON et al to **Samuel & Thomas WHITE** of Dartmouth. <Bristol Co.Deeds 36:405> ...1 Dec. 1748, Ephraim KIMTON & William KIMTON, shipwrights of Dartmouth and Joseph RUSSEL, cooper of Dartmouth, for Ł400 sold to Samuel WHITE, yeoman of Dartmouth & Thomas WHITE of Freetown...85 acre cedar swamp in the 16 acre Division of Cedar Swamp in Dartmouth...bounded on cedar swamp formerly laid out to John HATHWAY late of Dartmouth dec'd and Capt. Thomas TABER dec'd... it being laid out to Manassah KIMTON of Long Island dec'd. Witnesses: Thomas KIMTON, Stephen WEST Patience, wf of Ephraim, Marcy wf of William & Judith wf of Joseph, release dowers. Witness: Mary WITTINGTON(sp). <49:13>...20 Sept. 1762, Samuel WHITE, yeoman of Dartmouth, for Ł10.13s4d, sells to John WHITE, freeman of Freetown, his half of above. Witnesses: Rebecca WHITE, Elisha TOBEY. Rec. 28 Oct. 1765. <54:317,318>...30 Jan. 1770, Thomas WHITE, yeoman of Freetown, gives to sons Thomas WHITE Jr. & John WHITE, yeomen of Freetown...two sixths of the above, each. Witnesses: Peregrine WHITE, Thomas GILBERT. Rec. 11 Mar. 1772.

John WHITE of Lennister NH to **Thomas WHITE Jr.** of Freetown MA. <Bristol Co.Deeds 62:17> ...21 Nov. 1778, John WHITE of Lennister, Chester Co. NH, for Ł301.18s sells to Thomas WHITE Jr., yeoman...cedar swamp Boltons Cedar Swamp in Freetown...together with other lands that I own in Dartmouth. Witnesses: John GIFFORD Jr., Walter ALLEN. Rec. 18 Aug. 1783.

Thomas WHITE Jr. of Freetown MA to **John WHITE** of same. <Bristol Co.Deeds 50:128> ...30 Oct. 1752, Thomas WHITE Jr., laborer & wf Elizabeth, for Ł18.12s sold to John WHITE, laborer...one part of ye eight lot of cedar swamp and half of ye eight lot of upland in that called Swamp Lotts in Pocassett Purchase in Freetown...also half the 15th lot in sd purchase it being part of the land & swamp that belonged to Louis DEMORANVILLE of Freetown. Witnesses: Marcy WEST, Stephen WEST. Ack. 27 Apr.1 754 by Thomas WHITE Jr. Rec. 31 Oct. 1765.

Will of **John WHITE,** husbandman of Hopkinton NH. <Hillsborough Co.PR>
...dated 17 Apr. 1809...to wf **Mercy,** the note of hand that Jones BLANCHARD gave me bearing even date with this instrument...to sons **Liberty WHITE & Seth WHITE** and to daus **Jedidiah CLOUGH, Anna McMILLEN, Sarah McMILLEN, Experience BLANCHARD, Hope WHITE & Betty WHITE,** $5.00 each...wearing apparel & remainder of estate to wf **Mercy** (executrix). Witnesses: Aaron GREELEY, Cutteon(sp) FLANDERS, Rufus HATHAWAY.

Estate of **Melatiah WHITE** of Rochester MA. <Plymouth Co.PR #22592>
<2:104> Pr. 21 Sept. 1709, widow **Mercy WHITE** app'td admx. <2:112> Inventory taken 19 Sept. 1709. <3:198,199> Appraisal of estate, 17 Dec. 1712, by Samuel PRINCE, Lt. Peter BLACKMORE & James WINSLOW. (Capt. Isaac HOLMES & Roger HASCALL as "backups".) <3:199> Account of admx., 18 Dec. 1712; mentions the eldest son **Maletiah WHITE** and daus **Judah, Mercy & Margrett.** <3:380> On 22 Dec. 1715, widow **Marcy/Mercy JENKINS,** now wf of Thomas of Barnstable, states it was over 6 yrs since her husband's death, the children being then very young, the eldest not ten years and asks to have the children's share paid to her on account of their bringing up. <#22593> Bond 21 Sept. 1709, Samuel WINSLOW & Nathaniel WINSLOW of Rochester app'td guardians of the children. Witnesses: Joseph OTIS, Nathaniel THOMAS.

Samuel WHITE Sr.of Rochester MA to **Melatiah WHITE** of same. <Plymouth Co.Deeds 17:152> ...17 July 1697, Samuel WHITE Sr., for love & good will, to son Melatiah WHITE...upland in Rochester...being upon the Middle Branch of Mattapoisett River being 20 acres of or a third part of a lot of land...there being 62 acres & a half in the whole lot. Witnesses: Peter BLACKMER, Jonathan COB, Samuel WINSLOW...26 Oct. 1700, the sd Melatiah WHITE, for & in consideration of Housing & Lands already granted & delivered to me by way of exchange...by my Honoured Father Kenelm WINSLOW of Harwich...assigns all his rights in the above mentioned premises. Witnesses: Susanna WHITE, Peter BLACKMER. Both deeds ack. 21 Mar. 1704/5 & Rec. 4 Mar. 1723.

Estate of **Malatiah WHITE** of Rochester MA. <Plymouth Co.PR #22591>
<34:178> Letter/Bond 13 Mar. 1799, widow **Mercy WHITE** app'td admx. Sureties: Abraham HOLMES of

Rochester & Ephraim SPOONER of Plymouth. Witnesses: Nathaniel LOTHROP, Isaac LOTHROP. <36:514> Inventory taken 7 Mar. 1799 by Seth BLACKWELL, James FOSTER Jr., Timothy DAVIS; total estate, £95.9. <36:515> Insolvency. <36:515> Account of admx., 13 Mar. 1799.

Will of **Peter CRAPO** of Rochester MA. <Plymouth Co.PR 14:146>
...dated 20 Feb. 1756, mentions wf **Ann**; sons **Francis CRAPO, Peter CRAPO Jr., John CRAPO, Hezekiah CRAPO, Nicholas CRAPO, Seth CRAPO**; daus **Susanna DEMORANVILLE, Mary SPOONER, Elizabeth LUKE/LAKE/ LUCE, Rebecca MATHEWS**. Pr. 3 May 1756.

MICRO #7 OF 7

Will of **Samuel WHITE**, yeoman of Dartmouth MA. <Bristol Co.PR>
<18:14>...dated 25 Aug. 1762...to wf **Elizabeth** (executrix), one third of estate for life; to son **William WHITE**, 6s; to daus **Rebecca, Betty, Jemima & Mary**, remainder of estate. Witnesses: Abigail SPOONER, Francis CRAPOO, Thomas WEST. Pr. 2 Nov. 1762. <18:190> Inventory taken 29 Oct. 1762; total real estate, £300; sworn to 3 May 1763 by exx.

Rebecca WHITE of Dartmouth MA to **Elizabeth WHITE** of same. <Bristol Co.Deeds 47:164>
...11 June 1764, Rebecca WHITE, spinstress, for £40 sells to Elizabeth WHITE, widow...that part of ye homestead of my Honoured father Samuel WHITE late of Dartmouth dec'd set off to me...bounded by land of Seth SPOONER. Witnesses: Obed HATHWAY, Thomas WEST. Ack. 14 June 1764. Rec. 26 June 1764.

Will of **Jemima WHITE**, single woman of New Bedford MA. <Bristol Co.PR>
<29:496>...dated 5 Jan. 1788, all real estate to sisters **Betsey WHITE & Polly HOWLAND**; to neice **Hopestill HOWLAND**, two best gowns, silver shoe buckles, stone sleeve buttons; remainder to sister **Polly** to compensate for nursing of me in my sickness; Russell BAILEY, executor. Witnesses: Seth SPOONER, Rachel PETTY, Alden SPOONER. <30:59> Inventory taken 3 June 1788; incl. old house & barn <30:60> Account of admr., 2 Dec. 1788.

EDWARD WINSLOW

MICRO #1 OF 1

PLYMOUTH COUNTY DEEDS: (re: WINSLOW)

1803	Josiah	Bridgewater	adm.	#23200,	34:367;38:36,37,38,39
1804	David	Rochester	adm.	#23169,	34:381;40:204,212;42:99,100
1808	Nathaniel	Scituate	adm.	#23213,	39:167;42:517;60:477
1815	Isaac	Marshfield		#23185	
1816	Micah	Rochester	will	#23208,	48:61,62
1816	Richard	Rochester	adm.	#23221,	46:174;48:148
1818	Benjamin	Middleboro	adm.	#23168,	46:270;49:565,567;56:148-9
1818	Jirah et al	Middleboro	gdn.	#23190,	51:16
1819	Isaac	Marshfield	will	#23186,	("48 entries", see below)
1820	Lucy et al	Hanover	adm.	#23206,	51:107,359;53:280;54:152;63:30;66:43,44
1822	John	Marshfield/Hanover	adm.	#23194,	52:164;55:70;56:301,477;57:103,292;63:132,166-8;66:143,354;64:492
1825	Susan	Hingham	adm.	#23226,	52:399;55:359;59:417;60:40
1826	Sarah	Scituate	adm.	#23224,	61:39;62:55;63:23,24
1830	Nathaniel	Hanover	adm.	#23212,	61:356;68:110;69:205,335,547;70:11,163,164
1839	Lemuel	Rochester	will	#23205,	5T:127;10A:312;80:403;81:271,601
1846	Francis	Hingham	will	#23179,	2H:92;7V:246;88:530-2;93:33

Guardianship of Children of **Thomas WINSLOW Jr.** of Hanover MA. <Plymouth Co.PR #23206>
<51:107> Letter/Bond 4 Dec.1820, Barker RAMSDELL app'td gdn. of **Lucy Torrey WINSLOW & Ruth Gross WINSLOW,** minors under 14, chil. of **Thomas WINSLOW Jr.** & devisees of the will of **Ruth GROSS,** single woman of Hanover. Sureties: Benjamin D. FILLMORE & Turner STETSON of Hanover. Witnesses: Samuel WEBB, Seth WHITMAN. <53:280> Inventory taken 5 Mar. 1821, by Turner STETSON, Zacheus ESTES & Reuben ESTES of Hanover; total real estate, $130.00; total personal estate, $224.68. <54:152> Account of gdn., 4 Dec. 1821. <original> Request 2 Sept. 1826, of **Lucy T. WINSLOW,** about 18 yrs of age, that her present gdn. Capt. Barker RAMSDELL is about to remove from this part of the County & asks for the appointment of Richmond WINSLOW of Hanover. <63:30> Discharge 5 Sept. 1826, of Barker RAMSDELL as gdn. <51:359> Letter/Bond 5 Sept. 1826, Richmond WINSLOW app'td gdn. of **Lucy T. WINSLOW** (above 14) and **Ruth G. WINSLOW** (under 14). Sureties: Charles WINSLOW & Daniel BARSTOW Jr. of Hanover. Witness: G.W. WARREN. <66:43> Inventory taken 5 Dec. 1826 by Daniel BARSTOW Jr., Charles WINSLOW & Warren/Oren JOSSELYN of Hanover; total real estate, $78.00; total estate, $291.33. <63:30> Account of gdn., for the heirs of **Ruth GROSS** late of Hanover dec'd, allowed 5 Sept. 1826.

Will of **Isaac WINSLOW,** Physician of Marshfield MA. <Plymouth Co.PR #23186>
<50:396>...dated 25 Aug. 1815, mentions wf **Frances** and following chil., viz: **John WINSLOW** (executor), **Elizabeth WHITMAN, Ruth S. DINGLEY, Sarah CLAPP.** Codicil 14 Sept. 1819... children to contribute to the support of Mercy STOCKBRIDGE as I am obliged to do by the will of her father Dr. Benjamin STOCKBRIDGE. Witnesses (to both): Robert CUSHMAN, Joseph P. CUSHMAN, Ruth CUSHMAN. <50:397> Letter/Bond 15 Nov. 1819, **John WINSLOW** of Hanover app'td admr. Sureties: Kilborn WHITMAN of Pembroke & Henry WARREN of Plymouth. Witness: John TORREY. <50:444> Inventory, warrant dated 15 Nov. 1819 to Robert CUSHMAN, John THOMAS & Joseph P. CUSHMAN of Marshfield; total real estate, $22,891.00; total personal estate, $3240.74. <50:446> Notice. <56:73> Division, 3 Sept. 1822, of real estate, by David OLDHAM Jr., Robert CUSHMAN & John THOMAS, among the four children, viz: **John WINSLOW, Elizabeth WHITMAN** wf of Kilborn, **Ruth S. DINGLEY** wf of Thomas and **Sarah CLAPP** wf of Ebenezer. <54:384> Account of exr., 2 Apr. 1822. <original> Bond 21 Oct. 1822, **Kilborn WHITMAN** app'td admr. de bonis non. <original> Notice, mentions property of dec'd in Kennebeck Co.ME. <original> Petition of Kilbron WHITMAN for extension of time; **John WINSLOW** dec'd had property in Natchez, Miss. in which **Dr. Isaac WINSLOW**'s estate is involved. <63:165> List of Claims, 21 Oct. 1826: George PARTRIDGE, Chandler SAMPSON, William STANDISH, Gideon BARSTOW & wf, Edward CUSHING, Thomas CUSHING, Rachel CUSHING, Isaac CUSHING, estate of John CUSHING, Anna CUSHING, Ira THOMAS & wf Betsey, Belcher SYLVESTER, Jotham TILDEN. <63:514> Petition of creditors & discharge of Kilborn WHITMAN as admr., 14 Apr. 1827. <original> Bond 14 Apr. 1827, George P. RICHARDSON app'td admr. <64:114> Account of Kilborn WHITMAN, admr., 9 Apr. 1827. <64:188> Inventory of estate in Boston taken 21 June 1827. (Many other records pertaining to this estate are not of genealogical value and were not transcribed.)

Estate of **John WINSLOW,** Esq. of Marshfield/Hanover MA. <Plymouth Co.PR #23194>
<52:164> Letter 21 Oct. 1822, Horatio CUSHING of Hanover app'td admr. Sureties: Kilbron WHITMAN,

Thomas DINGLEY, Ebenezer CLAPP. <56:301> Inventory taken 21 Nov. 1822 by Robert CUSHMAN, John THOMAS & Peleg T. FORD of Marshfield; incl. dwelling house & one quarter acre near the Episcopal Church in Hanover; 130 acre homestead farm in Marshfield, being part of the ancient WINSLOW farm; 12 acres called wigwam point, formerly part of sd farm; 12 acre salt marsh in Marshfield; pew in Episcopal Church; total real estate, $4535.00; total personal estate, $795.50; 16 Dec. 1822, Horatio CUSHING is ordered to deliver to the widow **Susanna WINSLOW**, personal estate to amount of $500.00. <55:70> Notice. <56:477> Order to sell personal estate, 4 Mar. 1823. <57:103> Inventory, 14 Apr. 1823; additional personal estate, $59.60. <57:292;63:166> Insolvency. <63:167> List of Claims: Gideon BARSTOW & wf, Rachel CUSHING, Anna CUSHING, Edward CUSHING, Thomas CUSHING, Isaac CUSHING, Edward CUSHING for John CUSHING, Ira THOMAS & wf Betsey, Belcher SYLVESTER, Trustees of the Fund of the Episcopal Parish in Hanover, Carver WASHBURN & Co., John B. THOMAS, Sylvanus PERCIVAL, William STANDISH Jr., William TORREY, Daniel WRIGHT, Thomas DINGLEY, Nathaniel CLAPP, Anthony COLLAMORE, James CURTIS, Jabez HATCH, Allen DANFORTH, Charles WRIGHT, David OLDHAM, Chandler SAMPSON, Belcher SYLVESTER, Benjamin PERCIVAL, Jared WHITMAN, Kilborn WHITMAN as admr. de bonis non on estate of Isaac WINSLOW; balance due John WINSLOW exr. of Isaac WINSLOW's estate; Isaac WINSLOW's estate to the heirs of Elijah CUSHING for debts due from John WINSLOW's estate to sd CUSHING's heirs; claims allowed 20 Nov. 1826. <63:132> Petition to sell real estate to raise the sum of "$10.000", granted 20 Nov. 1826. <63:168> Account of admr., 20 Nov. 1826; incl. payment to Charles TURNER to bear his expenses to Natchez, $200.00; widow's allowance, $500.00. <66:157> Claim of Jared WHITMAN transmitted to the admr. at Natchez & by him paid, 16 June 1828. <64:492> Advertisement of sale, 10 Apr. 1827 by admr., at the late mansion house of **Dr. Isaac WINSLOW** dec'd in Marshfield; the following describes real estate of which **John WINSLOW** late of Hanover dec'd died seized...one undivided fourth part of land in Marshfield containing 305 acres being the easterly part of the farm formerly occupied by sd **Isaac WINSLOW**, bounded by heirs of Gen. John THOMAS, Rocky point woods, Samuel BAKER, Samuel FORD, Green Harbor River, Jethro TAYLOR and Joshua & David CARVER, excepting & reserving the improvement for life to the widow Joanna WINSLOW the late wife of Pelham WINSLOW in that part of the premises that was set off to her as her dower in sd Pelham's estate; excepting also 24 acres heretofore sold by **Dr. Isaac WINSLOW** to Peregrine & Hannah WHITE.

==========

Isaac WINSLOW of Marshfield MA. <Plymouth Co.PR #23185>
<original> Bond 10 July 1815, of Isaac WINSLOW, commissioner of wrecks. Sureties: John WINSLOW of Hanover & John B. THOMAS of Plymouth. Witnesses: Beza HAYWARD, Anna HALL.

==========

Estate of **Josiah WINSLOW**, housewright of Bridgewater MA. <Plymouth Co.PR #23200>
<original> Request 2 May 1803, of widow **Content WINSLOW**, for the appointment of her brother **Oliver HARVEY** of Bridgewater as admr. <34:367> Letter/Bond 2 May 1803, **Oliver HARVEY** app'td admr. Sureties: Ephraim SNELL & Samuel FORD of Bridgewater. <38:36> Inventory taken 2 May 1803 by Daniel SNOW, Zephaniah LOTHROP & Ephraim SNELL of Bridgewater; personal estate only, $136.39. <38:37> Notice. <38:38> Insolvency, 6 Feb. 1804; Creditors: Daniel HAYWARD, David HARVEY Jr., Maj. Daniel HARTWELL, Abiezer ALGER, Ichobod MACOMBER, Joshua GILMORE, George HOWARD, Zephaniah LOTHROP, George WILLIAMS, David HARVEY. <38:39> Account of admr., 1 Oct. 1804; delivered to the widow $124.00.

==========

Estate of **David WINSLOW** of Rochester MA. <Plymouth Co.PR #23169>
<34:381> Letter/Bond 18 Apr. 1804, widow **Betsey WINSLOW** app'td admx. Sureties: William SHERMAN & Allen MARSHALL of Rochester. Witnesses: Benjamin PICKENS, John BLACKMER. <40:204> Notice. <40:212> Dower set off to the widow, 25 May 1805, by Nathan WILLIS, Esq., Charles STURTEVANT, Esq. & John SIMMONS, yeoman, all of Rochester; part of homestead & part of the SHERMAN farm. <42:99> Inventory taken 18 Apr. 1804 by William SHERMAN, Joshua SHERMAN & Allen MARSHALL; 70 acre homestead in Rochester, $1500.00 and eight acres in Freetown, $100.00. <42:100> Account of admx., 5 Nov. 1806; Received from: Presbery CLARK, James CATHELL, Benjamin BROWN (for land sold), estate of Nathan DELENO, George WINSLOW; Paid to: Saulsbury BLACKMER, Nicholas CRAPO, Joseph CUNDALE, Mary HASKELL, Benjamin SPOONER, William SHERMAN, Samuel WELDEN, Abner VINCET/VINCENT, Abraham HOLMES, Micah WINSLOW, Abraham HOLMES, Seth POPE Jr., James HATHWAY, Hannah WINSLOW, Jeremiah CLAP, Isaac VINCENT, James CATHELL, Joshua SHERMAN, Cornelius SHERMAN, Thomas GIFFORD, Alden CUSHMAN, John HASS, Allen MARSHALL, John SIMMONS, Col. STURDAFANT/STURTEVANT, Benjamin TERRY, Thomas SHERMAN, Nathan WILLIS, Nathaniel GLOYD; also paid for sundry jobs done in the Tan Yard.

==========

Estate of **Nathaniel WINSLOW**, Esq. of Scituate MA. <Plymouth Co.PR #23213>
<39:167> Letter/Bond 18 Oct. 1808, Ebenezer COPELAND & Nathaniel WINSLOW app'td admrs. Sureties: Samuel CURTIS of Scituate & Josiah SMITH of Hanover. Witnesses: Elizabeth HAMMATT, J.B. THOMAS. <42:517> Inventory taken 18 Nov. 1808 by David STOCKBRIDGE, Esq. of Hanover and Samuel TOLMAN & Micah STETSON of Scituate; incl. homestead farm partly in Scituate & Hanover; 21 acres Wild cat pasture in Scituate; seven acre cedar swamp in Hanover; two & a half acre salt marsh in Marshfield; two & one quarter acre salt marsh in Scituate; five & a half fresh meadow in Scituate; 27 acres purchased of John TOLMAN; the 44 acre OLDHAM farm in Hanover. <60:477> Division, 17 July 1826, by Horatio CUSHING, Robert EELLS, David OLDHAM Jr.; to the following chil., viz: **Nathaniel WINSLOW, William WINSLOW, Nancy RIPLEY** dec'd wf of William P. of Plymouth, **Judith TOLMAN** wf of Elisha of Scituate, **Lydia COLLAMORE** wf of Anthony of Pembroke and **Sarah COPELAND** widow of Ebenezer of Scituate.

==========

Will of **Micah WINSLOW**, yeoman of Rochester MA. <Plymouth Co.PR #23208>
<48:61>...dated 30 Nov. 1804..entire estate to wf **Hannah** (executrix). Witnesses: Caleb MENDAL, Charles J. HOLMES, Abraham HOLMES. <48:62> Pr. 20 May 1816, widow **Hannah WINSLOW**, exx.

==========

Estate of **Richard WINSLOW** of Rochester MA. <Plymouth Co.PR #23221>
<46:174> Letter/Bond 19 July 1816, James CATHELL, yeoman of Rochester, app'td admr. Sureties: George B.N. HOLMES & Charles J. HOLMES of Rochester. Witness: Abraham HOLMES. <48:148> Inventory taken 19 July 1816 by George B.N. HOLMES, Esq., Allen MARSHALL & Martin SHERMAN of Rochester; incl. notes signed by Ichabod DAVIS, James CATHELL, Amos LEWIS & Nathaniel SEARS Jr.; personal estate only, $306.59.

Estate of **Benjamin WINSLOW**, yeoman of Middleborough MA. <Plymouth Co.PR #23168>
<46:270> Letter/Bond 28 May 1818, widow **Phebe WINSLOW** app'td admx. Sureties: Moses NICHOLS, blacksmith of Plymouth & Edmond ANTHONY, yeoman of Taunton. Witnesses: Beza HAYWARD, Mary W. HAYWARD. <49:565> Inventory taken 28 May 1818 by Edmond ANTHONY of Taunton and Oliver PEIRCE & Ethan PEIRCE of Middleborough; incl. 13 acre dwelling house bought of Seth CONE; land bought of Obid MIRICK; one undivided 6th part of 22 acres lying in common with Elizabeth & mother; half share of swamp in Assonet cedar swamp; woodland known as hunting house lot; land in Berkley; part of old dwelling house improved by Avery WINSLOW, about one third of sd house & corn house; salt meadow in Freetown; Notes against: James CHASE, Gilbert WINSLOW, Amos BRIGGS, Gilbert NICHOLS, John EATON, Edmond ANTHONY, Job WINSLOW, Joseph NICHOLS, Joseph ALLEN, Josiah HOLLOWAY, Abraham PIERCE, Avery WINSLOW, Gardner WINSLOW, David L. HATHAWAY, Samuel FRENCH, William CANEDY, Nathan BRIGGS, John HINDS, Nathaniel STAPLES, Abiel NICHOLS. <49:567> Notice. <56:148> Account of admx., 7 May 1822; the following names are written in the original with lines drawn through them, viz: **Phebe WINSLOW**, widow, **Jirah WINSLOW**, yeoman and **Tisdale WINSLOW**, minor; Paid to: Barzillo HATHEWAY, Charles STRANGE, Benjamin WEAVER, Obed MIRIC, Ethan PEIRCE, Avery WINSLOW, Robert POTTER, John EATON, Dean BURT, Calvin TILSON, Joseph JACKSON, Oliver PEIRCE, Samuel FRENCH, Nathan BRIGGS; to discount on notes of Josiah HOLLOWAY & Abiel NICHOLS. <56:149> Order for distribution, 7 May 1822, of $2207.92 in hands of the admx.; $735.94 (or one third) to the widow and a like sum to **Jireh WINSLOW & Tisdell/Tisdale WINSLOW.** <51:16> Guardianship, 4 Nov. 1818, **Phebe WINSLOW** app'td gdn. of **Jirah WINSLOW & Tisdell/Tisdale WINSLOW,** above 14. Sureties: Oliver PEIRCE, yeoman & Ethan PEIRCE, gent., of Middleboro. Witnesses: Samuel PICKENS, Beza HAYWARD.

ELIZABETH WINSLOW[2] (Edward[1])

Estate of **Capt. George CORWIN/CORWINE.** <Essex Co.Court Papers 44:96>
(The following is not dated but is among the papers of June 1685-Sept. 1685)
...A Liste of Severall Things Inventoried with the Estate of Capt. George CORWINE, which in Right belong to **Elizabeth,** his Relict Widdow, being Either reserved before, or Given to her, After Marriage, viz: a turkie carpet in the Hall, 15s; wicker basket, 5s; pomander basket in ye glas Chamber, 10s; turkie carpet in ye New Hall, £1.5s; "pilyon & clo:" (at 20s), £1; iron bound cheste in ye Chamber Entry, 5s; small Japan Trunke, 8s; soe much gold ye Capt. received of Mr. POPE pr the produce of an Indian boy sent me from Plimouth pr ye Governor & Councill, £8; skreen cover & a pair tobacco tongues; a large scretore & frame, given me soon after Marriage, now in ye Kitchin Chamber; pair of downe pillows; large callicoe quilt fringed; large callicoe quilt not fringed; large tankerd, plate, that was my former Husband's Mr. **Robert BROOKES** with our Armes; a plate sugar box given me by Gov. WINSLOW; a porringr sent John BROOK by Gov. WINSLOW; a smale hand silver candestick given John BROOK by **Herbert PELHAM;** 12 silver spoones 6 of them gilt & "runbd", given pr Mr. John BROOK Uncle to "R", one silver spoone given pr ye Lord Mayor; a large quarto bible with bezas notes; a silver watch; ye chaires in ye Glas Chamber and the chaires & Screetore of Gilded Leather in the Red Chamber which I bought with the produce of som Adventures the Capt. had Given me; a suit of damaske; one table clo:; one towill & 18 napkins given me by Capt. before Marriage; a chest of Linen at Plimoth which was my former husbands & was alwaies reserved to my selfe and kept in my possesion...The Severall particulers above...were granted by Capt. George CORWIN, my husband unto my selfe. Signed: **Elizabeth CORWIN.**

Estate of **Elizabeth CORWIN,** widow of Boston MA. <Suffolk Co.PR #2447>
<8:140> Pr. 23 Apr. 1698, son in law **Edward LYDE,** merchant of Boston, app'td admr. Sureties: Richard CRISP, merchant & Samuel PHILLIPS, bookseller. <8:278> Inventory exhibited 28 July 1698, (of estate of Madam Elizabeth CORWIN); Due from: Thomas WILKINS, Phillip KNIGHT & Henry WILKINS, all of Salem Village by bond, the sum of £27.15.8., plus interest of £2.4.4.; Due from: John GRAFTON of Salem on his bond bearing date of 12 Feb. 1685, £29.9. incl. interest. <14:87> Account of admr., 14 Sept. 1699; expenses incl. funerall charges, £56.11.4.; Doctor & nurses, £13.19.8. (The following appears to be a reference to an **Elizabeth CORWIN** who d. 23 Dec. 1717, Salem, viz: <22:804> Petition (no date), of Henry GIBBS, brazier of Boston & John COTTON, clerk of Newtown.)

Guardianship of Children of **Capt. John CURWIN** of Salem MA. <Suffolk Co.PR #1437>
Bond 9 Dec. 1685, widow **Margaret CURWIN** app'td gdn. of chil., viz: **George CURWIN, Elizabeth CURWIN & Lucy CURWIN.** Sureties: Edward WHARTON, John BLAKE. Witnesses: JOhn PARNELL, Samuel NEWMAN.

JOSIAH WINSLOW[2] (Edward[1])

Penelope WINSLOW of Marshfield MA to **Elizabeth BURTON.** <Bristol Co.Deeds 6:311>
...4 May 1688, Penelope WINSLOW, widow & sole executrix of the will of Josias WINSLOW, Esq. late of Marshfield dec'd...whereas the sd Josias by his will provided that all his lands outside of Marshfield should be at disposall of executrix to make part of the portion of his dau Elizabeth

...therefore I ye sd Penelope WINSLOW as executrix to make part of the Portion our our sd dau Elizabeth BURTON (now the wife of Stephen BURTON) to the value of fifty pound...convey...all that whole share of land...at Shawomet in the County of Bristol, viz: the 30th lot, containing 45 acres, in the 1st division, lying between the lots of Capt. Benjamin CHURCH & John JAMES...also the 30th lot, five acres in 2d division and the 25th lot, 36 acres, in 3d division, also lying between lands of CHURCH & JAMES...also one share of all the undivided land belonging to sd Purchase of land commonly called Shawomet. Witnesses: Nathaniel THOMAS, Esq., Isaac WINSLOW. Sworn to 3 Sept. 1709 by Nathaniel THOMAS and 20 Sept. 1710 by Isaac WINSLOW. Rec. 24 Nov. 1710.

Elizabeth BURTON of Marshfield MA to **Obadiah EDDY** of Swansea. <Bristol Co.Deeds 5:415>
...26 Mar. 1708, Elizabeth BURTON, widow of Stephen late of Bristol dec'd, for £20 silver money, sells to Obadiah EDDY, husbandman...10 acres in Shawomet Great Neck in the last division...bounded by the 12th lot, Swansea line, 14th lot and highway. Witnesses: Isaac WINSLOW, William CARVER. Rec. 7 Sept.1708.

Elizabeth BURTON of Marshfield MA to **John EDDY** of Swansea. <Bristol Co.Deeds 5:355>
...26 Mar. 1708, widow Elizabeth BURTON, for £10 currant money, sells to John EDDY...a little lott being the 30th lot, 5 acres in 1st Division at Shawomet. Witnesses: Isaac WINSLOW, William CARVER. Rec. 17 May 1708.

Elizabeth BURTON of Marshfield MA to **Ebenezer SHERMAN** of Swanzey. <Bristol Co.Deeds 5:360>
...26 Mar. 1708, widow Elizabeth BURTON, for £80 current money, sells to Ebenezer SHEARMAN/SHERMAN...a great lot #30, 45 acres in 1st Division. Witnesses: Isaac WINSLOW, William CARVER. Rec. 20 May 1708.

Elizabeth BURTON of Marshfield MA to **Jonathan BOWERS** of Shawomet. <Bristol Co.Deeds 7:103>
...7 Mar. 1708/9, Elizabeth BURTON, gentlewoman, for £90 sold to Jonathan BOWERS, shipwright... my two lots of land in the out lott of Shawomet...one containing 36 acres bounded by Taunton Great River & is 25th lot in 1st Division...the other contains 60 acres & is 22d lot in 2d Division. Witnesses: Isaac WINSLOW, Isaac THOMAS. Rec. 27 Oct. 1711.

Elisabeth BURTON Jr. of Duxbury MA to **Thomas BURTON** of same. <Bristol Co.Deeds 14:372>
...28 July 1722, Elisabeth BURTON Jr., for £400 sells to Thomas BURTON, yeoman...all my whole right...in all my lands & tenements in Bristol...divided or undivded in possession or revertion or as sd lands may at present ly in partnership or undivided between ye sd Thomas BURTON and myself. Witnesses: William RAND, Josiah WINSLOW. Rec. 7 Aug. 1722.

Thomas BURTON of Duxbury MA to **Nathaniel BYFIELD** of Bristol. <Bristol Co.Deeds 14:402>
...7 Nov. 1722, Thomas BURTON, Deputy Sheriff of Duxbury, for £15 sells to Nathaniel BYFIELD, Esq...one half of a common lott which came to him in right of his father Stephen BURTON late of sd Bristol dec'd, being the 118th lot...bounded by 117th lot in possession of Col. Henry McENTOSHE and 123rd lot belonging to Benjamin MUNROE, yeoman of Bristol. Witnesses: Benjamin SMYTON, Sarah CARY. Rec. same day.

<u>BRISTOL COUNTY DEEDS</u>: **(re: Stephen BURTON)**

<6:12> - 18 May 1681, S.B., merchant of Boston & wf Abigail, et al, land at Mt. Hope.
<1:2> - 29 May 1683, S.B., merchant of Bristol, et al, grantors.
<1:1> - 20 Feb. 1684, S.B., merchant, late of Boston now of Bristol, et al, grantors.
<1:37> - 17 Mar. 1686, S.B. & wf Elizabeth of Bristol to Simon LINDE of Boston, their house lot.
<1:38> - 26 Mar. 1687, Simon LYNDE of Boston leases to S.B. of Bristol.
<2:330> - 5 Aug. 1689, S.B. & wf Elizabeth to David CARY.
<1:101> - 10 Jan. 1689/90, S.B. & wf Elizabeth of Bristol to Nathaniel BYFIELD.
<1:215> - 10 May 1692, S.B. & wf Elizabeth to Samuel COBBETT.
<4:126> - 17 Dec. 1692, S.B. & wf Elizabeth of Bristol to Jeremiah BOSWORTH & Belamy BOSWORTH, yeomen of Bristol, land bounded partly by land of Nathaniel BOSWORTH dec.

Will of **Hon. Isaac WINSLOW** of Marshfield MA. <Plymouth Co.PR #23184>
<8:27>...dated 4 May 1736, mentions wf **Sarah**, sons **John WINSLOW & Edward WINSLOW** (youngest son), daus **Penelope WARREN** wf of James and **Elizabeth MARSTON** wf of Benjamin of Salem; mentions real estate at Marshfield, Pembroke, Middleborough & Rutland. Witnesses: Joshua SOUL, Palatiah WEST, Samuel WESTON, Nathaniel FISH; oath of witnesses, 6 Apr. 1739. Pr. 6 Apr. 1739, widow **Sarah WINSLOW, John WINSLOW & Edward WINSLOW,** executors. <8:29> <u>Inventory</u> taken 16 May 1739 by Edward ARNOLD, Kenelm WINSLOW & Jabez WHITTEMORE; sworn to 27 July 1739.

Will of **Sarah WINSLOW**, widow of Marshfield MA. <Plymouth Co.PR #23223>
<13:201>...dated 5 SEpt. 1753, mentions sons **John WINSLOW & Edward WINSLOW**; sister **Hopestill OLIVER**; dau **Elizabeth MARSTON**; grandchildren **Ann WARREN, Sarah WARREN & James WARREN Jr.**, chil. of dec'd dau **Penlope WARREN.** Witnesses: Ephraim COBB, Nathaniel GOODWIN, James CURTISS. Pr. 4 Feb. 1754, **James WARREN Jr.**, merchant of Plymouth, app'td exr. <13:327> <u>Inventory</u> taken 17 July 1754 by Perez TILLSON, John THOMAS & Jedediah BOURN. <14:59> <u>Account</u> of admr., 3 Apr. 1756; <u>Received from</u>: Edward WINSLOW, John WINSLOW, Mary TINKHAM; <u>Paid to</u>: Mrs. MARSTON, James, Ann & Sarah WARREN, Mr. WINSLOW, Mr. WHITE, Dr. John THOMAS, Madam OLIVER, John DINGLEY, Madam OLIVER for Mrs. HOLYOKE, Jedediah BOURNE, Jacob WESTON.

Estate of **John WINSLOW** of Marshfield MA. <Plymouth Co.PR #23193>
<23:52> Letter/Bond 6 June 1774, Pelham WINSLOW of Plymouth & Isaac WINSLOW of Marshfield app'td admrs. Sureties: David STOCKBRIDGE of Hanover & Joseph CUSHMAN of Duxborough. Witnesses: Edward HAWARD, Edward WINSLOW Jr.

Estate of **Pelham WINSLOW**, absentee of Plymouth MA. <Plymouth Co.PR #23218>
<27:30> Letter 1 Oct. 1779, Joshua THOMAS, Esq. of Plymouth app'td agent of estate of **Pelham WINSLOW**, who has absented himself for more than two years last passed with the enemies of the United States of America. <original> Bond 25 Oct. 1779 of agent. Sureties: William THOMAS, Physician & Abraham HAMMETT, gent. Witnesses: Lucy HAMMETT, I. LOTHROP. <25:458> Inventory taken 4 Dec. 1779 by William THOMAS, Thomas WITHERELL & Samuel BARTLETT Jr. of Plymouth; sworn to Feb. 1780 by Joshua THOMAS, agent.

Estate of **Pelham WINSLOW** of Plymouth MA. <Plymouth Co.PR #23219>
<original> Request 24 Apr.1784, of widow **Joanna WINSLOW**, who declines taking administration & asks that **Dr. Isaac WINSLOW**, brother of the dec'd, be app'td. <27:150> Letter 23 Apr. 1784, **Isaac WINSLOW** of Marshfield app'td admr. <original> Bond 22 Apr. 1784 of admr. Sureties: George WATSON & Thomas JACKSON, yeoman of Plymouth. Witnesses: Priscilla BURR, Isaac LOTHROP. <29:164> Inventory taken 6 May 1784 by Hugh ORR & Edward HOWARD of Bridgewater & John GRAY of Kingston; incl. land in Marshfield being the easterly end of the farm of the late **General WINSLOW** dec'd; half of 1200 acres in the Township of Winslow on Kenebeck River in the County of Lincoln. <original> Petition, 23 Apr. 1784, for partition of land held in common between **Isaac WINSLOW** & heirs of the dec'd, lying in Marshfield. <29:161> Division 6 May 1784, by above three appraisers; half to **Isaac WINSLOW**, half to heirs of the dec'd. <29:165> Insolvency, 22 June 1784. <29:165> Dower assigned to widow, **Joanna WINSLOW**, 7 May 1784; 110 acres in Marshfield. <29:256> Warrant 22 June 1784, to Briggs ALDEN & Gamaliel BRADFORD of Duxbury, to examine claims. <29:257> List of Claims, 15 Apr. 1785: Dr. Isaac WINSLOW, Stephen SAMPSON, Joseph CROSWELL, John TOBEY, Samuel BARTLETT, Capt. William WESTON, William H. JACKSON, John F. EDMUNDS, Thomas & John FLEET, Theophilus COTTON, John TORREY, William LeBARON, Samuel GOOLD, Joseph HOWLAND, John BARTLETT, Ichabod SHAW, Barnabas HEDGE,Joseph TRASK, Isaac BARKER, Samuel CLARK, Reginald McROATH, Thomas WETHRELL, William TRENHOLM, Nathaniel LITTLE, Lemuel DREW, Elisha FORD, Rufus ROBBINS, Isaac LeBARON, William COYE, Thomas DAVIS, Mercy HEDGE, Edward WINSLOW of Duxbury, William DREW, John WATSON, Abiel SHURTLEFF, Charles STOCKBRIDGE, estate of Gideon WHITE dec'd, DAVIS & HARLOW. <29:427> Account of admr., 3 Feb. 1786; land sold to Charles STOCKBRIDGE & John SOULE; Received of: Isaac SYMONS, Nathaniel SPRAGUE, Thaddeus RIPLEY, Richard HOLMES, Cephas WADSWORTH, Levi LORING, Cornelius SAMPSON, Stephen NYE, Noah FEARING, Levi BRADFORD, John GRAY, Simeon SAMPSON, Joseph DREW, Sylvanus DREW, Thomas BREWSTER, Joseph SOLE, Isaac BREWSTER, Seth DREW, Ebenezer FISH; Paid to: Hugh ORR, Asa WATERMAN, George KEITH. <29:428> Claims allowed, 23 May 1786.

INDEX